Canada

Mark Lightbody
Jeff Davis
Lisa Dunford
Steve Kokker
Susan Rimerman
Don Root
David Stanley

LONELY PLANET PUBLICATIONS
Melbourne • Oakland • London • Paris

CANADA

Churchill
Migrating polar bears and beluga whales pass by this historic northern settlement, one of the best spots to see the aurora borealis.

Nahanni National Park Reserve
Spectacular landscape ranges from the peaks of the Mackenzie Mountains to the canyons forged by the turbulent South Nahanni River.

Dawson City
This living museum of the gold-rush days is nestled at the confluence of the Yukon and Klondike Rivers, just 240km south of the Arctic Circle.

Vancouver Island
Wilderness meets civilization: tempestuous rain forests in Pacific Rim National Park Reserve, high tea in Victoria.

The Rockies
The spectacular mountains and valleys surrounding Banff and Jasper offer year-round adventure.

Dinosaur Provincial Park
Fossilized remnants of the previous inhabitants - dinosaurs - survive in southern Alberta's photogenic, desertlike badlands.

Wanuskewin Heritage Park
Nestled in the sacred Opamihaw Valley, the park highlights First Nations' life and traditions dating back over 6000 years.

Elevation

- 3000m
- 2400m
- 1800m
- 1200m
- 600m
- 300m
- 150m
- Sea Level

RUSSIA

ARCTIC OCEAN

Beaufort Sea
Sverdrup Islands
Axel Heiberg Island
Prince Patrick Island
Melville Island
Bathurst Island
Cornwallis Island
Viscount Melville Sound
Banks Island
Somerset Island
Prince of Wales Island
Victoria Island
Boothia Peninsula
Gulf of
King William Island
Amundsen Gulf

Alaska
Fairbanks
USA
Anchorage
Dawson City
Yukon Territory
WHITEHORSE
Watson Lake
JUNEAU
Coast Mountains
Mackenzie Mountains
Franklin Mountains
Mackenzie River
Anderson R.
Tuktoyaktuk
Inuvik
Beaufort Sea
Great Bear Lake
Northwest Territories
Nunavut
Arctic Circle
Thelon River
Baker Lake
YELLOWKNIFE
Lac la Martre
Great Slave Lake
Dubawnt Lake
Wood Buffalo National Park
Liard River
Peace River
Lake Claire
Lake Athabasca
Wollaston Lake
Reindeer Lake
Churchill R.
Churchill
Nelson R.
Spatsizi Plateau Provincial Wilderness Park
Prince Rupert
Williston Lake
Rocky Mountains
Lac la Ronge
Saskatchewan
Thompson
Manitoba
Queen Charlotte Islands
Prince George
British Columbia
Jasper National Park
Jasper
EDMONTON
Alberta
Athabasca River
Prince Albert
Lake Winnipeg
PACIFIC OCEAN
Vancouver Island
Kamloops
Banff National Park
Lake Louise
Banff
Calgary
Saskatoon
Moose Jaw
Yorkton
WINNIPEG
Nanaimo
Vancouver
Kelowna
Nelson
Swift Current
REGINA
Brandon
VICTORIA
Seattle
WA
Medicine Hat
USA
ND
Portland
OR
ID
MT
WY
NE
CA
NV
UT

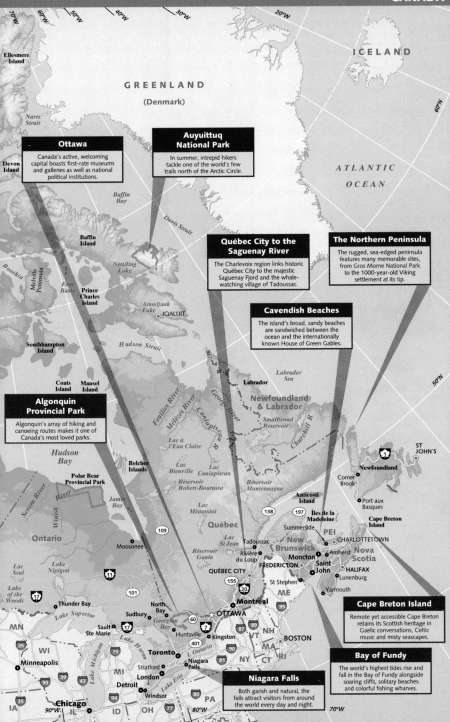

Ottawa

Canada's active, welcoming capital boasts first-rate museums and galleries as well as national political institutions.

Auyuittuq National Park

In summer, intrepid hikers tackle one of the world's few trails north of the Arctic Circle.

Québec City to the Saguenay River

The Charlevoix region links historic Québec City to the majestic Saguenay Fjord and the whale-watching village of Tadoussac.

The Northern Peninsula

The rugged, sea-edged peninsula features many memorable sites, from Gros Morne National Park to the 1000-year-old Viking settlement at its tip.

Cavendish Beaches

The island's broad, sandy beaches are sandwiched between the ocean and the internationally known House of Green Gables.

Algonquin Provincial Park

Algonquin's array of hiking and canoeing routes makes it one of Canada's most loved parks.

Cape Breton Island

Remote yet accessible Cape Breton retains its Scottish heritage in Gaelic conversations, Celtic music and misty seascapes.

Bay of Fundy

The world's highest tides rise and fall in the Bay of Fundy alongside soaring cliffs, solitary beaches and colorful fishing wharves.

Niagara Falls

Both garish and natural, the falls attract visitors from around the world every day and night.

Canada
8th edition – October 2002
First published – March 1983

Published by
Lonely Planet Publications Pty Ltd ABN 36 005 607 983
90 Maribyrnong St, Footscray, Victoria 3011, Australia

Lonely Planet Offices
Australia Locked Bag 1, Footscray, Victoria 3011
USA 150 Linden St, Oakland, CA 94607
UK 10a Spring Place, London NW5 3BH
France 1 rue du Dahomey, 75011 Paris

Photographs
Many of the images in this guide are available for licensing from
Lonely Planet Images.
W www.lonelyplanetimages.com

Front cover photograph
Canadian flags (Guy Grenier/Masterfile)

Wildlife, Parks & Heritage Sites title page photograph
The Waterton-Glacier International Peace Park (Rick Rudnicki)

ISBN 1 74059 029 5

Contents

INTRODUCTION　13

FACTS ABOUT CANADA　14

History 14
Geography 18
Climate 19
Government & Politics 21
Economy 22
Population & People 23
Education 25
Arts 25
Society & Conduct 30
Religion 30

WILDLIFE, PARKS & HERITAGE SITES　32

FACTS FOR THE VISITOR　42

Planning 42
Suggested Itineraries 43
Tourist offices 43
Visas & Documents 44
Embassies & Consulates . . 46
Customs 47
Money 48
Post & Communications . . 50
Digital Resources 51
Books 52
Newspapers & Magazines . 53
Radio & TV 53
Photography & Video 54
Time 54
Electricity 54
Weights & Measures 54
Laundry 55
Toilets 56
Health 56
Women Travelers 58
Gay & Lesbian Travelers . . . 59
Disabled Travelers 59
Senior Travelers 59
Travel with Children 60
Dangers & Annoyances . . . 60
Emergencies 61
Legal Matters 61
Business Hours 61
Public Holidays 62
Special Events 62
Activities 62
Courses 65
Work 65
Accommodations 66
Food 69
Drinks 70
Spectator Sports 71
Shopping 73

GETTING THERE & AWAY　74

Air 74
Land 77
Sea 77

GETTING AROUND　79

Air 79
Bus 80
Train 81
Car 83
Bicycle 87
Hitchhiking 88
Walking 88
Boat 88
Organized Tours 89

ONTARIO　91

Toronto 93
Around Toronto 130
Ottawa 133
Around Ottawa 146
Hull (Gatineau) 147
Around Hull 148
Eastern Ontario 150
Algonquin Provincial
Park East 150
South Algonquin Area . . . 150
Merrickville 152
Smiths Falls 152
Cornwall & Around 152
Morrisburg Area 153
Prescott 153
Brockville 153
Kingston 153
Around Kingston 159
Quinte's Isle 162
Trenton 163
Kawartha Lakes 164
Southwestern Ontario . . . 165
Hamilton 165
Welland Canal Area 169
Niagara-on-the-Lake 170
Around Niagara-on-the-Lake 174
Niagara Falls 176
Around Niagara Falls 185
Brantford 185
Six Nations Indian Reserve　186
Country Heritage Park . . . 186
Guelph 186
Kortright Waterfowl Park　188
Rockwood Conservation
Area 188
Kitchener-Waterloo 188
Around Kitchener-
Waterloo 191
Elora 192
Fergus 193
Stratford 194
St Marys 197

2   Contents

Tillsonburg & Delhi 198
Lake Erie Shoreline West . . . 198
London 199
St Thomas 203
Windsor 203
Amherstburg 206
Lake Huron Shoreline 206
Georgian Bay & Lakelands 207
Barrie 207
Wasaga Beach 207
Collingwood 208
Shelburne 209
Owen Sound 209
Port Elgin 211

Sauble Beach 211
The Bruce Peninsula 211
Manitoulin Island 214
Huronia Towns 215
Muskoka Towns 217
Algonquin Provincial Park 218
Georgian Bay Islands
National Park 220
Southeastern Georgian Bay
Provincial Parks 220
Parry Sound 221
Killbear Provincial Park . . . 221
Byng Inlet 221
Killarney Provincial Park . . 221

Northern Ontario 222
North Bay 222
Temagami 224
Sudbury 225
North of Sudbury 231
Timmins 231
Cochrane 232
Moosonee 233
West of Sudbury 234
Sault Ste Marie 235
Lake Superior Shoreline Area 242
Thunder Bay 245
West of Thunder Bay 253

QUÉBEC   256

Montréal **262**
Around Montréal **290**
Oka 290
Rivière Rouge 290
The Laurentians 290
Eastern Townships 296
Montréal to Québec City . 301
Québec City **305**
Around Québec City **320**
North Shore 320
South Shore 322
Charlevoix & Saguenay . . . **323**
Charlevoix 324
Saguenay 327
North Shore **330**
Tadoussac 330
Grandes Bergeronnes 333
Ste Anne de Portneuf 334
Baie Comeau 334
Godbout 334
Pointe des Monts 334

Pointe aux Anglais 335
Sept Îles 335
Havre St Pierre 336
Île d'Anticosti 336
Natashquan 337
Lower North Shore 337
Lower St Lawrence **338**
Rivière du Loup 338
Le Témis 340
Trois Pistoles 341
Parc du Bic 341
Rimouski 341
Gaspé Peninsula **342**
Ste Flavie 343
Grand Métis 343
Matane 344
Cap Chat 344
Ste Anne Des Monts 344
Parc de la Gaspésie 345
Mont St Pierre 345

Mont St Pierre to Forillon
National Park 346
Forillon National Park 346
Gaspé 347
Percé 348
The Bay Side 349
Matapédia Valley 351
Îles de la Madeleine **352**
Île du Cap aux Meules . . . 354
Île du Havre Aubert 354
Île du Havre aux Maisons 355
Grosse Île 355
Pointe de l'Est 356
Île de la Grande Entrée . . . 356
Île d'Entrée 356
Getting There & Away 356
Getting Around 356
Far North **357**
Abitibi-Témiscamingue . . . 357
James Bay 359
Nunavik 361

NEWFOUNDLAND & LABRADOR   363

St John's **367**
Around St John's **380**
South of St John's 381
Avalon Peninsula 382
Eastern Newfoundland . . . **385**
Bonavista Peninsula 386
Burin Peninsula 390
St Pierre & Miquelon **392**
Central Newfoundland . . . **394**
Gander 394
Notre Dame Bay Area 396
Lewisporte 398

Grand Falls & Windsor . . . 399
South of Grand Falls 400
Baie Verte Peninsula 401
Western Newfoundland . . . **401**
Deer Lake 401
Northern Peninsula 402
Corner Brook 411
Around Corner Brook 413
Stephenville 414
Port au Port Peninsula . . . 414
Barachois Pond
Provincial Park 414

Southwestern Newfoundland 414
Codroy Valley 415
Port aux Basques 415
Around Port aux Basques . 417
South Coast 418
Outports **419**
South Coast 419
Labrador **420**
Labrador Straits 422
Northern Coast 425
Central Labrador 426
Western Labrador 427

NOVA SCOTIA 430

Halifax 433
Around Halifax 447
South Shore 448
Peggy's Cove 448
Chester 449
Mahone Bay 450
Lunenburg 451
Bridgewater 454
Lahave 454
Lahave Islands 455
Liverpool 455
Seaside Adjunct Kejimkujik
National Park 456
Shelburne 457
Shelburne to Yarmouth . . . 458
Yarmouth to Windsor 458
Yarmouth 458
French Shore 461
Digby 461
Digby Neck 463
Kejimkujik National Park 465
Annapolis Valley 466
North of Kentville 469
Wolfville 469
Grand Pré 470
Windsor 471
Central Nova Scotia 473

Shubenacadie 473
Truro 473
Chignecto 474
Amherst & Around 477
Sunrise Trail 479
Tidnish Bridge 479
Pugwash 479
Wentworth 480
Caribou 480
Pictou 480
New Glasgow 482
Antigonish 482
Monastery 483
Eastern Shore 483
Lawrencetown Beach 483
Porters Lake 483
Musquodoboit Harbour . . . 483
Jedore Oyster Pond 484
Tangier 484
Taylor Head Provincial Park 484
Port Dufferin 484
Liscomb Mills 485
Sherbrooke 485
Country Harbour 485
Canso 485
Guysborough 486
Cape Breton Island 486

Port Hastings 486
Mabou 486
Inverness 487
Belle Côte 488
Chéticamp 488
Cape Breton Highlands
National Park 489
Pleasant Bay 491
Gampo Abbey 491
Cape North 492
Bay St Lawrence 492
Meat Cove 492
Around Neils Harbour 493
Ingonish 493
St Ann's 494
Big Bras d'Or 494
North Sydney 494
Sydney 495
Glace Bay 498
Louisbourg 498
Louisbourg National
Historic Site 499
Baddeck 499
Whycocomagh 501
St Peter's 501

PRINCE EDWARD ISLAND 503

Charlottetown 507
Eastern Prince Edward Island 514
Orwell 514
Wood Islands 514
Montague & Around 515
Souris 515
Basin Head 516
East Point 516
Elmira 517
St Peters 517
Greenwich 517

Central Prince Edward Island 517
Borden-Carleton 517
Victoria 518
Prince Edward Island
National Park 518
Brackley Beach 520
South Rustico 520
New Glasgow & St Ann . . 521
North Rustico 522
Cavendish 523
New London 524

Park Corner 525
Western Prince Edward
Island 525
Summerside 525
Région Évangéline 527
Tyne Valley 528
Lennox Island 528
Tignish to North Cape . . . 529
West Coast 529

NEW BRUNSWICK 531

Fredericton 534
Saint John River Valley . . . 540
Mactaquac 540
Woodstock 541
Hartland 541
Grand Falls 542
Edmundston 542
St Jacques 543
West Fundy Shore 544

St Stephen 544
St Andrews 547
Fundy Isles 549
Blacks Harbour 556
New River Provincial Park 556
Saint John 557
Central Fundy Shore 564
St Martins 565
Fundy Trail Parkway 565

Fundy National Park 565
Alma 567
Shepody Bay
Shorebird Reserve 568
Hopewell Rocks 568
Hillsborough 568
Moncton to Sackville 568
Moncton 569
St Joseph 574

4   Contents

Sackville 574
Fort Beauséjour
National Historic Site 575
Northumberland Shore . . . 575
Cape Jourimain 575
Bouctouche 576
St Louis de Kent 577

Kouchibouguac National Park 577
Northeastern
New Brunswick 578
Miramichi 578
Burnt Church First Nation . 579
Caraquet 580
Caraquet to Bathurst 581

Petit Rocher 582
Eel River First Nation 582
Dalhousie 582
Campbellton 582
Mt Carleton
Provincial Park 583

MANITOBA   585

Winnipeg 587
Around Winnipeg 601
Eastern Manitoba 602
Mennonite Heritage Village 602
La Broquerie 602
Whiteshell Provincial Park 602
Nopoming Provincial Park 603
Atikaki Provincial
Wilderness Park 603
Lake Winnipeg 603
Grand Beach 603
Netley Marsh 603

Winnipeg Beach 603
Gimli 604
Hecla Provincial Park 604
Snake Pits 604
Peguis & Fisher River 605
Lake Manitoba Shoreline 605
Northern Woods & Water
Route 605
Northern Manitoba 605
The Pas 605
Flin Flon 606
Thompson 607

Gillam 607
Churchill 607
Western Manitoba 615
Portage La Prairie 615
Spruce Woods Provincial Park 615
Brandon 615
Around Brandon 616
Neepawa 617
Riding Mountain
National Park 617
Around Riding Mountain 617

SASKATCHEWAN   619

Regina 622
Around Regina 629
Eastern Saskatchewan . . . 629
Yorkton 629
Crooked Lake
Provincial Park 630
Moose Mountain
Provincial Park 630
Estevan 630
Weyburn 631
Southwestern Saskatchewan 631
Moose Jaw 631

Chaplin Lake 632
Swift Current 632
Saskatchewan Landing
Provincial Park 632
Great Sand Hills 632
Maple Creek 633
Cypress Hills
Interprovincial Park 633
Eastend 633
Grasslands National Park 633
Big Muddy Badlands 634
Saskatoon 634

Manitou Beach 641
Northern Saskatchewan . . . 642
Prince Albert 642
Around Prince Albert 643
Prince Albert National Park 644
Lac La Ronge Provincial Park 644
Redberry Lake 645
Batoche National Historic Site 645
North Of Batoche 646
The Battlefords 646
Meadow Lake
Provincial Park 646

ALBERTA   647

Edmonton 651
Around Edmonton 664
Northern Alberta 667
Peace River & Around . . . 667
Mackenzie Hwy 667
Lake District 667
Wood Buffalo National Park 668
Calgary 668
Banff & Jasper
National Parks 684

Kananaskis Country 684
Canmore 685
Banff Townsite 686
Lake Louise 696
Icefields Parkway 699
Jasper Townsite & Around 701
Southern Alberta 709
Drumheller 709
Dinosaur Provincial Park . . 711
Medicine Hat 712

Head-Smashed-In
Buffalo Jump 712
Lethbridge 713
Writing-on-Stone
Provincial Park 715
Cardston 715
Waterton Lakes
National Park 715
Crowsnest Pass 717

BRITISH COLUMBIA   718

Vancouver 724
North of Vancouver 762

Vancouver Island 765
Victoria 768

Southeastern Vancouver Island 786
Nanaimo & Around 788

Port Alberni & Around . . . 792
Pacific Rim National Park
Reserve 794
Tofino & Around 796
Ucluelet 799
Parksville & Qualicum Beach 801
Denman & Hornby Islands 801
Courtenay & Comox 801
Campbell River 802
Quadra & Cortes Islands 803
Strathcona Provincial Park 804
Gold River 804
North Vancouver Island . . . 805
Southern Gulf Islands 807
Southwestern
British Columbia 813
Hope 814
Fraser River Canyon 814
Manning Provincial Park . . . 814
Kamloops 815

Wells Gray Provincial Park 818
Mt Robson Provincial Park 818
Kamloops to Williams Lake 819
Okanagan Valley 819
Osoyoos & Around 821
Penticton 822
Kelowna 825
Vernon 829
North of Vernon 830
Southeastern
British Columbia 831
Revelstoke & Around 831
Glacier National Park 835
Golden 835
Yoho National Park 836
Kootenay National Park . . . 838
Mt Assiniboine
Provincial Park 838
Radium Hot Springs 838
Invermere to Cranbrook . . . 839

Nelson & Around 840
Northeast of Nelson 841
West of Nelson 841
Northeastern
British Columbia 843
Prince George 843
Prince George to Smithers 845
Prince George to Dawson
Creek 846
Dawson Creek 846
Dawson Creek to the Yukon 846
South of Prince George . . . 847
Pacific Northwest 848
Prince Rupert 848
Prince Rupert to
New Hazelton 852
Cassiar Hwy 852
Queen Charlotte Islands . . 853

YUKON TERRITORY 858

Whitehorse 862
Alaska Hwy 867
Haines (Alaska) 872
Glacier Bay National Park
(Alaska) 874

Robert Campbell Hwy . . . 874
Klondike Hwy 874
Dawson City 877
Top of the World Hwy . . . 882
Dempster Hwy 883

Tombstone Territorial Park 883
Vuntut National Park 883
Ivvavik National Park 884
Herschel Island
Territorial Park 884

NORTHWEST TERRITORIES 885

Yellowknife 889
Around Yellowknife 895
Mackenzie Hwy to Fort
Providence 895
Fort Providence 896

North of Fort Providence 896
Hay River 897
Fort Smith 898
Wood Buffalo National Park 898
West of Great Slave Lake 899

Nahanni National
Park Reserve 900
Mackenzie River Valley . . . 902
Arctic Region 906

NUNAVUT 908

Baffin Region 911   Kitikmeot Region 913   Kivalliq Region 914

LANGUAGE 916

GLOSSARY 920

THANKS 922

CANADA MAP INDEX

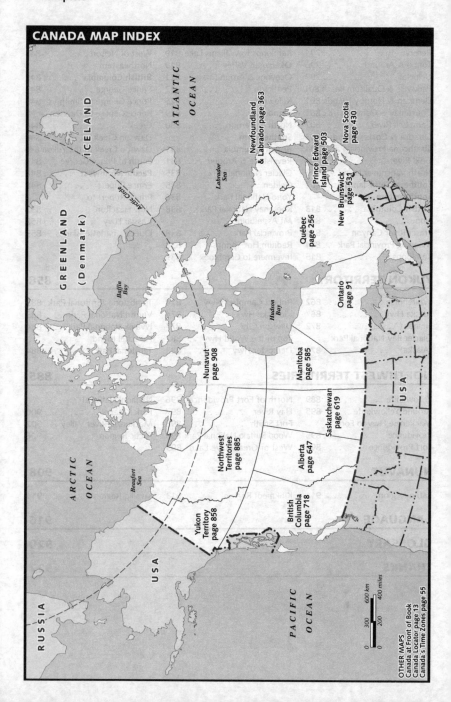

ATLANTIC OCEAN

ICELAND

GREENLAND (Denmark)

Baffin Bay

Labrador Sea

Newfoundland & Labrador page 363

Prince Edward Island page 503

Nova Scotia page 430

New Brunswick page 531

Québec page 256

Hudson Bay

Ontario page 91

Nunavut page 908

Manitoba page 585

Saskatchewan page 619

Alberta page 647

Northwest Territories page 885

Beaufort Sea

ARCTIC OCEAN

Yukon Territory page 858

British Columbia page 718

USA

USA

RUSSIA

PACIFIC OCEAN

Arctic Circle

0   300   600 km
0   200   400 miles

OTHER MAPS
Canada at Front of Book
Canada Locator page 13
Canada's Time Zones page 55

The Authors

Mark Lightbody

Mark was born and grew up in Montréal and was educated there and in London, Ontario. He holds an honors degree in journalism. Among a variety of jobs, he's worked in radio news and in the specialty graphics industry.

Mark has traveled in 50 countries, visiting every continent but Antarctica. He made his first foray across Canada at the age of four. Since then, he has made the trip numerous times, using plane, train, car and thumb.

In addition to his work on the Lonely Planet guide to Canada, Mark has written part of LP's *USA* and *Great Lakes* guidebooks. He has also contributed to *Travel With Children* and *Unpacked Again* (the latter – not the former – describing travel disaster stories). He has also worked on former editions of *Papua New Guinea, Australia, Malaysia, Singapore & Brunei* and *South-East Asia*.

He lives in Toronto with his wife and two children, all great travel companions.

Jeff Davis

Born in Alabama, Jeff grew up mostly in Columbus, Georgia. He attended college in Illinois and studied music, chemical engineering and finally, in a desperate bid to avoid the real world, writing. As an environmental engineer, Jeff travels the USA preparing oil spill prevention plans for truck stops. He now lives in Cincinnati, Ohio, with his wife and occasional travel companion, Rina. His Lonely Planet credits include work on the books *Georgia & the Carolinas, Central America on a Shoestring, USA* and *Chile*.

Lisa Dunford

Lisa was born in East Chicago, Indiana, but has been wandering ever since. She now calls Texas home, but previous residences have included Strathmore, Alberta, and Bratislava, Slovakia. Her degree in International Affairs from George Washington University led her, in a roundabout way, to newspaper work. When that became too confining, she quit to work freelance as a writer and editor. Lisa travels as much as money allows – which is never enough.

Steve Kokker

After growing up in Montréal, Steve received psychology and social work degrees at McGill University, then worked in mental health counseling for a few years before becoming film critic for the *Montréal Mirror* and *Hour* newspapers, which he did for eight years. Since 1996 he's divided his time between Montréal, Estonia and Russia. Since 1988 his numerous writing stints for Lonely Planet in all of these places have allowed him to appreciate more deeply each of his three homes. Recently he has also authored Lonely Planet's *Québec*.

Susan Rimerman

Susan joined Lonely Planet's US office as the Design Manager in 1999 and now serves as Series Publishing Manager for Micro-regional Guidebooks. Preferring extreme landscapes and spicy food, she has traveled extensively in Central and South America, the Caribbean and Southeast Asia. Her formal training includes a degree in journalism and international relations from the University of Southern California and a masters in creative writing from Sarah Lawrence College. She worked in broadcasting in Washington, DC, and in book publishing in New York City. Susan grew up in the San Francisco Bay area and now lives there with her husband, Andrew, and their cat, Flynn.

Don Root

On the long, strange trip to get here, Don has studied music, journalism, art and law; been a ski bum and a paralegal; played drums in a rock band, blues band and symphony orchestra; edited travel books and a rural weekly newspaper; published an underground literary 'zine; and frittered away untold years backpacking and mountaineering throughout the West. When not off on writing assignments, he holes up between the Golden Gate and the Wine Country in glorious Northern California.

David Stanley

David studied Spanish literature at schools in Canada, Mexico and Spain, ending with an honors degree from the University of Guelph, Ontario. He has spent much of the past three decades on the road, with visits to 176 of the planet's 244 countries and territories. He has crossed six continents overland.

During the 1980s David wrote pioneering travel guidebooks to Alaska/Yukon and the Pacific Islands. His *South Pacific Handbook*, now in its 7th edition, was the original guide to the South Seas. Just prior to the fall of the Berlin Wall, he led Lonely Planet into Europe with the first three editions of *Eastern Europe on a Shoestring*, which he researched and wrote single-handed. He also prepared the first two editions of Lonely Planet's *Cuba* from scratch.

FROM THE AUTHORS

Mark Lightbody I dedicate my portion of the book to my father, who died during its writing. On top of everything else, his eye for detail, broad knowledge and timely humor are irreplaceable. Who is going to keep me honest now?

I would like to thank all the Oakland Lonely Planet staff for unbelievable support, patience and encouragement. They are pros and great people besides.

In Canada, special thanks to Lloyd and Willa Jones and Jill and Konrad Sechley. A warm nod, too, to all the helpful residents and visitors I met while clocking untold thousands of kilometers researching. Your tips and conversations are a great part of the job.

As always, thank you to Colleen, Trevor and Ava for everything. Thanks, too, to my fellow writers on the project; they made work-sharing an agreeable and productive concept. Much appreciation is also due to all the travelers who take time to write with their wonderful, wacky, informative and inspiring tales and details. Keep them coming and see you next time.

Jeff Davis Thanks to the many Canadians and fellow travelers who helped me during my journey, especially Jamie Bastedo for feeding me at his house in Yellowknife; Kirt Ejesiak for the kayak tour of Frobisher Bay, Iqaluit; Michael Murphy for showing me around Pangnirtung; and Liz Dale for the tour of Norman Wells. Extra thanks go to Kate Hoffman, who introduced me to travel guidebook writing, and to David Zingarelli, who set up this complicated project in fine style. Most of all, thanks to my wonderful and patient wife, Rina, who caught my most potentially embarrassing mistakes. Because of her, coming home is the best part of any journey.

Lisa Dunford After putting more than 6000km worth of dirt on a rental car, I have an even greater appreciation for the rugged beauty of the prairie provinces than I did before this trek. I'm grateful to the residents of Saskatchewan for their incredible kindness, to fellow travelers like Cate Lynch and Diana Pyle for their shared wisdom, to Yaroslava Kojolianko for bringing the Ukraine a little closer and to the staff and owners of the Rahr Duck Camp for opening their home and their province to me.

I also want to thank David Zingarelli, Mark Lightbody, Susan Rimerman and Ryan Ver Berkmoes for words of support, encouragement and assistance and for bits of good advice. And I appreciate all the good catches and keen editorial work of Valerie Sinzdak and Wendy Smith. Justin Colgan and the LP cartography staff deserve special mention because I gave them so many additions that they had to decipher. Oh, and I can't forget CBC Radio: Thanks for the company, Sad Goat!

Steve Kokker I am indebted to a lot of great people whom I met along the way and who shared their knowledge about La Belle Province. Thanks to Dani Zbinden; Yvon Bélanger; Nathalie Decaigny; Paul L'Anglais; Guillaume Tétrault; Jacques Racine; Jean François Miousse; Lorraine Pes; Nicole, Oscar and Hélène; Martin Chouinard; Robert 'Mojo'; Philippe, Claire and Dominic Steinbach; and Nicholas Gaudet and Alex.

Thanks also to my friends and family who helped make the job a bit easier: Louise Treich; my mother and father, Michelle and Tony; Ingrid Thompson; Tom Waugh; Brent Beauparlant and Melanie; Stephanie Premji; Boris Romaguer; Pavel Sijanov; and James Roach.

At Tourisme Québec, huge thanks to Patrice Poissant, Johann Eustache, Christine St Pierre and especially Michel Bonato.

Thanks also to fellow LP authors Christine Coste, Mark Lightbody and Jeremy Gray. At LP, thanks to Robbie Reid, Tracey Croom, Christine Lee and many others at the US office!

Susan Rimerman Special thanks to David Zingarelli and Mariah Bear for providing this splendid opportunity to escape as far north as possible. Also to Margaret Livingston, Ruth Askevold, Daniel New and the Lonely Planet Oakland design team for handling guidebook production during my extended absence. The Visitor Reception Centres in Whitehorse, Dawson City and Carcross were essential in providing assistance, and Parks Canada helped with hiking and outdoor information in Haines Junction. Thanks, too, to Andy Tardiff for his enlightened perspective and hospitality on Herschel Island and to Val Drummond at Paddlewheel Adventures for pointing out the best running routes to avoid bears in Haines Junction.

Don Root A big thanks to all the super-friendly residents of BC and Alberta who made my time in their neck of the woods such a pleasure. From Calgary to Kelowna to Clayoquot Sound – you guys are tops! Huge appreciation also goes to fellow Lonely Planet authors Sara Benson, Julie Fanselow, Debra Miller and Chris Wyness, whose excellent research and writing for LP's *British Columbia* and *Vancouver* guides was used extensively in this book. And an extra-special well-fed thanks goes out to Andrew Hempstead and Dianne Melton in Canmore for their gracious hospitality and award-winning pumpkin soup! (Mmm, mmm good!)

David Stanley I'm grateful for having been given the opportunity to update the Maritimes chapters in *Canada*. As an Ontario boy, I'm a long-standing admirer of the gentler, friendlier lifestyle 'Down East,' where the almighty dollar hasn't yet been crowned king.

Special thanks to Cyndi Gilbert of the Sierra Club of Canada, Sharon Labchuk of Earth Action PEI, James R Culbert of Rainbow Lodge and Geoffrey Milder of Halifax, who pointed out areas worthy of attention. However, the one person whose advice and support made it all possible for me was my wife, Ria de Vos.

This Book

This 8th edition of *Canada* was written by a team of authors led by coordinating author Mark Lightbody, who also researched and updated all previous editions of the book. Mark wrote the introductory chapters and the Newfoundland & Labrador and Ontario chapters this time around. He was joined by fellow writers Jeff Davis (Northwest Territories and Nunavut), Lisa Dunford (Manitoba and Saskatchewan), Steve Kokker (Québec), Susan Rimerman (Yukon Territory and Inuvik in the Northwest Territories), Don Root (Alberta and British Columbia) and David Stanley (New Brunswick, Nova Scotia and Prince Edward Island).

Some of the text was based on work done for previous editions, whose writers included Mark Lightbody, Tom Smallman, Dorinda Talbot, Jim DuFresne, Thomas Huhti and Ryan Ver Berkmoes.

FROM THE PUBLISHER

A whole lot of people in Lonely Planet's Oakland office came together amid a lot of upheaval to produce this mammoth book. Valerie Sinzdak served as lead editor, with the expert guidance of senior editor David Zingarelli and immeasurable editing help from Susan Shook Malloy, Wade Fox, Wendy Smith, Rebecca Northen and Paul Sheridan. Working out the kinks were proofreaders Valerie, Susan, Wendy, Kathryn Ettinger, China Williams, Erin Corrigan, Don Root, Christine Lee and Tammy Fortin. Wade, Wendy, senior editor Michele Posner and managing editor Kate Hoffman helped with layout review.

A huge crew of cartographers pitched in to get all the maps drawn on time. Justin Colgan and Graham Neale led the cartography team, with senior cartographer Bart Wright making sure everything ran smoothly. Lee Espinole, Marji Hamm, Patrick Huerta, Rachel Jereb, Laurie Mikkelsen, Carole Nuttall, Don Patterson, David Ryder and Eric Thomsen did the mapping, with base-map editing help from Narinder Bansal, John Culp, Anneka Imkamp, Dion Good, Annette Olson, Terence Philippe, Kat Smith, Herman So and Sherry Veverka.

Joshua Schefers and Gerilyn Attebery headed up the design team, showing a lot of grace under pressure, with assistance from senior designer Tracey Croom and design manager Ruth Askevold, plus fellow designers Lora Santiago and Margaret Livingston. Gerilyn designed the sharp-looking color pages. In his final days at LP, illustrator Justin Marler applied his talents to one more book. Ken DellaPenta indexed this edition.

Hats off to all. A special thanks to Mark Lightbody and the rest of the Canada authors for staying in touch and making sure the job got done.

ACKNOWLEDGMENTS

Some of the maps in this book are derived from aerial photographs from the collection of the National Air Photo Library/Natural Resources Canada by right of Her Majesty the Queen in Right of Canada.

The excerpt from *I Married the Klondike*, by Laura Beatrice Berton, used in the Yukon Territory chapter, was reprinted with permission from the author's estate.

Foreword

ABOUT LONELY PLANET GUIDEBOOKS

The story begins with a classic travel adventure: Tony and Maureen Wheeler's 1972 journey across Europe and Asia to Australia. There was no useful information about the overland trail then, so Tony and Maureen published the first Lonely Planet guidebook to meet a growing need.

From a kitchen table, Lonely Planet has grown to become the largest independent travel publisher in the world, with offices in Melbourne (Australia), Oakland (USA), London (UK) and Paris (France).

Today Lonely Planet guidebooks cover the globe. There is an ever-growing list of books and information in a variety of media. Some things haven't changed. The main aim is still to make it possible for adventurous travelers to get out there – to explore and better understand the world.

At Lonely Planet we believe travelers can make a positive contribution to the countries they visit – if they respect their host communities and spend their money wisely. Since 1986 a percentage of the income from each book has been donated to aid projects and human rights campaigns, and, more recently, to wildlife conservation.

> Although inclusion in a guidebook usually implies a recommendation, we cannot list every good place. Exclusion does not necessarily imply criticism. In fact, there are a number of reasons why we might exclude a place – sometimes it is simply inappropriate to encourage an influx of travelers.

UPDATES & READER FEEDBACK

Things change – prices go up, schedules change, good places go bad and bad places go bankrupt. Nothing stays the same. So, if you find things better or worse, recently opened or long-since closed, please tell us and help make the next edition even more accurate and useful.

Lonely Planet thoroughly updates each guidebook as often as possible – usually every two years, although for some destinations the gap can be longer. Between editions, up-to-date information is available in our free, quarterly *Planet Talk* newsletter and monthly email bulletin *Comet*. The *Upgrades* section of our website (**W** www.lonelyplanet.com) is also regularly updated by Lonely Planet authors, and the site's *Scoop* section covers news and current affairs relevant to travelers. Lastly, the *Thorn Tree* bulletin board and *Postcards* section carry unverified, but fascinating, reports from travelers.

Tell us about it! We genuinely value your feedback. A well-traveled team at Lonely Planet reads and acknowledges every email and letter we receive and ensures that every morsel of information finds its way to the relevant authors, editors and cartographers.

Everyone who writes to us will find their name listed in the next edition of the appropriate guidebook and will receive the latest issue of *Comet* or *Planet Talk*. The very best contributions will be rewarded with a free guidebook.

We may edit, reproduce and incorporate your comments in Lonely Planet products such as guidebooks, websites and digital products, so let us know if you don't want your comments reproduced or your name acknowledged.

How to contact Lonely Planet:
Online: **e** talk2us@lonelyplanet.com.au, **W** www.lonelyplanet.com
Australia: Locked Bag 1, Footscray, Victoria 3011
UK: 10a Spring Place, London NW5 3BH
USA: 150 Linden St, Oakland, CA 94607

Introduction

Canada is big, spacious, rugged, uncluttered and tremendously varied. You can stand in places where perhaps nobody else has ever stood and, the next day, find yourself in the cosmopolitan mix of a world-class city.

From the Atlantic Ocean it's over 7000km to the Pacific coast. In between you can enjoy a coffee and a croissant at a sidewalk café or canoe on a silent northern lake. You can peer down from the world's tallest freestanding structure or over the walls of a centuries-old fort. You can spy moose and bears in the forests or seals and whales in the oceans. You can hike snowcapped peaks or watch the sunset on a distant horizon.

Four very different seasons can bring the cold, harsh winters Canada is known for but also sweltering summer days. Short, explosive springs and intensely brilliant autumns mean dramatic transitions.

It's said that the national personality has been shaped by the harsh realities of life on the northern frontier. Because the country is so young, Canadians are still discovering their modern identity – but it's there, and it's distinctly different from the character of Canada's neighbor to the south.

The cultural mix of Canada is often described as a mosaic, not the melting pot of the USA. This patchwork of peoples includes British, French and many others, ranging from Europeans to Asians as well as the original Native peoples. Despite the diverse communities present here, Canada has long enjoyed a reputation for peace and safety. More than ever, these are welcome qualities.

With its history, people, landscape and natural beauty, Canada offers an abundance of well-known sites, cities, attractions, parks and regions that make for wonderful destinations whether you're looking for a trip that's educational, inspiring or just plain fun. But don't pass up a chance to explore the less-traveled areas, too – at the fringes of the inhabited world, great challenges, eye-opening experiences and hospitable people await.

Facts about Canada

Canada has an international reputation for grand scenery, open spaces, cleanliness, wildlife, livable cities, peace and diversity. A visit to even just a portion of this sprawling land won't alter those preconceptions, but it will likely add some new, personal perceptions.

Canada is the second-largest country in the world – nearly as big as all of Europe. Only Russia is larger. The population of over 31 million works out to close to just two people per square kilometer. In the countryside the population is very thinly spread – the average Canadian farm is 200 hectares in size.

Nearly 90% of Canadians, though, huddle along the 6379km southern border with the USA. It's the longest unguarded national boundary in the world. The southern region is, of course, the warmest, most hospitable area of the country and also has the best land and waterways. Three-quarters of the population live in the towns and cities in this portion of Canada, where Toronto is the largest city.

The country is made up of 10 provinces and three northern territories. The four coastal provinces in the east – Newfoundland, Nova Scotia, Prince Edward Island and New Brunswick – are known as the Atlantic Provinces. (The Maritime Provinces – the Maritimes – are the Atlantic provinces minus Newfoundland.) Québec and Ontario are collectively termed central Canada, although Canadians will often refer to this area as eastern Canada. The three generally flat midwestern provinces – Manitoba, Saskatchewan and Alberta – are the prairies. British Columbia, between the Rocky Mountains and the Pacific Ocean, is generally called the West Coast. The territories are Nunavut, the Northwest Territories (NT) and the Yukon. The national capital is Ottawa, Ontario.

There are two official languages in the country: English and French. A movement within Québec, the one predominantly French province, to separate from Canada and form a new country has waxed and waned since the mid-1960s.

Canada is a young country with great potential and a people working to forge a distinct national identity, while struggling to hold the parts together.

HISTORY

Recorded Canadian history, while short relative to much of the world, is full of intrigue. Colorful, dramatic, tragic and wonderful occurrences and stories abound. Much of it has been well documented by historians and writers for those wishing to delve further – see the Books section in the Facts for the Visitor chapter for suggestions.

In under several hundred years there has been the discovery and exploration of the country by Europeans. Their voyages and those of the settling pioneers are fascinating tales of the unveiling of a large part of the globe.

The aboriginal cultures the Europeans met and dealt with through the years of the fur trade and beyond make up contrasting chapters of the story. Battles between the French and the British, and the British and the USA, are other major themes.

Canadians have come to appreciate and admire their nation's history. National and Provincial Historic Sites and buildings of every description found across the country are well worth exploring.

Original Inhabitants

When Columbus 'discovered' America in 1492, thinking he had hit the lands south of China, vaguely called 'the Indies,' he sensibly called the people he found 'Indians.'

Ironically, he was nearly correct, for the Native Indians had come from Asia, across the Bering Strait, after the last great ice age – about 15,000 years ago. The earliest known occupation site in Canada is the Bluefish Caves of the Yukon.

By the time Columbus arrived, the descendants of these people had spread throughout the Americas, from Canada's frozen north to Tierra del Fuego at the southern tip of Argentina and Chile.

The major Native Indian cultures – Maya, Aztec and Inca – developed in Central and South America. Although no comparably sophisticated Native Indian societies sprang up in Canada, partially due to the climate, the tribes in Canada had evolved dramatically through prehistory. When the Europeans arrived, Native Indian people across the country had developed a multitude of languages, customs, religious beliefs, trading patterns, arts and crafts, highly specialized skills, laws and governments.

At this time, around the early 1500s, six distinct groupings of people could be discerned, each with its own language family and customs. These six major groups are classified by their geographic location.

The Arctic peoples lived in the far north. The subarctic group was found across the country from Newfoundland to British Columbia. The Eastern Woodland tribes lived across the top of the Great Lakes, along the St Lawrence River and in what was to become Nova Scotia, New Brunswick and Prince Edward Island. The plains people roamed across the prairies from Lake Winnipeg to the foothills of the Rocky Mountains. The peoples of the plateau area lived throughout central-southern British Columbia, and the northwest group ranged from Vancouver to Alaska along the Pacific coast, including the ocean islands of British Columbia.

Most of these peoples depended on hunting, fishing and gathering. The more complex societies lived on the mild West Coast and around the fertile southern Ontario and St Lawrence Valley region in the east. The Eastern Woodland people had developed agriculture and lived in more-or-less permanent settlements. The tribes of the north and midwest lived a more hand-to-mouth existence. The Inuit (meaning 'people,' and once called the Eskimos) eked out an existence in a world virtually unchanged until the 1950s.

Within each grouping were numerous tribes that, in turn, comprised numbers of smaller bands who came together to winter or in times of celebration or hardship and when marriage partners were sought. While many have disappeared, 53 distinct languages are still spoken, and many of these have various dialects. The existing languages fall into 11 broader families, most of which are independent from all the others. North America is generally considered to be one of the most complex linguistic regions in the world. Today, though, less than half of Canada's Native Indian people can speak their tribe's original language.

The Inuit, who arrived from Asia after the forefathers of all other Native Indians, are a separate people. There are about 150,000 Inuit in the Arctic areas of the USA, Russia, Greenland (Denmark) and Canada. Canada is home to roughly 38% of the total population.

The peaceful Inuit had little to do with the more southerly Native Indian groups and, other than meetings with European explorers around the northeast coast, remained in relative isolation. They were the last group of Native Canadians to give up the traditional, nomadic way of life, although even with more modern housing, many remain primarily hunters. Despite having to face brutal weather conditions and frequent starvation, the Inuit were a remarkably healthy lot and the pristine conditions helped protect them from disease and sickness. The arrival of European infectious diseases dramatically reduced their numbers to the point where their very survival was in question.

Today, however, the Canadian Inuit population is at about 41,000, which is more than when the Europeans first showed up. The Beothuks of Newfoundland did not fare so well. They ceased to exist as a people when the last two women died in the early 1800s.

Across the rest of Canada, the explorers and pioneers, both intentionally and by accident, brought to an end the way of life of all Native Indian people. The eastern tribes, such as those of the Iroquois Confederacy, had to side against each other with the French or English in their seemingly never-ending battles and ended up losing all their land.

The plains people, such as the Cree and Blackfoot, with their teepees, horses, bows and arrows and spectacular feathered headdresses – perhaps the archetypal Native Indian of North America – were forced into the Europeans' world by the virtual extinction of the buffalo.

The West Coast tribes, such as the Haida, were more fortunate: their isolation, strong tradition of independence and long, stable history afforded some protection.

Overall, European discovery and settlement of the country reduced Native Indians from about 350,000 to 100,000. Through treaty arrangements, the formation of reservations (now called reserves), and strong policing, notably by the Royal Canadian

Mounted Police (RCMP), the remaining groups were provided some measure of protection. Canada never had the all-out wars and massacres that marred the clash of cultures in the USA.

European Exploration

The first European visitors to Canada were the Vikings from Iceland and Greenland. There is evidence that they settled in northern Newfoundland at the eastern edge of Canada around AD 1000. How long they stayed, how much they explored and what happened to them is unknown.

It was around AD 1500 that the action around the Americas started to heat up. The Spanish, French, British and Italians all wanted in.

In Canada, it was the French who got first licks. After a few earlier exploratory visits by the Europeans in 1534, Jacques Cartier of France, a subject of King Francis I, reached the gulf of the St Lawrence River and claimed all the surrounding area for France. It was probably from Cartier that Canada got its name. Originally *Kanata,* a Huron-Iroquois word for 'village' or 'small community,' its derivative showed up in Cartier's journal. The name was used for the St Lawrence area and eventually became the official name of the new country.

The French didn't bother much with this new colony throughout the 16th century, but the pattern of economic development that began then has continued through to the present. This is, put bluntly and simply, the selling of its resources to whoever is buying, thus enabling the country to pay for everything else it needs. The first commodities prized by the French were the fish of the East Coast and furs for the fashion-conscious of France.

Samuel de Champlain, another Frenchman, began further explorations in the early 1600s. He settled Québec City, and Montréal was founded soon after in 1642 as a missionary outpost. Throughout the 17th century fur-trading companies dominated this new world. In 1663 Canada became a province of France. There were about 60,000 French settlers by then – the ancestors of a good percentage of today's French Canadians.

Throughout the 1600s the French fought the Native Indians, who soon realized that they were getting a raw deal in the fur trade

and through development of their lands. The French kept busy, too, with further explorations. They built a long chain of forts down to Louisiana – another major settlement – in what is now southern USA. In the 1730s another of the major French explorers, Pierre Gaultier de Varennes, Sieur de la Vérendrye, was responsible for another series of forts. This one stretched across the south of what are now the provinces of Ontario, Manitoba and Saskatchewan.

The Struggle for Power

The British, of course, weren't just sipping pints through all this. Though concentrating on the lands of America's East Coast, the Hudson's Bay Company (still one of Canada's main department-store chains, but now known simply as The Bay) had moved into the Hudson Bay area in northern Ontario around 1670.

The British soon muscled into settlements on the Canadian East Coast. By 1713 they had control over much of Nova Scotia and Newfoundland. And then, for a while, there was peace.

In 1745 a British army from New England, in what is now the USA, moved north and captured a French fort in Nova Scotia. The struggle for control of the new land was on. What is known as the French and Indian War began in 1754, and the war in Europe, known as the Seven Years' War, began in 1756. The French held the upper hand for the first four years. In one of Canada's most famous battles, the British defeated the French at Québec City in 1759. Both General Wolfe, leader of the British, and the Marquis de Montcalm, who led the French, were killed in battle. After this major victory, the British turned the tide. At the Treaty of Paris, in 1763, France handed Canada over to Britain.

The British, however, didn't quite know how to manage the newly acquired territory. The population was nearly exclusively French, and at that time in Britain, Roman Catholics enjoyed very few rights – they couldn't vote or hold office. In 1774 the Québec Act gave the French Canadians the right to their religion, the use of French civil law in court and the possibility of assuming political office. The British, however, maintained positions of power and influence in both politics and business. It was during this period that the seeds of the Québec separatist movement were sown.

During the American Revolution (1775–83) against Britain, about 50,000 settlers – termed 'Loyalists' due to their loyalty to Britain – shifted north to Canada. They settled mainly in the Atlantic Provinces and Ontario.

This migration helped to balance the number of French and British in Canada. Soon after, Québec and Ontario were formed with their own governors. Throughout the late 1700s and into the 1800s Canada's frontiers were pushed farther and farther afield. Sir Arthur Mackenzie explored the northwest and the Mackenzie River, which was named after him, as well as much of British Columbia. Simon Fraser followed a river, which was later named after him, to the Pacific Ocean. David Thompson traveled the Columbia River, also in British Columbia. And in 1812, Lord Selkirk formed a settlement of Scottish immigrants around the Red River Valley near Winnipeg, Manitoba.

Also in 1812, the last war between Canada and the USA, the War of 1812, began. Its causes were numerous, but the USA's attempt to take over its northern neighbor was only part of the campaign against Britain. Each side won a few battles, and in 1814 a draw was declared.

Dominion Period

With the end of the US threat and the resulting confidence in themselves, many colonists became fed up with aspects of British rule. Some spoke out for independence. In both Upper (Ontario) and Lower (Québec) Canada, brief rebellions broke out. In 1840 both areas united under one government. But by this stage, the population in Upper (British, mainly) outnumbered that in Lower Canada (French) and wanted more than a half-say. The government became bogged down, with Britain attempting to work out something new.

Britain, of course, didn't want to lose Canada, as it had the USA, so it stepped lightly and decided on a confederation giving a central government some powers and the individual colonies others.

In 1867 the British North America Act (BNA Act) was passed by the British government. This established the Dominion of Canada and included Ontario, Québec, Nova Scotia and New Brunswick. The BNA Act became Canada's equivalent to a constitution, though it was far less detailed and all-inclusive than that of the USA.

John Alexander Macdonald (known as Sir John A) became Canada's first prime minister. The total population was 3½ million, nearly all living in the east and mostly on farms. It had been decided at the Act's signing in 1867 that other parts of the country should be included in the Dominion whenever possible.

The completion of the Canadian Pacific Railway – one of Canada's great historical sagas – joined the West Coast to the East, thereby linking the west with the Dominion. By 1912 all provinces had become part of the central government except Newfoundland, which finally joined in 1949.

In the last few years of the 19th century Canada received large numbers of immigrants, mainly from Europe. The government continued to grapple with French and British differences. These reached a peak during WWI, a conflict that Canada had entered immediately on Britain's behalf. In 1917, despite bitter French opposition in Québec, the Canadian government began a military draft.

Modern Era

After WWI Canada slowly grew in stature and prosperity, and in 1931 became a voluntary member of the Commonwealth.

With the onset of WWII, Canada once again supported Britain, but this time also began entering into defense agreements with the USA, and after the attack on Pearl Harbor, declared war on Japan.

In the years after WWII Canada experienced another massive wave of European immigration. The postwar period saw economic expansion and well-being right across North America. The 1950s were a time of unprecedented wealth, and the middle class mushroomed.

The 1960s brought social upheaval and social-welfare programs, with their ideals and liberalism. Canada's first Bill of Rights was signed in 1960. Nuclear-power generators and US nuclear warheads became major issues in Canada.

The Québec separatist movement attracted more attention. A small group used terrorism to press its point for an independent Québec.

In 1967 the country celebrated its 100th anniversary with the World's Fair (Expo 67), held in Montréal, as one of the highlights.

Internationally known politico Pierre Elliot Trudeau, a Liberal, became prime minister in 1968 and held power almost continually until his retirement in 1984. Despite great initial support, Trudeau was, to be kind, not a popular man at the end of his stay.

In 1976 the Parti Québecois (PQ), advocating separatism, won the Québec provincial election. But in 1980 a Québec referendum found that 60% of Québeckers were against independence and the topic faded.

Under Trudeau, the Canadian Constitution, one of the last steps in full independence from Britain, came into being in 1982, along with a Charter of Rights and Freedoms. Québec, wanting to be recognized as a 'distinct society' with special rights, never ratified the agreement and it was passed without its participation. Later talks to bring it into the fold, and thus make the agreement more national, have failed.

The 1984 election saw Brian Mulroney's Progressive Conservative party sweep into power with a tremendous nationwide majority, slamming the door on the Trudeau era. The 1988 World Economic Summit of the seven major industrial nations was held in Toronto, and the Winter Olympics were hosted in Calgary, each bringing greatly increased prestige and favorable attention to Canada's somewhat fragile international self-image. The government was reelected to another five-year term in 1988.

Following the customary pattern this government, too, fell from grace with a loud thump. Among the major issues through the later Mulroney years were the very controversial free-trade alliance with the USA and the attempt to reach a consensus, known as the Meech Lake Accord, on overhauling the distinctions between provincial and federal powers, rights and jurisdictions. Another live wire was the introduction of a Goods and Services Tax (GST).

In 1993 and again in 1997, the Liberals, led by Québecker Jean Chrétien, won elections handily. Chrétien, a one-time associate of Trudeau, and known for his strong French accent, has been around a long time, knows the ropes and appeals with his apparent lack of artifice and posturing.

The USA pushed for, and got, an extension to the Free Trade Agreement (FTA), which included Mexico in the North American Free Trade Agreement (NAFTA).

In 1995, under Premier Lucien Bouchard, another Québec independence referendum was held in Québec. Again it was voted down but a ballot could barely be wedged through the margin of victory. Since that narrow defeat separation enthusiasm has fallen in favor of Canadian unity. Though the possibility of Québec forming a distinct political entity at some point is always hovering over provincial-federal affairs, Bernard Landry, the new PQ leader and premier of Québec, isn't making any headway.

The late '90s and early new millennium have been uneventful politically, with the Liberals content to softly cruise without rocking anybody's boat. The huge deficit has been decreased. After the September 11, 2001, terrorist attacks in the USA the government began spending money on security and the Armed Forces, areas that had been ignored for decades. Immigration was tightened up and, controversially, police powers increased.

Current issues also include maintaining social programs such as a 'free' universal Medicare system, homelessness and the federal share of provincial and municipal social expenses. The country's high taxes are also a contentious matter. Skirmishes continue between Canada and the USA regarding trade, in both industry and culture.

Internationally, Canada maintains its position in NATO and as one of the so-called G-7 countries. (The G-7 group of Germany, France, the USA, the UK, Japan, Italy and Canada meets regularly to develop major economic policies.)

Canadian troops continue to be among the world's foremost peacekeepers, working not only in the Middle East and Cyprus, but also playing leading roles in Somalia, Kuwait and Yugoslavia. In early 2002, they went to Afghanistan in a more militaristic role to aid the Americans in tracking down Taliban fighters. Canadians also offered physical and monetary aid to New York City after the World Trade Center destruction.

GEOGRAPHY

Canada is about 7730km from east to west. The nation's only neighbor is the USA, which includes Alaska in the northwest. With such size the country can boast a tremendous variety of topography.

Though much of the land is lake- and river-filled forest, there are mountains, plains and even a small desert. Canada has (or shares with the USA) seven of the world's largest lakes and also contains three of the globe's 20 longest rivers. The country is blessed with the most freshwater of any country. About 25% of the country is covered in forest. Canada's highest mountain, Mt Logan, at 5951m, is found in the southwest Yukon.

Despite being bordered on three sides by oceans, Canada is not generally viewed as a maritime country. This is in part due to the large, central regions, which contain the bulk of the population and dominate in so many ways. Also, the Rocky Mountains and Niagara Falls, the country's two best-known and most-visited geographic features, are found inland.

From eastern Québec to the eastern edge of the country, the Atlantic Ocean plays a major part in the population's day-to-day life and offers the visitor much to discover and explore. The same can be said of the Pacific Ocean and British Columbia to the west.

Canada can be divided into seven geographic regions, each with its own characteristic scenery and landforms. The far eastern area, the Appalachian Region, includes Newfoundland, Prince Edward Island, New Brunswick, Nova Scotia and the part of Québec south of the St Lawrence River. The land is mainly hilly and wooded.

The St Lawrence–Great Lakes Lowland is roughly the area between Québec City and Windsor, Ontario, and includes most of the country's large towns, cities and industry. In all, about half of Canada's population lives here. The land, originally forested, later nearly all used for farming, is generally flat.

Centrally, south of the vast Hudson Bay, the most dominant characteristics of the Canadian map are the Hudson Bay–Arctic Lowlands. This region is mainly flat, bog or muskeg – little inhabited or visited, with the notable exception of Churchill, Manitoba.

Most of the north is taken up by the Canadian Shield, also known as the Precambrian Shield, formed 2½ billion years ago. This geographic area covers all of northern Manitoba, Ontario and Québec and also stretches farther east across Labrador and west across northern Saskatchewan to the northern boundary of Alberta. It's an enormous ancient, rocky, glacially sanded region of typical Canadian river-and-lake-filled timberland. It is also extremely rugged, cool and little-developed, with mining and logging the two primary ingredients in human settlement. This semi-remote area is best explored by visiting and/or camping in the government parks throughout the region.

The fifth region, the Great Plains, runs through southern Manitoba, Saskatchewan and parts of lower Alberta. The plains, formerly grasslands, make up a huge, flat region now responsible for Canada's abundant wheat crop.

The sixth geographic area is the Mountain or Western Cordillera Region covering British Columbia, the Yukon and parts of Alberta. Mountains dominate this region: the Rocky Mountains form the eastern edge of the area rising from 2000m to 4000m. Between them and the coastal peaks lie a series of lesser mountain ranges and valleys. Among the latter is the long, narrow valley called the Rocky Mountain Trench.

The interior of British Columbia consists of countless troughs, plateaus, hills, gorges, basins and river deltas. The province is by far the most scenically varied and spectacular in the country. Farther north, the 20 highest mountains in the country are found in the Yukon.

Lastly, there is the far north, the Arctic region. The northernmost section of the north is made up of islands frozen together for much of the year.

CLIMATE

Canada has four distinct seasons, all of which occur right across the country although their arrival times vary. The single most significant factor in climate, and even day-to-day weather, is latitude. In just a few hours traveling north by road, a drop (sometimes a considerable one) in temperature is often felt.

The warmest area of Canada is along the US border. It's no accident that nearly everybody lives in this southernmost region. The overall warmest areas of the country are British Columbia's south and central coast and southern Ontario particularly the area around the Niagara Peninsula. These

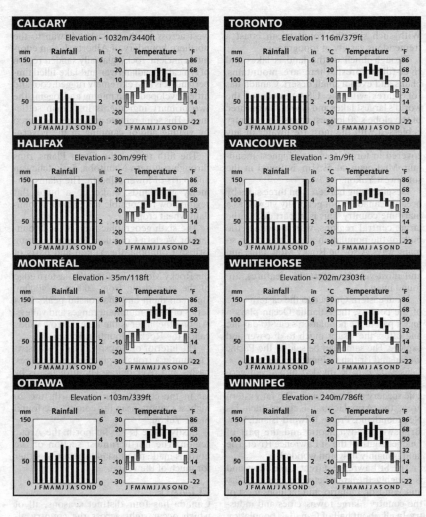

districts have the longest summers and the shortest winters.

July and August are the warmest months across the country and generally they are reasonably dry. Along the US border, summer temperatures are usually in the mid and upper 20°C range. Each year there are a few days in the 30°C range. Manitoba through to central British Columbia gets the hottest summer temperatures as well as the most sunshine. The west and east coasts are very wet with 2500mm of precipitation a year but much of that is through the winter

months. The prairies are fairly dry all year, but southeastern Canada including Montréal, Ottawa and Toronto can be quite humid in summer and damp in winter.

Ontario and Québec have warm summers without a lot of rain. Southern Ontario can be hot in midsummer. The east coast is generally cooler than the rest of the country and can have more summer rain as well.

Summers in the Yukon, the Northwest Territories and Nunavut can be pleasantly warm and have the added benefit of extremely long daylight hours. Outside the main cities, anywhere in Canada, nights are cool year-round.

Canadian winters are long. In more than two-thirds of the country the average January temperature is -18°C. The major cities are not consistently this cold, but temperatures are generally below freezing. Except in the warmest areas, snowfall can be heavy – especially from Toronto east. As a rule of thumb the farther north, the more snow. But only to a point: once past the central portion of the country, the dry conditions prevent snowfall of major accumulation. See the climate charts for more details on specific areas.

GOVERNMENT & POLITICS

Canada's form of the government is a constitutional monarchy.

Canada is ruled by a parliamentary system, with the head of state officially remaining the monarch of Britain. Within Canada the appointed governor general is the monarch's representative. The upper house, or Senate, also made up of appointees, is deemed to be the house of review (the home of 'sober second thought') regarding any potential legislation. Mostly it acts as a rubber stamp for the wishes of the elected lower house, or House of Commons. Senate reform, or its abolition, is an ongoing debate within the country.

The head of the political party with the most elected representatives in the House of Commons becomes the prime minister, the leader of the country. From the members of parliament within the governing party, the prime minister selects a cabinet that initiates legislation and, in effect, runs the country. Unlike in the USA, leaders can run for as long as they maintain popular support within their party. Governments are elected for five years, but elections can be called for earlier, either voluntarily by the prime minister, or, rarely, through a procedural motion following a lack of support in the House.

The 10 provinces are essentially self-governing and are presided over by premiers, elected provincially. Each province has a lieutenant governor appointed by the federal government. The three northern territories are, for the most part, the domain of the federal government, although more independence is being sought and some has

Symbols & Cymbals

Canada's current flag was selected in 1965 after 2000 public design entries were hotly debated in parliament. The side bars represent the ocean boundaries and are not blue because an important reason for the entire procedure was to show Canada's independence from Britain and France. Between 1924 and 1965, before the new flag was designed, the Red Ensign, which included a Union Jack, rippled over the country. Each province also has its own flag, few of which would be recognized by most Canadians. The white and blue 'fleur de lys' of Québec is probably an exception.

The national anthem, 'O Canada,' was composed by Calixa Lavalée in 1880.

been granted to Nunavut, formerly the eastern part of the Northwest Territories.

The constitution consists of both written proclamations under the Constitution Acts (1867 and 1932) and unwritten conventions. Updating, changing and clarifying constitutional matters and the balance of powers between the provinces, and between the provinces and the federal government, are long-running contentious issues.

Political Parties

From the middle of the 20th century until the 1990s, the party structure was somewhere between stable and staid. The three principal political parties were the Liberals (who for much of the country's history have virtually owned the reins of power), the Progressive Conservatives (not a lot unlike the Liberals, but without the success) and the New Democratic Party (NDP; known by its opponents as the 'socialist menace').

The Progressive Conservatives (Tories) were voted in every once in a while, apparently as an effort to keep the Liberals (Grits) somewhat humble and honest. The NDP has never formed a federal government and has always come up third. It has, however, ruled provincially (in several provinces) and generally accepts its opposition status, considering itself the 'conscience of the nation' keeping leftist initiatives on the burners.

After the 1993 Liberal landslide, the situation changed. The Conservatives and NDP were close to being wiped off the political map and haven't recovered.

The Reform party – based exclusively in the west and espousing strong right-wing social, economic and political policies – arose, took over second place and is now the Official Opposition. After much debate and mockery, the name was changed to the Canadian Alliance. They have embarrassed themselves consistently and made no inroads elsewhere in the country. So the country has pretty much become a one-trick show with no relief in sight.

The Bloc Québecois (BQ), the Québec independence-seeking party, is now ranked third. It has no members outside Québec and also presents the Liberals with no serious threat. There is a Green Party, but it does not have a significant profile. Prime Minister Jean Chrétien seems content to glide along indefinitely and most Canadians accept that with equanimity.

Provincially, the three main parties remain the Liberals, the Progressive Conservatives and the NDP. In British Columbia the Social Credit Party periodically forms a government. The provincial parties generally keep their distance from their federal cousins and act independently from them. The voters, too, treat them differently and have elected the NDP in four provinces since the mid-1980s. The Parti Québécois (PQ), a Québec provincial party, stresses Québec rights and fuels the diminishing dream of separation.

ECONOMY

Canadians enjoy the high standard of living that major Western countries are accustomed to and tend to take for granted. However, maintaining the wealth experienced by the previous generation is becoming ever more difficult, even elusive. The middle class is dwindling under high taxation, government and private downsizing and heavy debt. Today nearly half the workforce is women and by far the majority of households have two incomes, often by necessity.

The Canadian economy is based, as it always has been, on abundant natural resources. These natural renewable and non-renewable riches include fish, timber and wood products, minerals, natural gas, oil and hydroelectricity. Although only 5% of the land is arable, the agricultural sector – primarily in wheat and barley – accounts for much of the Canadian export total.

Manufacturing has long been a weak component of the economy and today employs just 14% of the country's workers. The most important manufactured product is motor vehicles. High-tech industries and developers in the space and computer fields (both software and hardware) are playing increasing roles in the economy.

By far the largest part of the economy, at a whopping 75%, is in services, which includes an enormous civil service. Banking, insurance, education, communication and consulting bring in foreign exchange. The rest of the service sector does not.

The country's major trading partner is the USA, although businesspeople are increasingly strengthening ties with Japan, China and all of the Pacific Rim. Mexico, too, is poised to become a major trading partner.

The high degree of foreign ownership of Canadian business has also been problematic, drawing profits away from the country. Overall, about 40% of the country's industry is owned by non-Canadians, led by US interests.

Currently unemployment hovers around 8%, with regional variations, and the inflation rate is under 2%. Canada's Gross Domestic Product (GDP; sometimes called the annual economic output) was $1,056,010 (in millions) for the year 2000. The Gross National Income (GNI), formerly called the Gross National Product, was US$21,050 per capita. This figure is made up of the GDP plus the income earned from investments abroad.

Canada has an immense 'underground economy.' This does not refer simply to various, more or less traditional, criminal activities, but the hidden transactions of legitimate businesses done in order to avoid paying tax. Estimates of the extent of this underground economy range to over 20% of the country's internal economic output. This is a staggering amount of taxes going unpaid, which means rates have to go up. This means people feel hard done by and so redouble their efforts to avoid paying. The car mechanic offers a tune-up, you offer to fix his plumbing; you stay at my B&B, I'll design you a brochure. The variations are infinite. There are even 'contra' or service-exchange clubs to join. All by word of mouth, of course.

Many transactions are done 'under the table,' meaning paid for in cash with no bills, receipts, written guarantees or paperwork generated. Offering to pay cash usually results in a lower price as well as the tax saving.

POPULATION & PEOPLE

Canada's population is 31,156,393 (2001). About 35% of Canadians are of British stock. French descendants of the original pioneers long made up about 30% of the

population, but this is now about 20% and falling. By far the majority of people of French descent live in Québec, but there are large numbers in New Brunswick, Ontario and Manitoba.

The English-speaking population has grown mainly by immigration from Britain and the USA. Over 3½ million Canadians are of Scottish or Irish ancestry.

Generally speaking, the French are Catholic, the British Protestant, but religion does not play a large part in Canadian life.

Early central and eastern European settlers went to the prairies, but can now be

---

Up with the Push-Up Bra, Down with the Zipper

Canadians can lay claim to quite an assortment of the products of human ingenuity, a real mixed bag of inventions and firsts. The Native Indians have given the world snowshoes and the birch-bark canoe; the Inuit developed the winter parka and accompanying boots known as mukluks, and the kayak. More recent Canadian inventions include the electron microscope and the manipulat-able space arm used on the US space shuttle. Canadians have also been active in the food arena. Important research developed strains of wheat suitable to a variety of world climates. Pablum, a baby cereal, was created in Canada. The country's most important, best-known fruit, the Mac-Intosh apple, comes from a wild apple tree found in Ontario that was reproduced through grafting. The chocolate bar was created by Ganong Brothers Ltd, which still produces bars and chocolates in St Stephen, New Brunswick. Canada Dry Ginger Ale is found throughout the world. Ice wine has gained international converts.

Other firsts include the paint roller (a simple yet great little device), the wireless photograph transmitter, the friction match, the chainsaw, lawn sprinklers, the horse-race starting gate and the snowmobile. To clear snow, the rotating snowplow was created in 1911, and 10 years later the snowblower was devised. Canadians have pioneered the development of short take-off and landing aircraft. For trains the observation car, known as the dome car, was designed in Canada. The use of calcium carbide-acetylene gas for light was discovered by Canadian Thomas Wilson. It replaced kerosene, another Canadian invention, and led to the formation of the giant Union Carbide Company. Standard Time, adopted around the world, was devised in Canada.

The push-up bra was created by Canadelle in Montréal in 1963 and will probably be the one invention in this list you'll remember. But Canada can also lay claim to the all-important clothes zipper. Insulin was discovered by Banting and Best in 1921. Cobalt, the radiation source stronger than X rays that is used to treat cancer around the world, was developed in Canada. The first battery-less radio was invented in Canada in 1925. The first all-electric, battery-less radio station followed two years later, in Toronto; called CFRB, it's still transmitting and to this day is the most listened to in the country. IMAX large-format films and technology were developed by a Canadian company.

Greenpeace, one of the world's predominant environmental groups, was founded in Vancouver. On the other hand, the green plastic garbage bag was also created in Canada. Two Canadians devised that 1980s classic, Trivial Pursuit, a board game that outsold Monopoly. The inexpensive Laser sailboat, globally popular, was designed by Canadians. Ice hockey was developed in the mid-1800s. And, to the chagrin of the country's US friends, it should be noted that the game of basketball was created by a Canadian. Lastly, let's praise the tuck-away handles on beer cases before toasting this list.

🍁 🍁 🍁 🍁 🍁 🍁 🍁 🍁 🍁 🍁 🍁 🍁 🍁 🍁 🍁 🍁 🍁 🍁 🍁

found everywhere, particularly in the large cities. Canada's third-largest ancestral ethnic group is German. Other major groups are Italian, Chinese, Ukrainian, Dutch, Greek, Polish and Scandinavian. In 1997, Chinese surpassed Italian as the third most common tongue in Canada.

Since 1990, other Asians and, to a lesser degree, Latin Americans and blacks from the Caribbean have been immigrating in larger numbers. Four out of five immigrants have neither English nor French as their mother tongue. Canada receives refugees from around the world. Unlike the early days of rapid expansion and settlement, today's arrivals head for the large cities. Toronto, the center for immigration, is one of the world's most cosmopolitan cities.

Aboriginal Peoples

There are about 554,000 Native Indians and 41,000 Inuit in Canada's population, vastly more than when Europeans first arrived. There are also about 210,000 Métis, the name used to denote those of mixed aboriginal and European ancestry. All together the three groups make up about 3% of Canada's total population. The majority live in the Yukon, the Northwest Territories and Ontario, but every province has some aboriginal communities. Native Indians and Inuit now have the highest birthrates in the country.

(Note: In North America, Indians from the Asian subcontinent are often called East Indians in order to distinguish them from the indigenous peoples. People from the Caribbean countries are sometimes referred to as West Indians.)

Inuit is the general name for the Eskimo peoples in Canada. This is their preferred name, as it distinguishes them from the Eskimo of Asia or the Aleuts of the Aleutian Islands.

Collectively the Native Indians, Inuit and Métis are also called Native Canadians. Another term that has gained currency is 'First Nations,' which recognizes the one-time independent status of individual aboriginal groups.

Since the early pioneering days the Native Indians' lot has been marked by sadness and tragedy. At first their numbers dropped dramatically with the influx of European diseases. Then they lost not only their power and traditions, but also their land and eventually, in many cases, their self-respect.

There are about 2250 reserves scattered across Canada and 600 government-registered Native Indian 'bands,' which has become a political and organizational term. Every Native Indian is officially affiliated with a band. Some bands own more than one reserve.

Over 70% of Native Indians live on these government reserves, most in poverty and on some form of government assistance. In the cities, with little education and few modern skills, many end up on the streets without a job or a place to live. Infant mortality, life expectancy, literacy, income and incarceration rates all compare unfavorably with those of other Canadians.

Native Indian leaders have, since the early 1980s, become more political, making stands on constitutional matters, land claims and mineral rights. A range of national organizations, such as the Assembly of First Nations, keeps Native Indian interests from being pushed aside. It is through these channels, however slow-moving, that the Native Indian voice will make the changes it feels necessary. Most Canadians feel the aboriginal peoples have had a raw deal and sympathize with many of their complaints.

This, however, has so far not resulted in the introduction of many concrete attempts to improve the situation. Sporadically ugly, highly publicized and potentially deadly confrontations arise across the country. Native Indian roadblocks and armed camps have erupted and disrupted the status quo. Accordingly, both provincial and federal governments are finding it less and less possible to ignore the state of affairs, and many issues regarding Native Indian rights and claims are currently before the courts. Among the issues to be dealt with is some form of self-government for aboriginal peoples. Native Indian schools to provide control over religious and language instruction and a Native Indian justice system are being discussed and slowly implemented on a district-by-district basis. Fishing and hunting rights and taxation are other debated subjects.

Native Indians have also become more active in revitalization movements that encourage spirituality, culture, language and a respect for their history. Celebratory powwows, to which non–Native Indians are welcome, are now a regular cultural occurrence.

EDUCATION

Under the jurisdiction of the provinces, Canada provides free education from elementary through secondary school. Beyond that tuition must be paid in what are known as community colleges (Cégeps in Québec) and universities, although the true cost is subsidized through taxes. Community colleges present one- to three-year programs in a range of fields from graphic design to jewelry-making to nursing. These are taught under the broad categories of arts, business, science and technology, and health services. Universities provide higher academic and professional training.

At the early levels, there are two basic school systems, known as the public and the separate. Both are free and essentially the same, but the latter is designed for Catholics and offers more religious education along with the so-called three 'Rs,' reading, (w)riting and (a)rithmetic. Anyone can join either one, but the two systems do split pretty much along religious denomination.

French-immersion programs, in which English-speaking children are taught all their courses in French, are an option in some urban schools across Canada.

There are also a number of private schools, but no real private system. Schools in this category include alternative educational methods, such as Waldorf and Montessori. The educational system has been under increased scrutiny in recent years. With many students leaving high school (the latter three to four years of secondary school) faring poorly in international testing, being called essentially illiterate by universities and, according to business leaders, poorly prepared for jobs in industry, education reform has been an ongoing topic.

In order to combat these shortcomings, a reemphasis has been placed on the fundamentals and on standardized curriculums and testing. Lack of government funding is a continuing concern.

About 85% of Canadians graduate from high school and 70% of them then go on to college or university. Students from around the world attend Canadian universities.

ARTS
Literature

Canada has produced an impressive body of writing. Most of it has appeared since the 1940s.

Among the best-known, most-read poets are EJ Pratt, Earle Birney, Gwendolyn McEwen, Irving Layton, Leonard Cohen (who also wrote the lesser-known novels *Beautiful Losers* and *The Favourite Game*), bp Nichol (for concrete poetry), Milton Acorn and Al Purdy. Montréaler Anne Carson, who wrote *Beauty of the Husband* (2001) and *Men in the Off Hours,* is gaining a major international reputation for her unique writing and intense themes. One of the world's favorite poems, the straightforward but poignant *In Flanders Fields* was written by Canadian soldier John McCrae in 1915.

Perhaps more familiar internationally are short-story writers and novelists including Margaret Atwood, Morley Callaghan, Robertson Davies, Marion Engel, Timothy Findley, Margaret Laurence, WO Mitchell, Alice Munro, Michael Ondaatje, Mordecai Richler and Rudy Wiebe. *Who has Seen the Wind,* Mitchell's best-known book, is about a boy growing up in Weyburn, Saskatchewan, the birthplace of the author.

Humorist Stephen Leacock's *Sketches of a Little Town,* based on Orillia, a town at the north end of Lake Simcoe in Ontario, has been called the most Canadian book ever written.

Elizabeth Smart's *By Grand Central Station I Sat Down and Wept* is slight in size but powerful in impact. Nancy Kilpatrick (also known as Amarantha Knight) writes horror, often about vampires, sometimes very sexual ones, with Canadian settings.

WP Kinsella writes of contemporary Native Indian life as well as baseball and is best known for *Shoeless Joe,* which was made into the film *Field of Dreams,* with Kevin Costner. Kinsella's *Dance Me Outside* was made into a film with a Native Indian cast. Brian Moore's *Black Robe* is about Native Indian–European relations in the 17th century and has been filmed, too.

Rohinton Mistry has been heaped with international praise for his novels *Such a Long Journey* and *A Fine Balance.* Nino Ricci's excellent books, including *Lives of the Saints,* deal partially with being an immigrant in Canada. Also from the 1990s like

Native Indian Literature

An intriguing branch of Canadian literature is the increasing voice of Native Indian writers. Born from a need to tell their side and truths and a desire to share and celebrate the wealth of their own cultures, Native Indian work produced since the 1980s or so includes some powerful and challenging novels, stories, plays and poetry. It's literature that breaks new ground and old rules, much of it drawing from the rich Native Indian tradition of oral storytelling.

Written initially as a letter to herself, Maria Campbell's autobiography *Halfbreed* was published in 1973 and became a best-seller. Like other Native Indian writers, Campbell emphasizes the need for authors to reclaim their own language. Many writers are angered at the appropriation of Native Indian stories by European authors. After having their land taken and their culture undermined, many saw the 'stealing' of their own stories as the last straw – the irony being that it is non–Native Indians who need those stories and the values they speak of the most.

The struggle for Native Indian self-determination was explored by Jeannette Armstrong in her internationally acclaimed novel *Slash*, published in 1985. Also successful was Beatrice Culleton's 1983 novel *In Search of April Raintree*, about the lives of two Métis girls. Another recommended novel is Ruby Slipperjack's *Honour the Sun*. Published in 1987, it charts the development of a young girl growing up in an isolated, fractured community. In 1992 she published *Silent Words* and in 2000 *Weesquachak & the Lost Ones*.

Thompson Highway has also been internationally recognized for his two very successful plays *The Rez Sisters* and *Dry Lips Oughta Move to Kapuskasing*. Though Highway, who sees theater as a natural extension of the storytelling medium, is perhaps the most widely known Native Indian playwright, he is just one of many working across the country. In 1998 his first novel, *Kiss of the Fur Queen*, appeared. In 2001 his first children's book, *Caribou Song* (part Cree, part English), was published. Ian Ross won the governor general's award for his play *FareWel*, which played in Toronto in 1998.

In 1996, Richard Van Kamp's *The Lesser Blessed* became the first Native Indian novel written in the Northwest Territories. He published short stories in 2001 in *Angel Wing Splash Pattern*. BC's Eden Robinson published her novel *Monkey Beach*, about a Native Indian woman's coming of age, to great reviews in 2000. The stories in her *Trapline's* lay bare the realities of reserve life. Robert Alexie's first novel, the semi-autobiographical *Porcupines & China Dolls*, was wonderfully received in 2002. He lives in Inuvik, NWT.

There are also excellent recent poetry and short-story anthologies. *Achimoona*, published in 1985, contains short fiction by younger Native Indian writers. *All My Relations*, published in 1990, is a large collection of short stories edited by writer Thomas King. The anthology *Seventh Generation*, edited by Heather Hodgson and published in 1989, contains a collection of contemporary Native Indian poetry. *Bent Box*, by Lee Maracle, published in 2000, was well received.

Ahtahkakoop (1999), the biography of a legendary Cree chief, by Deanna Christenson, is a powerful and tragic multidimensional work.

these, Carol Shields' *The Stone Diaries* met critical and popular success.

Largely unknown but internationally praised are Alistair MacLeod's *Island* (short stories, 2000) and *No Great Mischief* (novel, 1999).

Douglas Coupland in *Generation X*, *Shampoo Planet* and *Life After God* writes about the world of those in their 20s and 30s. William Gibson, in work such as *Neuromancer* and *Count Zero*, has a futuristic 'cyberpunk' perspective. His story *Johnny*

Mnemonic was made into a Canadian film in 1995. Anne Marie MacDonald's excellent *Fall On Your Knees* (1996), set in Cape Breton Island, is both weighty and emotional.

Newer, lesser-known writers to consider include Andrew Pyper, Russell Smith and Kenneth Harvey. *Concrete Forest* (1998), edited by Hal Niedzvieki, is a collection of stories by young urban writers.

English writer Malcolm Lowry spent most of his productive writing years in

British Columbia – many of them in a basic shack on the beach near Vancouver.

French Québec writers who are widely read in English include Anne Hebert, Marie-Claire Blais, Roch Carrier, Mavis Gallant and Gabrielle Roy. Extremely reclusive novelist Réjean Ducharme of Montréal is considered one of the major French-language writers. His latest book is *Va Savoir*.

Most good bookstores have a Canadiana section with both fiction and nonfiction works. Canada seems to produce writers who excel in the short story, so an anthology of these would make a good introduction to Canadian fiction. For a short-story collection, try one of the anthologies published annually by Oberon Press or by Penguin.

For more information, consult *The Oxford Companion to Canadian Literature*.

Music

Canadian musicians have become increasingly and deservedly well known in the past few decades, with many achieving international stature. The country has always tended to produce individualistic musicians who emphasize lyrics and personal sentiments.

Many of the most-established names have found it necessary to temporarily or permanently reside in the USA.

Canadians have perhaps been best known in the field of folk and folk rock. Among the top names are Leonard Cohen, Bruce Cockburn, Gordon Lightfoot, Joni Mitchell, Stompin' Tom and Neil Young.

Stretching this style are Jann Arden, the Barenaked Ladies, Blue Rodeo, the Cowboy Junkies and Kate & Anna McGarrigle.

Sarah McLachlan further adds both a poppy and rock flavor to wonderful effect. Nelly Furtado has come out of nowhere and become huge with her mega-hit 'I'm Like a Bird.' Chantal Kreviazuk has a thoughtful, personal style.

Vancouver's vocal group soulDecision has had some big pop hits *and* they play their own instruments. Wide Mouth Mason and 54 40 are solid pop-rock bands. Alanis Morissette, from Ottawa, is a distinctive pop-rock singer.

In rock, big names include Bryan Adams, Tom Cochrane, Amanda Marshall, Our Lady Peace and The Tragically Hip. The Rheostatics and Matthew Good Band make

edgy smart-rock. Nickelback has earned followers for its harder rock.

Jeff Healey and Colin James both play scintillating blues guitar. Blues artist Sue Foley has gained critical recognition as a singer-songwriter-guitarist and has opened for major blues players across North America.

In urban music (gaining widespread fans), check out hip-hop artists Kardinal Offishall, Swollen Members, Maestro and Rascalz. R&B artist Deborah Cox has had major success across North America. Jacksoul is a solid pop/R&B group.

In a country vein, Shania Twain, originally from Timmins, Ontario, is the reigning queen. Patricia Conroy, George Fox, kd lang, Anne Murray, Prairie Oyster, Rita McNeil, and Ian and Sylvia Tyson (both now solo artists) are others. Noncommercial is Fred Eaglesmith, who is great to catch live.

Among singers from Québec who are rarely heard outside that province, except perhaps in France, Gilles Vigneault could be the biggest name. Others are Michel Rivard and Daniel Lavois. Claude Leveillee and Isabelle Boulay are now very popular, but there are many more. Montréal's Lhasa, singing in Spanish, surprises with her passionate global sound. The province boasts its own successful pop, rock and semi-traditional folk bands and artists. Celine Dion, from Montréal, keeps rolling along with 'My Heart Will Go On' from the movie *Titanic* bringing superstardom.

The traditional Celtic-based music of the Atlantic Provinces remains popular in that region and efforts to hear some are recommended. *No Boundaries,* by fiddler Natalie MacMaster, is a fine album. The Barra MacNeils, the Rankins, Ashley MacIsaac, and the Irish Descendants bring this music to wider audiences. From Ontario are the Irish traditionalists, Leahy.

Loreena McKennitt has fashioned an Irish-based World Music sound all her own. Also in a global style is Jesse Cook playing flamenco guitar.

Buffy Sainte-Marie was the first in an increasing lineup of Native Indian musicians that includes Inuit singer Susan Aglukark. First Nations is a record label producing Native Indian musicians. Two contemporary acts are Kashtin and Lawrence Martin.

Pianist Oscar Peterson is the country's highest-profile jazz musician, followed by newcomer Diana Krall, a jazz pianist and vocalist who has been selling like a pop star.

Holly Cole sings a mix of jazz, pop and classic standards in a nightclubby style.

Saxophonist Jane Bunnett began playing a blend of jazz and Cuban music before it was popular and continues to make great music in that vein.

The Philosopher Kings play an amazing blend of jazz and R&B, dense music with sweet vocals.

In the classical field, Canada's best-known artists include guitarist Liona Boyd, the late pianist Glenn Gould, soprano Teresa Stratus and composer R Murray Schafer.

In opera, international star Ben Heppner is the country's best-known tenor.

Film

Canadian film is well respected abroad primarily through the work of the National Film Board (NFB; **w** www.nfb.ca), whose productions are, perhaps surprisingly, little viewed and scarcely known at home. Each year the film board, formed in 1939, releases a combination of animation, documentary and dramatic films. NFB offices can be found in some of the country's larger cities. Films are often screened at these centers and, increasingly, videos of the vast collection can be rented.

Canada also has a commercial feature-length film industry. Its output is relatively small and the quality varies. Generally, Québec has been the most prolific and artistically successful. The better-known movies are subtitled or dubbed into English. Denys Arcand's *Decline of the American Empire, Jesus of Montreal* and *Stardom* were major critical successes. Others from Québec include *Wind from Wyoming,* by Andre Forcier; gritty *Night Zoo,* directed by Jean Claude Lauzon; riotous *Perfectly Normal,* by Yves Simoneau; and *Maelstrom* (2000; narrated by a fish), by Denis Villeneuve. *Black Robe,* directed by Australian Bruce Beresford, tells a story set in 17th-century Québec.

Norman Jewison, the director of *Moonstruck,* could be considered the father of English-speaking Canadian film. Among other established English-language direc-

tors is David Cronenberg, known for *The Fly, Dead Ringers* and *Naked Lunch.* Another is Atom Egoyan, with a series of offbeat, challenging films including the highly praised *Exotica* and *Felicia's Journey* (2000). Bruce McDonald has done *Highway 61* and *Roadkill,* two rock and roll movies, and *Dance Me Outside* about contemporary Native Indian life. Ron Mann makes entertaining full-length documentaries such as *Grass* (2000), about the stuff you smoke, and *Twist. I've Heard the Mermaids Singing,* by Patricia Rozema, is a comedy-drama. *Margaret's Museum,* by Mort Ransen, takes place in Nova Scotia and won a handful of awards. *The Arrow,* by Don McBreaty, is based on the fascinating Avro Arrow fighter plane, featuring some documentary footage. *New Waterford Girl* (2000), about a Cape Breton teenager, was a deserving hit, and *waydowntown* (2000), a satire on Calgary office workers, is also worth seeing.

James Cameron, the director of *Titanic,* is Canadian. Lesser-known films and their makers can be seen at the major annual film festivals in Toronto, Montréal and Vancouver. Better video stores have a Canadian section.

Visual Art

Artists began painting Canada as early as the 1700s and their work has grown to encompass a wide variety of styles and international influences. One of the earliest distinctive Canadian painters was Cornelius Krieghoff, who used the St Lawrence River area of Québec as his subject matter. Out west Paul Kane was equally captivated by the Native Indians and their way of life. Landscape painters traveled and explored the country often following the laying of railway lines.

Tom Thompson and the Group of Seven beginning just before WWI established the style and landscape subject matter that was to dominate Canadian art for about 30 years. The Group of Seven members were Franklin Carmichael, Frank Johnston (later replaced by AJ Casson), Lawren Harris, AY Jackson, Arthur Lismer, JEH MacDonald and Frederick Varley. Their work, drawn from the geography of the eastern Canadian lakelands, is still the country's best known both inside and outside Canada. Emily Carr, in a similar tradition, painted

The Best-Known Canadian of Them All

It's not a politician. Not an astronaut. Nor the discoverer of insulin. Not even a singer or a hockey star. The best-known, most-recognizable and most-watched Canuck is Pamela Anderson (Lee), blonde bombshell, gracer of Playboy covers, feature of *Baywatch* reruns around the world and the world's first Internet superstar. There's even Porta-Pam, a program for your Palm Pilot! From Indiana to Italy to India, fans can't get enough of her films; the latest news on her breast implants; relationship misadventures with her ex, Mötley Crüe rock musician Tommy Lee, including their none-too-secret X-rated home movie; or tales of the newest lover.

We watch Pamela; Pamela watches the bay.

Now divorced with two kids, the girl born of Finnish ancestry in tiny Ladysmith, British Columbia, on Vancouver Island in 1967, was the first baby born on Canada's one-hundredth birthday, earning her the title of Centennial Baby. Maybe press coverage was in the stars. She has just signed to do more seasons of the campy *VIP* television series as Valery Irons, the head of a group of bodyguards (non-reality TV). After seeing other celebrity dudes, she took up with musician Kid Rock, who knows how to stir the pot himself.

After several years, her name still remains significant on the Internet. It's used like a brand name, such as Coke, to attract surfers to Web sites, regardless of what product or service is being sold. Ms Anderson generates thousands of hits a day. Reports indicate that there are 145,000 pages on the Internet citing Pamela – including everything from dubious marketers to building supply companies. That's a lot of drawing power. Despite fame and adulation, if not glory, her honest, self-deprecating reported quotes, such as 'It's not like I'm a great actress or anything,' and un-Hollywood-like demeanor indicate that the essential Canadian character remains intact.

the West Coast, its forests and Native Indian villages and totems.

In the 1950s, another group of painters, which included Jack Bush, Tom Hodgson and Harold Town, helped bring new abstract influences into Canadian painting. Michael Snow and the late Joyce Wieland, two of the best-known modern visual artists, grew out of this period. Well-known realists include Ken Danby, Alex Colville, Christopher and Mary Pratt and, for nature studies, Robert Bateman. Paterson Ewen, who died in 2002, was one of the country's most individual, unique painters, often using routed plywood for his large canvases of planetary subjects.

Attila Richard Lukacs and Charles Rea are challenging contemporary painters.

Micah Lexier is gaining broad recognition for his pieces using a range of materials.

As with the previous music and literature sections, the listing here is but a very brief overview of some of the country's artists.

Native Indian Art

Among the country's most distinctive art is that of the Inuit of the north, particularly their sculptures and carvings. These also represent some of the more affordable pieces, although many of their prices, too, can range into the stratosphere for larger works by some well-established artists.

Materials used for Inuit carvings include bone, ivory, antler and occasionally horn or wood. By far the most common, though, is a group of rock types known generically as soapstone. It includes the soft steatite and harder serpentine, argillite, dolomite and others. Quarried across the far north, the stone material can vary from black to gray to green and may be dull or highly polished.

Carving styles vary from one isolated community to the other across the far north, with some better known than others. Almost all work is done completely by hand with low-tech tools. Northern Québec tends to produce realistic, naturalistic work such as birds or hunting scenes. Baffin Island sculpture is more detailed and finer, often with varying depictions of people. The central Arctic area art embraces spiritual themes, and whalebone is often employed.

As a result of interest and appreciation in Inuit carvings there are now mass-produced imitations, which are widely seen and sold. Genuine works are always marked with a tag or sticker with an igloo symbol on it. Many are also signed by the artist. The type of retail outlet is also an indicator. A reputable store and not a souvenir kiosk will likely stock the real thing. Aside from the maker and the quality, imitations are not often even made of the true raw material and really are of no value or interest.

Inuit artists also produce prints that are highly regarded. Subject matter often is taken from mythology, but other works depict traditional day-to-day activities, events and chores. Prices are best in the Northwest Territories and the Yukon.

The best of Native Indian art is also expressed in printmaking, although there is some fine carving and basketry. Probably the country's best-known Indian paintings are those by artist Norval Morrisseau. The carvings and totems of Bill Reid and Roy Henry Vickers from the West Coast have established them as major international figures. Across the country much of what is sold as Native Indian art and craft is pretty cheap and tacky and a poor likeness to the work that was done at one time and to what can still be found with some effort.

Some of the most interesting and best-quality items from either Inuit or Native Indian artisans are the clothes: moccasins *(mukluks)*, knitted sweaters (from Vancouver Island, known as Cowichan sweaters) and parkas (warm winter coats). Some fine jewelry and beadwork are also created.

SOCIETY & CONDUCT

Anthropologists divide Native Indians into six cultural groupings, each with its own religion, language family, lifestyle and geographic area. (See Original Inhabitants in the History section, earlier in this chapter.)

All had a system of beliefs in which there was no sharp division between the sacred and the secular.

Europeans did their best to crush the original cultures and, together with disease, loss of land and means of livelihood, were largely successful. Despite somewhat intact traditions in the more remote communities, today the predominant religion is Christianity and English is the principal language.

Cultural rebirth, with revival of song, dance, language programs, healing and ritual, now accompanies the legal battles being waged across the country for land rights and political autonomy.

In pockets across the country there are followers of Pan-Indianism, a term used to describe the movement of resistance to white culture and its domination. It is essentially an intertribal political stand with some religious undercurrents.

Civil disobedience and confrontation with government occur sporadically across the country, usually instigated by differences of opinion over Native Indian rights. For more information, see the Population & People section, earlier in this chapter.

RELIGION

Canada was settled by Christians, primarily French and Irish Roman Catholics and English and Scottish Protestants. Even today the largest single religious group is Catholic.

Within the Protestant group, the Anglicans form the largest denomination, followed by the United Church. Montréal, Toronto and Winnipeg have considerable Jewish populations. More recent immigration has brought Hinduism and Islam to Canada. The Sikhs in Vancouver have a sizable community; it is, in fact, the largest Sikh population outside India's Punjab province. Among the Chinese populations of Vancouver and Toronto many people maintain the Buddhist tradition. Canada also has small but determined pockets of rural, traditional religious sects such as those of the Mennonites, Hutterites and Doukhobors.

Regardless, formal religion plays an ever-diminishing role in Canadian life. Attendance at the established churches has declined steadily since WWII. The lack of interest in religion by the children of immigrants, following in their peers' footsteps, seems cause for some family strife.

Among the Native Indian population, most list their religion as Catholic, an indication of the efficiency of the early Jesuits. There is, however, a small but growing movement back to the original spiritual belief systems.

Wildlife, Parks & Heritage Sites

Young moose gobble up greens in Newfoundland.

Arctic animals manage to survive amid the barren landscape of the far north.

Polar bears' fur coats help them blend in with the icy scenery in Nunavut.

Magnificent colors of tundra on Alexandra Fjord, Ellesmere Island, Nunavut

A field of purple wildflowers in Victoria, British Columbia

Peaks of the Kluane icefields in Kluane National Park, Yukon

Recreation of a sod viking hut at L'Anse aux Meadows, Newfoundland

JIM WARK

The spectacular scenery of Gros Morne National Park, Newfoundland

KEVIN LEVESQUE

Latin Quarter, Québec City, Québec

THOMAS HUHTI

Daisies abloom, New Brunswick

RICK RUDNICKI

The zinnia, a dahlia-like flower in Alberta

Wildlife

Flora

Canada's vegetation is considered young. Except for the West Coast, the entire country was under ice 15,000 years ago, making the forests across the country relatively new.

Canada comprises eight vegetation zones. In the far north is the **Arctic tundra**, which contains essentially no trees or shrubs. The most common plants are lichens and briefly blooming small wildflowers.

South of the tundra is the **boreal (northern) forest**, the largest vegetative zone and perhaps the most typical of Canada. White and black spruce trees predominate. In the east, balsam fir and jack pine are also common; in the west, alpine fir and lodgepole pine take their place.

In the east, the **Great Lakes–St Lawrence River forest zone** lies south of the boreal forest. Coniferous (evergreen, softwood) trees of the north mix with the deciduous (broadleaf, hardwood) trees of the south. In this region you'll see pines, including the majestic white pine and spruces, and you'll also see the maples, oaks, birches and others that supply the famous colors of Canadian autumns.

The fourth region, the **Acadian forest** of New Brunswick, Prince Edward Island and Nova Scotia is made up of red spruce, balsam fir, maple, yellow birch and some pine. The **parkland zone** is the area between the eastern forests and the western prairies, which begin in Manitoba. Trembling aspen is the dominant tree.

Manitoba, Saskatchewan and Alberta are best known for their flat **prairie grasslands**, the sixth zone, now mostly covered in cultivated grains. The grasslands once contained short, mixed and tall grass regions, but these have all but disappeared except for a few protected pockets.

British Columbia contains a richer variety of vegetation than elsewhere as well as some of the country's most impressive flora. The **Rocky Mountain forest** consists of subalpine species such as Engelmann spruce, alpine fir and larches, with lodgepole pine and aspen at higher elevations. Around the coastal areas, in the **Pacific Coast forest**, the truly awesome trees of the country grow, including the ancient, gigantic western red cedar, Douglas fir, western hemlock and Sitka spruce. Individual trees may be over 1000 years old.

Among the country's countless **wildflowers** is the trillium, which blooms in spring in shaded areas of the Ontario and Québec woods. The large white or pink flowers often carpet whole sections of the forest floor.

The pitcher plant – seen in bogs from Saskatchewan to Newfoundland and Labrador – is carnivorous (ie, it feeds on insects). The leaves collect rainwater, and insects – attracted to the plant by its purplish-red color and odor – fall down the slippery leaves into the water, where they drown; the plant then digests them.

The pickerel weed, with its deep purplish-blue spiked flower and narrow, long, green leaves, grows around ponds and shallow streams from Ontario to Nova Scotia. Loosestrife is a beautiful, waist-high, bright pinkish-purple plant seen along roadsides and in ditches and marshes across the country.

Across the Maritimes the lupine (blue, pink or somewhere in between) grows wild in fields and by the roadsides. Sea blush cast a pink glow over the rocks along the southern West Coast in spring. The bright red common Indian paintbrush supplies wonderful contrast to the blues and grays of the Rocky Mountains.

A delicious assortment of **wild berries** can be picked across the country. Blueberries are the most common and abundant, but if you're lucky, you may happen upon a patch of wild raspberries – one of life's exalted moments. The forests, meadows and marsh areas all contain plenty of other edible plants and mushrooms. They also have plenty of poisonous plants and mushrooms. Telling the difference is difficult at times, even with years of experience and a good book. If in any doubt at all, don't take a chance. Some species can be fatal.

Less deadly but more irritating is the three-leafed poison ivy, found in wooded southern regions of the country. A brush against this plant will irritate your skin, resulting in blisters and a maddening itch.

Fauna

Viewing animals in their natural element can be a highlight of a trip to Canada. While wandering through the woods here (or even driving the roads), you stand a good chance of coming across small mammals such as beavers, skunks and porcupines, which thrive in just about every province.

One of Canada's symbols, the **beaver** has become known for its industriousness – it spends much of its time chewing down trees and building its lodge home out of sticks and mud. You might spy a busy beaver in the early morning or early evening paddling across a stream or lake with its head just above water.

The **skunk** resembles a large black cat but with a white stripe down its back and a big, bushy tail. It's dangerous only in that it defends itself by spraying out of its nether regions the foulest, longest-lasting, most clothes-clinging smell imaginable. The cure is a bath in tomato juice. Watch out!

A curious animal, the **porcupine** manages to keep predators away by sporting hollow, barbed quills that project from its body like long hair. Many a dog has found itself with an unappetizing mouthful of them. The gray porcupine feeds mainly on bark and tree buds.

Of Canada's large land animals, the one you're most likely to see is the **deer**, whose numbers abound in the woodlands across the entire country. But you might also be lucky enough to spy some of the rarer wildlife, including the animals listed below.

Bears Canada's largest and most dangerous animals are widely dispersed, and, as there are four major types, most of the country is populated with at least one kind. For detailed information on the hazards of bears, see Dangers & Annoyances in the Facts for the Visitor chapter.

The **grizzly bear**, the most notorious, lives on the higher slopes of the Rocky and Selkirk Mountains of British Columbia, Alberta and the Yukon. The big grizzly can reach a standing height of 2.75m. To recognize a grizzly, look for brownish hair with white ends and a hump on the back behind the neck – not that it's a good idea to get too close. The grizzly can't see well but makes up for that with its excellent sense of smell and good ears. To make matters worse, it's fast, so be very happy that it can't climb trees.

The most common of bears, the **black bear** lives all across Canada; it's the variety you're most likely to see. Active during the day, the black bear often mooches around campgrounds, cottages and garbage dumps, sometimes scaling trees in search of food. Usually shorter than 1.5m high at the shoulders, it tends to weigh less than 90kg.

Actually a black bear but brown in color, the mostly nocturnal **brown bear** lives in British Columbia, Alberta and the Yukon. Don't confuse it with the brown bear of Europe and Asia, which is a close relative of the grizzly.

Thick, white fur distinguishes the very large **polar bear**, which can weigh in at 680kg. Found only in the extreme northern areas of the country, it can be viewed in Churchill, Manitoba and in zoos. A majestic animal, the polar bear looks graceful in the water despite its size and apparent awkwardness. Due to a reduction in numbers caused by hunting, it is now a protected animal.

Wolves & Coyotes The wolf looks like a large, silver-gray dog. Its ferocious reputation is more misconception than fact. Wolves usually hunt in packs and rarely harm people. Hunting has pretty well banished this animal from the southern populated regions, but you may hear the wolf's howl late at night if you're in the bush.

More widespread than the wolf, the coyote is smaller and cheekier, with an eerie howl or series of yaps used for communicating. More scavenger than hunter, the coyote sometimes falls prey to massive poison-bait campaigns by western ranchers and farmers.

Lynx & Cougars Nearly exclusive to Canada, the lynx is a gray cat about 90cm long with furry trim around its face and sharp pointed ears. Found all across the undeveloped Canadian woodlands, the mainly nocturnal cat eats small animals. But humans are its main enemy, mainly because people destroy its habitat.

Larger and rarer than the lynx, the regal cougar hunts the forests of British Columbia and the Rocky Mountains, mostly at night. Its favored prey is the Columbian blacktail deer. The cougar population is increasing on Vancouver Island, and the number of cougar attacks on people has risen (though such incidents are still infrequent).

Moose One of the largest animals lives in forests all across Canada, particularly around swamps. For the most part, moose range farther north than deer. You'll know them by their large, thick antlers and brown fur. The reclusive moose tends to keep to itself and sometimes takes to the water to escape biting bugs. However, there's little the animal can do to avoid hunters, who have made moose a favorite target. The male moose bellows in October and November in its search for a mate. At that time, the normally timid moose can become aggressive. Both deer and moose can be road hazards, especially at night. Watch for them and the roadside signs warning of their presence.

Caribou The barren-ground caribou lives in herds in the far north, though you might see some small groups of woodland caribou in more southern areas, such as the Gaspé Peninsula of Québec, the Lake Superior region of Ontario and Gros Morne National Park. Some Inuit still hunt caribou for food and for the hides, but the government now carefully monitors caribou numbers, since over-hunting and development have affected the population. A close relative of the North American caribou is the reindeer, found in Europe and Asia.

Above: The grizzly – a sight best seen from a distance

Elk Also called the wapiti, the elk populates the Rocky Mountains. This striking animal can appear quite tame, often allowing visitors to approach for picture taking. But be advised that people have been attacked, especially in the rutting or calving seasons. The elk is a cousin of the European red deer.

Rocky Mountain Goats As close as you'll get to an all-Canadian animal, the white and hairy mountain goat sports horns and looks like an old man. Found in British Columbia and the Yukon, it sometimes makes its home in populated areas, where it's quite tame, but it prefers the higher, more remote mountain regions. Clay aids the goat's digestive system, which explains why you might see one pawing at the ground and gobbling up clumps of earth.

Buffalo/Bison The huge, heavy-shouldered, shaggy herbivore that once roamed the prairies in vast herds now exists only in parks. The buffalo's near-extinction has come to symbolize the Europeans' effect on Native Indians and their environment. Technically, Canadian buffalo are bison, and there are two species, woodland and plains. Bison are now raised for their meat, which occasionally shows up on menus.

Whales A number of varieties of whales pass through the waters off the coast of British Columbia, in the St Lawrence River in Québec, and in the Atlantic Ocean off the country's East Coast. These include the humpback, finback, beluga and blue whale. For a detailed description of each of these types, see the boxed text 'Who Swims There?' in the Québec chapter. Throughout the coastal areas, whale-watching has become a very successful commercial enterprise. You'll find the names of companies offering whale-watching trips throughout the regional chapters.

Birds Five hundred species have been spotted in Canada, but many of them are quite rare. One of the most notable among the feathered residents is the **loon**, a waterbird with a mournful yet beautiful call that's often heard on the quieter lakes across the country (but particularly in northern Ontario) in early morning or evening.

The **great blue heron**, one of the country's largest birds, is a wonder to see when it takes off. The very timid bird lives in quiet marsh areas and takes flight at the least provocation.

The large, black-and-gray **Canada goose** can be aggressive, even around people. But much of the time you'll only see Canada geese from a distance, as they take to the skies in large, V-shaped formations during their spring and fall migrations.

Many species of **duck** dot the lakes of Canada, the mallard being the most common, the wood duck the most attractive and colorful.

The **whiskey jack**, or gray jay, found mainly in the Rockies, is a fluffy, friendly bird that will eat out of your hand. At the other end of the spectrum, the **bald eagle** and the **osprey** are large, impressive birds of prey – don't let them near your hand!

Around the coasts there's a fascinating array of marine birdlife, including the **puffin** and the **razorbill**. The puffin draws admirers with its brightly colored bill, high-speed flight and goofy expression. The chunky black-and-white razorbill with the hefty bill is Canada's answer to the penguin.

Fish Canada's waters also provide habitats for lots of animals, particularly fish. The most common freshwater fish include **northern pike**, **bass**, **walleye** and various **trout** varieties. In the Atlantic Provinces and Québec, the **Atlantic salmon** has become a highly sought-after catch for anglers, while humans' appetite for **Pacific salmon** has sent that fish into an alarming decline on the West Coast.

Parks & Heritage Sites

Canada's parks rank among its signature attractions. Every province boasts some unique natural areas, which belong to either the national or provincial park system. Some of the must-see spots, province by province, include Gros Morne National Park in Newfoundland, Cape Breton Highlands National Park in Nova Scotia, Fundy National Park in New Brunswick, Gaspésie Provincial Park in Québec, Algonquin Provincial Park in Ontario, Riding Mountain National Park in Manitoba, Prince Albert National Park in Saskatchewan, Banff National Park and Dinosaur Provincial Park in Alberta, Pacific Rim National Park and Yoho National Park in British Columbia, Kluane National Park in the Yukon, Nahanni National Park in the Northwest Territories and Auyuittuq National Park in Nunavut. See the regional chapters for more information on all of these.

National Parks

Canada has 39 national parks, which have been developed to protect, preserve and make accessible a special environment. All of them are well worth visiting. The parks are managed by the federal ministry department Canadian Heritage–Parks Canada (☎ 819-997-0055, 888-773-8888, ⓦ www.parkscanada.pch.gc.ca, 25 Eddy St, 7th floor, Hull, QC K1A 0M5). It doesn't provide detailed public information but does produce a free map brochure and booklets listing park locations and contact information. You can often find these booklets at tourist offices. The Parks Canada website offers complete details on the parks, camping reservations and costs.

Each province and territory includes parks, most with camping facilities. Several are close to major population centers and draw heavy crowds; others are more remote and offer good wilderness opportunities. Many manage to combine both characteristics.

Some parks rent canoes and/or rowboats. In parks with numerous lakes and rivers, a canoe is ideal; you can portage to different lakes. At other parks, you can rent bicycles. Many parks have established walking or longer hiking trails. A few parks even contain whole towns: Banff and Jasper National Parks both enclose the towns of Banff and Jasper.

Entrance fees to national parks vary from park to park and from nil to several dollars. Some parks offer free day use, but all charge for overnight camping. Some, such as Cape Breton and the Rocky Mountain parks, sell daily, multiday and yearly permits. The latter type is good for any park in the system.

Left: Bald eagles soar over Canada.

In addition to national parks, the system features 849 **national historic sites**, with 145 of special note (which means that you can expect to find interpretive centers and Parks Canada staff there). For day-use only, these sites preserve various artifacts of Canadian history, including forts, pioneer homesteads and battle sites. There are also seven nationally designated **heritage canals** and over two dozen **heritage rivers**. Three marine conservation areas, federal heritage buildings and heritage railway stations round out the program.

For information, contact Canadian Heritage–Parks Canada, which operates offices in some cities, such as Toronto. Most parks are covered in the regional chapters. Also see Camping under Accommodations in the Facts for the Visitor chapter.

Provincial Parks

Each province runs its own system of parks and reserves. These can vary dramatically. Some are developed for recreation, others to preserve something of historical interest, still others to protect wildlife or natural geographic features of particular beauty or uniqueness. Many are spectacular. They are much more numerous than national parks; Ontario, for example, has 280.

Some provincial parks provide camping and other conveniences. In many provinces day-use is free, and only those staying overnight have to pay an admission charge. At most parks, knowledgeable staff will answer questions and offer lectures, walks and other presentations. Some parks have a biologist or a naturalist on duty.

Provincial tourist boards and offices offer free material that provides some information on the parks under their jurisdiction. These outline camping facilities and basic features of the parks.

Some **provincial historic sites** also dot the country. Usually small, these spots are generally meant for short visits, anywhere from a half hour to a half day.

Territorial Parks

The parks in the territories tend to be small, simple and inexpensive to visit. They are often best used for overnight camping, although facilities may be minimal.

Crown Land, Reserves & Other Recreation Areas

Anyone can use undeveloped crown land (government-owned land) for hiking, canoeing and camping at no cost. Some crown land areas do have basic campsites carved out of the woods or lake edges and/or portage routes and hiking paths.

Generally, those seeking wilderness experiences can also use provincial nature reserves and designated wilderness areas. A careful scanning of provincial maps will often reveal some of these areas.

The BC Ministry of Forests produces a *Recreation Guide* and an excellent series of Forest District maps covering many undeveloped areas that fall outside any park system but that visitors are welcome to use. You can also inquire about such areas at regional tourist offices.

Local people will be able to help with advice and access information. Be well equipped and be especially careful with fire when enjoying these undeveloped areas.

World Heritage Sites

In a world of ever-increasing population and development, the permanent setting-aside of specific areas around the world for international protection and appreciation by humankind is particularly timely and politically noble. In 1972 the UN's United Nations Educational, Scientific and Cultural Organization (Unesco) adopted 'The Convention Concerning the Protection of the World Cultural and Natural Heritage.' Its mandate, now signed by 167 countries, is to identify and help preserve the world's most valuable cultural and natural wonders. Canada is one of the 21 representatives on the World Heritage Committee, which carries out the mission of the convention.

Amid growing threats of pollution, commercialization and even tourism, Unesco intends to maintain the integrity of the designated areas through educational, technical and financial assistance. To date, it has selected more than 700 sites in more than 120 countries. They include the USA's Grand Canyon, Australia's Uluru (Ayers Rock), Ecuador's Galapagos Islands, England's Stonehenge and India's Taj Mahal.

Canada has 13 sites designated by the World Heritage Convention. Nine are natural attractions, all either national or provincial parks: Gros Morne National Park, Wood Buffalo National Park, Dinosaur Provincial Park, Head-Smashed-In Buffalo Jump, Waterton Lakes National Park (part of the Waterton-Glacier International Peace Park), Rocky Mountain National Parks, Kluane National Park, Nahanni National Park and the new Miguasha Provincial Park.

Four sites involve human endeavor: Québec City, a European-style gem; L'Anse aux Meadows in Newfoundland, a thousand-year-old Viking camp; the seaside colonial town of Lunenburg, Nova Scotia; and SGaang Gwaii (formerly Anthony Island), home to the historic Haida Indian settlement of Ninstints. This last is part of Gwaii Haanas National Park Reserve, on the Queen Charlotte Islands in British Columbia, which also boasts outstanding natural features. All are definitely worth visiting.

The entire central downtown core of **Québec City**, the only walled city in North America, has been made a heritage site. Well-preserved stone ramparts, churches, houses and countless original buildings make for a vibrant, living museum overlooking the St Lawrence River. The future of Canada was decided here during the British-French colonial period in the 17th and 18th centuries.

Miguasha Provincial Park, designated by Unesco in 2000, holds amazing Devonian plant and animal fossil beds from 370 million years ago, the time when the Gaspé Peninsula of Quebec had a tropical climate.

Settled by Vikings, **L'Anse aux Meadows**, at the tip of Newfoundland's Northern Peninsula, is the oldest European habitation site in North America. But evidence suggests that the site was occupied 4000 years before that by Archaic people. Today, the wonderfully low-key national park set in rough, rocky northern environs doesn't look much different than when the Norse sailors first arrived. Some reconstruction brings the site alive.

Farther south along the same road is **Gros Morne National Park**. Its mountains and fjords make for scenic majesty, but Unesco has recognized the park for its outstanding geographic characteristics and the contributions they've made to scientific studies. The park's landscape shows major evidence of plate tectonics and glaciation – the creation of the surface of the earth, in other words. There are barren lands, sandy beaches, wildlife and ancient human history to discover within its borders.

The hilly, historic streets of **Lunenburg** edge back from a protective harbor on Nova Scotia's jagged south shore. The old, central district typifies an 18th-century British colonial town, as Lunenburg's tradition of wood-construction architecture has been maintained since the 1750s. In addition to the rows of fine homes, there are five central churches of note, including Canada's oldest Presbyterian church, dating from 1754, and the country's second oldest Anglican church. Not merely an architectural museum, Lunenburg serves as the base for Atlantic Canada's largest deep-sea trawler fleet, and it's home to the area's biggest fish-processing plant. It has also kept intact its stellar shipbuilding reputation, firmly established with the launching of the famous racing schooner *Bluenose* in 1921 and bolstered with its successor, *Bluenose II*, from the same yards in 1963.

In Alberta, way up north along the border with the Northwest Territories, lies the immense **Wood Buffalo National Park**, one of the world's largest parks. This wild, 45,000-sq-km reserve provides critical wildlife habitat. Home to about 4000 bison – the world's largest free-roaming herd – it's also the planet's only nesting site for the endangered whooping crane. The subarctic mix of bog, forest, caves, and salt plains offer shelter and sustenance for thousands of waterfowl and a range of northern mammals and birds. The delta of the Peace and Athabaska Rivers is among the world's largest inland deltas.

Set on the floor of an ancient tropical ocean, eastern Alberta's **Dinosaur Provincial Park** hardly looks like it belongs in Canada. The bizarre, convoluted, eroded terrain in dusty shades of ochre, sienna and brown contains secrets sunken and lost 75 million years past. Here in the glacially sculpted badlands of the Red Deer River Valley lies an unparalleled source of dinosaur fossils. Dozens of major museums around the world display specimens unearthed in this park region. Guided interpretation and walking trails make this fascinating area accessible.

In the foothills of southwest Alberta, in the traditional lands of the Blackfoot Indian, is the intriguing **Head-Smashed-In Buffalo Jump**, North America's oldest, largest and best-preserved bison jump. Where the rocky ledges of the Porcupine Hills meet the plains, generations of Native Indians ingeniously hunted the revered herds of bison. An excellent interpretation center and trails around the undisturbed site make this story of early Canada captivating.

The joint Canada-USA **Waterton-Glacier International Peace Park** straddles the Alberta-Montana border at the narrowest section of the Rocky Mountains. In Canada it runs westward to the British Columbia border. The joining of Canada's Waterton National Park with Montana's Glacier National Park in 1932 created the world's first international park. As a symbol for international cooperation in preserving places of global significance, it has helped inspire the creation of other such parks. The park uniquely combines prairie landscape with lofty, snowcapped peaks. Within a distance of just 1km, the dry, rolling hills of the southern Alberta plains rise dramatically to 3000m. The lowlands support antelope and coyotes; the alpine meadows and slopes sustain mountain goats and grizzly bears. The scenic Waterton Lakes, wedged between mountains, permit boat access to much of the park, including excellent walking trails that cover three vegetative zones. Originally the home of the Blackfoot people, the Waterton half has two national historic sites: western

Above: Bison used to meet their ends at Head-Smashed-In Buffalo Jump.

Canada's first commercial oil well and the Prince of Wales Hotel, a marvelous example of early mountain-resort lodging with a timber-frame interior. One of the USA's largest national parks, Glacier contains 50 smallish glaciers.

Best known among Canada's heritage sites are the **Rocky Mountain Parks**, which straddle the Alberta–British Columbia border. Internationally famous, Banff and Jasper National Parks get most of the attention, but the Rocky Mountain Parks also include smaller, towering Mt Assiniboine Provincial Park; diverse Yoho National Park, with the renowned Burgess Shale fossil beds; BC's Mt Robson (3954m), the highest peak in the Rockies; and Kootenay National Park. Alpine meadows, glaciers, hot springs, rushing rivers – the list of outstanding features is stunning.

Off the coast of British Columbia sit the Queen Charlotte Islands, sometimes referred to as the Canadian Galapagos for the rich variety of life in and among the West Coast rain forest. The southern half of Moresby Island has become South Moresby Gwaii Hanaas National Park, managed in part by the native Haida Nation. Tiny **SGaang Swaii** (Anthony Island), part of the park, is the most westerly of Canada's heritage sites. Ninstints, a former Haida village on the island, is regarded as the most significant of all Pacific Northwest Indian sites. Believed to have been an inhabited area for 2000 years, it contains still-standing totems and mortuary poles, as well as longhouse vestiges.

Unspoiled **Kluane National Park**, in the southwestern Yukon, belongs among the most untamed regions on earth. Together with the adjacent Wrangell–St Elias Park of Alaska, the Tatshenshini-Alsek Rivers of northern British Columbia and other areas, Kluane makes up one of the world's largest protected areas. The park contains the world's largest nonpolar icefields, with glaciers that date from the time when Canada was uninhabited. In one of the two mountain chains sits secluded, aloof Mt Logan (5951m), Canada's highest peak. Wildlife includes grizzly bears, moose, mountain goats, Dall sheep and sometimes caribou.

Tucked in the southwestern corner of the Northwest Territories is remote, mountainous **Nahanni National Park**, inaccessible by road. The turbulent South Nahanni River, classified as a Canadian heritage river, cuts through awe-inspiring canyons from the tundra zones of rocky peaks to the forested valleys at its mouth on the Liard River. At Virginia Falls, it plunges over 90m, twice the height of Niagara. With hot springs and abundant wildlife along the way, a once-in-a-lifetime river trip through this pristine wilderness is a dream for many.

Biosphere Reserves

The United Nations also has a program to designate biosphere reserves around the world. Mixed-use areas with human development, these reserves contain special features, often of a geographic nature. These areas act as models for responsible, community-based resource management and sustainable development.

Canada currently has 11, each of which is an interesting destination worth exploring if you're nearby. They are Niagara Escarpment and Long Point in Ontario; Charlevoix, Lac St Pierre and Mont St Hilaire in Québec; Southwest Nova in Nova Scotia; Waterton in Alberta; Riding Mountain in Manitoba; Redberry Lake in Saskatchewan; and Clayoquot Sound and Mount Arrowsmith in British Columbia.

Facts for the Visitor

PLANNING

When to Go

Spring, summer and autumn are all ideal for touring. The far north is best in summer, when the roads are open, ferries can cross rivers and daylight hours are long. Many of the country's festivals are held over the summer, one notable exception being the Québec Winter Carnival. If you're skiing and visiting the cities, a winter visit won't present any major hurdles. Winter tourism is increasing, with many outfitters offering dog-sledding, Nordic skiing and other winter outdoor activities. Also, Canada's ballet, opera and symphony season runs through the winter months.

The school summer holidays in Canada last from the end of June to Labor Day in early September. Most people take their vacations during this period. University students have a longer summer break, running from sometime in May to the beginning or middle of September.

March Break is a weeklong intermission in studies for elementary and high school students across the country; it falls sometime in March, though the actual dates vary by province and school board. Many people take the opportunity for a holiday, and all trains, planes and buses are generally very busy.

Note that outside the main summer season, which runs roughly from mid-June to mid-September, many visitor-oriented facilities, attractions, sights and even accommodations may be closed, particularly in the Atlantic Provinces. But the off-season has its advantages: lack of crowds, lower prices and perhaps better service (since those serving you aren't overworked). Spring and autumn make a good compromise between the peak season and the cold of winter. For campers, though, July and August are the only reliably hot months. For more details, see Climate in the Facts about Canada chapter.

Maps

Pick up good provincial road maps at the provincial tourist offices. Bookstores generally sell both provincial and city maps, and service stations often carry road maps as well.

The Canada Map Office (☎ 613-952-7000, 800-465-6277, **W** www.nrcan.gc.ca) produces topographic maps of any place in the country. Its website lists nationwide dealers.

World of Maps & Travel Books (☎ 613-724-6776, 800-214-8524, **W** www.worldofmaps.com, 1235 Wellington St, Ottawa, ON K1Y 3A3) stocks thousands of road maps and topographic maps and accepts online orders.

In Toronto, Federal Publications Inc (☎ 416-860-1611, 888-433-3782, **W** www.fedpubs.com, 165 University Ave) sells paper and CD-ROM maps, topographics, road maps and nautical charts. Also in the city, Open Air Books & Maps (☎ 416-363-0719, 25 Toronto St) carries a wide selection of maps of all kinds, including standard highway maps, city maps and topographic maps.

What to Bring

Those planning trips outside the summer season should bring a number of things to protect against cold. Layering of clothes is the most effective and the most practical way to keep warm. Pack clothes of varying thicknesses, such as thin and thick sweaters, short- and long-sleeved T-shirts and something more or less windproof. Don't forget the gloves, scarf and hat in winter.

Readers have suggested, however, that visitors planning to stay the winter need not bring bulky, warm clothes, especially those headed to the major cities, where secondhand clothing shops (such as Goodwill, Salvation Army and Value Village) sell good used wear of all sorts very cheaply.

Even in winter a bathing suit, which weighs next to nothing, is always good to throw in the pack, as you might want to make use of city or hotel pools (some heated), lakes or saunas. A collapsible umbrella is a very useful, practical accessory. A good, sturdy pair of walking shoes or boots is a good idea for all but the business traveler with no spare time.

English-language speakers who plan on spending some time in Québec might want to take a French/English dictionary or phrase book, although these are available in Montréal.

Drivers traveling long distances should carry a few basic tools, a spare tire that has been checked for pressure, a first-aid kit and a flashlight (torch). A few favorite tapes or CDs may help pass the hours driving in remote areas where there's nothing on the radio but static.

SUGGESTED ITINERARIES

It may seem obvious, but many visitors to Canada are shocked and overwhelmed by its size. Right away, those carefully made plans to skip from Toronto to Vancouver in a day or two, seeing all kinds of things along the way, turn out to be a pipe dream. If you've only got limited time (like most people), you'll be better off focusing on one region, exploring it well and then visiting again to take in another part of this vast country.

In the Maritimes, however, travelers can see a decent slice of three provinces (New Brunswick, Nova Scotia and Prince Edward Island) in two weeks, thanks to the manageably short distances. Some choose to tack on a visit to Newfoundland, but that island can easily justify a completely separate trip. You can squeeze in a great short visit (one week), though, if you stick to Newfoundland's west side and Northern Peninsula or if you head to St John's and investigate the Avalon Peninsula, maybe as far as Notre Dame Bay. Any itinerary that's more ambitious than those requires a lot of time-consuming land transportation.

If you're going to Québec, you can see Montréal, Québec City and the Gaspé Peninsula in a couple of weeks. Or you can combine parts of Québec, such as Montréal and the Gatineau area, with a trip to Ottawa and Kingston in Ontario.

Many people make a loop of Ottawa, Kingston, Toronto and Niagara Falls in two weeks or more, sometimes adding on a reasonable side trip to Georgian Bay or Algonquin Park. Other travelers focus on southern Ontario, including the entire Niagara region and Stratford and the cottage country above Toronto.

On the Prairies, your best bet is to do a circle from Winnipeg to Riding Mountain National Park to Saskatoon, Prince Albert, Regina, Moose Jaw and back to Winnipeg for a side trip to Churchill.

If you're starting off in Calgary, try a two-week circular trip through Banff and up to Jasper, spending plenty of time in the Rocky Mountains, then over to Edmonton and back to Calgary.

British Columbia can eat up a lot of time. You can spend several days in Vancouver alone, not even counting the numerous, enticing day trips from the city. A loop from Vancouver to Kamloops and through the Okanagan Valley requires at least a week. Plan on a similar time frame for the Kootenay area and the BC Rocky Mountain Parks. A week or more can easily disappear in Victoria and Vancouver Island, so a trip there and around Vancouver calls for at least two weeks total.

Northern Canada involves huge distances. A couple of weeks is enough to travel from Yellowknife to Dawson City, with a stop at Kluane National Park, but you'll do a lot of driving.

While the above itineraries cover many of the main cities and geographic highlights, it's not hard to spend *much* longer and travel less. Conversely, you *can* drive across the country in 10 days.

TOURIST OFFICES

There is no federal tourism department that supplies information to the public. The individual provinces handle all tourism information. The Canadian Tourism Commission (**W** www.travelcanada.ca), a combination of government and private businesses, produces a booklet with general information and addresses to contact for further information.

For basic help in planning a visit to Canada, see your closest Canadian embassy, consulate or high commission, listed later in this chapter under Embassies & Consulates. It can furnish details on entry requirements, weather, duty regulations and places to go for travel information.

Provincial/Territorial Tourist Offices

Each province has at least one major provincial tourist office within its borders. These offices can supply free maps and guides on accommodations, campgrounds and attractions, as well as information on major annual events. If you ask, they'll also furnish more specialized information on, for example, a particular activity or an organized wilderness tour; however, the staff probably don't have detailed information on any given area of their province or territory. For this information, contact a city tourist office in your area of choice.

Alberta
(☎ 780-427-4321, 800-661-8888, **W** www.travel alberta.com) Travel Alberta, PO Box 2500, Edmonton, AB T5J 2Z1

British Columbia
(☎ 250-387-1642, 800-435-5622, **W** www .hellobc.com) Tourism British Columbia, Parliament Buildings, Victoria, BC V8V 1X4

Manitoba
(☎ 800-665-0040, **W** www.travelmanitoba.com) Travel Manitoba, Dept SM5, 7th floor, 155 Carlton St, Winnipeg, MB R3C 3H8

New Brunswick
(☎ 800-561-0123, **W** www.tourismnbcanada.com) Tourism New Brunswick, PO Box 12345, Campbellton, NB E3N 3T6

Newfoundland & Labrador
(☎ 800-563-6353, **W** www.gov.nf.ca) Newfoundland Dept of Tourism, Culture & Recreation, PO Box 8700, St John's, NF A1B 4J6

Northwest Territories
(☎ 867-873-7200, 800-661-0788, **W** www.nwt travel.nt.ca) Northwest Territories Arctic Tourism, PO Box 610, Yellowknife, NT X1A 2N5

Nova Scotia
(☎ 902-425-5781, 800-565-0000, **W** www.explore .gov.ns.ca) Tourism Nova Scotia, PO Box 456, Halifax, NS B3J 2R5

Nunavut
(☎ 867-979-6551, 866-686-2888, **W** www.nunatour .nt.ca) Nunavut Tourism, PO Box 1450, Iqaluit, NU X0A 0H0

Ontario
(☎ 800-668-2746, 800-268-3736 in French, **W** www.ontariotravel.net) Ontario Travel, Queen's Park, Toronto, ON M7A 2E5

Prince Edward Island
(☎ 902-368-7795, 888-734-7529, **W** www.peiplay .com) Prince Edward Island Visitor Services, PO Box 940, Charlottetown, PE C1A 7M5

Québec
(☎ 877-266-5687, **W** www.bonjourquebec.com) Tourisme Québec, PO Box 979, Montréal, QC H3C 2W3

Saskatchewan
(☎ 877-237-2273, **W** www.sasktourism.com) Tourism Saskatchewan, 1922 Park St, Regina, SK S4P 3V7

Yukon
(☎ 867-667-5036, 800-789-8566, **W** www.touryukon .com) Yukon Dept of Tourism, PO Box 2703, Whitehorse, YT Y1A 2C6

Local Tourist Offices

Most Canadian cities and towns have at least a seasonal local information office;

many of these are mentioned in the regional chapters. The small, local tourist offices are the best places to find specialized information on a specific area. As a general rule the staff there will have little information on other parts of the country.

VISAS & DOCUMENTS

All visitors to Canada should have a photo ID and preferably two or three types of identification.

Passports

Visitors from all countries but the USA need a passport. Two minor exceptions include people from Greenland (Denmark) and St Pierre & Miquelon (France), who do not need passports if they are entering from their areas of residence. Absolutely everyone does need to have good identification, however, when visiting Canada.

For US and Canadian citizens, a driver's license has traditionally been all that was needed to prove residency, but often this is no longer sufficient. Bring a birth certificate or a certificate of citizenship or naturalization, if not a passport, to gain entry. US citizens arriving in Canada from somewhere other than the USA should present a passport.

Visas

For information, contact Citizenship and Immigration Canada (**W** www.cic.gc.ca). Visitors from nearly all Western and Commonwealth countries don't need visas, but South African citizens do. Tourists from Hong Kong and Taiwan also need visas, as do visitors from developing countries and residents of some Eastern European countries. Mexicans don't need visas, but most South Americans do.

Visitor visas ($75) are granted for a period of six months and are extendable for a fee. Extensions, at the same price, must be applied for at a Canadian Immigration Centre. Multiple entry visas are also available.

Visa requirements change frequently, and since visas must be obtained before you arrive in Canada, check before you leave – Europeans included. A separate visa is required for visitors intending to work or to go to school in Canada.

A passport and/or visa does not guarantee entry. Admission and the duration of your permitted stay is at the discretion of the immigration officer at the border. The decision is based on a number of factors, some of which you control, including: being healthy, obeying the law, having sufficient money and possibly possessing a return ticket out of the country. This latter requirement will not often be asked of any legitimate traveler, especially from a Western country.

If you're refused entry but have a visa, you have the right to appeal at the Immigration Appeal Board at the port of entry. Those under 18 years old should have a letter from a parent or guardian.

Visa Extensions An application for a visa extension must be submitted one month before the current visa expires. The fee for an extension is $75. For more information or an application, call or visit a Canadian Immigration Centre in one of the major cities. To obtain an extension, you must have a valid passport, an onward ticket and adequate finances.

Other Documents

US motorists traveling in Canada are advised to obtain a Canadian Nonresident Interprovince Motor Vehicle Liability Insurance Card, which is accepted as evidence of financial responsibility anywhere in Canada. US insurance companies issue these cards.

If you've rented a car, trailer or any other vehicle in the USA and you are driving it into Canada, bring a copy of the rental agreement to save any possible aggravation by border officials. The rental agreement should stipulate that taking the vehicle to Canada is permitted. Also, any visitor entering Canada with a vehicle registered in someone else's name should carry a letter from the owner authorizing use of the vehicle.

Side Trips to the USA

Visitors to Canada who are planning to spend some time in the USA should be aware of a few things to avoid disappointment. First, admission requirements to the USA when arriving by land can be significantly different than when arriving by air or sea from your country of origin. But the rules have one thing in common: they're all subject to rapid change, especially in the wake of the 2001 terrorist attacks, so check with the appropriate authorities before planning your visit.

Visitors to the USA from nearly all Western countries do not need visas, but there are exceptions, one being Portuguese citizens. For details on ongoing policy changes, consult the US State Dept (**w** www.travel.state.gov/visa_services.html).

Residents of countries for whom US visas are necessary should get them at home. Visitors can apply for US visas in Canada, but it's generally easier and quicker to do it at home and you're less likely to be refused. Visas cannot be obtained upon arrival in the USA. When getting a visa, ask for a multiple-entry one, as this may be useful.

People visiting the USA from countries whose citizens do *not* need a visa are subject to a $6 entry (visa waiver) fee at the border. It doesn't matter if you're going for an hour or a month. It also doesn't matter how you're arriving – you must pay even if you're entering on foot.

Also, most visitors to the USA (by air or sea) must present either a roundtrip or onward ticket. These tickets may be 'open' – that is, undated. Visitors entering the USA by land from Canada are not required to have any ticket, but they might have to offer some evidence of financial solvency, as well as proof of a residence abroad (ie, a document that shows you have a permanent address).

Commercial transportation services such as Amtrak and Greyhound face threats of heavy fines for carrying passengers without sufficient documentation and so have become more strict in requiring proper identification for crossing the border in either direction.

Check that your entry permit to Canada, whatever it may be, includes multiple entry, something that's generally granted for travelers holding passports from Western countries. But if not, you may find your afternoon side trip across the border to the USA involuntarily extended when Canadian officials won't let you back into Canada.

Anyone traveling with young children should be aware of the need for good documentation. Because of the fear of child abductions, parents can find themselves in the unenviable position of having to prove that the baby in their arms is in fact their own. This is particularly the case for male single parents but may affect anyone crossing the border without a spouse. In the latter case, consider taking along a letter of consent, preferably notarized, from the missing partner. Also, you might want to carry legal documents that establish custody.

Any time spent on a side trip to the USA will be included as time spent in Canada for the purpose of your time allotment upon arrival. For example, if you have been given a six-month stay in Canada and after three months you spend one month in California, upon your return to Canada you'll only be allowed to stay the remaining two months.

If you're planning to visit duty-free shops and take advantage of the prices, you must stay in the USA for at least 48 hours to be entitled to use them. The selection and prices at these shops have never been all that impressive, but smokers may find the cigarettes aren't a bad buy.

Border crossers should also note that foods such as meat, fish and eggs can be confiscated, so eat your picnic before meeting the customs agent.

For more information on border crossing and customs, consult **w** www.ccra-adrc.gc.ca.

Travel Insurance
A travel insurance policy covering theft, loss and medical problems is a wise idea. Consult your travel agent for options. The international student travel policies handled by STA Travel or other student travel organizations usually offer a good deal.

Check the small print, as some policies specifically exclude 'dangerous activities,' which can include scuba diving, motorcycling and even trekking. Also, a locally acquired motorcycle license may not be valid under some policies.

You might prefer a policy that pays doctors or hospitals directly rather than reimbursing you for your out-of-pocket expenses later. If you have to go the latter route, make sure you keep all documentation.

Check if your policy covers ambulances or an emergency flight home. If you have to stretch out, you'll need two seats and somebody has to pay for them.

Some policies give you a choice of medical-expense options; the higher coverage limits chiefly apply to countries like the USA, with its astronomical medical costs. Canada's hospital charges also tend to be steep; for nonresidents, the standard rate for a bed in a city hospital starts at $500 a day

and can top $2000. Make sure you examine the precise details, limitations and exclusions of your medical coverage.

The largest seller of medical insurance to visitors to Canada is Ingletrent Health (**☎** 416-340-0100, 800-387-4770, **w** www. trenthealth.com, 438 University Ave, Suite 1200, Toronto, ON M7Y 2Z1). Its hospital medical care (HMC) policies cover hospital rates, doctors' fees, extended health care and other features, but they won't pay to treat conditions you had prior to your arrival in Canada. Coverage ranges from a week to a year, with a possible renewal of one additional year. The 30-day basic policy costs $113 for an adult under the age of 55, $151 for ages 55 to 64 and $176 for 65 and over. Family rates are available.

Be sure to inquire about coverage details if you intend to make side trips to the USA, Mexico, Caribbean countries or other destinations.

Ingletrent also offers insurance policies for foreign students (at reduced rates) and for those visiting Canada on working visas. Its policies may be very beneficial in filling in coverage gaps before either a government policy kicks in, in the case of students, or the employers' paid benefits begin, in the case of foreign workers.

Contact Ingletrent, which operates offices in major cities across the country and has representatives in the northern territories, for an information pamphlet that includes an application form. It can often be found at post offices, banks, pharmacies, doctors' offices and some shopping centers. Read the information carefully; you should fully understand the conditions. Also, check the maximum amounts payable, as different policies allow for greater payments.

Many companies offer traveler's insurance, so consult the phone book.

EMBASSIES & CONSULATES
Canadian Embassies, High Commissions & Consulates
Australia
  High Commission: (**☎** 02-6270-4000, **w** www. canada.org.au) Commonwealth Ave, Canberra, ACT 2600
  Canadian Consulate General: (**☎** 02-9364-3000/3050) 111 Harrington St, Level 5, Quay West, Sydney, NSW 2000
  Consulate: (**☎** 03-9811-9999) 123 Camberwell Rd, East Hawthorn, Melbourne, Vic 3123

Consulate: (☎ 08-9322-7930) 267 St George Terrace, 3rd floor, Perth, Western Australia 6000

France
Embassy: (☎ 01-44-43-29-00, **W** www.amb-canada .fr) 35 Ave Montaigne, 75008 Paris

Germany
Embassy: (☎ 30-20-31-20, **W** www.dfait-maeci .gc.ca/~bonn) Friedrichstrasse 95, D-10117, Bonn

Ireland
Embassy: (☎ 01-478-1988) 65-68 St Stephen's Green, Dublin 2 (Note: the immigration section of this office has closed.)

Italy
Embassy: (☎ 06-44-59-81) Via G B de Rossi 27, Rome 00161

Japan
Embassy: (☎ 03-5412-6200, **W** www.dfait-maeci .gc.ca/ni-ka) 3-38 Akasaka 7-chome, Minato-ku, Tokyo 107

Netherlands
Embassy: (☎ 070-311-1600, **W** www.ocanada.nl) Sophialaan 7, 2514 JP The Hague

New Zealand
High Commission: (tel 04-473-9577, **W** www .dfait-maeci.gc.ca/newzealand) 61 Molesworth St, Thorndon, Wellington (Note: visa and immigration inquiries are handled by the Consulate General of Canada in Sydney, Australia.)

UK
High Commission: (☎ 020-7258-6600, **W** www .canada.org.uk) Macdonald House, 1 Grosvenor Square, London W1K 4AB

USA
Consulate General: (☎ 212-596-1790, **W** www .canadianembassy.org) 1251 Avenue of the Americas, New York, NY 10020-1175

Embassies & Consulates in Canada

The principal diplomatic representations to Canada are in Ottawa; these are listed here. Other offices can be found in major cities throughout Canada, and some of these are mentioned in the relevant sections of the regional chapters.

Australia
High Commission: (☎ 613-236-0841) 50 O'Connor St, Ottawa, ON K1P 6L2

France
Embassy: (☎ 613-789-1795) 42 Sussex Dr, Ottawa, ON K1M 2C9

Germany
Embassy: (☎ 613-232-1101) 1 Waverley St, Ottawa, ON K2P 0T7

Ireland
Embassy: (☎ 613-233-6281) 130 Albert St, Ottawa, ON K1A 0L6

Italy
Embassy: (☎ 613-232-2401) 275 Slater St, 21st floor, Ottawa, ON K1P 5H9

Japan
Embassy: (☎ 613-241-8541) 255 Sussex Dr, Ottawa, ON K1N 9E6

Netherlands
Embassy: (☎ 613-237-5030) 350 Albert St, Suite 2020, Ottawa, ON K1R 1A4

New Zealand
High Commission: (☎ 613-238-5991) 727-99 Bank St, Ottawa, ON K1P 6G3

Sweden
Embassy: (☎ 613-241-8553) 377 Dalhousie St, Ottawa, ON K1N 9N8

Switzerland
Embassy: (☎ 613-235-1837) 5 Marlborough Ave, Ottawa, ON K1N 8E6

UK
High Commission: (☎ 613-237-1530) 80 Elgin St, Ottawa, ON K1P 5K7

USA
Embassy: (☎ 613-238-5335) 490 Sussex Dr, PO Box 866, Station B, Ottawa, ON K1N 1G8

CUSTOMS

How thoroughly customs officials will check you out at a Canadian entry point depends on a number of things, including where you came from, what your nationality is and what you look like. If you're arriving from a country associated with the drug trade or with illegal immigration, don't be surprised by the extra scrutiny. After the terrorist attacks of September 2001, security has been tightened. People coming from countries where Islamic extremists are believed to operate can expect more attention, particularly if they have an Arabic background. Always make sure the necessary papers are in order.

Travelers may find that different border personnel interpret the rules differently. Regardless, arguing is of little use. If you're refused entry and you feel it's unjust, the best course is simply to try again later (after a shift change) or at a different border crossing.

If an agent wants to frisk or strip-search you, you're entitled to know the reason for his or her suspicion. If you wish to refuse the search, you can ask for legal counsel, which may be available at airports and larger entry points.

Don't get caught bringing drugs into Canada. This warning includes marijuana and hashish, as these qualify as narcotics in Canada. Sentences can be harsh. Note, too, that the USA has a zero tolerance policy: One marijuana seed can result in criminal prosecution.

Adults (generally anyone age 19 and older, though it varies by province) can bring in 1.1L (40ozs) of liquor or a case of 24 beers as well as 200 cigarettes, 50 cigars and 400g of tobacco (all cheaper in the USA). You can bring in gifts up to $60 in value.

Because of foot-and-mouth disease and mad cow disease, bringing in any meat products is not recommended, and carrying perishable food (such as fresh produce) and plant material of any sort may be a lot more trouble than it's worth. Inquire about current regulations before arrival.

Sporting goods, cameras and film and two days' worth of packaged or canned food can be brought in without trouble. But registering excessive or expensive sporting goods and cameras might save you some hassle when you leave, especially if you'll be crossing the Canadian-US border a number of times.

If you have a dog or cat, you'll need proof that it's had a rabies shot in the past 36 months. For US citizens, this is usually easy enough; residents of other countries might encounter more involved procedures. If you must bring a pet from abroad, check with the Canadian government or a representative before arriving at the border.

Boaters can bring pleasure craft into Canada either on a trailer or in the water for stays up to one year. Obtain the required entry permit from the customs office at or near the point of entry. All boats powered by motors over 10hp must be licensed.

Pistols, fully automatic weapons and any firearms less than 66cm (26 inches) in length are not permitted into the country. Most rifles and shotguns will be admitted without a permit.

MONEY
Currency
Canadian currency is much like that of the USA, with some noteworthy variations. Coins come in 1¢ (penny), 5¢ (nickel), 10¢ (dime), 25¢ (quarter), $1 (loonie) and $2 (twoonie, toonie) pieces. The loonie is an 11-sided, gold-colored coin known for the common loon (a species of waterbird) pictured on it. The twoonie is a two-toned coin

with a nickel outer ring and aluminum-bronze core featuring a polar bear. There is also a 50¢ coin, but you won't see it much.

Paper currency comes in $5, $10 and $20 denominations. The $50, $100 and larger bills are less common and could prove difficult to cash, especially in smaller businesses or at night. Service (gas) stations, for example, are sometimes reluctant to deal with larger bills. Canadian bills are all the same size but vary in their colors and images. Some denominations have two styles, as older versions in good condition continue to circulate.

All prices quoted in this book are in Canadian dollars, unless stated otherwise.

Exchange Rates
At press time, exchange rates were:

country	unit		Canadian dollar
Australia	A$1	=	$0.85
EU	€1	=	$1.38
Hong Kong	HK$10	=	$2.04
Japan	¥100	=	$1.20
New Zealand	NZ$1	=	$0.68
UK	UK£1	=	$2.27
USA	US$1	=	$1.59

Exchanging Money
Changing money is best done at companies such as Thomas Cook or American Express, which specialize in international transactions. In some of the larger cities these companies and other exchange houses operate small offices, booths and storefronts along main streets.

Banks and trust companies present a second option for changing money. Lastly, you can try hotels (always open at least), stores, attractions and service stations. The rates at the latter group are not likely to be in your favor.

Traveler's Checks If you're purchasing traveler's checks, buy them from American Express or Thomas Cook in either US or Canadian dollars. Some banks charge a couple of dollars to cash traveler's checks, so ask first. If you're being charged, be sure to cash several checks at once, as generally the charge remains the same no matter how many checks you cash. Despite this service charge, banks usually offer better rates than places such as hotels, restaurants and visitor attractions.

Personal checks are rarely accepted at any commercial enterprise.

Banks & ABMs Banking hours are generally shorter than regular store hours. Some banks offer evening hours a few times a week, while others, generally trust companies, are open on Saturday morning. For more information, see Business Hours, later in this chapter.

Automated banking machines (ABMs), often called ATMs (automatic teller machines) in other countries, are common throughout Canada, many of them affiliated with the Interac network. Interac permits cardholders to withdraw money from their account at any bank machine. More and more travelers have been using the Interac card – it's often the most convenient and quickest way to replenish your cash.

Bank machine locations include banks and some grocery stores, service stations, variety stores, shopping centers, bus and train stations, many of them accessible day or night, any day of the week. Most Canadian ABMs will take cards from most foreign countries, but before your visit, check with your bank to make sure your card will work.

Credit & Debit Cards Simply put, carry a credit card – you'll be able to use it almost everywhere, it'll save you the danger of taking large amounts of cash and you'll need a card to serve as a security deposit when you rent a car or even a bicycle. Also, credit cards allow you to make guaranteed reservations for accommodations; even Hostelling International (HI) hostels accept credit card reservations and payments. Plus, if you run out of cash, you can use your credit card to withdraw cash advances at bank machines.

Visa, MasterCard and American Express credit cards are honored in most places, particularly in cities. But in tiny, out-of-the-way communities, you might find that only cash and traveler's checks are accepted.

Most businesses that take credit cards also accept debit cards, which withdraw money directly from users' bank accounts to pay for purchases.

See Emergencies, later in this chapter, for help with lost/stolen cards.

Costs

Because of the widely different income levels in Canada, you'll find a range of housing, eating and entertainment prices. Inflation has been very low for several years, keeping prices fairly stable. In general, Ontario, Alberta and British Columbia are relatively costly. The three northern territories are pricier still. Your dollar will go farthest in Manitoba, Saskatchewan, Québec and all over Atlantic Canada. Cities are almost always more expensive than towns and rural areas, except in the far north.

For many visitors, the biggest expense will be accommodations. For information on lodging prices, see Accommodations, later in this chapter.

Food costs less in Canada than in much of Western Europe but more than in the USA and about the same as in Australia. For more about meal costs, see Food, later in this chapter.

For information on transportation prices (including gasoline costs), see the Getting There & Away and Getting Around chapters.

Most prices listed throughout this book do not include taxes, which can add significantly to your costs. It's a good idea to ask if tax is included when booking your room or buying your airline ticket. See Taxes, later in this chapter.

Tipping

Normal tipping is 10% to 15% of the bill. Tips are usually given to cabbies, waitstaff, hairdressers, barbers, hotel attendants and bellhops. Tipping helps get you better service in a bar, too, especially if you give a fat tip on the first order. After that, you won't go thirsty all night. A few restaurants have the gall to include a service charge on the bill. No tip should be added in these cases.

Taxes & Refunds

Provincial Tax In most of Canada, provincial consumer sales tax must be paid on all purchases. Alberta charges sales tax only on accommodations in hotels and motels, but the other provinces also tax most items bought in shops and food purchased at restaurants. The Yukon, Northwest Territories and Nunavut have no sales tax of their own.

Goods & Services Tax Also known as the Gouge and Screw Tax, the GST adds 7% to just about every product, service and transaction, on top of the usual provincial sales tax. In Ontario, for example, this total means an additional 15% on a bill, so remember to factor it in before reaching the cash register. Atlantic Canada provinces such as Newfoundland and Nova Scotia have combined their provincial tax with the GST to make one general or Harmonized Sales Tax (HST) of about 15%.

Visitors or travelers who prepare their own food, note that there is no tax applied to groceries.

Some tourist homes (the small ones), guesthouses and B&Bs don't charge GST for rooms, and foreign visitors should try asking for an exemption from the GST on their hotel bill when making payment. If paid, the GST is refundable.

Visitor Refunds Visitors can receive a GST tax rebate or refund on accommodations (including camping) and nonconsumable goods bought for use outside Canada, provided the goods are removed from the country within 60 days and cost over $50 each and total at least $200.

Tax paid on services, restaurant meals, transportation, car rentals and gas is not refundable. The *original* receipts and the goods must be verified at the border when you leave Canada. Credit card slips and photocopies are not sufficient. These rules may change at any time. For current details, check Revenue Canada (☎ 905-432-3332, W www.rc.gc.ca/visitors).

Most 'tourist' or duty-free shops and tourist information offices have a GST rebate booklet and mailing form; you can also contact Revenue Canada, Custom, Excise & Taxation, Visitors' Rebate Program, 275 Pope Road, Suite 104, Summerside, PE C1N 6C6, Canada. Beware the private rebate brokers with leaflets everywhere – they take a percentage, so you're better off dealing with the government directly by mail or website.

In addition, the provinces of Atlantic Canada, Manitoba and Ontario allow partial rebates on accommodation tax and provincial sales tax on goods. For Ontario (☎ 905-432-3332), separate forms are required; for the other provinces, you can submit your refund request on the GST application.

Check with a provincial tourist office for more information or for the necessary reimbursement forms – it's worth the trouble on a tent, camera or similarly large purchase.

Note that you need to send the original receipts to obtain the Ontario tax refund – a tricky detail because you also have to submit the originals for the GST refund. Get around this by applying first for the GST refund, as the original receipts will be returned and you can then apply for the Ontario refund.

POST & COMMUNICATIONS
Post
The mail service is neither quick nor cheap, but it's reliable. Canadian post offices will keep poste restante mail for two weeks, then return it to sender. Here's an example of how poste restante should be addressed: Recipient's Name, c/o General Delivery, Toronto, ON M5W 1A0, Canada.

A standard 1st-class airmail letter can only weigh 50g if it's going to a North American destination but can be as heavy as 500g for other international destinations.

Domestic postage costs 48¢ for a 1st-class letter (up to 30g) or a postcard, not including GST. A 1st-class letter (up to 30g) or postcard mailed to the US costs 65¢, not including GST. A 1st-class letter (up to 20g) or postcard sent to other destinations is $1.25, not including GST. Aerogrammes (which are not common) cost the same.

Suffice it to say, there are numerous methods for sending mail: via air, surface or a combination of these. For full details, go to a post office; full-page pamphlets explain all the various options, categories, requirements and prices.

Aside from the post offices themselves, stamps and postal services are often available at drugstores and some variety stores. Hotel concessions often stock stamps.

Telephone
Canada has an excellent telephone system. Rates tend to be low for local use and rather costly (but decreasing) for long distances. Overall, the rates are about the same as in the USA but probably more expensive (at least for long distances) than in Europe.

Public telephones are often readily available and can be found in hotel lobbies, bars, restaurants, large department stores and many public buildings. Telephone booths stand on street corners in cities and towns. The basic charge for a call at a pay phone varies but is generally 25¢ for a local connection. If you wish to speak to an operator, dial ☎ 0 and you'll be connected free of charge. It's also free to dial ☎ 411 (the telephone information number) or ☎ 911 (the emergency number).

Long-distance calls to anywhere in the world can be made from any phone, but the rate varies depending on what time of day it is and on how you make the call. It's cheapest and quickest not to ask for the assistance of an operator, but you have to know the area code as well as the number of the party to be reached.

If you're calling internationally, you also have to know the code for the country you're calling; most of these are listed in the front pages of the phone book. To make an international call direct, dial ☎ 011 + the country code + the area code + the phone number.

In Canada long-distance rates are cheapest from 11pm to 8am daily. The second-most-economical time slot is 6pm to 11pm daily, except Sunday, when this rate runs from 8am to 11pm. The most expensive time to call is 8am to 6pm Monday to Friday.

For those staying in hotels, motels, guesthouses and other such places, note that most establishments charge a service fee for the use of the phone on a per-call basis, even for local calls. If you're paying 50¢ per call, you might get a little bit of a shock when you see your final room bill.

Toll-Free Numbers Many businesses, ferries, hotels, hostels and tourist offices, etc, operate toll-free numbers that you can call at no cost, meaning that no long-distance charges apply. These numbers begin with 800, 888, 877, 866 and 855 (though new prefixes are being added all the time). When you call them, dial '1' first, as you would within an area code. Generally, you can call these numbers from anywhere in North America, but occasionally they'll only work within Canada or within a single province. You won't know until you try. Throughout this book, toll-free numbers (if available) are listed after the local phone numbers.

Phone Cards Phone cards can sometimes offer better per-minute rates than you'd get at a pay phone. You'll find a wide range of such cards for sale at drugstores, grocery stores and just about every convenience store. You purchase the card with a specified value – $5, $10, $20 or more – which buys you a specified number of 'units' (generally, minutes of calling). Every time you make a call, the value of the call is deducted from your balance.

eKno Communication Service

Lonely Planet's eKno global communication service provides low-cost international calls; for local calls, you're usually better off with a local card. eKno also offers free messaging services, email, travel information and an online travel vault, where you can securely store details of all your important documents. Register online at ⓦ www.ekno.lonelyplanet.com, where you'll find the local access numbers for the 24-hour customer service center. Once you've joined, always check the website for the latest access numbers and updates on new features.

Fax & Telegraph

Fax machines accessible to the public are available at major hotels, city post offices and at a range of small businesses in major towns. Check under 'Facsimile,' 'Stationers' or 'Mail Box Services' in the Yellow Pages. Facsimile messages often cost $1 to $2 per page.

To send a telegram anywhere in Canada or overseas, contact AT&T Canada, listed in the phone book.

Email & Internet Access

Email access is available at most corporate hotels and many hostels. In addition, most cities and some smaller towns now have Internet cafés or copy centers that offer online computer use at $3 to $10 an hour. Unfortunately, these places tend to come and go with regularity. More reliable are Canada's public libraries, which offer free Internet access for a limited time. You just sign up and wait your turn.

DIGITAL RESOURCES

The World Wide Web is a rich resource for travelers. You can research your trip, hunt down bargain airfares, book hotels, check on weather conditions or chat with locals and other travelers about the best places to visit (or avoid!).

There's no better place to start your Web explorations than the Lonely Planet website

(**W** www.lonelyplanet.com). Here you'll find succinct summaries on traveling to most places on earth, postcards from other travelers and the Thorn Tree bulletin board, where you can ask questions before you go or dispense advice when you get back. You can also find travel news and updates to many of LP's most popular guidebooks, and the subWWWay section links you to the most useful travel resources elsewhere on the Internet.

Throughout this book, you'll find websites for attractions and accommodations. Websites run by the provincial and territory tourist information offices are listed under Tourist Offices, earlier in this chapter. Other useful sites include:

Attractions Canada (**W** www.attractionscanada .com) – details and contact information for many of Canada's top tourist sites

Canada.com (**W** www.canada.com) – general news on all things Canadian

Canada WorldWeb Travel Guide (www.canada .worldweb.com) – hotel reservations, packages, maps and travel articles

Canada Travel (**W** www.canadatravel.ca) – reservations at major hotels, train bookings and travel packages

Canoe (**W** www.canoe.ca) – Canadian and international news, updated continually

BOOKS

For a brief guide to Canada's literature, see the Arts section in the Facts about Canada chapter.

Lonely Planet

If you'd like more information about some of the destinations featured in this book, Lonely Planet also publishes the city guides *Toronto, Montréal* and *Vancouver,* as well as the regional guides *British Columbia, Canada's Maritime Provinces* (covering Nova Scotia, New Brunswick and Prince Edward Island) and *Québec.* You might also find the *Alaska* and *Pacific Northwest* books useful, depending on your destination. The *French phrasebook* makes a good reference for visitors to Québec.

Travel

Canadian Lucy Izon's *Backpacker Journal* makes a handy, informative travel companion in which to keep your own diary and travel musings.

Jan Morris, a Welsh travel writer who has written about many cities around the world, published *City to City* in 1990, after she traveled Canada coast to coast; it's a highly readable collection of essays about 10 Canadian cities and their people. Note that this book was also published under the name *O Canada: Travels in an Unknown Country.*

In a similar vein, *Wild Is Always There: Canada Through the Eyes of Foreign Writers,* edited by Greg Gatenby, is a collection of pieces by various writers who have spent some time in the country.

Steven Brook has collected his quirky travel essays in *Maple Leaf Rag.* In *Welcome Home: Travels in Small-Town Canada,* Stuart McLean reveals much about the character of small-town life.

Kildare Dobbs depicts a bus trip across the country in *Ribbon of Highway: The Trans Canada Highway Coast to Coast.* John and Martha Stradiotta describe the many national and provincial parks across the country in *The Road to Canada's Wilds: Parks along the Trans Canada Highway. Canada's National Parks – A Visitor's Guide,* by Marylee Stephenson, is the most complete guide to the country's national parks and provides all the essential information.

Adventurers should check out Gary and Joanie McGuffin's *Where Rivers Run: A 6000-Mile Exploration of Canada by Canoe,* Eric Morse's *Freshwater Saga: Memoirs of a Lifetime of Wilderness Canoeing* and Richard Davids' *Lords of the Arctic: A Journey among the Polar Bears,* set in Churchill.

Farley Mowat writes about the north, wildlife and natural conservation in such books as *Never Cry Wolf.*

Additional Canadiana

Wordsmiths might like a peek at the *Canadian Oxford Dictionary,* with 2000 Canadianisms as well as biographies and geographic details. The *Dictionary of Newfoundland English* can seem almost foreign. In a few years the *Bilingual Canadian Dictionary* (French/English) will be published by the universities of Ottawa, Montréal and Laval.

The information-packed, one-volume *Canadian Encyclopedia* is available in book and CD formats and should be available in most libraries. The similar *Encyclopedia of British Columbia* offers a wealth of information.

John Robert Colombo has written a number of books of Canadian facts, figures and trivia, including *Canadian Literary Landmarks*. Mordecai Richler, well known for his fiction, has collected his essays on the country in *Home Sweet Home: My Canadian Album*.

Ralph Nader (yes, the famous US consumer advocate) has put together an interesting and sometimes surprising list of many of Canada's achievements in the book *Canada Firsts*.

History

Pierre Berton is Canada's prime chronicler of the country's history. He has written on a wide range of subjects, including the gold rush, the railways and the Depression, in an entertaining and informative way in such books as *Klondike, The National Dream* and *The Promised Land*.

Peter C Newman writes on Canadian business but has also produced an intriguing history of the Hudson's Bay Company, *Caesar's of the Wilderness,* beginning with the early fur-trading days.

A basic primer on the country's history is *The Penguin History of Canada*, by Kenneth McNaught.

American William Vollman is in the midst of writing a massive, seven-volume fictional but well-researched account of the clash of European and Native Indian cultures in Canada – these books are far more than dry history lessons. Within this multi-volume work is *Fathers and Crows,* which outlines French expansion from Acadia.

For more information on Canada's Native Indian people, try Allan Macmillan's *Native Peoples and Cultures of Canada,* which includes both history and current issues.

The classic book on Canada's Native Indian people, *The Indians of Canada,* was written in 1932 by Diamond Jenness. Originally from New Zealand, Jenness led a life that makes an amazing story in its own right, as he spent years living with various indigenous people across the country.

NEWSPAPERS & MAGAZINES

The *Globe & Mail* newspaper, sometimes termed Canada's newspaper, is published in Toronto but is available across the country daily; it provides a well-written record of national affairs from politics to the arts. The right-leaning *National Post* is also a good national paper; its emphasis is business news.

Other principal newspapers are the *Montréal Gazette, Ottawa Citizen, Toronto Star* and *Vancouver Sun.*

In Québec, readers of French should have a look at both the federalist *La Presse,* the largest circulation French daily, and the separatist-leaning *Le Devoir;* there are other French dailies as well.

Maclean's is Canada's weekly news magazine. The monthly *Canadian Geographic* features excellent articles and photography on a range of Canadian topics from wildlife to weather.

RADIO & TV

The Canadian Broadcasting Corporation (CBC), with both national and regional broadcasts on both radio (AM and FM bands) and TV, can be seen or heard almost anywhere in the country, including some of the more remote areas. It carries more Canadian content in music and information than any of the private broadcast companies. CBC Radio in particular is a fine service.

This Morning, a highly recommended show broadcast 9am to noon weekdays, offers listeners a well-rounded view of the nation's opinions in an entertaining and educational format. Highlights are rebroadcast nightly at 8pm.

The CBC also operates a French radio and TV network, both going under the name Radio-Canada. These can also be tuned into anywhere across the country.

Many private AM broadcasters in large cities have gone to so-called talk radio, which often features a baiting host and opinionated callers. Ask around and tune in for a quick earful of what some Canadians think of the day's hot topics. Two major stations to try are CFRB 1010 in Toronto and CJAD 800 in Montréal.

FM stations tend to have fewer advertisements and specialize in one form of music, be it rock or classical.

Besides the CBC the other major national TV network is the Canadian Television Network (CTV), the main commercial channel broadcasting a mix of Canadian, US and national programs. Its nightly national news show is seen across the country.

Canadians can readily tune into TV and radio stations from the USA and often do.

PHOTOGRAPHY & VIDEO

Camera shops in the major centers stock a range of products, including all kinds of film. Stores in larger cities also provide the freshest film (always check the expiration date) and the best prices. Black's, a good retail outlet with branches across the country (except in Québec), sells a good selection of film and offers quick processing, too.

Transparency film (slides) has become difficult to get without going to a good camera shop. It's best to buy plenty in a major city. The same goes for digital and video camera equipment and supplies. Tapes are available at Radio Shack, a cross-country electronic retailer. Drugstores (pharmacies, chemists), department stores and corner convenience shops generally carry only basic Kodak and Fuji print film.

When you buy most kinds of film in Canada, processing isn't included. However, Kodachrome can be purchased with processing included (the cheapest option). The Kodachrome processing plant is in the USA, and film can be mailed directly there, or you can leave the film at a camera store, which will arrange delivery for a modest fee.

Carrying an extra battery for your built-in light meter is a good idea because you know the one you're using will die at the most inopportune time.

For photographing wildlife, a 100mm lens is useful and can be handheld. To get serious, you will need a 200mm telephoto lens and a tripod. Early morning and evening are the best times of day to spy animals in the wild.

Canadian airports use X-ray scanning machines for security, which should pose no problems to most films. Any given roll should not be scanned more than half a dozen times to be on the safe side. With specialized film, for example film with an ISO (ASA) of 400 or higher, X-ray damage is a real threat. For those who do not want to take a chance with any film, good camera shops offer lead-lined pouches that can hold several canisters of film and that provide total protection. And, no, they are not unduly heavy.

TIME

Canada spans six of the world's 24 time zones. As shown on the map, the eastern zone in Newfoundland is unusual in that it's only a half hour different from the adjacent zone. The time difference from coast to coast is 4½ hours.

Canada uses Daylight Saving Time during summer. It begins on the last Sunday in April and ends on the last Sunday in October. Clocks are pushed forward an hour, which results in a seemingly longer summer day. Saskatchewan is the only large region that doesn't adopt Daylight Saving Time and instead uses Standard Time year-round, which means that the entire province falls in the Central Time Zone half the year (in winter) and the Mountain Time Zone the other half (in summer). Similarly, most of Nunavut does not change the clocks in spring and fall, with the exception of the tiny communities of Cambridge Bay and Kugluktuk. Nunavut falls within the Central Time Zone half the year and the Eastern Time Zone the other half. In Québec, too, half of Anticosti Island doesn't change with daylight saving time, nor does a portion of eastern British Columbia.

For details of each provincial time zone, see the Information section at the beginning of each province chapter. You can also get time-zone information from the website of the Institute for National Measurement Standards: **w** www.nrc.ca/inms.

ELECTRICITY

Canada, like the USA, operates on 110V, 60-cycle electric power. Visitors from anywhere besides North America should bring a plug adapter if they wish to use their own small appliances, such as razors, hairdryers, etc. Canadian electrical goods come with either a two-pronged plug (the same as a US one) or, increasingly, a three-pronger with the added ground. Most sockets can accommodate both types of plugs.

WEIGHTS & MEASURES

Canada officially changed from imperial measurement to the metric system in the 1970s. Most citizens accepted this change only begrudgingly, and even today you'll see that both systems remain for many day-to-day purposes.

All speed-limit signs are in metric – so do not go 100mph! Gasoline is sold in liters, but items such as hamburger meat and potatoes are still often sold by the pound. Canadian

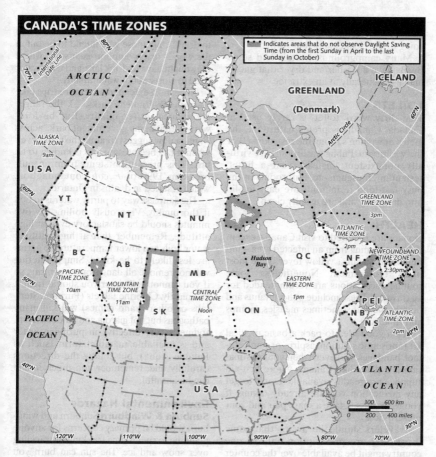

CANADA'S TIME ZONES

Indicates areas that do not observe Daylight Saving Time (from the first Sunday in April to the last Sunday in October)

ARCTIC OCEAN

ICELAND

GREENLAND

(Denmark)

ALASKA TIME ZONE
9am

USA

YT

NT

NU

GREENLAND TIME ZONE
3pm

ATLANTIC TIME ZONE
2pm

BC

AB

PACIFIC TIME ZONE
10am

MOUNTAIN TIME ZONE
11am

SK

MB

CENTRAL TIME ZONE
Noon

Hudson Bay

QC

NF

NEWFOUNDLAND TIME ZONE
2:30pm

EASTERN TIME ZONE
1pm

ON

PEI

NB

NS

ATLANTIC TIME ZONE
2pm

PACIFIC OCEAN

USA

ATLANTIC OCEAN

0   300   600 km
0   200   400 miles

---

radio stations often give temperatures in both Celsius and Fahrenheit degrees.

The expensive changeover has really resulted in a bit of a mess. The old system can never be eliminated completely as long as the USA, Canada's largest trading partner, still uses its version of British measurement.

For help in converting between the two systems, see the chart on the inside back cover of this book. Note that the US system, basically the same as the imperial, differs in liquid measurement, most significantly (for drivers) in the size of its gallons.

LAUNDRY

All cities and major towns have central storefronts known as laundromats (laundrettes for the Brits and Aussies), with rows of coin-operated washing machines and dryers. These establishments tend to be open every day until about 11pm (but there's usually an earlier cutoff time for starting new loads of laundry, so that you'll be done by the time the doors close).

You'll rarely find an attendant on the premises – so if you have any problems with the machines, good luck resolving them yourself. Many self-service laundries sell soap, but it's cheaper to bring some. A wash and dry costs a couple of dollars, most often in $1 or 25¢ coins.

Also common are dry cleaners, known simply as 'the cleaners,' where clothes can be cleaned and pressed in about a day, sometimes two or three. But you'll pay a lot more than at the laundromat.

The better hotels often offer an in-house laundry service, but it'll cost you more than going to the cleaners on your own.

Many campgrounds, hostels and some B&Bs have a washer and dryer that guests may use, generally at an extra fee.

TOILETS
That dirty word 'toilet' is rarely used in Canada. Canadians prefer bathroom, the men's or women's room, the restroom (!) or the washroom. Public washrooms are virtually nonexistent; instead, visit a hotel, restaurant, museum, etc. Bathrooms in the busy fast-food restaurants are easy to slip into discreetly and are usually clean.

HEALTH
No jabs are required to visit Canada, except if you're coming from an infected area – immunization against yellow fever is the most likely requirement. Nonetheless, some routine vaccinations are recommended for all travelers. These include polio, tetanus and diphtheria, and sometimes measles, mumps and rubella.

It's a good idea to pack a basic medical kit (antiseptic solution, aspirin or paracetamol, bandages, etc) even when your destination is a place like Canada, where first-aid supplies are readily available. Don't forget any medication you are already taking. If you wear glasses, take a spare pair and your prescription.

Travelers should be aware that some drugs that are prescription-only in one country might be available over the counter in Canada and vice versa. For example, the allergy medicines Allegra and Claritin and the muscle relaxant Roboxicet, all of which are prescription drugs in the US, can be bought by anyone in a drugstore in Canada.

Naughtier than the Image?

According to a 2000 poll, more than a third of Canadians admitted they had played hooky from work, claiming they were sick when they were fine. In Québec two-thirds of respondents fessed up to their devious ways. The main reason was wanting to be with a spouse or lover.

Water Purification
Canadian tap water from coast to coast is safe to drink. Only those who intend to be out in the woods or on outdoor excursions where they might have to drink lake and river water need to worry about water quality.

Since most extended adventure trips take place in government parks, ask the ranger about local water quality. But be forewarned that many government parks across Canada now suggest treating the water even when it has been tested and is known to be fine. This precaution stems from an outbreak in 1999 of *E coli* contamination, which resulted in deaths in Ontario.

The simplest way to purify water is to boil it thoroughly. Vigorously boiling for five minutes should be satisfactory even at high altitude. Remember that at high altitude water boils at a lower temperature, so germs are less likely to be killed. Simple filtering will not remove all dangerous organisms, so if you cannot boil water you should treat it chemically. Chlorine tablets (Puritabs, Steritabs or other brand names) will kill many pathogens but not giardia and amoebic cysts. Iodine is very effective in purifying water and is available in tablet form (such as Potable Aqua), but follow the directions carefully and, remember, too much iodine can be harmful.

Environmental Hazards
Sunburn & Windburn Sunburn and windburn should be primary concerns for anyone planning to spend time trekking or traveling over snow and ice. The sun can burn you even if you feel cold, and the wind can cause dehydration and chafing of skin. Use a good sunscreen and a moisture cream on exposed skin, even on cloudy days. A hat provides added protection, as do zinc cream or some other barrier cream for your nose and lips if you're spending any time on ice or snow.

Reflection and glare from ice and snow can cause snow blindness, so it's essential to use high-protection sunglasses for any sort of glacier visit or ski trip. Calamine lotion can help soothe a mild sunburn.

Hypothermia & Frostbite Though some think of Canada as a perpetually ice-bound wasteland, few people are likely to suffer health problems due to extreme cold. On winter days when frostbite is a possibility (due almost always to a combination of low temperature and high wind), you'll know it. Everybody will be discussing it, the radio will broadcast warnings about how many minutes of exposed skin is acceptable and…it will be bloody cold.

If you're in the mountains or the north, you should always be prepared for cold, wet or windy conditions even if you're just out walking or hitchhiking.

Hypothermia occurs when the body loses heat faster than it can produce it and the core temperature of the body falls. It's surprisingly easy to progress from very cold to dangerously cold due to a combination of wind, wet clothing, fatigue and hunger, even if the air temperature is above freezing. To protect yourself, dress in layers; silk, wool and some of the new artificial fibers are all good insulating materials. A hat is important, as a lot of heat is lost through the head. A strong, waterproof outer layer is essential for keeping dry. Carry basic supplies, including food that contains simple sugars so you can generate body heat quickly, and take lots of fluid to drink.

Symptoms of hypothermia are exhaustion, numb skin (particularly toes and fingers), shivering, slurred speech, irrational or violent behavior, lethargy, stumbling, dizzy spells, muscle cramps and violent bursts of energy. Sufferers may claim they're warm and try to take off their clothes – a sure sign that something's wrong.

To treat hypothermia, first get the person out of the wind and/or rain, remove his or her clothing if it's wet and replace it with dry, warm clothing. Give the person hot liquids – not alcohol – and some high-calorie, easily digestible food. Do not rub victims; instead, allow them to warm themselves slowly. This should be enough for the early stages of hypothermia, but if it's progressed further you might have to place victims in warm sleeping bags and get in with them.

Altitude Sickness Acute Mountain Sickness (AMS) occurs at high altitude and can be fatal. The lack of oxygen at high altitudes affects most people to some extent, some worse than others. To avoid the most severe symptoms, try to ascend slowly, with frequent rest days; spend two to three nights at each rise of 1000m. If you reach a high altitude by trekking, acclimatization takes

place gradually and you're less likely to be affected than if you fly directly there.

You should also drink extra fluids. In the dry, cold mountain air, you lose moisture as you breathe. Finally, you should eat light, high-carbohydrate meals for more energy, avoid sedatives, and skip alcohol, as it may increase the risk of dehydration.

Even with acclimatization, you may still have trouble adjusting. Headaches, nausea, dizziness, a dry cough, insomnia, breathlessness, fatigue, confusion, lack of coordination and loss of appetite are all warnings to heed. Mild altitude problems will generally abate after a day or so, but if the symptoms persist or become worse, the only treatment is to descend. Even 500m can help.

There is no hard and fast rule as to how high is too high: AMS has been fatal at altitudes of 3000m, although 3500m to 4500m is the usual range. It's always wise to sleep at a lower altitude than the greatest height reached during the day.

Infectious Diseases

Giardiasis If you're going to camp in the backcountry, you should take precautions against the intestinal parasite *(Giardia lamblia)*, which causes giardiasis, known colloquially as 'beaver fever.' This intestinal parasite is present in contaminated water.

The symptoms include stomach cramps, nausea, a bloated stomach, frequent gas and watery, foul-smelling diarrhea. Giardiasis can appear several weeks after you've been exposed to the parasite. The symptoms may disappear for a few days and then return; this can go on for several weeks.

You should seek medical advice if you think you have giardiasis or amoebic dysentery, but where this is not possible, tinidazole or metronidazole are the recommended drugs. Treatment is a 2g single dose of tinidazole or 250mg of metronidazole three times daily for five to 10 days.

Rabies This isn't a major problem, but rabies is something to be aware of when spending any time in the woods or undeveloped areas. Animals most likely affected are the squirrel, skunk, raccoon, bat and, particularly, the fox. Paradoxically, all of the above animals have learned to adapt quite well to populated regions and tend to frequent city parks and recreation areas, wooded areas around rivers and streams and even residential streets after dark. Especially on garbage nights!

Rabies is caused by a bite or scratch by an infected animal. Any bite, scratch or even lick from a mammal should be cleaned immediately and thoroughly. Scrub with soap and running water and then clean with an alcohol or iodine solution. If there's any possibility that the animal is infected, seek medical help immediately. Even if the animal is not rabid, all bites should be treated seriously, as they can become infected or can lead to tetanus.

You should consider a rabies vaccination if you're in a high-risk category – eg, if you intend to explore caves (bat bites could be dangerous) or work with animals.

Lyme Disease Lyme disease poses only a minor threat for those spending time in the woods. Since the late 1980s each summer has seen more cases of this disease, although the vast majority of North American cases have occurred in the USA.

Really more of a condition than a disease, it's transmitted by a species of deer tick, similar to a tick found on a dog but smaller. The tick infects the skin with the spirochaete bacterium, which causes the illness.

Symptoms vary widely, but the disease usually begins with a spreading rash at the site of the tick bite. Other symptoms include fever, headache, extreme fatigue, aching joints and muscles and mild neck stiffness. If untreated, these symptoms usually resolve over several weeks, but over subsequent weeks or months disorders of the nervous system, heart and joints may develop. Treatment works best early in the illness.

The best way to avoid the whole business is to take precautions in areas where it has been reported, such as Turkey Point, Ontario.

If walking in the woods, cover the body as much as possible, use an insect repellent containing diethylmetatoluamide (DEET) and at the end of the day check yourself, children or pets for the ticks. DEET is not recommended for children, so a milder substitute will have to do. Chances are that you will not feel the bite if it happens. Of course, most ticks don't transmit Lyme disease.

Sexually Transmitted Diseases (STDs)
STDs include gonorrhea, herpes and syphilis; sores, blisters or rashes around the genitals and discharges or pain when urinating are common symptoms. While abstinence from sexual contact is the only 100% effective prevention, using condoms is also effective. If you do contract a sexually transmitted disease, doctors will treat you with antibiotics.

HIV/AIDS Infection with the human immunodeficiency virus (HIV) may lead to acquired immune deficiency syndrome (AIDS), a fatal disease. Any exposure to blood, blood products or body fluids may put you at risk. The disease is often transmitted through sexual contact or dirty needles – vaccinations, acupuncture, tattooing and body piercing can be potentially as dangerous as intravenous drug use. Make sure all needles have been sterilized before they touch your body.

WOMEN TRAVELERS
Women can certainly travel safely by themselves in Canada, especially when heeding the following advice. When traveling alone, try to arrive at your destination before dark. If arriving at a bus or train station (bus stations in particular are often not in the best parts of town), take a taxi to the place where you're spending the night. In some of the larger cities, the bus and/or train station is connected to the subway system. Subways in Canada are clean and safe. Once close to your destination, catch a taxi from the subway stop.

If driving, keep your vehicle well maintained and don't get low on gasoline. If you do break down on the highway, especially at night, stick a large pre-made sign reading 'Call Police' in the window. Such a sign should quickly send the police your way. Away from busy areas, you shouldn't get out of your car and wait beside it, especially at night; rather, wait inside with the doors locked. In cities, avoid underground parking lots.

A woman alone shouldn't hitchhike. For more information, see Hitchhiking in the Getting Around chapter.

When booking rooms, some women suggest using only an initial with your surname. Hostels and B&Bs tend to be good, safe choices. In B&Bs and guesthouses, ask whether the rooms have locks – some do not. When checking into a motel, ask to see the room first and make sure the doors and windows can be secured. Most motel rooms come with a telephone.

Unaccompanied women in nightclubs or bars will often find they get a lot of attention (and possibly drinks) whether they want it or not. If you don't want the company, most men will accept a polite but firm 'no, thank you.'

If you plan to enjoy the outdoors, avoid using perfumes and fragrant cosmetics anywhere where bears might be.

In Toronto, the Women's Counselling Referral & Education Centre (☎ 416-534-7501, 525 Bloor St W) can offer advice on a wide range of problems and questions. For help with gynecological issues, contact Planned Parenthood (☎ 416-961-3200).

GAY & LESBIAN TRAVELERS
As a generally tolerant country, Canada doesn't present any particular problems for gays and lesbians. Laws in Canada protect against discrimination on the basis of sexual orientation.

Montréal, Toronto and Vancouver have sizable gay communities with support groups, associations and any number of clubs and bars. These same cities also host celebratory Gay Pride Days, which attract big crowds, including straights. In Toronto, the biweekly *Xtra* magazine offers a full range of information, including advertisements for lodgings and other businesses that cater primarily to gays. The same company publishes *Xtra West* in Vancouver and *Capitol Xtra* in Ottawa. Look for *Wayves* in Halifax and *Fugues* in Montréal.

Columbia Fun Maps (W www.funmaps .net) produces gay- and lesbian-oriented maps and brochures for cities across North America. The Montréal guide also includes information on Québec City.

The Male Accommodation Network (MAN; ☎ 514-933-7571) is a gay reservation lodging service with contacts around the country. In Toronto, Gay Services – TAGL (☎ 416-964-6600) offers information and counseling.

DISABLED TRAVELERS
Canada has gone further than the vast majority of the world's countries in making day-to-day life less burdensome to the physically disabled, most notably those in wheelchairs. This process continues.

Most public buildings are wheelchair accessible, including major tourist offices, major museums, art galleries and principal attractions. All the above and many restaurants also have washroom facilities suitable for wheelchairs. Major hotels are often equipped to deal with wheelchairs, and some less-expensive motel chains such as the countrywide Comfort Inn (frequently mentioned through the book) offer wheelchair access via ramps.

Many of the national and provincial parks have accessible interpretive centers, and often some of the shorter nature trails and/ or boardwalks have been developed with wheelchairs or self-propelled mobility aids in mind.

The VIA Rail system can accommodate the wheelchair-bound, but you should call at least 48 hours ahead. All bus lines will assist passengers and take chairs or any other aids providing they collapse to fit in the usual luggage compartments. Canadian airlines provide early boarding and disembarking for disabled passengers.

In major cities, parking lots all have designated parking spots for the physically disabled, usually marked with a painted wheelchair. These spots, located closest to the door or access point of the place being visited, cannot be used by others under threat of serious fine. Car rental agencies can provide special accessories such as hand controls with advance notice. Toronto's public transportation system, the TTC, runs a special bus service with lifts for wheelchairs.

The Canadian Parapalegic Association (☎ 416-422-5640, 520 Sutherland Dr, Toronto, ON M4G 3V9) can supply information on facilities for handicapped travelers in Canada.

SENIOR TRAVELERS
Visitors over the age of 65, and sometimes 60, should take advantage of the many cost reductions offered to seniors in Canada, including discounts on all means of transportation. Many of the government parks offer reduced rates, as do most of the country's attractions, museums, historic sites and even movie houses. Some hotels and motels may provide a price reduction – it's always worth asking.

Elderhostel (☎ 877-426-8056, W www.elder hostel.org) specializes in inexpensive, educational packages for those over 60. The standard type of program consists of mornings of lectures followed by afternoon field trips to related sights, focusing on such subjects as history, nature, geography and art. Participants stay in university dorms or the like. The length of the courses varies but can be several weeks. Full packages include meals, lodging and some transportation.

In Canada, a similar organization is Routes to Learning (☎ 613-530-2222, 877-475-5572, **w** www.routestolearning.ca, 213-4 Catarqui St, Kingston, ON K7K 1Z7).

TRAVEL WITH CHILDREN

Lonely Planet's *Travel with Children,* by Cathy Lanigan, includes all manner of advice on travel with children, including information on health and on kid-friendly activities in Canada.

Almost all attractions in Canada offer child rates. Some hotels/motels throw in free meals for kids, and some don't charge at all for those under 18 years old. Buses and trains generally offer child discounts.

Always fit children with lifejackets during any boating or canoeing excursions. While camping or in remote areas, be aware how quickly children can become disoriented and lost. Don't let kids stray where bears and cougars are known to exist. Ask park rangers if in any doubt. Never let children approach wild animals, no matter how cute and tame the animal appears (or how many other stupid people you see approaching it).

DANGERS & ANNOYANCES

Check the Health section, earlier in this chapter, for possible health risks. See also Road Rules & Safety Precautions in the Getting Around chapter for tips about driving.

Urban Problems

While everyone should take normal, commonsense precautions, street crime is minimal and shouldn't be a concern to visitors.

Since the mid-1990s, the number of people living on the streets has risen dramatically due to various social and political factors. The sheer volume of homeless people – in some cases the result of people with mental illnesses trying to cope without adequate services – often surprises both residents and visitors. But generally homeless people don't pose any danger.

Rural Problems

Fire When camping outside legitimate campgrounds, do not start a fire. This is extremely dangerous and could cause untold amounts of devastation during the dry summer months.

In designated campgrounds, make sure that anything that was burning is put out completely when you've finished with it, including cigarettes.

Bears Animals can present serious problems if you encounter them while you're camping in the woods. Bears – the most important danger – are always looking for an easy snack. Keep your food in nylon bags. Tie the sack to a rope and sling it over a branch away from your tent and away from the trunk of the tree, as most bears can climb (though grizzlies can't). Hoist it up high enough (about 3m) so a standing bear can't reach it. Don't leave food scraps around the site and never, ever keep food in the tent.

Don't try to get close-up photographs of bears and never come between a bear and its cubs. If you see any cubs, quietly and quickly disappear. If you do see a bear, try to get upwind so it can smell you and you won't startle it. While hiking through woods or in the mountains in bear country, some people wear a noisemaker, like a bell. Talking or singing is just as good. Whatever you do, don't feed bears – if you do, they will lose their fear of people and eventually lose their lives to park wardens.

Other Pests Campers are unlikely to encounter bears, but squirrels, chipmunks, mice and raccoons are common. They'll spend a lot of time tearing through bags of food or garbage and even smacking pots and pans around, making a heck of a clatter in the middle of the night. The best defense is not to feed them, no matter how cute, and to store all food securely.

All in all, though, bugs are the creatures most apt to torture you while you're in the woods. You might hear tales of lost hikers going insane from the blackflies and mosquitoes. This is no joke – they can make you miserable, though they can't do much physical harm beyond a handful of swollen bites.

June is generally the worst month, and as summer wears on, the bugs disappear. The bugs are at their worst deep in the woods, and they get worse the farther north you go. In clearings, along shorelines or anywhere there's a breeze you'll be safe, except from the buzzing horseflies, which are basically teeth with wings.

As a rule, darker clothes attract biting insects more than lighter ones. Perfume, too, evidently attracts the wrong kind of attention. Try to minimize the amount of skin exposed by wearing a long-sleeved shirt, long pants and a close-fitting hat or cap.

Take 'bug juice' – liquid or spray repellents such as Muskol and Off; the latter also has an extra-strength version known as Deep Woods Off. An ingredient often used in repellents known as DEET should not be used on children; some brands don't contain it. Lemon or orange peel rubbed on your skin will help if you're out of repellent.

Mosquitoes come out around sunset; building a fire will help keep them away. For campers, a tent with a zippered screen is pretty much a necessity.

Protect yourself from mosquitoes.

If you get lost and are being eaten alive, submerge your body in water if you are by a lake or river.

At least the bites and stings can't kill you – there are no poisonous spiders or insects in the country. Rattlesnakes do live in parts of Ontario, Alberta and British Columbia, but even serious hikers rarely see the generally timid animals. Still, if you're bitten, seek medical attention right away. If you're allergic to bees, wasps and hornets, carry a treatment kit outside of urban areas.

EMERGENCIES

In most of the country, particularly urban areas, call ☎ 911 for all police, fire and medical emergencies. In all other areas or when in doubt, call ☎ 0 and ask the operator for assistance. For nonemergency police matters, consult the local telephone book for the number of the station.

Should your passport get lost or stolen, contact your nearest consulate. For lost or stolen traveler's checks, contact the issuer or its representative. Upon purchase of the checks, you should have received a list of telephone numbers to call in case of loss. To expedite matters, keep a record of which checks you've cashed.

If you plan to make an insurance claim, be sure to contact the police, who will generate a record of the theft or incident. Ask for the reference number on the police report, as the insurance company will want it.

If you lose your credit card or traveler's checks, call the following emergency numbers: Visa (☎ 800-847-2911), MasterCard (☎ 800-361-3361) or American Express (☎ 800-221-7282).

LEGAL MATTERS

Visitors are unlikely to meet Canadian police officers. Spot checks on individuals and vehicles are not common. Drunk driving, however, is considered a very serious offense and random checks are held at bar closing time, notably around Christmas. You could find yourself in jail overnight, followed by a court date, heavy fine, suspended license and/or further incarceration.

Despite the fact that authorities might sometimes appear to be indifferent to drug use, recreational drugs are illegal and laws may be enforced at any time. Smuggling any drugs, including marijuana, is a serious crime. See Customs, earlier in this chapter, for more information.

BUSINESS HOURS

Most banks/trust companies are open 10am to 5pm Monday to Thursday, perhaps staying open to 6pm on Friday. Some are open until noon or 2pm on Saturday.

Canadian post offices are open weekdays, generally 9am to 5pm. Postal outlets in retail stores, often drugstores, have longer hours.

Shops are generally open from about 9am to about 6pm, sometimes staying open until 9pm Thursday or Friday. Shopping malls, plazas, large department stores and some downtown stores often remain open until 9pm every day. Convenience stores, some supermarkets and some drugstores are open 24 hours. In general, you'll be able to do some shopping on Sunday, except in eastern Canada (east of Québec). Nova Scotia remains closed up tight on Sundays by law.

Many restaurants generally close at about midnight, as Canadians do not dine particularly late, rarely eating out later than 10pm. Many of the better places serve lunch and dinner only, but smaller eateries and coffee shops open as early as 6am.

Most bars, pubs and lounges open at noon and close at 1am or 2am, but it varies by province. In Ontario last call is 2am. In Québec the more liberal laws allow bars to stay open until 3am or 4am. The larger cities usually have after-hours bars, which remain open for music or dancing but stop serving alcohol.

PUBLIC HOLIDAYS

Victoria Day and Labor Day are important holidays, as these long weekends (the holiday itself is always a Monday) unofficially mark the beginning and end of summer. They represent the opening and closing of many businesses, attractions and services, and the change of hours of operation for many others.

Thanksgiving (the same as the American holiday but held earlier) is really a harvest festival. The traditional meal includes roasted turkey.

Although not officially a holiday, Halloween (October 31) has become a significant celebration. Based on a Celtic pagan tradition, Halloween spawns countless costume parties. In larger cities, gays have adopted it as a major event, and nightclubs are often the scene of wild masquerades.

The following is a list of the main public holidays, when government offices, schools and banks are generally closed:

January 1 New Year's Day
3rd Monday in February Family Day (Alberta)
Monday nearest March 17 St Patrick's Day (Newfoundland)
March or April Good Friday and Easter Monday
Monday nearest April 23 St George's Day (Newfoundland)
Monday before May 24 Victoria Day (except in the Atlantic Provinces)
June 24 Fête Nationale, formerly known as St Jean Baptiste Day (Québec)
Monday nearest June 24 Discovery Day (Newfoundland)
July 1 Canada Day, called Memorial Day in Newfoundland
Monday nearest July 13 Orangeman's Day (Newfoundland)
1st Monday in August Civic Holiday
3rd Monday in August Discovery Day (Yukon)
1st Monday in September Labor Day
2nd Monday in October Thanksgiving
November 11 Remembrance Day
December 25 Christmas Day
December 26 Boxing Day

SPECIAL EVENTS

See the individual town sections of the regional chapters for information on particular special events.

The provincial governments publish annual lists of events and special attractions as part of their tourism promotion packages. Local tourist departments sometimes print up more detailed and extensive lists of their own, which include cultural and sporting exhibitions and happenings of all kinds.

Major provincial and national holidays are usually cause for some celebration, especially in summer, when events often wrap up with a fireworks display. During Canada Day festivities in July, skies light up from coast to coast.

ACTIVITIES

Canada's greatest attribute is its natural environment. Much of the country's appeal lies in the range of physical activities it makes possible, such as hiking, canoeing, fishing, skiing and exploring flora and fauna.

There are wilderness trips of all types, organized or self-directed. Provincial tourist offices have information on activities and on the hundreds of private businesses, operators and outfitters offering adventure tours and trips. All also distribute information on national and provincial parks, many of which can be highlights of a trip to Canada. Many of the national and provincial parks are detailed in the regional chapters (also see the special section on Canada's parks).

Cycling

In the east, some of the most popular cycling regions are the hilly Gaspé Peninsula in Québec and the Atlantic Provinces, excluding Newfoundland. You can expect nice, flat rides on Prince Edward Island. New Brunswick and Nova Scotia offer a fair bit of variety, plus pleasing scenery. Towns stand close together, so you can see a little bit of country and a little bit of city as you pedal.

In Ontario, try the Bruce Peninsula and the Thousand Islands Parkway area around Kingston. The other major cycling areas in Canada lie around the Rocky Mountains and throughout British Columbia.

Off-road mountain biking is popular across the country, particularly in resort areas such as the Laurentian Mountains of Québec and the Rockies. Rentals are available.

For information on bicycle rentals, some routes and events, see the Activities sections of the regional chapters. For further information, contact the Canadian Cycling Association (☎ 613-248-1353, **W** www.canadian -cycling.com, 702-2197 Riverside Dr, Ottawa, ON K1H 7X3), which can supply local contacts, trail information and much more.

Hiking

Canada offers a range of walks and hikes that are long or short, rugged or gentle, mountain or coastal. Almost all of the country's trails, and certainly most of the best, are found in either the provincial or national parks.

The majority of parks have some type of walking path, although some may be no more than a short nature trail. The larger the park, as a rule, the longer the trail. Conservation areas, wildlife reserves and sanctuaries often have marked trails.

Outside the federal and provincial park systems, some extended trails run through a mix of public and private lands.

Work is continuing on the **Trans Canada Trail**, a 15,000km crushed-stone path that winds from coast to coast with an offshoot from Calgary to Tuktoyaktuk on the Arctic Ocean. It will take about 300 days to cycle, 500 days to ride on horseback and 750 days to walk. For information on completed sections, call the trail foundation at ☎ 800-465-

3636 or visit **W** www.tctrail.ca. At the time of writing, the trail was 60% complete, with many usable sections.

Some of the prime spots for hiking include the Bruce Trail in Ontario, which runs from Lake Ontario 700km north to Georgian Bay; Killarney Provincial Park in Ontario; Pukaskwa National Park on Lake Superior, Ontario; Parc de la Gaspésie and Parc du Mont Tremblant in Québec; Gros Morne National Park in Newfoundland; the Fundy Trail in New Brunswick, which goes between St Martins and the Fundy National Park; the coastal hike in Pacific Rim National Park,

Going Green

Opportunities for outdoor recreation abound in Canada, a country full of remote, undeveloped areas and abundant wildlife that Canadians seem very committed to preserving. Long before the environmental movement came to the forefront, Canadian tour operators began to promote ecotourism, particularly at wilderness lodges, outdoor resorts and remote escapes.

Since the mid-1980s, respect for the country's natural wonders has grown markedly, not only within Canada but on the international scene. For example, celebrity activist Brigitte Bardot turned the world spotlight on the bloody slaughter of seal pups on Québec's Îles de la Madeleine (Magdalen Islands), and now people go out to the ice floes to photograph the baby seals, not to hunt them for their fur.

Recent years have seen further changes, innovations and growth in the ecotourism movement, resulting in a much wider range of possibilities. These include hiking the West Coast rain forest, whale-watching, whitewater rafting, photographing polar bears and exploring the culture of Native Indians; such trips often include instruction on subjects like plant ecology, geology and low-impact wilderness travel.

Many people assume that ecotours are costly, but this is no longer necessarily the case in Canada. An increasing number of good, small, inexpensive operators have sprung up; see the Organized Tours sections of the regional chapters for recommendations.

British Columbia; and the historic Chilkoot Trail in the Yukon.

Rock Climbing

Rock climbing has come out from under its rock and now draws plenty of participants, even novices. Group climbs, with instructors and equipment, are available across the country. Some areas to look into include Collingwood, Sault Ste Marie and Thunder Bay in Ontario, Banff and Jasper in Alberta and Squamish in British Columbia.

Canoeing & Kayaking

The possibilities for canoeing are almost limitless, whether you're interested in an easy half-day paddle or a battle with some of the most challenging whitewater. The government parks make a good place to start, and many of them are quite accessible. Some parks provide outfitters able to supply all equipment, while at other parks private operators do much the same thing from just outside the park boundaries.

In major cities operators organize trips and sporting-equipment stores sell all the supplies you'll need. Provincial and territorial tourist boards can provide information on canoeing areas and outfitters. Better bookstores and outdoor stores sell good guides to canoeing in Canada.

Some of the country's main canoeing areas include Kejimkujik National Park in Nova Scotia; La Mauricie National Park and La Verendrye Provincial Park in Québec; Algonquin Provincial Park and Killarney Provincial Park in Ontario; Prince Albert National Park in Saskatchewan; Bowron Lake Provincial Park and Wells Gray Provincial Park in British Columbia; Nahanni National Park in the Northwest Territories and Yukon River in the Yukon Territory.

Both whitewater and sea kayaking have increased markedly in recent years and rentals are widely available. Recommended areas include Bay Bulls in Newfoundland, Bay of Fundy in New Brunswick, Mingan Island National Park in Québec, Percé in Québec, the Ottawa River in Ontario, Lake Superior in Ontario and Vancouver Island and the Gulf Islands in British Columbia.

Fishing

Freshwater fishing is abundant and popular with both residents and visitors. Casting a line is one of the country's basic outdoor activities. In winter many northern areas set up and rent 'huts,' small wooden shacks, out on frozen lakes. Inside you'll find a bench, sometimes a heater, a hole in the ice and often more than a few bottles of beer.

Anglers must purchase fishing licenses, which vary in duration and price from province to province. Any tourist office can offer advice on where to buy one. At the same time, pick up a guide to the various 'open' seasons for each species and also a guide to eating fish. In southern regions there are recommended consumption guidelines due to natural contaminants and pollution such as mercury; it's important to follow the guidelines, especially for pregnant women and young children. Also, be sure to check on daily limits and any bait restrictions. In some areas live minnows or other bait is prohibited.

Skiing & Snowboarding

There are four main alpine ski centers: in Ontario, Québec, Alberta and British Columbia. The best spot to try in Ontario lies between the towns of Barrie and Collingwood. In Québec, skiers head to the Laurentian Mountains, about a two-hour drive north of Montréal and Québec City. South of Montréal ski centers are part of the Appalachian Mountains, known to skiers in Vermont and New Hampshire.

The Rocky Mountains provide truly international-class skiing at Banff and Lake Louise, Alberta, where runs are higher than any in the European Alps. Calgary is a two-hour drive to the east.

Whistler/Blackcomb, British Columbia, is a major resort that hosts international competitions. You'll also find good skiing in the Okanagan and Kootenay regions of the province.

Each of the above alpine regions offers cross-country skiing, although good trails or conditions can be found all across Canada.

The provincial tourist boards produce guides to skiing, and travel agents and many hotels/resorts can arrange full-package tours that include transportation, accommodations and lift tickets. As the country's major ski resorts are all close to cities, it is quite straightforward to travel on your own to the slopes for a day's skiing and head back to the city that same night.

Ice Skating

Lacing up the blades for a glide on frozen rivers and ponds and outdoor rinks is a Canadian tradition. You can rent skates at rinks in some major cities such as Montréal, Toronto and Winnipeg.

COURSES

Students wishing to study formally in Canada (eg, at a university) must get authorization within their own country. This can take six months. Obtain information from the Canadian embassy or other government representative in your country of residence.

Major cities have privately run schools specializing in teaching English as a second language (ESL). Some of these schools offer TOEFL English proficiency certificates, used to gain entry into Canadian universities. Montréal also has numerous schools where you can learn French. For courses over three months long, a student visa is required.

Also within the cities, a tremendous range of work and/or recreational courses are available, ranging from acupuncture to Web page design.

Many of the outdoor outfitters mentioned in the text offer short courses in canoeing, kayaking, rock climbing and the like.

WORK

Work authorizations must be obtained outside Canada and may take six months to acquire. A work permit is valid only for one specific job and one specific time, for one specific employer.

It is difficult to get a work permit; employment opportunities go first to Canadians. Those wishing to obtain a permit must get a validated job offer from an employer and take this to a Canadian consulate or embassy outside Canada.

Visitors to Canada are technically not able to work. However, employers hiring temporary service workers (hotel, bar, restaurant, resort) and construction, farm or forestry workers often don't ask for the permit. Visitors working here legally have Social Insurance numbers beginning with '9.' If you don't have this and you get caught, you may be told to leave the country.

Many young European women come to Canada as nannies. Japan has a program called Contact Canada, which includes one-year work permits with prearranged work, generally on farms. Many countries have student, employment or travel agencies where details on these programs can be obtained.

Student Work Abroad Program (SWAP)

Of particular interest to Australian and New Zealand students may be the SWAP. Organized by the international STA Travel (W www.statravel.com) and the Canadian Federation of Students (CFS), the program allows students between the ages of 18 and 25 to have a working holiday in Canada. Australians are entitled to stay for a year and New Zealanders for six months. The program has space for 200 people a year, and applicants must be enrolled in a post-secondary educational institution.

You'll be issued a one-year, nonextendable visa that allows you to work anywhere in the country. After you do an orientation program in Vancouver, you find your own job with help from the CFS. Most jobs are in the service area – as waiters, bar attendants, cleaners and maids – particularly in the snowfields over winter, although SWAP participants have worked in other kinds of jobs ranging from farmhands to hotel porters.

STA Travel arranges group departures at reduced fares from most major Australian and New Zealand cities in November and December. Independent departures leave throughout the rest of the year. Orientation information is provided on arrival in Canada.

For full details in Australia, contact an STA office or phone ☎ 300-733-035. In New Zealand, contact an STA office or phone ☎ 0508-782-872.

Working Holiday Program

This is another program that's open to people between the ages of 18 and 30 who need not be enrolled in a post-secondary educational institution (depending on nationality). Citizens of several Commonwealth, European and Asian countries are eligible. For information and application forms, contact a Canadian embassy or consulate. The minimum processing time for these applications is 12 weeks. For information, look at the government website W www .dfait-maeci.gc.ca/123go/workholiday-e.asp.

ACCOMMODATIONS

For many visitors, the biggest expense will be accommodations. There are, however, alternatives to the standard hotels, which can make paying for a bed nothing to lose sleep over. You'll generally find the more expensive lodging prices in the larger cities, while costs in country towns can be quite reasonable. In the far north, accommodation rates are a little more than in the south, sometimes outlandishly so.

In heavily touristed areas such as Niagara Falls and Québec City, the volume of places to stay tends to keep costs low, particularly when it's not peak season. However, Banff in the Rocky Mountains is pricey. As a rule, lodging prices are higher in the summer. At other times of the year, ask for a discount.

Accommodation rates quoted throughout the regional chapters are high-season prices unless otherwise stated. Rates may vary seasonally by $10 to $50 or more.

Camping

There are campgrounds all over Canada – federal, provincial and privately owned. Government sites – nearly always better and cheaper – fill up the quickest. Government parks tend to be quiet and scenic and often feature events and talks. Private campgrounds generally cater to trailers (caravans) and recreational vehicles (RVs). They often offer more services, plus swimming pools and other entertainment facilities.

In national parks, camping fees range from $10 to $22 for a site without hookups, to $26 for sites with water and electricity. There is usually a separate park entrance fee as well.

Provincial-park camping rates vary with each province but range from $10 to $26. Interior camping in the wilderness parks is always less, about $5 to $8. Commercial campgrounds are generally several dollars more expensive than those in either provincial or national parks.

Government parks start closing in early September for the winter. Dates vary according to the location. Some remain open for maintenance even when camping is finished, and you might be able to camp at a reduced rate. Other places are free in late autumn or early spring, when the gates are open but there's not a soul around. Outside of the main summer season, you have to investigate, but using the parks after official closing times can save the hardy a fair bit of money.

Many people travel around the country camping and never pay a dime. For those with cars or vans, using roadside rest areas and picnic spots can be quite convenient. If signs forbid overnight camping, don't set up a tent. If you're asleep in the car and a cop happens to wake you, just say you were driving, got tired, pulled over for a quick rest and fell asleep. For less chance of interruption, try one of the little side roads and logging roads off the highway. RVers (seniors note!) will find that gravelpit camping is frequently possible.

If you're driving the Trans Canada Hwy, you'll find campgrounds every 150km or so.

Hostels & Other Budget Lodging

Canada contains some excellent travelers' hostels, much like those found around the world. But here the term 'hostel' has some unfortunate connotations for travelers as well as hostel staff; it continues to refer to both government and private shelters for the underprivileged, sick and abused. There are, for example, hostels for battered women who have been victimized by their partners and hostels for recovering drug addicts. So, if you get a sideways glance when you say you're on the way to spend the night at the hostel, you'll know why.

Two hosteling groups in Canada cater to low-budget visitors (see subheadings below). They're the cheapest places to stay in the country, as well as the spots where you stand to meet the greatest number of travelers.

But in addition to these two organizations, totally independent hostels can be found around the country, albeit in small numbers. Ask around the backpackers' community for some names. The province of British Columbia has an informal network of privately run hostels that charge about the same rates as the 'official' ones. Québec, too, is most likely to contain some hostels of the unofficial variety.

Visitors to Québec are sometimes surprised to find the mixed-sex dorms common in Europe but not often seen elsewhere in Canada.

Hostelling International The nation's oldest and most established hosteling association is Hostelling International

(HI) Canada, a national organization that belongs to the internationally known hosteling association. The HI symbol is an evergreen tree and stylized house within a blue triangle. Throughout this book, these hostels are referred to as HI Hostels.

HI Canada includes about 80 hostels in all parts of the country. Nightly costs range from $12 to $25, with most around $17. At many, nonmembers can stay for an additional $2 to $5. A yearly international membership costs $27. An HI membership can quickly pay for itself and has now been built into the system, so after a few stays you automatically become a member.

Children under 17 stay free with a parent. Many hostels offer family rooms.

In July and August space may be a problem at some hostels, particularly in the large cities and in resort areas such as Banff, so reserving ahead is a good idea (call ☎ 800-663-5777). Reservations must be made more than 24 hours in advance, and you need a credit card to prepay. Outside July and August, getting a bed should not be difficult. Many hostels are closed in winter.

Note that reservations for some North American hostels can be booked through hostels in Europe, Australia, New Zealand and Japan using the hostel International Booking Network (IBN) systems or by going to the website ⓦ www.hostelbooking.com.

In addition to the lower nightly rates, members can often take advantage of discounts offered by various businesses – local hostels should have a list. Some of the regional offices and hostels organize outdoor activities such as canoeing, climbing, skiing, hiking and city walks.

For more information, contact Hostelling International–Canada (☎ 613-237-7884, fax 613-237-7868, ⓦ www.hostellingintl.ca, National Office, 400-205 Catherine St, Ottawa, ON K2P 1C3).

Backpackers Hostels The other main hostel group in Canada is a network of more than 100 independent (non-HI) hostels collectively known as Backpackers Hostels Canada (ⓦ www.backpackers.ca). Its symbol is a circled howling wolf with a map of Canada in the background.

Aside from typical hostels, the network includes campgrounds, campus and church facilities, organic farms, motels, retreats and tourist homes, all of which provide budget travelers with inexpensive accommodations. Several places offer an interesting work-for-stay system in which your labor means free room and board. The average price is about $17, and rooms for couples and families are often available.

A major benefit of Backpackers is that it offers lodging in both the main cities and in a range of smaller, out-of-the-way locations where nothing else of the sort is available. This loose network has no formal standards, so quality, atmosphere and approach vary a lot.

For information, contact Lloyd Jones at Longhouse Village Hostel (☎ 807-983-2042, fax 807-983-2914, RR 13, Thunder Bay, ON P7B 5E4).

A sort of subnetwork of Backpackers is the growing **Pacific Rim Network** (☎ 800-861-1366, ⓦ www.pacifichostels.net), which focuses on hostels of the North American Pacific Coast region. The network currently counts about 40 members, about half on Vancouver Island.

YMCA/YWCA For the most part these familiar institutions are slowly closing their accommodations operations and concentrating more on fitness, recreation and various other community-oriented programs. That said, many still offer decent lodging that falls somewhere between a hostel and a hotel, but prices have crept up. In YMCAs or YWCAs where complete renovations have occurred, costs can be as high as those of a mid-range hotel. One of the Vancouver Ys was built to be a hotel.

Clean and quiet, YMCAs and YWCAs often contain swimming pools and cheap cafeterias. They also, as a rule, enjoy very central locations – a big plus – and stay open all year. Some offer hostel-style dormitory accommodations throughout the summer. Throughout the book many are mentioned under Hostels in the Places to Stay sections.

The average price for a single room for men is $25 to $40; it's usually a bit more for women. Sharing a double can bring the price down to quite a reasonable level. Also, some places permit couples, and these doubles are a fair deal.

For information, contact YMCA Canada (☎ 416-928-9622, ⓦ www.ymca.ca, 42 Charles St E, 6th floor, Toronto, ON M4Y 1T4). Generally, the website offers more up-to-date information than the literature that YMCA Canada will mail to you.

University Residences Many Canadian universities rent beds in their dormitories during the summer. The 'season' runs approximately from May to some time in August, with possible closures for such things as large academic conferences. Campus residences are open to all, including families and seniors.

Rates average $30 a night, often with discounts for students. Reservations are accepted but aren't necessary. Sometimes the cost of a dorm room includes breakfast, but if not, you'll often find a cafeteria offering low-priced meals. The other campus facilities, such as the swimming pool, are sometimes available to guests.

Directories of the various residences are sometimes published and may be available on campus from the residence manager, the alumni association or the general information office.

Because this form of budget lodging remains somewhat unknown in Canada, finding a room, even in peak season, should not be a problem at most places. Though there's no reliable central information source, you can get some more information by calling ☎ 800-668-4908 or visiting the websites ⓦ www.umanitoba.ca/people/alumni/grads_in_res.html and ⓦ www.cuccoa.org.

Efficiencies
Basically hotel or motel rooms with cooking facilities, efficiency units are also called housekeeping units, serviced apartments or suites. They are often geared to businesspeople but can be especially helpful for traveling families.

Some motels have converted a few rooms into efficiencies, which cost a few extra dollars. You might also find a room or two with cooking facilities at a guesthouse or B&B. Some hotels also offer such rooms, usually calling them suites, although this broad term may not mean that there's a kitchen.

In the country's larger cities, some apartment complexes have also been set up to offer this type of lodging, but they're primarily aimed at businesspeople or visitors staying in town for a week or longer and might not offer per-night rates.

Guesthouses & Tourist Homes
The options in this category range from rooms in private homes to commercial lodging houses (the latter are more common than the former). You'll find them mainly in places with a large tourist trade, such as Niagara, Banff, Victoria, Québec City and Montréal.

Rooms range in size and feature varying amenities. Some include private bathrooms; many do not. Average doubles cost about $40 to $65.

Some so-called tourist homes are really rooming houses rented more often by the week or month; they usually have shared kitchens.

B&Bs
B&Bs, which continue to grow in number, offer a more personal alternative to the standard traditional motel/hotel. In many of the larger cities, associations manage B&Bs, while in other places tourist offices offer direct contact information for B&Bs. Some operate as full-time businesses, and others just provide their operators with part-time income for a few months in the summer.

Prices of B&Bs vary quite a bit, ranging roughly from $40 for a single to $160 for a double, with the average being $65 to $85 for two people. At the higher end you'll generally find more impressive furnishings and decor, sometimes in classic heritage houses.

Rooms, almost always in the owner's home, tend to be clean and well kept. Some places take children, and the odd one allows a pet. Breakfast can vary from light or continental to a full meal of eggs, bacon, toast and coffee. It's worth inquiring about the breakfast before booking.

Motels
In Canada, like the USA (both lands of the automobile), motels are ubiquitous – many dot the highways and cluster in groups on the outskirts of larger towns and cities. Mostly they're simple and clean, if somewhat nondescript.

Motel prices range from $40 to $85 for singles or doubles. Outside the cities, motel prices drop, so they can be a bargain, especially if there are two or more of you. Before entering a large city, you're better off exiting the main route and finding one of the secondary roads, where you'll find the cheapest spots.

Prices tend to go up in summer or during special events. Off-season bargaining is definitely worthwhile and acceptable; just a simple counteroffer sometimes works.

Many motels remain 'mom and pop' operations run by small businesspeople, but plenty of North American chains have opened up shop across the country. These include Comfort Inn (☎ 800-424-6423, W www.choicehotels.ca), Days Inn (☎ 800-329-7466, W www.daysinn.com/canada), Super 8 (☎ 800-800-8000, W www.super8 .com) and Travelodge (☎ 800-578-7878, W www.travelodge.com).

Hotels

Good, inexpensive hotels are not a Canadian strong point. Despite the wide range of hotel types, the word usually means one of two things to a Canadian – a rather expensive place to stay or a cheap place to drink. Most new hotels belong to international chains and cater to either the luxury market or businesspeople.

Established, big-name hotels in central downtown locations range in price from $125 to $225, but prices fluctuate widely with demand. At some, weekend and summer rates may be lower; at others, the opposite is true. Asking about special promotions is worthwhile.

Canadian liquor laws have historically been linked to renting beds, so the older, cheap hotels are often principally bars, and quite often low-class bars at that. For the impecunious who don't mind some noise and a somewhat worn room, these hotels can come in handy (note: they're not suitable for families or women traveling alone). Rates usually range from $25 to $40 per single, but more permanent guests usually take up the rooms on a monthly basis. This book covers some decent places in this category.

Between the new and the old hotels, you'll find a few good older, small hotels, particularly in the larger cities. Prices range from about $45 to $85 for singles or doubles.

Farm Vacations

Each province has a farm or ranch vacation program, enabling visitors to stay on working farms for a day, a week or even longer. The size and type of farm vary considerably, as do the activities offered, but you'll usually get chores to do or animals to tend. Rates range from roughly $40 to $55 for singles, $50 to $85 for doubles, depending on meals taken. There are also family rates and reductions for children. For details of these programs, contact the provincial tourist boards (see Tourist Offices, earlier in this chapter).

FOOD

Gastronomy in English-speaking Canada has long borrowed from the British 'bland is beautiful' tradition, but in recent times the large numbers of varying ethnic groups spread across the country have added some badly needed variety to the epicurean palate.

In most cities it's not difficult to find a Greek, Italian, Mexican or Chinese restaurant. Small bistro-type places all across the country emphasize freshness, spices and the latest trends; they tend to fill the gap between the low-end 'greasy spoons' (the equivalent of diners in the US) and the costliest restaurants.

In the country's largest cities, you'll come across some vegetarian restaurants, sometimes called natural-food or health-food restaurants. East Indian restaurants also offer a selection of vegetarian dishes.

At the opposite end of the spectrum, in the Atlantic Provinces on the East Coast, deep-fried food is common – all too common for many. It doesn't hurt to ask for an alternative cooking method or to pick from menus carefully.

You'll find a fair amount of fresh, locally grown produce in Canada, depending on the time of year. In summer the apples, peaches and cherries are superb. In June watch for strawberries; in August, blueberries. Throughout rural areas farmers set up stands alongside highways and secondary roads and sell fruit and vegetables at bargain prices.

Canada produces excellent cheeses, cheddars in particular – mild, medium and old. Oka from Québec is a more expensive, subtler and very tasty cheese developed by Trappist monks.

On both coasts, delicious and affordable seafood abounds. On the West Coast the salmon, fresh or smoked, is a real treat, and crab is plentiful. The East Coast boasts the lesser-known but highly esteemed freshwater Atlantic salmon. The Atlantic region is also famous for lobster and scallops. In the far north Arctic char is a specialty. The king of inland fish is the walleye, often called pickerel.

One truly Canadian creation must be mentioned – the butter tart. This delectable little sweet can best be described as…well, just get on the outside of one and you'll see.

French Food

Most of the country's few semioriginal repasts come from the French of Québec. French pea soup is thick, filling and delicious. The *tourtières* (meat pies) are worth sampling.

French fries in Québec, where they are known simply as *frites,* are unbeatable, especially those from the small roadside chip wagons. *Poutine* is a variation with gravy and cheese curds.

Québec is also the world's largest producer of maple syrup, made in the spring when the sap is running; pour some of the sweet stuff over pancakes or ice cream.

Farther east, in the Atlantic Provinces, the Acadian French carry on some of their centuries-old culinary traditions in such dishes as rapie pie *(paté à la rapure)* – a type of meat pie (maybe beef, chicken or clam) topped with grated, paste-like potato.

Native Indian Food

If the opportunity arises, sample some Native Indian foods based on wild game such as deer (venison) and pheasant. Buffalo meat, sold commercially in a few places, turns up on menus occasionally. It's lean and has more protein and less cholesterol than beef.

The fiddlehead is a distinctive green, only edible in springtime. It's primarily picked from the woodlands of the Maritime Provinces.

Wild rice, with its black husks and almost nutty flavor, is very tasty and often accompanies Native Indian–style meals. Most of it is picked by hand around the Ontario and Manitoba borders, but it's widely available in natural-food shops.

You also might want to try bannock, a simple, homemade bread that goes well with traditional corn soup.

Costs

As with most things, food is costlier than in the USA. If you're from Europe, though, or a country with a strong currency, you'll find prices are reasonable.

Generally, for dinner, any meal under $15 is a bargain, and $15 to $30 is a moderate price to pay. Wine, tax and tip are extra. Lunches cost a lot less, almost always under $10. Most of the places mentioned in this book fit into the budget and mid-range categories, but you'll also find some costlier places listed if you can afford to splurge.

DRINKS
Alcohol

Throughout much of Canada, you can only buy alcohol in government-run retail stores. In Alberta, however, private retailers sell all alcohol, and in Québec wine and beer can be bought at grocery stores and corner shops. West of Ontario, provinces permit 'off-sales,' meaning bars and hotels can sell takeaway beer.

The current drinking age across Canada is 19, except in Alberta, Manitoba and Québec, where it's 18. The drinking age is set by each province or territory and is subject to change.

Beer Canadian beer, in general, is good, not great. It's more flavorful and stronger than US brands and is always served cold. Lagers are by far the most popular beers, but ales, light beers, porters and stouts are available. Molson and Labatt are the country's biggest producers; Molson Export and Canadian and Labatt 50 and Blue are the most popular beers.

A welcome trend is the continuing success of small breweries producing real or natural beers and pubs brewing their own for consumption on the premises. Many of these are excellent.

In a bar the price of a draft beer ranges from about $2.75 for a 340ml glass to $5.50 for a pint. Draft beer by the glass or pitcher is the cheapest way to drink. In places with live music, prices usually go up after the night's entertainment arrives. At retail outlets beer bought in cases costs about $1.60 per bottle or can.

Wine Since the 1980s Canadian wines have improved steadily and considerably, yet the stigma of the early days often remains. True, the bottom-end wines taste as cheap as the price, but most of the Canadian wineries also take great care with at least some of their labels.

The country has two main wine-producing regions: Ontario's Niagara Peninsula, with by far the largest share of wineries, and British Columbia's Okanagan Valley. Wineries can also be found in southern Québec, elsewhere in Ontario (the Lake Erie Shoreline, and Pelee Island in Lake Erie) and in Nova Scotia.

In Ontario the Vintners Quality Alliance (VQA) grading and classification system sets and maintains standards for the better wines in much the same way as the Europeans do it. Wines sporting the VQA label are worth sampling. A similar grading system exists in British Columbia.

Canadian wineries produce red, white, dry, sweet and sparkling wines, but the dry whites and the very expensive ice wines are Canada's best. Import duties keep foreign wine prices up to protect the Canadian wine industry, but you can still get a pretty low-priced bottle of French or Californian wine.

Spirits Canada produces its own gins, vodkas, rums, liqueurs, brandies and coolers (sweet drinks flavored with fruits). But Canadian whiskey, generally known in the country as rye, is the best-known liquor and the one with the biggest reputation; it's been distilled since the mid-1800s. Canadian Club and VO rye whiskey are Canada's most famous drinks – good stuff. Rye is generally mixed with ginger ale or soda, but some like it straight with ice. Most of the high price of spirits in Canada is attributable to tax.

Other Beverages

The fruit-growing areas of Ontario, Québec and British Columbia produce excellent apple and cherry ciders, some with alcohol, most without. In Québec and the Atlantic Provinces visitors may want to sample a local nonalcoholic brew called spruce beer, which individuals make in small batches and sell in some local stores. It varies quite a bit and you can never be too sure what will happen when the cap comes off, but some people love the stuff.

Canadian mineral and spring waters are popular and readily available. Stores also sell bottled waters from Europe, especially France.

A cup of standard coffee in Canada is not memorable, but it isn't expensive either. If fresh, it can be fairly decent. Restaurant coffee is almost always a filtered brew. In the western provinces it's not uncommon to be offered free refills (sometimes multiple) with every purchased cup.

In the big cities a number of cafés serve espresso, cappuccino and the other European specialties, as well as high-quality regular coffee. You can also find a respectable cup at the ubiquitous doughnut shops across Canada.

Hot tea is also common; in restaurants, it's almost always made with tea bags.

SPECTATOR SPORTS

Technically, Canada's official national sport is lacrosse, a Native Indian game similar to soccer but played with a small ball and sticks. Each stick has a woven leather basket for catching and carrying the ball. Currently, this old sport's making a major comeback. The US-Canada National Lacrosse League (**w** www.be-lax.com), playing November to March, has 13 teams, five based in major Canadian cities (Calgary, Montréal, Ottawa, Toronto, Vancouver).

But the sport that really creates passion, and is the de facto national game, is ice hockey. This is especially true in Québec, home of the Montréal Canadiens, a hockey legend and one of the most consistently successful professional sports teams anywhere. If you're in Canada in winter, take time to see a National Hockey League (NHL; **w** www.nhl.com) game. The season runs from October to April. The league includes 30 teams altogether, six in Canadian cities (Calgary, Edmonton, Montréal, Ottawa, Toronto, Vancouver) and the rest in the US. Many smaller Canadian cities are home to minor-league teams.

The Canadian Football League (CFL; **w** www.cfl.ca) plays US-style football with some modifications. Although the Canadian game is faster and more interesting, the league is struggling, especially in Toronto. The other cities with teams are Calgary, Edmonton, Hamilton, Montréal, Ottawa, Regina, Vancouver and Winnipeg. The championship game, known as the Grey Cup, is played in late November.

Baseball is popular in Canada, and two Canadian teams are part of the US-based Major League Baseball (MLB; **w** www.major leaguebaseball.com): the Toronto Blue Jays in the American League and the Montréal Expos in the National League (though the

Hockey Night in Canada

For about 100 years ice hockey has brought out the passion in Canadians. No sport comes close to 'the world's fastest game' for a spot in a Canadian's heart. Now played in 20 countries, it is easily Canada's most important contribution to the world of sports.

The first match with rules (borrowed from field hockey, lacrosse and rugby) was played in Montréal in 1879 by McGill University students. Before that, a version of the game had been played as early as the 1850s by British soldiers stationed in eastern Canada. In the 1880s several leagues formed, but the game really gained national attention in 1892, when the Canadian governor general, Frederick Arthur, Lord Stanley of Preston, donated a trophy to be given annually to the top Canadian team. The pursuit of the Stanley Cup by teams of the National Hockey League (NHL), which came into existence in 1917, has since become an annual quest.

Although almost all of the players were Canadian, cities in the USA became home to several teams, with the Boston Bruins being the first to join the NHL in 1924. Eventually the league consisted of teams in Montréal, Toronto, Boston, New York, Detroit and Chicago. This six-team league existed until 1967, when it expanded to 12 teams; today there are 30.

In the 1950s and '60s, hockey announcer Foster Hewitt could be heard across the country every Saturday night as he called the game live from Maple Leaf Gardens in Toronto, first on the radio and later on TV. Hewitt's 'play-by-play' of Hockey Night in Canada helped to establish hockey as the national game. From then on, hockey stars became not just household names but Canadian legends. People still speak of the 1950s 'Rocket Richard riot,' when the city of Montréal went berserk after its Hall of Fame player, Maurice 'Rocket' Richard, was suspended by league president Clarence Campbell. Some even say that this was the catalyst for the Québec separatist movement!

During the 1980s superstar Wayne Gretzky became known around the world as he shattered every offensive record in the books. When he was traded from Edmonton to Los Angeles in 1988, one politician raised the matter in parliament, arguing that the trade should be prevented. Gretzky retired in 1999, spurring tears and homages across the country.

Today, the majority of players in the NHL remain Canadian, although increasingly the league has drafted excellent players from Sweden, Finland, the Czech and Slovak Republics, Russia and US colleges.

Women are also adding some diversity to Canada's unofficial national sport. Women have played hockey since its formative stages but in a much less organized fashion. Women players still lack a professional league today, though amateur leagues abound. Nonetheless, Canadian women have been making quite an impression on hockey fans over the last decade. In 1992 Manon Rhéaume from Québec City, a goalie, became the first woman ever invited to a NHL training camp when the Tampa Bay Lightning offered her a tryout. She didn't make the team but was offered a contract to play with its minor-league team.

In 1990 the Canadian team won the first-ever Women's World Championship, and, to top it all off, in 2002 Canada captured the gold medal in women's ice hockey at the winter Olympics.

To learn more, visit the Hockey Hall of Fame in Toronto or go to see a professional game in a major Canadian city (see the Spectator Sports section in this chapter). At any outdoor rink during the winter, you're likely to find a pick-up game in progress. If you've got skates and a stick, you're in the game and a part of a Canadian tradition.

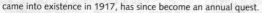

latter franchise might fold within the next few years). Toronto won the World Series Championship in 1992 and 1993. Minor-league teams play in many cities across the country.

In 1995 Canada gained entry into the American professional basketball league, known as the National Basketball Association (NBA; W www.nba.com). The Toronto Raptors have become part of the sport's increasing popularity.

Soccer and rugby, though growing, have never really caught on and are pretty small-time in Canada. But you might see a number of pick-up soccer games in parks, since many Canadians learn how to play in physical education classes in school. The country also supports amateur and semi-professional teams. The A League of the United Soccer Leagues (W www.united soccerleagues.com) includes 21 teams, three from Canada (Montréal, Toronto, Vancouver) and the rest from the US.

Rugby has its biggest following in British Columbia. Despite the sport's low profile elsewhere in the country, Canada has done well in international competition and the World Rugby Cup. For details on leagues and schedules, check W www.rugbycanada.ca.

Canadian women have excelled at the highest levels in skiing, skating, golf, curling and numerous Olympic events, but there are no major professional women's teams/leagues in Canada.

For more details on specific teams, see the Spectator Sports sections of the regional chapters.

SHOPPING

Despite being a Western consumer society largely filled with the goods of the international marketplace, Canada does offer the discriminating shopper a number of interesting and unique things to buy.

Outdoor or camping specialists may turn up something you haven't seen before, including particularly good outdoor clothing. Such products are not cheap, but they last forever.

If you're shopping for edible souvenirs, British Columbia's smoked salmon is a real treat. West Coast purveyors will also pack fresh salmon to take on flights home. In Québec maple syrup and maple sugar make different, inexpensive gifts. The wines of the Niagara region can be very good; ask for rec-

ommendations at liquor outlets in southern Ontario. Rye whiskey is a Canadian specialty.

Most good bookstores feature a Canadiana section for books on Canada or Canadian literature. Likewise, record shops offer CDs of Canadian music. Traditional, Celtic-based folk music is especially abundant in eastern Canada.

Art lovers can pick up prints of paintings done by Canadian painters in the gift shops of art galleries. Wood carving has enjoyed a long tradition in Québec, notably at the town of St Jean Port Joli. Another area for this, but to a lesser degree, lies along the French Shore of Nova Scotia. You can also find some fine handmade rugs in Nova Scotia, at Cheticamp.

Looking for something wearable? Try some jewelry with British Columbia jade. In Saskatchewan and Alberta you can outfit yourself like a cowboy; leatherwork for sale includes belts, vests, jackets, boots and hats.

Traditional Hudson's Bay blankets and coats made of 100% wool can be bought at one of The Bay department stores, run by Canada's oldest company – look for the tell-tale green, red, yellow and black stripes on a white background. Classic cloth lumberjack jackets in either red or blue checks are cheap and distinctive, if not elegant.

Roots, a high profile Canadian clothing company with outlets across the country and products in major department stores, offers a range of fashionable, quality garments and accessories; the company gained prominence during the 2002 Winter Olympics, when the US and Canadian Olympic teams made Roots their official clothing supplier.

Crafts shows, flea markets and specialty shops showcase the work of Canadian artisans. Potters, weavers, jewelers and other craftspeople turn out some fine work.

For information on the worthwhile Native Indian arts and crafts to consider as purchases, see Arts in the Facts about Canada chapter. These represent some of the most 'Canadian' souvenirs.

Beware the shops designed to serve tourists at the country's major attractions like Niagara Falls – they're not the place to look for a meaningful keepsake. Canadiana kitsch in the form of plastic Mounties, cheap pseudo–Native Indian dolls, miniature beavers and tasteless T-shirts are good for a smirk and nothing more.

Getting There & Away

AIR

Airports & Airlines

In Canada, the major air gateways are Montréal's Dorval Airport, Toronto's Pearson International Airport and Vancouver International Airport. To a lesser extent, Halifax International Airport in Nova Scotia acts as an entry point for eastern Canada. The following major European, Australian and American airlines all fly into Canada:

Air Canada
☎ 888-247-2262, **w** www.aircanada.com

Air France
☎ 800-667-2747, **w** www.airfrance.com

Alaska Airlines
☎ 800-252-7522, **w** www.alaskaair.com

Alitalia
☎ 800-361-8336, **w** www.alitalia.com

American Airlines
☎ 800-433-7300, **w** www.aa.com

America West
☎ 800-327-7810, **w** www.americawest.com

British Airways
☎ 800-247-9297, **w** www.britishairways.com

Iceland Air
☎ 800-223-5500, **w** www.icelandair.com

JetBlue
☎ 800-538-2583, **w** www.jetblue.com

Lufthansa
☎ 800-563-5954, **w** www.lufthansa.com

United Airlines
☎ 800-241-6522, **w** www.ual.com

Anyone traveling by air should be aware that new and tighter security procedures instituted after the 2001 terrorist attacks on New York City and Washington, DC, have made air travel a lengthier process. Arrive two to three hours in advance of your flight and expect relatively long and thorough check-ins. If you're traveling with anything that could be used as a weapon, including nail files, pack it in your checked baggage, not your carry-ons. Also, do *not* make any remarks or comments about bombs or terrorists. Bite your tongue and let the agents frisk you.

Buying Tickets

To get the lowest-priced tickets, you often have to fly out of an airline hub, such as New York, London, Amsterdam, Athens, Bangkok, Hong Kong, Manila and Sydney. Even if you can't depart from one of these locations, though, you can still save money by buying tickets far in advance and traveling at off-peak times. High season in Canada is July, August and around Christmas. Spring, early summer and fall offer better deals.

Sometimes you can save money by entering Canada via the USA. Many overseas flights to North America go first to the USA, with New York, San Francisco and Los Angeles being the major destinations. You can then either fly to a major Canadian city such as Montréal or Vancouver or catch a bus or train. Often, though, flying directly into Canadian gateway cities can be more or less the same price as first going to US cities.

In some places, notably the UK, the cheapest flights may be advertised by obscure 'bucket shops.' Some are reliable; others may not be. Paying by credit card generally offers protection, as most card issuers provide refunds if you can prove you didn't get what you paid for. Agents who accept only cash should hand over the

Warning

The information in this chapter is particularly vulnerable to change: prices for international travel are volatile, routes are introduced and canceled, schedules change, special deals come and go, and rules and visa requirements are amended. Airlines and governments seem to take a perverse pleasure in making price structures and regulations as complicated as possible. Check directly with the airline or a travel agent to make sure you understand how a fare (or any ticket you may buy) works. In addition, the travel industry is highly competitive and there are many lurks and perks.

The upshot of this is that you should get opinions, quotes and advice from as many airlines and travel agents as possible before you part with your hard-earned cash. The details given in this chapter should be regarded as pointers and are not a substitute for your own careful, up-to-date research.

tickets right away. After you've made a booking or paid your deposit, call the airline to confirm.

If you're looking for a dependable agency, try STA Travel (☎ 800-777-0112, W www.sta-travel.com), Flight Centre (W www.flightcentre.com) or Council Travel (☎ 800-226-8624, W www.counciltravel.com), all of which have offices around the world. In Canada, Travel Cuts (W www.travelcuts.com) is also a worthwhile choice.

You'll rarely find the best prices by contacting an airline directly, unless you book your ticket online. Many airlines offer discount fares (usually modest) on their websites, but you can turn up real bargains at websites that sell tickets for many different airlines, such as W www.cheaptickets.com, W www.expedia.com, W www.flightcentre.com, W www.lastminutetravel.com, W www.lowestfare.com, W www.orbitz.com, W www.travelclub.com and W www.travelocity.com.

Sales taxes and the GST may or may not be included in any airline ticket price quoted in Canada, so ask.

Round-the-World Tickets

If you are covering a lot of distance, a Round-the-World (RTW) ticket can be worthwhile. A good ticket includes a lot of stops in places all over the world, valid for up to a year of travel. Air Canada, in conjunction with other airlines, offers such tickets, with prices typically ranging from $3550 to $5520 depending on which countries you select. Cathay Pacific, Qantas and Singapore Airlines regularly participate in these deals. If you're going to Europe, side trips can be arranged at a reasonable cost.

Departure Tax & Airport Taxes

Passengers bound for international destinations must pay Canada's departure/airport tax, which is included in the price of almost all tickets, especially those purchased in Europe or Australia. If you bought a ticket in another country and it didn't include the $10 departure tax, you'll be asked to pay after you pass through customs and immigration, so make sure to check beforehand in order to have enough Canadian cash on hand.

Montréal, Toronto and Vancouver all have additional airport improvement taxes (AIT). Out of Toronto, the $10 fee is added to the cost of your ticket. But in Montréal ($10 at Mirabel, $15 at Dorval) and Vancouver ($10 North American flights, $15 international flights) you must pay the fee in cash as you are boarding. On your ticket, look for a box labeled 'AIT'; it should list the amount if it has been billed.

Passengers flying in Canada are also charged a $12 air traveler's security charge per flight. The fee offsets the recently implemented random use of air marshals and other safety measures.

Remember, too, that if you intend to apply for any GST rebate, the airport is your last chance to get a form (see Taxes in the Facts for the Visitor chapter for more details).

USA

Flights between US and Canadian cities are abundant and frequent but not necessarily direct. American discount (no-frills) airlines don't usually fly into Canada, but JetBlue, for example, gets as close as New York City and Buffalo, New York; Burlington, Vermont; and Seattle. America West flies into Vancouver.

Air Canada flies from Los Angeles to Vancouver and from New York City to Montréal and Toronto. American Airlines also serves the latter route.

Alaska Airlines serves the western Canadian cities of Victoria, Vancouver, Kelowna, Calgary and Edmonton.

UK

The UK is one of the busiest, most competitive air hubs in the world, and you'll have your pick of dozens of discount travel agencies in London – be careful that the one you choose will be there in the morning. You can also guard against fraud by buying a ticket from a bonded agent, such as one covered by the Air Travel Organiser's Licence (ATOL) scheme in the UK (W www.atol.org.uk).

For low-priced fares, contact STA Travel (see Buying Tickets), which maintains offices throughout the UK, or Trailfinders (W www.trailfinders.com), which operates in London, Manchester, Glasgow and Dublin.

To save money, think about departing from Heathrow International Airport instead of Gatwick and avoid traveling in the pricey summer months and around Christmas.

Iceland Air often offers the lowest rates to Canada, if you're willing to stop in Reykjavik. Also be aware that their only flight is to Halifax.

Air Canada flies from London direct to Montréal, Toronto, Calgary and Vancouver, but you are not likely to get much of a deal. Also, there are no student or standby rates offered on their international flights. Children under age 11 are entitled to discounts on some flights. If you want to visit Newfoundland while in Canada, you might consider traveling from London to St John's on Air Canada but returning from Toronto on a so-called open jaw itinerary, which in this case costs the same as a roundtrip ticket from London to Toronto and saves you the hassle and expense of finding transportation from mainland Canada to Newfoundland.

British Airways flies direct from London to Montréal. Alternatively, you can buy a cheaper British Airways ticket to New York City, then take an eight-hour bus ride or a 10-hour train ride to Montréal. Virgin Atlantic (☎ 800-862-8621, W www.virgin-atlantic.com) also offers good fares to New York (it doesn't fly to Canada).

Continental Europe
You can fly nonstop from Europe to a few Canadian cities. Air France serves Montréal, Toronto and Ottawa, while Alitalia goes to Toronto and Lufthansa offers flights from Frankfurt to Montréal, Vancouver, Calgary and Toronto. Air Canada flies out of Europe's major centers, such as Paris and Frankfurt (among others).

Amsterdam is a good place to find low-cost airfares. In Germany, STA Travel operates in Frankfurt, and Council Travel runs an office in Munich. For tickets for flights out of Paris, contact Council Travel (W www.counciltravel.com) or Nouvelles Frontières (W www.nouvellesfrontieres.com).

Charters Private Canadian charter companies operate flights to various European countries, generally through travel wholesalers or package tour companies. Several good charters travel between France and the province of Québec.

Some of the bigger, better established charter companies and tour wholesalers in Canada sometimes work in conjunction with major airlines. For example, Air Canada Vacations puts packages together for European visitors to Canada.

Many Canadian charter companies don't seem to have either an easy or a long life, so the names change frequently. Air Transat (☎ 866-847-1112, W www.airtransat.com) shows some staying power. In Canada or abroad, travel agencies and university student offices should be able to provide you with information on potential charter trips.

Australia & New Zealand
To get to Canada from this part of the world, you have to go to the USA first. It's easiest to travel from Sydney or Auckland to Los Angeles and then proceed to Canadian destinations such as Vancouver and Toronto. Qantas (☎ 800-227-4500, W www.qantas.com), Air New Zealand (☎ 800-262-1234, W www.airnewzealand.com) and United carry the bulk of passengers from Australia and New Zealand to the USA, but you might find better rates with Japan Airlines (☎ 800-525-3663, W www.japanair.com). Air Canada sometimes transfers passengers to Canadian destinations.

If you land in Los Angeles, San Francisco or Seattle, you can also reach Vancouver by train or bus.

To find good airfares, contact Flight Centre (see Buying Tickets), which originated in Australia, or STA Travel, the other main discount agency in Australia and New Zealand.

Asia
From Asia it's often cheaper to fly first to the USA rather than directly to Canada. Shop around in Singapore and in travel agencies and bucket shops in Bangkok and Kuala Lumpur. Singapore Airlines (☎ 800-742-3333, W www.singaporeair.com) and Korean Air (☎ 800-438-5000, W www.koreanair.com) run cheap flights around the Pacific, ending on the USA's West Coast. Korean Air flies from Hong Kong to Vancouver. You can also try Thai Airways (W www.thaiairways.com) and Malaysia Airlines (☎ 888-359-8655, W www.malaysiaair.com), both of which go to Los Angeles.

It's also easy to make connections to Canada from Tokyo. The STA Travel in Tokyo can help book tickets.

LAND
Bus

The Greyhound bus network (☎ 800-231-2222, www.greyhound.com) connects the major continental US cities with most major destinations in Canada, but you have to transfer to another bus at or near the US-Canadian border. Greyhound buses serve Montréal, Toronto and Vancouver. The trip from New York to Montréal (US$74 one way) takes eight hours; from Chicago to Toronto (US$77), 15 hours; from Seattle to Vancouver (US$20), four hours.

Note, however, that the multiday pass (Ameripass) available in the USA cannot be used in Canada. If you're using Ameripass, ask Greyhound how close you can get to your Canadian destination before having to buy a separate ticket. Greyhound's CanAm Pass is good for travel in either country for 15, 21, 30, 45 or 60 days. An adult pass costs US$513 to US$579, with substantial discounts for students and seniors (US$319 to US$359). You can also buy a West CanAm Pass and an East CanAm Pass, sold in 10- and 21-day versions. Prices for 10-day passes are adult/senior & student US$244/218, for 21-day US$324/288. There are also passes for Canadian and US citizens, as well as passes specifically for international travelers.

Other smaller US bus lines run directly to some Canadian cities with no stop or need for a bus change. Often the best approach for information on these routes is to call the bus station from which you intend to depart.

Alaska's Gray Line Alaskon buses connect Fairbanks, Anchorage, Skagway and Haines in Alaska with Whitehorse in the Yukon. Alaska Direct Busline does the same routes. See the Yukon Territory chapter for more information.

Train

Amtrak (☎ 800-872-7245, www.amtrak.com, 60 Massachusetts Ave NE, Washington, DC 20002, USA) operates four routes between the USA and Canada. In the east, Amtrak trains run from New York City to Montréal (US$54 to US$62 one way, 10 hours), New York City to Toronto (US$65 to US$99 one way, 12 hours via Niagara Falls) and Chicago to Toronto (US$98 one way, 11½ hours). On the West Coast, Amtrak connects Seattle to Vancouver (US$23 to US$34 one way, four hours).

The North America Rail Pass, good on Amtrak (USA) and Via Rail (Canada) provides you 45,000km of track for 30 days. In summer, the pass costs $1029/926 adult/senior & student.

Car

The highway system of the continental US connects directly with the Canadian highway system along the border at numerous points. These Canadian highways then meet up with the Trans Canada Hwy farther north.

During the summer months, Friday and Sunday can be very busy at major international border crossings, with shoppers, vacationers and visitors all traveling at the same time. Delays can be especially bad on the holiday weekends in summer. Waits at these times can be hours, so avoid them if possible. Crossings that are particularly prone to lengthy queues are those between Windsor (Ontario) and Detroit (Michigan); Fort Erie (Ontario) and Buffalo (New York State); Niagara Falls (Ontario) and Niagara Falls (New York State); Québec and Rouse's Point (New York State); and White Rock (British Columbia) and Blaine (Washington State). The small, secondary border points elsewhere are always quiet, sometimes so quiet that the officers have nothing to do except tear your luggage apart.

Between the Yukon Territory and Alaska, the main routes are the Alaska and Klondike Hwys and the Haines Rd.

Visitors with US or British passports are allowed to bring their vehicles into Canada for six months.

For important further information, see the Visas & Documents and Customs sections in the Facts for the Visitor chapter.

SEA
Ferry

On the East Coast, Canada is connected with the USA by several ferries. Two ferry routes link Yarmouth, Nova Scotia, to Bar Harbor, Maine, and Portland, Maine, in the USA. See the Yarmouth section in the Nova Scotia chapter for more details. From the south end of Deer Island, New Brunswick, in the Bay of Fundy, another ferry runs to Eastport, Maine. A ferry at the north end of Deer Island connects it to the New Brunswick mainland.

On the West Coast, ferries travel between Washington State and Victoria on Vancouver Island. From Port Hardy, on northern Vancouver Island, ferries also head north along the Inside Passage to Alaska. See the Getting There & Away sections for Port Hardy and Victoria in the British Columbia chapter.

Passenger Ship & Freighter

The standard reference for passenger ships is the *OAG Cruise and Ferry Guide,* published by the Reed Travel Group (☎ 01582-600-111, **W** www.oag.com, Church St, Dunstable, Bedfordshire LU5 4HB, UK). Another good source is their *ABC Passenger Shipping Guide.*

Since some cruise lines do not sell directly to the public, travel agents tend to be the best source of information about passenger ships.

Cunard's *Queen Elizabeth II* (**W** www.cunardline.com) sails 23 times a year between Southampton in the UK and New York; the trip takes six nights one way.

Princess Cruises (☎ 800-774-6237, **W** www.princess.com) travels from New York to the East Coast of Canada and up the St Lawrence River to Montréal.

Seabourn Cruise Line (☎ 800-929-9391, **W** www.seabourn.com, 6100 Blue Lagoon

Dr, Miami, FL 33126, USA) offers cruises to and around eastern Canada from Boston and New York. You can opt for seven- or 14-day trips, with stops in many Canadian ports before arrival in Montréal. These trips cost from about US$1000 a day and go way up.

American Canadian Caribbean Lines (☎ 800-556-7450, **W** www.accl-smallships.com) sails from New England up the Hudson River to Montréal and Québec City. Another cruise goes to Nova Scotia.

Many of the major lines cruise the British Columbia Inside Passage and Alaska, and these generally stop at either Vancouver or Victoria.

A more adventurous, though not necessarily cheaper, alternative is a freighter ship. More numerous than cruise ships, freighters offer a greater choice of routes. Passenger freighters typically carry six to 12 passengers (more than 12 would require a doctor on board) and, though less luxurious than dedicated cruise ships, give you a real taste of life at sea.

For information on freighters, contact TravLtips Cruise & Freighter Travel Organization (☎ 800-872-8584, **W** www.travltips.com, PO Box 580188, Flushing, NY 11358, USA) and Freighter World Cruises (☎ 800-531-7774, **W** www.freighterworld.com).

Getting Around

Whether using the train or bus network or a combination of both, visitors should remember that despite Canada's size, the population is small. In many ways this is an asset and part of the country's appeal, but it can also mean that transportation is not always frequent, convenient or even available. Hopping on a bus or train on a whim, as is possible in much of Europe, is not realistic here unless you're in one of the main population areas. However, as any traveler knows, the greater the hassle to get there, the less likely the place will be inundated by tourists.

Driving costs, although quite a bit higher than in the USA, are reasonable, with gasoline prices considerably lower than those in Europe.

Airfares are expensive, but for those with a little extra money and not much time, the odd flight may be useful.

AIR

The Canadian airline industry has been very turbulent recently, with several budget airlines folding and the market turning less competitive. The result is a generally lousy situation for travelers.

The country has just one major airline, Air Canada (☎ 888-247-2262, W www.air canada.com), which works with a number of regional carriers to form the domestic network. In 2001, Air Canada combined the smaller carriers that it owns – Air BC, Air Ontario, Air Nova (Atlantic Canada) and Canadian Regional Airlines – into one entity, called Air Canada Jazz. Independent carriers include Air Creebec (northern Ontario and northern Québec) and First Air (Northwest Territories). For details on these airlines, see the regional chapters.

A good alternative to Air Canada is the discount airline WestJet (☎ 800-538-5696, W www.westjet.com), serving an increasing number of national destinations, including Moncton, Hamilton, Ottawa, Toronto, Calgary, Edmonton, Kelowna, Vancouver and Victoria. WestJet can save you hundreds over Air Canada.

Also check Air Transat (☎ 877-872-6728, W www.airtransat.com), a charter airline

with well-priced flights and packages. The small, expanding airline Bearskin Air (W www.bearskinairlines.com) can take you from Toronto to Ottawa and Montréal, as well as on northern routes, if you're willing to ride in a nine-seater plane.

Tango (☎ 800-315-1390, W www.fly tango.com), a domestic, no-frills Air Canada spin-off, connects major Canadian cities.

Cross your fingers Canada 3000 and Royal Airlines can be brought back from the dead.

The Canadian aviation picture also includes some independent regional and local airlines, which tend to focus on small regions, particularly in the north. Together all these airlines cover most small cities and towns across the country.

Domestic flights tend to be costly, but shop around and you might find some good deals. If you want to fly across the country, you might want to consider taking a bus to the USA, getting a discount flight from New York City to Seattle, and then taking a bus back to Canada.

Another thing to consider is getting a ticket from point A to point B and stopping off in the middle. Often this can be done for little more than the straight-through fare.

Travel agencies offer economical charters and package tours to various Canadian cities, as well as to US destinations, especially during Christmas and through the summer holiday season. Book well in advance to take advantage of these specials.

Air Canada offers travelers 25 years of age and younger one-way standby fares that can be more than 40% cheaper than regular fares. These work best for short distances; for long hauls, a roundtrip flight is cheaper. If you call in the morning, the airline should be able to give you a good idea of what flight to try for. On smaller airlines it's worth inquiring about student rates, though you will need an International Student Identity Card (ISIC).

Quoted airfares within Canada generally don't factor in taxes, including the GST. Ticket agents will quickly total these for you, but you do need to ask. Make sure you do, so you can avoid a nasty surprise. Many major airports also add an airport improvement tax/fee that might have to be paid at the airport; inquire in advance about this, too.

BUS

Buses make up the most extensive transportation routes across the country. Normally cheaper than trains, they go nearly everywhere and usually offer clean, safe and comfortable traveling conditions. Also, buses generally run on time. Be forewarned, though, that bus schedules might not always be convenient. In some cases buses between two destinations might run only two or three times a week. In more out-of-the-way places there may be no service at all.

The largest carrier, Greyhound (☎ 800-661-8747, W www.greyhound.ca) runs from Ottawa westward. Other major companies include Voyageur in Ontario and Québec, Orleans Express in eastern Québec, SMT in New Brunswick, Acadian Lines in Nova Scotia and Roadcruiser in Newfoundland. See the regional chapters for information about these services. (See the Organized Tours section, later in this chapter, for information about alternative bus services that cater to budget travelers and hostelers.)

A one-way ticket on any of the major bus companies is usually good for 60 days, and a roundtrip ticket is valid for a year on most bus lines, but ask to be certain. A one-way ticket that allows stopovers might cost less than a pass and also last for a longer period of time.

If a destination is beyond one company's territory and involves switching bus lines at some point, the connection is generally free. Through tickets are sold for many routes in central and eastern Canada but generally not for westward destinations, which fall in Greyhound territory.

All bus lines (except in rare cases) use the same central bus station in any given Canadian city, so you can change bus lines or make connections at the same place. In a big city, if you have a choice of using the downtown station or a suburban stop, pick the downtown station. You stand a much better chance of getting a seat on the bus if you board at the point of origin. Seating is on a first-come, first-served basis.

You don't need a reservation for a bus ride. Arrive at the station about an hour before the departure to purchase a ticket. You can also buy tickets up to several days in advance, but beware that advance tickets do not apply to any specific bus and do not guarantee a seat. You still must arrive early and line up for your bus. For a small fee, some bus lines will book you the seat of your choice.

On holiday weekends, especially Friday night or around major holidays such as Easter, the bus stations can get pretty crowded and chaotic. At these times, buy your ticket beforehand and get there with plenty of time to spare.

On longer trips, always ask if there is a direct or express bus. On some routes some buses go straight through while others stop seemingly everywhere, which makes for an interminable trip. The price is generally the same, and you may save hours.

In summer, the air conditioners on buses can be far too effective. Take a sweater on board. Also, bring your own picnic whenever possible, as the long-distance buses stop at highway service-station restaurants where you pay an awful lot for plastic food. Smoking is not permitted on buses.

Passes & Discounts

In Canada you can buy some bus passes that work much like the famous Eurail pass. Greyhound's **Canada Travel Pass** allows for unlimited travel and comes in seven- ($264), 15- ($404), 30- ($474) and 60-day ($634) variations. Subtract 10% if you're a student or a senior. These are available all year except during major holiday times such as Christmas and Easter. The pass cannot be used on other bus lines, except if you're making a connection to Montréal on Voyageur.

If you're traveling with someone else, try Greyhound's **Companion Fare Pass**; one person pays full fare and the second person pays 50% of that. This applies to both one-way and roundtrip fares but must be purchased at least seven days prior to departure.

The **Route Pass**, purchased at bus stations, gives you access to numerous linked bus lines for (nearly) unlimited travel in Québec and Ontario, as far west as Sault Ste Marie. Choose among the seven- ($205), 14- ($233) and 18-day ($291) options; the 18-day pass also includes New York City. You can add on extra days at a daily rate. Some restrictions do apply, though – for example, you can't travel back and forth between two cities countless times. Also, the passes aren't valid during the Christmas season.

Travel agents in Europe may sell Canadian bus passes. Compare them carefully to those listed here. Representatives in Europe report that the bus passes sold in Canada are better options.

In addition to passes, there are several other specials to consider. Almost any one-way ticket can include four stopovers along the way, but you must specify them when buying the ticket and it must be used within 60 days. A roundtrip ticket, good for one year, usually permits any number of stopovers. Check with your bus company to verify details.

Some bus lines offer student fares (no age limit) on some routes, so ask. For example, Coach Canada provides student rates (ID required) for trips from Toronto to Montréal. Voyageur Colonial offers the same between Ottawa and Montréal. On some routes, students can get two free tickets with the purchase of four.

TRAIN

The railroad has played a major role in Canada's history, helping to spread European and other immigrants across the country. Because of the history of the Canadian Pacific Railway (CPR) and the Canadian National Railway (CNR), Canadians feel a special nationalistic attachment to the 'ribbons of steel' from coast to coast. Unfortunately, this does not mean they take the train very often. Both of these historic rail companies are out of the passenger business and operate freight trains only.

VIA Rail

Despite lack of domestic support and the slow dismemberment of the network, Canada still boasts a passenger train system extensive enough to be useful as well as appealing. VIA Rail (☎ 888-842-7245, **w** www.viarail.ca), a federal government agency, operates most passenger trains in

Canada, except for some worthwhile train lines mentioned below (or in the regional chapters) and some urban commuter trains. For the most part, the word 'VIA' has become synonymous with train travel and appears on the stations and their roadside direction signs. For train schedules and routes, pick up the *National Timetable* booklet at any VIA Rail station.

Most of the country's major cities are connected by rail; however, there are no passenger trains in Newfoundland (on the island) nor on Prince Edward Island. In other parts of the country, train routes provide the only overland travel option, allowing passengers a glimpse of otherwise unseeable countryside.

Train service is best in the so-called Québec City to Windsor, Ontario, corridor. In this densely populated area of the country, which includes Montréal, Ottawa, Kingston, Toronto and Niagara Falls, trains are frequent and the service is quick.

Generally, long-distance train travel is more expensive than taking the bus, and reservations are important, especially on weekends and holidays.

The pricing policy at VIA Rail is essentially that every trip is considered a one-way fare. A return trip between points A and B is billed as a one-way fare A to B plus a one-way fare B to A. Despite the lack of roundtrip fares, you can still find ways to reduce your costs considerably.

In the Québec City to Windsor corridor, tickets are 40% off with five days' notice, but you can't travel on Friday or Sunday. Everywhere else in Ontario and eastward, travel on any day is discounted 40% if the trip is booked at least seven days in advance. The discount does not apply to trains linking the Maritimes to Québec during the summer months but does include trains within each of these areas all year. Note that occasional sales may offer good discounts between Québec and the Maritimes during summer.

In the provinces west of Ontario, ticket reductions of at least 25% are available from the beginning of October to the end of May with at least seven days' advance notice (though it's wise to book farther ahead than that).

Call early, because only a limited number of seats are offered at the discount rates. Also note that discounts don't apply on or near major holidays, though children, seniors (over 60) and students with international ID cards are entitled to lower fares any time. People with children should inquire about family fares, which can mean substantial savings.

One final tip: quoted VIA fares, surprisingly, vary with the phone call, even by the hour! It's worth calling several times over a day or two, only buying a ticket when you hit a representative giving a low fare. For long trips you can save literally hundreds of dollars!

Long-Distance Travel By linking routes together, you can take a transcontinental train tour right across much of Canada, passing through nearly all the provinces in about five days. The journey rolls through vastly different scenery, some of it spectacular. This can be a very pleasant, relaxing way to go, particularly if you have your own room. During the summer months you should book this trip well ahead.

The longest continuous route in the country is from Toronto to Vancouver. VIA Rail calls this train the *Canadian,* in memory of CPR's original, and it looks like the 1950s stainless-steel classic, complete with the two-story windowed 'dome' car for sightseeing on the journey through Sudbury, Sioux Lookout, Winnipeg, Saskatoon, Edmonton, Jasper and the Rocky Mountains.

These four-day trips depart three times a week. The fare varies with the season. During high season (June to September), a coach seat costs $633 including tax, but in low season the fare is $411. Both rates require a seven-day advance booking.

If you want to begin farther east and cross the entire country, you can board a train in Halifax, but you'll have to change trains in Montréal and Toronto. The high-season fare from Halifax to Toronto is $202, so add that to the $633.

For all long-distance travel, VIA offers several types of cars and different sleeping arrangements ranging from semireclining seats to upper and lower pull-out berths to self-contained private roomettes of varying sizes. The price of any sleeping arrangement is added to the basic coach seat fare or Canrailpass. Discounts are also available on beds, with advance purchase.

Canadian Universities Travel Service

If you're on a budget or you're a young traveler, you might want to check out Travel Cuts (w www.travelcuts.com). Canada's student travel bureau offers a wealth of information from its offices in Halifax, Ottawa, Toronto, Saskatoon, Edmonton and Vancouver, among other places (in Montréal it's called Voyages Campus). You'll find some offices on university campuses and others in central downtown locations.

To obtain student discounts, you must present an International Student Identity Card (ISIC), available at Travel Cuts offices. You must have proper ID – this isn't Athens or Bangkok.

Travel Cuts specializes in getting travelers out of Canada cheaply, but the agency also sells European train passes, arranges working holidays and sets up language courses. And, although it deals mainly in international travel, it can provide tickets and advice for getting around Canada.

Within Canada, Cuts can arrange tours and canoe trips and help with domestic flights. The bureau's Discount Handbook, which lists over 1000 stores and service establishments, offers bargains to ISIC card holders.

Reservations for any type of sleeping arrangement beyond the basic seat should be made well in advance, several months ahead on popular routes such as Rocky Mountain trips. In the west, all meals are included if you book a sleeping setup; in the east, only breakfast is included.

Passes For those who intend to travel a lot, or far, or both, VIA Rail offers the **Canrailpass**. The pass allows 12 days of coach-class travel within a 30-consecutive-day period that begins on the day of the first trip.

The pass covers any number of trips and stopovers from coast to coast. Reserve your seats early, since there's only a limited number of seats on the train set aside for passholders.

The Canrailpass comes in two price versions – low season and high season. In low season – roughly January 6 to May 31 and October 1 to December 15 – you'll pay $423 including tax ($381 for ages 24 and under, students or those 60 and over). In high season – the rest of the year – the pass costs $678 ($610 for those in the discount age categories). You can purchase extra days at an additional cost.

You can buy the Canrailpass in Canada or in Europe (ask a travel agent or a VIA Rail outlet), but there's no difference in cost. Passholders may be entitled to discounts at a car rental agency, on Gray Line bus tours and at some hotels; inquire about these options.

The 10-day unlimited-use **Corridor Pass** is good between Québec City and Niagara Falls. Adults pay $228, with discounts for seniors, students and children – all in all, a great deal.

The **North America Rail Pass** is good across Canada, as well as for most Amtrak routes, collectively covering 900 cities and towns. From mid-October to June, the pass costs $725 ($652 for seniors and students); the rest of the year, it's $1029 ($926).

Other Train Lines

Amtrak is the US equivalent of VIA Rail. Many Canadian train stations sell Amtrak passes and offer information on its services. See the Train section in the Getting There & Away chapter.

The privately run *Rocky Mountaineer* is a tourist train operating through some of the country's finest western scenery. One route runs along the old CPR line through the southern Rockies to Banff – it's perhaps Canada's most spectacular stretch of track.

All trips run between Vancouver and Kamloops, with varying stops at Jasper, Banff and Calgary. The company offers a range of side trips and tours and operates from the beginning of May to the middle of October. Reservations should be made well in advance, but seats can be available at any time. Prices are discounted for brief periods at the beginning and the end of the season.

For more information, contact Rocky Mountaineer Railtours (☎ 604-606-7200, 800-665-7245, ⓦ www.rockymountaineer.com, 1150 Station St, 1st Floor, Vancouver, BC V6A 2X7) and see the Vancouver section in the British Columbia chapter.

Canada also has a few small train companies that offer touring opportunities. For example, the Algoma Central Railway in Sault Ste Marie, Ontario, provides access to a northern wilderness area. Ontario Northland runs north from Toronto and includes the *Polar Bear Express* up to Moosonee on Hudson Bay. The Québec North Shore & Labrador Railway travels from Sept Îles, Québec, north to Labrador. British Columbia Rail goes from Vancouver north to Whistler and Prince George. See the regional chapters for details on these.

CAR

In many ways, driving is the best way to travel (unless you're doing battle with rush-hour traffic in Montréal, Toronto and Vancouver). You can go where and when you want, use secondary highways and roads and leave the beaten track. It's particularly good in summer, when you can camp or even sleep in the car.

Canada keeps its roads in good condition and marks them well (though in Québec, non-French speakers may have some difficulty with the French-only signs). There are few toll roads in the country, although crossing some bridges requires a small payment.

The Trans Canada Hwy runs from St John's, Newfoundland, across more than 7000km to Victoria, British Columbia. You'll find campgrounds and picnic stops all along the route, often within 100km to 150km of each other. At the other end of the spectrum, rural routes meander through rural Canada. These small roads are marked RR1, RR7, etc.

Wherever your travels take you, make sure you find a decent provincial highway map. Provincial tourist offices can supply you with both provincial and national road maps – usually free. Service stations and variety stores sell similar maps.

Road Rules & Safety Precautions

A valid driver's license from any country is good in Canada for three months, but an International Driving Permit, available in your home country, is cheap and valid for one year almost anywhere in the world. You can't drive in Canada without auto insurance.

The use of seat belts is compulsory throughout Canada, and the fines for not wearing them are heavy. All provinces require motorcyclists to drive with the lights on and to wear helmets (which applies to passengers as well).

Traffic in both directions must stop when stationary school buses flash their red lights – this means that children are getting off and on. In cities with pedestrian crosswalks, cars must stop to allow pedestrians to cross.

Turning right at red lights (after first coming to a complete stop and checking that the way is clear) is permitted in all provinces except most of Québec. And all traffic violations in money-short Québec will cost you plenty, so take it easy there.

Sleeping at roadside parks, picnic spots or other areas on the highways is usually okay (signs may say otherwise); just don't set up a tent.

Try to avoid driving in areas with heavy snow, but if you must, you might have to buy snow tires. Many Canadian cars have four-season radial tires. If you get stuck, don't stay in the car with the engine going; every year people die of carbon monoxide suffocation by doing this during big storms. A single candle burning in the car will keep it reasonably warm.

When driving in the north of the provinces, the Yukon Territory and the Northwest Territories, you might have to travel long distances between service stations – try not to let your tank fall much below half-full and always carry extra gasoline. Make sure the vehicle you're driving is in good condi-

tion and take along some tools, spare parts, water and food.

On the gravel roads dust and flying stones kicked up by other vehicles pose the largest problems. Keep a good distance from the vehicle in front of you, and when you see an oncoming vehicle, slow down and stay well to the right (this also applies to vehicles overtaking you from behind). In case of damage, carry a spare tire, fan belt and hoses. Some people use a bug and gravel screen, and others also protect their gasoline tank and lights.

In much of the country, deer, moose and other wildlife on the road present potential hazards, especially at night, when animals are active and visibility is poor. In areas with roadside signs alerting drivers to possible animal crossings, keep your eyes scanning both sides of the road and be prepared to stop or swerve. Often a vehicle's headlights will mesmerize the animal, leaving it frozen in the middle of the road. Try flashing the lights or turning them off, as well as using the horn.

City driving comes with its own set of dangers, particularly during weekday rush hours in the big metropolitan areas. In Montréal, drivers possessing nerves of steel, abundant confidence and a devil-may-care attitude will fare best. To compound the fun, there are no lines painted on the roads in some places, and driving becomes a type of high-speed free-for-all. Guess what? The province of Québec has the highest accident rate in the country. All told, it's best to avoid city driving anywhere as much as possible, regardless of the time. Walking or taking the bus is generally cheaper than paying costly parking fees, and it's a lot easier on your nerves.

Rental

You'll find no shortage of car rental agencies across the country. Big companies such as Avis, Hertz, National and Budget operate counters at almost all the country's airports. To be certain of finding a car, make a reservation before you arrive.

Among the new-car agencies, Budget and Enterprise usually offer some of the best rates and also provide good service. The well-known used-car agency Rent-A-Wreck might give you a cheaper deal. Note that within each company rates vary from city to city, location to location. Searching for deals on the Internet, as opposed to telephoning offices, can often save you a lot of money.

Some companies rent vans, and, with a number of people sharing, this can work out to be quite economical. Reserve vans well in advance.

Most companies charge a daily rate of about $30 to $50 plus a per-kilometer fee. Others offer a flat rate, which is nearly always better if you're traveling far.

Weekend rates are often the cheapest and can include extra days, so a 'weekend' in car renting sometimes becomes three or even four days. Also, if you're renting for extended periods of time, ask for a discount beyond the weekly rate (the weekly rate generally saves 10% over the daily rate).

Beware that prices can be deceptive. The daily rate may be an enticing $29, but by the time you finish with insurance, gasoline (fill it up before taking it back or you pay the rental company's high per-liter prices plus a 'refilling fee'), the number of kilometers, provincial sales tax, GST and any other bits and pieces, you could wind up with a pretty surprising bill.

Count on needing a credit card to rent a car in Canada. There may be some companies here and there that will rent to those without plastic, but even after the hassle of finding one, expect more problems. First, the company will need a few days (at least) to check you out. If you're not working, things can be sticky; bring a letter from an employer or banker if you can, and lots of good identification. You may also need to leave a deposit, sometimes as much as several hundred dollars a day. After all that, you may still have to sign away your first child, too. It's not worth the headache.

Some companies require you to be over 21 years of age; others will only rent to those over 26. You might be asked to buy extra insurance depending on your age, but the required premiums are not high. Insurance is generally optional. Check to see if your car insurance at home includes rentals. If it does, you can skip the rental agency's pricey coverage.

Parents, note that children under 18kg (40lbs) are required to be in a safety car seat, which must be secured by a seat belt. The big-name rental companies can supply seats at a small daily rental fee. Outside the major cities it might take a couple of days for the rental agency to locate a child seat, so call ahead.

Recreational Vehicles Renting recreational vehicles (RVs) or various trailers (caravans) is another option. The RV market is big in the west, with specialized agencies in Calgary, Edmonton, Whitehorse and Vancouver (look them up in the Yellow Pages under 'Recreational Vehicles'). But RVs can also be rented in Toronto and other central and eastern cities.

Popular with European travelers, RVs should be booked before May for the summer. In high season mid- to large-size vehicles cost $180 to $220 per day. These can accommodate five to seven people and include six appliances. Make sure to ask for a diesel engine, as this will save considerably on running costs. Cheaper camper vans are also available, but these should be booked even earlier.

Canadream Campers (☎ 800-461-7368, ⊠ www.canadream.com) rents RVs in Calgary, Halifax, Montréal, Toronto, Vancouver and Whitehorse and offers one-ways. You can also try Go West Campers International (☎ 800-240-1814, ⊠ www .gowestcampers.com, 1577 Lloyd St, North Vancouver).

Buying a Car
Older cars can be bought quite cheaply in Canada. Look in the local newspaper or, in larger cities, the weekly *Buy & Sell Bargain Hunter Press, Auto Trader* or an equivalent, all of which can be bought at corner variety stores. Private deals are nearly always the most economical way to buy a car. Used-car businesses must mark up the prices in order to make a profit. Generally, North American cars cost less than Japanese and European cars.

Those who prefer a semiscientific approach to car buying should take a look at Phil Edmunston's excellent *Lemon-Aid,* an annual book published by the Canadian Automobile Protection Association. Available in stores and libraries, it details all the used cars on the market, rates them and gives rough price guidelines. Haggling over car prices, whether at a dealership or at someone's home, is the norm. Expect to knock off hundreds or even a thousand dollars depending on the value of the car.

If you only need to drive for a few months, a used car can be an excellent investment, especially if there are two of you. You can usually sell the car for nearly what you paid for it. A fairly decent older car should be available for under $4000. West Coast cars last longer because salt does not have to be used on the roads in winter, which means the cars rust less quickly.

To drive a car here, you'll need an international driver's license and Canadian insurance. Bring a letter from your current company indicating your driving record. Call an insurance broker (check the Yellow Pages in the phone book) in Canada, and the broker will find you a company offering temporary insurance for a few months. In order to get the insurance and then a plate for the vehicle, you'll need an address in Canada. That of a friend, relative, etc, will suffice. You should also have your passport.

Insurance costs vary widely and can change dramatically from province to province. As a rule, the rates for women are noticeably lower than for men of comparable age and driving records. If you're planning a side trip to the USA, make sure the insurance you negotiate is valid over the border, too. Also, remember that rates vary according to the age and type of car. A newer car may cost more to insure but may also be easier to sell.

Drive-Aways
One of the best driving deals is the uniquely North American drive-away system, in which someone hires you to drive his or her car to a specific destination. Usually, the car belongs to someone who has been transferred for work and has had to fly there or who doesn't have the time or ability to drive a long distance.

To participate in this system, make arrangements through a drive-away agency in one of the major cities. Look in the transportation section of the newspaper classifieds or in the Yellow Pages under 'Drive-Away Automobiles.' After the agency matches you up with a suitable car, you present a deposit of $300 to $600 (plus good identification and a couple of photos) and agree to deliver the car within a certain number of days. (If you don't show up with the car in the allotted time, the agency notifies the police.) Most drive-away outlets suggest a route to take.

You're not paid to deliver the car (but you may be if you really hit the jackpot and someone's in a rush) and generally you pay for gasoline, although sometimes a portion or all of the gasoline costs are paid by the owner. Try to get a smaller, newer car since that'll save you money on gas.

In summer, when demand is highest, cars can be harder to come by, and you might be asked for a nonrefundable administrative payment, perhaps $100. Though this increases the cost, it doesn't change the fact that drive-aways can turn out to be a great deal for two or more people traveling together.

The agencies typically allow eight days for a journey from the East to West Coasts. Some trips can take you across the border – Montréal to Florida is a common route.

Before you set out, make sure you know what will happen if the car breaks down. Get this information in writing if possible. Generally, you'll have to pay for minor car repairs of $150 or less, but keep the receipt and you'll be reimbursed upon delivery. If bad luck strikes and a major repair is required, the agency might get in touch with the owner and ask how to proceed, adding extra time and inconvenience to your trip.

Usually, drive-away cars are fairly new and in good working order. If not, the owner wouldn't be going to the bother and expense of transporting the car a long distance. Occasionally, you hear of a Jaguar or something similar available – a classy experience on a shoestring budget.

For more information on some drive-away agencies, see the Getting There & Away sections of the regional chapters.

Car Sharing
Allô Stop ([W] www.allostop.com) acts as an agency for car sharing. It unites people looking for rides with people who have cars and are looking for a companion to share gasoline expenses. A well-established service that's been in business for years, Allô Stop operates in Montréal, Québec City and other towns around Québec. See the Getting There & Away sections of the Québec chapter. Call a couple of days before your trip, and the agency will try to link you up with someone.

Sometimes commercial van shuttles ply the routes between major cities such as Montréal, Toronto and Ottawa on a regular, scheduled basis. These services charge far less than bus companies but are operating illegally. Also, they might not carry enough insurance coverage to protect against accident or emergency. But if you're willing to take the risk, they advertise in the classified sections of entertainment weeklies.

Canadian Automobile Association

The CAA (W www.caa.ca), like its counterpart the American Automobile Association (AAA), provides assistance to member motorists (check in your country of origin to see if there are reciprocal agreements). Its services include 24-hour emergency roadside assistance, trip planning and advice; the CAA also issues traveler's checks.

If you have a decent car, the association's help may not be necessary, but if you have bought an older car to tour the country, the annual membership fee ($85) may well be invaluable; after one or two breakdowns it will have paid for itself, as towing charges are high.

For information, contact the central Ontario office (☎ 800-268-3750, 60 Commerce Valley Dr E, Thornhill, ON L3T 7P9). Each province has its own regional office, and the CAA runs branches in most major cities and towns.

Gasoline

Gasoline (petrol), or simply gas (gaz in Québec), varies in price across the country, with the highest prices found in the far north and on the East Coast, particularly in Québec, Newfoundland and Labrador. Drivers approaching Québec from Ontario should top up the tank before the border. Alberta's prices, with fewer taxes, are fairly low, so it's a good idea to fill up there before hitting British Columbia. Those arriving from the USA should always have a full tank, as the low US prices will never be seen in Canada.

In general, the big cities have the best prices, so fill up in town. The more remote a place, the higher the cost of gas. Major highway service stations offer no bargains and often jack up the price on long weekends and at holiday times in order to fleece captive victims.

Gasoline is always sold by the liter. On average, a liter of gasoline costs about 65¢, or about $3.15 per imperial gallon. The Canadian (imperial) gallon is one-fifth larger than the US gallon.

BICYCLE

Though some cyclists do take on extensive tours in summer, the sheer size of Canada makes it difficult to cover much ground by bicycle alone. Most travelers use more efficient means of transportation to move between regions and bring their bikes only for recreational cycling and off-road mountain biking; see the Activities section of the Facts for the Visitor chapter for more information about these two popular sports. Some cyclists, however, do manage to cross the entire country by bike; see Hiking under Activities in the Facts for the Visitor chapter for information about the Trans Canada Trail.

If you're biking from place to place, go to the tourist offices and pick up provincial highway maps, which offer more detail and show more secondary roads than the usual service-station maps do. Large bookstores sell cycling guides. Provincial tourism offices and travel agencies can also provide information about companies that specialize in overnight and long-distance cycling trips.

Within the cities, the ease of getting around by bicycle varies. Edmonton, Montréal, Ottawa, Toronto and Vancouver all have bicycle routes, but some are much more extensive than others, ranging from Toronto's minimal system to Ottawa's good one.

For $15, VIA Rail allows passengers to take bicycles on trains with baggage cars – that is, pretty much any train going a fair distance (which excludes local and commuter trains). Sending bikes on buses is possible but expensive; you'll pay $10 for a bicycle box, plus a weight and mileage fee. A five-hour trip costs about $75. The major Canadian airlines charge a flat fee of $75 for a one-way flight, with just a bag supplied. In all cases you must perform some disassembly.

For further information, contact the Canadian Cycling Association (☎ 613-248-1353, W www.canadian-cycling.com, 702-2197 Riverside Dr, Ottawa, ON K1H 7X3), which can supply local contacts, trail information and much more.

Note that helmets are mandatory for those under age 18 and recommended for all cyclists.

HITCHHIKING

Readers' letters indicate there have been few problems hitchhiking in Canada; however, hitchhiking is never entirely safe in any country, and we don't recommend it. Travelers who decide to do it should understand that they are taking a small but potentially serious risk.

That said, hitchhiking is good in Canada. It's not the UK, which is a hitchhiker's dream, but thumbing a ride is still a worthwhile option. Many travelers depend on hitchhiking at least for a portion of their trip, and not just because it's cheap. The lack of buses or trains means the thumb can fill in a gap in the most convenient way.

Two people, one of each gender, is ideal for hitchhiking; it's safer, and it's often not difficult for drivers to take on two extra passengers. If you're three or more, or a single woman, forget it.

Outside of the big cities, stay on the main highways. Traffic can be very light on the smaller roads. Always get off where there's a service station or restaurant and not at a side road or farmer's gate. If you feel you've waited a long time to be picked up, remember that the ride you get may take you over 1500km.

Around towns and cities, pick your spots carefully. Stand where you can be seen and where a car can easily stop. A foreign T-shirt, like one with 'University of Stockholm' on it, might be useful. Some people find that a cardboard sign with large clear letters naming their destination is helpful.

If you're going into a large city, make sure the ride is going all the way. If it's not, get dropped off where you can catch a city bus, especially after dark. When leaving a city, it's best to take a bus out a little way, since hitchhiking in town is not recommended. Prostitutes employ this technique, and most drivers seem to feel that inner-city hitchhikers are a much less desirable breed than those out on the open road.

It's illegal to hitchhike within some city limits; fines can be steep. Generally, the scruffier you look, the more documents you should have to prove your identity should the police decide to question you.

You must stay off intercity expressways, though the feeder ramps are okay. In Toronto and Vancouver particularly, the police will stop you on the expressway.

Around the large cities you'll encounter heavy traffic leaving on Friday and returning on Sunday. Despite the volume of cars, hitchhiking is difficult at those times because most cars are full with families. Weekdays are best, as you'll encounter salespeople and truckers on the road. Many companies forbid truck drivers to pick up people, though some do anyway.

If you're in a hurry, going from Toronto to Vancouver shouldn't take longer than five days and has been done in three.

As early as the end of summer, nights can be very cold, depending where you are, and snow can fall in October in much of the country. Do not overestimate your luck.

One last tip – if you don't want to spend time in northern Ontario, get a ride straight through from Sault Ste Marie to Thunder Bay.

WALKING

See Activities in the Facts for the Visitor chapter for long-distance hiking trails, including the Trans Canada Trail.

BOAT

With oceans at both ends of the country and a lake- and river-filled interior, don't be surprised to find yourself in a boat at some point or other.

On the East Coast, major ferries link provinces and islands to the mainland. Boats connect Nova Scotia to Prince Edward Island. Two ferry routes link Nova Scotia to the US state of Maine and to New Brunswick, across the Bay of Fundy. Ferries also connect Nova Scotia to Newfoundland and run around the edges of Newfoundland and up to Labrador.

From Prince Edward Island, ferries travel to Québec's Îles de la Madeleine (Magdalen Islands) in the Gulf of the St Lawrence. Boats also run back and forth between the north and south shore of central Québec along the St Lawrence River.

On Canada's West Coast, ferries connect mainland British Columbia with Vancouver Island, the Gulf Islands and the Queen Charlotte Islands.

See the Getting There & Away and Getting Around sections of the regional chapters for particular ferry information.

ORGANIZED TOURS

If you want a general type of organized tour, the larger regional bus companies might be your best bet. They offer trips of varying lengths, including transportation, accommodations and possibly sightseeing.

Across the country small companies offer low-cost, often nature-based, tours and a variety of adventure trips; see the Organized Tours sections of the regional chapters for recommendations. Also see the Alternative Buses section, below. Good camping stores, hostels and tourist offices often carry pamphlets put out by such companies.

Throughout the Americas various private companies run tours aimed primarily at 18- to 38-year-olds. These trips should generally be organized before arriving. Travel agents in your home country can help. Most of the trips last two to five weeks and focus on cities and sights, but some are more slanted toward outdoor activities, with everything included but sleeping bags. A few trips may cover both Canada and the USA. If you're looking for a well-established outfit, try Trek America (☎ 800-221-0596, W www .trekamerica.com) and Suntrek (☎ 800-786-8735, W www.suntrek.com).

The Outward Bound Wilderness School (W www.outwardbound.ca), with offices in Vancouver and Toronto, runs good, rigorous outdoor adventure trips that are more like courses than holidays. Ranging from seven to 24 days, they take place in various rugged parts of the country; many programs include a solo portion. The Toronto branch (☎ 416-421-8111, 146 Laird Dr, Toronto, ON M7Y 5R1) will send out a pamphlet outlining its programs.

The Canadian Universities Travel Service, also known as Travel Cuts (W www.travel cuts.com), runs various trips that include activities like hiking, cycling and canoeing and can also arrange ski and sun-destination holidays. Travel Cuts maintains offices in every major city in Canada, including Toronto (☎ 416-979-2406, 187 College St, Toronto, ON M5T 1P7).

Hostelling International (HI) Canada also organizes some tours and activities

trips such as hiking, cross-country (Nordic) skiing, etc.

Major museums and art galleries also sometimes offer specialized educational/ recreational tours – to visit the Canadian Arctic and the Inuit carvers, for example – but these trips can also be very costly. If you have a particular interest, though, they can be worth the expense.

Always make sure you know exactly what sort of tour you're getting and how much it will cost. If you have any doubts about the tour company, pay your money into what is called the 'tour operators escrow account.' The law requires that this account number appear on tourist brochures (you may have to look hard). Doing this protects you and your money should the trip fall through for any reason. It's a good idea to pay by check because cash is always harder to get back; write the details of the tour, with destination and dates, on the front of the check. On the back, write 'for deposit only.'

Alternative Buses

Some well-established and innovative alternative transportation services cater to budget travelers and hostelers. These low-cost, high-convenience, good-fun companies first sprang up in western Canada but have spawned eastern counterparts. Services offered range from simple, point-A-to-point-B transportation to full-fledged tours. Most fall somewhere in between and last anywhere from a few hours to weeks.

The biggest player in this business is the national Moose Travel (☎ 888-816-6673 in Toronto, 888-388-4881 in Vancouver, W www .moosenetwork.com), an oft-recommended jump-on, jump-off adventure-travel/hostel-circuit transportation service that offers short- and long-trip packages in Ontario and Québec and in Alberta and British Columbia, with a train link between the east and west regions.

Moose picks up passengers in Montréal, Ottawa, Toronto, Banff and Vancouver and stops at cities, historic sites, provincial parks and other outdoor attractions, some of which would be difficult to reach without your own vehicle. Circuits range from a few days' duration to about two weeks.

Passengers pay for transportation only and add their selected activities, which can include adventure sports like whitewater rafting. Accommodation, not included in the price, is at hostels. The full East or West Pass costs $420.

Moose operates May to October. See the Toronto, Banff and Vancouver sections for more information.

Several companies pick up at Toronto hostels. Magic Bus (☎ 877-856-6610, W www.furtherstill.com) runs free-wheeling, anything-can-happen trips to Niagara Falls and cottage country. JoJo Tours (☎ 416-201-6465) advertises day trips around southern Ontario. Free Spirit (☎ 416-219-7562, W www.freespirit-tours.com) offers a rock-climbing and hiking package.

In Calgary, contact Hammerhead (☎ 403-260-0940, W www.hammerhead tours.com) for van day trips to fascinating sites around southern Alberta. Trips are not expensive, and they're even cheaper for hostelers.

Also based in Calgary is the Rocky Express, run by True North Tours (☎ 403-275-4979, 888-464-4842, W www.backpacker tours.com). The three- and six-day excursions to a series of hostels in the Rocky Mountains offer tons of opportunity for outdoor activities.

In Vancouver, check out Bigfoot Adventure Tours (☎ 888-244-6673, W www .bigfoottours.com) for trips around BC. In Victoria, look into Seagull Expeditions (☎ 800-580-3890, W www.backpacker tours.com) and Midnight Sun Adventure Tours (☎ 877-473-7669, W www.reserva tionsnow.ca) for Vancouver Island adventure bus trips.

You can sometimes purchase tickets for the above companies at travel agencies overseas, such as Travel Cuts (which operates a London office), STA Travel and Carlson Wagonlit. For more information on alternative bus tours, see the Organized Tours sections in the regional chapters.

Ontario

Smack in the middle of the country, Ontario is the center of Canadian politics and economics – and much of the arts as well. For this, it is not always loved. But the country's largest city, Toronto, is here, as are Niagara Falls and Ottawa, Canada's capital. These three places alone make the region one of the most heavily visited in the country.

And that's just for starters. Historic Kingston (between Ottawa and Toronto) and some of the middle-sized towns west of Toronto lure thousands of visitors with their country flavor and varying attractions, such as the Shakespearean Festival in Stratford and the Oktoberfest in Kitchener. Less known but equally representative of the province are the beaches of Lake Huron and Georgian Bay (the shorelines of these two bodies of water have been made archetypally Canadian by the country's best-known painters). Farther north, wilderness parks offer respite from the densely populated southern region and provide opportunities to see the northern transitional and boreal forests. The resource-based cities of Sudbury, Sault Ste Marie and Thunder Bay, each with their own attractions, are also good starting points for trips around the more rugged areas of Ontario, from the Lake Superior shoreline to as far north as legendary James Bay, with one of the province's oldest settlements, Moosonee.

Ontario is also the richest province, with as much manufacturing as all the other provinces combined. Despite that, agriculture is one of the most significant economic sectors. The north has tremendous mineral and forestry resources.

The province is traditionally conservative, politically and socially, but all manner of diversity thrives, and Ontario hosts the country's largest and most varied ethnic communities.

The name 'Ontario' is derived from an Iroquois word meaning 'rocks standing high near the water,' probably referring to Niagara Falls.

History
When Europeans staggered into this region, they found it settled and occupied by numerous

Highlights

Entered Confederation: July 1, 1867
Area: 1,068,587 sq km
Population: 11,874,436
Provincial Capital: Toronto

- Absorb Canada's capital, Ottawa, with its boggling array of museums and art galleries.

- Get soaked while whitewater rafting down the Ottawa River.

- Savor a meal and concert in the shadow of the CN Tower in cosmopolitan Toronto, the country's largest city.

- Peer over the edge of thundering Niagara Falls.

- Raise a glass in the Niagara wine region.

- Enjoy Shakespearean theater at Stratford or the works of George Bernard Shaw at Niagara-on-the-Lake.

OTHER MAPS
Ontario page 92
Niagara-on-the-Lake page 171
Georgian Bay & Lakelands page 208
TORONTO MAPS
Downtown Toronto page 96

Northern Ontario page 223

Thunder Bay page 247

Sudbury page 226

Sault Ste Marie page 236

Stratford page 195

London page 200

Toronto page 94

Ottawa page 135

Eastern Ontario page 151

Kingston page 155

Niagara Falls page 177

Southwestern Ontario page 166

Hudson Bay

QC

USA

Indian nations. The Algonquin and Huron Indians first dominated the southern portion of the province, but by the time of European exploration and trade in the early part of the 18th century, the Iroquois Confederacy, also known as the Five Nations, dominated the area south of Georgian Bay and east to Québec. The Ojibway covered the lands north of the Great Lakes and west to the Cree territory of the prairies in what is now Alberta and Saskatchewan.

French explorers and traders in the 17th century were the first Europeans to see much of Ontario, as they set up forts to link with the Mississippi. It wasn't until the arrival of the British Loyalists, around 1775, that large-scale settlement began. After the War of 1812, British immigrants began to settle in still larger numbers. By the end of the century, specialized farming, industry and cities were growing markedly. At the end of each of the world wars, immigration boomed.

Ontario now has a population of over 11 million, making it Canada's most populous province, and it is the first choice of immigrants from across the globe, with Toronto proving a powerful draw thanks to its strong economy and well-established support services for immigrants.

Information

Ontario Travel (☎ 800-668-2746, ⓦ www .ontariotravel.net) is the provincial tourism arm. It operates 10 year-round offices and several seasonal ones. Permanent offices

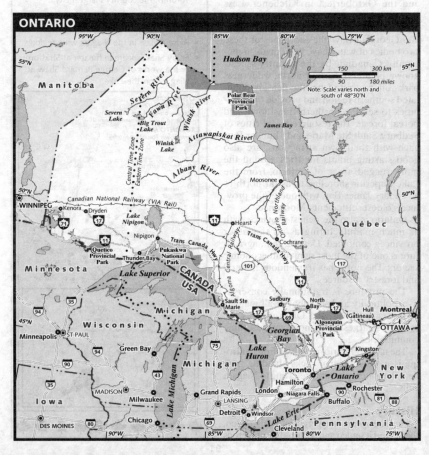

ONTARIO

can be found in Toronto, Niagara Falls, Windsor and at other major border crossings. Ontario Travel produces a range of free publications from accommodations to events. Its mailing address is Queen's Park, Toronto, ON M7A 2E5. City and regional tourist offices acting independently can be found around the province.

For emergency service dial ☎ 911 anywhere in the province.

Ontario is on Eastern Standard Time, except for the far western area which is on Central Time (matching neighboring Manitoba). Thunder Bay is on Eastern Time and Kenora on Central Time.

Ontario's provincial sales tax is 8%.

Activities

Ontario has 639 (some not yet developed) government parks ranging from simple dayuse beaches to huge wilderness tracts. Tourist offices should have an information booklet, or you can contact the Ministry of Natural Resources (☎ 416-314-2000, 800-667-1940, W www.ontarioparks.com). For camping reservations, call ☎ 888-668-7275; you'll need a credit card to reserve.

Despite urbanization and development there remains much uncluttered, wooded lakeland and many quiet country towns surrounded by small market garden farms. Within hours of Toronto and less time from Ottawa there are countless outdoor opportunities. The northern regions contain vast areas of wilderness. To get out into the woods or onto the water a good place to start is one of the many excellent government parks. Details are outlined in the text.

Ontario offers superb canoeing whether for a day or weeks. There are excellent routes in Algonquin and Killarney Provincial Parks, as well as around Temagami. Details can be found in the text.

Aside from the excellent walking in the provincial parks, long-distance trails are discussed in the text. See Bruce Trail under the Tobermory section and Voyageur Trail under the Sault Ste Marie section. Hike Ontario (☎ 416-426-7362, W www.hikeontario.com) at 1185 Eglinton Ave E, Suite 411, Toronto, ON M3C 3C6, can offer more information.

The Ottawa River in Eastern Ontario offers accessible river trips of the wild or mild variety. See the Ottawa section for complete details.

Downhill skiing can be found north of Toronto in the Barrie area and, with higher, steeper runs, at Collingwood. The Gatineau Hills area around Ottawa has downhill and excellent cross-country skiing. Northern Ontario also offers some downhill.

Southern Ontario has a number of bike paths on former train lines known as rail trails.

Toronto

pop 2.4 million

'T O' (or 'T dot' in hip-hop culture) is not only the capital of Ontario – it's the largest city in Canada. In fact, the sizes of its population, government and budget are greater than those of some Canadian provinces. Even so, the downtown area is manageably small and safe, and there are numerous compact neighborhoods and ethnic communities flaring out from the core, so visitors can and should explore much of the city on foot. Toronto's well-documented traditional stiffness has loosened up noticeably in recent years: restaurants and cafés sport outdoor patios for half the year; clubgoers and barflies party until 2am; and all manner of fashions and subcultures coexist.

Several major, dramatic architectural projects overseen by internationally prominent designers now in the works are sure to boost the city's presence and visual appeal. They include substantial expansions to the city's prime art gallery and the main museum. A new downtown opera house is being discussed, and the University of Toronto has hired renowned architect Sir Norman Foster to design a new pharmacy building.

In addition to being a primary focus for English Canadian arts and culture, Toronto is well entrenched as the nation's financial, communications and business hub (the Toronto Stock Exchange is one of North America's most important). It has the busiest Canadian port on the Great Lakes and is a major center for banking, manufacturing and publishing. Also, the city has been called Hollywood North – you may well wander unexpectedly into a movie shoot.

For all this, everybody in the country has an opinion on Toronto (which is almost always negative) and its supposed center-of-the-universe mentality. Still, its vitality,

ONTARIO

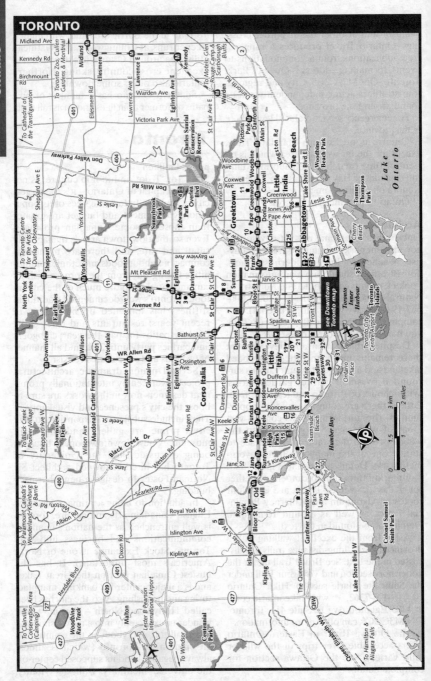

PLACES TO STAY
8 YWCA
11 Allenby
13 Queensway Motel
14 Four Points Sheraton
26 Leslieville Home Hostel
27 Beach Motel
28 Grayona Tourist Home
29 Candy Haven Tourist Home
33 Executive Motor Motel
35 Fourth St B&B

PLACES TO EAT
10 Big Carrot Natural Food Market
17 True Grits

19 Terroni
20 Dufflet's Pastries

ENTERTAINMENT
1 Yuk Yuks Superclub
2 St Louis Bar & Grill
16 Revue
18 Sneaky Dee's
21 Theatre Passe Muraille
25 Allen's
34 The Docks

OTHER
3 Oxygen Spa Bar

4 Ontario Science Centre
5 Montgomery's Inn
6 Casa Loma
7 Spadina House
9 Todmorden Mills Heritage
   Museum & Arts Centre
12 Brown's Sports & Cycle
15 Colbourne Lodge
22 St Paul's Basilica
23 Enoch Turner Schoolhouse
24 Librarie Champlain
30 Exhibition Place
31 HMCS *Haida*
32 Fort York

vibrancy and cleanliness are considerable assets. It may not be a warm, gregarious city, but it's way better than it was when it was known as Toronto-the-Good. Canadian Gen-X author Douglas Coupland described Toronto as '...a city with the efficient, ordered feel of the Yellow Pages sprung to life in three dimensions, peppered with trees and veined with cold water.' He should have been here 30 years ago.

The five cities surrounding and adjacent to the relatively small area of Toronto proper amalgamated in 1998. This enlarged Toronto has been dubbed 'the Megacity.' The urban sprawl beyond the new city boundaries is known as the Greater Toronto Area (GTA). The city and area continue to grow rapidly, partially fueled by new immigrants who arrive steadily from every corner of the globe.

There is a lot of central housing, part of an urban planning scheme that has kept a healthy balance between businesses and residences, making it a more livable city than many. Despite high costs, there are few areas of concentrated poverty. The streets are busy at night, and the downtown streetcars and subways are generally used without hesitation. Of course, some prudence is always wise. There are some rougher parts of town, but these tend to be away from areas of visitor interest.

History

In the 17th century, this was Seneca Indian land. Étienne Brûlé, on a trip with Samuel de Champlain in 1615, was the first European to see the site. The Native Indians did not particularly relish the visit. The chilly reception, ongoing suspicion and ill will temporarily impeded further French development. It wasn't until around 1720 that the French established a fur-trading post and mission in what's now the city's west end.

Eventually, the Brits, after years of hostility with the French, took over. John Simcoe, lieutenant governor of the new Upper Canada, chose the site as the capital in 1793, and it became known as York (Niagara-on-the-Lake had been the previous capital).

During the War of 1812, the USA held York and burned the Legislature. In retaliation, the British headed toward Washington and burned the US political headquarters; when the burn marks were painted over in white, it became known as the 'White House.'

In 1814, when the war ended, York began to expand, and stagecoaches first rolled on Yonge St in 1828. In 1834, with William Lyon Mackenzie as the first mayor, York was renamed Toronto, a Native Indian name meaning 'meeting place.' The city, controlled by conservative politicians, became known as 'Toronto the Good,' a tag that only began to fade in the 1970s. Religious restraints and strong anti-vice laws (it was illegal to hire a horse on Sunday) were largely responsible. Not all that long ago, curtains were drawn in department-store windows on Sunday, because window-shopping was considered sinful, and movies couldn't be screened on the holy day.

Like many big cities, Toronto has had its great fire. In 1904, about five hectares of the inner city burned, leveling 122 build-

DOWNTOWN TORONTO

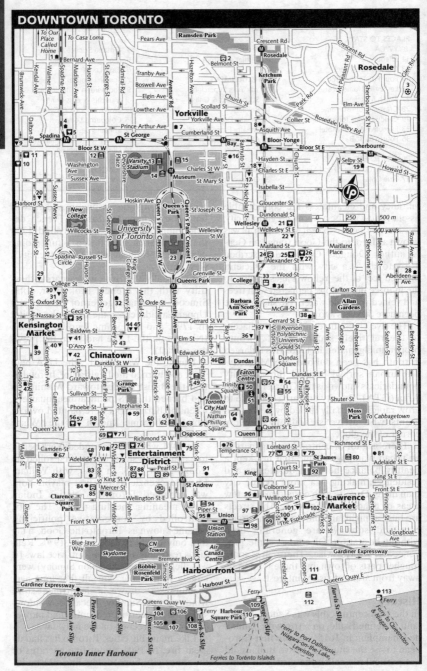

DOWNTOWN TORONTO

PLACES TO STAY
1 Havinn
4 Global Guesthouse
6 Park Hyatt
7 Four Seasons
19 Howard Johnson Selby Hotel & Suites
28 Aberdeen Guesthouse
32 Beverley Place
34 Days Inn
38 Neill-Wycik College Hotel
39 The Planet Traveler's Hostel
47 Grange Apartment Hotel
54 Bond Place Hotel
70 Canadiana Guesthouse & Backpackers
75 Hilton
78 HI Toronto
82 Global Village Backpackers
93 Strathcona
95 Royal York Hotel
96 Hotel Victoria

PLACES TO EAT
5 The Madison
9 By the Way Café
17 7 West Café
18 Green Mango
20 Kensington Kitchen
22 Zelda's
27 Bigliardi's
30 Peter's Chung King
31 Red Room
36 Swiss Chalet
37 Ryerson Polytechnic University Cafeteria
40 Phô' Hu'ng
41 Lee Garden
42 Swatow
43 Mata Hari Grill
44 Yung Sing Pastry Shop; Baldwin Natural Foods
45 Margarita's
57 Le Select Bistro
60 Queen Mother
68 Zupa's Deli
73 Alice Fazooli's
79 Young Thailand
86 Wayne Gretzky's
88 Peel Pub
100 Old Spaghetti Factory
101 Papillon

ENTERTAINMENT
2 Toronto Truck Theatre
10 Tranzac
11 Ye Olde Brunswick House
21 Slack Alice
24 Buddies in Bad Times Theatre
25 Tango
26 Woody's
29 Free Times Café
33 Cineplex Odeon Carlton Cinemas
35 Grossman's
52 Canon Theatre

56 Horseshoe Tavern
58 Bamboo Club
59 Music Gallery
66 Elgin & Winter Garden Theatre Centre
65 Massey Hall
67 Tri-tickets
69 Joker Club
71 Chicago's
72 Festival Hall
74 Montana's
81 Montreal Bistro & Jazz Club
85 Second City
87 Princess of Wales Theatre
89 Royal Alexandra Theatre
99 Hummingbird Centre
102 C'est What?
106 du Maurier Theatre
111 Guvernment

OTHER
3 Craigleigh Gardens
8 Metropolitan Toronto Reference Library
12 Bata Shoe Museum
13 Royal Ontario Museum
14 Children's Own Museum
15 Gardiner Museum of Ceramic Art
16 Manulife Centre
23 Provincial Parliament Buildings
46 Metro Toronto Coach Terminal
48 Art Gallery of Ontario; Cinémathèque Ontario
49 Textile Museum of Canada
50 Church of the Holy Trinity
51 Ontario Travel Centre; Flight Centre;
   Marchelino Restaurant
53 Toronto Currency Exchange
55 Mackenzie House
61 Canada Life Building
62 Campbell House
63 Osgoode Hall
64 Old City Hall; St Lawrence Market
76 Cloud Forest Conservatory
77 Post Office
80 First Post Office Museum
83 Mountain Equipment Co-op
84 Europe Bound Outfitters
90 Roy Thompson Hall
91 Toronto Stock Exchange
92 St James' Cathedral
94 Toronto Dominion Gallery of Inuit Art
97 Hockey Hall of Fame
98 GPO
103 Harbourfront Antique Market
104 Harbourfront Centre
105 Molson Place
107 Power Plant Art Gallery
108 Tourism Toronto; Premiere Dance Theatre;
    Queen's Quay Terminal; Tilley Endurables
109 Westin Harbour Castle
110 Toronto Island Ferry Terminal
112 Redpath Sugar Museum
113 Seflight Hydrofoil Jet Line

ings. Amazingly, no one was killed. The 1920s saw the first population boom, fueled by the end of the war and subsequent immigration. In 1941, 80% of the population was still Anglo-Celtic, but after WWII, the city began to change; close to one million immigrants have arrived since then, mainly Europeans. Italians make up the largest non-British ethnic group. This influx of new tongues, customs and food has livened up a place once thought to be a hopeless case of one-dimensional Anglo reserve.

Orientation

The land around Toronto is flat, and the city spreads like a spilled bucket of Lake Ontario water. Despite its size, the central city's grid-style layout, with nearly all the streets running north-south and east-west, means it's easy to stay oriented.

Yonge St (pronounced yung), the main north-south artery, is called the longest street in the world – it runs about 18km from Lake Ontario north to the city boundary, Steeles Ave, and beyond. The central downtown area is bounded by **Front St** to the south, **Bloor St** to the north, **Spadina Ave** to the west and **Jarvis St** to the east. Yonge St runs parallel to and in between Spadina Ave and Jarvis St, a few blocks from each of these. Street names change from 'East' to 'West' at Yonge St, and the street numbers begin there. Bloor St and **College St** (called Carlton St east of Yonge St), which is about halfway between Bloor St and the Toronto Inner Harbour, are the two main east-west streets.

Heading north from Union Station on Bay St to Queen St, you'll hit Nathan Phillips Square, the site of rallies and concerts, as well as the unique City Hall buildings. To the east, the Victorian building dating from 1899 is the old City Hall (check out the gargoyles), now used mainly for law courts. One block east is Yonge St, lined with stores, bars, restaurants and cinemas catering mainly to the young. On Yonge St between Dundas and Queen Sts is the enormous modern shopping complex known as the Eaton Centre.

On the west side of City Hall is Osgoode Hall, home of the Law Society. Queen St W between University Ave and Bathurst St (west of Spadina) is busy with many restaurants and antique, book, music and distinctive-clothing shops. A lot of young people involved in and on the fringes of the arts live in the area.

University Ave, lined with offices and trees, is Toronto's widest street and is the location of most major parades. The lit beacon atop the stately Canada Life Building, near the corner of University Ave and Queen St, is a guide to the weather. The light at the top is color coded: green means clear, red means cloudy, flashing red means rain, and flashing white means snow. If the tower lights are ascending, the temperature will rise; if they're descending, it will cool. Temperatures are stable if the lights are on and static.

Toronto is served by expressways on all four sides. Expect congestion. Along the lake, the Gardiner Expressway runs west into the Queen Elizabeth Way (QEW). The QEW goes to Hamilton and Niagara Falls. Just at the city's western border is Hwy 427, which runs north to the airport and Hwy 401. Hwy 401 runs east-west above the downtown area; east to the Toronto Zoo, Kingston and Montréal, and west to Windsor, which is opposite Detroit, Michigan. The often bumper-to-bumper segment of Hwy 401 between Hwy 427 and Yonge St has been called the busiest stretch of road in North America after California's Santa Monica Freeway. On the eastern side of the city, the Don Valley Parkway connects Hwy 401 to the Gardiner Expressway at the southern edge of the city.

See the Neighborhoods section, later, for more orientation information.

Information

Tourist Offices Tourism Toronto (☎ 416-203-2500, 800-363-1990, w www.tourism-toronto.com) is in the Queens Quay terminal, between Yonge and York Sts. It's open 9am to 5pm Monday to Friday. On weekends and holidays, staff will answer questions over the phone. To get to the office, take the elevator (midway down the mall) up to the Galleria offices, on Level 5. A second office in the Metro Convention Centre (225 Front St W) is open 8am to 8pm daily.

Much more convenient is the Ontario Travel Centre (☎ 416-314-0944, 800-668-2746, or ☎ 416-314-0956, 800-268-3736 for

French-speakers, 220 Yonge St, Level 1) in the Eaton Centre. It's open the same hours as the shopping center: 10am to 9pm weekdays, 9:30am to 6pm Saturday and noon to 5pm Sunday. It also has information on other areas of Ontario.

Money Toronto Currency Exchange (☎ 416-864-1441, 277 Yonge St) is central and open 9:30am to 9pm Monday to Saturday, 11am to 7pm Sunday. Yonge St has numerous banks.

Post & Communications Poste restante mail can be picked up at the GPO (☎ 416-365-0656, 25 The Esplanade) from 8am to 5:45pm weekdays. The mailing address is General Delivery, Postal Station A, Toronto, ON M5W 1A1. The post office near the Queen subway station (☎ 416-214-2353, 31 Adelaide St E) is good, and numerous drugstores around town have postal outlets.

Email & Internet Access The public library (see Libraries, below) offers Internet access, as does Insomnia Internet Bar Café (☎ 416-588-3907, 563 Bloor St W), considered the city's best Internet café. It's open 4pm to 2am Monday to Thursday, 4pm to 4am Friday, 10am to 4am Saturday and 10am to 2am Sunday.

Travel Agencies For the purchase of tickets around the country and out of Canada, Travel Cuts is recommended. It has six offices in town, the main one (☎ 416-979-2406, 187 College St) is central. The staff will shop around for the best deal and will offer even better rates for people under the age of 26 and students. For the latter two groups, youth and student identification cards can be issued.

The Flight Centre (☎ 888-840-6640), originally from Australia and with locations littered around town (there's one in the Eaton Centre) has consistently good prices. Agencies such as the Last Minute Club (☎ 416-441-2582), which specializes in the last-minute filling of flights and charters, may be worth a call. For flights to destinations such as Mexico or Florida, particularly during the Canadian winter, you could turn up a bargain.

Bookstores & Maps The World's Biggest Bookstore (☎ 416-977-7009, 20 Edward St), one block north of the Eaton Centre, is a browser's delight. Open Air (☎ 416-363-0719, 25 Toronto St) is the place to go for travel books, guides, maps and a range of books on nature, camping and outdoor activities. It is near the corner of Adelaide St E and Yonge St, and the door is downstairs, off Toronto St.

You can read about home at The Great Canadian News Co (☎ 416-975-9256, 561 Yonge St); there are newspapers from around the world and a vast periodical selection. Librarie Champlain (☎ 416-364-4345, 468 Queen St E) is a good French bookstore.

Libraries The Metropolitan Toronto Reference Library (☎ 416-395-5577, 789 Yonge St) is about a block north of Bloor St on the east side. It is open 10am to 8pm Monday to Thursday, 10am to 5pm Saturday and 1:30pm to 5:30pm Sunday, and offers free Internet access.

Medical Services Toronto General Hospital (☎ 416-340-4611, 200 Elizabeth St) is central, near University Ave.

Dangers & Annoyances Toronto's homeless people and beggars are generally harmless, but their numbers are appalling and come as a shock to many visitors.

The area east of Yonge St and between Jarvis and Sherbourne Sts is well known for prostitution. Women walking alone here at night are likely to be hassled by curb-crawlers. The southern section of Jarvis St (between Carlton and Queen Sts) and the streets nearby should be avoided by everyone late at night.

Viewpoints

The highest freestanding structure in the world, the **CN Tower** (☎ *416-868-6937*, **w** *www.cntower.com, 301 Front St; adult/child $16/11, extra $7 to top deck; open 9am-10pm Sun-Thur, 9am-11pm Fri & Sat)* has become a symbol and landmark of Toronto. The tower is in the southern end of the city, near the lake, south of Front St W at John St. The top antenna was put in place by helicopter, making the tower 533m high. Its primary function is radio and TV communications, but up at the top, there is a restaurant (see Places to Eat), a bar and two observation decks. The deck outside is windy, naturally, and not for those easily subject to vertigo. It's also worth bearing in mind that during the height of summer, you may have to stand in line for up to two hours – going up and down.

On a clear day, you can see for about 160km. At night, the tower provides a spectacular view of the city lights. A glass elevator whisks you up the outside of the tower. And for extra thrills, there is a section of glass floor on the main observation deck – stand on it and sweat! The time and weather display at ground level is worth a look. Also at the base of the tower are separate attractions directed toward the young. They include sophisticated simulator rides and a video arcade featuring the latest computer-generated games. See Places to Eat for information on eating at the revolving restaurant.

The **Park Hyatt** (*4 Avenue Rd*), **Manulife Centre** (*55 Bloor St W*) and the **Westin Harbour Castle** (*1 Harbour Square*) also offer great views and bars at which you can sip a cocktail while taking it all in.

Skydome

Beside the CN Tower, this dome-roofed sports stadium (*☎ 416-341-3663, for tours 416-341-2770,* **w** *www.skydome.com, 1 Blue Jays Way; adult/senior & youth/child $13/9/4; open for tours 11am-4pm daily; adults-only roof tour $25*) opened in 1989 and is best known for its fully retractable roof, the world's first such facility. The stadium, often referred to as simply 'the Dome,' is used primarily for professional baseball and football but also for concerts, trade shows and various other presentations.

Hotel Hijinks

The hotel that's part of the Skydome became instantly notorious when, during one of the first Blue Jays baseball games, a couple in one of the upper-field side rooms – either forgetfully or rakishly – became involved in some sporting activity of their own with the lights on, much to the crowd's amusement. Such a performance was later repeated at another game. Since then, the hotel has insisted on signed waivers stipulating that there will be no such free double plays.

Although far from eye-pleasing from the outside, the interior is strikingly impressive. It can be seen on the one-hour tour, which is offered several times a day, events permitting. The tours are a bit rushed but quite thorough, offering a look at one of the box suites, the view from the stands and press section, a locker room (without athletes), a walk on the field and all sorts of informative statistics and tidbits of information. Did you know that eight 747s would fit on the playing field, and that the stadium uses enough electricity to light the province of Prince Edward Island?

Another way to see the place (and a game) is via one of the three restaurants at the stadium (see the Places to Eat section). For those with money (lots of it), rooms can be rented in the adjacent Skydome Hotel, which has rooms overlooking the playing field.

A cheap seat to a Blue Jays baseball game is easily the least expensive way to see the Skydome (see Spectator Sports, later in this chapter).

Harbourfront

Harbourfront is a strip of lakefront land running from the foot of Bay St westward to roughly Bathurst St. Once a run-down district of old warehouses, factories and underused docklands, the area was originally slated for redevelopment primarily as parkland but with arts-oriented halls, theaters, galleries, workshops, etc included. Although this has happened to some degree, it is now generally acknowledged that construction was allowed to run amok, and that too much of the waterfront has been blighted by ugly condos.

For visitors, the center of activity is the attractive **Harbourfront Centre** (*☎ 416-973-3000,* **w** *www.harbourfront.on.ca, 235 Queens Quay*). Nearby is the **du Maurier Theatre** and **Molson Place**, a covered outdoor concert venue. There's a performance of some sort happening nearly every night, and some presentations are free. There are also a couple of nearby restaurants and a place or two for a drink. Boat tours depart from the shore here, and many private boaters moor around the area.

Just to the east is the impressive **Queens Quay terminal**, with its green-glass top. It's a refurbished 1927 warehouse containing some interesting specialty and gift shops, restaurants, the Premier Dance Theatre (see Entertainment) and, up above, offices and apartments. Contemporary art is displayed in the **Power Plant Art Gallery** (☎ 416-973-4949), an old power station near Queens Quay.

On weekends, the Harbourfront is popular for a walk along the pier or a browse in the **antique market**. Try the french fries from one of the many chip wagons.

To visit Harbourfront, first get to Union Station, the train station on Front St, a few blocks north of the lake. The subway will take you this far south. From here, either walk south on York St or take the LRT streetcar south to Spadina Ave. Service is continuous through the day and evening. Parking in the area can be difficult and costly, so seriously consider using public transportation.

Toronto Islands

From the foot of Bay St, you can take a 10-minute ferry ride out to the Toronto Islands. The three main ones are Ward, Centre and Hanlan's Point; they are connected by roads. Once mainly residential, the islands are largely public parklands and are very pleasant – particularly since there are no cars! The ferry rides (☎ 416-392-8193; adult/senior & child $5/3 round-trip) are as good as the harbor tour, and the cool breezes are great on a hot, sticky day.

Centre Island has the most facilities, many summer events and the most people. Boats can be rented, and there is a small animal farm and an amusement area for kids. Beaches line the southern and western shores, and there are two licensed restaurants and some snack bars.

Hanlan's Point, to the west, has the best beach, with a fine stretch of sand and good views. The water quality often precludes swimming, however. One word of warning about going to this beach: Don't leave your bicycle unlocked. At Hanlan's southwestern end is the city's first and only nude beach; there's a mix of people, but it's mainly a favorite haunt of gay men. Inland from the beach are picnic tables and some barbecue pits. Toward the city, on Hanlan's Point, is the small Toronto City Centre Airport.

Ward Island, on the east side, has quite a few houses. There is a small restaurant for snacks and light lunches. Because there is a year-round community living here, the ferries run through the winter (though less frequently), and between September and May service only Ward. The other islands can be reached on foot, but note that pretty much everything else on the islands is shut tight. Good thing, too, because the winter wind over here is none too hospitable.

Ontario Place

West of downtown, this 40-hectare recreation complex (☎ 416-314-9900, W www.osc.on.ca, 955 Lake Shore Blvd W; admission $11; entrance & ride pass adult/child $26/15; open 10:30am-1am Mon-Sat, 10:30am-midnight Sun mid-May–Oct) is constructed on three artificial islands just offshore from the Canadian National Exhibition (CNE) grounds. The lake-edge setting, the spacious design, numerous patios and outdoor activities can make for a pleasant summer escape from the hot, crowded downtown streets. A large, popular children's play area, where you can just let them go nuts, is included. Other activities and attractions, such as a water park with slides and a wading pool, must be paid for separately, or you can get the day pass. Also note that on rainy days, many of the activities, restaurants, etc may not operate.

The futuristic buildings and parkland contain restaurants, beer gardens, the **Molson Amphitheatre** for concerts and an **IMAX cinema** (admission $6), where 70mm films are shown on a six-story curved screen. In summer, there are nightly concerts at the amphitheater, with everything from ballet to rock at usual performance prices (a ticket permits site entry for the whole day). At the western end is another stage with a waterfall as a curtain, where amateurs or lesser names perform free shows. Nearby is the 700m-long flume water slide with simulated rapids and tunnels.

If you are driving, parking is a whopping $10 to $15. Instead, take a subway or streetcar to Bathurst St and then the streetcar south down Bathurst St to the CNE exhibition grounds, or catch the Harbourfront Station streetcar (No 509) from Union Station to the gate of Ontario Place. Take a sweater – even on a hot day, it gets cold at night down by the water.

Moored outside the eastern end of Ontario Place is the **HMCS** *Haida* (☎ 416-314-9755; admission $5; open May-Oct), a national historic site and Canada's most famous destroyer.

Museums & Galleries

Royal Ontario Museum This multidiscipline museum (☎ 416-586-5551, **W** *www.rom.on.ca*, *Queen's Park Ave at Bloor St W; adult/senior/student $20/13/12, slight reductions Mon-Fri, free 4:30pm-8pm Fri; open 10am-6pm Mon-Thur & Sat, 10am-9:30pm Fri, 11am-6pm Sun*) is Canada's largest and has exhibits covering the natural sciences, the animal world, art and archeology and, broadly, the history of humankind. The museum spans five floors, so a visit takes some time.

The collection of Chinese crafts, textiles and assorted arts is considered one of the best anywhere. The Egyptian, Greek, Roman and Etruscan civilizations are also represented. The dinosaur and mammalogy rooms are fascinating, with the latter containing a replica of part of an immense bat cave found in Jamaica. Another section outlines the history of trade between the east and west, from the ancient caravan routes to more modern times. The bird gallery – with a huge stuffed albatross and numerous display cabinets with pull-out drawers to explore – is very good.

The SR Perron Gem & Gold Room (actually four octagonal rooms) displays a dazzling collection of riches, including the 193-carat Star of Lanka sapphire; a 776-carat behemoth opal from Australia; and handfuls of rubies, diamonds and gold nuggets. They are made all the more appealing by the unique fiber-optic lighting system. In addition to these permanent exhibits, there are often in-depth touring exhibits – these are generally excellent, but a surcharge is added to the admission fee.

The subway is close by, but if you're driving, there is parking on Bedford Rd, west of Avenue Rd north of Bloor St. The museum has a restaurant that serves lunch.

Gardiner Museum of Ceramic Art

This very specialized museum (☎ 416-586-8080, 111 Queen's Park Ave; adult/senior & student $10/6, free 1st Tues of month; open 10am-6pm Mon, Wed & Fri, 10am-8pm Tues & Thur, 10am-5pm Sat & Sun) has pieces spanning centuries and continents. The collection is divided into four periods of ceramic history: pre-Columbian, Italian majolica from the 15th and 16th centuries, English delftware of the 17th century and English porcelain of the 18th century. The pre-Columbian pottery from Mexico and Peru is wonderful.

Art Gallery of Ontario

This is one of the top three art galleries in the country (☎ 416-977-0414, **W** *www.ago.net*, 317 Dundas St W; suggested donation $5; open 11am-6pm Tues, Thur & Fri, 11am-8:30pm Wed, 10am-5:30pm Sat & Sun), the others being in Ottawa and Montréal. Though not the Louvre, it is excellent, and unless you have a lot of stamina, you'll need more than one trip to see it all. The gallery houses works (mainly paintings) from the 14th century to the present. There is also a Canadian section and rooms for changing exhibitions, which can sometimes be the highlight of a visit. The AGO is best known for its vast Henry Moore sculpture collection – and the brand-new space made for it does it jusstice. The exhibit includes hands-on displays and many of his major sculptures of the human form.

There is a cafeteria and pricey restaurant if you need a break, as well as an excellent shop selling books, posters, crafts and jewelry. At the door, pick up a schedule of the gallery films, lectures, performances and concerts. Admission to the excellent special shows, which run very regularly, costs $10 to $12 and includes the regular gallery.

The Grange (☎ 416-977-0414, 317 Dundas St W; admission with AGO ticket; open 11am-6pm Tues, Thur & Fri, 11am-8:30pm Wed, 10am-5:30pm Sat & Sun) is a restored Georgian house adjoining the AGO. Authentic 19th-century furniture and workers in period dress represent life in a 'gentleman's residence' of the time. The Grange looks onto a pleasant city park, where Chinese people do their early morning Tai Chi.

Bata Shoe Museum Designed to resemble a large and very stylish, lidded shoebox, the Bata Shoe Museum (☎ 416-979-7799, W www.batashoemuseum.ca, 327 Bloor St W; admission $6, free first Tues of month; open 10am-5pm Tues, Wed, Fri & Sat, 10am-8pm Thur, noon-5pm Sun) has more to offer than you might imagine. Beginning with a set of footprints almost four million years old and incorporating some neat interactive displays, the general 'All About Shoes' exhibit provides a fascinating look at human history and culture. From the gruesome to the gorgeous, every type of footwear imaginable is here, including some celebrity leathers. Upstairs, there's a detailed look at 19th-century women's shoes and an excellent exhibit devoted to the central role of bootmaking in Inuit culture.

Textile Museum of Canada Obscurely situated and with no walk-in traffic at all, this excellent museum (☎ 416-599-5321, W www.museumfortextiles.on.ca, 55 Centre Ave; admission $5, free Wed after 5pm; open 11am-5pm Tues & Thur-Fri, 11am-8pm Wed, noon-5pm Sat & Sun) is highly recommended for anyone with the slightest interest in textiles. It's the only museum in the country to exclusively collect and display handmade textiles and tapestries from around the world. There are pieces from Latin America, Africa, Europe, Southeast Asia and India. The Tibetan collection is particularly fine, as is the one from Indonesia. In addition, there are changing shows of contemporary textiles.

The museum can be hard to find, as the door is tucked back from the street. It is on Centre Ave (running south off Dundas St W

between Bay St and University Ave), behind the Toronto City Hall.

Ontario Science Centre The science center (☎ 416-696-3127, W www.osc.on.ca, 770 Don Mills Rd; adult/senior & youth/child $12/7/6; open 10am-6pm daily) has an interesting assortment of scientific and technological exhibits and demonstrations, most of which you can touch. You might even learn something, although it's best for children (be warned – on weekends, there are hundreds of them).

The approachable yet detail-conscious 'Living Earth' exhibit includes a simulated rainforest; a limestone cave; and an ocean ecosystem designed to encourage respect, knowledge and awe for the real thing. The 'Information Highway' exhibit allows you to explore the Internet and take a look at virtual reality. There is also a large-format Omnimax cinema.

To get to the science center, which is located in a small ravine, take the subway to Eglinton, transfer to the Eglinton E bus and get off at Don Mills Rd. Ticket packages that include films are available too.

Hockey Hall of Fame Housed in the beautiful old Bank of Montréal building (1885) at the northwest corner of Front and Yonge Sts, the Hockey Hall of Fame (☎ 416-360-7765, W www.hhof.com, 30 Yonge St; adult/seniors/child $12/8/8; open 10am-5pm Mon-Thur, 10am-6pm Fri & Sat, 10am-5pm Sun) gives young and old fans all they could ask for and more. And for visitors unfamiliar with the game, enough background and history is presented to perhaps help explain Canadians' passion for this, the fastest of sports. Included is hockey's biggest prize – the Stanley Cup (sometimes it's a replica), a re-creation of the Montréal Canadiens' dressing room and all manner of interactive exhibits and activities. Evening hours are extended on Friday in summer.

Children's Own Museum This kids' museum (☎ 416-542-1492, 90 Queen's Park Ave; admission $4.75; open 10am-5pm daily), beside the ROM, focuses on active, fun learning for two- to eight-year-old children. The space is divided into various participatory areas (such as the garden and construction site), each with suitable play materials.

Police Museum Housed in the impressive headquarters building, the police museum (☎ 416-808-7020, **W** www.torontopolice .on.ca, 40 College St; admission free) displays a small collection of equipment, uniforms, etc from 1834 to the present. At press time, it was closed for renovations but was scheduled to reopen by fall of 2002. The confiscated weapons display has certainly given visitors pause over the years – let's hope it will be retained.

Redpath Sugar Museum Along the waterfront, this museum (☎ 416-366-3561, 95 Queens Quay W; admission free; open 10am-noon & 1pm-3:30pm Mon-Fri) is part of a large sugar mill. There is a film on the production of the sweet stuff, as well as exhibits of equipment. Before going, call to confirm access is possible – it is a working plant.

Toronto Dominion Gallery of Inuit Art Housed on the mezzanine floor of the Aetna Tower of the Toronto Dominion Centre, between Bay and York Sts, this gallery (☎ 416-982-8473, 66 Wellington St W; admission free; open 8am-6pm Mon-Fri, 10am-4pm Sat & Sun) displays a top-rate collection of far-northern art dating mainly from WWII to the present. It consists primarily of sculpture in stone and bone, which is the foremost form of Inuit art.

Occasionally, you may find a rope across the door of the gallery. Just take it down and go in; the gallery is still open, though there may well be no attendant. Free tours are given once a day on Tuesday and Thursday but can be arranged for any day – call and ask.

Market Gallery On the 2nd floor of the old City Hall, this gallery (☎ 416-392-7604; admission free; open 10am-4pm Wed-Fri, 9am-4pm Sat, noon-4pm Sun) is the city's exhibition hall and displays good, rotating shows (paintings, photographs, documents, artifacts) on Toronto's history.

Toronto Zoo

The huge zoo (☎ 416-392-5900, **W** www .torontozoo.com, Meadowvale Rd; adult/ senior/child $15/11/9; open 9am-7:30pm daily June-Oct; 9:30am-4:30pm daily rest of the year), which has an excellent reputation, is one of the country's largest and best, and

continues to expand. There are around 5000 animals on the 283 hectares, some in natural-setting pens the size of football fields. Of course, with enclosures so large, it takes a full day and a lot of legwork to see it. (Except for during the winter, a small train goes around the site, but walking is best.)

The animals are in five areas, each covering a major geographical zone. There are outdoor sections, as well as simulated climates in indoor pavilions. A clever idea is the blacklight area that enables you to observe nocturnal animals. Other good exhibits include those allowing for underwater viewing of beavers, polar bears and seals. One area has displays geared toward children, with some animals to touch and ponies to ride.

The zoo is north of Hwy 401, at the eastern edge of the city. To get there using public transportation, take the subway on the Bloor St line east to Kennedy, the last stop. From there, take the No 86A Scarborough bus to the zoo. It's quite a trip – about 20 minutes on the subway from the center of town and then about 40 minutes on the bus, plus waiting time.

Parking is $6 (free in winter). Call for the current schedule before visiting.

You may want to take your lunch, as McDonald's has an exclusive food contract for the grounds.

Paramount Canada's Wonderland

This family-oriented amusement park (☎ 905-832-7000, **W** www.canadaswonderland.com, Hwy 400; day pass for attractions adult/senior & child $51/30, grounds pass $30/20; open 10am-10pm daily early June-early Sept, 10am-10pm Sat & Sun May & Oct) boasts over 60 rides, including some killer roller coasters (one is a looping inverted jet coaster that travels at 90km/h) and at night is very popular with teenagers. There is also a 5-hectare water park (bring a bathing suit) and loads of Hanna-Barbera characters wandering around a huge kiddies' area – and every year, new attractions and rides are developed. Big-name concerts are held in summer at the Kingswood Theatre (tickets for these shows cost extra). Parking is another $7. The food is run-of-the-mill and expensive – bringing a picnic is not a bad idea.

Wonderland is away from the center of town, on Hwy 400. Exit at Rutherford Rd if you're traveling north; at Major Mackenzie Dr if you're going south. There are express buses from Yorkdale and York Mills subway stations.

Stock Market Place

The city's stock exchange (☎ 416-947-4676, 130 King St W; admission free; open 10am-5pm Mon-Fri) is Canada's largest and is one of the most modern anywhere. Stock worth $100 million is bought and sold each day, so it's a fairly hectic place. It is also one of the top 10 stock exchanges of the world – the only other North American exchange on the list is New York's.

There is no longer a trading floor, as it's all been computerized, but the visitors' center has interactive displays that help demystify and explain the process of stock transactions. There are also noon seminars called 'Lunch and Learn.' The stock exchange is on the northeast corner of King and York Sts, right in the center of the city's financial district.

Chess Games Corner

Also right in the heart of the city, on the corner of Yonge and Gould Sts, is the unofficial chess center. Here, through all kinds of weather, night and day, chess players and aficionados of every description gather to duel and bet. It all began with the late Joe Smolij in 1977, who was once listed in *Guinness World Records* as the world's fastest chess player.

Provincial Parliament Buildings

The attractive, pinkish sandstone Legislature (☎ 416-325-7500, University Ave; admission free; open 9am-5pm daily May-Sept, weekdays only rest of the year) sits in Queen's Park, just north of College St. The stately building was completed in 1892 and is kept in superb condition. Free tours are given frequently; call for a schedule. For some home-grown entertainment, head for the visitors' gallery when parliament is in session (roughly from October to December and February to June).

City Hall

In Nathan Phillips Square, this distinctive, three-part building (☎ 416-338-0338, cnr Queen & Bay Sts; open 9am-5pm Mon-Fri) represented the beginning of Toronto becoming a grown-up city. It was completed in 1965 to Finnish architect Viljo Revell's award-winning design. The twin clamshell towers, with a flying saucer–style structure between them at the bottom, are unmistakable. Free tours are given frequently Monday to Friday. The square out front is a meeting place and a location for concerts, demonstrations and office-worker lunches.

In winter, the attractive fountain pool becomes a popular artificial skating rink. Rental skates are available until 10pm daily. It's a lot of fun; don't feel intimidated if you are a novice – you won't be alone. Immigrants from around the world are out there gingerly making strides toward assimilation.

Queen St Streetcar

A simple way to rub shoulders with a real mix of locals is to hop the Queen St car and ride it from one end of the line to as far as you like. It cuts right through the heart of town, gliding past a range of neighborhoods, including High Park, Queen St W, Chinatown, Yonge St and The Beaches.

Historic Sites

There isn't a lot for history buffs, as the city is so new, but the few small sites are well presented, and the tourist office offers a printed guide to them. Many of these remaining old buildings stand where the old town of York was situated – in the southern portion of the city. See also The Grange, under the Art Gallery of Ontario, earlier in this chapter.

The large, red-brick houses found all over downtown Toronto were built around the 1920s. The taller, narrower ones, which often have more ornately decorative features, are Victorian and mostly date from 1890 to 1900 – a few are older.

Black Creek Pioneer Village A replica of an Ontario village a century ago, Black Creek Pioneer Village (☎ 416-736-1733, W www.trca.on.ca, Steeles Ave at Jane St; adult/child $9/5; open 10am-4pm daily May-Dec) is the city's top historic attraction. It's about a half-hour drive from the downtown area, in the northwest section of town, and is accessible by public transportation.

Restored buildings and workers wearing authentic dress give a feeling of what rural life was like in the 19th century. Crafts and skills of the times are demonstrated, using the old tools and methods. One reader raved about the herb garden. You can buy the results of the cooking and baking. In one of the barns is a large toy museum and a woodcarving collection. Special events are offered regularly through the season. There is parking, which is free – a rarity in Toronto.

Fort York The fort (☎ 416-392-6907, *Garrison Rd; adult/senior/child $5/3.25/3; open 10am-4pm Mon-Fri, 10am-5pm Sat & Sun*) was established by the British in 1793 to protect the town, which was then called York. It was largely destroyed at the end of the War of 1812 but was quickly rebuilt. Now restored, it has eight original log, stone and brick buildings. In summer, men decked out in 19th-century British military uniforms carry out drills and fire musket volleys. Free tours are given on the hour. Garrison Rd runs off Fleet St W (which in turn is near the corner of Bathurst and Front Sts). Take the streetcar south on Bathurst St. There is free parking here, too.

Casa Loma This 98-room medieval-style castle-cum-mansion (☎ 416-923-1171, W *www.casaloma.org, 1 Austin Terrace; adult/child $10/6; open 10am-4pm daily*) was built between 1911 and 1914 by Sir Henry Pellat, a very wealthy and evidently eccentric man. The mansion has been a tourist site since 1937, when the cost of upkeep became too much for its owner. The interior is sumptuous, built with the finest materials imported from around the world (note especially the conservatory). Pellat even brought in stonemasons from Scotland to build the walls around the estate.

In summer, the 2.5 hectares of restored gardens behind the castle are worth a visit in themselves. This area is open to the public (without the need to buy a ticket to the castle) on the first Monday of each month and every Tuesday from 4pm to dusk. At Christmastime, elaborate thematic indoor exhibits are put on, geared mainly toward children.

Parking at the site is $2.50 an hour. If you're lucky, you may find a spot in the surrounding neighborhood; alternatively, consider using the subway, which is within walking distance. The castle is found at Austin Terrace, which is off Spadina Ave. From the corner of Dupont and Bathurst Sts, it can be clearly seen, perched impressively above its surroundings.

Mackenzie House Owned by William Lyon Mackenzie, the city's first mayor and the leader of a failed rebellion against the government, this mid-Victorian home (☎ 416-392-6915, *82 Bond St; adult/child $3.50/2.50; open noon-4pm Tues-Fri, noon-5pm Sat & Sun*) is furnished with 19th-century antiques. In the basement is an old print shop where (it's said) the machines can be heard mysteriously working some nights. The house is a couple of blocks east of Yonge St, south of Dundas St E.

Spadina House This gracious mansion (☎ 416-392-6910, *285 Spadina Ave; adult/child $5/3.25; open noon-4pm Mon-Fri, noon-5pm Sat & Sun*) belonged to local businessman James Austin. Built in 1866, the impressive interior contains fine furnishings and art collected over three generations. About 10 of its 35 rooms are open to the public. The family gave the house to the historical board in 1982. The house is just east of Casa Loma.

Campbell House Downtown, this house (☎ 416-597-0227, *160 Queen St W; adult/child $4.50/3; open 10am-4:30pm Mon-Fri*) was once the residence of the chief justice of Upper Canada. It is a colonial-style brick mansion furnished in early 19th-century fashion.

Colborne Lodge Situated in High Park, the lodge (☎ 416-392-6916, *Colborne Lodge Dr; adult/child $3.50/2.50; open noon-4pm Tues-Sun, noon-5pm June-Sept*) is a Regency-style cottage built in 1836. It contains many original furnishings, including possibly the first indoor flush toilet in the province (now you want to go). Informative tours are offered by the costumed staff and may include baking or craft demonstrations.

Gibson House This Georgian-style house (☎ 416-395-7432, *5172 Yonge St; adult/child $3/2.25; open 9:30am-4:30pm Tues-Fri, noon-5pm Sat & Sun*), which belonged to a successful surveyor and politician, offers a glimpse of daily life in the 1850s. Costumed workers demonstrate crafts and cooking and offer a tour around the house. Special activities are planned regularly through the year. It's not far from the Sheppard subway stop in the far northern part of the city, and it is north of Sheppard Ave.

Montgomery's Inn Built in 1832 by an Irish military captain of the same name, Montgomery's Inn (☎ *416-394-8113, 4709 Dundas St W; adult/child $3/1; open 1pm-4:30pm Tues-Fri, 1pm-5pm Sat & Sun)* is a fine example of Loyalist architecture and has been restored to the period from 1830 to 1855. Afternoon tea is served, and costumed staff answer questions, bake bread and demonstrate crafts. It's near Islington Ave, in the city's far western end.

Enoch Turner Schoolhouse This school (☎ *416-863-0010, 106 Trinity St; admission free)* dates from 1848. It's a restored and simple one-room schoolhouse where kids are shown what the good old days were like. It was opened as the first free school so that the children of poorer citizens could learn the three Rs. You can visit it, free, when classes or other special events are not being held – call ahead and check the schedule. It is near the corner of King and Parliament Sts.

First Post Office Museum Toronto's first post office (☎ *416-865-1833, 260 Adelaide St E; admission free; open 9am-4pm daily)*, which dates from the 1830s, is one of only two original city buildings remaining in its original location (the other is the Bank of Upper Canada), and it has been designated a national historic site. Letters can still be sealed with wax by costumed employees and then sent from there.

University of Toronto The principal campus of this large, prestigious university (☎ *416-978-5000, University Ave)* is just west of the Queen's Park Parliament Buildings, off College St. The attractive grounds feature a range of architectural styles, from the University College building (1859) to the present. Free walking tours of the campus are given on weekdays through summer months, departing three times daily

(weather permitting) from Hart House, at 25 King's College Circle.

Todmorden Mills Heritage Museum & Arts Centre This historic site (☎ *416-396-2819, 67 Pottery Rd; adult/child $3/1.50; open 11am-4:30pm Tues-Fri, noon-5pm Sat & Sun May-Dec)*, near the location of an important 1794 sawmill and gristmill on the Don River, preserves two houses, complete with period furnishings, and a brewery dating from around 1825. It reveals the industrial history of the city. Also on the site is a train station (now a small railway museum) and a former paper mill (now used as a playhouse).

Churches The Anglican **Church of the Holy Trinity** (☎ *416-598-4521, 10 Trinity Square; admission free; open by chance)*, hidden right downtown behind the Eaton Centre on Trinity Square, is one of a kind. It's a funky, welcoming cross between a house of worship and a drop-in center – everything a community-oriented inner-city church should be. Opened in 1847, it was the first church in the city not to charge parishioners for pews. And it's been going its own way ever since. Don't miss the wonderful Christmas pageant tradition if you're in town in December. There is no charge (a donation is suggested), but tickets are required – call for information.

St James' Cathedral (☎ *416-364-7865, 65 Church; admission free; open by chance)* was built in 1853 and is the country's tallest church. This was originally the site of the town's first church, built in 1807.

Nearby, the first Catholic church was constructed in 1822. Now, stunning **St Paul's Basilica** (☎ *416-364-7588, 83 Power St; admission free; open 9am-4pm Mon-Fri, call for weekend hours)*, one of Toronto's most impressive Renaissance-style buildings, stands on this site. If the main doors are locked, go to the side door.

Neighborhoods

Because of Toronto's wide variety of ethnic groups, some of its more interesting neighborhoods offer glimpses of foreign cultures, while other neighborhoods simply preserve a distinctive character.

Harbourfront At the foot of Yonge St and nearby York St is the lake and the redeveloped waterfront area called Harbourfront. The old docks have given way to restaurants, theaters, galleries, artists' workshops, stores, condominiums and some parkland all along Queens Quay. The ferries for the Toronto Islands moor here.

St Lawrence Market & Entertainment District A few blocks north of Harbourfront is Front St, with Union Station (the VIA Rail terminal), the classic old Royal York Hotel and the performing-arts venue Hummingbird Centre. East from here is a renovated shopping, eating and club district, with the Saturday morning market as a neighborhood anchor. Two blocks west of Union Station is the CN Tower and, next door, Skydome, the sports stadium. A few blocks north of the Skydome, around Adelaide St W, Peter St and John St, is the Entertainment District. This is a very happening part of town, with restaurants and, more so, bars of every type (but mainly geared to the young) fighting it out for the weekend crowds. Take a look in the sidewalk for the Hollywood-like Walk of Fame honoring some of Canada's best-known artists. It is centered on King St W in front of the Royal Alexander Theatre.

Chinatown Toronto has a huge (and growing) Chinese population, and the principal Chinatown area is right in the center of town. The original old area runs along Dundas St W from Bay St, by the bus station, west to University Ave. There are many restaurants here, but this area is rather touristy and isn't really where the local Chinese shop.

The bigger and more interesting segment of Chinatown is farther west. Also on Dundas St W, it runs from Beverley St, near the Art Gallery of Ontario, to Spadina Ave and a little beyond. Most of Spadina Ave, from south of Dundas St all the way north to College St and then east and west for a bit along College St, is primarily Chinese.

Chinatown does have lots of restaurants, but there are also variety and grocery stores, street vendors, jobbers, herbalists, bakeries and places selling things recognizable only to the initiated. On weekends, the area is packed and sharp with sounds and smells. There are also a few Japanese and more and more Vietnamese businesses in the neighborhood.

Yorkville Once Toronto's small version of Greenwich Village or Haight-Ashbury, this old countercultural bastion is now the city's expensive boutique and gallery area. The district is central, just above Bloor St between Yonge St and Avenue Rd. It's centered around Cumberland St, Yorkville Ave and Hazelton Ave. Along the narrow, busy streets are many art galleries, cafés, restaurants, nightspots and glamorous shops. The boutiques of the enclosed Hazelton Lanes Shopping Centre are some of the most exclusive in the country.

The whole swish area can be pleasant in summer for its outdoor cafés and people-watching. It's worth a stroll, but the pretension and snobbery can grate. Still, there are some intriguing shops, and the galleries present a range of work – several display or sell Inuit pieces (for big dollars).

The Annex The area on Bloor St W roughly from Spadina Ave west to Manning Ave is a bustling, lively student area of bars, restaurants, cafés and interesting shops. A blend of immigrants, professors and other professionals add to the mix. Energetic and animated, the area is perfect for strolling.

At the corner of Bloor and Markham Sts (one block west of Bathurst St) stands an area landmark: the zany, gaudy Honest Ed's discount store, where giant signs say things like 'Don't just stand there, buy something.' Ed's subtlety is lost on no one – you won't believe the lines outside the door before opening time. With the money Eddie Mirvish has made, he has established a major reputation as a theater impresario/entrepreneur whose accomplishments have ranged to as far away as London, England.

Markham (Mirvish) Village, on Markham St south of Bloor St, is mostly Eddie's or his son's doing. The small district features restaurants, galleries, boutiques, bookstores and some interesting little specialized import shops.

Church St Also known as The Village, the area along Church St between Isabella and Grenville Sts is home to a thriving gay community. Around Wellesley St, there are quite a few cafés and restaurants and a range of nightspots, catering primarily but certainly not exclusively to the city's large homosexual population. It's generally a lively area but especially so on Saturday night. Many of the area's older houses along the residential side streets have been renovated, which helps to provide a town atmosphere just a stone's throw from Yonge St's bustle.

Cabbagetown This district, east of Parliament St, was settled by Irish immigrants fleeing the potato famine of 1841 and became known as Cabbagetown because the sandy soil of the area provided ideal growing conditions for cabbage. It's now both a working- to middle-class residential and commercial district. In addition to the differences between its denizens, the area is distinguished primarily by its Victorian terrace houses – which possibly constitute the richest concentration of such architecture in North America.

Since the 1970s, there has been considerable gentrification of this once run-down area. It's worth a stroll to peek at some of the beautifully renovated houses and their carefully tended gardens. Some of the area's highlights include Necropolis Cemetery (off Sumach St at Winchester St), one of the city's oldest and most interesting cemeteries, and Riverdale Farm, across Winchester St. A popular place for families and kids, it's run as a real working farm, with two barns to wander through and a selection of waterfowl and other animals, some of which may permit a pat or two.

Cabbagetown is bounded roughly by Gerrard St E to the south, Wellesley St E to the north, Parliament St to the west (which is the main business center) and Sumach St to the east.

Greektown In the east end of town along Danforth Ave, roughly between Pape and Woodbine Aves, is a large Greek community. Often called The Danforth, this has become one of the city's most popular dining areas, and warm summer nights in particular bring out smiling crowds. There are many restaurants; a few smoky cafés; and some big, busy, colorful produce and flower stores that stay open into the night.

Little India East of Greektown is the concentrated but intriguing Little India, with various worth-a-peek specialty stores, women in saris and the scent of spices in the air. There are also numerous restaurants situated here, many with laughably low prices. It's along Gerrard St E, just one block west of Coxwell Ave.

Corso Italia & Little Italy Italians, in quantity, are found in many parts of the city, but if there is one center of the community, it's probably on St Clair Ave W, east and west of the Dufferin St intersection – referred to as Corso Italia. Here you'll find Italian movies, espresso cafés and pool halls. Nearby, based along Dundas St W between Ossington and Dufferin Sts, is a Portuguese neighborhood.

A secondary primarily Italian area known as Little Italy, on College St west of Euclid Ave, is a livelier and trendier spot jammed with outdoor cafés, bars, small restaurants and people from all over town.

Rosedale One of the city's wealthiest areas is just northeast of the corner of Yonge and Bloor Sts. Driving or walking up Sherbourne St, north of Bloor St, leads to Elm Ave, where nearly every house on the north side is listed by the Historical Board as being of architectural or historical note. All the streets branching from Elm Ave contain some impressive domains, however. East along Elm Ave, Craigleigh Gardens is a small and elegant old park.

Parks
Around the corner from Yonge St, west a few doors on the south side of Richmond St W (beside little Temperance St) is the tiny **Cloud Forest Conservatory** (*Richmond St W; admission free; open 10am-3pm Mon-Fri*), an unexpected sanctuary in the downtown core. Built vertically as a 'modernist ruin,' it features exposed steel, creeping vines, a waterfall and a mural to construction workers.

Though short on city parks, Toronto does have some substantial, largely natural parks in numerous ravines formed by rivers and streams running down to the lake. Start in **Edwards Gardens** (*Lawrence Ave E at Leslie St*). It's a big, cultivated park with flower gardens, a pond and picnic sites. You can take a ravine walk from the gardens via **Wilket**

Creek Park. The Ontario Science Centre (see Museums & Galleries, earlier) backs onto the park here. Along Wilket Creek, you can walk for hours all the way down to Victoria Park Ave, just north of Danforth Ave. Much of the way is through woodland.

Not-So-Wild Animals

They're coming. Actually, many are already here. Ontario's wild animals are adapting to the modern urban world at an alarming rate. Downtown Toronto has been plagued for years by skunks and raccoons that tear up garbage, dig out garage floors or rip apart roofs in search of housing. But all of southern Ontario is now seeing foxes and coyotes in city parks and central neighborhoods. The latter have stealthily been grabbing pet cats and dogs and even hanging around schoolyards waiting for discarded sandwiches. In relatively developed Muskoka and Huronia, deer are commonplace, and recently, even wolves have been spotted along roadsides. They were formerly very reclusive and generally found farther north. Each summer, black bears are wandering into central and northern towns, snooping around for food and delighting kids and photographers but representing serious potential danger.

Above the Great Lakes, nighttime drivers should be very cautious of moose, which linger on the road, stunned by the lights. Hitting one is like slamming into a train.

What explains the ongoing incursion of wildlife into human territory? Various factors are at play. Habitats are disappearing, and road development is increasing. Animals are more frequently encountering humans, even in their deep-woods homes, and then losing their natural fear. Once accustomed to people, many animals find that getting food is easier in suburbia than in the wilds. Even global warming seems to play a part – weather and vegetation patterns are changing. Opossums, once exclusively of the southern USA, have now migrated to Ontario.

It's not uncommon to spend days hiking or canoeing in the bush only to see all the wildlife by the parking lot when you crawl back grubby and tired.

From the corner of Yonge St and St Clair Ave, walk east to the bridge and the sign for the nature trail. This leads down into the **Don River Valley**, another good walk.

High Park The city's biggest green area *(Bloor St W at Parkside Dr)* is popular for picnics, walking, cycling and jogging. There is a small children's zoo, a lake where people fish in summer and skate in winter, and a pool for swimming (which is free). Some parts of the park are manicured; other bits are left as natural woods. No cars are allowed on summer weekends.

Also in the park is Colborne Lodge (see Historical Sites, earlier), built by one of Toronto's first architects and now run as a historical site with costumed workers.

Tommy Thompson Park Formerly called and often still known as the Leslie St Spit, this landfill site is presided over by the Metro Toronto Conservation Authority *(☎ 416-661-6600, Unwin Ave at Leslie St; admission free; open 8am-6pm Sat, Sun & holidays).* It extends out into the lake and has unexpectedly become a phenomenal wildlife success. It was designed to both improve and develop shipping facilities but within a few years became the second-largest nesting place of the ring-billed seagull in the world. Terns and other bird species nest here too.

From April to October, a free shuttle runs from the nearest bus stop, on Leslie St at Commissioners Rd (about three long blocks from the main gate), through the gate at the spit and down about halfway. It runs every half hour from 9am to 5pm. At the far end (named Vicki Keith Point, after a local long-distance swimmer), out by the eastern edges of the Toronto Islands, there is a lighthouse and views of the city. No vehicles are permitted, but many people use bicycles – the Martin Goodman Trail runs by in both directions (see Cycling & Skating, under Activities, later).

At the gate, there is a map and a bird checklist. Portable toilets are positioned along the main path. Although some small sections are wooded, there is very little shade, so be prepared for sun in midsummer. Check the schedule at the gate for the free guided walks, which often have an ornithology or photography angle.

At the foot of industrial Cherry St, connected to Leslie St by Unwin St, the sandy, relatively quiet and poseur-free **Cherry Beach**, also called Clarke Beach, is popular with windsurfers and those seeking a cool breeze on hot days. There's a snack bar, a few barbecues among the trees and some shoreline footpaths.

Beaches & Bluffs To local residents, 'The Beach' is a rather wealthy, mainly professional neighborhood along Queen St E at Woodbine Ave, down by the lakeshore. To everyone else, it's part of **The Beaches** – meaning the area, the beaches themselves and the parkland along the lake.

The sandy beaches are good for sunbathing and picnicking, and the 3km boardwalk that edges the sand is used for strolling (or strutting, as the case may be). There's also a paved path for cycling and skating. Water quality inhibits swimmers, but you can rent sailboards, with or without lessons. At the west end, in Woodbine Beach Park, there's an excellent, Olympic-size public swimming pool. There are quite a few places to eat or quaff a brew nearby along Queen St E. To get to The Beaches from downtown, take the Queen St streetcar.

About 5km farther east are the Scarborough Bluffs, cliffs of glacial deposits known as till, set in parkland at the lake's edge. Erosion has created some odd shapes and has revealed layers of sediment that indicate five different glacial periods. There are paths here with good views over the lake. Below, in the lake itself, landfill has been used to form parkland (Bluffers Park) and boat-mooring space. To access Bluffers Park, turn south off Kingston Rd at Brimley Rd.

If you want to be atop the cliffs (and you do), there are several parks that afford excellent views of the bluffs and panoramas of Lake Ontario. For those with vehicles, to reach one area worth visiting, turn south off Kingston Rd onto Scarboro Crescent and then Drake Crescent. Park here; the bluffs are within walking distance. Another excellent vantage point at the highest section of the bluffs (about 98m) is at Cathedral Bluffs Park. It's still farther east along Kingston Rd; turn south at Cathedral Bluffs Dr.

Not far (by vehicle) east of the park is the defunct Guild (☎ 416-261-3331), with its large lakefront grounds and good views along the shoreline. In the garden, there's a collection of sculptures, columns and gargoyles rescued from condemned buildings. The Guild Inn is on Guildwood Parkway, south from Kingston Rd at Livingstone Rd.

Allan Gardens This park *(Carlton St; admission free; greenhouse open 10am-5pm daily)* is often mentioned but is rather overrated – most of it is nothing more than a city block of grass interspersed with a few trees and benches. The highlight is the large, old, round-domed greenhouse filled with huge palms and flowering trees from around the world. After dark, the entire place is unsavory enough to be not recommended, and that includes even taking a shortcut through the park.

Port of Toronto/Skyline View

Just south of Lake Shore Blvd, on Ploson St off Cherry St, not far from Tommy Thompson Park and Cherry Beach, is the Port. Freighters moor along the docks, but you can't get very close, and there is no public access. At the end of Poulson St you can see a very fine view of the harbor, islands and the city skyline.

Activities

Cycling & Skating For cyclists and inline skaters, the **Martin Goodman Trail** is the place to go to join the city fitness buffs. This recreation route along the waterfront stretches from The Beaches in the east end, past Harbourfront and the downtown area, to the Humber River, in the west end. From here, it connects with paths in parkland running northward along the Humber. This section is a really fine ride. You can go at least as far as Eglinton Ave, and that's quite a few kilometers.

If you fancy a longer trek, the Martin Goodman Trail links into the **Lake Ontario Waterfront Trail**, which stretches 325km from Hamilton to Trenton. Visit the tourist office for maps and pamphlets detailing sights along the way.

The Toronto Bicycling Network (☎ 416-766-1985) organizes short, medium and long weekend trips (some overnight) throughout summer.

Also, cycling along the Toronto Islands' **boardwalk** on the southern shores isn't a bad way to spend some time. You can take bicycles on some of the ferries, or rent them on Centre Island.

The most central place to rent bicycles (and inline skates) is **Wheel Excitement** (☎ 416-260-9000, 5 Rees St) in Harbourfront. There are also rentals on Centre Island at **Toronto Island Bicycle Rental** (☎ 416-203-0009), on the south shore, more or less straight back from the ferry landing. Farther out but cheaper is **Brown's Sports & Cycle** (☎ 416-763-4176, 2447 Bloor St W), near the Jane St subway station. It's not really that far from High Park or the Martin Goodman Trail for walkers and cyclists along Lake Shore Blvd.

Water Sports Free swimming in public pools (☎ 416-392-7838) can be found in High Park; the Gus Ryder Pool (known as Sunnyside pool), south of the park at the lake on Lakeshore Dr; and in Woodbine Park, at The Beaches, in east-end Toronto, at the foot of Woodbine Ave. Many other city parks include pools, but the aforementioned three are selected for their good locations, large size and popularity.

Sandy beaches, shady parks, a boardwalk and, on any hot summer day (especially on weekends), lots of people pack The Beaches district. Kew Beach is the most popular section, and the boardwalk goes through here. The same thing on a smaller scale can be enjoyed at Sunnyside Beach, in the west end, south of High Park. Work continues to make the water fit for swimming.

There is **windsurfing** at The Beaches too; rentals are available in the Ashbridges Bay area, at the western end of the beach.

The **Canoe & Kayak School** (☎ 416-203-2277, 283A Queens Quay W) rents canoes, which can be used for an enjoyable paddle out around the harbor.

Ice Skating In winter, there are good, free places to skate at **City Hall** and at **Harbourfront** – both with artificial ice and both with skate rentals. If it's been quite cold, there is also large, natural **Grenadier Pond** in High Park. Taking a whirl here is like being in a Brueghel painting.

Organized Tours

Bus Reliable **Gray Line** (☎ 416-594-3310, 610 Bay St) runs a basic two-hour inner-city tour (adult/senior/child under 13 $31/28/16) with hop-on/hop-off options at 20 places on its chopped-roof double-decker. Various other, more specialized tours lasting 2½ hours or more are offered, with site stops included. The full-day, $55 option goes to Midland and its attractions. Gray Line also offers an all-day Niagara Falls trip for $120. For Gray Line trips, passengers are picked up either from downtown hotels or the bus terminal at Bay St. Tickets can be bought on the bus or at the Gray Line desk in the Royal York Hotel, on York St across from Union Station.

Toronto Hippo Tours (☎ 416-703-4476) provides a 90-minute city tour (adult/child $35/23), then heads on to the lake for a shoreline cruise.

Olde Towne Niagara Tours (☎ 416-614-0999) offers a day-trip tour ($128) to Niagara Falls, which includes a ride on the *Maid of the Mist* or another attraction plus lunch. Pick-ups take place at major downtown hotels and by the airport. There is a booth at the Eaton Centre, but you can get a ticket on the bus; call beforehand to book.

Walking Tours of Toronto (☎ 416-966-1550) offers three summer walking tours of the city, focusing on history and architecture, with interesting asides thrown in. Tours ($12) run on weekends only and last about 1½ hours. Call to reserve a spot and to check meeting times and places.

Tours given by **A Taste of the World** (☎ 416-923-6813) delve into neighborhood nooks and crannies – one tries to unveil the mysteries of Chinatown – but the most popular tour is the cycling trip ($45 including bike) on the Toronto Islands. Walking tours cost $15 to $35.

An amazing range of informed, historical 'ROMwalks' are organized by volunteers from the **Royal Ontario Museum** (☎ 416-586-5513) from June to September. These free jaunts take place, rain or shine, on Sunday afternoons and Wednesday evenings. Call for details and starting points – look for the blue umbrella. Brochure are available at the ROM (see Museums & Galleries under Things to See & Do, earlier).

The **University of Toronto** (☎ 416-978-5000) runs free guided tours of the campus three times daily throughout the summer.

This is the country's largest university, and the campus has some fine buildings. Tours start from the map room in Hart House.

Boat Several companies run boat tours in and around the harbor and the islands. Most depart from Harbourfront around Queens Quay, John Quay and especially York Quay. Some privately owned sailing ships and schooners offer trips of varying duration as far as Niagara-on-the-Lake. Other boats are geared for fishing. If you look around the docks at Harbourfront, you'll see signs and/or captains advertising their charters. Keep in mind that the ferry to the Toronto Islands offers good city views and is very cheap (see Toronto Islands under Things to See & Do, earlier).

The harbor's main operator, **Mariposa Cruise Lines** (☎ 416-203-0178) has a variety of seasonal cruises. Besides the basic one-hour narrated tour of the harbor area (adult/senior/child $16/14/11), Mariposa offers more leisurely (and more expensive) evening trips, with a buffet, a bar and dancing. Tickets should be purchased in advance at Queens Quay Terminal, Pier Six.

Alternative There are quite a few Toronto-based companies offering out-of-town activities-based trips and wilderness tours. You can also refer to the Getting Around chapter for information on long-distance trips.

Great for budget travelers, **JoJo Tours** (☎ 416-201-6465, ☒ www.interlog.com/~jojotour) offers a tour that includes stops at wineries, Niagara-on-the-Lake and other highlights for $50. Tours operate all year, with a price drop in the off-season. Pick-ups occur at all hostels (tours can also be booked at the hostels). You also get a few hours to yourself at the falls. Ask about the other regional tours and outdoor-adventure possibilities that are offered Sundays.

Known for its anything-might-happen-and-usually-does adventures, **Magic Bus** (☎ 905-371-8747, ☒ www.furtherstill.com) offers one-of-a-kind trips on colorful buses (add a few brush strokes yourself). On the Niagara Falls day trip ($37), many of the top attractions are covered, including a winery (yes, there are samples), but with a spin. Departures are at 9am daily (May to mid-September) from several of the city's

hostels. The time of return varies, but it's a very full day. Magic Bus also offers a good trip northward to Bala, on Lake Muskoka in the heart of cottage country. This trip runs four times a week and costs $60, with an option of staying overnight at the Bala Bay Inn for $25. Most people feel it's worth staying over. Possible activities in Bala include swimming (beach or waterfalls), canoeing, hiking, waterskiing or just hanging out. There's a bar and a good club nearby with regular rock concerts.

Free Spirit Tours (☎ 416-219-7562, 705-444-3622, ☒ www.freespirit-tours.com) offers trips to the Bruce Peninsula near Collingwood. A one-day rock-climbing outing is $75. For $250, the two-day trip includes hiking, climbing and accommodations at a fine, alpine-like inn beside Blue Mountain. The trips run from May to October, and there are also winter programs. You can often arrange for pick-up in Toronto.

Moose Travel (☎ 905-853-4762, 888-816-6673, ☒ www.moosenetwork.com) is a fun but practical combination of bus company and tour operator for longer trips (see the website for details on pricing and options). It offers well-run, efficient, jump-on/ jump-off trips in and between Ontario and Québec and, secondly, in and around British Columbia, the Rockies and Alberta. A VIA Rail link between the two systems is available, too; Moose can offer a discount on this train ticket.

Passengers pay only for transportation and add their own costs for food and activities according to their own interests. The itineraries are well planned and researched, allowing for a range of experiences, from historical sites to bungee jumping. Each route includes stops at various geographic and cultural attractions and overnights at hostels, permitting a great deal of flexibility. The circuits' durations range from a minimum of four to 14 days, but you can take as long as you like. Most people go for the two-week trip. Service runs from May to October.

There are three options around Ontario and Québec that include regional highlights, such as Kingston, Algonquin Park, Montréal and Tadoussac. Prices range from $250 for a four-day Québec pass to $419 for the full east pass. Duration and price depend on the trip and mileage covered. There is also a day excursion to Niagara. Each year, new ideas and destinations are incorporated. Bargain rail links connect to eastern Québec. These trips are deservedly popular and generate a lot of positive feedback.

Special Events

Some of the major events in Toronto are the following:

May

Toronto International Powwow This two-day event celebrates Native Indian culture with dancers, costumes and crafts. It's at the Skydome in the middle of May.

June

Caravan This is a nine-day event of cultural exchange, during which ethnic groups offer music, dance and foods that are native to their homelands. A passport ($15) entitles you to visit the 50 or so different ethnic pavilions set up around the city. Buses travel between the pavilions. The event takes place during the middle or end of June. Ask at the tourist office for a complete list of events.

Queen's Plate The year's major horse race and one of North America's oldest (held since 1859) is run at the Woodbine Racetrack (☎ 416-675-7223) around the end of June.

Gay Pride Day Parade Always larger and wilder than the year before, Gay Pride Day culminates in an outrageous, no-holds-barred downtown parade and celebration of sexuality in just about all varieties (including S/M and fetishes). People of every persuasion come to watch floats and the participants and to party down; recent crowds were estimated at 100,000. Festivities take place on Church St toward the end of June.

Du Maurier Downtown Jazz Festival This excellent and ever-growing annual festival is held throughout the central city in June and early July, with a week of concerts held day and night. The jazz is varied, featuring local, US and European players. More gospel, blues and world-beat influences have been creeping into the mix. About a thousand musicians perform. Workshops, films and even jazz cruises are part of the event. Shows range from freebies on the streets, to nightclub performances, to concert-hall recitals. Prices vary considerably but for the most part are pretty reasonable.

July

Soul & Blues Festival This festival is conducted on weekends at Harbourfront.

International Picnic At the beginning of July each year, to welcome summer, this huge picnic is held on Centre Island. Admission is free, and there's music, dancing, contests and lots of food. It's very popular with the Italian community.

The Molson Indy This is Toronto's only major car race and is held in early or mid-July. Well-known names from the international circuit compete in front of large crowds during the two days of practice and qualifying trials, with the big race on the last day of the three-day event. It's held in and around Exhibition Place and Lake Shore Blvd, in the south-central portion of the city. Get tickets early; call ☎ 416-975-8000.

Fringe Theatre Festival With over 400 performances at six venues over a 10-day period (generally in July), the festival has become a major theatrical hit. The participants are chosen by lottery, so the performances vary widely in style, format and quality. Expect the unexpected. Drama, comedy, musicals and cabaret-style shows are all part of the event. Call ☎ 416-534-5919 for more information, or ask at the tourist office for a program guide.

Mariposa Folk Festival Begun in the early 1960s, Mariposa is a festival of mainly folk music but also includes bluegrass and Native music. Location and format vary annually; for current information, call the Mariposa Folk Foundation (☎ 416-588-3655). Jam sessions and workshops are generally part of the multiday event, which takes place in July or August.

August

Caribana This major West Indian festival held along Lake Shore Blvd W around the beginning of August is primarily a weekend of reggae, steel-drum, and calypso music and dance. The main attraction, however, is the huge parade featuring incredibly elaborate costumes à la Carnaval. The parade can have thousands of participants and takes five hours or more to pass by. Other events and concerts are spread over the two weeks prior to the parade.

Canadian National Exhibition The CNE claims to be the oldest (from about 1900) and largest annual exhibition in the world. It includes agricultural and technical exhibits, concerts, displays, crafts, parades, an air show, a horse show, all manner of games and rides, fireworks and free Ontario Place admission. The exhibition is held during the two weeks prior to, and including, the Labor Day holiday. The location is Exhibition Place on Lake Shore Blvd W.

September

International Film Festival The annual festival is a prestigious and major international cinematic event. Usually held in September, it lasts about a week and a half and features films of all lengths and styles, as well as gala events and stars. Check the papers for special guides and reviews. You can obtain tickets for individual screenings or buy expensive, all-inclusive packages. Tickets sell out very quickly.

October
International Festival of Authors Held in fall (usually October) at Harbourfront, this is the largest literary event of its kind in the world. Dozens of well-known novelists, poets and short-story writers gather to read and discuss their work. Each evening, three or four writers are presented. Readings are also held through the year on a weekly basis, generally featuring less-prominent authors.

Places to Stay
Rates in hotels fluctuate with demand and season; summer is the peak time. High-season rates are given in this section.

Camping There are several camping/trailer grounds within 40km of the city. The tourist office has a complete list.

Indian Line Campground (☎ 416-661-6600, fax 800-304-9728, Indian Line Rd) Tent sites $20. One of the closest campgrounds is this good place, which is part of Clairville Conservation Area. Indian Line Rd runs north-south on the east side of Pearson International Airport. The campground, with 224 sites, is near Steeles Ave, which marks the northern edge of the city limits. This is probably the best place for tenters.

Glen Rouge Camp (☎ 416-392-2541, Kingston Rd) Tent sites $22. Also close to the city, this place is on Hwy 2 (Kingston Rd) at Altona Rd, near Sheppard Ave E. It's on the lakefront, at the eastern border of Toronto and the town of Pickering. There are about 120 sites, and the grounds can be reached by public transit from downtown, though it's a long slow trip; call for directions. The camp is open from May to October.

Hostels At some hostels, discounts are offered to HI, ISIC and various other student cardholders – make sure to ask. The following listings are recommended places (most of the other hostels listed on the Internet are not).

HI Toronto (☎ 416-971-4440, 877-848-8737, fax 416-971-4088, ☒ www.hostellingint-gl.on.ca; 76 Church St) Dorm beds $19-23, doubles $30, private rooms $60. The recently finished (well, almost) renovations have made this central, downtown hostel with 185 beds contemporary and comfortable. It's organized, and the staff has worked hard to upgrade attitude and service. The hostel, which was formerly a hotel, is just north of

Adelaide St E, one block east of Yonge St. There are all the usual facilities (kitchen, laundry, lockers, etc), and a bonus is that it is air-conditioned. Their nearby travel store, Hits, sells memberships, guidebooks, maps, phone cards and the like.

Global Village Backpackers (☎ 416-703-8540, 888-844-7875, ☒ www.globalback packers.com, 460 King St W) Dorm beds/doubles $23-27/60; less with hostel or student cards and in winter. This independent hostel, with a great location (on the corner of Spadina Ave) by the edge of the Entertainment District, is the biggest in town. There are 200 beds, but they are spread over many rooms in the former hotel, so it's generally not cramped. There is a good lounge, a pleasant patio, Internet facilities and even a bar on the premises. For a big place, it is well organized, and management isn't loath to spending some money on design and maintenance. There are now sister hostels in Vancouver and Banff.

Canadiana Guesthouse & Backpackers (☎ 416-598-9090, 877-215-1225, ☒ www.canadianalodging.com, 42 Widmer St) Dorm beds $26, singles/doubles $45/60. Every time you turn around, this still new, well-run hostel in the heart of the Entertainment District has somehow grown. It may have 100 beds, but it feels smaller, because they are spread over a number of recently renovated, interconnected Victorian row houses. Features include air-conditioning, kitchen, free linens and patios. Weekly rates are offered in the off-season.

The Planet Traveler's Hostel (☎ 416-599-6789, ☒ www.theplanettraveler.com, 175 Augusta Ave) Dorm beds/doubles $20/50. Created out of a restored Victorian house smack-dab in the middle of bustling Kensington Market, this place was an instant success. It has just 20 dorm beds and two private doubles, which come with continental breakfast. There's a nice little patio out back and a brand-new restaurant/bar a few doors down.

Leslieville Home Hostel (☎ 416-461-7258, 800-280-3965, fax 416-469-9938, ☒ leslieville@sympatico.ca, 185 Leslie St) Dorm beds/singles/doubles $17/39/49. This cheaper, independent hostel consists of two houses in an east-end residential neighborhood 4km from downtown. Dorm capacity is 35, but there are six private rooms; weekly rates are available. It's small, very casual and homey. Kitchen and laundry facilities, free linens, parking and Internet access are all available. To get there, take the 20-minute streetcar ride along Queen St to Leslie St and walk north along Leslie St (the streetcar operates 24 hours). Reservations are suggested for summer.

Havinn (☎ *416-922-5220, 888-922-5220,* W *www.eol.ca/~havinn, 118 Spadina Rd*) Dorm beds/singles/doubles $25/45/60. This small, quiet place is more like a modest B&B than a hostel. It has just one dorm room and three private rooms, which include breakfast and are ideal for couples. For dorms, you get a real bed in a room with a maximum of three others. There are kitchen facilities (minus a stove but including a microwave) and a TV in each room. It's central (north of Bloor St) but residential, very clean and has parking – a good deal all around. In summer, reservations are suggested.

Our Place Called Home (☎ *416-972-7526,* e *opch3@hotmail.com, 366 Dupont St*) Singles $40; $10 for each additional person. Around the corner from the Havinn, Our Place is quite similar, with five pleasantly ascetic rooms and a full kitchen. The staff speak Japanese.

YWCA (☎ *416-923-8454, 80 Woodlawn Ave*) Dorm beds/singles/doubles $22/48/52. For women only, this place is central and near Yonge St. The private rooms have a shared bath but come with breakfast, and there's an inexpensive cafeteria here. Discounts for stays of a week or longer are offered.

University Residences *Neill-Wycik College Hotel* (☎ *416-977-2320, 800-268-4358, fax 416-977-2809,* W *www.neill-wycik.com, 96 Gerrard St E*) Beds start at $20 per person. Open early May-late Aug. This is a well located, recently renovated apartment-style student residence by Ryerson Polytechnic University. In summer, rooms are rented, and family rooms are also available. There are laundry facilities and a student-run cafeteria for breakfasts. However, the building isn't air-conditioned, so the small rooms can get very hot in mid-summer. But…the rooftop deck is fabulous.

University of Toronto (☎ *416-978-2477, fax 416-946-7169, www.utoronto.ca/visitnew-college/summer, 21 Classic Ave*) Room with breakfast $50. Open mid-May–late Aug. This place, at New College, also offers good weekly rates.

B&Bs & Tourist Homes Between June and November, reservations are suggested. In addition to the independent operators, there are B&B associations, which check, list and book rooms in the participating homes. Indicate where you'd like to be and any other preferences, and attempts will be made to find a particularly suitable host. A telephone call should get things sorted out. Prices range from $55 to $75 for singles to $75 to $140 for doubles.

The ***Downtown Toronto Association of B&B Guesthouses*** (☎ *416-410-3938,* W *www.bnbinfo.com, PO Box 190, Station B, Toronto, ON M5T 2W1*) specializes in rooms downtown, mainly in renovated Victorian houses.

Metropolitan B&B Registry (☎ *416-964-2566, 877-920-7842,* W *www.virtual cities.com*) is the largest outfit, with members in and out of town.

Across Toronto B&B (☎ *705-738-9449, 877-922-6522,* W *www.torontobandb.com, Box 269, 253 College St, Toronto, ON M5T 1R5*) has about 25 members.

Global Guesthouse (☎ *416-923-4004, 800-387-4788,* e *singer@inforamp.net, 9 Spadina Rd*) Singles/doubles with shared bath $54/64, with private bath $64/79. This place has a great location, just north of Bloor St W. The good-value rooms include parking, daily cleaning, cable TV, a telephone and maybe a painting by the owner. The 10 rooms fill up quickly. Beware of the noisy, ground-floor rooms by the subway.

Allenby (☎ *416-461-7095, 223 Strathmore Blvd*) Ⓜ Greenwood. Singles/doubles with continental breakfast $50/60. This spotless place is in the east end, near Greektown. There's a kitchen and deck for guests. Prices drop even lower during the nonsummer period. All rooms share bathrooms.

Candy Haven Tourist Home (☎ *416-532-0651, 1233 King St W*) Singles/doubles with shared bath $45/50. West of downtown is this simple place, right on the King St streetcar line; look for the sign right beside McDonald's. It's been around for decades and is quaintly old-fashioned. The elderly owner can tell you more than you want to know about the area.

Grayona Tourist Home (☎ *416-535-5443,
800-354-0244, 1546 King St W*) Singles/
doubles $55-60/65-80, family room $110.
Also west of downtown is this renovated old
house run by Marie Taylor, a friendly and
enthusiastic Australian. Every room has a
refrigerator and telephone, and all but one
has a TV. The marginally more expensive
rooms, which are good for families (there's
even a cot), have cooking facilities. The large
family room has a bathroom and kitchen.
Prices drop in the off-season. It's about 7km
from downtown, and although some of the
visitors walk, there is a streetcar along King
St that stops practically at the door.

Beverley Place (☎ *416-977-0077, fax 416-
599-2242, 235 Beverley St*) Singles/doubles
with breakfast $60-75/90-110. The 'Queen
Room' (with an impressive bed) costs more,
as does the 3rd-floor, self-contained apartment with its own balcony and city view. This
place is a little more upscale than others in
this category. Chinatown, Queen St W and
even the CN Tower are all within walking
distance. The house is a well restored, three-
story Victorian dating from 1877, with lots
of original features and wonderfully high
ceilings. The entire place is furnished and
decorated with interesting antiques and collectibles. An excellent breakfast is served at
the large kitchen table overlooking a secluded garden patio. The owner, Bill Ricci-
uto, also runs a similar house across the
street. Guests staying there go to No 235 for
breakfast. Aberdeen Ave runs west off Parliament St just north of Carlton St.

Aberdeen Guesthouse (☎ *416-920-8697,*
e *aberdeen@aol.com, 52 Aberdeen Ave*)
Singles/doubles with shared bath & breakfast $80-90/90-95. This is a small, renovated
Victorian home in the east-end area of Cabbagetown. There are three beautifully decorated rooms, breakfast is fabulous, the
house is air-conditioned, there's a shady
back garden and it's gay friendly.

Fourth St B&B (☎ *416-203-0771,*
e *fourthstbb@hotmail.com, 22 Fourth St*)
Two people with full breakfast $80. To be in
the city but in the country, try this flower-
shrouded cottage on Ward Island. It's a
short walk from the ferry and open all year.
Bicycles and weekly rates are available.

Efficiencies *Grange Apartment Hotel* (☎ *416-
603-7700, 888-232-0002, fax 416-603-9977,*

w *www.grangehotel.com, 165 Grange Ave*)
Rooms $90. These fully equipped studios are
central and reasonably priced. One week's
notice may be required in summer.

Motels For such a large city, Toronto is
short on motels. There are two main (but
skimpy) districts for motels in the city, and
others are scattered throughout the city and
around the perimeter.

On the west side of town, a shrinking
motel strip (due to redevelopment) can be
found along the lake on Lake Shore Blvd W,
informally known as 'the lakeshore.' Those
remaining are mostly between the Humber
River and Park Lawn Ave, just west of High
Park. This district isn't too far from the
downtown area (about 12km from Yonge
St), and the streetcar lines run the whole
way. To streetcar it, take the Queen St or
King St streetcar from downtown to Roncesvalles Ave and continue on the Queen St
streetcar to the Humber River. Switch (for
no charge) to the Humber streetcar, which
goes along the lakeshore. The motels edge
the shoreline, and several nearby parks on
the waterfront offer cool breezes in summer
and good views of the city and islands.

Also, several motels sit along Dundas St
W west of Hwy 427 (in suburban Missis-
sauga). From Lake Shore Blvd, go north up
Hwy 427 and turn left at Dundas.

Beach Motel (☎ *416-259-3296, 800-830-
8508, fax 416-503-0518, 2183 Lake Shore
Blvd W*) Rooms $65-75. The best choice is
this well-looked-after one that backs right
onto a huge, waterfront park with views to
downtown.

Queensway Motel (☎ *416-252-5821,638
The Queensway*) Doubles/twins $60/80. The
Queensway is sort of away from the main
routes and may have rooms when others are
full. Prices don't fluctuate so much, either.

Four Points Sheraton (☎ *416-766-4392,
800-463-9929, fax 416-766-1278, 1926 Lake
Shore Blvd W*) Rooms $130-165. This
upscale place is very conveniently situated,
looking across to the lake and before the
start of the motel strip itself. It has its own
restaurant and bar.

On the east side of town, on the old Hwy
2 to Montréal, motels start just east of
Brimley Rd. The Guildwood station of the
GO train (a commuter service) is just east of
the motel strip. It has parking, and trains run

frequently into downtown. Alternatively, public transit can get you into town, but it's very slow. Many of these motels are now used by the government as overflow social housing.

Park (☎ 416-261-7241, 3126 Kingston Rd) Doubles $65. This place is clean and decent.

Hotels You can't say Toronto and budget hotels in the same breath. Unlike Montréal, visitors simply will not find one. There are, though, some good moderate central places with a bit of character. Downtown, around the city's edges and around the airport, there is an abundance of large, modern hotels, many of which offer discount weekend packages.

Selby (☎ 416-921-3142, 800-387-4788, fax 416-923-3177, e reservations@hotelselby .com, 592 Sherbourne St) Rates $95-120 with breakfast. Situated north of Wellesley St, the Selby, recently bought by Howard Johnson, combines price with value. The turreted Victorian mansion, dating from 1882 and designated as a heritage site, has an interesting history. At one time, it was a girls' school. Later, Ernest Hemingway lived here when he worked for the *Toronto Star*, in his younger days, before heading to Paris. Rates for the upgraded rooms vary depending on size, features and date. Reservations are recommended from May to October. The long-running gay bar has closed, but the hotel's clientele remains a mix of straights and gays.

Strathcona (☎ 416-363-3321, 800-268-8304, fax 416-363-4679, w www.toronto .com/stratconahotel, 60 York St) Rooms $100-130. This is an upgraded older place with an excellent location, very near the train station. It has all the usual amenities and yet, for the downtown area, is moderately priced. There's a dining room, a coffee shop and a bar.

Hotel Victoria (☎ 416-363-1666, 800-363-8228, fax 416-363-7327, w www.toronto .com/hotelvictoria, 56 Yonge St) Singles/doubles with breakfast $120-155. This is one of the best of the small, old downtown hotels. Refurbished throughout, it maintains such features as a fine lobby. There are just 48 rooms.

Bond Place Hotel (☎ 416-362-6061, 800-268-9390, fax 416-360-6406, w www.bond

placehoteltoronto.com, 65 Dundas St E) Rooms with breakfast $95. This high-rise hotel has a great location near the Eaton Centre and is often busy with vacationers.

Executive Motor Hotel (☎ 416-504-7441, fax 416-504-4722, 621 King St W) Singles/doubles $119/129. More like a motel but perfectly good and with parking, this 75-room place is central, and the King St streetcar goes right by. Prices drop in the off-season.

Days Inn (☎ 416-977-6655, 800-329-7466, fax 416-977-0502, 30 Carlton St) Low-/high-season $120/150. This central place is reliable and has other locations around the city.

Westin Harbour Castle (☎ 416-869-1600, fax 416-869-1420, w www.westin.com, 1 Harbour Square) Rooms $260. The Westin has a fine location near the bottom of Yonge St, right at the edge of the lake, opposite the Toronto Islands. The revolving restaurant offers splendid views over the city and lake.

Royal York (☎ 416-368-2511, 800-441-1414, fax 416-368-9040, w www.fairmont .com,100 Front St) Rooms $260-300. The rates here rise depending on vacancy levels and the view. Among the top-class hotels, this hotel is the oldest and has served people from rock stars to royalty.

Hilton (☎ 416-869-3456, 800-445-8667, fax 416-869-3187, w www.hilton.com, 145 Richmond St W) Singles/doubles $300. This central, well-appointed hotel has a good reputation and a fine lobby area.

Four Seasons (☎ 416-964-0411, 800-268-6262, fax 416-964-2301, w www.fourseasons .com/toronto, 21 Avenue Rd) Rooms $400-600. The costliest rooms in town are found at this place, which is the celebrities' choice.

Places to Eat
Eating can be a real pleasure in this town. There are tasty choices in all price ranges, from ma-and-pa kitchens to dining rooms presided over by celebrity chefs. The many nationalities that are represented spice up the mix.

Not far from the swimming pool in High Park, on the main road through the park, there's the bustling **Grenadier Café** (☎ 416-769-9870), which serves a vast selection of quite good homemade meals at modest prices.

Markets There are some great self-catering options in Toronto. Two major health-food stores are the **Big Carrot Natural Food**

Market (☎ 416-466-2129, 348 Danforth Ave) and the more central **Baldwin Natural Foods** (☎ 416-979-1777, 20½ Baldwin St).

The city's prime outdoor market, **Kensington Market** (**W** www.kensingtonmarket.org) is a lively, multicultural, old-style market in a residential neighborhood squeezed along Baldwin St and Augusta Ave off Spadina Ave, just south of College St and east of Bathurst St. It's busiest on Saturday morning, but it's open all week during normal business hours. The cheese shops are good, and there's all manner of fresh fruit and vegetables. You can bargain over prices. There are some excellent restaurants in the area, too.

The *St Lawrence Market* (☎ 416-392-7219, 92 Front St E; open 7am-5pm Tues-Sun), in what was Toronto's first City Hall, dates from 1844. Here, nearly all the shoppers are of British ancestry, and the atmosphere is closer to sedate – there may even be classical musicians playing. It's best on Saturday, when farmers sell a superb range of high-quality produce – from fish to more rice varieties than you knew existed. Just north of the market building is **St Lawrence Hall**. This public meeting hall from the 19th century, topped with a clock tower, is considered one of the city's finest old buildings. Farmers pull trucks in here on weekends and sell right out of the back of them.

Yonge St Area Yonge St itself, though busy night and day, is not one of Toronto's prime restaurant districts. In the center, Yonge St has become swamped with fast-food franchises and cheap take-out counters. There are exceptions on and nearby the street, but many places are geared more toward lunch than dinner. That said, the strip south of Bloor St to Wellesley St has recently begun to show some real life.

Marchelino Restaurant (Level 1 food court, Eaton Centre) Dishes $5-8. Way above an average mall eatery, this attractive spot features a range of fresh, international dishes, all priced very reasonably.

Swiss Chalet (☎ 416-597-0101, 362 Yonge St) Dishes $7-12. This is an outlet of the popular Canadian roast-chicken and chips chain. It's nothing fancy but provides a sound and economical meal that almost everyone enjoys.

Ryerson Polytechnic University Cafeteria (☎ 416-979-5000, Jorgenson Hall, Gerrard St E at Victoria St) Dishes $5-10. This large, crowded, noisy cafeteria serves up reasonable meals at student prices. Food is served at mealtimes only.

Green Mango (☎ 416-920-5448, 707 Yonge St) Meals under $10. Open 11am-8pm Mon-Sat. With its excellent Thai food served fast and cheap, this place is a perennial winner of the 'best meal under $10' moniker.

7 West Café (☎ 416-928-9041, 7 Charles St W) Dishes under $10. Open 8am-3am. This three-story place, morphed from an old house, is an intimate, romantic candle-lit nook that's half café, half restaurant, half bar. Yes, it adds up beyond the components. The food is simple sandwiches and salads, but the atmosphere makes them taste like something special.

Young Thailand (☎ 416-368-1368, 81 Church St) Dishes $9-16. One of the city's most popular Asian choices (there are now three locations) has its original place here. It's moderately dressy and serves classic Thai cuisine at reasonable prices.

Bigliardi's (☎ 416-922-9594, 463 Church St) Dinner for two $120. Open 5pm-midnight. For a splurge on a good steak, try this established, traditional steak house. Reservations are suggested for weekends.

Farther north on Church in the Village are numerous places, some with very attractive patios.

Zelda's (☎ 416-922-2526, 542 Church St) Dishes $10. A fine example is this one, which is good for people-watching while nibbling straightforward items, like a chicken dish or salad, or sipping a cold one.

Entertainment District There are a clutch of new restaurants and nightclubs (some ferociously hip) to be found in this fickle, expanding galaxy to the north of the Skydome and containing the Mirvish theaters and Roy Thompson Hall.

Peel Pub (☎ 416-977-0003, 276 King St W) Daily special $5. Open 6:30am-2:30am daily. This cavernous tavern imported from Montréal draws crowds with its great prices, daily specials, cheap beer and loud, friendly atmosphere.

Alice Fazooli's (☎ 416-979-1910, 294 Adelaide St W) Dishes $12-20. Open noon-10pm.

This is a popular party place featuring crab and Italian fare with a huge wine list to help wash it down. The convivial atmosphere makes it a good place to go if you have a group.

Zupa's Deli (☎ 416-593-2775, 342½ Adelaide St W) Sandwiches $6-8. Open 6am-7pm Mon-Sat. For those in need of a smoked-meat sandwich in a small, busy, Jewish-style deli, check out this place east of Spadina. You'd have to be an alligator to get your mouth around one of these megasandwiches.

Wayne Gretzky's (☎ 416-979-7825, 99 Blue Jays Way) Dishes $8-15. Open 11am-2am daily. Owned by a hockey legend, this busy pub/bar/restaurant has something for everyone. The food – lots of pastas and burgers – gets the job done, but most people come for the busy, festive ambience, moderate prices and pleasant rooftop with a fine view.

Hard Rock Cafe (☎ 416-341-2388, Gate 1, Skydome) Dishes $7-14. Open 11am-1am daily. When no game is on, this café runs as the regular sports bar that it is; you can simply go in for a hamburger and a beer and have a look at the playing field. During games, tables with views must be paid for.

Possibly a better deal than the elevator/observation desk ticket at the CN Tower (see Viewpoints, earlier) is lunch or dinner at the *360 Revolving Restaurant* (☎ 416-362-5411), because the elevator ticket price is waived. Lunch prices start at $17, and dinner prices start at around $40, but there is no lunch in winter. Sunday brunch is also offered in summer. If you just want a drink in the bar (minimum $5), the elevator must be paid for.

St Lawrence Market Farther east, past the Hummingbird Centre, which is on Front St at Yonge St, is this other busy (but less so) eating, entertainment and nightclub area popular with both visitors and residents. For information on St Lawrence Market itself, see Markets, above.

Old Spaghetti Factory (☎ 416-864-9761, 54 The Esplanade) Dinner $8-11. Open 11am-10pm daily. Toronto, like many Canadian cities of any size, has its own version of this chain. The restaurant offers a good value. Meals are served in an eclectic, colorful atmosphere popular with everybody, including families and teenagers. The lunch menu is even cheaper.

Papillon (☎ 416-363-0838, 16 Church St) Mains $10-20. This is a very comfortable French crêperie. In winter, a fireplace adds ambience. It gets full when there are popular shows at the nearby Hummingbird Centre.

Queen St West Queen St W between Spadina and University is one of *the* lively central districts. Some places cater more toward trend than quality, but it's an interesting and varied area with some good and reasonably priced restaurants.

Queen Mother (☎ 416-598-4719, 208 Queen St W) Dinner $25-30. Open 11am-11pm daily. This comfortable place, a long-time city fave, is one of the better and more stable eateries in the area. It offers a varied menu with a Thai influence for full meals and serves coffee and snacks all day.

Le Select Bistro (☎ 416-596-6406, 328 Queen St W) Prix fixe $27. Open 11am-late (at least 11pm). Take a trip to Paris. There are a lot of repeat customers at this consistently good French bistro serving traditional meals.

Many of the area's younger residents and more impecunious artists have moved farther west to between Spadina Ave and Bathurst St and beyond. The local Goths and vampires/Edwardians stroll the area. Along here you'll find a range of new, small restaurants, clubs and specialty stores.

Terroni (☎ 416-504-0320, 720 Queen St W) Dishes $6-11. Open 9am-10pm daily. Cheap but stylish, this Queen St W mainstay has pizza, tasty focaccia sandwiches and some pastas. There's also a very nice back patio.

Dufflet's (☎ 416-504-2870, 787 Queen St W) Desserts $6. Dufflet's is the creator of Toronto's best-known desserts and has this small retail outlet with a couple of tables. The chocolate cakes are unreal.

Chinatown Area The city's large Chinatown is based around the corner of Spadina Ave and Dundas St W and is home to scores of restaurants and browser-friendly shops. Cantonese, Szechuan, Hunan and Mandarin food is all served. The district extends along Dundas St W, especially to the east of Spadina Ave and north up Spadina Ave to College St. To the west of Spadina Ave, the market area on Kensington Ave and particularly on Augusta Ave is busy during the day and has some small cheap *cafés*.

More and more Vietnamese places are springing up, as some Chinese are leaving the central core for more suburban areas.

Peter's Chung King (☎ 416-928-2936, 281 College St) Dishes $6-9. Open noon-10pm Sun-Thur, 1pm-11pm Fri & Sat. For tasty, inexpensive Chinese food in a variety of styles, including some fine spicy dishes such as orange beef, this restaurant gets high marks. The food is the draw; the decor isn't much, but at least the tablecloths aren't plastic. The hot peppered garlic chicken with peanut sauce and (believe it or not) the green beans are supreme.

Lee Garden (☎ 416-593-9524, 331 Spadina Ave) Dishes $7-15. Open 4pm-midnight daily. Long a Toronto fave, this institution in pastel green offers a consistently good and unusually varied Cantonese menu with lots of seafood. The adventurous can ask for explanations of the numerous items that are listed only in Chinese.

Swatow (☎ 416-977-0601, 309 Spadina Ave) Dishes $7-9. Open noon-10pm daily. This is another good choice, with an extensive menu covering different Chinese regions, notably Fukien with its clear soups and seafood specialties.

Phõ' Hu'ng (☎ 416-5934274, 350 Spadina Ave) Mains $5-7. Open 10am-10pm daily. This highly recommended place features an awesome array of soups (pho) that come with fresh greens. Some, featuring intestine, tendons and blood, may be too authentic, but many are delicious. Or try the bowls of vermicelli with your choice of ingredients – an outstanding meal at $6. Hint: consider the barbecued-pork version, toss on the greens and a squirt of hot sauce, and life is good. A fair-weather bonus is the patio.

An interesting street on the edge of Chinatown that not too many out-of-towners get to is Baldwin St, running east off Spadina Ave about two blocks north of Dundas St. About three blocks from Spadina Ave toward the east end of Baldwin St is a small, low-key commercial and international-restaurant enclave. Long a blend of Chinese and Western counterculture, Baldwin Village is now a green, leafy and busy block that's especially pleasant on summer evenings, when many of the varied restaurants have outdoor patios.

Margarita's (☎ 416-977-5525, 14 Baldwin St) Dishes $7-14. Open 11:30am-9:30pm Mon-Fri, noon-11pm Sat & Sun. This is a small, colorful Mexican cantina with the regular cheaper tortilla items and slightly more expensive authentic meals, such as moles. There is also a patio.

Mata Hari Grill (☎ 416-596-2832, 39 Baldwin St) Dinner for two $50. Open noon-10pm Tues-Sun. The long, narrow room is simple yet elegant and romantic, and the Malaysian food is exceptional. There's lots of seafood, but the satay is wonderful, and the mango chicken is a keeper too.

Yung Sing Pastry Shop (☎ 416-979-2832, 22 Baldwin St) Dishes under $5. Almost next door to Margarita's, this no-frills bakery and counter specializes in Chinese sweets. Help yourself to Chinese tea. It's strictly takeaway, but there's a shady picnic table in front of the shop.

Red Room (☎ 416-929-9964, 444 Spadina Ave) Dishes under $10. Open 7am-2am daily. Like being at the home of a favorite eccentric, artsy aunt, you can settle in amid the comforting atmosphere and relax with a simple meal of sandwiches or straightforward pastas. And then sip one of the 200 teas.

The Annex Area Bloor St W from Spadina Ave west to Bathurst St is a lively student area, with many restaurants, cafés, bookshops and the popular Bloor St Cinema.

The Madison (☎ 416-927-1722, 14 Madison Ave) Dishes under $15. Open daily. This is a fine, four-tiered pub with lots of outdoor space and very good pub food. The chicken wings' reputation flies.

By the Way Café (☎ 416-967-4295, 400 Bloor St W) Dishes $7-14. This is a small, comfortable bistro with an international menu. The salads and pita sandwiches are around $7; the main dishes a little more. Try the killer cakes, too.

Juice for Life (☎ 416-531-2635, 521 Bloor St W) Dishes $5-10. This is a city fave for its strictly vegetarian fare and absence of earnestness. The wholesome and tasty menu includes sandwiches, meatless burgers and pastas. There is also a vast array of smoothies and shakes to cure what ails.

True Grits (☎ 416-536-8383, 603 Markham St) Open 5pm-10pm Tues-Sun. Dinner $12-18. For some southern spice amid casual funk surroundings the tables here see a lot of regulars. If you want more upscale Cajun, the same owners operate Southern Accent a few doors down.

Kensington Kitchen (☎ 416-961-3404, *124 Harbord St*) Dishes $10-15. Casually elegant, this place offers meals with a Mediterranean slant. Lunches are inexpensive; dinner for two with wine is about $60. During fine weather, take advantage of the wonderful patio.

Little Italy Based along College St west of Bathurst, Little Italy is a cool (as in hot) spot for eating, meeting and hanging out. On weekend summer nights, there's a lot of good natured struttin' goin' on. But that doesn't mean there isn't well-prepared food, too.

Kalendar Koffee House (☎ 416-923-4138, *546 College St*) Mains $8-14. Open 11am-midnight. This intimate spot is great for a date and offers delicious things wrapped in pastry, fabulous salads, soups, pastas and can't-resist desserts. It also has a good selection of imported beer.

Bar Italia (☎ 416-535-3621, *584 College St*) Dishes $6-14. Open daily. Always crowded, this streamlined space has lots of atmosphere, excellent Italian sandwiches at good prices and pool tables upstairs. Complete dinners, including a glass of wine, start at $18. On weekends, there may be some live music thrown into the mix.

Café Diplomatico (☎ 416-534-4637, *594 College St*) Dishes $4-12. Open 8am-late daily. Everybody loves 'the Dip' for its casual, happening atmosphere, perfect patio and cheap tasty meals. Specialties are pizzas, salads and mussels, and the staff can steam up a good cappuccino as well.

Sicilian Ice Cream Co (☎ 416-531-7716, *712 College St*) Desserts under $6. Open 9am-midnight Mon-Sat, 11am-11pm Sun. For the best tartufo, sherbets and Sicilian ice cream in town, head farther west to this corner café, where you can eat in or take out.

Greektown/Danforth The Greek area along Danforth Ave, east of the city center between Pape and Woodbine Aves, is also a fun place to get a meal. Most of the restaurants get very busy on summer weekend nights, when there's a real festive air to the street. Casual, cheap souvlaki houses with a noisy, informal atmosphere but suitable for children are abundant. Eating early or after

9pm is recommended if you want to avoid the crowds. Some places serve until the very wee hours.

Astoria (☎ 416-463-2838, *390 Danforth Ave*) Dinner $15-16. Open 11am-midnight daily, later on weekends. This is a good, bustling, low-cost place – just look for the line and the charming patio. The kebab/rice/potato/salad combo is a fine, inexpensive meal. It's near the Chester subway stop.

Ouzeri (☎ 416-778-0500, *500A Danforth Ave*) Dishes $10-25. Open for lunch and dinner daily. This popular place presents a range of slightly more sophisticated main courses and tapas amid colorfully trendy surroundings and fellow diners. Fresh sardines in mustard sauce with a Greek salad and a cold beer will cost around $18.

Pan (☎ 416-466-8158, *516 Danforth Ave*) Dinner for two $70. Open 5pm-11pm daily, 5pm-midnight Fri & Sat. This comfortably upscale place is recommended for the very well-prepared meals featuring traditional Greek ingredients and flavorings.

Ellas (☎ 416-463-0334, *702 Pape Ave*) Mains $10-17. Open 11am-11pm Sun-Thur, 11am-midnight Fri & Sat. Since the 1960s, Ellas has carried on the tradition of the Greek standards, many of which are on view as you enter. It also offers a lot of seafood. It's dressy and has attentive service.

Little India There are good Indian restaurants scattered around town, but for a wallet-friendly place with a side order of cultural experience, you can't beat Little India, based on Gerrard St E just west of Coxwell Ave.

Madras Durbar (☎ 416-465-4116, *1435 Gerrard St E*) Dishes under $10. Open 11am-11pm daily. You're practically stealing the food at this tiny exclusively vegetarian South Indian eatery. The 10-item thali plate is a real exotic taste sensation and makes a complete meal for $6.50! Masala dosas so big they hang off the plate are $5.50.

Bar-Be-Que Hut (☎ 416-466-0411, *1455 Gerrard St E*) Dishes $6-11. Open noon-10pm Sun-Wed, noon-midnight Thur-Sat. This long-established place is plusher than most, has a selection of both meat and vegetarian dishes and provides live music Friday and Sunday nights. The half-chicken tandoori is $9; biryani is $11.

Haandi (☎ *416-469-9696, 1401 Gerrard St E*) Dishes $5-8. Lunch/dinner buffet $7/8. Open 11:30am-10:30pm daily. Large and sedate and with new owners, the Haandi serves very good dishes from the extensive menu and offers cheap all-you-can-eat buffets. There is also a good range of baked breads.

After dinner, pop into one of the nearby shops for a *paan* made to order at the counter. With or without tobacco, this is a cheap, exotic mouthful. Try to get the whole thing in your mouth; it's like a bite of India.

Entertainment

Toronto is busy after dark, with countless nightspots, concerts, films, lectures and the country's largest theater scene. The dance, symphony and opera seasons start in October or November and run through the winter.

The city's most complete entertainment guide is provided by *Now* magazine, a good weekly that's available free around town – at cinemas, restaurants, cafés, record stores and some street-corner newsboxes (where it must be paid for). *Eye* is similar. Also, all three of Toronto's daily newspapers provide weekly entertainment listings. Check either the Thursday *Star* or the Friday *Sun* for full listings; the Saturday *Globe & Mail* has film and theater listings.

Tri-tickets (☎ 416-504-7777, 29 Camden St) can usually get you a ticket for any show or event, sold out or not. The classified sections of the *Sun* and *Star* also list tickets available for every event in town, from opera to Rolling Stones and from hockey to baseball. For a price, any seat is yours.

Rush or same-day discounted tickets may be available at theaters for any given show. TO Tix (☎ 416-536-6468 ext 40) sells half-price leftover theater and dance tickets for shows the same day. It has a booth on the second level of the Eaton Centre. You must go in person. It's open afternoons only and is closed Sunday and Monday (buy tickets on Saturday for these days).

Performing Arts The city boasts plenty of first-rate theater. Only London and New York sell more tickets. Productions range from Broadway-type spectacles and musicals to Canadian contemporary dramas. Also big is dinner theater, where dinner and a show costs $40 to $60.

Many nonprofit theaters like *Theatre Passe Muraille* (☎ *416-504-7529, 16 Ryerson St*), *Tarragon* (☎ *416-536-5018, 30 Bridgman Ave*) and *Buddies in Bad Times Theatre* (☎ *416-975-8555, 12 Alexander St*) have one pay-what-you-can performance per week (usually Sunday afternoon). These are not the grand commercial spectacle venues.

Toronto Truck Theatre (☎ *416-922-0084, 94 Belmont*) The city's longest-running play, Agatha Christie's *The Mousetrap*, has been playing since 1976! A ticket is $16 to $24.

Royal Alexandra Theatre (☎ *416-872-1212, 260 King St W*) Perhaps the city's best-known theater, the impressive Royal Alex presents well-established plays and performers. Look for the Walk of Fame on the sidewalk out front.

Princess of Wales Theatre (☎ *416-872-1212, 300 King St W*) Next door to the Royal Alexandra is this lavish theater with one of the largest stages in North America. It was built to accommodate the musical *Miss Saigon* and presents spectacle shows from Broadway.

Canon Theatre (☎ *416-364-4100, 244 Victoria St*) This venue, a classic 1920s central theater worth visiting just for its gorgeous lobby, hosted the long-running *Phantom of the Opera*.

Elgin & Winter Garden Theatre Centre (☎ *416-314-2901, 189 Yonge St*) Also investigate this restored historic complex for its high-profile productions. Tours are offered on Thursday and Saturday.

The Dream in High Park (☎ *416-367-8243, Canadian Stage Co, High Park, Parkside Dr*) Requested donation $6. Make an effort to catch a wonderful outdoor performance (almost nightly July and August). Shows begin at 8pm, but go very early (with a blanket and picnic basket), or you'll be turned away.

Roy Thompson Hall (☎ *416-872-4255, 60 Simcoe St*) The Toronto Symphony (☎ 416-593-4828) plays here, along with a range of other, mainly classical concerts.

Hummingbird Centre (☎ *416-872-2262, 1 Front St E*) Both the Canadian Opera Company and the National Ballet of Canada call this home.

Trinity-St Paul's Centre (427 Bloor St W) At this venue, the world-renowned Tafelmusik orchestra (☎ 416-964-6337) performs baroque and classical music on period instruments.

Toronto Centre for the Arts (☎ 416-733-9388, 5040 Yonge St) The marvelous Recital Hall presents classical concerts by the world's top musicians and vocalists.

Massey Hall (☎ 416-872-4255, 178 Victoria St) The city's oldest concert hall has excellent acoustics and is a wonderfully intimate place to see a show, often folk or pop.

Premiere Dance Theatre (☎ 416-973-4000, 207 Queens Quay W) For dance, look into what's happening at this Harbourfront venue in the Queens Quay Terminal.

Comedy Clubs *Second City* (☎ 416-343-0011, 56 Blue Jays Way) Cover $20. This place has an excellent reputation for its sketch comedy and the people it develops. Dan Aykroyd, John Candy, Mike Myers and Gilda Radner all cut their teeth here.

Yuk Yuks Superclub (☎ 416-967-6425, 2335 Yonge St) Cover $5-15. The live acts here are sometimes funny, sometimes gross, sometimes a joke, but you might see future stars. Jim Carrey first performed in Toronto Yuk Yuks clubs. Admission is cheaper on some weekdays and more expensive on weekend nights, when there are two two-hour shows. Dinner packages are also available ($25).

Cinemas There are several repertory film houses around town. Prices are a couple of dollars less than those at first-run theaters and are much lower for those with an annual membership card, which is inexpensive.

Bloor Cinema (☎ 416-516-2330, 506 Bloor St W) This cinema is popular with the many students in the area. A wide variety of films is shown – US and European, old and new. Look for the festive midnight viewings.

Revue (☎ 416-531-9959, 400 Roncesvalles Ave) This ancient venue on an interesting street in the west end features different films nearly every night.

Cinémathèque Ontario (☎ 416-968-3456, Art Gallery of Ontario, Jackman Hall, 317 Dundas St W) This cinema at the AGO (see Museums & Galleries under Things to See & Do, earlier) also screens noncommercial films.

Ontario Place Cinesphere (☎ 416-314-9990, Ontario Place) IMAX movies are featured here.

Festival Hall (☎ 416-260-1440, 126 John St) The latest in movies, IMAX, video games and other technology is housed here.

Carlton Cinemas (☎ 416-598-2309, 20 Carlton St) This is a good spot for nonmainstream new releases.

Live Music Live-music clubs generally don't fill up until after 10pm.

Bamboo Club (☎ 416-593-5771, 312 Queen St W) Cover $5-10. This is a very popular club with lots of African and reggae sounds. It's always busy with a 30-something crowd. There's a rooftop patio to catch a breath and a kitchen serving tasty, spicy meals.

Horseshoe Tavern (☎ 416-598-4753, 370 Queen St W) Perhaps the city's most loved bar, this classic presents a mixture of alternative, rock, country, blues and rhythm and blues.

Chicago's (☎ 416-598-3301, 335 Queen St W) This place near Horseshoe Tavern features live blues. The kitchen is open daily until 1am, and there's often no cover charge.

Grossman's (☎ 416-977-7000, 379 Spadina Ave) Grubby and one of the cheapest spots in town (there's never a cover), Grossman's is also one of Canada's best-known venues and has hosted just about every big-name musician at one time or another. It's hit-or-miss, but there's usually an interesting, mixed crowd and, on a good night, it's pure magic.

Lee's Palace (☎ 416-532-1598, 529 Bloor St W) This place maintains its reputation for presenting up-to-the-minute rock and pop.

Healy's (☎ 416-703-5882, 178 Bathurst St) Owned by respected guitarist/vocalist/trumpeter Jeff Healy, this newish place consistently attracts excellent rock, blues and other bands and singers.

St Louis Bar & Grill (☎ 416-480-0202, 2050 Yonge St) No cover. This uptown neighborhood place often has good R&B with dancing, and the food's pretty good.

C'est What? (☎ 416-867-9499, 67 Front St E) Cover $3-10. For a range of quality noncommercial music, this downstairs haunt has a steady following.

Montréal Bistro & Jazz Club (☎ 416-363-0179, 65 Sherbourne St) The fairly dressy Montréal brings in some known jazz musicians regularly.

Music Gallery (☎ 416-204-1080, **W** www.musicgallery.org, 197 John St) Head here for experimental or free jazz. No liquor is served, and it's only open September to June.

Free Times Café (☎ 416-967-1078, 320 College St) There's regular live folk music at this traditional bastion.

Allen's (☎ 416-463-3086, 143 Danforth Ave) Look for live Celtic music on Tuesday and Saturday nights at this popular restaurant/bar. Sometimes there's a cover charge if the band is big.

Tranzac (Toronto Australia New Zealand Club; ☎ 416-923-8137, 292 Brunswick Ave) Those from Down Under may want to drop in here, where there is a bar open to all. It can be quiet, but look for the good, folk-related concerts, especially gypsy-style Django Reinhart music.

Dance Clubs A range of nightclubs can be found around town, but by far the most happening place is the booming Entertainment District near the Skydome. The areas between Richmond St W and Adelaide St W, and around the small Duncan, John and Peter Sts are packed with dance clubs. The area is jammed on weekends; the best way to find a place to your taste is to take a wander and check the people standing in line to get in. Other busy streets are Blue Jays Way, and from there, King St W to John St. For variety, some places in the area offer pool and more of a hip pub atmosphere.

Montana's (☎ 416-595-5949, 145 John St) No cover. Upstairs, there are various rooms with dancing and an outdoor deck at this popular mingling bar. Downstairs is a casual restaurant.

Joker Club (☎ 416-598-1313, 318 Richmond St W) Cover around $10. This megaclub has three floors of action, from pool tables to various rooms blasting hip-hop, house or Top 40.

Guvernment (☎ 416-869-0045, 132 Queens Quay E) Cover around $10. Huge and multiroomed with various music mixes, it's got something for everyone who wants to move.

The Docks (☎ 416-461-3625, 11 Polson St) Cover around $10. A great place on a hot summer night, there are indoor dance floors, outside bars, activities and a wonderful view of the city across the water.

Bars Bar hours are generally 11am to 2am, as they are all over Ontario. Numerous clubs stay open until 3am or 4am without

serving any more alcohol, and who knows how many illegal mercurial boozecans where pricey drinks can be had at all hours are in existence. Beer can be bought retail at Brewers Retail Stores, often marked as the Beer Store, and liquor and wine can be purchased at Liquor Control Board of Ontario (LCBO) outlets.

Park Hyatt rooftop bar (☎ 416-925-1234, Bloor St W at Avenue Rd) For a pleasant and free view of the city, head here – you can sit under the sun and sip a cool one 18 floors above the masses; there is an inside section too.

Panorama (☎ 416-967-0000, Manulife Centre, 55 Bloor St W) This lounge on the 51st floor is popular with a generally younger but mixed crowd. A beer costs around $5.

Ye Olde Brunswick House (☎ 416-964-2242, 481 Bloor St W) This bar, also known simply as 'Brunswick Tavern,' is best described as a funky student hangout; it's part pub, part frat house and often a bit crazy.

Sneaky Dee's (☎ 416-603-3090, College St at Bathurst St) This bar is cheap and colorful – and that goes for the clientele as much as for the decor. Slide into a booth here for casual atmosphere and a good place to just hang. Decent food is served all day.

Oxygen Spa Bar (☎ 416-322-7733, 2044 Yonge St) For a real gas, experimentalists will

Hit me again: how the locals breathe easier in Toronto

want to inhale the atmosphere of Canada's first oxygen bar, modeled after the I-need-a-boost stations of Japan. Get hooked up to a pure oxygen hose for 20 minutes ($16) and turn back the clock on the aging process.

Gay & Lesbian Venues Toronto is a major gay center, with numerous businesses and bars catering specifically to the queer community. Downtown, the focus of the action is Church St around Wellesley St E – a busy residential/commercial mix that draws crowds for strolling and people-watching on weekends. Plenty of cafés and restaurants have sidewalk tables, which adds to the open, relaxed atmosphere.

Woody's (☎ 416-972-0887, 467 Church St) For years this has been a very popular gay bar.

Slack Alice (☎ 969-8742, 562 Church St) This busy, primarily lesbian spot has a welcoming, fun vibe and good dance music.

Tango (☎ 416-972-1662, 510 Church St) is a popular women's club. There are many others in the area.

Spectator Sports

Skydome The Blue Jays, of Major League Baseball's American League, play ball at the Skydome (☎ 416-341-1111, W www.skydome.com, 1 Blue Jays Way). They won the World Series in 1992 and 1993 – the only times that baseball's top prize has been won by a non-US team. The season runs May to September, and tickets, which cost $7 to $44, can be bought by phone with a credit card (☎ 416-341-1234), at the box office (gate 9 at the stadium) or from a ticket outlet in the CIBC building (Bay St at King St).

The Toronto Argonauts (☎ 416-872-5000), part of the professional Canadian Football League (CFL), also play in the Skydome. Tickets cost $12 to $42, and the season runs July to November.

Tickets are always available from scalpers at the stadium just prior to the games. After the game has started, it is often possible to get tickets for less than face value. Note that food and drink, especially beer, is expensive, and that bottles or cans cannot be taken into the dome. Take a jacket, as things cool off down here at night if the roof is open.

Air Canada Centre From September to April, the Maple Leafs, of the National Hockey League, play at the Air Canada Centre (ACC; ☎ 416-977-1641, W www.theaircanadacentre.com, Bay St at Lake Shore Blvd), also known as The Hangar. Tickets are hard to get at the box office, as every game is pretty well sold out, but they can be bought without difficulty from scalpers outside the door just before the game. Tickets cost $22 to $360.

From October to April, the National Basketball Association's Toronto Raptors (☎ 416-366-3865) also play at the ACC.

The lacrosse season of the Toronto Rock (☎ 416-596-3075) lasts from November to March. This game, which is Canada's oldest, is back big-time – it's one of the hottest games around. It's cheap, fun, rough, fast and not too commercial. Tickets run $18 to $45.

Woodbine Racetrack The racetrack (☎ 416-675-7223, 555 Rexdale Blvd), northwest of downtown, features thoroughbreds and standardbreds (harness racing) and is home to the prestigious Queen's Plate. By public transportation, take the subway to Islington and then catch the direct 'Race' bus. Admission is free, and bets start at $2.

Shopping

Shops dot every part of the city, but you'll find concentrations of stores in huge malls like the **Eaton Centre** (220 Yonge St) or neighborhood marketplaces like Kensington Market, where you can scoop up some funky bargains among the used- and vintage-clothing shops, or St Lawrence Market, which hosts an antique and flea market every Sunday (see Markets under Places to Eat for more information). The Harbourfront **Antique Market** (☎ 416-260-2622, 390 Queens Quay W; admission free; open 10am-5pm Tues-Sun) features 100 booths selling collectibles, with an additional outdoor section on Sunday.

The Yorkville district and Bloor St W just west of Yonge house some of the country's toniest, most exclusive shops. Queen St W from University Ave west all the way to Bathurst boasts a fascinating mélange of stores from tattoo parlors and condom shops to music, book and clothing outlets.

For overviews of other neighborhoods with shops, see the Neighborhoods section, earlier.

Outdoor Gear Many travelers find that the city offers an excellent range of quality camping and outdoor gear at a reasonable price. Among them are *Mountain Equipment Co-op* (☎ 416-340-2667, 400 King St W), *Trailhead* (☎ 416-977-7031, 370 King St W) and *Europe Bound Outfitters* (☎ 416-205-9992, 383 King St W), which also does rentals. For fine outdoor clothing, *Tilley Endurables* (☎ 416-203-0463, Queens Quay Terminal, Harbourfront) turns out some of the toughest (but stylish) low-maintenance threads around. They're expensive, but they really last.

Getting There & Away

Air The airport, Pearson International, is about 24km northwest of the downtown area in a part of the city known as Malton. This is actually a separate city, but you wouldn't know it from the continuous urban landscape. The major Canadian airlines fly in and out of Toronto, as do many of the internationals. Pearson is by far the busiest airport in the country.

The third terminal, known as Trillium Terminal, was the first in Canada to be developed, owned and operated by private interests rather than by the government. Food, drink and parking are costly everywhere in the airport but particularly at the Trillium Terminal.

When departing from the airport or picking someone up at arrivals, be sure to find out the terminal number. Signs on the roads into the airport direct you to each terminal and indicate which airlines they serve.

Air Canada (☎ 416-925-2311) flies to Montréal, Halifax and Calgary. WestJet (☎ 800-538-5696), the country's most successful discount carrier, has begun connecting Toronto and Calgary ($190!! one way), Edmonton, Vancouver and Victoria, and new destinations may be added. Definitely give WestJet a call, as the company gets high passenger praise.

Small Toronto City Centre Airport, on the lake at the foot of Bathurst St, is used by Air Canada commuter aircraft and private planes. The commuter flights are a lot quicker than the major flights, because you're already downtown – and you get a better look at the city, too. There are flights to and from Montréal and Ottawa.

Depending on current conditions, it may be economical to skip over to Buffalo to take advantage of the periodically much cheaper US airfares. For example, a flight from Buffalo to Seattle could cost hundreds of dollars less than the fare from, say, Toronto to Vancouver. At either end, a short bus ride links the Canadian cities. In recent years, US fares and the difference in the exchange rate have not warranted the expense of getting to Buffalo.

Bus The Metro Toronto Coach Terminal, used for out-of-town destinations, is central, on the corner of Bay and Dundas Sts. It's the station for the numerous bus lines that cover Ontario from Toronto. Seniors and those with international student identification may get discounts. Lockers can be found on the lower level, and the upper floor has a restaurant. There's a bakery and café on the other side of Bay St. On the evening prior to a holiday or long weekend, expect crowds, and arrive early to ensure getting a ticket before departure time.

For destinations in Eastern Ontario and north of Toronto, call ☎ 416-393-7911. This number covers Voyageur, PMCL (Penetang-Midland Coach Lines), Canar, Ontario Northland and Trentway Wager bus companies. Collectively, these lines serve Barrie, Huntsville, Montréal, Niagara Falls, North Bay, Orillia and Parry Sound, as well as some US destinations, including New York.

Greyhound (☎ 416-367-8747) pretty much covers all of Ontario west of Toronto, including the Niagara region, Guelph, Kitchener, London, Windsor, Sudbury and beyond to western Canadian cities such as Winnipeg and Vancouver. It also operates the route to Peterborough and Ottawa and runs to Buffalo, Detroit and New York.

Smaller, local bus lines around Ontario connect to towns served by one or more of the above major carriers.

Some routes have both slow, milk-run trips, which stop frequently, and other express, direct trips, which can be hours quicker. Ask about roundtrip tickets – some bus lines offer these at reduced rates.

There are five departures for Ottawa daily, and the five-hour trip costs $54 one way. To Montréal, there are seven buses daily, one of them an overnighter that leaves at 12:30am. Tickets are $79. To Niagara Falls, the two-hour trip is $25. A discounted sameday roundtrip ticket is offered. To Thunder Bay, buses depart at 1am and 5pm ($155 one way, about 20 hours).

Adjacent to the terminal, on the western side, is the bus station for (among other runs) the GO buses (☎ 416-869-3200), a government line that services many of the nearby surrounding towns, stopping frequently along the way. It's mainly used by commuters but goes a relatively long way west of Toronto (to Hamilton, for example).

GO buses also go to the satellite communities of Barrie (to the north) and Oshawa (to the east), supplementing the regular bus service. Trips in these directions are not as frequent as the westbound ones, and the downtown bus terminal is not used as the departure point. For Barrie, catch the GO bus at the Finch subway station during evening rush hour. For Oshawa, catch the bus at the York Mills subway station, also during the end-of-day rush hour. In the morning, the buses come into town.

Quasi-legal van services ferrying people between Toronto and Montréal or Ottawa at deep discount prices spring up and then fade away regularly. Look for ads in *Now* or *Eye*. With these companies, it's just a matter of 'meet at a corner, pay cash, go.' Be aware that these companies may not have full insurance coverage.

Train Grand old Union Station, used for VIA Rail (☎ 416-366-8411) trains, is convenient. It's on Front St (which runs east-west), at the bottom of University Ave, York and Bay Sts. The subway goes right into the station (the stop is called Union). Remember that five days' notice (preferably more) will get you a considerably cheaper fare. Students and seniors also get good discounts. The full fare rates are listed here.

The station has several restaurants, some fast-food outlets and a bar. Sometimes, on the arrival level just as you come out the gate from the train, a travelers' aid booth is in operation to help with basic directions and to answer questions.

There are frequent daily departures for Kingston, Montréal and Ottawa but fewer on weekends. The one-way fare to Ottawa is $90 (four hours), and to Montréal, it's $99 (five hours). For Montréal, some trips are faster, with fewer stops than others. To Sudbury, there are three trips weekly, departing on Tuesday, Thursday and Saturday ($63, 7½ hours). Note that for Sudbury, the train actually goes to Sudbury Junction, a station about 10km from the center of town. Other cities that can be reached by VIA include Niagara Falls and London.

Ontario Northland (☎ 416-314-3750) runs the *Northlander* train to northern Ontario destinations, including Huntville, North Bay, Temagami and the *Polar Bear Express* to Moosonee. For the latter, take the *Northlander* to Cochrane (once daily except Saturday) and make connections there. For details, see Cochrane, later. Fares from Toronto to Cochrane are $128/115/108 adult/senior/student.

Amtrak (☎ 800-872-7245, ⬛ www .amtrak.com) trains link Toronto's Union Station with Buffalo, Chicago or New York City, with stops or other possible connections along the way. Reservations are needed for all trains.

GO trains also use the station; see Getting Around, later.

Car If you're planning on renting a car, be aware that many places require that you be at least 21 years old; for some places, the minimum age is 23. There are countless rental agencies in the city, but booking ahead, especially on holidays, is always recommended. The mandatory insurance costs extra, and goes up as the driver's age decreases (it can be over $20 per day). Remember, your own car insurance may cover rental, and many credit cards offer car rental insurance if payment for the rental is made on the card – call your bank to find out if your card is one of these.

Wheels 4 Rent (☎ 416-585-7782, 77 Nassau St), in Kensington Market, is central for used cars. If you have a credit card and are over 24, rates are excellent at $30 a day, including insurance, plus 9½¢ per kilometer over the first 150km.

Also worth a call is Economy Car Rental (☎ 416-961-7500, 374 Dupont St), between Spadina Ave and Bathurst St. New cars start at $33 a day with 200km free (plus 12½¢ per kilometer) for a compact vehicle. There are weekly and monthly rates, too.

National (☎ 416-364-4191, 800-227-7368), which has an office in Union Station as well as several other downtown locations and one at the airport, is a more standard rental company and offers new cars. Its average rates start at $43 per day for compact cars, with unlimited mileage. The company also offers weekend specials. Child seats and ski racks are available.

For long-distance trips, there are driveaway cars – about half a dozen places are listed in the Yellow Pages (under Automobile). One company is Auto Drive-Away Co (☎ 416-225-8790, ⬛ www.torontodriveaway

A sea kayak tour returning to Tofino, Pacific Rim National Park, British Columbia

Hiking through the Larch Valley, Banff, Alberta

Snowboarding in Calgary, Alberta

Climbers ascending to the summit of Mt Victoria (3464m), Banff National Park, Alberta

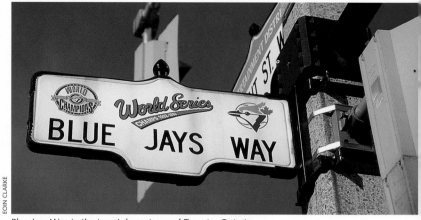
EOIN CLARKE

Blue Jays Way in the team's hometown of Toronto, Ontario

RICHARD CUMMINS

Thunderbird Park, BC

JON DAVISON

The CN Tower, Toronto, Ontario

THOMAS HUHTI

Point Riche Lighthouse, NF

RICHARD CUMMINS

Checking out the sights in a trolley, Vancouver, British Columbia

.com, 5803 Yonge St), which has cars for Canadian and US destinations. Also check the newspaper classified ads in either the *Toronto Sun* or the *Toronto Star* and the travel ads in *Now*. (Also see Drive-Aways in the introductory Getting Around chapter.)

Boat From the dock, at 225 Queens Quay E, Sea Flight Hydrofoil Jet Lines (☎ 416-504-8825, 877-504-8825) has boats that depart for a speedy, one-hour trip to the Queenston Dock, between Niagara Falls and Niagara-on-the-Lake. The $35 one-way fare includes a shuttle bus to either one. Call for schedule.

Hitchhiking Thumbing is illegal on the expressways in the city. On city streets, it's not done, except by women offering their company for a price. Safety should be a concern, but you can hitchhike on Hwy 401 out of town or on the lead-in ramps in town.

If you're heading east for Montréal, the best bet is to take city transit to roughly the corner of Port Union Rd and Hwy 401 in Scarborough, near the Toronto Zoo. To get there from downtown is a bit complicated, and the fastest way takes about 1½ hours. Take the subway east to the Kennedy stop. From there, catch the Scarborough LRT (light-rail transit) to the Lawrence East station. Transfer to the Lawrence East 54E bus. Go east to East Dr at Lawrence East. Transfer (free again) to the Rouge Hill No 13 bus to Hwy 401.

If you're going west, take the subway to Kipling. Transfer to the West Mall bus No 112 or 112B, and go to the corner of Carlingview Dr and International Blvd, almost at Hwy 401. This is just at the city limits, so you are okay on the highway, but it could be busy and difficult for cars to stop at rush hour. Public transit to this point takes about one hour from downtown.

If you're northbound, you're stuck. The best bet is to take the bus to Barrie and then hitchhike the rest of the way on Hwy 400 or Hwy 11, depending on your destination. The Trans Canada Hwy westbound can be picked up at Sudbury.

Getting Around
To/From the Airport There are several ways to get to the airport. The cheapest is to take the subway to Kipling on the east-west line. From there, transfer (free) to the *Airport Rocket* bus (No 192), which takes about 30 minutes. Or you can take the subway to the Lawrence West stop on the north-south Spadina-University line and catch the Malton No 58A bus from there.

The next method is to take the subway to either the Yorkdale or York Mills stations and catch the GO bus ($3.25) from there.

Lastly (and easiest and most costly), the Pacific Western Airport Express (☎ 905-564-6333) runs every 20 minutes to and from the airport and major hotels, such as the Royal York and Sheraton, as well as the bus and train stations and City Hall. The one-way fare is $15, and the trip takes about 80 minutes. These buses operate roughly between the hours of 5am and 10:30pm. The buses leave the airport terminals from outside the arrival levels.

Taxi fare from Yonge and Bloor Sts to the airport is $45; it takes about 45 minutes.

A shuttle bus, which is free for ticketholders for the City Centre Airport, runs from the Royal York Hotel to that airport. Otherwise there is TTC service: take the streetcar south on Bathurst St to Lake Shore Blvd (generally known as 'Lake Shore Rd' or 'The Lakeshore'). From there, the City Centre Airport is a two-block walk and then a short, *very* short ferry ride.

Toronto Transit Commission (TTC) The city has a good subway, bus and streetcar system. There's a 24-hour recorded route- and fare-information line (☎ 416-393-8663)and another line for more specific information (☎ 416-393-4636). Regular adult fare is $2.25 (cash), or 10 tickets (or tokens) for $18. Day passes ($7.50) are also available. Tickets or tokens are available in the subway and at some convenience and corner variety stores. Once one fare is paid, you can transfer to any other bus, subway or streetcar within one hour at no extra charge. One ticket can get you anywhere the system goes. Get a transfer from the driver, or in the subway from the machine inside the turnstiles where you pay the fare.

The subway system is clean and fast. There is one east-west line, which goes along Bloor St/Danforth Ave, and two north-south lines, one up Yonge St and one along Spadina Ave, where some of the stops are decorated with the work of Canadian artists.

The aboveground Scarborough RT train line connects the subway with the northeastern part of the city, from the Victoria Park stop to the Scarborough Town Centre. The Harbourfront LRT car runs above and below ground from Union Station (on Front St) to Harbourfront, along Queens Quay W to Spadina Ave and back again.

The subway runs until about 1:30am and begins at 6am (except on Sunday, when it starts at 9am). Bus hours vary; some run late but are infrequent.

The TTC system connects with bus routes in surrounding suburban cities such as Mississauga, Markham and Vaughan.

GO Train GO trains (☎ 416-869-3200) leave Union Station from 7am to 11:30pm daily, serving the suburbs of Toronto east to Whitby and west to Hamilton. Ticket inspection is random and on an honor system. Service is fast and steady throughout the day and frequent during weekday rush hours.

Streetcar Toronto is one of the few North American cities still using streetcars. They roll on St Clair Ave and on College, Dundas, Queen and King Sts, all of which run east-west, and Spadina Ave, which runs north-south.

Car All over Ontario, you can turn right on a red light after first having made a full stop. All vehicles must stop for streetcars, behind the rear doors, while the streetcar is loading or unloading passengers. Pedestrians use the painted crosswalks across the street, and traffic must stop for them. If you're driving, keep an eye out for these.

In Toronto, parking is expensive – usually about $3 to $4 for the first half hour, then slightly less. Most places have a flat rate after 6pm. Cheapest are the municipal lots, which are scattered around the downtown area and marked by green signs.

Rush hours are impossible, so try to avoid them. And watch where you park during rush hours, because the tow trucks show no mercy, and getting your vehicle back will cost a bundle in cash and aggravation.

Traffic is generally horrendous around the edges of town, and except for during winter, construction never ends. Always budget extra time for delays.

Hwy 407, running east-west from Markham to Mississauga for about 40km just north of the city, is an electronic toll road. Cameras record your license plate and the time and distance traveled. If you don't have a prepaid electronic gizmo on the car, a bill is mailed to you (bills are sent out of province and to some US states).

Bicycle The city has a very good website (W www.city.toronto.on.ca/cycling) for people planning on getting around Toronto by bicycle.

When cycling, be careful on the streetcar rails; cross at right angles or you'll land on your ear. Also watch for rain grates with slats *parallel* to the road! Riders under 18 years of age must wear a helmet.

See the Activities section, earlier, for places to rent bicycles.

Pedicab Pedicabs – deluxe bicycle rickshaws pedaled by sweating, fit young men – can be hired in summer along Yonge St, around the Entertainment District and in Yorkville. Prices are around $4 per person per block.

AROUND TORONTO

Within an approximate 1½-hour drive of the city are a large number of small, old towns that were once centers for local farming communities. Some of the country's best land is here, but working farms are giving way to urban sprawl, and many of the old downtown areas are now surrounded by modern housing developments. Still, desperate city dwellers make day trips around the district, especially on a Sunday, popular. There is still some nice rolling landscape and a few conservation areas (essentially parks), which are used for walking or picnicking. Quite a few of the towns attract antique hunters, and craft and gift shops are plentiful.

Northwest of Toronto, **Caledon** is one of the larger and closer examples and is set in the Caledon Hills. Not far southwest of Caledon, in **Terra Cotta**, is *Terra Cotta Inn* (☎ *905-873-2223, 175 King St*). It makes a good place to stop later in the day for an afternoon tea of scones, cream and jam. Call to check hours and dates of operation. Terra Cotta is also one of the closest points to Toronto for access to an afternoon's walk along part of the **Bruce Trail**, which runs for 780km north-south. The **Hockley Valley** area, near Orangeville, provides more of the same. The **Credit River** has trout fishing, and in winter, the area is not bad for cross-country skiing, although the hills aren't high enough for downhill skiing.

McMichael Collection

In Kleinburg, the McMichael Collection (☎ 905-893-1121, Ⓦ *www.mcmichael.on.ca, 10365 Islington Ave; adult/senior & student/family $12/9/25; open 10am-5pm daily June–mid-Oct, 10am-4pm Tues-Sun rest of the year*) is an excellent art gallery that consists of handmade wooden buildings in a pleasant rural setting and displays an extensive and impressive collection of Canadian paintings. Canada's best-known painters, collectively termed the Group of Seven, are well represented. If you're going to see northern Ontario, where much of the group's work was done, a visit to the McMichael Collection is all the more worthwhile. Other exhibits include Inuit and West Coast Native Indian art. Sculptures, prints and paintings are on display. Special changing exhibitions may feature photography or one particular artist or school of work. The surrounding wooded property is crossed with walking trails, where deer may be seen. The gallery has a book/gift shop and a restaurant. Schoolchildren often visit on weekday mornings.

Apart from its main attraction, Kleinburg is also home to numerous antique shops, small galleries, craft shops and places for a nosh.

The town is 18km north from the corner of Islington Ave and Hwy 401 in Toronto. To get there by car, go north up Hwy 427 to Hwy 27 and continue north. Turn right at Nashville Rd.

Public transportation is limited and a little awkward, but can be used. There is no service, though, on weekends or holidays. First, take the Toronto subway west to Islington on the east-west line. From there, catch bus No 37D north for around 35 minutes to Steeles Ave. At the intersection of Steeles and Islington Aves, transfer to the Route 13 York Region Transit bus. The only one of these of any use for those wishing to visit the gallery is at 8:45am, so you must make this connection. The bus will take you

The Magnificent Seven

The Group of Seven was a bunch of painters who came together in 1920 to celebrate the Canadian landscape in a new and vital way.

Fired by an almost adolescent enthusiasm, this men's group used paintbrushes to explore and capture on canvas the rugged wilderness of Canada. The energy they felt then can be seen today in some stunning paintings – vibrant, light-filled canvases of Canada's mountains, lakes, forests and townships.

This gung-ho group of painterly talent spent a lot of time traipsing the wilds of northern Ontario, capturing the landscape through the seasons and under all weather conditions. Favorite places included Algonquin Park, Georgian Bay, Lake Superior and Algoma. The Algoma Central Railway even converted an old boxcar into living quarters for the painters – a freight train would deposit them on a siding for a week or more, and the intrepid painters would set off, on foot or by canoe, to paint from morning till night.

The original seven members (the group later expanded to become the Canadian Group of Painters) were Franklin Carmichael, Lawren Harris, AY Jackson, Frank Johnston (later replaced by AJ Casson), Arthur Lismer, JEH MacDonald and FH Varley. Although he died before the group was officially formed, painter Tom Thompson was considered by other members as the group's leading light.

An experienced outdoorsman, Thompson drowned in 1917, just as he was producing some of his most powerful work. His deep connection to the land can be clearly seen in his vivid paintings. While the group took studios in Toronto (they sketched outside but produced finished work indoors), Thompson preferred working and living in his small rustic shack out back. And as soon as the winter ice broke, he'd be off to the great north.

The best places to see work by the Group of Seven are the McMichael Collection, in Kleinburg, north of Toronto; the Art Gallery of Ontario, in Toronto; and the National Gallery of Canada, in Ottawa.

to the gallery gate in about 20 minutes, from where it is a 10 minute walk in. On the way back, bus No 13 leaves at about 5pm and 6pm. To check details, call York Region Transit (☎ 905-762-2100).

Dunlap Observatory

Just north of the Toronto city limits, the Dunlap Observatory (☎ 905-884-2112, W www.ddo.astro.utoronto.ca, 123 Hillsview Dr, Richmond Hill; adult/student $6/4; call or see website for tour times) has what was once the world's second-largest telescope; it remains the biggest in Canada. A brief introductory talk is given to accompany a slide show, which is then followed by a bit of stargazing through the scope.

You must call ahead on a weekday for reservations. To reach the observatory, drive up Hwy 11 (the continuation of Yonge St) toward Richmond Hill; you'll see the white dome on the right. For public transportation, Go Transit buses from the Finch subway terminal stop at Hillsview Dr.

Cathedral of the Transfiguration

It seems nobody builds churches any more, especially on the grand old scale. But north of Toronto, straight up Hwy 404 from the city in the village of Gormley (near the town of Markham), there is one heck of an exception. Opened in 1987, this Slovak Byzantine Catholic cathedral (☎ 905-887-5706, 10350 Woodbine Ave; call for opening hours) is one of the country's largest, standing 62.7m high to the tip of its copper-topped spire. Based on a smaller version found in the Czech Republic, this is a 1000-seat church. One of the impressive features is the French-made main bell, ringing in at 16,650kg, second in size only to the one in Sacré Coeur in Paris. It's also the first cathedral in the Western Hemisphere to be blessed by a pope – John Paul II did the honors.

Pickering Nuclear Plant

About 40km east of Toronto on the Lake Ontario shoreline is this nuclear power station (☎ 905-837-7272, 839-1151, 1675 Montgomery Park Rd; admission free; open 9am-4pm Mon-Fri), which has portions open to the public. Whether you're pro or con on nuclear plants, you could find out something you didn't know. Free films and displays in

the visitors' center explain the operation. In-plant tours have been suspended since the September 11, 2001, terrorist attacks, and plans are uncertain. Look for the signs on Hwy 401 – the plant is at the foot of Liverpool Rd. If your kids are born glowing in the dark, don't blame Lonely Planet.

Cullen Gardens & Miniature Village

About a 45-minute drive east from Toronto on Hwy 401, in the town of Whitby, is a 10-hectare site of carefully tended gardens (☎ 905-668-1600, 300 Taunton Rd W; adult/senior/child/family $12/9/5/40; open 10am-10pm daily), which are interspersed with miniature models. A path, which will take two or three hours to walk if you're looking at all the impressive detail, winds through the gardens past a miniature village, modern suburban subdivision, farm and a scene from cottage country. The buildings, people and activities portrayed offer, in a sense, a glimpse of life in southern Ontario. The floral aspect of the gardens – although colorful and quite extensive – should not be confused with botanical gardens but rather should be viewed as the setting for the various scenes. The park appeals to a variety of people, particularly children.

The gardens are off Hwy 12, about 5km north along Hwy 401. When hunger strikes, there is a pleasant picnic and snack-bar area (bring your own food) or a fairly pricey sitdown restaurant.

Canadian Automotive Museum

Farther east, near Oshawa (a center for car assembly), this museum (☎ 905-576-1222, 99 Simcoe St S; admission $5; open 9am-5pm daily) has a collection of 65 cars. Included are a Redpath Runabout from 1890, a Model T (of course) and various automotive memorabilia.

Parkwood Estate

Also in Oshawa is the estate of RS McLaughlin (☎ 905-433-4311, 270 Simcoe St N, Parkwood; admission $6; call for hours), who once ran the Canadian division of General Motors. The property consists of a 55-room mansion with antique furnishings, set amid large gardens. The admission price includes a guide. Afternoon tea is served outside during summer and in the conservatory during winter. Call for hours and days closed – they vary.

Local Conservation Areas

Southern Ontario is urban. To offset this somewhat, the government has designated many conservation areas – small nature parks for walking, picnicking and (sometimes) fishing, swimming and cross-country skiing. The quality and characteristics of the areas vary quite markedly. While some protect noteworthy geographic areas, others are more historic in emphasis. Generally, they are not wild areas, and some are not even pretty, but they are close to major centers and do offer some relief from concrete. The tourist office has a list of those around Toronto and within a 160km radius of town. The Metro Toronto Conservation Authority (☎ 416-661-6600) is responsible for the development and operation of these areas, most of which are difficult to reach without a vehicle.

One place that makes a good, quick escape on a nice summer day is the large **Albion Hills Conservation Area** (☎ 905-880-4855, Hwy 50; admission $4; open 9am-dusk). It's primarily a quiet, wooded area with walking trails. In winter, it allows for decent cross-country skiing. It's on the west side of town; take Indian Line (by the airport) north. It becomes Hwy 50, which then leads to the park.

Also in this region, near Kleinburg, is the **Kortright Centre for Conservation** (☎ 905-832-2289, 9550 Pine Valley Dr, Woodbridge; admission $5; open 10am-4pm daily). There are trails here, too, but it's more of a museum, with displays and demonstrations on resources, wildlife, ecology, etc.

West of Toronto, near Milton, there are two conservation areas to consider visiting. **Crawford Lake** (☎ 905-854-0234, Steeles Ave at Guelph Line; admission $4; open 10am-4pm daily May-Oct) is one of the most interesting in the entire system. The deep, cool and pretty glacial lake set in the woods is surrounded by walking trails. Details on its formation and unique qualities are given in the well-laid-out interpretive center. Also on the site is a reconstructed 15th-century Iroquoian longhouse village. Crawford Lake is 5km south of Hwy 401, down a road called Guelph Line. There is a snack bar and some picnic tables at the site. The Bruce Trail (see Tobermory in the Georgian Bay & Lakelands section, later in this chapter) also runs through the park.

In about the same general area is the **Mountsberg Conservation Area** (☎ 905-854-2276, Millburough Line; admission $4; open 10am-4pm daily). To reach it, exit south off Hwy 401 at Guelph Line and continue to the No 9 Sideroad. Travel west to Town Line and turn north for 3.2km. It's 19km west of the town of Milton. The site provides a series of country-related educational programs throughout the year. One of the best is the maple-syrup/sugaring-off demonstration put on each spring; it explains in detail the history, collection and production of this Canadian specialty (for more information about maple syrup, see Eastern Townships in the Québec chapter).

Ottawa

pop 785,000

Ottawa arouses in Canadians the mixed emotions worthy of a nation's capital. It sits attractively on the south bank of the Ottawa River at its confluence with the Rideau River. The gently rolling Gatineau Hills of Québec are visible to the north.

The city attracts five million tourists a year, many just to see what the heck the capital is like. The abundance of museums and cultural activities is another enticement. And then, of course, in summer, you can see the traditionally garbed Royal Canadian Mounted Police (RCMP), also known as Mounties. You may be surprised by the amount of French you hear around town. Québec is just a stone's throw away, but the fact that most federal government workers are required to be bilingual is probably just as much of a factor. The government is the city's largest employer, and the stately, Gothic-style Parliament Buildings act as landmarks. Despite this, the city is now known as Silicon Valley North for its large and skilled computer, technology and telecommunications work force.

Ottawa has never been called an exciting city, but with the high-tech developments, steady growth, two universities, increasing nightlife, good food and progressive outlook, it's definitely ramping up. There's tons to do – and that's supplemented with an almost endless array of special events. The air is not fouled by heavy industry; the streets are wide and clean; and everywhere, people are jogging and cycling. Ottawa, a happening place? Who'd a thunk it?

History

The area's first inhabitants were the Algonquin Indians, followed by French fur traders. After 1759, British settlers started arriving, and in 1826, British troops founded a permanent base in present-day Ottawa in order to build the Rideau Canal (linking the Ottawa River to Lake Ontario). First called Bytown, Ottawa got its present-day name in 1855, and Queen Victoria made it the capital in 1857. After WWII, Paris city planner Jacques Greber was put in charge of plans to beautify Ottawa. The pleasant city is now dotted with parks, and most of the land along the waterways is for recreational use.

Orientation

Ottawa's central core is quite compact, making walking a feasible method of getting around. Downtown Ottawa is divided into eastern and western sections by the Rideau Canal. On the western side, Wellington St, the principal east-west street, is where you'll find Parliament Hill and many government buildings. The Ottawa River lies just to the north of Wellington, and one block south is Sparks St, a pedestrian mall with shops and fast-food outlets. Perpendicular to Wellington is Bank St, which is the main shopping street and home to many restaurants. Just to the west of the canal are Elgin St and Confederation Square, with the National War Memorial in its center. The large, French-looking palace is the Château Laurier hotel.

The Rideau Canal flows south through town, with walking and cycling paths at its edge. In winter, the frozen canal is used for skating.

Gladstone Ave roughly marks the southern boundary of the downtown area. About 8km from the Château Laurier, the canal joins Dows Lake. On the other side of the canal is Ottawa East, with Rideau St as the main street. The huge Rideau Centre, a three-level enclosed shopping mall with an overhead walkway across the street, is here. North, between George and York Sts, is Byward Market.

Along Wellington St and up Sussex Dr are many 19th-century buildings. Along Sussex Dr between George and St Patrick Sts, walking through the archways or alleys leads to a series of old connected courtyards, where you may find an outdoor café. North up Sussex Dr and to the left (west) is Nepean Point. The view is well worth the short walk.

Bank St south of the canal between Euclid and Cameron Aves has numerous antique and collectibles shops, as well as cafés where you can ponder your purchases.

There are four bridges across to Hull. The Portage Bridge, which leads into Wellington St on the Ottawa side, is the one to take to end up in downtown Hull.

Information

The museums and attractions of Ottawa are often in a state of flux and are frequently closed, either being renovated, repaired, upgraded or moved. If there is something you really wish to see, it's a good idea to call first to find out its current status. Also note that admission at many of them is free one day or evening of the week. Note that many of Ottawa's sites are closed on Monday.

Nearly all day and night, the market area of Ottawa is busy. Late at night, however, it does get a bit of an edge to it, with some drug and prostitution traffic. Walking alone in the quieter areas in the wee hours should probably be avoided.

The efficient tourist office, called Capital Infocentre (☎ 613-239-5000, 800-465-1867, W www.capcan.ca, 90 Wellington St), is opposite the Parliament Buildings. It's open 8:30am to 9pm daily from mid-May to the beginning of September and 9am to 5pm daily during the rest of the year. There's parking in the World Exchange Plaza (111 Albert St), one block south. If you need a travel agency, Travel Cuts (☎ 613-565-3555, 740 Bank St) has an Ottawa branch.

The World of Maps and Travel Books (☎ 613-724-6776, 1235 Wellington St) has an excellent selection of maps (including topographical ones) and guidebooks. Chapters (☎ 613-241-0073, 47 Rideau St) is a good general store and is open every day. The main branch of the Ottawa public library (☎ 613-236-0301, 120 Metcalfe St) has Internet access.

Several banks can be found along Sparks St. Accu-Rate Foreign Exchange (☎ 613-596-0612,

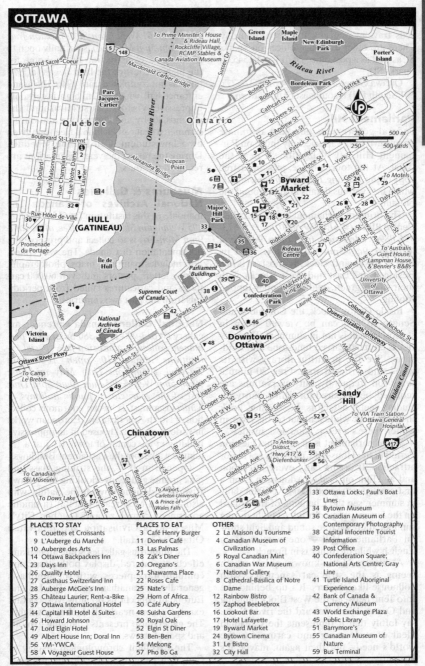

OTTAWA

PLACES TO STAY	PLACES TO EAT	OTHER
1 Couettes et Croissants	3 Café Henry Burger	2 La Maison du Tourisme
9 L'Auberge du Marché	11 Domus Café	4 Canadian Museum of
10 Auberge des Arts	13 Las Palmas	Civilization
14 Ottawa Backpackers Inn	18 Zak's Diner	5 Royal Canadian Mint
23 Days Inn	20 Oregano's	6 Canadian War Museum
26 Quality Hotel	21 Shawarma Place	7 National Gallery
27 Gasthaus Switzerland Inn	22 Roses Cafe	8 Cathedral-Basilica of Notre
28 Auberge McGee's Inn	25 Nate's	Dame
35 Château Laurier; Rent-a-Bike	29 Horn of Africa	12 Rainbow Bistro
37 Ottawa International Hostel	30 Café Aubry	15 Zaphod Beeblebrox
44 Capital Hill Hotel & Suites	48 Suisha Gardens	16 Lookout Bar
46 Howard Johnson	50 Royal Oak	17 Hotel Lafayette
47 Lord Elgin Hotel	52 Elgin St Diner	19 Byward Market
49 Albert House Inn; Doral Inn	53 Ben-Ben	24 Bytown Cinema
56 YM-YWCA	54 Mekong	31 Le Bistro
58 A Voyageur Guest House	57 Pho Bo Ga	32 City Hall

33 Ottawa Locks; Paul's Boat Lines	
34 Bytown Museum	
36 Canadian Museum of Contemporary Photography	
38 Capital Infocentre Tourist Information	
39 Post Office	
40 Confederation Square; National Arts Centre; Gray Line	
41 Turtle Island Aboriginal Experience	
42 Bank of Canada & Currency Museum	
43 World Exchange Plaza	
45 Public Library	
51 Barrymore's	
55 Canadian Museum of Nature	
59 Bus Terminal	

111 Albert St, 2nd floor), in the World Exchange Plaza, has longer hours than most and sells traveler's checks. It's open Saturday. There are other exchange offices on Sparks St, as well as a post office (☎ 613-844-1545, 59 Sparks St).

Ottawa General Hospital (☎ 613-737-7777, 501 Smyth Rd) is southeast of downtown.

Parliament Hill

Federal government buildings dominate downtown Ottawa, especially those on Parliament Hill, off Wellington St near the canal. At the tourist office, pick up a free copy of the *Walking Tour of Parliament Hill*, which lists various details in and around the buildings.

The primary Parliament Building, called **Centre Block** (☎ *613-239-5000, tours* ☎ *613-996-0896; admission free; open 9am-8pm Mon-Fri, 9am-5pm Sat & Sun)*, with its Peace Tower and clock, is most striking. Beside it are East and West Blocks, with their sharp, green, oxidized copper-topped roofing.

Inside Centre Block, the Commons and Senate sit and can be viewed when in session (which is not in summer). The interior is all hand-carved limestone and sandstone. See the beautiful library with its wood and wrought iron. Free 20-minute tours run frequently, but reservations are required; be prepared for tight security, including metal detectors. In summer, book the tour in the white tent out on the lawn; in winter, there's a reservation desk inside.

When parliament is in session, Question Period in the House of Commons is a major attraction. It occurs early every afternoon and at 11am on Friday. Admission is on a first-come, first-served basis. At 10am daily in summer, see the Changing of the Guard on the lawns – very colorful. At night during summer, there's a free sound and light show on Parliament Hill – one version is in English while the other is in French.

A bizarre, little-known quirk worth seeing is the stray-cat sanctuary, with dollhouse-like shelters. It's up behind the Info Tent, between the West Block building and Centre Block, toward the river. Some say loftily that it represents the Canadian ideal of welcoming and caring for the world's needy, but then again, maybe it's just nutty.

Supreme Court of Canada

This rather intimidating structure (☎ *613-995-5361, 301 Wellington St; admission free; open 9am-5pm Mon-Fri)* is partially open to nonlitigants. Construction of the home for the highest court of the land began in 1939 but was not completed until 1946. The grand entrance hall, which is 12m high, is certainly impressive. Visitors can stroll around the grounds, lobby and courtroom, and during summer, a visit can include a free tour given by a law student. Call for the schedule. During the rest of the year, reservations are required for tours.

Museums & Galleries

National Archives of Canada The mandate of this institution (☎ *613-995-5138, 395 Wellington St; admission free; open 9am-9pm Mon-Fri)* is to collect and preserve the documentation of Canada. The vast collection includes paintings, maps, photographs, diaries, letters, posters and even 60,000 cartoons and caricatures culled from periodicals from the past two centuries.

National Gallery Canada's premier art gallery (☎ *613-990-1985, 380 Sussex Dr; permanent collection admission free, special exhibitions about $10; open 10am-6pm Fri-Wed, 10am-8pm Thur May–mid-Oct; 10am-5pm Wed & Fri-Sun, 10am-8pm Thur rest of the year; closed public holidays in winter)* is a must. It has an enormous collection of North American and European works in various media, all housed in an impressive building in the center of town. It's just a 15-minute walk from the Parliament Buildings.

Opened in 1988, the striking glass and pink granite gallery overlooking the Ottawa River was designed by Moshe Safdie, who also created Montréal's Habitat (a unique apartment complex) and Québec City's Musée de la Civilisation and renovated Ottawa's City Hall.

The numerous galleries, some arched and effectively colored, display both classic and contemporary pieces, with the emphasis generally on Canadian artists. The US and European collections do, however, contain examples from nearly all the heavyweights. The gallery also presents changing exhibits and special shows.

The excellent chronological display of Canadian painting and sculpture not only gives a history of Canadian art but also, in a real sense, provides an outline of the development of the country itself, beginning with the depictions of Native Indian life at the time the Europeans arrived.

If you're in need of a recharging break, two pleasant courtyards offer the eyes a rest. Between them sits one of the gallery's most unusual and most appealing components, the beautifully restored 1888 **Rideau St Chapel**, which was saved from destruction a few blocks away.

On Level 2, along with the contemporary and international work, is the **Inuit Gallery**, and one room for the display of some of the extensive and fine **photography collection**.

The complex is large; you'll need a few hours, and you'll still tire before seeing all the exhibits, let alone the changing film and video presentations, lectures and concerts. There's a decent café, a restaurant, and a very fine shop with gifts and books. Underneath the gallery are two levels of parking.

Bytown Museum & Ottawa Locks Focusing on city history, Bytown Museum (☎ 613-234-4570; admission $5; open 10am-5pm Mon-Sat, 1pm-5pm Sun May–mid-Oct, call for rest of the year) is in the oldest stone building in Ottawa. It's east of Parliament Hill, beside the canal – go down the stairs from Wellington St and back to the locks at the river. Used during construction of the canal for storing military equipment and money, it now contains artifacts and documents pertaining to local history.

On the ground floor, Parks Canada runs an exhibit about the building of the canal.

The series of locks at the edge of the Ottawa River in the Colonel By Valley, between the Château Laurier and the Parliament Buildings, marks the north end of the 198km Rideau Canal, which runs to Kingston and the St Lawrence River. Colonel By, who was put in charge of constructing the canal, set up his headquarters here in 1826. Though never fulfilling any military purpose, the canal was used commercially for a while and then fell into disuse. The locks are now maintained by the government as heritage parks.

Canadian Museum of Contemporary Photography Wedged in between the Château Laurier and the canal in a reconstructed railway tunnel, the CMCP (☎ 613-990-8257, 1 Rideau Canal; admission free; open 10am-6pm Fri-Wed, 10am-8pm Thur May–mid-Oct; 10am-5pm Wed & Fri-Sun, 10am-8pm Thur mid-Oct–May) is the historic- and contemporary-photo museum. Originally part of the National Film Board, this is where the still photography division houses its photographic research departments and the country's vast photographic archives.

Unfortunately, gallery space is limited, and you may want to check what's on before visiting. Exhibits are not always of Canadians' work and may not be of very much interest to the casual viewer unacquainted with esoteric approaches to the photographic medium. Shows change quarterly.

Canadian War Museum & Vimy House This museum (☎ 613-776-8600, 330 Sussex Dr; adult/veteran/family $4/free/$9, admission free Sun morning; open 9:30am-5pm Fri-Wed, 9:30am-8pm Thur May–mid-Oct; 9:30am-5pm Tues-Wed & Fri-Sun, 9:30am-8pm Thur mid-Oct–May), with Canada's largest war-related collection, contains all manner of things military and traces Canadian military history. The life-size replica of a WWI trench is good. The museum also contains the country's largest collection of war art.

Renowned architect Raymond Moriyama has been selected to design the new war museum, which is scheduled to open in 2005, just west of Parliament Hill. He promises it will be unique and capture international interest.

Enthusiasts should ask about little-known Vimy House (same ☎ as museum, 221 Champagne Ave N; admission free; open 10am-4pm daily May-Oct, 10am-4pm Saturday Oct-May), a warehouse for heavy artillery, which is west along Wellington St (about 12 minutes by car).

Currency Museum If you like to look at money, you can see lots more of it at the Currency Museum (☎ 613-782-8914, Bank of Canada, 245 Sparks St; admission free; open 10:30am-5pm Mon-Sat, 1pm-5pm Sun June-Aug; closed Mon rest of the year). Various displays tell the story of money through the ages, from whales' teeth to collectors' banknotes.

Canadian Museum of Nature South of the downtown area, this museum (☎ 613-566-4700, 240 McLeod St at Metcalfe St; adult/senior/child/family $6/5/2.50/13, half-price Thurs, then free after 5pm; open 9:30am-5pm Fri-Wed, 9:30am-8pm Thur May-Labor Day; 10am-5pm Tues-Sun rest of the year) is housed in the attractive old Victorian building. The four-story museum is home to exhibits that foster an appreciation of nature, including a good section on the dinosaurs once found in Alberta. Also excellent are the realistic mammal and bird dioramas depicting Canadian wildlife. Major temporary exhibits on specific mammal, mineral or ecological subjects are a feature.

The **Viola MacMillan Mineral Gallery** is amazing, with some of the largest gems and minerals you're ever likely to see. The simulated mine comes complete with a shaky elevator. The East Coast tidal zone recreation is also very realistic. A separate section of the museum is geared toward children, and there's a cafeteria.

From Confederation Square, take bus No 5, 6 or 14 down Elgin St. Walking from the Parliament Buildings takes about 20 minutes.

Canada Aviation Museum This collection of over 100 aircraft is housed in a huge triangular building (about the size of four football fields) at Rockcliffe Airport (☎ 613-993-2010, 11 Aviation Parkway; adult/senior/child $6/4/2, free after 5pm Thur; open 9am-5pm Mon-Wed & Fri-Sun, 9am-9pm Thur May-Labor Day; 10am-5pm Tues, Wed & Fri, 10am-9pm Thur Labor Day-May). See planes ranging from the Silver Dart of 1909 to the first turbo-powered Viscount passenger carrier, right through to more recent jets. Peace- and wartime planes are equally represented; included is the renowned Spitfire. The Cessna Crane is the very one your author's father (Alexander Lightbody) trained in for the RCAF.

Other exhibits include aviation-related video games and audiovisual presentations.

Call to check opening hours, as they vary with attendance levels and the time of year. The museum is about 5km northeast (along Rockcliffe Parkway) from the downtown area, near the river and the Canadian Forces base.

Canada Science & Technology Museum This museum (☎ 613-991-3044, 1867 St Laurent Blvd; adult/senior/child/family $6/5/2/12; open 9am-5pm daily May-Sept, 9am-5pm Tues-Sun rest of the year), on the corner of Russell Rd southeast of downtown, has all kinds of participatory scientific learning exhibits. Try things out, test yourself, watch physical laws in action, see optical illusions. Also on display are farm machines, trains, model ships and stagecoaches. The bicycle and motorcycle collections are good. Higher-tech exhibits include computers and communication technologies. Make sure not to miss the incubator, where you can see live chicks in various stages of hatching.

The large display on space technology is interesting, with an assortment of Canadian space artifacts. An astronomy section has films and slides about the universe; on clear nights, take a peep through the large refracting telescope. Telephone reservations should be made for stargazing.

While popular with all age groups, this place is great for kids. Those without children may wish to avoid weekends due to the crowds and the increased numbers of young ones.

There's free parking at the museum.

Canada Agricultural Museum This government experimental farm (☎ 613-991-3044, 930 Carling Ave at Prince of Wales Dr; adult/child $5/3; open 9am-5pm daily Mar-Oct, reduced attractions rest of the year), southwest of downtown, includes about 500 hectares of flowers, trees, shrubs and gardens. The site is used for research on all aspects of farming and horticulture. There are tours, or you can go walking on your own. The farm also has livestock and showcase herds of cattle, an observatory, a tropical greenhouse and arboretum. The latter is good for walking or having a picnic and is also great in winter for tobogganing. The farm is linked to the rest of Ottawa's cycling routes. The museum is closed in winter, but the barn is open all year. Call regarding shows and special displays.

Canadian Ski Museum This is a small, specialized exhibit (☎ 613-722-3584, Trailhead Building, 1960 Scott St, 2nd floor; admission free; open 9am-5pm Mon-Sat,

11am-5pm Sun) with a collection of equipment and memorabilia outlining the history of skiing. To get to this site, west of downtown, take Laurier Ave to Scott St.

Byward Market
The Byward Market *(between George & York Sts; admission free)* is north of Rideau St. Opened in the 1840s, it's an interesting, busy renovated area where activity peaks on Saturday, which is market day. Farmers from west Québec and the Ottawa Valley sell vegetables, fruit and flowers, while specialty shops offer gourmet meats, seafood, baked goods and cheeses. Crafts are sold in the market building, and there are plenty of restaurants. The inviting neighborhood surrounding the actual market stalls is also referred to as Byward Market.

Royal Canadian Mint
Next door to the War Museum is the mint *(☎ 613-993-8990, 320 Sussex Dr; adult/senior & child $2/8; open 9am-9pm Mon-Fri, 9am-6pm Sat & Sun May-Aug, 9am-5pm daily rest of the year)*. No longer producing day-to-day coinage, it strikes special-edition coins, commemorative pieces, bullion investment coins and the like. Founded in 1908 and renovated in the mid-1980s, this imposing stone building has always been Canada's major refiner of gold. Tours are given by appointment; call to arrange one and see the process – from sheets of metal to bags of coins. Sorry, no free samples.

The main circulation-coin mint is in Winnipeg, Manitoba.

Cathedral-Basilica of Notre Dame
Built in 1839, this is one of the city's most impressive houses of worship *(Guigues Ave; admission free; open 7am-6pm daily)*. A pamphlet available at the door outlines the many features, including carvings, windows, the organ and the Gothic-style ceiling. The cathedral is across from the National Gallery, in the Byward Market area.

Prime Minister's House & Rideau Hall
You can view the outside of the present prime minister's house *(24 Sussex Dr)* and take a peek at the property. For security reasons, there is no strolling around the PM's grounds.

Around the corner and up from the river, Rideau Hall *(☎ 613-991-4422, 1 Sussex Dr; admission free; visitors' center open 9:30am-5:30pm daily May-Nov)*, the governor general's pad, was built in the early 20th century. There are 45-minute walking tours of the residence, with stories of some of the goings-on over the years. Tours are offered through the day, in summer only, or you can stroll the grounds all year.

At the main gate, the small changing of the guard ceremony happens on the hour throughout the day, from the end of June to the end of August.

Both houses are northeast along Sussex Dr. Rideau Hall is off Princess Dr, the eastern extension of Sussex Dr.

Rockcliffe Village
Farther east along Sussex Dr, Rockcliffe Village is one of the poshest, most prestigious areas in the country. Behind the mansion doors live some very prominent Canadian citizens and many foreign diplomats.

Laurier House National Historic Site
This Victorian home *(☎ 613-992-8142, 335 Laurier Ave; admission $2.50; open 9am-5pm Tues-Sat, 2pm-5pm Sun Apr-Sept, call for rest of the year)*, built in 1878, was the residence of two prime ministers, Wilfrid Laurier and the eccentric Mackenzie King. It's beautifully furnished throughout – don't miss the study on the top floor. Each of the two prime ministers is represented by mementos and various possessions.

It's best to visit in the early morning (that is, before the tour buses arrive); you'll have the knowledgeable guides all to yourself.

Turtle Island Aboriginal Experience
This intriguing new replica Indian village site *(☎ 613-564-9494, Victoria Island off Portage Bridge; adult/child $6/4; open 11am-6pm daily May-Sept)* offers glimpses into the original Native culture of the area. The demonstrations, music and dancing, canoes, longhouse and more are informative and entertaining. Turtle Island is walkable from downtown. Call for off-season activities.

Activities

In summer, there are **canoe** and **rowboat rentals** for trips along the canal at Dows Lake Pavilion (☎ 613-232-1001) at Dows Lake. The lake, a bulge in the Rideau Canal, is southwest of the downtown core; go south along Bronson Ave or Booth St.

The city has an excellent **parks** system, with a lot of inner-city green space. There are many **walking, jogging** and **cycling trails**, as well as picnic areas. You'll even find some **fishing**. The tourist office has a sheet, with map, of all the parks and a description of each. Bicycle paths wind all over town; get a map of them. For rentals, see Getting Around, later.

Surrounding the city on the east, south and west, and connecting with the Ottawa River on each side, is a broad strip of connected parkland known as the **Greenbelt** (☎ 613-239-5000). Within this area of woodlands, marsh and fields are nature trails, more bicycle paths, boardwalks, picnic areas and conservation areas.

For **whitewater rafting** trips, see the Activities section of Around Hull (Gatineau), later in this chapter.

In winter, there's **skiing** as close as 20km from town, in the Gatineau Hills. Two resorts with variously graded hills are **Camp Fortune** and **Mont Cascades**. Tow passes are more expensive on weekends. Gatineau Park (see the Around Hull, section, later) has excellent cross-country ski trails with lodges along the way. In warm weather, the park is good for walking and picnicking.

Again in winter, the Rideau Canal is famous for **ice skating**, with 5km of maintained ice. Rest spots on the way serve great doughnuts (known as beavertails) to go with the hot chocolate, although, judging by the prices, the beaver must be getting scarce. Ask at the tourist office about skate rentals.

Organized Tours

Moose Travel offers a popular budget-travel jump-on, jump-off bus service with an Ontario circuit, one in Québec and one combo trip. Ask at the hostels, or see Organized Tours under Toronto and the introductory Getting Around chapter for more details. The Ottawa International Hostel also sometimes organizes trips.

Gray Line (☎ 613-563-5463, Confederation Square) offers a two-hour tour ($20) of the city daily from May to November. Tickets are available at its office in Confederation Square beside the National Arts Centre. All tours depart from here, but there is hotel pick-up, too. It also does longer tours of the region and beyond.

Capital Double Decker & Trolley Tours (☎ 613-749-3666, Sparks St at Metcalfe St) has a few different options. Note that the trolley is just a bus decorated to look that way, and that the vehicle is the only difference between the tours. The narrated tour ($20) allows hop-on, hop-off privileges at 20 stops, including some in Hull. The route takes at least two hours, but you have the day to do it – a good way to get around. There's a sunset tour ($15) and a fall-colors trip ($20).

Paul's Boat Lines (☎ 613-235-8409, Ottawa Locks) runs cruises on the Ottawa River and the Rideau Canal. Each takes about 1½ hours and costs $13/7 adult/child. Also, for tickets and information, there's another dock at the Rideau Canal, across from the National Arts Centre.

The new, 90-minute tour offered by **Lady Dive** (☎ 613-223-6211, Sparks St at Elgin St) uses an amphibious vehicle that does a road tour and then plunges into the Ottawa River (adult/child $24/20).

Special Events

Some of Ottawa's major events are the following:

Winterlude This good and popular festival is held in early February. The three consecutive weekends of festivities center mainly around frozen Dows Lake and the canal. The ice sculptures are really worth seeing.

Canadian Tulip Festival This big annual event is held in late May, when the city is decorated with 200 types of tulips, mainly from Holland. Festivities include parades, regattas, car rallies, dances, concerts and fireworks.

Le Franco Festival Held in June, this festival is good fun and an opportunity to see some of the country's French culture through music, crafts and more.

International Jazz Festival This event lasts for 10 days at the end of July and features shows in Ottawa and Hull.

Central Canada Exhibition This annual event, held toward the end of August, involves 10 days of displays, a carnival and entertainment. The exhibition is held at Lansdowne Park.

Ottawa Folk Festival This annual two-day music festival at the end of August is increasingly popular.

Places to Stay

Camping Apart from the following two listings, there are other places to camp both east and west of town on Hwy 17, and there is camping in Gatineau Park (see Around Hull, later), across the river in Québec.

Camp Le Breton (☎ 613-724-6096, Fleet St at Booth St) Tent sites $8/person. Open June-Labor Day. This is an excellent campground that's practically right in the center of town, west along Wellington St past the Parliament Buildings. It's designed primarily for cyclists and hikers and has 200 tent sites with no electric or water hookups. Stays are limited to five nights. The city bus from the downtown area goes right to the campground, which is near the Ottawa River. Close to the campground are some rapids known as Chaudière Falls.

Camp Hither Hills (☎ 613-822-0509, fax 613-822-0196, 5227 Bank St, Hwy 31) Tent sites $18. Open mid-May–mid-Oct. The closest true campground to town is this one, 10km south of the city limits.

Hostels *Ottawa International Hostel* (☎ 613-235-2595, 800-663-5777, fax 613-235-9202, Ⓦ www.hostellingintl.on.ca, 75 Nicholas St) Dorm beds $18/22 members/nonmembers. Open year-round; 24-hour check-in Apr-Oct only. This HI hostel in the old Ottawa jail – see the gallows at the back – is one of the best-known hostels in the country. It has a very good, central location near the Parliament Buildings. There are 150 beds in the restored building, most of them in old cells – wake up behind bars. Management has made recent renovations, and facilities include a kitchen, laundry, parking and a shop. A bar is in the works. Reservations are recommended in midsummer and in February, when the Winterlude festival is on. The No 4 bus from the bus station on the corner of Arlington and Kent Sts, goes within two blocks of the hostel. From the train station, the No 95 bus does the same thing.

Ottawa Backpackers Inn (☎ 613-241-3402, 888-394-0334, Ⓦ www.ottawahostel.com, 203 York St) Dorm beds/doubles $18/55. Open year-round; check-in 7am-midnight. Right downtown in the market, this new, easygoing addition was instantly popular. There's Internet access, a kitchen and room for 35 in this converted 19th-century house, and it's often full.

YM-YWCA (☎ 613-237-1320, 180 Argyle Ave) Singles/doubles with shared bath $48/58, singles with private bath $58, quads with private bath ($78). Amenities include a cafeteria and a pool for guests.

Carleton University (☎ 613-520-5612/2600 ext 8401, 1233 Colonel By Dr) Rooms with breakfast $34/person. This university is pretty central but south of the downtown core, and it has a residence offering summer rooms from May to mid-August. Athletic facilities and full meal service (cafeteria) are available. Families are welcome.

B&Bs & Inns The places listed here are central, but those away from downtown may be a bit cheaper. Almost all prices include either a continental or full breakfast. Smaller places with just a few rooms do not have to charge tax. Some locations offer perks such as fireplaces or swimming pools, but nearly all have free parking. If Ottawa seems booked up or if you want to try staying across the river in Québec, there are a few guesthouses in Hull.

A Voyageur Guest House (☎ 613-238-6445, fax 613-236-5551, 95 Arlington Ave) Singles/doubles $39-49/54-59. There are six clean rooms with shared bathrooms here. Voyageur is on a quiet residential street right behind the bus terminal and is the best low-priced place in town. The manager, Khalid, is very welcoming.

There are two very good places in the convenient Byward Market area north of Rideau St.

Auberge des Arts (☎ 613-562-0909, 877-750-3400, 104 Guigues Ave) Singles $65, doubles with shared bath $75, doubles with private bath $100 with a small discount off-season. It's a collectible- and antique-filled home, but it's comfortable, not prissy at all, and has air-conditioning. English, French and Spanish are spoken, and the owner, Chantal, serves excellent healthy breakfasts. There's parking, too.

L'Auberge du Marché (☎ 613-241-6610, 800-465-0079, 87 Guigues St) Singles $65, doubles with shared/private bath $75/95. Across the street, this more modern, immaculate place with rooms in the private adjacent townhouse is a real bargain. There are three share-facilities rooms and one with private bath. Nicole gives you your own key to the separate entrance.

In the downtown area, just east over the canal and south of Rideau St, is a pocket where many of the central guesthouses are found. Many in this posher neighborhood are heritage houses or have some architectural distinction. It's a quiet, safe neighborhood – with all the embassies around, there's plenty of security. Amenities are more refined, and the prices generally higher. The No 4 bus runs along Rideau St from the downtown area.

Australis Guest House (☎ 613-235-8461, *35 Marlborough St*) Singles/doubles with shared bath $62/68, rooms with private bath $75. This comfy place is recommended for its excellent breakfasts and its helpful hosts, Carol and Brian Waters. The prices are also reasonable. The Waters offer a pick-up service from the train or bus station if arranged in advance. Marlborough St is south of Laurier, about a half-hour walk to the Parliament Buildings.

Lampman House (☎ 613-241-3696, 877-591-4354, fax 613-789-8360, e dgsy@compmore.net, 369 Daly Ave) Rooms $60-85. This Victorian house (12-foot ceilings) with a rooftop deck is a good bargain. One room has a private bath. Daly Ave is two blocks south of Rideau St.

Benner's B&B (☎ 613-789-8320, 877-891-5485, fax 613-789-9563, 539 Besserer St) Doubles with shared/private bath $85/95-105. Open year-round. Comfortably and tastefully decorated and one street south of Rideau in the Sandy Hill District, this place is just a 15-minute walk to downtown. Reservations are suggested for stays from May to October.

Gasthaus Switzerland Inn (☎ 613-237-0335, 888-663-0000, fax 613-594-3327, 89 Daly Ave) Rooms $88-148. This Swiss-style place enjoys one of the best locations in town, two blocks south of Rideau St and the market. The guesthouse has been created out of a large, old stone house and has 22 rooms, all with private bathrooms. Breakfast is Swiss style, with muesli, bread, cheese and coffee. Prices go down a few dollars

through the winter. The Swiss managers speak an impressive array of languages, including German and French.

Auberge McGee's Inn (☎ 613-237-6089, 800-262-4337, fax 613-237-6201, 185 Daly St) Rooms $95-200. In the deluxe inn category, this restored Victorian mansion includes 14 rooms. Rates increase with the number of features, and some rooms have private bathrooms.

Albert House Inn (☎ 613-236-4479, 800-267-1982, fax 613-237-9079, 478 Albert St) Rooms $88-175. On the downtown side of the canal, Albert House features 17 well-appointed rooms. Also expensive but with a good location, this heritage home from 1875 offers all the comforts, and the breakfast menu is extensive.

Efficiencies *The Business Inn* (☎ 613-232-1121, 800-363-1777, fax 613-232-8143, 180 MacLaren St) Rooms from $80 with continental breakfast. With 130 suites, from studios to two bedrooms, this is a full-service operation, including kitchens, restaurant and Internet access.

Doral Inn (☎ 613-230-8055, 800-263-6725, W www.doralottawa.com, 486 Albert St) Suites $100. This central inn has normal rooms and some suites with housekeeping units (kitchenettes).

Capital Hill Hotel & Suites (☎ 613-235-1413, fax 613-235-6047, 88 Albert St) Doubles $96, with kitchen $120. Similar to Doral Inn but much larger, this place offers some rooms with two double beds and others with kitchens. Prices vary by the month.

Motels There are two main motel strips, one on each side of the downtown area. On the east side, look along Rideau St and its extension, Montréal Rd, which leads east out of town.

Days Inn (☎ 613-789-555, 888-789-4949, fax 613-789-6196, 319 Rideau St) Doubles $110. This motel is close to downtown and has free parking.

Econo Lodge (☎ 613-789-3781, 800-263-0649, fax 613-789-0207, 475 Rideau St) Doubles $80-90 with breakfast. This place is not a bad deal, with a little breakfast shop and parking on the premises.

Howard Johnson Express Inn (☎ 613-746-4641, 888-891-1169, fax 613-746-6529,

112 Montréal Rd) Rooms $80-100. The place has just been totally renovated and is only a five-minute drive to downtown.

Concorde Motel *(☎ 613-745-2112, fax 613-745-2112, 333 Montréal Rd, Vanier)* Rooms $45-55. Don't book your mother in, but if the hostels are full or you're traveling cheap, this is the best bet. It ain't much to look at, but it's fine.

On the west side of Ottawa, check along Carling Ave, where there are numerous places about 10km from downtown. There are other, better ones closer to the center, but the price goes up. Both below have some kitchenettes.

Stardust *(☎ 613-828-2748, 2965 Carling Ave)* Singles/doubles $60/65. This place has 25 basic rooms.

Webb's Motel *(☎ 613-728-1881, 800-263-6725, fax 613-728-4516, 1705 Carling Ave)* Doubles $78. Cash is not accepted – only credit cards.

Hotels During summer, when Parliament is in recess and business traffic is light, many of the corporate-oriented downtown hotels offer daily and weekend specials.

Quality Hotel *(☎ 789-7511, 800-228-5151, 290 Rideau St)* Rooms $115-135, children free. In the middle price range, this is a straightforward place, recently renovated and close to downtown.

Howard Johnson *(☎ 613-237-2163, 877-436-5444, 123 Metcalfe St)* Rooms $70-90 with breakfast. This big-name outfit has just come to Ottawa.

Lord Elgin Hotel *(☎ 613-235-3333, 800-267-4298, fax 613-235-3333, 100 Elgin St at Laurier Ave)* Rooms from $150. This stately old place from 1941 has all the amenities.

Château Laurier *(☎ 613-241-1414, 800-441-1414, fax 613-562-7030, 1 Rideau St)* Rooms $250-400. The classic, castlelike place by the canal is the city's best-known hotel and is a landmark in its own right. The hotel has also a large indoor swimming pool.

Places to Eat
Byward Market Area The very popular central market provides bounteous options. During the warm months, many of the eateries have outdoor tables, and on weekend mornings, the place is hopping. In the Byward Market building, at the York St end,

look for the stand selling 'beavertails' – hot, flat doughnuts that first became popular when sold to skaters along the canal in winter.

Zak's Diner *(☎ 613-241-2401, 16 Byward St)* Dishes $4-8. It's got the '50s diner look, but it's young, hip and friendly. The club sandwich is dynamite, and the shakes and breakfasts are renowned, but wraps are also on offer, so it's not a total time warp. It stays open all night Friday and Saturday.

Oregano's *(☎ 613-241-5100, William St at George St)* Lunch/dinner special $9/11. For inexpensive pasta dishes, try this casual place. There is an all-you-can-eat lunch special or an early-bird dinner special (4:30pm to 8pm) of pasta, salad and soup. On Sunday, the menu changes slightly, and there's a brunch.

Las Palmas *(☎ 613-241-3738, 111 Parent Ave)* Dishes $9-14. Another international choice is this place, which had good Mexican food and a colorful interior courtyard. The fajitas especially are not to be missed.

Shawarma Place *(☎ 613-562-3662, 284 Dalhousie St)* Dishes under $7. Open 10am-4am daily. Familiar Lebanese standards (falafels, shawarmas) are good and very reasonably priced here.

Domus Café *(☎ 613-241-6007, 87 Murray St)* Lunch/dinner $12/23. Closed Sun evening. If you're looking for a splurge but want substance, not just style, you've found it. The kitchen uses fresh, local produce in creating excellent nouveau meals with an international slant.

Downtown Along Bank St and its side streets are numerous restaurants. The 800 block of Bank (not mapped) is a lively area with cafés, shops and more. All through downtown and around the market, look for the chip wagons frying excellent french fries and hamburgers.

Suisha Gardens *(☎ 613-236-9602, 208 Slater St)* Dishes $20-30. Near the corner of Bank St is this highly recommended Japanese place. The food is excellent (though somewhat Westernized), the environment authentic and the service perfect. The best room is downstairs and to the left. Dinner for two is $40 before drinks, and prices are lower at lunch.

Royal Oak *(☎ 613-236-0190, 318 Bank St)* Dishes $8. This is a friendly and a good place for British beer, an excellent burger or a beef-and-Stilton pie.

Kamal's (☎ *613-234-2703, 787 Bank St*) Dishes downstairs under $7, upstairs $9-18. Closed Sunday. Long-running Kamal's has good and inexpensive Lebanese classics downstairs and a more formal dining room upstairs; it's licensed to sell alcohol.

Flippers (☎ *613-232-2703, 823 Bank St*) Mains $16-18. No lunch Mon. For years, this upstairs restaurant by the corner of 4th Ave has satisfied seafood lovers. It does a blackened-fish dish every day.

Mexicali Rosa's (☎ *613-236-9499, 895 Bank St*) Dishes under $11. Well entrenched on the corner, this relaxed, rustic cantina-like spot cooks up tasty, moderately priced Tex-Mex food.

Roses Cafe (☎ *613-233-5574, 523 Gladstone Ave between Bay & Lyon Sts*) Dishes $6-9. Closed Sun lunch. Good, cheap, and mainly vegetarian Indian food is served at this small, casual but well-established restaurant.

Chinatown & Little Italy Ottawa has a small Chinatown with numerous restaurants within walking distance west of downtown. It's based around the corner of Bronson Ave and Somerset St W.

Ben-Ben (☎ *613-238-5022, 697 Somerset St W*) Dishes $6-11. Open 11am-11pm daily. Very popular with the community, this place serves good lunches of Szechuan and Cantonese cuisine.

Mekong (☎ *613-237-7717, 637 Somerset St W*) Mains $8-13. Open 11am-11pm daily. Mekong is recommended for good Vietnamese, as well as Chinese, dishes.

A few blocks west around Booth St are numerous Vietnamese places.

Pho Bo Ga (☎ *613-230-2931, 784 Somerset W*) Dishes $4.50-6.50. It's small and packed, but the menu is simple, sort of – 30 kinds of beef noodle soup. Throw on the greens, add some hot sauce, and it's a meal.

A little farther west, a few blocks beyond Bronson St, is Preston St's Corso Italia, Ottawa's Little Italy, absolutely lined with appealing Italian restaurants.

Paticceria-Gelateria Italiana (☎ *613-233-2104, 200 Preston St*) Desserts $5. What an amazing array of fresh pastries. Get a cappuccino and indulge. Have you ever seen a wedding-cake showroom?

Pub Italia (☎ *613-232-2326, 434 Preston St*) Dishes $10. Mama mia, a cross between a trattoria and an Irish pub…and it works! Enjoy the odd atmosphere with pizzas, pastas, and a range of British brews, either inside or on the patio.

Elgin & Rideau Sts A stroll along Elgin St between Somerset and Frank Sts always turns up a couple of places to eat, plus a popular nightspot or two. There are outdoor patios, cafés and pubs.

Elgin St Diner (☎ *613-237-9700, 374 Elgin St*) Dishes under $10. Open 24 hours. It's a bright and busy half-deli/half-diner, and it's good for breakfast, burgers and sandwiches.

Across the canal from Wellington St, the Rideau St area also has a number of eateries.

Nate's (☎ *613-789-9191, 316 Rideau St*) Dishes $4-7. This Jewish delicatessen, a local institution, is renowned far and wide for its low prices on basic food. The popular

breakfast special is the cheapest in the country ($2 for the works). Ask for the Rideau Rye – it's good bread for toast. Nate's also serves blintzes, latkes and smoked meat. The service is incredibly fast. It's open and busy on Sunday.

Horn of Africa (☎ *613-789-0025, 364 Rideau St*) Dishes $6-11. This local Ethiopian hangout is very cheap for exotic stews and dishes eaten with *injera*, an

African flatbread. Some vegetarian dishes are available. Call to check hours.

Entertainment

Bars & Live Music *Express* is the city's free entertainment weekly. *Capital Xtra* is similar and geared toward gays and lesbians. Also check Friday's *Ottawa Citizen* for complete club and entertainment listings.

Zaphod Beeblebrox (☎ 613-562-1010, 27 York St) This is a popular eclectic place for everything from New Age to rock to African music and rhythm and blues. Live bands play most nights, and cover charges are low. It also has a good selection of small-brewery beers.

Rainbow Bistro (☎ 613-241-5123, 76 Murray St) You can catch live blues, reggae or R&B upstairs at this popular place.

Hotel Lafayette (☎ 613-241-4747, Byward Market, York St) The 'Laff,' from 1849, is good for its cheap draft beer day or night. It's your old basic hotel beer parlor, but its character attracts a wide cross section of people.

Barrymores (☎ 613-233-0307, 323 Bank St) This longtime fave features mainly live rock and metal on weekends.

Irene's Pub (☎ 613-230-4474, 885 Bank St) Thankfully, no interior design work has been done at this funky, comfortable pub, which often has live Celtic, folk or blues to go with the great variety of imported beers.

Patty's Pub (☎ 613-730-2434, 1186 Bank St) Farther south than Irene's, this is a cozy Irish pub with music from Thursday to Saturday and an outdoor patio in summer.

Manx Pub (☎ 613-231-2070, 370 Elgin St) This small, casual, arty place offers single malts and microbrewery beers. There's some live weekend folk music.

Lookout Bar (☎ 613-789-1624, 41 York St) The market contains this gay fave.

Coral Reef (☎ 613-234-5118, 30 Nicolas St) It may be the oldest in town, but this lesbian bar is still hard to find. It's in the parking garage of the Rideau Center.

Performing Arts & Cinemas *National Arts Centre (NAC;* ☎ 613-755-1111, 53 Elgin St) This complex has theaters for drama and opera and is home to the symphony orchestra. It also presents a range of concerts and films. It's on the banks of the canal, in Confederation Square.

There are two repertory theaters showing two films a night: *Mayfair* (☎ 613-730-3403, 1074 Bank St), which charges $8 for nonmembers for the double bill, and *Bytown Cinema* (☎ 613-789-3456, 325 Rideau St), where nonmembers also pay $8.

Spectator Sports

The Ottawa Senators play NHL hockey at the *Corel Centre* (☎ 613-599-0300, tickets ☎ 613-755-1166, Hwy 17) in Kanata.

Lansdowne Park (☎ 613-580-2429, 1015 Bank St) is home again to the reborn Canadian Football League Ottawa team, now called the Renegades.

Getting There & Away

See Organized Tours under Toronto and the introductory Getting Around chapter for more details on budget hop-on, hop-off travel services like Moose Travel.

Air The airport is 20 minutes south of the city and is surprisingly small. Main airlines serving the city include Air Canada (☎ 800-247-2262), American Airlines (☎ 800-433-7300), British Airways (☎ 800-247-9297), Northwest Airlines and KLM (☎ 800-225-2525), US Airways (☎ 800-428-4322) and WestJet (☎ 888-937-8538).

Bus Central Station for buses (☎ 613-238-5900, 265 Catherine St near Bank St) is about a dozen blocks south of the downtown area. The principal bus lines are Voyageur and Greyhound. The one-way fare to Toronto is $60; to Kingston, $32; to Montréal, $29; and to Sudbury, $85. Students can get a third off the price for a book of tickets.

There are seven buses daily to Toronto, some of which are express, and 15 daily for Montréal. Buses depart frequently for Kingston, Belleville, Sudbury and others.

Train The VIA Rail station (☎ 613-244-8289, 200 Tremblay Rd) is 7km southeast of the downtown area, near the junction of Alta Vista Rd and Hwy 417, just east of the Rideau Canal.

There are four trains a day to Toronto and to Montréal. One-way fares Toronto $90, Kingston $42 and Montréal $41. By booking at least five days in advance, you can save between 25% and 35% if you avoid peak days like Friday.

For trips west, say, to Sudbury, there is no direct line, and connections must be made in Toronto, so it's a long trip.

Car Discount (☎ 613-310-2277, 427 Gladstone) car rental charges $40 per day for small cars.

Hitchhiking Hitchhiking is easy between Montréal and Ottawa but is convoluted if you're heading for Toronto. Going to Montréal, take the eastbound Montréal-Ogilvy bus on Rideau St; this leads to Hwy 17 East, where you can begin. For Toronto, take Hwy 31 south to Hwy 401 near the town of Morrisburg. The busy Hwy 401 (probably the most traveled route in Canada) connects Toronto with Montréal, and hitchhiking is fairly common along the way. For a more rural trip, take Hwy 7 and 37 to Tweed and then to Belleville, then Hwy 401 from there.

Getting Around

To/From the Airport The cheapest way to get to the airport is by city bus. Take bus No 97 from the corner of Slater and Albert Sts. The ride takes 17 minutes.

You can also try the Airport Shuttle Bus (☎ 613-260-2359), which leaves from many major hotels every half hour on the half hour from about 5am to midnight. The ride ($11) takes about 25 minutes. The bus is not as frequent on weekends; call about scheduling.

Bus Both Ottawa and Hull operate separate bus systems. A transfer is valid from one system to the other but may require an extra partial payment.

OC Transpo (☎ 613-741-4390) operates the Ottawa bus system, which tends to be volatile, with frequent changes in routes and fares. Call for assistance – the agents are very helpful. The standard fare is $2.35 cash, or cheaper tickets can be bought at corner stores around town. All Ottawa buses quit by around midnight; most quit earlier.

You can take the following buses from downtown to:

Bus terminal – No 4 south on Bank St; more frequently, the No 1 and No 7 stop within a block of the terminal

Train station – Transitway No 95 east on Slater St or the No 99 along Chamberlain

Museum of Nature – No 14 on Elgin St; Nos 99, 1, 4 and 7 all go within a block or so

Hull – No 8 west on Albert St but only during the day; the Outaouais bus service runs to Rideau St from Hull and continues at night

Car There is free parking in the World Exchange Plaza on weekends, and it's always the best place to park when visiting the downtown tourist office, one block away.

Bicycle Ottawa is the best city in Canada for cyclists, with an extensive system of paths in and around town and through the parks. You can get a bicycle route map from the tourist office.

For rentals, try Rent-A-Bike (☎ 613-241-4140) at the Château Laurier, in the rear parking area. It's open every day from May to September and charges $23 per day. ID is required.

AROUND OTTAWA

A unique site is the **Diefenbunker** (☎ 613-839-0007, 3911 Carp Rd, Carp; adult/child $12/10; open daily, call for hours and tour times), a secret underground fort built in the early 1960s as a military/government refuge. It has since been reopened as a Cold War museum. The huge shelter was built to house 300 personnel for 30 days in case of nuclear attack. Displays include air-raid sirens and bombs. It's about a 30-minute drive west of town, in the village of Carp. Admission includes a one-hour (or more) tour and parking.

Even the Mounties have to practice, and the **RCMP Stables & Practice Ground** (☎ 613-993-3751, Sandrich Rd; admission free; grounds open 9am-4pm daily May-Oct, 10am-2pm daily Nov-Apr) is where the musical ride pageant is perfected. The public is welcome to watch the practice sessions and the other equestrian displays held from time to time. Every evening for a week sometime prior to Canada Day (July 1), there's a full musical ride with a band. Otherwise, the daily evening practices are without the band and colorful uniforms. Also note that the ride is sometimes away on tour (call for details). Tours of the stables are given from 8:30am to 11am and 1:30pm to 3:30pm Monday to Friday during the summer season. If traveling by car, take Sussex Dr east to Rockcliffe Parkway. At Birch St, turn right to the grounds. To get there via public transit, take bus No 7.

The **Log Farm** (☎ 613-825-7551, 640 Cedarview Rd, Nepean; adult/child $5/4; open 8am-8pm daily May-Sept, 9am-5pm rest of the year), a re-creation of a 19th-century farm complete with costumed workers, is 20km southwest of Parliament Hill. There are historical exhibits and activities. Special events occur sporadically through the year.

Where the Rideau River meets the canal south of town (at the junction of Colonel By St and Hog's Back Rd) are the **Prince of Wales Falls** and walking and cycling paths. The falls, a local fave picnic spot with an adjacent set of locks, are also known as Hog's Back Falls.

HULL (GATINEAU)

pop 64,000

Across the river, in Québec, Hull is as much the other half of Ottawa as it is a separate city (that's why it's included in the Ontario chapter of this book). In late 2001, the name of Hull was changed to Gatineau as part of a political amalgamation agenda of various towns. At street level, this part will be called Hull for many years yet. The city has its share of government offices, and workers cross the river in both directions each day, but the Hull side remains home to most of the area's French population, and even the architecture (at least the older stuff) is different.

Hull is also the main city of the region of Québec known as Outaouais (which is pronounced basically as though you were saying Ottawa with a French accent). The Québec government has a booklet outlining the region's attractions and activities, mostly of the outdoor variety. There are some huge parks and reserves within a few hours' drive of town.

Orientation & Information

Promenade du Portage, easily found from either Portage Bridge or Alexandra Bridge, is the main downtown street.

The City Hall, known as Maison du Citoyen, is an attention-grabbing, dominating modern building with a 20m-high glass tower at 25 Rue Laurier. It also contains an art gallery and a meditation center (what English-speaking bureaucracy would do that?).

The tourist information office for Hull, La Maison du Tourisme (☎ 800-265-7822, 103 Rue Laurier at Boulevard St Laurent) is just over the Alexandra Bridge. It's open every day, all year.

The Ottawa city bus and trolley tours include Hull in their circuits (see Organized Tours under Ottawa, earlier).

Many of the sites in this section are shown on the Ottawa map.

Canadian Museum of Civilization

The area's best museum (☎ 819-776-7000, 100 Rue Laurier; adult/senior/child $8/7/4, half-price Sun; open 9am-6pm Fri-Wed, 9am-9pm Thur May-Oct; 9am-5pm Fri-Wed, 9am-9pm Thur Oct-Apr) is principally concerned with the history of Canada. It's in the large, striking complex with the copper domes on the river bank opposite the Parliament Buildings. Allow the best part of a day to seriously explore the place.

The **Grand Hall** of the lower level, with its simulated forest and seashore, explores Native Indian cultures and offers explanations of the huge totems and other coastal Native Indian structures.

The **Canada Hall**, on Level 3, presents displays and realistic re-creations tracing aspects of Canada's early history: the story of the European founding, the voyages of the country's explorers, settlement and historical developments through to the 1880s. The Basque ship section, complete with the sound of creaking wood in the living quarters, brings to life the voyages undertaken to reach the New World. Also particularly good are the Acadian farm model and the replica of the early Québec town square.

The entertaining and educational **Children's Museum** section, on Level 2, includes some excellent interactive exhibits.

The main level consists of three halls containing temporary exhibits on varying aspects of human history, culture and art. The **Native Indian & Inuit Art Gallery** usually, but not always, offers various shows by Native Indian artists – painting, dance, crafts and more. Don't miss the chance to see the art of British Columbian Native Indians, especially that of the Haida.

Cineplus shows realistic IMAX and OMNIMAX films. The ever-changing shows are extremely popular, with waits of two to three shows not uncommon, so arrive early for a ticket. A Cineplus ticket is in addition to the museum entry price; prices vary depending on the show but tend to be rather high. Again, it's less for kids and seniors.

There is a good *cafeteria* that offers, among other things, sandwiches and a salad bar or economical full meals all served within view of the river and Parliament Hill. The museum bookstore and gift shop are worth a browse. There's parking under the museum.

Casino du Lac Leamy
The other big site in Hull is the posh gambling hall (☎ 819-772-2100, 1 Boulevard du Casino; admission free; open 11am-3am daily), with parking, docking facilities and a helipad (gotta get those high rollers). A just-finished major expansion aims at turning this into a Las Vegas–style resort, complete with a huge hotel, 1000-seat theater, conference center, high-class restaurant and increased gambling facilities. The attire here is somewhat dressy. The casino is north of the center, off the third exit after going over Macdonald Cartier Bridge from Ottawa.

Places to Stay & Eat
The tourist office can help locate a B&B. Prices are lower than the Ottawa average. Motels can be found along Boulevard Alexandre Taché, which runs beside the river to the west of downtown Hull after you come across the bridge from Ottawa. There are also some business-oriented hotels downtown.

Couette et Croissants (☎ 819-771-2200, fax 819-771-4920, 330 Rue Champlain) Singles/doubles with shared bath $55/65. This is a small, attractive B&B northeast of downtown, about 10 blocks north of the Canadian Museum of Civilization.

Le Troquet (☎ 819-776-9595, 41 Rue Laval) Dishes under $14. The atmosphere and excellent food make this almost like a quick budget trip to Paris. Lunch on broccoli soup, baguette with brie, tomatoes and dijon followed by café au lait for $8.

Café Aubry (☎ 819-777-3700, 5 Rue Aubry) Dishes under $10. This café/bar serves light lunches and then heats up at night. It's located in a tiny pedestrian mall just off the Promenade.

Café Henry Burger (☎ 819-777-5646, 69 Rue Laurier) Dinner $50. This is one of the oldest and most elegant restaurants in Canada. The expensive French menu

changes with the seasons but always includes seafood and various meats.

Entertainment
After 2am, when the Ontario bars are closed, partygoers head across the river from Ottawa to Hull, where things are open until 3am and later. Narrow Rue Aubry, in the middle of downtown, has numerous nightspots, some with live music.

Le Bistro (☎ 819-778-0968, Rue Kent) At the Rue Aubry corner, this place attracts a casual and young crowd for music, food and drinks.

Les Raftsmen (☎ 819-777-0924, 60 Rue St Raymond) East of Boulevard St Joseph, this place has live music in a large, friendly, typically Québecois brasserie. It also offers a menu of standard beer-hall fare at good prices; food is served until 9pm.

Getting There & Away
The Outaouais Bus System (☎ 819-770-3242) has buses that operate along Rideau and Wellington Sts in Ottawa. From downtown Ottawa, bus Nos 33, 35 and 42 all go to Promenade du Portage.

A bicycle route over the Alexandra Bridge from Ottawa connects with a trail system that goes around much of central Hull and to Ruisseau de la Brasserie (Brewery Creek), a park area east of downtown.

AROUND HULL
Gatineau Park
Gatineau Park is a deservedly popular 36,000-hectare area of woods and lakes in the Gatineau Hills of Québec, northwest of downtown Hull. It's only a 20-minute drive from the Parliament Buildings in Ottawa.

The visitors' center (☎ 819-827-2020, 33 Scott Rd; open 9am-5pm daily) is 12km from Parliament Hill, off Hwy 5. On weekends, some roads may be closed to cars, and note that parking must be paid for at the more popular destinations, such as Lac Meech and the King Estate. The park is home plenty of wildlife, including about 100 species of birds, and features 150km of hiking trails and 90km of biking trails. Lac Lapêche, Lac Meech and Lac Phillipe have beaches for swimming (including a nude gay beach at Lac Meech) and thus are the most popular. The latter includes a *camp-*

ground, while there is canoe camping at Lac Lapêche (canoes can be rented). You can fish in the lakes and streams, and the hiking trails are good for cross-country skiing in winter. Small **Pink Lake** is pretty but is off limits for swimming. A boardwalk rims the lake for strolling. The lake is best during the week, when there are fewer people around.

Also in the park is **Kingsmere** (☎ 819-465-1867; admission $7; open 11am-5pm Mon-Fri, 10am-6pm Sat & Sun mid-May–mid-Oct), the summer estate of William Lyon Mackenzie King, who was prime minister in the 1920s, late 1930s and early 1940s. Here he indulged his hobby of collecting ruins, both genuine and fake. In 1941, King had bits of London's House of Commons brought over after the German blitz. His home, Moorside, is now a museum. An astute politician, King was much interested in the occult and apparently talked to both his dead dog and deceased mother. There's a pleasant tearoom at Moorside, with items such as cucumber sandwiches or black-forest ham on pumpernickel bread.

Occurring in September or October, **Fall Rhapsody** is a festival that celebrates the brief but colorful season when the leaves change – a time when the maples and birches of the Gatineau Hills are having their last fling before winter. An arts festival is part of the affair, as are hot-air ballooning and various concerts and competitions. Events are held in the park, with a few around town as well. During Fall Rhapsody, there are cheap buses from Ottawa-Hull to various spots in Gatineau Park.

There is no public transportation to the park, but the Ottawa-Maniwaki bus goes by.

Wakefield

Charming and scenic, small historic Wakefield, just outside the park, is a mix of heritage buildings, restaurants, cafés, lodgings and tourist-oriented shops. It's popular for day trips, but many stay longer.

The **Hull-Chelsea Wakefield Steam Train** (☎ 819-778-7246, 800-871-7246) connects Gatineau to Wakefield. The 1907 train travels alongside the park, making one-day roundtrips daily from early May to mid-October. Adult fare is $29 for the entertaining 64km round trip. Reservations are recommended. In Wakefield, there's enough

time for a meal or stroll. The station is at 165 Rue Deveault, north of central Hull.

Carman Trails (☎ 819-459-3180/2113, e carman@magma.ca, Carman Rd) Dorm beds $18/20 members/nonmembers. Open year-round. This HI hostel consistently gets great reviews, as does the affable, energetic, creative manager, Robert. It makes an excellent base for exploring the park and is a fine, always-evolving retreat in its own right. With 80 acres linked to the park, there is no end of outdoor possibilities here. Cycling, hiking, canoeing and cross-country skiing are all available (to really get into the bush, ask about the Haven). The hostel has its own licensed restaurant and organic greenhouses. Other features are a sauna, fireplace, family rooms and music nights. Book ahead, as capacity is only 40. You may be able to get picked up after getting off the Voyageur Ottawa-Maniwaki bus; call for details.

Black Sheep Inn (Mouton Noir) (☎ 819-459-3228, 753 Riverside Drive) Totally nondescript, this ragged country bar has deservedly earned an incredible reputation for the bands it brings in and is a fabulous place to hear good music.

Activities

Northwest of Gatineau Park, there are several outfitters who use a turbulent section of the Ottawa River for rafting adventures. The trips range from half-day to two-day adventures and run from roughly April to October. No experience is needed, and the locations are less than two hours from Ottawa. Book ahead for weekends, as the trips fill up. You can save money by going on weekdays.

Recommended **Esprit Rafting** (☎ 800-596-7238), just over the Québec border a few kilometers from Fort Coulonge, uses small, bouncy, 14-foot self-bailing rafts and provides pick-up and delivery from the Ottawa Hostel and Carman Trails. Esprit offers a one-day rafting trip with lunch ($85) and a whole range of other options, such as various canoe trips and kayaking courses. Good dormitory accommodations are available at its rustic Auberge Esprit lodge for $20, including breakfast and use of canoes and kayaks. You can also camp. All meals (the barbecue dinners are a treat) are offered.

Two other reliable organizations, both in Foresters Falls, Ontario, and with comparable prices are **Wilderness Tours** (☎ 800-267-9166) and **OWL Rafting** (☎ 800-461-7238), with both wild and mild trips, the latter being good for families; OWL's prices range from $60 to $90 for adults, $40 to $60 for children. Both companies offer meals, camping and more expensive cabin accommodations, which should be booked ahead.

Another option is a bungee jump or ripride ($30) – don't ask; it's high and fast – at **Great Canadian Bungee** (☎ 819-459-3714, 877-828-8170), just south of Wakefield.

Eastern Ontario

This region's highlights include the eastern side of Algonquin Park; the historic lakeside city of Kingston; lazy, quiet Quinte's Isle, with one of the province's favorite parks; and the cottage country around the Kawartha Lakes.

West from Ottawa, there are various routes through Ontario. Hwy 17, the Trans Canada Hwy, leads northwest to Pembroke, then continues to North Bay and on to Sudbury. This is the quickest way to western Canada.

From Pembroke there is another option. You can take Hwy 41 south to Hwy 60/62, which leads west through the southern portion of Algonquin Park to Huntsville, where Hwy 11 runs north to North Bay and south to Toronto.

The southern route from Ottawa goes to the more populated southern region of Ontario, the St Lawrence River, the Great Lakes and Toronto. From Ottawa, Hwys 31 and the fast, new 416 lead directly down to Hwy 401, the expressway to Toronto.

A prettier, though slower drive is to take Hwy 7 west out of Ottawa going through Perth and as far as Hwy 37. From here, Hwy 37 leads south through Tweed before dropping down to Hwy 401. This route is a standard itinerary and is a compromise between speed and aesthetics; it's about five hours from Ottawa to Toronto this way. Taking Hwy 7 any farther west really starts to add on the hours.

ALGONQUIN PROVINCIAL PARK EAST

The hilly eastern side of this park has some fine features, including the Barron Canyon,

which makes a great canoeing destination, and numerous waterfalls. There is a *campground* (☎ 705-633-5572, *reservations* ☎ 888-668-7275) at the Achray access point on Grand Lake and many interior sites, including some beauties with a beach just a 20-minute paddle away; sites are $22.

Algonquin Portage (☎ 613-735-1795), west of Pembroke on Route 28 (the road to Achray), rents tents, sleeping bags and canoes and has hostel accommodations, a shuttle service, food and gas.

Esprit Rafting (☎ 800-596-7238) is based near Pembroke, on the Ottawa River, east of Algonquin. It offers a one-day canoe trip down the Barron Canyon in Algonquin Park between May and October ($85, see Activities under Around Hull, earlier).

For more on Algonquin, see the Georgian Bay & Lakelands section, later in this chapter.

SOUTH ALGONQUIN AREA

This entire region has cottages for rent and lakeside resorts, but advance reservations are a very good idea. **Pembroke**, near the Québec border, is the closest town of any size.

If you are in the region, the small town of **Eganville** is worth a stop for the nearby **Bonnechere Caves** (☎ 613-628-2283, 800-469-2283; open May-Oct). The caves and passages, 8km southeast, were the bottom of a tropical sea about 500 million years ago and contain fossils of animals from long before the dinosaur age. Pathways lead through parts of the extensive system, past fossil banks and stalactites.

The old lumber town of **Barry's Bay** is now a supply hub for the cottagers in the area around **Lake Kaminiskeg**. It's also pretty close to Algonquin Park and is on the main highway to Ottawa. Odd as it may seem, this is the base for a sizable Polish population, attracted to the hilly, green topography, which is much like that along the Baltic Sea in northern Poland. The town of **Wilno** in this area was the first Polish settlement in Canada. Nearby **Killaloe**, toward Ottawa, is a small mecca for craftspeople and artisans.

The area that runs southwest to the Kawartha Lakes is a green, hilly, sparsely populated region known as the **Haliburton Highlands**.

EASTERN ONTARIO

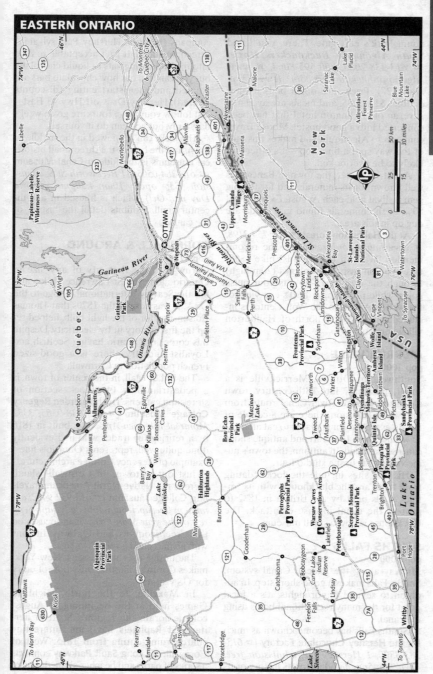

Maynooth is a small logging community about a 20-minute drive south of Algonquin Park's east gate. There, you'll find *South Algonquin Backpackers Hostel* (☎ 613-338-2080, 800-595-8064, W *www .algonquinbackpackers.com, Hwy 62 & Hwy 127*). Prices are dorm beds/singles/ doubles $17/25/35, and meals are available here, an old Arlington hotel that has been converted into a good hostel. Moose Travel connects to Algonquin and makes this out-of-the-way spot a fine stop – it's otherwise likely to be overlooked.

A district center, the town of **Bancroft** is well known for its minerals and for the big gem festival held each August. Examples of 80% of the minerals found in Canada are dug up in this area.

At the **Haliburton Forest** (☎ 705-754-2198, W *www.haliburtonforest.com*), the recommended 'Walk in the Clouds' hike ($65) takes you on suspended planks (20m high) through the tree tops – it gets your pulse going while providing a bird's-eye view of the woods. A visit to the Wolf Centre is included. The forest is north of Haliburton village on Route 7.

MERRICKVILLE
pop 1000
Southwest of Ottawa, Merrickville is a small, pleasant, late-18th-century town along the Rideau River/Canal route from Ottawa to Kingston. There are a couple of B&Bs, as well as some places to eat along St Lawrence St. A few craft and antique shops can also be found. In autumn, the town's numerous artists host a studio tour.

Historic sites include the **locks** (dating from 1830) and the **blockhouse**, with its 1m-thick walls built by the British in 1832 to protect the canal in case of attack. The blockhouse is now a small museum.

SMITHS FALLS
pop 9000
Midway along the Rideau Canal system, Smiths Falls makes a good short stop. In addition to several minor sights, it's a focal point for the many recreational boats using the canal.

Smiths Falls has become known as much for the **Hershey Chocolate Factory** (☎ 613-283-3300, 1 Hershey Dr; admission free; open 9am-5pm daily) as for its history or its canal location. A free tour of the Canadian branch plant of this famous USA chocolate company (based in Hershey, Pennsylvania) is recommended. It isn't acceptable to dive into the undulating vats of liquid chocolate, but you can find out how chocolate bars are created and then start eating (discounts offered). Hershey Dr is off Hwy 43 East – just follow your nose. Tours are given weekdays only, but you can do it yourself.

The locks can be viewed in the middle of town, and the best of the three small historical museums is the **Rideau Canal Museum** (☎ 613-284-0505, 34 Beckworth St S; admission $3; open 10am-4:30pm Victoria Day–mid-Oct), which is housed in a 19th-century mill. Exhibits detail the history of the canal.

CORNWALL & AROUND
pop 47,000
Cornwall is the first city of any size in Ontario along the St Lawrence Valley and has the Seaway International Bridge to the USA. It was here in the 1870s that Thomas Edison, creator of the light bulb, helped set up the first factory lit by electricity. Despite this corner of Ontario having Scottish and Loyalist ancestry, there is a good-sized French population in Cornwall.

The **Pitt St Mall**, in the center of town, is a pedestrian-only two-block section of stores and gardens. The **Inverarden Regency Cottage Museum** (☎ 613-938-9585, 3332 Montréal Rd; open Apr-Nov), built in 1816 by a retiring fur trader who had evidently done quite well, represents Ontario's finest example of Regency Cottage architecture.

Just out of town, on Cornwall Island, there is the **Native North American Travelling College Museum** (☎ 613-932-9452; admission free; open 8am-4pm daily June-Sept, rest of the year Mon-Fri), which focuses on the Cree, Iroquois and Ojibway Indians with artifacts and a replica village.

The bridge over to Massena, New York, makes Cornwall another busy port of entry for US visitors.

In **Maxville**, to the north, Highland Games held at the beginning of August commemorate the region's Scottish heritage. **St Raphaels** has some interesting church ruins dating from 1815. West of Cornwall, the **Long Sault Parkway** connects a series of parks and beaches along the river.

MORRISBURG AREA

Morrisburg is a small town that lies west of Cornwall on the St Lawrence River. Despite its small size, it's known far and wide for its good historic site, **Upper Canada Village** (☎ 613-543-4328, 800-437-2233; adult/child $16/7; open 9:30am-5pm daily mid-May–mid-Oct). This detailed re-creation of a country town from the 1860s consists of about 40 buildings, and costumed workers bring the past to life. There's a blacksmith's shop, inn and sawmill, as well as a working farm, all set by the river. You'll need at least several hours to fully explore the site. Without transportation, the village can be reached aboard buses running between Ottawa and Cornwall and on some buses that follow the Montréal to Toronto route. Many are direct, while others putt along, stopping at the smaller towns en route. Nearby **Crysler Battlefield Park** is a memorial to those who died fighting the USA in 1812.

Parks of the St Lawrence government agency (☎ 613-543-3704, 800-437-2233), based in Morrisburg, runs Upper Canada Village, the **Upper Canada Migratory Bird Sanctuary** (see below) and Fort Henry, in Kingston, as well as many of the campgrounds and parks along the river between Cornwall and Kingston.

Hwy 2 along the river is slower to travel but provides a more scenic trip than Hwy 401. It's used by many cyclists. There are numerous provincial parks along the way, especially east of town along the Long Sault Parkway. Going west, there is a seaway-viewing platform at **Iroquois**.

There are about half a dozen *motels* in Morrisburg and four *campgrounds*.

Upper Canada Migratory Bird Sanctuary Nature Awareness Campsite (☎ 613-543-3704, 800-437-2233, Hwy 2) Tent sites $19. This place is a little different from the average campground and is educational, too. Find it 14km east of town along Hwy 2. It has about 50 tent sites but few creature comforts.

PRESCOTT
pop 4000

Another 19th-century town, Prescott is the site of the International Bridge to Ogdensburg, New York. The harbor area has been overhauled and has a busy marina, but there isn't anything of note for the traveler.

Just to the east of the downtown area and walkable from the center is the **Fort Wellington National Historic Site** (☎ 613-925-2896; admission $3; open 10am-5pm daily May-Sept). The original fort was built during the War of 1812. It was rebuilt in 1838 and served militarily until the 1920s. Some original fortifications remain, as does a blockhouse and the officers' quarters from the 1830s. During summer, guides in costume supplement the interpretive displays. In the third week of July, the fort hosts the country's largest military pageant, which includes mock battles in full regalia. Outside the grounds are a few picnic tables with views of the river.

BROCKVILLE
pop 21,000

A small community along the river, Brockville is a particularly attractive town, with its many old stone buildings and the classic-looking main street. The courthouse and jail in the center of town date from 1842. During summer, many of the finest buildings are lit up, accentuating the slight resort flavor of this casual river port by the Thousand Islands. Cruises depart from the central waterfront area.

The **Brockville Museum** (☎ 613-342-4397, 5 Henry St; admission $3; open 10am-5pm Mon-Sat, 1pm-5pm Sun May-Oct; weekdays only rest of the year), in the historic Beecher House, provides a look at the area's history.

Fulford Place National Historic Site (☎ 613-498-3003, 287 King St E; adult/child $5/4; open 11am-4pm Wed-Sun June-Sept; weekends only rest of the year) is a 35-room Edwardian mansion from the 1900s. The other principal attraction, the **Brockville Railway Tunnel** (admission free; open May-Sept), the oldest train tunnel in the country, is for buffs only.

For the Thousand Island Parkway area west of Brockville, see Around Kingston, later in this chapter.

KINGSTON
pop 138,000

Kingston is a handsome town that retains much of its past through its preservation of many historic buildings and defense structures. Built strategically, where Lake Ontario flows into the St Lawrence River, it is a convenient stopping-off point almost exactly halfway between Montréal and

Toronto, and it's not difficult to spend an interesting and enjoyable day or three in and around town.

Once a fur-trading depot, Kingston later became the principal British military post west of Québec and was the national capital for a while. The many 19th-century buildings of local gray limestone and the streets of red-brick Victorian houses give the downtown area a distinctive charm. The attractive waterfront is also pleasant.

The city is home to Queen's University (founded in 1841) and the impressive cathedrals of St George (280 King St E) and St Mary (279 Johnson St). To all of this, add paradoxically that the city houses several large, (in)famous prisons.

Kingston was once a waterfront defense town; evidence of this is found in Confederation Park, which runs from City Hall down to the river, where yachts moor.

On Tuesday, Thursday, Saturday and Sunday, a small, open-air market takes place downtown, behind City Hall on King St.

Orientation & Information

Kingston lies a few kilometers south of Hwy 401. Princess St, the main street, runs right down to the St Lawrence River, along which are many fine old buildings. The whole city is low-rise, with few buildings higher than two or three stories, and there aren't many modern structures either.

At the bottom of Princess St, Ontario St runs along the harbor by the start of the Rideau Canal to Ottawa. This is the old, much restored area, with a tourist office, Victoria Battery and Shoal Tower (in Confederation Park), one of the four Martello towers in the city. There are views across the mouth of the canal to the Royal Military College.

King St leads out along the lake's shore toward the university. Here you'll see many fine 19th-century houses and parkland. A few blocks north of King St on Court St, the impressive limestone County Courthouse is near the campus, facing a small park. Farther out is Lake Ontario Park, with camping and a small beach.

The main downtown office of Kingston Tourism (☎ 613-548-4415, 888-855-4555, w www.kingstoncanada.com, 209 Ontario St) is across from City Hall in Confederation Park.

Away from the city center, the Fort Henry Information Centre (☎ 613-542-7388) is at the fort, near the junction of Hwys 2 and 15. It's open only from May to September.

The post office (120 Clarence St) is open 9am to 4pm weekdays.

The public library (☎ 613-549-8888, 130 Johnson St) has free Internet service.

Hotel Dieu Hospital (☎ 613-544-3310, 166 Brock St) is centrally located.

Indigo (☎ 613-546-7650, 259 Princess St) is a wide-ranging bookstore and has a café that even serves wine.

For all your quality outdoor/camping equipment and supplies, check out the selection at Trailhead (☎ 613-546-4757, 237 Princess St).

Fort Henry National Historic Site

This restored British fortification (☎ 613-542-7388, Fort Henry Dr; adult/student/child $11/8.50/5.25; open 10am-5pm daily late May-Oct), dating from 1832, dominates the town from its hilltop perch and is the city's prime attraction. The beautiful structure is brought to life by colorfully uniformed guards trained in military drills, artillery exercises, and the fife-and-drum music of the 1860s. Inside the fort, you can peek into, among other things, a fully furnished officer's room and the commandant's quarters. Admission includes a guided tour.

The soldiers put on displays periodically throughout the day. The best is the Garrison Parade, performed daily at 3pm. In addition, special events are held almost monthly.

Without a car, the fort is a little difficult to reach, as there is no city bus. You can walk – it's not that far over the causeway from town – but the last 500m or so is all uphill. Other than hoofing it, try to share a taxi, and maybe get a ride back with a fellow visitor. Or, if you have a few things to do around town, consider renting a bike for the day (see Getting There & Around, later in this section, for information on rentals).

City Hall

The grand City Hall (☎ 613-546-4251, 261 Ontario St) is one of the country's finest classical buildings – an excellent example of British Renaissance Tuscan Revival–style architecture! Built of limestone, it dates

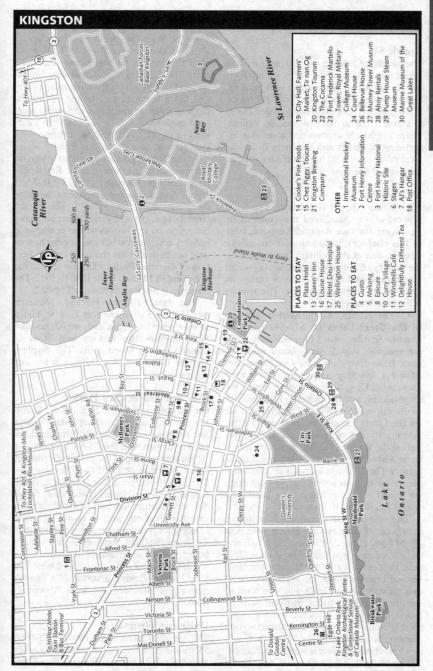

KINGSTON

St Lawrence River

Cataraqui River

Canadian Forces Base Kingston

Lundy's Lane

Constantine Dr

Mackenzie Cres

Navy Bay

Royal Military College

Frederick Dr

30 23

To Hwy 401

2

15

To Hwy 401 & Kingston Mills Lockstation Blockhouse

Concession St
Adelaide St
Stanley St
Pine St
Hamilton St

James St
Charles St
John St
Raglan Rd

Patrick St
York St
Quebec St
Plum St

Frontenac St

Victoria Park

Mack St
Brock St

Albert St

Nelson St

Victoria St

Toronto St

MacDonell St

Durham St
Park St

To Hilltop Motel, Train Station & Bus Terminal

2

Kingston Mills

Princess St

University Ave

Chatham St

Alfred St

Johnson St

Earl St

Collingwood St

Beverly St

Kensington St

Egde Hill

To Donald Gordon Centre

To Lake Ontario Park, Kingston Archaeological Centre & Correctional Service of Canada Museum

LaSalle Causeway

Anglin Bay

Inner Harbour

500 m
500 yards
0   250
0   250

Ferry to Wolfe Island

Kingston Harbour

Ontario St

Confederation Park

King St E

Wellington St

Rideau St

Bagot St

Montreal St

Bay St

Sydenham St

Wellington St

Clarence St

William St

Earl St

Gore St

Ontario St

Brock St

Queen St

Johnson St

Barrie St

Clergy St W

King St W

Queen's University

Queens Cres

Union St

Stewart St

City Park

Macdonald Park

Lake Ontario

Breakwater Park

20
19
21 22
13 14
15
12
10 11
18
9
17
8 6
5 7
16
24
4
26
30 29
28
27
25

McBurney Park

Ordnance St
Colborne St
Barrie St
Main St
Garrett St
Division St
Clergy St

Victoria Park

2

PLACES TO STAY
9   Plaza Hotel
13 Queen's Inn
16 Louise House
17 Hotel Dieu Hospital
25 Wellington House

PLACES TO EAT
4   Gusto
5   Mekong
8   Epicure
10 Curry Village
11 Windmills Café
12 Delightfully Different Tea House
14 Cooke's Fine Foods
15 Chez Piggy; Toucan
21 Kingston Brewing Company

OTHER
1   International Hockey Museum
2   Fort Henry Information Centre
3   Fort Henry National Historic Site
6   Stages
7   Al's Hangar
18 Post Office
19 City Hall; Farmers' Market; Tir nan Og
20 Kingston Tourism
22 The Cocama
23 Fort Frederick Martello Tower; Royal Military College Museum
24 Court House
26 Bellevue House
27 Murney Tower Museum
28 Ahoy Rentals
29 Pump House Steam Museum
30 Marine Museum of the Great Lakes

from 1843, when Kingston was capital of the then United Provinces of Canada.

Brock St

The middle of town in the 19th century was Brock St, and many of the original shops still stand along it. It's worth a walk around. Take a look in **Cooke's Fine Foods** (61 Brock St), a gourmet shop with old, wooden counters and a century-old pressed-tin ceiling. There are lovely aromas and a curious assortment of goods and shoppers, including local professors drinking the fresh coffee at the back of the store.

Museums

Apart from what is listed here, there are several other specialized museums in or near Kingston (see Around Kingston, later in this chapter), including one on county schools; one at the military base, detailing the history of military communications and electronics; and others on such things as geology, mineralogy and art. The tourist office has details.

On the waterfront is the **Marine Museum of the Great Lakes** (☎ 613-542-2261, 55 Ontario St; admission $4 for museum, $6.50 for museum, ship & pump-house museum; open 10am-5pm daily June-Oct, 10am-4pm Mon-Fri Jan-May; ship open Mar-Labor Day only). Kingston was long a center for shipbuilding, and the museum is on the site of the shipyard. In 1678, the first vessel built on the Great Lakes was constructed here. Among its list of credits are ships built during the War of 1812. The museum details these and other aspects of the Great Lakes' history. The 3000-ton icebreaker Alexander Henry can be boarded. In fact, you can sleep on board – it's operated as a B&B and hostel (see Places to Stay, later).

The one-of-a-kind, completely restored, steam-run **Pump House Steam Museum** (☎ 613-542-2261, 23 Ontario St; admission $4; open 10am-5pm daily May-Labor Day) was first used in 1849. It now contains several engines and some scale models, all run on steam. Train buffs will also want to see the 20 model trains from around the world displayed in a special exhibit room. (See the previous listing for information on combo museum tickets.)

Correctional Service is what Canadian bureaucrats call jails, and the **Correctional**

Service of Canada Museum (☎ 613-530-3122, 555 King St W; admission free; open 9am-4pm Mon-Fri, 10am-4pm Sat & Sun May-Sept) is about as close as you'll get to finding out what they're like without doing something nasty. The museum is located in the administration building across from the main prison and has a fascinating collection of articles, ranging from confiscated weapons to tools (and methods – like carved cafeteria trays) used in escapes. A visit is worthwhile – it's eye-opening, educational and free.

In the Fort Frederick Martello tower, on the grounds of the college, is the **Royal Military College Museum** (☎ 613-541-5010, Hwy 2 East; admission free; open 10am-5pm daily late June-Labor Day). This is the largest of the city's historic towers and has a collection on the history of the century-old military college. You have to wonder how or why, but here also lies the small arms collection of General Porfirio Diaz, who was the president of Mexico from 1886 to 1912. The museum is just east of town, off Hwy 2.

The **International Hockey Museum** (☎ 613-544-2355, Alfred St at York St; admission $4; open 9am-5pm daily mid-June–mid-Sept) honors the history and stars of Canada's most loved sport. The displays include lots of memorabilia, photos and equipment.

Macdonald & City Parks

On the corner of Barrie St and King St E is Macdonald Park, right along Lake Ontario. Just offshore, in 1812, the British ship Royal George battled with the USA's USS Oneida. At the western end of the park is the **Murney Tower Museum** (☎ 613-544-9925; admission $3; open 10am-5pm daily June-Sept), in the Martello tower from 1846. This round defense structure was part of the early riverside fortifications and is now a museum housing local military and historical tidbits. There are walking and bicycle paths along here and good swimming by the jetty.

On the corner of King St E and West St is City Park, featuring a statue of Canada's first prime minister, Sir John Alexander Macdonald.

Bellevue House

This national historic site (☎ 613-545-8666, 35 Centre St; admission $3; open June-Sept 9am-6pm daily; reduced hours spring & fall, *closed Nov-Apr)* is a superbly maintained Tuscan-style mansion, which apparently means a very odd-shaped, balconied, brightly painted architect's field day. It works though, and in the garden setting, this is an impressive and interesting house. It was once the home of Sir John Alexander Macdonald. The mansion houses many good antiques.

Kingston Archaeological Centre

If you've been out along Hwy 401, you probably noticed the sedimentary rock outcrops, one of the few interesting things along that highway's entire length from Montréal to Toronto. The Kingston Archaeological Centre *(☎ 613-542-3483, behind Tett Creativity Centre, 370 King St W; admission free; open 9am-4pm Mon-Fri)* has displays on the 8000-year human history of the area, featuring items dug from the surrounding landscape or found along the shoreline. Staff are helpful and may well show you items not on display.

Kingston Mills Lockstation Blockhouse

Away from the center, just north of Hwy 401, this restored blockhouse *(☎ 613-359-5377, Kingston Mills Rd; admission free; open 10am-4pm daily mid-May–mid-Oct)* dates from 1839. The purpose of the lock station and what it was like to operate are part of the explanatory exhibits.

Wolfe Island

It's possible to have a free minicruise by taking the car ferry from Kingston to Wolfe Island. The 20-minute trip affords views of the city, the fort and a few of the Thousand Islands. Wolfe Island, the largest in the chain at 30km by 11km, lies halfway to the USA and is basically flat farmland, although many of its inhabitants now work in town.

There is not a lot to see on the island, but there is the *General Wolfe Hotel (☎ 613-385-2611)*, a short walk from the dock, with its three busy and highly regarded dining rooms. Prices are moderate to slightly expensive. There are also some moderately priced *cabins* on the island, *B&Bs* and a *campground* (see Places to Stay) On the Kingston side, the ferry terminal is at the intersection of Ontario and Barrack Sts. The ferry runs continuously every hour or

so from 6am to 1am daily, taking about 50 vehicles at a time. From Wolfe Island, another ferry links to Cape Vincent, New York, but a toll is charged on this segment if you have a car.

Organized Tours

The tourist office has a pamphlet with map for a self-guided walking tour of the older part of town.

During summer and autumn, a **Haunted Walk** *(☎ 613-549-6366)*, a two-hour tour featuring stories of hangings and grave robbers ($10), leaves from the tourist information office every Tuesday to Saturday at 8pm.

On summer days, a trackless mini-train **Confederation Tour Trolley** *(☎ 613-548-4453)* departs regularly from the tourist office area for a 50-minute tour of the central Kingston area (adult/senior & student $10/8).

Boat tours will take you around some of the islands; a couple of companies run daily trips in summer. **Kingston 1000 Island Cruises** *(☎ 613-549-5544, 1 Brock St)* has several choices leaving from the Island Queen dock, on Ontario St at the foot of Brock St. The 1½ hour trip ($15) aboard the *Island Belle* takes you around the interesting Kingston shoreline with a commentary on some of the noteworthy sites. Throughout summer, it offers two or three trips a day. There are also three-hour cruises ($20), and dinner or sunset options on their other vessel, the *Island Queen* showboat.

See Thousand Islands Parkway, later in this chapter, for more cruises.

Places to Stay

Camping There are a few good camping options.

Lake Ontario Park (☎ 613-542-6574, fax 613-542-6574, King St W) Tent sites $20. Only 4km from downtown, this convenient campground is operated by the city's parks department. It's west, out along King St, and is green and pretty quiet. There's a small, weedy beach. A city bus runs from downtown right to the campground from Monday to Saturday until 7:30pm (Friday until 10:30pm).

Hi-Lo Hickory (☎ 613-385-2430, 877-996-7432, fax 613-385-1424, 260 Hogan Rd) Tent sites $20. This campground on Wolfe Island is reached by ferry from Kingston. The campground is about 12km east of the

Kingston ferry terminal and has a beach. A bridge on the island's other side connects to New York.

Kampgrounds of America (KOA; ☎ 613-546-6140, 800-562-9178, fax 613-546-6178, 2039 Cordukes Rd) Campsites $22-29. These campgrounds are seen all over North America, and there is a branch 1.6km north of Hwy 401, off Hwy 38. Generally, they are very plastic, having as little to do with camping as possible, and they are also expensive, big, and pretty busy. They cater mainly to trailers but have some tent sites.

Hostels Also see the *Alexander Henry*, under B&Bs, below.

Louise House (☎ 613-531-8237 ext 400, fax 613-531-9763, 329 Johnson St) Dorm beds $18, singles/doubles with breakfast $35/50. Open May-late Aug. Hostelling International operates this summer-only hostel downtown. The rest of the year, this house (dating from 1847) is a university residence.

B&Bs The tourist office can help with more choices.

Alexander Henry (☎ 613-542-2261, fax 613-542-0043, [W] www.marmus.ca, 55 Ontario St) Rates $20-70. Open May-Oct. In summer, you can stay at this unique B&B on a moored, retired 64m icebreaker. The ship is part of the downtown Marine Museum of the Great Lakes (see Museums, earlier). Beds are in the former crew's quarters, and a continental breakfast is served from the galley. You can wander all over the ship. It hasn't been gentrified at all – the vessel is plain, simple and functional, and the 19 rooms are pretty much like those on a working ship. This partially explains the good prices, from hostel bunks to the captain's quarters.

Wellington House (☎ 613-544-9919, 60 Wellington St) Singles/doubles $40/50 with shared bath & full breakfast. This central place offers a very good value and is open all year.

O'Brien House (☎ 613-542-8660, 39 Glenaire Mews) Singles/doubles with shared bath & breakfast $48/70, $85 with private bath & breakfast. This place, up near the train station and northwest of the downtown area, is a little less costly than the city norm. The owners seem particularly to like overseas visitors. There are reduced rates for children, and coffee or tea is available all day.

Motels If these motels are full, there are many other motels on Princess St, and some along Hwy 2 on each side of town.

Hilltop Motel (☎ 613-542-3846, 2287 Princess St) Rooms $35-55. This fine budget place is clean, quiet and friendly.

Comfort Inn (☎ 613-549-5550, 800-228-5150, fax 613-549-1388, 1454 Princess St) Rooms $85-135. The rooms downstairs are a few dollars more at this modern, equipped place with a continental breakfast.

Hotels There a a few good hotel options in Kingston.

Plaza Hotel (☎ 613-542-4921, 46 Montréal St) Singles/doubles with bath $30/35. This is the only remaining old cheapie and is on the corner of Queen St. It exists basically for the downstairs bar but is not badly kept. It's no family place and is not recommended for single women, but it is cheap.

Donald Gordon Centre (☎ 613-533-2221, 421 Union St) Singles/doubles $90/110. This place is totally different and is affiliated with (and very near) Queen's University. The center rents quiet, air-conditioned rooms.

Queen's Inn (☎ 613-546-0429, 866-689-9177, fax 613-546-7283, 125 Brock St) Rooms $79-99. The historic and central Queen's, from 1839, is one of the oldest hotels in the country but now offers modern facilities, style and services in its 17 rooms.

Places to Eat

Windmills Café (☎ 613-544-3948, 184 Princess St) Lunch/dinner $8/13. Contemporary Windmills serves very good vegetarian and meat dishes amid café-for-grownups surroundings. The menu may have Thai shrimp salad or warm goat-cheese torte. Wine is served.

Delightfully Different Tea House (☎ 613-546-0236, 222 Wellington St) Dishes under $7. Open 8am-4pm Mon-Fri. On the corner of Queen St, this sedate place turns out excellent fresh sandwiches, salads and bagels for lunch, or muffins and the like for breakfast. It is worth getting to for a light meal and is very inexpensive.

Epicure (☎ 613-536-5389, 291 Princess St) Dishes under $8. Open 8am-late. Amid increasingly yuppified downtown Kingston is this bit of funk, grit and fun, where you can read the paper, quaff a beer and wolf down a breakfast or sandwich any time of day. On Sunday nights, there's a special of bouillabaisse, bread and glass of wine for $10.

Kingston Brewing Company (☎ *613-542-4978, 34 Clarence St*) Dishes $6-10. This pub brews its own ales and lagers – try its Dragon's Breath Ale – and also has a good selection of nonhouse brands. It also makes its own wines and ciders, the first in Canada to do so. There are inexpensive tavern-style things to munch on and, interestingly, a daily curry.

Curry Village (☎ *613-542-5010, 169A Princess St*) Lunch/dinner $8/10. Open 11:30am-2pm & 5pm-9:30pm Mon-Sat, 2pm-9pm Sun. You can get a fine Indian meal at this upstairs restaurant. The menu includes biryanis, tandooris and a range of curries – and even classic but hard-to-find mulligatawny.

Mekong (☎ *613-549-5902, 394 Princess St*) Dishes under $8. Students and members of the local Vietnamese community enjoy this spotless new entry with great food and low prices. How about spicy chicken, shrimp and a heap of veggies with vermicelli for $7?

Chez Piggy (☎ *613-549-7673, 68 Princess St*) Lunch/dinner $8/25. Open 11:30am-2pm & 6pm-10pm daily. For a splurge, this is probably the city's best-known restaurant. It's in a renovated early-19th-century building down a small alley off King St between Brock and Princess Sts, and though it's been a local fave since 1979, standards have never slipped. There is also a Sunday brunch, with some items you don't see on a standard brunch menu (but again, it is definitely not for the budget-conscious). The restaurant is owned by a member of the 1960s US pop band The Lovin' Spoonful.

Gusto (☎ *613-536-5175, 425 Princess St*) Dishes $8-20. This stylish new place at the corner of Division St could be the hippest spot in town. The design, the food and even the customers are all very well turned out.

Entertainment
Cocama (☎ *613-544-1428, 178 Ontario St*) This is a huge dance bar down near the water. It's styled after the Limelight in New York City.

AJ's Hangar (☎ *613-547-3657, 393 Princess St*) This multileveled student place

has a mix of live rock, pool tables and dancing.

Stages (☎ *613-547-3657, 390 Princess St*) Stages is a popular dance club just across the road from AJ's.

Toucan (☎ *613-544-1966, 76 Princess St*) This Irish pub, down the alley near King St, often has live music.

Tir nan Og (☎ *613-544-7474, 200 Ontario St*) Most nights, you can hear live Celtic music here with no cover charge.

Getting There & Around
The bus terminal (☎ 613-547-4916, 175 Counter St) is a couple of kilometers south of Hwy 401, east off Division St. Services going to Toronto are frequent throughout the day (at least eight trips); to Montréal, buses are slightly less frequent. To Ottawa, there are buses each morning, afternoon and evening. Services also go to some of the smaller centers, such as Pembroke and Cornwall. The one-way fare to Montréal is $46; Ottawa costs $31 and Toronto $45.

For information on getting around by bus, call Kingston Transit (☎ 613-546-4291). For getting into town from the bus station, there is a city bus stop across the street. Buses depart at 15 minutes before and after the hour. From the train station, city bus No 1 stops on the corner of Princess and Counter Sts, just a short walk from the bus station.

The VIA Rail station (☎ 613-544-5600) is a long way northwest from the downtown area. There are five train services to Montréal daily, costing $60. To Ottawa ($39), there are four trains a day. To Toronto ($62), there are eight services daily. Discounts are offered on tickets purchased five days or more in advance.

The car rental company Discount (☎ 613-548-4004, 333 Barrie St) offers pick-up and drop-off.

Bicycle riders will be happy to note that the Kingston area is generally flat, and both Hwys 2 and 5 have paved shoulders. Rentals are available at Ahoy Rentals (☎ 613-539-3202, 23 Ontario St).

AROUND KINGSTON
North of Kingston is the Rideau Lakes region, an area of small towns, cottages, lodges and marinas with opportunities for fishing and camping. In a day's drive, you can

explore some of the smaller, rural Ontario villages.

Wilton has one of the many southern Ontario regional cheese factories with a retail outlet. In the little town of **Yarker**, straight up Hwy 6 from Hwy 401, the *Waterfall Tea Room* (☎ *613-377-1856, 2810 Country Rd 6*) is right on the river, by a waterfall, and has been recommended. The region has attracted 'back-to-the-landers' and counterculture people. Their influences show up in the number of health-food stores, craft outlets and bakeries. In **Tamsworth**, there is an arts-and-crafts outlet. **Marlbank** is another similar town.

West of town, along the coast, Hwy 33 has been designated the **Loyalist Parkway**. It retraces the steps of the Loyalists who settled this area some 200 years ago after fleeing the American Revolution. The parkway runs for 94km from Kingston to Trenton, passing over Quinte's Isle. To continue along Hwy 33 at Adolphustown, catch the continuously running, short and free ferry over to Glenora (on Quinte's Isle) and continue on to Picton.

Thousand Islands Parkway

To the east of Kingston, between Gananoque (gan-an-**awk**-way) and Mallorytown Landing, a small road – the Thousand Islands Parkway – dips south of Hwy 401, runs along the river for 35km and then rejoins the highway. It makes a scenic and recommended side trip when traveling Hwy 401 in either direction.

The route offers picnic areas and good views out to many of the islands from the pastoral strip of shoreline. For information on lodging or activities, call or visit the chamber of commerce (☎ 613-382-3250, 800-561-1595, 2 King St E) in Gananoque.

The waterfront here is lined with some tourist-oriented shops in replica 19th-century architecture.

The **Bikeway** bicycle path extends the full length of the parkway. Bicycles can be rented at several places, including the **1000 Islands Camping Resort** (☎ *613-659-3058, RR1, Landsdowne*), 8km east of Gananoque.

The St Lawrence Parks System maintains a series of recreational and historic places along this route and on Hwy 2 from Adolphustown to beyond Upper Canada Village at Morrisburg and all the way to Lancaster

near the Québec border. Boat cruises around the islands depart from the two small towns of Rockport and Gananoque.

Some 16km east of Kingston, in a log house in Grass Creek Park, you will find the **MacLachlan Woodworking Museum** (☎ *613-542-0543, 2293 Hwy 2; admission $3, open 10am-5pm daily Victoria Day-Labor Day, reduced hours in spring and fall, closed Dec-Apr*). The museum uses an extensive collection of tools to outline the development of working in wood.

Close to the town of Lansdowne, between Gananoque and Rockport, is the busy bridge to New York State. The **Skydeck** (☎ *613-659-2335, Hill Island; admission $6, open 8:30am-dusk daily May-Oct*) is a 125m observation tower between the bridge spans. Its three decks provide great views over the river area. There's a restaurant on the premises.

There is a bit of an **art colony** in the area, and in autumn, many of the local studios are open to the public. Ask the tourist office in Kingston or Gananoque for a list of the painters, sculptors, woodworkers, glass workers, weavers and other artisans.

Along the parkway are privately run *campgrounds*, *B&Bs*, numerous *motels* and some *cottages* to rent for longer stays.

Thousand Islands This scenic area just east of Kingston actually has more than 1000 islands, which dot the river between the two national mainlands. In spring, the islands undulate with the white blooms of the trillium, the provincial flower.

In Gananoque, the **Gananoque Boat Line** (☎ *613-382-2144, off King St*) has trips daily in July and August, and less often in May, June and September. A one-hour ride is $12; a three-hour tour is $18. At impressive **Boldt Castle**, one of the stops on the long trip, you can get off for a closer look and return to Gananoque on a later boat. Passengers stopping at the castle, which was built in 1904 for Boldt's wife, are subject to US Customs regulations, and non-Canadians may need a passport *and* visa.

In nearby Rockport, the **Rockport Boat Line** (☎ *613-659-3402, 800-563-8687*) also has trips out among the international islands at about the same prices. Boat trips depart from the dock 3km east of the Thousand Islands International Bridge

Toronto skyline seen from Centre Island, Toronto, Ontario

Toronto's diverse Kensington Market, Ontario

Flags representing all the provinces, Ottawa

The Changing of the Guard on Parliament Hill, Ottawa, Ontario

Camping out on Lake Superior, Ontario

Looking up at skyscrapers in downtown Toronto, Ontario

Niagara Falls (Horseshoe Falls), Ontario – 600,000 liters of water pour over every second.

frequently in peak season, less so in spring and autumn. **Heritage 1000 Island Cruises** (☎ 613-659-3151, 888-229-9913) has cruises on two vintage vessels – one from 1929, the other from 1952. Both the above have a trip stopping at the castle. The autumn cruises with the colored leaves as a backdrop are justly popular.

A different angle is to do it all yourself on a rented houseboat. This can be a lot of fun, but it is pricey unless you get several people together. If you want to look into it, try **Houseboat Holidays** (☎ 613-382-2842, RR3), in Gananoque, and see Rideau Canal, later in this section.

St Lawrence Islands National Park
Within the gentle, green archipelago is Canada's smallest national park (☎ 613-923-5261), consisting of 17 islands scattered along 80km of the river. At **Mallorytown Landing**, on the mainland, is the park headquarters, with the interpretive and information center, a walking trail and a beach. The center is open all year, but access to the islands is only from Victoria Day to Labor Day.

Many of the islands have picnicking, and 13 islands offer primitive *campsites* with minimal facilities, accessible only by boat ($10). Water taxis and boat rentals are available from the park headquarters and from many of the small towns along the parkway. Tourist offices or park headquarters will have information on what is available. National Park islands stretch from just off Mallorytown all the way down to Gananoque.

Frontenac Provincial Park
This park (☎ 613-376-3489, Route 19; admission $8.50; open year-round) straddles both the lowlands of southern Ontario and the more northern Canadian Shield, so the flora, fauna and geology of the park are mixed. The park is designed for overnight hikers and canoeists. There is no formal campground – rather, there are interior campsites scattered through the park, accessible only on foot or by water. Though the park is large, there are relatively few sites. Trails and canoe routes have been mapped out.

The entrance and the information center are at **Otter Lake**, off Route 19 north of Sydenham. The swimming is excellent, the bass fishing is pretty good, and there are no bears to worry about. **Frontenac Outfitters** (☎ 613-376-6220), near the main entrance, rents canoes.

Bon Echo Provincial Park
Northwest from Kingston up Hwy 41 is this park (☎ 613-336-2228; admission $8.50; open late May-lateOct). One of the largest parks in eastern Ontario, it's another good spot for canoeing. Some of the lakes are quite shallow and get very warm. There are walk-in and canoe-in campsites or roadside

---

Nothing New about Refugees

The issue of American independence from Britain divided the American colonies into two camps: the Patriots and the Loyalists. During the American Revolution (1775–83), the Loyalists maintained their allegiance to the British Crown. About one-third of the 13 colonies' population remained loyal to Britain. Severe laws were passed against them, forcing some 200,000 to leave during and after the revolution. Of those, between 50,000 and 60,000 fled to Canada, settling in the Maritimes, the Eastern Townships of Lower Canada (what's now known as Québec) and the St Lawrence–Lake Ontario region of Upper Canada (Ontario). Unknown to many today, not all were of British descent – they represented a mix of ethnic backgrounds. Regardless, their arrival strengthened Great Britain's hold on this part of its empire. In Nova Scotia, for example, the migration meant that the French no longer made up the majority of the population.

In this region, the Loyalists' arrival essentially led to the formation of the province of Ontario. Both the British and local governments were generous in their support, offering clothing, rations, and various aid and land grants.

Soon the Loyalists in Canada were not only self-sustaining but prosperous and powerful. Today their descendants make up a significant and influential segment of the Canadian population.

Loyalist sites can be seen in southern Québec, on Québec's Gaspé Peninsula and, in particular, at Saint John, New Brunswick, and Shelburne, Nova Scotia.

campgrounds with facilities. At Mazinaw Lake, there are Native Indian **rock paintings** on granite cliffs.

Rideau Canal

This 150-year-old, 200km-long canal/river/lake system connects Kingston with Ottawa. The historical route is good for boating or canoeing trips, with parks, small towns, lakes and many places to stop en route. When traveling from one end to the other, boats must pass through 47 lock systems. The old defense buildings along the way have been restored.

After the War of 1812, there was a fear that there could be yet another war with the Americans. The Duke of Wellington decided to link Ottawa and Kingston with a canal in order to have a reliable communications and supply route between the two military centers. Although the canal is just 200km in length, its construction was a brutal affair, involving as many as 4000 men battling malaria and the Canadian Shield, and working with some of the world's hardest rock. It climbs 84m from Ottawa over the Shield, then drops 49m to Lake Ontario. And guess what? Right! It never saw any military service.

It did prove useful later in the century for shipping goods around, but it is now used mainly for recreation. **Houseboat Holidays** (☎ 613-382-2842, RR3, Gananoque) rents houseboats for meandering along the canal. The boats sleep six to eight and come with all kitchen necessities (midweek/weekend/weekly rates start at $725/525/1000).

Roads run parallel with much of the canal, so walking or cycling is also possible.

Rideau Trail

The Rideau Trail is a 400km hiking trail system that links Kingston with Ottawa. It passes through Westport, Smiths Falls and many conservation areas, traversing forests, fields and marshes as well as some stretches of road along the way.

There are some historic sites on the route, and you'll see the Rideau Canal. There are also 64km of side loops. Most people use the route only for day trips, but longer trips and overnighting are possible. The main trail is marked by orange triangles; side trails are marked by blue triangles. The Rideau Trail Association (☎ 613-545-

0823) prints a map kit for the entire route. Between Kingston and Smiths Falls are numerous *camping* spots. The rest of the way, there is not as much provision for camping, but there are commercial accommodations. Camping on private land is possible, but get the owner's permission first.

QUINTE'S ISLE

Irregularly shaped Quinte's Isle provides a quiet and scenic retreat from the bustle of much of southern Ontario. The rolling farmland is reminiscent of Prince Edward Island, and in fact, Quinte's Isle is also known as Prince Edward County. Many of the little towns were settled in the 18th and 19th centuries. The cemeteries adjacent to the village churches reveal clues to these earlier times. The island has been somewhat rediscovered and is slowly being developed for visitors but hasn't changed very much yet.

Traffic is light on most of the island's roads, which lead past large old farmhouses and cultivated fields. The St Lawrence River is never far away, and many routes offer good views. **Fishing** is quite good in the Bay of Quinte and the locals use the waters for **sailing**. The island is popular for **cycling** – it's generally flat, and some of the smaller roads are well shaded. The excellent **strawberry-picking** in late June draws many outsiders.

There are three provincial parks, including **North Beach** (☎ 613-399-2030; day-use only) and the fine **Sandbanks** (☎ 613-393-3319), the only park that offers camping (see Places to Stay). The park is divided into two sections: the Outlet (with an excellent strip of sandy beach) and Sandbanks itself (containing most of the area's sand dunes, some over three stories high). There's a large undeveloped section at the end of the beach – good for walking and for exploring the dunes and backwaters.

On the other side of the island, **Lake on the Mountain**, the third park, is really nothing more than a picnic site but is worth a visit to see the unusual lake. It sits on one side of the road at a level actually higher than that of the road, while just across the street is a terrific view over Lake Ontario and some islands hundreds of meters below. Geologists are still speculating as to the lake's origins. The local Mohawk Indians have their own legends about the lake, which appears to have no source. One story has it that the lake is secretly fed by Niagara Falls.

The small town of **Picton** is the only town of any size on the island and has one of the six district museums. The main street's chamber of commerce (☎ 613-476-2421, 800-640-4717) has detailed maps of the island and some information on current accommodations. Get the Picton walking-tour guide, which leads you past some of the fine historic buildings in town. Another guide lists various island attractions, including **Bird House City**, with dozens of painted birdhouses (including a fire station and courthouse).

Belleville & Around

There's not much for the visitor in Belleville, across the Bay of Quinte – it's more a departure point for Quinte's Isle. But in July, the **Waterfront & Folklorama Festival** puts on three days of events, music and shows. Hwy 37 continues north through old Tweed to Hwy 7, which is the main route to Toronto from Ottawa. It's a bit slow, with only two lanes, but the scenery is good. There are a couple of parks along the way and several places to eat.

The **Tyendinaga Mohawk Territory** (a Native Indian reserve) is just off Quinte's Isle and is also mainly farmland. In mid-May, the original coming of the Mohawks is re-enacted in full tribal dress.

The **Native Renaissance II Gallery & Shop** (☎ 613-396-3255, Hwy 49, Deseronto), 29km east of Belleville on Tyendinaga Mohawk Territory, has a sizable collection of Native Indian arts and crafts and a section where new ones are created. It's open every day. At Shannonville, in the same direction but just 12km from Belleville, the **Mosport Speedway** is the site of motorcycle and drag racing periodically through summer. **Mapledale Cheese** (☎ 613-477-2454, RR1, Plainfield), sells excellent cheddar. It's north of Belleville up Hwy 37, roughly 10km north of Hwy 401.

Places to Stay

The area is best known for its camping. There are several commercial campgrounds near Sandbanks that are not as busy and worth atry if you can't get in there. There are numerous resorts, cottages, motels and B&Bs covering a range of prices. For a day or two, you're best off at a B&B, but for longer stays,

check into one of the simpler cabins or cottages. Some of the less costly places are situated in the Cherry Valley area. For accommodations information, contact the Picton chamber (listed earlier) or Belleville Tourism (☎ 888-852-9992). If all the accommodations options are booked out, try the motels around Belleville's perimeter – it's not far to return to the island the following day.

Sandbanks (☎ 613-393-3319, off Hwy 33) is the only park offering camping and is one of the most popular parks in the province; sites cost $16 to $22. Book ahead – reservations are definitely required, especially for weekends, when a fair bit of partying goes on.

Isiah Tubbs Inn & Resort (☎ 613-393-2090, 800-724-2393, West Lake Rd) is the most expensive place on the island and is costly even by Toronto standards (rooms are $120-300), but the luxury facilities and very fine design keep visitors coming back.

TRENTON

Small Trenton is known as the starting point of the **Trent-Severn Waterway**, which runs 386km through 44 locks to Georgian Bay, in Lake Huron. Yachties and sailors of every description follow this old Native Indian route each summer. The waterway cuts diagonally across southern Ontario cottage country, following rivers and lakes from Trenton (on Lake Ontario) to Georgian Bay, at the mouth of the Severn River (near Port Severn and Honey Harbour). It travels through or near many of the region's best-known resort areas, including the **Kawartha Lakes** and **Lake Simcoe**. Used a century ago for commerce, the system is now strictly recreational and is operated by Parks Canada. The water flow is regulated by a series of 125 dams along the route. The canal is opened for use in mid-May and closes in mid-October. A cruise ship plies the route, taking seven days. Shorter, four-day trips are also available. These are not cheap, but ask in Peterborough (see that section, later) for details.

Several companies along the route rent houseboats by the weekend, by the week or for longer periods. The boats come more or less fully equipped; some even have barbecues and can accommodate up to eight people (six adults), which makes for not only a good party but also a more reasonably priced one. The trips are good for families, too, with separate sleeping rooms for the kids. **Egan Houseboat Rentals** (☎ 705-799-5745, Egan Marine, RR4, Omemee), west of Peterborough on Route 7, is well established. Being right by the Kawartha Lakes gives you the option of hanging around the lakes or going all the way to Lake Simcoe.

Rates vary quite a bit, depending on timing, but start at about $550 for a weekend. On average, you will use about $140 worth of gasoline in a week.

Presqu'ile Provincial Park (☎ 613-475-4324) Tent sites $16-23. This park is west of Trenton and south of Brighton. A popular feature is the immense beach, but birdwatchers make up a sizable portion of the campers. The park has a large adjacent marsh, which is home to many species and represents a migration pit stop to many more in spring and autumn. Boardwalks allow access to portions of the wetlands. The camping is good, too, with large, treed sites. At Beach 3, you can rent boats, sailboarding equipment and bicycles.

Lake Ontario Waterfront Trail
Years of work through the 1990s by provincial and local governments, community groups and conservation authorities resulted in the opening of the 325km Lake Ontario Waterfront Trail, which stretches from Trenton through Toronto to Hamilton on the far western edge of Lake Ontario.

Suitable for walking, cycling and even inline skating, the trail links 160 natural areas, 126 parks and dozens of museums, galleries and historic sites. Hundreds of organized activities, from sidewalk sales to jazz festivals, take place along the trail during summer. The Waterfront Regeneration Trust (☎ 416-314-8572) in Toronto can provide maps and information on trail events, or ask at the Trenton tourist office (☎ 613-392-7635, 800-930-3255, 97 Front St).

KAWARTHA LAKES
Many of the pretty towns in the Kawartha Lakes vacation region have a good restaurant or two and, usually, a couple of antique dealers – **Bobcaygeon** and **Fenelon Falls** are two towns that are worth dropping into if you're up this way (the former also hosts a big fiddle contest each July).

Natural Areas
The district has some interesting parks as well. **Petroglyphs Provincial Park** (☎ 705-877-2552, off Hwy 28; admission $8.50; open mid-May–Thanksgiving) has probably the best collection of prehistoric rock carvings in the country. Rediscovered in 1954, there are reportedly 900 figures and shapes carved into the park's limestone ridges. The portions of the collection that are easy to view are much smaller than the figure 900 might suggest, and though interesting, it is not an overwhelming site. The most visible petroglyphs have been enclosed to protect the rock from acid rain, which is a serious problem over much of Ontario. The area and small lake within the park remain important spiritual sites for the local Native Indians.

Serpent Mounds Provincial Park (☎ 705-295-6879; off Route 34; admission $8.50; open May-Oct) is the site of an ancient Native Indian burial ground.

North up Route 38, the **Warsaw Caves Conservation Area** (☎ 877-816-7604) has hiking, swimming, camping and spelunking in eroded limestone tunnels and caves.

Peterborough & Around
pop 75,000
Peterborough is a middle-sized town more or less at the center of the Kawartha Lakes region. The older downtown area has some fine buildings; it's all very green, although the city seems in some danger of becoming a Toronto suburb. **Trent University** is another feature of the town's character.

The Trent-Severn Waterway passes through the large hydraulic-lift lock, a major landmark in town. A visitors' center shows how the locks along the system operate, and there is a working model. You can go on a trip through the locks into the Otonabee River or, if you're hooked, on a three- or five-day cruise through the locks and along part of the system.

Canoeing is a popular activity. Possibilities include easy trips on the canal or, in spring, tougher whitewater trips on rivers in the area. From Peterborough, you can get to Serpent Mounds Provincial Park (see the previous section); ask at the tourist office. The Ministry of Natural Resources publishes a map called *North Kawartha Canoe Routes*, which shows some possible trips and their portage distances.

The **Canadian Canoe Museum** (☎ 705-748-9153, 910 Monaghan Rd; admission $6.50; open 10am-5pm daily May-Oct; 10am-4pm Mon-Fri, 1pm-4pm Sat & Sun Nov-May) is excellent. It has a huge and fabulous collection with 200 canoes and kayaks on display, as well as other related exhibits in the well-designed and attractive space.

Southeast of Peterborough 10km is **Lang Pioneer Village** (☎ 705-295-6694, Hwy 7 to County Rd 34; adult/child $6/3; open noon-5pm Sun-Fri, 1pm-4pm Sat, late May-early Sept), with costumed workers, demonstrations and 20 buildings dating from 1800 to 1900.

A few kilometers north is **Lakefield**, a small town with a co-educational school. Formerly a boys-only school, Lakefield was the school to which Queen Elizabeth II sent Prince Andrew.

About 900 Ojibway reside on 400-hectare **Curve Lake Indian Reserve**, off Hwy 28, roughly 34km north of Peterborough. The reserve's *Whetung Ojibway Centre* (☎ 705-657-3661; admission free; open 9am-5pm daily year-round) has a vast collection of native crafts from around the country. The log building contains both new and old examples of Native Indian art, and the museum section has traditional pieces and valuable works from such artists as Norval Morrisseau. Some articles, including hand-made jackets and baskets, can be bought. The tearoom, open May to Thanksgiving, offers traditional foods such as buffalo burger and corn soup. The reserve, established in 1825, is off Curve Lake Rd, which runs out of Hwy 507. Continuing north you come to a less busy, less populated, hilly region known as the **Haliburton Highlands**. Bobcaygeon has some charm. Hwy 507 north through Catchacoma and Gooderham (which has a small waterfall) is perhaps the narrowest, oldest-looking highway in the province; it often seems more like a country lane.

Southwestern Ontario

This designation covers everything south and west of Toronto to Lake Huron and Lake Erie, which border the USA. For the most part, the area is flat farmland – the only area in Ontario with little forest – and population density is high. With the warm climate and long growing season, this southern tip of Canada was settled early.

Arching around Lake Ontario is a continuous strip of urbanization. This 'Golden Horseshoe' helps make the region one of the most industrialized and wealthy in the country. Hamilton, the largest city in the area, is a major steel town. Niagara, with its famous falls, is an important fruit-growing and wine-producing district.

Farther west, the soil becomes sandier, and the main crop is tobacco, although this is changing to ginseng, hemp and others as the Canadian cigarette market shrinks. Around Kitchener and London, the small towns are centers for the mixed farming of the region. Lake Erie and, especially, Lake Huron have sandy beaches. In some of the older country towns, crafts and antiques are available. Windsor – like Detroit, Michigan (its counterpart across the river) – is a hub for auto manufacturing.

Because the area is heavily populated and the USA is close by, attractions and parks do get busy in summer. In general, this is an area for people-related activities and pastimes, not for nature or rugged landscapes.

HAMILTON
pop 319,000
Hamilton, sometimes referred to as Steeltown, is a heavily industrialized city not high on many people's to-do list. As the center of Canada's iron and steel industry, with two major companies, Stelco and Dofasco, based here, it has a reputation for pollution.

Action has been taken to clean it up, and work in this direction continues. Although the air cannot be compared to that of the far north (what can?), these days, some of what one sees billowing from the many smokestacks is actually steam.

While Hamilton is obviously not a tourist mecca, there are nonetheless a few good things to see in and around town. As accommodations are modest, it's worth considering spending the night if you're planning a look around Niagara-on-the-Lake, which has high prices. Hamilton is halfway between Toronto and Niagara Falls. Its airport is increasingly important with the budget carrier WestJet using it as a less costly hub than Toronto.

The **Festival of Friends** takes place each August in Gage Park and features music, crafts and foods from many countries. Each June, in the town of Stoney Creek (south of Hamilton), there is an interesting spectacle – a re-enactment of a War of 1812 battle between British and USA soldiers. It's held at Stoney Creek Battlefield Park.

The **Hamilton Tiger Cats** (☎ 905-527-1508) play CFL football at **Ivor Wynn Stadium** (75 Balsam Ave) from July to November.

Orientation & Information
King St (one way going west) and Main St (one way going east, parallel to and one block south of King St) are the two main streets. King St has most of the downtown shops and restaurants. King and John Sts are the core of the downtown area. Jackson Square, on King St between Bay and James Sts, is a large shopping complex that includes restaurants, cinemas and even an indoor skating rink. James St, at Jackson Square Park with its fountain, divides the east and west street designations. The Con-

vention Centre (with an art gallery) is on the corner of King and McNab Sts. Just south across Main St is City Hall.

The downtown central tourist office (☎ 905-546-2666, 800-263-8590, 127 King St E) operates 9am to 5pm daily in summer and is otherwise closed Sunday. Other summer-only information booths are in busy visitors' centers around the city, such as the Royal Botanical Gardens or the African Lion Safari.

Royal Botanical Gardens
The Royal Botanical Gardens (☎ 905-527-1158, 680 Plains Rd W; adult/senior & child $8/7; open 9am-dusk daily), which consists of nearly 1000 hectares of flowers, natural park and wildlife sanctuary, is the big attraction in the area. It is one of the largest of its kind in the country and only one of five in the world to be designated 'Royal.' The grounds are split into sections, with trails connecting some areas.

During spring, the **Rock Garden** is a highlight, with its three hectares of rare trees and shrubs, waterfalls, ponds and 125,000 spring-flowering bulbs. From June to

SOUTHWESTERN ONTARIO

October, thousands of roses, including many antique varieties, bloom in the Centennial Rose Garden. The arboretum boasts the world's largest lilac collection (what an olfactory treat), which is best in May.

The sanctuary takes up nearly half of the grounds and consists of trails winding through marsh and wooded ravines – a paradise for bird-watchers and home to deer, fox, muskrat and coyotes. There is also an **interpretive center** and two *restaurants* at the gardens.

Coyote live in the Royal Botanical Gardens.

The site is between Hamilton and the suburban community of Burlington, on Plains Rd, near the junction of Hwys 2 and 6. It's open all year, but the outdoor areas have little to show from October to May.

Art Gallery of Hamilton
The art gallery (☎ 905-527-6610, 123 King St W; admission free; open 11am-5pm Tues, Wed & Fri-Sun, 11am-9pm Thur), the province's third largest, is spacious and has a good selection of Canadian and international paintings. It also runs an interesting film series, with screenings mainly on weekends.

Hamilton Place
In the same complex as the art gallery, this theater/auditorium for the performing arts (☎ 905-546-3100, 123 King St W) features shows of various types almost nightly, including regular performances by the Philharmonic and the Opera Company.

Dundurn Castle
One man's castle, Dundurn (☎ 905-546-2872, 610 York Blvd; adult/family $7/18; open 10am-4:30pm daily June-Sept, noon-4pm daily rest of the year), is actually a 36-room mansion that once belonged to Sir Allan Napier McNab, who was the prime minister from 1854 to 1856 of what was then the United Provinces of Canada. It's furnished in mid-19th-century style. The mansion is just out of town, about a 15-minute walk (or you can grab the York city bus).

Concerts are held on the grounds through the summer. Also at the site is a **military museum**, with weapons and uniforms dating from the War of 1812.

Whitehern
This elegant mansion (☎ 905-546-2018, 41 Jackson St W; admission $3.50; open 11am-4pm Tues-Sun mid-June–Labor Day, 1pm-4pm rest of the year), beside City Hall, was lived in by the prominent McQuesten family from 1852 to 1968. It contains original furnishings and art works and offers a peek into both the Victorian era and the life of the well-to-do. Also see the back garden.

Football Hall of Fame & Museum
Canadian football is commemorated and promoted at this museum (☎ 905-528-7566, 58 Jackson St W; admission $3; open 10am-4pm Tues-Sat, closed long weekends) through equipment, photos, trophies and the Grey Cup, football's top prize.

Canadian Warplane Heritage Museum
The spacious museum (☎ 905-679-4183, 9280 Airport Rd; adult/child/family $10/8/30; open 9am-5pm Fri-Wed, 9am-9pm Thur) is just east of the airport. Its impressive collection contains about 25 vintage planes, including a restored Lancaster bomber from WWII. All are in flying condition. There's also a *cafeteria* and gift shop.

Many of the planes, together with newer ones from a variety of sources, are part of an excellent two-day air show held in mid-June. Flights are available in some of the vintage aircraft.

Museum of Steam & Technology

The old pump house (☎ 905-546-4797, 900 Woodward Ave; admission $3; open 11am-4pm Tues-Sun June-Sept, noon-4pm Tues-Sun Oct-May), dating from 1860, was built to supply clean water when cholera and typhus menaced the city. These restored steam engines are among the largest in North America. Trimmed with mahogany and brass, they are rather attractive as objects. Also featured are photographs and engine exhibits.

African Lion Safari

About 1000 animals and birds roam this vast, cageless park (☎ 905-623-2620, 800-461-9453, RR1, Cambridge; adult/child $20/14; open 10am-5:30pm daily July & Aug, 10am-4pm daily May-June & Sept-Oct). You drive through, sometimes getting very close to lions, tigers and other animals. Monkeys and others climb and grope all over the car, and for this reason, those with particular pride in their vehicle are advised to use the park tour bus instead.

The park is not cheap, but the whole thing can take a full afternoon, and most people feel it's worth the money, especially if you have children with you. Try to make time for the live demonstrations, such as the one on birds of prey.

The park is between Hamilton and Cambridge, on Hwy 8.

Lake Ontario Waterfront Trail

This recreational trail follows the shoreline of Lake Ontario for 350km from Trenton to Hamilton. It's good for walking, cycling and inline skating, and in summer, there are dozens of organized outdoor activities and festivals along its length. Ask at the tourist office in Hamilton for a map and calendar of events, or look at W www.waterfront trust.com. It also connects to the Niagara Parkway & Recreational Trail; see the Around Niagara-on-the-Lake section for information on the trail.

Places to Stay

There are numerous local campgrounds; ask at the tourist office for further information.

Confederation Park (☎ 905-578-1644, 585 Van Wagner's Beach Rd) Campsites $18-22. This campground is just north of town on Centennial Parkway.

YMCA (☎ 905-529-7102, 79 James St) Singles $28. For low-budget lodgings, the Y has 172 rooms, for men only. Guests can use the pool and inexpensive cafeteria.

YWCA (☎ 905-522-9922, fax 905-522-1870, 75 McNab St) Singles $27. This hostel for women is comparable to the YMCA, although much smaller. It also has single rooms only and a pool and cheap cafeteria.

Haddo House (☎ 905-524-0071,107 Aberdeen Ave) Singles/doubles with full breakfast $80/85. About 1km from downtown, this is a late-19th-/early-20th-century home offering two rooms complete with private bathroom. It's for adults only.

Budget Motor Inn (☎ 905-527-2708, 737 King St E) Rooms $60. This adequate place is very central.

Visitors Inn (☎ 905-529-6979, 800-387-4620, 649 Main St W) Singles/doubles $75/80. Also downtown is this better choice.

Mountainview Motel (☎ 905-528-7521, 1870 Main St W) Rooms $50. This motel is farther out, close to McMaster University.

More motels can be found on the outskirts east or west of town.

Places to Eat

In the downtown area, King, John and James Sts offer numerous restaurants. The Jackson Square shopping mall includes many low-priced places. King St E is 'deal street,' with a few ethnic eateries and a café or two among its bars and skin-piercing parlors.

Taste of Bombay (☎ 905-522-2291, 234 King St E) Lunch buffet $8. A mix of vegetarian items is available daily here.

A more pleasant area is Hess Village, two blocks west of the Convention Centre.

Gown & Gavel (☎ 905-523-8881, 24 Hess St S) Dishes under $10. Get a light meal and beer under the umbrellas at this British-style pub.

Lazy Flamingo (☎ 905-527-0567, 19 Hess St S) Dishes $7-15. There's a choice of a nice patio, dining room or bar here, with a menu that includes Mexican, seafood, sandwiches and burgers. At night, there's music and always a good casual atmosphere.

Getting There & Away

The bus station (☎ 905-529-0196) is in the GO Centre, on the corner of James and Hunter Sts, about three blocks south of the center of town. Buses run to Toronto,

Niagara Falls and Brantford. Also here is the station for the GO commuter trains, which run to Toronto and points in between.

WELLAND CANAL AREA

The historic Welland Canal is a bypass of Niagara Falls that connects Lake Ontario with Lake Erie. A series of locks along the 42km-long canal overcomes the difference of about 100m in the lakes' water levels. The canal was initiated in 1829 by local businessmen to promote trade and commerce. Now in its fourth incarnation and part of the St Lawrence Seaway, it is a vital link in international freight service, allowing shipping into the industrial heart of North America from the Atlantic Ocean. The three principal cargoes that go through the canal are wheat, iron ore and coal. The average trip through the canal and its eight locks takes 12 hours. In St Catharines, remnants of the first three canals (built in 1829, 1845 and 1887) can be seen at various points. The fourth version, still in use but with some modifications and additions, was built between 1914 and 1932.

St Catharines
pop 141,000

Between Hamilton and the Niagara River, St Catharines is the major town of the Niagara fruit- and wine-producing district. In September, the **Niagara Grape & Wine Festival** (☎ 905-688-0212) is held with concerts, wine-and-cheese parties, a parade and more. In addition, activities are planned throughout the region over the week.

At **Mountain View Park** (*Mountain St at Bradley St*), there are locks at the escarpment from the second canal, along with some other 19th-century buildings. At Lakeside Park, along the waterfront in **Port Dalhousie** (dal-**oo**-zey), the early canals opened into Lake Ontario. This old harbor area is now a blend of the new and historic, with a reconstructed wooden lock, the oldest and smallest jail in the province and a lighthouse set alongside contemporary bars and restaurants. For hikers, there is the **Merritt Trail**, a walk that stretches from Port Dalhousie in St Catharines to Port Colbourne, mainly following the Welland Canal. It is detailed in the Bruce Trail guidebook; see Tobermory, later in this chapter. Local tourist offices also

have information; try the Welland chamber of commerce (see Welland, below).

For a more up-to-date look at the canal, visit the **Welland Canals Centre** (☎ 905-984-8880, 1932 Government Rd; adult/child $4/2; open 11am-4pm daily). It's at lock three of the currently used canal and includes a **museum** with exhibits on the canal and its construction, a viewing platform, and audiovisual displays on many aspects of the waterway. Ships from around the world may be seen on their way to and from the center of North America and the Atlantic Ocean. Fifty million tons of cargo are transported through the canal annually. There is also a **lacrosse museum** with details on Canada's oldest sport. The center is off Glendale Ave (which exits from the Queen Elizabeth Hwy). Follow the signs to the locks. You can get a bite to eat and something to drink while you watch the ships. A daily shipping schedule is posted.

Welland

Despite the predominance of agriculture in the region, Welland is primarily a steel town. A portion of the canal cuts right through town, with a larger bypass channel 2km from the downtown area; from there, international freighters can be viewed.

The city has become known for its more than two dozen painted **murals** depicting scenes from the history of the area and the canal. They can be seen around town on the sides of buildings, with the heaviest concentration along Main St E and the streets connecting it to parallel Division St, one block away. There are others along King and Niagara Sts. A pamphlet on the paintings can be picked up at one of the local tourist offices or at the chamber of commerce (☎ 905-732-7515, 32 Main St E).

The **Welland Historical Museum** (☎ 905-732-2215, 65 Hooker St; admission $2; open 10am-4pm Mon-Sat) offers more details on the canals.

In early June, the two-week **Rose Festival** celebrates the queen of flowers. There are displays, contests, a parade and other events.

Port Colborne

On Lake Erie at the southern end of the Welland Canal, Port Colborne has one of the largest water locks in the world. **Lock Eight Park**, south of Main St, obviously has the eighth lock, and the summer tourist-information booth is here too.

The quiet town doesn't really offer much to see or do. The **Port Colborne Historical & Marine Museum** (☎ *905-834-7604, 280 King St; admission free; open noon-5pm daily May-Dec*), laid out in a pioneer-village format, provides regional and canal history. There are some beaches in the area, and a number of cottage communities along the shoreline.

NIAGARA-ON-THE-LAKE
pop 13,000

This small, attractive village is about 20km downstream from the falls, and with its upscale shops and restaurants, well-known **George Bernard Shaw Festival** (see the boxed text) and curbs on development, it acts as a sort of foil to the hype and flash of Niagara Falls. The surrounding vineyards and history-filled parkland add to its appeal. Originally a Native Indian site, it was settled by Loyalists from New York after the American Revolution. In the 1790s, it was made the first capital of Ontario, and it is considered one of the best-preserved 19th-century towns in North America.

The lakeside location, tree-lined streets and old houses make Niagara-on-the-Lake a nice place to see before or after the falls. The village does get *very* busy on good summer days, though generally only on the main street. Stroll down the side streets and you'll get a taste of former quiet times in a small, prosperous Ontario town.

In Simcoe Park, right in town, there are often free classical music concerts on Saturday during the summer.

Orientation & Information

Queen St is the main street. On the eastern side of the downtown area, toward Niagara Falls, King St crosses Queen St at large Simcoe Park. Beyond that, Queen St becomes Picton St.

Staff at the chamber of commerce/tourist office (☎ 905-468-5012, accommodations ☎ 905-468-4263, **w** www.niagaraonthelake.com, 26 Queen St), around the side and downstairs, are friendly and helpful and will book lodging for you. From March to December, the office is open every day; later in the year, the hours are shortened and it's closed on Sunday.

Ask for the *Historic Guide*, a free pamphlet outlining in brief the town's history and providing a self-guided walking tour. It lists many of the noteworthy structures around town and indicates them on a map. Also ask about the **Garden Tour** put on by the Conservancy (usually on the third weekend in June), which allows visitors a peek around some of the splendid gardens in town. In October, the annual **B&B tour** gives you another chance to see behind the fences and doors around town.

Things to See & Do

The town's main street, Queen St, is the principal attraction. Restored and well-preserved wooden buildings and shops contain antiques, bakeries, various specialties, Scottish souvenirs and restaurants. Note particularly the **apothecary** (*Queen St at King St; admission free; open May-Oct*), dating from 1866. Now a museum, it is fitted with great old cabinets, remedies and jars.

If you've got a sweet tooth, don't miss getting a jam sample from the **Greaves store**

The Niagara Escarpment

An escarpment is a steep rock face, or cliff of great length. The Niagara Escarpment, often referred to in southern Ontario as a site for recreational activities, runs for 725km, with a maximum height of 335m. Once the shore of an ancient sea centered on what is now Michigan, USA, the escarpment begins in Ontario at the town of Queenston, on the Niagara River. On its way north to Tobermory and Manitoulin Island, it passes through or beside Hamilton, Collingwood and Owen Sound. A major outcropping of the escarpment can clearly be seen from Hwy 401 west of Oakville, at the Kelso Conservation Area.

The Niagara Escarpment Commission, through a series of parks and conservation areas, seeks to preserve the escarpment's natural beauty, flora and fauna. Now largely a recreation area, the escarpment is used for activities such as skiing and bird-watching, but it is best known for hiking along the Bruce Trail. For more details on the trail, see Tobermory in the Georgian Bay & Lakelands section.

(☎ 905-468-7831, 55 Queen St), run by fourth-generation jam-makers, or indulging yourself at a couple of obligatory **fudge shops**. The **renovated courthouse** (26 Queen St) is another impressive building now used for various functions, including the tourist office.

Historic Military Sites To the east of Niagara-on-the-Lake, toward the falls, is the **Fort George National Historic Site** (☎ 905-468-4257, Niagara Parkway; adult/child $6/4, free admission after 4:15pm; open 10am-5pm daily Apr-Nov) dating from 1797. The fort was the site of important battles during the War of 1812 and changed hands between the British and US forces a couple of times. Within the walls are the officers' quarters, a working kitchen, the powder magazine and storage houses. There isn't a lot to see, but the various costumed workers, particularly the soldiers performing different exercises, provide some atmosphere.

Tucked behind the fort is **Navy Hall**, at the water's edge. Only one building remains of what was a sizable supply depot for British forts on the Great Lakes during the

18th century. It was destroyed during the War of 1812. The US **Fort Niagara** is across the river.

In a fine location on the west side of town, at the opposite end of Ricardo/Front St are the minimal remains of **Fort Mississauga**. There are some plaques but no organized tours or facilities.

Also in town are **Butler's Barracks**. Admission is free, and pedestrians can reach it either from Mary St or along a trail leading from Fort George. First used by the British at the end of the War of 1812 as a storage and barracks site, the location has since been used for a variety of purposes by the Canadian military. Troops trained here for both World Wars and for the Korean War. Some buildings remain from the various periods of use, and markers lead visitors around on a mini Canadian-military-history tour.

Historical Museum This is the oldest local museum (☎ 905-468-3912, 43 Castlereagh St; admission $5; open 10am-5pm daily May-Oct, 1pm-5pm daily Nov-Dec & Mar-Apr, 1pm-5pm Sat & Sun Jan-Feb) in the province. It opened in 1907 and has a vast

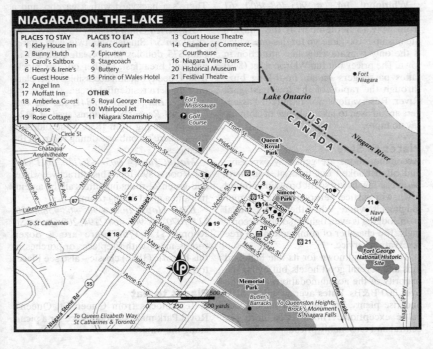

NIAGARA-ON-THE-LAKE

PLACES TO STAY
1 Kiely House Inn
2 Bunny Hutch
3 Carol's Saltbox
6 Henry & Irene's Guest House
12 Angel Inn
17 Moffatt Inn
18 Amberlea Guest House
19 Rose Cottage

PLACES TO EAT
4 Fans Court
7 Epicurean
8 Stagecoach
9 Buttery
15 Prince of Wales Hotel

OTHER
5 Royal George Theatre
10 Whirlpool Jet
11 Niagara Steamship

13 Court House Theatre
14 Chamber of Commerce; Courthouse
16 Niagara Wine Tours
20 Historical Museum
21 Festival Theatre

collection of early-20th-century items relating to the town's past, ranging from some Native Indian artifacts to Loyalist and War of 1812 collectibles.

Negro Burial Ground One of the routes of the Underground Railroad, which brought slaves from America across the border to freedom in Canada, ran from Buffalo across to Fort Erie and then along the Niagara River to Niagara-on-the-Lake and St Catharines. At 494 Mississauga St is a plaque on the site of what was a Baptist church and burial ground belonging to these early black settlers.

Organized Tours

Niagara Wine Tours (☎ 905-468-1300, 92 Picton St) offers various bicycle tours of area wineries ($55 to $75), which include visiting local wineries and tastings. Bikes are also available for rent ($25/day).

Niagara Steamship (☎ 905-468-8343, 800-250-4572) has cruises from the Navy Hall Dock at Fort George on a wood-fired steamship. Tours (adult/child $14/6) run hourly from mid-May to mid-October.

Whirlpool Jet (☎ 905-468-4800, 61 Melville St) departs opposite Delater St from May to September. If the Niagara Steamship is too tame, go for this one, which is the only Niagara Falls–like attraction in town. The pricey but fun Whirpool Jet ($49) takes passengers on an hour-long buzz through the rapids of the lower Niagara River. Reservations are required. Passengers are advised to take a change of clothing, say no more.

Places to Stay

Accommodations are generally expensive and often booked out to boot. For many people, a few hours spent browsing around town will suffice before finding cheaper lodging elsewhere. When the Shaw Festival is on, lodging is even tighter, so plan accordingly. The chamber of commerce has a free reservation service.

The town is known for its fine high-end inns and several good hotels, but by far the majority of the accommodations are in the over 300 B&Bs. Rates average about $100 and rise plenty, but there are some good-value exceptions. Those listed here are central and reasonably priced.

Rose Cottage (☎ 905-468-7572, 308 Victoria St) Singles/doubles $65 including breakfast. The cordial owner Elizabeth, not Rose, has one private room with an adjacent bathroom, and she is very close to downtown.

Bunny Hutch (☎ 905-468-3377, 305 Centre St) Room with shared bath & full breakfast $65. Open May-Oct. It's a nine-block walk to Queen St from this warm, friendly place with a big, quiet backyard and parking. It's not slick; it's just real people with two extra rooms.

Carol's Saltbox (☎ 905-468-5423, 223 Gate St) Doubles with full breakfast & shared/private bath $85/100. There are two small, cozy rooms with slanted ceilings at this very central choice from the 1820s. The rooms come with ceiling fans, mini-TVs and parking. The owner is well traveled and has a flair for tasteful decor.

Henry & Irene's Guest House (☎ 905-468-3111, 285 William St) Rooms with shared bath & full breakfast $60/70. This modern bungalow is quiet, air-conditioned and walkable from downtown. The owners speak German and will lend you bikes. There's a backyard with a gazebo, and a TV lounge.

Amberlea Guest House (☎ 905-468-3749, 285 John St) Singles $60, twin with shared bath $75, doubles with private bath $90, all with full breakfast. Farther out (six blocks from Queen) but still accessible is this place on a modern residential street.

Angel Inn (☎ 905-468-3411 fax 905-468-5451, 224 Regent St) Rooms start at $120. This inn, dating from 1823, is the oldest in town. There's a pub and dining room on the premises.

Moffat Inn (☎ 905-468-4116, 60 Picton St) Rooms $90-160. This attractive, white-and-green 22-room inn offers all the amenities and a good dining room.

Kiely House Inn (☎ 905-468-4588, 800-511-7070, fax 905-468-2194, 209 Queen St) Rooms $135-175. There are a dozen rooms, many with fireplaces or porches, at this historic (1832) classic – also see Places to Eat.

Places to Eat

A few blocks from Queen St, Queen's Royal Park makes a good place for a picnic along the water.

Stagecoach (☎ 905-468-3133, 45 Queen St) Dishes $4-8. This place is cheap, non-touristy and always busy. You can get a good-value breakfast before 11am.

Epicurean (☎ 905-468-0288, 84 Queen St) Meals $5-20. Highly recommended is this stylish, inexpensive lunch cafeteria that morphs into a bistro at night. A great range of tasty food includes a couple of vegetarian choices each day. There's also a small garden patio down the lane. In the evening, there are well-prepared fish, lamb and meat dishes.

Buttery (☎ 905-468-2564, 19 Queen St) Lunch $9-11. For a pub meal, try this place, which has a pleasant patio. On Friday and Saturday nights, a Henry VIII–style feast is put on, with entertainment, drink and victuals aplenty ($50).

Fans Court (☎ 905-468-4511, 135 Queen St) Lunch/dinner mains $8/15. Look here for some fine ethnic diversion in this most Anglo of towns. It serves Chinese and Asian dishes, such as Singapore noodles with curry. Apart from the pleasant dining room, there are also a few tables outside in a small courtyard. Prices are moderate at lunch, but the dinner menu is pricier.

Moving upscale, most of the inns and hotels have their own dining rooms.

Prince of Wales Hotel (☎ 905-468-3246, 6 Picton St) Dinner meals from $100 per person. This elegant hotel has a well-regarded, very formal dining room for fine contemporary French cuisine.

Kiely House Inn (☎ 905-468-4588, 209 Queen St) Dishes $8. Enjoy an afternoon

---

A Shaw Thing

The only festival in the world exclusively devoted to producing the plays of George Bernard Shaw and his contemporaries takes place in Niagara-on-the-Lake every year from April to October.

An internationally respected theater festival, the **Shaw Festival** (☎ 800-511-7429, ⊠ www.shawfest.com) was founded in 1962 by a group of local residents led by Brian Doherty, a lawyer and dramatist who had a passion for theater. The very first season consisted of eight performances of Shaw's *Candida* and *Don Juan in Hell,* from *Man and Superman.*

Doherty chose Shaw because he was 'a great prophet of the 20th century,' and because Shaw 'was the only outstanding playwright writing in English, with the obvious exception of Shakespeare, who produced a sufficient number of plays to support a festival.'

As well as producing Shaw's work, the festival aims to give space to a variety of plays not widely performed nowadays. These include Victorian drama, plays of continental Europe, classic US drama, musicals, and mystery and suspense plays.

The festival academy was established in 1985 primarily as a vehicle for the exchange of skills among the festival's ensemble of actors. Since then it has expanded to include various educational programs: there are specialized seminars held through the season and, on selected Saturdays, informal Lunchtime Conversations, where the public can join in discussions with members of the Shaw Festival company.

Ten plays are performed every season in three theaters around town – the **Court House Theatre,** the **Festival Theatre** and the **Royal George Theatre,** a onetime vaudeville house and cinema. All three theaters are within walking distance of the town center.

Tickets range from $25 to $75 for the best seats in the house on Saturday night at the Festival Theatre. Cheaper rush seats go on sale at 9am on the day of performance but are not available for Saturday shows. Students and seniors can get good reductions on some matinees, and weekday matinees are the cheapest. There are also brief lunchtime plays for $18.

The box office (☎ 905-468-2172) is open 9am to 8pm every day from mid-April to mid-January. If you're planning to see a play, call the toll-free telephone line from anywhere in Canada or the USA well in advance and ask for the Shaw Festival guide, or check the web. It will give you all the details, the year's performances and other useful information, as well as ticket order forms.

cream tea on the porch overlooking the gardens and golf course.

Getting There & Around

There are no direct buses between Toronto and Niagara-on-the-Lake. From Toronto, you must go to St Catharines or Niagara Falls (both daily) and then transfer. Charterways Bus Lines runs between the St Catharines bus terminal and Niagara-on-the-Lake three times a week. Here, the buses stop at Fort George. From mid-May to mid-October, a shuttle bus (☎ 800-667-0256) runs three times daily between Niagara-on-the-Lake and Niagara Falls for $10 or $15 roundtrip. From the middle of June to September, it stops at the Fort George parking lot, a 7-minute walk to downtown.

See Queenston, under Niagara Parkway & Recreational Trail, later in this chapter, for information on the high-speed hydrofoil from Toronto with a shuttle into Niagara-on-the-Lake.

Taxis to Niagara Falls charge about $30.

Cycling is a fine way to explore the area, and bicycles can be rented by the hour, half day or full day at **Niagara Wine Tours** (☎ 905-468-1300, *92 Picton St*) past the Moffat Inn.

AROUND NIAGARA-ON-THE-LAKE
Vineyards & Wine Tours

The triangle between Beamsville, Niagara-on-the-Lake and Niagara Falls is Canada's most important wine-producing area. The moderate microclimate created by the escarpment and Lake Ontario is a big part of the area's success. The ever-increasing number of wineries – there are now over two dozen – are producing some pretty fine wine. The better ones have a Vintner's Quality Alliance (VQA) designation.

Since the 1980s, wine producers have grown from operating essentially a small cottage industry to being internationally recognized vintners capable of turning out quality vintages. Many offer visitors a look around and a taste. A full day can be enjoyed touring the countryside and emptying glasses. Three of the principal wines are Riesling, chardonnay and gewürztraminer. Whites tend to dominate, but reds are also produced. The expensive ice wines (sweet and fruity) have gained a lot of favorable attention. Many of the wineries are open year-round. Some of the commercial tour operators include a winery or two on their bus excursions; most of these operate out of Niagara Falls.

Area tourist offices have lists of the 30-some wineries and their locations. The **Niagara Grape & Wine Festival** (☎ 905-688-0212), with scores of events over a week, takes place each September.

The following wineries near Niagara-on-the-Lake are among the best established.

The **Reif Estate Winery** (☎ 905-468-7738, *15608 Niagara Parkway; open 10am-6pm daily*), south of Niagara-on-the-Lake between Line 2 and Line 3 on the Niagara Parkway, conducts tastings and has a shop. Call for tour times.

Practically next door to Reif Estate, at Line 3, **Inniskillin Wine** (☎ 905-468-3554, *Niagara Parkway; open 10am-6pm daily*) has developed a good reputation and is the leading award winner of the region. A display outlines the production process and history of wine-making in Niagara.

Southwest of town, on Hwy 55, **Hillebrand Estates Winery** (☎ 905-468-1723, *1249 Niagara Stone Rd*) is another one with quality wines, tastings and tours.

Others to sample are: **Konzelmann** (☎ 905-935-2866, *1096 Lakeshore Rd*), **Marynissen** (☎ 905-468-7270, *RR6, Concession 1*), **Pillitteri** (☎ 905-468-3147, *1696 Niagara Stone Rd*) and **Stonechurch** (☎ 905-935-3535, *1242 Irvine Rd*).

Niagara Parkway & Recreational Trail

A slow, 20km trip along the two-lane **Niagara Parkway** to Niagara Falls is most enjoyable. Along the way are parks, picnic areas, good views over the river and a couple of campgrounds, all of which make up part of the Niagara Parks Commission park system. It runs pretty well the entire 56km length of the Niagara River, from Niagara-on-the-Lake, past the falls and to Fort Erie. A 3m-wide paved **recreational trail** for cycling, jogging, walking or skating runs the entire way, paralleling the parkway. It's excellent for either a short or long cycling excursion. The terrain is flat and the riverside scenery pleasant, and it's rarely very busy.

The trail can be easily divided into four sections, each of which would take around one to two hours of leisurely pedaling. Historic and natural points of interest are marked with plaques. Perhaps best of all, in season, are the fresh-fruit stands with cold cherry ciders and juices. Ask at the chamber of commerce for the Parks Commission's excellent *Recreation Trail Map*.

Queenston village is a quaint, sleepy historic throwback just before the Lewiston Bridge to the USA. The **Laura Secord Homestead** (☎ *905-262-5676, Queenston St at Partition St; admission $3; open every day May-Oct*) honors one of Canada's best-known heroines (partly because of the chocolate company that bears her name), who lived here during the War of 1812. At one point during the war, she hiked nearly 30km to warn the British soldiers of impending attack by the USA. The house can be visited and includes a chocolate sample. There's also a small candy shop on the premises. The rose garden out front is said to have been planted by Laura herself.

At the intersection of the Niagara Parkway and Queenston St (the main street in Queenston), by the War Memorial, sits the **Samuel Weir River Brink Gallery** (☎ *905-262-5676; admission free; open 10am-5pm Wed-Sat, 1pm-5pm Sun May-Oct*), a collection and library of art. Weir had the house built as a live-in gallery and library in 1916 to house his remarkably extensive art, book and antique collection. He formed a foundation to administer the estate for public access, provided that he was buried on the front lawn (which, in due time, he was).

Also on Queenston St, **Mackenzie House Printery** (☎ *905-262-5676; admission $2; open May-Oct*) has a collection highlighting printing and printing equipment as history. Displays detail historic newspapers, such as

For a good run, try the trail along the Niagara Parkway.

the *Colonial Advocate* edited by William Lyon Mackenzie, who later led the Upper Canada Rebellion.

Also in Queenston is the southern end of the Bruce Trail, which extends 780km to Tobermory on Georgian Bay. There are numerous access points in the Niagara and Hamilton areas. For more details on the trail, see Tobermory, later in this chapter.

From the Queenston Dock, **Sea Flight Hydrofoil Jet Lines** (☎ *877-504-8825*) boats depart for a speedy, one-hour trip to downtown Toronto ($35 one way). For passengers coming from Toronto, the price includes a shuttle bus to Niagara Falls or to Niagara-on-the-Lake. Call for a schedule.

A little farther along the parkway is **Queenston Heights Park**, best known for its large monument of Major General Brock (*open May-Oct*). The winding inside stairwell will take you up 60m to a fabulous view. Also in the area is the *Queenston Heights Restaurant* (☎ *905-262-4274*), where you can enjoy a summer beer on the balcony with grand views of the river. This is not a bad place for a meal, either, although it's not in the low-budget category. Dishes cost $15 to $35.

Near the restaurant is a monument to Laura Secord, and from here begins a 45-minute self-guided walking tour of the hillside detailing the Battle of Queenston Heights. Pick up a copy of the good walking-tour booklet at any of the information offices. It explains some of the historical background, outlines the War of 1812 and describes how the British victory here was significant in Canada's not becoming part of the USA. Interpreters are on hand at the huge Brock's monument, and the guidebook should be available there.

The Niagara Parkway continues through Niagara Falls and beyond, southbound. Attractions between Queenston and Niagara Falls, all of which can be reached on the

Niagara Falls *People Mover* buses during the summer season, are covered in the Niagara Falls section (next); see the Around Niagara Falls for details on the southern part of the route to Fort Erie.

NIAGARA FALLS
pop 79,000

The roaring falls make this town one of Canada's top tourist destinations. It's a busy spot – about 12 million people visit annually, and you'll hear and see people from all over the world.

The falls themselves, spanning the Niagara River between Ontario and upper New York, are certainly impressive, particularly the Canadian Horseshoe Falls. They look good by day and by night, when colorful spotlights flicker across the misty foam. Even in winter, when the flow is partially hidden and the edges frozen solid – like a freeze-framed film – it's quite a spectacle. (But, as one reader warned – the mist freezes on contact!) Very occasionally the falls stop altogether. The first recorded instance of this occurred on the morning of Easter Sunday 1848, and it caused some to speculate that the end of the world was nigh. An ice jam had completely cut off the flow of water. Some residents, obviously braver than we, took the opportunity to scavenge the riverbed beneath the falls!

It is said that Napoléon's brother rode from New Orleans in a stagecoach with his new bride to view the falls and that it has been a honeymoon attraction ever since. In fact, the town is sometimes humorously but disparagingly called a spot for newlyweds and nearly deads. Recently, it's been called Viagra Falls.

Supplementing the falls, the city has an incredible array of artificial attractions, which – together with the casino, hotels, restaurants and flashing lights – produce a sort of Canadian Las Vegas. It's a sight in itself, and it's growing. Another casino was being built during research.

Niagara Falls is about a two-hour drive from Toronto by the Queen Elizabeth Way (QEW), past Hamilton and St Catharines. Public transportation between Toronto and Niagara Falls is frequent and quick.

Orientation

The town of Niagara Falls is split into two main sections: the older commercial area, where the locals go about their business, and the other, largely tacky (but fun) part around the falls, which has been developed for visitors. The latter also has some pretty, green areas that offer some contrast.

In the 'normal' part of town, known as downtown, Queen St and Victoria Ave are the main streets. The area around Bridge St, near the corner of Erie Ave, has both the train and bus stations. The international hostels are nearby. Generally, however, there is little to see or do in this part of town.

About 3km south along the river are the falls and all the trappings of the tourist trade – restaurants, hotels, shops and attractions. In the vicinity of the falls, the main streets are the busy Clifton Hill, Falls Ave, Centre St, Victoria Ave and Ferry St. Going north along the river is scenic parkland, which runs from the falls downstream about 20km to Niagara-on-the-Lake. Many of the B&Bs are also between the two sections of town.

Information

The most central place for tourist information is at Horseshoe Falls, in the building known as Table Rock Centre. The Niagara Parks Commission runs the good but busy desk here (☎ 905-356-2241, W www.niagara parks.com). It's open daily from 9am to 6pm (until 10pm in summer).

The Niagara Falls Visitors & Convention Bureau (☎ 905-356-6061, 800-563-2557, W www.discoverniagara.com, 5515 Stanley Ave) is good for city information. It's open daily from 8am to 8pm in summer, with varying reduced hours during other months.

For information on anywhere in the province, visit the Ontario Travel Information Centre (☎ 905-358-3221, 5355 Stanley Ave), which is out of the center, about halfway between the Rainbow Bridge and Queen Elizabeth Way. To get there, go west on Roberts St (Hwy 420) from the bridge to Stanley Ave (Route 102). Ontario maps and information on destinations across the province can be picked up here. It's open from 9am to 8pm daily through summer.

Many of the free tourist-office booklets contain discount coupons for attractions, rides, etc. If you don't see any, ask. Also, many of the hotels and motels offer restaurant and other vouchers.

NIAGARA FALLS

OTHER
1 Niagara Helicopters
3 Niagara Spanish Aero Car
4 Ten Thousand Buddhas Temple
5 Great Gorge Adventure
8 Public Library
10 Post Office
11 Bus Station
12 VIA Rail Station
19 Ontario Travel Information Centre
23 Niagara Falls General Hospital
24 Niagara Falls Visitor & Convention Bureau
28 Casino Niagara
29 Niagara Falls Brewing Co
31 Lundy's Lane Historical Museum
33 Maid of the Mist
36 IMAX Theatre; Daredevil Gallery
36 Skylon Tower
38 Niagara Falls Convention & Civic Center
39 Minolta Tower
40 Table Rock Centre; Journey Behind the Falls
41 Niagara Parks Greenhouse
42 The *Old Scow*
43 Marineland
44 Niagara People Mover Depot

PLACES TO STAY
2 Niagara Glen View Campground
6 Days Inn
13 Europa
14 Niagara Falls International Hostel
16 Backpackers International Hostel & Inn
17 Butterfly Manor
18 Gretna Green
21 Glen Mhor Guesthouse
22 Eastwood Tourist Lodge
27 Econo Lodge
32 AAAA Royal Motel
34 Maple Leaf Motel

PLACES TO EAT
7 Xin Vego Café
9 Daily Planet
15 Simon's Diner; Dad's Diner
20 Jade Garden
25 Mama Mia's; Mai Vi
26 Tony's Place
30 Flying Saucer
37 Victoria Park Cafeteria

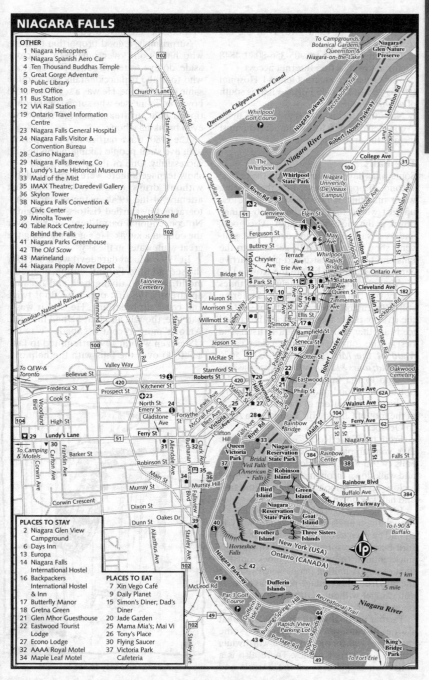

ONTARIO

The main post office (☎ 905-374-6667, Morrison St at St Clair Ave) is in the old section of town.

The public library (☎ 905-356-8080, 4848 Victoria Ave) has free Internet access.

The Greater Niagara General Hospital (☎ 905-358-0171, 5546 Portage Rd) is south of downtown.

Note that this is a 10-digit dialing area; even when dialing a local number, you must include the area code.

The Falls

Some wags have said the falls are the brides' second disappointment, but the roaring water tumbling 56m is a grand sight. Close up, just where the water begins to plunge down, is the most intense spot. Also good, and free, is the observation deck of the souvenir shop by the falls. (To get close to the falls and to get unobstructed photos, arrive early in the morning, before the crowds.)

After checking all the angles at all times of day, you can try several services offering still different approaches. Most close before the river partially freezes, but all the jagged ice is another marvelous sight in itself. The best of the four major tour services is the **Maid of the Mist** (☎ *905-358-0311, 5920 River Rd; tours $12.50)*, which takes passengers up to the falls for a view from the bottom – it's loud and wet. You can board the boat at the bottom of the incline railway at the foot of Clifton Hill. It sails from April to October.

From the Table Rock Centre, right at the falls, you can pay $7 at **Journey Behind the Falls** *(☎ 905-371-0254)*, don a plastic poncho and walk down through rock-cut tunnels for a close-up (wet) look from behind the falls and halfway down the cliff.

It's one way to cool off on a hot day, although the tunnels do get crowded, and you should be prepared to wait in line for a brief turn beside the spray. The wall of water is thick enough to pretty well block out the light of day. A million people each year see the falls from this vantage point – as close as you can get without getting in a barrel. It's open all year.

Farther north along the river is the **Great Gorge Adventure**, an elevator to some rapids and whirlpools. It's not a worthwhile way to spend your money. There also is a collection of pictures of the barrels and

vessels that many of the wackos attempting to shoot the falls have used.

Surprisingly, a good proportion of those who have gone over purposely, suicides aside, do live to tell about it. But only one who took the trip accidentally has had the same good fortune. He was a seven-year-old boy from Tennessee who surged over from a tipped boat upstream and did it without even breaking a bone.

The 1980s was a particularly busy period, with five stunt people taking the plunge, all successfully. One of them said he did it to show teenagers there were thrills available without drugs (yeah, right). The first attempt of the 1990s, witnessed and photographed by startled visitors, was original. No conventional barrel here – it was over the edge in a kayak. He's now paddling the great whitewater in the sky.

In 1993, a local daredevil went over for the second time. For this outing, he used a modified round diving bell, and became, apparently, the first person to do it twice and come up breathing. He said it was a bad one, though, and that he had hit hard. Among more recent escapades was the US citizen who in 1995 attempted to take a Jet Ski over the falls with the help of a

A dangerous way to see the falls

parachute. He might have made it if his parachute had opened.

A little farther downstream, about 6km or 7km from Horseshoe Falls, is the **Niagara Spanish Aero Car** (☎ *905-371-0254, Niagara Parkway*), the last of the big four attractions. You ride a sort of gondola stretched 550m between two outcrops, both on the Canadian side, above a whirlpool created by the falls ($6). It offers a pretty good angle of the river for a picture as it glides above the logs, tires and various debris spinning in the eddies below. It also operates until the end of October.

Tickets can be bought separately for each of the above three land-based views, or buy the Explorer's Passport, a ticket for all three, which costs less than the total of the three individual tickets (you don't have to visit all three in the same day). The Explorer's Passport Plus also includes the *People Mover* Bus Pass.

Other Viewpoints

Both the below also have restaurants. For details, see Places to Eat. The food served at both is not just an afterthought, and meals are well prepared, if straightforward.

The **Skylon Tower** (☎ *905-356-2651, 5200 Robinson St; admission $9; open 8am-11pm daily*) is the large, gray tower with yellow elevators running up the outside. There's an observation deck at about 250m, with both indoor and outdoor viewing. Aside from great views of the falls, both Toronto and Buffalo can be seen on clear days.

The **Minolta Tower** (☎ *905-356-1501, 6732 Fallsview St; admission $8; open 7am-11pm daily*) is close to the falls and virtually overlooks the lip. It has indoor/outdoor observation galleries and a revolving restaurant with spectacular views. An incline railway leads from the base of the tower down the hillside close to the falls.

Bridges

Two bridges run over the river to New York: the Whirlpool Rapids Bridge and, closer to the falls, the Rainbow Bridge, which celebrated its 50th year in 1991. You can walk or drive across to explore the falls from the USA side, but have your papers in order, and all those who don't need visas to enter the USA (Canadians excepted) will be charged a $6 fee. Both pedestrians and drivers have to pay a bridge toll. It's $1 each way for walkers, $4 for cars.

Lundy's Lane Historical Museum

This seemingly out-of-place, conspicuously low-key museum (☎ *905-358-5082, 5180 Ferry St; admission $1.50; open 9am-4pm daily May-Oct, noon-4pm Nov*), sitting on the site of the 1814 Battle of Lundy's Lane, catalogues local pioneer and military history, notably the War of 1812.

Clifton Hill

Clifton Hill is a street name but also refers more generally to the commercial part of the downtown area near the falls, which has given over (in sense-bombarding intensity) to artificial attractions in Disney-like concentration. You name it – museums, galleries, displays such as Ripley's Believe It or Not, Madame Tussaud's Wax Museum, Criminal's Hall of Fame (you get the drift) – they're all here. Looking is fun, but in most cases, paying the entrance fee will leave you feeling like a sucker. Most don't live up to their own hype. Also in this bright and busy section are dozens of souvenir shops and restaurants.

Casino Niagara

The immensely successful gambling hall (☎ *905-374-3598, 5705 Falls Ave; admission free (hope so!); open 24 hours year-round*) is never closed. Free shuttle buses run to the door from hotels and attractions all over town. A new casino was being constructed during research. The fate of the existing one is being debated.

Marineland

Of the many commercial attractions, this offers possibly the best dollar value. But Marineland (☎ *905-356-9565, 7657 Portage Rd; adult/child $30/20; open 9am-6pm daily July-Aug,10am-5pm daily mid-May–June, 10am-4pm daily Sept-Oct, closed rest of the year*) is an aquarium with captive dolphins, sea lions and killer whales and hasn't escaped controversy. Admission includes kid-pleasing shows and a wildlife park containing bison, bears, deer and elk. There are also rides, including a roller coaster, all covered in the cost of admission. You may, however, want to take a picnic lunch with you – the restaurants here are expensive and offer a limited selection. Marineland is roughly 2km from the falls, south on Portage Rd.

IMAX Theatre

The large-format (the screen is six stories high) IMAX cinema (☎ 905-374-4629, 6170 Buchanan Ave; admission $10; open 1pm-8pm daily) near the Skylon Tower, presents a 45-minute show about the history of the falls and some of the stunts that have been pulled in and over them. There are two other films as well. The price includes a **Daredevil Gallery** (go through the gift shop), which displays some of the barrels and contraptions that have been used to make the plunge.

Niagara Parks Greenhouse

Flowers and gardens are plentiful in and around Niagara Falls, which has moderate temperatures. The greenhouse and conservatory (☎ 905-371-0254; admission free; open 9:30am-5pm daily), less than 1km south of the Horseshoe Falls, provide a year-round floral display. A bonus is the tropical birds. Parking is $3.

The Old Scow

Across the street, rusting away in the river, the *Old Scow* is a steel barge that has been lodged on rocks waiting to be washed over the falls since 1918. So were the three men aboard when it broke free of the tug pulling it and drifted to within 750m of the brink. Without speedboats or helicopters, rescuing the men was some feat. Red Hill Senior, a local daredevil, climbed out hand over hand along a line that had been shot out from the roof of the waterside power-plant building. He was able to untangle the lines, allowing an attached buoy to reach the men, who climbed on and were pulled ashore.

Gardens & Nature Areas

Niagara Falls can be a fairly congested, urban experience, but there are some worthwhile quiet places to explore apart from the well-tended areas of plant life listed in this section.

Also free for browsing are the fastidiously maintained 40 hectares of the **Botanical Gardens & School of Horticulture Gardens** (☎ 905-371-0254, Niagara Parkway; open 11am-6pm daily) north along the

Parkway toward Queenston, about 9km from Horseshoe Falls. A farther 2.5km north is the **floral clock**, which is over 12m in diameter. Beside the floral clock, don't miss the Centennial Lilac Gardens, which are at their fragrant best in late May. In the **Butterfly Conservatory** (☎ 905-358-0025; adult/child $8.50/4.50; open 9am-4:30pm daily), at the Botanical Gardens, 2000 butterflies covering 50 species flutter about the flowers and visitors. Wearing white seems to attract them to land. In one area, they can be seen making their way out of chrysalides.

Other flower gardens are at **Queen Victoria Park**, right beside the Canadian falls, and at **Oakes Garden Theatre**, opposite the Maid of the Mist Plaza, near the falls. Opposite the USA falls, **Queen Victoria Park** also has varied and colorful floral displays through most of the year.

Niagara Glen Nature Preserve Top of the list and highly recommended, this preserve (☎ 905-371-0254, Niagara Parkway, 7km north of falls; admission free) is the only place where you can gain a sense of what the area was like before the arrival of Europeans. There are seven different walking trails here covering 4km, where the falls were situated 8000 years ago. The preserve is maintained by the Parks Commission, which offers free guided walks four times a day through summer (July to early September). The trails are always open to public use at no charge. The paths wind down the gorge, past huge boulders, icy cold caves, wildflowers and woods. Some people fish at the bottom from the shore. The river trail runs north to Pebbly Beach and south to the whirlpool, site of the Spanish Aero Car attraction. The whirlpool is an impressive sight from the Aero Car Terminal, but the size of the gorge itself isn't fully appreciated until seen from the shoreline. As noted above, there seems to be a lot of garbage trapped in the currents, mainly wood and tires, often from cottage docks and boathouses, but remember that everything that leaves Lake Erie has to pass into the whirlpool. Officially, the excellent trails end here.

Going farther is dangerous, and people have died. But some people do clamber over the rocks along the water's edge – to be safe, a good dozen or more meters back from the water – upstream toward the falls. The area where the river flows (or rather shoots) into the whirlpool can be reached and is very dramatic. This is not easy walking; the rocks can be slippery, and the river is hazardous. A local resident has said that from here, a further arduous 30 minutes leads to another set of even more overwhelming (and more dangerous) rapids. Twenty minutes beyond is the boardwalk for the Great Gorge Adventure. At this stage you can turn around, carry on for another five hours to a point close to the falls, or hop the Great Gorge elevator up to street level. Tickets evidently are not checked at the bottom because there are so few misfits who would take the time and effort to get down there on their own.

Walkers should take a snack and something to drink, for despite all the water, the Niagara is one river from which you do not want to drink – this region is one of the industrial centers of North America. The Niagara Glen Nature Preserve is 1km north of the Whirlpool Golf Course entrance on the Niagara Parkway (toward Niagara-on-the-Lake). The *People Mover* stops at the site, or in spring and autumn at the Spanish Aero Car, from where the glen is walkable (about 3km).

Dufferin Islands This series of small and interconnected artificial islands was created during the development of the hydro system. The area is green parkland, with walking paths and a short nature trail around the islands and through the woods. There are picnic tables, and a small area for swimming, which is best for children (though anyone can be a kid if it's hot enough). The islands are less than 2km south of the falls, on the west side of the road. Entry is free. Another 250m south is King's Bridge Park, with more picnic facilities and another small beach.

Ten Thousand Buddhas Temple
More tranquillity can be found at this totally out-of-context but intriguing Buddhist complex (*☎ 905-371-2678, 4303 River Rd; admission free; open 9am-5pm daily, main temple Sat & Sun only*). Visitors are welcome to view the various sculptures and artworks from China and enjoy the calm environment.

Niagara Falls Brewing Co
This local brewery (*☎ 800-267-3392, 6863 Lundy's Lane*) makes excellent beer (try

the Gritstone) and gives free tours Thursday and Saturday. Call for times.

Organized Tours
Double Deck (*☎ 905-374-7423, May-Oct*) offers two bus tours on British red double-decker buses. One includes admission to three of the city's major attractions and stops at other free sites ($47). You can stay on or get off at will, even taking two days to complete the tour. The second circles the same area but doesn't include any of the attractions ($21). Look for discount coupons. Tickets and boarding are at a booth by the foot of Clifton Hill.

More extravagant are the helicopter tours (a 9-minute flight including time over the falls) offered by **Niagara Helicopters** (*☎ 905-357-5672, 3731 Victoria Ave; adult/child $90/45*).

See Toronto, earlier, for sightseeing tours from that city.

Special Events
Call the tourist office for details on these free events. The **Blossom Festival** is held in early or mid-May, when spring flowers bloom, and parades and ethnic dances are featured. For winter visitors, the annual **Festival of Lights** is a season of day and night events stretching from the end of November to the middle of February. The highlight is a series of spectacular nighttime light displays set up along a 36km route.

Places to Stay
Accommodations are plentiful and, overall, prices aren't too bad, what with all the competition on both sides of the border. In summer, though, prices spike sharply upward. Outside the peak summer season, costs drop markedly, and through the winter, there are some very good bargains, with many of the hotels and motels offering two- or three-day packages, often including meals and discounts on attractions. Checking the travel section of weekend newspapers in town or in Toronto will turn up some deals. Since a room is a room, many places offer enticements such as waterbeds, saunas, heart-shaped Jacuzzis, FM stereos and movies for a 'dirty weekend' escape.

Prices vary by the day, season and demand and are higher on weekends and holidays (American *and* Canadian).

Camping There are campgrounds all around town. Three are on Lundy's Lane, leading out of Niagara Falls, and two are on Montrose Ave southwest of downtown. They are decidedly not primitive.

Niagara Glen View Campground (☎ 905-358-8689, Victoria Ave at River Rd) Sites $35-38. This campground, with tent and electrical sites, is closest to the falls. There are others along the Niagara Parkway farther north.

Hostels Both of the hostels listed here are open all year and are regularly full.

Niagara Falls International Hostel (☎ 905-357-0770, 888-749-0058, fax 905-357-7673, 4549 Cataract St) Dorm beds/private rooms $18/45. This popular HI hostel is in a former commercial building in the old town close to the train and bus stations. The hostel has room for about 90 people. There's a good-sized kitchen, laundry facilities, lockers and a large lounge. On offer are bicycle rentals and discounts for some of the museums and the Maid of the Mist.

Backpackers International Hostel & Inn (☎ 905-357-4266, 800-891-7022, fax 905-357-1646, Zimmerman St) Dorm beds/doubles $15/50. A very good alternative to the HI is this nearby inn in a huge, impressive house from 1896. There's a second entrance around the corner at 4219 Huron St. The upstairs rooms, like those in a small European hotel, are particularly charming. The price includes bed sheets, towels and a morning coffee and muffin. Guests have use of kitchen facilities. Bicycles can be rented, and there is pick-up at the train and bus stations (sometimes).

B&Bs The B&Bs often offer the best accommodations value. The Visitors & Convention Bureau (☎ 905-356-6061) is the best of the tourist offices to try for accommodations assistance. When booking a room, check if the breakfast is continental or full if that makes a difference to you.

There are quite a few B&Bs along convenient River Rd, which links the falls area with old Niagara Falls downtown, 3km downriver. Another advantage is views of the river across the street. Generally, they are cheaper than Niagara-on-the-Lake, at $90 average.

Glen Mhor Guesthouse (☎ 905-354-2600, fax 905-354-0255, 5381 River Rd) Rooms low/high season $60-70/70-100, with private bath & full breakfast. There are four rooms, and you can walk to the falls. Free pick-up at the bus and train station is offered.

Gretna Green (☎ 905-357-2081, 5077 River Rd) Rooms $65-110. This place, just a little north of Glen Mhor Guesthouse, has four rooms with private baths, TVs and air-conditioning. A full English breakfast is included, the warm English hostess is a plus, and sometimes, pick-up service is offered.

Butterfly Manor (☎ 905-358-8988, 4917 River Rd) Doubles with full breakfast $70-100. Nearby is this similar choice with four rooms.

Eastwood Tourist Lodge (☎ 905-354-8686, fax 905-354-8686, 5359 River Rd) Rooms $100-120 with full breakfast. More professional than the above, this full-time inn has been operating since the 1960s in the eye-catching rambling 1891 house with balconies overlooking the river. There are more rooms here than any other B&B, and each room is large with en suite bath. It's closed January to April. English, German and Spanish are spoken.

Motels There are millions of motels, including many on a 7km strip along Lundy's Lane, which leads west out from the falls and later becomes Hwy 20. There are scores more on Ferry, Murray and Stanley Sts. Prices vary from as low as about $40 in the off-season to as much as $120 in July and August. Prices also range with the various honeymoon rooms, double-size bathtubs, waterbeds and other price-bumping features. You may be able to strike a deal if you're staying two, three or more nights. The below are all budget choices.

AAAA Royal Motel (☎ 905-354-2632, fax 905-354-2632, 5284 Ferry St) Rates $40-85. This central motel is very near the lights of Clifton Hill and the restaurants, and is fewer than 30 minutes walk to the falls. The rooms are plain but fine (no phones), and there is a small pool. Meal vouchers are offered to guests for discounts at several nearby eateries.

Alpine Motel (☎ 905-356-7016, fax 905-356-6019, 7742 Lundy's Lane) Rooms $40-80. This small, tidy modest motel also has a pool and provides coffee and a muffin in the morning.

Maple Leaf Motel (☎ *905-354-0841, fax 905-354-2074, 6163 Buchanan Ave)* Doubles $40-90. This quiet, tucked-away motel is recommended. It's a friendly, well-run place fewer than two blocks from the falls.

Hotels Hotels tend to be new and expensive.

Europa (☎ *905-374-3231, Bridge St at Erie Ave)* Rooms $28. Across from the train station, this is a basic place with a nightclub downstairs that could be used by those traveling on the cheap in a pinch. It's not recommended for single women.

Econo Lodge (☎ *905-356-2034, 800-424-4777, fax 905-374-2866, 5781 Victoria Ave)* Doubles $65-150. Best buy among hotels is this establishment, where room prices are determined by demand. It has good amenities.

Days Inn (☎ *800-263-7073, fax 905-356-1800, 4029 River Rd)* Rooms $70-150. This chain, which has three locations in the area, is a reasonable and reliable choice. This branch is away from the center a little and has lower prices. It offers excellent off-season packages.

Places to Eat

Finding food in Niagara Falls is no problem, and while the dining isn't great, it isn't bad either; most places provide a pretty good value.

Victoria Park Cafeteria (☎ *905-356-2217, 6342 Niagara Parkway)* Dishes $5-8. Inexpensive meals can be found at this cafeteria opposite the US falls (in the building complex in the park of the same name, run by the Parks Commission). It's open daily. On the 2nd floor (open seasonally) is a more expensive sit-down version and an outdoor *beer garden* where you can get smoked-meat sandwiches and hamburgers ($9).

Around Clifton Hill and along Victoria and Stanley Aves, there are scads of restaurants. Japanese, German, Hungarian and, especially, the ever-popular Italian eateries abound. Many offer breakfast and/or lunch specials. Taking a leaflet from one of the hustlers on the street can lead to a good bargain.

Mama Mia's (☎ *905-354-7471, 5719 Victoria Ave)* Dishes $8-14. This comfortable place has been serving up standard Italian fare at moderate prices since the 1960s.

Mai Vi (☎ *905-358-0697, 5713 Victoria Ave)* Dishes $7-14. The food (and the presentation) in this neat little Vietnamese place is absolutely outstanding. It could hold its own in any big city anywhere. Just close your eyes and jab the menu – from pho to rice plates, you can't go wrong.

Flying Saucer (☎ *905-356-4553, 6768 Lundy's Lane)* Dishes $1-9. Open 6am-3am Sun-Thur, 6am-4am Fri & Sat. For fast food at any time of day and the cheapest breakfast in town, try this unmistakably shaped place.

There are also expensive restaurants in both the Skylon and Minolta Towers for meals with impress-everybody views.

Skylon (☎ *905-356-2651, 5200 Robinson St)* There are a couple of dining rooms at the top, the more expensive of which revolves once per hour. The other one offers buffet-style breakfasts, lunches and dinners at more moderate (but not inexpensive) prices. In the revolving restaurant, the early-bird dinner special (4:30pm & 5pm sittings) is $33. The *Minolta* (☎ *800-461-2492, 6732 Fallsview Blvd)* restaurant, in the Ramada Plaza Hotel complex, is similar. Reservations at both are recommended.

Tony's Place (☎ *905-354-7225, 5467 Victoria Ave)* Dishes $8-18. Between the falls and old downtown is this large, popular spot specializing in ribs, steak and chicken. There are regular a la carte dishes and a lower-priced children's menu.

Xin Vego Café (☎ *905-353-8346, 4939 Victoria Ave; closed Mon & Tues)* Dishes $8-14. This place is recommended for its innovative, eclectic international vegetarian menu, which features Thai and Japanese influences. It's a very inviting spot that provides an all-around enjoyable experience.

Jade Garden (☎ *905-356-0336, 5306 Victoria Ave)* Dishes $7-11. A pretty good Chinese meal for two can be had for $25 here, and it's open later than many places.

Daily Planet (☎ *905-371-1722, 4573 Queen St)* Dishes $5-7. In the slow part of town (old downtown), this place has pub grub and Mexican-accented snacks and is also a good place to grab a brew at non-tourist prices. There's dancing at night.

Simon's Diner (☎ *905-356-5310, 4116 Bridge St)*. Dishes $4-7. Down near the hostels, by the corner of River Rd, is the oldest restaurant in Niagara Falls (it looks it, with license plates and knickknacks everywhere). It offers funk and cheap basics.

Dad's Diner (☎ *905-354-1888, 4138 Bridge St)* Dishes under $7. Practically next door to Simon's, this diner is very good for low-cost, complete breakfasts.

Getting There & Away

See Toronto's Organized Tours section for information on trips to here from there.

Bus The bus station (☎ 905-357-2133, 4555 Erie Ave at Bridge St) is in the older part of town and away from the falls area, across the street from the train station. This is the station for buses to other cities, but a shuttle to the falls and even bus tours depart from here.

For Toronto, service is frequent, with a bus leaving at least once an hour from early morning (around 6am during the week) to about 10pm, although on weekends, there are fewer runs. The one-way fare is $25. The trip takes about two hours.

Shuttle buses run to Niagara-on-the-Lake three times daily during summer (see Niagara-on-the-Lake, earlier). Buses also depart for Buffalo, New York.

Niagara Airbus (☎ 800-268-8111) connects to airports in Toronto and Buffalo.

Train The VIA Rail station (☎ 888-842-7245, 4267 Bridge St at Erie Ave) is in the older part of town, close to this area's downtown section. There are two runs a day to Toronto: from Monday to Friday, trains leave at 6:45am and 5:15pm; on Saturday and Sunday, trains depart at 7:40am and 5:15pm. The trip takes about two hours, and the one-way fare is $27. There are substantially reduced fares if you book five days in advance and also very good prices on roundtrip tickets. There are two daily trains west to London and one southeast to New York City.

Getting Around

Walking is best for getting around; most things to see are concentrated in a small area.

Bus For getting around town and the area, there's the economical and efficient Niagara Parks *People Mover* bus system (☎ 905-371-0254), which operates from the end of April to mid-October. Note that the schedule is dictated by weather, demand, etc. It runs in a straight line from upstream beyond the falls, past the greenhouse and Horseshoe Falls, along River Rd, past both the Rainbow and Whirlpool Bridges, north to

the Niagara Spanish Aero Car attraction and, depending on the time of year, beyond to Queenston Heights Park. From there, it turns around then follows the same path 9km back. From the falls, it gets you close to either the bus or train station. One ticket is good for the whole day, and you can get on and off as much as you like at any of the stops. For a low extra charge, transfers can be made to the regular city-bus system. Such a connection will get you right to the door of the train or bus station. The *People Mover* ticket is a bargain at $5.50 and can be purchased at most of the stops. Throughout summer, the bus runs daily from 9am to 11pm, but after 9pm, it does not go farther out than the Rainbow Bridge. In spring and autumn, the schedule is somewhat reduced, and in winter, the system does not run at all.

Niagara Transit (☎ 905-356-1179) runs three similar shuttle services around town. One route, the Downtown Route, goes around the bus and train stations then to the falls. The Lundy's Lane Route goes around Clifton Hill and up Lundy's Lane, and the Marine Land Route runs from the falls area to the Rapids View depot (at the southern end of the *People Mover* route). The shuttles run half-hourly from 9am to 2am. Free transfers can be made from these shuttles to the others or to any city bus. All-day shuttle passes for $5 or one-way tickets can be bought from the driver. These routes cover many of the more popular sites and may be worth considering. The shuttles operate from May to October. After this time, the regular city buses must be used.

Car Driving in and around the center is nothing but a costly headache. Follow the signs to one of the several parking districts and stash the car for the day.

A good, free parking lot about a 15-minute walk from the falls is by the IMAX cinema, south off Robinson St, near the Skylon Tower. After leaving your car, walk to the concrete bridge on the north side of the parking lot. Go across the bridge to the top of the stairs, which lead down through some woods to the gardens and the river. Another parking place is the huge Rapids View Parking Lot, 3.2km south of the falls. It's off River Rd where the bus loop depot is situated but is a pay lot. From here, a pleasant walk leads to the falls.

AROUND NIAGARA FALLS

Refer to Around Niagara-on-the-Lake for details about the area between Niagara Falls and Niagara-on-the-Lake.

South from Niagara Falls, the Niagara Parkway, which begins at Niagara-on-the-Lake continues to Fort Erie, edged by parkland. The land along this strip is much flatter, the river clearly in view as the falls have not yet cut a gorge out of the river bed. But they are coming this way. Come back again in a few thousand years. There isn't much of interest here, as the road runs through residential districts, but there are certainly plenty of places to stop for a picnic or to rest in a shady spot by the water.

The town of **Fort Erie**, situated where the Niagara River meets Lake Erie, across from Buffalo, New York, is connected to the USA by the Peace Bridge. This is a major border-crossing point, and buses from Toronto connecting with many eastern US cities use it. On summer weekends, expect lines. Some air travelers find it worthwhile to go by bus to Buffalo from Toronto and its vicinity to take advantage of the sometimes cheaper US airfares.

The town is best visited for the reconstruction of **Historic Fort Erie** (☎ 905-871-0540, 350 Lakeshore Rd; adult/child $6.50/4; open 10am-6pm daily May-Nov), first built in 1764. The USA seized it in 1814 before retreating. At the fort, a museum, military drills and uniformed soldiers can be seen. Note it is also known as the Old Stone Fort. Take the guided tour; it's included in the price and well worthwhile.

The **Railroad Museum** (☎ 905-871-1412, 400 Central Ave; admission $2; open 9am-5pm daily May-Labor Day, weekends only in spring and fall) has articles and a locomotive relating to the steam era of train travel.

Fort Erie is also well known for its old, attractive **Fort Erie Race Track** (☎ 905-871-3200, 230 Catherine St; admission free). Races are held from May to October, and there are also slots. The track is off the Queen Elizabeth Way.

Slightly south of town is **Crystal Beach**, a small, rather rundown beach-cottage resort, which is too bad, because this is one of the warmest areas of the country, and the one with the longest summer.

BRANTFORD

pop 82,000

West of Hamilton and surrounded for the most part by farmland, Brantford has an old, somewhat frayed downtown that is now being upgraded. It is known for several things that make for an interesting visit. Tourism Brantford (☎ 519-751-9900, 800-265-6299, 1 Sherwood Dr) is downtown.

The district has long been associated with Native Indians – Chief Joseph Brant was based here. He led the Six Nation Indians,

Chief Joseph

who lived in an area stretching from here to parts of upper New York.

The **Brant County Museum** (☎ 519-752-2483, 57 Charlotte St; admission $2; open 10am-4pm Wed-Fri, 1pm-4pm Sat, 1pm-5pm Sun in July & Aug) has exhibits mainly on the white-settlers period through the 1930s. There is also information and artifacts on Brant and his people.

About three kilometers southeast of downtown are three Indian sites worth visiting. The **Woodland Cultural Centre Museum** (☎ 519-759-2650, 84 Mohawk St; admission $5; open 9am-4pm Mon-Fri, 10am-5pm Sat & Sun, closed holidays) has displays on the various aboriginal peoples of eastern Canada and offers some history of the Six Nations Confederacy. The confederacy, made up of the Mohawk, Seneca, Cayuga, Oneida, Onendaga and Tuscarora tribes, was a unifying cultural and political association that helped settle disputes between bands.

ONTARIO

A few minutes away is **Her Majesty's Chapel of the Mohawks** (☎ 519-758-5444, *291 Mohawk St; admission by donation; open 10am-6pm daily July-Labor Day, 1pm-5pm Wed-Sun rest of the year*), the oldest Protestant church in Ontario and the world's only Royal Indian Chapel. It sits on what was an original village site.

Northeast along Mohawk St leads to **Kanata** (☎ 519-752-1229, 440 Mohawk St; admission $4; open 8:30am-3:30pm Mon-Fri, 10am-4pm Sat & Sun), a replica 17th-century Iroquois village with a longhouse, demonstrations and trails. In the interpretive center, you can see a video on native life and artifacts.

Brantford was also the home of Alexander Graham Bell, inventor of the telephone. The **Bell Homestead National Historic Site** (☎ 519-756-6220, *94 Tutela Heights; admission $2; open 9:30am-4:30pm Tues-Sun*) displays some of his other inventions and is furnished as it was when he lived in it.

Myrtleville House (☎ *519-752-3216, 34 Myrtleville Dr; admission $2; open daily Victoria Day-Labor Day*), dating from 1837, is restored to reveal the early 19th century.

The town is also known for local son Wayne Gretzky, the greatest ice-hockey player the world has yet produced.

The bus station (☎ 519-756-5011, 64 Darling St) is central. Buses connect to Toronto, London and (via Hamilton) Niagara Falls.

SIX NATIONS INDIAN RESERVE

To the southeast of Brantford, and larger than the city itself, is Ohsweken, the Six Nations of the Grand Iroquois reserve. It is one of the best-known Indian communities in the country. Established in the late 18th century, it provides interested visitors with a glimpse of Native Indian culture.

Begin at **Odrohekta** (☎ *519-758-5444,* Ⓦ *www.sixnationstourism.com, junction Hwy 54 East & Chiefswood Rd; open 9am-4:30pm daily*), the gathering place. This center has information as well as a small, museumlike collection. For custom tours of the reserve and its Band Council House (seat of all decision-making), make an appointment at least two weeks ahead.

Practically across the street, the **Chiefswood National Historic Site** (☎ *519-752-5005; admission $3; open 10am-3pm Tues-Sun*

May-Oct) is the home of poet E Pauline Johnson. Her writing reflected the blending of European and Native cultures.

Various events are held through the year, including the **Six Nations Pageant**, a summer theater program established in 1948, and an annual **handicrafts sale** in November.

The **Grand River Pow Wow**, held for two days in late July at the Chiefswood Tent & Trailer Park, is a major event with hundreds of colorful dancers, traditional drumming and singing, as well as Native foods and craft sales. The park is adjacent to the historic site.

Camping (☎ *519-752-3969; open May-Nov)* Sites $20. There's camping too at the Chiefswood Tent & Trailer Park, which sits along the Grand River.

Also for overnighting, there is a good-value inn on the reserve.

Bear's Inn (☎ *519-445-4133, 4th Line Rd)* Rooms $54. Each of the 14 rooms in this white-pine log building has a different theme. Continental breakfast is included.

COUNTRY HERITAGE PARK

With 30 buildings on 32 hectares of land, this museum (☎ 905-878-8151, Tremaine Rd; adult/child $7/4; open 10am-5pm Sat & Sun July-Aug) brings to life the farming history of the area through demonstrations, displays and costumed workers in historical settings. It's near Milton, 52km southwest of Toronto, about a 45-minute drive. Leave Hwy 401 at exit 320 and follow the signs.

GUELPH
pop 94,000

Just north of Hwy 401 west from Toronto, Guelph is an old, attractive, middle-sized university town that's a nice place to live but does not have a lot to offer visitors. There are some fine houses along tree-lined streets, and the Speed River and downtown area is overseen by the dominant **Church of Our Lady**, on Norfolk St at Macdonell. The Guelph Centre shopping complex, on the corner of Douglas and Wyndam Sts, by historic St Georges Square, marks the middle of town. Wyndam St is the main shopping district and also offers restaurants and places for a drink. Try the local Sleeman Brewery beers.

The **Farmers' Market** (*7am-noon Sat)* takes place at the corner of Gordon St and Waterloo Ave. Almost 100 vendors come in from the surrounding countryside to sell their produce, and there's an assortment of local craftspeople, artists and booksellers.

The **Macdonald Stewart Art Centre** (☎ 519-837-0010, 358 Gordon St, on the campus; admission by donation; open noon-5pm Tues-Sun Sept-July) often has good shows in its seven galleries, which specialize in Inuit and other Canadian art.

McCrae House Museum (☎ 519-836-1482, 108 Water St; adult/student, senior & child $4/3; open 1pm-5pm Tues-Sun) is the birthplace of John McCrae, the author of an antiwar poem written during WWI, In Flanders Fields, which every Canadian kid reads in school.

South of town is the **Donkey Sanctuary of Canada** (☎ 519-836-1697, 6981 Puslinch Concession Rd; admission by donation, $4 suggested; open 9:30am-4:30pm Wed & Sun May-Nov, also Sat same hours July-Sept), a

peaceful, pastoral refuge for abused and neglected donkeys. Only the hardest of hearts could fail to be charmed by these remarkably friendly, gentle and amusing equines. It's off Hwy 6 north from Hwy 401.

University of Guelph Hostel (☎ 519-824-4120 ext 2694, Maritime Hall, Old Brock Rd, Hwy 6) Rates $22-43. From May to August, there's accommodations at the campus, at the corner of College Rd.

Bookshelf Café (☎ 519-821-3311, 41 Québec St) Dishes $6-15. This intelligentsia haven is near the main intersection of town – Wyndham and Québec Sts. The front area contains a good bookshop, while the side section is a tastefully austere restaurant with excellent food. Lunch could be a hummus and vegetable pita; dinner, Indonesian chicken with rice. It's a fine place for coffee too, and there is also a patio, a bar and, upstairs, a repertory cinema.

The Mennonites

The Mennonites are one of Canada's best-known yet least understood religious minorities. Most people will tell you that Mennonites wear black, ride in horse-drawn carriages and, eschewing modern life, work their farms in a traditional manner. And while basically true, these characteristics are only part of the story.

The Mennonites originated in Switzerland in the early 16th century as a Protestant sect among the Anabaptists. Forced from country to country due to their religious disagreements with the state, they arrived in Holland and took their name from one of their early Dutch leaders, Menno Simons. To escape persecution in Europe and to develop communities in rural settings, they trusted William Penn's promise of religious freedom and began arriving in North America around 1640, settling in southeastern Pennsylvania, where they are still a significant group. Most of North America's 250,000 Mennonites live in that state. In the early 19th century, lured by the undeveloped and cheaper land of southern Ontario, some moved northwards.

There are about a dozen Mennonite groups or branches in Ontario, each with slightly different approaches, practices and principles. The Mennonite Church is the middle ground, with the numerous other branches either more or less liberal. The majority of Mennonites are moderates. Most visible are the stricter, or 'plain,' groups, known for their simple clothes. The women wear bonnets and a long, plain dress; the men tend to wear black and grow beards. Automobiles, much machinery and other trappings of modern life are shunned.

The Old Order Mennonites are the strictest in their adherence to the traditions and most rigid in their practices and beliefs. They are similar in appearance to the well-known Amish, an ultra-conservative sect that also broke away from the Anabaptists in Europe several centuries ago. Distinguishing between the Mennonites and the Amish can be difficult, with their lifestyles varying slightly from one community to another. Both groups won't even wear buttons on their clothes, considering them a vanity. They don't worship in a church but hold rotating services in houses within the community. Homes are very spartan, with no carpets, curtains or wall pictures. And yet the Amish, who took their name from Jacob Ammon, a native of Switzerland, have long believed Mennonites to be too worldly. Some say traditional Amish are the plainest of the plain.

Latino's (☎ *519-836-3431, 51 Cork St E; closed Sun*) Dishes under $10. What a find! This family-run place with a welcoming atmosphere serves some incredibly good Chilean food at bargain prices. Everything is homemade; you can't go wrong, from the soups to the ceviche to the enchiladas.

KORTRIGHT WATERFOWL PARK

This park (☎ 519-824-6729, 305 Niska Rd; admission $4; open 10am-4pm Sat, Sun & holidays Mar-Oct) has a mainly captive collection of Canadian and exotic waterfowl – there are about 1000 birds representing several dozen species. The wooded setting allows for natural and close observation.

The park is beside the Speed River, south of Guelph. Niska Rd is just west of the intersection of Hwy 6 (Hanlon Expressway) and Kortright Rd W.

ROCKWOOD CONSERVATION AREA

About 10km east of Rockwood along Hwy 7, Rockwood Conservation Area (☎ 519-856-9543; admission $5; open May-Oct) makes a good destination for an afternoon outdoors. It's definitely one of the best conservation areas within the Toronto area. The park offers swimming, canoeing and picnicking, but of most interest is the landscape itself. There are woods, cliffs, caves and glacial potholes, all of which can be explored on foot. Trails wind all through the park, and canoes can be rented. There is also overnight *camping* available.

In the village of Rockwood, an hour can be spent strolling along the main street, with its antique and junk shops and craft boutiques.

Out-to-Lunch (☎ *519-856-1182, 203 Main St*) Dishes under $10. Open for lunch daily. Good, inexpensive food can be had at this restaurant.

KITCHENER-WATERLOO
pop 265,000

These twin cities – amalgamated to form one – are about an hour west of Toronto, in the heart of rural southern Ontario. About 55% of the inhabitants are of German origin (which explains why Kitchener was originally named Berlin). The city also acts as a center for the surrounding Amish and Mennonite farming communities.

It is these two factors that attract visitors and make the towns stand out from their neighbors. There is not a lot to see, and at a glance, things here are much the same as in any other large town. However, it's worth a short visit, particularly if your timing is right and you arrive for Oktoberfest (see Special Events, later). The towns share two universities and therefore have quite a large number of young people.

Orientation & Information

Kitchener is the southern portion of the twin cities and is nearly three times the size of Waterloo, but you can't really tell where one ends and the other begins. The downtown area refers to central Kitchener. King St is the main street and runs roughly north-south (even though it's called King St W and E); at the northern end, it runs to the two universities and beyond.

The farmers' market on the corner of King and Frederick Sts marks the center of downtown. This area of town has the train and bus stations, hotels and restaurants. King St runs south to Hwy 8, which continues to Hwy 401 – west for Windsor and east for Toronto. Hwy 8 W, at the junction of King St, heads to Stratford.

The Uptown (downtown) area of Waterloo along King St N from Bridgeport Rd north to William St W is a very pleasant district with various shops, restaurants, bars and nearby University of Waterloo.

It's 2.5km between the two downtown sections.

Maps and information are available at the Kitchener-Waterloo chamber of commerce (☎ 519-745-3536, 800-265-6959, 80 Queen St N). It's open 9am to 4:30pm Monday to Friday year-round.

Farmers' Market

The central market is held downtown (☎ *519-741-2287, 49 Frederick St; open 6am-2pm Sat*). It began in 1839 and features the products of the Amish and Mennonites – breads, jams, many cheeses and sausages, and handicrafts such as quilts, rugs, clothes and handmade toys. Whether they like it or not, it is the farmers themselves who are often the main attraction. Some of these religious people, whose ancestors were originally from Switzerland, live much as their grandparents did in the

19th century. There are also many merchants who aren't Mennonite.

Across the street, on the corner of King and Benton Sts, a **23-bell glockenspiel** rings at noon and 5pm.

Joseph Schneider Haus

This Heritage Canada site (☎ 519-742-7752, 466 Queen St S; admission $2.25; open 10am-5pm daily July & Aug, 10am-5pm Wed-Sat & 1pm-5pm Sun rest of the year) is the restored house of a prosperous German Mennonite. It's a museum depicting life in the mid-1850s, with demonstrations of day-to-day chores and skills.

Woodside National Historic Site

This site (☎ 519-571-5684, 528 Wellington St N, Kitchener; admission $3; open 10am-5pm daily mid-May–Dec) preserves the 100-year-old mansion where former prime minister William Lyon Mackenzie King (Canada's 10th prime minister) once lived. It has been restored and refurnished in upper-class 1890s style. The basement houses displays on the life of Mackenzie King.

Universities

In Waterloo, west off King St N on University Ave, the **University of Waterloo** and **Wilfrid Laurier University** sit right beside each other, and both have attractive, green campuses. The former is well regarded for its engineering department; the latter specializes in economics. Waterloo has an **art gallery** and the **Museum & Archive of Games** (☎ 519-888-4424, Burnt Matthews Hall, 200 University Ave; admission free), which depicts the history of games around the world. Hours vary depending on exhibits.

Doon Heritage Crossroads

This re-creation of a pioneer settlement circa 1914 (☎ 519-748-1914, Homer Watson Blvd; adult/student/senior/family $6/5/4/15; open 10am-4:30pm daily May-Labor Day, weekdays only rest of the year) is south of Kitchener (20 minutes by vehicle or call for transit information). The 23 buildings include a general store, workshops and a sawmill. There is also a model of an original Russian Mennonite village and a replica of an 1856 railway. To get to the site, go down King St, turn right on Fairway, left at Manitou St and left again at Homer Watson

Blvd. Special events are often held on weekends.

Centre in the Square & K-W Art Gallery

This performing arts complex (☎ 519-579-5860, 800-265-8977, Queen St at Ellen St) has an art gallery with changing exhibits and a 4000-piece collection. There's also a performance theater here.

Homer Watson House & Gallery

One of Canada's first notable landscape painters is the subject of this quite small, specialized museum (☎ 519-748-4377, 1754 Old Mill Rd; admission by donation; open noon-4:30pm Tues-Sun Apr-Dec). Watson (1855–1936) once lived here, and there are various pieces relating to his life and work.

Organized Tours

For getting around to some of the attractions just outside the area, like St Jacobs or Elora, consider the good, quite reasonably priced van trips offered by **Town & Country Tours** (☎ 519-743-3246, 519-894-4831); a half/full day $20/30).

Special Events

Some of the major events held here are the following:

Mennonite Relief Sale It is a large sale of homemade foods and crafts and also includes a quilt auction. It's held on the last Saturday in May in New Hamburg, 19km west of Kitchener-Waterloo.

Summer Music Festival This festival is four days of free or low-cost outdoor music concerts held at the end of June at venues around the downtown area.

Busker Carnival This is an annual festival of street entertainers that takes place in late August. Some of these performers are very good, and the whole thing is free.

Oktoberfest The event of the year, Oktoberfest, the biggest of its kind in North America and said to be the largest outside of Germany, attracts 500,000 people annually. The nine-day festival starts in early to mid-October and includes 20 beer halls, German music and foods, and dancing. A huge parade wraps up the festivities on the last day. For more information, call K-W Oktoberfest Inc (☎ 519-570-4267, 800-570-4267, w www.oktoberfest.ca). Upon arrival, visit one of the reception areas for a map, tickets, information and all the details on how to tie on your stein so you don't lose it. Reservations for accommodations during the festival should be made well in advance. For getting around, there is a free bus, in addition to the usual city buses.

Places to Stay

Hostels Although there's no true year-round hostel, the following help fill the gap.

Waterloo International Home Hostel (☎ 519-725-5202, 102B Albert St) Dorm beds $15. Backpackers' has a basic hostel here, very close to the University of Waterloo. It's open May to end of August, when students rent the rooms for the school year. The host, Joan, is a world-traveled author with a lot of unusual ideas she'll happily discuss.

University of Waterloo (☎ 519-884-5400, 800-565-5410, fax 519-746-7599, Ron Eydt Village, University Ave W) Singles/twins $42/29. University students and seniors get discounts. The university rents rooms May to late August. Meals are available on the campus at several places. Free parking and use of the swimming pool are included. Buses run frequently to the campus.

Wilfrid Laurier University (☎ 519-884-0710 ext 2771, fax 519-725-7574, 75 University Ave W) Singles/doubles $30/50. Rooms are available from May to mid-August but are generally used by those attending conferences. The dining room is open in the summer, too.

B&Bs The tourist office can help with current B&Bs. During Oktoberfest, many people rent out rooms. For information, call K-W Oktoberfest Inc (☎ 519-570-4267).

Austrian Home (☎ 519-893-4056, 90 Franklins St N, Kitchener) Singles/doubles $40/60 with breakfast. There are two rooms, a double and a twin with shared bath, at this Austrian-style B&B. It's one of the best bargains in town, and German is spoken.

Motels Motels are numerous, good and clean. Most of them are on Victoria St N (Hwy 7), which runs east-west off King St, just north of downtown Kitchener.

Mayflower (☎ 519-745-9493, 189 Victoria St) Rooms $45-85. This is one of the cheapest options in town.

Victoria Motel (☎ 519-742-7900, 175 Victoria St N) Rooms $55-70. The Vic is a bit

newer and more modern but still economical and has some kitchenettes.

Hotels For the dollar-conscious, a central hotel is not in the cards.

Walper Terrace Hotel (☎ 519-745-4321, 800-265-8749, fax 519-745-3625, 1 King St W) Singles/doubles $90/100. For those with a bit of cash to splash, this is a crackerjack central hotel. It's an old place that has been restored and has won a heritage award. It rents out over 100 rooms at rates that aren't bad compared to the other top-end places in town. And there's a good deli right in the hotel too.

Places to Eat

There are many restaurants on or near King St in Kitchener.

Williams Coffee Pub (☎ 519-744-7199, 198 King St W) Dishes under $10. For good java or a soup-salad-sandwich meal, it's hard to beat this eatery. Grab a newspaper and settle in, or have a game of chess out front on the sidewalk The food is fresh and plentiful.

Howl at the Moon (☎ 519-744-8191, 320 King St W) Meals $5-15.This easygoing pub/bar has something for everyone, with finger foods, chicken, beef, a kids' menu, a patio and live music. The wraps make a good lunch.

Fiedlers (☎ 519-745-8356, 197 King St E) Dishes $5-10. Closed Sun & Mon. Among the numerous European delis in Kitchener, this bustling one – stacked full of cheeses, rye breads, sausages and salamis – stands out.

Café Mozart (☎ 519-578-4590, 45 Queen St S) Desserts $5. Open 9:30am-10pm Sun-Thur, 9:30am-midnight Fri & Sat. After the nose gets a whiff of this place, the mouth will soon be munching on pastries, cakes or something covered with chocolate. It's not far from the bus station.

Concordia Club (☎ 519-745-5617, 429 Ottawa St S) Lunch/dinner $7/10-17. Closed Sun. For solid German fare, go where the locals go. Live entertainment is included on Friday and Saturday nights, and it's a very popular site during Oktoberfest. In summer, there is a *biergarten* too. It's away from downtown, but the genuine atmosphere is worth the effort.

The Uptown area in Waterloo on King St N has numerous eateries and bars.

Ali Baba (☎ 519-886-2550, 130 King St N) Dishes $20-30. Open daily, but dinner only on weekends. This steak house has been grilling since the 1960s. It's dark, formal and classy.

Entertainment

Echo is a free weekly with good club listings. There are numerous student-type bars on King St W in central downtown Kitchener.

Heuther Hotel (☎ 519-886-3350, 59 King St N, Waterloo) This is a good brewpub and place to eat, despite the one room featuring daytime strippers.

Circus Room (☎ 519-743-0368, 729 King St E, Kitchener) This venue draws a young crowd with live music Thursday to Sunday. It's a long way from downtown.

Sportsworld (☎ 519-653-4442, 800-393-9163, 100 Sportsworld Dr) This is a massive entertainment park containing, among other diversions, a waterslide, wave pool, go-kart track, video arcades and restaurants. Various tickets are available.

Bingemans Park (☎ 519-744-1555, 800-667-0833, 1380 Victoria St N) This park on the Grand River offers much the same thing as Sportsworld but also has 600 campsites ($26 to $36) for families going to this attraction.

Getting There & Away

The bus station (☎ 519-741-2600, 15 Charles St W, Kitchener) is a 5-minute walk from the center. There are very frequent services to Toronto and eight buses a day to London.

There are two VIA Rail (☎ 800-361-1235) trains a day to Toronto and one to London (Monday to Friday), with a change for Windsor. The station is on the corner of Victoria and Weber Sts, an easy walk north of downtown Kitchener.

AROUND KITCHENER-WATERLOO

For a nice local drive, take Hwy 401 past Kitchener (going west) to the Doon exit and go to New Dundee. From there, travel northwest to Petersburg, where you'll find the **Blue Moon Pub**. Then head on to St Agatha, with the church steeple, followed by St Clements and Lindwood – both are Mennonite towns with some interesting stores. Drive back east to Hawkesville, where there is a blacksmith's shop, and take a gravel road with fine scenery

to St Jacobs. Continue north up to Elmira and over to West Montrose.

St Jacobs

About 15km north of town (take King St N) is St Jacobs, a small historic village with a busy mix of traditional Mennonites and tourists. Numerous arts-and-crafts and gift shops housed in original buildings dating from the 19th century line the main street, King St. See the **Meeting Place** (☎ 519-664-3518, 1404 King St; admission by donation; open 11am-5pm Mon-Sat, 1:30pm-5pm Sun Apr-Dec; 11am-4:30pm Sat, 2pm-4:30pm Sun Jan-Mar), a very good interpretive center on the Mennonites and their history; it also acts as the tourist office.

The **Maple Syrup Museum & Antique Market** (☎ 519-664-1243, 8 Spring St; admission free; open 10am-6pm Mon-Sat, 12:30pm-5:30pm Sun) has an educational exhibit on the production of maple syrup, a Canadian specialty.

The **St Jacobs Farmers' Market** (☎ 519-747-1830, 800-265-3353, Farmer's Market Rd; open 7am-3pm Thur-Sat year-round) is a country version of the Kitchener farmers' market, with horse-and-buggy sheds still in place. It's 2km south of the village. There's also a **flea market** here, and on Tuesday and Thursday, cattle are auctioned next door at the Livestock Exchange. More authentic (and cheaper) is the less-touristy **Waterloo Market** (open 7am-2pm Sat year-round, 8am-1pm Wed June–mid-Oct), across the street.

If you like the town atmosphere, you can stay, but it will cost you.

Benjamin's (☎ 519-664-3731, 17 King St) Rooms $90-120. Right downtown, this renovated inn from 1852 has nine rooms, country charm and a good dining room. Dinner is about $25.

Jakobstettel (☎ 519-664-2208, 16 Isabella St) Rooms $150. This deluxe guesthouse in a stunning house is a high-end, well-established place to lay your head.

Stone Crock Bakery (☎ 519-664-3612, 1402 King St N) Whether you intend to stay overnight or not, a visit to this bakery/restaurant, near the corner of Albert St, should be on the agenda.

Elmira

Some 8km north of St Jacobs up Hwy 86 is Elmira. It's less touristy than St Jacobs;

ONTARIO

The Pub Crawl

Just west of Kitchener-Waterloo, four fine historic country taverns can be found in four neighboring villages. Each one dates from 1875 or earlier, and each offers atmosphere, good food and something to wash it down with. Begin in Petersburg at the **Blue Moon** (☎ 519-634-8405), a Georgian-style inn dating from 1848. It's off Hwys 7 and 8 at Regional Rds 6 and 12.

Next stop, to the west, is **EJ's** (☎ 519-634-5711) in Baden, again with some intriguing original decor, including hand-painted ceiling tiles. In fine weather, there is a patio as well. Beer from around the world is offered on tap.

Kennedy's Country Tavern (☎ 519-747-1313) is back east and north (not far from stop one – remember to designate a non-drinking driver; it's getting confusing). Kennedy's, in the village of St Agatha, has a bit of an Irish slant, although much of the food shows a German influence.

Last stop is the **Olde Heidelberg Restaurant & Brew Pub** (☎ 519-699-4413), in Heidelberg, north from St Agatha at the junction of Hwys 15 and 16. Here, in the middle of Mennonite country, a German country-style meal can be enjoyed with Bavarian beer brewed on the premises. The Heidelberg was built in 1838.

Stops one and two are closed on Sunday. Call any one of them and ask about the bus tours that sometimes do the circuit.

more a real, working country town, but with a significant Mennonite population.

Mennonite goods – including fine quilts, which are not cheap, and other crafts, such as furniture and antiques – are sold. The **Elmira Mennonite Church and cemetery** (58 Church St W) are oddly juxtaposed with the modern, suburban-like townhouses across the street.

In spring, the **Maple Syrup Festival**, with street activities and pancake breakfasts, is considered the province's biggest and best, and attracts thousands of visitors.

The area has quite a few B&Bs, many on farms and with owners who speak German. To locate one, call the Elmira chamber of commerce (☎ 519-669-2605, 877-969-0094, 5

First St). Rates start at $45/65 for singles/doubles.

There is no public transportation to Elmira.

About 7km east, in **West Montrose** is the only covered bridge remaining in Ontario. It was built in 1889 and is known as the Kissing Bridge.

Cambridge
pop 104,000

South of Kitchener, Cambridge is an old mill town now grown large, set alongside the Speed and Grand Rivers. There isn't much to see, but the redeveloped waterfront area known as **Riverbank** is pleasant and attracts shoppers. Many of the businesses once drawn by the power from the mill now contain factory outlets. Cambridge has a Scottish background, and this is celebrated with the annual July **Highland Games** (☎ 519-623-1340).

ELORA
pop 3500

Not far from Kitchener-Waterloo, northwest up Hwy 6 from Guelph, is this small, heavily touristed town. Named after Elora in India, with its famous cave temples, this was once a mill town that used the falls on the Grand River, which runs through town. The falls, the old mill, the pleasant setting and the nearby gorge and park make the town a popular day trip for both out-of-province visitors and Ontarians.

The main streets are Metcalfe, Mill and Geddes Sts, all right by the mill and river.

There is a chamber of commerce (☎ 519-846-9841, 877-242-6353, 152 Geddes St) downstairs in the library building.

Note that several regional towns have been amalgamated politically, including Elora and Fergus, and are known collectively as Wellington Centre.

The Greyhound bus connects north to Owen Sound and south to Toronto via Guelph. It stops at Little Katy Variety Store (☎ 519-846-5951), which is central, on Geddes St.

Things to See & Do

Not far from town at the **Elora Gorge Conservation Area** (☎ 519-846-9742, Wellington City Rd; admission $3.50; open May–mid-Oct), the Grand River flows through a deep limestone canyon. Much of the area is park, and trails lead to cliff views and caves at the water's edge. Riding the water in a tire tube is a fun way to spend a warm afternoon, and rentals are available. There are also picnic areas, *camping* and trout fishing.

Beginning near Georgian Bay, the **Grand River**, a Canadian Heritage River, winds its way south through Elora and continues just to the east of Kitchener-Waterloo, eventually emptying into Lake Erie. The Grand River watershed is the largest inland river system in the southern portion of the province. Aside from the gorge conservation area listed in Elora, there are many other parks and conservation areas located along the southern sections of the river, all offering access and information. Canoeing is possible in many sections (with rentals and shuttles); at others there are swimming facilities and walking trails. For more information, contact the Grand River Conservation Authority (☎ 519-621-2761) in Cambridge.

About a dozen blocks east of town along Mill St E, the **Elora Quarry Conservation Area** is worth a look and (better) a swim. There are no facilities other than a change room, but it's a very scenic place for kids of all ages to cool off on a hot day.

Plenty of small stores in Elora offer crafts, jewelry, paintings and pottery, much of which is produced by the numerous local artisans.

The **Elora Festival** (☎ 519-846-0331, 800-265-8977), an annual music festival, is held during the last weeks of July and into the first two weeks of August. The music is primarily classical (with an emphasis on choral works) or folk. Some of the concerts are held at the quarry, with performers playing in the middle of the water on a floating stage. On a warm summer night with the stage lit up, it really is an impressive experience. Other events include the annual September **Elora Fergus Studio Tour**, when local artisans open their workshops. Call the chamber of commerce for details.

Places to Stay
Elora Gorge Conservation Area & Campground (☎ 519-846-9742, Wellington City Rd) Campsites $11-14. This is a large campground that (though usually full on holiday weekends) has a number of sites that can be reserved one week in advance.

There are quite a few B&Bs in and around town. For accommodations assistance, call the chamber of commerce. Average price is $75 for two with breakfast.

Hornsby Home (☎ 519-846-9763, 231 Queens St) Singles/doubles $40/50. Considerably cheaper is this homey, friendly spot that always gets great reviews (mainly for its down-to-earth owners). A full breakfast is included in this real-life bargain. There are three rooms, one with private bath, the other two share a bath. If it's full, they can probably fix you up elsewhere.

Gingerbread House (☎ 519-846-0521, 22 Metcalfe St) Singles/doubles $60/80. This establishment's deluxe features, special breakfasts, fine furnishings and decor put it into a considerably higher price bracket. It's by the river over the bridge from town. Actor Nicolas Cage once used the suite.

Elora Mill Inn (☎ 519-846-5356, fax 519-846-9180, 77 Mill St W) Rooms $165-250. This is the prestigious place to stay in town; it offers a convenient location, views of the river, fireplaces and a dining room, but you may have to look in both pockets to pay the bill.

Places to Eat
Desert Rose Café (☎ 519-846-0433, 130 Metcalfe St) Dishes under $10. There's always a tasty choice of Mexican, Middle Eastern or Greek items on the menu at this local institution.

Shepherd's Crook (☎ 519-846-5775, 8 Mill St W) Dishes under $10. Watch the river flow from view behind a ploughman's lunch ($8) or meat pie baked with Guinness ($10) at this waterside pub.

Elora Mill Inn (☎ 519-846-5356, 77 Mill St W) Lunch/dinner $10/27. The swish dining room here offers lunches of sandwiches and salads, but at dinner, it gets serious, with Atlantic salmon, veal medallions and the like.

FERGUS
pop 9000
Fergus is Elora's neighbor and is a quiet farming town. As the name suggests, the heritage here is Scottish, and this is best appreciated at the annual **Highland Games** (Fergus Community Centre, 550 Belsyde Ave E; admission $15), which are held during the second week of August.

Included are Scottish dancing, pipe bands, food and sports events, such as the caber toss. It is one of the largest Scottish festivals and Highland Games held in North America. Call the chamber of commerce for details (☎ 519-843-5140, 877-242-6353, 400 Tower St S).

St Andrew St is the attractive main street. Many of the distinctive gray buildings are made of limestone, and a town oddity is the painted fire hydrants.

The central **Fergus Market Building**, off Bridge St, has various browser-friendly shops and is open on weekends.

Between Fergus and Elora Sts, the **Wellington County Museum** (☎ 519-846-0916, Route 18; admission $3; open 9:30am-4:30pm weekdays, 1pm-5pm weekends), a national historic site, has artifacts relating to the history of the county, art shows and gardens. Constructed in 1877, it is the oldest place in the country that was built as a shelter for the poor, aged and homeless.

Like Elora, Fergus is quite busy, and accommodations are not overly abundant. In general, costs are a little lower here.

The Thompson's (☎ 519-843-4065, 360 Provost Lane) Singles/doubles $45/55. This fine stone B&B is within walking distance of downtown. It's air-conditioned, and a full breakfast is part of the deal. Guests of the two rooms share the bath.

Riversedge Café (☎ 519-787-9303, Queen St W) Dishes under $8. Closed Mon & Tues. With a nice location behind the Market Building and a patio over the river, things could be worse than munching a sandwich, burger or one of the vegetarian pasta dishes here.

The Greyhound bus (☎ 800-661-8747), which goes to Guelph, where connections for Toronto can be made, stops at the *Highland Inn* (280 Bridge St), downtown. Have a beer while you wait; the inn's attractive pub is very tempting.

STRATFORD
pop 29,000
Surrounded by farmland, this is a fairly typical slow-paced, rural Ontario town, except that it's consciously prettier than most and is home to the world-famous Shakespearean Festival. Many of the numerous older buildings in the attractive, architecturally interesting central area have

been restored, and the layout along the river adds to the charm. Stratford's Avon River, with its swans and green lawns, together with the theaters, help the town deliberately and successfully resemble Stratford-upon-Avon, in England.

Some 12km east of Stratford along Hwy 8, the village of **Shakespeare** is geared toward visitors, with the main street offering numerous antique, furniture and craft shops. London (see that section, later) is about 60km or a 45-minute drive southwest, and Toronto is about a two-hour drive east.

Orientation & Information
Ontario St is the main street, and everything is close to it. At the foot of Huron St is the **Perth County Courthouse**, one of the town's most distinctive and dominant landmarks.

There is a friendly, helpful and well-informed tourist office (☎ 519-273-3352, York St at Erie St) in the heart of town. You can see pictures of guesthouses and peruse menus from many of the town's restaurants. Also, you can get a free parking sign for your car.

On fine days, **heritage walks** depart from the tourist office at 9:30am Monday to Saturday from July 1 to Labor Day. With one of the descriptive maps available, you could do your own walking tour. One map, put out by the Local Architectural Conservation Advisory Committee, details some of the history and architecture of the downtown area. Don't miss out on a walk along the river, where the park, lawns and theaters have been laid out in a soothing and visual manner.

Between November and May, information can be obtained from Tourism Stratford (☎ 800-561-7926, 88 Wellington St).

The public library (☎ 519-271-0220, 19 St Andrew St) has free Internet access.

Shakespearean Festival
Begun humbly in a tent in 1953, this Shakespeare festival (☎ 519-271-4040, ☎ 800-567-1600, ⓦ www.stratfordfestival.ca, PO Box 520, Stratford, ON N5A 6V2; tickets $39-80; May-Oct) attracts international attention. The productions are first-rate, as are the costumes, and respected actors are featured. Tickets go on sale mid-January and are available from

the box office at the Festival Theatre. Prices depend on the day, seat and theater.

By show time, nearly every performance is sold out. A limited number of rush seats are available at good reductions, and for some performances, students and seniors are entitled to discounts. Less-costly tickets are available to the concerts, lectures (including a fine series with well-known writers) and other productions, which are all part of the festival. Bargain-hunters should note that the two-for-one Tuesday performances offer a good value.

Write for the festival booklet, which gives all the details on the year's performances, dates and prices. Also in the booklet, or on the Web, is a request form for accommodations, so you can organize everything at once.

There are three theaters – all in town – that feature contemporary and modern drama and music; opera; and works by the Bard. Main productions take place at the **Festival Theatre** (*Queen St*), with its round, protruding stage. The **Avon Theatre** (*Downie St*), seating 1100 people, is the secondary venue, and the **Tom Patterson Theatre** (*Water St*) is the smallest theater.

Aside from the plays, there are a number of other interesting programs to consider, some of which are free; for others, a small admission is charged. Among them are postperformance discussions with the actors, Sunday-morning backstage tours, warehouse tours for a look at costumes, etc. In addition, workshops and readings take place.

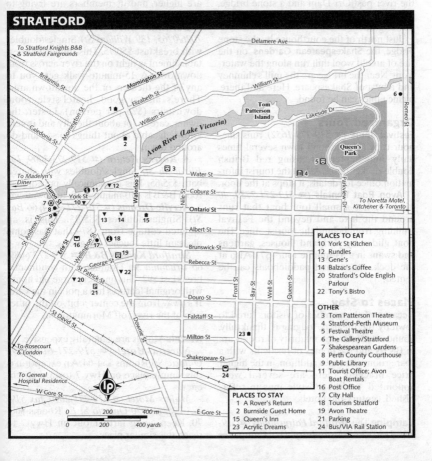

STRATFORD

PLACES TO EAT
10 York St Kitchen
12 Rundles
13 Gene's
14 Balzac's Coffee
20 Stratford's Olde English Parlour
22 Tony's Bistro

OTHER
3 Tom Patterson Theatre
4 Stratford-Perth Museum
5 Festival Theatre
6 The Gallery/Stratford
7 Shakespearean Gardens
8 Perth County Courthouse
9 Public Library
11 Tourist Office; Avon Boat Rentals
16 Post Office
17 City Hall
18 Tourism Stratford
19 Avon Theatre
21 Parking
24 Bus/VIA Rail Station

PLACES TO STAY
1 A Rover's Return
2 Burnside Guest Home
15 Queen's Inn
23 Acrylic Dreams

Things to See & Do

The **Gallery/Stratford** (☎ *519-271-5271, 54 Romeo St N; admission $5; open 10am-4pm Tues-Sun*) is a good art gallery in a fine old building near Confederation Park. Featured are changing international shows of modern painting, with the emphasis on Canadian works. Three shows are presented at any given time.

Articles collected around the region from the turn of the 20th century are on view at the small **Stratford-Perth Museum** (☎ *519-271-5311, 270 Water St; admission $3.75; open 10am-5pm Tues-Sat, noon-5pm Sun & Mon May-Oct, closed Mon rest of the year*).

Down by the river, near the Festival Theatre, **Queen's Park** is good for a picnic or a walk. Footpaths from the theater follow the river past Orr Dam and a stone bridge, dating from 1885, to the formal English flower garden.

Just north of the courthouse by the stone bridge, the **Shakespearean Gardens**, on the site of an old wool mill run along the waterfront. Near the bridge are the mill's chimney and a bust of Shakespeare. Here and there, picnic tables can be found.

Organized Tours

Festival Tours (☎ *519-273-1652*) runs one-hour trips ($10) around town several times daily June-September, using red British double-decker buses. Ask at the tourist information office for details; it stops at the door.

Avon Boat Rentals (☎ *519-271-7739, 40 York St*) has a small tour boat that runs around the lake and beyond the Festival Building, from behind the tourist office. The boat glides by parkland, houses, gardens and swans in a 35-minute tour ($7). Also at the dock, canoes and paddleboats can be rented.

Places to Stay

Because of the number of visitors lured to town by the theaters, lodging is, thankfully, abundant. By far, the majority of rooms are in B&Bs and the homes of residents with a spare room or two. In addition, in the higher price brackets there are several well-appointed, traditional-style inns in refurbished, century-old hotels.

Camping The *Stratford Fairgrounds* (☎ *519-271-5130, 20 Glastonbury Dr*) Campsites

$20. The farmers' market and a number of other events take place here, about seven blocks from the tourist office. There is also camping in St Marys (see that town's section, later in this chapter).

B&Bs A good way to find an economical bed is to book through the Stratford Festival Accommodations Department (☎ 519-273-1600, 800-567-1600, 55 Queen St). It will find a room in someone's home from as low as $50 if you have a ticket to a play. For a couple more dollars, breakfast can be included. Payment must be made in full when booking.

The Stratford & Area B&B Association (☎ 519-271-5644) does much the same thing, but not being part of the festival, its prices are higher, and its members are trying to run viable businesses.

Burnside Guest Home (☎ *519-271-7076/0265, 139 William St*) Singles/doubles with breakfast $50/75. This immaculate establishment is right on the river across from downtown. A 15-minute walk gets you to any of the theaters or the downtown area. There's also a good, hostel-style room downstairs ($25 per person). Lester, the owner, cares a lot about the city and is very knowledgeable about things to see and do around town.

A Rover's Return (☎ *519-273-3009, 132 Elizabeth St*) Singles/doubles with shared bath $55/65. This economically priced, five-room B&B is a 10-minute walk to downtown.

Acrylic Dreams (☎ *519-271-7874, 66 Bay St*) Singles/doubles $85/95. This is an updated cottage from 1879 that has some pleasant little touches for guests.

Stratford Knights B&B (☎ *519-273-6089, 66 Britannia St*) Doubles with continental breakfast $92. This fine very large old house with original features has a pool in the yard. It's away from the center a bit, on the other side of the river, off Mornington St.

Motels Motels are generally expensive.
Noretta Motel (☎ *519-271-6110, 691 Ontario St*) Rooms $54-64. An exception is this simple place on Hwy 7 toward Kitchener.

Majers Motel (☎ *519-271-2010, fax 519-273-79521, 2970 Ontario St E*) Rooms $60-70. Keep going farther out on Hwy 7 to reach this similar place.

Rosecourt (☎ 519-271-6005, 888-388-5111, fax 519-271-0236, 599 Erie St) Rooms $80. Close to town and with an appealing retro feel befitting its 1949 roots is this better choice, which is closed November to April.

Hotels *General Hospital Residence* (☎ 519-271-5084, 130 Youngs St) Singles/twins with breakfast $50/55. A possibility worth considering is a room here, and no, you don't have to get hit by a car to qualify. Similar to university dorms, the small, neat rooms come with single or twin beds, a fridge and a sink. Excellent weekly rates are offered. There are laundry and cooking facilities, a cafeteria and an outdoor swimming pool – all in all, a pretty fair bargain. They were having zoning problems at the time of research, so call to check on availability.

Queen's Inn (☎ 519-271-1400, 800-461-6450, fax 519-271-7373, 161 Ontario St) Doubles with bath $95. This historic inn with a wide range of rooms near Waterloo St, dates from the mid-19th century and is the oldest hotel in town. Management wrote the book on service. Prices are cut by up to half November to April, and good weekend packages are available. Many of the rooms are larger than some apartments (and feature more amenities).

Places to Eat
Balzac's Coffee (☎ 519-273-7909, 149 Ontario St) For the best coffee and hangout venue in town, get comfortable at this casually hip spot, with its old pressed tin ceiling and walls.

York St Kitchen (☎ 519-273-7041, 41 York St) Dishes under $10. Pretty much just a hole in the wall near the tourist office, the kitchen(ette) turns out excellent sandwiches ($5) and picnic plates, which might include a bit of smoked salmon or corn on the cob. There is a take-out order window, and the park by the river (right across the street) makes a good eating spot, or there are a few tables inside where you could try a lamb curry or pasta dish ($10).

As befits an English-style town, there are quite a few pubs about.

Stratford's Olde English Parlour (☎ 519-271-2772, 101 Wellington St) Dishes $8-20. For a pint and a traditional meal of shepherd's pie or steak 'n' kidney pie, this is a long-running fave. In summer, there's an outdoor patio.

Queen's Inn (☎ 519-271-1400, 161 Ontario St) Dishes $12-18. This inn, with several different eating rooms, has a pub, *Boar's Head*, for inexpensive and standard menu items, including a ploughman's lunch. The dining room has a continental menu, and the Sunday and Wednesday evening buffets are good.

Gene's (☎ 519-271-9678, 81 Ontario St) Dishes $7-10. Since 1970, this central place has provided the standard Cantonese options with some vegetarian selections.

Tony's Bistro (☎ 519-271-2991, 127 Downie St) Lunch/dinner $8/20. The small, simple, European-style dining room serves up very fine food, making for one of the best deals in town. The evening meal could be poached salmon or pork tenderloin with wild rice and apricots.

Rundles (☎ 519-271-6442, 9 Coburg St) Dinner $60 & up. Closed Mon. The Japanese-like design may be sparse, but the talent in the kitchen isn't. Entrées include duck, Atlantic salmon and lamb – all at the place that quite possibly has Stratford's best reputation.

Madelyn's Diner (☎ 519-273-5296, 377 Huron St) Dishes under $7. Closed Mon. This diner, away from the center and the visitors, over the bridge and down Huron St about 2km, is a friendly little place to have any meal. Breakfasts are served all day (from 7am) and are good, as are the roast-beef sandwiches and homemade pies. You may see an actor or two enjoying comfort food.

Getting There & Away
Several small bus lines servicing the region operate out of the VIA Rail station (101 Shakespeare St), which is quite central, off Downie St, about eight blocks from Ontario St. Cha-Co Trails (☎ 519-271-7870) buses connect Stratford with Kitchener daily, from where you can go to Toronto. They also run buses to London, with Windsor connections and some other southern Ontario towns.

VIA Rail (☎ 519-273-3234, 800-561-8630) runs two daily trains to Toronto. Trains also go west to London or Sarnia, with connections for Windsor.

ST MARYS
To the west of Stratford, St Marys is a small Victorian crossroads with a former opera house and some fine stone homes as reminders of its good times last century.

Several kilometers from town, off Hwy 7 and back toward Stratford, is the **Wildwood Conservation Area** (☎ 519-284-2292, Hwy 7; admission $7; open May-Oct). It isn't particularly attractive, but you can *camp* ($20) or go for a quick swim. For better swimming, try the spring-fed limestone quarry just outside St Marys (ask the locals for directions). It has change rooms and a snack bar.

TILLSONBURG & DELHI

These two small towns are in the center of a flat, sandy, tobacco-growing region. The number of smokers has been declining rapidly in Canada, so various crop alternatives (hemp, ginseng, oh how the worm turns) are being sought to keep the area productive.

On Hwy 3, west of Delhi, there is the **Ontario Tobacco Museum** (☎ 519-582-0278; admission $3; open 10am-4:30pm daily June-Sept, Mon-Fri rest of the year), with displays on the history and production of tobacco.

For males, casual work picking tobacco starts in mid-August. Ask at the Canada Manpower offices in these towns. Jobs last roughly a month. It's hard work, but room and board are often thrown in with the wage, and you can have a good time. Watch your valuables in the bunkhouse.

LAKE ERIE SHORELINE WEST

As the shallowest of the five Great Lakes, Erie long suffered the most with pollution. However, continuing environmental work has brought the waters back from the brink. Scattered along the lake's Canadian northern shoreline, from Windsor to Fort Erie, there are provincial government parks, some with camping, some for day-use only. Most are busy on summer weekends. This is a center for commercial lake fishing. Local restaurants specialize in Erie perch and walleye, although some people are leery of eating any of the lower Great Lakes catch due to possible chemical contamination.

Port Dover Area

The town of Port Dover is a busy little summer resort with a beach, boat tours, numerous tourist shops and a lighthouse.

The **Port Dover Harbour Museum** (☎ 519-583-2660, 44 Harbour St; admission by donation; open 10am-4:30pm Mon-Fri, weekends by chance) details the lake's fishing industry.

Harbour Princess Cruises (☎ 519-583-0202, Harbour St) offers several trips, including one to the Long Point Biosphere and weekend party trips with drinks and music. **CS Powell Charter** (☎ 519-426-1414, Dover Pier; $7) has cruises on the lake and upriver for an hour.

Turkey Point Provincial Park (☎ 519-426-3239, Route 10; admission $8.50 open mid-May–early Oct) and, even more so, **Long Point Provincial Park** (☎ 519-586-2133, Hwy 59; admission $8.50; open mid-May–early Oct) are good and popular. Despite an excellent beach at Long Point, the parks along the Lake Huron shoreline are superior for swimming. Also beware of deer ticks at Long Point; be sure to read the available information on these serious pests. Apart from these Lake Erie recreational areas, the region is mainly summer cottages, small towns and farmland. The shoreline itself is surprisingly scenic at points, with cliffs edging turquoise waters.

Erie Beach Hotel (☎ 519-583-1391, 19 Walker St) Rooms $80. This can't- miss- it, attractive hotel right in the heart of Port Dover contains popular dining rooms where the chef serves perch as well as the hotel's 'famous' celery bread.

Port Stanley Area

The town of Port Stanley has the agreeable atmosphere of an old, second-rate summer tourist town that doesn't care to be overly pretentious. It also has enough happening to not need to pander obsequiously to its visitors.

It has a fine summer program at the **Port Stanley Festival Theatre** (☎ 519-782-4353, 302 Bridge St), several low-key *restaurants*, *cafés* and a pleasing waterfront location. There's a sandy beach and a large dock with plenty of commercial fishing vessel traffic.

Port Stanley Terminal Rail (☎ 519-782-3730, 309 Bridge St; three times daily July-Aug, Sun all year) uses a 14km portion of the old London and Port Stanley Railroad track for one-hour trips (adult/child $10/5).

Some 11km west and 3km south of St Thomas, near the village of Iona, is the **Southwold Prehistoric Earthworks National Historic Site**, on Route 14 – watch for the sign. Surrounded by farmland are the earthwork remains of a double-walled Neutral Indian fort from around 1500-1650. It was once a village of about 600 people. There are no facilities at the site.

Wheatley Area

To the east, the town of Wheatley has some accommodations and **Wheatley Provincial Park** (☎ 519-825-4659, Hwy 3; admission $8.50; open mid-Apr–early Oct) where a violent storm swept much of the beach away in 1998. The *camping area* ($19-23) is good though. Be aware that during bird migration periods, this area is relatively busy.

Lakeside **Leamington** is Ontario's tomato capital and a major ketchup producer – now there's a claim to fame. There are several motels, B&Bs and a seasonal tourist office on the main street. It's about a 40km drive straight overland from Windsor, rather than around the lakeshore. For accommodations assistance, call the chamber of commerce (☎ 519-326-2721) Monday through Friday.

Farther west, **Point Pelee National Park** (☎ 519-322-2365, 407 Robson Rd; admission $4; open year-round), on the southernmost point of mainland Canada, is a top Lake Erie attraction. It's known for the thousands of birds that show up in spring and autumn on their migrations. As many as to 342 species have been observed here – about 60% of all the species known in Canada. The fall migration of monarch butterflies is a delightful spectacle of swirling black and orange. The region also contains some plants found nowhere else in the country, such as the prickly-pear cactus. There are numerous nature trails, a 1.5km boardwalk through the marsh, forest areas and sandy beaches within the park. Bicycles and canoes can be rented in summer. **Hillman Marsh**, on the shoreline north of Point Pelee, offers good bird-watching, a nature center and a walking trail.

Do Drop In (☎ 519-326-5558, 202 Seacliff Dr W) Singles/doubles $40/55. This is a Swedish/English B&B.

In Kingsville is the **Jack Miner Bird Sanctuary** (5km north of town, Division Rd; admission free; open Mon-Sat year-round).

Pelee Island From Leamington and Kingsville, ferries run to the largest island in the lake, Pelee Island. Pelee (**pee**-lee) is halfway across to Ohio. Ferries (☎ 519-724-2115, 800-661-2200) run from March to the beginning of December. Tickets cost $7.50 each way for adults; cars are $17. Reservations are a good idea, and check the schedule. From Pelee Island, ferries connect to Sandusky, Ohio.

Somnolent Pelee seems worlds away from much of southern Ontario. There's little going on, no glitz, no glamour, not much of anything. If you can't wind down here, give it up. Maybe that's why so many Americans are buying up waterfront lots. There are a couple of beaches (really warm water) and some small but well-known wineries.

There are tours, with tastings, at **Pelee Island Winery** (☎ 519-733-6551, 800-597-3533, 455 Seacliff Dr (County Rd 20); open May-Oct), the busiest spot on the island, and a very pleasant one, too. Quite a variety of wines are produced here, including Canadian champagne. Don't miss the almost gothic, atmospheric abandoned ruins of **Vin Villa Winery** and grounds and the old **lighthouse**.

There are a few restaurants on the island, inns, B&Bs and two campgrounds. *East Park Campground* (☎ 519-724-2931) This spot is basic and little used, though beachside and wooded and quiet, so the attendants at this campground on the east side of island may not even bother coming around to collect the money!

Bicycles can be rented. During midsummer, ferries and accommodations should be booked in advance. Note there is no bank or ATM on the island, and not a lot of groceries either. Contact the chamber of commerce in Leamington for information.

LONDON

pop 320,000

London is the most important town in the Lake Erie area and blends a fair bit of industry and manufacturing with its insurance-company head offices and one of the country's largest universities. The overall ambience is quiet, clean and conservative.

Even though the town has its own Thames River, Hyde Park and Oxford St, that's the extent of the London, England, resemblance. There are a few things to see in and around town, and it might prove a convenient stopover, as it lies roughly halfway between Toronto and the US-Canadian border at Detroit-Windsor.

Orientation & Information

The main east-west street is Dundas St; Richmond St is the main north-south street. The central area is bounded by York St to the south, Talbot St to the west, Oxford St to the north and Waterloo St to the east. The northern end of Richmond St is the hip strip, with a host of shops, eateries and cafés at which to hang out. There are some pleasant, tree-lined streets and elegant Victorian houses around the edges of the downtown area.

There is a downtown tourist office (☎ 519-661-5000, 800-265-2602, **w** www.city london.on.ca) on the main floor of City Hall, on Dufferin Ave, on the corner of Wellington St. It's open from 8:30am to 4:30pm Monday to Friday.

A second office (with the same telephone number) is at 696 Wellington Rd S, between Hwy 401 and Commissioners Rd, heading north into town from the highway. It's open daily from 8am to 8pm in summer (weekends only otherwise) and also has provincial information.

The public library (☎ 519-661-4600, 305 Queens Ave) has free Internet access.

Things to See & Do

Both an educational and a research facility affiliated with the university, the **London Museum of Archaeology** (*☎ 519-473-1360, 1600 Attawandaron Rd; adult/senior & student/child $3.50/3/1.50; open 10am-4:30pm daily*) displays materials and artifacts spanning 11,000 years of Native Indian history in Ontario. Adjacent to the museum building is an **active dig of a Neutral Indian village** (*May-Sept*) of about 500 years ago.

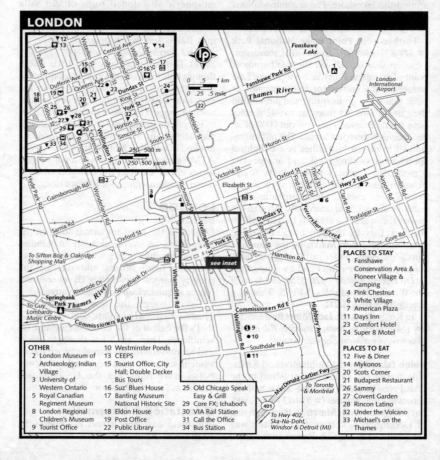

LONDON

OTHER
2 London Museum of Archaeology; Indian Village
3 University of Western Ontario
5 Royal Canadian Regiment Museum
8 London Regional Children's Museum
9 Tourist Office
10 Westminster Ponds
13 CEEPS
15 Tourist Office; City Hall; Double Decker Bus Tours
16 Suz' Blues House
17 Banting Museum National Historic Site
18 Eldon House
19 Post Office
22 Public Library
25 Old Chicago Speak Easy & Grill
29 Core FX; Ichabod's
30 VIA Rail Station
31 Call the Office
34 Bus Station

PLACES TO STAY
1 Fanshawe Conservation Area & Pioneer Village & Camping
4 Pink Chestnut
6 White Village
7 American Plaza
11 Days Inn
23 Comfort Hotel
24 Super 8 Motel

PLACES TO EAT
12 Five & Diner
14 Mykonos
20 Scots Corner
21 Budapest Restaurant
26 Sammy
27 Covent Garden
28 Rincon Latino
32 Under the Volcano
33 Michael's on the Thames

Parts of the village, including a longhouse, have been reconstructed. Special events are scheduled through the year, and some displays in the museum are changed regularly. A gift shop offers crafts such as baskets, quill boxes and pottery. The museum is northwest of the university. Take the Orchard No 31 bus from downtown.

At the 22-building **Fanshawe Pioneer Village** (☎ *519-457-1296, Fanshawe Park Rd; adult/student/child $5/4/3; open 10am-4:30pm Mon-Fri May-Thanksgiving)*, on the eastern edge of the city, staff in costume reveal skills and crafts and give a sense of pioneer village life in the 19th century. There is a tearoom at the site, or you can bring your own picnic. The adjoining **Fanshawe Park** is a conservation and recreation area with swimming, walking and picnicking areas. The entrance is off Fanshawe Park Rd, just east of Clark Rd.

Known as the RCR, the Royal Canadian Regiment is the oldest infantry regiment in Canada. The **Royal Canadian Regiment Museum** (☎ *519-660-5102, Wolseley Hall National Historic Site, Canadian Forces Base, Oxford St E at Elizabeth St; admission free; open 10am-5pm Tues-Fri, noon-4pm Sat & Sun)* has displays on its involvement in the North-West Rebellion of 1885 right through both World Wars and the Korean War. As well as the extensive displays, exhibits and dioramas, there is a gift shop with a range of military items. A visit takes about 1½ hours.

North of the downtown area, the beautiful campus of the **University of Western Ontario** (☎ *519-661-2111, 1151 Richmond St)* is pleasant to stroll around. Western is one of the country's larger universities and is known particularly for its business, medical and engineering faculties. The tourist office has a self-guided walking-tour pamphlet outlining some history.

Dating from 1834, **Eldon House** (☎ *519-661-5169, 481 Ridout St N; admission $4, admission free Wed & Sun; open noon-5pm Wed-Sun)* is the city's oldest house and is now an historical museum, with period furnishings from the Victorian era. Afternoon tea is served.

The **Guy Lombardo Music Centre** (☎ *519-473-9003, 205 Wonderland Rd S, Springbank Park; admission $3; open 11am-5pm daily May-Sept)* honors late musician and native son Guy Lombardo, who was well known across the continent for his New Year's Eve concerts. The collection of memorabilia and articles, including racing boats, outlines his career.

The **Banting Museum National Historic Site** (☎ *519-673-1752, 442 Adelaide St N; adult/senior & student/child $3/2/1; open noon-4pm Tues-Sat)* is in the house where Sir Frederick Banting, Nobel Prize winner and the co-discoverer of insulin, once lived and worked. The museum outlines the history of diabetes, and displays include a doctor's office from the 1920s.

Walkable from downtown, the **London Regional Children's Museum** (☎ *519-434-5726, 21 Wharncliffe Rd S; admission $5; open 10am-5pm Tues-Sat, noon-5pm Sun)* provides a variety of hands-on exhibits for kids to play and learn with.

The **Sifton Bog** is a site that is more than a little different – in fact, it's unique in southern Ontario. It's an acid bog that is home to a range of unusual plants and animals, including lemmings, shrews, the carnivorous sundew plant and nine varieties of orchids. Access to the bog is gained off Oxford St between Hyde Park Rd and Sanatorium Rd. There is also a pedestrian gate into the bog from the Oakridge Shopping Mall parking lot.

Also for nature-seekers, **Westminster Ponds** is an area of woods, bogs and ponds that supports a variety of wildlife, including foxes and herons. There is a viewing tower, and a boardwalk around some sections of the large undeveloped area. Two thousand years ago, indigenous people camped here. There is a trail into the area, heading east out of the tourist office on Wellington Rd S.

Some 32km west of the city, **Ska-Nah-Doht Indian Village** (☎ *519-264-2420, 8348 Longwoods Rd; admission $3; open 9am-4pm daily May-Sept, Mon-Fri rest of the year, closed holidays)* is a well-done recreation of a small Iroquois longhouse community from about 1000 years ago. Guided tours are available, or you can wander about yourself. The village structures are encircled by a palisade. Outside the walls, crops the Indians would have grown have been planted, and there are burial platforms. A **museum** supplies more information and contains some artifacts. The site, on Hwy 2, is in the wooded **Longwoods Road**

Conservation Area, which has some walking trails. From London, take Hwy 402 to interchange 86, and then follow Hwy 2 west. It's a good idea to call to confirm exact opening hours and dates.

Organized Tours

Double Decker Bus Tours (☎ 519-661-5000, City Hall, 300 Dufferin Ave) runs tours of the city aboard British double-decker buses. Two-hour tours ($9.50) depart twice daily from May to the beginning of September.

Departing from a landing in Springbank Park (off North St from Southdale Rd), **London Princess Cruises** (☎ 519-421-9277) does a number of different cruises along the river; a 45-minute tour is $8. There are also Sunday brunch trips and evening dinner cruises. Reservations are a good idea. The season runs from the end of May to October.

Special Events

Air Show Expect aeronautical acrobatics at this event (☎ 519-473-6444), held at the London International Airport the first week of June.

Home County Folk Festival In mid-July, watch for this free event (☎ 519-432-4310) in Victoria Park. Some pretty big names take to the stage over four days. Dance, crafts and a range of inexpensive foods are also featured.

Western Fair This 10-day agricultural and amusement event (☎ 519-438-3247) happens in Queens Park mid-month.

Places to Stay

The London & Area B&B Association (☎ 519-851-9988, **W** www.londonbb.ca) has a list of places, averaging $50 for singles and $65 to $75 for doubles. For many visitors, the most convenient area to look for motels will be along Wellington Rd, which leads north up from Hwy 401 to the center of town. Cheaper are the smaller, independent motels along the Dundas St E commercial strip, on the east side of town leading to Hwy 2. It's about a 10- to 15-minute drive into downtown.

Fanshawe Conservation Area & Campground (☎ 519-451-2800, 1424 Clarke Rd) Campsites $20-24. Open late Apr–mid-Oct. There is convenient camping within the city limits at this campground near the Pioneer Village. It's in the northeastern section of town, off Fanshawe Park Rd.

University of Western Ontario Alumni House (☎ 519-661-3814, 866-668-2267 ext 257, 1151 Richmond St) Singles student/non-student $29/39 with continental breakfast. The university rents rooms from May to partway through August. The residence is at the Richmond Gates. Be sure to call before arriving. The bus from downtown up Richmond St goes to the university gates, a few steps from the residence.

Pink Chestnut (☎ 519-673-3963, 1035 Richmond St) Rates $40-80 with breakfast. This place is easy to find, in the middle of things and very comfortable. The quiet garden is a plus, too. The bus stops almost at the door.

Days Inn (☎ 519-681-1240, 800-329-7666, fax 519-681-0830, 1100 Wellington Rd S) Rates $65-125. There's a heated pool, breakfast restaurant and bar on the premises.

Super 8 Motel (☎ 519-433-8161, 800-800-8000, fax 519-433-5448, 636 York St) Rooms with breakfast $70-80. This is a plain, no-frills place, but it's consistent and right downtown.

American Plaza (☎ 519-451-2030, 800-410-7115, 2031 Dundas St E) Rates $50-60. A low-cost choice is this motel with a pool and serviceable, clean, if basic rooms. Some have kitchenettes. But you can bet the honeymoon rooms aren't used by many newlyweds.

White Village (☎ 519-452-3176, 1739 Dundas St) Rates $50-70. This better place is a little closer to town and very well kept.

Comfort Hotel (☎ 519-661-0233, 800-228-5150, fax 519-661-0786, 374 Dundas St) Rooms $70-90. The free continental breakfast, parking and very central location are bonuses at this reliable outfit.

Places to Eat

Richmond St north of Dufferin to Oxford St, called Richmond Row, is absolutely lined with cafés and various casual eateries. At several places around town are colorful, carnival-like, semipermanent diner wagons. Parked in the heart of town, *Sammy* (Richmond St at Carling St) proffers cheap, fresh souvlaki and falafels. Get messy.

Covent Garden (☎ 519-439-3921, Richmond St at Dundas St) Open 8am-6pm Mon-Sat, 11am-5pm Sun. Wow! This market, remarkably right in the center of downtown (behind the Bay department store) is an excellent place to whet and satisfy the appetite.

There's plenty of fresh produce, as well as cheeses and breads. A number of small counters also prepare food.

Rincon Latino (☎ 519-645-2078, *398 Richmond St*) Dishes under $8. Open daily. This miniscule, barely-there kitchen with a few tables just south of Dundas St dishes up excellent and dirt-cheap authentic Salvadoran food with flair and care. Try the bean burrito and the genuine tamales wrapped in banana leaves.

Budapest Restaurant (☎ *519-439-3431, 346 Dundas St*) Lunch/dinner $9/15. Amidst traditional decor and textiles, this pleasant restaurant has been serving up Hungarian and European meals – such as goulash, schnitzels and chicken paprika – since the 1950s.

Scots Corner (☎ *519-667-2277, Dundas St at Wellington St*) Dishes under $11. This busy British-style pub serves burgers, meat pies and the like.

Mykonos (☎ *519-434-6736, 572 Adelaide St N*) Mains $10-17. For excellent Greek food and atmosphere, try this restaurant on the east side of town. Main courses include a range of vegetarian dishes and lots of seafood. There's an outdoor patio and Greek music in the evenings.

Under the Volcano (☎ *519-679-2296, 300 Colborne St*) Dishes $12-16. Comfortable yet not too casual, this converted house is named after Malcolm Lowry's great novel and is worth going to for its Mexican food.

Michael's on the Thames (☎ *519-672-0111, 1 York St*) Dinner $25. No lunch on weekends. Expensive, fine dining in a well-appointed, oak-lined room overlooking the Thames River can be enjoyed while the ivories tinkle in the background. For its setting and style, it is a good value. Specialties are seafood and chateaubriand.

Five & Diner (☎ *519-433-1081, 650 Richmond St*) Dishes under $9. Bright and nostalgic, with glistening chrome and tableside jukeboxes, this is a fun place for any meal.

Entertainment

London has always been a bit of a blues town, and though bars come and go, there is usually at least one place to hear some bar classics. Try ***Suz' Blues House*** (☎ 519-675-0153, 566 Dundas St) or ***Old Chicago Speak Easy & Grill*** (☎ 519-434-6600, 153 Carling St).

Core FX/Ichabod's (☎ *519-434-5698, 335 Richmond St*) The bar and dance club here attract similar, college-age crowds.

Call the Office (☎ *519-432-2263, 216 York St*) This venue features alternative bands.

CEEPS (☎ *519-432-1425, 671 Richmond St*) For decades, this place at Mill St has been a perennial favorite for the party-hearty under-30 crowd.

Getting There & Around

The Greyhound bus station (☎ 519-434-3991, 101 York St) is on the corner of Talbot St, in central downtown. Eight daily buses run to Toronto ($32) and four to Windsor ($30).

The VIA Rail station (☎ 519-672-5722) is nearby, on York St at the foot of Richmond St. It serves Toronto at least half a dozen times a day, two trips going via Stratford. The standard Toronto train fare is $43. In the other direction, the train goes to Chicago via Sarnia or Windsor.

As for getting around in London using public transportation, call London Transit Commission (☎ 519-451-1347) for fares and route information.

ST THOMAS

South of London, St Thomas is a small farming community made a little more interesting by its fine Victorian and other period architecture. In the downtown area, **City Hall** (*545 Talbot St*), the **Court House** (*2 Wellington St*) and **St Thomas Church** (*Walnut St*) are all worth a look.

Also for history buffs are two small museums, **Elgin County Pioneer Museum** (☎ *519-631-6537, 32 Talbot St; admission $2; open 9am-5pm Tues-Sat*), focusing on pioneer life, and next door, the **Military Museum** (☎ *519-633-7641, 30 Talbot; admission $2; open 9am-5pm Tues-Sun*), concentrating on the vicinity's military past.

St Thomas, though, has a tragic claim to fame – it was here in 1885 that Jumbo, that famous circus elephant, was hit and killed by a train. The life-sized **statue** at the west end of town pays tribute to him.

WINDSOR

pop 180,000

Windsor sits at the southwestern tip of the province, *south* across the Detroit River from Detroit, Michigan. Like its US counterpart, Windsor is primarily a car-making city. The inner cities, however, differ markedly. Though they're working on it, Detroit has long had deep problems. In contrast, the cute little downtown area of Windsor is neat and clean, with an abundance of parks and gardens, especially along the river. With the safe core, late-night bars, younger drinking age (not to mention Cuban cigars sold ostentatiously), it's a real party mecca in summer.

Windsor has another up on Detroit. In 1994, the city became home to the first casino in the province. Casino Windsor took in $100 million in its first three months of operation and has been attracting a daily attendance of about 20,000 ever since. Detroit has changed its laws to get in on the action, but Windsor remains popular, partially due to the good dollar exchange for Americans.

Apart from the gambling delights, Windsor doesn't have much specific to offer the visitor, but it is a major international border crossing, using either the Ambassador Bridge, or the tunnel that runs into Windsor's downtown. From here, it is about a two-hour drive to London and 4½ hours to Toronto. From Detroit, there are routes to Chicago.

The lively central area is around the junction of Riverside and Ouellette Sts. There are good views of the Detroit skyline, especially from Dieppe Gardens, which run right along the waterfront from the junction of these streets. Pitt and Chatham Sts are also important.

For information, there is a very helpful Ontario Travel Information Centre (☎ 519-973-1338, 800-265-3633, 110 Park St E), just a few minutes' walk from the bus station. It's open daily all year from 8:30am to 4:30pm, and until 8pm during summer.

The **Windsor-Detroit International Freedom Festival** (☎ 519-252-6274; admission free) combines Canada's July 1 national holiday with the July 4 celebrations in the USA for an event of parades, concerts and dances, with one of the continent's largest fireworks displays to end the affair. It begins the last week of June and takes place along the riverfront.

The two cities are connected by the Ambassador Bridge ($3) just west of downtown and the tunnel ($3.50) right downtown.

Casino Windsor

The huge, posh casino (☎ 519-258-7878, 445 Riverside Dr W) and hotel complex over-looking the river forms the base for the city's central renewal. It offers gaming tables, including blackjack and roulette, and slot machines gobbling anything from 25¢ to $500. The minimum age for entry is 19 years.

Art Gallery of Windsor

The striking AGW (☎ 519-977-0013, 401 Riverside Dr W, admission free; open 11am-7pm Tues-Thur, 11am-9pm Fri, 11am-5pm Sat & Sun), opened in 2001, presents challenging contemporary work.

Places to Stay

Most accommodations are in motels, with two main districts to check. Prices are higher on weekends but drop outside of summer. Huron Church Rd, leading off the Ambassador Bridge, is rich with choices.

University of Windsor (☎ 519-973-7074, 519-253-3000 ext 3276, Vanier Hall, University Ave) Rooms $25. From May through August, get a student's room, which are clean and quiet and very close to downtown at this residence beside the Ambassador Bridge. You may have to pay for parking or park blocks away on a residential street.

Nisbet Inn (☎ 519-256-0465, fax 519-256-0465, 131 Elliott St W) Singles/doubles $60/70 with breakfast. Just like an Old Country traditional, this English-style pub has rooms (four, with shared bath) upstairs. It's central, and there's a nice patio.

Diotte Bed & Breakfast (☎ 519-256-3937, 427 Elm Ave) Rooms $65 with full breakfast. This central B&B is about five blocks west of the casino and has air-conditioning, which can be a blessing in a Windsor summer.

Travelodge (☎ 519-258-7774, 800-578-7878, fax 519-258-0020, 33 Riverside Dr E) Rates $140-180. This downtown chain hotel is central and very close to the casino.

Apollo Motel (☎ 519-969-1828, 2080 Huron Church Rd) Rooms $65. Modest but good, this is a decent option.

Econo Lodge (☎ 519-966-8811, 800-553-2666, fax 519-966-3117, 2000 Huron Church Rd) Rooms $80-100. This lodge is 2km from the Ambassador Bridge.

The second area is in South Windsor on and around Division St, Howard St and Dougall Ave/Dougall Parkway. There are definitely some cheap options here but some real dogs, too.

ABC (☎ *519-969-5090, 3048 Dougall Ave*) Singles/doubles $60-65. There's a pool here.

Cadillac Motel (☎ *519-969-9340, 888-541-3333, fax 519-969-9340, 2498 Dougall St*). Rooms $65-90. Features include a pool and breakfast café at this very decent place.

Skyline (☎ *519-969-1060, 1425 Division Rd*) Rooms $50. Evidently the new owners are trying to upgrade, but check the rooms first. Swedish is spoken.

Places to Eat

There's no shortage of eateries along happening Ouellette St, which runs down to Riverside Dr. A good place for a meal is in the Via Italia neighborhood, along Erie St between Howard Ave and Lincoln Rd. Wyandotte St has scores of options from the university area through downtown and beyond, particularly Chinese and Middle Eastern places. Ottawa St, southeast of the core, has a multiethnic flavor, with a number of European restaurants, including Polish and Hungarian, and also an East Indian place or two.

Coffee Exchange (☎ *519-253-1923, 341 Ouellette St*) In the heart of town, this is a good café.

Under the Corner Restaurant (☎ *519-258-7191, 309 Chatham St W*) Dishes under $6. Down a few stairs at the corner of Dougall, this is a really nice little place with an attached bakery. It's good for any meal and is very low-priced, especially for breakfast.

Old Fish Market (☎ *519-253-7417, 156 Chatham St W*) Dishes $15-20. Try this place, two blocks east of the casino, for seafood.

Black Settlement in Ontario

The stories of the French, the English and the Natives that settled this region of Canada are well known. But to these stories must be added a fourth – that of the many blacks who came to the region prior to the American Civil War (1861–65).

Essex and Kent Counties, around Windsor and Chatham, make up one of the two regions of early black settlement in Canada (the other is around Halifax, Nova Scotia).

Windsor, as a terminal on the so-called Underground Railroad, was a gateway to freedom for thousands of former black slaves in pre–Civil War USA. The railway was really just a network of people ('conductors') who aided, directed and fed the fleeing slaves as, each night, they followed the north star to the next 'station.'

Aside from the museum in Amherstburg (see the Amherstburg section of the text), there are several sites in the region relating directly to this saga.

The **John Freeman Walls Historic Site** (☎ 519-258-5499) is located 1.5km north off Hwy 401, at exit 28 heading west from Windsor. The site includes the log cabin built in 1876 by Walls, a fugitive slave from North Carolina. The **Underground Railroad Museum** is also here.

Farther west, visit the **Buxton National Historic Site & Museum** (☎ 519-352-4799), near Chatham on County Rd 6 (exit Hwy 401 at Bloomfield Rd and go south). This museum concentrates on the lives of the black settlers who turned the Elgin Settlement into a new home and welcoming center for others following in their footsteps.

In the town of Dresden is **Uncle Tom's Cabin Historic Site** (☎ 519-683-2978). Uncle Tom was a fictional character in the controversial novel of the same name written by Harriet Beecher Stowe in 1852. It was based on the life of Josiah Henson, another southern black man. The site displays articles relating to the story and the salient history.

Just how much the tales of the Underground Railway are ingrained in the hearts of black Americans was suggested in the 1980s, when the Toronto Argonauts football team outbid several American teams for the services of hot new rookie Raghib 'Rocket' Ismail, just out of a US college. Ismail toured Toronto before deciding if he would join the Argonauts, and, sensing the region's racial tolerance, he struck a deal with them. After Rocket signed for an obscene amount of money, reporters at the obligatory news conference asked his mother what she thought of the agreement. Her reply was that they were going to ride that train north to freedom.

Patrick O'Ryan's (☎ 519-977-6227, 25 Pitt St) You can have Irish-type pub grub and wash it down with beer from the Emerald Isle.

Spago Trattoria (☎ 519-252-1626, 614 Erie St E) Dishes $7-13 Among the many Italian restaurants, try this casually classy one with an abundance of handsome, attentive waiters for excellent sandwiches, salads and pizza.

Getting There & Away
The bus station (☎ 514-254-7575) is central, on Chatham St, slightly east of Ouellette St. There are no long-distance buses for US destinations. Take the Tunnel bus to the Detroit inner-city bus terminal. From here, connections can be made for other cities.

The VIA Rail station (☎ 519-256-5511) is about 3km east of the downtown core, on the corner of Walker and Wyandotte Sts. There are frequent trains to Toronto via London.

AMHERSTBURG
pop 20,000
South of Windsor, where the Detroit River flowing from Lake St Clair runs into Lake Erie, sits small, historic Amherstburg.

Much of this history is outlined at the **Fort Malden National Historic Site** (☎ 519-736-5416, 100 Laird Ave; admission $4; open 10am-5pm daily May-Dec, call for other hours), situated along the river. There are some remains of the British fort of 1840. Beginning with the arrival of the fur traders, the area was the focal point for a lot of tension among the French, Native Indians and English and, later, the Americans. Here, during the War of 1812, General Brock (together with his ally, Shawnee Chief Tecumseh) discussed plans to take Detroit.

The **North American Black Historical Museum** (☎ 519-736-5433, 800-713-6336, 277 King St W; admission $5; open 10am-5pm Wed-Fri, 1pm-5pm Sat & Sun Apr-Oct) has displays on both black history in North America in general and the black settlement of the Windsor area in particular.

Park House Museum (☎ 519-736-2511, 214 Dalhousie St; admission $3; open 10am-5pm daily July-Aug, 11am-5pm Tues-Fri & Sun rest of the year), the oldest house in town, wasn't built here, but rather, it was ferried across the river in 1799 and is now furnished in 1850s style.

LAKE HURON SHORELINE
North of Windsor, on the southern tip of Lake Huron, industrial **Sarnia** is the hub of Chemical Valley, a large, modern, oil-and-chemical production and refining complex. Across the Bluewater Bridge, over the St Clair River, is Port Huron, Michigan. Southeast of Sarnia on Hwy 21 is the **Oil Museum of Canada** (☎ 519-834-2840, Hwy 21; admission $4; open 10am-5pm daily May-Nov, weekdays rest of the year), a national historic site and the location of the first commercial oil well on the continent. Producing wells can be seen in the area, and the search for more continues.

Along Lake Huron as far up as Tobermory on the Bruce Peninsula are numerous and popular parks, good sandy beaches, cottages and summer resort towns. The water is warm and clean; the beaches broad and sandy.

At **Kettle Point**, about 40km northeast of Sarnia, is a 350-million-year-old attraction. Along the shoreline are a series of spherical rocks called kettles (to geologists, concretions). Some of these calcite formations, which sit on beds of softer shale, are nearly 1m in diameter. The rare kettles are found in other countries but are often underground, and this collection is considered top rate.

Farther up the coast, south of Grand Bend, is the excellent **Pinery Provincial Park** (☎ 519-243-2220, Hwy 21; admission $8.50; open year-round), with 1000 *campsites* ($19 to $23). The beach is 10km long, and trails wind through the wooded sections. Farther north is smaller Point Farms Park.

Grand Bend is a Lake Huron resort town. It's a lively place in summer, with a few places for a drink along the shoreline.

Acting as the regional center, **Goderich** is a small, green and attractive town with a distinctive circular main street. It bills itself as the prettiest town in Ontario and has four museums. At dusk, view the 'world's best sunsets' from near the **Governor's House & Historic Gaol Museum** (☎ 519-524-6971, 181 Victoria St; admission $5; open 10am-4:30pm daily mid-May–Nov). It's set on a cliff on the town bluffs over the water. And these sunsets really are spectacular. The small **Marine Museum** (West St; admission $2; open 1pm-4:30pm daily July-Aug) has displays on shipping and the lake, while the **Huron County**

Museum (*☎ 519-524-2686, 110 North St; admission $2; open 10am-4:30pm Mon-Sat, 1pm-4:30pm Sun mid-May–Sept*) covers general history and pioneer days. The expensive, resorty **Benmiller Inn** (*☎ 519-524-2191, 800-265-1711, fax 519-524-5150, RR4*), not far east of Goderich in Benmiller village, has been an R&R retreat for many years; rooms start at $185.

The nearby village of **Blyth** is home to major summer theater, with the **Blyth Festival** (*☎ 877-862-5984; open July-Sept*), which features primarily Canadian plays, both new and old. **Blyth Station House** (*☎ 519-523-9826, 347 Dinsley St E*) Rooms $65-100. This unique B&B is in the converted train station; the highest-priced room has an en suite Jacuzzi. Several **restaurants** can be found along Queen St, the main street. Book ahead through the summer.

For details of the northern Lake Huron region as far as Manitoulin Island, see the following Georgian Bay & Lakelands section.

Georgian Bay & Lakelands

North of Toronto, the lakes and woods, towns, resorts, beaches and cottages – all presided over by magnificent Georgian Bay and its varied shoreline – make up the playground of southern Ontario.

The mostly wooded hills, scores of lakes and rivers, and numerous parks are scattered in and around prime farmland, making for fine summer fishing, swimming, camping and lazing – just what the doctor ordered. In winter, the area is busy with winter recreation: skiing, snowmobiling and lots of ice fishing. In September and October, people tour the region to see nature's annual, brilliantly colored tree show. Despite the emphasis on outdoor activities, this is generally a busy and developed area. For more space or wilderness, head farther north, or to the larger parks such as Algonquin, east of the bay.

The district around Barrie and Lake Simcoe to Orillia and northwest to Penetanguishene, and then around Georgian Bay west to Collingwood, is known collectively as **Huronia**. The area north of Orillia (roughly between the towns of Gravenhurst and Huntsville, along Hwy 11) and west to Georgian Bay is referred to as **Muskoka**, or (incorrectly) as the Muskokas. The name is taken from one of the larger lakes of the region.

West from Collingwood, along the south of Nottawasaga Bay, a smaller bay within Georgian Bay, is Owen Sound. At the southern entrance to the Bruce Peninsula, Owen Sound is the largest town in this area. The 'Bruce' is the narrow strip of land running north that divides Georgian Bay from the main body of huge Lake Huron. From the tip of the peninsula at Tobermory, you can take a ferry to Manitoulin Island, with connections to the mainland of northern Ontario.

The following text leads first from Barrie west and north to Manitoulin Island, around western Georgian Bay, and then from Barrie north and east through the Muskoka-Huronia region, around eastern Georgian Bay.

BARRIE
Barrie, about 1½ hours north of Toronto, is more or less the unofficial gateway to the big city's northward cottage country. On Friday afternoon, especially on holiday summer weekends, expect a lot of traffic on Hwy 400, at least to Barrie and often beyond. Coming back into Toronto, the traffic is heavy on Sunday night.

There is nothing of particular note in Barrie itself, although the popular beach at **Centennial Park**, on Kempenfelt Bay of large Lake Simcoe, is convenient and generally busy.

There's a large Ontario Travel Information Centre (*☎ 705-725-7280, 800-668-2746*) just south of Barrie at 21 Molson Park Dr (at Hwy 400), with details on regional points of interest. It's open all year.

The bus station (*☎ 705-739-1500, 24 Maple Ave*) is central. From here, buses go in all directions.

WASAGA BEACH
pop 14,000
Wasaga is the closest beach resort to Toronto. Around it and the strip of beaches (about 14km long) running up along the bay are hundreds of cottages and several private campgrounds. The center of activity is the decidedly unsubtle town of Wasaga Beach and its awesome beach with fine swimming

at **Wasaga Beach Provincial Park** (☎ 705-429-2516; admission $8.50; open year-round). The park, which is day-use only, also has some good inland hiking.

A popular weekend spot, and totally jammed on holidays, Wasaga Beach is nearly empty during the week. Some areas of the beach are more for families; others, like those around the snack bars, attract the younger crowd. You don't need to pay to hit the beach, but parking can be a hassle. An increasing array of manmade diversions are popping up.

The local chamber of commerce (☎ 705-429-2247, 866-292-7242, 550 River Rd) is open all year and is recommended for finding lodging. There are many *motels* around the district, including several along Main St or Mosley St. Rooms start at $80, more on long weekends, with cheaper weekly rates. Also check on Rural Route 1. Other places to stay are right on the beach. Lots of *cottages* with housekeeping facilities are also available, but these are generally for stays of a week or longer.

Four buses run daily between Toronto and Wasaga Beach. It's a 2½ hour trip, with a change of bus in Barrie. In Wasaga Beach, the bus travels right down the main road. The roundtrip fare is $49.

COLLINGWOOD
pop 16,000

In the center of the Blue Mountain ski area and right on the water, this little resort town has a reputation for being pretty, but it

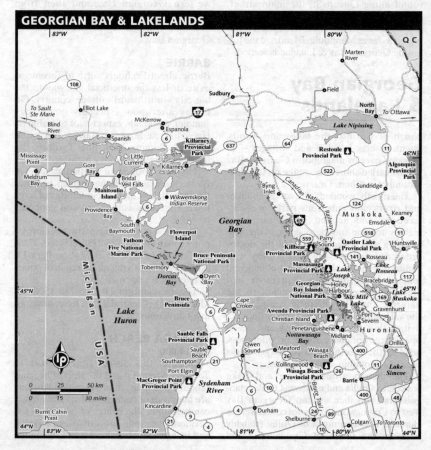

GEORGIAN BAY & LAKELANDS

really isn't. The surroundings are certainly scenic enough, with the highest sections of the Niagara Escarpment nearby, and omnipresent Blue Mountain and Georgian Bay lapping at the edges of town. The elevated rocky escarpment (a ridge) runs south, all the way to Niagara Falls. A major redevelopment is ongoing fueled by Intrawest's creation of a mega-, four-season, 'world-class' all-encompassing resort. Partially operational, it is already luring visitors for outdoor activities and pampered relaxation. The area is known for its 'blue' pottery, which is distinctive, but not cheap.

The informed tourist office (☎ 705-445-7722, 19 Mountain Rd) is slated to move. Things to do include **hiking**, **cycling** and **mountain biking**.

The **Scenic Caves** (*☎ 705-446-0256, Scenic Caves Rd; adult/child $9/6.50; open 10am-5pm daily mid-May–mid-Oct*) are not what most people expect of that term – they are really more like overhangs. Still, there is some good walking in and around (and between) rocks, limestone formations and the rugged terrain and excellent views.

For good-buy rock-climbing adventures and caving suitable for novices, call **Free Spirit Tours** (*☎ 705-444-3622/7723*). They offer one- and two-day guided trips. (See also under Toronto tours.)

There are many expensive places in the area, including resorts, lodges and inns with all the amenities.

Milestone Motel (*☎ 705-445-1041, 327 First St*) Rooms from $55. This place is between downtown and the ski area.

Blue Mountain Auberge & Hostel (*☎ 705-445-1497, Happy Valley Rd*) Hostel $25; rooms $90-150. Both price ranges are spanned here. It's a gorgeous place, like a Swiss alpine chalet, at the edge of the mountain and is run primarily as a hotel. But Clementine, the German owner, has a soft spot for hostelers and does take in *international* backpackers for just $25. We're not talking grubby bunkrooms – this is luxury on the cheap. It's usually booked during prime ski season by deep-pocketed hotel guests, but the rest of the year, hostelers can often get a spot – call first. The PMCL bus from Toronto connects to Collingwood and then to the Blue Mountain resort. From there, the lodge is walkable. Free Spirit Tours (see above) uses this as their accommodations connection.

Blue Mountain Resort (*☎ 705-445-0231, just west of town on Hwy 26*) Rooms from $150. Full condos are also available at the resort.

Several *restaurants* can be found on Hurontario St.

SHELBURNE
pop 4000

A rather nondescript small southern Ontario country town between Toronto and Owen Sound, Shelburne comes alive once a year when it hosts the **old-time fiddlers' contest** (*☎ 519-925-2600*). It's been held for two days in August since the 1950s. There's a parade, free music shows and ticketed concerts for the contest semifinalists, which should be reserved, as should accommodations.

OWEN SOUND
pop 21,000

Owen Sound is the largest town in the region, and if you're going north up the Bruce Peninsula toward Manitoulin Island, you'll pass by. It sits at the end of a deep bay, surrounded on three sides by the Niagara Escarpment.

Although still a working port, it is not the shipping center it was from the 1880s to the first years of the 20th century. In those early days, before the railway, the town rocked with brothels and bars, and was battled over by the believers – one intersection had a bar on each corner and was known as Damnation Corner; another had four churches and was called Salvation Corner. The latter seems to have won out, because the churches are still there. In fact, for 66 long years (from 1906 to 1972), you couldn't buy alcohol here. There aren't any merchant sailors on the waterfront now, but the pleasant town is busy throughout summer with visitors wandering and visiting the small but numerous museums.

The Sydenham River drifts through town, dividing it between east and west; the main street is Second Ave. There's a Visitor Information Centre (☎ 519-371-9833, 888-675-5555, 1155 1st Ave W) that's open daily from Victoria Day to Labor Day. Get a free parking pass and ask about the museum discount pass. A Saturday market is held beside City Hall, on Second Ave E.

Things to See & Do

The **Tom Thomson Memorial Art Gallery** (☎ *519-376-1932, 840 1st Ave W; admission by donation; open 10am-5pm Tues & Thur-Sat, 10am-9pm Wed, noon-5pm Sun June-Sept*) displays the work of Tom Thomson, a contemporary of Canada's Group of Seven and one of the country's best-known painters, as well as the work of other Canadian painters. Thomson grew up here, and many of his works were done nearby.

At the **County of Grey & Owen Sound Museum** (☎ *519-376-3690, 975 6th St E; admission $4; open all year, closed Mon*) are exhibits on the area's geology and human history. Outside (open mid-May to mid-August) are a half-sized replica of an Ojibway Indian village, an 8m birch-bark canoe, a log cabin and more.

Hometown boy Billy Bishop, who became a flying ace in WWI, is honored at the **Billy Bishop Heritage Museum** (☎ *519-371-0031, 948 3rd Ave W; admission $4; open Mon-Fri all year, Sat also May, Sept & Oct*), which is the Bishop home. Billy is buried in town at the Greenwood Cemetery.

In the old train station, the **Marine & Rail Museum** (☎ *519-371-3333, 1165 1st Ave W;*

Skiing & Snowboarding

Though the region north of Toronto tends to have milder winters and the topography is considerably less dramatic than in either Québec or around the Rockies, skiing is still a major winter activity. There are three main alpine centers, all offering daily equipment rental.

Closest to Toronto (about a two-hour drive) is **Horseshoe Valley** (☎ *705-835-2790, in Toronto ☎ 416-283-2988*). Take Hwy 400 up past Barrie to Horseshoe Valley Rd. Turn off, and the ski hill is 6km east. This is the smallest and lowest in elevation of the three and ideal for kids, families, the inexperienced or the merely out of shape. It's open every day and has night skiing until 10pm. The abundance of lifts (including a quad chair) means the lines move quickly, even on busy days. A plus here is that there is also a good system of nearly 40km of groomed cross-country trails. The trails close at 4:30pm.

Mt St Louis Moonstone (☎ *705-835-2112, in Toronto ☎ 416-368-6900*) is one of the province's top ski resorts and the largest (in terms of the number of ski slopes) in southern Ontario. It's at the village of Coldwater, about 10 or 15 minutes north of Horseshoe Valley on Hwy 400; take exit 131 to the right. Features include snowmaking and two licensed lodges (no accommodations). There are 42 runs, ranging from easy to difficult, with a 160m vertical drop.

Blue Mountain Resorts (☎ *705-445-0231, in Toronto ☎ 416-869-3799*), at Collingwood, is considered the most challenging of southern Ontario's ski centers and, being relatively far north, tends to have more natural snow and a longer season. The vertical drop here is 216m, with the maximum run length 1200m. The entire mountain area is undergoing a massive redevelopment and upgrading.

Collingwood is about a 2½-hour drive from Toronto. The slopes are 13km west of town on Blue Mountain Rd. There's daily bus service from Toronto.

Cross-country skiing is considerably less expensive; entrance fees to most places are in the range of $10 to $14 for the day. For cross-country skiing north of the city, there is the aforementioned Horseshoe Valley; or for a relatively wild, undisturbed winter wonderland, try **Awenda Provincial Park** (☎ *705-549-2231*), in Penetanguishene.

Close to Toronto are two good places to consider for cross-country skiing. **Albion Hills Conservation Area** (☎ *905-880-4855*) is 8km north of the town of Bolton, which is northwest of Toronto. Equipment can be hired, and there are 26km of trails winding through the woods. End a good day here with a snack in the coffee shop.

A second choice is to ski the grounds of **Seneca College** (☎ *905-833-3333 ext 5024, 13990 Dufferin St*) at its King Campus in King City. Snowshoes are available for rent. Call for trail conditions. When there is a lot of snow, the trails are open every day. Winding through the woods, they offer a good workout. There is no public transportation to the campus.

admission $3; open daily year-round), within the information center, details the town's transportation and shipbuilding history.

In spring and autumn, it's interesting to see the struggle that trout have to go through to reach their preferred spawning areas – the **Mill Dam and Ladder** were set up to help them on their swim upstream. It's a couple of blocks south of downtown, off 2nd Ave W near 6th St.

North of downtown is **Kelso Beach**, on Georgian Bay. Free concerts are held regularly here in summer.

Some 6km south of town, off Hwy 6, the Sydenham River falls over the Niagara Escarpment. The **Inglis Falls**, a 24m drop, are set in a conservation area that is linked to the Bruce Trail. The trail runs from Tobermory south to the Niagara River. See Tobermory, later in this chapter, for details. The segment by Owen Sound offers good views and springs, as well as the Inglis, Jones and Indian Falls. It makes a nice half-day walk.

Held in mid-August, the three-day **Summerfolk Music Festival** (☎ 519-371-2995) is a major North American festival. Musicians come from around the continent to perform in Kelso Park, right along the water; crowds can number 10,000. Admission is $25 per day. Call the tourist office for details and accommodations assistance.

Places to Stay & Eat
Most accommodations are motels. There are several on Ninth Ave.

Harrison Park (☎ 519-371-9734, 75 2nd Ave E) Unserviced tent sites $16. This large park right in town has picnic areas and fishing, and you can use the heated pool – Georgian Bay is known for its cold water.

Travellers Motel (☎ 519-376-2680, fax 519-371-3823, 740 Ninth Ave E) Rooms $40-45. This is the cheapest option.

Key Motel (☎ 519-794-2350, fax 519-794-2350) Rooms $50-60. A bit far, at 11km south of town on Hwys 6 and 10, this place is much better and yet still far undercuts the prices at the downtown chain hotels.

Marketside Café (☎ 705-371-7666, 813 2nd Ave E) Dishes $4-7. This is knock-your-socks-off good food on a shoestring. Unbelievable but true, it's delicious health food. Lentil soups, salads, Stilton and onion pie – anything. Great sweets, too. There are half a dozen tables and takeout.

Kelsey's (☎ 519-372-1992, Heritage Place Mall, 16th St) Meals $8-16. This place has a licensed patio and a range of finger foods and grilled meals.

PORT ELGIN
pop 7500
Port Elgin is a little resort town on Lake Huron, west of Owen Sound. There are sandy beaches, the warm waters of Lake Huron, cottages and camping. **MacGregor Provincial Park** (☎ 519-389-9056; day pass $8.50, open year-round), with *camping* ($16 to $20) and some walking trails, is 5km south. The **Saugeen River** has been divided up into canoeing sections ranging from 20km to 40km. Half-day and longer trips have been mapped out, with camping at several points along the river. A shorter trip is along the **Rankin River**. For information on paddling and outfitters, contact Bruce County Tourism Office (☎ 800-268-3838, **w** www.brucecounty.on.ca/tourism).

SAUBLE BEACH
Sauble Beach is a summer resort with an excellent, sandy, 11km beach; warm shallow waters; and entertainment diversions. The coast all along here is known for good sunsets.

There are plenty of hotels, motels and cottages for rent. Expect the many area campgrounds to be busy on summer weekends.

Sauble Falls Provincial Park & Campground (☎ 519-422-1952) Campsites $16-20. This is the best campground in the vicinity, so reservations are a good idea. Farther north along Route 13 are several commercial campgrounds, although some of them tend to be noisy at night with young partyers – check with the neighbors if this is a concern!

A walk around some of the side streets of the downtown area sometimes turns up a guesthouse sign or a seasonal B&B. Cottages tend to be cheaper than motels.

THE BRUCE PENINSULA
The Bruce, as it's known, is an 80km-long limestone outcropping at the north end of the Niagara Escarpment. Jutting into Lake Huron, it forms the western edge of Georgian Bay, splitting it away from the main body of the lake. This relatively undeveloped area of southern Ontario offers some

striking scenery, mixing rocky, rugged shorelines, sandy beaches, lakeside cliffs and green woodlands. The north end has two national parks. From Tobermory (at the tip of the peninsula), ferries depart for Manitoulin Island. For regional information, call the Bruce County Tourism Office (☎ 800-268-3838).

At Cape Croker, an Ojibway reserve north of Colpoy's Bay, about halfway up the peninsula, there's a secluded recommended *campground*. Nature tours are available, and Native Indian crafts sold.

Dyer's Bay

With a car, a good scenic drive goes via Dyer's Bay, which is about 20km south of Tobermory. From Hwy 6, take Dyer's side road into the village and then the road northeast along the coast. The road's not long, but with Georgian Bay on one side and the limestone cliffs of the escarpment on the other, it is impressive. The road ends at the Cabot Head Lighthouse. Before arriving there, you'll pass by the ruins of an old log flume, where logs were sent over the edge. The road south of Dyer's Bay is also good, leading down to a 'flowerpot' known as the Devil's Monument. Flowerpots are top-heavy standing rock formations created by wave erosion. This secondary road continues to Lion's Head, where you can connect back with the main highway.

Dorcas Bay

On Lake Huron, 11km south of Tobermory, there is a preserve owned by the Federation of Ontario Naturalists. This undeveloped area attracts many walkers and photographers for its wildflowers – up to 41 species of orchids can be spotted. To reach the site, turn west from Hwy 11 toward Lake Huron. You're there when you reach the parking lot with a few picnic tables and a toilet.

Bruce Peninsula National Park

The park (☎ 519-596-2233, Hwy 6; day-use $5; open May-Oct) protects and makes accessible some of the best features on the entire peninsula. For hikers, campers and lovers of nature, it's not to be missed. The park has several unconnected components, with segments on both sides of the peninsula, including Cypress Lake, some of the Georgian Bay coastline, the Niagara Escarpment between Tobermory and Dyer's Bay, and a great section of the Bruce Trail along the shoreline cliffs. Cypress Lake, with the campground ($18), swimming and some shorter walking trails, is the center of most activity. There is a visitors' center at Little Tub, Tobermory (next).

Tobermory
pop 900

This unpretentious fishing and tourist village sits at the northern tip of the Bruce Peninsula, which protrudes into Lake Huron. On one side of the peninsula are the cold, clear waters of Georgian Bay, and on the other, the much warmer waters of Lake Huron.

There is not much to see, but it is a busy place in summer. The Manitoulin Island ferry docks here. Aside from having its own subtle, tranquil charms, many people driving across Ontario and farther west cut through Manitoulin because it's quicker than driving around Georgian Bay. Tobermory marks the end of the 780km Bruce Trail, and it is also a diving center. The crystal-clear waters offshore contain more than 20 shipwrecks.

Activity is focused at the harbor area known as Little Tub. There's a Parks Canada center and a visitor information office (☎ 800-268-3838) just south of Little Tub on Hwy 6. Boats for tours of Flowerpot Island and all sorts of visiting yachts moor at Little Tub.

To reach Tobermory from the north, see Manitoulin Island, later in this chapter.

Fathom Five National Marine Park This is Ontario's first mainly underwater park (☎ 519-596-2233), developed to protect and make more accessible this intriguing offshore area, including the wrecks that lie in the park's waters, scattered between the many little islands.

About 5km offshore from Tobermory, Flowerpot Island is the best-known, most visited portion of the park and is more easily enjoyed than the underwater attractions. The island, with its unusual, precarious-looking rock columns formed through years of erosion, can be visited by boat from mid-May to mid-October. There are various trails on the island, taking from a little over an hour for the shortest one to 2¼ hours for the more difficult. Look for the wild orchids. The island has cliffs, some picnic spots and six basic campsites.

Reservations are needed for tenters, particularly on weekends, and you should bring all supplies with you, including water. Note that the mental image may not correspond with reality – there is little privacy, with boatloads of mainlanders arriving throughout the day. So much for the isolated island adventure.

Companies operating tugboats, a Zodiac and various other kinds of boats offer trips to the island, allowing visitors to hop off and catch a later boat back. The cost is about $16; just ask around the harbor area. The glass-bottomed boat is the best known, but the waters are so clear that wrecks can be seen simply by peering over the side of any boat. The last boat tours depart at around 5pm, but none run in poor weather.

Bruce Trail Tobermory marks the northern end of this 780km footpath, which runs from Queenston (on the Niagara River) to this point (on the tip of the Bruce Peninsula), over private and public lands. You can hike for an hour, a day or a week. The trail edges along the Niagara Escarpment, providing good scenery, though much of it is inaccessible from the road. Unesco (United Nations Educational, Scientific and Cultural Organization) has designated the Niagara Escarpment as a World Biosphere Reserve – an area that, although developed, preserves essential ecological features.

The most northerly bit, from Dyer's Bay to Tobermory, is the most rugged and spectacular. A good day's walk within the national park is possible. You may even get a glimpse of the rare Ontario rattlesnakes, though the chance of seeing one is slight, and they tend to be timid, so don't be deterred.

The Bruce Trail Association (☎ 800-665-4453, ｗ www.brucetrail.org) puts out a detailed guide of the entire route for $30, less for members. It's available in major bookstores. The mailing address is PO Box 857, Hamilton, ON L8N 3N9. Local tourist offices can tell you where there are access points.

Some parts of the trail are heavily used on summer weekends. Near Hamilton, at the southern end, there is a popular day walking area at Rattlesnake Point Conservation Area. Another southern one is at Terra Cotta, not far from Toronto. Yet another is at the forks of the Credit River.

There are designated areas for *camping* along the path, and in the gentler, busy southern sections, there are some huts where you can even take a shower. In other sections, there are accommodations in *B&Bs* or *old inns*. Prices start at $50/60 for singles/doubles. Remember the insect repellent, don't drink the water along the trail, and bring good boots – much of the trail is wet and muddy.

Activities The waters here are excellent for scuba diving, with many wrecks, geological formations and clear water. The water is

Take in some stunning scenery on the Bruce Trail.

also very, very cold. Even for snorkeling, a wet or dry suit is required. **G & S Watersports** (☎ *519-596-2200, Little Tub, Tobermory)* rents equipment and offers a variety of diving courses ($150 to $500). You can also rent equipment, including a wet suit ($60). The Ontario government puts out a pamphlet listing dive sites with descriptions, depths and recommendations. It's available free at the tourist office.

In 1993, a large section of well preserved, 8000-year-old underwater forest was discovered at Colpoy's Bay. It is thought to have been submerged hundreds of years after the retreat of the last Ice Age, when the lake levels rose.

Swimming in Georgian Bay in August can be good and warm, but not around here. Shallow Cypress Lake, in the park, is definitely a more sane choice.

Places to Stay There are a dozen or so motels in and around Tobermory, but prices are a little high in peak season, and reservations are recommended for weekends and holidays.

Cha Mao Zah (☎ 519-596-2708, Hwy 6; open May-Oct) Rates start at $30. New for this edition and recommended is staying on this Native Indian reserve, which has options from camping to sleeping in tipis with hides and furs ($30, and bring insect repellent) or cabins ($50 for two people; $75 for up to five people). Crafts are sold by the owner, a woodcarver. The reserve is 10km south of town.

Tobermory Village Campground (☎ 519-596-2689, Hwy 6) Tent sites $20, rooms with shared bath $40. This establishment, 3km south of the village, has camping and four basic rooms.

Harbourside Motel (☎ 519-596-2422, Carlton St, Little Tub) Rooms $80-100. This motel overlooks the harbor.

Peacock Villa Motel (☎ 519-596-2242, Hwy 6) Rooms $65. This nearby but sort of secluded spot is a short walk from the harbor.

MANITOULIN ISLAND

The world's largest freshwater island, Manitoulin Island is basically a rural region of small farms. About a third of the population is Native Indian. Tourism has become the island's main moneymaker, and many southerners own summer cottages.

The island is about 140km long and 40km wide, with a scenic coastline, some sandy beaches, 100 lakes (including some large ones), lots of small towns and villages and numerous hiking trails. It has remained fairly undeveloped. Visitors will soon find out that part of the reason for this is the difficulty of getting to the island and, once there, getting around. Transportation around the island is nonexistent, but ask at the tourist offices for any tours that may have started.

There are seasonal information offices in South Baymouth (where the ferry lands), Gore Bay, Mindemoya and Little Current (☎ 705-368-3021), the main one. West of the

ferry landing, at the village of **Providence Bay**, is the island's largest beach.

Two principal attractions of the island for many visitors are the fishing and boating. There are several fishing camps around the island. For cruising, the 225km North Channel is superb. The scenery is great – one fjord, **Baie Finn**, is 15km long, with pure white-quartzite cliffs. There are quite a few hiking trails; the tourist offices have information.

Beyond Meldrum Bay, at **Mississagi Point**, on the far western tip of the island, an old lighthouse (from 1873) provides views over the strait. Along the north side of the island, from Meldrum Bay to Little Current, is some of the best scenery.

Gore Bay, on the rocky north shore, has one of the island's five small museums. **Western Manitoulin Historical Museum** (*Dawson St; open daily June-Sept*) displays articles relating to the island's early settlers. See the prisoners' dining-room table from the jail. From the eastern headland at the edge of town, the lookout offers fine views. On the other side of town, the headland has a lighthouse. One of the main beauty spots, **Bridal Veil Falls**, is 16km east.

The largest community is **Little Current**, at the beginning of the causeway north to the mainland, toward the town of Espanola. The main tourist office for the island is here and can help with accommodations. Rates are not bad relative to the southern mainland. There are two viewpoints of note near town and one good walk. The **Cup & Saucer Trail**, 19km east of town, leads to the highest point on the island (351m), which has good views over the North Channel. Closer to town, 4km west and 16km south on Hwy 6, **McLeans Mountain** has a lookout with views toward the village of Killarney, on the mainland.

The **Wikwemikong Indian Reserve** (*Hwy 6*) is in the northeast part of Manitoulin Island. The interpretive center (☎ 705-859-2385), upstairs in the marina, has information on events and things to see on the reserve, known as Wiky. It hosts the largest **powwow** (loosely translated as 'cultural festival') in the province on the first weekend in August; it's a three-day civic holiday. Native Indians from around the country participate. It's an all-inclusive event, with dancing, music, food and crafts.

Getting There & Away

Getting to Tobermory or Manitoulin Island is difficult without a car. You must change buses in Owen Sound for the Bruce Peninsula. From Toronto and elsewhere, buses run frequently to Owen Sound, but from there, buses go to Tobermory on Friday, Saturday and Sunday in summer only. The complete trip takes almost the whole day. The schedule varies each year, so call. Greyhound goes all the way around Georgian Bay from Toronto to Espanola, and from there down to Little Current (on Manitoulin).

The island makes a good shortcut if you're heading to northern Ontario by car. Take the ferry from Tobermory, cross the island, and then take the bridges to the north shore of Georgian Bay. The route can save you a few hours of driving around the bay and is pleasant, although more costly.

From Tobermory, the *Chi-Cheemaun* (☎ 800-265-3163) ferry runs over to South Baymouth, on the southern edge of Manitoulin. It's not uncommon to have to wait for a crossing, so reservations are strongly suggested. There are four crossings daily in midsummer; two in spring and autumn. From Tobermory, departure times are 7am, 11:20am, 3:40pm and 8pm.

During the summer ferry season, mid-June to the beginning of September, the adult fare is $12. Cars cost $25. The 50km trip takes about 1¾ hours, and there is a cafeteria.

HURONIA TOWNS
Midland
pop 16,000

North of Barrie, on the eastern side of Georgian Bay, is the small commercial center of Midland, the most interesting of the Huronia region's towns. The Huron Indians first settled this area, and developed a confederacy to encourage cooperation among the neighboring Native peoples. The established Huron settlements attracted French explorers and, more critically, the Jesuit missionaries.

Midland has a number of worthwhile things to see. Downtown, look for the painted historic murals on walls everywhere. Unfortunately, even though the town is quite small, getting to the cluster of sites out of downtown is difficult without a vehicle. King St is the main street.

For information, see the chamber of commerce (☎ 705-526-7884, 800-263-7745, 208 King St), just south of the town dock.

For getting there and away, Penetang & Midland Coach Lines (PMCL) connects to Toronto and Penetanguishene. Get the bus at Dugger's Variety (☎ 519-526-3513, 551 Bay St).

Things to See & Do South of Yonge St, a short walk from downtown, **Little Lake Park**, with 100-year-old trees, a small lake and a sandy beach, also has two major sites: **Huronia Museum & Huron Indian Village** (☎ *705-526-2844, 549 Little Lake Park Rd; $6 for both; open 9am-5pm daily Apr-Dec*) is a good package. The village is a replica of a Native Indian settlements from 500 years ago (before the French Jesuits arrived on their soul-saving mission). The museum has a few Native Indian pieces but is mainly pioneer and later artifacts (check The Slenderizer, circa 1958), but there are also some paintings and sketches by members of the Group of Seven.

On Hwy 12 5km east of downtown, **Ste Marie Among the Hurons** (☎ *705-526-7838, Hwy 12; adult/student $10/7; open 10am-5pm daily mid-May–Oct*) is a well-done historic site that reconstructs the 17th-century Jesuit mission and tells the story of a rather bloody chapter in the book of Native Indian/European clashes. Graphic depictions of missionaries' deaths by torture were forever etched in the brains of older Canadians by now-discarded school history texts. Costumed interpreters answer questions and do demonstrations. There's a café on-site, and you may need it, because there is a lot to see.

Martyrs' Shrine (☎ *705-526-3788; admission $3; open May-Oct*), opposite the Ste Marie complex, is a monument to six martyred missionaries and is the site of pilgrimages each year. Even the pope showed up in 1984.

Right beside the Ste Marie site, the **Wye Marsh Wildlife Centre** (☎ *705-526-7809; admission $7; open 10am-4pm daily Sept-June, 10am-6pm daily July & Aug*) provides boardwalks, trails and an observation deck over the marsh and its abundant birdlife. Most notable of the feathered features are the trumpeter swans, once virtually wiped out in the area and now being brought back.

ONTARIO

The first hatching in the wild as part of this program occurred in 1993. Displays provide information on area flora and fauna. Guided walks are offered free with admission, and canoe trips through the marsh are also possible ($5). The site has a pleasant picnic area set amid indigenous gardens.

From the town dock, 2½-hour **boat tours** ($16) depart aboard the *Miss Midland* (☎ 705-526-0161, 888-833-2628, *off Bayshore Dr*) for the inside passage to Georgian Bay and the islands around Honey Harbour. Cruises run from mid-May to mid-October, with two trips daily during summer months.

Places to Stay & Eat The chamber of commerce lists local B&Bs.

B&B Galerie Gale (☎ *705-526-8102, 431 King St*) Singles/doubles $60-75/65-95. Central, just opposite the Huron village and museum, this convenient, comfortable place is owned by artists who can answer questions on the area. A good breakfast is included. One room has a private bath, and prices drop out of peak season.

Park Villa (☎ *705-526-2219, 888-891-1190, 751 Yonge St*) Rooms $62-90. This large motel has rooms with one, two or three beds, and prices are very good, especially if it isn't during the period from July to Labor Day.

Riv Bistro (☎ *705-526-9342, 249 King St*) Dishes $7-15. Open daily, dinner only Sat & Sun. Exceptional food with a Greek and Middle Eastern slant is the norm at this small but classy eatery.

Penetanguishene
pop 8000

Slightly north of Midland, this town (whose name is pronounced pen-eh-**tang**-wish-een, though it's often called just Penetang) is smaller but similarly historic, though with less to see. It has both a British and French population and past. Early French voyageurs (fur traders) set up around the British military posts, and both communities stayed. There is an information office (☎ 705-527-6484, 800-263-7745, 2 Main St).

Discovery Harbour (☎ *705-549-8064, Church St; admission $5.50 guided, $3.50 self-guided; open daily July-Labor Day*) is a reconstructed naval base slightly north of the center. The original base was built by the British after the War of 1812 in case the

USA forces came back for more, but they didn't. It features reconstructed ships; there are daily sailing programs aboard the two schooners *BEE* and *Tecumseth*. There are also 19th-century naval buildings and a theater program.

Between Penetanguishene and Parry Sound (to the north), the waters of Georgian Bay are dotted with 30,000 islands – the world's highest concentration. This and the nearby beaches make it somewhat of a boating and vacation destination, and the dock area is always busy in summer with locals and out-of-towners. Three-hour cruises, which are popular not only in summer but also in autumn, when the leaves are all reds and yellows, depart from here, Midland and Parry Sound.

Island Cruises (☎ 705-549-7797, 800-363-7447; *mid-May-Sept*) offers three-hour cruises aboard the MS *Georgia Queen* for $16/7 adult/child. Compared to the cruise from Midland, this one is longer, goes past more small islands and has a shorter season. The price is the same.

For somewhere to eat, try *Dock Lunch* (☎ *705-549-8111*), at the dock. It's just a fast-food joint, but it's got atmosphere and is open daily.

Awenda Provincial Park

Northward, Awenda (☎ *705-549-2231; admission $8.50; open mid-May–early Oct*), right at the end of the peninsula jutting into Georgian Bay, is relatively small but very good. It's busy with both day visitors and overnighters. The campsites are large, treed and private. There are four fine beaches connected by walking paths. The first one can be reached by car; the second and third are the sandiest. This is one of the few places around Georgian Bay where the water gets pleasantly warm. There are also a couple of longer, less-used trails through the park, one offering a good view of the bay.

Food and other supplies should be bought in Penetanguishene. Basic staples can be bought not too far from the park entrance, but a vehicle is still needed.

Sometimes, particularly after heavy rain, water contamination from shoreline-dwelling beavers can result in bathers experiencing a nasty 'swimmer's itch.' It's worth asking about by phone, as the beaches are a main attraction.

Reservations for the *campsites* ($20) are advised for summer weekends (or arrive Friday morning). The roadside signs on the approach indicating that the park campground is full are not always accurate, so persevering can be worthwhile. By evening on a Friday, however, it may well be chockablock until Monday morning. The park office has a list of commercial campgrounds in the district if it's booked out.

Orillia
pop 28,000

At the north end of Lake Simcoe, Orillia acts as the entrance to Muskoka and points beyond. Hwys 400 and 11 split just south of here and continue up to northern Ontario. It is also a major link in the Trent-Severn Canal System. From town, cruise boats ply the canal and Lake Couchiching.

With a few things to see, a well-regarded summer theater program and a preserved downtown on the edge of Lake Couchiching, a day or so here is enjoyable. Mississauga is the main downtown street, and there is a tourist office (☎ 705-326-3792, 150 Front St S).

Orillia was the home of Canada's well-known humorist Stephen Leacock. He wrote here and in 1919 built a lovely house, which is now the **Leacock Museum** (*☎ 705-329-1908, 50 Museum Dr; admission $5; open 10am-5pm daily June-Labor Day, otherwise Mon-Fri*). His Sunshine Sketches of a Little Town, based on Orillia, has been called the most Canadian book ever written.

The historic **Orillia Opera House** (*☎ 705-326-8011, 20 Mississaga St W*) is home to quality plays and performances, including productions by the Sunshine Festival Theatre Company (June to October).

Hugely successful **Casino Rama** (*☎ 888-817-7262, Rama Rd; open 24 hours daily year-round*), operated by the local Native Indian community just southeast of downtown, even provides a snowmobile parking area. Some big names perform.

The area around the north end of Lake Simcoe has three family-oriented provincial parks with camping. None of them offers much to do or dramatic scenery, but all are busy, easygoing places. In town are about a dozen standard inns and motels; several low-cost motels are along Laclie St.

Bass Lake Provincial Park (*☎ 705-326-7054*) Campsites $18-24. This place has a sandy beach, warm waters and a nature trail. There are boat and canoe rentals, as well as fishing in the lake.

HI Orillia Home Hostel (*☎ 705-325-0970, fax 705-325-9826, 198 Borland St E*) Dorm beds members/nonmembers $15/18. Open year-round. This small hostel in a home off Laclie St is set on a quiet, treed property and is walkable (1.2km) from the bus station. The owner, who speaks German, knows the area well and will happily offer advice and opinions.

Webers (*☎ 705-326-1919, 16 Front St N*) Dishes $5-16. For barbecued burgers, steaks or ribs, as well as pastas or excellent salads, this popular spot is central and open daily. For drivers heading north during summer on Hwy 11 and in need of a snack, stop at their burger outlet south of the Severn River. This joint is so popular that a pedestrian bridge had to be put up to enable patrons to cross the highway.

MUSKOKA TOWNS

The three following towns, discussed from south to north, are the principal centers of Muskoka. They supply this older, well-established and, in some sections, exclusive cottage country. All have numerous places to eat and many nearby motels and resorts. With some interesting if low-key attractions, various boat cruises and pleasant small-town atmosphere, they make a good tour of the region.

Gravenhurst
pop 10,500

Muskoka Rd is the main street in this least resorty working town with plenty of historic central buildings.

A main attraction is the **Bethune Memorial House** (*☎ 705-687-4261, 235 John St N; admission $3; open 10am-5pm daily mid-May–Oct, closed weekends rest of the year*), in honor of China's favorite Canadian, Dr Norman Bethune, who traveled throughout China in the 1930s as a surgeon and educator and who died there in a small village. The house details this and other aspects of his career and life.

Recommended is a trip on a restored 19th-century steamship, the ***Segwun*** (*☎ 705-687-6667, 820 Bay St, Sagamo Park*), with various cruises ($11 to $73, one to eight hours) around the big-three Muskoka Lakes (Lake

Muskoka; Lake Rosseau, with its 'millionaires' row' of summer retreats; and Lake Joseph). The wonderful ship is the oldest operating steamship in North America and delivered mail before the days of the automobile.

Through the summer, the professional **Muskoka Summer Theatre** (☎ 705-687-5550, 888-495-8888, Muskoka Rd S; admission $20-30) performs in the restored Opera House.

Bracebridge
pop 14,000

Bracebridge is a pretty town with a lively, resorty air for much of the year. Manitoba St is the main street, along which are pubs and restaurants. The *Lady Muskoka* (☎ 705-646-2628, 800-263-5239, at Riverside Inn, Eccelstone Dr; admission $15; May-Oct) cruises the Muskoka River and Lake Muskoka. Lunch and dinner is available on board.

Drop into the chamber of commerce (☎ 705-645-5231, 1 Manitoba St) and pick up their sheets on discovering the numerous trails and waterfalls (especially in spring) in and around town. High Falls is most dramatic.

Huntsville
pop 18,000

The region's largest town still retains a festive, welcoming ambience with its preserved core. As the last major place for supplies for those going into Algonquin Park or with summer places around the large Lake of Bays, it is a shopping headquarters that also caters to tourists and visitors. The chamber of commerce (☎ 705-789-4771, 8 West St N) is closed Sunday.

Spread over 90 acres, comprehensive **Heritage Place** (☎ 705-789-7576, 88 Brunel Rd; adult/child/family $18/16/60; open May-Oct) has two museums, a pioneer village and steam train, which collectively give some historical perspective to the region.

During the first three weeks of July, Huntsville hosts a **Festival of the Arts** (☎ 800-663-2787), which features classical music, jazz, theater, dance and literary events around town.

Ontario Northland (☎ 800-461-8558) runs buses from Toronto to Huntsville and Emsdale (near Kearney for canoeing). In Huntsville, the buses use Huntsville Travel (☎ 705-789-6431, 3 Main St E) as a depot.

ALGONQUIN PROVINCIAL PARK

Algonquin (☎ 705-633-5572/38, 888-668-7275, **w** www.algonquinpark.on.ca, Hwy 60; day-use $10; open year-round) is Ontario's largest park and one of Canada's best known. Established in 1893, it is also the oldest park in the province. Located about 300km north of Toronto, the park offers hundreds of lakes in approximately 7800 sq km of semiwilderness. There are 1600km of charted canoe routes to explore, many of them interconnected by portage paths. The one road through the park, Hwy 60, runs through the southern edge. Off it are lodges, hiking trails and eight campgrounds, as well as wilderness outfitters, who rent canoes and just about everything else. Maps are available at the park.

Camping reservations for campgrounds or backcountry are strongly recommended. Reserve ahead as much as possible. If you want some peace and quiet and a bit of adventure, the park is highly recommended. Algonquin and the Temagami area represent the two wilderness regions closest to Toronto and southern Ontario and provide a good opportunity to experience what much of Canada is all about. There is a lot of wildlife in the park, including bear, moose and wolves.

There are some interesting **hiking trails**, ranging from short, half-hour jaunts around a marsh to treks of several days in duration. Most of the short trails and lookouts are just off or near Hwy 60 and so can be enjoyed as part of a day trip.

Hwy 60 can be taken through the park free, but if you want to stop, the day fee is charged.

For more information, see Eastern Ontario, earlier in this chapter, for a section of the park near Ottawa.

Information

Located 43km from the west gate of the park on Hwy 60, overlooking Sunday Creek, is the very good visitors' center (☎ 705-637-2828), which is open 10am to 5pm daily May to November and 10am to 5pm Saturday and Sunday during the rest of the year. Various displays and dioramas illustrate the park's wildlife, history and geology. The center also contains an excellent bookstore, which includes cheap trail-guide brochures and a cafeteria.

On the reverse side of the canoe route map, there is camping advice and a lot of interesting information about the park. (It's handy reading material when you're inside the tent waiting for a storm to pass.)

Near the East Gate is a **logging museum** *(admission free; open 10am-6pm mid-May–mid-Oct).*

Be sure to read the pamphlet about bears thoroughly.

Canoeing

Summer weekends are a busy time for canoeing, so a system of admitting only a certain number of people at each canoe-route access point has been established. Arrive early or, preferably, book ahead. For reservations, call the park contact number above or write to the park at PO Box 219, Whitney, ON K0J 2M0.

At two canoe-route access points off Hwy 60 within the park, Canoe Lake and Opeongo Lake (see this section, next) renting canoes and gear. This is where most people begin a canoe trip into the park interior. To begin an interior trip from any other access point means transporting the canoe to it. (The interior refers to all areas of the park accessible only on foot or by canoe.) A good trip takes three to four days. The western access points – Nos 3, 4 and 5 on the Algonquin map – are good, with fewer people, smaller lakes and plenty of moose. The farther in you get by portaging, the more solitude you'll find. Also see the Eastern Ontario section, earlier, for information on the park's east side. Most rental places have ropes and mounting pads to enable renters to carry the canoes on the roof of their vehicles. To be safe, it is a good idea to bring enough of your own rope to secure the canoe. Different types of canoes are available. The heavy aluminum ones are the cheapest, but their weight makes them unsuitable for portaging. They are also noisy, and the seats get hot in the sun. For paddling around the main lakes, though, they are fine and virtually indestructible. If you want to get into the interior, where carrying weight becomes an issue, pay the extra to get a Kevlar canoe (which weighs in at about 30kg).

Water taxis can whisk you up huge Lake Opeongo, avoiding a long, rough paddle and getting you into the wilder areas. Make reservations through Algonquin Outfitters at Lake Opeongo (☎ 888-280-8886).

Outfitters & Organized Tours

The **Portage Store** (☎ 705-633-5622, W *www .portagestore.com*) is based at Canoe Lake, 14km from the west gate. It offers a full range of full or partial outfitting. Canoes rent from $20 per day; a complete rental package, with equipment and food for one day and night is available ($50), as are guided trips (from $40).

One of several outfitters based outside the park boundaries is **Algonquin Outfitters** (☎ 705-635-2243, W *www.algonquin outfitters.com*), with a base at Lake Opeongo in the park; another at Oxtongue Lake, just outside the western edge of the park on Hwy 60; and a gear store in Huntsville. It can rent you everything you need for a trip, sells supplies and even offers guided trips. Daily canoe rates vary with the type and weight ($20 to $26).

Also recommended is excellently priced **Canoe Algonquin** (☎ 705-636-5956), in Kearney, north of Huntsville. It rents kevlar canoes ($18/day), including paddles and life jackets. Tents, stoves and more can also be rented. Putting in at the nearby western access points gets you right into peace almost instantly. Book equipment in advance, especially in August. Call to find out about transportation from the Ontario Northland Toronto-Huntsville-Emsdale bus.

Call of the Wild (☎ 416-200-9453 in Toronto, 800-776-9453, W *www.callofthewild .ca*) has various all-inclusive trips, but the three-day, small-group guided canoe trip ($350) is the most popular. Meals, equipment and transportation from Toronto are included. Everyone helps with chores, setting up, etc. It also offers three-day winter trips (not in tents), with doing-your-own dog-sledding, snowshoeing and skiing options ($600).

Another reliable canoe-package operator is **Canadian Wilderness Trips** (☎ 416-960-2298, 45 Charles St E, Toronto). It is owned by Travel Cuts and has worked with international visitors for many years. Short and long trips to various Ontario locations are offered.

Voyageur Quest (☎ 416-486-3605) does similar trips at about the same price; you can contact this company through the Toronto HI hostel.

Moose Travel buses (see Organized Tours, under Toronto) make pick-ups/drop-offs in the park. See Eastern Ontario, earlier in this chapter, for other trip possibilities.

Also ask about the ranger-led programs, including 'the wolf howls.' These are offered throughout the summer season at various locations.

Places to Stay

Interior camping is $8 per person per night. At the campgrounds, where there are showers and real toilets, site prices range from $18 to $26. Among the highway campgrounds, Mew Lake is suggested. It has its own warm lake for swimming; some fairly attractive campsites by the far side of the lake, away from the highway; some trails nearby; and a store within walking distance.

The park also has a series of very comfortable lodges, but these are not in the budget category. There are numerous motels and cabins on Hwy 60 outside the park borders, especially on Hwy 60 before the west-side gate. Style and prices vary, but many are open only May to October.

Wolf Den Bunkhouse & Cabins (☎ 705-635-9336, ⓦ www.cottagelink.com/wolfden) Dorm beds $20. A work-in-progress, this great-looking, brand-new place has a ton of potential. Actually, it's a blend of new and restored old log cabins. It's 9km from the west gate.

Timber Trail (tel705-635-1097, 800-463-2995) Rooms $45-120. Across the street is this varied collection of rustic cabins fronted by a small store and restaurant.

Getting There & Away

For those without vehicles but who want to do it independently, the park is accessible by bus during summer months. Take the Ontario Northland (☎ 416-393-7911) bus from the Toronto bus station to Huntsville. Transfer to a Hammond Transportation (☎ 705-645-5431) bus into the park along Hwy 60. Also see Canoe Algonquin and Moose Travel in the Outfitters & Tours section, earlier.

According to one reader, it's relatively easy to hitchhike into Algonquin from Huntsville, particularly on weekends.

GEORGIAN BAY ISLANDS NATIONAL PARK

This park, consisting of 59 islands in Georgian Bay, has two completely separate sections. The principal segment is off Honey Harbour, north of Penetanguishene.

There's a park information office (☎ 705-756-2415) on the main street near the grocery store. In summer, a relatively inexpensive shuttle service runs over to Beausoleil, and water taxis go to other islands.

Beausoleil Island is the largest and the park's focal point, with campgrounds and an interpretive center. Several of the other islands have primitive camping facilities. The islands are home to the eastern Massasauga rattlesnake, which is actually rather small and timid – and now endangered, thanks to the proliferation of cottages and frightened men with axes.

Recreation includes swimming, diving, snorkeling and bass and pike fishing. Boating is also big in the area, what with all the islands and the Trent-Severn Canal system. Many boaters – and they range from those putting along in aluminum 14-footers (4m boats) to would-be kings in their floating palaces – tie up for a day or a night at the park islands, so they are fairly busy.

The park is really centered around the boating subculture and is otherwise not particularly interesting. For those seeking some sort of retreat, it is disappointingly busy and rather ostentatiously competitive. The water taxis are not cheap (starting at $30 one way) and, while providing some flexibility in destinations and schedules, still offer only limited access. Don't even think of taking a canoe out here – if the natural waves don't get you, one produced by a floating status symbol will.

Section two of the park, consisting of a number of smaller islands, is farther north up the bay, about halfway to Parry Sound. This section, although quieter, is inaccessible to those without their own vessels.

SOUTHEASTERN GEORGIAN BAY PROVINCIAL PARKS

Beginning with **Six Mile Lake** (☎ 705-756-2746, north of Port Severn; admission $8.50, open mid-May–mid-Oct), on Hwy 69, north of Port Severn, there is a series of very fine provincial parks (all with camping) along or near the bay. They make excellent stopping points on the way to Sudbury or fine destinations in themselves. Excellent **Massasauga** (use Oastler for information and rentals) is for canoeists only, while **Oastler** (☎ 705-378-2401, south of Parry Sound; admission $8.50; open mid-May–mid-Oct) has a beach.

PARRY SOUND
pop 6500

Parry Sound sits about midway up Georgian Bay and is the largest of the small district supply towns between southern Georgian Bay and Sudbury. There's a tourist office (☎ 705-461-4261) on the east side of Hwy 69, about a 10-minute drive south of town. In town, climb the lookout tower for views over the bay. The town bills itself as the birthplace of Bobby Orr, who, for the uninitiated, was a superb ice-hockey player. He was a Boston Bruins defenseman in the 1960s and '70s who changed the role of that position forever with his offensive prowess.

Boat cruises around the 30,000 islands on the *Island Queen* (☎ 705-746-2311, 800-506-2628, Bay St) push off from Government Wharf. The three-hour trips ($18) depart in the early afternoon and run from June to October.

Parry Sound is also known for its excellent and popular summer classical-music festival called the **Festival of the Sound** (☎ 705-746-2410); it runs mid-July to early August and features around 50 events.

There are dozens of motels and cottages for rent in the area, and the tourist office can help with local B&Bs.

Close to Parry Sound and accessible by a one-lane swing bridge is one of the largest of the Georgian Bay islands. **Parry Island**, 18km long and 59km around, is home to about 350 Ojibway Indians. At Oak Point, on the tip of the island, there's a small *campground* (☎ 705-746-8041), a marina, a restaurant and a craft shop. There are good views out to the surrounding islands and plenty of secluded coves to explore. Canoes are rented.

KILLBEAR PROVINCIAL PARK

Lake Huron's Georgian Bay is huge and grand enough to dwarf most of the world's waters. It's cool, deep, windy and majestic. The deeply indented, irregular shoreline along the eastern side, with its myriad islands, is trimmed by slabs of pink granite barely supporting wind-bent pine trees. This unique setting represents for many central Canadians the quintessential Canada. The works of the country's best-known painters, the Group of Seven, have linked this landscape to the Canadian experience.

Killbear (☎ 705-342-5492, north of Parry Sound; admission $8.50; open mid-May–mid-Oct) is one of the best places to see what it's all about. There is shoreline to explore, three short but good walking trails, numerous little hidden sandy beaches and camping ($18 to $23). Of course, it's popular; in July and August, call ahead to determine camping vacancies. To help ensure a quiet night, ask for one of the radio-free campgrounds. Harold's Point is good. In September, it may well be less than half full. During autumn, many visitors spend the day taking photographs and painting. May and June is also less busy. The park is highly recommended, even for just an afternoon. From Parry Sound east to Burk's Falls is more lake and timberland, with numerous cottages, both private and commercial. Out of season, things are quiet.

BYNG INLET
Packrat Lodge (☎ 705-383-0222, jennimac@ interlog.com, 2 Tansy Lane) Dorm beds/ rooms $15/30. Open June-Oct. This is a hostel and activity base with canoe, kayak and bike rentals. It also has a couple/family room.

KILLARNEY PROVINCIAL PARK

Killarney (☎ 705-287-2800, Hwy 637; admission $8.50; open year-round) is one of the province's most impressive parks, and a visit is highly recommended, even if only for a day's paddle. Its features are explored by foot or canoe. The members of Canada's Group of Seven artists worked in the park, and a provincial artists' association was instrumental in its establishment. Note the park is 60km from Hwy 69.

Because the lakes are relatively small, the maximum number of permitted overnight campers is low. The park's beauty is outstanding, so it's popular and often full. Try to go midweek, and make reservations, including booking a canoe, before arriving – call as far in advance as you can. Getting in on holiday weekends is nearly impossible.

The park is a uniquely mountainous forested area about 80km southwest of Sudbury, on the shores of Georgian Bay. It's one of Ontario's three wilderness parks and has few conveniences. There is excellent scenery, with birch and pine forest edged by the **La Cloche Mountains**. Some lakes are lined on one side by white-quartz mountains and on the other side by more typical reddish granite.

The lakes themselves offer astoundingly clear water with remarkable visibility, but unfortunately, this is in part due to acid rain. Indeed, some of the lakes were essentially dead, devoid of life, but recovery is under way.

Portaging from lake to lake is relatively easy, as the trails tend to be short, at least for the first few, most visited lakes. Two lakes could be explored from the dock at **Lake George**, making a fine day's outing for those without camping gear. The main campground is here ($11 to $23, season dependent), as is the park headquarters and information.

If you want to see more of the park, venture to the interior via portions of the 75km worth of portages. There are places for pitching a tent at most of the interior lakes.

Outfitters can be found along the road between the park and the village or in Killarney village. One to call is **Killarney Outfitters** (☎ 800-461-1117), which has package trips available too.

Killarney Village is tiny but has a couple of places to stay.

Sportsman's Inn (☎ 800-282-1913) Doubles motel/lodge $65/75. Open year-round. This rustic but comfortable lodge also has an adjacent motel-like section. There's a pub and sauna too.

Excellent fresh fish and chips can be had down at the dock area.

Northern Ontario

Northern Ontario is a vast, thinly populated region of lakes and forest. How large an area it is will quickly become evident if you're motoring around Lake Superior to or from Manitoba.

Commercial activity is almost all involved with natural resources – forestry and mining and their spin-offs. Sudbury is one of the world's major mining centers. Way up north beyond Sudbury, on James Bay, is the little town of Moosonee, one of the province's oldest European settlements, accessible by wilderness train. The big cities on the Great Lakes, Sault Ste Marie and Thunder Bay, are major shipping ports.

Outside the widely spaced towns, much of the land is wild, with clean waters and abundant wildlife. This is one of the best regions for really typically Canadian outdoor activities. The fishing, camping and canoeing attract visitors from southern Ontario and the USA. If you're planning on coming here, remember – summers are short.

NORTH BAY
pop 55,000
North Bay sits at the eastern end of big Lake Nipissing. At about 350km north of Toronto, it is the southernmost of the north's major towns.

The Trans Canada Hwy, which connects Sudbury to the west and Ottawa to the east, passes through town.

North Bay is also an access point to the many mining towns above it that straddle the Québec-Ontario border. There is some fine regional wilderness that attracts outdoor enthusiasts.

Orientation & Information
Main St is the main street; south of town it becomes Lakeshore Dr. The center of town is found between Cassells and Fisher Sts. Ferguson is the principal cross-street and runs from the waterfront east to the North Bay bypass (which connects Hwys 11 and 17). Lakeshore Dr going south turns into Hwy 11 for Toronto. Algonquin, leading north, becomes Hwy 11 for Timmins and also links to Hwy 17 east and west.

All along the shore in town is a sandy beach, with scattered parks and picnic tables. Sunset Park, just off Lakeshore Dr south of town, is good at the end of the day. At Canadore College (100 College Dr), northwest of downtown, one of several walking paths leads to Duchesnay Falls and good views.

The tourist office (☎ 705-472-8480, 800-387-0516) is south of downtown on Hwy 11, near the junction with Hwy 17 to Ottawa. It's open daily.

Things to See & Do
Beside the tourist office that is right on the North Bay bypass, the **Dionne Homestead Museum** (☎ 705-472-8480, 1757 Seymour St N; admission $3; open 9am-4pm Mon-Sat)

ONTARIO

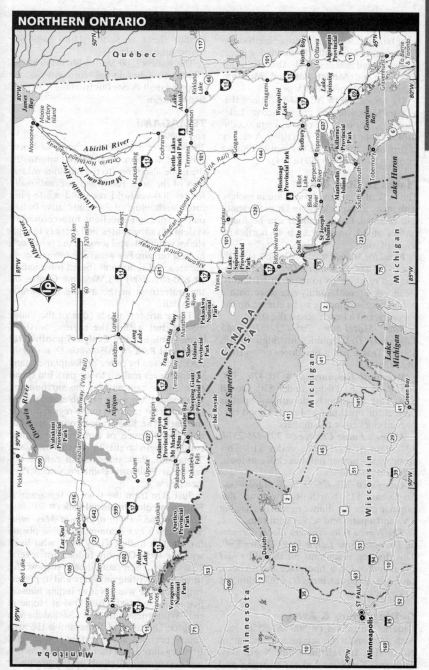

NORTHERN ONTARIO

contains articles relating to the Dionne quintuplets. Born in 1934, they became the most famous Canadian multiple-birth story. The museum is actually the family log farmhouse, moved and restored. Also at this location is the **Model Railroad Museum** (*admission $2; open May-Sept*).

The *New Chief* (☎ *705-494-8167, dock Waterfront/Memorial Dr*) cruises across Lake Nipissing, following the old voyageur paddle strokes, to the Upper French River. A variety of trips are offered (June to August), ranging from 1½ to five hours ($9 to $24).

Places to Stay & Eat

The bulk of accommodations are in motels, with many along Lakeshore Dr in the south end of town. Others motels can be found farther afield, on Hwy 11 both north and south of town.

Franklin Motel (☎ *705-472-1360, fax 705-494-9671, 444 Lakeshore Dr*) Rooms $45-60. You're close to town at this friendly, clean, economical, family-run place with a pool. There is camping and a stream on the property, and a beach across the street.

Star Motel (☎ *705-472-3510, 405 Lakeshore Dr*) Doubles low/high season $50/65. This is just a few doors down from the Franklin.

Windmill Restaurant (☎ *705476-2374, 168 Main St E*) Dishes under $10. Closed Sun. This neighborly downtown spot is perfect for breakfast and serves good barbecued chicken or fish dinners.

Moose's Loose Change (☎ *705-476-2374, 134 Main St E*) Dishes under $10. This rustic, hewn-timber pub has chili and toast, subs and pool tables.

Casey's (☎ *705-476-3373, 20 Maplewood St*) Dinner $15. North of downtown, this popular place for dinner or a drink has big TVs and a patio and serves until 1am.

The Navco (*Government Dock, Memorial Dr; open June-Labor Day*) Dishes $5-9. This floating restaurant on the old *Chief Commander I* is a fine place for a cheap, casual meal (pastas, burgers) while admiring Lake Nipissing.

Getting There & Away

Ontario Northland (☎ *800-461-8558*) runs both a rail and a bus service into and out of North Bay. Its rail lines link North Bay, Timmins, Kirkland Lake, Cochrane and Moosonee, as well as numerous smaller destinations in between. Connecting buses go farther afield, to Sudbury and Sault Ste Marie, for example.

The station (100 Station Rd) is near the tourist office, beside the Northgate Square shopping mall. A city bus from the mall goes to downtown.

TEMAGAMI
pop 1000

Temagami is a small town north of North Bay on Lake Temagami. More importantly, the name also refers to the fabulous wilderness of the area, renowned internationally for its 300-year-old red- and white-pine forest, archeological sites and Native Indian pictographs, an excellent interconnected system of canoe routes, and scenery that includes waterfalls and some of the province's highest terrain. For general information on the area, call Temagami Tourist Information (☎ *800-661-7609*). Its Welcome Centre, on the waterfront in the middle of town, is open daily.

There are few roads (one of the major assets), but within the region, north of Temagami, is **Lady Evelyn Smoothwater Provincial Park** (☎ *705-569-3622, no facilities*), accessed by canoe or floatplane. Many visitors never make it to the park but spend time canoe camping on the surrounding Crown land. Maps are available, and there's no charge for camping in the region outside the park. The local canoe routes are suitable for all levels of expertise, and some routes begin right in town, on Lake Temagami. Park information can be obtained at Finlayson Point Provincial Park (see below).

Just 2km from the town of Temagami is **Finlayson Point Provincial Park** (☎ *705-569-3205, 800-667-1940; open mid-May–mid-Sept*), which has a commemorative plaque for English author Grey Owl, who lived with the local Ojibway Indians for several years and then convinced the world, through his writing on nature and its preservation, that he was a Native Indian himself. See the boxed text 'Grey Owl at Home in the Wilderness' in the Saskatchewan chapter. The town of Temagami is the area supply center. Canoes can be rented, park trips organized, and there are B&Bs, motels and restaurants. A climb up the fire tower gets the blood going and provides a superlative view over the lake-filled forests.

For all your canoeing, fishing or camping needs, or for organizing trips into the region, visit **Smoothwater Outfitters** (☎ 705-569-3539, **W** *www.smoothwater.com*). The outfitter's comfortably rustic **Wilderness Lodge** is 14km north on Hwy 11, then 1km west, and has accommodations (camping $8, bunks $25, private double $92) and meals, plus access to trails and canoe routes. Staff can suggest trips based on your skill and available time and then supply gear and food. In winter, there are cross-country ski trails, some of which were being cut during research for this edition. The lodge hosts a busy schedule of workshops and packages incorporating music, painting, yoga, etc with wilderness trips. Smoothwater has an information cabin on the main street in Temagami.

Another outfitter is **Temagami Outfitting** (☎ 705-569-2595, **W** *www.icanoe.ca*), right in town, on the water. The company operates a shop, café and B&B and offers a fly-in service to get you to remote lakes. Or you can leave in a canoe right from the door!

Ontario Northland runs trains from Toronto to Temagami every day except Saturday. The fare is $76.

SUDBURY
pop 92,000
Sudbury sits on the rocky Precambrian Shield at the rim of the Sudbury Basin, a depression or crater formed two billion years ago. For over 100 years, it has been supplying the world with nickel.

Inco Ltd, one of the world's largest nickel producers, is the town's biggest employer and was once its lifeblood. While still vitally important, Inco and its rival Falconbridge have seen their fortunes decline with the drop in international demand and price. But Sudbury, to escape the precarious one-industry town scenario, has diversified. Provincial government decentralization has meant the relocation to Sudbury of several major departments, such as Energy & Mines, helping the move into new directions.

The city has long had a reputation for ugliness. The rough, rocky landscape was debased for years by the indiscriminate felling of trees and by merciless pollution from the mining and smelting operations. The result was a bleak, moonscape-like setting.

Much to Sudbury's credit, the worst of these characteristics have been (and are continuing to be) reversed. Indeed, the city has earned honors in environmental improvement, and with the development of parks and Inco's construction of a superstack to scatter emissions, the difference from years ago is impossible to miss. Some bleak areas do remain, and acid rain continues to be a problem. From up at the Big Nickel park, the views indicate how barren the terrain can be around the mines. The lack of vegetation is mainly due to industrial discharges, but the naturally thin soil covering the rocky Canadian Shield never helped.

Still, most of the town is no longer strikingly desertlike, and in fact, Sudbury is surrounded by a vast area of forests, hills and lakes, making it a center for outdoor and sporting activities. On the east side of town, away from the mining operations, the land is green and wild-looking. There are over a dozen lakes just outside town, including large, attractive Ramsey Lake, at the southeast edge of the city.

The downtown core, however, lacks character, and there really isn't much appeal. Sudbury isn't a place worth making a major effort to get to, but if you're heading across country, you'll probably pass through, and there are a few interesting things to see and do around the edges, mostly related to mining. Science North is a significant attraction.

The Sudbury Basin

The town of Sudbury sits on the southern rim of a ring of low hills outlining a unique and complex geological structure known as the Nickel Irruptive. The mines located around the outer rim of this boat-shape crater produce much of the world's nickel, platinum, palladium and related metals, as well as large amounts of copper, gold, tellurium, selenium and sulfur. The inner basin area is roughly 60km long and 30km wide. Possible explanations for its formation are a volcano or a giant meteorite.

ONTARIO

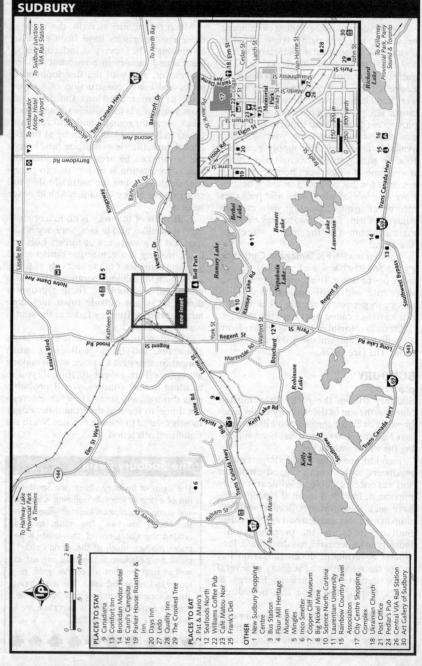

SUDBURY

PLACES TO STAY
9   Canadiana
13 Comfort Inn
14 Brockdan Motor Hotel
16 Carol's Campsite
19 Parker House Roastery &
    Inn
20 Days Inn
27 Ledo
28 Quality Inn
29 The Crooked Tree

PLACES TO EAT
2   Pat & Mario's
12 Seatoods North
22 Williams Coffee Pub
23 Café Matou Noir
25 Frank's Deli

OTHER
1   New Sudbury Shopping
    Centre
3   Bus Station
4   Flour Mill Heritage
    Museum
5   Mingles
7   Inco Smelter
8   Copper Cliff Museum
10 Big Nickel Mine
9   Science North; Cortina
11 Laurentian University
15 Rainbow Country Travel
    Association
17 City Centre Shopping
    Complex
18 Ukrainian Church
21 Post Office
24 Pedlar's Pub
26 Central VIA Rail Station
30 Art Gallery of Sudbury

The city has a large French population and a Scandinavian community.

Note that in July and August, the Sudbury region tends to be sunny and can be hot. However, it is generally dry, and nights can cool off sharply.

Orientation & Information

The main streets downtown are Elm St (running east-west) and Durham St (going north-south). The core runs along Elm St from Notre Dame Ave to Lorne St. On Elm St is the City Centre shopping complex and the Holiday Inn. The post office is across the street. The local bus routes start nearby.

Elgin St, running south off Elm St, divides Elm St E from Elm St W. At its southern end is one of the two VIA Rail stations. Heading east on Elm St, at Notre Dame Ave you'll see the unmistakable brown-bulbed Ukrainian church. Farther east, the street changes names several times. It passes a commercial strip of service stations, fast-food restaurants and motels, and eventually becomes Hwy 17 to Ottawa.

South of town, Regent St becomes Hwy 69 for Toronto. It also passes through a long commercial district. Going west, Lorne St leads to Hwy 17, one branch of the Trans Canada Hwy. Along the way, there are motels, the Big Nickel park, Inco Ltd, smelters and Copper Cliff. Hwy 11, running farther north over Lake Superior, is another branch of the Trans Canada Hwy.

Laurentian University, which features good views, lies on a hill on the far side of Ramsey Lake, southeast from downtown along Ramsey Rd.

The tourist office, the Rainbow Country Travel Association (☎ 705-522-0104, 800-465-6655, 1984 Regent St S), is inconveniently 10km south of town. It's open daily in summer but closed Sunday through the rest of the year.

Science North

The large, hands-on science center (☎ 705-522-3701, 800-461-4898, Ramsey Lake Rd; admission $13; open 9am-6pm daily in summer, 9am-5pm daily in spring & autumn, 10am-4pm daily Oct-May), at the southwestern end of Lake Ramsey, is a major regional attraction. This museum complex is conspicuously housed in two snowflake-shaped buildings built into a rocky outcrop

at the lake's edge, beside Alex Baumann Park (named after an Olympic swimmer native to Sudbury). Bell Park is adjacent to the north; the length of the park runs back toward downtown.

Inside, after you enter by tunnel through the 2.5-billion-year-old Canadian Shield, you'll find a collection of exhibits and displays on subjects ranging from the universe to insects, communications to fitness, animal life to rocks. Visitors are welcome to get involved with the displays through the many computers, the high-tech equipment and the knowledgeable staff, many of whom are from the university.

Some highlights are the white-quartz crystal displayed under a spotlight (looking like a lingam in an Eastern temple), the excellent insect section (how about patting a tarantula?) and the bed of nails. The fitness test is fun but can be humbling. The display about the Sudbury Neutrino Observatory, which is 2km underground, is fascinating. The 3-D film, presented in a pitch-black cave, is also quite remarkable. There are major changing exhibits and an IMAX movie theater.

Also in the complex are an inexpensive cafeteria, a restaurant, and a science and bookshop. At the swap shop, you can trade anything natural for anything else from nature's wonders.

There is a value combination ticket, which includes entry to the museum and to the IMAX films. The No 500 bus runs from the center of town to Science North frequently every day. Parking is $3.

Big Nickel Mine

Just west of town on Hwy 17, up on the hill, sits the Big Nickel, the symbol of Sudbury. The huge nickel, however, is actually made of stainless steel, and it has been temporarily moved to the Science Centre. A major new attraction called 'The Dynamic Earth,' is being planned for the Big Nickel site. It is to open in 2003. Previously you could go down the 20m mineshaft here, view equipment and see an exhibit of mining science, technology and history. How all this is to be incorporated into the new project remains to be seen, but going underground remains part of the scheme.

City bus No 940 goes to the site from downtown.

Copper Cliff Museum

This pioneering log cabin (☎ 705-674-3141 ext 2460, Balsam St, Copper Cliff; admission free; open 10am-4pm Tues-Sun June-Aug), where Inco has its operation, is filled with early-20th-century period furnishings and tools.

Flour Mill Heritage Museum

This is a similar place to the preceding listing – a 1903 pioneer house (☎ 705-673-

---

What Is It, Where Is It?

They bombard you every day. After journeying all the way from the sun, they penetrate your body in the billions, like bullets through butter. They are neutrinos – the miniscule, possibly massless, neutral elementary particles of the universe. They may be the world's most abundant bit, but they are also the smallest and are not easy to catch, let alone observe.

But in Inco's old Creighton mine, 2200m underground just outside Sudbury, a group of international physicists is doing just that. The Sudbury Neutrino Observatory (SNO) is collecting data that will provide revolutionary insight into the core of the sun, as well as the properties of neutrinos and their effect on the evolution of the universe. The sun produces over two hundred trillion trillion trillion neutrinos every second. Matter is virtually transparent to them. The elaborately designed SNO neutrino telescope, the size of a ten-story building, and the massive 1000-ton holding tank full of ultrapure, heavy water can catch (okay, can slow down) and monitor about 10 a day. Not bad, eh? You try to do better. Stephen Hawking, perhaps the world's best-known and certainly most recognizable physicist, visited and was given a complete tour in 1998. He thought it was pretty cool.

Data collection began in 1999, and in June 2001 the first results of the studies were released. They solved the mystery of the missing solar neutrinos and revealed new neutrino properties. You didn't think there was just one kind, did you? They come in three 'flavors.' They can change en route from the sun to us. The world never gets any simpler, but those doing the boggling work here hope to make it more understandable.

3141 ext 2460, 514 Notre Dame Ave; admission free; open 10am-4pm Tues-Sat, 11am-4pm Sun June-Sept) with period implements, artifacts and furnishings from the late 19th century. The museum is named after the three flour silos on the street.

Art Gallery of Sudbury

This art and museum center (☎ 705-675-4871, 251 John St at Nelson St; admission free; open noon-5pm Tues-Sun; closed holidays) is housed in a former mansion. It features changing art shows, often focusing on the work of local artists. There is also a permanent display of articles relating to the region's history.

Bell Park

After all the serious Sudbury sites, perhaps a bit of relaxation is in order, and Bell Park, walkable from downtown, fits the bill. This large green area with sandy beaches offers swimming practically in the center of town. It runs off Paris St south of downtown. Walk or drive toward Lake Ramsey and turn east on Facer St, beside the hospital. Walking paths follow the shore of the lake south all the way to Science North, and others continue north from the hospital.

Organized Tours

The *Cortina* (☎ 705-523-4629), a 70-seat passenger boat docked next to Science North, offers daily hour-long cruises (adult/child $12/6) around Ramsey Lake from May to September. The dock is part of the boardwalk that rims a portion of the lake.

Special Events

Northern Lights Festival This successful annual music event (☎ 705-674-5512) features unknowns and rising stars from around the country. It takes place in early July in Bell Park. Other concerts and theater are presented at Bell Park regularly through summer at the band shell, on the corner of Paris and York Sts, which overlooks Ramsey Lake.

Blueberry Festival Sudbury, with its rocky, sunny landscape, is prime blueberry territory. A walk off the road anywhere in the region will probably turn up a few berries. Locals come together to celebrate the berry at this mid-July festival (☎ 705-674-4030), which includes lots of outdoor events and public feedings such as blueberry-pancake breakfasts.

Places to Stay

Camping Sudbury is surrounded by rugged, wooded, lake-filled land. There are quite a few government parks within about 50km.

Windy Lake Provincial Park (☎ 705-966-2315) Campsites $20-23. This good campground, just 26km north of town off Hwy 144, is the best bet.

Carol's Campsite (☎ 705-522-5570) Campsites $18-22. This place, just 8km south of town on Hwy 69, is more commercial and designed for trailers.

Halfway Lake Provincial Park campground (☎ 905-965-2702) Campsites $20. This campground is about 90km northwest of town on Hwy 144.

University Residences *Laurentian University (☎ 705-675-4814, Ramsey Lake Rd)* Singles/doubles $30/45. The university rents rooms from mid-May to mid-August. The cafeteria is open weekdays. The problem is that the university is southeast of the downtown area, around the other side of Ramsey Lake. The views are good, though, and the area is pleasant and quiet. The No 500 bus from downtown runs to the university.

B&Bs *Parker House Roastery & Inn (☎ 705-674-2442, 888-250-4453, fax 705-674-8573, 259 Elm St)* Singles/doubles with shared bath $70/80, with private bath $80-115/90-130, all with continental breakfast. This central, clean, professional establishment with comfortable, well-appointed rooms (each with TV) includes a host of spa-like pampering possibilities. A very good continental breakfast is served at the main floor café, where the coffee beans are roasted daily.

The Crooked Tree (☎ 705-673-1352, 250 Edmund St) Singles/doubles with very full breakfast $45/55. More casual and homey than Parker House, this is another good B&B. It's between downtown and Science North. Renate is a congenial hostess, and the garden is a great place to plan the day.

Motels The bulk of Sudbury's accommodations are in motels found around the edges of town. Hwy 17 W is called Lorne St near town, and there are low-cost motels along it for a few kilometers. The better, newer motels are found south of town on Hwy 69. There are also other motels on Kingsway leading to Hwy 17 E.

Canadiana (☎ 705-674-7585, 965 Lorne St) Rates $45-55. This is a no-frills special, but it's okay if you're not prissy.

Comfort Inn (☎ 705-522-1101, 800-228-5150, 2171 Regent St S) Rooms $90-110. The to-be-expected standard franchise rooms are comfortable.

Brockdan Motor Hotel (☎ 705-522-5270, fax 705-522-5177, 1222 Pioneer Rd) Rooms $65-70. This small, modest motel is 5km south of town, right off Hwy 69.

Ambassador Motor Hotel (☎ 705-566-3601, fax 705-524-0433, 225 Falconbridge Rd) Rooms $80-90 with continental breakfast. This place is close to the airport.

Hotels *Ledo (☎ 705-673-7123, Elgin St)* Rooms $25. This bottom-end hotel surrounded by a lot of gritty urban life is opposite the train station. It can't really be recommended but may do for men looking hard for hostel rates. Ask in the bar about the rooms.

Days Inn (☎ 705-674-7517, 800-329-7666, fax 705-688-0369, 117 Elm St W) Rooms $70. This central place with clean, comfortable rooms is a good choice.

Quality Inn (☎ 705-671-1766, 800-461-1120, fax 705-673-5296, 390 Elgin St) Rooms $82. This is another reliable, no-surprises option, but it's on the other side of downtown.

Places to Eat

The Friday or Saturday *Sudbury Star* newspaper lists the weekend restaurant specials and Sunday brunches.

Frank's Deli (☎ 705-674-5428, 112 Durham St) Dishes $3-7. Closed Sun. Most towns have one of these old timeless counter-style joints good for breakfast or basic lunch.

Café Matou Noir (☎ 705-673-6718, 86 Durham St) Meals $5. Found at the back of the Black Cat Too magazine store, this quirky place serves up a good, cheap lunch of a homemade Cajun dish or two, a chili and baguette, or rice and beans.

Williams Coffee Pub (☎ 705-673-7598, 43 Elm St) Aside from good coffees and sweets, this café has a surprising array of fresh sandwiches, wraps and salads, and you can linger comfortably.

Seafoods North (☎ 705-522-4133, 1543 Paris St) Dinners under $10. For fresh seafood, this establishment in a small shopping plaza is recommended. The front of the place is a seafood store; the restaurant, tucked at the back and side, offers chowder, fish and chips or more complete dinners, such as pickerel, which is really walleye. Sunday, Monday and Tuesday evenings, you can partake of the all-you-can-eat fish and chips. Seafoods North is just south of Walford St – too far to walk from downtown.

Pat & Mario's (☎ 705-560-2500, *Lasalle Blvd at Barrydowne Rd*) Dishes $8-15. Away from the center, near the New Sudbury Shopping Centre, this is a nice, casual place, though slightly dressy. It's popular for Italian and finger foods and stays open late every night.

Landings Restaurant (☎ 705-522-0376, *100 Ramsey Lake Rd*) Lunch/dinner $8/10-20. For a bit of a splurge on seafood or a steak, consider this comfortable restaurant with a great view of Lake Ramsey from the inside of Science North. Main courses at dinner include Arctic char or chicken. It also has a full Sunday brunch.

Entertainment

Pedlar's Pub (☎ 705-669-1075, *63 Cedar St*) Here's a fine place for a pint – a friendly, Irishy pub with a good atmosphere and live music some nights. It's closed Sunday.

Mingles (☎ 705-524-6663, *762 Notre Dame Ave*) This is a very long-running dance club.

Getting There & Away

Air Air Canada (☎ 888-247-2262) serves the airport in the northeast corner of the city. Bearskin Airlines (☎ 705-693-9199) connects destinations in northern Ontario, including Timmins, Sault Ste Marie and Thunder Bay.

Bus The Greyhound depot (☎ 705-524-9900, 854 Notre Dame Ave) is about 3km north of the downtown core. This is also the station for Northland Ontario buses (same phone number), which run north to Timmins and south to Toronto.

There are three eastbound buses a day for North Bay/Ottawa/Montréal, four a day westbound for Sault Ste Marie/Winnipeg/Vancouver, and several a day southbound for Toronto; ask for the express trip.

The one-way fare to Ottawa is $85; to Sault Ste Marie, $50; and to Toronto, $63.

Train There are two VIA Rail stations servicing Sudbury, both at ☎ 800-361-1235. The original is conveniently on the corner of Minto and Elgin Sts, about a 10-minute walk from the center of town. It's in the low, gray building that is mostly black roof.

Unfortunately, there's only one train that uses this station. The 'Budd car' is the local nickname for the one-car train that makes the thrice-weekly trip from Sudbury through northern bush, past Chapleau to White River, north of Lake Superior. The one-way fare is $76, but it's 25% off if you book seven days in advance. The interesting eight-hour trip passes through sparsely populated forest and lakeland. For many villages and settlements, this is the only access. The train stops and starts, as people along the way – often wilderness seekers with their canoes and gear – flag it down. A moose or bear on the track also means an unscheduled stop. En route, you'll see lots of birdlife, including hill cranes and great blue herons. You might even do a bit of fishing or berry-picking if you're stuck waiting for a freight train to pass. The train trip is popular in autumn, when riders head out to see the leaves.

The other trains, such as those for Toronto or westbound, use a less central station known as Sudbury Junction, which is about 10km from the old downtown station. It is on Lasalle Blvd, past Falconbridge Hwy, in the northeast section of town. Buses only go to within 1km of the station.

There are three trips a week to Toronto, on Monday, Wednesday and Friday. The one-way fare is $70.

Going north and west, the train heads straight up through basic wilderness to Longlac, on to Sioux Lookout and eventually across the border to Winnipeg in Manitoba.

No direct route runs to Ottawa, so you must go via Toronto.

Car Renting a car may be useful in Sudbury. National (☎ 705-560-1000, 1150 Kingsway) has the best rates and will pick you up.

Hitchhiking Hwy 17, which becomes Kingsway (and then Elm St) in town, goes east to Ottawa. Regent St runs south from town into Hwy 69 S to Toronto. If westbound, head out along Lorne St, which eventually becomes Hwy 17 W.

Getting Around

For transit information, call ☎ 705-675-3333. The city buses collect at the downtown transit center, on the corner of Notre Dame Ave and Elm St. Bus No 940 goes to the Copper Cliff Mine smelter site and the Big Nickel site, at quarter to and quarter past each hour.

NORTH OF SUDBURY

Continuing north up Hwy 144 about two-thirds of the way to Timmins, you reach the Arctic watershed, at **Gogama**; from here all rivers flow north to the Arctic Ocean. Did you notice it was getting a bit cool?

Hwy 11 runs west from Cochrane (see that listing, below), eventually connecting with Thunder Bay. The province's most northerly major road, it cuts across rough, scrubby forest and passes through several mining towns. There are campgrounds en route.

The principal town is **Kapuskasing**, with its circular downtown center. **Hearst**, as noted in the Sault Ste Marie section, is the northern terminal of the Algoma Central Railway.

TIMMINS

pop 45,000

Way up here in northern Ontario is the largest city in Canada – in area, that is.

Originally the center of the most productive gold-mining area in the Western Hemisphere, Timmins still acts in the same capacity, but the local mines now work copper, zinc, silver, iron ore and talc, as well as gold.

Kidd Creek Mines is the world's largest producer of silver and zinc and is the main employer in town. One mine, now closed, was the country's deepest, going down nearly 2.5km. There are still over 2000km of underground workings in the area. Forestry products are also important in this rough, rugged, cold region.

There are hundreds of lakes within the designated city limits, as well as several dozen registered trap lines.

The first Europeans to settle were from Poland, Croatia and Ukraine, and many of their progeny are still here. To them must be added numbers of Italians, Finns and Scots, all of whom came with the lure of gold in the 1920s.

As in much of northeastern Ontario, there is quite a large French population, and Native Indians are a significant ethnic group.

Orientation

Timmins is actually made up of a number of small communities, the more important of which are Timmins proper, Schumacher, South Porcupine and Porcupine.

Hwy 101 passes through the center of town (where it is known as Algonquin Blvd) on its way west to Lake Superior and east to Québec. In town, the main streets are Third St (which runs parallel to the highway), Pine St and Cedar St. The central core is marked by the brick streets and old-style lamp posts.

The city's chamber of commerce (☎ 705-360-1900, 800-387-8466, 76 McIntyre) is in Schumacher.

Things to See & Do

Country star Shania is the queen of her hometown, and the new palace known as the **Shania Twain Centre** (☎ 705-360-8500, *Shania Twain Dr; adult/student & senior/family $8/6.50/30; open 9am-8pm daily*) showcases her life and music. There's memorabilia, guitars and concert footage, but the collection is somewhat dwarfed by the huge space. The site is between Timmins and Schumacher.

At the Shania Centre you can take an underground **gold mine tour** (*surface-tour admission $8, full tour adult/family $17/52; open Wed-Sat May, June, Sept & Oct; daily July & Aug*). The old Hollinger mine was discovered in 1909, and hundreds of millions of dollars worth of gold was dug out of here. Despite varied attractions at the complex, including panning for gold, the highlight remains the underground mine tour (in full gear), which takes visitors down 50m and includes a rail ride and a simulated dynamite blast. Call the chamber of commerce for full details on hours and for reservations. Pants and flat shoes are essential, and you should take a warm sweater.

The small but good **Timmins Museum** (☎ 705-235-5066, *70 Legion Dr near Algonquin Blvd E; admission $2; open 9am-5pm Mon-Fri, 1pm-5pm Sat & Sun May-Sept, rest of the year closed Mon*), in South Porcupine, doubles as an art gallery presenting changing exhibits, from paintings to performances. In the museum section, see the prospector's cabin, which gives an idea of the lives these people led. The history of the area is outlined with lots of photos, and

ONTARIO

there is some mining equipment outside, too.

The chamber of commerce serves as headquarters for four area **industrial tours** offered mid-June through August. There's an open pit mine tour, two sawmill tours and a forestry-nursery trip. Each is on a different day. Book through the chamber for these free glimpses into the local economy.

Places to Stay & Eat

There are several motels on each side of town and hotels in between.

Kettle Lakes Provincial Park (☎ 705-363-3511) East of town 35km and then north 3km is this recommended park. It's good for camping or a day trip to see the 20 or so small, round, glacial kettle lakes. You need a car to get here.

Regal (☎ 705-235-3393, Hwy 101 E) Rooms $45-55. On the east side, in South Porcupine, this motel is the cheapest place, and it's good.

Super 8 (☎ 705-268-7171, 888-483-6887, 730 Algonquin Blvd E) Doubles $70. Newer and larger, this place provides a light breakfast, and you can walk to a restaurant.

McIntyre Community Centre (☎ 705-360-1758, McIntyre Rd at Schumacher Dr, Schumacher) Dishes under $7. Also known as 'the arena,' this nontourist place at the hockey rink serves a good breakfast and sandwich lunch. The homemade pies and butter tarts are noteworthy, and you can look at pics of all the players who made the big leagues.

Kava House (☎ 705-267-5282, Pine St at Third St; open 7:30am-5pm Mon-Fri) Dishes $6-8. This cute little corner place, with staff in sort of traditional garb, serves up cheap, like-mother-made Ukrainian dishes, such as chicken Kiev and cabbage rolls.

Casey's (☎ 705-267-6467, 760 Algonquin Blvd E) Dishes $7-16. East of town, this is a popular chain restaurant with ribs, burgers, good salads and a place to have a beer.

Airport Hotel (☎ 705-235-3332, 151 Bruce Ave) Dishes $10-17. For a more expensive dinner out, try this historic lodge out by Porcupine Lake in South Porcupine. From the old lounge window, you can see the runway – the lake. At one time, this was a busy floatplane landing strip, and the bush pilots ate and slept here. A specialty is the fresh pickerel.

Getting There & Away

The train and bus stations (☎ 705-264-1377, 1 Spruce Ave) are in the same building, not far from Algonquin Blvd. Ontario Northland operates a daily bus service from Toronto via Sudbury. During summer, a bus runs from Timmins to Cochrane ($18), where you can catch the *Polar Bear Express* train. There is no train service into Timmins itself, although Ontario Northland does get as close as the town of Matheson. From there, a bus makes the one-hour trip into Timmins.

COCHRANE
pop 5500

Little Cochrane, roughly 100km north of Timmins, is the departure point for the *Polar Bear Express*. The large polar-bear statue at the entrance to Cochrane symbolizes the importance of the train to the town, where there's still a frontier feel in the wide streets.

The tourist association/board of trade (☎ 800-354-9948), can furnish you with more information from 9am to 4pm Monday to Friday.

Polar Bear Express

This is the best-known rolling stock of the Ontario Northland Railway (☎ 800-268-9281, 705-272-4228). The *Polar Bear* heads north from Cochrane through northern wilderness to Moosonee, the oldest permanent settlement in the province, on the edge of James Bay (part of vast Hudson Bay). Three hundred years ago, this was the site of an important fur-trading center.

Those taking the train have two choices. The *Polar Bear Express*, primarily for tourists or those in a hurry, provides a one-day roundtrip. It leaves early in the morning and returns late the same day, taking 4½ hours each way and allowing for a peek around Moosonee and Moose Factory.

A slower local train, the *Little Bear*, caters to an odd mix of tourists, Native Indians, trappers, geologists and serious paddlers. One car is specifically designed to transport canoes. It does not return the same day, meaning this is a minimum two-day trip.

The *Polar Bear Express* runs daily (except Friday) from about June 25 to September 5. The *Little Bear* operates all year but only three times a week. The summer fare on both trains is $55 roundtrip, with reservations required.

Out of summer, the regular train is $85. There are family, child and senior discounts. Trips can be booked from Ontario Northland Railway in Toronto, North Bay, Timmins or Cochrane or by phone. In Toronto, there is an information office in Union Station.

Simple lunches and snacks are sold on the train, but you're better off bringing your own. If you've driven to Cochrane, there is free parking beside the train station.

Ontario Northland also offers three-, four- and five-day tour packages (including some meals).

Visitors should know that despite the train's name, there are no polar bears in the region.

Other Attractions

The **Railway & Pioneer Museum** (☎ 705-272-4361, 210 Railway St; admission $3; open daily June-Labor Day) has some early railway, Native Indian and pioneer exhibits. The Tim Horton section is *not* about the now famous donut shops but about native son and hockey player Tim, who started the chain. The historical **Hunta Museum** (☎ 705-272-6300; admission free; open daily) is essentially a couple's stuff collection run rampant. It's well worth browsing and chatting, but call before going, since it's a little bit of a drive: 32km west on Hwy 668.

Courier du Bois (☎ 705-272-3273, Drury Park) offers tipi accommodations and tours in massive voyageur canoes.

Places to Stay & Eat

There are about 10 hotels/motels and camping. They tend to fill up in midsummer, so arrive early in the day or call ahead.

Greenwater Provincial Park & Campground (☎ 705-272-6335) Campsites $18. The park, 30km west of town, has numerous kettle lakes.

Drury Park & Campground (☎ 705-272-3223, 3rd Ave) Campsites $15-18. This park is right in town, close to the train station.

King George Hotel (☎ 705-272-2258, 101 Railway St) Singles/doubles $30/45. Shoe-stringers can consider this place, which is best known for its bar.

Commando Motel (☎ 705-272-2700, 5th Ave) Singles/doubles $52/60, less in winter. The train station is right across the street from this place.

Northern Lites Motel (☎ 705-272-4281) One bed $58. This motel has a handy restaurant/bar on the premises and is just south of town.

Spinning Wheel (☎ 705-272-4777, 3rd St) Dishes under $20. With seafood and steaks, this is the nicest place in town and is quite reasonable.

Getting There & Away

From Cochrane, the Ontario Northland Railway connects south with Timmins (via Matheson and a bus ride), North Bay and other regional towns. There are also buses between these points. The Ontario Northland train also runs between Toronto and Cochrane.

MOOSONEE
pop 2000

Moosonee, which sits near the tundra line with no road access, is as far north as most people ever get in eastern Canada. Once there, see the historic sites and the museums and, best of all, get out on the water on one of the boat tours. Moosonee is a mix of European and Native culture, while Moose Factory Island is Native. All sites operate in summer.

Ontario Northland can supply information on things to do and places to stay. For a look at the true north, with tundra and polar bears, see the Churchill section of the Manitoba chapter.

Two Bay Tours (☎ 705-336-2944, **W** www.twobay.com) offers several excursions in and around town that are good bets if you have just a day or two. Two Bay offers a $10 town bus trip with commentary. **Revillon Frères Museum** documents the Hudson's Bay Company's rival, the North West Company, which was based in Montréal. Nearby, the **Ministry of Natural Resources Interpretive Centre** has displays on the regional geography and fauna.

Moose Factory Island, out in Moose River, is the site of a Hudson's Bay Company trading post that was founded in 1672. It's 2km and 15 minutes from town by boat. Moose Factory itself is a community of about 1500 people, mainly Cree, at the far end of the island. Things to see include vestiges of the Hudson's Bay post and Centennial Park, with a small museum, a cemetery, and the Anglican church dating from 1860 (with moosehide altar cloths and Cree prayer books).

Two Bay (see that listing, earlier in this section) has roundtrips ($20) to the island that include a tour around with stops at the **Cree Village**, which has crafts for sale, and **Cree Cultural Centre**, the museum and other sites. Another trip via boat or freighter canoes ($18) takes people upstream to **Fossil Island**, where fossils over 300 million years have been found. More costly and extensive tours – which can include the Ship Sands Island Bird Sanctuary, the Moose River or James Bay and a walk on the muskeg – are also available.

Another attraction is the sometimes-visible **aurora borealis** (northern lights), but you're unlikely to see them from June to September, except possibly late at night. Also in winter, **dog-sledding trips** are offered.

On Tidewater Island, between the mainland and Moose Factory, is **Tidewater Provincial Park** (☎ 705-336-2987; day pass $6). Trips here can be arranged, and *camping* ($17) is possible. If camping, be prepared for a lot of mosquitoes and/or black flies.

There are a handful of places to stay, but they are not cheap. Reservations are pretty well a necessity. In Moosonee, right beside each other are the following two places, both with dining rooms.

Polar Bear Lodge (☎ 705-336-2345, 416-244-1495) Singles/doubles $75/90. The outside looks like a high school, but it is comfortable inside this lodge, which is open year-round.

Moosonee Lodge (☎ 705-336-2351) Singles/doubles $66/80. Unlike the Polar Bear, this lodge is only open in summer.

WEST OF SUDBURY

From Sudbury, Hwy 17 (the Trans Canada Hwy) runs along the north shore of Lake Huron. There are a few things to see if you wish to dawdle, and several smaller highways lead to more northern points. South of Espanola, Hwy 6 cuts across Lake Huron's North Channel to Manitoulin Island (see the Georgian Bay & Lakelands section, earlier).

Espanola

Espanola, the largest center between Sudbury and Sault Ste Marie, is a pulp-and-paper town and acts as a gateway for the Manitoulin Island ferry. The island can be reached by road on this side but connects with southern Ontario by ferry (see Tobermory in the Bruce Peninsula section, earlier in this chapter).

During July and August, **EB Eddy Forest Products Ltd** (☎ 800-663-6342) offers three different tours of its operations. Call for details and reservations, or visit its information center in Espanola. One trip lasts all day (nine hours) out in the bush, where you learn how the forest is managed. Good walking shoes are required.

Each of the other two tours is three hours in duration. One goes through the pulp mill to see the papermaking process; the other is through a sawmill – the biggest this side of the Rocky Mountains. These last two tours are not open to kids under the age of 12, and safety gear (supplied) must be worn. Not every tour is offered every day, so be sure to check the schedule. All the tours are free.

There are standard motels in town and a few places for a bite.

Deer Trail

The Deer Trail (Hwy 639) refers to a driving route north from the highway at Serpent River through Elliot Lake, around a little-developed region along the Little White River and back south to Hwy 17 at Ironbridge.

Mississagi Provincial Park (☎ 705-848-2806; open mid-May–mid-Oct) is about a third of the way around from Serpent River.

Did You Say What I Thought You Did?

The way Espanola got its name is an intriguing tale. In about 1750, the Ojibway Indians of the district went on a raid down south, in what is now the USA but which at the time was under Spanish control. They brought back a female captive who later taught her children Spanish. When French explorers arrived on the scene, you can imagine their surprise to hear the familiar Spanish being spoken. They called the settlement Espanole, which was subsequently anglicized to its present form.

At the park and at Flack Lake, there are nature trails, the latter with good examples of fossils and a feature known as ripple rock. There are other areas of geological interest along the way, such as the tillite outcrops, which were formed 1.5 million years ago; they're found 4km north of the Elliot Lake uranium symbol on Hwy 639.

Tourist offices in Serpent River or Blind River have a pamphlet/map indicating sites on the trail. There is also a lot of good canoeing in the district.

Elliot Lake

North of the Trans Canada Hwy, Elliot Lake is a mining town based mainly on uranium. It's a relatively new town, having been founded in 1954, when the ore was discovered. About a quarter of the population is French. With the tough times, the local mining industry has been suffering, and Elliot Lake has promoted itself as a fine retirement center, with a quiet, easy pace and low costs.

The **Nuclear & Mining Museum** (☎ 705-848-2084, Hwy 108; admission $2; open 9am-7pm daily May-Sept, 9am-5pm Mon-Fri rest of the year) features displays on the mining and applications of uranium but also has some area historical exhibits and a section on the wildlife of the region.

Good views over the North Channel can be had from the **Firetower Lookout**, north of town, 5km up the Milliken Mine access road.

Blind River

Blind River, sitting almost exactly halfway between Sudbury and Sault Ste Marie, is a good place to stop for a break. Though small, it's a neat and clean little town with a few good places to eat. On the east side of town is a large, helpful tourist office (☎ 800-263-2546) with information on the entire region.

Beside the information building is the **Timber Village Museum** (☎ 705-356-7544; open May-Oct), outlining the history of logging in the area. There are also some interesting items from the Mississagi people, the original Native Indian inhabitants.

The veneer mill south of town offers tours, and Huron Beach, 13km from Blind River, is a nice, sandy spot for **swimming**.

Camping is available near town; ask at the information office. Blind River also has five

motels, and it's not likely they'll all be full unless Brad Pit *and* Nicole Kidman are in town filming. For food, *JR's* chip stand, beside the highway, has good burgers and fries, but there are several sit-down restaurants to choose from as well.

St Joseph Island

St Joseph lies in the channel between Michigan and Ontario, 50km east of Sault Ste Marie. It's a rural island visited for swimming and fishing and for the **Fort St Joseph National Historic Site** (☎ 705-246-2664, Hwy 548; admission $3; open 10am-5pm daily end May-mid-Oct). The British fort ruins date from the turn of the 18th century and are staffed by workers in period costume. The reception center displays Native Indian, military and fur-trade artifacts. A large bird sanctuary surrounds the fort.

Also on the island is the **St Joseph Island Museum** (☎ 705-246-2672, 20th Side Rd at I Line Rd; admission $2; open daily May-Oct), which houses 4000 island articles exhibited in six historic buildings varying from an old general store to a log school. Another thing to keep an eye out for is the so-called pudding stones – red-, black- and brown-speckled white rocks. These jasper conglomerates (as they're known to rockhounds), found around the shoreline, were named by obviously hungry English settlers who felt they resembled suet and berry pudding.

St Joseph has several private campgrounds, motels and B&Bs. The island is reached by a toll-free bridge off Hwy 17.

SAULT STE MARIE
pop 79,000

'The Soo,' as the city is called, sits strategically where Lake Huron and Lake Superior meet. Once a fur-trading outpost, the Soo is an industrial town important as a shipping center, for here, on St Mary's River, is a series of locks that enable ships to navigate the seaway system farther west into vast Lake Superior.

Aside from the busy canal, the steel, pulp-and-paper and lumber mills are major but declining employers. The huge Algoma Steel mill, long one of the city's mainstays, has had to scale back considerably due to lost markets. Diversification has been assisted by the relocation of some provincial government offices from Toronto to the Soo, but times are still hard.

The International Bridge connects the city with its twin of the same name in Michigan, USA. Going west to Winnipeg is slightly shorter via Michigan and Duluth, Minnesota, than north of the lake, but this way is not as impressive.

With the bridge and the Trans Canada Hwy, the Soo is a convenient stopover and acts as a tourist supply center. It is the most appealing of the northern cities, and there are some fine outdoor possibilities within range to complement it. It's the last big town until Thunder Bay, to the west. Sudbury is 300km to the east, a drive of between three and four hours.

Orientation

The approach to Sault Ste Marie from the east or west is a long row of eateries, service stations and motels. Hwy 17 N (later west) becomes the Great Northern Rd and then Pim St in town. Hwy 17 E becomes Wellington St, which is the northern edge of the downtown core. If you're passing through, use the bypass to avoid traffic hassles.

For visitors, this is a dream town in terms of convenience. The downtown area is quite small and pleasant, with pretty much everything of interest either on or near the long, upgraded Queen St. South from Queen St is the restored waterfront area. This restoration process continues, and the slow, thoughtful approach taken by the city is paying dividends in creating a central core popular with residents and visitors alike.

Many of the city's attractions, the bus station, the Station Shopping Mall (a large shopping center) and several hotels are here, within walking distance of each other. Also in this general vicinity is the main tourist office.

A couple of buildings of particular note in town, in the middle of Queen St E, are the imposing courthouse and the Precious Blood Cathedral, constructed of local red-gray limestone in 1875 and originally a Jesuit mission. 'Queenstown' refers to the renovated downtown core.

Information

The huge Ontario Travel Information Center (☎ 705-945-6941, 261 Queen St W), near the

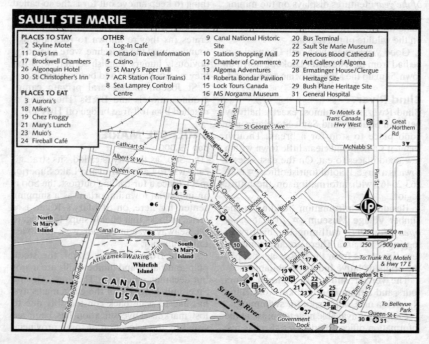

SAULT STE MARIE

PLACES TO STAY	OTHER	9 Canal National Historic	20 Bus Terminal
2 Skyline Motel	1 Log-In Café	Site	22 Sault Ste Marie Museum
11 Days Inn	4 Ontario Travel Information	10 Station Shopping Mall	25 Precious Blood Cathedral
17 Brockwell Chambers	5 Casino	12 Chamber of Commerce	27 Art Gallery of Algoma
26 Algonquin Hotel	6 St Mary's Paper Mill	13 Algoma Adventures	28 Ermatinger House/Clergue
30 St Christopher's Inn	7 ACR Station (Tour Trains)	14 Roberta Bondar Pavilion	Heritage Site
	8 Sea Lamprey Control	15 Lock Tours Canada	29 Bush Plane Heritage Site
PLACES TO EAT	Centre	16 MS *Norgama* Museum	31 General Hospital
3 Aurora's			
18 Mike's			
19 Chez Froggy			
21 Mary's Lunch			
23 Muio's			
24 Fireball Café			

International Bridge leading to the USA, can change money. It's open daily all year.

The Soo chamber of commerce (☎ 705-949-7152, 800-461-6020, 334 Bay St) is open Monday to Friday. The chamber also operates an information booth across the street in Station Mall, by the Sears department store.

For medical help, try the General Hospital (941 Queen St E), part of the Sault Area Hospital System.

For Internet access, the Log-In Café (☎ 705-942-5511, 229 Great Northern Rd), in the Ramada Inn, is excellent. And you can get a beer.

Parks

On the water, 2km east of town along Queen St E and close to the university, is **Bellevue Park**, the city's largest, with some gardens and picnic areas.

Kinsmen Park, known locally as Hiawatha Park, is about a 10-minute drive from Great Northern Rd, northwest of downtown Sault Ste Marie. It's on Fifth Line, 3.4km east off Great Northern. The wooded area has walking and skiing trails and is free.

Agawa Canyon & Algoma Central Railway

Together, these two make up the best-known and most-visited attraction in the area. The Agawa Canyon is a rugged wilderness area accessible only by the **ACR trains** (☎ 705-946-7300, 800-242-9287; Bay St at Gore St). The 500km rail line, which runs due north from town to Hearst, goes through a scenic area of mountains, waterfalls, valleys and forests. The route, constructed at the turn of the century, was originally built to bring raw materials into the industrial plants of Sault Ste Marie. The best views are from the seats on the left-hand side of the train.

There are two options for passengers seeking access to the canyon and its surroundings. The tourist train operates seasonally. The basic one-day visitor roundtrip to the canyon takes a full nine hours and costs $56/18 adult/child in summer, $75/45 in the fall; the train departs 8am daily from late May to mid-October. A two-hour stopover allows for a quick walk, fishing or lunch on the canyon floor. There is a dining car on board (modestly priced), and snacks

and drinks are also available. This is the most popular trip, so booking a couple of days (more in autumn) ahead is a good idea.

The trip is spectacular in autumn, when the leaves have changed color and the forests are brilliant reds and yellows. Normally, the colors are at their peak in the last two weeks of September and in early October. Yet another possibility is the winter snow-and-ice run, which is added (on weekends only) from January to March.

Secondly, there are trips that run the full length of the line to the town of **Hearst** (population 5500), about a nine-hour trip. Hearst, perhaps surprisingly, is essentially a French town, with under 15% of the population listing English as their mother tongue. The town remains primarily engaged in lumbering, although it has its own small university.

Beyond the canyon, the track travels over less impressive flat, forested lakelands, various bridges and northern muskeg. This is a two-day trip with an overnight stay at the northern terminal. Alternatively, it's possible to stay in Hearst as long as you wish and return when ready, or not at all (mind you, there's not a lot happening in Hearst). There are motels and B&Bs in Hearst; ask about them at the tourist information in Sault Ste Marie. From Hearst, buses can be caught east or westbound.

The Hearst train is used by anglers, trappers, painters, lodge operators and their guests, and various other local inhabitants

---

What I Did on My Holidays

In 1836 Anna Jameson (1794–1860), from Ireland, left Toronto, where she lived with her attorney-general husband Robert Jameson. She took off unescorted to the Detroit area; from there, she reached the Soo by boat, descended the rapids and attended a Native Indian assembly on Manitoulin Island. Through Georgian Bay and south to Lake Simcoe, she traveled back to Toronto and later home to Britain, where she published an account of the trip, entitled *Winter Studies and Summer Rambles in Canada*. And that was without a Lonely Planet guide.

and visitors. It stops anywhere you like or anywhere someone is standing and flagging it down, so obviously the going is slow, but some find the passengers a colorful lot, and the train provides the only true access into the region.

The fare on this train is calculated by zone; there are six zones for the entire 500km route. Trip (not zone) costs range from $12 to $102.

Information on backpacking, canoeing, swimming, camping and lodges in the canyon and beyond is available at the train station. All manner of supplies can be taken on board, including canoes, with 100lbs (30kg) free.

In Sault Ste Marie, the train station is by the Station Shopping Mall, in the center of town, and has free parking.

Canal National Historic Site

If Sudbury is rock city, the Soo is lock city. At the southwest corner of downtown, at the bottom of Huron St (by the International Bridge), are the locks linking Lake Superior to Lake Huron. Joining the two great lakes is the narrow St Mary's River, with its rapids. In 1895 the locks were built here, enabling lake freighters to make the journey hundreds of extra kilometers inland. Lake Superior is about 7m higher than Lake Huron.

The often continuous lake traffic (about 80 freighters a day in summer) can be watched from a viewing stand or from anywhere along the locks for no charge, but the boats are a long way out, mainly using the American locks. There are four US locks and one Canadian lock, found in the narrow channel between North St Mary's Island and South St Mary's Island. The Canadian lock, built in 1895, is the oldest and is used only for recreational vessels.

Walk over the locks to South St Mary's Island, where you will find the circular **Attikamek Walking Trail**. The paths, winding through the woods and under the International Bridge, make a nice retreat, with views of the shorelines, rapids and ships. It's a good picnicking spot. Just south is Whitefish Island, where the Ojibway Indians fished these plentiful waters for 2000 years. Fishing is still popular, and anglers are all over the place.

Boats from **Lock Tours Canada** (☎ 705-253-9850) depart downtown from behind

the Bondar Pavilion, beside the Holiday Inn. There are several trips daily in midsummer, fewer in spring and autumn. The two-hour tour ($20) goes through both the American and Canadian locks and is the only way to see the former from Canada. You also get a bit of a waterfront tour.

Sea Lamprey Control Centre

Down at the locks is this small research center (☎ 709-941-3000, 1 Canal Dr; admission free; open Mon-Fri July & Aug) where you can view some lamprey and the fish they victimize and learn more about these giant leeches. It's worth a stomach-turning look.

The Boardwalk

A boardwalk runs alongside the river off Bay St, behind the Station Shopping Mall, affording good views of the river and across to the USA. As well, there are places to fish and a number of city attractions to be found on or near the river. Near the foot of Elgin St, the large, white, tentlike structure is the **Roberta Bondar Pavilion**, built to honor the Soo's very own astronaut. Dr Roberta Lynn Bondar became Canada's first female astronaut aboard the space shuttle *Discovery* in 1992. The pavilion is the venue for regular concerts, exhibitions and a **farmers' market**, which takes place Saturday mornings in July and August.

MS *Norgama* Museum

The MS *Norgama* is now a museum (☎ 705-256-7447, Norgama Marine Park dock, foot of Spring St). It was the last ship built for overnight passenger use on the Great Lakes. The ship is moored at the dock near the Roberta Bondar Pavilion. Until it was vandalized in the summer of 2001, it was open for visitors throughout the summer. Finding the funds to reopen has been difficult and no date has been set.

Ermatinger House/Clergue Heritage Site

The Ermatinger House (☎ 705-759-5443, 831 Queen St E near Pim St; admission $2; open 10am-5pm daily June-Sept, 1pm-5pm Mon-Fri April-May & Oct-Nov) was built in 1814 by a British fur trader and his Ojibway wife. It's the oldest stone house west of Toronto and was where many explorers, including

Simon Fraser and Alexander Mackenzie, put up for the night. Inside, the house has been restored and contains 19th-century furnishings. Interpreters answer questions.

Beside it is the **Clergue Blockhouse**, a house built atop a former powder magazine, where one of the city's most influential citizens once lived.

Bush Plane Heritage Centre
This two-in-one museum (☎ 705-945-6242, *Bay St at Pim St; adult/senior/child $7.50/ 6.75/3.75; open 9am-9pm daily June-Sept, 10am-4pm daily Oct-May)* is in an old government hangar by the waterfront. The history of bush flying in Canada, a great story in itself, is tied closely to its role in forest-fire fighting. Many of the early small-plane pilots in the country were returning from the air force at the end of WWI. In addition to fighting fires, they also served in aerial mapping, surveying, medical assistance and rescuing. The museum has full-size planes on display, as well as some replicas, engines and parts. There are also maps, photographs and a tent that is set up as it would have been in the bush. Tours are offered.

Art Gallery of Algoma
This good local art gallery (☎ 705-949-9067, *10 East St; admission by donation; open 10am-5pm Mon-Sat)*, next to the public library, is worth a visit. There's an education room, a gallery workshop and two exhibition rooms of changing work.

Sault Ste Marie Museum
Housed in an Ontario heritage building, this small but well-put-together museum (☎ 705-759-7278, *690 Queen St E at East St; admission $3; open 10am-5pm daily June-Sept, 10am-5pm Mon-Sat rest of the year)* has various displays representing Native Indians, exploration, fur trading, lumbering, geology and other aspects of the area. The section on the Inuit is good. In the late-18th- and early-19th-century exhibits, the cigarettes recommended for asthma relief are a lark.

St Mary's Paper Mill
The large paper mill (☎ 705-942-6070 ext 2322, *Huron St)*, at the southwestern edge of downtown, offers free tours on demand weekdays. Call ahead, and then register at the security gate on arrival.

Tarentorous Fish Hatchery
Off Landslide Rd *(watch for signs on Great Northern Rd)* is this hatchery (☎ 705-949-7271; admission free; open 9am-4pm daily June-Labor Day, 9am-4pm Mon-Fri rest of the year), which raises chinook salmon, rainbow trout and brown

Bondar's Not Lost in Space

So what do you have to do to be the first and only woman on the Canadian astronaut team? If the life of remarkable Roberta Bondar is anything to go by, the answer is a lot.

Following Marc Garneau's achievement – he became the first Canadian in space, aboard a NASA shuttle flight in 1984 – Bondar became the first Canadian woman to enter space, aboard the *Discovery* in 1992.

Bondar was born in Sault Ste Marie in 1945. Besides getting top marks, she was athlete of the year in her last year at high school. At the university, she earned a degree in zoology and agriculture while getting her pilot's license and coaching the archery team. Continuing her education, she bagged a master's degree in experimental pathology, then a doctorate in neurobiology, and (just to stay well-rounded) finished off her doctor of medicine degree. For fun, she parachuted and got her scuba-diving certification.

Soon she was an assistant professor and head of a clinic treating patients with multiple sclerosis. But what she really wanted was to be an astronaut.

So, when the National Research Council of Canada decided to begin a space program, Bondar put her hand up, along with 4300 other Canadians. She was one of the six picked. You don't want to know about the training or the 12-hour days.

As a 'payload' scientist on board the shuttle, she carried out studies related to the effects of weightlessness on the human body. One finding she noted was that you needed Velcro to hold your head to the pillow (she's funny, too!). Upon returning to terra firma, she wrote a book about her experiences, *Touching the Earth*, which included many of her own photographs. Her new photography book captures Canada's national parks. She calls herself an 'organized tornado.'

trout and releases them into the river and surrounding waters, in an effort to develop and maintain major sport-fishing in the district. And it seems to be working. The region has a good reputation, and sizable fish are being taken right off the boardwalk in town.

Voyageur Hiking Trail

The partially completed Voyageur Hiking Trail will one day run between Manitoulin Island and Thunder Bay. The longest completed segment goes east from Gros Cap to Serpent River, a small village south of Elliot Lake on Hwy 108 along the North Channel of Lake Huron – a distance of about 200km. Another 300km are finished. The trail skirts the edge of Sault Ste Marie, but be forewarned that this is not an easy strolling path; obtain complete information from the Voyageur Trail Association (☎ 705-253-5353, 800-393-5353 and select message ☎ 9999 on your touch-tone phone, **w** www3.sympatico.ca/voyageur.trail).

Casino

The city has a new charity casino (☎ 800-826-8946, 30 Bay St) with 450 slots and gaming tables for roulette, blackjack, etc.

Organized Tours

Algoma Adventures (☎ 705-254-1500), with a ticket booth on the waterfront, next to the Holiday Inn, runs a sightseeing bus tour May to September. The 1¼-hour city tour ($12.50) is of historical and cultural sites. It runs four times daily in summer and with a diminished schedule in the spring. The company also runs various small group tours (☎ 705-945-5032) to cover area highlights, do horseback riding and see Indian rock paintings.

Experience North (☎ 888-463-5957, 488 Queen St E) offers a range of multiday kayak adventures, including in the Agawa canyon and on Lake Superior.

Special Events

Tugboat Race Held on the St Mary's River on the weekend closest to July 1, this is a bit of good, silly fun. Competitors from both sides of the river dress up their boats with flags and banners and putt for prizes and prestige.

Algoma Arts Festival This fall festival (☎ 709-949-0822) focuses on performing and visual arts.

Places to Stay

A quirk here is that while July and August are typically busy, September and October are peak season for autumn train trips.

Camping *Pointe des Chênes* (☎ 705-779-2696) Campsites $20-23. Open mid-May–mid-Sept. A little farther than the other choices, this is the best pick. The campground is at the mouth of the St Mary's River and features a good sandy beach and 82 sites. Go 12km west on Hwy 550 to Hwy 565, then 10km south past the airport to the community park. The drive takes about 25 minutes.

Bell's Point Beach (☎ 705-759-1561) About 15 minutes from town off Hwy 17 east, this is not a bad place, with camping beneath huge white pines. There's a beach on the river too.

KOA Tent & RV Park (☎ 705-759-2344, 800-562-0847, 501 Fifth Line) Tent sites $24. This park is 8km north of town on Hwy 17; turn west at the flashing amber light (Fifth Line). The park is on a river and is equipped with a laundry, store and pool.

Hostels *Algonquin Hotel* (☎ 705-253-2311, 888-269-7728, fax 705-942-0269, 864 Queen St E at Pim St) Singles/twins for members $21/30, nonmembers $23/31. This fine budget hotel, the only one in town, is an HI affiliate but is good for anyone who sleeps with his or her eyes closed. The rooms are very old and plain, with no extras, but they're clean, and each has at least a sink. If four of you want to share a room, it's the same price as two. A drawback is the lack of any common area or kitchen facilities. There's a bar downstairs for a cheap beer, but there's no music, so it's quiet in the rooms. The central location is superb, within walking distance of just about everything.

B&Bs *St Christopher's Inn* (☎ 705-759-0870, 923 Queen St E) Rooms $50-65 with breakfast. This large, somewhat gothic-looking Victorian place is conveniently central – just a short walk from the waterfront.

Brockwell Chambers (☎ 705-949-1076, 183 Brock St) Singles/doubles $65-85/75-95 with full breakfast. If you think the name implies style, you're right. This very swish restored 1905 home has all the comforts and then some. Downtown is just a short walk away.

Top O' The Hill (☎ *705-253-9041, 800-847-1681, 40 Broos Rd*) Singles/doubles with full breakfast $55/65. This B&B is in the northeastern section of the city, about a 10-minute drive from downtown. Reservations are suggested.

Motels Sault Ste Marie's location lends itself to a plethora of motels and a lot of people passing through. Most motels are on Hwy 17, either east or west of town, though some are downtown. Newer, more modern and pricier places can be found along Great Northern Rd, which leads north to the Trans Canada Hwy westbound. Prices fluctuate markedly with the seasons and traffic.

Shady Pines Motel (☎ *705-759-0088, 1587 Trunk Rd*) Singles/doubles $35/45. This is one of the cheapest motels in town, and though ugly at the front, it's actually good. Big rooms open onto a treed back yard with picnic tables and barbecues. It's 6km east on Hwy 17 E.

Travellers Motel (☎ *705-946-4133, 859 Trunk Rd*) Doubles from $39. This motel is closer to town than Shady Pines and has kitchenettes available.

Holiday (☎ *705-759-8608, 435 Trunk Rd*) Singles/doubles $43/45. Closer still to town, this vintage and pleasant-looking motel is another deal.

Skyline Motel (☎ *705-942-1240, 800-461-2624, fax 705-942-1240, 232 Great Northern Rd*) Rooms $55-75. Closer to downtown, this motel has a fridge in every room, and some have kitchenettes.

Comfort Inn (☎ *705-759-8000, 800-228-5150, fax 705-759-8538, 333 Great Northern Rd*) Rooms $80-120. This busy motel is part of a major chain.

Hotels See the Hostels section, earlier, for details on the budget-priced Algonquin Hotel.

Days Inn (☎ *705-759-8200, 800-329-7666, fax 705-942-9500, 320 Bay St*) Rates $80-115. Right by the river, this hotel is central and good. Facilities include a restaurant and a heated pool. Its Cellar Tap bar is the only brewpub in town.

Places to Eat

Most of the restaurants, many of which are the ubiquitous franchises, line the highway. However, those listed here are mainly local establishments found in the city center.

Queen St has a real assortment of good, atmospheric beaneries of the old lunch-counter type seemingly caught in time warps. Two town specialties are lake trout and whitefish, and both turn up on menus all over Sault Ste Marie.

Mary's Lunch (☎ *705-759-4836, 663 Queen St E*) Near the corner of East St, this inexpensive old-fashioned place serves its regulars lots of homemade stuff, including bread, and has the cheapest breakfast ($2!) in town, beginning at 6am.

Mike's (☎ *705-256-5484, 518 Queen St E*) Meals $4-7. Using just half a dozen stools, customers have been sitting, chatting and quaffing homemade Italian food since 1932. In a nod to the new century, there is now an outdoor patio in the back.

Fireball Café (☎ *705-949-8756, 746 Queen St E*) Dishes under $10. Now open for lunch Wednesday through Saturday, this hole-in-the-wall is a mini alternate arts center, with art, music and poetry presented some Friday nights. Having one of the daily specials here (it might be Thai or Indian) is like eating in an artist's kitchen.

Muio's (☎ *705-254-7105, 685 Queen St E*) Dishes $6-11. Try the fish specials here, surrounded by classic diner ambience and served by old-school waitresses in equal parts friendly and efficient. Muio's also offers daily specials, such as a complete meal of cabbage rolls ($10).

Chez Froggy (☎ *705-949-3764, 515 Queen St E*) Dishes $5-12. Open 9am-8pm weekdays only. This bilingual spot with a clean, simple interior serves up a blend of a few French-Canadian dishes, various vegetarian entrées and Canadian basics. Lunch specials ($5) are a deal and may include soup, a chicken wrap and tea. Dinner may be beef simmered in beer gravy or a cashew rice loaf.

Giovanni's (☎ *705-942-3050, 516 Great Northern Rd*) Lunch/dinner $7/12. Open noon-midnight Mon-Sat, Sun until 11pm. Italian food is hugely popular in the city, and this place packs them in for its extensive menu and don't-leave-hungry portions. Reservations are suggested weekend nights. Dinner includes an all-you-can-eat salad bar and bread.

Aurora's (☎ *705-759-1000, 384 McNabb St*) Dishes to $15. This is another long-term Italian favorite where the food has to be good just to take your attention from the decor. Various pastas, chicken dishes and good Italian sandwiches cost $7-8.

Entertainment
Queen St has a couple of pubs. Northern Breweries on Bay St is one of the country's oldest beer companies and has been operating in northern Ontario since 1876, so you may want to try one of the Northern brews in a bar of your choice.

The *Skylark Drive-In* (☎ 705-949-9292, 1323 Trunk Rd) is an old-style drive-in movie theater. Snuggle in the back seat and get nostalgic, as you relive the '50s.

Getting There & Away
There are regular Air Canada flights to the Sault Ste Marie airport, which is 13km west of town on Hwy 550, then 7km south on Hwy 565.

The bus station (☎ 705-949-4711, 73 Brock St) is downtown. There are three buses a day to Sudbury. From there, three buses daily depart for either Toronto or Ottawa. The through fare to Ottawa is $131; to Toronto, $112. There are also three buses daily to Winnipeg for $147. For buses to Detroit or Chicago, go to the city bus terminal and get over the bridge to the USA. For details, see Getting Around.

The Soo is a major drop-off point for those thumbing east and west. In summer, there are plenty of backpackers hanging around town. If you're going west, remember that it's a long way from Sault Ste Marie to Winnipeg, with little to see in between. Nights are cold, and rides can be scarce. Try to get a through ride to Thunder Bay (715km), and then go on to Winnipeg from there.

Getting Around
Buses run between the airport and major hotels.

At the city bus terminal (☎ 705-759-5438, Queen & Dennis Sts), you can catch the Riverside bus from downtown goes east to Algoma University, near Belvedere Park. Another city bus leaves from the terminal and goes over the bridge into the Soo, Michigan, USA. Taxis will also take you across the bridge. Once there, catch the one-hour shuttle bus (☎ 888-635-5830) to St Ignace, Michigan, where the long-distance US buses depart.

LAKE SUPERIOR SHORELINE AREA
From Sault Ste Marie to Thunder Bay, the Trans Canada Hwy is one of the few roads cutting through the thinly populated northern Ontario wilds. The highway to Wawa is particularly scenic. This huge area is rough, lake-filled timberland. Development has been slow to penetrate, and the abundant minerals and wildlife remain partially undisturbed. There are areas where there's logging, but these are rarely seen. But you may see signs of forest fires, which are common each year.

This quiet and beautiful part of the country is presided over by awesome Lake Superior – once known as Gitche Gumee (Big Sea Water) to the Ojibway Indians. The largest of the five Great Lakes (and one of the world's largest lakes), it's sometimes pretty, sometimes brutal. Even today, there are disastrous shipwrecks when the lake gets angry, and according to a Canadian folk song, Superior 'never gives up her dead.'

Several of the Canadian Group of Seven painters were inspired to work here, and descriptions that reached the poet Henry Wadsworth Longfellow had the same effect on him.

Along the highway are many provincial parks, which make good places to get a feel for the lake and surrounding forest.

Batchawana Bay
A relaxing afternoon or a full day can be spent north of town along the scenic shore of Lake Superior around Batchawana Bay. It's a 45-minute drive to **Chippewa Falls**, which is called the centerpoint of Canada, with trails and waterfalls. *Agawa Indian Crafts* (☎ 705-882-2311), a well-known landmark, is about 75km from the Soo in Pancake Bay. The stacks of animal pelts can be off-putting, but a browse here is a great excuse to get out of the car.

Right beside the highway, **Batchawana Provincial Park** (☎ 705-882-2209; day pass $8.50 per car) has *camping* ($20 to $24) and picnic spots, but just down the road, **Pancake Bay Provincial Park** (☎ 705-882-2209; day pass $8.50 per car), also with *camping* ($20 to $24), has a good trail and a better beach, although the water is cool. There are also motels, resorts and rental cottages in the area.

Bears often hang around the Montréal River **garbage dump**, about 25km northwest of Batchawana Bay, but it's gated most of the time, preventing vehicle passage. If you do go, don't leave your car to have a look around on foot.

Lake Superior Provincial Park

Hwy 17 runs for 80km through this large natural park north of Sault Ste Marie, so (luckily) you can't miss it. It's a beautiful park (☎ *705-856-2284; day pass $8.50; open all year*), with a few things to see, even if you don't stay. The rugged scenery is good, with rivers in the wooded interior and a shoreline featuring rocky headlands and sandy beaches. Several Group of Seven painters worked in the park.

The park has three *campgrounds* ($16 to $20), short and long hiking trails that are usually accessible from the highway (the coastal one takes six days), and seven canoe routes. Naturalists give talks and guided walks. The park also offers fishing. Mammals here include bears, and be wary of moose on the road at night.

At **Agawa Bay**, see the Native Indian pictographs on the shoreline rocks, believed to commemorate a crossing of the lake. Note the crevices in the rocks along the path. Farther along, stop at **Sand River** and walk down to the beach. Though the water is cold, the beautiful sandy beach, long and empty, looks as if it's been lifted from a Caribbean island.

For access to the less-visited, eastern side of the park, where there is no road, inquire about the train that runs along the far eastern edge. It can be caught at Frater (at the southern end of the park) or at Hawk Junction. The latter is a small village outside of the northern boundary of the park, east of the town of Wawa. The train line is part of the Algoma Central Railway.

Distance hikers and canoeists should hope for good weather – this is one of the wettest areas in Ontario. Trails are often enveloped in mist or fog, which lends a primeval, spooky air to the woods. Interior camping costs a few dollars less than the campgrounds with facilities.

Wawa
pop 460

The name is an Ojibway word meaning 'wild goose' and was bestowed on the town because of the thousands of geese that stop over on Lake Wawa during migrations. A huge steel goose by the tourist office marks the edge of town.

Wawa is in economic trouble, as the iron mine, its mainstay, closed in 1998. Outdoor-related tourism is picking up some of the slack, and the town acts as a supply center for the regional parks, but there's nothing much to see. East of town, on the highway near the OPP police station, **High Falls** is a scenic picnic spot. Ask at the helpful tourist office (☎ 800-367-9292 ext 260) about the numerous nearby hiking trails and treeless zone; it's open daily from May to Thanksgiving.

Motels are often full in summer, especially the ones right in town. Instead, go a few minutes west of town (locals say north), and look for the following great place right on the highway.

Northern Lights Motel (☎ *705-856-1900, 800-937-2414*) Singles/doubles $35-43/43-46. The rooms here have all been renovated, or there are individual chalets. Other features are a good licensed restaurant, a nearby waterfall (walkable) and…there's a nine-person outdoor hot tub.

Chapleau

Chapleau is a small logging and outdoors center that's inland from Wawa. There are numerous provincial parks in the area, three within 80km. Grey Owl lived in the vicinity for 15 years (for more on this fascinating character, please see the boxed text 'Grey Owl at Home in the Wilderness' in the Saskatchewan chapter).

Missinaibi Lake Park (☎ *705-864-1710; open early-May–mid-Sept*) is in the middle of **Chapleau Game Reserve**, the largest in the Western Hemisphere. The boreal forest is ideal for wilderness camping, canoeing or fishing. The regional tourist offices have a listing of canoe routes. There are 12 trips ranging from one to 14 days, with five to 47 portages. The longest one is a river-and-lake circle route going through part of the reserve; it's good for viewing moose. The tourist office can also help with information on the many lodges and fly-in camps.

The helpful Chapleau tourist office (☎ 877-774-7727), in the Township Museum (main street) has a good collection of mounted fauna and fish downstairs. See

Getting There & Away under Sudbury, earlier, for details on the Budd train.

White River

Back on the Trans Canada Hwy, this is called the coldest place in Canada, with temperatures recorded as low as -50°C. Get your picture taken near the thermometer. There are a couple of moderately priced motels, and VIA Rail connects the town to Sudbury. The station is on Winnipeg Rd, a short walk from the highway.

Pukaskwa National Park

Find out how tough you are. There is no road in Pukaskwa (**puk**-a-saw), and access is by foot or by boat. From Heron Bay, off the Trans Canada Hwy near Marathon, is a small road, Hwy 627, which goes to the edge of the park at Hattie Cove.

There is a visitor information center (☎ 807-229-0801) and a small, rarely full, 67-site *campground* ($15 to $18). For day-use ($3), there is a picnic area and swimming in a protected bay. In Superior itself, the water is cold, and swells can be hazardous, even for good swimmers.

The main attraction is the old 60km coastal **hiking trail** (one way), with primitive camping spots along the way. A shuttle can be arranged to take you one way. The terrain is rough but beautiful, and the weather is changeable, switching quickly from sun to storm. The trail is often wet and slippery, black flies and mosquitoes are guaranteed, and bears are often a bother. Even the mice can be trouble, digging into unattended supplies. Good luck.

And You Thought He Wasn't Real

White River was apparently the original home of the bear that inspired AA Milne's *Winnie the Pooh* books. Evidently, a Canadian soldier got an orphaned bear cub here before his departure to Europe. Feeling lonely, he named it Winnipeg, after his hometown. During WWI it ended up at England's London Zoo, where, with an abbreviated name, it became quite popular, and was subsequently immortalized in fiction.

The interior offers some challenging canoeing, including runs down the Pukaskwa and the less difficult, more accessible White River. Facilities are operational from early June to late September, though the park is open all year. For equipment rentals, try Pukaskwa Country Outfitters (☎ 807-229-0265, **w** www.pcoufitters.on.ca) in Marathon.

Slate Islands Provincial Park

Offshore from the small town of **Terrace Bay** is this cluster of islands, home to the highest density of woodland caribou anywhere. The islands, without natural predators, support several hundred caribou, which are studied by researchers looking into preserving the herds of mainland Ontario. Ask at the Terrace Bay Tourist Information Centre (☎ 800-968-8616) for people who do boat trips to the islands to see or photograph the caribou. Rough *camping* with no facilities is possible, but the islands are 13km offshore, so the trip is not cheap. While in Terrace Bay, a visit to **Aguasabon Falls and Gorge**, which has walking trails, is a worthwhile leg stretch.

Nipigon

Nipigon sits at the mouth of the Nipigon River, where Hwy 11 meets Hwy 17. There really isn't anything of note, but it is interesting that this was the first European settlement on Lake Superior's north shore. European traders established a fur-trading post here, in the middle of the traditional Ojibway lands. East of town along Hwy 17, look for the **Kama Lookout**, with good views of the Lake Superior shore. This segment of the highway is also known as the Terry Fox Courage Hwy.

Ouimet Canyon Provincial Park

About 45km west of Nipigon and 40km east of Thunder Bay, this park (☎ 807-977-2526; *admission by donation; open daily mid-May–Oct*) features an awesome canyon that's 3km long and 150m both wide and deep. The walls on either side of the chasm are virtually perpendicular. Fences and viewing stations have been built right at the sheer edges for good, heart-pounding views. The canyon was scoured out during the last Ice Age, and the bottom is home to some rare flora that are generally found only in Arctic regions. The canyon is definitely

The Legend of the Sleeping Giant

An Ojibway legend tells the story of the formation of the Sleeping Giant. In one version, Nana-bijou, the spirit of the Deep Sea Water, showed the Ojibway a mine where silver could be found as reward for their peaceful, spiritual way of life. But, he said, if anyone should ever tell the white people of its source, they would forever be turned to stone.

Upon seeing the fine articles and jewelry made of silver, the Sioux, the Ojibway's historical enemy, sought to discover the metal's origins. When even torture failed to reveal the secret, the Sioux decided to send a man in disguise to live as an Ojibway. Eventually, he was led to the mine. On his way back to his people with the great news, the Sioux stopped at a white man's encampment.

The white men were enthralled upon seeing the silver sample he had with him. After being plied with alcohol, the Sioux agreed to take several of the men by canoe to the mine. A great storm came up, drowning everyone but the Sioux, whose canoe the Ojibway later found floating around aimlessly. When the weather cleared, the open bay had been partially blocked by a huge rock formation, and the Ojibway knew that Nana-bijou's words had come to be.

worth a quick stop; most times, you'll find yourself alone. A 1km trail meanders around the top, and there are some interpretive displays. The park is 12km off the Trans Canada Hwy. Officially, there's no camping.

Sleeping Giant Provincial Park

Part of the Sibley Peninsula, this large and scenic park (☎ 807-977-2526; day pass $8.50, camping $20-24; open year-round) arcs 35km into Lake Superior. The setting and landscape are excellent, with woods, hills, shoreline and great views from several vantage points.

Look for foxes by the road on the way in at dusk. Moose also live in the park. Activities include swimming, fishing and camping, and there are some good walks, including one out along the top of the Sleeping Giant rock formation, where there are fine views. One hike, taking a minimum of two days, cuts across most of the west coast of the peninsula.

The park makes a good stop if you don't want to go into town (about 45km) to sleep.

On the way to the park, Pass Lake has *Karen's Kountry Kitchen* (☎ 807-977-2882, Route 587; open daily June-Sept, Wed-Sun Sept-Thanksgiving), where soups, salads, quiches, vegetarian pies are all under $10. It makes an exceedingly friendly and attractive lunch spot and has a deck overlooking a lake.

At the very end of the peninsula (watch the bumps in the road) is the tiny, remote, artsy community of **Silver Islet**, looking almost like a Newfoundland outport. The old mining store has been transformed into the *Silver Islet Store & Tea Room* (☎ 807-473-6310; open Thur-Tues May-Thanksgiving), where you can indulge in an irresistible cinnamon bun in a laid-back atmosphere; dishes are about $5.

East of Thunder Bay

Before you hit Thunder Bay, look for the sign that reads 'Smoked Fish, Seafood, Amethyst and Eggs,' 2.5km east of Lakeshore Dr on Hwy 17. The *Fish Shop* (☎ 807-983-2214; open 8am-8pm daily), presided over by a hoot of a Finnish woman, Hilkka, smokes and sells the best fish imaginable. And the prices are very good. Get the lake trout for a delicious taste of northern Ontario.

THUNDER BAY
pop 117,000

Edging the northern shores of Lake Superior and known as 'the Lakehead,' Thunder Bay is an amalgamation of Fort William and Port Arthur. Despite being so far inland, Thunder Bay is one of Canada's major ports and is as far westward as ships using the St Lawrence Seaway get this side of the border. The main cargo switching hands is prairie wheat going to market. Although much decreased in importance, the docks have long been one of the world's major grain handlers.

The city, halfway between Sault Ste Marie and Winnipeg (720km to either one), is a good stopping-off point. The place itself may not hold you long, but the setting is scenic and it makes a handy center for experiencing some of the things to see and do in northern Ontario's rugged timberland.

The first Europeans here were a couple of Frenchmen who reached the area in 1662. For hundreds of years, this was a fur-trading settlement. In 1869, the Dawson (the pioneer's road westward) was begun. In 1882, the Canadian Pacific Railway arrived, and soon the prairie's first shipment of wheat was heading east. Coming into town from the east on the Trans Canada Hwy, you'll pass mountains and see the city at the edge of the bay. Along the shoreline are pulp mills and grain elevators. Out in the harbor, ships are moored, and beyond is a long rock formation and an island or two. The unusually shaped mass of rock offshore, known as the **Sleeping Giant**, is important in Native Indian lore.

Orientation

Thunder Bay still has two distinct downtown areas, which are connected principally by Fort William Rd and Memorial Ave. The area between the two is pretty much a wasteland of fast-food outlets, the large Inter City Shopping Mall and little else.

Both downtown areas are rather drab, run-down and suffering from an economy long tied to dwindling resource-based industries, although on last visit, signs of improvement and hope were evident. In Port Arthur (Thunder Bay North), closer to the lakeshore, the main streets are Red River Rd and Cumberland St. Prince Arthur's Landing, off Water St, is a redeveloped waterfront area and includes parkland. The Pagoda tourist office is across the street. This half of Thunder Bay has a sizable Finnish population, which supports several specialized restaurants. Indeed, for a city its size, Thunder Bay has quite a large and varied ethnic population.

In Fort William (Thunder Bay South), the main streets are May St and Victoria Ave. The Victoriaville shopping mall is at this corner and is where most of the Fort William action occurs.

On each side of Thunder Bay is a commercial motel/restaurant strip.

Information

Tourism Thunder Bay (☎ 807-983-2041, 800-667-8386), at the Terry Fox Lookout and Memorial, about 6km east of town on Hwy 11/17, is open 9am to 5pm daily.

In Port Arthur, a central summer tourist office (☎ 807-684-3670) is in the 1910 Pagoda in the park on the corner of Red River Rd and Water St; it's open 9am to 5pm Monday to Friday. In Fort William, you can get some information at City Hall (500 Donald St E). There is also an information booth at Old Fort William. The tourist offices have pamphlets outlining architectural walking tours for both sections of town.

The Waverley Resource Library (☎ 807-344-3585, 285 Red River Rd) has free Internet access.

Thunder Bay Regional Hospital (☎ 807-343-6621, 460 Court St N) is in Port Arthur.

Old Fort William Historical Park

Some of Thunder Bay's best-known attractions are some distance from downtown, as is Old Fort William (☎ 807-473-2344; adult/child/family $10/8/31; open 10am-6pm daily mid-May–mid-Oct), the city's feature site.

The old fort settlement, with 42 historic buildings spread over 50 hectares west of town, not far past the airport and off Broadway Ave, is worth seeing.

From 1803 to 1821, Fort William was the headquarters of the North West Fur Trading Company. Here, the voyageurs and Native Indians did their trading, and settlers and explorers arrived from the east. In 1821, after much haggling and hassling, the company was absorbed by its chief rival, the Hudson's Bay Company, and Fort William declined in importance as a trading center.

The fort re-creates some aspects of the early, thriving days of the fur trade through buildings, tools, artifacts and documents. Workers in period dress demonstrate skills and crafts, perform historical reenactments and answer questions. Interesting displays include the Native Indian camp and the woodwork of the canoe building. The separate farm section has animals.

In summer, free special-event days are held regularly. In mid-July, the fort becomes the scene of the **Great Rendezvous**, a three-day festival that recreates the annual meeting of North West employees, voyageurs, Native Indians and traders. In August, keep an eye open for the **Ojibway Keeshigun**, a weekend festival of Native Indian culture.

THUNDER BAY

PORT ARTHUR

0   100   200 m
0   100   200 yards

PLACES TO STAY
2 Modern Motel
6 Travelodge Thunder Bay
13 Best Western Crossroads Motor Inn
14 Ritz Motel
15 Prince Arthur Hotel
18 Downtown Hostel
26 Archibald Arbor

PLACES TO EAT
1 Port Arthur Brasserie
7 Kelsey's
10 East Side Mario's
16 Kivelo Finnish Bakery
19 Hoito Restaurant
20 Prospector Steakhouse
24 Norma Jean's
27 Giorg
29 Good News Café
31 Cronos Café

OTHER
3 Thunder Bay Regional Hospital
4 Waverly Resource Library
5 Kanga's
8 Greyhound Bus Depot
9 Confederation College (Thunder Bay Art Gallery; HI Hostel)
11 Inter City Shopping Mall
12 International Friendship Gardens
16 Port Arthur Local Bus Terminal
17 Pagoda Tourist Office
21 Prince Arthur's Landing
23 Armani's
25 Thunder Bay Museum
28 City Hall
30 Inntowner Palace

FORT WILLIAM

0   100   200 m
0   100   200 yards

see Port Arthur inset

see Fort William inset

Thunder Bay Harbour

Port

0   5   1 km
0   .25   .5 mile

Keefer Terminal

Neebing-McIntyre Diversion

Kaministiquia River

McKellar Island

Mission Island

Victoriaville Mall

To Trowbridge Falls Campground, Pinebrook, Longhouse Village Hostel, KOA Campground & Sault Ste Marie

To Motels, Centennial Park, Boulevard Lake & Hwy 11 & 17 Trans Canada

To Kakabeka Falls, Winnipeg & Manitoba

To Thunder Bay Airport & Old Fort William Historical Park

To Mt Mackey, Chippewa Park & Duluth, Minnesota (USA)

Lakehead University

A thorough but relaxed visit to the fort can take half a day or more. Good, cheap home-made food (brick-oven bread and voyageur stew) is available in the fort's *canteen*.

Although the site is a long way out, the Neebing 10 city bus goes close to the fort, departing from the terminal in either Fort William or Port Arthur every hour; the last bus from the fort leaves at around 4:30pm, but check the schedules before setting out.

Terry Fox Monument

Overlooking the Sleeping Giant on Hwy 11/17 a few kilometers east of town, this 2.7m-high statue (and the segment of the Trans Canada Hwy northwest of town) honors the young Canadian who, in the early 1980s while dying of cancer, ran halfway across Canada to raise money for cancer research. After having one leg am-putated, he made it from Newfoundland to Thunder Bay, raising millions and becoming a national hero before finally succumbing. Each year, cities across the country and around the world hold Terry Fox Memorial Runs to raise further funds for his cause.

There is a good visitor information center here.

Thunder Bay Museum

This small historical museum (☎ 807-623-0801, 425 Donald St E; admission $3, free Sat; open 1pm-5pm Tues-Sun), housed in the former police station, contains Native Indian artifacts and an odds-and-ends col-lection of local history. Topics covered include fur trading, mining and the early pi-oneers. There's also an Albertosaurus replica. The museum is not extensive, but displays are well presented.

Thunder Bay Art Gallery

This gallery (☎ 807-577-6427, 1080 Keewatin St; admission $3; open noon-8pm Tues-Thur, noon-5pm Fri-Sun), at Confederation College campus off Balmoral St, collects, preserves and displays contemporary art by Native Indians. Works include paintings, prints, masks, sculptures and more. There are displays from the permanent collection, as well as traveling exhibits, which usually feature non–Native Indian artists. Norval Morrisseau, perhaps Canada's best-known Native Indian painter, was born in Thunder Bay, and some of his work is on view. The Northwood bus from Fort William goes to the campus door.

The Port

Thunder Bay Harbour is one of Canada's largest ports, according to tons handled, and it once claimed to have the greatest complex of grain elevators in the world. Ter-minals, elevators and other storage and docking facilities stretch along 45km of central waterfront. Some are no longer used. At the Port Arthur shipyards, the huge freighters are repaired.

In the middle of the waterfront is the Keefer Terminal complex, a cargo-handling facility where ships from around the world come and go. The terminal mainly handles resource materials and grains. Despite the industrial look of the port, there is life there among the terminals. On **Mission Island**, southeast of Arthur St, the Lakehead Region Conservation Authority has created a sanctuary for waterbirds. During the spring and autumn migrations, thousands of birds may be seen on the 40 hectares of wet-lands. To get there, cross the bridge off Syn-dicate Ave S and follow the signs.

Prince Arthur's Landing

Located in Port Arthur, by the lake opposite the Pagoda tourist office, the landing is a waterfront redevelopment zone. It contains the marina, the dock and a miniscule art gallery that is open casually. In the reincar-nated train station, on the 2nd floor, is a large layout created by the **Model Railroad Association** (admission $2.50; open 7pm-10pm Mon-Fri, 1pm-5pm Sat & Sun June-Labor Day).

Still, the site is primarily parkland. There are some walking paths that meander around three piers. The best is the one out to Wilson St Headland, with views of the lake and dock areas.

Mt Mackay

Mt Mackay (the Ojibway call it 'Thunder Mountain') is the tallest mountain in the area's northwestern mountain chain, rising to about 350m and offering good views of Thunder Bay and environs. The lookout is on an **Ojibway reserve** (☎ 807-622-3093; admission $5 per car; open 10am-5pm Mon-Fri, 10am-10pm Sat & Sun May–mid-Oct) and provides a good view of the city from the top of the winding road. But for seeing the Sleeping Giant, you're better off at the Terry Fox Lookout, off the Trans Canada Hwy.

Mt Mackay is southwest of downtown Fort William. Take James St south off Arthur St to City Rd, heading toward Chippewa Park, and follow the signs (look hard and turn right on Mission Rd). The road to Mt Mackay cuts through a portion of the residential area of the reserve. A walking trail leads farther up to the peak. No city bus gets close enough to make public transportation to the mountain a viable option.

Parks

For general information, call Parks & Recreation (☎ 807-625-2351); it's open Monday to Friday.

Centennial Park (☎ 807-683-5762) is a large, natural woodland park at the eastern edge of Port Arthur, near Hwy 17. It's alongside Current River, which flows into Boulevard Lake before entering Lake Superior. The park is over the Boulevard Lake Bridge, just off Arundel St. There are nature trails along the river and through the woods. On the grounds is a simulated logging camp of 1910 – not much to see, but the log cabins and buildings themselves are good. A **small museum** has a cross-cut section of a 250-year-old white-pine tree on display. Various dates in history are marked at the corresponding growth rings. It's amazing to think what has gone on while this tree quietly kept growing. Canoes and boats are rented. Up the road from the park is the **Bluffs Scenic Lookout**, offering a view of the lake and shore.

The **International Friendship Gardens** is a good-size city park west of downtown Fort William, on Victoria Ave near Waterloo St. Various local ethnic groups, such as the Finns and the Hungarians, have erected monuments and statues. There is a pond and some flowers but no extensive gardens.

On High St, just to the west of Waverley Park near Red River Rd, **Hillcrest Park** has a lookout point for views of the harbor and Sleeping Giant.

Amethyst Mines

Amethyst, a variety of quartz, is a purple semiprecious stone found around Thunder Bay. There are many superstitions sur-

rounding amethyst, including the early Greek one that it prevents drunkenness. The ever-practical Greeks therefore often fashioned wine cups from the stone. It is mined from veins that run on or near the earth's surface, so looking for the stone and digging it out are relatively easy. Within about 50km of the city are five sites where you can look for your own. Each site has some samples for sale if you should miss out on finding some yourself. The tourist office has a list of all the mines and can direct you to stores around town that sell a range of stuff produced with the finished stone – most of it, other than some jewelry, is pretty tacky. The stone generally looks better raw. Visits to all but one of the sites are free. You simply pay for the pieces you find and want to keep.

Thunder Bay Amethyst Mine Panorama (☎ 807-622-6908; admission $3; open 10am-5pm Mon-Sat May–mid-Oct) is a huge property off E Loon Lake Rd, which is east of Hwy 587 S, about 50km east of town. The site is about 7km north of the Trans Canada Hwy, and the road is rough and steep in places. Three of the mine sites, all much smaller, are on Rd No 5 N, a little farther east than E Loon Lake Rd. The three mine entrances can't be missed. You are given a pail and shovel and pointed in the right direction, then you're on your own – see what you come up with. Each site has a shop on the premises.

Activities

Finnish **saunas** are popular in the region. Try one at **Kanga's** (☎ 705-344-6761, 379 Oliver Rd, $15 for 2 people, 90 minutes; open 7am-11pm Mon-Fri, 8am-11pm Sat & Sun). This local fave also offers some Finnish eats and good desserts.

Wabakimi Canoe Outfitters (☎ 807-767-2022, ⓦ www.wabakimi.com; Dog Lake Rd), east of town off Hwy 527 N, offers canoe rentals and outfitting or expeditions of various lengths, which include wildlife, photography and fishing trips. Some go into Wabakimi, the large wilderness park northwest of Lake Nipigon; others go as far north as Hudson Bay. The outfitter now has its own new lodge.

The biologists at **Blue Loon Adventures** (☎ 807-767-6838, 888-846-0066, ⓦ www.foxnet.net/~blueloon) offer a range of day trips or longer outdoor adventures, including rafting, birding and biking outings, from their tent camp (tent sites $16), about 45 minutes south of town along Hwy 61. Meals are available.

Fishing charters into Lake Superior (for salmon and trout) are available from **Superior Fishing Charters** (☎ 807-683-8101). Call to make arrangements and organize pickup. Trout fishing is possible in nearby rivers and streams; the tourist office has a list of local fishing spots put out by the Ministry of Natural Resources.

From Thunder Bay to Kenora, near the Manitoba border, there are almost limitless fishing camps and lodges. Many people fly in to remote lakes. Tourist offices have more information on these wonderful-sounding but pricey trips.

Special Events
For details on all city events, call the tourist office.

First Nation Powwow Native Indian dancers hold a powwow on Mt Mackay around July 1.

Great Rendezvous For three days in mid-July, Old Fort William hosts a re-creation of the annual get-together of North West Company employees, voyageurs, Native Indians and traders who congregated at the fort to trade pelts and generally carouse. Hundreds of appropriately dressed characters take part.

Harbourfest Also held in July, this annual street festival features music, dancing, street theater, markets and a fireworks display, all centered around the marina.

Festa Italia In mid-August, this one-day event features food (of course), games and entertainment. It's held in the north-end, Italian section of town.

Places to Stay
Camping Thunder Bay is one of those happy places where good camping can be found close to town. For other camping options not listed here, see Sleeping Giant Provincial Park (earlier) and Kakabeka Falls Provincial Park (under West of Thunder Bay, later).

Trowbridge Falls Campground (☎ 807-683-6661) Campsites $14-18. This quiet, green campground is on the east side of the city off Hwy 11/17, about 500m north up Copenhagen Rd (near the Terry Fox Monument). It's run by the City of Thunder Bay, as is the adjacent Centennial Park.

KOA Campground (☎ 807-683-6221, Spruce River Rd) Sites $18-23. Three kilometers east of the monument and visible from the Trans Canada Hwy, this campground is more commercial than Trowbridge Falls and is geared toward RVs.

Chippewa Park (☎ 807-683-6661) Campsites $14-18. There's also camping southwest of the city at this park, a short drive from Old Fort William. From the junction of Hwys 61 and 61B, go 3.2km on Hwy 61B to City Rd and look for the signs. The peaceful park is right on the lake.

Hostels There are a few good budget options.

Thunder Bay International Hostel (☎ 807-983-2042, fax 807-983-2914, candu@ microage-tb.com, ⓦ www.backpackers.ca, 1594 Lakeshore Dr, PO RR13, Thunder Bay, ON P7B 5E4) Dorm beds $18, tent sites single/double $11/18. Open year-round. This hostel, at the Longhouse Village, is excellent. It's a fair distance from town – 18km east along Lakeshore Dr – but is well worth the effort. The location is green and quiet; the atmosphere, friendly and relaxed. The couple who run it, Lloyd and Willa Jones, are the driving force behind Backpackers Hostels Canada (see Accommodations in the Facts for the Visitor chapter for more information). The Joneses are knowledgeable about things to do around town.

There is swimming and walking near the hostel, and ask about McKenzie Point and the waterfall in the woods, where the brave or silly jump in. Basic food is available, and guests can use the kitchen. Rooms and beds are scattered all over the property in a variety of units, including a large mobile home, cabins, the main house and even a couple of buses. Tents can be set up on the lawn, and families can be accommodated. There are no city buses to the hostel, so take the eastbound Greyhound bus from the terminal (see Getting There & Away, later). For $8, the bus will take you along Lakeshore Dr to the hostel (or will at least let you off at Mackenzie Station Rd at the Trans Canada Hwy; from there it's a 1km walk south). Be sure to tell the driver where you're headed when you get on. There is a trip into town around noon and one back in the evening at around 7pm, but ask about up-to-date scheduling.

Downtown Hostel (☎ 807-683-3995, 139 Machar Ave) Dorm beds $15. During research, the Jones' daughter, Gail, opened her own hostel (as yet unnamed) downtown in central Port Arthur in a fine, old house.

Sibley Hall Confederation College (☎ 807-475-6381, fax 807-625-9596, 960 William St) Rooms $15/18 HI members/nonmembers. Open mid-May–mid-Aug. Hostelling International uses room in this college north of downtown Fort William. It's very institutional, with no common areas.

Lakehead University Residence (☎ 807-343-8612, 955 Oliver Rd) Singles/doubles $28/40. Open May–Aug 20. There are beds available at this university residence. It's between the two downtown areas and slightly west. The crosstown city bus goes past the campus.

B&Bs There are a couple of good B&B options.

Archibald Arbor (☎ 807-622-3386, fax 807-622-4471, nthall@norlink.net, 222 Archibald St S) Rooms $45-65 with continental breakfast. Open year-round. This B&B, in a renovated Fort William house, is very central.

Pinebrook (☎ 807-683-6114, fax 807-683-6114, Mitchell Rd) Rooms $55-100 with full breakfast. This rural B&B, on a large, wooded property, is near the Terry Fox Monument, east of town off Hwy 17. It's about a 15-minute drive. Features include nearby walking trails and a sauna. Some French and German are spoken.

Motels There are two areas of heavy motel concentration, one on each side of the city.

In Port Arthur, look along Cumberland St N, which leads from downtown into Hodder St, which then leads to the Expressway or Hwy 17 E. These economical motels are mainly found near the grain elevators along the lakefront.

Modern Motel (☎ 807-344-4352, 430 Cumberland St N) Doubles $40. Despite the low price, this is a very well-kept place – a real bargain.

The other motel district is along Arthur St, heading out of town from downtown Fort William past the airport.

Ritz Motel (☎ 807-623-8189, 2600 Arthur St E) Singles/doubles $60/62. On a spacious property close to town, this well-run motel offers some kitchenettes.

There are also a few motels side by side on Kingsway Ave off Arthur St E, but these are priced higher than they're worth.

Hotels The following are some decent hotel options.

Best Western Crossroads Motor Inn (☎ 807-577-4241, 800-265-3253, fax 807-475-7059, 655 Arthur St W) Rooms $75-95. This upgraded hotel in Prince Arthur is a good value, and kids stay free.

Prince Arthur Hotel (☎ 807-345-5411, 800-267-2675, 17 Cumberland St N) Rooms $85-100, often less on weekends. Newly renovated, this is the best business hotel in town, with some rooms overlooking the lake. It's right by the Pagoda tourist office and has several places to eat or drink, as well as an indoor pool.

Travelodge Thunder Bay (☎ 807-345-2343, 800-578-7878, fax 807-345-3246, 450 Memorial Ave) Rooms $80-90 with continental breakfast. This inn has a pool, and kids stay free.

Places to Eat

Port Arthur There are numerous restaurants on Memorial Ave, which links the two parts of the city.

Hoito (☎ 807-345-6323, 314 Bay St) Dishes $4-9. Open 7am-8pm Mon-Fri, 8am-8pm Sat & Sun. This Finnish place, set up around 1940, is known far and wide for its economical, homemade food served in plain surroundings. The large portions pack them in, especially for weekend lunches. There are a couple of other places in this Finnish neighborhood, and around the corner is *Kivela Finnish Bakery* (111 Second St), which is closed Sunday and Monday.

Prospector Steakhouse (☎ 807-345-5833, 27 Cumberland St S) Dishes $14-18. Open 4pm-9pm. If you win big at the nearby casino, you can wander over and be proudly carnivorous at this wood-lined serious steak cabin.

Port Arthur Brasserie (☎ 807-767-4415, 901 Red River Rd at Junot Ave) Dishes $8-12. Away from the central core is this popular brewpub, where – in addition to meals of pasta, burgers or fish – there's a major Sunday brunch. Work off the calories at the pub's volleyball court.

Kelsey's (☎ 807-345-0400, 805 Memorial Ave) Dinner $8-15. Open 11am-1am Mon-Sat,

ONTARIO

until 11pm Sun. This is a casual place geared toward a younger crowd and offering a good value for the money. There's seafood, chicken, some Greek dishes, burgers and more. Everything's served with all-you-can-eat pop music.

East Side Mario's (☎ 807-622-5500, 1170 Memorial Ave) Dinner $15. Open 11am-1am Mon-Sat, until 11pm Sun. This place, similar to Kelsey's, but with a more pseudo-Mediterranean look, specializes in Italian dishes. Steak is also available.

Fort William This side of town also has plenty on offer.

Norma Jean's (☎ 807-623-1343, 123 May St S) Dishes $4-12. Open 8am-8pm daily. This beautiful '50s-style diner has it down – the colors, the decor, the music. The classic diner menu is supplemented with some Italian fare. It's a great place for breakfast or a burger. The place achieved some infamy in the early 1990s, when Laurie 'Bambi' Bembenek, the popular protagonist in one of North America's most captivating criminal cases, waitressed here while on the run from US authorities, until a local tipped off the authorities as to her whereabouts.

Cronos Café (☎ 807-622-9700, 433 Syndicate Ave S) Dishes under $5. Open 11am-7pm Mon-Fri, noon-7pm Sat. Tucked away in an obscure corner of town, this arty, alternative sort of place is a welcome addition for lunch or dinner. It's good for inexpensive Greek or Middle Eastern fare or just a cappuccino.

Good News Café (☎ 807-623-5001, 116 Syndicate Ave S) Dishes $8-20. Open 10am-4pm Tues-Sun, dinner Fri & Sat. This little café just outside the Victoria Mall serves up meals with flair and an international twist. The owner gives cooking classes, and it shows – the grilled sandwiches, fresh flatbreads and salads all make very tasty lunches.

Giorg (☎ 807-623-8052, 114 Syndicate Ave N) Dishes $15-20. Closed Sun & Mon. Since 1989, this comfortably stylish open kitchen–style Italian spot has been serving fine food, wine and a touch of European class. All pasta is made on the premises. Reservations are suggested for weekends. The menu constantly changes; ask for recommendations.

Entertainment

Fort William has several places to consider.

Dewar's Pub (☎ 807-622-0777, 121 McKellar St) This pub has an array of beer and fish and chips.

Armani's (☎ 807-626-8002, 513 Victoria Ave E) Though the downstairs restaurant is dressy, the nightclub, with a rooftop bar in summer, is casual and attracts a young crowd.

Inntowner Palace (☎ 807-623-1565, Inntowner Hotel, Arthur St at Brodie St) Not for the piano-bar crowd, this popular hotel bar cranks up the volume for live rock.

Getting There & Away

Air Thunder Bay Airport is about a 15-minute drive southwest of town, at the junction of Hwy 11/17 (the Trans Canada Hwy) and Hwy 61 to Duluth, Minnesota. Air Canada (☎ 800-247-2262) offers flights to Winnipeg and Toronto. The discount carrier WestJet (☎ 888-937-8538) goes to Hamilton (Toronto) and Winnipeg, usually for less than Air Canada.

Bearskin Airlines (☎ 807-475-0006) serves the region and other northern parts of the province.

Bus The Greyhound bus depot (☎ 807-345-2194, 815 Fort William Rd) is closer to Fort William but lies in between the two downtown areas, near the Inter City Shopping Mall. It's a long walk north from central Fort William. To get there, grab a city bus; the Mainline bus goes past the door as it runs between Fort William and Port Arthur.

For Winnipeg ($101) and points farther west, there are three buses a day, beginning early in the morning and running until late.

For Sault Ste Marie ($115) and points east, such as Toronto, there are also three trips daily, and again, the schedule is evenly spaced. The same bus goes to Sudbury ($140).

Four times a week, Happy Time Tours (☎ 807-473-5955) buses go to Duluth, Minnesota.

The Grey Goose bus line runs to Fort Francis and, via the USA, to Manitoba. Get details at the Greyhound desk.

Car Enterprise (☎ 807-344-2800) has cars for $33 and up per day, with 200 kilometers free and great three-day weekend specials. There are several rental agencies at the airport.

A circular tour of northern Ontario can be made by car from Thunder Bay by backtracking to Lake Nipigon and following Hwy 11 (the most northerly provincial route) through Geraldton and Kapuskasing, returning south via Timmins, Sudbury or North Bay. Provincial parks are found at regular intervals along Hwy 11. Towns are small.

Hitchhiking Westbound travelers should head out to Arthur St; the airport bus will take you to a good spot. Alternatively, if you can get to Hwy 102 (Red River Rd/Dawson Rd), on the north edge of Port Arthur, you save a few kilometers along Hwy 11/17 before the turnoff to Winnipeg. If you're eastbound, anywhere on Hwy 17 is okay. For $8, the eastbound Greyhound bus will take you to the edge of town, but tell the driver upon boarding where you want to get off, because the drivers don't like making surprise unscheduled stops.

Getting Around
To/From the Airport The major hotels, such as the Prince Arthur, have complimentary airport shuttle buses for guests. If the buses have space and you wander over and smile nicely, the drivers might take you; they won't make special trips for nonguests. The ride takes about 15 minutes.

A city bus, the 'Arthur' route, also goes from the Fort William side of town right to the door of the airport. It's much slower, but it's only $2. Catch it anywhere on Arthur St.

Bus There is a good bus system (☎ 807-684-3744) that covers all areas of the city, and the drivers are some of the friendliest and most helpful in the country. Tell them we said so. The fare is $2.

In Fort William, the terminal for local buses is on the corner of May and Miles Sts. To get to the Port Arthur end of town, take the Memorial bus on May St, or the Mainline bus along Fort William St (same thing going the opposite way).

In Port Arthur, the terminal is on the corner of Water and Camelot Sts (just down from Cumberland St), by the waterfront. The Pagoda tourist office is next door.

The crosstown bus from either end of Thunder Bay goes to the university. The Neebing bus goes to Old Fort William from the Fort William terminal. City buses also go

to and from the motel and fast-food strips on both sides of town.

WEST OF THUNDER BAY
Beyond Kakabeka, the traffic thins appreciably, and the highway is not as scenic as east of Thunder Bay. At Shabaqua Corners, the highway forks, the south branch leading to Atikokan and Fort Frances, and the north branch heading for Kenora and the Manitoba border. The northern route is quicker. Along the Trans Canada Hwy from this point, moose are often seen, especially at night, so drive with caution and with your eyes frequently scanning the shoulders of the road. Near the town of Upsala, a sign indicates the Arctic watershed; from here, water flows north. Another marks the beginning of a new time zone – you save an hour going west. Also note that you won't get much on the radio until you pick up Ignace stations.

Kakabeka Falls
Set in a provincial park 25km west of Thunder Bay off Hwy 17, these waterfalls (☎ 807-473-9231; admission $2-8.50 per car; open year-round), about 40m high, are pretty. They're most impressive in spring, when the water in the river is at its highest, or after heavy rains. Sometimes the water flow is small, as it's dammed off for power. Walkways lead around and across the falls. Plaques tell the Ojibway legend of martyr Princess Green Mantle, who saved her village from the attacking Sioux by leading them over the falls.

Most people go to take pictures at the falls, but the park itself isn't bad, with *camping* ($20), swimming at small beaches and picnicking.

Northern Route
Ignace This town has a number of *motels* and a couple of *service station restaurants*. It also has a large tourist office (on the west side of town, beside the old fire tower), good for regional information and for details on fishing and canoe routes, including the White Otter Lake district.

Bears hang out at the garbage dump on the east side of town, 2km north up Hwy 599 just past the golf and country club on the right-hand side. Unfortunately, it's gated except noon to 5pm Thursday to Monday, and evening is the best time to see them. Although generally pretty blasé about the presence of people, they are unpredictable, so walking in is not recommended. Bears may look clumsy, but they can outdash any human – guaranteed.

South, between here and Atikokan, lies White Otter Lake, the site of **White Otter Castle**, a locally well-known oddity built in 1904 by a Scottish immigrant named Jimmy McQuat and now restored. He did it all by himself, and nobody knows why – he was a bachelor, yet this is a huge timber place with a four-story tower. It's on the northwestern arm of the lake, accessible only by canoe.

Dryden Like so many of the towns in the region, Dryden is fishing crazy – a service station may offer free minnows with every tank of gasoline. If you don't hunt or fish, there isn't much here for you. The Avenor paper mill, Dryden's major industry, offers interesting free tours on weekdays through summer. On the radio, listen for the Sunday-morning church sermon broadcast in Cree.

Kenora This pulp-and-paper town about 200km from Winnipeg is the closest town of any size to the Manitoba border. With a population of 15,800, it's a hub for much of the local tourist activity, which consists mainly of summer vacation cottages and fishing and hunting trips. Though slower, avoid the bypass and go through town to take in the pretty setting along the convoluted shores of Lake of the Woods. Watch for the traditional *inukshuks* (stone figures) beside area highways.

There is a visitors' center (☎ 800-535-4549, 1500 Trans Canada Hwy E) about five minutes east of the central core and another one about 20km west of town. Main St and Front St, along the water, are the main centers of activity.

The harborfront area of downtown has been redone to good effect; the marina is here, as are the docks, where you can catch two-hour **boat cruises** out on the lake. Less expensive is the little shuttle over to **Coney Island**, where you can take an afternoon's swim at the best sandy beach near town. There are other nearby beaches, such as popular **Norman Beach**, about 3km from downtown, at the junction of Parsons St and the Trans Canada Hwy.

The small but good **Lake of the Woods Museum** (☎ 807-467-2105, 300 Main St S, Memorial Park; admission $2; open 10am-5pm daily July & Aug, closed Sun & Mon rest of the year) features local history, notably focusing on the period around the start of the 20th century, when Kenora changed rapidly. Tours can be taken of the **paper mill** (504 Ninth St N). History-based wall murals dot the downtown area.

There's an international **sailing regatta** in late July, held in and around the 14,000 islands in the lake. An annual **folk festival** takes place in early July.

Many Ojibway Indians live in the area, and it is they who handpick the Canadian wild rice (manomin) that grows locally. It's easily available here or in health-food stores across the country and is delicious.

Many Native Indian pictographs have been found around the Kenora area. These paintings, done on rock using berry juices, tree gums and sap, depict history and legends. Visitors are able to take part in a number of Ojibway events, including regional powwows.

Anicinabe Park & Campground (☎ 807-467-2700, 877-318-2267, 140 Minto Crescent) Campsites $17-28. This campground, just a few blocks from the center of town, has showers and a beach. Other provincial parks are nearby.

There are motel options along the highway.

Whispering Pines (☎ 807-548-4025, fax 807-548-1342, Hwy 17) Rooms $50-60. This motel, 10km east of town, has low-priced rooms. A beach and camping are available across the street.

Days Inn (☎ 807-468-2003, 800-465-1123, fax 807-468-8551, 920 Hwy 17 E) Doubles $85. This link in the reliable chain is south of downtown.

Places to eat can be found along Main St, and look for the *chip wagons* around town and by the waterfront.

Southern Route
Mom's Way – the Manitoba, Ontario, Minnesota highway (Nos 11 and 12) – is the alternative between Thunder Bay and Winnipeg. It's less traveled and more scenic but slower.

Atikokan Once an iron-mining town, Atikokan is the supply center for Quetico Park, with a number of *motels* and *lodges* and plenty of casual places to find a meal. The ***Iron Mine*** (☎ *807-597-3915, 300 Main St*) is a good restaurant and pub; dishes run $4-11. Rockhounds may want to explore the interesting old mine sites of Steep Rock and Caland. Get a map at the tourist office, as the roads around the mines are rough and confusing.

Quetico Provincial Park This huge wilderness park (☎ *807-597-4602, reservations* ☎ *807-597-2737; day use $6; open year-round)*, 100km long by 60km wide, is linked to the Boundary Waters Canoe Area in Minnesota. Quetico is undeveloped for the most part but has one major organized ***campground***. It offers excellent canoeing (1500km of routes), primarily for those wanting peace and quiet. Portages tend to be short, averaging 400m. The use of motor boats is forbidden (except in a few areas by Native Indians), and you'll find no roads or logging within the park.

The park is a maze of lakes and rivers, with lots of wildlife and some Native Indian pictographs. Rocky shores and jack pines are typical of some parts, but there are large areas of bog in others and stands of red and white pine in others. The park can be accessed from several points, the principal one on the Canadian side being from the Dawson Trail campground, off Hwy 11, where there is an information pavilion. There are outfitters (for canoes and equipment) and maps available in and around the park. **Quetico Discovery Tours** (☎ *807-597-2621)* offers a variety of packages into the park.

Fort Frances Situated on Rainy Lake opposite International Falls, Minnesota, this is a busy border-crossing point into the USA. Both sides are popular outdoor destinations, with countless lakes, cottages, fishing, camping, etc. In town, you can visit a paper mill, the town's main business. A causeway across Rainy Lake to Atikokan offers great views of the lake.

The **Fort Frances Museum** (☎ *807-274-7891, 259 Scott St; admission free; open 10am-5pm daily mid-June–late Aug, closed Sun rest of the year)* examines Native Indian history and the fur trade, as well as more recent developments. At **Pither's Point Park**, on the shore of the lake, the museum also maintains Fort St Pierre (admission free, same hours as museum), a replica fur-trading post, a lookout tower and a logging boat.

Kay-Nah-Chi-Wah-Nung (☎ *807-483-1163, Shaw Rd; admission $7; open 10am-6pm daily June-Sept, 10am-5pm Wed-Sun rest of the year)* is a sacred Ojibway site 50km west of town on Hwy 11 at Emo. This site is historically significant as an early habitation location and as Canada's largest ancient ceremonial burial center. An interpretation center explains.

Grey Goose bus lines connects to Winnipeg or Thunder Bay. Hwy 71 N connects with Kenora and Winnipeg.

Sioux Narrows About 80km south of Kenora, on the eastern side of Lake of the Woods, Sioux Narrows is a resort town. In addition to the regional residents, many US citizens and Winnipegers spend time here during summer. The town and its surroundings have a range of cottages, lodges, motels, campgrounds and houseboats for rent. Lake of the Woods fishing is renowned far and wide. **Sioux Narrows Provincial Park** (☎ *807-226-5223; admission $6; open May-Sept)* has ***camping*** ($16 to $18) and contains some Native Indian pictographs.

Québec

Québec is Canada's largest province, a vast territory three times the size of France. This one province alone encompasses sparsely populated stretches of windswept Arctic tundra in the north, rich and wild boreal forests in the central areas, fertile agricultural land in the south and a maritime climate in the east. In between are majestic waterfalls, sand dunes, fjords, jagged mountain peaks and more meat *tourtières* (pies) than you can count.

Québec is not called 'La Belle Province' for nothing. The scenery in many areas is nothing short of breathtaking. Unspoiled Charlevoix is a protected area of natural beauty. The Laurentians boast splendid mountains and year-round resorts. The Eastern Townships, settled by Loyalists, comprise a gentle, quiet region of farms, lakes and rolling hills. The Gaspésie, with its rugged shoreline, wallops you with its splendor. The northern forests, home to huge and untamed parks, offer excellent and accessible wilderness. The delicate flowers and lichen on the rocks of the Far North add subtle notes of loveliness.

'Kebec,' an Algonquin Indian word meaning 'where the river narrows,' is also the heart of French Canada. The vast majority of the population speaks French, making Québec unlike the rest of North America. And the differences go far beyond language – the unique culture manifests itself in architecture, music, food and religion.

Even Montréal (pronounced **mor**-eh-al), where English is still widely used, has a decidedly different air than other Canadian cities, thanks to its joie de vivre and leisurely pace of life, while historic Québec City seems noticeably European.

Québec is generally at odds with the rest of English-speaking Canada, particularly in its politics. A sizable chunk of the population has long favored seceding from the rest of Canada (see History, below). Today, the French dominate the province. Outside of Montréal English residents are generally few, although parts of the Eastern Townships and the Gaspé and an area around the Ontario border near Hull still have English communities. Most immigrants arrive from

Highlights

Entered Confederation: July 1, 1867
Area: 1,540,687 sq km
Population: 7,333,283
Provincial Capital: Québec City

- Throw yourself into Montréal's multicultural mix and try a smoked meat sandwich.

- Wander the cobblestoned streets of Québec City.

- Thunder down some prime ski slopes, like Mont Tremblant.

- See where the Appalachians plunge into the sea at Forillon National Park.

- Gawk at the red cliffs of Québec's island paradise, the Îles de la Madeleine.

- Bike or ski one of North America's longest trails, the P'Tit Train du Nord.

- Do some whale-watching off the North Shore.

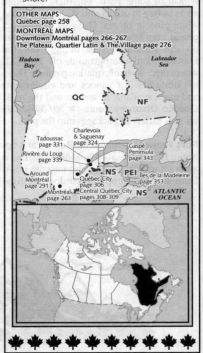

OTHER MAPS
Québec page 258
MONTRÉAL MAPS
Downtown Montréal pages 266-267
The Plateau, Quartier Latin & The Village page 276

Hudson Bay

Labrador Sea

QC

NF

Tadoussac page 331
Charlevoix & Saguenay page 324
Gaspé Peninsula page 343
Rivière du Loup page 339
Around Montréal page 291
Québec City page 306
NS
PEI
Îles de la Madeleine page 353
Montréal page 263
Central Québec City pages 308-309
NS
ATLANTIC OCEAN

French-speaking countries such as Haiti and Vietnam but line up with the anglophone group politically.

Québec's economy is made up of its pharmaceutical, aerospace, forestry, agricultural, hydroelectric, metallurgy, tourism, information technology and multimedia industries. Mining brings in $3.6 billion annually, agriculture $1.7 billion. The province's hydroelectric output is 14.4% of the global production.

Visitors should note that the farther east or north you travel the cooler the weather becomes. Even in midsummer an evening sweater may be required. By September temperatures drop noticeably everywhere but in the southeast.

For information about Hull, Chelsea, Wakefield and Gatineau Park, see the Ontario chapter.

History

At the time of European exploration, the region along the St Lawrence River from Ontario to Québec City was controlled by the Mohawks of the Iroquois Confederacy. North of and around Québec City, the Montagnais settled. Farther north lived the Crees, and beyond that the Labrador Eskimo, Naskapi and Inuit peoples. (The Montagnais and Naskapi are also known as Innu.) Around the southern portion of the Gaspé Peninsula, the Micmac (known as Mi'kmaq in the Maritime Provinces), found throughout Atlantic Canada, were the principal aboriginal group. They still live in the region, although their numbers are small. For more information on the Native Indians, see First Nations, later in this chapter.

French explorer Jacques Cartier landed in Québec City (then called Stadacona) and Montréal (then called Hochelaga) in 1534. Samuel de Champlain, also of France, first heard and recorded the word 'kebec' when he founded a settlement at Québec City some 70 years later, in 1608.

Through the rest of that century, the French and English skirmished over control of Canada, but by 1759 the English, with a final battle victory on the Plains of Abraham at Québec, established themselves as the winners in the Canadian colony sweepstakes. From this point on, French political influence in the New World waned.

When thousands of British Loyalists fled the American Revolution in the 1770s, the new colony divided into Upper (today Ontario) and Lower (Québec) Canada; almost all the French settlers congregated in the latter region. The inevitable struggles for power and status between the two language groups continued through the 1800s, with Lower Canada joining the Canadian confederation as Québec in 1867.

The early and middle portions of the 20th century saw Québec change from a rural, agricultural society to an urban, industrialized one whose educational and cultural base, however, still relied upon the Catholic Church, which wielded immense power. (About 90% of the population is Roman Catholic, though the Church's influence has declined sharply since the 1960s.) Under the control of Premier Duplessis in the 1940s and '50s, Québec became archly conservative.

The tumultuous 1960s brought the so-called Quiet Revolution, during which all aspects of French society were scrutinized and overhauled. Under the leadership of

Barely holding it together: Canada stays attached to Québec

Liberal premier Jean Lesage, a number of changes occurred. The provincial government instituted a mixed-sex (ie, coeducational) and free education system for everyone under 16, developed a system of social services (eg, government-funded medical care and pension benefits), gave more clout to unions, nationalized hydroelectric companies and celebrated the province's culture. Plus, intellectuals and extremists alike debated the idea of independence from Canada, as Québécois began to assert their sense of nationhood.

In 1960 the body Rassemblement pour l'Indépendance National (Assembly for National Independence) was founded, and in 1968 the Parti Québécois formed. From

1963 to 1970, the Front de la Libération du Québec (FLQ) committed a series of terrorist acts against symbols of English Canadian dominance, bombing mailboxes and other targets. When French president Charles de Gaulle visited Montréal in 1969 and made his infamous cry of *'Vive le Québec libre!'* ('Long live a free Québec!'), the Québécois crowd greeted him with wild cheers.

Things got very tense during the October Crisis of 1970, when members of an FLQ cell kidnapped British diplomat James Cross in Montréal, issuing their manifesto and a list of demands. Provincial cabinet minister Pierre Laporte was kidnapped by another FLQ cell five days later. Prime Minister Pierre Trudeau resorted to invoking the War Measures Act and sending military troops to Montréal to keep the peace. Laporte was murdered, Cross eventually sent free, and the army left in January 1971, but the political landscape had changed forever.

In 1976, the Parti Québécois came to power, headed by charismatic René Lévesque, and in 1980 the province held its first referendum on Québec separatism. The 'No' side won with about 60% of the vote. The Liberal party won elections in 1985 and 1989, for a time allaying federalist forces' fear of the country's breakup. However, Premier Bourassa fought for a 'special status' for Québec as a 'distinct society' in a Constitutional amendment in the Meech Lake Accord (1987). He got it.

The accord, however, died in 1990 because of disagreement by other provinces over this and other of its clauses. After that, Lucien Bouchard formed the Bloc Québécois party to further the separatist cause in the federal government.

In 1994 in the provincial government, the Parti Québécois returned to power under Jacques Parizeau and held another referendum in 1995 with a confusingly worded question on sovereignty. This one was a nail-biter, and the 'No' side won by less than 1%, a mere 53,000 votes – less than the number of spoiled ballots. Parizeau made headlines by declaring that they had lost, 'but by what? By money and the ethnic vote.' True, some 60% of francophones voted in favor of separation, while a vast majority of anglophone, Native Indians and immigrants sympathetic to the anglophone cause voted against it. However, Parizeau's ill-advised statement only amplified his opponents' allegations of xenophobia among the Parti Québécois.

By 2002 the issue of separation, while still officially advocated by the Parti Québécois under Bernard Landry, was no longer topical. Landry, not nearly as popular as Lévesque, saw support for his party slip in the wake of accusations of fiscal mishandling and social irresponsibility. While 43% of the population support sovereignty, the notion of an independent Québec is less attractive to a younger generation with more global concerns. Indeed, apprehension over globalization will have a greater effect on the future of the separatist cause than the strategies born from a very distant-seeming Quiet Revolution.

First Nations

Beginning in the late 1960s and increasingly throughout the 1990s, Canada's First Nations (the preferred term to describe all aboriginal groups) have been asserting their presence in the political and social spheres. They make up one of the most fascinating aspects of the Canadian cultural mosaic. A journey through Québec offers plenty of chances to get acquainted with the groups that have shaped the country's destiny more than most people know (for example, the names of six Canadian provinces and countless towns and geographical features come from Native Indian words, including 'Canada' itself!).

Eleven First Nations groups live in Québec. Eight of them belong to the Algonquin cultural and linguistic group and two to the Iroquois (Mohawks and Huron-Wendat), while the Inuit form a distinct group. Together they number 71,500, just under 1% of the total population. This number will skyrocket in the next generations, however, as half of all Native Indians living on reserves are under the age of 25; indeed, one of the striking aspects of these communities is the number of young children.

Innu Dubbed Montagnais ('mountain folk') by European explorers, the Innu have reclaimed their original name in recent years. Of the 14,300 Innu, 70% live in nine communities, mostly along the North Shore. A dynamic group, the Innu helped incoming Europeans set up fur-trading posts in the 17th century and in the 20th century they became one of the first Native Indian groups to assume control of their educational services and to set up outfitters, shopping malls, a museum and an ecotourism infrastructure. Many people around the world know of the Innu through the music of popular singer Kashtin.

QUÉBEC

Three Little Words

Many tourists wonder what the three words written on every license plate in the province, Je me souviens, mean. When they're told, 'I remember,' they usually go silent. As far as license-plate slogans go, it's not as straightforward as 'The Sunshine State,' that's for sure. What makes Québécois so proud of their good memories?

'Je me souviens' was first added to the provincial coat of arms in 1883. Author Eugène Taché, the architect of Québec City's Parliament Building, intended it to prolong the memory of a people and its hardships. Of course, it can be interpreted in various ways, but most agree that the phrase offers a permanent recognition, albeit unstated, of the marginalized status of Québec's French citizens, who have been victimized by colonization policies and denied nationhood.

In 1939, the provincial government officially adopted 'Je me souviens' as its slogan.

Cree In some ways the most visible First Nations group in the province, the Cree number some 13,100 in nine communities along James Bay and in the interior northwest of Lac St Jean. The Cree have achieved prominence through political activism, which began when the Québec government first approached the community in the 1970s to broach the subject of building the massive James Bay hydroelectric complex on traditional Cree hunting territory.

The community mobilized to defend its rights and in 1975 signed the historic James Bay and Northern Québec Agreement, which gave the Cree $135 million and exclusive use of, and hunting rights to, northern lands. More formidably, in the early 1990s, the Cree successfully blocked another Hydro Québec mega project on Rivière Grande Baleine (Great Whale River) in a brilliant campaign that brought Cree representatives to Ottawa and New York City.

Mohawk Another high-profile group, the Mohawks number about 11,000 in three communities in southwestern Québec: Kahnawake, just across the Mercier bridge from Montréal; Kanesatake, 53km west of Montréal at Oka; and Akwesane, straddling the Québec, Ontario and New York borders. Being so close to urban centers, many Mohawk have integrated to some degree with Québécois society.

In 1990, the Mohawks made headlines around the world when residents of Kanesatake took up armed resistance to fight the building of a golf club on land they considered sacred, near Oka. Residents of Kahnawake also participated in what became one of Canada's biggest land-claim crises; it led to military intervention.

Inuit Now 9200 members strong, the Inuit (which means 'person') survive in the most remote region of the province, Nunavik, in the far north. They live in 14 villages spread hundreds of kilometers apart with no roads to interlink them.

While the fur trade affected their lives beginning in the 18th century, the Inuit's general lack of contact with Europeans meant that they managed to preserve their traditional ways until the mid-20th century, when federal services began to play a dominant role in their everyday lives. They abandoned their traditional hunting weapons only in the last two generations.

In a short time, the Inuit have formed a cooperative that controls the distribution of food and goods in their territory. They also run their own airline and outfitters and have developed a system to promote and distribute their unique arts, crafts and clothing in the south.

National & Provincial Parks

The province oversees more than 40 areas dedicated to nature conservation, and visiting one of these spots can be a highlight of any trip to Québec. Some of the best parks in the province include Parc de la Gaspésie, Forillon National Park, La Mauricie National Park and Gatineau Park (see the Ontario chapter for Gatineau Park).

The provincial parks (Parc du Bic, for example), geared toward ecotourism, are open to the public for a small access fee; for extra fees, they offer recreational activities (usually canoeing, kayaking, rafting, hiking, cycling, camping in the wild) and events like full-moon hikes and campfire nature talks.

The *réserve fauniques* (wildlife reserves) have a mandate to conserve and protect the environment but also to make these spaces available to the public. The reserves are mostly known to hunters and fishers, who can practice their sport there with the appropriate license and permits, but more and more tourists are discovering them as less crowded alternatives to the provincial parks. The reserves offer the same gamut of activities as provincial parks but provide fewer services (information centers, canteens, guided tours). Both parks and reserves tend to be very well run, with clearly marked trails and clean facilities.

Both provincial parks and wildlife reserves are operated by the Société des Établissements de Plein Air du Québec (Sépaq; ☎ 418-890-6527, 800-665-6527, W www.sepaq.com).

Federally administered parks (Forillon National Park, for example) are run by Parks Canada (☎ 418-368-5505, 800-463-6769, W www.parkscanada.gc.ca). National parks often feature excellent educationally oriented events run by highly knowledgeable staff, plus a full range of outdoor activities.

Information

Québec has one of the best-organized tourism infrastructures in the country. Every large city and town as well as most small towns and villages have at least one tourist information office. Thick guide booklets are published every year for each region and are chock-full of information. The head office is in downtown Montréal. See Information in the Montréal section.

Be aware, though, that Québec's tourist offices – and the government tourist guides and websites – will only dispense information about those organizations that pay an annual membership fee to a provincial tourism association. Independent exploration will yield more surprises than you can find at the tourist offices.

The provincial sales tax is 6.5%.

Québec is on Eastern Time except for the far northeastern corner south of Labrador and the Îles de la Madeleine, which are on Atlantic Time.

For emergency service in Montréal and Laval, dial ☎ 911. Elsewhere call the operator on ☎ 0.

Activities

The Tourisme Québec offices can provide general information booklets on parks, historic sites, outdoor activities and adventure tour operators.

Cycling & Mountain Biking Cycling in Québec has exploded in popularity over the last 10 years. Today, the province is basking in its growing reputation as one of the best places for cycling in North America. Each year, the Tour de l'Île in Montréal attracts some 35,000 cyclists for a 64km long circuit.

Across the province, the Route Verte (Green Trail) is an ongoing system of bike trails on and off major roads that may become the world's longest bike trail when its 2400km are complete. Many sections are finished and are enjoyed by thousands each year; the main parts should be completed by 2004. The route takes in some of the loveliest sections of the Eastern Townships, the Laurentians and Charlevoix regions, among others.

There's some wicked mountain biking at Bromont (see the Eastern Townships section) and Mont Ste Anne (see North Shore under Around Québec City). Beginners can content themselves with Grey Rocks near Mont Tremblant.

Vélo Québec at the Maison des Cyclistes (☎ 514-521-8356, ⚐ www.velo.qc.ca, 1251 Rue Rachel Est), in Montréal, is the province's best place for those planning to make cycling a part of their trip. The organization rents bikes (from $25/day) and organizes events and guided excursions.

All bus companies will transport your bicycles, usually for a $15 surcharge. They must, however, be packed into a box or bag. At Pares, inside Montréal's main bus station, bike boxes are sold for $5. Limocar (☎ 450-435-6767), which serves destinations in the Laurentians between Montréal and Mont Laurier, does not require boxed bikes and transports them for free.

Canoeing & Kayaking If you head out on Québec's vast network of navigable waterways, you're virtually guaranteed some beautiful memories. Every national and provincial park and wildlife reserve offers canoe and kayak rental for about $20 to $30; if you plan on making this a main activity, you may save money by buying one. Many of the circuits are popular with canoe-campers and weekend nature-seekers, but others take you deep into wilderness and may necessitate portage from lake to lake.

Sea kayaking is increasingly popular along the North Shore of the far eastern St Lawrence River area, especially around the lovely Mingan archipelago.

In Montréal the Fédération Québécoise du Canot et du Kayak (☎ 514-252-3001, ⚐ www.canot-kayak.qc.ca, 4545 Ave Pierre de Coubertin) can provide tons of useful information and lists of organized group excursions, as well as French guides to canoeing in Québec.

Skiing & Snowboarding In winter, Québec is one of North America's prime ski meccas, with excellent slopes in the Laurentians north of Montréal and Québec City and also south of Montréal, close to the US border, at Mont Orford and Sutton (see the Eastern Townships section). Tourisme Québec publishes a *Ski Québec* guide and a *Winter Getaway* booklet, which list various hotel/ski packages.

The province boasts some 150 downhill ski hills, many small but some among the

QUÉBEC

continent's best. Mont Tremblant is Canada's second-busiest ski hill, after British Columbia's Whistler. Many resorts have lit runs for nighttime skiing. Equipment rental is always an option. Day tickets usually cost $25 to $50.

Snowboarding is wildly popular as well, and boards can be rented at nearly all downhill ski stations. One of the most popular places for snowboarding is at Mont Ste Anne, outside Québec City. The Snow Surfing World Cup takes place there each December.

Cross-country skiing is top-rate across the province. You'll find excellent trails at Gatineau Park (see the Ontario chapter) and along the Parc Linéaire du P'tit Train du Nord trail in the Laurentians. Trails usually charge an access fee, typically no more than $10.

Whale-Watching Although the highest concentration of whales has traditionally been found at the confluence of the Saguenay and St Lawrence Rivers, blue whales are more likely to be seen between Les Escoumins and Ste Anne de Portneuf. Belugas get as far west as St Siméon, and other whales travel all along the North Shore to the Mingan archipelago. Along the Gaspé Peninsula you also stand a good chance of spying whales, particularly off Forillon National Park. Tours that depart from Lower St Lawrence towns like Trois Pistoles all cross the river to the north side.

Whitewater Rafting Whitewater rafting is popular along the Rivière Jacques Cartier near Québec and the Rivière Rouge near Montréal. For information, contact these two organizations in Calumet: New World River Expeditions (☎ 819-242-7438, 100 Chemin Rivière Rouge) and Eau Vivre (☎ 819-242-6084, 120 Chemin Rivière Rouge).

Montréal

pop 3.4 million
Some cities take a bit of getting used to – you need time to know and appreciate them – but not Montréal. This city has an atmosphere all its own. It's a friendly, romantic place where couples kiss on the street and strangers talk to each other – an interesting and lively blend of things English and

French, flavored by the Canadian setting. More than three million people live in Greater Montréal – it's the second largest city in Canada after Toronto – and about 10% of all Canadians and 40% of Québec's population call this area home. Two-thirds of the population is French, but the downtown core seems surprisingly English.

To the visitor, it is the mix of old with new and the joie de vivre that are most alluring. French culture prevails, giving the atmosphere a European tinge, especially for visiting Americans, who often dub the city 'Paris without the jet lag' (although anyone who's been to Paris will scoff at that!). But Montréal is also a modern North American city, with great nightlife and 4000 restaurants.

Montréal exudes a warm, relaxed yet exciting ambience, as befits a city with confidence in its own worth. It's gained a reputation for fashion savoir-faire, but this is not limited to the moneyed – a certain flair (sometimes in the form of 'attitude') seems to come naturally to everyone.

History
Montréal makes up a prominent and colorful chapter in the history of Canada. Before the French hit the scene, the Algonquin, Huron and Iroquois shared the area, not always peacefully. Jacques Cartier first visited in 1535 and found Hochelaga, an Iroquois village at the foot of the mountain. The first permanent European settlement didn't begin until 1642, when sieur de Maisonneuve set up a religious mission named Ville Marie. The French named the mountain Mont Royal, which led to the city's present name. It soon became a fur-trading center. The Native Indians weren't too thrilled with these developments, and attacks on the European newcomers became a regular occurrence until just after 1700, when a treaty was signed. The fur trade boomed and Montréal served as an exploration base.

After a series of battles, the British took control of Québec City from the French in 1759. The French moved their capital upstream to Montréal, but that didn't last long. The British captured that, too, in 1760, and English settlers followed.

Soon the rebelling American colonies were after the city. In 1775, General Montgomery took Montréal without firing a shot. The American rebels retained control only

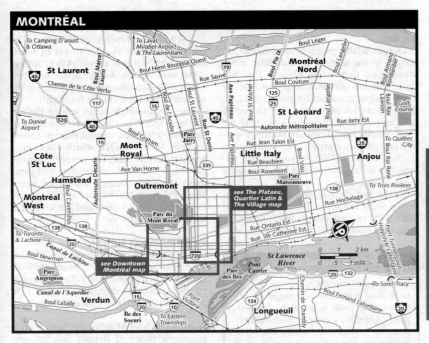

until the British beat back another group trying to take Québec City, which prompted the revolutionaries to flee Montréal.

In the mid-1800s, Montréal became the capital of the United Provinces of Canada. The late 1800s saw a big boom, with the shipping and rail lines bringing prosperity. By 1900, Montréal had turned into the commercial and cultural center of Canada. In the early part of the 20th century, it attracted a huge influx of Jewish Europeans – even today Montréal has the largest Jewish population in Canada.

From the 1920s to the '40s, Montréal gained a reputation as Sin City, due partially to Prohibition in the USA. Brothels, gambling houses and gangsters thrived; politicians and law-enforcers generally turned a blind eye. All this changed with the arrival of Jean Drapeau, who was elected mayor in 1954 and, except for a five-year period in the early '60s, remained mayor right into the mid-'80s. He cleaned up the city, encouraged redevelopment and staged the World's Fair and the Olympics. Though critics dubbed him 'Emperor,' claiming he was megalomaniacal, Drapeau remained

popular and helped to develop Montréal's international reputation.

In 1958, the city embarked on a huge redevelopment program, which included construction of a new subway system and the underground city (see the boxed text). The two tallest skyscrapers in Montréal, the 49-story Royal Bank of Canada Building and the 47-story Place Victoria, were built in the 1960s. (And the city's skyline won't get much taller, either: city law forbids new buildings from being taller than Mont Royal, which is 233m high).

As Old Montréal lost its function as a business center, the focus of downtown moved slightly north to around the Ville Marie shopping complex and Squares Dorchester and Victoria. Also in the 1960s, Montréal saw itself supplanted as Canada's economic capital by Toronto, which had been growing at a faster pace for decades.

New expressways were laid out and the Métro built in time to serve visitors to the 1967 World's Fair, which attracted over 50 million people during what's still considered Montréal's finest hour. In 1976, Montréal hosted the Summer Olympics, for which it built a grand new sports stadium whose troubled construction history continues to this day.

Despite all this progress, an economic recession in the early and mid-1990s made Montréal a depressing place – Rue Ste Catherine was plastered with 'For Sale' or 'Closed' signs; construction ground to a halt; the housing vacancy rate rose to nearly 10%; and spirits were sinking along with the employment rate. Tensions between supporters of separatism and federalism reached a peak in 1995, when a second referendum on separation was barely won by the federalist camp.

In the last decade, the gloom has reversed itself full force. By 2001, Montréal had a 0.7% vacancy rate, a lower unemployment rate than Toronto's, North America's highest percentage of college students (outstripping Boston) and over $1 billion of construction projects underway. The economy, despite another threat of recession in late 2001, was robust (4% growth in 2000), with multimedia, aerospace, telecommunications, biopharmaceutical and information technologies in the forefront.

The city routinely ranks among the top 20 places to live on the planet, according to the United Nations' annual Human Development Index (HDI), which takes into account factors such as literacy, environmental pollution, life expectancy and earnings. In 2000, *Details* magazine rated Montréal as the best city in the world to live in. Things haven't looked and felt so good in the city since Expo '67.

Population & People

With almost 3.4 million residents, Greater Montréal accounts for about 46% of Québec's total population. (The city proper numbers just over one million.) About 77% of Greater Montréal's residents were born in Canada.

About 60% of Montréalers have French ancestors; those of British descent now make up only 5% – less than half of what the figure was in the 1960s. Italians account for almost 7% of the total population. Other significant groups, from largest to smallest, are Jews, Greeks, Haitians, Chinese and Portuguese. More than one-quarter of Montréalers are descended from more than one group.

Though it no longer can boast its long-held title 'world's largest French-speaking metropolis outside Paris' (that has now passed to Kinshasa, capital of Zaire), Montréal is one of the most functionally bilingual cities in the world.

Orientation

The city sits on an island roughly 40km long and 15km wide where the Ottawa River flows into the St Lawrence River. Bridges connect all sides with the mainland; this reinforces the impression of really not being on an island at all. Despite the size of the city and the size of the island, it's easy to orient yourself and to get around Montréal.

In the middle of the island stands Mont Royal, a 233m-high extinct volcano. The core of the city, which is actually quite small,

---

The Underground City

When excited tourists ask residents questions about their famous underground city, the response tends to be, 'Huh? Oh yeah, that…' Essentially a string of office buildings, shopping centers, food courts and Métro stations extending about 3km north-south along 29km of corridors, the complex does provide a good alternative for pedestrians on cold winter days. And that's exactly how the locals look at it; they don't think of it as anything special.

Between the Monit Conference Center (1000 Rue Sherbrooke Ouest), opposite McGill University, and the Intercontinental Hotel (990 Rue St Antoine Ouest), near Old Montréal, you'll pass through shopping centers like Cours Mont Royal (which used to be the luxurious Mount Royal Hotel, gutted in 1988), Place Montréal Trust (with one of North America's highest water fountains), the 47-story Place Ville Marie (which opened in 1962) and Place Bonaventure (the continent's second-largest indoor trade mart, with an exhibition hall the size of four football fields).

A detailed map can be obtained at the tourist information center. You can also take a fun walking tour of part of the underground city with one of the original architects of the Métro system. Call Visite Jean Dumontier (☎ 514-388-8623) for schedules.

is at the base of the mountain, in the south-central section of the island.

Boulevard St Laurent, also known as 'The Main,' divides the city's eastern and western halves. East of Boulevard St Laurent, streets are given the Est (East) designation; west of St Laurent they include the Ouest (West) designation in their name.

The **downtown** area – a busy district of skyscrapers, shops, restaurants, offices and luxury hotels – is bounded by Rue Sherbrooke to the north, Ave Atwater to the west, Rue St Antoine to the south and Boulevard St Laurent to the east.

The small park Square Dorchester (formerly Dominion Square and often still called that) marks the center of downtown. The tourist office lies on the north side, along with the horse-drawn carriages, known here as *calèches,* which can be taken around parts of town or up the mountain. On the southwest corner you'll find the Windsor Station/Bell Centre complex, the hockey (and concert) arena built around the venerable old Canadian Pacific Railway terminal.

The wide Boulevard René Lévesque, known for its tall towers, runs past Square Dorchester. North, a block up Rue Peel from the square, is Rue Ste Catherine, the principal east-west artery, which is one-way eastbound. North of Rue Ste Catherine is Boulevard de Maisonneuve and then Rue Sherbrooke, the two other main east-west streets.

Running north and south off Rue Ste Catherine west of Rue Peel are Rue de la Montagne, Rue Crescent and Rue Bishop – together, they comprise a restaurant/nightlife district.

Walking uphill on Rue Peel for a number of blocks, you'll come to Ave des Pins, across which is the edge of Parc du Mont Royal. At the top of the staircase, the lookout provides excellent views of the city, the river and the surroundings to the south.

West of here, on Rue Sherbrooke, the city gives way to English residential areas, including the wealthy **Westmount**, at the foot of the mountain.

Old Montréal lies southeast of the downtown area; both Boulevard St Laurent and Rue St Denis lead into the historic heart of the city.

Just north of Old Montréal, you'll find a small but determined **Chinatown** clustered along Rue de la Gauchetière between Rue St Urbain and Boulevard St Laurent.

North of Chinatown on Boulevard St Laurent lies the engaging Plateau Mont Royal district. Known simply as **the Plateau**, it attracts the young and/or hip. Farther north along Boulevard St Laurent, between Ave Laurier and Rue Bernard, the **Mile End** district contrasts tradition with chic.

East of Boulevard St Laurent, the area remains predominantly French. About seven blocks east, Rue St Denis has become the center of a Paris-style café district sometimes called the **Quartier Latin** (Latin Quarter).

From Rue St Denis east along Rue Ste Catherine to Rue Papineau is Montréal's gay neighborhood, known as **the Village**.

Two blocks east of St Denis is Rue Berri. Station Centrale de l'Autobus, the city's main bus station, is on the corner of Rue Berri and Boulevard de Maisonneuve. A major transfer point in the Métro system, the Berri-UQAM station is also here; city buses roll in all directions from this subway stop.

For a great glimpse of Montréalers busy at life, take a stroll anywhere from lower Rue St Denis, north through the Plateau and up to Mile End. Saturday is the most lively day. For more information on the Latin Quarter, the Plateau, the Village and Mile End, see the Neighborhoods section, later.

Street Names Montréal is a bilingual, rather than French-speaking, city. Many squares, parks and other sites are known by their French names, but many of the streets were named by the British who dominated the city throughout its formative years. However, this book gives the Montréal street names in French. It may seem a little strange to read 'Rue McTavish' instead of 'McTavish St,' but this has been done for the sake of consistency.

Information
Tourist Offices Montréal and the Québec province maintain one central phone number for tourist information offices (☎ 514-873-2015, 877-266-5687, W www.bonjourquebec.com).

At the city's main tourist information office, Centre Infotouriste (1001 Rue Square Dorchester), near the corner of Rue Peel and Rue Ste Catherine, the friendly staff will supply you with information on all areas of Montréal and Québec, arrange guided tours and car rentals and

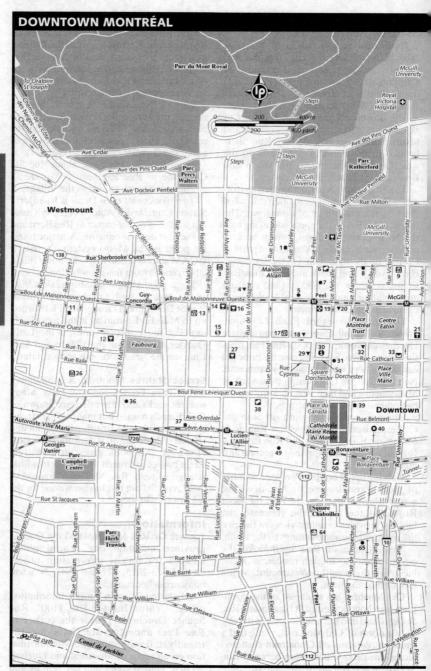

DOWNTOWN MONTRÉAL

DOWNTOWN MONTRÉAL

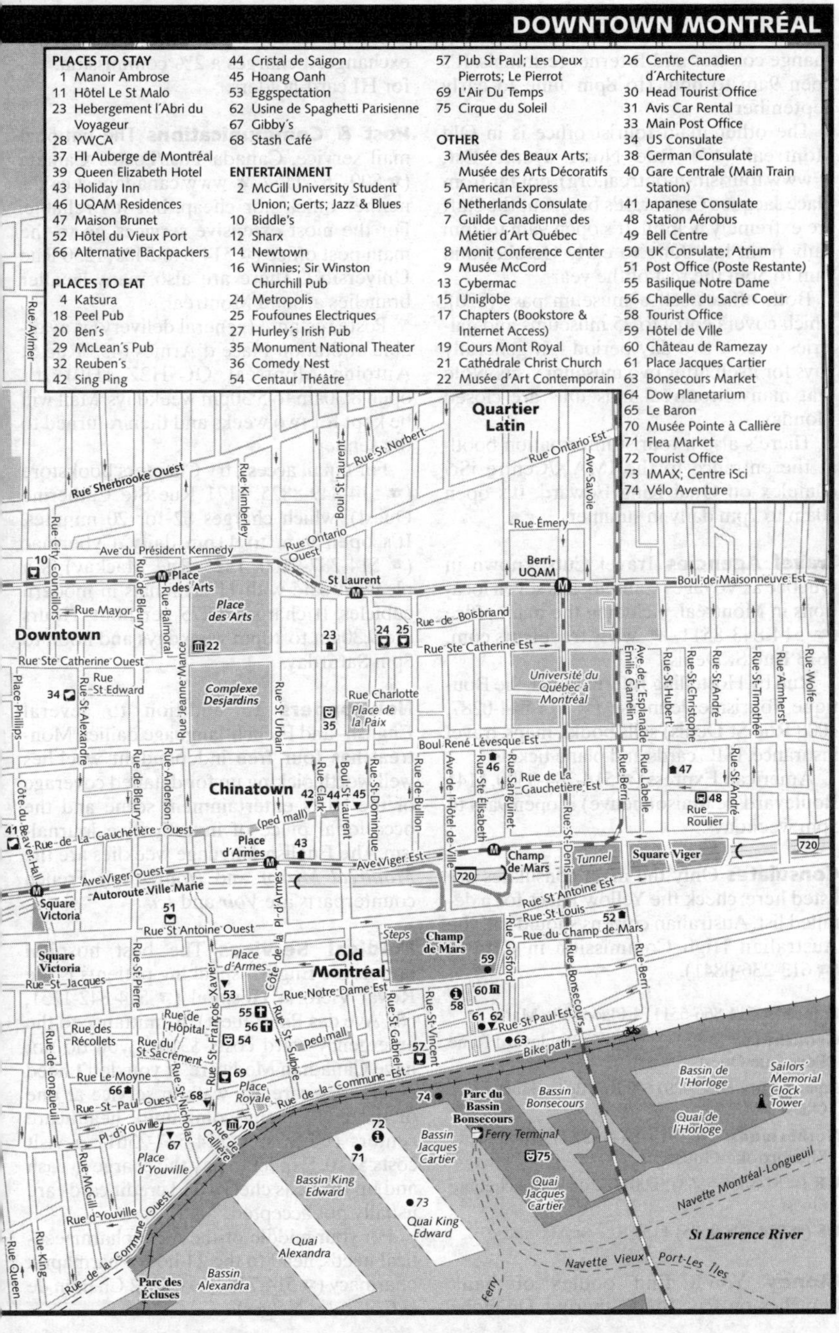

PLACES TO STAY
1 Manoir Ambrose
11 Hôtel Le St Malo
23 Hebergement l´Abri du Voyageur
28 YWCA
37 HI Auberge de Montréal
39 Queen Elizabeth Hotel
43 Holiday Inn
46 UQAM Residences
47 Maison Brunet
52 Hôtel du Vieux Port
66 Alternative Backpackers
PLACES TO EAT
4 Katsura
18 Peel Pub
20 Ben´s
29 McLean´s Pub
32 Reuben´s
42 Sing Ping
44 Cristal de Saigon
45 Hoang Oanh
53 Eggspectation
62 Usine de Spaghetti Parisienne
67 Gibby´s
68 Stash Café
ENTERTAINMENT
2 McGill University Student Union; Gerts; Jazz & Blues
10 Biddle´s
12 Sharx
14 Newtown
16 Winnies; Sir Winston Churchill Pub
24 Metropolis
25 Foufounes Electriques
27 Hurley´s Irish Pub
35 Monument National Theater
36 Comedy Nest
54 Centaur Théâtre
57 Pub St Paul; Les Deux Pierrots; Le Pierrot
69 L´Air Du Temps
75 Cirque du Soleil
OTHER
3 Musée des Beaux Arts; Musée des Arts Décoratifs
5 American Express
6 Netherlands Consulate
7 Guilde Canadienne des Métier d´Art Québec
8 Monit Conference Center
9 Musée McCord
13 Cybermac
15 Uniglobe
17 Chapters (Bookstore & Internet Access)
19 Cours Mont Royal
21 Cathédrale Christ Church
22 Musée d´Art Contemporain
26 Centre Canadien d´Architecture
30 Head Tourist Office
31 Avis Car Rental
33 Main Post Office
34 US Consulate
38 German Consulate
40 Gare Centrale (Main Train Station)
41 Japanese Consulate
48 Station Aérobus
49 Bell Centre
50 UK Consulate; Atrium
51 Post Office (Poste Restante)
55 Basilique Notre Dame
56 Chapelle du Sacré Coeur
58 Tourist Office
59 Hôtel de Ville
60 Château de Ramezay
61 Place Jacques Cartier
63 Bonsecours Market
64 Dow Planetarium
65 Le Baron
70 Musée Pointe à Callière
71 Flea Market
72 Tourist Office
73 IMAX; Centre iSci
74 Vélo Aventure
Quartier Latin
Rue Sherbrooke Ouest
Rue St Norbert
Rue Ontario Est
Ave Savoie
Rue Émery
Ave du Président Kennedy
Rue Ontario Ouest
Boul St Laurent
Rue Kimberley
Rue Aylmer
Rue City Councillors
Place des Arts
St Laurent
Berri-UQAM
Boul de Maisonneuve Est
Rue Mayor
Rue de Bleury
Rue Balmoral
Downtown
Rue-de-Boisbriand
Rue Ste Catherine Est
Rue Ste Catherine Ouest
Rue St Edward
Place Phillips
Rue Ste Alexandre
Rue Jeanne Mance
Complexe Desjardins
Rue St Urbain
Rue Charlotte
Place de la Paix
Université du Québec à Montréal
Ave de l'Esplanade
Emilie Gamelin
Rue St Hubert
Rue St Christophe
Rue St André
Rue St Timothée
Rue Amherst
Rue Wolfe
Boul René Lévesque Est
Rue Anderson
Côte du Beaver Hall
Chinatown
Rue Clark
Rue St Dominique
Rue de Bullion
Ave de l'Hôtel de Ville
Rue Ste Elisabeth
Rue Sanguinet
Rue de La Gauchetière Est
Rue Berri
Rue Labelle
Rue Roulier
Rue de La Gauchetière Ouest
(ped mall)
Place d'Armes
Ave Viger Est
Champ de Mars
Rue St Denis
Tunnel
Square Viger
Ave Viger Ouest
Autoroute Ville Marie
Square Victoria
Rue St Antoine Est
Rue St Louis
Rue du Champ de Mars
Rue St Antoine Ouest
Côte de la Pl d'Armes
Steps
Old Montréal
Rue Gosford
Rue Bonsecours
Rue St Pierre
Rue St Jacques
Rue St François Xavier
Rue Notre Dame Est
Rue St Gabriel
Rue St Vincent
Rue de l'Hôpital
Rue St Sulpice
Rue St Paul Est
Rue des Récollets
Rue du St Sacrément
ped mall
Bike path
Rue de Longueuil
Rue Le Moyne
Rue St Nicholas
Place Royale
Rue de la Commune Est
Rue St Paul Ouest
Parc du Bassin Bonsecours
Bassin Bonsecours
Bassin de l'Horloge
Sailors' Memorial Clock Tower
Quai de l'Horloge
Pl d'Youville
Rue de Callière
Ferry Terminal
Bassin Jacques Cartier
Place d'Youville
Rue McGill
Bassin King Edward
Quai Jacques Cartier
Navette Montréal-Longueuil
Rue d'Youville
Rue de la Commune Ouest
Quai King Edward
St Lawrence River
Rue King
Quai Alexandra
Navette Vieux Port-Les Îles
Rue Queen
Parc des Écluses
Bassin Alexandra
Ferry

QUÉBEC

make hotel reservations free of charge. The center contains a bookstore, currency exchange counter and Internet terminals. It's open 9am to 6pm (to 8pm June to early September).

The other main tourist office is in Old Montréal (174 Rue Notre Dame Est, **W** www.tourism-montreal.org), not far from Place Jacques Cartier. It's busy, but the staff are extremely helpful. It's open 9am to 7pm daily from late June to early October and 9am to 5pm the rest of the year.

Both offices sell a museum pass ($20), which covers entry to 25 museums and galleries over a two-day period – it generally pays for itself after two museum visits. Note that many Montréal museums are closed Monday.

There's also a tourist information booth at the entrance to the IMAX/Centre iSci complex on Quai King Edward. It's open 10am to 7pm daily in summer.

Travel Agencies Travel Cuts, known in Québec as Voyages Campus, has seven locations in Montréal, including the main office (☎ 514-843-8511, **W** www.travelcuts.com, 1613 Rue St Denis).

Run by Hostelling International, the Boutique Tourisme Jeunesse (☎ 514-844-0287, 4008 Rue St Denis) sells books, maps, travel insurance, ISIC cards and plane tickets.

American Express (☎ 514-284-3300, 1141 Boulevard de Maisonneuve) is open 9am to 5pm weekdays.

Consulates Only the main consulates are listed here; check the Yellow Pages for a detailed list. Australian citizens should call the Australian High Commission in Ottawa (☎ 613-236-0841).

France (☎ 514-866-6511) 1 Place Ville Marie

Germany (☎ 514-931-2277) 1250 Boulevard René Lévesque Ouest

Japan (☎ 514-866-3429) 600 Rue de la Gauchetière Ouest

Netherlands (☎ 514-849-4247) 1002 Rue Sherbrooke Ouest

UK (☎ 514-866-5863) 1000 Rue de la Gauchetière Ouest

US (☎ 514-398-9695) 1155 Rue St Alexandre

Money You'll find oodles of bank branches on Rue Ste Catherine. Uniglobe (☎ 514-845-5849, 1385a Rue Ste Catherine Ouest) is another good bet; for currency exchange, it charges a 2% commission, 1% for HI card-holders.

Post & Communications The national mail service, Canada Post/Postes Canada (☎ 800-267-1177, **W** www.canadapost.ca), is neither quick nor cheap, but it's reliable. For the most extensive services, go to the main post office (☎ 514-846-5401, 1250 Rue University). There are also many smaller branches around Montréal.

Poste restante (general delivery) is available at Station Place d'Armes (435 Rue St Antoine, Montréal, QC H2Z 1H0). It's open 8:30am to 5:30pm weekdays. Mail will be kept for two weeks and then returned to the sender.

For email access, try Chapters bookstore (☎ 514-849-8825, 1171 Rue Ste Catherine Ouest), which charges $2 for 20 minutes. It's open 9am to 11pm daily. Cybermac (☎ 514-287-9100, 1425 Rue Mackay) is a pleasant café with 11 terminals in modern cubicles. It charges $5.75 per hour. Hours are 9:30am to 10pm weekdays and noon to 8pm Saturday.

Newspapers In addition to several English- and French-language dailies, Montréal has four free independent weeklies well worth picking up for detailed coverage of the city's entertainment scene and the occasional piece of investigative journalism. The English-language weeklies are the *Montréal Mirror* and *Hour;* their French counterparts are *Voir* and *Ici.*

Medical Services The best hospital option for English-speaking patients is the Royal Victoria Hospital (☎ 514-842-1231, 687 Ave des Pins Ouest). Admittance to the emergency ward costs $310 if you do not have Canadian Medicare. If you don't need emergency care, try walk-in service at one of the city's many community healthcare centers (CLSCs; ☎ 514-527-2361); a visit costs $110. Expect to pay the charge in cash and up front, as checks and credit cards are usually not accepted.

For your middle-of-the-night pharmaceutical needs, head to the 24-hour Pharmaprix pharmacy (☎ 514-738-8464, 5122 Chemin de la Côtes des Neiges).

Old Montréal

The oldest section of the city dates mainly from the 18th century. Once the financial center of Canada, it now offers an attractive contrast to the modern-day downtown core. Vieux Montréal is a must for romantics and architecture lovers, who come to wander the narrow cobblestone streets, meandering past old stone houses and buildings that are now home to intimate restaurants and boutiques. The waterfront is never far away.

The main streets are Rue Notre Dame, which runs past the Basilique Notre Dame, and Rue St Paul. The Old Montréal tourist office is at the top of Place Jacques Cartier. Ask for the 36-page *Old Montréal Walking Tour* booklet (in English or French, $6), which points out noteworthy spots.

Place Jacques Cartier This square, now the area's focal point, fills up with visitors, vendors, horse-drawn carriages and musicians in summer. The plaza was laid out after 1803, the year a château on the site burned down and a public market was set up in its place. At its north end stands the Colonne Nelson (Nelson's Column), a monument erected by the British to the general who defeated the French and Spanish fleet at Trafalgar (it's actually a fiberglass replica).

One little oddity is the statue of an obscure French admiral, Jean Vauquelin, north of the square across Rue Notre Dame; it was put there later by the French as an answer to the Nelson statue.

Hôtel de Ville The Hôtel de Ville (☎ 514-872-1111, 275 Rue Notre Dame Est; free admission; open 8:30am-4:30pm Mon-Fri), Montréal's City Hall, towers over Place Jacques Cartier to the east. It was here, in 1969, that French leader Charles de Gaulle cried *'Vive le Québec libre!'* ('Long live a free Québec!') to the masses from the balcony, fueling the fires of the Québec separatist movement (and straining relations with Canada for years).

The design is pure Second Empire from 1878, though the building dates from much more recent times; after a fire destroyed the structure in 1922, it was remodeled after the city hall in Tours, France. There are occasional exhibits in the main corridor.

Château de Ramezay Opposite the Hôtel de Ville is the Château de Ramezay (☎ 514-861-3708, 280 Rue Notre Dame Est; adult/student $6/4; open 10am-6pm daily June-Aug, 10am-4:30pm Tues-Sun Sept-May), where Benjamin Franklin stayed during the American Revolution while fruitlessly attempting to convince the Canadians to join the cause.

The building is now a museum with a collection of 20,000 objects – paintings, engravings, costumes, photos, tools and other miscellany from Québec's early history.

Bonsecours Market Designed by architect William Footner and opened in 1847, this imposing old market (☎ 514-872-7730, 350 Rue St Paul Est; open 10am-6pm daily) was the main market hall until the 1960s, when local supermarkets effectively drove it out of business. Since 1992, it has served as a hall for exhibitions and shops selling arts and crafts, leather goods and designer clothing.

Place d'Armes & Basilique Notre Dame The other major square in the area is Place d'Armes, which features a monument to the city's founder – Paul de Chomedey, sieur de Maisonneuve – in the middle. On the south side of the square stands the famous Basilique Notre Dame (☎ 514-842-2925, 110 Rue Notre Dame Ouest; admission free; open 8:30am-5:30pm Mon-Sat, 1:30pm-5pm Sun; Sun mass 8am, 9:30am, 11am & 12:30pm).

Montréal's standout attraction, built in 1823, can hold 5000 people in a magnificently rich interior marked by an explosion of wood carvings and gilt stars painted in the ceiling vaults. The altar is backlit in weird and wonderful colors. The massive Casavant organ, with 5772 pipes, is used for concerts throughout the year, particularly during Christmastime. A new, religious multimedia sound and light show (*adult/child & senior $10/7; 6:30pm & 8:30pm Tues-Sat*) re-creates the history of the sacred building.

In the back, there's the small **Chapelle du Sacré Coeur** (Sacred Heart Chapel), which was added in 1888. It's also called the Wedding Chapel because of the countless nuptials held here – there's a waiting list of up to two years.

The Musée de la Basilique inside the basilica is closed indefinitely.

Place Royale In the west end of Old Montréal is the square where Ville Marie, Montréal's first small fort town, was built in 1642, at a time when the fighting with the Iroquois Confederacy was lengthy and fierce. During the 17th and 18th centuries, it served as a marketplace; it's now the forecourt of the Veille Douane (Old Customs House).

Opposite the square, the **Pointe à Callière Museum of Archaeology & History** (☎ 514-872-9150, 350 Place Royale; adult/student $9.50/5.50; open 10am-5pm Tues-Fri, 11am-5pm Sat & Sun) provides an excellent archeological and historical study of the beginnings of Montréal.

For the most part, the museum is underground, in the ruins of buildings and an ancient sewage/river system. Montréal's first European cemetery is here, established just a few years after the settlement itself.

Vieux Port The Old Port waterfront, part of a redevelopment district, is still evolving as construction and ideas blossom. Currently, it covers 2.5km of riverfront and centers around four *quais*, or piers. The **Promenade du Vieux Port**, a recreational path, runs along the river from Rue Berri west to Rue McGill. Cruise boats, ferries, jet boats and speedboats all depart for tours of the river from the various docks.

A summer tourist information booth (☎ 514-496-7678) stands at the entrance to **Quai King Edward** – pretty much in the center of things, at the foot of Boulevard St Laurent. This pier is also home to the **IMAX cinema** (☎ 514-496-4629; adult/student $10/9; open 10:15am-7:15pm daily) and the latest addition, the sparkling **Centre iSci** (☎ 514-496-4724; adult/student $10/9; open 10am-6pm Sun-Thur, 10am-9pm Fri & Sat), a science and entertainment center. Something of a cross between a workshop and a video arcade, the iSci features interactive games (eg, a 'fight' with a computer virus), a high-tech 'life lab' and lots of educational screen-based displays. Combined tickets with the IMAX are available. Check out the huge **flea market** (marché aux puces) here as well; it's open every day.

At the **Quai Alexandra** is a huge port and container terminal. Also here is the Iberville Passenger Terminal, the dock for cruise ships that ply the St Lawrence River as far as the Îles de la Madeleine. Nearby you'll find the **Parc des Écluses** (literally, Park of Locks), the site of open-air exhibitions; a bicycle path leads southwest along the pretty Canal de Lachine.

The **Quai Jacques Cartier** features restaurants, an open-air stage and a handicraft center. The Cirque du Soleil, Montréal's phenomenally skilled troupe of acrobats, performs here on occasion. Trolley tours of the port area depart from here, as does a ferry headed for Parc des Îles, particularly popular with cyclists (bikes can be taken on the ferry).

At Cité du Havre, a narrow promontory between Old Montréal and Île Ste Hélène, lies the city's most recognizable residential complex, **Habitat 67**. Designed by Moshe Safdie for the World's Fair as an experiment in residential modernism, this futuristic apartment block feels dated now, but the modular design (concrete blocks stuck together helter-skelter) was a bold, bizarre feat by any standards. The units sold for $50,000 each in 1967; they're now valued anywhere between $225,000 and $700,000.

Just east of Quai Jacques Cartier is the **Parc du Bassin Bonsecours**, a grassy expanse enclosed by a waterway crisscrossed with footbridges. In the summer, you can rent the cute paddleboats (equipped with a mock steamboat funnel) by the half hour for $4; in winter, the park draws ice-skaters.

At the northeastern edge of the historic port on the Quai de l'Horloge stands the striking white **Sailors' Memorial Clock Tower** (☎ 514-496-7678), now used as an observation tower and open to the public. The Tour d'Horloge also features a history exhibit.

Downtown

The city's modern downtown includes some of the city's best-known buildings, such as the 19th-century Cathedral Marie Reine du Monde and, at the other end of the spectrum, the Place Ville Marie, a contemporary shopping complex. Square Dorchester marks the center of downtown. A block north of the square lies the city's main shopping area, on Rue Ste Catherine. The Eaton Centre, a modern showpiece of a mall, is almost an attraction in its own right.

Running north off Rue Ste Catherine, Ave McGill College, once a narrow student ghetto, presents an imposing boulevard edged with some of the city's newest corporate and retail architecture. Structures aside, the channel of space leading from the city's main street to the campus of McGill University and beyond to the mountain and its landmark cross is certainly impressive. A substantial number of statues and sculptures, including the eye-catching *Illuminated Crowd,* line the avenue

If you head east along Rue Ste Catherine, you'll see Square Phillips, a meeting place where guitarists busk and bask. Farther east, just past Rue de Bleury, is Place des Arts, a complex for the performing arts. A few more blocks east lies Boulevard St Laurent (St Lawrence Blvd), the eastern border of downtown. One of the city's best-known streets, it boasts an interesting ethnic mix and lots of restaurants.

Musée des Beaux Arts The Museum of Fine Arts ('beaux arts' is pronounced **bose**-ar) is the city's main art gallery (☎ 514-285-2000, 1379 Rue Sherbrooke Ouest; temporary exhibits: adult/student $12/6, half-price 5:30pm-9pm Wed; permanent collection: admission free; open 11am-6pm Tues & Thur-Sun, 11am-9pm Wed).

The museum is split into two sections: the modern Jean Noël Desmarais Pavilion, on the south side of the street, and the Renata and Michael Ornstein Pavilion, on the north side. Also on the north side is the **Musée des Arts Décoratifs**, which features decorative art displays and handicrafts from the 20th century.

Both north and south sides offer a mix of exhibits from the permanent collection and temporary shows, but most visitors flock to see the more famous works by European and American artists in the Desmarais Pavilion, including paintings by Rembrandt, Picasso and Matisse and sculptures by Henry Moore, Alberto Giacometti and Alexander Calder. In the north wing, the older building (1912) (which used to constitute the entire museum) focuses on Inuit and other First Nations art.

There are guided tours in English 2:30pm and 5:30pm on Wednesday.

Musée d'Art Contemporain Located in the Place des Arts complex, the Museum of Contemporary Art (☎ 514-847-6226, 185 Rue Ste Catherine Ouest; adult/student/child $6/3/free, admission free 6pm-9pm Wed; open 11am-6pm Tues & Thur-Sun, 11am-9pm Wed) boasts more than 6000 works in its permanent collection. It's the country's only major gallery that focuses on contemporary art, and nearly two-thirds of the displays are dedicated to Québécois artists, such as Paul Émile Borduas. Other featured artists include Picasso, Max Ernst, Andy Warhol and Piet Mondrian. The temporary shows are often outstanding.

There's a free English-language tour at 6:30pm Wednesday and at 1pm and 3pm on weekends.

Centre Canadien d'Architecture You'll find both a museum and working organization promoting architecture, its history and its future in the impressive modern complex that houses the Canadian Centre for Architecture (☎ 514-939-7000, 1920 Rue Baile; adult/student $6/3, students free Thur, everyone free 5:30pm-8pm Thur; open 11am-6pm Tues-Wed & Fri-Sun, 11am-9pm Thur).

It may sound dry, but most people find at least some of the displays of interest; exhibits from years past have touched on the history of lawn care, among other offbeat topics. Part of the building has been created around **Shaughnessy House**, a wealthy businessman's residence built in 1874 (get a good view of the gray limestone annex from Boulevard René Lévesque out back). Highlights in this section include the solarium and a wonderfully ornate room with intricate woodwork and a fireplace.

Don't miss the **sculpture garden** on the south side of Boulevard René Lévesque. More than a dozen sculptures of varying styles and sizes – particularly impressive when lit up at night – are scattered about a terrace overlooking parts of south Montréal.

Musée McCord The city's main history museum, the McCord Museum of Canadian History (☎ 514-398-7100, 690 Rue Sherbrooke Ouest; adult/student/child $8.50/5/2, admission free 10am-noon Sat; open 10am-6pm Tues-Fri, 10am-5pm Sat & Sun) deals mostly with eastern Canada's early European settlement from 1700 onward. One room in the modest-size museum exhibits the history of Québec's indigenous people – one of the best of its kind in the province;

another displays highlights of the museum's collection, including Canadian costumes, textiles, decorative and folk art.

A highlight of the huge **photograph collection** is the work of William Notman, who, with his sons, photographed Canadian people, places and activities from 1850 to 1930.

The museum hosts children's workshops at 2pm Sunday.

Cathédrale Marie Reine du Monde The

Cathedral of Mary, Queen of the World (☎ 514-866-1661, *Boulevard René Lévsque Ouest at Rue de la Cathédrale; admission free; open 7am-7:30pm Mon-Fri, 8am-7:30pm Sat & Sun*) is a smaller but still magnificent version of St Peter's Basilica in Rome (scaled down to one-quarter size). Built between 1870 and 1894, this landmark provided another symbol of Catholic power in what was the heart of Protestant Montréal.

Inside, the neobaroque altar canopy is the main attraction, fashioned of copper and gold leaf and with fantastic swirled roof supports. This, too, is a replica of Gian Lorenzo Bernini's masterpiece in St Peter's. The overall impression is far more elegant than that of the more famous Basilique Notre Dame.

Cathédrale Christ Church Next to La

Baie department store, the Christ Church Cathedral (☎ 514-843-6577, *1444 Ave Union*) provides a much-needed dash of Victorian style (and a green lawn) on busy Rue Ste Catherine Ouest. Built from 1857 to 1859, the church was modeled on the Protestant cathedral in Salisbury, England – architect Frank Will's hometown. The stained-glass windows by William Morris' workshops add cheery relief to the otherwise sober interior.

McGill University McGill University

(☎ 514-398-4455, *845 Rue Sherbrooke Ouest*) is one of Canada's most prestigious learning institutions, with over 15,000 students. James McGill, a rich Scottish fur trader, founded the school in 1858, and in the last century and a half, it's earned a fine reputation, especially for its medical and engineering programs. Many campus buildings are showcases of Victorian architecture. The campus makes a picturesque place to stroll around or to stop for a midday picnic.

Dow Planetarium The Dow Planetarium

(☎ 514-872-4530, **w** *www.planetarium .montreal.qc.ca, 1000 Rue St Jacques; adult/ student/child/child under 6 $6/4.50/3/free*) offers 50-minute programs on the stars, space and solar system via a celestial projector in a 20m-high dome. English shows happen at 2:30pm Tuesday to Sunday and 7:15pm Thursday to Sunday.

Parc du Mont Royal The pride and joy

of Montréal is the Parc du Mont Royal (☎ 514-872-6559, **w** *www.lemontroyal.qc.ca*), known as 'the mountain.' On top of it, the **Chalet du Mont Royal** has become the city's most popular lookout point. About a kilometer northeast of the lookout stands Montréal's famous steel **Cross of Montréal**, erected in 1924 on the very same spot as the one set up in 1643 by city founder Paul de Chomedey, sieur de Maisonneuve. It's lit up at night and visible from all over the city.

Occasionally, big bands play on the huge balcony at the Chalet du Mont Royal in summer, bringing back memories of the 1930s. Meanwhile, every Sunday from early afternoon to late evening a scene more reminiscent of the 1960s unfolds around the **Georges Étienne Cartier monument** on Ave du Parc, one of the park's main entrances. Dubbed 'Tam-Tam Sundays,' these weekly events bring together several hundred people of the type grandma might not approve of and their tam-tams (bongo-like drums) for several hours of tribal playing and spontaneous dancing. It's become an institution. If the noise doesn't show you the way there, flare your nostrils and wait for the wafts of funny cigarette smoke to lead you to it.

The parking lot to the north at the **Observatoire de l'Est** serves as another major lookout. Also known as the Belvédere Camillien Houde, it's a popular spot for amorous couples (the parking lot fills up on summer nights) and students on grad night. You can walk between the two lookouts via the park trail in about half an hour.

To reach the park from downtown, enter via the staircase at the top of Rue Peel or behind the Georges Étienne Cartier monument on Ave du Parc. If you're in a car, there are paid parking lots off Boulevard Côte des Neiges. You can also take bus No 80 or 129 from the Place des Arts Métro stop to the Georges Étienne Cartier monument or bus No 11 from the Mont Royal Métro stop; the latter will drop you off near the Observatoire de l'Est.

Oratoire St Joseph The gigantic St Joseph's Oratory (☎ 514-733-8211, 3800 Chemin Queen Mary; admission free; open 6am-9pm daily), completed in 1960 and based on a 1916 church, honors St Joseph, Canada's patron saint, and also pays tribute to Brother André, a monk said to have healing powers; his heart is on view. The size of the Renaissance-style building is a marvel in itself. The oratory commands wonderful views on the northern slope of Mont Royal (the highest point in the city, at 263m).

Inside, there's a small **museum** (admission free; open 10am-5pm daily) dedicated to Brother André, who was beatified in 1982. From the Côtes des Neiges Métro, take bus No 16 to the oratory or walk.

Olympic Village
In the 1970s, the Olympics brought a host of attractions to the area that lies east of central Montréal, accessible from Rue Sherbrooke.

Olympic Park Ask any Montréaler and you'll find that scandal, indignation and tales of corruption envelop the buildings of Olympic Park in Parc Maisonneuve, in eastern Montréal. Still, the complex (☎ 514-252-8687, 4141 Ave Pierre de Coubertin; ⓜ Viau; adult/student $5.50/4.50), built for more than $1 billion for the 1976 Olympic Games, is magnificent.

The showpiece is the multipurpose **Stade Olympique** (Olympic Stadium). With a seating capacity of 80,000, it's often referred to as the 'Big O' – or, more recently, 'The Big Owe.' Finally completed in 1990, the complex has required a laughable litany of repairs (only a year later, a 55-ton concrete beam collapsed during a football game; in 1999, a section of the snow-covered roof caved in on top of an auto show). In theory, the 65-ton roof can be lifted via the tower cables, but you won't see it in action: High winds have torn holes in the roofing fabric, and the system, still undergoing repair, is plagued by mechanical problems. The stadium still manages to host baseball games (the Montréal Expos play here), concerts and trade shows.

A cable car runs up the tower of the **Olympic Stadium Funicular** (☎ 514-252-8687, 3200 Rue Viau; adult/student/child $10/7.50/5, with tour $12/8/8; open 10am-5pm daily). The world's tallest inclined structure (190m), the Montréal Tower, overhangs the stadium. Up top, the glassed-in observation deck affords outstanding views of the city and beyond for a distance of 80km.

The **Tourist Hall**, at the cable-car boarding station, is a three-story information center with a ticket office, restaurant and souvenir shop.

Swimmers should check out the **Centre Sportif**, an impressive complex with six pools, diving towers and a 20m-deep scuba pool. For more information, see the Activities section.

If you're seeing several attractions at Olympic Park, a combination ticket is the best value (adult/senior & student/child $15.75/11.75/8).

Guides offer a worthwhile English-language tour at 12:40pm and 3:40pm daily – if you join the tour, you'll appreciate having taken the time. It covers the Biodôme, Jardin Botanique, Insectarium and the Montréal Tower.

Biodôme Housed in the former Velodrome cycling stadium in the Olympic complex, the Biodôme (☎ 514-868-3000, 4777 Ave Pierre de Coubertin; adult/student/child $10/7.50/5; open 9am-5pm daily) re-creates four ecosystems and houses approximately 4000 animals and 5000 plants. Under one roof, you can amble through a rain forest, polar regions, the Laurentian Shield woodlands and the ocean environment of the Gulf of St Lawrence. Though some sections shine (the rain forest, for example), other sections are decidedly underwhelming.

A free shuttle runs between the Biodôme and the Jardin Botanique.

Jardin Botanique & Insectarium Though each of these attractions has its own entrance, they are both located on the same huge territory; one admission price is good for both.

Opened in 1931, the 81-hectare Jardin Botanique (☎ 514-872-1400, 4101 Rue Sherbrooke Est; adult/senior & student/child

QUÉBEC

$10/7.50/5; open 9am-5pm daily winter, 9am-7pm daily rest of the year) is now the world's third-largest botanical garden after those in London and Berlin. Some 21,000 types of plants are grown in 30 outdoor gardens and 10 climate-controlled greenhouses (where cacti, banana trees and 700 species of orchid thrive). The landscaped **Japanese Garden**, with its traditional pavilions, tearoom and art gallery, draws crowds; the grouping of bonsai is the largest outside Asia.

Whether you love or hate creepy crawlies, the collection of bugs from around the world at the **Insectarium** (*☎ 514-872-1400, 4551 Rue Sherbrooke Est),* located inside the Botanical Gardens, will intrigue you. Some popular ones include the tarantulas and scorpions, but don't miss the dazzling outdoor Butterfly House, which includes some of Québec's native species. Once a year, sometimes in spring, sometimes fall, biologists don chef hats for a popular Insect Tasting festival of gourmet bugs. Some 25,000 people come to munch on cooked locusts, ants and worms of varying degrees of plumpness!

Parc Jean Drapeau

One of Québec's biggest attractions, this park (*☎ 514-872-4537; admission free)* lies south of the city in the St Lawrence River. It consists of Île Ste Hélène and Île Notre Dame, the sites of the immensely successful

1967 World's Fair. You'll find an information kiosk near the park's only Métro stop.

If you're driving to the islands, one bridge, the Pont Jacques Cartier, leads to Île Ste Hélène, and another, the Pont de la Concorde, to Île Notre Dame. Consider taking the Métro to the Jean Drapeau stop instead. From the Métro stop, buses run to attractions on both islands – but walking is almost as fast.

Another option is the Water Shuttle (*☎ 514-281-8000),* across the river from the Vieux Port at Quai Jacques Cartier. The shuttle ($3.50 one-way) takes pedestrians and bikes on the 15-minute trip. The first crossing from Quai Jacques Cartier is at 10:35am, with more departures on the hour; the last return trip from Île Ste Hélène leaves at 7:10pm daily (11:10pm Fri-Sun June-Aug.)

Alternately, you could bike all the way from Old Montréal on the bike path for free, via Pont de la Concorde.

Île Ste Hélène At the northern end of this island you'll find the largest amusement park in the province, **La Ronde** (*☎ 514-872-4537; full/limited admission $29/15.75; open 10am-9pm Sat & Sun May, 10am-9pm daily June-early Sept).* The assortment of bone-shaking rides includes *le monster,* an impressive roller coaster. For the less adventurous, the gentle minirail offers good views of the river and city. A variety of concerts and shows are held throughout the summer.

Near La Ronde stands an old fort where the British garrison was stationed in the 19th century. Inside the remaining stone ramparts, uniformed soldiers in period dress give demonstrations at the **Musée Stewart** (*☎ 514-861-6701; adult/student, senior & child/child under 7 $6/4/free; open 10am-6pm daily mid-May–early Sept, 10am-5pm Wed-Sun early Sept–mid-May).*

Walkways meander around the island, past gardens and among the old pavilions from the World's Fair. One of them, the American pavilion (in the spherical Buckminster Fuller Dome) has become the **Biosphère** (*☎ 514-283-5000, 160 Chemin Tour de l'Île; adult/senior & student/child $8.50/6.50/5; open 10am-5pm Wed-Mon).* Using a range of exhibits and so-so interactive displays, this center explains the Great Lakes-St Lawrence River ecosystem, which

At the Insectarium: not your everyday meal

makes up 20% of the globe's water reserves. There's a great view of the river from the upstairs Visions Hall.

Île Notre Dame Created from 15 million tons of earth and rock excavated when the Métro was built, this artificial island is laced with canals and pretty garden walkways. Things really light up here during the wildly popular Le Mondial international fireworks competition (**W** www.lemondialsaq.com) in July and August.

The rest of the year, the main draw is the huge, spaceship-like **Casino de Montréal** (☎ 514-392-2746; admission free; open 24 hrs), the former French pavilion from the World's Fair. Opened in 1993, the casino drew so many people (and earned so much money) that expansion occurred almost instantly. Bridges link the pavilion to an attractive garden called the **Jardin des Floralies**, a wonderful place to stroll.

Five thousand people can fit on the nearby artificial beach, the **Plage du Parc Jean Drapeau** (☎ 514-872-6093; adult/child $7.50/3.75, discounts after 4pm; open 10am-7pm daily June 24-late Aug, weather permitting). The water is filtered and treated with chemicals, but many residents remain squeamish about splashing about there. That the beach is often cramped to capacity doesn't help. Take bus No 167 from the Jean Drapeau Métro.

Île Notre Dame is also home to the **Pavilion des Activitées Nautique** (Water Sports Pavilion; ☎ 514-392-9761; admission free; open 9am-9pm daily), based around the former Olympic rowing basin adjacent to the beach. Events held here include the Dragonboat rowing races in late July. You can rent sailboards and paddleboats; in winter, the area becomes a huge skating rink. There's also some cross-country skiing; equipment can be rented. The annual Formula 1 Grand Prix race takes place every June at the **Circuit Gilles Villeneuve**, the racetrack named after the Québec racecar driver. The rest of the year, the track is popular with inline skaters.

Neighborhoods

Quartier Latin Rue St Denis between Boulevard de Maisonneuve and Rue Sherbrooke is the center of a café, bistro and bar district with lots of open-air places and music spots. Though originally an all-student area, the neighborhood has added some more expensive establishments to the mix, but the number of young people continues to make the nights especially lively. Snoop around in the side streets, too, where little bars can be discovered. You might want to stay in some of the good small hotels in the area.

Going south along Rue St Denis will lead you into Old Montréal.

The Plateau Away from tourist haunts, the Plateau area is a multiethnic district full of inexpensive housing, outdoor cafés, restaurants, discos, bars and interesting, funky shops. The 19th-century homes with ornate wooden or wrought-iron balconies, pointy Victorian roofs and exterior staircases make for a charming atmosphere – wander around and see what you discover.

The loosely defined area runs from Rue Sherbrooke north to about Boulevard St Joseph. Rue St Denis and Ave du Parc mark the east and west edges. Known by many as The Main, the always interesting Boulevard St Laurent is the principal commercial strip of the district. Running north-south, it divides the city into east and west (historically French and English, respectively) and has long reflected various nationalities. Both St Denis and St Laurent pass through a mix of French, English, Portuguese and other communities with abundant bookstores, clothing stores, coffee shops and restaurants.

The area around and along Rue Prince Arthur is good for strolling and eating, as is the section farther north, on and around Ave Duluth.

If you're looking for offbeat apparel, you'll find numerous vintage and secondhand clothing shops on Ave du Mont Royal, in the 10 blocks west of the Mont Royal Métro station.

Mile End Upper Rue St Laurent leads into this unusual neighborhood bounded by Ave Laurier to the south, Rue Bernard to the north, Ave du Parc to the east and Boulevard St Laurent itself to the west. French and Greek residents and traditional Hassidic Jews make for an interesting cultural mix.

Many upper-class French, a growing segment of Montréal's population, live in the Outremont neighborhood just to the

THE PLATEAU, QUARTIER LATIN & THE VILLAGE

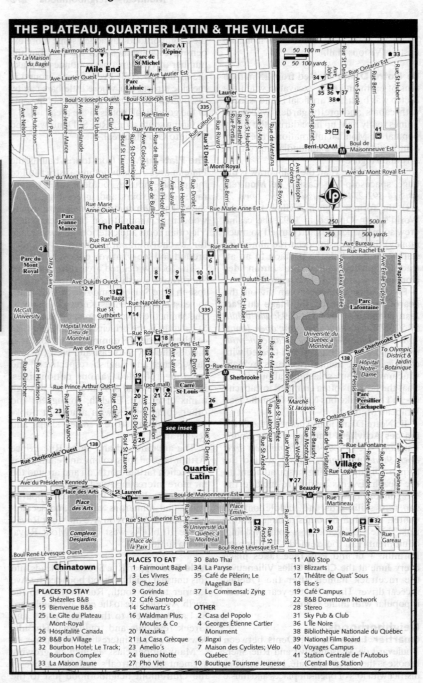

PLACES TO STAY
5 Shézelles B&B
15 Bienvenue B&B
25 Le Gîte du Plateau
   Mont-Royal
26 Hospitalité Canada
29 B&B du Village
32 Bourbon Hotel; Le Track;
   Bourbon Complex
33 La Maison Jaune

PLACES TO EAT
1 Fairmount Bagel
3 Les Vivres
8 Chez José
9 Govinda
12 Café Santropol
14 Schwartz's
16 Waldman Plus;
   Moules & Co
20 Mazurka
21 La Casa Grècque
23 Amelio's
24 Bueno Notte
27 Pho Viet

30 Bato Thai
34 La Paryse
35 Café de Pèlerin; Le
   Magellan Bar
37 Le Commensal; Zyng

OTHER
2 Casa del Popolo
4 Georges Étienne Cartier
   Monument
6 Jingxi
7 Maison des Cyclistes; Vélo
   Québec
10 Boutique Tourisme Jeunesse

11 Allô Stop
13 Blizzarts
17 Théâtre de Quat' Sous
19 Café Campus
22 B&B Downtown Network
28 Stereo
31 Sky Pub & Club
36 L'Île Noire
38 Bibliothèque Nationale du Québec
39 National Film Board
40 Voyages Campus
41 Station Centrale de l'Autobus
   (Central Bus Station)

east of Parc du Mont Royal. A smattering of pricey boutiques and restaurants dot a portion of Ave Laurier. Farther north, Rue Bernard has some noteworthy restaurants, bars and cafés. Ave du Parc is the center of the Greek community.

Little Italy Still farther north, Boulevard St Laurent leads into this slowly upgrading traditional Italian area. From the southern edge at Rue St Zotique, several restaurants and cafés line Boulevard St Laurent for a couple of blocks northward. Rue Jean Talon marks the northern boundary; Boulevard St Denis, the east; and Rue Clark, the west.

Bustling Jean Talon Market has become a Montréal favorite – it's really a cool place to be on Saturday, sipping cappuccino.

The Village The city's gay community has revitalized Rue Ste Catherine Est between Rue St Hubert and Ave Papineau. New restaurants and stores, plus bars and night-clubs that cater to gays and lesbians, continue to open in this once neglected part of town, which runs from Boulevard René Lévesque north to Rue Sherbrooke. The area around Rue Amherst and Boulevard de Maison-neuve features an increasing array of antique and specialty shops worth a browse.

Recently, some popular mixed and straight clubs have entered into the area, and the comfortable confluence of people from all walks of life and of all sexualities adds some complexity to the surroundings. The area still retains, however, a bit of a run-down feel.

Suburbs

Lachine The suburb of Lachine, which sur-rounds the Canal de Lachine, is worth a visit for its history, architecture and general ambience. Not touristy, it reveals a little of Montréal's roots and culture. The side streets behind the impressive College Ste Anne nunnery and City Hall, both along Boulevard St Joseph, make for good wandering.

Built between 1821 and 1825, the **Canal de Lachine**, southwest of Montréal, allowed boats to circumvent the Lachine Rapids of the St Lawrence River. It closed in 1970, but the area has been transformed into a 14km-long park that's terrific for cycling and walking. The city of Montréal is also building

a marina along the canal near downtown, at the bottom of Rue Peel, which will reopen the canal to pleasure boats. Each summer, sections of the canal become living art spaces with exhibitions and outdoor sculptures.

The **Fur Trade & Lachine Canal National Historic Site** (☎ 514-637-7433, 1255 Boule-vard St Joseph; adult/student $2.50/1.50; open 1pm-6pm Mon, 10am-6pm Tues-Sun April-early Sept, 9:30am-5pm Wed-Sun early Sept-Nov), in an old stone house on the wa-terfront, tells the story of the fur trade in Canada. Trading was done right here because the rapids made further river navi-gation impossible.

Outside, a small interpretation center (open 1pm-6pm Mon, 10am-6pm Tues-Sun April-early Sept) explores the canal's history. Guided tours are conducted along the canal – you should call ahead to confirm. For more information about the Lachine Canal, call the administrative offices at ☎ 514-283-6054.

A nearby shop on the canalfront, **Claude Brière** (☎ 514-639-7466, 833 Boulevard St Joseph; open 9am-6pm daily) rents out canoes ($12/hour) and paddleboats ($8/hour).

The Lachine waterfront is accessible from Old Montréal via the cycling route beside the canal. You can also take the Métro to Angrignon and then the No 195 bus to 12th Ave. To get to Lachine by car, take Hwy 20 east from downtown and exit at 32nd Ave.

Cosmodrôme Multimedia exhibits focus on the solar system, satellite communica-tions and space travel at the Cosmodôme Space Science Centre (☎ 450-978-3600, 2150 Autoroute des Laurentides; adult/student/child $9.75/6.50/7.50; open 10am-6pm Tues-Sun) in Laval, north of the island of Mon-tréal. At this interactive museum of space and new technologies, you'll find lots of models of rockets, space shuttles and planets. The multimedia show 'Reach for the Stars' simulates space travel with cool special effects on a 360-degree screen.

The center is about a 20-minute drive from downtown Montréal on Hwy 15 north. By public transportation, take bus No 60 or 61 from Henri Bourassa Métro.

Parc des Îles de Boucherville A green oasis at Montréal's doorstep, this Sepaq-run park (☎ 450-928-5088; admission $3.50; open

8am-7pm daily mid-May–early Sept, 9am-5pm daily Apr–mid-May & early Sept-early Oct) makes a great respite from downtown (which, only 10km away, is visible from some spots), especially for canoe-lovers. Five interconnected islands feature 22km of hiking and cycling trails, plus a pleasant canoe circuit. Day rentals of bikes/canoes/kayaks cost $21/29/35.

By car, take Hwy 20 exit 1. A ferry departs from Quai Jacques Cartier in the Vieux Port hourly in the summer (☎ 514-281-8000 for more information).

Activities

Boating One of the most beautiful spots for boating, canoeing and kayaking is the **Parc Mille Îles** (☎ 450-622-1020, W *www.parc-mille-iles.qc.ca, 345 Boulevard Ste Rose; adult/child $3/1; open 9am-6pm daily)* in Laval, north of Montréal. Located on the Rivière des Mille Îles, the park includes 10 islands where you can disembark on self-guided water tours. About 10km of the river (including calm inner channels) are open for paddling. You can rent canoes and kayaks ($28/day) or rowboats ($35/day). In wintertime, sports types come here for cross-country skiing and skating.

Take the Métro to Henri Bourassa and transfer to the STL bus No 72, which takes you to the park entrance. By car, take Hwy 15 north to exit 16, Boulevard Ste Rose – the park is four blocks east.

Cycling With about 350km of bike paths, Montréal has been voted the best city in North America for cyclists by several magazines. You can buy cycling maps at bookstores, but also ask at tourist offices for freebies. One very fine 14km route leads southwest from the edge of Old Montréal all the way to Lachine along the old canal, with a lot of history en route. Picnic tables are scattered along the way, so pack a lunch. Another route covers the Vieux Port area, and yet another the Parc Jean Drapeau. All three are connected.

The lighthearted, good-time Tour de l'Île, on the first Sunday in June, is a major event that attracts about 45,000 cyclists. A week earlier, some 10,000 children participate in the Tour des Enfants.

For all things bike, your first stop should be at Vélo Québec's **La Maison des Cyclistes** (☎ 514-521-8356, W *www.velo.qc.ca, 1251 Rue Rachel Est).* Not only can you rent bikes there (from $25/day), you can also pick up invaluable tips on planning your trip anywhere in the province.

Vélo Aventure (☎ 514-847-0666), at the Vieux Port, charges $7/22 per hour/day for bicycles ($8/25 on weekends). Children's trailers and inline skates are also available. A major bike path runs right near the shop and goes for miles.

Ice Skating & Inline Skating You can do year-round indoor ice skating at the gigantic **Atrium** (☎ 514-395-0555, 1000 Rue de la *Gauchetière Ouest; adult/senior & child $5/3; skate rental $4; open 11:30am-6pm Tues-Fri & Sun, 10am-10pm Sat).* There are various children's and adult sessions.

The **Patinoir du Bassin Bonsecours** (☎ 514-496-7678; admission $2, skate rental *$6; open 10am-7pm daily),* inside the Parc du Bassin Bonsecours at the Vieux Port, is one of Montréal's most popular outdoor skating rinks in winter.

The **Lac aux Castors** (☎ 514-872-6559, *Parc du Mont Royal; admission free; skate rental $6)* is another excellent place for skating in winter – it's nestled in the woods near the large parking lot and pavilion.

Swimming The best place to do laps is at Olympic Park's **Centre Sportif** (☎ 514-252-4622, 4141 Ave Pierre de Coubertin; adult/ *student $3.79/3.23; open 6:30am-10pm Mon-Fri, 9am-4pm Sat & Sun),* which has six indoor pools, wading and diving pools and a waterslide.

Organized Tours

Walking For worthwhile walking tours of Old Montréal, contact **Guidatour** (☎ 514-844-4021; adult/student $12/10), whose strolls depart at 11am and 1:30pm daily from late June through September. **Old Montréal Ghost Trail** (☎ 514-868-0303; adult/student $12/10) offers evening tours focused on crimes and ghosts; they're led by guides in period costume (read: hard-up local actors).

Bus & Boat The old standby of tour companies, **Gray Line** (☎ 514-934-1222), at the tourist office on Square Dorchester, operates 11 sightseeing jaunts, including the 1½-hour basic city-orientation tour (adult/

child $18.50/10). The six-hour deluxe bus trip (adult/child $45/25), a better value, includes admission to the Biodôme and Jardin Botanique. Yet another trip goes to the Laurentian Mountains north of Montréal ($69/47). Buses depart from Square Dorchester.

The **Amphi Tour** (☎ *514-849-5181*) offers a surprise: fitted with a backboard propeller, this bus tours the Old Port area for half an hour and then drives into the river to cruise the port area for another half hour. The tour (adult/child $18/15) departs from Quai King Edward daily from May to October. Reservations are essential.

A couple of companies offer bouncing, soaking jet-boat trips through the nearby Lachine Rapids. **Lachine Rapids Tours** (☎ *514-284-9607*) leads 90-minute trips (adult/child 13-18/child 6-12 $49/39/29) leaving from Old Montréal. **Rafting Hydro-jet** (☎ 514-767-2230) will take you on rubber-raft trips through the rapids for $34.

AML Cruises (☎ *514-842-3871*) also runs river tours from the Quai de l'Horloge, at the foot of Rue Berri in Old Montréal.

Calèche These picturesque horse-drawn carriages meander around Old Montréal and Mont Royal; at $35/60 per half hour/hour, this kind of ride isn't the most cost-effective way to get around, but it can be scenic. Calèches line up, among other places, at the Vieux Port and at Place d'Armes. In winter, sleighs are used for trips up and around Mont Royal; they charge similar rates. Drivers usually provide running commentary, which can serve as a pretty good historical tour.

Special Events

Montréal is known as the 'City of Festivals.' Nary a week goes by without some type of festival, cultural or artistic, and many are well organized and a lot of fun.

January

Fête des Neiges From the end of January to the beginning of February, two weekends of fun and games celebrate the ubiquitous snow at the Parc des Îles.

June

Grand Prix Player's du Canada The Circuit Gilles Villeneuve (☎ 514-350-4731, ⓦ www.grand prix.ca), a Formula 1 circuit, brings thousands of

tourists to Île Notre Dame for this early June event, rare in North America. Tickets are virtually impossible to get unless you purchase them well ahead of time.

L'International Benson & Hedges This international fireworks competition takes place twice a week from mid- to late June and features splendid displays from around the world. It's held at La Ronde but is visible from many places around the Jacques Cartier bridge.

International Jazz Festival At the end of the month, this festival (☎ 514-871-1881, 888-515-0515, ⓦ www.montrealjazzfest.com) and its rival, L'Off Festival de Jazz (ⓦ www.loff festivaldejazz.com), make the city explode in jazz and blues.

July

Just for Laughs Comedy Festival For nearly two weeks in mid-July, just about everyone in town gets giddy at this festival (☎ 514-845-3155, ⓦ www.hahaha.com), which draws top, middle and bottom acts from around the world. Most performances are in English.

Les Francopholies de Montréal More than 200 music concerts pay tribute to French-language artists at this late-July festival (☎ 514-876-8989), which often features excellent bands and singers in fun-filled shows.

August

Festival des Films du Monde The city's biggest, though far from only, film festival (☎ 514-848-3883, ⓦ www.ffm-montreal.org) had its heyday in the 1970s and '80s, before big bad Toronto started a bigger one. Hundreds of great films screen over 10 days, beginning in late August.

September

Marathon de Montréal This mid-month race is all embracing, with contestants ranging from the very young to those in wheelchairs.

Places to Stay

Booking Agencies If you arrive in town without reservations, the Centre Info-touriste (☎ 514-873-2015, 877-266-5687) will do bookings for free. For discounted reservations throughout Québec and discount train fares within Canada, contact Hospitalité Canada (☎ 514-287-9049, 800-665-1528, ⓦ www.hospitality-canada.com, 405 Rue Sherbrooke Est).

B&B Downtown Network (☎ 514-289-9749, 800-267-5180, 3458 Ave Laval) deals with over 50 private homes. Singles/doubles start at $40/50.

Camping *Camping D'Aoust* (☎ *450-458-7301, 3844 Route Harwood*) Tent sites $22.

Open mid-May–mid-Oct. Nearly an hour's drive west of Montréal, this bucolic site lies on Route 342 in Hudson. Hiking is good around the site, which includes a small farm. Take exit 26 coming from Montréal or exit 22 coming from Ottawa on Hwy 40; then it's 3km down the road on the right.

Hostels & University Residences HI

Auberge de Montréal (☎ 514-843-3317, fax 514-934-3251, W www.hostellingmontreal .com, 1030 Rue Mackay) Dorm beds $21/25 members/nonmembers, private doubles $52/64. Check-in 9:30am-2am. This large, central and well-organized hostel south of Boulevard René Lévesque features air-conditioned dorm rooms with four to 10 beds in each. Amenities include breakfast in the summer and Internet access. The hostel organizes activities and offers free daily shuttle service to the Mont Tremblant hostel (see Mont Tremblant in The Laurentians section, later).

Alternative Backpackers (☎ 514-282-8069, W www.auberge-alternative.qc.ca, 358 Rue St Pierre) Dorm beds peak season/off-season $18/16, doubles $50. Located in a quiet street about a 10-minute walk from the Old Port, this hostel contains 48 beds spread over two very colorful, unusually laid-out floors in a converted commercial space.

Le Gîte du Plateau Mont-Royal (☎ 514-284-1276, W www.hostelmontreal.com, 185 Rue Sherbrooke Est) Dorm beds $23, private rooms $45-55. A hostel with a B&B feel, this place is very clean and close to the downtown core; it offers some self-contained units with cooking facilities.

YWCA (☎ 514-866-9941, fax 514-861-1603, W www.ydesfemmesmtl.org, 1355 Boulevard René Lévesque Ouest) Doubles $69 June-Sept, $62 Oct-May. Montréal's YMCA no longer provides accommodations, yet the YWCA allows both men and women in the residences (only women have access to the gym, though). There's a kitchen on every floor. Groups of at least five can bring their sleeping bags and stay for $10 per person in dorm facilities. Dorm rooms, not air-conditioned, have four beds.

McGill University Residence Halls (☎ 514-398-8299, e reserve@residences .lan.mcgill.ca, 3935 Rue University) Singles $33/40 student/nonstudent. Staying in student housing gives you access to both cafeterias and laundry rooms. For an extra fee, you can buy entry to McGill's superb gym. The residences, in a wooded area, are a steep walk uphill.

UQAM Residences (☎ 514-987-6669, 303 Boulevard René Lévesque) Singles/doubles $35/45, studio apartments $50. Readers have raved about these modern, bright rooms.

B&Bs

Bienvenue B&B (☎ 514-844-5897, 800-227-5897, W www.bienvenuebb.com, 3950 Ave Laval) Singles & doubles without bath $65/75, singles/doubles with bath $75/85. This B&B near Carré St Louis features 12 nicely furnished rooms in a lovely stone Victorian house with wrought-iron balconies.

Shézelles B&B (☎ 514-849-8694, fax 514-528-8290, W www.bbcanada.com/ 2469.html, 4272 Rue Berri) Studio $120, doubles without/with bath $70/90. Paneled walls and a large fireplace make this place a bastion of warmth and hospitality. The 'love nest' studio apartment is superb, sumptuously furnished and occupying the entire ground floor. Upstairs are two rooms, one of which has a Japanese sliding door and a skylight directly over the bed.

La Maison Jaune (☎ 514-524-8851, fax 514-521-7352, W www.maisonjaune.com, 2017 Rue St Hubert) Singles/doubles without bath $45/65. This B&B offers five rooms appointed in different colors in a pretty yellow Victorian-era building. The quietest room has a balcony overlooking the garden.

B&B du Village (☎ 514-522-4771, 1279 Rue Montcalm) Doubles $70-90, self-contained apartments $130. This pleasant, gay-friendly place features an enclosed courtyard and balconies. There's even a resident masseur for those stressed by shopping and happy hours galore! The larger rooms come with TV and bathroom; all are air-conditioned.

Hotels

Maison Brunet (☎ 514-845-6351, fax 514-848-7061, 1035 Rue St Hubert) Rooms without/with bath $58/68. The garrulous owner of this hotel can be found behind the counter holding forth amid old-fashioned decor with touches of sugary rococo. Breakfast is served in the garden, next to a cute little fountain.

Hôtel le St Malo (☎ 514-931-7366, fax 514-931-3764, e stmalo@colba.net, 1455

QUÉBEC

Rue du Fort) Singles/doubles $50/68-78. In the western part of downtown, this pleasant place with modern furnishings offers a good deal.

Hebergement l'Abri du Voyageur (☎ 514-849-2922, fax 514-499-0151, W www.abri voyageur.ca, 9 Rue Ste Catherine Ouest) Singles/doubles from $52/57; additional guests $10. One of the best low-budget places around, this totally renovated hotel with original pine floors and exposed brick has 30 rooms – each with a sink, fan and TV. Some might find the red-light district too seedy, however.

Manoir Ambrose (☎ 514-288-6922, fax 514-288-5757, W www.manoirambrose.com, 3422 Rue Stanley) Singles $40-50. Doubles without/with private bath $65/85-125. Compared to the sterile international hotels, this fine place in a quiet, central residential area is a real bargain, even if the decor in its 22 rooms (some of which are air-conditioned) borders on kitsch.

Bourbon Hôtel (☎ 514-523-4679, 800-268-4679, W www.bourbon.qc.ca, 1574 Rue Ste Catherine Est) Doubles/triples/quads $105/115/135, suites $130-230. Located in the huge Bourbon Complex, a gay emporia of bars and diners, this gay-friendly hotel can be a good value for the money – the suites fit four to eight people. It can be noisy and cruisy till the breakfast hours, though.

Hôtel du Vieux Port (☎ 514-844-0767, 756 Rue Berri) Doubles $135, suites $240. This hotel offers special rates for long stays. The modish, 27-room inn lodged in an 1882 warehouse sits above a fine pub/restaurant in the heart of Old Montréal. Buffed floors, original wooden beams and views of the Vieux Port set the tone. Prices include access to a pool and small gym.

Holiday Inn (☎ 514-878-9888, 99 Ave Viger Ouest) Doubles from $129. This four-star place is on the edge of Chinatown – you can't miss the fake pagodas on the rooftop. It offers above-average luxury for the price, with a health club, indoor pool and sauna. Prices, though, can change from day to day, depending on the demand and the time of year.

Queen Elizabeth Hotel (☎ 514-861-3511, 900 Boulevard René Lévesque Ouest) Doubles $209-299, suites from $300. The 'Queen E' is world famous as the site where John Lennon and Yoko Ono wrote 'Give Peace a Chance' during their 1969 nude love-in; in fact, part of their suite is now a room (No 1742) that can sometimes be had for as little as $79 (the bed's a pullout, you know), but only when the hotel is full. Prices vary considerably depending on dates, occupancy, etc.

Places to Eat

Some people say it's the French background, while others put it down to the sin-and-repent mentality of a predominantly Catholic city – whatever the reason, Montréalers do love to eat out. The city's reputation for culinary excellence has Gallic roots, but its more recent cosmopolitanism makes for a veritable United Nations of cuisine. Dining can be such a pleasure in this city; in fact, some gourmands come to Montréal for the sole purpose of eating. The choice is bewildering: there are some 4500 restaurants – more per capita than anywhere else on the continent, except New York.

The downtown and Plateau areas have the greatest concentration of restaurants. Spanning the two districts are two major dining strips along Boulevard St Laurent and Rue St Denis, both of which enjoy a wide range of reasonably priced, high-quality food. The farther north you go, the smaller and more innovative the establishments become. Two smaller streets, Rue Prince Arthur Est and Ave Duluth Est, intersect those two major strips; a lot of restaurants line these side streets.

In Chinatown, a bevy of low-cost eateries cluster close together. Greek places are ubiquitous, with a high concentration on Rue Prince Arthur Est. On Ave Duluth Est, the Portuguese reign with their wonderful roasted meats and seafood. A vibrant Little Italy features a decent choice of Italian restaurants. The many Vietnamese restaurants scattered throughout the city are renowned for their authenticity. Add that to the excellent Indian, Lebanese, Thai and even Ethiopian cuisine readily found in the city…and you have a slice of paradise.

Many restaurants have a policy of *apportez vôtre vin* (bring your own wine; BYOW).

Markets The city's two biggest markets are open 8am to 6pm Monday to Wednesday and Saturday, 8am to 9pm Thursday and

QUÉBEC

Friday and 8am to 5pm Sunday year-round. Both have indoor and outdoor sections.

Atwater Market (☎ 514-935-5716, 138 Ave Atwater) Near the Canal de Lachine, this tidy, chichi market features scores of vendors outside and high-class delis, bak-eries and specialty shops inside, in the tiled, vaulted hall under the clock tower.

Jean Talon Market (☎ 514-277-1588, 7075 Rue Casgrain) Located in the heart of Little Italy, this place is more ethnically varied than Atwater Market and is the city's

Essential Montréal Experiences

Aside from other of the city's culinary delights, bagels and smoked meat sandwiches form quin-tessential Montréal experiences; it would be plainly sinful not to indulge during your visit.

The Little 'O' Ever since Isadore and Fanny Shlafman, Ukrainian Jews, opened their first bakery in Montréal in 1915 (which ultimately grew into the legendary Fairmount Bagel), making yeast rings from a recipe they'd brought with them from Kiev, bagels have been part of local lore. A competitor, Myer Lemkomwicz, a Polish Jew, opened his own shop in 1957 (now the Maison du Bagel), and aficionados now debate whether he outstripped the original (many think so!).

Fairmount Bagel (☎ 514-272-0667, 74 Ave Fairmount Ouest) Ⓜ Laurier. You'll find oodles of variations, including pumpernickel and cumin, sun-dried tomato and cinnamon raisin bagels. The Fairmount bakery also makes matzoh boards, New York pretzels (which taste like they've been soaked in the Dead Sea) and 'bozo bagels,' which are triple normal size.

La Maison du Bagel (☎ 514-276-8044, 263 Ave St Viateur Ouest) Here's the real deal. A dozen freshly made plain, poppy-seed or sesame-seed bagels cost $4.25, and they are perfectly crusty, chewy and slightly sweet – worthy of their international reputation. Take bus No 55 north along Boulevard St Laurent.

Smoked Heaven on Rye Debates over bagels seem trite compared to the heated disputes over the origins and authenticity of the other Montréal staple: smoked meat. Termed 'pastrami' outside of Mon-tréal (and don't even dare to put corned beef in the same category!), smoked meat is made by curing a beef brisket with salt, garlic, herbs and spices, then smoking it for several days and finally steaming it.

By all accounts, it was created in 1908 in Montréal's garment district by one Ben Kravitz, a Lithuanian Jew who arrived in Canada in 1899; he used his grandparents' recipe for curing beef in order to make it last longer without refrigeration. Eventually, Ben's became a legend.

But it's Schwartz's (also called the Montréal Hebrew Delicatessen) that holds the nation's smoked meat crown. Reuben Schwartz, a Romanian Jew, opened his first restaurant in 1927, and today the landmark deli still uses his recipe, serving sandwiches by the dozens. The staff at Schwartz's claim to be the only ones who still smoke their own briskets, using only fresh meat (there are no freezers in the place!) The frequent line-ups outside the place, which hasn't changed decor in decades, attest to its popularity.

Schwartz's (☎ 514-842-4813, 3895 Boulevard St Laurent) Lunch dishes $5-9. Open 9am-12:30am Sun-Thur, 9am-1:30am Fri, 9am-2:30am Sat. Don't bother with the lean cut – medium is what you need for the best taste. While the meat here is a bit drier than at other places, that's only because the cooks use no chemicals to make it artificially juicier. Here you get the full flavor, the real thing.

Ben's (☎ 514-844-1000, 990 Boulevard de Maisonneuve Ouest) Average dishes $5-11. Open 7:30am-3am Mon-Fri, 7:30am-4am Sat & Sun. Celebrity photos line the walls at this other fixture on the Montréal dining landscape, in this location since 1949. The waiters are creaking old wise-crackers, and the kindergarten color-coordination of the decor plays tricks with your eyes.

Reuben's (☎ 514-866-1029, 1116 Rue Ste Catherine Ouest) Dishes $6-13. Open 6:30am-2am Sun-Thur, 6:30am-5am Fri-Sat. With rows of pickled peppers in the window, Reuben's does its eponymous sandwich (smoked meat, sauerkraut and melted cheese) for $7; it's one of the best smoked-meat variations around.

largest, most interesting market, with an overwhelming selection. You're expected to haggle over the fruits, vegetables, potted plants, herbs and (of course) maple syrup.

Waldman Plus (☎ 514-285-8747, 76 Rue Roy Est) Open 9am-6pm Mon, 9am-9pm Tues-Sun. For fresh fish, there's no beating this Montréal landmark, which supplies many of the city's hotels and restaurants. The volume and variety – if not the smell – will make your head spin. Waldman Plus also runs a restaurant next door, *Moules & Co* (☎ 514-496-0540) Open 11am-10pm Tues-Sun. It serves fish delicacies from mussels to sushi. Lunch specials start at $7.99.

Old Montréal Old Montréal is a fine place to splurge. In fact, it might be a good idea to spend as much as you can. Although this beautiful area contains some of the city's finest restaurants, it also draws lots of tourists, and many of the mid-priced places make delicious-sounding but essentially assembly-line dishes at marked-up prices.

Usine de Spaghetti Parisienne (☎ 514-866-0963, 273 Rue St Paul Est) Dishes $6-17. Open 11am-10pm daily. Come here for cheap eats in a friendly atmosphere. Meals include fettucine with baby clams or curried beef-filet medallions (both $14), with all the bread and salad you can eat.

Eggspectation (☎ 514-282-0119, 201 Rue St Jacques) Average dishes $8. Open 6am-4pm Mon-Fri, 6am-5pm Sat & Sun. For omelets, crêpes or burgers, try this place.

Stash Café (☎ 514-845-6611, 200 Rue St Paul Ouest) Dishes $11-18. Open 11:30am-11pm daily. This place serves hearty Polish cuisine in an intimate setting achieved by church pews and low-hanging ceiling lamps. A good set meal including standards such as pierogi and borscht costs $14.

Gibby's (☎ 514-282-1837, 298 Place d'Youville) Dinner $30-50 per person. Open 4:30pm-11pm daily. A snazzy, popular place in a 200-year-old converted stable serves such specialties as steak and roast beef, although the lobster and scampi also warrant a visit. Reservations are suggested, especially on weekends.

Downtown & Chinatown You'll find eateries every few steps in the downtown core. The choice is good, as is the variety, though prices tend to be slightly higher and the food slightly more conservative than in the restaurants outside the center core.

Peel Pub (☎ 514-844-6769, 1107 Rue Ste Catherine Ouest) Average dishes $3-9. Open 8am-3am daily. This spot has become a favored hangout of McGill students – indeed, it's big enough to accommodate the entire student body and feels as crowded as if did! The atmosphere is fun and lively, but the star is its bargain-basement food (eg, a quarter chicken and ribs with salad for $7).

Amelio's (☎ 514-845-8396, 201 Rue Milton) Dishes $6-12. Open 11:30am-8:45pm Tues-Fri & Sun, 4pm-8:45pm Sat & Mon. In the so-called 'McGill ghetto,' this has been a popular student draw for decades. The portions of pizza and pasta are generous; a medium pizza with salad ($11) is enough to stuff two people. Lunch specials are $5.

McLean's Pub (☎ 514-393-3132, 1210 Rue Peel) Dishes $6-15. This has managed to maintain an air of old-style pub (the wood panels, impressive ceiling and fireplace help). The mostly English clientele sure love their Reubens or McLean's Sub ($7 to $9).

Katsura (☎ 514-849-1172, 2170 Rue de la Montagne) Lunch $8-14, dinner $27-37. Open for lunch 11:30am-2:30pm Mon-Fri, dinner 5:30pm-10pm daily. Amid a blaze of kimonos and stylish decor, sample the excellent lunch, popular with businesspeople. Your best bet is an evening table d'hôte at the monumental sushi bar. The Nipponese delicacies are prepared with the greatest care, but the ambience is glacial.

Bueno Notte (☎ 514-848-0644, 3518 Boulevard St Laurent) Table d'hôte lunch $12-18, dinner $25-30. More often than not, this elegant place is filled with strutting fashion victims. Because of – or perhaps despite – its poseur clientele, the chefs serve up excellent Italian and international fare, from delicate, savory pastas to sizzling Angus steaks.

Cristal de Saigon (☎ 514-875-4275, 1068 Boulevard St Laurent) Dishes $6-13. Open 11am-10pm daily. This Vietnamese diner specializes in satisfying Tonkinoise soups (meals in themselves) and draws crowds of local Chinatown residents.

Hoang Oanh (☎ 514-954-0051, 1071 Boulevard St Laurent) Average dishes $5-10. Across the street from Cristal de Saigon, this place is famous for Vietnamese submarine sandwiches.

Sing Ping (☎ 514-397-9598, *74 Rue de la Gauchetière Ouest*) Dishes $8-15. Open noon-2am daily. Sing Ping enjoys an excellent reputation. Its huge tables are ideal for a good meal with friends before hitting the clubs along Rue St Denis.

Quartier Latin & the Village In the last few years, the eating options in this area have improved dramatically. The lively clientele these restaurants attract can be as noteworthy as the food.

La Paryse (☎ 514-842-2040, *302 Rue Ontario Est*) Average dishes $5-10. Open 11am-11pm Mon-Fri, noon-11pm Sat & Sun. The thickest, juiciest burgers in town come with an array of toppings at this spot with neo-retro, bright rooms. The homemade fries ($2) and vegetable soups ($2.50) are terrific.

Café de Pèlerin (☎ 514-845 0909, *330 Rue Ontario Est*) Dishes $7-14. You won't feel like leaving this unassuming space, and you'll probably find yourself returning, even if your stay in town is short. Decent food, good service and a laid-back atmosphere (try the terrace out back) are all you need for a good night out. You can also eat in the attached wood paneled bar, Le Magellan.

Pho Viet (☎ 514-522-4116, *1663 Rue Amherst*) Appetizers $2-4, dishes $7-14. Open 11am-3pm & 5pm-9pm Mon-Fri, 5pm-9pm Sat. Excellent Vietnamese food at affordable prices have made this a very popular place. A Vietnamese fondue for two will set you back just $21.

Bato Thai (☎ 524-6705, *1310 Rue Ste Catherine Est*) Dishes $7-17. Open 11am-3pm & 5pm-10pm Mon-Fri, 5pm-10pm Sat & Sun. The ever-fresh ingredients and boat-shaped bar here get rave reviews. Daily specials cost $8, and all dishes are inexpensive (beef curry with coconut milk and basil leaves goes for $9).

The Plateau This is the dining area of choice for many Montréalers and tourists alike. As you head north from the Quartier Latin, a slightly seedy, bohemian air gives way to the chichi crowd of upper Rue St Denis and Boulevard St Laurent, where you'll find some of the city's slickest dining establishments. Just north of there, the pedestrian Rue Prince Arthur is a favorite 'restaurant row' full of mid-priced eateries, 1 BYOW.

Farther north, Ave Duluth is a narrow old street (once a red-light district) that has been redone as a restaurant center, and with its painted, graffitied walls and ethnically mixed populace, it's more charismatic than Rue Prince Arthur. Between the two, Boulevard St Laurent has many great food stops, whether you're hungry for Polish sausage or smoked meat, bagels or something fancier.

Chez José (☎ 514-845-0693, *173 Ave Duluth Est*) Dishes $4-6. Open 7am-8pm Mon-Fri, 8am-7pm Sat & Sun. This cramped little place serves up fresh empanadas for just $3. It's known for its brunchtime crêpes and omelets, but the daily soups ($3) are a real treat. The ambience is the real draw here, though, with marine-theme walls, friendly service and an eccentric, bilingual clientele.

Mazurka (☎ 514-844-3539, *64 Rue Prince Arthur Est*) Average dishes $5-13. Open 11:30am-midnight daily. Some of the best comfort food in the Plateau can be had here, and it's dirt cheap. The daily specials, featuring pierogi and meat or cheese blintzes, cost around $6. Mazurka sprawls over four levels decorated by paintings from the Old Country.

Café Santropol (☎ 514-842-3110, *3990 Rue St Urbain*) Average dishes $6-12. This is the ideal spot for reading, writing postcards or just plain procrastinating in a cozy interior or on the garden-like terrace. For over 25 years, this mainly vegetarian café has also been known for its huge, bizarre sandwiches, served with an orchard's worth of fruit and salad.

La Casa Grècque (☎ 514-842-6098, *200 Rue Prince Arthur Est*) Dishes $7-18, lunch specials $4-14. Open 11am-11:30pm daily. One of the city's legendary eateries serves tasty, if unadventurous, dinners.

Les Vivres (☎ 514-842-3479, *4434 Rue Ste Dominique*) Brunch $7.25, dishes $6-8. Open noon-midnight Mon-Fri, 11am-midnight Sat-Sun. A granola paradise, a decked-out garage, a diner for tree-hugging lefties – call it what you will, but this vegan co-op serves up delicious food, considering vegans' limited diet. Try the Indian plate.

Govinda (☎ 514-284-5255, *263 Rue Duluth Est*) Lunch $7, dinner $9. Open 11:30am-9pm Sun-Wed, 11:30am-11pm Thur-Sat. Located in the city's Hare Krishna Center, Govinda offers a mini-buffet with standard Krishna fare, plus a Québécois accent (veggie tortière and Shepherd's Pie, for example).

Le Commensal (☎ 514-845-2627, 1720 Rue St Denis) Average dishes $9-15. Open 11am-11pm Sun-Thur, 11am-11:30pm Fri & Sat. Set up buffet-style, the excellent food is priced by weight and always turns out to be way more expensive than it should be. Another outlet is at 1204 Rue McGill College.

Zyng (☎ 514-284-2016, 1748 Rue St Denis) Dishes $10-15. Open 11:30am-10pm daily. Soup-lovers wax lyrical here, where a bowl of delicious noodle, meat or veggie costs $5 (your choice of ingredients). The bright, peppy interior make the flavors even more vivid. Have chocolate-covered lychees for dessert.

Elsewhere in Montréal A bit of exploring can really pay off in Montréal, as several of the city's best places to eat are in out-of-the-way areas.

Il Mulino (☎ 514-273-5776, 236 Rue St Zotique Est) Ⓜ Jean Talon. Dishes $20-35. Open noon-3pm Tues-Fri, 5pm-11pm Tues-Sat. Perhaps the top Italian restaurant in town, this spot right in Little Italy offers a breathtaking array of specialties. Try the vegetarian starter plate ($10) before moving on to baby lamb chops, so tender they practically cut themselves.

Le Troquet (☎ 514-271-6789, 106 Ave Laurier Ouest) Ⓜ Laurier. Average dishes $10. Open 9am-midnight daily. People come to this Mile End restaurant for terrific mussels ($9 to $11) and the very French ambience. The menu also features panini, soups and salads. There's live jazz and blues on weekends.

Pho Lien (☎ 514-735-6949, 5703 Chemin Côte des Neiges) Ⓜ Côte des Neiges. Dishes $5-11. Open 5pm-11pm Wed-Mon. In a city with so many excellent Vietnamese restaurants, this is regarded as one of the best. The energy not spent on decor went into the great food here – huge meal soups and authentic pho keep customers lining up outside.

Pushap Sweets (☎ 514-737-4527, 5195 Rue Paré; Ⓜ De la Savane) Dishes $5-10. Open 11am-9pm daily. Out of the way, this little place could be mistaken for a *dépanneur* (convenience store) from its unassuming appearance. Yet connoisseurs say that this family restaurant is the city's top Indian eatery. The vegetarian *thali* is superb.

Entertainment

Even rival Torontonians admit it: Montréal's nightlife is the liveliest in Canada. Nightclubs serve alcohol until 3am – the longest opening hours in the country – and the variety of these establishments is astounding. Most places don't start buzzing until after 11pm. Expect to line up and be checked out to make sure you pass muster.

Traditionally, the area around Rue Crescent and Rue Bishop downtown has been anglo territory, with francophones gathering farther east; however, for several years already, Boulevard St Laurent has become party central for all types and persuasions. Certainly, it is an endlessly more energetic and interesting alternative to the often tacky pick-up cruising bars on Rue Crescent.

See the *Mirror* and *Hour* free weeklies for complete listings of what's on. Places des Arts also publishes the monthly *Calendrier des Spectacles*, a guide to performing arts events. *La Scena Musicale* is a free monthly devoted to the classical arts. The monthly *Nightlife* is your best bet for hot clubs and music trends. *Fugues* is a free, partially bilingual monthly booklet for the gay and lesbian scene.

Call Info-Arts Bell (☎ 514-790-2787) for details of theater, shows and other events. For major pop and rock concerts, shows, festivals and sporting events, purchase tickets from the box office or call Admission (☎ 514-790-1245, 800-361-4595). Ticketmaster (☎ 514-790-1111) sells tickets to concerts and theater shows.

Clubs *Les Deux Pierrots* (☎ 514-861-1686, 104 Rue St Paul Est) Cover charge around $3. Open Thur-Sat, occasionally other nights. This huge two-story club that's been around for the better part of three decades features live rock bands on Friday and Saturday nights in summer. The public is encouraged to sing along to the French chansons.

Foufounes Electriques (☎ 514-844-5538, 87 Rue Ste Catherine Est) Café/bar open 3pm-3am daily, dance floor open at 10pm. Students, alternafreaks and all manner of trendies go here, a renowned bastion of underground music (the name means 'electric buttocks'). This place has some bizarre touches – Egypto/sci-fi art, weird back-lighting in the aquarium room and a pit (don't ask).

Metropolis (☎ *514-844-3500, 59 Rue Ste Catherine Est)* Open 10pm-3am Fri & Sat. Metropolis boasts Canada's largest dance floor (capacity 2500). Housed in a former art deco cinema, this place features live bands and DJs, bars spread over three floors and dazzling sound and light shows.

Newtown (☎ *514-284-6555, W *www .newtown.ca, 1476 Rue Crescent)* Restaurant and lounge bar open 11am-1am, disco open 9pm-3am daily. Jacques Villeneuve's schmooze emporium is a trendy spot that's injected new life into Rue Crescent, attracting a well-to-do crowd in the 25-35 range. The food is decent (dishes $6-17).

Stereo (☎ *514-282-3307, 858 Rue Ste Catherine Est)* Open 2am-10am Sat & Sun. The after-hours club of choice for years, Stereo owes its popularity to the wicked in-house and imported DJs, excellent sound system and the 60/40 gay/straight mix. It gets pretty hot around 5am.

In the Plateau, you'll find plenty of clubs along Boulevard St Laurent between Rue Sherbrooke and Ave Mont Royal. The crowds tend to be young and hipper-than-thou. Some hot Plateau spots include the following.

Café Campus (☎ *514-844-1010, 57 Rue Prince Arthur Est)* Open Mon-Sat. One of the most popular student clubs features '80s hits, French rock and live bands. Happy hour ($1 a beer) starts at 8:30pm. Expect youngins who can't hold their liquor.

Jingxi (☎ *514-985-5464, 410 Rue Rachel Est)* Open Wed-Sat, sometimes Sun. A landmark of the Montréal house music scene, Jingxi attracts legions of 20-somethings to be freeze-framed by the terrific light shows. Jingxi's local and imported DJs have great reputations among those in the know.

Blizzarts (☎ *514-843-4860, 3956a Boulevard St Laurent)* Open 8pm-3am daily. There's no sign out front, but this is a cool, discreet bar where good music is the thing, not pretentious posing. Inventive DJs serve up jazz, funk, hip-hop, roots and dub. Hit the small dance floor or hang out on all the sofas.

Sky Pub & Club (☎ *514-529-6969, 1474 Rue Ste Catherine Est)* A fixture in the gay community, this two-part space includes a cruisy, fashion-conscious pub that gets crowded during Sunday 'tea dance' afternoons and Tuesday evening drag shows, and

an upstairs club that takes off very late on weekends.

Le Track (☎ *514-521-1419, 1584 Rue Ste Catherine Est)* Open 3pm-3am daily. In the Bourbon Complex (see Places to Stay on the map), this popular disco/bar with a leather boutique sprawls over three floors. The crowds pack in on Wednesday night.

Pubs & Bars *Pub St Paul* (☎ *514-874-0485, 124 Rue St Paul Est)* Cover charge $5. Old Montréal isn't the greatest place to go pub-crawling – it's touristy and expensive. Bucking the trend is the Pub St Paul, with a terrific view of the port, a comfortable ambience and several pool tables.

Winnies (☎ *514-288-0623, 1455 Rue Crescent)* This sprawling, split-level place draws crowds with its thumping disco music. Local author Mordecai Richler used to knock back cold ones in the *Sir Winston Churchill Pub* upstairs. It serves so-so food all day (dishes $10-16), and drinks are half-price from 5pm to 8pm.

Hurley's Irish Pub (☎ *514-861-4111, 1125 Rue Crescent)* Open noon-3am daily. At this cozy place, the live music (usually rock and folk, with great Celtic fiddlers) starts at 9pm most nights. As in many pubs, football and soccer matches are shown on big screens – prepare to join in.

Gerts (☎ *514-398-3319, 3840 Rue Mc-Tavish)* Open 9am-1am Mon-Wed, 9am-3am Thur & Fri, 5pm-3am Sat. Gerts, in the McGill University student union building, plays DJ-driven R&B, hip-hop, blues and house, with an 'oldies night' thrown in for good measure.

Le Magellan (☎ *514-845-0909, 330 Rue Ontario Est)* Attached to the great Café de Pèlerin (see Places to Eat), this relaxed place plays canned jazz and chansons amid a sprinkling of maritime doodads. The house specialty is rum, and they've got a dozen different kinds.

L'Île Noire (☎ *514-982-0866, 342 Rue Ontario Est)* Open 4pm-3am daily. Connoisseurs will be dazzled by the Scotch selection here. Extremely friendly, even vivacious, staff contrast with the low-key ambience and slightly upscale vibes to make this a true delight.

Else's (☎ *514-286-6689, 156 Rue Roy Est)* Open 11am-3am daily. You seep into the relaxed feel of this great local bar with candlelit tables to chat over and finger food to keep you going.

Casa del Popolo (☎ *514-284-3804, 4873 Boulevard St Laurent*) This great space combines a comfortable bar/café serving healthy meals with an English-language performance space (poetry readings, film screenings). Check out the schedule of the Casa's concert hall, La Sala Rossa, across the street, for unusual, interesting fare.

Sharx (☎ *514-934-3105, 1606 Rue Ste Catherine Ouest*) Open 11am-3am daily. Sharx features pool and billiard tables everywhere you look ($9/hour), rows of TV screens and a post-apocalyptic feel.

Jazz & Blues *Biddle's* (☎ *514-842-8656, 2060 Rue Aylmer*) This is *the* fixture on the jazz scene. Run by venerable bassist Charles Biddle, it's a tad touristy but fun, with *fin-de-siècle* decor and musical paraphernalia hanging from the ceiling. Prepare to stand in line if you haven't reserved. There's no cover charge, but there is usually a fee to sit at a table (as opposed to standing or sitting at the bar) – ask in advance.

L'Air du Temps (☎ *514-842-2003, 191 Rue St Paul Ouest*) This place, with a smoky, spotlit stage girded by a wooden balcony and bar, is the stuff legends are made of. Small groups or solos start at 5pm, and the bigger names come on around 9:30pm, when a $5 cover kicks in.

Jazz & Blues (☎ *514-398-3319, 3840 Rue McTavish*) In the McGill Student Union building, this spot usually holds concerts by good student bands. The schedule's on the university's website: W www.mcgill.ca.

Performing Arts For modern dance, check local listings to see what's on at *Espace Go* (☎ *514-845-4890, 4890 Boulevard St Laurent*). For classical music, check out concerts held at McGill University; they tend to be very good. Or see what's on at Montréal's main performing arts center, *Place des Arts* (☎ *514-842-2112,* W *www.pda.qc.ca, 175 Rue Ste Catherine Ouest*).

Orchestre Symphonique de Montréal (☎ *514-842-9951*) The renowned Orchestre Symphonique de Montréal, under the direction of Swiss conductor Charles Dutoit, performs at the Place des Arts from September to May.

Les Ballets Jazz de Montréal (☎ *514-982-6771*) This modern-dance troupe has earned a sterling reputation for its experimental forms.

Centaur Théâtre (☎ *514-288-3161, 453 Rue St François Xavier*) The center of English-language theatre, the Centaur has a hit-and-miss repertoire of classics and experimental fare.

Monument National Theater (☎ *514-871-2224, 1182 Boulevard St Laurent*) Admission $5. This place holds regular rehearsals of dramatic plays by students of the National Theatre School. Mostly in French, the programs cover a range of genres, from Shakespeare to Sam Shepard.

Théâtre de Quat' Sous (☎ *514-845-7277, 100 Ave des Pins Est*) This is a wonderful venue for intellectual and experimental drama.

Comedy Nest (☎ *514-932-6378, 1740 Boulevard René Lévesque*) Cover charge $3-15 (discounts for students). Shows 9pm Wed & Thur, 9pm & 11:15pm Fri & Sat. The Comedy Nest features talent from all over North America. Expect a dash of cabaret – with singers, dancers, musicians, female impersonators and more.

Cinemas Check W www.cinemamontreal .com for the latest on what's playing where.

National Film Board (☎ *514-283-9000, 1564 Rue St Denis*) Open noon-9pm Tues-Sun. Paradise for serious cinephiles, the NFB hosts regular screenings, but the real attraction is the **Cinérobothèque** – make your choice, and a robot housed in a glass-roofed archive pulls your selection from one of 6000 videodiscs. Then settle back into individual, stereo-equipped chair units to watch your personal monitor (students/non-students $2/3 per hour).

Spectator Sports

Hockey and Catholicism are regarded as national religions in Québec, but baseball also attracts a fair number of fans. Ironically, although the internationally renowned Habs and Expos have fallen upon hard times in their leagues, Montréal's dark-horse football team, the Alouettes (☎ 514-254-2400), is riding an unexpected wave of popularity in a new home at McGill University's *Molson Stadium* (*1255 Rue University*).

Tickets for most sporting events are available from the Admission ticket service

QUÉBEC

QUÉBEC

(☎ 514-790-1245), which operates various outlets around town, including one in the Berri-UQAM Métro station.

The Montréal Canadiens hockey team (affectionately dubbed 'Habs') have won the Stanley Cup 24 times, but the last time was in 1993 – and the Molson family did the unthinkable by selling the team in 2000. Still, Montréalers have a soft spot for the Habs, and if you're in town during the season, don't miss the opportunity to see a match.

The Habs play at the **Bell Centre** (☎ 514-932-2582, w www.centre-molson.com, 1260 de la Gauchetière Ouest), formerly the Molson Centre. Tickets go on sale in advance during the season, which runs from October to April, with playoffs until June. List prices range from $17 for a seat in the rafters to $130 for rink-side seats. Seats are also available through the legions of scalpers who begin lingering about noon on game days. Scalpers tend to charge much more than face value, but after the game starts, you can often negotiate them down to half-price. If you're going to purchase tickets from a scalper, it's better to be discreet about it, since scalping may be frowned on by the authorities.

Outdoor hockey games are some of Québec's most memorable sporting affairs – you won't soon forget the earsplitting cries of *but* (goal) fueled by thermoses of mulled wine. Informal matches take place just about wherever a pond has frozen over and public rinks are set up – for example, at Parc La Fontaine or at the Olympic rowing basin of Île Notre Dame, in the Parc des Îles.

The Montréal Expos (☎ 514-253-3434, 800-463-9767, w www.exposmlb.com), Montréal's major-league baseball team, has fallen on hard times, and few fans bother to attend games at the **Stade Olympique** (Rue Pie IX at Rue Sherbrooke) anymore. The survival of the club has been in question for several years. If you want to go to a game, tickets ($7 to $23) are very available from the box office or from Admission from April to September.

Shopping

Guilde Canadienne des Métier d'Art Québec (☎ 514-849-6091, 2025 Rue Peel) Open 10am-6pm Tues-Fri, 10am-5pm Sat. The city's first art gallery carries a small and somewhat expensive collection of work by Québec artisans, as well as Inuit prints and carvings and other Canadiana. Rotating exhibits drawn from the country's best artisans feature prints, sculptures and crafts.

Le Baron (☎ 514-866-8848, 932 Rue Notre Dame Ouest) For survival, sporting and leisure gear, this is the top address in town. Backpack buyers should set aside a few hours just to look. Prices are high.

Getting There & Away

Air Montréal has two airports. Dorval, 20km west of downtown, serves most domestic, US and overseas flights. Mirabel, 55km northeast of downtown, serves cargo and charter flights.

Montréal's sickly-looking Dorval Airport levies an airport improvement tax of $15 on all international flights before you leave, a major irritant to locals who haven't seen much improvement since 1996, when this supposedly temporary tax was levied. Mirabel Airport charges a $10 improvement tax.

For airport information, call ☎ 514-394-7377 or 800-465-1213 or visit the website w www.admtl.com.

Bus Buses to the airports and to Canadian and US destinations depart from the Station Centrale de l'Autobus (Central Bus Station; ☎ 514-842-2281, 505 Rue de Maisonneuve Est).

Buses to Québec City ($42, three to four hours) come in express, local and long-distance varieties. More than 30 buses shuttle from Montréal to Québec City daily. The locals stop elsewhere along the way, like Trois Rivières ($26, 1¾ to 2¼ hrs, eight daily); long-distance buses continue beyond to farther destinations, like Tadoussac ($81, 5½ hours, twice daily). From Québec City you can connect to many other places.

In winter, ask about companies providing ski-shuttle day trips to the Laurentians for either downhill or cross-country skiing. Limocar (☎ 450-435-8899) offers well-priced trips to Mont Gabriel (with connections to nearby resorts) from the main bus station. Tickets include lift passes.

Moose Travel, an alternative bus service that mainly caters to hostelers, runs to various points in Québec, as well as Ottawa, Toronto and elsewhere in the province. For more information about the company, which stops in Montréal, see Alternative Buses in the Getting Around chapter of this book.

Train Montréal's Gare Centrale (Central Station; 895 Rue de la Gauchetière Ouest), below the Queen Elizabeth Hotel, is the local hub of VIA Rail (☎ 514-366-8411, W www.viarail.ca). Service is best along the so-called Québec City–Windsor corridor, which includes Montréal, Ottawa, Kingston, Toronto and Niagara Falls.

VIA Rail's overnight service between Montréal and Toronto is a treat. Trains leave at 11:30pm nightly except Saturday, arriving at 8am with a complimentary breakfast included. Standard one-way fares in a sleeper cabin start at $90.

Amtrak (☎ 514-215-824-1600, 800-872-7245, W www.amtrak.com.) runs a daily train between New York City and Montréal (US$52 to US$65, 10 hours), arriving at Gare Centrale.

Car & Motorcycle Continental US highways link directly with their Canadian counterparts along the border at numerous points. These roads meet up with the Trans Canada Highway (Hwy 40), which runs directly through Montréal. From Boston to Montréal, it's about 490km (4½ hours); from Toronto, it's 540km (five hours). Québec City is 2½ hours away.

Allô Stop (☎ 514-985-3032, W www.allostop.com, 4317 Rue St Denis) offers lots of rides to destinations in Québec and to the US. Membership for passengers is $6; you also pay a portion of the ride cost to the agency three hours before the trip, and the rest goes to the driver. Ride sharing can yield good deals; to Québec City it's $15, to Ottawa $16, to Toronto $35, to New York (from Montréal) $65 and to Gaspé $50.

Autotaxi (W www.autotaxi.com), a Web-based bulletin board for ride sharing in all corners of Québec, offers great deals.

Getting Around
To/From the Airports The cheapest way downtown from Dorval Airport is via bus and Métro. Outside the Dorval arrivals hall, catch bus No 204 Est to the Dorval Bus Transfer Station and switch to No 211 Est, which delivers you 20 minutes later at the Lionel Groulx Métro station. Buses usually

leave every 15 minutes, and the entire journey should take about an hour. Both buses run 5am to 1am. You can make the trip with only one ticket ($2).

The Québécois Bus Company (☎ 514-931-9002, 842-2281) runs Aérobus shuttles from Dorval to downtown, stopping at Station Aérobus (777 Rue de la Gauchetière Est; ⓜ Champ de Mars) and the Station Centrale de l'Autobus (Central Bus Station). The 20-minute trip is offered every half-hour daily from 5am to 11pm. One-way/roundtrip tickets cost $11/20. Buses leave from gate No 19. At the Station Aérobus, a smaller shuttle will pick you up and drop you anywhere in central downtown free of charge – an excellent service.

Aérobus shuttles also serve Mirabel Airport; tickets for the one-hour journey downtown cost $20/30 one way/roundtrip. From the bus station downtown, buses leave from gate No 17 three to four times a day on weekdays, nine times daily on weekends.

Bus & Métro Montréal has a modern and convenient bus and Métro system run by STCUM (☎ 514-280-5653, W www.stcum.qc.ca). The Métro is the city's subway system, which runs quickly and quietly on rubber tires, just like the one in Paris. It operates until at least 12:30am, and some buses provide service all night.

One ticket can get you anywhere in the city. Transfers, good for a connecting bus or Métro train, are valid for 90 minutes. Individual tickets are $2.25; a pack of six costs $9. A weekly card ($14), valid from Monday to Sunday, is a good deal. Monthly passes cost $50. Tourist cards are $7 for one day or $14 for three days.

Car & Motorcycle Montréal drivers possess nerves of steel, and you should too if you wish to drive in this town. If you drive downtown, you'll have to pay for metered street parking (25¢ for 10 minutes in the center city) or for the public parking lots (about $3 per half hour).

At Dorval Airport, several car rental companies have placed representatives in the arrivals hall, including Alamo, Avis, Budget, Hertz, National and Thrifty. Budget (☎ 514-938-1000) also runs several locations in town, including a counter at the Gare Centrale. You should be able to get a subcompact for under $50 per day with unlimited mileage, taxes and insurance. You'll probably find similar rates at Avis (☎ 514-288-9934, 1225 Rue Metcalfe).

Rent-a-Wreck (☎ 514-328-9419, 10625 Rue St Gertrude), in North Montréal, charges $46/284 per day/week for its most basic models (stick shift or automatic). You get 250km/1500km free per day/week and pay 10¢ per additional kilometer. Despite the name, the firm rents out recent models. If you call ahead, Rent-a-Wreck will pick you up at the Sauvé or St Michel Métro stops.

Around Montréal

Just a short drive from Montréal, several destinations can give you a glimpse of the kind of scenic landscapes and cultural mix that exist farther afield in the province. All of these spots are best accessed by car.

OKA

This small town, at the confluence of the Ottawa and St Lawrence Rivers, about 50km west of Montréal, is known for the 1880s-era Oka Monastery (☎ 450-479-8331, 181 Rue des Anges; adult/child $2/free; open 10am-5:30pm daily). Some 70 Trappist monks still live here, where they make cheese, and they open their home to visitors, who come to see the religious artworks and several old stone buildings. Guided tours take place 10am to 5pm Tuesday to Sunday from late June to early September; for the rest of September and October, tours happen 10am to 5pm on weekends.

In 1990, Oka was the arena of a major, armed confrontation between Mohawk people and the federal and provincial governments, after the government officials opened the door for developers to build a golf course on land the Mohawks considered sacred. At first a local land squabble, this issue soon came to represent outstanding issues, such as land claims and self-government, that Native Indians across the country would like to see properly resolved.

On the edge of the large Lac des Deux Montagnes, the Parc d'Oka (☎ 514-479-8365, 2020 Chemin Oka; admission $3.50; open 9am-7pm daily) offers a bunch of activities, including sunbathing on a sandy beach, swimming, sailing, canoeing, kayak-

ing and cycling. The *campground* ($22-30) contains a staggering 800 places that draw swarms of campers.

You can also head to the public beach in nearby Pointe Calumet, 5km west of Oka. From Montréal, take Hwys 15 or 13 to Route 640 west, which leads to Route 344 and Oka.

RIVIÈRE ROUGE

About an hour's drive northwest of Montréal is the Rouge River, one of the best whitewater rivers in North America. New World River Expeditions (☎ 819-242-7238, W www.newworld.ca, 100 Chemin Rivière Rouge), based in Calumet, Québec (near Hawkesbury, Ontario), offers five-hour trips from April to October; reserve ahead. Trips cost $84 Monday to Saturday, $89 on Sunday, including a hot dog lunch. The company also offers longer trips (two to five days), plus sportyaking in inflatable rubber kayaks and horseback riding. There's a restaurant/lodge and pool, so you're not exactly roughing it. Staff can explain directions to this place – the route's a bit tricky.

THE LAURENTIANS

Between 80km and 150km north of Montréal, this section of the ancient Laurentian Shield is a mountainous and rolling lake-sprinkled playground. The land proved a failure for lumber and mining, but when skiing caught on, the whole place became resort-land. Today people flock here not only for the best in eastern skiing but also for camping, fishing and swimming in summer.

Cycling draws lots of enthusiasts, with good distance trails and rougher mountain biking in many areas. The Parc Linéaire du P'Tit Train du Nord (☎ 450-436-8532; cycling permit adult/child $5/free, cross-country ski permit adult/child $7/free) is a 200km-long system of bike and cross-country ski trails – it's one of the province's best-maintained routes. The park stretches from St Jérôme all the way up to Mont Laurier, following an old railway line and passing streams, rivers, rapids, lakes and unbeatable mountain scenery, along with rest stops, information booths (some in old train stations), restaurants, B&Bs and bike rental and repair shops.

The many picturesque French towns dominated by their church spires also make the Laurentians popular for just lazing in the sun. Plentiful accommodations and restaurants provide a wide range of services, from elegant inns with fine dining rooms to modest motels.

The Autoroute Laurentienne, also known as Hwy 15, is the fastest route north from Montréal; it's the way the buses go. The old Route 117 north is slower but much more pleasant.

The better-known towns and resorts are all clustered near the highways. Cottage country spreads out a little farther east and west. In general terms, the busy area ends at Mont Tremblant Provincial Park. The smaller villages on the upper areas of Route 117 are quiet and typically 'Laurentian.'

To find less-developed areas or to camp, you pretty much have to head for the big parks, as most of the region is privately owned. Outside the parks, campgrounds are generally privately owned, too, and tend to be small and busy. The lodges in the area are generally (but not always) quite pricey, but motels are more affordable.

The busiest times in the Laurentians are July, August, around Christmas, February

and March. At other times, prices tend to fall. Autumn is a good season to visit – the hills are colorful and the cooler air is ideal for walking. In all seasons, the whole area enjoys a festive, relaxed atmosphere.

Year-round tourist information offices, which can assist with accommodations, can be found in the villages of St Sauveur des Monts, Ste Adèle, Ste Agathe and St Jovite and at Mont Tremblant Village. The region's main tourist office (☎ 450-436-8532, 800-561-6673, **w** www.laurentides .com, 14142 Rue de la Chapelle) is in Mirabel; you'll see signs for the turnoff on Hwy 15.

Limocar (☎ 450-446-8899) buses leave from Montréal's main terminus and stop in most main towns in the Laurentians. In ski season, special buses operate to various hills; see Bus in Montréal's Getting There & Away section, earlier.

Taxi de la Rouge (☎ 819-275-3113) offers a brilliant service to facilitate your travel. For $7, the company will transport your baggage to any campground, B&B, motel or hotel of your choice between St Jérôme and Mont Laurier, enabling you to

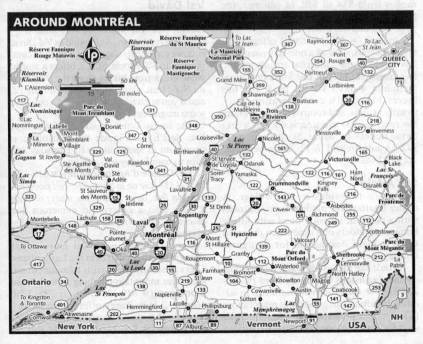

hike or cycle without the added weight of your belongings.

St Sauveur des Monts

Founded in 1854, St Sauveur is the busiest village in the Laurentians, just 60km from Montréal; it's a packed, popular destination year-round. There are five major ski hills around the village and in nearby Morin Heights. Many pretty side roads meander nearby, notably Chemin Rivière du Simon, accessible via Chemin du Village. The residential village of **Piedmont**, just 4km east of St Sauveur on the east side of Hwy 15, offers good alternate places to stay and eat and in some ways has become an extension of St Sauveur.

The main tourist office (☎ 450-227-4072, 605 Chemin des Frênes), in Piedmont (exit 60 off Hwy 15), is open year-round.

Mont St Sauveur (☎ 450-227-4671, W *www.montsaintsauveur.com, 350 Rue St Denis; open 9am-10:30pm Mon-Sat, 8:30am-9pm Sun)* is the area's largest ski station, with 29 runs and facilities suitable for snowboarding, snow-tubing, snow-rafting and snowshoeing. A day pass ranges from $34 to $40. In summer, the place turns into a giant (but so-so) water park with endless lines.

Limocar (☎ 450-446-8899) offers some great specials, such as a one-day roundtrip bus ticket from Montréal to any of the five major ski hills in the St Sauver area, including a day's ski-lift pass. The bus leaves Montréal's central station early, usually at 7am, and returns late afternoon. No reservations are necessary. On weekdays, tickets to Mont St Sauveur cost $42/33 adult/child 6-12; on weekends, they're $48/36.

Ste Adèle

There are two sides to this village. A rather unattractive modern core contrasts with a pleasant lakeside lined with lovely homes, reminders of a time when this used to be a main destination for bourgeois holiday-seekers.

If you'd like to do whitewater river rafting, contact **Excursions Rivière du Nord** (☎ 450-224-2035, W *www.riviere-du-nord.ca)*. In addition to rafting, this good outfit rents canoes ($36 for two persons) and bikes ($12/half day) for combo canoe-bike trips. Excursions

begin from the parking lot at the end of Rue St Joseph (Hwy 15 exit 67).

Val Morin

Nestled among lush mountains is this lovely village whose downtown consists of just a few houses. The excellent cross-country skiing is famous here. The **Centre de Ski Far Hills** (☎ 800-567-6636, *Chemin du Lac LaSalle)* administers the 96km of trails, which curve around mountains, cross frozen lakes and pass through magnificent scenery. There's a $10 access fee.

In town, drop into **Centre LauRentian** (☎ 819-322-1668, 5991 Rue Morin), a combination bike rental shop ($25/day, $75/week), cross-country ski rental shop, used bookstore and café.

At the **Sivananda Ashram Yoga Camp** (☎ 800-263-9642, 673 8-ème Ave), outdoor and indoor yoga and meditation courses take place in sumptuous surroundings throughout the year. Accommodations range from tents ($35) to summer chalets ($45) to very serene doubles ($70) inside the main building, which is made out of straw bales.

Val David

Also nestled at the foot of mountains, Val David, like Val Morin, is surrounded by beautiful landscapes. As languid as Val David is, however, it feels larger and rushed in comparison to Val Morin. Still, it offers a worthwhile break from biking along the P'tit Train du Nord trail, which whizzes right through it, and if you need to spend the night, you'll find some magnificent places to stay.

The tourist office (☎ 819-322-2900, 2501 Rue de l'Église), inside the post office, is open 9am to 5pm Sunday to Thursday and 9am to 6pm Friday to Saturday.

The **Galerie d'Art Inuit Baffin** (☎ 819-322-2632, 1337 Rue de la Sapinière, 2nd floor; admission free; open 10am-5pm daily) is more a store than a gallery, but numerous fine pieces of Inuit soapstone carvings are displayed.

Rock climbing is to Val David what skiing is to other villages in the Laurentians. There are many rocky cliffs to mount in the area. The mountain-climbing school **Passe Montagne** (☎ 819-322-2900 ext 235, 1760 Montée 2-ème Rang) offers introductory courses. The sports shop **Phénix Sports et Aventures** (☎ 819-322-1118, 2444 Rue de l'*Église*) rents climbing gear, as well as mountain bikes and canoes. For $44, you can paddle down the Rivière du Nord for two hours and bike back.

Le Chalet Beaumont (☎ *819-322-1972, 1451 Rue Beaumont*) Dorm beds $18, doubles without/with private bathroom $23/27 per person. Perched atop a forested hill, this hostel has the look and feel of a luxury country chalet. It's only 1km from biking and skiing trails (people ski from the front door). The dorm rooms can accommodate two to four people. Hostel staff will pick you up from the bus station – call first.

Ste Agathe des Monts

Sitting on the edge of the pretty Lac des Sables, the village exudes some of the old-world Anglo-Saxon charm of the English settlers who built it up as an ideal hideaway, beginning in the mid-1890s. A number of villas and stately homes around the lake and in the village harken back to this era while the center feels lackluster and run-down.

The tourist office (☎ 819-326-0457, 24 Rue St Paul Est) is open year-round.

There are three **public beaches** right in the center of town, all of which offer access for $4.

Maple Syrup & the Sugar Shack

Intimately tied to the very notion of Canada is the country's most recognized export, maple syrup. And nowhere is maple syrup more deeply tied to traditional ways than in Québec. Some 75% of the world's maple syrup comes from Québec, where it brings in over $100 million annually.

It was the Native Indians who first taught Europeans how to make the sweet syrup from maple sap (they would bring it to a boil by tossing hot rocks from a fire into a pot full of sap). Each tribe has its own legend concerning the discovery of the sweet stuff. Algonquins say that a wife who decided to cook her husband's meat in maple sap found the sugary elixir; Micmacs say that a lazy wife who left a pot of maple sap boiling too long accidentally happened on maple syrup; the Iroquois have it that a nice but dim-witted wife cooked her husband's meat in maple sap, thinking it was water – the sweet result so pleased hubby, he decided to look into it more…

Whites began making maple syrup in the early 18th century. By the 19th century, cultivating the sap and transforming it into syrup had become a part of Québécois heritage.

Every summer, starches accumulate in maple trees. When the temperature dips below zero, these are turned into sucrose. The sugar maple (native to North America) has more of an enzyme that transforms starch to sucrose than other species of maple.

To tap the sugar inside the tree, inventive types have come up with a system that sucks out the sap through a series of tubes called Sysvacs, which snake through a maple grove to machines that cook the sap into a syrup. The different grades produced depend on how long it is cooked and to what temperature (to make taffy, for example, it must cook to 26°C above boiling point).

Sugar shacks became part of the Québécois experience in the early 20th century. They remain places to experience the maple tradition at its best. The 'taffy pull' is the most fun – you scoop up some snow, put it on a plate and have some steaming syrup from a piping caldron poured onto it. The syrup hardens as it hits the snow, and it can then be twisted onto a Popsicle stick and sucked and chewed until you feel the need to do it all over again.

In addition to the taffy pull and a look around the syrup-making operations, you can be treated to a hearty Québécois meal.

Sugar shacks are only open for a month or so, in February and March. Some are mentioned throughout this book. Any tourist information office can recommend others. One worth highlighting is the **Cabane à Sucre Jean Renaud et Fils** (☎ *450-473-3943, 1034 Boulevard Arthur Sauvé*), located on Route 148 in Ste Eustache, just west of Hwy 13. It sits on the site of a family-run maple grove that's operated since 1865. The cafeteria-style dining room here is not what you'd call rustic, but the enormous variety of food makes up for it in a big way. There's a huge buffet table or set meals of traditional Québécois meat-heavy food (turkey, beef, chicken and a 'sausage cocktail') and ten kinds of desserts.

At the maple-sugar shack **Cabane à Sucre Millette** (☎ *819-688-2101, 1357 Rue St Faustin; adult/child $7/5; open 9am-6pm daily Mar-Apr*), you can see production in action – sap is still culled in horse-drawn carts – and sample the results.

The **Centre Touristique et Éducatif** (☎ *819-326-1606, 5000 Chemin du Lac Cordon; adult/student $5/4; open 8am-4:30pm Sun-Thur, 8am-8pm Fri & Sat June-Oct*), about 13km west of town in the county of St Faustin/Lac Carré, is a marvelous, protected area that showcases local flora and fauna. You can take a hike on the walking trails or rent canoes and kayaks. At the excellent *campground* (☎ *819-326-9072*), sites cost $16. To get there from town, head west on Chemin Tour du Lac, which turns into Chemin du Lac Manitou, then turn left onto Chemin du Lac Caribou until it becomes Chemin du Lac Gordon.

Relais de la Sauvagine (☎ *819-326-5228, 10 Chemin Tour du Lac)* Doubles $80. A good deal for the price, this British-style country inn features comfortable rooms, each with its own bathroom, and faces the lake.

Auberge Le St Venant (☎ *819-326-7937, 234 Rue St Venant)* Doubles $86-136. Boasting one of the best lake views in town, this small hotel with nine tastefully decorated and spacious rooms is one of the most attractive places to stay in the Laurentians.

Ville de Mont Tremblant

The Mont Tremblant area is the jewel of the Laurentians, drawing almost three million tourists each year. Ville de Mont Tremblant is a new moniker for a group of villages fused administratively, including the town of St Jovite, Mont Tremblant Village and the area around the famous Station Tremblant, the second-busiest ski hill in Canada after BC's Whistler.

The largest tourist information office is in St Jovite (☎ *819-425-3300, 305 Chemin Brébeuf)*; it's open 9am to 7pm daily from late June to early September, 9am to 5pm daily the rest of the year. Near Mont Tremblant Village, you'll find an office (☎ *819-425-2434, 1001 Montée Ryan)* at the corner of Route 327 (which becomes Chemin Principal). Another tourist information kiosk is at Station Tremblant (☎ *819-681-3000 ext 46642*) on the Place des Voyaguers.

The most popular of all of the area's events is the **Festival International du Blues**, the country's biggest blues festival, held in mid-July. Look out also for the **Molson Ex Pro Challenge** in early April, four days of competitions in snowboarding and 'freeskiing' (think Jonny Moseley).

Mont Tremblant Village is a sweet, tiny village that barely spreads beyond Chemin Principal. The P'tit Train du Nord bike trail slithers along the village's west side, along the shores of Lac Mercier, where you can take a break on a **public beach**.

Station Tremblant (☎ *888-736-2526,* W *www.tremblant.com)*, now under the administration of Intrawest (the Vancouver company responsible for putting Whistler on the map) has become one of the best-known ski hills in North America. It boasts 92 slopes (10 expert) and a vertical drop of 650m; the longest run extends 6km. Accordingly, weekend day passes are considerably higher than at other places: adult passes cost $55/47 per full day/half day; for children 13 to 17, it's $40/35. Prices are 30% lower on weekdays. Detractors say that the glitter and glam outshine the slopes at Tremblant and that the prices aren't justified. Others just have a good time.

A fake, pedestrian 'tourist village' of shops, restaurants and condos has been built at the foot of the south side of the mountain, re-creating the feel of a 19th-century village but with 20th-century style and excess. Some original buildings (from the way-back days of the 1950s or so) remain close to the mountain, but all others were constructed later, some recalling architecture in Old Québec City.

Places to Stay The tourist offices can help you find a place if everything seems booked.

Camping Labellet et Rouge (☎ *819-686-1954, Kilometer 98.3 of P'tit Train du Nord trail)* Tent sites $16. You'll come across this good campground just off the bike trail 7km north of Mont Tremblant Village. The staff can also arrange to drive your luggage to other campgrounds farther north or south.

International Youth Hostel (☎ *819-425-6008,* W *www.hostellingtremblant.com, 2213 Chemin Principal)* Dorm beds $18/21/23 HI member/Canadian nonmember/other nonmember, doubles $48/58 HI member/nonmember, free for children under 12. This popular, often crowded hostel features a kitchen, laundry room, small but lively bar, Internet access and a nice view of the surrounding mountains. A free shuttle service connects to the main hostel in Montréal.

Le Lupin (☎ *819-425-5474, 127 Rue Pinoteau)* Singles/doubles $79/109. A combo B&B and hotel, this impeccable log house is only a few minutes' walk from the beach on Lac Tremblant, halfway between the village and the resort.

Getting There & Away Limocar (☎ 450-435-6767) runs buses from Montréal to St Jovite, Station Tremblant and Mont Tremblant Village ($24, two to three hours, at least four times daily). Limocar's special deals include a one-day roundtrip bus ticket from Montréal to the ski hill plus a day's ski-lift pass. On weekdays, the deal costs $64/48 adult/child under 17; on weekends, it's $68/49.

From St Jovite, a free shuttle bus (Bus No 1) travels to Station Tremblant.

By car from Montréal, take Hwy 15 to its end north of Ste Agathe, then Route 117. Turn north on Montée Ryan, 2km past St Jovite, to head toward Mont Tremblant.

Parc du Mont Tremblant

One of the province's most spectacular parks (☎ *819-688-2281, Chemin du Lac Supérieur; admission $3.50; open 8am-9pm daily)* is also the province's first – it opened in 1894. Covering 1510 sq km of gorgeous Laurentian lakes, rivers, hills and woods, the park boasts a number of distinctive features, including rare vegetation (silver maple and red oak, for example), hiking and biking trails, canoe routes and wildlife. Some of the park's many *campgrounds* come with amenities, but most are basic. Pitching a tent costs $17 to $20. In busy periods, it's best to reserve a spot.

This vast park is divided into three sectors. The most developed area is the Diable sector, home to beautiful Lac Monroe. The main entrance and information center is but 18km east of Station Tremblant. Roads are paved in Diable, and some of the campgrounds have showers. The incredible trails here range from an easy, 20-minute stroll past waterfalls to day-long hikes that take in stunning views of majestic

valleys. You can also take your bike out on some trails or rent canoes – a highly rated canoe trip goes down the very winding Rivière Diable.

Farther east, the Pimbina sector is accessible from St Donat. Here you'll also find an information center, canoe and kayak rentals and campgrounds with some amenities. Activities include swimming at Lac Provost and hiking and biking trails nearby. A highlight in this sector is the Carcan Trail, a 14.4km trail to the top of the park's second-highest peak (883m), which passes by waterfalls and lush scenery on the way.

Farther east still is the Assomption sector, accessible via the town of St Côme, with more trails, secluded cottages and remote camping options. In winter, you can't access this sector by car, as nobody plows snow off the roads.

The wilder interior and eastern sections are accessible by dirt roads, some of which are old logging routes. Some campsites can only be reached by foot or canoe. The off-the-beaten-track areas abound in wildlife, including bear and moose. With some effort, it's possible to have whole lakes to yourself, except for the wolves whose howls you hear at night. By late August, nights are cold.

St Donat

Located in the neighboring Lanaudière region, St Donat, just 32km northeast of Ste Agathe along Route 329, shares a similar landscape of lakes and vast mountains with its Laurentians neighbor. However, it tends to be much less crowded and cheaper than the villages along Route 117, and it might make a good alternative destination thanks to its many places to stay and eat.

There are several hiking trails of note, most starting from the southern edge of Lac Archambault. The **Sentier Inter-Centre de la Montagne Noire** leads you past the remains of a cockpit of a military plane that crashed here. A steep 7km trail climbs to the mountain's summit (900m) for some stupendous views.

Rawdon

Known as one of Québec's most multiethnic towns, Rawdon, also in the Lanaudière region 20km west of Joliette, was first settled by Loyalists and Irish immigrants in 1799. Scottish and British followed, and, in the 1920s, an influx of Slavic immigrants (Russians, Poles and Ukrainians) settled here. Reflecting this mix is the **Centre Multiethnique** *(☎ 450-834-3334, 3588 Rue Metcalfe; open 1pm-4pm Fri-Sun),* which exhibits arts and crafts representing all these groups.

Bordering the Rivière Ouareau, the **Parc des Chutes Dorwin** *(☎ 450-834-2282; adult/child $3/2; open 9am-7pm daily),* on Route 337 at the edge of town, makes a lovely spot for a picnic or brief hike.

EASTERN TOWNSHIPS

The Eastern Townships (Cantons de l'Est in French), the 'Garden of Québec,' extend roughly from Granby south and east to the Vermont, New Hampshire and Maine borders in the US. The area, nestled in the foothills of the Appalachian mountains, contains some of the province's most scenic countryside. Because of this, and due to its proximity to Montréal (the nearer townships are only 45 minutes away by car), the region has become a popular destination for urbanites seeking country respites. On summer and fall weekends, the main villages fill up with city folk seeking local produce, antiques, local art and fresh air.

The Eastern Townships boast Québec's most fertile soil. Agriculture has always played an important role here, and the area is the province's apple and wine country. Maples groves also grow in abundance.

In spring, 'sugaring off' – the tapping of trees for maple syrup and then boiling and preparing it – takes place in the region. Summer brings fishing and swimming in the numerous lakes. During autumn, a good time to visit, the leaves change into vibrant colors and farmers start plucking apples off the trees and making some tasty cider. In winter, the ski season draws crowds to Mont Orford and Sutton.

Cycling is extremely popular in the region, with nearly 500km of trails taking in sumptuous landscapes of rolling hills. Pick up the free guide *Cycling the Eastern Townships* and other cycling maps at any of the tourist offices in the area. Whether on bike or in a car, you can spend many pleasant afternoons meandering along country roads from one village to another, sampling local produce as you go.

The area's main tourist office (☎ 450-375-8774, 800-263-1068), just off exit 68 of Hwy 10, is open year-round. There are also 23 smaller offices spread out across the region, some of which are open May to September only.

The main route through the Eastern Townships is Hwy 10.

Granby

This town is mainly known as the home of the province's most famous zoo: the **Granby Zoo** *(☎ 450-372-9113, 525 Rue St Hubert; adult/child 5-12/child 2-4 $20/15/9; open 10am-7pm daily June-Aug, 10am-6pm Sat & Sun May & Sept),* off Hwy 10 exit 68. More than 1000 animals (250 species) live here, most in cages but some roaming 'free.' The zoo's expansion project has added a small aquapark with wave pool and a controversial dolphin show (even Brigitte Bardot wrote a letter to zoo officials begging them to cancel their plans).

Bromont

This town seems to revolve around Mt Brome's **Ski Bromont** resort *(☎ 450-534-2200, W www.skibromont.com, 150 Rue Champlain).* Summertime, its 100km of trails have made it a magnet for serious mountain bikers (the place has hosted world championships), while families flock

Winter wonderland in the Eastern Townships

to the hugely popular aquapark on the premises. Wintertime, Ski Bromont comes alive again as one of the area's top slopes. Mountain-bike and ski rentals are available onsite.

Lac Brome (Knowlton)

Lac Brome is the name of seven amalgamated towns, with Knowlton being the biggest and best known. Situated just south of Lac Brome (the lake, that is), Knowlton has a long historical connection to this scenic, small body of water. Settled by Loyalists in the early 19th century, the town turned into an upper-class residence and retreat by the end of the century thanks to a successful flourmill and sawmill, which drew on the local water supply.

It still retains a chic-er than thou air, evidenced by the shiny cars paraded down the main street, the pricey art, antique and souvenir shops and fashionable restaurants. It's worth driving around the side streets to look at the stately homes and manors. Otherwise, the town has a sterile, cold feel to it.

The main tourist office (☎ 450-242-2870, 696 Chemin Lakeside) is in the Foster section, just north of the lake.

To get to **Lac Brome**, follow Route 243 or Route 215. You can go **swimming** just off Chemin Lakeside on the south tip of the lake.

Besides its body of water, the town is also famous for Brome Duck, essentially Peking duck bred only here since 1912 and fed a special diet including soya and vitamins. The result is a tasty bird that's lower in nasty things like sodium, cholesterol and fat than other meats. You can visit the shop at the **duck breeding farm** (☎ 450-242-3825, 40 Rue Center; open 8am-5pm Mon-Fri, 10am-4pm Sat & Sun).

The **Musée Historique du Comté de Brome** (☎ 450-243-6782, 130 Rue Lakeside; adult/child $3.50/1.50; open 10am-4:30pm daily mid-May–mid-Sept), set up in six historic houses, focuses on the Loyalist history of the area and, oddly, features a WWI Fokker DVII German war plane on display.

You'll find a number of places to stay and eat here, including the following.

Majuka (☎ 450-243-1239, 266 Stage Coach) Singles/doubles $75/90. Made of wood, this dreamy place nestled in woods overlooks Sutton's mountains and boasts a freshwater pond good for a brisk swim after a hot sauna. From Knowlton, head 6km west to Route 215 and drive 2km south to Brome, then another 2km along Chemin Stage Coach.

Auberge Knowlton/Le Relais (☎ 450-242-6886, 286 Chemin Knowlton) Doubles from $90. At the Auberge, stay in very pretty rooms in a Victorian hotel. Le Relais, a reputed restaurant on the 1st floor, serves very fine regional and international cuisine. There's a nice terrace. Appetizers go for $3 to $7, dishes for $15 to $22.

Sutton

One of the region's most popular destinations, the Sutton township dates from the late 18th century, when British Loyalists made their homes around the Sutton Mountains, a string of velvety, round mountains whose highest peak (Sommet Rond) is 950m. Today Sutton fills up on weekends throughout the year – summer for the hiking, fall for the leaf peeping, winter and spring for the skiing.

The tourist office (☎ 450-538-8455, 11b Rue Pincipale Sud) stays open year-round.

Some 80km of popular hiking trails have been cleared in the thickly forested mountains, in a conserved area called the **Parc d'Environnement Naturel** (☎ 450-538-4085; adult/child $3/2; open daily June-Oct). If you're **camping** you can sleep in a refuge ($10) at 840m (foam mattresses are supplied) or at one of three campgrounds with no services ($5 per person). The one at Lac Spruce is particularly nice. Get your passes at the tourist office or at the start of the trails, high up Chemin Maple, past Mont Sutton ski hill.

If you want to combine hiking with kayaking, snowshoeing, backcountry skiing or other activities, the folks at **Au Diable Vert** (☎ 450-538-5639, 169 Chemin Staines) will ensure a memorable stay. You can rent equipment and go at it alone or take guided kayaking or hiking tours ($25 to $35), camp out ($20 per site), stay in a refuge ($25) or chalet ($85), get a fine meal ($15) or take a combination package. Again, the views are staggering from the trails and campsites. From Sutton, take Chemin Scenic all the way until 1km before the pretty village of Glen Sutton.

Mont Sutton (☎ 450-538-2545, W www.montsutton.com, 671 Chemin Maple; day

QUÉBEC

ticket adult/child 6-17 $39/28), the ski station, features 55 trails and a bumpy 'Skill Zone' for snowboarders. You can rent equipment onsite.

Willow House (☎ *450-538-0035, 30 Rue Western)* Singles/doubles $30/50. Near the center of town, the least expensive B&B around is in a large home that could use a few repairs but is perfectly comfortable.

Passiflore Inn (☎ *450-538-5555, 55 Rue Principale Sud)* Doubles $60-75. The spotless interiors of this B&B's rooms are gorgeous, some with wood-paneled floors. The Passiflore is right on the main street, but you don't hear much traffic from inside.

Valcourt

Vistitors come to the relatively unattractive Valcourt, on Route 243 (exit 90 off Hwy 10), for two well-known sites that stand on opposite ends of the social spectrum.

Joseph Armand Bombardier, the inventor of the Ski-Doo (snowmobile), was born here and made his first test models in Valcourt. His name is now on many jets and heavy machinery around the world. At the **Musée J Armand Bombardier** (☎ *450-532-5300, 1000 Ave J-A Bombardier; adult/student $5/3; open 10am-5pm daily May-early Sept, 10am-5pm Tues-Sun early Sept-Apr)*, you can see early models of his famous Ski-Doo (and see amusing clips of how they looked in action) and get a tour of the factory that still churns out snowmobiles.

Valcourt's other residents of world-wide renown ('infamy' might be a more accurate term) are the Raelians – quite an intriguing bunch, actually. On a dusty lot outside town, they've set up a funky museum of sorts, **UFOland** (☎ *450-532-6864, 1382 Rang 7; adult/child $10/7.50; open 10am-5pm Sat & Sun June, 10am-5pm Wed-Sun July-Aug)*, which was constructed out of straw bales in accordance with messages that the movement's leader, Rael, received from extraterrestrials. You'll get a 90-minute tour, visit a life-size UFO replica, find out why genetics and cloning are salient to the Raelians (there's an 8m DNA model to marvel at) and be guided to the kitschy souvenir shop.

Magog

New Englander Ralph Merry III arrived here in 1797 and founded several flour and saw mills, launching the settlement of the surrounding area. The tourist office (☎ 819-843-2744, 55 Rue Cabana) is a busy place, within walking distance of the wharf and city beach. Here you'll find photographs and details of accommodations and restaurants in the area, and you can make free local calls.

The real attraction in Magog, off Hwy 10, is the lake. In the middle of town, there's a small, free **beach** that's often unbearably crowded. At the wharf, 200m south of the beach, a number of companies rent equipment for water sports. **Tribord** (☎ *819-868-2222)* has a kiosk there and offers parasailing, Sea-Doo (personal watercraft) rides, waterskiing and a bumpy trip on a Big Banana raft. Big boat cruises also ply Lac Memphrémagog from here.

Sea-Doos and their land-locked cousins Ski-Doos can be rented at **Centre Mécanique Magog** (☎ *819-868-2919, 9 Boulevard Bourque)*, a five-minute drive from the center of town. The company will transport your rented equipment free of charge.

A 23.5km **bicycle trail** begins from Magog and ends up at the entrance to the Parc du Mont Orford.

La Belle Victorienne (☎ *819-847-0476, 142 Rue Merry Nord)* Doubles $75-95. A daintily elegant and large Victorian house in the town center, this is reputed to be one of the best places in town. You can have your morning coffee in the garden.

Hotel Union (☎ *819-843-3363, 259 Rue Principale)* Doubles $30-50. Central location and cheap rates – that's about all it has going for it, but sometimes that's all you need.

Domaine des Pins/Ranch du Spaghetti (☎ *819-847-4091, 3005 Chemin Miletta)* Singles/doubles $70/95. Your best choice in Magog is this motel/restaurant combo on the west tip of the lake. Away from the town bustle, you're treated to excellent views, comfortable rooms and a very good dining room where, as you can tell by the name, pasta rules supreme. Dishes go for $8 to $15.

Lac Memphrémagog

Private owners have snapped up most of the lakefront property around the largest and best-known lake in the Eastern Townships. Legend has it that a prehistoric creature nicknamed Mephré lives in Lac Mephrémagog. Sadly, however, just like its feisty cousins in Loch Ness, Lake Champlain and other lakes around the world in which monsters supposedly reside, this sneaky bugger has eluded photographers and researchers who could reliably prove its existence.

Halfway down the west side of the lake at St Benoît du Lac is a **Benedictine monastery** (☎ *819-843-4080; admission free; open 5am-9pm daily year-round*) where monks continue the tradition of the ancient Gregorian chant. Visitors can attend services and even stay here: there's a men's hostel here and a women's hostel at a nearby nunnery. You can practically make a meal out of the various cheeses made and sold on the premises. Also try to taste the cider the monks make.

Parc du Mont Orford

Just a 10-minute drive north of Magog lies this 58-sq-km park (☎ *819-843-9855, 3321 Chemin du Parc; admission $3.50; open daily*), one of the province's best and most diverse parks, partially due to an arts center and excellent ski station in its territory. Even thousands of people with no interest in outdoor activities come here. Surprisingly, there's no public transportation from Magog to Parc du Mont Orford, so you'll have to rely on your own wheels – car or bike – to get here.

Flanked by two mountains, Mont Orford (853m) and Mont Chauve (600m), the park is a forested paradise with a major lake (Lac Stukely), rivers and numerous walking trails. An 11.5km trail leads to the summit of Mont Orford and some very dramatic views – on a clear day you can see Vermont. Canoe trips up the Étang aux Cerises are popular.

The **Centre d'Arts Orford** (☎ *819-843-9871, 3165 Chemin du Parc*) hosts the **Festival Orford**, a series of highly reputed classical music concerts, theater and dance performances held in July and August. Tickets cost $20 to $30. At other times, you can drop into the pleasant space to see occasional free exhibits.

The ski station **Mont Orford** (☎ *819-843-6548; open 9am-4pm daily*) is a massive one, with 52 slopes and a 540m vertical drop. Maniacal thrill-seekers might want to stay away, though: 75% of the slopes are not classed as difficult. The complex also includes 56km of cross country trails. During the last week of September and the first week of October, you can take a panoramic chair-lift ride to see the splendid foliage colors (adult/child $9.50/7.50). Held in early October, Octoberfest is a much-loved Bavarian singing and drinking festival.

Camping du Parc (☎ *819-843-9855, 3321 Chemin du Parc*) Tent sites $19-30, refuges $13. Camping on a site with services can get pricey here, depending on whether you require electricity – plus, you must pay $5 to reserve in advance! Parking is another $5. Despite the gouging, the park does have lovely campgrounds, though you're just as well to pitch a tent in the wild ($19).

Auberge du Centre d'Arts Orford (☎ *819-843-8595, 3165 Chemin du Parc*) Dorm beds $15/18 HI member/nonmember, doubles $89. Located on the grounds of the Centre d'Arts, this hostel enjoys one of the nicest locations in the province. Spacious, rustic cabins are available from May through October. There's also a lovely, peaceful onsite hotel, mostly for art lovers who arrive for the concerts and show. Off-season (spring and fall), these rooms can sometimes be had for as low as $21 each.

North Hatley

On a beautiful spot at the northern tip of Lac Massawippi, this is the cutest of all the cute Eastern Township towns. Full of art galleries and antique shops, North Hatley is where the upper classes with artistic inclinations come to shop. Consequently, there's fine dining too.

The stately homes attest to the town's past as a vacation spot for rich Americans who used to partake of the charming ambience via a passenger rail service that once linked Sherbrooke with Vermont. As early as 1880, it could be called a resort town. An American influence still makes itself felt (there are as many cow paintings and scented candles here as anywhere in New England!) Rue Principale is even sometimes still referred to as Main St.

The tourist office (☎ 819-842-2223, 300 Rue Mill) sells the $10 pass you're supposed to buy to use the bike trails in the region. **Les Sports D'Eau** (☎ *819-842-2676, 240 Rue Mill*), adjacent to the parking lots in front of the tourist office, rents bikes/canoes/kayaks/paddleboats for $7/15/10/12 per hour. **Équitation Massawippi** (☎ *819-842-4249, 4700 Route 108*) offers two-hour horseback rides for $35.

QUÉBEC

This is not the place to find inexpensive accommodations, but many of the B&Bs and lodges offer sumptuous surroundings and boast very pretty views. The tourist office has photos and descriptions of all lodging types.

Serendipity (☎ 819-842-2970, 680 Chemin de la Rivière) Singles/doubles $70/90. The least-expensive B&B still provides pleasant views and agreeable decor.

Abenaki Lodge (☎ 819-842-4455, 4030 Chemin Magog) Doubles $159-179. This four-star mini-palace features impressive, wood-paneled interiors and spacious rooms decorated with fine rugs and arts and crafts.

Getting There & Away North Hatley is only 17km east of Magog along Route 108; however, there's a longer, scenic route. From Magog, take Route 141 12km south, then head north on Chemin de la Montagne, which runs parallel to Lac Massawippi; at Ste Catherine de Hatley, head east on Chemin de North Hatley-Magog until it rejoins Route 108. North Hatley is just 2km farther east.

From Sherbrooke, head south on Route 143 until Route 108; proceed 9km.

There is no bus service.

Sherbrooke

The administrative and industrial capital of the Eastern Townships is a pleasant, bilingual city that combines an old downtown of slightly run-down 19th-century charm with newer sectors featuring modern conveniences and riverside parks.

For general information, stop at the tourist office (☎ 819-821-1919, 3010 Rue King Ouest). **Réseau Riverain**, the 18km walking and cycling path along Rivière Magog, makes an agreeable stroll. It begins at the edge of Parc Blanchard (☎ 819-822-5890), where there's also a **public beach**. For window-shopping in the old part of town, where you'll find low-key antique shops, try along Rue Wellington Nord.

The **Centre d'Interprétation de Sherbrooke** (☎ 819-821-5406, 275 Rue Dufferin; adult/student $4/2.50; open 9am-5pm Tues-Sun) has a lot to offer. You can view an exhibit on the city's history, book a guided city tour or head out on your own with a recorded version ($7). You'll also find one of the province's best-kept archives here, and you can see

many people researching their genealogies or going through old newspapers.

At the **Musée des Beaux-Arts** (☎ 819-821-2115, 241 Rue Dufferin; adult/student $4/3; open 11am-5pm Tues & Thur-Sun, 11am-9pm Wed late June-early Sept; 1pm-5pm Tues & Thur-Sun, 1pm-9pm Wed early Sept-late June), decent temporary exhibits share space with a permanent display of work by regional artists and sculptors.

Close enough to be a suburb of Sherbrooke but so far away in spirit that it might be another country, Lennoxville is the region's English bastion, thanks to the Anglican **Bishop's University** (☎ 819-822-9600, Rue du Collège). Founded in 1843 and styled architecturally after both Oxford and Cambridge in England, it has managed to retain an air of the mother country.

You'll find a number of motels on Rue King Ouest at the western entrance of the city.

Bishop's University Residences (☎ 819-822-9600 ext 4, Rue du Collège) Singles/doubles $16/25 with communal washroom, $19/33 with washroom shared between two rooms. Somewhat austere but clean student residences are available from mid-May to late August. Register at MacKinnon Hall.

Hôtel Le Président (☎ 819-563-2941, 3535 Rue King Ouest) Singles/doubles starting at $50/80. Not a bad choice for mid-price hotels, this one stands on a main thoroughfare and contains an indoor pool and sauna.

Antiquarius Café (☎ 819-562-1800, 182 Rue Wellington Nord) Dishes $7-14. Open 10am-5:30pm Mon & Tues, 10am-10pm Wed-Sun. This is a truly amazing place – half antique store, half restaurant – where you can eat surrounded by – even on! – nice works of art and old furniture.

Getting There & Away From the bus station (☎ 819-569-3656, 20 Rue King Ouest), buses go to Montréal (2¼ hrs to 3½ hrs, $26) ten times a day from Monday to Thursday and on Saturday, with an additional six buses on Friday and Sunday. Local buses (Nos 2 and 82) go from the bus station to Bishop's University in Lennoxville from 6am to 1am daily; the ride costs $2.25.

Sherbrooke lies along Hwy 10, east of Magog. Allô Stop (☎ 819-821-3637, 1204 Rue King Ouest), the ride-sharing organization, offers rides to Montréal/Québec City for $9/15.

South of Sherbrooke

The entire area around **Coaticook**, on Route 147, is particularly scenic. You can cross the longest suspended bridge in the world (169m) in the **Parc de la Gorge** (☎ 819-849-2331, 135 Rue Michaud; adult/child $7/4; open 10am-5pm daily May-late June & early Sept-Nov, 9am-7pm daily late June-early Sept, 9am-4pm Mon-Wed & 9am-9pm Thur-Sun Dec–mid-Mar). It towers 50m above an impressive gorge created by the Rivière Coaticook coursing through it. You'll find 10km of hiking paths and 18.5km of biking trails, as well as other surprises, inside this wild, lovely and very worthwhile park.

East of Sherbrooke

This region, bordering the US states of Maine and New Hampshire, boasts the highest elevations in the Eastern Townships, with mountains topping 1000m. The least-visited and less-developed part of the Townships boasts superb scenery and more breathing space. **Parc du Mont Mégantic** (☎ 819-888-2941, 189 Route du Parc; admission $3.50; open 9am-11pm daily June-early Sept, 9am-5pm early Sept-May), some 60km east of Sherbrooke along Routes 108 and 212, features rocky, mountainous scenery, showing off yet another facet of the area.

Farther east is the **Parc de Frontenac** (☎ 418-422-2136, 599 Chemin des Roy; admission $3.50; open daily 8am-9pm May-Sept), one of the province's least-visited provincial parks. Canoe enthusiasts rave about the circuits and scenery here. The park offers *camping* at several campgrounds ($19 to $23), as well as refuges for overnight canoeing or hiking trips. To get to the park's northern St Daniel sector, take Hwy 112 from Sherbrooke to the town of Disraëli. From there, take Chemin du Barrage Allard (Rang 6), then Route 267.

MONTRÉAL TO QUÉBEC CITY

Leaving Montréal behind and traveling east on Route 138, you begin to get a sense of what small-town Québec is like: stone houses with light-blue trim and tin roofs, silver-spired churches, ubiquitous chip wagons called *cantines* and main streets with shops built right to the road. The best

section is from Trois Rivières onward to the northeast.

A much quicker route is Hwy 40, a four-lane expressway that can get you from Montréal to Québec City in 2½ to three hours.

South of the river, you can take the less interesting Route 132, which more or less follows the south bank of the river, or the faster, duller Hwy 20; despite its tedium, Hwy 20 does pass by Drummondville, the site of a famous annual festival (see Drummondville section, later).

Berthierville

The birthplace of world-famous racecar driver Gilles Villeneuve, Berthierville is also known for its proximity to the Îles de Berthier (comprising the northern parts of the Unesco-designated Lac St Pierre World Biosphere Reserve). Visitors come to take in the air of faded 19th-century bourgeoisie along the town's once-rich waterfront.

On the southwest corner of Routes 138 and 158 stands the oldest Anglican church in Québec, the **Chapelle Cuthbert** (1785), home to the summer tourist information bureau (☎ 450-836-7336). From early September to the end of May, the tourist bureau opens up shop inside the Days Inn (☎ 450-836-1621, 760 Rue Gadoury). No matter where the bureau staff may be, they offer travel packages, including cruises, ice-fishing and wildlife excursions.

The **Gilles Villeneuve Museum** (☎ 450-836-2714, 960 Ave Gilles Villeneuve; adult/student $6/4; open 9am-5pm daily) pays homage to Villeneuve, who became legendary after his death in a 1982 crash, and also features his brother Jacques, a well-known racer in his own right. Displays include model racecars, simulators and lots of photos.

While most of the cruises around the Lac St Pierre Biosphere Reserve depart from the south bank of the St Lawrence (see the Sorel-Tracy section, later), the **Pourvoirie du Lac St Pierre** (450-836-7506, 2309 Rang St Pierre) offer two-hour bird-watching excursions in medium-size boats for $15 per person with a reservation. Boats leave from the outfitter's headquarters in St Ignace de Loyola.

To take a six-minute ferry ride to Sorel-Tracy, follow Rue de Bienville south to the road's end in the village of St Ignace de

Loyola. From there, the ferry (☎ 450-836-4600) leaves once or twice an hour year-round. The fare is $2 each way; taking a car costs $3.35

Louiseville

In this town on Route 138, you'll find one of the most impressive churches in Canada. An opus of marble, **St Antoine de Padoue** *(50 Rue St Laurent)*, built in 1917, boasts 67 intricate stained-glass windows and a magnificent cupola painted to represent the seven virtues. Note the wooden statue of St Antoine de Padoue out front – it miraculously survived a major fire in 1926.

Trois Rivières

Local hyperbole aside, Trois Rivières can lay claim to being one of the oldest towns in North America north of Mexico, but you'd never know it now – it looks more like a forgotten city in the US Midwest than one born of a 1634 European outpost. And as for the name, don't bother looking for three rivers – the town's moniker refers to the number of branches of the Rivière St Maurice at its mouth, where islands split its flow into three channels.

The attractive **old section**, based around Rue Notre Dame and Rue des Forges, is small but good for a stroll. Cafés and bars abound in this lively area. Rue des Ursulines and Rue Radisson are also main streets. The St Lawrence River borders the southern edge of the area. The tourist office (☎ 819-375-1122, *1457 Rue Notre Dame*) is open year-round.

To go on a cruise, buy tickets at the kiosk run by **Croisières/Cruises** (☎ 819-375-3000), along the waterfront promenade at the foot of Boulevard des Forges. One-day cruises leave for Montréal and the St Maurice, Saguenay and Outaouais Rivers, among other destinations. You can also opt for the 90-minute regional cruises (adult/child $12/6), offered once or twice daily.

Among the land-based attractions, the **Musée des Arts et Traditions Populaires du Québec** (☎ 819-372-0425, *200 Rue Laviolette; adult/student $6/4; open 9am-7pm daily mid-June–early Sept, 10am-5pm Tues-Sun early Sept–mid-June*) presents a good collection of traditional domestic objects, plus material from archeological digs of Amerindian settlements in the area. The

nearby **old prison** (1822) contains a small exhibit.

The **Musée des Ursulines** (☎ 819-375-7922, *734 Rue des Ursulines; adult/student $2.50/1.50; open 9am-5pm Tues-Fri, 1:30pm-5pm Sat & Sun May-Nov; 1:30pm-5pm Wed-Sun Mar-Apr*) chronicles the history of Ursuline nuns in Québec; the first group arrived from Italy in 1639. The former hospital houses a small museum with a fine collection of textiles, ceramics, books and prints related to religion.

The **Pulp and Paper Industry Exhibition Center** (☎ 819-372-4633, *800 Parc Portuaire; adult/child $3/1.50; open 9am-6pm daily June-Aug; 9am-5pm Mon-Fri, 11am-5pm Sat-Sun Sept*) explains why the city was the world capital of pulp and paper for so long, from the late 19th century to about the 1930s.

The only North American cathedral done in the Westminster style is the 1858 neo-Gothic **Cathèdrale de l'Assumption** (☎ 819-374-2409, *363 Rue Bonaventure; admission free; 7am-noon & 2pm-5pm daily*). Built on an even grander scale, **Basilica Notre Dame du Cap** (☎ 819-374-2441, *626 Rue Notre Dame; admission free; open 8am-8pm daily*), in nearby Cap de la Madeleine, is a major pilgrimage stop. Though it looks somewhat like a spaceship about to lift off, the interiors are both magnificent and garish, with gold and calacatta marble its principal elements.

La Flottille (☎ 819-378-8010, *497 Rue Radisson*) Dorms $16.50-19.50, private doubles $46. This HI hostel is relatively lackluster, though not far from the center of things.

Gîte Universitaire (☎ 819-374-4545, *1550 Rue Père Marquette*) Singles/doubles $25 per person. Open May-Aug only. About a 10-minute drive from the center of town, this university residence building offers clean accommodations and access to the sports complex. It's best to reserve in advance.

Getting There & Away A bridge connects Trois Rivières with the south shore of the St Lawrence. The city is easily accessible via Hwys 40 and 20 or Routes 138 and 132. The bus station (☎ 819-374-2944, *275 St Georges*) is located behind the Hôtel Delta. Orléans Express runs eight daily buses to Montréal ($26, two hours) and six daily to Québec City ($35, 1¾ hrs).

Shawinigan & Grand Mère

These medium-size industrial towns, on Hwy 55 farther north up the Rivière St Maurice, are rather bleak, with little to hold the visitor. Both reflect the area's dependence on pulp and paper mills, and both contain power-generating plants.

At Shawinigan, you can visit the falls and see **Cité de l'Énergie** (City of Energy; ☎ 819-536-8516, 1000 Ave Melville; adult/student/child $14/12/8; open 10am-5pm Tues-Sun mid-June–early July & early Sept-early Oct, 10am-6pm daily early July-early Sept). A small town in and of itself, this theme park incorporates a river cruise, city guided tour, a 'time machine' and a truly stunning view of the river valley from the 115m-high observation tower lying atop an old hydroelectric pylon. Guided tours are only in French, however.

Between 5th and 6th Aves in Grand Mère, you'll find the rock in the shape of an old lady's head that gave the town its name. Boat tours on the river are available. If you're heading for any of the northerly parks, stock up here because the food and supply selection doesn't get any better farther north.

Between here and La Mauricie National Park there isn't much in the way of accommodations, so you're pretty much stuck with one of the few ordinary motels in Grand Mère or Shawinigan. In both places, you can fortify yourself with a decent meal before or after venturing out with the canoe.

La Mauricie National Park

This very well may be Québec's best-run and best-organized park (☎ 819-538-3232, 888-855-6673; adult/student $3.50/1.50). As such, it is also one of its most frequented. The arresting beauty of the nature here, whether seen from a canoe or from one of the many walking trails, is everyone's eye candy but particularly suits those who don't want to feel completely disconnected from 'civilization.' The services offered include a convenience store and two cafés. Some of the campgrounds contain as many as 219 spaces. You'll find information centers at the park's entrances at St Jean des Piles and St Mathieu.

The park covers 550 sq km, straddling northern evergreen forests and the more southerly hardwoods of the St Lawrence River Valley. The low, rounded Laurentian Mountains, among the world's oldest, are part of the Canadian Shield, which covers much of the province. Between these hills lie many small lakes and valleys. The Canadian government created the park in 1970 to protect some of the forest that the paper industry was steadily chewing up and spitting out – at one point, two sawmills were operating in the park's current territory.

The numerous **walking trails**, which can take you anywhere from a half hour to five days to complete, offer glimpses of the indigenous flora and fauna, brooks and waterfalls (the Chutes Waber in the park's western sector are particularly worth the hike to see them), as well as panoramic views onto delicate valleys, lakes and streams. The longest trail, Le Sentier Laurentien, stretches over 75km of rugged terrain in the park's northern reaches. There are refuge chalets along the way, but you must arrange to get back to the starting point after finishing the trail (30km along Route de la Promenade). Plus, you must pay $40 to complete the trail (reservations ☎ 819-533-7272).

The park is excellent for **canoeing**. Five canoe routes, ranging in length from 14km to 84km, can accommodate everyone from beginners to experts. Canoes ($18/day) can be rented at three sites, the most popular being Lac Wapizagonke, which has sandy beaches, steep rocky cliffs and waterfalls. You can also go **fishing** for trout and bass here.

In winter, some visitors come for **cross-country skiing** (adult/child $5/2.50) or winter camping in heated huts.

Also offered for a small fee are a variety of activities geared toward children, demonstrations and talks about nature.

If you want to stay here, *camping* at designated sites costs $22/26 without/with electricity; camping in the wild during canoe trips costs $14/18 without/with campfire. You can also sleep in one of two large *chalets* (☎ 819-537-4555) for $22 to $24 per person in shared rooms that accommodate four to 10 people.

No public transportation reaches the park, so you'll need a car. The main entrance is at St Jean des Piles (Hwy 55 exit 226), but there's another at St Mathieu (Hwy 55 exit 217). Both are well indicated and are connected by the 63km-long Route Promenade, which runs through the park.

QUÉBEC

Réserve Faunique du St Maurice

The 784 sq km of this wildlife reserve (☎ 819-646-5687, Route 155) offer a more secluded variation on the theme found in La Mauricie National Park. For general information, stop at the visitor's center at Rivière Matawin, 90km north of Trois Rivières. The park's centerpiece is **Lac Normand**, a crystal-clear lake where a rare species of salmon called kokani live. **Hiking** trails snake around the lake, offering impressive views. If you're *camping,* you can pay $19 for a site with showers near the lake.

Canoeing ($18/day) is most popular on the long, thin Lac Tousignant, along which you'll find isolated spots to pitch your tent ($13.50) and several comfortable refuges ($22.50) with bunk beds and wood stoves. After a small portage, you can continue on Lac Soucis and make an 18km (one-way) trip over several days.

Most people come here for **hunting** and **fishing,** so the trails and lakes are marvelously uncrowded. The only downside is the $12 it'll cost you to cross the tiny bridge over the St Maurice river – Canada's most expensive toll bridge by length. The drive from Trois Rivières, however, is especially scenic. Be sure to stop off at the flea market **Marcé aux Puces** (☎ 819-646-5005, 3660 Route 155), south of Rivière Matawin – an outdoor extravaganza of old furniture, toilets, funky dishes and outlandish owners.

Sorel-Tracy

Originally two towns now fused as one, Sorel-Tracy is primarily an industrial area, with the Sorel side being the only half worthy of any interest. Most visitors to Sorel use it as a stepping stone to the Îles de Sorel and the Lac St Pierre World Biosphere Reserve (designated by Unesco in 2000). From Sorel, it's possible to take **eco-cruises** of the largest archipelago in the St Lawrence (103 islands), which boasts the largest heron colony in North America, rare plants and fish and 288 species of observed birds (116 of these nest in the region). It's hard to believe that such pristine beauty lies within view of factories and metal industries.

For help planning your stay, contact the tourist bureau (☎ 450-746-9441, 92 Chemin des Patriotes). The **Centre d'Interpretation de Sorel** (☎ 450-780-5740, 6 Rue St Pierre; adult/student $3/1.50; open 10am-7pm daily July & Aug; 10am-5pm Wed-Fri, 1pm-5pm Sat & Sun Sept-May) serves as a general introduction to the Lac St Pierre region, offering information on the area's flora and fauna and the industrial history of Sorel.

Nature Cruises (☎ 450-780-5740, 6 Rue St Pierre; adult/child $30/15) runs three three-hour excursions a day. The last, which leaves at 6:30pm, catches a usually spectacular sunset and includes a light supper; the most popular of the lot, it costs $10 more. The company can also organize overnight stays on the islands.

The ferry (☎ 450-743-3258) to St Ignace de Loyola leaves from Sorel (see the Berthierville section, earlier).

Odanak

One of only two Abénaki Native Indian reservations, this small village on Route 132 north of Sorel-Tracy is also home to the only museum dedicated to their culture and traditions. The *Musée des Abénakis* (☎ 450-568-2600, 108 Rue Waban-Aki; adult/student $4/2; open 10am-5pm Mon-Fri, 1pm-5pm Sat & Sun May-Oct) tells the story of the Abénaki through masks, videos, artifacts and handicrafts. The sculptures placed outside on pretty parkland are particularly interesting. On the first Sunday in July, the Abénaki hold their annual pow-wow here.

Nicolet

Continuing north on Route 132, you'll come to Nicolet, founded in 1672. Now a major religious center, it's sometimes dubbed the 'town of bells' for all its churches and cathedrals. The attractions here range from the austere *Cathédrale de Nicolet* (☎ 819-293-5492, 671 Boulevard Louis Fréchette), frightening in its 1960s modernity, to the far more interesting *Musée des Religions* (☎ 819-293-6148, 900 Boulevard Louis Fréchette; adult/student $4.50/1.75; open 10am-5pm daily June-Sept, 10am-5pm Tues-Sun Oct-May). The museum's permanent collection consists of 5000 religious objects and artifacts, including flashy altar pieces. The temporary exhibits, on loan from museums around the world, tend to be excellent.

Drummondville

This semi-industrial town of 45,000 people, just off Hwy 20, has carved an interesting niche for itself by becoming home to the Mondial des Cultures festival, one of the province's most renowned cultural gatherings. Artists and performers from around the world converge on this unassuming spot at the beginning of July.

For more information on this festival, contact the tourist bureau (☎ 819-477-5529, 1350 Rue Michaud), open daily year-round; it's accessible from Hwy 20 exits 175 or 177.

Le Village Québécois d'Antan (☎ 819-478-1441, 1425 Rue Montplaisir; adult/student/child $17/11/7; open 10am-6pm daily June 1-Sept 30) is a reconstruction of 19th-century pioneer villages spread over 7km. Guides in period costume put on bread-making and crafts displays, while visitors sample traditional food and kids feed the animals. From June through August, the village hosts nightly performances of **Legendes Fantastiques** (☎ 800-265-5412; adult/child $33.50-37.50/16.75-18.75), a dazzling, multimedia show that mixes circus, drama and comedy to re-create folklore, legends and timeless tales for all ages. Over 50,000 people see it each year.

Québec City

pop 672,000

Québec City is the cradle of French culture in North America, the historic heart of Québec. Moreover, it is also its jewel. Since 1985, the entire old town has been placed on the UN's prestigious World Heritage list. This walled old city is a living museum, each street a page in the book of French Canada's struggle for survival, even dominion, in British North America. The old part of Québec remains the only walled city in the USA and Canada.

Yet it is also a lively capital with a vibrant population of 672,000 if you include outlying areas and townships (Québec City itself only counts 167,000 people). Home to some of the country's best museums, Québec City can also lay claim to being the most 'European' city on the continent. Old Montréal shares this feel to some degree, as does the French Quarter in New Orleans, but nowhere in North America is the picture as complete. Because of this, Québec City is a year-round tourist mecca. Each year, some four million tourists pass through, a quarter

of them from outside Canada. It regularly figures in the top ten most-visited spots in North America on numerous surveys.

The city is also an important port, lying where the Rivière St Charles meets the Rivière St Laurent. It sits on top of and around a cliff, a wonderful setting that affords views over the river and the town of Lévis (pronounced **lev**-ee) across the river.

Although many people are bilingual, the vast majority are French-speaking and 94% can claim French ancestors. But because this is a tourist town – ranking with Banff and Victoria as one of the country's most-visited destinations – plenty of shopkeepers and at least some of the staff at attractions can communicate in English.

History

One of the continent's earliest settlements, the site of Québec City was already an Indian village called 'Stadacona' in Huron Indian when the French explorer Jacques Cartier landed here in 1535 on his second voyage to the New World. He returned in 1541 with the notion to start a post upstream at Cap Rouge, but this plan turned out to be a failure that set back France's colonial ambitions in the region for more than half a century.

Explorer Samuel de Champlain finally founded the city for the French in 1608, calling it Kebec, from the Algonquin Indian word meaning 'the river narrows here,' and built a small base at Cap Diamand.

The English successfully attacked in 1629, but Québec was returned to the French under a treaty three years later and it soon became the center of New France. Repeated English attacks followed. In 1759, General Wolfe led the British to victory over Montcalm on the Plains of Abraham (although both generals died in the battle). One of North America's most famous battles, this event virtually ended the long-running conflict between Britain and France. In 1763, the Treaty of Paris gave Canada to Britain. In 1775, the American revolutionaries had a go at capturing Québec but were promptly pushed back.

In the 19th century, the city lost its status and importance in the shadow of Montréal. When the Great Depression burst Montréal's bubble in 1929, Québec City regained some stature as far as government

QUÉBEC

matters were concerned. Some business-savvy locals launched the now-famous Winter Carnival in the 1950s in order to incite a tourism boom.

In April 2001, the city was the site of the Summit of the Americas, which exploded into mass demonstrations and protests against globalization. Images of 6000 police and 1200 soldiers using water cannons, tear gas, clubs and rubber bullets on protesters were broadcast around the globe.

Orientation

The city itself is surprisingly small, covering 93 sq km, with nearly all things of interest packed into one compact corner.

Part of the city sits on top of the cliffs of Cap Diamant (Cape Diamond), and part lies below. Québec is thus divided into Haute Ville (Upper Town) and Basse Ville (Lower Town), each with old and new sections. The Citadelle, a fort and famous landmark, stands on the highest point of Cap Diamant overlooking the city. Together, the 10 sq km of these historic upper and lower areas form the appealing Vieux Québec (Old City). Rue St Jean is a main street with many bars and restaurants.

A well-known landmark in Old Québec is the copper-topped, castle-style Château Frontenac hotel dating from 1892. Behind the château, a large boardwalk called the Terrasse Dufferin edges along the cliff, providing good views over the river. From here, the boardwalk leads to the Promenade des Gouverneurs, a path that runs between the

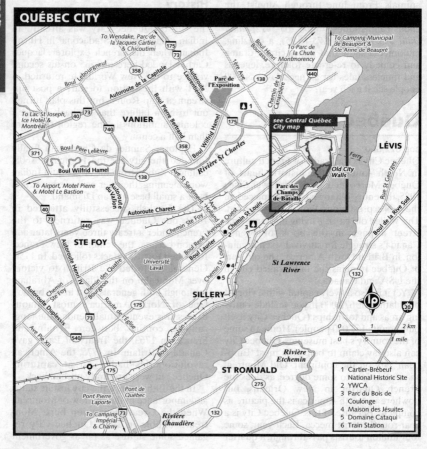

QUÉBEC CITY

To Wendake, Parc de la Jacques Cartier & Chicoutimi

To Parc de la Chute Montmorency

To Camping Municipal de Beauport & Ste Anne de Beaupré

Parc de l'Exposition

1

see Central Québec City map

To Lac St Joseph, Ice Hotel & Montréal

VANIER

LÉVIS

Boul Wilfrid Hamel

Rivière St Charles

Old City Walls

To Airport, Motel Pierre & Motel Le Bastion

Parc des Champs de Bataille

Autoroute Charest

STE FOY

Chemin Ste Foy

Chemin St Louis

3

Université Laval

Boul Laurier

St Lawrence River

4

5

SILLERY

To Camping Impérial & Charny

ST ROMUALD

Pont Pierre Laporte

Pont de Québec

Rivière Etchemin

Rivière Chaudière

6

0   1   2 km
0   .5   1 mile

1 Cartier-Brébeuf National Historic Site
2 YWCA
3 Parc du Bois de Coulonge
4 Maison des Jésuites
5 Domaine Cataraqui
6 Train Station

cliff's edge and the Citadelle. Beyond that lies the huge park called Parc des Champs de Bataille.

Below the Château Frontenac is Old Lower Town, the oldest section of the city, sitting mainly between the St Lawrence and St Charles Rivers and hugging the cliffs of Cap Diamant.

The focal point of this small area, at the northeastern edge of Old Québec, is Place Royale. From here, you can walk or take the funicular to the top of the cliff of Upper Town. Rue Sous le Cap and Rue du Petit Champlain, which are only 2.5m across, are two of the oldest streets in North America.

The wider area of Lower Town, which surrounds Upper Town on the north, south and west, contains residential, business and industrial areas, as well as some vibrant and newly developing social sectors like St Roch. Much farther north in Lower Town are the highways leading north, east and west. To the extreme southwest of the city you'll see signs for either Pont de Québec or Pont Pierre Laporte. Both bridges lead to the south shore.

Outside the wall in Upper Town are some places of note, including the National Assembly (Legislative Buildings) and some restaurants. The two main streets heading west from Old Upper Town are Boulevard René Lévesque and, to the south, Grande Allée, which eventually becomes Boulevard Wilfrid Laurier. Grand Allée, in particular, is busy at night, as bars and numerous places to eat draw crowds.

A smart place to get oriented is at the Édifice Marie Guyart, where the Obsérvatoire de la Capitale offers great views of the lay of the land; see the Outside the Walls section, later, for more information.

Information

You'll find tourist information offices throughout Greater Québec. On the Web, check out **W** www.quebecregion.com. The main office is Centre Infotouriste (☎ 418-649-2608, 800-363-7777, 12 Rue Ste Anne), on Place d'Armes, opposite the Château Frontenac. From June to September, it's open 8:30am to 7:30pm daily; at other times it closes at 5pm. You can book various city tours here.

A second, equally large but less crowded tourist office (☎ 418-649-2608, 835 Ave Wilfrid Laurier) is at the entrance to the Plains of Abraham. Kiosk Frontenac, a booth on Terrasse Dufferin facing the Château Frontenac, makes reservations for all city activities and is the starting point for some tours.

Old Upper Town

Citadelle The French started to build here in 1750, when bastions were constructed for storing gunpowder. The fort (☎ 418-694-2815, Côte de la Citadelle; adult/child $5.50/4; open 9am or 10am to 5pm or 6pm Apr-Sept, 10am-3pm Oct) was completed by the British in 1820 after 30 years' work and served as the eastern flank of the city's defense system against invading Americans.

Today the Citadelle is the home base of Canada's Royal 22s (known in bastardized French as the Van Doos), a French regiment that developed quite a reputation through WWI, WWII and the Korean War. A museum outlines the group's history. The entrance fee includes admission to this museum and a guided tour, offered April to October. The changing-of-the-guard ceremony takes place at 10am daily in summer. The 'beating of the retreat,' which features soldiers banging on their drums as they leave the grounds at shift's end, happens at 6pm on Tuesday, Thursday, Saturday and Sunday during July and August, followed by the last tour. It's a bit of Canadiana in the heart of Québec.

Parc des Champs de Bataille The huge Battlefields Park runs southwest from the Citadelle. Its hills, gardens, monuments and trees take up 108 hectares and make perfect spots for strolling, biking, in-line skating and cross-country skiing. Despite its present-day pleasantness, though, the park was once a bloody battleground, the site of a conflict that determined the course of Canadian history. The part closest to the cliff is known as the **Plains of Abraham** – it was here in 1759 that the British finally defeated the French, with both generals, Wolfe of Britain and Montcalm of France, dying in the process. A **monument** to Wolfe stands in front of the Musée du Québec and a **monument** to Montcalm stands on Grande Allée west of the military manège.

Walking or bus tours of the park depart from the **Discovery Pavilion** (☎ 418-648-

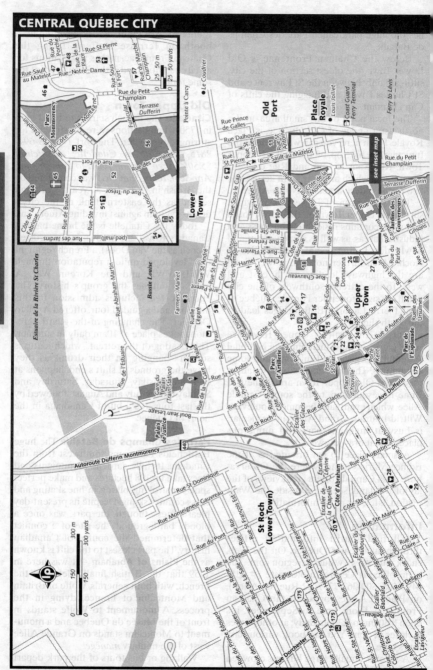

CENTRAL QUÉBEC CITY

QUÉBEC

CENTRAL QUÉBEC CITY

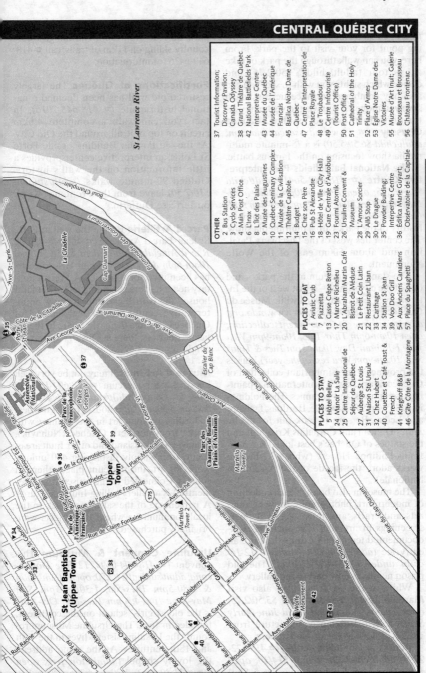

OTHER
2 Bus Station
3 Cyclo Services
4 Main Post Office
6 L'Inox
9 L'Îlot des Palais
10 Québec Seminary Complex
11 Musée de la Civilisation
12 Théâtre Capitole
14 Budget
15 Chez son Père
16 Pub St Alexandre
18 Hôtel de Ville (City Hall)
19 Gare Centrale d'Autobus
23 Fourmi Atomik
26 Ursuline Convent & Museum
28 L'Amour Sorcier
29 Allô Stop
30 Le Drague
35 Powder Building; Interpretive Centre
36 Edifica Marie Guyart; Observatoire de la Capitale
37 Tourist Information; Discovery Pavilion; Canada Odyssey
38 Grand Théâtre de Québec
42 National Battlefields Park Interpretive Centre
43 Musée du Québec
44 Musée de l'Amérique Français
45 Basilica Notre Dame de Québec
47 Centre d'Interpretation de Place Royale
48 Le Troubadour
49 Centre Infotouriste (Tourist Office)
50 Post Office
51 Cathedral of the Holy Trinity
52 Place d'Armes
53 Eglise Notre Dame des Victoires
55 Musée d'Art Inuit, Galerie Brousseau et Brousseau
56 Château Frontenac

PLACES TO EAT
1 Aviatic Club
7 Piazzetta
13 Casse Crêpe Breton
17 Marché Richelieu
20 L'Abraham Martin Café
21 Bistrot de Méduse
22 Le Petit Coin Latin
22 Restaurant Liban
33 Carthage
34 Station St Jean
39 Voo Doo Grill
54 Aux Anciens Canadiens
57 Place du Spaghetti

PLACES TO STAY
5 Hôtel Belley
24 Manoir La Salle
25 Centre International de Séjour de Québec
27 Auberge St Louis
31 Maison Ste Ursule
32 Chez Hubert
40 Couettes et Café Toast & French
41 Krieghoff B&B
46 Gîte Côte de la Montagne

QUÉBEC

4071, 835 Ave Wilfred Laurier; admission free; open 9am-5:30pm daily), a good starting point for your visit to the park. From here, you can walk through the park or take a bus tour (adult/child $3.50/2.75) and decide which sights you wish to see. You can also buy combined entrance tickets, which save you money if you wish to visit many attractions. In the same building, **Canada Odyssey** (W *www.odysseecanada.com; adult/child $6.50/5.50)* is a 75-minute multimedia show focusing on the famous battle.

The National Battlefields Park Interpretive Centre (☎ 418-648-5641; *adult/child $3.50/2.75; open 10am-5:30pm daily mid-May–mid-Oct, 10am-5:30pm Tues-Sun mid-Oct–mid-May)* focuses on the dramatic history of the park with a multimedia show. The center lies west of the Discovery Pavillion and about 500m east of the Wolfe Monument.

The standout museum in the park – and one of the city's finest – is just west of the Interpretive Centre. The worthwhile **Musée du Québec** (☎ *418-643-2150,* W *www.mdq.org; admission free for permanent collection; open 10am-6pm Thur-Tues, 10am-9pm Wed June 1-Labour Day; 10am-5pm Tues & Thur-Sun, 10am-9pm Wed rest of the year)* houses the province's most important collection of Québécois art, as well as international paintings, sculptures and ceramics. The holdings include work by Riopelle, Borduas, Dallaire and Leduc. Be sure to look out for art by James Duncan and Cornelius Krieghoff and the statues of Québec's best-loved sculptor, Louis-Philippe Hébert (whose 22 bronze works adorn the facade of the Assemblée Nationale).

The museum also boasts a rich collection of modern art, photographs, drawings and arts and crafts, and most weeks it hosts screenings of art films. The incisive, well-documented temporary exhibits require an entry fee *(adult/senior/student/child 12-16/child under 12 $10/9/5/3/free).* The old prison nearby is now part of the gallery.

While in the park, you can also visit **Martello Tower 1** *(adult/child $3.50/2.75; open 10am-5:30pm daily mid-June–early Sept),* a British defensive structure from 1812. Kids love to run around in here.

Rent skates for **inline skating** (☎ *418-522-2293; adult/child 2hr rental $14/10; open 10am-9pm Mon-Fri, 10am-6pm Sat & Sun)*

from a kiosk at the western entrance of the park, off Rue Montcalm. You can go **cross-country skiing** on 11km of trails; call ☎ 418-649-6476 for information.

Fortifications of Québec The largely restored old wall has been deemed a national historic site (☎ *418-648-7016).* In fact, you can walk a complete 4.6km circuit on top of it, all around the Old City. At the old Powder Building beside Porte St Louis, an interpretive center provides a little information on the wall's history. Guided 90-minute walks *(adult/student $10/7.50)* leave from the Frontenac Kiosk on Terrasse Dufferin.

Parc d'Artillerie Beside the wall at Porte St Jean, Parc d'Artillerie (☎ *418-648-4205, 2 Rue d'Auteuil; adult/student $3.50/3; open 10am-6pm daily),* a National Historic Site, has been used for centuries. A French military headquarters beginning in 1747, it later housed the British garrison. It's now an interpretive center with a scale model of Québec City circa the early 1800s. In the officers' quarters, there's a history lesson for children.

Musée d'Art Inuit It may not be very well known, but this museum (☎ *418-694-1828, 39 Rue St Louis; adult/student $6/4; open 9:30am-5:30pm daily)* houses one of the best collections of Inuit art in the country, with works from northern Québec (Nunavik), Nunavut, Baffin Island and other Inuit areas. Aside from simply displaying 450 unique works of art, the museum places them in context. Connected to the museum (conveniently!) is a gallery selling Inuit sculptures. A percentage of the sales goes back to the local communities where the objects were originally purchased.

Ursuline Convent & Museum This convent (☎ *418-694-0694, 12 Rue Donnacona; adult/student $4/2.50; open 10am-noon & 1:30-5pm Tues-Sat, 1:30pm-5pm Sun May-Sept; 1pm-4:30pm Tues-Sun Oct-Apr)* is the oldest girls' school on the continent, founded in 1641. The Ursuline Museum recounts the Ursuline sisters' lives in the 17th and 18th centuries. At the same address, the lovely **chapel** *(admission free; open 10am-11:30am & 1:30pm-4:30pm Tues-Sat,*

QUÉBEC

1:30-4:30pm Sun May-Oct) dates from 1902 but has retained some interiors built in 1723. Buried here are the remains of both Marie de l'Incarnation, the founder of the convent, and General Montcalm. Talk about strange bedfellows!

Cathedral of the Holy Trinity Built in 1804 and modeled on St Martin in the Fields in London, this elegantly handsome church (☎ 418-692-2193, 31 Rue des Jardins; admission free; open 9am-6pm daily May-June, 9am-8pm daily July-Aug, 10am-4pm daily Sept–mid-Oct) was the first Anglican cathedral built outside the British Isles. The bell tower, 47m up, has an eight-bell chime that competes for attention with the nearby Basilica Notre Dame.

Latin Quarter The Latin Quarter refers to a section of Old Upper Town that surrounds the large **Québec seminary** complex, with its stone and wooden buildings, grassy, quiet quadrangles, a chapel and museum. The seminary originally served as the site of Laval Université, which outgrew the space here and moved to Ste Foy in the 1960s. Some faculties remain, however, including the School of Architecture, the largest of its kind in Canada.

The focus of the area is the towering **Basilica Notre Dame de Québec** (☎ 418-694-0665, 20 Rue De Buade; admission free; open 7:30am-4:30pm daily). Samuel de Champlain erected a chapel on this site in 1633, but it was destroyed in 1640, and a stone church was built in its place in 1650. Over the next century the simple structure was enlarged and promoted to rank of cathedral, but several fires damaged it before its reconstruction in 1925. The grandiose interiors faithfully re-create the spirit of the 18th century. A tacky multimedia show ($7), held five times a day, tells the story of the church in sound and light.

Next door is the excellent **Musée de l'Amérique Francaise** (*Museum of French America*; ☎ 418-692-2843, 2 Côte de la Fabrique; adult/student $4/2; open 10am-5pm daily July-early Sept, 10am-5pm Tues-Sun rest of the year). Purported to be Canada's oldest museum, this entertaining and educational institution contains artifacts relating to French settlement and culture in the New World. Your admission fee grants you

entrance into some of the seminary buildings, where religious and other temporary exhibits are mounted. The free guided tours will get you into the oldest buildings. If the gates to the left of the Basilica are closed, enter the seminary grounds at 9 Rue de l'Université.

Musée des Augustines Situated on the grounds of a monastery, this museum (☎ 418-692-2492, 32 Rue Charlevoix; admission by donation; open 9:30am-noon & 1:30pm-5pm Tues-Sat, 1:30pm-5pm Sun) describes the lives of the religious nuns who arrived in a harsh, nearly unpopulated Québec in 1639. Three brave sisters originally came to New France to found a hospital, Hôtel Dieu, which for over 350 years has never stopped functioning as a caregiving center. The interesting exhibit features paintings, antique furniture and other works of art.

Château Frontenac It's said to be the world's most photographed hotel. The Château Frontenac (*1 Rue des Carrières*) was built in 1893 by the Canadian Pacific Railway as the most striking of the CPR's series of luxury hotels across Canada. During WWII, Prime Minister MacKenzie King hosted Winston Churchill and Franklin Roosevelt here.

Tours (☎ 418-691-2166; adult/child $6.50/3.75; 10am-6pm daily May–mid-Oct, 1pm-5pm Sat & Sun rest of the year) leave every hour on the hour and last 50 minutes. They depart from the base of the staircase next to Bar St Laurent on the main floor.

Facing the hotel along Rue St Louis is the **Jardins des Gouverneurs**, a small park that was part of the Château St Louis, which once stood in Château Frontenac's place. You'll find a small monument to both Wolfe and Montcalm here.

Terrasse Dufferin This is the most popular meeting spot in the city, a given on any visitor's agenda. Outside the Château Frontenac along the riverfront, this 425m-long esplanade provides dramatic views over the Rivière St Laurent, perched as it is 60m high on a cliff. Its western extremity leads to the Citadelle, and on the eastern end stands a statue of de Champlain – a popular place to arrange meetings. A Unesco monument placed on the Terrasse in 1985 honors the city's placement on the World Heritage List.

Champlain stands facing **Place d'Armes**, a small square in front of the main tourist information office. Once a military parade ground, it's now a handy city orientation point.

Hôtel de Ville At the end of Rue de Buade stands the **Hotel de Ville** (City Hall; ☎ 418-691-6467, 2 Rue des Jardins), built in 1895 on the site of a destroyed college for Jesuits (the Brits closed them down in 1759). The present building is interesting architecturally for its mix of styles, with American neo-Roman the predominant one. Tours (adult/student $3/2) leave at 9am, 3pm and 3:45pm from the end of June to August. From mid-May to late June and from September to mid-October, they go at 3pm and 3:45pm.

Old Lower Town

This section covers the Old Town areas of the Lower Town. You can get down to the area several ways – for example, by taking Côte de la Canoterie from Rue des Ramparts to the Old Port and Train Station. Most, however, walk down the charming and steep Rue Côte de la Montagne. About halfway down on the right there is a shortcut – the escalier Casse-Cou (Break-Neck Staircase) – that leads down to Rue du Petit Champlain. A busy, attractive street, Rue du Petit Champlain is said to be, along with Rue Sous le Cap, the narrowest in North America and is also one of the oldest.

Parc Montmorency You'll see this small expanse of green on your way down Côte de la Montagne. In the center stands the statue of Sir Georges Étienne Cartier, one of the fathers of Confederation. Site of the first cemetery in North America north of Mexico, this spot was later used to hold government assembly meetings. After the building burned down in 1883, a memorial park then sprang up in its place.

Place Royale The central and principal square of the Lower Town area has 400 years of history behind it. In 1690, cannons placed here held off the attacks of the English naval commander Phips and his men. When de Champlain founded Québec, it was this bit of shoreline that was first

settled. Today the name 'Place Royale' often refers to the district in general.

The new **Centre d'Interpretation de Place Royale** (☎ 418-646-3167, 27 Rue Notre Dame; adult/student $3/2; open 10am-5:30pm daily late June-Oct) touts the area as the cradle of French history on the continent. Also on the square are many buildings from the 17th and 18th centuries, overpriced tourist shops and a statue of Louis XIV (in the middle).

Église Notre Dame des Victoires Dating from 1688, this modest house of worship (Our Lady of Victories Church; ☎ 418-692-1650, 32 Rue Sous le Fort; admission free; open 9:30am-4:30pm daily) on the square is the oldest stone church in the US and Canada. It stands on the very spot where de Champlain had set up his 'Habitation,' a small stockade, 80 years prior to the church's arrival. Inside are copies of works by Rubens and Van Dyck. Hanging from the ceiling is a replica of a wooden ship, the Brézé, thought to be a good-luck charm for ocean crossings and battles with the Iroquois.

Old Port

Built around the old harbor in Lower Town north and east of Place Royale, the Vieux Port (Old Port) is a redeveloped multipurpose waterfront area still undergoing changes and growth. It's a large, spacious assortment of government buildings, shops, condominiums and recreational facilities with no real focal point but a few things of interest to the visitor.

Musée de la Civilisation Arguably the province's best museum, this is not to be skipped, no matter the excuse! The first striking aspect of the museum (☎ 418-643-2158, 85 Rue Dalhousie; adult/student $7/4, Tues free Sept-May; open 10am-7pm daily late June-early Sept, 10am-5pm Tues-Sun early Sept-late June) is its architecture. Built in 1988, the ensemble was conceived by Moshe Safdie, who not only incorporated some existing old buildings into the whole (the Estèbe house dates from 1752) but also used traditional elements of Québécois architecture (slanted roof, stylized garret windows). The exterior staircase is a work of art in its own right.

Inside the museum, things get even better. Of the two permanent exhibits, one focuses on the cultures of Québec's 11 First Nations, and another ('Mémoires/Memories') offers an excellent chronology of life in the province via the objects that defined different eras. You'll see everything from old bars of soap to spinning wheels to a huge neon Tavern sign.

The temporary exhibits are usually well-organized and memorable, mainly dealing with very contemporary concerns (globalization, genetics, cloning, etc). A number of displays are interactive and many truly innovative (a surprising rarity in our age of technological complexity!).

Antique Shop District Rue St Paul, northwest of the Place Royale near the Old Port Interpretation Centre, lies at the heart of an expanding antique quarter. From Place Royale, take Rue St Pierre toward the harbor and turn left at Rue St Paul. About a dozen shops here sell antiques, curiosities and old Québécois relics.

You'll also find some good little cafés along this relatively quiet street. Farther along, at the waterfront on Rue St André, is the **farmers' market**, where you can buy dozens of local specialties, from wines and ciders to honeys, chocolates, herbal hand creams and, of course, maple syrup products. Beyond the market is the **Gare du Palais** train and bus station, constructed in the château style. It's well worth walking inside just for a gander at its Old World splendor.

If you walk toward the wall from the station, in a few minutes you'll come upon the **L'Îlot des Palais** (☎ 418-691-6092, Rue Vaillier; adult/student $3/2; open 10am-5pm daily late June-early Sept), an exhibition set up around actual archeological digs. Platforms lead over foundations, firepits and outlines of several buildings that Laval Université students uncovered and explored.

Outside the Walls
Assemblée Nationale Back in Upper Town, just across from the Porte St Louis, is the home of the Provincial Legislature (☎ 418-643-7239, Ave Honoré Mercier at Grande Allée Est; admission free; open 9am-4:30pm daily late June-early Sept, 9am-4:30pm Mon-Fri early Sept-late June). Better known as the National Assembly, it's a Second Empire structure dating from 1886, built to replace the old parliament building that had burned down in present-

day Parc Montmorency. The facade is decorated with 22 bronze statues of important figures in Québec's history, from politicians and cardinals to explorers and colonists. Free tours are given in English and French.

Édifice Marie Guyart At this structure, the **Obsérvatoire de la Capitale** (☎ 418-644-9841, 675 Boulevard René Lévesque; adult/student $4/3; open 10am-5pm daily July–mid-Oct, 10am-5pm Tues-Sun rest of the year) offers great views from the 31st floor and should help you get your bearings. You can also bone up on local history by reading the information panels.

St Jean Baptiste & St Roch These two regions flank the Old Town to its west and northwest, respectively; they're both worth exploring on foot. The heart of St Jean Baptiste, part of the Upper Town, is Rue St Jean, which extends from the Old Town. Good restaurants, hip cafés and bars and interesting shops, some of which cater to a gay clientele, line Rue St Jean between Ave Dufferin and Rue Racine, but the down-to-earth ambience is proof that you're way out of the traditional tourist zone. You're more likely to see locals in this laid-back region than in the Old Town.

From Rue St Jean, take any side street and walk downhill (northwest) to the narrow residential streets like Rue D'Aiguillon, Rue Richelieu or Rue St Olivier. Just as long, outside staircases are trademarks of Montréal architecture, so are these miniature, scrunched-together houses, some with very nice entrances, typical of Québec City's residential landscape.

Walking down Côte Ste Geneviève, you'll get to a steep staircase, the Escalier de la Chapelle, which takes you down to Lower Town and to the interesting St Roch area. Traditionally a residential district for factory and naval workers, it's been slowly going through a gentrification process. Along the main artery, Rue St Joseph, are junk shops, secondhand clothes stores and used bookstores along with spiffy new cafés. Check out the art galleries on Rue St Vallier Est.

Cartier-Brébeuf National Historic Site On the St Charles River, north of the central walled section of the city, this park (☎ 418-648-4038, 175 Rue de l'Espinay;

QUÉBEC

adult/student $3/2.25; open 10am-6pm daily mid-June–mid-Sept) marks where Cartier and his men were nursed through the winter of 1535 by the local Native Indians. You'll find a full-scale replica of Cartier's ship and a reproduction of a Native Indian long-house in the park's green (but rather inauthentic-looking) riverside setting.

Parc du Bois de Coulonge Not far west of the Plains of Abraham lie these colorful gardens (☎ *418-528-0773, 1215 Chemin St Louis; admission free)*, a paean to the plant world. Now open to the public, this wood-land full of extensive horticultural displays used to be the private property of a succes-sion of Québec and Canada's religious and political elite.

Maison des Jésuites The historic Jesuit House site (☎ *418-688-8074, 2320 Chemin du Foulon; admission $2; open 11am-5pm Tues-Sun June-Sept, 1pm-5pm Tues-Sun Oct-May)*, south of town along the river in Sillery, dates back 3500 years, when Native Indians lived here. The Jesuits started a mission at this location in 1637, but the site continued to function as a meeting place for the Native Indians and acted as a focal point for their relations with Europeans. Low-key displays illustrate the story and clash of cultures.

Domaine Cataqui The provincial premier holds official functions to bedazzle VIPs at this site (☎ *418-681-3010, 2141 Chemin St Louis; adult/child $5/4; open 10am-5pm daily Mar-Dec, 10am-5pm Tues-Sun Jan-Feb)*, home to a million square feet of lovely gardens. There are nine buildings on the sprawling grounds, all elegant, and it's easy to see how this place was the epicenter of high-class social life in the 1930s. In the main villa, several rooms serve as exhibition halls, mostly focusing on the site's history. You can come here year-round, but it's really something to see when the gardens are in full bloom, in spring and summer.

Organized Tours

Walking Affable archeologist Paul Gaston gives the city's best and most thematically diverse walking tours when not zipping around town researching on his bike. Contact **Paul Gaston l'Anglais** (☎ *418-529-*

3422; tours $8-12) for such tours as Beer Brewing, Cemeteries of Old Québec, Mili-tary Walks, Women's Struggle to Get the Vote and the Parks of the City. All last about two hours and are highly worthwhile. His English is a bit rusty, but he manages.

La Compagnie des Six Associes (☎ *418-802-6665; tours $12-15)* boasts a great staff and very good walking circuits like the ever-popular Vice and Drunkeness, which creaks opens the rusty door on the history of alcohol and prostitution in the city. Other tours, done in English and French, focus on epidemics, disasters, crimes and prisons in Québec's past. A cheery bunch, they are. Make reservations at the company's kiosk at the main tourist office.

If you don't want a live guide, you can rent a CD player at any tourist office for $10 to $15 and walk different circuits yourself, while listening to tours on disc. Call ☎ 418-990-8687 for more information.

Boat Québec City is not a particularly good place to take a boat cruise: the choice is limited, and the views aren't much better than what you'd get from the cheap ferry to/from Lévis on the south shore. Near Place Royale at the river's edge you'll see the MV *Louis Jolliet* and other vessels offering cruises downriver to the waterfalls Chute Montmorency and to Île d'Orléans.

Another company with a smaller vessel, *Le Coudrier* (☎ *418-692-0107)*, does 90-minute cruises around Québec City and down the river for $15 and cheaper one-hour trips, too. You can also do full-day trips with a meal; the itinerary includes Grosse Île. For information, call or visit the vessel at quay No 19, along the Old Port dock opposite the Agora.

Bicycle If you want to pedal your way around town, **Cyclo Services** (☎ *418-692-4052, 160 Quai St André; tours $28)*, inside the farmers' market near the Old Port, rents bikes and organizes excellent bike tours of the city and outskirts for small groups. The knowledgeable and fun guides frequently give tours in English.

Calèche Horse-drawn carriages (calèches) make for a nice ride but cost $60 for about 40 minutes. Drivers offer a good tour of the historic district. You can usually find some calèches lined up on Rue St Jean, inside the gates to Old Town.

Special Events

Winter Carnival This famous annual event (W www.carnaval.qc.ca), unique to Québec City, bills itself as the biggest winter carnival in the world, with parades, ice sculptures, a snow slide, boat races, dances, music and lots of drinking during the first half of February. Activities take place all over Old Town (many at the Parc de l'Esplanade), and the famous slide is on the Terrasse Dufferin behind the Château. If you want to go, organize the trip early, as accommodations fill up fast, and bring lots of warm clothes.

Fête Nationale de la St Jean Baptiste On the night of June 23, Québec City parties hard. Major festivities begin on the Plains of Abraham at 8pm. For more information, visit W www.snqc.qc.ca.

Summer Festival This festival (☎ 888-992-5200, W www.infofestival.com), held in the first half of July, features some 500 free shows and concerts, including drama and dance. Most squares and parks in the Old City host some activity daily, especially the Parc de la Francophonie (behind Hôtel de Ville) at noon and in the evening.

Les Grands Feux Loto-Québec This major fireworks show (☎ 800-923-3389) takes place at the Chutes Montmorency at the end of July.

Places to Stay

There are many, many places to stay in Québec City, and generally the competition keeps the prices down to a reasonable level. Most budget accommodations are in small European-style hotels. Motels and larger downtown hotels tend to be expensive. As you'd expect in such a popular city, the best cheap places are often full. Look for a room before 2pm or phone ahead for a reservation. Midsummer and Winter Carnival time are especially busy, particularly weekends.

Camping *Camping Municipal de Beauport* (☎ 418-666-2228, 95 Rue Sérénité) Tent sites $18. This excellent campground north of Québec City is green, peaceful and just a 15-minute drive from the Old City. To get there, take Hwy 440 or Hwy 40 toward Montmorency, get off at exit 321 and turn north.

Camping Impérial (☎ 418-831-2969, 888-831-2969, 152 Route du Pont) Tent sites $21. On the south shore, just 1km west from the Québec bridge, this small, intimate campground (only 36 places) comes with all the conveniences. If it's full, you'll find many private campgrounds on this south shore road, particularly west of Québec City.

Hostels & University Residences *Centre International de Séjour de Québec* (☎ 418-694-0775, W www.cisq.org, 19 Rue Ste Ursule) Dorm beds $17/21 members/nonmembers, doubles $50. A friendly, lively place, this HI hostel is the most central and popular in town. Despite its great size (233 beds), it's usually full in summer. Rooms are off creaky, wooden-floored corridors that go on forever. The pleasant cafeteria serves three economical meals. Some travelers report better luck finding a room by showing up in person than by calling.

YWCA (☎ 418-683-2155, 855 Ave Holland) Singles/doubles $29/52. The Y takes couples or single women in its 15 rooms. Because of the limited space, be sure to reserve ahead. Facilities include a cafeteria and pool. Take bus No 7 along Chemin Ste Foy to Ave Holland, then walk south.

Université Laval (☎ 418-656-2921, 5030 Rue de l'Université) Singles/doubles $25/35, discounts for students (about 10%). Open May–mid-Aug. The university offers decent, if small, quarters on a campus that stays pretty lively even in summer. It's west of the center of town, at the point where Boulevard René Lévesque merges with Boulevard Wilfrid Laurier. Bus No 800 or 801 from the corner of Ave Dufferin and Boulevard René Lévesque will get you there in about 15 minutes.

B&Bs *Chez Hubert* (☎ 418-692-0958, e bheber@microtec.net, 66 Rue Ste Ursule) Singles/doubles $85/110. This smoke-free B&B on one of Old Town's prettiest streets is decorated in smart colors and tasteful furniture.

Krieghoff B&B (☎ 418-522-3711, 1091 Ave Cartier) Doubles $80. Run by the Krieghoff bar downstairs, this modern B&B retains an intimate air. You'll find it on a nice street far enough from the busy center of town to make for a respite but close enough to be walkable, too.

Couettes et Café Toast & French (☎ 418-523-9365, 1020 Ave Cartier) Singles/doubles $75/85. Away from the crowds but close to Grande Allée, this nice place offers tastefully decorated rooms. The owner takes

Canada's Coolest Hotel

Spending hundreds of dollars to sleep on a bed of ice might not sound terribly appealing, but North America's first Ice Hotel was a smashing success with hardy thrill-seekers in its first year, the winter of 2000-1 – so much so that it was back, bigger, better, and icier, in the 2001-2 season.

It's hard to wrap your head around the idea, but everything here is made of ice: the reception desk, the pen you sign the guest book with, the working sink in your room, your bed, dishes, the shot glasses, which frequently come in handy...

Okay, not *everything* is made of ice. There are no ice hot tubs, ice stoves or ice fireplaces, for example. But once inside, no one feels like nit-picking. Visitors say that the bed of ice is not as chilly as it sounds – you sleep in thick sleeping bags on lush deer pelts.

Some 350 tons of ice go into the five-week construction of this perishable hotel. One of the most striking aspects is its size – over 3000 sq meters of frosty splendor. As soon as you set foot in the entrance hall, it feels strangely overwhelming – tall, sculpted columns of ice support a ceiling where a crystal chandelier hangs, and carved sculptures, tables and chairs line the endless corridors.

Located about a half-hour drive from central Québec City at Lac St Joseph's Station Écotouristique Duchesnay, it is well placed to combine an exotic stay with outdoor activities – skiing, snowshoeing, dog-sledding, igloo-building and ice-fishing. There's also a luxury hotel nearby, so you can enjoy indoor comforts too.

Oh yes, you pay through the nose for all this exoticism. There are many packages, but expect to spend no less than $229 per person per night, based on double occupancy. The larger suites fit up to eight people, making them marginally cheaper. For more information, contact the **Ice Hotel** (☎ 875-4522, 143 Route Duchesnay, Ste Catherine de la Jacques Cartier). It's off exit 295 of Hwy 40, west of Québec City via Route 367.

special delight in guests who wish to perfect their French over morning toast and coffee.

Motels You'll find concentrations of motels in several areas, including Beauport, northeast of the city. To get there, head north along Ave Dufferin, then take Hwy 440 until the exit for Boulevard Ste Anne/Route 138; head to the 500-1200 blocks. A bike trail from the city passes nearby. A second area is west of the center on Boulevard Wilfrid Hamel (Route 138). To get there, head west on Hwy 440 to the Henri IV exit. Neither are far or difficult to reach. City buses run to these districts, so whether you have a car or not, they may be the answer if you find everything booked up downtown. Prices generally are higher than you'd pay for motels in other regions.

Motel Pierre (☎ 418-681-6191, 1640 Boulevard Hamel) Singles/doubles $76/88. This place tries hard – the staff go out of their way to be helpful – but it remains standard stuff. Choose from a range of room sizes.

Motel Le Bastion (☎ 418-871-9055, 3825 Boulevard Hamel) Singles/doubles $40/60. With comfortable rooms and decent prices, this is a good bet, though it's farther out of the city, close to Route 73 (which becomes the Pont de Québec farther south).

Hotels *Hôtel Belley* (☎ 418-692-1694, 249 Rue St Paul) Singles/doubles $80/110. A great place for the young and hip who still like their comfort and chic, this place offers spacious, tastefully decorated though sparse rooms with brick walls or wood paneling. On the first floor is a wonderful bar, the Belley Tavern.

Maison Ste Ursule (☎ 418-694-9794, 40 Rue Ste Ursule) Doubles $47-87. One of the best deals in the Old Town, this small hotel on a quiet street occupies a house built in 1756. The place includes a range of rooms, with shared or private bath, as well as a nice courtyard out back and a 1st-floor art gallery with a talkative parrot.

Auberge St Louis (☎ 418-692-2424, 48 Rue St Louis) Singles/doubles from $69/89 including full breakfast. This is one of the better deals in the Old Town, with 27 rooms at reasonable rates. Parking costs extra.

Manoir La Salle (☎ 418-692-9953, 18 Rue Ste Ursule) Singles/doubles $35/50-75. The prices in this nine-room place haven't

risen in years. Some may prefer the upstairs rooms to avoid having to go through the lobby to the bathroom (which you have to do if you're staying in the ground-floor rooms). Some kitchenettes are available.

Gîte Côte de la Montagne (☎ 418-694-4414, 54 Côte de la Montagne) Doubles $150, loft $300. Some rooms here come with a view onto Château Frontenac. The gorgeous loft (which fits six) is the standout, with fireplace, views of the river and the Château, and even a sink that swivels around into a toilet!

Places to Eat

Restaurants are abundant and the quality generally high. A number of Old Town eateries try to pack in the crowds and serve an odd mix of high- and low-brow cuisine. Many restaurants do boast unbeatable locations, however.

Rue St Jean outside the Old Town and other excellent places in St Roch offer good alternatives, though without the Old World charms.

For self-catering, try the supermarket *Marché Riche-lieu (1097 Rue St Jean),* which offers breads from the in-house bakery, fruits, cheeses and even bottles of wine with screw-top lids.

Old Upper Town *Restaurant Liban* (☎ 418-694-1888, 23 Rue d'Auteuil) Dishes $3-6. This is a popular spot for a quick *shish taouk* (chicken sandwich) and other Lebanese fast-food favorites.

Le Petit Coin Latin (☎ 418-692-2022, 8½ Rue Ste Ursule) Breakfast $4-8, dishes $12-16. For a French-style breakfast, try this spot near Rue St Jean. Open every day, the small café serves croissants, muffins, eggs and low-priced lunch specials. In summer, you can eat on the outdoor patio.

Casse Crêpe Breton (☎ 418-692-0438, 1136 Rue St Jean) Dishes $6-11. Near Côte du Palais, this small restaurant specializes in crêpes of many kinds, starting as low as $3.25. Some diners like to sit right up at the counter and watch the chefs put the tasty crêpes together.

Aux Anciens Canadiens (☎ 418-692-1627, 34 Rue St Louis) Dishes $11-23.

Housed in the historic Jacquet House, which dates from 1676, this noteworthy spot relies on traditional dishes and typically Québécois specialities. Here one can sample such provincial fare as apple wine, pea soup, duck or trout followed by dessert of maple-syrup pie. The special table d'hôte menu, offered from noon to 6pm, starts at the fair price of $14 and includes a glass of wine or a beer.

Old Lower Town Rue St Paul is the main restaurant row in this district. This old quiet street contains several inexpensive places away from the main bustle.

Aviatic Club (☎ 418-522-3555, 450 Rue de la Gare du Palais) Appetizers $6-12, dishes $15-24. Sumptuously set inside the already grand train station, this was *the* hot spot in town in 2001. Set up like a lounge, the dimly lit interior comes complete with on-site DJs. The world cuisine melts in your mouth, including the famous sushi. Wednesday nights, the sushi starts at $1.25 a pop!

Place du Spaghetti (☎ 418-694-9144, 40 Rue de Marché Champlain) Dishes $8-15. One of the best bargains in town serves various pasta dishes, which include bread and salad, for $10 and up ($8 at lunch). It boasts an attractive patio beneath the Château Frontenac.

Piazzetta (☎ 418-692-2962, 63 Rue St Paul) Breakfast $3-8, dishes $7-16. Now *this* is a pizza parlor! With beautiful high ceilings, wood-paneled floor and large stone oven in which some 25 types of pizzas get cooked, this is heaven. The surprise is Piazzetta's breakfasts – all eggs and omelettes are cooked in the stone oven, so there's not a dab of grease.

Outside the Walls If you head west along Grande Allée from Old Québec, you'll find a popular and lively strip of more than a dozen alfresco restaurants. All have complete lunch specials for $7 to $10 (from soup to coffee), and at most places, dinners range from $12 to $22.

L'Abraham Martin Café Bistrot de Méduse (☎ 418-647-9689, 595 Rue St Vallier

Est) Dishes $7-11. Open 9am-11pm daily. Good for a quick bite or a bit of lounging, this café boasts an unusual locale, perched on the staircase leading down to St Roch at the bottom of Côte Ste Geneviève. It serves mainly sandwiches and salads and good hot, light meals. The artistic co-op Méduse lies below.

Carthage (☎ *418-529-0576, 399 Rue St Jean)* Lunch $8, suppers from $12. Open 11:30am-2:30pm & 5:30pm-11pm daily. This split-level BYOW Tunisian restaurant offers couscous, meat and vegetarian specials, most agreeably spicy. The atmosphere is even more memorable than the food, with high ceilings and low tables before which you kneel on cushions.

Station St Jean (☎ *418-529-6672, 481 Rue St Jean)* Dishes around $7. Open 8am-11pm daily. These folks understand the rhythm of the night – breakfasts (over 30 choices) are served until 4pm! And they're copious servings at that. Otherwise, the hamburgers are inventive (with smoked meat or salmon), and the fries are great.

VooDoo Grill (☎ *418-647-2000, 575 Grande Allée Est)* Dishes $8-17. Described by the owners as a 'restaurant/museumm,' it's even more than that. An experience just to walk through, the complex merges two discos, a bar, a splendid dining room that stretches the concept of exotic decor to its fullest, and a laid-back patio overlooking busy, fashionable Grande Allée. Specialties include wok meals, huge Asian soups, mega-salads, and many meat dishes with, er, exotic sauces.

Entertainment

Though Québec City is small, its plenitude of nightspots keeps it active after dark, although many of these places change faster than editions of this book. The French entertainment paper *Voir,* published each Thursday, offers complete listings. Folk clubs known as *boîtes à chanson* are more popular here than in Montréal and can be found along and around Rue St Jean. Generally inexpensive, they enjoy a casual, relaxed atmosphere in which it's easy to meet people.

Chez son Père (☎ *418-692-5308, 24 Rue St Stanislas)* One of the best boîtes à chanson for years, this spot boasts great atmosphere. You can catch some newcomers here, plus occasional big-name concerts.

L'Inox (☎ *418-692-2877, 38 Rue St André)* In the Old Port area, the city's only brewpub draws beer lovers to its pleasant outdoor patio. A must-visit, the spot includes a small museum where you can learn about the craft of beer-making. Then, until the wee hours, you can put that knowledge to practical use.

Le Troubadour (☎ *418-694-9176, 29 Rue St Pierre)* Set cozily in the cave cellar of one of the city's oldest surviving houses (dating from 1754), this great tavern pours out plenty of local brew. For $4 you can sample four different kinds. The imported beers available come from 11 countries. You could do a lot worse than spending a few hours here.

Pub St Alexandre (☎ *418-694-7075, 1087 Rue St Jean)* This busy pub has 200 kinds of beer (ever tried Chinese, Portugese, New Zealand or Lebanese beer?) and an array of pub-type grub ($4 to $7).

Fourmi Atomik (☎ *418-694-1473, 33 Rue d'Auteuil)* The underground set grooves to music that alternates between grunge, rock, punk and sometimes ambient.

Le Drague (☎ *418-649-7212, 815 Rue St Augustin)* The city's gay and lesbian scene is pretty small, and this is its star player, a relaxed bar where the mostly male crowd spills out into an alleyway when things get busy. On weekends, disco takes over the basement.

L'Amour Sorcier (☎ *418-523-3395, 789 Côte Ste Geneviève)* Open 2pm-3am Thur-Sun. The most pleasant bar on the gay circuit, this spot is mainly frequented by women, but it's not exclusive.

Grand Théâtre de Québec (☎ *418-643-8131, 269 Boulevard René Lévesque Est)* The city's main performing arts center presents classical concerts, dance and theater, all usually of top quality. The Opéra de Québec often performs here.

Théâtre Capitole (☎ *418-694-4444, 972 Rue St Jean)* A smaller spot to catch performing arts, this theater/restaurant sometimes offers cabaret and musical revues.

Getting There & Away

Air The airport is west of town, off Hwy 40, near where Hwy 73 intersects Hwy 40 on its way north. Air Canada (☎ 418-692-0770, 800-630-3299) serves Montréal, Ottawa and other major Canadian cities. The Air

Canada subsidiary Air Canada Jazz (☎ 888-247-2262), formerly Air Nova, offers daily flights connecting to Montréal and the Îles de la Madeleine.

Bus You'll find the station (☎ 418-525-3000, 320 Rue Abraham Martin) next to the main train station, Gare du Palais. Orléans Express (☎ 514-842-2281) runs buses to Montréal ($42) nearly every hour during the day and evening. Buses also regularly go to Rivière du Loup and then on to Edmundston, New Brunswick. From Rivière du Loup, you can take SMT buses to destinations in Atlantic Canada. The Intercar bus line (☎ 418-617-9108, 888-861-4592) runs up the north coast to Tadoussac ($33).

There are no direct buses to or from the USA. They go via Montréal.

Train Odd as it may seem, small Québec City has three train stations (☎ 418-692-3940, 800-361-1235), all with the same phone numbers. In Lower Town, the renovated and simply gorgeous Gare du Palais, complete with bar and café, is central and convenient, off Rue St Paul. Daily trains go to Montréal ($38) and destinations farther west. Bus No 800 from Place d'Youville runs to the station.

The Ste Foy station (3255 Chemin de la Gare), southwest of the downtown area, is used by the same trains and is simply more convenient for residents who live on that side of the city.

Also of interest to travelers is the third station; it's inconveniently located across the river in the town of Charny. Trains at this station mainly serve eastern destinations, such as the Gaspé Peninsula and the Maritimes, but some serve Montréal as well. Buses connect to Ste Foy. Overnight trains go Moncton, New Brunswick ($111), every day except Tuesday, departing at 10:30pm and arriving 12 hours later.

Car Allô Stop (☎ 418-522-0056, ⓦ www.allostop.com, 467 Rue St Jean) gets drivers and passengers together for rides to other parts of Québec. See Montréal's Getting There & Away section for more details.

Ferry The ferry (☎ 418-644-3704) between Québec City and Lévis runs constantly – all day and most of the night. The one-way fare is $2.50/1.75 per adult/child, and $5.60/2.50 for a car/bike. Fares are about 25% cheaper from October to March. You'll get good views of the river, cliffs, the Québec skyline and Château Frontenac even if the cruise only lasts a few minutes. The terminal in Québec City is at Place Royale in Lower Town.

Getting Around

To/From the Airport Autobus La Québecoise (☎ 418-872-5525) shuttles between downtown and the airport for $9. It leaves from major hotels but will make pickups around town if you call at least one hour before flight time. La Québecoise also offers daily service to both Montréal airports. A taxi to Vieux Québec or Ste Foy is $24.50. Try Taxi Coop (☎ 418-525-5191).

Bus A ride on the recommended city bus system (☎ 418-627-2511) costs $2.25 (or eight tickets for $15.25), with transfer privileges. The buses go out as far as Ste Anne de Beaupré on the north shore. The terminal, Gare Centrale d'Autobus (225 Boulevard Charest Est), in Lower Town, will supply you with route maps and information.

Many buses serving the Old Town area stop in at Place d'Youville, just outside the wall on Rue St Jean. Bus No 800 goes to Gare Palais, the central long-distance bus and train station. Bus Nos 800 and 801 go from downtown to Laval Université.

Car In Québec City, driving isn't worth the trouble; you can walk just about everywhere, the streets are narrow and crowded, and parking is an exercise in frustration. But if you're stuck driving, the tourist office can give you a handy map of city-operated parking lots that don't gouge too much. You'd be wise to use the parking lots in St Roch, which charge nearly half the price as those in Upper Town. There are a few off Rue St Vallier Est. Parking there means a 10-minute hike (up lots of stairs), but you can buy yourself a treat with the money you save.

All car rental agencies suggest booking two days ahead. Budget (☎ 418-692-3660, 29 Côte du Palais) operates in town and at the airport. Discount (☎ 418-692-1244, 800-263-2355) often offers cheaper rates; call for locations.

QUÉBEC

Bicycle Many bike paths run through and around the city. The tourist information office sells a detailed map, *Greater Québec Cycling Trails*, for $3. Cyclo Services (☎ 418-692-4052, 160 Quai St André) rents bikes; see Organized Tours, earlier.

Around Québec City

As charming as Old Québec may be, and as tempting as it may be to wander around for days, the larger Québec region is well worth exploring. Not only will you find some of the province's top slopes, but you can also check out a Huron-Wendat sweat lodge and one of the tackiest religious sites in Canada.

NORTH SHORE
Wendake
The small town of Wendake, about 15km northwest of the city via Hwy 73 (exit 154), has attracted interest with its reconstructed Huron-Wendat village, the curiously spelled **Onhoúa Chetek8e** (☎ 418-842-4308, 575 Rue Stanislas-Kosca; adult/student & child $7/6; open 9am-5pm daily May–mid-Oct). The 'letter' 8 in Huron-Wendat is pronounced 'oua,' like the 'wh' in 'what.'

A guided tour takes you through a traditional longhouse and into a sweat lodge, while you learn about Native Indians' liberal child-rearing practices and their beliefs in the meaning of dreams. Call ahead to make sure there are English-speaking guides on duty the day you want to visit. An onsite restaurant serves up bison, caribou, succotash and linguini (for the timid) for $13 to $28. The gift shop sells souvenirs and crafts all done by locals. The money you spend stays in the community.

St Gabriel de Valcartier & Stoneham
St Gabriel de Valcartier, accessible via Route 371 north from Wendake, is a large military base you can drive through. Also there is the popular **Village Vacances** (*Holiday Village;* ☎ 418-844-2200, 1860 Boulevard Valcartier), a mini-city in itself that offers a gamut of summer fun. The most popular section is the huge **Aqua Park** (adult/child $22/14; open 10am-5pm early-late June, 10am-7pm late June-early Sept), which is packed to capacity on hot summer

days. At Holiday Village, you can also do some horseback riding, rafting and the water luge.

At Stoneham, the **Station Touristique** (*Mountain Resort;* ☎ 418-848-2411, 800-463-6888, 1420 Chemin du Hibou) offers an array of summer and winter activities. There's a good downhill ski station here, used for mountain biking in the summer. The resort recently underwent a $200 million facelift in an effort to turn it into one of the province's main ski centers.

Auberge du Jeune Voyageur (☎ 418-848-7650, 24 Montée des Cassandres) Dorm beds $18, singles/doubles $35/50. Our readers rave about this combo B&B/hostel, just north of the village of Stoneham. The comfortable place is a lot of fun, with bike rentals and organized activities. It's only a few minutes' drive from the Parc de la Jacques Cartier, where you'll find great opportunities for hiking and canoeing; a ride there costs $3.

Parc de la Jacques Cartier
This huge wilderness park (☎ 418-890-6527; admission $3.50), just off Route 175 about 40km from Québec City, is ideal for a quick escape from the city. In less than an hour's time, you can be camping, hiking or biking trails or canoeing along the long, narrow and exceptionally scenic Rivière Jacques Cartier. The only drawback is that the park's main road follows the river, and unless you go farther inland, cars and vans whiz by as you're canoeing. Near the entrance, an information center provides details on the park's activities and services. Camping equipment, canoes and bikes can all be rented. Simple overnight cabins are scattered throughout the park, and there are campgrounds ($18 to $20). In winter you can go cross-country skiing; shelter huts lie along some of the routes.

Réserve Faunique des Laurentides
Go a little farther north and you'll reach the entrance to this wildlife reserve (☎ 418-848-2422, Route 175; admission $3.50), 7861 sq km with scores of wooded hills and mountains with scores of lakes and streams. You can hike and fish and stay overnight; you'll find campgrounds ($18 to $20) along the road through the park. There are also very good canoe-camping possibilities, some in regions

that tend to be less crowded than the Parc de la Jacques Cartier.

Île d'Orléans

An uncontestable highlight of the region, this island will make you feel eons away from Québec City, even though it is visible from many spots. This special feel has attracted hundreds of urbanites who keep summer, country and permanent homes here.

While it's no longer a sleepy, pastoral farming region, it remains agricultural and boasts some beautiful scenery and views onto either shore. One road circles the island, with two running north-south. Most of the services are concentrated on the western tip, in St Pétronille, but restaurants, B&Bs and attractions are spread out everywhere. You'll spot a few windmills and lots of artistic workshops and galleries. Some of the villages contain houses that are 300 years old, plus other wooden or stone cottages in the Normandy style. Parts of it feel like a well-off city suburb that have been transplanted into a forest.

The tourist information office (☎ 418-828-9411, 490 Côte du Pont), visible as soon as you cross the bridge, will tell you what's left in terms of accommodations on the island. The staff can also set you up with bike rentals.

Auberge le P'tit Bonheur (☎ 418-829-2588, 183-186 Côte Lafleur) Dorm beds $18. This HI hostel in a gorgeous stone manor lies in the middle of the south side at St Jean. You can also rent bikes and cross-country skis here.

Domaine Steinbach (☎ 418-828-0000, 2205 Chemin Royal) Singles/doubles $65/75. This combination apple orchard and cider house is one of the most charming places to stop on the island – whether you sleep in the 300 year-old manor or not. The fine ciders, jams and vinaigrettes, on sale in the main house, are obviously made with love. Sampling is encouraged. The rooms are extremely comfortable, and the views across to Charlevoix's mountains are stunning.

Parc de la Chute Montmorency

These waterfalls, about 7km east of Québec City, have been turned into a tourist trap. Yes, these are higher than the Niagara Falls but not nearly as impressive, though they look particularly good in winter. They are

perfectly visible from the main road. They can also be seen for free, but many pay hefty fees inside the park (☎ 418-663-3330, 2490 Ave Royale). There's no entrance fee per se, but parking from the end of April to the end of October is $7.50, and a roundtrip on the cable car up the mountain is another $7.50.

Be forewarned: the cable car doesn't provide the best views – the suspended footbridge right above the falls does. If you're feeling ambitious, you can climb the 487 steps up the mountain.

The park lies along Route 138 in Beauport, just past the bridge for Île d'Orléans. To get there for free, either park your car in the church parking lot in neighboring Beauport and walk the 1km to the falls or catch the No 800 at Place d'Youville in Québec City and transfer at the Beauport terminal, taking bus No 50 to the top of the falls or No 53 to the bottom. You can also bike from Québec City.

Ste Anne de Beaupré

This gaudy little tourist town, a kind of religious theme park, is justly renowned for its immaculate and mammoth **basilica** (☎ 418-827-8227, 10018 Ave Royale; admission free; open 8:30am-4:30pm daily). Since the mid-1600s, the village has been an important religious site. An annual pilgrimage takes place here in late July, attracting thousands of people; any nearby space becomes part of a huge camp – check out the camper trailer park across the street.

The basilica, begun in late 1920s, replaced earlier chapels. Note the many crutches inside the door, all cast off by the legions allegedly healed by God. The church features good tile work on the floor, stained glass and ceiling mosaics and more chapels in the basement, but somehow the sermons bellowing out of loud speakers and the TV monitors flashing instructions (eg, 'Kindly Keep Silent') detract from the religious atmosphere. Not to mention the souvenir kiosk outside and the Blessings Bureau next door – line up to have a priest bless the Jesus keychain you've just bought. Those holding up the line are trying to slip in a spontaneous confession.

Check the hotel across the street. It's designed like a chapel, stained glass included – yuk – yet it does have an inexpensive cafeteria. Nearby is the **Cyclorama of**

Jerusalem (☎ 418-827-3101, 8 Rue Régina; adult/child $6/3; open 9am-6pm end Apr-end Oct), not an indoor cycling track, but a 360-degree painting of Jerusalem on the day Jesus died.

Intercar bus line runs up the north shore from Québec City and stops in town. See the Getting There & Away section under Québec City.

Mont Ste Anne

A little farther east, 50km from Québec, Mont Ste Anne (☎ 418-827-4561, 2000 Boulevard Beau Pré) is best known as a ski area – it's the number one hill near Québec City and one of the top slopes in the province. Amateur and expert skiers and snowboarders alike rave about its 56 trails and 13 lifts. In summer, you can ride a gondola to the mountain's summit. Or if you're up to it, bicycle and hiking trails wind to the top. All of April there's a giant sugar shack set up here.

If you want to do **cross-country skiing**, you find 224km of excellent trails just 8km from Mont Ste Anne along Route 360, around the village of St Ferreol les Neiges.

Camping Mont Ste Anne (☎ 418-827-5281, Rang St Julien) Tent sites $22-28. More expensive than usual because it includes an onsite water and beach slide, as well as walking trails, this campground is one of several places you'll pass on Route 138 going east from Québec City through the Ste Anne de Beaupré area.

The Hiver Express (☎ 418-525-5191) offers express bus service from several Québec City hotels to Mont Ste Anne ($22 roundtrip) and other winter destinations, leaving in the morning and returning late afternoon.

Canyon Ste Anne

Some 6km northeast of Beaupré on Route 138, in a deep chasm, are the 74m-high Ste Anne waterfalls (☎ 418-827-4057, 206 Route 138; adult/child $6.50 including parking; open May-late June & Sept-Oct 9am-5:30pm, late June-Aug 8:30am-6:30pm). You can walk around and across them via a series of steps, ledges and bridges. Though busy, this is quite a pleasant spot – less developed and more dramatic than the falls at Montmorency.

Cap Tourmente National Wildlife Area

Along the riverside beyond Cap Tourmente village lies this bird sanctuary (☎ 418-827-4591, 570 Chemin du Cap Tourmente; adult/child $4/2; open 9am-5pm daily) run by Parks Canada. Flocks of snow geese come here in spring and autumn, but many other species, as well as a range of animals and plants, make these wetlands home. Besides the birds themselves, the attractions include an interpretation center (watch for the hummingbirds) and meandering walking paths. The refuge is south of Cap Tourmante, off Route 138.

SOUTH SHORE
Lévis

A cross between a smallish town and a suburb of Québec City, Lévis doesn't offer much for the visitor, but the ferry ride over makes a mini-cruise that features good views of Québec. In town, the main shops and restaurants are along Rue Bégin.

The **Terrasse de Lévis**, a lookout point inaugurated in 1939 by King George VI and the future Queen Elizabeth II, offers excellent vistas of Québec City and beyond from the top of the hill on Rue William-Tremblay.

Between 1865 and 1872, the British built three forts on the south shore cliffs to protect Québec. One, known as **Fort No 1** (☎ 418-835-5182, 41 Chemin du Gouvernement; adult/student $3/2.25; open 9am-5pm daily May-Aug, 1pm-4pm Thur-Sun Sept), has been restored and operates as a national historic site with guided tours. It's on the east side of Lévis in Lauzon.

Berthier sur Mer

This small, riverside village founded in 1672 serves mainly as the departure point for the best tours to Grosse Île, given by **Croisières Lachance** (☎ 418-259-2140, 110 Rue de la Marina; tours adult/child $42/34). Tours depart from the marina one to four times daily from May to mid-October. The price includes a round trip to Grosse Île, as well as a Parks Canada–guided excursion of the island. Other tours cruise through the Îles aux Grues archipelago.

A trip to **Grosse Île**, which served as the major quarantine station for immigrants arriving from Europe from 1832 to 1937, is without a doubt one of the most interesting excursions in the province. It sheds much light on a little-known aspect of North American history. The tragic histories lived out on the island are cleverly, at times movingly, explained by guides. The tour includes visits to the disinfection chambers, the original hospital and living quarters of the immigrants, and the memorial burial area. Many of those who died were of Irish descent. In 1909, a 48-foot Celtic cross – the tallest one in the world! – was erected in their memory. You'll also be told about the 600 species of flora on the island (21 of them rare).

The water in the Rivière St Laurent here begins to get salty – the concentration is about 23% and increases gradually farther east.

Montmagny

This first town of any size east of Lévis is a good launching point for a visit to **Île aux Grues**. This is the only inhabited island in the 21-island archipelago, as well as the biggest (10km long), with North America's largest unspoiled wetland on its eastern tip. Bird-watchers come here and to Montmagny in spring and autumn, as snow geese stop nearby on their migration route. Two or three ferries (☎ 418-248-6869; free) leave daily from the marina in the center of town. Other excursions to the archipelago are also possible.

In Montmagny is the **Centre Éducatif des Migrations** (*Migration Educational Center;* ☎ 418-248-4565, *45 Rue du Bassin Nord; adult/student $4/3.50; open 9:30am-5pm daily June-Nov*), an interpretive center with exhibits on migration, both bird and human. The first portion features a display on the Great White Goose. The second presents the history of European migration at Grosse Île and the surrounding south shore through a sound and light show.

St Jean Port Joli

This small but spread-out town, with a big two-spired church right in the middle, is a famous center for the Québec art of woodcarving. Locals call it the world capital of wooden sculpture, and they can make a good case to support it.

To see excellent examples of the woodcarvers' art, go to the **Musée des Anciens**

Canadiens (☎ *418-598-3392, 332 Ave de Gaspé Ouest; adult/child $4.50/2; open 9am-5:30pm daily May-June & Sept-Oct, 8:30am-9pm daily July-Aug*). Ask for a guide booklet in English. The museum displays work done by some of the best known local sculptors, past and present.

Campgrounds lie in both directions outside town, with the closer ones to the east. Numerous motels line Route 132.

Camping de la Demi Lieue (☎ *418-598-6108, 800-463-9558*) Tent sites $19-23. This huge campground (over 300 places) features a heated pool and all the amenities. At least you won't feel alone!

La Boustifaille (☎ *418-598-3061, 547 Ave de Gaspé Ouest*) Appetizers $3-7, dishes $5-11. A veritable institution, renowned far and away, this restaurant serves Québécois food. After huge portions of pork ragout, meat tortière and cheese quiche, topped off with maple syrup cake, you won't need to eat for several days.

Orléans Express buses stop right in the center of town at the SOS convenience store across the street from the church. Three buses go to Québec City daily ($22, 2¼ hours).

Charlevoix & Saguenay

As you head east along the St Lawrence River from Québec City, you'll be treated to some of the most scenic landscapes in the province, as the shoreline becomes more typical of that found in eastern Canada. With neat small farms and little villages dominated by churches – usually topped by silver spires – this is rural Québec, where life has changed little for well over a century. You won't hear much English spoken in this part of the province.

Charlevoix is a beautiful, exciting region with endless possibilities for total wilderness immersion, while the Saguenay's fjord landscape ranks among the most stunning and dramatic in the province.

There are ferries across the river at various points. The farther east you go, the wider the river becomes and the more costly the ferry. Be sure to reserve your place on the ferries well ahead of time, especially in summer, when they fill up.

CHARLEVOIX

Beyond Mont Ste Anne (see the North Shore section, earlier) is the scenic coastal and mountain district known as Charlevoix. Its 6000 sq km are home to only 30,000 people. For 200 years, this pastoral strip of hilly, flowery farmland wedged between northern wilderness and the river has been a summer retreat for the wealthy and privileged. Though vestiges of this remain and prices are still on the high side, it's become a more democratic destination.

Unesco has classified the entire area as a biosphere or a heritage site, which has resulted in worthwhile restrictions on the types of permitted developments – as well as a palpable sense of pride on the part of residents.

Aside from rolling hills, glacier-carved crevices, cliffs and jagged rock faces, the most unique geographical feature of the area is the immense valley from Baie St Paul to La Malbaie, formed from the impact of a prehistoric meteor. A space rock weighing 15 billion tons, with a diameter of 2km, smashed into the earth here at 36,000 km/hr some 350 million years ago. The point of impact was the present-day Mont des Éboulements, halfway between Baie St Paul and La Malbaie, some 10km inland. The crater the meteor left in the earth measures 56km in diameter.

Baie St Paul

As you head east along Route 138, the first urban stop after Québec City is Baie St

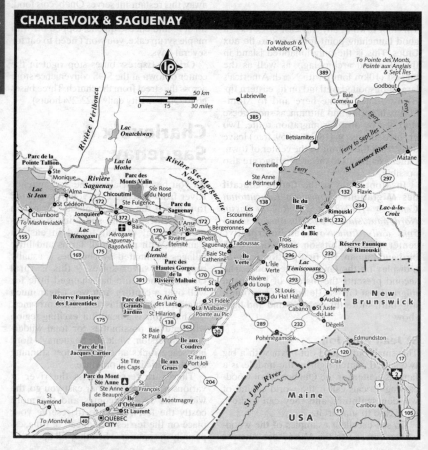

CHARLEVOIX & SAGUENAY

Paul, with its old streets and big church. The year-round tourist office (☎ 418-435-4160, 444 Boulevard Mgr de Laval) is on Route 138 just west of town. The attached **Centre d'Histoire Naturelle de Charlevoix** (☎ *418-435-6275; admission free; open 9am-5pm daily late May–mid-Oct, 10am-4pm Sat & Sun mid-Oct–late May*) features displays on flora and fauna and the geography of the Charlevoix district, explaining in detail the meteorological impact and the area's seismic proclivities.

The town's main street, Rue St Jean Baptiste, is lined with historic houses, some of which have been converted into galleries and restaurants. Artists' studios and craft shops are scattered around the side streets.

The bus station (☎ 418-435-6569, 2 Route de l'Équere at Boulevard Mgr de Laval) is at the restaurant La Grignotte, about a 20-minute walk to downtown. Three buses a day go to/from Québec City ($15, 1¼ hrs), with an extra Friday service. There are also three buses daily to/from La Malbaie ($7, 45 minutes) and two buses daily going as far east as Baie Comeau ($54, 5½ hrs).

Places to Stay & Eat *La Balcon Vert* (☎ *418-435-5587, 22 Côte du Balcon Vert*) Tent sites $17, dorm beds $17, rooms/chalets for two $45. Open mid-May–mid-Oct. This is an excellent place for spending the night. With its restaurant, bar, woodsy setting, chalets, dorms and campground, it's a retreat, hotel and hostel all in one. Check out the fabulous view overlooking the town and surrounding mountains. This spot lies east out of the center of town, off Route 362.

Camping du Gouffre (☎ *418-435-2143, 439 Chemin St Laurent*) Tent sites $16-23, chalets from $65. On the banks of the shallow Rivière du Gouffre outside of town, this heavily wooded campground is reminiscent of a farm, with numerous services.

Motels-Chalets Chez Laurent (☎ *418-435-3895, 1493 Boulevard Mgr de Laval*) Motel rooms from $50, fully equipped chalet cottages $125. This decent choice lies among a strip of hotels and motels right on Route 138, about 20 minutes' drive north of the center.

Le Saint Pub/Microbrasserie Charlevoix (☎ *240-2332, 2 Rue Racine*) Dishes $7-13, full-course meals $13-21. Beer lovers will be foamy at the mouth in this half-brewery,

half-pub, where many meals are infused with the locally-brewed malt (eg, beer-marinated smoked meat, salads with beer vinaigrette). For $4.50, you can try four regional brews in sample sizes. Local cheeses are on the menu, too. The friendly atmosphere makes it a popular hangout.

Around Baie St Paul

The **Parc des Grands Jardins** (☎ *418-439-1227; admission $3.50; open 8am-8pm daily June-Aug, 9am-5pm daily Sept-May*) covers 310 sq km of territory, much of it taiga (a kind of forest dominated by conifers). Caribou roam freely here and munch on lichen. You can rent canoes and kayaks and stay at campsites or in chalets. The tireless among you might want to take up the challenge of one of the province's longest and most difficult continuous trails, **La Traversée**, which stretches 100km from the Parc des Grands Jardins, snaking down the great valleys in the Parc des Hautes Gorges and winding up in the Parc du Mont Grands Fonds. If you can hike or ski about 18km a day, it will take you seven days and six nights to cross. To get to the Parc des Grands Jardins, take Route 381 north of Baie St Paul; it's 30km to the visitors' center and 46km to the main entrance.

The scenery is superb around **Les Éboulements**, with farms running from the town's edge to the river. You may have to stop while a farmer leads cattle across the highway. Note the piles of wood used for the long winters and the many carving outlets. Also note the unusual rock formations – these are the result of a powerful 1663 earthquake. The village is worth a stop just to soak up its atmosphere.

Île aux Coudres

Quiet, rural Île aux Coudres is what many people disappointed in better-known Île d'Orléans are looking for. It's the kind of gentle, easygoing place where you go to spend an afternoon and end up staying for days. There are a few museums, but the real pleasures here are in lazy walks along the beach or drives around the island.

The tourist office (☎ 418-438-2930, 21 Rue Royale Ouest) sits near the crossroads just beyond the port. The **Musée de l'Île aux Coudres** (☎/fax 418-438-2753, 231 Chemin des Coudriers; adult/student $3.50/3; open

QUÉBEC

8:30am-7pm daily May-Oct) makes for a pleasant stop, with its antique-shop feel. It chronicles the settlement of the island and features displays on the local flora and fauna.

For some **sea kayaking**, head to **Kayak de Mer** (☎ *418-438-4388, 783 des Coudriers)*, on the south side of the island. The options here range from simple rentals ($29 for a half day) to excursions such as the 90-minute sunset trip. The more adventurous five-hour excursion includes lots of explanations about the island's marine and bird life.

La Malbaie–Pointe au Pic

The community of La Malbaie is now an amalgamation of five previously separate villages on both sides of the Rivière Malbaie. The main sector, on the west side of the river, is called La Malbaie–Pointe au Pic, designating the two most important towns, now fused together.

The tourist office (☎ 418-665-4454, 630 Boulevard de Comporté) is in La Malbaie.

Seemingly a small, insignificant village, Pointe au Pic was a holiday destination for the wealthy at the beginning of the 20th century, drawing the elite set from as far away as New York. One of its famous residents was US president William Howard Taft, who had a summer home built there. Some of these large, impressive 'cottages' along Chemin des Falaises have now been converted into comfortable inns.

Attesting to the area's glory – past and present – is the splendor of the **Manoir Richelieu**. The sprawling, romantic hotel dating from 1928 got a $140 million facelift in 1999 and resembles Québec City's Château Frontenac. Today, it's mainly filled with bus-loads of gamblers rabidly partaking of the adjacent, posh **casino** (☎ *418-665-5322; admission free; open 10am or 11am to midnight or 3am daily)*, but it's still worth a look.

Parc des Hautes Gorges de la Rivière Malbaie

This provincial park (☎ *418-439-1227, 800-665-6527; admission $3.50; open 7am-9pm daily May-early Oct)* is still somewhat of an undiscovered gem – relative to other provincial parks, that is. A paved road joined it only in 2000. This 233 sq km park boasts several unique features, including the highest rock faces east of the Rockies; sheer rock plummets (sometimes 800m) to the

calm Rivière Malbaie, which snakes off at right angles at times.

There are several vigorous trails here, to be attacked by the fit and adventurous. One is a 4.5km walk straight up through several vegetation zones, from a maple grove to permafrost. Like other provincial parks, this one offers canoe rental and numerous camping options ($19 to $24).

To get there from Québec City, drive east along Route 138, head north at St Hilarion and follow the signs (it's about a 35km drive from Route 138); if you're in La Malbaie, head back west along Route 138, then head north at the cutoff for St Aimé des Lacs and keep going to the park.

St Siméon

This generally unremarkable town calls itself an ecological village, mainly because of **Les Palissades Centre Éco-forestier** (☎ *418-638-3333, 502 Rue St Laurent; adult/child $3/2; 9am-8pm daily June-Sept, 9am-6pm Thur-Sun Oct)*, 13km outside of the village itself. At this forest center, you can walk on several trails to admire the unusual geological formations.

You can take an hour-long ferry ride (☎ 418-638-2856) from St Siméon to Rivière du Loup, on the south shore of the St Lawrence. The ferry runs from mid-April to January 2. Throughout the summer, there are four or five departures a day. The fare is $11.30/7.50 per adult/child. You must pay an extra $4 to take a bike, $29 for a car.

Baie Ste Catherine

This attractive dot on the map is in many ways Tadoussac's poorer sister (for information about Tadoussac, see that heading in the North Shore section, later). A number of the same activities offered in Tadoussac are also possible from here. Some of the large **whale-watching** cruises that depart from Tadoussac pick up passengers from Baie Ste Catherine's pier as well. The **Groupe Dufour Croisières** (☎ *418-692-0222, 22 Quai St André; tours from $45)* offer excursions on boats carrying anywhere from 48 to 489 passengers.

Azimut Aventure (☎ *418-237-4477, 185 Route 138)* is one of the best places to organize **kayaking** expeditions. This friendly, professional bunch tends to attract a clientele who are serious about their water sports. The range of possible excursions includes a memorable two-day trip to L'Anse St Jean ($95). You can also simply rent kayaks ($35/day) and make your own itinerary.

The main point of interest on this side of the river is the **Pointe Noire Observation Centre** (☎ *418-237-4383 or 235-4703, Route 138; admission $2; open 9am-6pm daily mid-June–mid-Oct)*, up the hill from the ferry landing. This whale-study post where the two rivers meet features an exhibit, a slide show and films, and an observation deck with a telescope for views over the mouth of the river. This is one of the best places to see belugas – you can often spy them in the Saguenay very close to shore, especially when the tide is coming in.

At the northern end of town, you can catch a free, 10-minute ferry to Tadoussac; it runs around the clock. The boat departs every 20 minutes from 8pm to 10pm weekdays and from 1pm to 8pm on Saturday; at all other times, it runs once or twice an hour.

SAGUENAY

There are two main areas of this region. The first hugs the Rivière Saguenay, close to the fjord, and consists of tiny, scenic villages on both the north and south sides of the river. The second is an urban, industrialized center with Chicoutimi as its pivot. Both depend on the same lifeline: the majestic Rivière Saguenay, fed by Lac St Jean.

The fjord itself is 100km long, stretching from Ste Fulgence, just northeast of Chicoutimi, to Tadoussac. Formed during the last Ice Age, the fjord is the most southern in the Northern Hemisphere. As deep as 270m in some places, the riverbed rises to a depth of only 20m at the fjord's mouth at Tadoussac due to a narrowing of the glacier at that point. This makes the relatively warm, fresh waters of the Saguenay jet out atop the frigid, salt waters of the St Lawrence, leading to some unique marine phenomena. The entire waterway now enjoys a protected status. The cliffs, some 500m high, are the real stars of the area, jutting dramatically over the river.

L'Anse St Jean

Considered one of the loveliest villages in Québec, this is also the departure point for some scenic cruises along the fjord.

The **Croisière Personnalisée Saguenay** (☎ *418-272-2739, 15 Rue du Faubourg)* offers four types of cruises on a 24-foot motorboat, including some island exploration and stopovers at Tadoussac or Ste Anne du Rose.

If you want to get your own oars wet, head to **Fjord en Kayak** (☎ *418-272-3024, 4 Rue du Faubourg; tours starting at $39)*, which offers great excursions that last from three hours to five days.

Auberge Chez Monika (☎ *418-272-3115, 12 Chemin des Plateaux)* Dorm beds $10. Perched atop a steep hill (even by car it's a challenge – if walking, prepare for a long, tough hike), this is a medicinal plant farm doubling as a hostel. Run like a commune by a multilingual herbalist and her students, the place includes dorm rooms and a shared kitchen. It's 4.7km from Route 170; follow the signs for the Centre Équestre (Equestrian Center), which is almost next door.

Rivière Éternité

The town itself might be rather moribund, but there's a lot going on nearby, including main entrances to both the Saguenay-St Lawrence Marine Park and Parc du Saguenay (see below). Don't miss the **Halte des Artistes**, a free, drive-through exhibit of wood sculptures on the west side of town.

You might also want to take a gander at the 8.5m-tall statue of the **Virgin Mary** perched atop Cap Trinité, the peak on the westernmost edge of the Baie Éternité. It looms there, ominously, on one of the highest cliffs on the fjord, protecting the sailors and boats that pass under it. It was erected in 1881 by Charles Robitaille, who had narrowly escaped death the previous winter after his horse crashed through the ice over the waters below the cliff. He vowed to honor the Virgin Mary for having saved his life and commissioned the work from Louis Jobin, a well-known sculptor. It took over a week to cart and assemble the towering figure.

Saguenay-St Lawrence Marine Park & Parc du Saguenay

Both these parks overlap somewhat and extend into the Saguenay, Charlevoix and North Shore regions, with various entry points.

The Saguenay-St Lawrence Marine Park (☎ *418-235-4703, 800-463-6769)* was the first

QUÉBEC

conservation project in Québec to be jointly administered by the federal and provincial governments. It covers 1138 sq km of water and coastline from the Baies des Ha! Ha! (near La Baie) to the St Lawrence River, then stretches north to Les Escoumins and south to St Fidèle. The park's Rivière Éternité visitors' center (☎ 418-272-3027, 877-272-5229, 91 Chemin Notre Dame) offers canoe and kayak rental and numerous guided activities.

The Parc du Saguenay (☎ 418-272-3008, 877-272-5229) borders most of the fjord on both sides of the river. It's a hiker's delight, with over 100km of splendid trails that sometimes open onto striking views of the fjord, plus a number of trailside refuges where you spend the night. One of the park's entrances is at Rivière Éternité (☎ 418-272-1509/3008, 91 Chemin Notre Dame). In winter, there are frequent ice-fishing excursions in this area; contact the park for information about the trips it offers.

Ste Rose du Nord

Located on the Saguenay River's less-frequented north side, 45km from Chicoutimi, one of Québec's prettiest villages seamlessly blends in with the surrounding natural world. It's a pleasure to wander around here, letting the gentle pace of the village envelop you.

Camping Descente des Femmes (☎ 418-675-2581, 154 Rue de la Montagne) Tent sites $12-17. You can pitch your tent on a hill here and wake up to a view over the village and onto the fjord. The showers and toilets are in a converted grange, and the owner's a hoot.

Pourvoirie du Cap au Leste (☎ 418-675-2000, Chemin du Cap à l'Est) Singles/doubles from $96/144. This outfitter offers dramatic views over a large stretch of the fjord and can organize hiking, canoeing, kayaking, snowmobiling, snowshoeing and other sporting activities. The onsite restaurant serves superb regional cuisine. This spot lies at the end of a side road off Route 172 between Ste Anne du Rose and St Fulgence.

Chicoutimi

This city is quite pleasant thanks to its pedestrianized port area (a magnet for cyclists and skateboarders) and its young pop-

ulation (it's home to a university and Cégep, which is Québec's equivalent of a junior college). Originally the site of a 1676 fur trading post, it became the world's pulp and paper capital in the early 20th century, along with Trois Rivières.

Administratively, the city has been fused with Jonquière and is known alternately as Ville de Saguenay, though locals hate the new name.

For general information, contact the tourist office (☎ 418-698-3167, 800-463-6565, 295 Rue Racine Est).

La Pulperie (☎ 418-698-3100, 300 Rue Dubuc; adult/student $8.50/6; open 9am-6pm daily late June-early Sept) was once the world's biggest pulp mill. Although it no longer operates, a guided tour and exhibition explain the mill's history and its role in the development of the city. Your tour will include most of the city's main sites, all in the same area as the mill, a part of town that's been dubbed the 'Bassin.' All tours begin at the Chambre de Commerce (☎ 418-698-3100, 194 Rue Price Ouest).

The tour also features the **House of Arthur Villeneuve**, containing his now famous depictions of the town and landscape. Villeneuve's former home has become a museum known not so much for the paintings it contains but for the painting it is. The entire house has been painted inside and out like a series of canvases in Villeneuve's bright, naive folk style.

The **Petite Maison Blanche** (Little White House), which held steady against a devastating flood of 1996 and which news photographs made famous, can also be seen on the same premises. Across the street is the mid-19th-century **Église Sacré Coeur** (Sacred Heart Church; ☎ 418-543-4302, Rue Bossé; admission $3.50; open 10am-5pm daily), which has a small exhibit on local history inside.

Places to Stay & Eat *Cégep* (☎ 418-549-9520, 534 Rue Jacques Cartier Est) Singles/doubles $21/29 with bedding, $17/25 without. Open year-round, this is an adequate college dormitory 1.5km from the bus station. It's in the sinister gray building to the far left of the college's general entrance.

Auberge Centre Ville (☎ 418-543-0253, fax 418-693-1701, 104 Rue Jacques Cartier

Est) Singles/doubles $40/65. This is a good, centrally located place with no frills.

Numerous cafés, bistros and bars dot Rue Racine Est. Chain restaurants mainly lie on Boulevard Talbot and Boulevard Saguenay.

Bistro La Cuisine *(☎ 418-698-2822, 387A Racine Est)* Appetizers $4-12, dishes $8-14. Feast on mussels, pasta and burgers in a slick, relaxed atmosphere. The specials offer a good deal.

La Piazzetta *(☎ 418-549-4860, 412 Boulevard Saguenay Est)* Dishes $7-16. Pizzas are the main attraction here, and they come in a wide variety.

La Bougresse *(☎ 418-543-3178, 260 Ave Riverin)* Appetizers $3-10, dishes $14-26. Fine French cuisine is fastidiously prepared and served in elegant surroundings.

Getting There & Away Air Canada (☎ 692-0770, 800-630-3299) operates five daily flights from Montréal to Chicoutimi. The airport is located at Bagotville.

Intercar bus line (☎ 418-543-1403, 55 Rue Racine Est) connects to Québec City, Montréal, Jonquière and Tadoussac. Local buses run by CITS (☎ 418-545-2487) link Chicoutimi, Jonquière and La Baie. Buses also go to Tadoussac. L'Autobus L'Anse St Jean (☎ 418-543-1403) runs a van down the Saguenay to L'Anse St Jean.

Jonquière

A friendly but nondescript place of limited interest, Jonquière lies west of Chicoutimi along Routes 170 or 372. It is home to the enormous Alcan aluminum smelter and two paper mills. Just south of the city (follow Rue Ste Dominique) is the more appealing **Lac Kénogami**, with some 50km of scenic walking trails and several campgrounds.

The closest thing you'll find to a downtown core in Jonquière is Rue St Dominique between Boulevard du Royaume and Boulevard Harvey – look for a smattering of tacky nighclubs, dive bars and some eateries.

Worth a gander is the **Pont d'Aluminum** (Aluminum Bridge), bridging both banks of the Rivière Saguenay at the end of Route du Pont near the Shipshaw hydroelectric dam. Built in 1950, it weighs one-third as much as a comparably sized steel bridge; it's said to be the only one of its kind in the world.

Lac St Jean

The Lac St Jean region refers to the ring of towns surrounding the lake of the same name, whose coastline forms a wobbly circle 210km long. Fairly flat, the region is defined almost entirely by the 1053-sq-km lake. While much less scenic or interesting than neighboring regions, it does feature numerous worthwhile attractions.

Lac St Jean touts itself as the heart of Québec nationalism and as the province's blueberry and meat pie *(toritière)* capital, though all of these elements can be found elsewhere in equally large quantities.

The 256 km of **cycling** trails around the lake combine to form the Véloroute des Bluets (Blueberry Bike Trail), and nearly every town along the way has some facilities to make the trip easier – rental and repair shops, B&Bs that cater to cyclists and rest areas. For maps and a list of helpful stops along the way, contact the Véloroute (☎ 418-668-0849, 1671 Ave du Pont Nord) in Alma.

Mashteuiatsh is one of the best-organized Native Indian villages in the province. The **Musée Amérindien de Mashteuiatsh** *(☎ 418-275-7494, 1787 Rue Amishk; adult/student $6/4.50; open 10am-6pm daily mid-May–mid-Oct, 9am-noon & 1pm-4pm Mon-Fri rest of the year)* features good exhibits with multimedia displays on the history and way of life of the Pekukamiulnuatsh.

Village Historique Val Jalbert *(☎ 418-275-3132, Route 169; adult/child 7-14/child under 7 $12/5/free; open 9am-5pm daily mid-May–mid-June & Sept-Oct, 9am-7pm daily mid-June–Aug)* is not a village per se but a ghost town come to life. It re-creates life at the beginning of the 20th century in a town revolving around the pulp and paper industry. As you visit the remains of the old mill, the old religious school and log residences, guides in period costume explain the history and really get into the act, singing old folk tunes, waving rulers like the strict old schoolteachers used to do and carting logs for a fire.

Places to Stay *Camping Plage Desbiens* *(☎ 418-346-5436, Route 169)* Tent sites $15-22. This large campground off the main road includes a sandy beach and all the facilities.

Auberge Île du Repos *(☎ 418-347-5649, 105 Route Île du Repos)* Tent sites $15, dorm beds $17/19 member/nonmember, singles/

doubles from $45. Taking up an entire little island between Ste Monique and Péribonka, this HI resort features hostel dorms, kitchen facilities, private chalet rooms, camping, a rather pricey restaurant, bar with pricey live music and a beach with swimming in murky water. It's popular with Québécois looking for some rest and recreation, though there's no public transportation here. The atmosphere depends a lot on who the other guests are.

North Shore

The Côte Nord (North Shore) comprises two large regions, Manicouagan (stretching from Tadoussac to just east of Godbout) and Duplessis (east to the Labrador border). Statistics here are a bit overwhelming. The two regions together encompass an awesome 328,693 sq km (the size of New Zealand, Belgium and Switzerland together) and 1250km of coastline. In this vast expanse live only some 106,800 hardy souls (1.4% of Québec's population), almost all along the coast, making the area's population density a meager 0.3 persons per square kilometer.

The farther east you go, the greater the distance between villages, the fewer the people, the deeper the isolation, and the wilder the nature. Inland is a no-man's land of hydroelectric power stations, outfitter resorts, dense forest and labyrinthine rivers. This part of the Canadian Shield was heavily glaciated, resulting in a jumble of lakes and rivers. All rivers flow south toward the St Lawrence River or east toward the sea. Relatively flat, the land rarely rises higher than plateaus 500m to 900m above sea level (the Groulx mountains north of Baie Comeau being the exception).

Whale-watching is the major attraction in the area around Tadoussac, where the Saguenay River flows into the St Lawrence. While a spectacular activity in and of itself, it has sadly eclipsed all other facets of the area. The possibilities for adventure tourism are endless here.

TADOUSSAC

This tiny village of under 1000 people explodes with life in the summer, when thousands of people visit to catch sight of the main tourist draw – whales. However, unlike other single-purpose tourist towns, Tadoussac has much more to offer, including walks along sand dunes, boat trips up the Rivière Saguenay, sea-kayaking expeditions, several-day hikes and other adventure sports. The attractive town (marred by tacky signs with whale fins advertising cruises) also makes a good social spot, as it's home to a wild youth hostel and several bars where you can relax or let it all hang out after a day's activities.

Tadoussac became the first fur-trading post in European North America in 1600, eight years before the founding of Québec City. When the Hudson's Bay Company closed its doors in the mid-1850s, Tadoussac was briefly abandoned, only to be revived as a resort with the building of the garish Hotel Tadoussac in 1864. The town was also reinvented as an important cog in the pulp and paper wheel, spun enthusiastically by British industrialist William Price.

The tourist information office (☎ 418-235-4744, 197 Rue des Pionniers), in the middle of town, is open 8am to 9pm daily from June to August and 8:30am to 5pm weekdays from September to May. All the sites and boat trips operate seasonally, and November to May Tadoussac shuts down.

The **Centre d'Interpretation des Mammiféres Marins** (CIMM; ☎ 418-235-4701, 108 Rue de la Cale Sèche; adult/child $5.50/3; open 9am-8pm daily mid-June–late Sept, noon-5pm mid-May–mid-June & late Sept-late Oct) gives visitors excellent background information on local sea creatures through video clips and exhibits. You can also listen to whale songs.

The mini-museum **Maison Chauvin** (☎ 418-235-4657, 157 Rue du Bord de l'Eau; adult/student $3/2; open 9am-9pm daily mid-June–mid-Sept, 9am-5pm daily late May–mid-June & mid-Sept–early Oct) is a replica of the continent's first fur-trading post and offers some history on the first transactions between Native Indians and Europeans. Exhibits are in French, but ask for an English guide book.

Built in 1747 by the Jesuits, **La Vielle Chapelle** (☎ 418-235-4324, Rue du Bord de l'Eau; adult/children $2/50¢; open 9am-9pm daily mid-June–mid-Oct) is one of the oldest wooden churches in the country. This small house of worship is also known as the Indian Chapel.

The provincial government operates a **fishbreeding station** (☎ 418-235-4569, 115 Rue du Bateau Passeur; adult/child $5/4; open 10am-6pm mid-May–Aug) to provide fish for the restocking of Québec's salmon streams and rivers. You can see its operations and get a firsthand look at the fish.

Activities

You'll find some fine green areas around town for **hiking**. A walking trail beginning and ending at the Rue du Bord de l'Eau leads around the peninsula at Pointe de l'Islet park; spying whales from the shore is sometimes possible here.

You can also go hiking at the Parc du Saguenay (see separate heading, earlier); one of the park's entrances is located in Ta-

doussac. The park's **Maison des Dunes Interpretation Centre** (☎ 418-235-4238; adult/child $3.50/1.50; open 9am-5pm daily June–mid-Oct) is 5km out of town at the end of Rue des Pionniers. An exhibit explains why what everyone calls 'dunes' in the area are actually marine terraces, formed by waves, not wind, as dunes are. Trails go from here down to the beach and to a small waterfall.

At Lac de l'Anse à l'Eau, the 43km hiking trail to Baie Ste Marguerite begins; this trip requires overnighting in the refuge huts, so contact the Parc du Saguenay before heading out.

Whale-watching is an industry here. Check out the possibilities carefully – you want to get the kind of tour that's right for

QUÉBEC

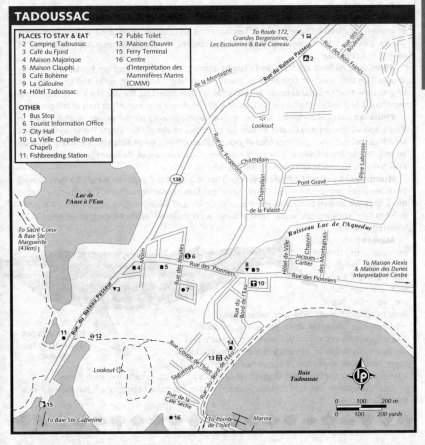

TADOUSSAC

PLACES TO STAY & EAT
2 Camping Tadoussac
3 Café du Fjord
4 Maison Majorique
5 Maison Clauphi
8 Café Bohème
9 La Galouïne
14 Hôtel Tadoussac

OTHER
1 Bus Stop
6 Tourist Information Office
7 City Hall
10 La Vielle Chapelle (Indian Chapel)
11 Fishbreeding Station

12 Public Toilet
13 Maison Chauvin
15 Ferry Terminal
16 Centre d'Interprétation des Mammifères Marins (CIMM)

To Route 172, Grandes Bergeronnes, Les Escoumins & Baie Comeau

Rue du Bateau Passeur
Rue des Bois Francs
Rue des Bouleaux
de la Montagne
Rue des Forgerons
Lookout
Champlain
Champlain
Pont Gravé
Père Labrosse
de la Falaise
138
Lac de l'Anse à l'Eau
Ruisseau Lac de l'Aqueduc
To Sacré Coeur & Baie Ste Marguerite (43km)
Morin
Rue des Jésuites
Rue des Pionniers
Hôtel-de-Ville
Jacques-Cartier
des Montagnais
Chauvin
To Maison Alexis & Maison des Dunes Interpretation Centre
Rue des Pionniers
Rue du Bord de l'Eau
Rue Coupe de l'Islet
Saguenay
Rue-du-Bord-de-l'Eau
Rue de la Cale sèche
Lookout
Baie Tadoussac
To Baie Ste Catherine
To Pointe de l'Islet
Marina
0   100   200 m
0   100   200 yards

you. Generally, the smaller the boat, the better. Expect to pay at least $35 per person for a three-hour trip. Tickets are available all over town.

For the adventurous, **Tayaout** (☎ *418-235-1056, 148 Rue du Bord de l'Eau)*, offers some sea-kayaking whale-watching expeditions. Claude Morneau is a captain who runs **Impacct** (☎ *877-904-1964)*, a small charter company. He takes people in groups no larger than 12 on his fishing vessel and promises relaxed, personalized tours, mainly up the Saguenay fjord. He charges $10 an hour per person, usually for three- to four-hour trips.

Places to Stay

Camping Tadoussac (☎ *418-235-4501, 428 Rue du Bateau Passeur)* Tent sites $21. During summer the 200 places fill up nightly; arrive early in the morning to get one of the sandy sites. The campground lies on Route 138, 2km from the ferry.

Maison Majorique (☎ *418-235-4372, 158 Rue du Bateau-Passeur)* Tent spaces

---

Who Swims There?

Aside from many smaller cetaceans like white-sided Atlantic dolphins and white-beaked dolphins, there are five species of whales you are most likely to see swimming and surfacing in the St Lawrence River.

Beluga (*béluga*) whales are the smallest species of whale, typically measuring about 4.5m long and weighing over 1000kg. They usually live in groups of 20 to 100. Part of the toothed subgroup of whales, they feed on capelin, smelt, herring, crabs and shrimp. To distinguish them from other whales, look for a pale beige or white color, a protuberant forehead and a mouth that looks like it's caught in a perpetual grin.

Blues (*rorqual bleu*) are the planet's largest animals. Those in the northern hemisphere, slightly smaller than their southern counterparts, reach 27m in length and weigh up to 150 tons, nearly as long as three train cars and as heavy as 30 elephants. Their hearts are the size of a VW Beetle. In one mouthful, a blue whale can take in 45 tons of water. Each one eats about four tons of krill per day.

Finbacks (*rorqual commun*) are the second-largest animals on the planet, reaching 24m in length and weighing up to 60 and 80 tons (at birth they're already 6m long!) The spray from their breath can jet out 7m high. They feed in groups when preying on small fish, alone when filling up on krill. To identify a finback, look for the asymmetrical coloring of the lower jaw – white or yellowish on the right side and black on the left side.

Humpbacks (*rorqual à bosse*) average 15m in length and typically weigh 30 tons. Dorsal protuberances and denticulated (finely serrated) tails characterize them. Though slow swimmers, they are known to fly through the air at times, and during mating season, they'll engage in lobtailing, slapping the water several times with their tails while holding themselves in an inverted position.

Minkes (*petit rorqual*) can grow to 10m in length and weigh as much as eight tons. Fast swimmers, they are also the most likely to approach boats (fishermen swear young minkes do so whenever there are young children aboard) and love to show off by hurling themselves out of the water. Their slender, streamlined bodies make acrobatics easier. Minkes' other physical characteristics include pointed heads, whitish bellies, darker backs and diagonal white bands on the upper surface of each flipper.

Humpbacks put on an acrobatic show.

Sperm (*cachalot*) and **right** (*baleine franche*) whales have also been spotted, but they're rare in these waters.

$6, dorm beds $15/18 members/nonmembers, double rooms $39. Anything goes at this red-roofed big house with an attached bar that's full of energy. Good, informal banquet-style dinners cost $6. The mini-bus service ($7 for two people) drives you northwest to hiking trails up the Saguenay; you return on your own along the fjords.

Maison Alexis (☎ 418-235-4372, 389 Rue des Pionniers) Dorm beds $15/18. Run by the owners of the above hostel, and only a three-minute drive from town, it still feels eons away from the busy center, nestled in woods and supposedly haunted. Aside from that, it's a quiet, creaky, great old place with rooms for four.

Maison Clauphi (☎ 418-235-4303, 188 Rue des Pionniers) B&B singles/doubles $69/76, motel doubles $89. Choose among accommodations in a motel, in a nearby B&B or in a more luxurious suite. The staff here can set you up with cruise tickets and more adventurous package trips, including mountain biking and surf biking (which entails riding the waves on a bike-like apparatus).

La Galouïne (☎ 418-235-4380, 251 Rue des Pionniers) Singles/doubles $35/45. Very friendly owners run this very good B&B in a centrally located home. The boutique on the 1st floor sells amazing sand-made objects from the Îles de la Madeleine.

Hotel Tadoussac (☎ 418-235-4421, 165 Rue du Bord de l'Eau) Doubles from $80, suites $150-255. Looking, feeling and smelling like a sanatorium, this seemingly out-of-place, huge luxury resort was built in 1864 and has been renovated several times since. A walk through the lobby and around the grounds is an experience.

Places to Eat

Café du Fjord (☎ 418-235-4626, 152 Rue du Bateau Passeur) Lunch buffet $13, dinner buffet $16. Open 11am-3pm & 6pm-11pm daily. A convivial atmosphere and succulent food help make this cabinlike space a winner. There is only a buffet (all you can eat or by weight), but the choice is splendid. After the restaurant closes, the bar keeps rocking until the wee hours.

Café Bohème (☎ 418-235-1180, 239 Rue des Pionniers) Dishes $4-9. Open 7am-11pm daily. A great hangout, this bohemian café serves healthy sandwiches and quiches, delicious breakfasts and equitable (ie, fairtrade) coffee. Some evenings there are poetry readings or talks by naturalists.

Getting There & Away

Tadoussac is right off Route 138. The 10-minute ferry from Baie Ste Catherine in Charlevoix is free and runs around the clock. The terminal is at the end of Rue du Bateau Passeur.

Intercar (☎ 418-235-4653, 433 Route 138) bus line connects Tadoussac with Montréal (7½ hours) and Québec City ($33, four hours) twice a day and runs as far as Baie Comeau. The bus stop is opposite the campground. Buses also go to Chicoutimi ($16, 1½ hours) Sunday through Friday.

GRANDES BERGERONNES

With excellent whale-watching opportunities and two superb attractions, Grandes Bergeronnes might provide a quieter alternative for those who wish to avoid the bustle of Tadoussac, 22km southwest.

Archéo Topo (☎ 418-232-6695, 498 Rue de la Mer; adult/child $5.50/2.50; open 10am-5pm late May–mid-Oct) is a research and exhibition center dedicated to archeological findings along the North Shore. Outside, trails lead down to the coast.

A few kilometers farther east is the **Cap de Bon Désir Interpretation Centre** (☎ 418-232-6751, 162 Rue de l'Église; adult/child $5/2; open 8am-8pm daily June-Aug, 9am-6pm daily Sept), run by Parks Canada. At this worthwhile stop, you'll find excellent marine life exhibits and scheduled activities, but the real attractions are the large rocks by the shore – it's almost always possible to spot passing whales.

At nearby Les Escoumins, 12km north of Bergeronnes on Route 138, the **Essipit Centre** (☎ 418-233-2202, 888-868-6666, 1087 Rue de la Réserve) is an Innu organization that sells excellent local crafts in its boutique and makes reservations for stays in the Innu's campground and chalets. The center also offers very good whale-watching cruises at slightly lower prices than in Tadoussac. From Les Escoumins, a ferry goes to Trois Pistoles in the Gaspésie two or three times daily from mid-May to mid-October. The fare is $11.50/7.25 per adult/child. Taking a bicycle costs $4; a car is $29.

STE ANNE DE PORTNEUF

The best reason to stop in this small town is to partake of one of the best whale-watching expeditions in the entire region. Among its unusual offerings, **Crosières du Grand Héron** (☎ *418-587-6006, 888-463-6006, Rue du Quai; adult/child 6-13/child under 6 $38/25/free*) boasts a unique night-time bioluminescence tour. At this distance from the Saguenay River, the company's Zodiac (for up to 12 people) is often the only boat in a vast expanse of water.

Though there may be fewer whales here than around Tadoussac, your chances of seeing some up close are excellent. The Swiss Whale Society (**W** www.isuisse.com/cetaces) has set up a research camp nearby and runs two-week scientific expeditions. For about $1200 (course, accommodations and equipment included), you can join the Society for a 14-day bioacoustic research project.

BAIE COMEAU

This unattractive city owes its existence to Robert R McCormick, former owner of the *Chicago Tribune,* who, in 1936, decided to build a colossal pulp and paper factory here. This enterprise necessitated harnessing the hydroelectric power of the Manicouagan and Outardes Rivers. This in turn begat other hydro-dependent industries like aluminum processing. The immense Reynolds company still produces its famous foil here, among other products.

Baie Comeau is useful as a road gateway to Labrador. You'll find many services here, as well as canoeing, kayaking, swimming and biking possibilities, but to want to stay here, you'd have to profess an interest in strange smells and at times surreal and larger-than-life industrial landscapes.

The tourist information office (☎ 418-296-8178, 3503 Boulevard Laflèche) is near the western limits of the city. Several motels also dot Boulevard Lasalle.

A year-round ferry (☎ 418-294-8593) makes the 2½-hour journey to Matane one or two times a day from May to September, less frequently at other times of the year. The fare is $13 per adult, $30 per car.

From Baie Comeau, Hwy 389 runs north past the Manicouagan projects and then beyond to Wabush and Labrador City, on the border of Québec and Labrador. For details of these similarly awesome towns

and Labrador, see the Labrador section in the Newfoundland chapter. This section also contains some more information on traveling the road to Labrador. This is a fascinating landscape with lake-filled barrens, tundra and the **Groulx Mountains**, about 120km northwest of the hydroelectric complex Manic Cinq; peaks reach as high as 1000m.

GODBOUT

This tiny town occupies a lovely, sleepy, windswept spot on the St Lawrence. Originally a 17th-century trading post, it flourished thanks to its salmon-filled rivers, Godbout and Trinité. It remains one of the best spots in the province for salmon fishing.

The old general store serves as the tourist information office (☎ 418-568-7647, 100 Rue Pascal Comeau), which has a small exhibit on local history and some great antiques. The **Musée Amérindien et Inuit** (☎ *418-568-7306, 134 Rue Pascal Comeau; adult/child $3/2; open 10am-7pm daily June-Sept*) owns a nice collection of Inuit and Native Indian sculptures. If you feel like **swimming**, dive into the Rivière Godbout, at the western end of the village.

The **Dépanneur Proprio** (☎ *418-568-7535, 156 Rue Pascal Comeau*), a convenience store, sells fishing permits for non-residents, and rents out plain, neat rooms on the 2nd floor (singles/doubles $28/34).

A ferry (☎ 418-568-7575) links Godbout with Matane (see the Gaspé Peninsula section, later, for details).

POINTE DES MONTS

This marks the point where the St Lawrence graduates from river to gulf. The 1830 lighthouse here, one of the oldest in Québec, has lorded over dozens of shipwrecks over the past century, despite its function. The 28m-tall structure sits on a picturesque spit of land and has been converted into a **museum** (☎ *418-939-2400, 1830 Chemin du Vieux Phare; admission $2.50; 9am-7pm daily mid-June–mid-Sept*) that explains the lives of the keepers and their families, who lived inside it. A restaurant onsite serves first-rate local specialties, and the B&B here (same ☎ as museum) offers good dinner-room-sea excursion (or diving) packages for about $130 for two. This could make an exotic, relaxing and fun stop.

POINTE AUX ANGLAIS

A few kilometers east of this tiny village lies a long public beach where people can pitch their tents in the wooded dunes for free and spend a day sighting whales offshore. The beach is sandy, sprawling and clean – one of the finest on the North Shore – and while there are no services whatsoever here (not even a toilet), you can shower for $4 at the nearby restaurant *Le Routier de Pentecôte* (☎ *418-799-2600, 2767 Route 138)* from 6am to 9:30pm daily. You can also rent a cheap room here. There are also two official campgrounds around the village of Rivière Pentecôte, 8km north of Pointe aux Anglais on Route 138.

SEPT ÎLES

The last town of any size along the North Shore, Sept Îles boasts several worthwhile stops. Despite the rather isolated location, this is Canada's second-busiest port as measured by tonnage.

For general information, go to the main tourist information office (☎ 418-968-0022, 1401 Boulevard Laure Ouest) or the smaller one at the Parc du Vieux Quai (port).

There are two Innu reserves in the area: Uashat, in the western sector of the city, and Maliotenam, 14km east. Though these look rather depressed and colorless, the well-organized Innu here run several enterprises, including the **Musée Shaputuan** (☎ *418-962-4000, 290 Boulevard des Montagnais; adult/ student $3/2; open 9am-5pm daily late June-early Sept, 9am-5pm Mon-Fri & 1pm-5pm Sat early Sept-late June).* The museum covers Montagnais (Innu) history, culture, traditions and superstitions. Temporary exhibits of local artists' work are also held in the circular exhibition hall, itself divided into four sections, symbolizing the seasons.

Another worthwhile stop is **Le Vieux Poste** (☎ *418-968-2070, Boulevard des Montagnais; adult/student $4/3; open 9am-5pm daily late June-late Aug),* an old fur-trading post built in 1661. It's been reconstructed as a walk-through series of buildings, each with its own exhibit to show the lifestyles of the hunters who used to call the forest home.

There is a small island archipelago off Sept Îles. The largest, **Île Grande Basque**, is a pretty spot to spend a day, walking on the 12km of trails or picnicking on the coast. La

Petite Sirène (☎ *418-968-2173; adult/child 6-13 $15/9)* runs 10-minute boat crossings from Sept Îles' port to/from the island ten times a day and also organizes guided trips there. Tickets are available at the Parc du Vieux Quai (port), where other companies offer similar trips. For guided **kayaking** tours of the islands, contact **Vêtements des Îles** (☎ *418-962-7223, 637 Ave Brochu).* Île du Corosol is a bird refuge.

You'll find several motels along Route 138 (Boulevard Laure).

Le Tangon (☎ *418-962-8180, 555 Ave Cartier)* Tent sites $10, dorm beds $16/19 member/nonmember, singles/doubles with shared bathroom $26/42. This HI youth hostel contains basement rooms with six to eight beds each; the private rooms on the 2nd floor often fill up with fishermen. The hostel area is fairly cramped, and there's little room to socialize, but it's very clean.

Gîte des Îles (☎ *962-6116, 50 Rue Thibault)* Singles/doubles $40/50. This is a welcoming B&B in a quiet sector north of Route 138.

Getting There & Away

Intercar (☎ 418-962-2126) runs a daily bus to/from Baie Comeau ($27, 3½ hours) and a daily bus to/from Havre St Pierre ($25, 2½ hours). The bus station is at 126 Rue Mgr Blanche.

The Relais Nordik in Rimouski (☎ 418-723-8787, 800-463-0680) operates a ferry that travels along the Lower North Shore to Blanc Sablon once a week. From Sept Îles, it leaves the Quai Mgr Blanche and travels to Île D'Anticosti.

QNS&L Railway (☎ 418-968-7808, 100 Rue Retty) operates a train service to Schefferville, 568km north, one of the province's most remote spots; it was once a thriving mining town. The train goes once a week and costs $138 roundtrip. A separate service runs once or twice a week to Labrador City for about the same price and treats passengers to phenomenal scenery. Cutting through forests, the tracks pass over gorges, dip inside valleys, curve around waterfalls and rapids, dive through a section of mountain and jut along stretches of lakes, rivers, hills and forest as far as the eye can see. The train crosses a 900m-long bridge, 50m over Rivière Moisie and past the 60m-high Tonkas Falls.

QUÉBEC

HAVRE ST PIERRE

Immediately east of Sept Îles, the scenery changes dramatically. Villages cease to appear with regularity, the trees become progressively smaller, some hilltops lead to stretches of muskeg, and river after river reaches its destination, some by creeping humbly, others by tumbling forcefully into the St Lawrence, sometimes off a rocky cliff, sometimes in the torrents of stunning rapids.

On the way to Havre St Pierre, **Mingan** is definitely worth a stop. Populated by a dynamic Innu community (who call it Ekuanitshit), the village occupies a lovely spot where wind and waves have carved out strange monoliths and figures by the coast. Not to be missed is the **Église Montagnaise** (☎ 418-949-2272, 15 Rue de l'Église; admission free; open 8am-7pm daily), a little church with Native Indian motifs inside, which makes for a striking mix of Catholicism and aboriginal culture. A teepee form enshrines the crucifix, and the stations of the cross are painted on animal skin parchment.

The sizable fishing town of Havre St Pierre has a lot of charm, though its highly developed tourist industry feels out of place in this otherwise laid-back region. It's also an industrial zone, where iron oxide and titanium rich rock are extracted (in mines near Lac Allard) and then shipped to processing plants in Tracy-Sorel. If you're up early enough, you can catch the miners heading for their break-of-dawn train, which takes them 43km north to the mines.

Havre St Pierre was founded in 1857 by six Acadian families who had left the Îles de la Madeleine and set up here in traditionally Inuit territory. At the tourist information office (☎ 418-538-2512, 957 Rue de la Berge), a small exhibit has been mounted in the old general store.

The region's main attraction is the **Mingan Archipelago National Park** (☎ 418-538-5264, 975 Rue de l'Escale), a protected zone made up of an 85km-long string of 40 main islands near the mainland. These stretch from Longue Pointe de Mingan to 40km east of Havre St Pierre. The islands' distinguishing characteristics are the odd, erosion-shaped stratified limestone formations along the shores. They've been dubbed 'flowerpots' for the lichen and small vegetation that grow on top of them. Perched atop them might be the puffin (macareux moine), a striking mix between a parrot and penguin and one of some 200 bird species you can see here.

Several kiosks lined up at the marina each offer a variety of excursions. Comparison shop to find the one that suits you. In general, the smaller the boat, the better the experience. Count on $30 to $50 per excursion. **Agaguk** (☎ 418-538-1588, 1062 Rue Boréale) is run by a young dynamic team that rents kayaks, canoes and bikes and runs excellent guided kayak tours of the archipelago.

Places to Stay

Camping is allowed on some of the islands for $6 to $9 per night, but you must register first at the visitors' center of the national park.

Auberge de la Minganie (☎ 418-538-1538, 3908 Route 138) Tent sites $8, dorm beds $15. The minus is that it's located an inconvenient 17km west of Havre St Pierre and there's no transportation from town (though the Orléans bus will stop if you ask, and you'll have to walk the remaining 700m). The plus is that this isolated hostel sits on a beautiful, quiet bay, surrounded by trails through woods. You can rent a canoe here and immerse yourself in the surrounding serenity. Beds are in separate cabins, and there are laundry and kitchen facilities.

Auberge Boréale (☎ 418-538-3912, 1288 Rue Boréale) Singles/doubles $46/56. This large B&B in the eastern end of town rents out bikes and boasts a pretty sea view (ask if your room has one).

ÎLE D'ANTICOSTI

Only in the last few years has this island's 7943 sq km of nature begun to unfold its beauty before an ever-growing number of visitors. Until recently, the only people who've been able to appreciate the land and its riches have been lazy deer hunters with good connections – lazy because, with over 120,000 deer on the island, it doesn't take much looking to find one, and good connections because, for much of the island's modern history, it has been private land.

A French chocolate maker named Henri Menier (his choco empire turned into Nestle!) bought the island in 1895 to turn it into his own private hunting ground (people have come from far and wide to shoot the deer here). Only recently have small parts of the island been turned into a wildlife reserve.

It's a heavily wooded, cliff-edged island with waterfalls, canyons, caves and good salmon rivers. The **hiking** and **biking** trails are limitless; the island is a paradise for outdoors adventurists. **Port Menier**, inhabited mainly by employees of the wildlife reserve and those in the service industry, is the closest thing to a village on the island. It's from here that the island's lone road ventures to the interior. A tourist information office (☎ 418-535-0250) is on Chemin des Forestiers.

The **Écomusée D'Anticosti** (☎ 418-535-0250, Rue Dr Schmidt), in Port Menier, is a free exhibit of the flora and fauna found on the island. Nearby, you can see some houses dating from Menier's time on the island. There are also a few restaurants and B&Bs in the area, but accommodations should be arranged before arrival.

Though it's possible to get to the island yourself, camp, rent a bike or ATV and wander around, it requires much planning. One campground, *Camping Baie Ste Claire* (☎ 418-533-0155), is not far from Port Menier, but you don't want to find yourself stuck in this sector of the island. Because the distances to the eastern sector of the island are so great, you need a vehicle. Nearly every visitor chooses to go with one of the many small-group package tours. Get more information at the tourist office at Havre St Pierre.

Among the tour companies, **Safari Anticosti** (☎ 418-538-1414) is probably the best bet. Its well-organized tours of two or more days take in all the sites and concentrate on the wilder eastern sector of the island. The company's helicopters depart daily from Havre St Pierre. Count on paying about $229 for two days.

The only regular transportation service is the once-weekly boat from Havre St Pierre operated by the Relais Nordik (☎ 418-723-8787, 800-463-0680), but it is not the most convenient. It arrives in Port Menier at midnight every Monday morning and leaves again every Wednesday at 3:45pm.

NATASHQUAN

Natashquan is still getting used to its recent connection to the rest of the province. Route 138 only joined it to Sept Îles in 1996,

and only since 1999 has it been paved. Romantics are drawn here for the experience of going to the end of the road and for the peaceful, windswept beauty. Others treat a trip here as a pilgrimage to the birthplace of Gilles Vigneault, a singer-songwriter of great stature in Québec.

You can direct your questions to the small tourist information office (☎ 418-726-3756, 33 Allée des Galets), but because the tourism infrastructure is not so well developed here, your best bet is to just ask around if you'd like to go on a fishing, canoeing or kayaking trip. Just like in the old days, things get done here via word of mouth and out of a genuine desire to be helpful.

Les Galets is a small collection of small white houses with bright red roofs huddled together on a small peninsula. Fishermen used to sort and dry their catch here. It's now an abandoned, lovely area.

Aside from enjoying the endless, sandy beaches, you might want to spend some time here **hiking** inland. You can feel completely isolated and peaceful on the 15km of trails through unspoiled woods full of numerous waterfalls, lookouts and obscenely beautiful spots to sit and picnic.

LOWER NORTH SHORE

The string of tiny villages in the far eastern corner of the province remains an enigma for most Québécois, mere names on the weather report. Because no roads connect them to the rest of the province and because you can only reach the towns via a weekly boat, the area remains a challenging destination for all but the most determined. Snowmobilers, however, can travel on a trail that links Natashquan with Blanc Sablon.

The Relais Nordik boat is the region's main lifeline, setting sail every week of the year (except from mid-January through early April) from Rimouski, bringing supplies, the odd curiosity-seeker and, for the brief while the boat remains docked in each port of call, a few hours of fresh conversation to the locals. During the two to three hours in each port, passengers can disembark and sniff around. Most of the villages are spread around the ports, but even the inland ones can be visited by hopping a lift with friendly locals.

Kegasta is an anglophone village known for its crushed-seashell-covered roads. The one outfitter in the area, **Pourvoirie Leslie Forman** (☎ *418-726-3738*), sets up lobster, crab and scallop fishing excursions. **Harrington Harbour**, the next town, is living eye candy. Considered one of Québec's ten prettiest villages, this anglophone community has made much of its rocky terrain and small, wind-sheltered bay. All the brightly colored houses are perched atop rocks. A popular place is *Amy's B&B & Craft Shop* (☎ *418-795-3376*).

Blanc Sablon is the end of the line, 2km west of the Labrador border. A ferry (☎ 418-461-2056) links it to St Barbe in Newfoundland (less than an hour's ride), and a paved road connects it to several coastal villages in Labrador. A dynamic, mainly anglophone fishing community lives in this historic area where numerous archeological digs have turned up a European presence since the 16th century and an aboriginal one stretching back over 7000 years.

Lower St Lawrence

This region *(Bas St Laurent)* extends from La Pocatière to just west of Ste Flavie at the start of the Gaspé Peninsula. Tourists often zip along the coast through the region, making brief stops in Rivière du Loup or Rimouski, the last large population centers before the Gaspésie. Yet aside from the spectacular views of the North Shore's mist-covered, layered mountains from the region's coastline, surprises await inland.

RIVIÈRE DU LOUP

This town has a way of weaving itself into your heart. While it boasts nothing of particular grandeur, visitors often leave saying, 'There's *something* I like about that place.' Built on a rocky ridge (which gives it several extremely steep hills) at the mouth of the Rivière du Loup, it has benefited from its position as gateway to the Maritime provinces (Edmundston in New Brunswick is 122km away). A ferry also connects it to the St Siméon, in the Charlevoix region.

The tourist information office (☎ 418-862-1981, 189 Boulevard de l'Hôtel de Ville) is open year-round.

The lively **Musée du Bas St Laurent** (☎ *418-862-7547, 300 Rue St Pierre; adult/ student $5/3; open 10am-6pm daily early June-early Oct, 1pm-5pm Tues, Thur-Sun & 6pm-9pm Mon & Wed early Oct-early June)* offers a good mix of regional history and contemporary art exhibits.

Eccentricity is alive and well at **Les Carillons** (☎ *418-862-3346, 393 Rue Témiscouata; adult/child $5/2; open 9am-8pm daily late June-early Sept, 9am-5pm daily early-late June & early Sept-early Oct)*, the self-proclaimed largest museum in the world dedicated to bells. Spread out over sprawling gardens are some 200 bells saved from metal smelters, the largest weighing 1000kg.

At the small **Parc des Chutes**, a few minutes' walk from downtown at the end of Rue Frontenac, some picnic tables and a 2.3km trail offer a chance to admire the 30m waterfalls that power a small hydroelectric power station.

A short drive up to the hilly areas of town leads you to the tiny **Park de la Croix Lumineuse**, where an illuminated cross guards a nice lookout. To get there from downtown, take Rue Joly south until the underpass leading to Rue Témiscouata. Make a left on Chemin des Raymond, then turn left at Rue Alexandre, right at Rue Bernier and left at Rue Ste Claire.

The nonprofit group **La Société Duvetnor** (☎ *418-867-1660, 200 Rue Hayward)*, founded in 1979 by marine biologists keen to preserve the fragile ecosystem on offshore islands, offers a range of bird-watching and nature excursions that last anywhere from a few hours to several days. Sighting belugas is common. Prices range from $20 for a 90-minute trip to and around the Îles du Pot à l'Eau de Vie, to $30 for a day trip to Île aux Lièvres ($15 for kids), to $180 for overnight stays in cottages or an old lighthouse, including meals. Boats leave from the marina.

Places to Stay & Eat

International Youth Hostel (☎ *418-862-7566, fax 418-862-1843, 46 Boulevard de l'Hôtel de Ville)* Dorm beds $16.50/19 member/nonmember, doubles $21/22. This old yellow house boasts a central location and a placid atmosphere as far as hostels go. Cheap breakfasts are also served, and activities around the city are sometimes organized.

Cégep Student Residence (☎ *418-862-6903 ext 282, 325 Rue St Pierre*) Singles/doubles $20/40. Clean and quiet, this college housing might not give the most authentic picture of how students really live. Sparsely equipped kitchens are at your disposal.

Au Vieux Fanal (☎ *418-862-5255, 170 Rue Fraser*) Doubles $70/80 without/with river view. One of the best motels on the strip is this simple place with great views of the river, a heated swimming pool and charming owners.

Le Chateau Grandville (☎ *418-868-0750, 94 Rue Lafontaine*) Singles/doubles $80/95, with breakfast $85/105. There's Old World

elegance galore in this mid-19th-century grand home. The three restaurants on the premises, also excellent, feature an outdoor terrace and cozy bar.

L'Estaminet (☎ *418-867-4517, 299 Rue Lafontaine*) Dishes $6-10. Open 10am-midnight or 1am daily. You can feast on good salads, paninis and pasta in a publike atmosphere, then wash them down with some of 100 types of beers. Mussels with fries, the house specialty, start at $7.

Les Sucreries de Jojo (☎ *418-862-2671, 340 Rue Lafontaine*) Dishes $5-11. Open 8am-6pm Mon-Wed, 8am-10pm Thur & Fri, 9am-5pm Sat & Sun. This country kitchen–style café is renowned for its sweets (pastries and Belgian chocolate), but the breakfasts in particular are killer.

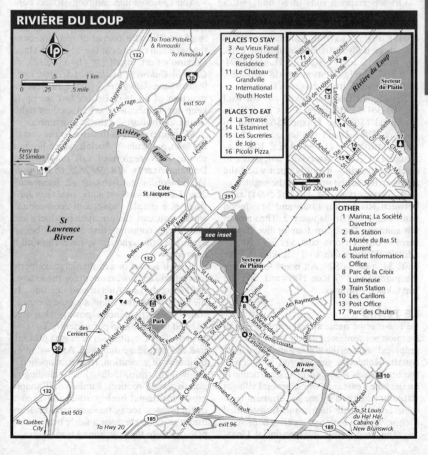

RIVIÈRE DU LOUP

PLACES TO STAY
3 Au Vieux Fanal
7 Cégep Student Residence
11 Le Chateau Grandville
12 International Youth Hostel

PLACES TO EAT
4 La Terrasse
14 L'Estaminet
15 Les Sucreries de Jojo
16 Picolo Pizza

OTHER
1 Marina; La Société Duvetnor
2 Bus Station
5 Musée du Bas St Laurent
6 Tourist Information Office
8 Parc de la Croix Lumineuse
9 Train Station
10 Les Carillons
17 Parc des Chutes

QUÉBEC

La Terrasse *(☎ 418-862-6927, 171 Rue Fraser)* Dishes $7-14. The specialty of this restaurant inside the Hôtel Levesque is what almost everyone comes here for – the smoked salmon, smoked by the owners and every bit as succulent as it's rumored to be.

Picolo Pizza *(☎ 418-868-1671, 371 Rue Lafontaine)* Appetizers $3-10, dishes $9-18. Despite the word 'pizza' in the name, make no mistake – this is fine cuisine. The pastas and pizzas are creative, the specialties well seasoned and the beer cocktails offbeat – try some brews mixed with cranberry juice or iced tea!

Getting There & Away

Highway 20 (exit 503), Route 132 and Hwy 185 lead directly into Rivière du Loup.

Orléans Express runs three daily buses to/from Montréal ($68, 5½ hours), seven daily to/from Québec City ($34, 2½ to four hours), six daily to/from Rimouski ($19, 1¼ hrs), three daily to/from Edmundston ($18, two hours) and two to/from Halifax ($94, 11½ hrs). The bus station (☎ 418-862-4884, 83 Boulevard Cartier) has coin lockers.

Rivière du Loup is linked by Via Rail (☎ 800-361-5390) three times a week to Montréal ($68), to Gaspé ($65) and to Halifax ($96). Don't bother going to the train station (☎ 418-867-1525, Rue Lafontaine at Rue Fraserville) unless it's to catch your train – it's only open when the trains arrive, in the middle of the night.

A ferry service (☎ 418-862-5094) runs between Rivière du Loup and St Siméon from mid-April to January 2. Throughout the summer, there are four or five departures a day. Tickets cost $11.30/7.50 per adult/child ages five to 11. Taking a bike costs $4; a car is $29. All boats leave from the marina at 199 Rue Hayward, and the trip takes 65 minutes.

LE TÉMIS

Le Témis is the name affectionately given to a region concentrated around its main geographical feature, the 40km-long Lac Témiscouata. Relatively unexplored in Québec, the area holds a few surprises, particularly on the lake's east side, where several villages slated to be closed by the government took their fate in their hands and transformed themselves into busy and creative communities. The **Petit Témis Interprovincial Linear Park** makes a scenic bike and walking trail, mainly flat, which runs along an old train track for the 135km from Rivière du Loup to Edmundston, New Brunswick.

Hwy 185, with its pulp and paper mills and forests interspersed with farms, provides a foretaste of New Brunswick. If you go this route, you'll always be able to say you've been to **St Louis du Ha! Ha!**. Its odd name could come from the Hexcuewaska Indian language, referring to something unexpected, or from a 15th-century French expression for 'dead end'; others say it reflects the exclamation of wonder the area's first colonizers uttered upon seeing such beauty. Considering the town's relative lack of attractiveness, we'd have to vote for one of the former explanations.

You can do some camping around here. Near **Cabano**, a number of motels offer a typical Québec amenity: a bar. In Cabano itself, you'll find a couple of restaurants on the one main street near the edge of the lake. Cabano's **Fort Ingall** *(☎ 418-854-2375, 81 Chemin Caldwell; adult/child $6.50/4; open 9:30am-6pm daily June-Sept)* is a 1973 reconstruction of an 1839 British fort set up to keep out Americans who had set their sights on the south shores of the St Lawrence.

Most interesting is the area to the east of the lake, particularly **Auclair**, which lies in a scenic, hilly region of tall maples. The **Domaine Acer** *(☎ 418-899-2825, 65 Route du Vieux Moulin; guided visit $2; open mid-Mar–Dec 24 9am-5pm daily, until 6pm July-Aug)* is a maple grove-cum-ecomuseum, where you can taste maple products and sample the country's first alcoholic beverage made from a maple sap base. The stuff is heavenly.

Auclair is part of a multivillage cooperative called JAL (an acronym for the villages of St Juste du Lac, Auclair and Lejeune). In the early 1970s, the villages joined forces to stand up to provincial powers that had decided to close them permanently. The cost of providing essential services was prohibitive, the government argued. After winning their stay of execution, residents opened a number of mini-industries, including a potato seed producer, lumber mill, maple grove, medicinal herb garden and even a coffin builder. Today, these creative endeavors have made the area a fairly burgeoning place, despite the enveloping tranquility.

TROIS PISTOLES

Just east of Rivière du Loup, Hwy 20 ends, and, except during its brief reappearance around Rimouski, you must continue on Route 132.

In rendering homage to the Basque fishermen who used to fish in the St Lawrence centuries before the arrival of Europeans, the **Parc de l'Aventure Basque en Amérique** (☎ 418-851-1556, 66 Ave du Parc; adult/student $6/3.50; open 9am-8pm daily June–mid-Oct) opens the door onto a part of history few are familiar with. The exhibits are in French only, but an English booklet is available, and English tours can be booked in advance. On the first weekend in July, the museum hosts the International Basque Festival, with music, games and a small parade.

Behind the museum is a large fronton. A fronton? It's a rectangular, marked court with a large wall on one end, and it's used to play a game of Pelote Basque, one of the world's oldest ball games. With a ball velocity of up to 300km/h, it's also the world's fastest ball and bat game. Visitors can try playing Pelote for themselves (or rent the court for $10/hour).

Guided excursions to the offshore **Îles aux Basques** (☎ 418-851-1202, 11 Rue du Parc; $15 per person; open daily June-early Sept) touch upon the social history of the island as well as its present status as a protected bird sanctuary.

Camping & Motel des Flots Bleus Sur Mer (☎ 418-851-3583, Route 132, Rivière Trois Pistoles) Tent sites $15, singles/doubles from $40/60. This campground, 5km west of town on the banks of the Rivière Trois Pistoles, is a small, quiet affair with toilets and showers. The neighboring motel is barebones, but it's the cheapest around and decent enough.

A passenger ferry operated by Compagnie de Navigation des Basques (☎ 418-851-4676, 11 Rue du Parc) runs to/from Les Escoumins on the North Shore two or three times daily from mid-May to mid-October. The fare is $11.50/7.25/free per adult/child 5-16/child under 5. Taking a bicycle costs $4; a car is $29.

PARC DU BIC

One of the smaller provincial parks is nonetheless one of Québec's most striking. At times, the landscape seems surreal, especially with thousands of eiders flying overheard. The Parc du Bic (☎ 418-869-3333, 33 Route 132; adult/child $3.50/1.50) covers 33 sq km of islands, bays, jagged cliffs, lush, conical mountaintops and rocky shores covered with plump grey and harbor seals. The plethora of activities here includes organized minibus tours, sea-kayaking excursions, specialized walks, bike rental ($18/day) and hiking, biking, skiing and snowshoe trails.

The friendly, flexible and knowledgeable staff at **Kayak Rivi-Air Aventure** (☎ 418-736-5252, 3257 Route 132), in Le Bic, offer good kayaking options, including half-day, full-day or sunset outings for $30 to $60.

The park's campground is nice but too close to traffic to be peaceful.

RIMOUSKI

Rimouski is a fairly large, growing industrial and oil-distribution town made lively in part by a sizable student population. The main street is Rue St Germain, which runs east and west from the principal cross street, Ave Cathédrale. At the intersection of Rue St Germain and Ave Cathédrale is the Place des Veterans square, where you'll find the helpful tourist office (☎ 418-723-2322, 50 Rue St Germain Ouest).

A pretty stone church (1826) houses the **Musée Régional de Rimouski** (☎ 418-724-2272, 35 Rue St Germain Ouest; adult/student $4/3; open 10am-9pm Wed-Sat, 10am-6pm Sun-Tues June-Sept; noon-5pm Wed-Sun Oct-May). The hit-and-miss exhibits usually include a display of local, contemporary art.

Just 5km east of Rimouski is the **Musée de la Mer** (☎ 418-724-6214, 1034 Rue du Phare; adult/student $6/4; open 10am-5pm daily June & late Aug–mid-Oct, 9am-7pm daily July-late Aug), which tells the story of the sinking of the Empress of Ireland in 1914 – after the Titanic, it's the worst disaster in maritime history. In the 14 minutes it took for the boat to sink after being rammed inadvertently by a Norwegian boat, 1012 people lost their lives.

For hiking, mountain biking and a view of a canyon and waterfalls from the province's highest suspended bridge (62m), head to the **Portes de l'Enfer** (☎ 418-735-6063, Chemin Duchénier) in St Narcisse de Rimouski, some 30km south of Rimouski along Route 232.

QUÉBEC

Places to Stay & Eat

Cégep Residences (☎ 418-723-4636, 320 Rue St Louis) Students: singles/doubles $18/25, without bedding $12/18; nonstudents: singles/doubles $21/28. This college rents standard student rooms year-round, on a daily, weekly or monthly basis. Considering the paper-thin walls, you'd better ask for as quiet a floor as possible.

Auberge de la Vielle Maison (☎ 418-723-6010, 35 Rue St Germain Est) Singles/doubles $45-60/55-70. Somewhere between a B&B and hotel, this large house styled after a country home features eight comfortable rooms, all with hardwood floors, shared bathrooms and lots of privacy. Plus, it's right on the main street. Breakfast is included.

Maison Bérubé (☎/fax 418-723-1578, 1216 Boulevard St Germain Ouest) Singles/doubles $40/50. A farm house on Route 132, halfway between Bic and Rimouski, this charming place offers a bit of country living near the city. Bike rentals are available.

Central Café (☎ 418-722-4011, 31 Rue de l'Évêché Ouest) Dishes $7-13. Off the main street you'll find the city's best hangout, a great bistro in a two-story old house with a terrace shaded by maples. The food is standard (pasta, smoked meat, burgers) but tasty.

Maison du Spaghetti (☎ 418-723-6010, 35 Rue St Germain Est) Appetizers $3-8, dishes $8-14. A Rimouski institution for 20 years, this place serves up the city's best pasta dishes in copious portions. Definitely get the garlic bread ($4), done on pizza crust.

Le Crêpe Chignon (☎ 418-724-0400, 140 Ave de la Cathédrale) Dishes $5-10. This bright light on the Rimouski dining scene serves delicious meal and dessert crêpes, quesadillas ($8), and lunch specials ($6 to $9), all in a relaxed, friendly atmosphere.

Getting There & Away

Air Satellite (☎ 418-722-6161) flies from Rimouski to Baie Comeau twice a day Monday to Friday.

Buses link Rimouski three times a day with Montréal ($80, 7½ hours), five times a day with Rivière du Loup ($19, 1½ hours) and Québec City ($38, four hours). Four buses a day go to Gaspé ($36), two each along the south (nine hours) and north (seven hours) coasts of the peninsula. All buses depart from the bus station (☎ 418-723-4923, 90 Rue Léonidas).

The VIA Rail station (☎ 418-722-4737, 57 Rue de l'Évêché Est) is only open when trains pull in, usually past midnight. Six trains a week go to/from Montréal ($81, eight hours).

Allô Stop (☎ 418-723-5248, 106 Rue St Germain) hooks up drivers with those needing lifts to Québec City or Montréal. The agency is open 10am to 5:30pm Saturday to Wednesday, 10am to 9pm Thursday and Friday.

A ferry service (☎ 418-725-2725) links Rimouski with Forestville on the North Shore. From late April to early October, two to four boats make the 55-minute journey every day. The one-way fare is $14/9 per adult/child. A bicycle costs an extra $4; a car is $34.

The Relais Nordik (☎ 418-723-8787, 800-463-0680, 17 Ave Lebrun) takes passengers on its weekly cargo ship en route to Sept Îles and villages along the North Shore. It departs Rimouski at 12:30pm every Tuesday from early April to mid-January, and gets to Blanc Sablon at 7pm Friday. There are different classes of cabins, and prices vary accordingly. A Rimouski–Blanc Sablon roundtrip in a four-berth cabin with three meals a day is $745. A Natashquan–Blanc Sablon roundtrip in the same class is $356.

All boats and ferries leave from the marina, just north of the city.

Gaspé Peninsula

The rounded chunk of land that juts out north of New Brunswick into the Gulf of St Lawrence is known locally as 'La Gaspésie.' East of Matane, the characteristic features of the region really become evident: the trees and woods thicken into forests, the towns dwindle in size, the North Shore slowly disappears from view, the wind picks up the salt air, and you sense remoteness more and more. The landscape, particularly on the north coast, also becomes breathtakingly spectacular, as rocky cliffs plunge into the sea and layers of mountains and hills stretch for miles.

Some of the province's best hiking trails and possibilities for adventure tourism are here. Tourists will have no problem finding services, though tourism is less developed than in the province's metropolitan centers.

For the traveler who finds French a bit of a struggle, English communities at the eastern tip and around the south shore make a petit respite!

STE FLAVIE

On Route 132 in Ste Flavie, a large information center for the Gaspésie offers help to travelers year-round. If you're here late in the season, pick up one of the pamphlets listing facilities that remain open until mid-October.

Ste Flavie's **Centre d'Art Marcel Gagnon** (☎ *418-775-2829, 564 Route de la Mer; admission free; open 8am-11pm daily May-Sept, 8am-9pm daily Oct-Apr*) is definitely worth a visit. It's an inn, restaurant and art school based around an exhibit of over 80 life-size concrete statues by prolific sculptor, painter and writer Marcel Gagnon. The figures, all with different faces, march out to sea, appearing and disappearing with the tide. You'll also see other artwork on display and for sale.

The center includes a restaurant and café, and the *Auberge (same ☎ & address)* offers comfortable singles/doubles from $50/100, including breakfast. A double room, full-course dinner, breakfast and entrance to the Jardins de Métis (see Grand Métis, below) costs only $130 for two.

GRAND MÉTIS

One of the province's most revered attractions, the **Jardins de Métis** (☎ *418-775-2222, 200 Route 132; adult/student/child 6-13/child 5 & under $12/11/3/free; open 8:30am-6pm daily June–mid-Oct*) comprises 40 acres of immaculately tended gardens boasting over 2000 varieties of plants. Begun in 1910, the gardens are also known as the Reford Gardens (after Elsie Reford, who inherited the land from her uncle Lord Mount Stephen, founder of the Canadian Pacific Railway). Streams, paths and bridges add variety to the landscape, as does a 37-room mansion doubling as a museum. International floral exhibits happen here every summer.

About 10km east of town are the villages of **Métis Beach** and **Métis sur Mer**, with nice sandy beaches. This area has traditionally been a country retreat for bourgeois, wealthy English families. It's worth taking a

QUÉBEC

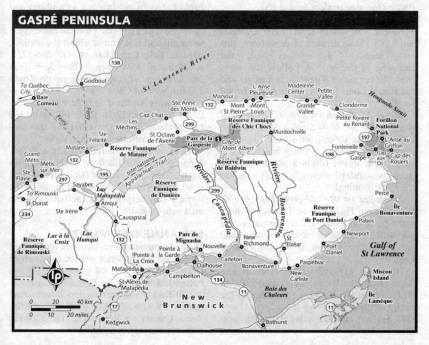

GASPÉ PENINSULA

detour through the towns to see the large houses with Anglo-Saxon names emblazoned on their front lawn signs.

MATANE

Matane, 42km east of Métis sur Mer, is a commercial fishing port known for its famous shrimp (the Festival de la Crevette, or Shrimp Festival, takes place around June 20 every year). Salmon go up the river here to spawn in June, and it's possible to do some fishing right from downtown. Take the Promenade des Capitaines road off Route 132, and you'll see salmon fisherfolk in action.

For help planning your stay, go to the tourist information office (☎ 418-562-1065, 968 Ave du Phare Ouest).

Absolu Aventure (☎ 418-562-8112, W www.absoluaventure.com) organizes one- to five-day guided hikes for beginners or advanced hikers on part of the International Appalachian Trail, which cuts through the Réserve Faunique de Matane. Reserve via the website.

You can buy fish, fresh or smoked, at several fish markets in town. Try **Poissonnerie Boréalis** (☎ 418-562-7001, 985 Ave du Phare Ouest; open 9am-6pm daily).

Camping de la Rivière Matane (☎ 418-562-3414, 150 Route Louis Félix Dionne) Sites $13-19. Southwest of downtown, this huge place (144 sites) offers good, quiet camping in the woods. Follow the signs from the corner of Rue Parc Industriel and the Route Louis Félix Dionne and proceed for 3km.

Motel Le Beach (☎ 418-562-1350, 1441 Rue Matane sur Mer) Singles/doubles from $40/45. About 100m from Route 132 – and thus a bit quieter than other hotels on the strip – this motel offers a good sea view from its standard rooms. It's very close to the ferry terminal.

Le Rafiot (☎ 418-562-8080, 1415 Ave de Phare Ouest) Dishes $7-14. This yellow-and-white place on Route 132 is a casual sort of pub with marine decor, plenty of seafood and good prices on shrimp dinners all summer long.

Buses (☎ 418-562-4085) arrive at and depart from the Irving gas station, 521 Ave du Phare Est (Route 132), 1.5km east of the center of town. Two buses a day go to Gaspé ($42, 5¼ hrs), and four a day go to Rimouski ($16, 1½ hrs).

The ferry terminal (☎ 418-562-2500, 877-562-6560) here provides the easternmost link to the north shore. Passenger ferries carrying 126 cars run year-round to Baie Comeau and Godbout several times a day from May to September. Service is less frequent other times of the year. Both trips take about two hours and 20 minutes and cost $13/30 per adult/car. Bikes are free.

The ferry terminal is off Route 132, about 2km west of the town center.

CAP CHAT

A completely surreal sight awaits you here. After nearly 200km of not much more than rocky coastline, scattered villages and forested hills, suddenly giant white windmills appear perched on hilltops, stoically twirling their propellers. This is the largest windmill park in Canada, with 133 of the dreamlike critters producing 100 MW of electricity, all used locally. It was meant to be a first experiment in harnessing wind power in the province, but the idea hasn't progressed much since the windmills were installed. The world's largest vertical axe windmill (110m) is here, too – alas, it's broken, but freeze-frame it in a photo and your friends will never know!

If you'd like to take a tour of the biggest windmill and learn more about the project, contact **Éole Cap-Chat** (☎ 418-786-5719; adult/student $5/3; open 8:30am-5pm daily late June-Sept). Look for the signs on Route 132 just west of Cap Chat.

Camping Au Bord de la Mer (☎ 418-786-2251) Tent sites $12-16. Right off Route 132 east of the bridge at Cap Chat, this standard campground offers some nice views.

Gîte Vents et Marées (☎/fax 418-786-5065, 38 Rue des Écoliers) Singles/doubles from $40/55. This elegant B&B off the main road is perfectly comfortable, and the owners can help arrange activities in the area year-round.

STE ANNE DES MONTS

Home to numerous restaurants, motels and shops, Ste Anne is not one of the prettier towns, but it is a good place to stock up before heading into the Parc de la Gaspésie. You'll find a summer tourist information bureau (☎ 418-763-5832, 90 Boulevard Ste Anne Ouest) on Route 132. The Orléans Express bus stop is next door.

L'Échouerie (☎ 418-763-1555, 295 1-ère Ave Est) Dorm beds $19. A converted school, this hostel offers a kitchen, a café, bike rental, transportation to Gaspésie Park – the works. To get there from the bus stop, cross the street, go east to Route de Parc, heading toward the church, then east along the river road. It's a 2km walk.

PARC DE LA GASPÉSIE

From Ste Anne des Monts, Route 299 runs south to the excellent Parc de la Gaspésie *(☎ 418-763-3181; admission $3.50)*, 802 sq km of spectacular scenery dotted by lakes and two of the province's most beautiful mountain ranges, the Chic Choc and McGerrigle Mountains, which together include 25 of the 40 highest summits in Québec. One of the province's best camping spots is here, as well as some of the best hiking (the International Appalachian Trail passes through). What's more, the only herd of caribou south of the St Lawrence River lives in the park.

At the Parc de la Gaspésie's **Interpretation Centre** *(☎ 418-763-7811; admission free; open 8am-8pm daily early June-end Sept)*, the staff are extraordinarily helpful in planning a schedule to match your time and budget. They also rent out hiking equipment.

Mont Jacques Cartier (1270m) is the highest peak in the Gaspésie. Hiking the mountain takes about 3½ hours roundtrip and makes for a very worthwhile trip – the alpine scenery and views are fantastic, and it's fairly common to see some of the herd of woodland caribou munching on lichen near the barren peaks.

Overnight *camping* costs $23 in one of the four campgrounds. The busiest one is across the road from the Interpretation Centre, but try for a spot at the 39-site campground at Lac Cascapédia. Throughout the park, *chalets* for rent start at $80 a day.

Gîte du Mont Albert (☎ 418-763-2288) Doubles $155, chalets from $100. This large, comfortable lodge next to the Interpretation Centre is for those who like their nature spiced with luxury. The facilities include a pool (open to campers, too) and a first-class restaurant – if you want to treat yourself, here's the place to do it.

A bus runs from the Ste Anne des Monts tourist information center to the Interpretation Centre. It leaves at 8am daily; the roundtrip fare is $6/3/free per adult/child 6-12/child 5 and under. Another shuttle ($13 roundtrip) runs hikers to the La Galène campground, the closest one to Mont Jacques Cartier. From there, another shuttle ($5) takes hikers the final 4km to the beginning of the hiking trail that leads up the mountain; that shuttle departs five times daily. The buses operate from the end of June to the end of September.

The **Réserve Faunique des Chic Chocs** *(☎ 418-797-5214; admission $3.50)* surrounds and bleeds into the Parc de la Gaspésie. Mainly a site for hunting and fishing, it also attracts geological expeditions. The reserve runs a gem-collecting trip (adult/child under 14 $20/10). In general, the area is less impressive than the Parc de la Gaspésie. To reach the main entrance, go south on Route 299, 12km past the Gîte du Mont Albert, then east for 1.5km on the Route du Lac Ste Anne toward Murdochville.

MONT ST PIERRE

The scenery becomes ever more spectacular east of Ste Anne des Monts: the North Shore disappears from view, and the road winds around rocky cliffs and waterfalls, every curve unveiling a stretch of mountains cascading down to the sea.

Mont St Pierre appears after a dramatic bend in the road. The town takes its name from a 418m mountain with a cliff that people regularly fling themselves from: **hang-gliding** and **para-gliding** enthusiasts come here in droves to enjoy one of the best spots on the continent for the sport. At the end of July, the international, 10-day hang-gliding festival **Fête du Vol Libre** *(☎ 418-797-2222)* turns the skyline multicolored with hundreds of sails. Near the eastern end of town, a rough road goes to the summit of Mont St Pierre, where there are takeoff stations and excellent views. If you're not hoofing it up the mountain – which takes an hour – you must have a 4WD vehicle.

If you feel like running off a cliff, your best bet is to do it with **Pilot Yvon Volé** *(☎ 418-797-2896, 34 Rue Prudent Cloutier)*. The tandem jump with Yvon costs a cool $100 for a 10- or 15-minute ride, but if you've never done it, it's worth it.

QUÉBEC

At the town of **Mont Louis**, just 6km east, the **Parc et Mer Mont Louis** (*☎/fax 418-797-5270, 18 10-ème Rue Est; admission free; open 8am-10pm daily late June-Sept*) comes highly recommended. A combination hip Internet café (the only place on the peninsula where you can sip espresso, read *Wallpaper* and surf the Web for $5/hour!), restaurant, nature trail, crafts boutique and concert hall (featuring lively bands on weekends), it's also an ideal place to camp. Ten sites by the beach cost $18 each.

The Parc de la Gaspésie can be reached via unpaved roads (watch for logging trucks!) from behind Mont St Pierre, but having a good map is helpful, as the routes are not marked well.

Camping du Pont (*☎ 418-797-2951, 120 Rue Prudent Cloutier*) Tent sites $16. The smaller of two campgrounds in Mont St Pierre is slightly more pleasant, though near the main road.

Auberge Les Vagues (*☎ 418-797-2851, 84 Rue Prudent Cloutier*) Dorm beds $15, singles/doubles $25/42, motel rooms $30/45. This hostel/motel has tiny rooms, but the place includes all you'll need, with a restaurant/bar and communal kitchen on the premises. The motel rooms have undergone slightly more renovations than the hostel accommodations.

MONT ST PIERRE TO FORILLON NATIONAL PARK

As you head east, the landscape keeps increasing in majesty. As the road winds and then dips into and out of towering green valleys around **Grande Vallée**, look for unusual, even playful, patterns etched by glaciers onto the planet's oldest rock. At L'Anse Pleureuse, turn south to **Murdochville** for tours of its impressive, yet somewhat unappealing, copper mine (*☎ 418-784-3335, 345 Route 198; adult/child $8/5; open 10am-4pm daily mid-June–mid-October*).

Petite Vallée is a particularly attractive village that bursts to life with the **Festival en Chanson** (*☎ 418-393-2222*) at the end of June. Founded in 1982, this has become one of the most popular and important folksong festivals in the province, launching the careers of popular singers Daniel Boucher and Richard Séguin. It usually lasts about ten days and, despite its status, has retained

an intimate feel – kids and even the local butcher participate impromptu on stage.

For those not visiting Forillon, Route 197 runs south just past Petite Rivière au Renard, avoiding the end of the peninsula.

At **Cap des Rosiers**, the gateway to Forillon National Park, a **graveyard** on the cliff tells the town's history: how the English came from Guernsey and Jersey; how the Irish settlers were Kavanaghs, O'Connors, etc; and how both groups mingled with the French. Generations later, the same names live on.

FORILLON NATIONAL PARK

Well worth a stop for its rugged seaside terrain and wildlife, this park (*☎ 418-368-5505; adult/child 6-16/child under 6 $3.75/2/free; open 9am-9pm daily June-early Oct*) lies at the extreme northeastern tip of the peninsula. Run by the ever-efficient Parks Canada, it offers a wealth of organized activities (at least one day in English). In the woods, you might come across moose, deer, fox and an increasing population of black bears (many tourists report sightings – take necessary precautions). The shoreline cliffs attract seabirds (including the great blue heron), and whales and seals make frequent appearances offshore.

There are two main entrances with visitors' centers where you can pick up maps: one at L'Anse au Griffon (east of Rivière au Renard), on Route 132, and another on the south side of the park at Fort Péninsule.

The northern coast consists of steep limestone cliffs – some as high as 200m – and long pebble beaches. **Cap Bon Ami** showcases the best of this topography. You can do some whale-watching through the telescope there. In the north sector, beyond Cap des Rosiers, you'll find a great picnic area with a small, rocky beach. The south coast features more beaches, some sandy, with small coves. **Penouille Beach** is said to have the warmest waters.

The good trails that meander through the park range from easy, 30-minute walks to a rigorous 18km trek that takes six hours one way. The hike along the southern shore to **Cap Gaspé** is easy and pleasant, with seashore views. The International Appalachian Trail ends here, as the Appalachians plunge into the sea once and for all.

Boat tours offer an opportunity for **whale-watching**.

Places to Stay

Forillon Campgrounds (☎ *418-368-6050*) Tent sites $16.50-20. The park contains 367 campsites in four campgrounds, and these often fill to capacity. Petit Gaspé is the most popular organized campground, as it is protected from sea breezes and has hot showers. The smallest campground (41 sites) is at Cap Bon Désir.

Auberge de Jeunesse de Cap aux Os (☎ *418-892-5153, 2095 Boulevard Grande Grève*) Price $15/17 members/nonmembers. Open 24 hours May-Oct. One of the most established places in the province features a fine view overlooking the bay. This friendly spot can accommodate 80 people. Breakfast and dinner are available, as are kitchen facilities. The main bus that runs along the north coast of the peninsula from Rimouski to Gaspé stops at the hostel throughout the summer. A drawback for those without vehicles is that it's a long way to any of the hiking trails, although bicycles can be rented.

GASPÉ

After a few hundred kilometers of tiny villages, Gaspé may seem like a mini-metropolis. Yet after hours of stunning scenery, it also feels dirty, dull, and run-down. Still, if you need some nightlife, you'll find some good choices here (much better than in Percé).

This was where Jacques Cartier first landed in June 1534 and, after meeting with the Iroquois of the region, boldly planted a wooden cross, claiming the land for the king of France.

The **Musée de la Gaspésie** (☎ *418-368-1534, 80 Boulevard Gaspé; adult/student $4/3; open 9am-7pm daily end June-early Sept, 9am-5pm Tues-Fri & 1pm-5pm Sat & Sun early Sept–mid-Dec & mid-Jan–end June*) depicts the lives of the region's settlers and features some maritime exhibits, crafts and a section on traditional foods. It also familiarizes you with Cartier's voyages. Six bronze plates outsides comprise the **monument** commemorating his landing.

The **Site Historique Micmac de Gespeg** (☎ *418-368-6005, 783 Boulevard Pointe Navarre; adult/student $4/3; open 9am-5pm daily mid-June–mid-Sept*) teaches visitors about the disappeared Micmac Indian culture in a re-created village setting with a good gift shop.

Cégep de la Gaspésie (☎ *418-368-2749, 94 Rue Jacques Cartier*) Singles/doubles $22/37, rooms for six $74. This central, regional college is worth checking for a cheap bed during the summer. There are laundry and kitchen facilities.

Motel Adams (☎ *418-368-2244, 20 Rue Adams*) Singles/doubles from $54/59. The rooms tend to be large, if otherwise standard, at this centrally located spot. The staff can help arrange fishing expeditions.

A small airport south of town links Gaspé with Montréal and the Îles de la Madeleine daily. For flights, contact Air Canada Jazz (☎ 888-247-2262).

The Orléans Express bus stop is at the Motel Adams. Four buses a day travel to Rimouski, two along the north coast (seven hours), two along the south coast (nine hours) of the peninsula. Either way costs $36.

The International Appalachian Trail

The continent's longest, most ambitious hiking trail is the International Appalachian Trail (IAT), which stretches from Mt Springer in Georgia to Cap Gaspé and covers the mainland portion of the Appalachian mountain chain, one of the world's oldest. In combination with other trails in the southern US, the IAT makes it possible to walk on cleared trails from Key West, Florida, to Cap Gaspé – 7616km! In the US, more than 30 million people a year use their Appalachian Trail. In June 2001, the Canadian leg of the trail (making it 'international') officially opened. The trail winds about 672km through some of the most spectacular portions of the Gaspé peninsula.

Although there are portions that should only be attempted by experienced hikers, the trail is well-marked, with 21 shelters along the way and 18 campgrounds with some services. For more information, see **w** www.internationalat.org.

QUÉBEC

VIA Rail (☎ 418-368-4313) offers service three times a week to/from Montréal ($118, 17½ hours), with trains traveling along the Matapedia Valley and along the south coast of the peninsula.

PERCÉ

This town owes its fortunes entirely to a huge chunk of limestone with a hole in it. The 88m-high, 475m-long Rocher Percé (Pierced Rock), one of Canada's best-known landmarks, is truly stunning in person; photos could never do its majesty justice. The many activities possible here and the killer new hostel are enough to warrant a several-day stay. Unfortunately, the town's allure is greatly undermined by the sheer numbers of tourists who flock to it each summer.

The tourist office (☎ 418-782-5448, 142 Route 132), in the center of town, is open 9am to 7pm daily from the end of May to the end of October.

The town's most famous attraction, **Rocher Percé**, is accessible from the mainland at low tide only (a timetable is posted at the tourist information office and by the stairs leading down to the rock). Signs

MARK LIGHTBODY

Rocher Percé

warning of falling rocks should be taken seriously – each year, some 300 tons of debris detach from the big rock. In fact, there used to be two holes in it, but one arch came crashing down in 1845. To get there, take Chemin du Mont Joli to the end and descend the staircase.

The boat trips to green **Île Bonaventure**, an island bird sanctuary with over 200,000 birds (including the continent's largest gannet colony) make for highly recommended excursions. Along Route 132, you'll be accosted by many companies offering trips – select carefully, and ask if you can tour the island or just sail around it. The bigger boats can't get close to the attractions.

Les Traversiers de l'Île (☎ 418-782-2750, 9 Rue du Quai) offers good 90-minute cruises, as well as stopover tours that give you time to walk some of the beautiful trails on the island. It's best to leave early to make the most of your day.

Better still are **underwater diving** expeditions at **Club Nautique de Percé** (☎ 418-782-5403, 199 Route 132), where the offerings include thematic dives to explore marine biology, underwater seal observation tours and even whale observation tours when possible. Count on spending about $75 for a full day with two dives. The club also rent kayaks ($55 for half-day). The pool onsite might suit those who don't want to brave the seas.

The **Centre d'Interprétation** (☎ 418-782-2721, Route d'Irlande; admission free; open 9am-5pm daily June–mid-Oct) is a good place to learn about the local flora and fauna in bilingual exhibits. The center is 2km from the center of town; to get there, turn right onto Route des Failles, then left onto Route d'Irlande.

Behind the town are some interesting walks, for which the map from the tourist office is useful. Hike up to **Mont Ste Anne** to take in a great view and to see the cave along the 3km path, which begins behind the church. Another area walking trail (3km) leads to the **Great Crevasse**, a deep crevice in the mountain near the Camping Gargantua campground.

Places to Stay

Accommodations here are fair bargains, although prices can spike sharply upward during midsummer, when traffic is very heavy. On the cheap end of the spectrum, numerous campgrounds lie close at hand. The tourist office can help you find a place: the choice is large.

Camping Gargantua (☎ 418-782-2852, 222 Route des Failles) Sites $18, motel singles/doubles $65/75. Perched at the highest point around Percé (if you're biking, it'll be quite a climb!), this complex features great views, nearby walking trails and, in the motel section, an excellent dining room. Far from the touristy center, this is a great place.

La Maison Rouge (☎ 418-782-2227, 125 Route 132) Dorm beds $20, singles/doubles $40/60. The best place in town, it comprises a converted red grange-cum-hostel with three 10-bed rooms, plus a central, stately home with fine and spacious accommodations. The owners rent kayaks and encourage guitar-playing and building bonfires.

Maison Ave House (☎ 418-782-2954, 38 Rue de l'Église) Singles/doubles from $25/35. This B&B enjoys an excellent location off the main street in the middle of town. The owner, Ethel, is adorable and discreet. The comfy rooms come with sinks.

Gîte le Presbytère de Percé (☎ 418-782-5557, 47 Rue de l'Église) Singles/doubles $50/60-80. On the same quiet street but closer to the church, this place features a peaceful, contemplative atmosphere.

Places to Eat

La Maison du Pêcheur (☎ 418-782-5331, 155 Place du Quai) Pizzas $10-21, dishes $14-22. An obvious choice for a little splurge, this maritime-theme dining room serves 16 types of fantastic pizza (even octopus pizza!) baked in its maplewood-heated stove, as well as other succulent dishes. All this and a view of the rock to boot.

Les Fous de Bassans (☎ 418-782-2266, 162 Route 132) Dishes $9-16. This casual, recommended café just off the main street is good anytime – for just a coffee or a meal in warm atmosphere. The menu includes seafood dishes and vegetarian items.

Resto-bar Le Matelot (☎ 418-782-2569, 7 Rue de l'Église) Dishes $7-15. You can get a very good evening meal at this candlelit place that features seafood in the mid-price range (lobster's the specialty). Later at night, you can just have a beer and catch the night's entertainment.

For picnic breads, try the **bakery** (9 Rue Ste Anne).

Getting There & Away

Orléans Express (☎ 418-782-2140) buses link Percé to Rimouski ($46, 8½ hrs) twice a day. A trip to Cap aux Os (Forillon National Park) requires a transfer in Gaspé. The Petro Canada service station and dépanneur (convenience store) at the north end of the main street serve as the bus station.

VIA Rail (☎ 418-782-2747) serves the south side of the peninsula three times a week from Montréal (via Charny at Québec City). The one-way fare from Charny to Percé, an 11-hour ride, is $92. The station is 10km south of town at Anse à Beaufils. A taxi there costs about $11.

THE BAY SIDE

The south shore of the Gaspé Peninsula along the Baie des Chaleurs is quite different from the north coast. The land is flatter and less rocky, the weather warmer. Villages are more run-down. The coast is harder to see from the road. There are also a few English towns (residents have charming accents, and pronounce Gaspé 'Gaspi' and Percé 'Percy'!). Much of the French population descended from the original Acadian and Basque settlers. The inland area is virtually uninhabited.

New Carlisle

One of the area's English towns, New Carlisle was founded by Loyalists and boasts some grand colonial homes. The three Protestant churches in town recall New England 19th-century architecture. René Lévesque, the provincial premier who worked the hardest for Québec separatism, was born here and lived at 16 Rue Sorel.

Hamilton House (☎ 418-752-6498, 115 Rue Gérard Lévesque; adult/student $3.50/3; open 10am-4:30pm daily June-Sept) is a highlight of the area. Dating from 1852, it once housed the local member of Parliament and his family. Since 1983, it's blossomed into a museum in the hands of owner Katherine Smollett, a lovely dear. The two-story mansion has been lovingly stuffed to the brim with old photographs, scrapbooks, antiques and costumes of all kinds, placed thematically in the 14 rooms. Visits include a trip to the 'haunted basement.' Tea and scones are served in the sitting room most afternoons.

Bonaventure

A pleasant town founded by Acadians in 1791, Bonaventure boasts the region's most interesting attractions.

The **Musée Acadien** (☎ *418-534-4000, 95 Ave Port Royal; adult/student $5/4; open 9am-6pm daily end June-early Oct; 9am-5pm Mon-Fri, 1pm-5pm Sun rest of the year*) merits a visit. Its bilingual booklets explain some of the tragic yet fascinating Acadian history. The museum hosts great Acadian music evenings at 7:30pm on Wednesday.

North of town, the **Grotte de St Elzéar** (☎ *418-534-4335, 198 Route de l'Église; adult/child $37/27; open 8am-4pm daily June–mid-Oct*) offers four-hour tours of one of Québec's oldest caves. You descend into the cool depths (it's one way to escape summer heat, but bring warm clothes!) and view the stalactites and stalagmites. English tours must be booked in advance. To get there, take Chemin de la Rivière and follow the signs.

The well-run outfit **Cime Aventure** (☎ *418-534-2333,* **w** *www.cimeaventure.com, 200 Chemin Arsenault*) leads a large variety of canoe/kayak trips – either a few hours along the scenic, tranquil Rivière Bonaventure or several days around the tip of the Gaspésie. Excursions cost $20 to $1260, but day trips cost less than $70. On Cime Adventure's site, you'll find a camping-supply store (with vegetarian food), bike rental, a sauna and one of the province's nicest campgrounds (tent sites $20, teepee sites $40). Take Chemin de la Rivière, which extends from Ave Grand Pré.

Bonaventure has some charming, if eccentric, places to stay and a good selection of eateries.

Gîte du Foin Fou (☎ *418-534-4413, 204 Chemin de la Rivière*) Singles/doubles $40/55. Ask the owner why he calls his B&B 'Crazy Hay': 'Because there's hay all around, and a nut in the middle – me!' There are creative surprises to be found everywhere in this spacious house that attracts a young, artistic, laid-back crowd. Anything goes here.

Auberge du Café Acadien (☎ *418-534-4276, 168 Rue Beaubassin*) Meals $8-15. Singles/doubles $50/60. The specialty here is the owners' own smoked salmon (marinated in light maple sauce and smoked with maple wood) – the delicious stuff comes alongside

other excellent, Cajun-style meals in the restaurant. Upstairs, guests stay in a few comfortable rooms with shared bathroom.

Bistro Bar le Fou du Village (☎ *418-534-4567, 119 Ave Grand Pré*) Dishes $4-8. This pub serves good snacks, but it mainly attracts people with live music, which keeps the place lively from Thursday through Sunday nights. The cover charge varies.

New Richmond

Nestled in the bay near the mouths of two rivers, New Richmond is another small Loyalist (read: English-speaking) center. The **British Heritage Centre** (☎ *418-392-4487, 351 Boulevard Perron Ouest; adult/student $5/3.50; open 9am-6pm daily June-Aug*) re-creates a Loyalist village of the late 1700s. It consists of an interpretive center, houses, a general store, a lighthouse and other buildings. The center also covers the influence of later Irish and Scottish immigrants.

Carleton

The people of the Gaspésie come here for a day at the beach. You'll find a tourist office (☎ *418-364-3544, 629 Boulevard Perron*) in the Hôtel de Ville.

From the docks, boats depart for **fishing** or sightseeing excursions. At the **bird sanctuary** at the Baie du Barachois, right in the center of town, you can see herons, terns, plovers and other shore birds along the sandbar. Walking paths and a road also lead behind the town to the top of Mont St Joseph (555m), which provides fine views over the bay and across to New Brunswick. The blue metal-roofed oratory at the top can be visited – after the climb, the snack bar is a welcome sight.

Camping de Carleton (☎ *418-364-3992, Pointe Tracadigash*) Tent sites $14-18. Set on a jutting spit of land in front of town, this campground gives you access to miles of beach. You can go swimming here, too. Rent canoes nearby to do some birding or just to explore the calm inner bay.

The Orléans bus stops at 561 Boulevard Perron; get tickets inside the restaurant Le Héron (☎ *418-364-7000*). Buses go to Rimouski and Montréal twice daily. The train station is 1km from the center of town, back against the mountains on Rue de la Gare. A train goes to Montréal three times a week.

Parc de Miguasha

The small peninsula south of Route 132 near Nouvelle is renowned for its fossils, so much so that it is one of Canada's 13 Unesco world heritage sites. According to Unesco's description, no other fossil site does a better job of illustrating the Devonian period (342 to 395 million years ago): in this small region are 'the greatest number and best preserved specimens found anywhere in the world of the lobe-finned fishes that gave rise to the first four-legged, air-breathing terrestrial vertebrates – the tetrapodes.'

Inquire at the **Information Centre** (☎ 418-794-2475, 231 Route Miguasha Ouest; adult/child $4/2; open 9am-6pm daily June–mid-Oct) about guided walks that take visitors through the museum and along a trail to the fossil-filled cliffs, where you can see fish and insects that existed here so long ago. Do not collect your own fossils!

For those headed to Dalhousie, New Brunswick, a ferry (☎ 506-684-5107) just down the road from the park leaves hourly for the two-minute trip, which costs $12 for car and driver.

Pointe à la Garde

There is no village here, just a castle. Yes, a castle, a modern one built by someone fulfilling a life-long dream to live in fairy-tale surroundings. Good news for others: it has been transformed into what may be Québec's most memorable hotel after Québec City's Ice Hotel. Ironically, the grandiose premises include an excellent, year-round HI hostel.

Chateau Bahia (☎ 418-788-2048, 152 Boulevard Perron) Dorm beds $17, shared rooms for 3-5 $20 per person, doubles $45/59 without/with private bath. The château emerges through the trees as if from a dream, particularly if you are not expecting it. All rooms come with their own staircase and small balcony, allowing you your night in a castle tower – and for a fraction of the price you might have to pay in Europe. The onsite restaurant serves only banquet-style dinners ($12) at 8:30pm, but these are stupendous. The Orléans bus will stop 100m from the door if you ask the driver.

Pointe à la Croix/Listuguj

The scenery becomes more lush and green at this point, while the bay slowly peters out in a swampy mix of mist-covered islands and weeds. A largely Micmac Indian community survives around Pointe à la Croix, where they've lived for centuries; Listuguj is the Micmac part of town. A bridge crosses over to Campbellton, New Brunswick. Some people live on New Brunswick time here (one hour ahead), as so many people work in that province, and businesses tend to accommodate both time zones.

A few kilometers west of the bridge from Pointe à la Croix, the Parks Canada-run **Battle of the Restigouche National Historic Site** (☎ 418-788-5676, Route 132; adult/child $3.75/2; open 9am-5pm daily June-early Oct) details the 1760 naval battle of Restigouche, which finished off France's New World ambitions. An interpretive center explains the battle's significance to the British and displays salvaged articles and even parts of a sunken French frigate.

MATAPÉDIA VALLEY

Between the village of Matapédia and the coast of the St Lawrence River lies this peaceful, pretty valley that's unlike any other portion of the Gaspésie. The broad-leafed maple and elm trees that cover the valley add a lot of color in autumn. The Rivière Matapédia has become famous for its salmon fishing, but expensive permits are required – in the past, Presidents Nixon and Carter managed to find the funds for them.

Matapédia

A gateway for those embarking on the International Appalachian Trail, this tiny village also offers opportunities for some beautiful canoe/kayak expeditions. **Nature-Aventure** (☎ 418-865-2100, 9 Rue du Vieux Pont) leads a range of rugged and worthwhile canoeing, mountain biking and hiking trips along and near the Rivières Restigouche and Matapédia.

Causapscal

A pretty picture, the traditional look of this little town comes from a beautiful stone church and many older houses with typical Québécois silver roofs. Sometimes the odors of nearby sawmills make things unpleasant, but generally people come here to enjoy the outdoors. Over 25km of walking and observation trails meander through the surrounding hills. Salmon is king here, as

QUÉBEC

you can tell by the outlandish salmon statue on the main road.

There are a couple of covered bridges south of town and, in the center, a pedestrian-only suspension bridge across the Matapédia – anglers go there to cast their lines where the Rivières Causapscal and Matapédia meet. If you want to try your luck at **fishing**, a permit here only costs $35/day; farther up the Causapscal where salmon are plenty, you'll pay $200/day, while farther up the Matapédia it's only $5/day (you gets what you pays for!). Ask at the tourist office (☎ 418-756-6048, 53 Rue St Jacques) for more information.

The Orléans Express bus, linking New Brunswick to the Lower St Lawrence, stops at 122 Rue St Jacques.

Îles de la Madeleine

Only higher temperatures and a few palm trees separate the world's island paradises from this string of islands in the Gulf of St Lawrence. Arguably the province's most attractive region, these islands bewitch the visitor with their sense of isolation and unspoiled natural beauty (there's no polluting industry here beyond a salt mine). The stretches of red cliffs on the islands burn into the memory of all who see them firsthand.

The Îles de la Madeleine, or Magdalen Islands as they're known in English, are a dozen islands stretched out over some 100km. They're 215km southeast from Gaspé and 105km from Prince Edward Island. Six islands are linked over 65km by long sand spits. Where sandy beaches don't greet the Gulf (sand covers 30% of the islands), iron-rich red cliffs do. Wind and sea have shaped the cliffs into fantastic shapes that seem to take on new forms in changing light; one never tires of looking at them.

In complement to the landscape's unusual hues, many of the island's houses and fishing boats sport smart, audacious colors. A can of paint goes a long way here, where small, modern villages are alight in purples, yellows, greens and reds. It's the kind of laid-back place where people don't lock their doors. The contented locals are not overly sociable

or solicitous, but they're friendly and respectful of each other's privacy.

Most surprising of all, in summertime the place bubbles with life. Where the Gaspésie is overwhelmingly beautiful but socially limp, the islands are teeming with the energy of young, free-minded travelers who come here for days or months at a time. In fact, the place has been a magnet for artists, hippies, drifters and free-thinkers since the 1960s, when beatniks are credited with having 'rediscovered' the islands. This influence continues to be felt today, thanks to a new generation of adventurous travelers into eating healthy foods, relishing the outdoors and letting it all hang out in bars livelier than you'd find on Rue St Denis in Montréal.

Apart from the social scene, most of the islands' activities and sights revolve around the sea. Beach-strolling, and exploring lagoons, tidal pools and cliff formations can take up days, but so can poking around the fishing villages and going on nature excursions. Swimming is possible in the open sea or, preferably, in some of the shallow lagoons – water is warmest in August and September. Currents are strong and venturing far from shore is not advisable.

The sea and wind, which is nearly always very strong, combine to create a powerful draw for active types. Kite surfing is popular, as are kite-buggying and windsurfing. On land, the islands make a spectacular place for cycling – the main roads are paved and in good condition.

Windsurfing is popular in the Magdalen Islands.

Kayaking in the St Lawrence River from Québec City, Québec

Facade of Hotel de Ville, Vieux Montréal

Shops on Rue de la Commune, Montréal

Îles de la Madeleine in the Gulf of St Lawrence, Québec

THOMAS HUHTI

Detail from the colorful houses in the fishing village of Rose Blanche, Newfoundland

THOMAS HUHTI

Lobster traps along the harbor in Norris Point, Gros Morne National Park, Newfoundland

JIM WARK

A waterfall spilling through unspoiled terrain in Gros Morne National Park, Newfoundland

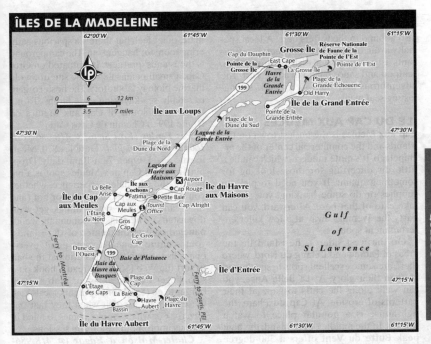

ÎLES DE LA MADELEINE

Still other visitors come here for the wildlife: in early spring, former seal hunters now take tourists out on the ice to see and photograph baby seals.

About 95% of the population is francophone, but anglophones with Scottish and Irish ancestry, descendants of shipwrecked sailors, live on Île d'Entrée and Grosse Île. Until very recently, these English communities mixed very little with the French, despite sharing only 222 sq km. This is changing slowly; reported sightings of English islanders socializing in Cap aux Meules have trickled in – there's even been talk of intermarriage.

In case you're wondering about the name, the islands took their moniker, supposedly, from the wife of the first French governor, Madeleine Fontaine, in the late 17th century.

The islands fall in the Atlantic Time Zone, one hour ahead of mainland Québec. The main road, Route 199, runs through the six connected islands. Île d'Entrée is only accessible by boat.

The tourist office (☎ 418-986-2245, 128 Chemin du Débarcadère) is near the ferry terminal; it's open year-round.

Except for Cap aux Meules, villages here are spread out and without traditional centers; the names refer more to regions than to towns.

Special Events

In addition to the events listed here, various music, crafts and sporting festivals take place from mid-June through mid-September.

Sand Castle Contest This competition (☎ 418-986-6863) takes place in mid-month along a 2km stretch of beach on Havre Aubert.

Traditions Maritimes en Fête This festival focuses on the islands' folklore and history in songs, races, shows and exhibits for three weeks beginning at the end of August.

Canadian Professional and Amateur Windsurf Competition This contest is usually held here in late August and early September.

Fête du Vent This festival of wind, held in mid-September, showcases islanders' inventions that run on wind power.

Food

Sampling fresh seafood is a memorable experience, especially if you try the local mussels. The main catch, though, is lobster;

QUÉBEC

the season runs from mid-May to mid-July. Snow crabs, scallops, mussels, perch and cod also abound in the waters here. A local specialty available at many of the better restaurants is *pot-en-pot*, a dish of mixed fish, seafood and sauce baked in a pie crust. The adventurous may want to try dark, strong-tasting seal meat.

ÎLE DU CAP AUX MEULES

Cap aux Meules is the busiest town on the islands and the commercial center of the archipelago. It's quite modern, which can be a little disconcerting for those looking for something quaint. If you need to pick up supplies or do some banking, you should take care of that here. Afterward, you can party the evenings away at a few killer entertainment spots.

On the west side of the island lie the areas of **Fatima** and **L'Étang du Nord**, where there are some excellent spots to see the red cliffs in their glory. At **La Belle Anse**, you can walk along the cliffs to gape at their patterns of erosion. At **Cap du Phare**, the lighthouse is a popular place to watch sunsets. In the middle of the island, the high peak **Butte du Vent** offers a 360-degree panorama. The road leading there, Chemin des Buttes, is also very scenic. At **Anse de l'Étang du Nord**, you'll find a small harbor, a concentration of boutiques and cafés, a public square for festivities and an unusual sculpture of seven hauling fishermen.

Young, enthusiastic sportsmen who can ensure your outdoors thrills run the excellent **Aerosport Carrefour d'Aventures** (☎ 418-986-6677, 1390 Chemin Lavernière) in the Gros Cap area. Most people sign up for the kayak expeditions, which include cave visits, but when the wind is right, you'll have a more unforgettable experience if you opt for the power kites – you'll sail along the beaches in a kite-pulled buggy. You can also go kite-surfing.

Places to Stay & Eat

Camping Le Barachois (☎ 418-986-4726, Chemin du Rivage) Tent sites $15-20. The largest campground on the islands (180 places) feels crowded; it's popular with trailers.

Auberge Internationale des Îles (☎ 418-986-4523, 74 Chemin du Camping) Tent sites $15-20, dorm beds $23/25 member/nonmem-

ber, doubles $46. Now *this* is a hostel! With room for only 30, the place boasts an intimate, quiet feel, but there's a spacious gathering room for hanging out. The campground is the islands' prettiest. It's situated on Gros Cap, a small peninsula on the site of an old marine biology laboratory. The hostel organizes daily sea-kayaking expeditions. To get there, head south of Cap aux Meules on Route 199 to Chemin de Gros Cap.

Pas Perdus (Lost Steps; ☎ 418-986-5151, 160 Chemin Principal) Doubles $70. Meals in café $5-11. Open 7am-10pm daily. Dropping into this Cap aux Meules spot is a big part of the Magdalen experience, whether you sleep in the upstairs rooms or not (and they can be noisy when things get wild downstairs). The relaxed, bohemian, wood-paneled café is the center of the islands' youth-culture scene. At some point, everyone rolls through to have a drink at the bar, to surf the Web ($6/hour), read a book on a sofa, linger over breakfast or grab a shark burger to go ($5). Monday nights, locals kick the energy up a notch when they belt out jazz, rock or whatever else comes to mind in famous impromptu fusion jam sessions.

Chalet-Maison à Edgar (☎ 418-986-5214, 49 Chemin Thorne) Doubles $85-120, weekly $550-850. Located on a quiet stretch of road in Fatima, the chalet offers two separate housing units to choose from, with all the conveniences.

Café Théâtre Wendell (☎ 418-986-6002, 185 Chemin Principal) Dishes $5-10. Enjoy light, healthy meals in a relaxed atmosphere at this perfect hangout in Cap aux Meules. The in-house Cinéma Parallel screens films most weekends at 9pm.

La Factrie (☎ 418-986-2710, 521 Chemin du Gros Cap) Dishes $7-19. Its name is a play on the word 'factory,' as this restaurant is in a lobster processing plant (for proof, just peer through the huge window that overlooks the workings!). Cafeteria-style, it serves up fresh seafood with no pretensions. Try the homemade soup ($3) and coquilles St Jacques ($5).

ÎLE DU HAVRE AUBERT

The archipelago's largest island lies south of Cap aux Meules, connected by long strings of sand at points barely wider than the road.

The most lively area of the town of **Havre Aubert** is known as La Grave, an old section by the water at the southeastern tip of the island. Small craft and gift shops, some restaurants and many old houses line the main street. Here you feel the rustic charm of an old-time fishing community.

On any rainy day, the interesting **aquarium** (☎ 418-937-2277, 146 Chemin de la Grave; adult/child $4/2; open 10am-6pm daily June–mid-Oct) is packed with visitors disturbed from their seaside activities. The 'petting pool' makes a popular stop.

The **Musée de la Mer** (☎ 418-937-5711, 1023 Route 199; adult/child $4/2; open 9am-6pm daily end June-Aug, 9am-5pm Mon-Fri & 1pm-5pm Sat & Sun Sept-end June) features displays on shipwrecks and various aspects of the islands' transportation and fishing history.

A must-visit spot is the **Artisans du Sable** (☎ 418-937-2917, 907 Route 199), a workshop and boutique specializing in creations (vases, lamps, frames and clocks) made entirely of sand.

L'Istorlet (☎ 418-937-5266, 100 Chemin de l'Istorlet) Tents $10-15, singles/doubles $20-30/25-35. This complex rents bikes ($18/ day) and watersports equipment like snorkels, canoes, sailboards and kayaks; staff also give lessons and guided tours. You can pitch a tent or stay in the comfy wooden tents or in rooms in the main complex.

La Maison de Camille (☎ 418-937-2516, 946 Chemin de la Grave) Singles/doubles $45/55. This B&B in the heart of La Grave is a real charmer. A garden out back lines the waterfront, the wood paneled interior exudes real warmth, and your barefooted host is a true winner (so laid-back that you might have to make your own breakfast).

Café de la Grave (☎ 418-937-5765, 969 Route 199) Dishes $7-9. Your island experience wouldn't be complete without a visit to this grand ex–general store, transformed into a blissful café serving nachos, sandwiches, soups, salads, daily specials and pot en pot.

ÎLE DU HAVRE AUX MAISONS

Probably the most scenic of the Magdalen Islands, Havre aux Maisons is an explorer's paradise. Heading north from Cap aux Meules, take the first left from Route 199 to Chemin de la Petite Baie and Chemin des Cyr, which curves around **Butte Ronde**, a steep, high hill worth the climb. Even more impressive is the east coast of the island,

which you can see by following Chemin de la Pointe Basse and Chemin des Montants. Best approached from the north along Chemin des Montants, the landscape is ridiculously scenic, with rolling hills, isolated houses and a cute lighthouse guarding a dramatic view onto rocky cliffs and the rugged sea.

GROSSE ÎLE

Scottish pioneers settled this, the principal English section of the islands. Despite generations of isolation on a mainly French island chain, many of the locals barely speak a word of French, a touchy subject for the francophone locals. Pointe de la Grosse Île, East Cape and Old Harry are the main communities. At Old Harry (named in honor of Harry Clark, who was for a long time the area's only inhabitant), walruses used to be slaughtered for oil. Sea Cow Lane is the site of the former walrus landing.

The **Gateway to the East Interpretation Center** (☎ 418-985-2931, 56 Route 199; admission free; open 10am-6pm daily May-Sept) features an excellent exhibit on the rare flora and geological peculiarities of the islands. The center is near the salt mine, which excavates at a depth of over 200m below sea level.

In Pointe de la Grosse Île, check out **Trinity Church**, known for its stained glass depicting Jesus the fisherman. Through the windows, the eye captures the graves, the piles of lobster traps, some solitary houses and then the sea – the island's world in microcosm.

At the **Council for Anglophone Magdalen Islanders** (☎ 418-985-2116, 787 Route Principale; admission free; open 8am-4pm Mon-Fri, 1pm-4pm Sat & Sun), in Old Harry, you can visit an old schoolhouse, which housed grades one through six for 52 years (take a look at what they had to use as a toilet!). Other thematic exhibits also focus on the English community.

About 16km north off La Grosse Île lies **Île Brion**, an ecological reserve once but no longer inhabited by humans. It remains home to 140 species of birds and much interesting vegetation. L'Istorlet in Havre Aubert (see Île du Havre Aubert, earlier) organizes snorkeling trips there; check at the tourist office for other ways to get there and possibly stay overnight.

POINTE DE L'EST

Linking Grosse Île and Île de la Grande Entrée, this wild region boasts the archipelago's most impressive beach. **Plage de la Grande Échouerie**, a curving sweep of pale sand, extends for about 10km from Pointe Old Harry. A short road with parking areas and trails stretching down to the beach begins near Old Harry's harbor. From Route 199, a few turnoffs lead to hiking paths. Other than the beach, Pointe de l'Est is entirely a national wildlife refuge area.

ÎLE DE LA GRANDE ENTRÉE

This island begins beyond Old Harry and leads to a beautiful, isolated section of the archipelago not as frequently visited. People have only lived here since 1870.

Just past Old Harry on Route 199, stop in at **St Peter's by the Sea**, a beautiful, peaceful little church overlooking the sea and bounded by graves of the Clark and Clarke families. It's open to the public and well worth a visit. On a breezy day, the inside offers a quiet stillness broken only by creaking rafters. Made entirely of wood, the church includes a richly carved door honoring drowned fishermen.

The locus of activity on this island is the excellent **Club Vacances des Îles** (*☎ 418-985-2833, 377 Route 199*), which focuses on ecotourism and research. Knowledgeable guides lead 2- to 10km nature walks ($5-10), ornithological expeditions in kayaks and cave exploration excursions ($27) that give you the chance to swim, in a wetsuit, through caves and grottos – even mud baths are an option! All can be done in English, but it's best to ask ahead. The club includes a cafeteria open to all, rooms for rent and a lovely campground, but you can only get accommodations with tour packages.

Gîte L'Émergence (*☎ 418-985-2801, 122 Chemin des Pealey*) Doubles $60. Right at the tip of the island, in a remote sector near a beach and small harbor, this little B&B is comfortable and quiet.

Délices de la Mer (*☎ 418-985-2831, 907 Chemin Principal*) Dishes $6-15. One of the best restaurants on the islands is this unassuming but atmospheric diner at the end of Route 199. Sit with the fishermen and try the delicious chowder or cod.

ÎLE D'ENTRÉE

The one inhabited island not connected by land with the others attracts fewer tourists. A twice-daily ferry run by SP Bonaventure (*☎ 418-986-8452*) links it to the port at Cap aux Meules from Monday to Saturday. The one-hour ride costs $16. Board in front of the Coast Guard building at Cap aux Meules. It's possible to leave Cap aux Meules at 8am, explore the island and return on the 4pm ferry. The tourist office can tell you about other boat tour options.

GETTING THERE & AWAY

The airport (*☎ 418-969-2888*) is on the northwest corner of Île du Havre aux Maisons. Air Canada Jazz (888-247-2262), formerly Air Nova, offers twice-daily flights from Montréal via Québec City, Mont Joli and Gaspé. Flights from Halifax arrive once or twice a week.

The cheapest and most common way to get to the Îles de la Madeleine is by ferry from Souris on Prince Edward Island to Île du Cap aux Meules. Traversier CTMA (*☎ 418-986-3278*), whose boat holds 300 passengers and 90 vehicles, makes the five-hour, 223km cruise from April through January. From July to early September, boats go once or twice a day; at other times, service is less frequent. In midsummer, reservations are strongly recommended. If you don't have reservations, arrive at least two hours ahead of time. The fare is $37/10 per adult/child ages five to 12. Bikes cost $9 extra, cars $70.

CTMA also operates a weekly passenger service from Montréal via Québec City and Matane, with a whale-watching stop in Tadoussac. It takes about 48 hours for the journey, but it's a great way of seeing the St Lawrence River, and you can always boat one way and return by car. In 2002, the country inaugurated this route with a new, large boat; prices were not available at press time.

GETTING AROUND

There is no public transportation on the islands. Le Pédalier (*☎ 418-986-2965, 365 Chemin Principal*), in Cap aux Meules, rents cycles for $18/day.

Thrifty (*☎ 418-969-9006*) rents cars from an office near the airport, but it's essential to book as far ahead as possible.

MA Poirier (☎ 418-986-4467) runs a seven-hour guided bus tour of the islands; it leaves from the tourist office.

Far North

Wherever you are in Canada, the 'north' or 'far north' are ambiguous terms. For the vast majority of people, two hours north of Montréal – or a few hours' drive north from almost any of the country's major cities – is considered the north. In Québec, certainly, straying more than a couple of hundred miles beyond the main population centers puts you in the land of the boreal forest. And yet, if you travel as far north as possible on the most remote route in the middle of nowhere, you might get halfway up the province. The north is an immense and sparsely populated region, the most northerly sections of which are dotted with tiny Inuit and Native Indian settlements accessible only by bush plane. The developed areas owe their existence to massive industrial operations – mining, forestry and hydroelectricity.

While accessing the *really* far north (the Inuit communities in Nunavik) requires expensive flights, other areas of the Abitibi-Témiscamingue and James Bay regions can easily be reached by car and bus and will give you a taste of Canada's True North.

ABITIBI-TÉMISCAMINGUE
In over 65,140 sq km, people barely outnumber the lakes, by a margin of 155,000 to 100,000. But despite the shortage of humans, this sparsely populated area occupies a special place in the Québécois imagination. The last area to be settled and developed on a major scale, it stands as a symbol of dreams and hardships.

The traditional land of Algonquin Native Indians, Abitibi-Témiscamingue is an amalgamation of two distinct areas, each named after different tribes. Témiscamingue, accessible only via northern Ontario and one long road south of Rouyn-Noranda, does not see many tourists.

Abiti-Témiscamingue was colonized following the usual pattern of resource exploitation. Before the 19th century, the only Europeans in the area were hunters and fur traders. Then forestry and copper mining brought more development.

In the 1920s, however, the desolate area took on new life, thanks to gold fever. The precious mineral was found first near present-day Cadillac, and as thousands flooded the region in search of fortune, the first mine opened in 1927. Others mines opened as more deposits were discovered, with boom towns blooming around them. Many of these mines have closed; the larger ones of Val d'Or (meaning Valley of Gold) and Rouyn-Noranda survived.

Today, this sector of Québec retains an exotic air, partially due to its remoteness. Most of Abitibi's terrain is flat, which makes the stunning valleys and cliffs of Parc d'Aiguebelle all the more striking in contrast. Témiscamingue is more diversified in its vegetation and landscape, with valleys and the majestic Lac Témiscamingue.

Réserve Faunique la Vérendrye
Because of its immensity (13,615 sq km) and its remoteness, this provincial park (☎ 819-736-7431, Hwy 117; admission $3.50; open daily mid-May–mid-Sept) offers some of the best wilderness opportunities in the province. Though the landscape might not be as grandiose and imposing as in other wildlife reserves, canoers and campers revel in the vast spaces that put the 'wild' back in wildlife.

Flora and fauna abound here – there are moose, black bears, foxes, wolves and 35 other mammals, 150 species of birds and thousands of gray trout. The waterfalls at Lac Roland are worth seeing. You can rent canoes to explore the 4000 lakes. There are several camping possibilities ($16) and chalets for rent inside the reserve.

You can access the reserve at four points, all on Hwy 117. Coming from the Laurentians, you'll reach the information post Le Domaine (☎ 819-435-2541) 58km past the village of Grand Remous. During the 180km drive across the reserve to Val d'Or, there are no villages – make sure your tank is full.

Val d'Or
Born in 1933 around the Sigma gold mine, Val d'Or today looks like a mining boom town of yesterday, with wide avenues and a main street (3-ème Ave) that one can easily imagine being frenzied in the gold rush days. That main street still has a rough edge to it. The Sigma mine still operates, though

it's no longer the city's economic engine. The tourist office (☎ 819-824-9646, 20 3-ème Ave) is on Hwy 117 at the eastern end of town.

La Cité de l'Or (☎ 819-825-7616, 90 Ave Perreault; adult/student $20/16; underground tours 8:30am-5:30pm daily late June-early Sept) offers guided excursions 91m underground to show what gold mining's all about. On the same site is the **Village Minier de Bourlamaque** *(adult/student $10/8)*, a restored mining village with 80 log houses. Call to reserve tours in advance and bring warm clothes if you're going underground.

Centre Plein Air Arc-en-Ciel (☎ 819-824-1414, 600 Chemin des Scouts) Tent sites $14, dorm beds in chalets $17. This complex features a pond where you fish for your trout meal (which will be cooked for you) and lots of fresh air. Follow Chemin de la Baie Carrière south of town.

Aux 3 Tilleuls (☎ 819-825-4765, 106 Rue Champlain) Doubles $50-60. This modern, comfortable B&B includes an outdoor pool. Two rooms come with private bathrooms.

Val d'Or is well served by air. Air Creebec (☎ 800-567-6567, **w** www.air creebec.ca) flies Sunday through Friday from Montréal. Air Canada flies from Montréal to Val d'Or, direct or via Rouyn-Noranda. Three daily buses go to/from Montréal ($72, seven hours). Two daily buses travel to/from Amos ($14, one hour), and one bus per day runs to Rouyn-Noranda ($20, 1½ hrs), Matagami ($38, 3½ hrs) and Chibougamau via Senneterre ($107, six hours). All buses depart from the bus station (☎ 819-874-2200, 851 5-ème Avenue).

Parc d'Aiguebelle

As the Abitibi landscape can be a tad on the dull side, the stunning scenery in this provincial park (☎ 819-637-7322, 1737 Rang Hudson; admission $3.50; open year-round) comes as a doubly pleasant surprise. Suddenly there are magnificent canyons and gorges, massive rocky cliffs with fascinating geological formations and excellent, rugged hiking trails flanked by trees 200 years old.

This small park (only 268 sq km) has three entrances – via Mont Brun (well marked on Hwy 117 between Val d'Or and Rouyn-Noranda; this is the closest to the suspended bridge), via Destor (off Route 101 between Rouyn-Noranda and La Sarre) and via Taschereau (south from Route 111 between La Sarre and Amos). You'll find lovely campgrounds near all three ($19), as well as canoe and kayak rental.

Rouyn-Noranda

The area's most interesting town is made up of two distinct sectors. At Noranda (in the city's northwest) the successful mines were set up; it was run, settled and organized by American and British industrialists. The French established Rouyn (in the southeast part of the city) as a frontier town; it was chock-full of brothels, bars, hotels and shops. To this day, you can see the difference between Rouyn's more helter-skelter setup and Noranda's elite, orderly feel.

Your first stop should be the **Maison Dumulon** *(☎ 418-797-7125, 191 Ave du Lac; tours $3; open 9am-8pm daily late June-early Sept, 9am-5pm Mon-Fri early Sept-late June).* The town's first general store and post office opened here in 1924, and it later turned into a residence, which has been charmingly transformed to re-create the look and feel of the old general store. On the fun guided tour, friendly staff in costume explain the town's interesting history. At the tourist office (☎ 418-797-3195), also housed here, you can pick up free day parking permits for the city.

If you're looking to stay overnight, you'll find a number of nondescript, cheap motels along Ave Larivière.

Cégep de l'Abitibi-Témiscamingue (☎ 418-762-0931 ext 5250, 555 Boulevard de Collège) Rooms $20. Located east of tiny Lac Edouard in the Rouyn sector of town, this college offers student rooms for rent from mid-May to mid-August.

Highway 117 runs right through Rouyn-Noranda. Buses go to/from Val d'Or ($20, 1½ hours) twice daily Monday to Friday, once daily Saturday and Sunday. Each weekday, one bus runs to/from La Sarre ($14, one hour). Also, once a day a bus travels to/from North Bay, Ontario ($45, 3½ hours). Buses depart from the bus station (☎ 418-762-2200, 52 Rue Horne).

Amos

The first town to be founded in Abitibi, in 1910, Amos became a center of the forestry and agriculture industries. Despite this history, it's a pleasant, languid town that enjoys some of the cleanest water of any urban area in the world! A natural source of springwater emerging from a nearby glacier-formed esker constitutes the town's water source – it's so pure, it's bottled commercially under the name of Périgny in the same form as it pours from the city's faucets and taps.

For general information, go to the tourist office (☎ 819-727-1242, 892 Route 111).

The **Refuge Pageau** (☎ *819-732-8999, 3991 Chemin Croteau; adult/student/child 3-12 $10/8/6; open 1pm-5pm Tues-Fri, 1pm-8pm Sat & Sun late June-Aug; 1pm-5pm Sat & Sun Sept)* makes a highly worthwhile stop, especially – though not only – for the kids. Before he opened his animal shelter in the 1970s, Michel Pageau was a hunter and trapper, but he had a change of heart, deciding to put his energies into nursing and helping wounded animals. His shelter takes in mammals and birds who've been hit by cars, hurt by hunters or fallen sick, and they can be seen healing in this outdoor compound. The tour guides don't know English, but if you can understand French, the touching stories of how these animals came to be here add to the experience.

JAMES BAY

Comprising 350,000 sq km (nearly 1½ times the size of the UK), James Bay *(Baie James)* is the largest administrative municipality in the world. Only 30,000 people live here, almost half of them Cree Indians living in eight reserves separated by hundreds of kilometers in both the western section bordering James Bay and in the eastern sectors north and west of Chibougamau.

This area truly represents Québec's final frontier, with the seeming endlessness of unpopulated boreal spruce forests giving way to the taiga, where trees become visibly shorter the farther north you go.

The near-mythic Route de la Baie James road ends at Radisson, a small village 1400km north of Montréal, 800km north of Amos. A 100km extension branches westward to Chisasibi, a Cree reserve near James Bay. This area is defined by the immense James Bay hydroelectric project, a series of hydroelectric stations that produce half of Québec's energy resources.

It goes without saying that, while temperatures have been known to pass 30°C here in July or August, it is essential to bring warm clothes to protect from chilly summer evenings. The usual July daytime temperature is around 17°C. In winter – which can come as early as October – the temperatures are often below -15°C and can reach -40°C at night.

Most people access the region via Abitibi. Route 109 runs 183km north to Matagami, the last town before Route 109 becomes the Route de la Baie James and continues 620km to Radisson. To reach the eastern sector, where Chibougamau is the largest town, you're better off starting from the Lac St Jean region. From Chibougamou, a grueling 424km gravel road (Route du Nord) joins the Route de la Baie James at Kilometer 274. It's also possible to drive from Senneterre to Chibougamau (351km) on the paved Route 113, passing through several Cree villages.

Matagami

For a dreary town in the middle of nowhere, this place sure feels busy. Since 1963, when the town was founded, it has been the site of a copper and zinc mine, and it's also Québec's most northerly forestry center – both of these industries are still going strong here, and shift workers are always coming and going. Finally, almost everyone driving through on Route 109 on the way to Radisson stops here for the night. Because both workers and travelers want a good night's rest, nightlife here is, to say the least, limited – unless you consider 5am still 'night,' as that's when restaurants open for breakfast.

Hôtel-Motel Matagami (☎ *819-739-2501, 99 Boulevard Matagami)* Singles/doubles $72/82. Considered the top place in town, it's decent enough and always seems to be crowded – mainly because of the restaurant, which is open from 5am to 10pm daily. Breakfasts run about $10, with other meals costing $10 to $20.

Motel Le Caribou (☎ *819-739-4550, fax 819-739-4552, 108 Boulevard Matagami)* Singles/doubles $40/65. A bit more run-down than the Hôtel Matagami, it's still fine for a night. Each room has its own bathroom. A dingy bar in front draws long-faced, jowly clientele.

Every day but Saturday, a bus travels to/from Val d'Or (3½ hrs), and it stops at the Hôtel Matagami.

Route de la Baie James

This road, an extension of Route 109 heading *way* north was built in the 1970s to facilitate the construction of the James Bay hydroelectric project (also known as La Grande). As such, the road is paved, wide and kept in good shape.

At Kilometer 6, a tourist office (☎ 819-739-2030) operates 24 hours a day throughout the year. You must at least slow down here and announce yourself through a speaker – for safety reasons, everyone traveling north is registered. It's worthwhile to stop and go inside, however, as you can pick up several booklets and pamphlets that detail the geological and geographical features along the way and offer information about the forest fires that destroyed huge swaths of land. There are bilingual information panels all along the road and emergency telephones at Kilometers 135, 201, 247, 301, 361, 444 and 504.

At Kilometer 37, you'll reach the route's only *campground (reservations ☎ 819-739-4473)*.

Everyone needs to stop at Kilometer 381, the so-called *Relais Routier,* the only gas station and service stop on the road. It's open 24 hours a day. There's a *cafeteria (☎ 819-638-7948)* and a *motel* of sorts, where singles/doubles cost $56/81.

Radisson

Named after explorer Pierre-Esprit Radisson, the village was set up in 1973 to house the workers on the James Bay hydroelectric project. It looks and feels larger than its population of 350 would suggest, partly because it was built to accommodate fluctuating numbers of workers (who work there for eight days, then fly home for six) and because about 20 families have decided to settle permanently here and create a real village.

The scenery around Radisson is spectacular, with views of the majestic Rivière La Grande from the built-up area around the larger-than-life Robert Bourassa hydroelectric power station (also called LG2), just outside town.

The tourist office (☎ 819-638-8687, 198 Rue Jolliet), at the village's entrance, can help you organize your stay. It's open 8am to 8pm daily June through September. At other times, contact the Town Hall (☎ 819-638-7777, 101 Place Gérard Poirier).

Everyone who makes it up here takes a free, guided tour of the power station. The main offices of **Hydro Québec** (☎ 819-638-8486) are in the Pierre Radisson Complex. After an introduction to hydroelectricity, you'll be taken inside and outside the massive LG2 (also called Robert Bourassa, after the Québec premier who oversaw its construction). This, together with LG2A, the world's largest underground power station (as tall as a 15-story building but buried 140m deep in the bedrock), produces 1/4 of the province's energy and ranks as the third-largest hydroelectric plant in the world.

Eight power stations stretch out over the 800km length of Rivière La Grande; thus, the same water is used eight times, for a total energy output of 15,244 megawatts. It took 20 years, 185,000 laborers and 70 million work hours to complete construction at a cost of some $23.5 billion. The most impressive element is the Robert Bourassa spillway, backed by the enormous Réservoir Robert Bourassa, which is three times the size of Lac St Jean. Stretching out almost 1km in length, this 'giant staircase' of a spillway features a series of 10 steps blasted out from rock, each 10m high with a landing the size of two football fields.

You'll find several motels, two- and three-star, in town.

Camping Radisson (☎ 819-638-8687, 198 Rue Jolliet) Tent sites $15-17. Located on a hill behind the tourist office, this campground includes modern toilet and shower facilities.

Chisasibi

Located near where Rivière la Grande meets Baie James, 100km west of Radisson, Chisasibi is a Cree village well worth visiting. The surrounding nature, windswept taiga doused by the Arctic breezes from James Bay, is haunting.

The town as it looks now has existed only since 1981. Before this, the residents lived on the Island of Fort George, 10km from town, where the Hudson's Bay Company had set up a fur-trading post in 1837. A vestige of the old-fashioned way of life survives in the many teepees seen in backyards here – mainly these are used for smoking fresh fish.

Margaret and William Cromarty (☎ 819-855-2800) offer excellent guided excursions of varying lengths to Fort George, where most of the original structures, including churches, schools and cemeteries remain. Traditional meals can be ordered. A two-hour tour costs $25.

The **Mandow Agency** (☎ *819-855-3373*) also arranges excursions to the island of Fort George, as well as fishing trips, canoe trips and winter activities. Expect to pay about $60 per person per outing (with snacks included), though the different guides the agency works with charge different prices. The company also acts as middleman for nearby outfitters.

LG1, another hydroelectric station, is 81km west of Radisson on the way to Chisasibi. While it's less monumental than Robert Bourassa (LG2), enough concrete went into its construction to pave a road from Montréal to Miami. Five lookouts near the complex provide stunning views of Rivière La Grande. Contact Hydro Québec in Radisson to take a tour of this station.

Chibougamau

Built around a series of copper and gold mines, Chibougamau is a dreary place indeed, but as northern Québec's largest settlement, it offers a number of services. About 800km from Radisson and 232km north of the Lac St Jean region, it occupies a remote area shared by several Cree villages, notably **Oujé Bougoumou** and **Mistassini**, 90km north near the banks of the largest freshwater lake in the province, Lac Mistassini.

There are two tourist offices in town: a year-round outpost at the Economic and Tourist Commission (☎ 418-748-6060, 600 3-ème Rue) and another summer-only office (☎ 418-748-7276, 512 Route 167 Sud), open June to September.

The **Réserves Fauniques Assinica & des Lacs Albanel-Mistassini et Waconichi** (☎ *418-748-7748, Route du Nord; admission $3.50*), two adjacent wildlife reserves north of Chibougamau, are truly wild places. There are chalets to rent ($43 for two people) and sites for rustic camping ($19 to $26), as well as canoe rental. You can register at the Centre du Plein Air du Mont Chalco (☎ 418-748-7162), 4km north of Chibougamau on Route 167; it's open 7am to 10pm daily June to September.

NUNAVIK

The territory of Nunavik stretches from the 55th to the 62nd parallel, bordered by the Hudson Bay to the west, the Hudson Strait to the north and Ungava Bay and the Labrador border to the east. At 507,000 sq km, it's a tad smaller than France, yet fewer than 10,000 people live here, in 14 villages separated from each other by several hundred kilometers of mainly tundra, with no roads to join them. Almost 90% of the population is Inuit; the remainder includes Native Indian (Cree and Naskapis) and white Québécois.

Though much of Nunavik is classified as tundra, there is a great diversity to its geography. Even tundra has many rich shades of beauty – the region is far from being merely a desolate plain of snow and ice. In the southwest, sandy beaches and large sand dunes stretch as far as the eye can see. In the northeast, the formidable Torngat Mountains extend in a series of bare, rocky peaks and untamed valleys 300km along the border of Labrador. The province's highest peak, Mont d'Iberville (1652m), is here.

There are also five meteorite-formed craters in Nunavik (of the 144 known on Earth). The largest – indeed one of the largest on the planet – is called **Pingualuit**, a 1.4-million-year-old cavity with a diameter of 3.4km and a depth of 433m (the height of a 145-story building) in parts. The lake that's formed inside the crater is 267m deep. Its water is considered among the purest in the world – in terms of transparency, it's second only to Japan's Lake Masyuko. Pingualuit lies 88km south of Kangiqsujuaq.

Floating above this terrain are the magical Northern Lights (aurora borealis), which can be seen an average of 243 nights in the year.

Socially, the villages hold great interest. The Inuit are generally friendly and approachable – and it's their adaptability that's helped them make such a radical transition in their lifestyles in so short a time. But the differences between Inuit communities and contemporary North American towns may give the unprepared a jolt of culture shock.

The villages range in population from an unimaginable 159 (Aupaluk) to 2050 (Kuujjuaq). Half the population is under 18, as you might guess by the sheer number of little ones running around. Everybody gets by all right here, money-wise, but some struggle with the serious social problems of domestic violence, drug abuse and alcoholism (even though most villages are 'dry'), as in many modern communities. There are 4.4 persons per household in Nunavik, compared to 2.6 in the rest of the province.

Because Nunavik can only be accessed by plane, few casual tourists make the trip. Yet those willing to make their own local contacts can do independent travel in the region. One should be prepared for the high prices for goods and services, however. On average, food prices are 69% higher here than in Québec City. A liter of milk costs $5.65, a 24-can case of Coke $33 (versus $7 elsewhere). Don't expect your precious ISIC card to be of help here!

After Inuktitut, the second language here is English. More youngsters are learning French than their parents did, but elders can rarely speak anything other than Inuktitut.

Getting There & Away

Unless you're willing or able to make a long snowmobile trek north of Radisson, the only way to get to Nunavik is by plane. First Air (☎ 800-267-1247) provides service between Montréal and Kuujjuaq. The full fare is $2210 roundtrip, but a seven-day advance purchase knocks the price down to $1440. During occasional sales, you might find fares for $700.

Air Inuit (☎ 800-361-2965) flies from Montréal to Puvirnituq for $2560 full fare or $1545 with seven-day advance purchase. From there, flights go to other villages such as Kuujjuarapik-Whapmagoostui (a roundtrip flight from there to Purvinituq costs $1000!). Air Inuit's Montréal-Kuujjuak fares are similar to First Air's.

Air Creebec (☎ 800-567-6567) flies into Whapmagoostui (Kuujjuarapik). An Air Creebec roundtrip flight from Montréal costs $1720 full fare or $890 with seven-day advance purchase.

Newfoundland & Labrador

Two distinct geographic areas make up this singular political entity, but the residents will remind you that Newfoundland (new-fen-**land**) is Newfoundland and Labrador is Labrador. The former is the island section of the province, the latter the larger northern mainland portion, and each is always referred to separately. Though these areas have much in common, there are cultural, historical, geological and developmental differences. In late 2001 the province's name, for the first time, officially included Labrador.

By far the majority of the population lives in more accessible Newfoundland, and this is the region most visitors see. Newfoundland has a unique character, and even a brief encounter with it is gratifying. It's a rugged, remote, weather-beaten land at the edge of Canada, heavily influenced by the sea and the conditions of the not-too-distant far north. From the often foggy shores, generations of fishers have headed out to sea and the waters legendary for cod and dozens of other kinds of fish. This more than anything has determined the life and culture of the province.

On the Grand Banks, lying southeast off the most populated region (the Avalon Peninsula), fishing boats gather from around the world, as they have done since just a few years after Columbus saw the 'New Land.' Unfortunately, the huge, modern, hi-tech, floating factories used by some nations, together with illegal practices, are a far cry from the traditional Newfoundland family trawler. The 1990s saw the inevitable result of fish factories, with drastically reduced catches and the end of work for tens of thousands of Newfoundlanders. It is hoped the decimated cod schools will return. In the meantime, other species, particularly lobster, are helping tide people over. Fish farming is also being attempted, but for many people, the old way of life, relying on the sea, is gone for good. Developing oil riches off the coast has meant work, and tourism has increased considerably in the past five years. In 2000, for the first time in many years the population didn't decrease; in fact, it went up. Though

Highlights

Entered Confederation: March 31, 1949
Area: 404,520 sq km
Population: 533,761
Provincial Capital: St John's

- Walk the hilly streets of St John's, the oldest city in North America.

- Enjoy traditional music and satirical theater at local venues around the province.

- View the icebergs and whales around Twillingate and Notre Dame Bay.

- Photograph stunning historic seaside villages.

- Hike along the fjords in Gros Morne National Park.

- Visit a 1000-year-old Viking settlement at L'Anse aux Meadows National Historic Park.

- Discover isolated fishing communities.

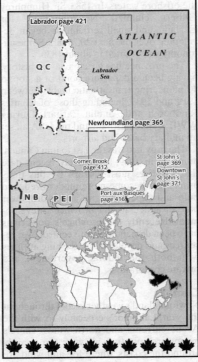

NEWFOUNDLAND

363

the increase was only by a couple of hundred people, it struck a hopeful chord.

All of Labrador and the northern portions of the island are part of the Laurentian Shield, one of the earliest geological formations on earth – possibly the only area unchanged from times predating the appearance of animals on the planet.

Across the province, in both sections, the interior is mostly forested wilderness with many peat bogs and countless lakes and rivers. Almost all the people live along the coast, with its many isolated fjords, bays and coves.

History

In 1497, John Cabot sailed around the shores of Newfoundland in the employ of Henry VII of England. Not long after, explorers under the flags of France and Portugal were also in the area. By the 15th and 16th centuries, thanks to tales of cod stocks so prolific that one could nearly walk on water, fishers from those countries, as well as Basques and Spaniards, regularly plied the offshore waters. In 1583, Sir Humphrey Gilbert claimed Newfoundland for England, and small settlements began developing over the next 200 years. Some autonomy was granted in about 1830.

The province has a rich aviation history, having been a departure point or a stop in 40 pioneering transatlantic flights between 1919 and 1937, including those of Charles Lindbergh and Amelia Earhart. During WWII, Canada, Britain and the USA all set up military bases and airports.

The province was the last to join Canada, doing so in 1949, a relatively recent date that surprises most visitors. By this time, fishing had become more modernized, and pulp and paper, iron ore and hydropower had all added to the province's development. Recently the province's politicians have been demanding more control over resources and development, clashing at times with both the federal government and private corporations.

Climate

Newfoundland's weather is cool throughout the year, Labrador's especially so, with the Arctic currents and north winds. There's heavy precipitation all year too, mainly around the coasts, where fog and wind are common. Summer is short, but July and August are generally quite warm. The sunniest and driest places are the central, inland areas.

Economy

The economy experienced upheaval in the 1990s. Years of overfishing depleted the essential cod stocks to the point that, in 1992 and 1993, bans were implemented. This devastated a province that was already enduring a 20% unemployment rate. More than 30,000 fishers were put out of work, and in many small coastal villages, as many as 80% of the families were on government assistance. The moratorium has now been lifted, but serious concern lingers over the long-term prospects of the cod industry.

Tempering the bad news were major oil and mineral discoveries. In Labrador's Voisey's Bay, near Nain, massive deposits of nickel, copper and cobalt have been located. Development of these resources has so far been impeded by political and economic debate as well as Native Indian concerns. The vast oil fields of Hibernia, located offshore near the Grand Banks southeast of St John's, began production in the late 1990s. Nearby Terra Nova began pumping in 2002.

Population & People

The people of Newfoundland and Labrador are of mainly English and Irish descent. The distinct culture they have developed is perhaps most noticeable in the language, with its strong lilting inflections, distinctive accent, unique slang and colorful idiom. A look at the map reveals descriptive and lighthearted names such as Nick's Nose Cove, Come-by-Chance, Main Tickle and Cow Head. Residents of 'The Rock' are known humorously as Newfies to people in the rest of the country, and they're often the butt of Canadian jokes. No malice is meant, however, as it's generally accepted that Newfoundlanders are among the friendliest and most quick-witted of Canadians (which is not to say they always appreciate the jokes or the term 'Newfie.')

Other peoples have played prominent roles in the development of this land. The Vikings landed and established a settlement in AD 1000. Inuit and other Native Indian bands were calling the area home long before that, and historic sites mark some of these settlements. Newfoundland proper, the island portion of the province, was the site of one of the most tragic of all North American encounters between the early Europeans and the original inhabitants. The Beothuk lived and traveled across much of the province for about 500 years. In the early 1800s, the last of the group died, victims of hostility, diseases brought by Europeans, and bad luck. Today, Labrador is still inhabited by Inuit and, in smaller numbers, Innu people.

Information

The Department of Tourism, Culture and Recreation (☎ 800-563-6353, fax 709-729-0057, e info@tourism.gov.nf.ca, public.gov .nf.ca/tourism) oversees tourism promotion

and publishes a series of guides. Its mailing address is Visitor Services Section, PO Box 8730, St John's, NF A1B 4K2.

Tourist or visitor information centers found across the province are often called 'chalets.' They sell good provincial highway maps ($3).

In Atlantic Canada there is a Harmonized Sales Tax (HST). It's a consumer tax that includes provincial sales tax and the federal GST. In Newfoundland and Labrador, this tax totals 15%.

The island portion of the province is on Newfoundland Time, which is 30 minutes ahead of Atlantic Time. The southeastern portion of Labrador, south of Cartwright and down along the Strait of Belle Isle, falls in Newfoundland time. Northern (from

NEWFOUNDLAND

Cartwright northward), central and eastern Labrador are all on Atlantic Time.

The expression '…and a half hour later in Newfoundland,' taken from the central Canadian broadcast media schedules, has become a regularly used comic interjection, with an infinite number of possible applications.

For emergency service in the St John's and surrounding area dial ☎ 911. Elsewhere, call the operator on ☎ 0.

Activities

Outdoor possibilities are wide ranging, and the tourism department publishes a guide outlining many of them. There is excellent hiking and camping in the national and provincial parks. Trail creation was a priority across the province in the 1990s. Most visitors' centers will have local trail information. Some trails, such as the East Coast Trail, are discussed in the text. The Trailway Provincial Park (☎ 709-256-8833) is a 900km-long gravel park stretching from Port aux Basques to St John's along an abandoned rail line used by walkers, cyclists, ATV riders and snowmobilers.

Whale- and iceberg-watching are ever popular on the north and east coasts. Note that iceberg season is generally mid-April through mid-June, and whales appear mid-July and after. Many regions provide excellent wildlife observation, with moose and caribou two of the most interesting animals to observe. Freshwater fishing can be enjoyed across the province. Hydrophiles have begun to discover the nearly unlimited kayaking and canoeing opportunities.

Sometime between April and June each year the province celebrates St George's Day.

Traditional Celtic-style music remains popular, and numerous folk festivals are held around the province during the summer months.

Accommodations

Accommodations prices are much like those in the rest of Canada, but there are often fewer options in any given place. Labrador's prices tend to be higher and the choices more limited. Scattered about the province are small, family-run guesthouses known as 'hospitality homes.' These are often the best choices for travelers, for both price and fun. Often, hospitality homes are the only choice, and many are just an extra room in a family's home.

Generally, tourist offices publish lists of accommodations, but these are rarely complete. All provincial tourist chalets – and an increasing number of local information offices – provide free phones to arrange lodging. In some of the small, out-of-the-way spots the pub manager might be able to suggest a couple of names.

Motels are generally fairly new and reliable, but they're more expensive than hospitality homes and fairly uniform. The larger towns offer hotels as well.

Opportunities to camp are pervasive. Facilities at parks are often minimal, often lacking showers or hookups for recreational vehicles. A provincial camping reservation hot line (☎ 800-866-2267) has been set up for provincial parks.

There are also some privately run campgrounds, and it is rarely a problem to find a decent place to camp; however, potential tenters should have reasonably decent equipment, as the weather doesn't allow for a casual hammock-in-the-tree style of camping.

Getting Around

Getting around the province presents some peculiar problems. The ever-growing road network connects major towns and most of the regions of interest to visitors but remains sketchy in many areas. Outside the two cities of St John's and Corner Brook and a few large towns, such as Gander and Port aux Basques, communities are small and the visitor traffic is light. Except for the one trans-island route, the public bus system consists of a series of small, regional services that usually connect with one or more major points. Although not extensive, this system works pretty well and will get most people to where they want to go. There is no train service on the island, but one line in western Labrador still operates.

The 905km-long Trans Canada Hwy is the only road linking St John's, the capital, to Port aux Basques on the other side of the island. It is a long haul, a 10- to 12-hour drive, but there are a few places worth stopping and several towns break up the trip.

For many of the small, isolated coastal villages known as 'outports,' the only means

Not a Swiss Watch

Like Newfoundland's icebergs, you need to go with the flow here. This province is not anal about efficiency, practicalities and profits. Many places don't have addresses or even street names. Opening hours change with the weather, the demand, local finances and various other factors, like if someone is ill. Times and schedules change often and seemingly without reason. Travel connections, if there are any, are not always smooth or convenient. For many urban visitors with a plan, all this can be frustrating, annoying and challenging. But the rewards are many.

In Canada it's a bit of a cliché, but it's true. The people here are among the friendliest, most generous and helpful you are likely to meet. Conversations come easy and are sprinkled with local idioms and humor. You may have a business operator provide his or her service and ask for nothing but an IOU, telling you 'just mail me a check when you get home.' Many others seem almost apologetic about asking for money. A guesthouse may unexpectedly throw in breakfast. Indeed, it has been well documented that the relatively thin-walleted population here donates more to charity per capita and per income than any other Canadians.

Ask someone in town where you can buy smoked fish, and he or she may telephone someone at home and set up a deal for you. Similar stories are commonplace.

There is little to no advertising, marketing, hype or neon. Inflated prices are as rare as hen's teeth. The only national franchises of consequence are Tim Horton's donut shops, and with their good deals they have become almost like community drop-in centers.

If you're thinking of covering a lot of ground, remember that, while distances are relatively small, the driving tends to be slow. Other than the Trans Canada, most roads are narrow and winding, and along the northern bays many pass through countless villages. To get between places, you must wind around bays and inlets, and in places the topography is surprisingly mountainous. And always there is more to see than imagined.

There really is nowhere like this in North America. Rules and regulations are few. Generally you can park where you want, walk where you want, even set up a tent in some places. Thousands of Canadians say they have always wanted to go to Newfoundland but haven't made it. Enjoy the trip and go with the flow.

of transportation and connection with the rest of the province is by boat. Some of these villages are connected by a surprisingly inexpensive ferry service that runs regularly in a couple of areas and is for passengers and freight only. A trip along one of these routes provides a chance to see some of the most remote communities in North America. Visitors are few, but mainstream culture is seeping in at an ever-increasing rate.

St John's

pop 175,000

St John's, the province's capital and largest center, is a city that manages to feel like a town – invigorating yet warm, busy yet homey – a modern city with its fishing village roots showing. Its splendid geo-graphical location and its tumultuous, romantic history make St John's an inviting tourist destination.

As the oldest city in North America and Britain's first overseas colony, St John's has been called the birthplace of the British Empire.

The city rises in a series of steps, sloping up from the waterfront. Everywhere there are stairs, narrow alleys and winding streets. Several of the downtown roads are lined with colorful, pastel clapboard townhouses.

The land is inhospitable, the weather not much better and the economy still pretty much dependent on the whims of the sea. This will undoubtedly alter with the oil fields' exploitation (see Economy, earlier in this chapter), and the past few years have seen some quickening of controversial downtown development.

Sure I'll Try It. What Is It?

Having a 'scoff,' to use a local term for eating, can be a bit of an adventure across the province, with many unfamiliar terms showing up on menus. Most of these unknown dishes have something to do with the sea and are well worth sampling.

Brewis is a blend of fish, onion and bread (see 'hardtack,' below) that's soaked overnight and then cooked. Cod tongues are actually tender, fleshy bits that are really closer to cheeks. They're often served deep-fried with very unimpressive results, but if you can, try them pan-fried. Doughboys are the provincial version of dumplings. Figgy duff is a thick fig pudding that is boiled in a cloth bag and is also the name of a well-known rock band. Fishcakes are a blend of cod, potato and onion mushed together and fried – delicious. Flipper pie is a pie made with seal flippers. Hardtack is hard bread, usually oval-shaped pieces, that is often used to make brewis. Scruncheons is a nice word to say, and one perfectly suited to fried bits of pork fat. They are often served with brewis or fish. Toutons (**towt**-ins – don't say too-**tohns** because that's what all the visitors say) are pieces of bread dough fried in pork fat. When you're done eating you can rightfully say in local parlance, 'I'm full as an egg.'

History

In 1497, John Cabot became the first European to find the excellent and protective harbor that led to the city's development. As Newfoundland is the closest point to Europe in the New World and because the famous Grand Banks teemed with fish offshore, a European settlement sprang up in 1528.

Unfortunately, this brought to an end not only the lifestyle but the very existence of the Beothuk Indians.

From its inception, the settlement was the scene of battles, raids, fires, pirating, deprivations and celebrations. The Dutch attacked in 1665. The French ruled on three occasions, but each time the English regained the settlement from them. The settlement's location has inspired more than trade, warfare and greed, however.

The first transatlantic wireless telegraph message was received here, 40 pioneering airplane crossings – including Earhart's and Lindbergh's – used the site, and even Pan Am's inaugural transatlantic flight touched down here. The wharves have been lined with ships for hundreds of years and still are, acting as service stations to fishing vessels from around the world. As befits a port of adventurers and turbulent events, the tradition of raising a glass is well established. Eighty taverns were well in use as long ago as 1775, and in the early 1800s, rum was imported to the tune of over a million liters annually. Today, the city might well still lay claim to having the most watering holes per capita (likely disputed by Halifax).

In 1892, the Great Fire, lit by a dropped pipe, burned down more than half the town. In 1992, another major downtown fire burned a considerable section of Harvey Rd and its many old houses.

The city has a housing policy stipulating that new housing be designed to blend in with the existing historic character of the street. Examples of this may be seen on New Gower St east of the city hall.

Orientation

The main streets are Harbour Dr running right along the bay; Water St, lined with shops, restaurants and bars, one street up; and Duckworth St, farther up still from the waterfront. The rest of the city continues to rise, rather steeply, up the hill away from the sea. It's said that everyone in town has strong legs.

In town, the east end of Gower St is noted for its many multicolored Victorian terrace houses. These attractive old English- and Irish-style houses are now protected for their historic character. Although central, Gower St – not to be confused with New Gower St – is a little tricky to find. It runs parallel to and in between Duckworth St and Queen's Rd immediately behind the Anglican Cathedral and then northeastward.

Beside city hall, located on New Gower St near Adelaide St, is the oft-photographed 'Mile 0' sign marking the start of the Trans Canada Hwy.

At the northeastern end of Water St is the small Harbourside Park, with a monument to Sir Humphrey Gilbert. His landing near here on August 5, 1583 marked the

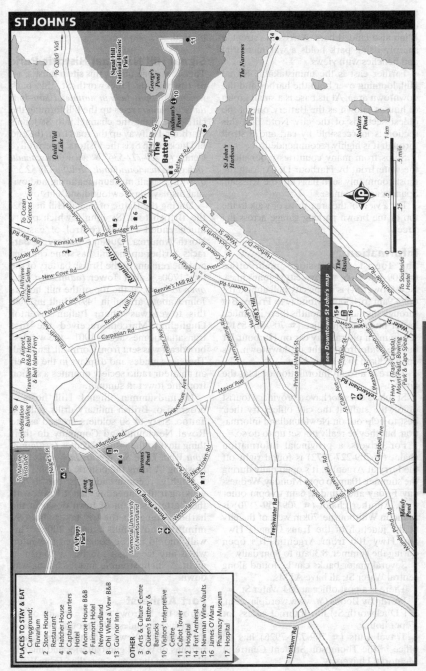

ST JOHN'S

Signal Hill National Historic Park

George's Pond

The Narrows

Soldiers Pond

Quidi Vidi Lake

To Quidi Vidi

Deadman's Pond

Signal Hill Rd

The Battery

Battery Rd

St John's Harbour

Forest Rd

The Boulevard

Rennie's River

Kenna's Hill

King's Bridge Rd

Torbay Rd

Logy Bay Rd

To Ocean Sciences Centre

New Cove Rd

To Hillview Terrace Suites

Portugal Cove Rd

Rennie's Mill Rd

Elizabeth Ave

Carpasian Rd

Circular Rd

Military Rd

Prescott St

Gower St

Cower St

Duckworth St

Water St

Harbour Dr

The Basin

Southside Rd

To Southside Hostel

Rennie's Mill Rd

Queen's Rd

Harvey Rd

Long's Hill

Empire Ave

Merrymeeting Rd

Prince of Wales St

Mayor Ave

Bonaventure Ave

To Airport, Traveller's B&B Hostel & Bell Island Ferry

To Confederation Building

To Marine Institute

Nagle's Pl

Allandale Rd

Springdale St

New Gower St

Hamilton Ave

LeMarchand Rd

Pleasant St

St Clare Ave

To Hwy 1 (Trans Canada); Mount Pearl, Bowring Park & Cape Spear

Campbell Ave

Cashin Ave

Prince of Wales St

Newtown Rd

Elizabeth Ave

Prince Philip Dr

Westerland Rd

Freshwater Rd

Mundy Pond Rd

Thorburn Rd

Mundy Pond

Long Pond

Burtons Pond

CA Pippy Park

Memorial University of Newfoundland

Water St

see Downtown St John's map

1 km

.5 mile

.5

.25

0

0

PLACES TO STAY & EAT
1 Campground;
   Fluvarium
2 Stone House
   Restaurant
4 Hatcher House
5 Captain's Quarters
   Hotel
6 Monroe House B&B
7 Fairmont Hotel
   Newfoundland
8 Oh! What a View B&B
13 Guv'nor Inn

OTHER
3 Arts & Culture Centre
9 Queen's Battery &
   Barracks
10 Visitors' Interpretive
   Centre
11 Cabot Tower
12 Hospital
14 Fort Amherst
15 Newman Wine Vaults
16 James O Mara
   Pharmacy Museum
17 Hospital

founding of Newfoundland and Britain's overseas empire. Lord Nelson and Captain Bligh also landed here. Across the street, a sharply rising park holds a war memorial and benches with views.

Farther east is the unmistakable Signal Hill, looming over both the harbor and the downtown area. At its base is a small group of houses known as the Battery, one of the oldest sections of the city. Note that this section is inaccessible by car, and a stroll through it is highly recommended.

Ships from many countries moor along the waterfront by Harbour Dr. Among the most commonly seen flags are the Russian, Spanish and Japanese.

For a view of the area, drive or walk to the top of the brown parking garage across the street.

Information

The Tourist Commission's main office (☎ 709-576-8106, W www.city.st-johns.nf.ca, New Gower St) is in the city hall annex. It's open 9am to 4:30pm Monday to Friday. But through the summer months there is a much better information office (☎ 709-576-8514) set up in an old railway car on Harbour Dr on the waterfront right in downtown. It's open 8:30am to 5:30pm daily.

There is also an information desk at the airport.

St John's does *not* have a provincial tourist office; the staff at the city offices try their best to help out on Newfoundland information, but they're really not set up to do so.

For drivers, a provincial information chalet (☎ 709-227-5272) is found right off the ferry at Argentia. It's open daily during the summer 10am to 6pm Monday, Wednesday, Friday and Sunday, 6am to 6pm other days. Another chalet (☎ 709-759-2170) is found in Whitbourne, 70km west of the city at the junction of the Trans Canada Hwy and Hwy 100 from Argentia. It's open during the summer, 8:30am to 8pm daily.

Several major banks can be found along central Water St; all have ATMs.

There is a post office at 354 Water St.

Wordplay Books (W www.wordplay.com, 221 Duckworth St) has Internet access for $7 per hour.

Travel Cuts (☎ 709-737-7926) has an office in the Thompson Student Centre at Memorial University.

St Clare's Mercy Hospital (☎ 709-778-3111, 154 LeMarchant Rd) is centrally located.

Signal Hill National Historic Park

The view alone makes this site a must. East of town along Duckworth St, this park *(open 8am-8pm daily in summer, 10am-4pm daily in winter)* rises up the hill forming the cliff edge along the channel into St John's Harbour. Halfway up the road from the end of Duckworth St is the Visitors' Interpretive Centre (☎ 709-772-5367, W www.parkscanada .pch.gc.ca/newfoundland; adult/family $2.55/ 6) with a small **museum** featuring audiovisual displays on Newfoundland's history.

During the Battle of Signal Hill in 1762, the British took St John's, which pretty much ended French control of eastern North America. **Queen's Battery & Barracks**, farther up the hill, has some cannons and the remains of the British battery of the late 1700s. **Cabot Tower** *(admission free; open to 9pm),* at the top of the hill, honors John Cabot's arrival in 1497. Built in 1900, this tower was where Italian inventor Guglielmo Marconi received the first transatlantic message in 1901 – the wireless broadcast was sent from Cornwall, England. There are guides and displays in the tower; an amateur radio society operates a station from the tower in summer.

In midsummer, Signal Hill hosts a program of British military drills called a Tattoo. Sixty to 80 soldiers dressed as the Royal Newfoundland Company do their thing next to the visitors' center *(3:30pm & 7pm Wed, Thur, Sat & Sun July–mid-Aug),* finishing by firing the historic cannons.

Highly recommended is the 1.7km walking trail connecting Cabot Tower with the Battery section of town down in the harbor. Going up, the trip takes about 90 minutes and climbs almost 200m. This walk should not be considered in winter, when any ice lingers, in heavy fog or at night. A slight stumble and it's a long way down.

Fort Amherst

Across the Narrows are the remains of this fort, which includes a lighthouse from 1810, the first light in Newfoundland. There are also remains of WWII gun batteries and incredible views of the rugged coastline. From Water

St, head west and turn south at the first light to cross Waterford River. Follow the signs to Fort Amherst. Park just before Amherst and walk through the cliffside village about 200m to the fort. Also here is the **Lighthouse Tearoom and Museum** (☎ 709-754-0619; admission $1; open 1pm-5pm daily June-Sept).

Newfoundland Museum
This small but decent museum (☎ 709-729-2329, Ⓦ www.nfmuseum.com, 285 Duckworth St; admission $3; open 9am-5pm daily, closed holidays) has a few relics and a skeleton – the only remains anywhere – from the extinct Beothuk tribe who once lived here. Also on display are exhibits about the Vikings and the history of St John's, and a life jacket worn by a steward on the *Titanic*.

Murray Premises
The fully renovated Murray Premises, on Water St at Beck's Cove, is one of the oldest warehouses in the city. It was built in the 1840s, somehow escaped the fire of 1892 and today is a national historic site, where the original timber and brick can be seen. Tucked among the shops and restaurants is the **Newfoundland Science Center** (☎ 709-754-0823; adult/student & senior $4.50/3.50; open 10am-5pm Mon-Fri, 10am-6pm Sat, noon-5pm Sun), a hands-on science experiment for kids. Exhibits change three times yearly.

James O'Mara Pharmacy Museum
The pharmacy museum (☎ 709-753-5877, 488 Water St; admission free; open 11am-5pm

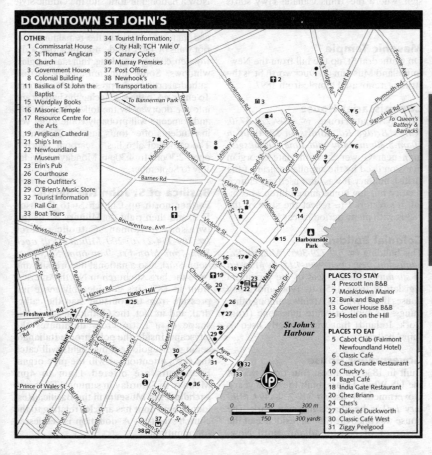

DOWNTOWN ST JOHN'S

OTHER
1 Commissariat House
2 St Thomas' Anglican Church
3 Government House
8 Colonial Building
11 Basilica of St John the Baptist
15 Wordplay Books
16 Masonic Temple
17 Resource Centre for the Arts
19 Anglican Cathedral
21 Ship's Inn
22 Newfoundland Museum
24 Erin's Pub
26 Courthouse
28 The Outfitter's
29 O'Brien's Music Store
32 Tourist Information Rail Car
33 Boat Tours

34 Tourist Information; City Hall; TCH 'Mile 0'
35 Canary Cycles
36 Murray Premises
37 Post Office
38 Newhook's Transportation

PLACES TO STAY
4 Prescott Inn B&B
7 Monkstown Manor
12 Bunk and Bagel
13 Gower House B&B
25 Hostel on the Hill

PLACES TO EAT
5 Cabot Club (Fairmont Newfoundland Hotel)
6 Classic Café
9 Casa Grande Restaurant
10 Chucky's
14 Bagel Café
18 India Gate Restaurant
20 Chez Briann
24 Ches's
27 Duke of Duckworth
30 Classic Café West
31 Ziggy Peelgood

NEWFOUNDLAND

daily mid-June–mid-Sept) in Apothecary Hall, an original art nouveau building, is a replica of an 1885 drugstore (chemist's), complete with vintage fixtures, cabinets, equipment and medicines.

Courthouse
Near the Newfoundland Museum, the working courthouse on Duckworth St dates from 1904. In the late 1980s it had a major facelift and now appears pretty much as it did when it first opened. It is one of the more imposing buildings in town.

City Hall
On New Gower St, five blocks west of the courthouse (Duckworth St runs into New Gower St), is the new city hall and Mile 0 sign, where the Trans Canada Hwy starts westward on its 7775km-long journey across Canada to Victoria, British Columbia.

Masonic Temple
On Cathedral St, up the hill from the Newfoundland Museum on Duckworth St, is the striking, renovated temple from 1897.

Commissariat House
Commissariat House (☎ *709-729-6730, King's Bridge Rd; admission $2.50; open 10am-5:30pm daily mid-June–Thanksgiving)*, near Gower St, is the late-Georgian mansion used by the supplies officer of the British military. It was later used as a church rectory, nursing home and children's hospital. It's restored to reflect the style of the 1830s, with many period pieces.

Colonial Building
This building (☎ *709-729-3065, Military Rd; admission free; open 9am-4:15pm Mon-Fri in summer)* was the seat of the provincial legislature from 1850 to 1960 and today houses the Provincial Archives among other things. It's built of white limestone (from Cork, Ireland) that was formerly used as ships' ballast.

Government House
Built in 1830 (at a cost four times that of the US White House, built the same year), Government House (☎ *709-729-4494, Military Rd)* is beside Bannerman Park. The house was once the official residence of the governor of Newfoundland, until Newfoundland became part of Canada. Since then the lieutenant governors have called it home. Tours aren't available, but you can sign the guest book.

Newman Wine Vaults
These recently reopened vaults (☎ *709-739-1892, 440 Water St; admission free; open noon-4pm daily Aug-Sept)*, in one of the oldest buildings in town, were used to store and age port from Portugal from 1679 to 1996.

Anglican Cathedral
Across the street from the Masonic Temple is the Anglican Cathedral of St John the Baptist (☎ *709-726-5677, 22 Church St; open 10am-2pm Mon-Fri, 11am-noon Sat, 11am-3pm Sun)*, serving Canada's oldest parish (1699). Now a national historic site, the Gothic-style church had its cornerstone laid in 1834. The church was gutted in the Great Fire of 1892 and then rebuilt within the remaining exterior walls by 1905. Inside, note the stone walls, wooden ceilings and long, thin stained-glass windows. Some museum-quality British cathedral artifacts are preserved in one room. To enter, go to the side facing the harbor and into the doorway by the toilet. Ring the bell and someone will probably come to let you in. Students offer tours June to September. The cathedral also has a tearoom, which is open 2:30pm to 4:30pm Monday to Friday July to September.

Basilica of St John the Baptist
Farther north up Church St to Garrison Hill, and then right on Military Rd, is this twin-spired Roman Catholic church (☎ *709-754-2170, 200 Military Rd; open 8am-4pm Mon-Fri, 9am-6pm Sat, 9am-noon Sun)*, also a national historic site and once the largest church in North America. Built in 1855, it's considerably more impressive from the outside than the cathedral, and in fact, the Gothic facade in the shape of a Latin cross dominates the cityscape. Inside, the polychrome Italianate ceiling with gold-leaf highlights will catch the eye's attention, as will the pipe organ. Free tours are offered 11am to 4pm Monday to Saturday in summer. The small **Archdiocesan Museum** in the Basilica Residence next door has articles relating to the church's history. A donation is requested for admittance.

NEWFOUNDLAND

St Thomas' Anglican Church

Opened in 1836, this wooden church (☎ 709-576-6632, *Military Rd at King's Bridge Rd; open 10am-4pm Mon-Fri, various hours weekends*) is the oldest in St John's and is famous for surviving both of the city's 19th-century conflagrations.

CA Pippy Park

The dominant feature of the northwestern edge of downtown is the huge, feature-filled 1343-hectare CA Pippy Park (☎ 709-737-3655). Recreational facilities here include walking trails, picnic areas, playgrounds and a campground. The park also has a snack bar. **Memorial University**, the province's only university, is here, too.

The university's **botanical garden** (☎ 709-737-8590; admission $2; open 10am-5pm daily May-Nov) is at Oxen Pond, at the western edge of the park off Mt Scio Rd. It's both a cultivated garden and nature reserve. Together, these and the park's **Long Pond** marsh provide visitors with an excellent introduction to the province's flora and varying natural habitats, including boreal forest and bogs. At Long Pond the bird-watching is good, and mammals such as moose can sometimes be spotted in the park.

Freshwater Resource Centre

Also in CA Pippy Park is this striking hexagonal balconied building across the street from the campground. The main feature is the 25m **fluvarium** (☎ 709-754-3474; adult/senior/child $5/4/3; open 9am-5pm daily, closed Wed Sept-June, call to confirm hours), a glass-sided cross-section of a 'living' river. Viewers can peer through large windows to observe the natural, undisturbed goings-on beneath the surface of Nagle's Hill Brook. Numerous brown trout and the occasional eel can be seen. If the weather has been unsettled with high winds or if there has been any rain, the water becomes so cloudy that virtually nothing can be seen through the murkiness.

Within the center are a demonstration fish hatchery and exhibits that closely examine plants, insects and fish of freshwater ecosystems. Outside there are interpretive trails; it's possible to walk all the way to Quidi Vidi Lake from here. Feeding time is scheduled at 4pm, and tours are offered hourly except at 4pm.

Arts & Culture Centre

The Arts & Culture Centre complex (☎ 709-729-3900, Ⓦ www.artsandculturecentre.com/stjohns, *Prince Phillip Dr*), about 2km northwest from the downtown area, beside the university, contains the **Art Gallery of Newfoundland and Labrador** (☎ 709-737-8209; admission free; open noon-5pm Tues, Wed, Sat & Sun, noon-5pm, 7pm-10pm Thur & Fri). The art gallery displays mainly contemporary Canadian painting and sculpture. There is also a **theater**, which hosts events during summer.

Confederation Building

Just off Prince Phillip Dr, northeast of the arts center, is the 12-story home of the provincial government, which houses a small **military museum** (☎ 709-729-2300; admission free; open 9am-4pm Mon-Fri).

Marine Institute

Those with a special interest may want to visit this university facility (☎ 709-778-0200, 155 Ridge Rd; admission free; tours 1:30pm, 2:45pm Mon-Fri July-Aug). It's an educational unit for studying all things marine, from waves and shipping to new fishnet materials. The hour-long tour includes a huge flume tank and, of most interest, a sophisticated navigation simulator that lets you try steering a boat through the Narrows.

Ocean Sciences Centre

This research facility (☎ 709-737-3706, *Marine Lab Rd; admission free; open 10am-5pm daily June-Sept*) is operated by Memorial University's science department. Ongoing work in the lab area (no public access) examines the life cycle of salmon, seal navigation, ocean currents and many other aspects of life in the colder ocean regions. In the visitor area, you can handle various sea creatures in a touch tank, or check out some seals in outdoor tanks.

The center is about 8km north of town just before Logy Bay, at the end of Marine Lab Rd on the ocean. From town take Logy Bay Rd (Route 30) and then follow Marine Dr. There is no public transportation.

Bowring Park

Southwest of the downtown area off Pitts Memorial Dr on Waterford Bridge Rd, this is another popular large city park. A couple of streams and walkways meander through the park. The Peter Pan statue is a replica of the famous one in Kensington Gardens in London, England, and was made by the same sculptor.

Cape Spear

A 15-minute drive southeast of town leads you to the most easterly point in North America. The area is preserved as the Cape Spear National Historical Site (☎ 709-772-5367, Blackhead Rd; adult/senior/child 6-16/family $2.50/2/1.50/6; open 10am-6pm daily mid-June–mid-Oct) and includes the refurbished 1835 lighthouse (one of the oldest in Newfoundland), an interpretive center and the heavy gun batteries and magazines built in 1941 to protect the harbor during WWII. A trail leads along the edge of the headland cliffs, past 'the most easterly point' observation deck and up to the lighthouse. You can continue all the way to Maddox and Petty Harbour if you wish. The coastal scenery at this spot is spectacular, and through much of the summer, there is an opportunity to spot whales. You reach the cape from Water St by crossing the Waterford River west of town and then following Blackhead Rd for 11km.

Quidi Vidi

Over Signal Hill, away from town, is the tiny, picturesque village of Quidi Vidi (kidee-vi-dee). This little fishing port has the oldest cottage in North America. Mallard Cottage (☎ 709-576-2266, 2 Barrows Rd; admission free; open 10am-5pm in summer, call otherwise) dates back to the 1750s and is now a national heritage site and a very cluttered antique/junk shop. Buy something to help maintenance.

Built in 1762, Quidi Vidi Battery (☎ 709-729-2977, Cuckhold's Dr; admission $2.50; open mid-June–Thanksgiving) is up the hill from the village, guarding the bay. The French built it after taking St John's. It was later taken by the British and remained in military service into the 1800s. Interpreters in costume answer questions.

Inland from the village, Quidi Vidi Lake is the site of the St John's Regatta, which is held on the first Wednesday in August. Started in 1818, it's probably the oldest continuing sporting competition in North America. The Royal St John's Regatta Museum (☎ 709-576-8058, Lakeview Ave at Clancy Dr off Forest Rd; admission free) is on the 2nd floor of the boathouse at the lake. The Rennies River flowing into the west end of the lake is an excellent trout stream. A popular trail leads around the lake.

Quidi Vidi Brewing (☎ 709-738-4040, 15 Barrows Rd; tours hourly 10am-4pm Tues-Sat; admission $1 with tastings) is a microbrewery in an old fish processing plant with half a dozen brews. You'll either love or hate the unique cherry beer.

You can walk to the village from Signal Hill in about 20 minutes or go around by road from St John's. Take Forest Rd, which runs along the lake and then turns into Quidi Vidi Village Rd. Locals would rather you parked on the outskirts and walked in.

Activities

The Grand Concourse is an ambitious 100km-long network of trails all over town and linking St John's with Mt Pearl and Paradise via downtown sidewalks, trails, river corridors and old railway beds. The system,

---

St John's on Ice

A sight that almost equals seeing a 40-ton humpback whale breaching is a five-story iceberg silently sailing past St John's Harbour. Greenland glaciers produce up to 40,000 icebergs annually, and the prime viewing area in Newfoundland is around Twillingate Island in Notre Dame Bay; an average of 370 icebergs drift as far south as St John's each year, in some years even more. In 1984, a total of 2200 reached the city.

The typical iceberg is 30m high and weighs 204,000 tons, with only one-eighth of it appearing above the water. Icebergs are often classified as 'slob ice,' a thick slush of small ice pieces; 'bergy bits,' or small icebergs; and 'growlers,' icebergs that are particularly dangerous because of their low profile and instability. The iceberg season in St John's extends from May to June, with an occasional iceberg appearing in early July. The best places to see them are at Signal Hill and Cape Spear. A big one nearby puts a noticeable chill in the air.

largely completed in 2000, is a nifty piece of forward urban thinking. Most hiking is done in the CA Pippy Park or Quidi Vidi Lake areas. Buy the map at Water St Pharmacy (☎ 709-579-5554, 335 Water St) or magazine stands. Some street signs are color-coded to map trails, and signs and plaques can be seen all over town.

Sea kayaking is now also possible out of St John's. **Eastern Edge Outfitters** (☎ 709-782-5925) has one-day tours ($120) as well as a number of multiday tours and courses.

Take a paddle near St John's.

Organized Tours

For a relatively small city, St John's has an extraordinary number of tours available.

Bus British Island Tours (☎ 709-738-8687) does three-hour double-decker bus tours ($20) departing at 9:30am and 1:30pm that include Signal Hill and Quidi Vidi. The company offers free shuttle service to and from lodgings.

Legend Tours (☎ 709-753-1497, 66 Glenview Terrace) covers St John's, Cape Spear and the Marine Dr area and has received many favorable reviews for its city tours ($30). The commentary is richly woven with humor, historical tidbits and information on the people and province.

Discovery Tourist Services (☎ 709-722-4533, Fairmont Newfoundland Hotel) has city tours and half-day tours of the Avalon Peninsula ($95) and further afield to Trinity and overnight packages to the Burin Peninsula.

On Your Own Tours (☎ 709-753-5353, 112 Duckworth) will design an itinerary for you – anything from a one-day walking tour

to monthlong adventures. The company can organize car rentals, accommodations and tours as well.

Walking Terry's Tours (details at the tourist railway car) offers fascinating walking tours for just $5, and you'll learn some little-known stories.

Boat Boat tours depart from near the railroad car information office or from communities south of St John's along the coast. Most charge around $25 to $35, though some do offer student and senior discounts, so shop around. For whale-watching, try to pick a calm day, as it allows the boat to travel farther and spot whales easier. The sea can get rough and cold, so take warm clothes – it may be balmy in the protected harbor, but it's quite a different story once outside the Narrows. A sip of the Screech (legendary local rum) may help.

Dee Jay Charters (☎ 709-753-8687, on the harbor by the rail car tourist chalet) runs a good-value 2½-hour trip from the waterfront out to sea in search of icebergs in June, whales in July and August and seabirds any time (adult/child $25/16). If the big highlights are not in the neighborhood there is still bird-watching and sightseeing along the coast, including Quidi Vidi. Three trips are offered daily.

Island Rendezvous (☎ 709-747-7253, 800-504-1066), based in suburban Mt Pearl but operating out of the village of Garden Cove two hours from town, has a one-of-a-kind trip ($140). Popular with residents, the two-day adventure visits an abandoned outport. Visitors are taken to Woody Island, virtually a ghost town except for some people who use it as a base for seasonal fishing, and put up in a large old house run as a hospitality home. The days are spent poking around the old town and island and on a boat tour of Placentia Bay. It's a glimpse into the traditional fishing village way of life and an escape from what has replaced it. Meals, entertainment and accommodations are included, making the tour a pretty fair bargain.

There are several charters in St John's offering 'tall ship' outings from the waterfront. Both **J&B Schooner Tours** (☎ 709-753-7245, Pier 6) and **Adventure Tours** (☎ 709-726-5000, Pier 7) offer several daily tours for more than two hours ($35) on different boats.

Special Events
Only major festivals are listed here.

Discovery Days Two days of celebrations beginning around June 18 commemorate the city's birthday. Festivities include concerts (any Newfoundland event includes music), a parade, street dance and sporting events.

Craft Fair The Newfoundland and Labrador craft fair is held twice annually, at the end of July and November, in St John's Memorial Stadium.

George Street Festival Featuring music of all kinds, this festival on central George St is held around the end of July.

The Provincial Folk Festival This three-day event, which takes place annually around the first week of August, has great music and should not be missed. Dancers and storytellers also perform in their respective traditions.

Royal St John's Regatta What probably began as a bet among a few fishers to see who could row faster is now the oldest continuous sporting event in North America. The regatta officially began in 1825 and is held on the first Wednesday of August. The entire town closes up that day and everybody heads to the shores of Quidi Vidi Lake to watch.

Places to Stay
Camping *CA Pippy Park* (☎ 709-737-3669, 877-477-3655, *Nagles Place*) Sites with/ without hookups $20/14. Open May 1-Sept 30. This campground is conveniently located right in the city by the university. It is off Higgins Line at the northwestern side of the park near the Confederation Building. For a campground in town it is quite green and quiet. In summer, it does fill up, especially weekends, when there is some partying.

Butter Pot Provincial Park (☎ 709-685-1853, 800-563-6353, *Route 1*) Sites without hookups $10. The park, 30km west along the Trans Canada Hwy, has a very pleasant wooded setting, a beach, an interpretive center and trails, including an easy climb up Butter Pot Hill. It is often full on summer weekends.

Hostels There are currently several hostels open, a relative cornucopia. The situation here is always volatile, so confirm if possible.

Hostel on the Hill (☎ 709-754-7658, cellular ☎ 709-682-0718, e oboag@yahoo.com, 65 Long's Hill St) Shared/doubles $15/30. This welcome addition is central, comfortable, open all year and has a great deck with harbor view. A breakfast of bagel and coffee is included – all in all a fine deal. There are only spaces for eight people.

Southside Hostel (☎ 709-753-9480, e southsidehostel@hotmail.com, 621 Southside Rd) Single $15. The location is nowhere near as convenient, but if you want quiet and a reason to visit a somewhat obscure residential neighborhood, this fits the bill. Dave, the manager, may be able to get you a lift from downtown.

Hatcher House (☎ 709-737-7933, *Memorial University*) Singles student/nonstudent $15/20. Open mid-May–mid-Aug. It is a bit bureaucratic, and you may have to phone several people to get current details (try office hours Monday to Friday), but there are rooms at the campus with doubles and weekly rates offered. Meals are available. There are buses to town, but you can walk in less than half an hour, even if the roads are not direct. From the campus Newtown Rd leads downtown.

Travellers B&B Hostel (☎ 709-437-5627) Rooms with breakfast $25. The owners of this hostel, who have traveled on the cheap themselves, rent out a couple of rooms in their house on a large property about a 10-minute drive north of downtown on Pine Line by Torbay. There's no public transportation but if you play your cards nicely someone may pick you up. The grounds are large enough to accommodate tents. Call Donna or Jerry, who were in New Zealand during research, for exact location.

Tourist Homes & B&Bs Aside from these established tourist homes and B&Bs, the tourist office should have a list of places in homes, which are generally not mentioned in the accommodations guides.

Gower House (☎ 709-754-0047, 800-563-3959, 180 Gower St) Singles with shared/ private bath $40/50, doubles with shared/ private bath $55/65 with breakfast. Centrally located near the Anglican Cathedral, this favorite Victorian place has good rooms. Half come with private bathroom, and one has a balcony. Other benefits include the use of kitchen, laundry and parking facilities.

Monkstown Manor (☎ 709-754-7324, 888-754-7377, fax 709-722-8557, 51 Monkstown Rd) Rates $55-75. This recommended B&B in a downtown 1890 house is run by two well-known personalities: a folklorist and a traditional fiddler. They can tell you pretty much anything you want to know and can help you suss out some interesting events. With a good breakfast and comfortable rooms, this is a bargain.

Oh! What a View (☎ *709-576-7063, 184 Signal Hill Rd*) Rooms with breakfast $60-70. This establishment is recommended as a neat, clean B&B with a spectacular view over the harbor and city from two decks. There are four rooms, and all include a continental breakfast of bread and homemade muffins. Two of the rooms are in the basement, but they are modern and comfortable. City buses run nearby, but it's only a 10-minute walk into town. It's open May-October.

The Prescott Inn (☎ *709-753-7733, 888-263-3768, fax 709-753-6036, 19 Military Rd*) Rooms start at $50, kitchen suites $105. An excellent hot breakfast is included. This long-running B&B with luxury touches is centrally situated on the northeastern side of downtown in a well-kept old house with balconies looking out over the harbor. Seniors get a 10% discount.

Monroe House (☎ *709-754-0610, 877-754-0610, 8A Forest Rd*) Rooms $80-100. This upscale establishment, behind the Fairmont Hotel Newfoundland, was once the home of the Newfoundland prime minister. The six rooms are spacious and tastefully decorated; the breakfasts are substantial; and in the evening there's complimentary wine. If you are seeking some creature comforts and a little pampering, this fits the bill.

Motels & Hotels *Guv'nor Inn* (☎ *709-726-0092, 800-961-0092, 389 Elizabeth Ave*) Rooms $70-90. This motel, recently renovated, has a restaurant and pub and is near the university.

Greenwood Lodge & Motel (☎ *709-364-5300*) Rooms $65. This motel, toward Mt Pearl off Route 60, is close to town. It has a game room and laundry facilities.

Crossroads Motel (☎ *709-368-3191*) Singles/doubles $55/66. This standard motel is at the junction of Routes 1 and 60.

Hotels are not St John's strong point, but with good guesthouses this shouldn't pose problems.

Captain's Quarters (☎ *709-576-7173, fax 709-738-2002, 2 King's Bridge Rd*) Singles/doubles with shared bath $45/50. Other rooms have private bath. This is a central, low-cost inn across the street from the Commissariat House. There are 20 small, clean rooms, and a light breakfast is included. On the 1st floor there is a small pub with dartboards and fireplaces.

Hotel St John's (☎ *709-722-9330, 800-563-2489, fax 709-722-9231, 102 Kenmount Rd*) Rates $80-115. A third of the 85 rooms come with kitchen facilities at this hotel about 6km from downtown.

Best Western Travellers Inn (☎ *709-722-5540, 800-261-5540, fax 709-722-1025, 199 Kenmount Rd*) Singles/doubles $90/100. This is a fairly standard, reliable mid-range chain hotel. There is a dining room, and children stay free.

Fairmont Hotel Newfoundland (☎ *709-726-4980, 800-866-5577, fax 709-726-2025, Cavendish Square*) Rates $189-300. The city's large, historic hotel, with the imposing stone facade at the end of Duckworth St, is the top-end classic in town. Ask about the discount weekend rates.

Efficiencies *Hillview Terrace Suites* (☎ *709-754-9822, 888-754-9822, fax 709-754-9047, 3 Wedland Crescent*) Rates $80. There are 80 good value, full housekeeping, furnished units here in low-rise buildings at the edge of town. It's like having your own apartment – dishes, pictures on the wall, everything. The two-bedroom units offer long-term rates, too.

Places to Eat
The city has a tasty array of restaurants, with Duckworth and Water Sts in particular having many eateries.

Bagel Café (☎ *709-739-4470, 183 Duckworth St*) Prices $5. Get an all-day breakfast here, including various omelets and fish cakes, or a budget bagel-and-coffee lunch. The café has a snug little interior and a few tables outside.

Classic Café West (☎ *709-579-4444, 364 Duckworth St*) Lunch specials $6-8, dinner $12-18. Open 24 hours daily. This is an excellent place featuring a wide selection of seafood, fresh-baked goods with local berries and value prices. Menu items include coffee and a giant muffin ($2.50), a small basket of steamed mussels and a beer ($9) and lunch specials like grilled salmon. It also has a great patio. There's a second location at 73 Duckworth, but it isn't open all night.

Chucky's (☎ *709-579-7888, 10 King's Rd*) Prices $4-15. At this busy, friendly spot with

NEWFOUNDLAND

eye-catching decor, there is plenty of seafood, but of more interest may be the wild game selection. You can try caribou or moose steak ($15) or stew ($10) or just have a soup and sandwich.

Keep in mind that many of the pubs, including those on George St, serve very reasonable midday meals.

Duke of Duckworth *(☎ 709-739-6344, 325 Duckworth St)* Prices $6-8. Local workers pile in here for pub grub such as meat pies, sausages and sauerkraut or soup-and-sandwich combinations.

Ziggy Peelgood *(Water St at Ayres Cove)* is a chip wagon/institution that fires up top-rate fries daily.

There are some fine ethnic options, too.

Casa Grande *(☎ 709-753-6108, 108 Duckworth St)* Dishes $8, full dinner $14. This nicely decorated Mexican restaurant holds about 10 small wooden tables encircled by wicker chairs and serves Tex-Mex standards.

India Gate *(☎ 709-753-6006, 286 Duckworth St)* Lunch buffet 11am-2pm Mon-Fri $8, menu dishes $11. For an East Indian meal, try the all-you-can-eat weekday lunch buffet or the meat, vegetarian and tandoori options at dinner.

Not everywhere is casual. The following restaurants are a bit fancier.

Chez Briann *(☎ 709-579-0096, 290 Duckworth St)* Lunch $8-14, dinner mains $25. A French restaurant featuring seafood and meat, particularly lamb, has been carved from this heritage house. The private rooms with fireplaces are more than comfortable, and the place isn't snobby at all.

The World's First Flush Toilet

The digs at Ferryland have turned up some interesting artifacts, including, say archeologists, what is probably the world's first flush toilet, dating back to the 1620s. Among the remains that have turned up from Lord Baltimore's colony is a privy that was strategically situated on the shoreline with a hole above the sea. Twice a day the high tide came in and 'flushed' the contents away into the ocean, leaving nothing but a little saltwater on the seat.

Stone House Restaurant *(☎ 709-753-2425, 8 Kenna's Hill)* Dinner $100 & up for two. This has long been considered the city's number one choice for fine dining. Specialties are seafood, game and traditional Newfoundland dishes. It's in one of the city's oldest homes. Reservations are recommended.

Cabot Club *(☎ 709-726-4980, Fairmont Hotel Newfoundland, Cavendish Square)* Dinner $100 & up for two. Head to this elegant hotel dining room for dinner with the best view in the city. Watching the lights emerge around the harbor at dusk is spectacular.

Fish & Chips Shops St John's has some of the best fish and chips anywhere, bar none. People often bad-mouth cod, but it is *the* fish in this part of the world, and fresh out of the sea it's excellent. Despite the depleted cod stocks, the moratorium of the '90s is over and getting fresh fish is usually possible. That this needs mentioning given the once boundless local stocks is enough to make you wince.

Forget about downtown and get to fish and chips central at the junctions of Harvey, LeMarchant and Freshwater Rds, where there are numerous time-tested outlets.

Ches's *(☎ 709-722-4083, 9 Freshwater Rd)* At this favorite the fish is like biting into a steak, but it melts in your mouth and the fries match up (under $8).

Entertainment

St John's is a lot of fun at night. Political correctness in the sphere of alcohol is pleasantly absent and makes a refreshing change from the ever-present moralism found in much of Canada. The elsewhere often-forbidden 'happy hour' here becomes stretched to a laughable misnomer lasting from as early as 11am to as late at 7:30pm. Two-for-one specials abound, and establishments are busy through the day, especially on weekends.

George St, which is pretty crazy with crowds and queues at a variety of bars, is closed nightly at 10pm to vehicle traffic, with the exception of the police and taxis. These raucous places party on till 3am, and there's something for adults of all ages.

Corner Stone *(☎ 709-754-1410, 16 Queen St at George St)* This is a video dance bar.

Sundance *(☎ 709-753-7822, George St at Adelaide)* Sundance has a large outdoor deck, indoor pool tables and a popular happy hour.

Fat Cat *(☎ 709-722-6409, 5 George St)* Young crowds head here for blues.

There are some big-time fun pubs offering live Irish and traditional music, including the following:

O'Reilly's *(☎ 709-722-4853, 15 George St)* Packed on weekends, this is a great place for music and lively crowds.

Erin's Pub *(☎ 709-722-1916, 186 Water St)* Another of this type, Erin's has live music most nights.

Ship's Inn *(☎ 709-753-3870, 265 Duckworth St)* Attracting an arty crowd, the Ship is a good place, and gay-friendly too. It sporadically offers live music, including jazz on Sunday. The entrance is down the steps beside the arts council on tiny Solomon Lane.

Masonic Temple *(☎ 888-754-7377, Cathedral St)* Kick up your heels here 8pm to 10pm Wednesday, Friday and Sunday in July and August. You get a lesson in Newfoundland set dancing and then a chance to practice with superb live music for $10.

Schroeder's Piano Bar *(☎ 709-753-0807, 10 Bates Hill)* Tucked away on a side street, this is a quiet, romantic little spot where you may get some interesting live music.

If you want to take in some culture, try the following performing arts venues.

Arts & Culture Centre *(☎ 709-729-3900, Confederation Parkway)* Live theater and dance performances are staged regularly.

Resource Center for the Arts *(☎ 709-753-4531, LSPU Hall, 3 Victoria St)* The center presents work by local playwrights.

Shakespeare by the Sea Theatre *(☎ 709-576-0980)* Live outdoor productions are presented at 6pm ($10) at the Bowring Park amphitheater. No advance sales.

Shopping
O'Brien's Music Store *(☎ 709-753-8135, 278 Water St)* is a great source for recorded traditional music, instruments, and information on upcoming events.

Getting There & Away
Air Air Canada (☎ 709-726-7880) to Halifax costs $649 one way, to Montréal $853.

For flights solely within the province try Air Nova (which is affiliated with Air Canada), Interprovincial Airlines (☎ 709-576-1666) or Air Labrador (☎ 709-753-5593, 709-896-3387).

Bus The bus system is a little confusing, but if you can track things down, it can work fairly well. Unlike in other provinces, buses are not monopolized by one or two companies but are run by a lot of small, local and regional services. For destinations not listed below, ask around or at the tourist office. Some operators use vans or cars, sometimes called 'share taxis.' In town there isn't even a bus station! Call the various bus companies to find out where to meet, if they don't pick you up.

DRL (☎ 709-738-8088) operates just one route, but it's the province's main one, running across Newfoundland along the Trans Canada Hwy to Port aux Basques and stopping at most every place along the way. To Port aux Basques, there's one bus daily ($97 one way, 13 hours) at 7:45am from the university's education building.

For Argentia, Placentia and Freshwater, there is Newhook's Transportation (☎ 709-726-4876, 709-227-2552 in Placentia, 13 Queen St), which runs buses daily down to the southwest Avalon Peninsula ($20 to Argentia, 1½ hours); buses are supposed to await ferry arrivals but call first. In Argentia you can make dockside arrangements for getting to St John's.

Share Taxi Molloy's Taxi (☎ 709-722-4249) runs down the east coast of the Avalon Peninsula to Trepassey. Fleetline Bus Service (☎ 709-722-2608) goes to Carbonear ($11) and the lower Conception Bay area daily except Sunday. Call first as this schedule changes at a whim.

Shirran's (☎ 709-722-8032) runs up to the Bonavista Peninsula and right into Bonavista ($20). Venture Bus Lines (☎ 709-727-4990) goes to the peninsula as far as Lethbridge.

North Eastern (☎ 709-747-0492) goes to Twillingate ($50).

Bonavista Cab (cellular ☎ 709-682-5776) can get you to Trinity.

On the Burin Peninsula, Cheeseman's Bus Service (☎ 709-753-7022) goes to Marystown ($30) at 3:30pm daily, and Foote's Taxi (☎ 709-832-0491, 800-866-1181) goes all the way to Fortune ($35) at 4pm. North Shore Bus Lines (☎ 709-722-5218) runs up to Old Perlican.

Ferry The Marine Atlantic ferry for North Sydney, Nova Scotia, docks at Argentia on the southwest coast of the Avalon Peninsula. There are three runs a week in each direction from mid-June to mid-September and then one weekly in fall. There are no ferries on this route from early October to mid-June. During peak period, it departs Argentia on Monday (11pm), Thursday (8am) and Saturday (8am). It leaves North Sydney Monday (6am), Wednesday (6am) and Friday (3:30pm). In fall, there are only Monday departures. The crossing time is 15 hours, less if seas are calm. An adult ticket is $60, a bicycle $20, and a car $135. Rooms are extra, dorm beds $22. You can take the less expensive ferry to Port aux Basques and then drive across the province twice, but with gasoline costs, calculate the savings first. From Argentia to Nova Scotia – and on the afternoon ferry from Port aux Basques to Nova Scotia – you arrive around midnight and definitely need to make a reservation for a room in advance.

Passengers can enjoy movies, a bar with live band, a children's play area, even miniature golf on the top deck – in short, the works. Sleeping all over the place has been disallowed (bummer!), so you're in a chair all night.

In July or August, reservations are a good idea in either direction; in the USA or Canada, call ☎ 800-341-7981, 902-794-8109 in North Sydney or 709-227-2431 in Argentia. The website is W www.marine-atlantic.ca. Usually one or two days' notice is all that is necessary, though at that point you may not get a cabin or dorm berth.

If you're in a car, you may get a free car wash as you board the ferry back to the Canadian mainland. This is to get rid of two bug varieties harmful to potatoes and found only in Newfoundland.

Getting Around
To/From the Airport There isn't a city bus to the airport, which is about 6km north of town on Route 40 going toward Portugal Cove. Because of federal regulations, a taxi to the airport is $12; from the airport it's $17.50. The official airport service is by Dave Gulliver Cabs (☎ 709-722-0003). Inquire about sharing, and if you're lucky, it may be cheaper.

Bus The St John's Transportation Commission runs the Metrobus (☎ 709-722-9400)

city bus system. Schedules are printed in the Yellow Pages phone book. There are a few bus routes in and around town, and together they cover most areas. No 3 covers the central area. By transferring from this route to an adjoining loop, say the No 12 going west, you can get a pretty good city tour for just a couple dollars. For hitchhiking south on Avalon Peninsula, catch Nos 150 or 8, which will take you to Bay Bulls Rd. For the Trans Canada Hwy, take No 3 out to Avalon Mall, then the No 9.

The fare is $1.50 per ride. If you're in town for a while, get a 10-ride Metropass ($13.50).

Car If you want a rental car when arriving at the airport (or in town), make sure you reserve. Rates are about the same as anywhere else in Canada. Major companies include Budget (☎ 709-747-1234, 954 Topsail Rd) and Enterprise (☎ 709-739-6570, 835 Topsail Rd). Rent-A-Wreck (☎ 709-753-2277, 43 Pippy Place), with cheaper used cars, has compacts for $32 a day plus 100km free; it also has free pickup and delivery.

If you drive a rental car one way between St John's and Port aux Basques, you'll have to pay a drop-off fee of about $200.

Bicycle Hills and crazy intersections are not a cyclist's only nightmare in the city. The sewer grates run *parallel* with the road; thus, unless you want a bent rim and broken arm, pay strict attention.

To rent two wheels, try Canary Cycles (☎ 709-579-5972, 294 Water St). Top-of-the-line mountain bikes are $12 for two hours, $30 for a weekend.

Around St John's

NORTH & WEST OF ST JOHN'S
Marine Dr, north of St John's toward Torbay, goes past sweet coastal scenery. There are rocky beaches at both Middle Cove and Outer Cove – good for a walk or picnic. Offshore around **Torbay** is a fine whale-watching area; one or two lost puffins may also be around. Marine Dr ends at Pouch Cove, but a gravel road continues to Cape St Francis for good views. West of town, head to Topsail for a great view of Conception Bay and some of its islands.

West of St John's is **Bell Island**, which is worth a day trip. It's about a 20-minute drive and a 20-minute ferry ride (every hour 7am to 11pm; $5 car and driver, passenger $3) from town. The island sports a pleasant mélange of beaches, coastal vistas, lighthouses and trails. Miners here used to work in shafts under the sea at the world's largest submarine iron mine. **Iron Ore Mine & Museum** (☎ 709-488-2880; adult/senior/child $7/6/3; open 11am-7pm daily June-Sept) details the operation. The museum includes mining equipment, tools, and prints by the renowned portrait photographer Yousuf Karsh.

There are several places to stay on the island. One of the better ones is *Island Hideaway* (☎ 709-488-2846, fax 709-722-5526, Long Harry Rd), which has a dining room and good walking nearby. Singles/doubles are $50/55.

SOUTH OF ST JOHN'S

Some 10km south of St John's is **Petty Harbour**, filled with weathered boats, wharves and sheds on stilts and surrounded by high rocky hills. Production companies have used it for movie settings.

Orca Inn (☎/fax 709-747-9676, ☎ 877-747-9676, Main Rd) Singles/doubles $50/60. Each of the three rooms has a private bath, and the rate includes a full breakfast.

In **Goulds**, at the junction of Hwy 10 and the road to Petty Harbour in Bidgood's Plaza, don't miss *Bidgood's* (☎ 709-368-3125; open 9am-9pm Mon-Sat, noon-5pm Sun), a supermarket with a twist. It's known for its Newfoundland specialties, especially with locals, who stock up on their favorite items before returning to jobs on the mainland. Where else can you buy caribou steak, moose in a jar or seal-meat pie? Depending on the time of year, the selection may also include cod tongues, saltfish or lobster. And there are jars of the province's distinctive jams – try partridgeberry or the elite of the island's berries, bakeapple.

Bay Bulls & Witless Bay

This is a prime area for **whale-, iceberg- and bird-watching**. Three islands off Witless Bay and southward are preserved as the **Witless Bay Ecological Reserve** and represent one of the top seabird breeding areas

in eastern North America. Every summer, more than a million pairs of seabirds gather to breed, including puffins, kittiwakes, murres, cormorants and storm petrels.

No one is permitted on the islands, but tour boats do get close enough for you to consider taking earplugs as well as a camera and binoculars. The din overhead is incredible. The best months for visiting are June and July, which are also good for whale-watching – humpback and minke are fairly common here. Whales are seen into early August, and the humpback, with its acrobatics, is the most spectacular of all whales for its breaching performances. If you really hit the jackpot, in early summer, an iceberg might be thrown in too.

From May to October, numerous operators run highly recommended trips out to the colonies and the bays where whales congregate. The boats closest to the reserve are cheapest, because they all end up here anyway. The boats departing from farther away offer longer trips. You can't miss the operators – just look for signs off Route 10. Reservations are suggested.

Gatherall's (☎ 800-419-4253, Northside Rd) in Bay Bulls has several trips daily that include whale-watching and the bird colonies ($30, 2½ hours). Another here is **O'Brien's** (☎ 709-753-4850) out of Bay Bulls; tours ($30 to $35) depart several times daily during summer. O'Brien's also runs a shuttle bus from major hotels in St John's for $10.

In Witless Bay, **Murphy's Bird Island Tours** (☎ 709-334-2002, 888-783-3467) has good shorter trips ($25, 2 hours).

One of the cheaper and quicker ways to see aquatic life is farther south, through either **Molly Bawn Tours** (☎ 709-334-2621) in Mobile or **Ocean Adventure Tours** (☎ 709-334-3998), operating out of Bauline East, south of Tors Cove. These one-hour tours ($15/10 adult/child under 12 years) operate 8am to around 8pm and head for Great Island, just a 10-minute water jaunt from the docks.

Something new is the increasing availability of kayak tours. Seeing a whale from a kayak is certainly a thrill. **Bay Bulls Kayaking Tours** (☎ 709-334-3394) has three-hour trips at $45. **Wilderness Newfoundland** (☎ 709-747-6353), south in Cape Broyle, offers half-day ($50) and full-day ($105) trips with lunch.

NEWFOUNDLAND

On Hwy 10 in Witless Bay, there is a visitor information center (☎ 709-432-2820), open 9am to 8pm daily.

AVALON PENINSULA

The peninsula, more like an island hanging on to the rest of the province by a thin strip of land, is the most densely populated area of Newfoundland, with nearly half its population.

Conception Bay is lined with scores of small communities, but fishing villages dot the entire shoreline.

At Argentia, in the southwest, is the depot for the ferry connecting with Nova Scotia.

For hikers, the epic **East Coast Trail** stretches 520km from Cape St Francis all the way to Cape Race, making use of existing coastal trails and bucolic rural paths. It is part easy coastal walking, part tough wilderness trail. A 50km segment also connects with the 50km D'Iberville Trail in the Avalon Wilderness Area (see the following Southern Avalon section). The East Coast Trail Association (☎ 709-738-4453, W www .eastcoasttrail.com) has information. Maps are available at **The Outfitters** (☎ 709-579-445, 220 Water St), a camping and gear shop in St John's.

Southern Avalon Peninsula

Despite its proximity to St John's, this section of the province is very good for viewing wildlife and has several good parks. Routes 10 and 90, together comprising what's known as the Irish Loop, make for a good tour of the region.

La Manche Provincial Park There is excellent camping at this park (☎ 709-685-1823, 800-563-6353, fax 709-729-1100, Route 10) 53km south of St John's. It has 70 campsites ($10), many of them overlooking La Manche Pond, along with a day-use area and beach. It can fill up on weekends.

There are also two scenic trails that begin in the campground. The first is a 15-minute walk from the day-use area to a small waterfall. The second follows the fire-exit track from site No 59 to the remains of La Manche, a fishing village that was destroyed in 1966 by a fierce winter storm. It's about a 30-minute hike one way.

Fisherman's Landing (☎ 709-432-2450, Route 10) Prices $4-10. At Cape Broyle, this straightforward eatery with fabulous views serves up cheap but excellent seafood as well as sandwiches and other standard fare. Also note the historical murals on the walls.

Ferryland South a few kilometers along Hwy 10 is marvelously picturesque Ferryland, site of one of the earliest English settlements in North America. It dates to 1621 when Sir George Calvert, who later became Lord Baltimore, established a village, the Colony of Avalon. The town lasted for a few years before the long cold winters sent Calvert to Maryland in search of warmer weather. Other English families later arrived here, however, and maintained the colony until 1673, when a Dutch raid destroyed most of the town.

Aside from wandering and absorbing the seaside aesthetics, don't miss the **Colony of Avalon** site and museum (☎ 709-432-3200; adult/student & senior $5.75/3.50; open 9am-7pm daily June-early Sept, 9am-5:30pm daily May & mid-Sept–Oct). Displayed inside are many of the artifacts that have been recovered and preserved. It's a short walk to the four main dig areas and the field laboratory where everything from axes to bowls are being recovered and restored. Workers are at the dig sites 8am to 4:30pm Monday to Friday and 8am to 12:30pm some Saturdays, and the plaques really bring the site alive. Beyond the dig sites a very rough dirt road (it's walkable) leads to the 1870 **lighthouse**.

The village's former courthouse is now the small local **Historic Ferryland Museum** (☎ 709-432-2155, Route 10; admission $2; open 9am-5pm daily June-Sept) or you can climb the Gaze. This towering hill sits behind the museum and was so named by early settlers who used to climb it to watch for approaching warships or to escape the frequent pillages by the Dutch or the French. The view on a clear day makes mounting the hill worth the trouble.

Downs Inn (☎ 709-432-2808, 877-432-2808, fax 709-432-2659, Irish Loop Dr) Rooms $50-75. Once a convent, this inn has four rooms that come with full breakfast, and everything is close at hand.

Colony Cafe (☎ 709-432-2508, Route 10) Prices under $10. This small friendly café by the colony site serves carefully prepared meals with some seafood. It's open daily from May to September.

Avalon Wilderness Reserve In the interior of the peninsula is the huge Avalon Wilderness Reserve, with an increasingly large herd of woodland caribou, now numbering about 100,000. Permits, available at the La Manche Provincial Park office, are required to visit the area for hiking or canoeing. Caribou, however, can sometimes be seen right at the edge of Hwy 10. There are two posted areas for caribou crossings. The first is a 30km stretch between Chance Cove Provincial Park and Portugal Cove South, and the second is a 20km stretch between Trepassey and St Stephens. The former section near Portugal Cove South is particularly rife with caribou; one local reportedly stopped counting at 85 one morning. Unfortunately, days are rarely without thick fog; the Portugal Cove area holds an unofficial world record for most foggy days in a row. As migrating animals, caribou tend to move en masse, and often you spot the animals grazing in groups of 10 to 30. Even spotting a lone individual is a real treat, as they are impressive beasts rarely seen by those not living in the far north of Canada, Russia or Finland.

Mistaken Point Ecological Reserve At Portugal Cove South, taking the Cape Race exit brings you, after 16km, to the 5km-long Mistaken Point Ecological Reserve (☎ 709-729-2424; open all year), in which 620-million-year-old multicelled marine fossils – easily the oldest in North America – have been found. It's being considered for world heritage site status by Unesco. At the end of the road, to the east, is Cape Race, where a lighthouse keeper received the fateful last message from the *Titanic*.

Chance Cove Provincial Park (☎ 709-729-2424, Route 10) How about free camping! The campground here, south of Cappahayden, almost 7km toward the coast from Hwy 10, is little more than a gravel parking area for those with recreational vehicles. But tenters can walk up the bluff overlooking the cove to one of the most scenic regional campsites.

Trepassey Trepassey was the launching place of Amelia Earhart's renowned first-woman-across-the-Atlantic flight in 1928. The diminutive **Trepassey Museum** (admission $2; open July & Aug) has local histori-cal artifacts. Caribou are often seen on the road west from town.

Northwest B&B (☎ 709-438-2888, 877-398-2888) Rooms $45-60. There are two rooms with private bath and two without. A continental breakfast is included with the room.

Trepassey Motel (☎ 709-438-2934, fax 709-438-2722, Main Rd) Singles/doubles $55/59. This small motel has just 10 rooms but does offer a restaurant.

Along Hwy 90 The area from St Vincent's to St Mary's provides an excellent chance of seeing whales, particularly the humpback, which feeds close to shore. Halfway between the two villages is **Point La Haye Natural Scenic Attraction**, a sweeping pebbled beach overlooking St Mary's Bay. The lighthouse isn't much more than a light atop scaffolding. There are no official campsites here, but people occasionally set up on the beach.

On Hwy 90, **Salmonier Nature Park** (☎ 709-229-7888, Salmonier Line; admission free; open 10am-6pm daily June-Labor Day, 10am-4pm to Thanksgiving) is in the center of the Avalon Peninsula, 12km south of the junction with Hwy 1. A 2.5km trail through the woods takes you past indigenous fauna – moose, caribou, beaver – in their natural setting. There is also an interpretive center with exhibits and touch displays for children.

Conception Bay

Like the rest of eastern Newfoundland, Conception Bay is rich in history and coastal scenery (and well populated as befits its name). Much of the early history of Canada was played out here. **Bay de Verde** in the north can be reached in half a day's drive from St John's. Fleetline Bus Service (☎ 709-722-2608) connects St John's to Carbonear with a daily bus, except Sunday, and makes stops along the way.

Brigus Despite its small size, Brigus, set amid rocky cliffs 80km west from St John's, has a deserving reputation for its agreeable atmosphere. A former resident, Captain Robert Bartlett, was renowned as one of the foremost Arctic explorers in the 20th century. He made more than 20 expeditions into the Arctic region, including one in 1909 during which he cleared a trail in the ice that enabled US commander Robert Peary to make his celebrated dash to the North Pole.

NEWFOUNDLAND

Bartlett's house, **Hawthorne Cottage**, is a national historic site and museum (☎ *709-528-4004, Irishtown Rd; admission $2.55; open 10am-8pm daily mid-May–Nov)*.

Also in town is **Ye Olde Stone Barn Museum** (☎ *709-528-3391, 4 Magistrate's Hill; admission $1; open noon-6pm daily)*, which has a set of displays on Brigus' 200-year history. Nearby is the Brigus Tunnel, which was cut through rock in 1860 so Bartlett could easily access his ship in the deep cove on the other side.

In July and August, Sunday walking tours are presented with costumes, dancing and skits – worth catching for $5. Ask at the historic site for details.

There are more accommodations here than anywhere else on Conception Bay.

The Brittoner (☎ *709-528-3412, fax 709-528-3412, 12 Water St)* Singles/doubles with full breakfast $50/55. This Victorian home right in the middle of things provides private bathrooms.

Captain Bob's (☎ *709-685-5438, fax 709-834-6000, 6 Forge Rd)* Rates $50-55. Also right in the center, Bob's has three rooms.

North St Café (29 North St) Prices $2-7. Head to this quaint little cottage for a bite (fish cakes, quiche) or afternoon tea; it's open daily.

North along Hwy 70 is the turnoff to **Hibbs Cove**, 9km to the east at the end of Port de Grave Peninsula, another picturesque harbor and home of the **Fishermen's Museum** (☎ *709-786-3912; admission $2; open 10am-noon, 1pm-5pm Mon-Sat, 1pm-5pm Sun late June-early Sept)*. The small complex consists of a museum with pictures and artifacts depicting the trade at the start of the 20th century, a fishermen's home built in 1900 and a one-room schoolhouse. In **Port de Grave**, on the way to Hibbs Cove, the *fish market* sells everything from cod tongues and crab to salt fish, salmon and scallops.

Harbour Grace Up past Cupid's, where the first official English settlement of Newfoundland was attempted in 1610, Harbour Grace is where the Spanish and French, and pirates, had holed up since the early 1500s. There are several historic sites and a heritage district along Cochrane and Water Sts boasting various architectural styles. The old customs house was once the site of an erstwhile pirate headquarters.

The SS *Kyle* from 1913 can be viewed in the harbor.

Many of the first attempts to fly across the Atlantic departed from Harbour Grace, beginning in 1919. In 1932, four years after her flight from Trepassey on the Avalon Peninsula to Europe, Amelia Earhart took off from here and became the first woman to cross the Atlantic solo. The **Harbour Grace Airfield** (☎ *709-596-5901, Earhart Rd; open all year)* is designated a historic site.

Carbonear Island This island has had a tumultuous history, with international battles, pirate intrigues, shipwrecks and more recently, seal-hunt controversy. Carbonear Island is designated a historic site, and there are many examples of old architecture in town. The annual **Conception Bay Folk Festival** at the end of July is not to be missed. This three-day event (☎ *709-596-7877)* features traditional Newfoundland, Irish and folk music.

EJ Pratt (1883–1964), one of Canada's best-known poets, was born in Western Bay, and a national historic plaque here commemorates him.

Farther north up the coast, **Northern Bay Sands Park** (☎ *709-584-3465)*, an ex-provincial park, has beautiful beaches and camping. On the inland side is a good spot for freshwater swimming, as the ocean is far too cold. Tent sites $9.

At Bears Cove, near **Bay de Verde**, a short walk leads to dramatic views. **Baccalieu Island Ecological Reserve** *(inaccessible due to the cliffs and sanctuary status)* offshore hosts 11 species of seabird that breed here, including three million pairs of Leach's storm petrel, the largest such colony in the world. Where Hwy 70 ends at the tip of the peninsula, the countryside around **Grates Cove** features hundreds of rock walls used to wall vegetable gardens and pen livestock; the entirety is now a designated national historic site.

Trinity Bay

On the other side of the peninsula along Trinity Bay are several towns that exemplify the often wonderful place names of Newfoundland. How about the absolutely lovely Heart's Delight or Heart's Content?

Heart's Content The **Cable Station Provincial Historic Site** (☎ *709-583-2160, Hwy*

Fiery-red sunset over Cape Breton Island, Nova Scotia

Part of the fishing fleet, South Shore, Nova Scotia

Halifax architectural aesthetics: a mural on the wall of a brick building, Nova Scotia

Sand meeting grass near St Peters, Prince Edward Island National Park

Boat scenes, North Rustico, Prince Edward Island

Lighthouse at dusk, Prince Edward Island

Folksy spot to a sit a spell, North Rustico, Prince Edward Island

80; admission $2.50; open 10am-5:30pm daily June-Labor Day) tells the story of when the first transatlantic cable was laid here in 1866 and how the community played an important role in transatlantic communications for the next 100 years.

Legge's Motel (☎ 709-538-2929, fax 709-583-2939, near the historic site) Rates $45-60. This small establishment has seven self-contained housekeeping units, two cheaper simple motel-style rooms and a restaurant.

Dildo At the bottom of Trinity Bay, pretty Dildo (when you stop sniggering) is a good spot for whale-watching. Pothead (more sniggering) whales come in by the school, and humpbacks, a larger species, can also be seen in summer. Both can be viewed from the shore. The **Dildo Interpretation Center** *(☎ 709-582-2687; admission free; open daily July-Sept)* has exhibits on the area's 19th-century codfish hatchery, as well as the ongoing Dorset Eskimo archeological dig on Dildo Island.

In South Dildo is the **Whaling and Sealing Museum** *(☎ 709-582-2282; admission $2; open 11am-5pm Mon-Fri June-Sept)* has artifacts, photos and a stuffed seal.

Argentia

The southwest portion of the Avalon Peninsula is known primarily for Argentia, which has the large ferry terminal for boats to Nova Scotia. For ferry information, see the St John's section earlier. Newhook's Transportation (☎ 709-227-2552) connects both Argentia and Placentia with St John's by road. It's 130km to St John's or a good 90-minute drive.

The ferry arrives around 5am, so you shouldn't need to get a room since there's not much to see.

Fitzgerald's Pond Park (☎ 709-227-4488) Tent sites $10. This park is 25km north along Hwy 100.

Placentia

Nearby in Placentia, settled in 1662, are the remains of a French fort at **Castle Hill National Historic Site** *(☎ 709-227-2401; admission $2.50; open 8:30am-8pm daily July-Sept, 8:30am-4:30pm daily rest of year)*, with a visitors' center and fine views. In the early 1800s, Placentia – then Plaisance – was the

French capital of Newfoundland, and French attacks on the British at St John's were based from here.

The old **graveyard** by the Anglican church offers more history, as does **O'Reilly House Museum** *(☎ 709-227-5568, 48 Riverside Dr; admission $2; open 9am-8pm Mon-Fri, noon-8pm Sat & Sun mid-June–Sept)*. In a home built in 1902 and restored in 1989, it acts as a local museum offering details of both the house and the area. The **courthouse** and **Roman Catholic church** are other notable historic buildings. A boardwalk runs along the waterfront, and there is a beach.

Near Placentia, there is a section of the coast that is forested, a rather unusual sight here as so much of the entire provincial coastline is barren and rocky. Placentia has one hotel and two B&Bs.

Harold Hotel (☎ 709-227-2107, fax 709-227-7700, Main St) Rooms $50-90. This plain, central hotel, 5km from the ferry terminal, also has a restaurant.

Cape St Mary's

At the southern tip of the peninsula is **St Mary's Ecological Reserve**, a top-rate place for glimpsing seabirds. An unpaved road leads the 16km from Route 100 into the sanctuary, where there is an interpretive center *(☎ 709-729-2431; adult/child/family $3/2/7; open 9am-7pm daily May-Nov)* and a lighthouse. A 30-minute walk takes you to views of Bird Rock, the third-largest gannet-nesting site in North America. Its near-vertical cliffs rise more than 100m from the sea and provide ideal nesting conditions during summer for nearly 60,000 seabirds, including kittiwakes, murres and razorbills. During summer, guides are present to answer questions. Commercial boat trips cruise the coast and islands for birds and whales.

Eastern Newfoundland

This is the province's smallest region and consists of the area just west of the Avalon Peninsula on the edge of the main body of the island. Geographically it is also distinguished from the central portion of the province by the jutting peninsulas at each end: the Bonavista to the north and the Burin to the south.

The ferry for the islands of St Pierre and Miquelon departs from Fortune in the south. To this day, the islands are French possessions.

BONAVISTA PENINSULA

The Bonavista Peninsula has many flyspeck traditional fishing communities, including some of the oldest in the province. Some people claim that historic Trinity is the oldest town in North America. Terra Nova National Park preserves a section of the peninsula in its natural state.

Contact the Discovery Trail Tourism Association (☎ 709-464-3704, **W** www.the discoverytrail.org) for information on their fine walking trails around the peninsula.

Clarenville

This is the access point to the peninsula, and it's best to pass right through. The town does have a full range of services for travelers, including large food stores, a laundromat and a handful of hotels and B&Bs.

Island View Hospitality Home (☎ 709-466-2062, fax 466-2331, 128 Memorial Dr) Singles/doubles $39/45. Breakfast and evening snacks are included at this place with an ocean view just north of Clarenville on Hwy 230.

Southern Bay

Along the edge of Southern Bay, Hwy 235 has some splendid water views and a picnic spot with a view at Jiggin' Head Park. On the beaches here and around the Avalon Peninsula in late June and early July, millions of capelin – a small silver fish – get washed ashore by the tides. This is partially due to the spawning cycle and partially to being chased by hungry cod. People go down with buckets and bags to scoop up a free meal.

Bonavista
pop 5000

Strung out along the shore, Bonavista, at the end of the peninsula, offers history and charm. It was here where John Cabot landed on June 24, 1497, first seeing the 'new found land.' Later he drifted down to St John's harbor and stopped there. For his troubles, King Henry VII of England rewarded him

with the royal sum of £10. It wasn't until the 1600s that Bonavista became a permanent village, and from then on through the 1700s, the British and French battled over it as they did for other nearby settlements. Most visitors come for the **Ryan Premises National Historic Site** (☎ 709-468-1600, Ryans Hill Rd; adult/senior/family $2.50/2/6; open 10am-6pm daily mid-May–mid-Oct), an assemblage of six refurbished 19th-century outport fishing buildings originally used to grade, cure, barrel and store salted fish. An interpretive center features displays and frequent concerts and demonstrations.

In the center of town, the **Mockbeggar Property** (☎ 709-468-7300, Mockbeggar Rd; admission $2.50; open 10am-5:30pm daily mid-June-Thanksgiving) is the restored home of F Gordon Bradley, Newfoundland's first representative to the Canadian senate. A number of buildings dot the premises.

Just up the road at the waterfront is The Matthew (☎ 709-468-1493; adult/family $3/8; open 9am-8pm daily), a gorgeous replica of the ship Cabot sailed into Bonavista. Around the corner at the old courthouse is a whipping post where instant justice could be meted out.

The **Cape Bonavista Lighthouse** (☎ 709-468-7444, Hwy 230; admission $2.50; open 10am-5:30pm daily mid-June–Thanksgiving), dating from 1843, has been restored and is a provincial historic site with period-garbed guides. Don't miss the puffins zooming on and off the little island (best in morning and evening) beside the lighthouse.

On the way from town is **Landfall Park** (Cape Shore Rd), with its statue of John Cabot.

Dungeon Provincial Park (free admission) is the site of an unusual rock formation on the shoreline. The park itself is little more than a parking area and an interpretive display, but from the top of these headland cliffs you can view a handful of sea stacks along the coastline of Spillar's Cove. More impressive is the Dungeon, a hole along the shoreline that is 250m in circumference, 15m deep and has two channels where the sea roars in and out. In early summer, whales may be seen off the coast.

Outside of town at the village of Maberly on Hwy 238, you can get views of an offshore island where thousands of seabirds roost. Principal species are puffins, kittiwakes and murres. There is an excellent 17km coastal hiking trail from Maberly to Little Catalina.

If you want to stay here, you can stake a tent or hole up in a B&B. Camping is not allowed officially at Dungeon Provincial Park, but there is *Paradise Farm Trailer Park* (☎ 709-468-1150) It's 7km away on Hwy 230 on a 65-acre farm. Sites are $9 to $15. At *White's B&B* (☎ 709-468-7018, 21 Windlass Dr), rooms cost $45 to $55. This place with an ocean view rents bikes and provides a full breakfast.

Shirran's (☎ 709-722-7741) and Bonavista Cabs (☎ 709-468-2457) charge $25 from St John's. Marsh Taxi (☎ 709-468-7715) and Venture Bus Lines (☎ 709-722-4249) also cover parts of the peninsula, including Southern Bay. Between them all, there are trips every day except weekends.

Port Union

The Fisherman's Protective Union was formed here in 1910, and a monument honors its founder. At this ice-free port, fish-processing plants and one of the province's largest trawler fleets are struggling to survive the slight cod stocks. For history, check out the **Port Union Historical Museum** (☎ 709-469-2159, Main St; admission $2; open 11am-5pm daily mid-June–mid-Sept) in the former train station. The home of Sir William Ford Coaker, founder of the union, is now a small museum known as the **Bungalow** (☎ 709-469-2728, Bungalow Hill; admission $4; open 10am-5pm daily mid-June–mid-Sept). It's full of period artifacts.

Trinity

Walkable and very historic Trinity is one of the province's most eye-pleasing communities. Though somewhat isolated, it generates a fair bit of summer visitor traffic.

First visited by Portuguese explorer Corte-Real in 1500 and established as a town in 1580, Trinity might be the oldest town on the entire continent. Many buildings along the narrow streets have been restored, and much of the diminutive town has national heritage designation. There are about half a dozen historic sites or museums to visit.

Trinity Museum (☎ 709-464-2244, Church Rd; admission $2; open 10am-7pm daily mid-June–mid-Sept) has over 2000 local artifacts, as well as the oldest fire engine in North America, dating to 1811.

West St has several sites virtually side by side. The **Lester Garland Premises** (☎ 709-464-2042; admission $2.50; open 10am-5pm daily mid-June–Thanksgiving) is a Georgian brick house and home of the first speaker of the House of Assembly. The **Interpretation Centre** (☎ 709-729-0592; admission $1; open 10am-5pm daily June-Oct) has information on the history, houses and buildings in town. From there swing past **Green Family Forge**, a blacksmith museum (admission $1; same hours as above). They have been forging iron pieces here for shipbuilders since 1750, with the present building dating back to 1895.

Hiscock House Provincial Historic Site (☎ 709-464-2042, Church Rd; admission $2.50; open 10am-5pm daily mid-June–Thanksgiving) is a restored merchant's home, furnished to the 1910 period.

Ryan Building (same telephone, admission and hours as the Hiscock House) is another provincial historic site. It has been restored to portray the general store owned by the Ryan family from 1902 to 1952. Finally, venture out to **Fort Point**, where you'll find four cannons embedded in the ground, the remains of the British fortification from 1745.

In New Bonaventure, 14km down the road from Trinity, is the **Cape Random Film Set** (admission free; open 9am-7:30pm daily June-Oct), where the international television miniseries was shot in 2000. The site re-creates a fishing community of the early 1800s.

The **Skerwink Trail** is a fabulous coastal walking path from the end of Dogberry Rd (also called Dog Cove Rd) in Port Rexton, affording spectacular views. Get a map at the Dockside Restaurant and Gallery.

Organized Tours For a good, entertaining and inexpensive ($8) overview of local history, try **Trinity Walking Tours** (☎ 709-464-2042).

Ocean Contact (☎ 709-464-3269), a whale-watching and research organization working out of the Village Inn on Taverners Path, offers whale-watching expeditions ($55) in a 9m rigid-hull inflatable and all-inclusive, more expensive multiday trips in its larger boat.

More economical is **Atlantic Adventures** (☎ 709-781-2255), using a sailboat for its

NEWFOUNDLAND

whale-watching tours. Several tours a day are offered ($35, 2½ hours). Contact the company at the Dock Restaurant (see Places to Stay & Eat).

Boat tours should be booked at least a day ahead.

Places to Stay & Eat *Lockston Path Provincial Park* (☎ 709-464-3553, Route 236, Port Rexton) Tent sites $11. Campers can head 5km up Hwy 236 to this park.

Trinity Loop Fun Park (☎ 709-464-2171, Route 239, look for signs) Camping free. This strange place has Ferris wheels, pony rides, a miniature train and large gravel areas where it allows anybody, especially RVers, to camp. Within the complex is a store, restaurant and a laundromat in a boxcar.

Village Inn (☎ 709-464-3269, fax 709-464-3700, Taverner's Path) Singles/doubles start at $60. Ocean Contact operates from this historic and popular inn. Films and slides on whales and other sea life are screened.

Trinity Cabins (☎ 709-464-3657, fax 709-464-3764, Route 239) 2-person cabins $50-55. The housekeeping cabins (with cooking facilities) here, which date from 1948, are said to have been the first tourist accommodations in the province. For the brave, there's a beach nearby.

There are about a half-dozen B&Bs.

Beach B&B (☎ 709-464-3695, Church Rd) Rooms $55-65. Right in the center of town, the Beach provides a full breakfast.

Campbell House (☎/fax 709-464-3377, ☎ 877-464-7700, High St) Rooms $80-100. More upscale is this beautifully restored historic house from 1840. Others can be found in nearby Trinity East, Port Rexton and Trouty.

Eriksen Premises (☎ 709-464-3698, fax 709-464-2104, West St) Rooms $80-110. Meals $10-20. The best meal in town can be found at this inn. The delightful little gourmet restaurant on the 1st floor consists of two small rooms, offering lunch, afternoon tea or dinner.

Cheaper seafood can be found at the casual *Dock Restaurant* (☎ 709-464-2133, beside the town wharf), from where the Atlantic Adventures sailboat embarks.

Entertainment *Rising Tide Theatre* (☎ 888-464-3377, by the ocean near the Lester Garland Premises) Tickets $10/14/33 day/night/with dinner. Performances 2pm Wed, Sat & Sun. This theater performs an entertaining outdoor drama on the history of Trinity, with a Ryan slant. The show is part of 'Theatre in the Bight,' a three-month-long historical pageant (June to October) of different theatrical forms in and around Trinity.

Rocky's Place (☎ 709-464-3400, High St) Enjoy traditional music and dancing here every Tuesday at 10pm.

Terra Nova National Park

The Trans Canada Hwy 240km west of St John's and 80km east of Gander splits this park (☎ 709-533-2801; adult admission $3.25/9.25 one/four days, family $6.50/19.50 one/four days, free mid-Oct–mid-May) that typifies the regional geography. The admission fee includes the interpretation center and access to all the trails, beach, picnic sites, etc.

The rocky, jagged coastline on beautiful Bonavista Bay gives way to long bays, inland lakes, ponds, bogs and hilly woods. There's canoeing, kayaking, fishing, hiking, camping, sandy beaches, even swimming in Sandy Pond. Lots of wildlife – moose, bear, beaver, otter and bald eagles – may be seen, and from May to August, icebergs are commonly viewed off the coast.

Unfortunately, for information you have to get halfway into the park, to **Saltons Marine Interpretation Centre** (Hwy 1; open 9am-9pm daily June-Sept, 9am-5pm daily May & Oct) north of Newman Sound. Hands-on exhibits and other displays can take up a morning. The touch tank with sea creatures is fun, if you can stand the cold water. The center also has the Starfish Eatery, with light meals and some seafood.

Hiking & Canoeing Terra Nova has 14 trails, totaling nearly 100km. The Malady Head Trail is a roundtrip of 4km to the edge of a headland cliff with stunning views of Southwest Arm and Broad Cove. Sandy Pond Trail is an easy 3km loop around the pond and through a bog. From Newman Sound Campground you can hike the Coastal Trail and see marine life along the shoreline. There's also the 9km Old Trails network of small trails from Sandy Cove to the historic fishing community of Salvage, a mixture of gentle and demanding hikes.

There are eight backcountry areas, six accessible via trail, canoe or water taxi from the interpretation center; another two are canoe-in only, via the Sandy Pond–Dunphy's Canoe Route, a 10km paddle that has one short portage. Canoes can be rented at Sandy Pond, where the canoe trails begin. Two more canoe trails exist, totaling 17km one way. There are campsites ($8 per party), and you must obtain a backcountry permit from the interpretation center or the administration building in the off-season. Reservations are a good idea, particularly for the Sandy Pond–Dunphy's route. Ocean Watch

will also drop backpackers at the Newman Sound outports during its regular trips. That would reduce the hike to South Board Cove to 17.5km and to Minchin Cove to 14km.

The granddaddy of all backpacking opportunities is the Outport Loop, a 50km epic trail now completed – or as completed as it gets. This is a serious trail, with topo map and compass required. Parts are unmarked – not to mention mucky and wet. Only serious and prepared hikers should try the whole loop. It is possible to cheat via a water taxi. Certainly get ranger advice before setting off on this rugged but recommended adventure.

Moose on the Loose

Though the moose is a fairly common animal across Canada, it is mainly found in the less populated, heavily forested northern regions. Nowhere in Canada are you as likely to see one as in Newfoundland. There are some 40,000 of them here, and many of them live close to towns and roads, including the Trans Canada Hwy. This, of course, increases the chances of getting a good look at one but also presents some hazards. There is more than one moose-vehicle collision per day across the province, and smacking into a beast the height of a horse weighing 400kg, with antlers nearly 2m across, is more wildlife than most people care for.

Moose tend to like the highways for a number of reasons. The open space makes walking easy; there is usually more breeze, meaning fewer insects; and in spring the salt from winter de-icing makes a nice treat. For these reasons, they also enjoy the train tracks, a habit that decreased their population at the rate of some 2000 per year until the train service was discontinued.

The areas of heaviest concentration are well marked, and signs should be heeded, particularly when traveling after dark, which is when most accidents occur. About 90% of the run-ins take place between 11pm and 4am. If you do see a moose on or beside the road, slow down and, if it doesn't want to move, approach slowly with the lights off, as they seem to get mesmerized by the beams.

Get out and take pictures if you like; moose are generally not aggressive and are very impressive, if unusual-looking, animals. They can be unpredictable, however, and anything of this size should not be approached too closely or startled. During rutting (mating) season in October and November, the males (bulls) can become very belligerent and downright ornery; it's a good time to stay in the car and well out of their way.

Calves are born in spring, and throughout the summer, it is not uncommon to see a cow moose with her young. Females and their young do not have antlers. An adult male grows a 'rack' of antlers each summer, only to have it fall off each autumn.

Organized Tours Excellent day trips offered by **Ocean Watch Tours** (☎ 709-533-6024) depart from behind the interpretation center. The three-hour trip ($40), departing 9am daily, may include working researchers and specializes in wildlife, seeking out whales, seals and birds. The company's fjord tour ($32) explores the fjords and islands and sometimes stops in at old abandoned outports. It leaves Newman Sound at 1pm and 4pm. An outport sunset cruise ($28) departs at 7pm.

Also here is **Terra Nova Adventures** (☎ 709-533-9797, 888-533-8687), with popular 2½-hour kayak tours ($45) twice daily. There are also full-day coastal tours ($120). All tours are May to October and subject to demand. Reservations are advised.

Fifteen kilometers from the west gate of the park in Burnside are the archeological sites administered by the **Burnside Heritage Foundation** (☎ 709-677-2474). These are popular with parkgoers. The Quarry is the largest aboriginal quarry ever found, and the Beaches is the largest Beothuk settlement discovered. The latter has the only Beothuk grave ever found. Tour boats to the sites take 20 minutes; while waiting, you can visit the field laboratory and museum in Burnside, open 10am to 8pm daily. If you book early, you can even help scientists dig.

Places to Stay Even though Terra Nova has nearly 600 sites, on weekends in summer travelers should arrive a bit early or book a site at ☎ 866-533-3186.

Newman Sound Campground Tent sites $14-18. This is the park's main campground. The Campground Hiking Trail is good for moose viewing. Also here is **Newman Sound Service Center** (☎ 709-533-9133), with groceries, a laundromat and bicycle rentals.

Malady Head Campground Tent sites $12. This more basic campground is at the north end of the park.

Commercial lodging can be found outside the park, most notably at Eastport at the north end and Port Blandford in the south.

White Sails Inn & Cabins (☎ 709-677-3400, 38 Beach Rd, Eastport) Rates $40-80. There are standard, hotel-like rooms or eight individual units.

BURIN PENINSULA

This southern peninsula has been the base for European fishing boats since the 1500s. The Grand Banks off the peninsula (part of the continental shelf) teem with fish, or at least they did until the early 1990s, when stocks plummeted.

Sadly, the southern coast ferry route from Port aux Basques to Terrenceville was shortened in the mid-1990s. Terrenceville, already depressed from the depleted cod fishery, was hit hard by the loss of the ferry business and subsequently lost its St John's bus service.

But from the capital, Cheeseman's Bus Service (☎ 709-753-7022) goes to Marystown ($30) at 3:30pm daily; the return trip is at 8am. Foote's Taxi (☎ 709-832-0491, 800-866-1181) goes all the way to Fortune ($35) at 4pm; the return trip is at 8am.

The MV *Northern Whale* ferries passengers and freight between Bay L'Argent, Recontre East and Pool's Cove across Fortune Bay. But Bay L'Argent is far north of the highlights on the Burin Peninsula and Pool's Cove is very far from Harbour Breton, or anything else really. If you do go, no buses serve Pool's Cove; you'll have to contact Hickey's Bus Service (☎ 709-885-2523), which serves Harbour Breton and Grand Falls/Windsor. The ferry is daily in summer; all told, getting to Pool's Cove from Bay L'Argent would take over three hours and cost $6.50.

Marystown

Although this is the largest town on the peninsula, there is not much for the visitor unless you're desperate for a McDonald's. There is also a tourist center (☎ 709-279-1211) on Hwy 210. It's open 8:30am to 9pm Monday to Friday, 10am to 9pm weekends.

Dock Point B&B (☎ 709-279-4570, fax 709-279-3224, 16 King's Rd) Rooms $45-55. Breakfast is included at this two-room place close to the shoreline.

Frenchman's Cove Provincial Park (☎ 709-826-2753, Route 213) Tent sites $9. You can camp and swim at this park 11km away at Garnish.

Burin

Settled by fishers from Europe in the 1700s, Burin is one of the oldest towns on the south coast. It is actually a picturesque series of villages sparsely scattered around coves and lumpy, treeless hills.

Burin is still struggling to maintain its important role in the Grand Banks and has a major trawler repair facility as well as a processing plant. Crab and lobster fishing have kept many of the trawlers afloat since the cod collapse.

In the town of Burin itself, there is **Burin Heritage Museum** (☎ 709-891-2217, Main at Union St; admission $2; open 10am-8pm daily mid-June–Oct), which consists of two historical homes and a small park dotted with marine engines and winches. Nearby is **Captain Cook's Lookout Trail**, picked up by turning off Main St at St Patrick's Elementary School and following the side street to its end. It's a 20-minute walk to the lookout view.

St Lawrence

St Lawrence is a mining town with the only deposits of fluorspar in Canada. It was once the world's largest producer. Although this is no longer the case, the mine still operates, and the **St Lawrence Miner's Museum** (☎ 709-873-2222, Route 220; admission $2; open 9am-9pm daily) outlines its history.

From St Lawrence to Lawn, Hwy 220 rises steadily over a series of hills and ridges to provide some grand views of the coast and numerous opportunities to hike to the top of rocky knobs for even better views. There are small community parks with *free camping* at both Point au Gaul and Point May. **Point May Park** is an especially scenic spot to spend the night. Located right on Hwy 220 north of the town toward Grand Bank, the small park overlooks the French islands. The only facilities here are a pair of outhouses and a parking lot.

Grand Bank

Its role now diminished, this was one of the main centers of the early Grand Banks fishery. The Burin Peninsula long served as the base for the famous Grand Banks fishing grounds. You can pick up the brochure *Grand Bank Heritage Walk* for a self-guided tour through town that will explain the varied 1880s vintage architecture of the homes, churches and Water St storefronts. Hikers will like the **Marine Hike**, a 6km trail leaving from Christian's Rd off Hwy 220 and tracing Admiral's Beach. Another 5km trail climbs 108m to the top of Bennett's Hill and proffers grand vistas.

The **Southern Newfoundland Seamen's Museum** (☎ 709-832-1484, Marine Dr; admission $2.50; open 9am-4:30pm daily May-Oct), at the edge of town, depicts both the

The Grand Banks

The fabulous portion of the Atlantic Ocean known as the Grand Banks, lying just southeast and southwest of Cape Race, is the southern part of the Avalon Peninsula, is one of the prime reasons why anybody ever bothered with the New World. It was in 1497 that John Cabot, an Italian working for England, first put down a net and couldn't believe his eyes when he saw it bulging with fish. It wasn't long before other Europeans began to arrive and set up fishing communities on the shores of Newfoundland. After 500 years of serious plundering, it remains one of the world's best fishing grounds. However, in the early 1990s the warning bells finally went off, when everybody realized that the dominant species, cod, had finally been reduced to alarmingly small numbers. Biologists, fishers and the government are now working on allowing the stocks to replenish.

The Banks are a series of submarine plateaus stretching from northwest to southeast about 80km out to sea from Cape Race. They cover an area about 500km long by 300km wide, with a depth ranging from 5m to 350m. Though mostly in the Labrador Current, the waters are met by the Gulf Stream, and this blending of the warm and cold gives rise to the legendary fogs. It also helps plankton (tiny marine plants and animals) to thrive, and this food source results in the millions of fish. The main catch has always been cod, but there are also halibut, flounder and herring, among others. Boats come from around the world to fill their hulls, notably from Norway, Japan, Portugal, Spain and Russia. Canada has imposed restrictions and regulations but has an impossible task in trying to enforce its limits and authority.

As well as the fog, nasty storms and marauding icebergs are hazards that fishers have had to contend with through the centuries. In the 1980s oil was discovered in parts of the Banks, raising another potential threat to this unique biological resource.

NEWFOUNDLAND

era of the banking schooner and the changes in the fishery over the years. Its collection of model sailing ships is impressive. Also in town is **George C Harris House** (☎ 709-832-1574, 16 Water St; admission $2; open 10am-8pm daily July-Sept), with rooms housing local artifacts.

The Grand Bank Heritage Society runs the **Summer Theatre Festival** (☎ 709-832-1574, Route 220), with historical drama performances ($8) and dinner theater performances ($20). Performances are Wednesday through Sunday in July and August.

Thorndyke (☎ 709-832-0820, 33 Water St) Rooms $55-65. This imposing but pleasant designated historic home makes a fine place to stay. It's busy, so call for reservations. From the roof, there are views of the town and bay.

Fortune

Fortune is the jumping-off point for trips to St Pierre and Miquelon, and 20,000 people a year pass through on their way to the islands. Aside from looking after visitors, many of the townspeople are employed at the large fish-processing plant. There is also a shipbuilding and repair depot.

Fair Isle Motel (☎ 709-832-1010, 888-275-1098, fax 709-832-0009, Grandview Blvd) Singles/doubles $59/64. This recently renovated motel, with 10 rooms, is currently your only option for lodging.

St Pierre & Miquelon

Once called the Islands of 11,000 Virgins, these two dabs of land, lying 16km west off Newfoundland's Burin Peninsula, belong to France. The tiny islands represent the only French holdings left in North America. The 6000 residents drink French wine, eat baguettes and pay for it in euros.

First claimed by France in the 1500s, the islands were turned over to the British along with Cape Breton after the Seven Years' War. They were then ceded to the French by the British in 1783 under the Treaty of Paris. Battles over fishing rights continued with Newfoundland, and the islands changed hands a couple more times until 1815. Since

then, they have remained under French control. The disputes over territorial fishing and resource rights have continued though, becoming notably acrimonious periodically from the 1960s to the mid-'90s. Negotiations in the past decade have given France control of a zone that extends for 24 miles off St Pierre and Miquelon, as well as a 17km-wide corridor running south 300km toward international waters.

An interesting aside is St Pierre's role during the Prohibition period in the USA. In the 1920s, Canada would legally export what amounted to oceans of booze to the French island, where US rumrunners would pick it up to take home.

As in so much of Atlantic Canada, the main source of livelihood has always been fishing and the supplying of fishing boats. The region's decreased fishery, most notably the depleted and now more regulated cod industry, has seriously undermined the economic viability of the islands. France has paid some compensation to those put out of work and aims to boost the tourism industry. The mother country is also putting money in the new airport and other public-works programs.

The archipelago consists of numerous islands. St Pierre, although not the largest, is the principal one; it's the most populated, and its town of the same name is the largest on the islands.

Miquelon is actually two islands separated by a narrow isthmus of sand. The northern section, Great Miquelon, has most of the people and a small town. The southern island, called Langlade or Little Miquelon, is quite wild. The remaining islands are all very small.

Canadian and US visitors need neither passports nor visas for a visit, but a good ID such as a birth certificate or driver's license with photograph is recommended. For citizens of the European Union (EU), Switzerland and Japan, passports are required. All other nationals need both a passport and a visa. These details should be confirmed prior to arrival.

Note that the time on the islands is half an hour ahead of Newfoundland time. Also keep in mind that making a phone call from Newfoundland to the islands is an international call as far as the long-distance carriers are concerned. The area code for the French islands is ☎ 508. Note also that Canadian and US calling cards are not valid. Local cards can be bought.

Merchants gladly take Canadian money on the islands, but prices are usually quoted in euros (€). The islands are more expensive than Newfoundland. On the plus side is the duty-free shop for alcohol, cigarettes, etc. Also, you may need a 220-volt electrical adapter, and French plugs are round. Beware that there are no cash machines on the islands.

Lastly, note that some stores are closed on Saturday afternoons, most are closed on Sunday, and many are closed between noon and 1:30pm every day. Restaurants and bakeries remain open. Gotta love that Latin attitude.

Information

The St Pierre Tourist Office (☎ 508-412384, 800-565-5118 off the islands, **w** www .st-pierre-et-miquelon.com) can provide a complete accommodations listing. Calling the islands is like calling overseas. Other than any 800 numbers, you must dial ☎ 011 508 (the country and area codes) before the local number.

While French is widely spoken, many people are bilingual. Most importantly, French wine can be bought at the corner stores.

Several annual holidays and festivals occur in July and August. Bastille Day is on July 14. On August 4, Jacques Cartier's arrival in the islands in 1536 is celebrated. The following week, a two-day festival on Miquelon recalls the Acadian heritage, and later in the month, another two-day event on St Pierre celebrates the Basque heritage. From mid-July to the end of August, folk dances are often held in St Pierre's square.

Things to See & Do

In St Pierre, you can see the small **museum**, which outlines the island's history, and the **cathedral**. Also, visit the interesting **French cemetery**.

Outside town, there is a lighthouse at **Gallantry Head** and good views from Cap aux Basques. Out in the harbor, a 10-minute boat ride away, is **Île aux Marins**, with a another small museum. You can take a bilingual guided tour around the island,

which had its own fishing village at the start of the 20th century. For details on this and other tour possibilities, see the Information Centre on Place du Général de Gaulle.

Miquelon, 45km away, is less visited and less developed. The people here are largely of Acadian background, while St Pierre's inhabitants are French (mainly from Brittany and Normandy) and Basque.

The village of **Miquelon**, centered around the church, is at the northern tip of the island.

From nearby **l'Étang de Mirande**, a walking trail leads to a lookout and waterfall. From the bridge in town, a scenic 25km road leads across the isthmus to **Langlade**. The island of Langlade remains pretty much the same as it has always been. There are some summer cottages but no year-round inhabitants – human ones, that is. There are some wild horses and smaller animals such as rabbits, and around the rocky edges and lagoons you'll see seals and birds.

Places to Stay & Eat

St Pierre has around a dozen hotels and guesthouses (pensions). The latter tend to be more reasonably priced and often provide breakfast. Accommodations can be tight in the high season, so you may want to check before you go.

Le Paris Madrid (☎ 508-412933, fax 508-414899, 14 Rue du 11 Novembre) Singles/doubles €26/30. One of the cheapest places to stay around, this white two-story hotel has 11 rooms that come with a complimentary breakfast.

Hotel Robert (☎ 508-412419, 888-959-8214, 10/12 Rue du 11 Novembre) Singles/doubles €84/111. Situated on the waterfront right next door to Le Paris Madrid, the Hotel Robert is the largest hotel in St Pierre, with 54 rooms, and it is quite spiffy as well.

Pension Roland Vigneau (☎ 508-413867, 12 Rue des Basques) Singles/doubles €28/31. This modest B&B has four rooms, and meals are available.

Miquelon has its own tourist office (☎ 508-416187) and several places to stay.

Maxotel (☎ 508-416457, fax 508-416594, 42 Rue Sourdeval) Singles/doubles €54/58. This place by the sea has some rooms with kitchens.

Hotel-Bar l'Escale (☎ 508-416456, fax 508-416050, 30 Rue Victor Briand) Singles/doubles €34/37. This central hotel has six rooms, each with private bath. Rooms include breakfast.

There are small **campgrounds** at l'Étang de Mirande and Le Cap near town.

As might be expected on French islands, restaurants are numerous relative to the size of the population, and the food is good. In both St Pierre and Miquelon, there are several places serving traditional French food. St Pierre has more choice and a number of less expensive places for sandwiches, pizza and the like. There are also several bakeries and pastry shops.

Le Maringouin'fre (☎ 508-419125, 22 Rue Général Leclerc) has burgers and good crêpes.

Le Feu de Braise (☎ 508-419160, 14 Rue Albert Briand) has both traditional French and Italian dishes. Both are open daily.

Getting There & Away
Air Air Saint-Pierre (☎ 508-410000) flies from St John's ($123, 45 minutes), Montréal, Halifax and Sydney (Nova Scotia) April through October. Information and reservations can be had through Air Canada.

Ferry There is one ferry company, SPM Express (☎ 888-959-8214 in Newfoundland), but tour companies such as St Pierre Tours (☎ 709-832-0429 in Fortune) and Lake's Travel (☎ 709-832-2006 in Fortune) use the company's boats and book its tickets, too.

From Fortune, the MV *Maria Galanta* departs at 1:30pm every Friday and Sunday from April to November and daily in July and August for the one-hour crossing. The roundtrip fare is $73/37 adult/child. It leaves St Pierre at 2:45pm. Definitely double-check the schedule ahead of time.

During July and August, there is a special one-day roundtrip excursion service offered that leaves Fortune early in the morning and returns late in the afternoon. It is available through St Pierre Tours, and the price is the same as a regular ticket, although it is a different (slower) vessel. If you have a special interest, you may be able to get a day trip to Miquelon alone in peak season, but ask for current status.

St Pierre Tours, with offices in both St John's (☎ 709-722-3892, 888-959-8214, 116 Duckworth St) and Fortune (☎ 709-832-0429, 5 Bayview St) offers various package tours that include ferry crossings, room and continental breakfast. The price is $135 per person, based on double occupancy of a room for a night at Hotel Robert. For roundtrip transportation from St John's, it's another $100 each person.

Getting Around
From May to mid-October the MV *Maria Galanta* travels to and from Miquelon Tuesday, Friday and Sunday twice daily. The rest of the year there is only one trip daily. The roundtrip fare is €20, less for children, and the trip takes about an hour. Other ferries ply the hour-long route to Langlade (€16 roundtrip) and Île aux Marins (€3 roundtrip).

In St Pierre rent a 'rosalie,' a four-wheeled bicycle that comes in two sizes; two- and four-person models are available. There are regular bicycles as well, or small motorbikes. In both St Pierre and Miquelon, tours on horseback are offered.

Also on St Pierre, there are tours by bus and mini-train, and on Miquelon a bus trip takes visitors around the island and across the isthmus to Langlade. In a couple of days much can be seen on foot.

Central Newfoundland

The vast, little-populated central area is the largest geographic region of the island portion of the province. Gorgeous, village-packed Notre Dame Bay is a Newfoundland highlight.

From Lewisporte, ferries depart for Labrador. The southern area is mostly inaccessible, lake-filled woodland. One road leads down to the coast, linking many small remote villages to the rest of the province.

GANDER
pop 13,000
Gander is at the crossroads of the east-west Trans Canada Hwy and Hwy 330, which leads to Notre Dame Bay. It is a convenient stopping point but is one of the province's least attractive places. It's a suburb with no downtown.

Gander served the first regular transatlantic flights and then, during WWII, was a major link for planes on their way to Europe. The first formation of bombers made in the USA for the UK left here in February 1940. The location was chosen because it is close to Europe but far enough inland to be free of the coastal fog that often plagues St John's.

Numerous US and Canadian airlines also used Gander for transatlantic flights beginning in the 1930s. The airport, a major Aeroflot refueling stop, was long known as the site of thousands of defections from Russia, Cuba and former Eastern Bloc countries – the plane touched down and passengers asked for political asylum. These days it is more likely the hopeful arrivals will seek refugee status, which permits them to stay in Canada until their case is heard. Recently many flights were rerouted here after the 2001 terrorist attacks in the USA.

There is a tourist chalet (☎ 709-256-7110) on the Trans Canada Hwy at the central exit into town, and it's open 9am to 9pm daily during summer.

Gander is a main stop for the buses of DRL (☎ 709-651-3434), which has a ticket office at the airport. A bus for St John's departs at 5pm daily, and the bus for Port aux Basques departs at 12:48pm daily.

Things to See & Do
Aviation attractions have all been consolidated just west of the tourist chalet at the **North Atlantic Aviation Museum** *(☎ 709-256-2923, Trans Canada Hwy; adult/senior/child $3/2/2; open 9am-9pm daily in summer, 9am-5pm off-season)*. Exhibits detail Newfoundland air contributions to WWII, the history of navigation and the Battle of Britain, and there are numerous reconstructions of planes and controls.

At the airport (☎ 709-256-3905) is a small aviation display and a huge tapestry depicting the history of flight. The display is in the passengers' waiting lounge, but if you don't have a ticket, ask the security officials – they might let you in. Some people have received an impromptu tour of the ATC Tower or Gander Flight Training, though advance notice is requested.

The **Silent Witness Monument**, just east of town, south off the Trans Canada Hwy, tenderly marks the site of a horrendous early morning crash in December 1985, in which 248 US soldiers returning home from the Middle East for Christmas were killed along with eight crew members. The swath of forest taken out by the crash is astounding. The possible causes are still debated.

Just east of the tourist chalet off the highway is the **Thomas Howe Demonstration Forest** *(☎ 709-256-4693; admission free; open daily)*, with 2km of trails through forest and wetlands revealing the life and importance of the native boreal forest.

Places to Stay & Eat
Jonathan's Pond Campground *(☎ 709-424-3007, Route 330)* Tent sites $10. Though 15km north of town, this is a fine wooded campground with swimming. Beware of moose on the highway at night.

Square Pond Park *(☎ 709-533-2738)* Tent sites $10. East of town 28km is this second choice for campsites.

There are numerous motels, mostly chains, on the highway but they're decidedly pricey.

Country Inn Motel *(☎ 709-256-4005, 877-956-4005, 315 Gander Bay Rd)* Rooms $44-50. With just nine rooms north of the highway, this is a quiet, inexpensive choice.

Friend's B&B *(☎ 709-256-4560, 877-256-4560, 66 Bennett Dr)* Singles/doubles $45/55. A complete breakfast is included with the four rooms at this very hospitable place.

The usual fast-food outlets are on Airport Dr. In the shopping center on the corner of Elizabeth St and Airport Dr, the lavishly decorated Chinese **Highlight** *(☎ 709-256-3347)* is better, offering meals

---

What Are You Talking About?

Unique words and expressions pepper the language here, sometimes even confounding residents. But then, it's said there are about 60 dialects. The authoritative source is the *Dictionary of Newfoundland English*, but numerous slimmer volumes provide examples of many of the most fun and colorful examples. A 'streel' is an untidy person; 'whizzgigging' is a mix of whispering and giggling. Many other unusual words are seen and heard in the place names across the province.

NEWFOUNDLAND

for $4-8. Beware that the restaurant closes at 8pm daily.

Giovanni's Café (☎ 709-651-3535), down a few doors, has good coffee, wraps and some vegetarian and Mexican-style items all under $5.

NOTRE DAME BAY AREA

This coastal area north of Gander is the jewel of Central Newfoundland. About 80 little villages are found around the bay nestled in small coves or clinging to the rocky shoreline. From Gander there are two road loops – one through Lewisporte, the other eastward to Wesleyville – which make good circular tours.

Offshore is a large cluster of islands, including Fogo, New World and Twillingate, which should not be missed and where whales and icebergs may be seen.

Boyd's Cove

The Birchy Bay area of timber and farming districts was once roamed by the Beothuk Native Indians. The recently opened **Beothuk Interpretation Centre** (☎ 709-656-3114, off Hwy 340; admission $2.50; open 10am-5:30pm daily June–mid-Oct) features displays, exhibits and a video explaining the archeological discoveries of a nearby Beothuk village. Walk the short trail to the dig sites of this extinct tribe. From Hwy 340, head along the road 2km to South Boyd's Cove to reach the center. There's a picnic table, too.

Change Islands

These two islands, reached by ferry from Farewell at the end of what seems a long road from the main highway, don't change much, name notwithstanding. There are five 25-minute trips in each direction daily costing $13.50 per car and driver and $4.50 per person roundtrip. From Farewell, the first ferry leaves at 7:45am, the last at 8pm, with the others scattered evenly through the day. Check schedules at the ferry office (☎ 709-627-3492) or one of the B&Bs on the islands, as the times change *often*.

The two main Change Islands, with a population of just 500 or so, are connected by a short causeway at the northern end, where the largest village is located. The islands are quiet, with many traditional wooden houses and some old fishing-related buildings painted in a red-ochre color common to the area.

Boat tours are available from **Change Islands Adventure Tours** (☎ 709-621-3106, 94 Main Rd), which has four two-hour cruises ($20) daily and sunset cruises if enough people show interest.

Seven Oaks Island Inn & Cottages (☎ 709-621-3256, fax 709-621-3256) Rooms $55-75, 2-bedroom cottages $90. This well-regarded establishment is one of two places to stay at the northern end of the island. Meals are available and boat tours can be arranged. There is also a small store in the vicinity.

Hart's B&B (☎ 709-621-3133, in Change Islands village) Singles/doubles $44/48. In addition to breakfast, an evening snack is included, and other meals are available at extra charge.

Fogo Island

Fogo, just to the east of Notre Dame Bay, is only 25km long. Nevertheless, it's the largest of the area's islands. Tread carefully though, because the Canadian Flat Earth Society has stated that Fogo is at the edge of the world. Indeed, it's claimed that Brimstone Head is one of the four corners of the earth. Standing here looking out to sea it's not difficult to agree.

Like the Change Islands, Fogo is reached by ferry from Farewell. There are five boats daily from 9am to 8:30pm. The fare is $16.50 for car and driver, $5.50 for adult passengers roundtrip. This trip takes about 50 minutes. Again, check with the ferry office (☎ 709-627-3492) as the schedule's flexible.

The island has an interesting history, having first been settled by Europeans in the 1680s. There are about 10 villages on the island, together holding a population of about 4500. There are a couple of fine walking trails, a sandy beach at Sandy Cove, a small herd of caribou and some free-roaming ponies on the island. At Burnt Point is a lighthouse. At several fish plants, visitors can have a look around.

Icebergs can often be seen, and in July there's a folk festival. A heritage house has been converted into the small **Bleak House Museum** (☎ 709-226-2237, Route 333; admission free; open daily July-Sept) in Fogo. The town also has the reconstructed **School House Museum** (☎ 709-266-2237; admission *free; open July-Sept)*. Little Seldom has two buildings at the marina that house the **Marine Interpretation Centre** (☎ 709-627-3366; admission $2; open daily May-Oct), full of local heritage displays. Picking berries is a treasured island pastime.

Payne's Hospitality Home (☎ 709-266-2359, north side of island) Singles/doubles $28/56. A light breakfast is included at this longtime favorite.

Quiet Canyon Hotel (☎ 709-627-3477, fax 709-627-3340) Rooms start at $60. You can also get a meal in the dining room at this place near the ferry terminal in Man O'War Cove.

Two or three more **B&Bs** and a **motel** round out the options. It's a good idea to book ahead before arriving in July and early August.

Beaches Bar & Grill (☎ 709-266-2750) Prices under $12. This establishment serves up seafood and traditional Newfoundland dishes.

New World Island

From the mainland, causeways almost imperceptibly connect Chapel Island, tiny Strong's Island, New World and Twillingate Islands.

At **Newville** the visitors' center (☎ 709-628-5343) is open 9am to 6pm daily from early-June to September and has maps of the area and a sheet describing some of the fine district trails and walks.

Pretty **Dildo Run Provincial Park** (☎ 709-629-3350, Route 340, Virgin Arm) has **camping** (tent sites $11) and picnicking set in a wooded area by a bay. Due to currents, swimming is not recommended.

The western section of New World Island is far less visited. The small fishing villages clinging to the rough, rocky edges of the sea hold some of the area's older houses. At **Moreton's Harbour** is the small **Moreton's Harbour Community Museum** (☎ 709-684-2355;$2; open 10am-8pm daily mid-June–Sept), in an old-style house furnished in much the manner it would have been when the town was a prosperous fishing center.

There are several very small parks around where picnicking and even camping are possible, although facilities are minimal. One of them is **Wild Cove Park**, 2km north of Moreton's Harbour on the road to Tizzard's Harbour. The facilities amount to a single picnic table and a pair of doorless outhouses, but the cove is extremely scenic.

To the east, Pike's Arm has the new **Pike's Arm Museum** (open 10am-6pm Mon-Sat late June-Oct), which is like someone's grandmother's house and reveals a typically traditional outport home. At the end of the road is a new stepped trail leading to a fabulous viewpoint.

Twillingate Island

Actually consisting of two barely separated islands, North and South Twillingate, this area of Notre Dame Bay gets the most attention, and deservedly so. It's stunningly beautiful, with every turn of the road revealing new ocean vistas, colorful fishing wharves or tidy groups of pastel houses perched on cliffs and outcrops.

Held each year during the last week of July, the **Fish, Fun & Folk Festival** is a 'don't miss' event. The four-day festival (call the visitors' center for information) features traditional music and dance, some of which goes back to the 16th century. There are fishing exhibits, lots of food and crafts as well. This is a busy time of year, with the possibility of whales and icebergs lurking offshore, so book early if possible.

The **Long Point Lighthouse** (☎ 709-884-5755; admission free; open 10am-8pm Mon-Sat, 4pm-7pm Sun) is a spectacular place, with dramatic views of the coastal cliffs. Visit the 114-year-old lighthouse, and a guide will lead you up the winding stairs to the top for a 360-degree view or to watch the light flashing. This is an ideal vantage point to watch for icebergs, which are fairly common in May and June and not unusual in July. Places even sell the ice; you can get it in your drinks.

In the town of Twillingate is the **Twillingate Museum** (☎ 709-884-2825, off Main St; admission $1; open 10am-8pm daily late May-Oct), in what was formerly the Anglican rectory. Twillingate, one of the oldest towns in this part of the province, was settled by British merchants in the mid-1700s. One room of the museum displays articles brought back from around the world by local sea captains and includes a cabinet from India, a hurdy-gurdy from Germany and an Australian boomerang. Another room details the seal hunt and its controversy.

NEWFOUNDLAND

Next door is **St Peter's Church** (*open 1pm-6pm daily*), which dates from 1844 and is one of the oldest wooden churches in Newfoundland.

An absolute must is the **Fishing Museum** (☎ 709-884-2485, *Walter Elliott Causeway; admission $2; open 10am-8pm daily mid-June–Sept*). You can't miss the place, with the vivid mural just off the main road. The varied contents, great setting and gregarious owner/guide can easily turn an expected quick stop into a considerable and worthwhile visit.

Badger's Day Park (*near Herring Neck, east of the visitors' center; admission free*) has swimming and two good trails, one with views.

Toward Durrell, the **Iceberg Shop** (☎ 709-884-2242, *Main St; admission free; open 9am-9pm daily*), in a barn from the 1860s, has an iceberg interpretation center on the 1st floor and a craft shop on the top floor.

Don't neglect to tour around unbelievably scenic Durrell. Many of the two-story, boxlike wooden houses are over 100 years old. The **Durrell Museum** (☎ 709-884-5537; *adult/child $1/50¢; open 11am-9pm daily June-Oct*) is perched atop Old Maid Hill. It has displays on the fishing community in the early 1900s and the unfortunate polar bear (now stuffed) who wandered into the area in 2000. Bring your lunch; there are a couple of picnic tables alongside a spectacular view.

Organized Tours Twillingate Island Tours (☎ 709-884-2242), operating from the Iceberg Shop, offers three highly recommended boat trips per day to view icebergs and whales along the jagged local shores (adult/child $30/15).

Twillingate Adventure Tours (☎ 709-884-5999, 888-447-8687, *off Main St*) is an exceedingly friendly operation, with two-hour iceberg tours (possibly whales and seabirds too) departing from the wharf; generally three tours depart daily ($30).

Places to Stay *Sea Breeze Municipal Park* Tent sites $4. Beside the Long Point Lighthouse, right by the sea, is this glorious, very inexpensive – though primitive – place to bed down. You may have the place to yourself. It's wonderful, and there are fabulous hiking trails to high points overlooking the coast.

The Hillside B&B (☎ 709-884-5761, *5 Young's Lane*) Singles/doubles with light breakfast $45/50. This B&B, just up the hill from the Iceberg Shop, is in a house from 1874. It features fine views of the harbor and lighthouse.

Toulinguet Inn (☎ 709-884-2080, 877-684-2080, *56 Main St*) Singles/doubles $55/60. At this three-room inn in a traditional house right on the water, rates include a good breakfast.

Anchor Inn (☎ 709-884-2776, fax 709-884-2326, *N Main St*) Rooms $58-75. This motel/inn with views has some rooms in the lodge and motel-style rooms (some with cooking facilities). There is also a dining room.

Harbour Lights Inn (☎/fax 709-884-2763, *189 Main St*) Rooms with light breakfast $60-85. This historical house, renovated in 1995, is more upscale with a list of amenities including private bathrooms and TVs and a whirlpool. It's located right on the harbor and is popular, so call ahead.

Beach Rock B&B (☎ 709-884-2292) Singles/doubles $40/45. The Beach is a modest, homey B&B south of town, away from the limited action at Little Harbour.

Places to Eat *R&J* (☎ 709-884-5566, 709-884-5421, *Main St*) Prices $8 or less. This busy place has fish and chips, breakfasts, burgers and a great view of one of the many harbors.

Anchor Inn (☎ 709-884-2776, *north side of town*) Prices $8-15. The inn has a large dining room and bar with views over the ocean.

Marg's Kitchen (☎ 709-884-2292, *Beach Rock B&B*) Prices $15. For a good, fresh homemade meal of cod or halibut, this is a good choice.

Golden (☎ 709-884-2747, *60 Main St*) This Chinese place is open daily and has dishes for $5 to $8.

Twillingate Dinner Theatre (☎ 709-884-5423, *Crow Head*) Dinner & show $22. A complete dinner of stuffed, baked cod is followed by a humorous show, at 7pm Monday to Saturday.

LEWISPORTE
pop 4500

Stretched out Lewisporte, known primarily for its ferry terminal, is the largest town along the coast. Other than the boats, there really isn't much reason to visit – though as a distribution center it does have all the goods and services.

The **Bye the Bay Museum & Craft Shop** (☎ 709-535-2844, Main St; admission $1; open 9am-noon, 1pm-5pm Mon-Sat May-Oct), in the large wooden Women's Institute Building, displays articles from the area's history, including a long, multihued rug depicting various facets in the life and times of Lewisporte.

Several people offer **boat trips** to the quiet, rocky **Exploits Islands**, where local people have summer cottages. One to try is **Beothuk Indian Adventure Tours** (☎ 709-535-3344), which uses a pontoon boat. **Caribou Adventure Tours** (☎ 709-535-8379, 19 Premier Dr) runs a safari-like trip to observe woodland caribou. Canoe, mountain bike and hiking trips are also offered.

Woolfrey's Pond Campground (☎ 709-541-2267; open June-Sept) Tent sites $10. Practically downtown, the campground has swimming and a boardwalk trail.

Notre Dame Provincial Park (☎ 709-535-2379) Tent sites $9. This campground is 14km from town on the Trans Canada Hwy. Keep in mind it sometimes fills up during summer.

There are three guesthouses right on Main St.

Northgate B&B (☎ 709-535-2258, 106 Main St) Singles/doubles $40/50 with full breakfast. Northgate is a short walk from the ferry terminal. German is spoken.

Brittany Inns (☎ 709-535-2533, 800-563-8386, fax 709-535-2533, Main St) Rooms $60. This establishment, on the way into town from Hwy 341, has 34 renovated rooms with some housekeeping units, a dining room and bar.

Oriental Restaurant (☎ 709-535-6993, 131 Main St) Prices $5-9. Though pretty straightforward, you get a chance at a few vegetables – by now you know that finding veggies can be a challenge in these parts.

For groceries, head to *Riteway* (68 Main St; open daily 8am-11pm).

Getting There & Away
Bus The DRL bus running between Port aux Basques and St John's stops at Notre Dame Junction at the Edison Irving gas station (☎ 709-535-6749) south of town on the Trans Canada Hwy. The bus for St John's departs at 3:54pm daily and the one

for Port aux Basques leaves at 1:25pm. The gas station is about 16km from town and the ferry dock. Taxis meet the bus arrivals.

Ferry The ferries out of Lewisporte, which go to Happy Valley–Goose Bay, Labrador, are run by Woodwards. Information and reservations for them can be obtained through the provincial tourism information office (☎ 800-563-6353).

The ferry goes to Cartwright on the Labrador coast, then on through Hamilton Inlet to large Lake Melville (which the Vikings may have visited) and finally to Happy Valley–Goose Bay in the heart of Labrador, where there is an important military base.

With a vehicle, you can go from here across central Labrador to Churchill Falls and beyond to Labrador City at the Québec border. The road continues south through Québec to Baie Comeau.

The ferry to Goose Bay is a serious ride, taking about 38 hours and only making the one stop en route. A variation is the direct trip with no stop in Cartwright. This knocks about three hours off the total travel time.

A one-way ticket is $97 (seniors $87, children five to 12 $49); add $160 for a car. Cabins are available at additional charge; the cheapest dorm berth is $38. There are two ferries a week in each direction (one direct, one with the stop), from mid-June to approximately September, that depart every four days: first the direct, then the one with the stop four days later, etc. The direct boat leaves at 10pm (no meal the first night, so eat first), the latter at 4pm.

Tickets might be available on the same day, but the company make no promises (especially in summer), and if you have a car you're likely out of luck.

If you are driving, you can leave your car at the ferry terminal in Lewisporte. There is a security guard, but a waiver must be signed discounting responsibility.

Arrive 90 minutes before departure in either Lewisporte or Happy Valley–Goose Bay.

GRAND FALLS & WINDSOR
These two small towns sit in pulp and paper country. Actually Windsor seems more like a suburb of Grand Falls, and the latter is of more interest to the visitor. Grand Falls' city

center is Church Rd and High St, but most of the commercial district is now on the north side of the Trans Canada Hwy along Cromer Ave. Here you will find the fast-food chains, large food stores and malls.

There's a visitor information center (☎ 709-489-6332) on the highway about 2km west of town. It's open 8am to 8pm daily late-May to late September.

DRL bus company (☎ 709-489-0625) has its own office and stop at 20 Cromer Ave, north off the Trans Canada Hwy, opposite Tim Horton's donuts.

The **Mary March Museum** (☎ 709-292-4522, Cromer Ave at St Catherine St; admission $2.50; open 9:30am-4:30pm daily May-Oct) is particularly worthy. Among other things, it outlines the life of the extinct Beothuk tribe.

Set in the woods behind the museum is a re-creation of a **Beothuk Indian village**

Beothuk Indians

Scattered around much of north-central Newfoundland, the Beothuks, a distinct cultural group, inhabited the area from about 500 years ago until 1829, when the last woman died. It was the Beothuk, their faces painted red with ochre, who were first dubbed 'red men' by the arriving Europeans, a name that was soon to be applied to all the Native Indian peoples of North America.

Seminomadic, they traveled the rivers, notably the Exploits, in birch-bark canoes between the inland lakes and the sea at Notre Dame Bay. They were not a violent people, and there weren't large numbers of them. As a result of hostility, firepower and diseases brought by white people, the ultimate tragedy unfolded. Before anybody had enough gumption or time, just a handful of Beothuk Indians were left. By the early 1800s, there were only two women alive to leave what knowledge they could. Both the Mary March Museum and a re-created village in Grand Falls outline what is known of the Beothuk. The Newfoundland museum in St John's also has a display, including a skeleton – the only known remains anywhere. The Beothuk Trail, Hwy 380, leads through some of their former lands.

(☎ 709-489-3559; admission $2; open 10am-5pm daily mid-June–Labor Day)

Overlooking the Grand Falls (a series of rapids and small cascades) is the **Salmonid Interpretation Centre** (☎ 709-489-7350; admission $3; open 8am-dusk daily mid-June–mid Sept) Reach the center from the downtown area by crossing the Exploits River from Scott St then following the signs. There are exhibits and displays covering the biology and history of the Atlantic salmon and an observation deck where you can watch the fish struggle upstream during their spawning run.

Not far west of town, at Beothuk Park, is the **Loggers' Exhibit** (☎ 709-292-4522, exit 17 Trans Canada Hwy; admission $2.50; open 9am-4:30pm daily mid-May–mid-Sept), with an outdoor exhibit simulating a late 19th-/early 20th-century logging camp.

Places to Stay & Eat
Beothuk Park (☎ 709-489-9832, Trans Canada Hwy) With/without hookups $17/12. This treed park is 2km west of town and has swimming and trails, some used by all-terrain vehicles (ATV's).

Poplar Inn (☎ 709-489-2546, 22 Poplar Rd) Singles/doubles $45/50. As the town's economical lodging, this B&B fills up fast. Poplar Rd runs off Lincoln Rd behind the Mt Peyton Hotel.

Hotel Robin Hood (☎ 709-489-5324, 78 Lincoln Rd) Rooms $70/80. Central and overlooking the Exploits River, the inviting Robin Hood, with rustic charm and just 20 rooms, is a bargain.

There are also a couple of fairly expensive motels in town.

Tai Wan (☎ 709-489-4222, 15 High St) Dishes $6-10. Open 11am-11pm daily. This Asian restaurant is in the heart of Grand Falls.

SOUTH OF GRAND FALLS
Hwy 360 runs 130km through the center of the province to the south coast. It's a long way down to the first settlements at the end of **Bay d'Espoir**, a huge fjord. The cliffs at **Morrisville** offer the best views. **St Alban's** is the main town and is connected with Grand Falls by bus. **Conne River** is a Mi'kmaq First Nations town. There are a few motels and a campground around the end of the bay.

Farther south is a concentration of small, remote fishing villages. The scenery along

Hwy 364 is particularly impressive, as are the aesthetics around **Harbour Breton**. Shutterbugs, try not to shoot all your film.

Jipujikuek Kuespem Park *(☎ 709-882-2470, Conne River Indian Reserve)* Tent sites $9. This small park is near the junction to Head Bay d'Espoir and is unlikely to be full. Ask about the old-growth forest.

Southern Port Hotel *(☎ 709-885-2283, fax 709-885-3111)* Rooms $60-65. There are only 10 rooms here, but this hotel has the only dining room in Harbour Breton.

A better choice is found in little English Harbour West, a town noted for its knitted sweaters. ***Olde Oven Inn*** *(☎ 709-888-3461, 709-877-888-2244, Main Rd)* has four rooms in a house from the 1920s that looks out over the bay. Singles/doubles are $40/50.

Getting There & Away

The Bay d'Espoir Bus Service (☎ 709-538-3429 in St Alban's) links Grand Falls to St Alban's. A bus leaves St Alban's at 8am Monday, Wednesday and Friday and arrives at Grand Falls at 11am. The return trip leaves Grand Falls at 4pm. Hickey's Bus Service (☎ 709-885-2523 in Harbour Breton) does pretty much the same run on the same days from Grand Falls to Harbour Breton.

At Pool's Cove, you can board Rencontre East Ferry (☎ 709-292-4327), which makes one trip daily, except Wednesday, to Bay L'Argent on the south side of Fortune Bay. This mini outport trip would save a considerable amount of backtracking for travelers without a car. The cost is $7 and includes a stop at Rencontre East; all told the trip takes three hours. At Bay L'Argent, you can hike or hitch to Country Lodge on Hwy 210 to pick up bus transportation either to the Burin Peninsula or to St John's.

BAIE VERTE PENINSULA

Little-visited Baie Verte (Green Bay), northwest of Grand Falls, has a long history of human habitation. **Springdale**, the largest community in the area and gateway to the region, has half a dozen choices for accommodations.

George Huxter Memorial Park *(☎ 709-673-4313)* Tent sites $9. This place is 3km from Springdale. To the east, short ferry trips connect several of the islands.

At **Baie Verte**, a relatively sizable town at the northwest end of the peninsula, check

out the **Miners' Museum** *(☎ 709-532-8090; admission $2; open 9am-8pm daily June-Sept)* and tunnel. It doubles as the tourist office. Just out of town, open-pit asbestos mining can be seen from an observation point off the main highway. The peninsula also has deposits of copper, gold, silver and zinc, though much of it has been mined out. Some of the many **abandoned mines** can be visited (get details at the Miners' Museum). In the past, 5% of the world's nickel was mined at little **Tilt Cove**.

Flatwater Pond Park *(☎ 709-532-4472)* Tent sites $9. This park with 25 sites is 15km south of Baie Verte on Hwy 410.

The Maritime Archaic Native Indians originally settled the edges of the peninsula and were followed by the Dorset Inuit, who had a camp at or around **Fleur de Lys** for several hundred years starting around 1000 BC. There is a soapstone outcrop here from which the Inuit gouged the material for carvings and for household goods such as lamps. You can visit archeologists and the new interpretation center at the **Dorset Soapstone Quarry Site** *(☎ 709-253-2126, Route 410; open May-Nov)*, now classed as a national historic site. Icebergs drift by in early summer.

Remote **La Scie** is another good place to see an iceberg; boat trips are available.

The only transportation in the district is Guy Bailey's Bus Service (☎ 709-532-4642), which has one trip per week to/from Corner Brook. The bus goes to Corner Brook at 9am, returning at 2pm. The one-way fare is $25.

Western Newfoundland

Relatively accessible from the mainland, diverse Western Newfoundland offers fabulous natural and cultural sites. Corner Brook is the province's second-largest city, while the Northern Peninsula is lined with attractions of international renown. The quiet Port au Port region is home to the province's French communities.

DEER LAKE

There's little in Deer Lake for the visitor, but it's a convenient jumping-off point for trips up the Northern Peninsula. A good tourist chalet (☎ 709-635-2202), open 8am to 9pm daily, sits right on the Trans Canada Hwy.

Deer Lake Municipal Park (☎ *709-635-5885, 33 Nicholasville Rd*) Tent sites $9. This campground has showers and 30 sites without hookups.

Driftwood Inn (☎ *709-635-5115, 888-635-5115, fax 709-635-5901, 3 Nicholasville Rd*) Rooms $58-72. In town, 2.5km from the bus stop, this large, white, green-trimmed wooden building – an easy walk from Main St – is a good place to stay.

Most of the town's restaurants are fast-food chains on the Trans Canada Hwy, but there is *Tai Lee Garden* (☎ *709-635-5364, Main St*) in the middle of town. It's a simple, cheap Chinese eatery, with prices from $6 to $9.

North of town, **Newfoundland Insectarium** (☎ *709-635-4545, Hwy 430, Reidville; open daily July-Sept, closed Mon rest of year*) is a major new attraction with live and preserved insects from around the globe.

The daily DRL bus stops in Deer Lake at the Irving Big Stop (☎ 709-635-2130) on the Trans Canada Hwy; the fare to and from St John's is $75. If you're coming from the east, the bus gets in at around 5pm, 20 minutes too late to pick up the Viking Express bus (Mon, Wed, Fri) north up the peninsula. In this case, you should call Viking (☎ 709-634-4710) in advance and let the staff know you're coming; be forewarned that the bus won't wait long if you're late. *But,* for Rocky Harbour only, catch the Pittman's bus at the Big Stop at 5:15pm Monday to Friday.

If you're coming from Port aux Basques and going north, see Getting There & Away under Corner Brook.

NORTHERN PENINSULA

From Deer Lake, the immense Northern Peninsula extends 430km northward along one of the most extraordinary, eye-catching roads in eastern North America. Called the Viking Trail, Hwy 430 extends between the coast and the Long Range Mountains to two Unesco world heritage sites, another national historic site, two provincial parks, wonderfully barren far-north topography and views over the history-filled Strait of Belle Isle to the coast of remote Labrador. Wildlife abounds, from large mammals to specialized fauna, and the area boasts unbelievably various and abundant – and huge – edible berries and ex-

cellent salmon fishing. And there are spectacular fjords, small coastal fishing villages and exceedingly friendly people.

Even for those without a lot of time, a trip from Port aux Basques to the Northern Peninsula, if only as far as Gros Morne, makes a visit to Newfoundland memorable. Many people make this region the focus of their trip to 'The Rock' and never go farther east than Deer Lake. L'Anse aux Meadows, a 1000-year-old Viking settlement (by far the oldest European landing site in North America, centuries ahead of Christopher Columbus) has become somewhat of a pilgrimage site, drawing visitors from all over the USA and, to a lesser extent, Europe.

All of this has led to a growing number of tourists in recent years, which has meant an increase in services along the way. Motels, cabins and B&Bs are generally sufficient in number (though they can still fill up in peak summer periods). Complementing these accommodations are several wonderfully simple, rough, natural campgrounds. This can be a wet, cool region, with a lot of bugs as well, so if you're tenting, be prepared for the odd night in a motel.

It's roughly a five- to six-hour drive from Deer Lake to St Anthony, with the price of gas increasing as you go (although it's not as exorbitant as it once was).

Bus transportation is possible, if a bit spotty along the entire route.

Gros Morne National Park

Gros Morne National Park (☎ *709-458-2066; open all year*) is a must for its magnificent, preternaturally varied geography, which has earned it status as a Unesco world heritage site, not to mention the moniker 'Galapagos of Geology.' Special features include fjords that rival Scandinavia's, the majestic barren Tablelands, unrivaled mountain hiking trails, sandy beaches and adjacent historic little fishing communities. There is plenty of wildlife, including caribou and moose, whales and offshore seals. Part of the UN designation is due to the park's Precambrian, Cambrian and Ordovician rock and the evidence this rock supplies researchers for the theory of plate tectonics. Another factor was the site's 4500 years of human occupation.

Woody Point, Norris Point and Rocky Harbour villages are the principal commercial centers. Rocky Harbour is the main community, where you'll find all the amenities, including a laundromat and grocery stores. In the southern portion of the park, Hwy 431 leads to Woody Point and beyond to the Tablelands, Green Gardens and, at the end of the highway, **Trout River**, a small, picturesque fishing community.

Woody Point makes a good center for seeing the southern portion of the park, but keep in mind it's more than an hour's drive back to the main visitors' center along winding roads around Bonne Bay.

There is enough to do in and around the park to easily fill several days, but campers take note, this is a heavy rainfall area, so cross your fingers and be prepared.

Information The park has two visitor information centers. At either one, purchase the entrance permit (adult/senior/child/family $5/4/2.50/10 per day, or the four-day pass for $15/12/7.50/30). A seasonal pass is also offered. Admission includes the trails, Discovery Centre, all day-use areas, exhibits, displays and day-hike trails. It also goes toward the cost of a campsite.

The main center (☎ 709-458-2066; open 9am-9pm daily July-Aug, 9am-5pm daily rest of year) is 25km from the entrance on Hwy 430, at the exit to Norris Point. Maps, books and backcountry permits are available at both information centers, and the main center also has an impressive interpretive area that includes a slide show, restaurant and other services.

The smaller information center (☎ 709-458-2066; open 9am-8pm daily mid-June–early Sept, 9am-5pm spring and fall, closed Oct-May) is by the park entrance on Hwy 430 as you approach Wiltondale.

The new oversized **Discovery Centre** (☎ 709-458-2066) in Woody Point has some interactive exhibits and a multimedia theater explaining the ecology of the park and its world heritage status. There's a helpful information desk, daily interpretive activities in summer and a small café too.

Things to See & Do In the southwest corner of the park are the compelling **Tablelands**, by the road's edge not far from Woody Point. This is a barren 80km flat-topped ledge of rock, 700m high, shoved up from beneath the ocean floor – a glimpse of

the earth's insides. You can view the vegetation-free, golden phenomenon from points along Hwy 431, and there's a short trail to the base of the barren mountains.

Farther west, **Green Gardens** is a volcanic coast that features sea caves and sea stacks. It's an hour hike from the second trailhead of the Green Garden Trail to the coast.

Several **boat tours** are offered. Tableland Boat Tours (☎ 709-451-2101, Trout River; open mid-June–mid-Sept) runs three trips daily up Trout River Pond past the Tablelands ($25). From the government wharf in Norris Point, Bon Tours (☎ 709-458-2730, 800-563-9887, Main St, Rocky Harbour) runs two-hour boat trips of **Bonne Bay** ($25). They depart at 10am and 2pm daily and stop over in Woody Point for more people to board before cruising the Arms. If you do this trip and the Western Brook Pond boat tour, the operator may give a discount on one or the other (see the Western Brook Pond section).

Near Rocky Harbour is **Gros Morne Swimming Pool** recreation complex (☎ 709-458-2350, Hwy 430; adult/child $3/2; open daily), with a 25m swimming pool and hot tub, ahhh. Call, as the schedule is complicated.

Above Norris Point toward Rocky Harbour, definitely stop at **Photography Lookout**, which has a great view over Bonne Bay and across to the golden-hued Tablelands. In Norris Point, a marine biology station with public aquarium was being built during research.

Farther up the coast past Sally's Cove, parts of the wreck of the SS *Ethie*, which ran aground in 1919, can be seen on the beach. The storm and subsequent rescue sparked the writing of a song about the incident.

Western Brook Pond This is the park's feature fjord, with dwarfing cliffs nearly 700m high running vertically from the cool waters. Boat tours of the 15km-long fjord are offered and definitely recommended. Bon Tours (☎ 709-458-2730, 800-563-9887, Main St) runs a 2½-hour trip that takes you past sheer cliffs towering at the water's edge. The trips are very popular, and you usually need to make reservations in summer at least a day in advance.

The tours run from June to the end of September, with three trips daily, at 10am, 1pm and 4pm (and 6pm if demand warrants it), each taking up to 40 passengers (adult/family $30/66). The dock is reached after an easy 3km walk from the road along the Western Brook Pond Trail; keep in mind it takes 40 minutes.

Just north of here in Cow Head are the perennially popular theatrical presentations of the summerlong **Gros Morne Theatre Festival** (☎ *709-243-2899, 877-243-2899, various locations; tickets $7-15; performances most days July & Aug)*. Performances may be outdoors or in.

The gentle, safe, sand-duned beach at **Shallow Bay** at the other end of the geographic spectrum seems almost out of place – as if transported from the Caribbean by some bizarre current. The water, though, provides a chilling dose of reality, rarely getting above 15°C.

For history visit the **restored fishing camp** *(admission free; open 10am-6pm daily early June–late Sept)* at Broom Point depicting the inshore fishery of the 1960s. The three Nudge brothers and their families fished here from 1941 to 1975, when they sold the entire camp, including boats, lobster traps and nets, to the national park. Everything has been restored and is now staffed with interpretive guides. Another fine site is the still-operating **Lobster Head Cove Lighthouse** *(admission free; open 10am-6pm daily early June–mid-Oct)* with various exhibits; the rocky shore here is great for tidal pool exploration.

The park staff host interpretive programs, guided walks and evening presentations throughout summer.

Activities The park maintains over 20 trails that total 80km and feature seven backcountry camping areas for what arguably could be some of the best hiking in Newfoundland. The gem of the park's trail system is **James Callahan Gros Morne Trail** to the peak of Gros Morne, the highest point in the area at 806m. The 16km roundtrip hike is said to be a seven- to eight-hour hike, but many people can cover it in less time. The trail is well maintained, with steps and boardwalks, but is still a tough hike, especially the steep rock gully that must be climbed to the ridgeline of the mountain. This is not a trail for tennis shoes. The views at the top and of 10-Mile Pond, a sheer-sided fjord, make the effort well worth it. There is

backcountry camping in Fern Gulch along the trail, and a popular strategy is to set up there for a couple of nights and scale the mountain without the packs.

Green Gardens Trail is almost as scenic and challenging. The 18km loop has two trailheads off Hwy 431, with each one descending a valley to the Green Gardens, a volcanic coastline. Plan on seven to 10 hours for the entire loop, or book one of the three backcountry camping areas, all of them on the ocean, and turn the hike into an overnight adventure.

Shorter but just as scenic are **Tablelands Trail**, which extends 2km to Winterhouse Brook Canyon for a 4km roundtrip hike; **Lookout Trail** near Woody Point, a 5km loop to the site of an old fire tower above the tree line; and **Western Brook Pond Trail**, the most popular trail in the park, which is an easy 6km roundtrip hike to the western end of the fjord.

Other overnight hikes include **Stanleyville Trail**, a roundtrip of 4km to the site of an old logging camp where there is backcountry camping. This easy trail begins in the Lomond day-use area off Hwy 431. Western Brook Pond Trail and **Snug Harbour Trail** can be combined for a 7km one-way hike to backcountry campsites in the famous fjord. Or book your passage on the tour boat and have it drop you off at the head of Western Brook Pond, where there are several more backcountry campsites.

The granddaddies are the **Long Range Traverse** and **North Rim Traverse**, serious multiday treks over the mountains for the experienced. Permits and orientation are required.

Backcountry campsites ($10 per person per night) must be booked in advance at the visitors' centers. If you plan to do several trails, invest $10 in a copy of *Gros Morne National Park Trail Guide*, a waterproof map of the park with trail descriptions on the back.

Many of the hiking trails are used as cross-country skiing trails in winter, but in recent years the park has undertaken an ambitious ski-trail construction program; many trails in the impressive 55km system were designed by Pierre Harvey, Canadian Olympic champion. The best place to start is the main visitors' center, with its ski chalet, rentals, loop trails, and lighted night trails.

Organized Tours Well-organized **Gros Morne Adventure Guides** (☎ *709-458-2722, 800-685-4624)* is found where the road ends in Norris Point. Popular half-day sea kayak tours of Bonne Bay leave three times daily from 9am to 6pm ($45/105 half/full day). Multiday trips or trips to Western Brook Pond can be arranged. There also are day-long or multiday hiking, skiing and snow-shoeing trips (starting at $75). Reservations are required.

A small new business, **Base Camp** (☎ *709-458-3311)*, on the road into Rocky Harbour from Hwy 430, rents kayaks and even hiking boots. They also offer kayak instruction and a couple of two-hour guided paddles ($45).

Atlantic Canada Adventure (☎ *709-458-3089)* in Norris Point offers guided hikes to your specifications. The two owners speak English, French, German and Italian.

Places to Stay Within Gros Morne National Park are five *campgrounds* (☎ *800-563-6353,* W *www.parkscanada.gc.ca/grosmorne)*. Fees are $15.25 at all but Green Point, which has less-developed facilities (no showers) and is $11. Reservations are taken. None of the campgrounds have sites with water or electricity. Only Green Point is open all year. Lomond and Berry Hill operate from the end of May to early October. Trout River and Shallow Bay are open mid-June to mid-September.

Berry Hill, the largest campground, is most central; Shallow Bay has ocean swimming; Trout River is isolated; and Lomond is closest to Hwy 430.

Rocky Harbour is easily the busiest of the tiny, seaside villages and offers the most tourist services, including many places to stay.

Juniper Campground & Hostel (☎ *709-458-2917, West Link at Pond Rd, Rocky Harbour)* Camping $11-16, dorm beds $12. Open mid-May–end Sept. Beside the campsites is the popular, recently expanded 15-bunk hostel, in a large cabin that includes a kitchen and showers. Central Rocky Harbour is walkable.

Major's Hospitality (☎ *709-458-2537, 888-999-2537, Pond Rd, Rocky Harbour)* Rates $15 or $20 for two people in one bed with no breakfast. Virtually next door to Juniper is Major's, a fun cross between a B&B and a hostel. It's presided over with a

touch of good-natured cynicism by Violet, the owner.

Evergreen B&B (☎ *709-458-2692, 800-905-3494, Rocky Harbour)* Singles/doubles with shared bath $40/45. This is a pleasant four-room place with laundry facilities and a full breakfast featuring homemade goodies.

Gros Morne Cabins (☎ *709-458-2020, fax 709-458-2882, Main St, Rocky Harbour)* Cabins start at $75. These 22 beautiful individual log cabins come with wood-lined kitchens and views of the ocean. A one-bedroom place is large enough for up to two adults and two kids. Inquire next door at Endicott's variety store.

Ocean View Motel (☎ *709-458-2730, 800-563-9887, fax 709-458-2730, Main St, Rocky Harbour)* Rooms $60-85. In the heart of town, this modern, 44-room place has a dining room and an agent for organizing tours.

Quiet Woody Point presents more choices, including a second hostel – two hostels in one region is a dizzying, unheard of array for this part of the world.

Woody Point Hostel (☎ *709-453-7254, 709-453-2470, School Rd, Woody Point)* Dorm beds $15, private rooms $20/35. Open all day mid-May–Oct. The small, casual hostel has a kitchen and 10 beds. It is on School Rd, at the rear of the clinic. From the Western Petroleum gas station, where the bus stops, go up the hill, then turn right and take the first left to the top of the hill. Unfortunately, the hostel's future has been threatened by the dicey tenancy situation.

Victorian Manor (☎ *709-453-2485, in Woody Point)* Rooms in house $50-70, cabins $60-75. This hospitality home has three rooms in the nice old house or newer two-bedroom efficiency cabins. The rooms include a light breakfast.

Across the bay in Norris Point there are more choices.

Eileen's B&B (☎ *709-458-2427, 3 Gill's Lane, Norris Point)* Singles/doubles $35/45 with shared bath, $45/50 with private bath. This B&B with a fine view has three rooms that come with breakfast and evening snack.

In Trout River, *Crocker's Efficiency Unit* (☎ *709-451-5220, Main St)* is actually a rental house – three bedrooms, kitchen – that costs $60 for the works. It's available July to September. Look for it right beside the gas station, across the street from the sea.

Places to Eat There are sufficient places for getting something to eat around Gros Morne National Park, with restaurants in all the villages and grocery stores everywhere but Trout River.

Java Jack's (☎ 709-458-3004, *Main St, Rocky Harbour*) For a munch, don't miss this minuscule but bustling community center of a café with excellent coffees, sweets, wraps ($6) and a few well-prepared seafood and vegetarian items. It's open 7:30am to 9pm daily.

Jackie's (☎ 709-458-2649, *Main St, Rocky Harbour*) This place has cheap burgers and sandwiches and an ocean-view deck. It's open 9am to 11pm daily.

Lighthouse Restaurant (☎ 709-453-2213, *Woody Point*) Prices $4-14. Open daily. In the center of Woody Point, across from the dock, is this gregarious low-cost, all-purpose place for light meals and seafood. You may even see a whale from the window.

Seaside Restaurant (☎ 709-451-3461, *Main St, right on the water, Trout River*) Dishes $10-16. Open noon-10pm daily. For a minor splurge, head directly to this well-regarded dining room. At dinner, try one of the scallop or shrimp dishes. At lunch, try the chowder and sandwich for $8. Dinner reservations are recommended.

Getting There & Around Martin's Bus Service (☎ 709-453-2207 in Woody Point, 709-634-4710 in Corner Brook) connects Woody Point with Corner Brook via daily runs Monday to Friday. It departs Trout River at 9am, Woody Point at 9:30am and Corner Brook for the return trip at 4:30pm. The one-way fare between Woody Point and Corner Brook is $12. In Woody Point, Martin's uses the Western Petroleum gas station as its depot, which is not far from the hostel.

You can also arrange for bus transportation to anywhere in the park.

Also good for connecting Rocky Harbour and Corner Brook is Pittman's Bus Service (☎ 709-458-2084 or cellular ☎ 709-458-7198 in Rocky Harbour, 709-634-4710 in Corner Brook), but the buses run only on weekdays. They leave Rocky Harbour at 9am; no set stops exist, so call and they'll pick up and drop off around Rocky Harbour, including at the hostel. In Corner Brook, buses depart from Millbrook Mall (see Corner Brook, later in this chapter). The fare is $12.

The Viking Express bus (☎ 709-634-4710 in Corner Brook) departs Corner Brook for St Anthony via Deer Lake at 3pm on Monday, Wednesday and Friday. The bus overnights at St Anthony and then makes a return run the following day. It stops at Norris Point (across Bonne Bay from Woody Point) and at Ocean View Motel in Rocky Harbour on demand for those who want to continue north. Call in Corner Brook to be sure of pick-up.

A water taxi shuttles across Bonne Bay (watch for whales) between Norris Point and Woody Point three times a day, departing Norris Point at 9am, 12:30pm and 5pm and Woody Point at 9:30am, 1pm and 5:30pm. A one-way ticket is $5. For an additional $5, you can ride the connecting bus from Woody Point to Trout River. This is a good, cheap way to get a look at the Tablelands and the only way to get to Trout River.

The Arches

Out of the park back northward on Hwy 430, the Arches is worth a stop for a stroll down to the beach, which is littered with beautiful, smooth, colored rocks about the size of footballs. The main attractions, though, are the three extant limestone arches and the remains of maybe three or four more formed some 400 million years ago. The shoreline is a good place to spy starfish.

Table Point Ecological Reserve

North of Bellburns along the shore, there are protected sections of 470-million-year-old limestone containing abundant fossils.

River of Ponds Park

On the Pond River, which is good for salmon and swimming, there is a simple *campground* (☎ 709-225-3421, *Hwy 430*) offering 40 good sites with showers but no hookups for $9.

Hawke's Bay

Halfway to St Anthony from Deer Lake, Hawke's Bay was a whaling station at the turn of the 20th century. There are some excellent salmon waters and a salmon ladder, a device to aid the fish in getting upstream. The town has a motel and two B&Bs.

Just behind the tourist office, which is open 10am to 7pm daily in summer, is **Torrent River Nature Park** (☎ 709-248-5344, *Hwy 430; open June-Sept)*. Campsites at the park are $9. Nearby, the **Hogan Trail** begins along the Torrent River. Most of the 3km walking trail is on a boardwalk and leads over marsh and through the woods to the salmon ladder.

Port au Choix

Busy and interesting Port au Choix, one of the biggest towns between Gros Morne and St Anthony, and a major fishing port, is well worth a stop.

The principal attraction is **Port au Choix National Historic Site** (☎ *709-861-3522, Point Richie Rd; admission $2.75; open 9am-7pm daily mid-June–early Oct)*. The site is away from the town center near the ocean; just follow the signs. The visitors' center features a reconstructed house along with touch-screen exhibits and artifacts outlining the various ancient groups of people who lived here thousands of years ago. There are good walking trails around the digs and free guided tours. In 1999, archeologists found the living site of the Maritime Archaic Indians at Gargamelle Cove.

From the center you can walk or drive to **Phillip's Garden**, which has vestiges of Paleo-Eskimo houses. Paleo-Eskimo people settled on the Cape Riche Peninsula between 1500 and 2200 years ago. The road continues to the 1871 **Point Riche lighthouse**. A walking trail leads from the north side of town to the lighthouse, then you can loop around via the road to the visitors' center. The complete stroll would be close to 6km.

Downtown, the **Heritage Centre** *(Fisher St; open noon-4pm Mon-Sat; admission free)* has some artifacts from the adjacent Maritime Archaic Indian cemetery dating from 3200 to 4300 years ago. The remains of 110 individuals, as well as tools, weapons and ornaments, were discovered here accidentally in 1967.

For a little more recent history, just out of town is a plaque outlining some of the tussles between the French and British for the fishing rights in the area, which continued from the 1600s into the 1900s. In 1904, yet another treaty was signed in which the French relinquished their rights here in ex-change for the privilege in Morocco (ah yes, the days when all the world was a Monopoly board).

Lastly, don't miss **Studio Gargamelle/ Museum of Whales** (☎ *709-861-3280, Hwy 430; admission $4; open June-Sept)*, the workshop of artist Ben Ploughman. His very engaging, knowledgeable and humorous manner complements the fascinating and evolving whale museum he's creating. A highlight is the impressive whale skeleton with the bones from an entire whale wired together.

Places to Stay & Eat *Jeannie's Sunrise B&B* (☎ *709-861-2254, 877-639-2789, Fisher St)* Rooms $35-55. The economical choice in Port au Choix is this four-room B&B with an ocean view.

Sea Echo Motel (☎ *709-861-3777, 888-861-3777, Fisher St)* Singles/doubles $68/75. This more expensive motel has been upgraded, but look at more than one room. For the money, they missed a few spots. The dining room is quite good, friendly and has good lunch specials.

The Anchor Café (☎ *709-861-3665, Fisher St; open 11am-10pm or later daily Apr-Oct)* You can't miss this place – the front half is the stern of a boat – and don't, because it has the best meals in town. There's a wide selection of seafood dinners (starting at $10), locally cultured mussels ($8) and soups, like a big bowl of excellent seafood chowder, with bread ($5).

Three Mile Lake Campground Tent sites without hookups $10. About 50km north of town, just north of the turnoff for Shoal Cove West (a village), is this very quiet, wooded, private campground with a beach. It has just reopened with new owners.

North of Port au Choix

Close to town, the mountains veer off to the east and aren't as imposing. The landscape becomes more and more barren, until it appears pretty much like that found in the far Canadian north – an essentially flat, pond-filled primeval expanse. There is probably no other place in the country where this type of rugged terrain is as accessible.

At Plum Point a gravel road connects with the eastern shore; this is a part of Newfoundland that even travel hardy natives rarely see.

NEWFOUNDLAND

Tuckamore Country Inn (☎ 709-865-6361, 888-865-6361, fax 709-865-2112, 1 Southwest Pond, Main Brook) Rooms $80, suites $120 with breakfast. There are five rooms and three suites, a dining room, fireplace and sauna. Call ahead before driving across the peninsula, because the lodge is mainly used as a base for package adventure tours that include trips to see birds, caribou, etc. It's also often used by hunters and anglers.

The main town over on the peninsula's eastern side is **Roddickton**, and here, as in Main Brook, there are outfitters for hunting and fishing. There is also some hiking, and a trip up Cloud Hill affords good views of the islands offshore.

Betty's B&B (☎ 709-457-2371, fax 709-457-3271) Singles/doubles $35/45. There are three rooms and it's open all year.

Back on Hwy 430, **St Barbe** has a ferry to Labrador (see Labrador later). From here on, the coast of Labrador is visible on clear days.

Dockside Motel (☎ 709-877-2444, fax 709-877-9459) Rooms $55-65, cabins $65. This modern place literally right beside the ferry landing has 15 rooms, 10 cabins and a restaurant.

Pistolet Bay Provincial Park

With 30 sites in a wild but wooded area 20km from the main road and 40km from the Viking site, this is a good place to stay if you're camping (☎ 709-454-7580, Route 437). Tent sites are $11. Be prepared for the mosquitoes and blackflies; they seem to have a real mean streak. But there's a sandy beach, and the comfort station at the park has hot showers and laundry facilities, and it's even heated. What luxury!

Cape Onion

The closest town for milk and bread (and beer) is the fishing village of **Raleigh**, and another 8km farther north the road ends at Cape Onion. The cape reveals dramatic coastal scenery of islands, coves and 'tickles,' which in Newfoundland refer to narrow passages of water between two land formations.

Tickle Inn (☎ 709-452-4321, fax 709-452-4321, Cape Onion; open June-Oct) Rooms $50-65. This delightful seaside inn, built in 1890, features four rooms, a parlor warmed by a Franklin woodstove, and excellent home-cooked meals of local seafood and

Newfoundland dishes. Rate includes a light breakfast. Other meals are by request, and boat tours of the coastline or a nearby shipwreck can be arranged.

St Lunaire to Straitsview

There are five small, old fishing villages on the way to the historic site of L'Anse aux Meadows. You may see kids by the road's edge selling berries collected out on the barrens. In mid-August, these will include the queen of all Newfoundland berries, the golden bakeapple, sold here for $30 per gallon (4.5L – the people here still use imperial measurements, unlike those in much of the country) and fetching as much as $50 farther south.

Smith's Restaurant (☎ 709-623-2539) Prices $5-15. In St Lunaire-Griquet, this restaurant by the sea serves traditional meals of cod tongue, salt fish and brewis or scallops and also nonseafood Canadian standards.

Valhalla Lodge (☎ 709-623-2018 summer only, fax 709-623-2144) Rooms $50-65. In Gunner's Cove, this recommended lodge is 5km from the historic park. Rates for the six Scandinavian-themed rooms include a light breakfast. Maybe you can stay in the room where Pulitzer Prize–winning author E Annie Proulx stayed while writing *The Shipping News*. Also here is *Northern Delight (☎ 709-623-2220)*, a restaurant with lots of regional dishes and iceberg ice for your drink. The portions are enormous, and prices are under $10.

Marilyn's Hospitality Home (☎ 709-623-2811, 877-865-3958) Singles/doubles $35/40. At Hay Cove, this highly recommended lodging is practically across the street from the entrance to the national park. Rates include a full breakfast; other meals by request.

L'Anse aux Meadows National Historic Park

This fascinating park (☎ 709-623-2608, Hwy 436; adult/child/family $5/3/10; open 9am-8pm daily mid-June–Labor Day, 9am-4:30pm daily May–mid-June & Labor Day-Oct, closed rest of year), 43km from St Anthony's, is made all the more special by the unobtrusive, low-key approach of the park developers. In an unspoiled, waterside setting – looking pretty much as it did in AD 1000 – are the remains of the settlement created by Vikings from Scandinavia and Greenland who became the first Europeans to land in North America. Replicas of sod buildings complete with costumed docents, demonstrations and simulated fires almost transport you back in time.

The Vikings, led by Leif Eriksson, son of Erik the Red, built their own boats, sailed all over the North Atlantic, landed here, constructed houses (vestiges of which still remain), fed themselves – and they were practically all just 20-something years old. Oops, let's not forget they smelted iron out of the bog and forged nails with it – 1000 years ago!

Allow two to three hours to browse through the interpretive center, with its artifacts, see the film and walk around the remains of eight original wood and sod buildings and the three reconstructions.

Also captivating is the story of Norwegian explorer Helge Ingstad, who discovered the site in 1960, ending years of searching. His tale and that of his archeologist wife is told in the interpretive center. A short path behind the replica buildings leads to a small graveyard where the body of local inhabitant George Decker, who made Ingstad's day by pointing out the mounds in the terrain, lies.

Take time to walk the 3km trail that winds through the barren terrain and along the coast that surrounds the interpretive center.

For those without transportation, the taxi ride to the site from St Anthony's costs about $30.

If you're totally captivated by the Viking experience, nearby is **Viking Boat Tours** (☎ 709-623-2100, *Noddy Bay; open May 24–mid-Sept*), which offers two-hour boat tours ($30) on a replica Viking ship. You don't have to row, but you can't sail either; the Canadian Coast Guard won't allow it. So you motor around the bay looking at shipwrecks, icebergs and coastal scenery. Be prepared for cold and wet.

L'Anse aux Meadows

There is no camping in the historic park, but just past the entrance is a small roadside picnic park where occasionally cyclists or hitchhikers will pitch a tent. It's worth going to the top of the cape to pretty L'Anse aux Meadows village, with its hand-scribbled signs advertising iceberg ice. Also here is the recommended **Norseman Gallery & Café** (☎ 709-623-2018). There's nothing deep-fried, and the menu has other items like spaghetti and chili ($6). Seafood is $16 to $19.

On the way is the brand new **Norstead** (☎ 709-623-2828; *adult/family $7/14; open 10am-6pm daily June-Oct),* a commercial site set up to present Viking life as it was here 1000 years ago. There are four building re-creations, demonstrations on food, textiles, etc, and a ship replica.

St Anthony
pop 3500

You made it! Unfortunately, it's a little anticlimactic. As the largest town in the north of the northern peninsula, it's functional and an important supply center and fish-processing depot. It's not what you'd call pretty, but it has a rough-hewn charm. Hwy 430 becomes North St and then West St in the center of town.

Grenfell is a big name around here. Sir Wilfred Grenfell was a local legend and, by all accounts, quite a man. Born in England and educated as a doctor, he first came to Newfoundland in 1892 and, for the next 40 years, built hospitals and nursing stations and organized much-needed fishing cooperatives along the coast of Labrador and around St Anthony.

The Grenfell Historic Properties subsumes a number of local sites pertaining to him. The **Grenfell Interpretation Centre** (☎ 709-454-4004, *West St, opposite the hospital; adult/family $6/12; open 9am-8pm daily May-Nov)* is a bit pricey for the admittedly thorough displays about his life. There is also a general visitor information desk here (☎ 709-454-4011), open 10am to 8pm daily.

The **Grenfell Museum** (☎ 709-454-2281, *behind the hospital; admission $3; open 9am-8pm daily May-Nov),* near the interpretation center in Grenfell's former home, is perhaps more worthwhile. The fine old house with a large wraparound porch has displays that outline his life and work.

Back beside the interpretation center is the **Dockhouse Museum** (☎ 709-454-4010; *admission free; open daily June-Oct),* where Grenfell Mission boats used to be repaired. It's now restored to its original 1920s look.

The main road through town ends at **Fishing Point Park**. The towering headland cliffs here are very impressive, and there are a handful of short trails, with names like Iceberg Alley and Whale Watchers Trail, that head to observation platforms on the edge of the cliffs. Admission is free.

The St Anthony Municipal Building *(West St; open 8:30am-4:30pm Mon-Fri)*, opposite Woodward Motors (car dealership) has a huge stuffed **polar bear** in the lobby. This guy showed up on pack ice in 1984 and scared the willies out of locals, but it died of natural causes in the harbor before it could cause any mischief.

There are a few craft outlets in town, including quality **Grenfell Handicrafts**, with parkas embroidered by hand, whalebone and ivory carvings, and other articles at the Grenfell Interpretation Centre. The mukluks (a traditional Inuit soft winter boot made of sealskin or caribou hide and sometimes fur lined) make a good albeit pricey souvenir.

Northland Discovery Tours *(☎ 709-454-3092, daily trips June-Oct)* offers boat cruises for whale- or iceberg-viewing. This is a prime area for both.

For some good, casual fun get to the **Legion** building *(☎ 709-454-2340, East St, leaving town)* on Wednesday night, when some local musicians play traditional stuff and snacks are available.

Places to Stay & Eat *Triple Falls RV Park (☎ 709-454-2599, fax 709-454-2245, Hwy 430)* Tents $10, trailers $14-18. Just 7km from St Anthony, this is convenient, but there are only four tent sites.

Wildberry Country Lodge (☎ 709-454-2662, Hwy 430) Rates $15-75. Also north of town, about 15 minutes away, this new addition has everything from low-cost bunk rooms to comfortable rooms with two double beds. Breakfast is included. It's got a fine, quiet setting and a restaurant with seafood, too.

Howell's Tourist Home (☎ 709-454-3402, 1 Spruce Lane, off East St) Singles/doubles $33/39. The four rooms all have private bath. Meals are available, and it's open all year.

Trailsend Hospitality Home (☎ 709-454-2024, 1 Cormack St) Singles/doubles with full breakfast $35/45. Guests can use the kitchen and laundry.

Vinland Motel (☎ 709-454-8843, 800-563-7578, West St) Rooms from $71. This is a sizable motel in the center of town.

The Lightkeeper's Café (☎ 877-454-4900, Fishing Point Park) Prices $5-11. Open summer 9am-10pm daily. The motels have restaurants, but it's almost obligatory to try a cup of chowder at the former lightkeeper's house, which has a fabulous location. Enjoy dinner while watching icebergs float by.

Leifburdir (same ☎ as Lightkeeper's Café) Dinner most nights June-Oct. Adult/senior/teen/child $32/27/25/15. For a more social, zany meal, try the Leifburdir next door. You enter a sod house and find yourself at a Viking banquet complete with participatory skits and a full meal, from salad to dessert, that might include moose stew or baked salmon.

At the Viking Mall downtown is a *Foodlands (☎ 709-454-8475)* grocery store for stocking up if you're taking the boat north.

Getting There & Away Flying to St Anthony is technically possible, but the airport is nearly an hour away. In 1998, a road was paved from the St Anthony Airport around Hare Bay to Main Brook, thus opening Main Brook and Roddickton to obviate backtracking. Trouble is, there is still an unpaved (but maintained) segment from Main Brook to Roddickton.

St Anthony is the final stop for Viking Express (☎ 709-454-8843), with the bus pulling into the Vineland Motel in the middle of town. The bus departs St Anthony for Corner Brook at 10am Sunday, Tuesday and Thursday. To Corner Brook it's $55. From Corner Brook connections can be made for the DRL bus to either Port aux Basques or St John's.

Cruising Labrador runs a passenger and freight-only ferry service – no cars – to Labrador. For information and reservations contact the provincial tourism information office (☎ 800-563-6353).

The ferry connects to Cartwright, Happy Valley–Goose Bay and then heads up the coast, linking a series of small, remote outports. Other than Goose Bay–Happy Valley, there is no road access to these villages, and that is part of their appeal. For car ferries see Getting There & Away under Lewisporte, earlier in this chapter.

It's approximately a 12- to 14-day roundtrip to Nain, the northernmost point, about 1038 nautical miles from St Anthony. (A nautical mile is 6076 feet, a standard mile 5280 feet.) The ferries run from the first week of July to around mid-October, not long before the coastal ice meets the Arctic pack ice, and everything is sealed up until the summer thaw.

Toward the end of the season, even though November storms are a month away, the weather can play havoc with the schedule, and the one-way trip can take twice as long. With high winds and waves close to 15m high, the ship is often harborbound for days at a time.

Normally, the ferry is a comfortable ship with four meals a day (you didn't forget about 'night lunch' did you?) and a selection not unlike that found in any mainland restaurant but with prices that are slightly higher.

Fares are low and determined by the number of nautical miles traveled. The rate is roughly 25¢ per nautical mile and an additional 12¢ per nautical mile for an economy two-berth cabin (better cabins are available). Children and seniors pay less. To Red Bay, it's 64 miles, thus $16, and to Goose Bay it's 570 miles or $142.50. To head to Nain and back with an economy cabin would be $765.

There are 46 possible ports of call along the entire route, and the number of stops partially determines the length of the trip. You can get off at the village of your choice, but keep in mind that most of the stops are not set up for tourists and there's not a whole lot to do while waiting for the ferry to return. At most ports, the ship usually needs one to two hours to unload, and that is enough time for a good look around.

The low prices make the trip a bargain. Because of that, and the chance to visit some of the country's most remote settlements and view fine scenery, the trip has become popular with visitors. Less than half the tickets are for tourists, as most are required for local residents and their supplies.

Be prepared when making a reservation to pay a 25% deposit. There are three trips a month in July and August, and two in September and October.

CORNER BROOK
pop 22,500

This is Newfoundland's second-largest town, after St John's. Up high beside the waters of Humber Arm, it is fairly attractive despite the often pervasive smell – a reminder that the focus of the town is the huge pulp and paper mill. The Corner Brook area is likely the sunniest region of the province, and the warm, clear skies of summer can be a real treat.

The downtown area consists of Main St by Remembrance Square and up along maplelined Park St toward the Heritage District.

The large tourist office (☎ 709-639-9792) and craft shop can't be missed, just off the Trans Canada Hwy near the turnoffs into town. Hours are 8am to 8pm during summer.

The Family Bookstore (☎ 709-639-9813) in the Corner Brook Plaza has a tremendous selection of Newfoundland books.

The public library (☎ 709-634-0013, Mt Bernard Ave), in the Sir Richard Squires Building, has free Internet access.

Things to See & Do

Northwest of downtown, up on cliffs overlooking the Humber Arm, is a national historic site, the **Captain James Cook Monument** (*Crow Hill Rd, off Atlantic Ave*). Get a map from the tourist office, as the roads are pretty convoluted. Mr Cook certainly got around. He surveyed this entire region in the mid-1760s, and his names for many of the islands, ports and waterways, such as the Humber Arm and Hawke's Bay, remain. His work here was so successful it led to voyages to New Zealand and Australia.

Known as the **Heritage District**, the older section of town, dating from 1925 to 1940, surrounds Central St. It's primarily a residential area, though there are some shops and a few restaurants.

The historic **Humbermouth Depot** (*Station Rd, off Humber Rd; admission $2; open 10am-8pm daily June 15-Sept 15*) sports the handsome steam locomotive and narrow-gauge rolling stock that chugged across the province from 1921 to 1939. In the station is a photographic exhibit.

An arm of Memorial University, the **Corner Brook Arts & Culture Centre** (☎ 709-637-2580, University Dr) features a 400-seat performing-arts facility and an art gallery (*admission free; open 9am-5pm daily*), which displays the works of local artists as

NEWFOUNDLAND

well as touring art shows. Culture is fine, but many people head to the center because of the **swimming pool** (☎ 709-637-2584; admission $3). Call ahead, because the public swim times vary.

Places to Stay & Eat
Prince Edward Park (☎ 709-637-1580, North Shore Hwy) Tent sites $9. The closest place to set up a tent is a five-minute drive from the tourist center, with 40 sites without hookups in a wooded setting. Take the Riverside Dr exit as you approach Corner Brook from the east and follow the signs along and over the Humber River.

Blow Me Down Provincial Park (☎ 709-681-2430, fax 709-681-2238, Route 450) Tent sites $11. This park at the end of Route 450

(which leads from town along the Humber Arm) is farther away but more scenic. Out here at the tip of the peninsula there are 28 sites, showers and laundry facilities, along with hiking trails and some good views of the Bay of Islands.

Memorial University (☎ 709-737-8000) Residence dorms are sometimes available in summer, but availability changes each year; call for details.

Corner Brook has a handful of tourist homes with prices lower than the numerous motel chains.

Bide-A-Nite Hospitality Home (☎ 709-634-7578, 877-934-7578, 11 Wellington St) Singles/doubles with breakfast $35/45. This central home with two rooms is the most affordable choice.

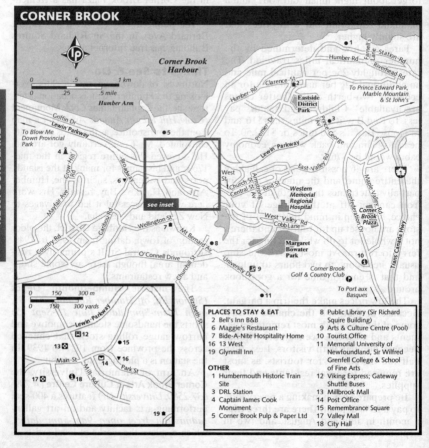

CORNER BROOK

PLACES TO STAY & EAT
2 Bell's Inn B&B
6 Maggie's Restaurant
7 Bide-A-Nite Hospitality Home
16 13 West
19 Glynmill Inn

OTHER
1 Humbermouth Historic Train Site
3 DRL Station
4 Captain James Cook Monument
5 Corner Brook Pulp & Paper Ltd

8 Public Library (Sir Richard Squire Building)
9 Arts & Culture Centre (Pool)
10 Tourist Office
11 Memorial University of Newfoundland, Sir Wilfred Grenfell College & School of Fine Arts
12 Viking Express; Gateway Shuttle Buses
13 Millbrook Mall
14 Post Office
15 Remembrance Square
17 Valley Mall
18 City Hall

Bell's Inn (☎ 709-634-5736, 888-634-1150, 2 Ford's Rd) Rooms $56-90 with full breakfast. This antique-decorated central B&B is within walking distance of downtown. It has eight rooms and is open all year.

Glynmill Inn (☎ 709-634-5181, 800-563-4400, fax 709-634-5106, 1 Cobb Lane) Rooms start at $75, suites $165. For more gracious accommodations, this downtown inn is recommended. It's a large, 80-room Tudor-style inn set off by surrounding lawns and gardens and offers a good dining room as well.

Maggie's (☎ 709-637-6627, 26 Caribou Rd) Prices under $8. Call for hours. At the edge of a small mall, Maggie's has outstanding Newfie pea soup, a few veggie items, seafood and sandwiches.

Glynmill Inn Mains $25. Corner Brook's mainstay for a splurge has long been the dining room and wine cellar of this landmark inn.

13 West (☎ 709-634-1300, 13 West St) Mains $25. One of the province's most well-received bistros is around the corner from Remembrance Square. This creative eatery features an eclectic menu of meat, seafood and pasta. Main courses rarely miss the mark in quality, and the wine list is extensive.

Getting There & Away

Corner Brook is a major hub for bus service throughout Newfoundland. Most – but not all – regional operators use a bus station (☎ 709-634-4710) in the center of town, adjacent to the Millbrook Mall shopping center, not far from Main St. Unfortunately, DRL, for points east and west along the Trans Canada Hwy, uses Pike's Irving station (☎ 709-634-7422), about 3km from the city center on the highway. It has a bus heading west at 5:55pm daily and a bus east at 11:25am. The fare to Port aux Basques is $32, to St John's $79. No city buses link the two bus depots.

Gateway (☎ 709-695-3333, 888-695-3322) has a shuttle to and from Port aux Basques ($30). This service goes to the bus office in Millbrook Mall and makes Viking Express/Pittman's connections for Rocky Harbour and northward. From here, the Viking Express bus goes up the northern peninsula, leaving Monday, Wednesday and Friday at 4pm for St Anthony. One-way fare to St Anthony is $55. This bus makes stops in Rocky Harbour for Gros Morne National

Park. Pittman's also departs here for Rocky Harbour, leaving Monday to Friday at 4:30pm.

Martin's Bus Service goes to Woody Point and Trout River in Gros Morne National Park. The bus departs at 4:30pm Monday to Friday and the ticket is $12. Eddy's Bus Service (☎ 709-634-7777) runs to Stephenville three to four times daily. Its office is at 9 Humber Rd, and the one-way fare is $10. Finally, if you need to reach Burgeo on the south coast, Devin's Bus Line (☎ 709-634-7777, 709-634-8281) provides service with an afternoon bus Monday through Friday. Sunday trips depend on demand. For all trips reservations are necessary.

AROUND CORNER BROOK
Marble Mountain

This major downhill ski center (☎ 709-637-7616) is in the Humber Valley 8km east of town on Hwy 1. The 500m Steady Brook Falls Trail leads from the ski area's rear parking lot to a cascade that tumbles more than 30m. Marble Mountain Ski Area Trail is 3.5km one way to the 500m summit of Skill Hill, where there are good views.

For more serious walkers, including overnighters, there are numerous hikes in the **Blomidon Mountains** (also spelled 'Blow Me Down'), south of the Bay of Islands along Hwy 450 to Lark Harbour. These mountains were formed about 500 million years ago from brownish peridotite rock pushed up from the earth's mantle when the geographic plates of both North America and Europe bumped together. What makes this special is that Newfoundland is one of the few places in the world where this type of rock is exposed.

Other features are the great views of the bay and islands and a small caribou population. Some of the trails, especially ones up on the barrens, are not well marked at all, so bring topographical maps and proper equipment. For a general description of the area, purchase a copy of *Best Hiking Trails in Western Newfoundland,* by Keith Nicol.

One of the easiest and most popular trails begins at a parking lot on the left side of Hwy 450 (500m from the bridge that crosses Blow Me Down Brook). The trail can be taken for an hour or so, or for more avid hikers, it continues well into the mountains, where you're on your own. At **Blow**

NEWFOUNDLAND

Me Down Park (☎ 709-681-2430, 800-563-6353, Route 450, Lark Harbour), near the end of Hwy 450, there are also well-used marked trails that provide fine views of the coastline.

STEPHENVILLE
pop 10,000

Formerly a large military-base town, with the decaying evidence still visible, Stephenville now relies mainly on the Abitibi-Price pulp mill. The town sits on St George's Bay between Corner Brook and Port aux Basques and acts as entrance to French Port au Port. The chamber of commerce tourist chalet (☎ 709-643-5854) is on the Trans Canada Hwy south of the exit, Route 490, for downtown Stephenville. Stephenville is possibly the least appealing town in Newfoundland, and festival time aside, there is no compelling reason to stop.

The Stephenville Festival is a three-week English theater event (with Shakespeare to modern Newfoundlanders' plays), usually held in late July with local and internationally known participants.

Indian Head Park (☎ 709-643-8368, Golf Course Rd; open July-Labor Day) Sites $11. This wooded campground has 30 sites and a swimming pool but no showers. To reach it, turn onto Massachusetts Ave from Hwy 460 and follow it around the airport to the coast.

Hotel Stephenville (☎ 709-643-5176, fax 709-643-5381, 19 Oregon Dr) Rates $59-74. Conveniently central, this 50-room place once hosted Elvis Presley and US president Eisenhower. The only hint of those golden years now is the American-state street names around town.

PORT AU PORT PENINSULA

The large peninsula west from Stephenville is the only French area of the province and has been since the early 1700s, when it became known as the French Shore. It was used by the French for fishing in the **Strait of Belle Isle** right up until the early 1900s. **Red Island** was at one time France's most important fishing base in the New World.

Today, the farther west you go the stronger the French culture is. At the southwest tip of the Port au Port Peninsula in **Cape St George**, area children still go to French school, preserving their dialect, which is now distinct from the language spoken in either France or Québec. Mainland, Lourdes and Black Duck Brook are also very French. In late July or early August each year, there is a major French folk festival held in Cape St George, with lots of music and other events.

In **Port au Port West**, a small community not far from Stephenville, **Our Lady of Mercy Church** (☎ 709-648-2632, open mid-June–early Sept) is worth a look. Begun in 1914, it is the largest wooden building in Newfoundland. During July and August, a guide provides details and stories about the church. On the way there from Stephenville, after going across the small bridge, continue straight on the small road. Don't follow the road around to the left or you'll miss the church like everybody else does. There is also the **Lady of Mercy Museum** (☎ 709-648-2632; admission $2; open 10am-5pm daily June-Sept), with a craft shop, tearoom and collection of local artifacts.

At **Piccadilly Head Park** you'll find a rugged stretch of coast, hiking trails and 50 campsites without hookups.

BARACHOIS POND PROVINCIAL PARK

Right on the Trans Canada Hwy near the exits to Stephenville, this large park (☎ 709-649-0048, open mid-May–mid-Sept) is one of the few in Newfoundland that offers a backpacking opportunity. From the campground, a trail heads 4.5km one way to the top of Erin Mountain, a peak of almost 400m. On top there are backcountry campsites and excellent views of the surrounding area.

Plan on two hours for the climb. There are no fees for hiking or camping on the mountain. The park also has a swimming area, canoe rentals, showers, laundry facilities, a small store and a 150-site campground ($11). This is one of the busiest campgrounds in the province and one of just a couple that can be full, especially on weekends.

Southwestern Newfoundland

Within the small southwestern corner of the province, the visitor is offered a remarkable variety of geography and history. It is well worthwhile spending some time exploring it rather than just doing the usual mad dash to or from the ferry. Hilly Port aux Basques, built up and around a jutting, jagged peninsula and offering all the services, including a major tourist office, is the center of the region.

CODROY VALLEY

North of Port aux Basques beyond Cape Ray, the broad green, fertile Codroy Valley runs from the coast northeast alongside the Long Range Mountains for about 50km. This is one of the prime farming regions of the province, and compared with the generally rugged, rocky landscape, it looks positively lush. A good spot for a view of the valley (accessible by car) is down near the sea by the town of **Searston**.

Farther along, the road goes up a mountain at **Cape Anguille**, with views as far as the mainland on a clear day. Back at the inlet, the estuary of the Grand Codroy River is an important wetland area for birds. It's impressive at migration times, when thousands of geese, black ducks and other species make a pit stop.

Despite the valley's long period of settlement and the many quiet farms, it does have a nasty side to it. Codroy Valley can be the windiest place in Newfoundland – and that's saying something. Along the highway winds can reach 200km/h. They used to have to stop the trains at times to prevent them from blowing off the tracks.

PORT AUX BASQUES
pop 6100

When approached by ferry from Nova Scotia, the rocky, barren, treeless landscape here – the first glimpse of Newfoundland for most – can look a little forbidding, but it is also immensely appealing for its rough, undeveloped character.

The town itself, at least the older section built on and around the hills to the left of the ferry as it approaches, is very attractive. The narrow, winding roads edged with traditional wooden houses are fun to walk, offering different views and angles at every turn.

Port aux Basques was named in the early 16th century by Basque fishers and whalers who came to work the waters of the Strait of Belle Isle, which separates the province from Québec.

Today, Port aux Basques is a principal terminal for the Marine Atlantic ferry. The ferry company is the largest employer in town, though there are also freight-handling and fish-packing industries. The town is also sometimes known as Channel Port aux Basques.

The town center is to the southeast of the ferry landing and back the way you came in on the ferry. To get to this old section of town, cross the bridge after leaving the ferry and turn left.

For the new, uninteresting part of town, turn right along the Trans Canada Hwy. Go past a number of gasoline stations and turn left at the Hotel Port aux Basques on the corner of Grand Bay Rd and High St. This leads to the shopping mall, the center of the new district.

The tourist chalet (☎ 709-695-2262), with information on all parts of the province, is on the Trans Canada Hwy a few kilometers out of town on the way to St John's. Hours are 6am to 11pm daily during summer. Adjacent to the Hotel Port aux Basques is the Railway Heritage Center (☎ 709-695-7560), which houses the city's information office, open from 9am to 9pm daily in summer. Outside are antique railroad cars (tours $2).

Gulf Museum

Downtown, across from the town hall, is this two-story museum (☎ 709-695-7604, 118 Main St; adult/family $4/7; open 10am-7pm daily early July–late Aug). Most of the collection is maritime artifacts – many from shipwrecks.

The showpiece of the museum is its astrolabe. This navigational instrument from the 17th century is a striking brass contraption, about 17.5cm in diameter, made in Portugal in 1628. The design is based on a principle discovered by the ancient Greeks to allow for charting of the heavenly bodies. Variations on it have been used for nautical navigation since 1470. The astrolabe is in remarkable condition and is one of only about three dozen in the world. It was found by a diver off Isle aux Morts along the south coast from town in 1982 and is believed to have been on board either a Portuguese or Basque fishing boat.

Grand Bay West Beach

To hit the beach in Port aux Basques, head down Grand Bay West Rd and turn onto

Klye Lane just before crossing the third bridge. At the end of Klye Lane is a small park overlooking a wide, sandy beach. This is also the start of the Cormack Trail to JT Cheeseman Provincial Park.

Places to Stay

With all the ferry traffic, reservations are a good idea unless you arrive very early in the day.

JT Cheeseman Provincial Park (☎ 709-695-7222, fax 709-695-9384, Route 408) Tent sites $10. This is a fine place, and it's close enough to town to be convenient when arriving late or leaving early. It has 102 sites and is 12km along the Trans Canada Hwy north of town. There are no showers, but the park features a wide sweeping beach, hiking

trails and boat rentals. A few whale bones found on the beach are on display.

Heritage Home (☎ 709-695-3240, 11 Caribou Rd; open May-Oct) Singles/doubles with continental breakfast $40/46. At this five-room guesthouse, you can stay in bed almost until the ferry, literally across the street, blows the horn. Bathrooms are shared except in the family suite.

Four Seasons B&B (☎ 709-695-3826, 82 High St) Singles/doubles $40/50. This modest four-room B&B is near Heritage Home but closer to the mall.

St Christopher's Hotel (☎ 709-695-7034, 800-563-4779, fax 709-695-9841, Caribou Rd) Rooms start at $70, suites with kitchen start at $90. This establishment, with a fine view from its hilltop location, is a commercial

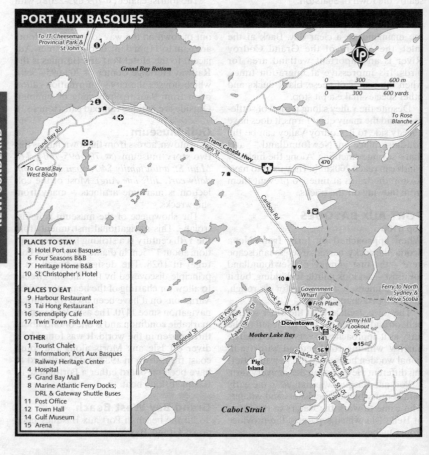

PORT AUX BASQUES

To JT Cheeseman
Provincial Park &
St John's

Grand Bay Bottom

Grand Bay Rd

To Grand Bay
West Beach

Trans Canada Hwy

High St

To Rose
Blanche

470

1

Caribou Rd

Government
Wharf   Fish Plant

Ferry to North
Sydney &
Nova Scotia

1st Ave
2nd Ave

Brook St

Downtown

Main St

Army Hill
Lookout

Regional St

Lakes Shore Dr

Mother Lake Bay

Pig
Island

Charles St

Main St

Reed St

Reet St

Baird St

Cabot Strait

0   300   600 m
0   300   600 yards

PLACES TO STAY
3 Hotel Port aux Basques
6 Four Seasons B&B
7 Heritage Home B&B
10 St Christopher's Hotel

PLACES TO EAT
9 Harbour Restaurant
13 Tai Hong Restaurant
16 Serendipity Café
17 Twin Town Fish Market

OTHER
1 Tourist Chalet
2 Information; Port Aux Basques
   Railway Heritage Center
4 Hospital
5 Grand Bay Mall
8 Marine Atlantic Ferry Docks;
   DRL & Gateway Shuttle Buses
11 Post Office
12 Town Hall
14 Gulf Museum
15 Arena

NEWFOUNDLAND

hotel offering more amenities and a dining room and bar.

Hotel Port aux Basques (☎ *709-695-2171, 877-695-2171, fax 709-695-2250, 1 Grand Bay Rd*) Singles start at $65, suites are available and kids stay free. The hotel is just off the Trans Canada Hwy on the way out of town eastbound and has a restaurant offering seafood.

Places to Eat
Harbour Restaurant (☎ *709-695-3238, 121 Caribou Rd*) Prices under $10. Open 6am-1am and all night weekends. The location is tempting, with superlative views and close proximity to the ferry, but even the breakfast (under $4) is not well executed. The menu is mainly fried chicken or fish and chips.

Richard's (☎ *709-695-3813, Grand Bay Mall, Grand Bay Rd*) Closed Sunday. This simple but cheap family place in the tatty mall has breakfast specials for $3.

Serendipity Café (☎ *709-695-2088, 88 Main St*) Prices under $8. Closed Sunday. This recommended spot is cozy and tidy. With its urbane, sophisticated design, it seems somewhat out of context.

Tai Hong (☎ *709-695-7548, 116 Main St*) Dishes $5-9. Open 11am-10pm daily. For standard Chinese, try this place that at least offers vegetables and some Canadian basics to round out the menu.

Twin Town Fish Market (*Charles St*) Closed Sunday. If you're heading for a campsite and want some seafood, this market perched at the end of the street has it all.

Getting There & Away
Bus The DRL bus service (☎ 709-695-4216) leaves once a day at 8am from the ferry dock terminal for the 904km trip to St John's ($97, 14 hours). You can stop at any of the towns along the way (and there are plenty of stops). Connections can be made in other towns with other, more local, bus companies that serve destinations other than those on the main route to St John's.

Note that the DRL bus to Corner Brook ($32) does *not* stop where buses for Gros Morne depart. The Corner Brook departure point for buses to Gros Morne is across town from the DRL stop. If you're going to Gros Morne, or beyond, you're better off catching the Gateway Shuttle Service (☎ 888-695-3322) to Corner Brook ($30), which goes to

Millbrook Mall. (See the Corner Brook section for connections.) Gateway also departs at 8am, but only Monday through Friday. From Corner Brook, a number of smaller lines fan out to smaller destinations.

Ferry Marine Atlantic (☎ 800-341-7981, w www.marine-atlantic.ca) operates both the ferry routes from Nova Scotia to Newfoundland, one going to Argentia and this one to Port aux Basques.

From the beginning of June to the middle of September there are one to three trips daily on a wildly staggered schedule. Printed schedules are ubiquitous around Nova Scotia and Newfoundland. In midsummer, reservations are recommended. Generally one or two days' notice is sufficient unless you require a berth in a cabin, in which case the earlier the better. Early morning or late-night trips are usually less busy and, if you're walking or cycling, there shouldn't be any trouble. If you'll be arriving in Port Aux Basques or North Sydney on a late ferry, you definitely should have a room booked before you arrive.

The fare is $22, less for children and seniors, $67 per car, more with a trailer or camper. The night ferry, departing at 11:30pm, saves you the cost of lodging, but passengers are no longer allowed to lay out a blanket anywhere, including the floor, so you are stuck sitting in a chair all night. The chairs in the TV lounge do recline, so there is a rush for those upon boarding. If you feel like a bag of dirt with a stiff neck in the morning, at least there are free showers. In the reasonably priced cafeteria, there is a microwave oven, if you're pinching pennies and want to use your own tea bag.

For those with extra cash, berths and cabins are also available. A dorm bunk is $14, a four-berth cabin $90, but remember, you're getting up very early.

The crossing takes five to six hours in summer and up to 7½ hours in winter.

AROUND PORT AUX BASQUES
Cape Ray
Fourteen kilometers north of the Marine Ferry Terminal and adjacent to JT Cheeseman Provincial Park is Cape Ray. The coastal scenery is engaging, and the road leads up to the windblown **Cape Ray lighthouse complex** (☎ *709-695-2262*). A

plaque commemorates the first transatlantic cable, which was laid in 1856. There is also information on the archeological **Dorset Paleo-Eskimo site** here dating from 400 BC to AD 400. Thousands of artifacts have been uncovered from this, the southernmost known Dorset site, and dwelling sites can be seen. The lightkeeper's house across the street is now a *craft shop* open mid-June to mid-September.

Hiking

The Port aux Basques/southern Codroy area offers some interesting hikes, due in part to the Long Range Mountains. The **Cormack Trail** is a long trail under development that will stretch from Port aux Basques north to Flat Bay near Stephenville. In Port aux Basques, you can pick up the trail at Grand Bay West Beach, where there is a trail map. From there, it's an 11km hike along the coast to JT Cheeseman Provincial Park. Signs direct you through Cape Ray, and the trail resumes at the lighthouse, reaching the Red Rocks area in 4km.

Table Mountain Trail begins on the Trans Canada Hwy opposite the exit to Cape Ray, where a Table Mountain Digital Project sign marks a rough dirt road. The 6km trail is actually this rugged road (don't even think about driving up it) that leads to the top of the 518m-high flat-top mountain. On top are the ruins of a radar site, airstrip and buildings that the USA put up during WWII. The hike is not hard, but plan on three to four hours for the 12km roundtrip walk.

Starlite Trail is another access route into the Long Range Mountains. It's 31km north of Port aux Basques on the Trans Canada Hwy near the community of Tompkins and is a one-way hike of 2km to a high point where there are views of the Codroy Valley.

SOUTH COAST

The often ignored Hwy 470, which heads east out of Port aux Basques for about 50km, is a fine short excursion. If you've got your own transportation and an afternoon or a day waiting for a ferry, this is an ideal little side trip. Edging along the shoreline, the road rises and falls over the rounded, eroded windswept terrain, looking as though it's following a glacier that plowed through yesterday. Visible along the other side of the road are half a dozen evenly spaced fishing towns.

Isle aux Morts (Island of the Dead) came by its name through the many shipwrecks just offshore that have occurred over some 400 years. Between Burnt Islands and Diamond Cove you pass stunning Barachois Falls plunging out of the hills north of Hwy 470. Look for a small 'Scenic Hike' sign for the start of a boardwalk that winds to almost the base of the falls.

The highlight is the last village along the road, **Rose Blanche**, an absolutely splendid, traditional-looking village nestled in a little cove with a fine natural harbor – a perfect

Rose Blanche, a classic Newfoundland village

example of the classic Newfoundland fishing community. To reach the **Rose Blanche Lighthouse** (☎ 709-695-7411; adult/family $3/7; open 9am-9pm May-Oct), turn left at the town hall and fire station and follow the side road to the H&P Lounge. Bear left up that imposing gravel road that winds its way up the rocky slopes nearly to the historic structure. Restorations to the original stone lighthouse of 1873 were completed in 1999. The *Hook, Line & Sinker* (☎ 709-956-2005, open seasonally) café is right next door and is a delightful spot for a light lunch. You can walk up here right past people's front doors.

For those who long to go that one step further, a trip can be taken by boat (ask around the docks) across the bay to the smaller village of **Petites**, which has a population of about 30 families. Here, and visible from the Rose Blanche Lighthouse, **Bethany United Church** is probably the oldest wooden church in North America (although now the Anglicans have taken over), dating from 1859. It's a plain and simple church kept in excellent condition and has registers of births, deaths and marriages to pore over for details of local history. Before going, ask if someone is around to open it.

For those without a vehicle, Gateway Transportation (☎ 709-695-3333) in Port aux Basques offers flexible tours of the South Coast and Rose Blanche. These aren't scheduled, but a two-hour tour is about $60 for one to four people; call and make a deal.

Outports

'Outport' is the name given to any of the tiny coastal fishing villages accessible only by boat. Some are on one of the major intraprovincial coastal ferry lines; others are not. These little communities represent some of the most remote settlements left in North America. Change is coming at an ever quickening pace, but for the moment, these outports harbor the rough Newfoundland life at its most traditional. These villages clinging to the rocky coastlines are perhaps the best places to see the unique culture of the Newfoundland people of European blood born in Canada.

Coastal Labrador Marine Services has runs up the coast of Labrador. But one heads directly to Happy Valley–Goose Bay, which is hardly an outport, with soldiers from a handful of countries stationed there. This ferry takes vehicles and passengers. The other run, from St Anthony, is for passengers only and leapfrogs from one outport to the next. This is the boat to be on. For details, see the Labrador, St Anthony and Lewisporte sections in this chapter.

For places to stay on the north coastal trip, there are some established lodgings, or you can ask around about alternatives beforehand or just take a chance on arrival. You can always stay on the ferry if you're continuing on without a stopover. This can be tiring if you're doing it on the cheap; sleeping on the floor or in a chair can be pretty uncomfortable after a few days, espe-

cially if the sea is rough. On a longer trip, consider a cabin as the prices actually are quite fair. Ask about stopovers and how long the ticket is good for. For details and schedules, call the provincial tourism information office (☎ 800-563-6353). It also makes reservations.

SOUTH COAST

At the moment, you can cobble together a number of ferries to bop across the South Coast. This is a more accessible trip than cruising northern Labrador, and the area gives a more typical view of traditional Newfoundland life than the more Inuit and Native Indian–influenced villages of Labrador. It's also cheaper. Currently, you can go from Rose Blanche east as far as Hermitage, a total of eight stops. There are also a few outports with ferry service around the Burin Peninsula, but these are not connected in a longish linear fashion, more just go-and-return-style trips. Be forewarned however that ferry services and schedules change frequently.

Departing from Rose Blanche – not Port Aux Basques – you can hopscotch to Lapoile and Grand Bruit. From Grand Bruit, you can continue to Burgeo, where yet another ferry will link up with Ramea, Grey River, Francois, McCallum, Gaultois and, finally, Hermitage. From here, you'll have to suss out transportation back to the main highway and possible bus transportation. Up-to-the-minute ferry schedules can be found at the provincial tourist office in Port aux Basques, or contact the Department of Works, Services, and Transportation (☎ 709-635-4100).

There is one ferry daily except Tuesday and Thursday from Rose Blanche to Lapoile ($3). Note the times are not the same each day, and the schedule changes in the winter (November to March). The same number of ferries go on to Grand Bruit for another $2.75.

From Grand Bruit, the next ferry goes to Burgeo ($4.50). It leaves Tuesday morning. – That's it, once a week, so don't get caught waiting unless you want to.

From relatively large and road-linked Burgeo, you've got various options. Devin's Bus Line Limited (☎ 709-886-2955 in Burgeo) has service back to Corner Brook. It leaves 8am or 9am Monday through

NEWFOUNDLAND

Friday. Monday, Wednesday and Friday it is scheduled to wait for the ferry, but by the time you read this it could have changed. There is no bus service on weekends.

Burgeo also offers three ferry options. The MV *Gallipoli* runs passengers and vehicles between Burgeo, lovely Ramea and Grey River. It just shuttles back and forth every day, with one to three departures daily on a fairly complicated schedule. Passenger-only fare is $3 to Ramea and $3.25 more to Grey River.

Another boat, the MV *Marine Voyager*, leaves at 2:15pm Sunday, Monday, Wednesday, Friday and Saturday for Grey River ($4.25, 2½ hours), continuing to very, very tiny Francois ($3.75, two hours) at 5:15pm.

From Francois, eastbound, the ferry frequency drops markedly, with a trip to McCallum at 7am Thursday ($3.75, 2½ hours), continuing on to Hermitage ($1.75, 1½ hours) via Gaultois. Whew! Are you getting this? The point is, it is all possible, as long as you are relaxed and flexible. Also keep asking the locals and call the Department of Transportation.

Lastly, the MV *Terra Nova* does the McCallum-Gaultois-Hermitage run daily, but this service may be cut back. All these ferries are subject to decreasing government largesse.

Places to Stay

Accommodations are hassle-free in larger Burgeo, but along the way you should have little trouble lining up something, even if it's just with a family. The locals are very helpful and do see a few (not many) strangers lugging backpacks passing through. If you're concerned, the phone book or tourist information in Port aux Basques could help, but informal boardinghouses may not be registered with the tourism department.

Blue Mountain Cabins (☎ 709-492-2753) Singles/doubles $60. There are just two cottages at this place in Grand Bruit. Meals are offered at modest prices.

Sandbanks Provincial Park (☎ 709-886-2331) Campsites $11. In Burgeo, this park has an excellent campground that is comfortably equipped with heated washrooms and showers. The rangers are knowledgeable and helpful, and the beach is stunning.

Burgeo Haven B&B (☎ 709-886-2544, 888-603-0273, 111 Reach Rd) Singles/doubles start at $45/55. This large house in Burgeo has four guestrooms. It's open from mid-May to the end of September and offers Internet access.

Gillett's Motel (☎ 709-886-1284, fax 709-886-3304, 1 Inspiration Rd), Singles/doubles $65/70. Another option in Burgeo, Gillett's is modern, has a dining room and is close to the ferry.

Although Francois is small, there are at least half a dozen boardinghouses where you can stay. Just ask around.

Labrador

Labrador is the part of the province – three times the size of Newfoundland – that is adjacent to the Québec mainland. The Strait of Belle Isle separates Labrador from the island. This vast, rugged land is one of the last incompletely explored areas in the country and one of the largest, cleanest, natural areas anywhere (at least, cynics and environmentalists sneer, away from the resource development sites or until the mineral extraction companies get their way).

The geological base of Labrador is the ancient Laurentian Shield – possibly the oldest unchanged region on the earth. It's thought the land looks much the same as it did before life on the planet began – expect primeval-looking, undulating, rocky, puddled expanses with little vegetation. Four great caribou herds, including the world's largest with some 750,000 head, migrate across Labrador to their calving grounds each year.

Until the 1960s, small numbers of Inuit, other Native Indians and longtime European descendants known as 'liveyers' were the only human residents in Labrador. They lived in little villages dotted along the rocky coasts as they had done for centuries, eking out an existence fishing and hunting. The interior was virgin wilderness.

Through the past few decades, a new people, with a completely different outlook and lifestyle, has arrived. White southerners have been lured by the overwhelming and nearly untouched natural resources.

And so, not far away from the more or less traditional way of life of the original inhabitants lie some of the world's most modern, sophisticated industrial complexes. So far, most of the development has been far inland, near the border of

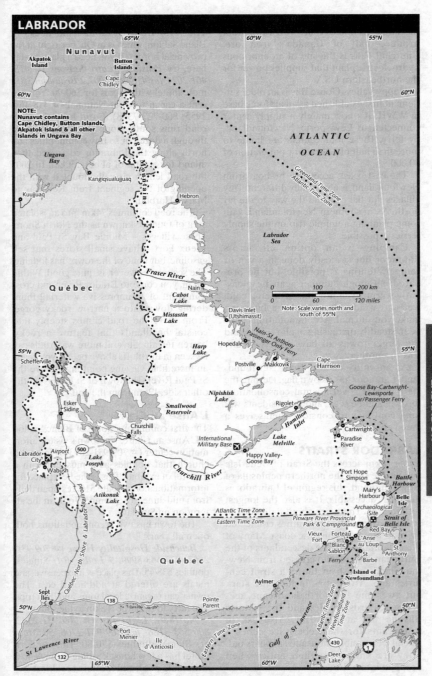

LABRADOR

Nunavut

Akpatok Island

Button Islands

Cape Chidley

NOTE:
Nunavut contains Cape Chidley, Button Islands, Akpatok Island & all other Islands in Ungava Bay

Ungava Bay

Kangiqsualujjuaq

Kuujjuaq

Québec

Torngat Mountains

ATLANTIC OCEAN

Greenland Time Zone
Atlantic Time Zone

Hebron

Labrador Sea

Fraser River

Nain

Cabot Lake

Mistastin Lake

Davis Inlet (Utshimassit)

Nain-St Anthony Passenger Only Ferry

Harp Lake

Hopedale

0   100   200 km
0   60   120 miles
Note: Scale varies north and south of 55°N

Schefferville

Postville   Makkovik

Cape Harrison

Esker Siding

Nipishish Lake

Smallwood Reservoir

Rigolet

Goose Bay-Cartwright-Lewisporte Car/Passenger Ferry

Churchill Falls

International Military Base

Lake Melville

Hamilton Inlet

Cartwright

Labrador City

Airport

500

Lake Joseph

Happy Valley-Goose Bay

Paradise River

Wabush

Churchill River

Port Hope Simpson

Atikonak Lake

Mary's Harbour

Battle Harbour

Atlantic Time Zone
Eastern Time Zone

Belle Isle

Archaeological Site

Strait of Belle Isle

Pinware River Provincial Park & Campground

Red Bay

Vieux Fort

Forteau

L'Anse au Loup

Blanc Sablon

St Barbe

St Anthony

Ferry

Québec

Island of Newfoundland

Aylmer

Atlantic Time Zone
Newfoundland Time Zone

Sept Iles

138

Pointe Parent

Eastern Time Zone

430

1

Port Ménier

Ile d'Anticosti

Gulf of St Lawrence

Deer Lake

St Lawrence River

132

LABRADOR

Québec. Labrador City and Wabush, with the latest technology, are two towns that produce half of Canada's iron ore. Churchill Falls is the site of an enormous hydroelectric plant that supplies power for the northeastern USA.

Happy Valley–Goose Bay is an older settlement first established as an air force base in WWII. It's now mainly a supply center connected to Lewisporte, Newfoundland, by ferry. These four centers are home to more than half of Labrador's population of 30,000.

The east coast, accessible by boat from Newfoundland, is also totally different. Tiny villages dot the coast all the way to the far north. As in southern Newfoundland, with some planning a unique trip on the supply ferries is possible.

Camping is an option all across Labrador but is mostly done in a van or camper. Tenting is possible, but be prepared; although summers can be pleasantly warm, even hot, this is often a cold, wet and windy place. And the bugs can make you suicidal. Accommodations have been steadily increasing in all regions, and the larger towns all have hotels of one sort or another.

As an entity distinct from Newfoundland, Labrador has its own flag. Despite the 2001 official governmental consolidation, this will still be seen, and the residents will long continue to consider themselves a breed apart.

LABRADOR STRAITS

Lying 18km across the Strait of Belle Isle and visible from the northern peninsula of Newfoundland, this region of Labrador is the most accessible. It is also the longest settled area. There are about half a dozen small, permanent communities connected by road along the historic coast. Many of the inhabitants are the descendants of the European fishers who crossed from Newfoundland to fish in the rich strait centuries ago. Attractions include the stark but awesome far north landscape, icebergs, seabirds, whales and the historic Basque site at Red Bay. Also ask in restaurants for the iceberg ice cubes – glacial ice possibly thousands of years old. They are known for their antics when dropped into a drink.

Blanc Sablon

The ferry from Newfoundland docks at Blanc Sablon, which is in Québec right at the provincial border. If you need a place to stay here, try *Pension Quatre Saisons* (☎ 418-461-2024, fax 418-461-2007, 2 Beaudoin St), a motel/hotel with rooms for $60-90. You can rent a car in town at National (☎ 418-461-2955, 800-227-7368). From here the only road runs south along the Québec coast through a dozen or so tiny communities and north along the Labrador coast and then inland for a total of about 150km. In 2001 the road length virtually doubled with the opening of the segment from Red Bay to Mary's Harbour.

The road continues 74km into an isolated area of Québec known as the North Shore. Three villages – Middle Bay, St Paul and Vieux Fort – have small stores that sell gasoline, but none of the towns has lodging. The scenery, however, is quite good. Within 19km, you come to Brador River and cross it in front of an impressive waterfall thundering down into a narrow rocky gorge. From there the road climbs steeply into coastal headlands that feature a rocky, barren terrain. Several more waterfalls can be seen in the bluffs above before you reach an incredible viewing point high above the St Paul River. The town of St Paul is on the other side, 12km from the end.

L'Anse au Claire

The first community north of Blanc Sablon is L'Anse au Claire. The town's visitor information center (☎ 709-931-2013) is in an old church that doubles as a museum with a handful of exhibits. This is the best place for information along Route 510. It's open daily from mid-June to September (only in the afternoon on Sunday).

The town has two accommodations, both open all year.

Beachside Hospitality Home (☎ 709-931-2662, 877-663-8999, 9 Lodge Rd) Singles/doubles $38/45. This place is inexpensive, and meals are offered at additional cost. The owner can organize local tours and boat trips. The ferry to St Barbe is 8km to the south.

Northern Light Inn (☎ 709-931-2332, 800-563-3188, fax 709-931-2708, 58 Main St) Singles/doubles $70/80. This modern motel has a few housekeeping rooms and a swimming pool, and it offers breakfast.

Forteau & Beyond

Forteau, the largest community along the coast here, is home of the annual Bakeapple Festival in mid-August, a three-day event of music, dance, food and crafts.

Grenfell Louis Hall B&B (☎ 709-931-2916, fax 709-931-2189, 3 Willow Ave) Singles/doubles $40/50. This five-room B&B is in an old nursing station near the trailhead for the Overfill Brook Trail.

Seaview Cabins (☎ 709-931-2840, fax 709-931-2842, 33 Main St) Rates $50-75. Seaview has a restaurant, grocery store and laundry facilities.

On the way to L'Anse au Loup along Route 510 is the **Labrador Straits Museum** (☎ 709-931-2067; admission $2; open 10am-8pm daily in summer), with exhibits on the early local residents and others that outline the region's traditional way of life, especially the contributions of women. It doubles as a visitors' center and *craft shop*.

L'Anse Amour

L'Anse Amour Burial Mound (☎ 709-458-2417) is a Maritime Archaic Indian stone-covered burial site dating from about 7500 years ago, the earliest burial mound of its type known in North America.

Continue along the side road, past some impressive rocky bluffs, and you'll end up at the **Point Amour Lighthouse Provincial Historic Site** (☎ 709-927-5825, L'Anse Amour Rd; admission $2.50; open 10am-5pm daily June-Thanksgiving). The renovated site features the furnished lightkeeper's house, the tower, costumed interpreters and a craft shop. The light was first illuminated in 1858, after four years' work building the 36m tower. Today, you can climb to the top. It's a 127-step climb, however the 360-degree view of the coastline is spectacular. Beware – signs warn of unexploded WWII-era ordnance in the area.

Lighthouse Cove B&B (☎/fax 709-927-5690) Singles/doubles $35/40. In town at this bargain B&B, dinner is available. The homemade food is excellent, and the couple who run the place are extremely knowledgeable about the area.

L'Anse au Loup

L'Anse au Loup, like many of the coastal villages, has a French name, but the people here (about 625 of them) are of English ancestry. Groceries, alcohol and gas are available and together with the town's wide sweep of sandy beach make a stop worthwhile, maybe even for overnight.

Pinware River Provincial Park (☎ 709-729-2424) Tent sites $9. Between L'Anse au Loup and Red Bay, this park has 15 campsites and some picnic tables. Don't forget the insect repellent.

Barney's B&B (☎ 709-927-5634, fax 709-927-5609, 122 Main St) Rooms $30/38. This three-room hospitality home offers the best accommodations deal around. Rates include a light breakfast, and seafood meals are available at additional cost, or you can use kitchen facilities.

The scenery from Pinware River Provincial Park to Red Bay is some of the best along Route 510. First you skirt the west side of the river, then cross over on a one-lane iron bridge, and then run along the east side, high above the rushing whitewater. This stretch of the Pinware is renowned for its salmon fishing, and there are lodges with guiding service. About 10km from Red Bay is a barren, rocky area that is full of blueberries and bakeapples (and pickers) in August.

Red Bay

Red Bay is marked by the rusting Québec freighter in the harbor that ran aground in 1966. The **Red Bay National Historic Site** (☎ 709-920-2051, Route 510; admission $3; open 9am-6:30pm Mon-Sat, noon-8pm Sun, mid-June–early October) is the prime attraction of the region. It chronicles the discovery in the late 1970s of three Basque whaling galleons from the 1500s on the sea bed just off Red Bay. The ice-cold waters have kept them well preserved, making the area an underwater museum. Subsequent research has found that this was the largest whaling port in the world in the late 16th century, when more than 2000 men resided here. On display is one of those Basque whaling vessels that was pulled from the murky, icy depths, and there is an hour-long explanatory video. Some of the excavated land sites can be visited by boat, including a cemetery on nearby **Saddle Island**, where there is a self-guided interpretive trail. The historic site also runs the **Saddle Boat tours**. Passage for the short ferry ride is $2.

Red Bay's accommodations amount to a few cabins that are rented out at the restaurant.

Whaler's Cabins (☎ 709-920-2156) Single or double $65. The few cabins come with kitchenettes, but *Whaler's Restaurant* itself is a very pleasant place to have a bowl of seafood chowder.

Beyond Red Bay

Traveling the brand-new road provides a sense of real remoteness rather than outstanding beauty. Formerly a winter-only road passable when everything is frozen, it leaves the coast and travels inland about 80km to Mary's Harbour. The latter was created in 1955 after a fire wiped out the centuries-older settlement of Battle Harbour. Some of the historic fishery buildings, as old as 200 years, escaped the flames and have been restored. They can be reached by boat in summer from Mary's Harbour. The *Riverview Hotel* (☎ 709-921-6948, fax 709-921-6376) has eight rooms ($65-80) and a restaurant. It's open June to October.

Hiking

There are a handful of pleasant day hikes between Forteau and Cape Diable. The first is **Overfall Brook Trail** in the town of Forteau. The 4km trail is a one-way hike along the coast with views of the Point Armour Lighthouse in the distance. It ends at a 30m waterfall. East of the town is **Schooner Cove Trail**, a 3km trek from Route 510 to the cove that was once the site of Archaic Indians thousands of years ago and then a whaling factory.

On the west side of L'Anse au Loup is the **Battery Trail**, a 2km or 30-minute hike through a stunted tuckamore forest to the summit of the Battery, where a spectacular view of the Strait of Belle Isle can be enjoyed. Finally near Cape Diable is another marked hiking trail that climbs 2km to a high point along a bluff.

Getting There & Away

Those traveling by car should be aware that the road running up and down the coast from Blanc Sablon is not connected to farther destinations in either Québec or Labrador.

Air Air Canada Jazz (☎ 888-247-2262), the Air Canada subsidiary, has flights from Deer Lake, Newfoundland, to Blanc Sablon. Also try Provincial Airlines (☎ 800-563-2800) from Corner Brook, Deer Lake or Happy Valley–Goose Bay. Air Labrador (☎ 800-563-3042) links St John's to Goose Bay and numerous coastal communities. Blanc Sablon is also connected to Québec destinations such as Sept-Îles and Québec City by Air Canada (☎ 888-247-2262).

Ferry From early May to some time in January the MV *Apollo* – a vehicle and passenger ferry – runs from St Barbe, Newfoundland, to Blanc Sablon, Québec. It is operated by Labrador Marine (☎ 866-535-2567) out of St Barbe. From the beginning of July to the end of August, when things are at their busiest, the boat runs two or three times a day; at other times service drops to once or twice daily. In peak season, the ferry leaves St Barbe at 8am, 12:30pm and 5pm on Tuesday, Thursday and Saturday, at 10:15am and 2:45pm on Monday and Wednesday, at 10:15am and 4:15pm on Friday, and at 2pm and 6:30pm on Sunday.

From Blanc Sablon, the ferry leaves at 10:15am and 2:45pm Tuesday, Thursday and Saturday, at 8am, 12:30pm and 5pm Monday and Wednesday, at 8am, 1:30pm and 6:30pm Friday, and at 11:45am and 4:15pm Sunday. But don't take our word for it. Be sure to check ahead of time. The rest of the season there are fewer trips.

The two-hour trip from St Barbe to Blanc Sablon is $9 per person, $18.50 for a car and more for trailers, etc. Reservations are advisable, but it's not unknown to arrive 15 minutes prior to departure in August and still get a place. The problem then is getting back. Only half the spaces on the ferry for autos are allowed to reserve, and these are usually gone a week or more ahead of time; thus, you need to get to the ferry office way before it opens to line up and get a number. And keep in mind the time difference – Blanc Sablon is a half-hour behind Labrador, which is on Newfoundland time.

A coastal freight service, the *Nordic Express*, operated by Relais Nordik Inc (☎ 418-968-4707 in Sept-Îles, 800-463-0680 from anywhere in northwestern Québec) runs up the Québec coast from Sept-Îles on the Gulf of St Lawrence to Blanc Sablon with stops along the way. There is one trip a week, and it should be booked a month ahead in July and August.

Woodwards operates the Coastal Labrador Adventure Cruises ferry from St Anthony, Newfoundland, up the Labrador coast. It makes a call at Red Bay as well, but it's a passenger-only service. For details see St Anthony earlier.

NORTHERN COAST

Beyond Mary's Harbour all the way up to **Ungava Bay** are dozens of small semitraditional communities and settlements accessible only by sea or air along the rugged, largely unspoiled mountainous coast. This area of Labrador doesn't get a lot of visitors but offers the persistent a look at some of the most remote regions of North America.

Living off the land completely has pretty much disappeared, especially now that the fishing industry has all but gone belly up. Between government moratoriums and lack of fish, making a wage from the sea is almost impossible. Some hunting and trapping is still carried on, but these days unemployment is high and many people rely on government funds. Still, the lifestyle remains unchanged in many ways due simply to the isolation and the small size of the villages. The people are a determined lot – they have to be.

The accommodations situation is a bit of an unknown; most travelers use the ferry as a floating hotel. For those wishing to get off and hang around until the next boat, it usually means winging it for a room, though larger places should have something.

Coastal Labrador Marine Services' passenger-only ferry from St Anthony plies the Labrador coast from Red Bay up into Goose Bay and then as far north as Nain. Private vessels can be hired to reach still farther north. See the St Anthony section, earlier in this chapter.

Makkovik, an early fur-trading post, is a traditional fishing and hunting community. Both new and old-style crafts can be bought. In **Hopedale**, a historic site presided over by the Avituk Historical Society (*☎ 709-923-2262; open June-Sept*) preserves the old wooden Moravian mission church from 1782. The site includes a store, residence, some huts and a museum collection.

At the 12-room *Amaguk Inn* (*☎ 709-933-3750, fax 709-933-3764,*) in the area, singles/doubles cost $85/95. The inn also serves meals, and you can get a beer in the lounge.

The Moravian Church

The Moravians developed in the mid-1400s as the Church of the Brotherhood. They broke from the Church of Rome and fled persecution in their place of origin, the then largely German-speaking provinces of Bohemia and Moravia, in what is now the Czech Republic. A strong evangelical movement, the Moravians set up missions in Asia, Africa, the West Indies and North and South America.

Starting in the late 1700s, members began ministering to the Inuit of the New World, doing some good but attempting to diminish the Native Indian spirituality and culture at the same time. They were a prominent European group all along the Strait of Belle Isle on both the Newfoundland side and, most notably, on the coast of Labrador. They maintained an extensive mission community here until the 1950s. Many of their former buildings are still in use, some as historical sites.

The Innu community of Utshimassit, long-called **Davis Inlet**, has a terrible history of misery and major social and economic problems. They want to move to Sango Bay, where they believe they will be able to have the kind of more traditional life they want.

Close to the northern tip of Labrador, the wild **Torngat Mountains** are popular with climbers because of their altitude (some of the highest peaks east of the Rockies) and their isolation.

Nain
pop 1000

This is the last stop on the Coastal Labrador Marine Services ferry, and it is the last town of any size as you go northward. Fishing is the main industry, but the potentially massive Diamond Fields nickel, cobalt and copper mine in discussion stages nearby at Voiseys Bay will obviously affect this community. After the fishing season, hunting and trapping continue as they have for centuries.

The **Piulimatsivik-Nain Museum** burned down in 1999, but ask around to find out where the remaining artifacts are.

Atsanik Lodge (*☎ 709-922-2910, fax 709-922-2815, Sand Banks Rd*) Singles/doubles

Boundless Riches – Maybe

Despite all the early fish stocks, nobody has ever called Newfoundland a wealthy place. Yet resources may finally offer some hope of employment, economic stability and a measure of financial independence.

In Labrador's Voiseys Bay, near Nain, geologists have located stunningly rich concentrations of copper, cobalt and especially nickel. Thus far, bickering between the government and private interests over production and operations (the government wants it done provincially as much as possible), not to mention environmental concerns and the impact on the native Inuit and Innu, have kept it all theoretical.

Offshore oil has been discovered in Newfoundland's Terra Nova region, and the huge Hibernia oil field off St John's has begun producing. Still, there are a lot of ifs and debts to be paid before this potential of billions materializes. Many of the 600,000 provincial residents, long tired of being the butt of jokes told by mainland Canadians (not to mention being the subject of misconceptions about federal assistance policy), may yet experience a windfall of sorts. St John's is starting to see some trickle-down loose change from Hibernia. Sociologists, reporters and especially politicians have already noted a nascent 'Newfie nationalism,' which to some may be more important than hard cash.

$87/98. This is Nain's only hotel. It offers a dining room and laundry.

You may find a guesthouse as well.

Webb's Gifts and Souvenirs (☎ 709-922-2960) has local and area crafts.

CENTRAL LABRADOR

Making up the territorial bulk of Labrador, the central portion is an immense, very sparsely populated and ancient wilderness. Paradoxically, it also has the largest town in Labrador, Happy Valley–Goose Bay.

Happy Valley–Goose Bay
pop 7000

Goose Bay was established during WWII as a staging point for planes on their way to Europe and has remained an aviation center.

Today there is a Canadian military base used by pilots from around both Canada and Europe for testing high-tech planes, in particular controversial low-flying jets that the Innu say disturb their way of life.

The town has all the services, including hotels, but for the outsider there is not a lot to see or do and it is very isolated. The remote, forested landscape, however, attracts many anglers and hunters, and there are numerous fly-in possibilities for camping.

The **Labrador Interpretation Centre** (☎ 709-497-8566, Hillview Dr, North West River; admission $3; open afternoons Tues, Wed, Sat, Sun; mornings Thur, Fri; closed Mon) reveals the history of the region across 9000 years with oral presentations, dioramas and artifacts.

The **Labrador Heritage Museum** (☎ 709-497-8858, off Route 520; admission $2; open 8:30am-4:30pm Wed-Fri all year) outlines some of the history of the area through photographs and includes a trapper's traditional shelter, samples of animal furs, some of the minerals found in Labrador and details on the ill-fated Wallace-Hubbard expedition into Labrador's interior. The museum, incorporating a 1923 Hudson Bay store, is on the north side of town on the former Canadian Forces base.

At the **Northern Lights Military Museum** (☎ 709-896-5939, 170 Hamilton River Rd; admission free; closed Sun) some of the military history of the city is displayed. Also here see the Trappers Brook animal displays, with lifelike depictions of much of the fauna found in the region.

The city has three fair-size hotels and a handful of B&Bs.

TMT B&B (☎ 709-896-4404, fax 709-896-2990) Rates $25-40. With seven rooms, this is the cheapest lodging in town. Call for directions.

Davis' B&B (☎ 709-896-5077, 14 Cabot Crescent) Singles/doubles $40/50 with light breakfast. Both of the two rooms have private bath, and there is a sitting room with TV.

Royal Inn (☎ 709-896-2456, fax 709-896-5501, 3 Royal Ave) Singles/doubles $57/67, housekeeping units $87. This is the city's most economical hotel. It also offers a free light breakfast.

Getting There & Away Goose Bay is well served by air. Provincial Airlines serves

Blanc Sablon and Goose Bay from Newfoundland's major towns. Labrador Airways connects to St Anthony and covers all the small communities along the Labrador coast.

If you are traveling by car, from Happy Valley–Goose Bay, Hwy 500, which is a gravel road, runs westward through the heart of Labrador to Churchill Falls and then forks. Hwy 500 continues south to Wabush, Labrador City and Fermont, Québec.

The road makes the entire inland area auto accessible. Drivers can take vehicles on the ferry from Happy Valley–Goose Bay to Newfoundland, allowing for a complete circuit of the region. This road should only be traveled between June and October, and services are minimal. In fact, between Happy Valley–Goose Bay and far western Labrador, services are available only at towns. There are no roadside service stations. This makes for some pretty long stretches without a coffee or any other critical requirements. And the roads can be bad. Still, travelers have made it in passenger cars, though to quote one: 'I don't know that I'd do it again.'

The drive from Goose Bay to Labrador City takes about 10 hours. The section between Goose Bay and Churchill Falls is rough and slow. The provincial government continues to discuss paving the entire route, but don't hold your breath – this concept has been airborne for years. At present, epic washouts can close the road down completely, to the dismay of local truckers. Government agencies can provide you with road information, but anything they say should be taken with a grain of salt; assume conditions will be worse.

Cars can be rented in Happy Valley–Goose Bay at Budget and National, both with desks at the airport, but not for travel on Hwy 500, due to its rough conditions.

The car ferry from Lewisporte makes the trip to Goose Bay direct or with just a stop at Cartwright on the way. See Lewisporte, earlier in this chapter, for details on this marathon 35- to 38-hour ferry ride. For the passenger-only ferry from St Anthony, see Getting There & Away under St Anthony earlier.

WESTERN LABRADOR

Accessible from Québec, everything in this area of Labrador is oversized in the extreme – mega-developments in a mega-landscape that the visitor is able to explore relatively easily. Remember that there is a one hour time difference between Québec and Labrador City.

Labrador City/Wabush
pop 12,000

These twin mining cities just 15km from Québec represent modern, industrial Labrador. They are generally referred to collectively as Labrador West. The largest **open-pit iron ore mine** in the world is in Labrador City, operated by Iron Ore Company. A modern town has developed around it since it opened in 1958. Another, **Wabush Mines**, operates in Wabush. You can tour both facilities by contacting Labrador West Tourism (*☎ 709-944-7631, open Wed & Sun July-Oct*).

All the resource development in this part of the world is colossal in scale, as the tours will reveal. Dump trucks 18m long with 3m-high tires are almost like absurd works of art.

There is a Destination Labrador information office (*☎ 709-944-7788, 800-563-6353*) at 118 Humphrey Rd, Bruno Plaza. Or call *☎ 709-944-7132*, the tourist chalet.

Things to See & Do The **Height of Land Heritage Centre** (*☎ 709-944-2284, 1750 Bartlett Dr, open May-Oct*), in a former bank, is now a museum. Also, the Labrador City Town Hall has paintings by Tom Thompson.

Most people want to see the land away from town, and you don't have to go far to do that. The landscape, a vast expanse of low, rolling, forested mountains interspersed with areas of flat northern tundra, was scraped down by glaciers.

The **Wapusakatto Mountains** are just 5km from town, and parts have been developed for skiing. From Wabush 39km east on the Trans-Labrador Hwy is **Lac Grand Hermine Park** (*☎ 709-282-5369; admission $12*) for camping, a beach and some fine scenery. It's open June 1 to Sept 15.

The 15km **Menihek hiking trail** goes through wooded areas with waterfalls as well as open tundra. Outfitters can take anglers to excellent fishing waters.

Bus tours of the towns or surroundings are available.

A real treat is the free light show – the aurora borealis (also called the northern lights) – about two nights out of every three. Northern Canada is the best place in the world to see them because the magnetic north pole is here. Evidently these otherworldly colored, waving beams are charged particles from the sun that are trapped in the earth's magnetic field.

Inuit belief is that the shimmering lights are the sky people playing a game of ball. Another belief is that the lights are unborn children playing. The Ojibway called the lights *Waussnodae* and believed them to be torches held by their dead grandfathers to light the way along the Path of Souls. The souls of the recently deceased walked this path, the Milky Way, to their final resting place.

Note that in summer, with the extremely long daylight hours, the show may not be visible.

Places to Stay & Eat There are several somewhat pricey hotels and motels, some with dining rooms. Advance booking is recommended for all places. Ask around for guesthouses, but don't bet on finding one. The places below are in Labrador City.

Carol Inn (☎ 709-944-7736, 888-799-7736, fax 709-944-7110, 215 Drake Ave) Singles/doubles $87/92. All 20 rooms are housekeeping units with cooking facilities.

Two Seasons Inn (☎ 709-944-2661, 800-670-7667, fax 709-944-6852, Avalon Dr) Singles/doubles $90/92. This larger, more-upscale place has nearly 50 rooms, a dining room and a bar.

Tamarack B&B (☎ 709-944-6003, 835 Tamarack Dr) Rate $40/50. This house has three rooms with shared bath.

Most of the eight or so restaurants are in Labrador City and include a couple of *pizza places* and *Jed's Pub* (☎ 709-282-5522, Grenfell Dr). Fish and sometimes caribou show up on menus. *Breadbasket Bakery & Café* (☎ 709-944-5355, 208 Humber Ave) in the Carol Lake Shopping Center is a chance to get away from grease if you're on a budget.

Churchill Falls

Not quite halfway to Goose Bay is modern Churchill Falls. It is built around one of the largest hydroelectric generating stations in the world. Developed in the early 1970s, **Churchill Falls Hydro-Electric Facility** (☎ 709-925-3335) offers free 2½-hour tours

Monday to Friday that must be booked in advance. The diverted Churchill River, falling over a 300m ledge, powers the underground turbines that kick out 550 megawatts, enough to supply almost the entire needs of the New England states. It's quite a piece of engineering.

The town is connected by Hwy 500 to Goose Bay to the east and Wabush to the west.

Banking, laundry, car repair and gasoline can all be taken care of in Churchill. This is the only place between Goose Bay and Labrador City with supplies, so stock up.

Churchill Falls Inn (☎ 709-925-3211, 800-229-3269, fax 709-925-3285) Singles/doubles $82/92. This central inn has a coffee shop and bar; booking ahead is recommended.

Black Spruce Chalet (☎ 709-925-3241, fax 709-925-3241) Rate $44. This choice has six rooms.

Getting There & Away Transportation can be an adventure in itself. Several airlines – including Air Canada, with its regional partner Air Canada Jazz, from Newfoundland – connect with Labrador City and the rest of Canada.

Hwy 500 from Happy Valley–Goose Bay continues from just west of Churchill Falls south to Wabush and Labrador City and then to Fermont, Québec. From there it becomes the mainly paved (with some fine gravel sections) Hwy 389 and then continues for 581km south through the little-developed northern Manicougan District of Québec, past Manic 5 with its huge dam to Labrador City. It can be driven in one day, but it's a long day. Some sections are slow due to roughness or the narrow winding road, but it is generally smoother and in better shape than the road from Goose Bay to Churchill Falls. Some small bridges are one-way traffic only.

There are motels and campgrounds along the way, for example at Manic 5, and a motel, restaurant and service station at Bassin Manic 5. For those going north from Baie Comeau, road conditions can be checked with the provincial police in that town. For those going south, if you are in any doubt or are wondering about updates or road improvements, the police in Labrador can help.

Back at the Hwy 500 fork at Churchill Falls, a northern branch, Hwy 501, continues to Esker, which is halfway between Labrador City and Schefferville, where the road ends. Esker is really nothing more than a train station. This road is not maintained by the province.

National and Budget have offices in Wabush, but rental cars may not be driven on Hwy 500.

Western Labrador is also accessible by rail. The route begins at Sept-Îles, Québec (even farther east than Baie Comeau). From there, catch the Québec North Shore and Labrador railway to Labrador City or beyond to Esker and Schefferville back in Québec .

There are no other train routes in Labrador. The road from Happy Valley–Goose Bay to Labrador City/ Wabush makes the train accessible to the eastern portion of Labrador.

In Labrador City, the Québec North Shore and Labrador train station (☎ 709-944-8205) is at Airport Rd. The one-way adult fare to Sept-Îles is $56. Through the summer, there are three departures weekly – Tuesday, Wednesday, and Friday at noon. The train has a snack car for light lunches.

See the Sept-Îles section in the Québec chapter for more details.

Nova Scotia

In Nova Scotia you're never more than 56km from the sea, a feature that has greatly influenced the character of the province. For generations the 7400km of rugged coastline, with its countless bays and inlets, has provided shelter for small fishing villages, especially along the southern shores.

The typical Maritime scenes and towns dotted along the coast give way to Halifax-Dartmouth, one of Canada's most attractive major metropolitan areas – a modern, cosmopolitan urban center that retains a historic air.

Inland, much of the province is covered with forest, while low hills roll across the north. The Annapolis Valley, famous for its apples, is gentle, bucolic farm country – resplendent in spring with lovely pink and white blossoms.

The Bay of Fundy region lays claim to the world's highest tides. Along the impressive Northumberland Strait are wide sandy beaches washed by the warmest waters around the province.

Visiting rugged and mountainous Cape Breton Island, which shows another side of the varied topography, is another highlight of a trip to Nova Scotia.

History

When Europeans first arrived in what was to become Nova Scotia, they encountered the Mi'kmaq Indians, the dominant people of the Maritimes.

The French created the first European settlement at Port Royal in 1605, calling the region Acadia. Although the area changed hands between the French and English several times over the following 100 years, there were no major British communities until the founding of Halifax in 1749. A contingent of Germans arrived at Lunenburg a few years later. The ethnic balance changed in 1755 when the Acadian population was uprooted by the British (see 'The Acadians' boxed text). Highland Scots landed in familiar-looking Cape Breton in 1773, and over the next century many more Scots followed to settle Nova Scotia, which means 'New Scotland.' In the late 1700s

Highlights

Entered Confederation: July 1, 1867
Area: 55,491 sq km
Population: 941,000
Provincial Capital: Halifax

- Visit Halifax, with its well-preserved history, fine dining and lively music scene.
- Enjoy the charm of coastal villages such as Lunenburg and Peggy's Cove.
- Watch the whales at Digby Neck or Pleasant Bay.
- Explore Annapolis Valley, with its fascinating Acadian history.
- Forage the fossil-laden shoreline of Parrsboro.
- Drive the Cabot Trail to see dramatic coastal scenery.
- Experience early French Canada at Louisbourg National Historic Site.

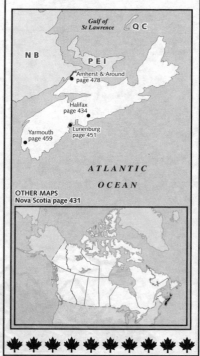

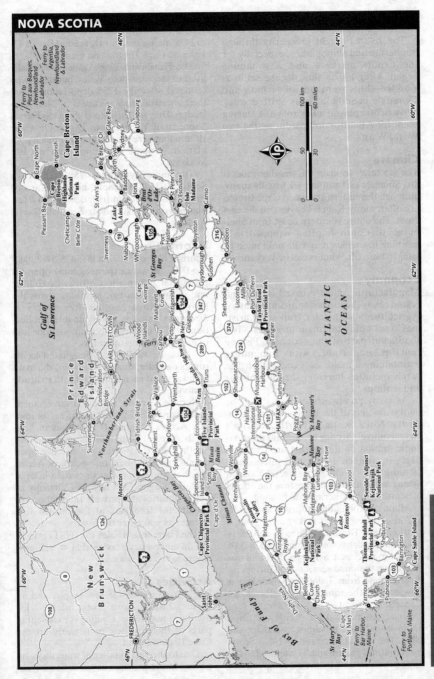

NOVA SCOTIA

thousands of Loyalists from the USA swelled the population.

The 1800s brought prosperity through lumbering and shipbuilding, especially for the export markets, and coal mining began. After 1867 a slow decline set in as wooden ships went out of fashion and Canada's economic focus shifted west. Nova Scotia played a key role as a staging point for Atlantic convoys during the two World Wars.

Climate

The sea tends to keep the weather moderate. Summer and autumn are usually sunny, although the eastern areas and Cape Breton are often windy. Rain is heaviest on the east coast. The entire southern coast from Shelburne to Canso is often wrapped in a morning fog, which may take until noon or later to burn off. Winters can be very snowy.

Economy

Manufacturing, mostly based on natural resources, is the most significant industry. Agriculture – with dairy, fruit and Christmas trees being the main products – is a significant part of the economy. Fishing remains important, with Lunenburg maintaining a major east coast fleet. The catch includes herring, shrimp, lobster and scallops.

At many points offshore you'll see the buoys and nets of the local aquaculture industry. Nova Scotia is North America's largest mussel-farming center, and most Atlantic salmon on the market are reared in cages in protected bays and inlets. Fishfarming may eventually overtake ocean fishing as the natural stocks show the effects of centuries of indiscriminate hauling.

Mining, shipbuilding, tourism and crafts are also major moneymakers. For over a century Cape Breton produced a soft, dirty coal that was dangerous to mine, and in 2001 the last mine closed. Sydney's steel mill was shut down the same year, and the former industrial zone from Sydney to Glace Bay is now among the most depressed areas in Canada.

Undersea natural gas fields off Cape Sable Island feed pipelines bound for the USA. The benefits received by Nova Scotia for its natural gas are small compared to the huge profits earned by the oil companies.

Population & People

About 12,500 Mi'kmaqs live in Nova Scotia in 14 communities, mostly around Bras d'Or Lake on Cape Breton and near Truro.

The French-speaking Acadians originally lived in the Annapolis Valley, but those who returned after the 1755 deportation found their ancestral lands occupied by New Englanders. They settled instead along the French Shore from Yarmouth to Digby. On Cape Breton there are predominantly French populations around Chéticamp and on Isle Madame.

The majority (about 75%) of Nova Scotia's 941,000 people, however, are of English, Scottish and Irish descent. In a few places you can still hear Scottish Gaelic spoken.

Information

Tourism Nova Scotia (☎ 902-425-5781, 800-565-0000, ⓦ www.explorens.com) operates provincial information offices in Halifax and six other strategic locations across the province. Nova Scotia's free *Doers & Dreamers* guide is an invaluable publication. Use it to check accommodations and to find guided-trip operators.

There are 10 different designated scenic routes on older, smaller roads, not the main highways, and each is marked with roadside symbols.

Service Canada, a federal government agency, provides Internet access at Community Access Program (CAP) sites in hundreds of rural communities around Nova Scotia. The CAP sites are usually open during business hours on weekdays. Access is either free or a dollar or two an hour at these well-signposted facilities. Virtually all public libraries also provide Internet access, usually for free. Ask at the information counter as you enter the library.

The Harmonized Sales Tax (HST) is 15%.

For emergency service dial ☎ 911 anywhere in the province.

Activities

Aside from its seaside topography and intriguing history, Nova Scotia offers varied outdoor possibilities. Cycling is excellent in parts of the province, particularly around Cape Breton Island.

Due to the vast number of waterways, canoeing in the province is good. Sea kayaking is becoming increasingly popular and outfitters are found at numerous coastal towns around the province.

For hiking, the national and provincial parks contain both easy and strenuous trails.

Also popular is whale-watching in the Digby Neck area and along the north shore of Cape Breton. In July and August, reserving boat tickets up to a week in advance might be necessary.

Other outdoor pursuits include birdwatching, rockhounding, fossil-searching, surfing, and freshwater and deep-sea fishing.

Accommodations

Nova Scotia has a wide range of lodgings – from backcountry campsites to fine, historic inns to banal motels. July and August are by far the busiest months, and accommodations can be scarce then in much of the province. From late September to late May many attractions, campgrounds and guesthouses are closed.

For nature lovers, the provincial parks of Nova Scotia (W parks.gov.ns.ca) rent campsites for $14 to $18 depending on whether showers and flush toilets are provided. Because electrical hookups are not available, these parks are pleasantly uncrowded and among the most convenient for tenters in Canada. The only times when you might have to reserve are Friday and Saturday from mid-July to mid-August, in which case you should call the park directly. Day use of all parks is free.

Getting Around

The largest bus company is Acadian Lines (☎ 800-567-5151, W www.acadianbus.com). For information on the Maritime Bus Pass accepted by Acadian Lines see Getting Around in the introduction to the New Brunswick chapter. The main routes are Amherst-Truro-Halifax, Halifax-Truro-Baddeck-Sydney, Halifax-Truro-St Peter's-Sydney and Halifax-Kentville-Digby-Yarmouth.

Bus routes on the south shore are operated by DRL Coachlines (☎ 888-263-1852, W www.drlgroup.com), running from Halifax to Yarmouth via Lunenburg, and the Zinck Bus Company (☎ 902-468-4342), heading east to Sherbrooke. Transoverland (☎ 902-248-2051) has a bus from Sydney to Chéticamp. Private minibus shuttles operate between Charlottetown and Halifax.

Halifax

pop 114,000 (metro area 335,000)

The Nova Scotia capital, Halifax sits on one of the world's most extensive natural harbors, midway along Nova Scotia's south Atlantic shore. Although Halifax is the largest Canadian city east of Montréal, its historic central district, never more than a few blocks from the water, is pleasingly compact. Modern buildings nestle among heritage structures interspersed with numerous green areas and parks.

The port is the busiest on Canada's east coast partially because it's a year-round harbor – ice forces most others to close in winter. Canada's largest naval base is here; other major industries are manufacturing, oil refining and food processing.

Residents are known as Haligonians.

History

The area was first settled by Mi'kmaq Indians, and Halifax itself was founded in 1749 as a British stronghold counterbalancing the French fort at Louisbourg on Nova Scotia's northeast tip.

The harbor was used as a British naval base during the American Revolution (1775–83) and the War of 1812. During both World Wars, Halifax was a distribution center for supply ships heading for Europe – a function that brought many people to the city.

In 1917 the *Mont Blanc,* a French munitions ship carrying a cargo of TNT, collided with another ship in the harbor. The result, known as the Great Explosion, was the world's biggest man-made explosion prior to A-bombs being dropped on Japan in 1945 (see the 'A Christmas Tree for Boston' boxed text).

The city was the home of Canada's first representative government, first Protestant church and first newspaper.

Orientation

This hilly city lies on a peninsula between the harbor and an inlet called the North West Arm. The downtown area, dating from the earliest settlement, extends west from Lower Water St to the Citadel, a star-shaped fort on a hill. Cogswell St to the north and Spring Garden Rd to the south mark the other boundaries of the capital's

HALIFAX

PLACES TO STAY
41 YMCA
42 Lord Nelson Hotel
57 Dalhousie University,
   O'Brien Hall
59 Waverley Inn
61 Halifax Heritage House
   Hostel
65 Garden Inn B&B
66 Westin Hotel

PLACES TO EAT
7 Harbourside Market
9 O'Carroll's Irish Pub
14 Bluenose II Restaurant
22 Café C'est Si Bon
25 Midtown Tavern & Grill
29 McKelvie's
33 Satisfaction Feast
39 Mediteraneo Café
45 Your Father's Moustache
47 Tu Do Restaurant
48 Thirsty Duck Pub & Eatery
49 Second Cup
58 Kinh-Do
62 Trident Booksellers & Café

OTHER
1 US Consulate
2 Police Headquarters
3 Transit Terminal
4 Hertz
5 Historic Properties
6 Lower Deck
8 Split Crow
10 Double Decker Tours
11 Halifax Ferry Terminal
12 Halifax Metro Centre
13 City Hall
15 Transit Terminal
16 McNabs Island Ferry
17 Cable Wharf; Murphy's on
   the Water; Peggy's Cove
   Express
18 Old Town Clock
19 The Dome
20 Grafton St Dinner Theatre

21 St Paul's Church
23 Province House
24 Art Gallery of Nova Scotia
26 Neptune Theatre
27 Diamond Bar
28 Post Office
30 Harbour Hopper Tours
31 Maritime Museum of the
   Atlantic; Bluenose II
32 Tourism Nova Scotia
34 The Eagle Pub & Eatery
35 Khyber Centre for the Arts
36 Tourism Halifax
   International Visitor Centre
37 Reflections Cabaret
38 Halifax Trading and Guide
   Post; Vertigo Climbing
   School
40 Book Room
43 Birmingham Bar & Grill
44 Lawtons Drugs
46 American Express
50 Air Canada
51 Halifax Public Library
52 Halifax Feast
53 St Paul's Cemetery
54 Keith's Brewery Building;
   Brewery Market
55 Impark
56 Government House
60 Bearly's Bar & Grill
63 Discount Car Rentals
64 All Saints Cathedral
67 VIA Rail Station; Enterprise
   Rent-a-Car
68 Pier 21 Centre

NOVA SCOTIA

core. Conveniently, much of what is of interest to visitors is concentrated in this area, making walking the best way to get around.

From this central area the city spreads in three directions from the harbor. Sackville St and Spring Garden Rd lead west up from the shoreline. Dartmouth, a twin city, lies east across the harbor and has business and residential districts of its own.

Two bridges span Halifax Harbour, connecting Halifax to Dartmouth and leading to highways north (for the airport) and east. The MacDonald Bridge at the eastern end of North St is closest to downtown. You can walk across, but bicycles cannot be ridden. Farther north is the MacKay Bridge. The toll for cars on either bridge is 75¢. A passenger ferry ($1.65) also links the downtown areas of Halifax and Dartmouth.

The airport is 40km northwest of town on Hwy 102.

If you'll be staying long in Halifax, you should check the arrival dates of cruise ships. These huge vessels call about 10 times a month in July and August, and almost every other day in September and October. When they do, the waterfront, downtown and all the main tourist sites become hopelessly overcrowded. Save Point Pleasant Park or McNabs Island for such a day.

Information

Tourist Offices Tourism Nova Scotia has an information office (☎ 902-424-4248, 1655 Lower Water St) next to the Maritime Museum right down by the water. It's open year-round, 8:30am to 8pm daily in summer, 8:30am to 4:30pm Wednesday to Sunday mid-October to May.

The Tourism Halifax International Visitor Centre (☎ 902-490-5946, Sackville St at Barrington St) is centrally located and geared to the city. It's open 8:30am to 7pm daily from late May to September (until 8pm in July and August), 8:30am to 4:30pm weekdays only the rest of the year.

Money Halifax has numerous banks, but the only one open on Saturday (9am to 3pm) is TD Canada Trust (☎ 902-422-7471, 6239 Quinpool Rd) west of the center.

The exchange office at Halifax International Airport is open 6am to 9pm daily and charges a $5 fee per transaction.

American Express (☎ 902-423-3900, City Center Atlantic, Box 44, Suite 205, 5523 Spring Garden Rd, Halifax, NS B3J 1G8) is the only full-service American Express office east of Montréal. It will cash traveler's checks and the personal checks of cardholders, and accept mail for those with American Express credit cards or traveler's checks. It can also replace lost or stolen checks and is open 9am to 5pm weekdays.

Post The post office (☎ 902-494-4670, 1680 Bedford Row) is between Sackville St and Prince St. Mail sent c/o General Delivery, Halifax, NS B3J 2L3, is held here. It's open 7:30am to 5:15pm weekdays.

The post office inside Lawtons Drugs (☎ 902-429-0088, 5675 Spring Garden Rd) stays open 8am to 9pm Monday to Friday, 9am to 6pm Saturday and noon to 5pm Sunday.

Email & Internet Access The Halifax public library (☎ 902-490-5700, 5381 Spring Garden Rd) is open 10am to 9pm Tuesday to Thursday, 10am to 5pm Friday and Saturday. You can book a time slot for free Internet access. The Second Cup outlet nearby on Spring Garden Rd, mentioned later under Places to Eat, also provides Internet access.

Bookstores The Book Room (☎ 902-423-8271, 1546 Barrington St at Blowers St) has been around for nearly 160 years.

The Halifax Trading and Guide Post (☎ 902-492-1420, 1586 Granville St near Sackville St) sells specialized hiking, canoeing and kayaking guides in Nova Scotia, plus canoe-route maps.

Medical Services In medical emergencies you can resort to the Halifax Infirmary (☎ 902-473-3383/7605, 1796 Summer St), which is the emergency department of the Queen Elizabeth II Health Services Centre. It's open 24 hours. Persons without health insurance are charged a basic fee of $300 (!) to be seen here, with any medical tests or specialist consultations extra. The minimum charge for anyone hospitalized is $3200 a night.

If you are without health insurance and it's not a life-threatening situation, ask your hotel to try to set up an appointment with a private doctor on your behalf, which should cost about $25. Most private doctors are swamped with work and won't accept new patients, but your hotel or hostel manager may be able to find one who will make an exception. There are no general walk-in clinics in Halifax, and health-spending cut-backs by the federal government have left the entire system reeling. If you can't find a doctor willing to see you in Halifax and it's not urgent, take a minibus shuttle to Charlottetown, PEI, where walk-in clinics *do* exist.

Historic Properties

The Historic Properties is a group of restored buildings on Upper Water St constructed between 1800 and 1905. Many of these buildings – long two-story places designed for easy storage of goods and cargo – now house shops, boutiques, restaurants and bars.

Privateer's Warehouse, dating from 1814, is the oldest stone building in the area. The privateers were government-sanctioned and -sponsored pirates who fed off the 'enemy'; the booty was hidden here. Among the other vintage buildings are the wooden **Old Red Store** – once used for shipping operations and as a sail loft – and **Simon's Warehouse**, built in 1854.

The green **Cable Wharf** building, along the pier by the Dartmouth ferry terminal, is a center for handicrafts and souvenirs. It holds offices for boat tours and the McNabs Island ferry. Also nearby is the ferry to Dartmouth.

Maritime Museum of the Atlantic

This large museum (☎ 902-424-7490, *1675 Lower Water St; adult/senior/child/family $6/5/2/15; admission free 5:30pm-8pm Tues & daily mid-Oct–Apr; open 9:30am-5:30pm Mon-Sat, till 8pm Tues, 10:30am-5:30pm Sun),* south of the Historic Properties, warrants a peek not only for boat buffs. It's spacious and contains lots of models, photographs and historical explanations. The lens from a Halifax lighthouse is impressive, as are the painted figureheads taken from various ships, many of them wrecks. There's a wildly popular display on the *Titanic* and another on the Great Explosion. The Titanic 3D Theater is $2.50 per person extra.

Outside at the dock you can explore the CSS *Acadia,* a retired hydrographic vessel from England. Also docked here is the WWII corvette HMCS *Sackville,* the last of 122 warships of its kind. Admission to each ship is included with admission to the Maritime Museum, or $1 for each separately.

Often moored at the wharf by the museum is *Bluenose II,* a replica of Canada's best-known boat. The original *Bluenose* schooner was built in 1921 in Lunenburg and never lost a race in 20 years. In tribute, the 10¢ coin bears the schooner's image. The *Bluenose* has become nearly as familiar a Canadian symbol as the maple leaf.

The *Bluenose II* was launched in 1963 and now has a permanent berth at the Maritime Museum when not on display at other Canadian ports. Two-hour harbor tours are given on the schooner, but when it's docked you can walk on board to look at this beautiful piece of work for free.

Brewery Market

Also part of the restored waterfront, this complex is in the Keith's Brewery Building (dating from 1820) at 1496 Lower Water St. It now contains boutiques, restaurants and a couple of pubs. A farmers' market is held on the lower level from 7am to 1pm Saturday year-round (from 8am in winter).

The lively **Keith's Brewery Tours** (☎ *902-455-1474; adult/child $9/7; every half hour noon-8pm Mon-Thur, noon-9pm Fri & Sat, noon-4pm Sun, Sat & Sun only Oct-May)* is led by a costumed guide and includes two mugs of beer.

Pier 21 Centre

Pier 21 was to Canada what Ellis Island was to the US. Between 1928 and 1971 over a million immigrants entered Canada through Pier 21, including 48,000 war brides (mostly from the UK) and their 22,000 children. In addition, nearly half a million troops departed from here for Europe during WWII. In 1999 this national historic site reopened as a museum featuring a large pavilion with information displays, boutiques, cafés and multimedia exhibits detailing the travails of refugees and immigrants hoping to call Canada home.

Pier 21 (☎ *902-425-7770,* w *pier21.ns.ca, 1055 Marginal Rd; adult/senior/child $6.50/ 5.50/3.50; open 9am-5pm daily June-Aug,*

9am-5pm Tues-Sat Sept-May) is somewhat hidden behind the VIA Rail station. To reach it, go around the side of the Westin Hotel on Terminal Rd. Or better yet, follow the waterfront boardwalk a kilometer south from Historic Properties and you'll bump right into it.

Historic Downtown

Government House, with its venerable edifice, is between Hollis St and Barrington St, near the corner of Bishop St. Government House has been the residence of the provincial lieutenant governor since 1807 and is not open to the public. It was built for Governor John Wentworth.

Also known as the Old Burying Ground, **St Paul's Cemetery**, first used in 1749, is across the street from Government House on Barrington St. By the time it closed down in 1844 more than 12,000 people had been buried here.

Since 1819 **Province House** (☎ 902-424-4661, *Hollis St between George & Prince Sts; free guided tours; open 9am-5pm Mon-Fri, 10am-4pm Sat & Sun July & Aug)*, a fine example of Georgian architecture, has been the home of Canada's oldest provincial legislature. In the off-season the staff will show you part of the building if you visit 9am to 4pm weekdays.

The provincial **Art Gallery of Nova Scotia** (☎ 902-424-7542, **W** *www.agns.gov.ns.ca, 1723 Hollis St; adult/student $5/2, by donation Tues; open 10am-6pm Tues-Fri, noon-5pm Sat & Sun year-round, also noon-5pm Mon July & Aug)* is housed in the restored heritage Dominion Building of 1868 (once used as the post office) across from Province House. Provincial and other Canadian works make up much of the large collection of 5000 pieces. There are both permanent and changing exhibits, and free tours are given at 2pm Sunday.

The Anglican **St Paul's Church** (☎ 902-429-2240, *1749 Argyle St; admission free; open 9am-4:30pm Mon-Fri Sept-May, 9am-5pm Mon-Sat June-Aug)*, near Prince St, was the first Protestant church in Canada (dating from 1749). A guide is on hand to answer questions. One of the intriguing curiosities is the piece of metal lodged above the door in the north wall, inside the porch. This is part of a window frame from another building implanted here during the

---

A Christmas Tree for Boston

Few cities have experienced such a sudden and unexpected turning point in their history as Halifax did with the Great Explosion. The day it occurred, December 6, 1917, was bright and clear, and WWI was raging somewhere overseas in Europe, not in Canada. At 8:30am, out in the harbor, the *Mont Blanc*, a French munitions ship, and the *Imo*, a Belgian relief ship, struck each other due to human error.

Even after the two boats collided in The Narrows adjacent to the city, the *Mont Blanc* – filled with 300 rounds of ammunition, 10 metric tons of gun cotton, 200 tons of TNT, 2100 tons of picric acid (used in explosives) and 32 tons of highly flammable benzol stacked in barrels on the deck – did not immediately explode. Instead it caught fire, and its crew, only too aware of the cargo, took to lifeboats and rowed to Dartmouth. The ship then drifted unattended toward Halifax, drawing bystanders to the waterfront to watch the spectacle.

At 9:05am the ship exploded in a blinding white flash, the largest man-made explosion before the nuclear age; more than 1900 people were killed and 9000 injured. Almost all of the northern end of Halifax, roughly 130 hectares, was leveled. Most of the buildings and homes that were not destroyed by the explosion burned to the ground because of winter stockpiles of coal in the cellars.

All 2830 tons of the *Mont Blanc* were shattered into little pieces. The barrel of one of its guns was found 5km away, and the anchor shank, which weighed more than a ton, flew 3km in the other direction. The blast was felt as far away as Sydney on Cape Breton and was heard on Prince Edward Island. The misery was compounded when Halifax was hit the next day by a blizzard that dumped 40cm of snow on the city.

Relief efforts were immediate and money poured in from as far away as New Zealand and China; but most Haligonians remember the generosity of the US state of Massachusetts, which donated $750,000 and instantly sent an army of volunteers and doctors to help in the recovery. Halifax was so grateful for the assistance in its hour of despair that the city still sends a Christmas tree to the city of Boston every year as a token of appreciation.

1917 explosion of the *Mont Blanc*, 3km away in Halifax Harbour.

Built in 1890 at the opposite end of the sunken courtyard from St Paul's Church, Halifax's **City Hall** is a true gem of Victorian architecture.

At the top of George St, at Citadel Hill, stands one of the city's most beloved symbols, the **Old Town Clock**. The inner workings arrived in Halifax in 1803 after being ordered by Prince Edward, the Duke of Kent, then the commander.

Khyber Centre for the Arts

This artist-run center (☎ 902-422-9668, ⓦ *www.khyberarts.ns.ca, 1588 Barrington St; admission free; open 11am-5pm Tues-Sat, until 10pm Thur*) includes several galleries, plus the studio of noted potter Shana Salaff. The center's Artist's Club is worth joining ($10) if you're at all interested in the Halifax art scene, as you'll be allowed into the members' bar and invited to attend lectures, cabarets, raves and other events. Show openings are usually at 8pm Monday and accompanied by dancing to DJ music. Another DJ spins the discs from 10pm on Wednesday. All in all, the Khyber Centre is a great place to touch base with emerging artists.

Halifax Public Gardens

The public gardens may be small – if seven hectares is small – but they're regarded as the finest Victorian city gardens in North America. They're found on the corner of South Park St and Spring Garden Rd. Oldies bands perform off-key concerts in the gazebo 2pm to 4pm Sunday from late June to early September.

Citadel National Historic Site

Canada's most visited national historic site, the Citadel (☎ *902-426-5080, off Sackville St; adult/senior/child/family $6/4.50/3/14.75 May-Oct, grounds free rest of the year but exhibits closed; open 9am-6pm daily July & Aug, 9am-5pm daily Sept-June),* a huge, oddly angled fort on top of Halifax's big central hill, has always been the city's towering landmark.

In 1749, with the founding of Halifax, construction of a citadel began; this version is the fourth, built from 1818 to 1861. Halifax was originally a military base intended to

checkmate the French, and the great grandson of a fort we see today was meant to defend Canada from the Americans.

The excellent guided tours explain the fort's shape and how, despite appearances, it was not very well designed or constructed. For a freebie, come by for the hourly changing of the fully kilted guard in ostrich feather hats.

Also in the compound is the Army Museum, with exhibits relating to Atlantic Canada's military history.

Nova Scotia Museum of Natural History

This museum (☎ *902-424-7353, 1747 Summer St; adult/family $4/12, free mid-Oct–May; open 9:30am-5:30pm Mon-Sat, 9:30am-8pm Wed, 1pm-5:30pm Sun June–mid-Oct; 9:30am-5pm Tues-Sat, 1pm-5pm Sun mid-Oct–May*) west of the Citadel is considered the headquarters of the provincial museum system. History, wildlife, geology, people and industry are all covered. The three-dimensional animal and fish exhibits are excellent, and there's a good history section with an old stagecoach and a working model of a late-1800s sawmill.

Point Pleasant Park

Some 39km of nature trails, picnic spots, a restaurant, a beach and the Prince of Wales Martello Tower – a round 18th-century defensive structure – are all found within this 75-hectare wooded sanctuary. Good views are to be enjoyed all the way around the perimeter. No cars are allowed.

The park is at the far southern end of town, at the tip of the peninsula. If you're walking, the park begins 2km south of Spring Garden Rd. The No 9 bus connects Point Pleasant with downtown's Scotia Square until 9pm, or you can drive to the park's edge. There's ample free parking at Harbour Lookoff and another lot off Point Pleasant Dr.

York Redoubt

The remains of a 200-year-old fort make up this national historic site (☎ *902-426-5080; admission free; grounds open 9am-8pm daily mid-May–Aug, 9am-7pm Sept, 9am-6pm Oct, 9am-5pm Nov–mid-May, buildings open 10am-6pm mid-June–early Sept*). It overlooks the harbor from a bluff just south of the North West Arm (south of the center). Designed to protect the city from attack by sea, it was built at the narrowest point of the outer harbor. The site was used in various capacities by the military from 1793 to as late as 1956.

Aside from the view, there are mounted guns, a Martello tower and historical information and displays; the underground tunnels are cool enough.

York Redoubt is off Hwy 253 6km south of Sir Sandford Fleming Park. Bus No 15 comes directly here.

McNabs Island

Out in the harbor and easily seen from York Redoubt, this long island makes a good break from the city. There are guided walks, beaches, picnic tables and hiking trails, and a teahouse serves basic snacks or seafood. Between 1888 and 1892 a fort was built at the south end of the island to defend Halifax Harbour.

Boats depart from the Halifax dock area at 9am and 2pm from June to mid-September; tickets ($12.50) can be bought from Murphy's on the Water (☎ 902-420-1015) by Cable Wharf.

Activities

Kayaking Ocean kayaking tours and rentals are available through **Sea Sun Kayak School & Adventures** (☎ 902-471-2732, W *www.paddlenovascotia.com, St. Mary's Boat Club, 1741 Fairfield Rd, off Jubilee Rd)* west of the center. Rental of a single kayak is $35/50 a half/full day, doubles $50/78. From May to October full-day guided kayaking tours ($99 plus tax) are offered on Wednesday, Friday and Sunday. Trips of two, three and four days are also arranged.

The Trail Shop (☎ 902-423-8736, 6210 Quinpool Rd; single/double kayaks $25/35 a day, $20/25 each additional day, $45/55 Fri morning-anytime Mon) has kayaks for rent, also west of downtown.

Rock Climbing The **Vertigo Climbing School** (☎ 902-492-1492, W *www3.ns.sympatico .ca/vertigo, 1586 Granville St)* at Halifax Trading & Guide Post offers an introduction to rock climbing for $85. It also runs rope courses, hikes and custom trips.

Diving There are about 50 wrecks at the mouth of Halifax Harbour, and more good diving is available along the coast. For information and equipment rentals, try **Nautilus Aquatics** (☎ 902-454-4296, 6162 Quinpool Rd). From late May to early September it runs dive charters every Sunday, costing $45 per person for the boat plus $12 per tank. A complete equipment package including one tank is $50.

Cycling For cycling information or to join a bicycle tour of the city or region, contact the nonprofit **Velo Bicycle Club** (☎ 902-423-4345, W *www.velohalifax.ca).*

Bicycles can be rented from **Peddle and Seat Ventures** (☎ 902-497-3092). They don't have an office, but if you call them, a pick-up or delivery point will be arranged. Hybrid bikes including helmets and locks are $22/100 plus tax a day/week, and panniers and racks another $3 a day. Owner Dana Gallant will help with bicycle-touring arrangements and can be hired as a tour leader.

Organized Tours

No shortage exists here. The tourist office has a complete list, but some of the more established and interesting ones follow. Most have discounts for seniors, children and/or students.

Harbour Hopper Tours (☎ 902-490-8687, W *www.harbourhopper.com, near the Maritime Museum)* offers 55-minute tours around town and out into the harbor in a seaworthy Lark 5 tour bus/boat. The tours ($23) depart every 1½ hours May to mid-October.

Double Decker Tours (☎ 902-420-1155) runs 1½-hour city tours in London-style buses. The tours (adult/senior/child $18/17/6) leave from the corner of Duke and Water Sts at 10:30am and 12:30pm daily mid-June to mid-October (also at 2:30pm in July and August).

Halifax Ghost Walk (☎ 902-469-6716, e *macrev@ns.sympatico.ca)* features tales of pirates, buried treasure and ghosts from the old city's lore. The two-hour walk, offered July to mid-September, leaves at 8:30pm every couple of days from the Old Town Clock and winds through town to the docks. Cost is $8.50/5 adult/senior or child.

The beauteous *Bluenose II* takes visitors out on **harbor sailing cruises** (☎ 800-763-1963, W *www.bluenose2.ns.ca, Lower Water St near the Maritime Museum),* at least

NOVA SCOTIA

when it's in town or not being worked on. If you're lucky enough to be around when it's operating, don't miss the chance for the too-cheap-to-be-true $20 sailings. Trips are usually at 9:30am and 1:30pm from June to September but they're canceled if there's rain, wind or fog.

Murphy's on the Water (☎ 902-420-1015, ⓦ www.murphysonthewater.com, *Cable Wharf at Historic Properties)* offers another way to get out on the water, with as many as 17 boat tours throughout the day from May to October. The two-hour narrated trip aboard the *Harbour Queen* goes past both new and old city landmarks and at $16 is a pretty good value. The boat carries 200 people and has both open and closed decks, a snack counter and a bar. From mid-June through August there are three to four runs daily. Out of peak season there are two trips daily, and in winter it closes down completely. Dinner cruises ($37) are another option. Murphy's also operates the *Mar II*, a very handsome sailboat, for trips around the harbor. The 1½-hour sailing trips cost $18. Some trips include whale-watching, but this is not a prime area for that possibility.

From mid-June to early October **Peggy's Cove Express** (☎ 902-422-4200, ⓦ www.peggyscove.com, *Cable Wharf)* has a 4½-hour boat/bus tour to Peggy's Cove. Cost is $50 including a chowder lunch (or $69 with a lobster meal).

Also offering a Peggy's Cove tour is **Markland Tours** (☎ 902-499-2939). The four-hour tour is $30 and picks up at the HI Hostel (10% discount for HI cardholders). Other tours include Annapolis Valley ($62), Lunenburg ($60) and a city tour ($24). These tours are available year-round and are booked by phone.

The **Halifax Heritage House Hostel** (☎ 902-422-3863, *1253 Barrington St)* runs minibus tours that are inexpensive because only transportation is included (meals and lodging are paid separately). There are day trips to Digby and the South Shore ($40), an overnight trip to Fundy National Park ($80) and a three-day trip to Cape Breton and the Cabot Trail ($120). The tours generally operate from mid-June to early September, depending upon demand. A reservations list is kept at the hostel reception and you don't need to be staying there to sign up. It's a great value and a lot of fun.

Special Events

Some of the major events held in Halifax in summer are:

Gay Pride Parade On a Saturday afternoon in late June gays and straights assemble in downtown Halifax for the biggest coming out of the year.

Canada Day Canada's birthday on July 1 is celebrated in high style in Halifax with parades, live entertainment, rock concerts and fireworks.

Nova Scotia Tattoo Every year this event is held in Halifax during the first week of July (or close to it). You'll see vast formations of Scottish bagpipers on parade.

Halifax Natal Day A major event held at the end of July or early August with a parade, street parties, boat races, a bridge walk, concerts and a fireworks display.

Atlantic Jazz Festival This festival (ⓦ www .jazzeast.com) takes place at the end of July.

Halifax Atlantic Fringe Festival This festival in August draws hundreds of performers, from musicians and actors to comics and mimics, for a variety of events that are staged throughout the metro area. Buskers arrive in Halifax en masse around this same time.

Places to Stay

Camping There's no campground in Halifax itself. See Places to Stay in the Dartmouth section for information on camping at Shubie Park, accessible by city bus from Halifax. For a campsite west of town, see Places to Stay in the Peggy's Cove section, later in this chapter.

Hostels & University Residences *Halifax Heritage House Hostel* (☎ 902-422-3863, fax 902-422-0116, ⓦ www.hostellingintl.ns.ca, *1253 Barrington St)* Dorm beds $18/22 for members/nonmembers, private singles/doubles $40/47. Check-in 4pm-11pm Nov-Apr; 4pm-1am May-Oct. This HI hostel is perfectly located in a fine historic house erected in 1864. The hostel is an easy walk from the VIA Rail station and to downtown and the waterfront. There's room for 70 guests, and features include cooking facilities and an outdoor patio. Double and family rooms with shared bath are available. The maximum stay is seven nights. From the airport, the Airbus goes to the nearby Westin Hotel. From the bus depot, take the No 7 bus south from the corner of Robie and Almon to the corner of Barrington and South Sts. No parking is available.

Halifax Backpackers Hostel (☎ 902-431-3170, W *www.halifaxbackpackers.com, 2193 Gottingen St*) Dorm beds $18-22 per person, private singles/doubles $35/50. This storefront place has recently expanded to 30 beds. Though it's in a dodgy part of town (use caution at night), it's attractive and well run.

YMCA (☎ 902-423-9622, fax 902-425-3180, 1565 South Park St) Singles $30/130 daily/weekly. The 45-room YMCA accepts men only and bathrooms are shared. Facilities include a gym and swimming pool. The location is excellent, across from the Public Gardens and near Citadel Hill. Free parking is available after 6pm only.

Dalhousie University (☎ 902-494-8840, fax 902-494-1219, W *www.dal.ca/confserv*) Singles/doubles $39/59, students $27/46, seniors $35/53. From mid-May to late August, Dalhousie's massive summer accommodations program is your best bet for an inexpensive room in Halifax. Rooms are available at Fenwick Place, Howe Hall, O'Brien Hall and Shirreff Hall, and the front desks of these residences are staffed 24 hours a day. You can go directly there, but it's a good idea to call ahead as groups sometimes reserve entire buildings. The bathrooms are generally shared but the rates usually include parking, taxes, breakfast and use of the athletic facilities. A common fridge and microwave may be provided on your floor. Laundry services are $1. The reduced student rate doesn't include parking ($7 a night extra, if required). If you stay a week, you pay for only six nights.

Two of the residences are on the campus about 1km from the waterfront: *Howe Hall* (☎ 902-494-2108, 6230 Coburg Rd at LeMarchant St) is a four-story stone building adjacent to the main campus. *Shirreff Hall* (☎ 902-494-2428, 6385 South St at Oxford St) is a stone building erected in 1919 behind a magnificent portico with four pillars.

The other two residences are much closer to downtown. *O'Brien Hall* (☎ 902-494-2013, fax 902-494-6955, 5217 Morris St) has a location on the corner of Barrington St, around the corner from the HI hostel, that just can't be beat.

Fenwick Place (☎ 902-494-3886, fax 902-494-2213, 5599 Fenwick St) is a 33-story skyscraper with 200 apartments ($56/80 for a two-/three-bedroom unit). It's the most

upscale of the Dalhousie residences and tends to be full when the others still have rooms.

B&Bs & Tourist Homes *Fountain View Guesthouse* (☎ 902-422-4169, W *browser.to/fountainviewguesthouse, 2138 Robie St*) Singles/doubles/triples $24/30/35 & up. A room with two double beds for four persons is $50. This plain, straightforward place is the only inexpensive tourist home near town. It's the bright blue house with white trim, between Compton Ave and Williams St. All seven rooms have TV. It's also quite popular, so try in the morning after guests have left. Only three parking places are available and credit cards are not accepted.

Garden Inn B&B (☎ 877-414-8577, fax 902-492-1462, W *www.gardeninn.ns.ca, 1263 South Park St*) Doubles $109 May-Oct, $89 Nov-Apr. All 23 rooms are air-conditioned. This 1875 Victorian house with an attached annex is well located, and ample parking is available.

Bob's Guest House (☎ 877-890-4060, fax 902-454-2060, W *www.sjnow.com/bobs, 2715 Windsor St*) Doubles $75-99 June-Oct, $59-79 Nov-May. Along Windsor St, northwest of Quinpool Rd, Bob's has a variety of rooms – the attic suite is cozy – along with nice gardens and a hot tub. Same-sex couples are welcome here. It's near a large Sobeys Supermarket and walking distance from the bus station. Take bus Nos 82 or 17.

Motels As with the B&Bs, there's a serious shortage of budget motels around Halifax, and the few places that do exist take advantage of the situation by charging more than they're worth. The main motel strip is far from the center along the Bedford Hwy (Hwy 2), northwest of town. Bus Nos 80 and 82 go into the city, a 15-minute drive away.

Travellers Motel (☎ 800-565-3394, fax 902-835-6887, 773 Bedford Hwy) Cabins/units $45/69 & up. The 18 simple, unheated duplex cabins are available from May to October only, but from November to April, the 25 motel rooms are only $52.

Hotels *Waverley Inn* (☎ 800-565-9346, fax 902-425-0167, W *www.waverleyinn.com, 1266 Barrington St*) Doubles $95-249 May-Oct, $79-199 Nov-Apr with breakfast. For a bit of a splurge, you might try this historic place, with 32 rooms that haven't lost a bit of their circa-1866 charm. You're quite close to downtown and parking is provided.

Lord Nelson Hotel (☎ *800-565-2020, fax 902-423-7148,* **w** *www.lordnelsonhotel.com, 1515 South Park St*) Rooms $89-199. The cost of the 174 rooms varies daily, from $89 single or double around Christmas to $199 if a conference is on. Yet even in July and August you should be able to get a bed at the Lord Nelson for $129 if you call ahead and ask for the summer special. The location is ideal and the elegance of a grand hotel of the 1920s is included in the price.

Places to Eat

Halifax has a good selection of restaurants offering a variety of foods in all price ranges, and generally the quality is high.

Downtown The ***Harbourside Market*** at Historic Properties on Upper Water St comprises six separate cafeteria-style restaurants where you can get self-service seafood, Italian

Dig in!

dishes, salads and deli-style meals for around $10. You place your order at the counter and carry your tray out onto a deck overlooking Halifax Harbour. It's cheap, convenient and reasonable quality (not fast food).

O'Carroll's Irish Pub (☎ *902-423-4405, 1860 Upper Water St*) Mains $18 & up. Open 11am-11pm daily (pub until 1am). O'Carroll's is a sort of a low-key genteel pub (away from the boisterousness of other Halifax pubs) with superb steak and seafood. There's good traditional Maritime music here nightly from 10pm. Dinners are pricey, but nondiners can absorb the atmosphere for the price of a drink.

McKelvie's (☎ *902-421-6161, 1680 Lower Water St*) Dinner mains around $10-12. Open 11:30am-9:30pm daily. Famous for its seafood, this huge place in an old firehouse is an institution of sorts. Reservations are advisable.

Bluenose II Restaurant (☎ *902-425-5092, 1824 Hollis St at Duke St*) Breakfast including coffee $5-6, lunch specials under $6, dinners from $7. Open 6:30am-10pm Mon-Fri, 8am-10pm Sat & Sun. This long-standing restaurant is packed with locals at lunch. The menu ranges from Greek and Italian to full lobster dinners, and there is beer on tap.

Café C'est Si Bon (☎ *902-425-5799, 1717 Barrington St*) Lunch dishes around $5. Open 6am-11pm Mon & Tues, 6am-2am Wed-Fri, 7am-2am Sat, 7am-11pm Sun. This café is a pleasantly informal place to order a fettuccine, quiche, salad or goulash lunch. In the evening you can listen to local musicians (check the notices taped to the door).

Mediteraneo Café (☎ *902-423-4403, 1571 Barrington St*) Breakfast under $3, mains $5-10. Open 7am-10pm Mon-Sat, 7am-9pm Sun. For breakfast, try this place – all morning you'll find it jammed with people who know a good deal. Mediteraneo is also extremely popular for the many Lebanese dishes, such as cabbage rolls, grapevine leaves and *shawarma*. HI cardholders get a 10% discount here.

Satisfaction Feast (☎ *902-422-3540, 1581 Grafton St*) Sandwiches $5, dinners $9 & up. Open 11am-10pm daily. In a pale blue building, this is a well-established vegetarian restaurant for lunch or dinner. The Indian curry of the day ($10) is definitely worth considering.

Midtown Tavern & Grill (☎ *902-422-5213, 1684 Grafton St at Prince St*) Meals $7. Open 11am-10pm Mon-Sat. This is a national treasure – a good example of the Canadian workers' tavern. It's packed with friendly locals at lunch, most of them enjoying dishes like *poutine* ($3), large Caesar salad ($5), pizza ($5-7), fish and chips ($7) or steak and eggs ($7) and washing it down with draft beer. The steak is great for the money, and from 4:30pm until closing, a glass of draft beer is only $1.99.

Highlife Café (☎ *902-422-7050, 2011 Gottingen St off Cogswell St next to Staples*) Mains $9-11. Open 7:30am-5pm Mon, 7:30am-10pm Tues-Fri, 1pm-10pm Sat &

Sun. The music and decor are straight out of Ghana, and the food is as African or Caribbean as anything you'll find in Accra or Kingston. Entrées include *jollof* rice ($10), curry goat ($9-11) and stewed beef ($9-11), or you can just order roti with sauce ($4). Highlife's breakfast and lunch specials are also around $4. This is one of the only authentic African restaurants in the Maritimes.

Spring Garden Rd *Second Cup* (☎ *902-429-0883, 5425 Spring Garden Rd at Queen St)* Coffee just over $1. Open 7am-midnight daily. This is the largest version of this chain in Canada. A great feature is the availability of computers for free Web surfing.

Tu Do Restaurant (☎ *902-421-0081, 1541 Birmingham St)* Main meals $6-7. Open until 10pm Mon-Thur, until midnight Fri & Sat (closed 3pm-5pm daily). The good, inexpensive Vietnamese food available here makes this place worth seeking out. There's only one entrée over $10 on the easily understood menu. You'll like the linen tablecloths, fresh ingredients and pleasing decor.

Thirsty Duck Pub & Eatery (☎ *902-422-1548, 5470 Spring Garden Rd)* Meals $5-8. Open 11am-11pm Mon & Tues, 11am-midnight Wed, 11am-2am Thur-Sat, 11am-9pm Sun. To get to this place, go into the store and up the stairs to the rooftop patio. It's got burgers, fish and chips, sandwiches and salads, and draft beer at low prices. You could strike gold and get live music with your food and drink.

Your Father's Moustache (☎ *902-423-6766, 5686 Spring Garden Rd)* Main meals $7-14. Open 11am-midnight Sun-Wed, 11am-1am Thur-Sat. Just up the street, this place also features a rooftop patio and live music. The food menu includes pastas ($7-8), steaks and ribs ($8-14) and grilled haddock ($10).

Farther South *Kinh-Do* (☎ *902-425-8555, 1284 Barrington St)* Lunch special $5. Open 11:30am-9:30pm Tues-Fri, 4:30pm-9:30pm Sat & Sun. For Vietnamese food, try this casual place. It offers tasty dishes, an extensive menu and low prices.

Trident Booksellers & Café (☎ *902-423-7100, 1256 Hollis St)* Coffee/tea under $2. Open 8:30am-5pm Mon-Sat, noon-5pm Sun. This somewhat bohemian café, with the large stained-glass piece in the window, is the place to linger over a 'fair trade' coffee or a pot of herbal tea, sandwiches and pastries. When you've finished with the newspaper, check out the other half of the café, which has a fine selection of books, new and used.

Sobeys Supermarket (☎ *902-422-9884, 1120 Queen St at Fenwick)* Open 24 hrs from 7am Mon to midnight Sat; closed Sun. Come here for splendid picnic fare or groceries to carry back to the hostel.

Entertainment

Live Music Halifax has an astonishing number of pubs (55 at last count) and nightlife options. Doing the 'pub pinball' is a local pastime. For a complete rundown of the music scene grab a copy of *The Coast*, Halifax's entertainment newspaper. Offered free at restaurants and pubs, this publication provides a full schedule of music, film and stage performances in the city.

Lower Deck (☎ *902-425-1501, 1869 Upper Water St)* Open 11am-12:30am. On the lower level of the Privateer's Warehouse at the Historic Properties on the waterfront, Lower Deck presents Maritime folk music nightly at 9pm ($3 cover). Nothing on the food menu is over $10 (only the seafood plate is over $7). A caveat: Go early or you won't get a seat.

Split Crow (☎ *902-422-4366, 1855 Granville St)* Open 11am-12:30am or later daily. This is the best known of the pubs in the old fashioned Granville St Mall off Duke St. Lunch specials like clams and chips are under $5; come for the live Maritimes music daily from 9pm to midnight (weekends until 1am). The Saturday matinee from 3:30pm to 6:30pm also packs them in ($3 cover).

Bearly's Bar & Grill (☎ *902-423-2526, 1269 Barrington St)* Open 11am-midnight Mon & Tues, 11am-1:30am Wed-Sun. From Thursday to Sunday more live music, especially bluegrass and blues, can be enjoyed at this place near the HI Hostel.

Birmingham Bar & Grill (☎ *902-420-9622, 5657 Spring Garden Rd)* Open 11am-10pm Sun-Thur, 11am-11pm Fri & Sat. This large bar near the Public Gardens presents hot jazz from 8pm Wednesday to Sunday. The list of imported beers is extensive.

Clubs *The Dome* (☎ *902-422-5453, 1740 Argyle St)* Open 11am-3:30am daily. Dubbed the 'Liquordome,' there are four establishments under one roof here. At *My Apartment*

NOVA SCOTIA

and *Lawrence of Oregano* a DJ spins Top 40 music nightly from 10:30pm. Upstairs in *Cheers* a live band plays cover music from 10:30pm Tuesday to Saturday.

The Attic (☎ 902-423-0909, 1741 Grafton St) Open 10pm-3:30am Thur, 9pm-3:30am Fri & Sat. This is the fourth and most exclusive unit at The Dome, where top rock bands cater to a smart younger crowd. A single cover charge of $3 Thursday, $5 Friday and Sunday and $6 Saturday includes admission to all four venues. Be aware of the dress-code ban on athletic or camouflage wear, numbered shirts, ripped clothes and hats.

Reflections Cabaret (☎ 902-422-2957, 5184 Sackville St) Open 4pm-4am daily. In the basement below Tourism Halifax, Reflections began as a mainly gay disco and has developed into an 'in' place where plenty of straights also come. There's live music after 9pm, and the drink prices are good.

Bars *Diamond Bar* (☎ 902-423-8845, 1663 Argyle St) Open 11am-2am daily. This is another establishment with multiple coolly named rooms. The middle room right behind the trendy sidewalk terrace is *Backstage*. To the right is gay-friendly *Diamond* and to the left is *Economy Shoe Shop*, which James Cameron reportedly frequented while filming *Titanic* in Dartmouth. There's live jazz in the Shoe Shop every Monday from 9:30pm (no cover charge). The section straight back from Backstage is the *Belgian Bar* because Belgian beer is on tap.

The Eagle Pub & Eatery (☎ 902-425-1889, 1565 Grafton St near Blowers St) Open 3pm-2am Mon-Fri, noon-2am Sat & Sun. The Eagle is Halifax's most famous gay bar. Nothing on the food menu is over $9.

Theater *Neptune Theatre* (☎ 902-429-7070, 1593 Argyle St) In 1997 this two-stage complex was rebuilt at a cost of $25 million and it's now the city's leading theatrical venue. During the regular season from September to May you might see musicals, drama or comedy here, with tickets averaging $37. The building also contains the *du Maurier Studio Theatre* which presents more avant-garde programs from October to April. From mid-July to mid-August the Neptune stages a musical comedy for summer visitors from Tuesday to Sunday with tickets ranging $15-30 depending on the seat.

Shakespeare by the Sea (☎ 902-422-0295, Oceanside Parking Lot off Point Pleasant Dr) There's nothing quite like Shakespeare by the sea, and in July and August that's exactly what you get in performances of the Bard's works in Point Pleasant Park. Performances in the Summer House on the east side of the park are at 7pm Tuesday to Saturday and also at 2pm Saturday and Sunday, with tickets costing $8.

Grafton St Dinner Theatre (☎ 902-425-1961, 1741 Grafton St) Open 6:45pm-10pm Tues-Sun. Tickets $37. At the Grafton St Dinner Theatre you get a three-course meal (drinks not included) and a lighthearted musical comedy. Seating is at large banquet-style tables with 10 to 18 seats, so singles won't feel out of place. Reserve well ahead for a Friday or Saturday night – other nights are less heavily booked.

Halifax Feast (☎ 902-420-1840, Maritime Center, 1505 Barrington St) Open 7pm-9:45pm Tues-Sat Feb-Dec. Tickets $40. The seating here is more intimate than at Grafton St – the tables have just six to 10 seats and are on three levels – and the jokes are slightly more risqué. If you enjoyed one theater, take in the show at the other another night. As lots of locals also come to these places, both theaters change the show three or four times a year.

Spectator Sports

In winter, the Halifax Mooseheads face off against visiting hockey teams at the 9000-seat *Halifax Metro Centre* (☎ 902-451-1221, 5284 Duke St at Brunswick St), across from the Old Town Clock. At other times, the center hosts international performing artists and bands. The box office is open 11am to 5pm weekdays.

Getting There & Away

Air Air Canada (☎ 888-247-2262, 1559 Brunswick St, near Spring Garden Rd; open 9am-5pm Mon-Fri) has domestic flights from Halifax to Calgary, Edmonton, Montréal, Ottawa, St John's, Toronto, Vancouver and Winnipeg. Outside Canada, it flies directly to Boston, London and Newark. Its subsidiary, Air Canada Jazz, also provides connections to most airports around the Maritimes, including Charlottetown, Fredericton, Moncton, Saint John, Sydney and Yarmouth.

Air Canada is not the only show in town! In the past, the following have also flown into Halifax: Air Labrador, Air St-Pierre, Air Transat, American Airlines (Eagle Air), Continental Airlines and Icelandair. The $10 'airport improvement fee' levied at Halifax should be included in your ticket.

Bus The principal bus line is Acadian Lines, which connects with New Brunswick's SMT Lines at Amherst. There are also a couple of smaller, regional lines which service the south coast. They all use the Acadian Lines bus station (☎ 902-454-9321, 6040 Almon St). Almon runs south off Robie St, northwest of the Citadel. The station is open from 6:30am to 7pm daily, plus all bus arrival times, and $2 coin lockers are available. This station is not in the best part of town and some care should be taken if you arrive late.

Following are the one-way fares to several destinations. To North Sydney (one express service daily and other milk runs) it's $59, to Yarmouth (via Digby) $52, Moncton $45, Saint John $68 and Fredericton $75. The 7am bus from Halifax connects in Moncton for Montréal daily and for New York on Friday and Saturday.

DRL Coachlines (☎ 902-450-1987) offers a cheaper service from Halifax to Yarmouth ($38, via Lunenburg). The route runs right along the South Shore, leaving Halifax at 6:25pm daily.

Zinck's Bus Co (☎ 902-468-4342) runs a service along the Eastern Shore from Halifax to Sherbrooke ($15), stopping at all the small villages along the way. It runs once a day (except Sunday) eastbound and Tuesday to Saturday westbound. The departure from Halifax is at 5:30pm.

Shuttle To reach Prince Edward Island by scheduled bus you must connect through Moncton. Minibus shuttles do the Halifax-Charlottetown run far more quickly and directly than the bus, completing the journey in four hours.

The Halifax-based PEI Express Shuttle (☎ 877-877-1771) and Go-Van (☎ 866-463-9660) both charge $45 one-way with front door pick-ups provided around Halifax between 6:30am and 7:30am.

The Charlottetown-based Advanced Shuttle (☎ 877-886-3322) and Square One Shuttle (☎ 877-675-3830) do the reverse,

leaving Halifax in the afternoon. Advanced Shuttle can carry up to three bicycles on its service at $10 each if you let the office know beforehand.

Kiwi Kaboodle's Tradewind Shuttle (☎ 902-463-4244) offers one-way transportation to Lunenburg for $30. Pick-ups can be arranged anywhere in Halifax around 9:30am.

Try Town Transit (☎ 877-521-0855) also does daily van shuttles between Halifax and Lunenburg at $22 one-way. They'll also pick up at your hostel door but will only go if they have at least four bookings.

Train The VIA Rail station (☎ 888-842-7245, 1161 Hollis St) is six blocks south of the downtown area. It's off Terminal Rd by the huge Westin Hotel and is one of the few examples of monumental Canadian train-station architecture left in the Maritimes. No coin lockers are available at the station.

The train is more useful for reaching out-of-province destinations than for getting around Nova Scotia. A train to Moncton, New Brunswick ($52), and eventually Montréal, departs at 12:55pm daily (except Tuesday) along a route through eastern New Brunswick that includes stops at Amherst, Sackville, Miramichi, Bathurst and Campbellton.

The fare to Montréal is $197, but if you book a week in advance the price goes down to $147. You can reserve up to 331 days in advance and it's definitely a good idea to do so as only a limited number of cheap seats are sold for each train.

Getting Around
To/From the Airport Halifax International Airport is 39km northeast of town on Hwy 102 toward Truro. There are no city buses to the airport but there is the Airbus (☎ 902-873-2091). It runs between the airport and the downtown center, with stops at major central hotels such as the Westin (near the HI hostel) and the Lord Nelson. The fare is $12/20 one-way/roundtrip. The bus makes 23 trips daily with the first run at 6am and the last bus leaving the airport at 11:15pm. Allow 90 minutes before flight time.

An alternative is Share-A-Cab (☎ 800-565-8669). Call at least four hours before flight time and it will find other passengers and pick you up. The price is $24.

The Halifax-Charlottetown minibus shuttles offer pick-up/drop-off at Halifax

NOVA SCOTIA

International Airport for an additional $3 to $5 fee. Some will pick you up right at the airport door while others make you take a taxi to the Airport Hotel (ask). See Shuttle, in the earlier Getting There & Away section, for the numbers to call.

Bus Metro Transit (☎ 902-490-6600) runs the good, inexpensive city bus system. The fare is $1.65, or $30 for a 20-ticket booklet. Transfers to ferries are included. Perk's News Stand near the transit terminal at the foot of George St sells booklets. Another transit terminal is on both sides of Barrington St outside Scotia Square. Call for route and schedule information or pick up a free *Metro Transit Riders' Guide* from Tourism Halifax.

The No 7 city bus on Robie St goes from the bus station into town. 'Fred' is a free city bus running a circuit along South St, Lower Water St, Barrington St, Spring Garden Rd and South Park St back to South St. It runs every 30 minutes from 11am to 6pm daily from June to August with 18 stops along the route.

Hitchhikers heading north toward Truro or west toward Windsor will want to pick up bus Nos 80 or 82 to the Cobequid Terminal near the junction of Hwys 101 and 102 north of Bedford. Those heading west can use bus No 21 which ends at the village of Timberlea on St Margarets Bay Rd (Hwy 3). Eastbound toward Sherbrooke, take bus No 62 from the Dartmouth ferry terminal to Cherry Brook on Hwy 7 (no service Sunday).

Car In Halifax be on the lookout for pedestrians, who have priority at crosswalks. They'll sometimes step out into the road without looking and the driver is held responsible should an accident occur. Pedestrians are far less common elsewhere in the Maritimes, so you really do need to make a mental effort to be on guard.

The car rental companies represented at Halifax International Airport are Avis, Budget, Dollar, Hertz, National and Thrifty. Due to high operating costs at the airport, car rentals from there are much more expensive than those in town. To get around this, take the Airbus into town and rent your car there.

Enterprise Rent-a-Car (☎ 902-492-8400, 1161 Hollis St), inside the VIA Rail station, has cars at $37 a day including 200 free kilo-

meters (extra kilometers 14¢ each). Insurance is $19 a day (zero deductible). The weekly rate is $200 with 1400 free kilometers. Ask about reduced weekend and monthly rates.

Discount Car Rentals (☎ 902-423-7612, 1240 Hollis St) has four different price seasons, starting at $39/99/259 a day/weekend/week in midwinter, increasing to $50/125/320 in midsummer. Unlimited kilometers in the three Maritime provinces are included (you're not supposed to take the car to Maine, Québec or Newfoundland). Insurance is $22 a day extra ($300 deductible), and as usual, add 15% tax. If you can show a youth hostel card, you'll get a 10% discount on the weekly rate only.

Rent-a-Wreck (☎ 902-434-4224, 130 Woodlawn Rd, Dartmouth) has some of the lowest rates in town. Their office is way out near exit 7 from Hwy 111, but if you call they'll probably offer to pick you up. Prices start at $35 a day with 200 free kilometers. A weekend of Friday to Monday or Saturday to Tuesday will be $100 with 800 free kilometers. Weekly it's $240 with 1600 free kilometers. In the off-season these rates go down to $29/89/199 a day/weekend/week and you can get a 10% discount anytime by showing an HI card. In all cases, extra kilometers are 12¢ each. Insurance is $13 a day.

Parking in the downtown area can be a real hassle. For a central place to stash the wheels, go to Impark (☎ 902-423-0680, 1505 Lower Water St) – look for the red signs near Salter St opposite Brewery Market. Impark also has a couple of other locations around town.

Impark has an all-day ticket for $8. After 5pm and all day Saturday and Sunday the flat rate is $5. The daily and evening flat rates are valid until 6am the next morning, when a new parking period begins.

Impark will take RVs during the day but campers must vacate the lot by 10pm. There's a $2000 fine for sleeping overnight in an RV parked in a commercial parking lot or on the street.

Halifax parking meters are enforced from 8am to 6pm Monday to Friday. The fine for ordinary parking violations is around $15.

Ferry Ferries run continuously from the Halifax ferry terminal near the Historic Properties dock. One boat heads across the bay to the city of Dartmouth, the other is a peak-period service to Woodside, just south of Dartmouth. A ticket is $1.65 one way and the ride makes a nice, short mini-tour of the harbor. From Monday to Saturday the Dartmouth ferries run every 15 minutes at peak times, otherwise every 30 minutes. The last one is at 11:30pm. On Sunday they run from noon to 5:30pm but only June through September. Bicycles are welcomed.

AROUND HALIFAX
Dartmouth
pop 65,000

Founded in 1750, one year after Halifax, Dartmouth is Halifax's counterpart just across the harbor. However, the similarities end with the waterfront location of the central area. Compared with Halifax, Dartmouth is more residential and its city center less commercial. The downtown area lacks the history, charm and bustle of Halifax. Suburban Dartmouth is mostly highways and shopping malls.

Having said that, Dartmouth does make for a cheap afternoon side trip and even a scenic one, thanks to the ferry. The Halifax-Dartmouth ferry, operated by Metro Transit (the bus people), is said to be the oldest saltwater ferry system in North America, dating back to 1752 when it was just a rowboat.

Orientation & Information Alderney Gate houses the ferry terminal, the Dartmouth public library, city offices, a food court and some shops. The farmers' market in the ferry complex operates from 7am to 2pm on Saturday year-round.

A tourist desk (☎ 902-490-4433) with brochures and staff to answer questions is at the ferry complex (open 9am-6pm mid-May to October).

For free Internet access, the Dartmouth public library (☎ 902-490-5745, 60 Alderney Dr), just outside the ferry terminal, is open 10am to 9pm Tuesday to Thursday, 10am to 5pm Friday and Saturday and 2pm to 5pm Sunday.

Things to See & Do The **Dartmouth Heritage Museum** (☎ 902-464-2300, Alderney Dr at Wyse Rd; admission $2; open 10am-5pm Tues-Sun mid-June–Aug, 1:30pm-5pm Wed-Sat Sept–mid-June) is adjacent to the Police Community Office and Leighton Dillman Park, about a 15-minute walk to the left from

the Halifax ferry. It houses an eclectic collection pertaining to the city's natural and human history and includes some First Nations artifacts and crafts, various tools and fashions and industrial bric-a-brac. The $2 admission fee also includes entry to Quaker Whaler House if you visit both on the same day.

A short walk from the ferry is the **Quaker Whaler House** (☎ 902-464-2300, 59 Ochterloney St; admission $2; open 10am-5pm Tues-Sun mid-June–Aug), the oldest house in the Halifax area, having been built in 1786. The Quakers came to the region as whalers from New England. Guides in costume lead visitors around the house.

Just outside Dartmouth is a major government marine research center, the **Bedford Institute of Oceanography** (☎ 902-426-2373, 1 Challenger Dr; admission free; open 9am-4pm Mon-Fri), Canada's leading oceanographic facility. The surprisingly interesting exhibits cover fisheries and various ocean studies, and the self-guided tour is a rewarding way to put in an hour. Other features include a video, an exhibit on the *Titanic* and some aquarium specimens to see. From May to August student guides are available. The inexpensive cafeteria makes it worth coming at lunchtime. To get there from Dartmouth by car, take Windmill Rd to Princess Margaret Dr, which is near the MacKay Bridge, or take bus No 51 from the Dartmouth ferry terminal.

Places to Stay & Eat *Shubie Campground* (☎ 902-435-8328, ☒ www.shubiecampground.com, Jaybee Dr off Waverley Rd) Without/with hookups $19/21. Open mid-May–mid-Oct. Owned by the municipality but privately operated, Shubie Park is the only campground accessible from Halifax on public transportation. The location, near the Shubenacadie Canal, is convenient, although the site is just a grassy field with little shade. Facilities include showers and a laundromat. Bus No 55 stops within two blocks of the entrance, but it doesn't run on Sunday, in which case head to the Micmac Mall via a local trail and pick up the No 10 bus to Halifax.

See Porters Lake in the Eastern Shore section for an excellent camping possibility just east of Dartmouth.

Caroline's (☎ 902-469-4665, 134 Victoria Rd) Singles/doubles $40/50 with continental

NOVA SCOTIA

breakfast. Open Apr-Dec. This friendly three-room place is beyond the Dartmouth Heritage Museum and not far from the Macdonald Bridge, a kilometer from central Dartmouth.

Seasons Motor Inn (☎ 902-435-0060, fax 902-435-0060, **W** home.istar.ca/~garson, 40 Lakecrest Dr) Singles/doubles $58/63 mid-June–mid-Sept, $53/58 other months. Off Main St near exit 6 from Hwy 111, Seasons Motor Inn offers 33 rooms in a solid brick two-story building. Facilities include a communal kitchen, laundromat and free parking. Frequent bus service is available to Halifax.

Alderney Bar & Café (☎ 902-469-0787, 69 Alderney Dr) Sandwiches/mains $6/8 & up. Open 11am-10pm Mon-Fri, 11am-3pm Sat & Sun. Opposite the ferry and to the right, the Alderney Bar features spacious interiors and pub grub like pizza, pastas and fish and chips.

Queen of Cups Teahouse (☎ 902-463-1983, 44 Ochterloney St) Lunch $4-7. Open 10am-5pm Mon-Sat. This cozy place, more or less opposite Quaker Whaler House, is fine for a good healthy lunch of soup ($5), salad ($4-7), wrap ($5-7) or sandwich ($4-5). Otherwise drop in for tea for two ($3). Owner Shelley Goodson does Tarot readings, if you call ahead for an appointment.

South Shore

The 'South Shore' refers to the area south and west of Halifax stretching along the coast to Yarmouth. It contains many fishing villages and several small historic towns. Some of the coastal scenery is good – typically rocky, jagged and foggy.

The first one-third of the area, closest to Halifax, is the city's cottage country and is quite busy. The tourist route through here is called the Lighthouse Route and is probably the most visited region of Nova Scotia.

DRL Coachlines buses service the area daily, leaving Halifax westbound at 6:25pm and Yarmouth eastbound at 6:25am (at 11:30am on Sunday). This schedule makes it more convenient for bus travelers to move east than west.

PEGGY'S COVE

Canada's best-known fishing village lies 43km west of Halifax on Hwy 333. It's a pretty place, with fishing boats, nets, lobster traps, docks and old pastel houses that all seem perfectly placed to please the eye. The 415-million-year-old granite boulders (known to geologists as erratics) littering the surroundings add an odd touch. Even the horror of Swissair Flight 111, which crashed not far offshore in September 1998, has not dimmed the village's quintessential picture-postcard feel.

The smooth shoreline rock all around the lighthouse just begs to be explored (but do not get too close – every year visitors are swept into the cold waters by unexpected swells). Count on the fog, too. It enshrouds the area at least once every three days and is present most mornings.

The village, which dates from 1811, has just 60 residents, most of whom are fishers. The lighthouse is now a small post office that uses its own lighthouse-shaped stamp cancellation mark.

Peggy's Cove is one of the most visited attractions in the Maritimes – and it's close to the capital too, so there are crowds which detract from its appeal. The best time for a visit is before 10am. Many tour buses arrive in the middle of the day and create what has to be one of the worst traffic jams in the province. Whenever a cruise ship is in Halifax – as happens a couple of times a week in summer – Peggy's Cove becomes a carnival as passengers are bused en masse to the touristy Sou'wester Restaurant near the lighthouse. To help ease the problem, there's a free parking area with washrooms and a tourist information office (but no picnic tables) on the left as you enter the village. By all means stop there and walk the last few hundred meters.

Things to See & Do

Across the street from the parking area is the **deGarthe Gallery** (☎ 902-823-2256; admission $1; open 9am-5pm daily mid-May–mid-Oct) with paintings by local artist William deGarthe (1907–83), who also sculpted the magnificent Fishermen's Monument in front of the gallery. From here it's just a five-minute walk past the much photographed fishing harbor to the rock formations and lighthouse.

A poignant, tasteful **memorial** to the 229 individuals who perished aboard Swissair Flight 111 has been created off Hwy 333

1.8km north of the turnoff to Peggy's Cove. A panel at the entrance indicates the precise crash site on the horizon. After a lengthy investigation, it was determined that a ceiling fire in the cockpit area led to the crash of the Geneva-bound flight an hour after it departed from New York.

Novashores Adventures (☎ 902-449-1726, W www.novashores.com, 10295 Hwy 333, Glen Margaret), based at Wayside Camping Park, offers ocean kayaking tours on scenic St Margaret's Bay at $40/75 a half/full day in a single kayak or $60/95 for two in a tandem, snack or lunch included.

Places to Stay

Wayside Camping Park (☎ 902-823-2271, fax 902-823-1119, 10295 Hwy 333, Glen Margaret) Without/with hookups $15/20. Open Apr–mid-Oct. This large campground 10 km north of Peggy's Cove and 36km from Halifax has lots of shady sites available up on the hill. You may find a good one except in midsummer, when it's crowded and people tend to stay for a few days.

Lover's Lane Housekeeping Cottages (☎ 902-823-2670, 8388 Hwy 333) Singles/doubles $50/75, extra persons $10. Open June-Sept. Just 500m north of the Swissair Memorial, there are five attractive cottages right on the ocean here.

Cliffy Cove Motel (☎ 902-823-3178, 8444 Hwy 333) Rooms $40-75. Open May-late Oct. The 11 motel rooms in a long block are 200m north of Lover's Lane. There's one small room at $40 single or double, four with queen beds at $69 and six larger rooms at $75.

CHESTER
pop 1200

Overlooking Mahone Bay, the old village of Chester was established in 1759. It's had a colorful history as the haunt of pirates and Prohibition-era bathtub-gin smugglers.

The center of town is along Pleasant St between King and Queen Sts, and the picturesque harbor lies along Water St. A large regatta is held here in mid-August. The tourist office (☎ 902-275-4616) is in the old train depot on Hwy 3 north of town. It's open May to October.

The DRL Coachlines bus to Halifax ($11) and Yarmouth ($32) stops at Hammond Kwik Way (☎ 902-275-5203, 3711 Hwy 3), a kilometer outside of town.

A fine example of Georgian architecture dating from 1806, the **Lordly House Museum** (☎ 902-275-3842, 133 Central St; admission free; open 10am-5pm Tues-Sat, 1pm-5pm Sun mid-May–mid-Oct) contains three period rooms illustrating 19th-century upper-class life, plus displays on the history of Chester. There's a genealogy research area you can use if any of your ancestors are from the area, and free Internet access is available to all.

For boat and bicycle rentals, try **Captain Evan's Wharf** (☎ 902-275-2030, W www .chesterahoy.com, 233 Pig Loop Rd; open mid-May–mid-Oct). At the north end of the harbor, this outlet rents single kayaks ($12/35/50 for one/four/eight hours), double kayaks ($15/40/65) and canoes ($10/15/18). Captain Evan also rents bicycles at $20/75 per day/week. One-hour harbor tours in an open boat called *Osprey 210* are $30/45/60 for one/two/three people.

Places to Stay & Eat

Graves Island Provincial Park (☎ 902-275-4425, W parks.gov.ns.ca, 3km northeast of Chester) Sites $18. Open mid-May–early Oct. Sixty-four wooded and open campsites are available on an island in Mahone Bay, a kilometer off Hwy 3 and connected by causeway. RVs usually park right in the middle of the area, but some nice shady, isolated tent sites are tucked away on the flanks of the central plateau. A hiking trail and beach are available, and Graves Island is very popular in midsummer. It will be full Friday and Saturday nights.

Mecklenburgh Inn B&B (☎ 902-275-4638, W www.atlanticonline.ns.ca/meck, 78 Queen St) Singles/doubles $65/75-85 with breakfast. Open mid-May–Oct. This large two-story inn next to the post office was built in 1890. There's a breezy 2nd-floor verandah, and some rooms have private adjacent balconies. It's casual and full of character.

Windjammer Motel (☎ 902-275-3567, 4070 Hwy 3) Singles/doubles $60/65 mid-June–early Sept, $50/55 other months. Just 300m from the tourist office, the 18 rooms are in several long wooden blocks. A restaurant is on the premises.

Julien's Pastry Shop Bakery (☎ 902-275-2324, 43 Queen St near Pleasant St) Sandwiches $4. Open 8am-5pm Tues-Sun (7am-5:30pm in July & Aug). For a casual bite, Julien's features healthy sandwiches and fresh baked croissants daily. Tea or coffee on the sidewalk terrace will be under $2.

Luigi's Café (☎ *902-275-5185, 19 Pleasant St*) Prices $4-6. Across the street from the Chester Playhouse, this is the place for soups ($2.50-5.50), salads ($4.50-8.50) and sandwiches ($4.50). Breakfast is available all day ($4-7 without coffee).

Entertainment
Chester Playhouse (☎ *902-275-3933, 22 Pleasant St*) Tickets $13-25. This theater runs comedies, musicals and dramas through July and August. Performances are at 8pm Wednesday to Saturday.

Fo'c'sle Tavern (☎ *902-275-3912, Queen St at Pleasant St*) Open 11am-11pm (until midnight or later on weekends). This rollicking local pub has an air of authenticity.

MAHONE BAY
A little piece of eye candy, Mahone Bay, with its islands and history, has become a sort of city escape. It's a popular destination for a Sunday drive from Halifax, about 100km away, or for an afternoon tea. The town has antique and craft shops and a decided tourist orientation. You can see fine examples of Victorian gingerbread-house architecture around town.

Along Hwy 3 on the east side of town is the tourist information office (☎ 902-624-6151, 165 Edgewater St), which is open mid-May to September. Among the many handouts are the walking-tour brochures of Mahone Bay. Baywater Cemetery behind the tourist office contains the tombs of many early settlers of this area.

DRL Coachlines stops at the Irving gas station (☎ 902-624-6311) on Edgewater St in the center of Mahone Bay, right next to the three churches.

Things to See & Do
In a row along Edgewater St facing the waterfront are three historic **churches** belonging to the Anglican, Lutheran and United denominations.

The **Settlers' Museum & Cultural Centre** (☎ *902-624-6263, 578 S Main St; admission by donation; open 10am-5pm Tues-Sat, 1pm-5pm Sun June-Oct*) deals mainly with the first German settlers to the area. Displays in two rooms cover the 1850s.

Amos Pewter (☎ *800-565-3369,* W *www .economusee-atl.com/pewter/english, 589 Main St; admission free*), across the street from the Settlers' Museum, demonstrates and explains the art of pewter-making. It's open year-round (closed Sunday from January to April).

The MV **Summer Bay** (☎ *902-521-4300; adult/child $30/17 plus tax*) does two-hour harbor cruises from Mahone Bay's Government Wharf four times a day in July and August.

Sea kayaking is excellent in island-studded Mahone Bay. **Mahone Bay Kayak Adventures** (☎ *902-624-0334, 619 S Main St; single/double kayak rentals $58/83 per day; open mid-May–early Oct*), right on the harbor, is a friendly operation with a good reputation. It also has canoes and offers a shuttle service up and down the coast.

For novices, there are half-day introductory lessons for $45. A half-day trip to Indian Point is $55/75 single/double, while full-day trips to Blue Rocks and Stonehurst near Lunenburg (where you can see seals) are $105/170. Two-day customized B&B tours where you kayak from one inn to the next can be arranged. All equipment, lodging and meals are included in the cost of such tours.

Places to Stay & Eat
Fairmont House B&B (☎ *902-624-8089,* e *fairmonthouse@sympatico.ca, 654 S Main St*) Singles/doubles $60/85 including breakfast. Open mid-May–early Oct. This large gray wooden house near the Government Wharf has three rooms with private bath.

The Red Door B&B (☎ *902-624-8479,* e *reddoor@auracom.com, 381 W Main St*) Singles/doubles/triples $55/65/75 mid-May–mid-Nov, $50 single or double other months. Breakfast is included. The three rooms with shared bath are in a white house opposite Mahone Bay's liquor store, 500m from the center of town. The backyard garden is nice.

Jo-Ann's Deli Market and Bake Shop (☎ *902-624-6305, 9 Edgewater St*) Open 9am-6pm daily May-Oct. In the very heart of Mahone Bay, Jo-Ann's Deli is the place to come for organic veggies, sinfully rich cakes and pastries and all manner of other edible goodies. For the healthiest loaves of bread you'll ever find, go next door to

LaHave Bakery (☎ 902-624-1420, 3 Edge-water St; open year-round), in the former train station.

Mimi's Ocean Grill (☎ 902-624-1342, 662 S Main St) Lunch mains around $10, dinner $11-20. Open noon-2:30pm & 5:30pm-8:30pm Mon-Fri, noon-9pm Sat & Sun May-June & Sept-Oct, noon-9pm daily July & Aug. For nouvelle cuisine with Thai and Italian over-tones, try this place. For lunch there's Tuscan *panini* ($10) or chicken pot pie ($11), while dinner brings such dishes as ocean primavera ($17) and Atlantic potlatch ($18).

LUNENBURG
pop 2600
This attractive town, known for the *Bluenose* sailing schooner built here in

1921, is the region's only Unesco world her-itage site. Always a shipbuilding town, this well-preserved historic gem is still the linch-pin of the provincial fishing industry, with one of the major fleets of the north Atlantic seaboard. The largest fish-processing plant in North America is here, producing High-liner frozen seafood products.

Lunenburg was founded in 1753 when the British encouraged Protestants to emi-grate from Europe. It became the first largely German settlement in the country.

On the second weekend in July, a craft festival is held, and in mid-August the equally popular **Folk Harbour Festival** (☎ 902-634-3180) is a weekend of traditional music and dance. In early October the town tips a few pints during its **Oktoberfest**.

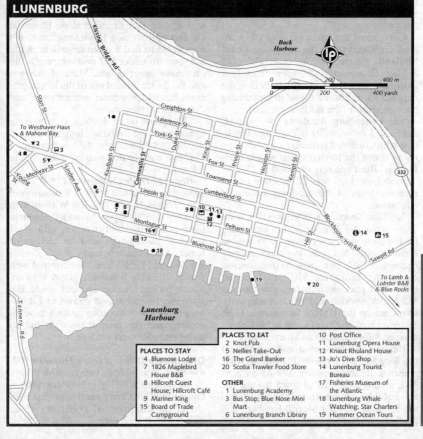

LUNENBURG

To Westhaver Haus & Mahone Bay
Back Harbour
Lunenburg Harbour
To Lamb & Lobster B&B & Blue Rocks

PLACES TO STAY
4 Bluenose Lodge
7 1826 Maplebird House B&B
8 Hillcroft Guest House; Hillcroft Café
9 Mariner King
15 Board of Trade Campground

PLACES TO EAT
2 Knot Pub
5 Nellies Take-Out
16 The Grand Banker
20 Scotia Trawler Food Store

OTHER
1 Lunenburg Academy
3 Bus Stop; Blue Nose Mini Mart
6 Lunenburg Branch Library
10 Post Office
11 Lunenburg Opera House
12 Knaut Rhuland House
13 Jo's Dive Shop
14 Lunenburg Tourist Bureau
17 Fisheries Museum of the Atlantic
18 Lunenburg Whale Watching; Star Charters
19 Hummer Ocean Tours

NOVA SCOTIA

Information

The Lunenburg Tourist Bureau (☎ 902-634-8100) is up on Blockhouse Hill Rd, with a great view of the area. It's open 9am to 7pm daily May to October.

The Lunenburg branch library (☎ 902-634-8008, 19 Pelham St) provides free Internet access 1:30pm to 5:30pm Tuesday, Wednesday and Friday, 9am to 9pm Thursday and 9am to 5pm Saturday.

Things to See & Do

The well-executed **Fisheries Museum of the Atlantic** (☎ 902-634-4794, 68 Bluenose Dr; admission $8; open 9:30am-5:30pm June-late Oct) houses an aquarium and exhibits on fishing and fish processing. It also screens various films on marine life and has two ships – a dragger and a fishing schooner – in the water for inspection. If you purchase your ticket after 4pm, it's good for the next day (ask).

Considered the finest example of Georgian architecture in the province, **Knaut Rhuland House** (☎ 902-634-3498, 125 Pelham St; admission $3; open 10am-5pm daily June–mid-Sept), erected in 1793, is the only authentic historic house in Lunenburg open to visitors (the B&Bs excluded).

The **Lunenburg Academy** (☎ 902-634-2220, 97 Kaulbach St) is the huge black-and-white turreted structure on a hill seen rising above the town on your way in from Halifax. Built entirely of wood in 1895 as a prestigious high school, it is one of the rare survivors of the academy system of education.

Jo's Dive Shop (☎ 800-563-4831, Ⓦ www.jodive.ns.ca, 296 Lincoln St) has everything for the diver including rentals. From June to early October, Jo's runs dive charters upon request at $50 per person (four-person minimum). Tanks are $10, otherwise an equipment package including two tanks is $52 (mask, snorkel and fins not supplied). Dives are on the HMCS Saguenay, a 112m destroyer sunk in 27m of water in 1994. You'll also see walls, pinnacles and harbor seals.

Bicycles can be rented and repaired at the **Bicycle Barn** (☎ 902-634-3426, Ⓦ www.tallships.ca/bikelunenburg, 579 Blue Rocks Rd), almost 2km east of town toward the Blue Rocks neighborhood. Hybrid bikes are $20 a day. Owner Merrill Heubach will gladly help you plan your trip.

Organized Tours

From June to mid-October **Lunenburg Whale Watching** (☎ 902-527-7175, Bluenose Dr) offers three-hour whale-watching trips departing from the Lunenburg harbor for $38 per person.

Star Charters (☎ 902-634-3535, Bluenose Dr) schedules four sailing trips daily on its wooden ketch Eastern Star for $22 a person for a two-hour tour ($25 sunset tour). All trips will be running in July and August, while in June and September there's a reduced schedule.

Hummer Ocean Tours (☎ 902-521-0857) does coastal cruises (adult/child $25/12) from the Lunenburg Railway Wharf, off Bluenose Dr, four times a day from June to September.

Places to Stay

Lunenburg is no Peggy's Cove, but in mid-season, tour buses rumble along Bluenose Dr and tourists clog the intersections. It's impossible to find a room anywhere in the old town for under $50, and camping is the only low-budget option. Most of the inns and B&Bs are formed out of the larger, gracious, historic properties around town, and that doesn't come cheap.

The tourist office doubles as a booking agency for all the B&Bs and hotels, and late in the day they'll know who still has vacancies.

If you want to do some camping, try the following spot.

Board of Trade Campground (☎ 902-634-3656, fax 902-634-3194, Ⓔ LBT@auracom.com, 11 Blockhouse Hill Rd) Without/with hookups $16/21. Open May-Oct. Right in town beside the tourist office, with great views, is this campground for trailers or tenters. Unfortunately, many of the 55 sites are designed for RVs and are covered with gravel, while the remaining grassy sites are closely packed together and lack shade. The convenient location and glories of Lunenburg make it worth putting up with these inconveniences this time. It does get full, so arrive early. Showers are free.

Downtown Hillcroft Guest House (☎ 902-634-8031, Ⓦ www.bbcanada.com/1369.html, 53 Montague St) Singles/doubles $50/65. Open May-Oct. Continental breakfast is included in the price of Hillcroft's three rooms with shared bath.

Mariner King (☎ 800-565-8509, fax 902-634-8509, W www.tallships.ca/marinerking, 15 King St) Doubles $75-109 mid-May–mid-Oct, $60-88 mid-Oct–mid-May, including full breakfast. This ornate three-story house (1830) is opposite the post office in the middle of the old town.

1826 Maplebird House B&B (☎ 888-395-3863, fax 902-634-3863, W www3.ns.sympatico.ca/barry.susie, 36 Pelham St) Rooms $90 Mar-Oct, $75 Nov-Feb, including full breakfast. This four-room house overlooking the harbor has a lovely rear garden with a swimming pool.

West & East of Downtown *Bluenose Lodge* (☎ 800-565-8851, fax 902-634-8851, e bluenose@fox.nstn.ca, 10 Falkland St) Rooms $85-90 ($5-10 less at beginning and end of season). Open mid-May–Oct. This big place on the corner of Lincoln St is about 125 years old. A breakfast buffet is included in room rates.

Westhaver Haus (☎ 902-634-4937, fax 902-634-8640, 102 Dufferin St) Singles/doubles $50-60/60-70 including breakfast. Open May-Oct (off-season by reservation). Here is yet another magnificent Lunenburg house with stately columns supporting an upper deck. The lower price makes the short uphill walk worthwhile.

Lamb & Lobster B&B (☎ 902-634-4833, fax 902-634-3195, W www.bbcanada.com/3232.html, 619 Blue Rocks Rd) Singles/doubles $45/55 with shared bath. Open June-Oct. This B&B 2km from town is appropriately named since the owner, William Flower, is a lobster fisherman and a shepherd. In the evening guests may be shown how the family collies round up the sheep.

Places to Eat

Sampling the fish here is an absolute must. As well, try some off-beat Lunenburg specialties. Solomon gundy is pickled herring with onions. Lunenburg pudding – pork and spices cooked in the intestines of a pig – goes well with Scotch and water. Fish cakes with rhubarb chutney are also much appreciated here. The famous Lunenburg sausage and sauerkraut reflects the town's German roots.

Nellies Take-Out (26 Lincoln St) Meals $3-7. Open 11am-6pm daily May-Sept. This converted bus parked near the Esso gas station at the west entrance to town serves some of the cheapest and best take-out food in town. A large order of french fries is $3, fish and chips is $5-7 and a cheeseburger is $3. There are even two picnic tables at your disposal.

Knot Pub (☎ 902-634-3334, 4 Dufferin St) Meals $8. Open 11:30am-9:30pm Mon-Sat, noon-9:30pm Sun (the bar stays open later). Good pub food is on hand at this place, including pots of mussels ($4.50/8.50 small/large), fish and chips ($8) and nachos. Happy hour with beer specials runs from 4:30pm to 7pm.

Hillcroft Café (☎ 902-634-8031, 53 Montague St) Mains $13-20. Open 5:30pm-9pm daily mid-Apr–Oct. Lunenburg has a handful of casually upscale bistros, such as this one which provides two vegetarian options.

The Grand Banker (☎ 902-634-3300, rear entrance at 82 Montague St) Meals $10. Open 8am-9:30pm Sun-Wed, 8am-10pm Thur-Sat. This pub facing the waterfront has half-price seafood happy hours from 4pm to 5:30pm daily. Items like scallops, mussels, shrimp, calamari and Solomon gundy go for under $4 at that time (and the bargain continues all winter).

Scotia Trawler Food Store (☎ 902-634-4914, 266 Montague St) Open Mon-Sat. Visit this supermarket to check out local delicacies such as the Lunenburg pudding and Lunenburg sausage in the meat section, Solomon gundy, sauerkraut, fresh mussels and live lobsters with the seafood, and veggie plates in the bakery. If you're camping, investigate the barbecue situation at the campground before buying items that need to be cooked.

Entertainment

Lunenburg Opera House (☎ 902-634-4010, 290 Lincoln St) Tickets $5-20. Numerous Maritime music concerts are held here – check the placards in the window.

Getting There & Away

DRL Coachlines buses pull in at Blue Nose Mini Mart (☎ 902-634-8845), a convenience store at 35 Lincoln St. A bus leaves at 10:20am Monday to Saturday and 3:15pm Sunday for Halifax ($15), and at 8pm daily for Yarmouth ($32).

NOVA SCOTIA

For vans to/from Halifax, see Shuttles under Getting There & Away in the Halifax section.

BRIDGEWATER

Bridgewater, an industrial town with a big Michelin tire plant, is the largest center on the South Shore, with a population of over 7000. Though located right on the LaHave River, Bridgewater isn't a picture-perfect museum town like Chester, Mahone Bay or Lunenburg. Rather, it's the regional service center with large shopping malls and fast-food outlets. Still, quaint corners remain on the back streets.

The **South Shore Exhibition**, held each July, is a major five-day fair with traditional competitions between Canadian and US teams in such events as the ox pull.

The helpful Bridgewater Tourist Office (☎ 902-543-7003, 45 Aberdeen Rd) is across the highway from Atlantic Super Store. It is open 9am to 7pm daily July and August, 9am to 5pm other months.

The **Wile Carding Mill** (☎ *902-543-8233, 242 Victoria Rd; admission free; open 9am-5pm Mon-Sat, 1pm-5pm Sun June-Sept)* is an authentic water mill dating from 1860. Carding is the straightening and untangling of wool fibers in preparation for spinning.

DRL Coachlines uses the Irving gas station (☎ 902-543-2447) on North St, 400m south of exit 12 from Hwy 103. It's 2.3km from here to the Fairview Inn in central Bridgewater. Bus fares are $16/30 to Halifax/Yarmouth.

Places to Stay & Eat

Fairview Inn (☎ *877-671-0777, 25 Queen St)* Singles/doubles $40/45 shared bath, $50/55 private bath, $60/65 suite. This magnificent three-story wooden hotel has been operating since 1863, and unlike the fancy B&Bs of Lunenburg, the Fairview also caters to local residents. Twenty-one rooms have shared bath, the other eight have private bath. The Fairview is brimming with atmosphere and makes a great base for touring this area.

Deluxe Delight Café (☎ *902-543-4450, 25 Queen St)* Main meals $8. Open 6:30am-4pm Mon-Thur, 6:30am-8pm Fri & Sat, 9am-8pm Sun (reduced hours in winter). This unpretentious café occupies the main dining room of the historic Fairview Inn. Things haven't changed much here since the 1940s, and it's mostly local residents ordering breakfast ($3-5 including coffee), sandwiches ($4-5) or dinner (pork chops $8, roast beef $8, haddock $9). It's real Down East food!

LAHAVE

LaHave is just a tiny village on the south bank of the LaHave River. The only HI hostel on the South Shore is here, plus an excellent bakery, a historic site and kayaking possibilities. The LaHave Ferry near the hostel is very handy for anyone driving along the coast (see Getting There & Away, later).

On the outskirts a kilometer west of the village is Fort Point, a national historic site. It was here in 1632 that the first group of French settlers soon to be known as Acadians landed from France. A fort, Ste Marie de Grâce, was built later the same year but very little of it remains today. The site was supplanted by Port Royal in the Annapolis Valley and never became a major center. The **Fort Point Museum** (☎ *902-688-2696, Fort Point Rd; admission free; open 10am-5pm daily June-Aug),* in the former lighthouse keeper's house at the site, tells the story of this early settlement and its leader, Isaac de Razilly.

Near Crescent Beach, 8km southwest, is **Crescent Sea Kayak Tours** (☎ *902-688-2806,* W *www.lairdadventures.com, 5008 Hwy 331)*. Three-hour tours among the LaHave Islands are $35 for a single kayak and $60 for a double.

Places to Stay & Eat

LaHave Marine Hostel (☎ *902-688-2908, fax 902-688-1083,* W *www.hostellingintl.ns.ca, 3421 Hwy 331)* Members/nonmembers $12/15. Open June-Sept. This historic wooden building erected in 1900 was a warehouse back in the days when LaHave was a center for trade with the West Indies. Today it's a simple HI hostel ideal for cyclists, backpackers or any like-minded soul looking for a low-budget place to spend the night. The hostel has two double rooms, one single and one triple, and couples and even individuals can often get a room to themselves. Sheets are $2 extra (if needed). There's a sitting room, a library and a well-equipped kitchen where you can prepare complicated meals. The riverside dock behind the hostel is a great place to linger.

LaHave Bakery (☎ 902-688-2908, 3421 Hwy 331) Lunches $4-5. Open 10am-5pm daily Sept-June, 9am-5:30pm July & Aug. The LaHave Bakery below the HI hostel is one of the best in eastern Canada, if not the whole country. When passing through LaHave, be sure to stop for a soup and sandwich lunch, or just a 'fair trade' coffee/ tea. Bread is baked daily on the premises – stock up.

Getting There & Away
The LaHave Ferry connects Hwys 332 and 331, saving motorists a 40-km drive up and down the river to use the bridges of Bridgewater. The five-minute cable ferry trip goes every half hour, costing $3 for a car and all occupants. Pedestrians can ride back and forth as often as they like for free.

Try Town Transit (☎ 902-521-0855) operates a van shuttle between Halifax and LaHave at $31 one-way.

LAHAVE ISLANDS
Just southwest of LaHave are the LaHave Islands, a handful of small, pleasant-to-look-at islands connected to the mainland by a 2-km causeway along Crescent Beach and to each other by one-lane iron bridges. You're allowed to drive a car along the sands of Crescent Beach!

On Bell Island just past the Government Wharf is the **Marine Museum** *(☎ 902-688-2973, 100 Bell Island; admission free; open 10am-5pm daily June-Aug)*. The museum is in St John's Anglican Church and services are occasionally still held among the marine artifacts.

Rissers Beach Provincial Park (☎ 902-688-2034, W parks.gov.ns.ca, 5463 Hwy 331) Campsites $18. Open mid-May–early Oct. A kilometer west of the causeway to the LaHave Islands and 10km from LaHave is Rissers Beach, which features a very busy (in July and August) campground and an excellent long, sandy beach, although the water is none too warm. There's also a saltwater marsh with a boardwalk trail. A good interpretive display with information on the natural environment is here. The 92-site campground has two sections, one along the beach and another inland. Rissers Beach is close enough to Halifax/Dartmouth to get rather crowded on midsummer weekends.

Thomas Raddall Provincial Park, near Port Joli to the southwest, gets a lot less traffic, and the campsites are larger and more private (see the Seaside Adjunct Kejimkujik National Park section).

LIVERPOOL
Situated where the Mersey River meets the ocean, Liverpool is another historic English-style town with an economy based on forests and fish. British privateers were active in this area in the early 1800s, protecting the British trade routes from incursions by the USA, and Liverpool's shipbuilding industry dates from those days. The many excellent free attractions in Liverpool should put it squarely on your list. Privateer Days at the end of June is a major event here.

The very helpful tourist office (☎ 902-354-5421, 28 Henry Hensey Dr), just off Main St near the river bridge, has a walking-tour pamphlet and brochures of scenic drives. The center is open daily mid-May to September.

The DRL Coachlines bus to Halifax ($22) and Yarmouth ($27) stops at the Irving gas station (☎ 902-354-2048, corner of Bristol Ave and Milton Rd), an easy 10-minute walk into town.

Things to See & Do
The impressive **Sherman Hines Museum of Photography & Galleries** *(☎ 902-354-2667, 219 Main St; admission free; open 10am-5:30pm Mon-Sat, noon-5pm Sun May–mid-Dec)* has a name that pretty much says it all. Six – count 'em, six – galleries run the gamut of media, including the only photographic museum east of Montréal. It's housed in the massive wooden town hall erected in 1901.

Perkins House *(☎ 902-354-4058, 105 Main St; admission free; open 9:30am-5:30pm Mon-Sat, 1pm-5:30pm Sun June–mid-Oct)*, built in 1766, is now a museum with articles and furniture from the colonial period. It's named for well-known Loyalist Simeon Perkins, whose story is told here.

Next door, the **Queen's County Museum** *(☎ 902-354-4058, 109 Main St; admission free; open 9:30am-5:30pm Mon-Sat, 1pm-5:30pm Sun year-round)* has First Nations artifacts and more materials relating to town history, as well as some writings by early citizens.

At **Fort Point**, a cairn marks the site where Samuel de Champlain landed from

France in 1604. The **lighthouse** (☎ 902-354-5260, 21 Fort Lane at the end of Main St; admission free; open 10am-6pm daily late May-early Oct) is accessible to the clambering public; you can even blow the lighthouse's hand-pumped foghorn. The displays and panels in and around the lighthouse offer some fascinating insights into Nova Scotia's early history. From Fort Point you get a lovely view of the US-owned Bowater Mersey pulp mill at Brooklyn, 3km north of Liverpool.

Rossignol Surf Shop (☎ 902-354-3733, W www.outdoorns.com/surfshop, 216 Main St; open 10am-5pm Mon-Sat), opposite the Museum of Photography, offers two-hour surfing lessons every Wednesday and Saturday morning year-round at the White Point Beach Resort. The $50 fee includes use of a board. Mid-August to November is the prime surfing season along the South Shore, and Rossignol's website is a good source of information.

Places to Stay & Eat

Geranium House (☎ 902-354-4484, W www.eucanect.com/tourism/geranium.html, 87 Milton Rd) Doubles $40. Open May–mid-Oct. This B&B on a large wooded property next to the Mersey River has three rooms with shared bath. It's near exit 19 from Hwy 103 and only 400m from the DRL Coachlines bus stop.

Transcotia Motel (☎ 902-354-3494, fax 902-354-3352, 3457 Hwy 3, Brooklyn) Singles/doubles $44/50 June-Sept, $39/45 Oct-May. Transcotia offers 22 tastefully designed motel rooms behind a thicket of coniferous trees a kilometer north of the Bowater Mersey pulp mill. The motel has an inexpensive restaurant.

Morningside Café (☎ 902-354-2411, 236 Main St) Breakfast or lunch $5. Open 8am-3:30pm Mon-Fri, 9am-2pm Sat. This restaurant inside Home Hardware directly opposite the tourist office serves breakfast at $4-5 including coffee. For lunch there are sandwiches ($3-5), salads ($5) and quiche or pot pie (both under $7).

Liverpool Pizzeria (☎ 902-354-2422, 155 Main St) Medium pizza $9, pasta $6. Open 8:30am-11pm Sun-Thur, 8:30pm-midnight Fri & Sat. This workaday place serves the usual Italian fare such as lasagna.

SEASIDE ADJUNCT KEJIMKUJIK NATIONAL PARK

This undeveloped region of the South Coast between Port Joli Bay and Port Mouton (ma-**toon**) Bay is part of a larger national park in the interior northwest of Liverpool. Created in 1988, the 'Keji Adjunct' protects a beautiful, wild stretch of shoreline and its fauna.

Services are nonexistent – no camping or fires are allowed, no toilets or drinking water are available. What you will find is pristine coastline, with two great beaches, coves, vistas, rock formations, wildflowers and an abundance of bird life. Admission is free.

The only access from Hwy 103 is along a 6.5km gravel road. From the parking lot, the 3km **Harbour Rocks Trail** follows an old cart road through mixed forest to Harbour Rocks, where seals are often seen. St Catherines Beach just beyond is closed to visitors because it's a nesting area of the endangered piping plover.

The Port Joli Basin also contains the **Point Joli Migratory Bird Sanctuary** where birders will find waterfowl and shorebirds in great numbers, especially during migration periods. It's at the top end of Port Joli Harbour and is only easily accessible by kayak. Liverpool's **Rossignol Surf Shop** (☎ 902-683-2550) has a beach house at 604 St Catherines River Rd on the road to the Seaside Adjunct, which serves as a base for sea kayaking tours ($55/95 a half/full day) from mid-May to early October. Kayak rentals are $30/45 a half/full day.

Places to Stay

Thomas Raddall Provincial Park (☎ 902-683-2664, W parks.gov.ns.ca) Sites $18. Open early June-early Oct. Across Port Joli Harbour from Keji Adjunct, Thomas Raddall Park is 4km off Hwy 103, then 3km down an access road to the park gate. The park's large, private campsites – including eight walk-in sites – are in a lovely shady forest. The campground includes showers, and a 5km-long trail system (bikes welcome on a couple of trails) extends out onto awesome beaches – the real attraction here. Plenty of nesting birds and even seals are found in this area, and it's far enough away from Halifax not to be overcrowded.

SHELBURNE

pop 2200

This is one of the most attractive and interesting towns anywhere on the South Shore. The whole place is pretty much like a museum, with fine buildings and historic sites at every turn – in fact it casually displays Canada's largest concentration of pre-1800 wooden homes. Disney even filmed *The Scarlet Letter* here in 1995. Relics from the filming include the steeple on the Sandspit Artisans Cooperative on Dock St and the Shakespearean-style Guild Hall behind it.

Shelburne, like many towns in the Fundy region, was founded by Loyalists, and in 1783 it had a population of 16,000, making it the largest community in British North America. Life in the USA was not easy for those loyal to the British crown, and thousands left for Canada; many of those who came here were from the New York aristocracy.

Water St, the main street, has many houses that are 100 to 200 years old, and quite a few of the two-story wooden homes are marked with dates.

Dock St along the harbor features several historic buildings and museums, plus the tourist office (☎ 902-875-4547, **W** www .auracom.com/~tnshelb), which is open daily from mid-May to early October. A collective ticket to four museums is $8.

Shelburne is still a major port. Clearwater Continental Seafoods has a large packing plant on the wharf, though recent cutbacks in fishing quotas have resulted in a marked decline in fishing activity. A little farther out are the shipyards where repairs to regional ferries and other vessels are carried out.

This shipbuilding town is known as the birthplace of yachts. As well as prize-winning yachts, it produces other types of boats.

The biggest festival is **Founders' Days** on the last weekend of July.

DRL Coachlines connects Shelburne to Halifax ($30) and Yarmouth ($16). Buses stop at the Irving gas station (☎ 902-875-3033, 41 Falls Lane at Water St), near Hwy 103 1.3km north of town.

Things to See & Do

Built in 1784, the **Ross-Thompson House** (☎ 902-875-3141, 9 Charlotte Lane; admission $3, free until noon Sun; open 9:30am-5:30pm daily June–mid-Oct), with its adjacent store, belonged to well-to-do merchants who arrived from Britain via Cape Cod. It now acts as a small museum where furniture, paintings, artifacts and original goods from the store can be viewed. The house is surrounded by gardens, as it previously would have been.

Nearby is a Loyalist house dating from 1787. Now the **Shelburne County Museum** (☎ 902-875-3219, 8 Maiden Lane at Dock St; admission $3, free until noon Sun; open 9:30am-5:30pm daily June–mid-Oct, 9:30am-noon & 2pm-5pm Tues-Sat other months), it holds a collection of Loyalist furnishings, displays on the history of the local fishery and other articles from the town's past. The oldest fire engine in Canada, a wooden cart from 1740, is quite something. There's also a small collection of Mi'kmaq artifacts, including typical porcupine-quill decorative work.

Shelburne has long had a reputation for its dories, small boats first used for fishing from a mother schooner and in later years for inshore fishing and as lifeboats. Many were built from the 1880s until the 1970s. At the museum called the **Dory Shop** (☎ 902-875-4003, 11 Dock St; admission $3, free until noon Sun; open 9:30am-5:30pm daily June–mid-Oct), you can see examples still being made in the workshop upstairs.

Ocean Breeze Kayak Adventures (☎ 902-875-2463, **W** www.oceanbreeze3.com; open Apr-Oct), inside the Muir-Cox Shipbuilding Interpretive Centre at the south end of Dock St, rents kayaks ($35/60 half/full day) and bicycles ($20 a day including helmet). This company also offers half-/full-day kayak tours ($45/90) to The Islands Provincial Park.

Al Keith (☎ 902-875-1333, **W** www .studio14.ns.ca) leads 2½-hour guided walking tours around town whenever at least four people are interested. The tourist office takes bookings, or call him up. The $10 price includes admission to two museums – which makes it a great deal – and Al knows all there is to know about Shelburne.

Places to Stay & Eat

The Islands Provincial Park (☎ 902-875-4304, **W** parks.gov.ns.ca, off Hwy 3) Sites $18. Open mid-May–Aug. Less than 2km from the Irving gas station in Shelburne (where the DRL bus stops), this provincial park offers a view of the Shelburne waterfront across the harbor. The 65 campsites, some quite nice, are in mature forest, and there is swimming nearby. The campground has showers.

Loyalist Inn (☎ 902-875-2343, fax 902-875-1452, 160 Water St) Rooms $54 for up to four people year-round. This older three-story wooden hotel right in the middle of town has 18 rooms with bath. There's sometimes live music in the dining room downstairs.

Bear's Den (☎ 902-875-3234, W www .bearsden.ns.ca, Water St at Glasgow St) Singles/doubles $45/55, including breakfast. Open Apr-Nov. This small and economical B&B is just 200m from the DRL Coachlines stop. You'll pass it on the way into the center of town. The owner was considering retiring and moving to California, so be sure to call ahead.

Claudia's Diner (☎ 902-875-3110, 149 Water St) Main meals under $10. Open 8am-8pm Mon-Fri, noon-7pm Sun May-Oct, 9am-3pm Mon-Fri, noon-7pm Sun Nov-Apr. This is a low-priced restaurant with style and standard fare. The cinnamon rolls are good and the lobster chowder ($5.50) comes in a large bowl. A full breakfast with coffee will be $4 here.

Shelburne Pastry & Tea House (☎ 902-875-1164, 151 Water St) Lunch $4-7. Open 10am-8pm Mon-Sat July & Aug, 10am-5pm Mon-Sat other months. The atmosphere here is a tad trendier than at Claudia's, and it's great for a healthy soup and omelet lunch, or coffee and cakes midmorning or afternoon.

Sea Dog Saloon (☎ 902-875-2862, 1 Dock St) Main meals $8-16. Open 11am-8pm Mon-Sat, noon-8pm Sun May-Sept, until 9pm in July & Aug. Lots of cheap pub snacks like wings, nachos, chowder and steamed mussels are available here (around $6), but you can also order seafood dinners ($16), steaks ($9-16), haddock and chips ($8-10) and pork chops ($9). The Sea Dog Caesar salad ($8) is recommended. There's an outdoor terrace beside the water, and live music Saturday nights from 9pm. From October to April when the downstairs section is closed, The Wreck Room sports bar upstairs remains open with a limited menu.

SHELBURNE TO YARMOUTH
Barrington, 32 km southwest of Shelburne, dates back to 1760 when Cape Cod settlers

erected their meetinghouse here. The town has four museums, all within walking distance of one another. Cape Sable Island and Pubnico were both once Acadian settlements and each has a small general museum. Pubnico remains French and is considered the oldest non-native village in Canada still inhabited by the descendants of its founders.

Yarmouth to Windsor

This region of Nova Scotia stretches northward from Yarmouth and along the south shore of the Bay of Fundy to Windsor and the Minas Basin. It consists, primarily, of two very distinct geographical and cultural regions.

The coast between Yarmouth and Digby is where many of the Acadians ended up after their deportation from the Annapolis Valley. The 'French Shore' and its history are still very much in evidence today.

Even better known, however, is the scenic valley of the Annapolis River, which runs more or less from Digby to Wolfville. Populated largely by the descendants of New Englanders, it's famous for apples, and in springtime the blossoming valley is at its best.

YARMOUTH
With a population of nearly 8000, Yarmouth is the largest town in western Nova Scotia. It's a transportation center where ferries from Portland and Bar Harbor in Maine dock. Two tourist routes from Halifax – the Evangeline Trail through the Annapolis Valley and the Lighthouse Route through Lunenburg – terminate here.

The huge provincial tourist office (☎ 902-742-5033) near the ferry docks offers both local and provincial information and has a money exchange counter. It's open 8:30am to 5pm daily May to October and 8am to 9pm July and August.

The Yarmouth public library (☎ 902-742-2486, 405 Main St) provides free Internet access 10am to 9pm Monday to Friday and 10am to 5pm Saturday.

Things to See & Do
The **Yarmouth County Museum** (☎ 902-742-5539, 22 Collins St; adult/family $2.50/5; open 9am-5pm Mon-Sat, 2pm-5pm Sun

June–mid-Oct, 2pm-5pm Tues-Sat mid-Oct–May) is in a gray stone building that was formerly a church. Most of the five period rooms have to do with the sea – ship models and a large collection of paintings of sailing ships dating from the 1840s to 1910, for example.

The **Firefighters' Museum** (☎ 902-742-5525, 431 Main St; adult/family $2.50/5; open 9am-5pm Mon-Sat, 10am-5pm Sun June-Aug, 9am-4pm Mon-Fri, 1pm-4pm Sat rest of year) has a collection of beautiful fire engines dating from 1819 to 1935.

The lighthouse **Yarmouth Light** (☎ 902-742-1433, Hwy 304; admission free; open daily mid-May–mid-Oct) is 12km from the ferry terminal at the end of Cape Forchu. From Main St, turn left on Hwy 304 (Van-couver St) when you see the Golden Horse Fountain. The view from the lighthouse is spectacular as the rocks of Nova Scotia sweep down into the sea. There's a small but good interpretive center with gregarious guides.

Places to Stay & Eat
Murray Manor B&B (☎/fax 902-742-9625, ⓦ www.murraymanor.com, 225 Main St) Singles/doubles $65/75, including breakfast. Just a block from the ferry is this stately two-story house on spacious grounds surrounded by a stone wall. There are three rooms.

Clementin's B&B (☎ 902-742-0079, 21 Clements St) Singles/doubles $50/70. Open May-Nov. This impressive two-story mansion in the upper town is 700m back from the

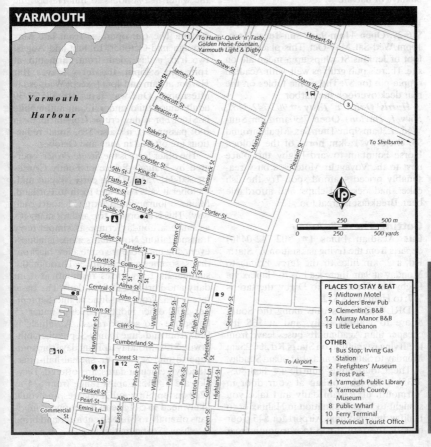

YARMOUTH

Yarmouth Harbour

To Harris'-Quick 'n' Tasty, Golden Horse Fountain, Yarmouth Light & Digby

To Shelburne

To Airport

250   500 m
250   500 yards

PLACES TO STAY & EAT
5   Midtown Motel
7   Rudders Brew Pub
9   Clementin's B&B
12 Murray Manor B&B
13 Little Lebanon

OTHER
1   Bus Stop; Irving Gas Station
2   Firefighters' Museum
3   Frost Park
4   Yarmouth Public Library
6   Yarmouth County Museum
8   Public Wharf
10 Ferry Terminal
11 Provincial Tourist Office

NOVA SCOTIA

tourist office and only 250m from the County Museum.

Midtown Motel (☎ 877-742-5600, fax 902-742-3433, **W** *nsonline.com/midtown .htm, 13 Parade St)* Singles/doubles $65/65-75 July & Aug, $50-55/55-60 in shoulder seasons. Open June-Oct. This two-story motel block is central and you get a free coffee in the morning. There are a couple of efficiency units with kitchens too.

Little Lebanon (☎ 902-742-1042, 100 *Main St)* Meals $5-7. Open 11:30am-8pm Mon-Fri, 4pm-8pm Sat. The Lebanese food is excellent at this place across from Food-master, 500m south of the tourist office. Light meals like shawarma, falafel and hummus are $4. There's a large choice of Lebanese entrées, and great desserts such as baklava or halvah.

Rudders Brew Pub (☎ 902-742-7311, 96 *Water St)* Pub menu $5-14, dinner entrées $16-29. Open 11am-9pm Sun-Tues, 11am-10pm Wed-Sat May-Oct. This place at the foot of Jenkins St whips up a mean ale on site. There's pub grub as well, with Acadian rappie pie for $7. The picnic tables on the rear deck overlook the harbor.

Harris' Quick 'n' Tasty (☎ 902-742-3467, *Hwy 1, Dayton)* Open 7:30am-8pm Sun-Wed, 7:30am-9pm Thur-Sat. Meals around $8. On Hwy 1 3km north of the Golden Horse Fountain toward Digby, this place next to the Voyageur Motel is a busy, reasonably priced seafood spot. Try the fish cakes, haddock and chips, and affordable beer. Breakfast is great too.

Getting There & Away

Bus Acadian Lines (☎ 902-742-0440) departs from the Irving gas station, 65 Starrs Rd, a 2.5km hike to the ferry. Friday to Monday at 9am there's a bus to Halifax via Digby and Kentville. To Digby, the fare is $17; to Halifax it's $52.

DRL Coachlines runs along the South Shore to Halifax daily, and at $38 it's cheaper than Acadian. Its buses leave from the Irving gas station on Starrs Rd at 6:25am Monday to Saturday and at 11:30am Sunday.

The Cloud Nine Shuttle (☎ 888-805-3335) will pick you up at your door in Yarmouth at 7:30am daily and take you straight to your destination in Halifax or to Halifax International Airport for $45 (four hours). The return trip to Yarmouth from Halifax starts around 2pm and they pick up anywhere in town.

Ferry There are two major ferry routes in and out of Yarmouth, both to the state of Maine in the USA; one connects with Bar Harbor (via a high-speed super catamaran) and the other with Portland. Fares are high (for Canadians) because they're based on US dollars, whereas Americans will comment on how cheap this cruise is for them. (The prices below have been converted into Canadian dollars, but all fares listed in the company brochures are in US currency, a situation that isn't prominently noted in the brochures themselves.)

The Bay Ferries' *Cat* (☎ 888-249-7245, **W** fun.catferry.com) literally skates across the water in 2¾ hours to Bar Harbor; the 9500-horsepower engines are truly incredible, as is the computerized ride-control system. The *Cat* operates from late May through mid-October. In July and August two trips a day zoom from Yarmouth, at 1pm and 8:45pm; the ferry leaves Bar Harbor at 8am and 4pm (except Wednesday afternoon). One-way fares are $85/77/39 adult/senior/child under 13; an automobile is $146. For a day cruise (roundtrip for a foot passenger), it's also $85. Small reductions are offered in June and October.

The other ferry is the *Scotia Prince,* operated by Maine's Prince of Fundy Cruises (☎ 800-341-7540). From early May to mid-October it sails back and forth to Portland, Maine, a journey of 320km (11 hours each way). This is a popular trip and for many it's as much a holiday cruise as simple ferry transportation. Note that service is almost every day, but there are quite a few blackout dates, so check in advance. Through the summer the ferry leaves Yarmouth at 10am daily and Portland at 9pm daily. The basic fare is $132 from mid-June to mid-September, $102 other months, children under 15 half-price (no senior rates). A vehicle is $162 from mid-June to mid-September, otherwise $131. Monday to Thursday from mid-June to mid-September, special half-price, standby vehicular fares are offered. Bicycles are $11-15. Cabins range from $34 to $270 on top of the other charges, and you'll likely need to call ahead to get one. Americans often fly to Maine, rent a car and bring it to Nova Scotia on this ferry.

Call ahead for either ferry, as vehicle reservations ($8 extra) will probably be necessary. Walk-on passengers should be okay anytime. In Maine, an additional $5 departure tax is collected.

FRENCH SHORE

Up the coast along St Mary's Bay toward Digby is the Municipality of Clare, an area also known as Old Acadia. This is the heartland of the province's French-speaking Acadian population. It's an interesting region where traditional foods and crafts are available, a few historic sites can be seen and, in summer, festivals are held in some of the small villages. Because the towns are small, a visit through the area can be done quite quickly.

As you travel through the region you'll see crafts being offered out of people's houses. The best among them are the quilts and the woodcarvings.

Cape St Mary

A long wide arch of fine sand, just 900m off Hwy 1, **Mavilette Beach** is marvelous. The marsh behind the beach is good for birdwatching.

Cape View Motel (☎ 902-645-2258, fax 902-645-3999, **w** nsonline.com/capeview/index.html, off Hwy 1) Rooms $66 & up. Open mid-May–early Oct. This motel just above Mavilette Beach has both regular motel rooms and self-contained cottages.

Cape View Restaurant (☎ 902-645-2519) Dinner mains $10-18. Open 11am-8pm May-June & Sept-Oct, 10am-10pm July & Aug. Across the street from the motel (but under separate ownership), this place serves mainly seafood – clams are a local specialty – but also available is rappie pie ($6.50), an old Acadian dish (for details see Church Point). The beach looks great at sunset from here.

Church Point

The **Église Ste Marie** (☎ 902-769-2808, Hwy 1; admission $2; open 9am-5pm daily mid-May–mid-Oct) towers over the town (also commonly referred to as Pointe de l'Église) and most other churches too. Built between 1903 and 1905, it is said to be the tallest and biggest wooden church in North America. Near the altar is a reliquary with a fragment of the True Cross and a piece of the skull of St Anne. The small museum in the corner by the altar contains articles from the church's history, including various vestments and chalices. A guide will show you around and answer any questions.

Adjacent is the **Université Ste Anne**, the only French university in the province and a center for Acadian culture. Two hundred to 300 students attend classes here.

The oldest of the annual Acadian cultural festivals, Festival Acadien de Clare, is held during the second week of July. In July and August the musical *Évangéline* is presented every Tuesday and Saturday at 8pm in the **Théâtre Marc-Lescarbot** (☎ 902-769-2114) at Church Point.

Rapure Acadienne (☎ 902-769-2172, 1443 Hwy 1) Large rappie pie for two people $6. Open 8am-5:30pm Sept-June, 8am-9pm July & Aug. A bit over a kilometer south of the church toward Yarmouth is a place where all the local establishments get their rappie pie *(paté à la rapure)*. Look for the Acadian flag outside. Inside, several women are always busy preparing the three varieties: beef, chicken or clam. The result is difficult to describe but it's a type of meat pie topped with grated pastelike potato from which all the starch has been drawn. They are bland, filling and inexpensive and can be bought piping hot. Weather permitting, there's a picnic table under a tree beside the building where you can gorge on rappie pie.

Belliveau Cove

Roadside Grill (☎ 902-837-5047, 3334 Hwy 1) Dishes $6-12. Open 8am-9pm daily July & Aug, 9am-7pm daily rest of year. This pleasantly old-fashioned and comfortable local restaurant/diner has sandwiches ($3.50) and light foods but also lots of seafood – try the steamed clams ($7-12), a local specialty, or the rappie pie ($5-7). All prices include tax. Roadside Grill rents three small cabins with fridge and microwave behind the restaurant at $45 single or double. These unheated cabins are only rented from June to mid-October.

DIGBY

An old, attractive town with 2200 residents, Digby was built around a hill in the Annapolis Basin, an inlet of the Bay of Fundy. It's famous for its scallop fleet and busy with its terminal for the *Princess of Acadia* ferry, which plies the waters between Digby and

Saint John, New Brunswick. The town is also well known for its 'Digby chicks,' a pungent type of salty smoked herring sold at fish markets but not available in restaurants. The huge circular enclosures in the sea out toward the Digby ferry dock are commercial salmon farms.

The town was founded by United Empire Loyalists in 1783, and since then its life has been based on fishing. Up Mount St from Water St is Trinity Anglican Church and its graveyard. A couple of blocks away, at the south edge of the downtown section, is the old Loyalist cemetery (1783) on Warwick St.

From the ferry landing, it's about 5km to Water St in downtown Digby. The main draw is Water St, which becomes Montague Row near the tourist office.

Information

In the center of town is the local tourist office (☎ 888-463-4429, 110 Montague Row), which is open from mid-May to mid-October.

Along Shore Road 2.5km from the ferry terminal is the much larger provincial tourist office (☎ 902-245-2201) with information about Digby and all of Nova Scotia. It is open from 8am to 8:30pm daily May to mid-November. There's a great view of the Annapolis Basin from the parking lot opposite this tourist office.

The Western Counties Regional Library (☎ 902-245-2163, 84 Warwick St) opposite the general hospital offers Internet access. It's open 12:30pm to 4:30pm and 6pm to 8pm Tuesday to Friday and 10am to 2pm Saturday.

Admiral Digby Museum

This small museum (☎ 902-245-6322, 95 Montague Row; adult/child $2/free; open 9am-5pm Tues-Sat, 1pm-5pm Sun June-Aug; 9am-5pm Tues-Fri Sept–mid-Oct; 9am-5pm Wed & Fri mid-Oct–May) displays articles and photographs pertaining to the town's marine history and early settlement.

Places to Stay

Digby Campground (☎ 902-245-1985, fax 902-245-1985, w www.angelfire.com/biz2/DigbyCamping, 236 Victoria St) Without/with hookups $15/18-23, overnight shelters $20. Open mid-May–mid-Oct. This campground is centrally situated between the roads to downtown Digby, Digby Neck and the Saint John ferry (4km from the ferry). What is unique here are the five overnight shelters holding three adults or a family of four. Basically they're just set tents with a door and two plywood platforms (you must supply all your own bedding) but it saves you the trouble of putting up your tent and protects you from mosquitoes and the rain.

Bayside Inn (☎ 888-754-0555, w www3.ns.sympatico.ca/bayside, 115 Montague Row) Singles/doubles/triples $50/69/84, breakfast included. This renovated three-story building is opposite a park right on the Digby waterfront. The 11 rooms have private bath and TV, and there's a guests' lounge.

Siesta Motel (☎ 902-245-2568, fax 902-245-2560, w www.valleyweb.com/siesta, 81 Montague Row) Doubles $53 & up. Adjacent to the Irving gas station where the Acadian Lines bus arrives, the 15 rooms at Siesta Motel are in an L-shaped block – it's a good combination of location and price.

Places to Eat

Royal Fundy Fish Market (☎ 902-245-5411, on Prince William St by the docks) Open 10am-6pm Mon-Sat May-June & Sept–mid-Oct, 9am-9pm daily July & Aug. Half restaurant, half market, the Royal Fundy has the best selection of fresh seafood in town. If you're camping or have cooking facilities, a bag of fresh scallops can make a remarkably delicious dinner. They cost $10 a pound. You can also get them precooked. Digby chicks, the heavily smoked herring for which the town is well known, will last up to two weeks and usually cost $1 each. There are also tables at the Royal Fundy where you can order scallops, shrimp or clams and chips for $10 or fish and chips for $7.50. It's the best deal in town.

Kaywin Restaurant (☎ 902-245-5543, 51 Water St) Main meals $7-13. Open 11am-10pm Mon-Fri, noon-10pm Sat, noon-9pm Sun. This is a good place to sample the local scallops ($13), haddock ($10) and clams ($12.50). Chinese combos are under $8 and there's a $10 Chinese buffet from 5pm to 7pm Friday to Sunday.

Entertainment

Fundy Dockside (☎ 902-245-4950, 34 Water St) This upscale pub downstairs at the Fundy

Restaurant presents live music (blues, rock, folk, etc) Friday and Saturday nights. *Club 98* upstairs is a glitzy disco with a DJ. It's open from 10pm to 2am Wednesday to Saturday. Both places charge $3 admission.

Red Raven Pub (☎ 902-245-5533, *100 Water St*) Open 11am-9pm daily May–mid-Oct. Local bands often play in this lively tavern on weekend evenings.

Getting There & Away
The Acadian Lines bus stops at the Irving gas station (☎ 902-245-2048), 77 Montague Row at Warwick St, a short walk from the center of town but 6km from the ferry. There's a bus to Halifax ($38) at 10:45am daily, and one to Yarmouth ($17) at 10:35pm Thursday to Sunday.

Bay Ferries (☎ 902-245-2116, ☎ 888-249-7245, Ⓦ www.nfl-bay.com) operates year-round between Digby and Saint John, New Brunswick, with three trips daily from late June to early October, except Sunday when there are only two. Summer departure times are 5am, 1pm and 8:45pm (no 5am trip on Sunday). The crossing takes a little more than 2½ hours. Prices are steep – $35 per adult passenger and $70 per car, with bicycles $25. Vehicle reservations ($5 extra) are a good idea for this trip, and you should arrive at the dock an hour before departure.

DIGBY NECK
The long, thin strip of land that protrudes into the Bay of Fundy from just north of town is known as Digby Neck. It's visible from much of the French Shore. At the far west end are Long and Brier Islands, two sections of the peninsula that have become separated from the main arm. Short ferry rides connect them, and a road links Westport (on Brier Island, at the far end) to Digby.

Whale-Watching
What draws most people to this area is the sea life off Long and Brier Islands. From June to October whale- and bird-watching boat cruises run from East Ferry, Tiverton, Freeport and Westport. Conditions make it a good location for seeing whales; the season is relatively long, beginning in May,

building up in June and remaining steady, with a good population of three whale species – finback, minke and humpback – as well as dolphins, porpoises and seals, through August. The whale-watching trips here are the best and most successful of any in Nova Scotia.

There are now over a half-dozen operators who run whale-watching tours with surely more to come. Still, reservations are a good idea and can be made by phone (credit card guarantee required). Many places will give you 10% off if you're a senior or have a CAA/AAA card or student card.

In Westport, **Mariner Cruises** (☎ 902-839-2346, Ⓦ *www.marinercruises.ns.ca; adult/child $35/17.50; open mid-June–mid-Oct*) has a booking office just to the left of the ferry, but you board the boat a kilometer along the waterfront. The trips can last anywhere from 2½ to five hours depending on where the whales are.

Brier Island Whale & Seabird Cruises (☎ 902-839-2995, 800-656-3660; *4-hour tour $40*) runs five trips daily in July and August. In May, June and September it may operate only once a day, whereas in midseason the trips are often fully booked. The office is below Brier Island Backpackers in Westport, 700m to the left as you leave the ferry.

Across Grand Passage in Freeport there's **Whale & Seabird Tours** (☎ 902-839-2177; *$28/25/15 adult/senior/child*), based at Lavena's Catch Café. The 3½-hour tours run from mid-June to September.

Hopeful passengers should bring along plenty of warm clothing (regardless of how hot a day it seems), sunblock and binoculars, if possible. A motion-sickness pill taken before leaving the dock may not be a bad idea either.

Minke Whale

Long Island
It's almost 18km between the Tiverton and Freeport ferry landings along the length of Long Island. Tiverton is a small village with

NOVA SCOTIA

a couple of whale-watching operations and a local fishing community. The **Island Museum** (☎ *902-839-2853, 3083 Hwy 217; admission free; open 9:30am-4:30pm daily late May-June & Sept–mid-Oct, 9:30am-7:30pm daily July & Aug)*, 2km west of the Tiverton ferry, also contains a tourist information desk.

The most interesting sight on Long Island is **Balancing Rock**. The trailhead is well posted along Hwy 217, 2km southwest of the Island Museum. The roundtrip walk is close to 4km along a trail that includes rope railings, boardwalks and an extensive series of steps down a rock bluff to the bay. It's very slippery. At the end there is a viewing platform that puts you within 15m of this 7m-high stone column perched precariously on the edge of a ledge just above the pounding surf of St Mary's Bay.

Near the center of Long Island is **Central Grove Provincial Park**, where a hiking trail leads to the Bay of Fundy (2km roundtrip, admission free). This trail is less known, so it won't be as crowded in midsummer.

Places to Stay & Eat *Long Island Campground* (☎ *902-839-2327, fax 902-839-2327, 524 Hwy 217)* Tent sites/RVs $12/15. Open mid-June–mid-Sept. This campground on Hwy 217, 2.5km before the Freeport ferry, has 15 sites in an open field with no shade.

Lavena's Catch Café (☎ *902-839-2517, 15 Hwy 217)* Main meals $7-10. Open 9am-8pm daily mid-May–June & Sept-early Oct, 9am-11pm July & Aug, 11am-8pm Fri-Sun early Oct–mid-Dec. The terrace on this casual restaurant directly above the wharf at Freeport offers the best sunset views on Digby Neck. If you're staying in Westport, take the ferry over for dinner (foot passengers travel free). Lavena's Catch serves fresh seafood, such as haddock burgers ($4), scallop rolls ($5) and the haddock/scallop sampler ($7). For dinner, there's haddock ($8) or Digby scallops ($10). The food is all pan-fried (not deep fried). Whale-watching can be arranged, and Internet access is available on a donation basis.

Brier Island

Brier Island has the best selection of places to stay and eat, the most whale-watching cruises, the finest scenery and numerous excellent, if rugged, hiking trails. Westport is a quaint little fishing village still relatively unspoiled by tourism.

Columnar basalt rocks are seen all along the coast, and agates can be found on the beaches. The island has three lighthouses, and there are countless seabirds.

Places to Stay & Eat *Brier Island Backpackers Hostel* (☎ *902-839-2273, fax 902-839-2410,* **w** *www.brierislandhostel.com, 223 Water St)* Beds $12. To get to the hostel turn left as you come off the ferry at Westport and go 700m along the waterfront to RE Robicheau Store. Above a gift shop, the hostel has 18 brand-new beds, squeaky clean washrooms, a full kitchen, an adjacent laundromat and even Internet access in the lobby. The comfortable place is run by a friendly Dutchman and his wife, who's from the area. They also run the large grocery store next door. The hostel is open year-round and has to be one of the nicest in Canada.

Dock and Doze Motel (☎ *902-839-2601, fax 902-839-2601,* **w** *www.canadianinnsite .com/000368.html)* Doubles $60 ($10 extra with kitchen). Open May–mid-Oct. Directly opposite the ferry landing at Westport, just to the right as you get off, are these three units – two downstairs and one above.

Westport Inn (☎ *902-839-2675, fax 902-839-2245)* Singles/doubles $50/55. Open May-Oct. This place is 300m from the ferry, to the right as you get off, then left up the hill. The three rooms above the restaurant are available year-round, but the restaurant is open only mid-May to September. It offers good home cooking, with fish and chips or pork chops for $11, scallops scampi for $14, a seafood platter for $19 and many other choices.

D&D Grill (☎ *902-839-2883)* Main meals $8-10. Open 10am-8pm May-June & Sept–mid-Oct, 7am-11pm July & Aug. This small lunch counter between the ferry and the hostel serves a full breakfast ($5.50), fish and chips ($8.50), clams and fries ($10) and burgers ($3-5).

Getting There & Away

Two ferries connect Long and Brier Islands to the rest of Digby Neck. The Petit Passage ferry leaves East Ferry (on Digby Neck) on the half hour, and Tiverton on the hour; they are timed so that if you drive directly from

Tiverton to Freeport there is no wait for the Grand Passage ferry to Westport. The ferry leaves Freeport on the hour, Westport at 25 minutes after the hour.

Both ferries operate 24 hours a day year-round. In midsummer when the traffic is heavy, the ferries run almost continuously. Roundtrip passage is $3 for a car and all passengers. Pedestrians ride free.

If you've booked a whale-watching trip at Westport, you'll need to allow a minimum of 90 minutes to drive there from Digby.

There's no public transportation along Digby Neck so you'll need a car or will have to rely on hitchhiking. This is also a good area for bicycling.

KEJIMKUJIK NATIONAL PARK

This park, located well away from the tourist areas of the seacoast, contains some of Nova Scotia's most pristine wilderness and best backcountry adventures. Less than 20% of Kejimkujik's 381 sq km is accessible by car; the rest is reached either on foot or by paddle. Canoeing, in particular, is an ideal way to explore this area of glacial lakes and rolling hills, and the park is well set up for extended, overnight paddles.

Kejimkujik is 46km south of Annapolis Royal via Hwy 8. At the visitors' and interpretive center (☎ 902-682-2772, fax 902-682-3367, Hwy 8; park admission adult/senior/child/family one-day pass $3.25/2.50/1.75/7.50, four-day pass $9.75/7.50/5.25/22.50; visitors' center open 8:30am-8pm daily mid-June–early Sept, 8:30am-4:30pm Mon-Fri rest of year), you can reserve backcountry sites and purchase maps and books. It's at the main entrance, just south of Maitland Bridge. Ask about the Atlantic Pass, which allows entry to seven national parks in eastern Canada for the entire season.

Hiking & Canoeing

More than 40 backcountry campsites are scattered along the trails and among the lakes of Kejimkujik. The main hiking loop is a 60km trek that begins at the east end of Peskowesk Lake and ends at the Big Dam Lake trailhead. Most backpackers take three to four days to cover it, with September to early October being the prime time for such an adventure. A shorter loop, ideal for an overnight trek, is the 26km Channel

Lake Trail that begins and ends at Big Dam Lake. The Hemlocks and Hardwood Trail is the best day hike.

The park also features more than a dozen lakes connected by a system of portages for flatwater paddling. Extended trips of up to seven days are possible in Kejimkujik with portages ranging from a few meters to 2.4km in length.

You must stay in backcountry sites and book them in advance by calling or stopping at the visitors' center. The sites are a hefty $16.25 per night, plus a $4.25 reservation fee for each backcountry trip; there's a 14-day maximum, and you can't stay more than two nights in any site. A topographical map ($5) may be required (the park staff may insist that you use a topo map if you plan a very ambitious trip).

Canoes and bicycles can be rented in the park at **Jakes Landing** (☎ 902-682-5253, 8km from park entrance), which recently changed ownership; call for new hours and prices.

You can also rent canoes at **Loon Lake Outfitters** (☎ 902-682-2220, Hwy 8; canoes $20/100 per day/week) just north of the park entrance. Loon Lake also rents tents at $6-13 a day, depending on size, as well as canoe packs, stoves and other such gear at $4, and bicycles at $20.

Places to Stay

Jeremy's Bay Campground (☎ 902-682-2772, fax 902-682-3367, ☒ parkscanada.pch.gc.ca/keji) Sites $14. (Camping fees are in addition to park entry fees.) Open year-round. Jeremy's Bay has 360 campsites, including a handful of walk-in sites near the shoreline for those who want to put a little distance between themselves and those RVers running their generators or playing a radio.

You can reserve a site at Jeremy's Bay for an additional $7.50 by calling ☎ 800-414-6765 at least three days in advance, but you cannot request a specific site. You just have to accept whatever you're given when you arrive. Thirty percent of the sites at Jeremy's Bay cannot be booked over the phone and are assigned on a first-come, first-served basis. All of these will be taken by midafternoon Friday on any midsummer weekend.

Whitman Inn (☎ 800-830-3855, fax 902-682-3171, ☒ www.whitmaninn.com, 12389 Hwy 8) Singles/doubles from $55/60. About

4km south of the park in Caledonia is this comfortable place to stay for noncampers. It's a restored house built around 1912 and has an indoor swimming pool, saunas – the works – yet the simplest of the rooms are moderately priced. All meals are available.

Raven Haven Hostel & Family Park (☎ 902-532-7320, fax 902-532-2096, W www .annapoliscounty.ns.ca, 2239 Virginia Rd) Beds $14/16 members/nonmembers. Open mid-June–early Sept. Raven Haven is 25km south of Annapolis Royal and 27km north of the national park. From exit 22 on Hwy 101, go 17km south on Hwy 8 to Maitland, then right 2km on Virginia Rd. This community-run place is a unique combination of HI hostel and small family campground right on Sandy Bottom Lake. The six-bed hostel is in a housekeeping cabin near the beach, then there's an inexpensive canteen, a row of five RV sites with hookups ($16) and finally six tent sites ($14) nicely ensconced in the forest. It's a scenic location, and you can rent a canoe for $4/25 an hour/day.

ANNAPOLIS VALLEY

The Evangeline Trail through the valley via Hwy 1 is not as scenic as might be expected, although it does pass through or by all the major towns and the historic sites. To really see the valley and get into the countryside it's necessary to take the smaller roads parallel to Hwy 1. From here the farms and orchards, generally hidden from the main roads, come into view.

For those seeking some work in late summer, there should be jobs available picking apples. Check in any of the valley towns such as Bridgetown, Lawrencetown and Middleton. Line things up a couple of weeks before picking time, if you can. McIntosh apples arrive first, at the end of August, but the real season begins around the first week of September.

Annapolis Royal

One of the valley's prime attractions, Annapolis Royal is a picture-postcard place with many historic sites and great places to stay and eat.

The site of Canada's first permanent European settlement, founded by Samuel de Champlain in 1605, is nearby at Granville Ferry. As the British and French battled over the years for the valley and land at the mouth of the Annapolis River, the settlement often changed hands. In 1710, the British had a decisive victory and changed the town's name from Port Royal to Annapolis Royal (in honor of Queen Anne).

Despite the town's great age (in Canadian terms) the permanent population is under 600, so it's quite a small community and easy to get around. It's a busy place in summer with most things of interest on or near long, curving St George St. There is a waterfront boardwalk behind King's Theatre on St George St, with views over to the village of Granville Ferry.

A farmers' market is held every Saturday morning from mid-May to mid-October, as well as on Wednesday afternoon in July and August.

A Nova Scotia Tourism Information Centre (☎ 902-532-5769) is at the Tidal Power Project site by the Annapolis River Causeway. It's open mid-May to mid-October. Pick up a copy there of the historic-walking-tour pamphlet.

Fort Anne National Historic Site Right in the center of town, this park preserves the memory of the early Acadian settlement plus the remains of the 1635 French fort, the mounds and moats intact. An eight-room museum (☎ 902-532-2397, off Upper St George St; admission $2.75; open 9am-6pm daily May-mid-Oct) has replicas of various period rooms, artifacts, uniforms and weapons; the Acadian room was transferred from an old homestead and the four-panel tapestry is extraordinary. The admission fee is only for the museum – entry to the extensive grounds is free.

If you're around on a Tuesday, Thursday or Sunday at 9:30pm from June to mid-September, join the fort's special Candlelight Tour of the Garrison Graveyard. Your park guide will be dressed in black and sport an undertaker's top hat and cape, and everybody on the tour is given a candle lantern. Then you all troop through the graveyard, viewing the headstones in the eerie light and hearing tales of horror and death. The tour is $5 per person and very entertaining.

Tidal Power Project At the Annapolis River Causeway, this project (☎ 902-532-5454, 236 Prince Albert Rd; admission free;

open 10am-5:45pm mid-May–June & Sept–mid-Oct, 8am-8pm July & Aug) offers visitors the chance to see a hydroelectric prototype that has been harnessing power from the Bay of Fundy tides since 1984. There's an interpretive center on the second floor that uses models, exhibits and a short video to explain how it works. This center also provides lots of useful information on the ecology and history of the area. Tidal power may come into its own in a few decades when cheaper fossil fuels begin to run out, but as yet the cost of building the dams is prohibitive.

Places to Stay & Eat *Turret B&B* (☎ 902-532-5770, 372 St George St) Doubles $60 & up. Open mid-May–Oct. This Victorian mansion with an actual turret has three rooms for rent.

The Grange Cottage (☎ 902-532-7993, fax 902-532-7993, e ron.marshall@ns.sympatico.ca, 102 Ritchie St) Singles/doubles $45/60. There are half a dozen upscale B&Bs and inns in historic buildings on St George St southeast of Prince Albert Rd. For better value (and a quieter location) check out the three rooms with shared bath at The Grange Cottage. This three-story house with an enclosed porch stands on spacious grounds.

Helen's Cabins (☎ 902-532-5207, 106 Hwy 201) Singles or doubles $50. Open mid-May–Nov. One km east of town, these five vintage cabins built in 1950 have hot plates for cooking. The same folks run Tom's Pizzeria next door (pizzas $4-23).

Fort Anne Café (☎ 902-532-5254, 298 St George St) Lunch $3-6, dinner $8-10. Open 8am-8pm daily July & Aug, 8am-3pm Mon-Sat other months. This is where the local people go. Breakfast is around $5 including coffee. For lunch, there are burgers ($3-4), sandwiches ($3-6) and haddock, clams and scallops with fries ($8-9). At dinner you can get Digby scallops for $10 or a complete seafood platter for $14. Since smoking was banned, this place has become a lot nicer.

Ye Olde Towne Pub (☎ 902-532-2244, 9 Church St) Pub meals under $10. Open 11am-11pm Mon-Fri, 10am-11pm Sat, noon-8pm Sun. This busy place just off St George St by the wharf is okay for lunch and a brew. The menu includes salads ($4-7), sandwiches ($4-7), burgers ($5-10), fish and chips ($6-9) and seafood ($9-16).

Entertainment *King's Theatre* (☎ 800-818-8587, 209 St George St) Tickets $11-14. Across from the Fat Pheasant Restaurant is this theater, which presents musicals, dramas and concerts most evenings at 8pm in July and August. Other shows are staged occasionally throughout the year, and Hollywood films are screened most weekends ($5-6).

Getting There & Away The Acadian Lines bus stops at the Port Royal Wandlyn Inn (☎ 902-532-2323, 3924 Hwy 1), 1.2km southwest of Annapolis Royal. Daily buses leave at 11:15am to Halifax ($33) and at 10:05pm to Digby ($6), but service to Yarmouth ($22) is only Thursday to Sunday at 10:05pm.

The highway police are especially vigilant around Annapolis Royal. The 50km/h and 60km/h zones extend far out from town and should be observed.

Around Annapolis Royal

The **North Hills Museum** (☎ 902-532-2168, 5065 Granville Rd, Granville Ferry; adult/child $2/1; open 9:30am-5:30pm Mon-Sat, 1pm-5:30pm Sun June–mid-Oct), halfway to Port Royal, has a superb collection of Georgian antiques displayed in a farmhouse dating from 1764.

Some 14km northwest of Annapolis Royal, the **Port Royal National Historic Site** (☎ 902-532-2898, 53 Historic Lane; adult/child $2.75/1.35; open 9am-6pm daily mid-May–mid-Oct) is the actual location of the first permanent European settlement north of Florida. It's a replica, reconstructed in the original manner, of de Champlain's 1605 fur-trading habitation, destroyed by the English eight years after it was begun. Costumed workers help tell the story of this early settlement.

Bridgetown

Farther northeast along the Annapolis Valley, Bridgetown has many trees and some fine examples of large Maritime houses. A seasonal tourist office is in Jubilee Park, near the post office on Granville St.

Valleyview Provincial Park (☎ 902-665-2559, w parks.gov.ns.ca) Sites $14. Open early June-Aug. Valleyview is 5km straight up Church St from Bridgetown. It's right on the northern rim of the Annapolis Valley with a fabulous view from near sites 18 and

19. All sites are nicely separated and have adequate shade – check No 23 if you value privacy. It is a very steep climb up by bicycle. Valleyview is nowhere near as crowded as many other campgrounds around here.

Kentville

Kentville is a functional town that marks the east end of the Annapolis Valley. Unfortunately, there aren't any true budget accommodations in downtown Kentville, although a few possibilities exist in the outskirts.

The tourist office (☎ 902-678-7170, 125 Park St), 1.3km west of the center, is open 9:30am to 5:30pm daily June to early October (9:30am to 7pm in July and August).

In town, local artifacts, history and an art gallery can be seen at the **Old King's Courthouse Museum** (☎ 902-678-6237, 37 Cornwallis Ave; admission free; open 9:30am-4:30pm Mon-Sat year-round). The courthouse was the seat of justice from 1903 to 1979. Ask to see the 30-minute Parks Canada video about the 1760 migration of the New England planters to take up lands from which the Acadians had been forcibly expelled.

At the eastern end of town 2km from the center is the **Agriculture Research Station** (☎ 902-678-1093, off Hwy 1; admission free; open 8:30am-4:30pm daily June-Aug). The Blair House Museum here holds exhibits related to the area's farming history and particularly to its apples. Guided museum tours are offered during summer. The **Nature Trail Foot Path** (which is also known as the Kentville Ravine Trail) begins from the gravel parking lot immediately east of the entrance to the research station. No bicycles are allowed on this pleasant walking trail through the old-growth woods, one of the few areas in the province with original forest.

Places to Stay & Eat
Grand Street Inn (☎ 877-245-4744, fax 902-679-1991, e grand streetinn@ns.sympatico.ca, 160 Main St) Doubles from $65, including breakfast. A kilometer out of the downtown area toward New Minas, this is a very attractive old three-story Queen Anne revival house. Guests can use the outdoor swimming pool.

Allen's Motel (☎ 902-678-2683, fax 902-678-1910, w www.allensmotel.ns.ca, 384 Park St) Doubles $55 & up. Open Feb-Dec.

This attractive 10-room motel faces a small park, 2.5km west of central Kentville.

Sun Valley Motel (☎ 902-678-7368, fax 902-678-5585, w www.svmotel.com, 905 Park St) Doubles $55 & up. Just off Hwy 101 at exit 14 toward Kentville and 2km west of Allen's Motel, Sun Valley offers a row of rooms facing the road on attractively landscaped grounds. A free continental breakfast is included.

King's Arms Pub (☎ 902-678-0066, 390 Main St) Dishes $5.25 and up. Open 11am-10pm Mon-Sat, 11am-9pm Sun. You can have a drink next to a fireplace or outside on the patio at this classic pub. Available meals include steak and kidney pie or a pot of mussels. Happy hour is from 4:30pm to 6:30pm daily, with pints at $3.25 and half pints under $2. There's live music on weekends.

Paddy's (☎ 902-678-3199, 30 Aberdeen St) Dinners $8-15. Open 11am-9pm Sun-Wed, 11am-10pm Thur-Sat. Near the King's Arms, this place doubles as an Irish pub and a small brewery producing such gems as Annapolis Valley Ale. Try the Paddy's Irish stew ($5.50) made with Paddy's Porter. **Rosie's** next door is part of the same complex and offers Tex-Mex favorites like chicken chimichangas ($10).

Getting There & Away
Acadian Lines (☎ 902-678-2000, 66 Cornwallis St) is at the old train station in the center of town. The bus to Yarmouth ($37) leaves Thursday to Sunday at 8:35pm. To Halifax ($18) it leaves at 10:30am Monday to Friday and at 1:05pm and 6:30pm daily.

Kings Transit (☎ 888-546-4442, also at 66 Cornwallis St) operates an excellent regional bus service between Bridgetown and Wolfville with a flat fare of $2. The service runs in three stages: Bridgetown to Greenwood, Greenwood to Kentville and Kentville to Wolfville, with a change of buses necessary at each stage. Free transfers are available. Thus if you wanted to go from Bridgetown right through to Wolfville, it would cost $2 and you'd need to ask for two transfers as you boarded. The buses run hourly, leaving the transfer points on the hour. At Kentville you can catch them from 6am to 7pm Monday to Friday, 8am to 3pm Saturday (no service on Sunday).

NORTH OF KENTVILLE

The area up to Cape Blomidon, on the Bay of Fundy, makes for a fine side trip, offering good scenery, a memorable view of much of the Annapolis Valley and a couple of beaches. At Cape Split a dramatic hiking trail leads high above the Minas Basin and Channel.

The Look-off

From the road's edge at nearly 200m high, this could well be the best view of the soft, rural Annapolis Valley, its rows of fruit trees and farmhouses appearing like miniatures.

Look-off Family Camping Park (☎ 902-582-3022, fax 902-582-1334, W *www.lookoff camping.com)* Without/with hookups $20/27. Open mid-May–mid-Oct. This place is across the street from the Look-off 6km north of Canning on Hwy 358. The sites with hookups are in the middle of a large grassy field, while the tent sites around the perimeter get some shade.

Scots Bay

The road continues north from the Look-off to Scots Bay, which has a large pebbled beach. From the end of the road, a spectacular 13km hiking trail leads to the cliffs at Cape Split, the tip of a 100km basalt ridge along the Bay of Fundy with cliffs 200m high. This is not a loop trail, so you must retrace your steps.

Blomidon

Blomidon Provincial Park (☎ 902-582-7319, W *parks.gov.ns.ca, off Hwy 358)* Sites $18. Open early June–early Oct. Blomidon, 27km from Kentville, is on a different road than The Look-off, beginning 3.5km back toward Canning. From the junction it's 14km to the campground, dramatically set atop the red cliffs you see as you arrive. The beach and picnic area are at the foot of the hill, just before the final 2km climb up to the campground. The water can get quite warm. Blomidon's hiking trails skirt dramatic 183m red shoreline cliffs. It's a pleasant place to stay, though it does fill up on summer weekends as Halifax isn't that far away. On Friday try to arrive by noon.

WOLFVILLE

Wolfville (**woof**-el) is a quiet, green university town best known as the home of artist Alex Colville. With its art gallery, comfortable inns and impressive historic homes, there's more than a wisp of culture in the air. This is manifested by the summerlong Atlantic Theatre Festival (☎ 902-542-4242), with four classics performed virtually every day June through September.

The tourist office (☎ 902-542-7000, 11 Willow Ave) is in Willow Park, at the east end of Main St, and is open May to early October.

The Wolfville Memorial Library (☎ 902-542-5760, 21 Elm Ave), in the former train station, offers free Internet access. It's open 11am to 5pm and 6:30pm to 8:30pm Tuesday, Thursday and Friday, 11am to 5pm Wednesday and Saturday, and 1pm to 5pm Sunday.

Waterfront Park

This park *(Gaspereau Ave at Front St; admission free; always open),* behind Tim Hortons, offers a stunning view of the tidal mudflats, Minas Basin and the red cliffs of Blomidon. Panels explain the tides, dikes, flora and fauna, legends, culture, history and ecology of the area. It's a top sight, not to be missed.

In a house dating from the early 1800s, the **Randall House Museum** (☎ *902-542-9775, 171 Main St near the tourist office; admission by donation; open 10am-5pm Mon-Sat, 2pm-5pm Sun mid-June–mid-Sept)* deals with the early New England planters and colonists who replaced the expelled Acadians, and the history of Wolfville up to the 1960s. Afternoon tea ($3) is served from 2:30pm to 4pm on antique china with homemade cookies – great!

The **Acadia University Art Gallery** (☎ *902-585-1373; Main St at Highland Ave; admission by donation; open 1pm-4pm Tues-Sun),* in the Beveridge Arts Centre building, exhibits mainly the works of Maritime artists. It also has a collection of the work (mostly serigraphs) of Alex Colville, some of which is always on display.

From May to late August, birds known as **chimney swifts** collect by the hundreds to glide and swoop en masse at dusk. There's a full explanation of the phenomenon at the **Robie Tufts Nature Centre**, on Front St opposite the public library, which features outdoor displays and a tall chimney where the birds display their acrobatic talents.

Places to Stay & Eat

Blue Shutters B&B (☎ *902-542-3363,* W *www.bbcanada.com/blueshutters, 7 Blomidon Terrace)* Rooms $60 & up. Open May-Oct.

Three hundred meters directly up the steep hill from the tourist office, this modern home is worth calling. One room has a private bath.

Garden House B&B (☎ *902-542-1703,* e *gardenhouse@ns.sympatico.ca, 150 Main St*) Singles/doubles $50/65. This big old house 400m east of the tourist office has a backyard overlooking the bay.

This being a college town, you will find a few pizza and sub shops along Main St. There are also a couple of good coffee shops.

The Anvil Lounge (☎ *902-542-4632, Gaspereau Ave near Waterfront Park*) Meals $6-9. Open 10am-1am daily. This large sports bar with cheap beer and occasional live music also serves gigantic portions of spaghetti ($6), vegetarian nachos ($5), steaks ($6-9) and some seafood at prices better than anywhere else in town. The grilled chicken Caesar ($7) is fantastic. Wednesday after 5pm chicken wings are 20¢ each. The Anvil isn't noted for its high cuisine but it sure is filling. Be aware that the kitchen closes at 8pm (the bar stays open until late). Friday and Saturday nights there's a DJ.

Joe's Food Emporium (☎ *902-542-3033, 292 Main St*) Meals $10. Open 7:30am-midnight Sun-Thur, 7:30am-2am Fri & Sat. A step up from The Anvil, Joe's is a lively place with an outdoor patio and a wide-ranging menu: a medium pizza is $10-15, nachos supreme cost $7, and a quiche and salad will set you back $6. There's beer and wine as well.

Getting There & Away
The Acadian Lines buses stop at Acadia University in front of Wheelock Hall, at the top of Horton Ave. If you're arriving on one, be sure to disembark there as the next stop may be far from town. Bus tickets are available at the information counter (☎ 902-585-2110) in the university's Student Union Building off Highland Ave. Fares are Halifax $16, Yarmouth $39.

The easternmost terminus of the Kings Transit bus is in front of Billy Bob's Pizza, 209 Main St (note that of the four pizzerias in Wolfville, Billy Bob's is the least appealing). For information on this bus service, see Getting There & Away in the Kentville section.

GRAND PRÉ
Now a very small English-speaking town, Grand Pré was the site of one of the most tragic but compelling stories in eastern Canada's history, detailed at the national historic site, 5km east of Wolfville and 1km north of the main highway. (See the boxed text 'The Acadians' for more information on the expulsion.)

Grand Pré National Historic Site
Grand Pré means 'great meadow' and refers to the farmland created when the Acadians built dikes along the shoreline, as they had done in northwest France for generations. There are 1200 hectares below sea level. It's a beautiful area and you'll easily understand why the Acadians didn't want to leave, especially after all the labor they'd invested. The park (☎ *902-542-3631, 2242 Grand Pré Rd; adult/family $2.50/7; open 9am-6pm daily mid-May–Oct*) is a memorial to the Acadians, who had a settlement here from 1675 to 1755 and then were given the boot by the British.

The park consists of an information center, gardens, space and views, and free tours of the site are offered. A new stone church, built in the Acadian style, sits in the middle of the site as a monument to the original inhabitants. Inside, the history of those people is depicted in a series of colorful paintings done in 1987 by New Brunswick painter Claude Picard.

In the gardens are a bust of Henry Wadsworth Longfellow, honored for his poem that chronicles the Acadian saga, and a statue of the poem's fictional Evangeline, who is now a romantic symbol of her people.

Acadian Days, an annual festival held sometime toward the middle of July, consists of music, storytelling, and arts and crafts. In winter, the site can be visited for free.

Places to Stay
Evangeline Motel (☎ *888-542-2703,* w *www .evangeline.ns.ca, 11668 Hwy 1*) Doubles $59 & up. Open May-Oct. Overlooking the turnoff to Grand Pré National Historic Site, this well-established motel is on attractive grounds, and its restaurant is popular.

Blomidon View Motel (☎ *902-542-2039, 127 Evangeline Beach Rd*) Doubles $48. Open mid-May–Sept. This 10-room motel right on muddy Evangeline Beach, 4km beyond the Grand Pré National Historic

Site, is one long wooden building with five rooms on each side. An RV-crowded *campground* is across the road.

WINDSOR

A small town on the Avon River, Windsor was once the only British stronghold in this district of French power and Acadian farmers.

Hwy 1 becomes Water St in town, and the main intersection is with Gerrish St.

Just off exit 6 from Hwy 101 is the helpful tourist office (☎ 902-798-2690), open every day of week from mid-May to mid-October. Be sure to go up on the dike beside the tourist office for a view of the tidal river flats.

The Acadians

When the French first settled the area around the Minas Basin on the southern shore of the Bay of Fundy in the early 17th century, they named the land Acadia. By the next century these settlers thought of themselves as Acadians. To the English, however, they were always to be 'the French.' The rivalry and suspicion between these two powers of the New World began with the first landings and was only to increase in hostility and bitterness.

The population of Acadia continued to grow throughout the 17th and 18th centuries and, with various battles and treaties, control changed hands from French to English and back again. Finally, in 1713 with the Treaty of Utrecht, Acadia became British Nova Scotia. The Acadians refused to take an oath of allegiance, though for the most part they weren't much interested in France's point of view either and most of them just wanted to be left alone. Things drifted along in this state for a while and the area around Grand Pré became the largest Acadian community. By this time the total regional population was close to 10,000, with 3500 more people in Louisbourg and still others on Prince Edward Island.

Unfortunately for the Acadians, tensions once again heated up between England and France, with squabbles and standoffs taking place all over the east coast. When a new hard-line lieutenant governor, Charles Lawrence, was appointed in 1754, he quickly became fed up with the Acadians and their supposed neutrality. He didn't trust them and decided to do something about it. He demanded an oath of allegiance to England and, as in past, the Acadians said forget it. This time, though, the rules had changed.

In late August 1755, with France and England still locked in battle in Europe and paranoia increasing, what was to become known as the Deportation or the Expulsion began. All told, about 14,000 Acadians were forced out of this area. Villages were burned and the people boarded onto boats.

The sad, bitter departure was the theme for Longfellow's well-known, lengthy narrative poem *Evangeline*, titled after its fictional heroine. Many Acadians headed for Louisiana and New Orleans, where the name became Anglicized to 'Cajun.' The Cajuns, some of whom still speak French, have maintained aspects of their culture to this day. Others went to various Maritime points, New England, Martinique, Santo Domingo or back to Europe, and a few even made their way to the Falkland Islands. Nowhere were they greeted warmly with open arms. Some hid out and remained in Acadia. In later years many of the deported people returned.

Today, most of the French people in Canada's Atlantic provinces are descendants of the expelled Acadians, and they're holding tight to their heritage. In Nova Scotia, the Chéticamp area in Cape Breton and the French Shore north of Yarmouth are strongholds. A pocket in western Prince Edward Island and the Port au Port Peninsula in Newfoundland are others. New Brunswick has a large French population stretching up the east coast past the Acadian Peninsula at Caraquet and all around the border with Québec.

There has recently been an upsurge in Acadian pride and awareness; in most of these areas you'll see the Acadian flag and museums dealing with the past and the continuing Acadian culture. The Université de Moncton, especially, is a current stronghold of Acadian culture. Festivals held in the Acadian areas provide an opportunity to see traditional dress, sample foods and hear some of the wonderful fiddle-based Acadian music.

NOVA SCOTIA

Things to See & Do

Off King St, there's an old wooden block-house and earthen mounds still intact amid portions of the **Fort Edward National Historic Site** (☎ 902-532-2321; admission free; open 10am-6pm daily mid-June–early Sept), a British fort dating from 1750. The fort was used as one of the assembly stations during the expulsions of the Acadians and claims to be the oldest blockhouse in Canada. The grounds are accessible year-round.

The **West Hants Historical Society Museum** (☎ 902-798-4706, 281 King St; admission free; open 10am-6pm Tues-Sat mid-June–Aug, 10am-4pm Mon-Fri Sept), a couple of blocks from Fort Edward, is in an old Methodist church. Among the exhibits are a high-wheel bicycle from the 1870s, a crazy quilt from 1905 and an Acadia stove from 1911.

Haliburton House (☎ 902-798-2915, 424 Clifton Ave; adult/child $2/1; open 9:30am-5:30pm Mon-Sat, 1pm-5:30pm Sun June–mid-Oct) was the home of Judge Thomas Chandler Haliburton (1796–1865), one of the founders of written American humor. He created the Sam Slick character in Mark Twain-style stories. Although these aren't read much now, many Haliburton expressions, such as 'quick as a wink' and 'city slicker,' are still often used. Haliburton's large estate is in the eastern section of town off Grey St, which itself leads from Gerrish St.

Windsor Hockey Heritage Society

Windsor calls itself the birthplace of ice hockey, though this has created a heated debate with Kingston, Ontario, which makes the same claim. They say the boys of King's College School here in Windsor began playing the game on Long Pond around 1800. In 1836, Haliburton even referred to 'playing ball on ice' in his book *The Clockmaker*. These tidbits and more (the first pucks were slices of a thick pine branch, and the Mi'kmaq Indians supplied handmade hockey sticks to the North American market well into the 1930s) can be gathered at the **Windsor Hockey Heritage Society** (☎ 902-798-1800, 128 Gerrish St; admission free; open 10am-4:30pm Mon-Sat), a souvenir shop and museum. Ask the attendant to put on the

eight-minute video about Windsor's claim to have invented hockey.

The first hockey game?

Founded in 1972, the **Mermaid Theatre** (☎ 902-798-5841, 132 Gerrish St; admission free; open 9am-4:30pm Mon-Fri) is one of Canada's most famous children's theaters. The four-person troupe is on tour during winter but the office remains open year-round. You're welcome to peruse the large collection of puppets, costumes and sets used for previous shows, and one of the staff may offer to take you upstairs where you can see the next batch being made.

Places to Stay

Smiley's Provincial Park (☎ 902-757-3131, W parks.gov.ns.ca, McKey Section Rd) Sites $18. Open early June-Aug. Smiley's is 20km east of Windsor, off Hwy 14. There are nice wooded campsites and you can swim in the river.

Meander In B&B (☎ 877-387-6070, 153 Albert St at Grey St) Singles/doubles $50/60. This historic 1898 mansion in the center of town has three rooms with shared bath.

Avonside Motel (☎ 902-798-8344, 2116 Hwy 1, Falmouth) Singles/doubles $44/49 & up. This place is convenient for bus passengers as it's directly across the road from the Irving gas station where the Acadian Lines bus stops and less than a kilometer north of central Windsor. The 19 rooms are in two long blocks.

Downeast Motel (☎ 800-395-8117, 4212 Hwy 1 at Hwy 14) Singles/doubles/triples $45/55/65. This first-rate motel 3km south of Windsor, near exit 5 from Hwy 101, offers 20 spacious rooms with double brick walls between each unit (super quiet).

Getting There & Away

Acadian Lines buses from Halifax to Windsor continue on to Kentville or Digby, making stops throughout the Annapolis Valley. Service to Yarmouth is only Thursday to Sunday at 7:35pm. The one-way fare to Yarmouth is $43, to Halifax $12. In Windsor the bus stops at Irving Mainway gas station (☎ 902-798-2126, 2113 Hwy 1), toward Falmouth. This station is just across the Avon River from downtown Windsor, a six-minute walk.

Central Nova Scotia

The central part of Nova Scotia, in geographic terms, essentially takes in the corridor of land from Halifax up to the New Brunswick border. For those coming by road from elsewhere in Canada, this is their introduction to Nova Scotia. But don't turn against the province because of what you see from the Trans Canada Hwy, as it passes through flat, uninteresting terrain on the way to Truro. Parrsboro is a worthwhile stop southwest of Amherst and there is some superb scenery along the shores of the Bay of Fundy.

SHUBENACADIE

Shubenacadie, or simply 'Shube,' is best known for the **Shubenacadie Provincial Wildlife Park** (☎ 902-758-2040, 149 Creighton Rd off Hwy 2; adult/family $3/7.50; open 9am-7pm daily mid-May–mid-Oct, 9am-3pm Sat mid-Oct–mid-May). This unusual provincial park houses abundant examples of Nova Scotia's wildlife, including birds, waterfowl, foxes and deer, in large enclosures. Only animals that cannot be released into the wild are kept, and you'll find it fascinating even if you're not a zoo person. Turn off Hwy 102 at exit 11 and follow Hwy 2 to the park entrance, 38km south of Truro and 67km north of Halifax, just north of the town of Shubenacadie.

Wild Nature Camping Ground (☎ 902-758-1631, 20961 Hwy 2) Without/with hookups $12/17. Open late May-Sept. A kilometer northeast of the Provincial Wildlife Park, this friendly, clean and well-maintained campground has lots of space and is not dominated by RVs. It's over a hill from the highway so there's not much traffic

noise. Lots of tent sites are available at the back of the campground, some in a forest, others in a grassy field. A lake is adjacent and there are hot showers.

TRURO
pop 12,000

Truro, with its central position in the province, is known as the hub of Nova Scotia. The Trans Canada Hwy passes through the north and east of town; Hwy 102 runs south to Halifax. The VIA Rail line goes by, and Truro is also a bus transfer point.

The main part of town is around the corner of Prince and Inglis Sts, where some redevelopment has gentrified the streets. Other parts are interminable malls. Still, Truro offers a glimpse of authentic Maritimes life not dominated by tourism. Almost a tenth of the area's population is Native Indian.

The tourist office (☎ 902-893-2922) is on the corner of Prince and Commercial Sts. It's open late May to October and provides free Internet access.

The best time to visit is the second weekend in August when there's a big Mi'kmaq powwow at Millbrook First Nation.

Colchester Museum

In the center of town, this large museum (☎ 902-895-6284, 29 Young St; adult/child $2/50¢; open 10am-5pm daily July & Aug, 10am-noon & 2pm-5pm Tues-Fri, 2pm-5pm Sat other months) has exhibits on the founding of Truro, the region's human history and Elizabeth Bishop, a noted poet who grew up in the area.

Tidal Bore

The Bay of Fundy is known for having the highest tides in the world, and an offshoot of these is a tidal bore, or wave, that flows up the feeding rivers when high tide comes in. The advancing wave is often only a ripple, but with the right phase of the moon it can be a meter or so in height. It runs upstream, giving the impression of the river flowing backward.

One of the most popular tidal-bore viewing points in Nova Scotia is the lookout on the Salmon River, off Hwy 236, just west of exit 14 from Hwy 102 on the northwest side of Truro. A video on this phenomenon plays continuously from May to October at the **Truro Tidal Bore Interpretive Centre** *(no phone, S Tidal Bore Rd opposite the Palliser Motel; admission free)*. The folks in the gift shop at the adjacent Palliser Motel will gladly tell you exactly when the next tidal bore will arrive.

Places to Stay

Nova Scotia Agricultural College *(☎ 902-893-7519, fax 902-893-6545,* **W** *www.nsac .ns.ca, College Rd, off Main St)* Singles/doubles $35/46 daily, $115/173 weekly. Just 2km northeast of the VIA Rail station, the college rents 126 rooms with shared bath in the student dorms from May to August. Apply to the NSAC Conference Office in Fraser House between 8:30am and 10:30pm. There's a cafeteria on campus.

Willow Bend Motel *(☎ 888-594-5569, 277 Willow St)* Singles/doubles $55/69 mid-June–mid-Sept, $45/50 other months, continental breakfast included. Right across the street from the Acadian Lines bus station is this pleasant 27-room motel.

Stonehouse Motel *(☎ 877-660-6638, fax 902-897-9937, 165 Willow St)* Rooms $55 single or double mid-June–mid-Sept, $45 other months. This possibility is halfway between the Acadian Lines bus station and the VIA Rail station.

Palliser Motel *(☎ 902-893-8951, fax 902-895-8475,* **e** *palliser@auracom.com, S Tidal Bore Rd)* Singles/doubles $41/59, extra persons $7. Rates include a full buffet breakfast. Open May-Oct. This motel is off Hwy 236, very near exit 14 from Hwy 102. It's 5km from the Acadian Lines station and directly opposite the tidal-bore viewing area. The staff will wake you up if you want to see a nocturnal bore. In July and August the Palliser is usually full by 5pm, so call ahead for a reservation. A 10% CAA/AAA discount is available.

Keep in mind that the *Wentworth Hostel* is not quite halfway to Amherst via Hwy 4 (see the Sunrise Trail section, later in this chapter).

Places to Eat

Engine Room *(☎ 902-895-5151, 160 Esplanade St)* Sandwiches $4-7, dinners $8. Open 11am-9pm Mon-Sat, noon-8pm Sun for food (bar open later). In the train station mall along Esplanade St, this large sports bar also presents live music some evenings,

as advertised on signs outside. Main meals include lasagna ($7) and steaks ($8-15).

Murphy's Fish & Chips *(☎ 902-895-1275, 88 Esplanade St)* Main meals $5-9. Open 11am-7pm Mon & Tues, 11am-8pm Wed-Sat, noon-8pm Sun. On the opposite side of the ticket office at the train station, Murphy's is always packed with local residents who rave about the fish and chips.

Fletcher's Restaurant *(☎ 902-895-8326, 337 Prince St)* All meals under $10. Open 7am-11pm Mon-Sat, 7am-10pm Sun. Friendly Fletcher's offers home cooking, including fish and chips ($5-7), clam or fish chowder ($4) and scallops and fries ($9). It's also very popular at breakfast.

There's a *farmer's market* near the VIA Rail station between Havelock and Outram Sts every Saturday from June to October.

Getting There & Away

The Truro Acadian Lines bus station (☎ 902-895-3833, 280 Willow St) is one of the largest in the province. It's less than 2km from the VIA Rail station via Willow and Arthur Sts. Coin lockers ($2) are available. The station is open 8am to 11pm daily.

There are six buses a day to Halifax ($15) and three a day, with different stops, to Sydney ($48). To Saint John, New Brunswick ($54), buses leave at 8:20am and 2:15pm daily, with a change in Amherst; two other buses go to Amherst ($21). There are also four runs per day to Antigonish ($17).

The VIA Rail station (☎ 888-842-7245) is in town at 104 Esplanade St, near the corner of Inglis Place. Trains in and out of Nova Scotia pass through Truro, so connections can be made for Halifax, Montréal and various points in New Brunswick. Trains to Halifax ($21) are daily except Wednesday; to Moncton ($35) and Montréal ($183) trains run daily except Tuesday. Purchasing tickets five days in advance for travel within the Maritimes, or seven days in advance to Québec, usually saves you 30% or more, although these reduced-fare seats are limited in number.

CHIGNECTO

This region west of Truro is named after the bay and the cape at the western tip. This is one of the least visited, least populated areas of the province. The road network is minimal, although the Glooscap Trail tourist route goes through the eastern portion. It's an area with some very interesting geology and ancient history, which attracts dinosaur detectives, fossil followers and rock hounds. The Minas Basin shore has some good scenery and shoreline cliffs. The tides of the Minas Basin are high even by Fundy standards. Unfortunately, there's no bus service along this coast.

Economy

The **Cobequid Interpretation Centre** (☎ 902-647-2600, 3248 Hwy 2 near River Phillip Rd; admission free; open 9am-4:30pm Mon-Fri, 9am-6pm Sat & Sun July & Aug) features good exhibits on the ecology and history of the area. A WWII observation tower offers great views of the surrounding area.

There are two main trail systems near Economy. The **Economy Falls Trail** in the Cobequid Mountains begins 7km north up River Phillip Rd and leads 4km into the Kenomee Canyon, ending at a stunning 20m cascade. This is one of the best hikes in the area. The trailhead for the **Devils Bend Trail** is only 3km up the road. These trails link up, as the Kenomee hiking map ($2) available at the interpretation center shows. The **Thomas Cove Coastal Trail** is down Economy Point Rd, 1.5km east on Hwy 2 from River Phillip Rd.

Silver House B&B (☎ 902-647-2022, fax 902-647-2459, e silver.house@ns.sympatico.ca, 3289 Hwy 2) Singles/doubles $64/69. Near the corner of River Phillip Rd, this large farmhouse makes a good base for hikers using the nearby trails.

Morrisons Takeout (☎ 902-647-2823, 3397 Hwy 2) Meals $6-8. Open noon-8pm Wed-Sun late May-early Sept. This is a great place to pick up some picnic food, such as scallops, clams or fish and chips. The fried clams are dug locally and are among the best to be had in the Maritimes, no doubt because of their freshness. Tax is included in all posted prices.

Five Islands Provincial Park

This park (☎ 902-254-2980, w parks.gov.ns.ca, 618 Hwy 2; open early June-early Oct), on the west flank of Economy Mountain, 9km west of Economy and 25km east of Parrsboro, offers camping, a beach and picnic spots. The park is by the sea, 3km off Hwy 2. Walking trails traverse the varied terrain; some lead to the 90m-high cliffs at the edge of the Minas Basin, with views of the islands. Nearby tidal flats are good for clam-digging.

The campground at Five Islands has 90 sites ($18), most in a semi-open area with good views of the bay. You'll find some huge grassy campsites in the lower area, whereas in the forested upper area the sites are a bit closer together.

Parrsboro

Parrsboro is the largest of the small towns along the Minas Basin shore and is a place to stay for a day or two. There are several museums, a fossil-laden shoreline to explore and a half dozen B&Bs and inns. In the center of town, beside the town hall, is the tourist office (☎ 902-254-3266, 4028 Eastern Ave), open mid-May-early Oct. Among other things, this office has tide information for visiting rock hounds. Free Internet access is provided.

The area is interesting geologically and is known for its semiprecious stones, fossils and dinosaur prints. People scour the many local beaches and rock faces for agates and amethyst and attend the annual Gem & Mineral Show in mid-August. This get-together for rock, mineral and fossil collectors began in the 1970s and features displays, demonstrations, guided walks and boat tours.

Fundy Geological Museum At the museum (☎ 902-254-3814, 162 Two Islands Rd; adult/student & senior/family $4/3.25/10; open 9:30am-5:30pm daily June–mid-Oct, 9am-5pm Tues-Sat mid-Oct–May) you can find out why the Parrsboro beaches have been dubbed 'Nova Scotia's own Jurassic Park.' It features a glittering collection of minerals and fossils, of course, but also has models, hands-on exhibits and computer-aided displays that explain the fascinating geological history of the area. Naturalists on staff also lead special tours to the nearby beaches.

Partridge Island This is not only the most popular shoreline to search for gems but also a place steeped in history. Among others, Samuel de Champlain landed here in 1607 and took away (what else?) amethyst rocks from the beach. The island is 4km south of town on Whitehall Rd. An interpretive display explains how the powerful

Fundy tides break up the layers of rock and expose new gemstones every year. More than likely there will be a dozen people searching the pebbled shoreline or the bluffs for agate, jasper, stilbite and other stones.

Just before the beach is **Ottawa House Museum** (☎ 902-254-2376, 1155 Whitehall Rd; admission $1; open 10am-6pm June–mid-Sept), which preserves Sir Charles Tupper's summer home. Tupper was the premier of Nova Scotia and later prime minister of Canada. The museum helps finance maintenance of the building by selling ice cream cones, a good excuse to indulge.

From the end of the beach a hiking trail with explanatory panels climbs to the top of Partridge Island (which is connected to the mainland by an isthmus), ending at a spectacular viewpoint; it's a 45-minute walk each way. The views of Blomidon and Cape Split across Minas Basin are superb.

Ship's Company Theatre All the world's a stage or in this case, an entire boat is. The MV *Kipawo*, built in the Saint John Shipyard in 1926, was the last of the Minas Basin ferries. In July and August a variety of plays are performed here, most of them new works from Maritime writers. The box office (☎ 902-254-3000) is in town at 198 Main St (tickets $20) but the *Kipawo* itself is at the south end of downtown by the shore.

Organized Tours Dinatours (☎ 902-254-3700, 237 Main St) offers three-hour guided mineral- and fossil-collecting tours ($20) from May to October. Departure times vary with the tides. Numerous specimens from previous trips can be seen (and bought) at the main office.

Places to Stay & Eat *Glooscap Campground* (☎ 902-254-2529, fax 902-254-2313, 1380 Two Island Rd) Without/with hookups $12/18. Open mid-May–Sept. This attractive municipality-owned campground by the shore (5km south of town) offers some nice secluded tent sites.

Knowlton House B&B (☎ 902-254-2773, 2330 Western Ave) Singles/doubles $60/65. Open mid-June–mid-Sept. Three rooms are available here in a fine Parrsboro mansion.

Riverview Cottages (☎ 902-254-2388, 3575 Eastern Ave) Singles/doubles $32/40 & up ($40/50 with a woodstove). Open mid-

Apr–mid-Nov. On Hwy 2, 1km east of the center, Riverview offers 18 cottages of various types. Some have light housekeeping, others are unheated. None have telephones or televisions. Guests enjoy free use of the rowboats and canoes on the river behind the cottages. Weekly rates are possible. This is probably your best bet in Parrsboro, but it's often full.

John's Café (☎ 902-254-3255, 151 Main St) Lunches $3-8. Open 7:30am-6pm Mon-Sat, 8:30am-6pm Sun May-Nov. This unpretentious little café serves a variety of coffees and teas, plus healthy sandwiches, salads, soups, chili and quiche.

Berry's Restaurant (☎ 902-254-3040, 29 Two Island Rd) Main meals $8-9. Open 7am-9pm daily (to 10pm in summer). Try the fish chowder ($4.25), burger plate ($6.50), flounder dinner ($8.25) or scallop dinner ($9). Berry's is right in town.

Diligent River

At Diligent River is the **Wards Falls Hiking Trail**, a 3.5km one-way hike up a river gorge. The trail is well maintained but steep in some places, and toward the end it passes the 7m cascade. The trailhead is opposite 10726 Hwy 209, 10km west of Parrsboro.

Cape Chignecto Provincial Park

Opened in 1998, this is now the crown jewel of the peninsula and one of the best hiking experiences in the Maritimes. The highlight here is the very challenging yet-to-be-completed 45km **Bay of Fundy Coastal Hiking Trail** with wilderness – nay, old-growth – campsites. At the time of writing, 35km had been finished, beginning and ending at Red Rocks in West Advocate (and they're hacking more every day). The trail from Red Rocks to Cape Chignecto is rugged and only for those in shape; rounding the bend from here the views are simply magnificent, with occasional breathtaking drop-offs of 200m in some canyons.

Some hikers have tried to avoid the ups and downs of the trail by taking shortcuts along the beach at low tide. While it's possible to use the beach if you're only doing a short day hike from Red Rocks, it's extremely dangerous to try to go from Mill Brook toward Cape Chignecto along the beach as the distances between the entry/exit points are just too long. Hikers have had to be rescued from the cliffs by helicopter! At the moment hikers must return to Red Rocks along a logging road from Eatonville, but the last section of the trail may already have been finished, making this unnecessary.

For a day hike, you can go halfway to Mill Brook then walk back to Red Rocks along the beach. Of course, double-check the tide status with the wardens before you set out as you could also be cut off by a rising tide here. All told, those in shape should be able to do it in around two hours. Everyone using these trails must register at the Interpretive Centre at Red Rocks and pay a $3 hiking fee. This gives the wardens a way of controlling what people are doing along the trail, understandable in light of the danger from the tides just mentioned.

If you plan on camping in the backcountry, reservations are a necessity; contact the park office (☎ 902-392-2085, ⓦ www .capechignecto.net). There are 39 wilderness campsites at six points along the coastal trail, plus 25 walk-in sites near Red Rocks. Reservations are essential for the wilderness sites as only hikers with campsite reservations are allowed to spend a night on the trail. Campsites are $18. The campsites (and by extension the trail) are closed from early October to mid-May.

West Advocate itself has a magnificent long sandy beach piled high with driftwood.

If you'd like to stay in the area, try the following.

Lands End Retreat B&B (☎ 902-392-2835, *1219 West Advocate Rd*) Singles/doubles $35/45. Open May–mid-Nov. This large two-story house near Chignecto Variety Store is just 500m from the Red Rocks trailhead.

Reid's Century Farm Tourist Home (☎ 902-392-2592, fax 902-392-2523, *1391 West Advocate Rd*) Singles/doubles $40/50. Open June-Sept. Three rooms are available in this farmhouse on a real country farm just off Hwy 209, 1.3km from the Red Rocks trailhead.

AMHERST & AROUND
pop 10,000
Amherst is the geographic center of the Maritimes and a travel junction. For almost anyone heading into Nova Scotia, passing through is a necessity. From here, Hwy 104 leads south toward Halifax and then cuts

east for Cape Breton Island. Also from Amherst, it's not far to the Northumberland Shore and the Sunrise Trail along the north coast. Hwy 16, which leads to the bridge to Prince Edward Island, is just across the border in New Brunswick.

Information
Just off exit 1 of Hwy 104 is a huge provincial welcome center (☎ 902-667-8429) that is open March to mid-December. The center features information for all of Nova Scotia, an interpretive area and gardens out front. Behind the center is the **Fort Lawrence Interpretive Centre** (☎ 902-667-1756, 9am-5pm *June–mid-Oct*), which includes a scale model of a British fort built near here in 1750. In those days the border between British and French territory was the Nova Scotia/New Brunswick border of today. Fort Beauséjour – clearly visible to the north – was the corresponding French fort.

Cumberland County Museum
This museum (☎ 902-667-2561, *150 Church St; admission $1; open 9am-5pm Mon-Sat, 2pm-5pm Sun May-Sept; 9am-5pm Tues-Sat Oct-Apr*) is in the erstwhile home (erected 1838) of the Father of Confederation, RB Dickey. The most interesting displays are the articles made by prisoners of war at the Amherst Internment Camp during WWI. (Leon Trotsky was one of the POWs.)

Amherst Point Migratory Bird Sanctuary
This bird sanctuary is 6km west of central Amherst. Go west on Victoria St, past the Wandlyn Inn Hotel. A few hundred meters beyond the Inn veer left toward Amherst Point when the road divides. The poorly marked trailhead becomes apparent if you watch for a parking lot in the forest on the left.

Over 200 bird species are seen in this 490-hectare sanctuary. A loop trail circles and crosses several ponds and lakes, through the fields and marsh. It's always open and free, but bicycles are prohibited.

Places to Stay & Eat
Loch Lomond Park (☎ 902-667-3890, fax 902-667-0309, *off Hwy 2 just south of exit 4 from Hwy 104*) Without/with hookups $16/20. Open mid-May–mid-Oct. Loch Lomond has

NOVA SCOTIA

a variety of reasonable tenting sites near the shore of Blair's Lake.

Victorian Motel (☎ 902-667-7211, 150 E Victoria St) Singles/doubles $52/60. This motel offers 20 rooms in two long blocks a few minutes walk from the center of town.

Brown's Guest Home (☎ 902-667-9769, fax 902-667-2055, **w** home.istar.ca/~dnallen, 158 E Victoria St) Singles/doubles $45/55. Open May-Oct. The three rooms in this stately three-story house are an alternative to the motel.

Treen Mansion (☎ 902-667-2146, 113 Spring St) Singles/doubles/triples $35/50/60. This large Victorian house with a porch and tower was built in 1907. There are three rooms; rates include breakfast in the sunroom.

Hampton Diner Open Kitchen (☎ 902-667-3562, 21386 Fort Lawrence Rd) Main meals $10. Open 7am-9pm Tues-Sun mid-May–Sept. This classic diner, 700m south of the Amherst tourist office and 3km north of downtown Amherst, has been around since 1956. You can't miss it as you come into town. It's recommended for good, cheap food and quick, courteous service. Breakfast with bacon and coffee is $4.50 (or $2.25 for two eggs, potatoes and toast), while meals served include T-bone steak ($12.50), fish platter ($10) and scallops and fries ($10). Sandwiches and hamburgers are $3.

Getting There & Away
The ticket agent and station for Acadian Lines is the Irving Mainway gas station

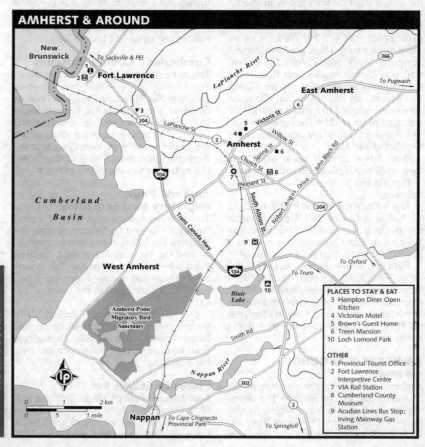

AMHERST & AROUND

PLACES TO STAY & EAT
3 Hampton Diner Open Kitchen
4 Victorian Motel
5 Brown's Guest Home
6 Treen Mansion
10 Loch Lomond Park

OTHER
1 Provincial Tourist Office
2 Fort Lawrence Interpretive Centre
7 VIA Rail Station
8 Cumberland County Museum
9 Acadian Lines Bus Stop; Irving Mainway Gas Station

(☎ 902-667-8435, 213 S Albion St), 2.3km south of the VIA Rail station. There are three buses a day for Halifax, at 12:05am, 3:20pm and 9:35pm; fare is $35. SMT will take you north to Moncton daily at 10am, 3:55pm and 6:35pm for $10 (also from the Irving station).

Amherst's VIA Rail station (☎ 800-561-3952), built in 1908, is on Station St, a few minutes' walk from the center of town. Trains run to Halifax ($39) daily except Wednesday, and to Moncton ($16) and Montréal ($170) daily except Tuesday. Coin lockers ($1) are available in the station, but the building is open limited hours, closing at 5pm daily.

Eastbound motorists should be aware of a toll section of the Trans Canada Hwy between Amherst and Truro. The toll is only $3 but it's an incentive to use scenic Hwy 2 through Parrsboro instead of dull – but fast – Hwy 104. The appealing Sunrise Trail (Hwy 6) through Pugwash and Tatamagouche to Pictou also avoids the toll.

Sunrise Trail

This tourist route crosses the north coastal region of the province, from the New Brunswick border to Cape Breton Island.

The Northumberland Strait between Nova Scotia's north shore and Prince Edward Island has some of the warmest waters north of the US Carolinas. Summer water temperatures average slightly over 20°C. Hwy 6 runs along a strip of small towns and beaches on the Northumberland Shore.

TIDNISH BRIDGE
At Tidnish Bridge, Hwy 970 from Port Elgin, New Brunswick, joins Hwy 366, which leads east to Hwy 6 and the Sunrise Trail. A tourist information office (open July and August) is right at the junction as you enter Nova Scotia.

Amherst Shore Provincial Park (☎ 902-661-6002, **W** parks.gov.ns.ca, 6596 Hwy 366) Sites $18. Open early June-Aug. The campsites are nicely separated in mixed forest, 15km east of Tidnish Bridge. A few hiking trails are available. **Northeast Beach Provincial Park**, 6km east of Amherst Shore, has no camping but does offer abundant picnic facilities and a pleasant beach.

PUGWASH
Two of Pugwash's claims to fame are the large salt mine, which produces boatloads of Windsor salt to be shipped from the town docks, and the colorful Gathering of the Clans festival, which takes place each year on July 1. Street names in town are written in Scottish Gaelic as well as in English.

There are several craftspeople in town, and their wares are sold along the main street and also at tables set up at the former Pugwash train station on Saturday. Built in 1888, the station is one of the oldest in Nova Scotia and today serves as a tourist office and library. **Seagull Pewter** (☎ 902-243-2516, 9926 Hwy 6) has a shop and factory just west of town.

Pugwash is perhaps best known for the events that took place in the prominent white house at 247 Water St, on a point jutting into the bay. In July 1957 industrialist Cyrus Eaton (1883–1979) brought together a group of 22 leading scientists from around the world to discuss disarmament issues and science. The meeting was sponsored by Bertrand Russell, Albert Einstein and others, though they themselves did not attend. The Pugwash Conference laid the groundwork for the Partial Test Ban Treaty of 1963, and since 1957 there have been over 200 Pugwash conferences at different venues. In 1995 the Pugwash Conferences on Science and World Affairs received the Nobel Peace Prize. The Pugwash Conference (**W** www.pugwash.org) still uses the house, which is now known as the **Cyrus Eaton's Thinkers Lodge**, for occasional meetings, and the building cannot be visited.

Hillcrest Motel (☎ 902-243-2727, fax 902-243-2704, 11054 Hwy 6) Singles/doubles $38/46. Six motel-style rooms are available in a long block, 2km east of Pugwash. The motel's *restaurant* (open 7am-7pm, until 8pm in summer) serves a full breakfast for $5. The fish and chips ($6-7) are better than average; for dinner try the pan-fried haddock ($11).

Caboose Café (no phone, Durham St) Main meals $10. Open June–mid-Sept. Next to the old train station in the center of Pugwash, the Caboose Café provides lunch options such as a cabooseburger ($5), fish burger ($5) and lobster roll ($9). Dinner starts at $10 for a fish platter and rises to $23 for lobster.

WENTWORTH

The shortage of budget accommodations along the north shore may warrant a detour to Wentworth, 25km south of Wallace via Hwy 307. Wentworth is also not quite halfway between Truro and Amherst on Hwy 4.

Wentworth Provincial Park (☎ *902-548-2379, fax 902-548-2389,* W *parks.gov.ns.ca, 1525 Valley Rd)* Sites $14. Open mid-May–early Oct. This provincial campground, just 500m off Hwy 4 between Truro and Oxford, has 49 sites scattered through the forest. It's managed by the same folks who run the HI hostel up on the hill beyond the park.

Wentworth Hostel (☎ *902-548-2379, fax 902-548-2389,* W *www.hostellingintl.ns.ca, 249 Wentworth Station Rd)* Beds $18/22 members/nonmembers. Open year-round. To reach the hostel, go 1.3km west on Valley Rd off Hwy 4, then straight up Wentworth Station Rd till you see the HI hostel on the right. The last 700m are a bit steep if you're on foot carrying a backpack. This big rambling farmhouse was built in 1866 and has been used as a hostel for half a century. There are 15 dorm beds, a five-bed family room and one double room called the Livingston Room (the family and double rooms cost $2 per person extra). Wentworth has kitchen facilities, showers and parking, and 75km of mountain-bike trails are accessible from a trailhead just outside the door. A good one-hour roundtrip hike from the hostel is to The Lookoff, a bluff with a great view. Downhill and cross-country skiing are practiced here in winter.

All Seasons B&B (☎ *888-879-5558,* W *www.bbcanada.com/1628.html, 14371 Hwy 4)* Doubles $45 & up. Just 700m south of the turnoff to Wentworth Park and the hostel, this modern bungalow above the highway is another worthy option.

CARIBOU

From May to mid-December the ferry to Prince Edward Island leaves from the Caribou ferry terminal, 7km north of Pictou on Hwy 106. For ferry details see Getting There & Away in the introduction to the Prince Edward Island chapter. A PEI tourist information counter (☎ 902-485-6483) is inside the Servicenter at the terminal. It's open 10am to 8pm daily July and August.

You can do a three-hour roundtrip on the ferry as a walk-on passenger for just $11 per person (seniors $9, kids under 13 free). You pay at the cafeteria aboard ship. For departure times, call ☎ 888-249-7245; be careful not to take the last ferry of the day if you want to come right back! Free parking is available at the Caribou ferry terminal. This cheap excursion is well worth considering if you aren't planning to visit the island.

The beach at **Caribou/Munroe's Island Provincial Park** (☎ *902-485-6134,* W *parks .gov.ns.ca, 2119 Three Brooks Rd),* 3.7km southeast of the Caribou ferry terminal (turn left as you leave the ferry), is sandy with gradually deepening water. It's possible to cross the sandbar to Munroe's Island. Picnic tables sit along a small ridge above the beach. Admission is free, and the water here is as warm as any in Nova Scotia. The park's *campground* is open early June to August and has 95 campsites ($14). The 18 sites numbered 78-95 in the overflow area are gravel and only suitable for RVs, but all of the others are grassy and well shaded.

PICTOU

Pictou (**pik**-toe), one of the most attractive and engaging towns along the North Shore, is where the Highland Scots first landed in 1773, to be followed by thousands in the settling of 'New Scotland.' In town, among the many older structures, are several buildings and historic sites relating to the early Scottish pioneers.

Water St is the main street and reflects the architectural style of the early Scottish builders. Above it, Church, High and Faulkland Sts are lined with some of the old, capacious houses for which the town is noted.

Pictou, with its stone buildings and scenic waterfront, is a haven for artists. Throughout town there are various art studios and craft shops, with most of them clustered along Water and Front Sts.

The **Lobster Carnival**, a three-day event at the beginning of July, marks the end of the lobster season. The four-day **Hector Festival** in mid-August celebrates the area's Scottish heritage and includes concerts. Just across the water at Pictou Landing, there's a Mi'kmaq powwow the second weekend in June.

The large provincial tourist office (☎ 902-485-6213) at the Pictou Rotary (traffic circle), northwest of the town center, stocks loads of brochures. It's open 9am to 7pm daily May to mid-December and 8am to 9pm July and August.

Things to See & Do

Hector Heritage Quay, part of the waterfront, has been redeveloped to preserve both history and access. The interpretive center (☎ 902-485-4371, 33 Caladh Ave; adult/family $5/12 for center & boatyard; open 9am-6pm Mon-Sat, noon-6pm Sun mid-May–early Oct) has a re-created blacksmith shop, a collection of shipbuilding artifacts and varied displays and dioramas depicting the life of the Scottish immigrants.

At the boatyard, a full-size replica of the first ship to bring Scottish settlers, the three-masted *Hector*, is being reconstructed. Begun in 1993, it will take a few more years to complete. Guides tell the story of the crossing and settlement.

In the old train station (1904), the **Northumberland Fisheries Museum** (☎ 902-485-4972, 71 Front St; admission $3; open 9am-7pm Mon-Sat, noon-7pm Sun late June-early Oct) tells the story of the area's fishing heritage. A prize exhibit is the spiffy *Silver Bullet*, an early 1930s lobster boat.

The **Visitors Marina Centre** (☎ 902-485-6960, 37 Caladh Ave; open late May-early Oct) on the waterfront rents bicycles at $5 for four hours or $10 a day. The same office has kayaks at $10/35/55 an hour/four hours/day for a single, or $15/40/60 for a double. From the Marina Centre the **Jitney Trail**, a former railway route, runs 3km west along Pictou Harbour.

Places to Stay & Eat

Hostel Pictou (☎ 902-485-8740, e alouise macisaac@hotmail.com, 14 Chapel St) Dorm beds $17. Open June-Sept. Part of the Backpackers Hostels chain, this cozy hostel is just a block off the Pictou waterfront. It occupies a historic house dating from 1848, and the beds are in three shared double rooms. There's a large TV room/lounge and a common kitchen. Going out in the evening is no problem as there's no curfew.

Miles Away Inn (☎ 902-485-4799, e miles away@ns.sympatico.ca, 106 Front St) Doubles $48 & up. Miles Away offers nine rooms with shared bath in a heritage building.

Linden Arms B&B (☎ 902-485-6565, 62 Martha St) Doubles $50, including breakfast. Open June-Sept. This attractive two-

story house is in a residential area seven short blocks above the waterfront.

The Lionstone Inn (☎ 902-485-4157, fax 902-485-4157, 241 W River Rd) Motel rooms $59 single or double mid-June–mid-Oct, $40-49 mid-Oct–mid-June; cabins $54 & up, or $59 & up with cooking facilities. Away from the downtown area and near the Pictou Rotary (behind KFC), Lionstone Inn has 14 well-maintained motel units in two long wooden blocks, as well as 13 spartan, older individual cabins with their own kitchens. The unheated cabins come in a variety of sizes and are closed in winter. At the beginning or end of the season you might get one for $45.

Fougere's Restaurant (☎ 902-485-1575, 89 Water St) Main meals $10. Open 11:30am-9pm Tues-Sun May–mid-Nov. Lunch is a good value with dishes like pork schnitzel ($8), hamburgers or chicken fingers ($7) and pastas ($6-10). At dinner try the seafood chowder ($7) and halibut steak ($19).

Down East Family Restaurant (☎ 902-485-4066, 12 Front St) Breakfast with coffee $4. Open 7am-7pm daily. This untouristy local favorite does some real home cooking.

Entertainment

deCoste Entertainment Centre (☎ 902-485-8848, 91 Water St) Box office open 11:30am-5pm Mon-Fri. This impressive performing arts center stages a range of live shows, from plays and comedies to the leading Celtic musicians in Canada.

Relics Public House (☎ 902-485-5577, 50 Caladh St) Open 11:30am-8pm Mon-Thur, 11:30am-9pm Fri & Sat, noon-8pm Sun May-June & Sept-Oct, 11am-9pm daily July & Aug. This friendly pub on the waterfront opposite Hector Heritage Quay presents traditional Maritime music every Saturday at 9pm ($2 cover charge). From mid-June to August there's also an open-mike session on Wednesday nights and karaoke on Friday. Typical pub food like poutine ($4), chicken fingers ($6) and nachos ($8) is available, and for bigger appetites, there's the seafood platter ($12) or the daily special advertised on the blackboard outside.

Getting Around

Unfortunately Pictou has no bus service. A water taxi (☎ 902-396-8855, $10/18 one-way/roundtrip) makes two runs per day to and

NOVA SCOTIA

from New Glasgow in July and August. In Pictou it leaves from beside the Salt Water Café (opposite the *Hector*) at 1:30pm and 6:30pm; in New Glasgow it departs from the Riverfront Marina in town at noon and 5pm.

NEW GLASGOW
pop 10,000
New Glasgow is the largest town on the Northumberland Shore. It originally was, and remains, a small industrial center, and there's little to see in town. Frank Sobey opened his first supermarket here in 1917, genesis of the family-owned Sobey chain that still dominates the grocery business throughout the Maritimes.

The Acadian Lines buses stop at the Irving Mainway gas station (☎ 902-755-5700, 5197 E River Rd), near exit 25 from Hwy 104, 2km south of central New Glasgow. Service is available three or four times a day to Truro ($10), Halifax ($25) and Sydney ($39). There's no bus to Pictou (19km) or Caribou (27km), so this stop is only convenient if someone is picking you up or you're willing to continue by thumb.

The **Crombie Art Gallery** (☎ *902-755-4440, 1780 Abercrombie Rd; admission free*), between New Glasgow and Abercrombie Point, is a private gallery open only on Wednesday in July and August. You must join one of the free guided tours given every hour on the hour from 9am to 4pm (reservations not necessary). Other months, call ahead and you may be able to arrange a private visit if staff are available. The Crombie is housed in the personal residence of Frank Sobey (1902–85), founder of the Sobey supermarket chain, and it has an excellent collection of 19th- and early-20th-century Canadian art, including works by Cornelius Krieghoff and the Group of Seven.

ANTIGONISH
pop 5000
Pleasant Antigonish (an-tee-guh-**nish**) is an agreeable stopping place for anyone passing this way. It's a university town, with good places to stay, a nearby beach and no industry. The hiking possibilities north of town could keep you busy for a day, at least.

Antigonish is known for its annual **Highland Games**, held in mid-July. These Scottish games have been going on since 1861. You'll see pipe bands, drum regiments, dancers and athletes from far and wide. The events last a week. **Festival Antigonish** is a summer theater festival, with all performances held at one of the university auditoriums.

The tourist office (☎ 902-863-4921), just off the Trans Canada Hwy at the junction with Hwy 7, is open 9am to 6pm late June to early October and 9am to 8pm July and August.

The Antigonish public library (☎ 902-863-4276, 274 Main St), in the town hall (entrance off College St), provides public Internet access from 10am to 9pm Tuesday and Thursday and from 10am to 5pm Wednesday, Friday and Saturday.

Things to See & Do
In the classic Antigonish Depot that was built in 1908 by the Intercolonial Railway, the **Heritage Museum** (☎ *902-863-6160, 20 E Main St; admission free; open 10am-5pm Mon-Sat July & Aug, 10am-noon & 1pm-5pm Mon-Fri other months*) features displays pertaining to the early days of Antigonish. The most interesting exhibit is the 1864 hand-hauled fire engine the town once used to put out blazes.

A 4km hiking/biking trail to the nature reserve at **Antigonish Landing** begins just across the train tracks from the museum, then 400m down Adam St. The Landing's estuary is a good bird-watching area where you might see eagles, ducks and ospreys.

The attractive campus of 125-year-old **St Francis Xavier University** is behind St Ninian's Cathedral (1874) near the center of town. It's a pleasant place to stroll.

Places to Stay & Eat
Whidden's Campground & Trailer Court (☎ *902-863-3736, fax 902-863-0110, ⓔ whiddens@ant.auracom.com, Main St at Hawthorne St*) Without/with hookups $22/26, without car $11, mobile home $72 & up plus $10 for each additional person. Open May-Oct. This unusual accommodations complex right in town offers a real blend of choices. It's a large place renting campsites and 16 mobile homes with complete facilities. Facilities include a swimming pool and laundromat. Notice the greatly reduced camping rate for persons arriving by bicycle or on foot.

St Francis Xavier University (☎ *902-867-2855, fax 902-867-3751, ⓦ www.stfx.ca, West St*) Singles/doubles $29/40. Office open 9am-

9pm Mon-Sat, 10am-4pm Sun mid-May–mid-Aug. Under a kilometer from the bus station, St Francis Xavier has 30 rooms with shared bath for rent in summer. Apply to Conference Services in the side of Morrison Hall facing the Angus L Macdonald Library. After 4pm on Sunday, go to the Security Office in the basement of MacKinnon Hall to rent a room. Rates include use of the university facilities, such as the laundromat and pool, and free parking.

The Yellow Door B&B (☎ 902-863-1385, *38 Highland Dr*) Singles/doubles $40/55. Open July & Aug. Only a few hundred meters west of the university, this modern two-story house has three rooms for rent.

Sunshine on Main Café (☎ 902-863-5851, *332 Main St*) Light mains/full dinner $9/13. Open 7am-9:30pm Sun-Thur, 7am-10pm Fri & Sat. This café has a bistro feel, and vegetarians aren't ignored. The menu includes sandwiches ($7, or $9 with soup), soup and salad ($10), gourmet burgers ($9) and pasta dishes ($11).

Wong's (☎ 902-863-3596, *232 Main St*) Open 11am-10pm Tues-Thur & Sun, 11am-11pm Fri & Sat. Full dinners $8-11. This friendly place provides the local Chinese option. Combination plates are $9-12, Cantonese specialties $10-19.

Getting There & Away
The Acadian Bus Lines terminal (☎ 902-863-6900) is on the Trans Canada Hwy at the turnoff for James St into town. It's on the west side of the city and within walking distance of the downtown area. Buses include those to Halifax (four a day, $34) and to Sydney (one midday and two early evening trips, $31). It's $10 to New Glasgow and $19 to Truro. The station is open daily until 10:30pm and $2 coin lockers are available.

MONASTERY
Thirty-two kilometers east of Antigonish in the village of Monastery, the Augustine Order now occupies a Trappist monastery established by French monks in 1825. The access road to **Our Lady of Grace Monastery of the Monks of St Maron** is on the right after a small bridge just off the Trans Canada at exit 37. Two kilometers up the valley, beyond the main monastery, a trail along a stream leads to the **Shrine of the Holy Spring**. It's a palpably spiritual place.

Eastern Shore

The 'Eastern Shore' is the area east from Dartmouth to Cape Canso, at the extreme eastern tip of the mainland. It's one of the least visited regions of the province; there are no large towns and the main road is slow, narrow and almost as convoluted as the rugged shoreline it follows. Marine Dr, the designated tourist route, is the only route through the area. There are some campgrounds and good beaches along the coast, but the water on this edge of the province is prohibitively cold.

LAWRENCETOWN BEACH
Lawrencetown, a wide Atlantic surfing beach, is perhaps the best beach near Halifax. It's on Hwy 207, which begins in downtown Dartmouth as Portland St.

Seaboard B&B (☎/fax 902-827-3747, **W** *www.bbcanada.com/5112.html, 2629 Crowell Rd*) Singles/doubles $45/60 & up. Open June–mid-Oct. This stylish two-story house on a slope above an inlet is in East Lawrencetown near the junction with Hwy 207, a kilometer from Lawrencetown Beach.

PORTERS LAKE
From Lawrencetown Beach it's just 8km along Crowell Rd to *Porters Lake Provincial Park* (☎ 902-827-2250, **W** *parks .gov.ns.ca, 1160 Crowell Rd, 4km south of Hwy 107 from Dartmouth*) Sites $18. Open early June-Aug. This campground is on a peninsula and small island in Porters Lake, and the 158 nicely separated campsites have lots of shade. It's best to reserve for Friday or Saturday nights from mid-July to mid-August, otherwise there should be no problem getting a site. It's easily the most attractive campground around Halifax.

MUSQUODOBOIT HARBOUR
The **Musquodoboit Harbour Railway Museum** (☎ 902-889-2689, *7895 Hwy 7; admission free; open June-Sept*), in a former train station built in 1918, also dispenses tourist information. The **Musquodoboit Trailway**, a 15-km section of the Trans Canada Trail, follows an old rail bed to Gibraltar Rock, leaving from the museum. Another trailhead is 500m up Hwy 357 off Hwy 7, not far from the museum, and ample

parking is available there. The Trailway is ideal for bicycling. (Musquodoboit is pronounced musk-o-**dob**-it.)

Martinique Beach Provincial Park, 12km south of the village of Musquodoboit Harbour down E Petpeswick Rd from Hwy 7, boasts the longest beach in the province. The Atlantic breakers roll right in here. Camping is not allowed.

JEDORE OYSTER POND

Quite the name for a town. See the small **Fisherman's Life Museum** (☎ *902-889-2053, 58 Navy Pool Loop; adult/child $2/1; open 9:30am-5:30pm Mon-Sat, 1pm-5:30pm Sun June-mid-Oct*) – it's a model of a typical 1900s fishing-family's house, now with costumed guides and eternal tea-time.

Golden Coast Seafood Restaurant (☎ *902-889-2386, 10320 Hwy 7*) Dinner $8-15. Open 11am-9pm daily June-Sept, 11am-7pm Sun-Thur, 11am-8pm Fri & Sat other months. Across the street from the Fisherman's Life Museum, Golden Coast Seafood gives you the option of buying fresh fish to take away or enjoying a seafood dinner in the restaurant. Its seafood chowder ($5.50), with chunks of lobster, scallops and haddock, is excellent.

TANGIER

Up the coast in Tangier is **Coastal Adventures Sea Kayaking** (☎ *902-772-2774,* W *www.coastaladventures.com, off Hwy 7, open mid-June-early Oct*). It offers kayak courses, rentals ($35/50 half/full day) and guided trips. Its day trip ($100) is an introduction to kayaking and includes a tour to offshore islands. It also has canoes and double kayaks. The company has a small B&B called **Paddlers Retreat** next to the office. The three rooms with shared bath (singles/doubles $40/55) are intended mostly for people taking Coastal Adventures trips.

Murphy's Camping on the Ocean (☎ *902-772-2700,* W *www.dunmac.com/~tangiercap/ murphy, Murphy's Cove*) Without/with hookups $15/18. Open mid-May–mid-Oct. Down a side road 1.5km off the highway and 7.5km west of Tangier is this campground, where you should be able to find a secluded tent site. On rainy nights you can relax in a cozy lounge area called 'Sailors Rest.' There's great kayaking (bring your own) among the small islands just offshore,

and Murphy's rents canoes, rowboats and bicycles at $15/25 a half/full day. The owner, Brian Murphy, runs scenic boat trips at $50 an hour, plus $10 per person, for the whole boat – good value if five or more people want to go. Brian can also drop you off on an uninhabited island where you can stay overnight in an abandoned sea shanty.

TAYLOR HEAD PROVINCIAL PARK

A little-known scenic highlight of Nova Scotia, this spectacular park (☎ *902-772-2218, 20140 Hwy 7; admission free; open mid-May–early Oct*), just east of the village of Spry Harbour, encompasses a 6.5km peninsula jutting into the Atlantic. On one side is a long very fine, sandy beach fronting a protected bay. (Unfortunately, the water doesn't seem to warm up much.)

Some 17km of hiking trails cut through the spruce and fir forests. The Headland Trail is the longest at 8km roundtrip and follows the rugged coastline to scenic views at Taylor Head. It's a three- to four-hour walk. Shorter is the Bob Bluff Trail, a 3km roundtrip hike to a bluff with good views. In spring you'll encounter colorful wildflowers, and this is a great bird-watching venue.

The main parking lot is 5km off Hwy 7 on a good gravel road, but if the gate is closed or you're on a bicycle or walking, note that one end of the Bull Beach Trail is just 800m from the main highway. Camping is not allowed, so stay elsewhere, pack the picnic cooler and plan on spending a full day hiking, lounging and (maybe) swimming here.

PORT DUFFERIN
pop 157

Port Dufferin is approximately a two-hour drive from Halifax, Antigonish or the Halifax International Airport.

Marquis of Dufferin Seaside Inn (☎ *902-654-2696, fax 902-654-2970, 25658 Hwy 7*) Singles/doubles $60/65 in the new block, $41/47 in the old block. Open end of May–mid-Oct. Tiny Port Dufferin is mentioned solely for this inn, a highly regarded retreat featuring coastal views, breezes and tranquillity. The nine new rooms are in a motel-like strip next to the original house, while the five older rooms are in a block across the street. Larger housekeeping and family rooms are $71. The **dining room** in the restored 1859 house serves outstanding Maritime-style seafood meals. Breakfast is $4-6, dinners $11-17.

LISCOMB MILLS

Several well-developed hiking trails begin near the fancy Liscomb Lodge at Liscomb Mills, 52km east of Port Dufferin on Hwy 7. The **Mayflower Point Trail** to the coast begins from the parking lot on the east side of the Liscomb River bridge. You join the nearby **Liscomb Trail** by going up the driveway of the house at 2993 Hwy 7, then turning right. This trail follows the river's east bank 9.5km upstream through the forest to a fish ladder and suspension bridge. You can return down the other side of the river. Many picturesque cascades appear along the way, and signboards explain the ecology of the area.

SHERBROOKE

Inland toward Antigonish, 26km east of Liscomb Mills, the pleasant little town of Sherbrooke is overshadowed by its historic site, which is about the same size and one of the province's top attractions.

The local tourist office is at Sherbrooke Village (see paragraph below) and is open the same hours. Zinck's Bus Co (☎ 902-468-4342) has a bus leaving the Acadian Lines terminal in Halifax for Sherbrooke at 5:30pm Monday to Saturday. The return trip leaves St Mary's River Lodge, Sherbrooke, at 8am Tuesday to Saturday and at 6pm Sunday ($15 to Halifax).

Sherbrooke Village (☎ 902-522-2400, Hwy 7; adult/family $7.25/21; open 9:30am-5:30pm daily June–mid-Oct) re-creates life 125 years ago through buildings, demonstrations and costumed workers. It's called a living museum and all of the 28 houses, stores and workshops are the original ones (not replicas). The green, quiet setting helps to evoke a real sense of stepping back in time.

St Mary's River Lodge (☎ 902-522-2177, fax 902-522-2515, **W** www3.ns.sympatico.ca/lodge, 21 Main St) Singles/doubles $52/62 with private bath, breakfast included. Open Apr-Dec. This stylish place with five rooms and two suites is adjacent to the re-created village in the center of town. The Zinck's Bus Co service to Halifax leaves here at 8am Tuesday to Saturday, 6pm on Sunday.

Vi's B&B (☎ 902-522-2042, 8140 Main St) Singles/doubles $44/48. Open June-Sept. On the main road in Sherbrooke, this large B&B has a good location and fair prices.

COUNTRY HARBOUR

North of Port Bickerton, Hwy 211 is cut by Country Harbour. The Country Harbour ferry runs hourly, 24 hours a day year-round. It departs the Port Bickerton side on the half hour, and the Goldboro side on the hour (in July and August the ferry runs every half hour). It's $3 per car.

Salsman Provincial Park (☎ 902-328-2999, **W** parks.gov.ns.ca, Hwy 316 between Goldboro and Goshen) Sites $18. Open mid-May–early Oct. Near Stormont, 9km northwest of the turnoff to the Country Harbour ferry, Salsman has campsites on a peninsula in Country Harbour (site No 18 is nicely isolated on a point). There are showers. It could be full the last weekend in July and the first weekend in August; at other times you should be okay.

CANSO

With a population of just 1200, this town at the edge of the mainland is probably the largest on the whole eastern shoreline. Since the first attempted settlement in 1518, Canso has seen it all: Native Indian battles, British and French landings and captures, pirates, fishing fleets and the ever-present difficulties of life ruled by the sea.

The **Whitman House Museum** (☎ 902-366-2170, Main St at Union St; admission free; open 9am-5pm daily late May-Sept) holds reminders of parts of the town's history and offers a good view from the widow's walk on the roof. The 1885 house doubles as the tourist office.

An interpretive center on the waterfront tells the story of **Grassy Island National Historic Site** (☎ 902-366-3136, Union St; admission $2.50; open 10am-6pm daily June–mid-Sept), which lies just offshore and can be visited by boat. In 1720, the British built a small fort here to offer some protection from the French, who had their headquarters in Louisbourg. This outpost, however, was extremely vulnerable to military attacks and was totally destroyed in 1744. Among the ruins today there's a self-guided hiking trail with eight interpretive stops explaining the history of the area. The boat to

Grassy Island (included in admission) departs from the center upon demand.

The **Chapel Gully Trail** is a 10-km boardwalk and hiking trail along an estuary and out to the coast. It begins near the lighthouse on the hill behind the hospital at the east end of Canso. A large map is posted at the trailhead. Allow three hours for the hike.

GUYSBOROUGH

Guysborough is the county seat. The **Old Court House Museum** (☎ 902-533-4008, 106 Church St at Queen; admission free; open 9am-5pm Mon-Fri, 10am-4pm Sat & Sun June-Sept) contains the area's tourist office and stocks leaflets on the many local hiking trails.

Carritt House B&B (☎ 902-533-3855, 20 Pleasant St) Singles/doubles/triples $50/60/70. Open mid-May–mid-Oct. This two-story frame house on Hwy 16 opposite the public library in Guysborough has three rooms with shared bath.

Boylston Provincial Park (☎ 902-533-3326, **w** parks.gov.ns.ca, off Hwy 16) Sites $14. Open early June-Aug. Boylston is on a hilltop above Guysborough Harbour, 4km north of Guysborough village. The 36 campsites in this well-wooded park are never all taken. From the picnic area on the highway below the campground, a footbridge leads to a small island. A display near the park office records the visit of a Norwegian earl, Henry Sinclair of Orkney, in 1398!

Cape Breton Island

Cape Breton, the large island at the northeast end of Nova Scotia, is justly renowned for its rugged splendor. It's the roughest, highest, coolest and most remote area of the province. The coast is rocky, the interior a blend of mountains, valleys, rivers and lakes. The Cabot Trail, the nearly 300km-long highway around Cape Breton Highlands National Park, is one of Canada's grandest and best-known roads, winding and climbing to 500m between mountain and sea.

The island offers more than natural beauty – it has a long and captivating human history encompassing the Mi'kmaq, the British, the French and, especially, the Scots, who were attracted because of the terrain's strong resemblance to the Scottish Highlands. Many people around Chéticamp speak French, while a good part of Nova Scotia's Mi'kmaq community lives around Bras d'Or Lake.

The Cabot Trail, understandably the island's most popular attraction, can be busy, even a little crowded in July and August. The sketchy public transportation system makes getting around Cape Breton without a vehicle difficult. Acadian Lines runs from Halifax and Antigonish to Sydney, stopping at Baddeck along the way. Transoverland Ltd runs a bus route from Sydney and Baddeck to Chéticamp through the Margaree Valley. Alternatively, a variety of tours are offered from Halifax.

PORT HASTINGS

Cape Breton ceased to be a true island when the Canso Causeway was built in 1955. A big and busy provincial tourist office (☎ 902-625-4201) is on the east side of the causeway in Port Hastings. Here you can pick up information on all parts of Cape Breton or book rooms with the help of an agent. It's open 8:30am to 8:30pm daily April to mid-January.

South of neighboring Port Hawkesbury is an industrial area with gypsum loading, oil storage, a pulp mill and natural gas processing. Nova Scotia Hydro has a huge generating station here.

MABOU

From the Canso Causeway, Hwy 19, known as the Ceilidh (**kay**-lee) Trail, goes up the western side of the island to the highlands. The first part of this route is not very interesting but it still beats the Trans Canada Hwy (Hwy 105), which goes straight up the middle.

At Mabou, things pick up. It's a green, hilly region with valleys following numerous rivers and sheltering traditional towns. Here Scottish Gaelic is still spoken and actually taught in the schools. One of Cape Breton's most renowned bands, the Rankin Family, is from Mabou. On July 1 a Scottish picnic is held, with music and dancing.

Cape Mabou Highlands

An extensive network of hiking trails extends between Mabou and Inverness toward the coast west of Hwy 19. The main trailhead is at Mabou Post Rd, reached by following Mabou Harbour Rd 4.5km west from the large white St Mary's Church in Mabou and then heading 7.7km northwest on a gravel road signposted 'Mabou Coal Mines.' A second trailhead is at MacKinnon's Brook, 3.8km beyond Mabou Post Rd on a narrowing gravel track.

There's very limited parking at the trailheads, and in midsummer you should arrive early, if possible. If you plan to do some hiking, buy a copy of the *Cape Mabou Highlands Hiking Trails* map ($2.50) at the Mabou River Hostel. Maps are also posted at the trailheads. There are numerous alternative routes.

Places to Stay & Eat

Mabou River Guest House & Hostel (☎ 888-627-9744, fax 902-945-2605, **W** *www.mabouriverhostel.com, 19 Mabou Ridge Rd*) Dorm beds $20, singles $29-34, doubles $42-48, family room $45-53, suite $85-95, plus tax. Open year-round, by reservation Nov-Apr. This well-run 37-bed guesthouse, just 100m off Hwy 19 right in town, offers eight private rooms, two suites and five dorms. There's a kitchen, barbecue, laundry facilities ($3 a load), Internet access ($1 per 10 minutes), a games room and ample parking. The self-service continental breakfast from 8am is $3 per person. Ceilidhs and step-dance workshops are held in summer. Pick-ups can be arranged from the bus stop in Whycocomagh ($10), and the hostel offers tours of the Cabot Trail ($40) and Louisbourg Fortress ($30) if at least three people are interested. There's kayaking in the harbor near the hostel, and kayaks are for rent at $10/50 an hour/day. Bicycles are also available.

Beaton's B&B (☎ 902-945-2806, fax 902-945-2340, **W** *www.bbcanada.com/370.html, 11311 Hwy 19*) Singles/doubles/triples $40/55/70 plus tax. Three rooms are for rent in this two-story house by the road just south of Mabou.

Shining Waters Bakery & Eatery (☎ 902-945-2728, *Hwy 19*) Breakfast $4-5. Open 6:30am-7pm Mon-Sat, 9am-7pm Sun. Start the day at this healthy, inexpensive place near the Mabou River Bridge. The homemade bread is $2.75 a loaf, and you can get a full breakfast featuring thick slices of it. The salads or sandwiches are $4-6, fish dishes $5.

Entertainment

The Red Shoe Pub (☎ 902-945-2626, 11531 Hwy 19) Open noon-11pm Mon-Wed, noon-1am Thur-Sun (closed Tues in winter). Thursday is wing night, often with live music. There's always a group playing from 9:30pm on Saturday ($6 cover charge), and on Sunday from 4pm to 8pm there's a jam session ($6 cover charge). It's Mabou's favorite venue.

Mabou Hall (☎ 902-945-2093, 11538 Hwy 19) From late June to mid-September there's a ceilidh at this hall opposite the Red Shoe Pub every Tuesday night at 7:30pm (admission $5).

INVERNESS

The first town of any size on the northern shore is this old coal-mining center. Beginning near the fishing harbor there are miles of sandy beach with some nice secluded spots and few people. Surprisingly, the water

Miners dug up the coal under Inverness.

temperature is not too bad, reaching 19°C to 21°C in summer, which is about as warm as it gets anywhere around the Maritimes – cool but definitely swimmable. Pilot whales can sometimes be seen off the coast.

A boardwalk runs a kilometer along the beach. Up closer to town, the **Inverness Miners' Museum** (☎ 902-258-3822, 62 Lower

Railway St; adult/child $1/50¢; open 9am-7pm daily mid-June–early Sept), in the old train station, has mementos from the former Inverness coal mines. Lower Railway St is next to the Fire Department off Hwy 19.

Ceilidh Café *(☎ 902-258-3339, 15896 Hwy 19)* Breakfast/lunch $4/5. Open 7am-11:30pm daily. This café is on Hwy 19 toward the north end of town, next door to a laundromat. It's a local hangout with breakfast for $4 and burgers with fries for $5, though fancier tourist food is offered in midsummer. The cigarette smoke may be a deterrent.

BELLE CÔTE

From Belle Côte, where the Cabot Trail meets the coastline, northward to Cape Breton Highlands National Park, French culture adds a different interest to the island. Descendants of the Acadians settled the area – and the area north of Yarmouth – in the 1750s after being expelled from the mainland by the British during the Seven Years' War.

The strength of this culture in Cape Breton is remarkable because of its small size and isolation from other French-speaking people. Almost everyone, it seems, speaks English, although an accent is often detectable. Among themselves, they switch to French, keeping the language very much alive. Aside from the language, the French food, music and dance are worth sampling.

Six kilometers north of Belle Côte watch for **Joe's Scarecrow Theatre** *(☎ 902-235-2108, 11842 Cabot Trail; open mid-June–early Oct),* by the highway next to Ethel's Takeout restaurant. It's a humorous, quasi-macabre outdoor collection of life-size stuffed figures. Several other folk-art shops are along the highway between here and Chéticamp.

CHÉTICAMP

pop 3000

Busy Chéticamp is the center of the local Acadian community and the gateway to nearby Cape Breton Highlands National Park. From Chéticamp the Cabot Trail becomes more scenic, with superlative vistas and lots of hills and turns as you climb to the highest point just before Pleasant Bay.

The **Church of St Pierre** dominates the town, as churches so often do in French centers. It dates from 1893 and has the characteristic silver spire and colorful frescoes.

The Acadians have a tradition of handicrafts, but in this area one product, hooked rugs, has long been seen as of particular beauty and value. Many of the local women continue this craft; their wares are displayed and sold in numerous outlets in and around town. A good rug costs $250 to $650 or more. Each is made of wool, and to complete the intricate work takes about 12 hours per 30 sq cm.

Co-op Artisanale de Chéticamp

Don't miss this cultural center *(☎ 902-224-2170, 15067 Main St; admission free; open mid-May–late Oct)* near the large church in the middle of Chéticamp. The museum downstairs has a limited but fascinating display of artifacts, furniture and some older hooked rugs. Demonstrations of rug making are given. This operation is supported through the sale of quality local handicrafts at the large craft shop upstairs and by the restaurant, which closes an hour or two later than the museum and craft shop.

Les Trois Pignons

At the north end of town, this museum *(☎ 902-224-2642, 15584 Main St; admission $3.50; open 9am-5pm daily May-June & Sept–mid-Oct, 8am-7pm daily July & Aug)* shows, among other things, the rugs and tapestries of many local people, including those of Elizabeth Lefort, who has achieved an international reputation. Her detailed representational rugs and portraits in wool hang in the White House, the Vatican and Buckingham Palace. Internet access is available here at $2 an hour.

Whale-Watching

From Government Wharf, across and down from the church, whale-watching cruises are run. The most common species in the area is the pilot whale, also called the pothead, but fin whales and minkes are also seen, as are seals, bald eagles and a couple of seabird species. Demand is high in midsummer, so reserve your trip the day before.

The three-hour boat excursions by **Whale Cruisers** *(☎ 902-224-3376, 800-813-3376, W www.whalecruises.com, Government Wharf; adult/child $29/12)* are a pretty good value. The company runs three trips daily – at 9am, 1pm and 5 or 6pm – from mid-May until mid-October.

Acadian Whale Cruise (☎ *902-224-1088,* W *www.whalecruise.com, Quai du Phare; trips $26*) has an office below the lighthouse along the boardwalk from the tourist office. Cruises are offered from mid-May to September.

Farther along the waterfront opposite Salon Le Gabriel, **Seaside Whale & Nature Cruises** (☎ *902-224-2400, 800-959-4253, 15407 Main St; adult/child $27/13.50; open June-Sept*) does whale-watching on the *Love Boat*.

Places to Stay

Though quite a few rooms are available around town, accommodations are tight throughout July and August, so calling ahead or arriving early in the afternoon is advisable.

Seashell Cabins (☎ *902-224-3569, 125 Chéticamp Island Rd, Île de Chéticamp*) Singles/doubles $48/58. Open mid-June–mid-Oct. On the tip of the island, just 700m off the Cabot Trail, this row of three small rustic cabins is worth a try. There are basic cooking facilities at this gay-friendly spot near the beach.

Albert's Motel (☎ *902-224-2077, 15068 Main St*) Singles/doubles $55/60. Open mid-May–mid-Oct. This block of four clean wooden rooms is almost opposite the Co-op Artisanale de Chéticamp in the heart of town.

Merry's Motel (☎ *902-224-2456, fax 902-224-1786,* W *www.capebretonisland.com/cheticamp/merrysmotel, 15356 Main St*) Singles/doubles $50/65. Open May-Oct. Also try this motel with eight units in a long block right in town.

Les Cabines du Portage (☎ *902-224-2822, 15660 Main St*) Two-bed cabins $70 for two persons, $10 each additional person; two-bedroom cabins $80 a double or $90 for up to four. Weekly rates are $400/450 for a small/large unit. Off-season rates are discounted $10 a day or $50 a week. Just before the park, this place is ideal if there are three or more of you. Each of the six two-bed cabins and four bigger, two-bedroom units has a kitchen.

Places to Eat

Co-op Artisanale Restaurant (☎ *902-224-2170, 15067 Main St*) Dinners under $9.

Open 7am-9pm daily mid-May–Oct (10am-7pm toward the beginning and end of the season). This outstanding restaurant's large menu offers many fine choices, but it excels in Acadian dishes like *poulet fricot* (potato and chicken soup) at $5, *pâté à la viande* (meat pie) at $5, blood pudding (pork custard) at $5, *chiard* (potato and meat stew) at $7 and fish cakes at $9 (here, as in Newfoundland, fish means cod; other types are called by name). For dessert, the gingerbread with hot sauce and the fruit pie are both under $3. The women who run the place and do the cooking and baking wear traditional dress.

Seafood Stop (☎ *902-224-1717, 14803 Main St*) Main meals $6-8. Open 11am-9pm daily May–mid-Oct. This large fish market and restaurant out on the highway south of town sells all manner of take-away seafood for that special picnic. A complete lobster dinner in the dining room will be $20 with dessert and coffee, or just take the fish and chips for $6-8.

In July and August, **LM Chéticamp Seafoods Ltd** (☎ *902-224-1688*) runs a fish market opposite the Royal Bank on Main St.

Getting There & Away

Chéticamp is connected to Baddeck ($10) and Sydney ($12) by Transoverland Ltd (☎ *902-248-2051*). In Chéticamp the company's minibus departs from Cormier's Esso gas station (☎ *902-224-2315, 15437 Main St*) at 7:30am Monday, Wednesday and Friday. Tickets are sold by the driver. Unfortunately, there's no bus service through or around the national park.

CAPE BRETON HIGHLANDS NATIONAL PARK

This spectacular national park includes some of the grandest terrain in the Maritimes. It stretches right across Cape Breton's noble northern finger with dramatic cliffs on one side, and rocky coves and sandy beaches on the other. Established in 1936, Cape Breton Highlands was the region's first national park, and at 950 sq km it's one of the largest in eastern Canada. You've got an excellent chance of seeing moose, whales and bald eagles, and the possibilities for day hikes and car camping are many.

The Cabot Trail, one of the best-known roads in the country, gets its reputation from

NOVA SCOTIA

the 106km national park segment of its Cape Breton loop. The drive is at its best along the northwestern shore and then down to Pleasant Bay. The road winds right along the shoreline, across barren plains, to **French Mountain**, the highest point (459m). Then it zigzags through switchbacks and descends to Pleasant Bay, just outside the park. If you're driving, make sure your brakes are good and can afford to burn off a little lining.

Toward Ingonish, the **Grand Anse Valley** contains virgin forest; the short **Lone Shieling Trail** leads through 300-year-old maple trees to a replica of a Scottish Highland crofter's hut, a reminder of the area's first settlers.

If possible, save the trip for a sunny day when you can see down the coastline. Summer conditions tend to be rather rainy, foggy and windy even while remaining fairly warm. The driest month is generally July, with June and September the runners-up. Maximum temperatures during mid-summer usually don't exceed 25°C, and minimums are around 15°C.

Both of the entrances, Chéticamp and Ingonish, have information centers where you purchase your motor-vehicle entry permit. A one-day pass is $3.50, four days $10.50, less for seniors and children; family passes are $8 for one day, $24 for four. An Atlantic Pass valid at seven national parks in Atlantic Canada is also available. One-day passes are good until noon the next day.

The **Chéticamp Information Centre** (☎ 902-224-2306, 16646 Cabot Trail; open 9am-5pm daily mid-May–June & Sept–mid-Oct, 8am-8pm daily July & Aug) has displays, a relief map and a 10-minute slide show. The bookstore sells maps (including topographical ones), and the helpful staff dispense hiking brochures and good advice.

The **Ingonish Information Centre** (☎ 902-285-2535, 37677 Cabot Trail; open 8am-6pm daily mid-May–June & Sept–mid-Oct, 8am-8pm daily July & Aug) is much smaller and only sells park entry tickets, hands out brochures and answers questions. Wheelchair-accessible trails are indicated on the free park map available at either entrance.

Hiking

For as big and rugged as Cape Breton Highlands National Park is, the hiking is surprisingly limited. Legitimate multiday trails are

now nonexistent since the Lake of Islands trail closed in 1998. The park has 25 trails and only one of them leads to backcountry campsites.

The **Fishing Cove Trail** is an 8km one-way walk that descends 330m to the mouth of rugged Fishing Cove River. You must pre-register for one of the eight backcountry campsites there at the Chéticamp Information Centre. The two trailheads for Fishing Cove are 4.5km apart on the Cabot Trail. The southern trail is a gentle 8km descent along a stream; the northern trail makes a steep 2.8km drop down the hillside to the beach. This is your best opportunity to experience the true wilderness of Cape Breton Highlands National Park and is highly recommended.

Most of the other trails are shorter and close to the road. Many trails take you to ridge tops for impressive views of the coast. The best is probably **Skyline Trail**, a 7km loop that puts you on the edge of a headland cliff right above the water. This trail is posted along Cabot Trail 5.5km above Corey Brook Campground. Other trails with ocean views from mountaintops include Aspy, Glasgow Lake and Franey Mountain Trail.

Cycling

The park is a popular cycling destination. However, it is not suggested that it be your inaugural trip. The riding is tough but the views are spectacular when cycling through the park or other coastal roads in the area. Despite the high numbers of motorized tourists and steep hills, considerable biking takes place here.

If you need to rent a bicycle, try **Sea Spray Cycle Centre** (☎ 902-383-2732, 1141 White Point Rd; bicycle rentals $25/35 half/full day; open 9am-5pm daily June–mid-Oct) in Smelt Brook. Sea Spray is an especially good outfitter that sells maps with suggested coastal routes for self-guided tours. It also leads organized tours and does bicycle repairs.

Camping

Cape Breton Highlands National Park campgrounds (☎ 902-224-2306, fax 902-224-2445, ☒ parkscanada.pch.gc.ca) Without/with hookups $15/21; discounts after 3 days. The park entry fee is extra. There are seven campgrounds in the park, some for tenters only. Reservations are not generally accepted at any of the campgrounds – most sites are first-come, first-served. Exceptions are the wheelchair-accessible sites, group campsites and backcountry sites, which can be reserved. The park motto is 'We always have room,' but don't be surprised if it's tight on peak-season weekends. The campgrounds away from the park entrances tend to be small, with 10 to 20 sites. In these, pick a site, self-register and set up.

The 162-site **Chéticamp Campground** is behind the information center at the west entrance to the park, 3km north of Chéti-camp. Wheelchair-accessible sites are available. When the main campground is full, an overflow area is opened. However, there are no 'radio free' areas, so peace and quiet is not guaranteed. You register at the information center.

Self-registration applies at Corney Brook (20 sites), MacIntosh Brook (10 sites) and Big Intervale (10 sites). **Corney Brook**, 10km north of Chéticamp Campground, has only open unprotected sites around a parking area. It's popular for its great views, sea breezes and nearby trails. **MacIntosh Brook**, 3km east of Pleasant Bay, offers sites in an open field with some shade (and lots of mosquitoes in spring). **Big Intervale**, 11km west of Cape North, offers sites along a river, along with barbecues and a covered picnic shelter. A 9.6km hiking trail is nearby.

On the east side of the park, you have a choice of the 256-site **Broad Cove Campground** at Ingonish and the 90-site **Ingonish Campground**, 37437 Cabot Trail near Keltic Lodge at Ingonish Beach. Special sites with a fireplace (but no hookups) are available at these for $17, firewood $3 extra, and both have wheelchair-accessible sites. Because these large campgrounds are near the beach they tend to be crowded with local families in midsummer and can be noisy.

From late October to early May, you can camp at the Chéticamp and Ingonish campgrounds for $10, including firewood.

PLEASANT BAY

Pleasant Bay is best known for its whale-watching tours; various companies have kiosks along the wharf. **Pleasant Bay Whale & Seal Tour** (☎ 902-224-1316; adult/child $25/12; open June–mid-Oct) offers 1½-hour cruises at 9:30am, 1pm, 3pm and 5pm, with the 3pm and 5pm cruises replaced by one at

4pm at the beginning and end of the season. Weather conditions and demand can alter this schedule.

Captain Mark's Whale and Seal Cruise (☎ 888-754-5112, **W** www.whaleandseal cruise.com; adult/child $25/12; open June–Sept) promises a whale sighting or your money back.

Wesley's Whale Watching (☎ 902-224-1919, **W** www.cabottrail.com/whalewatching; adult/child $25/12; open mid-May–mid-Oct) also guarantees a whale sighting or the tour is free. In addition to their Cape Island-style boat, they do whale-watching from zodiacs at $30/15.

The **Whale Interpretive Centre** (☎ 902-224-1411, **W** www.cabottrail.com/whales, 104 Harbour Rd; adult/family $4.50/14; open 9am-6pm daily mid-May–Oct), next to the whale-watching boats at Pleasant Bay, opened in 2001 with informative exhibits on marine mammals. Internet access is available at the CAP site here.

GAMPO ABBEY

From Pleasant Bay, a paved road continues 4.5km north along the coast to the small village of Red River. The road then becomes gravel and extends another 3.3km north to Gampo Abbey (☎ 902-224-2752, **W** www.gampoabbey.org), in a stunning location on this remote north coast. This is one of the only authentic Tibetan monasteries in North America intended mostly for Western followers, and students come from all across Canada and the USA for extended meditation programs. The noted Buddhist author Ani Pema Chödrön spends six months of each year here.

Just beyond Gampo Abbey is a circular **Stupa for World Peace**, then after another kilometer or so, the gravel road ends. Here the real journey starts as a rough track continues 10km north to **Pollett's Cove**, an old fishing settlement now abandoned. It's a three-hour hike each way and the views are superb. The soaring cliffs mark another outer edge of the continent.

Cabot Trail Hostel (☎ 902-224-1976, **W** www.cabottrail.com/hostel, 23349 Cabot Trail) Dorm beds $20. Open mid-May–Sept. A kilometer west of the turnoff to Pleasant Bay and 700m north of the Rusty Anchor Restaurant, this eight-bed hostel is behind the Celtic Vision Café. The café is worth a stop for baked goods; there's Internet access for $3 per 15 minutes. Ask about the 'moose tour.' The van does pick-ups at the Mabou River Hostel at $20 per person (minimum of three).

Mountain View Motel (☎ *902-224-3100,* **w** *themountainview.com, 23659 Cabot Trail)* Doubles $60 & up, cottages $100. Open May-Oct. Mountain View is a new motel, 500m east of the turnoff to Pleasant Bay, with one block of 10 rooms and another of eight rooms, plus four cottages. A large restaurant is on the premises.

CAPE NORTH

Don't confuse the village of Cape North, just outside the park, with the extreme northern portion of Cape Breton, which is also called Cape North. Cape North village at the junction of the Cabot Trail and Bay St Lawrence Rd has the **North Highlands Community Museum** (☎ *902-383-2579; admission free; open 10am-6pm daily June-early Oct),* behind Morrison's Restaurant on the corner.

North of here on Bay St Lawrence Rd, **Cabot's Landing Provincial Park** on Aspey's Bay is the location where John Cabot is believed to have landed in 1497. Every June 24 a reenactment is held on the beach at Sugarloaf Mountain. This long sandy beach is among the best in Nova Scotia but there's no camping. For that, continue 8km north to Bay St Lawrence.

MacDonald's Motel (☎ *902-383-2054, fax 902-383-2200, 2 Bay St Lawrence Rd)* Singles/doubles $55/60. Open mid-May-Oct. At the junction of Cabot Trail and Bay St Lawrence Rd opposite Morrison's Restaurant, this motel has 12 rooms in a long block, plus a few cabins behind.

Morrison's Restaurant (☎ *902-383-2051, Cabot Trail)* Seafood dinner $17-21. Open 11am-8pm daily mid-May-June & Sept-Oct, 8am-9:30pm daily July & Aug. This casual café at the junction of Cabot Trail and Bay St Lawrence Rd offers super seafood specialties and old-fashioned atmosphere. Lunch could be a grilled salmon sandwich ($8), while for dinner consider the braised halibut, poached salmon or lobster. It's very popular.

BAY ST LAWRENCE

Bay St Lawrence is a picturesque little fishing village where you can camp or go

whale-watching. Several whale-watching operators are based here. **Captain Cox** (☎ *902-383-2981; adult/child $25/12; open July–mid-Sept)* has been doing these trips since 1986. You could see minke, pilot, fin, humpback or sei whales on your trip, plus seals, dolphins and perhaps even a moose standing by the shore. During the peak season there's also **Captain Fraser's Oshan Whale Cruise** (☎ *902-383-2883; tours $25; open mid-July–Aug).* Both captains leave at 10:30am, 1:30pm and 4:30pm and stay out between two and three hours.

Jumping Mouse Campground (☎ *902-383-2914,* **w** *www.cabottrail.com/BaySt .Lawrence/DoubleCrow/camp.htm, 3360 Bay St Lawrence Rd)* Sites $15, cabin $30. Open mid-May–Sept. Directly above the harbor at Bay St Lawrence, this is one of the most spectacular campgrounds in the Maritimes, perched on a high cliff above the open sea where fin whales come up to blow. The 10 campsites are large but fully exposed to the wind. If the weather forecast is negative, ask about storm sites in the nearby forest. There's also a four-bed barebones cabin with shared bath. The showers here are free, and this place is quiet.

Highlands by the Sea B&B (☎ *902-383-2537, 3014 Bay St Lawrence Rd)* Singles/doubles $50/65. Open June-Oct. The large white house is adjacent to the St Margaret Village post office, 2km before Bay St Lawrence.

MEAT COVE

The northernmost road in Nova Scotia ends at Meat Cove village, 13km northwest of Bay St Lawrence (the last 7km gravel). From Meat Cove, **hiking trails** continue west to Cape St Lawrence lighthouse and Lowland Cove. If you're not planning to camp and want to hike to the cape, leave your car at the **Meat Cove Welcome Center** (☎ *902-383-2284)* at the entrance to the village and walk the last kilometer, as there's no parking right at the trailhead. The center is open 8am to 7pm daily June to October.

Meat Cove Campground (☎ *902-383-2379/2658, 2475 Meat Cove)* Sites $15. Open June-Oct. These are some of the most scenic sites in Cape Breton; you can actually watch whales from your tent perched on a grassy bluff directly above the sea. The sites are not as far apart as they are at Jumping Mouse and are similarly unsheltered. However, this is a great base for hiking as the trail to Cape St Lawrence begins just 200m up the road and there's an ocean beach just below the campground.

Meat Cove Lodge (☎ *902-383-2672, 2305 Meat Cove)* Doubles/quads $40/60 including breakfast. Open June-Sept. This modernistic wooden lodge installed in a narrow valley is at the entrance to Nova Scotia's northernmost community, 1km before the end of the road. The Fraser Trail begins opposite the lodge. A complete lobster/crab dinner ($13/11) is served from 4pm to 8pm, or get seafood chowder for $6.

AROUND NEILS HARBOUR

On your way down from Cape North to Ingonish, it's worth leaving the Cabot Trail and following more scenic White Point Rd via Smelt Brook to Neils Harbour, an attractive little fishing village. Down at the wharf you can buy fish and lobster.

Back on the Cabot Trail 5km south of the Neils Harbour turnoff is **Black Brook Beach**, a great place to swim because a freshwater stream tumbles over the high granite cliffs at the left end of the beach, allowing you to rinse off the saltwater.

South Harbour B&B (☎ *902-383-2615, 210 White Point Rd)* Singles/doubles $35/45. Open June–mid-Oct. Two rooms with shared bath are available at this B&B 1km off the Cabot Trail on the scenic loop to Neils Harbour. Rates include a full breakfast, and no tax is added.

Two Tittle B&B (☎ *902-383-2817,* w *www.capebretonisland.com/whitepoint, 2119 White Point Village Rd)* Singles/ doubles $40/60. This bungalow is directly above the harbor in the quaint fishing village of White Point. The hosts offer whale-watching trips (adult/child $25/10) at 10am, 1:30pm and 4:30pm from July to September. Good hiking is nearby.

Chowder House (☎ *902-336-2463, Neils Harbour)* Meals $7. Open 11am-6pm daily mid-June–Sept (11am-9pm in summer). This wildly popular place on the point next to the lighthouse (just down from the harbor) serves to-die-for clam or seafood chowder for under $4 and a haddock platter for just $7. The plastic plates and self-service at the counter help keep down costs. It's just 1.2km off the Cabot Trail and worth the detour.

INGONISH

At the eastern entrance to the national park are Ingonish and Ingonish Beach, two small towns with accommodations and basic supplies.

Keltic Lodge, a theatrical Tudor-style complex erected in 1940, shares Middle Head Peninsula with the famous Cape Breton Highland Links golf course and the Ingonish Campground. The lodge is well worth visiting for its setting and the breathtaking hiking trail to the tip of the peninsula just beyond the resort.

The beach at **Ingonish Beach** is a wonderful place, with a long, wide strip of sand tucked in a bay surrounded by green hills. The water can get pleasantly warm after a few sunny days.

Activities

Several kayak outfitters operate tours or rent supplies for do-it-yourself kayaking. Among them is **Cape Breton Sea Coast Adventures** (☎ *902-929-2800, 877-929-2800,* w *www.members.tripod.com/adventure_4u, 42314 Hwy 19; half-/full-day tour $49/89 plus tax; open June–mid-Oct).* Tour leader Mike Crimp meets clients at a hut opposite the Muddy Rudder Seafood Shack in Ingonish Beach.

Whale-watching tours are run by **SeaQuarium** (☎ *902-285-2103/2401, off Cabot Trail; tours $25)* from North Bay, Ingonish, with three sailings daily from mid-June to September.

SeaVisions (☎ *902-285-2628, based at Knotty Pine Cottages, 39126 Cabot Trail; adult/child $30/15)* at Ingonish Ferry also does whale tours three times daily from June to early September.

Places to Stay & Eat

Driftwood Lodge (☎ *902-285-2558,* e *driftwood.lodge@ns.sympatico.ca, 36125 Cabot Trail, Ingonish)* Rooms $20-70. Open from June-Oct. This recommended place, 100m south of Sea Breeze and 8km north of the Ingonish park entrance, is run by great hosts, Wanda and Kersti Tacreiter. All of the rooms in their three buildings are different in size, amenities, views and price, which can be confusing, so ask to see a few before deciding. Cheapest are the four rooms with shared bath in the Red House at $20-40 single and $30-45 double, or slightly less in early June and from early September to October. A panoramic beach is just below the lodge.

Knotty Pine Cottages & Tourist Home (☎ 800-455-2058, fax 902-285-2576, **w** *ingo nish.com/knotty, 39126 Cabot Trail)* Cottages $50-115, house rooms $45 & up. This place in Ingonish Ferry has 10 cottages with varying levels of amenities. All but one have cooking facilities, and some have balconies with views. There are also three rooms with shared bath in a house across the road.

Coastal Waters Restaurant (☎ *902-285-2526, 36404 Cabot Trail)* Main meals $9-14. Open 8am-9pm daily May-Oct. A kilometer south of Driftwood Lodge, this sit-down place serves sandwiches ($6), burgers ($3-7), seafood ($13-14) and pastas ($9). The breakfast specials start at $4.

Muddy Rudder Seafood Shack (☎ *902-285-2280, 38438 Cabot Trail)* Appetizers $5-6, seafood dinners $15-17. Open 11am-8pm daily June-Sept. This small eatery on the Cabot Trail just before you cross the Ingonish River is only a handful of tables out on a terrace. If it's rainy, you go into a 'shelter' designed like an old fisherman's beach hut. The food is prepared with flair by master chef Pearl, and features steamed lobster, mussels, crabs and clams. It's all so unorthodox, you'll probably like it.

ST ANN'S

The **Gaelic College of Celtic Arts & Crafts** (☎ *902-295-3411, 51779 Cabot Trail; admission $2.50, children under 12 yrs free; open 8:30am-5pm daily mid-June–late Sept),* at the end of St Ann's Bay, is the only Gaelic college in North America. Founded in 1938, it offers programs in the Scottish Gaelic language, bagpipe playing, Highland dancing, weaving, kilt making and other things Scottish. Students of all ages from across the land are welcome. Drop in any time from mid-June to early September and the chances are you'll hear a student sing a traditional Gaelic ballad or another play a Highland violin piece; mini-concerts and recitals are performed throughout the day. You can stroll around the grounds, see the museum with its historical notes and tartans, or browse the gift shop for books, recorded music or kilts.

North River Kayak Tours (☎ *888-865-2925, Murray Rd; open late May–mid-Sept)* does half-/full-day kayak tours at $55/95, and 2½-hour introductory tours at $50. Day rentals are $30/50 a half/full day for a single, $40/60 a double or $25/40 for a canoe. Go about 8km north of St Ann's, then it's another 3.5km south on a side road.

BIG BRAS D'OR

After crossing the long bridge over an arm of Bras d'Or Lake on the way toward Sydney, a secondary road branches off and leads north to the coast and the village of Big Bras d'Or. Offshore are the cliff-edged **Bird Islands** of Hertford and Ciboux. The islands are home to large colonies of razorbills, puffins, kittiwakes, terns and several other species.

Bird Island Tours (☎ *902-674-2384, 800-661-6680,* **w** *fox.nstn.ca/~birdisld, 1672 Big Bras d'Or Rd, 6km off Hwy 105; tours $32)* runs 2½-hour boat tours to the islands from mid-May to mid-September. The Bird Islands are about 1.5km off Cape Dauphin and take 40 minutes to reach. In June and July some 300 to 400 pairs of nesting puffins will be present, so those are the prime months for a visit. Binoculars are handy and can be rented, but they're not necessary as the tour boat goes to within 20m or so of the islands.

Mountain Vista Seashore Cottages (☎ *902-674-2384, 800-661-6680, fax 902-674-2742,* **w** *fox.nstn.ca/~birdisld, 1672 Big Bras d'Or Rd)* Cottages $35-150 July & Aug, $30-130 shoulder seasons. Without/with hookups $18/20. Open May-Oct. The same folks who run the Bird Island boat tours rent three cottages at their base. The smaller cabin with cooking facilities but no shower is $30/35 off-/in-season single or double. The two larger cottages can each be divided into two separate units by locking a connecting door, and rooms without cooking facilities start at $50/60 off-/in-season single or double. An entire two-bedroom housekeeping cottage with all facilities goes for $130/150 for up to four people. The 16 grassy campsites are a good bet in midsummer.

NORTH SYDNEY

Nondescript North Sydney is important as the Marine Atlantic terminal for ferries to Port aux Basques and Argentia in Newfoundland. There isn't much to see in town, but it's a convenient place to put up if you're using the ferry.

Tourist information is dispensed from a kiosk (☎ 902-539-9876), on the right as you leave the ferry, 9am to 5pm June to mid-October and 9am to 7pm July and August.

The main street in town is Commercial St. For drivers, there's free parking behind the public library, on Commercial St near the corner of Blowers St, close to the ferry terminal.

The small **North Sydney Heritage Museum** (☎ 902-794-2524, 299 Commercial St; admission free; open 10am-3pm Mon-Fri Apr-Oct, noon-4pm Mon, 10am-6pm Tues-Fri, 10am-2pm Sat June-Aug) is also here, with a collection of historical marine detritus.

Places to Stay & Eat

If you're coming in on a late ferry, you'll likely need advance room reservations – budget motels are in short supply. Several pricey B&Bs are on Queen St, a southward extension of Commercial St, a bit over 1km southwest of the ferry terminal. If you decide to spend the night in the car, there's a large shopping mall up King St where numerous RVs park for the night. A 24-hour (except Sunday) Sobeys Supermarket is there as well.

Alexandra Shebib's B&B (☎ 902-794-4876, 88 Queen St) Singles/doubles/triples $40/60/70. This large house opposite the harbor is the least expensive B&B near town.

MacNeil's Motel (☎ 902-736-9106, fax 902-736-8070, 1408 Hwy 105) Singles/doubles $50/67 mid-June–mid-Sept, $50/55 shoulder seasons. Open Apr-early Dec. This motel on Hwy 105 at Bras d'Or, exit 17, 5km from the Newfoundland ferry, has a total of 17 rooms in one duplex and three blocks of five units each.

Robena's 2000 Family Restaurant (☎ 902-794-8040, 266 Commercial St) Full breakfast $4. Open 7am-9pm daily June-Sept, 7am-7pm other months. If it's breakfast you're looking for, you'll find it here until noon weekdays, 1pm weekends. Lunch and dinner specials are posted on boards in the window.

Getting There & Away

Bus There's no bus depot in North Sydney; the depot proper is in Sydney. However, the Acadian Lines bus between Sydney and Halifax via Baddeck can be picked up at the Best Western North Star Hotel (☎ 902-794-8581, 39 Forrest St). It runs twice a day and costs $59 to Halifax. (The North Star is the long two-story hotel with a prominent red roof on the hill directly above the Marine Atlantic ferry terminal.)

Transit Cape Breton's No 5 bus runs back and forth between North Sydney and Sydney a few times a day for $3.25. It can be caught along Commercial and Queen Sts at around 7:15am, 9:15am, 1:15pm, 3:15pm and 6:15pm Monday to Saturday (no 7:15am bus on Saturday). To confirm these times, call the dispatcher at ☎ 902-539-8124.

Ferry North Sydney is the terminus of all ferry crossings between Nova Scotia and Newfoundland. The service to Port aux Basques operates daily year-round, with up to four departures a day in midsummer ($22/11 adult/child plus $67/10 per car/bicycle). To Argentia, the ferry operates three times a week from late June to mid-September, and weekly from mid-September to early October ($60/30 adult/child plus $135/20 per car/bicycle). Cabins, dorm beds and reclining seats are extra.

Vehicle reservations are recommended in midsummer; call Marine Atlantic (☎ 902-794-8109, 800-341-7981) in North Sydney. Foot passengers can buy tickets on the spot. You can also make reservations by mail; write to Marine Atlantic Reservations Bureau, 355 Purves St, North Sydney, NS B2A 3V2.

The ferry terminal is near the center of North Sydney at Commercial and Blowers Sts. The Trans Canada Hwy (Hwy 105) leads straight into or out of the ferry terminal. The Newfoundland tourist information counter (☎ 902-794-7433) in the ferry terminal is open from mid-May to mid-October.

SYDNEY
pop 26,000

Sydney is the only real city on Cape Breton and the embattled core of the island's collapsed industrial belt. As the heart of a coal-mining district, this old town has seen its share of grief and hardship. Long a drab, rather grim place with a hard-drinking, warm and friendly population, the city has managed without much spare money to modestly upgrade the downtown districts.

Tourism may help to offset the shutdown of the steel mill and coal mines that were the region's largest employers.

The main street downtown is Charlotte St, which has many stores and restaurants. Several large malls have also popped up around town. There's a lot to do, and with the ferry to the north and Louisbourg to the south, many people pass through. The choice of places to stay is good.

There's a local tourist office (☎ 902-563-4636, 800-565-9464, 320 Esplanade) inside the Civic Centre on the waterfront, but it's more of a chamber of commerce. It's open 8:30am to 5pm weekdays year-round.

The McConnell Memorial Library (☎ 902-562-3279, 50 Falmouth St at Charlotte) offers Internet access. It's open 10am to 9pm Tuesday to Friday and 10am to 5:30pm Saturday.

Northend

The oldest Roman Catholic Church in Cape Breton (1828) is across from the ferry terminal. **St Patrick's Church Museum** *(☎ 902-562-8237, 87 Esplanade; admission free; open 9:30am-5:30pm Mon-Sat, 1pm-5:30pm Sun June-Aug)* features the stone church, with its meter-thick walls and a variety of interesting artifacts inside, including the town's whipping post from the mid-19th century.

Cossit House *(☎ 902-539-7973, 75 Charlotte St; admission free; open 9:30am-5:30pm Mon-Sat, 1pm-5:30pm Sun June–mid-Oct)* dates from 1787. The oldest house in Sydney, it's now a museum with period furnishings. Just down the road is the **Jost Heritage House** *(☎ 902-539-0366, 54 Charlotte St; admission free; open 9:30am-5:30pm Mon-Sat June-Oct)*, built in 1790 and now a museum housing a marine exhibit.

In the old neoclassical Lyceum building is the **Cape Breton Centre for Heritage & Science** *(☎ 902-539-1572, 225 George St; admission free; open 10am-4pm Tues-Fri, 1pm-4pm Sat)*. The museum details the human and natural history of this region and houses an art gallery.

Action Week is an annual event held in the first week of August. Festivities include music, sports and various other goings-on.

Sydney Tar Ponds

Just three blocks east of the Charlotte St museums is North America's largest toxic waste site, the notorious Sydney Tar Ponds. From Kia Auto Mall, at the corner of Prince and Dodd Sts, go 700m north on Dodd and Intercolonial Sts keeping right toward Ferry St, which runs directly into the site (entry forbidden). From the gate at the east end of Ferry St you'll get a good view (and smell) of this poisonous pool and the now defunct steel mill, visible beyond a long hill of slag known as the 'High Dump.' The 'Tar Pond' is actually the tidal estuary of Muggah Creek, and toxic wastes are carried out to sea with every tide. A kilometer beyond the mill ruins is a 51-hectare coke-oven site, now just a field of coal-black rubble contaminated to depths of 25m. It's a scene of utter desolation you'll only want to see once in your life.

From the founding of the Sydney steel mill in 1901, some of the world's dirtiest coal was burned to produce coke, and wastes simply accumulated. After the mill became unprofitable in 1967, a Crown corporation took over. The first cleanup attempt began in 1986 but was abandoned after absorbing $55 million in federal and provincial funds. The coke ovens closed in 1988. In 1996 a $20-million scheme to bury the Tar Ponds under a mountain of slag was canceled when alarmingly high levels of PCBs (polychlorinated biphenyls) were discovered. In 2001 the mill was finally shut down, leaving behind 700,000 metric tons of sludge, including an estimated 45,000 tons contaminated with deadly PCBs.

The Nova Scotian and Canadian governments are well aware of the billions of dollars it will cost to clean up the mess, but instead of action, there have been repeated 'studies' to buy time and deflect criticism. Sydney has one of the highest cancer rates in Canada by far, and in May 2001 Canada's minister of health announced that $7 million had been budgeted to evacuate those most affected. Some houses along Intercolonial St carry banners from residents begging to be relocated away from the toxic brew flowing beneath their lawns and leaking into their basements. This disaster zone is right in the middle of Nova Scotia's third-largest city, and the scale of the problem becomes clear after the briefest of visits.

Places to Stay & Eat

University College of Cape Breton (☎ 902-563-1792, fax 902-563-1449, Ⓦ www.uccb.ns.ca,

1250 Grand Lake Rd) Singles/doubles $33/40, students $27, parking $1. Open mid-May–mid-Aug. The college is on the highway to Glace Bay (bus No 1 hourly from Sydney). Sixty rooms with shared bath are available in a student dorm at MacDonald Residence, and the receptionist is on call 24 hours a day during the season.

Royal Hotel (☎ 902-539-2148, 345 Esplanade opposite the Civic Centre) Singles/doubles/triples $40/50/60 with shared bath, singles/doubles $50/55 with private bath, $65 double suite plus $8 for extra persons. This three-story wooden hotel dating from the early 20th century is nicer on the inside than the exterior suggests. There are eight rooms with shared bath, one with private bath and three two-room suites. A small communal kitchen is available for guests. Parking is provided at the rear.

*Park Place B&B (☎ 902-562-3518, fax 902-567-6618, **w** www.bbcanada.com/81 .html, 169 Park St near Brookland St)* Singles/doubles $45/60. Open May-Oct. This B&B in an old Victorian home is located only a few blocks from the Acadian Lines bus station.

Century Manor B&B (☎ 902-567-1300, 212 Whitney Ave) Singles/doubles $45/60. Open May-Oct. Another two-story house, two blocks from Park Place B&B, this one is on an even nicer tree-lined street.

Soup's on Café (☎ 902-539-6483, 16 Pitt St) Breakfast with coffee $3. Open 8am-5pm Mon & Tues, 8am-7pm Wed, 8am-8pm Thur & Fri, 8am-3pm Sat, 9am-2pm Sun. Between Esplanade and Charlotte, this is a popular breakfast place.

Joe's Warehouse Food Emporium (☎ 902-539-6686, 424 Charlotte St) Meals $17-22. Open 11:30am-10pm Mon-Sat, 4pm-10pm Sun (until 11pm July & Aug). This large restaurant has a varied menu featuring steak and seafood. The outdoor back patio has views of the water, and inside there's a cozy little bar called *The Front Office* with plush seating. Joe's is much nicer than the plain exterior lets on.

Jasper's (☎ 902-539-7109, 268 George St at Dorchester) Meals $8-13. This inexpensive 24-hour family restaurant has a large menu.

Entertainment

Smooth Herman's Cabaret (☎ 902-539-0408, Esplanade at Falmouth St) Open 8pm-3:30am Sat-Thur, 4:30pm-3:30am Fri. This huge bar often presents a live band Thursday to Saturday nights ($5 cover charge).

Getting There & Away

Air Air Canada Jazz flies between Sydney and Halifax year-round, while Air Canada flies to Toronto from June to mid-September only. Air St-Pierre (☎ 902-794-4800) flies to the tiny French island of St Pierre near Newfoundland.

An 'airport improvement fee' of $10 (not included in the ticket price) must be paid at a separate counter by all departing passengers.

Bus The Acadian Lines bus depot (☎ 902-564-5533) is away from the center a bit (walkable if necessary), across the street from the big Sydney Shopping Centre Mall on Terminal Dr. It can be hard to find the first time as it isn't visible from Prince St. If you're on foot, go around behind KFC at Prince Street Plaza and you'll see it next to the Ford dealer. It's open 6:30am to 11pm Monday to Friday, 6:30am to 7pm Saturday and Sunday. The infamous Sydney Tar Ponds are adjacent to the station. Coin lockers ($2) are available.

There are buses to Halifax ($60) at 7am, 8:30am and 4:30pm. The two services via Baddeck stop at the ferry terminal in North Sydney. Acadian Lines sometimes has specials on the 8:30am bus to Halifax via St Peters that bring the price down to $41.

To Charlottetown the fare is $89 and a change of buses is required in Truro and Moncton. These connections only work on Friday, Saturday and Sunday. To Moncton ($72) the bus leaves daily at 7am.

Transoverland Ltd (☎ 902-248-2051 in Chéticamp) runs minibuses from Sydney to Baddeck and then north through the Margaree Valley and up the coast to Chéticamp ($12). The buses depart Monday, Wednesday and Friday at 3pm.

Getting Around

There's no city bus service to Sydney Airport (other than the hourly Glace Bay buses which pass on the highway 1.5km from the terminal). A taxi to Sydney is $14 for the whole car, or $7.50/9 to a hotel/residence for a shared taxi. Avis, Budget, Hertz and National have car rental desks at the airport, but they are only open if reservations have been made.

Transit Cape Breton (☎ 902-539-8124) operates several bus routes around the region between North Sydney and Glace Bay. Those of most interest to travelers are the No 5 bus to North Sydney (four or five a day) and hourly bus No 1 to Glace Bay via the University and Dominion. The corner of Dorchester and George Sts is the beginning point in Sydney (no buses on Sunday).

You can rent a car from Budget (☎ 902-564-2610, 501 Esplanade), near the Civic Centre.

A caveat: Sydney's parking sentinels are thought to be omniscient. They will ticket you. The meters take 50¢ an hour from 8am to 6pm weekdays; at other times, parking is free.

GLACE BAY

As part of the Sydney area's industrial region, the difficulties of the Cape Bretoners are reflected here. The district has a long, bitter history of work with low pay and poor conditions – when there is any work at all – and it regularly has one of the highest unemployment rates in the country. Glace Bay's coal-mining tradition is over. The mines are now shut and the population has decreased.

The **Miners' Museum** (☎ 902-849-4522, 42 Birkley St; complete tour $8; open 10am-6pm daily June-Aug, 9am-4pm Mon-Fri other months), off South St, less than 2km east from the town center in Quarry Point, provides a look at the history of local coal mining. It features equipment displays and a re-created village depicting a miner's life at the beginning of the 20th century. The highlight, though, is an hour-long underground tour led by a retired miner that includes walking in the tunnel. It costs less if you forgo the mine visit, but don't.

The **Marconi National Historic Site** (☎ 902-842-2530, Timmerman St, Table Head; admission free; open 10am-6pm daily June–mid-Sept) marks the place where, in 1902, Italian Guglielmo Marconi sent the first wireless message across the Atlantic, to Cornwall, England. The site has a model of the original transmitting station along with other information on the developments in communications that followed.

LOUISBOURG
pop 1300

At the edge of the ocean on an excellent harbor sits Louisbourg, the largest of the region's fishing towns and now famous for its adjacent historic fort. There are a couple of other things to see in the village as well.

In July and August there's usually a shuttle service between Sydney and Louisbourg costing $25 per person roundtrip. The contact details and schedule vary from year to year, but tourist information offices may know something. Otherwise you'll need to hire a taxi or rent a car for the trip.

The **Sydney & Louisbourg Railway Museum** (☎ 902-733-2720, 7336 Main St; admission free; open 9am-5pm daily June & Sept–mid-Oct, 8am-7pm daily July & Aug), which includes the tourist office, is at the entrance to the town. The museum has displays pertaining to the railway, which ran up to Sydney from 1895 until 1968, shuttling fish one way and coal the other.

Places to Stay & Eat

Mira River Provincial Park (☎ 902-563-3373, **w** parks.gov.ns.ca, off Brickyard Rd, 2km east of the bridge at Albert Bridge) Sites $18. Open mid-May–early Oct. This campground between Louisbourg and Sydney offers the closest nature camping to either place. There's a beach on the Mira River, but the motorboats can be noisy. A half-dozen small private campgrounds are along Hwy 22 from Sydney.

Louisbourg Motorhome RV Park (☎ 902-733-3631, fax 902-733-3140, **w** louisbourg.com/motorhomepark, 24 Harbourfront Crescent) Without/with hookups $10/15. Open mid-May–Oct. This place is right on the harbor just below the Louisbourg Playhouse. Most sites are for RVs, but there's also a grassy tenting area with covered picnic tables.

Stacey House B&B (☎ 888-924-2242, **e** geraldine.beaver@ns.sympatico.ca, 7438 Main St) Singles/doubles $50/65. Open June-Oct. Four rooms are available in this attractive two-story house with green shutters near the east entrance to town.

Greta Gross B&B (☎ 902-733-2833, **e** bantama@atcon.com, 48 Pepperell St) Singles/doubles $35/45. Open May-Oct. This two-story house is directly back from Stacey House B&B.

Kathy's B&B (☎ 902-733-2264, 18 Upper Warren St) Singles/doubles $40/45. Open June-Sept. Kathy's is just up from the post office. It's the large two-story house with a widow's walk on the roof.

Garden Sanctuary B&B (☎ 902-733-3497, 7590 Main St) Singles/doubles $40/45. This large yellow two-story house is at the west end of town toward the fortress.

Fortress View Restaurant (☎ 902-733-3131, 7513 Main St) Meals $6-7. Open 8am-8pm daily mid-May–June & Sept–mid-Oct, 7am-9pm July & Aug. This place looks upscale from outside, but you can get fish and chips for $6-7 and hamburgers for $4-5.

Entertainment

Louisbourg Playhouse (☎ 902-733-2996, 11 Lower Warren St) On the waterfront, behind the fire station, is this theater built as a set for the Walt Disney movie *Indian Warrior* in 1993. The playhouse is now Louisbourg's permanent performing arts center and hosts a variety of plays during the year. The musical *Spirit of the Island* runs weeknights at 8pm from July to mid-September (adult/senior/child $14/12/5), with various guest vocalists and other performances on weekends.

LOUISBOURG NATIONAL HISTORIC SITE

This extraordinary historic site (☎ 902-733-2280, 259 Park Service Rd; adult/family $11/24.50 June-Sept, $4.50/11.25 May & early Oct; open 9:30am-5pm daily June & Sept, 9:30am-5pm daily May & early Oct, 9am-7pm daily July & Aug) is about 50km south of Sydney on the southeast tip of Cape Breton Island and is well worth the trek. The entrance to the fortress is 2.5km beyond the Railway Museum tourist office in town.

After the Treaty of Utrecht in 1713, the French lost their bases in Newfoundland and mainland Nova Scotia. This left them Prince Edward Island, the islands of St Pierre and Miquelon, and Cape Breton Island, which became the conduit for exporting cod to France and, later, a new military base. Louisbourg, a massive walled fort and village complex, was worked on continually from 1719 to about 1745. It looked daunting but was poorly designed, and the British took it in 46 days during 1745 when it was barely finished. It would change hands twice more. In 1760, after British troops under the command of General James Wolfe (leader of the Louisbourg onslaught) took Québec City, the walls of Louisbourg were destroyed and the city was burned to the ground.

In 1961, with the closing of many Cape Breton coal mines, the federal government began a make-work project – the largest historical reconstruction in Canadian history – and Louisbourg rose from its ashes. Today the site depicts in remarkable detail what French life was like here in the 1700s. All the workers, in period dress, have taken on the lives of typical fort inhabitants. Ask them anything – what the winters are like, what that tool is for, who they had an affair with – and they'll tell you. (And Anglophones are 'harassed' as spies by the French guards at the gates!)

You'll need a lot of time to see the park properly – plan on spending a minimum of half a day at the site. The best times to visit are in the morning, when there's more going on and fewer tourists, and during June or September. Take in the movie in the interpretive center first. Free guided tours around the site are offered through the day; cannons are fired four times daily.

The weather here is very changeable and usually bad. Take a sweater and raincoat even if it's sunny when you start out, and be prepared for lots of walking. As well as the fort area itself, there are hiking trails around the grounds and out to the Atlantic coast.

Admission seems steep but the fort is well worth it. This isn't just one museum or historic house but an entire town! The revenue Parks Canada collects from visitors is barely sufficient to maintain the large complex.

Three restaurants here serve food typical of the time. One place has hamburgers or sandwiches for $4, but it's worth splurging on a real 18th-century meal at the **Grandchamps House** ($7-10, including tea or coffee). The servers will be dressed in period costume, and in midsummer you'll need to wait awhile just to get a table. Otherwise buy a 1kg loaf of soldiers' bread at the **Destouches Bakery**. It's delicious; one piece with cheese makes a full meal.

BADDECK

An old resort town in a pastoral setting, Baddeck is on the north shore of the saltwater Bras d'Or Lake, halfway between Sydney and the Canso Causeway. The name Baddeck comes from the Mi'kmaq word

Apatakwitk, and Bras d'Or is French for 'Golden Arm.' Chebucto St is the main thoroughfare, but the lake itself is what makes Baddeck special.

An excellent tourist office (☎ 902-295-1911) sits on the corner of Chebucto and Twining Sts in the center of Baddeck. It's open 9am to 5pm daily June to mid-October and 9am to 8:30pm July and August.

The Baddeck public library (☎ 902-295-2055, 520 Chebucto St) offers Internet access for a donation. It's available 1pm to 5pm Monday, 1pm to 5pm and 6pm to 8pm Tuesday and Friday, 5pm to 8pm Thursday and 10am to noon and 1pm to 5pm Saturday.

Alexander Graham Bell National Historic Site

Alexander Graham Bell, the inventor of the telephone, had a summer home called Beinn Bhreagh near Baddeck. It's visible to the left across the bay from the present historic site but cannot be visited as Bell's descendants still live there. Alexander Graham himself is buried at Beinn Bhreagh.

Parks Canada operates this large museum (☎ 902-295-2069, Chebucto St; admission $4.25; open 9am-8pm daily July & Aug, 9am-6pm June & Sept, 9am-5pm Oct-May) covering all aspects of this remarkable man's inventions and innovations. Written explanations, models, photographs and objects detail his varied works. On display are his medical and electrical devices, telegraphs, telephones, kites and seaplanes. You'll need at least two hours if you want to view all three exhibit halls.

Kidston Island

This micro-island just offshore serves as a park for Baddeck. It has a fine swimming beach, some nature trails and a lighthouse dating from 1915. In July and August the Baddeck Lions Club operates a free pontoon boat that makes the short trip between Government Wharf and the island. The boat leaves every 20 minutes from 10am to 6pm on weekdays and noon to 6pm on weekends.

Organized Tours

On Water St, along the waterfront, Government Wharf is lined with pleasure craft, sailing boats and tour boats offering cruises around Bras d'Or Lake. One of them,

Amoeba Sailing Tours (☎ 902-295-2481; tours $20; open May-Sept), offers four tours daily on its tall-mast sailboat. **Loch Bhreagh Boat Tours** (☎ 902-295-2016; adult/child $20/10; open June-mid-Oct) offers the same on a powerboat.

Places to Stay & Eat

KOA Kampground (☎ 800-562-7452, fax 902-295-2288, ⓦ www.koa.com/where/ns/54104.htm, off Hwy 105) Without/with hookups $19/24-26, cabins $38. Open mid-May–mid-Oct. This attractive campground 9km west of Baddeck on Hwy 105 and 1km east of the beginning of the Cabot Trail is 700m off the highway. Facilities include a store, restaurant, pool and laundromat, and there's lots of shade. The three camping cabins are a good value. In July and August KOA fills up.

Heidi's B&B (☎ 902-295-1301, 64 Old Margaree Rd) Rooms $50. Open June-Oct. Just past the hospital, this castlelike house is a long block up the hill from the tourist office.

Sarah Jean's B&B (☎ 888-515-0552, fax 902-295-3162, ⓔ mary.macdonald@ns.sympatico.ca, 18 High St) Rooms from $50, including a full breakfast. This large two-story house is up Twining St from the tourist office.

Restawyle Tourist Home (☎ 902-295-3253, 231 Shore Rd) Doubles $55. Open mid-May–mid-Oct. Just west of town, this large three-story restored house with a deck in front has four rooms.

Village Kitchen Café (☎ 902-295-3200, 474 Chebucto St) Breakfast/dinner $4/8. Open 7am-9pm daily June-Sept, 11am-9pm or 11am-7pm other months. Just off the main street, this is a spot for an eggs-and-toast breakfast, or in the evening the 'Fish & Stein.' It's good home cooking at local prices, and this is one of the few places that stay open all winter.

Highwheeler Café/Deli/Bakery (☎ 902-295-3006, 486 Chebucto St) Open 6am-7pm daily May–mid-Oct. Deli sandwiches $5. This Baddeck eatery offers some inexpensive possibilities while maintaining high standards. The menu lists a mouthwatering selection of sandwiches, salads and bakery items. It's a good choice for breakfast, as it opens at 6am with coffee and a vast array of baked goods.

Getting There & Around

All buses out of town depart from the Irving gas station (☎ 902-295-1616) on Hwy 105, 2.5km west of central Baddeck via Shore Rd.

Acadian Lines buses serve Baddeck along their Halifax to Sydney run. Buses arrive from Sydney daily at 8:35am and 5:50pm, continuing on to Antigonish, Truro and Halifax. Toward Sydney, the bus leaves at the inconvenient hour of 7:30pm daily. Fares are $24 to Antigonish, $13 to Sydney, $55 to Halifax.

Also from Baddeck, Transoverland Ltd buses run north through the Margaree Valley and then up the coast to Chéticamp on Monday, Wednesday and Friday. They leave for Sydney around 9:30am, toward Chéticamp around 3:30pm year-round.

WHYCOCOMAGH

The **Negemow Basket Shop** (☎ 902-756-3491, 9217 Hwy 105), at the Waycobah First Nation just west of Whycocomagh, sells Mi'kmaq crafts. Rod's One Stop next door pumps some of the cheapest gas on Cape Breton Island.

In Whycocomagh the Acadian Lines buses stop at Vi's Restaurant (☎ 902-756-2338), at the junction of Hwys 105 and 252 opposite the Irving gas station. The Mabou River Hostel will pick you up here for $10 if you let them know in advance (the 1:30pm bus from Halifax arrives here at 7pm).

Whycocomagh Provincial Park (☎ 902-756-2448, W parks.gov.ns.ca, 9729 Hwy 105) Sites $18. Open early June-Aug. Just 2km east of Whycocomagh, this is the only provincial park offering camping on this side of Cape Breton Island. There are some nice sites on the hillside above the Trans Canada, as well as a cooking shelter and a trail to the Look-Off. Sites are usually available, even in midsummer.

ST PETER'S

pop 730

This bustling little town is on a narrow strip separating the Atlantic Ocean and Bras d'Or Lake along Hwy 4. A variety of stores and places to eat are along the main street.

The Tourism Cape Breton information office (☎ 902-535-2185) is open 9am to 5pm daily mid-June to September. It's on Hwy 4, 700m east of the St Peter's Canal.

The daily Acadian Lines bus from Sydney stops at Joe Pops Store (☎ 902-535-3349, 9982 Hwy 4), in the center of St Peter's, less than a kilometer west of the bridge over the canal.

The **St Peter's Canal** (☎ 902-535-2118; admission free), built in the 1850s, includes a 91m, double-gate lock to allow vessels to move between the different water levels of the lake and the ocean. Parks Canada provides an outdoor exhibit explaining the lock and the history of the canal.

The best view of the canal is from the platform opposite the **Nicolas Denys Museum** (☎ 902-535-2379, 46 Denys St; admission 50¢; open 9am-5pm daily June-Sept). The museum has old photos of the area and a few artifacts.

Treasure Hollow Gift Shop (☎ 902-535-3212, 9856 Hwy 4; open 10am-5pm Mon-Sat, 1pm-5pm Sun May-Sept), in the center of town, rents sit-on-top kayaks at $7/20/35 an hour/half day/full day plus tax for a single, or $10/25/40 for a double.

Battery Provincial Park (☎ 902-535-3094, W parks.gov.ns.ca, 10110 Hwy 4) Sites $14. Open early June-Aug. This uncrowded park occupies the east side of the St Peter's Canal. The park has no showers but does have hiking trails, a small beach and some nice shady sites. It's seldom full, even in midsummer, and makes a great base for canoeists and kayakers, who can paddle through the locks at no charge weekdays from mid-May to October.

MacDonald Hotel (☎ 902-535-2997, fax 902-535-3686, 9383 Pepperell St) Rooms with one bed $40 single or double ($30 off-season), with two beds $50 for up to four people. Open mid-June–early Oct. This historic three-story hotel is behind the Irving gas station on Hwy 4 in the center of St Peter's, a two-minute walk from the Acadian Lines bus stop. Aside from the six rooms and nice little bar, the hotel restaurant serves lunch specials in the $7 range. The dinner menu features scallops ($16), salmon ($15) and halibut ($15).

NOVA SCOTIA

Getting There & Around

All buses out of town depart from the bus station (☎ 902-295-1610) on Hwy 105, 2.5km west of central Baddeck, via Sheep Rd.

Acadian Lines buses serve Baddeck along their Halifax to Sydney run. Buses arrive from Sydney daily at 9.20am and 6.30pm, continuing on to Antigonish, Truro and Halifax. Inbound Sydney, the bus leaves at the inconvenient hour of 12.40pm daily. Fares are $24 to Antigonish, $43 to Sydney, $55 to Halifax.

Also from Baddeck, Transoverland Ltd buses run north through the Margaree Valley and then to the coastal Cheticamp on Monday, Wednesday and Friday. They leave for Sydney around 8.30am to Ingonish around 3.45pm year-round.

WHYCOCOMAGH

The Reezanov Basket Shop (☎ 902-756-2911, Hwy 105), at the Waycobah First Nation, just west of Whycocomagh, sells gift items crafts, Rod's. One stop next door pumps some of the cheapest gas on Cape Breton Island.

In Whycocomagh, the Acadian Lines bus stop at Vi's Restaurant (☎ 902-756-2581), at the junction of Hwys 105 and 252, opposite the Irving gas station. The Mabou River Hostel will pick you up here for $10 if you let them know in advance (the 4.40pm bus from Halifax arrives here at 7pm).

Whycocomagh Provincial Park (☎ 902-756-2448, ☎ parkscanvse 723v Hwy 105) offers 94 sites. Open early June–Aug. The 30km part of Whycocomagh this is the only provincial park offering camping on this side of the whole Breton Island. There are some nice sites but the inlands are a bit distant to reach, as are the secluded shelters and a trail to the Look-Off. Sites are usually available even in mid-summer.

ST PETER'S

pop 229

This bustling little town is on a narrow strip separating the Atlantic Ocean and Bras d'Or Lake around Hwy 4. A variety of stores and places to eat are along the main street.

The Tourism Cape Breton Information office (☎ 902-535-2185) is open 9am to 9pm daily mid-mid-June to September. It's on Hwy 4, 30m east of the St Peter's Canal.

The daily Acadian Lines bus from Sydney stops at the Kwik-Stop (☎ 902-535-3133, 9842 Hwy 4) in the center of St Peter's less than a kilometer west of the bridge over the canal.

The St Peter's Canal (☎ 902-535-2118, off on the Hwy), built in the 1850s includes a 91m-long stone lock to allow vessels to move between the different water levels of the lake and the ocean. Parks Canada provides an outdoor exhibit explaining the lock and a history of the canal.

The Reserve near of the canal is upon the hill top opposite the Nicolas Denys Museum (☎ 902-535-2379, 46 Denys Street, admission $2/ entry time 9am-5pm daily June). The museum has old photos of the area and a few artifacts.

Treasure Hollow Gift Shop (☎ 902-535-2772, 9836 Hwy 4) offers 18-member Main Sat 9am–5pm Sun Hwy Sept) in the center of town, rents ski on-top kayaks at $7/$9.50 an hour/half day) and lay pays tax for a single or $11/$24.00 for a double.

Battery Provincial Park (☎ 902-535-3094, www.parkscanv.caz, Hwy 4 Hwy) Sites $14. Open early June, Aug. This uncrowded park occupies the east side of the St Peter's Canal. The park has no showers but does have fishing trails, a small beach and some nice shady sites. It's seldom full, even in mid-summer, and makes a great base for a paddlers and kayakers who can paddle through the locks at no charge weekdays from mid-May to October.

MacDonald Hotel (☎ 902-535-3676, 902-535-2935, 9909 Hwy 4, 10-15 Pepperell St). Rooms with one bed $40 single or double $50 or two-persons with two beds $50-kin up to four people. Constructed at dawn from a Cape Town, has four three-story hotel's behind the Irving gas station on Hwy 4 in the center of St Peter's. A two-minute walk from the Acadian Lines bus stop (☎ 902-535-2) from the six rooms and after little lively-bar, the hotel restaurant serves lunch specials at $6-8? value. The dinner menu features scallops ($16) salmon ($15) and halibut ($16).

Prince Edward Island

A tenth the size of Nova Scotia, Prince Edward Island (PEI) is Canada's smallest and most densely populated province. You'd never guess it, however, since it's rural and the towns aren't big at all, though countless little-used roads crisscross every segment of land. This province fits the image of the English countryside: roads winding gently between bright red fields and through manicured villages of neat wooden houses and gardens.

Away from the tourist centers, the pace of life is slow. Laws prohibiting billboards further add to the old-country flavor of the island. Indeed, in some ways it has changed little from the descriptions in the internationally famous novel *Anne of Green Gables*, written here by Lucy Maud Montgomery in the early 20th century.

Three equal-size counties make up the island: Prince in the west, Queens in the middle and Kings in the east. Each county has a scenic road network mapped out by the tourist bureau. Though far from the only options, these routes do take in the better-known attractions and the historical and geographical points of note. The 'Kings Byway' circles the east side of the island, the 'Blue Heron' loops around the center and the 'Lady Slipper' reaches the westernmost shores of PEI.

As in the other Maritime provinces, the visiting season is short. Many attractions, tour operations and guesthouses are open only during the two midsummer months of July and August. From early September to mid-June facilities are closed, signs are taken down and access roads to many parks and sights are blocked with barriers.

Yet those who go during spring (until mid-June) and fall (after the first week of September) will find discounted room prices, a serene atmosphere and fairly mild temperatures – quite a contrast to July and August, when for eight short weeks the island is suddenly jam-packed. Toward the end of July and in early August, all accommodations will be full and reservations become almost essential.

History

Aboriginal peoples arrived here about 11,000 years ago, before the island separated

Highlights

Entered Confederation: July 1, 1873
Area: 5700 sq km
Population: 138,900
Provincial Capital: Charlottetown

- Spend time in Charlottetown, the birthplace of Canadian confederation.

- Take in a ceilidh with traditional music and dance.

- See the House of Green Gables at Cavendish, the setting for the novel *Anne of Green Gables*.

- Enjoy a summer day on a north coast beach.

- Dine out on casual, delicious lobster suppers, often held in church halls.

- Hike or peddle along the Confederation Trail, an old railway line that is now a bicycle route.

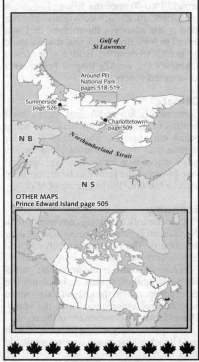

from the mainland. The Mi'kmaq, a branch of the Algonquin nations, arrived at about the time of Christ.

In 1534 Jacques Cartier of France was the first European to record seeing the island. Settlement didn't begin for another 200 years. The initially small French colony grew somewhat with the British expulsion of the Acadians from Nova Scotia in the 1750s. In 1758 the victorious British also expelled 3000 Acadians from Île St Jean, the former French name for Prince Edward Island.

After the Treaty of Paris in 1763, the island became British and was renamed Island of St John. In 1769 St John became self-governing, and in 1799 the name was changed to honor Edward, duke of Kent (son of King George III and father of Queen Victoria). In the early 1800s there was a marked rise in population, with immigrants from the British Isles.

Prince Edward Island joined Confederation in 1873, deciding to forgo its independence for the economic benefits of union. The population has remained stable at around 140,000 since the 1930s.

In 1997, after much debate and protests among the islanders themselves, PEI was linked to New Brunswick and the mainland by the Confederation Bridge – at almost 13km, it's the world's longest bridge over ice-covered waters.

Climate

Conveniently, July and August are the driest months of a fairly damp year. The warm ocean currents give the island a milder climate than most of Canada, and the sea gets warm enough for swimming in midsummer. In winter the snow can be meters deep and can last until the beginning of May.

Economy

PEI is primarily a farming community, with the main crop, potatoes, being sold all over the country. The rich, distinctively red, soil is the secret, the locals say.

Fishing, of course, is also important, particularly for lobsters, oysters and herring. The lobster suppers held throughout the province have become synonymous with the island. Mussel farms are common along the coast.

The quiet, gently rolling hills edged with good beaches have made tourism a reliable moneymaker.

Population & People

Europeans of French, Scottish and Irish background make up nearly 90% of the population. French-speakers live in the area from Miscouche to Mont Carmel. Some 1000 Mi'kmaqs also live on Prince Edward Island.

Information

Tourist Offices For useful information, contact the head office of Tourism PEI (☎ 902-368-5540, 888-734-7529, ⓦ www.peiplay.com, PO Box 940, Charlottetown C1A 7M5). There are 11 provincial tourist offices around the island, open 9am to 4:30pm daily June to mid-October (8am to 9pm in July and August). From mid-October to May the only offices open are in Charlottetown and the ersatz 'traditional' PEI Gateway Village complex at the foot of Confederation Bridge.

Taxes The provincial sales tax is 10%, added to the 7% GST.

Email & Internet Access A dozen Access PEI offices around the province provide free Internet access on a first-come, first-served basis. You can also obtain free Internet access at all public libraries.

Emergency For emergency service dial ☎ 911 from anywhere in the province.

Activities

Cycling With its winding country roads, gently rolling hills and short distances between towns, PEI is one of Canada's most popular destinations for cyclists. Hills rarely exceed a 30-degree incline or 1km in length, and the highest point on the island, at Springton, is only 142m.

The grandaddy of trails in the Maritimes is the Confederation Trail, a 350km stone dust multiuse trail stretching from Tignish to Elmira along railway lines abandoned in 1989. The prevailing winds on PEI blow from the west or southwest, and you should also cycle in that direction if possible.

See the Charlottetown Getting Around section, later in this chapter, for bike rental information.

Kayaking Ocean kayaking has taken off around PEI in recent years. From mid-June to mid-September kayak tours are offered

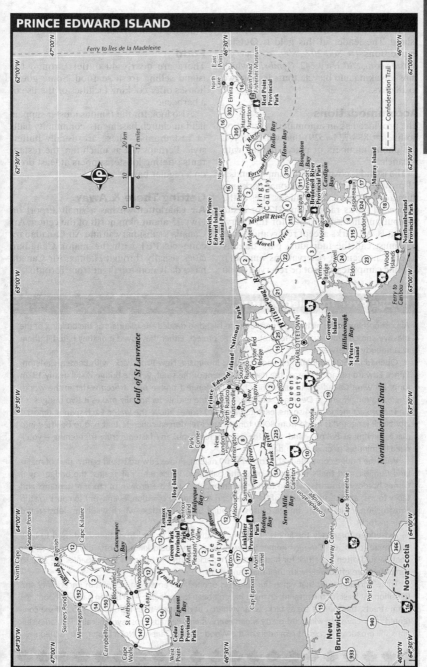

at North Rustico, South Rustico, Brudenell River Provincial Park, Souris and Lennox Island. The leader in this field is **Outside Expeditions** (☎ *800-207-3899*, W *www.get outside.com, 890 Hwy 242, Cymbria*) which runs kayaking and bicycle tours lasting two to 18 days.

Accommodations
The province has an automated reservation hotline (☎ 888-734-7529) that will give you the phone numbers of places to stay with vacancies.

The island is covered with campgrounds – 13 provincial parks, one national park and numerous private campgrounds. Fees at the provincial parks range from $17 for a site without any hookups to $23 for fully serviced sites. All parks accept reservations, but you must call the individual park directly (there's no central reservations number). Specific campsites cannot be reserved – you have to accept whatever site happens to be available upon arrival.

Food
There are nearly 40 outlets around the island selling fresh seafood. Some guesthouses offer cooking facilities or the use of a barbecue.

Also look for the famous lobster suppers held in church basements, community halls or restaurants – these are usually buffet-style. Perhaps not as much fun, the restaurants offering lobster suppers at least do so on a regular basis.

Getting There & Away
Air Charlottetown has a small airport on Hwy 15 about 6km north of the center. Air Canada's subsidiary airline Air Canada Jazz connects PEI with the major Canadian cities, usually through Halifax. Air Canada has a daily nonstop flight from Toronto.

Bridge over Troubled Waters

Almost nothing in the history of Prince Edward Island so divided the islanders as the building of the massive and controversial Confederation Bridge project. Either they loved it or they hated it; there was nobody in between.

Opened in 1997, the bridge connects Cape Jourimain, New Brunswick, with Borden-Carleton, Prince Edward Island. It crosses the narrowest point of the strait, yet the bridge is still nearly 13km long, allowing Canadians to claim they have the longest bridge over frozen water in the world. There is a longer one in Denmark, but an island in the middle technically makes it two bridges.

The project includes 44 spans, each towering 20 stories above the water. Each span is almost a city block long and is made from 8000 tons of steel-reinforced concrete that had to be lifted into place. Driving at 80kph – and, with the wind behind you, any faster is truly frightening – you'll need 12 minutes to cross the bridge.

With the bridge completed, at a cost of $900 million, Prince Edward Island is now part of mainland Canada, and that's the source of all the ballyhoo. Those who rail against the bridge say it carries hordes of tourists, who in turn bring crime, litter and the growth of chain restaurants and tacky tourist attractions. Friends of the Island, an anti-bridge coalition, even went to court to stop construction, claiming the bridge causes ice build-up in the strait, which will harm lobster and scallop stocks.

Pro-bridge forces say the link is necessary because travel to and from the island used to be a nightmare for locals. During summer the wait for a ferry would kill most of a day, and in winter boats would often get stuck for hours in the ice pack. With the bridge, PEI companies are able to compete more effectively with their mainland rivals.

There's no argument that when the toll gates opened, PEI entered a new era of uncertainty and transition. At least for the present, changes haven't been too palpable – no brazen packs of hoodlums roam streets, the tourists are as tacky as anywhere but no worse than before and you still see contented moo-cows chewing cud pretty much everywhere. Perhaps most symbolically, PEI radio stations still broadcast incessant reminders of the Wood Islands–Caribou, Nova Scotia, ferry schedule.

Bus See the Charlottetown Getting There & Away section for information on the SMT bus service from Moncton and the various van services from Halifax.

Car & Motorcycle Confederation Bridge (☎ 902-437-7300, w www.confederationbridge .com) makes getting there faster, easier and cheaper. Traffic can access the bridge 24 hours a day, seven days a week; sadly, the 1.1m-high guardrails steal away any panorama you'd hoped for. The toll is $37 per car and all passengers and is only collected as you leave PEI.

Bicycle riders and pedestrians are banned from the bridge and must use a free, demand-driven shuttle service. On the PEI side, go to the Bridge Operations Building near the toll gates; on the New Brunswick side, look for the Bridge Facility Building at the junction of Hwys 16 and 955. You're not supposed to have to wait more than two hours for the shuttle at any time.

Ferry The remaining ferry service to PEI links Wood Islands (in the eastern section of PEI province) to Caribou, Nova Scotia. It doesn't operate from mid-December to April. The 22km trip takes 1¼ hours and costs $49 for a car and all passengers, $11 per person for pedestrians or $20 for a bicycle and cyclist. In summer there are eight runs in each direction daily; boats leave seven times a day in September. You only pay as you're leaving PEI; the trip over from Nova Scotia is free. Contact Northumberland Ferries Ltd (☎ 888-249-7245, w www.nfl-bay.com) for information. It's first-come, first-served (no reservations taken).

The other ferry service is from Souris to the Îles de la Madeleine in Québec. For information about it, see Getting There & Away in the Îles de la Madeleine section of the Québec chapter.

Charlottetown

pop 33,000

Charlottetown – or 'Ch'town' – is an old, quiet country town that also happens to be the historic provincial capital. Established in 1763, it's named after Charlotte, Queen of Great Britain and Ireland (1744–1818).

In 1864 discussions to unite Canada were first held here. An agreement was reached in 1867, when the Dominion of Canada was born, and Charlottetown later became known as the birthplace of Canada. It's Canada's smallest provincial capital, with a downtown area so compact that everything is within walking distance. The slow-paced, tree-lined colonial and Victorian streets make Charlottetown the perfect urban center for this gentle and bucolic island. In July and August the streets are bustling with visitors, but things are rather quiet out of season.

Orientation

University Ave is the city's main street; it ends at the entire block taken up by Province House and the Confederation Centre of the Arts complex.

A block west along Grafton St is Queen St, parallel to University Ave. This is the other main street of Charlottetown and of more interest to visitors. During summer the first block of Richmond St east of Queen St becomes a gentrified pedestrian mall called Victoria Row.

From Richmond St south to the waterfront is Old Charlottetown. A number of buildings sport plaques giving a bit of their history and the date of construction. Great George St, running downhill from Province House, is Charlottetown's most monumental street, lined with late-19th-century mansions.

At the foot of Great George St, south of Water St, is Peake's Wharf and Confederation Landing. This redeveloped waterfront area is often the focal point of city festivals. The main tourist information center is nearby.

West of town is the large Victoria Park, with a broad promenade running along its edge and the bay.

Information

Tourist Offices The tourist office (☎ 902-368-4444, 178 Water St) for Charlottetown and the main office for the whole island is in the Stone Cottage, near Founders Hall at the foot of Hillsborough St. It's one of the few tourist offices in the Maritimes open year-round: 8am to 10pm daily July and August, 9am to 6pm daily in the shoulder seasons, 9am to 4:30pm weekdays from early October to mid-May. Inside are courtesy phones to make local reservations.

Money In addition to regular banking hours, TD Canada Trust (☎ 902-629-2265, 192 Queen St at Kent St), is open 9am to 3pm Saturday; it's the only bank in town open weekends.

Post The central post office (☎ 902-628-4400, 135 Kent St, Charlottetown C1A 1M0) holds general delivery mail. It's open 8am to 5:15pm weekdays.

Email & Internet Access The Confederation Public Library (☎ 902-368-4642, Queen St between Victoria Row and Grafton St) provides free Internet access; it's possible to book a time slot. It's open 10am to 9pm Tuesday to Thursday, 10am to 5pm Friday and Saturday, 1pm to 5pm Sunday.

Laundry Downtown Convenience (☎ 902-368-1684, 54 Queen St), has a satellite TV–equipped laundromat in the basement. It's $1.25 to wash or dry. Check out the 99¢ ice cream cones upstairs. The store's open 10am to 10pm weekdays, 11am to 10pm Saturday, 11am to 9pm Sunday.

Other laundromats (with easier parking) are at 236 and 251 University Ave on the north side of town.

Medical Services The Polyclinic Professional Center (☎ 902-629-8810, 199 Grafton St) is an after hours walk-in medical clinic open 5:30pm to 8pm Monday to Friday and 9:30am to noon Saturday. Any Canadian provincial health card will be accepted here, but foreigners must pay a $40 fee. Appointments are not required. The tourist office will know about other walk-in clinics of this kind.

Province House

This neoclassical, three-story, sandstone building (☎ 902-566-7626, 165 Richmond St; admission free; open 9am-5pm daily June-Sept, 9am-5pm Mon-Fri Oct-May) is both a national historic site and the seat of the current Provincial Legislature. The Confederation Chamber on the 2nd floor is known as the 'birthplace of Canada,' for it was here in 1864 that the 23 representatives of the British North American colonies began working out the details for forming the Dominion of Canada.

This room and a couple of others have been restored to what they looked like in 1864. Inside or perhaps out at the entrance, you may also see workers in period costumes, each representing one of the original founders. At 11:15am, 2:15pm and 4:15pm daily from July to early September, there is a 'fathers of confederation' reenactment. A 15-minute film can be seen on the 1st floor.

St Dunstan's Basilica

This large neo-Gothic basilica (☎ 902-894-3486, 45 Great George St at Dorchester; free admission; open 8am-5pm daily) is south of Province House. Built in 1898, the town's main Catholic church is unexpectedly ornate inside, painted in an unusual style.

Founders Hall

This new attraction (☎ 902-368-1864, ⓦ www.foundershall.ca, 8 Prince St; adult/senior/youth/family $7.50/6/4/19; open 8:30am-8pm daily June-early Oct, 10am-4pm Tues-Sat early Oct-May) opened in 2001 in a former railway building at the foot of Prince St. The multimedia exhibits showcase Canada's history since the 1864 Charlottetown Conference.

Beaconsfield House

This beautiful yellow Victorian mansion (☎ 902-368-6603, 2 Kent St; admission $3.50; open 9am-5pm Tues-Sun mid-June–early Sept, 10am-4pm Tues-Sun rest of the year) was built in 1877. It is now the headquarters of the PEI Museum and has 11 historically furnished rooms. During summer guided tours are given and afternoon tea is served on the large verandah.

Government House

Across Kent St is Victoria Park and Government House, another beautiful old mansion. This one has been used as the official residence of PEI's lieutenant governor since 1835. No visitors are allowed.

From here, follow the wooden boardwalk to **Old Battery Point**, where six cannon point toward the entrance to Charlottetown harbor. This is one of the city's most beautiful corners.

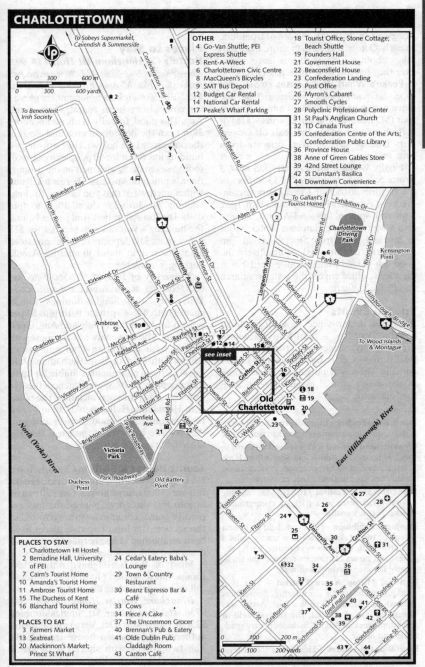

CHARLOTTETOWN

To Sobeys Supermarket, Cavendish & Summerside

To Benevolent Irish Society

To Gallant's Tourist Home

Charlottetown Driving Park

Kensington Point

To Wood Islands & Montague

North (Yorke) River

East (Hillsborough) River

Victoria Park

Duchess Point

Old Battery Point

Old Charlottetown

see inset

OTHER
4 Go-Van Shuttle; PEI Express Shuttle
5 Rent-A-Wreck
6 Charlottetown Civic Centre
8 MacQueen's Bicycles
9 SMT Bus Depot
12 Budget Car Rental
14 National Car Rental
17 Peake's Wharf Parking
18 Tourist Office; Stone Cottage; Beach Shuttle
19 Founders Hall
21 Government House
22 Beaconsfield House
23 Confederation Landing
25 Post Office
26 Myron's Cabaret
27 Smooth Cycles
28 Polyclinic Professional Center
31 St Paul's Anglican Church
32 TD Canada Trust
35 Confederation Centre of the Arts; Confederation Public Library
36 Province House
38 Anne of Green Gables Store
39 42nd Street Lounge
42 St Dunstan's Basilica
44 Downtown Convenience

PLACES TO STAY
1 Charlottetown HI Hostel
2 Bernadine Hall, University of PEI
7 Cairn's Tourist Home
10 Amanda's Tourist Home
11 Ambrose Tourist Home
15 The Duchess of Kent
16 Blanchard Tourist Home

PLACES TO EAT
3 Farmers Market
13 Seatreat
20 Mackinnon's Market; Prince St Wharf
24 Cedar's Eatery; Baba's Lounge
29 Town & Country Restaurant
30 Beanz Espresso Bar & Café
33 Cows
34 Piece A Cake
37 The Uncommon Grocer
40 Brennan's Pub & Eatery
41 Olde Dublin Pub; Claddagh Room
43 Canton Café

Organized Tours

Bus trips around the island are offered by Abegweit Tours (☎ 902-894-9966) from June to early October. The north shore trip ($60) takes about six hours. Buses leave whenever they have at least three passengers.

Peake's Wharf Boat Cruises (☎ 902-566-4458, 1 Great George St) depart from the marina at the wharf for a 70-minute harbor tour ($15), the 6:30pm sunset cruise ($15) or a 2½-hour tour to see the seals off Governors Island ($21). Cruises operate from June to August.

Finally, **walking tours** (☎ 902-368-1864, 8 Prince St; adult/child under 12 $3.50/free) of the historic district of Charlottetown commence at Founders Hall at 10am, 11am, 1pm, 3pm and 4pm in July and August. There's also a 'Merchants & Mansions' walking tour at 2pm and 'Waterfront Storytelling' at 7pm (same price and months). Alternatively, the good self-guided tour brochure available at the tourist office covers the waterfront area and Peake's Wharf.

Special Events

All across the province, look for the local ceilidhs (**kay**-lee) – mini-festivals where there's always some music (usually of the traditional Celtic-based variety) and dancing. There's usually one a week. Some of the major annual events here include the following:

Jazz & Blues Festival – Bigger every year, this early-May festival features major Canadian performers.

Charlottetown Festival – This festival kicks off in mid-June and lasts until mid-September. It's a theatrical event with free outdoor performances, a children's theater and dance programs.

Blue Grass Music Festival – This two-day camping event takes place at a park or campground. Tickets are not costly.

Provincial Exhibition – This event, held in the first week or two of August, features tractor pulls, a carnival with rides, harness racing, entertainment and games of chance along with the traditional horse and livestock shows.

National Milton Acorn Festival – This is a unique event worth considering. Sometimes known as Canada's People's Poet, Acorn was born and raised on PEI. The festival, held in the third week of August, includes poetry readings and music.

Festival of the Fathers – Held along the historic waterfront in late August, this festival celebrates Charlottetown's history with street musicians, dances, traditional food and a 10-tavern pub crawl.

Places to Stay

Hostels *Charlottetown HI Hostel* (☎ 902-894-9696, fax 902-628-6424, **W** www.isn.net/peihostel, 153 Mount Edward Rd) Beds $15.50/18.50 members/nonmembers plus $1 for compulsory linen rental. Open June-Aug. This good, friendly HI hostel is about 3km from the downtown area and close to the university (see below). The barn-shaped building has room for 50 people in dorms of four to seven beds, with men on the upstairs floor, women downstairs. There's a kitchen with a microwave that you can use for light cooking. The hostel is closed 10am to 4pm daily. The Confederation Trail passes behind the building – you can rent bicycles for $15 a day (plus $10 deposit) or walk into town along the trail in about 30 minutes. Ample parking is available.

University of PEI (☎ 902-566-0486, fax 902-566-0793, **W** www.upei.ca/~housing, 550 University Ave) Singles/doubles $34/39 shared bath, $46/49 private bath, plus $4 per person for breakfast in July and Aug. Open May-Aug. The university offers rooms with shared bath at Marian Hall and larger rooms with twin beds in Bernadine Hall. Two-bedroom apartments suitable for up to four people are $79. Shared kitchenettes are available, and parking is included. The office is in Bernadine Hall (open 24 hours), and reservations are a good idea in July and August. The main disadvantage is the distance from town.

Tourist Homes & B&Bs In Charlottetown B&B-type places that don't provide breakfast are called tourist homes. Over 70 places fit into this category; some of the less expensive homes closer to town are covered in this section. But lots of upscale places have been established in fine heritage homes and decorated with antiques and collectibles.

Most of the B&Bs have only a few rooms, and some don't have signs outside – call up before heading their way.

Blanchard Tourist Home (☎ 902-894-9756, 163 Dorchester St) Singles/doubles $25/30. Open May-Oct. Very central is this authentic old wooden house from 1909. The two rooms with shared bath are a bargain. Daytime parking is rather limited around here, but you're allowed to park overnight on the street.

Ambrose Tourist Home (☎ 902-566-5853, 800-665-6072, 17 Passmore St) Singles/doubles $32/38 ($45 with two beds). Open May-Oct. Six rooms with shared bath are available in this duplex house near downtown. There's also a self-contained apartment ($65).

Amanda's Tourist Home (☎ 902-894-9909, 130 Spring Park Rd) Rooms $30. There are two rooms with shared bath in this large two-story house with ample parking.

Cairn's Tourist Home (☎ 902-368-3552, 18 Pond St) Singles/doubles $24/30. This spotless and friendly place in a modern bungalow has three rooms with shared bath available. It's on a residential street just two blocks from the SMT bus station.

Gallant's Tourist Home (☎ 902-892-3030, fax 902-368-1713, **w** www3.islandtelecom .com/~st.clair.gallant, 196 Kensington Rd) Singles/doubles/triples $20/25/35. This single-story bungalow beyond Belvedere Golf Course is a couple of kilometers northeast of the city center, but the four rooms with shared bath are priced to fill. The proprietors will pick you up free at the airport or bus station if you call ahead, and they'll run you into town in the morning.

The Duchess of Kent (☎ 902-566-5826, 800-665-5826, fax 902-368-8483, **w** www .bbcanada.com/5155.html, 218 Kent St) Doubles from $85. Open May-Nov. Period furnishings decorate this central B&B is in a large heritage house from 1875. There are four spacious rooms or suites with private baths. Guests can make use of the common kitchen and living room.

Motels **Sherwood Inn Motel** (☎ 902-892-1622, 800-567-1622, fax 902-892-2358, **e** ping@isn.net, 281 Brackley Point Rd) Rooms from $42 mid-June–mid-Sept, $35 other months. Almost opposite the airport and less than a kilometer from the terminal, this motel has a variety of rooms. Six rooms in an older two-story block are $42/47 singles/doubles in July and August ($35 rest of year). The 20 rooms in two long blocks cost $57 in July and August ($40 other months). The 18 new rooms in the main block are $83 ($50). A laundromat is on the premises.

Places to Eat

Markets **Farmers Market** (☎ 902-626-3373, 100 Belvedere Ave between University Ave and Mt Edward Rd) Open 9am-2pm Sat year-round, 9am-2pm Wed July & Aug. This is a fun place to go for breakfast, lunch, organic vegetables, island foods and genuine handicrafts. It's right beside the Confederation Trail.

The Uncommon Grocer (☎ 902-368-7778, 123 Queen St) Open 8am-6pm Mon & Tues, 8am-9pm Wed-Fri, 9am-6pm Sat. This is the only vegetarian deli on PEI and the best place on the island to get a loaf of real healthy bread or organic vegetables. There are five different sandwiches ($4), two soups ($3), a choice of salads ($4) and hot meals, plus vegan items. The small café here serves specialty coffees.

Mackinnon's Market (☎ 902-894-9311, Prince St Wharf) Open 8:30am-8:30pm Mon-Sat, 11am-8:30pm Sun May-Oct. Down at the edge of Confederation Landing on Charlottetown's waterfront is Mackinnon's, where you can buy fresh mussels, clams and oysters, as well as live or cooked lobster.

Cafés **Beanz Espresso Bar & Café** (☎ 902-892-8797, 38 University Ave) Sandwiches or salads under $5. Open 6:30am-6pm Mon-Fri, 8am-6pm Sat, 9am-5pm Sun. Charlottetown is rich in pubs and poor in cafés, and even Beanz is more of a sandwich-and-salad place. Still, it's okay for a specialty coffee or a cup of Newfoundland tea.

Cows (☎ 902-892-6969, 150 Queen St) It's not a large place, but Cows is an island institution turning out good homemade ice cream ($3-4). There are also outlets, open from May to early October only, in Borden-Carleton, Cavendish and Summerside, plus one in Charlottetown at Peake's Wharf (☎ 902-566-4886). People across Canada can be seen sporting the colorful, humorous Cows T-shirts ($22).

Pubs **Olde Dublin Pub** (☎ 902-892-6992, upstairs at 131 Sydney St) Meals from $8. Open 11am-2am Mon-Sat, 4pm-midnight Sun (closed Sun in winter). This place has an agreeable outside deck and live Irish and Maritimes music beginning at 10pm Thursday, Friday and Saturday night ($5 cover charge). Beers on tap include Guinness,

Harp, Killkenny Cream and Smithwick's Amber Ale. Pub grub like fish and chips, shepherd's pie and steak cost $8. And if that's not good enough, the upscale **Claddagh Room** downstairs has pricey but tasty seafood.

Brennan's Pub & Eatery (☎ *902-892-2222, 132 Richmond St*) Dinners $10-22. Open 11am-2am Mon-Sat, 11am-midnight Sun (in winter open at 4pm). This lively, gay-friendly pub boasts a menu that ranges from fettucine primavera to steaks and nachos. In the afternoon folk musicians serenade the crowd outside, while at night there's live jazz and blues.

Restaurants ***Town & Country Restaurant*** (☎ *902-892-2282, 219 Queen St*) Breakfast special $4. Open 9am-10pm daily. For breakfast, a simple meal or a snack, this cheap and unpretentious place fits the bill with its basic Canadian and Lebanese menu. The excellent breakfast special is served until noon, in summer on a small outdoor patio.

Seatreat (☎ *902-894-5678, 202 University Ave at Euston St*) Dishes $5-13. Open 9am-10pm daily. Here you'll find the most affordable seafood in town, including baskets of steamed mussels ($5), salmon or haddock dinners ($13), bowls of fish chowder ($4.25) and, of course, lobster dinners.

Canton Café (☎ *902-892-2527, 73 Queen St at Dorchester*) Lunch/dinner specials $6/7. Open 11am-2am Mon-Wed, 11am-3:30am Thur-Sat, 11am-12:30am Sun. Good deals, the Chinese specials are available from 11am to 9pm, with a choice of dishes and tea or coffee included. Otherwise, lobster is $19.

Cedar's Eatery (☎ *902-892-7377, 81 University Ave*) Dinners $8-14. Open 11am-midnight Mon-Thur, 11am-1am Fri-Sat, 4pm-11pm Sun. This fine little place is right in the middle of town. The specialty is Lebanese food, ranging from falafels ($8) to more expensive kabobs ($16), but there's also standard Canadian fare: salads, sandwiches and steaks, plus a number of vegetarian dishes. Cedar's is one of the few places that stays open late.

Piece A Cake (☎ *902-894-4585, upstairs at 119 Grafton St*) Lunch dishes from $7, dinner from $10. Open 11am-10pm Mon-Sat (closed Mon evening in winter). Next to the Confederation Court Mall, this casual bistro in a pleasant, open locale offers salads, pastas and creative dishes with Asian overtones.

Entertainment

For a complete rundown on the plays, dinner theater and band appearances, get hold of *The Buzz,* the free entertainment guide for PEI.

Confederation Centre of the Arts (☎ *902-566-1267, 800-565-0278, Queen St at Grafton St*) Evening show $22-40, matinee $20-36. The architectural style of this large modern structure is at odds with the rest of town, which has made it controversial since construction began in 1960. Each year *Anne of Green Gables,* dubbed 'Canada's favorite musical,' is performed here. Show times are at 8pm Monday to Saturday from mid-June to early September; in July and August there's also a matinee on Monday, Wednesday and Saturday at 2pm. Special guest appearances may displace the musical on Thursday and Friday nights in July and August.

42nd Street Lounge (☎ *902-566-4620, 125 Sydney St*) Open 4:30pm-midnight Mon-Sat. At this cocktail lounge above the Off Broadway Restaurant, you can sip a martini while relaxing on a comfy sofa. It's gay-friendly and the gregarious server behind the long bar makes everyone feel at home.

Myron's Cabaret (☎ *902-892-4375, 151 Kent St*) Open 11am-3am daily. Off University Ave, Myron's is the largest nightclub on the island, with two dance floors. There's live music downstairs starting around 9pm Wednesday to Saturday. The disco upstairs cranks up at 11pm Thursday to Saturday. Admission is free on Wednesday; Thursday to Saturday it's around $5 for entry to both sections.

Baba's Lounge (☎ *902-892-7377, 81 University Ave*) Cover $3-5. Open 11am-2am Mon-Sat, noon-midnight Sun. This bar above Cedar's Eatery presents live modern rock and blues nightly. It's a slightly alternative scene where you can hear well-known local groups playing their own original music.

Benevolent Irish Society (☎ *902-963-3156, 582 North River Rd*) Admission $7. Nearly every Friday at 8pm mid-May through late October the Irish Hall on the far north side of town presents a ceilidh with traditional Irish, Scottish and PEI music and dance – great fun. Arrive early, as parking and seating are limited.

Spectator Sports
Just north of the center, *Charlottetown Driving Park* (☎ 902-892-6823, 46 Kensington Rd) offers you a chance to soak up some of the excitement of the races at no cost. As elsewhere in the Maritimes, it's harness racing you'll see here – a horse pulling a small buggy with a driver. Admission is free because these folks make their money on the gambling. Races take place from 7:30pm to 10:30pm Saturday from May to early January and 7:30pm to 10:30pm Thursday from June to September.

Shopping
Anne of Green Gables Store (☎ 902-368-2663, 110 Queen St) Open 9am-7pm Mon-Wed, 9am-8pm Thur & Fri, 9am-5pm Sat, noon-5pm Sun Apr-Dec. Here you'll find enough Green Gables kitsch to last a lifetime.

Getting There & Away
Air The Air Canada subsidiary Air Canada Jazz flies between Halifax and Charlottetown five or six times a day and directly to Montréal and Toronto at least daily. A $10 passenger facility charge (not included in the ticket price) is collected from each passenger over the age of two. Before buying a plane ticket to Ch'town, compare the price of flying into nearby Moncton and renting a car there.

Bus SMT Bus Lines uses the Confederation Bridge to/from Moncton, New Brunswick. The company also picks up and drops off passengers in Kensington and Summerside. In summer there are two trips daily, except for Friday and Sunday, when there are three. A ticket to Moncton is $35. In Moncton this service connects to numerous other buses, plus the train to Montréal. The SMT depot (☎ 902-566-9744, 330 University Ave) has $2 coin lockers; it's open 8:30am to 6pm weekdays, 7am to 2:30pm and 5pm-6pm weekends.

Shuttle If you're headed to Halifax, Nova Scotia, or any point along the way, private van shuttles are a better bet than the bus.

The seven-passenger Go-Van Shuttle (☎ 902-456-5678, 866-463-9660) operates daily upon request, leaving Halifax around 7:30am and Charlottetown at noon. In Halifax you can get picked up and dropped off anywhere in the city; in Charlottetown, there's pick-up in the parking lot between KFC and Dollarama, on University Ave near Nassau St. You must book by phone (of course, the shuttle only goes when there are bookings). Between Charlottetown/Summerside and Halifax the fare is $45 one-way (students and seniors $40) – pretty standard for this route.

The Halifax-based PEI Express Shuttle (☎ 877-877-1771, W www.peishuttle.com) works exactly the same as the Go-Van, except that it picks up at 11:30am from Burger King, on University near Belvedere Ave in Charlottetown. It operates daily year-round, but you need to book in advance.

Two Charlottetown-based companies, the Square One Shuttle (☎ 877-675-3830) and the Advanced Shuttle (☎ 877-886-3322), do the reverse route, leaving Charlottetown at 8am or 8:30am and Halifax at 2pm or 3pm. Advanced Shuttle will pick up at Halifax International Airport for an extra $3 and can carry up to three bicycles at $10 each if you let the drivers know beforehand.

Getting Around
To/From the Airport Charlottetown Airport is 8km north of the city center at Brackley Point Rd and Sherwood Rd. A taxi to town costs $10/12 for one/two, plus $4 per additional person. Taxi fare to Summerside is $60. Car rental companies with desks at the airport include Avis, Budget, Hertz and National, although staff may only be there when there are advance bookings.

Bus There's no city bus service or other public transportation on PEI, but the 15-passenger Beach Shuttle (☎ 902-566-3243) shuttles between Charlottetown and the north coast beaches of the national park. Beach Shuttle leaves from the tourist office in the Stone Cottage at 8:50am, 10:55am, 3:05pm and 5:05pm from early June to late September (at 9:35am and 3:10pm only, early and late in the season). It stops at the HI hostel at 9am and 11:05am (at 9:45am only, early and late in the season), then proceeds on to the Cavendish Visitor Centre, at the junction of Hwys 6 and 13. The fare is $10/18 one-way/roundtrip.

Car A car, for better or worse, is the best and sometimes the only means of seeing much of the island. The supply of rental cars is limited and in summer, getting a car is not easy. You could be told they're all taken for the next week or two, so reserve well ahead.

At National Car Rental (☎ 902-368-2228, University Ave at Euston St), the least expensive compacts start at $39 per day, plus $16 insurance and 17% tax, with 200km free. In midsummer National bumps the basic price up to $72.

Rates at Budget Car Rental (☎ 902-566-5525, 215 University Ave) start at $38 per day, plus $21 insurance and tax, jumping to $75 a day in July and August.

There's also Rent-A-Wreck (☎ 902-566-9955, 57A St Peters Rd), where you pay $40 a day in summer, $30 in winter, with 200km included. Insurance costs $13 a day. The office is open 8am to 5:30pm weekdays, 8am to 1pm Saturday.

Parking meters cost 50¢ an hour from 8am to 6pm Monday to Friday but are free evenings, weekends and holidays. Parking at Peake's Wharf, at the foot of Prince St, is $6 a day ($12 for RVs). You'll find free on-street parking on the back streets of the old town if you look for it.

Traffic around Charlottetown doubles in July and August, with gridlock on University Ave all day and parking at a premium throughout the city.

Bicycle Smooth Cycles (☎ 902-566-5530, W www.smoothcycle.com, 172 Prince St at Kent St) rents hybrid bicycles for $24/85 a day/week and sells the excellent *PEI Cycling Guide* for $15. All manner of bicycle repairs are done here.

MacQueen's Bicycles (☎ 902-368-2453, fax 902-894-4547, W www.macqueens.com, 430 Queen St) has road bikes for $25/100 a day/week. Both shops rent panniers ($25) and helmets, while MacQueen's also arranges bicycle tours.

Eastern Prince Edward Island

The eastern third of the province, Kings County, is a lightly populated, rural region of farms and fishing communities. Much of

this section of PEI is peopled by descendants of Scottish settlers rather than by the French of the western side or the Irish of the central district. There's a 374km circular sightseeing route east of Charlottetown known as the **King's Byway Scenic Drive**, which follows the route described here.

ORWELL

Just 28km east of Charlottetown via Hwy 1 is the **Orwell Corner Historic Village** (☎ 902-651-8510, off Hwy 1; admission $4; open 9am-3pm Tues-Fri mid-May–late Oct; 9am-5pm daily mid-June–Aug), a restored and preserved 19th-century community. Originally settled by Scottish immigrants in 1766, the village includes a farm, blacksmith, post office and store, among other buildings, still in their original settings. Concerts ($8) are held at 8pm four nights a week in July and August, Wednesdays only in September.

A kilometer beyond is the **Sir Andrew MacPhail Homestead** (☎ 902-651-2789, 271 Fletcher Rd; admission free; open 10am-8:30pm Sun-Fri, 10am-6pm Sat July & Aug; 10am-6pm Mon, Tues & Thur, 10am-8:30pm Wed, Fri & Sun, 10am-4pm Sat late June-Oct). This national historic site preserves the farm where MacPhail and his brother started the island's seed potato industry. It features a restaurant on the wrap-around porch of the MacPhail home and a few nature trails.

Maclean's Century Farm Tourist Home (☎ 902-659-2694, W www.2hwy.com/pe/m/macefath.htm, 244 New Cove Rd) Singles/doubles $35/38. Just 2km off Hwy 1 at Orwell Cove, three rooms are available in a large farmhouse on a hill overlooking the sea.

Rachel's Motel & Cottages (☎ 902-659-2874, 800-559-2874, W www.holidayjunction.com/canada/pei/cpe0014.html, 4827 Hwy 1) Doubles $50 mid-June–mid-Sept, $40 shoulder seasons. Open May–mid-Oct. Just west of the turnoff to Lord Selkirk Provincial Park in Eldon, Rachel's consists of eight rooms and four cottages. It's clean and neat and set a bit back from the highway.

WOOD ISLANDS

Down on the south coast, 'Woods' is where you'll find the PEI–Nova Scotia ferry terminal, and as such it's sometimes busy (see Getting There & Away in the introduction to this chapter for details). The Nova Scotia mainland is 22km (75 minutes) across the Northumberland Strait. For a cheap scenic cruise, do a three-hour roundtrip on this ferry as a 'walk-on passenger' for only $11 (seniors $9, children under 13 free). Don't leave on the last ferry of the day if you want to come right back, however!

The PEI tourist office (☎ 902-962-7411) is just outside the ferry terminal (keep sharp right as you leave the terminal). It's open 8am to 6:30pm from June to mid-October (until 10pm in July and August). At the harbor mouth beyond it is the free day-use **Wood Islands Provincial Park** with a nice lighthouse (1876).

Northumberland Provincial Park (☎ 902-962-7418, W *www.gov.pe.ca/visitors guide/explore/parks, Hwy 4)* Sites $17/20 without/with hookups. Open mid-June–late Sept. This park, 3.5km east of the Wood Islands ferry wharf on Hwy 4, offers nice sheltered campsites in a coniferous forest right on the coast.

MONTAGUE & AROUND
Montague is a bustling little town with shopping malls, supermarkets, fast-food outlets and traffic jams. Do your grocery shopping at the large Sobeys Supermarket on Main St.

A local tourist office (☎ 902-838-4778, Station St) is in the former train station, adjacent to the Montague marina. Trains arrived here from 1906 to 1984, and now it's a terminus of the Confederation Trail. The office is open from mid-May to October.

There is a larger provincial tourist office (☎ 902-838-0670) at Pooles Corner, the junction of Hwys 3 and 4, 5km north of Montague. In addition to the racks of brochures and information, there's an extensive set of museum-quality displays and exhibits on PEI and a small video theater. It's open 9am to 4:30pm in June and from September to early October, 8am to 7pm in July and August.

Back in town, the **Garden of the Gulf Museum** (☎ 902-838-2467, 564 Main St S; adult/child $3/free; open 9am-5pm Mon-Fri mid-June–late Sept & 9am-5pm Sat in July & Aug) is just across a small bridge from the local tourist office. This museum in the ornate brick former Post Office & Custom House (1888) was established in 1958 and is the oldest museum on PEI.

From the Montague marina **Cruise Manada** (☎ 902-838-3444, 800-986-3444; adult/child $18/9; open mid-June–Sept) offers highly rated boat tours to PEI's largest seal colony. It departs from the wharf right in front of the local tourist office.

Brudenell River Provincial Park (☎ 902-652-8966, W *www.gov.pe.ca/visitorsguide/ explore/parks, off Hwy 3)* Sites $17/20-23 without/with hookups. Open mid-June–early Oct. This provincial park is part of a well-developed resort complex with two golf courses, a golf academy, horseback riding, upscale cottages, a marina, a conference center, a resort and restaurants. Everything other than camping is very expensive. Happily, the RV park and campground are nicely separated, and the tent sites are well laid out in a coniferous forest. The Confederation Trail passes the park.

Cardigan Lobster Suppers (☎ 902-583-2020, 5445 Hwy 321) Supper $28. Open 5pm-9pm daily late June-Sept. Cardigan, an old shipbuilding port north of Brudenell River Provincial Park, has a lobster supper house where the meal includes chowder, salad bar and dessert, as well as the lobster.

SOURIS
With a population of 1300, Souris feels like a real town after you've passed through so many small villages. First settled by the Acadian French in the early 1700s, it was named Souris, meaning 'mouse', due to several plagues. It's pronounced like the English name **Sur**-rey. The town is an important fishing port and the departure point of the ferry to the Îles de la Madeleine in Québec.

There's a provincial tourist office (☎ 902-687-7030, Main St) next to the CIBC Banking Centre. It's open 9am to 5pm daily from mid-June to early October, with extended hours in July and August (8am to 7pm).

St Mary's Catholic Church, built of red island sandstone in 1901, rises above town on Longworth St, up Chapel Ave from Main St. It's the dominant structure in town, but the Town Hall on Main St and several other buildings are also worth a look on the way by.

Venture Out Cycle & Kayak (☎ 902-687-1234, W *www.peisland.com/ventureout; open July-Sept)* is at Souris Beach Park, the wide sweeping beach at the west entrance to town on Hwy 2. Rentals of single kayaks cost $12/25/40 for one/three/seven hours; doubles are $17/35/60. Bicycles cost $5/12/20. Take a guided kayak tour for $30/48 for two/three hours.

Places to Stay & Eat

A Place To Stay Inn (☎ 902-687-4626, 800-655-7829, 9 Longworth St) Dorm beds $20, singles/doubles $50/60 including continental breakfast. Located right beside landmark St Mary's Church, this absolutely superb facility includes dorm rooms, as well as 12 guestrooms. It has full kitchen and laundry facilities, a lounge and TV room, mountain bikes for rent ($4/12/22 per hour/half day/ day) and many more extras.

Church Street Tourist Home (☎ 902-687-3065, 8 Church St) Singles/doubles $35 including a light breakfast. Open Apr-Jan. This B&B in the center of town, 10 minutes on foot from the ferry, is simple but good. It's an older two-story house with three shared bathrooms. The proprietor, Jimmy Hughes, is the mayor of Souris!

Dockside B&B (☎ 877-687-2829, fax 902-687-4141, ⒲ www.colvillebay.ca, 37 Breakwater St) Doubles $45/55 without/with bath including breakfast. Open mid-June–mid-Oct. This modern two-story house directly above the ferry terminal has a wonderful sea view from the front lawn.

Bluefin Restaurant (☎ 902-687-3271, 10 Federal Ave) Dishes $8-13. Open 7am-8pm Mon-Sat, 8am-8pm Sun, closing at 7pm mid-Sept–May. The Bluefin is a little hidden, down a side street that begins opposite the CIBC Banking Centre in the middle of town. This local favorite offers large portions of fish and chips ($8), pork chops ($11), halibut steak ($13) and seafood platters ($16). The noon special is available from 11am to 1pm. The attached *Black Rafter Lounge* (☎ 902-687-3271; open 11am until late, closed Sun Sept-May) is a large sports bar worth checking out in the evening.

Getting There & Away

From April to September the car ferry MV *Madeleine* (☎ 888-986-3278) connects Souris with the Îles de la Madeleine in Québec, five hours and 134km north in the Gulf of St Lawrence. It leaves Souris daily at 2pm, with no Monday departure from April to June and in September. From mid-July to mid-August there's an additional 2am departure on Saturday, Sunday and Monday. The one-way adult/child passenger fare is $36/18; cars/bicycles cost $68/8.50 each way.

A branch of the Confederation Trail leads through town directly to the Souris Marine Terminal.

BASIN HEAD

Not really a village, Basin Head is the site of the **Basin Head Fisheries Museum** (☎ 902-357-7233, off Hwy 16; adult/child $3.50/free; open 9am-5pm daily June-Sept, until 6pm July & Aug), at the ocean's edge 3km northeast of Red Point. This provincial museum traces the history of the island's fishing industry and features an interpretive center, boat sheds with vessels on display and the Smith Fish Cannery, which now houses a coastal ecology exhibit including saltwater aquariums. An excellent golden beach is just below the museum; its sands are famous for the squeaking sound they make as you walk on them.

Red Point Provincial Park (☎ 902-357-3075, fax 902-357-3076, ⒲ www.gov.pe.ca/ visitorsguide/explore/parks, off Hwy 16) Sites $17/20 without/with hookups. Open mid-June–Sept. Ten kilometers northeast of Souris, Red Point is a small park with a sandy beach and some pleasant shaded tent sites. Choose your site carefully, as changes are not allowed.

EAST POINT

At East Point, the northeast tip of the island, the cliffs are topped by a **lighthouse** (☎ 902-357-2106; adult/child $2.50/1; open 10am-6pm daily mid-June–Aug), which can be climbed as part of a little tour. The assistant's old house nearby has a restored radio room and a gift shop. It's expected that in a few years the house will have to be moved (as the lighthouse has been moved previously) because of the creeping erosion of the shoreline.

The north shore area of Kings County all the way along toward Cavendish is more heavily wooded than much of the island, but that doesn't mean the end of farms and potatoes altogether. There's a lot of fishing done along this coast – you could join a charter boat in search of tuna. Many are based at North Lake and Naufrage.

The people of the northeastern area have a fairly strong, intriguing accent not unlike that heard in Newfoundland.

ELMIRA

Railway buffs won't wish to miss the **Elmira Railway Museum** (☎ *902-357-7234, Hwy 16A; adult/child $2/free; open 10am-6pm daily July & Aug, 10am-5pm Fri-Wed mid-June–mid-Sept)*, in the original terminal at this end of the island. The Confederation Trail starts right here. The museum has a scale model of the railway and outside is an old Canadian National Railway mail car.

ST PETERS

The nets for commercial mussel farming can be seen stretched around St Peters Bay. A provincial tourist office (☎ 902-961-3540) is beside the bridge at St Peters, just where the Confederation Trail crosses Hwy 2. It's open 9am to 4:30pm daily in June and from September to early October, 8am in 7pm daily in July and August.

St Peters Park (☎ *902-961-2786,* W *www .isn.net/~stpeters, Hwy 2)* Sites $15/20 without/with hookups. Open mid-June–Sept. This is the closest campground to the national park's Greenwich section (see below). St Peters Park is a grassy field next to Hwy 2, 1.5km west of the bridge in St Peters. The Confederation Trail passes just below it.

Midgell Centre (☎ *902-961-2963, 6553 Hwy 2)* Beds $15. Open mid-June–mid-Sept. Set up principally for the guests of a Christian center, this complex opens its doors to overnight visitors. Five dark green wooden buildings sit beside the highway 4km west of St Peters. There are 60 beds, plus showers, a lounge and a kitchen for light cooking. The center is a good base for visiting Greenwich but is often closed, so call ahead.

GREENWICH

In 1998 Parks Canada opened another rather incredible section of Prince Edward Island National Park along the peninsula north and west of St Peters. Do check this place out for the rare parabolic dunes – found only here and in one spot along Germany's North Sea coastline; 3% of the planet's piping plovers are found here too. Big developments are planned for this last strip of wilderness on the island.

In 2001 the **Greenwich Interpretation Centre** (☎ *902-961-2514; adult/families $6/15; open 9am-5pm daily May-Oct, until 8pm mid-June–Aug)*, 9km west of St Peters on Hwy 313, opened in a huge barn-shaped facility at the entrance to this section of the park. The national park entry fee ($3.50) is not included in the interpretation center admission charge, though you can get a combined ticket at $8/19. The center has exhibits on the park and a 12-minute audiovisual presentation.

The 373 hectares in the national park's Greenwich section are crossed by 7km of trails. You'll find trailheads a kilometer west of the interpretation center. The beach is a kilometer north. Camping is not allowed at Greenwich.

Central Prince Edward Island

The area north of the capital in Queens County is where all the action is on Prince Edward Island. The national park is here, with its camping and beaches, as are many of the island's most touted attractions. To feed and house the vacationers, scores of lodging and dining establishments have popped up not far from the north coast. The **Blue Heron Scenic Drive** circles the center of the island, taking in all the main sights.

BORDEN-CARLETON

Gateway Village (☎ *902-437-8570, Hwy 1; admission free; open 8am-10pm daily July & Aug; 9am-8pm daily June & Sept, 9am-6pm daily rest of year)*, at the PEI end of the Confederation Bridge, is worth visiting for free maps and brochures, restrooms and an exhibit called Our Island Home. The usual assortment of shops and restaurants is here too, though most are closed outside of July and August.

The **Confederation Trail** begins near the corner of Dickie Rd and Industrial Dr, 1.5km from Gateway Village. Ask someone to point you in the right direction. Staff at Gateway Village will give you a free map of this famous bicycle trail.

Duchess Gateway B&B (☎ *902-855-2765,* W *www.peibedandbreakfast.com/duchess/ duchess.htm, 264 Carleton St)* Rooms with shared bath $40 mid-June–mid-Oct, $30 mid-Oct–mid-June, including cooked breakfast. Duchess Gateway is directly opposite the Irving gas station on Hwy 1 as you leave Borden-Carleton and is the cheapest place to stay in this part of PEI.

Carleton Motel (☎ 902-437-3030, **W** *www.bestofpei.com/carletonmotel.html, Hwy 1)* Rooms $50-60 July & Aug, $45 rest of year. This motel on Hwy 1, just 1.3km beyond the Irving gas station in Borden-Carleton, has 24 rooms in a long wooden block facing the highway. Seven units have kitchens, and there's a coffee shop.

VICTORIA

Straddling Queens and Prince Counties is this picturesque fishing village just off Hwy 1 35km west of Charlottetown. Victoria is something of a haven for artists and features a number of studios and art galleries, as well as Island Chocolates, a shop that produces excellent Belgian chocolates. The community center becomes the ***Victoria Playhouse*** (☎ 902-685-2025; *adult/youth & senior $17/15)* in July and August. It presents concerts on Monday and theatrical productions other nights, always beginning at 8pm. In September the program varies, and you'll need to call for information.

Simple Comforts B&B (☎ *902-658-2951, 877-658-2951, 20287 Hwy 1)* Hostel beds $20, B&B rooms from $35 including a hearty breakfast. Outside town on Hwy 1 is this B&B, which also bills itself as a 'bicycle hostel.' Indeed, the top floor is a 13-bed hostel, with three hostel rooms at one end of the building and three nicer B&B rooms with shared bath at the other. This ramshackle complex is full of character, piled high with priceless relics from the days when it was an Anglican Church camp. The owners rent bicycles at $10/20 a day for an old/new bike ($20 for a tandem). Simple Comforts does airport pick-ups at $20 per trip for guests.

PRINCE EDWARD ISLAND NATIONAL PARK

Just 24km north of Charlottetown, this is one of Canada's smallest national parks, but it has 45km of varied coastline. Sand dunes and red sandstone cliffs give way to wide sandy beaches (widest at Cavendish).

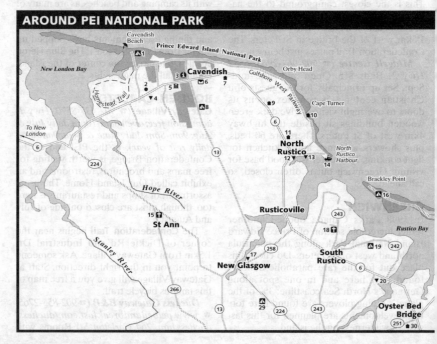

A day pass to the park costs $3.50 per person or $8 per family; from mid-September to early June it's free. You can also get a combination pass for the park and Green Gables or even a seasonal Atlantic Pass accepted at seven national parks in eastern Canada. The park maintains an information desk and exhibits in the Cavendish Visitor Centre (see Cavendish, later in this chapter). Failing that, there's the Brackley Visitor Centre (☎ 902-672-7474), open June to early October, at Brackley Beach and the Dalvay Administration Office (☎ 902-672-6350), open 8am to 4pm weekdays year-round, off Gulfshore Parkway behind the Dalvay by the Sea Hotel. The park's website is **W** www.parkscanada.gc.ca/pei.

The coverage that follows is organized from east to west, first dealing with the park and park-run facilities, then with private businesses both in and out of the park.

Beaches

There are several long stretches of beach in the park, and they are all good. **Dalvay Beach** is the easternmost beach, and a couple of short hiking trails begin in the area. **Stanhope Beach**, opposite the campground of the same name, has no cliffs or dunes; the landscape is flat and the beach is wide. A boardwalk leads to the beach. Long, wide **Brackley Beach**, in the middle of the park, is backed by sand dunes and more visited than the previous two. (Stanhope and Brackley have lifeguards on duty through the day in midsummer.) **Cavendish Beach**, edged with large sand dunes at the west end of the park, is the widest of them all. It's easily the most popular beach and gets pretty busy in peak season.

Take care while swimming off the north coast, as undertows and riptides are all too common. Every year people get sucked out by the undertow, and windy days when there's surf are the riskiest. All the coast beaches tend to have red jellyfish, known locally as bloodsuckers – but don't worry; they're not. Most are much smaller than a closed fist and, while unpleasant, are not really dangerous, although brushing against one can irritate the skin. There's virtually no shade to be had at any of the beaches.

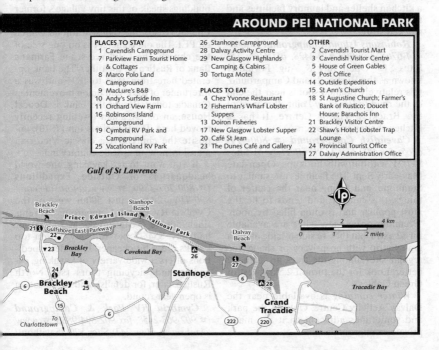

AROUND PEI NATIONAL PARK

PLACES TO STAY		
1 Cavendish Campground	26 Stanhope Campground	OTHER
7 Parkview Farm Tourist Home & Cottages	28 Dalvay Activity Centre	2 Cavendish Tourist Mart
8 Marco Polo Land Campground	29 New Glasgow Highlands Camping & Cabins	3 Cavendish Visitor Centre
9 MacLure's B&B	30 Tortuga Motel	5 House of Green Gables
10 Andy's Surfside Inn		6 Post Office
16 Orchard View Farm	PLACES TO EAT	14 Outside Expeditions
16 Robinsons Island Campground	4 Chez Yvonne Restaurant	15 St Ann's Church
19 Cymbria RV Park and Campground	12 Fisherman's Wharf Lobster Suppers	18 St Augustine Church; Farmer's Bank of Rustico; Doucet House; Barachois Inn
25 Vacationland RV Park	13 Doiron Fisheries	21 Brackley Visitor Centre
	17 New Glasgow Lobster Supper	22 Shaw's Hotel; Lobster Trap Lounge
	20 Café St Jean	24 Provincial Tourist Office
	23 The Dunes Café and Gallery	27 Dalvay Administration Office

Gulf of St Lawrence

Brackley Beach

Stanhope Beach

Prince Edward Island National Park

Gulfshore East Parkway

21

22

23   Brackley Bay

24

Brackley Beach   25

6

15

To Charlottetown

6

Coyehead Bay

Stanhope

Dalvay Beach

26

27

6

28

Grand Tracadie

Tracadie Bay

222   220

0   2   4 km

0   1   2 miles

Camping

The national park operates three official campgrounds, and as you might expect, all are in heavy demand during summer. Eighty percent of the sites at all three campgrounds are reservable for an additional $7.50 fee, but you must do so at least three days in advance by calling ☎ 800-414-6765. You cannot request a specific site and must accept whatever is available when you arrive. Park entry fees are extra.

Only 20% of sites are first-come, first-served, and these go early in the day in summer. A waiting list of 30 names is kept, and any unoccupied sites are issued to those on the list around noon. To obtain an unreserved site in midsummer, you should arrive early and get on the waiting list right away. The staff will tell you when they'll begin issuing unreserved sites, and you have to be there in person when your name is read out.

Stanhope Campground *(☎ 800-414-6765, fax 902-629-2428, off Hwy 6)* Sites $17/19 without/with hookups. Open mid-June–mid-Oct. Across the road from Stanhope Beach, this campground has showers, a kitchen shelter and laundry facilities and features a wooded setting and a well-stocked store.

Robinsons Island Campground *(☎ 800-414-6765, fax 902-629-2428, off Hwy 15)* Sites $15. Open July & Aug. Formerly known as the Rustico Island Campground, this relatively isolated spot is near the end of the road to Brackley Point, 4km west of the Brackley Visitor Centre. It has a kitchen shelter and showers.

Cavendish Campground *(☎ 800-414-6765, fax 902-629-2428, off Hwy 6)* Sites $17/21 without/with hookups. Open late May-early Sept. The facilities are similar to Stanhope, and, being near the center of things, this campground tends to be the most popular and is often filled by noon. 'Premium ocean-view' sites are available for $2 extra, but they're side by side along a grassy strip with no privacy or shade; the regular sites among the trees are actually better. Look for the turnoff 2.5km west of Green Gables.

Winter camping is available near the Dalvay Activity Centre. Outside the park and sometimes adjacent to it are many private campgrounds.

BRACKLEY BEACH

There's a provincial tourist office (☎ 902-672-7474) at the junction of Hwys 6 and 15, 4km before the national park. It's open from 9am to 4:30pm daily in June and from September to early October, 8am to 9pm daily in July and August.

From June to early October Shaw's Hotel (☎ 902-672-2022), just outside the park at Brackley Beach, rents bicycles for $5/17 an hour/day.

The Dunes Café and Gallery *(☎ 902-672-2586, Hwy 15)* Lunch/dinner $18/30. Open 9am-9pm daily July–mid-Sept. You can't miss the striking architecture of this ceramics showroom and rather pretentious café on Hwy 15 just outside the park.

Lobster Trap Lounge *(☎ 902-672-2769, off Hwy 15)* Cover $2. Open 8pm-midnight daily mid-June–early Sept. Adjoining Shaw's Hotel near Brackley Beach, the Lobster Trap is a fairly rollicking spot with shindigs a couple nights a week.

SOUTH RUSTICO

The Acadian settlement at South Rustico dates back to 1700, and several fine historic buildings speak of this tiny village's former importance. Most prominent is **St Augustine Church** (1830), the oldest Catholic church on PEI. The old cemetery is on one side of the church, the solid red-stone **Farmer's Bank of Rustico** on the other. The bank operated here from 1864 to 1894 and was a forerunner of the credit union movement in Canada today. Beside the bank is **Doucet House**, an old Acadian dwelling recently moved here. The **Barachois Inn** (1870), opposite the church, is a classic Victorian mansion, now an upscale country inn.

If you want to try **kayaking**, the world headquarters of **Outside Expeditions** (☎ 800-207-3899, **W** www.getoutside.com, 890 Hwy 242) is just 500m west of the Cymbria RV Park & Campground. It rents single/double ocean kayaks at $43/55 per half day, $54/77 per full day. Sit-on-top kayaks are a bit cheaper. Outside Expeditions offers a wide variety of kayaking, canoeing and bicycling tours (see North Rustico, later, for details), and this location is open year-round.

Cymbria RV Park & Campground *(☎ 902-963-2458, fax 902-894-9888, **W** www .cymbria.ca, Hwy 242)* Sites $20/25 without/

with hookups. Open mid-May–mid-Oct. Some nice tent sites are at the very back of the property, and the friendly young owner, Trent Howlett, will help you find one. Cymbria is a bit off the beaten track (about 3km off Hwy 6) and therefore less likely to be full in midsummer.

Tortuga Motel (☎ 902-621-2020, 25 Hwy 251) Rooms $45-75. Open July & Aug. This affordable motel near the intersection of Hwys 6 and 7 in Oyster Bed Bridge has 20 rooms in a long strip with a coffee shop in the middle. It's pretty basic and far from the beaches if you don't have a car.

Café St Jean (☎ 902-963-3133, 5033 Hwy 6) Lunch under $10. Open 11:30am-10pm daily mid-June–mid-Sept. Besides all the lobster suppers, this upscale café at South Rustico is a consistent, creative bistro with a Cajun and regional flair. It presents live traditional music, often at 7pm on Tuesday and

Friday (cover $3-5). You can get lunch dishes like sandwiches or fish and chips ($9). Dinner brings chicken, beef and fish dishes ($17-21) or lobster ($25), all served on a large deck overlooking Rustico Bay.

NEW GLASGOW & ST ANN

Two famous lobster-supper houses are south of Rusticoville, one in the village of New Glasgow and another 7km away in St Ann on Hwy 224. Both offer lobster plus all-you-can-eat chowder, mussels, salads, breads and desserts. You may even get some live music to help the food go down.

St Ann's Church Lobster Supper (☎ 902-621-0635, Hwy 224) Lobster dinner $25. Open 4pm-8:30pm Mon-Sat mid-June–late Sept. The St Ann supper house is an original and still operates in the St Ann's Church basement, as it has done for the past few decades. It's busy, casual and friendly.

That Crazy Mixed-Up Lobster

Unfortunately for this mottled greenish, bluish or blackish prehistoric wonder, somebody realized it tasted bloody good. This has meant that we've learned a lot about it, although the facts on this 100-million-year-old crustacean read like a joke book: it tastes with its feet, listens with its legs (of which there are 10) and has teeth in its stomach (which is found just behind the head). The kidney is in the head, the brain in the neck and the bones (shell) on the outside.

Lobster is widely associated with the East Coast of Canada, but perhaps Prince Edward Island, with its famous lobster suppers, is most closely linked with this symbol of gourmet dining. It's now hard to believe, but there wasn't much interest in the delicate meat until a good way into the 20th century. In fact, islanders used to use lobster as fertilizer for the island's farms.

There are two fishing seasons, one in the spring, ending in late June, and one in the winter. To catch lobster, wooden or metal traps baited with herring bits are dropped overboard to rest on the bottom and checked soon after. The trap's ingenious cage design allows the lobster's claws to narrow on the way in, but once the lobster's inside, the claws spread apart again and crawling back out is impossible. The older wooden traps are available for purchase around the island at about $5 each and will one day be museum pieces.

Lobsters can be baked, broiled or barbecued, but the usual method is to boil them alive. They're cooked in boiling, salted fresh water for 12 to 15 minutes for the first pound, plus four minutes for every additional pound (500g). When done, the lobster sports the characteristic orange-red shell, not unlike that of some bathers at Cavendish beach. Most meaty is the tail, followed by the larger claws. Though most people quickly discard it, the green mushy liver, known as tomalley, is considered a delicacy and one of the choicest parts to savor.

New Glasgow Lobster Supper *(☎ 902-964-2870, Hwy 258)* Lobster dinner $25. Open 4pm-8:30pm daily June-early Oct. The supper house in New Glasgow is a bit more commercial than that in St Ann and is open on Sunday.

New Glasgow Highlands Camping & Cabins *(☎ 902-964-3232, fax 902-964-3232, W www.town.cavendish.pe.ca/newglasgow highlands)* Campsites $24/26 without/with hookups, cabins $45/50 doubles/triples. Open Apr-Oct. This is probably the nicest campground on PEI, with 15 sites properly spaced in the forest, 1.7km east of the PEI Preserve Company on Hwy 224. Each campsite has a fire pit, and there are also 22 cabins, each with two bunks, a double bed, sofa and picnic table; you share a bath. Light cooking facilities are provided in the lodge. A laundromat, small store and heated swimming pool are on the premises. Canoe rentals are $15 per canoe for up to five hours including drop-off at a nearby lake. It's all immaculately maintained; in fact, this place is so good you should certainly call ahead to reserve if you plan to be here in July or August. Before mid-June and after early September, the cabin prices drop to $30 single or double, a real bargain. Rowdy behavior is not allowed here.

NORTH RUSTICO

North Rustico is the home of probably the best-known, busiest restaurant in the province. There's a post office here, as well as two supermarkets and a bank. Whereas nearby Cavendish is purely a tourist town, North Rustico has some local life.

The Rustico area is the base for one of the province's largest fishing fleets. Prince Edward Island's fishing industry is inshore (as opposed to offshore), meaning that the boats head out and return home the same day.

North Rustico Harbour is a tiny fishing community with a lighthouse that you can drive to from town or walk to along the beach once you're in the national park.

Kayaking

Kayaking trips in the national park are offered by **Outside Expeditions** *(☎ 902-963-3366, 800-207-3899* W *www.getoutside.com, 374 Harbourside Dr)*, PEI's leading adventure tourism provider. The 1½-hour introductory 'Beginner Bay' tour ($39) begins with a lesson in kayaking techniques. The most popular trip is the three-hour 'Harbour Passage' tour ($50), which operates three times daily, at 9am, 1pm and 5pm, from mid-June to mid-September. Before and after season the company will run a trip whenever at least four people want to go. Look for the office at the end of the road in North Rustico Harbour, 1.5km from Fisherman's Wharf Lobster Suppers (see Places to Eat).

Fishing

A few captains at North Rustico Harbour take visitors out on deep-sea fishing trips in summer. Follow the road beside Fisherman's Wharf Lobster Suppers down to the wharf and you'll see signs for **Barry Doucette's Deep Sea Fishing** *(☎ 902-963-2465)*, **Bearded Skipper's Deep Sea Fishing** *(☎ 902-963-2334)*, **Aiden's Deep Sea Fishing Trips** *(☎ 902-963-2442)* and **Peter Gauthier's Deep Sea Fishing** *(☎ 902-963-2129)*. **Court Bros Deep Sea Fishing** *(☎ 902-963-2322)* is farther down, at the end of the road near Outside Expeditions.

Most of these trips are offered in July and August only, although Court Bros goes from June to mid-September. The actual period when these trips operate depends not only on the tourist season but also on government fishing seasons. The price is usually $20/10 adult/child for three hours of fishing. On a typical trip, six to 10 people will take turns fishing for cod, mackerel and several other species, and the catch belongs to the boat.

Places to Stay & Eat

Andy's Surfside Inn *(☎ 902-963-2405, fax 902-963-2405, Gulfshore West Parkway)* Doubles $45-55 July & Aug, $35 June & Sept-Nov, including a light breakfast. Andy's is inside the national park, 2.7km from North Rustico on the way to Orby Head. This large rambling house overlooking Doyle's Cove has been an inn since the 1930s. Andy's offers eight rooms with shared bath. The kitchen is open to those who want to bring home a few live lobsters. The view from the porch is simply stunning.

Orchard View Farm *(☎ 902-963-2302, 800-419-4468,* W *www.peionline.com/al/orchard, 7602 Hwy 6)* Singles/doubles $45/55, cottages $150 July & Aug, $60 other months. Open

May–mid-Nov. Away from the beach on the road to Cavendish, 2km west of North Rustico, there are four B&B rooms with shared bath and a communal kitchen in a large farmhouse, plus 12 housekeeping cottages (with kitchenettes). Prices are negotiable, especially if you stay a few nights.

MacLure's B&B (☎ 902-963-2239, W *www.2hwy.com/pe/m/metehata.htm, 7920 Hwy 6)* Singles/doubles $45/50 July & Aug, $40/45 other months including breakfast. Halfway between North Rustico and Cavendish, MacLure's offers three rooms with shared bath in a large farmhouse in lovely peaceful surroundings.

Fisherman's Wharf Lobster Suppers (☎ *902-963-2669, 7230 Main St)* Lobster dinners $27 & up. Open 4pm-9pm daily mid-May–mid-Oct. This huge place gets crowded in peak season, with lines from 6pm to 8pm. It's a fun, casual, holiday-style restaurant offering good meals for your money. For $27 a pound you are served a lobster and can help yourself to an impressive salad bar, unlimited amounts of chowder, some good local mussels, rolls and a variety of desserts. If you get really lucky, along the back wall are tables with a view of the ocean.

Doiron Fisheries (☎ *902-963-2442, Harborside Dr)* Market price. Open 8am-6pm daily May–mid-Oct. At the wharf in North Rustico you can get fresh seafood ranging from lobsters and mussels to scallops, hake and cod. If there are two of you, consider feasting on a four- or five-pound lobster (2.5kg), available live or cooked. The prices here are less than half those of the restaurants.

CAVENDISH

At the junction of Routes 6 and 13, this tourist center is the area's commercial hub. You're in the heart of things when you see the service station, wax museum, church, cemetery and assorted restaurants. Also situated at the junction, alongside the police station and municipal offices, is the **Cavendish Visitor Centre** (☎ 902-963-7830). This outlet has a wealth of information on the area, along with a craft shop, exhibits on the national park and a courtesy phone to make reservations. It's open 9am to 6pm daily from late May to late October, with extended hours in July and August (8am to 10pm).

East of Cavendish is a large amusement park, and close by are go-cart tracks, waterslides, golf courses, miniature golf, fairy castles, petting farms, a palace of the bizarre, a planetarium, West Coast totem poles, a Ripley's Believe It or Not Museum and other tacky diversions, including a life-size replica of the space shuttle *Columbia.* The growing number of these manufactured attractions is sad and definitely an eyesore in this scenic region of PEI.

Numerous tourist homes, motels and cottages can be found around Cavendish. Remember that this is the busiest and most expensive area that you can stay. Almost all of the motels, restaurants, shops and attractions of Cavendish are closed from November to April, and most open only from late June to early September. Off-season many businesses take their signs down and almost vanish from sight, but in July and August this area is inundated with tourists, and price gouging goes on. Come in spring or fall, and you'll easily find a cottage at 50% off.

House of Green Gables

Cavendish is the hometown of Lucy Maud Montgomery (1874–1942), author of *Anne of Green Gables,* and the House of Green Gables here is administered by Parks

Lucy Maud Montgomery

Canada as a heritage site. Apart from the Prince Edward Island National Park, this house (☎ 902-672-6350, Hwy 6; adult/family $5/12; open 9am-8pm daily late June–mid-Sept, 9am-5pm daily May-Oct, noon-4pm Wed-Sun Nov, Dec, Mar & Apr) is the most popular tourist attraction in the province.

The life of the real Lucy Maud Montgomery has become thoroughly entwined with that of her fictional character, Anne of Green Gables. Everything relating to either the story or the author anywhere on the island has now pretty well become part of the Green Gables industry.

The House of Green Gables is known as the place where Anne, the heroine of Montgomery's 1908 novel, lived. The warm-hearted book tells the story of a young orphan, Anne, and her childhood tribulations in late-19th- and early-20th-century Prince Edward Island in a way that makes it a universal tale.

Aside from celebrating Lucy and Anne themes through exhibits and audiovisual displays, the house presents farm demonstrations and period programs throughout summer. The trails leading from the house through the green, gentle creek-crossed woods are worthwhile. 'Lover's Lane,' particularly, has maintained its idealistic childhood ambience.

Organized Tours

All tour operators have an Anne-themed tour (they'd be nuts not to), including **Cavendish Tours** (☎ 902-963-2031), whose three-hour tour ($35) is convenient, as its schedule follows the arrival of the Beach Shuttle (see Getting Around in the Charlottetown section). Another much longer tour ($60) starts in Charlottetown.

Places to Stay & Eat

Marco Polo Land Campground (☎ 902-963-2352, 800-665-2352, fax 902-963-2384, ⓦ www.marcopololand.com) Sites $24/28 without/with hookups. Open June-early Oct. This campground, near Cavendish 1km south of the visitor center on Hwy 13, has a range of amenities over its 100 acres, including two swimming pools. Sites in the 300 and 400 series are spread through a shady forest, while most of the others are RV parking plots in an open field. The campground accepts reservations by phone.

Parkview Farm Tourist Home & Cottages (☎ 902-963-2027, 800-237-9890, fax 902-963-2935, ⓦ www.peionline.com/al/parkview) Singles/doubles/cottages $45/55/135-220. Tourist home open year-round, cottages mid-May–mid-Oct. The four B&B rooms are in a sizable farmhouse on a working dairy farm that overlooks the ocean 2km east of Cavendish on Hwy 6. Across the road there are also seven two- or three-bedroom cottages with kitchens, which you can get for $60 outside July and August.

Chez Yvonne Restaurant (☎ 902-963-2070, 8947 Hwy 6) Dishes $8. Open 7:30am-9pm daily June-Sept. Opposite the Cavendish Tourist Mart, Chez Yvonne has been serving upscale steak and seafood dinners to tourists since the 1970s. This place is well known for its home cooking, especially the bread and rolls baked on the premises.

Cavendish Tourist Mart (☎ 902-963-2370, 8934 Hwy 6) Open 8am-9pm daily mid-May–Sept. This grocery store 1.5km west of Green Gables stocks all essential supplies. It also features a laundromat ($1.25 to wash).

Getting Around

The Cavendish Red Trolley runs from the Marco Polo Land Campground at the top of every hour from 10am to 6pm; it stops at Cavendish Country Inn, the Cavendish Visitor Centre, Cavendish Beach and Green Gables. For $3 you can use the ticket all day.

NEW LONDON

New London, some 10km southwest of Cavendish, is the birthplace of Lucy Maud Montgomery, author of Anne of Green Gables. The house where she was born in 1874 is now a **museum** (☎ 902-886-2099, Hwy 6 at Hwy 20; admission $2; open 9am-5pm daily late May-early Oct) that contains some personal belongings.

Blue Winds Tea Room (☎ 902-886-2860, 10746 Hwy 6) Lunch under $10. Open 11am-6pm daily June-early Oct. Just 500m southwest of the Lucy Maud Montgomery birthplace, this well known café with a nice view is a good choice for lunch. Try the soup and salad combo ($7.25), quiche ($8.50), chicken dishes ($9.50) and desserts ($3.50). Afternoon tea ($4.50) is served anytime.

PARK CORNER

About 10km northwest of New London in the village of Park Corner is the **Lucy Maud Montgomery Heritage Museum** (☎ 902-886-2807, 4605 Hwy 20; admission $2.50; open 9am-5pm daily June–mid-Sept), in the home of Lucy Maud's grandfather. The site has a lot of Anne paraphernalia. Take a guided tour; there's a guarantee that if you're not absolutely fascinated, you don't pay the admission.

At Silver Bush, 500m down the hill from here, is a house that was owned by Montgomery's uncle when Lucy Maud was just a girl. This was one of her favorite places – she was married in the parlor in 1911. The home is called the **Anne of Green Gables Museum** (☎ 902-886-2884, 4542 Hwy 20; adult/family $2.75/6; open 9am-5pm daily May–mid-Oct) and contains such items as her writing desk and autographed first-edition books. A path leads down from the house to the famed Lake of Shining Waters.

Beds of Lavender B&B (☎ 902-886-3114, **W** www.bbcanada.com/3367.html, 4606 Hwy 20) Singles/doubles/triples $30/40-50/60 including breakfast. Open June–mid-Oct. This pleasant house with a deck overlooking the Lake of Shining Waters, directly opposite the Lucy Maud Montgomery Heritage Museum, is an ideal place for Anne aficionados to stay. Call ahead, as the three rooms are often full.

Western Prince Edward Island

The western third of the island is made up of Prince County. The county's northern section is, like so much of the province, pretty farm country. The southernmost area, along Egmont and Bedeque Bays, retains some evidence of its Acadian French history. Lennox Island offers the best opportunity on PEI to learn something about the province's Mi'kmaq people.

The **Lady Slipper Scenic Drive** (named for the provincial flower) around Prince County is 288km long. This is the least visited part of the island – and, because of that, perhaps the most stimulating – but outside the camping season, budget accommodations are pretty scarce here.

SUMMERSIDE
pop 15,000

At one time residents of the capital would move to this side of the island in the hot months. The approach to 'S'side' along Hwy 1A is much like the approach to Ch'town; it's lined with motels and hamburger joints. But centrally, Summerside is a quiet village with quaint old homes on streets trimmed with big trees. You'll find most of the commercial establishments on the one main street, Water St. The Confederation Trail runs right through Summerside, crossing the street opposite the Ultramar gas station on Harbour Dr.

For a week in mid-July Summerside hosts the Lobster Festival, with nightly feasts, contests, games and music. A hydroplane regatta is held at the end of the month.

Information

The provincial tourist office (☎ 902-888-8364) is on Hwy 1A 4km east of Summerside. It's open 9am to 4:30pm daily from June to early October, with extended hours in July and August (8am to 9pm). Pick up the walking-tour pamphlet, which details some of the town's finer buildings dating back to the 1850s.

Rotary Regional Library (☎ 902-436-7323, 192 Water St) provides free Internet access. Go in early to reserve a time slot for later in the day. It's open 10am to 9pm Tuesday, 10am to 5pm Wednesday to Saturday, 1pm to 5pm Sunday. (The library is housed in the old Summerside train station and the Confederation Trail passes the back door.)

Spinnaker's Landing

This boardwalk area along Summerside's waterfront includes the usual overpriced gift shops and the Deckhouse Pub, as well as the city's **Lighthouse Lookout** (☎ 902-436-6692; admission free; open 9:30am-5:30pm daily mid-June–late Sept), which houses a tourist office on the 1st floor and observation platform at the top. From mid-May to late September you can rent **bicycles** at **Fogarty's Cove Café** (☎ 902-888-3918) for $16/24 per half day/full day.

Spinnaker's Landing also contains a small outdoor stage area for free live music in summer.

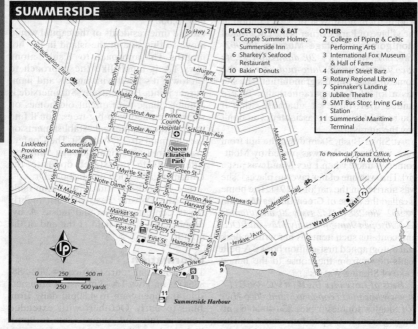

SUMMERSIDE

PLACES TO STAY & EAT
1 Copple Summer Holme;
  Summerside Inn
6 Sharkey's Seafood
  Restaurant
10 Bakin' Donuts

OTHER
2 College of Piping & Celtic
  Performing Arts
3 International Fox Museum
  & Hall of Fame
4 Summer Street Barz
5 Rotary Regional Library
7 Spinnaker's Landing
8 Jubilee Theatre
9 SMT Bus Stop; Irving Gas
  Station
11 Summerside Maritime
  Terminal

International Fox Museum & Hall of Fame

The controversial story of island fox farming is told at this museum (☎ 902-436-2400, 286 Fitzroy St; admission $2; open 10am-5pm daily mid-June–Aug), one block from Water St. In 1890 a local man successfully bred two wild silver foxes captured on the island, marking the first time wild, fur-bearing animals had been bred in captivity. The principles learned are now used around the world. Through the 1920s fortunes were made in Summerside through shipbuilding and fur farming. For a time, the latter was PEI's most important economic activity.

The museum is arranged in Holman Homestead (1855), a beautiful historic house with a lovely garden. Holman himself was a fox breeder, and there are still fox farms on the island today.

College of Piping & Celtic Performing Arts

The school (☎ 902-436-5377, 619 Water St E; admission free; open 11am-5pm Mon-Fri late June-Aug) provides visitors with free mini-concerts weekdays at 11:30am, 1:30pm and 3:30pm – expect bagpipes, singing and dancing. There are also exhibits in the main hall and a Celtic gift shop open year-round. A ticket is $12 for the special two-hour Scottish ceilidh shows at 7pm Monday to Thursday (they're outdoors – bring a sweater). Watch for the International Highland Gathering at the end of June (day passes $10).

Places to Stay

Linkletter Provincial Park (☎ 902-888-8366, fax 902-432-2707, w www.gov.pe.ca/ visitorsguide/explore/parks) Sites from $17/20 without/with hookups. Open mid-June–Sept. The 84 campsites at the end of Linkletter Rd off Hwy 11 are in an open grassy field on a ho-hum beach 5.3km west of Summerside.

Clark's Sunny Isle Motel (☎ 902-436-5665, 877-682-6824, w www.sunnyislemotel .mainpage.net, 720 Water St E) Rooms $46/56 one/two beds. Open May-Oct. Summerside's motel strip starts here, 2.5km east of the center. The nicest rooms are at the back, facing a large garden and away from the road.

Cairn's Motel (☎ 902-436-5841, 877-224-7676, **W** www.cairnsmotel.pe.ca, 721 Water St E) Doubles $46. Open May-Oct. Across the street from Sunny Isle and not quite as nice, Cairn's features 12 rooms in a long wooden block. The Confederation Trail passes behind the motel.

Baker's Lighthouse Motel (☎ 902-436-2992, 877-436-2992, 802 Water St E) Doubles $46-56 June-Sept, $36-49 Oct-May. A kilometer farther east, near the entrance to town, Baker's offers some rooms in a two-story block; it's the least desirable of the three motels mentioned in this section.

Copple Summer Holme (☎ 902-436-3100, fax 902-436-2055, **W** www.copplesummer holme.com, 92 Summer St) Singles/doubles $65/85 including breakfast. Open mid-May–Oct. There are three rooms with bath in this elegant, antique-filled mansion built in 1880.

Summerside Inn (☎ 902-436-1417, 877-477-1417, fax 902-436-1730, **W** www.peisland .com/summersideinn, 98 Summer St) Doubles $75-85 June-Oct, $65-75 other months. This is another huge mansion, directly across from Copple Summer Holme.

Places to Eat
Bakin' Donuts (☎ 902-436-3201, 48 Water St E) Full breakfast special $4, muffins 85¢. Open 4:30am-midnight daily. On the way into the city center from the east, this is the best place to go for breakfast. The muffins are huge, and two full breakfast specials are offered daily (served anytime). Ask for the 'muffin of the day' and pay only 60¢.

Sharkey's Seafood Restaurant (The Little Mermaid; ☎ 902-436-8887, 240 Harbour Dr) Dishes $7-10. Open 11am-9pm daily mid-May–mid-Sept. This recommended place on the waterfront has fine views of the harbor. It offers standard fare of mainly fried foods, such as burgers, but there are also seafood dishes such as fish and chips ($6-9), lobster rolls ($7), lobster burgers ($9), clam dinners ($9) and scallop dinners ($10). Fresh fish, mussels and lobster can be purchased, too.

Entertainment
Jubilee Theatre (☎ 800-708-6505, Harbour Dr) In July and August the Jubilee presents a dinner theater package beginning at 5pm from Tuesday to Saturday. The $50 ticket in-cludes a lobster or steak dinner with chowder, dessert and tea or coffee, plus a vaudeville-style musical program. It's guaranteed to please vacationers (what's offered varies from year to year).

Fogarty's Cove Café (☎ 902-888-3918, **W** www.summersidewaterfront.com, off Harbour Dr) Open 9:30am-5:30pm daily June-late Sept, 8am-10pm daily July & Aug, to 10:30pm Tues & Wed. This earthy café at Spinnaker's Landing presents local musicians, serves organic food and has information on untouristy local events. The folk club (cover $2), 8pm on Tuesday, is a great opportunity to hear local talent, and you can join the drum circle for free on Wednesday at 8pm. Spinnaker's Landing is the venue for a free outdoor folk concert from 6pm to 8pm Friday to Sunday, mid-June to early September.

Summer Street Barz (☎ 902-436-7400, 12 Summer St) Open 11am-2am Mon-Sat. This is Summerside's top night spot, with two disco dance floors. Bourbon Street, downstairs, pumps out high-energy dance music for the 19 to 25 crowd; a slightly older clientele heads upstairs to Mustang, which plays country music and rock. Friday and Saturday are the big nights ($4 cover charge). From 8pm to 11pm Sunday there's an alcohol-free teen dance ($5 cover charge).

Getting There & Away
The SMT bus stops at the Irving gas station (☎ 902-436-2420, 96 Water St) in the center of town. The fare to Charlottetown is $10, to Moncton $25, to Halifax $47. See Getting There & Away in the Charlottetown section for information on the Halifax van shuttles, which also pick up in Summerside upon request.

RÉGION ÉVANGÉLINE
Most of the descendants of the early French settlers live in the section of the province between Miscouche and Mont Carmel. Six thousand still speak French as a first language, and serious efforts are made to preserve Acadian culture as a way of life. The red, white and blue flag with a single yellow star is a proud symbol of these people. (See the Nova Scotia and New Brunswick chapters for more information on the Acadians.)

Miscouche

West of Summerside, the **Acadian Museum** (☎ 902-432-2880, Hwy 2; adult/child $3.50/1.75; open 9:30am-7pm daily July & Aug; 9:30am-5pm Mon-Fri, 1pm-4pm Sun rest of year) in Miscouche has a collection of early Acadian memorabilia relating the engrossing history of the Acadians before and after the mass expulsion from Nova Scotia in 1755 by the British. An audiovisual exhibit provides more information. A visit to learn something of this tragic story is worthwhile. It was at the Second Acadian Convention in Miscouche in 1884 that the Acadian flag and the Ave Maris Stella anthem were adopted. Several monuments around the museum and the nearby Church of St John the Baptist recall these events.

TYNE VALLEY

North along Hwy 2, the village of Tyne Valley is worth a stop. There are a few handicraft workshops to visit, including a pottery place.

Six kilometers north of Tyne Valley along Hwy 12 is Green Park Provincial Park, which includes a mediocre beach, campground and the worthwhile **Green Park Shipbuilding Museum** (☎ 902-831-7947, off Hwy 12; admission $4; open 9am-5pm daily June-Sept). PEI's 19th-century shipbuilding industry consisted of almost 200 small shipyards where 20-person teams could build boats in six months or less. On the grounds there's an interpretive center, a re-created shipyard with a partially constructed 200-ton brigantine in it, and Yeo House, the renovated home of a wealthy ship owner in the 1860s.

Places to Stay & Eat

Green Park Provincial Park (☎ 902-831-7912, fax 902-831-7941, W www.wavesonthe green.com, off Hwy 12). Sites $17/23 without/with hookups, cabins $35/225 day/week. Open late June-early Sept. The 58 campsites are in a mixed forest. Inside the park beyond the camping area are 12 camping cabins with shared bath. Known as 'Waves on the Green,' these cabins are an excellent value.

Doctor's Inn (☎ 902-831-3057, W www .peisland.com/doctorsinn, 32 Allen Rd) Singles/doubles $45/60 with shared bath including breakfast. This is a fine country B&B in Tyne Valley whose superlative dining room is able to take full advantage of its surrounding organic garden. The four-course dinner costs $50 per person including wine and is by reservation only. The inn also sells its organically grown vegetables and potatoes.

The Landing Oyster Bar (☎ 902-831-3138, 1327 Port Hill Station Rd) Open 11am-9pm daily, to 10pm Fri & Sat March-Dec. Meals $7-9. Between the general store and post office in the center of Tyne Valley, The Landing serves seafood with organic vegetables from the Doctors Inn. The specialty is 15 deep-fried oysters for $12. The bar stays open a couple of hours later than the restaurant, and in July and August you can hear live Maritimes music at 9pm four nights a week (cover $3-5). In the off-season the music is only on Friday. Four local craft beers are on tap.

LENNOX ISLAND

A group of about 50 Mi'kmaq families (350 people) live on Lennox Island in Malpeque Bay. The scenery is good, and the island is easily accessible by road from the west side of the bay near the village of East Bideford, north of Tyne Valley. The reserve is 7km down East Bideford Rd off Hwy 12, connected by a bridge.

The people earn a living from blueberry production and lobster fishing. There's a big powwow the last weekend in June. The main holiday here is the last Sunday in July, St Ann's Day.

St Ann's Church, dating from 1898, can be visited. Opposite it is the **Lennox Island Mi'kmaq Cultural Centre** (☎ 866-831-2702; admission $3; open late June-Aug), with exhibits on Malpeque Bay. Paintings and artifacts deal with the history of the first indigenous people in Canada to be converted to Christianity. Ask for the ecotourism walking map of the self-guiding trail.

Just down from the Cultural Centre is a **Craft Shop** (☎ 902-831-2653; open June-early Oct) with a good array of items, including ash splint baskets made by the local people. Finally, there's a pottery workshop called **MicMac Productions** (☎ 902-831-2277; open March-early Oct) in the village.

Charlie Greg Sark's **Mi'kmaq Kayak Adventures** (☎ 902-831-3131, 877-500-3131, fax 902-831-2390, W www.minegoo.com, 4

Eaglefeather Trail), based at the Craft Shop, offers three-hour trips to an island at 9am, 1pm and 5pm ($50), sunset paddles ($50) and full-day trips to several islands ($95). A 24-hour trip (noon to noon), including camping on an island and two meals, is $200. All this happens daily in July and August and by appointment in May, June and September.

TIGNISH TO NORTH CAPE

Tignish is a friendly, natural town, remote from the tourist hot spots of central PEI. The towering **Church of St Simon and St Jude** (1859) has an impressive pipe organ built in Montréal and installed here in 1882. It employs 1118 pipes. The church itself is beautifully decorated in white and blue.

The **Confederation Trail** begins (or ends!) on School St, two blocks south of the church. The **Tignish Cultural Centre** (☎ 902-882-1999, 305 School St; free admission; open 8am-4pm Mon-Fri), near the church, provides a good exhibition of old maps and photos, tourist information and a library with Internet access.

North Cape

Lovely if windblown North Cape is a promontory with a lighthouse. The Atlantic Wind Test Site wind turbine station has been set up to study the efficacy of wind-powered generators. The **interpretive center** (☎ 902-882-2991, north end of Hwy 12; adult/senior & student $2/1; open 10am-6pm daily mid-May-early Oct, 9am-8pm daily July & Aug) provides information and features a small aquarium. Upstairs there's a rather pricey restaurant. Even more interesting is the rock seabed at North Cape, which can be explored at low tide – look for sea life in the pools and watch for coastal birds and even seals.

For a bit of fun, check out **Captain Mitch's Boat Tours** (☎ 902-882-2883, Hwy 12; adult/child $20/10; open July & Aug), leaving from Seacow Pond Harbour, 6.5km south of North Cape. Seals and seabirds are often seen off North Cape, where the tides of the Gulf of St Lawrence and Northumberland Strait meet.

Places to Stay & Eat

Gulf Side Park (☎ 902-882-3262, 20460 Hwy 12) Sites $14/18 without/with hookups. Open May–mid-Oct. Here you pitch your tent in an open grassy field beside the road, 3.5km south of Seacow Pond Harbour.

Murphy's Tourist Home & Cottages (☎ 902-882-2667, 325 Church St) Cottages & rooms from $50, rooms including continental breakfast. Open mid-May–early Oct. Almost adjacent to the massive redbrick church in Tignish, Murphy's offers four rooms in the main house and five housekeeping cottages with one or two bedrooms and kitchenettes. Extra people are $15 each. It's comfortable, welcoming and the best value west of Summerside.

Tignish Heritage Inn (☎ 877-882-2491, fax 902-882-2500, W www.tignish.com/inn, off Maple St) Doubles from $65 (from $55 beginning & end of season) including breakfast. Open mid-May–mid-Oct. The four-story brick convent (1868) behind the church is now a 17-room inn. All rooms have private bath.

Co-op Lunch Bar (☎ 902-882-2020, Church St at Central St) Breakfast $3, lunch $4-5. Open 8:30am-6pm Mon-Sat (until 8pm Thur & Fri). This lunch bar in the Tignish Co-op, behind the Irving gas station in town, is definitely your best bet for breakfast or lunch, with sandwiches ($2-3), hamburger deluxe ($4) and fish and chips ($5). It's always crowded with locals.

Cousins Diner & Restaurant (☎ 902-882-5670, 276 Phillip St) Dishes $7-13. Open 7am-10pm daily (until 11pm in summer). Cousins is 1.5km south of the center of town on Hwy 2. The diner side of this establishment opens at 7am daily for breakfast ($3-5), burgers ($6-7) and club sandwiches ($7). At 11am the restaurant side (where you can order alcohol) begins serving things like clam dinner ($7), nachos ($8), fish and chips ($9) and sautéed scallops ($13). The restaurant closes at 10pm, the diner at 11pm. Gunner's Pub at Cousins is a good evening venue.

WEST COAST

About midway down the coast on the western shore along Hwy 14 is the village of Miminegash, in one of the more remote sections of the province. The **Irish Moss Interpretative Centre** (☎ 902-882-4313, Hwy 14; admission $1; open 10am-7pm Mon-Sat, noon-8pm Sun early June-late Sept) was begun by local women whose families have long been involved in the collecting or harvesting of the moss, a type of seaweed.

Almost half the world's supply of Irish moss comes from PEI. If you're dying to savor seaweed, the **Seaweed Pie Cafe** at the center has a standard lunch menu but also serves a special seaweed pie ($3.25 a slice). The moss is in the middle layer of cream.

Cedar Dunes Provincial Park (☎ 902-859-8785, fax 902-859-3900, W www.gov .pe.ca/visitorsguide/explore/parks, off Hwy 14) Sites $17/20 without/with hookups. Open late June–mid-Sept. There is tent space in an open grassy field adjacent to West Point Lighthouse. The beach is nice.

West Point Lighthouse (☎ 800-764-6854, fax 902-859-1510, W www.peisland.com/west-point/light.htm, off Hwy 14) Doubles $80-95 July & Aug, $70-85 June & Sept. Open late June-Sept. The lighthouse, dating from 1875, has been restored, and part of the former lightkeeper's quarters has been converted into a nine-room inn. The restaurant is famous for its clam chowder ($5/7 cup/bowl).

New Brunswick

At 73,400 square km, New Brunswick is the largest province in the Maritimes. It's quite different from bucolic Prince Edward Island or coast-oriented Nova Scotia: New Brunswick's defining characteristic is that it remains largely forested. Yet, for most visitors, the areas apart from the vast woodlands have the most appeal.

From the Québec border the gentle, pastoral farming region of the Saint John River Valley leads to the Bay of Fundy with its cliffs, coves and tidal flats caused by the world's highest tides. The eastern shore offers warm, sandy beaches and strongholds of Acadian culture. The wooded highlands of the north contain one of the highest mountains in eastern Canada.

Saint John, the largest city, and Fredericton, the capital, both have intriguing Loyalist histories. Moncton is Canada's largest partly French-speaking city east of Québec.

History

What is now New Brunswick was originally the land of the Mi'kmaq and, in the western and southern areas, the Maliseet First Nations.

The French first attempted settlement in the 1600s. The Acadians, as they came to be known, farmed the area around the Bay of Fundy using a system of dikes. In 1755 they were expelled by the English, whose numbers rose by some 14,000 with the arrival of the Loyalists after the American Revolution. The Loyalists settled the Saint John and St Croix river valleys and established Saint John. Through the 1800s, lumbering and shipbuilding boomed, and by the start of the 20th century other industries, including fishing, had developed. That era of prosperity was ended by the Depression. Attempts have been made since then to create jobs in such areas as high tech, filmmaking and call centers.

Climate

Summers are mild and winters are very snowy and cold. The driest month of the year is August. Generally, there is more rain in the south.

Highlights

Entered Confederation: July 1, 1867
Area: 73,400 sq km
Population: 756,600
Provincial Capital: Fredericton

- Explore the Saint John River as it eases its way through the province-long valley.
- Be amazed by the world's highest tides along the Bay of Fundy.
- Visit Grand Manan, a rugged island offering hiking and whale-watching.
- Step back in time in gracious St Andrews, one of Canada'a most alluring towns.
- Sample a dozen gourmand delights at the Saturday morning Moncton Market.
- Take a trip back in time at the Acadian Historic Village near Caraquet.
- Hike through huge, undeveloped Mt Carleton Provincial Park.

Fredericton page 535
Moncton page 569
St Stephen page 546
Saint John page 558
Fundy Isles page 550
OTHER MAPS
New Brunswick page 533

531

Economy

Lumber and pulp and paper operations, are two of the main industries. Some 28,000 jobs depend directly or indirectly on forestry, and pulp and paper exports are worth a billion dollars a year. Almost 99% of the tree harvesting involves clearcutting.

Manufacturing and mining are also important, as are mixed farming and fishing. Large scale lead and zinc mining continues near Bathurst, and potash is mined near Sussex.

Population & People

Just over 10,000 Native Indians live in New Brunswick, with the Maliseet along the upper Saint John River in the west and the Mi'kmaq in the east. A majority of the population of 756,600 has British roots. People with Irish ancestry are the biggest single group in places like Saint John and Miramichi.

Around 37% of the population have French ancestors and 16% speak French only. The French-speaking areas are Edmundston (85% French), the Acadian Peninsula (especially Caraquet), the coast from Miramichi to Shediac (mixed English and French) and Moncton (40% French).

In 1969 New Brunswick became Canada's only officially bilingual province (on the provincial level, English is not an official language in Québec, and French isn't official in the other eight provinces).

Information

Tourism New Brunswick (☎ 800-561-0123, **W** www.tourismnbcanada.com) handles provincial tourist information. Its mailing address is New Brunswick Tourism, PO Box 40, Woodstock, NB E3N 3G1.

The province has six primary visitor information centers at strategic entry points: St Jacques, Woodstock, St Stephen, Aulac, Cape Jourimain and Campbellton. These are open from mid-May to mid-October only. From mid-June to early September they're open until 9pm daily, the rest of the year until 6pm.

The Harmonized Sales Tax (HST) is 15%.

For emergency service dial ☎ 911 anywhere in the province.

Activities

A copy of the tourist office's *Adventures Left & Right* or *Craft Directory* may be helpful. New Brunswick has good bird- and whale-watching, particularly in the southern regions. Note that in summer whale tours in some areas may fill up a week in advance.

Fundy National Park and Mount Carleton Provincial Park have numerous hiking trails and there is more walking in the eastern Bay of Fundy region, notably along the new Fundy Trail. Bicycle routes exist along the Saint John River above Fredericton and in the national parks. The tourist office can help locate canoeing waters and give advice on fishing.

Accommodations

The province has a complete range of accommodations, and Tourism New Brunswick's provincial tourist offices can help with reservations. Aside from national and provincial campgrounds and motels, there are B&Bs, country inns, farm vacations and sports lodges and cabins. Accommodations are required to post a sign in the room listing officially approved prices.

Getting Around

Bus New Brunswick's SMT bus lines (☎ 800-567-5151, **W** www.smtbus.com) link up with Orleans Express in Rivière du Loup, Québec, three times a day. Direct connections from North Bay, Toronto, Ottawa, Montréal and Québec City right through to Moncton are possible. SMT also connects to Orleans Express in Campbellton daily.

On Friday and Saturday, SMT buses from Saint John go as far as Bangor, Maine, where they connect with Vermont Transit to/from Boston and New York. Eastbound, a bus leaves New York just after midnight on Saturday and Sunday connecting right through to Halifax with changes in Bangor, Saint John, Moncton and Amherst – a 24-hour trip! For information on the daily bus service between Bangor and Calais, see Getting There & Away in the St Stephen section.

The main SMT routes include Bangor to Saint John to Moncton, Moncton to Fredericton to Miramichi, Rivière du Loup to Edmundston to Fredericton to Moncton, Campbellton to Miramichi to Moncton, Moncton to Summerside to Charlottetown and Moncton to Sackville to Amherst.

The Maritime Bus Pass is valid on all SMT and Acadian Lines services in the Maritimes

NEW BRUNSWICK

($201/259/380 for 7/10/14 consecutive days). It can only be purchased at the bus stations in Antigonish, Campbellton, Charlottetown, Edmundston, Fredericton, Halifax, Moncton, New Glasgow, Saint John, Sydney, Truro and Yarmouth. Although the pass is valid on SMT services to/from Rivière du Loup, Québec, and Bangor, Maine, it cannot be purchased in those cities. If you have time, you can order one in advance over the phone at ☎ 800-567-5151 and have it mailed to you, otherwise just take the train from Montréal to Campbellton, or a ferry from Maine to Yarmouth, Nova Scotia, and purchase your bus pass there.

Train VIA Rail (☎ 888-842-7245, **W** www .viarail.ca) operates a passenger service between Montréal and Halifax six times a week. For schedules, pick up the *National Timetable* booklet at any VIA Rail station. Train travel is more expensive than taking the bus and reservations are important, especially on weekends and holidays.

Tickets are available from Montréal to Campbellton ($114, 11 hours), Bathurst ($127, 13 hours), Miramichi ($134, 14 hours), Moncton ($163, 15½ hours), Sackville ($167, 16½ hours), Amherst ($170, 17 hours), Truro ($183, 18½ hours) and Halifax ($197, 20 hours).

Between the Maritimes and Québec, travel is discounted 40% if the trip is booked seven or more days in advance. Only a limited number of seats are offered at the discount rates. Children, seniors (over 60) and students with international cards are entitled to discounts any time.

Fredericton

pop 47,000
Fredericton remains the queen of New Brunswick's towns. Unlike most of its counterparts, it is non-industrial and a very pretty, genteel, quiet place. This is one of the only major cities in the Maritimes not reached by tidal waters (the city is 16m above sea level). This is the province's capital, and about a fifth of its residents work for the government. The small, tree-lined central area has some visible history to explore. Abundant benches grace the streets of this welcoming city.

History
Three hundred years ago, Maliseet and Mi'kmaq Native Indians lived and fished in the area. The French followed in 1732 but were eventually burned out by the British, who brought in 2000 Loyalists fleeing the United States after the American Revolution.

Fredericton really came into its own the next year when the British Government decided to form a new province by splitting New Brunswick away from Nova Scotia. Lieutenant-governor Thomas Carleton visited then Ste Anne's Point and was impressed with its strategic location on the Saint John River, suitable for receiving large ships and practically in the center of the new province. In 1785, he not only made it the provincial capital and the base for a British garrison but renamed it 'Frederick'stown' in honor of Sir Frederick, Duke of York and the second son of King George III.

Orientation
The city center is on a small, rounded peninsula that juts into the Saint John River. The Westmorland St Bridge connects the downtown area with the north shore residential areas. Farther east, Hwy 8 crosses the river on the Princess Margaret Bridge. Coming into town from the west on the Trans Canada Hwy, take Regent St straight down to the heart of town.

Information
The Visitors Centre (☎ 506-460-2129, 397 Queen St) in City Hall is open Monday to Friday year-round from 8am to 4:15pm and until 8pm during summer.

If you're driving in, the visitors center should be your first stop as they'll give you a pass to park free at some municipal parking lots (including the one behind City Hall) and all parking meters. It's the sort of friendly gesture you remember.

The main post office (☎ 506-444-8602, 570 Queen St) is open 8am to 5pm Monday to Friday. General Delivery mail addressed to Fredericton, NB E3B 4Y1, is kept here.

Fredericton Public Library (☎ 506-460-2800, 4 Carleton St) offers free Internet access upstairs on a first-come, first-served basis 10am to 5pm Monday, Tuesday, Thursday and Saturday, 10am to 9pm Wednesday and Friday.

Paragon Laundromat (☎ 506-458-5852, 256 Regent St at Charlotte), open 9am to 9pm weekdays, 9am to 6pm weekends, charges $1.25 to wash.

If you need to see a doctor you can visit the After Hours Clinic (1015 Regent St) 6pm to 10pm weekdays, 1pm to 5pm weekends. It's beside Shoppers Drug Mart. No appointment is required. Canadians/foreigners without health insurance are charged $25/35.

Officers' Square
This is the city's central park – on Queen St between Carleton and Regent Sts. The square was once the military parade ground and it still sits among military buildings.

At 11am and 7pm weekdays from mid-July to the third week in August, you can see the full-uniform Changing of the Guard ceremony here.

Also in the park during summer is the Outdoor Summer Theatre, which performs daily at 12:15pm weekdays and 2pm weekends. This free theater-in-the-square is performed by a local group known as the Calithumpians, whose skits of history are laced with a good dose of humor.

On Tuesday and Thursday evenings in summer at 7:30pm, free band concerts attract crowds. There might be a marching, military or pipe band, and sometimes classical music is played too. In the park is a statue

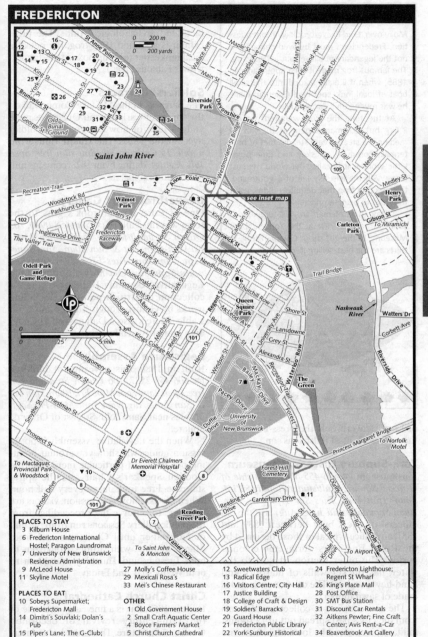

FREDERICTON

Saint John River

see inset map

PLACES TO STAY
3 Kilburn House
6 Fredericton International
  Hostel; Paragon Laundromat
7 University of New Brunswick
  Residence Administration
9 McLeod House
11 Skyline Motel

PLACES TO EAT
10 Sobeys Supermarket;
  Fredericton Mall
14 Dimitri's Souvlaki; Dolan's
  Pub
15 Piper's Lane; The G-Club;
  Upper Deck Sports Bar
25 Cravings Café

27 Molly's Coffee House
29 Mexicali Rosa's
33 Mei's Chinese Restaurant

OTHER
1 Old Government House
2 Small Craft Aquatic Center
4 Boyce Farmers' Market
5 Christ Church Cathedral
8 After Hours Clinic;
  Shoppers Drug Mart

12 Sweetwaters Club
13 Radical Edge
16 Visitors Centre; City Hall
17 Justice Building
18 College of Craft & Design
19 Soldiers' Barracks
20 Guard House
21 Fredericton Public Library
22 York-Sunbury Historical
  Museum
23 Officers' Square

24 Fredericton Lighthouse;
  Regent St Wharf
26 King's Place Mall
28 Post Office
30 SMT Bus Station
31 Discount Car Rentals
32 Aitkens Pewter; Fine Craft
  Center; Avis Rent-a-Car
34 Beaverbrook Art Gallery
35 New Brunswick Legislative
  Assembly Building

NEW BRUNSWICK

Fredericton's Famous Frog

Move over, Lord Beaverbrook. Without question, Fredericton's most beloved character is not the legendary publisher but a 19kg frog. The famous frog made its first appearance in 1885, when it literally leaped into the small boat of local innkeeper Fred Coleman while he was rowing on Killarney Lake.

At the time the frog weighed a mere 3.6kg but Coleman kept it at the inn by feeding it a steady (very steady) diet of buttermilk, cornmeal, whiskey and june bugs. Little wonder it became the world's largest frog. With the leisurely life of a gourmand, this was one frog that definitely didn't want to return to being a prince.

Today the Coleman frog is forever enshrined in a glass case at the York-Sunbury Museum. In the gift shop, Coleman frog T-shirts are the best-selling items.

of Lord Beaverbrook, the press baron and the province's most illustrious son.

York-Sunbury Historical Museum

This museum (☎ 506-455-6041, *west side of Officers' Square; adult/student/family $2/1/4; open 1pm-4pm Tues-Sat Apr–mid-Dec, 10am-5pm daily mid-June–Aug*) is in the old officers' quarters built between 1839 and 1851, an edifice typical of those designed by the Royal Engineers during the colonial period. The older section, closest to the water, has thicker walls of masonry and hand-hewn timbers. The other, newer end is made of sawn timber.

The museum has a collection of items from the city's past spread out in 12 rooms: military pieces used by local regiments and by British and German armies from the Boer and both World Wars; furniture from a Loyalist sitting room and a Victorian bedroom; Native Indian and Acadian artifacts and archaeological finds. The prize exhibit is a stuffed 19kg frog, the pet of a local innkeeper (see the boxed text 'Fredericton's Famous Frog').

Soldiers' Barracks

The barracks in the Military Compound on the corner of Carleton and Queen Sts gives you an idea of how the common soldier lived in the 1820s. The **Guard House** (*no phone, 15 Carleton St; admission free; open July & Aug*), dating from 1828, contains military memorabilia.

Beaverbrook Art Gallery

One of Lord Beaverbrook's gifts to the town was this gallery (☎ 506-458-0970, *703 Queen St; adult/family $5/10; open Mon-Fri 9am-6pm, Sat & Sun 10am-5pm June-Sept, 9am-5pm Tues-Fri, 10am-5pm Sat, noon-5pm Sun Oct-May*), opposite the Legislative Assembly Building. There's a collection of British paintings including works by Gainsborough, Turner and Constable. There's also a Dalí as well as Canadian and provincial works.

Legislative Assembly

Built in 1880, this government building (☎ 506-453-2527, *706 Queen St; admission free; open 9am-7pm Mon-Fri, 10am-5pm Sat & Sun June-Aug, 9am-5pm Mon-Fri Sept-May*) is near Saint John St, east of Officers' Square.

When the Legislative Assembly is not in session, guides will show you around, pointing out things of particular merit, like the wooden Speaker's Chair and the spiral staircase. Free tours leave every half hour. When the assembly is in session, visitors are welcome to observe the proceedings from the public gallery. Sessions run from the end of November until Christmas and from March to June, with sittings from 1pm to 6pm Tuesday and Thursday and 10am to 6pm Wednesday and Friday.

Christ Church Cathedral

Built in 1853, this is a fine early example of the 19th-century revival of decorated Gothic architecture. The cathedral is interesting because it's very compact – tall for the short length of the building, yet with a balance and proportion that make the interior seem both normal and spacious.

There is some good stained glass, especially around the altar. Free tours are offered daily mid-June to Labor Day. The church is just off Queen St at Church St, by the river, east of town.

Boyce Farmers' Market

The farmer's market (☎ 506-451-1815, 665 George St between Regent & Saint John Sts; open 6am-1pm Sat year-round) has nearly 150 stalls selling fresh fruit, vegetables, meat and cheese, as well as handicrafts, homemade desserts and flowers. There is a restaurant, too, open for breakfast and brunch.

Old Burial Ground

The Loyalist cemetery (Brunswick St, at Carleton St; open 8am-9pm daily), dating from 1784, is an easy walk from downtown. This area was settled by Loyalists who arrived from the 13 colonies after the American Revolution, and many of them were eventually buried here. It's interesting to look around the grounds.

Old Government House

This magnificent stone palace (☎ 506-453-6440/2505, 51 Woodstock Rd; admission free; open 10am-5pm daily mid-June–mid-Sept, 10am-4pm Mon-Fri rest of the year) was erected for the British governor in 1826. The representative of the queen moved out in 1893, after the province refused to continue paying his expenses, and during most of the 20th century the complex was an RCMP headquarters. In 2000 it was converted into a tourist attraction of the first order, and from mid-June to mid-September guided tours are led by staff in period costume (other months it's best to call ahead). New Brunswick's lieutenant governor presently lives on the 3rd floor, and the official black limousine with a single crown for a license number is often parked on the west side of the building.

Activities

If you'd care to drift along the river, the Small Craft Aquatic Center (☎ 506-460-2260, off Woodstock Rd; open mid-May–early Oct), near Old Government House on the Saint John River behind the Victoria Health Centre, rents canoes, kayaks and rowboats

at $9 an hour. A much better deal is to pay $30 for a weekly pass, which allows you to paddle up and down the river as much as you like for the entire week! The catch is, they only loan their equipment for two hours at a time, but you can report back and begin another two hours right away. The center also offers guided canoe tours, from one-hour outings to three-day river ecology trips, and instruction in either canoeing or kayaking. Two-hour paddles depart upon request at $25 for the first person, $20 for the second and $15 for those under 18. They'll even go if you're alone, but you should call ahead to make sure a guide will be available.

Organized Tours

The first thing to do is head to the information office to pick up the excellent Tourrific Tours brochure from the city. There are literally dozens of tours of all sorts available, free or otherwise.

In July and August, a member of the Calithumpian actors' group wearing a historic costume leads a good, free hourlong walking tour around town, beginning at City Hall at 10am and 6pm weekdays, 10am weekends. Ultra-popular are the **Haunted Hikes** ($12), given by the same, suddenly ghoulish, thespians at 9pm on Monday, Tuesday, Thursday and Friday.

To see Fredericton from the water, the **Carleton** (☎ 506-454-2628, Regent St Wharf) has riverfront cruises on the Saint John River. Afternoon and evening departures happen daily in July and August, at 2pm and 7pm Saturday and Sunday in June and September. A one-hour tour costs $7/3 adult/child. The tour boat is basically a houseboat.

Special Events

Some of the major events and festivals celebrated in the city between July and September are listed here.

New Brunswick Highland Games Festival This two-day Scottish festival with music, dancing and contests on the Old Government House grounds is held each summer in late July.

New Brunswick Summer Music Festival Four days of classical music held at Memorial Hall at the University of New Brunswick campus in late August.

Handicraft Show This juried craft show is held in Officers' Square on the first weekend in

September. All types of handicrafts are exhibited and sold.

The Fredericton Exhibition This annual six-day affair starts on the first weekend in September. It's held at the exhibition grounds, on the corner of Smythe and Saunders Sts. The exhibition includes a farm show, a carnival, harness racing and stage shows.

Harvest Jazz & Blues Festival This weeklong event transforms the downtown area into the 'New Orleans of the North' in early September when jazz, blues and Dixieland performers arrive from across North America.

Places to Stay

Hostels *Fredericton International Hostel at Rosary Hall* (☎ *506-450-4417, fax 506-462-9692, 621 Churchill Row)* Rooms $20/22 members/nonmembers. Office open 7am-noon & 6pm-10pm daily. This HI-affiliated hostel set up in a capacious older residence hall is oozing with character. In summer it's fully a hostel, but even in other seasons when students return the management keeps rooms open for hostelers. Travelers are often shocked to find that rates given here get them their own room on most nights. A common kitchen and laundry facilities are available, and free parking is provided.

University of New Brunswick (☎ *506-453-4800, fax 506-453-3585,* ᴡ *www.unb.ca/housing/conf/accomodations.html, 20 Bailey Dr)* Singles/doubles $30/44 tourists, $19/31 students. Only students can get the weekly rate of $84. From June to mid-August the university has 120 rooms available, most with shared baths (the 22 rooms with private baths are usually full). The rooms are in McLeod House, 81 Montgomery St, but to get one you must first go to the Residence Administration, 20 Bailey Dr, 1km away in the lower campus (or 1.2km southeast of the hostel). This office is open daily from 8am to 11pm. Common kitchens are on the 5th and 6th floors of the residence, and there's a pool. The campus is within walking distance of the downtown area to the southeast.

Tourist Homes & Motels *Kilburn House* (☎ *506-455-7078, fax 506-455-8192,* ᴡ *www.bbcanada.com/2282.html, 80 Northumberland St)* Singles/doubles from $55/70. This three-story red frame house on the west edge of downtown has three rooms.

Skyline Motel (☎ *506-455-6683, 502 Forest Hill Dr)* Singles/doubles $46/49 ($55 with two beds), $175 a week single. This motel on the east side of town operates as a student residence from September to April. From May to August the 27 units are available to tourists.

Norfolk Motel (☎ *800-686-8555, 815 Riverside Dr)* Singles/doubles $42/48 June–mid-Sept, $40/46 rest of the year. A kilometer east of Princess Margaret Bridge in North Fredericton, the Norfolk has 20 rooms back-to-back in a long wooden block (ask for one of the quieter units on the back side). It's on the old road to Moncton, 5km from the center of town.

Places to Eat

There has been a small explosion of outdoor cafés and restaurants featuring outdoor decks in Fredericton. The best place to head for supper and fresh air is *Pipers Lane*, a courtyard of sorts between King and Queen Sts, west of York St. The alley between Nos 358 and 362 Queen St will take you directly there. Surrounding this open area are almost a dozen restaurants, coffee shops, pubs and ice-cream parlors, half of them with outdoor seating.

Dimitri's Souvlaki (☎ *506-452-8882, 349 King St)* Mains $12. Open 11am-10pm Mon-Sat. Dimitri's in Pipers Lane is good for an inexpensive Greek lunch or dinner of souvlaki, pita, brochettes, moussaka and the like. The traditional shish kebab is $12, and you can enjoy it on the restaurant's rooftop patio. Vegetarians can order a Caesar salad ($6), a deluxe Greek salad ($5) or a super vegetarian pita ($3.25).

Cravings Café (☎ *506-452-7482, 384 King St opposite Pipers Lane)* Lunches under $5. Open 7:30am-6pm Mon-Fri, 8am-5pm Sat. Until 11am you can enjoy a hearty breakfast for $3.50, then it's tasty lunch fare like pitas, wraps and *donairs* (gyros). It's self-service, but arty and informal, light years from the fast-food places in nearby King's Place Mall.

Mexicali Rosa's (☎ *506-451-0686, 546 King St)* Mains $6-12. Open 11:30am-11:30pm Sun-Thurs, 11:30am-1am Fri & Sat. More outdoor dining can be enjoyed here, with nachos ($7), cheese quesadillas ($6), chimichangas ($12) and a burrito dinner ($10).

Mei's Chinese Restaurant (☎ 506-454-2177, 74 Regent St) Full dinners $13-15. Open 11:45-2pm Tues-Fri, 5pm-9pm Tues-Sun. Mei's is the best Chinese restaurant in town. It offers Szechuan and Taiwan-style dishes and has some combination plates (egg roll, fried rice and main course) for $7. There's a lunch buffet on Thursday and Friday ($11).

Molly's Coffee House (☎ 506-457-9305, 554 Queen St) Dishes under $7. Open 9:30am-midnight Mon-Fri, noon-midnight Sat & Sun. In addition to lighter fare and good coffee, Molly's has a few vegetarian options. Its specialty is baked meals such as lasagna, casserole and shepherd's pie.

Sobeys Supermarket (☎ 506-458-8891, on Prospect St West off Regent St South) Open 24 hrs. Away from the center, this supermarket at the Fredericton Mall is a good source of picnic fare. Saturday mornings, the farmers' market previously mentioned is even better.

Entertainment
Upper Deck Sports Bar (☎ 506-457-1475, Piper's Lane) Open 5pm-2am Mon-Thurs, noon-2am Fri-Sun. Sports freaks have their choice of bars in Fredericton, including this one. There are cheap pitchers of beer, lots of billiards and live music on the weekends ($4 cover).

Dolan's Pub (☎ 506-454-7474, Piper's Lane) Open 11:30am-midnight Mon-Wed, 11:30am-2am Thur & Fri, 10am-2am Sat. Dolan's presents live Celtic music on Thursday, Friday and Saturday nights beginning around 10pm ($5 cover).

The G-Club (☎ 506-455-7768, 377 King St off Pipers Lane) Open 8pm-2am Wed-Sun. This is Fredericton's only gay/alternative club. There's no sign. Just look for the door with the number 377 on it beside Corleone's Pizza and go up to the 3rd floor. A $3 cover charge is collected.

Sweetwaters Club (☎ 506-444-0121, 339 King St) Open 8pm-2am Thurs-Sat. This large bar and restaurant with disco dancing caters to teens and 20s ($5 cover charge).

Shopping
Fredericton is a hot spot of the old craft of pewter smithing. Examples can be seen at *Aitkens Pewter* (☎ 506-453-9474, 65 Regent St). Other craftspeople in the town

do pottery and woodcarving. *The Fine Craft Center* (☎ 506-450-8989, 87 Regent St) often displays artistic pottery and sculpture.

The *College of Craft & Design of New Brunswick Community College* (☎ 506-453-2305, 457 Queen St) behind Soldiers Barracks provides another chance to buy artistic pottery.

Getting There & Away
Air Fredericton is a small city, but as the provincial capital it does get a fair bit of air traffic. Many flights in and out are stopovers between various other points. Air Canada or its subsidiary Air Canada Jazz has at least one nonstop flight daily from Montréal, Ottawa, Toronto and Halifax. A $12 'airport improvement fee' must be paid separately at the airport restaurant (not included in the ticket).

Bus The SMT bus station (☎ 506-458-6000, open 7:30am-8:30pm Mon-Fri, 9am-8:30pm Sat-Sun) is at 101 Regent St at Brunswick St. Coin lockers are $2. Schedules and fares to some destinations include: Moncton ($30) at 11:15am and 6pm daily; Campbellton ($33) and then Québec City ($80) at 11:30am, as well as at 2:50pm and 8:15pm via Edmundston; and Halifax ($73) and Amherst ($40), which are both at the same times as Moncton. It also goes to Summerside and Charlottetown, PEI ($61), at the same times as to Moncton. There's a bus west to Bangor, Maine ($34), on Friday and Saturday at 11:20am via Saint John.

Getting Around
To/From the Airport Fredericton Airport is on Hwy 102, 14km southeast of town. A taxi to the airport costs $16 for the first person, then another $1 for each additional person. Avis, Budget, Hertz and National have car rental desks at the airport.

Bus The city has a good public transportation system, Fredericton Transit (☎ 506-460-2200), and the $1.45 fares include free transfers. Service is halved on Saturday and no buses run on Sundays and holidays.

Most Fredericton city bus routes begin at King's Place Mall, on King St between York and Carleton. To facilitate connections, all buses leave together.

The university is a 15-minute walk from the downtown area; if you want to take the bus, take No 16S south on Regent St. It runs about every 20 minutes.

For hitching on the Trans Canada Hwy you want the Fredericton Mall bus, which is No 16S or 11S.

For heading back into the city from these places catch the No 16N.

Car Discount Car Rentals (☎ 506-458-1118), 580 King St at Regent, has compact cars starting at $44 a day with 200km or $49 with unlimited mileage, plus $13 a day collision insurance and 15% tax. The 'weekend special' of $123 (plus tax and insurance) gives you a car for any three days with unlimited mileage, so long as one of the days is a Saturday. In midsummer, prices could be higher.

Avis (☎ 506-454-2847), also downtown at 81 Regent St, is more expensive.

Bicycle Rentals are available at Radical Edge (☎ 506-459-3478), 386 Queen St, at $5/25 per hour/day. The tourist office or Radical Edge can give you help on myriad trails around the area; you can pick up the colorful free *Trail Guide* brochure.

Saint John River Valley

The Saint John River winds along the western border of the province past forests and beautiful lush farmland, through Fredericton between tree-lined banks, and then around rolling hills to the Bay of Fundy. The valley's soft, eye-pleasing landscape is particularly picturesque from just north of Saint John to Florenceville. Most of New Brunswick's Maliseet Indians live along its banks.

There are bridges and ferries across the river at various points. The Trans Canada Hwy (Hwy 2) follows the river up to Edmundston and then crosses into Québec.

Because the main highway connecting the Maritimes with central Canada runs along the river, it's a busy route in summer. There's a choice of two routes, the quicker Trans Canada Hwy mostly on the west side of the river, or the more scenic Hwy 105 on the east. The slower route goes right through many of the smaller villages.

MACTAQUAC

The **Mactaquac Power Dam**, 25km west of Fredericton on Hwy 102, has created a lake of 84 square km called Head Pond that extends as far as Nackawic. The concrete dam built in 1968 is 43m high, the tallest in the Maritimes. The six turbines generate 600,000 kilowatts of electricity, though only in spring when the station is working at capacity. It's possible to visit the generating station (☎ 506-462-3814, 451 Hwy 105; admission free; open 9am-4pm daily May-Sept) and take a 45-minute tour, which includes a look at the turbines and an explanation of how they work.

Mactaquac Provincial Park

Mactaquac is New Brunswick's most developed provincial park. To get there from Fredericton go 24km west on Hwy 102, cross the hydroelectric dam and continue another 6km around on Hwy 105. This park (or resort) along the north side of Head Pond offers swimming, fishing, hiking, picnic sites, camping and boat rentals. There's also a golf course where you play for $40 (plus $15 club rentals). Day use is $5 per vehicle.

The *campground* (☎ 506-363-4747, Ⓦ *www.tourismnbcanada.com/web/english/outdoor_network, 1256 Hwy 105; open mid-May–early Oct)* is huge, with 305 sites at $21 for tents or $23 with electricity. This place is busy and through much of the summer it will be full on Friday and Saturday nights. The lakeside campground has a swimming beach, grocery store and kitchen shelter.

King's Landing Historical Settlement

This re-created early 19th-century Loyalist village (☎ 506-363-5090; adult/family $12/30; open 10am-5pm daily June–mid-Oct) is 36km west of Fredericton, on the way to Woodstock. Take exit 253 off the Trans Canada Hwy. Here you can get a glimpse (and taste) of pioneer life in the Maritimes. A community of 100 costumed staff inhabits 11 houses, a school, church, store and sawmill typical of those used a century ago. The **King's Head Inn** serves traditional food and beverages. The children's programs make King's Landing ideal for families.

A provincial tourist office (☎ 506-363-4994, 10 Prince William Rd; open 10am-6pm daily mid-May–early Oct, 8am-9pm July & Aug) is at exit 253 off the Trans Canada Hwy near King's Landing.

WOODSTOCK

A small town set in a rich farming area, Woodstock acts as a tourist crossroads. The Trans Canada Hwy passes the town, as does Hwy 95 to Interstate 95 in Maine (which runs south to Boston and New York). The center of Woodstock has some fine old large Maritime houses.

If you're arriving from the USA, a large provincial tourist office (☎ 506-325-4427, open 10am-6pm daily late May-early Oct, 8am-9pm July & Aug) is off Hwy 95, 5km east of the border crossing from Houlton, Maine, on the way to Woodstock and the Trans Canada Hwy.

HARTLAND

Hartland is an attractive little town with a nice setting, and it does have the grandaddy of New Brunswick's many wooden covered bridges. The 74 such bridges dotted around the province on secondary roads were covered to protect the timber beams used in the construction. With such protection from

rain and sun, a bridge lasts about 80 years. They are generally high and wide because cartloads of hay pulled by horses had to pass over them.

The **Hartland Covered Bridge** over the Saint John River was erected in 1897 and is 390m long. The summer-only tourist office (☎ 506-375-4075; open 9am-6pm daily late May-early Oct) at the east end of this bridge has a complete listing of covered bridges, if you're interested.

Places to Stay & Eat

Ja-Sa-Le Motel (☎ 800-565-6433, fax 506-375-8860, on Trans Canada Hwy) Singles/doubles $56/60 mid-June–mid-Sept, $46/50 rest of the year. This 14-room place, north of town 2km from the bridge, is the only local motel. In July and August the motel rents rooms in a farmhouse diagonally across the highway at $45/50.

21st Century B&B (☎ 506-375-6786, 5 Monty St) Rooms $45 single or double with shared bath year-round including breakfast. This new two-story wooden house is in the upper town, 1km from the bridge.

Campbell's B&B (☎ 506-375-4775, e campbb@nbnet.nb.ca, 7175 Hwy 105) Singles/doubles $40/50 including breakfast. This large, quaint two-story wooden house

NEW BRUNSWICK

A River under Siege

The Saint John River begins in Maine, USA, in the northwestern corner of New Brunswick and flows south for over 700km before entering the Bay of Fundy at Saint John. It has been likened to the Rhine for its strong inexorable flow, the various industries within sight of its banks and the transportation corridors that follow its broad course.

Like so many North American rivers, the Saint John has experienced the impact of human activities. Chemical pollution from cities and factories falls in the headwaters as acid rain, and pesticides sprayed on agricultural lands are carried into the river by runoff. The clearcutting of forests increases the level of sediments in the province's rivers, covering the spawning areas of fish with silt and depleting the oxygen supply.

New Brunswick Hydro's Mactaquac Dam, west of Fredericton, blocks the migration of Atlantic salmon and other species up the river. To compensate for this, a salmon hatchery has been built next to the dam and other species are carried around it in tanker trucks.

All along the Saint John's banks, huge pulp mills pump liquid wastes directly into the river's flow. Excluding the mills upriver in Maine, three of New Brunswick's largest pulp and paper mills abut the Saint John: Fraser Papers at Edmundston, Irving Pulp & Paper at Saint John and the St Anne-Nackawic Company at Nackawic. McCain Foods has large potato-processing plants at Grand Falls and Florenceville.

By the time the Saint John reaches the Bay of Fundy, the history of its long journey is flowing between its banks. The river we borrowed is being returned in a less than pristine state.

overlooks the Saint John River and is just 3km north of the famous covered bridge on Hwy 105. The New Brunswick Trail passes the door. It's the nicest place to stay around Hartland.

Peter's Family Restaurant (☎ 506-375-4935, 362 Main St) Meals under $10. Open 11am-10pm Mon-Fri, noon-10pm Sat & Sun. This Chinese place in an old wooden church near the covered bridge offers lunch specials weekdays from 11am to 2pm. At $7, the combination plates are good value.

GRAND FALLS
pop 7000

Although this town consists essentially of one main street, the falls on the Saint John River make it an interesting short stop. The falls are best in spring or after a heavy rain. In summer, much of the water is diverted for generating hydroelectricity. The hydro dam also takes away from the rugged beauty this site once had. The area at the bottom of the gorge reached by a staircase is more scenic than the falls themselves.

In a park in the middle of town, the falls drop about 25m and have carved out a 1½km-long gorge with walls as high as 70m. Overlooking the falls is the **Malabeam Reception Centre** (☎ 877-475-7769, Madawaska Rd; admission free; open 10am-6pm daily June & Sept; 9am-9pm July & Aug) that doubles as a tourist office. Among the displays inside is a scale model of the gorge showing the extensive trail system that follows the edge of it.

A 253-step stairway down into the gorge begins at **La Rochelle** (☎ 877-475-7769, 1 Chapel St; adult/family $3/7; open June-early Sept), across the bridge from the Malabeam Reception Center and left on Victoria St. You can also take a 45-minute **boat ride** (adult/family $10/25) up the gorge. They run up to eight times a day but only in midsummer when water levels are low (it's too dangerous when the river is in full flood). Buy the boat ticket first as it includes the stairway to the base of the gorge.

Places to Stay & Eat

Maple Tourist Home (☎ 506-473-1763, ⓦ www.bbcanada.com/4029.html, 142 Main St) Doubles $70-90 mid-June–mid-Sept, $50-65 rest of the year, breakfast included. This two-story house with three rooms is

conveniently located right in the center of town near the SMT bus stop.

La Bouffe Margarit's Restaurant (☎ 506-475-1818, 262 Broadway Blvd) Breakfast $5. Open 6am-9pm Mon-Sat, 7am-9pm Sun. Right in the center of town, La Bouffe serves café latte and filled croissants. It's popular with the locals.

Getting There & Away

The SMT bus stops at the Irving gas station (☎ 506-473-5704), 315 Broadway, right in the center of town. Daily buses to Edmundston and Fredericton call here.

Hwy 108, the Plaster Rock Hwy, cuts across the province from here to the east coast, slicing through forest for nearly its entirety. Deer and moose aren't much used to traffic here, so take care.

EDMUNDSTON
pop 11,000

If you're coming from Québec there's a good chance this will be your first stop in the Maritimes, as the border is only about 20km away. From here it's a three-hour drive to Fredericton. An international bridge on St Francois St at the south end of town connects Edmundston to Maine just across the river.

Edmundston is an industrial pulp and paper center. The Fraser Papers Pulp Mill was founded by Archibald Fraser in 1918. The town is pretty well split in half by the Madawaska River. The old central district on the west side of the river is built around low hills that give it some character. Some 85% of the population is French-speaking, though most also speak English.

Clustered around exit 18 from the highway is the tourist office, a shopping mall, some fast-food restaurants and the university.

The Madawaska Maliseet First Nation has a large reserve along Queen St south of town and Indian craft shops by the road sell wallets, belts and moccasins.

Information

The local tourist office kiosk (☎ 506-739-2115; open July & Aug) is next to the Forum opposite the university on Blvd Hébert. You get an excellent view of town and the smelly pulp mill from here.

The Royal Bank (☎ 506-735-5518, 48 St Francois St) has a branch right beside Canada Customs at the border crossing that's open 10am to 3pm Monday to Wednesday and 10am to 5pm Thursday and Friday. Otherwise TD Canada Trust (☎ 506-735-8843) is across the street and open 9am to 5pm Monday to Wednesday and Friday, 9am to 7pm Thursday.

The Edmundston Public Library (☎ 506-735-4714, open variable hours Tues-Sat), off Queen St near the Ford dealership, offers free Internet access (identification required).

Madawaska Museum
This museum (☎ 506-737-5282, 195 Blvd Hébert at 15 August St; admission $3.50; open 9am-8pm daily July & Aug, 7pm-10pm Wed & Thur, 1pm-5pm Sun rest of year) outlines the human history of the area. The museum also has displays on local industries such as the timber trade.

Places to Stay & Eat
Camping Iroquois (☎ 506-739-9060, 1318 Main St) Tent/trailer sites $16/21 for two persons ($5 for a third person). Open mid-May–mid-Sept. Four kilometers south of Edmundston along Queen St, sites Nos 43 to 46 down by the river are the nicest for tents, though farthest from the shower blocks. It's seldom full.

University of Moncton (☎ 506-737-5016, W www.cuslm.ca, 171 Blvd Hébert) Singles/doubles $23/33 plus tax. Open mid-June–late August. In summer 44 rooms are available at the Residence Louis Cyr, across the street from KFC and 500m up a steep hill from the bus station. At times you get your own washroom and fridge (a steal). No cooking facilities are provided. A cheap laundromat is in the building.

Praga Hotel (☎ 506-735-5567, fax 506-736-6315, W www.sn2000.nb.ca/comp/praga-hotel, 127 Victoria St) Singles/doubles $50/55 mid-June–mid-Sept, $40/45 rest of the year. This three-story hotel opposite the Fraser Marina has 20 rooms. It's the closest place to the bus station.

Motel Rose (☎ 506-739-9492, fax 506-739-5334, 625 Blvd Acadie) One-bed rooms $35 single or double low season, $45 'when it starts getting busy.' Two-bed rooms $45/60 triple slow/busy seasons. The nine motel rooms are in a long block facing old Hwy 2. Three small cabins are available in summer. This no-frills place is the cheapest motel in town. Motel Rose is two kilometers north of Edmundston and 13½km south of the Québec border.

Bel Air (☎ 506-735-3329, 174 Victoria St) Chinese dinners $6-8, other dinners under $14, breakfast special $3. Open 24 hours. Bel Air, on the corner of Victoria St and Blvd Hébert, with a sign that can't be missed, has been here since the 1950s and has become a city landmark. The extensive menu offers Italian, Chinese, seafood or basic Canadian fare. The portions are pretty filling.

Praga Hotel (☎ 506-735-5567, 127 Victoria St) Lunch/dinner buffet $5.95/8.75. Chinese buffet 11:15am-2pm Mon-Fri, 5pm-9pm Tues-Sun. There's also Sunday brunch from 11am to 2pm ($8.25). The food isn't as good as that at the Bel Air but you can take all you want.

Getting There & Away
The SMT terminal (☎ 506-739-8309) is across the street from the Bel Air restaurant, at 169 Victoria St near the corner of Blvd Hébert at the bridge.

You can catch buses here for Québec City and points east such as Fredericton, Moncton or Halifax. For trips to Maine or other US destinations, departures are from Saint John.

To Moncton and Amherst there are two services daily on SMT Bus Lines from which a transfer can be made to Halifax. One-way fares are Fredericton $42, Saint John $58, Moncton $69, Amherst $78 and Halifax $111. For Moncton, the local bus is at 7am, the express at 2:15pm.

There are three buses daily to Québec City, which includes transferring to the Orleans Express bus line at Rivière du Loup. Orleans is the company that covers eastern Québec. One-way fares are Rivière du Loup $19, Québec City $51.

ST JACQUES
Seven kilometers north of Edmundston, about halfway to the Québec border, is the small community of St Jacques. The Trans Canada Hwy enters Québec here and becomes Hwy 185, a slender strip of bitumen linking the Maritimes with the rest of the country.

A large provincial tourist office (☎ 506-735-2747) is right on the New Brunswick/Québec border, 9km north of Les Jardins de la Republique. It's open 10am to 6pm daily mid-May to early October and 8am to 9pm in July and August. Across the street from this office is Edmundston Airport with an authentic WWII Lancaster four-engine bomber on display outside the terminal. The Trans Canada Trail passes directly behind the bomber and enters Québec 20m north.

Les Jardins de la Republique Provincial Park *(☎ 506-735-2525, fax 506-737-4445,* **W** *www.tourismnbcanada.com/web/english/ outdoor_network)* Without/with hookups $20/23. Open mid-May–mid-Sept. Located between Hwy 2 and the Madawaska River, this park gets a lot of traffic noise.

West Fundy Shore

Almost the entire southern edge of New Brunswick is presided over by the ever-present, constantly rising and falling, always impressive waters of the Bay of Fundy.

The fascinating shoreline, the resort town of St Andrews, the quiet Fundy Isles, the city of Saint John and Fundy National Park make this easily one of the most appealing and varied regions of New Brunswick.

ST STEPHEN

Right on the US border and across the river from Calais in Maine, St Stephen is a busy entry point for US visitors coming east. It's a small, old town that forms the northern link of what is known as the Quoddy Loop – a circular tour around southeastern New Brunswick and northwestern Maine around Passamaquoddy Bay. From St Stephen the loop route goes to St Andrews and then on to Deer Island and lastly to Campobello Island, which is connected by bridge to Maine. It's a popular trip that takes anywhere from a day to a week, and includes some fine seaside scenery, interesting

---

The Tides of Funnel-Shaped Fundy

The tides of the Bay of Fundy are the highest in the world. This constant ebb and flow is a prime factor in the life of the bay, the appearance of the shoreline and even how residents set shipping and fishing schedules.

An old Mi'kmaq legend tells how the demigod Glooscap was looking for somewhere to have a bath. To be helpful, his friend Beaver built a massive dam across the mouth of a river, creating a huge pool. Yet just as Glooscap was stepping in, Whale appeared from the sea and demanded to know why water was being withheld from her realm. Glooscap quickly returned to dry land, and at that, Whale demolished the dam with a kick of her mighty tail, sending saltwater surging up the river. So powerful was her blow that the water has continued sloshing back and forth ever since.

A more prosaic scientific explanation for these record tides is in the length, depth and gradual funnel shape of the bay itself. As the high tide builds up, the water flowing into the narrowing bay has to rise on the edges. It is pushed still higher by the shallowing seabed. A compounding factor is called resonance. This refers to the rocking back and forth from one end to the other of all the water in the bay as if in a giant bathtub. When this mass swell is on the way out of the bay and meets a more powerful incoming tide head on, the volume of water increases substantially.

The contrasts between the high and ebb tide are most pronounced at the eastern end of the Bay of Fundy and around the Minas Basin, where tides of 10 to 15m occur twice daily about 12½ hours apart. The highest tide ever recorded anywhere was 16.6m, the height of a four-story building, at Burncoat Head near the village of Noel, Nova Scotia.

All tides, large and small, are caused by the rise and fall of the oceans due to the gravitational pull of the sun and the moon. Consequently, the distance of the moon and its position to the earth relative to the sun determine tidal size. When the moon is full or new, the gravitational forces of the sun and moon are working in concert, not at cross purposes, and the tides at these two times of the month are higher than average. When one of these periods coincides with the time when the moon is at its closest to earth (perigee, once every 27½ days) the tides are at their most dramatic.

The times and heights of the tides change around the bay and local schedules are available at many tourist offices in the region.

history and a number of pleasant, easy-going resort-style towns.

In St Stephen the Festival of International Cooperation is held in August, with concerts, parades and street fairs.

Information

In the former train station at the corner of Milltown Blvd and King Sts is a large provincial tourist office (☎ 506-466-7390). It offers currency exchange and other services 10am to 6pm daily June and September and 8am to 9pm July and August.

International Currency Exchange (☎ 506-466-3387, 128 Milltown Blvd), two blocks from Canada Customs, will cash Canadian dollar traveler's checks at face value without commission. Their rates are competitive for US/Canadian exchanges. It's open 8am to 6pm daily December to April and 8am to 8pm other months.

Behind the tourist office is the St Croix Public Library (☎ 506-466-7529), open 9am to 5pm Wednesday, Thursday and Saturday, 1pm to 5pm and 7pm to 9pm Tuesday, 1pm to 9pm Friday, for free Internet access.

Ganongs' Chocolate Museum

St Stephen has quite a reputation as a chocolate mecca because it is the home of Ganong's, a family chocolate business since 1873 whose products are known all around eastern Canada. It's believed that the five-cent chocolate nut bar was invented by the Ganong brothers in 1910, and they are also credited for developing the heart-shaped box of chocolates seen everywhere on Valentine's Day. The old factory on the main street of town is now a museum (☎ 506-466-7848, 73 Milltown Blvd; adult/family $4/10; open 10am-5pm Mon-Sat) displaying everything from boxed chocolates to bars such as Pal O'Mine, a very sweet little number. The Ganong Chocolates Store at the front of the complex can be visited free.

Milltown

Milltown is the most monumental part of town with many large mansions along the 3km of Milltown Blvd. About 2.6km west of the main border crossing is the **Charlotte County Museum** (☎ 506-466-3295, 443 Milltown Blvd; admission free; open 9:30am-4:30pm Mon-Sat June-Aug). There are displays on shipbuilding and lumbering, as well as on other local industries, and the town's ties to the USA. The museum is in an impressive mansion built in 1864.

Nearby and right on the river is **Salmon Falls Park**. This delightful little spot overlooks the rapids in the St Croix River and a fish ladder that helps spawning salmon continue upstream. A gravel path connects the park to **Cotton Mill Park**, the site of a cotton mill that operated from 1880 to 1959. Both overlook the **Milltown Generating Station**, one of the continent's oldest hydroelectric plants (1881), operated by New Brunswick Power. Due to insurance constraints, tours are no longer given.

Places to Stay

Oak Bay Campground (☎ 506-466-4999, fax 506-466-5472, ⓦ www.oakbaycampground .com, 742 Hwy 1) Without/with hookups $18/21. Open mid-Apr–Oct. Oak Bay is on Hwy 1 9km east of St Stephen and 5km west of the St Andrews access road. Many of the sites experience highway noise but there's an interesting shoreline to explore at low tide.

White Swan Motel (☎ 888-659-9399, 186 King St) Rooms $55 single or double ($60 two beds) mid-June–mid-Sept, $49 single or double ($55 two beds) rest of the year. This clean and quiet motel is the least expensive place to stay close to town.

Scoodic Motel (☎ 506-466-1540, fax 506-466-9103, 241 Hwy 1, 4km east on Hwy 1) Rooms $52 single or double ($56 with two beds) mid-June–mid-Sept, singles/doubles $35/40 ($45 with two beds) rest of the year. The price includes toast and coffee at the office in the morning. This reasonable motel is within sight of the SMT bus stop.

Busy Bee Motel & Cabins (☎ 800-890-0233, fax 506-465-8165, 419 Hwy 1) Rooms $35/43 single or double low/high season. Busy Bee is 2km east of the Scoodic and 3km west of Oak Bay Campground. The eight housekeeping cabins and 12 motel rooms are the least expensive in town, though the price charged could depend on how busy it is and even the weather (the price posted on the sign facing the highway may or may not be accurate).

Places to Eat

St Jerome Restaurant (☎ 506-466-3027, 73 Milltown Blvd) Dinner $9-11. Open 9am-9pm Sun-Thurs, 9am-10pm Fri & Sat. This

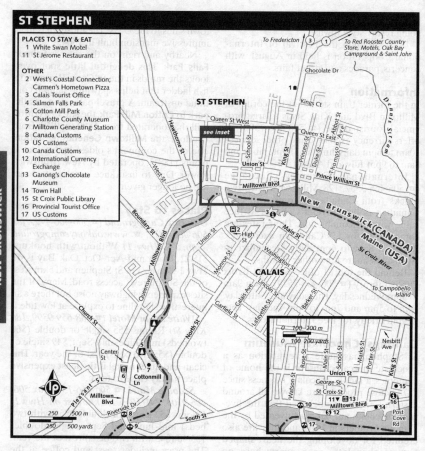

ST STEPHEN

PLACES TO STAY & EAT
1 White Swan Motel
11 St Jerome Restaurant

OTHER
2 West's Coastal Connection;
   Carmen's Hometown Pizza
3 Calais Tourist Office
4 Salmon Falls Park
5 Cotton Mill Park
6 Charlotte County Museum
7 Milltown Generating Station
8 Canada Customs
9 US Customs
10 Canada Customs
12 International Currency
   Exchange
13 Ganong's Chocolate
   Museum
14 Town Hall
15 St Croix Public Library
16 Provincial Tourist Office
17 US Customs

meat-and-potatoes restaurant, which you'll find next to the Chocolate Museum, specializes in barbecue chicken and ribs. The menu includes a half chicken or ribs ($11) and two pork chops ($9). The all-day breakfast is $3.

Red Rooster Country Store (☎ 506-466-0018, Hwy 1 at Old Bay Road, 4km east of town) Main meals $7-14. Open 6am-10pm daily. The Cook House Restaurant serves hearty meals, such as chicken dishes ($7-9), steaks ($12) and fish ($10-14). The country dinner plates are good values at $8-9. Breakfast is also good and it's worth visiting for the healthy whole wheat bread fresh from the Homestead Bakery. It's pleasant and friendly – as popular with the locals as it is with visitors.

Getting There & Away

The SMT bus stops at Red Rooster Country Store (☎ 506-466-2121), on Hwy 1 at 5 Old Bay Road, 4km east of town. There's a daily bus to Saint John ($19) at 4:10pm, connecting to Moncton ($38) and Halifax ($73) on Friday, Saturday and Sunday. To Bangor ($15), the bus only goes on Friday and Saturday at 3:30pm. In Bangor immediate connections are available to Boston and New York.

Across the border in Calais, Maine, West's Coastal Connection (☎ 800-596-2823) has a bus leaving for Bangor daily at 9:30am (US$18). The bus picks up from Marden's parking lot behind **Carmen's Hometown Pizza** (☎ 207-454-8400), 63 Main St, Calais, three blocks straight ahead from US Customs. In Bangor buses use the

Greyhound terminal and leave at 3:30pm (also stopping at Bangor Airport). Bus passes are not accepted.

ST ANDREWS

Also known as St Andrews by-the-Sea, this is a summer resort of some tradition and gentility. Together with a fine climate and picturesque beauty, St Andrews has a long, charming and often visible history – it's one of the oldest towns in the province and for a long period was on equal terms with Saint John. Loyalists founded the town in 1783.

Orientation & Information

Water St, the main street, is lined with restaurants, souvenir and craft shops and some places to stay. King St is the main cross street; one block from Water St, Queen St is also important.

There's a local information office (☎ 506-466-4858) near the junction of Hwys 1 and 127 North that's open 10am to 6pm daily July and August. A second tourist office (☎ 506-529-3556, 46 Reed Ave) is next to the arena and open 9am to 5pm daily mid-May to early October and 8am to 8pm July and August. Pick up the walking guide from the tourist office – it includes a map and brief description of 34 particularly interesting places.

Many companies offering boat trips have offices at the Adventure Destinations complex beside Market Square at the foot of King St. They're only open during the peak season from mid-June to early September.

Email & Internet Access

Seafarers' Internet Café (☎ 506-529-4610, 233 Water St) has five computers providing access at $2 per 20 minutes. You can get online 9am to 10pm daily in July and August and 9am to 9pm Tuesday to Sunday the rest of the year.

Laundry

Washboard Laundry (☎ 506-529-3048, 241 Water St) has new machines and charges $2 to wash or dry. It's open 8am to 11pm daily.

Historic Buildings

Sheriff Andrew House (☎ 506-529-5080, cnr of King & Queen Sts; admission by donation; open 9:30am-4:30pm Mon-Sat, 1pm-4:30pm Sun July-Sept) is a restored middle-class home that dates from 1820. It has been redecorated in period style and is attended by costumed guides.

Charlotte County Court House (☎ 506-529-4248, 123 Frederick St; admission free; open 9am-5pm Mon-Fri June–mid-Oct, 1pm-4pm Mon-Fri mid-Oct–May), erected 1840, displays a royal coat of arms carved on the façade in 1858. The adjacent old jail is now the County Archives (with a gift shop).

Greenoch Presbyterian Church (no phone, cnr Edward & Montague Sts), dating from 1824, is named for the relief carving of a green oak on the steeple.

Also worth a look is the classic 1889 Algonquin Hotel, with its verandah, gardens, tennis courts and pool. Inside, off the lobby, are a couple of places for a drink, be it tea or gin. In 1914 workers tarring the roof started a fire that seriously damaged the 234-room resort hotel, but it was rebuilt the next year.

Blockhouse Historic Site

The restored wooden guardhouse (☎ 506-529-4270, Water St; admission free; open 9am-8pm daily June-Aug, 9am-5pm early Sept) is the only one left of several that were built here for protection in the War of 1812 and it almost didn't survive the 20th century. In 1993 arsonists set fire to the historical structure, resulting in the floors and ceiling being rebuilt out of white pine. The original hand-hewn walls survived, distinguished inside by the dark hue of their timber. There are some good views through the gun holes on the 2nd floor. The park is at the northwest end of Water St. If the tide is out, there's a path that extends from the blockhouse out across the tidal flats. Centennial Park opposite the blockhouse has a cozy picnic pavilion with electrical outlets.

Sunbury Shores Arts & Nature Centre

This is a nonprofit educational and cultural center (☎ 506-529-3386, www.sunbury shores.org, 139 Water St; admission free; open 9am-4:30pm Mon-Fri, noon-4pm Sat year-round, also noon-4pm Sun May-Sept) offering instruction in painting, weaving, pottery and other crafts, as well as natural science courses. Various changing exhibits run through summer. It is based in Centennial House, an old general store.

NEW BRUNSWICK

The center also maintains the 800m **Twin Meadows Walking Trail**, a boardwalk and footpath through fields and woodlands beginning opposite 165 Joe's Point Road beyond the blockhouse.

Huntsman Aquarium Museum

Two kilometers northwest of the blockhouse and past the Algonquin Golf Course, right next to the Fisheries & Oceans Biological Station, is the Huntsman Marine Science Centre with research facilities and labs. It's part of the Federal Fisheries Research Centre – St Andrews' most important business. Some of Canada's leading marine biologists work here.

The Huntsman lab also maintains its museum (☎ 506-529-1202, 1 Lower Campus Rd; adult/child $5.75/3.75; open noon-4:30pm Mon & Tues, 10am-4:30pm Wed-Sun late May-Oct, 10am-6pm July-Sept) that features displays of most specimens found in local waters, including seals. There's a good seaweed display and one pool where the various creatures can be touched, even picked up, which is great for kids. The high point of the day at the aquarium is feeding of the center's harbor seals, usually done at 11am and 4pm. The center is west of town on Brandy Cove Rd.

Minister's Island Historic Site

Minister's Island was purchased and used as a summer retreat by William Cornelius van Horne, builder of the Canadian Pacific Railway across the country and the company's first president and later chairman of the board. The island, his cottage of 50 rooms and the unusual bathhouse with its tidal swimming pool can now be visited.

Minister's Island is accessible at low tide, even by car, when you can drive on the hard-packed sea floor. A few hours later this route is under 3m of water. You can only visit the island on a guided tour through **Friends of Minister's Island** (☎ 506-529-5081; adult/child $5/2.50; open May-Oct). The two-hour tours are offered once or twice a day, depending on the tides. Call to hear a recording with exact departure times. You meet at the end of Bar Rd, 1½km off Hwy 127 East to Saint John, where a guide then leads the caravan across the tidal flats. You have to have your own vehicle.

St Croix Island Viewpoint

On Hwy 127 North, 8km from town and 9km off Hwy 1, is a viewpoint (admission free; always open) overlooking the tiny island in the St Croix River where in 1604 French explorer Samuel de Champlain spent his first winter in North America. The island itself is in Maine, but a series of panels explain the significance of this National Historic Site. (In 2004 there will be massive celebrations in this region to mark the 400th anniversary of the first continuous French settlement in North America.)

Activities

Eastern Outdoors (☎ 506-529-4662, W www .easternoutdoors.com, 165B Water St; open mid-May–Oct) is a St Andrews-based outfitter that offers three-hour kayak trips at $35. It also rents kayaks ($25/35 half/full day single, $45/55 double), canoes ($25/35) and mountain bikes ($7/15/25 an hour/half day/full day).

Organized Tours

From late June to September several companies at the market wharf run $50 **sightseeing cruises** that include whale-watching. Because the ideal waters for watching these beasts are farther out in the bay, it's better to take this tour from either Deer Island or Campobello if you happen to be visiting those places, where you'll spend more time actually watching the whales. Yet even without the whales, the scenery here is lovely and seabirds are abundant.

Heritage Discovery Tours (☎ 506-529-4011, W personal.nbnet.nb.ca/sheilaw/hdt) offers a 'Magical History' walking tour (adult/family $15/40) with costumed guides at 10am daily from May to October. There's also a 'Mysteries of the Night Ghost Walk' at 8pm, which is great for families with children ($10/30). All tours begin from the Algonquin Resort, and they're often sold out a week in advance, especially during the 'bus tour months' of September and October. Most bookings are done by phone.

In July and August **HMS Transportation** (☎ 506-529-4443, 260 Water St;) has two-hour bus tours (adult/child $12/6) of the town leaving the Algonquin Resort at 10am.

Places to Stay

Camping Kiwanis Oceanfront Camping (☎ 877-393-7070, fax 506-529-3246,

W www.kiwanisoceanfrontcamping.com, 550 Water St) Tent site $19, with electricity $23. Open mid-May–mid-Oct. At the far east end of town on Indian Point is this facility, run by the Kiwanis Club, for tents and trailers. It's mostly a gravel parking area for trailers although some grassy spots are found. There are picnic tables and good views but no shade.

Tourist Homes Salty Towers (☎ 506-529-4585, e steeljm@nbnet.nb.ca, 340 Water St) Rooms from $30, doubles with bath & efficiencies with kitchen $65. You could call this a Victorian tourist home with a hostel complex; even the proprietor dubs it 'Chateau Alternatato.' Although it has been an inn since 1921, Salty Towers is unlike anything else in St Andrews, if not Canada. Run by Jamie Steel, a local naturalist, it's a sprawling 1840s mansion turned into an offbeat, very casual place for wanderers to call home – you'll also find local students on the premises. There are 16 rooms of every conceivable size and fashion, so take a look at lots. Five have private baths, the others share baths. This is not for those looking for gingerbread Victorian quaint. It's just a short walk from the bus station and town.

B&Bs & Motels Eider Shore Guesthouse (☎ 506-529-4795, W www.charlottecounty online.com/esgh.htm, 100 Queen St) Singles/doubles $65/80 July & Aug, $50/65 spring & fall. Open Apr-Nov. This central guesthouse is a modest but very appealing place that has been serving guests for many years.

A Seascape B&B (☎ 506-529-3872, e mac@nbnet.nb.ca, 190 Parr St) Singles/doubles $65/75. Open June-Sept. Similar in price to Eider Shore Guesthouse, this place is in an 1860s Cape Cod home.

Blue Moon Motel (☎ 877-534-5271, fax 506-529-3245, 310 Mowatt Dr) Rooms $55 single or double July & Aug, singles/doubles from $45/50 shoulder seasons. Open May-Oct. This 39-room single-story motel serves the purpose. The Greenside Motel next door is similar.

Places to Eat
From June to mid-October Market Square downtown hosts a Thursday morning *farmer's market*.

Waterfront Takeout (no phone, 40 King St at Water St) Lunch $5. Head here for cheap eats. It has fish and chips from $5 and cheeseburgers from $3.

Historic Chef's Café (☎ 506-529-8888, 178 Water St) Meals $12-26. Open 6:30am-10pm daily. For a burger and a dose of Elvis, there's Chef's Café, with its 1950s decor and classic jukebox. Super deluxe burgers are $8, and regular meals of chicken, steak or seafood vary. Note that all prices on the menu include tax.

Entertainment
The Tidal Pool (☎ 506-529-4282, 248 Water St) Open 3pm-1am Mon-Wed, noon-1am Thurs-Sun. This is the only place in town with live music. There's blues and folk on weekends, sometimes also during the week. Local events are advertised on posters outside.

Getting There & Around
SMT Bus Lines departs HMS Transportation (☎ 506-529-3101, W www.hmstrans .com) at 260 Water St at 4pm daily for the 1½ hour trip to Saint John ($14). It goes the other way toward Bangor, Maine, Friday and Saturday at 2:45pm ($18).

HMS Transportation also rents cars at $48 a day including 200km, plus tax and $14 insurance.

FUNDY ISLES
Deer Island
Deer Island, the closest of the three main Fundy Isles, is a modest fishing community. Lobster is the main catch. Around the island are half a dozen wharves and the net systems used in aquaculture. Narrow, winding roads run down each side toward Campobello Island (drive defensively). This 16-by-5-km island has been inhabited since 1770 and a thousand people live here year-round. It's well wooded and deer are still plentiful. Most land is privately owned so there are no hiking trails.

There's a summertime tourist information booth at the ferry landing. At **Lamberts Cove** is a huge (it could well be the world's largest) lobster pound used to hold live lobster. Another pound is at Northern Harbor down the road.

At the other end of the island is the 16-hectare **Deer Island Point Park** where Old

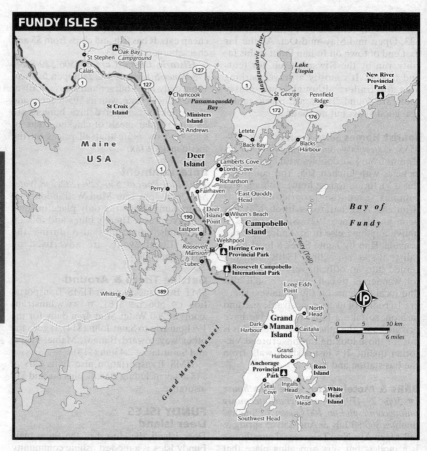

FUNDY ISLES

Sow, the world's second largest natural tidal whirlpool, can be seen offshore a few hours before high tide. Whales pass occasionally.

Kayaking The **Piskahegan River Company** (☎ 506-755-6269, 800-640-8944, W www.piskahegan.com) offers island day tours ($60/95 a half/full day), and supper and moonlight paddles ($45 and up). To get to the Deer Island base, take Leaman Rd to the left 1.3km from the ferry. The sea kayak shack will be 500m ahead. Call ahead as the shack tends to be staffed only when there are reservations.

Eastern Outdoors (☎ 800-565-2925, W www.easternoutdoors.com, Brunswick Square, 39 King St, Saint John) operates Deer Island kayak tours ($59) throughout

the year. Participants meet at the northern ferry wharf on Deer Island and see numerous marine mammals, seabirds, islands and beaches during the six hours. There's no minimum number of people required to run a tour, and for an extra $10 they'll throw in roundtrip transfers from Saint John.

Whale-Watching The whale-watching is good here, thanks to the island's location. The whales arrive in large numbers in mid-July and stay right through October. **Cline Marine Inc** (☎ 506-747-0114, 800-567-5880, W www.clinemarine.com, 99 Richardson Rd) offers whale-watching tours on the 60-passenger Cathy & Trevor at 9:30am, 12:30pm and 3:30pm in July and August (2½ hours, adult/child $50/25). The 12:30pm tour is sometimes full, but you can usually squeeze on the other two. In June only the 12:30pm departure goes, and in September and October there's a special 4-hour tour at 12:30pm costing $60/30. They depart from Richardson Wharf. From Letete ferry, go 2.8km, turn left and continue another kilometer to the office.

Lambert's Outer Island Tours (☎ 506-747-2426, 506-754-5115; *adult/child/family $43/25/120*) also offers whale-watching tours at 10am, 1pm and 4pm in July and August. It's a smaller operation than Cline with a smaller boat. They leave from Lord's Cove, 2km straight ahead from Letete ferry.

Places to Stay & Eat *Deer Island Point Park* (☎ 506-747-2423, fax 506-747-1009, W www.angelfire.com/biz/dipointpark, 195 Deer Island Point Rd) Tent sites $15. Open June-Sept. The best place to spend a night on the island is this park run by the Deer Island Recreational Council. You can set up your tent on the high bluff and spend an evening watching the Old Sow whirlpool. The campground includes nice grassy sites, showers, laundry facilities and even a small store. It's directly above the Campobello ferry landing.

Gardner House B&B (☎ 506-747-2462, Lambert Rd) Singles/doubles $50/60. Open May-Sept. This large farm house 1km beyond the lobster pound at Lambert's Cove features a small but charming steak and seafood restaurant (open 11am-10pm in summer) on the first floor and three rooms on the second floor.

45th Parallel Motel (☎ 506-747-2231, fax 506-747-1890, W www.angelfire.com/biz2/parallel45, 941 Hwy 772) Singles/doubles $46/60 May-Oct, $40/50 Nov, Dec, March & Apr, closed Jan & Feb. The summer rate includes breakfast. This motel in Fairhaven, 5km north of the Campobello ferry and 10½km south of Letete ferry, has a row of 10 rooms in a block behind the restaurant.

45th Parallel Restaurant (☎ 506-747-2231, 941 Hwy 772) Main meals $9-14. Open noon-2pm Tues & Thurs, 5pm-10pm Fri & Sat, noon-7pm Sun mid-Sept-early June, 11am-9pm early June-mid-Sept. Of course, their specialty is seafood, such as fish and chips ($9) and scallops and fries ($14). In summer they also serve lobster rolls ($10), clam chowder ($8) and lobster dinners ($22-25).

Getting There & Away A free 25-minute government ferry runs to Deer Island from Letete (L'Etete in French), 14½km south of St George on Hwy 172 via Back Bay. The ferries run year-round every half hour 7am-7pm, hourly 7pm-10pm. Get in line early on a busy day.

In July and August a privately operated ferry leaves Deer Island Point for Campobello Island, costing $13 for a car and driver plus $2 per passenger. It's a scenic 25-minute trip past numerous islands. There are 10 trips a day between 8:30am and 6:30pm.

The same company runs another ferry that connects Deer Island Point to Eastport, Maine, an attractive seaside town where you may see freighters moored. It leaves for Eastport every hour on the hour from 9am to 6pm, and is $10 for car and driver plus $2 each passenger.

Campobello Island

Campobello, a scenic, tranquil island, has long been enjoyed by the wealthy as a summer retreat. Due to its accessibility and proximity to New England, the island has always felt as much a part of the USA as a part of Canada. Like many moneyed families, the Roosevelts bought property in this peaceful coastal area at the end of the 1800s and it is for this that the island is best known. Today you can see the 34-room 'cottage' where Franklin D Roosevelt grew up (between 1905 and 1921) and which he visited periodically throughout his time as US president (1933-45).

The atmosphere on Campobello is remarkably different from that on Deer Island. It's more prosperous and gentler, with straight roads and better facilities. A third of Campobello is parkland and the golf course occupies a bit more. Most of the tourists here are Americans. There isn't even a gas station on the island and to fill their tanks the 1200 residents of Campobello must cross the bridge to Lubec, Maine. They generally use the same bridge to go elsewhere in New Brunswick as the Deer Island ferry only runs in summer.

From the bridge at the southwestern tip of the island, it's 84km to St Stephen by road. On the Campobello side, 500m from the bridge, is a tourist office (☎ 506-752-7043) with currency exchange that is open

10am to 6pm daily late May to early October and 9am to 7pm July and August.

Things to See & Do The ferry from Deer Island arrives at Welshpool, which is halfway up the 16km-long island and about 3km from the Roosevelt mansion. The southern half of Campobello is almost all park and the southernmost portion of this green area is taken up by the 1200-hectare **Roosevelt Campobello International Park**, the site of the Roosevelt mansion and a visitor center (☎ 506-752-2922, W *www.fdr.net, Hwy 774; admission free; open 10am-6pm daily late May-Oct*). Aside from an interesting photo exhibition on the Roosevelts, the visitor center proudly displays an original birchbark canoe (1890) once owned by Roosevelt himself.

Free guided tours of the Roosevelt mansion are offered, and adjacent **Hubbard House** (1898) can also be visited. The grounds around these buildings are open all the time, and you can peek through the windows when the doors are closed. The park is just 2½km from the Lubec bridge, and from the Roosevelt mansion's front porch you can look directly across to Eastport, Maine. You'd hardly know you were in Canada.

Unlike the manicured museum area, most of the international park has been left in its natural state to preserve the flora and fauna that Roosevelt appreciated so much. A couple of gravel roads meander through it, leading to beaches and 7½km of nature trails. It's a surprisingly wild, little-visited part of Campobello Island. Deer, moose and coyote are among the mammals in the park, and seals can sometimes be seen offshore on the ledges near Lower Duck Pond, 6km from the visitor center via a gravel road. Among the many birds along the shoreline are eagles, ospreys and loons.

Along the international park's northern boundary is **Herring Cove Provincial Park** (admission free). This park has another 10km of walking trails as well as a campground and a picnic area on an arching 1½km beach. It makes a fine, picturesque place for lunch.

Ten kilometers north of Roosevelt Park, **Wilson's Beach** has a large pier where fish can be bought, and a sardine-processing plant with an adjacent store. There are various services and shops here in the island's biggest community.

Four kilometers north of Wilson's Beach, **East Quoddy Head** with its lighthouse at the northern tip of the island is the second busiest visitor spot. Whales can often be seen from here and many people put in some time sitting on the rocky shoreline with a pair of binoculars enjoying the sea breezes.

Activities From June to mid-September the **Piskahegan River Company** (☎ 506-755-6269, 800-640-8944, W *www.piskahegan.com*) operates out of Pollock Cove Cottages, 2455 Hwy 774, Wilson's Beach. It offers kayaking tours ($60/95 a half/full day) around Campobello, but you must call ahead for reservations as the staff isn't always there.

The **Campobello Whale Watch Company** (☎ 506-752-2359) on North Road Wharf 3km north of Welshpool ferry has two-hour tours (adult/child $42/25). Departures are at 10am, 1:30pm and 4pm from July to mid-September. You've a chance of seeing finback and minke whales, as well as porpoises.

Cline Marine (☎ 800-567-5880) will pick up passengers for its whale-watching trips at Head Harbor Wharf upon request. See the Deer Island section for details.

Places to Stay *Herring Cove Provincial Park* (☎ 506-752-7010, fax 506-752-7012, W *www.tourismnbcanada.com/web/english/outdoor_network, 136 Herring Cove Rd*) Without/with hookups $21.50/24. Open mid-May–early Oct. This 76-site park on the east side of the island, 3km from the Deer Island ferry, has some nice secluded sites in a forest setting. It's preferable to Deer Island Point Park and makes a good base for visiting the adjacent international park. A long sandy beach is nearby and there's ample hiking. The park runs the golf course (☎ 506-752-7041; open May–mid-Oct) opposite, which charges $18.50 to play nine holes plus $15 club rental.

Friar's Bay Motor Lodge (☎ 506-752-2056, 802 Hwy 774; open Apr-Dec) Singles/doubles from $35/40. This simple motel 1km from the Deer Island ferry landing in Welshpool consists of a long row of basic wooden units.

Lupine Lodge (☎ 506-752-2555, W *www.lupinelodge.com, 610 Hwy 774*) Singles/doubles $50/70-99. Open June-Oct. This unusual hotel, 800m from Roosevelt Cam-

Whale-Watching Galore

Whales, the great mammals of the depths, have become major attractions around the Maritimes. Tours that go out to sea to photograph the awesome creatures depart from ports in places ranging from New Brunswick's Grand Manan Island to Nova Scotia's Cape Breton. From most accounts, the trips are usually successful and well worth the $20 to $40 cost for a couple of hours.

Some of the best areas for such a trip are around the Fundy Isles in New Brunswick or from the tip of Digby Neck in Nova Scotia. Also in Nova Scotia, the north shore of Cape Breton up around the national park is excellent. The sightings are so regular here that many captains offer a full refund if no whales emerge, or at the very least a rain check.

Around the Bay of Fundy the most commonly seen whales are the fin (or finback), the humpback, the right (less commonly seen) and the minke. In addition, porpoises and dolphins are plentiful. The humpback, one of the larger whales of the Maritimes, puts on the best show, breaching and diving with tail clearly visible above the surface. In this area the best whale-watching begins in early August and lasts until September.

From Westport at the tip of Digby Neck the season seems to begin a little earlier, with good sightings reported in late June, and by mid-July there are good numbers of all species.

Up around Cape Breton the smaller pilot or pothead whales, also sometimes known as blackwhales, are common and they're sometimes even seen from shore. Finbacks frequent these waters as well. Operators here run trips in July and August.

Research continues to investigate whether whale-watching itself is detrimental to the always vulnerable whale populations. Regulations now suggest that no boat approach too closely as the whales have enough problems to deal with.

A whale of a time on the Fundy Isles, baby!

pobello International Park on the way from Welshpool, has 11 rooms in two large log cabin-style blocks. A third such block contains the reception desk and restaurant.

Grand Manan Island

South of Campobello Island, Grand Manan is the largest of the Fundy Isles – a peaceful, relaxed and engaging island. The island offers spectacular coastal topography, excellent bird-watching, fine hiking trails, sandy beaches and a series of small fishing villages along its 30km length. The only thing missing is inexpensive accommodations.

In 1831, James Audubon first documented the many birds which frequented the island. About 312 species, including puffins and Arctic terns, live here or pass by each year, so bird-watchers come in numbers as well. Offshore it's not uncommon to see whales feeding on the abundant herring and mackerel. Whale species include the humpback, finback, minke and pothead, arriving here in June when the waters warm up sufficiently.

The relative isolation and low-key development mean there are no crowds and little obvious commercialization, making it a good place for cyclists. It's small enough to do as a day trip with your own bike; they can also be rented on the island, if you wish to leave your car in Blacks Harbour.

Something to sample on the island is the dulce (also spelled dulse), an edible seaweed for which Grand Manan Island is renowned. It's a very popular snack food around the Maritime provinces and most of it (and the best, say connoisseurs) comes from this island. Dulce is sold around the island mostly from people's homes. Watch for signs.

Grand Manan's Visitor Information Centre (☎ 506-662-3442) is well hidden behind the Grand Manan Museum at Grand Harbour. It's open 10am to 4pm Monday to Saturday and 1pm to 5pm Sunday in July and August.

North Head The ferry terminal is at North Head. There are a few crafts shops and touristy stores along the main drag but of most interest is the **Whale & Sea Bird Research Station** (☎ *506-662-3804, 24 Hwy 776; admission by donation; open 10am-4pm daily mid-May–Sept, 8:30am-5pm July & Aug*) directly across the street from the ferry terminal. It provides a lot of good information on the marine life of the surrounding waters. Exhibits include skeletons and photographs, and there are some books on whales and the island in general. The station has a harbor porpoise release program.

North End Some of the most popular of the numerous short walking trails around the island are in this area. Highly recommended is the somewhat pulse-quickening (especially in the fog) trail and footbridge out to the lighthouse at **Swallows Tail** on a narrow cliff-edged promontory. To get there, turn right as you leave the ferry – it's only 1km to the footbridge. The views of the coast and sea are great.

Grand Harbour On the north side of Grand Harbour, 11km south of North Head, is the **Grand Manan Museum** (☎ *506-662-3524, 1141 Hwy 776; adult/ student $4/2; open 10am-4:30pm Tues-Sat June-Sept*). Recently expanded, it has a marine section, displays on the island's geology, antiques and reminders of the Loyalist days, but the highlight is the stuffed-bird collection with examples of species seen on the island. There's a good selection of books for sale, and bird checklists for the island.

Seal Cove Seal Cove flourished during the epoch of the smoked herring (1870-1930),

and many wooden structures remain from that time including numerous smokehouses along the harbor. They're now used as warehouses but the outer structures have been preserved. Purse seiners still fish for herring here, but the biggest catch is lobsters. Connors Brothers has a cannery at Seal Cove.

Anchorage Provincial Park south of Seal Cove is good for bird-watching – wild turkeys and pheasant are common.

Southwest Head The 9km drive south from Seal Cove to the lighthouse and a walk beyond along the edge of the 180m cliffs should not be missed. Unlimited hiking possibilities extend in both directions.

Activities Grand Manan features more than 18 marked and maintained foot paths that cover 70km of some of the finest hiking in New Brunswick. The most extensive system of trails is found at the north end of the island near Long Eddy Point Lighthouse and several can be linked for an overnight trek.

Note that the trails may change with property decisions by landowners; find out before you go. For more information buy a copy of *Heritage Trails and Foot Paths on Grand Manan* ($5) at the Grand Manan Museum in Grand Harbour.

Adventure High (☎ *506-662-3563,* W *www.adventurehigh.com, 83 Hwy 776, North Head; open mid-May–Oct*), 600m to the left of the ferry wharf, does sea kayak tours at $50/95 a half/full day. Their two-hour sunset tour is $35. Adventure High also rents bicycles at $16/20 a half/full day (9am-3pm is half a day).

Organized Tours The **Island Coast Boat Tour** (☎ *506-662-8181, 199 Cedar St*) company runs trips from the North Head's Fisherman's Wharf, offering four-hour whale-watching tours (adult/child $44/22) in a 12m vessel daily at 7:30am and noon July through mid-September. Whale sightings are guaranteed or your money back.

A little bit different are the tours from **Sea-View Adventures** (☎ *506-662-3211, North Head*); these trips (adult/child $43/24) offer not only whales, porpoises, etc on the surface, but also video of bottom-life for those onboard; kids can get their hands on sea life. In July and August tours go out daily at 7:45am and 12:45pm.

Sea Watch Tours (☎ 506-662-8552, W www.seawatchtours.com) in Seal Cove has been around for 25 years and knows these waters. Most of the company's wildlife viewing tours are long (up to six hours), so take a lunch, a motion sickness pill and a warm sweater. Peak whale-watching begins in mid-July and continues through September. Whale sightings on these trips (adult/youth/child/infant $46/36/26/16) are guaranteed, and you often get to see the endangered northern right whale. In midsummer these tours are often fully reserved several days in advance.

Places to Stay There are over two dozen places to stay but prices are among the highest in the Maritimes and there are no significant off-season discounts. Aside from seeing Grand Manan as a day trip by ferry, the only low budget way to go is camping.

Hole in the Wall Park (☎ 506-662-3152, 866-662-4489, fax 506-662-3593, W www.grandmanancamping.com, 42 Old Airport Rd, North Head) Sites $20-24. Open mid-May–Oct. The entrance to this park is 1km from the ferry (to the right as you exit). Some of the sites are rather rocky for tents and they're all different, so have a look first.

Anchorage Provincial Park (☎ 506-662-7022, fax 506-662-7035, W www.tourism nbcanada.com/web/english/outdoor_network, between Grand Harbour and Seal Cove) Tent site $21.50, with electricity $24. Open mid-May–early Oct. Anchorage is 16km from the ferry, 4km north of Seal Cove and 1km off the island highway. If you have your own transportation, this is the best camping on the island by far, and most guests are tenters. It's a spacious place with 101 grassy sites that catch the ocean breeze. If you arrive early, there are some particularly nice sites edged into the woods. A kitchen shelter is provided for rainy days, and there's a playground, laundromat and long sandy beach. It's possible to reserve but the staff never turns anyone away. Anchorage adjoins some marshes which comprise a migratory bird sanctuary, and there are several short hiking trails. Non-campers are welcome to use these trails for free.

Swallowtail Inn (☎ 506-662-1100, W www.angelfire.com/nb/swallowtail, 50 Lighthouse Rd, North Head) Singles/doubles $69/85. Open May-Sept. This B&B is the prominent white house on the point next to the lighthouse you see from the ferry as you're arriving on Grand Manan – the erstwhile lighthouse keeper's residence. It's 1km to the right from the ferry and has commanding views in three directions.

Marathon Inn (☎ 506-662-8144, W www.angelfire.com/biz2/marathon) Singles/doubles $94/99 July-Sept, $74/79 June & Oct, $50 May, $44/49 mid-June–mid-Sept with shared bath. Open May-Oct. The inn's three wooden Victorian-era buildings are just a few hundred meters from the ferry terminal up Marathon Lane from the post office. The original inn was established in 1871 and it's still impressive, although this three-story complex has obviously seen better days. The 15 rooms with baths in the first building are the best, while the 13 unheated shared-bath rooms on the top two floors of the annex are not approved by the Department of Tourism. For that reason, they're the best buy on the island and Elderhostel groups often book them solid. Don't expect luxuries such as a lock on your door at the Marathon Inn.

Shorecrest Lodge (☎ 506-662-3216, fax 506-662-3507, W www.angelfire.com/nb/shorcres, 100 Hwy 776, North Head) Rooms with breakfast $99 in July & Aug, $65 in May, June, Sept & Oct, $50 without breakfast in March, Apr & Nov. This cozy 10-room guesthouse, 700m to left from the ferry, is well managed.

Surfside Motel (☎ 877-662-8156, fax 506-662-9191, e kcheney@nb.sympatico.ca, 123 Hwy 776, North Head) Singles/doubles $70/80. This is the only motel on Grand Manan, with 24 rooms in long motel blocks, 900m to the left from the ferry.

Amble Inn Cottages (☎ 506-662-8107, 2262 Hwy 776, Seal Cove) Singles/doubles/triples $70/75/75. The Amble Inn office, 4km south of Seal Cove, handles bookings at these six duplex cottages, 700m farther down the road from the office.

Places to Eat North Head village has the widest selection of dining options with a couple of takeout places, two or three regular restaurants and a finer dining room in the **Shorecrest Lodge** serving dinner entrées at $15-19.

Griff-Inn (☎ *506-662-8360, 121 Rte 776, North Head*) Meals under $10. Open 7am-9pm daily year-round (until 10pm in summer). This place behind the Surfside Motel charges a bit more than similar restaurants on the mainland. The food is good, with breakfast at $3-5, sandwiches $3-5, salads $6 and fish and chips $7-10.

North Head Bakery (☎ *506-662-8862, 199 Hwy 776, North Head*) Open 6am-6pm Tues-Sat Apr-Dec, also Mon in July & Aug. Do visit this outstanding bakery opposite Grand Manan Hospital, 1.7km to the left from the ferry, for healthy rolls, pastries, cakes and pies. Coffee is served.

Fundy House Restaurant (☎ *506-662-8341, 1303 Hwy 776, Grand Harbour*) Meals $9. Open 7:30am-11pm Mon-Sat, noon-11pm Sun June-Sept; 11am-9pm Mon-Sat Oct-May. This good local restaurant beside the highway on the south side of Grand Harbour, 2km north of Anchorage Provincial Park, serves pizza as well as clams and chips.

Getting There & Away Coastal Transport Ltd (☎ *506-662-3724, 506-456-3842, North Head*) operates the ferry service from Blacks Harbour, south of St George on the mainland, to North Head on Grand Manan Island. Actually, there are two ferries – one old and one new. The 64-vehicle, 300-passenger MS *Grand Manan V* built in 1990 is larger and quicker, knocking half an hour off the two-hour trip. The older MV *Grand Manan* is only used at peak periods. Both ferries have cafeterias, outdoor decks and inside chairs. Seeing a whale is not uncommon.

For either boat the roundtrip fare is $8.75 per adult, $4.40 for children under 13 and $26.20 for a car. For campervans and trailers you pay according to their length. Bicycles are $3. The trip is free on the way over to Grand Manan – just board the boat in Blacks Harbour and go. A ticket is needed to return to the mainland. Advance-ticket sales are available at North Head only for the first trip of the day. Trucks with perishable cargoes (fresh seafood) get priority on the ferry.

In July and August there are seven trips Monday through Saturday and six on Sunday, but there are still usually lines if you have a car, and there's no reservation system. For walk-ons, bicycles, etc there is

never a problem. From September to the end of June the number of trips drops to three or four a day. The service is heavily subsidized by the province, and when the money isn't there, crossings listed in the timetable may be canceled.

If the line of cars at Blacks Harbour is endless, consider doing Grand Manan as a day cruise. There's lots of free parking near the wharf at Blacks Harbour, though the parking lot can be crowded in midsummer. Depending on the season, you'll have between four and 10 hours on the island between ferries, plenty of time to do the Swallows Tail walk, visit the Whale & Sea Bird Research Station and explore North Head. Summer is the best time to do this as you'll be able to stand out on deck, whales will be in the area, everything in North Head will be open and you'll have a better choice of ferries for your return.

BLACKS HARBOUR
The jump-off spot for Grand Manan Island is Blacks Harbour. Sardine lovers will note that this seaport is also home of Connor Brothers, one of the world's largest producers of the delectable little fish-in-a-can. Two thousand people work here. Connor Brother's trademark brand is Brunswick Sardines and the company runs a factory outlet store (☎ 506-456-3897) behind Silver King Restaurant in the center of town. Load up!

Bayview B&B (☎ *506-456-1982,* W *www.bbexpo.com/nb/bayview.htm, 391 Deadmans Harbour Rd*) Singles/doubles $45/50. This family house opposite a bay, 4km from the Grand Manan ferry, offers three rooms with shared bath.

Smith's Motel (☎ *506-755-3034,* W *www .sn2000.nb.ca/comp/smiths-motel, 5254 Hwy 1, Pennfield Ridge*) Singles/doubles $49/54 mid-June–mid-Sept, $42/47 shoulder seasons. Open Apr-Dec. Just 2½km east of the Hwy 176 turnoff to Blacks Harbour, Smith's has 27 rooms in three blocks. There's a restaurant; otherwise ***Pennfield Take-Out*** next door has cheap takeout ice cream, hamburgers and lobster rolls.

NEW RIVER PROVINCIAL PARK
Just off Hwy 1, about 35km west of Saint John on the way to St Stephen, this large park has one of the best beaches along the

Fundy Shore, a wide stretch of sand bordered on one side by the rugged coastline of Barnaby Head.

You can spend an enjoyable few hours hiking Barnaby Head along a 6km network of nature trails. The **Chittick's Beach Trail** leads you through coastal forest and past four coves, where you can check the catch in a herring weir or examine tidal pools for marine life. Extending from this loop is the 2½km **Barnaby Head Trail**, which hugs the shoreline most of the way and at one point puts you on the edge of a cliff 15m above the Bay of Fundy. Some spots can be wet and slippery.

During the camping season the park charges a $5 fee per vehicle for day use which includes parking at the beach and Barnaby Head trailhead.

The park *campground* (☎ *506-755-4042, fax 506-755-4063,* **W** *www.tourismnb canada.com/web/english/outdoor_network, 78 New River Beach Rd; open late May-early Oct)* is across the road from the beach and features 100 secluded sites, both rustic and with hookups, in a wooded setting. Camping is $21.50 for tents and $24 for sites with electricity. Drawbacks are the gravel emplacements and traffic noise from the nearby highway. Many sites are reserved but some are kept open on a first-come, first-served basis.

Saint John

pop 73,000
Historic Saint John (whose name is always spelled out in full, never abbreviated, to avoid confusion with St John's, Newfoundland) is the province's largest city and main industrial center. Sitting on the bay at the mouth of the Saint John River it is also a major year-round port. The dry dock is one of the world's largest. The huge JD Irving conglomerate is headquartered here.

Saint John's refurbished downtown area reflects its proud past. It's known as the 'Loyalist City' for the thousands of late 18th-century refugees who settled here, and evidence of this background is plentiful. The central city and surrounding residential side streets have some very fine architecture and a stroll past the impressive facades is well worthwhile.

History
The Maliseet Indians were here when the British and French began squabbling about furs. Samuel de Champlain had landed in 1604, however the area remained pretty much a wilderness until 1783, when about 7000 people loyal to Britain arrived from republican America.

The Loyalists were the true founders of Saint John, turning a fort site into Canada's first legal city, incorporated in 1785. Between 1844 and 1848 some 35,000 Irish immigrants fleeing a famine in Ireland passed through Saint John, and today they comprise the city's largest ethnic group.

By the mid-19th century Saint John was a prosperous industrial town, important particularly for its wooden shipbuilding enterprises. Though it now uses iron and steel rather than wood, shipbuilding is still a major industry. In 1877, two-thirds of the city, including most of the mercantile district, was reduced to ashes by fire. It was soon rebuilt.

Orientation
Downtown Saint John sits on a square peninsula between the mouth of the Saint John River and Courtenay Bay. Kings Square marks the nucleus of town. Its pathways duplicate the pattern of the Union Jack. Brunswick Square, a modern shopping mall, is on the corner of King and Germain Sts. One block farther west at Water St is the redeveloped waterfront area and Market Square. Don't confuse Market Square with the Old City Market three blocks away.

The district below Kings Square is known as the South End with Queens Square at its heart. On Courtenay Bay, to the east, are the dry dock, shipbuilding yards and much heavy industry. North of town is Rockwood Park, a recreational area with a campground.

West over the Harbour Bridge (25¢ toll) is Saint John West. Many of the street names in this section of the city are identical to those of Saint John proper, and to avoid confusion, they end in a west designation, such as Charlotte St West.

Saint John West has the landing for ferries to Digby, Nova Scotia, and the city container terminals. The famous Reversing Falls are just to the north. Farther west going out of town is the motel district with the Irving Nature Park to the south.

SAINT JOHN

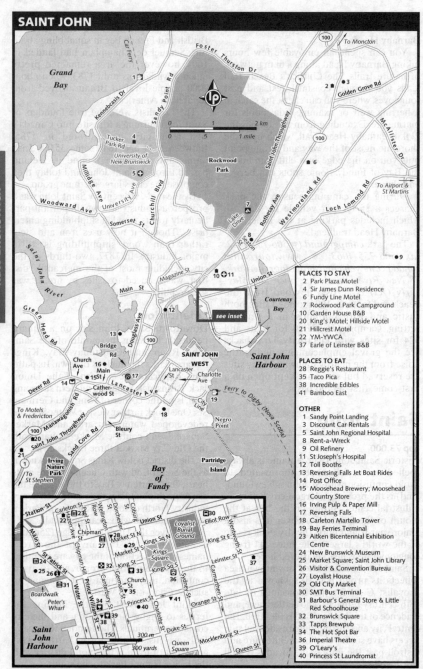

PLACES TO STAY
2 Park Plaza Motel
4 Sir James Dunn Residence
6 Fundy Line Motel
7 Rockwood Park Campground
10 Garden House B&B
20 King's Motel; Hillside Motel
21 Hillcrest Motel
22 YM-YWCA
37 Earle of Leinster B&B

PLACES TO EAT
28 Reggie's Restaurant
35 Taco Pica
38 Incredible Edibles
41 Bamboo East

OTHER
1 Sandy Point Landing
3 Discount Car Rentals
5 Saint John Regional Hospital
9 Oil Refinery
11 St Joseph's Hospital
12 Toll Booths
13 Reversing Falls Jet Boat Rides
14 Post Office
15 Moosehead Brewery; Moosehead
   Country Store
16 Irving Pulp & Paper Mill
17 Reversing Falls
18 Carleton Martello Tower
19 Bay Ferries Terminal
23 Aitken Bicentennial Exhibition
   Centre
24 New Brunswick Museum
25 Market Square; Saint John Library
26 Visitor & Convention Bureau
27 Loyalist House
29 Old City Market
30 SMT Bus Terminal
31 Barbour's General Store & Little
   Red Schoolhouse
32 Brunswick Square
33 Tapps Brewpub
34 The Hot Spot Bar
36 Imperial Theatre
39 O'Leary's
40 Princess St Laundromat

Information

The Visitor & Convention Bureau (☎ 506-658-2990, 888-364-4444) in Market Square has knowledgeable, friendly staff and all the printed matter you'll need. Ask for the self-guided walking tours. It's open daily year-round 9am to 6pm (until 8pm mid-June to August).

The main post office with General Delivery is in Saint John West (☎ 506-672-6704; 41 Church Ave West, Postal Station B, E2M 4X6). Its hours are 8am to 5pm Monday to Friday.

The Saint John Library (☎ 506-643-7220, 1 Market Square) provides free Internet access 9am to 5pm Monday and Saturday, 10am to 5pm Tuesday and Wednesday and 10am to 9pm Thursday and Friday.

Princess St Laundromat (☎ 506-652-7064, 106 Princess St) has a remarkably pleasant atmosphere with comfortable chairs and TV. You'll pay $1.50 a wash 8am to 7:30pm Monday to Friday, 8am to 4:30pm Saturday and Sunday.

There aren't any after-hours walk-in medical clinics in Saint John. If you need to see a doctor you'll have to go to the emergency room at one of the two hospitals, St Joseph's Hospital (☎ 506-632-5555, 130 Bayard Dr), on the north side of downtown, or the Saint John Regional Hospital (☎ 506-648-6000, 400 University Ave), off Sandy Point Road 6km north of the center.

Unless you have valid travel health insurance, you should approach these facilities with caution as absurdly high fees are asked of non-Canadians. Just to register at St Joseph's is $200 and any treatment will be extra. Saint John Regional collects a $110 hospital charge, plus $90 to see a doctor. In non-life-threatening circumstances, it's better to try to persuade a private doctor to see you. Ask your hotel to call around on your behalf.

New Brunswick Museum

Relocated in 1998 to Market Square, this is an eclectic, worthy place (☎ 506-643-2300; adult/student/family $6/3.25/13; open 9am-5pm Mon, Tues, Wed, & Fri, 9am-9pm Thur, 10am-5pm Sat, noon-5pm Sun mid-May–Oct, closed Mon rest of the year) with a mixed collection. There's a very good section on marine wildlife, with some aquariums and information on lobsters, and an outstanding section on whales. There's a collection of stuffed animals and birds, mostly from New Brunswick. The displays on the marine history of Saint John are good, with many excellent models of old sailing ships.

Barbour's General Store & Little Red Schoolhouse

This is a renovated old general store (☎ 506-658-2939, Market Square; admission free; store & museum open 9am-6pm daily mid-June–mid-Sept). It's packed with the kind of merchandise sold 100 years ago, including old stoves, drugs, hardware and candy. Most items are not for sale. The Little Red Schoolhouse alongside is a small museum. Guided walking tours ($5) depart from here twice daily in July and August.

Aitken Bicentennial Exhibition Centre

The center (☎ 506-633-4870, 20 Hazen Ave; admission free; open 10am-5pm daily July & Aug; noon-4pm Wed-Sun rest of the year), which includes the City of Saint John Gallery, is across from the YM-YWCA in an attractive rounded sandstone building dating from 1904. It has six galleries that offer changing displays on art, science and technology. There's also a very good children's interactive gallery called ScienceScape.

Loyalist House

Loyalist House (☎ 506-652-3590, 120 Union St at Germain St), dating from 1810, is the city's oldest unchanged building. The Georgian-style place is now a museum (admission $3; open 10am-5pm Mon-Sat, 1pm-5pm Sun July & Aug, 10am-5pm Mon-Fri June) depicting the Loyalist period and contains some fine carpentry. The monument to the Loyalists next to the house is striking.

Old City Market

On Market St between Germain and Charlotte Sts is this colorful, interesting market (☎ 506-658-2820, 47 Charlotte St; open 7:30am-6pm Mon-Thur, 7:30am-7pm Fri, 7:30am-5pm Sat), which has been in this building since 1876. Outside the door on Charlotte St, see the plaque outlining some of the market's history.

Inside, the atmosphere is friendly but busy. Apart from the fresh produce stalls, most active on Saturday when local farmers come in, there are several good eating spots, a deli and some antique stores. Good bread is sold, and dulce and cooked lobster are available.

Loyalist Burial Ground

This attractive site is just off Kings Square, in a park-style setting in the center of town. Here you can see tombstones dating from as early as 1784.

Reversing Falls

The Bay of Fundy tides and their effects (see Tidal Bore Park under Moncton later in this chapter) are unquestionably a predominant regional characteristic. The falls here are part of that and are one of the best known sites in the province. However, 'reversing falls' is a bit of a misnomer. When the high Bay of Fundy tides rise, the current in the river reverses, causing the water to flow upstream. When the tides go down, the water flows in the normal way.

The **Reversing Falls Visitor Centre** (☎ 506-658-2937, 200 Bridge Rd; open 8am-7pm daily mid-May–early Oct) next to the bridge over the falls can supply a *Reversing Falls Tide Table* brochure which will explain where in the cycle you are. You can also watch a film at the touristy observation deck (admission $2) above the tourist office. The frequent east-west buses from Kings Square pass here.

The **Irving Pulp & Paper Mill** adjacent to the Reversing Falls is one of New Brunswick's dirtiest mills. In recent years stricter government regulations have forced Irving to try to clean up their act, although they've still got a long way to go, as you can smell. If you'd like to arrange a free tour of the mill, call ☎ 506-635-7749 during business hours and ask for Gail. You can see smoke rising from the mill from almost anywhere in the city.

Moosehead Brewery

Moosehead Brewery used to claim it was the country's oldest independent beer maker, dating back to 1867, the year of Confederation. Now it bills itself as the largest Canadian-owned brewery, in contrast to Labatt (purchased in 1995 by a Belgium conglomerate) and Molson (hefty slices of which are owned by Carlton & United Breweries of Australia and Miller Brewing

of the USA). The Moosehead plant, just up the road from the Reversing Falls center, offers public tours at 1pm and 3pm daily mid-June through August. They include a movie and beer tasting, and can be booked by calling the Moosehead Country Store (☎ 506-635-7020, 49 Main St West; admission free; open 9am-5pm Mon-Wed, 9am-9pm Thur & Fri, 10am-5pm Sat year-round). The country store has great logo attire for all you mooseheads.

Carleton Martello Tower

In Saint John West, this national historic site (☎ 506-636-4011, 545 Whipple St cnr Fundy Dr; adult/family $2.50/6.25; open 9am-5pm daily June-early Oct) is just off Lancaster Ave, which leads to the Digby ferry terminal. Look for the signs at street intersections. A Martello tower is a circular two-story stone coastal fortification. They were first built in England and Ireland at the beginning of the 19th century. In North America the British built 16 of them during the early 1800s, including several at Halifax. Inside you can explore the restored powder magazine, barracks and the upper two levels that were added during WWII for the defense of the Saint John Harbour. Guides will show you around and provide background information. Go when there's no fog because the promontory sits on one of the highest points in the city and the view is outstanding.

Irving Nature Park

For those with vehicles and an appreciation of nature, this park (☎ 506-653-7367, west end of Sand Cove Rd; admission free; open 8am-dusk early May-early Nov) is a must (well worth the 15-minute drive southwest from the center) for its rugged, unspoiled coastal topography. It's also a remarkable place for bird-watching, with hundreds of species regularly reported. Seals may be seen on rocks off-shore, and the Irving oil storage tanks and pulp mill are visible in the distance.

Though the park is said to be on Taylors Island, this is not an island at all but rather a 245-hectare mountainous peninsula protruding into the Bay of Fundy. Seven trails of varying lengths lead around beaches, cliffs, woods, mudflats, marsh and rocks. Good footwear is recommended. The perimeter can be driven on a 6½km dirt road.

To reach the park take Hwy 1 west from town and turn south at Exit 107, Bleury St. Then turn right on Sand Cove Rd and continue for 2km to the entrance. The No 11 Fundy Heights bus from Simms Corner comes close to the park (no service on Sunday). Maps are posted throughout the park and toilets are provided. Other facilities include free gas barbecues, picnic tables, observation decks and binoculars. Worthwhile free tours are given on weekends (call ahead for times).

Rockwood Park

On the northeast edge of the city center, this 870-hectare park is Canada's largest park contained within a city. Recreational facilities include picnic spots, wooded hiking trails, swimming areas, campground, interpretive center, golf course, canoe rentals, horse stable, a children's farm and zoo. The park is open from 8am to 8pm and admission is free.

Activities

Eastern Outdoors (☎ 800-565-2925, W *www .easternoutdoors.com, 3rd floor, Brunswick Square, 39 King St; open 10am-6pm Mon-Sat, until 9pm Thur & Fri*) rents bicycles ($25 a day), kayaks ($35) and canoes ($35). This is fine if you're in for a day of peddling around Rockwood Park or the Irving Nature Park, or a paddle out to Partridge Island. Don't risk paddling over the Reversing Falls, however! Eastern Outdoors also runs daily kayaking tours to Dipper Harbour and Deer Island at $59, plus $10 for transfers from Saint John.

Organized Tours

Many have asked and even more are surprised – whale-watching is not an attraction in Saint John, save for the very occasional, very wayward minke.

The **Saint John Transit Commission** (☎ 506-658-4700) has 2½-hour bus tours (adult/child $16/5) around the city from mid-June to early October. Departures and tickets are from Reversing Falls Visitor Centre, Barbour's General Store at Market Square and Rockwood Park Campground. Two tours daily depart. At 9:30am the bus leaves Reversing Falls, and takes 15 minutes to get to each of the other two stops. The trip is reversed from 12:30pm to 1pm.

Also from Barbour's, in July and August, are guided walking tours around the historic portions of downtown offered by **Aquila Tours** (☎ *506-633-1224*). Tours cost $5 and depart at 2pm daily. Similar walking tours are offered by **Helyar Productions** (☎ *506-657-5244*) from the Atrium Fountain at Market Square departing at 7pm Monday to Saturday from June to August. These cost $5/15 adult/family.

Reversing Falls Jet Boat Rides (☎ *506-634-8987*, W *www.jetboatrides.com*) offers two types of trips from June to mid-October. The one-hour slow boat trips (adult/child $26/20) to the Reversing Falls and around the harbor depart from Market Square. There are also 20-minute jet boat rides through the whitewater at the Reversing Falls departing from Fallsview Park. Count on getting soaked on these, but rain gear and life jackets are provided.

Special Events

Loyalist Days This eight-day event during the second week of July celebrates the city's Loyalist background. Featured are a re-creation of the first arrival, period costumes, parades, arts and crafts, music recitals, lots of food and fireworks on the last night of the festival.

Festival by the Sea For 10 days this very popular, highly regarded performing arts event presents hundreds of singers, dancers and other performers from across Canada in concerts and shows put on throughout the city night and day. Many of the performances staged in parks and along the harborfront are free.

Grand Ole Atlantic National Exhibition Held at the end of August in Exhibition Park, this event includes stage shows, livestock judging, harness racing and a large midway (fairground).

Places to Stay

Camping *Rockwood Park Campground* (☎ *506-652-4050, fax 506-642-6304,* W *www.sn2000.nb.ca/comp/rockwood-park-campground, Crown St*) Campsites $15/20 without/with electricity, less for stays of a week or more. Open mid-May–early Oct. Just north of Rothesay Ave, a couple of kilometers north of the downtown area, is huge Rockwood Park, with its small lakes, picnic area, golf course and part of the University of New Brunswick's campus. It's an excellent place to camp, with pleasant campsites and a view of the city. Bus No 6 Mount Pleasant from Kings Square comes within a few blocks of the campground Monday to Saturday.

Hostels *YM-YWCA (☎ 506-634-7720, fax 506-634-0783, 🅦 www.saintjohny.com, 19-25 Hazen Ave)* Singles $35/30/25 adult/student/ HI member, weekly $100 member & non-member. The HI-affiliated YM-YWCA features 16 single rooms with single beds and use of a clean shared bath. (There's no dormitory and no doubles – couples must rent two rooms.) Each occupant gets a room key and has full use of facilities such as the swimming pool, common room and exercise rooms. A free washer and drier are in the bathroom. The lobby is always open and the snack bar is inexpensive. Parking is free except from 8am to 6pm weekdays when it's 50¢ an hour. It's all a little threadbare but you can't beat the price.

University of New Brunswick Saint John Campus (☎ 506-648-5755, fax 506-648-5762, 🅦 www.unbsj.ca/hfs, off Sandy Point Rd near the Rockwood Park Golf Course) Singles/doubles $29.50/43.50 (students $18.75/35.65). The 71 rooms at the Sir James Dunn Residence, 6km north of the city center (Bus No 15 from Kings Square), are available from May to August.

B&Bs *Earle of Leinster B&B (☎ 506-652-3275, 🅔 leinster@nbnet.nb.ca, 96 Leinster St)* Singles/doubles $61/70 with one bed, $74 double with two beds. There's a $5 discount if you pay cash. This inn, a short walk from Kings Square, is in a three-story Victorian town house (1878) with seven rooms, each with a private bath. Rates include laundry facilities and a VCR with videos and popcorn. It's strictly no smoking. Calling ahead is a good idea as the place tends to fill up in summer.

Garden House B&B (☎ 506-646-9093, 🅔 ghouse@nbnet.nb.ca, 28 Garden St) Singles/doubles $60/85 July & Aug, $50/60 rest of the year. From Kings Square walk north on Coburg St to Garden St on the left. This large wooden Victorian home has four rooms and there are laundry facilities.

Motels Saint John may have more motels than any place in the Maritimes. Many of them are along Manawagonish Rd and its continuation Ocean West Way, the old Hwy 100 west of town, parallel to and north of Hwy

1. A few more motels are on Rothesay Ave (Hwy 100 eastbound), and though slightly more expensive, they're closer to town.

Many of these motels offer low weekly rates, though perhaps not in July and August. Even if you only intend to stay five or six nights, it's well worth considering taking a weekly as Fredericton and much of the coast is within commuting distance by car, and you won't need to worry about finding accommodations every night.

The main problem with Manawagonish Rd is that it's 7km west of the downtown area and Ocean West Way is another 4km west of that. Yet the No 14 Fairville bus comes and goes into town from this strip (last bus back at 6:07pm weekdays), and in a car it's just a 15-minute trip. The motels that follow are a selection – there are more.

King's Motel (☎ 506-672-1375, 1121 Manawagonish Rd) Singles/doubles/triples $42/46/51. King's has six units in a long block overlooking the highways. The larger *Hillside Motel (☎ 888-625-7070)* next door is a few dollars more expensive.

Hillcrest Motel (☎ 506-672-5310, 1315 Manawagonish Rd) Singles/doubles/triples $42/46/51. Hillcrest has 17 rooms in a long wooden block closer to the road (and thus a bit noisier) than the other places.

Terrace Motel & Cottages (☎ 506-672-9670, 2131 Ocean West Way) Rooms $49-79 single or double, cabins $40-59, depending on how busy it is. In winter the six motel rooms with fridge and microwave are rented at $150 a week, and in summer the seven duplex cabins go for $175 a week. Several similar motels are nearby.

Fundy Line Motel (☎ 506-633-7733, fax 506-633-1680, 532 Rothesay Ave) $48 for singles & doubles June-Sept, $45 Oct-May. The 51 rooms are in a two-story block, 5km east of town. No weekly rates are offered.

Park Plaza Motel (☎ 800-561-9022, fax 506-648-9494, 607 Rothesay Ave) Singles/ doubles $52/62 mid-June–mid-Sept, $52/58 rest of the year (one bed). A kilometer east of the Fundy Line Motel, there are 84 units in three one- and two-story blocks. Weekly rates of $160 single or double are available year-round

Places to Eat

Reggie's Restaurant (☎ 506-657-6270, 26 Germain St) Dinners under $7, most sandwiches under $4. Open 6am-6pm Mon & Tues, 6am-7pm Wed-Fri, 6am-5pm Sat & Sun. For cheap eats there's Reggie's, which has been around since 1969. Near the Loyalist House, this is a classic downtown no-nonsense diner that specializes in smoked meat from Ben's, a famous Montréal deli. Also on the menu are chowders at $4.25 or less and other fare. It opens at 6am for breakfast when you can have Reggie's Favorite – three sausages, an egg, home fries, toast and hot mustard – for $4 (coffee extra), served all day. Place your order at the counter when you arrive.

Incredible Edibles (☎ 506-633-7554, 42 Princess St) Pasta $10, specials $10; dinner for two $50 & up. Open noon-9:30pm Mon-Sat, 5pm-9:30pm Sun. This is a nice spot for a bit of a splurge. It offers crepes, curries, pastas, seafood and a few vegetarian choices. Friday from 6:30pm to 9:30pm you can get the amazing hip of beef dinner special for $13.

Taco Pica (☎ 506-633-8492, 96 Germain St) Mains $10-17. Open 10am-10pm Mon-Sat. Perhaps the best ethnic cuisine in Saint John is the fusion of Guatemalan and Mexican at Taco Pica. An economical introduction to the cuisine is the *pepian* ($9), a simple but spicy beef stew that is as good as you'll find in any Guatemalan household.

Bamboo East (☎ 506-634-1661, 136 Princess St) Weekday lunch buffet $8 noon-2pm, weekend dinner buffet $12 5pm-8pm. Open 11am-11pm Mon-Fri, 4:30pm-11pm Sat & Sun. The best way to sample the Chinese food at Bamboo East is to attend a buffet.

Entertainment

Imperial Theatre (☎ 506-674-4100, 24 Kings Square South) Box office open 10am-7pm Mon-Fri, noon-4pm Sat. This performing arts center reopened in 1994 after having been restored to its original 1913 splendor. Performances range from classical music to live theater. Call for schedule and ticket information.

The Hot Spot Bar (☎ 506-657-9931, 112 Prince William St) Open 9pm-2am Thur, 7pm-2am Fri, 8pm-2am Sat. Most of the action at night is around the corner of Princess and Prince William Sts; The Hotspot is right on the corner and has them hopping. The live entertainment and cheap

drinks have made it very popular among the city youth.

O'Leary's (☎ 506-634-7135, 46 Princess St) Open 11:30am-11pm Tues, 11:30am-1:30am Wed-Fri, 11am-1:30am Sat. This is a good old-fashioned Irish pub with plenty of British and Irish brews as well as live music on Thursday, Friday and Saturday evenings. On Wednesday it's open-mic night. Take a stab, you could be a star.

Tapps Brewpub (☎ 506-634-1957, 78 King St) Open 11am-midnight Mon-Thur, 11am-2am Fri & Sat, 4pm-10pm Sun. On King St between Germain and Charlotte Sts is Tapps Brewpub, with decent India pale ale and a *weissbier* made on the premises. It also has pub grub sandwiches ($7), steaks ($9-14) and live music during the week.

Getting There & Away

Air Air Canada or its subsidiary Air Canada Jazz has flights to Montréal, Toronto and Halifax three or four times a day. A 'passenger facility charge' of $10 must be paid at the gate by all passengers aged two and over (not included in the ticket).

Bus SMT Bus Lines (☎ 506-648-3500) has a large station at 300 Union St on the corner of Carmarthen St, a five-minute walk from the town center. It's open 7:30am to 9pm Monday to Friday and 8am to 9pm Saturday and Sunday; $2 coin lockers are available.

To Fredericton there are two trips daily at 9:30am and 6:15pm, costing $18. That same bus is used for connections for passengers carrying on to Québec City, for which the fare is $80. The bus to Moncton leaves at 8:30am and 3:15pm and the fare is $24; you'll have to go there to get to Charlottetown, for which the fare is $55 all the way through. The same schedule holds for buses to Halifax ($66).

SMT Bus Lines connects with Orleans Express lines in Rivière du Loup, Québec, for Québec destinations. For cities in Nova Scotia, SMT connects with Acadian Bus Lines. There's also a direct service to Bangor, Maine, on Friday and Saturday.

Ferry The Bay Ferries' *Princess of Acadia* (☎ 506-649-7777, 888-249-7245, **w** www.nfl-bay.com) sails between Saint John and Digby, Nova Scotia, across the bay year-round. Depending on where you're going, this can save a lot of driving around the Bay of Fundy through Moncton and then Amherst, Nova Scotia, but the ferry is not cheap. Adult/child fares are $35/15 one way from late June to mid-October, $20/10 the rest of the year. The all season fare for cars/motorcycles/bicycles is $70/45/25. There's a passenger-only roundtrip fare ($35) if you want to make a day cruise out of it.

Crossing time is about three hours. From late June to mid-October there are three services daily from Digby: 5am, 1pm and 8:45pm, except for Sunday when there is no 5am crossing. From Saint John, times are 12:45am, 9am and 4:45pm with no 12:45am trip Sunday. During the rest of the year ferries go once or twice a day. Arrive early or call ahead for vehicle reservations ($5 additional fee), as the ferry is very busy in July and August. Even with a reservation, arrive an hour before departure or your space may be given away. Walk-ons and cyclists should be OK anytime. There's a restaurant and a bar on board.

Hitchhiking Hitching toward Moncton on Rothesay Ave is a bummer as it's mostly local traffic – a destination sign is a big help. Take the frequent Nos 1 and 2 buses from Kings Square to the corner of Rothesay Ave and McAllister Dr to get started. It's easier to hitch north or west as you can take the No 14 Fairville bus out on Manawagonish Rd to a ramp leading onto Hwy 7 for Fredericton, or a little farther east to Hwy 1 to St Stephen. For St Martins, take bus No 22 Loch Lomond out past the airport.

Getting Around
To/From the Airport The airport is east of town on Loch Lomond Rd between Saint John and St Martins. There's an airport shuttle (☎ 506-648-8888) costing $10 that leaves approximately 1½ hours before all flights, from top hotels like the Hilton on Market Square and the Delta Brunswick on Brunswick Square. For a taxi call Vets (☎ 506-658-2020); it costs $25 for the first person plus $2 each additional person. City bus No 22 goes to the airport from Kings Square at 6:25am, 7:50am, 9:25am, 12:35pm, 2:30pm, 4:10pm and 5:30pm weekdays (for departure times from the airport, add around 30 minutes to these times).

Bus Saint John Transit (☎ 506-658-4700) has 30 routes around the city. The most important is the east-west bus, which is called Nos 1 & 2 eastbound to McAllister Dr and Nos 3 & 4 westbound to near the ferry terminal in Saint John West. It stops at Kings Square in the city center every 10 or 15 minutes from 6am to 7pm, every half hour from 7pm to midnight, Monday to Saturday. On Sunday it's every 45 minutes from 10am to 6pm. Another frequent bus is Nos 15 & 16 to the University. It leaves from Kings Square from 6:10am to 9:10am and 2:25pm to 5:55pm weekdays. At other times you catch it on Metcalfe St. On Saturdays all of the University buses leave from Metcalfe St, but on Sunday they all leave from Kings Square. The bus fare is $1.75.

Car There are several choices for car rentals. Discount Car Rentals (☎ 506-633-4440), 622 Rothesay Ave, is opposite the Park Plaza Motel. Rent-a-Wreck (☎ 506-672-2277), 2 Seaton St, is near the junction of Rothesay and Thorne Aves. Call and they may send a driver to pick you up. Avis, Budget, Hertz and National all have car rental desks at the airport.

Parking meters in Saint John take $1 an hour from 8am to 6pm weekdays only. You can park free at meters weekends, holidays and in the evening, but note the time limits. The parking meters on Sydney St south of Kings Square allow up to 10 hours free parking on weekends and holidays. You can park free anytime on back streets such as Leinster and Princess Sts, east of Kings Square. The city parking lot at 11 Sydney St is free on weekends.

Central Fundy Shore

The Central Fundy Shore from Saint John to Hopewell Cape has only recently been discovered by tourism. It's still not possible to drive directly from St Martins to Fundy National Park – that road has yet to be built – and a detour inland through Surrey is necessary unless you're prepared to hike. Indeed, hikers, cyclists and nature lovers will all be enchanted by this coast. Kayakers can put in from several points and the cliffs and tides are a big attraction.

ST MARTINS

A one-hour hour drive east of Saint John will take you to the worthy destination of St Martins, one of the province's historic towns, situated on the Bay of Fundy. It's a small, pretty, out of the way place that was once the center of the wooden shipbuilding trade. The two covered bridges date back to 1935. Now with the opening of the Fundy Trail Parkway, this place is becoming a hotspot.

Century Farm Family Campground (☎ 506-833-2357, Ⓦ www.sn2000.nb.ca/ comp/century-farm-campground, 67 Ocean Wave Dr) Without/with hookups $14/18, cabins $35/40 without/with bath. Open May–mid-Oct. Near the center of St Martins, Century Farm hosts the usual rows of trailers but there are also grassy sites for tents. There's no shade but there is a beach. Call ahead if you want a camping cabin. Four don't have private baths but hold up to four persons; only one has a toilet and sink.

Nostalgia's Nook B&B (☎ 506-833-4957, Ⓦ www.bbcanada.com/3999.html, 16 West Quaco Rd) Rooms $65 mid-June-mid-Sept, $50 rest of the year. This B&B is in an old-style house just down the coastal road to the right as you enter St Martins.

Maple Miniatures Minihorse Farm B&B (☎ 506-833-6240, Ⓦ www.worldis.com/kathi, 280 West Quaco Rd, 2½km west of Nostalgia's Nook) Rooms $55 including breakfast. Open May-Oct. Two rooms are for rent in a wooden house and pony rides can be arranged for the kids.

Seaside Restaurant (☎ 506-833-2394, 81 Macs Beach) Main meals $8-13. Open 11am-8pm daily. Right on the beach near the caves just east of the covered bridge, Seaside serves dishes like fish and chips, scallop dinner, seafood dinner and seafood casserole. Lobster in the shell costs $25.

FUNDY TRAIL PARKWAY

The cliff-edged coastal region between St Martins and Fundy National Park and inland toward Sussex is a rugged section of the province which is said to be the only remaining coastal wilderness between Florida and Newfoundland. In recent years efforts have been made to develop the area for tourism, and in late 1998 a drivable 11km parkway and adjoining littoral hiking/biking trail were opened to the public.

Currently, the road and trails go as far as the Big Salmon River, a lovely (and easy) stretch with 10 viewpoints and picnic areas. Eventually this network will extend east to Fundy National Park and north to Sussex.

At Big Salmon River is an interpretive center with exhibits and a 10-minute video presentation. Remains of a sawmill that existed here from the 1850s to the 1940s can be seen at low tide in the river directly below the interpretive center.

A suspension bridge leads to a vast wilderness hiking area beyond the end of the road, and it's possible to hike from Big Salmon River to Goose River in Fundy National Park in three to five days. At last report, no permits or permissions were required to do so. Beyond Big Salmon River, you'd better be prepared for wilderness, rocky scree and even a rope ladder or two. Some beach sections are usable only at low tide and the cliffs are unsafe to climb.

The entrance to the parkway (☎ 506-833-2019, Ⓦ www.fundytrailparkway.com; admission $5.75 per car; open 6am-8pm daily mid-May–Oct) is 8½km west of St Martins. Pedestrians and cyclists can enter free. In the off season the main gate is closed, but you can always park at the entrance and hike or peddle in. On Saturdays, Sundays and holidays an hourly shuttle bus operates from noon to 6pm ferrying hikers up and down the trail between the parkway entrance and Big Salmon River. The shuttle is free if you paid the vehicular fee or $2 if you didn't. The coast of Nova Scotia is visible across the bay.

FUNDY NATIONAL PARK

Fundy National Park (☎ 506-887-6000; entry permit $3.50/10.50 per person 1 day/4 days, family $7/21) is one of the country's most popular parks. Aside from the world's highest tides, this park on the Bay of Fundy has an extensive network of hiking trails. Irregularly eroded sandstone cliffs and the wide beach at low tide make a walk along the shore interesting. There's lots of small marine life to observe and debris to pick over. The park even has a covered bridge!

Fundy is also home to one of the largest concentrations of wildlife in the Maritimes, including black bears, moose, beavers and peregrine falcons. The ocean is pretty bracing here, so there's a heated saltwater

Mountain bikers take to the trails throughout Fundy National Park.

swimming pool (☎ 506-887-6014; admission $2/1.50 adults/children; open 11am-6:30pm daily late June-early Sept) not far from the eastern entrance to the park.

You can reach the park, 129km east of Saint John and about halfway to Moncton, by following Hwy 114 from Hwy 1. Entering from the north you first reach the **Wolfe Lake Information Centre** (☎ 506-432-6026, Hwy 114; open 10am-6pm daily late June-early Sept). At the south entrance is the park's **visitors' center** (☎ 506-887-6000; open 10am-6pm daily mid-June–early Sept, 9am-4pm rest of the year). Both have bookstores and information counters where you can purchase your entry permit. If you'll be visiting any of the other national parks in the Maritimes and Newfoundland, ask about the Atlantic Pass, which covers entry to seven parks for the entire season.

Hiking & Cycling
Fundy features 120km of walking trails where it's possible to enjoy anything from a short stroll to a three-day backpack. The most popular backpacking route is the **Fundy Circuit**, a three-day trek of 48km through the heart of the park. Hikers generally spend their first night at Marven Lake and their second at Bruin Lake, returning via the Upper Salmon River. First stop at

the visitors' center to reserve your wilderness campsites ($3 per person per night; call ahead for reservations if possible).

Another overnight trek is to hike the **Goose River Trail**, an old cart track that extends from Point Wolfe 7.9km to the mouth of Goose River, where there's backcountry camping. The Goose River Trail links up with the Fundy Trail, accessible by road from St Martins. This three-day trek is one of the most difficult in the province and is not at all as well developed as the trails in the national park. Note that while you can cycle to Goose River, the trail beyond can only be done on foot. For more information on the section from Goose River to the suspension bridge over the Big Salmon River, see the previous Fundy Trail Parkway section.

Enjoyable day hikes in Fundy National Park include **Coppermine Trail**, a 4.4km loop to an old mine site, as well as **Third Vault Falls Trail**, a challenging one-way hike of 3.7km to the park's tallest falls. Note that several of the park's trails require river fordings, so be prepared.

The only wheelchair-accessible trail is the 500m boardwalk portion of the **Caribou Plain Trail** in the center of the park, 10½km from the visitor center. The boardwalk passes a beaver pond and is a good nocturnal hike.

Mountain biking is allowed on six trails: Goose River, Marven Lake, Black Hole, Bennett Brook (partially), East Branch, and Maple Grove. Surprisingly, at last report there were no bicycle rentals in Fundy National Park or in nearby Alma. Call the visitors' center for current information on this.

On a lighter note, Fundy has a popular **Fundy Night Life Hike** with a ranger; it's great, if spooky, fun. It takes place Saturdays at 8pm in July and August (3 hrs, $8/12/33 child/adult/family) and reservations should be made well in advance at the visitors' center.

Places to Stay
The park has four campgrounds with individual sites and a fifth for groups; there are also 13 wilderness sites. Reservations can be made via the national park hotline (☎ 800-414-6765). A reservation fee of $7.50 is added to the cost. You must do this at least three days in advance and you cannot request a specific site. The park entry fee is extra and is paid upon arrival.

Arriving from the Trans Canada Hwy, you first reach the *Wolfe Lake Campground* which is just an open field at the northwest entrance to the park. Wolfe Lake has the advantages of a covered cooking area and few other campers. You could have it almost to yourself even in midsummer. The 20 tent sites are $10 and there are no showers.

In the interior, 16km from the Wolfe Lake entrance and 3½km northwest of the visitor center, is the 264-site *Chignecto Campground* with sites with hookups ($17 to $19) and tent sites ($12).

The 131-site *Headquarters Campground* is near the visitor center and has sites with hookups ($19) and tent sites ($12). Along the coast, 8km southwest of the visitor center down Point Wolfe Rd, is the *Point Wolfe Campground* with 181 tent sites ($12). Expect sea breezes and cooler temperatures at the coastal campgrounds.

The 13 backcountry campsites consist of one at Chambers Lake, two at Marven Lake, four at Goose River, three by the Point Wolfe River, one at Tracey Lake and two at Bruin Lake. This means that only 13 groups of one to four persons can camp in the backcountry on any given night and only one tent per site is allowed. To reserve a backcountry site, call the visitors' center at ☎ 506-887-6000 (no additional reservation fee).

Fundy HI Hostel (☎ 506-887-2216, fax 506-887-2226, 129 Devils Half Acre Rd) Members/nonmembers $12/17, plus $1 for sheets (if required). Open June–Sept, closed 11am-5pm. In addition to the camping possibilities, there's this HI hostel, a convenient facility close to the golf course just off Point Wolfe Rd, 1½km from the park visitor center. It's just past the Devil's Half Acre Trail. There are two eight-bed dorms, a family room with two double beds separated by a partition and a separate group dorm. These facilities are in five wooden buildings remaining from what was once an art school. The hostel has excellent cooking facilities, a separate lounge area and ample parking. Beds are usually available but call to be sure.

Fundy Park Chalets (☎ 506-887-2808, **W** www.fundyparkchalets.com, off Hwy 114) Chalets $78 ($50 off-season). Open May-Oct. These nice little cottages are in a small forest between the golf course and the visitors' center. Each accommodates up to four people.

ALMA

In the village of Alma, just east of the park on Hwy 114, are a motor inn, hotel and restaurants, along with a few tourist services: small food market, liquor store and laundromat. Most facilities close in winter and Alma becomes a ghost town.

Fresh Air Adventure (☎ 800-545-0020, **W** www.freshairadventure.com, 16 Fundy View Dr; open late May–mid-Sept), just up the street that begins by the bridge at the entrance to the park in Alma, offers myriad kayaking tours in and around Fundy, including estuary and harbor tours (2 hrs, $45) and bay tours (4 hrs, $55). It also runs multiday trips in July and August, including a three-day coastal paddle to the Big Salmon River ($390).

Places to Stay & Eat

Parkland Village Inn (☎ 506-887-2313, **W** www.parklandvillageinn.com, 8601 Hwy 114) Singles/doubles/triples $65/75/85 mid-June-mid-Sept, $50/60/65 beginning and end of season. Open mid-May–early Oct. This three-story hotel is a two-minute walk from the park entrance. It has a restaurant, takeout and laundromat.

Alpine Motor Inn (☎ 506-887-2052, **e** alpinegroup@auracom.com) Rooms $75. Open June–mid-Sept. On Hwy 114, 200m from the park entrance, the Alpine Motor Inn contains 34 rooms.

Tides Restaurant (☎ 506-887-2313, 8601 Hwy 114) Main meals $11-18. Open 11:30am-9pm Mon-Fri, 8:30am-9pm Sat & Sun mid-May–early Oct. At the Parkland Hotel, the main dining room is pricey at $4-6 for chowder, $11 mussels, $13 trout, $16 haddock, $18 salmon and $19 seafood platter. The Parkland's adjacent take-out section is also pricey at $8-9 for fish and chips, $10 clam dinner and $11 scallop dinner. If these prices put you off, the small grocery store across the street has upscale sandwiches and coffee.

Kelly's Bake Shop (☎ 506-887-2460, 8587 Hwy 114). Open 10am-5pm Mon-Fri, 9am-6pm Sat & Sun May-early Oct, 7am-8pm July & Aug. The sticky buns are legendary here. They cost about a dollar each and one is enough for breakfast and possibly lunch. There are also sandwiches and subs ($3-6).

NEW BRUNSWICK

Collins Seafood Lobster Shop (☎ 506-887-2054, 20 Ocean Dr) Collins Seafood behind Kelly's sells live or cooked lobsters, plus fresh scallops, shrimps and mussels. Smoked salmon may also be available. For the price of a meal at any of Alma's over-priced eateries you can buy the makings of a real feast here.

SHEPODY BAY SHOREBIRD RESERVE

At Mary's Point on the Bay of Fundy, another 22km east of Cape Enrage on Hwy 915, is the Shepody Bay Shorebird Reserve *(no phone, Mary's Point Road, off Hwy 915; admission free)*. From mid-July to mid-August this is a gathering place for literally hundreds of thousands of shore birds, primarily sandpipers.

Nature trails and boardwalks have been built along the dikes and marsh. The interpretive center is only open from late June to early September, but you can use the 6½km of trails anytime. The village of Harvey and small town of Riverside-Albert are just north of here.

Places to Stay

Sandpipers Rest B&B (☎ 506-882-2744, W *www.sandpipersrest.nb.ca, 15 Mary's Point Road, Harvey)* Singles/doubles $45/50 shared bath, doubles $60 private bath. Open May-Oct. This quiet two-story house with a nice garden is 4km south of Riverside-Albert via Hwy 915.

Cailswick Babbling Brook B&B (☎ 506-882-2079, W *bay-of-fundy.com/cailswick, 5662 Hwy 114, Riverside-Albert)* Singles/doubles/triples $45/55/65. This imposing two-story farmhouse stands on spacious grounds.

Peck Colonial House B&B (☎ 506-882-2114, W *www.peckcolonial.com, 5566 Hwy 114)* Singles/doubles/triples $45/55/65. Less than 1km east of Cailswick Babbling Brook, this two-story colonial-style house next to the highway contains three rooms for rent. If you're just passing by, meals (seafood chowder, clam chowder, chili) are served and baked goods (bread and pies) are sold in their tea room (open noon-8pm).

HOPEWELL ROCKS

The **Hopewell Rocks Ocean Tidal Exploration Site** (☎ 877-734-3429, *off Hwy 114;* admission $5/12 adult/family, shuttle $1 extra; open 9am-5pm daily mid-May–early Oct; 8am-8pm late June–mid-Aug) is at Hopewell Cape, the place where the Petitcodiac River meets the Fundy waters in Shepody Bay. The 'rocks' are unusual erosion formations known as 'flowerpots.' The shore is lined with these irregular geological forms, as well as caves and tunnels, all of which have been created by erosion from the great tides.

This former provincial park is being heavily promoted as a tourist attraction, and it can be extremely crowded in midsummer. However, an exploratory walk along the beach at low tide is still worthwhile – check the tide tables at any tourist office. You can't hit the beach at high tide, but the rock towers are visible from the trails above. In either event, morning is best for shutterbugs.

From late June to early September **Baymount Adventures** (☎ 506-734-2660, W *www.baymountadventures.com, adult/child $45/40)* offers two-hour kayak tours. Their office is 100m beyond the café inside the Exploration Site.

HILLSBOROUGH

Fourteen kilometers north of Hopewell Rocks and 20km southeast of Moncton, Hillsborough is a small town overlooking the Petitcodiac River. From here a restored steam engine of the **Salem-Hillsborough Railroad** (☎ 506-734-3195, *off Hwy 114)* pulls antique coaches beside the river to Salem 8km away (adult/child $8.50/4.50; roundtrip 1 hour). The train departs at 2pm every Wednesday, Saturday and Sunday in July and August.

Moncton to Sackville

This corner of New Brunswick is the geographical heart of the region, a transportation crossroads most Maritime travelers will transit at least once. At the center of it all is Moncton, whose two principal attractions are places where nature appears to defy gravity. Southeast of the city is a memorial to the Acadians, and Sackville, a small town almost on the Nova Scotia border that will satisfy anyone from a university milieu.

MONCTON
pop 60,000

Moncton is the second city of the province and a major transportation and distribution center for the Maritime provinces. It's only 96km west of the Confederation Bridge to Prince Edward Island, and the train to Nova Scotia passes through. Next to Halifax, Moncton has the region's busiest airport by far. And due to a couple of odd attractions – Magnetic Hill and a tidal bore – it's worth a brief stop on your way by.

If you happen to be passing through Moncton in early May you can check out the Acadian Art Festival. And in July a bluegrass and old-time fiddle-music festival takes over town.

History

The present city of Moncton is at the southwestern end of an old Mi'kmaq portage route from Shediac. In the 1740s the first Acadians settled at this strategic bend of the Petitcodiac River, which they called Le Coude (The Elbow). Their situation became precarious in 1755 after troops led by Lt-Colonel Robert Monckton captured Fort Beauséjour to the southeast, and in 1758 the British deported all Acadians from the area.

In 1766 a party of Protestant German immigrants from Pennsylvania resettled 'The Bend.' The place was of little significance until 1846 when Nova Scotian Joseph Salter established a major shipbuilding industry here. However in the early 1860s falling

NEW BRUNSWICK

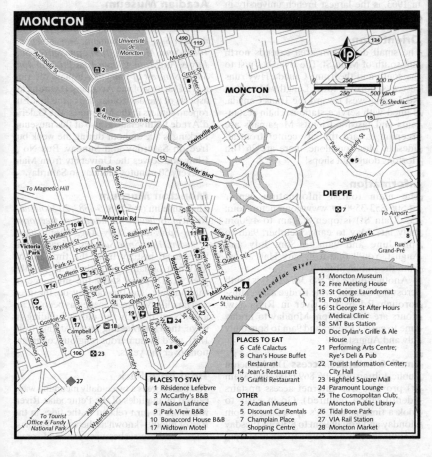

MONCTON

PLACES TO STAY
1 Résidence Lefebvre
3 McCarthy's B&B
4 Maison Lafrance
9 Park View B&B
10 Bonaccord House B&B
17 Midtown Motel

PLACES TO EAT
6 Café Calactus
8 Chan's House Buffet Restaurant
14 Jean's Restaurant
19 Graffiti Restaurant

OTHER
2 Acadian Museum
5 Discount Car Rentals
7 Champlain Place Shopping Centre
11 Moncton Museum
12 Free Meeting House
13 St George Laundromat
15 Post Office
16 St George St After Hours Medical Clinic
18 SMT Bus Station
20 Doc Dylan's Grille & Ale House
21 Performing Arts Centre; Rye's Deli & Pub
22 Tourist Information Center; City Hall
23 Highfield Square Mall
24 Paramount Lounge
25 The Cosmopolitan Club; Moncton Public Library
26 Tidal Bore Park
27 VIA Rail Station
28 Moncton Market

demand for wooden ships led to the closure of Moncton's shipyards.

The town might have ceased to exist entirely had the Intercolonial Railway not arrived in 1871. This company eventually became the Canadian National Railways, which chose Moncton as the site of its main locomotive repair shops for all of eastern Canada. During WWII the city served as a transportation hub and the airport was developed as a training facility for pilots from many Allied countries.

Moncton still thrives as a main service center for the Maritimes. Although the early Acadians were forced out, many of their descendants returned in later years, and nearly half the population is French-speaking today. The Université de Moncton, founded in 1963, is the largest French university in Canada outside Québec.

Orientation

The small downtown area extends north and south of Main St. The river lies just to the south and the Trans Canada Hwy runs east-west north of town. Lengthy Mountain Rd, leading west toward the Trans Canada, is lined with service stations, chain restaurants and fast-food joints. Megamalls are creeping toward the city center from all sides. In Moncton alone, there are 26 Tim Hortons doughnut shops!

Information

The main tourist information center (☎ 506-853-3590, W www.gomoncton.com; 655 Main St) is open 8:30am to 4:30pm daily late May to early October, 9am to 7pm June and 9am to 8pm July and August. You'll find it in City Hall across from the public library.

Another office (☎ 506-387-2053) is south across the Gunningsville Bridge along Hillsborough Rd by the river in Riverview. Hours are 9am to 5pm Monday to Friday June to early October and 9am to 8pm daily July and August.

Email & Internet Access The Moncton Public Library (☎ 506-869-6037, 644 Main St) provides free Internet access upstairs (identification required). Go in early to book a time, or call. It's open 9am to 5pm Monday and Friday, 9am to 8:30pm Tuesday to Thursday July and August; 9am to 8:30pm

Tuesday to Thursday, 9am to 5pm Friday and Saturday rest of the year.

Laundry To use the machines at St George Laundromat (☎ 506-854-6761, 64 St George St) you must buy a token at the adjacent convenience store ($1.50). Wash and dry 8:30am to 8:30pm Monday to Saturday, 9:30am to 8:30pm Sunday.

Medical Services You can see a doctor without making an appointment at the St George St After Hours Medical Clinic (☎ 506-856-6122), 404 St George St, next to Jean Coutu Pharmacy. It's open from 5:30pm to 8pm Monday to Friday and noon to 3pm Saturday, Sunday and holidays.

Acadian Museum

On the university campus this museum (☎ 506-858-4088, Clement Cormier Bldg; admission $2/1 adults/students, Sun free; open 10am-5pm Mon-Fri, 1pm-5pm Sat & Sun July & Aug; 1pm-4:30pm Tues-Fri, 1pm-4pm Sat & Sun rest of year) has displays offering a brief history of the Acadians. It chronicles aspects of the day-to-day life of the first European settlers in the Maritimes. The Galerie d'Art de l'Université is also at this museum. Parking is 50¢ an hour during the week but free on Saturday and Sunday. Bus No 5 Elmwood serves the University from Main St every 50 minutes Monday to Saturday.

Moncton Museum

This museum (☎ 506-856-4383, 20 Mountain Rd near Belleview St; admission free; open 10am-8pm daily July-Aug, 9am-4:30pm Mon-Sat, 1pm-5pm Sun rest of year) outlines local history from the time of the Mi'kmaq Indians and early settlers to the present. Displays show the influence of shipbuilding and the railway on the area and an old-style street scene has been recreated. Next door is the oldest building in town, the **Free Meeting House** dating from 1821, used by numerous religious congregations over the years.

Tidal Bore Park

The tidal bore is a twice-daily incoming wave caused by the tides of the Petitcodiac River, which are in turn related to the tides in the Bay of Fundy – known as the world's highest tides. The bore rushes upstream and some-

Extremely Boring

A feature related to the tides is the tidal bore, a daily occurrence in some of the rivers flowing into the Bay of Fundy, most notably the Petitcodiac River in Moncton and the Salmon River in Truro, Nova Scotia.

As the tide advances up a narrowing bay it starts to build up on itself, forming a wave. The height of this oncoming rush can vary from just a few centimeters to about 1m. The power behind it forces the water up what is normally a river draining to the sea. This wave flowing upstream is called a tidal bore.

The size and height of the bore is determined by the tide, itself regulated by the moon. In the areas where the bore can be most interesting it is not difficult to get hold of a bore schedule. As with the tides, there are two bores a day, roughly 12 hours apart. While this is an interesting occurrence, especially in theory, the bores are not often overwhelming experiences to observe.

times raises the water level in the river by 6m in a few minutes. The wave itself varies in height from a few centimeters to over 30cm.

A good place to watch for it is in Tidal Bore Park at the east end of Main St where a large clock displays the time of the next bore. Note that there's no free parking right at Tidal Bore Park, so allow time to find a spot elsewhere. The unsightly, litter-filled parking lots adjacent to Tidal Bore Park are owned by the RCMP, which has posted large 'no parking' signs.

Moncton Market

This is a year-round food market (*no phone, 120 Westmorland St south of Main St; open 7am-1pm Sat*). The weird sign outside says 'Degen Deli' but the market is through the door. Although some organic fruits and vegetables are sold, it's not really a farmer's market as most items are ready to eat. The array of food items, mostly local specialties sold in small packages, is mind-boggling, and the market is always packed with locals who come every week. Plan on having your breakfast or lunch here. It's a must if you're in Moncton on a Saturday morning.

Magnetic Hill

Incredibly, this is said to be Canada's third most visited natural tourist attraction (☎ 506-858-8841, *corner of Mountain Rd and the Trans Canada Hwy; $3 per car; open 8am-8pm mid-May–mid-Sept*). Gravity here seems to work in reverse – start at the bottom of the hill in a car and you'll drift upward. It looks like uphill, but it's actually downhill, an optical illusion. The car fee may be worth it if there are several of you in the vehicle, otherwise you can park free at the adjacent Wharf Village Shoppes and walk over to watch the paying customers coast back. Late at night and in the off season it's free. The fact that hundreds of thousands of tourists a year could be attracted by this gimmick is the most impressive aspect of it all.

In recent years the hill has become the center of a variety of attractions, which now include the city-operated **Magnetic Hill Zoo** (☎ 506-384-0303, *100 Worthington Ave; adult/family $6.50/20, open 10am-6pm Mon-Fri, 9am-7pm Sat & Sun May-Oct; 10am-5pm Sun Nov-Apr*) with over 400 animals, a rather expensive **water park** (☎ 800-331-9283; *adult/family $19.50/64; open mid-June–early Sept*) with slides of various sorts, restaurants, stores and even a golf course. A mini-train links the different diversions in midsummer.

Places to Stay

Camping & Hostels *Camper's City* (☎ 877-512-7868, *fax 506-855-5588,* W *www.sn2000.nb.ca/comp/camper_city, 138 Queensway Dr*) Without/with hookups $20/26. Open June-Sept. This is the nearest campground to the city, at the Mapleton Rd exit from Hwy 2. They cater mostly to RVs but have some nice grassy sites for tents at the back of the campground. In midsummer it will be packed with nothing between you and your neighbors.

Université de Moncton (☎ 506-858-4008, *fax 506-858-4620,* W *www.umoncton.ca; off Archibald St*) Singles/doubles $48/60 adult, $34/48 student & senior. From May to late August the university rents rooms in two of the residences. The 170 in the 11-story Maison Lafrance near the Acadian Museum have private baths, microwaves and fridges. There are also cheaper rooms with shared baths in the Résidence Lefebvre up the hill at \$32 single (\$19 for students), but they don't like to give them to tourists and you may have to beg. All bookings are handled by Housing Services at Résidence Lefebvre (open 8am-midnight).

Tourist Homes *Park View B&B* (☎ 506-382-4504, 254 Cameron St)* Singles/doubles/triples \$45/55/65. Three rooms are available in an elegant modernistic brick house facing Victoria Park.

Bonaccord House B&B (☎ 506-388-1535, fax 506-853-7191, W www.bbcanada.com/4135.html, 250 Bonaccord St at John St)* Singles/doubles \$45/55. Within walking distance of the center is the four-room Bonaccord House. It's the appealing yellow-and-white house with stately Doric columns on the porch and a yard surrounded by a white picket fence.

McCarthy's B&B (☎ 506-383-9152, 82 Peter St)* Singles/doubles \$45/55 mid-June–mid-Sept, \$35/45 shoulder seasons. Open May-Oct. This place, with four rooms, is a longtime favorite of travelers. Peter St is near the university just under 2km north of the downtown center. It's often full so call ahead. Smokers are not admitted.

Motels *Midtown Motel* (☎ 506-388-5000, fax 506-383-4640, W www.atyp.com/midtown, 61 Weldon St)* Rooms \$69/79 one/two beds mid-June–mid-Sept, \$59/69 rest of the year, extra persons \$5. This two-story motel is right in the center of town within walking distance of the bus and train stations.

Scenic Motel (☎ 506-384-6105, 47910 Hwy 128)* Singles/doubles \$55/60 mid-June–mid-Sept, \$30/35 rest of the year. Open May-Oct. The 20 motel rooms in a two-story block face the highway, 3.3km west of Magnetic Hill. Go up the hill on Ensley Dr (Hwy 126 North), which begins next to McDonalds.

Restwell Motel (☎ 506-857-4884, W www.restwellmotel.com, 12 McFarlane Rd)* Singles/doubles \$45/55 mid-June–mid-Sept, \$35/45 rest of the year, \$195 single weekly. Restwell Motel, 600m west of Scenic Motel on Hwy 128, has 12 rooms in one back-to-back block, with a few rooms upstairs above the office. All rooms have a fridge and the weeklies above the office have kitchenettes. It's a little hard to see from the road as it's hidden behind a hill.

Places to Eat

Café Calactus (☎ 506-388-4833, 179 Mountain Rd at Robinson)* Lunch \$5-6. Open 10am-2pm Mon, 10-8pm Tues-Sun. This colorful café offers healthy California-style vegetarian food, such as 'flutes' made with tortillas (\$5), pelizzas (a type of pizza; \$6), burritos (\$6), soup (\$2-4), salads (\$3-7), whole grain bread and metaphysical teas and coffees. It's a good place to touch base with the local counterculture.

Rye's Deli & Pub (☎ 506-853-7937, 785 Main St)* Specials from \$6. Open 8am-9pm Sun-Thur, 8am-midnight Fri & Sat. This deli, on Main St near Westmorland St, has great bagels and nightly specials listed on a blackboard on the wall, such as spaghetti on Monday and steaks on Thursday. It also has a happy hour from 4pm to 9pm featuring tall 20oz glasses of draft for \$3.50, pitchers for \$7.75 and shots for \$2.75. There's live music Saturday from 7pm to 11pm.

Graffiti Restaurant (☎ 506-382-4299, 897 Main St)* Main meals \$8-12. Open 11am-11pm Sun-Thurs, 11am-midnight Fri & Sat. Graffiti is upscale in everything but price. The French-speaking staff offer tastefully presented dishes with a Mediterranean or 'new Greek' flair, including seafoods (\$8-12), grilled dishes (\$9-11), moussaka (\$8) and daily specials (\$8-11).

Jean's Restaurant (☎ 506-855-1053, 371 St George St)* Main meals \$9. This 1950s-style diner is a Moncton institution and local residents really pack Jean's stools and booths. It's great for breakfast until 11am (\$3 including coffee), then there's fish and chips (\$8), fried clams (\$9) and fried scallops (\$9).

Chan's House Buffet Restaurant (☎ 506-858-0112, 80 Champlain St)* Lunch/dinner \$8/11. Open 11am-midnight Mon-Thur, 11am-1am Fri & Sat, 11am-11pm Sun. Chan's continuous Chinese and Vietnamese buffet runs all day every day from 11am to 9pm, with the dinner price kicking in at 3:30pm. It's just east of the Champlain Place Shopping Centre.

Entertainment

Look for a free copy of *Action* magazine giving a lengthy rundown on Moncton's vibrant nightlife. Central Main St has several bars catering to the young with live bands and dancing.

Performing Arts Centre (☎ *506-856-4379, 811 Main St, Mon-Fri 9am-5pm, Sat 9am-1pm)* The impressive Capitol Theatre, a 1920s vaudeville house, has been restored and is now the city's Performing Arts Centre. Call the theatre box office for a schedule of performances, which include both Theatre New Brunswick and Symphony New Brunswick on a regular basis throughout the year. The Acadian group Grand Dérangement plays here occasionally.

The Cosmopolitan Club (☎ *506-857-9117, 702 Main St at Botsford)* Open 8:30pm-2am Wed-Sun. Cosmopolitan is the largest dance club in Moncton with a capacity for 1100 persons. It's mostly the 19-25 crew that attends this disco ($4 cover charge). Friday from 4pm to 10pm there's jazz downstairs and the crowd tends to be over 30ish.

Paramount Lounge (☎ *506-860-6927, 800 Main St at Church)* Open 8pm-2am Tues-Thur, 4pm-2am Fri, 8pm-midnight Sat. Paramount is more of a sitdown scene than 'the Cosmo' but it can also be loud, danceable and packed with gyrating bodies. It's Moncton's gay-friendly venue. The cover charge varies.

Doc Dylan's Grille & Ale House (☎ *506-382-3627, 841 Main St)* Open 11:30am-2am Mon-Fri, 10:30am-2am Sat & Sun. More live music can be enjoyed at Doc Dylan's, on the corner of Main & Foundry Sts. The pub features live music two or three times a week.

Getting There & Away
Air Greater Moncton Airport is New Brunswick's busiest airport by far, and flights to other parts of Canada tend to be cheaper here than those out of Halifax. You can fly Air Canada to Halifax, Montréal, Ottawa and Toronto.

A possibility worth investigating if you want to save money is Westjet to and from Hamilton, Ontario. It's got numerous onward connections to cities all across central and western Canada from there, and Westjet's one-way Hamilton-Moncton fare varies from $349 plus tax to as little as $149 if you book at least 10 days ahead. Check for specials.

An 'airport improvement and reconstruction fee' of $10 (not included in the ticket price) must be paid at a separate counter by all departing passengers at Moncton.

Bus SMT Bus Lines (☎ 506-859-5060) has a large station at 961 Main St on the corner of Bonaccord St between town and the train station. Some schedules with one-way ticket prices are: Fredericton, 11:45am and 5:40pm daily ($30); Saint John, 11:30am and 6pm daily ($24); Halifax, 11am, 2:15pm and 8:30pm daily ($43); and Prince Edward Island, 2:25pm daily, and an extra trip at 8:40pm Friday, Saturday and Sunday ($35). The bus station itself is open from 7:30am to 8:30pm Monday to Friday, 9am to 8:30pm Saturday and Sunday. A good little café is in the bus station and there are $2 coin lockers.

Train The VIA Rail station (☎ 506-857-9830) is southwest of the downtown area near Cameron St, 200m off Main St. Look for it behind the building at 1234 Main St or behind Sobeys Supermarket at the Highfield Mall. The station is open from 9am to 6pm daily and luggage storage is $2.50 per piece.

The *Ocean* goes through northern New Brunswick, including Campbellton, and into Québec, on its way to Montréal daily at 5:45pm, except Tuesday. The train to Halifax departs daily at 11:35am, except Wednesday. Regular one-way fares are $52 to Halifax and $163 to Montréal. If you purchase your ticket a week in advance you save 25%, providing discount seats are available.

Hitchhiking Hitching north or east from Moncton is a hassle as there are numerous diverging roads and lots of local traffic. Hitching west to Saint John or Fredericton is a bit easier. In either case, bus No 5 Elmwood from Main St will take you to the corner of Elmwood Dr and Hennessey Rd, very near the Elmwood Dr exit from the Trans Canada. A destination sign will be helpful. To hitch to Fundy National Park, take the No 12 Riverview East bus to the corner of Hiltz and Hillsborough Sts (this bus is infrequent but one leaves Highfield Square Monday to Saturday at 8:25am).

Getting Around
To/From the Airport Greater Moncton Airport, about 6km east of Champlain Place Shopping Centre via Champlain St, is served by bus No 20 Champlain from Champlain Place nine times on weekdays. A

taxi to the center of town should cost $12. Avis, Budget, Hertz and National have car rental desks at the airport.

Bus Codiac Transit (☎ 506-857-2008) is the local bus system running daily, except Sunday. Fares are $1.50. There's no bus right to Magnetic Hill and some services are infrequent, so try to check bus times beforehand.

Car Discount Car Rentals (☎ 506-857-2323, open 8am-6pm Mon-Fri, 9am-1pm Sat), 566 Paul St, opposite Champlain Place Shopping Centre, has cars from $39 daily with unlimited mileage, plus $19 collision insurance and tax. This price may be higher in midsummer.

Parking can be a hassle in Moncton – the parking meters ($1 an hour) and 'no parking' signs extend far out from downtown. Parking meters are free evenings and on weekends, although this information isn't posted. The municipal parking lot at Moncton Market on Westmorland St charges $1/7 an hour/day from 7:45am to 6pm Monday to Friday and is free on Saturday, Sunday and evenings after 6pm. Highfield Square Mall on Main St between the train and bus stations provides free parking for its clients, and who's to say you aren't one?

ST JOSEPH

Here, 25km southeast of Moncton, is the **Monument Lefebvre National Historic Site** (☎ 506-758-9783, 480 Central St; adult/senior/ child/family $2/1.50/1/5; open 9am-5pm June-mid-Oct), which tells the enthralling but difficult story of the Acadians, the early French settlers of the Bay of Fundy region, most of whom were expelled by the British in 1755. The exhibits, including paintings, crafts and life-size models, are well done and, unlike those at many such history-based sites, also devote some attention to the subjects' lives through the years to the present.

St Joseph is in the Memramcook Valley, the only area near the Bay of Fundy where some Acadians live on what was the land of their forebears before the mass deportations.

The site is between Moncton and Dorchester off Hwy 106.

SACKVILLE

Sackville is a small university town that's in the right place for a pit stop. In Octagon

House (1855), just off East Main St, is a tourist office (☎ 506-364-4967; 6 King St). It has the usual brochures and a few picnic tables; open 9am to 5pm daily late May to mid-October.

Mt Allison University

This top-rated small university features monumental buildings on a compact park-like campus in the center of town. Mt Allison was the first Canadian university to accept a female student (in 1862), and the first in the British Empire to award a bachelor's degree to a woman (in 1875). Among the facilities open to the public is a swan pond, a library and the **Owens Art Gallery** (☎ 506-364-2574, 61 York St; admission free; open 10am-5pm Mon-Fri, 1pm-5pm Sat & Sun) founded in 1984.

Sackville Waterfowl Park

Across the road from the university, off East Main St, is the Sackville Waterfowl Park on a major bird migration route. Boardwalks have been built over portions of it and there are interpretive signs. The Wildlife Service (☎ 506-364-5044, 17 Waterfowl Lane off East Main St; admission free; open 8am-4pm Mon-Fri) has a Wetlands Display in their office at one of the entrances to the park and information for those wishing to see more.

Places to Stay

Mt Allison University (☎ 506-364-2250, fax 506-364-2688, W www.mta.ca/conference, 155 East Main St) Singles/doubles $26/46, students $20. Open May-Aug. The university, right in the center of town, offers rooms to overnight guests. To get one go the Conference Office in Windsor Hall between 8:30am and 4:30pm Monday to Friday. After hours, call ☎ 506-364-7546. The dorms have shared bathrooms and cooking facilities.

Harbourmaster's House B&B (☎ 506-536-0452, 30 Squire St) Singles/doubles/ triples $60/70/85 mid-June–mid-Sept, $40/50/60 rest of the year. This two-story house in a nice neighborhood is just 400m from the center of town via Bridge St.

Tantramar Motel (☎ 800-399-1327, fax 506-364-1306, W www.tantramar.com/motel, 4 Robson Ave) Singles/doubles from $45/49 mid-June–mid-Sept, $42/45 rest of the year. Just off Hwy 2 at the Cattail Ridge exit, 20 rooms are available in a V-shaped motel with the office in the middle. The eight-room **Bordens Motel** (☎ *506-536-1066)*, a few hundred meters away at 146 Bridge St, 1½km east of the center, is under the same management and charges exactly the same prices.

Places to Eat

Mel's Tea Room (☎ *506-536-1251, 17 Bridge St)* Meals $6-9. Open 8am-midnight Mon-Sat, 10am-11pm Sun. The favorite among locals is this 'tea room' in the center of town, which has the charm of a 1950s diner with the jukebox and prices to match. Operating since 1919, Mel's has ice cream, pies, sandwiches and breakfast specials for $2-3, while major à la carte dishes include fish and chips ($6), pork chops ($7) and T-bone steaks ($9).

Patterson's Family Restaurant (☎ *506-364-0822, 16 Mallard Dr)* Main meals $7-12. Open 7am-10pm daily. Patterson's is well hidden down the road that runs between the Irving gas station and Tim Horton on Main St, near the Main St exit from Hwy 2. The locals line up here for big breakfast specials costing $5-6 with coffee, or hamburger lunches for under $7. A seafood dinner or a steak shouldn't be over $12, and there are several inexpensive vegetarian choices.

Getting There & Away

The SMT bus stops at the Irving gas station (☎ 506-364-4383), East Main St and Mallard, 800m north of the university. Buses between Moncton and Amherst with connections to Halifax stop here three times a day.

The VIA Rail station (☎ 888-842-7245) is on Lorne St, 1.3km south of the university. One-way, same-day adult fares from Sackville are $17 to Moncton, $43 to Halifax and $167 to Montréal. Advance booking can reduce these prices.

FORT BEAUSÉJOUR NATIONAL HISTORIC SITE

Right by the Nova Scotia border, this park (☎ *506-536-0720, 1½km west of the provincial tourist office at Aulac; adult/child $2.50/1.50; interpretive center open 9am-5pm daily June–mid-Oct)* preserves the remains of a French fort built in 1751 to hold the British back. It didn't work. Later it was used as a stronghold during the American Revolution and the War of 1812. Only

earthworks and stone foundations remain, but the view is excellent, vividly illustrating why this crossroads of the Maritimes was fortified by two empires. A visitors' center tells the tale.

The New Brunswick Visitor Centre (☎ 506-364-4090, 158 Aulac Rd) is open 10am to 6pm daily mid-May to early October and 9am to 9pm July and August. It's off Hwy 2 in Aulac, at the junction of roads leading to all three Maritime provinces.

Northumberland Shore

New Brunswick's half of the Northumberland Shore stretches from the Confederation Bridge to Kouchibouguac National Park – in Nova Scotia this coast is called the 'Sunrise Trail.' Folks here, like those farther north on the Acadian Peninsula and in northern Prince Edward Island, claim their waters are the warmest north of either Virginia or the Carolinas in the USA, having been warmed by spin-off currents of the Gulf Stream.

A good part of the population of this coast is French-speaking, and Bouctouche especially is an Acadian stronghold. Farther north, Kouchibouguac National Park protects a variety of littoral environments and their natural flora and fauna.

CAPE JOURIMAIN

The opening of the Confederation Bridge at Cape Jourimain in 1997 coincided with the closing of the ferry terminal at nearby Cape Tormentine. These days most motorists zip straight onto the bridge from Hwy 16 and the nearby coast is relatively quiet.

If you're arriving from PEI, it's worth stopping at the New Brunswick Visitor Centre (☎ *506-538-2133, Hwy 16)* at the New Brunswick end of the Confederation Bridge for free brochures. It's open 9am to 6pm daily mid-May to early October and 8am to 9pm July and August.

If you're headed for PEI, there's no charge to use the Confederation Bridge eastbound – you pay when you come back. If you're on a bicycle or walking you must pick up the free shuttle across the bridge at the Bridge Facility Building at the junction

NEW BRUNSWICK

of Hwys 16 and 955. It leaves every two hours upon request.

Nova Scotia–bound, there's a shortcut along Hwy 970 from Port Elgin to Tidnish Bridge, which is useful if Cape Breton is your destination.

BOUCTOUCHE

This small town is a cultural focal point with several unique attractions. You can learn about Acadian culture, hike or kayak along a dune, go bicycling or just enjoy the beach. KC Irving (1899-1992), founder of the Irving Oil empire, was from Bouctouche, and there's a large bronze statue of him in a park beside Hwy 475 in town.

The Visitor Information Centre (☎ 506-743-8811, Hwy 134), at the south entrance to Bouctouche, features a boardwalk that explains the oyster industry of this area and is open 10am to 5pm Wednesday to Sunday June to September and 9am to 9pm daily July and August.

The SMT bus stops at the Irving gas station (☎ 506-743-6047, 130 Irving Blvd), 700m west of center of Bouctouche. The daily Moncton-Campbellton bus stops here.

Le Pays de la Sagouine

This appealing attraction (☎ 800-561-9188, W www.sagouine.com, 57 Acadie St; adult/senior/student/family $8/6/4/20; open 10:30am-4pm daily mid-June–Sept, 10am-6pm July & Aug), 1km south of the center of Bouctouche, consists of a cluster of buildings on a small island in the Bouctouche River. The admission is valid for two days. In July and August there's a supper theater daily at 7pm except Sunday with a variety of musical programs ($40 including dinner). In June and September, the dinner show is usually on Saturdays only (most programs are in French). Dedicated to Acadian writer Antonine Maillet, Le Pays de la Sagouine is an immersion course in Acadian history and culture.

Kent Museum

The Kent Museum (☎ 506-743-5005, 150 Hwy 475; adult/child $3/1; open 9:30am-noon & 1pm-4pm Mon-Fri mid-June–mid-Oct, 9am-5pm Mon-Fri, noon-6pm Sat & Sun July & Aug) is in the former Convent of the Immaculate Conception (1880), 2km east of the center of Bouctouche. The ex-

hibits cover Acadian culture, and the chapel can also be visited.

Irving Eco Centre

The Irving Eco Centre (☎ 506-743-2600, 1932 Hwy 475; admission free; interpretive center open noon-5pm Mon-Thurs, noon-6pm Fri, 10am-6pm Sat & Sun mid-May–Oct, 10am-8pm daily July & Aug), on the coast 9km northeast of Bouctouche, opened in 1997. 'La Dune de Bouctouche' is a long sandspit pointing out into the Northumberland Strait. The interpretive center has displays on the flora and fauna, but the highlight here is a 2km boardwalk above the dunes. The peninsula itself is 12km long and four to six hours are required to hike to its end and back over the loose sand. Few visitors go beyond the boardwalk, so even a short walk will leave the crowds behind.

To reduce the impact of the large numbers of visitors in July and August, only the first 2000 persons to arrive each day are allowed onto the boardwalk. It reopens to everyone after 5pm. Otherwise, the boardwalk is accessible anytime year-round. Saturdays at 8am there's a free bird-watching tour. Bicycles are not allowed on the dune, but there's a separate 12km hiking/cycling trail through mixed forest to Bouctouche town which begins at the Eco Center parking lot. These excellent facilities are sponsored by the Irving Oil Company as a public relations gesture.

Kayaking

KayaBéCano (☎ 888-529-2232, W www.kayabecano.nb.ca, 1465 Hwy 475; open mid-May–early Sept), 2½km south of Irving Eco Centre, runs two-hour kayak trips (adult/child $25/10) that explore the cultured oyster industry of the area. Three-hour kayak trips out to the dunes cost $30/15. KayaBécano rents trimarans for sailing on the Bay of Bouctouche at $35 for the first 1½ hours, plus $10 each additional hour and $10 per extra person after the first. You can also do the oyster trip by trimaran for $25.

Places to Stay & Eat

Bouctouche Bay Campground (☎ 888-530-8883, fax 506-743-8883, W www.sn2000.nb.ca/comp/bouctouche-bay-camping, 2239 Hwy 475) Sites $20. Open May-Sept. This place 1½km north of the Irving Eco Centre is typical of the many small private campgrounds along this coast. The scarce shady sites are usually occupied by seasonal RVs and overnighters generally end up in a crowded open field divided into 'sites.'

Aux P'tits Oiseaux B&B (☎ 506-743-8196, fax 506-743-8197, e oiseau@nbnet.nb.ca, 124 Hwy 475) Singles/doubles $50/55 plus $10 per additional person in the family room, or $50 single or double in the smaller room. Both have a shared bath. Breakfast is included and no tax is charged. This friendly B&B near the Kent Museum features a collection of 500 carved birds mounted through the house. Book ahead as it's full all summer.

Jalbert B&B (☎ 800-338-2755, w www .sn2000.nb.ca/comp/jalbert-b&b, 2309 Hwy 475) Doubles $55. Two kilometers north of the Irving Eco Centre, Jalbert is just across the road from the beach.

Restaurant Le Vieux Presbytère de Bouctouche (☎ 506-743-5568, opposite the Kent Museum on Hwy 475) Lobster dinner $35. Open 5:30pm-8:30pm daily June-early Oct. This large restaurant in an old religious residence does PEI-style lobster suppers. Reservations are required.

ST LOUIS DE KENT

This small village provides a few services for those visiting nearby Kouchibouguac National Park and offers another kayaking possibility.

Kayakouch (☎ 506-876-1199, w www .kayakouch.com, 10617 Hwy 134; open mid-June–Aug), just 4km south of the national park, rents kayaks at $18/28/45 for 2/5/24 hours for a single, or $30/45/75 a double. They also offer guided kayaking tours at $50 per person. Co-owner Nicole Daigle will arrange women-only two-night kayak camping trips upon request.

Places to Stay & Eat

Daigle's Park (☎ 506-876-4540, fax 506-876-3399, w www.campingdaigle.com, 10787 Hwy 134) Without/with hookups $17/20-26. Open mid-May–mid-Sept. If the national park campgrounds are full, a good alternative is this private campground, 2½km south of the park entrance. There are some well wooded sites for tenters.

Kouchibouguac Motel (☎ 506-876-4317, fax 506-876-4318, w www.kouch.com, 10983

Hwy 134) Rooms from $60 single or double with one bed, chalets from $95, $10 less in the off-season. This motel 400m south of the national park entrance also has a restaurant with a $6 lunch special weekdays.

Oasis Acadienne B&B (☎ 506-876-1199, fax 506-876-1918, w www.kayakouch.com, 10617 Hwy 134) Singles/doubles $39/75 including full breakfast. Open May-Oct. In the off-season rooms are $5 cheaper. This six-room B&B 4km south of Kouchibouguac National Park is run by the Kayakouch people who do kayak rentals and organized kayaking tours. They have a wharf on the Kouchibouguasis River right in their own backyard.

KOUCHIBOUGUAC NATIONAL PARK

The highlights of this park are the beaches, lagoons and offshore sand dunes stretching for 25km. The sands are good for strolling, bird-watching and clam-digging. At the south end of the main beach, seals are often seen offshore.

Kouchibouguac (KOOSH-e-boo-gwack), a Mi'kmaq word meaning 'river of long tides,' also has populations of moose, deer and black bear as well as some smaller mammals. Other features are the birdlife around the salt marsh and a bog where there's an observation platform.

For swimming, the water is warm. The lagoon area is shallow and safe for children, while adults will find the deep water on the ocean side bracing. To be near the beach many local families spend their annual holidays camping in the park, which explains why the campgrounds are in such high demand. There's also a 'gay beach' in the park, a 45-minute walk to the right from the end of the boardwalk at Kellys Beach.

The park is 100km north of Moncton with an entrance just off Hwy 11. The visitors' center (☎ 506-876-2443, 186 Hwy 117; park admission $3.50/7 per adult/family 1 day, $10.50/21 4 days; open 9am-5pm daily mid-May–mid-Oct, 8am-8pm July & Aug) features interpretive displays and a small theater as well as an information counter and gift shop. Before buying a day pass, remember that you can also get an Atlantic Pass valid at seven national parks for the entire season.

Check with the center for the variety of programs offered at the park, including a three-hour tour in a large Voyageur canoe where you paddle to offshore sand bars to view birds and possibly seals. The tours are offered four times a week from late June to early September and are $25 for adult, $15 for children.

The visitors center has a special all-terrain wheelchair with oversized wheels that park staff loan free upon request. Thus equipped, physically challenged persons can cover most of the trails in the park. Otherwise, the 600-meter boardwalk to Kellys Beach is wheelchair-accessible.

The excellent **Bog Trail** is a boardwalk beyond the observation tower, and only the first few hundred meters from the parking lot are crushed gravel. This trail tends to be crowded around the middle of the day and is best done early or late. The **Cedars Trail** is less used.

Cycling

Kouchibouguac features hiking trails and canoe routes but what really sets it apart from other national parks is the 40km network of bikeways – crushed gravel paths that wind through the heart of the park's backcountry. In July and August the **Ryan Rental Center** (☎ 506-876-3733) rents bicycles at $5.50/28 an hour/day and canoes/kayaks at $30/48 per day. From its day-use area, it's possible to cycle a 23km loop and never be on the park road.

Camping

Kouchibouguac has two drive-in campgrounds and three primitive camping areas totaling 359 sites. The camping season is from mid-May to mid-October and the park is very busy throughout July and August, particularly on weekends. Reservations ($8 extra fee) are taken for 60% of the sites; call ☎ 506-876-1277. Otherwise, you'll have to get on a very lengthy 'roll call' waiting list – which can take two or three days to clear.

South Kouchibouguac is the largest campground, located 13km inside the park near the beaches and featuring 311 sites along with showers and a kitchen shelter. The rate is $16.25 to $22 a night during summer. The park entry fee is extra.

Cote-a-Fabien is on the north side of Kouchibouguac River, away from the bike trails and beaches, and does not have showers. A site here is $14 a night. The three primitive campgrounds in the park have only vault toilets and a pump for water and are $10 a night for two people.

Northeastern New Brunswick

North of Fredericton and Moncton lie vast forests. Nearly all of the province's towns are along the east coast or in the west by the Saint John River near the US border. The interior of northern New Brunswick is almost inaccessible rocky, river-filled timberland.

Inland, highways in this area can be quite monotonous with thick forest lining both sides of the very straight roads. In the eastern section the coastal roads are where pretty much everything of interest lies.

MIRAMICHI

In late 1995, the towns of Chatham and Newcastle, the villages of Douglastown, Loggieville and Nelson, and several 'local service districts' along a 12km stretch of the Miramichi River were amalgamated to form the city of Miramichi with a combined population of around 20,000. Like Bathurst farther north, Miramichi is an English-speaking enclave in the middle of a predominantly French-speaking region.

Information

Miramichi is 50km northwest of Kouchibouguac National Park via Hwy 11, and as you approach Chatham from the south, you pass a tourist office (☎ 800-459-3131) that is open daily from 9am to 9pm late May to early October (9am to 6pm at the beginning and end of the season).

Another second seasonal tourist office (☎ 506-623-2152, open June-Aug) is in downtown Newcastle at Murray House, an 1826 edifice moved to Ritchie Wharf in 1993.

The Newcastle public library (☎ 506-623-2450, 100 Fountain Head Lane), just down from Ritchie Wharf, and the Chatham Public Library (☎ 506-773-6274, 30 King St), next to Elm Park, provide free Internet access. Both are open 1pm to 8pm Tuesday and Wednesday and 10am to 5pm Thursday to Saturday.

Newcastle

Though surrounded by two huge paper mills and a couple of sawmills, central Newcastle is pleasant. Here in the central square park is a **statue to Lord Beaverbrook** (1879-1964), one of the most powerful press barons in British history and a statesman and philanthropist of no small reputation. Among the many gifts he lavished on the province are the 17th-century English benches and the Italian gazebo in this square. His ashes lie under the statue presented as a memorial to him by the town.

Beaverbrook spent most of his growing years in Newcastle. **Beaverbrook House** (☎ 506-624-5474, *518 King George Highway; admission free; open 9am-5pm Mon-Fri, 10am-5pm Sat, 1pm-5pm Sun mid-June–Aug*), his boyhood home (erected 1879), is now a museum.

A riverfront boardwalk park nearby, the **Ritchie Wharf** has playgrounds for kids, cafés, a lighthouse, an information center and summer boat tours to **Beaubears Island**. This island in the river has been a Mi'kmaq camp site, a refugee camp for Acadians during the expulsion and a shipbuilding site. Today it's a little known national historic site. Boat tours ($8) to the island leave between noon and 3pm on Tuesday and Thursday in July and August when at least five paying passengers are present.

Places to Stay & Eat

Enclosure Campground (☎ 506-622-8638, fax 506-622-8638, **W** www.sn2000.nb.ca/comp/enclosure-campground, *8 Enclosure Rd*) Without/with hookups $15/19-24. Open May-Oct. Southwest of Newcastle off Hwy 8 is another of Lord Beaverbrook's gifts – a former provincial park called The Enclosure. This riverside park is now privately run and a nice wooded area with spacious 'wilderness' sites is available for tenters. A $3 fee per group is collected from non-campers wishing to use the park's day-use area or swimming pool.

Miramichi Hotel (☎ 506-622-1201, *83 Newcastle Blvd, Newcastle*) Singles/doubles $25/30. The massive four-story Miramichi Hotel was erected just off Newcastle's central square in 1905. Most guests in the 26 rooms are permanent residents who pay by the month, and the Miramichi doesn't go after the tourist trade. For male backpackers and budget-conscious couples, however,

it's great as the SMT bus station is only 900m away. Lone women travelers might feel uncomfortable here. A huge bar called the Black Horse Tavern is downstairs.

Fundy Line Motel (☎ 506-622-3650, fax 506-622-8723, *869 King George Highway, Newcastle*) Singles/doubles $45/55 mid-June–mid-Sept, $40/49 rest of the year. The three long rows of rooms at the Fundy Line are 2km east of central Newcastle.

Governor's Mansion (☎ 877-647-2642, fax 506-662-3035, **W** www.governorsmansion.ca, *62 St Patrick's St, Nelson*) Singles/doubles with shared baths from $40/50, $75-85 double with private baths. On the south side of the river near Nelson-Miramichi Post Office is the Victorian Governor's Mansion (1860), onetime home of J Leonard O'Brien, first Irish lieutenant governor of the province. The nine bedrooms are on the second and third floors. A continental breakfast is included.

Scoreboard Sports Restaurant (☎ 506-622-6556, *295 Pleasant St, Newcastle*) Main meals under $10. Open 11am-11pm Mon-Fri, 9am-11pm Sat, 9am-7pm Sun. Just off Newcastle's main square, the unpretentious Scoreboard serves items like cheeseburgers ($4), fish and chips ($6-9), a dozen wings ($10) and sirloin steak ($17). All prices on their menu include tax. From September to early May there's live music on Fridays from 9pm to midnight.

Sobeys Supermarket (☎ 506-622-2098, *261 Pleasant St, Newcastle*) Open 24 hours a day. The picnic fare you purchase here can be consumed at the picnic tables of Ritchie Wharf.

Getting There & Away

The SMT bus station (☎ 506-622-0445, open 8:30am-5pm Mon-Fri, 1pm-3pm Sat & Sun) is at 60 Pleasant St in downtown Newcastle, 1km from Ritchie Wharf. There are no coin lockers. Daily buses leave here for Fredericton ($17), Saint John ($35), Moncton ($14) and Campbellton ($21), with the later two requiring a change in Chatham.

The VIA Rail station (☎ 800-561-3952) in Newcastle is on Station St at George St, 600m up the hill from Sobeys Supermarket. Trains from Montréal and Halifax stop here.

BURNT CHURCH FIRST NATION

The Mi'kmaq Nation at Burnt Church on Miramichi Bay, 40 km east of Miramichi city, has witnessed violent clashes in recent years between federal fisheries officials seeking to restrict Native Indian access to the lucrative lobster fishery and Mi'kmaq warriors. These events have made this small reserve a household word across Canada and the struggle is ongoing. The name itself harks back to the destruction of an Acadian village here by the British in 1758.

CARAQUET

The Acadian Peninsula, which extends from Miramichi and Bathurst out to two islands at the edge of the Baie des Chaleurs, is a predominantly French area that was first settled by the unhappy Acadian victims of colonial battles between Britain and France in the 1700s. The descendants of Canada's earliest French settlers proudly fly the Acadian flag around the region, and many of the traditions live on in the music, food and language, which is different from that spoken in Québec.

The oldest of the Acadian villages, Caraquet, was founded in 1757 by refugees from Nova Scotia. It's now the main center of the peninsula's French community. Caraquet's bustling fishing port off Blvd St Pierre Est, is colorful, with a large variety of ships. The Acadian Festival in August includes a variety of events.

Acadian Museum

In the middle of town, with views over the bay from the balcony, is this museum (☎ 506-726-2682, 15 Blvd St Pierre Est; adult/student $3/1; open 10am-6pm Mon-Sat, 1pm-6pm Sun June–mid-Sept; until 8pm July & Aug) with a neatly laid out collection of artifacts donated by local residents. Articles include common household objects, tools, photographs and a fine wood stove. Most impressive is the desk/bed, which you can work at all day and then fold down into a bed when exhaustion strikes. It belonged to a superior at the Caraquet Convent in 1880.

Activities

The tourist office (☎ 506-726-2676, 51 Blvd St Pierre Est, open daily mid-June-mid-Sept) and all of the local tour operators are at the Day Adventure Center, down on the waterfront near the fishing harbor.

Sea of Adventure (☎ 800-704-3966; open July & Aug) offers three-hour whale-

watching tours in 12-passenger rigid-hull Hurricane zodiacs at $50 plus tax.

The boat Île Caramer (☎ 506-727-0813) runs deep-sea fishing trips ($20) from Caraquet three times a day June to mid-October, leaving the fishing harbor at 5:45am, 1pm and 6pm. A minimum of six persons is required to go, so call ahead.

Places to Stay & Eat

Camping Caraquet (☎ 506-726-2696, fax 506-727-3610, ⓦ www.sn2000.nb.ca/comp/camping-caraquet, 619 Blvd St Pierre Ouest) Without/with hookups $15/19-22. Open mid-June–mid-Sept. This former provincial park overlooking the sea is just west of the Ste Anne du Bocage sanctuary. The core of the campground is now a solid phalanx of RVs, but there are plenty of tent sites around the perimeter.

Gîte Chez ma Tante Estelle (☎ 506-727-7879, 70 Blvd St Pierre Est) Doubles $50. Open June-Sept. This modern bungalow overlooks the fishing port.

Gîte à Rita (☎ 506-727-2841, 116 Blvd St Pierre Est) Doubles $40. Open June-Aug. This characteristic Acadian house is only a few hundred meters from the fishing harbor.

Motel Landry (☎ 506-727-5225, 11665 Hwy 11, Pokemouche) Singles/doubles $45/50. This six-room motel is 12km south of Caraquet.

Restaurant Le Caraquette (☎ 506-727-6009, 89 Blvd St Pierre Est) Main meals $6-25. Open 6am-11pm Mon-Sat, 7am-11pm Sun. Next to the Shell gas station directly above the port, La Caraquet is extremely popular with the locals. It's a good choice for breakfast ($3-4 with coffee), and for dinner there's chicken ($6-8) and a large seafood selection ($7-25). Smoking is not allowed.

Carapro Fish Market (☎ 506-727-3462, 60 Blvd St Pierre Est) Open 10am-6pm Apr-Dec, 9am-9pm July & Aug. Opposite the dock area is a big fish market with fresh, salted and frozen seafood for sale.

Getting There & Away

Public transportation around this part of the province is very limited as the SMT buses don't pass this way. A couple of van shuttles do exist, but these are used most by local residents wishing to connect with the bus or train in Miramichi or Bathurst and are unlikely to be of much use to other travelers.

CARAQUET TO BATHURST
Ste Anne du Bocage

Six kilometers west out of town is Ste Anne du Bocage (☎ *506-727-3604, 579 Blvd St Pierre Ouest; admission free; open 8am-9pm daily May-Oct*), one of the oldest religious shrines in the province. On this spot Alexis Landry and other Acadians settled soon after the infamous expulsion of 1755, and the graves of some of them are on the sanctuary grounds. Down a stairway by the sea is a sacred spring where the faithful come to fill their water bottles.

Motel Bel-Air (☎ *506-727-3488, fax 506-727-3065,* W *www.sn2000.nb.ca/comp/motel-bel-air, 655 Blvd St Pierre Ouest*) Doubles/quads \$40/50. This block of back-to-back rooms is opposite an Irving gas station, 1km west of Ste Anne du Bocage.

Maison Touristique Dugas (☎ *506-727-3195, fax 506-727-3193,* W *www.maison touristiquedugas.ca, 683 Boulevard St Pierre Ouest*) Without/with hookups \$10/19, singles/doubles \$35/40 with shared bath, \$50-60 double with cooking facilities, cabins \$50 double. This large red wooden house with a rear annex, 1½km west of Ste Anne du Bocage, dates back to 1926. A variety of accommodations are available, from 11 rooms with shared baths and two apartments with private cooking facilities in the main house to five cabins with private baths and cooking facilities in the backyard. Breakfast and tax are extra.

Acadian Historic Village

The Acadian Historic Village (*Village Historique Acadien,* ☎ *506-726-2600, 14311 Hwy 11; adult/senior/child/family \$12/10/6/30; open 10am-6pm daily early June-Sept*), 15km west of Caraquet, is a major historic reconstruction set up like a village of old, with 33 buildings and workers in period costumes reflecting life from 1780 to 1880. The museum depicts daily life in a typically post-expulsion Acadian village and makes for an intriguing comparison to the obvious prosperity of the British King's Landing historic village west of Fredericton.

A good three to four hours is required to see the site, and you'll want to eat. For that there are five choices: two snack bars, two restaurants and the *Dugas House*, the latter serving Acadian dishes.

The site is on Hwy 11 between Bertrand and Grande-Anse. The village has a program (\$30) for kids which provides them with a costume and seven hours of supervised historical 'activities.' If you don't have time to see everything, ask the receptionist to stamp your ticket for reentry the next day. In September only five or six buildings are open and village admission is reduced to \$6/15 adult/family. Facing the village parking lot is a **wax museum** which costs an additional \$7 to visit (audio guide included).

Grande Anse

This small town boasts a unique **Popes Museum** (☎ *506-732-3003, 184 Hwy 11; adult/family \$5/10; open 10am-6pm daily mid-June–Aug*), which houses images of 262 popes from St Peter to the present one, as well as various religious articles. There is also a detailed model of the Basilica and St Peter's Square in Rome.

A beach and picnic spot are at the foot of the cliffs behind the large church in Grande Anse. To get there, go down the road marked 'Quai' beside the church to the fishing port.

West of Grande Anse

All along the route from Grande Anse to Bathurst, the rugged, shoreline cliffs are scenic, and across Baie des Chaleurs you can easily see the outline of the Gaspé Peninsula in the province of Québec. There are some beaches and picnic sites.

At **Pokeshaw Community Park**, 5½km west of the Popes Museum, you can witness a rare sight. Atop an isolated sea stack created by coastal erosion, thousands of double-crested cormorants nest in summer. In late fall, the birds fly south to their winter home in Maryland. From the parking lot you can look straight across at the birds which are on the same level as you, although a great gulf separates you. It's a terrific place to photograph the coastal cliffs, and you can also picnic and swim. Admission is \$1 per car.

Bathurst is yet another industrial town, but based on some extremely rich lead/zinc mines and buttress lumber. It's an English-speaking enclave in a predominantly French region. VIA Rail and SMT both have stations near downtown at the south end of

Nepisiguit Bay, but there's really nothing to detain you here.

PETIT ROCHER

Some 20km north of Bathurst in Petit Rocher is the **New Brunswick Mining & Mineral Interpretation Centre** (☎ *506-542-2672, 397 Hwy 134; admission $5.50; open 10am-6pm daily late June-Aug*). This mining museum has various exhibits on the local zinc-mining industry. The tour includes a simulated descent in a mining shaft and takes about 45 minutes.

Le Vieux Couvent (☎ *506-783-0587, fax 506-783-5587,* W *www.sn2000.nb.ca/comp/ auberge-d'anjou, 587 Hwy 134*) Rooms from $40 including breakfast. This place is part of the upscale Auberge d'Anjou and the 11 cheaper rooms are in an old convent behind the main building. It's near the large church in the center of town, on the corner of the road to the wharf.

Motel Château Maritime (☎ *506-783-4297, fax 506-783-7363,* W *www.sn2000.nb.ca/comp/ chateau-maritime, 495 Hwy 134*) Singles/doubles $40/45. The 22 attractive rooms are in a well constructed brick block between the highway and the beach. When things are slow, the price drops to $35 single or double.

EEL RIVER FIRST NATION

The people of the Eel River First Nation have created an **Aboriginal Heritage Garden** at Eel River Crossing, just southeast of Dalhousie. This botanical garden has two greenhouses displaying regional plants, especially native herbs. The garden only opened in the spring of 2002, and admission fees and hours were still unknown at press time. The garden is just south of Eel River First Nation, straight up Hwy 280 (Cove Road) from Chaleur Beach on Hwy 134 at the south end of the causeway along the sandbar. The Eel River Bar Powwow is held on the reserve the last weekend of July.

The barrage on Eel River just below the garden was built in the 1960s to supply water to the Dalhousie pulp mill, but it's no longer used for that purpose. What it has done is destroy the aboriginal clam fishery on the nearby sandbar by restricting water flows in and out of the bay.

DALHOUSIE

Dalhousie is a small, industrial town on the northeast coast of New Brunswick on the Baie des Chaleurs opposite Québec. The huge Bowater pulp mill runs along the north side of town. Dalhousie is about half the size of nearby Campbellton. William St and parallel Adelaide St near the dock are the two main streets.

On the corner of Adelaide St is the **Restigouche Regional Museum** (☎ *506-684-7490, 115 George St; admission free; open 9am-5pm Mon-Fri, 9am-1pm Sat, 1-5pm Sun*) with local artifacts and history.

From mid-May to September the cruise boat *Chaleur Phantom* (☎ *506-684-4722*) departs from the marina at the west end of Adelaide St on a nature cruise in the bay at 9am ($15), and a scenic cruise along the Restigouche River at 2pm and 7pm ($15). The cruises spot birds, seals and porpoises.

Anne's Restaurant (☎ *506-684-2276, 109 Brunswick St*) Main meals $5-14. Open 7am-6pm Mon-Fri, 9am-11pm Sat. Anne's is known for its large portions and a friendly staff. Breakfast with coffee is $2.25-4.25, and for lunch there are hamburgers ($4), sandwiches ($2-6) and a good daily special.

The former car ferry from Dalhousie to Miguasha, Québec, was discontinued in 2000 when the subsidies were withdrawn.

CAMPBELLTON

Campbellton, located on the Québec border, is the second-biggest highway entry point to the Maritimes from the rest of Canada. It's in the midst of a scenic area on the edge of the Restigouche Highlands. The Baie des Chaleurs is on one side and rolling hills encompass the town on the remaining sides. Across the border is Matapédia and Hwy 132 leading to Mont Joli, 148km into Québec. A huge pulp mill is 3½km west of Campbellton.

The last naval engagement of the Seven Years' War was fought in the waters off this coast in 1760. The Battle of Restigouche marked the conclusion of the long struggle for Canada between Britain and France.

Main streets in this town of about 9,000 residents are Water St and Roseberry St, around which the commercial center is clustered. Campbellton is a truly bilingual town with store clerks saying everything in both French and English.

Information

There's a large provincial tourist office (☎ *506-789-2367, 56 Salmon Blvd*) next to the City Center Mall near the bridge from Québec. It's open 10am to 6pm daily mid-May to early October and 8am to 9pm July and August. A park opposite features a huge statue of a salmon surrounded by man-made waterfalls.

The Campbellton Public Library (☎ 506-753-5253, 2 Aberdeen St at Andrew) provides free Internet access 10am to 5pm Monday to Friday July and August and 10am to 5pm Tuesday to Saturday other months.

Things to See & Do
Sugarloaf Provincial Park (☎ 506-789-2366, 596 Val d'Amours Rd; admission free; open year-round), off Hwy 11 at exit 415, is dominated by Sugarloaf Mountain, which rises nearly 400m above sea level and looks vaguely like its namesake in Rio. From the base, it's just a half-hour walk to the top and you're rewarded with excellent views of the town and part of the Restigouche River. Another trail leads around the bottom of the hill.

A unique attraction of Sugarloaf Provincial Park is the **Alpine Slide** which involves taking a chairlift up another hill and sliding back down a track on a small sled. The slide operates from late June to early September and costs a mere $3.50 a ride. It closes down if there's been any rain as the brakes on the sleds won't hold when they're wet. A nearby office rents mountain bikes at $15/25 a half/full day. In winter you can ski here.

Places to Stay & Eat
Sugarloaf Provincial Park (☎ 506-789-2366, Ⓦ www.tourismnbcanada.com/web/english/outdoor_network, 596 Val d'Amours Rd) Without/with hookups $18/21-24. Open mid--early Oct. There are 76 sites in a pleasant wooded setting at this park 4km from downtown Campbellton.

Campbellton Lighthouse Hostel (☎ 506-759-7044, fax 506-759-7403, Ⓔ julie.jardine@campbellton.org, 1 Ritchie St) Dorm beds $15/19 members/nonmembers. Open mid-June–Aug. This distinctive HI hostel is in a converted lighthouse by the Restigouche River, just up from the provincial tourist office. The 20 beds are in two large dorms, one with 12 beds, the other eight beds. You can only check in from 8 am to 10am or 4pm to midnight, but there's ample parking and the SMT bus stop is just 200m away.

McKenzie House B&B (☎ 506-753-3133, Ⓦ www.bbcanada.com/4384.html, 31 Andrew St) Singles/doubles from $50/60. This large two-story house with an impressive verandah is four blocks south of the tourist office.

Sanfar Cottages (☎ 506-753-4287, Ⓦ www.sanfar.bizland.com, 35 Restigouche Dr, Tide Head) Cottages $46/50 for 2/4 persons, $54/58 for 3/6 with cooking facilities. Open June-Sept. Sanfar is at Tide Head on Hwy 134, 7km west of Campbellton. The 11 neat little cottages vary in size and number of beds, and not all include cooking facilities. The café here doesn't generally serve breakfast, but you can get lunch from 11am to 2pm weekdays and dinner nightly from 5pm. This cozy complex is recommended.

Little Saigon (☎ 506-753-2501, 144 Water St) Average mains $7-10. Open 11am-8:30pm Tues-Fri, noon-8:30pm Sat-Sun. Little Saigon has friendly owners and good Vietnamese-Chinese food.

Getting There & Away
The SMT bus stop is at the Pik-Quik convenience store (☎ 506-753-3100) on Water St near Prince William St. The SMT bus departs Campbellton daily at 11am for Fredericton and Moncton ($33 to either). Twice a day (once in the morning and once in the afternoon) an Orleans Express bus leaves Campbellton for Gaspé ($52), Québec City ($61) and Montréal ($95).

The VIA Rail station (☎ 800-561-3952) is conveniently central at 113 Roseberry St. There's one train daily, except Wednesday, going south to Moncton and Halifax, and one daily, except Tuesday, heading the other way to Montréal ($114). The station is open from 5:45am to 10:30am and 5:45pm to 10pm (closed Tuesday afternoon and Wednesday morning). No coin lockers are available.

If you'll be driving southwest toward Saint Léonard on Hwy 17 beware of moose and deer on the road. Collisions with these animals are an almost daily occurrence here.

MT CARLETON PROVINCIAL PARK
This 17,427-hectare park is the Maritime's only really remote, sizable nature park, offering visitors mountains, valleys and rivers in a wilderness setting. It's the New Brunswick equivalent of Ontario's famous

Algonquin Park, and you'll have your best chance in the region of seeing large mammals (moose, deer, bears) in the wild. Because it's not a national park, Mt Carleton is little known and relatively unvisited, even in midsummer.

The main feature of the park is a series of rounded glaciated peaks and ridges, including Mt Carleton, which at 820m is the highest in the Maritimes. This range is actually an extension of the Appalachian Mountains, which begin in the state of Georgia.

At the entrance to the park is a visitors' center (☎ 506-235-0793, off Hwy 385; open 8am-8pm Mon-Fri, 10am-10pm Sat & Sun May-Oct) for maps and information. In the past an entry fee of $5 per car was charged, but lately the park staff have decided the fee isn't worth the trouble it takes to collect and have allowed free entry. This may change again in the future. Hunting and logging are prohibited in the park, and all roads are gravel-surfaced.

Activities

Day hiking is the best way to explore Mt Carleton. The park has a 62km network of trails, most of them loops winding to the handful of rocky knobs that are the peaks.

The easiest peak to climb is the **Mt Bailey Trail**, a 7½km loop to the 564m hillock that begins near the day-use area. Most hikers can walk this route in three hours. The highest peak is reached via the **Mt Carleton Trail**, a 10km route that skirts over the 820m knob, where there's a firetower. Along the way is a backcountry campsite, located near three beaver ponds and in full view of the mountain. Plan on three to four hours for the trek and pack your parka. The wind above the tree line can be brutal at times.

The most scenic hike is the **Sagamook Trail**, a 6km loop to a 777m peak with superlative vistas of Nictau Lake and the highlands area to the north of it. Allow three hours for this trek. The **Mt Head Trail** connects the Mt Carleton and Sagamook trails, making a long transit of the range possible.

All hikers intending to follow any of these long trails must register at the visitor center or park headquarters before hitting the trail. Outside the camping season from mid-May to mid-September, you should call ahead to

make sure the main gate will be open as the Mt Carleton trailhead is 13½km from the park entrance. Otherwise, park your car at the entrance and walk in – the Mt Bailey trailhead is only 2½km from the gate.

Canoeing and **kayaking** on the chain of lakes in the center of the park are very popular. If you don't have your own equipment, you can try renting from **Nictau Lodge** (☎ 506-356-8353, fax 506-356-8354, **W** www.tobiquenordic.com; open mid-Apr–Nov) inside the park on the south side of Nictau Lake. Rates for one/three days are $30/55 for a bicycle, $30/75 for a single kayak or $40/100 for a canoe or double kayak. The lodge also has five cabins with shared baths at $80 double and three lodges with baths at $150 for up to six. A bunkhouse with 11 beds is $30 per person. Reservations are essential as the staff is not always there.

Places to Stay

Armstrong Brook Campground (☎ 506-235-0793, fax 506-235-0795, **W** www.gnb.ca/0078/carleton, off Hwy 385) Campsites $11 Sun-Thur, $14 Fri-Sat. Open mid-May–Sept. This large campground on the north side of Nictau Lake 3km from the park entrance has toilets, showers and a kitchen shelter, but no sites with hookups. Because of this, the RV drivers often have their noisy generators running, so camp well away from them. Check the eight tent-only sites along Armstrong Brook on the north side of the campground where you're unlikely to be bothered. This campground is never full.

Aside from Armstrong Brook, there are two walk-in campgrounds and one backcountry spot. The **Williams Brook Campground**, a few kilometers beyond Armstrong Brook on the north side of Nictau Lake, has only eight walk-in sites, each with a wooden tent platform. It's great if you want to be alone. The **Franquelin Campground** on the south shore of the lake has nine walk-in campsites and is better situated for hiking as it's just 1½km from the Mt Bailey trailhead (10km from Mt Carleton). The **Headwaters Campsite** up on Mt Carleton itself has just three sites, and it's a good idea to call ahead and try to reserve one if you're sure you want to sleep there. Camping at Williams Brook and Franquelin costs $9 a night; at Headwaters it's $5 a night.

Manitoba

Manitoba, Canada's fifth province, probably gets its name from the Algonquian Indian languages – in Lake Manitoba there is a strait where the water hits the limestone edges, making an odd echoing sound; the Native Indians associated this sound with the Great Spirit *(manito)* and named the spot Manito Waba (meaning 'Manito Strait'). Manito Waba became Manitoba.

The province is the first of the three prairie provinces as you head westward. The southern half is low and flat; the western edge is best for farming. The Canadian Shield, which covers about half the country, cuts across northern Manitoba, making this rocky, hilly, forested lake land.

Winnipeg, the capital, has a long and interesting history that greatly influenced the development of the west in general. The city is a major cultural center and offers plenty of choice in entertainment and eating out. Neighboring St Boniface is the largest French community in western Canada.

Scattered across the province are large parks, ideal for exploring the terrain. Way up on Hudson Bay, Churchill with its intriguing wildlife is one of the destinations most alluring to visitors.

Manufacturing is the province's most significant economic sector. Wheat is the major agricultural product, with various other grains and cattle following closely behind. In the north, there are rich deposits of gold, copper, nickel and zinc.

History

The Assiniboine and Cree First Nations were the principal groups inhabiting the region upon the arrival of Europeans. The Dene of the northern sections and around Hudson Bay soon became involved with the fur traders. The Ojibway, found mainly across Ontario, also moved as far west as the great lakes of Manitoba.

Unlike in much of the rest of the country, early European exploration and settlement occurred not in the more hospitable south but along the cold coasts of Hudson Bay. By the early 17th century fur-trading posts had been set up. Much of Manitoba, first called

Highlights

Entered Confederation: July 15, 1870
Area: 650,090 sq km
Population: 1,113,898
Provincial Capital: Winnipeg

- Visit the polar bears of Churchill in fall, and the beluga whales in summer.

- Take part in the cultural life of Winnipeg's St Boniface neighborhood, western Canada's largest French community.

- Look into settlers' lives at Winnipeg's historical museums.

- Drive past fields of nodding sunflowers in the southeastern part of the province.

- Explore the multitude of forests, lakes, rivers and meadows in the 3000-sq-km Riding Mountain National Park.

Churchill page 608
Around Churchill page 611
Greater Winnipeg page 588
Central Winnipeg page 591
OTHER MAPS
Manitoba page 586

MANITOBA

585

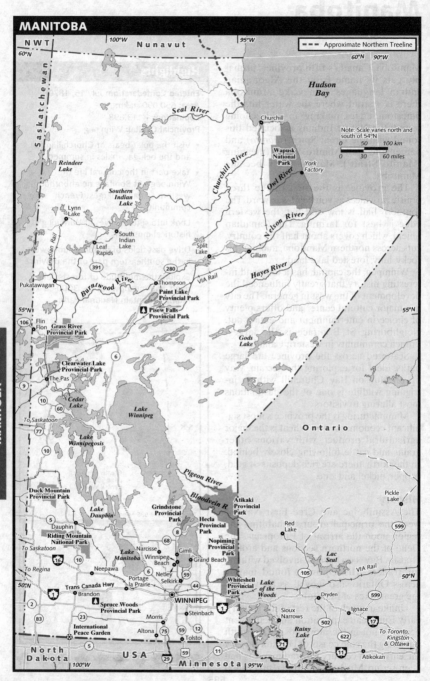

MANITOBA

Note: Scale varies north and south of 54°N

Rupert's Land, was granted by Charles II of England to the Hudson's Bay Company.

Led by Lord Selkirk, agricultural settlement began in 1812 in the area that is now Winnipeg. Conflict between farm expansion and land rights of the Métis resulted in two major rebellions against the federal authorities in 1869 and 1885. Louis Riel, who is still a controversial figure, led the Métis uprisings. He is considered the father of Manitoba.

In the late 19th century, waves of European settlers – mostly English, Scottish and Ukrainian – arrived to grow wheat, and Winnipeg became the economic center of the region. Immigration abated during the Depression, and has continued at a slower pace since. The most recent groups to arrive are those from Somalia and the Philippines. Since the 1950s the north has opened up, and mining and hydroelectricity have become important factors in the province's development.

Provincial Parks

Manitoba's parks provide an excellent way to experience the land and enjoy outdoor activities. The well-forested eastern provincial parks, on the border with Ontario, provide recreational opportunities such as hiking, fishing, boating and skiing, as nearby as an hour and a half from Winnipeg. As you travel north through the parks – Whiteshell, Nopiming, Atikaki – each gets successively wilder with fewer people and fewer facilities.

The 'Manitoba Magic Provincial Parks Guide' is available from the province's parks department (☎ 800-217-6497, Ⓦ www.manitobaparks.com). An annual pass ($20) is a good deal if you plan to visit more than one. Unless otherwise noted, a day pass costs $5. You can buy annual and day passes at park gates in the summer. Area businesses sell day passes off-season when gates are closed (and enforcement is light). Campsites often fill up, call the Parks Reservation System (☎ 888-482-2267) to book a spot.

Information

Information and brochures are available from Travel Manitoba (☎ 800-665-0040, Ⓦ www.travelmanitoba.com), the provincial tourist agency. Offices can be found in Winnipeg and at major border crossings. Towns also have their own city tourist offices, which often have some provincial information in addition to local guides.

The provincial sales tax is 7%. Manitoba is on Central Time.

Activities

The province offers abundant **canoeing** possibilities. Travel Manitoba has an excellent guide detailing canoe routes, including some wilderness trips.

The province is renowned for excellent **fishing**, which attracts many visitors, especially from the USA. The northern lakes offer trout, pike and others. Travel Manitoba produces several publications with lists of areas and outfitters.

Riding Mountain National Park offers good **hiking** and **horseback riding**. Whiteshell Provincial Park has developed trails of varying difficulty.

Churchill offers excellent opportunities for **wildlife viewing**; you can see polar bears, beluga whales and possibly caribou, in addition to the typical Canadian mammals, which may be spotted in provincial parks. Churchill is also a destination for serious birders.

Winnipeg

Winnipeg is a tall town on a flat prairie. Situated halfway between the coasts, it is surrounded by cultivated fields. With 667,000 residents, this is the metropolitan heart of the province but don't remind northern residents that, they don't like it.

Somewhat like a miniature Chicago – its midwestern-US, culturally-sophisticated farm center counterpart – Winnipeg stages a wide variety of plays, performances and concerts. Baroque chamber orchestra concert anyone? The city also has some fascinating history that visitors can explore in museums and at various sites.

Summers are very hot and winters very cold. The corner of Portage Ave and Main St is said to be the windiest corner of the continent.

History

The Cree called the area Winnipeg, meaning 'muddy water.' They shared the land now occupied by Winnipeg with the Assiniboines, before the first European trader, de la Vérendrye, arrived in 1738. In the early 19th century the area was the center of fur-trading rivalry between the Hudson's Bay Company and the North West Company.

GREATER WINNIPEG

1 McPhillips St Station Casino
2 Seven Oaks House
3 Holy Trinity Ukranian Orthodox Cathedral
4 Western Canadian Aviation Museum
5 CanadInns Stadium; Winnipeg Arena
6 Living Prairie Museum
7 Grant's Old Mill
8 Historical Museum of St James-Assiniboia
9 Assiniboine Park Zoo
10 Armstrong Point
11 Royal Canadian Mint
12 Fort Whyte Centre
13 Riel House
14 University of Manitoba; Travel Cuts

MANITOBA

In 1812 Lord Selkirk led Scottish and Irish immigrants to the area to create the first permanent colonial settlement. Later, Fort Garry was built. Louis Riel, a native son from St. Boniface and one of Canada's most controversial figures, led the Métis in voicing concerns over their way of life. The railway arrived in Winnipeg in 1881.

The 1970s saw urban redevelopment upgrade the provincial capital and Hudson's Bay Company moved its headquarters here from London. In the 1980s, the main street, Portage Ave, underwent a massive change, with the building of a mega-mall complex taking over several blocks. The wide downtown streets, edged with a balance of new and old buildings, give a sense of permanence as well as of development and change.

Orientation

As you approach Winnipeg from the east on the Trans Canada Hwy, a sign marks the longitudinal center of Canada.

Once in Winnipeg, Main St is the north-south corridor. Portage (pronounced 'port-**idge**') Ave, a major southeast-northwest artery, leads westward towards the airport and eventually to the westbound Trans Canada Hwy. Most of the hotels and restaurants and many of the historic sites are within a 10-block square around this point. The railway station is central, on the corner of Main St and Broadway Ave. The Legislative Building and other government buildings are on Broadway Ave, too.

Northeast of the city core is the old warehouse area known as the Exchange District.

North along Main St, the Centennial Centre is an arts and cultural complex. The small Chinatown is also in this area.

North of Rupert St on Main St is an area of cheap bars and dingy hotels. Farther north on Main St, you'll find some evidence of the many ethnic groups, primarily Jews and Ukrainians, who once lived here in greater numbers.

South of the downtown area, across the Assiniboine River on Osborne St, is Osborne Village, a popular area with boutiques, stores and restaurants. South of Osborne Village, west along Corydon Ave, is a small Italian district that has a little café and restaurant scene. It's particularly good for a stroll in summer, when many of the places have outdoor patios along the street.

Information

Tourist Offices The main tourist office is Travel Manitoba Centre (☎ 204-945-3777, 800-665-0040) in the Johnstone Building at The Forks, the historic riverside market behind the train station. The office is open 10am to 6pm daily.

Travel Manitoba operates another office (☎ 204-945-5813) in the Legislative Building on Broadway Ave. During summer it's open 8am to 7pm daily; winter hours are 8am to 4:30pm Monday to Friday.

Tourism Winnipeg (☎ 204-943-1970, 800-665-0204, 279 Portage Ave) is open 8:30am to 4:30pm Monday to Friday. There's also a booth on the main floor of the airport, open 8am to 9:45pm daily.

Money The Custom House Currency Exchange (☎ 204-987-6000, 245 Portage Ave) has better rates and longer hours than the banks. ATMs are widely available.

Post & Communications The main post office is at 266 Graham Ave. Centennial Library (☎ 204-986-6450, 251 Donald St) has Internet stations.

Travel Agencies Travel Cuts (☎ 204-783-5353, 499 Portage Ave) has a branch downtown and one at the University of Manitoba (☎ 204-269-9530, 225 University Centre), which is south of downtown.

Bookstores A large selection of Canada-related books and authors are available

McNally Robinson (☎ 204-943-8376, 393 Portage Ave) on the ground floor of Portage Place. Those who like hunting for used books will love the piles at Red River Books (☎ 943-956-2195, 92 Arthur St).

Medical Services The Health Sciences Centre (☎ 204-787-3167) is located at 820 Sherbrooke St.

The Forks

The fetching location at the confluence of the Red and Assiniboine Rivers, behind the VIA Rail Station off Main St near Broadway Ave, has in one way or another been the site of much of Manitoba's history. Native Indians first used the area some 6000 years ago. The early explorers and fur traders stopped here; forts were built and destroyed; and Métis and Scottish pioneers later settled The Forks.

Behind the Children's Museum, the Orientation Circle has a history exhibit. The Riverwalk is a path with historic notes written on plaques in English, French and Cree. Parts of the trail also provide views of the city along the way.

The site, however, is essentially a riverside park and recreation area. The Market Building buzzes with shoppers at the produce stands, international art and craft shops, multiethnic food stalls and restaurants. The Johnston Terminal is similar, though with less-exotic wares.

In July and August, costumed guides offer walking tours of the historic area on Wednesday through Sunday afternoons. On Thursday evenings from 7pm to 11pm, live swing bands perform under a canopy for dancers. For more information on events, call ☎ 204-957-7618. Canoes can be rented from a little stand here May to September, contact Travel Manitoba (☎ 204-945-3777) for more information.

Crossing the river or cruising over to Osborne Village, making a stop at the dock behind the Legislature, is easy with the **Splash Dash Water Taxi** (☎ 204-783-6633; one-way $2; 11am-8pm Mon-Fri). On the water taxi you can look around at the city from a new perspective without having to drive between sights. In winter there is skating on the river or you can walk over the ice to St Boniface Basilica, with it's impressive-looking facade. Cross-country ski trails are groomed along the river.

City buses connect the downtown area to the site near the Market Building, but it's quite walkable. The No 99 or No 38 bus runs from here to Broadway Ave and around by the Art Gallery and Portage Ave.

Manitoba Children's Museum A whole range of hands-on exhibits that encourage play and learning are set up especially for those between the ages of three and 11 years at the Manitoba Children's Museum (☎ 204-956-5437, The Forks; admission adult/child $5/4; open 9am-4:30pm Mon-Wed, 9am-8pm Thur & Fri, 11am-8pm Sat, 10am-5pm Sun). Included are a fully functional television studio, an exhibit on exploring computer technology and a tree that preschoolers can climb to spot life-sized animals and birds.

St Boniface

Primarily a residential neighborhood, St Boniface, across the Red River on Boulevard Provencher, is one of the oldest French communities in Canada. The tourist office has a booklet on the area, which includes a map and self-guided walking tour. To get there from downtown, take the bus east along Portage Ave across the bridge and then walk along the river to the church and museum.

Taché Promenade follows the Red River along Rue Taché, past much of St Boniface's history. A few plaques indicate the major points of interest and provide some details about the Grey Nuns, a pioneering order that traversed the wilderness in the late 1800s in canoes before landing and setting up their convent on the banks of the Red River.

The imposing facade of the **St Boniface Basilica** (151 Ave de la Cathédrale), dating from 1908, is worth a look. The rest of the old church was destroyed by fire in 1968. The current church, in the rear, is the fifth incarnation since 1818. Louis Riel, the Métis leader, was born in St Boniface and is buried in the cemetery in front of the facade, facing the river.

Next door, the circa-1850 convent contains the **St Boniface Museum** (☎ 204-237-4500, 494 Rue Taché; admission adult/child $2/1.50; open 9am-noon Mon-Fri, 10am-5pm Sat, 10am-8pm Sun mid-May–Sept; 9am-noon Mon-Fri, noon-4pm Sun Oct–mid-May). This is the oldest building in Winnipeg and evidently is the largest oak-log construction on the continent. It houses odds and ends pertaining to Riel and to other French, Métis and Native Indian settlers as well as to the Grey Nuns, who lived and worked here after arriving by birch-bark canoe from Montreal, a trip of nearly 3000km.

There's also some information on Jean Baptiste Lagimodière, one of the best-known of the *voyageurs* (early French fur traders/explorers) who canoed between here and Montreal. There is an example of the famous wooden Red River Cart. Ox-drawn, it could be floated across rivers by repositioning the wheels. Because of the dust of the trails, the axles were not oiled, and it's said that the creaking and squeaking of a caravan of settlers could be heard for miles. Also in the museum are some articles that were saved from the destroyed basilica.

Used as the setting for some of the author's works, literature buffs might enjoy seeing the **Gabrielle Roy House** (☎ 204-231-8503, 375 Rue Deschambault) after its renovation.

The **Centre Culturel Franco-Manitobain** (☎ 204-233-8972, 340 Boulevard Provencher; open 9am-8pm Mon-Fri, 12-5 Sat & Sun) has a small gallery with rotating exhibits. *Le Café Jardin* serves French-Canadian lunches Monday to Friday, and hosts a happy hour on Friday. The organization sponsors a number of cultural events throughout the year.

Museum of Man & Nature

Exhibits of history, culture, wildlife and geology are on view at the Museum of Man & Nature (☎ 204-956-2830, ⓦ www.manitobamuseum.mb.ca, 190 Rupert St; adult/child galleries $6.50/5, science center $5/4, planetarium $5/4, combined ticket $15/10; open 10am-6pm daily July & Aug; 10am-4pm Tues-Fri, 10am-5pm Sat & Sun Sept-June). In the museum galleries, the dioramas of Native Indian life and animals are realistic. A re-creation of a 1920s town comes complete with an old cinema that plays Chaplin movies. You can also climb aboard a full-sized replica of the *Nonsuch*, a large 17th century wooden boat.

The newest exhibit showcases the 300-year history of the Hudson's Bay Company with artifacts, historical videos and a trading post replica. The parklands ecological display is slated to open in early 2003.

Also onsite, the hands-on science center is great for kids. On weekends throughout the year, the planetarium has showings three

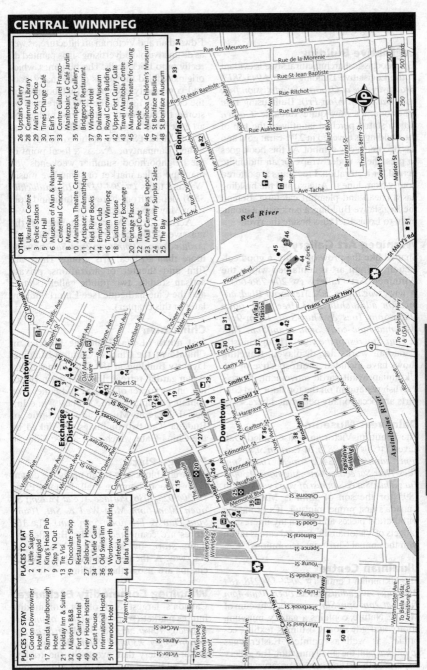

CENTRAL WINNIPEG

PLACES TO STAY
15 Gordon Downtowner Hotel
17 Ramada Marlborough Hotel
21 Holiday Inn & Suites
32 Masson's B&B
40 Fort Garry Hotel
49 Ivey House Hostel Guest House
50 Old Swiss Inn International Hostel
51 Norwood Hotel

PLACES TO EAT
2 Little Saigon
4 Marigold
7 King's Head Pub
9 Step 'N Out
13 Tre Visi
19 Chocolate Shop Restaurant
27 Salisbury House
34 La Vieille Gare
36 Old Swiss Inn
38 Wordsworth Building Cafeteria
44 Barba Yiannis

OTHER
1 Ukrainian Centre
3 Police Station
5 City Hall
6 Museum of Man & Nature; Centennial Concert Hall
8 Mezzo
10 Manitoba Theatre Centre
11 Artspace; Cinémathèque
12 Red River Books
14 Empire Club
16 Tourism Winnipeg
18 Custom House
20 Currency Exchange
22 Portage Place
23 Travel Cuts
24 Mall Centre Bus Depot; United Army Surplus Sales
25 The Bay
26 Upstairs Gallery
28 Centennial Library
29 Main Post Office
30 Times Change Café
31 Earl's
33 Centre Culturel Franco-Manitobain; Le Café Jardin
35 Winnipeg Art Gallery; Bridgeport Restaurant
37 Windsor Hotel
39 Dalnavert Museum
41 Royal Crown Building
42 Upper Fort Garry Gate
43 Travel Manitoba Centre
45 Manitoba Theatre for Young People
46 Manitoba Children's Museum
47 St Boniface Basilica
48 St Boniface Museum

St Boniface

Red River

MANITOBA

times daily. In summer there are more offerings; call ☎ 204-943-3139 for a recorded listing.

Legislative Building
The neoclassical architectural style is evident at the Legislative Building (☎ 204-945-5813, *Broadway Ave at Osborne St; admission free; open 9am-6pm Mon-Fri*). Built using rare limestone, it's now quite valuable. *Golden Boy*, a statue perched jauntily at the top of the building, is covered in 23½-carat gold and has become a city symbol. As this book goes to press, he is under wraps for an indefinite period for restoration. Free tours are offered hourly from June to August, and the building has a cheap and pleasant cafeteria. Behind the Legislative Building, a park with a monument to Louis Riel runs beside the river.

Winnipeg Art Gallery
Shaped like the prow of a ship, a good collection of Inuit art is contained within the Winnipeg Art Gallery (☎ 204-786-6641, W *www.wag.mb.ca, 300 Memorial Blvd; admission adult/child $4/3, free Wed; open 10am-5pm Tues & Thur-Sun, 10am-9pm Wed mid-June–early Sept; 11am-5pm Tues & Thur-Sun rest of the year*). Though mostly Canadian works are displayed, traveling shows have included a retrospective of the Ukrainian avant-garde movement. There's a stylish restaurant on the top floor and concerts are occasionally performed here.

Dalnavert Museum
The beautiful Victorian house called Dalnavert (☎ 204-943-2835, 61 Carlton St; admission adult/child $4/3; open 10am-5pm Tues-Thur, Sat & Sun June-Aug; noon-4:30pm Tues-Thur, Sat & Sun rest of year) was built in 1895 for the son of John A Macdonald, Canada's first prime minister. It's brimming with period pieces and the many interesting gadgets of Victorian life. Special care is taken with the annual Christmas decorations.

Ukrainian Centre
The Ukrainian Centre (☎ 204-942-0218, 184 *Alexander Ave; admission $2; open 10am-4pm Tues-Sat, 2pm-5pm Sun*), near the Museum of Man & Nature, contains a gallery, museum, library and gift shop. Costumes, textiles, ceramics, as well as painted Easter eggs (*pysankas*), fill the small museum. The gallery displays both old and contemporary works.

Exchange District
In this 20-block area, you'll find substantial Edwardian and Victorian architecture, as well as distinctive old advertising signs painted directly onto brick walls. The buildings, which originally filled the needs of the many stock and commodity exchanges that boomed in the city from 1880 to the 1920s, are now restored for scattered restaurants, nightclubs, art galleries, a few shops and other businesses.

Old Market Square, at the corner of King St and Bannantyne Ave, is a focal point of the neighborhood; summer weekends you may find a flea market or some live music. Walking tours (☎ 204-942-6716; adult/child $5/3) depart from here at 11am and 2pm from May to September.

Across from Market Square is the massive **Artspace** (☎ 204-947-0984, 100 *Arthur St; open 9am-6pm Tues-Sat*), housing more than 20 local arts groups There are film and theater organizations, private artisan studios, two public gallery spaces and the Cinémathèque (see Entertainment, later in this chapter).

Chinatown
Just north of the Exchange District, in **Chinatown**, the Chinese Cultural Building/Dynasty Building, at 180 King St, has a tiny Asian garden retreat. The Mandarin Building, on the corner of King St and James Ave, contains a replica of the Chinese Nine Imperial Dragon Mural and a statue of Buddha. The two buildings are linked by the China Gate, which runs above King St.

Portage Place
Three city blocks are taken up by the downtown indoor shopping mall, Portage Place (☎ 204-925-4636, Portage Ave at Vaughn St; open 10am-6pm Mon-Wed & Sat, 10am-9pm Thur & Fri, noon-5pm Sun). The 160 stores are connected to The Bay department store by an enclosed overhead walkway. A theater company and IMAX cinema are also in the building.

Winnipeg Commodity Exchange
Canada's largest and oldest commodity futures market (☎ 204-925-5000, Commodity Exchange Tower, 5th floor, 360 Main St; admission free; open 9:30am-1:20pm Mon-Fri) has a visitor's gallery that overlooks the trading area. Call the receptionist to schedule a tour.

Holy Trinity Ukrainian Orthodox Cathedral

Within this church with bulbous Byzantine domes is the provincial branch of the Ukrainian Museum of Canada (☎ 204-582-1018, 1175 Main St; admission $2; open 10am-4pm Mon-Sat July & Aug) Examples of traditional arts and crafts are displayed.

Upper Fort Garry Gate

In the small park on Main St is the ruin of the old stone gate and some remaining wall (restored in 1982) of Fort Garry, with interpretive signs. Since 1738, four different forts have stood on this spot, or nearby. The gate dates from 1835 and was part of the Hudson's Bay Company's fort system.

Royal Canadian Mint

Canada's coinage – as well as coins for many other, especially Asian, countries – is produced southeast of town at the Mint (☎ 204-257-3359, 520 Lagimodière Boulevard; admission $2; open 9am-5pm Mon-Fri May-June, 9am-5pm Mon-Fri & 10am-2pm Sat July & Aug, 10am-2pm Mon-Fri Sept-Apr). Watch the state-of-the-art procedures used in cranking out two billion coins a year from the gallery of this pyramid-shaped glass building. Free tours are offered daily.

Western Canadian Aviation Museum

In a hangar opposite the Winnipeg international airport, the WCAM (☎ 204-786-5503, 958 Ferry Rd; admission adult/child $5/3; open 10am-4pm Mon-Sat, 1pm-4pm Sun) has a good collection of planes. About five minutes west by car, at the end of Sharpe Blvd, is the **Air Force Heritage Park** (☎ 204-833-2500 ext 5993, Airforce Way; admission free; open 8am-4pm Mon-Fri) with about 10 aircraft mounted outside.

Riel House

In a residential area known as St Vital, the Riel House (☎ 204-257-1783, 330 River Rd; admission by donation; open 10am-6pm daily mid-May–Labor Day) details the man's life here in the 1880s. The restored, fully-furnished, French-Canadian–style log farmhouse, built in 1881, belonged to Riel's parents. A staff interpreter offers information on Riel and on the Métis in general.

Louis Riel, Hero of the Métis

The Métis are people of mixed Native Indian and French blood, almost always the result of unions between white men and Native Indian women. Many Métis can trace their ancestors to the time of western exploration and fur trading, when the French voyageurs traveled the country, living like (and often with) the Native Indians. The term *métis* is also used more generally to include English-Indian mixed bloods, in order to avoid the term half-breed.

As time passed and their numbers grew, many Métis began to use the St Boniface/Winnipeg area as a settlement base, living a life that was part European, part traditionally Native Indian. This unique juxtaposition soon became an identity. The ensuing rebellions against the political authorities were the almost inevitable product of this consciousness.

Born in St Boniface in 1844, Louis Riel led the Métis in an antigovernment uprising in 1869, partly to protest the decision to open up what they saw as their lands to new settlers and partly to prevent possible assimilation. When complaints went unheeded, he and his men took Upper Fort Garry. Government troops soon reversed that and, to the Canadian government, Riel became a bad guy. Land was allotted to the Métis, however, and the province of Manitoba was created. As part of the turning twists of Riel's fate, he was then elected to the House of Commons, but was forbidden to serve.

There is some question about what transpired in the next few years. Riel may have spent time in asylums. In any case, he took refuge in Montana for several years from the stress of personal persecution and political machinations. Later he returned to lead the again-protesting Métis in their 1885 struggle in Saskatchewan, where they had fled in search of greater autonomy. They again lost the battle. Riel surrendered and, after a dramatic trial, was called a traitor and hanged. The act triggered French anger and resentment towards the British that has not been forgotten. Riel's body was returned to his mother's house in Winnipeg and then buried in St Boniface. Ironically, Riel is now considered a father of the province.

🍁 🍁 🍁 🍁 🍁 🍁 🍁 🍁 🍁 🍁 🍁 🍁 🍁 🍁 🍁 🍁 🍁 🍁 🍁 🍁

MANITOBA

Seven Oaks House
This log homestead (☎ 204-339-7429, 115 Rupertsland Blvd; admission adult/child $3/2; open 10am-5pm daily late May–Labor Day) was built (without nails) in 1851 and now contains settlers' history.

Historical Museum of St James-Assiniboia
This small museum (☎ 204-888-8706, 3180 Portage Ave; admission by donation; open 10am-5pm daily Apr–Labor Day; 10am-5pm Mon-Fri rest of the year) has a collection of Native Indian, Métis and pioneer belongings from the turn of the last century. On site, there's a 100-year-old log house with authentic furnishings.

Ross House
The first post office in the west, Ross House (☎ 204-943-3958, Joe Zuken Heritage Park, 140 Mead St N; admission free; open 11am-6pm Wed-Sun June-Aug) is an example of Red River log construction, furnished with period pieces.

North End/Selkirk Ave
Selkirk Ave has long been the commercial center of the city's North End and the first home of a range of immigrant groups. The area is north along Main St, just past the junction of Hwy 42 (in town it's known as Henderson Hwy), which leads over the river and north out of town. Many of the houses are more than 100 years old. From May to August, free walking tours of the area depart at 10am and 2pm from the Bell Tower, four blocks west of Main St on Selkirk Ave. For more information, call ☎ 204-586-3445.

Assiniboine Park
Assiniboine is reportedly the largest city park (2355 Corydon Ave; admission free; open 9am-dusk daily). A 40-hectare zoo (☎ 204-986-6921) has animals from around the world. See the statue of Winnie the Bear, a bear purchased in White River, Ontario, by a soldier from Winnipeg on his way to England to serve in WWI. The bear ended up at the London Zoo and is said to have been the inspiration for AA Milne's Winnie the Pooh.

There's an English garden and the historic **Pavilion** (☎ 204-888-5466), with an art gallery and two restaurants. Other features include a **conservatory** (204-986-5537), with some tropical vegetation, and the **Leo Mol Sculpture Garden** (☎ 204-986-6532).

At the beginning of July, watch for the free evening outdoor Shakespearean performances in the park.

Assiniboine Forest
South of the Assiniboine Park, between Shaftsbury and Chalfont Aves, this largely undeveloped forest area is even larger than the park itself. In the middle is a pond with an observation area for bird watching, and deer may be seen from the winding trails, open from dawn to dusk.

Grant's Old Mill
Grant's, near Sturgeon Creek, is a reconstruction of an 1829 water mill (☎ 204-986-5613, 2777 Portage Ave; admission by donation; open 10am-6pm daily May–Labor Day). Grist (grain) is ground and offered for sale as souvenirs.

Living Prairie Museum
North of Grant's Mill, a preserve with walking trails and an interpretive center form the Living Prairie Museum (☎ 204-832-0167, 2795 Ness Ave; admission free; open 10am-5pm Sun Apr-Jun, 10am-5pm daily July & Aug). In this 12-hectare area, the now-scarce original, unploughed tall prairie grass is protected and studied. Approximately 200 native plants are represented, as well as a variety of animal and birdlife. Naturalists are on hand to answer questions or lead walks.

Fort Whyte Centre
Walking trails, exhibits, demonstrations and slide shows on local wildlife are part of Fort Whyte (☎ 204-989-8355, 1961 McCreary Rd; admission adult/child $5/4; open 9am-5pm Mon-Fri, 10am-5pm Sat-Sun). In addition to the conservation area with a marsh, lake and woods, there's a kid-friendly museum and a freshwater aquarium representing the province's different aquatic life. Canoe lessons and rental, as well as a small restaurant and shop, round out the offerings.

Activities
The city's parks and recreation department (☎ 204-986-3700) operates several indoor

swimming pools. One of the country's largest is the **Pan-Am Pool** (☎ 204-986-5890, 25 Poseidon Bay; admission free; public hours vary), which was built for the Pan-American games. Three pools, including one for kids, are onsite.

Organized Tours
Gray Line and **Paddlewheel River Rouge Tours** (☎ 204-944-8000, 78 George Ave; open May-Oct), working together, offer five boat and bus tours ranging in length and price. The basic downtown doubledecker bus tour ($20/12). lasts 3½ hours. Boat tours depart from a dock at the end of Alexander Street. Basic two-hour along-the-river cruises (adult/child $12.75/7) or more costly three-hour evening dinner-dance cruises ($13.75, $14.50-22 with meals), on a replica paddlewheeler. Another travels down to Lower Fort Garry (adult/child $21.95/12, 7½ hours).

Special Events
Le Festival du Voyageur Held mid-February, this 10-day festival in St Boniface commemorates the early French voyageurs with concerts, a huge winter street party, a Governor's Ball with period costumes, arts and crafts displays and lots of outdoor activities.

The Red River Exhibition In late June at Red River Exhibition Park (3977 Portage Ave), this festival is a week-long carnival, with an amusement park and lots of games, rides and exhibits.

Gay Pride Day Watch for the big parade held at the end of June.

Winnipeg Folk Festival This annual festival (☎ 204-231-0096) takes place for three days in early July, with more than 200 concerts plus a craft and international food village. The festival is held at Birds Hill Park, about 20km north of downtown.

Winnipeg Fringe Festival This is a nine-day event held in the Exchange District in late July, featuring international fringe theatre, comedy, mime, music and cabaret.

Folklorama The city's big, popular festival of nations celebrates the city's surprising number of ethnic groups. Two weeks of August are filled with music, dance, and food in pavilions throughout downtown Winnipeg.

Places to Stay
Camping There are a few places to camp around town but most are a long way out, off the main highways or up at the beach areas around Lake Winnipeg.

Conestoga Campsites (☎ 204-257-7363, 1341 St Anne's Rd) With/without hookups $18/12, open May–mid-Oct. This basic facility is near the crossroads of Perimeter Hwy 100 and Route 150.

Traveller's RV Resort (☎ 204-864-2721, fax 204-253-9313, 870 Murdock Road) With/without hookups $25/16, open May–mid-Oct. This grassy campground is family-friendly, with a swimming pool and mini-golf.

Hostels Both hostels can be full (or close to it) in July and August, so calling ahead is not a bad idea.

Guest House International Hostel (☎ 204-772-1272, 800-743-4423, fax 204-772-4117, 168 Maryland St) Dorm beds $16, doubles $38; open by appt only Dec-Mar. The slightly worn backpackers' hostel can accommodate about 40 people in a variety of rooms (including four for couples) and has a kitchen, laundry facilities and Internet access. *X-Files* aficionados should know that the woman who played Fox Mulder's sister once stayed here. She may or may not have been abducted from a 2nd-floor bedroom. No membership is required.

Ivey House Hostel (☎ 204-772-3022, fax 204-784-1133, 210 Maryland St) Dorm beds $17/21 members/nonmembers, singles $20/27; reception open 8am-midnight daily June-Nov, 8am-10am & 4pm-midnight daily Dec-May. This HI hostel – in an old turreted house near the corner of Broadway Ave and Sherbrooke St – is not far from the bus station. The place sleeps 40 in a variety of small rooms. Facilities include a kitchen, laundry room, TV lounge and credit-card Internet access. Linens can be rented for $1. Nearby, at 194 Sherbrooke St, is the HI regional office (for memberships, sleep sacks, etc).

From the airport, catch the No 15 bus to the corner of Sergeant and Maryland Sts. From there, take No 29 bus to the corner of Broadway Ave and Maryland St. From the train station, walk west along Broadway Ave, or take the No 29 bus to the corner of Broadway Ave and Sherbrooke St and walk a block west.

University of Manitoba (☎ 204-474-9942, 26 MacLean Crescent, Pembina Hall) Rooms $20 per person; mid-May–mid-Aug. These university rooms, south of downtown inside the Perimeter Hwy, get cheaper the longer you stay. A month's stay costs $300.

B&Bs About 30 B&Bs rent rooms in Winnipeg, most of which are listed in the Travel Manitoba accommodations guide. The provincial B&B Association (☎ 204-661-5218, W www.bedandbreakfast.mb.ca) produces its own list as well. Facilities vary widely but most have shared bathrooms. Reserving ahead is recommended.

Twin Pillars (☎ 204-284-7590, fax 204-453-4925, W www.escape.ca/~tls/twin.htm, 235 Oakwood Ave) Singles/doubles $35/45-55. Guests at Twin Pillars have privacy – a separate entrance to their side of the house, along with a TV in each room – but can also socialize in the guest-only kitchen/laundry room. The historic home is walking distance to Osborne Village and is on major bus routes.

Masson's B&B (☎/fax 204-237-9230, 181 Rue Masson) Singles/doubles $40-45/50-55. In the heart of the French St Boniface district, this place is a 15-minute walk to The Forks and a half a block from city bus service. The three rooms have Victorian furnishings. French and English are spoken here.

Free Spirits (☎ 204-475-7603, 825 Grosvenor Ave) Singles/doubles $45-60/50-70. The rate for these colorful, modern rooms with a French flair includes tax. In addition to the B&B, there are also spa services, including professional massage, facials and a meditation room.

West Gate Manor (☎ 204-772-9788, fax 204-772-9782, W www.escape.ca/~jclark, 71 West Gate) Singles/doubles $48-64/64-69. Of the several B&Bs in the historic, mansion-filled Armstrong Point area, West Gate Manor is one of the longest running. The many wooden-floored rooms have been decorated with charming antiques. The helpful proprietors are very knowledgeable about the city. A short walk takes you from here to the Cordyon Street restaurant row; a much longer walk takes you downtown (a portion of this route is not recommended at night). Credit cards are accepted.

Motels A number of good mid-price alternatives are available, but they are farther out from the center.

Assiniboine Garden Inn on The Park (☎ 204-888-4806, fax 204-897-9870, 1975 Portage Ave) Rooms for up to 4 people $45. Closest to downtown is this recommended inn, with a dining room offering food at good prices – especially breakfast. The place is popular with families.

Palimino Plains Motel (☎ 204-837-5831, 3740 Portage Ave) Singles $42-52, doubles $46-56. At night you can't miss the kitschy neon sign with a horse at this classic, drive-up-to-your-door motel. Don't expect frills (no coffee, no Kleenex); do expect low prices.

Super 8 Motel (☎ 204-837-5891, fax 204-254-7019, 1485 Niakwa Rd E/Hwy 1) Singles/doubles $56-66/65-79. This simple but friendly motel, east of the city on the Trans Canada Hwy, is super cheap with super clean, modern rooms.

Comfort Inn (☎ 204-269-7390, fax 204-783-5661, 3109 Pembina Hwy) Singles/doubles $69-76/77-88. Near the Perimeter Hwy, Comfort Inn is farther out than the other places, but it is immaculate with big rooms. The front-desk staff is welcoming and continental breakfast is $3.

Canad Inn Fort Garry (204-261-7460, fax 204-275-2187, W www.canadinns.com) Singles/doubles $72-89/84-99. This Canadian chain is made for families with restless children. The Fort Garry branch not only offers a family-oriented restaurant and a waterslide, but it also has kid (and adult) theme suites ($119).

Hotels For grit seekers, there are several skid row specials with very basic amenities north of Portage Ave on Main St. The downstairs bars are the primary features of these establishments, which are not recommended for women. Up the scale a bit are several old, slightly musty hotels that are well located and not terribly unsafe. Each has an active bar, restaurant, and carry-out beer service, as well as free parking.

Osborne Village Inn (☎ 204-452-9824, fax 204-452-0035, 160 Osborne St) Singles/doubles $48/58. New cable televisions and mini-fridges in each room make up for the mismatched, sagging furniture at this place with no nonsmoking rooms. The setting can't be beat – it's right in the midst of the funky shops and restaurants of Osborne Village

Gordon Downtowner Motor Hotel (☎ 204-943-5581, fax 204-943-5581, 330 Kennedy St) Singles/doubles $56/61. This freshly painted, purple hotel is quite central, just a few blocks from Portage Place.

If you have a CAA or AAA (US) card, it's worth mentioning. Many hotels and motels in the mid-range offer a 10% discount for members.

Norwood Hotel (204-233-4475, fax 204-231-1910, W www.norwood-hotel.com, 112 Marion St) Singles/doubles $74/82. A friendly, family-owned boutique hotel, Norwood has clean, comfortable rooms. The restaurant is highly regarded (including room service), but the pub offers food just as good for less money. It's close to downtown, just over the Main St S bridge, off St. Mary's Street.

Ramada Marlborough Hotel (204-942-6411, fax 204-942-2017, 331 Smith St) Rooms $67-83. This historic property has a neat old lobby and renovated guest rooms. Free parking and a free airport shuttle are included. It's on the edge of the Exchange District.

Watch for specials at the top-end hotels. Prices fluctuate unbelievably, especially off season, and these can be a real luxury bargain.

Holiday Inn & Suites (204-786-7011, 204-772-1443, W www.sixcontinentshotels .com, 360 Colony St) Rooms/suites $89-94/109-139. The Holiday Inn connects to the bus station and is a favorite with older travelers. This is one of the few new properties downtown.

Sheraton Four Points (204-775-5222, fax 204-775-5333, 1999 Wellington Ave St) Rooms $99-139. The 7th-floor rooms are the best in this sleek, stylish airport hotel. Look for the local artist's gallery-quality photographs of Winnipeg architecture that decorate the walls.

Fort Garry Hotel (204-942-8251, 800-665-8088 fax 204-956-2351, W www.fortgarry hotel.com, 222 Broadway Ave) Rooms $99-140 with breakfast. This attractive establishment, built in 1913, is the city's classic old hostelry and one of the grand hotels built by the wealth of the Canadian railroads. All the room rates include a buffet breakfast (brunch on Sunday).

Places to Eat

Winnipeg has a wide variety of cuisines and good values for the money. Don't be put off if the decor is slightly less than posh – the culinary talent outshines often the ambience. Many of the better downtown hotels have Sunday brunches at noon. The cheapest places to eat breakfast and lunch on

weekdays are the cafeterias in government office buildings.

Wordsworth Building Cafeteria (204-944-8927, 405 Broadway Ave) Meals $2-6. A large salad bar and an open, airy lunchroom are the highlights of this cafeteria.

Golden Boy Cafeteria (204-275-5955, Broadway Ave at Osborne St) Meals $3-6. This small cafeteria in the basement of the Legislative Building has daily specials like stir-fry chicken and rice, in addition to grilled offerings.

Salisbury House (204-956-1714, 354 Portage Ave) Meals $5-8. This local chain, with outlets around the city, serves cheap, plain food in a florescent, cafeteria-style setting. Downtown on a Sunday most things are closed, but this branch is open early and closes late every day.

Chocolate Shop Restaurant (204-942-4855, 268 Portage Ave) Meals $5-15. The original '40s to '50s style and the popular afternoon teacup and tarot-card readings draw people to this likeable, moderately priced downtown eatery.

Bridgeport Restaurant (204-948-0085, top floor, Winnipeg Art Gallery, 300 Memorial Blvd) Meals $7-10. Entrees are artfully arranged at this colorful restaurant. Lunch is served from 11:30pm to 2:30pm, but soups – like lobster bisque – and sumptuous desserts are available from 11am to 4pm.

Old Swiss Inn (204-942-7725, 207 Edmonton St) Lunch/dinner $8-11/12-21. Classic Central European dishes like Wiener schnitzel and cheese fondue are served in this intimate downtown restaurant.

The Forks historic site is a pleasant place for a bite. Along with the multiethnic food stalls and the small cafés of the Market Building, there is **Barba Yiannis** (204-948-0015) for a substantial, creative Mediterranean meal. Main dishes cost $7 to $15.

In the Exchange District and Chinatown there are a few eating spots.

Marigold (204-944-9400, 245 King St) Meals $6-10. It's best to come here on weekends, when dim sum is served from steam carts and much more Chinese than English is spoken at the tables. On weekdays, a small buffet is popular with office workers.

Little Saigon (204-947-3999, 333 William Ave) Meals $6-11. In addition to filling rice and vermicelli dishes, Little

Saigon offers 33 vegetarian items on its Vietnamese/Chinese menu.

King's Head Pub (☎ 204-957-7710, 120 King St) Meals $6-12. This busy British-style pub is a private club, but tourists can sign in as guests.

Tre Visi (☎ 204-949-9032, 173 McDermot Ave) Meals $8-18. A stylish white-table atmosphere, combined with excellent Italian food, make reservations a must here – even at lunch.

Step 'N Out (☎ 204-956-7837, 283 Bannatyne Ave) Lunch/dinner $9-12/18-24. Twinkly lights and cozy tables give this restaurant its romantic touches. The eclectic food mixes Asian and Western cuisines; only organically grown vegetables are served.

There are plenty of good restaurants with a range of prices in Osborne Village and along Corydon Ave (the Italian area); both are south of the downtown area.

Urban Ojas (☎ 204-953-1812, 684 Osborne) Lunch/dinner $6-11/16-22. This organic bistro is above the Ambrosia aromatherapy spa. The Continental menu boasts dishes like free-range chicken and crab risotto.

Carlos & Murphy's (☎ 204-284-3510, 129 Osborne St) Meals $8-12. This is a well-established Mexican place with an outdoor patio, a big menu and moderate prices

Wasabi Sushi Bistro (☎ 204-474-2332, 121 Osborne St) Meals $8-12. A 2nd-floor restaurant, this smaller, second location of the Wasabi restaurant has ultrafresh sushi in a minimalist setting.

Sofia's Caffé (☎ 204-452-3037, 635 Corydon Ave) Dishes $7-15. Sofia's serves linen-napkin quality pasta at paper-napkin prices. Try the fettuccini with shrimp in a spicy, creamy sauce.

La Vielle Gare (☎ 904-237-7072, 630 Rue des Meurons) Lunch/dinner $9-15/18-28. In the St Boniface area, this restaurant, housed in a 1914 train car, can be summed up in three words: elegant, French and expensive. Frog legs provençal? Bien sur!

Green Gates (☎ 204-897-0990, 6945 Roblin Blvd) Meals $10-20. The Wow! hospitality group is well regarded locally for its excellent restaurants and chefs. Green Gates, one of its properties, is a little ways out (off the Perimeter Hwy) but worth the trip for the Canadian ingredients and garden-grown herbs.

Rae and Jerry's (☎ 204-775-8154, 1405 Portage Ave) Meals $18-30. This Winnipeg institution, west along Portage Ave away from the center, is a steak and roast beef house that's been serving up its classic panache for many years.

Entertainment
To find out what's going on in the city, check the Winnipeg Free Press on Thursday for complete bar and entertainment listings.

Casinos Winnipeg pioneered permanent legal gambling houses in Canada. (Yes, the government also allocates money to gambling-addiction programs.) Both large casinos have live music on weekends, regular concert events and separate smoking and nonsmoking gaming areas. You must be 18 or older to enter.

McPhillips St Station Casino (☎ 204-957-3900, 484 McPhillips St) The Old West train-station motif carries throughout the sprawling building. An odd, multisensory ride called the Millennium Express takes you on a regional history lesson for $5. Most of the games are nickel, quarter or loonie slots, interspersed with very few blackjack/poker tables. The electronically enhanced Bingo area is extensive, and Kino and sports betting are also available. Liquor is allowed in the bar areas only. There's a sit-down restaurant and two MickeyDs onsite.

Club Regent (☎ 204-957-2700, 1425 Regent Ave) This huge casino is in the eastern suburb of Transcona. A neon palm tree sign is part of the Caribbean island paradise theme, which includes a large, walk-through aquarium, vast open areas and replicas of Mayan ruins. Except for the decor, the Regent is very similar to McPhillips Street in its offerings – though it feels a little newer.

Bars & Live Music Osborne Village and Cordyon Ave have many cafés and bar/restaurants to hang out at. Just stroll along and pick one.

Earl's (☎ 204-989-0103, 191 Main St) This is the 'in' place for happy hour. It's a big chain bar/restaurant with a popular patio, near The Forks. The food's okay but not great; it's the place, the people and the drinks that make it work.

Royal Crown Building (☎ 204-947-1990, 83 Garry St) $5 minimum. The bar on the

30th floor of this building has great views and there is a revolving restaurant one floor up.

Times Change Café (☎ 204-957-0982, *Main St & St Mary Ave*) Close to the railway station, this inexpensive café is good for jazz and blues. Live shows are on Friday, Saturday and Sunday nights.

Windsor Hotel (☎ 204-942-7528, 187 *Garry St*) Hear the blues belted out live downtown at the Windsor. If you're looking to escape the overly young-looking dance scene, this is the place.

Rogue's Gallery (☎ 204-947-0652, 432 *Assiniboine Ave*) This gay-friendly coffeehouse often hosts singer/songwriters.

Bella Vista (☎ 204-775-4485, 53 *Maryland*) A neighborhood hangout and pizzeria near Armstrong Point, Bella Vista has live folk music most nights.

Dance Clubs Much of the dance music scene is downtown near The Forks or in the Exchange District.

Mezzo (☎ 204-987-3391, 291 *Bannatyne Ave*) The patrons at Mezzo are as cool and as beautiful as the dance club's sleek polished steel exterior. Don't forget to wear black.

The Empire (☎ 204-943-3979, 436 *Main St*) Latin and European dance beats pulse the night away in this historic bank building. There's live music some nights, and one lounge is nonsmoking.

Performing Arts Though not well known, Winnipeg is, on a per-capita basis, one of the top performing arts capitals of North America. The season generally runs from September through May. Many tickets can be purchased through Select-A-Seat (☎ 204-976-SEAT) and student discounts are often available.

Manitoba Theatre Centre (☎ 204-942-6537, ⓦ www.mtc.mb.ca, 174 *Market Ave*) Thought-provoking dramas and comedies are preformed by the same company that runs the local fringe festival.

Prairie Theatre Exchange (☎ 204-942-5483, 393 *Portage Ave*) Billed as the only theater company in a shopping center, this group is located on the 3rd floor of Portage Place. Shows are fairly traditional.

Manitoba Theatre for Young People (☎ 204-942-8898, ⓦ www.mtyp.ca, 2 *Forks Market Rd*) Performances include produc-

tions for teens, for three to five year olds, and for those nine to adult.

Winnipeg's Contemporary Dancers (☎ 204-453-0229, 109 *Pulford St*) New choreographers are given a chance to shine in performances by this modern company.

Royal Winnipeg Ballet (☎ 204-956-2792, 800-667-4792, ⓦ www.rwb.org, *Graham Ave & Edmonton St*) This ballet troupe has an excellent international reputation and offers both traditional performances, like *Giselle*, as well as more modern works.

Centennial Concert Hall (☎ 204-956-1360, 555 *Main St*) Near the Museum of Man & Nature, the Centennial Hall is the home of the *Winnipeg Symphony Orchestra* (☎ 204-949-3999, ⓦ www.wso.mb.ca) and the *Manitoba Opera* (☎ 204-942-7479, ⓦ www.manitobaopera.mb.ca).

Musik Barock (☎ 204-453-4946, 525 *Wardlaw Ave*) This baroque orchestra performs concerts, more frequently around Christmas, in a United Methodist Church.

Centre Culturel Franco-Manitobain (☎ 204-233-8972, 340 *Boulevard Provencher*) The center presents all kinds of interesting shows, concerts and productions in St Boniface. Some performances require a knowledge of French, some transcend language and still others use French and English.

Cinemas *Cinémathèque* (☎ 204-925-3457, 100 *Arthur St*) This cinema has daily showings of Canadian and international films – from art flicks to Monty Python comedies.

IMAX Cinema (☎ 204-956-4629, 363 *Portage Ave*) Adventure-oriented features are shown on a 5½-story screen in Portage Place mall.

Spectator Sports

In summer and fall, the Winnipeg Blue Bombers (☎ 204-784-2583, ⓦ www.bluebombers.com), almost Grey Cup–champions, play professional Canadian League football in the *Canad Inns Stadium* (1430 *Maroons Rd*).

The Manitoba Moose (☎ 204-780-7328, ⓦ www.moosehockey.com) of the American Hockey League (AHL) face off at the *Winnipeg Arena* (1430 *Maroons Rd*) for now. A new venue is scheduled to open in late 2003.

The **Winnipeg Goldeneyes** (☎ 204-982-2273, *Mill St*) play Northern League – almost professional – baseball at *CanWest* near the Exchange District.

Shopping

Between Stradbrook Ave and Donald St, along Osborne St, *Osborne Village* has funky, artistic shops with genuinely one-of-a-kind gifts, tchotchkes and jewelry.

United Army Surplus Sales (☎ 204-786-5421, *460 Portage Ave*) If you're looking for cheap camping equipment before heading out to the provincial parks, stop here.

The Bay (☎ 204-783-2112, *Portage Ave at Memorial Blvd*) Newer sporting goods are available at this department store, as is almost everything else. Hudson's Bay Company is the oldest incorporated trading company still in business. It was chartered May 2, 1670, and the headquarters moved from London to Winnipeg in 1970. In the basement there's a trading post with souvenirs and wool coats made to look like the traditional, colorful Hudson's Bay blankets once traded with the Native peoples.

If you're not heading any farther north, Winnipeg is a good place to shop for Native art from the tundra areas. Prices are incredibly high: A tiny sculpture can sell for hundreds of dollars.

Northern Images (☎ 204-942-5501, *Portage Place, 393 Portage Ave*) This company sells Dene and Inuit crafts at this and other outlets throughout Canada.

Upstairs Gallery (☎ 204-943-2734, *266 Edmonton St*) The carvings of animals and humans by northern craftspeople are stunning, if expensive.

Bayat Inuit Gallery (☎ 204-475-5873, *163 Stafford St*) Bayat has a fairly good selection of Inuit arts.

Getting There & Away

Air The international airport is about 15 to 20 minutes northwest of the city center.

Air Canada (☎ 800-247-2262, Ⓦ www.aircanada.ca) flies to points in Canada and the US. In partnership with Calm Air, it also makes trips to Churchill (more frequent in October and November).

Northwest Airlines (☎ 800-225-2525, Ⓦ www.nwa.com) can take you to US destinations, usually transferring in Minneapolis.

The smaller WestJet Airlines (☎ 888-937-8538, Ⓦ www.westjet.com) serves Calgary, Hamilton and Saskatchewan destinations,

while Bearskin Airlines (☎ 800-465-2327, Ⓦ www.bearskinairlines.com) flies to Flin Flon, The Pas and points in Ontario.

Bus The station is the Mall Centre Bus Depot (☎ 800-661-8747 for bus information, 487 Portage Ave); it's open from 6:30am to midnight. There are left-luggage lockers, and the station has a restaurant.

Greyhound (☎ 204-982-8747, Ⓦ www.greyhound.ca), Grey Goose (☎ 204-784-4500) and the short-distance Beaver bus line all operate from the same counter. Their phone numbers each access a central, semi-automated reservation center that can handle any route. Three daily buses run to Thunder Bay ($102, nine hours) and three to Regina ($65, seven to nine hours). A ticket to Brandon (three hours) costs $26 and one to Thompson (9½ hours) is $83. Daily buses also go to Riding Mountain National Park and West Hawk Lake.

Train In summer there's a tourist information booth for the central VIA Rail Station (☎ 800-561-8630, Ⓦ www.viarail.ca, Broadway Ave & Main St). A train departs at 4:55pm Wednesday, Friday and Sunday stopping in Saskatoon ($108) at 2am on its way to Edmonton ($160). The eastbound train leaves Tuesday, Thursday and Sunday at 12:10pm, going north over Lake Superior en route to Toronto ($233, 30 hours). There is no train to Regina or Calgary. For information on the northern train to Churchill, see that section, later in the chapter.

Leaving your car at the station for extended periods can be risky, as break-ins are common. A reasonable substitute is the multi-leveled lot downtown on Edmonton St near St Mary Ave.

Hitchhiking For hitchhiking west out of town, take the express St Charles bus along Portage Ave. After 6pm take the Portage Ave–St Charles bus. If you're going east on Hwy 1, catch the Osborne Hwy 1 bus or the Southdale bus on Osborne St South, on the corner of Broadway Ave.

Getting Around

To/From the Airport The Sargent No 15 city bus runs between the airport and Vaughan St on the corner of Portage Ave every 20 minutes; the fare is $1.65.

A taxi from the airport to the center of town costs about $20. An airport limo, which runs to and from the better hotels from 9am to nearly 1am, costs more than a cab.

Bus All city buses cost $1.65, and you'll need exact change. Routes are extensive and transit information is available from ☎ 204-986-5700 and ⓦ www.winnipegtransit .com. If you're changing buses, you'll need to get a transfer from the driver.

Car For car rental, Executive (☎ 204-478-7283, 104 Pembina Hwy) is an okay value, with rates from $29 per day with 150km free. With 14 days notice, a week's rental at one or another of the airport-based chain companies can be found for about $200, with unlimited mileage. The clerks at the Thrifty (☎ 204-949-7600) counter are especially friendly.

Bicycle There are bicycle routes through town and some out of town. Ask at the tourist office for details. The hostels rent bicycles.

AROUND WINNIPEG
Birds Hill Provincial Park
Just 24km northeast of downtown, is a great city escape – Birds Hill (☎ 204-222-9151, Park Rd off Hwy 59; admission $5; open dawn-dusk). Highlights are miles of well-forested and fairly level hiking trails, bike and cross-country ski paths, a small beach, and deer and wild turkeys.

Lower Fort Garry
Thirty-two kilometers north of Winnipeg, between Lockport and Selkirk on the banks of the Red River, is a restored Hudson's Bay Company fort dating back to the 1830s (☎ 204-785-6050, Hwy 9; admission adult/child $5.50/2.75; open 9am-5pm daily mid-May–Labor Day). It's the only stone fort from the fur-trading days that is still intact. In later times it was used as a police training center, a penitentiary, a 'lunatic asylum,' a Hudson's Bay Company residence and a country club.

The buildings are historically furnished and the grounds are busy with costumed workers who'll answer questions. There's a *restaurant* and a picnic area. To get here, take the Selkirk bus from the main station

and tell the driver you're going to the fort – the fare is about $10 roundtrip.

Selkirk
Beyond the fort, halfway to Lake Winnipeg, is Selkirk, the 'Catfish Capital of the World.' Prime eating in these parts and a big lure for US anglers are the lunkers that are taken out of the Red River. The **Marine Museum of Manitoba** (☎ 204-482-7761, Queen Ave & Eveline St; admission adult/child $3/2; open 9am-5pm Mon-Fri & 10am-6pm Sat & Sun May-Sept) has six large historic ships, including a restored steamer and an icebreaker.

Oak Hammock Marsh
Southern Manitoba has several important, very large marshes. These critical wetlands are home to thousands of waterfowl and other birds and act as way stations along major migration routes for thousands more.

North of the city, about 8km east of Stonewall, and 15km west of Selkirk is one of the best bird sanctuaries on the continent, Oak Hammock Marsh (☎ 204-467-3300, Route 200 at Hwy 67; admission adult/child $4/3; open 10am-8pm daily May-Aug, 8:30am-dusk daily Sept-Oct, 10am-4:30pm daily Nov-Apr). More than 280 species can be seen from the boardwalks or through the scopes on viewing platforms and at windows in the interpretive center. Interactive displays and computer games help children learn about the local wildlife.

Dugald
Dugald, not far east of Winnipeg along Route 15, is home to the **Costume Museum of Canada** (☎ 204-853-2166, Dugald Rd at Route 206; admission adult/child $4/3; open 10am-5pm Tues-Fri, noon-5pm Sat & Sun May-Oct), a collection of 35,000 items of dress and accessories dating from 1765 to the present. The various garments are displayed on soft mannequins in realistic settings. There's also a tea room and a gift shop.

South of Winnipeg
South and slightly west of Winnipeg and bordered by North Dakota is an area known as the **Pembina Valley**. The Red River flows northward through this prime farming region.

MANITOBA

Morris is the site of a major annual rodeo, second in size only to Calgary's Stampede. It takes place for five days at the beginning of August.

This is also sunflower country, and a festival to mark this is held in **Altona** on the last weekend in July. The Mennonites of the area supply some very fine homemade foods for the occasion.

Three kilometers east of the village of Tolstoi, not far from the Minnesota border, is the **Tall Grass Prairie Preserve** (☎ 204-425-3229, Route 209; admission free; open dawn-dusk). The Manitoba Naturalists' Society oversees the protection of the 2000-hectare area of increasingly rare south prairie ecosystem. A 1.6km interpretive trail is accessible year-round.

Eastern Manitoba

The border region of Manitoba has the same rugged woodland terrain as neighboring Ontario. Toward Winnipeg this begins to give way to the flatter expanse more typical of the southern prairies. In the northeast, the sparsely populated timberlands continue through a series of gigantic government parks; the southeast is primarily farmland.

MENNONITE HERITAGE VILLAGE

Southeast of Winnipeg, about an hour's drive down through sunflower country, is the town of Steinbach. Steinbach is a center for the Mennonites, a religious utopian group that originated in Europe and reached Manitoba via Pennsylvania and Ontario. The Mennonite museum complex (☎ 204-326-9661, Hwy 12; admission adult/child $5/3; village open 10am-4pm Mon-Fri May-Sept; information center/gift shop open 10am-4pm Mon-Fri year-round) is 2km north of town.

Most of the site is a re-created late-19th-century Mennonite village with some century-old buildings. A restaurant on the grounds serves good, fresh, traditional Mennonite food.

The information center gives some of the history of the movement, and has a quilting exhibit and workshop. For more information on Canada's Mennonite com-

munities, see the Kitchener section in the Ontario chapter.

LA BROQUERIE
Just outside Steinbach, this little village with a population descended from French and Belgian pioneers celebrates its Gaelic roots on June 24 with the Fête Franco-Manitobaine de la St Jean Baptiste.

WHITESHELL PROVINCIAL PARK
An hour and a half east of Winnipeg along the Ontario border is this 2590 sq km park containing 200 lakes. Outdoor activities are available year-round. There are hiking trails – some are short, others are as long as 60km – and numerous canoe routes, including the popular one through the tunnel on Caddy Lake.

The roads through the park are the Trans Canada Hwy in the south, Hwy 44 in the center and Route 309 in the north. Most of the larger recreation areas have park offices, including in the village of Rennie (☎ 204-369-5232, 800-214-6497, Hwy 44; Mon-Fri 8am-noon & 1-4pm). Offices have hiking information, as do the entrance gates, which are open in the summertime.

The area around Falcon and West Hawk lakes has the most services: A few restaurants, gas stations, laundry and an ice-cream parlor, in addition to marinas and cross-country ski rental.

Park highlights include the Alf Hole Goose Sanctuary, which is worth a visit during spring and autumn migrations. At Bannock Point, not far north of Betula Lake, are centuries-old Native Indian petroforms – rock formations in the shapes of fish, snakes and birds.

West Hawk Lake Resort (☎ 204-349-2244, 3km north of Hwy 1 on Hwy 44; rooms for 2-4 people $75-90; open year-round) offers clean, large two-bedroom cabins. **Falcon Trails Resort** (☎ 204-349-8273, Falcon Lake Rd; rooms/cabins $45-55/125) has comfy B&B rooms as well as expensive hot-tub cabins right on the water.

There are hundreds of **campsites** for trailers and tents in the park. To book a site ahead of time, contact the Park Reservation Service (☎ 888-482-2267,

[W] *www.manitobaparks.com; with/without hookups $17-20/7-16)*. Bays 1 and 4 in the Falcon Lake campground have much more cover than the tent sites at Falcon Beach and West Hawk Lake.

NOPOMING PROVINCIAL PARK

Offering a taste of the true northern wilderness is the quiet and less-accessible Nopoming Provincial Park (☎ 204-534-7204, Route 314), north of much busier Whiteshell. There are some woodland caribou, though you are unlikely to see them in summer months.

This park has a sketchy road system and three campgrounds. Spruce and jack pines line the waterbanks at **Black Lake Campground** (☎ 888-482-2267, [W] *www .manitobaparks.com, Route 314; with/ without hookups $17/10)*. Here is the trail-head for the 9km roundtrip Black River hike, and it is only 7km away from the Walking on Ancient Mountains trail.

ATIKAKI PROVINCIAL WILDERNESS PARK

Heading north, the province quickly becomes rather wild: There's no direct road access, nor any designated campsites in this wilderness park (☎ 204-277-5212). Atikaki is usually visited by canoe with loops from three days to several weeks long. Canoe-access can be gained from Wallace Lake, which is reached by rough road and then portaging. For information on outfitters that can fly you in, contact Travel Manitoba for its lodging and fishing guides.

One area of interest in the park is along the Bloodvein River, where there are remnants of Native Indian cliff paintings thought to date back 6000 years, and Pigeon River churns up whitewater.

Lake Winnipeg

Lake Winnipeg, Canada's fifth-largest lake, is by far the dominant geographic feature of the province. It begins just beyond suburban Winnipeg, with its southern tip lying about 50km north of the city, and it ends in virtually untouched northern wilderness. Manitobans take day trips to the easily accessible southern

region in summer. The prime recreational features are the fine sandy beaches and the numerous parks and wetlands, which are ideal for bird-watching and other wildlife observation.

The region north of Winnipeg, wedged between massive Lake Winnipeg to the east and Lake Manitoba to the west, is known as the Interlake. It contains several National and Provincial Parks as well as smaller lakes. In the northern Interlake region, east of Lake Winnipeg, the population thins markedly, the cottage communities disappear and the real north begins.

GRAND BEACH

Lake Winnipeg's eastern shore is lined with beaches, including the unofficial center of summer fun, Grand Beach, which is very popular in season and a ghost town out of season. Dunes reach as high as 8m. The lagoon behind the dunes is home to hundreds of birds species.

Grand Beach Provincial Park & Campground (☎ 204-754-2212, 888-482-2267, Hwy 12; with/without hookups $17/10) is one of the busiest campgrounds in the province, especially popular with college-age patrons. The cedar cabins at **Northwind Cabins** (☎ 204-783-1980, Grand Beach Rd; 1–3-bed cabins $300/ week) are nicer looking than some in cottage country, and they have flush toilets! Patricia Beach, closer to Winnipeg, is for day use only.

Much of the land on the west side of the lake is privately owned, but there are larger towns and more services, many of which are open year-round.

NETLEY MARSH

At the southern tip of the lake, 16km north of Selkirk, is Netley Marsh, formed where the Red River drains into the southern end of Lake Winnipeg. This is a major waterfowl nesting area. In the fall, hunters and bird-watchers bring their conflicting points of view to enjoy the 18 species of duck and the flocks of geese.

WINNIPEG BEACH

This is the southernmost recreation area on Lake Winnipeg. A provincial park protects the best strip of sand for public use and there is good windsurfing out in the bay. In and around Winnipeg Beach there's an abundance of services. *Bye the Lake B&B* (☎ 204-389-5657, *Winnipeg Beach Rd; rooms $65/75 winter/summer*) has two clean, motel-like rooms overlooking the lake. Both have a mini-fridge, cable TV, and one has a private entrance.

Jane & Walter's Restaurant (☎ 204-389-5473, *Hwy 9; meals $10-14*), a few kilometers north of town, serves huge portions of homecooked favorites like chicken and ribs. It's open daily in the summer.

GIMLI

On the western shore of Lake Winnipeg, 90km north of Winnipeg, and marked by the Viking statue, this fishing and farming community is made up largely of the descendants of Icelandic pioneers. The area, once known as the Republic of New Iceland, was settled around 1880.

New Iceland Heritage Museum (☎ 204-642-4001, *94 1st Ave; admission free; open 10am-6pm daily mid-May–Labor Day*) outlines the area's history with some artifacts of the local settlement. Every summer, around the beginning of August, the **Islendingadagurinn** (Icelandic Festival) is held here, with three days of games, contests, parades and folk music.

Part of the Lakeview Inn & Suites chain, *Lakeview Resort* (☎ 204-642-8565, 877-355-3500, fax 204-642-4200, *10 Centre St; rooms $109/129 in winter/summer*) is a modern resort with a shopping arcade on the 1st floor. There are also several older, standard motels in town.

Across 1st St, the long-time tradition *Whitecap's Restaurant* (☎ 204-642-9735, *72 1st Ave*) serves everything from burgers ($6.25) to main dishes like pickerel – a flaky white lake fish (also known as walleye) that shouldn't be missed – for $17.

HECLA PROVINCIAL PARK

Farther north is Hecla Provincial Park (☎ 204-378-2261, *Hwy 8*), which comprises several islands jutting into and almost across Lake Winnipeg. A causeway leads to the principal Hecla Island; Hecla Village was the site of an Icelandic settlement in 1876.

The **Heritage Home Museum** (*no phone , Village Road; admission free; open 10am-4pm daily mid-May–Labor Day*) and self-guided interpretive trail detail some of the historical highlights.

The island is well populated with moose, and deer and smaller mammals are commonly seen. The **Grassy Narrows Marsh** teems with waterfowl including pelicans. Numerous hiking trails wind through the woods and along shorelines.

The queen bedroom at *Solmundson Gesta Hus* (☎ 204-279-2088, Ⓦ www.heclatourism.mb.ca, *Village Rd; singles/ doubles $50-55/55-75*) has a great view of the lake. There are many animals on the property: ducks, geese, dogs, cats....

Outside the village, a golf course, hiking and cross-country skiing trails, tennis court, swimming pool are available at *Gull Harbor Resort* (☎ 204-279-2041, fax 204-279-2000, *Hwy 8*), which has rooms for $72/107 in summer/winter. *Gull Harbour Campground* (☎ 800-482-22-67, Ⓦ www.manitobaparks.com; *sites $10*) is at the northern tip of the island.

SNAKE PITS

Snake lovers, you're in luck. Here in Manitoba is the world's largest population of red-sided garter snakes, concentrated in wiggling mega-dens of up to 10,000 of the little funsters.

The mating ritual, when tens of thousands emerge from their limestone sinkhole lairs to form masses of entwined tangles, takes place around the last week of April and the first two weeks of May, or when the weather has warmed enough to perk up the slitherers. Early in September, after a fancy-free summer, the snakes return to their dens but remain at the doors until the cold autumn weather forces them to crawl inside for the winter. The snakes are not dangerous.

The **Narcisse Wildlife Management Area** (☎ 204-642-6070, Ⓦ www.gov.mb.ca/ conservation, *Hwy 17; admission free; open dawn-dusk*) protects one area of the snake pits. It's just under a two-hour drive from Winnipeg – follow Hwy 17 6km north of Narcisse. A 3km walking trail has a few interpretive signs. There are bathrooms near the parking, but not much else. Packing a lunch (or at least a snack) and something to drink is not a bad idea, although well water is available.

Other locations for snake pits are around Chatfield and Inwood. In nearby **Komarno**, there's a statue of the world's largest mosquito.

PEGUIS & FISHER RIVER

North of Narcisse, Hwy 17 leads to two fairly isolated Native Indian Reserves: Peguis and Fisher River. The **Peguis Powwow** is a five-day event featuring games, song, crafts and various activities, to which the Cree and Ojibway of the reserves invite the public. Call the Manitoba Association of Friendship Centres (☎ 204-943-8082) for exact dates. This is an undeveloped area, with little in the way of tourist development. Hecla Provincial Park is just over 40km to the east.

LAKE MANITOBA SHORELINE

Much less commercial than Lake Winnipeg but with a series of small towns and some cottage communities, Lake Manitoba also has some fine sandy beaches, particularly at Twin Lakes (in the south), around the town of Lundar and at Silver Bay (west of Ashern). St Laurent, a predominantly French and Métis community, is a regional supply town.

The area between the lakes is important for beef cattle, and some of the farms take in overnight guests. For more information, contact the Manitoba Country Vacations Association (☎ 204-776-2176, W www.countryvacations.mb.ca).

NORTHERN WOODS & WATER ROUTE

This is a series of roads connecting Winnipeg with British Columbia, running across northern portions of Saskatchewan and Alberta. Most of the roads are surfaced, though there are stretches of gravel. There are no cities, but many small communities, nine provincial parks and numerous campgrounds along the way. You'll find lots of lakes and woods up here, as well as fishing areas and wildlife. Nights are cool.

From Winnipeg, the route heads to The Pas (in the northwest of the province), continues to Prince Albert, Saskatchewan, then into Alberta ending at Dawson Creek, British Columbia. The road is marked on signs as 'NWWR.'

Northern Manitoba

Two thirds of the province still lies north of The Pas, above the two big lakes at the 53rd parallel. Northern Manitoba is rugged, lake-filled timberland that slowly evolves into the treeless tundra of the far north. Flin Flon, The Pas and Thompson are the main towns.

Way up on Hudson Bay is Churchill; it's remote but one of the province's top draws and boasts historical significance.

THE PAS

Once an important meeting site for Native Indians and British and French fur traders, The Pas is now a district center and acts as the 'gateway to the north.' Lumber is important, and this is a rich agricultural area as well. During the short summer, days are long and sunny.

The small **Sam Waller Museum** (☎ 204-623-3802, 306 Fischer Ave; admission adult/child $2/.75; open 1pm-5pm daily) has an eclectic collection of indigenous wildlife, curios, coins and more.

Built in 1896, **Christ Church** (☎ 204-623-2119, Edwards Ave at Saskatchewan River) was founded by Henry Budd, the first Native Indian ordained by the Anglican Church. On one wall, the Lord's Prayer and the Ten Commandments can be seen written in Cree. Call and someone will arrange to let you visit.

Also of interest is **Opaskwayak Indian Days**, an annual festival in mid-August put on by the local Cree Nation who live across the Saskatchewan River from town. Call the Pas Friendship Centre (☎ 204-623-6459) for exact dates.

Within Clearwater Lake Provincial Park, deep crevices and huge chunks of rock fallen from cliffs can be seen along the Caves Trail. It's called Clearwater for a reason – the bottom can be seen from more than 10m.

There are about half a dozen motels or hotels in town, so finding a vacancy shouldn't be a problem. Across the road from the bus station, the ***Wescana Inn*** (☎ 204-623-5446, fax 204-623-3383, 459 Fischer Ave; singles/doubles $62/74) is a clean and comfortable motel. ***Campers Cove*** (204-624-5525 or 888-482-2267,

W *www.manitobaparks.com, Clearwater Lake Provincial Park, Route 284; with/without hookups $10/17)* has 35 sites near the water; there are several showers and a boat launch.

Getting There & Away

The Pas is connected to Winnipeg by air with Calm Air (☎ 800-839-2256) and Bearskin Airlines (☎ 204-624-5190). Grey Goose (☎ 204-623-9999) runs buses, and VIA Rail (☎ 888-839-2256) has train service. Driving from Winnipeg takes about eight hours if you take Route 327 and Hwy 6. The bus takes a longer route. VIA Rail continues on to Thompson and Churchill.

FLIN FLON
pop 10,500

Farther north, right on the Saskatchewan border, Flin Flon is a copper- and zinc-mining center. The unusual name is taken, it's said, from the protagonist of a novel some prospectors found up here in 1915. A goofy statue of the character, Josiah Flintabbatey Flonatin, greets visitors at the edge of town. The town is built on the rocky Canadian Shield, meaning you'll be going up and down hills as you make your way around town.

Flin Flon has recently been in the news as the site (below ground) of Canada's first legalized, government-run marijuana growing operation. The high-tech, quality-controlled product is distributed across the country to those requiring it for legitimate medicinal purposes. No tours.

As you enter town, you can't miss the statue and the *Flin Flon Tourist Bureau & Campground* (☎ 204-687-2946, fax 204-687-5133, Hwy 10; open 8am-8pm mid-May–mid-Sept). Twenty steps away is the *Flin Flon Station Museum* (☎ 204-687-2946, Hwy 10; admission adult/child $2/.50; open 10am-8pm Mon-Fri & 11am-5pm Sat-Sun mid-May–mid-Sept). Have a look at the examples of birch-bark biting: This is an old Cree women's craft that has almost disappeared. Using their teeth, they etch patterns, often of animals, into the bark.

The **Hudson Bay Mining & Smelting Company surface mine** (☎ 204-687-2050; admission free; open by appointment) can be toured from June to August; call for directions. Copper, zinc, gold and silver are mined.

The city is surrounded by typical northern rocky, wooded lakeland. There are canoe and camping outfitters in town. Between The Pas and Flin Flon, the huge **Grass River Provincial Park** (☎ 204-472-3331, 888-482-2267, W *www.manitobaparks.com; Hwy 10 at Route 39)* is not far east. With about 150 lakes strung along

The Mighty Canadian Shield

The 'Shield' is one of Canada's most dominant physical characteristics. This mass of ancient, stable rock surrounds Hudson Bay on the east, south and west in a vast U pattern, forming a shield-like shape around the perimeter. In the north, it runs from the Atlantic Ocean on the coast of Labrador 3000km west past Lake Winnipeg northwest to Lake Athabasca, to Great Slave Lake, Great Bear Lake and on to the Arctic Ocean. From the Hudson Bay areas, it stretches south from Lake Superior to the St Lawrence River around Kingston.

And just what is it? The Shield was the first region of the continent raised permanently above the sea. It is made of predominantly igneous, fossil-free, stratified rock from the Archaeozoic period, and is among the world's oldest rock. The entire region was scraped and gouged by glaciers, resulting in an almost uniformly flat to undulating rocky surface very sparsely and intermittently covered with soil. Rarely across its expanse does it rise more than 500m above sea level. Many of the dips, dents, cracks and pits in the surface are filled with water – lakes, rivers and ponds of every shape and size. In several sections, as much as 40% of the surface is freshwater.

The southern sections tend to be forested and, in Manitoba, these boreal woodlands extend as far north as Churchill. Farther north the trees begin to diminish, and eventually disappear entirely, leaving lichen and mosses as the principal vegetation.

the river, the Grass River system is ideal for canoeing and the fishing is excellent.

Flin Flon has a couple of older hotels in the center, on Main St, and a couple of motels around the edges. *Royal Hotel* (☎ *204-687-3437, fax 204-687-5354, 93 Main St; singles/doubles $35/60)* is a basic hotel with a Chinese restaurant onsite. The northern chain motel, *Victoria Inn* (☎ *204-687-7555, fax 204-687-5233, W www.vicinn.com, Hwy 10 N; singles/doubles $45/87)* is more expensive but has a range of facilities including hot tub, exercise room and laundry.

Bearskin Airlines (☎ 204-687-8941) serves Flin Flon from Winnipeg. Grey Goose (☎ 204-687-8239, 63 3rd Ave E) buses run to The Pas and Winnipeg.

THOMPSON
pop 15,000
The last town northwards connected by surfaced road, Thompson is a nickel-mining center. There is virtually nothing but wilderness on the long road up here, whether you've come from The Pas or along Lake Winnipeg. And just out of town in any direction, civilization disappears quickly. If driving, make sure you have the necessary supplies, water and fuel, as services are few to nil, especially on Hwy 6 north of Lake Winnipeg.

The minimum eight-hour trip is pretty tedious, but one worthwhile stop, 50km shy of Thompson, is **Pisew Falls Provincial Park**. A short boardwalk leads to the falls, and a 22km backcountry hike leads to Kwasitchewan Falls – the highest in Manitoba. **Paint Lake Provincial Park**, 30km south of Thompson, has *Pat's Paint Lake Lodge* (☎ *204-677-9303, fax 204-677-5573, Hwy 6)* with cabins going for $60 to $90; it's open year-round.

You can visit the **Inco nickel mine** (☎ *204-778-2454; admission free; open by appointment)* but the tour only shows surface operations; call for directions. The **Heritage North Museum** (☎ *204-677-2216, 162 Princeton Drive; admission adult/child $3/2; open 10am-6pm July-Aug, 1pm-5pm Sept-May)*, in two impressive log buildings, has exhibits relating to natural history, the fur trade and early white settlement. The **Thompson Folk Festival** is held annually on the weekend

closest to the summer solstice, usually around June 22.

Places to Stay
McReedy Campground (☎ *204-778-8810, fax 204-677-3567, 114 Manasan Drive)* Sites $15; open mid-May–Sept. This campground, less than 2km from town north on Hwy 6, caters mostly to RVs. It offers vehicle storage and a free shuttle to the train.

Northern Lights B&B (☎ *204-677-4111, fax 204-677-8027, 204 Wolf St)* Singles/doubles $50/60. Two common areas, guest kitchen, Internet access and rooms with private bath and cable TV are the assets of this modern house.

Getting There & Away
The VIA Rail (☎ 888-842-7245) trip from Thompson to Churchill departs Monday, Wednesday and Friday evenings and gets in the next morning. An economy seat with advance notice is $62, a sleeper for one is $250.

Grey Goose Bus Lines (☎ 204-778-8867) makes the trip from Winnipeg to Thompson for $73. If you drove to Thompson and are planning to travel onward to Churchill you can park at City Hall, which is free and more secure than leaving the car at the train station away from the center.

Calm Air (☎ 800-839-2256) flies to Churchill ($338) Monday, Wednesday and Friday.

GILLAM
Situated about halfway to Churchill on the train line, Gillam exists because of its major hydropower development along the Nelson River. A gravel road now runs from Thompson, and Grey Goose provides transportation.

CHURCHILL
pop 800
Despite its forbidding, remote location and extremes of weather – July and August are the only months usually snow-free – Churchill has always been of importance to the region. In terms of European exploration, the area is one of the oldest in the country. The first Hudson's Bay Company outpost was set up here in 1717;

MANITOBA

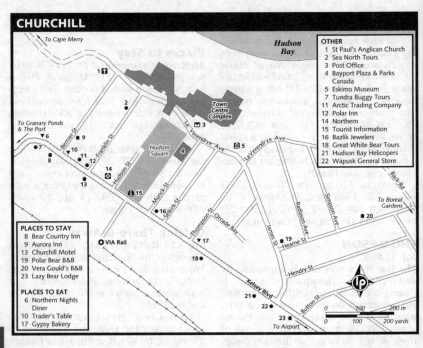

CHURCHILL

To Cape Merry

Hudson Bay

Town Centre Complex

To Granary Ponds & The Port

Hudson Square

La Verendrye Ave

La Verendrye Ave

Bernier St

Franklin St

Hudson St

Munck St

Selkirk St

Thompson St

Orcade Bay

Radisson Ave

Simpson Ave

Back Rd

James St

Hearne St

Kelsey Blvd

Hendry St

Button St

To Boreal Gardens

VIA Rail

To Airport

OTHER
1 St Paul's Anglican Church
2 Sea North Tours
3 Post Office
4 Bayport Plaza & Parks Canada
5 Eskimo Museum
7 Tundra Buggy Tours
11 Arctic Trading Company
12 Polar Inn
14 Northern
15 Tourist Information
16 Bazlik Jewelers
18 Great White Bear Tours
21 Hudson Bay Helicopers
22 Wapusk General Store

PLACES TO STAY
8 Bear Country Inn
9 Aurora Inn
13 Churchill Motel
19 Polar Bear B&B
20 Vera Gould's B&B
23 Lazy Bear Lodge

PLACES TO EAT
6 Northern Nights Diner
10 Trader's Table
17 Gypsy Bakery

0   100   200 m
0   100   200 yards

the outpost was named after Lord Churchill, Governor of the HBC and later the first Duke of Marlborough, who died trying to find the Northwest Passage. The company's influence in the region was so widespread and that it's been said the initials HBC stand for 'Here Before Christ.'

The railway was completed in 1929, connecting the prairies to an ocean port that's closer to Europe than Montreal. Churchill was once one of the largest grain-handling ports in the world. After some years of decline, grain handling is again increasing under new management. A launching and monitoring station for communications satellites, built about 20km east of town on the site of the former Churchill Research Range at a cost of $250 million, was, unfortunately, a bust after one launch.

Today, the town relies mostly on tourism, billing itself as the 'Polar Bear Capital of the World.' It sits right in the middle of a migration route, which means the great white bears often wander into the township. During October and early November, visitors are taken out on the frozen tundra in tall specialized buses to see the huge and very dangerous bears.

Churchill is definitely not a cheap place to visit, but it's worth it to see the animals. For most people, a three-day stay will suffice; those with a special interest will often visit for five days. To get the most out of a trip, consider going out on a bay or tundra tour more than one day. Many visitors get off the morning train, dump their gear and head out on one of the tours without pause. The return train leaves at night, so you can take a tour on your last day, too.

Bring a camera, lots of film and binoculars. Mosquitoes and black flies are ferocious in July and August, so be prepared to do battle. Repellent-saturated jackets and head-nets can be bought in town but are often sold out. The United Army Surplus store in Winnipeg sells this gear (usually cheaper) – the nets make for a good investment.

Average temperatures in Churchill are -2.3°C in May, 6.1°C in June, 12°C in July, 11.5°C in August, 5.7°C in September and -1°C in October. You don't want to know

Dense, early morning mist on the Saint John River, Fredericton, New Brunswick

A house and boat at Acadian Historic Village near Caraquet, New Brunswick

Bay of Fundy's Hopewell Rocks, New Brunswick, site of the highest tides in the world

JOHN MCINNES

Dramatic sky over Cape Merry, Churchill, Manitoba

JOHN MCINNES

Polar bear alert sign in Churchill, Manitoba

MARK LIGHTBODY

Pisew Falls near Thompson, Manitoba

MARK LIGHTBODY

The rocky Hudson Bay coastline at Churchill, Manitoba

about the rest of the year – let's just say that -50°C is normal. Even though temperatures can get to the high 20s in July, it's advisable to bring warm clothing – sweaters and reasonable footwear – for any visit. Winter seems to be coming a little later each year (pushing the polar-bear migration back), but by October the snow is usually flying.

Particularly hardy visitors might like to participate in the July **Dip In the Bay** event, part of which requires relay team members to jump into the not-so-balmy Arctic waters.

Orientation & Information

The raggedy township sits at the juncture of the Churchill River and Hudson Bay. It feels small and naked coupled with the vastness all around and the immense Arctic sky above. Facilities are minimal; there is no luxury, no pavement, no traffic lights and no trees. The whole town site can be walked easily.

There is a tourist information office (☎ 204-675-2022) on Kelsey Blvd at Hudson St, opposite the train station. Towards the Town Centre Complex, in the same building as the Royal Bank, Parks Canada (☎ 204-675-8863) operates a visitor's center and a small museum of northern frontier history. It's open 1pm to 9pm daily from June to November. Films on Churchill and the polar bears are shown. The knowledgeable park staff can answer questions in depth.

Overlooking Hudson Bay at the north end of town, the large Town Centre Complex houses a high school, a library and recreational facilities, which include a swimming pool and a movie theater. Getting work in the hotels and restaurants in season is possible.

Flora & Fauna

The area around Churchill is wild and starkly beautiful. The coastline is heaped with huge quartzite boulders worn smooth by the retreating glaciers, and in summer the tundra is covered in red, orange and violet wildflowers. There is an incredible variety of wildlife to see, from polar bears to beluga whales, and during winter it's one of the best places in the world for watching the aurora borealis (northern lights). Other wildlife in the Churchill area includes seals, beaver, caribou, gray wolves, lemmings, snowy owls and Arctic foxes. Apart from all that, the air itself is so unbelievably clean it'll make the hairs in your nostrils stand up and sing.

Polar Bears The township is an attraction for the animals (food and fun), but it's also thought that the older bears force the younger ones to move inland and that this could be why they sometimes lumber into town. Local police and government authorities maintain a 24-hour vigil from September to November to protect bears and humans from each other. An alert system has been set up – if you see one, call ☎ BEAR (2327) – and if bears do come into town in the daytime, they're tranquilized and moved out of town by helicopter. Gunshots at night are usually authorities firing into the air to shoo off townbound bears. Persistent trespassers are trapped and carted off to the polar bear 'jail,' where they may be held through winter.

To see polar bears at close range, a tour (booked well in advance) is the only sure, safe option; see Organized Tours.

Beluga Whales During summer, from around mid-June until the end of August, up to 3000 beluga whales move into the Churchill River. It's thought that the whales are drawn by the warmer water temperatures. They spend summer feeding on large schools of capelin, calving, mating and checking out *Homo sapiens*.

Adult belugas are glossy white and about 3m to 5m long. Though they're easily spotted from the shore of Hudson Bay, a boat trip is the best way to see them. The whales come right up to the boat and a special microphone dropped over the side allows passengers to hear their extraordinary song. Early whalers who heard them through the hulls of their ships called them sea canaries. Belugas were heavily hunted right up until 1968; now only Inuit hunters are allowed to take a small number.

Birds From the end of May to mid-June, it's possible to see up to 200 species of

MANITOBA

Fluffy White Killers

Most of the world's population of polar bears – thought to be between 21,000 and 28,000 strong – live in the Arctic regions of Canada. Since the bears gained protection in the early 1970s, numbers steadily increased, particularly along the coasts of Manitoba and Ontario. In 1983, polar bears were reclassified from 'endangered' to 'vulnerable.'

The bears' continued survival depends on a protected habitat and, perhaps more than anything else, an abundant and healthy population of seals – their primary food source and the reason they are supremely adapted to life in the Arctic. The bears' huge rounded bodies, thick fur and heavy layers of fat help to conserve heat and keep them buoyant in the water. The undersides of their enormous paws, which are bigger than a man's face, are covered in hair so that they don't slip and slide (and look silly) on the ice.

Though the average male weighs around 600kg, polar bears can run incredibly fast across rough ice, leap over tall hurdles and clamber up steep ice cliffs. They're also able to gently lower themselves backwards into the sea, swim underwater or on the surface with only their noses showing, and then come barreling out again at top speed.

The bears of Manitoba spend winter on the pack-ice of Hudson Bay, hunting seals. Their sense of smell is so good they can detect dinner under a meter of ice and snow. Mating takes place during April and May. When the sea ice melts, they head inland for the summer, where they laze about nibbling on berries and grasses and patiently waiting for the ice to re-form. In October they begin to make their way to coastal areas where the ice first freezes. Pregnant females stay behind to look for sites to build maternity dens where the cubs are born – tiny, blind and helpless – in December or January. In March the small family (there are usually two cubs) moves onto the ice in search of seal pups.

The main migration route followed by the bears of northern Manitoba runs along the coast between Nelson River, about 200km south of Churchill, and Cape Churchill, about 25km east of Churchill. Up to 300 bears have been sighted on the Cape during the migration season (October to November).

Though bear numbers are increasing, their survival is far from assured. Warmer, shorter winters in the past few years seem to be having a negative effect on the bears around Churchill. The ice has been slow to freeze and breaks up faster than previously, disrupting the main hunting season. Weight loss is being reported and long-term health may be in jeopardy. Other threats include oil exploration, oil spills and general pollution of the oceans. Despite living in the remote Arctic, polar bears have been found to carry excessively high levels of insecticides in their tissue.

birds in and around Churchill. The rare Ross's gull, whose breast turns pale pink in the mating season, nests in Churchill. More common visitors include Pacific and red-throated loons, Smiths' longspurs, Arctic terns, yellow warblers and snow geese. From late June to mid-August it's also possible to see up to 40 species of rare tundra butterflies.

Cape Merry, the Granary Ponds by the port, Bird Cove and Akudlik Marsh, 4km south of Churchill, are all excellent bird-watching spots.

Eskimo Museum
Inuit artwork is the specialty of the museum (☎ 204-675-2030, La Verendrye Ave at James Ave; admission by donation; open 1pm-5pm Mon, 9am-noon & 1pm-5pm Tues-Sat June-Nov, 1pm-4:30pm Mon & Sat June-Nov, 10:30am-noon & 1pm-4:30pm Tues-Fri Dec-May). Intricate, stylized carvings of northern life are made from antlers, bones, and stone – audio programs explain their history. Northern fauna displays include a narwhal whale tusk and a polar bear fetus. Books and artworks are for sale.

Thanadelthur's Cairn
With the establishment of the Hudson's Bay Company outpost in this area, Lord Churchill got to be the Duke of Marlborough. The Dene woman who arranged a peace treaty between the warring tribes of the region, which made the post possible,

got this small cairn behind the Anglican church in 1967.

National Historic Sites
Fort Prince of Wales This is one of four national historic sites in the Churchill area administered by Parks Canada. The partially restored stone fort (☎ 204-675-8863; tour $5; open 1pm-5pm & 6pm-10pm daily June-Oct), on the peninsula head opposite Cape Merry, was originally built to protect the fur-trading business of the Hudson's Bay Company from possible rivals. It took 40 years to construct but was surrendered to the French without a shot being fired because it was never seriously manned. In summer Parks Canada runs a boat from Cape Merry to the site, and the fort is included on commercial boat itineraries.

Sloop's Cove Four kilometers upriver from the fort, Sloop's Cove is a stop on many of the summer boat tours. The cove was used by European vessels out on whaling excursions and on trading trips with the local Inuit. Names of some of the early Hudson's Bay Company people, including that of Samuel Hearn, the local 18th-century governor, can be seen carved into the seaside rocks.

Cape Merry Just 2km from town at the end of the gravel road on the headland northwest of Churchill, Cape Merry (☎ 204-675-2026; admission free; open 1pm-5pm & 6pm-10pm daily June-Oct) has the remains of a stone battery built in 1746; there's a small information booth with guides on hand. In summer the large, flat rocks are a good spot for whale-watching; along the way you'll see dozens of species of birds. Don't forget the repellent, and be aware of the bear situation.

York Factory Much farther afield (250km southeast of Churchill), York Factory was a fur-trading post that operated for more than 250 years. In the 18th and 19th centuries it was one of the Hudson's Bay Company's most significant trading posts. The remaining wooden building (☎ 204-675-8863, near Hanes River; tours $5; open varying hours June-Aug), built around

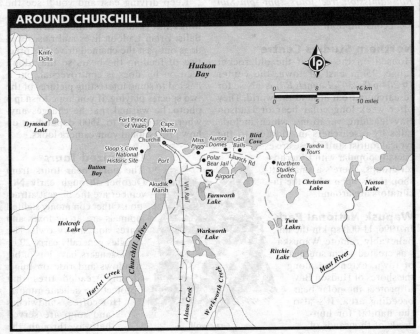

AROUND CHURCHILL

MANITOBA

1832, has no foundations so it can 'ride' the permafrost. Also at the site are other ruins, some recovered artifacts and a cemetery. Situated deep in polar- and black-bear country, and with limited facilities and unpredictable weather conditions, York Factory is accessible only by air or (for the very determined and experienced) by canoe.

Bird Cove

Bird Cove, about 15km east of town and accessible by vehicle (tours are available), is one of the best spots for viewing birdlife. Along the way (and with a short hike), you can see the wreck of the *Ithaca*, a freighter that went down in a storm in 1961 at the western edge of the cove. Visitors are advised to take care when walking on the beach because the tides rise and fall very quickly. The decks of the freighter are rusted through and are not safe to walk on.

Boreal Gardens

About 1.5km east of town, the gardens and greenhouses (☎ 204-675-8866, *Shore Rd; admission free; tours 2pm-4pm Sun July-Aug*) here produce some food for local consumption.

Northern Studies Centre

Housed on the site of the old rocket range, 25km east of town, the center (☎ 204-675-2307, *Launch Rd*) is a base for researchers from around the world. They offer week-long polar bear or Hudson Bay learning vacations, which include talks by researchers in addition to the typical tourist stuff. These are especially popular with Elderhostel groups. There's a small gift shop that's open when the facilitators are around.

Wapusk National Park

In 1996, 11,000 sq km the unbelievably remote Wapuska was created 45km southeast of town, extending along the shores of Hudson Bay, to protect the polar bear breeding area. It's also the habitat for hundreds of thousands of

birds. It's hard to get to Wapuska without one of the approved tour operators; contact Parks Canada office (☎ 204-675-8863) or the Churchill Chamber of Commerce (☎ 888-389-2327) to obtain more information.

Other Attractions

The simple **graveyard** behind the Anglican church on Shore Road, at the western edge of town, has some far-north–related epitaphs and is worth a stroll. There's a **beach** behind the Town Centre Complex; stick a toe in the Arctic Ocean.

If you rent a truck, you can drive east out of town on the only road. Near the airport is the town dump, otherwise known as the Polar Bear dining room. If you do see bears here, please keep a great distance – they can run 50km/h. Across from there is **Miss Piggy**, the 1979 wreckage of a C46 airplane – it's quite ominous when spied while flying in. Next are the observation skylights of **Aurora Domes** (☎ 800-265-8563) that are rented out from January through March for watching the northern lights.

Keep driving east and you'll see the former rocket range radar system that looks like what's its called: **Twin Golf Balls**. Brian Ladoon lives and raises sled dogs out past the chained drive. His practice of feeding the bears so they don't feed on his dogs is controversial, but it has led to some interesting pictures of the two species playing. If you hope to snap a photo, be warned that he charges anywhere from $25 to $500 depending on how professional your camera looks.

Organized Tours

The polar bear tours from October through early November are the biggest attraction. Other commonly sighted animals are arctic foxes and hares and snowy owls. The buggies generally carry 20 or so passengers, have lots of big windows and ride on huge, deeply treaded tires that protect the delicate tundra. Hot coffee, sandwiches and soup are served halfway through the

Gray wolf

eight-hour excursion ($161). Both companies pick you up at your hotel, and the offices have gift shops.

Great White Bear Tours (☎ *204-675-2781, 800-765-8344, Kelsey Blvd between Selkirk & Thompson Sts*) is the smaller company, but most of its buggies are newer and custom-made with a see-through grate on the floor of the observation deck. Bears can walk up underneath you and blow your toque (hat) off. Make sure to tie your shoes well!

The best-known operator, **Tundra Buggy Tours** (☎ *204-675-2121, 800-544-5049, Kelsey Blvd at Bernier St*), is also known as International Wildlife Adventures. This company can arrange complete trips, including airfare. Some very expensive itineraries include an overnight stay out with the bears in a Tundra Buggy lodge. In summer, without the bears, prices drop: A four-hour tour costs $75.

In warmer months, **Sea North Tours** (☎ *204-675-2195, 39 Franklin St*) specializes in boat and sealife tours. A 2½-hour boat tour ($65) includes Fort Prince of Wales and, most likely, dozens of whales at close range (no guarantee).

A variety of naturalist-led walking tours are offered from May through October by **Adventure Walking Tours** (☎ *204-675-2147, Box 1166*) in Churchill. Call ahead for information. The small-group walks are a half day ($54) or full day ($107) and can take in four distinct eco-zones – marine, sub-Arctic forest, tundra and boreal forest.

From May to November, **Hudson Bay Helicopters** (☎ *204-675-2576, Kelsey Blvd at Thompson St*) offers flights for $195/390 per person for a half/full hour, with a four-person minimum. The hour-long tour comes with a bear sighting or refund.

Dog-sled rides are available year-round (in the summer using wheeled 'sleds') through the Wapusk General Store (☎ *204-675-2887, Kelsey Blvd*). A half-hour trip is $45.

Places to Stay

There are a number of accommodations and, in polar bear season, October through early November, all of them are vastly overpriced for what you get. Lower

your expectations and feel lucky to be seeing polar bears. Most of the rooms are reserved in advance by tour groups. At the beginning of September, tour companies release back the rooms they don't really need. So you'll either have to book a year in advance or less than a month before your trip. **Uniglobe Travel** (☎ *204-675-2811, 140 Kelsey Blvd*) may be able to help if it starts to feel like there's no room at any inn.

Backcountry lodges are an insanely expensive option; outfitters are listed in the Travel Manitoba accommodations guide.

B&Bs As well as the options listed below, during bear seasons other homes may rent out rooms. Tour companies sometimes know which have openings.

Vera Gould's B&B (☎ *204-675-2544, 87 Hearne St*) Singles/doubles $65/95 in bear season, $35/65 out of season, with breakfast. This B&B is the oldest and hardest to book. Rates include a very full breakfast, which often consists of pancakes with Québec maple syrup or toast with homemade jams.

Polar Bear B&B (☎ *204-675-2819, Hearne St at James St*) Singles/doubles $60/90 in bear season, $40/60 out of season. These tiny rooms are serviceable, and certainly cost less than a hotel. One room sleeps four people in bunk beds ($160). Bicycles are available for free.

Hotels Most hotels rates include transportation to and from the airport.

Churchill Motel (☎ *204-675-8853, fax 204-675-8828, Kelsey Blvd at Franklin St*) Singles/doubles $75/85 year-round. The cheapest and most basic option, this place also has a greasy spoon.

Bear Country Inn (☎ *204-675-8299, fax 204-675-8803, 126 Kelsey Blvd*) Rooms $120/70 in bear season/out of season, with toast and coffee. This motel-like building is simple with no phones and little furniture, but the proprietors (including the German shepherd) are extremely friendly and rooms have cable TV.

Lazy Bear Lodge (☎ *204-675-2869, fax 204-675-2408, Kelsey Blvd at Burton St*) Singles/doubles $150/160 in bear season, $75/85 out of season. This two-story inn was built with whole timber logged in the area. The small rooms have at least one wall with the interesting woodwork exposed.

Aurora Inn (☎ 204-675-2850, fax 204-675-2850, 24 Bernier St) Singles/doubles $149/169 in bear season, $85/105 out of season. The Aurora was converted from an apartment building, so all the rooms at Aurora have full kitchens and laundry service. The rooms, which are lofts, can sleep from four to six people. Each additional person more than two costs $20.

Places to Eat

Gypsy's Bakery (☎ 204-675-2322, Kelsey Blvd at Thompson St) Meals $4-10. The bakery serves very good soups, sandwiches and homemade pastries from a walk-up counter from 7am to 9pm daily.

Northern Nights Diner (☎ 204-675-2403, 101 Kelsey Blvd) Meals $7-18. At the lodge of the same name, this modern restaurant is where the buggy drivers eat. A few vegetarian options stand out on the menu.

Trader's Table (☎ 204-675-2141, Kelsey Blvd at Bernier St) Mains $24-32. Caribou and Arctic char (the local fish) are served in a cozy, rustic atmosphere with a fireplace. Ask about desserts featuring locally grown berries. It's only open for dinner.

Northern (☎ 204-675-8891, Kelsey Blvd at Franklin St). This grocery/department store sells produce, meats and dried goods Monday to Saturday – in addition to clothes and toys.

Shopping

Kelsey Boulevard has a bunch of very similar souvenir shops selling everything from polar bear pajamas to genuine Inuit art. Off the strip, the *Eskimo Museum* has the widest variety of Inuit carvings.

Arctic Trading Company (☎ 204-675-8804, Kelsey Blvd) sells a fair amount of winter clothing.

Gold polar bear charms at *Bazlik Jewelers (☎ 204-675-2397, 219 Kelsey Blvd)* might do if you're looking for a souvenir of a different ilk.

Getting There & Away

There is no road to Churchill; access is by plane or train only.

Air Air Canada (☎ 888-247-2262), in conjunction with Calm Air (☎ 204-675-2913) heads to Churchill from Winnipeg. Advance-purchase tickets range from $490 to $612 in bear season. The planes are small and luggage space is limited. Bags sometimes (sometimes often) get 'bumped' and don't arrive on your flight. This is true heading back to Winnipeg as well. Pack essentials in your carry-on.

Train Three trains a week leave for Churchill from Winnipeg, departing at 10pm on Sunday, Tuesday and Thursday. They arrive two days later at 8:30am. Return trips are Saturday, Tuesday and Thursday evenings. The Churchill station (☎ 800-561-8630), down a short street opposite the tourist information office off Kelsey Blvd, is only open for arrivals and departures.

During peak season, an economy roundtrip ticket – just a seat – costs $275 to $350 with advance purchase. Single private rooms are $625 to $700 and a double room is $725 to $800 per person. Private rooms sell out for the two night, 1600km trip a year advance. Dining car meals are offered ($8 to $10) at dinner or there is a sandwich takeout counter. Packing drinks and snacks is a good idea.

Leaving your car at the train station in Winnipeg while you travel to Churchill can be risky as break-ins are common. A reasonable substitute is the multileveled lot downtown on Edmonton St near St Mary Ave. Another option is to drive or bus to Thompson and take the train from there. This cuts down on time spent in transit as the train is excruciatingly slow.

Getting Around

Walking the length and breadth of town is quite easy. Polar Inn (☎ 204-675-8878, 15 Franklin St) rents bicycles for $15. (They also rent down-filled parkas, wind pants and boots).

If it gets too cold, Churchill Taxi (☎ 204-675-2345) will take you around. For out-of-town excursions, Tamarack Rentals (☎ 204-675-2192, Kelsey Blvd at Button St) has half-ton pick-ups for $65 a day plus gas, which will cost you dearly. Be aware that the road only goes 22km.

Western Manitoba

From Winnipeg westward toward the Saskatchewan border, the mostly flat prairie landscape dominates. Get used to it – it lasts until halfway through Alberta! That said, the terrain is neither totally barren nor treeless, and there are a couple of government parks in this section of the province to visit.

Not far out of Winnipeg along the Trans Canada Hwy, where Hwy 26 runs north off the highway, is a statue of a white horse. Native Indian legend has it that a Cree rode this way on his white horse with his new bride, hotly pursued by his failed rival in love, a Sioux. Eventually overtaking the couple, the scorned Sioux man killed both bride and groom. The young woman's spirit entered the horse, which continued to roam the prairie for years, a living reminder of the tragic couple.

PORTAGE LA PRAIRIE

Portage is a farm center. Look for the crop identification markers by the highway indicating wheat, flax, mustard, etc. Other common crops include barley, sunflowers and canola. The latter two are grown for their oils, used in cooking and prepared-food production. The Trans Canada has a summer tourist office, but the bulk of the town is on Hwy 1A (Saskatchewan Ave).

Explorer Pierre de la Vérendrye built a fort here in 1738. On the original site is a replica, **Fort La Reine Museum & Pioneer Village** (☎ 204-857-3259, Hwy 1A at Hwy 26; admission adult/child $3/2; open 9am-6pm Mon-Fri & 10am-6pm Sat-Sun May-Sept).

With rooms running $68 to $89, the *Westward Inn & Conference Centre* (☎ 204-857-9745, 2401 Saskatchewan Ave W) has restaurants, a pool and a giant aluminum Coke can in the parking lot.

North of town, along the southern shores of Lake Manitoba between Routes 242 and 430, is another of the province's essential wetlands. Thirty-two kilometers long, **Delta Marsh** is internationally known. There's camping near the eastern edge at *St Ambroise Beach Provincial Park Campground* (☎ 888-482-2267, W www.manitobaparks.com, Route 430; tenting sites $7-10).

The Trans Canada Hwy splits into two segments 11km west of Portage. The Yellowhead Route (Hwy 16) runs north along the southern edge of Riding Mountain National Park and on to Edmonton, Alberta. The southern portion (Hwy 1), the original, heads due west to Brandon and on to Calgary, Alberta.

SPRUCE WOODS PROVINCIAL PARK

Thirty kilometers south of the highway, this 27,000 hectare park (☎ 204-827-8850, Hwy 5; parking $5 for 3 days) features an area of desert-like sand dunes as high as 30m. This terrain supports the northern prairie skink (Manitoba's only lizard), the western hognose snake and two species of cacti not found elsewhere in the province. Walking trails lead to some of the more interesting sections of the park, including the dunes known as Spirit Sands (1.6km to first overlook) and beyond to underground-fed pools like the Devil's Punchbowl (3.5km). Alternatively, horsedrawn covered wagons (additional charge) can be taken to these attractions from May to September.

Other areas such as the *Kiche Manitou campground* (☎ 888-482-2267, W www .manitobaparks.com, Hwy 5; tent sites $14) offer woods and lakes. Weekends are busy; call ahead.

BRANDON

The second largest city in the province, with a population of a little more than 42,000, is considered a good place to live. Primarily a commercial center, it's 4km south of the highway. Tourist information is available at the **Riverbank Discovery Centre** (☎ 204-729-2141, 545 Conservation Drive).

Everything from cattle breeding to barley pasture weed control is investigated at the **Agriculture Canada Research Centre** (☎ 204-726-7650, Route 459; admission free; tours Tues & Thur by appointment). This experimental farm has been operating, in one form or another, since 1886 .

When the Bison Reigned Supreme

In the days before the European arrival in the west, huge herds of bison roamed from what is now Manitoba to the Rocky Mountains, and from Texas to the shores of Great Slave Lake. On the wide, open, grassy plains of the prairies, herds could number in the hundreds of thousands.

The name buffalo is very commonly, if not nearly always, used in relation to the North American bison, though this is technically incorrect. A buffalo is a type of heavy oxen found across Africa and Asia.

The bison is a large, shaggy form of wild cattle. An old bull can weigh as much as 900kg, and full-grown females average over 500kg. To the western Indians, the bison were stores with legs, but were also beings with spirits, to be respected. Bison were the principal source of food. Native groups from more-northern areas added currants, berries and boiled fat to the dried meat to form pemmican, a nutritious mix that kept many a fur trader and explorer alive. Clothes, tents and bedding were made from the hides and hair. Horns were used in crafts and rituals, the bones as knives. Nothing went to waste – even the 'chips' (dried excrement) were burned as fuel.

Bison were hunted first with arrows on foot, then later, on horseback, after the Spanish brought horses to the content. At places like Head-Smashed-In, Alberta, or the Stott Site in Grand Valley Provincial Recreation Park, hunters would herd the bison over cliffs.

Through the late 19th century, Europeans with rifles and horses slaughtered the immense herds to near extinction, often for nothing more than amusement. For the Plains Indians, the demise of the bison led to starvation and meant the end of their way of life. In Canada, the largest remaining wild herd is found at Wood Buffalo National Park (see the Northwest Territories chapter).

Daly House Museum (☎ 204-727-1722, 122 18th St; admission adult/child $3/2; open 10am-noon & 1pm-5pm Tues-Sun) is chock-full of Victoriana and local history. An addition contains the whole Brandon pharmacy, circa 1915.

Outside of town at the airport, the **Commonwealth Air Training Museum** (☎ 204-727-2444, Hangar 1, Hwy 10; admission adult/child $3.50/2; open 10am-4pm daily May-Sept, 1pm-4pm daily Oct-Apr) tells the story of the thousands of recruits from around the British Commonwealth who trained from 1939 to 1945 before heading over to Europe. There are 13 original training planes housed in the old Brandon hangar. A number of small training centers such as this one dotted the prairies.

The main street, Rosser Ave, has a few places to eat. *Sweet Temptations* (☎ 204-727-1601, 459 23rd St) serves good homemade breads and soups. The *YWCA* (☎ 204-727-0643, 148 11th St; room $35) offers cheap downtown accommodations, with meals, to both sexes. *Braeview B&B* (☎ 204-727-4594, 23 Hanbury Place; singles/doubles $40/50) has eat-off-the-floor-clean, new rooms with cable TV and telephone. The chain *motels* are on the Trans Canada, near the large, kitschy *Harry's Ukrainian Kitchen* (☎ 204-725-4020, 1120 Service Rd; meals $7-15).

The Greyhound Bus Depot (☎ 204-727-0643, 141 6th St) is just south of Rosser Ave.

AROUND BRANDON

Uniforms, guns, ammunition, vehicles and more – dating from 1796 – are collected at the **Royal Canadian Artillery Museum** (☎ 204-765-3000, Hwy 340, Shilo; admission free; open summer 8am-4pm Mon-Fri, 1pm-4pm Sat & Sun; 8am-4pm Tues-Fri rest of the year).

Ten kilometers west of Brandon is the **Stott Site** (open May-Sept), a Native Indian bison kill area dating back some 1200 years. Displays offer information on how it was used, and a Native Indian encampment has been re-created.

From Brandon west to the border, you'll see derricks pumping oil. Remember that during summer, clocks move back one hour at the Saskatchewan border because Saskatchewan, unlike the rest of the country, does not use Daylight Saving Time.

NEEPAWA

Northeast of Brandon is Neepawa, a town that hosts the annual Lily Festival the third week in July. *Garden Path B&B* (☎ 204-476-3184, 536 Second Ave; rooms $49-79) is a stop on the festival garden tour, and the antique quilt- and cat-filled B&B is a homey place to stay. To buy lily bulbs in spring and fall, head 4km south of town to **The Lily Nook** (☎ 204-476-3225, Hwy 5). During July, its fields are open for viewing.

The **Margaret Laurence Home** (☎ 204-476-3612, 312 First Ave; admission $2/1; open 10am-6pm daily June-Sept, noon-5pm daily Oct-May), also in Neepawa, has been turned into a mini-museum. A gift shop sells the author's work and gives out a map of the nearby cemetery where the 'Stone Angel' of eponymous book fame resides.

RIDING MOUNTAIN NATIONAL PARK

Due north of Brandon, 300km northwest of Winnipeg, Riding Mountain National Park (☎ 800-707-8480, Hwy 10; daily pass single/family $3.50/7.50; open year-round) is the major attraction of western Manitoba. Covering nearly 3000 sq km, it's a huge island of a park rising above the surrounding plains. Much of it is highland, set on a forested escarpment that runs from North Dakota to Saskatchewan. Within the park are deciduous forests, lakes, rivers and meadows. Elk, moose and bear are plentiful and not uncommonly seen from the road.

Most of the park is wilderness, but **Wasagaming**, on the south shore of Clear Lake, is a casual resort town featuring log construction with stores, cabins, restaurants and a cabin. Most businesses close from Thanksgiving to Labor Day. The park **Visitors Centre** (☎ 204-848-7275, Wasagaming Rd; open 9:30am-5:30pm daily May-June & Sept-Thanksgiving, 9:30am-8pm daily June-Aug) is also here, with natural history displays and movies.

The park has more than 400km of **walking**, **cycling** and **horseback riding** trails, providing access to various sections of interest. One long trail leads to a cabin once used by the naturalist Grey Owl. At

Lake Audy, about 40km from Wasagaming, is a fenced herd of 30 bison. The park is patrolled by rangers on horseback. If you want to go for a ride, Elkhorn Resort (☎ 204-848-2802, Mooswa Drive W) has two-hour trips for $30 per person in the summer.

Canoeing is good in parts, and rentals are available from Clear Lake Marina (☎ 204-867-7298, Wasagaming Rd). Canoeing on Clear Lake itself, with winds and motorboats, is not recommended.

Grey Goose Bus connects the park to Winnipeg and Dauphin. It runs from Winnipeg to Wasagaming once daily, except Saturday, through the summer.

Places to Stay

Backcountry camping is possible, check with the visitor's center. Motels and cabins are plentiful in Wasagaming, but most close for winter.

Wasagaming Campground (☎ 800-707-8480, fax 204-848-2596, Columbine Rd at Ta-wa-pit Drive) With/without hookups $19.50/6.50. In the forested south side of Wasagaming, the main campground is within walking distance of the town center.

Moon Lake Campground (☎ 800-707-8480, fax 204-848-2596, 33km south of Dauphin on Hwy 10) Tent sites $10.50. More remote, this beautiful setting is a great place for spotting moose in the misty mornings.

Manigaming Motel Resort (☎ 204-848-2459, 137 Ta-wa-pit Drive) Rooms $69. The pleasantly grungy, two-room motel units each have two double beds, and a mini-fridge. The property also has newer, pricier chalets.

New Chalet (☎ 204-848-2892, fax 204-848-4515, 116 Wasagaming Drive) Singles/doubles $70/90. If you arrive in winter, this shiny new property is your only option.

AROUND RIDING MOUNTAIN

North of the park up Hwy 10, **Dauphin** is one of many Ukrainian centers found all across the prairie provinces. **Canada's National Ukrainian Festival** (☎ 204-622-4600, 119 Main St) office has a gift shop and tea room and organizes the festival held at

MANITOBA

the beginning of August each year. Folk dancing, traditional costumes and cultural displays are part of the celebration, but the reason most people come is the food: pierogies (potato or cabbage stuffed dumplings topped with sour cream and sautéed onions), cabbage rolls (stuffed with rice or meat) and kielbasa are among the favorites.

Farther to the north, **Duck Mountain Provincial Park** *(Blues Lake office ☎ 204-546-5000, Routes 367 & 366)* is wilder, less busy and has better fishing than Riding Mountain.

Saskatchewan

Saskatchewan is a Cree Indian word that refers to the Saskatchewan River and means 'river that turns around when it runs.' Prior to the arrival of Europeans – first fur traders and explorers, then farmsteading settlers – the region was primarily Cree territory. They were a seminomadic people whose life was inextricably linked with the herds of bison that roamed the vast plains.

Tourism is not a major industry in Saskatchewan. Most people pass through and find the scenery along the Trans Canada Hwy monotonous: mercilessly flat, often without a tree in sight. But such wide-open space can be stunning, with golden ripening wheat or pale blue flax rippling to the horizon as the sunrise colors play in the fields. In such openness, sunsets, thundercloud formations and night skies are all spectacular.

If you get off the Trans Canada Hwy, the landscape becomes more varied. The northern half of Saskatchewan has more than 100,000 lakes and few roads. Prince Albert National Park is accessible Canadian timberland. Between this area and the prairie of the south is a transition zone stretching across the province, covering the lower middle section of Saskatchewan in rolling hills and cultivated farmland. Dozens of canoe routes have been mapped within these two regions.

South of the highway, around Grasslands National Park, is dramatic desertlike topography, which is home to endangered species like the burrowing owl. To the southwest, tree-covered Cypress Hill Provincial Park rises like an island above the prairie – the highest point between here and the Rockies. Tough nature is the biggest draw, but the two major cities have a few sights worth a stopover.

Economically, Saskatchewan and wheat are pretty much synonymous. The province is North America's greatest wheat grower and, with more than a third of Canada's farmland, produces two-thirds of Canada's crop. In addition to wheat, grains such as barley and rye are important, as are sunflowers and beef cattle. The province also

Highlights

Entered Confederation: September 1, 1905
Area: 651,903 sq km
Population: 1,021,762
Provincial Capital: Regina

- Watch the seemingly endless skies put on a show at sunset or during an approaching storm.

- Visit Wanuskewin Heritage Park to gain an appreciation of Native Indian culture and history.

- Float weightless in Little Manitou Lake, with 13 times more salt content than the Dead Sea.

- Canoe and hike in Prince Albert National Park, once the home of famous naturalist Grey Owl.

- Discover historic Moose Jaws' underground secrets.

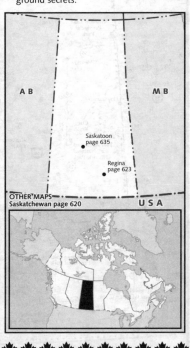

OTHER MAPS
Saskatchewan page 620

SASKATCHEWAN

110°W   N W T   105°W   N T   100°W

60°N   60°N

Fort Smith

Slave River

Wood Buffalo National Park

Uranium City

Lake Athabasca

Stony Rapids   *Black Lake*

▲ Athabasca Sand Dunes Provincial Wilderness Park

Winter Access Only

Wollaston Lake

Manitoba

Note: Scale varies north and south of 54°N

0   50   100 km
0   30   60 miles

955

Reindeer Lake

905

Fort McMurray

Clearwater River Provincial Park

Lynn Lake

La Loche

Southend

102

391

Pukatawagan

Alberta

Mountain Time Zone / Central Time Zone

55°N   55°N

Meadow Lake Provincial Park

155

Lac La Ronge Provincial Park

Lac la Ronge

La Ronge

106

Amisk Lake

Flin Flon

Bonnyville

55

Meadow Lake

Cumberland Lake

The Pas

N Saskatchewan R

To Edmonton

16

4

Prince Albert National Park

120

55

Narrow Hills Provincial Park

Saskatchewan River

60

Lloydminster

55

Prince Albert

55

Melfort

Wildcat Hill Provincial Wilderness Park

3

Hudson Bay

77

14

40

Cut Knife

North Battleford

40

Redberry Lake

Batoche National Historic Site

10

Lake Winnipegosis

Fort Battleford National Historic Park

16

11

Duck Mountain Provincial Park

Veregin

41

14

Biggar

Saskatoon

5

Quill Lakes

Yellowhead Hwy

Good Spirit Provincial Park

10

5

9

Kindersley

7

Rosetown

44

11

Manitou Beach

Last Mountain Lake

Yorkton

Crooked Lake Provincial Park

Oyen

S Saskatchewan R

Leader

The Great Sand Hills

Lake Diefenbaker

Last Mountain House Provincial Historic Park

10

10

16

To Calgary

21

Saskatchewan Landing Provincial Park

Trans Canada Hwy

Lumsden

Fort Qu'Appelle

1

To Winnipeg

50°N   50°N

Medicine Hat

1

Swift Current

4

Chaplin Lake

Moose Jaw

REGINA

35

Moose Mountain Provincial Park

Moosomin

Cypress Hills Provincial Park

Maple Creek

Old Wives Lake

2

6

Weyburn

13

Carlyle

2

41

Eastend

13

Assiniboia

39

9

Estevan

83

18

Wood Mountain Post Provincial Park

Big Muddy Badlands

Grasslands National Park

110°W   Montana   105°W   USA   North Dakota

SASKATCHEWAN

has the richest potash deposits (used in fertilizer) in the world.

Driving is the best way to see the province. You should watch for the Mohawk service stations, which sell a blended gas made partly from wheat, said to cut emissions by as much as 40%. Drivers should also be aware of the temptation to speed presented by the straight, uncluttered highways. Police regularly pick off visitors and hand out heavy fines.

The weather in Saskatchewan is usually changeable and extreme, but drought has been all too common in recent years.

History
Evidence of aboriginal inhabitation dates from at least 10,000 BC. When Europeans first arrived in the late 17th century, the region was divided among Native Indians of three distinct language groupings. Most prominent among them were the Dene (Chippewa), Cree and Assiniboine. They aided the first explorers and traded furs. White settlers homesteaded in significant numbers from about 1880 and the plains were converted from bison range to farmlands. After 1890, most of the Native people had been confined to reserves and the traditional way of life was pretty much over.

By 1930 the developing agricultural area, together with the railway, led to the immigration of nearly a million Europeans to the prairie provinces. Saskatchewan is home to the socialist movement in Canada and has maintained its allegiance to those ideals more or less since the 1930s.

After WWII the significance of wheat production increased. Farms had to be huge to make mass cultivation viable, and from there urbanization began. The economy diversified as mineral and energy reserves were exploited.

In recent years, the population has remained constant. The number of farmers continues to decline and the towns and cities can't fill the employment gap. Saskatchewan is now mainly urban, with less than 25% of residents living on farms. Regina and Saskatoon, about equal in size, are by far the largest centers. The British, Ukrainian, German, Austrian and Scandinavian ethnic background of most residents is readily noticeable in the numbers of fair-skinned blondes.

Provincial Parks
The parks provide a good chance to see the nonurban areas of the province. Most of Saskatchewan's parks are situated above or below the level of the plains and many contain townsites and residential areas. Parks are open year-round and entry at the gate is usually $7. For more information and camping reservations, contact Saskatchewan Environment and Resource Management (☎ 306-787-2700, 800-667-2757, W www .serm.gov.sk.ca). Cypress Hills and Meadow Lake Provincial Parks are hugely popular with campers in the summer because of the respite from the heat that their forests provide.

Information
Tourism Saskatchewan (☎ 877-237-2273, W www.sasktourism.com) is the provincial body that supplies the public with visitor information. It offers a series of thorough booklets. The accommodation guide is particularly good. In addition, each town has its own small tourist office open daily from June through August and Monday to Friday the rest of the year.

Saskatchewan is on Central Time and, unlike the rest of the country, does not go on summer Daylight Saving Time.

The provincial sales tax is 6%.

Activities
The principal outdoor activities in the province are canoeing and fishing, both of which are done primarily north of Saskatoon in the woodlands. Tourism Saskatchewan's *Vacation Guide* outlines some outdoor possibilities and lists some outfitters.

Whooping cranes, battling extinction, migrate through Saskatchewan on their way between Wood Buffalo National Park and Texas; they're often seen in the southern portions of the province, which means you'll find some good **bird-watching** there. Call the Canadian Wildlife Service in Saskatoon (☎ 306-975-5595) to report sighting information. Last Mountain Lake (north of Regina), Chaplin Lake (west of Moose Jaw) and Galway Bay (west of Kyle) are major waterfowl migration observation points.

Tourism Saskatchewan has a general leaflet suggesting **canoeing** possibilities, as well as detailed booklets on mapped canoe routes from novice to advanced. Prince

SASKATCHEWAN

Albert National Park has designated routes. In Saskatoon, consult the Meewasin Valley Authority (☎ 306-665-6887) for details on canoeing the South Saskatchewan River.

With 100,000 lakes in Saskatchewan, there are bound to be a few hungry fish. Walleye, pike and trout are prime species, and they often attract visitors from the United States. Remote sights require guide service or floatplane transportation. Tourism Saskatchewan produces a great **fishing** and **hunting** guide that lists most outfitters.

If you're interested in **berry-picking**, blueberries, saskatoons (similar to blueberries), raspberries, strawberries and chokecherries are only a few of the fruits that can be culled at farms throughout the province during summer months. Signs along the highways direct you to these delicious stops (and tell you if the place is open). For a map of berry-picking farms, contact the Saskatchewan Fruit Growers Association (☎ 306-645-447, 877-973-7848, **W** www.saskfruit.com).

Regina

pop 200,000

Regina is Saskatchewan's capital. It acts as the commercial, financial and industrial center of the province but is still a relatively quiet prairie town that pretty much closes down after dark. Two interesting facts about the city: Regina is the sunniest capital in Canada and, oddly, every single tree you see here was planted by hand.

History
Cree Indians originally lived in this area, butchering bison and leaving the remains along the creek. It became known as Wascana, a Cree word meaning 'pile of bones.' Later, European settlers were prompted to dub the settlement Pile O'Bones. In 1882 the city was made capital of the Northwest Territories, and its name was changed to Regina in honor of Queen Victoria. The Northwest Mounted Police used the city as a base from the 1880s, and in 1905 it became the capital of the newly formed Saskatchewan.

In 1933, the Cooperative Commonwealth Federation (CCF), a socialist party, held its first national meeting in Regina and called for the end of capitalism. In 1944 it became the first socialist party to form a Canadian provincial government. The CCF merged with the New Democratic Party (NDP) in 1961 to form Canada's left-wing party.

Orientation
The city's two main streets are Victoria Ave, running east-west, and Albert St, going north-south. Both streets are lined with fast-food restaurants and service stations. East of the downtown area, Victoria St becomes Hwy 1 east (the Trans Canada Hwy), bound for Winnipeg. South of the downtown area, Albert St leads to both Hwy 6 (southbound) and Hwy 1 west. Albert St north leads into Hwy 11, which goes to Saskatoon. Black-and-white eyeball street signs around town direct visitors to the city's principal attractions.

The downtown core is bounded by Albert St to the west, 13th Ave to the south, Osler St to the east and the railway tracks to the north.

Victoria Park sits in the middle of the downtown area. Scarth St and 12th Ave, which edge the park, are important shopping streets. Scarth St between 11th and 12th Aves has been converted into a small, pleasant pedestrian mall with trees and benches. On the park's northeast corner is the old city hall, which houses a theater, shops and the Regina Plains Museum. The large Cornwall Shopping Centre, a major mall, is perpendicular to the pedestrian mall on 11th Ave.

Wascana Centre, a 1000-hectare park, is the city's dominant feature and, in addition

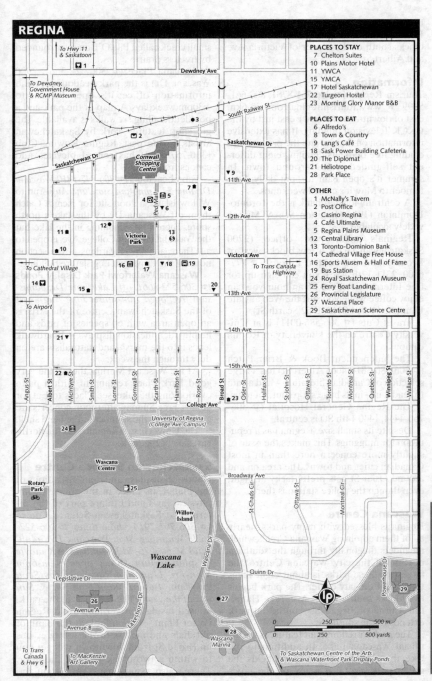

REGINA

To Hwy 11 & Saskatoon

Dewdney Ave

To Dewdney, Government House & RCMP Museum

South Railway St

Saskatchewan Dr

Saskatchewan Dr

Cornwall Shopping Centre

11th Ave

12th Ave

Victoria Park

Victoria Ave

To Cathedral Village

To Trans Canada Highway

To Airport

13th Ave

14th Ave

15th Ave

Angus St · Albert St · McIntyre St · Smith St · Lorne St · Cornwall St · Scarth St · Hamilton St · Rose St · Broad St · Osler St · Halifax St · St John St · Ottawa St · Toronto St · Montreal St · Quebec St · Winnipeg St · Wallace St

College Ave

University of Regina (College Ave Campus)

Wascana Centre

To Trans Canada & Hwy 6

To MacKenzie Art Gallery

Rotary Park

Wascana Lake

Willow Island

Legislative Dr

Avenue A

Avenue B

Lakeshore Dr

Wascana Dr

St Chads Cir · Ottawa St · Montreal Cir

Broadway Ave

Quinn Dr

Powerhouse Dr

Wascana Marina

To Saskatchewan Centre of the Arts & Wascana Waterfront Park Display Ponds

0   250   500 m.
0   250   500 yards

PLACES TO STAY
7   Chelton Suites
10 Plains Motor Hotel
11 YWCA
15 YMCA
17 Hotel Saskatchewan
22 Turgeon Hostel
23 Morning Glory Manor B&B

PLACES TO EAT
6   Alfredo's
8   Town & Country
9   Lang's Café
18 Sask Power Building Cafeteria
20 The Diplomat
21 Heliotrope
28 Park Place

OTHER
1   McNally's Tavern
2   Post Office
3   Casino Regina
4   Café Ultimate
5   Regina Plains Museum
12 Central Library
13 Toronto-Dominion Bank
14 Cathedral Village Free House
16 Sports Musem & Hall of Fame
19 Bus Station
24 Royal Saskatchewan Museum
25 Ferry Boat Landing
26 Provincial Legislature
27 Wascana Place
29 Saskatchewan Science Centre

SASKATCHEWAN

to its natural appeal, contains many of Regina's primary attractions. It lies four blocks south of the corner of Victoria Ave and Albert St.

Information

Tourism Regina (☎ 306-751-8781, 800-661-5099, **w** www.tourismregina.com) is 6km east of downtown on Hwy 1 east just by the CKCK Television building. It has extensive information on the city and the province, including free booklets detailing eight different self-guided walks around town. In summer it's open 8am to 5pm daily; September to May, it's closed weekends.

A centrally located bank is the Toronto-Dominion (1914 Hamilton St). ATMs are widely available.

Regina's main post office (2200 Saskatchewan Dr) is a few blocks west of Broad St. At the Central Library (☎ 777-6000, 2311 12th Ave), you can sign up for free Internet time. For $6 an hour you can enjoy coffee while you surf the Web at Café Ultimate (☎ 584-2112, 1852 Scarth St).

Travel Cuts (☎ 306-586-0011) is at University Centre on the University of Regina campus.

The independent Book & Briar Patch (☎ 306-586-5814, 4065 Albert St) has a large selection of Canadian literature – and a café to read it in – in its huge shop south of town.

The Regina General Hospital (☎ 306-766-4444, 1440 14th St) is central.

Despite its small size, Regina has a reputation for muggings. This makes the issue of slightly more concern here than in most Canadian cities and towns. The area on and around Osler St gets pretty tacky at night, even though the police station is there.

Wascana Centre

Regina is blessed with many parks, nearly all of them adjoining Wascana Creek, which meanders diagonally through the southern portion of the city. Wascana Centre, the largest of these parks, is about eight times the size of the city center. The park begins five blocks south of 12th Ave. Take Hamilton, Lorne or Broad Sts south; the park extends to the southeast.

The park's predominant feature is the artificial Wascana Lake. In addition to the lake, the picnic areas and sports fields, the green park contains many of the city's points of interest. It's hard to imagine, but originally there was nothing here but a small creek called Pile O'Bones surrounded by treeless prairie.

Wascana Place (☎ 306-522-3661, 2900 Wascana Dr) is the park headquarters and information office; it's open 9:30am to 4:30pm weekdays. A map of the park and a booklet detailing six walks is available. The gift shop features work by Saskatchewan artists. In the past, Regina Rowing Club (306-757-0928) has rented bicycles and canoes from here.

Ferry **boat tours** (☎ 306-347-1810, Wascana Dr; tour $2; 1pm-4pm Sun June-Aug) run to Willow Island, a good site for picnics. Catch them off Wascana Dr by the lake's north shore. There's no swimming in the lake but the Wascana Pool, off College Ave, is open to all. There are flower gardens in the section north of the Provincial Legislature building.

Wascana Waterfowl Park Display Ponds (☎ 306-522-3661, off Lakeshore Dr; admission free; open 7am-sunset June-Aug), east of the Saskatchewan Centre of the Arts, is an open area with 60 species of birds and helpful identification displays. A boardwalk leads into the marsh, and naturalists are on duty through the week.

At the Wascana Marina, there's the very good Park Place restaurant with a patio overlooking the lake; see Places to Eat for details. Free Sunday afternoon concerts are given through the summer at the band shell.

The University of Regina is on the northeast side of the park.

Saskatchewan Science Centre

Hands-on displays and demonstrations of the planet, its place in the solar system, physical laws and life are part of the offerings at Saskatchewan Science Centre (☎ 306-791-7914, show times ☎ 306-522-4629, Winnipeg St at Wascana Dr; adult/child $6.50/4.75, $12/9 with IMAX movie or planetarium show; open 9am-6pm Mon-Fri, 11am-6pm Sat-Sun May-Sept; 9am-5pm Tue-Fri, noon-6pm Sat & Sun rest of the year). The center is in the park, housed inside an overhauled old Regina Power Plant – take a look at the bank of old dials and meters in the lobby. A bus up Broad St from downtown will get you to within a two-block walk of the door. There's also a snack bar, a restaurant and a nifty little store. A large-format IMAX movie theater and the Kalium Observatory are other features of the center. Stargazing nights are held two or three times a month at the observatory.

Royal Saskatchewan Museum
State-of-the-art displays snake around this newly renovated museum (☎ 306-787-2815, 2445 Albert St; admission $2/1; open 9am-6pm daily July-early Sept; 9am-5pm Mon-Fri, 11am-4pm Sat & Sun early Sept-June). The First Nations Gallery presents thousands of years of Saskatchewan's Native Indian history with interactive narration and realistic scenes, in addition to films on topics like Native dances. Upstairs there are exhibits of animals native to Saskatchewan, with good accompanying explanations.

MacKenzie Art Gallery
Specializing in Canadian artists, this first-rate museum (☎ 306-522-4242, 3475 Albert St; admission by donation; open 11am-6pm Fri-Tues, 11am-10pm Wed & Thur) evinces a definite contemporary flair. Shows change every few months; recent exhibitors have included the three-dimensional artist Gathie Falk. The gallery hosts a range of events, including film screenings, meet-the-artist sessions and Sunday afternoon tours.

Provincial Legislature
Built in 1919 in loose English Renaissance style at a cost of $3 million, the legislature building (☎ 306-787-5357, Legislative Dr; admission free; open 8am-9pm daily May-Aug, 8am-5pm Sept-Apr) is on the park's west side. Inside, 34 kinds of marble were used. There are free tours on the hour (except at lunchtime) from June to Labor Day. Take a look at the Native Heritage Foundation Gallery, in the east wing, which exhibits and promotes Native Indian art.

Regina Plains Museum
There is life away from the park. The 2nd floor of the old City Hall building downtown is home to the tiny Regina Plains Museum (☎ 306-780-9435, 1835 Scarth St; admission free; open 10am-4pm Mon-Fri). A field made of 14,000 individual stalks of clear-glass wheat set in front of a mirror is the main attraction. You can buy glass wheat souveniers from the reception desk.

Government House
Saskatchewan's current lieutenant governor works (but doesn't live) in this house (☎ 306-787-5717, 4607 Dewdney Ave; admission free; open 10pm-4pm Tues-Sun). The restored home originally belonged to the lieutenant governor of the Northwest Territories and Saskatchewan from 1891 to 1945. The territorial government was set up in 1870 to oversee the huge tract of land that was passing from the control of the fur-trading companies.

The Government House contains furnishings from the turn of the last century. Public tours are offered and sometimes high tea is served in the Victorian ballroom – call for times. The site is northwest of the town center.

RCMP Centennial Museum & Depot
The history of the Royal Canadian Mounted Police, from 1874 onward, is detailed at this museum (☎ 306-780-5838, Dewdney Ave W; admission free; open 8am-6:45pm daily May-Sept, 10am-4:45pm daily Oct-Apr). It was in this part of the country that their slogan 'we always get our man' became legend. On display are uniforms, replicas and stories of some of the famous and notorious exploits of the force. The training facilities and barracks, known as the depot, can also be viewed. Tours run hourly in summer.

At the depot, you can also watch the Sunset Ceremony, a formal drill spectacle of drumming and marching surrounding the flag-lowering – on Tuesday only, at 6:45pm, in July and August.

Sports Museum & Hall of Fame
In the former Land Titles building, a heritage site across from Victoria Park, is a small provincial museum (☎ 306-780-9232, 2205 Victoria Ave; admission by donation; open 9am-5pm Mon-Fri, 1pm-5pm Sat & Sun mid-May–Labor Day). It honors local athletes and teams, with a tribute to Gordie Howe, a local boy made good as one of the greatest players in hockey history.

Antique Mall
For a mooch around on a rainy day or on Sunday, when things are pretty quiet, try the Antique Mall (☎ 306-359-3383, 1175 Rose St; admission free; open 10am-6pm Mon-Sat,

noon-5pm Sun). This grouping of 25 or so antique booths and dealers north of downtown provides plenty to rummage through.

Other Attractions

The **Devonian Pathway** is 11km of paved bike routes through four city parks. It begins and ends at Rotary Park, off the Albert St bridge.

The **Saskatchewan Wheat Pool** (☎ *306-569-4411)* can help you plan a visit to a grain elevator or a livestock sale yard.

Special Events

Saskatchewan Indian Federated College Powwow
Held over a weekend in April, the powwow (☎ 306-779-6328) in the Agridome of the Exhibition Grounds features dancers from around North America, as well as traditional Native Indian crafts and foods.

Buffalo Days This six-day celebration (☎ 306-781-9200) is a big annual event held at the end of July/beginning of August. Stores put up special decor and some workers wear pioneer garb. A talent stage offers free entertainment and the days are filled with competitions, pancake breakfasts, a beard-growing contest and parades, peaking with a big concert and barbecue in Wascana Park on what is known as Pile O'Bones Sunday. The amusement park features rides, music shows, a casino and various displays and exhibits.

Regina Folk Festival This three-day festival (☎ 306-757-7684) is based in Victoria Park but includes concerts elsewhere around town. It's held on a weekend in mid-August.

Agribition A five-day agricultural and livestock show (☎ 306-565-0565) takes place at the end of November.

Places to Stay

Camping Camping in Regina is limited; there are much better spots in the Qu'Appelle Valley, about an hour's drive northeast.

King's Acres (☎ *306-522-1619, Trans Canada Hwy)* Sites $16-24. You'll come to King's Acres as you approach Regina from the east on Hwy 1, near the tourist office. It's geared mainly to trailers and recreational vehicles but has some tent sites.

Hostels *Turgeon Hostel* (☎ *306-791-8165, 2310 McIntyre St)* Dorm beds $17/22 members/nonmembers. This very good HI hostel is in a fine old house once belonging to William Turgeon, an Acadian Frenchman

who was attorney general in 1907. The hostel is quite central – McIntyre St is a residential street near Wascana Centre. It has 50 beds, as well as cooking and laundry facilities, and stays open until midnight.

Canadian Means Quality

Since it's all you're looking at, a word about the golden grain is in order.

Wheat, brought to the New World by European settlers, was largely responsible for the development of the Canadian prairies. It is the primary crop across the provinces of Manitoba, Saskatchewan and Alberta, but by far the bulk of it is grown in Saskatchewan.

So productive are the fields here that Canada is the world's sixth-largest producer, after Russia, China, the USA, India and France. The majority of wheat is produced for the export market. Russia, despite its own massive wheat production, is one of Canada's most important clients. Canadian wheat is sought after for its quality and high protein content.

Because of the cold climate, the principal variety grown is hard red spring wheat, a bread wheat that is planted in spring and harvested in August and September. The other main type is durum wheat, its characteristics making it especially suitable for the production of pasta.

In late summer, when the ripened wheat is golden brown, it is not uncommon to see the huge self-powered combines cutting and threshing through the fields at any hour of the night or day, often in teams. At night in particular, with the bright light beams skimming across the fields from the droning machines, it's quite a memorable sight.

The Canadian Wheat Board markets the crop. This organization represents the farmers, the consumers and the government in buying, selling, setting quotas and regulating export.

Farmers are paid when they deliver their bushels to the grain elevators (see the boxed text 'Wheat Castles of the New World'), where the crop is pooled and sold by the board. Once that is accomplished, the wheat is carried to ports by train and loaded onto freighters for destinations far and wide.

YMCA (☎ 306-757-9622, 2400 13th Ave) Singles $24. The men-only Y rents small single rooms. There's a cheap cafeteria and a pool you can use. Note that in summer it's not unusual for all the rooms to be booked.

YWCA (☎ 306-525-2141, 1940 McIntyre St) Singles $35. For women only, the YWCA is spiffier than the YMCA. There's a kitchen and an Internet room.

B&Bs **Daybreak Bed & Breakfast** (☎ 306-586-0211, 316 Habkirk Dr) Singles/doubles around $24/36. Daybreak is a 12-minute drive southwest of town. There are two rooms, plus a friendly dog and cat in residence. Free transportation both to and from the airport or bus terminal is offered.

Morning Glory Manor B&B (☎ 306-525-2945, 1718 College Ave) Singles/doubles $45-55/55-65. This 1923 home with a country decor is near Wascana park. It has really comfortable beds (two per room).

Motels The east side of town along Victoria St has the cheapies.

Sherwood House Motel (☎ 306-586-3131, fax 306-584-7490, 3915 Albert St) Singles/doubles $57/60. The modern-if-boring rooms at the Sherwood are on the cheaper side of what's available in town.

Days Inn (☎ 306-522-3297, fax 306-522-0807, 3875 Eastgate Dr E) Singles/doubles $63-89/67-89. Newer and less flimsy furnishings than most motels fill up the rooms at the Days Inn on the Trans Canada. There's a laundry room and an indoor pool with waterslide.

North Star (☎ 306-352-0723, Hwy 1 E) Rooms $33. It's basic in the extreme and in need of work, but the rooms are clean and the beds are okay.

Hotels **Plains Motor Hotel** (☎ 306-757-8661, fax 306-525-8522, 1965 Albert St at Victoria Ave) Singles/doubles $39-41/43. A decent budget hotel, the Plains is central. Each room has its own bath. There's a restaurant and free parking. When turned on, the neon tower atop the hotel sign indicates the weather forecast – blue means clear, green means precipitation and orange means unsettled weather. If the lights are running up, the temperature will rise, and vice versa.

Chelton Suites (☎ 306-5549-4600, fax 306-569-3531, 1907 11th Ave) Rooms $65-95. Right downtown, near the casino, this 'suite' hotel really just has slightly larger than normal rooms with a mini-fridge and microwave.

Hotel Saskatchewan (☎ 306-522-7691, fax 306-757-5521, 2125 Victoria Ave) Rooms $99-149. This historic business-oriented hotel has a grand lobby. The restaurant serves high tea Friday and Saturday afternoons.

Places to Eat

Most options listed here are in the central area, many of which are closed on Sunday nights. That said, most of the eateries around the outskirts remain open, and the Saturday newspaper is full of ads for Sunday brunch buffets. A hearty one is served at the **Regina Hungarian Cultural & Social Club** (☎ 306-522-8182, 1925 McAra St; brunch $8), east of downtown off Victoria Ave.

Sask Power Building Cafeteria (☎ 306-566-2553, 2025 Victoria Ave) Breakfast $2-$4, lunch $2.75-$5.25. The 13th floor of the central office building provides great views of the city. The inexpensive cafeteria is open for breakfast and lunch Monday to Friday. A little gallery lines the walls from the elevator to the dining room.

Town & Country (☎ 306-757-0915, 1825 Rose St) Dishes $4-8. This is a basic, friendly place, good for breakfast.

Lang's Café (☎ 204-757-5655, 1745 Broad St) Dishes $5.50-8.50. The decor is plastic, but the food is cheap. Vietnamese and Thai dishes are especially good.

Heliotrope (☎ 306-569-3373, 2204 McIntyre St) Dishes $5-12. Interesting world cuisine is served in this casual whole-food vegetarian house. Soups, like the squash coconut, are quite tasty.

Alfredo's (☎ 204-585-3838, 1801 Scarth St) Dishes $7-14. On the downtown pedestrian mall, this eatery has two dining rooms. The wine bar with streetfront patio allows smoking, the restaurant in the rear doesn't. Standard pastas and pizzas are done well.

Park Place (☎ 306-522-9999, 3000 Wascana Dr) Dishes $10-20. The location of this restaurant – overlooking Wascana Lake – means that reservations are suggested for both lunch and dinner. It's open every day.

The Creek in Cathedral Bistro (☎ 306-352-4448, 3414 13th Ave) Lunch dishes $6-9, dinner dishes $17-20. Jazz music, steel cable lighting and old pictures of the area set the stage, but the food performs. Dishes like venison sirloin with sundried cranberries and spaetzle (dumplings), or seafood ragout in a leek and vermouth sauce, are as dramatic as they are delicious.

The Diplomat (☎ *306-359-3366, 2032 Broad St*) Lunch dishes $8-12, dinner dishes $20-24. For a quality steak, the Diplomat is a well-established upscale tradition.

Farmers' market (*Scarth St at Victoria Ave; open 11am-4pm Wed, 8am-1pm Sat June-Aug*) This smallish seasonal market is set up on the east side of Victoria Park. Produce and baked goods (including jams and pies), as well as some crafts, are offered for sale. Call the tourist office for more information.

Entertainment

For a list of events, browse *Prairie Dog*, the free local entertainment monthly.

McNally's Tavern (☎ *306-522-4774, 2226 Dewdney Ave*) Irish bands and 24 beers on tap make this a lively evening hangout. The shepherd's pie isn't bad either. There are a few other nightspots on this street north of the town center, so parking is tough. A taxi is a good idea.

Cathedral Village Free House (☎ *306-359-1661, 2062 Albert St*) Local microbrews are served in a sunny courtyard during summer, in a cozy pub the rest of the year.

The Break & Voodoo Lounge (☎ *306-546-3666, 2540 Victoria Ave E*) Dance music and pool tables are the two different sides of this nightclub. Friday and Saturday nights the place is open extra, extra late.

Casino Regina (☎ *306-565-3000, 1880 Saskatchewan Dr*) The fine, defunct old train station houses a casino and restaurant. You can try your luck from 9am to 4am seven days a week.

If you're looking for more upscale entertainment, Regina offers a number of performing arts options.

MacKenzie Art Gallery (*tickets* ☎ *306-584-8890, 3475 Albert St*) A theatrical dramatization of the 1885 court battle, *The Trial of Louis Riel* is enacted at the art gallery. One of Canada's most famous historical figures, the leader of the French Métis, Riel led two uprisings against the British government. The re-creation of the trial highlights issues that are still relevant. Shows are Wednesday to Friday mid-July to

mid-August. Tickets ($11) are available at the tourist office or at the door.

Globe Theatre (☎ *306-525-6400,* **W** *www .globetheatrelive.com, 1801 Scarth St*) This theater in the round presents classic plays and experimental works from August to April.

Saskatchewan Centre of the Arts (☎ *306-565-4500,* **W** *www.centreofarts.sk.ca, 200 Lakeshore Dr*) The concert hall in the park hosts a variety of performances, from folk to rock to opera. It's also home to the symphony orchestra.

There's also a *repertory cinema* (☎ *306-777-6104, 2311 12th Ave*) showing art films in the lower level of the Central Library.

Spectator Sports

In summer and autumn, the Saskatchewan Roughriders (☎ *306-525-22181,* **W** *www .saskriders.com*) play Canadian Football League (CFL) games at *Taylor Field* (*2940 10th Ave*).

Curling is a major winter sport on the prairies, and the Curlodrome at *Exhibition Park* (☎ *306-781-9300,* **W** *www.regina exhibition.com, 1700 Elphinstone St*) holds major competitions, known as bonspiels, through the snowy months. Best described as shuffleboard on ice, curling involves one member throwing the 'rock,' as teammates sweep the path with a broom to increase friction and influence the rock's course.

Getting There & Away

Air Canada (☎ *888-247-2262,* **W** *www.air canada.ca*) has flights throughout the country and on to international destinations. WestJet (☎ *888-937-8538,* **W** *www .westjet.com*) serves Vancouver, Calgary, Edmonton and Thunder Bay from Regina.

The bus station (2041 Hamilton St) is downtown, just south of Victoria Ave. There are luggage-storage lockers and a quick-lunch counter. Greyhound and Saskatchewan Transportation Company buses share the same number (☎ *306-787-3360*) – together they cover the province and country. Four Greyhound buses make the ride west to Calgary ($94, 10 hours) and east to Winnipeg ($65, 7½ to nine hours). Three Saskatchewan buses a day head to Saskatoon ($34, three hours). The hostel has cheap bus tickets available to members.

There's no train service in or out of the city.

For hitching east, take the No 4 bus from downtown; going west, grab the No 79 Albert Park.

Getting Around

The airport is about a 15-minute drive southwest of downtown, and the only way to get there is by taxi, which costs about $9. Try Capital Cabs (☎ 306-791-2225).

Regina Transit (☎ 306-777-7433, **w** www .reginatransit.com) operates the bus routes around the city. Buses run from 6am to midnight Monday to Saturday and from 1:30pm to 8:30pm on Sunday. The fare is $1.60.

The car rental company Thrifty (☎ 306-525-1000) has an outlet in the airport and one centrally located in the Holiday Inn (1975 Broad St). Other chain companies have offices at the airport as well.

AROUND REGINA
Lumsden

Northwest of Regina, Lumsden sits nestled and protected in a convoluted, lumpy, hilly little valley on the main road (Route 11) to Saskatoon. The Franciscan monks here run St Michael's Retreat (☎ 306-731-3316), which offers weekend and weeklong guided retreats and programs including food and accommodations.

Qu'Appelle Valley

The Qu'Appelle Valley runs east-west from the town of Fort Qu'Appelle, northeast of Regina, and makes a good contrast to the prairies. Following the Qu'Appelle River and interspersed with lakes, this valley is one of Saskatchewan's green and pretty playgrounds.

There are several provincial parks and historic sites along the glacially formed valley. Only 37km northwest of Regina, Craven is an easy day trip. Nearby, you can tour a fur-trading post in **Last Mountain House Provincial Historic Park** (☎ 306-787-2700, Hwy 20; admission $7; open noon-5pm Fri-Mon July–Labor Day). Staff, displays and reconstructed buildings tell the story of the site, which dates around 1870.

The **Kinsmen Big Valley Jamboree**, held annually in the middle of July, is one of the province's big country-music festivals, drawing acts from around Canada and the USA. Beer gardens, free camping and booths selling all manner of western garb are part of the three-day event.

In August, the **Craven Valley Stampede** is worth catching. Chuck-wagon races, roping contests and country and western music are some of the features.

Fort Qu'Appelle
pop 2200

Fort Qu'Appelle lies northeast of Regina by the Qu'Appelle River. The **Fort Qu'Appelle Museum** (☎ 306-332-6643, Bay Ave at Third St; admission $3/2; open 1pm-5pm mid-May–early Sept) has a collection of Native Indian artifacts, pioneer articles and some things from the old Hudson's Bay Company post (1864), which is adjacent to the museum.

Each year in early or mid-August a large **Native Indian powwow** takes place at the Standing Buffalo Reserve, 9km west of town. Dance competitors come from far and wide. Call the Qu'Appelle Valley Friendship Centre (☎ 306-332-4685) for more information.

Also west of town is the **Echo Valley Provincial Park** (☎ 306-332-3215, Route 220) with a *campground*, swimming and trails around the valley.

Eastern Saskatchewan

VEREGIN

Veregin lies near the Manitoba border, north of Yorkton and 265km northeast of Regina. A series of mainly reconstructed buildings and homes reveal aspects of settlers' lives in a religious community circa 1900 at the **Doukhobour Heritage Village** (☎ 306-542-4441, Hwy 5; admission $3/1.50; open 10am-6pm daily mid-May–mid-Sept, 10am-4pm Mon-Fri rest of the year). Houses and the Prayer Home are decorated in typical traditional fashion and include some attractive textiles. You can sometimes buy bread baked in the old-style brick ovens.

YORKTON

This area, with its strong Ukrainian and Eastern European heritage, is a good spot for the branch of the Western Development

SASKATCHEWAN

Museum that depicts the struggles of the various immigrant groups in the province. **WDM Story of People** (☎ *306-783-8361, Hwy 16 W; admission $5; open 10am-5pm daily May-Sept, 1pm-5pm Tues-Sun Oct-Apr*) is a great indoor/outdoor museum of daily life.

On the ceiling of the church dome at **St Mary's Ukrainian Catholic Church** (☎ *306-783-4549, 155 Catherine St*), Stephen Meuhsh painted a fresco that rivals the work of artists in Europe. The doors are always open for inspiration, and donations are accepted.

Every May the town hosts the **Yorkton Short Film and Video Festival** (☎ *306-782-7077*, **W** *www.yorktonshortfilm.org*), the oldest continuously running short-film festival in North America.

Veregin & the Doukhobours

Veregin is a small, essentially unknown town, more or less in the middle of nowhere, but it has a rather unexpected, intriguing history. The town and its surrounding area were settled between 1898 and 1899 by the Doukhobours, a determined and somewhat extraordinary religious sect from Russia.

At the turn of the 20th century, with help from writer Leo Tolstoy, many of these people left their homeland and the persecution there to come to Saskatchewan in search of religious freedom and seclusion. Here, under the leadership of Peter Veregin, they created a small but successful community. Bliss was not to last, however, and soon the Doukhobours were once again in trouble with their neighbors and the government.

The problem? The Doukhobours were known to resist any type of mainstream authority. Partially based on fact, though somewhat exaggerated, are the well-known tales of nude demonstrations and arson that have, rightly or wrongly, come to be closely associated with the group.

After about 20 years here, many of the Doukhobours moved to British Columbia, where there's still a community. In the 1950s some of them returned to Russia or once again headed to new lands, this time settling in Paraguay.

Broadway St has standard restaurants and several motels. With rooms running $70 to $100, **Patrick Place** (☎ *306-641-0119, 88 5th Ave N*) has more character. The elegant white house is full of history that the owners will gladly share.

Within an hour's drive are **Good Spirit Provincial Park**, with beaches and sand dunes, and the larger **Duck Mountain Provincial Park**, on the border of Manitoba. Dauphin is two hours away.

CROOKED LAKE PROVINCIAL PARK

Due south of Yorkton, 30km north of the Trans Canada, Crooked Lake Park (☎ *306-728-7480, Route 247*) can make a pleasant overnight camping stop under the elms. The park is along the eastern stretches of the rolling Qu'Appelle Valley and Qu'Appelle River.

MOOSE MOUNTAIN PROVINCIAL PARK

South of the Trans Canada Hwy, Moose Mountain (☎ *306-577-2600, Hwy 9*) provides an oasis of aspen on a plateau. If you're looking for activities, you've found them. ***Kennosee Inn Resort Hotel*** (☎ *306-577-2099, Hwy 9*) is the park lodge. On-site or nearby are waterslide parks, golf courses, mini-golf, horseback riding, baseball diamonds, hiking, biking, and cross-country trails.

Twenty-six kilometers southeast of the park is **Cannington Manor Historic Park** (☎ *306-787-2700, Route 603; adult/child $2.50/2; open 10am-6pm Wed-Mon May-Sept*). English settlers built a limestone mansion here unlike anything seen on the 1890s prairie. All that remains of the utopian community are a few restored buildings.

ESTEVAN
pop 10,900
Near the US border, Estevan is one of the largest towns in southern Saskatchewan. It's a town with energy – it has the world's largest deposits of lignite coal, three electrical generating stations and some natural gas pockets and is surrounded by oilfields.

Local attractions include the sandstone rock formations at **La Roche Percée**, once a site of Native Indian religious observance, and the **Estevan Brick Wildlife Display**, which has samples (stuffed and live) of most local species, including bison and antelope.

Ask at the tourist office about rock hounding (rock collecting) or visiting the dam and coal mines. There are about half a dozen standard motels.

South of town in North Portal, the **Cadillac Hotel** used to play host to infamous Chicago gangster Al Capone – this was a huge booze-smuggling area during the Prohibition days (1920–33) in the USA.

WEYBURN
pop 10,100

From Weyburn, a farming supply center, the so-called CanAm International Hwy leads northward to Regina and beyond, and southward through North and South Dakota and Wyoming in the US. Weyburn is the birthplace of Canadian author WO Mitchell and the setting for his best-known book, *Who Has Seen The Wind*, about a boy growing up.

The **Soo Line Historical Museum** (☎ *306-842-2922, 411 Industrial Lane; admission $1; 9am-8pm Mon-Sat, 1-8pm Sun May-Sept; 1pm-5pm Mon-Fri Oct-Apr*) has some Native Indian artifacts and articles from the pioneer days.

Southwestern Saskatchewan

Running across the southern section of the province is the Red Coat Trail, a highway route from Winnipeg, Manitoba to Lethbridge, Alberta. The trail is named after the Mounties and roughly parallels the route they took in coming to tame the west. Tourist offices have a pamphlet highlighting the historical and geographical points of interest along the way. Here, as in much of the province, the government parks have areas of geographic, historic or cultural significance.

The sights in this section form a circular drive (east to west, south and then west to east), and it's possible to follow this route and continue up Route 2 to Saskatoon without doubling back.

MOOSE JAW

Situated halfway between the former railway towns of Winnipeg and Calgary,

Moose Jaw was selected as a major Canadian Pacific Railway terminal in the late 19th century. Theories on the origins of the once-heard, never-forgotten name are numerous and nebulous; *moosegaw* is a Cree word meaning 'warm breezes,' so this possibility has some credence. The town center has a historic character to it, with many surviving brick buildings from the town's boom days in the 1920s. Around town 33 large murals illustrate the past. History and several not-to-miss sights – like the spa and the tunnels – make Moose Jaw one of the most interesting towns in the province.

The chamber of commerce operates a substantial information office (☎ 306-693-8097) on the Trans Canada Hwy, beside the statue of the moose. It's open 9am to 5pm daily in July and August, 9am to 5pm weekdays from September to June. Out-of-province cars can park free at meters in town.

The downtown Greyhound station (☎ 306-692-2345) is on High St, one block east of Main St. There are numerous trips daily to Regina and one for Saskatoon.

Things to See & Do
The **Temple Gardens Mineral Spa** (☎ *306-694-5055, 24 Fairford St; admission $7; open 9am-11pm daily*), in the downtown Temple Gardens Resort Hotel, draws a lot of visitors. The heated mineral pool is the main attraction, but there's a lengthy list of pampering services offered. Extended hours are available to hotel guests.

Highly recommended is the stranger-than-fiction **Tunnels of Moose Jaws** (☎ *306-693-5261, office: 108 Main St; adult/child $12/6 for one tour, $19/9 for both tours; open 10am-5:30pm Mon-Thur, noon-7:30pm Fri-Sun*). Millions of dollars have gone into creating two different tunnel tours. The 'Chicago Connection' is a re-creation of 1920s gangster Al Capone's hideout (he's really thought to have lived down here). A whole city comes to life underground – with tommy-gun toting actors leading the way. The 'Passage to Fortune' tells the somewhat more somber and strictly historic tale of Chinese immigrants in Moose Jaw who lived in the tunnels before prohibition. They came to Canada seeking a better life but encountered racism and worked in deplorable conditions to raise the money required to become citizens. For some, the only housing they could afford was hidden in these basements and passageways. Again live actors, animatronics and re-created and historic settings tell the story. Each tour takes about an hour and they are both worth seeing.

The development of transportation, from horse-drawn conveyances onward, is chronicled in the **Western Development Museums – History of Transportation** (☎ 306-693-5989, 50 Diefenbaker Dr; admission $6/2; open 9am-6pm daily). In addition to old carts, antique autos, train cars and small planes, look for the Lorch Snowplane: a propeller-driven ski bus that could reach speeds of 100km on the ice.

The **Burrowing Owl Interpretive Area** (☎ 306-692-1765, 250 Thatcher Dr; admission $3; open 9am-5pm daily May-Sept) at the Exhibition Grounds offers a glimpse of these little-known endangered birds.

Curiosity seekers might enjoy the **Sukanen Ship & Pioneer Village Museum** (☎ 306-693-7315, Hwy 2 S; admission $3; open 10am-5pm Mon-Fri May-Oct), 13km out of town, with plenty of pioneer relics and remains and a ship built here for sailing on the sea.

You can take a tour of the town and its murals with the **Moose Jaw Trolley Company** (☎ 306-693-8537, 24 Fairford St E).

Moose Jaw is also home to the famous Snowbirds, an aerial acrobatic squadron that performs at air shows across the continent. The **Saskatchewan Air Show**, the largest on the prairies, is held here each July.

Places to Stay
Prairie Oasis Complex (☎ 306-692-4894 or 1-800-854-8855, Thatcher Dr E at Hwy 1) Sites $16-20, rooms $48-120. This is a family-oriented recreation center (it has water-slides, restaurant, laundry, etc) with mobile homes, rooms with kitchens, motel rooms and campsites.

Capone's Hideaway Motel (☎ 306-692-6422, 1 Main St. N) Singles/doubles $40-45/45-50. Across from the tunnels and the old rail station, this motel, marked by an antique car as a sign, even has a few 1920s theme rooms. Rates include continental breakfast.

Temple Gardens Resort Hotel (☎ 306-694-5055, fax 306-694-8310, 24 Fairford St E) Rooms $80-140. The best thing about this hotel is the complimentary big fluffy bathrobes and flip-flops you can wear to pad down to the spa pool. The rooms aren't bad either.

CHAPLIN LAKE
West of Moose Jaw, stop at the Interpretive Site here beside the mounds of snowlike sodium sulphate produced by Chaplin Lake. Like other salty lakes in the province, this one supports brine shrimp (sea monkeys!), which in turn attracts thousands of shorebirds, many of them endangered. For bird-watchers, a dusty road encircles the lake and tours are offered from the **Chaplin Nature Center** (☎ 306-395-2770, Hwy 1; tour prices vary; open May-Sept). Farther west on the Trans Canada, watch for the American white pelicans at Reed Lake beside Morse.

SWIFT CURRENT
A bed or a meal in transit can be found without difficulty in the farm center of Swift Current off the Trans Canada Hwy. It's a good base for day trips to Eastend (see separate heading, later). The **Mennonite Heritage Village** (☎ 306-773-7685, Kinetic Park; open May to Sept) reveals something of this Christian sect. You can also tour through the religious Hutterite community off Hwy 4 north of town; call ☎ 306-778-2327 for an appointment.

SASKATCHEWAN LANDING PROVINCIAL PARK
Straight north from Swift Current, the section of the Saskatchewan River here was used as a crossing point by the early European explorers and, later, the white settlers. **Goodwin House** (☎ 306-375-5525, Hwy 4; open 8am-4:30pm Mon-Fri, 10am-6pm Sat-Sun May-Sept), built by the North West Mounted Police, is the visitors' center, with historical details and information on Native Indian sites within the park. There's also camping and hiking.

GREAT SAND HILLS
Just west of Swift Current (north of Gull Lake and Maple Creek) is a semidesert area with dunes and near-arid vegetation. The best viewing area is about 10km south of the little village of **Sceptre**, in the northwestern section of the hills near the town of Leader.

MAPLE CREEK

At the edge of Cypress Hills (see that section, below), 20km north of the park, Maple Creek is worth a stop during the **Cowboy Poetry Gathering** weekend (usually in September). Begun in 1989, the event attracts storytellers and singers who carry on the tradition. You can also see the work of artisans such as saddle-makers and silversmiths. On Saturday night there's a big Western dance. Call the Jasper Centre (☎ 306-662-2434) for more information. The other reason to visit this town is to stock up on provisions at the shiny new co-op grocery store before heading into Cypress Hills.

CYPRESS HILLS INTERPROVINCIAL PARK

Straddling the provincial border, the park (☎ *306-662-4411*) typifies this region of small lakes, streams, trees and green hills up to 1400m high; it offers a great place for camping and hiking.

The western block sector is larger and more natural, while the services are mostly on the Alberta side. A dirt road links this area to the national historic site **Fort Walsh** (☎ *306-662-3590, Park Rd; adult/child $6/3; open 9:30am-5:30pm May-Thanksgiving)*. The fort, built in the late 1870s as a North West Mounted Police base, is a remnant of the district's rich but sad history. The hills, always a sanctuary for animals, were at one time also a welcoming retreat for the Plains Indians. Information at the old fort tells the story of the time when 'a man's life was worth a horse and a horse was worth a pint of whiskey.'

The center block sector has many facilities: bicycle and rowboat rental, pony rides, a store, resort, restaurant, swimming pool. Camping in the four shady campgrounds is so popular that summer weekends are often booked as soon as advance reservations open on January 1. For more information, call ☎ 306-662-5411. The *Cypress Park Resort Inn (☎ 306-662-4477, Park Rd; rooms/cabins $65-75/$55-75; open year-round)* is another busy option.

EASTEND

Quiet Eastend, 1½ hours southwest of Swift Current on Hwy 13, is surrounded by badlands, which, early in the morning or at dusk, offer panoramas of pinks and golds, textures and shadows. Pick up the 'Guide to the Valley of Hidden Secrets' for a self-guided driving tour of the nearby geographical highlights. Jones Peak is good at sunset. Nearby, Sioux chief Crazy Horse once camped.

In 1994 excavations unearthed the first *Tyrannosaurus rex* skeleton discovered in Saskatchewan. It proved to be one of the most complete found anywhere. Visit the **T Rex Discovery Centre** (☎ *306-295-4009, Hwy 13; admission by donation; open 9am-5pm Mon-Fri, 11am-4pm Sat & Sun May-Sept; closed lunchtime rest of the year)* to see parts of it. The center is a working lab, but a larger museum is underway. In summer you can reserve a spot to go out on a dig ($75).

GRASSLANDS NATIONAL PARK

Not yet developed, this park preserves noteworthy flora and fauna, as well as remarkable geological and historical features. It's a two-section park lying between Val Marie and Killdear, south of Swift Current and west of Assiniboia. The eastern block consists of the Killdeer Badlands west of Wood Mountain Post Provincial Park. The park's western section lies along the Frenchmen River Valley southeast from the town of Val Marie, at the junction of Hwy 4 and Hwy 18.

Information and the latest details on the park are available at the park's service office and visitors' center (☎ *306-298-2257, Hwy 4)* in Val Marie, as are all the area services; it's open 8:30am to 5pm daily June to August, 8:30am to noon and 1pm to 4:30pm weekdays the rest of the year. There are no toilets, potable water or formal campsites or trails in the park (aside from the antelope and mule deer tracks). Guided hikes are offered in summer months and no-trace camping is allowed. There's a driving route with an interpretive pamphlet.

Surrounded by ranchland, the park protects a section of original, natural, short-grass prairie land. Features include the badlands, 70-Mile Butte (the second-highest point in the province), cliffs and coulees (gulches, usually dry), a prairie-dog town (near where endangered burrowing owls nest) and some historic Native Indian sites.

Val Marie is tiny but contains one of the best places to stay in the province if you're into character. *The Convent B&B (☎ 306-289-4515, Hwy 4; singles/doubles $37-45/54-61)* is actually in a restored convent. The wood-work is impressive and the white duvet covers complement the rich oak tones of wall-unit cupboards. Full breakfast is included, and exquisite dinners are available by reservation. Tender pork medallions in a soy-orange redux are far from the ordinary, prevalent fried food. A huge lounge with overstuffed furniture and a left-book library provide a great place to relax after a hike.

Also in town is a good museum/gallery/ literary bookstore in **The Brick School House** (☎ 306-298-4910, Center St).

BIG MUDDY BADLANDS

Off Hwy 34 south of Regina and Moose Jaw, near the US border, this hot area of sandstone formations, hills and valleys was once used by stagecoach robbers, cattle rustlers and all the other bad-guy types you see in Western movies. In fact, the outlaw Butch Cassidy used to ride here.

These badlands are more spread out and harder to explore than those in southern Alberta. Here, many of the most interesting formations are on private lands. If you really want to explore, try **Cornach & District Tours** (☎ 306-267-3312, Box 722, Cornach), which offers tours of the Big Muddy. The conspicuous **Castle Butte**, 4km west off Hwy 34 and 25km north of Hwy 18, is a sort of elaborate upside-down bowl sticking up on the prairie.

Small, musty old hotels are available in Benough and Cornach. The ***Big Beaver Regional Park*** (☎ 306-267-4520, 1st at Main St; open June-Sept; sites $8-12) is a basic campground.

Farther east, two provincial parks may be of interest. **Wood Mountain Post Historic Park** (☎ 306-266-2016, Hwy 18; admission $5; open 10am-5pm Thur-Mon June–mid-Aug) covers more-recent history, with displays on the North West Mounted Police and the Sioux people. Wood Mountain was where Chief Sitting Bull brought his Sioux warriors after their victory against Custer at the famous 1876 Battle of Little Bighorn (in what is now Montana, USA). There are some reconstructed buildings and tours are given.

At **St Victor's Petroglyphs** there are prehistoric Native Indian carvings in the rock. At press time, the site was closed for archeological work. Call ☎ 306-787-2700 to check on it.

Saskatoon

pop 232,000

Saskatoon is a small, slow-paced city sitting smack in the middle of the Canadian prairies. The clean, wide streets, low skyline and flat surroundings give the city a Western flavor. The South Saskatchewan River meanders through the center, banked by parkland that provides a welcome touch of greenery and shade. Seven bridges link the city across the river. The largest employer in town is the university, and Saskatoon has pretty much become the provincial cultural center, with an active arts community.

History

In 1883, 35 members of the Temperance Colonization Colony from Ontario founded a settlement on these Cree lands. The town stayed (though the ban on alcohol didn't), taking its name from the Cree word *misaskwatomin,* for one of the indigenous berries still enjoyed today in pies and jams. (The saskatoon berry is similar to, but a little more fibrous than, a blueberry.) In 1890 the railway hit town and growth continued until the Depression. The city has had its ups and downs since then but is now well established and diversified beyond its agricultural roots. Uranium mines and some of the world's largest potash deposits are found nearby.

Orientation

The South Saskatchewan River cuts through the city diagonally from northeast to southwest. The main downtown area lies on the west bank; the university is on the opposite side.

Idylwyld Dr divides the city's streets into their east and west designations. Out of town in each direction, Idylwyld Dr becomes Hwy 16, the Yellowhead Hwy. The city is split into north-south sections by 22nd St, and the streets on either side are marked accordingly. Streets run east-west, avenues north-south.

The main street is 2nd Ave. Another important street is 21st St E, with its blend of new and old architecture and lots of stores, bookended by the Delta Bessborough at one end and Midtown Plaza, the old CN train station, at the other.

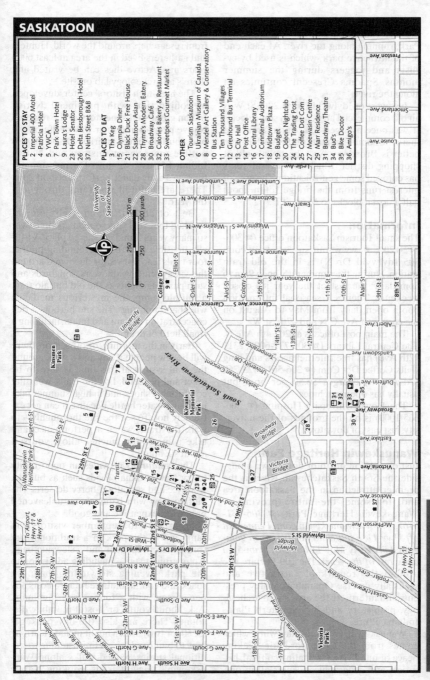

SASKATOON

PLACES TO STAY
2 Imperial 400 Motel
4 Patricia Hotel
5 YWCA
7 Park Town Hotel
9 Laura's Lodge
23 Hotel Senator
26 Delta Bessborough Hotel
37 Ninth Street B&B

PLACES TO EAT
3 The Keg
15 Olympia Diner
21 Black Duck Free House
22 Saskatoon Asian
28 Thyme's Modern Eatery
30 Broadway Café
32 Calories Bakery & Restaurant
33 Sweetpeas Gourmet Market

OTHER
1 Tourism Saskatoon
6 Ukrainian Museum of Canada
8 Mendel Art Gallery & Conservatory
10 Bus Station
11 Ten Thousand Villages
12 Greyhound Bus Terminal
13 City Hall
14 Post Office
16 Central Library
17 Centennial Auditorium
18 Midtown Plaza
19 Budget
20 Odeon Nightclub
24 The Trading Post
25 Coffee Dot Com
27 Meewasin Centre
29 Marr Residence
31 Broadway Theatre
34 Bud's
35 Bike Doctor
36 Amigo's

SASKATCHEWAN

Behind the Delta Bessborough is one of the city's large parks, Kiwanis Memorial Park, running along the river. At each end of the attractive park, which is used by cyclists and joggers during the summer months, Spadina Crescent continues on along the river.

Just west of Idylwyld Dr on 20th St W is an old commercial area, now in some decay. It was once a largely Ukrainian area, and there are some remnants of this past. Faring better is Broadway Ave, the town's oldest shopping district, which for several years has enjoyed some gentrification. The area of interest runs from the bridge south about half a dozen blocks to Main St E.

Information

The small Tourism Saskatoon office (☎ 306-242-1206, W www.tourismsaskatoon.com, 305 Idylwyld Dr N) is in the old train station. During the summer it's open 9am to 5pm daily; the rest of the year it's closed weekends. There's a seasonal information booth open daily from May to August on the corner of Ave C N and 47th St W.

The main post office is at 202 4th Ave N. The Central Library (☎ 306-777-6000, 2311 12th Ave) has free Internet access and long waits. Coffee Dot Com (☎ 306-561-2923, 269 3rd Ave S) charges $6.50 per hour but usually has open machines.

The Royal University Hospital (☎ 306-665-1000) is on the grounds of the university, just east of downtown.

Wanuskewin Heritage Park

Just over 17km north of downtown alongside the South Saskatchewan River is the premier attraction in the Saskatoon area and, for some, the entire province – Wanuskewin Heritage Park (☎ 306-931-6767, W www.wanuskewin.com, Penner Rd off Hwy 11; adult/child $6.50/4; open 9am-9pm daily early May-Labor Day, 9am-5pm daily rest of the year). The 100-hectare site around the remarkably attractive and scenically diverse Opamihaw Valley presents and interprets the area's rich archeology, prehistory and the Northern Plains Indian culture.

Wanuskewin (wah-nus-**kay**-win), which comes from the Cree word for 'seeking peace of mind,' is a fascinating cultural, historical and geographical center all in one.

Two dozen prehistoric archeological sites have been unearthed, attracting attention from researchers around the world. Hunters and gatherers lived in the area at least 6000 years ago. Active digs can be visited and there's an archeology lab on-site.

The high-tech visitors' center, developed in conjunction with provincial Native Indian groups, tells the story of the regional Native peoples and their way of life on the once buffalo-filled prairies. Displays also outline more-recent history and Native Indian life as it is now. During summer there are daily dance performances at 2pm. There are cultural programs throughout the year.

Best of all is the land itself, left untouched to reveal why so many people over so many years found it a sacred place. Virtually invisible from the surrounding prairie, four trails lead the visitor down and around the valley amid wildflowers, songbirds and such park highlights as the old buffalo trail, a buffalo jump, the mysterious medicine wheel and tipi rings. The site harbors a rich concentration of flora and fauna, including a small herd of deer.

Early in the morning, or off-season, there will be few people if any and a walk around the trail system at this time is sure to be quiet and peaceful. For the trails, wear flat comfortable shoes, and in high summer take juice or a water bottle because it can get extremely hot. To see the site thoroughly – to walk the trails, watch a performance, and take a break for lunch – allow yourself about six hours.

The *restaurant* provides an opportunity to try Native Indian foods such as buffalo, wild rice and saskatoon-berry desserts. The buffalo stew with bannock, an unleavened bread, is inexpensive and good.

From June to September visitors can camp out in the park in a traditional *tipi* (bring insect repellent and a sleeping bag). An overnight stay – including admission to the park, evening storytelling, bannock snack and continental breakfast – costs $69 per person, with a four-person minimum. Ask about youth or hostel-member discounts. There are also full-day packages ($250 for two), which might include learning how to build and raise a tipi, listening to traditional stories, guided walks along Wanuskewin's ancient trails, cooking Native

[handwritten margin notes: 5/29/04 – very interesting, but a bit "white-washed" – still worth the visit. Selective memories. Trail of the Buffalo – beautiful.]

Indian foods and making crafts such as dream catchers.

Airport pick-up and drop-off can be arranged. Otherwise, getting to the site presents some difficulties for those without a car. Pretty much the only option is an expensive cab ($20 one way). The Lawson Heights No 18 bus only gets you to within about 8km. If you're staying at the Patricia Hotel or area B&Bs, mention to the managers that you'd like to go to Wanuskewin and they may be able to arrange transportation, especially if there's a bunch of you.

Western Development Museum

You open the door of the re-created 1910 boomtown (☎ 306-931-1910, 2610 Lorne Ave S; adult/child $6/2; open 9am-5pm daily) and you're looking down Main St. It looks like a movie set: stores, workshops, a hotel, rooming houses, a printing shop and other establishments outfitted with all manner of period goods and costumed mannequins. You can take your friend's picture in an antique car or have yours professionally snapped (for a fee) in the photographer's studio on the block. There's also a cafeteria on-site that has a historic dining room, which is part of the set.

The museum is quite a way south of town. The No 1 Exhibition bus brings you here from 2nd Ave downtown. When leaving the museum, get on the bus going the same way as when you arrived; it loops around.

Ukrainian Museum of Canada

Preserving and presenting Ukrainian heritage through articles donated by Ukrainian immigrants is the mission of this museum (☎ 306-244-3800, 910 Spadina Crescent E; adult/child $2/1; open 10am-5pm Mon-Sat, 1pm-5pm Sun May-early Sept, closed Mon rest of the year). A highlight is the collection of colorful textiles used in formal and everyday dress and for other household purposes. Other items are the painted eggs (pysanka) and a brief history of the pioneers' arrival. There are branches of this museum, affiliated with the Ukrainian Orthodox church, in other Canadian cities, such as Winnipeg and Edmonton, but this is the main one.

Ukraina Museum

This slightly smaller museum (☎ 306-244-4212, 202 Ave M S; adult/child $2/1; open 11am-5pm daily) has examples of Ukrainian crafts and dress, and exhibits that portray aspects of Ukrainian culture from prehistoric times to the mid-20th century. All in one large room, it seems more lively than the other museum, despite similarities. The staff members, of Ukrainian descent, still visit that nation frequently and are quite knowledgeable about the history. They can open the Ukrainian-Catholic Cathedral of St George next door for you – and it's a must-see. Every surface in the onion-domed, Byzantine church is intricately painted with icons of saints and Mary or Jesus. Arches, domes, walls – the building is an art museum in stunning deep colors.

Marr Residence

A block from the river in the historic Nutana neighborhood sits Saskatoon's oldest building (☎ 306-665-6887, 326 11th St E; admission by donation; open 10am-5pm weekends July-Aug), still in its original location. Built in 1884, it was used as a hospital the following year, during the North West Rebellion.

Meewasin Valley & Centre

The pretty, green Meewasin Valley follows the South Saskatchewan River down the middle of the city. (Meewasin is a Cree word meaning 'beautiful valley.') From behind the Bessborough Hotel, the valley park runs in both directions and on both sides of the river for a total of 17km.

The Meewasin Valley Trail is good for walking and cycling, and picnic tables are scattered among the trees, where black-and-white magpies flit. Bridges span the river at several places and the trail follows the banks on both sides.

The Meewasin Centre (☎ 306-665-6888, 402 3rd Ave S; admission by donation; open 9am-5pm daily) is really a mini-museum about the river and the city's history, with an informative slide show. Although it's hard to imagine, the river is melted glacier ice from a section of the Rockies far to the west near Lethbridge, Alberta. The Meewasin Centre also has good maps of the trail.

Mendel Art Gallery & Conservatory

A short walk along the river from the downtown area brings you to the Mendel Art

Gallery (*☎ 306-975-7610, 950 Spadina Crescent E; admission by donation; open 9am-9pm daily*). Recent exhibits have been quite, um, contemporary (in other words: out there). The small conservatory has a few palms, among other plants.

Saskatchewan Indian Cultural Centre

Vibrant Native art is on display at this 2nd-floor interpretive center (*☎ 306-244-1146, 120 33rd St E; admission free; open 9am-noon & 1pm-5pm Mon-Fri*). The only drawback is that there are no labels explaining the origin of the colorful paintings, clothing and sculpture. You can buy language instruction tapes, and videos on Native dance and on building a birch-bark canoe.

University of Saskatchewan

Parking on campus is tough, especially at the Place Riel information center (☎ 306-966-4343, Wiggins Rd). Here you can get maps of the campus and sights like the **Diefenbaker Centre** (*☎ 306-966-8384, Diefenbaker Place; admission free; open 9:30am-8pm Tue-Thur, noon-5pm Sun*). The museum details aspects of former prime minister's Diefenbaker's life and career.

Forestry Farm Park & Zoo

This park (*☎ 306-975-3382, 1903 Forest Dr; park admission $2/vehicle, zoo admission adult/child $4.50/2.50; open 10am-4pm daily Apr-Sept*) is 8km northeast of the downtown area. The zoo inside the park is home to around 300 animals, mostly those found in Saskatchewan and other parts of Canada: wolves, lynx, caribou and bison. There are also gardens, picnic sites, a restaurant and a fishing lake. In winter the park has a ski trail.

Beaver Creek Conservation Area

Follow Lorne Ave S 13km from Idylwyld Bridge in the Meewasin Valley to the Beaver Creek Conservation Area (*☎ 306-374-2474, Hwy 219; admission by donation; open 9am-9pm daily June-Aug, noon-5pm Sat & Sun Sept-Oct & Feb-May*), a large park protecting some of the river valley and its wildlife. Walking trails run through the area and the information center provides geographical and historical background.

Saskatchewan Railway Museum

The province's railway history is spread out at this museum yard (*☎ 306-382-9855, 2km south of Hodgson Rd on Hwy 60; adult/child $2/1; open 1pm-6pm Sat & Sun early May-early Sept*). There are engines, cabooses and even transplanted railway buildings.

Berry Barn

On a working farm 11km southwest of town, the Berry Barn (*☎ 306-978-9797, 830 Valley Rd; open 11am-5pm Apr-Sept, 11am-8pm Fri-Tues Oct-Christmas*) sells a range of foods made with the saskatoon berry. Light, berry-filled meals are offered at tables overlooking the Saskatchewan River. Try the Belgian waffles with complimentary topping bar. There's also a substantial gift shop. In season, you can go into the fields and pick your own berries.

Organized Tours

Shearwater Boat Cruises (*☎ 306-549-2452, 950 Spadina Crescent E; open May-Sept*) has frequent one-hour trips (adult/child $10/6) along the river departing from behind the Mendel Art Gallery.

Canoeski Discovery (*☎ 306-653-5693, W www.canoeski.com, 1618 9th Ave N*) offers canoe and ski tours, including three- to four-day packages around the province ($450). **Canada Ways Canoeing** (*☎ 306-373-2671, 318 Wollaston Rise*) has three-hour get-your-feet-wet canoeing lessons ($20) on demand, as well as Saskatchewan River day outings ($30) and overnight trips ($125).

Special Events

All of Saskatoon's crowd-drawing events happen in the summer.

Shakespeare on the Saskatchewan Each year, one play by the Bard is presented June through August in a tent near the river by the Mendel Art Gallery. Performances are in the evening and advance tickets are advised; call ☎ 306-652-9100 for bookings.

Saskatchewan Jazz Festival This festival (☎ 306-652-1421) is held at the end of June or beginning of July and takes place at various locations around town. Most of the concerts and performances are free.

Louis Riel Day This is a one-day event held in the first week of July, with various outdoor activities and contests taking place by the Bessborough Hotel.

The Exhibition Held over eight days in mid-July, The Exhibition features livestock competitions, exhibits, concerts, rides and parades.

International Fringe Festival At the end of July, look for this weeklong festival, showcasing varied, experimental and inexpensive theater, including drama, mime, comedy and dance.

Folkfest This three-day festival (☎ 306-931-0100) takes place in mid-August. The $10 fee gets you into 25 multicultural pavilions set up around the city, where you'll find food, crafts, music and dances. A free shuttle bus does the circuit.

Places to Stay

Camping *Gordon Howe Campground* (☎ 306-975-3328, Ave P south of 11th St) Serviced/unserviced $19/12. Open May-Sept. Operated by the City Parks Department, it's fairly green and, although geared to campervans, there are some tent sites. It's often full on weekends. There's a small store for basic supplies.

Saskatoon 16 West RV Park (☎ 306-931-8905, Hwy 16 at 71st St) Serviced/unserviced $22/17. Open Apr-Oct. This RV park with a laundromat and convenience store is just a five-minute drive northwest of town on Hwy 16.

Hostels *University of Saskatchewan* (☎ 306-966-8600, 131 Saskatchewan Hall) Singles/doubles $23/28. Open May-Aug. Accommodation is available during summer at the university, a 25-minute walk northeast of town along the river. There's a three-day minimum.

Laura's Lodge (☎ 306-934-7011, 1026 College Dr) Singles/doubles $30/40. Across the street from the university and hospital, Laura's mainly attracts guests who are visiting loved ones. This is a great, reasonable place to stay. The recently renovated, private rooms have twin or double beds with shared bath. Each room has a calling-card phone. The common areas are large: a TV lounge, a full kitchen, a laundry room. Reserve ahead.

YWCA (☎ 306-244-2844, 525 25th St E) Singles $39. The YWCA rents small rooms to women. There's a pool and a shared kitchen on-site.

Patricia Hotel (☎ 306-242-8861, 345 2nd Ave N) Dorm beds $14, singles/doubles $40/50. The Patricia is right downtown, an easy walk to the bus station. Unfortunately, the inexpensive bar downstairs can be very, very noisy until late.

B&Bs *Chaplin's Country B&B* (☎ 306-931-3353, 7km E of Hwy 11 on Route 354) Singles/doubles $40/55. This wonderful 40-hectare farm, about 11km southeast of town, comes complete with cows, pigs, sheep and goats. The wood-paneled home has country decor and comfy tall beds in rooms with shared bath. Big breakfasts often include garden treats like fresh tomatoes or homemade apple syrup.

Ninth St B&B (☎ 306-244-3754, **W** www.bbcanada/949.html, 9th St E) Singles/doubles $52/56-60. The three rooms in this stylish old home are tastefully decorated – and they have private baths! A short walk across the river from the historic Nutana district takes you to the city center. There is free airport transportation and bicycle loaners are available.

Brighton House (☎ 306-664-3278, fax 306-664-6822, **W** www.bbcanada/567.html, 1308 5th Ave N) Singles/doubles $50-60/60-70. Adorned with gingerbread detailing, the partially pink Brighton house features a garden hot tub, a guest laundry, bicycles to use, and for a small fee transportation can be arranged. Rooms come with telephone. The house is about 2km north of downtown on a major bus line.

Motels *Colonial Square Motel* (☎ 306-343-1676, fax 306-956-1313, 1301 8th St E) Rooms $62-69. On busy, commercial 8th St, the Colonial is near many restaurants and shops. The rooms are pleasant and predictable but entirely clean and safe.

Imperial 400 (☎ 306-244-2901, fax 306-244-6063, 610 Idylwyld Dr N) Rooms $69. This motel is a member of a reliable, province-wide chain. Most, including the Saskatoon version, have laundry rooms, waterslides and pools.

Hotels *Hotel Senator* (☎ 306-244-6141, fax 306-244-1559, 243 21st St E) Singles/doubles $62/72 for new rooms, $52/62 for old rooms. The historic downtown Senator is the oldest operating hotel in Saskatchewan. The highly ornamented lobby, restaurant and pub reflect this status. Upstairs don't let the worn hallway carpet fool you; half the rooms have brand-new furniture.

Park Town Hotel (☎ 306-244-5564, fax 306-665-8698, 924 Spadina Crescent E) Singles/doubles $70/78. Moving up the scale

↳ stayed 8/26 – 8/28/04 nice.

is the Park Town, which overlooks the river close to the Ukrainian Museum. Rooms are standard hotel issue, but the views are great, and on weekdays a courtesy van will take you anywhere you need to go in town.

Delta Bessborough (☎ 306-244-5521, fax 306-244-5521, 601 Spadina Crescent E) Rooms $99-200. The classic Bessborough is a city landmark, one of Canada's grand railroad hotels. The large, expensive, chateau-like place can't be missed at the bottom of 21st St, by the river.

Places to Eat

Olympia Diner (☎ 306-244-1513, 120 2nd Ave N) Dishes $4-14. Open 24 hours. This is a basic, all-purpose restaurant, but it has a varied menu. Breakfasts are a good deal and will hold you long past lunch.

Saskatoon Asian (☎ 306-665-5959, 136 2nd Ave S) Dishes $6-10. The menu offers mainly Vietnamese dishes, but there are also some Thai-influenced items and Chinese plates to round out the options.

Black Duck Free House (☎ 306-244-8850, 154 2nd Ave S) Dishes $6-15. Beer is the staple at this pub, but the fish and chips are good too.

The Keg (☎ 204-653-3633, 301 Ontario Ave N at 24th St) Dishes $11-16. The Keg (a national chain), on the corner of 24th St, is a medium-priced place serving good steaks. There's an outdoor patio and a popular bar adjoining the restaurant.

Broadway Ave, with its variety of eateries and a couple of coffee shops, is worth strolling at feeding time.

Thyme's Modern Eatery (☎ 306-477-7774, 626 Broadway Ave) Dishes $4-7. At this primarily vegetarian café, the offerings are mostly light, like sandwich wraps.

⊛***Broadway Café*** (☎ 306-652-8244, 818 Broadway Ave) Dishes $5-10. This is a busy 1950s-style burger-and-sandwich joint.

⊛***Calories Bakery & Restaurant*** (☎ 306-665-7991, 721 Broadway Ave) Lunch dishes $6-9, dinner dishes $12-18. Once primarily a bakery, Calories is now a popular restaurant. Inventive salads and incredible breads are lunch highlights. ⤳ excellent!

Around the outskirts, 8th St E and 22nd St W both offer abundant choices:

Poverino's (☎ 306-955-7319, 1625 8th St E) Dishes $6-10. Large portions of cheap pasta are this chain restaurant's specialty.

Touch of the Ukraine (☎ 306-382-7774, 2401 22nd St W) Dishes $5-11. If you get a craving for good pierogies and cabbage rolls, come here. Many customers still speak Ukrainian.

Granary (☎ 306-373-6655, 2806 8th St E) Meals around $20. For a choice of prime rib, steak or seafood, and a prairie-artifact-filled atmosphere, try the Granary. ⤳ $ $!

Taunte Maria's Mennonite Restaurant (☎ 306-931-3212, Faithful Ave at 51st St) Dishes $4-14. Open Mon-Sat. Toward Wanuskewin, this restaurant, a block or so off Idylwyld Dr N, offers basic healthy farm food for any meal of the day. The soups are excellent.

Entertainment

Broadway Ave has a multitude of bars and cafés, so if you're looking for evening entertainment, just take a stroll.

Bud's (☎ 306-244-4155, 817 Broadway Ave) Live rhythm and blues nightly and a Saturday afternoon jam are highlights.

Odeon Nightclub (☎ 361-651-1000, 241 2nd Ave S) The dance beat pulses at this stylish downtown haunt in the old Royal Bank building. ⤳ music starts late llpm

Amigo's (☎ 306-652-4912, 632 10th St E) This Tex-Mex bar features alternative local and regional bands.

Jax Nightclub (☎ 306-934-4444, 302 Pacific Ave) The old warehouse area around the corner of 24th St and Pacific Ave near Ontario Ave has become a mini-nightlife district. Jax is one of the places that's jumpin'.

Centennial Auditorium (☎ 306-938-7800, 35 22nd St E) The Saskatoon Symphony plays regularly from September to May at its home venue. Large-scale theatrical productions and dance performances are also held here.

Persephone Theatre (☎ 306-384-7727, 2802 Rusholme Rd) This theater puts on less-than-commonplace shows.

Broadway Theatre (☎ 306-652-6556, 715 Broadway Ave) This historic cinema shows cult classics and art films.

Spectator Sports

The Saskatoon Blades (☎ 306-938-7800, w www.saskatoonblades.com) play Western League (which includes four Canadian provinces and two US states) junior hockey from September to March at ***Saskatchewan Place*** (3535 Thatcher Ave).

great for breakfast

Camping site at Wanuskewin Heritage Site, Saskatchewan

Grain silos in the early morning light, Saskatchewan

Traditional Native dancing at Wanuskewin Heritage Site, Saskatchewan

RICK RUDNICKI

Taking a wild ride at the Calgary Stampede, Alberta

ROSS BARNETT

Rough-and-tumble badlands scenery in Dinosaur Provincial Park, Alberta

RICK RUDNICKI

Racing down the bobsled track at Canada Olympic Park, Calgary, Alberta

ANDREW BROWNBILL

Moraine Lake, surrounded by the Rocky Mountains in Banff National Park

Shopping

Broadway Ave has some cute and quirky little shops among its restaurants and bars. There are also a few interesting shops downtown, including:

Trading Post (☎ *306-653-1769, 226 2nd Ave S*) This shop specializes in crafts and souvenirs, with an emphasis on Native Indian goods. There's some junk but also some fine Cowichan-style wool sweaters and British Columbian jade.

Ten Thousand Villages (*143 2nd Ave N*) A North America–wide chain, Ten Thousand Villages is a nonprofit run by the Mennonite Central Committee, which hires native craftspeople in small places all over the world to create the pieces that are sold in these stores.

Getting There & Away

The airport is 8km from the center, in the northeast of the city, off Idylwyld Dr. Air Canada (☎ 888-247-2262, W www.air canada.ca) connects to international destinations through Winnipeg and Calgary. WestJet (☎ 877-952-4638, W www.westjet .com) is an alternative for domestic destinations like Winnipeg and Calgary. Transwest Air (☎ 306-665-2370, 800-667-9356, W www .transwestair.com) serves Prince Albert and various small northern towns from Saskatoon and Regina.

The big Greyhound bus depot (☎ 306-933-8000, 23rd St E at Ontario Ave) serves various destinations throughout Saskatchewan from the Transit Terminal. Buses run to Regina ($35), Prince Albert ($21), Watrous ($17), and Waskesiu ($32) from June to August. The trip to Calgary (seven to 11 hours) and the trip to Winnipeg (11 to 16 hours) both cost about $85. The station has a cafeteria and the washrooms even have showers, which people with tickets can use.

This station's is way out, a long drive west from downtown on Chappell Dr. The taxi fare is about $15. You'll be even less happy with the Saskatoon timetable. Trains run to Edmonton ($61, six hours) and on to Jasper and Vancouver three times a week, on Monday, Thursday and Saturday at 2:35am. Trains also run three times a week, to Winnipeg ($87, 9½ hours) and on to Toronto on Monday, Wednesday and Saturday at 2:25am. There's no train service to Regina.

Getting Around

A taxi to the airport costs about $14. Alternatively, catch the No 1 bus from the Transit Terminal, a section of 23rd St E between 2nd and 3rd Aves N that is blocked off to all traffic but the buses. Tell the driver you're going to the airport because you'll need to transfer to a No 21 en route. There's a bus every half hour through the day.

All routes and schedules can be accessed through the city bus information line (☎ 360-975-3100). Many of the bus routes begin at the Transit Terminal. There are signs for all the bus routes, benches to sit on and lots of people milling about waiting. One of the drivers will be able to help you with any destination questions. Bus fare is $1.60.

Budget (☎ 306-244-7925, 234 1st Ave S) offers car rental. Rates vary wildly depending on promotions. There are other local and well known companies, including Avis and Thrifty, around town and at the airport.

Bicycles can be rented at the Bike Doctor (☎ 306-664-8555, 623 Main St) for about $15 a day.

MANITOU BEACH

Six kilometers north of the town of Watrous, about 120km southeast of Saskatoon, Little Manitou Lake contains mineral water 13 times denser than that of the Dead Sea. It was called Lake of Healing Waters by the Plains Indians and in the 1930s and '40s became a bustling Canadian resort. Today, small Manitou Beach isn't as fashionable, but you can still swim in the very buoyant, pungent-smelling lake for free. Everything in town is walking distance.

The **Manitou Springs Resort & Mineral Spa** (☎ *306-946-2233, Lake Ave at Watrous St; single bath $8.50; rooms $75-105*) has three large indoor pools heated to different temperatures. The minerals in the water (and the reflection off the cedar ceiling) make your bath the color of watery brown mustard. Don't be turned off by the color; the buoyancy is too much fun – like being a weightless astronaut twirling about. Buy an inflatable travel pillow at the entrance and you can float as flat as if you were in bed. While you soak, you're alleviating the pressure on your joints and giving your skin a nourishing mineral oil treatment.

You can take the waters in a more private atmosphere at **Mineral Bath House**

(☎ 306-946-4174, Lake Ave at Unwin St; single bath $8.50 per person). One-, two-, four- and six-person tubs are available. You have control of the water temperature and bubble jets.

If you're feeling too relaxed, head over to **Danceland** (☎ 306-946-2743, Lake Ave at Hunler St; buffet & dance $20; 5pm-late nightly June-July, 5pm-late Fri & Sat rest of the year) and swing to live big bands. The original 1920s dance floor 'floats' on a horsehair bed.

The white-sided, garden-set **Lakeside Country Inn** (☎ 306-946-3456, Winnipeg St at MacLachlan Ave; rooms $49-69 with full breakfast) is a pleasant place to stay. Rooms come with either baths en suite or private baths down the hall. A TV lounge room has complimentary tea and coffee and snacks for a small fee. Another option is **Manitou Nu-Inn** (☎ 306-946-3350, MacLachlan Ave at Winnipeg St; rooms $49-90), with basic nonsmoking motel rooms on the beach.

The **Jemm Minimart** (☎ 306-946-2833, Hwy 365 at Lake Ave) serves as the bus station in Manitou Beach. Buses to/from Regina ($24) run on Tuesday and Thursday.

On Hwy 2, at the north end of Last Mountain Lake, the Canadian Wildlife Service runs the **Last Mountain Lake National Wildlife Area** (☎ 306-836-2022, Hwy 15; admission by donation; open dawn-dusk). This is a great spot to watch migrating sandhill cranes in fall. There's a little unattended interpretive building that's always open. You can get driving maps here.

Northern Saskatchewan

The area north of Saskatoon seems like the northern portion of the province and it's referred to that way, but really this is central Saskatchewan. Geographically speaking, Prince Albert National Park isn't even halfway to the northern border, so technically north begins somewhere beyond that point.

From Saskatoon, Hwy 16 (the Yellowhead Hwy) runs northwest through North Battleford on its way to Edmonton and British Columbia. Between Saskatoon and Prince Albert is a rolling farm belt that runs the width of the province. Prince Albert

seems a long way north and the growing season is indeed short. At Prince Albert the land begins to change, and Prince Albert National Park, just north of town, marks the start of the vast boreal (northern) forest that takes up the northern half of Saskatchewan.

Saskatchewan has more than 100,000 lakes, and a good percentage of these are in the wilderness regions north of Prince Albert. This rugged region of the province is much like the north of the country everywhere from Newfoundland westward. It forms part of the rough, rocky Canadian Shield. The national park and several others in the region are about as far north as most visitors (or residents) get.

In the summertime, Native Indian dance competitions are held throughout the area on weekends. For more information on the Pow Wow trail, call the Indian Métis Friendship Centre (☎ 306-764-3431) in Prince Albert.

PRINCE ALBERT
pop 39,000

Prince Albert is the most northerly town of any size in the province. Forests lie to the north, the flat grain fields to the south. It also sits right in the middle between Alberta and Manitoba. Known as PA, it serves as the jumping-off point for trips into the huge Prince Albert National Park. In 1776 a fur-trading post was built here among the Cree. The town was founded in 1866 by a churchman who came to set up a mission, and was named after Queen Victoria's husband.

In 1988 the South African diamond company De Beers staked a claim on some land 40km or so from Prince Albert. Since then, with obvious respect for De Beers' expertise, millions of hectares nearby have been staked for diamond searching, and processing of ore has begun at some of the sites.

The Tourism and Convention Bureau (☎ 306-953-4385, 3700 2nd Ave W) has a lot of information on the park and points north, as well as the town.

There are a couple of quite minor attractions. The **Historical Museum** (☎ 306-764-2992, Central Ave At River St E), in the old fire station, has displays on the city's past and a tearoom overlooking the North Saskatchewan River.

Prince Albert is the location of a major three-part prison. (The locals could have opted for a university but they chose a penitentiary instead.) The **Rotary Museum of Police & Corrections** and the **Evolution of Education Museum** (☎ 306-953-4385, 3700 2nd Ave W; admission $2; open 10am-8pm May-Sept) are on the tourist office property.

In mid-August, Prince Albert hosts a large powwow at the Exhibition Grounds and in mid-September there's a Métis Fall Festival.

Places to Stay & Eat

Super 8 Motel (☎ 306-953-0088, fax 306-763-8388, 4444 2nd Ave W) Singles/doubles $40/45. This clean motel is owned and run by the Peter Balantyne Cree Nation.

Carry's Bed and Breakfast (☎ 306-922-7474, **W** www.bbcanada.com/careybb, 1904 1st Ave E) Singles/doubles $50/60. Freshly painted rooms and new queen beds add a touch of modern comfort to a 1904 home – as do the private cable TVs and Internet access.

Amy's on Second (☎ 306-763-1515, 2990 2nd Ave W) Dishes $6-16. Known far and wide for excellent food, Amy's serves tasty specialties like grilled pickerel or steaming hot wild-rice soup. Don't miss the cheesecake. There's a cozy fire and local art on the walls.

Tannin's Restaurant & Wine Bar (☎ 306-763-4252, 2685 2nd Ave W) Dishes $10-20. Tannin's serves tapas and a large selection of wines by the glass in addition to Continental fare.

Getting There & Away

Transwest Air (☎ 800-667-9356, **W** www.transwestair.com) flies to Saskatoon and La Ronge.

The bus station (☎ 306-953-3700, 99 15th St E) is downtown. There's one bus a day for Saskatoon ($18) and one a day (the Lac La Ronge bus) to Waskesiu ($12) in the national park (May to September).

AROUND PRINCE ALBERT

The area north of town is known as the lake district, a relatively undeveloped area of woods, bush, lakes and cottages. In addition to those found within the national park, other mega-lakes of the region are Candle Lake, with a provincial park, and Montreal Lake.

Land of the Loon Resort (☎ 306-982-4478, on Christopher Lake; rooms/cabins

Grey Owl at Home in the Wilderness

Naturalist Grey Owl was somewhat of a legend through the 1930s for his writings and lectures on conservation and for his love of the wilderness. He toured widely across North America and the United Kingdom, encouraging preservation and appreciation of the environment. His first book, *The Men of the Last Frontier*, was published in 1931. *Tales of an Empty Cabin*, published in 1936, is possibly his best-known work.

Upon his death in 1938 in Prince Albert, it was discovered that he had assumed a false identity and lifestyle as a Native Indian and that in fact he was Archibald Stansfield Belaney of Hastings, England. This only enhanced his reputation. He had emigrated to Canada, become a trapper and guide, married an Iroquois woman and been adopted as a brother by the Ojibway tribe.

His wife, Anahereo, who died in 1986, was awarded the Order of Canada for her work in conservation. Her ashes are buried by the graves of Grey Owl and their only daughter, beside the cabin where they lived and worked in Prince Albert National Park. Much of his research was done in the park.

The small, simple, one-room cabin on Ajawaan Lake has become a pilgrimage site of sorts. From here, the couple worked to restore the nearly obliterated beaver population. The cabin, known as Beaver Lodge, sits right on a beaver lodge by the lake's edge.

It is still a fairly inaccessible spot, but it can be reached one of two ways. First is the Grey Owl Trail, a 20km hike along Kingsmere Lake. Alternatively, you can canoe from the end of the road, on Kingsmere River upstream to Kingsmere Lake. From there, paddle across the lake to the northern end, where there is a choice of either a 3km walking trail or a 1km portage to Ajawaan Lake; from there you can paddle to the cabin.

SASKATCHEWAN

$75/85-130) is a destination itself. The buildings are all new-log construction and the dining hall has entertainment on weekends. Here you can rent sailboats, small horse-power motor boats, canoes, kayaks and cross-country skis, depending on the season.

PRINCE ALBERT NATIONAL PARK

The national park (☎ 306-663-5424, Route 263 or Route 264; admission $4 per day, $18 for 3 days; open year-round) is a huge, primarily wilderness tract of softly rolling terrain where the prairie of the south turns to the woodland of the north. Among the geographic features are huge, cool lakes, spruce bogs and forested uplands. There are trails of greatly varying lengths and good canoe routes providing access to much of the park. There's fishing, a range of camping possibilities and, in winter, cross-country ski trails.

Other highlights are **Lavallee Lake** (with the second-largest white-pelican colony in the country), the herd of **wild bison** in the southwestern grassland portion of the park and the four-hour hike to a cabin occupied for seven years by the controversial conservationist **Grey Owl**. The top of the Shady Lake lookout tower is a great place to see a sunset.

The park's southern border is about 50km north of Prince Albert. The resort village of **Waskesiu**, on the huge lake of the same name, acts as the park's focal point. Here you'll find the information center, lodging, restaurants, groceries, gasoline and a sandy beach with swimming. In season, don't expect peace and quiet in the busy townsite; out of season pretty much everything closes up. The natural expanse is hard to explore without a car, as the trailheads and marinas are outside of the town.

The three **marinas** (☎ 306-663-5994) within the park rent canoes. Waskesiu Lake is way too big and rough for most paddlers – you need to transport the canoe to one of the smaller lakes. The office can recommend good three-day ventures.

There are many **campgrounds** (☎ 888-333-7267 for reservations) in the park. Beaver Glen and the trailer park are about a 20-minute walk from where the bus stops in Waskesiu. These are popular and fill up on midsummer weekends; it's best to arrive as early as possible on a Friday or reserve in advance. Other camping areas are geared to tenters. The smaller campgrounds are simple and quiet, or there's backcountry camping for canoeists and hikers.

Among the 10 or so accommodation possibilities in town, **Skyline Motel** (☎ 306-663-5373, fax 306-663-1928, Waskesiu Dr at Balsam St; rooms $50-60; open May-Thanksgiving) is among the lowest priced, though there are no nonsmoking rooms. **Lakeview Hotel** (☎ 306-663-5311, fax 306-663-5543, Lakeview Dr at Willam St; rooms $54-74) is one of the few open year-round.

Outside of town is the most alluring accommodation. **Kapasiwin Bungalows** (☎ 306-663-5225, fax 306-663-5225, 2500 Northshore Rd; cabins $85-105; open May-Sept) is the only one on the lake. You're much more likely to find peace here.

LAC LA RONGE PROVINCIAL PARK

The park (☎ 800-772-4064, Hwy 2; admission $7), which completely surrounds enormous, island-filled Lac la Ronge, is Saskatchewan's largest provincial park. Aside from the main lake, it contains about 100 more and a portion of the Churchill River known for its falls and rapids. Here the trees are shorter, more scattered and mostly pine. Floatplanes are the transportation of choice for trips farther north. See the Tourism Saskatchewan brochure on hunting and fishing for a list of outfitters.

On the west side of the park is the small village of **La Ronge**. In town, **Robertson's Trading Post** (☎ 306-425-2080, La Ronge Ave) is an attraction as well as a supply store. In addition to selling groceries, winter moccasins and handmade birch toboggans, Robertson's still actively buys and sells wild fur. The pelts and trophies in the back of the store are reminiscent of an earlier time.

Free tours are given of the **La Ronge Wild Rice Corporation** (☎ 306-425-2283, 1210 Poirier Rd; tours by appt weekdays mid-Aug–mid-Oct), which processes the rice gathered by local producers. If you are not familiar with Canadian wild rice, don't miss giving it a taste. Long used by Native peoples, it's black-hulled and has a mild, nutty flavor. It's also sold in local stores.

In the lobby of **Mistasinihk Place** (La Ronge Ave at Louis Rd; admission free;

open 7:30am-5pm Mon-Fri), a governmental office building, there are displays on the life, crafts and history of the people of the north.

You can rent a canoe for $25 a day from Sundance Marina (☎ 306-425-5000, Hwy 2 S, behind Lakeshore Esso), which also offers boat tours; prices vary depending on duration, destination and number of people.

Nut Point Campground (☎ 800-772-4064, eastern end of La Ronge Ave; serviced/unserviced sites $20/15) can be found at the trailhead to the Nut Point Hike, 1.6km from town.

Among the four or five motels, the *Waterbase Inn (☎ 306-425-2224, 303 La Ronge Ave; singles/doubles $70/75)* has doors opening out onto the stark-looking lake.

Transwest Air (☎ 800-667-9356, W www.transwestair.com, 303 La Ronge Ave) has regular service to Prince Albert and Saskatoon and offers charter service in floatplanes to points north. Although there are no scheduled one-hour sightseeing floatplane rides, you could probably talk the pilots into it for a price – if there are no fishermen chartering the planes.

An hour north of town on less-than-paved road is **Stanely Mission**, the oldest standing building in Saskatchewan. This church can be seen from across a narrow waterway.

REDBERRY LAKE
About an hour's drive northwest of Saskatoon off Hwy 40, Redberry Lake is a prime bird-watching location. The lake and its islands are protected as a federal bird sanctuary. Of greatest interest are the large, white pelicans and the small, scarcer piping plover, but there are many others.

BATOCHE NATIONAL HISTORIC SITE
Northeast of Saskatoon, 80km up Hwy 11 and off Hwy 312 from the town of Rosthern, is the site of the 1885 Battle of Batoche (☎ 306-423-6227, Route 225; adult/child $4/3; open 9am-5pm daily early May-Sept), fought between the government and the Métis (led by Louis Riel). Batoche was the center of a Métis settlement and its provisional government in the late 19th century; many of these people had left Manitoba after running into difficulties over land there. The visitors' center tells the story of the battle and includes an audiovisual display on the Métis from the 1860s to the present.

Wheat Castles of the New World

The unique, striking, columnar red, green or gray grain elevators seen along rail lines across the province are the classic symbols of midwestern Canada. These vertical wheat warehouses have been called the 'castles of the New World' and to this day are the artificial structures most visible across the plains.

Simple in design and material and built solely for function, they have been described as Canada's most distinctive architectural form. Western painters, photographers and writers have used them as sources of inspiration and turned them into objects of art.

Across much of the province grain elevators have come to represent the economic life of the town and district. Indeed, they have topped in size, if not in importance, that other traditional landmark, the church.

The first grain elevators were built in the 1880s. As Canada became the 'breadbasket of the world' at the start of the 20th century, the number of elevators mushroomed, reaching a peak of nearly 5800 in 1938. Consolidation and changing conditions have brought that number down to just 700. Their destruction concerns many individuals and groups who hope to prevent (not just lament) their disappearance.

Formerly made entirely of wood, they are now built from materials such as steel and cement. The classic shape, about 10m square and 20m high, is being experimented with as well, in an attempt to improve efficiency.

The stark beauty of elevators catching the light or looming out of the horizon is certainly an unmistakable part of the prairie landscape.

NORTH OF BATOCHE

Just north of Batoche on Hwy 11, **Duck Lake** is worth a brief stop. Throughout the town, which has been revamped with antique street lamps and brick sidewalks, painted murals tell some of the area's cultural and historical stories. One outlines the tale of a Cree, Almighty Voice, and how he and a white policeman ended up dying over the killing of a cow.

Twenty-six kilometers farther west, **Fort Carlton Historic Park** (☎ 306-787-2700, *Route 212; adult/child $2.50/2; open 10am-6pm early May-early Sept*) provides more information on the fur trade, the treaties signed with the Plains Indians and the Riel rebellion.

THE BATTLEFORDS

The Battlefords refers to two towns linked by bridge across the North Saskatchewan River and the adjacent district, about 140km northwest of Saskatoon off the Yellowhead Hwy.

Located in North Battleford is the interesting **Western Development Museum – Heritage Farm & Village** (☎ *306-445-8083, Hwy 16 at Hwy 40; adult/child $6/2; open 9am-5pm daily early May-early Sept, 12:30pm-4:30pm Wed-Sun rest of the year*). The outdoor village with wooden sidewalks includes fully outfitted houses, from a modest Ukrainian hut to an upscale French doctor's brick house. Other buildings you can enter include the general store, pharmacy, livery stable, dairy barns – all are linked by an old-fashioned crank telephone system so you can talk to people in other buildings.

Also in town, some of the best-known Cree artwork is on display at the **Alan Sapp Gallery** (☎ *306-445-1760, 1 Railway Ave; admission by donation; open 1pm-5pm daily June-Sept, 1pm-5pm Wed-Sun Oct-May*).

In 1876 the North West Mounted Police built what is now **Fort Battleford National Historic Site** (☎ *306-937-2621; adult/child $4/2; open 9am-5pm daily mid-May–mid-Sept*), 5km south on Hwy 16. Guides in costume help you explore the five buildings full of police and Native Indian artifacts, tools and memorabilia.

Turn Stone Manor B&B (☎ 306-445-5122, Ⓦ *www.bbcanada.com/4804.html, 1391 97th St; singles/doubles $69/79*) is an elaborate Queen Anne revival house furnished with antiques, including a circa-1912 pool table in the top-floor guest lounge. More than 300 campsites can be found north of the Battlefords on Jackfish Lake in **Battlefords Provincial Park** (☎ *306-386-2212, Park Rd off Hwy 4; seviced/unserviced $20/15*).

Cut Knife, 50km west of Battleford on Hwy 40, was the site of a battle between the government authorities and the Native people in the early summer of 1885. About 15km north of town through the Poundmaker Reserve, plaques mark the site of Chief Poundmaker's grave and outline the story of the skirmish. In Cut Knife itself, you can't miss the huge eight-ton tomahawk.

MEADOW LAKE PROVINCIAL PARK

About 200km northwest beyond the Battlefords, Meadow Lake (☎ *306-236-7680; park admission $7; seviced/unserviced campsites $20/15*) is a popular place for **camping**. The park landscape, running along a chain of lakes by the Alberta border, has boreal forest similar to that of Prince Albert National Park but is less dramatic without the Canadian shield lands. Nature trails and a series of longer hiking trails allow for wildlife viewing. In addition to the campgrounds, visitors can stay in simple, privately operated rental **cabins**.

The park is north of Meadow Lake off Hwy 55 and is part of the Northern Woods & Water Route, a road system that begins in Manitoba and ends in British Columbia.

Alberta

Not so long ago Alberta was a vast, sparsely inhabited wilderness. Today, thanks to the discovery here of rich oil and gas resources, the province has two of Canada's largest cities – Edmonton and Calgary. For the visitor, however, Alberta's main attractions are its wildlife, historic sites, diverse scenery and the wide range of recreational pursuits it offers. Banff and Jasper National Parks in the Rocky Mountains attract visitors from around the world for their beauty, wilderness and winter sports.

Westernmost of the prairie provinces, Alberta is bordered in the north by the Northwest Territories, in the east by Saskatchewan, in the south by Montana and in the west by British Columbia. Prairie lands cover east and central Alberta. The rugged and largely inaccessible north is filled with rivers, lakes and forests. The southwestern edge of the province rises from foothills into the Rocky Mountains, while much of the rest of the south is dry and flat, with badlands (barren, convoluted arid land) in some areas.

Although Edmonton is the most northerly of Alberta's major cities, it is geographically in the center of the province. Set among the northern woodlands, it's the provincial capital and home to the oil-and-gas industry's scientists, blue-collar technicians and the wells (some 7000 within a 160km radius). Calgary has all the industry's head offices, corporate wealth and white-collar management types, but it's aesthetically burdened by seas of charmless suburbs stretching over the arid hills. Most other sizeable cities in Alberta are service centers for the huge wheat farms and cattle ranches that contribute significantly to the provincial economy.

History
From 9500 to 5500 BC, Alberta – particularly the southern portion – was occupied by the Plains Indians. For millennia they lived a nomadic life, walking great distances hunting the vast herds of bison they used for food, clothing and shelter.

The Plains Indians included the Blackfoot, Blood, Peigan, Atsina (also called Gros

Highlights

Entered Confederation: September 1, 1905
Area: 661,185 sq km
Population: 3,064,200
Provincial Capital: Edmonton

- Explore the spectacular high-alpine trails of Banff and Jasper National Parks – on skis in winter or on foot in summer.
- See for yourself the surreal turquoise waters of Peyto Lake.
- Follow the dinosaur trail around Drumheller and Dinosaur Provincial Park.
- Do the pub-crawl boogie in Edmonton's Old Strathcona district.
- Don your spurs and Stetson and swagger on down to the Calgary Stampede.
- Commune with a moose at Elk Island National Park.

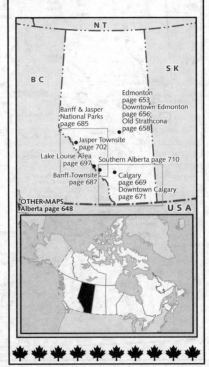

ALBERTA

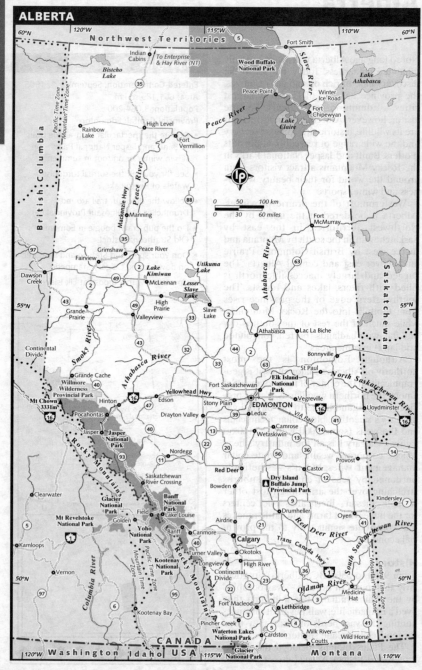

The Naming of Alberta

The province of Alberta was named after the fourth daughter of Queen Victoria, Princess Louise Caroline Alberta (1848–1939), who was married to Canada's fourth governor general, the Marquis of Lorne.

Ventre), Cree, Tsuu T'ina (Sarcee) and Assiniboine. The Sioux came from the south in the late 1800s.

The first Europeans in Alberta were fur traders who arrived around the middle of the 17th century. They were followed in the 18th century by the Hudson's Bay Company and its main rival, the Northwest Company; both set up trading posts throughout the region. The two companies amalgamated in 1821 as the Hudson's Bay Company, which administered the area until 1870, when the territory became part of the Dominion of Canada. Settlers were then encouraged to migrate to Alberta by the government's offers of cheap land.

The 1870s saw the establishment of the Northwest Mounted Police (NWMP), later to become the Royal Canadian Mounted Police (RCMP), as a response to the lawlessness caused by the whiskey trade, in which the Plains Indians were given cheap alcohol in exchange for bison hides.

The coming of the railway in the 1880s made access to the West easier and led to a rapid expansion of the population. Wheat farming and cattle ranching formed the basis of the economy, but coal mining and timber were also important. The discovery of natural gas and oil in the early 20th century added to Alberta's wealth.

In 1905 Alberta became a fully fledged province of Canada, with Edmonton as its capital.

Between WWI and WWII the economy and immigration slowed down. However, in 1947 further deposits of oil and natural gas were discovered. Then, with the oil crisis of the early 1970s, people and money began to pour in from all parts of the country. Calgary and Edmonton became booming, modern cities – today the country's fifth and sixth largest cities, respectively.

In the mid-1980s, with the fall in the price of oil and grains, the boom ended and hard times came quickly to many people. Some Albertans left the province, but most of those leaving were Easterners returning to the homes they'd left during the Alberta boom. Since then, oil and gas remain the biggest contributors to provincial coffers, but the manufacturing and service sectors have gained ground, leading to a healthier economic diversity. The province's per-capita GDP grew by over 27% from 1992 to 2000, and the provincial economy has now surpassed British Columbia's as the country's third largest (after Ontario and Québec).

Climate

Alberta has about 2000 hours of sunshine per year – more than any other province. Summers are warm, with the southern areas reaching temperatures of around 25°C in July and August. The average annual rainfall is about 450mm, a good portion of which falls between June and early August. The generally dry, warm weather in August and September makes these months particularly good for traveling. In the mountains summers are short and it's always cool at night.

Snowstorms can sweep down from the north beginning in early October. Temperatures can go for weeks in the subzero Celsius range and you'll soon understand why cars have cords for engine block heaters poking through their grills. In the south the harshness of winter is reduced by the chinook winds – warm, dry westerlies that can quickly raise temperatures by as much as 20°C.

They Call the Wind Chinook

The chinook is a warm, dry southwesterly wind that blows off the eastern slopes of the Rocky Mountains in winter. These winds can change the snowy streets of Calgary, for example, to slush and puddles within hours. The name is derived from the Chinook Indians, who lived along the northwest Pacific coast, mainly in what is now Washington State in the US.

National & Provincial Parks

Alberta has five national parks, of which three – Banff, Jasper and Waterton Lakes – are in the Rocky Mountains. Wood Buffalo National Park, the largest and least accessible, is in the far northeast, while Elk Island National Park, the smallest, is just east of Edmonton. Camping in the parks operates on a first-come, first-served basis, and sites cost between $10 and $24, depending on facilities. For more information on the national parks see the specific park sections in this chapter.

In addition, the province maintains scads of parks and recreation areas – over 500 sites in all. Many have campgrounds that charge anywhere from $5 to $20 per night, and reservations are accepted for many of those. Backcountry camping in the provincial parks costs $3 per person per night; reservations (☎ 403-591-7075) are required in Kananaskis Country. For more information, visit W www3.gov.ab.ca/env/parks/gateway.

Information

Tourist offices are run by Travel Alberta (☎ 780-427-4321, 800-661-8888, fax 780-427-0867, W www.travelalberta.com, PO Box 2500, Edmonton, Alberta T5J 2Z4). The association can supply general information as well as contact information for the provincial regional and local tourist offices.

Alberta is on Mountain Time, seven hours behind Greenwich Mean Time. The province has no sales tax but does levy a 5% accommodations tax.

Activities

With its mountains, rivers, lakes and forested wilderness areas, Alberta provides plenty of opportunities for independent or guided outdoor recreational activities. Travel Alberta's free *Alberta Vacation Guide* lists companies offering guided fishing, horseback riding, cycling, canoeing, whitewater rafting, hiking, rock climbing, mountaineering and more. It's available from any visitors' center.

Hiking & Cycling Hiking and cycling trails abound in the national and provincial parks and provincial recreation areas. Two of the more spectacular cycling routes are the Icefields Parkway, between Banff and Jasper,

and the Bow Valley Parkway, between Banff and Lake Louise. Edmonton and Calgary have hiking and cycling trails within their city boundaries.

Canoeing & Kayaking Some of the more popular places for canoeing are the lakes and rivers in Banff, Jasper, Waterton Lakes and Wood Buffalo National Parks, as well as Writing-on-Stone Provincial Park. In Jasper National Park, whitewater kayakers and rafters tackle the Athabasca, Maligne and Sunwapta Rivers. Guide companies are plentiful in all of these places – see the individual sections for details.

Good sources of information for paddlers include the Alberta Whitewater Association (☎ 780-427-6717, W www.abkayaker.com, 11759 Groat Rd, Edmonton T5M 3K6), the University of Alberta's Campus Outdoor Centre (☎ 780-492-2767, W www.per.ualberta.ca/outdoorcentre, P-153 Van Vliet Centre, Edmonton T6G 2H9), and the University of Calgary's Outdoor Program Centre (☎ 403-220-5038, W www.kin.ucalgary.ca/campusrec, 2500 University Dr NW, Calgary T2N 1N4).

Skiing & Snowboarding The best downhill ski areas are Nakiska in Kananaskis Country; Mt Norquay, Sunshine Village and Lake Louise in Banff National Park; and Marmot Basin in Jasper National Park. Many of the hiking trails in the national and provincial parks become cross-country ski trails in winter.

Rock Climbing & Mountaineering The Rocky Mountains provide plenty of challenges for the climber, from beginner to advanced. Organizations based in Banff, Calgary, Canmore and Jasper offer instruction and guided climbing. One good source of information is Yamnuska (☎ 403-678-4164, W www.yamnuska.com, Suite 200, 50-103 Bow Valley Trail, Canmore T1W 1N8), a well-known mountaineering school.

Accommodations

Campers should get a copy of *Alberta Campground Guide*, a free Travel Alberta booklet available at visitors' centers. It gives an alphabetical listing of towns and their campgrounds, both government and private. In national and provincial parks, sites cost from around $10 to $24, and in private campgrounds anywhere from $5 to $30, depending on facilities. Also available is the *Alberta Accommodation Guide,* which lists hotels, motels, B&Bs, lodges, guest ranches and farm stays in the province. Both guides are published annually.

Hostelling International (HI; **w** www .hostellingintl.ca/alberta) has 16 hostels in Alberta; reservations can be made online. For information about HI hostels in northern Alberta contact Hostelling International – Northern Alberta (**☎** 780-432-7798, fax 780-433-7781, **e** nab@hostellingintl.ca, 10926 88th Ave, Edmonton T6G 0Z1). For southern Alberta, contact Hostelling International – Southern Alberta (**☎** 403-283-5551, fax 403-283-6503, **e** sab@hostellingintl.ca, 203-1414 Kensington Rd NW, Calgary T2N 3P9).

Edmonton

Edmonton, which is Canada's sixth-largest city, sits astride the banks of the North Saskatchewan River. The city was founded on the abundant resources of the surrounding area and these remain the basis of the economy. As an early aviation center, Edmonton was once known as 'The Gateway to the North,' but that title changed to 'Oil Capital of Canada' in the 1970s, when the entire province boomed and shrugged off its cowboy image. The city experienced explosive growth, and the downtown area was totally modernized.

Since those heady days the fluctuating fortunes of the oil and gas industries have meant a series of minor ups and downs for the city. The 1990s brought more diversity, stability and a manageable, ongoing prosperity. Today the city continues to develop, albeit at a more modest pace.

Visitors are attracted to Edmonton for its proximity to Jasper and other national parks, its transportation links to the far north and its range of attractions and shopping.

The city has an average of over six hours of sun per day. Summers are short, generally dry and warm, with daytime temperatures averaging 22°C. In January, the coldest month, the average daytime high is 11°C. Ouch!

History

When European explorers and fur traders arrived in the late 18th century, the area had been populated by the Cree and Blackfoot nations for over 5000 years.

In 1795 the Hudson's Bay Company built Fort Edmonton, which grew as a fur-trading center until about 1870, when the Canadian government bought the land from the company and opened up the area for pioneers. By 1891 the railway had arrived from Calgary, and in 1892 Edmonton was officially incorporated as a town. In 1905, with the creation of Alberta, Edmonton – then numbering 8000 residents – became the capital.

With the discovery of gold in the Yukon in 1897, Edmonton was the last outpost of civilization for many gold seekers heading north to the Klondike. In 1938 North America's first mosque was built here. WWII brought a large influx of people, many to work on the Alaska Hwy. Though the province's population is mainly of British descent, many residents have German backgrounds. Ukrainians, too, have had a large hand in the region's development, and for this reason the city is sometimes humorously referred to as Edmonchuk.

The greater Edmonton area now has an ethnically diverse population approaching one million, as well as a busy cultural calendar. Rivalry with Calgary continues unabated.

Orientation

From Edmonton the Rocky Mountains are about 300km west, the lake country and Alaska Hwy (Hwy 97) are north, Lloydminster in Saskatchewan is 250km east and Calgary is 300km south. The North Saskatchewan River, which starts in the Columbia Icefield in the Rocky Mountains, drifts through the town center, separating downtown, on the north bank, from the lively and more interesting Old Strathcona district to the south. Between them, the river bottom is taken up by a series of beautiful parks. Note that many streets and avenues have both number designations and names, used interchangeably (eg, 82nd Ave/Whyte Ave).

North of the River The small, walkable **downtown**, bounded roughly by 104th Ave to the north, 100th Ave to the south, 109th

St to the west and 95th St to the east, consists of many mirrored, 1970s-design, highrise buildings. Above and below the downtown streets, pedestrian walkways (called pedways) connect shopping malls, hotels and restaurants. The area bustles with office workers and shoppers during the day and early evening but, apart from the theaters, tends to be quiet at night and on weekends.

At the heart of downtown is Sir Winston Churchill Square, bounded by 102nd and 102A Aves and 99th and 100th Sts. It's surrounded by City Hall, the Edmonton Art Gallery, the Francis Winspear Centre for Music, the Citadel Theatre, the excellent Stanley A Milner Public Library and the big Edmonton Centre shopping mall.

The eastward redevelopment of the city center during the 1970s and '80s stopped at 97th St, and for a few blocks east of there some of the streets are sleazy, especially 96th St. The bars and hotels in this area aren't recommended.

Jasper Ave (101st Ave) is Edmonton's long main thoroughfare, loaded with stores and restaurants. At its west end it jogs over onto 102nd Ave, which leads west from downtown through the **West End**, a wealthy district of fine homes, then leads on through subdivisions and strip malls to Stony Plain Rd, a commercial strip that becomes the Yellowhead Hwy to Jasper.

Six kilometers north of the center, the Yellowhead Trail (Hwy 16) is an industrial beltway that bypasses downtown for travelers heading east to Saskatoon or west to Jasper. Note that this road is especially scenically challenged. You're better off opting for the more interesting 101st Ave (Hwy 16A) through the center.

South of the River Across the river, the historic **Old Strathcona** district runs along 82nd Ave (also called Whyte Ave) several blocks east and west of 104th St. This lively area is the hippest place to be in Edmonton (see Old Strathcona, later in this section).

Heading south, 104th St joins the Calgary Trail (Hwy 2), which leads to the international airport, Red Deer and Calgary.

Information
Tourist Offices Edmonton Tourism (☎ 800-463-4667, W www.tourism.ede.org)

has three offices. The downtown office (☎ 780-426-4715, fax 780-425-5283, 9797 Jasper Ave NW), in the Shaw Conference Centre, is open 8am to 5pm Monday to Friday year-round and has tons of flyers and brochures. At the town's south approach, the Gateway Park Visitor Information Centre (☎ 780-496-8400, fax 780-496-8413, e gateway@ede.org, 2404 Calgary Trail SW), on the median between the north- and southbound sides of Hwy 2, handles inquiries from out-of-towners and is open 8am to 9pm daily in summer, 8:30am to 4:30pm Monday to Friday and 9am to 5pm weekends the rest of the year. The third office is on the western approach to town, along Hwy 16A in the Spruce Grove & District Chamber of Commerce office (☎ 780-962-2561, fax 780-962-4417, 99 Campsite Rd, Spruce Grove T7X 3B4). It's open 8:30am to 4:30pm Monday to Friday.

Parking is a problem in downtown Edmonton, but you can get free parking permits and a map of parking lots from the tourist offices June to August.

Money Major banks have branches on Jasper Ave. American Express (☎ 780-421-0608, 10180 101st St) is open 8:30am to 6pm Monday to Friday and 10am to 5pm Saturday. Foreign currency exchange services include Custom House Currency Exchange (☎ 780-423-6000, 10250 101st St) and Money Mart, which has 16 offices in greater Edmonton, including 10024 82nd Ave (☎ 780-433-8073), open 24 hours, and 10756 Jasper Ave (☎ 780-425-2275), open 8am to 10pm Monday to Friday, 9am to 9pm Saturday, 11am to 6pm Sunday.

Post The main post office (☎ 780-944-3271, 9808 103A Ave) is open 8am to 5:45pm Monday to Friday.

Email & Internet Access Naked Cyber & Espresso Bar (☎ 780-433-9730, 10442 82nd/ Whyte Ave), in Old Strathcona, is open 24 hours and charges $6 an hour for Internet access. Another Naked location, also open 24 hours, is at 10354 Jasper Ave (☎ 780-425-9730). The downtown library (see Libraries, below) has excellent free Internet facilities.

Travel Agencies For inexpensive airfares, check out The Adventure Travel Company

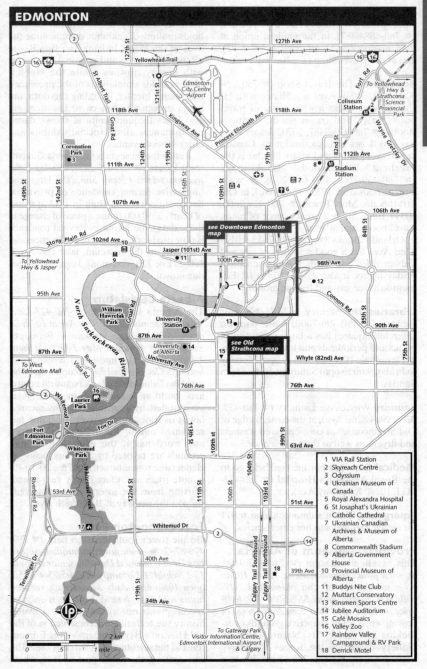

EDMONTON

see Downtown Edmonton map

see Old Strathcona map

1 VIA Rail Station
2 Skyreach Centre
3 Odyssium
4 Ukrainian Museum of Canada
5 Royal Alexandra Hospital
6 St Josaphat's Ukrainian Catholic Cathedral
7 Ukrainian Canadian Archives & Museum of Alberta
8 Commonwealth Stadium
9 Alberta Government House
10 Provincial Museum of Alberta
11 Buddys Nite Club
12 Muttart Conservatory
13 Kinsmen Sports Centre
14 Jubilee Auditorium
15 Café Mosaics
16 Valley Zoo
17 Rainbow Valley Campground & RV Park
18 Derrick Motel

To Gateway Park
Visitor Information Centre,
Edmonton International Airport
& Calgary

(☎ 780-439-3096, 8103 104th St) and Travel Cuts, which has offices at 10127A 124th St (☎ 780-488-8487), in the student union at the University of Alberta (☎ 780-492-2592), and at the Travel Shop (see Bookstores).

Bookstores The Travel Shop (☎ 780-439-3089, 10926 88th Ave) is affiliated with HI Canada and stocks a wide range of travel books, maps and travel goods. Audrey's Books (☎ 780-423-3487, 10702 Jasper Ave) has two floors of books including Canadiana, travel guides and maps. Similar is the excellent Greenwoods' Bookshoppe (☎ 780-439-2005, 800-661-2078, W www.greenwoods.com, 10355 82nd Ave), in Old Strathcona. Map Town (☎ 780-429-2600, 10344 105th St) is a great source of maps, travel books and atlases.

Orlando Books (☎ 780-432-7633, 10123 82nd Ave) has a good selection of gay and lesbian titles and holds readings on most Friday nights. It also carries *Times.10*, Edmonton's free gay and lesbian monthly.

Libraries The Stanley A Milner Public Library (☎ 780-496-7000, 7 Sir Winston Churchill Square) has a large collection of books and periodicals and lots of free Internet terminals. It's open 9am to 9pm Monday to Friday, 9am to 6pm Saturday, 1pm to 5pm Sunday.

Laundry Whyte Ave Laundry (☎ 780-439-0285, 9904 82nd Ave), at the eastern edge of Old Strathcona, has coin-operated washers and dryers, as well as drop-off service.

Medical Services For medical help, go to the Royal Alexandra Hospital (☎ 780-477-4111, 10240 Kingsway Ave).

Emergency Within Edmonton, dial ☎ 911 for police, medical and fire emergencies.

Provincial Museum of Alberta

This excellent museum (☎ 780-453-9100, W www.pma.edmonton.ab.ca, 12845 102nd Ave; adult/senior 65 and older/child 7-17/child 6 & under/family $8/6.50/4/3/20, half-price on Tues; open 9am-5pm daily), west of downtown, is set in attractive grounds overlooking the river. Its Natural History Gallery describes the forces that have shaped Alberta and its life forms. It has a large display of fossils and minerals. The must-see Gallery of Aboriginal Culture holds multimedia exhibits documenting the lives of the Plains Indians. The Bug Room offers an up-close-and-personal encounter with creepy-crawlies, while the Habitat Gallery holds simulations of the province's four major biomes, including the flora and fauna encountered in each. The museum also hosts frequent cultural shows, dance performances, films, special exhibits and other special events.

Beside the museum is the **Alberta Government House** (☎ 780-427-2281, 780-452-7980; free tours 1pm-4:30pm Sun), the large and impressive former residence of provincial lieutenant governors. Built in 1913 at a cost of nearly $350,000 (quite a piece of change in those days), the Jacobean Revival residence is now used for government conferences.

To get to the museum, take bus No 1, 100, 111 or 120 west along Jasper Ave from downtown.

Alberta Legislature

The Alberta Legislature (☎ 780-427-7362, W www.assembly.ab.ca, 97th Ave at 107th St; open 8:30am-5pm weekdays, 9am-5pm weekends & holidays May 1-Oct 15; 9am-4:30pm weekdays, noon-5pm weekends & holidays Oct 16-April 30) occupies the original Fort Edmonton site. A beautiful beaux-arts building completed in 1912, it is surrounded by fountains and manicured lawns overlooking the river. Its dome has remained one of Edmonton's landmarks, and word has it the expansive 57-acre grounds are favored by amorous locals for clandestine romantic activity. Free 30- to 40-minute tours are offered daily year-round, starting from the interpretive center/gift shop in the pedway at 10820 98th Ave.

Fort Edmonton Park

On the river's south side, this park (☎ 780-496-8787, W www.gov.edmonton.ab.ca/fort, Fox Dr at Whitemud Dr; adult/senior & youth 13-17/child 2-12/family $7.75/5.75/4/23.50; open 10am-6pm daily July & Aug, reduced hours mid-May–June & Sept, open only for special events rest of the year) is a living-history site featuring a reconstruction of the old Hudson's Bay Company's Fort Edmonton and the surrounding town circa 1885. The fort contains the entire post of 1846, which was built to promote the fur trade (not as a military fort).

Outside the fort are streets re-creating different periods in Edmonton's history, from the frontier days of 1885 to the turn of the 20th century (circa 1905) to Edmonton's version of the Roaring Twenties. Costumed interpreters help bring the scenes to life. In summer, admission includes rides on a steam train and streetcar. Wagon tours are offered in September. To get to the fort, take bus No 104 or 105 from downtown.

Beside the fort is the **John Janzen Nature Centre** (☎ 780-496-2939/2910; *adult/senior & youth /child/family $1.25/1/75¢/3.75; open 9am-4pm Mon-Fri, 11am-4pm Sat & Sun late May-June; 10am-5pm Mon-Fri, 11am-5pm Sat & Sun July & Aug; 9am-4pm Mon-Fri, 1pm-4pm Sat & Sun Sept-late May; closed Dec 25-31),* where you'll find an exhibit room housing a few examples of both living and taxidermied local animals, insects and reptiles – best of the lot is the demonstration beehive. Outside are 4km of interpretive nature trails. Kid-friendly instructional programs take place year-round.

Valley Zoo

Northeast of Fort Edmonton Park, this zoo *(reception ☎ 780-496-6912, information ☎ 780-496-8787,* **w** *www.gov.edmonton.ab.ca/valley zoo, 13315 Buena Vista Rd/87th Ave; adult/ senior & youth 13-17/child 2-12/family $5.75/4.25/3.25/18 early May-early Oct, reduced prices rest of the year; open 9:30am-8pm daily July & Aug, closing hours vary rest*

The Mall That Ate...

Sprawled over 48 hectares, the **West Edmonton Mall** (☎ 780-444-5330, 800-661-8890, **w** *www.westedmontonmall.com)* bills itself as 'the world's largest shopping and entertainment centre.' Big it certainly is; how entertaining is another matter. From its roots as a humble suburban shopping mall, 'West Ed' has metastasized into a commercial monster that has sucked zillions of dollars out of the rest of Edmonton's retail life.

If you are drawn by the spectacle of the world's largest shopping mall, be forewarned that all is not what it seems. There's less diversity than the claim of 'over 800 stores and services' implies. The collection of stores will be familiar to North American mall rats everywhere; the numbers have been padded by counting numerous outlets of the same store scattered throughout the labyrinth. Fans of Orange Julius, the ubiquitous purveyor of a treacly orange drink, will be cheered that West Ed has three.

Much of the recent construction at the mall – like Canadian airports, the West Edmonton Mall is never complete – has been for entertainment, rather than retail, attractions. The frostbitten denizens of the Canadian Plains have flocked to West Ed's artificial climate, where a growing number of diversions await those looking for more in life beyond browsing the 30 moderately priced shoe stores. Again, hype often outpaces substance. 'Bourbon Street' has all the allure of a watered-down Hurricane cocktail and features the non–New Orleans native Hooters.

Elsewhere, a slew of attractions is ready to prove that West Ed isn't just the mall that ate Edmonton but is also the mall ready to eat your wallet. Among them (prices given are admission per adult/child): **Deep Sea Adventure**, a submarine ride ($12/5); the **Ice Palace** skating rink ($5.50/3); **Galaxyland** amusement park ($29.95/21.95); and **World Waterpark**, a huge enclosed beach and waterslide area where you'll never need sunscreen ($29.95/21.95).

If your spending spree leaves you tuckered out, West Ed also has the **Fantasyland Hotel** (☎ 780-444-3000, 800-737-3783), *complete with theme suites such as the evocatively named 'Truck Room,' where you can bed down in the back of a pickup under the romantic glow of a stop light. Standard rooms start at $175 a night; the theme rooms start at $235.*

West Ed is open daily. Hours for the main retail area are 10am to 9pm weekdays, 10am to 6pm Saturday, noon to 6pm Sunday. The entertainment attractions keep different hours, which vary throughout the year, while the restaurants and clubs stay open later at night. The complex is bounded by 87th Ave and 170th St. From downtown, take bus No 1, 2, 100, 111 or 112.

ALBERTA

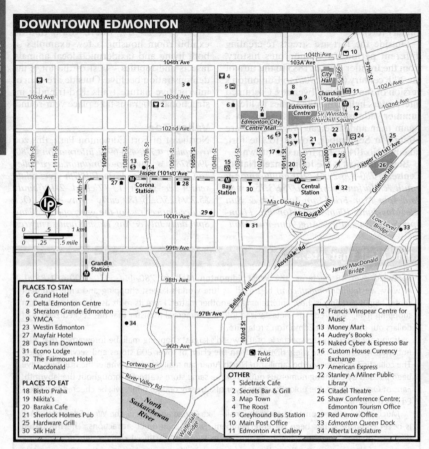

DOWNTOWN EDMONTON

PLACES TO STAY
6 Grand Hotel
7 Delta Edmonton Centre
8 Sheraton Grande Edmonton
9 YMCA
23 Westin Edmonton
27 Mayfair Hotel
28 Days Inn Downtown
31 Econo Lodge
32 The Fairmount Hotel Macdonald

PLACES TO EAT
18 Bistro Praha
19 Nikita's
20 Baraka Cafe
21 Sherlock Holmes Pub
25 Hardware Grill
30 Silk Hat

OTHER
1 Sidetrack Cafe
2 Secrets Bar & Grill
3 Map Town
4 The Roost
5 Greyhound Bus Station
10 Main Post Office
11 Edmonton Art Gallery

12 Francis Winspear Centre for Music
13 Money Mart
14 Audrey's Books
15 Naked Cyber & Espresso Bar
16 Custom House Currency Exchange
17 American Express
22 Stanley A Milner Public Library
24 Citadel Theatre
26 Shaw Conference Centre; Edmonton Tourism Office
29 Red Arrow Office
33 Edmonton Queen Dock
34 Alberta Legislature

of the year), in Laurier Park at the southern end of Buena Vista Rd, holds about 500 animals – from addax to zebu. In summer, kids will enjoy the petting zoo, camel and pony rides, miniature train, carousel and paddleboats.

Muttart Conservatory

South of the river off James MacDonald Bridge, the Muttart Conservatory (*reception ☎ 780-496-8735, recorded information ☎ 780-496-8755, 9626 96A St; adult/senior, student & youth 13-17/child 2-12/family $5/4/2.50/15; open 9am-6pm Mon-Fri, 11am-6pm Sat, Sun & holidays, extended hours in summer*) comprises four glass pyramids sheltering hundreds of plant species from the area's seemingly endless

winters. One pyramid holds a tropical jungle, another the plants of arid desert regions, and a third showcases temperate-forest vegetation. The fourth pyramid is used for changing exhibitions (Easter lily fans, take note!). Get there via bus Nos 85 or 86.

Edmonton Art Gallery

This art gallery (☎ 780-422-6223, **w** *www .eag.org, 2 Sir Winston Churchill Square at 99th St & 102A Ave; adult/senior & student/ child 6-12 $5/3/2, free Thur after 4pm; open 10:30am-5pm Mon-Wed & Fri, 10:30am-8pm Thur, 11am-5pm Sat, Sun & holidays*) has a collection of over 5000 works of art by Canadian and international artists in all media, of which roughly 150 are on display at any one time. The gallery also hosts regular traveling exhibitions.

Odyssium

The futuristic-looking Odyssium (☎ 780-451-3344, W www.odyssium.com, 11211 142nd St; adult/senior & student/child 3-12/ family $10/8/7/39, admission plus IMAX $16/13/11/60; open 10am-9pm daily July & Aug; 10am-5pm Mon-Thur, Sun & holidays, 10am-9pm Fri & Sat Sept-June) holds six galleries full of exhibits. Four areas focus on space, the human body, forensic science and the environment. A fifth gallery is especially for kids ages two to eight and features, among other exhibits, a 'construction zone' and a working beehive. The sixth gallery hosts rotating and traveling exhibits. Techies will find a ham radio station and computer lab, while budding astronomers will enjoy the observatory and the big planetarium presenting programs on the solar system and universe. Not surprisingly, there's an IMAX theater as well; rock-music laser shows are offered frequently. Take bus No 125 from downtown to Westmount St next to Coronation Park.

Ukrainian Heritage Sites

North of downtown lies an area rich in Ukrainian cultural sites. The imposing **St Josaphat's Ukrainian Catholic Cathedral** (☎ 780-422-3181, 10825 97th St at 108th Ave; admission free; open by appointment) has good examples of colorful Ukrainian decorative art.

Close by, the **Ukrainian Canadian Archives & Museum of Alberta** (☎ 780-424-7580, 9543 110th Ave; admission by donation; open 10am-5pm Tues-Fri, noon-5pm Sat) has more Easter eggs and other Ukrainian artifacts.

The **Ukrainian Museum of Canada** (☎ 780-483-5932, 10611 110th Ave; admission free; open 9:30am-4:30pm Mon-Fri May-Aug, rest of year by appt), in St John's Parish School & Hall, has a small collection of costumes, pysanky (Easter eggs), dolls and fine tapestries.

Old Strathcona

This charming and vibrant area south of the river along 82nd/Whyte Ave was once the town of Strathcona. Though now absorbed into the city, Old Strathcona is rich in histor-ical buildings dating from the 1890s. Its proximity to the University of Alberta, which lies within walking distance to the west, gives it a buzz of young, artsy energy. Funky shops, restaurants, theaters and nightclubs are plentiful, making Old Strathcona the perfect antidote for those dazed by the mall.

Leave the car and explore on foot. For added context, pick up a copy of the pamphlet *Strathcona Historical Walking & Driving Tour* at the Old Strathcona Foundation (☎ 780-433-5866, 401-10324 82nd Ave). From 105th St east, 82nd Ave has been spruced up with brick sidewalks and old-style lampposts, and several small attractions dot the district.

The **Old Strathcona Farmers' Market** (☎ 780-439-1844, 10310 83rd Ave at 103rd St; open 8am-3pm Sat year-round, also noon-5pm Tues July & Aug) hosts some 130 vendors. This not-to-be-missed indoor market offers everything from organic food to vintage clothing to crafts. *Everyone* comes here Saturday morning – it's quite the scene.

Anyone with a hang-up for phones will enjoy the **Telephone Historical Centre** (☎ 780-433-1010, 441-2077, W www.telephone historicalcentre.com, 10437 83rd Ave; adult/ senior, student & child/family $3/2/5; open 10am-4pm Tues-Fri, noon-4pm Sat). The small museum holds a collection of antique phones and several interesting interactive exhibits (one on switching technologies is a behind-the-scenes eye-opener).

Antiques aficionados can browse the 22,000-sq-foot **Old Strathcona Antique Mall** (☎ 780-433-0398, 7614 103rd St), occupied by over 200 vendors.

Activities

For information on park and recreation facilities like outdoor swimming pools, skating and skiing areas, and bicycle paths, contact **Edmonton Parks & Recreation** (☎ 780-496-4999, 9803 102A Ave).

The huge **Kinsmen Sports Centre** (☎ 780-944-7400, 496-7300, W www.gov.edmonton .ab.ca/kinsmen, 9100 Walterdale Hill; adult/ senior & youth 13-17/child 2-12/family $6/4/3/12; open 5:30am-10pm Mon-Fri, 7am-10pm Sat & Sun) has public swimming pools, court sports, fitness centers, saunas and more.

Edmonton has an extensive network of bicycle routes; the best area to cycle is along the river. *Cycle Edmonton* is an excellent

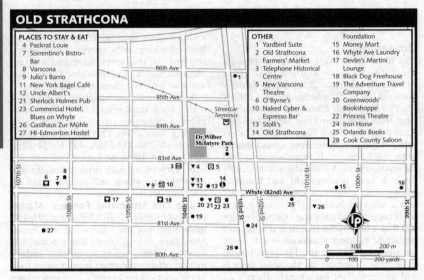

OLD STRATHCONA

PLACES TO STAY & EAT
4 Packrat Louie
7 Sorrentino's Bistro-Bar
8 Varscona
9 Julio's Barrio
11 New York Bagel Café
12 Uncle Albert's
21 Sherlock Holmes Pub
23 Commercial Hotel; Blues on Whyte
26 Gasthaus Zur Mühle
27 HI-Edmonton Hostel

OTHER
1 Yardbird Suite
2 Old Strathcona Farmers' Market
3 Telephone Historical Centre
5 New Varscona Theatre
6 O'Byrne's
10 Naked Cyber & Espresso Bar
13 Stolli's
14 Old Strathcona
15 Money Mart
16 Whyte Ave Laundry
17 Devlin's Martini Lounge
18 Black Dog Freehouse
19 The Adventure Travel Company
20 Greenwoods' Bookshoppe
22 Princess Theatre
24 Iron Horse
25 Orlando Books
28 Cook County Saloon

Foundation

free map showing these routes and is available from the tourist offices.

Organized Tours

Several companies offer half-day tours of Edmonton (around $35-40) or longer tours exploring the outlying areas. Try **Magic Times Tours** (☎ *780-940-7479*, **W** *home .istar.ca/~itsmagic*), **Out an' About** (☎ *780-909-8687*, **W** *www.outanabouttours.com*) or **Peter's Edmonton Tours** (☎ *780-469-2641, 904-6973*).

You can get out on the river on the *Edmonton Queen* (☎ *780-424-2628*, **W** *www .edmontonqueen.com, 9734 98th Ave; closed in winter*), a modern sternwheeler riverboat. The one-hour sightseeing cruises ($15) leave from Rafter's Landing, across from the Shaw Conference Centre, on the river's south bank, and cruise either up or down the river at the captain's discretion. Live onboard entertainment is often scheduled. Lunch cruises cost $45; dinner cruises are $50.

Special Events

Edmonton has many festivals throughout the year. Some of the larger ones include the following:

June

Jazz City International Music Festival This week-long event (☎ 780-433-4000, 432-7166) at the end of June is marked by concerts all over town, many outside and free.

The Works: A Visual Arts Celebration Also in late June and spilling over into early July, this major arts celebration (☎ 780-426-2122, **W** www .theworks.ab.ca) features two weeks of exhibits and events around town, including some in city parks.

July

International Street Performers Festival Amazing buskers bring the streets alive during this multi-day event (☎ 780-425-5162) around the second week of July.

Klondike Days Edmonton's biggest festival (☎ 780-423-2822), held late in July, celebrates a less than honorable period in the city's history. In the gold-rush days, unscrupulous entrepreneurs lured gold seekers to the city with false tales of a trail from Edmonton to Dawson City in the Yukon. Many died trying to find the trail; others gave up and returned to settle in Edmonton. Festival events include locals in period costume, roadside stages alive with singers and dancers, parades through the streets and nightly concerts.

August

Edmonton Heritage Festival This three-day Hawrelak Park festival (☎ 780-488-3378) celebrates the city's ethnic diversity in the first week of August.

Edmonton Folk Music Festival Gallagher Park, just east of the Muttart Conservatory, hosts four days of blues, jazz, country & western, bluegrass and traditional folk music during this festival (☎ 780-429-1899) in the second week of August.

The Klondike Days is Edmonton's biggest festival.

Edmonton Fringe Theatre Festival Well worth catching, this event (☎ 780-448-9000, [w] www .fringe.alberta.com) features an 11-day program of live alternative theater, with over 1000 performances in 13 theaters, on three outdoor stages, in the parks and on the streets. Many shows are free and no ticket costs more than $10; there's no booking – you choose a theater and stand in line. The festival draws half a million people each year to Old Strathcona around the middle of August.

November

Canadian Finals Rodeo Canada's major indoor rodeo (☎ 780-471-7210, 888-800-7275) boasts the biggest money prizes for roping, riding and the rest. The main event at Skyreach Centre is held concurrently with Farmfair International, a huge agricultural show at Agricom next door. It all runs for 10 days early in the month. Rodeo tickets cost $15 to $40.

Places to Stay

Old Strathcona is by far the best place to stay in Edmonton. Downtown hotels are plentiful but short on character. If for some ungodly reason the West Edmonton Mall is the reason for your visit, you can choose from among a plethora of both chain and indie motels near the mall on Stony Plain Rd.

Camping Several good campgrounds are close to town.

Rainbow Valley Campground & RV Park (☎ 780-434-5531, 888-434-3991, fax 780-436-5479, [w] www.rainbow-valley.com, 13204 45th Ave; open mid-April–mid-Oct) Sites $16-21, weekly rates available. Enjoying a great location right in central Whitemud Park is the municipal Rainbow Valley Campground, off Whitemud Dr. Amenities include laundry and washroom facilities, free hot showers, cook shelters with wood-burning stoves, horseshoe pits, a playground, convenience store and

access to the park's nature trails. To get there, take the 122nd St/119th St exit, go south on 119th and make the first right; the driveway starts a block down on the south side of Whitemud and goes under the freeway to the campground, on the north side.

Glowing Embers Travel Centre & RV Park (☎ 780-962-8100, fax 780-962-8162, 26309 Hwy 16A, Spruce Grove; open Apr–mid-Oct) Sites $24. A reasonable choice for RVers heading to the West Edmonton Mall, this large west-side park at the junction of Hwys 16A and 60 has laundry and shower facilities, a store, car wash and propane sales.

Half Moon Lake Resort (☎ 780-922-3045, fax 780-922-3646, 21524 Township Rd 520, Sherwood Park; open May–early Oct) Sites $15-21. This large resort, 29km southeast of Edmonton, offers lake swimming, paddleboat rentals, mini-golf, a fish pond, horseback riding, showers, laundry, a playground, store and more. From Edmonton, follow 23rd Ave east, passing Hwy 21 and continuing another 10km (23rd Ave becomes Township Rd 520).

Hostels *HI-Edmonton Hostel* (☎ 780-988-6836, 877-467-8336, fax 780-988-8698, [e] eihostel@hostellingintl.ca, 10647 81st Ave) Dorm beds $18-20 for members, $23-25 for nonmembers, private rooms available. This hostel sits on a quiet residential street in Old Strathcona, easy walking distance from the action. It has two kitchens, a laundry, library, Internet access, mountain bike rentals and more. Take bus No 7 or 9 south from downtown.

YMCA (☎ 780-421-9622, fax 780-428-9469, 10030 102A Ave) Dorm beds $20 (three-night maximum stay), singles/doubles from $35/52 (weekly rates available). The central Y is downtown, opposite Edmonton Centre mall, next to the Sheraton Hotel and close to the Greyhound bus station. It takes in men and women and has a TV room, gym facilities (including a pool) and a cheap cafeteria.

University of Alberta (☎ 780-492-4281 Housing & Food Services, fax 780-492-7032, 44 Lister Hall, at 87th Ave & 116th St) Singles/doubles $31.50/42. Open May-Aug. The university, in southwest Edmonton, rents out rooms in summer. It has good facilities and cheap cafeterias. Weekly and monthly rates are available.

B&Bs The *Bed & Breakfast Association of Greater Edmonton* (☎ 780-432-7116, fax 780-462-9651, 3230 104A St) maintains a list of member establishments and can make bookings. Rooms range from $45 to $80. Tell the staff where you want to be and what you're looking for, and they'll match you up with the appropriate choice.

Motels Motels are concentrated in two areas near town. One is along Stony Plain Rd and the Yellowhead Hwy (Hwy 16) west of downtown in the suburban sprawl around West Edmonton Mall. Here you'll find the following two places:

Travelodge Edmonton West (☎ 780-483-6031, 800-578-7878, fax 780-484-2358, W www.travelodge.com, 18320 Stony Plain Rd) Rooms from around $70. A good choice for mallsters with kids, the newish Travelodge is not only close to the West Edmonton Mall, it has in-room Super Nintendo and a gigantor water slide.

Sandman Hotel West Edmonton (☎ 780-483-1385, 800-726-3626, fax 780-489-0611, W www.sandmanhotels.com, 17635 Stony Plain Rd) Singles/doubles from $69/74. The Sandman makes up for a complete lack of charm with a large indoor pool that will keep the kids wet and wild for hours. A 24-hour Denny's Restaurant is on site.

The other motel strip is along the Calgary Trail south of the city, with mostly reasonably priced motels, including the following:

Derrick Motel (☎ 780-438-6060, 866-303-6060, fax 780-461-5170, 3925 Calgary Trail North) Singles/doubles from $49/59. This motel has 28 newly renovated rooms and suites.

Chateau Motel (☎ 780-988-6661, fax 780-988-8839, 1414 Calgary Trail Southwest) Singles/doubles from $40/50. The friendly Chateau, about 3km south of 23rd Ave, offers satellite TV and kitchenettes.

Hotels Edmonton is not blessed with a great selection of low-end hotels.

Grand Hotel (☎ 780-422-6365, 888-422-6365, fax 780-425-9070, 10266 103rd St) Rooms from $55. Downtown, the Grand is opposite the bus terminal and sits atop a dive bar and a restaurant with cheap breakfasts. If you come in on the bus late and just can't think about moving, this might be your choice, but even then you're only a five-minute walk from the YMCA, which actually has a nicer vibe.

Commercial Hotel (☎ 780-439-3981, fax 780-439-5058, 10329 82nd Ave) Singles/doubles $34/38 with shared bath, $42 & up with private bath. In Old Strathcona, this bare-bones place is friendly, decent and has live blues in the bar downstairs.

Mayfair Hotel (☎ 780-423-1650, 800-463-7666, fax 780-425-6834, 10815 Jasper Ave) Rooms from $60. Downtown, the Mayfair is a handsome older hotel that also holds residential apartments. It's a good value and has a friendly, professional staff.

Downtown holds several other uninspiring mid-range chain hotels. You might try *Econo Lodge* (☎ 780-428-6442, 800-613-7043, fax 780-428-6467, 10209 100th Ave), with singles/doubles starting at $64/70 with breakfast; or *Days Inn Downtown* (☎ 780-423-1925, 800-267-2191, fax 780-424-5302, e daysinn@compusmart.ab.ca, 10041 106th St), with singles/doubles for $80/90 and good Internet specials often available.

The following are some top-end choices.

Varscona (☎ 780-434-6111, 888-515-3355, fax 780-439-1195, W www.varscona.com, 8208 106th St at 82nd Ave) Rooms $110-125. In the wonderful Old Strathcona district, the Varscona is *the* place to stay in Edmonton. This delightful little boutique hotel offers every plush amenity, including a business center, fitness center, morning paper, continental breakfast and evening wine-and-cheese tasting, as well as a perfect location for exploring the city's best neighborhood. Leave your car parked in the free covered parking lot and stroll right out the door to a kaleidoscope of nearby pubs, clubs and restaurants. You can't go wrong here.

The Fairmont Hotel Macdonald (☎ 780-424-5181, 800-441-1414, fax 780-429-6481, W www.fairmont.com, 10065 100th St) Singles/doubles from $199/219. This regal establishment is Edmonton's oldest and most elegant hotel. Have your driver pull the carriage up to the grand entry and walk through the doors into a different era. The main part of the hotel dates from 1915, when the Canadian Pacific Railway built a string of plush palaces like this to attract high-society hoity-toits, who would naturally arrive by rail. The legacy of this fine business strategy remains, though the Macdonald is now part of the Fairmont chain. The hotel commands a prime spot overlooking the river; enjoy the view while your diamond tiara is being polished.

The city's other top-dollar hotels, while nice, are also-rans compared to the above two establishments. They include the *Sheraton Grande Edmonton* (☎ 780-428-7111, 800-263-9030, fax 780-441-3098, ⓦ *www .sheratonedmonton.com, 10235 101st St*), with rooms starting at $154; the *Westin Edmonton* (☎ 780-426-3636, 800-228-3000, fax 780-428-1454, ⓦ *www.westin.com, 10135 100th St*), with rooms starting at $180; and the *Delta Edmonton Centre* (☎ 780-429-3900, 800-268-1133, fax 780-428-1566, ⓦ *www .deltahotels.com, 10222 102nd St*), with singles/doubles starting at $234/244. Weekend rates are generally substantially less.

Places to Eat
Budget It's not hard to find good, cheap eats in Edmonton. Downtown try the following:

Silk Hat (☎ 780-425-1920, 10251 Jasper Ave) Lunch specials $6-9. Silk Hat dates from 1940. It still has the small wall juke-boxes at the booths and movie posters on the walls. It's fully licensed to sell booze and serves breakfast all day. The shakes are made with real ice cream.

Baraka Cafe (☎ 780-423-1819, 10088 Jasper Ave) Sandwiches $3-4, dishes $6-7. Open to 11pm Sun-Thur, to midnight Fri & Sat. This is a good coffee bar with various bakery treats.

Old Strathcona has its share of good eating places.

Café Mosaics (☎ 780-433-9702, 10844 82nd/Whyte Ave) Dinners $6-13. This hip spot offers fresh food and a good array of veggie dishes. It's open Monday to Saturday for breakfast, lunch and dinner and Sunday for brunch.

Uncle Albert's (☎ 780-439-6609, 10370 82nd/Whyte Ave) Prices $4.50-12. This busy place is open for breakfast, lunch and dinner. On the menu are pancakes ($5) and fish and chips (around $6.25).

New York Bagel Café (no phone, 8209 104th St) Bagel platters & specials $7-11. This laid-back and cozy spot serves excellent bagels, cappuccinos and light deli-style foods.

Near West Edmonton Mall you'll find the following:

Hap's Hungry House (☎ 780-483-2288, 16060 Stony Plain Rd) Breakfast & lunch $5-8. Open 6:30am-4pm daily. This unadorned diner is loved by locals for its great breakfasts and lack of chain affiliation. It's also smoke-free.

Mid-Range Where 101A Ave and 100A St meet, right in the center of town, a small pedestrian-friendly zone is home to several popular restaurants, most with outdoor seating.

Bistro Praha (☎ 780-424-4218, 10168 100A St) Dishes $14-18. This European-style spot has a lot of dark wood and a quiet clubby atmosphere. Salads go for around $5 and main meals like schnitzel for about $14. During nonmeal hours it's pleasant for a good coffee with cake or a pastry and a flip through a newspaper.

Nikita's (☎ 780-414-0606, 10162 100A St) Dishes $7.50-19. Down a couple of doors from Bistro Praha is Nikita's, which has pub fare, pizza and more substantial items and is generally a cool place to hang out.

Nearby, on Rice Howard Way (the cool, overgrown alley) you'll find an outlet of Sherlock Holmes Pub (see description below).

Old Strathcona teems with moderately priced restaurants.

Gasthaus Zur Mühle (☎ 780-432-1838, 8109 101st St) Dishes $10-14. Edmonton's German community comes to 'The Mill' to load up on Jäger schnitzel and live accordion music (weekends).

Julio's Barrio (☎ 780-431-0774, 10450 82nd Ave) Dinner dishes $10-16. This is a popular Mexican place filled with noisy college students slamming tequila shots and tossing down classics like burritos and enchiladas.

Sherlock Holmes Pub (☎ 780-433-9676, 10341 82nd Ave) Meals $9-12. Though part of a small chain, the Sherlock Holmes has not only a great beer selection but also truly outstanding pub fare. The wide-ranging menu includes traditional English favorites like steak and kidney pie, bangers and mash and fish and chips, as well as calamari, curries, quesadillas and chicken cordon bleu. A bright, spic-and-span interior and convivial atmosphere add to the experience. Look for the red British phone booth out front.

Top End *Hardware Grill* (☎ 780-423-0969, W *www.hardwaregrill.com, 9698 Jasper Ave*) Dishes \$24-37. Nationally recognized and widely regarded as Edmonton's finest restaurant, this smoke-free downtown dining room sits quietly behind huge windows in a restored historic building that once housed a hardware store. The menu changes regularly and features dishes with native Canadian food, such as seafood, game, berries and whole grains. The signature cedar-plank-cooked salmon (\$23) is a perennial favorite. Adding to the draw is an outstanding wine list – several-time honoree of the Wine Spectator Award of Excellence – that includes over 500 top-quality selections at fair prices; many are available by the glass.

Sorrentino's Bistro-Bar (☎ 780-434-7607, *10612 82nd Ave*) Dishes \$11-21. Run by a famous local family of restaurateurs, this Old Strathcona eatery features a bustling open kitchen turning out unusual Italian dishes, scrumptious fresh pastas and char-grilled steaks in an always crowded and stylish dining room. It's a popular date place.

Packrat Louie (☎ 780-433-0123, *10335 83rd Ave*) Dinner dishes \$19-24. Also in Old Strathcona, this casually elegant place serves steak, seafood and chicken dishes, as well as creative pizzas, soups and salads. The small outdoor patio could use a little work, but the interior is spacious and comfortable. It's a good bet for lunch or dinner.

Entertainment

See and *Vue* are free local alternative weekly papers with extensive arts and entertainment listings. For daily listings, see the entertainment section of the *Edmonton Journal* newspaper.

Performing Arts Edmonton offers a busy performing-arts calendar.

Citadel Theatre (☎ 780-425-1820, 888-425-1820 tickets, W *www.citadeltheatre.com, 9828 101A Ave*) Adult tickets usually \$35-50, seniors \$25-40, students \$23-33. Edmonton's foremost playhouse, the Citadel is actually a five-theater complex hosting mainstream drama, comedy, experimental productions, concerts, lectures and films. Its season is from September to May.

Jubilee Auditorium (☎ 780-451-8000, *11455 87th Ave*) This is the venue for the Edmonton Opera (☎ 780-429-1000, W www .edmontonopera.com) during its October to April season. Opera tickets run \$22 to \$83 for adults, \$20 to \$56 for seniors and students. The Auditorium also hosts concerts and special performances.

New Varscona Theatre (☎ 780-433-3399, *10329 83rd Ave*, W *www.varsconatheatre .com*) The Varscona often stages edgy, fringe productions. Tickets are typically around \$15 for adults, \$12 for seniors and students, but ask about specially priced matinees and two-for-one performances. The season runs September to May.

Francis Winspear Centre for Music (☎ 780-428-1414, 800-563-5081, *4 Sir Winston Churchill Square*) The Edmonton Symphony Orchestra (☎ 780-428-1414, tickets ☎ 800-563-5081, W www.edmontonsymphony.com) plays here September to June; tickets run \$20 to \$60 (5% off for seniors, 10% off for students).

Clubs & Pubs For concentrated club- and pub-hopping, Old Strathcona is the place. Here are a few favorites among the many.

Black Dog Freehouse (☎ 780-439-1082, *10425 82nd Ave*) Friendly and popular, this pub features ancient wooden furniture, well-poured pints and occasional live rock. Check out the 'Wooftop' patio.

Blues on Whyte (☎ 780-439-3981, 10329 *82nd Ave*) This 12-bar bastion presents live, hurts-so-good blues in the old Commercial Hotel, an appropriately world-weary venue that throughout its long history has no doubt inspired a blues lyric or two.

Cook County Saloon (☎ 780-432-2665, *8010 103rd St*) Open Wed-Sat nights. Visiting cowboys and cowgirls, urban or otherwise, stampede to Cook County Saloon for country music and dancing.

Devlin's Martini Lounge (☎ 780-437-7489, *10507 82nd Ave*) This coolest of the cool martini bars attracts a sophisticated, young professional crowd. Its big open windows facing the sidewalk make for the best people-watching on Whyte.

Iron Horse (☎ 780-438-3710, 8101 103rd *St*) Occupying the cavernous former 1907 CP rail station, the Iron Horse has plenty of room for dancing (lots of live music), drinking, shooting pool and scoping the studs and studmuffins. But this place also has a fantastic side patio, where they fire up the barbecue when weather permits – a great place to hang out for lunch or a summer's-eve dinner.

O'Byrne's (☎ *780-414-6766, 10616 82nd Ave*) A popular Irish pub, O'Byrne's offers the requisite Guinness on tap, along with superb Irish food and music.

Stolli's (☎ *780-438-4848, 10360 82nd Ave*) Dance clubs are everywhere in Old Strathcona, but if you're under 25, this small upstairs place has the perfect vibe. Until midnight you can lounge on the sofa in back and do some quiet cooing with your lovely inamorata. After midnight, the line goes down the stairs and out onto the sidewalk, and you'll need to suck in that beer belly to get out on the jam-packed dance floor.

Yardbird Suite (☎ *780-432-0428,* W *www .yardbirdsuite.com, 11 Tommy Banks Way near 103rd St & 86th Ave*) This large, low-key jazz club, in Old Strathcona, is the labor of love of the nonprofit Edmonton Jazz Society. Big names play here when they're in town, and ticket prices are always reasonable. Night owls, take note: shows often start and end early.

Also check out Sherlock Holmes Pub (see Places to Eat, earlier).

Sidetrack Cafe (☎ *780-421-1326, 10333 112th St*) This old roadhouse-style cafe, on downtown's west side, features blues as well as local rock groups.

Gay and lesbian clubs in Edmonton include *Secrets Bar & Grill* (☎ *780-990-1818, 10249 107th St*), catering primarily to women; *Buddys Nite Club* (☎ *780-421-0992, 11725B Jasper Ave*), catering primarily to men; and *The Roost* (☎ *780-426-3150, 10345 104th St*), accommodating men and women.

Cinemas *Princess Theatre* (☎ *780-433-0728, 10337 82nd Ave*) Adult/student & youth 12-17/senior & child 4-11 $8/6/5, all seats $5 on Monday and for weekend matinees. This is Edmonton's main outlet for good, varying films, including foreign and art flicks. The cinema itself is a historic site – it was the first marble-fronted building west of Winnipeg and at one time showed first runs of Mary Pickford films.

Spectator Sports

If you're here during ice hockey season (from October to April), try to see a home game of the National Hockey League's Edmonton Oilers (☎ 780-414-4625, 866-414-4625, W www.edmontonoilers.com) at *Skyreach Centre* (*7424 118th Ave NW*). Tickets cost $24 to $118.

The Edmonton Eskimos (☎ 780-448-3757, 800-667-3757, W www.esks.com) play Canadian Football League football from July to October at *Commonwealth Stadium* (*11000 Stadium Rd*). Tickets run $23 to $41 for adults, $12.50 to $21.50 for kids.

The Edmonton Trappers (☎ 780-414-4450, W www.trappersbaseball.com) of the Pacific Coast Baseball League are a farm team for the Minnesota Twins. They play their home games at *Telus Field* (*10233 96th Ave*) from April to August. Tickets cost $5 to $11.

Getting There & Away

Air Edmonton International Airport (YEG) is about 30km south of the city along the Calgary Trail, about a 45-minute drive from downtown. Major carriers serving the airport include Air Canada (☎ 888-247-2262, W www.aircanada.ca), with frequent flights to major cities such as Vancouver, Calgary and Toronto; Northwest Airlines (☎ 800-225-2525, W www.nwa.com), with flights to Minneapolis–St Paul; WestJet (☎ 800-538-5696, W www.westjet.com), a discount carrier serving western Canada; and Horizon Air (☎ 800-547-9308, W www .horizonair.com), offering commuter flights to Seattle.

Edmonton City Centre Airport (YXD), 3km north of downtown off 97th St near 118th Ave, is used by private planes and several commuter airlines.

For a complete list of airlines serving Edmonton, go online to W www.edmonton airports.com.

Bus The large Greyhound bus station (☎ 780-413-8747, 10324 103rd St at 103rd Ave) is central. It's open 5am to 12:30am and has luggage-storage lockers ($2) and a fast-food restaurant. Greyhound goes east to Winnipeg twice a day ($154, 19 to 20 hours) and west to Vancouver three times a day ($139, 16 to 17 hours). There are four daily trips to Jasper ($52, five hours) and two to Prince George ($100, 10 hours). A web of services goes north as far as Hay River ($137, 16 hours) and Whitehorse ($254, 29 hours). At least 11 buses a day run to Calgary ($42, from 3½ hours).

Another bus line serving Calgary is Red Arrow (☎ 780-425-0820), with its office in the Howard Johnson Plaza Hotel (10010 104th St). It offers four to seven buses a day leaving from outside the hotel; the one-way fare is $46. The deluxe buses have free soft drinks, power ports for laptop computers and other niceties.

Train The small VIA Rail station (fares and reservations ☎ 888-842-7245, depot ☎ 780-448-2575, 12360 121 St) is on the west side of City Centre Airport. It has a convenience shop, luggage-storage lockers ($1) and a Hertz car rental booth.

The *Canadian* travels three times a week east to Saskatoon, Winnipeg and Toronto and west to Jasper, Kamloops and Vancouver. At Jasper, you can connect to Prince George and Prince Rupert. VIA Rail services and fares are constantly in flux, so confirm details in advance.

Getting Around

To/From the Airport City buses don't go as far south as the international airport. The cheapest option is Sky Shuttle Airport Service (☎ 780-465-8515, 888-438-2342), which runs vans on three routes serving hotels downtown, in the West End and in the university area. Rates are $11/5.50 adult/child. The downtown route operates at least every 30 minutes; the ride takes 35 minutes from the last downtown stop to the airport.

Cab fare to downtown will run about $42 to $44 (see Taxi, later).

Bus & LRT Edmonton Transit System (ETS) operates city buses and the short 10-stop tram system, the Light Rail Transit (LRT). The LRT runs northeast from the university, east along Jasper Ave, north along 99th St and then northeast all the way to 139th Ave in Clareview. Between Clareview station and Stadium station the LRT travels above ground; from Churchill station to Grandin station it runs underground.

A single one-way fare on the LRT or buses is $1.75/1.25 adult/child six to 17. You can transfer from one to the other, but you must get a transfer receipt when you pay your fare and you must use the transfer within 90 minutes. You can also buy a day pass for $6. On weekdays from 9am to 3pm and on Saturday from 9am to 6pm, travel

between the five subway LRT stations between Churchill and Grandin is free.

An information center, open from 8:30am to 5:30pm weekdays, is in the Churchill LRT station (99th St at 102A Ave). Transit telephone operators (☎ 780-496-1611) are available weekdays from 6:30am to 9pm, and weekends and holidays from 8am to 5:30pm. Automated schedule information (☎ 780-496-1600) is available 24 hours. Buses on most routes operate at 30-minute intervals throughout the day, though they may be more or less frequent depending on the route and time of day. The LRT line operates from about 5:30am to 1:30am Monday to Saturday and until 12:30am Sunday. Late-night bus service is limited.

Streetcar The High Level Bridge is quite a sight just to look at, but between mid-May and early October you can actually ride across it on a streetcar. Thanks to the efforts of the Edmonton Radial Railway Society (☎ 780-437-7721, 🌐 www.edmonton-radial-railway.ab.ca), who refurbished the old CPR line and got it going again, you can board one of the vintage beauties on the river's north side next to the Grandin LRT station (109th St between 98th & 99th Aves) and take it across the bridge right into the heart of Old Strathcona (103rd St at 84th Ave). The roundtrip fare is $3, and the streetcars normally run twice an hour from 11am to 4pm.

The society also operates restored streetcars in Fort Edmonton Park.

Car All the major car rental firms have offices at the airport and around town. Among those at Edmonton International Airport are Avis (☎ 800-879-2847), Budget (☎ 800-268-8900), Hertz (☎ 800-263-0600) and Thrifty (☎ 800-367-2277). Check the Yellow Pages for other agencies around town.

Taxi Two taxi companies are Yellow Cab (☎ 780-462-3456) and Alberta Co-Op Taxi (☎ 780-425-8310). The fare from downtown to the West Edmonton Mall is about $20. The flagfall is $2.50, then it's $1.10 every kilometer.

AROUND EDMONTON
Alberta Railway Museum

This museum (☎ 780-472-6229, 🌐 www.railwaymuseum.ab.ca, 24215 34th St; adult/

senior & student/child 3-12 $4/2.50/1.25; open 10am-5pm daily mid-May–early Sept), on the northeast edge of Edmonton, has a collection of over 50 railcars, including steam and diesel locomotives and rolling stock, built and used between 1877 and 1950, as well as a collection of railway equipment, old train stations and related buildings. On weekends, volunteers fire up some of the old engines and you can ride along for $3 (the diesel locomotives run every Sunday in season; the 1913 steam locomotive gets fired up only on holiday weekends). To get there, drive north on 97th St (Hwy 28) to Hwy 37, turn right and go east for 7km to 34th St, then turn right and go south about 2km.

East of Edmonton

In the northern Beaver Hills, 45km east of Edmonton on the Yellowhead Hwy, is a 194-sq-km tract of original aspen forest that is preserved as **Elk Island National Park** (☎ 780-922-5790, ⓦ *www.parkscanada.gc.ca/elk, adult/senior/child 6-16 $4/3/2).* The park holds a high concentration of animals, including free-roaming herds of elk and plains bison and a small herd of threatened wood bison. Bison can often be seen from the road and will almost certainly be spied along the walking trails.

About 35 other mammal species also inhabit the park, and many can be sighted on early morning or evening hikes. Autumn is a particularly good time for wildlife viewing, as much of the vegetation has thinned out. Beavers are abundant in the many boggy areas, and the park holds large numbers of moose.

The park is a popular weekend spot, with camping, hiking, cycling and canoeing in summer and cross-country skiing and snow-shoeing in winter. It can be reached in under an hour from Edmonton and makes a good day trip. The information office near the entrance off Yellowhead Hwy (Hwy 16) distributes an excellent free guide to the park's features and wildlife. Read the guide to bison viewing, as these animals can be aggressive. The park's interpretive center schedules a variety of special programs and walks during the summer.

Some of the park's facilities close from early October to May. *Campsites* cost $14 a night; primitive camping costs $5 a night. A campfire permit costs an additional $4 a

night. For detailed information contact the superintendent (☎ 780-992-2950, Elk Island National Park, Site 4, RR 1, Fort Saskatchewan T8L 2N7).

The **Ukrainian Cultural Heritage Village** (☎ 780-662-3640, 8820 112th St; adult/senior/child 7-17 $6.50/5.50/3 peak season, half-price rest of the year; open 10am-6pm daily mid-May–early Sept, then 10am-4pm daily until mid-Oct, 10am-4pm Mon-Fri rest of the year), 50km east of Edmonton on Hwy 16 (3km east of Elk Island National Park), pays homage to the 250,000 Ukrainian immigrants who came to Canada in the late 19th and early 20th centuries. Many settled in central Alberta, where the landscape reminded them of the snowy steppes of home. Among the exhibits are a dozen or so structures, including a restored pioneer home and an impressive Ukrainian Greek Orthodox church. Docents in period costume add historic flavor.

South of Edmonton

Heading south toward Calgary, take Hwy 2A from Leduc to reach **Wetaskwin.** It's home to the **Reynolds-Alberta Museum** (☎ 780-361-1351, 800-661-4726, Hwy 13; adult/child $9/5; open 9am-5pm daily late-May–June, 9am-7pm daily July & Aug, 9am-5pm Tues-Sun & holiday Mondays rest of the year), an 83-acre complex 1km west of town devoted to celebrating the machine: in aviation, transportation, agriculture and industry. Among the collection highlights are a 1929 Duesenberg Phaeton Royale and a 1913 Chevy. The museum also houses **Canada's Aviation Hall of Fame.**

As you continue south, halfway between Edmonton and Calgary on Hwy 2 is **Red Deer,** a town of 69,000 in the heart of grain and cattle country. The compact downtown area has a sprinkling of structures dating from the pioneer days. Annual events include Westerner Days in mid-July and an international air show in early August. During either Calgary's Stampede or Edmonton's Klondike Days, travelers might consider Red Deer as a base. It's about 1½ hours away from either city, and accommodations here will not be as tight or expensive. For more information, contact the Red Deer Visitor & Convention Bureau (☎ 403-346-0180, 800-215-8946, ⓦ www.tourism reddeer.net, 30 Riverview Park).

Map Maker, Bible Reader & Tireless Trekker

From 1784 to 1812 David Thompson mapped much of the Canadian Rockies and the surrounding region while leading four major expeditions for fur-trading companies. He discovered the source of the Columbia River in British Columbia, helped map the border with the USA and found Athabasca Pass near Jasper, which for 40 years was the only route used by traders across the Rockies.

Though he was an energetic leader who covered about 130,000km by canoe, foot and horse, his daring exploits were not matched by an unbridled lifestyle. He extolled the virtues of soap in his meticulous journals, refused to use alcohol for trade with the Native peoples he met and enjoyed reading the Bible to the crustier members of his parties around the evening campfire.

His relations with Native Indians were generally good; he understood the value of their knowledge and readily adopted their advice for survival on his lengthy treks. His wife was part Cree, and he came to understand the Native Indian beliefs in the spirituality that was inherent in the land.

Thompson died at the age of 86 in 1857, and 59 years later material from his 77 notebooks was published in a volume simply titled *Narrative*. This caused a minor sensation, as Canadians and Americans began to realize the scope of Thompson's accomplishments. At the same time modern map-making techniques revealed the remarkable accuracy of the maps he had carefully drawn on his journeys 100 years before.

As you travel in Alberta, you'll often run into Thompson's name. In the town of Rocky Mountain House, 80km west of Red Deer, **Rocky Mountain House National Historic Site** (☎ 403-845-2412) preserves the site of fur-trading posts that were used at different times from 1799 to 1875 and that were a base for Thompson's explorations early in the 19th century. The park site is open year-round, but the excellent visitors' center is open only 9am to 5pm daily from May to September. The site is 5km west of the modern town on Hwy 11A. The 180km stretch of Hwy 11 from Rocky Mountain House west to the Icefields Parkway in the Rockies has been named the David Thompson Hwy.

One of the best books on Thompson is Jack Nisbet's *Sources of the River*. It places his accomplishments in the context of both historical and modern times.

Southeast of Red Deer on the way to Drumheller, **Dry Island Buffalo Jump** is an isolated provincial park that begins on a dramatic bluff overlooking the Red River Valley, near the town of Huxley. The initial view is like that of a mini-\Grand Canyon, whose multihued walls have been exposed by 63 million years of geological history. Among the many fossils that have been found here are those of the enormous and carnivorous *Tyrannosaurus rex*. Some 2000 years ago, aboriginal tribes drove bison over the edge of the 45m bluffs. Today the park site is seldom crowded and almost eerie when the wind howls down the river valley. To reach the park, which has no entrance gate or office, take the well-marked part-gravel road that runs 19km east of Hwy 21 just north of Huxley.

West of Edmonton

Heading west from Edmonton toward Jasper, the Yellowhead Hwy is a gorgeous drive through rolling wooded hills that are especially beautiful in fall. Accommodations are available along the way.

Hinton is the home of the Athabasca fire lookout tower, which offers a spectacular view of the Rockies. To get to the lookout tower, take Hwy 16 2km west from Hinton, then Hwy 40 18km north. Around the tower are a hang-glider launch area and the 960-hectare Athabasca Lookout Nordic Centre, which offers wintertime visitors beautifully groomed ski trails up to 25km long. It also has lighted night skiing on a 1.5km trail, plus a 1000m luge run. There's a use fee of $5. For more information, contact the Hinton Ranger Station (☎ 780-865-8264, 3rd floor, Government Centre, 131 Civic Centre Rd).

Hinton's well-marked tourist information center (☎ 780-865-2777, 309 Gregg Ave) is right alongside the Yellowhead Hwy. It's open daily in summer, weekdays only the rest of the year.

Northern Alberta

The land north of Edmonton is a vast, sparsely populated region of farms, forests, wilderness areas, lakes, open prairies and oilfields. The Cree, Slavey and Dene were the first peoples to inhabit the region, and many of them still depend on fishing, hunting and trapping. The northeast is virtually no roads and is dominated by Wood Buffalo National Park, the Athabasca River and Lake Athabasca. From its headwaters in British Columbia, the mighty Peace River makes its way to Lake Athabasca in the northeast of the province. The northwest is more accessible, with a network of highways connecting Alberta with northern British Columbia and the Northwest Territories.

PEACE RIVER & AROUND

From Edmonton, Hwy 43 heads northwest to Dawson Creek, British Columbia, (a distance of 590km), the official starting point of the Alaska Hwy. Numerous campgrounds and several provincial parks line the route. The scenery is generally flat or gently undulating, with dairy and cereal farms and with grain silos in nearly every town. **Grande Prairie**, a large, sprawling community, is an administrative, commercial and agricultural center. Most of the accommodations are centered on 100th St and 100th Ave. The visitors' information center (☎ 780-539-0211, 11330 106th St) is open in summer; for information the rest of the year, call the Grande Prairie Regional Tourism Association (☎ 780-539-7688).

Hwy 2, heading north directly out of Edmonton, is a more interesting route than Hwy 43; it follows the southern shore of **Lesser Slave Lake** part of the way. On the northern edge of the town of McLennan, the **Kimiwan Birdwalk and Interpretive Centre** (*in summer* ☎ *780-324-2004, in off-season* ☎ *780-324-3010*) is a special place for bird-watchers. The lake and surrounding marsh stand in the middle of three migratory routes, and nearly 300,000 birds pass through each year. The interpretive center is open 10am to 5:30pm five to seven days a week (it varies) from May through August, but the paths are open year-round.

The Peace River is so named because the warring Cree and Beaver Indians made

peace along its banks. The town of **Peace River** sits at the confluence of the Heart, Peace and Smoky Rivers. The visitors' information center, open May to September, is in the old train station, or you can stop by the **Museum of Peace River** (☎ 780-624-4261), at the end of Main St, for information. The town has several *motels* and two *campgrounds*. Greyhound buses leave daily for the Yukon and Northwest Territories. West of town, Hwy 2 leads to the Mackenzie Hwy.

MACKENZIE HWY

The small town of **Grimshaw** is the official starting point of the Mackenzie Hwy (Hwy 35) north to the Northwest Territories. The relatively flat and straight road is paved for the most part, though there are stretches of loose gravel or earth where the road is being reconstructed.

The mainly agricultural landscape between Grimshaw and Manning gives way to endless stretches of spruce and pine forest. Come prepared, as this is frontier territory and services become fewer (and more expensive) as the road cuts northward through the wilderness. A good basic rule is to fill your tank any time you see a gas station from here north.

High Level, the last settlement of any size before the Northwest Territories border, is a center for the timber industry. Workers often stay in the motels in town during the week. The only service station between High Level and Enterprise (in the Northwest Territories) is at Indian Cabins.

LAKE DISTRICT

From St Paul, over 200km northeast of Edmonton, to the Northwest Territories border lies Alberta's immense lake district. Fishing is popular (even in winter, when there is ice-fishing) but many of the lakes, especially farther north, have no road access and you have to fly in. St Paul, gateway to the lake district, is a trading center, with a **flying-saucer landing pad**, which is still awaiting its first customer. The region around St Paul has lots of provincial parks and campgrounds.

Hwy 63 is the main route into the province's northeastern wilderness interior. The highway, with a few small settlements and campgrounds along the way, leads to

Fort McMurray, which is 439km north of Edmonton. Originally a fur-trading outpost, it is now home to one of the world's largest oilfields. The story of how crude is extracted from the vast tracts of sand is told at the **Oil Sands Discovery Centre** (*☎ 780-743-7167, junction of Hwy 63 & MacKenzie Blvd; adult/child $3/2; open 9am-5pm daily mid-May–early Sept; 10am-4pm Tues-Sun rest of the year*). At the Fort McMurray Visitor's Bureau (*☎ 780-791-4336, 800-565-3947, 400 Sakitawaw Trail*), you can make reservations to tour the enormous oil-sand-production facilities ($15; children under age 12 not admitted).

WOOD BUFFALO NATIONAL PARK

You can access this huge park from Fort Smith in the Northwest Territories; see that chapter for information on the park.

In Alberta, the only access is via air to Fort Chipewyan, where there's a Visitors Reception Centre (*☎ 780-697-3662*). In winter, an ice road leads north to Peace Point (which connects to Fort Smith), and another road links the park to Fort McMurray.

Calgary

Calgary protrudes conspicuously from the flat plains of south-central Alberta. Farms are minutes away, and the rising foothills of the Rockies are just visible to the west, yet the streets of the city center, headquarters of the oil industry, are lined with office towers. Calgary is young and modern, with a metropolitan-area population approaching 1 million. It's an economic center with a university, professional sports franchises and an increasingly diverse cultural life. It is now also second only to Toronto as the home for major Canadian corporations.

The city's residents generally are educated and well paid and work in high-tech, energy and resource-based industries. The previously popular cowboy boots and hats have become vestiges of the recent past.

Calgary's climate is dry and sunny. It gets hot in summer but remains amazingly cool in the shade. In winter the warm chinook winds periodically blow off the mountains, drastically raising temperatures – at least temporarily.

Banff National Park is 120km west. Edmonton is 294km north.

History

The name Calgary, meaning 'clear, running water' in Gaelic, comes from Calgary Bay on Scotland's Isle of Mull. The area was initially home to the Blackfoot, but they were joined in the 18th century by the Sarcee and the Stoney. In the 1800s, as a result of intertribal conflicts and troubles between the tribes and European trappers, the Northwest Mounted Police were sent in to cool things down.

The NWMP established Fort Calgary in 1875. The Canadian Pacific Railway got here in 1883. Settlers were offered free land, and the population jumped to 4000 by 1891. Soon, cattle herders from the USA were pushing north, looking for better grazing. Calgary became a major meat-packing center and cowboy metropolis. Slowly, with moderate growth, it became a transportation and distribution point and is still Canada's cattle center. But since the late 1960s the city has had to deal with some dramatic changes, exploding from a fair-size cow town to a brand-new city of steel and glass.

The reason for Calgary's changeable fortunes is simple: oil. Oil had been discovered as far back as 1914, but it wasn't until the late 1960s that the black gold was found in vast quantities across Alberta. This discovery, coupled with the energy crisis of the 1970s, which bumped prices up sharply, saw the industry boom. The city took off, becoming the headquarters of 450 oil companies and home to more US citizens than any place outside of the USA.

After a brief, breath-catching period, the city's cultural side began to develop as well. However, during the 1980s the bottom fell out of the oil market and, with 70% of the workforce dependent on that industry, times quickly became tough. But Calgary's fortunes and reputation were boosted when it hosted the Winter Olympics in 1988, and by 1993 the oil and gas industries had rebounded. The city now has a broader economic base.

Orientation

Calgary lies on flat ground. It began at the confluence of the Bow and Elbow Rivers and has spread equally in all directions; the

CALGARY

1 Jubilee Auditorium
2 Peters' Drive-In
3 Greyhound Station
4 Calgary Zoo
5 Inglewood Bird Sanctuary
6 Firefighters Museum

city is the country's second largest area. The downtown core is still bounded by the Bow River to the north. The Elbow River runs through the city's southern portions. In the north, the Trans Canada Hwy cuts east-west across the city along 16th Ave NE and 16th Ave NW. The international airport is to the northeast, off Barlow Trail; the University of Calgary is to the northwest, off Crowchild Trail (Hwy 1A).

The city is divided into four geographical quadrants: northwest (NW), northeast (NE), southwest (SW) and southeast (SE). These abbreviations are important, as they're marked on street signs and included in addresses. The Bow River and Memorial Dr divide the city between north and south. Centre St (in the north) and Macleod Trail (in the south) split the city into east and west. It's fairly easy to figure where you're going, since most streets and avenues are numbered. Streets run north-south, and avenues run east-west.

The street-numbering system on the avenues is slightly nontraditional. For example, if you are on a stretch of street with a 2nd St crossing at one end and a 3rd St at the other, the street numbers begin at 300 at the 2nd St end and climb to the high 300s at the 3rd St end, where they begin at 400. Good luck.

Downtown Around the downtown center, a network of enclosed pedestrian bridges and over-the-street walkways connects buildings and shops. It's called the 'Plus 15' system, as the walkways are all at least 15 feet (5m) above ground. Eighth Ave between 3rd St SW and 1st St SE is a long pedestrian mall called Stephen Ave Walk. It's lined with trees, benches, shops (including large department stores), restaurants and fast-food places. Vendors sell crafts and souvenirs.

The western downtown area mainly has offices and businesses. The eastern section was the last to undergo redevelopment. It used to be the savior of the impecunious with its cheap bars and tatty hotels, of which there are a few remnants, but generally it's pretty cleaned up.

Stone lions guard each side of the Centre St Bridge over the Bow River, which has the grayish-green color of Rocky Mountain waters. The river marks the downtown area's northern edge. West of the bridge is Prince's Island Park, a pleasant natural area for strolling or dog-walking. On the north side of the bridge, stairs on both sides lead up to the cliff. A footpath along the cliff provides good city views, especially from atop the west-side stairs. Note that most points of interest downtown are within walking distance of each other.

Other Districts Just northwest of downtown over the river, off Memorial Dr, is the agreeable older district of **Kensington**, which has restaurants, cafés and nightclubs. You can walk here from downtown, crossing the river at 10th St, or take the LRT to Sunnyside Station.

South of Calgary Tower, over the railway tracks, are **Uptown** and the **4th St/Mission** districts, vibrant areas popular with young people and single professionals. Uptown is focused on 17th Ave SW between Centre St and 10th St SW. The 4th St/Mission district is focused on 4th St SW south of 17th Ave SW. Both areas have pubs, clubs, boutiques, galleries and restaurants.

Follow 17th Ave east to reach Stampede Park, east of which is the funky district of **Inglewood**, a cozy neighborhood of bookstores, antique shops and friendly pubs and restaurants.

Information

Tourism Calgary (☎ 403-263-8510, 800-661-1678, fax 403-262-3809, **W** www.tourism calgary.com, 220 8th Ave SW) operates a visitors' center in the Riley & McCormick

store on Stephen Ave Walk. It has city maps (including walking-tour maps that highlight various historic buildings) and lots of brochures. The staff will help you find accommodations. Hours are 8am to 5pm daily (until 8pm June to August). Information booths are also available at both the arrivals and departures levels of the airport.

Banks dot Stephen Ave Walk, and many are open Saturday. Most large branches will exchange foreign currency, as will American Express (☎ 403-261-5982, 421 7th Ave SW).

The main post office (☎ 403-974-2078, 207 9th Ave SW) is open 8am to 5:45pm Monday to Friday.

Wired Cyber Cafe (☎ 403-244-7070, 1032 17th Ave SW) has full Internet access for $10 an hour. It's open 9:30am to 10pm Monday to Friday, 10am to 9pm Saturday, 11am to 8pm Sunday. The downtown library (see Libraries) also offers Internet access.

The Hostel Shop (☎ 403-283-8311, **W** www .hostelshop.com, 1414 Kensington Rd NW) has travel and outdoor activity guides and maps, as well as travel goods. Map Town (☎ 403-215-4060, 400 5th Ave SW) has travel guides and a wide range of maps.

The WR Castell Central Library (☎ 403-260-2600, **W** www.calgarypubliclibrary.com, 616 Macleod Trail SE) is open 10am to 9pm Monday to Thursday and 10am to 5pm Friday and Saturday year-round, as well as 1:30pm to 5pm Sunday from mid-September to mid-May. It offers visitor Internet access for $2 an hour; demand is high for the 20 or so terminals, so you might have to wait. Check the website for branch libraries.

Avenue Coin Laundry (☎ 403-262-8777, 333 17th Ave SW) is in a modern apartment tower.

Hospitals include Foothills Hospital (☎ 403-670-1110, 1403 29th St NW), Peter Lougheed Centre of the Calgary General Hospital (☎ 403-291-8555, 3500 26th Ave NE), Rockyview General Hospital (☎ 403-541-3000, 7007 14th St SW) and Alberta Children's Hospital (☎ 403-229-7211, 1820 Richmond Rd SW).

Within Calgary, dial ☎ 911 for police, medical and fire emergencies.

Calgary Tower

This 1968 landmark (☎ 403-266-7171, **W** www .calgarytower.com, 101 9th Ave SW; elevators $8/5/3 adult/senior & youth 13-17/child 3-12;

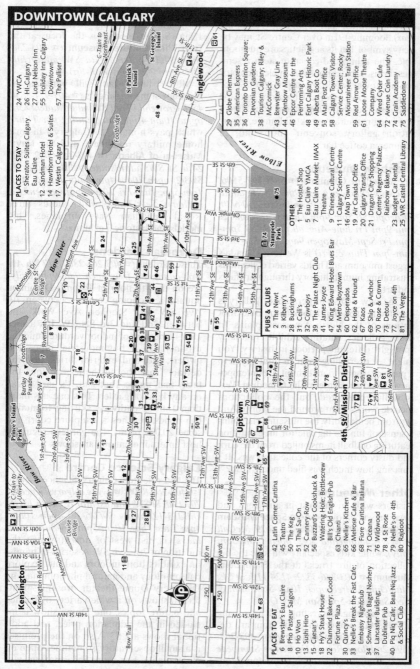

observation gallery open 7:30am-11:30pm daily in summer, 8am-10pm daily rest of the year), looming 191m over Centre St, may be a city symbol, but its aesthetics are questionable. The reinforced-concrete stem resembles a prison blockhouse or nuclear-reactor cooling tower, while the top is '60's Space Age à la *The Jetsons*. Elevators take 62 seconds to reach the top, where you'll find a revolving restaurant, cocktail lounge, observation gallery, souvenir shop and, in summer, a coffee bar.

Glenbow Museum

The excellent Glenbow (☎ 403-777-5506, W www.glenbow.org, 130 9th Ave SE; adult/senior/student & youth/family $10/7.50/6/30, all people $6 5pm-9pm Thur year-round & 5pm-9pm Fri June-Aug, all people $3 5pm-9pm Fri Sept-May; open 9am-5pm Sat-Wed, 9am-9pm Thur & Fri) is Western Canada's largest museum and holds varied collections illustrating human history through artifacts and art.

One new 740-sq-m permanent gallery is devoted to an in-depth look at the Blackfoot nations of the North American plains. In other galleries, rotating exhibits regularly spotlight different periods in history. You might see everything from an Inuit kayak to a pioneer wagon to an exhibit of contemporary Canadian painters. The Canadian West is well represented, but the collections include works from around the world. And far from being stuffy, the museum maintains a sense of fun; its tag line for an exhibition featuring oddball items pulled from the dark and dusty corners of the collection was, 'It's amazing how much was filed under "Huh?"'

Other Museums

Visitors with an interest in airplanes and aviation will enjoy the **Aero Space Museum of Calgary** (☎ 403-250-3752, 4629 McCall Way NE; adult/child $6/2; open 10am-5pm daily), while kids especially will love the big collection of fire trucks at the **Firefighters Museum** (☎ 403-246-3322, 4124 11th St SE; adult/child $2/free; open 10am-5pm Mon & Wed-Sat, noon-5pm Sun May-Oct).

The growing, harvesting and processing of Alberta's amber waves of grain are detailed at the **Grain Academy** (☎ 403-263-4594, 2nd floor, Round-Up Centre, Stampede Park; admission free; open 10am-4pm Mon-

Fri year-round, also noon-4pm Sat Apr-Sept), while the history of the local Tsuu T'ina (Sarcee) people is the focus at the **Tsuu T'ina Culture Museum** (☎ 403-238-2677, 3700 Anderson Rd SW; adult/child $3/1; open 9am-4pm Mon-Fri).

Military-history buffs will appreciate the **Museum of the Regiments** (☎ 403-974-2850, 4520 Crowchild Trail SW; adult/student $5/2; open 10am-4pm daily, until 9pm Thur), which pays homage to Calgary's historic home miltary regiments, and the **Naval Museum of Alberta** (☎ 403-242-0002, 1820 24th St SW; adult/student/child under 12 $5/3/2; open 10am-4pm daily July & Aug; 1pm-5pm Tues-Fri, 10am-6pm weekends & holidays Sept-June), which holds three Royal Canadian Navy airplanes, ship models and historical exhibits.

Devonian Gardens

These gardens (☎ 403-268-2300, 317 7th Ave SW; admission free; open 9am-9pm daily) are on the 4th floor of Toronto Dominion Square, a shopping complex between 7th Ave SW and Stephen Ave Walk and between 2nd and 3rd Sts SW. It's a nice idea – a hectare of indoor verdure amid the urban jungle – but industrial pipes and girders, tile, and exterior brick flooring detract from the aesthetics, as does the tacky mall music. That said, it's hard to rag on any kind of garden. This one has more than 1km of pathways skirting fountains, fish ponds, benches, a sculpture court and some 20,000 plants. The gardens regularly host entertainment and art shows.

Calgary Science Centre

The kid-oriented Calgary Science Centre (☎ 403-268-8300, W www.calgaryscience.ca, 701 11th St SW; adult/senior & youth 13-18/child 3-12/family $9/7/6/32; open 10am-4pm Tues-Thur, 10am-5pm Fri-Sun & holidays) is just west of downtown at the junction of 7th Ave SW. A series of hands-on exhibits, both indoors and out, explore paleontology and natural phenomena. The Discovery Dome theater presents giant-screen shows on a wide variety of science and nature topics; one Dome show is included in the admission price, and additional shows are $3. Also on the premises is a small observatory, sometimes open on clear nights. For more information, you might check out the website, but for a science museum, the site is truly awful.

Chinese Cultural Centre

This cultural center (☎ 403-262-5071, 197 1st St SW; admission free; open 9am-9pm daily), built in 1993 by skilled Chinese artisans, is the impressive landmark building blocking 2nd Ave at the edge of Chinatown. Inside you'll find a magnificent 21m-high dome ornately painted with 561 dragons and other imagery. Its design was inspired by Beijing's Temple of Heaven. The 2nd and 3rd floors frequently house changing art and cultural exhibitions. Downstairs, the **museum** (adult/senior & child $2/1; open 11am-5pm daily) holds Chinese art and artifacts, including a collection of replica terra-cotta soldiers.

Prince's Island Park

This pretty park, on an island in the Bow River north of downtown, is connected to both sides of the river by pedestrian bridges. It's a cool, quiet spot with lots of trees and flowers, picnic tables and jogging and cycling paths – a good antidote to a hot summer's day in Calgary. As the signs say, the water in the Bow River is too swift and cold to be safe for swimming. The bridge to the island from downtown is at the north end of 3rd St SW.

Heritage Park Historical Village

This 26-hectare living-history park (☎ 403-259-1900, W www.heritagepark.ab.ca, 1900 Heritage Dr SW at 14th St SW; adult/child 3-17/family $11/7/41, plus $8 per person for train & boat ride; open 9am-5pm daily mid-May–early Sept, 9am-5pm Sat & Sun mid-Sept–mid-Oct; limited operation rest of the year), southwest of downtown, sits on a peninsula jutting into the Glenmore Reservoir. The park re-creates life in a western Canadian town during three different eras: the 1860s, the 1880s, and around 1910.

The reconstructed frontier village includes a Hudson's Bay Company fort, a working grain mill, an 1896 church and many stores full of artifacts and antiques. The well laid-out grounds also hold a ranch house, teepee, trapper's cabin and schoolhouse. Be sure to take a look at the two-story outhouse, for which the phrase 'look out below!' has special meaning. An excellent collection of horse-drawn vehicles includes stagecoaches, traps and surreys, and you'll also see old cars, railway coaches and a working steam engine. But you won't be Huck Finnished until you hop aboard the SS *Moyie* sternwheeler for a cruise on the reservoir.

Admission includes a pancake breakfast served between 9am and 10am daily in season. If you miss that, you'll find several eating places around the grounds, and you can buy fresh bread from the bakery. In the off-season, October to May, you can come for Sunday brunch (adult/child $11/6). To get there, take C-Train to Heritage station, then bus No 20.

Fort Calgary Historic Park

This 16-hectare national and provincial historic site (☎ 403-290-1875, W www.fort calgary.com, 750 9th Ave SE; adult/child 7-17 $6.50/3; open 9am-5pm daily May-early Oct), just east of downtown, preserves the spot where Calgary's original settlement began. In 1875 the first detachment of the Northwest Mounted Police arrived here, where the Bow and Elbow Rivers meet. They built Fort Calgary, which was occupied by a police post until 1914. All that remains of the fort are a few foundations; a replica is under construction, with workers using period tools and materials. Plaques give some of the history.

An interpretive center tells the story of Calgary's development with displays and a video on the Northwest Mounted Police, as well as streetscapes re-creating Calgary from 1875 to the 1940s. The fort site is pleasant and has good views, and costumed interpreters are present all season. Paths lead down to the river and across a footbridge to St Patrick's Island and on to the Calgary Zoo.

To the east, across the Elbow River, is **Hunt House**, probably the oldest building on its original site in the Calgary area. It was built by the Hudson's Bay Company in 1876 for one of its employees. Next door, the larger **Deane House** was built in 1906 for the commanding officer of Fort Calgary. It now operates as a restaurant (☎ 403-269-7747).

Calgary Zoo

The zoo (☎ 403-232-9300, 800-588-9993, W www.calgaryzoo.ab.ca, 1300 Zoo Rd NE; adult/child 2-17 $11/5.50, seniors half-price Tues-Thur; open 9am-5pm daily), one of

Canada's largest and best zoos and Calgary's most popular attraction, is east of downtown on St George's Island and the northern bank of the Bow River. It brings together over 1100 animals representing 227 species of mammal, bird, reptile, amphibian, fish and invertebrate, many in enclosures simulating their natural habitats. Call ahead to check on feeding times. A huge new Africa exhibit is scheduled to open in 2003.

Besides the animals, the zoo has a **Botanical Garden** with changing garden displays, a tropical rain forest, a good butterfly enclosure and the 6½-hectare **Prehistoric Park**, featuring fossil displays and life-size dinosaur replicas in natural settings. Picnic areas dot the zoo and island, and a café is on-site.

During winter, when neither you nor the animals will care to linger outdoors, the admission price is reduced. To get there, take C-Train east to Zoo stop.

Inglewood Bird Sanctuary

This 32-hectare nature reserve (☎ 403-269-6688, 2425 9th Ave SE; admission free; open 9am-5pm daily, until 8pm Fri-Sun June-Aug) is southeast of downtown at the end of 9th Ave, on a forested section of the Bow River flats. The area is home to at least 260 bird species and is a resting spot for those on the migratory trail. It's a good resting spot for migrating humans as well – the serenity here makes a perfect antidote to city noise and traffic.

Trails lead through the sanctuary; they're open during daylight hours year-round. A small **interpretive center** (admission free, donations appreciated; open 10am-5pm daily May 1-Sept 30, 10am-4pm Tues-Sun rest of the year) has kid-friendly interactive exhibits describing the local birdlife.

Bus No 411 goes within a few blocks of the sanctuary on weekdays only; weekends, you can take bus No 1 from downtown, which stops a bit farther away.

Fish Creek Provincial Park

On Calgary's southwest edge, this huge tract of land (☎ 403-297-5293; admission free; open 8am-dark daily year-round) protects Fish Creek, which flows into the Bow River, and its surrounding valley. It acts as a shelter for many animals and birds and is

the country's largest urban park. Park interpreters present slide shows and lead walking tours to explain some of the local ecology. Dogs must be kept on a leash.

For details, contact the administration office or go online to ⓦ www3.gov.ab.ca/env/parks/prov_parks/fishcreek. There are numerous access points to the park, which stretches 20km between 37th St in the west and the Bow River in the east. From downtown, take bus No 3 via Elbow Dr.

Calaway Park

This large amusement park (☎ 403-240-3822, ⓦ www.calawaypark.com; adult & youth/child 3-6/senior 50 & up/family $19.50/14/12/60; open 10am-8pm daily July-Aug, reduced schedule mid-May-June & Sept-early Oct, closed rest of the year), 10km west of town on the Trans Canada Hwy (Hwy 1) at the Springbank Rd exit, features 27 rides, mini-golf, a trout-fishing pond, children's playground, restaurants and live entertainment daily. If you can't drag yourself (or the kids) away, you can stay in the park's own **RV park/campground** (☎ 403-249-7372, fax 403-242-3885); it's $15 for a tent site, $25 for full hookups.

Canada Olympic Park

Calgary hosted the 15th Winter Olympics in 1988, a first for Canada. At Canada Olympic Park (☎ 403-247-5452, ⓦ www.coda.ab.ca, 88 Canada Olympic Rd SW; open daily), a 15-minute drive west of town on the Trans Canada Hwy to the Bowfort Rd exit, you can see the 70m and 90m ski jumps – from the top you realize how crazy those guys are – and the concrete bobsled and luge runs. (You can ride a bobsled on the actual track, winter or summer, for $45.) Some of the facilities are now used as an Olympic training center. The **Olympic Hall of Fame** has three floors of exhibits honoring athletic achievements, and simulators that re-create the sensation of bobsledding and skiing. Facility hours vary throughout the year; call or go online for a schedule.

You can look around the park yourself ($7 per person) or take a two-hour guided tour that includes a bus around the grounds and admission to the Hall of Fame ($10 per person).

The Olympic skiing events actually took place 55km west of town in Kananaskis

Country (see that section, later in this chapter). But both downhill skiing (full-day adult lift ticket $30/25 weekend/weekday) and cross-country skiing (day pass $6 for ages seven and older) are offered here in winter. Ski rentals are available.

In summer, the park is popular for lift-served mountain biking; a day pass is $7.

Activities

Calgary holds an incredible 400km of **cycling** and **hiking** trails, many in the parks and nature areas. The city's excellent *Calgary Pathway and Bicycle Route Map* is available for $1 from the Calgary Parks and Recreation Department office (☎ 403-268-3888, 205 8th Ave SE, 3rd floor). The map is also sold at Canadian Tire stores and bike shops around town.

Two leisure centers run by Calgary Parks & Recreation have giant wave pools, year-round skating, racquetball courts, hot tubs, climbing walls and more. They are: **Village Square Leisure Centre** (☎ 403-280-9714, 2623 56th St NE) and **Southland Leisure Centre** (☎ 403-251-3505, 2000 Southland Dr SW at 19th St SW). Downtown, the big, beautiful **Eau Claire YMCA** (☎ 403-269-6701, 101 3rd St SW; adult/student/senior/youth 14-17/child 2-13/family $8/6/5/4/3.25/17; open 5:30am-10:30pm Mon-Fri, 7am-7pm Sat, Sun & holidays) has the latest in keep-fit facilities.

And don't forget **fishing**. The Bow River begins as clean, clear, barely melted ice in Bow Lake in the Rockies, not far from Banff, and flows swiftly through Calgary. From Calgary it slows and warms and eventually reaches Medicine Hat, near the Saskatchewan border. The 60km stretch from Calgary east to Carseland is considered one of North America's best trout-fishing rivers, thanks to its abundance of big brown and rainbow trout. Numerous fishing-guide services and sporting goods stores in town offer fishing tackle and information. One place that combines the two is **Country Pleasures** (☎ 403-271-1016, 10816 Macleod Trail S).

Organized Tours

The cheapest way to tour town is to take the No 10 bus from along 6th Ave. For $1.75 this bus goes on a 2½ hour circular route past old and new areas and the city's highest point, with views to the foothills,

the university and some wealthy districts in the northwest.

Brewster Gray Line (☎ 403-221-8242, 800-661-1152, W www.brewster.ca, 808 Centre St S) runs traditional bus tours of Calgary and various Rocky Mountain locations from Calgary. The Calgary tour ($43) takes about four hours and covers about 50km. It includes Fort Calgary, Canada Olympic Park and the downtown area, with admission prices included in the ticket. Guides give a history of the city. The 'Beautiful Banff' tour takes nine hours ($80/60 summer/rest of the year).

Two small tour companies have a delightfully informal approach. **Hammerhead Tours** (☎ 403-260-0940, W www.hammerhead tours.com) operates two trips, one east to the Drumheller badlands and Royal Tyrrell Museum ($60) and another south to Head-Smashed-In Buffalo Jump ($60). Both are full-day trips with a small group in a van and take in various attractions along the way. The tour picks up at several locations, including HI-Calgary and Calgary Tower. Trips are run from May to November. HI members get 15% off.

Working in conjunction with HI-Calgary hostel is **True North Tours** (☎ 403-912-0407, 888-464-4842 in Canada), which operates the Rocky Express, a six-day trip to Banff, Lake Louise and Jasper with accommodations in various hostels along the way (around $215 plus hostel rates). Vans are used, and the optional group meals can really keep costs down. There is also a three-day trip with shorter hikes. Reservations should be made about two or three weeks in advance. Trips run from mid-May to early October.

Moose Travel Network runs a tour-bus loop between Banff and Vancouver, BC, stopping at great destinations all along the way (see Getting There & Away in the Banff section).

Special Events

For a year-round list of the city's events, go online to W www.tourismcalgary.com/festivals1.html. Calgary's two biggest events both take place in July.

Calgary Stampede This wild, 10-day festival (☎ 403-261-0101, 800-661-1260, W www.calgary stampede.com), which dates from 1912, starts with a huge parade in the second week of July each year. Most organized events take place in

Stampede Park southeast of downtown, but many of the streets are full of activity, too. Stampede Park comes alive with concerts, shows, exhibitions, dancing and eating, attracting over 100,000 people each day. An amusement area features rides, a gambling hall and lots of contests. Highlights are the chuck-wagon races and the rodeo, which is said to be North America's biggest and roughest. Events include calf-roping, branding and riding bucking broncos and bulls. At night the Stampede Stage Show takes over, with singers, bands, clowns, dancers and fireworks; tickets for the main events go early. Gate admission is $10/5 adult/senior & child. The town and nearby countryside are packed for the duration of the celebrations, so it's a good idea to book accommodations well in advance or arrive early. For more information, write to Calgary Exhibition & Stampede, Box 1060, Station M, Calgary, AB T2P 2K8.

The Wild West takes over town during the Calgary Stampede in July.

Calgary Folk Music Festival The main events of this festival (☎ 403-233-0904, **W** www.calgary folkfest.com), held in late July, take place on Prince's Island and include performances by big-name local, national and international artists. Past performers have included the Cowboy Junkies, David Byrne, Tom Cochrane, Kathy Mattea and Buckwheat Zydeco, among many many others. A one-day pass runs $35 to $40. Four-day adult passes, available by advance purchase only, cost about $90 to $100. The festival also brings free lunchtime performances on Stephen Ave Walk and evening performances in various venues around town.

Places to Stay

The prices quoted in this section are normal for summer; some rise during the Stampede, while others fall during winter. Tourism Calgary's visitor service center will make free bookings (see Tourist Offices under Information, earlier).

Camping Several campgrounds suitable for both RVs and tents are near the city.

Mountain View Farm Campground (☎ 403-293-6640, fax 403-293-4798) Sites $18-26. Open year-round. Mountain View Campground is on a farm 3km east of the Calgary city limits on the Trans Canada Hwy. It has showers, laundry, a barbecue, mini-golf, even a petting zoo. German is spoken.

Calgary West KOA (☎ 403-288-0411, 800-562-0842) Sites $25-30. On the Trans Canada's south side at the western city limits, near Canada Olympic Park, the KOA has 350 sites (including pull-throughs), a pool, laundry facilities, a game room and shuttle service to downtown.

Calaway Park (☎ 403-249-7372, fax 403-242-3885) Sites $15-25. Calaway Park, 10km west of Calgary on the Trans Canada Hwy (Springbank Rd exit), has full facilities, including showers and laundry but no pull-throughs.

Hostels *HI-Calgary* (☎ 403-269-8239, fax 403-266-6227, **W** www.hostellingintl.ca/ alberta, 520 7th Ave SE) Dorm beds $16/20 members/nonmembers. Open 24 hours. This popular hostel is on the east side of downtown, not far from Fort Calgary. It's a large place, complete with laundry, kitchen, Internet access and snack bar, but it still often gets full in summer. Reservations are recommended. The hostel organizes a lot of events and activities and offers a variety of cost-saving ideas.

YWCA (☎ 403-263-1550, fax 403-263-4681, 320 5th Ave SE) Singles $40/50 without/with bath, doubles $50/60. The central YWCA is for women only. It has clean rooms, a pool and gym. The exterior must have been a pork-barrel project to appease the concrete union.

University of Calgary (☎ 403-220-3203, University Housing Office, Cascade Hall, Room 104, 3456 24th Ave NW, Calgary T2N 4V5) Dorm beds $20, apartments $50-100.

The university rents dorm rooms and apartments from early May to the end of August. Facilities on campus include a gym and a cheap cafeteria. The university, northwest of the center off Crowchild Trail, is served by the C-Train.

B&Bs The visitors' center keeps a list of B&Bs and makes bookings, as does the *Bed & Breakfast Association of Calgary* (☎ 403-277-0023, fax 403-295-3823, w www .bbcalgary.com). The *Alberta Accommodation Guide* lists over 40 B&Bs in Calgary; rates average around $50/75 for singles/ doubles.

Motels Most of the good moderately priced accommodations lie outside the city center in motels. Calgary has dozens of them in all parts of the city, but there are some areas of heavy concentration, making it easy to shop around.

One of these is south of the city along Macleod Trail, a commercial strip with service stations, fast-food restaurants, motels and furniture shops.

Econo Lodge South (☎ 403-252-4401, 888-559-0559, fax 403-252-2780, 7505 Macleod Trail S) Singles/doubles from $79/89. This motor hotel has laundry facilities, a pool, sauna and a licensed restaurant and lounge.

Travelodge Calgary Macleod Trail (☎ 403-253-7070, 877-530-9206, fax 403-255-6740, 9206 Macleod Trail S) Singles/doubles from $79/99. The Travelodge offers a pool, spa and sauna, laundry facilities and a free newspaper.

'Motel Village,' as it's been dubbed, is a motel area in northwest Calgary on and just off 16th Ave (the Trans Canada Hwy). Southeast of the University of Calgary, 16th Ave meets Crowchild Trail; linking the two on a diagonal, forming a triangle, is Banff Trail (Hwy 1A). The area is thick with independent and chain lodgings, and although it is a fair way from downtown, Motel Village is well linked by C-Train service (Banff Trail stop).

Several budget offerings here have basic, no-frills rooms starting at around $65 in summer. These include: *Holiday Motel* (☎ 403-288-5431, fax 403-247-3018, 4540 16th Ave NW), *Traveller's Inn* (☎ 403-247-1388, fax 403-247-4220, 4611 16th Ave NW) and *Budget Host Motor Inn* (☎ 403-288-

7115, 800-661-3772, fax 403-286-4899, 4420 16th Ave NW).

Econo Lodge Motel Village (☎ 403-289-2561, 800-917-7779, fax 403-282-9713, w www .econolodgecalgary.com, 2440 16th Ave NW) Singles/doubles from $79/89. This is one of two Econo Lodges in Motel Village. The other (☎ 403-289-1921, 800-917-7779, fax 403-282-2149, 2231 Banff Trail) has similar rates. Both are relatively nice for the chain.

Holiday Inn Express (☎ 403-289-6600, 800-465-4329, fax 403-289-6767, 2227 Banff Trail NW) Singles/doubles from $81/91. This newish property has comfortable, well-equipped rooms, a pool, spa, sauna and free newspapers.

Other good choices around town include the following:

Holiday Inn Calgary Downtown (☎ 403 266-4611, 800-661-9378, fax 403-237-0978, w www.holidayinn-calgary.com, 119 12th Ave SW) Singles & doubles from $119. Though convenient to downtown, the Holiday Inn is a well-kept secret. It sits quietly off by itself on the south side of the tracks, in a hip block of pubs and restaurants not far from the Uptown action. Note, however, that east of here, between the hotel and Stampede Park, you might run into some scantily clad, stiletto-heeled women acting extremely eager to meet you. If that makes you uncomfortable, head west on your evening constitutionals.

Best Western Airport Inn (☎ 403-250-5015, 877-499-5015, fax 403-250-5019, w www.bestwesternairportinn.com, 1947 18th Ave NE) Singles/doubles from $79/89. Out near the airport and northeast of downtown, this Best Western is a straightforward place with decent rooms, a restaurant, bar, pool and free airport shuttle.

Delta Calgary Airport Hotel (☎ 403-291-2600, 800-268-1133, fax 403-250-8722, w www.deltahotels.com, 2001 Airport Rd NE) Rooms $239. In the airport itself, and connected to the terminals, this place is almost luxurious and features a health club, among other amenities. The rooms are suitably soundproofed. Should jet lag get you down, there's a masseuse on call.

Hotels Lodgings downtown are mostly modern business-oriented hotels linked to the Plus 15 walkways. Many of these places drop their rates on weekends.

Lord Nelson Inn (☎ 403-269-8262, 800-661-6017, fax 403-269-4868, 1020 8th Ave SW) Rooms from $115. On downtown's west side, the modest Lord Nelson has full facilities and free parking.

Sandman Hotel (☎ 403-237-8626, 800-726-3626, fax 403-290-1238, **W** www.sandman hotels.com, 888 7th Ave SW) Singles/doubles $111/121, weekend specials as low as $80 single or double. This is a good, standard mid-range hotel with a gym, swimming pool, on-site restaurant and cocktail lounge.

Hawthorn Hotel & Suites (☎ 403-263-0520, 800-661-1592, fax 403-262-9991, **W** www.hawthorncalgary.com, 618 5th Ave SW) Rooms from $155. All rooms have kitchenettes at this modern all-suites hotel.

Westin Calgary (☎ 403-266-1611, 800-937-8461, fax 403-233-7471, **W** www.westin.com, 320 4th Ave SW) Rooms starting at $190 weekdays, as low as $120 weekends. This hotel has 525 large and luxurious rooms, as well as a complete business center.

Sheraton Suites Calgary Eau Claire (☎ 403-266-7200, 800-325-3535, fax 403-266-1300, **W** www.sheraton.com, 255 Barclay Parade SW) Rooms from around $260 weekdays, $165 weekends. The 325-suite Sheraton enjoys a great location right by Eau Claire Market. Its design, both inside and out, embodies a touch more class than most of the concrete corporate monstrosities downtown. Amenities are abundant for both the business and pleasure traveler.

The Palliser (☎ 403-262-1234, 800-441-1414, fax 403-260-1260, **W** www.fairmont .com, 133 9th Ave SW) Rooms from $178. When Queen Elizabeth drops by Calgary, she stays at this grand Canadian Pacific Railway hotel dating from 1914. Now a Fairmont, the hotel offers 405 elegantly updated rooms and suites varying greatly in size.

Places to Eat

Steaks still figure prominently in the 'Old West' image of Calgary, but the growing number of ethnic groups is reflected in the variety of restaurants.

Breakfast Coffee and muffin? Or eggs and bacon? Either way, Calgary's got you covered. All these places are options for a light lunch, too.

Schwartzie's Bagel Noshery (☎ 403-296-1353, 513 8th Ave SW) Bagels $1 or less;

'bagelwiches' $4-6. Near Stephen Ave Walk, this is part of a local chain good for coffee and a wide range of bagels and toppings.

Nellie's Break the Fast Café (☎ 403-265-5071, 516 9th Ave SW) Prices $6.50-9. A popular down-home breakfast place now affiliated with the Nellie's empire (see below), this upstairs café has tasty omelets, pancakes and such, as well as Ukrainian-style breakfast and lunch specials. On nice days you can read the paper on the rooftop deck.

Nellie's Kitchen (☎ 403-244-4616, 738B 17th Ave SW) Breakfast $5-9. This small, pleasant café has fantastic breakfasts and a patio out back. The Nellie's dynasty also includes *Nellie's on 4th* (☎ 403-209-2708, 2308 4th St SW) and brand-new Nellie's Cosmic Café (not yet open at press time).

Steaks & Seafood Alberta in general, and Calgary in particular, has long had a reputation for steak – this is the heart of cattle country after all. Several steak houses in town serve a mean hunk of cow – at a mean price. Carnivores on a budget can sample the local cattle less expensively, with a city lunch specialty known as beef dip. This consists of thinly sliced roast beef served plain in a long bun, usually with fries and a bowl of 'sauce' to dip the meat into. In the better places this dip is nothing but juice from the roast – it should not be like gravy. Prices are about $5 to $7.

Quincy's (☎ 403-264-1000, 609 7th Ave SW) Steaks $23-37, other Continental cuisine dishes $26-36. Quincy's has an attractive

Calgary meals: more than a mouthful

wood-lined dining room and several other rooms catering to group functions.

Hy's Steak House (☎ 403-263-2222, 316 4th Ave SW) Steaks & prime rib $25-35. Hy's has changed little from when it opened in 1955. It's a classic plush steak house where the carpets are as dark and thick as the prime Alberta beef.

Other local favorites for a slab of steak include *Caesar's* (☎ 403-264-1222, 512 4th Ave SW) and *The Keg* (☎ 403-266-1036, 1101 5th St SW).

Cannery Row (☎ 403-269-8889, 317 10th Ave SW) Most dinner dishes $15-20 (upstairs $24-35). For seafood, the casual Cannery Row (or its elegant upstairs affiliate, McQueen's, ☎ 403-269-4722) is the place. Downstairs, your bucket of steamers or platter of prawns comes with live R&B on Friday and Saturday nights; upstairs, the lobsters love jazz. Up or down, choose from the same excellent wine list.

Oceana (☎ 403-245-8787, 1800 4th St SW) Dinner dishes $15-25. A promising newcomer on the seafood scene, Oceana has a menu stuffed to the gills with fish of every description.

Other Canadian Fare From California cuisine to a quintessential burger, Calgary restaurants provide plenty of choices for casual Canadian- and American-style meals.

Lancaster Building (☎ 403-206-6400, 304 8th Ave SW) If you're on Stephen Ave Walk around lunch or dinner, check out the 2nd floor of the Lancaster building, on the corner of 2nd St SW. Around a dozen kiosks serve cheap chicken, pizza and other fast-food fare. You get street views, too.

Peters' Drive-In (☎ 403-277-2747, 219 16th Ave NE) Burgers $2.50-4. Peters' is a Calgary institution that's been flipping out flame-broiled burgers since 1962. At dinnertime, huge hungry hordes pile up in front of the walk-up window, while a long line of cars idles away in the extra-long drive-up lane. Look for the big lawn with picnic tables out front.

Buzzard's Cookshack & Watering Hole (☎ 403-264-6959, 140 10th Ave SW) Sandwiches $4-10, lunch dishes $8-20, dinner $11-26. Next to (and affiliated with) Bottlescrew Bill's pub, this thoroughly casual eatery with a busy Western decor offers sandwiches (including a good beef dip),

burgers and wraps at lunch, plus steaks and other entrées at dinner. And you get the same great beer selection available in the pub. The patio is a nice place to hang in summer.

Piq Niq Cafe (☎ 403-263-1650, 811 1st St SW) Lunch $10-13, dinner $12-25. This gourmet café downtown packs in the customers for its panini sandwiches at lunch and its beef, seafood, chicken and pastas for dinner. The restaurant's funky bar, Beat Niq (see Live Music, later), hosts weekend jazz.

4 St Rose (☎ 403-228-5377, 2116 4th St SW) Mains $11-17. California cuisine and wine are the focus of this comfortable 4th St bistro. The wide-ranging menu includes tapas, salads, burgers, sandwiches, personal-size gourmet pizzas and noodle dishes, as well as substantial entrées such as mango-chipotle chicken and five-spice seared salmon.

Brewster's Eau Claire (☎ 403-265-2739, 101 Barclay Parade) Lunch dishes $13-14, dinner dishes $11-20. Brewpub lovers will be in heaven here. Brewster's – a small chain but no relation to the Banff tour bus kings – brews a wide selection of fine beers on the premises, including some nice, subtle fruit beers that even guys might drink. And the kitchen serves creative fare that's far too tasty to be called 'pub grub.' For lunch, try the pepper-seared tuna sandwich with wasabi mayo, sliced fresh tomatoes, sweet pickled ginger and sunflower sprouts. For dinner, maybe it's the Irish ale salmon or cabernet sirloin. Yum.

Melrose Cafe & Bar (☎ 403-228-3566, 730 17th Ave SW) Pizzas $7-9, dinner dishes $9-15. A trendy spot in a trendy neighborhood, the Melrose might be the epitome of 17th Ave style. Readers of *Calgary Straight* voted its terraced patio best in town; the beer from the 16 taps is treated with TLC, including chilled lines and a special glass rinser; and the menu offers gourmet pizzas from a wood-burning oven, as well as fresh and healthy sandwiches, salads, seafood and more.

Wildwood (☎ 403-228-0100, 2417 4th St SW) Dinner dishes $17-33. The beers are as carefully brewed as the food is prepared at this upscale microbrewery/restaurant. Both the upstairs restaurant and downstairs pub offer gorgeous, casually elegant ambience. The innovative 'Canadian Rocky Mountain' cuisine features lots of meat, including caribou, elk, lamb and your basic beef. Tours of the brewery are available.

Asian The city's vibrant, teeming Chinatown, centered around 2nd and 3rd Aves at Centre St, is particularly lively on Sunday around noon, when lots of fresh pastries are on offer. Good Chinese bakeries include *Diamond Bakery* (☎ 403-269-1888, 111A 3rd Ave SE), downstairs in Good Fortune Plaza, and *Rainbow Bakery* (☎ 403-234-9909, 328 Centre St S), in the Dragon City Shopping Centre.

Ho Won (☎ 403-266-2234, 115 2nd Ave SE) Dishes $6-12. With 180 items on the menu, you'll certainly find what you want at this small, older Chinese place with a large following.

Regency Palace (☎ 403-777-2288, 328 Centre St SE) Average dishes $10-16. The cavernous but pleasant Regency Palace, in the Dragon City Shopping Centre, offers Chinese classics such as Peking duck and shark's-fin soup on its extensive, 150-item menu.

Sushi Hiro (☎ 403-233-0605, 727 5th Ave SW) Dinner sushi plates $10-20. This spacious and popular Japanese restaurant offers a nice atmosphere and well-prepared sushi, sashimi, teriyaki, nabemono and tempura.

Thai Sa-On (☎ 403-264-3526, 351 10th Ave SW) Lunch specials around $5, dinner dishes $7-13. The menu at this authentic Thai restaurant has a large vegetarian section with a couple dozen different selections. The pleasant atmosphere includes wood parquet floors and Thai art on the walls.

Pho Pasteur Saigon (☎ 403-233-0477, 207 1st St SE) Soups $4-5. This rudimentary Vietnamese restaurant is famous for its 18 kinds of beef noodle soup. Toss on the plate of vegetation that comes with it, add some sauce and you have a great meal for around $5 or less.

Italian Got a craving for garlic and red wine? No problem.

Fiore Cantina Italiana (☎ 403-244-6603, 638 17th Ave SW) Pastas $6-9, specialties $10-13. With a busy patio and an always-packed dining room, this place is a hub of activity in a lively neighborhood. The menu offers a long list of fresh pastas.

Teatro (☎ 403-290-1012, 200 8th Ave SE) Dinner pizzas & pastas $12-27, seafood &

meats $25-40. Across from the performing-arts center (hence the name), the stylish Teatro occupies a stately 1911 bank building complete with pillars and high ceilings. The menu is equally stunning, employing fresh regional ingredients in creative recipes. Try the seared sea bass served with slow-cooked fennel and leeks, olive tapenade and red-wine sauce ($29) or perhaps the whole roasted rack of lamb with mascarpone scalloped potatoes and gingered quince sauce ($37).

Chianti (☎ 403-229-1600, 1438 17th Ave SW) Dinner dishes $8-16. More accessible to those on a budget is this well-liked and modestly priced chain serving a wide menu of respectable pastas, seafood, chicken and, yes, veal dishes.

Other Ethnic Food Among the other international restaurants, the following two stand out:

Latin Corner Cantina (☎ 403-262-7248, 109 8th Ave SW) Dinner dishes $14-19. From Brazil to Argentina, Mexico City to Madrid – this small but stunning place celebrates Latin culture from around the world with an exciting menu and ambience to match. Order a tapa or two and a glass of Rioja while you wait for your heavenly paella. Live Latin music (often big-name touring acts) is presented Thursday to Saturday nights year-round.

Rajdoot (☎ 403-245-0181, 2424 4th St SW) Dishes $8-15. Sometimes you just get a hankering for a good *channa chandi chowk* or perhaps some scrumptious *methi chaman braham bhojan*. If you can't get to India, this award-winning restaurant is the next best place. Vegetarians will be most pleased.

Entertainment

For complete entertainment guides, pick up a copy of *ffwd*, the city's largest entertainment weekly, or the music-oriented *Calgary Straight*. Both are available free around town. The Friday edition of the *Calgary Herald* has a pull-out called 'What's Up' that does a good job of outlining the pleasures of the weekend and beyond.

Performing Arts The city has several venues for drama, opera, symphony and major concerts.

Epcor Centre for the Performing Arts (☎ 403-294-7455, 205 8th Ave SE) Known as

The Centre, this five-venue complex is home to six resident theater companies, among them *Alberta Theatre Projects* (☎ 403-294-7402), *Theatre Calgary* (☎ 403-294-7440) and *One Yellow Rabbit Performance Theatre* (☎ 403-264-3224). Its Jack Singer Concert Hall also hosts the *Calgary Philharmonic Orchestra* (☎ 403-571-0849), maybe; the CPO is currently experiencing financial woes and its fate is uncertain.

Loose Moose Theatre Company (☎ 403-265-5682, 269-1444, 1229 9th Ave SE) Loose Moose, in Inglewood just east of the downtown area, puts on comedy and drama – old and new.

Pumphouse Theatres (☎ 403-263-0079, 2140 9th Ave SW) The Pumphouse stages experimental plays.

Jubilee Auditorium (☎ 403-297-8000, 1415 14 Ave NW) is where the *Alberta Ballet* performs; tickets (starting at $20) often go fast. Big-name concerts are also presented here.

Live Music *King Edward Hotel* (☎ 403-262-1680, 438 9th Ave SE) Downtown, the King Eddy is the city's prime blues bar. A quintessential dive, it's been around as long as some of the ancient musicians who play here. Even the cigarette burns have cigarette burns. Lord have mercy, in the key of G.

Kaos (☎ 403-228-9997, 718 17th Ave SW) For nightly live jazz – and some blues for good measure – Kaos is the place.

Beat Niq Jazz & Social Club (☎ 403-263-1650, 811 1st St SW) Below Piq Niq bistro, this downtown basement club hosts great live jazz Friday to Sunday nights.

Buckingham's (☎ 403-233-7550, 1000 9th Ave SW) Buckingham's is a big downstairs dive with pool tables, dartboards, live rock and good bar chow like burgers and fries.

The Newt (☎ 403-283-1132, 107 10A St NW) North across the river in Kensington is this hip bar with a vast selection of martinis, and live music that runs the gamut from folk to Latin to classic rock.

Dance Clubs *Cowboys* (☎ 403-265-0699, 826 5th St SW) This big two-story club boasts bands and bevies of beautiful bodies boogying out on the large dance floor. If you don't have a Stetson, don't worry – the Western theme is only window dressing here; rock, country and dance music are all

on the schedule. It's open Wednesday to Saturday nights.

Desperados (☎ 403-263-5343, 1088 Olympic Way SE) Smaller than Cowboys but drawing a good crowd as well, Desperados has a small dance floor, DJ dancing Thursday to Sunday and occasional live music.

Embassy Nightclub (☎ 403-213-3970, 516C 9th Ave SW) Good drinks specials help get people dancing at Embassy, a local favorite featuring three dance floors, a rooftop patio and regular retro nights.

The Palace Night Club (☎ 403-263-9980, 219 8th Ave SW) This Stephen Avenue mall venue is great for live comedy, concerts and DJ dancing.

Gay & Lesbian Venues For club and entertainment listings, pick up a copy of *Outlooks* (☎ 403-228-1157, W www.outlooks.ab.ca), a gay-oriented monthly newspaper distributed throughout the province. The website offers an extensive gay resources guide to Calgary and beyond.

Detour (☎ 403-244-8537, 318 17th Ave SW) Doing double duty as the Arena Coffee Bar by day, Detour attracts a mixed crowd of gays and lesbians at night.

Metro-Boyztown (☎ 403-265-2028, 213 10th Ave SW) As the name suggests, this is a popular spot for boys, boys, boys.

The Verge (☎ 403-245-3344, 4A 2500 4th St SW) The Verge is predominantly a lesbian bar, although its clientele includes some gay men as well. It's a cozy, classy kind of place with a nice mahogany bar and occasional dancing, drag shows and live acoustic music.

Pubs Irish pubs are as ubiquitous here as green in Ireland, making Guinness the pint of choice. Have two pints and you'll be Dublin your pleasure!

James Joyce (☎ 403-262-0708, W www .jamesjoycepub.com, 114 8th Ave SW) Like Molly Bloom, you could spend a whole book in this pub one day, the foam slowly descending the side of your pint glass and your own Leopold there yes that look in his eyes asking you yes furtively at first will you yes then with a little more confidence his eyes sparkling and yes you know you will say yes but you want to linger a moment as the sun glances in the window yes and the bartender polishes a glass and he's yes still there yes staring longingly at you and asking yes do you like this pub heart pounding and yes you say ever so coyly yes you say yes you do. Yes! Also try the equally superb *Joyce on 4th* (☎ *403-541-9168, 4th St & 24th Ave SW*).

Dubliner Pub (☎ *403-234-8831, 304 8th Ave SW*) Downstairs in the Lancaster Building, this agreeable Irish pub is a busy, friendly place to quaff a pint.

Ceili's (☎ *403-508-9999, 126-513 8th Ave SW*) Less an Irish pub than a place to see and be seen, this trendy spot is a magnet for beautiful people, primarily downtown's movers and shakers. Fridays and Mondays get particularly jammed with the after-work crowd. Grab one of the tables outside in good weather.

Kilberry's (☎ *403-283-2262, 302 10th St NW*) Over in Kensington, this Celtic pub pours well over 100 different single malt whiskies.

Ship & Anchor (☎ *403-245-3333,* W *www .shipandanchor.com, 534 17th Ave SW*) King of Calgary's English-pub scene, the Ship & Anchor is a neighborhood pub extraordinaire, drawing a mixed crowd for its good beer selection, food, music (both live and canned) and social ambience. Sit out on the patio and gape at passersby, or stay inside and watch footy matches on the telly.

Bottlescrew Bill's Old English Pub (☎ *403-263-7900, 140 10th Ave SW*) Just across the tracks from downtown, Bottlescrew Bill's boasts a selection of over 150 beers from around the world.

Hose & Hound (☎ *403-234-0508, 1030 9th Ave SE*) Cozy Inglewood's funky neighborhood pub occupies a converted firehouse and offers two patios, one covered and heated. The kitchen serves good pub food – wings, salads, pastas, burgers, sandwiches, personal-size pizzas and even substantial entrées (most $6-8).

Rose & Crown (☎ *403-244-7757, 1503 4th St SW*) This huge British-style pub has an excellent beer selection and an outdoor patio.

Cinemas *Plaza Theatre* (☎ *403-283-3636, 1113 Kensington Rd NW*) The repertory Plaza Theatre has two different shows each night, plus midnight performances on Friday and Saturday. It presents offbeat US and foreign films.

Globe Cinema (☎ *403-262-3308, 617 8th Ave SW*) The Globe screens an interesting schedule of foreign and revival movies.

IMAX Theatre (☎ *403-974-4629, 132-200 Barclay Parade SW*) Calgary's IMAX is in the Eau Claire Market, just south of the Bow River. Next door is the *Cineplex Odeon* (☎ *403-263-3166*), a multiplex theater.

Spectator Sports

The Calgary Flames (☎ 403-777-0000), archrival of the Edmonton Oilers, play ice hockey from October to April at the *Saddledome* in Stampede Park. Tickets cost $12 to $50.

The Calgary Stampeders (☎ 403-289-0258) of the Canadian Football League play from July to September at *McMahon Stadium* (*1817 Crowchild Trail NW*) in northwest Calgary. Tickets run $25 to $50.

Shopping

Many visitors are taken by the Western apparel seen around town at Stampede time or in country music bars.

Alberta Boot Co (☎ *403-263-4605,* W *www .albertaboot.com, 614 10th Ave SW*) You can visit the factory and store run by the province's only Western boot manufacturer and pick up a pair made from your choice of kangaroo, ostrich, python, rattlesnake, lizard, alligator or boring old cowhide; prices range from $235 to $1700.

Riley & McCormick (☎ *403-262-1556, 403-266-8811, 220 8th Ave SW*) For cowboy hats, shirts, skirts, vests, spurs and other Western gear, check out this store, with locations on Stephen Ave Walk and elsewhere.

Eau Claire Market (☎ *403-264-6460,* W *www.eauclairemarket.com, 2nd St & 2nd Ave SW*). The town's most interesting shopping center is a large two-story enclosed mall with shops, restaurants, a produce market, nightspots, a multiplex theater and an IMAX theater.

Getting There & Away

Air Calgary International Airport (YYC; ☎ 403-735-1372, W www.calgaryairport.com) is about 15km northeast of the center off Barlow Trail, a 25-minute drive away.

Air Canada (☎ 888-247-2262, 333 5th Ave SW) flies to cities throughout Canada, the USA and Europe. Discount carrier WestJet (☎ 403-250-5839, 888-937-8538) serves Alberta and British Columbia.

US airlines serving Calgary include Horizon Air (☎ 800-547-9308), American Airlines (☎ 800-433-7300), Continental Airlines (☎ 800-231-0856), Delta Air Lines (☎ 800-221-1212), Northwest Airlines (☎ 800-225-2525) and United Airlines (☎ 800-241-6522).

A number of regional companies serve small markets in BC, Alberta and the northern territories.

Bus The Greyhound bus station (☎ 403-265-9111, 850 16th St SW) isn't far from the center, but it's a navigational nightmare to reach. It's walkable from downtown, but most people opt for the free city shuttle bus from the C-Train 10th St SW stop, which goes to the door. The station has luggage-storage lockers ($2 small, $4 large) and is open 5:30am to 12:30am daily.

A sample of destinations served include Banff ($20, two hours, six buses daily), Edmonton ($40, from 3½ hours, 13 or more daily), Kamloops ($80, nine hours, four daily), Regina ($93, 11 hours, four daily), Saskatoon ($79, nine hours, two daily), Vancouver ($115, 15 hours, five daily) and Winnipeg ($145, 20 hours, four daily).

Red Arrow (☎ 403-531-0350, 800-232-1958, ⓦ www.redarrow.pwt.ca) runs six luxury buses a day to Edmonton from its Calgary terminal at 205 9th Ave SE. The one-way fare is $46.

In summer, Giddy Goat Adventures (☎ 403-609-9992) runs a daily shuttle to HI-Banff from HI-Calgary; one-way fare is $25.

Train You can travel by train from Calgary to Vancouver via Banff with the privately owned Rocky Mountaineer Railtours (☎ 800-665-7245, ⓦ www.rockymountaineer.com). The peak season one-way fare to Vancouver is $784/1458 single/double, including some food and an overnight stop in a hotel in Kamloops. The service, which is like a cruise ship on rails, runs from May to mid-October. The station is underneath the Calgary Tower, on the corner of 9th Ave and Centre St.

Getting Around
To/From the Airport The Airporter (☎ 403-531-3907/3909) runs every half hour from around 6:30am to 11:30pm between all the major downtown hotels and the airport, and charges $9/15 one-way/roundtrip. Airport Shuttle Express (☎ 403-

509-4799, 888-438-2992, ⓦ www.airportshuttleexpress.com) offers on-demand shared shuttle service for around $12 to any of the downtown hotels.

You can also go between the airport and downtown on public transportation (see Bus & LRT, below). From the airport, take the No 57 bus to the Whitehorn stop (northeast of city center) and transfer to the C-Train; or just reverse the process coming from downtown. This costs only $1.75 but takes about an hour.

A taxi to the airport costs about $25.

Bus & LRT Calgary Transit (☎ 403-262-1000, ⓦ www.calgarytransit.com) operates the bus and Light Rapid Transit (LRT) rail system. Its office (240 7th Ave SW) has route maps, information and tickets and is open 8:30am to 5pm Monday to Friday. Maps are also available at Tourism Calgary.

The Calgary LRT train is known as the C-Train. One fare entitles you to transfer to other buses or another C-Train. The C-Train is free in the downtown area along 7th Ave between 10th St SW and 3rd St SE. If you're going farther or need a transfer, buy your ticket from a machine on the C-Train platform (it helps to have extra coins with you, as the machines reject about every other one, seemingly at random). Most of the bus lines run at 15- to 30-minute intervals daily. There is no late-night service.

The single fare for the C-Train and buses is $1.75/1.10 adult/child. A book of 10 tickets costs $14.50/9, and a day pass is $5/3. Transfers are free and are good for 90 minutes. When going from the C-Train to a bus, present your ticket to the driver. If you plan to go from a bus to the C-Train or another bus, you must request a transfer from the bus driver when you pay your initial fare.

Car All the major car rental firms are represented at the airport and downtown, including Avis (☎ 403-269-6166), Budget (☎ 403-226-1550), Discount Car Rentals (☎ 403-299-1224), Hertz (☎ 403-221-1300), National (☎ 403-263-6386), Rent-A-Wreck (☎ 403-287-1444) and Thrifty (☎ 403-262-4400).

Taxi For a cab, call Alberta South Co-Op Taxi Lines (☎ 403-531-8294) or Yellow Cab

(☎ 403-974-1111). Fares are $2.50 for the first 160m, 20¢ for each additional 160m and 20¢ for each 30 seconds of elapsed time.

Bicycle The car rental company Budget (☎ 403-226-1550, 140 6th Ave SE) rents basic mountain bikes for $12 a day with a $200 deposit. Sports Rent (☎ 403-292-0077, 4424 16th Ave NW, W www.sportsrent.ca) has a large selection of mountain bikes and road bikes at prices ranging from $22 to $45 per day.

Banff & Jasper National Parks

Much of the Rocky Mountains area of Alberta, running along the British Columbia border, is contained and protected within two huge, adjacent national parks: Banff to the south and Jasper to the north. The Icefields Parkway links the two, though there is no real boundary. Adjoining the southern boundary of Banff National Park is Kananaskis Country, a provincial recreation area.

The entire area is one of spectacular beauty with some of the world's best scenery, climbing, hiking and skiing. The national parks offer jagged, snowcapped mountains, peaceful valleys, rushing rivers, natural hot springs and alpine forests. The opaque emerald-green or milky-turquoise color of many Rocky Mountains lakes will have you doubting your eyes. The parks also have both modern conveniences and backcountry trails to choose from, and wildlife abounds, particularly in Jasper National Park.

Canada's first national park, Banff was established in 1885 and named for Banffshire, Scotland, the home of two Canadian Pacific Railway (CPR) financiers. Built around the thermal sulfur springs at what has become the Cave & Basin National Historic Site, Banff today covers 6641 sq km and is by far the best known and most popular park in the Rockies. With 25 mountains of 3000m or higher, Banff is world famous for skiing and climbing, though most visitors just come to view the astonishing scenery. Jasper National Park is larger, wilder and less explored but, like Banff, offers excellent hiking trails.

Orientation & Information

The small townsites of Banff, Lake Louise, Jasper and Canmore act as focal points for orientation, supplies and information. In Banff National Park, accommodations during summer are expensive and hard to find. It's worth booking ahead or staying in one of the towns outside the park, such as Canmore in Alberta or Field, Golden, Radium Hot Springs, Windermere or Invermere in British Columbia, and making day trips.

On entering Banff or Jasper National Park, you will be given the excellent *Mountain Guide*, with information and maps about both parks, as well as Kootenay, Yoho, Glacier and Mount Revelstoke National Parks in BC. For information before you arrive, go online to W www.parkscanada.gc.ca.

The one-day park entry fee is $5/4/2.50 adult/senior/child; the passes are good until 4pm the following day. An annual pass entitling the bearer to unlimited admission to all 11 national parks in western Canada costs $35/27/18, and you can upgrade your day pass to one of these. For more information, call ☎ 800-748-7275.

The backcountry hiking and wilderness camping fee is $6 per night, with a maximum charge of $30. Passes are available from all park visitors' centers. Note that there may be a limit on the number of backcountry passes to some popular areas. Check with the relevant park visitors' center for details.

Dangers & Annoyances

In the backcountry, assume all water sources harbor *Giardia,* an intestinal parasite spread through human and animal feces. Filter all water, boil it for at least 10 minutes or treat it with purification tablets before drinking it.

If you're heading into wilderness regions, read the pamphlet *You are in Bear Country,* which gives advice on how to steer clear of bears and what to do if this becomes unavoidable. It's available at the visitors' centers.

The trails heavily used by horse trips are a real mess; long-distance hikers will want to avoid them. Ask at the park-warden offices or the visitors' centers about which trails are used most by the horses.

KANANASKIS COUNTRY

Adjacent to the southeastern corner of Banff National Park and 90km west of Calgary,

BANFF & JASPER NATIONAL PARKS

1 Miette Hot Springs
2 Snaring River Campground
3 HI-Jasper
4 HI-Maligne Canyon
5 Marmot Basin
6 HI-Mount Edith Cavell
7 HI-Athabasca Falls
8 Mt Kerkeslin Campground
9 Honeymoon Lake Campground
10 Jonas Creek Campground
11 HI-Beauty Creek
12 Icefield Centre
13 Columbia Icefield; Wilcox Creek
   Campground
14 Athabasca Glacier
15 HI-Hilda Creek
16 HI-Rampart Creek; Rampart
   Creek Campground
17 The Crossing
18 Num-Ti-Jah Lodge
19 Waterfowl Lakes Campground
20 HI-Mosquito Creek; Mosquito
   Creek Campground
21 Protection Mountain Campground
22 Castle Mountain Campground
23 Johnston Canyon
24 Johnston Canyon Campground

Kananaskis Country (☎ 403-673-3985, W www3.gov.ab.ca/env/parks/prov_parks/ kananaskis) is an outdoor recreational area consisting of a contiguous cluster of provincial parks and reserved multiuse areas. Its 4250 sq kilometers hold excellent opportunities for skiing, climbing, cycling, hiking, golfing, horseback riding, boating, camping and picnicking.

Skiing & Snowboarding

In winter, skiing is top on the list. Kananaskis Country holds two downhill resorts: **Nakiska** (☎ 403-591-7777, 800-258-7669, snow report ☎ 403-244-6665; W www.skinakiska.com; adult full-day pass $46; ski season early Dec–mid-Apr), where the alpine skiing events of the 1988 Winter Olympics were

held, and smaller **Fortress Mountain** (☎ 403-591-7108, 800-258-7669, snow report ☎ 403-244-6665, W www.skifortress.com; adult full-day pass $34; ski season early Nov-late Apr), home of the Canadian National Freestyle Team. Both are off Hwy 40 south of the Trans Canada Hwy. Cross-country skiing in Kananaskis Country is also good, with trails throughout the area, as well as the nearby Canmore Nordic Centre, built for the 1988 Olympic cross-country skiing events.

CANMORE

Unhindered by the growth limits imposed on Banff, 26km west, fast-growing Canmore is a popular alternative to the resorts inside the national parks. Just off the Trans Canada Hwy (Hwy 1) and squeezed between Banff

National Park and Kananaskis Country, Canmore has a pleasant downtown that has not yet been buried under tourism.

Travel Alberta's well marked provincial tourist office (☎ 403-678-5277, 2801 Bow Valley Trail) is just off the Trans Canada Hwy. It's open 8am to 8pm daily June to August, 9am to 6pm or 7pm the rest of the year. Canmore Public Library (☎ 403-678-2468, 950 8th Ave) is open daily and offers limited free Internet access. For a good look at the underbelly of life from Canmore to Jasper, pick up a copy of *Wild Life*, a free indie monthly with an unbridled take on the area. Better yet, go by the office (129 Bow Meadows Crescent) and toss Mark a toonie or six-pack of Kokanee for his efforts.

Activities
The town is a base for **Alpine Helicopters Ltd** (☎ *403-678-4802*, W *www.alpine helicopter.com, 91 Bow Valley Trail)*, which offers 'flightseeing' (starting at $130 per person) and heli-hiking (starting at $235 per person) trips in the Rockies. If you'd rather get high on your own, contact **Yamnuska** (☎ *403-678-4164*, W *www.yamnuska.com, 50–103 Bow Valley Trail, Suite 200)*, an established mountaineering school offering a full slate of peak experiences. Whitewater rafting is the specialty at **Mirage Adventure Tours** (☎ *403-678-4919*, W *www.mirage tours.com, 999 Bow Valley Trail)*.

Canmore is also home of the superb **Canmore Nordic Centre Provincial Park** (☎ *403-678-2400, 100–1988 Olympic Way)*, built for the 1988 Olympic cross-country skiing and biathlon events. In winter, ski the Centre's 60km trail system (adult/senior & youth/child $5/4/3); in summer you can mountain-bike it. Lessons and rentals are available for both activities.

Places to Stay & Eat
Canmore Clubhouse (☎ *403-678-3200, fax 403-678-3224*, W *www.alpineclubofcanada.ca, Indian Flats Rd)* Dorm beds $17/21 club members/nonmembers. About 5km southeast of town (a 45-minute walk), the Alpine Club of Canada's beautiful hostel sits on a rise overlooking the valley. There are laundry facilities, a library, kitchen, sauna and an almost tangible aura of mountaineering history. The Alpine Club offers classes in

mountaineering and maintains several back-country huts.

Bow Valley Motel (☎ *403-678-5085, 800-665-8189, fax 403-678-6560*, W *www.bow valleymotel.com, 610 8th/Main St)* Rooms from $95 in peak season. Canmore has a heap of chain places along busy, striplike Bow Valley Trail (Hwy 1A), which parallels the Trans Canada. In a better location downtown is this friendly independent motel with basic rooms.

Grizzly Paw Brewing Company (☎ *403-678-9983, 622 8th/Main St)* Dinner dishes $8-16. This local microbrewery has good soups and burgers, but the homebrew is uninspiring.

BANFF TOWNSITE
Banff townsite, 138km west of Calgary, attracts several million visitors a year. Yet the small, rustic alpine-style village consists essentially of one main street, so it can get crowded. In July and August, the normal population swells by 25,000. Although this can cause problems, the many vacationers create a relaxed and festive atmosphere.

History
Banff townsite was created solely as a tourist destination. The Canadian Pacific Railway wanted a health spa here to attract wealthy, well-traveled Victorians who would arrive – as paying passengers – on CPR trains. And come they did, ready to relax in the rejuvenating hot springs or hire one of the many outfitters to take them up the mountains.

In 1912, the decision to allow cars in Banff opened up the area to people other than rich Victorians, and the town began pushing its boundaries. The south side of the river, with the Banff Springs Hotel, catered to the wealthy crowd. The north side of the river resembled more of a prairie town, with small lots zoned in a grid system. This class-distinctive boundary is still evident today.

Banff continues to face conflicts over its growth. Many people complain that the townsite is too crowded and argue that more hotels and streets should be built to accommodate all the camera-clicking tourists. Others think there's far too much building already. To control growth, the federal government has decreed that only

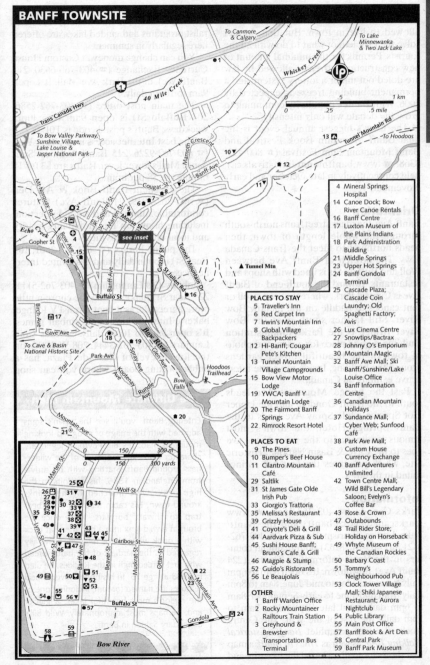

BANFF TOWNSITE

PLACES TO STAY
5 Traveller's Inn
6 Red Carpet Inn
7 Irwin's Mountain Inn
8 Global Village
  Backpackers
12 HI-Banff; Cougar
   Pete's Kitchen
13 Tunnel Mountain
   Village Campgrounds
15 Bow View Motor
   Lodge
19 YWCA; Banff Y
   Mountain Lodge
20 The Fairmont Banff
   Springs
22 Rimrock Resort Hotel

PLACES TO EAT
9 The Pines
10 Bumper's Beef House
11 Cilantro Mountain
   Café
29 Saltlik
31 St James Gate Olde
   Irish Pub
33 Giorgio's Trattoria
35 Melissa's Restaurant
39 Grizzly House
41 Coyote's Deli & Grill
44 Aardvark Pizza & Sub
45 Sushi House Banff;
   Bruno's Cafe & Grill
46 Magpie & Stump
52 Guido's Ristorante
56 Le Beaujolais

OTHER
1 Banff Warden Office
2 Rocky Mountaineer
  Railtours Train Station
3 Greyhound &
  Brewster
  Transportation Bus
  Terminal

4 Mineral Springs
  Hospital
14 Canoe Dock; Bow
   River Canoe Rentals
16 Banff Centre
17 Luxton Museum of
   the Plains Indians
18 Park Administration
   Building
21 Middle Springs
23 Upper Hot Springs
24 Banff Gondola
   Terminal
25 Cascade Plaza;
   Cascade Coin
   Laundry; Old
   Spaghetti Factory;
   Avis
26 Lux Cinema Centre
27 Snowtips/Bactrax
28 Johnny O's Emporium
30 Mountain Magic
32 Banff Ave Mall; Ski
   Banff/Sunshine/Lake
   Louise Office
34 Banff Information
   Centre
36 Canadian Mountain
   Holidays
37 Sundance Mall;
   Cyber Web; Sunfood
   Café
38 Park Ave Mall;
   Custom House
   Currency Exchange
40 Banff Adventures
   Unlimited
42 Town Centre Mall;
   Wild Bill's Legendary
   Saloon; Evelyn's
   Coffee Bar
43 Rose & Crown
47 Outabounds
48 Trail Rider Store;
   Holiday on Horseback
49 Whyte Museum of
   the Canadian Rockies
50 Barbary Coast
51 Tommy's
   Neighbourhood Pub
53 Clock Tower Village
   Mall; Shiki Japanese
   Restaurant; Aurora
   Nightclub
54 Public Library
55 Main Post Office
57 Banff Book & Art Den
58 Central Park
59 Banff Park Museum

those people who can demonstrate a valid need (such as owning a business) will be allowed to live in town. But that doesn't solve the problem of what to do with all the tourists. Permits for the minimal amount of new construction currently allowed by law are doled out under a lottery system, and a permanent building freeze is expected by 2006. With Banff's popularity continuing to grow, the debate will only intensify.

The town's biggest annual event is the dual Banff Mountain Book Festival and Banff Mountain Film Festival (☎ 800-413-8368, **W** www.banffmountainfestivals.ca), held consecutively in late October and early November.

Orientation

Banff Ave, the main street, runs north-south through the whole length of town, then heads northeast to meet the Trans Canada Hwy. The stretch of Banff Ave between Wolf and Buffalo Sts is lined with shops and restaurants. Toward the south end of Banff Ave is Central Park, where you can stroll or rent canoes to paddle on the mellow Bow River. Still farther south over the Bow River Bridge is the Park Administration Building, a good place for a view and photo of town or the beautiful flower gardens around the building. Inside are some interactive exhibits on Canada.

Past the bridge, Mountain Ave leads south to the Banff Gondola and the Upper Hot Springs, while Spray Ave leads to the Banff Springs Hotel, the town's most famous landmark. To the west, Cave Ave goes to the Cave & Basin National Historic Site, which preserves the first hot springs found in the area.

Information

Parks Canada (☎ 403-762-1550, **W** www .parkscanada.gc.ca/banff) and the Banff/ Lake Louise Tourism Bureau (☎ 403-762-8421, fax 403-762-8163) both maintain counters in the Banff Information Centre (224 Banff Ave), downtown. It's open 8am to 6pm daily from mid-May to mid-June, 8am to 8pm daily from mid-June to early September, 8am to 6pm daily until late September, 9am to 5pm daily the rest of the year. The Centre stocks the free pamphlet *Banff Historical Walking Tour*, as well as *Trails in Banff*, a map that shows footpaths around the townsite and

immediate vicinity. (For trails farther afield, see Hiking under Activities, later.) Free naturalist programs and guided hikes are offered here regularly in summer.

You can change money at Custom House Currency Exchange (☎ 403-760-6630, 211 Banff Ave), in the Park Ave Mall. It's open 9am to 10pm daily.

The main post office (☎ 403-762-2586, 204 Buffalo St) is open 9am to 5:30pm weekdays; Banff's postal code is T0L 0C0.

The best Internet access is at Cyber Web (☎ 403-762-9226, 215 Banff Ave), on Sundance Mall's lower level. Rates are $3 for 15 minutes or $8 per hour.

The excellent Banff Book & Art Den (☎ 403-762-3919, 94 Banff Ave) features comfortable quarters and a good selection, including books on the mountains, history and local outdoor activities.

The public library (☎ 403-762-2661, 101 Bear St) is open daily and has limited Internet access.

Johnny O's Emporium (☎ 403-762-5111, 223 Bear St) makes doing the chore a little more agreeable, as it contains a TV lounge, bakery, Internet kiosk and pinball games. It's open 9am to 10pm daily. Cascade Coin Laundry (☎ 403-762-3444, 208 Wolf St), on the lower level of Cascade Plaza, has a public posting board where you can shop

---

The Ultimate Mountain Man

Entering Banff, you'll see the town's signs adorned with the image of a rugged-looking mountain man. It's Bill Peyto, a legendary character who explored much of the wilderness around Banff. Starting with his arrival from England in 1886, his exploits in the high peaks were matched by his hijinks around town. His cabin featured a set bear trap to thwart burglars. And once he brought a wild lynx into a bar, then sat back with a drink while chaos reigned. Generally regarded as the hardiest of the hardy breed who first settled high in the Rockies, he died in 1943 at age 75. In his honor several local features are named for him, including one of the region's most beautiful lakes, a glacier and, perhaps most appropriately, Wild Bill's Legendary Saloon in Banff.

for used ski gear, find a ride to Jasper or maybe snag a place to live. It's open 8am to 10pm daily (until 11pm in summer).

Mineral Springs Hospital (☎ 403-762-2222, 301 Lynx St) offers medical treatment.

Dial ☎ 911 for police, medical, fire or backcountry emergencies. For nonemergency backcountry problems, you can call the Banff Warden Office dispatch line (☎ 403-762-1470), which operates 24 hours year-round.

The police are strict in Banff; after 1am they often check cars for drunk drivers and drugs. Fines are heavy.

Banff Park Museum

Near the Bow River Bridge is the park museum (☎ 403-762-1558, 93 Banff Ave; adult/child $2.50/1.50; open 10am-6pm daily in summer, 1pm-5pm daily rest of the year). It occupies an old wooden CPR building that dates from 1903, before Banff had electricity. Now a national historic site, the museum contains a taxidermied collection of animals found in the park, including grizzly and black bears, plus a tree carved with graffiti dating from 1841. In summer, a free half-hour guided tour of the museum takes place at 11am weekdays and 3pm weekends.

Whyte Museum of the Canadian Rockies

The must-see Whyte Museum complex (☎ 403-762-2291, W www.whyte.org, 111 Bear St, adult/senior & student $6/3.50, special shows may be higher; open 10am-5pm daily) features an art gallery and a vast collection of photographs telling the history of early explorers, artists and the Canadian Pacific Railway. Special shows – such as a recent one on bears – focus on a particular aspect of mountain life around the world. Heritage walking tours of town ($5) are offered twice daily in summer and on Sunday the rest of the year; call for times. The museum foundation also presents films, lectures and concerts regularly.

Luxton Museum of the Plains Indian

The fortlike wooden building on the southwest side of the Bow River Bridge is Luxton Museum (☎ 403-762-2388, 1 Birch Ave; adult/senior & student/child 6-12 $6/4/2.50;

open 10am-5pm daily in summer, reduced hours rest of the year). The museum illustrates the history of Alberta's indigenous peoples, with life-size displays, models and re-creations depicting various aspects of traditional cultures.

Banff Springs Hotel

Since it was completed in the 1920s, this 800-room baronial palace, on Spray Ave 2km south of downtown, has posed for thousands of postcards and millions of snapshots. The spectacular design includes towers, turrets and cornices, giving the impression that the hotel (now part of the Fairmont chain) is full of hidden secrets. Within its thick granite walls are myriad public spaces, bars and restaurants. Even if you're not staying here, it's a fascinating place to wander around.

Banff Centre

Dance, theater, music and the visual arts are all on tap at the Banff Centre (☎ 403-762-6100, 403-752-6301, 800-413-8368 tickets, W www.banffcentre.ca, 107 Tunnel Mountain Dr), up on the hill east of downtown. One of Canada's best-known art schools, the Centre regularly schedules public exhibits, concerts and other events throughout the year. The Banff Information Centre can provide you with a complete schedule, or you can check the website.

Banff Gondola

For spectacular views over the surrounding mountains, Bow River and Banff townsite, ride up the Banff Gondola (☎ 403-762-2523, Mountain Ave; adult/child 6-15 $20/10; open daily, until 9pm May-Aug, closed Dec 25 & Jan 7-18. The gondola zips you to the 2285m summit of Sulphur Mountain in about eight minutes. An observation terrace, restaurants and a historic weather station are on top. Alternatively, you can hike up the mountain's steep east side – about two hours one way – and get a free gondola ride down (tickets are only needed going up). The trail starts from the Upper Hot Springs parking lot.

The gondola's lower terminal, adjacent to the Upper Hot Springs pool, is just about 4km south of Banff on Mountain Ave. You can hitch a ride from town fairly easily. You can also take the Brewster bus (☎ 403-762-6767), though it costs $27/13.50 adult/child, including the gondola fare (the bus fare portion is $7 per person); if there's more than one of you, it's cheaper to take a cab, which costs about $9 for up to four or five people. The Brewster bus runs May to October, departing from the depot every hour on the hour and from the Banff Springs Hotel every hour on the quarter hour.

Cave & Basin National Historic Site
Banff was born with the discovery of hot sulfur springs in a cave at what is now the Cave & Basin National Historic Site (☎ 403-762-1566, Cave Ave; adult/child $2.50/1.50; open 9am-6pm daily mid-May–Sept; 11am-4pm weekdays, 9:30am-5pm weekends rest of the year). Today's swimming pool and complex, southwest of town, has been rebuilt in the original 1914 style, but you're not allowed to bathe at the site. Visitors can see (and smell) the cave and sulphurous waters, as well as view exhibits and a 30-minute film.

It's free to stroll around the attractive grounds, where you'll see both natural and artificially made pools. Picnic tables, a fine view and a snack bar make this a good place for an alfresco lunch. Several pleasant short trails begin here.

Upper Hot Springs
You'll find a soothing hot pool, steam room and spa at Banff Upper Hot Springs (☎ 403-762-1515, end of Mountain Ave; adult/student $7.50/6.50; open 9am-11pm daily in summer; 10am-10pm Sun-Thur, 10am-11pm Fri & Sat rest of the year), near the Banff Gondola, 4km south of town. The water emerges from the spring at 47°C; in winter it has to be cooled before entering the pool, but in spring the snowmelt does that job. In addition to the pool, you can indulge in a massage or an aromatherapy wrap. Bathing suits, towels and lockers can be rented.

Lake Minnewanka
The park's largest reservoir, Lake Minnewanka, is 11km east of Banff townsite. Forests and mountains surround this scenic recreational area, which features plenty of hiking, swimming, sailing, boating and fishing opportunities. From mid-May to early October, Lake Minnewanka Boat Tours (☎ 403-762-3473) offers a 90-minute cruise on the lake to Devil's Gap ($28/12

adult/child). To get to the lake from the townsite, take Banff Ave east over the Trans Canada Hwy to Minnewanka Rd and turn right. From May to October, **Brewster** (☎ 403-762-6767) runs a three-hour bus tour to the lake, which includes the 90-minute boat cruise ($44/22 adult/child).

Activities
Hiking Before doing any hiking, check in at the Banff Information Centre; Parks Canada staff will tell you about specific trail conditions and hazards. They can also provide you with a couple of excellent free brochures.

Day Hikes in Banff National Park outlines hikes accessible from the townsite. You'll find many good short hikes and day walks right around the Banff area. You can take a pleasant, quiet stroll by **Bow River**, just three blocks west of Banff Ave beside Bow Ave. The trail runs from the corner of Wolf St along the river under the Bow River bridge and ends shortly after on Buffalo St. If you cross the bridge, you can continue southeast through the woods along a trail to nearby **Bow Falls**.

For a good short climb to break in your legs and to view the area, walk up stubby **Tunnel Mountain**, east of downtown. A trail leads up from St Julien Rd; you can drive here, but it's not a long walk from downtown to the start of the path.

From the southern end of Buffalo St, a short interpretive trail between Bow River and Tunnel Mountain heads north and east to the **Tunnel Mountain hoodoos**. The term 'hoodoo' refers to the distinctive vertical pillar shapes carved into the rock face by rainfall and glacial erosion.

Just west of downtown, off Mt Norquay Rd, is the 2km **Fenland Trail** loop, which goes through marsh and forest and connects the town with First Vermilion Lake.

For longer, more remote hiking, get the Backcountry Visitors' Guide, which contains a simple map showing trails and backcountry campgrounds throughout the park, as well as recommended two- to five-day treks. Anybody hiking overnight in the backcountry must sign in and buy a wilderness permit ($6 per night per person).

If you can't make it to the Information Centre, get up-to-date trail reports in a recorded telephone message (☎ 403-760-

1305) or on the park website (**W** www
.parkscanada.gc.ca/banff).

Canoeing You can go canoeing on **Lake Minnewanka** and nearby **Two Jack Lake**, northeast of Banff. The **Vermilion Lakes**, three shallow lakes connected by narrow waterways, attract lots of wildlife and make excellent spots for canoeing. To get to the lakes, head northwest out of town along Lynx St and follow signs toward Hwy 1. Just before the highway, turn left onto Vermilion Lakes Dr, and you'll soon come to small parking areas for the lakes.

If you're car- or canoe-less and want to stay close to town, your best bet is the **Bow River**. You can rent a canoe from **Bow River Canoe Rentals** (*☎ 403-762-3632, Bow Ave & Wolf St; open 10:30am-6pm daily mid-May–Sept*) for $16/40 per hour/day.

Cycling You can cycle on the highways and on some of the park trails. Two good, short cycling routes close to Banff run along **Vermilion Lakes Dr** and **Tunnel Mountain Dr**. For a longer trip, try the popular and scenic 24km **Bow Valley Parkway**, which connects Banff and Lake Louise. **Snowtips/Bactrax** (*☎ 403-762-8177, 225 Bear St*) runs excellent two- to four-hour mountain biking trips that cost $15 an hour. Parks Canada publishes the brochure *Mountain Biking & Cycling Guide – Banff National Park*, which describes trails and regulations. (For information on renting bikes, see Getting Around, later.)

Horseback Riding Operating out of the Trail Rider Store, **Holiday on Horseback** (*☎ 403-762-4551, **W** www.horseback.com, 132 Banff Ave*) offers a variety of horseback-riding trips on trails around town. An hour-long ride along Spray River costs $30; the three-hour Bow Valley Loop is $61; a full-day ride up Sulphur Mountain, including down-home barbecue, costs $120.

Rock Climbing Banff's rocky crags and limestone peaks present almost endless opportunities for good climbing. In fact, many of the world's best climbers live in nearby Canmore so that they can enjoy easy access to this mountain playground. This is not terrain for unguided novice climbers; even experienced climbers wanting to go it alone

should first talk to locals, read books and get the weather lowdown before venturing out.

Inexperienced climbers will find quite a few companies offering climbing courses and organized tours into the mountains. **Mountain Magic** (*☎ 403-762-2591, 224 Bear St*) holds indoor classes that'll teach you some basics for $45 per person. In Canmore **Yamnuska** (*☎ 403-678-4164, **W** www.yamnuska.com, 50–103 Bow Valley Trail, Suite 200*) offers a lengthy list of mountaineering classes and adventures for all skill levels around Banff and throughout the Canadian Rockies. Also in Canmore the **Alpine Club of Canada** (*☎ 403-678-3200, **W** www.alpineclubofcanada.ca, Indian Flats Rd*) can provide information and/or a guide.

Skiing & Snowboarding Three excellent mountain resorts, all with spectacular scenery, are near Banff. **Ski Banff @Norquay** (*☎ 403-762-4421, 866-464-7669, **W** www.banffnorquay.com, Mt Norquay Rd; adult full-day ticket $47*), just 6km north of downtown Banff, is the area's oldest resort. **Sunshine Village** (*☎ 403-762-6500, 877-542-2633, snow conditions ☎ 403-277-7669, **W** www.skibanff.com; adult full-day ticket $56*), off Hwy 1 22km southwest of Banff, rises to 2730m and boasts 92 runs. Its four high-speed quad chairlifts zip you up the mountain in no time, and a new gondola went on line for the 2001–02 season.

Lake Louise (*☎ 403-522-3555, 800-258-7669, **W** www.skilouise.com; adult full-day ticket $59*), 60km west of Banff near the Samson Mall, ranks among Canada's largest ski areas, with 17 sq km of skiable terrain spread over four mountain faces.

A three-day pass, usable at all three resorts, is $175. Other multiday packages are also available. For more information, contact the **Ski Banff/Sunshine/Lake Louise** office (*☎ 403-762-4561, 800-661-1431, 223 Banff Ave*), in the Banff Ave Mall.

Heli-Skiing Canadian Mountain Holidays (*CMH; ☎ 403-762-7100, 800-661-0252, **W** www.cmhski.com, 217 Bear St*) specializes in four- to 10-day heli-skiing trips to some of the best and most remote areas in the western mountain ranges. These superb trips start at around $4000 per week. **RK Heli-Ski** (*☎ 403-762-3771, 403-760-2824, 800-661-6060, **W** www.rkheliski.com, Banff*

Springs Hotel or 124 Banff Ave) offers one-day trips starting at $600 per person, as well as longer packages. Both companies use ski areas in BC.

Organized Tours

Brewster Gray Line (☎ *403-762-6767,* W *www.brewster.ca, 100 Gopher St)* offers a number of bus tours from Banff through the Rockies parks. For complete information, visit the website. The three-hour 'Discover Banff' tour ($47/23.50 adult/child) goes to the hoodoos, Tunnel Mountain Dr, Sulphur Mountain (gondola ride not included in tour price) and Cave & Basin National Historic Site. Brewster also runs tours to Lake Louise, the Columbia Icefield and Jasper.

A couple of companies offer budget-oriented tours, with overnight stays at HI hostels along the way. These tours are generally geared for younger, backpacker types (usually ages 18 to 30), but they are open to anyone. **True North Tours' Rocky Express** (☎ *403-912-0407, 888-464-4842,* W *www .backpackertours.com/truenorth)* offers a six-day, five-night trip starting in Banff and slowly traveling through Lake Louise, along the Icefields Parkway, up through Jasper and returning to your choice of Banff, Lake Louise or Calgary. The price of $215 includes tax and park fees but doesn't include hostel accommodations (another $80) or food ($20 donation to the food kitty).

Bigfoot Adventure Tours (☎ *604-772-9905, 888-244-6673)* offers a two-day tour from Banff to Jasper and back again for $95, also not including accommodations and food. Its two-day, one-way trip from Banff to Vancouver, with an overnight stop in Squilax (near Shuswap Lake), costs $106.

Places to Stay

Accommodation is fairly costly and, in summer, often hard to find. The old adage of the early bird catching the worm really holds true here, and booking ahead is strongly recommended. The rates listed here apply to the peak season (basically July and August); rates fall considerably at other times of the year. If you're not camping or staying at hostels, B&Bs and private tourist homes can be a reasonably priced alternative, and they're usually good sources of local information.

The Banff/Lake Louise Tourism Bureau tracks vacancies on a daily basis; check the listings at the Banff Information Centre. You might also try Banff/Lake Louise Central Reservations (☎ 403-705-4015, 877-542-2633, W www.banffreservations.com), which books rooms for more than 75 different lodgings.

Some people stay in Canmore or Golden (in BC) just outside the park, where the rates are lower, and enter the park on a day-trip basis.

Camping Banff National Park contains 13 front-country campgrounds, most of which lie right around the townsite or along the Bow Valley Parkway. Most are open only between May or June and September. They are all busy in July and August, and availability is on a first-come, first-served basis, so check in by noon or you may be turned away. Campgrounds with showers always fill up first. Camping is permitted only in designated campgrounds. For more information, call Parks Canada at ☎ 403-762-1550.

Tunnel Mountain Village Campgrounds Sites $17-24. Open year-round. This complex at the top of Tunnel Mountain Rd includes three separate campgrounds: two primarily cater to RVs needing electrical hookups, and one accommodates only tents, with a whopping 618 tenting sites. All are close to town and have flush toilets and showers.

Two Jack Lakeside Campground Sites $17. Open mid-May–mid-Sept. Twelve kilometers northeast of Banff on Lake Minnewanka Rd, this campground has showers and 80 sites on Two Jack Lake.

Two Jack Main Campground Sites $13. Open mid-May–mid-Sept. About 1km north of Two Jack Lakeside, this one features 381 sites, flush toilets and running water but no showers.

Johnston Canyon Campground Sites $17. Open early June–mid-Sept. About 26km along the Bow Valley Parkway west of Banff, this 140-site campground is wooded and fairly secluded, though trains whistle by at night. Facilities include flush toilets and showers.

Castle Mountain Campground Sites $13. Open mid-May–early Sept. A smaller campground without showers, Castle Mountain is 2km north of Castle Junction on the Bow Valley Parkway.

Hostels *HI-Banff* (☎ 403-762-4122, 866-762-4122, fax 403-762-3441, W www .hostellingintl.ca/alberta, 801 Coyote Dr) Dorm beds $21/25 members/nonmembers; private rooms available. Three kilometers from downtown via Tunnel Mountain Rd, this hostel contains 216 beds, Cougar Pete's Kitchen, the Storm Cellar pub, laundry facilities, a game room and a common room with a fireplace. At this hub of activity, you can arrange everything from ski trips and tours to mountain bike rentals. This hostel acts as the central reservations service for all the other HI hostels in the region (except the one at Lake Louise), including the seasonal hostels along the Icefields Parkway.

HI-Castle Mountain (☎ 403-762-4122, 866-762-4122, fax 403-762-3441, Bow Valley Parkway) Dorm beds $15/19 members/nonmembers. This rustic 28-bed hostel between Banff and Lake Louise has pit toilets.

Y Mountain Lodge (☎ 403-762-3560, 800-813-4138, fax 403-760-3202, W www.ywca banff.ab.ca, 102 Spray Ave) Dorm beds $22, private rooms from $55. The centrally located Y Mountain Lodge accommodates both men and women in its 120 dorm beds and 45 private rooms. The pleasant and comfortable facilities include a bistro. Reservations are accepted and recommended.

Global Village Backpackers (☎ 403-762-5521, 888-844-7875, fax 403-762-0385, W www.globalbackpackers.com, 449 Banff Ave) Dorm beds from $25, semiprivate rooms from $64. This addition to Banff's hostel scene is just a two-minute walk from downtown and has a hot tub, sauna, game room and Internet access.

B&Bs & Tourist Homes The Banff/Lake Louise Tourism Bureau, in the Banff Information Centre (see Information, earlier), keeps a complete list of B&Bs. To obtain information in advance, write to the bureau at PO Box 1298, Banff T0L 0C0. Most B&Bs provide private rooms and full breakfasts, while 'tourist homes' – basically B&Bs without the breakfast – offer rooms in houses or small separate cabins. Summer rates range from $65 to over $100.

Motels & Hotels Banff has no cheap motels or hotels, especially in the busy summer months. About 20 places line Banff Ave north of Elk St; generally fairly large,

they cater to tour groups and entice visitors with numerous perks like saunas and hot tubs. Many places are geared toward skiers and boarders, offering kitchens and rooms with two beds, which can be a good value for groups of four or more. Remember, the following are peak summer rates – expect significantly lower prices at other times.

Red Carpet Inn (☎ 403-762-4184, 800-563-4609, fax 403-762-4894, 425 Banff Ave) Rooms from $125. The Red Carpet is close to town, and guests can use the pool next door at the High Country Inn.

Irwin's Mountain Inn (☎ 403-762-4566, 800-661-1721, fax 403-762-8220, W www .irwinsmountaininn.com, 429 Banff Ave) Rooms from $145. Amenities here include covered parking, a hot tub, sauna and fitness center.

Bow View Motor Lodge (☎ 403-762-2261, 800-661-1565, fax 403-762-8093, W www.bowview.com, 228 Bow Ave) Rooms from $155. The Bow View's name suggests its greatest asset. It's a comfortable place steps from the Bow River. Amenities include a restaurant, pool and hot tub.

Traveller's Inn (☎ 403-762-4401, 800-661-0227, fax 403-762-5905, W www.banff travellersinn.com, 401 Banff Ave) Rooms from $185. This place features a friendly staff and a good location close to the center. The rooms have large balconies; other amenities include an outdoor hot tub, heated underground parking and Internet access.

Rimrock Resort Hotel (☎ 403-762-3356, 800-661-1587, fax 403-762-4132, W www .rimrockresort.com, Mountain Ave) Rooms from $255. Near the Upper Hot Springs 3km from town, this large upscale resort offers a free shuttle service, excellent mountain views and large, luxurious rooms.

The Fairmont Banff Springs (☎ 403-762-2211, 800-441-1414, fax 403-762-4447, W www.fairmont.com, 405 Spray Ave) If, somewhere along the way, you win the lottery or simply want to super-splurge, the historic Banff Springs, 2km south of downtown, is the place. It's geared primarily to package deals that include everything from meals to golf at summer rates starting at – are you ready? – $1019 a night. Just a room with breakfast and gratuities included will set you back about $625. And if you really *just* want a room and nothing more, well, the hotel sets aside a few broom closets for folks like you ($175).

ALBERTA

Places to Eat

Like any resort town, Banff has plenty of restaurants. Some of the better ones are listed below.

Budget *Cougar Pete's Kitchen* (☎ 403-762-4122, 801 Coyote Dr) Breakfast, lunch & dinner starting at $4-7. For reasonably priced meals, try Cougar Pete's, in the HI-Banff hostel. It even attracts longtime residents with its awesome breakfasts and superb mountain atmosphere.

Evelyn's Coffee Bar (☎ 403-762-0352, 201 Banff Ave) The best local coffee place, this spot at the Town Centre Mall serves good sandwiches and excellent baked goods made on the premises.

Sushi House Banff (☎ 403-762-4353, 304 Caribou St) Sushi plates $3-5. At Sushi House, next door to Bruno's in the same building, a mini-train chugs around the sushi counter and you take your pick from its cargo.

Sunfood Café (☎ 403-760-3933, 215 Banff Ave) Lunch $5-9, dinner dishes $10-14. On the upper level of Sundance Mall, this place offers a great vegetarian menu of organic soups, salads, sandwiches, hot dishes and desserts for lunch and dinner. It's also a quiet place to sit and write a postcard.

Shiki Japanese Restaurant (☎ 403-762-0527, 110 Banff Ave) Soups $7. Shiki, in the Clock Tower Village Mall, specializes in large and warming ramen soups.

Aardvark Pizza & Sub (☎ 403-762-5500, 304A Caribou St) Medium pizzas $10-15. This is the town's best pizza-and-sub place. It's open until 4am daily.

Mid-Range *St James Gate Olde Irish Pub* (☎ 403-762-9355, 205 Wolf St) Sandwiches $9-12, Irish classics $10-14. This wonderful pub has great food and fun Irish music and atmosphere. But pub aficionados come for the 35 taps – with Guinness and many other European favorites – plus 55 Scotch and 10 Irish whiskeys. The pub is named after the Dublin address of the original (and still operational) Guinness Brewery, founded by 34-year-old Arthur Guinness in 1759.

Melissa's Restaurant (☎ 403-762-5511, 218 Lynx St) Burgers $7-8, pizzas $16, steaks $15-25. A major local favorite (especially at breakfast), Melissa's occupies a log building

from 1928 that looks like a wood cabin inside and an English cottage outside. The menu includes pizza, burgers, steaks and more. The bar stays open from 7am to 10pm daily. Don your fleece vest and blend in with the locals on Tuesday, when highball cocktails are only $1.50.

Old Spaghetti Factory (☎ 403-760-2779, Cascade Plaza, Banff Ave at Wolf St) Meals $8.25 & up. For lively atmosphere, head here to carbo-load on pasta meals that include bread, salad, ice cream and coffee. It's an excellent value.

Magpie & Stump (☎ 403-762-4067, 203 Caribou St) Lunch $7-13, dinner $11-15. Minimal windows give this Tex-Mex place a cozy, barlike atmosphere.

Bruno's Cafe & Grill (☎ 403-762-8115, 304 Caribou St) Most meals $7-11. Open 7am-midnight daily. Bruno's offers a wide-ranging menu, including good salads, burgers, chicken and fish.

Coyote's Deli & Grill (☎ 403-762-3963, 206 Caribou St) Dinner dishes $14-24. If you want inventive Southwestern cuisine, try Coyote's, where the open kitchen gives you a chance to see the chefs in action. The hip and lively setting is as refreshing as the menu. Coyote's serves breakfast, lunch and dinner, when it's a good idea to book a table.

Cilantro Mountain Café (☎ 403-760-3008, Tunnel Mountain Rd) Pizzas $13-15, pastas $14-16, steaks & seafood $24-26. You can sit out on the patio or inside at this pleasant bistro at Buffalo Mountain Lodge, near the HI-Banff hostel. The specialties here are gourmet pizzas and fresh pastas, prepared with fresh seasonal ingredients.

Two Italian restaurants both have die-hard regulars:

Giorgio's Trattoria (☎ 403-762-5114, 219 Banff Ave) Pastas $12-14.50, pizzas $13-26. Giorgio's probably has the nicer atmosphere, and the food is good, too.

Guido's Ristorante (☎ 403-762-4002, 116 Banff Ave) Mains $11-23. Some Banffonians prefer the food at this upstairs place.

Top End *Le Beaujolais* (☎ 403-762-2712, ⓦ www.info-pages.com/beaujolais, Banff Ave at Buffalo St) À la carte dishes $30-45, three-course dinner $52-58, six-course dinner $85. The acclaimed Beaujolais employs regional ingredients in its gourmet French cuisine.

ALBERTA

Saltlik (☎ 403-762-2467, 221 Bear St) Lunch $10.50-20, steaks $20-29, other dinner dishes $15-24. This newish upscale steak house has a trendy, elegant atmosphere. Besides beef selections, the menu offers seafood, chicken, pork and venison.

Grizzly House (☎ 403-762-4055, 207 Banff Ave) Four-course fondue dinners $32-48. Seating until midnight. A local institution, the Grizzly House achieves a romantic atmosphere with dark lighting and secluded booths. The menu centers on fondue, and adventurous eaters can sample buffalo, rattlesnake, caribou and other exotic meats.

Bumper's Beef House (☎ 403-762-2622, 603 Banff Ave) Steaks $20-33. Though north of downtown, Bumper's remains one of Banff's busier restaurants. Carnivores can chomp into Alberta beef steaks, prime rib and barbecued ribs, while vegetarians can enjoy the good salad bar.

The Pines (☎ 403-760-6690, 537 Banff Ave) Dishes $17-32. Reservations suggested. North of downtown in the Rundlestone Lodge, this is one of Banff's finest restaurants. Fresh Canadian ingredients such as salmon and venison get the full artistic treatment. The extensive wine list features Canadian vintners.

Entertainment

Banff is the social and cultural center of the Rockies. You can find current entertainment listings in the 'Summit Up' section of the weekly *Banff Crag & Canyon* newspaper, or in the monthly *Wild Life*.

Rose & Crown (☎ 403-762-2121, 202 Banff Ave) This British-style upstairs pub and restaurant has live rock music, darts and pool. A rooftop patio opens in good weather.

Barbary Coast (☎ 403-762-4616, upstairs at 119 Banff Ave) The bar at Barbary Coast steak house is a friendly, locals' place featuring live rock and jazz on Friday and Saturday nights.

Tommy's Neighbourhood Pub (☎ 403-762-8888, 120 Banff Ave) A local crowd comes here for the sunken patio – perfect for Banff Ave people-watching.

Wild Bill's Legendary Saloon (☎ 403-762-0333, 201 Banff Ave) Dedicated to the memory of legendary Bill Peyto (see the boxed text 'The Ultimate Mountain Man'), Wild Bill's, upstairs in the Town Centre

Mall, is crammed any night of the week with folks hoping to re-create some of its namesake's wilder exploits.

Outabounds (☎ 403-762-8434, 137 Banff Ave) This downstairs club is a hot dance bar.

Aurora Nightclub (☎ 403-760-5300, 110 Banff Ave) Another place to groove and sweat is the Aurora, downstairs in the Clock Tower Village Mall.

Lux Cinema Centre (☎ 403-762-8595, 229 Bear St) The local movie house screens first-run films.

Getting There & Away

The bus terminal is at 100 Gopher St. Greyhound (☎ 403-762-1092, 800-661-8747) operates five buses a day to Calgary ($21, 1¾ hours), Vancouver ($112, 14 hours) and points in between. Greyhound also serves Canmore ($8) and Lake Louise ($12); call for a schedule.

Brewster Transportation (☎ 403-762-6767) operates one express bus a day to Jasper ($51, 4½ hours) from April to October. It also runs buses to Lake Louise ($11).

VIA Rail no longer serves Banff, but the privately owned *Rocky Mountaineer* stops at Banff on its way between Calgary and Vancouver. The basic one-way fare from Banff to Vancouver in summer is $669 per person based on double occupancy. The fare includes breakfast, lunch and an overnight stop at a hotel in Kamloops. The service runs between mid-April and mid-October, with three departures a week in June, July and August. For more information, contact Rocky Mountaineer Railtours (☎ 604-606-7245, 800-665-7245, fax 604-606-7250, w www.rockymountaineer.com, 1150 Station St, 1st floor, Vancouver, BC V6A 2X7).

In summer, SunDog Tour Co (☎ 780-852-4056) runs a shuttle between Banff and Jasper daily, stopping at all the hostels along the way; one-way fare for the whole distance is $51 (or $58 to/from the Maligne Lake hostel). Fares to points in between are based on length of trip. For an extra charge, you can arrange to take bikes on the shuttle.

Also in summer, Giddy Goat Adventures (☎ 403-609-9992) runs a daily shuttle to HI-Banff from HI-Calgary; one-way fare is $25.

Moose Travel Network (☎ 888-388-4881, w www.moosenetwork.com) offres a backpacker-oriented minibus shuttle service that loops between Vancouver and Banff,

ALBERTA

stopping at hostels in great destinations along the way. Buses depart each stop at least three times a week. For around $400, you can get on and off at will anytime during the May-to-October season. Price includes transportation only.

Getting Around

To/From the Airport Shuttle buses run daily year-round from Calgary International Airport to Banff. Buses run most frequently in winter, less often in summer and least often in spring and fall. Companies include Rocky Mountain Sky Shuttle (☎ 403-762-5200, 888-762-8754), Brewster Transportation (☎ 403-762-6767, 800-661-1152) and Banff Airporter (☎ 403-762-3330, 888-449-2901). The adult fare with all three companies is around $40/75 one-way/roundtrip.

Bus Banff Transit (☎ 403-760-8294) operates two trolley bus routes through town. One route follows Spray and Banff Aves between the Banff Springs Hotel and the RV parking lot north of town; the other goes from the Luxton Museum along Banff Ave, Wolf St, Otter St and Tunnel Mountain Rd to the hostel and Tunnel Mountain Village Campgrounds. Both stop at the Banff Information Centre. Buses operate every 30 minutes from 7am to midnight, mid-May to September, and from noon to midnight the rest of the year. The fare is $1/50¢ adult/child.

Car All of the major car rental companies have branches in Banff. During summer, all the cars might be reserved in advance, so call ahead. If you're flying into Calgary, reserving a car from the airport (where the fleets are huge) may yield a better deal than waiting to pick up a car when you reach Banff. The agencies include Avis (☎ 403-762-3222, 800-879-2847, Cascade Plaza on Wolf St), Banff Rent-A-Car (☎ 403-762-3352, 204 Wolf St), Budget (☎ 403-762-4565, 800-268-8900, 208C Caribou St), Hertz (☎ 403-762-2027, 800-263-0600, in the Fairmont Banff Springs hotel) and National (☎ 403-762-2688, 800-227-7368, Lynx & Caribou Sts).

Taxi For cab service, try Taxi Taxi & Tours (☎ 403-762-3111, 101 Owl St) or Mountain Taxi & Tours (☎ 403-762-3351, 230 Lynx St).

Bicycle Bike rental places are plentiful. Banff Adventures Unlimited (☎ 403-762-4554, 800-644-8888, ⓦ www.banffadventures.com, 211 Bear St) rents standard mountain bikes for $7/24 per hour/day and full-suspension bikes for $12/40. Snowtips/Bactrax (☎ 403-762-8177, ⓦ www.snowtips-bactrax.com, 225 Bear St) also offers rentals, ranging from $6 to $10 per hour and $22 to $36 per day.

LAKE LOUISE

About 57km northwest of Banff is Lake Louise, known as the jewel of the Rockies. Before you get to the lake you'll come to the uninspiring village of Lake Louise, which is really nothing more than the small Samson Mall shopping center, a service station, and a few lodgings. The lake itself is 5km away. In summer Parks Canada runs a shuttle bus from the village to Lake Louise and Moraine Lake (see Getting There & Around, later). If you'd rather walk, it'll take you about 45 minutes from the village to Lake Louise on the footpath.

Lake Louise itself is a much-visited and stunning lake sitting in a small glacial valley, surrounded by snowcapped mountains. Visit early in the morning, when it's less crowded, and your chances of seeing the classic reflection in the water are better. Some fine walks and hikes are possible nearby. The humongous Chateau Lake Louise sits at the lake's north end; the Fairmont folks, who own the chateau, are building a controversial convention center for the hotel in grizzly bear habitat – good goin', guys.

The Bow Valley Parkway is a slightly slower but much more scenic drive than the Trans Canada Hwy between Banff and Lake Louise.

Information

The visitors' center (☎ 403-522-3833) in the village is open 8am to 8pm daily from June to September, 9am to 5pm the rest of the year. It has information from both Parks Canada and Banff/Lake Louise Tourism. It also has good exhibits on the geological and natural history of the Rocky Mountains. Next door in Samson Mall, Woodruff & Blum bookstore (☎ 403-522-3842) stocks general guides to the Canadian Rockies, as well as hiking, cycling and climbing guides and maps.

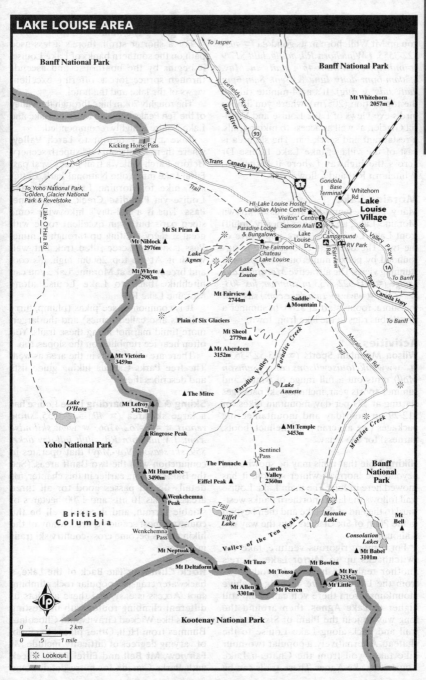

LAKE LOUISE AREA

To Jasper

Banff National Park

Banff National Park

Icefields Pkwy

Bow River

93

Kicking Horse Pass

Trans Canada Hwy

1

Mt Whitehorn
2057m ▲

Gondola
Base
Terminal

Whitehorn
Rd

Lake
Louise
Village

To Yoho National Park,
Golden, Glacier National
Park & Revelstoke

Lake O'Hara Rd

Trail

HI-Lake Louise Hostel
& Canadian Alpine Centre

Visitors' Centre

Paradise Lodge
& Bungalows

Samson Mall

Lake
Louise
Dr

Campground

RV Park

Bow Valley Pkwy

1A

Mt St Piran ▲

Mt Niblock ▲
2976m

Lake
Agnes

The Fairmont
Chateau
Lake Louise

Fairview
Rd

To Banff

Mt Whyte ▲
2983m

Lake
Louise

Trans Canada Hwy

To Banff

Mt Fairview ▲
2744m

Saddle
▲ Mountain

Plain of Six Glaciers

Mt Sheol ▲
2779m

Mt Aberdeen ▲
3152m

Paradise Valley

Paradise Creek

Lake
Annette

Moraine Lake Rd

▲ Mt Victoria
3459m

The Mitre ▲

Trail

Mt Lefroy ▲
3423m

Lake
O'Hara

Ringrose Peak ▲

Yoho National Park

Sentinel
Pass

Mt Temple ▲
3453m

Moraine Creek

The Pinnacle ▲

Mt Hungabee ▲
3490m

Eiffel Peak ▲

Larch
Valley
2360m

Banff
National
Park

Wenkchemna
Peak ▲

British
Columbia

Trail

Eiffel
Lake

Moraine
Lake

Mt
Bell ▲

Wenkchemna
Pass

Valley of the Ten Peaks

Consolation
Lakes

Mt Neptuak ▲

Mt Deltaform ▲

Mt Tuzo ▲

Mt Tonsa ▲

Mt Bowlen ▲

▲ Mt Babel
3101m

Mt Fay
3235m

Mt Allen ▲
3301m

Mt Perren ▲

Mt Little ▲

Kootenay National Park

0   1   2 km
0   .5   1 mile

LP

☀ Lookout

Lake Louise Sightseeing Gondola

In summer Lake Louise Ski Area will scoot you up Mt Whitehorn in its gondola (☎ 403-522-3555, 1 Whitehorn Rd; adult/child $17/9 roundtrip; open 9am-4pm daily in May, 8:30am-6pm daily June & Sept, 8am-6pm daily July & Aug). It's a 14-minute ride to the top station (2057m), where you'll have bird's-eye views of Lake Louise and Victoria Glacier, as well as access to hiking trails, a restaurant and snack bar. The ski area is east of the village; take Lake Louise Dr across the highway (where it turns into Whitehorn Rd) and follow signs.

Moraine Lake

Many people consider the lesser-known Moraine Lake, about 15km (mostly uphill) from Lake Louise, the more impressive of the two. The deep-teal-colored lake is surrounded by peaks; numerous trails provide stunning views. The attractive *Moraine Lake Lodge* (☎ 403-522-3733 in summer, fax 403-522-3719, W www.morainelake.com) sits near the shore; rooms start at $260. In summer a shuttle bus runs to the lake from town.

Activities

Wilson Mountain Sports (☎ 403-522-3636, W www.lakelouisewilsons.com, Samson Mall) rents out a full range of winter and summer sports gear, including ski packages starting at $29 per day, mountain bikes for $12/29 an hour/day and mountaineering packages (ice ax, crampons, helmet, boots, harness) for $35 a day.

Hiking Note that trails may be snowbound beyond the 'normal' winter season; it has snowed here in July! The main Lake Louise trail follows the lake's northern banks westward to the end of the lake and then beyond to the **Plain of Six Glaciers**. On the way is a teahouse.

For a more rigorous venture, take the switchbacks up to **Mirror Lake**. There's another teahouse here and good views from the **Little Beehive** and **Big Beehive** mountains. From there you can climb still higher to **Lake Agnes**, then around the long way to join the Plain of Six Glaciers trail and back along Lake Louise to the chateau. Alternatively, a popular two-hour hike takes you from the Chateau Lake Louise to Lake Agnes. These trails can be

followed for a couple of hours or turned into a good day's walk.

For a shorter stroll, there's a less-used path on the southern banks of Lake Louise; it begins by the boathouse and ascends through spruce forest, offering excellent views of the lake and the hotel.

The roughly 20km hike through the **Valley of the Ten Peaks** between Moraine Lake and Lake Louise is highly recommended.

Take a quick detour to **Larch Valley**, where there's a stream and superb scenery. Before Larch Valley a trail heads west past **Eiffel Lake** into Yoho National Park. Better still, hike to Moraine Lake from Lake Louise via **Paradise Creek** and **Sentinel Pass**. This is a full-day's hike with some steep parts but is an excellent route with great scenery. Getting up through Sentinel Pass is a long, scree-filled trek but well worth it. At the top, 2600m high, it's cool and breezy. Once at Moraine Lake you can hitchhike back to Lake Louise along Moraine Lake Rd.

It is common to see pikas (plump, furry animals also called conies) and the larger, more timid marmot along these trails. You often hear ice rumbling on the slopes, too.

There are other trails in the area as well. The free Parks Canada hiking guide lists and describes them.

Skiing & Snowboarding Lake Louise has a large ski area (☎ 403-522-3555, snow report ☎ 403-762-4766, W www.skilouise .com, 1 Whitehorn Rd; adult full-day ticket $59; ski season Nov-May) that operates in conjunction with the two Banff areas. (See the Banff section, earlier in this chapter, for details on ski passes good for all three areas.) It has 10 lifts and 1700 hectares of skiable terrain, and it could well be the country's most scenic ski area. Many of the hiking trails become cross-country ski trails in winter.

Rock Climbing The **Back of the Lake**, a backwater crag, is a popular rock climbing spot. Access is easy, and there are lots of different climbing routes with interesting names like Wicked Gravity and Chocolate Bunnies from Hell. Other places to climb, of varying degrees of difficulty, include **Mt Fairview**, **Mt Bell** and **Eiffel Peak**. Check with Parks Canada for more details. One locally recommended guide is Mark Klassen of **Corax Alpine** (☎ 403-760-0609, **W** www.ascentguides.com).

Places to Stay

Unless you camp or get a bed at the hostel, you'll have to pay a lot of loonies to stay in Lake Louise. Eat at your hotel (or someone else's).

Lake Louise's two campgrounds (☎ 403-522-3833) are run by Parks Canada, and both are right off the Trans Canada Hwy. The *tenting campground* (Fairview Rd), with sites for $17, is open mid-May to Sept 30; the *RV campground*, with sites for $21, is open year-round. Both have flush toilets and showers.

HI-Lake Louise Hostel & Canadian Alpine Centre (☎ 403-522-2200, fax 403-522-2253, **W** www.hostellingintl.ca/alberta, Village Rd) Dorm beds $24/28 members/nonmembers; private rooms available. This 150-bed hostel, a joint project of Hostelling International and the Alpine Club of Canada, is a short walk north of Samson Mall. For a hostel, it's a palace. It has two kitchens, Bill Peyto's Café, laundry facilities, a sauna, ski and bike workshops and a large mountaineering library. Reservations are essential.

Lake Louise Inn (☎ 403-522-3791, 800-661-9237, fax 403-522-2018, **W** www.lakelouiseinn.com, 210 Village Rd) Rooms from $159. This comfortable 230-room place in the village area has an indoor heated pool, two hot tubs, ski storage and repair areas, laundry facilities and three restaurants.

Paradise Lodge & Bungalows (☎ 403-522-3595, fax 403-522-3987, **W** www.paradiselodge.com, 105 Lake Louise Dr) Bungalows from $165, lodge suites from $250. This cute choice, neat as a pin, offers both lodge rooms and individual bungalows on flower-filled, manicured grounds. It's just a short walk from the lake.

Post Hotel (☎ 403-522-3989, 800-661-1586, fax 403-522-3966, **W** www.posthotel.com, Village Rd) Rooms from $305. If you need to spend a lot of money, this is the place to do it. In the village, this Relais & Chateaux lodging is the epitome of mountain elegance. The timbers-and-stone architecture conveys a warm and cozy lodge ambience, while dining and amenities – including goose-down duvets, fireplaces and Jacuzzi tubs – are all first-rate.

The Fairmont Chateau Lake Louise (☎ 403-522-3511, 800-441-1414, fax 403-522-3834, **W** www.fairmont.com, Lake Louise Dr) Summer B&B packages from $788 per night. This gargantuan lakefront chateau doesn't have the classic charm of its sibling, the Banff Springs Hotel. Moreover, it seems unconscionable for a hotel of this size (or any size) to even *be* here. Save your money.

Getting There & Around

The bus terminal (☎ 403-522-3870) is at Samson Mall. See the Banff section, earlier in this chapter, for bus service details.

In summer, Parks Canada runs the Vista shuttle bus from the village to both Moraine Lake and Lake Louise. The shuttles run to/from Lake Louise every half hour between around 8:15am and 7:30pm and to/from Moraine Lake every hour between 8:15am and 7pm, making several stops en route. The service is currently free, although a token charge is being discussed. For more information, inquire at the vistors' center (see Information, earlier).

ICEFIELDS PARKWAY

This 230km road (Hwy 93) linking Lake Louise with Jasper opened in 1940 and is one of Canada's most spectacular stretches of asphalt. The highway follows a lake-lined valley between two chains of the Eastern Main Ranges, which make up the Continental Divide. The mountains here are the highest, most rugged and maybe the most scenic in all the Rockies. To best appreciate this if you're on the bus, sit on the left side going from Lake Louise to Jasper. The highway is good but slow, as animals such as goats, bighorn sheep and elk are often beside or even on it.

You can drive the route in a couple of hours, but stopping at the many vista points, picnic spots and sights, or hiking on one of the many trails, can take a full day or longer. Visitors' centers have trail details. Cycling the Icefields Parkway is popular. Because of the terrain it's easier to go from Lake Louise to Jasper than vice versa.

The tabloid-size *Mountain Guide,* which Parks Canada hands out at all the entrances to the mountain national parks, has excellent maps detailing sights en route. Parks Canada also has a useful brochure, *The*

Icefields Parkway, which offers further details about the route.

The best time to see **Peyto Lake**, one of the world's most beautiful glacial lakes, is early in the morning, between the time the sun first illuminates the water and the time the first tour bus arrives. Farther north, around **Waterfowl Lake**, moose are plentiful.

Athabasca Glacier

About halfway between Lake Louise and Jasper is the Athabasca Glacier, a tongue of the vast **Columbia Icefield**. The icefield itself covers 325 sq km, and parts of it are over 300m thick. Its meltwaters flow into the Mackenzie, North Saskatchewan and Columbia Rivers.

Icefield Centre (☎ 780-852-6288; admission free; open 9am-6pm May–mid-Oct), opened in 1996, is across the highway from the glacier and a public/private joint venture between Parks Canada and Brewster. It holds numerous well-designed displays explaining glaciers – one of the best is a time-lapse film showing a glacier altering the ground beneath it – and a Parks Canada information desk offering trail details, ecology information and backcountry trek planning. Commercial elements include the obligatory gift shop, several pricey but mediocre restaurants and a small *hotel* (☎ 877-423-7433) with rooms starting at $185 in peak season, $90 in spring and fall.

You can walk or drive to the toe of the glacier from the Icefield Centre. To hike onto the glacier, you'll need a guide. **Athabasca Glacier Icewalks** (☎ 780-852-6550, 800-565-7547, W *www.telusplanet.net/public/iceman1*), with an office in the Icefield Centre, offers a three- to four-hour guided glacier hike (adult/child $40/20) and a deluxe five- to six-hour trip taking in the icefalls of the glacier ($45/22).

You'll find it impossible to miss the hype and hard-sell for the 'snocoach' ice tours offered by **Brewster** (☎ 877-423-7433, W *www.brewster.ca*). The 90-minute tours (adult/child $28/14) drive out on the ice and reach the vast areas of the glacier that can't be seen from the road.

Athabasca Glacier to Jasper

Other points of interest are **Sunwapta Falls** and **Athabasca Falls**, closer to Jasper. Both are worth a stop, though you may be appalled by the bonehead decision to put an ugly utility-road bridge over the most scenic part of Athabasca Falls.

At Athabasca Falls Hwy 93A sneaks quietly off to the left. By all means, take it. Literally the road less traveled, this old route into Jasper offers a blissfully traffic-free experience as it slips serenely through deep dark woods and past small placid lakes and meadows.

Places to Stay

The Icefields Parkway is lined with a good batch of rustic HI hostels. Most are close to the highway in scenic locations; they're small and without showers, but there's usually a 'refreshing' stream nearby.

Contact the HI-Banff hostel (☎ 403-762-4122, fax 403-762-3441, W www.hostelling intl.ca/alberta) for details on the following choices:

HI-Mosquito Creek Dorm beds $15/19 members/nonmembers. Closed the first two weeks of May, early Oct–early Nov, Mon & Tues early Nov–mid-Dec. This excellent

---

Glaciers Are Cool, But Icefields Are Awesome

The Columbia Icefield contains about 30 glaciers and is up to 350m thick. This remnant of the last ice age covers 325 sq km on the plateau between Mt Columbia (3747m) and Mt Athabasca (3491m), off the parkway connecting Banff to Jasper. It's the largest icefield in the Rockies and feeds the North Saskatchewan, Columbia, Athabasca, Mackenzie and Fraser River systems with its meltwaters.

The mountainous sides of this vast bowl of ice are some of the highest in the Rocky Mountains, with nine peaks over 3000m. One of its largest glaciers, the Athabasca, runs almost down to the road and can be visited on foot or in specially designed buses. The water you'll see at the toe of the glacier fell as snow on the icefield about 175 years ago.

32-bed hostel is on the Icefields Parkway about 26km north of Lake Louise, next to the Mosquito Creek campground. Set in woods by a creek, it has cooking facilities and a sauna.

HI-Rampart Creek Dorm beds $14/18 members/nonmembers. This 24-bed hostel, 11km north of the Saskatchewan River Crossing, also has a sauna and closes during the same periods as the Mosquito Creek hostel plus Wednesday from early November to mid-December. It's a sunny site with a nice community campfire pit. Good bouldering opportunities are available right behind the hostel.

HI-Hilda Creek Dorm beds $14/18 members/nonmembers. Closed the first two weeks of May, late Oct–early Dec, Mon-Wed early-\mid-Dec. The 21-bed Hilda Creek hostel, 8km south of Icefield Centre, enjoys a spectacular, high-altitude setting at the base of a cirque below Mt Athabasca.

The following two rustic HI hostels are also on the Icefields Parkway and can be booked through HI-Jasper (☎ 780-852-3215, 877-852-0781, fax 780-852-5560, Ⓦ www.hihostels.ca/alberta):

HI-Beauty Creek Dorm beds $12/17 members/nonmembers. Operates on a reduced schedule from Oct-Apr. This 22-bed hostel is 17km north of Icefield Centre and 87km south of Jasper. It's easy to miss, on the west side of the highway just north of Beauty Creek. From here you can easily hike to Stanley Falls and seven other waterfalls along Beauty Creek.

HI-Athabasca Falls Dorm beds $13/18 members/nonmembers. Closed Tues Oct-Apr. The 40-bed Athabasca Falls hostel is 32km south of Jasper. In summer the Athabasca Falls area swarms with tourists.

Along Icefields Parkway you'll also pass **campgrounds**, as well as the beautiful, rustic **Num-Ti-Jah Lodge** (☎ 403-522-2167, fax 403-522-2425, Ⓦ www.num-ti-jah.com), where rooms start at $150 with shared bath, $170 with private bath.

Also en route, **The Crossing** (☎ 403-761-7000, fax 403-761-7006, Ⓦ www.thecrossingresort.com) includes a comfortable motel with singles/doubles for $92/97, a restaurant and bar at Saskatchewan Crossing, where Icefields Parkway intersects Hwy 11.

JASPER TOWNSITE & AROUND

Jasper, 369km west of Edmonton, is Banff's northern counterpart. It's smaller, with fewer things to see and do, and its setting is less grand, but some people prefer its quieter streets and less tourist-oriented attitude.

It's a good connecting point, with the Yellowhead Hwy and VIA Rail running east to Edmonton and west to Prince George, and the Icefields Parkway going south to Lake Louise. The town is a good supply center for trips around Jasper National Park.

Some of the most apparent wildlife in Jasper are the elk, which hang out downtown during the autumn rutting and spring calving seasons. They emit haunting cries and occasionally charge disrespectful tourists.

Orientation

The main street, Connaught Dr, has virtually everything, including the bus terminal, train station, banks, restaurants and souvenir shops. Outside the train station is a 21m totem pole carved by a Haida artisan from British Columbia's Queen Charlotte Islands. Nearby is an old CN steam engine. The address numbers throughout town, when posted at all, are difficult to follow.

Off the main street, small wooden houses bedecked with flower gardens brighten the alpine setting.

Information

Tourist Offices Right downtown is Parks Canada's Jasper Information Centre (☎ 780-852-6176, Ⓦ www.parkscanada.gc.ca/jasper, 500 Connaught Dr), easily one of Canada's most eye-pleasing tourist offices. It's a stone building covered in flowers and plants. The large green out front is a popular meeting spot, often with people and backpacks lying all over the place. Occasionally, elk can be spotted mowing the lawn. The building also holds a Friends of Jasper gift shop and, in summer (June to mid-October), a Jasper Tourism desk.

The center has information on trails in the park and will offer suggestions to fit your specifications. It distributes two good publications on area hiking, *Day Hikes in Jasper National Park* and *Backcountry Visitors' Guide,* and a list of tourist homes in town. It's open 9am to 5pm daily from April to mid-June, 8am to 7pm daily from

ALBERTA

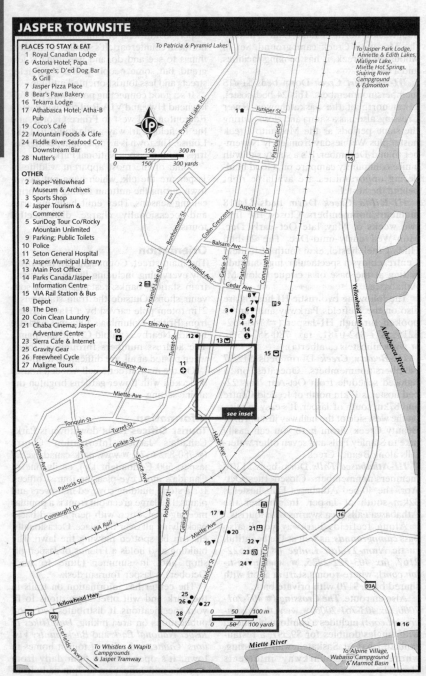

JASPER TOWNSITE

PLACES TO STAY & EAT
1 Royal Canadian Lodge
6 Astoria Hotel; Papa George's; D'ed Dog Bar & Grill
7 Jasper Pizza Place
8 Bear's Paw Bakery
16 Tekarra Lodge
17 Athabasca Hotel; Atha-B Pub
19 Coco's Café
22 Mountain Foods & Cafe
24 Fiddle River Seafood Co; Downstream Bar
28 Nutter's

OTHER
2 Jasper-Yellowhead Museum & Archives
3 Sports Shop
4 Jasper Tourism & Commerce
5 SunDog Tour Co/Rocky Mountain Unlimited
9 Parking; Public Toilets
10 Police
11 Seton General Hospital
12 Jasper Municipal Library
13 Main Post Office
14 Parks Canada/Jasper Information Centre
15 VIA Rail Station & Bus Depot
18 The Den
20 Coin Clean Laundry
21 Chaba Cinema; Jasper Adventure Centre
23 Sierra Cafe & Internet
25 Gravity Gear
26 Freewheel Cycle
27 Maligne Tours

To Patricia & Pyramid Lakes

To Jasper Park Lodge, Annette & Edith Lakes, Maligne Lake, Miette Hot Springs, Snaring River Campground & Edmonton

Juniper St
Patricia Circle
Pyramid Lake Rd
Aspen Ave
Colin Crescent
Bonhomme St
Balsam Ave
Pyramid Ave
Geikie St
Patricia St
Connaught Dr
Cedar Ave
Elm Ave
Turret St
Maligne Ave
Miette Ave
Yellowhead Hwy
Athabasca River

0   150   300 m
0   150   300 yards

see inset

Tonquin St
Turret St
Pine Ave
Willow Ave
Geikie St
Spruce Ave
Hazel Ave
Patricia St
Connaught Dr
VIA Rail
Yellowhead Hwy
Icefields Pkwy

To Whistlers & Wapiti Campgrounds & Jasper Tramway

Robson St
Geikie St
Miette Ave
Patricia St
Connaught Dr

17
18
20
21
22
23
24
25
26
27
28
19

0   50   100 m
0   50   100 yards

93A

93

16

Miette River

To Alpine Village, Wabasso Campground & Marmot Basin

mid-June to early September, 9am to 6pm daily the rest of September and October, 9am to 4:30pm daily from November to March.

Jasper Tourism & Commerce (☎ 780-852-3858, fax 780-852-4932, W www.jasper canadianrockies.com, 409 Patricia St) offers information on the town and is open 9am to 5pm weekdays.

Post & Communications The main post office (☎ 780-852-3041, 502 Patricia St & Elm Ave) is open 9am to 5pm Monday to Friday.

The Jasper Municipal Library (☎ 780-852-3652, 500 Robson St) has Internet access for $5 an hour, and for a small fee you can also use its fax machine and copier. It's open 11am to 9pm Monday to Thursday, 11am to 5pm Friday and Saturday. Better for Internet access is Sierra Cafe & Internet (☎ 780-852-1199, 610 Connaught Dr), which offers the added blessing of having iMacs for terminals. Rates are $1.50 for the first 10 minutes and $1 for the next 10. What's more, there's good coffee, food and atmosphere, too.

Laundry Clean yourself and your clothes at Coin Clean Laundry (☎ 780-852-3852, 607 Patricia St). It has coin-op showers ($2 for 10 minutes) and is open 8am to 9:30pm.

Medical Services For medical help, go to Seton General Hospital (☎ 780-852-3344, 518 Robson St).

Museums

The small **Jasper-Yellowhead Museum & Archives** (☎ 780-852-3013, 400 Pyramid Lake Rd; adult/senior & student $3.50/2; open 10am-9pm daily in summer; 10am-5pm daily in fall, 10am-5pm Thur-Sun rest of the year) has some interesting displays on the town's history and development. One documents the story of the two Harragin sisters, the park's first women mountain guides (hired by Brewster in the 1920s).

Downstairs at the Whistlers Inn, a small wildlife museum called **The Den** (☎ 780-852-3361, Connaught Dr & Miette Ave; adult/senior & student/family $3/2/6; open 9am-10pm daily) houses a collection of stuffed animals representing the park's wildlife in natural-like settings.

Jasper Tramway

The lower terminal of the Jasper Tramway (☎ 780-852-3093, W www.jaspertramway.com, Whistlers Mountain Rd; adult/child $18/9; open 8:30am-10:30pm in summer, reduced hours in spring & fall) is about 7km south of Jasper along Whistlers Mountain Rd off the Icefields Parkway. The busy gondola goes up Whistlers Mountain in seven minutes and offers panoramic views 75km south to the Columbia Icefield and 100km west to Mt Robson in British Columbia. The upper terminal is at an altitude of 2500m; here you can get a bite in the restaurant and hit the hiking trails. It's a 45-minute walk to the summit, above the tree line, where it can be cool.

SunDog Tour Co (see Organized Tours, later) operates a shuttle from town to the tramway. The price ($25/15 adult/child) includes roundtrip transportation and the tram ticket. Buses leave from the totem pole in front of the train station.

Patricia & Pyramid Lakes

These lakes, about 7km northwest of town along Pyramid Lake Rd, are small and relatively quiet. They have hiking and horseback-riding trails, picnic sites, fishing and beaches; you can rent canoes, kayaks and windsurfers. In winter there's cross-country skiing and ice skating. It's not uncommon to see deer, coyotes or bears nearby.

Lakes Annette & Edith

Off the Yellowhead Hwy, 3km northeast of town along Lodge Rd, Lake Annette and Lake Edith are at about 1000m altitude and can be warm enough for a quick swim. The woodsy day-use area around them holds beaches, hiking and biking trails, and picnic areas. Boat rentals are available. This is a mellow, slightly off-the-beaten-path place to kick back and soak in the beauty surrounding you.

Jasper to Maligne Lake

About 11km east of Jasper on the way to Maligne (ma-**leen**) Lake, you pass **Maligne Canyon**, a limestone gorge about 50m deep at its deepest but just a couple of meters wide at its narrowest. From the teahouse, a trail leads down the canyon past views of waterfalls, springs, crystalline pools and interesting rock formations. Note that the tour-bus hordes all start at the teahouse, walk down the canyon a short distance and take the obligatory smiling-head photo, then turn around and head directly back up to tea and scones. But *you* can park at the bottom and walk *up* toward the teahouse, through the equally spectacular and blissfully uncrowded lower canyon, until you run into *them*. Turn off the main road at the sign for 5th Bridge.

Continuing another 21km up the road to Maligne Lake, you'll come to **Medicine Lake**, whose level rises and falls due to the underground drainage system; sometimes the lake disappears completely.

Maligne Lake

At the end of Maligne Lake Rd, 48km southeast of Jasper, is the largest of the glacier-fed lakes in the Rockies and the second largest in the world. The lake is promoted as one of the most scenic of mountain lakes, but this is perhaps unwarranted. It's a commercial, busy destination, and the classic view with the island is some kilometers out in the lake, accessible only by boat.

Maligne Tours (☎ *780-852-3370*, **W** *www.malignelake.com, 627 Patricia St*) is the concessionaire for the variety of activities available at and around the lake. Maligne Lodge, the building at the end of the road, is the activity center and has a restaurant and souvenir shop. It's open May to October. The most popular activity offered is the 1½-hour **boat tour to Spirit Island** (adult/senior/child $35/30/17.50). It leaves hourly between 10am and either 4pm or 5pm from June to late September, with a reduced schedule from season opening (sometime in May) until early June. If you'd rather go self-propelled, you can rent a canoe ($15 per hour) or sea kayak ($20 per hour). **Horseback trail rides** leave from the lodge twice a day from mid-June to September; the 3½-hour trips cost $55. It's free to avail yourself of the fine hiking trails and, in snow season, cross-country ski trails, that lace the area.

The company offers a shuttle bus between the town of Jasper and the lake from May to early October. The bus runs three to five times a day in each direction and costs $12 per person each way.

Miette Hot Springs

A good spot for a soak is the remote Miette Hot Springs (☎ *780-866-3939, 800-767-1611,*

W *www.parkscanada.gc.ca/hotsprings, Miette Rd; adult/senior & child/family $6/5/17; open daily mid-May–mid-Oct; 8:30am-10:30pm in summer, 10:30am-9pm in spring & fall*), 61km northeast of Jasper off the Yellowhead Hwy, near the park boundary. Miette has the hottest mineral waters in the Canadian Rockies, emerging from the ground at 54°C and cooled to around 40°C. The modern spa features two hot pools and a refreshing cool pool. You can rent a bathing suit for $1.50 and a towel for $1.

Activities

Hiking Wildlife is more plentiful and hikers are generally fewer in Jasper than in Banff. If the weather has been wet, you may want to avoid the lower trails, where horseback trips are run: they make the path a mud bath. Topographic maps are available at the Friends of Jasper shop in the Jasper Information Centre.

The leaflet *Day-hikers' Guide to Jasper National Park* has descriptions of most of the park's easy walks, while the *Backcountry Visitors' Guide, Jasper National Park* details longer trails and backcountry campsites and suggests itineraries for hikes of two to 10 days. If you're hiking overnight, you must obtain a backcountry permit from Parks Canada in the Jasper Information Centre. These cost $6 per person per night up to a maximum of $30. For detailed information and reservations for routes that have capacity restrictions, call the Parks Canada Trail Office at ☎ 780-852-6177.

Off the Icefields Parkway, about 10km southeast of Jasper, is the small **Valley of the Five Lakes**. The 8km loop around the lakes is mostly flat and makes a pleasant two- to three-hour stroll. Alternatively, you can take the trail that heads off north from the loop to **Old Fort Point**, about 2km from Jasper. The **Mt Edith Cavell** and **Miette Hot Springs** areas also have good day hikes. For a good two- or three-day hike, try the 45km **Skyline Trail**, which starts at the northwestern end of Maligne Lake and finishes on Maligne Lake Rd about 13km from Jasper. Approximately 26km of the trail is at or above the tree line and has great scenery. The trail has plenty of wildlife, too; watch out for grizzlies.

Cycling Bicycling is permitted on the highways and on designated park trails. Cycling is not allowed off the trails. Journeys of a few hours, a day or several days (with overnight stops at campgrounds, hostels or lodges) are all possible. For more information, get a copy of *Mountain Biking Guide, Jasper National Park* from the Jasper Information Centre.

A good cycling route that's close to town is along **Maligne Lake Rd** to Maligne Canyon or farther to Medicine Lake. A popular, scenic but fairly tough trail ride goes through the Valley of the Five Lakes to Old Fort Point, a distance of about 23.5km. For bicycle rentals, see Getting Around, later.

Rock Climbing Climbing classes and guided climbs are available from **Paul Valiulis/ICPeaks** (☎ 780-852-4161, W *www.icpeaks.com*) and from **Peter Amann** (☎ 780-852-3237, W *www.incentre.net/pamann*). Climbing gear is available at **Gravity Gear** (☎ 780-852-3155, 618 Patricia St).

Horseback Riding Pyramid Riding Stables (☎ 780-852-7433) offers rides through the stunning hills above Jasper (one-/two-/three-hour rides $25/43/65). To reach the stables, follow Pyramid Lake Rd 4km uphill from the town center and watch for the signs.

Whitewater Rafting Calm to turbulent rafting can be found on the **Maligne River**, **Sunwapta River** and the **Athabasca River** near Athabasca Falls. Numerous companies offer trips of varying lengths. **Maligne**

Rafting Adventures (*book tickets at Maligne Tours,* ☎ 780-852-3370, W *www.mra.ab.ca, 627 Patricia St*) offers half-day, Class III whitewater trips on the Sunwapta ($65 per person), as well as easier and harder trips. **Whitewater Rafting Ltd** (☎ 780-852-7238, 800-557-7238) leads 3½-hour trips to Athabasca Falls and two-hour rides on the Maligne or Sunwapta Rivers (all starting at $50); trips can be booked all over town, including at Freewheel Cycle (618 Patricia St).

Skiing & Snowboarding Jasper National Park's only ski area is **Marmot Basin** (☎ 780-852-3816, W *www.skimarmot.com, Marmot Basin Rd; adult full-day pass $49; ski season Dec-May*), which lies 19km southwest of town off Hwy 93A. The 607-hectare area has 75 downhill runs, beginner through expert, served by six chairlifts and two T-bars. New for 2001–02: the Eagle Ridge area, encompassing two mountain faces with 20 new runs, served by a new quad chair. Marmot Basin also features plenty of scenic cross-country trails and a chalet. Call for a snow report.

Near Maligne Lake, the **Moose Lake Loop** (8km) and the trail in the **Bald Hills** (11km) are easy introductions to the park's 200km of cross-country ski trails.

Organized Tours
Three main companies in town book tickets for various tours and activities, including train rides, boat cruises, air tours, hiking, rafting, horseback riding, shuttle service and more.

Ride the rapids in the Rockies.

They are: **Maligne Tours** (☎ 780-852-3370, W www.malignelake.com, 627 Patricia St), **SunDog Tour Co/Rocky Mountain Unlimited** (☎ 780-852-4056, fax 780-852-9663, 888-786-3641, W www.sundogtours.com, 414 Connaught Dr) and **Jasper Adventure Centre** (☎ 780-852-5595, 800-565-7547, W www.jasperadventurecentre.com, 604 Connaught Dr), in the VIA Rail station.

Brewster Gray Line (☎ 780-852-3332, 607 Connaught Dr), in the VIA Rail station, offers a three-hour 'Discover Jasper' tour to some of the local sights, including Patricia and Pyramid Lakes and Maligne Canyon (adult/child $45/22.50). Its Maligne Lake cruise takes five hours ($63/31.50). It also runs 7½-hour Icefields Parkway tours to Lake Louise ($88/44 one way, $120/60 two-day roundtrip, not including accommodations in Lake Louise). Prices are lower in spring and autumn.

Places to Stay

In general, prices here are lower than in Banff.

Camping Jasper's 10 park campgrounds are generally open from mid-May to late September or early October, although a few stay open until the first snowfall (which may not be that much later). All are first-come, first served. For information, contact Parks Canada (☎ 780-852-6176, 500 Connaught Dr). Notable among the 10 are the following:

Whistlers Campground Sites $15-24. The closest campground to town, Whistlers is about 3km south, off the Icefields Parkway on Whistlers Rd. It has electricity, showers and flush toilets, but even with 781 sites it gets crowded. In summer films and talks are presented nightly.

Wapiti Campground Sites $13-18. About 2km farther south from Whistlers Campground, on the Icefields Parkway and beside the Athabasca River, Wapiti is the only campground in the park open during winter. It offers flush toilets and electricity year-round but has showers only in the summer season.

Snaring River Campground Sites $10. Snaring River Campground is 17km north on the Yellowhead Hwy. A good argument could be made that this 66-site primitive campground enjoys the most spectacular

setting in the park. It lies at the foot of the Palisades – a long, sheer cliff band. Across the highway, the Colin Range thrusts its pristine rock walls heavenward in an area that will have rock climbers salivating.

Wabasso Campground Sites $13. Wabasso Campground is 17km south on beautiful Hwy 93A. It's peaceful down this way. This 228-site campground has flush toilets but no showers. It opens in late June.

Hostels *HI-Jasper* (☎ 780-852-3215, 877-852-0781, fax 780-852-5560, W www.hostelling intl.ca/alberta, Whistlers Mountain Rd) Dorm beds $18/23 members/nonmembers. This large HI hostel is 7km southwest of Jasper near the Jasper Tramway; the last 2km are uphill. It has a barbecue, laundry facilities, a large kitchen and Internet access. The search is on for a new site in town; stay tuned. In summer, SunDog Tour Co (see Organized Tours, earlier) operates a shuttle bus from town to the Jasper Tramway; drivers will drop you at the hostel for $3 one way.

HI-Jasper is also the contact for the following two rustic hostels:

HI-Mount Edith Cavell Dorm beds $13/18 members/nonmembers. Open mid-June–mid-Oct. A mountaineer's delight, this little hostel is walking distance from the parking area/trailhead beneath 3363m Mt Edith Cavell – a stunning peak. It's south of Jasper, 13km off Hwy 93A up Mt Edith Cavell Rd. The road closes in winter, and though the hostel officially closes along with it, groups can cross-country ski up and stay at the hostel in winter; call for more information.

HI-Maligne Canyon Dorm beds $13/18 members/nonmembers; closed Wed Oct-Apr. The Maligne Canyon hostel, 11.5km east of town up Maligne Lake Rd, has 24 beds in two cabins. It's a short walk from the Maligne Canyon teahouse and trailhead.

Tourist Homes The Parks Canada information center and the Jasper Tourism & Commerce office (see Information, earlier) both have lists (call Jasper Tourism to request a copy by mail) of over 100 tourist homes that are usually centrally located and open all year. Bizarre national park regulations forbid breakfast being served (that's why you won't find any B&Bs in Jasper), but some places may offer you a muffin with a cup of tea.

You can also just cruise the streets close to town center, where almost every house has a sign offering rooms. In summer many of these places fill up early, so it's a good idea to book ahead. Rates run anywhere from $30 to $80 or more per night (no tax).

Motels, Hotels & Bungalows Numerous motels line Connaught Dr on the approaches to Jasper. Downtown holds more lodgings – all convenient, but none particularly special. A concentration of higher-end places is on Geikie St, within walking distance of downtown. And several places outside town proper offer bungalows (usually wooden cabins) that are only open in summer. The prices listed here are summer rates; at other times you can get significant discounts.

Athabasca Hotel (☎ 780-852-3386, 877-542-8422, fax 780-852-4955, W www .athabascahotel.com, 510 Patricia St) Rooms starting at $75 with shared bath, $109 with private bath. Downtown's Athabasca Hotel has basic rooms, a pub and a restaurant.

Astoria Hotel (☎ 780-852-3351, 800-661-7343, fax 780-852-5472, W www.astoriahotel .com, 404 Connaught Dr) Rooms from $168. The comfortable Astoria has nicely appointed rooms and a popular pub and restaurant. Note: room Nos 114–117 and 132–135 face a noisy back alley and are best avoided.

Royal Canadian Lodge (☎ 780-852-5644, 800-661-9323, fax 780-852-4860, W www .charltonresorts.com, 96 Geikie St & Juniper St) Rooms from $315. This place is a quiet and refined motel with large rooms, a gourmet restaurant and an indoor hot tub and heated pool.

Patricia Lake Bungalows (☎ 780-852-3560, 888-499-6848, fax 780-852-4060, W www.patricialakebungalows.com, Patricia Lake Rd off Pyramid Lake Rd) Rooms from $81, cottages from $132. Open May–mid-Oct. A quiet family atmosphere pervades tidy Patricia Lake Bungalows, about 5km north of town on Patricia Lake. More parklike than rustic, the resort features manicured grounds, canoe and boat rentals, nature trails, a Laundromat, outdoor hot tub and well-equipped cottages and motel rooms.

Pyramid Lake Resort (☎ 780-852-4900, 888-852-4900, fax 780-852-7007, W www .pyramidlakeresort.com, Pyramid Lake Rd)

Rooms from $209. Open year-round. This bustling place is a little farther north along Pyramid Lake Rd from Patricia Lake Bungalows. It's a larger, fancier resort, with a licensed dining room, stunning mountain views and boats, canoes and kayaks to take out on the gorgeous lake. But it doesn't have the feeling of remote tranquility you'll get at Patricia Lake Bungalows.

Tekarra Lodge (☎ 780-852-3058, fax 780-852-4636, W www.tekarralodge.com, Hwy 93A) Lodge rooms from $154, cabins from $164. Open May-Oct. Tekarra Lodge is 1km south of Jasper off Hwy 93A at the confluence of the Miette and Athabasca Rivers. It's a great site out of the tourist fray, and the rustic lodge has been elegantly updated.

Alpine Village (☎ 780-852-3285, fax 780-852-1955, W www.alpinevillagejasper.com, Hwy 93A) Log cabins from $150. Open May-Oct. Near the Tekarra, just a bit farther south on Hwy 93A, the Alpine Village is a neat and friendly place with nicely renovated older cabins and deluxe newer cabins. The landscaped grounds include a swimming pool and mountain-view deck. On nice evenings, guests take their lawn chairs out on the riverbank and watch the sunset.

The Fairmont Jasper Park Lodge (☎ 780-852-3301, 800-441-1414, fax 780-852-5107, W www.fairmont.com, 1 Old Lodge Rd) Rooms from $479. Fairmont's deluxe Jasper Park Lodge is a class act with a country-club feel. Its amenity-filled cabins and chalets are scattered across expansive grounds that include a championship golf course. The lodge's main lounge is open to the public and is the best place in town to write a postcard over a quiet cocktail.

Places to Eat
Many of the hotels and lodges have their own dining rooms. Additional selections include the following:

Bear's Paw Bakery (☎ 780-852-3233, 4 Cedar Ave) Wholesome homemade baked goods are the specialty at this welcoming little bakery. The aromas of delicious croissants, muffins and whole-grain breads waft out onto nearby Connaught Dr; follow your nose.

Coco's Café (☎ 780-852-4550, 608 Patricia St) Prices $4-7. For breakfast, this small, hip café offers eggs, waffles, muesli, muffins and more. Lunch brings delicious sandwiches and burritos. Vegetarians will appreciate the menu's many vegan items, and solo travelers will find plenty of essential reading material, like old copies of *Climbing* magazine. Save room for the heavenly peanut butter Nanaimo bar.

Sierra Cafe & Internet (☎ 780-852-1199, 610 Connaught Dr) Breakfast & lunch specials $5-7. A great place to start the day, Sierra Cafe offers affable proprietor Dieter's homemade touch on fresh-baked scones, muesli, granola and more. Breakfast is served all day. The atmosphere is mellow and jovial, and you can check your email, too (see Post & Communications, earlier).

Papa George's (☎ 780-852-3351, Astoria Hotel) Breakfast & lunch $5-11, dinner $13-24. Papa George's serves classics for breakfast, burgers and sandwiches for lunch, and regional specialties like grilled caribou sausage with apple fennel slaw ($18) for dinner.

Mountain Foods & Cafe (☎ 780-852-4050, 606 Connaught Dr) Breakfast $3-7, lunch & dinner $4-9. This place is open all day and serves good breakfasts, vegetarian foods, burgers, and homemade soups and muffins. Order at the counter and take it back to your table.

Jasper Pizza Place (☎ 780-852-3225, 402 Connaught Dr) Pizzas $10-13.50. Locals love Jasper's, which has a rooftop patio and excellent pizza.

Fiddle River Seafood Co (☎ 780-852-3032, 620 Connaught Dr) Dishes $13-38. The town's best seafood place has a fine view from its 2nd-floor location. The salmon and trout ($19-24) couldn't be any fresher if they flopped right onto your plate.

For a wide selection of bulk and natural foods, check ***Nutter's*** (☎ 780-852-5844, 622 Patricia St).

Entertainment

Downstream Bar (☎ 780-852-3032, downstairs at 620 Connaught Dr) The newish Downstream Bar, below Fiddle River Seafood Co, is a comfortable, mostly non-smoking place with a good beer selection and pool tables.

Atha-B Pub (☎ 780-852-3386, Athabasca Hotel) This pub regularly has live rock bands and dancing.

De'd Dog Bar & Grill (☎ 780-852-3351, Astoria Hotel) This venue is famous for its imported draft beers. You can play pool and

darts with the colorful locals who like to hang out here.

Chaba Cinema (☎ 780-852-4749, 604 Connaught Dr) Opposite the VIA Rail station, this cinema shows first-run movies.

Getting There & Away

Bus The Greyhound bus station (☎ 780-852-3926, 607 Connaught Dr) is in the VIA Rail station. Four buses daily serve Edmonton ($52, from 4½ hours). Two buses a day go to Prince George ($52, five hours), Kamloops ($60, six hours) and Vancouver ($105, from 11½ hours).

Brewster Transportation (☎ 780-852-3332), at the same station, has one daily express bus to Lake Louise ($44, 4½ hours) and Banff ($51, 5½ hours).

Train VIA Rail (☎ 888-842-7245, 607 Connaught Dr) offers tri-weekly train service west to Vancouver and east to Toronto. In addition, there is tri-weekly service to Prince George, where the train continues to Prince Rupert after an overnight stay. Basic fares are usually a bit more than the bus, although the train is more comfortable, if slower. With the gutting of rail funding by the Canadian government, these trains are geared mostly toward sightseeing tourists. Call or check at the VIA Rail station for exact schedule and fare details.

The private Rocky Mountaineer Railtours train (☎ 800-665-7245, **w** www.rockymountaineer.com) runs between Jasper and Vancouver via Kamloops. It operates from May to mid-October, and the number of trips varies each month. The peak-season one-way fare to Vancouver is $724/1338 single/double, including some meals and an overnight stay in Kamloops.

Getting Around

Car rental in Jasper is available through the following: Avis (☎ 780-852-3970, Petro Canada station, 300 Connaught Dr), Budget (☎ 780-852-3222, Shell station, 638 Connaught Dr), Hertz (☎ 780-852-3888, VIA Rail station, 607 Connaught Dr) and National (☎ 780-852-1117, VIA Rail station, 607 Connaught Dr).

If you're in need of a taxi, call Heritage Cabs (☎ 780-852-5558).

Freewheel Cycle (☎ 780-852-3898, 618 Patricia St) and Sports Shop (☎ 780-852-

3654, 406 Patricia St) rent mountain bikes for around $20 to $35 a day, depending on suspension.

Southern Alberta

Southern Alberta is cattle-ranching country, although wheat is important, too. Here you can visit the badlands, with their unusual rock formations and vestiges of prehistoric beasts around Drumheller and Dinosaur Provincial Park, or see Head-Smashed-In Buffalo Jump, where the Blackfoot used to hunt herds of buffalo. In the southeastern corner rising out of the prairies is Cypress Hills Provincial Park. In Writing-On-Stone Provincial Park you can see hoodoos and ancient petroglyphs. To the west are the spectacular Alberta Rockies, which you may see beckoning on clear days.

The Rockies extend south across the border into the US. Butting up against the border, a portion of the range is preserved in Waterton Lakes National Park, a gorgeous mountain realm offering stunning scenery equal to that found in Banff and Jasper National Parks but without the crowds.

DRUMHELLER

About 150km northeast of Calgary in the Red Deer River Valley, Drumheller is a small city in a strange setting. Approaching town, you begin to see badlands – steep-walled canyons eroded out of the prairie and revealing millions of years of the earth's geological history. Then suddenly the highway plummets into one of these canyons and slides into Drumheller, 122m below prairie level.

The area is renowned for its dinosaur fossils. More complete dinosaur skeletons of the Cretaceous period (from 64 to 140 million years ago) have been found in this region than anywhere else on the planet. The city has caught on to the tourism potential of dinosaurs, and statues and symbols of the extinct critters are all over town; most are eyesaurs. Kids and dinosaur buffs might find this amusing, but others might find it cloying. The outstanding Royal Tyrrell Museum, reason enough to come here on a day trip from Calgary, sits a short distance outside town, as if a wee bit embarrassed to be seen with all the dino-schlock.

The tourist information center (☎ 403-823-1331, 60 1st Ave W), marked by a huge *T rex* looking hungrily toward Calgary, is open 9am to 9pm daily in July and August and 9am to 6pm daily the rest of the year.

Dinosaur Trail, Horseshoe Canyon & Hoodoo Drive

Drumheller is on the Dinosaur Trail, a 48km loop that runs northwest from town and includes Hwys 837 and 838. The loop takes you past **Midland Provincial Park** (no camping), where you can take a self-guided hike, across the Red Deer River on the free, cable-operated **Bleriot Ferry**, which has been running since 1913, and to vista points overlooking the area's impressive canyons.

Horseshoe Canyon, the most spectacular area chasm, is best seen on a short drive west of Drumheller on Hwy 9. An interpretive center on the canyon rim explains the area geology, while trails lead down into the canyon for further exploration.

The Hoodoo Drive, about 25km long (it only goes one way so you must return by the same route), takes in the **hoodoos**, about 18km southeast of Drumheller on Hwy 10. Here are the best examples of these weird, eroded, mushroom-like columns of sandstone rock. This area was the site of a once prosperous coal-mining community. The Atlas Mine is now preserved as a provincial historic site. Take the side trip on Hwy 10X (which includes 11 bridges in 6km) from Rosedale to the small community of Wayne, where you can stop for a beer at the fabled Last Chance Saloon.

Royal Tyrrell Museum of Palaeontology

This excellent museum (☎ 403-823-7707, 888-440-4240, **w** www.tyrrellmuseum.com; adult/senior/youth/family $8.50/6.50/4.50/20; open 9am-9pm daily mid-May–Labor Day, 10am-5pm daily Labor Day–mid-Oct, 10am-5pm Tues-Sun & holiday Mondays rest of the year) is set in a fossil-rich valley along Dinosaur Trail (Hwy 838) 6km northwest of town. It uses displays, videos, films and computers to outline the study of early life on earth. Fossils of ancient creatures, including flying reptiles, prehistoric mammals and amphibious animals, help trace the story of evolution; best of all is the extensive display of over 35 complete dinosaur

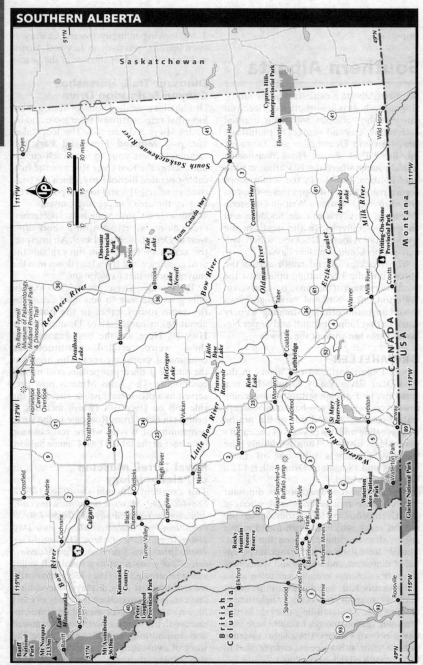

SOUTHERN ALBERTA

Saskatchewan

Oyen

Dinosaur Provincial Park

Patricia

Tide Lake

Brooks

Lake Newell

Bassano

Deadhorse Lake

Red Deer River

To Royal Tyrrell Museum of Palaeontology, Midland Provincial Park & Dinosaur Trail

Horseshoe Canyon Overlook

Drumheller

Strathcona

Carseland

McGregor Lake

Vulcan

Little Bow River

Bow River

Medicine Hat

Trans Canada Hwy

South Saskatchewan River

Crowsnest Hwy

Elkwater

Cypress Hills Interprovincial Park

Wild Horse

Pakowki Lake

Milk River

Writing-On-Stone Provincial Park

Coutts

Milk River

Warner

Taber

Ettkom Coulee

Oldman River

Little Bow Lake

Travers Reservoir

Keho Lake

Monarch

Coaldale

Lethbridge

Cardston

Carway

St Mary Reservoir

CANADA

USA

Montana

Crossfield

Airdrie

Calgary

Cochrane

Black Diamond

Okotoks

High River

Longview

Nanton

Claresholm

Fort Macleod

Stavely

Turner Valley

Kananaskis Country

Peter Lougheed Provincial Park

Mt Assiniboine 3618m

Elkford

Sparwood

Rocky Mountain Forest Reserve

Coleman

Blairmore

Frank

Bellevue

Hillcrest Mines

Crowsnest Pass

Frank Slide

Head-Smashed-In Buffalo Jump

Pincher Creek

Waterton River

Waterton Lakes National Park

Waterton Park

Glacier National Park

Fernie

Roosville

British Columbia

Banff National Park

Mt Norquay 2133m

Banff

Lake Minnewanka

Canmore

Bow River

0 15 25 50 km
0 30 miles

skeletons. A Burgess Shale Exhibit shows the many wild and weird creatures that died and became part of the shale. In summer, with advance reservations, you can participate in a fossil dig (adult/youth 10-15 $85/55) or join an expert-led guided hike to a dig site (adult/child $12/8). The museum is named for Joseph Tyrrell (**teer**-ell), a geologist who made the first discovery of dinosaur bones in the area in 1884.

Places to Stay

River Grove Campground & Cabins (☎ 403-823-6655, fax 403-823-3132, ⓦ www .virtuallydrumheller.com/rivergrove, 25 Poplar St) Sites $20-25, cabins from $60. In town the River Grove Campground enjoys a pleasant shady spot on the river's north bank. It has showers, a laundromat, a store and cabins.

Badlands Motel (☎ 403-823-5155, fax 403-823-7653, 801 N Dinosaur Trail) Singles/doubles $60/65. Drumheller has several cheap motels. The Badlands, just north of town on the Dinosaur Trail, offers decent rooms, none nonsmoking. Its best asset might be Whif's (see Places to Eat).

Heartwood Manor (☎ 403-823-6495, 888-823-6495, fax 403-823-4935, ⓦ www.discover alberta.com/heartwoodmanor, 320 N Railway Ave E) Rooms from $110. This small, friendly inn offers luxuriously appointed rooms and an optional, extra-charge gourmet breakfast. Massage, aromatherapy and other spa services are available. The only downside might be the inn's proximity to the railroad tracks; when the train goes by, you'll think of Alvy's boyhood home under the Coney Island roller coaster in Woody Allen's *Annie Hall*. Light sleepers might prefer the inn's sister property, Heartwood Haven.

Super 8 Motel (☎ 403-823-8887, 888-823-8882, fax 403-823-8884, 680 2nd St SE) Rooms from $119. Behind the McDonald's at the junction of Hwys 9 and 10, the newish Super 8 has a nice pool with a water slide.

Places to Eat

Whif's Flapjack House (☎ 403-823-7595, 801 N Dinosaur Trail) Meals $4-7. At the Badlands Motel, Whif's is a good bet for a down-home breakfast or lunch.

Sizzling House (☎ 403-823-8098, 160 Centre St) Dinners $8-11. Sizzling House is a

perennial local favorite for its surprisingly good Chinese food.

Stavros (☎ 403-823-6362, 1103A Hwy 9) Dinner dishes $10-24. When locals go fancy, many go to Stavros in the Best Western Jurassic Inn. The wide-ranging dinner menu offers Greek specialties, calzones, pizzas and pastas, steaks, seafood and more. It's open for three meals daily.

Shopping

The Fossil Shop (☎ 403-823-6774, ⓦ www .thefossilshop.com, 61 Bridge St) This shop, immediately north of the Hwy 9 bridge at the north end of 2nd St, is worth visiting for a look around and perhaps a purchase of a 75-million-year-old souvenir. Its knowledgeable staff can help make sense of all kinds of bones and dinosaur fragments. Some of these ancient treasures aren't even all that expensive.

Getting There & Away

Buses run from the Greyhound bus station (☎ 403-823-7566, 308 Centre St) to Calgary daily ($25, two hours) and to Edmonton twice a week ($50, 5½ hours).

Hammerhead Tours (☎ 403-260-0940 in Calgary, ⓦ www.hammerheadtours.com) runs a full-day tour ($60) from Calgary to the Drumheller badlands and Royal Tyrrell Museum from May to November.

DINOSAUR PROVINCIAL PARK

This isn't Jurassic Park, but, as a Unesco world heritage site, it's the next best thing. Dinosaur Provincial Park (☎ 403-378-4342, toll-free in Alberta ☎ 310-0000 ext 403-378-4342, ⓦ www3.gov.ab.ca/env/parks/prov_parks/dinosaur, off Hwy 544; admission free; open year-round) is a 76½-million-year-old dinosaur graveyard roughly halfway between Calgary and Medicine Hat, some 48km northeast of Brooks. From the Trans Canada Hwy (Hwy 1), take Hwy 36 or Secondary Hwy 873 to Hwy 544.

The park's dry, convoluted lunar landscape was once a tropical rain forest on the shores of an inland sea. Dinosaurs thrived here; archaeologists have uncovered more than 300 complete skeletons, many of which now reside in museums around the world.

A full day can easily be spent exploring the 73-sq-km park, which is full of wildlife, wildflowers and wild rock formations (known as hoodoos) – photographers will have a field day here. In summer, take plenty of water (walking in the valley can be as hot as hell), a hat, sunscreen and insect repellent.

Five interpretive hiking trails and a driving loop run through part of the park, but to preserve the fossils, access to 70% of the park is restricted. The off-limits areas may be seen only on guided hikes and bus tours (adult/child $4.50/2.25), which operate from late May to October. The tours are popular, and you should reserve a place by calling ☎ 403-378-4344 or toll-free in Alberta ☎ 310-0000 ext 403-378-4344 after May 1 for the following season.

The park's **Royal Tyrrell Museum Field Station** (☎ *403-378-4342, toll-free in Alberta* ☎ *310-0000 ext 403-378-4342, adult/child $2.50/1.50; open 8:30am-9pm daily mid-May–early Sept, daily with reduced hours early Sept-early Oct, 9am-4pm Mon-Fri early Oct–mid-May)* has four display areas where nearly complete skeletons have been encased in glass. Archaeologists are on hand to answer questions during summer.

The park's two good *campgrounds* are by a creek, which makes a small, green oasis in this stark place. A tent site costs $15, a powered site costs $18, and laundry facilities and hot showers are available. These sites fill up regularly, so you should phone for reservations (☎ 403-378-3700, toll-free in Alberta ☎ 310-0000 ext 403-378-3700; $6 reservation fee). Motel accommodations are available in Brooks.

MEDICINE HAT

Knowing this city's nickname is 'The Gas City' may or may not entice you here. Sitting on the banks of the South Saskatchewan River, at the junction of the Trans Canada and Crowsnest Hwys (Hwys 1 and 3, respectively), the city was formed in 1883 when the Canadian Pacific Railway, drilling for water, hit natural gas. Enough gas was subsequently found to prompt Rudyard Kipling to label it 'the city with all hell for a basement.' Even today the downtown street lamps are lit by gas.

The visitors' center (☎ 403-527-6422, 800-481-2822, 8 Gehring Rd SW) is south of downtown, off the Trans Canada Hwy at Southridge Dr. It's open 8am to 9pm daily in summer, 9am to 5pm Monday to Saturday the rest of the year. The Greyhound bus station (☎ 403-527-4418, 557 2nd St SE) is downtown and open daily.

From the visitors' center or the highway, you can see the **Saamis Tepee** (☎ *403-527-0073*), a tribute to Canada's indigenous peoples. The 20-story-high metal structure was used ceremonially at the 1988 Winter Olympics in Calgary. The sight has a small interpretive center. Medicine Hat is also notable for its parks and walking trails, some of which line the South Saskatchewan River, and the downtown's fine, old redbrick buildings.

Southeast of the city, straddling the Saskatchewan border off Hwy 41, **Cypress Hills Interprovincial Park** is an oasis of forest surrounded by seemingly endless prairie. See the Saskatchewan chapter for details.

HEAD-SMASHED-IN BUFFALO JUMP

About 18km northwest of Fort Macleod and 16km west of Hwy 2, Head-Smashed-In Buffalo Jump (☎ *403-553-2731*, **w** *www .head-smashed-in.com, Spring Point Rd/ Secondary Hwy 785; interpretive center $6.50/3 adult/child; center open daily 9am-6pm mid-May–mid-Sept, 10am-5pm mid-Sept–mid-May)* is a Unesco world heritage site. For thousands of years, Blackfoot peoples stampeded bison over the cliff here. They then used the meat, hide, bone, horns and nearly everything else for their supplies and materials. The site was last used for this purpose in the early 19th century. According to legend, a young brave wanted to view a killing from beneath the cliff but became trapped and was crushed by the falling bison, hence the name Head-Smashed-In.

The excellent interpretive center, built into the hillside, provides explanations of how the Blackfoot hunters used the site. Outside are nearly 2km of outdoor trails. A 10-minute film, a dramatized reenactment of the buffalo hunt, is shown regularly during the day, and sometimes Native Indians give lectures on the lives of their ancestors. Allow an hour for the trails and 1½ hours for the indoor displays. A snack bar serves bison, chicken and sandwiches. The site gets busy by late morning so arriving early is advisable; also you may see deer and more birds on the trails before the sun gets too hot. See Organized Tours in the Calgary section, earlier in this chapter, for tours to here.

How Head-Smashed-In Buffalo Jump got its name

LETHBRIDGE

Lethbridge, on the Crowsnest Hwy, is the largest town in southern Alberta, the third largest in the province and a center for the local agricultural communities. The town straddles the beautiful, undeveloped Oldman River Valley, here known as simply 'the coulee.' Downtown and most commercial businesses are on the coulee's east side, while the University of Lethbridge and residential districts are on the west. Linking the two sides is the High Level Bridge, supposedly the world's longest (1.6km) and highest (96m) railway trestle. It's easily visible from Hwy 3. Down in the coulee, the parkland along the Oldman holds 62km of walking and cycling trails.

The pleasant downtown centers around a nice little park. To its west the appropriately named Scenic Dr runs along the coulee rim. To its east busy Mayor Magrath Dr is a chain-store-infested drag that could be Anywhere, North America.

Information

Lethbridge has two visitors' centers. The main office (☎ 403-320-1222, 800-661-1222, 2805 Scenic Dr S at Mayor Magrath Dr S) is open daily year-round. The other office (☎ 403-320-1223) is on Brewery Hill at the western end of 1st Ave S. It's open Tuesday to Saturday March to mid-May, daily mid-May to Labor Day, Tuesday to Saturday Labor Day to October 31 and is closed the rest of the year.

To buy stamps or send mail, you can go to the main post office (☎ 403-382-4604, 704 4th Ave S). Internet access is available at Esquire's coffeehouse (☎ 403-380-6747, 621

4th Ave S) for $12 per hour, and it's free at the Lethbridge public library (☎ 403-380-7310, 810 5th Ave S).

Things to See & Do

The **Nikka Yuko Japanese Garden** (☎ 403-328-3511, 7th Ave S at Mayor Magrath Dr S; adult/youth 6-17 $5/3; open daily mid-May–early Oct, 9am-9pm in summer, 10am-4pm in spring & fall), in Henderson Park, was built to honor Japanese-Canadian friendship. Its authentic Japanese gardens consist of ponds, rocks and shrubs. The buildings and bridges were built in Japan and reassembled here on the 1.6-hectare site. Young women in traditional Japanese kimonos greet you and provide background information.

In the coulee between the east and west sides of the city, beside Oldman River, is **Indian Battle Park** (3rd Ave S, west of Scenic Dr), named after a famous 1870 battle between the Blackfoot and the Cree. Within the park is **Fort Whoop-Up** (☎ 403-329-0444, ⓦ www.fortwhoopup.com; adult/child $5/3; open 10am-6pm Mon-Sat, noon-5pm Sun in summer; 1pm-4pm Tues-Fri & Sun rest of the year), a replica of Alberta's first and most notorious illegal whiskey trading post. Around 25 of these outposts were set up in the province between 1869 and 1874 for the purpose of trading whiskey, guns, ammunition and blankets for buffalo hides and furs from the Blackfoot tribes. Their existence led directly to the formation of the Northwest Mounted Police, who arrived in 1874 at Fort Macleod to bring law and order to the Canadian West.

Nearby, on the north side of the High Level Bridge, is the **Helen Schuler Coulee Centre and Lethbridge Nature Reserve** (☎ *403-320-3064; admission free*), which contains a small interpretive center (open daily in summer, Tuesday to Sunday afternoon the rest of the year) and nature trails on the reserve's 80 wooded hectares along the river. It's quiet and cool in the coulee, and you'll see a range of flora and fauna.

The small but well-run **Sir Alexander Galt Museum** (☎ *403-320-4258/3898, 320 Galt; admission by donation; open 10am-4pm daily*), at the west end of 5th Ave S, presents well-documented exhibits of art and artifacts focusing on various aspects of southern Alberta history. Exhibits rotate regularly, and the museum often hosts impressive visiting exhibitions. In the back a fantastic observation gallery overlooks the coulee.

Places to Stay & Eat

Bridgeview Campground (☎ *403-381-2357, 1501 2nd Ave W*) Sites $22-32. This 100-site park enjoys a beautiful location on the river bottom, 'underlooking' the High Level Bridge. Amenities include showers, a Laundromat, a store and a heated pool.

Henderson Lake Campground (☎ *403-328-5452, 3419 Parkside Dr S*) Sites $20-31. Next to the lake in Henderson Park, this place also has 100 sites and full amenities but no pool.

YWCA (☎ *403-329-0088, fax 403-327-9112, 604 8th St S*) Singles/doubles $22/40. The YWCA is for women only. It has laundry facilities, a gym, hot tub and sauna.

University of Lethbridge (☎ *403-329-2244, fax 403-329-5166, ☒ home.uleth.ca/anc-con, 4401 University Dr, Lethbridge T1K 3M4*) Dorm beds $15-20, shared apartments $35 per person. Available May-Aug. The university, southwest of downtown over Oldman River, offers summer accommodations to the general public.

Lethbridge Community College (☎ *403-329-7218, fax 403-327-9062, 3000 College Dr S*) Dorm beds $20, two-bedroom suites $40, townhouses $80. Available May–mid-Aug. Not to be outdone, the local community college also rents out accommodations. From downtown, follow Scenic Dr to College Dr and turn right.

Motels downtown include the following:

Lethbridge Lodge (☎ *403-328-1123, 800-661-1232, fax 403-328-0002, ☒ www.lethbridgelodge.com, 320 Scenic Dr S*) Rooms from $94. A large, full-service hotel on the rim of the coulee, the Lethbridge Lodge hosts a lot of conferences and business travelers.

Holiday Inn Express (☎ *403-394-9292, 866-494-9292, fax 403-394-9202, ☒ hiel@telusplanet.net, 120 Stafford Dr S*) Rooms from $109. Along with a great downtown location and the chain's usual comforts, the Holiday Inn Express, opened in November 2000, still boasts that fresh, new-car smell.

Among the scads of motels lining busy Mayor Magrath Dr are the following:

Pepper Tree Inn (☎/fax *403-328-4436, ☎ 800-708-8638, 1142 Mayor Magrath Dr S*) Singles/doubles from $59/64. The friendly Pepper Tree has well-equipped rooms with fridges and VCRs.

Parkside Inn (☎ *403-328-2366, 800-240-1471, fax 403-328-5933, 1009 Mayor Magrath Dr S*) Singles/doubles from $62/67. Across the street from Henderson Park, the Parkside is relatively charmless but reasonably priced. It has an on-site restaurant and lounge.

Lethbridge is no culinary capital. You might try the following:

Treat's Eatery (☎ *403-380-4880, 1104 Mayor Magrath Dr S*) Lunch $7-11, dinner dishes $15-18. This moderately priced lunch and dinner place is hugely popular with locals for its pasta platters, stir-frys and large sandwiches.

Brewster's Brewing Co (☎ *403-328-9000, 1814 Mayor Magrath Dr S*) Burgers & sandwiches $7-9, dishes $12-15. Good beer and good food in a casual atmosphere mark this link in the small Brewster's chain.

Getting There & Around

The Lethbridge airport (☎ *403-329-4474, 417 Stubb Ross Rd*), a short drive south of town on Hwy 5 (Mayor Magrath Dr), is served by commuter affiliates of Air Canada (☎ 888-247-2262). Six or seven flights a day go to Calgary.

Greyhound (☎ *403-327-1551, 411 5th St S*) has service to Calgary ($32, from three hours) and Regina ($75, from 13 hours).

For detailed information about local bus service, call the Lethbridge Transit Infoline

(☎ 403-320-4978/3885). The downtown bus terminal is on 4th Ave at 6th St. Local bus fare is $1.85.

WRITING-ON-STONE PROVINCIAL PARK

This park (☎ *403-647-2364; admission free; open year-round*) is southeast of Lethbridge and close to the US border; the Sweetgrass Hills of northern Montana are visible to the south. To get to the park, take Hwy 501 42km east of Hwy 4 from the town of Milk River. The park is named for the extensive carvings and paintings made by the Plains Indians over 3000 years ago on the sandstone cliffs along the banks of Milk River.

Some of these **petroglyphs and pictographs** can be seen along a 2km trail open to self-guided hiking, but the best art is found in a restricted area (to protect it from vandalism), which you can only visit on a guided tour (free) with the park ranger. Other activities possible here include canoeing and swimming in the river in summer and cross-country skiing in winter. Park wildlife amounts to more than 160 bird species, 30 kinds of mammals, four kinds of amphibians and three kinds of reptiles, not to mention the fish in the river. The park is always open; the tours are available daily from mid-May to September. Pick up tickets from the naturalist's office one hour before tour time.

The *campground* (☎ *403-647-2877, 877-877-3515 in Canada*) by the river has sites ($16 to $20) with running water, showers and flush toilets and is popular on weekends; it's open April to September.

On the way to the park from Lethbridge, dinosaur enthusiasts may want to stop at **Devil's Coulee**, near Warner, where dinosaur nests and eggs were uncovered in 1987. Here you can visit a museum (☎ 403-642-2118) and an active dig (tours available).

CARDSTON

Mormons founded Cardston, 70km southwest of Lethbridge at the junction of Hwys 5 and 2, in 1887. Their large, geometrically blocky **Alberta Temple** (☎ *403-653-1693, 348 3rd St W*) was erected in 1923 and looks like something Frank Lloyd Wright might have built with Legos. Although only Mormons can enter the impressive temple, visitors can roam the grounds and check out the small

visitors' center, open 9am to 9pm daily May to September.

The **Remington-Alberta Carriage Centre** (☎ *403-653-5139,* W *www.remingtoncentre .com, 623 Main St; adult/senior/youth 7-17/ family $6.50/5.50/3/15; open 9am-6pm daily mid-May–mid-Sept, 10am-5pm daily rest of the year*) records the history of horse-drawn transportation in the 19th and early 20th centuries. It has over 250 buggies, wagons and sleighs and includes a museum, carriage factory, blacksmith and stable.

WATERTON LAKES NATIONAL PARK

Established in 1895 and now part of a Unesco world heritage site, Waterton Lakes, a 525-sq-km national park, (*in summer* ☎ *403-859-5133, in winter* ☎ *403-859-2224, emergency* ☎ *403-859-2636,* W *www.parkscanada.pch .gc.ca/waterton; adult/senior/child $4/3/2*) lies in Alberta's southwestern corner, 130km from Lethbridge. Here the land rises from the prairie into rugged, beautiful alpine terrain with many valleys, lakes and waterfalls. The spectacular landscape continues uninterrupted across the 49th Parallel into the US, where it is protected in Glacier National Park. Together the two parks comprise Waterton-Glacier International Peace Park.

Though backpackers get to savor the park's best scenery, even those who don't venture far from the Winnebago can marvel at Upper Waterton Lake, the deepest lake in the Rockies (146m), and Cameron Falls, which cascade across rock 600 million years old. Spotting wildlife is common – cougars, grizzlies, black bears and elk all roam the park – and more than 800 wildflower species grow here.

A highlight for many visitors is a boat ride across Upper Waterton Lake, whose far shore is in Montana, USA. **Waterton Shoreline Sightseeing Cruises** (☎ *403-859-2362*) operates cruises on the lake, with boats holding up to 200 passengers. A limited operation (with no stops in the USA) begins in May; the full schedule operates in July and August, with most cruises stopping at Goat Haunt, Montana. The roundtrip costs $24/12/8 adult/youth 13-17/child.

A great half-day trip can be made by taking the boat one way ($14/8/6) and walking the 13km trail back. Or join

ALBERTA

One Park, Two Nations

Waterton Lakes National Park has joined with Glacier National Park in the US to form the Waterton-Glacier International Peace Park. Although the name evokes images of binational harmony, in reality each park is operated separately, and entry to one does not entitle you to entry to the other.

Glacier National Park was created in 1910 and comprises over 400,000 hectares. The park is open year-round; however, most services are only open from mid-May to September. Entry to the park costs US$5 per person or US$10 per car. From Waterton Lakes, take Hwy 6 22km south to the US border, where the road becomes US Hwy 17. Follow this 23km south to US Hwy 89 and continue 21km south to the park entrance at St Mary, Montana. The road into the park here is sometimes closed in winter. The main services for the park are on the southwestern side at West Glacier, Montana.

For more information on Glacier National Park, contact the US National Park Service (☎ 406-888-7800, fax 406-888-7808, **w** www.nps.gov/glac/home.htm, PO Box 128, West Glacier, MT 59936). For campground reservations, call ☎ 800-365-2267; for hotel reservations in the park, call ☎ 406-892-2525.

rangers on the not-to-be-missed 'International Peace Park Hike,' an eight-hour guided hike (which includes a lunch stop) from Waterton Village to Goat Haunt. The hike is offered every Saturday at 10am from the end of June to Labor Day, and it's free, but hikers must pay for their boat ride back.

Lacing the park are 255km of hiking trails, some of which are also good for cycling and horseback riding, while in winter many become cross-country skiing/snowshoeing trails. Among the many hikes, the 8.7km **Crypt Lake Trail** is one of the most popular in Canada. The route is both challenging and exhilarating – hikers negotiate a ladder, a precipitous ledge and a tunnel – and from town, the only way to reach the trailhead is by boat (Waterton Shoreline Sightseeing Cruises; adult $13 roundtrip).

The park is open year-round and gets considerably fewer visitors than Banff and Jasper. It's blissfully low on tour buses, and the village of Waterton is smaller and much more low-key than Banff. Spring and fall are great for storm-watching, as high winds regularly kick up whitecaps and even full-on waves on the lake.

The park's visitors' center (see main park contact information, listed above) is across the road from the Prince of Wales Hotel. It's open daily from mid-May through early October.

Places to Stay

The park has three Parks Canada vehicle-accessible campgrounds, none of which take reservations. Backcountry campsites are limited and can (and should) be reserved; call the park's main number, listed above.

Waterton Townsite Campground Sites $17-23. Open mid-May–mid-Oct. This 238-site campground, on Hwy 5 at the southern end of town, is the park's largest and has full facilities, but open fires are prohibited.

Open fires are permitted at the other two campgrounds: 129-site ***Crandell*** ($13), northeast of town on Red Rock Parkway, and 24-site ***Belly River*** ($10), in the southeast corner of the park on Chief Mountain Hwy. Both of these are open mid-May to early- or mid-September. Neither one has showers.

Just outside the park are a few privately owned campgrounds, including ***Waterton Springs Campground*** (☎ *403-859-2247, fax 403-859-2249, Hwy 6)*, with sites for $16 to $23; and ***Crooked Creek Campground*** (☎ *403-653-1100, Hwy 5)*, with sites for $11 to $16.

HI-Waterton (☎ *403-859-2151, 888-985-6343, fax 403-859-2229, **w** www.hostelling intl.ca/alberta, Cameron Falls Dr at Windflower Ave)* Dorm beds $21/25 members/nonmembers; private rooms available. Closed Dec-Jan. The newish 21-bed hostel shares facilities with the Lodge at Waterton Lakes; hostelers get a discount at the lodge spa.

El Cortez Motel (☎ 403-859-2366, 208 Mountview Rd) Rooms from $75. Open May-Oct. The El Cortez looks like a '50s-style road motel. It's humble but has prices to match.

Northland Lodge (☎/fax 403-859-2353, 408 Evergreen Ave) Rooms from $85. Open mid-May–Sept. This nine-room lodge is a pleasant 10-minute walk from the village center past Cameron Falls.

Kilmorey Lodge (☎ 403-859-2334, fax 403-859-2342, W www.kilmoreylodge.com, 117 Evergreen Ave) Rooms from $98. The historic lakefront Kilmorey dates from the late 1920s and has a comfortable, home-away-from-home feel to it. Its ambience is upscale-rustic; the 23 rooms are nicely furnished with antiques and down comforters but without TVs or phones. Think quiet. The lodge restaurant is excellent.

Bayshore Inn (☎ 403-859-2211, 888-527-9555, 604-708-9965 off-season, fax 403-859-2291, W www.bayshoreinn.com, 111 Waterton Ave) Rooms from $100. Open Apr–mid-Oct. The Bayshore is your basic motel, but it's got a prime lakefront location 'downtown.' Get a room overlooking the water.

Waterton Lakes Lodge (☎ 403-859-2150, 888-985-6343, fax 403-859-2229, W www .watertonlakeslodge.com, 101 Clematis Ave) Rooms from $195. New and glitzy, the nine two-story lodging units here look like modern suburban condos. Amenities include a restaurant and pool/health club/recreation center.

Prince of Wales Hotel (in season ☎ 403-859-2231, other times ☎ 406-756-2444, fax 403-859-2630, Prince of Wales Rd) Rooms from $269. Open mid-May–Sept. The vener-able Prince of Wales Hotel, a national historic site, perches on a rise overlooking the lake. Though incredibly photogenic from a distance, up close the hotel looks smaller and much more 'venerable.' Nevertheless, the views alone are almost worth the price. To get there, turn in across the road from the park visitors' center.

CROWSNEST PASS

West of Fort Macleod the Crowsnest Hwy (Hwy 3) heads through the prairies and into the Rocky Mountains to Crowsnest Pass (1396m) and the BC border. At the beginning of the 20th century this was a rich coal-producing region, which gave rise to a series of small mining towns. In 1903 one of these, Frank, was almost completely buried when 30 million cubic meters of nearby Turtle Mountain – some 82 million tons worth – collapsed and killed around 70 people. This and other mining disasters, plus a fall in demand for coal, eventually led to the demise of the coal industry, although a mine at Bellevue operated until 1961 (summertime tours available; ☎ 403-564-4700; adult $6). Today the Pincher Creek area is a center for a different form of energy: windmill farms are a growing presence.

Frank Slide Interpretive Centre (☎ 403-562-7388, W www.frankslide.com; adult/child $6.50/3; open daily 9am-5pm), 1.5km off Hwy 3 and 27km east of the British Columbia border, overlooks the Crowsnest Valley. As well as displays on the slide's cause and effects, it has exhibits on the coming of the railway and on late-19th- and early-20th-century life and mining technology.

British Columbia

British Columbia, known simply as BC, is Canada's westernmost province. It's bordered in the north by the Yukon and the Northwest Territories; in the east by Alberta; in the south by the US states of Montana, Idaho and Washington; in the northwest by Alaska; and in the west by the Pacific Ocean.

The province contains some of the world's most varied and spectacular scenery. The magnificent Canadian Rockies are primarily in the southeast, and the northern interior is full of mountain ranges, forests, lakes and wilderness. The southern interior has a small desert, while the lush Pacific coastal area has rainforests and countless inlets and islands. In short, the range of landscapes provides a wide range of habitat for wildlife, as well as opportunities for outdoor activities to suit every taste.

Victoria, the provincial capital, is at the southern tip of Vancouver Island, which lies off the southwest coast of the mainland. Vancouver, the province's business center and by far BC's largest city, sits alongside the Strait of Georgia near the mouth of the Fraser River.

BC culture, particularly on the southwest coast, is slightly different from that of the rest of Canada. More lifestyle-conscious than in the east, it partially reflects California's influence. Tourism – in a province with many lucrative industries – is the second-largest moneymaker (after timber).

History

BC's earliest-known inhabitants are believed to have arrived from Asia 12,000 years ago, after the end of the last Ice Age. Some settled along the Pacific coast while others settled in the interior east of the Coast Mountains.

The Pacific coast First Nations included the Bella Coola, Cowichan, Gitskan, Haida, Kwakiutl, Niska, Nootka, Salish and Tsimshian groups. With plenty of animal, marine and plant life available, they were able to evolve a highly sophisticated culture and an intricate trade network.

Inland, with its greater climate extremes, the people led a nomadic, subsistence way

Highlights

Entered Confederation: July 20, 1871
Area: 948,596 sq km
Population: 4,095,900
Provincial Capital: Victoria

- Stroll the streets and parks of Vancouver, where the wilderness meets the metropolis.

- Kayak among the whales on Vancouver Island's wild west coast.

- Hit the slopes at Whistler, a world-class ski resort that also boasts a hopping nightlife.

- Take a soothing soak in one of BC's many regional hot springs.

- Taste fruit right off the tree in the sunny Okanagan Valley.

- Hear an avalanche's rumble on Rogers Pass.

- Gaze at haunting totem poles on the Queen Charlotte Islands.

OTHER MAPS
British Columbia pages 720-721
Southern Gulf Islands page 809
Southwestern British Columbia page 814

VANCOUVER MAPS
Downtown Vancouver
& Around pages 728-729

Prince Rupert page 849
Prince George page 844
Southeastern British Columbia page 832
Vancouver Island pages 766-767
Okanagan Valley page 820
Kamloops page 816
Vancouver page 726
Kelowna page 825
Nanaimo page 789
Victoria page 769
Downtown Victoria & Inner Harbour page 772

PACIFIC OCEAN

of life. To the north they followed migratory herds of animals such as the caribou and the moose; to the south they followed the bison. In the south, around the Fraser, Columbia and Thompson Rivers, salmon was also an important resource. Most of these people were Athabaskans (now called Dene, pronounced de-**nay**), which included such groups as Beaver, Chilcotin, Carrier, Sekani and Tahltan. Other important groups were the interior Salish (divided into the Lillooet, Okanagan, Shuswap and Thompson) and the Kootenay (or Kootenai).

Near the end of the 18th century, European explorers appeared off the West Coast in search of new sources of wealth. The Russians and Spanish came first and were soon followed by British explorer Captain James Cook, who was looking for a water route across North America from the Pacific to the Atlantic – the legendary Northwest Passage. He was unable to find it, but his account of the riches to be had from furs brought traders eager to cash in on the lucrative market. The most famous of these fur traders/explorers were Alexander Mackenzie, Simon Fraser and David Thompson, who explored routes overland from the east. The fur companies established a series of trading posts that, by the 1820s, came under control of the Hudson's Bay Company.

In the meantime, initially to counter the Spanish presence, Captain George Vancouver had explored and claimed Vancouver Island for Britain. In 1849, following years of dispute with the USA, Vancouver Island became a Crown colony.

The discovery of gold along the Fraser River in 1858 brought in a flood of people seeking their fortune and led to mainland BC also being declared a Crown colony. A second wave of fortune hunters came when gold was discovered farther north in the Cariboo region. Although the gold rush lasted only a few years, many of those who came in the wake of the miners remained behind to form more permanent settlements. In 1866 the two colonies were united and, after much discussion, joined the Canadian Confederation in 1871 as the province of British Columbia.

The arrival of the transcontinental railway in 1885 opened up BC to the east; and the settlement of the prairies around

this time created demand for the province's resources, particularly timber. The building of the Panama Canal, which was completed in 1914, meant easier access to markets in Europe and along North America's East Coast. This brought about a boom for the BC economy.

Following WWI, an economic downturn led to industrial unrest and unemployment, and the Wall St crash of 1929 brought severe depression and hardship. Prosperity only returned with the advent of WWII and was sustained after the war with the discovery of new resources and the development of a manufacturing base.

At the beginning of the 1990s, BC experienced an economic boom led by Vancouver, which enjoyed its links to then-thriving Asia as well as a large influx of moneyed immigrants fleeing Hong Kong ahead of the handover to China. But these economic ties to Asia were both a blessing and a curse. The crash of the Asian economies in the late 1990s sent a chill through Vancouver and devastated the lumber industries, which counted on Asian exports. This, coupled with the collapse of fishing stocks, resulted in a recession stretching from the metropolitan southwest to the rural towns of the far north. Today, BC's economy has diversified, with high-tech and tourism playing bigger roles. In absolute dollars the province has Canada's fourth-largest economy. But the GDP growth per capita has been abysmally low – between 1992 and 2000 it was the worst in Canada – and many economists bemoan BC's inability to rebound from the 'dismal decade' of the '90s, blaming a poor investment climate as one of the major contributing factors.

Climate

BC's climate is varied. On the coast it is mild with warm, mostly dry summers and cool, wet winters. The interior is much drier, particularly in the south along the Okanagan Valley; summers are hot and winters cold. In the mountains, summers are short and often wet, and winter snowfalls are heavy.

Unless you're coming for winter activities like skiing, the best time to visit is from early June to early October. During this period, rainfall is less, temperatures are warm, daylight hours are long and all the transport routes are open.

National & Provincial Parks

BC has six national parks and more than 400 provincial parks covering a total area about twice the size of Switzerland. Four of the national parks are close to each other in the southeast – Yoho, Kootenay, Glacier and Mt Revelstoke. Yoho and Kootenay adjoin Alberta's Banff National Park in the Rocky Mountains, while Glacier and Mt Revelstoke are farther west in the Columbia Mountains. Pacific Rim National Park Reserve stretches along Vancouver Island's west coast. It's divided in two by Barkley Sound and includes the Broken Group Islands. Gwaii Haanas National Park Reserve, inaccessible by road, is in the Queen Charlotte Islands.

The provincial parks are all listed in Tourism BC's *Road Map & Parks Guide*, available free at Visitor Info Centres. Most of the parks can be reached on paved or gravel roads in conventional vehicles, though you'll need a 4WD vehicle to reach some, and others have no road access at all – you'll have to hike in. A few can be reached only by ferry.

Some national and provincial parks are open all year, but most are open only from April or May to September or October. Many have vehicle (RV) and tent campsites, picnic areas and toilets and offer activities such as hiking, swimming, boating and fishing. At most of them a camping fee between $5 and $19 is charged during the peak visiting season.

Some places considered historically significant have also been set aside as parks. Examples of these are Barkerville east of Quesnel, Fort Rodd Hill near Victoria and Fort Steele in the southeast near Cranbrook.

Much of the land in the provincial forests can be used for recreation and camping at low cost ($8 to $10 per night, or $27 for an annual pass). Because these areas are not well publicized they are generally not busy, and camping spots may be found when others in the area are fully booked. Most tourist information centers around the province will have maps of the local forest districts.

Information

Tourism BC operates the province's impressive and comprehensive tourism infrastructure and produces a mountain of literature covering just about everything the visitor

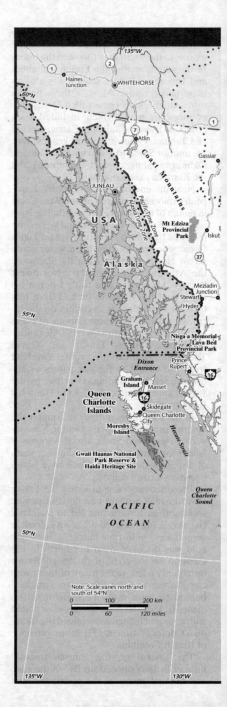

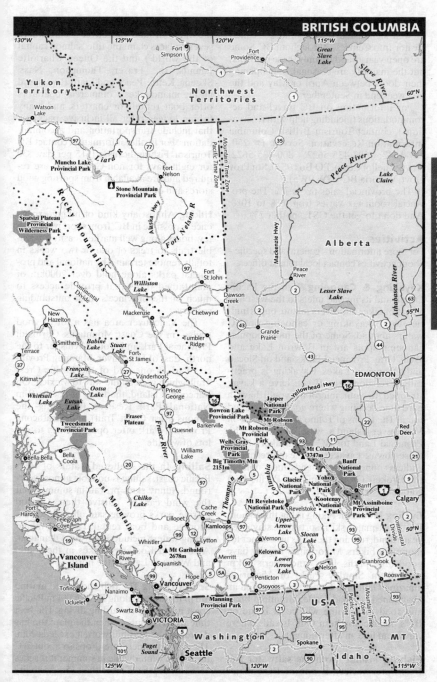

BRITISH COLUMBIA

needs to know. It oversees a broad network of well signposted tourist offices – called Visitor Info Centres – throughout BC. Some are open year-round (mainly those in towns) but the majority are seasonal, only opening their doors between April or May and the first weekend in September.

For information on BC travel and accommodations (including help with reservations), contact Tourism British Columbia Information/Reservation Service (☎ 250-387-1642, 604-435-5622, 800-435-5622, w www.hellobc.com, PO Box 9830, Stn Prov Govt, Victoria BC V8W 9W5).

The provincial sales tax is 7%. The provincial room tax varies from 8% to 10%. And don't forget the GST, another 7%.

Activities

For more information – general and specific – about activities contact local tourist offices.

Kayaking & Canoeing With the Pacific Ocean and its myriad inlets to the west and a host of lakes and rivers inland, opportunities to go kayaking or canoeing on BC waters abound. Some of the more popular canoeing spots are in Bowron Lake and Wells Gray Provincial Parks, and on Slocan and Okanagan Lakes. Kayaking is practically a religion here. If you have a kayak strapped to your microbus, you'll have a hard time deciding where *not* to pull off and use it. The towns of Tofino and Ucluelet, on Vancouver Island's west coast, are the Promised Land for BC sea kayakers. From these towns, kayakers can explore nearly endless sounds full of islands, most notably the Broken Group Islands in Pacific Rim National Park Reserve.

Cycling Mountain biking is big throughout BC. Most major ski resorts now stay open year-round, running their lifts in summer for mountain bikers. Major cities usually have good bike paths, like Vancouver's 10km seawall in Stanley Park, or Victoria's amazing Galloping Goose Trail, built on an abandoned railroad grade. Mountain bikes and road bikes alike will be at home on BC's bucolic Southern Gulf Islands, where cars seem like an afterthought.

Fishing Fishing, both the saltwater and freshwater variety, is one of BC's major tourist attractions. Particularly popular are the waters around Vancouver Island (where several places claim the title 'salmon capital of the world') and the Queen Charlotte Islands; the Fraser, Thompson, Nass, Skeena, Kettle, Peace and Liard Rivers; and all the inland lakes. Commercial operators offer boat rentals or charters, and many fishing lodges offer all-inclusive packages that include transportation and accommodations. For further information contact BC Tourism. Fishing licenses ($15 per day, $30 for eight days for non-Canadians) are required and are available from sporting good stores and outfitters.

Hiking Almost any kind of hiking experience is possible in BC: from short walks of a few hours along well marked, easily accessible trails to treks of one or two weeks in totally remote terrain. The national and provincial parks alone hold over 2000km of maintained trails that provide access to much of the province's most outstanding scenery.

The Vancouver area has a lot of good trails – in the Coast Mountains, Garibaldi Provincial Park and around Whistler to the north. East of Vancouver, Manning Provincial Park is one end of the Pacific Crest Trail, which goes all the way to Mexico! On Vancouver Island, the trails in Pacific Rim National Park Reserve (including the famous West Coast Trail) and Strathcona Provincial Park offer opportunities to see lots of wildlife.

Sailing In the sheltered waters of BC's Pacific coast, sailing is possible almost year-round. Sunny skies prevail in summer, but the wind can be elusive then. Coastal marine parks provide safe all-weather anchorage and boat rental. Favored inland sailing waters include Harrison, Okanagan, Arrow and Kootenay Lakes in the south, and Williston Lake in the north.

Scuba Diving The rich and varied marine life in the waters along BC's 7000km Pacific coast makes for rewarding diving. The best time to go is winter, when the plankton has decreased and visibility often exceeds 20m. The water temperature drops to about 7°C to 10°C in winter while in summer it reaches 15°C. At depths of more than 15m, visibility

The Endangered BC Salmon

As does the rest of the Pacific Northwest, BC confronts the issue of wild salmon depopulation in its rivers. The threats to salmon in BC are much the same as in Oregon and Washington: decades of overfishing; pollution of streams and rivers; the practice of clear-cutting forests; and hydroelectric dams that stop migrating fish. However, BC salmon – and the governmental bodies and environmentalists who work to protect the salmon population spawned in BC rivers – face one unique adversary: Alaska.

The states of Oregon and Washington, the province of BC, and most of the region's First Nations tribes (who often have treaty rights to fish for salmon) have largely worked together to preserve the salmon population by restricting catches and improving watersheds. The government and fishing industry in Alaska, however, have been almost totally uncooperative. Alaska has refused to adopt the fishing restrictions advocated by the other governments in the region, continuing to fish the waters of the Gulf of Alaska with what seems like environmental abandon.

This is a particular problem for BC. Adult salmon – which will later enter Canadian waters to spawn – spend most of their lives in the waters of the Northern Pacific, where Alaskan trawler boats harvest fish in great numbers. Alaskan fishers take a huge bite out of the BC fish population before the fish enter Canadian jurisdiction and protection. The animosity between Canadian and Alaskan fishers is often very intense, highlighted by the 1996 standoff at Prince Rupert, when BC fishers blockaded an Alaska ferry in the Prince Rupert harbor for over a week.

Salmon numbers continue to dwindle in BC. In 1998 the federal government completely banned fishing for Coho salmon, in response to evidence pointing to the species' imminent extinction. For instance, in the Skeena and Thompson Rivers, Coho stocks are down to 1% of what they were just a few decades ago. (Other species of salmon are still harvested in BC, though in greatly restricted numbers.)

Most Canadian anglers, charter and commercial fishers, and First Nations groups grudgingly accept the government-enforced ban. Their anger is reserved for the Alaskans, who continue to harvest Coho and other salmon by the thousands as those fish swim through US waters on their way toward Canadian rivers.

is good year-round, and temperatures rarely rise above 10°C.

The best dive spots are off Pacific Rim National Park Reserve on Vancouver Island's west coast; in the Strait of Georgia (particularly around Nanaimo); and in Queen Charlotte Strait off Vancouver Island's northeast coast.

Skiing BC's climate and mountainous terrain provide great conditions for downhill (alpine) and cross-country (Nordic) skiing in the many ski resorts and provincial and national parks. Most of the downhill ski resorts are equipped with chair lifts that serve vertical rises ranging between 400m and 700m, plus a few around the 1100m mark. The cross-country resorts offer thousands of kilometers of groomed and ungroomed trails. It's also possible to go heli-skiing in the remoter parts of the province. Pick up a copy of Tourism BC's brochure *Ski/Winter Adventure*, which details the scores of major downhill and cross-country skiing centers in the province. Most of these centers are in the south, from Vancouver Island east to the Rocky Mountains.

Surfing In Pacific Rim National Park Reserve on Vancouver Island, Long Beach – where the waves come rolling in right off the tempestuous north Pacific – reputedly has BC's best surfing. A substantial surf scene exists there, and you'll find surfers, surf shops and surf camps ready to get you up and hanging as many as you can, if not 10.

Whale-Watching Vancouver Island is the place for whale-watching. Killer whales (orcas) inhabit the waters off Victoria in the south of the island and around Telegraph Cove in the northeast; tours are available

BRITISH COLUMBIA

from those cities. Pacific grey whales migrate between Baja California and Alaska, traveling north in spring and south in fall. They may be seen anywhere around the island, but the best tours are out of Ucluelet and Tofino, on the west coast.

Whitewater Rafting Favored rafting rivers include the Fraser, Thompson and Chilliwack close to Vancouver; the Adams and Clearwater near Kamloops; the Kootenay, Kicking Horse and Illecillewaet in the Rockies; the Chilko and Chilcotin in the Cariboo region west of Williams Lake; and the Skeena, Spatsizi, Stikine, Alsek and Tatshenshini in the north. Competent guide companies are plentiful.

Accommodations

Nearly all provincial and national parks charge a fee for camping during the summer season – generally anywhere from $5 to $19 per night. BC Parks has a reservation service (☎ 604-689-9025, 800-689-9025) for camping at the most popular provincial parks. The non-refundable service fee is $6 a night up to a maximum charge of $18, plus the 7% GST. The service operates from March to mid-September, and reservations may be made up to three months in advance.

Hostels are plentiful throughout the province, but are certainly found in ski areas and other places of heavy backpacker interest. Hostelling International (☎ 604-684-7111, W www.hihostels.bc.ca), Pacific Rim Hostels (W www.pacifichostels.net) and SameSun Hostels (☎ 250-862-8940, 877-562-2783, W www.samesun.com) are major networks, each with many affiliated BC hostels.

The Tourism BC publication *Approved Accommodations,* published annually, is an encyclopedic listing of places to stay, including motels, hotels, hostels and campgrounds – both public and private. Tourism BC can make reservations for you at the properties listed (see the earlier Information section).

Vancouver

pop 2.1 million

One of Canada's most spectacularly scenic cities, Vancouver lies nestled between the sea and mountains in BC's southwest corner. The natural world intrudes on the city's busy urban life at every turn: Vancouver's impressive high-rise center is dwarfed only by the snowclad mountains rising immediately to the north; inlets of the Pacific reach far inland, isolating parts of the city on thumblike peninsulas; and sandy beaches dot the shoreline. Parks are numerous and large. One, Stanley Park, an extension of downtown, equals the size of the downtown business area.

But Vancouver has a lot more to offer than postcard good looks. One of North America's most cosmopolitan cities, it is still a city of new immigrants – wander the streets and you'll hear a dozen languages (the city is now the most Asian in North America). Vancouver also attracts young professionals and artists from the eastern provinces, who come here to enjoy the city's recreation and easygoing sophistication. Yet for all the bustle of these newcomers, the city also provides an old-fashioned cultural refinement reflecting its British heritage. With over two million people in its metropolitan area, Vancouver is Canada's third-largest city (behind Toronto and Montréal).

Vancouver is a national center for the arts, business, fashion, sports and politics. It's one of Canada's filmmaking centers and a progressive place known for liberal politics and recognition of alternative lifestyles.

The port, the busiest on North America's West Coast, operates year-round in the beautiful natural harbor of Burrard Inlet, and it handles nearly all of Canada's trade with Japan and Asia. The frequent take-offs and landings of floatplanes are reminders of the vast wilderness just to the north.

History

The Vancouver area was first inhabited by the Salish people. The first European to see the region was Spanish explorer José Maria Narváez in 1791.

As a condition of confederation with the rest of Canada, Ottawa promised BC in 1870 that it would build a transcontinental railroad. However, for the Canadian Pacific Railway (CPR) to link east and west, BC would need to build a mainland coastal terminus, since the new province's population center and capital, Victoria, was on an island. Railroad engineers picked a site on sheltered Burrard Inlet, which at that time was sparsely lined with a ragtag collection of saloons, lumber mills and farms. The first train arrived from Montréal in 1886, stopping at a thrown-together, brand-new settlement called Vancouver. A year later, the first ship docked from China, and Vancouver began its boom as a trading center and transportation hub. In 1890, just four years after it was founded, Vancouver had already outpaced Victoria in population.

The building of the Panama Canal, which was completed in 1914, meant easier access to markets in Europe and along North America's East Coast. This brought about a boom for the BC economy and for its main trade center, Vancouver.

Large numbers of Chinese moved to the province and were instrumental in building the CPR; they later established their own Chinatown just east of downtown. Japanese settlers came slightly later, establishing truck farms and becoming the area's principal commercial fishermen.

WWI and the Wall Street crash of 1929 brought severe economic depression and hardship to Canada. Prosperity only returned with the advent of WWII, when both shipbuilding and armaments manufacturing bolstered the region's traditional economic base of resource exploitation. After the war the city changed rapidly. The western end became the high-rise apartment center it now is. In 1974 Granville St became a mall. Redevelopment included housing as well as office buildings and this set the foundation for the modern, livable city Vancouver is today. In 1986 the city hosted Expo 86, a successful world's fair. A few prominent structures from the fair remain.

In advance of China's takeover of Hong Kong in 1997, tens of thousands of wealthy Hong Kong Chinese emigrated to the Vancouver area. Unlike previous waves of immigrants, the Chinese who came to Vancouver were from the wealthy business classes. As a result Vancouver real estate prices shot through the roof, with cost-of-living figures suddenly rivaling those of Paris, London and Tokyo. New suburbs sprang up, particularly around Richmond, which are now essentially single-race enclaves of ethnic Chinese.

In the late 1990s problems with Asian economies and the generally poor state of the BC economy slowed the meteoric economic development seen earlier in the decade. But globalization and technological growth, especially among high-tech and biotech industries, have buffered Vancouver's fortunes, and the city entered the 21st century among the Pacific Rim's economic and cultural capitals.

Climate

It rarely snows in Vancouver and it's not often oppressively hot. The only drawback is the rain, particularly in winter when it rarely stops and the cloud cover obliterates the view of the surrounding mountains. Even in summer a rainy spell can last for weeks. But when the sun shines and the mountains reappear, most people here seem to forget all the soakings they've endured.

Orientation

Greater Vancouver is built on a series of peninsulas bounded on the north by Burrard Inlet and on the south by Fraser River and Boundary Bay. The Coast Mountains rise directly behind the city to the north, while to the west the Strait of Georgia is cluttered with islands. The many bays, inlets and river branches, as well as the Pacific coastline, are major features of the city. Much of the city's recent growth has pushed suburbs far up the Fraser River to the east.

Hwy 99, the continuation of I-5 from Washington State, enters the city on Oak St, which unfortunately doesn't have a bridge to downtown. If you're heading to downtown, you'll need to detour west to Granville St or east to Cambie St, which have bridges. The Trans Canada Hwy (Hwy 1) bypasses Vancouver proper to the east; from it, E Hastings St leads to downtown.

Generally, the avenues run east-west and the streets go north-south. Some streets downtown, as well as many of avenues in the Greater Vancouver area, are given east or west designations, so Hastings St, for example, is divided into W Hastings St and E Hastings St. As a general rule the dividing cross street is Main St. However, for numbering purposes, the downtown east-west streets begin numbering at Carrall St, near Chinatown; on the West Side they start with Ontario St. North-south streets begin numbering at Waterfront Rd, along Burrard Inlet. As a reference in downtown addresses, Robson St begins the 800 block. In

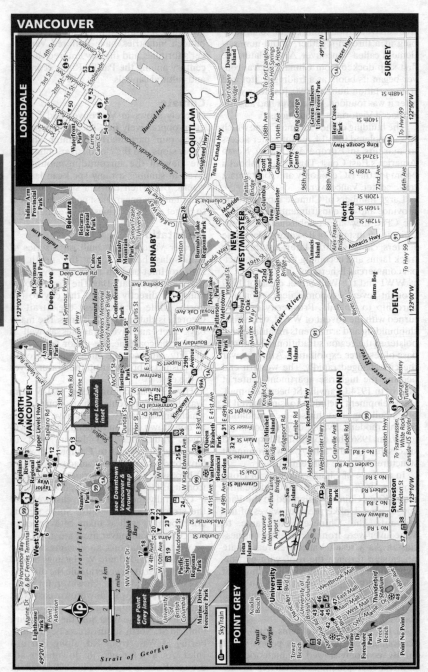

VANCOUVER

BRITISH COLUMBIA

PLACES TO STAY
2 ThistleDown House B&B
5 Beachside B&B
8 Park Royal Hotel
9 Capilano RV Park
10 The Grouse Inn
11 Canyon Court
12 Holiday Inn Express
17 HI Vancouver Jericho Beach
28 Burnaby Cariboo RV Park
33 Fairmont Vancouver Airport;
   Globe@YVR
34 Holiday Inn Express
35 The Met Hotel
36 Richmond RV Park
43 Gage Residence
   & Conference Centre

PLACES TO EAT
1 Salmon House on the Hill
6 Beach House at Dundarave Pier
7 Beach Side Café
15 The Teahouse

20 Montri's Thai Restaurant;
   Cellar Jazz Café; Kitsilano's
   Cyber-Café
22 Nyala Restaurant; The Green V
23 Acropol
30 Seasons in the Park
31 Zeenaz Restaurant
32 All India Sweets & Restaurant
50 Thai House Restaurant
52 Gusti di Quattro

OTHER
3 Capilano Suspension Bridge
4 Lynn Canyon Ecology Centre
13 BC Rail Station
14 The Raven Public House
16 Vancouver Aquarium Marine
   Science Centre
18 Ecomarine Ocean Kayak
   Centre; Cooper Boating Centre
19 1 Hot Box Internet Lounge
21 Great West Coin Laundromat
24 Ridge Theatre
25 Kino Cafe

26 Vancouver Little Theatre
27 Van East Cinema
29 Bloedel Conservatory
37 Gulf of Georgia Cannery
   National Historic Site
38 Steveston Museum; Steveston
   Landing
39 Travel InfoCentre
40 Museum of Anthropology
41 Nitobe Memorial Garden
42 UBC Main Library
44 Student Union Building (SUB)
45 Bus Loop
46 UBC Aquatic Centre
47 UBC Bookstore
48 UBC Botanical Garden
49 Sailor Hagar's Brewpub
51 Travel InfoCentre
53 Rusty Gull
54 SeaBus Terminal
55 Lonsdale Quay Market;
   Lonsdale Quay Hotel;
   Cheshire Cheese Inn
56 Visitor Information Centre

BRITISH COLUMBIA

the Kitsilano area, numbered avenues don't predict the street addresses.

Downtown & Around Vancouver's city center is itself on a peninsula, cut off from the city's southern portion by False Creek and from the northern mainland by Burrard Inlet. This peninsula's tip is preserved as Stanley Park, one of Vancouver's greatest treasures. Three bridges – Burrard, Granville and Cambie – link the southern part of the city, known confusingly as the West Side, with downtown. Only one bridge, the high-flying Lions Gate Bridge, links downtown to the northern suburbs, resulting in traffic nightmares.

Pacific Centre, a three-block complex of offices, restaurants, shops and theaters, beginning on the corner of Robson and Howe Sts, is pretty much the center of downtown. Robson St and Georgia St, just north, are the two principal northwest to southeast streets. Robson St is lined with boutiques and restaurants. Davie St, between Burrard St and Stanley Park, is a secondary commercial and shopping street. Only Georgia St, which becomes the Stanley Park Causeway, continues through Stanley Park to Lions Gate Bridge.

The main northeast to southwest streets are, from west to east: Burrard, Howe, Granville and Seymour. North of Georgia

St, bordered by Howe and Burrard Sts, is the main office, banking and financial district. At the water's edge, at the foot of Howe St, is the impressive Canada Place, the convention center, with its jagged white 'sails.' Much of Granville St, from Nelson St north to W Hastings St, is closed to cars. It's not a true pedestrian mall as trucks and buses are still permitted and it has never worked well as a central showcase.

The high-density area west of the downtown shopping area is known as the **West End** – *not* to be confused with West Vancouver on the North Shore, or with the West Side, south of downtown.

Three districts in the downtown vicinity are worth noting. **Yaletown**, on Hamilton and Mainland Sts between Davie and Nelson Sts, is a 'hot' part of town where old warehouses have been converted into hip bars, restaurants and loft apartments. **Gastown**, along Water St, north of W Hastings St between Richards and Columbia Sts, is the historic center of old Vancouver, with many restored Victorian buildings. Bustling **Chinatown** is just to the southeast, in the area more or less bordered by Carrall and Gore Sts and E Hastings and Keefer Sts.

Other Districts Don't let the name confuse you: The **West Side** comprises the

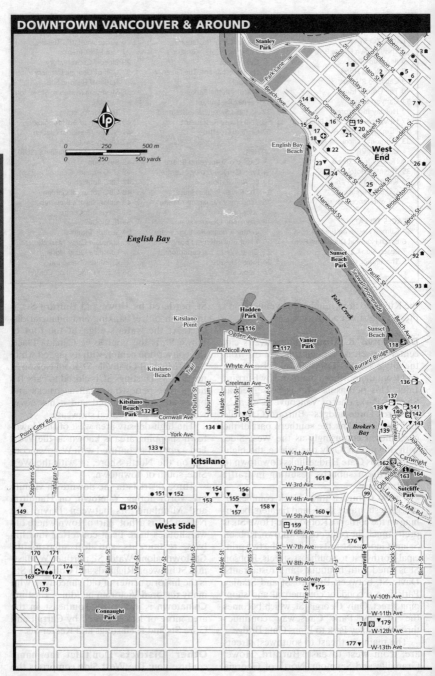

DOWNTOWN VANCOUVER & AROUND

Stanley Park

Chilco St
Gilford St
Robson St
Alberni St
3
4
1
Barclay St
2
5
6
Haro St
Nelson St
Denman St
7
Comox St
Beach Ave
14
Comox St
Pendrell St
16
19
West End
15
17
20
18
21
Bidwell St
Cardero St
26
English Bay Beach
22
West End
23
Pendrell St
24
Davie St
25
Nicola St
Burnaby St
Broughton St
Harwood St
Jervis St

Park Lane

English Bay

92
93

Sunset Beach Park
Pacific St
Seawall Promenade
False Creek

Kitsilano Point
Hadden Park
116
Ogden Ave
117
Vanier Park
Sunset Beach
118
Burrard Bridge

Kitsilano Beach
McNicoll Ave
Whyte Ave
Creelman Ave
136

Trail
Arbutus St
Laburnum St
Maple St
Walnut St
Cypress St
Chestnut St
137
141
138
140
142
143
139
Duranleau

Kitsilano Beach Park
132
Cornwall Ave
135
Broker's Bay
Johnston

Point Grey Rd
134
York Ave
133
Kitsilano
W 1st Ave
162
Cartwright
163
164
Sutcliffe Park

Stephens St
Trafalgar St
W 2nd Ave
161
W 3rd Ave
99
Old Bridge
Lamey's Mill Rd

151
152
154
156
W 4th Ave
160
153
155
149
150
157
158
W 5th Ave
159
W 6th Ave
West Side

W 7th Ave
176

170
171
174
W 8th Ave
Granville St
Hemlock St
Birch St
169
172
Larch St
Balsam St
Vine St
Yew St
Arbutus St
Maple St
Cypress St
Burrard St
Fir St
173
W Broadway
Pine St
175

Connaught Park
W 10th Ave
W 11th Ave
178
179
W 12th Ave
177
W 13th Ave

0   250   500 m
0   250   500 yards

DOWNTOWN VANCOUVER & AROUND

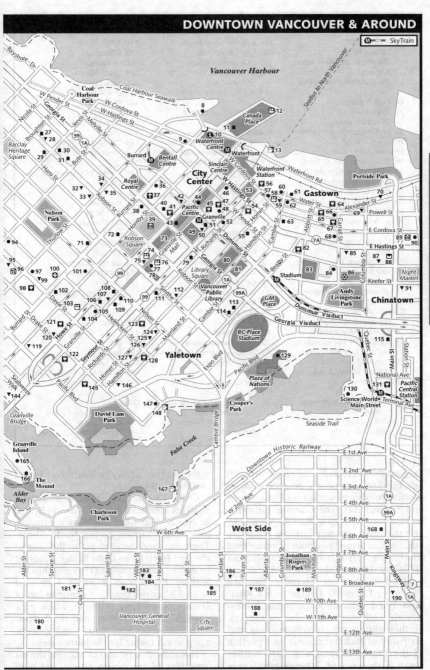

DOWNTOWN VANCOUVER & AROUND

PLACES TO STAY
1 Buchan Hotel
3 The Westin Bayshore Resort & Marina
11 The Pan Pacific Hotel; Five Sails
14 English Bay Inn
15 Sylvia Hotel
16 Oceanside Hotel
22 Best Western Sands Hotel
26 Nelson House
27 Greenbrier Hotel
29 Listel Vancouver; O'Doul's
30 Pacific Palisades Hotel; Zin
31 Blue Horizon Hotel
38 Hotel Vancouver; 900 West
40 Crowne Plaza Hotel Georgia
43 Four Seasons Hotel
51 St Regis Hotel
55 Victorian Hotel
63 Cambie International Hostel
71 YMCA
72 Wedgewood Hotel; Bacchus
79 Kingston Hotel
92 Parkhill Hotel
93 HI Vancouver Downtown
102 Burrard Motor Inn
104 Holiday Inn Hotel & Suites - Downtown Vancouver
106 Bosman's Motor Hotel
108 Royal Hotel; The Royal Pub
109 Global Village Backpackers
110 Comfort Hotel; Fred's Uptown Tavern; BaBaLu
111 Dufferin Hotel
113 YWCA
114 The Georgian Court Hotel; William Tell
115 C&N Backpackers Hostel
134 Maple House B&B

166 Granville Island Hotel
168 City Centre Motel
180 Shaughnessy Village
182 Ramada Vancouver Centre; Fairview Pub
184 Holiday Inn Vancouver Centre
188 Windsor Guest House

PLACES TO EAT
2 True Confections; Poncho's
6 De Dutch Pannekoek House
7 Robson Public Market
18 Raincity Grill
20 Delilah's
21 Brass Monkey
23 Krishna Pure Vegetarian Restaurant
25 Romano's Macaroni Grill
28 Il Domo; Ezogiku Noodle Café
32 Cin Cin
33 Thai House Restaurant
34 Joe Fortes
35 Café Il Nido
42 Diva at The Met
50 Gotham
59 Water Street Café
69 Incendio
70 The Alibi Room
75 Kitto Japanese House
85 The Only Seafood Restaurant
87 Buddhist Vegetarian Restaurant
91 The Gain Wah
95 Stepho's Souvlaki
99 Kam's Place; Joe's Grill; The Fountainhead Pub
107 Goulash House Restaurant & Pastry Shop

112 Subeez Cafe
119 Il Giardino
120 La Bodega
124 Urban Monks
125 Soup Etc
126 blue water
127 Brix
133 Tangerine
135 Deserts; Flying Wedge Pizza
138 Bridges
143 The SandBar; Diane Sanderson Silk Studio
144 C
146 Rodney's Oyster House
149 The Naam
152 Bishop's
153 Joe's Grill
154 Taka Sushi
155 Las Margaritas
157 Roti Bistro
158 Annapurna
160 The Lazy Gourmet
170 Greens & Gourmet
173 Nat's New York Pizzeria
174 Lumiere
175 Szechwan Chongqing Seafood Restaurant
176 Paul's Place
177 Ouest
179 Vij's
181 Bali
183 Tojo's
186 Rasputin
187 Nice 'n Spicy Reggae Cafe
190 SoMa; Monsoon

OTHER
4 Spokes Bicycle Rentals
5 Alley Cat Bike Rentals
8 Seaplane Terminal

long-established residential neighborhoods and bustling commercial centers *south* of downtown Vancouver across False Creek and English Bay. The Cambie, Granville and Burrard Bridges lead to the West Side, and the main east-west arterial roads are 4th Ave and Broadway, both of which lead to the University of British Columbia (UBC) at the tip of the peninsula.

Head west after crossing Burrard Bridge or Granville Bridge to see **Kitsilano**, filled with students, young professionals and now-successful ex-hippies. Farther south is the rapidly growing municipality of **Richmond**, built on a portion of the Fraser River Delta. Still farther south is the port of **Tsawwassen**, where

you can catch a ferry to Vancouver Island and the Gulf Islands.

Over Lions Gate Bridge and Iron Workers Memorial Second Narrows Bridge lie North Vancouver and West Vancouver, collectively known as the **North Shore**. There are three ways to get to this side of Burrard Inlet: Lions Gate Bridge, accessed by way of the causeway (Hwy 99) through Stanley Park; Iron Workers Memorial Second Narrows Bridge, a continuation of Trans Canada Hwy (Hwy 1), which goes through East Vancouver; and the SeaBus from Waterfront Station to Lonsdale Quay, a trip worth taking for the harbor views.

Horseshoe Bay marks the northwest boundary of the North Shore, and here

DOWNTOWN VANCOUVER & AROUND

9 Marine Building	73 Eatons	129 Yuk Yuk's; The Rage
10 Tourist InfoCentre	74 Granville Cineplex Odeon	130 Science World; Alcan
12 CN IMAX Theatre	76 Capitol 6; The Lennox Pub	OMNIMAX Theatre
13 SeaBus Terminal	77 The Commodore; The	131 Cobalt
17 Care Point Medical Centre	Granville Book Company	132 Kitsilano Outdoor Pool
19 Denman Place Discount	78 Orpheum Theatre	136 Aquabus Stop
Cinema	80 Main Post Office	137 False Creek Ferries
24 Balthazar	81 Queen Elizabeth Theatre;	139 Ecomarine Ocean Kayak
36 American Express	Vancouver Playhouse	Centre; Cooper Boating
37 Christ Church Cathedral;	82 Honey Lounge; Milk Bar;	Centre
Canadian Craft Museum	Lotus Sound Lounge; Lotus	140 Granville Island Public
39 Vancouver Art Gallery	Hotel	Market
41 Element Sound Lounge	83 Cinemark Tinseltown	141 Aquabus
44 Thomas Cook	84 World's Narrowest Office	142 New Revue Stage;
45 Railway Club	Building	Backstage Lounge; Arts Club
46 Henry Birks & Sons; Birks	86 Dr Sun Yat-Sen Classical	Theatre/Granville Island
Clock	Chinese Garden & Park	Stage
47 Malone's Bar & Grill;	88 Post Office	145 Wett Bar
Piccadilly Pub	89 Vancouver Police Centennial	147 Reckless The Bike Store
48 Travel Cuts	Museum	148 Aquabus Stop
49 The Bay	90 Firehall Arts Centre	150 Chivana
52 International Travel Maps &	94 Gay & Lesbian Centre	151 Duthie Books
Books	96 Internet Coffee	156 Wanderlust
53 SFU Harbour Centre; The	97 Davie Laundromat	159 Fifth Avenue Cinemas
Lookout; Harbour Centre	98 Numbers	161 Reckless The Bike Store
Tower	100 St Paul's Hospital	162 Waterfront Theatre
54 Naked	101 Rent-A-Wreck	163 Information Centre
56 Steamworks Brewing	103 Pacific Cinémathèque	164 Crafthouse
Company; The Landing	105 Lo-Cost Car Rental	165 Emily Carr Institute of Art &
57 Shine	116 Vancouver Maritime	Design
58 Blinding Light	Museum	167 Aquabus Stop
60 Gastown Steam Clock	117 Gordon MacMillan Southam	169 Khatsahlano Medical Clinic
61 Hill's Native Art	Observatory; Vancouver	171 Banyen Books & Sound
62 Inuit Gallery of Vancouver	Museum; HR MacMillan	172 The Travel Bug
64 The Purple Onion	Space Centre	178 Stanley Theatre
65 Sonar	118 Vancouver Aquatic Centre	185 International Travel Maps
66 Gassy Jack Statue; Maple	121 Odyssey	& Books
Tree Square	122 The Yale	189 Mountain Equipment Co-op
67 The Irish Heather	123 Richard's on Richards	
68 The Brickyard	128 Yaletown Brewing Co	

BRITISH COLUMBIA

you'll find another BC Ferries Terminal. Just north of Horseshoe Bay is the tiny residential community of Lions Bay.

Information

Tourist Offices The Tourist Info Centre (☎ 604-683-2000, 800-435-5622, fax 604-682-6839, Plaza Level, Waterfront Centre, 200 Burrard St) is open 8am to 6pm daily in summer and 8:30am to 5pm weekdays, 9am to 5pm Saturday the rest of the year.

The staff can help you book accommodations, tours, transportation and activities. You can also obtain transit tickets, schedules and passes here and a free copy of *The Vancouver Book,* the official visitor's

guide, which has information on shopping, accommodations, entertainment, local transportation and more.

There's also an Info Centre at Vancouver International Airport (☎ 604-303-3601).

Gay and lesbian resources include the Gay & Lesbian Centre (☎ 604-684-5307, 1170 Bute St) near Nelson Park and the free biweekly publication *Xtra West,* widely available around town.

The British Columbia Automobile Association (BCAA; ☎ 604-268-5555, 4567 Canada Way) in Burnaby provides car-club members with travel information, maps, travel insurance and accommodations reservations. For 24-hour emergency road service, call ☎ 604-293-2222.

Money The major national banks, such as Toronto Dominion, Bank of Montreal, Canada Trust and CBIC, have branches throughout the city; some are open on Saturday. ATM machines are liberally sprinkled throughout all the shopping and business districts.

Thomas Cook has a number of offices in Vancouver, including one (☎ 604-687-6111) at 777 Dunsmuir St. American Express (☎ 604-669-2813) is at 666 Burrard St. Robson St has a number of exchange bureaus open until late at night. Vancouver International Airport provides banking and money-changing facilities too.

Post & Communications The main post office (☎ 604-662-5723, 349 W Georgia St) is open 8am to 5:30pm weekdays.

HI hostels offer Internet access to guests, and access is available at the Vancouver Public Library's central branch ($5 per 55 minutes; see Libraries). Internet cafés include Internet Coffee (☎ 604-682-6668, 1104 Davie St), Kitsilano's Cyber-Café (☎ 604-737-0595, 3514 W 4th Ave) and 1 Hot Box Internet Lounge (☎ 604-228-8266, 4446 W 10th Ave).

Travel Agencies Travel Cuts, the student travel organization, has seven Vancouver offices (☎ 604-659-2830, 567 Seymour St; ☎ 604-659-2887, 120 W Broadway; ☎ 604-822-6890, UBC Student Union Building; ☎ 604-659-2860, 203-5728 University Blvd, UBC Village; ☎ 604-659-2820, 1516 Duranleau St, Granville Island; ☎ 604-659-2845, 1114 Burnaby St, HI-Downtown; ☎ 604-659-2850, MBC 2280, Simon Fraser University).

Bookstores Duthie Books (☎ 604-732-5344, 2239 W 4th Ave) is Vancouver's longest-running book and magazine retailer. It's in Kitsilano and it's big.

The independent Granville Book Company (☎ 604-687-2213, 850 Granville St) overflows with magazine racks and free local newspaper bins, while The Travel Bug (☎ 604-737-1122, 2667 W Broadway) neatly packs myriad travel titles, maps and travel accessories into a tiny storefront.

Check International Travel Maps & Books (☎ 604-687-3320, 552 Seymour St) for maps covering just about every region of the world. There's also a West Side location

(☎ 604-879-3621, 530 W Broadway). If guidebooks, maps and travel literature aren't enough, Wanderlust (☎ 604-739-2182, 1929 W 4th Ave) has a separate luggage department next door.

At Banyen Books & Sound (☎ 604-732-7912, 2671 W Broadway), you enter an oasis of incense and sacred music, where yoga mats are stacked against the walls. Categories like Tibetan Buddhism, herbalism, organic gardening and the like get entire rows here.

Libraries The huge, architecturally controversial Vancouver Public Library (☎ 604-331-3600, Ⓦ www.vpl.vancouver.bc.ca, 350 W Georgia St) looks somewhat like the Roman Colosseum. It's open 10am to 8pm Monday to Thursday, 10am to 5pm Friday and Saturday and 1pm to 5pm Sunday. Twenty-one other branches are scattered around town.

Newspapers & Magazines The city's two daily newspapers are the *Vancouver Sun* (Ⓦ www.vancouversun.com) and the *Province* (Ⓦ www.vancouverprovince.com).

Among the free publications widely distributed throughout the city are the *Georgia Straight,* a news and entertainment weekly that's the best source of information on what's going on in town; and *Xtra West,* which serves Vancouver's gay and lesbian community.

Laundry Coin laundries around town include Davie Laundromat (☎ 604-682-2717, 1061 Davie St), in the West End, and Great West Coin Laundromat (☎ 604-734-7993, 2955 W 4th Ave), in Kitsilano.

Medical Services Walk-in clinics include Care Point Medical Centre (☎ 604-681-5338, 1175 Denman St), downtown; and Khatsahlano Medical Clinic (☎ 604-731-9187, 2689 W Broadway), in Kitsilano.

Hospitals include BC Children's Hospital (☎ 604-875-2345, 4480 Oak St), BC Women's Hospital (☎ 604-875-2424, 4490 Oak St), St Paul's Hospital (☎ 604-682-2344, 1081 Burrard St) and Vancouver General Hospital (☎ 604-875-4111, 855 W 12th Ave).

Emergency For police, fire or a medical emergency, call ☎ 911.

Dangers & Annoyances Violent crime is unusual but theft is common. Lock your car and secure valuables in the trunk, and always lock your bicycle.

Hastings St east from about Homer St is downtrodden, especially near Main St. Don't dawdle here at night.

Panhandlers are the greatest annoyance in Vancouver. Areas where you'll likely be hassled by beggars include Granville St (especially between Pender and Davie Sts) and Gastown.

Downtown

Downtown Vancouver is bordered on two sides by water, and on a third by the enormous Stanley Park. This constriction has forced the city upward. While none of the business towers are startlingly high, the cumulative effect of so many skyscrapers makes Vancouver seem modern and somewhat forbidding. Another anomaly of downtown Vancouver is that most of the high-rises in the West End, the area near Stanley Park, are residential towers erected in the 1950s. A *lot* of people live right downtown, and this has kept small markets and other neighborhood facilities in operation. Downtown has a real lived-in quality unusual in a North American city of this size.

For travelers, the center of the city is **Robson St**. A collage of tourist shops, fashion boutiques, coffee shops and restaurants, Robson St is a great place for people-watching. Locals, international tourists and recent immigrants all throng here, giving the street the feeling of a mini United Nations. Shops and restaurants stay open late at night, often till midnight in summer.

Landmarks Completed in 1895, **Christ Church Cathedral** (☎ 604-682-3848, 690 Burrard St; open daily, times vary depending on services and events) is the city's oldest surviving church. Inside, the Gothic-inspired sandstone structure features timber framework and stained-glass windows.

The spectacular art deco **Marine Building** (355 Burrard St; open 8am-6pm Mon-Fri) was completed in 1930 and is a 22-story tribute to Vancouver's maritime history. Sea horses, waves and marine fauna are depicted on a frieze that wraps around the front of the building, while a ship's prow sails forth over the Burrard St entrance.

Step inside the ornate lobby to see the maritime theme continued with blue and green tiles and an array of sea creatures on both the walls and the brass doors. For more than 10 years this was the tallest building in the British Empire.

Vancouver's most famous timepiece is the **Birks clock**, at the southeast corner of Hastings and Granville Sts. Built in 1905, Vancouver's first public clock has been at three locations along with its owner, jeweler Henry Birks & Sons. The clock, which has its original wooden movement, is hand-wound every Tuesday morning.

At 174m, the unattractive **Harbour Centre Tower** (☎ 604-689-0421, 555 W Hastings St) is the tallest building in BC. The 360-degree views from the top are everything you'd expect and just about worth the money it costs to be whisked up in the glass 'Skylift' elevators (adult/senior/student $9/8/6; open 8:30am-10:30pm daily in summer, 9am-9pm daily in winter) to 'The Lookout' restaurant and observation gallery.

Vancouver Art Gallery Between Robson Square and W Georgia St is the Vancouver Art Gallery (☎ 604-662-4700, 750 Hornby St; adult/senior/student $10/8/6, children under 12 free, admission by donation on Thur; open 10am-5:30pm Mon-Wed & Fri-Sun, 10am-9pm Thur).

The gallery building was originally the Vancouver Provincial Courthouse, designed in the early 1900s by Francis Rattenbury, who also designed Victoria's Parliament Buildings and Empress Hotel. In the 1970s, noted architect Arthur Erickson designed Robson Square and at the same time turned the courthouse into this world-class art gallery.

Among its broad holdings, the museum boasts Canada's largest permanent collection of works by renowned BC artist Emily Carr (see the boxed text 'The Life & Work of Emily Carr' elsewhere in this chapter).

Rotating exhibitions include both contemporary and historical painting, sculpture, graphic arts, photography and video by distinguished regional, national and international artists.

Canadian Craft Museum This excellent museum (☎ 604-687-8266, 639 Hornby St; adult/senior & student $5/3, children under

12 free; open 10am-5pm Mon-Sat, 10am-9pm Thur, noon-5pm Sun & holidays) is dedicated to the role of craft, both historical and contemporary, in human culture. The museum's exhibits – works in glass, wood, clay, metal and fiber – blur the line between 'craft' and 'art.' The gift shop is wonderful.

Canada Place & Waterfront Station
Jutting into the harbor at the foot of Howe St, Canada Place was built to house the Canada pavilion at Expo 86. Its stridently modern design invites comparisons. Does it resemble an ocean liner with tentlike sails, the white exoskeleton of a large spiny insect or just the Sydney Opera House? In any case, the building has become a city landmark. It's home to the World Trade Centre, the Vancouver Convention & Exhibition Centre, a cruise-ship terminal, The Prow Restaurant, the Pan Pacific Hotel, retail shops, a food court and the CN IMAX Theatre.

Just a block away from Canada Place is Waterfront Station, the grand old CPR station. Opened in 1915, this was the CPR's western terminus from where transcontinental passenger trains either ended or began their journeys. The deteriorating building was restored and is now a transportation hub for SkyTrain and SeaBus services (see Public Transportation under Getting Around).

BC Place Stadium & GM Place
Concerts, trade shows, sporting events and other large-scale gatherings are held at BC Place Stadium (☎ *604-669-2300, 777 Pacific Blvd S*), unmistakable for its translucent dome-shaped roof. The roof is 'air-supported,' which means it's inflated by huge fans (no, not sports fans) and kept in place by criss-crossed steel wires, hence its quilted appearance. The 60,000-seat stadium is home field for the BC Lions of the Canadian Football League (CFL).

Also here is the BC Sports Hall of Fame & Museum (☎ *604-687-5520, Gate A; adult/other $6/4, children under 5 free, family ticket (up to 4 people) $15; open 10am-5pm daily*).

Adjacent to BC Place Stadium, GM Place (☎ *604-899-7889*) is another large arena that's home to the Vancouver Canucks professional hockey team and the Vancouver Ravens pro lacrosse team.

Gastown & Around
Vancouver's Victorian-era business district, Gastown takes its name from 'Gassy' Jack Deighton, an English sailor who forsook the sea to open a bar here in 1867. When a village sprang up around his establishment it was called Gassy's Town. (A statue of Gassy Jack stands in Maple St Square, where Cordova and Water Sts meet.)

After the center of Vancouver moved elsewhere, Gastown gradually became a skid row. But in the 1970s it was restored and renovated, simply pushing Vancouver's seedier characters a little farther south to Hastings St.

The old Victorian buildings now house restaurants, bars, boutiques and galleries, many of which sell expensive First Nations art. The brick streets have been lined with trees and old streetlamps, and sidewalk vendors and buskers add a festive air.

Water St is the main thoroughfare, holding most of the attractions. On the corner of Water and Cambie Sts, the **Gastown Steam Clock** is among the city's most photographed attractions. The clock stands on a vent of steam lines formerly used to heat local businesses. You can see the steam works through glass panels. The clock blows off steam and whistles every 15 minutes, and it chimes every hour. Though it looks old, the clock was built in 1977.

To learn more about this colorful area, take the free guided walking tour (☎ 604-683-5650) offered daily mid-June to September. The 1½-hour tour meets at the statue in Maple Tree Square at 2pm.

Vancouver Police Centennial Museum
Between Gastown and Chinatown, this unusual museum (☎ *604-665-3346, 240 E Cordova St; adult/senior & child age 7-13 $5/3; open 9am-3pm Mon-Fri year-round, 10am-3pm Sat in summer*), in the old Coroner's Court Building, illustrates the history of law enforcement in Vancouver.

Displays include a gruesome autopsy room, forensic laboratory, jail cell and radio dispatch room. You'll see old uniforms, police cars and motorcycles, a huge weapons display, counterfeit money and re-creations of famous crime scenes.

Chinatown & Around
About 35,000 people of Chinese descent live in the area around Pender St, a neighbor-

hood roughly bordered by Abbott St and Gore Ave; thousands of others come here to shop, making this one of North America's largest Chinatowns.

In this real Chinese market and business district, nearly all signs are in Chinese, including the street signs, and English is rarely spoken. The colors, smells, signs and occasional old Chinese-style balcony are reminiscent of Hong Kong. Throughout the day the streets bustle with people going in and out of shops that sell hanging ducks, bales of strange dried fish, exotic fruit and Eastern remedies. Numerous Chinese restaurants and bakeries tempt the hungry tourist.

Now that newer arrivals from Hong Kong have colonized Richmond, the center of Chinese Canadian business and culture has at least in part relocated there. But there's still plenty of vitality here.

In summer, a great **night market** (*Pender & Keefer Sts, east of Main St; open 6:30pm-11:30pm Fri-Sun May-Sept*) captures all the fun, food, noise and excitement of its counterparts in Asia. And don't forget the Chinese New Year celebrations if you're here during the Lunar New Year (see Special Events).

The **Sam Kee building** (*8 W Pender St*), the world's narrowest office building, has made it into *Ripley's Believe It or Not!* and *The Guinness Book of Records*. In 1906 Chang Toy, owner of Sam Kee Co, bought land here, but in 1926 the city expropriated all but a 1.8m-wide strip of it. Chang thumbed his nose at City Hall by building the world's narrowest office building.

Modeled after the classical gardens of the Ming Dynasty, the **Dr Sun Yat-Sen Classical Chinese Garden** (☎ *604-662-3207, 578 Carrall St; adult/senior/student $7.50/6/5; open 9:30am-7pm June 15-Sept 15, 10am-6pm Sept 16-June 14*) is an urban sanctuary incorporating Taoist principles of yin and yang – rugged and hard balanced by soft and flowing, dark balanced by light, large balanced by small. Admission includes a guided tour.

Next to the classical garden is the walled **Dr Sun Yat-Sen Park** (*admission free; 9:30am-5:30pm May 1-June 14 & Sept 30, 9am-6:30pm June 15-Aug 31, 9:30am-4pm Oct 1-April 30*), a beautiful Chinese garden around a large fish pond. The entrance is behind the bust of Dr Sun Yat-Sen in the cultural center courtyard.

Science World & Alcan OMNIMAX Theatre Just south of Chinatown at Terminal Ave is Science World (☎ *604-443-7440, 1455 Quebec St; adult/senior & child age 4-18 $14.75/9.25; open 10am-5pm Mon-Fri, 10am-6pm Sat, Sun & holidays*). This gleaming geodesic dome 'golf ball' houses interactive exhibits on science, technology and natural history.

Its huge OMNIMAX Theatre (☎ *604-443-7443*) has a domed screen five stories high and a 28-speaker wraparound sound system. Theater-only tickets ($11.25/9) are available for selected screenings, but for most shows you must purchase a museum-and-theater combination ticket ($19.75/14.25).

Stanley Park

Vancouver's largest and most-beloved green space, Stanley Park is a 405-hectare cedar forest flanked by beaches that extend north and west of downtown.

The park was established in 1888 and named after the governor general of Canada, Lord Stanley, the same man who lent his name to the National Hockey League's prestigious trophy. Today it's estimated that eight million visitors come to the park each year, making it the city's most popular attraction.

Hiking, cycling and jogging trails meander through the woods. The Seawall Promenade winds 10.5km along the park's shoreline and is one of the world's great urban walks. And the park's three beaches are popular in summer for sunbathers and swimmers. From various points there are nice views of downtown Vancouver, the North Shore and out to sea toward the islands.

Canada's largest aquarium and one of the city's premier destinations, Stanley Park's **Vancouver Aquarium Marine Science Centre** (☎ *604-659-3474; adult/senior & youth age 13-18/child age 4-12 $14.95/11.95/8.95; open 10am-5:30pm daily early Sept-late June, 9:30am-7pm daily late June-early Sept*), houses nearly 9000 sea creatures representing 250 species. Among the denizens of the deep on view here are dolphins, sea lions, sharks, beluga whales, octopuses, eels and otters.

A standout aquarium exhibit is the Amazon Gallery, a re-creation of a tropical rain forest, complete with sloths, crocodiles, toucans, piranhas, tree frogs and hourly rainstorms. The Vancouver Aquarium is also Canada's largest marine mammal rescue-and-rehabilitation center. Inquire about the 40-minute behind-the-scene tours with naturalist guides that take place daily ($20/15).

Granville Island

On the south side of False Creek, under the Granville Bridge, this one-time industrial 'island' (actually a peninsula) has been re-developed into a busy blend of businesses, restaurants, galleries and theaters.

The Granville Island Information Centre (☎ 604-666-5784, 1398 Cartwright St; open 9am-6pm daily) has pamphlets, free maps and a change machine for parking.

The island's center of activity, and a food lover's dream come true, is **Granville Island Public Market** (☎ 604-666-6477, Johnston St; open 9am-6pm daily, closed Mon in Jan). Greengrocers, fishmongers, butchers, bakers, cheese makers and other food merchants squeeze into the bustling market, making it a great place to appreciate the region's natural bounty.

Granville Island is also an artisans' mecca with working studios and commercial galleries. **Emily Carr Institute of Art & Design** (☎ 604-844-3800, 1399 Johnston St) presents frequent exhibits in its galleries. Boaters will find chandleries and kayak rental places on the island.

The old **Downtown Historic Railway**, once part of Vancouver's tram-car system, travels between Granville Island and E 1st Ave and Ontario St every 30 minutes from 1pm to 5pm on Saturday, Sunday and holidays, mid-May to mid-October. The trip takes about 15 minutes; roundtrip fare is $2/1 adult/senior & child. If you take the train from Ontario St, you can park free at the E 1st Ave railcar barn. At Granville Island catch the train near W 2nd Ave below the Granville Bridge.

At night, the island's focus shifts to the performing arts as theaters and nightclubs open their doors. And with a choice of nine restaurants on the island, there is no shortage of places to eat.

To get to the island, take bus No 50 from Waterfront Station, or take a mini-ferry (see Getting Around).

Vanier Park

On English Bay below the Burrard Bridge, Vanier Park comprises 15 hectares of lawn, ponds and pathways and is home to several museums. When the weather's fine you'll see people strolling, jogging, cycling, walking their dogs or simply sitting and watching the ships anchored in English Bay. On windy days, the park is an ideal and popular place to fly kites.

The fine **Vancouver Museum** (☎ 604-736-4431, 1100 Chestnut St; adult/senior & youth/child under 4/family $8/5.50/free/25; open 10am-5pm Mon-Wed & Fri-Sun, 10am-9pm Thur) vividly recounts both distant and recent Vancouver history. Exhibits include a look at the everyday life of First Nations people, plus artifacts of Vancouver at work and play – everything from an 1869 'bone-shaker' bicycle to a 1967 black-light poster from the Retinal Circus nightclub. Changing exhibits often have a scope far beyond Vancouver.

The **HR MacMillan Space Centre** (☎ 604-738-7827, 1100 Chestnut St; adult/senior & youth/child age 5-10 $12.75/9.75/8.75, child under 5 free or $5.25 including simulator, family ticket $40; open 10am-5pm daily, closed Mon Sept-June), at the Vancouver Museum, has displays on space science and the mechanics of space exploration. It's all hands-on with interactive displays, computer games – even a moon rock you can touch. One highlight is a full-motion flight-simulator 'ride,' included with admission. The HR MacMillan Star Theatre presents 40-minute space-related shows on a 19m-diameter dome. On Wednesday to Saturday evenings this theater is used for laser-music shows (separate admission $8.65); come early or make reservations.

Adjacent, the **Gordon MacMillan Southam Observatory** (☎ 604-738-2855, 1100 Chestnut St; admission free; open noon-5pm & 7pm-11pm Fri & Sat) features a telescope open for public viewing when the weather's clear and volunteers are available.

The **Vancouver Maritime Museum** (☎ 604-257-8300, 1905 Ogden Ave; adult/senior & youth age 6-19 $7/4, family $16; open 10am-5pm daily May-Sept, 10am-5pm Tues-Sat & noon-5pm Sun rest of year), at the foot of Cypress St, is a five-minute walk west from the Vancouver Museum. Exhibits include wooden models, old rowboats, information on shipwrecks and pirates, the reconstructed bridge of an actual tugboat and a children's discovery center with hands-on displays.

The maritime museum also features the *St Roch*, a 1928 RCMP Arctic patrol sailing ship that was the first vessel to navigate the legendary Northwest Passage in both directions. Guided tours of the ship are offered.

Kitsilano

The south shore of English Bay, extending west roughly from Burrard to Alma Sts, and south as far as about W 16th Ave, is the neighborhood of Kitsilano. The area west from Alma St to UBC is Point Grey, a mostly affluent residential neighborhood.

During the 1960s and '70s, Kitsilano was a hippie enclave and center of countercultural sympathies and lifestyles. As times changed, the hippies turned into professionals and the neighborhood became genteel; the old single-family homes here are now unaffordable to the students who once gave the area its élan.

But Kitsilano, usually referred to as 'Kits,' is still fun to explore, particularly along W 4th Ave and W Broadway, which are lined with unusual shops, bookstores and ethnic restaurants. The old counterculture atmosphere can still be found here, but today the organic-food stores and cheap vegetarian restaurants of the hippie days are sandwiched between upscale bistros and European clothing boutiques.

One thing that hasn't changed over the years in Kitsilano are the beaches. Kits faces onto English Bay, and the sandy strands that flank the water are gathering spots for sun-worshippers in summer. **Kitsilano Beach**, near Vanier Park, and **Jericho Beach**, farther west on W 4th Ave, are two of the most popular.

University of British Columbia

The University of British Columbia (*UBC;* ☎ *604-822-4636*) is at Vancouver's westernmost point, on a peninsula jutting into the Strait of Georgia. The huge 402-hectare campus and adjacent 763-hectare Pacific Spirit Regional Park make up the University Endowment Lands, much of which is still forest.

This area was heavily logged from 1861 to 1891, but it wasn't clear-cut, mostly because many of the trees were too difficult to reach. This allowed the remaining trees to generate substantial regrowth. The remarkable forests here today are part of Vancouver's legacy; with the 1988 creation of Pacific Spirit Regional Park, an area almost twice the size of Stanley Park has been preserved for future generations.

Museum of Anthropology This excellent museum (☎ *604-822-3825, 6393 NW Marine Dr; adult/senior/student $7/5/4, family $20, free 5pm-9pm Tues; open 10am-5pm Wed-Mon & 10am-9pm Tues May-Sept, 11am-5pm Wed-Sun & 11am-9pm Tues rest of year*) exhibits art and artifacts – including a renowned collection of totem poles – from cultures around the world. Emphasis is on BC's coastal First Nations people.

The building's exhilarating design was inspired by the post-and-beam longhouses of many coastal indigenous groups. Its fabulous use of glass allows the exhibits to be set off against a backdrop of mountains and sea.

Nitobe Memorial Garden Designed by a leading Japanese landscape architect, this beautiful garden (☎ *604-822-6038, 1903 West Mall; adult/senior & student $2.75/1.75 in summer, free rest of year; open 10am-6pm daily Mar-Oct, 11am-3pm Mon-Fri rest of year*) is near Gate 4 at the foot of Memorial Rd, near the museum. Aside from some traffic noise, it's a tranquil retreat perfect for quiet meditation.

UBC Botanical Garden A real gem, the 28-hectare UBC Botanical Garden (☎ *604-822-9666, 6804 SW Marine Dr; adult/senior & student $4.75/2.50 in summer, free in winter; open daily 10am-6pm in summer, 10am-2:30pm in winter*), near W 16th Ave, holds 10,000 different trees, shrubs and flowers in several different thematic plantings. The Botanical Garden Centre (free admission) has a gift shop, nursery and scenic overlook.

Pacific Spirit Regional Park This huge park – a long, wide strip stretching from Burrard Inlet on one side of the peninsula to the North Arm of the Fraser River on the other – acts as a green zone between campus and the city.

It's a fantastic area to explore, with 35km of walking, jogging, cycling and equestrian trails through forests of giant cedar and fir little changed since the time the first Europeans arrived.

In the park you'll find 12,000-year-old **Camosun Bog**, a unique wetland that's home to many native birds and plants. Reach the bog by a boardwalk starting at Camosun St and W 19th Ave. The Park Centre (☎ 604-224-5739, W 16th Ave; open 8am-4pm Mon-Fri), near Blanca St, is where you'll find information and maps.

Wreck Beach Vancouver's busiest nude beach is this famous stretch of sand along NW Marine Dr. Heading south past the Museum of Anthropology you'll see markers for trails into the woods; take trail No 4, 5 or 6 down to the beach. People do swim here, but the water's full of Fraser River industrial effluent and none too appetizing. For beach history, organized events and other details, check out W www.wreckbeach.org.

Queen Elizabeth Park & Around

This 53-hectare park (☎ 604-257-8584) is between Cambie and Ontario Sts and W 29th and W 37th Aves. It holds Vancouver's highest point and offers great city views from almost every direction. The park features a mix of sports fields, manicured lawns, formal botanical gardens, tennis courts, a pitch-and-putt golf course, lawn-bowling greens, the city's only Frisbee golf course, the Bloedel Conservatory and one of Vancouver's top restaurants, Seasons in the Park (see Places to Eat). The main route going into the park is W 33rd Ave.

On the park's east side is Nat Bailey Stadium, home to the single-A Vancouver Canadians; on a warm summer afternoon or evening, there aren't many places in the city where you can have a more enjoyable beer and hot dog while being entertained at the same time (see Spectator Sports).

Crowning the hill at Queen Elizabeth Park is the Buckminster Fuller–inspired, 'triodetic'-dome **Bloedel Conservatory** (☎ 604-257-8584; adult/youth age 13-17/senior/child age 6-12 $3.75/2.85/2.25/1.85; open 9am-8pm Mon-Fri year-round, 10am-9pm Sat & Sun Apr-Sept, 10am-5pm Sat & Sun Oct-Mar). This 'garden under Plexiglas' has three climate zones supporting 400 species of plants and 150 free-flying tropical birds.

VanDusen Botanical Garden This 22-hectare park (☎ 604-878-9274, 5251 Oak St; adult/senior/youth age 13-18/child age 6-12 $6.50/5/4/3.25, family $15; open 10am-9pm in summer, 10am-dusk rest of year) is between W 33rd and W 37th Aves, about four blocks west of Queen Elizabeth Park. It holds a small lake, a sculpture collection, an Elizabethan hedge maze and ornamental plants from around the world. In December a section of the garden is illuminated with 19,000 Christmas lights.

Richmond

Bordered by the Fraser River's North and South Arms, the island city of Richmond is almost exclusively Chinese, to such an extent that it's often referred to as 'Asia West.' A slice of Hong Kong, the city's shopping centers are filled with Chinese stores, Chinese products and Chinese shoppers, and most of the signs are in Chinese. You'll find excellent Chinese food here at reasonable prices.

Richmond began as an agricultural and fishing community. Even today, it still has some of the Lower Mainland's best farmland, much of it made usable by the many dikes that have been built to hold back the river. It's also home to BC's largest fishing fleet at Steveston.

Steveston In Richmond's southwest corner is the old fishing village of Steveston, Canada's largest commercial fishing port. Today it's tame compared to the late 1800s, when a fishing-season population of 10,000 people lived here, and a dozen or so canneries lined the river. Today, only BC Packers' Imperial Cannery, started in 1893, remains in operation.

The history of Steveston is detailed at **Steveston Museum** (☎ 604-271-6868, 3811 Moncton St; admission by donation; open 9am-1pm & 1:30pm-5pm Mon-Sat). Moncton St runs through the center of the old village that fronts on to the South Arm of the Fraser River. The charming village has a selection of shops, good restaurants and pubs.

Local history is also the focus at **Gulf of Georgia Cannery National Historic Site** (☎ 604-664-9009, 12138 4th Ave; adult/senior & student/child age 6-16 $6.50/5/3.25, family $16.25; open 10am-5pm daily June-Aug;

10am-5pm Thur-Mon April, May, Sept & Oct, closed rest of year). The cannery operated from 1894 to 1979 and was the largest on the Fraser River. Inside are exhibits and a theater showing a film about West Coast fishing history.

Down on the busy waterfront you can buy fresh fish right off the boats docked at **Steveston Landing**, or wander around the complex with its restaurants and shops.

North Vancouver

North Vancouver extends west from Indian Arm to West Vancouver, with the Capilano River approximating the western boundary.

You can take in the shops and restaurants at Lonsdale Quay, hike or ski on Grouse Mountain, walk across a suspension bridge or explore some of North Van's fabulous parks. Plus, the various train services offered by BC Rail leave from its station at the foot of Pemberton Ave running south off Marine Dr.

To get to North Van, take the SeaBus from Waterfront Station to Lonsdale Quay. At the quay, buses leave on various routes throughout North Van. Buses also travel to North Van west along W Georgia St to Lonsdale Quay, and east on Pender St to Phibbs Exchange (near the north end of the Iron Workers Memorial Second Narrows Bridge), where you can connect with other buses.

Lonsdale Quay Market Aside from being a transportation hub, Lonsdale Quay Market *(☎ 604-985-6261, 123 Carrie Cates Court; open 9:30am-6:30pm Mon-Thur & Sat-Sun, 9:30am-9pm Fri)* features food stalls, specialty shops and restaurants with good views. Inside the PGE building, just east of the market, is a Visitor Information Centre *(☎ 604-984-8588; open 9am-6pm daily May-Sept)*, or walk up the hill to the Travel InfoCentre *(☎ 604-987-4488, 131 E 2nd St; open 9am-5pm Mon-Fri)*.

More shops, cafés, restaurants and businesses line Lonsdale Ave north of the quay.

Capilano Suspension Bridge You might ask yourself, why do people spend money to walk on a bridge that goes nowhere? But visitors arrive here by the busload to do just that. The bridge *(☎ 604-985-7474, 3735 Capilano Rd; adult/senior/student/child age 6-12 $10.75/8.75/6.75/3.25; open 8am-9pm daily May-Sept, 9am-5pm daily Oct-Apr)* spans the Capilano River for almost 135m at a height of 69m.

George Mackay built the first bridge here in 1888, to gain access to some of his 2400 hectares. Made of cedar planks and hemp rope, it became a popular destination for thrill seekers. Though no longer made of rope and planks, the suspension bridge is still *very* popular, and the crowds can be oppressive. Also here are history and forestry exhibits, a totem-pole and nature park, the First Nations Carving Centre, a gift shop and restaurants.

Grouse Mountain On the northern extension of Capilano Rd, Grouse Mountain *(☎ 604-984-0661, 6400 Nancy Greene Way)* is the city's most convenient ski and boarding area, and it's great for walking and hiking in summer (take bus No 236 from Lonsdale Quay). The Observatory *(☎ 604-998-4403)* offers the best views of any restaurant in Greater Vancouver. Go when the weather's clear, and consider going up in late afternoon so you can see the city's lights come on.

Grouse Mountain is famous for its Swiss-built **Skyride** *(adult/senior/youth age 13-18/ child age 7-12 $17.95/15.95/11.95/6.95, family $49.95; departs every 15 min 9am-10pm)*. This aerial tramway whisks you from the base to the chalet, 1100m above sea level, in about eight minutes. Prices are slightly higher if you are going up to ski, but it's free if you have reservations at the Observatory restaurant.

If you'd rather hike up, try the **Grouse Grind**, probably the most popular alpine hike in the Vancouver metro area. The steep, 2.9km route gains 853m in elevation – a good cardio workout. Athletic people make it up in about an hour, lesser mortals do it in 90 minutes. The trailhead is in front of the chalet. It's free to hike up, and you can catch the Skyride down for $5.

Lynn Canyon Park Set in thick woods, this 250-hectare park provides a good example of the temperate rain-forest vegetation found throughout the coastal Pacific Northwest. The park has many hiking trails you can take to find your own picnic spots and swimming spots in deep-water pools.

One park highlight is a vintage-1912 **suspension bridge** that crosses Lynn Canyon some 50m above the river. Though not as big as the Capilano Suspension Bridge, this one is similar and it's free. Near the bridge, an **Ecology Centre** has interactive displays, films and slide shows about the area's biology.

To get here, take bus No 228 or 229 from Lonsdale Quay. If driving, take the Trans Canada Hwy to Lynn Valley Rd and follow it north to Peters Rd; turn east (right) and continue to the parking lot.

Mt Seymour Provincial Park Just 16km from Vancouver, this park (☎ 604-986-2261) sits at an altitude of about 1000m and has hiking trails (varying in difficulty and length) that pass 250- to 800-year-old Douglas firs. Some areas are rugged, so backpackers should register at the park office, where trail maps are available. There's also skiing in winter (see Activities).

RVs can park in the parking lot, but no tent campgrounds are available here. Public transportation doesn't serve the park, but from Phibbs Exchange, bus No 215 will get you to the bottom of Mt Seymour Rd, where you might be able to hitch a ride on up. A shuttle bus operates in ski season. If you're driving, take the Trans Canada Hwy (Hwy 1) to Mt Seymour Parkway (near the Second Narrows Bridge) and follow it east to Mt Seymour Rd.

Deep Cove/Indian Arm While you're in the area, you might want to go to **Cates Park**, on the Dollarton Hwy overlooking Indian Arm. What is now a relatively small park is where writer Malcolm Lowry, best known for his novel *Under the Volcano*, lived with his wife from 1940 to 1954. A walk dedicated to him leads to the former site of his squatter's shack (ironically, when Lowry was squatting here the authorities did everything in their power to have him removed). In the park you will also find the remains of the Dollar Lumber Mill (in operation from 1916-42), a 15m First Nations war canoe, forest walks and a sandy beach.

Farther along is the small village of Deep Cove, where you can rent kayaks and canoes to explore Indian Arm. For a drink or a meal here, try the Raven Public House (see Bars & Pubs under Entertainment).

To get to Deep Cove or Cates Park, take bus No 212 from Phibbs Exchange. If driving, take the Trans Canada Hwy (Hwy 1) to the Dollarton Hwy (near the Second Narrows Bridge) and follow it east.

West Vancouver

Between the Capilano River and Horseshoe Bay, West Vancouver, or 'West Van,' is home to some of the Lower Mainland's wealthiest neighborhoods.

The main artery of West Van is Marine Dr, which passes through the communities of **Ambleside** and **Dundarave**, collectively known as 'The Village.' This is the commercial center of West Vancouver, and here you'll find designer shops, cafés and restaurants.

Marine Dr winds its view-filled way past expensive waterfront homes, rocky beaches and small coves hidden from the road. Eventually it reaches Horseshoe Bay, where you can wander around the marina or catch the ferry to Bowen Island, the Sunshine Coast or Nanaimo.

Lighthouse Park Off Marine Dr about 10km west of the Lions Gate Bridge, this 75-hectare park (☎ 604-925-7200) offers easy access to virgin forest. Some of the 500-year-old Douglas firs here stand as tall as 60m. You'll also see the unusual arbutus, a wide-leaf evergreen with orange peeling bark.

The park has about 13km of hiking trails, the most popular of which leads to Point Atkinson Lighthouse. Park maps are available in the parking lot. Catch bus No 250 west on W Georgia St.

Horseshoe Bay The small community of Horseshoe Bay enjoys great views across the bay and up Howe Sound to distant glacial peaks. Several places to eat and shop line the waterfront, but the town is really about the BC Ferries terminal, from where ferries travel to Nanaimo on Vancouver Island, Langdale on the Sunshine Coast (Sechelt Peninsula) and Bowen Island.

Just beyond town, at the end of Marine Dr, is lovely little **Whytecliff Park**, a great place to watch the ferries, play on the rocky beach or go for a swim. An underwater reserve makes the park a divers' favorite.

To get to Horseshoe Bay, take bus Nos 250 or 257 (express) west on W Georgia St.

Activities

With Vancouver's forested parks, ski slopes, ocean and sports centers, you'll always have something to do.

Hiking Hiking opportunities abound in the Lower Mainland's many regional and provincial parks.

For a serious hike on the North Shore, take the **Baden-Powell Trail**, which extends 41km from Horseshoe Bay on Howe Sound to Deep Cove on Indian Arm, joining together most of the area's major mountainous trails. **Cypress Provincial Park**, just 8km north of West Vancouver off Hwy 99, has eight hiking trails through forests of huge Douglas fir, yellow cypress and cedar. **Mt Seymour Provincial Park**, 13km northeast of downtown, has 10 trails varying in difficulty and length. At both parks you should be prepared for continually changing mountain weather conditions. On clear days both parks offer magnificent views.

For general information about the parks administered by the Greater Vancouver Regional District, call ☎ 604-432-6350. For information about provincial parks in the Vancouver area, call the BC Parks Lower Mainland District (☎ 604-924-2200).

Skiing Some excellent downhill skiing/snowboarding areas and cross-country ski trails are just minutes from downtown.

Cypress Mountain Ski Area (☎ *604-926-5612, 604-419-7669 for snow information*), at Cypress Provincial Park in West Vancouver, has 23 runs, rentals, instruction, night skiing, cross-country ski trails, a tobogganing slope and snowshoe tours. A shuttle bus (☎ 604-878-9229, adult/youth under 18 $10/7; call for times) operates daily from Lonsdale Quay and other places. A downhill day pass costs adult/youth age 13-18/child age 6-12/senior $36/30/17/15, and $2 for kids under five.

Grouse Mountain (☎ *604-980-9311, 604-986-6262 for snow information*), in North Vancouver, has 22 runs, rentals, instruction, night skiing, a snowshoe park, cross-country ski trails and an outdoor skating rink. A downhill day pass is adult/youth age 13-18/senior & child age 7-12 $32/24/17.

Seymour Ski Country (☎ *604-986-2261, 604-879-3999 for snow information*), at Mt Seymour Provincial Park in North Vancouver, has 21 runs, rentals, instruction, night skiing, snowshoe and cross-country trails and a tobogganing slope. A shuttle bus (☎ 604-718-7771; adult/other $7/5; call for times) operates daily during the ski season from Lonsdale Quay, Phibbs Exchange and the Mohawk Gas Station at the foot of Mt Seymour Rd. A downhill pass for adult & youth/senior/child age 6-12 costs $22/19/12 weekdays, $29/19/14 weekends.

Cycling Vancouver's 16 designated bicycle routes total nearly 129km. One favorite, the 39km Seaside Route, takes in the seawall around Stanley Park, False Creek, Kitsilano and Locarno Beach. Look for the *Cycling in Vancouver* brochure or call the Bicycle Hotline at ☎ 604-871-6070 for more information. It's mandatory to wear a helmet while cycling.

See Getting Around for information on bicycle and in-line skate rental.

Swimming Vancouver has 11 fine swimming beaches, and from late May to early September, seven of them are patrolled by lifeguards. These include Third Beach and Second Beach (Stanley Park), English Bay Beach (West End), Kitsilano Beach, Jericho Beach, Locarno Beach and Spanish Banks Beach (all on the West Side). Wreck Beach (see the University of British Columbia, earlier) is the city's nude beach.

The water this far north is never exactly warm; it reaches a high in summer of around 21°C (70°F). Sometimes the bacteria count in the water off the city beaches can get too high for healthy swimming; check the newspapers for daily reports. For information regarding city beaches call ☎ 604-738-8535.

You can also swim in pools around town. Although the main aquatic centers in Greater Vancouver are open year-round, two of the more central outdoor pools are open summers only. Admission to any is about $4/3/2 adult/youth & senior/child.

Vancouver Aquatic Centre (☎ *604-665-3424, 1050 Beach Ave*), at Sunset Beach beside the Burrard Bridge, has a 50m pool, whirlpool, diving tank, gym and sauna. **UBC Aquatic Centre** (☎ *604-822-4521*), off University Blvd, has a 50m pool, saunas and public exercise areas.

The heated 137m **Kitsilano Outdoor Pool** (☎ *604-731-0011, Cornwall Ave & Yew St;*

open May-Sept), at Kitsilano Beach Park, is the only one in the city to use saltwater. The **Second Beach Pool** (☎ *604-257-8370, Stanley Park; open May-Sept)* is beside the beach and has lanes for laps as well as a children's area with waterslides.

Boating From kayaking to sailing to windsurfing, Vancouver's waterways offer it all.

Ecomarine Ocean Kayak Centre (☎ *604-689-7575, 1668 Duranleau St)* rents single/double kayaks for $22/32 for two hours or $42/62 for a full day on Granville Island. It has another outlet at the Jericho Sailing Centre at Jericho Beach near the hostel. Ecomarine also offers courses and educational tours.

Experienced sailors can rent sailboats from, among others: **Blue Pacific Yacht Charters** (☎ *604-682-2161, 1519 Foreshore Walk)* and **Cooper Boating Centre** (☎ *604-687-4110, 1620 Duranleau St)*, both on Granville Island. A skipper can be provided if you're not confident about your skills. Three- to four-hour sailing cruises on English Bay are also offered.

Windsure Windsurfing School (☎ *604-224-0615, 1300 Discovery St)*, at the Jericho Sailing Centre, rents boards and offers lessons.

Scuba Diving Popular diving areas include Cates Park in North Vancouver; Lighthouse and Whytecliff Parks in West Vancouver; and Porteau Cove on Hwy 99, 24km north of Horseshoe Bay, a provincial marine park with an artificial reef and a campground with showers.

Outfitters include **International Diving Centre** (☎ *604-736-2541, 2572 Arbutus St)* and **The Diving Locker** (☎ *604-736-2681, 2745 W 4th Ave)*, both in Kitsilano.

Organized Tours

In Vancouver you can do city tours by bus, trolley, taxi, boat, seaplane, bicycle or on foot. You can take a dinner cruise in the harbor or ride a horse-drawn carriage through Stanley Park. If you want to leave the city for the day, you can hop a steam train to Squamish, or have dinner on a train that goes as far as Porteau Cove, about halfway between Horseshoe Bay and Squamish. Following is a list of just some of the tours available.

Bus Gray Line (☎ *604-879-3363)* offers several different city tours on big buses. Probably the most popular is the Deluxe Grand City Tour, a 3½-hour tour of the best the city has to offer for about $40/38/29 adult/senior/child. With the company's double-decker bus tour ($22/21/11) you can hop on and off at any of 20 stops from 8:30am to 6:30pm over two days.

Vancouver Trolley Company (☎ *604-801-5515)* operates replicas (on wheels) of the famous San Francisco trolleys. You can get on or off the trolley at 23 different attractions and hotels throughout the day from 9am to 6pm. The trolley starts and finishes in Gastown at 157 Water St and stops at such places as Canada Place, the Vancouver Art Gallery, the Vancouver Aquarium, English Bay, Vanier Park, Granville Island and Chinatown. The entire circuit takes two hours and the trolleys depart every half-hour. The cost is $24/12 adult/child.

Boat Harbour Cruises (☎ *604-688-7246)*, at the north foot of Denman St in Coal Harbour, by Stanley Park, offers a variety of boat tours. Its MPV *Constitution*, Vancouver's only authentic paddlewheeler, operates 75-minute sightseeing tours around the harbor every day between mid-May and mid-September and from November to mid-April. The tour costs $18/15/6 adult/senior/child. Lunch and dinner cruises are also available.

Vancouver Champagne Cruises (☎ *604-688-8072)* offers a three-hour sunset cruise departing daily from Granville Island. The cruise takes in the Stanley Park beaches, Ambleside Beach in West Vancouver and English Bay. It departs at 5:30pm and costs $55 with dinner, $30 without.

False Creek Ferries (☎ *604-684-7781)* offers scenic harbor tours in summer aboard its small passenger ferries. The tours depart from the Granville Island dock next to Bridges restaurant daily in summer and weekends during the winter. The 40-minute tour costs $8/6/5 adult/senior/child.

Starline Tours (☎ *604-272-9187)* offers a unique boat tour from Steveston late March to mid-May, when as many as 700 sea lions take up residence on the Steveston jetty to gorge themselves on Fraser River fish. If you're fortunate you may see some orcas on the trip. The 90-minute tour costs $25/20/12 adult/senior & student/child. Call for schedule.

Train The *Royal Hudson* steam train, one of the last operating steam trains in Canada, runs between the BC Rail Station in North Vancouver and Squamish, at the head of Howe Sound. The train operates from late May to mid-September, leaving North Vancouver at 10am and returning at 4pm, with a two-hour stop in Squamish. Another option is to take the MV *Britannia*, operated by Harbour Cruises, one way to Squamish and the *Royal Hudson* the other way. The MV *Britannia* departs at 9:30am and returns at 4:30pm. A shuttle service between the BC Rail Station and Coal Harbour is provided. The train roundtrip costs $50/43/13 adult/senior & youth/child; the train/boat combination costs $70/65/22. Another option is to travel Parlour Class both ways on the train for $83/78/60. This includes lunch on the way up and afternoon tea on the return trip. Call ☎ 604-984-5246 for information.

The *Pacific Starlight* Dinner Train is another tour offered by BC Rail from early May to late October, plus on special occasions such as New Year's Eve and Valentine's Day. The train has nine vintage cars, including three dome cars and six salon cars, which have been refurbished in art deco style. The train leaves the BC Rail Station in North Vancouver at 6:15pm and travels along the scenic route to Porteau Cove, on Howe Sound not far from Squamish, with dinner served on the way. After a 45-minute stop at Porteau Cove the train returns to North Vancouver, arriving at 10pm. The rates are $86 for salon seating and $110 for dome seating. Call ☎ 604-984-5246 for information.

Walking & Cycling Walkabout Historic Vancouver Tours (☎ 604-720-0006) offers the Downtown Vancouver/Gastown and Granville Island tours, both of which explore the city's architecture and history with a guide dressed in 1890s period costume. The daily tours cost $18.

Spokes Bicycle Rentals (☎ 604-688-5141, 1798 W Georgia St) offers two cycling tours daily between mid-May and mid-September. The Stanley Park Seawall Tour takes about 1½ hours and costs $30. The Granville Island Tour – which includes the Seawall, Beaver Lake, English Bay and a lunch break at Granville Island – takes about 3½ hours and costs $60.

Other Tours Stanley Park Horse-Drawn Tours (☎ 604-681-5115) is a leisurely and informative way to see the park. The daily one-hour narrated tours in a 20-passenger carriage depart every 20 to 30 minutes from beside the information booth on Stanley Park Dr, east of the rowing club. The cost is $17/16/11 adult/senior & student/child. A free shuttle bus runs from downtown to the park about six times a day.

If you are into kayaking and can get at least four people together, **Ocean West Expeditions** (☎ 604-688-5770, 800-660-0051), in the English Bay bathhouse at the foot of Beach Ave and Denman St, will take you on a three-hour escorted tour of the waterfront and Stanley Park. The cost is $75 per person.

Lotus Land Tours (☎ 604-684-4922) will take you on a wilderness experience not that far from the city. The four-hour tour to North Vancouver, which is described as being for the 'inexperienced and the unfit,' includes a guided kayaking trip in Indian Arm off Deep Cove, a barbecued salmon lunch on Twin Island, and a chance to explore the forest and beach for $135. It also offers orca-watching tours, as well as cycling and hiking trips.

Harbour Air (☎ 604-688-1277, 800-665-0212) offers a number of seaplane tours, such as the 20-minute Panorama tour of the city for $76 a person. The terminal is on Coal Harbour Rd, about one block west of Canada Place.

Special Events

Any month you visit Vancouver you'll find a festival of some sort taking place. Following is a list of some major events. For up-to-date information get a copy of *The Vancouver Book* from the Travel Info Centre, or pick up a copy of *Visitor's Choice*, available free at many tourist attractions and hotels.

January

Polar Bear Swim This popular, chilly affair has been taking place on English Bay Beach annually on New Year's Day since 1819, and it might just be the ultimate cure for a hangover. Up to 2000 people charge into the ocean at 2:30pm. Not many dally for long, but some swim the 90m to a buoy and back to the beach. If you can't handle the water, watching is allowed. Call ☎ 604-665-3424 for information.

Chinese New Year The date of the lunar new year varies from late January to early February each year, but the fireworks crackle in Chinatown for days before and days after. The festivities take place over 15 days and feature the Dragon Parade, good food and music, dancing, art exhibits and storytelling. Call ☎ 604-415-6322 for information.

May

Vancouver International Children's Festival The red-and-white tents go up in Vanier Park on the last Monday of the month and stay up for seven days while 70,000 people enjoy Canadian and international acts dedicated to keeping the young, and young of heart, totally entertained. Call ☎ 604-708-5655 for information or check W www.youngarts.ca.

June

Bard on the Beach Shakespeare Festival Starting around the second Tuesday of the month and going through to the end of September, this summerlong celebration of all things 'Bill' takes place in a 500-seat tent at Vanier Park, with English Bay acting as a backdrop. Usually two plays are performed throughout the summer. Call ☎ 604-739-0559 for more information or check W www.bardonthebeach.org.

Alcan Dragon Boat Festival The third weekend of the month, about 2000 competitors from around the world take part in the Dragon Boat races on False Creek. Call ☎ 604-688-2382 for information.

Vancouver International Jazz Festival Some of the biggest names in jazz take the stage at 25 venues in the Vancouver area. In addition, a two-day New Orleans–style street festival takes place in Gastown. The festival starts on the third Friday of the month and runs for 10 days. Call ☎ 604-872-5200 for information or check W www.jazzvancouver.com.

July

Canada Day Celebrations Canada Place is the main location for the celebrations marking the country's birthday on July 1, which includes music, food and fireworks. Call 604-666-8477 for information or check W www.canadaplace.ca.

VOX – Vancouver Outdoor Art Exhibition Located around the Vancouver Art Gallery, between Robson and Georgia Sts, this is Western Canada's largest outdoor art exhibition. Call ☎ 604-984-6756 for information.

Vancouver Folk Music Festival Jericho Beach Park is the venue for this festival, which has musicians performing on seven stages throughout the third weekend of the month. Call ☎ 604-602-9798 for information.

Celebration of Light This, the world's largest musical fireworks competition, starts at the end of July and goes to the beginning of August. Three competing countries (which change each year) put on their most spectacular display of fireworks over three nights, with all of them coming together to put on a dazzling display on the final night. The displays are held at English Bay; get to the beach early to claim your spot. Call ☎ 604-641-1193 for information or check W www.celebration-of-light.com.

August

Abbotsford International Air Show Held on the second weekend of the month, this is known as 'Canada's national air show.' If it flies, you'll probably find it here. The show takes place in Abbotsford, 56km southeast of the city near the Canadian-US border. Call ☎ 604-852-8511 for information or check W www.abbotsford airshow.com.

Gay Pride Day Held on the first Sunday, watch for the outrageous main parade drawing 130,000 spectators along Denman St. Call ☎ 604-687-0955 for more information or check W www.vanpride.bc.ca.

Pacific National Exhibition Known simply as the PNE, this fair takes place for two weeks starting in the middle of August and ending on the Labour Day Monday in September. Along with the traditional agricultural exhibitions and home displays there are concerts, car derbies, loggers shows, an amusement park and all the junk food you can stomach. Call ☎ 604-253-2311 for information or check W www.pne.bc.ca.

September

Vancouver International Fringe Festival This popular theater event presents drama, musical theater, comedy and dance from around the world. It takes place over 10 days starting at the beginning of the month and is held in various venues at and around Granville Island. Call ☎ 604-257-0350 for information.

Vancouver International Film Festival Although it doesn't have the star-studded glamour of some other film festivals, this is the third-largest one in North America, with 400 screenings of 300 films from 50 countries. The festival takes place over 17 days from the end of September to mid-October in seven city theaters. Call ☎ 604-685-0260 for information or check W www.viff.org.

December

Christmas Carolship Parade This is a uniquely Vancouver tradition, which takes place from around the 5th to the 23rd. About 100 boats of all sizes, lit up and decorated like Christmas trees, take part in a flotilla that on different nights sails past False Creek, English Bay, Point Grey, West Vancouver, or up Burrard Inlet to Port Moody. On many of the boats carolers sing through sound systems, while other boats play taped music. Whether you're lucky enough to be on one of the boats or simply hear the carols from the shore, this is a great way to help bring on the Christmas spirit. Call ☎ 604-878-8999 for information.

Places to Stay

Vancouver is unusual in that a great many inexpensive and moderately priced hotels and motels remain in the otherwise high-rent downtown area, so there's no reason not to stay right in the center of things.

Summer is busy in Vancouver, so make reservations early. The Tourist Info Centre (☎ 604-683-2000, **W** www.tourismvancouver .com) and the Super Natural British Columbia reservation service (☎ 800-435-5662) can be a great help in finding reasonably priced accommodations.

Camping No public campgrounds lie in Vancouver proper. The following campgrounds are close to the city.

Burnaby Cariboo RV Park (☎ 604-420-1722, fax 604-420-4782, **W** www.bcrvpark .com, 8765 Cariboo Place) Sites $23-35. East of the city, off Hwy 1 at the Cariboo exit in Burnaby, this place has an indoor pool, lounge, laundry facilities and convenience store.

Capilano RV Park (☎ 604-987-4722, fax 604-987-2015, **W** www.capilanorvpark.com, 295 Tomahawk Ave) Sites $25-35. Off Capilano Rd in North Vancouver, this park has everything, including a Jacuzzi.

Richmond RV Park (☎ 604-270-7878, fax 604-244-9713, **W** www.richmondrvpark.com, 6200 River Rd) Sites $17-23. Open Apr-Oct. South of the Middle Arm of the Fraser River in Richmond, near Hollybridge Way, this is one of the closest campgrounds to town.

ParkCanada RV Park and Campground (☎ 604-943-5811, fax 604-943-0093, **W** www .parkcanada.com, 4799 Hwy 17, Delta) Sites $18.50-21.50. This park northeast of the Tsawwassen ferry terminal has free showers.

Hostels Most of the good hostels are full in summer and busy the rest of the year, so it's a good idea to make reservations.

HI-Vancouver Downtown (☎ 604-684-4565, 888-203-4302, fax 604-684-4540, **e** vandowntown@hihostels.bc.ca, 1114 Burnaby St) Dorm beds members/nonmembers $20/24, private doubles $55/64. Open 24 hours. At the corner of Thurlow St, this hostel has 212 beds with no more than four in a room. Facilities include a patio, library and games room. It's conveniently walkable from anywhere in the downtown area. A free shuttle runs to the HI Vancouver Jericho Beach hostel and Pacific Central Station.

Global Village Backpackers (☎ 604-682-8226, 888-844-7875, fax 604-682-8240, **e** gvbp@interlog.com, 1018 Granville St) Dorm beds members/nonmembers $21/24, private doubles with shared bath $59/65, triples with private bath $57/60. Brightly painted and lively, this place strikes a nice balance between the near-stodginess of the HI facilities and the grunginess of some other Vancouver hostels. Features include a rooftop patio, nightly pub runs, good apartment and job boards, lockers, a bike-storage room and a lounge with pool table.

C&N Backpackers Hostel (☎ 604-682-2441, 888-434-6060, **e** backpackers@ sprint.ca, 927 Main St) Dorm beds/singles $14/35. Office open 8am-11pm, no curfew. This hostel has a laundry, Internet room and bike rentals. It's not in the best area but is walking distance from downtown and not all that far from the SkyTrain Science World–Main St Station and Pacific Central Station. Take bus Nos 3, 8 or 19 from downtown along Main St.

Cambie International Hostel (☎ 604-684-6466, fax 604-687-5618, **e** info@ cambiehostels.com, 300 Cambie St) Dorm beds $15. This centrally located hostel provides bedding and rooms with shared bath. Amenities include laundry facilities and bicycle storage, but no cooking facilities (though the first breakfast is on the house). A bakery, café and bar on the ground floor make it a convenient but potentially noisy place to spend the night. Ask about free pick-ups from Pacific Central Station or the airport. The Cambie also operates a second, more sedate location downtown (☎ 604-684-7757, 515 Seymour St), but only double rooms are available at $20.

YMCA (☎ 604-681-0221, fax 604-681-1630, **W** www.vanymca.org, 955 Burrard St) Singles/doubles $47/57, private family rooms $90. Parking $7 per night. The Y is right downtown. Women and couples are allowed, and many travelers stay here. The only drawback is the constant sound of unlocking doors. Bathrooms are down the hall. Gym and pool facilities are available, and a small, inexpensive restaurant serves breakfasts and sandwiches that are good values.

YWCA (☎ 604-895-5830, 800-663-1424, fax 604-681-2550, **W** www.ywcahotel.com,

733 Beatty St) Singles/doubles with shared bath $56/70, doubles with private bath up to $111. The 155 rooms come in various configurations, from simple singles to rooms that sleep five. Seniors, students and YWCA members get about 10% off. Between W Georgia and Robson Sts near BC Place Stadium, this is more like a hotel, and it accommodates men, women, couples and families. Each room has a refrigerator, but there are also communal kitchens, plus TV lounges and a laundry. Fitness facilities are available but are off-site. The SkyTrain Stadium Station is a five-minute walk.

HI-Vancouver Jericho Beach (☎ 604-224-3208, fax 604-224-4852, e van-jericho@ hihostels.bc.ca, 1515 Discovery St) Dorm beds members/nonmembers $17.50/20, private doubles $45. Open 24 hours. Although away from town center, the original Vancouver HI hostel is in a great location and with 286 beds is the largest in Canada. It's close to the beach, not far from the restaurants and bars on W 4th Ave and about 20 minutes from downtown by bus (take bus No 4 south on Granville St).

University Residences *Gage Residence & Conference Centre* (*University of British Columbia;* ☎ 604-822-1010, fax 604-822-1001, w www.conferences.ubc.ca, Gage Towers, 5961 Student Union Blvd) Singles/doubles with shared bath $24/48 & up, self-contained apartments $99 & up. You don't have to be a student to stay in UBC's student housing during summer break, from May to late August; its 47 condominium-style apartments are available year-round. The pleasant campus has a cafeteria, some cafés, a laundromat, pub and sports facilities.

B&Bs Vancouver's B&Bs are numerous and popular. Two services that book rooms in all price ranges are Old English B&B Registry (☎ 604-986-5069, fax 604-986-8810, e vicki@ bandbinn.com) and Town & Country B&B (☎/fax 604-731-5942, w www.townand countrybedandbreakfast.com).

A few popular choices are listed below.

Nelson House (☎ 604-684-9793, e bestinvan@lightspeed.ca, 977 Broughton St) Rooms $88-178. This three-story 1907 house has six rooms and a top-floor suite. Close to Robson St, it offers a full breakfast, fireplaces and a lovely garden.

English Bay Inn (☎ 604-683-8002, fax 604-683-8089, e inn@aebc.com, 1968 Comox St) Rooms start at $180, suite $375. Each of the eight rooms in this gem of a B&B has a private bathroom and nice touches like a four-poster bed. The inn has an elegant parlor, a formal dining room and a small garden. Be sure to book well in advance.

Windsor Guest House (☎ 604-872-3060, 888-872-3060, fax 604-873-1147, e info@ dougwin.com, 325 W 11th Ave) Rooms $75-105. Beside City Hall and City Square just off Cambie St, this 1895 home has 10 rooms, some with private bath and all with cable TV. Rates include a full breakfast and free off-street parking.

Maple House B&B (☎ 604-739-5833, fax 604-739-5877, e info@maplehouse.com, 1533 Maple St) Rooms $85-130. Just off Cornwall Ave close to the beach and Vanier Park, this 1900 heritage home has five rooms.

ThistleDown House B&B (☎ 604-986-7173, 888-633-7173, fax 604-980-2939, e davidson@helix.net, 3910 Capilano Rd) Rooms $125-220. North of the Upper Levels Hwy (Hwy 1), this B&B is an exceptional value. The 1920s house on a half-acre lot has a country inn feel. The gourmet breakfast is scrumptious, and homemade cakes and pastries are served for afternoon tea. All five rooms have private bath.

Beachside B&B (☎ 604-922-7773, 800-563-3311, fax 604-926-8073, 4208 Evergreen Ave) Rooms $150 & up. This West Vancouver B&B is right on the beach, with views of Point Grey and the Lions Gate Bridge. It offers a seaside whirlpool, good breakfasts and the feeling that the city is far away (though a bus on Marine Dr gets you there in about 20 minutes).

Motels & Hotels – Downtown *Kingston Hotel* (☎ 604-684-9024, 888-713-3304, fax 604-684-9917, w www.KingstonHotel Vancouver.com, 757 Richards St) Singles/ doubles $45-80/55-95. Parking $10 per night. The town's best low-cost hotel was also the city's first B&B hotel. It still offers a morning meal of coffee, juice and toast. Extras include a sauna, guest laundry and TV lounge.

Victorian Hotel (☎ 604-681-6369, 877-681-6369, fax 604-681-8776, e victorian hotel@hotmail.com, 514 Homer St) Singles/ doubles with shared bath $59/69, private bath $89/99. Fenced parking $8 per night. This is a real find in Vancouver – a 27-room European-style pension in a beautifully renovated historic building, *with* reasonable prices. Some rooms have kitchenettes and all have phones and small TVs. Continental breakfast is included. The Victorian also offers hostel-style accommodations in a separate building for $35/45 singles/doubles.

Dufferin Hotel (☎ 604-683-4251, 877-683-5522, fax 604-683-0611, **e** *reservations@ dufferinhotel.com, 900 Seymour St)* Singles/doubles with shared bath $55/65, with private bath $80/85. Free parking. This good choice has a dining room and pub.

Royal Hotel (☎ 604-685-5335, 877-685-5337, fax 604-685-5351, **e** *frontdesk@ attheroyal.com, 1025 Granville St)* Rooms with shared bath $99, with private bath $129. Rates include continental breakfast plus welcoming cocktails in the hotel pub. A guest laundry is available.

Both the Dufferin and the Royal pubs serve a primarily gay clientele, though they're straight-friendly.

Bosman's Motor Hotel (☎ 604-682-3171, 888-267-6267, fax 604-684-4010, **e** *bosmans@ telus.com, 1060 Howe St)* Singles/doubles $119/129. Free parking. One of the city's best deals, Bosman's is central, has an outdoor pool and is everything most people will ever need in a moderately priced lodging.

Holiday Inn Hotel & Suites – Downtown Vancouver (☎ 604-684-2151, 800-663-9151, fax 604-684-4736, **e** *hidtvan@ intergate.bc.ca, 1110 Howe St)* Singles/doubles $159/179. Near Davie St, this place is a class act for a chain hotel, with large rooms, a pool, health club, restaurant and bar. Some rooms have kitchens.

Crowne Plaza Hotel Georgia (☎ 604-682-5566, 800-663-1111, fax 604-642-5579, **e** *hgsales@hotelgeorgia.bc.ca, 801 W Georgia St)* Rooms $169 & up. Built in the 1930s, and complete with wooden paneling, chandeliers and ornate brass elevators, this is a real charmer. Rooms are a good value.

St Regis Hotel (☎ 604-681-1135, 800-790-7929, fax 604-683-1126, **w** *www.stregishotel .com, 602 Dunsmuir St)* Rooms $125 & up. Considering the location, right in the heart of the city, the basic rooms here are a good value.

Georgian Court Hotel (☎ 604-682-5555, 800-663-1155, fax 604-682-8830, **e** *info@ georgiancourt.com, 773 Beatty St)* Singles/doubles $195/215. This nicely decorated European-style hotel offers fabulous service in the center of the entertainment district.

In the city center you'll find new luxury hotels and elegant older hotels.

Hotel Vancouver (☎ 604-684-3131, 800-441-1414, fax 604-662-1907, **e** *reserve@ hvc.cphotels.ca, 900 W Georgia St)* Rooms $289 & up. Completed in 1939, the Hotel Vancouver is a fine example of the château-style hotels built by Canada's railways. Its green copper roof remains a city landmark. Check out the fine relief work, Renaissance detail and the gargoyles, supposedly reproductions of 11th-century cathedral carvings. The hotel offers all the creature comforts, including an excellent fitness facility and indoor pool. Even if you're not staying here you can enjoy one of the three afternoon teas served daily.

Four Seasons Hotel (☎ 604-689-9333, 800-268-6282, fax 604-689-3466, **e** *ian.maw@ fourseasons.com, 791 W Georgia St)* Rooms start at $290. Vancouver's highest-rated hotel is above the Pacific Centre shopping complex.

Wedgewood Hotel (☎ 604-689-7777, 800-663-0666, fax 604-608-5348, **e** *info@ wedgewoodhotel.com, 845 Hornby St)* Rooms $240 & up. If you want a more personalized experience, try this fantastic vintage boutique hotel with luxurious rooms, homemade cookies, cordless phones and a health club.

The Pan Pacific Hotel (☎ 604-662-8111, 800-663-1515 in Canada, 800-937-1515 in USA, fax 604-662-3815, **e** *reservations@ panpacific-hotel.com, 300-999 Canada Place)* Rooms $415 & up. This deluxe convention hotel has three restaurants, a health club and an outdoor heated pool open year-round. It's worth going in just to see the eight-story atrium, complete with totem poles, and the lounge with 12m-high glass walls (through which the harbor views are spectacular).

Motels & Hotels – West End *Sylvia Hotel* (☎ 604-681-9321, fax 604-682-3551, 1154 Gilford St)* Rooms start at $65, suites $145. Parking $7 per day. Next to Stanley Park, the well-loved, if slightly faded, Sylvia enjoys a marvelous location on English Bay and is close to both Davie and Denman Sts.

The ivy-covered hotel was built in 1912 (the new low-rise wing was added in 1986) and has been declared a heritage building. The 119 rooms all have private bath, and 23 have kitchens.

Buchan Hotel (☎ 604-685-5354, 800-668-6654, fax 604-685-5367, e buchanhotel@bc.sympatico.com, 1906 Haro St) Singles/doubles with shared bath $69/75, with private bath $85/95. This nicely appointed older hotel is also next door to Stanley Park.

Burrard Motor Inn (☎ 604-681-2331, 800-663-0366, fax 604-681-9753, e burrardres@aol.com, 1100 Burrard St) Singles $84-94, doubles $104, plus $5 for kitchenette. Free parking. This moderately priced motel is convenient and a favorite of families and budget travelers.

Oceanside Hotel (☎ 604-682-5641, 877-506-2326, fax 604-687-2340, e oceansidehotel@hotmail.com, 1847 Pendrell St) 1-bedroom suites with or without kitchens start at $130. Free parking. Close to Stanley Park, this hotel in a former apartment building has suites that are good values, some with kitchens.

Robson St, west of the busy shopping district, has some good hotel deals in a prime area.

Greenbrier Hotel (☎ 604-683-4558, 888-355-5888, fax 604-669-3109, e greenbrierhotel@aol.com, 1393 Robson St) Rooms $149-169. Free parking. A former apartment building transformed into a suite hotel, the Greenbrier is nicer than it looks from the outside. Each room has a full kitchen and sitting area.

Blue Horizon Hotel (☎ 604-688-1411, 800-663-1333, fax 604-688-4461, e info@bluehorizonhotel.com, 1225 Robson St) Rooms $159 & up. This place has great views, balconies, an indoor pool, restaurants and a bar.

Davie St holds a couple of moderately priced hotels.

Parkhill Hotel (☎ 604-685-1311, 800-663-1525, fax 604-681-0208, e prkhillres@aol.com, 1160 Davie St) Rooms $160 & up. Just north of Thurlow St, the Parkhill is a convention hotel with two restaurants.

Best Western Sands Hotel (☎ 604-682-1831, 800-661-7887, fax 604-682-3546, e sands@rpdhotels.com, 1755 Davie St) Rooms start at $169. At the far end of Davie St near Denman St, this hotel has a lounge,

the Bayside Room, that's a good place to catch an English Bay sunset.

The Westin Bayshore Resort & Marina (☎ 604-682-3377, 800-937-8461, fax 604-687-3102, e bayshore.sales@westin.com, 1601 Bayshore Dr) Rooms $259 & up. At Coal Harbour, the Westin offers high-quality amenities right on the waterfront and close to Stanley Park and Denman St. Aside from having doormen dressed in Beefeater outfits, the hotel is famous for having the billionaire recluse Howard Hughes as a guest for three months in 1972.

Pacific Palisades Hotel (☎ 604-688-0461, 800-663-1815, fax 604-688-4374, e sales@pacificpalisadeshotel.com, 1277 Robson St) Rooms start at $275, suites $325. Different from the usual selection, this hotel has bright retro decor and late-afternoon 'soul flow' receptions (an updated, healthier take on the happy-hour concept). Perks include an on-site health club and pool complete with kids' play area.

Listel Vancouver (☎ 604-684-8461, 800-663-5491, fax 604-684-7092, e moreinfo@listel-vancouver.com, 1300 Robson St) Rooms start at $240. This 'art hotel' features original artworks on the 4th and 5th 'gallery floors.' The restaurant is good, too.

Motels & Hotels – West Side

City Centre Motel (☎ 604-876-7166, 800-707-2489, fax 604-876-6727, e ctcmotel@intergate.bc.ca, 2111 Main St) Rooms $75. Free parking. One of the more central motels, the City Centre is a 10-minute walk south of the SkyTrain Science World–Main St Station and Pacific Central Station.

Shaughnessy Village (☎ 604-736-5511, fax 604-737-1321, e info@shaughnessyvillage.com, 1125 W 12th Ave) Single/double studio rooms start at $60/70, 2-room suites $99/109. This high-rise complex is a B&B, hotel, resort, apartment building and amusement center all rolled into one. The least-expensive rooms, tiny shiplike studio cabins, come packed with every amenity. Guests get a free breakfast in the on-site restaurant.

Holiday Inn Vancouver Centre (☎ 604-879-0511, 800-465-4329, fax 604-872-7520, e info@holidayinnvancouver.com, 711 W Broadway) Rooms $149 & up. This large complex has a pool, restaurant, casino and great views.

Ramada Vancouver Centre (☎ *604-872-8661, 800-663-5403, fax 604-872-2270,* e *ramada@direct.ca, 898 W Broadway)* Rooms $150 & up. Just 10 minutes from city center, the Ramada has a restaurant and a pub where you'll hear some good R&B.

Granville Island Hotel (☎ *604-683-7373, 800-663-1840, fax 604-683-3061,* e *reservations@granvilleislandhotel.com, 1253 Johnston St)* Rooms $219 & up. In a top location right on False Creek with great downtown views, this hotel is near the island's famed market, art and craft galleries and theaters, and it's just seconds away from the mini-ferries to downtown or Kitsilano. A brewpub is on the main floor.

Motels & Hotels – North Shore
A cluster of motels lies close to the Lions Gate Bridge, not far from Grouse Mountain. Look along Marine Dr and north up Capilano Rd. The motels along here are similar in terms of facilities and rates, starting at about $120. Ask about kitchenettes. All have free parking. Examples include The Grouse Inn (☎ *604-988-7101, 800-779-7888, fax 604-988-7102, 1633 Capilano Rd),* ***Canyon Court*** (☎ *604-988-3181, 888-988-3181, fax 604-990-2755,* e *canyonct@direct.ca, 1748 Capilano Rd)* and ***Holiday Inn Express*** (☎ *604-987-4461, 800-663-4055, fax 604-984-4244,* e *teja1@istar.ca, 1800 Capilano Rd).*

You can also try these two more-noteworthy lodgings:

Park Royal Hotel (☎ *604-926-5511, 877-926-5511, fax 604-926-6082,* w *www .parkroyalhotel.com, 540 Clyde Ave)* Rooms $159 & up. In West Vancouver, beside the north section of Park Royal Shopping Centre just off Taylor Way, this small 30-room hotel has the feel of an English country inn, complete with pub.

Lonsdale Quay Hotel (☎ *604-986-6111, 800-836-6111, fax 604-986-8782,* e *sales@ lonsdalequayhotel.bc.ca, 123 Carrie Cates Court)* Rooms $150 & up. In North Vancouver, this hotel has an unbeatable combination: great city view, the SeaBus close at hand and the Lonsdale Quay Market to explore.

Motels & Hotels – Richmond/Airport
If you want to stay close to the airport, or simply like the idea of staying in Richmond, numerous hotels will fit the bill.

Holiday Inn Express (☎ *604-273-8080, 888-831-3388, fax 604-214-8488,* e *info@ hi-express.bc.ca, 9351 Bridgeport Rd)* Rooms start at $109. This one is beside Hwy 99.

Fairmont Vancouver Airport (☎ *604-207-5200, 800-441-1414, fax 604-248-3219,* w *www .fairmont.com, Vancouver International Airport)* Rooms start at $189. You can't stay any closer to the airport than this. Accessed by a walkway next to the US departure hall, this hotel offers soundproofed state-of-the-art rooms, plus a restaurant and lounge.

Places to Eat
In Vancouver, you can journey gastronomically around the world just by wandering down the street. Powerhouse chefs flex their muscles at top dining rooms downtown, while cozy neighborhoods preserve their roots with Chinese noodle shops, European cafés and hippie vegetarian havens. Add in the West Coast's natural bounty of farm, garden and sea, and you've got the makings of a culinary capital.

Unless otherwise stated, all of the following restaurants are open for lunch and dinner daily, although some may cut back their opening hours in winter, and are listed in ascending order of price.

Downtown *Kitto Japanese House* (☎ *604-687-6622, 833 Granville St)* Dishes $6 & up, combination dinner $8. Kitto has beautiful shoji lanterns and wooden booths, and it's perfect for late-night sushi or noodles.

Goulash House Restaurant & Pastry Shop (☎ *604-688-0206, 1065 Granville St)* Dishes $8.50-12.50. The neighborhood is seedy, but the food – like stuffed cabbage

Table for two

rolls, beef goulash and vegetable ragout – is great.

Gotham (☎ 604-605-8282, 615 Seymour St) Mains $26-50. Open 11:30am-2:30pm Mon-Fri, dinner from 5pm daily. This snazzy steakhouse features a heated 'urban garden' patio.

Diva at the Met (☎ 604-602-7788, **e** reservations@divamet.com, 645 Howe St) Breakfast $8-14, lunch $13-18, dinner $32-44. The Metropolitan Hotel's premier dining space provokes only one question: Is there anything these culinary maestros can't do?

Five Sails (☎ 604-662-8111, 300-999 Canada Place) Mains $28-38, prix-fixe dinner $70. Open 6pm-10pm daily. The Pan Pacific Hotel's five-diamond restaurant has views to match the bill you'll get at the end of the evening.

Eateries near Robson St run the gamut from bowls of noodles to elaborate French cuisine.

De Dutch Pannekoek House (☎ 604-687-7065, 1725 Robson St) Dishes $6.50-13.50. Open 8am-3:30pm Mon-Fri, 8am-3pm Sat & Sun. Try the enormous oven-baked pancakes, massive omelets or specialty Dutch platters.

Thai House Restaurant (☎ 604-683-3383, 1116 Robson St) Mains $6-15, lunch specials $8. This excellent Thai restaurant is trussed up with palm trees and Southeast Asian art.

Ezogiku Noodle Café (☎ 604-685-8606, 1329 Robson St) Dishes $5-8.50. Tiny Ezogiku specializes in big bowls of steaming ramen in a dozen-plus varieties. You might have to wait for a seat, but it's worth it.

Robson Public Market (1610 Robson St) Pick up fresh fruit and vegetables, cheese and bread for a Stanley Park picnic here.

Zin (☎ 604-408-1700, 1277 Robson St) Lunch $10-14, dinner $12-22. Open 7am-midnight daily. At the Pacific Palisades Hotel, artful Zin features an eclectic menu ranging from sake-cured salmon to the mysterious 'global soup.'

Joe Fortes (☎ 604-669-1940, 777 Thurlow St) Most mains $20-25. For steaks, oysters, grilled fish and other traditional Northwest cooking, go to chummy Joe's.

Café Il Nido (☎ 604-685-6436, 780 Thurlow St) Lunch $12-16, dinner mains $15-32. Tucked into a leafy courtyard, this well-loved Italian restaurant cooks tempting pastas, as well as meat, fish and fowl entrées.

Cin Cin (☎ 604-688-7338, 1154 Robson St) Meals $16-40. Open for lunch Mon-Fri,

dinner daily. Cin Cin's beautiful Gaudi-esque circular stairway spirals up to the top-floor dining room, where prices for such one-of-a-kind dishes as octopus salad or honey-braised rabbit are only moderately extravagant.

O'Doul's (☎ 604-661-1400, **w** www.odouls restaurant.com, 1300 Robson St) Breakfast $4-10, lunch $7-17, dinner mains $21-35. Now into its third decade at the Listel Vancouver hotel, O'Doul's offers Asian-accented Pacific Rim cuisine. Seafood tapas and fine whiskeys are served until late at the sweeping 65-foot-long mahogany bar. Live jazz plays nightly.

West End & Stanley Park Close to Stanley Park, beware of touristy places. Farther south toward English Bay Beach, the choices and views just keep getting better.

Poncho's (☎ 604-683-7236, 835 Denman St) Dishes $10-14. Closed Mon. Try Poncho's for authentic Mexican dishes like carne a la tampiqueña (marinated beef).

Krishna Pure Vegetarian Restaurant (☎ 604-688-9400, 1726 Davie St) Buffet $7-10. Krishna offers a 35-item all-you-can-eat Indian buffet.

Brass Monkey (☎ 604-685-7626, 1072 Denman St) Mains $16-24. Open from 5pm daily. Adorned with hanging lamps, artwork and a large fireplace, this romantic neighborhood favorite offers a small menu of pasta and seafood, as well as ultra-hip house cocktails.

Delilah's (☎ 604-687-3424, 1789 Comox St) 2-/3-course dinner $24/32. Open from 5:30pm daily. The kitsch factor here will leave you speechless while you watch people odder and more famous than yourself down martinis from the city's original snazzy cocktail list.

Raincity Grill (☎ 604-685-7337, 1193 Denman St) Lunch $12-16, dinner $21-32. Raincity has time and again been voted the best West Coast cuisine in Vancouver. The service is friendly and unpretentious.

The Teahouse Restaurant (☎ 604-669-3281, 800-280-9893, Ferguson Point) Lunch $14-23, dinner $21-29. This gracious restaurant, hidden by a grove of Douglas fir, is the kind of place Vancouverites save for special occasions, especially since the terrace affords wonderful sunset views over the ships moored in English Bay. Innovative

West Coast cuisine focuses on fresh seafood draped in creative sauces.

Romano's Macaroni Grill (☎ 604-689-4334, 1523 Davie St) Meals $10-20. Set in a beautiful Queen Anne stone mansion, this Italian restaurant's bag of tricks includes opera singers, cooking exhibitions and pay-what-you-drink jugs of wine.

Yaletown & Around

Soup Etc (☎ 604-689-4505, 1091 Hamilton St) Soup combinations from $5. Open 7am-5pm daily. This sparkling clean joint serves up bowls of stews and soups with recipes from around the globe.

Urban Monks (☎ 604-669-1311, 328 Nelson St) Dishes $7-12. This young Yaletown café offers delightfully pure vegetarian cuisine.

Subeez Cafe (☎ 604-687-6107, 891 Homer St) Mains $9-13. Subeez counts artists and lofters among its regulars. Some come for the ultimate hangover cure: the $10 'Big-Ass Breakfast.'

Rodney's Oyster House (☎ 604-609-0080, 1228 Hamilton St) Rodney's offers up to 20 varieties of oysters from the east and west coasts. The service is informal – to say the least.

Brix (☎ 604-915-9463, 1138 Homer St) Lunch $9-12, dinner $15-24. Open 11:30am-2:30pm Mon-Fri, dinner from 5pm daily. Looking like the back streets of Paris, Brix bistro offers lamp-lit courtyard tables and imaginative food.

blue water (☎ 604-688-8078, 1095 Hamilton St) Set lunches $20-25, dinner mains $30. This high-concept seafood restaurant represents the pinnacle of Yaletown dining. Fresh fish entrées often come straight from Granville Island, while over a dozen kinds of oysters are flown in from the Gulf Islands, Atlantic Canada and France.

C (☎ 604-681-1164, Ⓦ www.crestaurant .com, 1600 Howe St) Dinner mains $24-35, 8-course tasting menu $85. Open 11:30am-2:30pm Mon-Fri & Sun, dinner 5:30pm-11pm daily. Nowhere is seafood prepared more adventurously than at the cutting-edge kitchens of C. On weekdays, the West Coast dim sum lunch ($18.50 per person, minimum two people) would be a bargain at twice the price.

Il Giardino (☎ 604-669-2422, 1382 Hornby St) Pastas $12-16, dinner entrées $30. Open noon-2:30pm Mon-Fri, 5:30pm-11pm Mon-Sat. The city's best Tuscan cooking is enlivened by fresh infusions of berries, local produce and wild game.

Joe's Grill (☎ 604-682-3683, 1031 Davie St) Meals $5-10. Joe's is the kind of diner they just don't make anymore, with items like two-egg breakfasts for $3.50 or burgers for $6. There's another location in Kitsilano (604-682-3683, 2061 W 4th Ave).

Stepho's Souvlaki (☎ 604-683-2555, 1124 Davie St) Dishes $8-12. This is a local Greek favorite, but come early as there's often a line to get in.

La Bodega (☎ 604-684-8814, 1277 Howe St) Tapas $3-8, mains $16. Open from 5pm daily. Vancouver's most authentic Spanish restaurant draws Spanish expats for tapas, paella and sangria.

Gastown & Chinatown

If you look hard, Gastown offers some delectable deals among the tourist traps. Most of Chinatown's restaurants take up residence along Pender St, while you'll find dirt-cheap cafeterias and diners on rough E Hastings St – if you can stomach the surroundings, that is.

Buddhist Vegetarian Restaurant (☎ 604-683-8816, 137 E Pender St) Items around $3. Meals under $12. This place serves deluxe vegetarian dishes and all-day dim sum.

The Gain Wah (☎ 604-684-1740, 218 Keefer St) Dishes from $4. Come here for dozens of varieties of congee and noodle soups.

The Only Seafood Restaurant (☎ 604-681-6546, 20 E Hastings St) Most dishes $8-11. Open 10am-8pm daily. In the same location since 1912 (look for the vintage neon seahorse), this tiny restaurant serves up great fresh seafood at reasonable prices.

The Irish Heather (☎ 604-688-9779, 217 Carrall St) Dishes $6-14. This bar not only pours the best Guinness in town, but also serves hearty Irish country fare.

Incendio (☎ 604-688-8694, 103 Columbia St) Pizzas $8-21. Open for lunch Mon-Fri, dinner daily. A refuge from the mean streets outside, this boldly painted Italian café makes its own wood-fired pizzas, calzones and gorgeous salads.

Water Street Café (☎ 604-689-2832, 300 Water St) Mains $13-23. Elegant Water Street Café serves up warm focaccia bread along with fresh pasta and seafood at streetside tables right in the center of Gastown.

The Alibi Room (☎ 604-623-3383, *157 Alexander St*) Dishes $7-18. The stylish fare at this film-industry hangout should win an Academy Award.

Granville Island Granville Island's *public market* (☎ 604-666-6477, *Johnston St; open 9am-6pm daily*) overflows with fresh fish, vegetables, fruit, meats, cheeses, fresh-baked goods and everything else you might need for a picnic.

The SandBar (☎ 604-669-9030, *1535 Johnston St*) Meals $11-18. At the stylish SandBar, over 1800 wines are ready to complement the seafood tapas or substantial Pacific Northwest cuisine offered at bargain prices.

Bridges (☎ 604-687-4400, *1696 Duranleau St*) Pub fare $9-15, dinner entrées $25-35, prix-fixe menu $50. On a warm summer evening, there's no place better than Bridges overlooking False Creek. Choose the casual bistro downstairs (over two dozen wines by the glass) or the more formal dining room upstairs.

West Side An international grab bag of inexpensive ethnic restaurants offers amazing $6 (or less!) lunchtime deals between Cambie and Granville Sts on West Broadway. This area is primarily a small Asian enclave.

Nice 'n Spicy Reggae Cafe (☎ 604-877-0189, *382 W Broadway*) Meals under $10. They make the tastiest Jamaican coco bun sandwiches ($3) and all-you-can-eat jerk chicken on Tuesday.

Bali (☎ 604-731-8281, *1016 W Broadway*) Mains $7-13. Bali keeps the true aromas and spicy flavors of the archipelago alive with indigenous and Dutch cooking.

Rasputin (☎ 604-879-6675, *457 W Broadway*) Mains $13-25. Start off with fresh Caspian Sea caviar, then feast on blinis, cabbage rolls and perhaps a little chicken Kiev.

Szechwan Chongqing Seafood Restaurant (☎ 604-734-2668, *1668 W Broadway*) Most dishes around $10. This Chinese favorite serves up searing-hot delicacies (mainly seafood, with a staggering 200 plus dishes on the menu).

Where Granville St meets West Broadway, you'll find plenty of creative upstarts and proven favorites.

Paul's Place (☎ 604-737-2587, *2211 Granville St*) Dishes $5-9. Open 8am-3pm Mon-Fri, 8am-4pm Sat & Sun. This perfect breakfast place has a short but sweet menu of hotcakes and omelets.

The Lazy Gourmet (☎ 604-734-2507, *1605 W 5th Ave*) Mains $8-10. Open 11:30am-3pm daily, 5:30pm-9:30pm Thur-Sat. This creative bistro turns everyday pizzas, burgers and salads into something special.

Adventurous new restaurants also keep popping up along South Main (also known as SoMa) and Cambie St.

Monsoon (☎ 604-879-4001, *2526 Main St*) Dishes $3-13. Hip Monsoon's pan-Asian menu draws heavily from the subcontinent: Try the Indian-spiced fries with hot banana chutney or chai brulee for dessert. There's a cool hipster coffeehouse, *SoMa*, next door.

Vij's (☎ 604-736-6664, *1480 W 11th Ave*) Mains $17-24. Dinner from 5pm daily. The star of Indian cuisine in Vancouver, modern Vij's doesn't take reservations. But with food so excellent and lotus ponds out front, it's hard to complain about the wait.

Ouest (☎ 604-738-8938, *2881 Granville St*) Mains $23-36. Open from 5:30pm daily. With an awards list longer than the waiter's apron, Ouest looks as sophisticated as it tastes. Changing menu selections focus on contemporary French cuisine with West Coast stylings, and over 3000 bottles of wine line the walls.

Tojo's (☎ 604-872-8050, *Suite 202, 777 W Broadway*) Mains $12-20. Open 5pm-10:30pm Mon-Sat. Tojo's has no competition when it comes to sushi, or views of downtown Vancouver after dark. Expect to spend about $75 for a seat at the sushi bar, where one simply surrenders to Tojo's mastery of seasonal ingredients and fresh seafood.

Seasons in the Park (☎ 604-874-8008, *800-632-9422, Cambie St at W 33rd Ave*) Lunch $13-22, dinner entrées $17-28. Open 11am-2:30pm Mon-Fri, dinner from 5:30pm daily. Set amid the gardens of Bloedel Conservatory in Queen Elizabeth Park, with the North Shore mountains as a backdrop, this restaurant has hosted world leaders. Make reservations to enjoy the zesty Pacific Northwest cuisine, such as Chilean sea bass in a prickly pear sauce or rack of lamb marinated with a martini.

Kitsilano *Deserts (1935 Cornwall Ave)* Dishes under $5. This Middle Eastern vegetarian take-out joint makes its own spinach pies, falafel pita sandwiches and racks of honeyed sweets.

Flying Wedge Pizza (☎ 604-732-8840, 1937 Cornwall Ave) Slices $4. It's possibly Vancouver's best thick-crust pizza, and slices may feature anything from vegetarian pesto to honey-curried chicken.

Annapurna (☎ 604-736-5959, 1812 W 4th Ave) Meals $8-13. This vegetarian Indian restaurant is full of great surprises, including nearly a hundred glowing paper lanterns hanging from the ceiling.

The Naam (☎ 604-738-7151, 2724 W 4th Ave) Dishes $3.50-10. Open 24 hours. A relic of Kitsilano's hippie past, this vegetarian health-food restaurant has the charm of a big old farm kitchen. Live guitar music – including folk, jazz, classical and flamenco – is presented nightly, which is good because lines tend to be long and the service unhurried.

Greens & Gourmet (☎ 604-737-7373, 2681 W Broadway) Buffet dishes $1.59/100g. Open 11am-10pm daily. Vegetarians (and vegans) enjoy flavor-friendly buffet dishes, as well as non-dairy desserts and a separate breakfast menu.

Nat's New York Pizzeria (☎ 604-737-0707, 2684 W Broadway) Slices $4. Closed Sun. Thin-crust pizza lovers, rejoice. Nat's does the real thing.

Roti Bistro (☎ 604-730-9906, 1958 W 4th Ave) Meals $6-12. True West Indian roti is hard to come by in Vancouver, but not here. Chairs are few, but great Caribbean music plays while you wait for your jerk chicken and pone.

Taka Sushi (☎ 604-734-4990, 2059 W 4th Ave) Dishes $3-19. Open 5pm-11pm Tues-Sun. This stylish sushi bar rarely has a seat to spare.

Las Margaritas (☎ 604-734-7117, 1999 W 4th Ave) Lunch $8-14, dinner entrées $11.50-17. This Mexican cantina's patio often overflows with people drinking sangria.

Nyala Restaurant (☎ 604-731-7899, 2930 W 4th Ave) Dishes $8-13. Vegetarian buffet adult/child $11/6 Mon. Open from 5pm daily and Sunday lunch. Richly spiced Ethiopian food eaten with *injera* (flatbread) is finished off with a traditional coffee ceremony. Occasionally there's live world music.

Tangerine (☎ 604-739-4677, 1685 Yew St) Dishes $6-15. Open from 5pm Tues-Sun, weekend brunch 9am-3pm. Tangerine is a cool underground lounge with a fusion tapas menu that never bores.

Acropol (☎ 604-733-2412, 2946 W Broadway) Mains $13-18. Combination platters $35-40. Open 11:30am-11:30pm Mon-Sat. Relax with a decanter of wine while breezes blow by the outdoor tables at this elegant little taverna.

Montri's Thai Restaurant (☎ 604-738-9888, 3629 W Broadway) Meals $10-15. Open for dinner daily. Perhaps the city's best Thai restaurant, Montri's offers superb pad thai and a deft range of curries.

Bishop's (☎ 604-738-2025, ⓦ www .bishopsonline.com, 2183 W 4th Ave) Mains $28-36. Open from 5:30pm daily. John Bishop has cooked for celebrities and visiting diplomats. His menu at this intimate dining room mingles Thai, Chinese, French and Italian cuisine – all with absolutely fresh ingredients, strong yet complementary flavors and ingenious presentation. Service is flawless, and the man himself often ushers guests in the door.

Lumiere (☎ 604-739-8185, 2551 W Broadway) 4-course tasting menus $55-75, plus $40 for wine. Open from 5:30pm daily. One of the most highly regarded restaurants in Canada, Lumiere embraces a kind of French-fusion cooking that takes the best of world cuisine and drapes it in wonderful sauces.

Punjabi Market This Indian neighborhood – complete with street signs in Punjabi – runs south along Main St from E 48th to E 51st Aves.

Zeenaz Restaurant (☎ 604-324-9344, 6460 Main St) Veg/nonveg buffet $8/10. Closed Tues. You can also select items off the regular menu for around $12, but with a smorgasbord as good as this one, why bother?

All India Sweets & Restaurant (☎ 604-327-0891, 6505 Main St) Buffet $6. Not to be outdone, this place sets out a 45-item all-you-can-eat vegetarian buffet with endless trays of Indian sweets.

Lonsdale Quay *Cheshire Cheese Inn (☎ 604-987-3322, level 2, Lonsdale Quay Market, 4585 Dunbar St)* Meals $6-12. This cozy pub offers traditional British fare like bangers and mash at unbeatable prices.

Thai House Restaurant (☎ 604-987-9911, *180 W Esplanade*) Dishes around $10. Lunch buffet Sat & Sun $7.50. Uphill from Lonsdale Quay, the lovely premises here feature hand-cut wood posts and floor-to-ceiling windows.

Gusti di Quattro (☎ 604-924-4444, *1 Lonsdale Ave*) Dinner mains $15-28, chef's tasting menu $55. Open 11:30am-2:30pm Mon-Fri, dinner from 5pm daily. This nouvelle Italian nook is breathtakingly romantic.

West Vancouver *Beach Side Café* (☎ 604-925-1945, *1362 Marine Dr*) Lunch $8-15, dinner $15-33. This West Van hideaway offers an excellent wine list and a wealth of Pacific Northwest–style seafood, as well as views of the marina off a heated outdoor deck.

Beach House at Dundarave Pier (☎ 604-922-1414, *150 25th St*) Lunch $12-18, dinner $17-30. Set in the sands with spectacular views of the downtown lights across the water, the Beach House takes West Coast seafood and creatively adds berries, citrus and fresh herbs.

Salmon House on the Hill (☎ 604-926-3212, *2229 Folkestone Way*) Lunch $10-15, dinner $23-28. The Salmon House ranks among Vancouver's finest culinary experiences, especially with all the city lying at your feet. First Nations art sets off the Pacific Northwest cuisine beautifully.

Entertainment

The best source for arts and nightlife coverage is *The Georgia Straight,* a free weekly newspaper widely available around town. Tickets for many concerts and other performances are available through Ticketmaster (☎ 604-280-3311, **W** www.ticketmaster.ca).

Performing Arts For an up-to-date performing-arts schedule, call the Arts Hotline (☎ 604-684-2787, **W** www.alliance forarts.com).

Ballet British Columbia (☎ 604-732-5003, **W** www.balletbc.com) Vancouver's top dance troupe performs at the Queen Elizabeth Theatre (see Theater, below). The season runs September to June.

Vancouver Opera (☎ 604-683-0222, **W** www.vanopera.bc.ca) The city's opera company stages four annual productions at the Queen Elizabeth Theatre between October and May.

Vancouver Symphony Orchestra (☎ 604-876-3434) The symphony performs at the *Orpheum Theatre* (☎ 604-665-3050, *884 Granville St*).

Theater Theater, from mainstream to fringe, flourishes in Vancouver. The main performance season runs fall through spring. The Greater Vancouver Professional Theatre Alliance (☎ 604-608-6799, **W** communicopia.net/services/calendar1) publishes a quarterly theater guide.

Vancouver Playhouse (☎ 604-873-3311, *600 Hamilton St*) At the Vancouver Playhouse, part of the Queen Elizabeth Theatre complex, the Vancouver Playhouse Theatre Company showcases original Canadian and international works.

Firehall Arts Centre (☎ 604-689-0926, **W** www.firehall.org, *280 E Cordova St*) Inside a historic fire station, this intimate venue is home to local theater, dance and cultural arts groups.

Vancouver Little Theatre (☎ 604-876-4165, *3102 Main St*) This tiny place stages bold new experimental, often controversial productions and improv.

Arts Club Theatre (☎ 604-687-1644, **W** www.artsclub.com) Famous for its 'talk back' matinees, this theater company gave Michael J Fox and many other Canadian actors their starts. It has two main stages: the *Granville Island Stage* (*1585 Johnston St*) and the refurbished 1930s *Stanley Theatre* (*2750 Granville St*).

Performance Works (☎ 604-606-6425, *1218 Cartwright St*) This multipurpose venue in a converted warehouse puts together the electrifying Kiss Project each February. Check the Web site **W** www.dancearts.bc.ca/kiss.htm for details.

Waterfront Theatre (☎ 604-685-1731, *1410 Cartwright St*) Local theater companies perform new works by BC playwrights here on Granville Island.

Live Music From mild to wild – live music is everywhere in Vancouver.

Piccadilly Pub (☎ 604-682-3221, *620 W Pender St*) The Pic books local rock and blues bands almost nightly.

Railway Club (☎ 604-681-1625, *579 Dunsmuir St*) The Railway hosts local songwriters and musicians and offers jams every Saturday afternoon.

The Commodore (☎ 604-739-4550, 868 Granville St) Up-and-coming local bands know they've made it when they play the old Commodore Ballroom, now managed by the House of Blues group.

The rough Lower East Side is a breeding ground for punk, hard-core metal and the extreme alternative scene, especially at *The Cobalt* (☎ 604-255-2088, 917 Main St) and *The Brickyard* (☎ 604-685-3922, 315 Carrall St).

For a complete list of jazz and blues venues, call the Coastal Jazz & Blues Society (☎ 604-872-5200, W www.jazzvancouver.com).

The Yale (☎ 604-681-9253, 1300 Granville St) The entry to this great blues bar is adorned with photos of Koko Taylor, Junior Wells and other stars who've played here.

Fairview Pub (☎ 604-872-1262, 898 W Broadway) Inside this dimly lit pub at the Ramada, local blues and jazz bands take the stage nightly.

Cellar Jazz Café (☎ 604-738-1959, W www.cellarjazz.com, 3611 W Broadway) Open Wed-Sat. This underground club showcases great local jazz.

Kino Cafe (☎ 604-875-1998, 3456 Cambie St) Flamenco, rumba, salsa and Latin jazz find a home here.

Dance Clubs For current club listings, tune into 'The Fox' 99.3 FM or 'Zed' 95.3 FM. Savvy clubbers can print out free VIP passes (no line, no cover) at W www.clubvibes.com.

The downtown area has a number of happening spots.

BaBaLu (☎ 604-605-4343, 654 Nelson St) Open Wed-Sat. BaBaLu is the city's slickest Latin club, so feel free to salsa away, martini in hand, or drop by the Cuban cigar lounge.

Richard's on Richards (☎ 604-687-6794, 1036 Richards St) Vancouver's longest-running dance venue is still alive and bursting at the seams with lithe young divas and gangsta wanna-bes.

Wett Bar (☎ 604-662-7707, 1320 Richards St) Open Wed-Sat. More visually stimulating than all the other downtown clubs put together – think hot dancing in an aquamarine aquarium.

Element Sound Lounge (☎ 604-669-0806, 801 W Georgia St) Open Wed-Sun. A svelte basement lounge featuring a mix of trip hop, tribal, sexy and soulful house. The enormous gilt mirror behind the bar

Vancover rocks!

is perfect for catching that alluring stranger's eye.

The Purple Onion (☎ 604-602-9442, 15 Water St) Alcoves at this split-level club/lounge in Gastown have sheltered stars like Harry Connick Jr and Benicio del Toro.

Sonar (☎ 604-683-6695, 66 Water St) In Gastown, this is the city's premier club for experimental DJs and live club shows from all over the globe. On any given night you may find progressive house, jazz fusion, soul, hip-hop, reggae or perhaps electronica.

Shine (☎ 604-408-4321, 364 Water St) Open Tues-Sun. Some call this Vancouver's sexiest club. An elite crowd grooves to funk, deep house and live hip-hop at this Gastown spot.

Chivana (☎ 604-733-0330, 2340 W 4th Ave) This sleek resto-lounge in Kitsilano stays open late, making it almost irresistible for drinks or Asian-Cuban tapas out on the balcony.

Gay & Lesbian Venues Take a look at the listings in *Xtra! West* for pub and club venues. A good place to start is Davie St, Vancouver's rainbow flag district.

The Fountainhead Pub (☎ 604-687-2222, 1025 Davie St) It's just the 'local,' but many people start the night off here on the patio.

Numbers (☎ 604-685-4077, 1042 Davie St) This intense multilevel men's cruise bar has a few pool tables and strict bouncers.

Odyssey (☎ 604-689-5256, W www .theodysseynightclub.com, 1251 Howe St) Near Davie St, this long-running dance space has a reputation for being the wildest gay men's nightclub.

Dufferin Hotel (☎ *604-683-4251, 900 Seymour St*) Skip the go-go boys, but come for drag karaoke.

Lotus Hotel (☎ *604-685-7777, 455 Abbott St*) Upstairs the new ***Milk Bar*** and ***Honey Lounge*** are particular faves for FlyGirl! DJ nights.

Bars & Pubs Almost all bars and pubs are open daily, with last call heard sometime between midnight and 2am.

The Lennox Pub (☎ *604-408-0881, 800 Granville St*) Poised at a coveted intersection of Granville and Robson, this sleek pub keeps a few Belgian beers on tap.

Naked (☎ *604-609-2700, 432 Richards St*) This sexy lounge has an eye-catching wrought-iron fence covering the window-ledge patio. The crowd is young and savvy.

Bacchus (☎ *604-689-7777, 845 Hornby St*) In the Wedgewood Hotel, this decadent lounge has a heady air of sophistication and nightly jazz piano.

900 West (☎ *604-684-3131, 900 W Georgia St*) At the Hotel Vancouver, who can resist sinking into plush lounge chairs like these? Dashingly dressed patrons eye the stellar wine list (or perhaps the torch singer).

Yaletown Brewing Co (☎ *604-681-2719, 1111 Mainland St*) This classic brewpub has an enormous patio, pool tables and a casual crowd enjoying the fine microbrews.

Cardero's Marine Pub (☎ *604-669-7666, 1583 Coal Harbour Quay*) Cardero's juts out over the West End waterfront, in between the yachts. At night you can drink in the North Shore lights.

Balthazar (☎ *689-8822, 1215 Bidwell St*) Flaming torches lead the way into this West End fin-de-siècle resto-lounge, where well-heeled locals rejuvenate with Mediterranean food and blood-red wine.

Steamworks Brewing Company (☎ *604-689-2739, 375 Water St*) In Gastown, admire the tall wooden timbers inside Vancouver's outstanding original brewpub, where you can play pool or lounge by the fireplace. Outside on the patio the scent of hops mixes with the inlet breezes.

The Irish Heather (☎ *604-688-9779, 217 Carrall St*) This Gastown pub pours the best Guinness in town and offers excellent Irish country fare and live music most weekdays.

The Alibi Room (☎ *604-623-3383, 157 Alexander St*) This is where the city's film-makers and Hollywood stars hang out. Deep house, jazz and R&B DJs spin in the underground lounge while upstairs there's amazing food.

The Cambie (☎ *604-684-6466, 300 Cambie St*) At the seamy edge of Gastown, the Cambie International Hostel's outdoor picnic tables overflow with folks from all walks of life who come for good conversation and cheap pitchers of beer.

Backstage Lounge (☎ *604-687-1354, 1585 Johnston St*) On Granville Island, this breezy deck overlooking False Creek features live music almost nightly, buskers outside during the day and a variety of local beers on tap (Granville Island Brewery is just down the street).

Sailor Hagar's Brewpub (☎ *604-984-7669, 86 Semisch Ave*) A short walk uphill from Lonsdale Quay, this popular brewpub offers good views of the city skyline, over a half dozen beers on tap and plenty of good pub grub.

Rusty Gull (☎ *604-988-5585, 175 E 1st St*) Reminiscent of a well-kept pub in Dublin or Boston, the Rusty Gull pleases patrons with both its beer and food menus. A tiny heated back patio at this North Shore spot commands major views of downtown Vancouver and the shipyards.

The Raven Public House (☎ *604-929-3834, 1052 Deep Cove Rd*) If you've been for a stroll along Malcolm Lowry's Walk in Cates Park, come here and pay your respects to the great man, who was known to enjoy a drink or two himself. There are 26 beers on tap, reputedly excellent food and a toasty fireplace.

Cinemas Off-beat and independent film festivals, such as ***Cinemuerte*** (Ⓦ *www.cinemuerte.com*) and ***Out on Screen*** (Ⓦ *www.outonscreen.com*), pop up year-round here. For information on the Vancouver Film Festival, see Special Events.

Capitol 6 (☎ *604-669-6000, 820 Granville St*) This central cinema's Theatre One can seat up to 1000 people on star-studded opening nights, but skip the upstairs theaters, which have small screens and narrow seats.

CN IMAX Theatre (☎ *604-682-4629, 201-999 Canada Place*) Adult/child $10.50/8.50. On the waterfront at Canada Place, this IMAX cinema offers a 'make-your-own-double-feature' option: See any two shows on the same day and get the second ticket half-price.

Pacific Cinémathèque (☎ 604-688-3456, W *www.cinematheque.bc.ca, 1131 Howe St*) Annual membership $6 (required). First movie $3.25 (regularly $6.50). Double features $7.50. This nonprofit repertory cinema is like an ongoing film festival.

Denman Place Discount Cinema (☎ 604-683-2201, *1737 Comox St*) This West End second-run theater shows three films for $3 on Tuesday.

Cinemark Tinseltown (☎ 604-806-0799, *88 W Pender St*) Vancouver's most technically advanced first-run cinema has giant screens, stadium seating and underground validated parking.

Blinding Light (☎ 604-684-8288, W *www .blindinglight.com, 36 Powell St*) Annual membership (required) $3. All seats $5. Serious film junkies flock to this 100-seat lounge cinema for cutting-edge glimpses of the avant-garde, the underground or the just plain weird.

Van East Cinema (☎ 604-299-9000 ext 3278, *2290 Commercial Dr*) Tues $2.50. This balconied theater shows an eclectic schedule of critically acclaimed new and classic films.

Fifth Avenue Cinemas (☎ 604-734-7469, *2110 Burrard St*) Vancouver's premier art house shows foreign films and indie favorites.

Ridge Theatre (☎ 604-738-6311, *3131 Arbutus St*) Double features $3-5, seniors free Mon. This neighborhood second-run theater has double-bill pairings that are often hilariously tongue-in-cheek.

Comedy Clubs ***Yuk Yuk's*** (☎ 604-687-5233, *750 Pacific Blvd*) Cover Tue-Thur $5, Fri-Sat $10. Stand-up comics from across North America perform here.

TheatreSports (☎ 604-738-7013) Tickets $8-14.50. This wildly popular improv group performs on Granville Island's ***New Revue Stage*** (*1585 Johnston St*).

Spectator Sports
Owned by the major-league Oakland A's, the Vancouver Canadians (☎ 604-872-5232, W www.canadiansbaseball.com) play single-A baseball at ***Nat Bailey Stadium*** (*4601 Ontario St*), beside Queen Elizabeth Park. The season runs from June to September. Tickets cost $7 to $10.50. Take bus No 3 south on Main St to E 30th Ave.

Winners of the 2001 Grey Cup championship, the BC Lions (☎ 604-589-7627, W www.bclions.com) play CFL football from June to November at ***BC Place Stadium*** (*777 Pacific Blvd*). Tickets are $13.50 to $45.

The Vancouver Canucks (☎ 604-899-4625) of the National Hockey League (NHL) play at ***GM Place*** (*800 Griffiths Way*). Tickets run $38 to $75. The season lasts from October to April.

Shopping
On **Robson St**, the busiest shopping street and a major hangout and people-watching area, you can buy everything from couture to condoms, from Italian newspapers to fresh crab. The trendiest section is between Burrard and Jervis Sts. Even if you don't find what you were looking for, you won't be bored.

The other major focus for downtown shopping is Pacific Centre, which runs from Robson to Pender Sts between Granville and Howe Sts. Most of the stores are national and international chains; the major department-store anchor is ***Eatons***, and the Hudson's Bay Company – ***The Bay*** – is just a block south.

If you like furniture, home furnishings and interior decorating, Yaletown is a good place to check out. The old warehouse-district-gone-lofts is loaded with stylish design shops.

Try looking around the Gastown area for First Nations art.

Inuit Gallery of Vancouver (☎ 604-688-7323, *206 Cambie St*) Some of the foremost collections of Inuit and Northwest Coast art are found in this government-licensed gallery. Crafts are also sold at its sister shop, ***Images for a Canadian Heritage*** (☎ 604-685-7046, *164 Water St*).

Hill's Native Art (☎ 604-685-4249, *165 Water St*) Begun in 1946 as a small trading post on Vancouver Island, Hill's flagship store has many carvings, prints, ceremonial masks, cozy Cowichan sweaters, traditional music and books of historical interest. Artists are often found at work in the 3rd-floor gallery.

Next to Robson St, there's nowhere else in Vancouver more fun to shop than Granville Island. Merchants at the ***public market*** (☎ 604-666-6477, *Johnston St; open 9am-6pm* *daily)* sell fancy jams, syrups and other preserved foods that make good gifts; the fishmongers can pack fish for air shipment.

Granville Island blooms with high-quality craft shops, especially clustered around the Net Loft building.

Crafthouse (☎ 604-687-7270, **w** www.cabc .net, *1386 Cartwright St)* This nonprofit art gallery run by the Crafts Association of British Columbia (CABC) keeps schedules of provincial craft shows.

Both Broadway and W 4th Ave are lined with shops, many reflecting both the area's old hippie past and its hip, upscale present. However, for a concentrated shot of shopping, go to South Granville, across the Granville Bridge from downtown, between W 4th Ave to W 16th Ave. In many ways a microcosm of Vancouver, you'll find high-end boutiques, Asian groceries, art galleries and antique stores.

West Broadway has a lot of outdoor stores.

Mountain Equipment Co-op (☎ *604-872-7858, 130 W Broadway)* You just about need overnight gear to get around Canada's largest outdoor-equipment store. MEC is a hip, ecologically sensitive company with an in-house line of backcountry gear. You must pay the $5 lifetime membership fee to make a purchase.

Getting There & Away

Vancouver is Canada's Pacific gateway to Asia, the Pacific Northwest and the Americas. It boasts an international airport, three seaplane terminals, a helicopter terminal and a large train and bus station close to the city center.

Air Vancouver International Airport (YVR; ☎ 604-207-7077, **w** www.yvr.ca) is 13km south of the city center in Richmond. The main airport has two terminals: international and domestic. Most major airlines offer flights to Vancouver. For information on airlines serving Canada, see the Getting There & Away chapter of the book.

The extensive facilities include tourist information counters on each level (where you can be assisted in 10 languages), foreign currency exchange kiosks, ATMs, six Royal Bank branches and three full-service spas.

The smaller Airport South Terminal, off Inglis Dr, handles regional airlines and floatplanes. To get to it take bus No 425 from Airport Station or take a taxi, as it's definitely too far to walk.

For information about getting to/from the airport, see the Getting Around section.

If you are on a flight leaving Vancouver to destinations in BC or the Yukon, the departure fee is $5; to other destinations in Canada, the USA (including Hawaii) or Mexico the fee is $10; and to all other international destinations the fee is $15. Children under the age of two and passengers connecting with other flights on the same day are exempt. This tax is not included with the ticket price and must be paid at the airport booths or automatic ticket sales machines.

Seaplane Harbour Air Seaplanes (☎ 604-688-1277, **w** www.harbour-air.com) offers regularly scheduled seaplane flights to the Southern Gulf Islands ($74 one-way) and to Victoria ($99 one-way) and Nanaimo ($54 one-way) on Vancouver Island. The company's Vancouver Harbour terminal is on Coal Harbour Rd about a block west of Canada Place.

Bus The bus station is part of Pacific Central Station, 1150 Station St, southeast of the city center, and here you'll find Greyhound, Pacific Coach Lines and Malaspina Coach Lines.

Greyhound (☎ 604-482-8747) links Vancouver with Seattle and other US cities, as well as points east and north in Canada. Greyhound does not have service to Victoria but does travel to Nanaimo ($12, including the ferry); 3½ hours). Some other examples of one-way fares (including tax) from Vancouver are Banff ($105, 14 hours), Calgary ($123, 15 hours), Jasper ($105, 12 hours), Kamloops ($50, five hours), Kelowna ($55, six hours), Prince George ($96, 13 hours), Squamish ($8.25, 1¼ hours), Whistler ($20, 2½ hours) and Whitehorse ($315, 45 hours). Children under 11 travel for half-price.

Pacific Coach Lines (☎ 604-662-8074) has daily services to Victoria, leaving the bus station every hour at 15 minutes to the hour from 5:45am to 8:45pm. The one-way fare (including ferry) is $28 from Pacific Central or $32 from Vancouver International Airport. From Pacific Central the journey takes about three hours. The bus will pick up on its route along Cambie St, but reservations are required.

Malaspina Coach Lines (☎ 877-227-8287) has two services a day to the Sunshine Coast. Sample one-way fares, which include the ferry, are: Gibsons Landing ($15.25, 1¾ hours), Sechelt ($18.50, 2¼ hours) and Powell River ($30, 5¼ hours).

Perimeter (☎ 604-266-5386) operates a shuttle between Vancouver International Airport and Whistler for a one-way fare of $53/30 adult/child (five to 11).

Quick Coach Lines (☎ 604-940-4428) operates a daily shuttle to downtown Seattle for $34 one-way; the bus also makes stops at Seattle's Sea-Tac airport ($44).

You can also catch a TransLink city bus to White Rock, close to the US border. Take bus No 351, 352 or 354 south on Granville St.

Bigfoot Adventure Tours/Moose Travel Network (☎ 888-244-6673, W www.bigfoot tours.com) runs funky multiday bus tours that schedule time for outdoor activities and stop overnight at hostels (accommodations costs aren't included in the tour prices). Available tours (most offered April to November) include a four-day jaunt around Vancouver Island with stops in Victoria, Tofino and Nanaimo and opportunities for hiking, kayaking, whale-watching and bungy jumping ($205); two-day ($100) and six-day ($280) one-way tours to Banff; a six-day loop to Banff and Jasper and back ($287); and a grand 10-day loop through western Canada ($373) that includes Whistler, Kamloops, Valemount, Jasper, Banff, Revelstoke and Kelowna (you can pause at any stop and rejoin the next bus one week later). The company also runs shuttles from Vancouver to Seattle ($32 one-way, $59 roundtrip) and to Whistler in ski season (November to April; $27 one-way, $49 roundtrip).

Train Trains operating out of Vancouver travel across the country, to the Rockies, through the province or into the USA.

Vancouver is the western terminus for VIA Rail. The magnificent Pacific Central Station is off Main St at 1150 Station St, between National and Terminal Aves. For 24-hour information on train fares and reservations call ☎ 888-842-7245, or visit W www.viarail.ca. The ticket office is open daily. The luggage storage room is open 8:30am to 5pm Tuesday, Friday and Sunday.

The VIA Rail route east goes through Kamloops, Jasper and Edmonton. Trains leave Tuesday, Friday and Sunday at 5pm. Stopovers are permitted but you must reserve again.

Amtrak (☎ 800-872-7245) connects Vancouver to Seattle with one train daily leaving Pacific Central Station at 6pm. In addition, Amtrak runs three buses a day from Vancouver to Seattle. The one-way train or bus fare ranges from US$25 to US$34.

The privately owned Rocky Mountaineer Railtours trains travel through some of the country's most scenic landscapes from BC to Banff and Calgary (VIA Rail does not provide service along this route). This isn't really a service for people just trying to get from place to place, unless you have a lot of money to spend. Most tickets come with accommodations (there's an obligatory overnight stay in Kamloops) and meals, with more extensive packages available on both the Vancouver and Alberta ends. The summer-season fare from Vancouver to Banff, Jasper or Calgary is $720; a basic four-day package runs $999.

The services run from mid-April to mid-October. For information contact a travel agent or Rocky Mountaineer Railtours (☎ 800-665-7245, W www.rockymountaineer .com), 130-1150 Station St, in Pacific Central Station.

British Columbia has its own railway system, BC Rail (☎ 604-984-5246, 800-663-8238), which operates the *Cariboo Prospector* from North Vancouver to Squamish, Whistler, Lillooet, 100 Mile House, Williams Lake, Quesnel and Prince George, where it connects with VIA Rail. One train leaves daily at 7am with service as far as Whistler and Lillooet; the one-way fare to Whistler is $39/35/23/8 adult/senior/child/infant, and the trip takes about 2½ hours (the train departs Whistler for North Vancouver at 6:10pm). Three days a week – Sunday, Wednesday and Friday – the train continues on to Prince George; one-way fare to Prince George is $212/191/127/43 and the trip takes about 13 hours. Reservations are required.

Trains leave from North Vancouver, at BC Rail Station, 1311 W 1st St, at the southern end of Pemberton Ave. To get to the station take bus No 239 west from the SeaBus terminal at Lonsdale Quay. During the summer, from June 4 to October 28,

TransLink operates one shuttle bus ($2.50) a day to the station, leaving Pacific Central Station at 6:05am with pickups along W Georgia St.

Car & Motorcycle If you are coming from the USA (Washington State) you'll be on US I-5 until the border town of Blaine, then on Canada Hwy 99. It's about an hour's drive from the border to the city center. Hwy 99 continues through downtown Vancouver, over Lions Gate Bridge and north by way of the Upper Levels Hwy (Hwys 1 & 99) to Horseshoe Bay, Squamish, Whistler and beyond.

If you're coming from the east, you'll almost certainly be on the Trans Canada Hwy (Hwy 1), which snakes through the city's eastern end, eventually meeting with Hastings St. It continues over the Iron Workers Memorial Second Narrows Bridge to North Vancouver and eventually on to West Vancouver (where it also becomes Hwy 99) and Horseshoe Bay. If you want to go downtown, turn left onto Hastings St and follow it into the city center.

If you are coming from Horseshoe Bay in the north, the Trans Canada Hwy (Hwy 1) heads through West Vancouver and North Vancouver before going over the Second Narrows Bridge into Burnaby. If you're heading downtown, leave the highway at the Taylor Way exit in West Vancouver (it's also a part of Hwy 99) and follow it over the Lions Gate Bridge into Stanley Park and into the city center.

Ferry BC Ferries (☎ 888-223-3779, 1112 Fort St, Victoria, BC V8V 4V2, ⓦ www .bcferries.com) operates the ferry routes in BC's coastal waters. Two main routes link greater Vancouver with Vancouver Island: Tsawwassen (about an hour's drive south of Vancouver city center) to Swartz Bay (a 30-minute drive north of Victoria), and Horseshoe Bay (a 30-minute drive north of Vancouver city center) to Nanaimo. From Tsawwassen, ferries also go to Nanaimo and the Gulf Islands. From Horseshoe Bay, ferries also go to Bowen Island and the Sunshine Coast.

During the summer months there are hourly sailings from 7am to 10pm between the mainland and Vancouver Island. The rest of the year it's usually every two hours,

except during holidays. The crossing takes 90 minutes to two hours. Friday evening, Sunday afternoon and evening, and Monday holidays are the busiest times, and if you have a car there is often a one- or two-ferry wait. To avoid long delays it's worth planning your crossing for less busy times.

The one-way fare on all mainland-to-Vancouver Island routes in the summer, or peak season (end of June to the middle of September), is $9.50/4.75 adult/child (five to 11), $33.50 for a car (driver not included), $54.50 for a vehicle over 7ft high and up to 20ft long, $16.75 for a motorcycle (or $25.25 if it has a sidecar and/or trailer), $2.50 for a bicycle and $4 for a kayak or canoe. These rates are slightly lower if you travel midweek (Monday to noon Friday, unless one of these days is a public holiday) and are substantially lower in the winter, or low season.

To get to Tsawwassen by city bus, catch the southbound bus No 601 (South Delta), from either Howe St or from the corner of Granville St and W 4th Ave, to the Ladner Exchange. From the exchange take bus No 640 (Tsawwassen Ferry) to the ferry terminal. A quicker way is to catch the SkyTrain to Scott Road Station and there catch bus No 640. The fare either way is $1.75, or $3.50 if you travel in peak traffic time. From Swartz Bay you can take bus No 70 into Victoria. To get to the Horseshoe Bay ferry terminal from Vancouver take the West Vancouver Blue Bus No 250 or 257 (Horseshoe Bay) northbound on W Georgia St. The bus stops in front of The Bay department store, between Granville and Seymour Sts.

Getting Around

To/From The Airport The quickest option is the Vancouver Airporter bus (☎ 604-946-8866), which runs to/from Pacific Central Station and all major central hotels for $12/9/5/24 adult/senior/child age six to 12/family; roundtrip prices are $18/17/10/36 with no time limit. Purchase tickets from the airport ticket office, the driver or from the hotels. Buses run every 30 minutes between about 6am and midnight.

By city bus, take the 98 B-Line, which starts at Waterfront Station then travels along Burrard, Howe and Granville Sts to the Airport Station. The buses are wheelchair-accessible and have bike racks. Total travel time is about 35 minutes and the fare is $1.75 ($3.50 during peak traffic time). You need exact change.

A taxi from the airport to the city center takes about 25 minutes and costs around $35.

Public Transportation Vancouver's public transit service, TransLink (☎ 604-521-0400, W www.translink.bc.ca), administers the operation of buses, the SkyTrain light-rail system and SeaBus passenger ferries. Fares range $1.75 to $3.50, depending on distance traveled and time of day.

The fare is good for travel on buses, the SkyTrain and the SeaBus and is valid for 90 minutes from time of purchase. Service on most routes ends at about 1am daily.

If you start your journey on a bus, be sure to get a transfer from the driver as proof of payment. Before boarding the SkyTrain or SeaBus purchase a ticket from machines in the terminal/station; they accept coins, $5 and $10 bills; return change; and will issue a fare receipt automatically (which serves as a transfer).

DayPasses good for one day's unlimited travel cost $7 for adults. Get them at SeaBus terminals, SkyTrain stations or shops displaying the 'FareDealer' sign. You can also save money by purchasing a book of 10 'FareSaver Tickets.'

The *Transportation Services Guide for Greater Vancouver* is a map showing the bus, SkyTrain and SeaBus routes, plus information on fares and schedules. It costs $1.50 and is sold at convenience stores and bookstores.

The wheelchair-accessible SkyTrain connects downtown Vancouver with Burnaby, New Westminster and Surrey. Trains depart downtown's Waterfront Station about every three to five minutes, and a trip to King George Station at the other end takes about 40 minutes.

The SeaBus catamarans zip back and forth across Burrard Inlet between Waterfront Station and Lonsdale Quay in North Vancouver. The two 400-passenger ferries take about 12 minutes to make the trip; a worthwhile journey if only for the fabulous views. The ferries are wheelchair accessible and take bicycles at no extra charge.

Car & Motorcycle Congestion is a big problem, especially along the city's bridges (probably best avoided during weekday rush hours). Few downtown streets have left-turn signals, and traffic can back up for blocks during peak traffic hours. Most of the north-south streets in city center are one-way, Burrard St being the exception.

Metered parking downtown is difficult to find and usually short-term, costing around $2 an hour. In lots or garages the rate is about $3.75 an hour or $10 a day. Many downtown hotels provide parking to guests.

Generally the daily rate for car rental starts at around $35 a day for a small car, but if you rent by the weekend, week or month, it'll cost less. Weekend rates are often the cheapest and can include three or even four days.

Check the Yellow Pages for a complete listing of car rental companies. Following is a small selection with their downtown addresses and an example of starting daily rates:

Budget
☎ 604-668-7000, 800-268-8900
501 W Georgia St; $34

Enterprise
☎ 800-736-8222
585 Smithe St; $35

Hertz
☎ 604-606-4711, 800-263-0600
1128 Seymour St; $35

Lo-Cost Car Rental
☎ 604-689-9664, 888-556-2678
1105 Granville St; $30

Rent-A-Wreck
☎ 604-688-0001, 800-327-0116
1083 Hornby St; $33

Thrifty
☎ 604-647-4599, 800-847-4389
1400 Robson St; $32

Renting recreational vehicles (RVs), camper vans or various trailers (caravans) is another option. These should be booked early in the year as they are popular, especially with European visitors. The summer season is the most expensive, with mid- to large-size vehicles costing around $200 a day. These are good for five to seven people and include appliances. Cheaper camper vans are also available for around $150 a day but these should be booked even earlier. Two companies to try are Candan RV Rentals (☎ 604-530-3645, 800-922-6326, W www.candan.com, 20257 Langley Bypass, Langley) and Go West (☎ 604-987-5288, 800-661-8813, W www.go-west.com, 1577 Lloyd Ave, North Vancouver).

Taxi Meters start at $2.30 and run at 10¢ for each 15 seconds. Companies include Black Top & Checker Cabs (☎ 604-731-1111), Vancouver Taxi (☎ 604-871-1111) and Yellow Cab (☎ 604-681-1111). Vancouver Taxi has about 30 wheelchair-accessible taxis that can be used by travelers with lots of luggage.

Bicycle Riding on the sidewalk is illegal and bicycle helmets are mandatory. Designated bicycle routes lace the city; try the popular 9km Seawall route around Stanley Park.

The map *Cycling in Vancouver* is available at libraries and bicycle stores or by calling the Bicycle Hotline (☎ 604-871-6070) or Cycling BC (☎ 604-737-3034).

Bicycles are permitted on the SeaBus but not on the SkyTrain. Many buses have bike racks. For more information call ☎ 604-521-0400 or check ⓦ www.translink.bc.ca.

Rental shops include Alley Cat Bike Rentals (☎ 604-684-5117, 1779 Robson St), Reckless The Bike Store (☎ 604-648-2600, 110 Davie St or 604-731-2420, 1810 Fir St) and Spokes Bicycle Rentals (☎ 604-688-5141, 1798 W Georgia St).

Mini-Ferry Two companies operate mini-ferries around False Creek. False Creek Ferries (☎ 604-684-7781) runs from the Aquatic Centre on Sunset Beach to Granville Island and Vanier Park ($2/1 adult/senior & child), and from Granville Island to Stamps Landing (near Cambie St Bridge), Science World ($5/4/3 adult/senior/child from Granville Island) and Plaza of Nations, a waterfront public plaza regularly hosting events and entertainment.

Aquabus (☎ 604-689-5858) travels from the foot of Hornby St to Granville Island, Stamps Landing, Yaletown and Science World. Fares are similar to False Creek Ferries.

NORTH OF VANCOUVER
Sea to Sky Hwy

From Horseshoe Bay north to Whistler, the Sea to Sky Hwy (Hwy 99) affords mountain scenery to rival the Rockies. Alas, the area's blessing – its proximity to the Vancouver metro area – is also its curse: It can get damned crowded up here.

After leaving Horseshoe Bay, Hwy 99 spectacularly edges along Howe Sound. At Brittania Beach, the **BC Museum of Mining** (☎ 604-688-8735, ⓦ www.bcmuseumof mining.org; adult/student & senior/child under 5 $9.50/7.50/free; open 9am-4:30pm daily mid-May–Thanksgiving for self-guided tours) covers the time early in the 20th century when this area had the largest copper mine in the British Empire. Admission includes a mine tour. A bit farther along, **Shannon Falls** tumbles over a 335m cliff just off the road.

Some 48km from Horseshoe Bay, **Squamish** is noted for its rock climbing. The granite cliffs here are some of the world's longest unbroken rock faces; pull over and watch for climbers hanging from the rock like colorful spiders. Windsurfing and mountain biking are also popular. Thousands of bald eagles winter around town. And at **West Coast Railway Heritage Park** (☎ 604-898-9336, 39645 Government Rd; adult/senior & student/family $6/5/18; open 10am-5pm daily), you can see a large collection of historic railroad cars, many of which have been converted to a walk-through museum of railroad history and restoration. Weather permitting, staff run a miniature railway for kids ($2). The Squamish Visitor Info Centre (☎ 604-892-9244, ⓦ www .squamishchamber.bc.ca, 37950 Cleveland Ave) is open daily year-round.

Budget lodging is available at:

Squamish Hostel (☎ 604-892-9240, 800-449-8614, ⓔ hostel@mountain-inter.net, 38490 Buckley Ave) Shared rooms $15 ($40 for 3 nights), private rooms $30. This basic hostel is a short walk from downtown, and amenities include bikes to borrow, a small rock-climbing wall, fully equipped kitchen, laundry and rooftop deck.

Just northeast of Squamish is immense **Garibaldi Provincial Park** (☎ 604-898-3678, fax 604-898-4171), a 195-sq-km mountain wilderness. Most of the park is undeveloped; it is known mostly for its hiking areas covered by more than 67km of developed trails. The trails become cross-country ski runs in winter. Five park access roads lie along Hwy 99 between Squamish and Pemberton.

Whistler & Around

Whistler is one of North America's top ski resorts and has plenty of recreation options in summer as well. Don't assume you can't ski in summer – Whistler has runs that remain open nearly year-round.

Whistler Creekside, the original Whistler base, is the first area you will come to either by road as you approach from the south, or by train. The Visitor Info Centre (☎ 604-932-5528, **W** www.tourismwhistler.com, cnr Lake Placid Rd & Hwy 99; open 9am-6pm daily) offers detailed hiking maps and information on outdoor activities.

A bit farther up the highway is **Whistler Village** (turn off the highway at Village Gate Blvd). Built almost entirely from scratch starting in the 1980s, the resorts, hotels and stores here blend together like one big ultramodern outdoor shopping mall, mountain-style. The massive hotels look like castles, and many of the buildings are faced with quarried stone. The commercial center of Whistler Village resembles a European-like pedestrian village with winding streets, brightly lit shops, fine restaurants and boisterous après-ski pubs. It all has a sort of contrived Disney-esque feel about it, but the skiers, shoppers and hikers who gather here are having fun and lend the place a light, relaxed atmosphere.

Skiing The whole ski complex here is owned and run by Intrawest (☎ *604-932-3434, 800-766-0449,* **W** *www.whistler-blackcomb.com; adult full-day pass good at both mountains $61; season mid-Nov–early June*). The usually reliable snowfall, mile-high vertical drops (1609m on Blackcomb, 1530m on Whistler) and mild Pacific air combine to provide some of the most pleasant skiing to be found anywhere. Snowboarders consider Whistler Mountain, with banked runs and rocky bluffs, to be a boarder's dream come true. Nordic fans will find cross-country trails as well. In summer, glacier skiing, hiking and mountain-biking keep the resort hopping.

Places to Stay You won't get one of the cookie-cutter condo or hotel rooms for much under $100 a night; the average is closer to $175, especially if you want to be in the heart of things. Substantial discounts are usually offered in summer and shoulder seasons. To make general accommodations reservations, call ☎ 604-664-5625 or 800-944-7853, or visit **W** www.tourismwhistler.com.

HI-Whistler (☎ *604-932-5492, fax 604-932-4687,* **e** *whistler@hihostels.bc.ca, 5678 Alta Lake Rd*) Dorm beds $19.50-23.50. It's rather remote, but the hostel enjoys a beautiful setting on Alta Lake. Perks include canoes, bike rentals, Internet access and a dead-on view of Blackcomb Mountain. To get to the hostel, you can hoof it from the village (a 45-minute walk), or ride one of several daily local buses. The BC Rail train will stop at the hostel upon request.

Shoestring Lodge (☎ *604-932-3338, fax 604-932-8347,* **w** *www.shoestringlodge.com, 7124 Nancy Greene Dr*) Dorm beds/motel rooms start at $21/80. The place can get rowdy, with exotic dancers and bands in the on-premises Boot Pub, so ask for a room well down the hall if you want some peace and quiet.

Many budget ski lodges operate in the Nordic Estates area off Hwy 99, with dormitory-style accommodations starting at $25 (bring your own linens, toiletries and sleeping bag). They include *Fireside Lodge* (☎ *604-932-4545, 2117 Nordic Dr*) and *UBC Lodge* (☎ *604-932-6604, 604-822-5851 in Vancouver,* **e** *whistler@ams.ubc.ca, 2124 Nordic Dr*).

Places to Eat Like everything else in Whistler, dining is quite expensive, though inexpensive options can be found.

Peak's Coffee House (☎ *604-905-6818, 26-4314 Main St, Whistler Village*) In addition to serving good coffee drinks, Peak's offers Internet terminals and great Adirondack chairs outside when the weather's nice.

Moguls (☎ *604-932-4845, Village Square*) Snacks & sandwiches under $6. Experience the true Whistler attitude at this coffee shop, where snowboarders make smoothies, grilled panini and veggie rolls.

Auntie Em's (☎ *604-932-1163, 4340 Lorimer Rd*) Meals from $6. This is a simple café selling fresh baked goods, sandwiches and salads.

Ingrid's Village Cafe (☎ *604-932-7000, 4305 Skiers Approach*) Meals under $7. Just off Village Square, this makes a great stop for breakfast or lunch, with several varieties of vegetarian burgers, and the prices are a steal.

The Brewhouse (☎ *604-905-2739, 4355 Blackcomb Way*) Burgers and sandwiches $9-11, pizzas $13-14. This microbrewery offers splendid suds and sophisticated pub grub.

Rimrock Cafe (☎ *604-932-5565, 2117 Whistler Rd*) Meals $24-45. This well loved place is one of Whistler's top dining rooms, though without undue pretension. Fresh seafood is the specialty.

Entertainment In Whistler, there are plenty of pubs worth warming yourself up in.

Black's (☎ 604-932-6408, Mountain Square) Black's has a great little bar upstairs with almost a hundred local and imported beers and an even better selection of whiskies. Downstairs the family restaurant makes pizza and pasta.

Dubh Linn Gate (☎ 604-905-4047, 4320 Sundial Crescent) This low-key Irish pub was hand-built in the old country. There's a traditional menu of country cooking and often live music.

As far as clubs go, you'd expect Canada's top ski resort to be a partying place, and it is. Check the free Whistler This Week newspaper for listings.

Maxx Fish (☎ 604-932-1904, 4232 Village Stroll) The most progressive ('Come in if you dare!') nightclub in town, where DJs spin hip-hop, deep house and electrafunk.

Tommy Africa's (☎ 604-932-6090) and the **Savage Beagle** (☎ 604-938-3337), under the same roof at 4222 Village Square, both draw a younger crowd with DJs.

Buffalo Bill's (☎ 604-932-6613, 4122 Village Green) This venue attracts the 30-and-older set with live touring acts and comedy nights.

The Boot Pub (☎ 604-932-3338, 7124 Nancy Greene Dr) Live bands play frequently at this pub in the Shoestring Lodge, but the most popular performers here are the naked dancers of 'Das Boot Ballet,' appearing several nights each week.

Getting There & Away Greyhound (☎ 604-482-8747, 800-661-8747) offers about seven daily trips from Vancouver's Pacific Central Station to Whistler; the fare is $20/40 one-way/roundtrip.

Bigfoot Adventure Tours (☎ 604-777-9905 in Vancouver, or 888-244-6673) runs a shuttle between central Vancouver and Whistler three times daily. The fare is $27/49 one-way/roundtrip (with open-ended return) for students and hostel cardholders of any age, $42/79 for everyone else. Add $10 for service to/from Vancouver International Airport.

BC Rail (☎ 604-984-5246, 800-339-8752 within BC, 800-663-8238 outside BC) runs one train daily each morning from North Vancouver to Whistler, with a return run in the evening. The trip takes about 2½ hours. The one-way fare (including breakfast or dinner) is $39/35/23/8 adult/senior/child age two to 12/children under age two. Reservations are recommended.

Sunshine Coast

The name refers to the coastal area north of Horseshoe Bay to Lund, 24km north of Powell River. It's a narrow strip of land separated from the mainland by the Coast Mountains. The scenery is excellent: hills, mountains, forests, inlets, harbors and beaches. And yes, this maritime region really does enjoy more sunshine annually than anywhere else on the mainland.

Slow and winding Hwy 101, edging along the coast, is broken at two separate points where you'll need to take a ferry – from Horseshoe Bay to Langdale and from Earls Cove to Saltery Bay. The highway ends completely at Lund. From Powell River ferries run to Comox on Vancouver Island, as well as to Texada (pronounced tex-**ay**-da) Island, a former strip-mining center. For information about the ferries, call BC Ferries (☎ 888-223-3779, **w** www.bcferries.com) or pick up a schedule and fare information at any of the area Visitor Info Centres.

Visitors can make the Sunshine Coast part of an interesting driving circuit from Vancouver, around Vancouver Island and back. BC Ferries offers a circular ferry ticket known as the Sunshine Coast Circle-Pac that includes all four ferries around the loop – to Vancouver Island via Horseshoe Bay or Tsawwassen, then across to Powell River, and then down the Sunshine Coast with ferries at Egmont and Gibsons – at a good reduction from full fare. The normal fare is $22/79.75 adult/car, CirclePac fares are $18.70/67.80.

Malaspina Coach Lines (☎ 877-227-8287) runs two buses a day from Vancouver along the Sunshine Coast. Some examples of one-way fares, which include the ferry, are Gibsons Landing ($15.25, 1¾ hours), Sechelt ($18.50, 2¼ hours) and Powell River ($30, 5¼ hours).

Sechelt and Powell River are the commercial and activity centers of the coast. Aside from the good hiking, camping and fishing in the area, these towns are bases for some of the world's best diving, although it's not for novices and local guides should be used.

In Powell River, the Visitor Infomation Centre (☎ 604-485-4701, 877-817-8669, W www .discoverpowellriver.com, 4690 Marine Ave; open year-round) can recommend kayaking, mountain biking and scuba diving outfitters. Ask about a nearby 65km canoeing circuit, and get information on **Desolation Sound Provincial Marine Park**, which has abundant wildlife, diving, canoeing and wilderness camping.

Places to Stay & Eat Accommodations around Powell River include hotels, motels and campgrounds.

Willingdon Beach Campsite (☎ 604-485-2242, 4845 Marine Ave) Walk-in tent sites $15, full hookups $20. Facilities include showers and a laundry.

Old Courthouse Inn & Hostel (☎ 604-483-4000, e oldcourthouseinn@armourtech.com, 6243 Walnut St) Dorm beds $17, singles/ doubles $27/35, with private bathroom $35/44. In the Townsite section, this hostel has a great little café on the ground floor. Low-cost pick-ups from the bus or ferry can be arranged.

Captain Billy's Old Fashioned Fish and Chips Two pieces $6.45. Captain Billy has been dishing up fish near the ferry terminal for more than 25 years.

Little Tea Pot Euro Café (☎ 604-485-5955, 4582 Willingdon Ave) Homemade soups about $4, lunch specialties around $8. This quaint café also hosts Sunday afternoon poetry readings.

Shinglemill Pub (☎ 604-483-2001, 6233 Powell Place), on Powell Lake. Mains from $12. This pub offers good, moderately priced bistro food and great views.

Vancouver Island

The attractions of Vancouver Island, the largest island off the West Coast of the Americas, range from its rugged wilderness to the grand rooms of its provincial legislature.

The island is 450km long and has a population of nearly 700,000 people, most of whom live along the southeastern coast.

The geography is scenically varied. A mountain range runs down the center of the island, its snow-capped peaks setting off the woods and many lakes and streams. The coast can be either rocky and tempestuous or sandy and calm.

South of the island, across the Strait of Juan de Fuca, the sea is backed by the substantial Mt Olympus (2428m) in Washington State's Olympic National Park.

Across the Strait of Georgia, which runs along the island's eastern shore, the mainland's Coast Mountains form the skyline. The open western coast is fully exposed to the Pacific. The waters around the island are filled with marine life, much of which is commonly seen and some, like the salmon, eaten. Crab is a BC culinary delicacy and the world's largest octopuses are found here.

Vancouver Island also has diverse birdlife, with more than 440 different species. The bald eagle is widespread and can be seen near rivers and lakes; the golden eagle is an endangered species but can still be seen along the coast.

The central north-south mountain chain divides the island into distinct halves. The sparsely populated west coast is rugged, hilly, forested and cut by deep inlets. The more gentle eastern side is suitable for farming. The island's industries – forestry, mining and fishing – and nearly all of the principal towns are found along this side of the ridge. Up the east coast the resort towns and villages have plenty of campgrounds, motels, hotels and guesthouses. However, don't imagine the entire east coast to be urban sprawl. It's still quite undeveloped in places, especially north of Campbell River.

Evidence of Vancouver Island's history of logging is everywhere in defoliated hillsides. However, the collapse of lumber prices in the late 1990s has decimated logging towns like Gold River and caused much misery in the lives of long-term residents. So too, the collapse of fishing stocks has hit communities like little Alert Bay hard and there have been a rash of suicide attempts and other tragedies.

The tourist industry is fast becoming a primary income-producer for the island, but this is little consolation to the towns that supported themselves by exploiting their natural resources and now have few left to exploit for tourists.

The island has the mildest climate in the country. It's particularly moderate at the southern end, where the northerly arm of

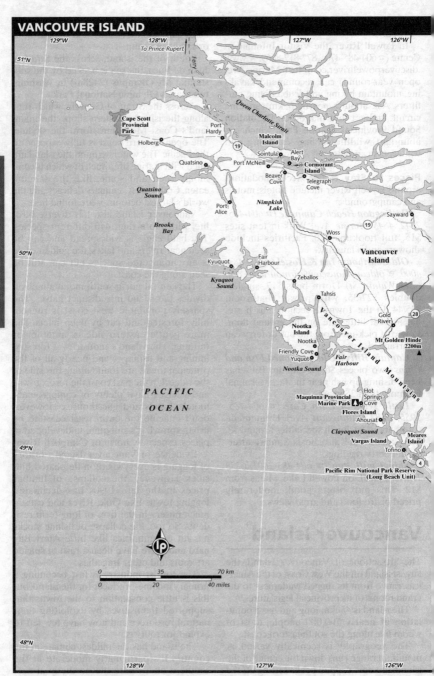

VANCOUVER ISLAND

To Prince Rupert

Queen Charlotte Strait

Cape Scott Provincial Park

Holberg

Port Hardy

Malcolm Island

Sointula   Alert Bay

Port McNeill   Cormorant Island

Beaver Cove

Telegraph Cove

Quatsino

Quatsino Sound

Port Alice

Nimpkish Lake

Sayward

Brooks Bay

Woss

Vancouver Island

Kyuquot

Fair Harbour

Kyuquot Sound

Zeballos

Tahsis

Gold River

Vancouver Island Mountains

Mt Golden Hinde 2200m

Nootka Island

Nootka

Friendly Cove
Yuquot

Fair Harbour

Nootka Sound

PACIFIC OCEAN

Maquinna Provincial Marine Park

Hot Springs Cove

Flores Island

Ahousat

Clayoquot Sound

Vargas Island

Meares Island

Tofino

Pacific Rim National Park Reserve (Long Beach Unit)

0   35   70 km
0   20   40 miles

BRITISH COLUMBIA

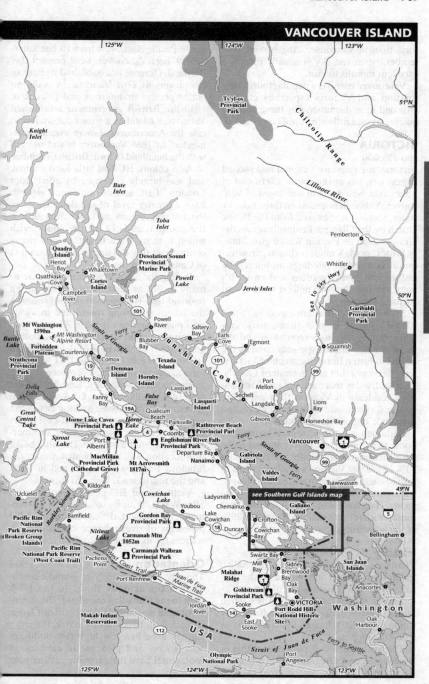

VANCOUVER ISLAND

see Southern Gulf Islands map

BRITISH COLUMBIA

Washington State protects it from the ocean. There is substantially less rain in Victoria than in Vancouver. August and September, when the sky is usually blue, are excellent months to visit.

Vancouver Island is a popular tourist destination and Victoria especially can get crowded in midsummer. For those seeking quieter spots, a little effort will be rewarded.

VICTORIA
pop 335,000

Victoria, the province's capital and second largest city, lies at the southeastern end of Vancouver Island, 90km southwest of Vancouver. Although bounded on three sides by water, Victoria is sheltered from the Pacific Ocean by the Olympic Peninsula across the Strait of Juan de Fuca in Washington State.

With Canada's mildest climate, architecturally compelling buildings, an interesting history and famed gardens and parks, it's not surprising that two million tourists visit Victoria annually.

Many people come here expecting to find a kind of Olde English theme park; certainly that is the city's reputation and the point of much of the hype generated by the tourist industry. In reality, much of Victoria feels like any other city in western Canada. That said, today there are still more British-born residents in Victoria than anywhere else in Canada, and they have entrenched their style rather than forgotten it.

Although it is the provincial capital and home to an important university and naval base, Victoria is not an industrial city. About 30% of greater Victoria's residents work in tourist- and service-oriented businesses, while another 20% work in the public sector. The island is also a major retirement center, with retirees making up around 20% of the population.

History

Victoria's first residents were the Salish Indians, who fished and hunted on the protected bay. The felicitous site of future Victoria was not colonized until 1843, when James Douglas, acting for the Hudson's Bay Company (HBC), founded Fort Victoria as a fur-trading post.

The history of BC departed from that of Washington and Oregon in 1846 when the British and US governments fixed the US-Canadian border at the 49th parallel. The HBC, which heretofore had controlled the entire Pacific Northwest from its headquarters at Fort Vancouver, near present day Portland, Oregon, re-established its base of operations at Fort Victoria. In order to better protect its interests and citizens, in 1849 the British government established Vancouver Island as a crown colony, just in case the Americans got more expansionist-minded. In 1866 Vancouver Island merged with the mainland to form British Columbia.

As a colony, BC had little local control, and was largely governed by edict from London. If BC and its population were to have a greater level of self-determination, the growing colony had two choices: join the prosperous USA to the south, with which it shared much history and many commercial ties, or join the new Dominion of Canada far to the east.

Joining the USA made a lot of sense to many in BC, as there were already strong regional ties. The political debate raged in the colony's drawing rooms and in Victoria's pugnacious newspapers. After Ottawa promised to build a railroad to link eastern and western Canada in 1870, delegates from BC voted to join Canada in 1871 with Victoria as capital of the new province.

For Victoria, without a land link to the rest of Canada or the USA, industrial growth was not an issue and the city didn't experience the same boom-and-bust cycles that many of the manufacturing and mercantile cities of the west did. The city's beautiful location was an early attraction – the fabulous Empress Hotel opened in 1908, and the tourist trade began in earnest.

Victoria and BC generally prospered after WWII. With its solid base of government employment, the city has avoided the problems of over-reliance on natural resources for its economic base.

Orientation

The city lies at Vancouver Island's southeastern tip, actually closer to the USA than to the Canadian mainland. The downtown area is simply laid out and not large. Bounded on two sides by water, the city's central area has few high-rise buildings and is easy and pleasant to explore on foot; you'll have little trouble getting your bearings.

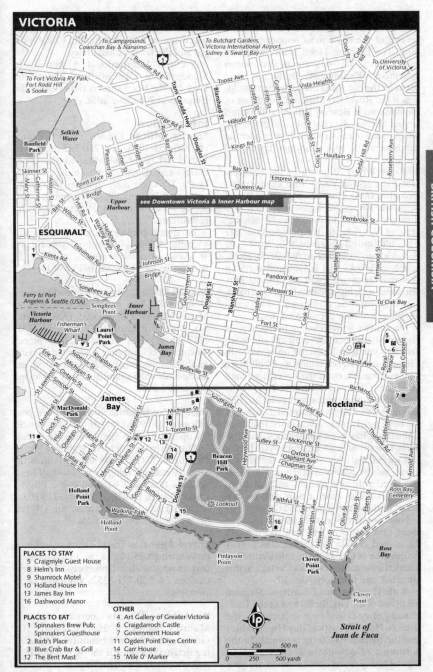

VICTORIA

BRITISH COLUMBIA

To Campgrounds, Cowichan Bay & Nanaimo

To Butchart Gardens, Victoria International Airport, Sidney & Swartz Bay

To University of Victoria

To Fort Victoria RV Park; Fort Rodd Hill & Sooke

Burnside Rd E

Trans Canada Hwy

Gorge Rd E

Topaz Ave

Vista Heights

Blanshard St

Quadra St

Graham St

Prior St

Fifth St

Cook St

Cedar Hill Rd

Hillside Ave

Rock Bay Ave

Douglas St

Kings Rd

Haultain St

Cook St

Cedar Hill Rd

Roseberry Ave

Selkirk Water

Banfield Park

Skinner St

Mary St

Catherine St

Ashton St

Bay St

Point Ellice

Bridge

Queens Av

Empress Ave

Pleasant St

Turner St

Bridge St

Tree Rd

Wilson St

Upper Harbour

see Downtown Victoria & Inner Harbour map

Pembroke St

Chambers St

Fernwood St

Harbour Rd

Walking Path

ESQUIMALT

Esquimalt Rd

Songhees Rd

Johnson St

Government St

Douglas St

Blanshard St

Pandora Ave

Johnson St

To Oak Bay

Kimta Rd

Bridge

Ferry to Port Angeles & Seattle (USA)

Songhees Point

Inner Harbour

Fort St

Cook St

Victoria Harbour

Fisherman's Wharf

Laurel Point Park

James Bay

Belleville St

Rockland Ave

Rockland

5

4

Royal Terrace

Joan Crescent

6

Kingston St

Superior St

Michigan St

Ontario St

Southgate St

Fairfield Rd

Richardson St

7

Erie St

St Lawrence St

Montreal St

Simcoe St

James Bay

8

9

Michigan St

Oscar St

Sutlej St

Oxford St

Oliphant Ave

Chapman St

Thurlow Rd

Lotbiniere Ave

Arnold Ave

MacDonald Park

Dock St

Pilot St

Oswego St

Niagara St

Menzies St

10

Toronto St

12

13

14

1

McKenzie St

Heywood Ave

Beacon Hill Park

11

Dallas Rd

Boyd St

S Turner St

Clarence St

Government St

Battery St

Douglas St

Lookout

May St

Faithful St

Cook St

Linden Ave

Wellington Ave

Moss St

Olive St

Joseph St

Eberts St

Dallas Rd

Ross Bay Cemetery

Holland Point Park

Walking Path

15

16

Holland Point

Finlayson Point

Clover Point Park

Ross Bay

Clover Point

Strait of Juan de Fuca

PLACES TO STAY
5 Craigmyle Guest House
8 Helm's Inn
9 Shamrock Motel
10 Holland House Inn
13 James Bay Inn
16 Dashwood Manor

PLACES TO EAT
1 Spinnakers Brew Pub;
  Spinnakers Guesthouse
2 Barb's Place
3 Blue Crab Bar & Grill
12 The Bent Mast

OTHER
4 Art Gallery of Greater Victoria
6 Craigdarroch Castle
7 Government House
11 Ogden Point Dive Centre
14 Carr House
15 'Mile 0' Marker

0   250   500 m
0   250   500 yards

The focal point is the Inner Harbour, a section of Victoria Harbour surrounded by several of the city's most important structures. The Empress Hotel faces the waterfront. Across the way are the enormous provincial Parliament Buildings, and between the hotel and the parliament buildings is the Royal BC Museum. Southeast of the museum is Beacon Hill Park, the city's largest. Surrounding the park and extending down to the ocean are well kept residential neighborhoods with attractive lawns and gardens.

Along Wharf St, north of the Empress Hotel, the central Visitor Info Centre overlooks the Inner Harbour. Following Wharf St north along the water will take you through Old Town, the restored original area of Victoria, to Bastion Square, the city's old central square and the site of old Fort Victoria. Parallel to Wharf St and a couple of blocks east is Government St, a principal shopping street and tourist hub, also lined with historic buildings. One block east is Douglas St, downtown's main thoroughfare and busy commercial center.

Downtown's northern boundary is Fisgard St, between Government and Store Sts. Here you'll find a small Chinatown with Chinese-style street lamps and buildings, Chinese characters on the street signs and, of course, Chinese restaurants. The area is remarkably neat, clean and colorful, due mainly to the brightly painted facades of the buildings. Fan Tan Alley, in the middle of Chinatown, has a few small shops and connects Fisgard St with Pandora Ave. In the 1860s when this alley – Canada's first Chinatown – was in its heyday and much bigger, it was lined with opium dens and gambling houses. It's a lot quieter now with no evidence of those early vice-filled days.

Following Fort St east up the hill and then along Oak Bay Ave will lead you through the 'tweed curtain' to the wealthier, very British area of Oak Bay. The Info Centre has detailed information on walks to take in this attractive and traditional district.

Both Douglas and Blanshard Sts lead north out of the city, the former to the Trans Canada Hwy (Hwy 1) and Nanaimo, the latter to Hwy 17 (Patricia Bay Hwy), Sidney and the Swartz Bay ferry terminal. To the northwest of downtown is Gorge Rd, an area of heavy motel concentration. It forms part of Hwy 1A, which cuts across Douglas St, runs along the northern side of the gorge and meets up farther west with Craigflower Rd and the Trans Canada Hwy.

Victoria International Airport is in Sidney, about 19km north of Victoria on Hwy 17. The bus station is right behind the Empress at 700 Douglas St.

Information

Tourist Offices The Visitor Info Centre (☎ 250-953-2033, fax 250-382-6539, 812 Wharf St) is by the water at the Inner Harbour, diagonally opposite the Empress Hotel. It's open daily and has pamphlets, maps and information on shopping, sightseeing, transportation, accommodations and restaurants.

For pre-trip planning, contact Tourism Victoria (☎ 250-414-6999, fax 250-361-9733, w www.tourismvictoria.com, 4th floor, 31 Bastion Square, Victoria, BC V8W 1J1).

Money Major banks have branches along Douglas St. You can change money at Money Mart (☎ 250-386-3535, 1720 Douglas St), American Express (☎ 250-385-8731, 1213 Douglas St or many other places downtown. US currency is accepted in many establishments but usually at a worse exchange rate than found at money-exchange offices or banks.

Post & Communications The main post office (☎ 250-935-1351) is at 714 Yates St. It's open 8:30am to 5pm Monday to Friday.

The Greater Victoria Public Library (☎ 250-382-7241, 735 Broughton) offers Internet access, charging $3 for two half-hour sessions that can't be used consecutively. Cyber Station (☎ 250-386-4687, 1113 Blanshard St) has Internet access for $10 per hour, as well as coffee drinks.

Travel Agencies Travel Cuts has an office downtown (☎ 250-995-8556, 1312 Douglas) and another at the University of Victoria campus (☎ 250-721-8352, Student Union Building).

Bookstores The city's best bookstore is Munro's Books (☎ 250-382-2464, 1108 Government St), in a beautiful old building originally built for the Royal Bank. It is now classified as a heritage building; the atmosphere inside is almost ecclesiastical and is worth a look even if you aren't shopping for a book.

Crown Publications (☎ 250-386-4636, 521 Fort St) sells maps, charts, federal and provincial publications on Canadiana, books on First Nations culture, nature and travel guides.

Among a number of secondhand bookstores downtown is Renaissance Books (☎ 250-381-6469, 579 Johnson St), where you just might be able to find a dog-eared copy of Richard Brautigan's *Willard and his Bowling Trophies*. Probably not, but you never know.

Newspapers & Magazines The daily paper is the *Times Colonist*. Arts and entertainment news is featured in the weekly *Monday Magazine*.

Laundry A small coin-op laundry and showers are under the main Visitor Info Centre, on the waterfront level (convenient for yachties). The Maytag Homestyle Laundry (☎ 250-386-1799, 1309 Cook St) has self-service machines, drop-off service and dry cleaning.

Medical Services If your medical needs aren't grave, head to Mayfair Walk-In Clinic (☎ 250-383-9898, 3147 Douglas St), in the Mayfair Shopping Mall. If your whole life is flashing before your eyes, you'll want Royal Jubilee Hospital (☎ 250-370-8000, 1900 Fort St), east of downtown.

Emergency Dial ☎ 911 for police, fire or ambulance.

Dangers & Annoyances At night, Broad St between Yates and Johnson Sts is often occupied by prostitutes and drunks. Some lowlifes also hang out in the area near the corner of Yates and Douglas Sts. Panhandlers work downtown Victoria day and night.

Inner Harbour
Many attractions, from the schlocky to the sublime, ring the Inner Harbour.

Royal British Columbia Museum This acclaimed museum (☎ 250-356-7226, 888-447-7977, **w** *rbcm1.rbcm.gov.bc.ca*, 675 Belleville St; adult/senior & student/family

$9/6/24; open 9am-5pm daily) is a must-see, even for those weary of museums. The complex includes the National Geographic IMAX theater (screenings until 8pm), for which combined discount admission tickets are available.

The First Peoples exhibit hall is packed with carvings, canoes, beadwork, basketry and more; hushed tones prevail as visitors wander through the totem pole displays, a replica of a 19th-century Haida village and Nawalagwatsi, 'the cave of supernatural power.' Elsewhere on the 3rd floor, learn about BC's immigrant history via a walk-through model of Captain Vancouver's *Discovery* or by visiting an old-time movie theater and the gold rush exhibit. If you can't get to a tide pool in person, the 2nd-floor 'Living Land, Living Sea' gallery is a good place to mingle with sea stars, anemones and the like.

Outside the museum are two historical buildings: **Helmcken House** (☎ 250-361-0021; adult/senior & student/child $5/4/3; open 10am-5pm daily May-Oct, noon-4pm Thur-Mon during winter), the one-time residence of an early town doctor; and one of Victoria's oldest buildings, **St Anne's Pioneer Schoolhouse**, dating from the mid-1800s (open for group tours only). If you visit in summer, you may be able to speak with First Nations artists at work in the carving shed in adjacent **Thunderbird Park**, the site of several traditional totem poles.

Parliament Buildings The multiturreted Parliament Buildings (☎ 250-387-3046, 501 Belleville St; open 8:30am-5pm daily), facing the Inner Harbour, were designed by Francis Rattenbury and finished in 1898. On top of the main dome is a figure of Captain George Vancouver, the first British navigator to circle Vancouver Island. Rattenbury also designed the Empress Hotel as well as the Parthenon-like Royal London Wax Museum, once a Canadian Pacific railway ticket office. Free 35-minute guided tours are offered daily in summer.

Paintings in the lower rotunda depict scenes from Canadian history. The Legislative Chamber is where all BC laws are made. You can view the debates from the public gallery when the legislature is in session. The buildings are lit spectacularly at night by more than 3000 lightbulbs; one

DOWNTOWN VICTORIA & INNER HARBOUR

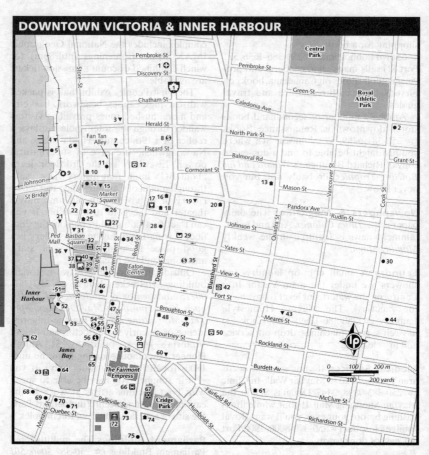

local wag said the lights made the Parliament look like 'a Disney caricature of itself.'

Pacific Undersea Gardens A sort of natural aquarium, the gardens (☎ 250-382-5717, 490 Belleville St; adult/senior/youth age 12-17/child age 5-11 $7.50/6.50/5/3.50; open 10am-7:30pm daily in summer, 10am-4:30pm rest of year, closed Tues & Wed Jan & Feb) are on the Inner Harbour. Visitors descend beneath the water's surface to view a range of corralled sea creatures such as octopuses, eels, crabs, etc. Children especially find it intriguing.

Royal London Wax Museum This museum (☎ 250-388-4461, 470 Belleville St;

adult/senior/youth & student/child age 6-12 $8.50/7.50/6.50/4; open daily 9am-7:30pm in summer, 9:30am until 5pm or 6pm rest of year), in front of the Parliament Buildings, contains more than 300 wax models of historical and contemporary figures. Kids love the dungeon.

Miniature World At Miniature World (☎ 250-385-9731, 649 Humboldt St; adult/students/child $9/7/6; open daily 8:30am-9pm in summer, 9am-7pm May & Sept, 9am-5pm rest of year), beside the Empress Hotel, you'll find over 80 scenes depicting (in exact detail) various themes, such as historical sites, fairy tales and the world of Dickens. The highlight is a large model train representing the development of the Canadian

DOWNTOWN VICTORIA & INNER HARBOUR

PLACES TO STAY
10 Swans Suite Hotel
  & Brewpub
13 Victoria Backpackers Hostel
16 Hotel Douglas
18 Best Western Carlton Plaza
20 Ocean Island Backpackers Inn
24 Isabella's Guest Suites
25 HI Victoria Hostel
48 Strathcona Hotel; Legends
61 Abigail's Hotel
74 Crystal Court Motel

PLACES TO EAT
 3 Herald St Caffe
 4 Harbour Canoe Club
 7 Foo Hong Chop Suey
15 Green Cuisine
19 John's Place
21 Chandler's Seafood
  Restaurant
22 Il Terrazo Ristorante
23 Willie's Bakery
31 Süze
33 Re-Bar
36 Wharfside Eatery; Boom
  Boom Room
39 Siam Thai
40 Camille's Fine Westcoast
  Dining
43 Blue Fox Café
53 Blackfish Cafe

57 Sam's Deli
60 Millos

OTHER
 1 Mayfair Walk-In Clinic
 2 Kingfisher Charters
 5 Russian Submarine; Island
  Boat Rentals
 6 Level Nightclub
 8 Money Mart
 9 E&N Railiner Station
11 Dragon Song Music Co
12 McPherson Playhouse
14 Ocean River Sports
17 BJ's Lounge
26 Renaissance Books
27 Steamers Public House
28 Travel Cuts
29 Main Post Office
30 Maytag Homestyle Laundry
32 Maritime Museum of British
  Columbia
34 Sasquatch Trading Ltd
35 American Express
37 D'Arcy McGee's
38 Victoria Bug Zoo
41 Munro's Books
42 Cyber Station of Victoria
44 BC Ferries Office
45 Crown Publications
46 The Whale Store
47 Canadian Impressions

49 Greater Victoria Public
  Library
50 Royal Theatre
51 West Coast Air/Kenmore Air
  Seaplanes
52 Victoria Marine Adventure
  Centre; Harbour Air
  Seaplanes; Victoria Kayak
  Tours
54 Custom House Currency
  Exchange
55 Cycle Treks
56 Visitor Info Centre; Prince of
  Whales
58 Miniature World
59 The Vic Theatre
62 Inner Harbour Ferry Terminal
63 Royal London Wax Museum
64 Pacific Undersea Gardens
65 Victoria Harbour Ferry;
  Ticket Centre
66 Bus Station
67 Crystal Garden
68 Hotel Grand Pacific
69 Victoria Carriage Tours
70 Tally-Ho Sightseeing Tours
71 Parliament Buildings
72 Royal British Columbia
  Museum
73 Thunderbird Park
75 Helmcken House; St Anne's
  Pioneer Schoolhouse

BRITISH COLUMBIA

Pacific Railway from 1885 to 1915. Watch out for the tour-bus hordes.

Crystal Garden Conservation Centre
This indoor garden (☎ 250-381-1213, W www.bcpcc.com/crystal, 713 Douglas St; adult/senior/child $8/7/4; open daily 8:30am-8pm July-Aug, reduced hours rest of year) holds a colorful profusion of tropical plants and flowers, free-flying butterflies and 65 varieties of endangered animals and birds from around the world. The original building, designed by Francis Rattenbury after London's Crystal Palace, was completed in 1925. It was restored and reopened in 1980.

Bastion Square
Along Wharf St between Yates and Fort Sts, Bastion Square was the former site of Fort Victoria and held the courthouse, jail, gallows and brothel. The whole area has been restored and redeveloped. The square is pleasant for strolling and people-watching.

Maritime Museum of British Columbia
Inside an 1889 building that once housed BC's provincial law courts, this museum (☎ 250-385-4222, 28 Bastion Square; adult/senior/student/child $6/5/3/2; open 9:30am-4:30pm daily) explores Vancouver Island's seafaring past and present. It has more than 400 ship models dating back to 1810; displays on piracy, shipwrecks and navigation; and the Tilikum, a converted dugout canoe that John Voss sailed almost completely around the world from 1901 to 1904.

Victoria Bug Zoo
The Victoria Bug Zoo (☎ 250-384-2847, 1107 Wharf St; adult/senior & student/child age 3-16 $6/5/4; open 9:30am-5:30pm Mon-Sat, 11am-5:30pm Sun) holds displays you'll either love or want to step on. You'll see everything from fist-sized beetles to the perpetually pregnant Australian stick insect. The leaf-cutter ants going about their business inside the meters of Plexiglas tubes are mesmerizing.

Russian Submarine

Docked in front of the Harbour Canoe Club at the foot of Swift St, the hulking black *Cobra*, a 1970s-vintage nonnuclear Soviet submarine, is open as a tourist attraction (*☎ 250-382-3022, Swift St, adult/child $10/8; open daily 9am-9pm summer, 9am-5:30pm rest of year*). The 85m-long vessel was built in Leningrad and carried a crew of 78. A creepy assignment, no doubt; one of the factoids you'll learn here is that the crewmen typically spent a third of their shore leave in government sanatoriums.

Carr House

South of the Inner Harbour, a short walk or bus ride (No 5 or 11 from downtown) leads to the birthplace of Emily Carr, one of Canada's best known painters. The Carr House (*☎ 250-383-5843, ⓦ www.emilycarr .com, 207 Government St; adult/senior/child $5/4/3; open 10am-5pm daily late May–mid-Oct*) shows something of her background and displays some of her work, both in painting and literature.

Scenic Marine Dr

Starting from Fisherman's Wharf on the west and Beach Dr on the east, the Scenic Marine Dr is the name applied to the picturesque route that skirts the Strait of Juan de Fuca (mainly on Dallas Rd). Along the way you'll have great views over the sea, and you'll pass parks, beaches and some of Victoria's wealthiest neighborhoods.

Fisherman's Wharf Just west of the Inner Harbour, around Laurel Point, is Fisherman's Wharf. Fishing boats and pleasure craft come and go, and you can sometimes buy fresh seafood from the boats. A picturesque mix of houseboats is moored at one end of the dock, and a green overlooking the area makes a nice picnic spot.

Beacon Hill Park Southeast of the Inner Harbour, along Douglas St, this gorgeous

---

The Life & Work of Emily Carr

Emily Carr was born in Victoria in 1871. After her parents died when she was young, she was discouraged from pursuing her love of painting because it was 'unladylike.' Eventually, she was forced to forsake her vocation entirely and work as a teacher.

Her career as an artist took a pivotal turn when, in 1898, she accompanied a cleric on his mission at Ucluelet on Vancouver Island. The life and arts of the First Nations village had a profound effect on Carr. Inspired by what she saw, she began using both the landscape and the people as her subject matter. However, she felt that the power of both nature and First Nations culture was missing from her painting. A trip to Paris at age 39 gave her new insights, and her work took on a unique use of color, brush stroke and subject matter.

Back home her new paintings were not taken seriously. At age 42, after a disastrous exhibition of paintings that scandalized the staid values of the time, she became a social outcast. To make ends meet she became a landlady in central Victoria. It wasn't until the late 1920s, when her scorned paintings were shown in eastern Canada, that she began to get the respect she deserved. Carr returned to painting with renewed energy and until the latter 1930s she painted some of her best-known works.

As her health failed she wrote several books about her life. Her book *Klee Wyck* is a collection of stories recalling her life among the First Nations people. Its title means 'The Laughing One.'

Carr's house in Victoria is open to the public, and her paintings can be viewed at the Art Gallery of Greater Victoria and other galleries across Canada.

61-hectare park is Victoria's largest. The park is an oasis of tall trees, flowers, ponds and pathways – a walker's or jogger's delight. The park's southern edge overlooks the ocean and offers good views of the Strait of Juan de Fuca. At the park's southwest corner, the path along the water meets the **'Mile 0' marker**, the Pacific terminus of the Trans Canada Hwy.

Rockland

East of downtown Victoria, Rockland, which lies between Fort St and Fairfield Rd, and extends east to Moss St, is a wealthy neighborhood filled with handsome old homes and a number of civic buildings.

Art Gallery of Greater Victoria Often overlooked, this substantial art gallery (☎ 250-384-4101, W www.aggv.bc.ca, 1040 Moss St; adult/senior & student $5/3, children under 12 free; open 10am-5pm Mon-Sat, until 9pm Thur, 1pm-5pm Sun) has excellent collections of Asian, pre-Columbian and Latin American art, as well as contemporary Canadian paintings. Emily Carr's works are on permanent display and there are some good Inuit pieces; take bus No 10, 11 or 14.

Government House This is the official residence of the province's lieutenant governor, but only the impressive gardens (☎ 250-387-2080, 1401 Rockland Ave; admission free; open dawn-dusk) are open to the public. You can reach them on bus No 10, 11 or 14.

Craigdarroch Castle Near Government House, but off Fort St, this opulent four-story mansion (☎ 250-592-5323, W www .craigdarrochcastle.com, 1050 Joan Crescent; adult/student/child age 6-12 $10/5.50/2.50; open daily 9am-7pm summer; 10am-4:30pm rest of year) was built in the mid-1880s by Robert Dunsmuir, a coal millionaire. He died before it was completed. The castlelike, 26,000-sq-foot house has 39 rooms and 17 fireplaces. It's been completely restored and is open to the public (take bus No 11 or 14).

Fort Rodd Hill National Historic Park

Soulfully scenic, this 18-hectare park (☎ 250-478-5849, 603 Fort Rodd Hill Rd; adult/child $3/1.50; opening hours vary),

about 12km northwest of the city off Ocean Blvd, is the only national historic site on Vancouver Island. It was built in the late 1890s to protect Esquimalt Harbour and the Royal Navy yards, as signs on the self-guided walking trails tell visitors.

Fisgard Lighthouse, western Canada's first, has been in continuous use since 1860; incidentally, the causeway was built for the convenience of visitors only after the last lighthouse keeper departed. On a slow day, you'll have the delightful museum inside the lighthouse all to yourself – feel free to curl up for a nap while listening to the waves roar all around you.

Bus No 50 from downtown comes within 2km of the fort site.

Butchart Gardens

Roses are red, Tibetan poppies are blue and tulips are yellow and pink and white – all is well at Butchart Gardens (☎ 250-652-5256/4422, 866-652-4422, W www.butchart gardens.com, 800 Benvenuto Ave, Brentwood Bay; in summer, adult/youth age 13-17/children 5-12 $19.25/9.50/2, reduced prices rest of year; open daily at 9am, closing times vary by season). The gardens, 21km northwest of Victoria, are probably the city's most famous attraction. Built around a former limestone quarry, the 20-hectare gardens were created by Jennie Butchart and her husband Robert, a cement magnate, beginning in 1904. Among the various plantings here are a rose garden, Italian garden and a sunken garden with water features.

You can walk through in about 1½ hours, but plant lovers will want to linger much longer. The best time to come is after 3pm, when the crowds have thinned. From June to September and in December the gardens are open until 9pm or 10pm and are illuminated after dark. On Saturday nights during July and August, a spectacular fireworks display set to music is presented at no extra charge.

The gardens are in Brentwood Bay. If you're driving, follow Hwy 17 north toward Sidney. City bus No 75 serves the gardens from downtown Victoria; call 250-382-6161 for schedule information. More popular is the Gray Line shuttle (☎ 250-388-6539/5248, 700 Douglas St; $4 each way).

Note that if you drive here and are planning to head up-island after visiting the gardens, you needn't come all the way back to Victoria to head north. The **Brentwood–Mill Bay Ferry** crosses Saanich Inlet from Brentwood Bay, just north of the gardens, to Mill Bay, well up-island toward Duncan. The ferry takes cars and provides a huge shortcut.

Western Shore

West of Victoria, Hwy 14 takes you from the city's manicured parks and gardens to the pristine wilderness of Vancouver Island's west coast. The highway runs through Sooke (35km west of Victoria) then along the coast overlooking the Strait of Juan de Fuca to Port Renfrew, at the south end of the popular West Coast Trail (see Pacific Rim National Park Reserve later in this chapter). Along the way are parks and beaches for walking, beachcombing and picnicking.

Before you reach Sooke follow the signs from Milnes Landing up Sooke River Rd to the **Sooke Potholes**, where you can go swimming, picnicking and hiking. Sooke's Visitor Info Centre (☎ 250-642-6351, 2070 Phillips Rd at Hwy 14) and local museum are housed in the same building. Victoria's bus network extends to Sooke – take bus No 50 to the Western Exchange then change to No 61.

East Sooke Regional Park (☎ 250-478-3344; admission free; open during daylight hours) makes a great day trip from town for its 50km of hiking trails crisscrossing 1400 hectares of beautiful coastland. From Hwy 14 westbound, turn left on Gillespie Rd and right on E Sooke Rd.

Farther along Hwy 14, the windswept **French Beach** and **China Beach** Provincial Parks both offer hiking trails and swimming. You can camp at French Beach (☎ 250-391-2300).

At **Port Renfrew**, a good day trip from town, the main attraction is **Botanical Beach**, a sandstone shelf, which at low tide is dotted with tidal pools containing all manner of small marine life: starfish, anemones, etc. To return to Victoria without retracing your tracks, take the logging road across the island to Lake Cowichan, from where better roads connect to Duncan and Hwy 1.

The West Coast Trail Express (☎ 250-477-8700) runs a shuttle from Victoria to Port Renfrew. You can use it for an interesting day trip to the west coast beaches along the Strait of Juan de Fuca or to begin the hiking trail to Bamfield (for details see West Coast

Trail under Pacific Rim National Park Reserve later in this chapter).

If you were hoping to hike the West Coast Trail but can't get a permit, try the increasingly popular 47km **Juan de Fuca Marine Trail**, which runs from China Beach to Botanical Beach; for more information call BC Parks South Vancouver Island District (☎ 250-391-2300).

Activities

One easy place to check out an array of possible activities is **Victoria Marine Adventure Centre** (VMAC; ☎ 250-995-2211, 800-575-6700, W www.marine-adventures.com, 950 Wharf St). Here you'll find kayak, bike and scooter rentals, whale-watching excursions, seaplane flightseeing tours, fishing charters and more. While you're there, kick back with a beer at the Blackfish Cafe (see Places to Eat).

Whale-Watching Scores of excursion operators offer trips out into the Strait of Georgia to watch orcas, or killer whales (three-hour trip $70-80 adult, $50-55 child). Other wildlife you may see on these trips are bald eagles, seals and sea lions, and many kinds of seabirds.

Going on a whale-watching trip is as easy as walking to the waterfront and signing up for the next excursion. Among the many companies are **Ocean Explorations** (☎ 250-383-6722, 888-442-6722, 532 Broughton St), at the Whale Store; **Prince of Whales** (☎ 250-383-4884, 888-383-4884, 812 Wharf St), just below the Visitor Info Centre; and **Cuda Marine Adventures** (☎ 250-995-2832, 866-995-2832, 463 Belleville St), in the Hotel Grand Pacific.

Kayaking You'll see plenty of paddlers poking about the harbor in kayaks. It's a nice way to get away from the crowds and see the city from out on the water. Several places rent kayaks for around $40-45 a day. Among the best are **Ocean River Sports** (☎ 250-381-4233, 1437 Store St), which also sells equipment and runs courses; **Harbour Rentals** (☎ 250-995-1661, 450 Swift St), by the Russian sub at Heritage Quay; and **Victoria Kayak Tours** (☎ 250-216-5646, W www.kayakvictoria.com, 950 Wharf St), at VMAC, which also offers lessons and tours.

Scuba Diving The Strait of Georgia provides opportunities for world-class diving.

Several excellent shore dive sites are found near Victoria, including Saanich Inlet, Saxe Point Park, the Ogden Point Breakwater, 10-Mile Point and Willis Point for deep diving. Race Rocks, 18km southwest of Victoria Harbour, offers superb scenery both above and below the water.

Diving charters and dive shops in Victoria provide equipment sales, service, rentals and instruction. Try **Ogden Point Dive Centre** (☎ 250-380-9119, w www.divevictoria.com, 199 Dallas Rd).

Fishing The waters around Victoria are renowned for deep-sea fishing, with salmon being the top prize. Many freshwater lakes and streams within an hour or two of Victoria are good for trout and/or salmon fishing. Saanich Inlet often has high concentrations of salmon.

Scores of charter companies offer deep-sea fishing trips of varying lengths. Most supply all equipment, bait and even coffee. Get a complete list of outfitters from the Info Centre. **Kingfisher Charters** (☎ 250-479-8600, 888-479-8600, 2nd floor, 1821 Cook St) offers half-day ($400 for up to 4 adults) or full-day ($800) trips.

Hiking & Cycling Victoria has a lot of nice quiet areas for hiking or biking. Beacon Hill Park is a great place to start. From there,

---

The Galloping Goose

Stretching from Swartz Bay to the Sooke area, the 100km Galloping Goose/Peninsula trail system ranks among the best cycling/pedestrian routes in BC.

The trail, named for a noisy gas railcar that ran between Victoria and Sooke in the 1920s, is built mostly on abandoned Victoria & Sidney and Canadian National railway beds. Four bus lines along the route – Nos 50 (Goldstream), 61 (Sooke), 70 (Pat Bay Hwy) and 75 (Central Saanich) – are bike-rack equipped. For a brochure with maps or more information, ask at area Visitor Info Centres or call Capital Region District Parks (☎ 250-478-3344). The Greater Victoria Cycling Coalition's website, w www.gvcc.bc.ca, is a good place to look for regional cycling information.

---

cyclists could explore the beautiful James Bay neighborhood, with its many quiet tree-lined streets, or make a loop around Scenic Marine Dr. Those up for more adventure could tackle all or part of the 100km Galloping Goose Trail. See 'The Galloping Goose' boxed text for more information.

Organized Tours

Gray Line Bus Company (☎ 250-388-6539/5248, 800-663-8390, w www.grayline.ca/victoria, 700 Douglas St) offers a variety of tours. Its city tour on double deckers (1½ hours, $18/9 adult/child) takes in some of the major historical and scenic sights. Buy tickets and catch the bus in front of the Empress Hotel. Other popular offerings include a Butchart Gardens tour ($26/7) and their newest tourist temptation, the 'LarcNess MonsTour': a 70-minute harbor tour in an amphibious craft ($25/13).

When friends and relatives come to visit, locals refer them to **Enchanted Tours of Victoria** (☎ 888-475-3396, 3408 Seymour Place). It uses smaller air-conditioned minibuses and has commentary and itineraries that are less canned than others. The tours pick-up from local hotels and start at $25.

There's no more romantic way to see the city than in a horse-drawn carriage with **Tally-Ho Sightseeing Tours** (☎ 250-383-5067). A 30-minute clip-clop around the waterfront in your own personal carriage costs $60. Follow your nose to the corner of Belleville and Menzies Sts, where all the horses await you. **Victoria Carriage Tours** (☎ 250-383-2207) offers essentially the same service and lines up on the opposite side of Menzies.

Victoria Harbour Ferry Co (☎ 250-708-0201; open Mar-Oct) operates a fleet of little toy ferry boats resembling something you'd find in a giant's bathtub. Hop on one at the Empress dock for a 45-minute loop tour around the harbor ($12/6 adult/child under 12; season May-Oct). For one price you can get on and off as you like at regular stops such as Fisherman's Wharf and Spinnakers Brewpub. On Sunday morning in summer, look for the free 'Harbour Ferry Ballet,' which entails five of the little ferries doing a choreographed putt-putt to the music of Strauss' 'Blue Danube Waltz.' It takes place in the Inner Harbour facing the Empress Hotel, and while it's oh so silly and touristy, what the heck, it's really cute.

Victoria Bobby Walking Tours (☎/fax 250-995-0233, W www.walkvictoria.com) is a 75-minute city walk led by a retired, uniformed London police officer. It departs from the Visitor Info Centre at 11am daily, May through September. Tours cost $10; reservations recommended.

Seagull Expeditions (☎ 250-360-0893, 800-580-3890, W www.backpackertours.com/ Seagull, 213-951 Topaz Ave) operates backpacker-style, hostel-stay bus tours of Vancouver Island. The offerings are subject to change but have included a five-day tour ($186, not including hostel accommodations) taking in Victoria, the murals at Chemainus, bungy jumping in Nanaimo, and Pacific Rim National Park Reserve/ Tofino; and a three-day trip out to Pacific Rim National Park Reserve/Tofino ($129).

Midnight Sun Adventure Travel (☎ 250-480-9409, 800-255-5057, fax 250-370-7871, W www.midnightsuntravel.com, 843 Yates St) offers adventure activities on its guided van tours of the island. The 14-day Nootka West Coast Trail trip ($1490) includes a five-day hike on Nootka Island and visits to Tofino and Alert Bay. The four-day West Coast Adventure ($375) includes a kayak trip from Tofino to Vargas Island and back. The tours leave from Victoria, and rates include either motel accommodations or camping.

Special Events
Major events in Victoria include the **Terrif-Vic Jazz Party** (W www.terrifvic.com) in mid-April; the **Victoria Day Parade** and **Swiftsure International Yacht Race** in late May; the **Victoria Flower and Garden Festival** in mid-June; **Jazzfest International** and **Folkfest**, both held in late June and early July; **Canada Day** celebrations on July 1; the **Victoria Shakespeare Festival**, which lasts from mid-July through mid-August; **First People's Festival**, held the second weekend in August; the **Vancouver Island Wine Festival** in early September; and special Christmas and New Year celebrations starting as early as November through January.

Places to Stay
Lodging in Victoria can be expensive and, in summer, hard to find. Reserve as soon as you know your travel plans. In the downtown area, several renovated older hotels provide good value; to stay in the prime locations on

the Inner Harbour will take a bite out of your budget. If you're looking for inexpensive lodgings, you'll need to stay at one of the hostels, or else head out of the downtown area to one of the motel strips in the suburbs. Prices for accommodations are seasonal; if you travel outside of the main summer season, you'll save considerably on rooms.

If you're having trouble finding a room, Tourism Victoria's room reservation service (☎ 800-663-3883) may be able to help.

Camping *Fort Victoria RV Park* (☎ 250-479-8112, fax 250-479-5806, W www.fortvicrv .com, 340 Island Hwy 1A) Sites $28-29, including full hookups and free hot showers. Closest to town is this RV park, off Island Hwy 1A, 6km northwest from the city center. A bus stop is at the gate (take bus No 14 or 15 from downtown). The park caters mainly to RVs. It does have a few tent sites but there are no trees, and open fires are not allowed.

Thetis Lake Campground (☎ 250-478-3845, fax 250-478-6151, 1938 W Park Lane) Site $16, plus $2 electricity, $1 water, $1 sewer. Open year-round. A little farther out is this campground, on Rural Route 6 off the Trans Canada, 10km northwest of the city center. All facilities are available, including a store and coin-op showers, and you can swim in the nearby lake.

Goldstream Provincial Park (☎ 250-391-2300, fax 250-478-9211, Sooke Lake Rd) Sites $18.50. Open year-round. The best campground is at this park, on the Trans Canada Hwy 16km northwest of downtown Victoria on bus No 50 from Douglas St. You can go swimming, fishing or hiking.

The Visitor Info Centre can tell you of other campgrounds not too far from town.

Hostels *HI-Victoria Hostel* (☎ 250-385-4511, 888-883-0099, fax 250-385-3232, 516 Yates St) Dorm beds $17/21 members/nonmembers; private rooms $38-46. This HI hostel is in the old part of town just up from Wharf St. It has room for over 100 people, a large common area, kitchen, laundry, 24-hour check-in, no curfew and a good notice board. In summer, you can join other hostlers for some rooftop volleyball. In peak season it's advisable to check in before 4pm. The hostel may soon be moving to a quieter location on the southeast side of downtown.

Ocean Island Backpacker's Inn (☎ *250-385-1788, 888-888-4180, fax 250-385-1788,* **w** *www.oceanisland.com, 791 Pandora Ave*) Dorm beds $18-22, private doubles start at $45, weekly rates available, 24-hour check-in. Ocean Island is more than a hostel, it's an experience – an experience akin to being kidnapped by 100 of your closest friends and cajoled into partying till you explode. That may not appeal to some inhibited staid types, but Aussies will feel right at home here. The large exuberantly friendly place has about 150 beds and spacious common areas. Amenities include organized hiking trips, parties and pub crawls, a licensed café, Internet access, bike rentals and 24-hour staffing.

Victoria Backpackers Hostel (☎ *250-386-4471, fax 250-386-5539,* **e** *turtlerefuge@hotmail.com, 1608 Quadra St*) Dorm beds $15, private rooms $40. Also known as the Turtle Refuge, this friendly and relaxed hostel gets a cool crowd of international travelers, who often pitch in and help make improvements around the place. Amenities include luggage storage, kitchen and laundry facilities, no curfew, and probably by now, a killer sundeck.

University of Victoria (*Housing & Conference Services;* ☎ *250-721-8395, University of Victoria; rooms available late May–late Aug*) Singles/doubles $38/50. The university rents dorm rooms over summer (bus No 14 from Douglas St).

B&Bs Victoria is packed with B&Bs, with rates starting around $75. For help finding one, inquire at the Visitor Info Centre.

Craigmyle Guest House (☎ *250-595-5411, 888-595-5411, fax 250-370-5276,* **w** *www.bctravel.com/craigmyle, 1037 Craigdarroch Rd*) Singles/doubles $65/80 & up. About 1km east of downtown by Craigdarroch Castle, this beautiful inn has 13 rooms with private bath and four with assigned bath. Family suites available.

Holland House Inn (☎ *250-384-6644, 800-335-3466,* **w** *www.hollandhouse.ca, 595 Michigan St*) Rooms $100-295, most $175-250. Near the Inner Harbour in a beautiful neighborhood between the Parliament Buildings and Beacon Hill Park, the delightful Holland House occupies a 1932 Victorian-style place and a 1988 addition. Each of the 17 rooms and suites is opulently appointed and has its own bathroom, phone and TV. A full breakfast is served in the bright conservatory or out on the patio in good weather. This is a nice place.

Dashwood Manor (☎ *250-385-5517, 800-667-5517, fax 250-383-1760,* **w** *www.dashwoodmanor.com, 1 Cook St*) Rooms $125-345, most $245-285. The beautiful Dashwood enjoys an excellent location by the ocean and Beacon Hill Park. Each of the 14 handsome rooms has its own bathroom; breakfast comes from the stocked in-room refrigerator, with fresh croissants delivered each morning.

Spinnakers Guesthouse (☎ *250-386-2739, 877-838-2739, fax 250-384-3246,* **w** *www.spinnakers.com, 308 Catherine St*) Rooms $179 & up. On the harbor's northwest side, Spinnakers Brewpub offers upscale rooms in three nearby guest houses. Many rooms have Jacuzzi tubs and fireplaces, and all are close to the pub so you'll be just hops away when 'beer:30' rolls around.

Motels & Hotels The Inner Harbour is ringed by the Empress Hotel and many other lodgings, both modern and aging. You'll pay top dollar for the location, but other than the view you won't necessarily get much character. The following selections (among the plentiful lodgings in town) offer good value or character or both. All are within walking distance of the Inner Harbour and other downtown attractions.

Crystal Court Motel (☎ *250-384-0551, fax 250-384-5125, mbscott@vanisle.net, 701 Belleville St*) Singles/doubles $80/84 (add $2 for a kitchen). One of the best values in the town center, the Crystal Court is humble but lovable. The location – right across from the bus station and Crystal Garden – is central, though a bit busy with traffic. The staff is superfriendly, and while the Queen wouldn't stay here, for her subjects the rooms are just fine.

Hotel Douglas (☎ *250-383-4157, 800-332-9981, fax 250-383-2279,* **w** *www.hoteldouglas.com, 1450 Douglas St*) Rooms with shared bath $50, with private bath $95 & up. This centrally located budget hotel dating from 1911 is popular with international travelers. It's definitely not luxurious, but the old lady is far more fresh than flophouse. Downstairs, the bright and popular Cafe de la Lune is open until 1am weekdays and until 3am on Friday and Saturday.

BRITISH COLUMBIA

Strathcona Hotel (☎ 250-383-7137, 800-663-7476, fax 250-383-6893, **W** www.strathconahotel.com, 919 Douglas St) Rooms start at $89. The Strathcona is an older hotel with a young energetic vibe. A nightclub (Legends) and a plethora of bars and restaurants keep it bustling into the wee hours – if quiet is a priority, ask for a room away from the action. In summer, check out the rooftop pub and beach volleyball courts. Parking is $4 per night.

Shamrock Motel (☎ 250-385-8768, 800-294-5544, fax 250-385-1837, 675 Superior St) Singles/doubles $120/140. Enjoying a great location across from Beacon Hill Park, the Shamrock charms at first sight with its bright, Irish-green paint job and flower-bedecked premises. All rooms have kitchenettes so you can cook your own spuds. The only downside is some traffic noise, which scares the leprechauns away.

Helm's Inn (☎ 250-385-5767, 800-665-4356, **W** www.helmsinn.com, 600 Douglas St) Rooms $110-145, suites up to $165. A reader recommendation led us to this spotless, comfortable and friendly inn a block from the Royal BC Museum, two blocks from the Inner Harbour and kitty-corner from Beacon Hill Park. It was a great recommendation – the place is absolutely superb. A modest, low-rise exterior belies the beautiful, immaculately maintained spaces inside. Rooms are plushly appointed and all have kitchenettes. The inn is 100% nonsmoking, and the service is impeccable and ever-smiling. This one's a keeper.

James Bay Inn (☎ 250-384-7151, 800-836-2649, fax 250-385-2311, **W** www.james bayinn.bc.ca, 270 Government St) Singles/doubles $108/121 & up. A few blocks from the Inner Harbour in the quiet and lovely James Bay neighborhood, this inn occupies a handsome heritage building dating from 1911. Though a hotel for most of its life, the building was operating as St Mary's Priory in 1945, when one of the priory's patients, Emily Carr, died here. Guests can choose from among standard rooms, luxury suites or a two-bedroom cottage. A café and pub are on site. The inn also has a hip sense of humor: Visitors to its website hear a rendition of the Stones' 'Gimme Shelter.'

Best Western Carlton Plaza (☎ 250-388-5513, 800-663-7241, fax 250-388-5343, **W** www.bestwesterncarlton.com, 642 Johnson St) Rooms start at $119. This refurbished 1912 heritage hotel is convenient to the historic Old Town district and has been nicely updated with spacious amenity-filled rooms. Kitchen suites are available, and the staff is notably cheerful and friendly. All things considered, it's a pretty good value.

Abigail's Hotel (☎ 250-388-5363, 800-561-6565, fax 250-388-7787, **W** www.abigails hotel.com, 906 McClure St) Rooms start at $120. This romantic Tudor-style mansion – a cross between a B&B and a boutique hotel – has exquisitely furnished rooms with fresh flowers and goose-down duvets. Rates include evening hors d'oeuvres and a three-course breakfast.

Isabella's Guest Suites (☎ 250-381-8414, **W** www.isabellasbb.com, 537 Johnson St, entrance on Waddington Alley) Suites $150 a night or $800 a week, including breakfast. This unique choice features an excellent off-street location and modern romantic verve in one of Victoria's busiest shopping and dining areas. The two apartment-like suites include huge beds, complete kitchens, clawfoot tubs and enclosed showers, wood floors and classy furnishings. Il Terrazo next door will deliver room-service dinners on request. And Victoria's best coffeehouse/café, Willie's Bakery, is right next door. This is definitely among the coolest digs in town.

Swans Suite Hotel & Brewpub (☎ 250-361-3310, 800-668-7926, fax 250-361-3491, **W** www.swanshotel.com, 506 Pandora Ave) Suites $159-249, penthouse $695. In a landmark-yellow, flower-covered gem of a building near the waterfront, Swans is absolutely sensational. Dating from 1913, the former granary and feed store has been transformed into 30 big suites that retain the interesting old post-and-beam architecture but surround it with clean hip styling. The outrageously wonderful 3000-plus-sq-ft split-level penthouse – you'll want to move in permanently – features a private rooftop hot tub and enough great art to be its own gallery. If all that's not enough, Swans also runs a microbrewery downstairs, and the pub is one of the best places in town for eating, drinking and people-watching. If you stay here, you may stay in Victoria longer than you planned.

The Fairmont Empress (☎ 250-384-8111, 800-441-1414, fax 250-381-4334, **W** www.fairmont.com, 721 Government St) Rates from around \$239 for a room facing the city, more for a harbor view. Last but not least is Victoria's first hotel, the Empress – one of the grand château-style hotels built across Canada by the Canadian Pacific Railway around the turn of the 20th century. For the hotel's design, the CPR turned to the brilliant young English architect Francis Rattenbury (1867–1935), who had come to BC in 1892. Rattenbury designed the Empress in 1903, a decade after his famous Parliament Buildings and well before he left his wife for a much younger woman, took her back to England and was subsequently murdered by her clandestine lover, Rattenbury's young chauffeur. A scandal worthy of the Empire, indeed.

Rattenbury and the CPR's glory days are long gone, but the Empress remains the symbol and centerpiece of Victoria. They just don't build them like this anymore, as several cheap modern imitations in the vicinity make abundantly clear. Today the hotel is part of the Fairmont chain – the folks with the annoying Web site – and continues to attract honeymooners, bus-tour groups and well-heeled travelers. It certainly still embodies a sense of good old-fashioned British imperialism; High Tea at the Empress (\$46) is an upper-crust tradition, and if you hang out in the hotel's Bengal Lounge much you'll be donning your pith helmet and tiger-hunting togs in no time. Apart from that, this is, after all, just a luxury hotel with some view rooms. It's up to you to decide whether history is worth the big mark-up.

High Tea at the Empress

English-style high tea at the Empress Hotel is so mandatory an experience for most visitors as to be a cliché. While high tea isn't usually considered a meal in itself, this extravagance of clotted cream, berries, scones and biscuits will surely ruin your appetite for an evening meal. The tearooms at the Empress are lovely, but high tea isn't cheap – you'll spend \$46 per person for the honor. Reservations are a good idea in all but the dead of winter.

🍁 🍁 🍁 🍁 🍁 🍁 🍁 🍁 🍁 🍁

Places to Eat

Though a small city, Victoria has a variety of restaurants, due in part to its many visitors, and prices are generally good.

Budget *Willie's Bakery* (☎ 250-381-8414, 537 Johnson St) Breakfast \$4.25-8, lunch \$3.75-7.75. In funky Old Town, Willie's is a cool coffeehouse and bakery with a sophisticated breakfast and lunch menu. In addition to great pastries, baguettes and croissants, breakfast choices might include homemade granola or brioche french toast with local berries and maple mascarpone cream. At lunch, the menu offers high-style sandwiches such as Tofino shrimp with avocado, cucumber and red-curry mayo. The atmosphere is warm, with lots of brick and some interesting fruit sculptures, and you might hear jazz on the sound system. Outside, the beautiful brick patio, adorned with flowers and a fountain, is a tranquil Old Town oasis – the perfect place to sip a café mocha and write a postcard.

John's Place (☎ 250-389-0711, 723 Pandora Ave) Breakfast \$4-10. Locals come to this off-the-tourist-track spot for large portions of good hearty grub at breakfast or lunch. The atmosphere is busy and casual, with an eclectic mix of framed posters on the walls and mellow rock music on the stereo.

Blue Fox Café (☎ 250-380-1683, 101-919 Fort St) Breakfast \$5.50-9, lunch \$7-8.50. This place offers a more creative, healthier menu than John's, with veggie elements and international influences.

Sam's Deli (☎ 250-382-8424, 805 Government St) Sandwiches, soups & salads, most under \$7. Despite its location at Tourist Ground Zero, Sam's offers good food at reasonable prices. Sit outside, away from the noise and crowds. It's open 7:30am to 7pm Monday to Friday, 8am to 7pm Saturday, 9am to 7pm Sunday.

Green Cuisine (☎ 250-385-1809, 5-560 Johnson St) Vegetarians will love this place. It lays out a 100% vegan buffet (\$1.59 per 100g) and has fresh squeezed juices, healthy desserts and other delights. It's open 10am to 8pm daily.

Foo Hong Chop Suey (☎ 250-386-9553, 564 Fisgard St) Meals \$5-8. This place is small and basic, yet has good, simple Cantonese food.

The fish and chips are excellent in Victoria. Two good places include:

Blackfish Cafe (☎ 250-385-9996, 950 Wharf St) Breakfast $7-9, lunch $8-12, dinner $15-17. In the Victoria Marine Adventure Centre, right down on the docks, this little place gets an A for atmosphere. Snag a table outside and watch the seaplanes, ferries, whale-watching boats, kayaks, seagulls and occasional curious seal cruise by.

Barb's Place (☎ 250-384-6515, 310 St Lawrence St) Fish & chips around $8. Barb's at Fisherman's Wharf, west of downtown, is in a wooden shack down on the dock. It's not worth a special trip, but would make a good stop if you're taking the Harbour Ferry tour or meandering along the Scenic Marine Dr. You might be able to buy fresh crabs from the boats nearby.

Mid-Range *Süze* (☎ 250-383-2829, 515 Yates St) Meals $12-23. Suze offers a small, Asian-influenced menu and a hip bar scene. Look for creative gourmet pizzas like the Thai prawn version, with spinach, cilantro, curry and scallions. The lounge, with exposed brick and a vintage 7.5m-long mahogany bar, is one of the coziest and coolest places in Victoria.

Re-Bar (☎ 250-361-9223, 50 Bastion Square) Breakfast $5-10, weekend brunch $6-10, lunch & dinner $8-13. One of the most happening places in town, the Re-Bar features an eclectic contemporary international menu, heavy on the vegetarian side, and artsy decor to match. The staff is young and hip, and claustrophobes will appreciate the nicely spaced tables.

Wharfside Eatery (☎ 250-360-1808, 1208 Wharf St) Lunch $7-15, dinner $16-30. If the weather's good and dining on a outdoor deck is appealing, then the Wharfside Eatery is a good bet. While fresh seafood is the specialty, the menu also offers various wraps, steaks, pastas and wood-fired pizzas. The atmosphere is festive and exuberant.

Il Terrazo Ristorante (☎ 250-361-0028, 555 Johnson St) Lunch $8-13, dinner $15-25. Bustling and popular, Il Terrazo is a local favorite for Italian pastas, grilled meats and tempting pizzas. The atmosphere is nice, and you can dine alfresco in good weather.

Millos (☎ 250-382-4422/5544, 716 Burdett Ave) Lunch $7-10, dinner $10-20. Victoria has a number of good Greek restaurants, but Millos has the reputation for the best roast lamb ($15); stay late for belly dancers on Friday and Saturday night.

Swans Brew Pub (☎ 250-361-3310, 506 Pandora Ave) Average mains $8-13. Both a brewpub and a great place for lunch or light dinner, Swan's has great beer, good burgers and sandwiches, and one of the city's most appealing, art-filled barrooms.

Herald St Caffe (☎ 250-381-1441, 546 Herald St) Lunch $10-12, dinner $16-27. This small Italian bistro serves delicious pastas, as well as vegetarian dishes and great desserts. Oenophiles take note: The wine list has some 400 selections, with about 20 available by the glass.

Harbour Canoe Club (☎ 250-361-1940, 450 Swift St) Lunch $9-11, weekend brunch $6-12, dinner $11-22. Near Chinatown on the Upper Harbour, this beautifully done renovation of an 1894 building houses a microbrewery and a restaurant with excellent beer and tasty casual fare a cut above pub grub. In nice weather, sit outside for harbor views (dominated by the Russian submarine).

The Bent Mast (☎ 250-383-6000, 512 Simcoe St) Dinner entrées $9-17. Out in the James Bay neighborhood, this neat little spot in an old 1884 house is open late every night and has a nice outdoor patio, a warm cozy bar and regular live music.

Siam Thai Restaurant (☎ 250-383-9911, 512 Fort St) Dinner entrées $10-19. Crowds pack Siam Thai for excellent Thai food at reasonable prices. It's casually elegant, and the service is friendly and efficient. The kitchen gets extra kudos for agreeing to make something not on the menu, then doing a stunning job of it.

Top End In addition to the places below, you can always book a table at the Empress, but go by the bank first.

Chandler's Seafood Restaurant (☎ 250-385-3474, 1250 Wharf St) Lunch $10-13, dinner $15-46. This long-established dining room draws tourists and locals alike for superbly prepared fresh fish. The atmosphere is clubby and comfortable.

Blue Crab Bar & Grill (☎ 250-480-1999, 146 Kingston St) Dinner $20-30. Superb views and fine seafood are a winning combination at the upscale Blue Crab, west of downtown in the Coast Harbourside Hotel. The atmosphere is elegant and dressy. Reservations are requested.

Camille's Fine Westcoast Dining (☎ 250-381-3433, 45 Bastion Square) Dinner $17-27. Camille's has the reputation of being Victoria's most inventive restaurant, its fusion cooking combining the best of Northwest ingredients with eclectic, international recipes. The menu is big on fish and game. Open for dinner only, nightly.

Entertainment

Monday Magazine, the weekly entertainment paper available free around town, has extensive coverage of what's going on.

Performing Arts Classical-music organizations in Victoria include **Victoria Symphony Orchestra** (☎ 250-385-6515 or 250-386-6121; season Sept-May), which performs at the Royal Theatre and **Pacific Opera Victoria** (☎ 250-385-0222 or 250-386-6121; season Oct-May), which offers three productions a year at the Royal Theatre.

Theater Victoria has a number of theatres that provide venues for plays, concerts, comedies, ballets and operas.

McPherson Playhouse (☎ 250-386-6121, 3 Centennial Square) This playhouse, on the corner of Pandora Ave and Government St, regularly puts on plays and comedies.

Royal Theatre (☎ 250-386-6121, 805 Broughton St) The elegant Royal hosts a range of performances, including ballet, symphony, dance and concerts.

Other theaters worth checking are the **Belfry** (☎ 250-385-6815, 1291 Gladstone Ave) northeast of the downtown area, and the **Phoenix Theatre** (☎ 250-721-8000) on the University of Victoria campus.

Live Music Though Victoria isn't as happening as Vancouver after dark, you can still find places to hear live music.

Legends (☎ 250-383-7137, 919 Douglas St) This longstanding nightclub in the Strathcona Hotel books an eclectic mix of good live bands several times a month. In the meantime, it's Top 40 DJ dancing.

Steamers Public House (☎ 250-381-4340, 570 Yates St) Just below Government St, Steamers is a good pub that brings in both local and touring bands.

Other places to check for live music include **Swans Brewpub** (see Pubs), **D'Arcy McGee's** (☎ 250-380-1322, 1127 Wharf St)

and **James Bay Inn** (☎ 250-384-7151, 270 Government St). Check out the calendar in *Monday Magazine* to see what's happening when you visit.

Dance Clubs The Bastion Square area and Old Town have several dance clubs, which come and go with the tides.

Boom Boom Room (☎ 250-381-2331, 1208 Wharf St) Regular theme nights draw a young crowd here.

Level Nightclub (☎ 250-380-2733, 1630 Store St) This cavernous club is a good place to get lost on the dance floor, or anywhere else for that matter.

Gay & Lesbian Venues Victoria's gay and lesbian scene is not what you'd call thriving. To find out what's going on in town, go chat up the bartender at **BJ's Lounge** (☎ 250-388-0505, 642 Johnson St, entrance on Broad St), a gay bar around the corner from the Best Western Carlton Hotel.

Pubs *Spinnakers Brew Pub & Restaurant* (☎ 250-386-2739, 308 Catherine St) Across the blue bridge, Spinnakers makes great beer and also has a deck with views of the Inner Harbour.

Swans Brewpub (☎ 250-361-3310, 506 Pandora St) Swans takes up half the main floor of Swans Hotel. Visit Thursday for Celtic music.

Sticky Wicket Pub (☎ 250-383-7137, 919 Douglas St) It doesn't make its own beer, but the Sticky Wicket, in the Strathcona Hotel, offers an extensive selection of international beer on tap, as well as creative food, seating for families and a rooftop patio with beach volleyball courts.

Cinemas Several first-run cinemas are scattered around downtown. For more interesting fare try **Vic Theatre** (☎ 250-383-1998, 808 Douglas St), which schedules a lot of foreign films, or **Cinecenta** (☎ 250-721-8365), the University of Victoria's cinema, which screens recently released and classic independent films in the Student Union Building.

Shopping

On Government St between Pandora and Fisgard, the street is closed off every Sunday in summer for a big arts and crafts market. Don't miss this quintessential Victoria scene.

A number of craft shops along Douglas and Government Sts sell First Nations art and craftwork such as sweaters, moccasins, carvings and prints. The good stuff is expensive.

Canadian Impressions (☎ *250-953-7790, 921 Government St)* This shop stocks some quality First Nations crafts.

Sasquatch Trading Ltd (☎ *250-386-9033, 1233 Government St)* Sasquatch stocks a good selection of Cowichan sweaters. These hand-spun, hand-knit sweaters are warm and should last a decade or more.

Eaton Centre (☎ *250-382-7141)* Victoria's mall rats scurry around Eaton Centre, a large enclosed shopping center on Government and Douglas Sts between Fort and View Sts. The complex includes five floors and 100 shops, plus restaurants, fountains and a rooftop garden.

Dragon Song Music Co (☎ *250-385-4643, 16 Fan Tan Alley)* If you go check out this nifty little shop full of drums and lots of other cool instruments, you'll also get to see Fan Tan Alley, one of Chinatown's interesting attractions. Fan Tan Alley isn't easy to find, but discovering it is half the fun.

Getting There & Away

Air Victoria International Airport (YYJ) is in Sidney, about 26km north of the city off the Patricia Bay Hwy (Hwy 17). Airlines serving Victoria include Air Canada (☎ 888-247-2262, W www.aircanada.ca); Horizon Air (☎ 800-547-9308, W www.horizon air.com), with service between Victoria and Seattle, Port Angeles and Bellingham; North Vancouver Air (☎ 800-228-6608, W www.northvanair.com), with flights to Vancouver, Whistler, Tofino, Campbell River and Powell River; and WestJet Airlines (☎ 888-937-8538, W www.westjet .com), with flights to Vancouver and other Western Canadian cities.

West Coast Air (☎ 250-388-4521, 800-347-2222, W www.westcoastair.com) and Harbour Air Seaplanes (☎ 250-384-2215, 800-665-0212, W www.harbour-air.com) offer seaplane flights to Vancouver Harbor. Kenmore Air (☎ 800-543-9595, W www.kenmoreair.com) flies seaplanes to Seattle daily. Harbour Air leaves from in front of VMAC; Kenmore and West Coast share a terminal one dock north.

Bus The bus station is at 700 Douglas St. Pacific Coach Lines (☎ 250-385-4411, 800-661-1725, W www.pacificcoach.com) operates buses to Vancouver (the bus depot, cruise ship terminal or airport) every hour between 6am and 6pm (until 9pm on Friday and Sunday) during July and August and every two hours from 6am to 8pm the rest of the year; the adult peak-season fare, which includes the ferry, is $28.50/55 one-way/roundtrip to Vancouver depot, or $32.50/63 to the airport; children five to 11 are half-price.

Laidlaw Coach Lines (☎ 250-388-5248, 800-318-0818 in Canada, 800-663-8390 in the USA, W www.grayline.ca/victoria) covers Vancouver Island from Victoria all the way to Port Hardy and out to Tofino. Six or seven buses a day travel to Nanaimo. From there, four buses go west to Port Alberni, with two continuing to Tofino; and four or five go north to Campbell River, with one or two continuing to Port Hardy.

Although Greyhound has no service on Vancouver Island or from Victoria to the mainland, you can get fare and schedule information and purchase tickets for buses departing Vancouver at the Victoria bus depot (☎ 250-385-4411).

Train The Esquimalt & Nanaimo Railiner, or E&N Railiner, operated by VIA Rail (☎ 250-383-4324, 888-842-7245, W www .viarail.ca, 450 Pandora Ave), connects Victoria with points north, including Duncan, Nanaimo, Parksville and Courtenay. There is one train in each direction per day – northbound from Victoria at 8:15am, southbound from Courtenay at 1:30pm. The scenic journey takes about 4½ hours. Adult fare to Courtenay is $44/88 one-way/roundtrip. For a nice day trip, take the train as far as Qualicum Beach, get off and have lunch (you'll have a couple of hours), then catch the southbound train back to Victoria. Roundtrip adult fare to Qualicum Beach is $60. The *Malahat,* as the train is known, is popular, so book ahead. Seven-day advance purchases are about 35% cheaper, and ask about various promotional fares.

Full schedules are available online or at travel agencies, the Visitor Info Centre or the small Pandora Ave train station, at the east end of the Johnson St bridge (the blue bridge). To get there, take bus No 6, 24 or 25.

Ferry BC Ferries (☎ 250-386-3431, 888-223-3779 in BC, W www.bcferries.com) operates service to the mainland from Swartz Bay, 27km north of Victoria via the Pat Bay Hwy (Hwy 17). Ferry schedules are widely available around town. BC Ferries' information office, 1112 Fort St, is open 8:30am to 4:30pm weekdays.

The trip between Swartz Bay and Tsawwassen near Vancouver takes 95 minutes, with sailings every hour between 7am and 10pm in July and August; slightly reduced schedule rest of year. The peak-season one-way fare is $9.50/4.75/33.50 adult/child age 5-11/car. To reserve a spot for your vehicle, call ☎ 888-724-5223 in BC or 604-444-2890 outside BC, or visit the website.

BC Ferries also operates between Swartz Bay and five of the southern Gulf Islands: Galiano, Mayne, Saturna, Salt Spring and North Pender. Schedules vary by season and destination, with more frequent sailings in July and August. The peak-season roundtrip fare is $6.25/3.25 adult/child (25¢ less to Salt Spring island); a car is $21.50 ($19.25 to Salt Spring Island).

Several ferries serve Washington State from the Inner Harbour ferry terminal at 430 Belleville St.

The Victoria Clippers, a small fleet of sleek space-age catamaran ferries run by Clipper Navigation (☎ 250-382-8100, W www.clippervacations.com), sail from Victoria to the San Juan Islands (Friday Harbor, 1¾ hours, peak season adult fare US$29/49 one-way/roundtrip) and Seattle (2½ hours, from US$66/109).

The car ferry MV *Coho,* operated by Black Ball Transport (☎ 250-386-2202, Port Angeles ☎ 360-457-4491, W www.north olympic.com/coho), sails to Port Angeles, just across the Strait of Juan de Fuca. The fare is US$30 for a car and driver. Extra passengers and walk-on passengers pay US$8/4 adult/child age 5-11. Canadian currency is accepted. The trip takes about 1½ hours. Mid-June through mid-September, four boats a day leave Victoria. The rest of the year, boats leave two to three times a day.

The passenger-only Victoria Express (☎ 250-361-9144, 360-452-8088 in Port Angeles, 800-633-1589 in the US, W www.victoriaexpress.com) also goes to Port Angeles from the Inner Harbour terminal, departing two to three times daily from late May through early October; the one-way/roundtrip adult fare for the one-hour journey is US$12.50/25.

Visitors who are arriving in Port Angeles without their own transportation can take a direct bus to either Seattle or Sea-Tac Airport on Olympic Bus Lines (☎ 360-417-0700, 800-457-4492, W www.olympicbuslines.com). The one-way/roundtrip adult fare is US$29/49 to Seattle (about 2¾ hours) and US$43/58 to Sea-Tac (about 3½ hours). Buses leave twice a day on the scenic trip, which includes a ferry crossing.

Washington State Ferries (Sidney ☎ 250-381-1551 or 250-656-1531, Seattle ☎ 206-464-6400, recorded information ☎ 800-843-3779 in Washington, ☎ 888-808-7977 in Washington, W www.wsdot.wa.gov/ferries/index.cfm) operates a car ferry between Sidney, BC, north of Victoria, and Anacortes, Washington, north of Seattle, via the San Juan Islands. The trip takes at least three hours. One-way peak-season fare for a vehicle and driver is US$41. Extra passengers and walk-on passengers pay US$11/7.70/5.50 adult/youth/senior. If you're going from Sidney to Anacortes, you can stop off on the San Juans and get back on later for no extra charge.

Getting Around

Airporter Shuttle Bus (☎ 250-386-2525, 877-386-2525) provides shuttle service between the airport and all area hotels and B&Bs. The buses run every half-hour from 4:30am to midnight daily and cost $13/11.70 adult/senior & student. City bus No 70 comes to within 1km of the airport at its McTavish Park 'n Ride stop; if you're coming from the airport, the Airporter will drop you there for $2.

BC Transit buses (☎ 250-382-6161, W www.bctransit.com) run frequently and cover a wide area. The normal one-way fare is $1.75 ($2.50 if you travel into a second zone, such as the suburbs of Colwood or Sidney). Have exact change ready. All-day passes ($5.50/4 adult/senior & student) are not sold on buses but are available from convenience stores and the Visitor Info Centre. Bus No 70 goes to the BC Ferries terminal at Swartz Bay. Bus No 75 travels to the Washington State Ferry dock in Sidney.

Major car rental companies have offices at the airport and in and around the downtown area. Downtown area offices include Avis (☎ 250-386-8468, 1001 Douglas St), Budget (☎ 250-953-5300, 757 Douglas St); Enterprise (☎ 250-475-6900, 2507 Government St), National (☎ 250-386-1213, 767 Douglas St) and Thrifty (☎ 250-383-3659, 625 Frances Ave).

Call Empress Taxi (☎ 250-656-5588), Victoria Taxi (☎ 250-383-7111), Blue Bird Cabs (☎ 250-382-4235), or, for a two-seat human-powered pedicab ride, Kabuki Kabs (☎ 250-385-4243).

Cycle Treks (☎ 250-386-2277, 811 Wharf St) rents bikes for $8 to $10 per hour or $35 to $40 per day.

Victoria Harbour Ferry (☎ 250-708-0201) provides frequent service (every 15 minutes in peak summer season) to the Empress Hotel, Visitor Info Centre, Ocean Pointe Resort, Fisherman's Wharf, Spinnakers Brewpub and other stops on the Inner Harbour and Gorge waterway. Fares start at $3/1.50 adult/child under 12; prices vary depending on how far you travel.

SOUTHEASTERN VANCOUVER ISLAND

For information on provincial parks in this region, contact the BC Parks South Vancouver Island District (☎ 250-391-2300, fax 250-478-9211, 2930 Trans Canada Hwy, Victoria, BC V9B 6H6).

Duncan & Cowichan Valley

About 60km north of Victoria along the Trans Canada Hwy is the small town of Duncan. It marks the beginning of the Cowichan Valley, which runs westward and contains large Cowichan Lake. This is the land of the Cowichan people, BC's largest First Nations group.

A good day trip from Victoria, for those with wheels, is to head up to Chemainus, back to Duncan, then over to Lake Cowichan, across to Port Renfrew and down the west coast back to town. It's a lot of driving but if you're in no hurry and can stop a lot it makes an interesting, full day. For information, ask at the Visitor Info Centres. The well used logging road from Lake Cowichan to Port Renfrew is gravelled and in good shape; with a basic map, you shouldn't have any difficulty.

Duncan's Visitor Info Centre (☎ 250-746-4636, www.duncancc.bc.ca, 381A Trans Canada Hwy) is in the strip mall on the corner of Coronation St. It's open daily in summer, reduced hours the rest of the year. There really isn't much to see in Duncan (although the old part of town is worth a look around) or the township of Lake Cowichan, but the valley and lake are good for camping, hiking, swimming, fishing and canoeing. The turnoff for Lake Cowichan is about 4km north of Duncan, left (east) of the Trans Canada Hwy; from the turnoff the lake is another 22km.

Since 1985, Duncan, the 'City of Totems,' has developed a project with the Cowichans to have totem poles carved and displayed around town. You'll see many examples of this west Coast art form.

Quw'utsun' Cultural & Conference Centre This center (*☎ 250-746-8119, 200 Cowichan Way; adult/senior & student/child/family $10/8/6/25; open daily 9am-6pm in summer; 10am-5pm rest of year)* has exhibits on Cowichan craftwork and carvings (you can often watch carvers and weavers at work) as well as a gift shop and a restaurant serving Cowichan cuisine. The admission price includes a 22-minute movie about the center and Cowichan people.

BC Forest Discovery Centre About 3km north of Duncan is the BC Forest Discovery Centre (*☎ 250-715-1113, W www.bcforestmuseum.com, 2892 Drinkwater Rd; adult/senior & student/child $7/6/4, reduced in off-season; open daily 10am-6pm in summer, 10am-4pm rest of year)*. The 40-hectare site holds a stand of original-growth Douglas firs, 55m tall, that were present before Captain Cook arrived in 1778. Included in the price in summer is a ride around the site in a small steam train. You can visit a bird sanctuary or view a replica of an old logging camp and logging equipment. Inside are more displays and movies of old logging operations.

Activities Many hiking trails surround Cowichan River and Cowichan Lake. One is the **Cowichan River Footpath**, an 18km-long trail with a good variety of scenery along the way. You can either do it in a day or camp en route. The path goes to Skutz Falls; from there you can head back to Duncan or keep going upriver. Maps of the trail are available at sporting stores. Cowichan Lake gets warm enough to swim in. You can also go fishing and canoeing in the lake and river.

Places to Stay The area has a hostel and plenty of campgrounds and motels.

Cowichan River Provincial Park (☎ 250-391-2300, *Riverbottom Rd*) Sites $12. East of the town of Lake Cowichan on Riverbottom Rd (take Skutz Falls Rd off Hwy 18), this park has two riverside campgrounds: Stoltz Pool, 18km east of the town, is open year-round; Skutz is 14km east and open summers only.

Lakeview Park Municipal Campground (*seasonal campground* ☎ 250-749-3350, *year-round town/reservations phone* ☎ 250-749-6681, *town fax 250-749-3900, 885 Lakeview Park Rd*) Sites $17-20; open May-Sept. This campground is on Cowichan Lake's south shore about 3km west of the town. It has showers, toilets and free firewood.

Gordon Bay Provincial Park (☎ 250-391-2300, 800-689-9025, fax 250-478-9211, *Walton Rd, off South Shore Rd*) Sites $18.50. Open year-round, with reduced fees and services Sept-Mar. Farther west along the lake, this beautiful campground has 126 sites for trailers and tents, as well as showers and flush toilets. Reservations are accepted.

River's Edge Hiker's Hostel (☎ 250-701-7616 or 250-749-6563, 160 Cowichan Lake Rd, Lake Cowichan) Dorm beds $18. This basic hostel is by the Cowichan River.

Duncan Motel (☎ 250-748-2177, fax 250-748-2289, 2552 Alexander St) Singles/doubles $36/42 & up. One of the cheapest motels in this area is the Duncan, which has some kitchenettes. It's a block off the main drag.

Falcon Nest Motel (☎ 250-748-8188, fax 250-748-7829, 5867 Trans Canada Hwy) Singles/doubles $44/50. Falcon Nest is another basic option and has a seasonal outdoor heated pool.

Best Western Cowichan Valley Inn (☎ 250-748-2722, 800-927-6199, fax 250-748-2207, 6474 Trans Canada Hwy) Singles/doubles $79/85 & up. The parklike Cowichan Valley Inn is convenient to the BC Forest Discovery Centre and Quw'utsun' Centre and has a pool, restaurant and pub.

Getting There & Away Laidlaw Coach Lines buses travel between Duncan and Victoria for $11 including tax, one-way. The 70-minute train trip between Duncan and

Victoria on the E&N Railiner costs $15/30 one-way/roundtrip including tax; there is one a day in each direction. The station is downtown at 120 Canada Way; purchase tickets from the conductor (see Getting There & Away in the Victoria section for more information).

Carmanah Walbran Provincial Park

Take logging roads from Lake Cowichan to reach this majestic wilderness park, which contains 2% of BC's remaining old-growth forest. The 16,450-hectare park was created after years of bitter fighting over logging rights. The rich rainforest here holds some of the world's tallest trees, including a giant Sitka spruce 94.5m high. The park has some basic tent sites, drinking water, limited marked trails and an information office.

Trails extend beyond the park north into the Carmanah Valley, which has wilderness camping. The rough trails can often be muddy. Though the park is adjacent to the West Coast Trail, no access between the Trail and the park is available. The road from Lake Cowichan takes at least 2½ hours by car, and watch for trucks! Along the way is Nitinat Lake, the 'confused sea,' renowned for windsurfing, and another road leading to the Didtidaht Nation Centre, where limited services are available. The Info Centre in Duncan has some information on the park. For further details, contact the BC Parks South Vancouver Island District (☎ 250-391-2300).

Duncan to Nanaimo

About 16km north of Duncan on Hwy 1A is the small town of **Crofton**, from where you can catch ferries to Vesuvius Bay in the north of Salt Spring Island (see the Southern Gulf Islands section later in this chapter).

Chemainus

Chemainus, 10km north of Crofton, had a novel and interesting way of putting itself on the tourist map. In 1983 the town sawmill shut down, and to counter the inevitable slow death, an artist was commissioned to paint a large outdoor mural relating to the town's history. People took notice, more murals were painted and now there are over 30 of them. A bustling and prosperous community developed and the sawmill reopened.

The brightly painted Chemainus Theatre has been restored and is the most striking building in town. It hosts community theater (☎ 800-565-7738, W www.ctheatre.bc.ca). Lots of craft shops and restaurants make a short visit a worthwhile proposition. The Visitor Infomation Centre (☎ 250-246-3944, W www .chemainus.bc.ca) is at 9796 Willow St.

Off the coast of Chemainus are **Thetis Island** and **Kuper Island**. Kuper Island is a First Nations reserve for which you need permission from the chief to visit. Thetis Island is primarily geared to boaters and has two marinas; Thetis Island Marina has a pub. At Pilkey Point, some interesting sandstone formations line the beach.

Ferries for these islands leave from Oak St; the ticket office is opposite the Hot Java Kafe (good coffee and free Internet access). Roundtrip fare is $5.25 per person, plus $13.50 for a car.

Chemainus Hostel (*☎ 250-246-2809, 9694 Chemainus Rd*) Dorm beds $15. Once an old mill-workers' dorm, the Chemainus features separate sleeping areas for men and women, a laundry room and secure bike storage.

Fuller Lake Motel (*☎ 250-246-3282, 888-246-3255, fax 250-246-3445, 9300 Smiley Rd*) Singles/doubles $55/65. This place is on a frontage road along the west side of the Trans Canada Hwy, just south of the Henry Rd stoplight. It has pleasant rooms and some kitchenettes.

Chemainus is largely a town of B&Bs. One to try is *Bird Song Cottage* (*☎ 250-246-9910, fax 250-246-2909, W www.birdsong cottage.com, 9909 Maple St*) Singles/doubles start at $80/105. Rooms are nostalgic at this Victorian cottage, which sits in a nice neighborhood with water views.

Ladysmith & Around

A postcard-pretty small town about 26km north of Duncan on the Trans Canada Hwy, Ladysmith is perched on a steep hillside looking east to the Coast Range on the mainland. Originally built as a coal-shipping port by industrialist James Dunsmuir, the town was named after the South African town of the same name. The warmest seawaters north of San Francisco are said to flow at **Transfer Beach Park**; it's right in town and you can camp there. Many restored late 19th- and early 20th-century buildings give

the town considerable charm. The Visitor Info Centre (☎ 250-245-2112, 26 Gatacre Ave) is open Monday to Friday 9am-4pm.

North of town, turn off on Yellow Point Rd, a beautiful bucolic route to Nanaimo that passes a couple places of interest.

Yellow Point Lodge (*☎ 250-245-7422, W www.yellowpointlodge.com, 3700 Yellow Point Rd*) Singles $64-120, doubles $115-190, including three meals. At Yellow Point Lodge, it's hard to say which is more stunning: the setting – on a rock shelf jutting out into the Strait of Georgia – or the gorgeous log lodge itself, which sits right over the water and is backed by 66 hectares of woods. Cabins of various sizes and luxury levels dot the woods, making ideal retreats for holing up and writing the Great Canadian Novel.

Crow & Gate (*☎ 250-722-3731, 2313 Yellow Point Rd*) Farther north, the Crow & Gate is an authentic British-style pub, right down to the steak-and-kidney pie or oysters and Guinness. Set on a big spread in the middle of nowhere, it's well worth the detour for a meal or just a pint out in the sun.

NANAIMO & AROUND
pop 85,000

Nanaimo, about 110km north of Victoria, is Vancouver Island's second major city. It's an appealing place with a diverse cross section of people, a busy little downtown and a visitor-oriented waterfront. It's also a transportation hub; two BC Ferries terminals connect the city with the Horseshoe Bay and Tsawwassen terminals outside Vancouver.

Orientation & Information

The entire waterfront area off Front St along the harbor has been redone with a seaside walkway, docks, shops, restaurants, coffee bars and pubs. Behind the harbor lies the central core. Most of the restaurants and shops are on Commercial and Chapel Sts and Terminal Ave, which run more or less parallel to the harbor. To the south, Nicol St, the southern extension of Terminal Ave, leads to the Trans Canada Hwy. To the north, Terminal Ave forks – the right fork becomes Stewart Ave and leads to the BC Ferries terminal in Departure Bay; the left fork becomes Hwy 19A, the Oceanside Route, which heads up-island to Courtenay, Campbell River and Port Hardy. The

Nanaimo Parkway/Hwy 19, the speedy Inland Island Highway, bypasses the entire town on the west side.

The waterfront promenade links several parks. **Georgia Park** has a few totem poles, a display of First Nations canoes, including a large war canoe, and a fine view of Nanaimo Harbour. **Swy-A-Lana Lagoon** is good for children to splash in, and **Mafeo-Sutton Park** is where you'll find ferries to Newcastle Island.

The Visitor Info Centre (☎ 250-756-0106, 800-663-7337, fax 250-756-0075, ⓦ www .tourismnanaimo.com, 2290 Bowen Rd) is between Hwys 19 and 19A off Northfield Rd, north of downtown. Watch for the many large signs. Located in a 60-year-old mansion, the center has local and regional

information and is open daily year-round. It stocks a walking-tour guide describing historical buildings around downtown. In summer, an information office in the Bastion historical site on the waterfront is open daily. Downtown also has its own small Downtown Nanaimo Information Centre (☎ 250-754-8531, ⓦ www.nanaimo downtown.com, 150 Commercial St), open daily in summer and Monday to Saturday the rest of the year. It has lots of flyers and information about the downtown area.

The Old City Quarter, a small section of downtown around Bastion, Fitzwilliam, Selby and Wesley Sts (on the west side of Hwy 19A, up the hill), is being rejuvenated. The impressive **Port Theatre** performing-arts complex (☎ 250-754-8550, 125 Front

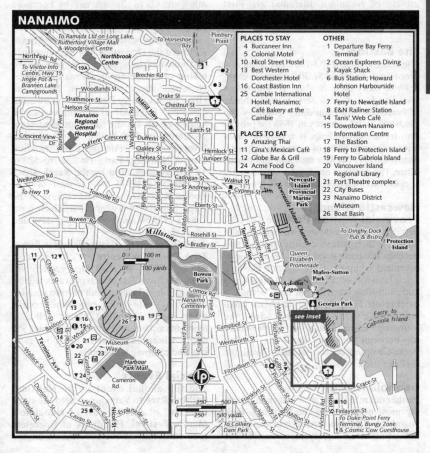

St), down by the waterfront, also includes the big Vancouver Island Regional Library (☎ 250-753-1154, 90 Commercial St), which offers Internet access.

The downtown post office is at Harbour Park Mall, between Front St and Gordon St at Terminal Ave. Tanis' Web Cafe (☎ 250-714-0302, 139 Bastion St) offers Internet access for $5.50 an hour. Nanaimo Regional General Hospital (☎ 250-754-2141) is at 1200 Dufferin Crescent, northwest of the downtown area.

Nanaimo District Museum

This small museum (☎ 250-753-1821, 100 Cameron Rd; admission $2; open 9am-5pm daily in summer, 9am-5pm Tues-Sat rest of year) displays items of significance in the growth of Nanaimo. Included are First Nations, Hudson's Bay Company and coal-mining artifacts.

The Bastion

The Bastion (☎ 250-753-1821, cnr Bastion & Front Sts; adult/child $1/50¢; open 10:30am-4:30pm daily July & Aug, 10:30am-4pm Wed-Sun May, June & Sept) is the highlight of Nanaimo's old buildings. Built by the Hudson's Bay Company in 1853 for protection from local Indians, it was never used but for the odd firing of a cannon to quell a disturbance. It's now a museum and tourist office. The cannons are fired over the water at noon on open days, June to September.

Newcastle Island Provincial Marine Park

Just offshore from downtown is Newcastle Island, which offers cycling, hiking and beaches. It's also a good place for a picnic or overnight camping. Cars are not allowed. The island was once dotted with mineshafts and sandstone quarries but later became a quiet resort. From April to October, a small ferry (☎ 250-753-5141; $5/2 adult/bike roundtrip) leaves hourly on the 10-minute trip between the island and Mafeo-Sutton Park. Camping on the island is available ($12 per site).

Gabriola Island

Farther out into the strait is Gabriola Island, the most northerly of the Southern Gulf Islands. A fine day can be had exploring, but you'll need a bicycle or car. It has

several beaches and three provincial parks offering swimming, shoreline walking and tidal pool examination. At **Malaspina Galleries**, the wind and tides have carved some unusual shapes into the sandstone. Accommodations and camping are available on the island, which is accessed by ferry from the Harbour Park Mall (see the Getting Around section). For more information contact the Gabriola Island Visitor Info Centre (☎ 250-247-9332, W www.gabriola island.org, 575 North Rd).

Activities

Nanaimo divers are trying to make the city the provincial **scuba diving** capital. Two different junked navy ships have been sunk in the area to create artificial reefs, and many other great dive sites are nearby. For more information contact **Ocean Explorers Diving** (☎ 250-753-2055, 800-233-4145, W www .oceanexplorersdiving.com, 1956 Zorkin Rd), near the Departure Bay ferry terminal.

Three nearby spots where you can go **hiking** or **canoeing** are Nanaimo Lakes, Nanaimo River and Green Mountain. Hikes from **Colliery Dam Park** southwest of downtown (take Albert St southwest to 4th St, go west on 4th and turn southwest again on Harewood Rd) lead to Harewood and Overton Lakes. For more information contact Nanaimo Parks (☎ 250-765-5200). To go **kayaking**, stop by the **Kayak Shack** (☎ 250-753-3234, 15-1840 Stewart Ave), at Zorkin Rd in Sealand Market, next to the Departure Bay ferry terminal, which rents kayaks ($35/50 single/double per day) and offers classes and tours.

Thrill seekers head immediately to **Bungy Zone Adrenalin Centre** (☎ 250-753-5867, 888-668-7874, W www.bungyzone.com, Nanaimo River Rd), which operates, legally, off a 42m-high bridge south of town (call for directions). This long-established outfit offers bungy jumping ($95) as well as a flying-fox zip line and high-speed swing ($50 each). A licensed café and a hot tub are on-site, and camping is available.

Special Events

The top annual event is the **Nanaimo Bathtub Race** to Vancouver, held the third weekend of July as part of **Nanaimo's Marine Festival**. Hundreds of fiberglass tubs start out, about 100 sinking in the first five minutes. Winners complete the 58km passage of the Strait of Georgia Strait's wild waters to reach the beaches at Vancouver.

Places to Stay

Camping *Newcastle Island Provincial Marine Park* (☎ 250-391-2300, fax 250-478-9211) Sites $12. For tranquility, you can't beat this small walk-in campground on Newcastle Island, a short ferry ride from Nanaimo. It has 18 tent sites; no reservations.

Jingle Pot RV Park & Campground (☎ 250-758-1614, fax 250-758-7170, 4012 Jingle Pot Rd) Sites $14-21. Jingle Pot is on the north side of Nanaimo off Hwy 19. It has showers, laundry facilities, tent sites and flowers, oh, the flowers!

Brannen Lake Campsites (☎ 250-756-0404, 866-756-0404, 4220 Biggs Rd) Sites $17-20. Near Jingle Pot west of the Nanaimo Parkway, this tidy campground is on a working ranch. It has a petting farm for the kids, and you can rent canoes for paddling on Brannen Lake.

Hostels *Nicol Street Hostel* (☎ 250-753-1188, 800-861-1366, fax 250-753-1185, W www.nanaimohostel.com, 65 Nicol St) Dorm beds $17, private rooms $34, cottage $50, tent sites $10 per person. The folksy and central Nicol Street Hostel is a small friendly place that will make you feel at home. It has all the usual hostel amenities, plus available camping and some nice views from its hilltop site.

Cosmic Cow Guesthouse (☎ 250-754-7150, W www.cosmiccow_guesthouse.tripod.com, 1922 Wilkinson Rd) Dorm bed $18. If rural is your thing, moooove on down to the Cosmic Cow, a riverside farm 10 minutes south of town. Amenities include a free breakfast, Internet access, laundry facilities, bike rentals and storage, nature trails, a pool table and volleyball court. Nanaimo city bus No 11 will get you close.

Cambie International Hostel, Nanaimo (☎ 250-754-5323, 877-754-5323, fax 250-754-5582, W www.cambiehostels.com, 63 Victoria Crescent) Dorm beds $20; first breakfast free. Affiliated with the Cambie in Vancouver, this downtown hostel has room for about 50 people in small dorm rooms, each with double-size bunks, a bathroom with shower and lockers. At street level, the hostel has a bakery/café and probably *the* most happening bar and grill in town, thanks to cheap beer, live music on weekends and an international crowd.

Hotels Many basic budget motels are on the highway north and south of the city, while downtown holds the more expensive chain places.

Colonial Motel (☎ 250-754-4415, fax 250-753-1611, 950 N Terminal Ave) Singles/doubles start at $54/60. The Colonial Motel is along the busy main drag at the north end of downtown, not far from the Departure Bay ferry terminal. Some rooms have kitchenettes, and kayak rentals are available.

Buccaneer Inn (☎ 250-753-1246, 877-282-6337, fax 253-753-0507, W www.thebuccaneer inn.com, 1577 Stewart Ave) Singles/doubles $59/64 & up. Also north of downtown but along the waterfront, the Buccaneer is just three blocks from the ferry terminal and a great value. It's diver friendly and has clean, comfortable rooms and suites, most with ocean views.

Best Western Dorchester Hotel (☎ 250-754-6835, 800-661-2449, fax 250-754-2638, W www.dorchesternanaimo.com, 70 Church St) Rooms start at $75. The historic downtown Dorchester is a handsomely refurbished hotel featuring rooms and suites overlooking the harbor.

Coast Bastion Inn (☎ 250-753-6601, 800-663-1144, fax 250-753-4155, W www.coast hotels.com, 11 Bastion St) Rooms from $87. This luxurious downtown high-rise has well-appointed rooms with panoramic views.

Ramada Ltd on Long Lake (☎ 250-758-1144, 800-565-1144, fax 250-758-5832, W www.longlakeinn.com, 4700 N Island Hwy) Singles/doubles from $109/119. About 5km north of town, the Ramada has a swimming beach, canoe rentals, a fitness center, hot tub and sauna. The balconied rooms all overlook Long Lake, which is pretty despite its proximity to the highway.

Places to Eat

The *pub* at the Cambie hostel (see Places to Stay) is popular for budget food and drink.

Amazing Thai (☎ 250-754-7818, 486A Franklyn St) Mains $6-9. Closed Sun-Mon. Up the hill in the Old City Quarter, Amazing Thai is a good place for your Gai Phad Mamuanghimmapan fix.

Dinghy Dock Pub & Bistro (☎ *250-753-2373, 8 Pirates Lane*) Lunch $5-10, dinner entrées $8.50-15. Another fine place for a meal is the pleasantly casual Dinghy Dock, a small floating pub on the dock at Protection Island, an eight-minute trip from downtown on a small ferryboat. Seafood and pastas are offered at dinner; sandwiches, burgers and fish and chips star at lunch. The great outdoor patio has views across the harbor to Nanaimo, and after dinner you can stroll the small, quiet residential island. Live music happens regularly on weekends. It's all very cool. Get the ferry (☎ 250-753-8244; $4.75 roundtrip) from the docks below the big condo tower at Front St and Promenade.

Gina's Mexican Café (☎ *250-753-5411, 47 Skinner St*) Mains $8-14. Gina's offers inexpensive Mexican food, casual fun atmosphere and views. But when the menu lists 'chili rellanos,' you get nervous.

The Globe Bar & Grille (☎ *250-754-4910, 25 Front St*) Dinner entrées $10-15. Inside the beautifully restored 1886 Globe Hotel, this place offers unquestionably the best dining experience in town. The wide-ranging menu features upscale sandwiches, burgers, pastas, stirfries, seafood, steak and chicken. It's full of locals who come to dine or hang out in the upstairs bar, which has a large-screen TV and a custom-made pool table. Live music is presented Thursday to Saturday night.

Acme Food Co (☎ *250-753-0042, 14 Commercial St*) Dinner entrées $14-17. Time will tell whether this new place catches on, but it looks pretty good out of the blocks. It's a trendy, artful affair, where a jazzy soundtrack accompanies your martini and sushi appetizer. Dinner entrées tend toward steak, seafood and chicken, though you can also order pastas and build-your-own pizzas.

Getting There & Away

Laidlaw Coach Lines (☎ 250-753-4371, 800-318-0818 in Canada, 800-663-8390 in the US, ⓦ www.grayline.ca/victoria) connects Nanaimo with points north and south; the one-way fare to Victoria is $19.25. The station is behind the Howard Johnson Harbourside Hotel at 1 Terminal Ave, north of the center near Comox Rd.

The E&N Railiner (☎ 888-842-7245) passes through once a day in each direction

on its way between Victoria and Courtenay; the fare to Victoria is $23/46 one-way/roundtrip. The station (321 Selby St) has no ticket office; you can purchase tickets from the conductor.

Two ferry routes link Nanaimo with the mainland. The ferry trip from the Departure Bay terminal (at the north end of Stewart Ave, near downtown) to Horseshoe Bay, north of Vancouver, takes about 1½ hours. The longer trip between the Duke Point terminal (south of town; take the Duke Point Hwy off the Island Hwy) and Tsawwassen, south of Vancouver near the airport, takes two hours. Both ferries make at least eight departures daily in each direction between late June and early September; reduced schedule rest of year. The peak-season fare for each is $9.50/4.75 adult/child age 5-11, plus $33.50 for a car. For more information, contact BC Ferries (☎ 250-386-3431, 888-223-3779 in BC, ⓦ www.bcferries.com).

Getting Around

For information about local city buses call Nanaimo Regional Transit (☎ 250-390-4531) or pick up their transit guide at the tourist office. All city buses stop on Gordon St near Harbour Park Mall. Bus No 2 goes to the Departure Bay ferry terminal. The fare is $1.75/1.50 adult/youth. A day pass costs $4.50/3.50.

The Nanaimo Seaporter (☎ 250-753-2118) bus will shuttle you between the Duke Point, Departure Bay or Gabriola Island ferry terminal and anywhere in Nanaimo.

The ferry to Gabriola Island leaves from near the Harbour Park Mall on the 20-minute crossing. Roundtrip fare is $5.25/2.75 adult/child age 5-11, plus $13.50 for a car; bikes are free.

PORT ALBERNI & AROUND

Just outside Parksville, Hwy 4 splits off from Hwy 19 and leads west toward the Pacific. Halfway across the island at the head of Alberni Inlet, a 35km-long fjord, pleasant and scenic Port Alberni is built on forestry and fishing. Commercial fishing boats work out of the area, most catching salmon, and the waterfront offers a nice mix of working docks and tourist development.

The Alberni Valley Chamber of Commerce (☎ 250-724-6535, fax 250-724-6560, w www.avcoc.com) operates a Visitor Info Centre at the junction of Hwys 4 and 4A – the town's east entrance. It's open daily year-round.

Internet access and a good cuppa joe are available at the Web Grind Cafe (☎ 250-720-0358, 3131 3rd Ave).

shops, restaurants, an observation/clock tower and a farmers' market on Saturday year-round. On the Quay's south side (look for the red and white lighthouse) is **Port Alberni Maritime Discovery Centre** (☎ *250-723-6164/841, adult/child $2/free, open 9am-5pm daily mid-May–Sept),* where you

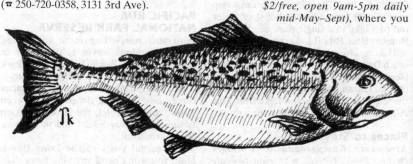

Port Alberni is touted as the 'salmon capital of the world.'

Things to See & Do

Port Alberni's big draw is **Lady Rose Marine Services** (☎ *250-723-8313, 800-663-7192 Apr-Sept,* w *www.ladyrosemarine.com, 5425 Argyle St),* which runs day-long trips up Barkley Sound to Bamfield, Ucluelet and the Broken Group Islands and back on the 100-passenger *Lady Rose* and 200-passenger *Frances Barkley.*

The working packet freighters make numerous stops en route to deliver mail and supplies, with a 60- to 90-minute layover in Bamfield. Taking a ride on one of them is an enjoyable, scenic way to spend a lazy day, as well as a practical means of returning from the West Coast Trail's north end at Bamfield. There's a coffee shop on board. Bring a sweater or jacket, even if it's warm in Port Alberni.

The Bamfield run goes three to five times a week year-round and costs $23/45 one-way/roundtrip. The company makes a separate run to Ucluelet ($25/50) and the Broken Group Islands ($20/40) three times a week in summer, and the rest of the year, kayakers and canoeists can request a stop at the islands. The company runs the *Sechart Whaling Station Lodge* on the islands (from $70 per person per day, including meals) and also rents canoes and kayaks ($35-50 per day).

Both vessels leave from **Harbour Quay**, at the foot of Argyle St, a tourist area with

can get a feel for the town's seafaring heritage.

Port Alberni has several other heritage attractions (w www.alberniheritage.com). Local cultural history is the focus of **Alberni Valley Museum** (☎ *250-723-2181, 4255 Wallace St, admission by donation; open 10am-5pm daily & until 8pm Thur, May-Sept; open same hours Mon-Sat rest of year).* Exhibits include beautifully woven goods and a spectacular Chinese paper lion headdress.

McLean Mill National Historic Site (☎ *250-723-1376, 5633 Smith Rd; adult/youth & senior/family $6.50/4.50/14; open 10am-6pm daily mid-May–Sept)* preserves a steam-powered sawmill dating from 1926. Get there on the restored 1929 **Alberni Pacific Railway Steam Train** (☎ *250-723-2118/1376; roundtrip fare adult/youth & senior/child under 6/family $20/15/7/45, including mill admission; operates Thur-Mon June-Sept),* which makes several trips a day in season. Trains depart the restored 1912 E&N station at the entrance to Harbour Quay.

Natural wonders nearby include **Cathedral Grove**, east of town in MacMillan Provincial Park, which is right by Hwy 4 at the west end of Cameron Lake. This grove – a must-see half-hour stop – is regarded by local First Nations people as a sacred place. The grove is virgin forest with huge Douglas firs and red cedars, some 800 years old. Trails lead through the delicate, ancient ecosystem of towering trees. It's a popular spot and the roadside parking can be horrendous.

About 15km west of Port Alberni, huge **Sproat Lake** is home base for the impossibly huge Martin Mars water bombers used to fight forest fires. These leviathans can scoop over 27,000 litres (7000 gallons) of water out of a lake in a single pass. See them on Bomber Base Rd off Lakeshore Rd.

Hikers also come to Port Alberni to reach **Della Falls**, Canada's highest waterfall (see Strathcona Provincial Park later in this chapter) by an alternative route – canoeing the length of Great Central Lake from Port Alberni and taking the trail up from there.

Places to Stay

Arrowvale Campground & Cottages (☎/fax 250-723-7948, **w** www.arrowvale cottages.com, 5955 Hector Rd) Sites $15-18; luxury cottages $115-150. On the Somass River, 6km west of Port Alberni, Arrowvale has showers, swimming, a playground, farm tours and laundry.

Stamp River Provincial Park (☎ 250-954-4600, fax 250-248-8584, Beaver Creek Rd) Sites $12. This small wooded campground with 23 primitive sites, 14.5km northwest of Port Alberni, is near Stamp Falls and open year-round. From August to December you can watch salmon fight their way up the fish ladders here.

Sproat Lake Provincial Park (☎ 250-954-4600, fax 250-248-8584, Hwy 4) Sites $15-17.50. Thirteen kilometers west of town on the north shore of massive Sproat Lake, this park also features some prehistoric petroglyphs.

Personal Touch Hostel (☎ 250-723-2484, 4908 Burde St) Dorm beds $15. This humble home hostel is an option if your tent leaks.

Alberni Inn (☎ 250-723-9405, 800-815-8007, 3805 Redford St) Singles/doubles $61/71. All rooms at the Alberni have kitchenettes or full-size kitchens.

Esta Villa Motel (☎ 250-724-1261, 800-724-0844, fax 250-724-0833, **w** www.alberni .net/estavilla, 4014 Johnston Rd) Singles/ doubles $75/92. The simple but delightful Esta Villa has friendly management, beautifully kept parklike grounds and a forest for a backyard. You can walk down to a creek and might spy deer or the occasional black bear along the way.

Getting There & Away

Laidlaw Coach Lines (☎ 250-724-1266, 800-318-0818 in Canada, 800-663-8390 in the US, **w** www.grayline.ca/victoria, 4541 Margaret St) runs buses from Port Alberni to Ucluelet ($16.50) and Tofino ($19.25).

PACIFIC RIM NATIONAL PARK RESERVE

With rain forests of huge cedar and fir trees, and tremendous waves rolling in from across the ocean, Pacific Rim National Park Reserve has become one of BC's top attractions. The 50,000-hectare park includes three units: the Long Beach area between Tofino and Ucluelet, the Broken Group Islands in Barkley Sound and the famous West Coast Trail.

For casual visits to the Long Beach Unit, you won't need anything more than a stop at the park information center. It's just inside the park's southern boundary, 108km west of Port Alberni on scenic but often serpentine Hwy 4; the drive takes about an hour and a half. Parking at the Long Beach Unit costs $3 per vehicle for two hours or $8 per vehicle per day, good until 11pm; obtain permits at the Wickaninnish Centre or trailhead parking lots. If you plan to stay more than a few days, an annual parking pass is available for $42 per vehicle ($31.50 for seniors). Parks Canada's Great Western Pass is also honored. There's no charge to drive through the park to Tofino.

For trips to the Broken Group Islands or the West Coast Trail, or more information on the park in general, contact Parks Canada, Pacific Rim National Park Reserve (☎ 250-726-7721, fax 250-726-4720, **w** www.parkscan.harbour.com/pacrim, 2185 Ocean Terrace Rd, PO Box 280, Ucluelet, BC V0R 3A0).

Long Beach Unit

Easily accessed by Hwy 4, the Long Beach Unit attracts the largest number of visitors in the park. Start with a stop at the **Wickaninnish Centre**, which holds interpretive exhibits on the park's cultural and natural history, as well as a nice restaurant (see Places to Eat under Ucluelet, later in this chapter). Then try one or more of the trails that range in length from 100m to 5km. They include:

Long Beach Easy walking at low tide and great scenery along the sandy shore

Radar Hill 100m climb to a former WWII installation

Bog Trail 800m interpretive loop around a moss-layered bog

Rain Forest Trail Two 1km interpretive loops through old-growth forest

South Beach 1km roundtrip through forest to a pebble beach, accessed behind the Wickaninnish Centre

Spruce Fringe 1.5km loop trail featuring hardy Sitka spruce trees

Schooner Cove 2km trail through old- and second-growth forests, with beach access

Wickaninnish Trail 5km shoreline and forest trail, accessed behind the Wickaninnish Centre

The safest place to swim is the north end of Long Beach, where surf guards patrol the beach during July and August.

Camping *Green Point Campground* (☎ 800-689-9025 *for reservations*) Semi-serviced sites $20, primitive walk-in sites $14. Open mid-Mar–Oct. This park-run campground is 18km from Tofino and 20km from Ucluelet along Hwy 4. The 94 drive-in sites can be reserved up to three months ahead; it's first-come, first-served for the 20 walk-in sites.

Long Beach Golf Course Campground (☎ 250-725-3332, *fax* 250-725-3302, **W** *www.longbeachgolfcourse.com*, *1850 Pacific Rim Hwy*) Sites $20, including a bundle of firewood. Open May-Oct. Near Grice Bay, this primitive 53-site campground will happily get you teed off. It has a washroom and pit toilets, picnic tables and firepits, but no showers or hookups.

Broken Group Islands

This unit includes about 100 islands at the entrance to Barkley Sound. The islands are an increasingly popular **kayaking** destination, but visitors must know what they're doing – or sign on with a guided trip. Get a list of outfitters from the park office.

Toquart Bay is the principal launching spot, accessed via a 16km gravel logging road off Hwy 4, 12km northeast of the Pacific Rim Hwy junction. You'll also find a BC Forest Service campsite at the launch.

Lady Rose Marine Services (☎ 250-723-8313, 800-663-7192 Apr–Sept) transports kayakers and their gear from both Toquart

Bay and Port Alberni to Sechart Whaling Station Lodge, the company's base in the Broken Group Islands. There, rooms with shared baths are available from June through September (from $70 per person per day, including meals). The company also runs a water taxi from Sechart and Toquart Bay to several of the Broken Group Islands for $20 to $45 per person, depending on the pick-up and drop-off points. You can rent canoes and kayaks at Sechart, too.

West Coast Trail

The third and most southerly section of the park is the 75km West Coast Trail, one of Canada's best-known and toughest hiking routes. Originally constructed as an escape route for shipwreck survivors, the trail runs between Pachena Bay (Information/Registration Centre ☎ 250-728-3234), near Bamfield on the north end, and Gordon River (Information/Registration Centre ☎ 250-647-5434), near Port Renfrew on the south. Hikers must be able to manage rough terrain, rock-face ladders, stream crossings and adverse weather conditions. Plan on six to eight days to hike the entire route.

Some people do a day hike or even hike half the trail from Pachena Bay (considered the easier end of the route), but each overnight hiker must have a permit, and only 52 people can begin the trail on any given day, 26 in each direction. To apply, call the Super Natural British Columbia Reservation Service (☎ 250-387-1642, 604-663-6000 in Greater Vancouver, ☎ 800-663-6000). Hikers can call March 1 and request any starting date in May; April 1 for any start date in June; May 1 for July; June 1 for August; and July 1 for September. When you call, be ready with an intended start date and two alternate dates, the name of the trailhead from which you intend to start, the number of hikers in your party (maximum 10) and a Visa or MasterCard number. The nonrefundable reservation fee ($25 per hiker) includes a trail guide and map.

Permits also are available through a waiting-list system; six of each day's 26 available spaces are set aside to be used on a first-come, first-served basis at each trailhead. Waiting-list spaces are allocated at 1pm each day from both of the registration centers, and people who land the spaces can start hiking that day. But from July to mid-September, hikers sometimes wait up to three days to get a permit via the waiting list. Day hikers are allowed on the trail from each end, but they must obtain a free day-use permit, available from the registration centers.

In addition to the $25 reservation fee, you'll pay a $70-per-person trail use fee plus two ferry fees totaling $25, payable when you sign in at the registration center. Hikers can sign in as early as 3:30pm the day before they start; if they plan to arrive after 1pm of their start date, they must notify the registration center before 1pm to save their space.

Hikers can camp at any of the designated sites along the route, most of which have solar-composting outhouses. Those who want to hike only the easier half of the trail from Pachena Bay to Nitinat Narrows can leave from Nitinat Lake. Make advance arrangements for a ride from West Coast Trail Express (see Getting There & Away, below).

A few companies lead guided through-hikes on the West Coast Trail; Parks Canada keeps a list.

It takes 90 minutes to drive from Port Alberni to Bamfield (Pachena Bay) on a gravel logging road. It's a two-hour drive on paved Hwy 14 from Victoria to Port Renfrew (Gordon River). West Coast Trail Express (☎ 250-477-8700, W www.trailbus.com) offers daily roundtrip shuttle-bus service May 1 to Sept 30 from Victoria, Nanaimo and Port Alberni to all West Coast Trail trailheads. Lady Rose Marine Services (☎ 250-723-8313, 800-663-7192 Apr-Sept) runs a passenger ferry between Port Alberni and Bamfield ($23 one-way).

TOFINO & AROUND
The most appealing end-of-the-road town on Vancouver Island, Tofino sits at the end of Hwy 4, 122km west of Port Alberni. Its population doubles in summer as people come to visit nearby Pacific Rim National Park Reserve, Hot Springs Cove and other natural attractions. It seems the coolest visitors often end up staying; the town's young, environmentally aware population gives Tofino a great vibe. Healthy food and smiles are ubiquitous here.

Tofino sits on Clayoquot Sound, a Unesco Biosphere Reserve and one of Vancouver Island's most scenic areas. Dotted with

islands and rimmed by mountains, Tofino's setting is both serene and spectacular. And if you want to see whales, sea lions and other marine life, this is a top place to go.

Information
The Visitor Info Centre (☎ 250-725-3414, fax 250-725-3296, W www.island.net/~tofino, 121 Third St) is open daily, May to September. The *Long Beach Maps* brochure offers helpful listings for Tofino, Ucluelet and Pacific Rim National Park Reserve.

Hot Springs Cove
One of BC's best day-trip destinations, Hot Springs Cove is the best-known part of Maquinna Provincial Marine Park, 37km north of Tofino. Most sojourners travel by Zodiac boat, watching for whales and other sea critters en route, though seaplane service is available. From the boat landing, you can hike 2km over boardwalks to a series of natural hot pools perfect for soaking.

Many outfitters make the run to Hot Springs Cove. **Remote Passages** (☎ 725-3330, 800-666-9833, W *www.remotepassages.com*, 71 Wharf St) is one of the more ecologically minded companies, with guides well-versed in the natural history of Clayoquot Sound. Its six- to seven-hour Hot Springs Explorer trip costs $89/59 adult/child.

A few primitive campsites are near the hot-springs boat landing. The Hesquiaht First Nation operates *Hot Springs Lodge* (☎ 250-670-1106), in the community of Hot Springs Cove. Its six rooms cost $115 each. The innkeepers will take you to the Hot Springs Cove boardwalk at your convenience, and you can also enjoy a private beach. You can only get to the lodge by water taxi from Tofino ($60/25 adult/child age 5-15 roundtrip).

Meares Island
Visible from Tofino, Meares Island is home to the Big Tree Trail, a 400m boardwalk stroll through old-growth forest, including a red cedar tree that's been standing for 1500 years. Everybody does that trail, but few hike the great trail ringing the whole island; it's a two- to 2½-hour jaunt. The island was the site of a key 1984 anti-logging protest that kicked off the modern environmental movement in Clayoquot Sound. **Rainforest**

BRITISH COLUMBIA

Boat Shuttle (☎ 250-725-3793) runs a 2½-hour shuttle trip from the Fourth St wharf to Meares Island and back for $20/5 adult/child under 12. Sea Trek Tours (☎ 250-725-4412, 800-811-9155, W www.seatrektours.bc.ca, 441B Campbell St) offers 90-minute trips that feature a glass-bottom boat ride for $25/20/15/5 adult/senior & student/child age six to 12/child age two to five.

Ahousat

Located on remote Flores Island north of Tofino, Ahousat is a First Nations reserve. It's known for the Wild Side Heritage Trail ($20 per person trail fee), a moderately difficult path that traverses 16km of old-growth forests, beaches and headlands between Ahousat and Cow Bay. Walk the Wild Side (☎ 250-670-9586, 888-670-9586), a First Nations business, leads guided hikes on the route ($30 per person including the trail fee). It's a 40-minute water taxi ride from Tofino to Ahousat; Cougar Island Water Taxi (☎ 250-670-9692, 800-726-8427) makes the run on demand for around $90 per boat (up to six or seven passengers) one-way. Wild Side Trail hikers may get a discount.

If you want to spend the night, check out Hummingbird Hostel (see Hostels under Places to Stay).

Tofino Botanical Gardens

These beautiful 5-hectare gardens (☎ 250-725-1220, 1084 Pacific Rim Hwy; adult/student/child $10/6/2; open 9am to dusk daily) feature the native plants of Clayoquot Sound and several theme gardens, along with bird-watching blinds, a frog pond and sculpture garden. Anyone arriving without a car gets a dollar off admission.

Activities

Remote Passages (☎ 250-725-3330, 800-666-9833, W www.remotepassages.com, 71 Wharf St), near the intersection of Second and Main Sts, is a well-respected company offering kayak day trips ($44 and up) and overnights with experienced guides. The tours always maintain an ecology-conscious, educational emphasis. Tofino Sea Kayaking Company (☎ 250-725-4222, 800-863-4664, W www.tofino-kayaking.com, 320 Main St) offers kayak tours ($44 and up), rentals, lessons, the End of the Road espresso bar

and a great bookstore. Rainforest Kayak Adventures (☎ 250-725-3117, 877-422-9453, W www.rainforestkayak.com, 316 Main St) specializes in three- to six-day guided tours and instructional courses for beginner and intermediate paddlers; prices start at $580.

Tofino is the island's Surf City. Inner Rhythm Surf Camp (☎ 250-726-2211, 877-393-7873, www.innerrhythm.net, 2490 Pacific Rim Hwy) features a variety of adult and youth surf classes and camps. Surf Sister (☎ 250-725-4456, 877-724-7873, W www.surfsister.com) is BC's only all-female surf school, with two-day courses for $195, including gear rentals. Live to Surf (☎ 250-725-4464, W www.livetosurf.com, 1180 Pacific Rim Hwy) rents boards and gear and offers information and insight on the local scene.

You're likely to see whales on any trip to Hot Springs Cove or Flores Island or sometimes even from shore in Tofino, but you can also book a trip devoted to their pursuit. They migrate through the area from March to May, though like the cooler tourists, many of them linger here through summer and even into fall. Many local outfitters run two- to three-hour trips (about $50-70), including Jamie's Whaling Station (☎ 250-725-3919, 800-667-9913, W www.jamies.com) and Remote Passages (☎ 250-725-3330, 800-666-9833, W www.remotepassages.com).

Places to Stay

Tofino's budget lodging scene has brightened in recent years, but you still won't find many rooms under $100 from May through September, so you'll want to book way ahead.

Camping You'll find several good, albeit pricey, choices a few kilometers south of Tofino on Mackenzie Beach. Also see Camping under Pacific Rim National Park Reserve, earlier in this chapter.

Mackenzie Beach Resort (☎ 250-725-3439, 1101 Pacific Rim Hwy) Sites $15-30. Open year-round. This park has an indoor heated pool, Jacuzzi and showers.

Crystal Cove Beach Resort (☎ 250-725-4213, fax 250-725-4219, W www.crystal covebeachresort.com, 1165 Cedarwood Place) Sites $20-45. Open year-round. Amenities here include firepits, picnic tables, free hot showers and laundry facilities to wash your duds.

Bella Pacifica Resort & Campground (☎ 250-725-3400, fax 250-725-2400, w *www .bellapacifica.com, 400 Mackenzie Beach Rd)* Sites $27-36. Open Mar-Oct. Bella Pacifica has forested and beachfront sites, nature trails, flush toilets, hot showers and laundry facilities.

Hostels ***HI-Tofino Whalers on the Point Guesthouse*** (☎ 250-725-3443, fax 250-725-3463, w *www.tofinohostel.com, 81 West St)* Dorm beds $22/24 members/nonmembers, private rooms & suites $66-70 members, $99-109 nonmembers. The Ritz Hotel of hostels, Whaler's sits right by the ocean in Tofino's west end. Built specifically as a hostel, this handsome newish place features a game room, sauna, surfboard lockers and spacious common areas.

The Wind Rider (☎ 250-725-3240, fax 250-725-3280, whole@island.net, 231 Main St) Dorm beds from $25, private rooms from $60. This place is a nonprofit, women-only retreat house with a great vibe. Kitchen facilities and linens are provided, and there's a deck and Jacuzzi. The premises are strictly drug and alcohol free.

Hummingbird Hostel (☎ 250-670-9679, w *www.hummingbird-hostel.com)* Dorm beds $20. In a restored 1904 house on the waterfront in Ahousat, on Flores Island, the Hummingbird is accessible by water taxi twice a day from Tofino ($15 each way). The taxi ride adds to the cost of staying here, but guests can hike the Wild Side Heritage Trail free, and if you're really looking for remote, this'll do it. And yes, you'll see hummingbirds – possibly a bear or wolf, too.

B&Bs ***Paddler's Inn B&B*** (☎ 250-725-4222, 800-863-4664, w *www.tofino-kayaking.com, 320 Main St)* Singles/doubles $55/65, shared bath. The best budget choice is the Paddler's Inn, which is run by the Tofino Sea Kayaking Co and sits right above its store. Rates include continental breakfast.

Inn at Tough City (☎ 250-725-2021, 877-725-2021, fax 250-725-2088, w *www.tough city.com, 350 Main St)* Rooms from $140. This place is unique. Though relatively new, it was built using a lot of recycled materials, which give it a warm, lived-in feel. And though thoroughly modern in a cool artsy way, it's spiced with off-the-wall antiques (not the kind your grandma has). Finally,

the amenities and views are splendid. It all comes together superbly.

Motels & Resorts ***Dolphin Motel*** (☎ 250-725-3377, fax 250-725-3374, 1190 Pacific Rim Hwy) Rooms $79 & up. About 3km south of town near Chesterman Beach, the Dolphin is a basic but tidy road motel. All rooms have refrigerators.

Schooner Motel (☎ 250-725-3478, fax 250-725-3499, 311-321 Campbell St) Singles/ doubles $95/115 & up. Another nice basic motel, this one is downtown overlooking the bay.

Middle Beach Lodge (☎ 250-725-2900, fax 250-725-2901, w *www.middlebeach.com, Hwy 4).* Rooms start at $105, including continental breakfast. On the highway 3km south of Tofino, the contemporary Middle Beach Lodge sits on 16 magnificent oceanfront hectares. The two-lodge complex was built using lots of recycled wood (including teak off a 1925 ocean liner) and has an enlightened guest-management policy: You and WC Fields can hole up in the adults-only lodge 'At the Beach,' while the Partridge Family and Brady Bunch duke it out in the separate all-ages lodge 'At the Headlands.' Both lodges are beautiful and luxuriously appointed.

Maquinna Lodge (☎ 250-725-3261, 800-665-3199, fax 250-725-3433, 120 First St) Rooms $110 & up. Some rooms here come with views of the sound, and all have TV and telephone. The lodge also has a popular pub.

Best Western Tin Wis Resort (☎ 250-725-4445, 800-661-9995, fax 250-725-4447, w *www.tinwis.com, 1119 Pacific Rim Hwy)* Rooms start at $175. The Tin Wis, which is First Nations–operated, offers the usual high-standard chain rooms, along with beach access, a fitness room (like you really want to be exercising *indoors* in Tofino!) and hot tub.

Duffin Cove Resort (☎ 250-725-3448, 888-629-2903, fax 250-725-2390, w *www .duffin-cove-resort.com, duffin@island.net, 215 Campbell St)* Studios $165, suites $245, cabins $300. Near the water and downtown, this resort sits on a quiet cul-de-sac overlooking its own private cove. The cozy beachside cabins would make for an incredibly romantic getaway, but all accommodations here are first-class.

Wickaninnish Inn (☎ 250-725-3100, 800-333-4604, fax 250-725-3110, w *www.wickinn*

.com, Osprey Lane) Rooms start at $340. South of town at Chesterman Beach, the Wickanninnish is Tofino's top-end option. The intimately sized Relais & Châteaux property offers full spa facilities and 46 exquisitely furnished rooms with push-button gas fireplaces, two-person tubs and private balconies. The inn's Pointe restaurant is one of BC's best.

Clayoquot Wilderness Resort (☎ 250-726-8235, 888-333-5405, W www.wild retreat.com, PO Box 130, Tofino, BC V0R 2Z0) Rooms start at $489 per person per night, 2-night minimum. Rates include three gourmet meals a day and water taxi to/from the resort. On Quait Bay, 30 minutes by boat northeast of Tofino, this remote floating 'adventure lodge' specializes in horseback riding and fishing. Ask about the even more remote 'Wilderness Outpost' on the Bedwell River ($575 per night per person, all-inclusive).

Places to Eat

Jupiter Juicery & Bakeshop (☎ 250-725-4225, 451 Main St) For a healthy pick-me-up, come to this hip, hidden haven beneath the 'Big Yellow Building' and grab yourself a delicious fruit smoothie or a hot homemade chai.

Common Loaf Bake Shop (☎ 250-725-3915, 180 First St) This low-key local gathering spot has second-floor atrium seating and tasty homemade muffins, cookies, breads and cakes. It also makes pizza for dinner. It's a great place to hang out and read Melville on a rainy day.

Salals Co-op (☎ 250-725-2728) By now hopefully in its new digs at Campbell & Fourth Sts, this organic grocery and cafe is a focus of Tofino's health-conscious, socially enlightened community. The back of the café menu holds an impressive 'Manifesto' laying out the progressive principles upon which the coop was founded. Support this place.

Alleyway Café/Costa Azul (☎ 250-725-3105, Rear 305 Campbell) Breakfast $7-10.25, dinner $7.25-12. Tucked in the yard behind the corner of First and Campbell Sts, the Alleyway serves a range of all-day breakfasts and various vegetarian lunches. At dinnertime, it transforms into its alter ego, the Costa Azul, and serves Mexican-style fare.

Café Pamplona (☎ 250-725-1237, W www .cafepamplona.com, 1084 Pacific Rim Hwy) Most mains $10-23. This fine-dining haven at the beautiful botanical gardens features lots of fresh seafood with Asian-accented recipes, using fresh produce right out of the adjacent garden. The menu changes regularly, and suggested wine pairings are offered. The atmosphere is relaxed and artful. Open for lunch and dinner; dinner reservations suggested.

Raincoast Café (☎ 250-725-2215, 120 Fourth St) Meals $12-24. The Raincoast offers Pacific Rim cuisine also featuring local seafood. It's a small snappy bistro with a great reputation for fine dining.

Pointe Restaurant (☎ 250-725-3100) In the Wickanninnish Inn, this place ranks among BC's best, with both fixed-price dinners ($70; $50 vegetarian) and à la carte main dishes ($24 to $39). Reservations are essential at dinner. Lunch is less expensive ($10 to $21), with such fare as a grilled wild sockeye salmon BLT on black-currant cornmeal toast ($14).

Getting There & Around

North Vancouver Air (☎ 800-228-6608, W www.northvanair.com) flies to Tofino from Vancouver ($185/355 one-way/roundtrip) year-round, and from Victoria ($235/460) summers only. The Tofino Airport is south of town off the Pacific Rim Hwy.

Laidlaw Coach Lines (☎ 250-725-3431, 800-318-0818 in Canada, 800-663-8390 in the US, W www.grayline.ca/victoria) operates daily bus trips to Tofino's station, 450 Campbell St. The one-way fare is $33 from Nanaimo, $53 from Victoria.

In summer, Long Beach Link (☎ 250-726-7790, 866-726-7790, W www.longbeach link.com) runs a once-daily shuttle between Tofino and Nanaimo ($54 roundtrip). The company also shuttles passengers between Tofino and Ucluelet ($9/12 one-way/roundtrip), with stops at several points in between.

UCLUELET

Ucluelet doesn't match Tofino's charm, but it's a bustling place with plenty of visitor services at generally cheaper prices than in Tofino. The Visitor Info Centre (☎ 250-726-4641, fax 250-726-4611, W www.ucluelet info.com, 100 Main St) is open year-round.

A second office at the Hwy 4 junction is open June through August.

Attractions in town include **Big Beach**, with tide pools, shells, kelp beds and a gazebo shelter; access the beach via a 600m trail from Bay St. The **Wild Pacific Trail** winds past the scenic lighthouse at Amphitrite Point and connects with a boardwalk trail at He-Tin-Kis Park.

Majestic Ocean Kayaking (☎ 250-726-2868, 800-889-7644, **W** www.majestic.bc.ca, 125 Garden St) offers three-hour kayak tours of Ucluelet Harbour ($49), as well as longer trips on Barkley Sound and Clayoquot Sound.

Laidlaw Coach Lines (☎ 800-318-0818 in Canada, 800-663-8390 in the US, **W** www.grayline.ca/victoria) provides bus service to Ucluelet from Nanaimo ($30.25 one-way) and Victoria ($49.50). See Tofino, earlier, for more transportation options.

Places to Stay

Ucluelet Campground (☎ 250-726-4355, 260 Seaplane Base Rd)Sites $16 & up. It's humble, but it has hot showers and flush toilets.

Ucluelet Hotel (☎ 250-726-4324, fax 250-726-1215, 250 Main St). Rooms $30 & up with shared bath. It's basic and cheap. If all you need is a place to crash, this'll do.

West Coast Motel (☎ 250-726-7732, 247 Hemlock St) Singles $79, doubles $85 & up. The West Coast offers rooms and suites (some with kitchenettes) overlooking the harbor, plus an indoor pool, gym and sauna.

Canadian Princess Resort (☎ 250-726-7771, 800-663-7090, fax 250-726-7121, **W** www.canadianprincess.com, 1943 Peninsula Rd) Onboard shared-bath staterooms start at $70/80 singles/doubles, on-shore lodge rooms start at $125. The Canadian Princess is a 70-year-old retiree who, in her working years as a survey ship for the Royal Canadian Navy, was known as the William J Stewart. In 1979, she was purchased by Victoria's creative Oak Bay Marine Group, which turned William into the Canadian Princess, a floating hotel. A lady at last, the liberated vessel now holds fine shipboard lodging and a fun little bar frequented by the town's eclectic mix of characters. On a recent visit to said bar, one totally pissed bloke in a see-through blouse and miniskirt fell head over high-heels into an unsuspecting travel writer's table, nearly spilling a perfectly good martini onto the laptop. I say. The resort's higher rates are for the adjacent on-shore lodge rooms, but why? Get yourself a tiny but charming stateroom onboard.

Roots Lodge (☎ 250-726-2700, 888-594-7333, **W** www.livehotels.net, 310 Seabridge Way) Rooms $150 & up. Part of the ongoing Reef Point development, Roots Lodge (right along Peninsula Rd east of town) is endorsed by the increasingly omnipresent Canadian clothing conglomerate that shares its name. It's obviously a high-dollar endeavor – a self-billed 'adventure-travel lodge' that offers lots of activities and comfortable accommodations.

Tauca Lea by the Sea (☎ 250-726-4625, 800-979-9303, **W** www.taucalearesort.com, 1911 Harbour Dr) Rooms $230 & up. The upscale Coast Hotels chain manages this fancy place out on a peninsula off Seaplane Base Rd. You can launch a kayak practically from your door, and the suites – each with kitchen, living room, dining room, fireplace and deck – and common areas are in plush 'rustic elegant' style. The resort's Boat Basin restaurant offers 'fresh Pacific cuisine.'

Places to Eat

Blueberries Café (☎ 250-726-7707, 1627D Peninsula Rd) Breakfast $5-9, lunch $7-9, dinner $12-21. This cozy café offers a great creative menu. Breakfasts are especially nice; try the slurpacious waffle with warm strawberry-blueberry compote. Next door, the **Blue Raven Coffee Bar** has great espresso drinks and Internet access for $6 an hour.

Matterson House Restaurant (☎ 250-726-2200, 1682 Peninsula Rd) Breakfast $4-9, lunch $5-9, dinner $11-19. Great breakfasts with homemade baked goods draw a nice local crowd to the licensed Matterson House. Try the build-your-own omelets. In nice weather, you can hang out on the porch.

Wickaninnish Restaurant (☎ 250-726-7706, Wick Rd) Dinner entrees $8.50-13. Not to be confused with Tofino's upscale Wickaninnish Inn, this fine restaurant is north of Ucluelet in Pacific Rim National Park Reserve's Wickaninnish Interpretive Centre. It offers a fine changing menu of

Shopping for delicacies in Vancouver's Chinatown, British Columbia

Ross Fountain in Butchart Gardens, Victoria, BC

Parliament Buildings and Victoria Harbour, BC

Downtown Vancouver skyline seen from Stanley Park

SUSAN RIMERMAN

Structure at the Tr'ondëk Hwëch'in Cultural Centre in Dawson City, Yukon

SUSAN RIMERMAN

Wide-open spaces along the Dempster Hwy in the Yukon

SUSAN RIMERMAN

Traditional storefronts from the gold-rush era, Dawson City, Yukon

Pacific Northwest cuisine, a cozy bar and terrific views of Long Beach.

PARKSVILLE & QUALICUM BEACH

Back on the island's east coast, these towns and the coast toward Comox are known for their long stretches of beach, but Cancún this is not. If time is limited, you can stay on the Inland Island Hwy and zoom right by without missing much.

The Parksville area is dotted with provincial parks. For information on any of them, call the BC Parks Strathcona District office (☎ 250-954-4600).

Horne Lake Caves Provincial Park attracts spelunking (caving) enthusiasts, who can explore limestone caves here, 16km west of Qualicum Beach off Hwy 19 (northbound). Some caves are open to self-guided exploration, and several different guided tours are available in summer. No camping.

Take a trip to the dark side: exploring the caves under BC

Rathtrevor Beach Provincial Park (☎ 800-689-9025, W www.discovercamping.ca) Sites $12-18.50. Open year-round. This popular park, 3km southeast of Parksville off Hwy 19, has a large campground with 175 forested sites, flush toilets, free hot showers, a playground and an RV dump station. The big draw is 2000m of beautiful sandy beach. Reservations are accepted.

Englishman River Falls Provincial Park Sites $15. About 13km southwest of Parksville at the end of Errington Rd, this park has a nice 30-minute hiking trail through the woods past waterfalls and emerald pools that are great for swimming.

Little Qualicum Falls Provincial Park Sites $15. About 13km west of Parksville on Hwy 4, this is another heavily forested park with the namesake falls and camping.

DENMAN & HORNBY ISLANDS

Farther north up the coast are two lesser-known Gulf Islands – Denman and Hornby. There's good birdwatching on Hornby Island, and both islands have provincial parks, hiking, swimming, fishing, scuba diving and beaches.

Fillongley Provincial Park (☎ 250-954-4600, fax 250-248-8584) Campsites $15. This park on Denman Island's north shore is the only provincial park on the islands that allows camping. It has 10 primitive sites fronting Lambert Channel.

Denman Island Guesthouse & Hostel (☎ 250-335-2688, W www.earthclubfactory .com, 3806 Denman Rd) Bunks $20, private double $40. This unique hostel is run by the Earth Club Factory, a company dedicated to 'celebrating sustainable products & ideas.' Among the various accommodations options here is the beautiful but weird 'tree sphere' – a treehouse that looks like a giant wooden eyeball.

Bradsdadland Campsite (☎ 250-335-0757, fax 604-925-1453, 2105 Shingle Spit Rd) Sites $23-32. This beachfront campground on Hornby Island is a small, family-oriented resort that emphasizes quiet.

The ferry for Denman Island leaves from Buckley Bay, about 20km south of Courtenay, and takes 10 minutes. For Hornby Island you take another ferry from Gravely Bay on Denman Island. The roundtrip fare for each is $4.75/2.50 adult/child age 5-11, $11.75 for a car.

COURTENAY & COMOX

Courtenay is the larger of these two essentially joined towns – commercial centers for the local farming, logging and fishing industries. The Visitor Info Centre (☎ 250-334-3234, 888-357-4471, W www.comoxvalley chamber.com, 2040 Cliffe Ave), in Courtenay, serves both. The towns themselves don't hold much of visitor interest, but the Powell

River ferry to/from the mainland docks near here, and Vancouver Island's premier ski area is a short drive to the northwest.

Mt Washington

In winter, island ski bums flock to **Mt Washington Alpine Resort** (☎ *250-338-1386, 888-231-1499, snow report ☎ 250-338-1515,* **W** *www.mtwashington.bc.ca, Strathcona Pkwy; season Dec-Apr; adult full-day pass $45),* which gets an average annual snowfall of 860cm. The resort offers 50 runs served by five chairlifts and three surface lifts, plus night skiing, Nordic skiing (on a 55km track system), snow-tubing, snowshoeing, two snowboard terrain parks and a big lodge. There are great hiking and mountain biking opportunities in summer. If you're coming from down south and want to bypass Courtenay/Comox, take exit 130 off the Inland Island Hwy. Shuttle bus service operates from Courtenay (☎ 250-337-2294).

Lodging is available on the mountain, including at the new *Mt Washington Guest House/Hostel* (☎ *250-898-8141,* **W** *www .mtwashingtonhostel.com, 1203 Fosters Place)* Dorm beds $20, private rooms from $55. This convenient ski-in/ski-out hostel has kitchen and laundry facilities, ski/bike storage and an outdoor hot tub.

Getting There & Away

Comox Valley Airport (YQQ; **W** www .comoxairport.com) is served by Pacific Coastal Airlines (☎ 800-663-2872), Air Canada (☎ 888-247-2262) and WestJet (☎ 888-937-8538). The airport is in Lazo, north of Comox on the way to the ferry terminal.

VIA's E&N Railiner (☎ 888-842-7245) runs between Victoria and Courtenay once daily ($44/88 one-way/roundtrip). The station is at 899 Cumberland Rd; purchase tickets from the conductor. The buses of Laidlaw Coach Lines (☎ 250-334-2475, 800-318-0818 in Canada, 800-663-8390 in the US, **W** www.grayline.ca/victoria, 9-2663 Kilpatrick St) stop in Courtenay on their run between Nanaimo and Port Hardy.

BC Ferries (☎ 250-386-3431, 888-724-5223 in BC, **W** www.bcferries.com) connects Comox with Powell River, on the mainland. The ferry terminal is in Little River, 13km north of Comox (follow signs). The crossing takes 75 minutes and the one-way fare is $7.50/2.75/25 adult/child age 5-11/car.

CAMPBELL RIVER

Campbell River is the self-proclaimed 'Salmon Capital of the World.' Sportfishing is king here, and the town is also the main departure point for Strathcona Provincial Park and Quadra and Cortes Islands.

The Visitor Info Centre (☎ 250-287-4636, 800-463-4386, fax 250-286-6948, **W** www .campbellrivertourism.com, 1235 Shoppers Row) is open 9am to 7pm daily in summer, 9am to 5pm Monday to Saturday the rest of the year. Internet access is available at the public library (☎ 250-287-3655, 1240 Shoppers Row) and at On Line Gourmet (☎ 250-286-6521, 970 Shoppers Row).

The well-done **Museum at Campbell River** (☎ *250-287-3103,* **W** *www.crmuseum .ca, 470 Island Hwy; adult/student & senior $5/3.75; open 10am-5pm Mon-Sat, noon-5pm Sun mid-May–Sept, noon-5pm Tues-Sun rest of year)* sits above the highway on the town's south side. It features a good collection of First Nations masks, an 1890 pioneer cabin and video footage of the Ripple Rock explosion. (Ripple Rock, a submerged mountain in the Seymour Narrows north of Campbell River, caused more than 100 shipwrecks before it was blown apart in 1958. An overlook on Hwy 19 shows what's left of it.)

Most visitors come here to fish for one or more of five salmon species – Coho, Chinook, sockeye, humpback (or pink) and chum. Fishing guides are plentiful; get a list from the Visitor Info Centre. For a different perspective, call **Paradise Found Adventure Tour Co** (☎ *250-923-0848, 800-897-2872,* **W** *www.paradisefound.bc.ca),* which offers Campbell River snorkel tours that let you get a fish's-eye view of the migrating salmon. The tours run daily July to late October and cost $79. The company also offers hiking tours in the area.

Scuba diving is excellent off the coast in Discovery Passage. For more information, call **Beaver Aquatics Ltd** (☎ *250-287-7652, 760 Island Hwy).*

Places to Stay

Elk Falls Provincial Park (☎ *250-954-4600, fax 250-248-8584)* Sites $12. About 3km northwest of Campbell River on Hwy 28, this 1100-hectare park has a huge riverside campground with 122 sites and flush toilets. Elk Falls is a beautiful 25m cascade.

Loveland Bay Provincial Park, about 19km northwest at Campbell Lake, and **Morton Lake Provincial Park**, 19km north off Hwy 19, are both small and secluded and have primitive sites for $12.

Above Tide Motel (☎ 250-286-6231, fax 250-286-0290, 361 Island Hwy) Singles/doubles $64/69 & up. This quiet place is a good value. All rooms have water views.

Rustic Motel (☎ 250-286-6295, 800-567-2007, fax 250-286-9692, ₩ www.rusticmotel .com, 2140 N Island Hwy) Singles/doubles start at $60/80. Right in town, this motel has standard rooms, kitchenettes and full kitchens, suites and cabins. It's basic but clean and friendly.

Coast Discovery Inn & Marina (☎ 250-287-7155, 800-663-1144, fax 250-287-2213, ₩ www.coasthotels.com, 975 Shoppers Row) Singles/doubles start at $135/145. The big chain hotel downtown is the Coast, an ugly mid-rise convenient to the ferry terminal. It has a private marina, restaurant, pub and health club.

Painters Lodge (☎ 250-286-1102, 800-663-7090, fax 250-286-0158, ₩ www.painters lodge.com, 1625 McDonald Rd) Rooms $179 & up. In a previous incarnation, this fishing lodge was a big favorite among both anglers and the Hollywood set, when guests included Bob Hope, Bing Crosby, John Wayne and Susan Hayward. The old lodge burned down in 1985, and the new version is the lap of luxury for the rod-and-reel set. Fishing packages include boats, guides, foulies and fishing gear. But you don't have to fish to come here. As the ritziest accommodations in Campbell River, the lodge draws a diverse clientele. If you *did* come here to fish, also ask about the affiliated **April Point Resort** on Quadra Island.

Places to Eat
Java Shack (☎ 250-287-9881, 1281 Tyee Plaza) One of the coolest coffeehouses on Vancouver Island, Java Shack knows how to make a truly superior cafe mocha, as well as healthy sandwiches incorporating fresh produce. Photos of rock-climbing and other outdoor adventures line the walls. This place is a real find. It's also conveniently right across the street from the ferry dock.

Bee Hive Cafe (☎ 250-286-6812, 921 Island Hwy) Breakfast $6-9, lunch $7-9, dinner $8-17. The Bee Hive blends modern food and contemporary decor with historical photos of Campbell River. It's down by the waterfront on the south side of downtown.

Fusilli Grill (☎ 250-830-0090, 4-220 Dogwood St) Dinner entrées $11-22. Up on the hill out of the tourist zone, the Fusilli Grill offers good Italian food in a casual setting.

Riptide (☎ 250-830-0044, 1340 Island Hwy) Sandwiches $10-14, pizzas $14-18, dinner entrées $16-36. This big upscale pub has a nice bar with several good beers on tap, as well as an interesting menu including pastas, steaks and creative entrées like hazelnut-encrusted lamb tenderloin and black peppercorn pressed salmon. The central fireplace takes the chill off, and views of the marina are great out the big front windows.

Harbour Grill (☎ 250-287-4143, 112-1334 Island Hwy) Dinner entrées $19-28. In Discovery Harbour Mall, this elegant white-linen place specializes in steaks, but also offers chicken, duck, lamb and veal dishes.

Getting There & Around
Laidlaw Coach Lines (☎ 250-287-7151, 800-318-0818 in Canada, ☎ 800-663-8390 in the US, ₩ www.grayline.ca/victoria, 509 13th Ave) offers service north to Port Hardy ($49 one-way) and south to Victoria ($44). For information about local buses call Campbell River Transit System (☎ 250-287-7433).

QUADRA & CORTES ISLANDS
On Quadra Island, just offshore, you can see marine and birdlife or visit the First Nations' **Kwagiulth Museum** (☎ 250-285-3733) at Cape Mudge in the south. The island also has hiking trails, including a strenuous two-hour trail up Chinese Mountain, and beautiful **Rebecca Spit Provincial Park** – an appealing park the author would find even more appealing if he didn't have a friend named Rebecca who chewed tobacco. Accommodations and camping are available on the island.

Tsa-Kwa-Luten Lodge – The Resort at Cape Mudge (☎ 250-285-2042, 800-665-7745, fax 250-285-2532, ₩ www.cape mudgeresort.bc.ca, Lighthouse Rd) Rooms start at $120. This place, by the beach and surrounded by a vast tract of forest, is a beautiful upscale resort run by the Kwagiulth First Nations people, whose art, architecture and food prevail as a theme.

Cortes Island, east of Quadra Island, has plenty of deserted beaches and lots of wildlife. It's about an hour, and two ferries, from Campbell River. It also has accommodations, food and camping.

Ferries to Quathiaski Cove on Quadra Island leave Campbell River regularly from Discovery Crescent (across from Tyee Plaza); the roundtrip fare is $4.75/2.50 adult/child age 5-11, plus $12 for a car. Another ferry departs Heriot Bay on Quadra Island for Whaletown on Cortes Island; the roundtrip fare is $5.75/3, plus $14.50 for a car. Ask about the van service to Cortes four times a week from the Laidlaw Coach Lines depot.

STRATHCONA PROVINCIAL PARK

Basically a 250,000-hectare wilderness area, the island's largest park is Strathcona Provincial Park (☎ 250-954-4600; open year-round). Hwy 28 between Campbell River and Gold River cuts across the park's most developed portion, providing access to campgrounds and some well marked trails. All trails in the park are for hiking only: no horses or mountain bikes.

In the Buttle Lake district, two well-known hikes are the **Elk River Trail** and the **Flower Ridge Trail**. Both lead to fine alpine scenery. Like other developed trails, these two are suitable for all age groups. This area also has a number of short trails and nature walks. Other less-developed trails demand more preparation and lead to remote areas.

In the south part of the park the **Della Falls Trail**, for example, is a tough two- or three-day trek but is great for scenery and ends at the country's highest waterfall (440m). You need a good map. (Many people get to the falls from Port Alberni; for details, see that section earlier in this chapter.) Other fine walks are those in the **Beauty Lake** area and one crossing the **Big Interior Massif** up to Nine Peaks. From the highest peaks, such as Golden Hinde (at 2200m, the highest on the island), Colonel Foster and others, you can see the ocean to the west and the Strait of Georgia to the east. One thing you won't have to look at is a grizzly bear, as there aren't any on Vancouver Island.

On the park's east side, accessed from Mt Washington Alpine Resort west of Courtenay, **Forbidden Plateau** holds another popular trail network, with a 15km (one-way) trek to the top of Mt Albert Edward (2093m) being among the most popular hikes.

The park has two serviced *campgrounds* with running water and pit toilets. Buttle Lake Campground ($15) is near the park's north entrance and is the nicer of the two. Ralph River Campground ($12) is at the south end of the Buttle Lake, on the eastern shore. Both are open April through October. Wilderness camping in the park costs $5 per person per night.

Strathcona Park Lodge (☎ 250-286-3122, fax 250-286-6010, **W** www.strathcona.bc.ca, Hwy 28)x Rooms with shared bath start at $58, with private bath at $88, cabins at $149; call for minimum-stay requirements. Begun in 1959 as an outdoor education center, this family-run lodge just outside the park still takes teaching as its mission. For most of the year, the lodge welcomes schoolchildren for weeklong introductions to the natural world. But in summertime, the lodge becomes a base camp for travelers – especially families – eager to experience the outdoors with few distractions.

Strathcona runs a variety of programs, including hiking, canoeing and sea-kayaking trips to remote locales. Most visitors stay on weeklong packages, but overnight accommodations are usually available. You can rent kayaks and canoes or spend your time sampling the nearby hiking trails. The lodge also operates a chalet at Mt Washington.

GOLD RIVER

In the center of the island, west of Strathcona Provincial Park, Gold River, accessed by Hwy 28, is the last stop on surfaced roads. The little town is a caving capital and is the headquarters of BC's Speleological Association. Visitors can join spelunking trips to **Upana Caves** and to **Quatsino Cave**, the deepest vertical cave in North America. Kayakers can try their luck on the whitewater section of the river known as the **Big Drop**. For more information, ask at the Visitor Info Centre (☎ 250-283-2418, fax

250-283-7500, cnr Hwy 28 & Scouts Lake Rd); it's open mid-May to early September.

The working freighter MV *Uchuk III* (☎ *250-283-2325,* W *www.mvuchuck.com, Government Wharf),* a converted WWII minesweeper, cruises through a maze of fjordlike inlets to some of the remote villages and settlements in **Nootka Sound** and **Kyuquot Sound** on the Pacific coast. Day trips are offered to Tahsis (adult/senior/child age 7-12 $45/41/22.50: Jan-June) and to the Mowachaht village of Friendly Cove, visited by Capt Cook in 1778 ($40/37/20, plus $9/7/4 landing fee; July–mid-Sept). Also available, year-round, are two-day trips to Kyuquot (single/double/child $195/310/70, including accommodations) and the former gold-mining town of Zeballos ($160/250/70). Government Wharf is south of town at the end of Hwy 28.

Ridgeview Motor Inn *(☎ 250-283-2277, 800-989-3393, fax 250-283-7611, 395 Donner Court)* Rooms $89 & up. This 48-room motel is near the Visitor Info Centre. It has cable TV, laundry facilities and available kitchens.

NORTH VANCOUVER ISLAND

Less populated and less visited than the south, the northern half of the island is a rugged area with lots of good opportunities for outdoor activities. Heading north from Campbell River, Hwy 19 cuts inland and urbanization all but disappears. It's a scenic 198km drive (about 2½ to three hours) from Campbell River to Port McNeill, the largest town on the north island. On the way you'll see forests, mountains, lakes and rivers, but little in the way of 'civilization.'

The Telegraph Cove–Port McNeill area is of most interest with its whale-watching and First Nations sites. Many of the travelers you meet will be heading north to Port Hardy to catch the ferry to Prince Rupert.

Telegraph Cove

About 8km south of Port McNeill (190km north of Campbell River), a road turns east off Hwy 19 and leads 10km to this small community, one of the best of the West Coast's so-called boardwalk villages (villages in which most of the buildings are built over the water on wooden pilings). Formerly a sawmill village, it has good fishing, but the killer whales are its main at-

traction. Johnstone Strait, between Sayward and Alert Bay, is one of the best places in Canada to see them.

Stubbs Island Whale Watching *(☎ 250-928-3185/17, 800-665-3066,* W *www.stubbs island.com, Beaver Cove Rd; adult/child age 1-12 $65/59; trips daily June-Sept, reduced schedule late May & early Oct)* runs three-hour whale-watching tours out of Telegraph Cove. Reservations are required, and warm clothing is strongly advised.

Port McNeill

pop 2850

This logging center is the departure point for Alert Bay on Cormorant Island and Sointula on Malcolm Island. The Visitor Info Centre (☎ 250-956-3131, fax 250-956-3132, 351 Shelley Crescent) is about two blocks from the ferry terminal. It's open daily in summer, weekdays only the rest of the year.

The town has a few private campgrounds, B&Bs and modest motels. Don't head up this way without a reservation.

Haida-Way Motor Inn *(☎ 250-956-3373, 800-956-3373, fax 250-956-4710,* W *www .portmcneillhotels.com, 1817 Campbell Way)* Singles/doubles $80/96. This downtown motor inn is the biggest place in town. Amenities include a pub, restaurant and Internet access.

Having a Whale of a Time

Using sonar to track the fish, over a dozen pods of killer whales (each pod containing about 20 members) come to Johnstone Strait in summer to feed on migrating salmon. Many of the whales swim in Robson Bight, along one of its beaches, rubbing their sides and stomachs on the pebbles and rocks that have been smoothed and rounded by the action of the water. No one knows quite why they do this, but the whales obviously get a lot of pleasure from it and maybe that's reason enough. Who would want to tangle with a pleasure-seeking killer whale?

The Johnstone Strait killer whales are featured in David Attenborough's documentary *Wolves of the Sea.*

Alert Bay

Alert Bay, on 5km-long Cormorant Island, is a fascinating blend of old fishing settlement and First Nations village. The **U'Mista Cultural Centre** (☎ 250-974-5403), a 2km walk from the BC Ferries dock, shows off Kwakiutl art, mainly masks, a ceremonial bighouse and a 52m-tall totem pole (the world's tallest).

Seasmoke Whalewatching/Sea Orca Expeditions (☎ 250-974-5225, 800-668-6722 in BC, [W] www.seaorca.com) offers whale-watching trips aboard its classic wooden sloop, the SV *Tuan*. Imagine watching orcas without the roar of gas engines in your ears. Nice. Cost is $70/40 adult/child age 3-12. The company also has available onshore lodging (singles/doubles $85/100).

Sunspirit Hostel (☎ 250-974-2026, [e] tours@midnightsun.com, 549 Fir St) Dorm beds $17 & up. This hostel occupies a former church near the beach. It has a full kitchen, huge common area, fireplace and a TV/VCR.

Ferries between Alert Bay and Port McNeill take 45 minutes. The roundtrip fare is $5.75/3/14.50 adult/child age 5-11/car.

Port Hardy

This small town at the northern end of Vancouver Island is best known as the departure point for the ferry trip through the famed Inside Passage to Prince Rupert aboard the *Queen of the North*. The terminal is 3km south of town across Hardy Bay at Bear Cove, which is one of two sites where evidence of the earliest human occupation of the central and northern coastal areas of BC – around 8000 to 10,000 years ago – was found. (The other site is Nanamu, now a canning town on the eastern shore of Fitzhugh Sound.)

The Visitor Info Centre (☎ 250-949-7622, fax 250-949-6653, [W] www.ph-chamber.bc.ca, 7250 Market St) is open daily in summer and weekdays only the rest of the year.

The area around Port Hardy has good salmon fishing and scuba diving. **North Island Diving & Water Sports** (☎ 250-949-2664, 8665 Hastings St) rents and sells equipment and runs courses. You can also rent canoes and kayaks at the end of the jetty.

In and around Port Hardy are campgrounds, hotels, motels and about 20 B&Bs. Several of the campgrounds are near the ferry terminal.

Wildwoods Campsite (☎ 250-949-6753, cnr Forest Development Rd & Hwy 19) Sites $12-18. This campground, on the ferry terminal road, is one of the closest campgrounds. Others are *Sunny Sanctuary Campground* (☎ 250-949-8111, 866-251-4556, 8080 Goodspeed Rd) and *Quatse River Campground* (☎ 250-949-2395, fax 250-949-9021, 8400 Byng Rd).

Quarterdeck Inn (☎ 250-902-0455, 877-902-0459, fax 250-902-0454, [W] www.quarterdeckresort.net, 6555 Hardy Bay Rd) Singles/doubles start at $65/75. The beautiful new Quarterdeck sits right on the waterfront and all rooms have water views. Amenities include a restaurant, pub, marina, hot tub and fitness center.

Glen Lyon Inn (☎ 250-949-7115, 877-949-7115, fax 250-949-7415, [W] www.glenlyoninn.com, 6435 Hardy Bay Rd) Rooms start at $85. Another nice hotel is the Glen Lyon Inn, with riverview rooms, some new, overlooking the marina. Amenities include guest fitness and laundry facilities, Internet access, a restaurant and pub.

The town fills up the night before a ferry is due to depart so it's worth booking ahead.

Getting There & Around Laidlaw Coach Lines (☎ 250-949-7532, 800-318-0818 in Canada, 800-663-8390 in the US, [W] www.grayline.ca/victoria, 7210 Market St) has one or two buses a day to Victoria for $93. North Island Transportation, operating out of the same office, runs a shuttle bus to/from the ferry terminal for $5.25 one-way. The bus will pick you up or drop you off wherever you're staying.

BC Ferries (☎ 250-386-3431, 888-223-3779 in BC, [W] www.bcferries.com) sails the *Queen of the North* up the Inside Passage to Prince Rupert on daylight sailings (15 hours) from mid-May to early October. The voyages are spectacular for scenery and wildlife. Reservations for vehicles are an excellent idea. The fare is $106/53/218 adult/child age 5-11/car.

'Discovery Coast' ferries serve Bella Coola on the BC mainland from Port Hardy from June to September. Again, the sights

The Inside Passage to Prince Rupert

BC Ferries (**W** www.bcferries.com) runs the 15-hour, 440km trip along the coast, around islands and past some of the province's best scenery. The classic *Queen of the North* ferry leaves every other day at 7:30am (check in by 6:30am, if you have already booked a place) and arrives in Prince Rupert at 10:30pm. (In winter the ferry leaves just once a week.)

There's a short stop at Bella Bella, about a third of the way up, which is mostly for the locals but also as a drop-off point for kayakers. The one-way fare is $106/53/218/362 per adult/child 5-11/car/RV up to 6m long. Outside the summer peak period (late May to the end of September) the fares can be half as much.

If you're taking a vehicle in summer you should reserve well in advance. Call BC Ferries in Victoria (☎ 250-386-3431) or from any place else in BC (☎ 888-223-3779). However, it's possible to go standby. To do so put your name on the waiting list as early as possible and be at the ferry terminal by 5:30am at the latest on the day of departure. Binoculars are useful as you're often close to land and the wildlife viewing is good: the possibilities include bald eagles, porpoises, sea lions and humpback and killer whales.

Once in Prince Rupert you can continue on Alaska State Ferries farther north to Juneau and Skagway; catch BC Ferries to the Queen Charlotte Islands; or go by land into the BC interior and up to the Yukon and Alaska.

are great and from Bella Coola you can take rugged Hwy 20 456km to Williams Lake and Hwy 97 (see the Southwestern British Columbia section). The fare is $110/55/220 adult/child age 5-11/car.

Cape Scott Provincial Park

About 64km west of Port Hardy over an active logging road (gravel), this remote park (☎ 250-954-4600, fax 250-248-8584, open year-round) offers challenging hiking, wilderness camping ($5 per person per night) and exploring along pristine beaches. Most accessible is the undisturbed expanse of sandy beach at San Josef Bay, under an hour's walk along a well maintained trail from the trailhead at the park boundary.

Beyond this, things get serious. The eight-hour, 24km slog to wild Cape Scott, an old Danish settlement at the park's far end, weeds out the Sunday strollers. Just submit totally to the 'goddess of mud' and rewards will come to you. Nels Bight Beach, at six hours and with camping, is one of them. Wildlife is abundant.

Note that the west coast of this northern tip of the island is known for strong winds, high tides and heavy rain. You'll need to take all supplies and equipment if you're camping. Also, it's suggested that water be purified.

Southern Gulf Islands

When Canadians refer to British Columbia as 'lotus land,' the Gulf Islands are often what they have in mind. Lying northeast of Victoria, and southwest off Tsawwassen on the mainland, this archipelago of nearly 200 islands in the Strait of Georgia spills over into the San Juan Islands of Washington State.

The mild climate, abundant flora and fauna, relative isolation and natural beauty combine to make these small and mostly uninhabited islands an escapist's dream destination. Traditionally, they've attracted retirees, artists and other countercultural types who shun the 9-to-5 grind of mainland life.

Vessels of all descriptions cruise in and out of bays, harbors and marinas much of the year. Scuba diving, fishing, sailing and kayaking are all popular pastimes, but the five islands serviced by BC Ferries also offer such land-based pleasures as hiking, horseback riding and gallery hopping.

Lodging is tight, so reservations are mandatory, especially in peak summer season. Canadian Gulf Islands Reservations (☎ 250-539-3089, 866-539-3089) handles bookings for more than 100 B&Bs, inns, cottages and other accommodations. Most restaurants on the Gulf Islands are associated with lodges, resorts and B&Bs, so they're not cheap. Campers should carry propane stoves (fires are not usually allowed) and their own cooking supplies. Many of the islands do not have ATMs. See the links at W www.gulfislands.com for more sneak previews.

Getting There & Around

BC Ferries' (☎ 888-223-3779, W www.bcferries.com) services to the islands are fairly good, though potentially very confusing. In general, there are more ferries, to more places, in the morning than in the afternoon, so make sure you know how and when you're getting back if you're planning a day trip. If you're coming from Vancouver Island, it's easy to stop over on at least one of the islands on the way back to the mainland. Be sure to pick up a ferry schedule, available at any Visitor Info Centre.

Ferries from Tsawwassen on the mainland go to Saturna, Mayne, Galiano, Pender and Salt Spring Islands. A one-way pedestrian passage is $9, or $35.50 for a car, but the return trip to Tsawwassen costs about half as much. Ferries from Swartz Bay to all of the above islands cost $6.25 one-way for a passenger, or $21.50 for a vehicle. For all of these runs, reservations for cars are strongly advised in high season.

Once on the islands, interisland ferries cost $3 per passenger, $7 for a car. Bicycle and scooter rental is usually available near the ferry terminals, marinas or main towns. Cycling the quiet island roads is a very popular pastime, but check out a topographic map first. On Salt Spring the roads are narrow, winding and sometimes almost impossibly steep!

Salt Spring Island
pop 12,000

The largest and most populous Southern Gulf island has about 12,000 permanent residents and about three times that number of people in summer. Local farms produce everything from apples to organic cheese to some of Canada's best lamb and wool. In fact, sheep serve as the unofficial mascot of Salt Spring Island; they graze in pastures, and sheep signposts point the way to local artists' and craftspeople's studios.

For many centuries, First Nations people hunted and gathered on the island and called it 'Klaathem' ('salt spring') for the salt springs on the island's north end. In the 19th century, the first settlers arrived; they were pioneering African Americans seeking escape from prejudice and social tensions in the USA. Their small group formed a community at Vesuvius Bay, began farms and set up schools. Despite conflicts with First Nations tribes, they survived and were later joined by British and Irish colonists.

The principal village of **Ganges** is not far from the Long Harbour ferry landing. The Visitor Info Centre (☎ 250-537-5252, 866-216-2936, fax 250-537-4276, W www .saltspringtoday.com, 121 Lower Ganges Rd; open daily year-round) keeps listings of special events and maps of galleries and artists' studios open to the public. A vibrant Saturday morning market (8am-4pm Apr-Oct) for artists, craftspeople and farmers is probably the best of its kind on the islands. ArtSpring (☎ 250-537-2102, 100 Jackson Ave) boasts a full calendar of performing arts events. The island's Festival of the Arts takes place in July. Nearby, Mouat Park has walking trails and a frisbee golf course.

Mt Maxwell Provincial Park offers sweeping views and horseback riding (call Salt Spring Guided Rides at ☎ 250-537-5761). Ranking among the Gulf Islands' best parks, **Ruckle Provincial Park** (☎/fax 250-653-4115, Beaver Point Rd), set on a historic farmstead 10km east of the Fulford Harbour ferry terminal, offers easy forest and shore hikes, as well as fishing and primitive *camping* ($12).

At Fulford Wharf, **Salt Spring Kayaking** (☎ 250-653-4222, 2923 Fulford-Ganges Rd)

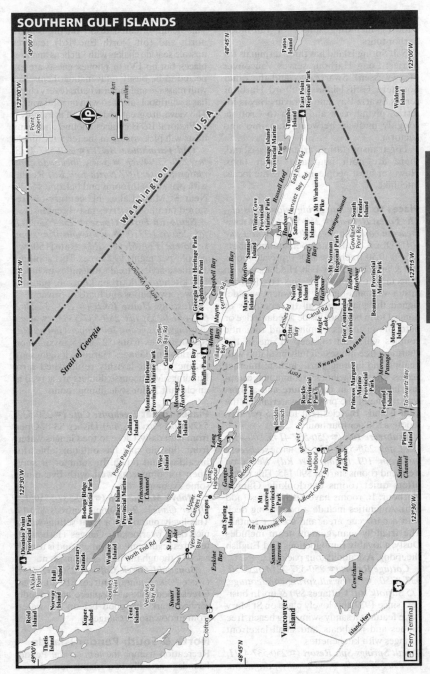

SOUTHERN GULF ISLANDS

BRITISH COLUMBIA

Strait of Georgia

Washington U.S.A.

Point Roberts

Patos Island

Waldron Island

Tumbo Island

East Point Regional Park

Cabbage Island Provincial Marine Park

East Point Rd

Russell Reef

Winter Cove Provincial Marine Park

Lyall Harbour

Narvaez Bay Rd

Saturna

Saturna Island

Mt Warburton Pike

Plumper Sound

South Pender Island

Gowlland Point Rd

South Point Rd

Breezy Bay

Mt Norman Regional Park

Bedwell Harbour

Beaumont Provincial Marine Park

Browning Harbour

Prior Centennial Provincial Park

Magic Lake

Canal Rd

North Pender Island

Amies Rd

Otter Bay

Bennett Bay

Campbell Bay

Fernhill Rd

Samuel Island

Horton Bay

Mayne Island

Village Bay

Georgia Point Heritage Park & Lighthouse Point

Miners Bay

Mayne

Sturdies Bay

Bluffs Park

Galiano Bay Rd

Galiano Island

Montague Harbour Provincial Marine Park

Montague Harbour

Parker Island

Prevost Island

Beddis Beach

Ruckle Provincial Park

Beaver Point Rd

Swanson Channel

Ferry to Vancouver

Ferry

To Swartz Bay

Princess Margaret Marine Provincial Park

Portland Island

Piers Island

Moresby Island

Moresby Passage

Satellite Channel

Fulford Harbour

Fulford Harbour

Fulford-Ganges Rd

Mt Maxwell Provincial Park

Mt Maxwell Rd

Beddis Rd

Long Harbour

Long Harbour Rd

Upper Ganges Rd

Ganges

Ganges Harbour

Salt Spring Island

St Mary Lake

Wise Island

Trincomali Channel

Porlier Pass Rd

Bodega Ridge Provincial Park

Wallace Island Provincial Marine Park

Wallace Island

Secretary Islands

Alcala Point

Hall Island

Norway Island

Reid Island

Dionisio Point Provincial Park

North End Rd

Vesuvius Bay

Vesuvius Bay Rd

Erskine Bay

Sansum Narrows

Stuart Channel

Southey Point

Kuper Island

Tent Island

Thetis Island

Crofton

Island Hwy

Vancouver Island

Cowichan Bay

Ferry Terminal

0   1   2   4 km
0   1   2 miles

offers kayak rental and guided introductory paddles, including sunset or full-moon harbor tours.

Salt Spring Island has three terminals for ferries: Long Harbour serves Vancouver (Tsawwassen), Swartz Bay and the other Southern Gulf Islands; Fulford Harbour serves Swartz Bay; and Vesuvius Bay is for ferries plying back and forth to Crofton, roughly midway between Nanaimo and Victoria.

For transportation around the island, there are both land and water taxis. However most people, including the locals, hitchhike.

Places to Stay

Saltspring Island Hostel – The Forest Retreat (☎ 250-537-4149, W www.beacom.com/ssihostel, 640 Cusheon Lake Rd) Dorm beds members/nonmembers $15.50/19.50, treehouse $60/70, private rooms $40 & up. Closed Nov-Feb. Hidden away on 4 hectares of woodlands, this HI-affiliated hostel was hand-built by its owners, who designed the place with all the comforts of home. Dorm beds are inside a cedar lodge or outdoors in tepees. Families and romantic couples will want to sleep in one of the charming tree houses, all fully insulated with heating and lighting. Perks include Internet access, kitchen facilities, a communal campfire, baby goats in the pasture and a short trail to one of the prettiest waterfalls in the Gulf Islands. Bicycles rent for $15 per day, scooters $30 per four hours.

Seabreeze Inn (☎ 250-537-4145, 800-434-4112, fax 250-537-4323, W www.seabreeze inns.com, 101 Bittancourt Rd) Weekday/weekend rooms start at $90/145. This motel offers quiet rooms overlooking Ganges Harbour; 16 rooms have kitchenettes (add $10). Amenities include a pool, a big deck with a barbecue area, and scooter rentals. The friendly management team includes Dusty, a lovably rambunctious Old English sheepdog. Ask about tour packages.

Cottage Resort (☎ 250-537-2214, fax 250-537-8750, W www.saltspring.com/cottage, 175 Suffolk Rd) Cottages $90 & up. In business since 1932, this lovely place on St Mary Lake features a sandy swimming beach, free canoes and rowboats, and small lakefront cottages with kitchenettes.

Salt Springs Spa Resort (☎ 250-537-4111, fax 250-537-2939, W www.saltysprings.com, 1460 North Beach Rd) Chalets start at $239. This health-oriented resort on the island's north end (off North End Rd) features upscale seaside chalets with kitchens and fireplaces, but no TVs or phones; guests are expected to be busily rejuvenating themselves with massage and mineral baths (every chalet has a whirlpool tub filled with mineral water). The views are great and the staff is friendly.

Pastoral B&B choices abound and many hosts will pick you up at the ferry terminals.

Old Farmhouse B&B (☎ 250-537-4113, fax 250-537-4969, W www.bbcanada.com/oldfarmhouse, 1077 North End Rd) Rooms with private bathrooms and balconies $170. Near St Mary Lake, this century-old restored farmhouse serves tasty breakfasts.

Seido-En Forest House (☎ 250-653-2311, fax 250-653-2310, W www.saltspring.com/seido-en, 124 Meyer Rd) Rate $150/two people per night, $900/week. This soothing Japanese-style retreat's amenities include a full kitchen, indoor sunken tub, outdoor shower, two patios and loads of privacy.

Hastings House B&B (☎ 250-537-2362, 800-661-9255, fax 250-537-5333, W www.hastingshouse.com, 160 Upper Ganges Rd) Rooms/suites from $275/315 in summer. Overlooking Ganges Harbour, lodgings are in one of four lavishly refurbished farm buildings. Multicourse dinners are served in an elegant Tudor-style dining room.

Places to Eat

Treehouse Café (☎ 250-537-5379, 106 Purvis Lane) Dishes $3-8. Open from 8am daily. Close to the Ganges waterfront, this hip spot has outdoor tables for breakfast and lunch. In summer, it stays open for dinner as well, with live music some evenings.

Moby's Marine Pub (☎ 250-537-5559, 124 Upper Ganges Rd) Dinner entrées $10-17. This lively pub offers a great setting with a nice deck overlooking Ganges Harbour. It features regular entertainment and is usually a scene, though the food is inconsistent.

Bouzouki Greek Cafe (☎ 250-537-4181, Grace Point Square) Entrées $10-20. Great Greek food, nice atmosphere and friendly service mark this good bet on the waterfront in downtown Ganges.

North & South Pender Islands

Recreation trumps the arts on the Pender Islands – actually two islands joined by a short bridge. The more than 2000 islanders prefer to spend their time playing in the glorious natural surroundings, where the sea, sky and neighboring islands all seem close enough to touch. Wherever you go, watch out for the more-or-less tame deer wandering the islands.

For **beaches**, try Hamilton in Browning Harbour on North Pender and Mortimer Spit on South Pender. Close to Medicine Beach at Bedwell Harbour, North Pender's **Prior Centennial Provincial Park** has several walking trails and campsites *($12; reservations ☎ 604-689-9025, 800-689-9025,* w *www.discovercamping.ca).* On South Pender good views are the reward for the hour-long hike up **Mt Norman** (255m).

To get out on the water, look up **Kayak Pender Island** *(☎ 250-629-6939, 2319 Mac-Kinnon Rd),* at Otter Bay Marina. The company offers tours (from $35), lessons and rentals.

Places to Stay *Otter Bay Marina (☎ 250-629-3579, fax 250-629-3589, 2311 MacKinnon Rd)* Tents/cabin $35/75. Close to the North Pender ferry terminal, the marina offers carpeted waterproof tents with cots that sleep up to four people. There are showers, laundry facilities, a swimming pool and a store.

Cooper's Landing (☎ 250-629-6133, 888-921-3111, w *www.cooperslanding.com, 5734 Canal Rd)* Dorm beds, members $20-22; family rooms, members/nonmembers start at $60/80. If you subscribe to the local belief that the Penders are the center of the universe, then Shark Cove – where the two islands meet – must be nirvana. This HI hostel, near the Mt Norman trailhead, offers an enticing combination of reasonably priced accommodations, along with sauna and massage. Bring your own linens, or pay the hostel's small rental fee.

Betty's B&B (☎ 250-629-6599, e *bettysb-b@direct.ca, 4711 Buccaneer Rd)* Rooms peak/off-peak $75/60. Sitting on the shores of North Pender's Magic Lake, rates include large home-cooked breakfasts and the use of mountain bikes and a rowboat. Phone in advance for free pick-ups from the ferry terminal.

Inn on Pender Island (☎ 250-629-3353, 800-550-0172, fax 250-629-3167, w *www.innonpender.com, 4709 Canal Rd)* Basic

rooms (no phone or TV) $70-90, cabins $130. This small inn in the woods is popular with cyclists. A few cabins have private hot tubs or porches with good views; these are stocked with kitchen gear, a wood-burning stove and small TV/VCR. The inn also does door-to-door delivery of continental breakfast and has an excellent restaurant.

Oceanside Inn (☎ 250-629-6691, w *www.penderisland.com, 4230 Armadale Rd)* Rooms $159 & up, including full breakfast. Closed Nov–mid-Dec. This plush oceanfront B&B offers incredible views and romantic ambience. All rooms have private bath, hot tub and deck. Dinner is also available.

Bedwell Harbour Island Resort & Marina (☎ 250-629-3212, 800-663-2899, fax 250-629-6777, w *www.bedwell-harbour.com, 9801 Spalding Rd)* Rooms $120, cabins $160 & up, villas $270 & up. On South Pender, this large resort on small tranquil Bedwell Harbour feels well out of the tourist fray. Yachties love to pull up at the marina and hang for a while. The resort is undergoing a transformation into 'Poet's Cove at Bedwell Harbour.'

Galiano Island

Despite its proximity to Tsawwassen, long and narrow Galiano Island has fewer than 1000 residents, most living on the island's southeast side near Sturdies Bay. Keep in mind that many locals like to keep very much to themselves. The information center (☎ 250-539-2233, w www.galianoisland.com) is on the right-hand side as you leave the ferry terminal. Call Go Galiano Island Shuttle (☎ 250-539-0202) for pick-ups from the ferry or trips around the island.

About 75% of the island is forest and bush, from the sheer rock cliffs below Bodega Ridge to the many small islands just off Galiano's coast. The island has excellent beaches, especially at **Montague Harbour Provincial Marine Park**. Kayakers like to camp at **Dionisio Point Provincial Park**, at the island's far northwest end; the park can be reached only by boat or via the hiking trail from Devina Dr. You can hike almost the length of the east coast and climb either **Sutil Mountain** (323m) or **Mt Galiano** (342m) for panoramic views of the Olympic Mountains.

There's good **scuba diving** at Alcala Point, home to friendly wolf eels; anemone walls at Race Point and Baines Bay; a swim-through cave at Matthews Point; and the sunken Point Grey tugboat. Contact Galiano Diving (☎ 250-539-3109, **w** www.galianodiving.com) for equipment and charters.

Dive in at Alcala Point.

Montague Harbour Provincial Marine Park (*reservations* ☎ *604-689-9025, 800-689-9025,* **w** *www.discovercamping.ca*) Sites $15. Primitive campsites are 10km from Sturdies Bay ferry terminal.

Bodega Resort (☎/*fax 250-539-2677, 120 Cook Rd*) Cottages start at $60, add $20 each additional person. This favorite family resort offers horseback-riding trails and a trout-fishing pond. Fully furnished log cottages can sleep up to six people. Ask about 'Weekends for Readers' hosted by Celia Duthie, of Vancouver independent bookseller fame.

For other inns, B&Bs and hotels, check out the links at **w** www.galianoisland.com.

Max & Moritz Spicy Island Food House (☎ *250-539-5888, Sturdies Bay Rd*) Dishes under $10. Arrive early at the ferry so you can sample the delicious Indonesian and German food – yes, that's right – offered here.

The ***Hummingbird Pub*** (☎ *250-539-5472, 47 Sturdies Bay Rd*) features live entertainment on summer weekends and an outdoor picnic and barbecue area.

Mayne Island
pop 900

Active Pass, the narrow channel that separates Mayne and Galiano Islands, presents the tightest squeeze on the Tsawwassen-Swartz Bay ferry route. The human history of the island is also distinctive: in the 19th century, gold-rushers stopped here halfway between Vancouver Island and the Fraser River to fortify themselves for the rest of their trip.

Village Bay, on the southwestern side of Mayne Island, is the ferry terminal, although there are docking facilities for boaters at other points. About two dozen **artists' studios** operate on Mayne and there are late-19th-century **heritage buildings** at Miners Bay, including the Plumper Pass Lock-up, now the island's museum.

There are plenty of **beaches**, and Mayne's back roads offer some of the best **cycling** in the Gulf Islands. It'll take hikers about an hour roundtrip to conquer Mt Parke. Mayne Island Canoe & Kayak Rentals (☎ 250-539-2667), at Seal Beach near Miners Bay, offers **kayaking** instruction and *camping* ($10 per person), with hot tub and showers.

Tinkerers B&B and ***Till Eulenspiegel Guesthouse B&B*** (☎ 250-539-2280, **e** *tinkerers@gulfnet.pinc.com, 417 & 421 Sunset Place*) Rates $75-105. These spots in Miners Bay share ownership as well as an international clientele. Spanish and German are spoken (and taught), or you can simply laze around the hammock and enjoy the sea views.

Springwater Lodge (☎/*fax 250-539-5521,* **w** *www.gulfislands.com/springwaterlodge*) Rooms with shared bathroom $40, 2-bedroom cabins with stove, refrigerator & sun deck $95. Built on Miners Bay in the 1890s, this is the oldest continuously operating hotel in the province – and it's showing its age. But it's an okay place to sleep for a night (and an even better place to eat).

Oceanwood Country Inn (☎ *250-539-5074, fax 539-3002,* **w** *www.oceanwood.com, 630 Dinner Bay Rd*) Deluxe rooms $160-330. All of the uniquely outfitted rooms have views of Navy Channel, some with whirlpool tubs and private balconies. The restaurant is one of the best in the Gulf Islands, serving Northwest cuisine (four-course dinner $44). Check the website for package deals and a taste of the innkeepers' unforgettable hospitality.

Saturna Island
pop 350

The most lightly populated island, Saturna is a bit harder to reach than the other main Gulf Islands. To many people, however, this inaccessibility makes it all the more attractive as a remote and tranquil escape for a few days or more. For more information, visit W www.saturnatourism.bc.ca.

At Saturna Point by the ferry terminal in Lyall Harbour, there's a store and a pub. **Winter Cove Provincial Marine Park** has a good sandy beach and swimming, fishing, boating and hiking. At the top of **Mt Warburton Pike** (497m) is a wildlife reserve with feral goats and fine views, though you'll also have to look at a mess of telecommunications equipment. Saturna Sea Kayaking (☎ 250-539-5553), in Boot Cove (only a five-minute walk from the ferry), offers kayaking lessons and rentals, along with good paddling advice.

Saturna, like the other Gulf Islands, has its share of resident artists. See the annual map brochure (available on the ferries and around the island) for a listing of those who invite visitors to their studios, usually by appointment. A short stroll from Saturna Lodge (see below) is **Saturna Island Vineyards** (☎ 250-539-5139, W www.saturna vineyards.com; open 11am-4:30pm daily May-Sept, Sat & Sun Oct & Nov). This winery offers free tours and tastings.

There are no campgrounds on Saturna Island and no more than a dozen places to stay indoors, so be sure to book in advance.

Breezy Bay B&B (☎ 250-539-5957, e breezybay@gulfislands.com, 131 Payne Rd) Singles/doubles $60/75. This B&B is in an 1890s farmhouse about 2km from the ferry terminal, with a long verandah overlooking orchards and a pond. In the morning, guests can look forward to a filling country breakfast of delicious local ingredients.

East Point Resort (☎ 250-539-2975) Cottages $80 & up. This resort offers six cottages on the waterfront, with private sandy-beach access and forested trails, plus whale-watching near East Point Park. There is usually a seven-day minimum stay in high season.

Saturna Lodge (☎ 250-539-2254, 888-539-8800, fax 250-539-3091, e saturnalodge@ hotmail.com, 130 Payne Rd) Rooms $135-195, including a gourmet breakfast. All guests at this upscale yet unpretentious lodge enjoy access to a garden hot tub, bicycles, bocce, badminton and croquet. Its restaurant offers fine dining (three-course dinner $30) and culinary theme nights on Thursday. The vineyards are close by.

Southwestern British Columbia

The heavily populated area immediately surrounding Vancouver is known as the Lower Mainland. Most people see this region as something to get through on the way to somewhere else. We won't quibble with this, but there are a few places to break up the trip and once into the Fraser Canyon, BC's legendary topography takes over.

East from Vancouver to Chilliwack, the road is uninterestingly flat and straight; more or less an expressway right into the city. There's no point trying to hitch along this stretch, as it's illegal for cars to stop. Note that this entire area is a hotbed of police speed traps.

At the small town of Hope, 150km east of Vancouver, the road splits. The Trans Canada Hwy follows the Goldrush Trail (the route the old wagon trail took to the Cariboo gold rush) north up the Fraser River Valley toward Cache Creek. As the road follows the river, which winds and twists through the canyon, there are many points of interest and viewing areas. The farther north you go, the drier the land becomes and the fewer trees there are, until around Cache Creek the landscape resembles that of a cowboy movie.

Northeast of Hope the Coquihalla Hwy heads to Kamloops. It's a wide, straight 195km express route with a $10 toll. Service stations are few, so leave with a full tank. The scenery along the way is pleasant and there are plenty of places to stop and view it.

The Crowsnest Hwy (Hwy 3) east of Hope heads first southward through Manning Provincial Park and then into the Okanagan Valley – the dry, beautiful fruit-growing region of BC. The green hills of the

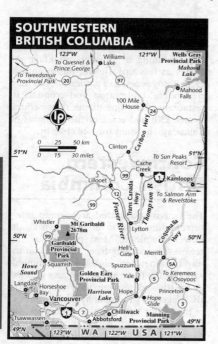

SOUTHWESTERN BRITISH COLUMBIA

Hope area fade to brown as the road heads toward Osoyoos.

HOPE

There's not much in Hope itself but it's a good access point for the Fraser River Canyon and southern BC. Several lakes and more than a dozen provincial parks are close by. If you have a bit of time, the **Othello Tunnels**, 15 minutes by car from Hope, are worth the trip. Situated in the Coquihalla Canyon Recreation Area and running alongside the river of the same name, a series of tunnels were cut for a railway line between 1911 and 1919. It's an interesting hour stroll along the gorge and unique enough to have been used in several movies, including *First Blood,* which you may recall was the first 'Rambo' movie. Obviously, the scenery is better than the film.

Southeast of town, a 15-minute drive on the Crowsnest Hwy, are the remains of the infamous 'Hope slide.' In 1965 four people were killed when a small earthquake caused a huge part of a mountain to slide off, burying the highway below.

The Visitor Info Centre (☎ 604-869-2021, fax 604-869-2160, **w** www.hopechamber.bc.ca, 919 Water Ave), near the river, is a good place to collect information. There's plenty of *camping* in the area as well as both long and short hiking trails. *Motels* can be found on the Old Princeton to Hope Rd as well as downtown, with singles or doubles starting around $45.

FRASER RIVER CANYON

One of the province's principal rivers, the swift-flowing historic Fraser, pours out of central BC into the ocean at Vancouver. The Thompson River, a major tributary, joins it at Lytton. A trip along Hwy 1 by the steep-sided canyon offers some of the province's more impressive scenery.

Several provincial parks lie along the canyon. **Emory Creek Provincial Park**, just north of Hope, has camping, fishing and hiking. A good picnic stop is **Alexander Bridge Provincial Park**, 1km north of Spuzzum. The open-grate suspension bridge, built in 1926, spans the Fraser River and is free to cross.

Whitewater rafting down the Fraser and its tributaries' fast-flowing rapids is popular and a number of companies offer trips. The Visitor Info Centres in Hope (see above) and Lytton (☎ 250-455-2523, fax 250-455-6669, 420 Fraser St) have information on the scores of trips available. Those with motorized rafts allow more time for watching the ever-changing scenery, while paddle rafts where you have to work are more exciting. Either way you'll get soaked. In Yale, **Fraser River Raft Expeditions** (☎ 604-863-2336, ☎ 800-363-7238) is a major operator. A one-day trip costs around $105.

About 25km north of Yale on Hwy 1 is the **Hell's Gate Airtram** (☎ 604-867-9279, **w** www.hellsgate.bc.ca; tickets $11/7 adult/youth age 6-18), a widely advertised cable-car system that goes down to the rushing Fraser River daily late March to late October. Look it over before buying the hype.

Lytton is a pleasant town sitting where the clear Thompson waters meet the cloudy Fraser River. Hwy 1 goes north to Cache Creek.

MANNING PROVINCIAL PARK

This 70,000-hectare provincial park is habitat for over 200 species of birds and mammals (you're likely to see black bears, but no grizzlies) and glorious summer wildflowers. Manning also marks the end of the 4240km **Pacific Crest Trail** from Mexico to Canada. The visitor center (☎ 250-840-8836; open 8am-4pm daily in summer) has information on hikes and interpretive programs. Across the road from the center, *Manning Park Resort* (☎ 250-840-8822, 800-330-3321, fax 250-840-8848, W *www.manningpark resort.com, Hwy 3)* has a lodge (rooms start at $129), café and general store. In autumn Pacific Coast Trail through-hikers swap tales inside the Bear's Den bar. And plenty of people use the park's four *campgrounds* (sites $12-18.50).

The visitor center and resort are 64km east of Hope on Hwy 3.

KAMLOOPS
pop 87,000
Sitting at the point where the North Thompson, South Thompson and Thompson Rivers meet, Kamloops has always been a service and transport crossroads. In fact the town was once called 'Kahmoloops,' a Shuswap word meaning 'meeting of waters.' The Trans Canada Hwy cuts east-west through town, the Yellowhead Hwy (Hwy 5) heads north, Hwy 5A heads south and the Coquihalla Hwy heads southwest to Vancouver. With this strategic location, the city is the major service and industrial center in the district. That said, the economy here is far from robust. It's a blue-collar town trying to get by – an honest place with a lot of character.

The city is surrounded by some 200 lakes, making it a good watersports area. The dry, rolling hills make interesting scenery and excellent ranching territory. Summers can be extremely hot with temperatures of 40°C.

Kamloops is spread over a wide area, with motels, restaurants and other services lining the Trans Canada Hwy. The core itself is quiet, clean and pleasantly strollable.

Orientation & Information
Train tracks separate the Thompson River's edge from the downtown area. Next to the tracks, running east-west, is Lansdowne St, one of the main streets. The other principal streets are Victoria, the main shopping street, and Seymour, both parallel to and south of Lansdowne. The Trans Canada

Hwy is several blocks farther south. On the northwestern corner of the city, along Lorne St, is Riverside Park, a pleasant spot for picnicking and swimming. The North Thompson River meets the Thompson River across from the park's shoreline.

The Visitor Info Centre (☎ 250-374-3377, 800-662-1994, fax 250-828-9500, W www .kamloopschamber.bc.ca/tourism.php, 1290 W Trans Canada Hwy), at exit 368, is open 8am to 8pm daily in summer, 9am to 5pm weekdays the rest of year. The main post office (☎ 250-374-2444) is at 301 Seymour St.

Kamloops Library (☎ 250-372-5145, 465 Victoria St) has free Internet access, but you only get a half hour and you'll probably wait at least that long for a terminal. A better bet is PC Doctor's Digital Café (☎ 250-372-5723, 463 Lansdowne St), one block over, which has loads of terminals for 10¢ a minute, $5 an hour.

The Royal Inland Hospital (☎ 250-374-5111) is at 311 Columbia St. McCleaners coin laundry (☎ 250-372-9655) is at 437 Seymour St.

Things to See & Do
The **Kamloops Museum** (☎ 250-828-3576, W *www.city.kamloops.bc.ca/parks/museum .html, 207 Seymour St; admission by donation; open 9:30am-4:30pm Tues-Sat year-round, extended hours July-Aug)* has three floors of exhibits covering the town's history and people. Among the displays are pioneer implements and Shuswap tools and ornaments. The museum also publishes a Heritage Walking Tour guide to Kamloops.

Kamloops Art Gallery (☎ 250-828-3543, W *www.galleries.bc.ca/kamloops, 465 Victoria St; adult/child $3/2; open 10am-5pm Tues, Wed, Fri, Sat, 10am-9pm Thur, noon-4pm Sun)* is in the library building. It's not huge but has a good broad collection that doesn't shy away from the avant garde.

Secwepemc Museum & Heritage Park (☎ 250-828-9701, W *www.secwepemc.org, 355 Yellowhead Hwy; general/senior & child age 7-12 $6/4; open 8:30am-8pm Mon-Fri, 10am-6pm Sat & Sun in summer, 8:30am-4:30pm Mon-Fri Sept-May)*, northeast of the center, is the most interesting site in town. The five-hectare site holds re-created traditional Secwepemc (Shuswap) winter and summer houses and has an indoor museum that outlines the history and the

BRITISH COLUMBIA

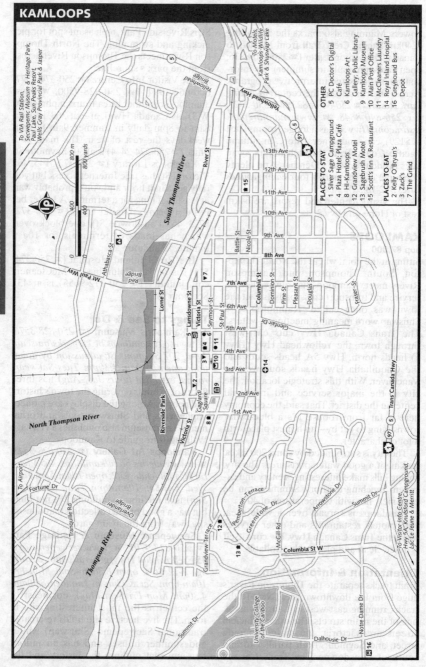

KAMLOOPS

To VIA Rail Station,
Secwepemc Museum & Heritage Park,
Paul Lake, Sun Peaks Resort,
Wells Gray Provincial Park & Jasper

To Motels,
Kamloops Wildlife
Park & Shuswap Lake

Yellowhead Hwy

Yellowhead
Bridge

South Thompson River

River St

13th Ave
12th Ave
11th Ave
10th Ave
9th Ave
8th Ave
7th Ave
6th Ave
5th Ave
4th Ave
3rd Ave
2nd Ave
1st Ave

Battle St
Nicola St
Columbia St
Dominion St
Pine St
Pleasant St
Douglas St
Fraser St

Lansdowne St
Victoria St
Seymour St
St Paul St

Lorne St

Athabasca St

Mt Paul Way

Red Bridge

Glenfair Dr

Riverside Park

North Thompson River

Gaglardi
Square

Victoria St

To Airport

Fortune Dr

Tranquille Rd

Overlander
Bridge

Thompson River

Pemberton Terrace

Greenstone Dr

Grandview Terrace

McGill Rd

Columbia St W

Arrowstone Dr

Summit Dr

Trans Canada Hwy

To Visitor Info Centre,
Hwy 5A, Knutsford Campground,
Lac Le Jeune & Merritt

Summit Dr

University College
of the Cariboo

Notre Dame Dr

Dalhousie Dr

0   400   800 m
0   400   800 yards

PLACES TO STAY
1 Silver Sage Campground
4 Plaza Hotel; Plaza Café
8 Grandview Motel
12 Sagebrush Motel
13 Scott's Inn & Restaurant
15 Hi-Kamloops

PLACES TO EAT
2 Kelly O'Bryan's
3 Zack's
7 The Grind

OTHER
5 PC Doctor's Digital
   Café
6 Kamloops Art
   Gallery; Public Library
9 Kamloops Museum
10 Main Post Office
11 McCleaners Laundry
14 Royal Inland Hospital
16 Greyhound Bus
   Depot

culture of the Secwepemc Nation. Unfortunately, there is no city bus to the park.

Kamloops Wildlife Park (☎ 250-573-3242, W *www.kamloopswildlife.org, Hwy 1 exit 390/391; adult/youth age 13-16/child age 3-12 $7/5/4; open 8am-8pm daily July & Aug; 8am-5pm daily Sept-June)* has many animals found in Canada's west as well as critters from foreign lands – 70 species in all. The 48-hectare spread is 15 minutes east of Kamloops on Hwy 1.

Sun Peaks Resort
Off the Yellowhead Hwy 53km northeast of Kamloops, Sun Peaks Resort (☎ 800-807-3257, *snow information* ☎ 250-578-7232, W *www.sunpeaksresort.com, 3150 Creekside Way; adult day pass $49; ski season Nov-Mar)* offers downhill and even cat skiing, as well as 40km of cross-country trails. This place is huge – 1363 hectares covering three mountains – and has good vertical (881m). Nine lifts serve 94 runs, including many long, dry powder runs. The resort also boasts over 2000 hours of sunshine a year and a large base-area village. A shuttle to Kamloops runs six times daily in ski season ($29 one-way). In summer, the resort stays open for hiking, mountain biking and golf. Accommodations are available at Sun Peaks, including at *Sun Peaks International Hostel* (☎ 250-578-0057, W *www.sunpeaks hostel.com, 1140 Sun Peaks Rd),* where dorm beds cost $20 per person and a private double is $45.

Places to Stay
Camping *Silver Sage Campground* (☎ 250-828-2077, 877-828-2077, 771 Athabasca St E) Sites $16-25. This facility, northeast over the river, is nothing special, but it's quiet and offers views across the river to downtown, which is walkable from here. It has a coin laundry and showers.

Knutsford Campground (☎ 250-372-5380, e *knutsfordcamp@hotmail.com, Hwy 5A)* Sites $18-28. This RV park is 12km southwest of town on Hwy 5A toward Merritt, about 6km south off the Trans Canada Hwy. All facilities are available, including showers and a coin laundry.

You can also camp in two nearby provincial parks: *Paul Lake Provincial Park*, 24km northeast of Kamloops, which has sites for $12; and *Lac Le Jeune Provincial Park,*

37km southwest of town, which offers more developed sites for $15. For more information on either park, contact the BC Parks Thompson River District office (☎ 250-851-3000, 1210 McGill Rd) in Kamloops.

Hostels *HI-Kamloops* (☎ 250-828-7991, fax 250-828-2442, W *www.hihostels.bc.ca, 7 W Seymour St)* Dorm beds $16/20, private rooms available. Office open 8am-1pm & 5pm-10pm in summer, 8am-noon & 5pm-10pm rest of year. This spacious HI hostel is in a beautiful former courthouse close to downtown. It has a lounge and dining room in the original courtrooms. The 73 beds are usually all taken in summer. From the Greyhound bus depot take local bus No 3 ($1.50) to the corner of Seymour St and 3rd Ave, then walk two blocks west, or you can walk the entire way in about 30 minutes.

Hotels & Motels The two main areas for motels are Columbia St, west of the downtown area, and on the Trans Canada Hwy, east of town.

Thrift Inn (☎ 250-374-2488, 800-661-7769, fax 250-374-2488, 2459 Trans Canada Hwy) Singles/doubles $37/39 & up. Thrift has a heated swimming pool, satellite TV and free continental breakfast.

Sagebrush Motel (☎ 250-372-3151, 888-218-6116, fax 250-372-2983, 660 W Columbia St) Singles/doubles $50/55 & up. One of the cheapest on Columbia St is the basic Sagebrush Motel, which has a seasonal heated pool and sauna.

Grandview Motel (☎ 250-372-1312, 800-210-6088, fax 250-372-0847, W *www.grand viewmotel.com, 463 Grandview Terrace)* Singles/doubles start at $66/72. Among the many others in this area, Grandview has large outdoor gardens and a pool. Oddly, the views here are largely obstructed and hardly grand.

Scott's Inn & Restaurant (☎ 250-372-2281, 800-665-3343, fax 250-372-9444, W *www.scottsinn.kamloops.com, 551 11th Ave)* Singles/doubles start at $66/70. Down in town, Scott's has an indoor pool and hot tub, as well as a welcoming café.

Plaza Hotel (☎ 250-377-8075, 877-977-5292, fax 250-377-8076, W *www.plaza heritagehotel.com, 405 Victoria St)* Rooms $139-199; deep discounts often available. Now in her mid-70s, this restored grande dame downtown has a few wrinkles and can't hear too well, but she's had a life. If you stay here and listen closely, maybe she'll tell you a tale or two.

Places to Eat

Along and around Victoria St there are numerous places for a meal or just coffee.

The Grind (☎ *250-828-6155, 705 Victoria)* Recently relocated a few blocks away from the center of downtown, this great coffeehouse sets the standard for Kamloops Cool.

Plaza Café (☎ *250-377-8675, 405 Victoria St)* Breakfast $2-10, lunch $5-10, dinner $10-20. This café in the Plaza Hotel is open 7am to 2pm and 5pm-9pm daily and serves good breakfasts and lunch specials.

Zack's (☎ *250-374-6487, 377 Victoria St)* Soups & sandwiches $3-5. Open 7am-11pm daily. This mellow coffeehouse bakes its own bagels and offers light fare.

Kelly O'Bryan's (☎ *250-828-1559, 244 Victoria St)* Dinner entrées $12-25. This merry Irish-style pub/restaurant offers good burgers, hearty Irish stew and well-poured pints of Guinness.

Getting There & Around

Kamloops Airport (YKA; ☎ 250-376-3613, 3035 Airport Dr) is 7km northwest of town on Kamloops' north shore. Air Canada Regional (☎ 888-247-2262) flies to Kamloops daily from Vancouver.

The Greyhound bus depot (☎ 250-374-1212, 725 Notre Dame Dr), southwest of the downtown area off W Columbia St, has a cafeteria and luggage-storage lockers. Buses depart daily to Vancouver, Calgary, Jasper, Edmonton, Prince George and Kelowna.

VIA Rail (☎ 888-842-7245) offers three trips weekly either east to Jasper, Edmonton and beyond or south to Vancouver. For Prince George you must transfer in Jasper. The Kamloops station is 11km north of town off the Yellowhead Hwy and is only open 30 minutes prior to departures.

The privately operated *Rocky Mountaineer* tour train stops here overnight on its various trips. (See the Getting There & Away section in Vancouver for details).

For information about local bus routes call Kamloops Transit System (☎ 250-376-1216). A one-way fare is $1.50. For a taxi call Yellow Cabs (☎ 250-374-3333).

WELLS GRAY PROVINCIAL PARK

In the Cariboo Mountains about halfway between Kamloops and Jasper, and off the Yellowhead Hwy (Hwy 5), is this huge, undeveloped and relatively little-visited 541,000-hectare wilderness park. In Clearwater, the Visitor Info Centre (☎ 250-674-2646, fax 250-674-3693, 425 E Yellowhead Hwy), on the corner of the Yellowhead Hwy and Clearwater Valley Rd, has lots of useful information and maps on the park.

You can hike along more than 20 trails of varying lengths, go mountain biking, canoeing on the lakes and rivers, whitewater rafting on Clearwater River, mountain climbing, downhill or cross-country skiing, and horseback riding. Canoeing often provides the only access to hiking trails and only experienced, fully equipped mountaineers should attempt climbing or venture onto the snowfields and glaciers. Wildlife is plentiful. Of the park's many scenic waterfalls, **Helmcken Falls**, where the Murtle River plunges 137m, is the most spectacular.

Wells Gray has five designated *campgrounds* with sites costing $12, plus plenty of wilderness camping ($5 per person per night) along the shores of the larger lakes.

There are three access points to the park. From Clearwater to the south, the Clearwater Valley Rd enters the park at Hemp Creek; from Blue River a 24km gravel road and 2.5km track lead to Murtle Lake in the southeast; and from 100 Mile House off Hwy 97 it's 88km on paved road to Mahood Lake in the southwest.

For more information, contact the BC Parks Thompson River District office in Kamloops (☎ 250-851-3000, 1210 McGill Rd).

MT ROBSON PROVINCIAL PARK

Skirting the Fraser River, the Yellowhead Hwy and the railway run along the valley of this 217,000-hectare park, which adjoins Alberta's Jasper National Park. At the park's west end is Mt Robson (3954m), highest point in the Canadian Rockies. When the clouds aren't hugging it, it's visible from the highway.

At the base of the mountain the visitors center (☎ 250-566-4325, fax 250-566-9777; open May-Oct), 17km east of Tete Jaune Junction on Hwy 16, has park information and runs interpretive programs during summer. Like Wells Gray, the park offers the full range of activities as well as picnic areas, *campgrounds* ($12-17.50) and lookout points. In August and September you can see salmon spawning on the river at Rearguard Falls.

KAMLOOPS TO WILLIAMS LAKE

West of Kamloops, the Trans Canada Hwy heads to **Cache Creek**, where Hwy 97 (the Cariboo Hwy) leads north to Williams Lake. The dry, scrub-covered hills around the crossroads of Cache Creek give way to endless forest as you head north from Clinton. At 100 Mile House (named after the roadhouse located at this distance from the start of the original Cariboo Wagon Rd) you can turn off the highway and travel northeast to Mahood Lake in Wells Gray Provincial Park.

Williams Lake is a transport and industrial center best known for the Williams Lake Stampede, which takes place at the beginning of July. It's BC's answer to the Calgary Stampede and is a wild time that lasts four days. The Visitor Info Centre (☎ 250-392-5025, fax 250-392-4214, 1148 S Broadway), on Hwy 97, can give you details.

West of Williams Lake, Hwy 20 leads to huge, undeveloped **Tweedsmuir Provincial Park**, which has excellent canoeing opportunities, as well as *campgrounds* ($12) and backcountry camping ($5 per person per night). You might see bighorn sheep en route. The park is open mid-June to mid-September. For more information, contact the BC Parks Cariboo District office (☎ 250-398-4414, 281 1st Ave N) in Williams Lake.

Okanagan Valley

The Okanagan, a beautiful and unique area of Canada, is a series of valleys running about 180km north-south in south-central BC. To the east are the Monashee Mountains, to the west the Cascade Mountains. The valleys were carved out by glaciers and are linked by a series of lakes, the largest of which is Okanagan Lake. The varied and interesting landscape makes the entire region scenic.

The northern end is gentle green farmland that climbs to woods of evergreens. The farther south you get, the drier the terrain becomes. Near Osoyoos, close to the US border, cactuses grow on desert slopes that get only 250mm of rain a year. And everywhere are rolling, scrubby hills, narrow blue lakes and clear sky.

The Okanagan is a significant retirement area. This, in some measure, is responsible for the growth of the area's major towns, which are increasingly popular with seniors from not only BC but all over Canada. The entire region is also a vacation mecca for those searching for some hot summer sun when it's wet or gloomy in the mountains or on the coast. Through July and August expect all types of accommodations to be tight.

Fruit Orchards & Vineyards

The hot, dry summers, in combination with the fertile soil and heavy irrigation, has made the region the country's top fruit-growing area. About 100 sq km of orchards blanket the Okanagan.

During April and May the entire valley springs to life with blossoms from thousands of fruit trees. In late summer and autumn the orchards drip with delicious fresh fruit. Stands dotting the roads sell Canada's best and cheapest produce. Grapes are the last fruit of summer to ripen, but one of the most important; the valley has a national reputation for its high-quality wine, and several of the area's 30-odd vineyards offer tasting rooms.

The drive north along Hwy 97 from Osoyoos is an almost endless succession of orchards, farms, fruit stands and the like. Slow-moving tourists and retirees on this route will give you plenty of time to smell the apples, peaches, and, yes, the roses.

If you wish to tie your trip to a specific fruit, the approximate harvest times are as follows:

harvest times	fruit
June 25-July 25	cherries
July 15-August 10	apricots
July 20-September 10	peaches
August 1-October 20	apples
August 15-September 15	pears
August 28-September 30	tomatoes
September 1-September 20	prunes
September 9-October 18	grapes

There's work picking fruit; it's hard and the pay isn't great, but you don't always need a work permit and you'll meet lots of young people. Arrive early and shop around. The

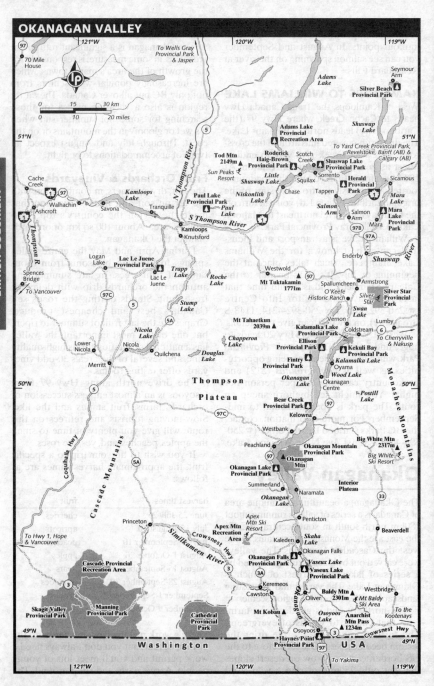

OKANAGAN VALLEY

To Wells Gray
Provincial Park
& Jasper

70 Mile
House

To Yard Creek Provincial Park,
Revelstoke, Banff (AB) &
Calgary (AB)

Adams
Lake

Silver Beach
Provincial Park

Adams Lake
Provincial
Recreation Area

Shuswap
Lake

Seymour
Arm

Cache
Creek

Walhachin

Ashcroft

Kamloops
Lake

Savona

Tranquille

Kamloops

Knutsford

Logan
Lake

Lac Le Jeune
Provincial Park

Lac Le
Jeune

Trapp
Lake

Roche
Lake

Stump
Lake

Spences
Bridge

To Vancouver

Nicola
Lake

Lower
Nicola

Nicola

Quilchena

Chapperon
Lake

Douglas
Lake

Merritt

Tod Mtn
2149m

Sun Peaks
Resort

Paul Lake
Provincial Park

Paul
Lake

S Thompson River

Roderick
Haig-Brown
Provincial Park

Little
Shuswap Lake

Niskonlith
Lake

Scotch
Creek

Squilax

Chase

Shuswap Lake
Provincial Park

Sorrento

Tappen

Herald
Provincial
Park

Sicamous

Mara
Lake

Salmon
Arm

Salmon
Arm

Mara

Mara
Lake
Provincial
Park

Westwold

Mt Tuktakamin
1771m

Spallumcheen

O'Keefe
Historic Ranch

Armstrong

Enderby

Shuswap
River

Silver
Star

Silver Star
Provincial
Park

Mt Tahaetkun
2039m

Vernon

Swan
Lake

Lumby

To Cherryville
& Nakusp

Katamalka Lake
Provincial Park

Ellison
Provincial Park

Coldstream

Kalamalka
Lake

Kalamalka Lake
Provincial Park

Kekuli Bay
Provincial Park

Fintry
Provincial
Park

Oyama

Wood Lake

Thompson
Plateau

Okanagan
Lake

Okanagan
Centre

Postill
Lake

Monashee Mountains

Bear Creek
Provincial Park

Westbank

Kelowna

Okanagan Mountain
Provincial Park

Big White Mtn
2317m

Big White
Ski Resort

Peachland

Okanagan
Mtn

Okanagan Lake
Provincial Park

Summerland

Naramata

Interior
Plateau

Okanagan
Lake

Apex Mtn
Ski Resort

Penticton

Cascade Mountains

Coquihalla Hwy

To Hwy 1, Hope
& Vancouver

Princeton

Apex Mtn
Recreation
Area

Crowsnest Hwy

Kaleden

Skaha
Lake

Okanagan Falls
Provincial Park

Vaseux Lake

Beaverdell

Simikameen River

Keremeos

Cawston

Okanagan Falls

Vaseux Lake
Provincial Park

Baldy Mtn
2301m

Oliver

Westbridge

Mt Baldy
Ski Area

To the
Kootenays

Cascade Provincial
Recreation Area

Skagit Valley
Provincial Park

Manning
Provincial Park

Cathedral
Provincial
Park

Mt Koban

Osoyoos
Lake

Osoyoos

Anarchist
Mtn Pass
1234m

Crowsnest Hwy

Haynes Point
Provincial Park

To Yakima

Washington

USA

BRITISH COLUMBIA

0   15   30 km
0   10   20 miles

season starts first around Osoyoos, where the weather is warmer. Many towns have agricultural employment offices.

OSOYOOS & AROUND

At the south end of the Okanagan Valley, small Osoyoos sits at the edge of dark-blue Osoyoos Lake, surrounded by stark, dry rolling hills. The skies are sunny and the waters warm.

With its hot, dry weather, the Osoyoos region produces Canada's earliest and most varied fruit and vegetable crops. Look for roadside stands selling cherries, apricots, peaches, apples and other fruit. Many vineyards also dot the area.

On the lake's east side lies a small desert, known as a 'pocket desert,' that runs about 50km north to Skaha Lake and is about 20km across at its widest point.

Averaging less than 200mm of rain a year, the area has flora and fauna uncharacteristic for Canada, including the calliope hummingbird (Canada's smallest bird), rattlesnakes, painted turtles, coyotes and cacti.

In a province where all the superlatives describing scenery work overtime, the stretch of landscape between Osoyoos and Penticton on a clear day has to rank as one of the more deserving.

Orientation & Information

Osoyoos is at the crossroads of Hwy 97 heading north to Penticton (past several provincial parks where you can camp) and the Crowsnest Hwy running east to the Kootenay region and west to Hope. The US border, cutting through Osoyoos Lake, is just 5km to the south.

The Visitor Info Centre (☎ 250-495-7142, 888-676-9667 in Canada, fax 250-495-6161, **W** www.osoyooschamber.bc.ca) is slightly northwest of town, at the junction of Hwys 3 and 97. It is open daily in summer, weekdays only the rest of the year.

The Greyhound bus stop (☎ 250-495-7252, Hwy 3 at Hwy 97) is at the Husky station at the highway junction west of town. Buses run to/from Vancouver, Calgary and north up the valley.

Things to See & Do

The climate makes **Osoyoos Lake** the warmest in the country. That together with the sandy beaches means great swimming.

The small **Osoyoos Museum** (☎ 250-495-2582, Park Place; adult/child age 6-14 $3/1; open 11am-5pm daily mid-May–mid-Sept), in Gyro Community Park off Main St, has displays on natural history, the Inkameep people, orchards, irrigation and the provincial police.

The **Desert Centre** (☎ 250-495-2470, 877-899-0897, **W** www.desert.org, 146th Ave; adult/senior & student/child age 2-12/family $5/4/2/12), north of town off Hwy 97, is a 27-hectare site devoted to study and preservation of the area's desertlands. A boardwalk trail winds through the arid vegetation to observation points with interpretive information. It's open daily mid-April to mid-October; reduced schedule rest of year.

The **pocket desert**, off Black Sage Rd, is on the Inkameep people's reserve but you can visit by first asking permission from their office there. If you follow Black Sage Rd north from there to Oliver you'll pass several **wineries**. From Oliver, rough Camp McKinney Rd goes east to the **Mt Baldy ski area** (☎ 250-498-4086, Mt Baldy Rd), which has cross-country trails and 11 downhill runs with a vertical drop of 420m.

East of Osoyoos, on Hwy 3, the **Anarchist Mtn Lookout** at 700m, offers a superb view of the town, valley, desert, lake and US border. You need a car or a ride to reach it. You can also reach the ski area off Hwy 3 (turn left on Mt Baldy Rd before Canyon Bridge).

West of town, Hwy 3 runs up the Similkameen Valley, a beautiful quiet place one step removed from the well-trod tourist track. Surrounded by orchards, **Keremeos** is noted for its fruit and wines. And about 30km west of Keremeos is **Cathedral Provincial Park**, a 33 sq km mountain wilderness characterized by unusual rock formations and the beautiful Cathedral Lakes. Mule deer, mountain goats and California bighorn sheep inhabit the park, which is accessed by a gravel road off Hwy 3, 3km west of Keremeos. The park has no campgrounds, but backcountry camping is possible. For more information, contact the BC Parks Okanagan District office (☎ 250-494-6500), 11km north of Summerland on Hwy 97.

Places to Stay & Eat

Haynes Point Provincial Park (☎ 250-494-6500, fax 250-494-9747, 32nd Ave; open Apr-Oct) Sites $17.50. Jutting into the lake 2km south of downtown off Hwy 97, the Haynes Point campground has the most sought-after sites. Reservations (☎ 800-689-9025) are available and necessary.

Nk'mip (Inkameep) Campground *(☎/fax 250-495-7279,* **W** *www.campingosoyoos .com, 45th St; open year-round)* Sites $18-29. To reach this good alternative on the Indian Reserve, go 4km east of town on Hwy 3 to 45th St, then 1km north. Sites are usually available, and amenities include a beach, showers, laundry facilities, a store with ice and a marina with boat rentals.

Cabana Beach Campground *(☎ 250-495-7705, fax 250-495-6031,* **W** *www.cabana beach.com, 2231 E Lakeshore Dr)* Sites $19-29. This well developed campground 3km southeast of downtown has small cabins, as well as tent and trailer space.

Sun Beach Motel *(☎ 250-495-7766, fax 250-495-7766,* **e** *sunbeachmotel@otvcablelan .net, 7303 Main St)* Rooms $45 & up. One of the many beachside motels lining 'motel row' on Main St, this one has barbecues, boat docks and patios.

Plaza Royale Courtyard Inn *(☎ 250-495-2633, 800-700-0092, fax 250-495-5140,* **W** *www .plaza-royale.com, 8010 Valiant Lane)* Singles/ doubles $55/60 & up. This motor inn, west of town at the junction of Hwys 3 and 97, has kitchenettes, a pool and some king beds.

The Ridge Brewpub *(250-495-7679, 9907 Hwy 3)* Dinner entrées $7-15. At the junction of Hwys 3 and 97, this gorgeous new brewpub makes a variety of superb beers on-site, and its restaurant serves delicious salads, sandwiches and pastas, as well as dinner entrées after 5pm. The atmosphere is casually elegant, even in the pub section. It's a nice place to cool off.

PENTICTON
Penticton, the southernmost of the three Okanagan sister cities, sits directly between Okanagan Lake and Skaha Lake, which are connected by the Okanagan River. The sun shines for an average of 600 hours in July and August – about 10 hours a day – and that's more than it shines in Honolulu! It's not surprising, then, that the number-one industry is tourism.

Orientation
The downtown area lies just south of Okanagan Lake. It's a pleasant place for

strolling and window shopping, either during the day or at night, when twinkling streetlights make it look like Disneyland. Most of the land alongside the lake is park, the notable exception being the view-blocking Penticton Lakeside Resort & Casino, which looms over the beach. Compared to the other valley towns, Penticton has more vibrant buzz than Osoyoos or Vernon, but it can't touch Kelowna.

Lakeshore Dr runs west beside the lake from the downtown area to Riverside Dr and Hwy 97. The main street is fittingly Main St, running north-south; at the southern end it continues straight on to S Main St, and to the right it forks off to become Skaha Lake Rd, which then turns into Hwy 97. The downtown area extends about 10 blocks south from the lake. Most of the restaurants and bars are in this area.

Information
The Visitor Info Centre (☎ 250-493-4055, 800-663-5052, fax 250-492-6119, **W** www .penticton.org, 888 Westminster Ave W) is open daily year-round. Sharing the space is the British Columbia Wine Information Centre (☎ 250-490-2006, **W** www.bcwine info.com), which sells just about every wine made locally.

The main post office (☎ 250-492-5717, 56 Industrial Ave W) is south of downtown off Main St. A more convenient downtown postal outlet is at Gallop's Flowers (☎ 250-492-8394, 187 Westminster Ave W). Penticton Public Library (☎ 250-492-0024, 785 Main St) offers Internet access.

Penticton Regional Hospital (☎ 250-492-4000) is south of downtown at 550 Carmi Ave.

Things to See & Do
When the mercury climbs, the **beaches** start looking pretty good. Close to the downtown area, Okanagan Beach is about 1300m long. It's sandy, and in summer the water temperature is about 22°C. At the town's south end, Skaha Beach is about 1.5km long and has sand, trees and picnic areas.

Okanagan Lake here offers some of the best windsurfing conditions in the Okanagan Valley. You'll find all manner of activities – including **windsurfing, sailing,** and **parasailing** – available down on the water next to Lakeside Resort.

The river between the lakes is popular for **inner tubing**, though not all that interesting. Coyote Cruises (☎ 250-492-2115, 215 Riverside Dr) rents inner tubes that you can float on all the way down to Skaha Lake, about a two-hour trip. Coyote offers a shuttle service between the lakes.

Mountain biking is great in summer up on Apex Mountain (see Apex Mountain Ski Resort, below). Also popular with cyclists is the Kettle Valley Railway Trail, which runs 41km up Okanagan Lake's east side to Chute Lake, on the east side of Okanagan Mountain Provincial Park. For information or bike rental, try the Bike Barn (☎ 250-492-4140, 300 Westminster Ave W).

Rock climbing is phenomenal on Skaha Bluffs, a climbing area southeast of town with more than 400 bolted routes. For directions (and maybe a lesson), call Skaha Rock Adventures (☎ 250-493-1765, 113-437 Martin St).

At the **Okanagan Inland Waters Marine Museum** (☎ 250-492-0403, **w** www .sssicamous.com, 1099 Lakeshore Dr W; adult/child age 5-12 $4/1; open 9am-9pm daily in summer; 10am-4pm Mon-Fri rest of year) you can go aboard two restored historic ships, both built in 1914. The SS *Sicamous*, a steam-powered sternwheeler, carried passengers and freight on Lake Okanagan from 1914 to 1936. The SS *Naramata* operated as a barge tug until 1965.

Penticton Museum (☎ 250-490-2451, 785 Main St; admission by donation; open 10am-5pm Mon-Sat in summer, reduced hours rest of year), at the library complex, is an excellent small-town history and culture museum. Displays are varied, well presented and pleasingly eclectic.

Of the many area wineries, one of the closest is **Hillside Estate Winery** (☎ 250-493-6274, 888-923-9463, 1350 Naramata Rd; free tasting; open 10am-5pm daily May-Oct, 10am-5pm Fri-Sun Nov-Dec, Jan-Apr by appointment), northeast of downtown. Continue north up the road to others.

Apex Mountain Ski Resort

This resort (☎ 250-292-8222, 877-777-2739, snow report ☎ 250-492-2929 ext 2000, **w** www .apexresort.com, Green Mountain Rd; adult full-day ticket $44; ski season late-Nov–mid-Apr), 37km west of Penticton, off Green Mountain Rd, has 67 downhill runs for all ability levels, plus cross-country trails. Numerous packages are available with Penticton motels, but you can also stay on the mountain, including at the ski-in, ski-out **Apex Double Diamond Hostel** (☎ 250-292-8256, 866-273-9737, **w** www.doublediamond hostel.com; dorm bed $19, private doubles $49). The resort runs a shuttle bus from town ($7/12 one-way/roundtrip) and is open for hiking, mountain biking and horseback riding in summer.

Special Events

Don't miss the funky **Beach Blanket Film Festival** in late July. You bring your lawn chair to the beach to watch the films, which are projected onto a screen out in the lake.

The city's premier annual event is the **Peach Festival** (☎ 250-493-7385/4055, 800-663-5052), a weeklong event that has taken place around the beginning of August since 1948. There are sports activities, novelty events, music and dance, nightly entertainment, and a major parade held on Saturday. At about the same time is the annual **BC Square Dance Jamboree** (☎ 250-492-5856). It goes on for six nights from 8pm to 11pm, and about 3500 dancers take part. There's an enormous dance floor in Kings Park. There are also street dances, dances held at both lakes – in the water! – pancake breakfasts and other activities.

At the end of August athletes are put through their paces in the **Ironman Canada Triathlon** (☎ 250-490-8787). In early October for 11 days the **Okanagan Wine Festival**, centered in Penticton, takes place throughout the valley (☎ 250-490-2464, 250-861-6654, **w** www.owfs.com).

In early September, look for the **Pentastic Jazz Festival** (☎ 250-770-3494, **w** www .pentasticjazz.com).

Places to Stay

The Info Centre has complete lists of all types of lodging, including the many area B&Bs.

Camping Many tent and trailer parks are south of town, around Skaha Lake. Most charge about $18 to $22 for two people in a tent. Try:

Camp-Along Resort (☎ 250-497-5584, 800-968-5267, fax 250-497-6652, **w** www .campalong.com, Hwy 97 S) Sites $18-28. This full-service family campground overlooks

Skaha Lake 6km south of the city limits. Amenities include pool, showers, laundry and store.

Waterworld RV & Campground (☎ 250-492-4255, 🖥 www.waterworld.bc.ca, 185 Yorkton Ave) Sites $22-25. Kids will love this campground near Skaha Lake, which is part of a big waterslide park. Campers get a discount at the water park. Tent sites and full-hookup sites are available, and the park has all the usual amenities.

Hostels *HI-Penticton* (☎ 250-492-3992, fax 250-492-8755, 🖥 www.hihostels.bc.ca, 464 Ellis St) Dorm beds $16/20 members/non-members; private rooms available. Office open 7am-12:30pm, 4pm-midnight daily. This excellent hostel occupies a 1901 house that has the dignified look of a US consulate in some Third World backwater. It's mightily convenient, downtown just south of the Greyhound depot, and has the usual amenities: kitchen, laundry, patio, bike rental and discounts in town. It also has details about finding fruit-picking work.

Motels Penticton is chock full of motels. Lakeshore Dr/Riverside Dr and S Main St/Skaha Lake Rd are the two main areas.

Valley Star Motel (☎ 250-492-7205, fax 250-492-0977, 🖥 www.valleystar.penticton.com, 3455 Skaha Lake Rd) Singles/doubles $66/68 & up. The Valley Star, at the town's south end, has pleasant rooms and a pool.

Log Cabin Motel (☎ 250-492-3155, 800-342-5678, fax 250-492-8468, 🖥 www.logcabinmotel.penticton.com, 3287 Skaha Lake Rd) Singles/doubles $65/85 & up. This motel has nice grounds, a pool and nice rooms.

Slumber Lodge Penticton (☎ 250-492-4008, 800-663-2831, 274 W Lakeshore Dr) Singles/doubles start at $88/98. Fronting the lake close to the downtown area is the restful Slumber Lodge Penticton.

Penticton Lakeside Resort Conference Centre & Casino (☎ 250-493-8221, 800-663-9400, fax 250-493-0607, 🖥 www.rpbhotels.com, 21 Lakeshore Dr W) Rooms start at $189. This glitzy lakefront mid-rise houses many of the gamblers losing money in the downstairs casino.

Places to Eat

Nearly all the downtown restaurants are on or near Main St, and the revival of the downtown core has brought an increase in choice.

Blueberry Patch (☎ 250-493-8911, 413 Main St) Breakfast special $3. Open daily at 8am, the Blueberry Patch gives you a plate of eggs, hash browns, bacon or sausage and toast for a mere $2.99. Such a deal.

Barley Mill Brew Pub (☎ 250-493-8000, 2460 Skaha Lake Rd) Mains $7-16. For great homebrew and good pub fare, this British-style place is a local favorite.

Theo's (☎ 250-492-4019, 🖥 www.eatsquid.com, 687 Main St) Dinner entrées $11-37. With a lighthearted style and a courtyard atmosphere vaguely reminiscent of a Greek village, Theo's is a fine place to get your feta, baklava or whatever. You might catch some Greek dancing if the staff gets into the ouzo.

Granny Bogner's (☎ 250-493-2711, 302 Eckhardt Ave W) Dinner entrées $19-25. A European-trained chef and large wine list mark this place, in an old mansion two blocks west of Main St. The menu features steak and seafood, as well as some exotic meats.

Entertainment

Element (☎ 250-493-1023, 535 Main St) This hot dance club also has pool tables and a sports lounge with big-screen TV.

The Blue Mule (☎ 250-493-1819, 218 Martin St) The Blue Mule, near the corner of Westminster Ave, has country music and dancing.

Barking Parrot (☎ 250-493-9753, 21 W Lakeshore Dr) A local crowd lounges around at the outdoor tables at this place in the Penticton Lakeside Resort.

Getting There & Around

Penticton Airport (YYF; ☎ 250-492-6042, 🖥 www.cyyf.org, Airport Rd off Hwy 97S) is served by Air Canada Regional (☎ 888-247-2262), with scheduled flights to Vancouver.

The Greyhound bus depot (☎ 250-493-4101, 307 Ellis St), on the corner of Nanaimo Ave one block east of Main St, has a cafeteria and luggage-storage lockers. Buses depart daily for Vancouver ($54; seven hours), Kelowna ($13; 1¼ hours), Vernon ($19; 2½ hours) and Calgary ($91; 12 hours).

For local bus information contact Penticton Transit (☎ 250-492-5602), or visit the Visitor Info Centre and pick up a copy of the *Rider's Guide*, which lists routes and fares. The one-way adult fare is $1.50, $3.25 for a day-pass.

KELOWNA
pop 150,000
Kelowna, founded in 1892, sits halfway down Okanagan Lake, midway between Vernon and Penticton. It's encircled by the rounded, scrubby hills typical of the valley, but closer to town the hills become greener, with terraced orchards lining the slopes. The town itself is greener still, with many parks and gardens. Beneath skies that are almost always clear, sandy beaches rim the lake's dark blue water.

The 150,000 people in Kelowna's metropolitan area make it the Okanagan Valley's major city. Summer days are usually dry and hot, the nights pleasantly cool, and winters are mild. With nearly 2000 hours of sunshine each year, Kelowna is not only an ideal agricultural area but a popular tourist destination. It's a lively place with a distinct resort feel. The town's big event is the 10-day Okanagan Fall Wine Festival (☎ 250-861-6654), which runs from the end of September into early October.

Orientation
The large City Park on the lake's edge forms the town's western boundary. Starting from the big white modern sculpture 'Sails' and the model of Ogopogo, the mythical lake monster, at the edge of City Park, Bernard Ave runs east and is the city's main drag. Other important thoroughfares are

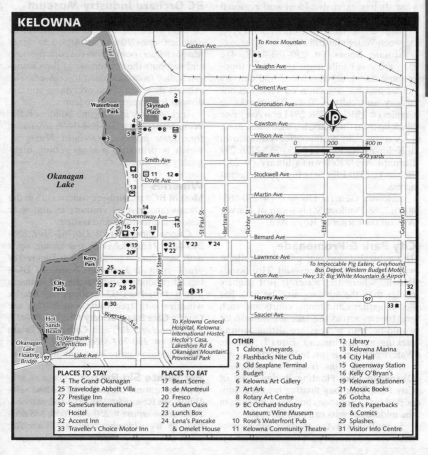

KELOWNA

PLACES TO STAY
4 The Grand Okanagan
25 Travelodge Abbott Villa
27 Prestige Inn
30 SameSun International Hostel
32 Accent Inn
33 Traveller's Choice Motor Inn

PLACES TO EAT
17 Bean Scene
18 de Montreuil
20 Fresco
22 Urban Oasis
23 Lunch Box
24 Lena's Pancake & Omelet House

OTHER
1 Calona Vineyards
2 Flashbacks Nite Club
3 Old Seaplane Terminal
5 Budget
6 Kelowna Art Gallery
7 Art Ark
8 Rotary Art Centre
9 BC Orchard Industry Museum; Wine Museum
10 Rose's Waterfront Pub
11 Kelowna Community Theatre
12 Library
13 Kelowna Marina
14 City Hall
15 Queensway Station
16 Kelly O'Bryan's
19 Kelowna Stationers
21 Mosaic Books
26 Gotcha
28 Ted's Paperbacks & Comics
29 Splashes
31 Visitor Info Centre

BRITISH COLUMBIA

Water, Pandosy and Ellis Sts, all running north-south. South of town Pandosy St becomes Lakeshore Rd. Hwy 97, called Harvey Ave in town, is the southern edge of the downtown area; it heads west over the bridge toward Penticton.

Eastward, along roughly a 15km stretch, Harvey Ave is a slightly restrained commercial strip lined with service stations, junk food restaurants, motels and the rest of the usual suspects.

Information
The Visitor Info Centre (☎ 250-861-1515, 800-663-4345, fax 250-861-3624, ⓦ www .kelownachamber.org, 544 Harvey Ave), on Hwy 97 near the corner of Ellis St, is open daily in summer, weekdays the rest of the year. It has extensive local and regional information.

Most of the banks are on Bernard Ave, between Water and Ellis Sts.

Mosaic Books (☎ 250-763-4418, 411 Bernard Ave) sells maps (including topographic ones), atlases, travel and activity guides and has a section on First Nations history and culture. Ted's Paperbacks & Comics (☎ 250-763-1258, 269 Leon Ave), one block up from City Park, is a used-book store.

A convenient postal outlet is downtown at Kelowna Stationers (☎ 250-762-2276, 297 Bernard Ave). Kelowna's library (☎ 250-762-2800, 1380 Ellis St) offers free Internet access.

Kelowna General Hospital (☎ 250-862-4000, 2268 Pandosy St) is south of Harvey Ave, on the corner of Royal Ave.

City Park & Promenade
The central downtown park is excellent, with lots of shade trees and 'Hot Sands Beach,' where the water is just slightly cooler than the summer air. The park has flower gardens and tennis courts and such great views across the lake it's no wonder would-be fruit pickers are sitting around picking guitars instead. Equally bucolic Waterfront Park is just to the north.

The beach runs from the marina to **Okanagan Lake Floating Bridge**, west of City Park. This long floating bridge is supported by 12 pontoons and has a lift span in the middle so boats can pass through.

From Bernard Ave, the lakeside promenade extends north past the marina and is

good for a stroll or jog in the morning or evening.

Kelowna Arts District
Kelowna's arts district lies around the intersection of Water St and Cawston Ave. Here you'll find the enormous **Art Ark** gallery (☎ 250-862-5080, 135-1295 Cannery Lane), **Skyreach Place** (see Entertainment, later), the new **Rotary Art Centre**, a mixed-use performing-arts studio and theater space, and the light and airy **Kelowna Art Gallery** (☎ 250-762-2226, 1315 Water St; admission by donation; open 10am-5pm Tues-Sat, 10am-9pm Thur, 1pm-4pm Sun), which features the work of many local artists. This district is pleasant to explore on foot.

BC Orchard Industry Museum
Also downtown, the Orchard Museum (☎ 250-763-0433, 1304 Ellis St; admission by donation; open 10am-5pm Mon-Sat; closed Mon in winter) occupies an old packinghouse and recounts the conversion of the Okanagan Valley from ranchland to orchards. The exhibits show just about everything you can do with fruit, from seeds to jam.

Tucked away in the same building is the **Wine Museum** (☎ 250-868-0441; admission free; same hours as Orchard Museum), which is primarily a shop selling high-quality BC wines.

Wineries
Most of BC's multiplying wineries are in the Okanagan. Several vintners in and near Kelowna offer tours and tasting.

Calona Vineyards (☎ 250-762-9144, 888-246-4472, 1125 Richter St; free tasting; open daily 9am-7pm in summer, 10am-5pm rest of year), right in Kelowna, is one of BC's largest producers and was the Okanagan's first; it started in 1932. Among other nearby wineries with free tours and tasting are **Quail's Gate Estate Winery** (☎ 250-769-4451, 3303 Boucherie Rd) and **Cedarcreek Estate Winery** (☎ 250-764-8866, 5445 Lakeshore Rd). The Info Centre has a complete list.

Big White Ski Resort
With a summit elevation of 2319m, Big White Ski Resort (☎ 250-765-8888, 800-663-2772, snow report ☎ 250-765-7669, 888-663-6882, ⓦ www.bigwhite.com, Big White Rd; adult full-day tickets $52; season Dec-Apr),

55km east of Kelowna off Hwy 33, gets dumped on with deep dry powder in winter. The resort offers over 1000 hectares of skiable terrain, as well as three snowboard parks, 25km of cross-country trails, a tube park and night skiing. A shuttle bus runs to/from Kelowna ($13/17 one-way/roundtrip) Numerous inns and lodges at the resort can be reserved through the central office. Hostels in the base village area include:

Bumps (☎ 250-765-2100, 888-595-6411, fax 250-765-3035, W *www.bumpshostel.com*, *7500 Porcupine Rd*) Dorm beds $17-18, private singles/doubles $19.50/39. Close to restaurants and nightlife, 34-bed Bumps offers ski/snowboard lockers, laundry and Internet access.

SameSun Big White Hostel (☎ 250-765-7050, 877-562-2783, W *www.samesun.com*, *Alpine Centre*) Dorm beds $20, private singles/doubles $50/60, ski packages available. Known for its party atmosphere, this ski-in, ski-out place has Internet access, outdoor hot tubs and a free pancake breakfast. Also ask about SameSun's Hostel 2, formerly Bumps Too, which boasts deluxe rooms with kitchen and private bath for $79 single or double.

Activities

Kelowna has lots of good trails to explore on foot or bicycle. History buffs can pick up a *Heritage Walking Tour* brochure at the Info Centre. Also well worth asking about is the **Kettle Valley Railway Trail**, a scenic 8km loop around Myra Canyon through tunnels and over old trestles. **Okanagan Mountain Provincial Park** (☎ 250-494-6500), south of Kelowna off Lakeshore Rd on the lake's east side, is a popular spot for hiking and horseback riding. Many of the trails date from the fur-trade days.

Fishing is possible on Okanagan Lake and many of the 200 other lakes near Kelowna. You'll need a license, available from sporting goods stores and gas stations. From Kelowna Marina you can take fishing trips or cruises. Windsurfers leave from the old seaplane terminal near the corner of Water St and Cawston Ave. Parasailing is offered daily in summer by Kelowna Parasail Adventures Ltd (☎ 250-868-4838, 1310 Water St), in front of the Grand Okanagan Hotel. Sports Rent (☎ 250-861-5699, 3000 Pandosy St) rents all sorts of watercraft, plus bikes and backpacking equipment.

About 8.5km northwest of Kelowna, **Bear Creek Provincial Park** (☎ 250-494-6500) offers windsurfing, fishing, swimming, hiking and wilderness camping.

Kelowna Land & Orchard Co (☎ 250-763-1091, 3002 Dunster Rd; $5.25/2 adult/child age 12-16, under 12 yrs free) is one of many local places with orchard tours. It also has fruit products and baked goods available. Admission includes a wagon tour.

Organized Tours

Okanagan Wine Country Tours (☎ 250-868-9463, 866-689-9463, W *www.okwinetours .com*) offers half-day or longer wine-tasting tours starting at $35.

Monashee Adventure Tours (☎ 250-762-9253, 888-762-9253, W *www.monashee adventuretours.com, 1591 Highland Dr N*) leads hiking and bicycling tours of the Kettle Valley Railway route and other local trails.

Places to Stay

As in the rest of the Okanagan Valley, accommodations here can be difficult to find in summer; it's best to book ahead or arrive early in the day.

Camping Camping is the cheapest way to stay in the area, though you'll be outside town.

Bear Creek Provincial Park (☎ 250-494-6500 information, ☎ 800-689-9025 reservations, Westside Rd; open Apr-Oct) Sites $18.50. Bear Creek, 9km west of Kelowna off Hwy 97S, on the lake's west side, offers 122 sites close to the beach. Sites fill up fast.

Willow Creek Family Campground (☎ 250-762-6302, 3316 Lakeshore Rd) Sites $18-22. Close to shops and restaurants, Willow Creek boasts a beach, fire pit and free hot showers. It's about 3km south of downtown.

Numerous other private campgrounds ($18-28) are in Westbank and south along Lakeshore Rd.

Hostels *Kelowna International Hostel* (☎ 250-763-6024, fax 250-763-6068, W *www .kelowna-hostel.bc.ca, 2343 Pandosy St*) Dorm beds $16-18, private doubles $37-40. A short walk from the beach and 12 blocks from the downtown core, this hostel in an old, spiffed-up house feels relaxed and neighborly. Amenities include laundry, Internet access, a clean kitchen and a large outside deck.

SameSun International Hostel (☎ 250-763-9814, 877-562-2783, fax 250-763-9815, W www.samesun.com, 245 Harvey Ave) Dorm beds $20, private singles/doubles $49/59. SameSun caters to the young backpacker/skier crowd with lots of organized activities, including pub crawls and cruises on SameSun's private houseboat, *Jaws*. This gorgeous, modern 120-bed hostel looks nicer than almost all motels in town. Perks include volleyball courts, pool tables, Internet access, a barbecue area and bike rentals. SameSun also provides a ski shuttle ($8) to Big White Ski Resort, where it also runs a hostel (see Big White Ski Resort, earlier).

B&Bs Kelowna has more than 60 B&Bs, which range from luxurious lakeside retreats to farmhouses in the middle of vineyards. The Visitor Info Centre keeps a substantial list.

Motels & Hotels Many motels lie along Hwy 97 north of the downtown area.

Western Budget Motel (☎ 250-763-2484, 2679 Hwy 97 N) Singles/doubles $43/46 & up. Cheapest of the cheap, the Western Budget is also farthest from the lake (about six or seven kilometers).

Traveller's Choice Motor Inn (☎ 250-762-3221, 800-665-2610, fax 250-762-7261, W www.travellerschoice.kelowna.com, 1780 Gordon Dr) Rooms $99 & up. If you choose this one, you'll get a decent room, morning coffee and pastries, and use of a pool and Jacuzzi. Bike rentals available.

Accent Inn (☎ 250-862-8888, 800-663-0298, fax 250-862-8884, W www.accentinns.com, 1140 Harvey Ave) Singles/doubles start at $119/129. This modest, well-run place has comfortable rooms, a seasonal outdoor pool, an indoor hot tub, sauna and exercise room. Guests get a discount at the adjacent restaurant.

Travelodge Abbott Villa (☎ 250-763-7771, 800-663-2000, 800-578-7878, W www.travelodge.com, 1627 Abbott St) Rooms start at $109. This Travelodge is especially nice for the chain and a great deal. Right across Abbott St from the lake, it's in about

the same charmed location as the Prestige Inn, but here you'll pay a lot less.

Prestige Inn (☎ 250-860-7900, 877-737-8443, fax 250-860-7997, W www.prestigeinn.com, 1675 Abbott St) Singles/doubles $150/160. This upscale place has a restaurant, pool, hot tub and fitness center, and it's right across the street from City Park and the lake.

The Grand Okanagan (☎ 250-763-4500, 800-465-4651, fax 250-763-4565, W www.grandokanagan.com, 1310 Water St). Rooms start at $259. If you can afford it, this luxurious lakeside hotel is a good choice. It takes up a couple of city blocks and contains everything from shops to a gym, spa, pools, restaurants and a casino.

Places to Eat

The Bean Scene (☎ 250-763-1814, 274 Bernard Ave) Start your morning off with a coffee and muffin at the Bean Scene, just a block from City Park. It's a scene all right. You'll find great coffee and a crowd of hip and happenin' locals hanging around.

Lena's Pancake & Omelet House (☎ 250-861-5531, 533 Bernard Ave) Breakfast $5-8. Lena's makes a mean eggs Benedict in several variations, along with all types of pancakes and omelets.

Impeccable Pig Eatery (☎ 250-762-0442, cnr Burtch & Harvey) Breakfast $7-9. This other locally famous breakfast nook is tucked away in a strip mall behind Blockbuster.

Lunch Box (☎ 250-862-8621, 509 Bernard Ave) Sandwiches $5-8. Sit inside or out here and enjoy excellent breakfasts, salads and sandwiches, including the house-specialty Montréal smoked-meat sandwich. More substantial entrées are also available.

Urban Oasis (☎ 250-762-2124, 1567 Pandosy St) Most items $4-6. An excellent choice for health-conscious travelers, Urban Oasis has a hip, friendly staff who will hook you up with fresh juices, power shakes, delicious veggie wraps and other yummables.

Hector's Casa (☎ 250-860-3868, 2911 Pandosy St) Entrées $10-16. Canada can be a pretty depressing place for Mexican-food fans. But you won't need Prozac at Hector's, where even the most discerning enchiladeros will find reason to celebrate. This is the real thing, amigo – so superb and authentic, you'll weep tears of joy. Or is that the jalapeños?

de Montreuil (☎ 250-860-5508, 368 Bernard Ave) Prix-fixe dinners $30-41. This excellent restaurant has dedicated itself to buying whatever it can from local growers. The menu offers steak, seafood, lamb, chicken and a token veggie item or two. It's open for lunch weekdays and for dinner nightly.

Fresco (☎ 250-868-8805, 1560 Water St) Mains $19-32. New kid on the fine-dining scene, Fresco benefits from the culinary passion of owner-chef Rod Butters, who uses the best regional ingredients and seasonally fresh produce in his recipes. Try the four-course chef's special dinner ($42). The atmosphere, in a historic exposed-brick building, is warm and comfortable. Open for dinner Tuesday to Saturday; reservations recommended.

Entertainment
Rose's Waterfront Pub (☎ 250-860-1141, 1352 Water St) This popular beer-swilling spot has lively atmosphere, a great lakeside patio and standard pub fare.

Kelly O'Bryan's (☎ 250-861-1338, 262 Bernard Ave) Kelly's features a popular upstairs 'paddy-o' and good Guinness on tap.

Flashbacks Nite Club (☎ 250-861-3039, 1268 Ellis St) In a former cigar factory, Flashbacks brings back '80s-style live music.

Splashes (☎ 250-762-2956) and *Gotcha* (☎ 250-860-0800), across the street from each other in the 200 block of Leon Ave, are two dance clubs that draw crowds.

The Sunshine Theatre Company (☎ 250-763-4025) stages a range of productions at the *Kelowna Community Theatre*, on the corner of Water St and Doyle Ave.

The 'Parks Alive!' *free concerts*, featuring everything from rock to classical music, take place several times a week in summer at downtown's Kerry Park, Waterfront Park and City Park. For the line-up, call ☎ 250-868-3307.

Skyreach Place (☎ 250-979-0888, W www.skyreachplace.com, 1223 Water St) is a new 6000-seat coliseum that hosts big events.

Getting There & Around
Air Kelowna International Airport (YLW) is about 20km north of town on Hwy 97. Air Canada (☎ 888-247-2262) has daily flights to Vancouver, Calgary and Edmonton. Discount carrier WestJet (☎ 250-491-5600, 888-

937-8538) serves those same cities plus Victoria. Horizon Airlines (☎ 800-547-9308) flies nonstop to Seattle.

The Kelowna Airport Shuttle bus (☎ 250-765-0182) runs between town and the airport; fare is $12.

Bus Greyhound (☎ 250-860-3835, 800-661-8747, 2366 Leckie Rd) is north of downtown, off Hwy 97. Buses run up and down the Okanagan Valley daily, as well as to Kamloops (three hours, $26), Prince George (11½ hours, $93), Calgary (10 hours, $83) and Vancouver (six hours, $57).

For information about city buses call Kelowna Regional Transit System (☎ 250-860-8121, W www.kelownatransit.com) or pick up a copy of the *Kelowna Regional Rider's Guide* from the Visitor Info Centre. Basic fare is $1.50-1.75. A day pass costs $4.25. Bus services are centered downtown on Queensway St between Pandosy and Ellis Sts.

VERNON
Vernon, the most northerly of the Okanagan's 'Big Three,' lies in a scenic valley encircled by three lakes. Unlike Kelowna and Penticton, it's a blue-collar town with few attractions, but some excellent parks and recreation opportunities lie not far outside town.

The town has two Visitor Info Centres. The main one (☎ 250-542-1415, 800-665-0795, W www.vernontourism.com) is at 701 Hwy 97S, just outside downtown to the south. It's open daily year-round. The other (☎ 250-545-2959, fax 250-542-3623) is about 5km north of town at 6326 Hwy 97 N, near the southeastern shore of Swan Lake, and open daily May to October.

The downtown library (☎ 250-542-7610, 3001 32nd Ave) is open Monday to Saturday and has limited Internet access. Polson Park, off 25th Ave and next to 32nd St, is a pleasant and shady flower-filled park with a small creek running through it. If it's hot this is a good rest spot.

The Greyhound bus depot (☎ 250-545-0527) is at 3102 30th St.

O'Keefe Historic Ranch
North of Vernon 12km, this old 8000-hectare cattle ranch (☎ 250-542-7868, W www.okeeferanch.bc.ca, 9380 Hwy 97; adult/child $6.50/4.50; open 9am-5pm May-Oct) was

home to the O'Keefe family from 1867 to 1977. Among other things you'll see the original log cabin, a general store and St Ann's, the oldest Roman Catholic church in the province. It's a good introduction to life in the valley before it was taken over by fruit.

Provincial Parks

Several provincial parks are in the area. For more information on any of them contact the BC Parks Okanagan District office (☎ 250-494-6500, fax 250-494-9737), 11km north of Summerland on Hwy 97.

The 8.9-sq-km **Kalamalka Lake Provincial Park**, south of town on Kalamalka Lake's east side, offers swimming, fishing, hiking and picnicking. **Ellison Provincial Park**, 25km southwest of Vernon on Okanagan Lake, is western Canada's only freshwater marine park; scuba diving is popular. **Silver Star Provincial Park** is 22km northeast of Vernon; take 48th Ave off Hwy 97. The park offers good hiking in summer, with views possible all the way west to the Coast Mountains.

Silver Star Mountain Resort

Ten lifts, including two high-speed quads, serve over 1000 hectares of skiable terrain at Silver Star Mountain (☎ 250-542-0224, 800-663-4431, snow report ☎ 250-542-1745, W www.skisilverstar.com, Silver Star Rd; full-day adult ticket $49; season Nov-Apr), 22km northeast of Vernon via 48th Ave and Silver Star Rd. Shuttle service is available. The resort also offers 105km(!) of cross-country skiing, as well as night skiing, tubing and halfpipes and a terrain park for boarders. In summer, the resort opens for hiking and mountain biking. Accommodations are available on the mountain, including:

SameSun Ski-in Lodge (☎ 250-545-8933, 877-562-2783, W www.samesun.com, Pinnacles Rd) Dorm bed $20, private singles/doubles $49/59. SameSun has pulled out all the stops once again at this custom-designed ski-in, ski-out hostel. The huge 140-bed place has pool tables, Internet access, huge kitchen and dining areas, a comfortable lounge and outdoor hot tubs. It even offers a free pancake breakfast.

Places to Stay & Eat

Accommodations are available in all price ranges. The Info Centres have information on local B&Bs.

Ellison Provincial Park (☎ 250-494-6500, fax 250-494-9737; open Apr-Oct) Sites $15. This is by far the best campground. It has 71 sites and is often full, so call ahead. To get there, take 25th Ave west from downtown Vernon 16km.

HI-Vernon – Lodged Inn (☎ 250-549-3742, 888-737-4927, fax 250-549-3748, W www.hihostels.bc.ca, 3201 Pleasant Valley Rd) Dorm beds $15/19 members/nonmembers, private rooms available. This 30-bed hostel is close to downtown in an 1894 Queen Anne. It has Internet access, bike and ski storage, laundry and kitchen facilities, a ride board and a library and lounge with TV/VCR.

Travelodge (☎ 250-545-2161, 800-578-7878, fax 250-545-5536, W www.travelodge.com, 3000 28th Ave) Singles/doubles $59/69. The reliable, downtown Travelodge has standard rooms and is fairly priced.

Best Western Vernon Lodge (☎ 250-545-3385, 800-663-4422, fax 250-545-7156, W www.rpbhotels.com, 3914 32nd St) Singles/doubles start at $99/109. Farther north from the Travelodge is Vernon Lodge, on the corner of 39th Ave. The hotel has an indoor pool and tropical garden, a restaurant and a pub.

For a small town, Vernon has lots of eateries – particularly little coffee shops and sandwich places.

Bean Scene (☎ 250-558-1817, 2923 30th Ave) The hub of what's happening in town, this café offers good coffees and teas served by a friendly staff.

Johnny Appleseed (☎ 250-542-7712, 3018 30th Ave) Breakfast $3-5, lunch $5-6. This popular downtown place serves good soups, sandwiches, juices, smoothies and wraps.

Eclectic Med (☎ 250-558-4646, 3117 32nd St) Most entrées $13-20. A favorite with locals, Eclectic Med lives up to its name with foods from around the world – everything from Thai chicken salad to Moroccan lamb.

NORTH OF VERNON

At Sicamous, Hwy 97A meets the Trans Canada Hwy (Hwy 1). From there the Trans Canada heads west past Shuswap Lake to Salmon Arm and Kamloops; east, the highway goes to Revelstoke then past Mt Revelstoke, Glacier and Yoho National Parks to Lake Louise in Alberta.

Shuswap Region

The district around **Shuswap and Mara Lakes** is picturesque, with green, wooded hills and farms. The grazing cattle and lush, cultivated land make a pleasant change of scenery no matter which direction you're coming from. Of the region's many provincial parks, four – Shuswap Lake, Herald Park, Silver Beach and Yard Creek – have vehicle campsites.

At the Okanagan Valley's north end, on the tip of one of Shuswap Lake's 'arms,' **Salmon Arm** is mainly a resort town, although timber and fruit-growing are also important. If you're here in October head 46km northwest to **Roderick Haig-Brown Provincial Park** (☎ 250-851-3000; open year-round), where you'll see between 25,000 and 2.5 million sockeye salmon migrating up the Adams River to spawn. Haig-Brown (1908–76) was a Canadian naturalist and angler who wrote many books that remain in print. The park access road turns north off Hwy 1 at Squilax.

One way to explore the Shuswap and Mara Lakes is by houseboat, which can be rented in the town of **Sicamous**, the self-styled 'houseboat capital of Canada.' You can also rent them in Salmon Arm. The Sicamous Chamber of Commerce (☎ 250-836-3313, fax 250-836-4368, **W** www .sicamouschamber.bc.ca, 110 Finlayson St) has area information.

HI-Shuswap Lake – Squilax General Store and Hostel (☎/fax 250-675-2977, **W** www.hihostels.bc.ca, Hwy 1) Dorm beds $15/19 members/nonmembers, private rooms available. About 10km east of Chase on the northwest tip of Shuswap Lake, this hostel makes a rural hub for area explorations. Accommodation is in old cabooses.

Southeastern British Columbia

Southeastern BC is dominated by the Rocky, Selkirk, Purcell, Monashee, and Columbia Mountains. National and provincial parks throughout the area preserve and make accessible much of the varied terrain. Wedged between the parallel mountain chains is an incredibly scenic series of lakes, rivers and thinly populated valleys.

The Purcell Mountain region below Golden, west from the Rockies and including Kimberley, is known as the East Kootenays. The West Kootenays run in and around the Selkirk Mountains west of Creston to Grand Forks and include Nelson, Nakusp and the Kootenay, Slocan and Arrow Lakes. This is a gorgeous area of mountains and valleys generally overlooked by visitors and definitely worth considering for a few days of exploration, especially along Hwys 3A and 6. It's an outstanding region for outdoor activities: camping, hiking and climbing in summer, and some of North America's best skiing in winter.

Several ferries across lakes and rivers connect highways throughout the region. They generally run from about 6am to midnight and are mostly free. The southeastern corner of BC is on Mountain Standard Time, while most of the rest of the province is on Pacific Standard Time, a difference of an hour.

REVELSTOKE & AROUND
pop 8500

This small town, on the Trans Canada Hwy (Hwy 1) 70km east of Sicamous, is a mountaineer's dream come true. Its quiet streets are lined with neat wooden houses and tidy gardens, and snowcapped peaks pierce the sky in every direction. Mt Revelstoke National Park is just outside town, and Glacier National Park is just a short drive down the highway. Revelstoke is also a busy railway center.

The Visitor Info Centre (☎ 250-837-5345, 800-487-1493, fax 250-837-4223, **W** www .revelstokecc.bc.ca, 204 Campbell Ave) is open daily in summer, weekdays only the rest of the year. A second well-marked location (☎ 250-837-3522) lies on the Trans Canada Hwy at the junction of Hwy 23N. It's open daily May to September.

Parks Canada (☎ 250-837-7500, 301 W 3rd St) has information about Mt Revelstoke and Glacier National Parks. It's open 7:30am to noon and 1pm to 4:30pm weekdays. In the same building, the Friends of Mt Revelstoke & Glacier (☎ 250-837-2010) has books and maps of the parks. The post office (☎ 250-837-3228) is next door.

The public library (☎ 250-837-5095, 605 Campbell Ave) has good free Internet access. For outdoor equipment (or a good

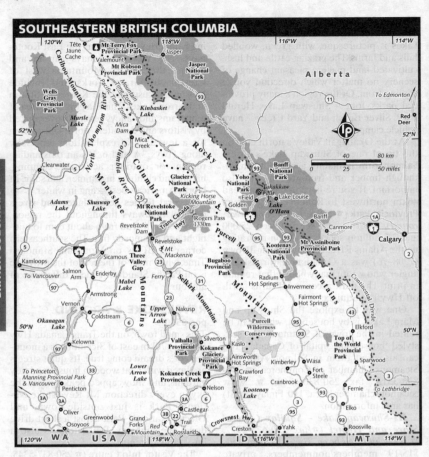

SOUTHEASTERN BRITISH COLUMBIA

cuppa joe) check out Bertz Outdoor Equipment & Café (☎ 250-837-6575, 217 Mackenzie Ave).

The Greyhound bus depot (☎ 250-837-5874, 1899 Fraser Dr) is west of town, just off the Trans Canada Hwy.

Railway Museum

The railway museum (☎ *250-837-6060*, W *www.railwaymuseum.com, 719 Track St W; adult/senior/youth age 7-16 $6/5/3; open 9am-8pm daily July-Aug; reduced hours rest of year*), in a beautiful building downtown right off Victoria Rd, has a 1948 steam locomotive and other rail cars, as well as good displays on the CPR (Canadian Pacific Railway; see the 'The Iron Link – an Engineering Marvel' boxed text).

Revelstoke Firefighters Museum

Take the kids to this museum (☎ *250-837-2884, 227 W 4th St; admission free; open 8am-5pm daily*) full of shiny old fire trucks and firefighting paraphernalia and big strong handsome firemen. (Guys, better leave your wife at the motel.)

Mt Revelstoke National Park

This relatively small national park, just northeast of Revelstoke in the Selkirk Mountains, is known for jagged, rugged peaks and steep valleys. The view of these from Mt Revelstoke is excellent. Access to the mountain is along the 26km Meadows in the Sky Parkway (1.5km east of Revelstoke, off the Trans Canada Hwy), which leads through cedars, alpine meadows and near-

A moss-covered pingo, a huge mound of ice formed by weather, Tuktoyaktuk, Northwest Territories

Lac la Martre, a large lake 150km west of Yellowknife, Northwest Territories

Ice floes between Greenland and Canada near the Northwest Territories

Kapitan Khlebnikov breaking ice, Ellesmere Island, Nunavut

Iceberg floating in Resolute Bay, Nunavut

Ivory gull, Nunavut

Aerial view of an iceberg, Nunavut

The Iron Link: An Engineering Marvel

British Columbia had an almost separate existence from the rest of Canada until 1885, when the Canadian Pacific Railway across the Rockies was completed. These rails for the first time linked the disparate territories of the west and east and were instrumental in cementing the unity of the nation.

Running the rails through the Rockies was an enormous challenge that was accomplished by the labor of thousands of immigrant workers, who endured harsh conditions to complete the dangerous work. Hundreds were killed by disease and accident, including the horrific avalanches of Rogers Pass, which swept away men and trains like toys. Eventually huge tunnels and snow sheds were laboriously constructed to protect the trains.

East of Field, the gradients were so steep that any braking problem caused trains to run away down the hill, where they would eventually fly off the tracks with terrible loss of life. To solve this problem, two huge spiraling tunnels were built inside the granite mountains, reducing the grade to a much more manageable 2.2%. These remain in use and are an internationally recognized engineering marvel.

Along with the trains, Canadian Pacific built grand hotels in Calgary, Banff, Lake Louise, Vancouver and elsewhere to encourage tourists and business travelers to ride the line and explore the region. The line was completed on November 7, 1885 and carried passengers for over 100 years. Today it is still traversed by Canadian Pacific Railway freight trains and the occasional Rocky Mountaineer Railtours cruise train. West from Calgary, much of the route is paralleled by the Trans Canada Hwy (Hwy 1).

There are three excellent places to learn about the history of this rail line in BC.

A lookout from the Trans Canada Hwy 8km east of Field gives a good vantage of the lower of the two spiral tunnels. It has interesting explanatory displays.

A museum area inside the Rogers Pass Visitor's Centre in Glacier National Park shows the hazards of avalanches. The free publication *Snow War* details the railway's efforts to beat the winter. See Glacier National Park in this chapter for details.

The railway museum in Revelstoke documents the history of the entire Canadian Pacific Railway line through the mountains. See Revelstoke in this chapter for details.

BRITISH COLUMBIA

tundra to Balsam Lake, within 1.5km of the 1920m summit. A trail continues to the top. (You can also hike to the top from the base of Meadows in the Sky Parkway; it's 10km [four to five hours] one-way.)

Several good hiking trails lead from the summit, with backcountry camping permitted. No other camping is allowed. You are required to have a backcountry camping permit ($6 per person per night, in addition to the park pass), available from Parks Canada in Revelstoke (☎ 250-837-7500, w www.parkscanada.gc.ca/revelstoke, 301 W 3rd St) or from the Rogers Pass Centre (☎ 250-814-5232) in Glacier National Park. There's good skiing in the long winters. Much of the summer is rainy so check that tent for leaks.

Admission to Mt Revelstoke and Glacier National Parks (the two are administered jointly) is $4/3/2 adult/senior/child age 6-16 per day. This pass is good until 4pm the next day and will get you into all the mountain national parks, so if you want to make a whirlwind tour up to Banff and Jasper, go for it (information on Banff and Jasper is in the Alberta chapter).

Parks Canada provides two useful publications about the park. The free *Selkirk Summit* provides general information on Glacier and Mt Revelstoke National Parks, while *Footloose in the Columbias* ($1.50) provides detailed information on hiking in the two parks.

Canyon Hot Springs

These springs (☎ 250-837-2420, w www.canyonhotsprings.com, Hwy 1; adult/child age 4-14 $6.50/5.50, day pass $8.50/7; open 9am-9pm daily May-Sept, until 10pm July-Aug), 35km east along the Trans Canada Hwy between Revelstoke and Glacier National Parks, consist of a hot pool (40°C) and a larger, cooler swimming pool. Admission includes a locker and shower. You can rent a bathing suit and towel. Camping and cabins are available (see Places to Stay).

Skiing

Five kilometers southeast of Revelstoke, **Ski Powder Springs** (☎ *250-837-5151, 800-991-4455,* W *www.catpowder.com, Camozzi Rd; adult full-day ticket $28/32 weekday/weekend; season Dec-Mar*) is a downhill and cross-country ski resort on Mt Mackenzie. It's run by the Cat Powder folks, so naturally offers cat skiing (packages from $1000), as well as a double chairlift and a handle tow. The base lodge has rentals, a lounge and dining room.

Revelstoke serves as a winter base for helicopter-skiing. Try **CMH Heli-Skiing** (☎ *800-661-0252,* W *www.cmhski.com*) or **Selkirk Tangiers Heli Skiing** (☎ *800-663-7080,* W *www.selkirk-tangiers.com*).

For cross-country skiing, head 7km south of Revelstoke on Hwy 23 to Mt MacPherson ski area, where a 22km trail system is set by the local Nordic club. Other good areas include the Revelstoke Golf Course, the Meadows in the Sky Parkway in Mt Revelstoke National Park and the Columbia River Flats. For more information call ☎ 250-837-7041/6168.

Places to Stay

Blanket Creek Provincial Park (☎ *250-422-4200, fax 250-422-3326, open May-Oct*) Sites $12. This park, 25km south of Revelstoke on Hwy 23, has running water but no showers. Reservations are accepted (☎ *800-689-9025*). **Martha Creek Provincial Park** (*same contact information; open May-Sept*), 20km north of Revelstoke on Hwy 23, has similar facilities.

Canyon Hot Springs (☎ *250-837-2420, fax 250-837-3171, Hwy 1; open May-Sept*) Sites $20-27, cabins $95 & up. This full-facility campground, 35km east of Revelstoke (see Canyon Hot Springs, earlier) has showers, toilets and a grocery store. Camping rates do not include admission to the hot pools.

HI-Revelstoke – Traveller's Hostel & Guest House (☎ *250-837-4050, 877-562-2783, fax 250-837-6410,* W *www.canadianskihostels.com, 400 2nd St W*) Dorm beds $20, private singles/doubles available (call for rates). This immaculate hostel has free

Internet access, bicycle rentals, several kitchens and much more. It has a ski package in winter for only $29.

Monashee Lodge (☎ *250-837-6778, 800-668-3139, fax 250-837-5111,* W *www.catpowder.com, 1601 3rd St W*) Singles/doubles $48/53 & up. The Monashee can arrange snow-cat skiing and offers ski, fishing and golf packages.

Regent Inn (☎ *250-837-2107, 888-245-5523, fax 250-837-9669,* W *www.regentinn.com, 112 E 1st St*) Singles/doubles start at $99/109, including continental breakfast. Right in the heart of downtown, the Regent is a stylish restored heritage place with a great restaurant and pub.

Coast Hillcrest Resort Hotel (☎ *250-837-3322, fax 250-837-3340,* W *www.hillcresthotel.com, 2100 Oak Dr*) Rooms start at $120. The fanciest place in town is the new Hillcrest, 3km east of downtown off the Trans Canada (turn at the KOA). The big lodge building has an appropriate mountain atmosphere with lots of exposed timbers and great views. The rooms (all nonsmoking) are large and amenity-laden. Other perks include a restaurant, lounge, hot tub, sauna and fitness center.

Durrand Glacier Chalet (☎ *250-837-2381, fax 250-837-4685,* W *www.selkirkexperience.com*) Weeklong summer hiking packages $1300. The ultimate Alpine accommodations are offered by Revelstoke's Selkirk Mountain Experience. The folks at this company will fly you in a helicopter up to a Swiss-style mountain chalet perched in nosebleed territory at 1900m, 40km northeast of Revelstoke. Summer hiking and winter ski-mountaineering packages are offered. All include gourmet meals, the helicopter ride and guides for your hikes.

Places to Eat

Woolsey Creek Café (☎ *250-837-5500, 212 Mackenzie Ave*) Dinner entrées $8.50-11. This hip cafe has a casual artsy atmosphere and World Beat food like curries and Thai wraps. It's open for breakfast and lunch on Monday and all three meals the rest of the week.

Manning's Restaurant (☎ *250-837-3200, 302 Mackenzie Ave*) Most entrées $7-9. Manning's is a popular Chinese place that also has some Western items on the menu.

Tony's Roma (☎ *250-837-4106, 306 Mackenzie Ave*) Pastas $9-12. Come to

Tony's for all your -ettis, -ines and -onis. The pizzas are good too.

River City Pub (☎ *250-837-2107, 112 E 1st St*) Sandwiches $6-8. The pub at the Regent Inn has a good selection of beers, above-average pub grub and a nice patio. If you're feeling more formal, try the Inn's ***112 Restaurant*** for steak, seafood and more.

GLACIER NATIONAL PARK

In the Columbia Mountains, about halfway between Revelstoke and Golden, lies this 1350-sq-km park (☎ *250-837-7500, day pass $4/2 adult/child age 6-16; open year-round*) containing more than 430 glaciers. If you think the other mountain parks have been wet then you'll like this place. It only rains here twice a week – once for three days and then again for four. It's the same in winter; it snows nearly every day. The annual snowfall can be as much as 23m. Because of the sheer mountain slopes, this is one of the world's most active avalanche areas. For this reason skiing, caving and mountaineering are closely regulated; you must register with the park warden. Around Rogers Pass you'll notice the many snowsheds protecting the highway. With the narrow road twisting up to 1330m, this is a dangerous area, sometimes called Death Strip – an unexpected avalanche can wipe a car right off the road. Still, the area is carefully controlled, and sometimes snows are brought tumbling down with artillery before they fall by themselves.

At the park's east side is the dividing line between Pacific Standard and Mountain Standard time zones.

The Rogers Pass Centre, Parks Canada's interpretive center (☎ *250-814-5232*), is open daily from 8am to 7pm in summer; reduced hours rest of year. It has films on the park and in summer organizes guided walks. Displays document the railway's efforts to conquer the pass and vice-versa. A cafeteria and service station are next door.

Not far from here are the park's only two campgrounds: ***Illecillewaet River*** and ***Loop Brook***. Both have running water and flush toilets and charge $13 a night per site, in addition to the park pass. They're open June to September.

Parks Canada provides two useful free publications about the park. *Selkirk Summit* (free) provides general information on Glacier and Mt Revelstoke National Parks, while *Footloose in the Columbias* ($1.50) provides detailed information on hiking in the two parks.

GOLDEN
pop 8000

As you travel along the Trans Canada Hwy from Alberta, this town is the first of any size in BC. It's also at the junction with Hwy 95, which connects the town with Radium Hot Springs and Invermere to the south.

If you don't get off the highway here, Golden looks like nothing more than a commercial strip of motels, fast food restaurants and service stations. But down in the heart of town, 2km south of the highway, Golden has some charm.

One attraction the town is proud of is a new **Kicking Horse Pedestrian Bridge**, a covered timber-frame bridge over the Kicking Horse River. The beautiful work of art, a major community effort, crosses the river at 8th Ave.

The Visitor Info Centre (☎ 250-344-7125, 800-622-4653, fax 250-344-6688, 500 10th Ave N) is open daily in July and August, weekdays the rest of the year.

Rafting

Golden is the center for whitewater rafting trips on the turbulent Kicking Horse River. These trips are bumpy, with lots of Class-III and -IV rapids.

Wet 'n' Wild Adventures (☎ 250-344-6546, 800-668-9119, **w** www.wetnwild.bc.ca) has exciting trips ($55/83 half/full day) and quality guides.

Wildlife-observing float tours of the major Columbia Valley wetlands are offered by **Kinbasket Adventures** (☎ 250-344-6012, **w** www.rockies.net/~kbasket, adult/child $40/20).

Skiing

Golden's local ski area, **Kicking Horse Mountain Resort** (☎ 250-439-5400, 866-754-5425, **w** www.kickinghorseresort.com, 5400 Kicking Horse Trail; full-day adult ticket $48.75) is still in its infancy since the big money showed up with grand plans. The resort offers 64 runs and a hellacious vertical drop (1240m). So far it has just three lifts, but one is a super-duper high-speed gondola that ascends to a fancy restaurant and minilodge at an elevation of 2450m.

Heli-Skiing & Hiking

South of Golden, in the Purcell Mountains, is the world's center for helicopter skiing – in districts such as the Gothics, Caribous and, perhaps best known, the Bugaboos. The last named is a region of 1500 sq km of rugged, remote mountains accessible only by helicopter during the winter months. This dangerous, thrilling sport attracts rich visitors from around the world each winter and spring.

The skiing is superb but a portion of the appeal is the danger. Avalanches are not uncommon, tumbling snows claim lives on a regular, though not frequent, basis – just often enough to give the run down that extra kick. A one-week package costs around $4500 and up. Companies include Golden's own **Purcell Helicopter Skiing** (☎ 250-344-5410, 877-435-4754, **W** www.purcellhelicopterskiing.com) and Banff's **Canadian Mountain Holidays** (CMH; ☎ 403-762-7100, 800-661-0252, **W** www.cmhski.com, 217 Bear St).

During summer months you can visit some of the area lodges and enjoy hiking. Mountaineers, too, come from around the world to test their skills on the sheer rock faces and granite pinnacles in **Bugaboo Provincial Park** (☎ 250-422-4200; road pass-

Thrill-seekers enjoy the Golden area's heli-skiing opportunities.

able late spring through fall), 45km west of Hwy 95 from Brisco, 62km south of Golden.

Places to Stay

Golden Municipal Campground (☎/fax 250-344-5412, 1407 S 9th St; open mid-May–mid-Oct) Sites $13-15. This wonderful low-key campground lies right beside the river. It's basic but quiet (when trains aren't passing). Amenities include coin-op hot showers (but no laundry), nearby pool and recreation facilities and a riverbank trail. The Kicking Horse Grill & Mad Trapper Pub are within walking distance. If you don't need hookups, go for the highest-numbered site available, way upriver away from 'civilization.'

Kicking Horse Hostel (☎ 250-344-5071, **W** www.kickinghorsehostel.com, 518 Station Ave) Dorm beds $20. This casual place has a nice backyard, but the *front* yard is so close to the railroad tracks that sleepwalkers had better tie themselves into bed at night.

Mary's Motel (☎ 250-344-7111, fax 250-344-7321, 603 8th Ave N) Singles/doubles $74/84. Down in town, a short walk from the pedestrian bridge, Mary's has pools, hot tubs, a sauna, and a riverside walking trail.

Golden Super 8 Motel (☎ 250-344-0888, fax 250-344-7288, 1047 Trans Canada Hwy) Singles/doubles $81/85.50. One of many motels up on the highway, this one serves a free continental breakfast and has nice rooms.

YOHO NATIONAL PARK

Yoho National Park in the BC Rockies, adjacent to the Alberta border and Banff National Park to the east and Kootenay National Park to the south, offers mountain peaks, river valleys, glacial lakes and beautiful meadows – a bit of everything. Yoho is not as busy as Banff and has campground vacancies when Banff is full. A possible drawback is the often wet or cloudy days. Still, Yoho is more accessible and the weather better (not saying much) than at Glacier. The name is a Cree word expressing astonishment or wonder. The rushing Kicking Horse River flows through the park.

Field

Very small Field, lying in the middle of the park, is the first town in BC as you head west along the Trans-Canada Hwy (which follows the Kicking Horse River). Many of its buildings date from the early days of the railways.

The park information center (☎ 250-343-6783, W www.parkscanada.gc.ca/yoho), next to the highway, is open daily 8am to 7pm in summer, 9am to 4pm or 5pm the rest of the year. BC Tourism and Alberta Tourism both have desks here in summer. The free *Backcountry Guide* is an excellent resource for park exploration.

Greyhound buses stop at Field.

Lake O'Hara

Nestled high in the mountains, this somewhat exclusive beauty spot more than lives up to its exalted reputation. It's definitely worth the sizable hassle to reach. Compact wooded hillsides, alpine meadows, snow-covered passes, mountain vistas and glaciers are all concentrated around the stunning lake, and a web of trails perfect for daylong and half-day hikes, most fairly rigorous, makes it all accessible. A simple day trip is well worthwhile, but overnighting makes hiking more trails possible. The fine Alpine circuit trail (12km) offers a bit of everything.

To reach the lake, you can either walk 13km from the parking area or take a bus ($12/5 adult/child age 6-16) that runs daily from mid-June to early October. The bus leaves from the Lake O'Hara parking lot, 15km east of Field on the Trans Canada Hwy. Places on the bus are limited, as are permits for the popular backcountry *camping* ($6 per person per night). You may reserve for both up to three months in advance of your visit by calling ☎ 250-343-6433 from 8am to noon and 1pm to 4pm weekdays mid-March to early October. The reservation fee is $10 and given the popularity of Lake O'Hara, reservations are basically mandatory. However, if you don't have advance reservations, six day-use places and three to five campsites are obtainable by showing up in person at the park information center in Field the day *before* you want to go. In high season there's often a line long before the doors open at 9am. The area around Lake O'Hara is usually snow-covered or muddy until mid-July. Also see Lake O'Hara Lodge under Places to Stay.

Activities

Near Field is the turn-off for **Takakkaw Falls** – at 254m, one of Canada's highest waterfalls. From here, **Iceline**, a 20km hiking loop, passes many glaciers.

The beautiful green **Emerald Lake**, 10km off the Trans Canada Hwy, has trails around it, and the water in the lake is just warm enough in late summer for a quick swim.

The **Burgess Shale World Heritage Site** protects the amazing Cambrian-age fossil beds on Mt Stephen and Mt Field. These 515 million-year-old fossils preserve the remains of marine creatures that are some of the earliest forms of life on earth. The Royal Tyrrell Museum in Drumheller, Alberta, has a major display on these finds. The only way to see this area is by guided hikes ($45). For information on these strenuous jaunts, call the Yoho–Burgess Shale Foundation (☎ 250-343-6006, 800-343-3006).

Also east of Field by the Trans Canada Hwy are the famous **spiral tunnels**, the feats of engineering that enable Canadian Pacific trains to navigate the challenging Kicking Horse Pass.

Places to Stay & Eat

Yoho has five campgrounds, open from May or June to September or October. Only the *Kicking Horse Campground* ($18) has showers, making it the most popular. *Chancellor Peak* ($13) has the river and good views. Other campgrounds are the wooded *Hoodoo Creek* ($13), quiet *Monarch* ($13) and *Takakkaw Falls* ($13). The last named, a five minute walk from parking, is especially beautiful and tents-only.

Field has several B&Bs; the Info Centre has details.

HI-Whiskey Jack Hostel (☎ 403-762-4122, fax 403-762-3441, W www.hihostels.bc.ca, Yoho Valley Rd) Dorm beds $13/17 members/nonmembers. Open June-Sept. Phone reservations are via the Banff International Hostel. This hostel is 15km off the Trans Canada Hwy on Yoho Valley Rd, just before the Takakkaw Falls campground. Don't tell anyone about this place – it's way too cool.

Kicking Horse Lodge (☎ 250-343-6303, 800-659-4944, fax 250-343-6355, W www.kickinghorselodge.net, 100 Centre St) Rooms $124 & up. This modern lodge up in town has nice rooms with some kitchenettes, as well as a guest laundry, licensed dining room and lounge.

BRITISH COLUMBIA

Cathedral Mountain Lodge & Chalets (☎/fax 250-343-6442, ⓦ *www.cathedral mountain.com, Yoho Valley Rd; open May-Oct)* Cabins $145 & up. Near Field 1km down Yoho Valley Rd, this pleasantly rustic lodge at the base of Cathedral Mountain offers magnificent views, a store, a great dining room and a friendly mountain experience.

Lake O'Hara Lodge (☎ 250-343-6418 summer/winter; ☎ 403-678-4110 Oct-Jan & mid-Apr–mid-June, ⓦ *www.lakeohara.com)* Rooms $395, cabins $525 & up, including all meals, afternoon tea and the bus ride up the hill. A superlative splurge, the historic, upscale-rustic Lake O'Hara Lodge probably shouldn't be here. But it is, so you might as well enjoy it. In winter, you can ski (or dogsled) up the road and stay here for $215 per person per night.

Across the tracks in town, the cool little ***Truffle Pigs Café*** (☎ 250-343-6462, 318 Stephen Ave) is a good place for a cup of coffee or a light bite, and the adjacent store sells supplies and booze.

KOOTENAY NATIONAL PARK

Kootenay National Park is solely in BC but is adjacent to Banff National Park and runs south from Yoho National Park. Hwy 93 (the Banff-Windermere Hwy) runs down the center and is the park's only major road. From the north entrance at Vermillion Pass to Radium Hot Springs at the park's south end there are campgrounds, points of interest, hiking trails and views of the valley along the Kootenay River.

Kootenay has a more moderate climate than the other Rocky Mountain parks and in the southern regions especially, summers can be hot and dry. It's the only national park in Canada to contain both glaciers and cacti.

The Kootenay Park Visitor Centre (☎ 250-347-9505, 7556 Main St E, ⓦ www .parkscanada.gc.ca/kootenay), in Radium Hot Springs, is the main Parks Canada facility. It's open daily 9:30am to 4:30pm in spring, 9am to 7pm in summer; closed the rest of the year. The Vermillion Crossing Visitor Centre (no phone), 8km south of the pass, is open from 10am to 7pm daily in summer, 11am to 6pm spring and fall; closed mid-October to mid-April.

Stop at **Marble Canyon** for the 30 minute walk – it is a real adrenaline rush. The trail follows the rushing Tokumm Creek, crisscrossing it frequently on small wooden bridges with longer and longer drops below as you head up to the waterfall.

MT ASSINIBOINE PROVINCIAL PARK

Between Kootenay and Banff National Parks is this lesser known, 39 sq km provincial park, part of the Rockies World Heritage designated area. The craggy summits of Mt Assiniboine (3561m), often referred to as Canada's Matterhorn, and its near neighbors are a magnet for climbers. The park also offers hiking and all the usual activities.

From Hwy 93, two hiking trails start from near the highway at Vermillion Crossing in Kootenay National Park. From Banff National Park in Alberta, a gravel road takes you close to the park through the ski resort of Sunshine Village. Another road leads from Spray Reservoir south of Canmore to the trailhead near Shark Mountain. The trails all meet at Lake Magog where there is the park headquarters (☎ 250-422-4200), a walk-in ***campground*** ($5 per person per night), some ***cabins*** and the commercially operated ***Mt Assiniboine Lodge*** (☎ 403-678-2883, fax 403-678-4877).

RADIUM HOT SPRINGS

At Kootenay National Park's south edge, where Hwy 93 joins Hwy 95, is the town of Radium Hot Springs. The Visitor Info Centre (☎ 250-347-9331, 800-347-9704, fax 250-347-9127, 7556 Main St E), is open April to October. The hot springs (☎ 250-347-9485; $6/5 adult/child), 3km north of the town, are always worth a visit, though they can be busy in summer, when they're open daily from 9am to 11pm.

If you're here in fall, look for the Headbanger's Ball – otherwise known as bighorn sheep rutting season. The rams have been known to practice their WWF head-butts right in town. And to think they do it just for ewe.

The park has four ***campgrounds*** ($13-22); call the park for information. Radium Hot Springs has lots of motels, many in alpine style.

Motel Tyrol (☎ 250-347-9402, 888-881-1188, fax 250-347-6363, ⓦ *www.moteltyrol .com, 5016 Hwy 93)* Rooms $69 & up. Typical of the many motels is this friendly and tidy place, which has a heated pool, hot tub and balconies.

INVERMERE TO CRANBROOK

South from Radium Hot Springs, Hwy 93/95 follows the Columbia River between the Purcell and Rocky Mountains.

Invermere to Wasa

On the west side of Windermere Lake, 14km south of Radium, **Invermere** is a small resort town with a beautiful setting. The town itself is just quaint enough, but not too much. The Visitor Info Centre (☎ 250-342-2844/6316, fax 250-342-3261, W www .columbiavalleychamber.com) is out on the highway, just south of the turnoff into town. It's open daily May to September, weekdays only the rest of the year.

Places to stay in Invermere include **Wandering Rogue Hostel** (☎ 250-342-3445, W www.wanderingrogue.com, 1010 12th St) Dorm beds $20, private rooms $35 per person, including a free pancake breakfast. It doesn't look like much from the outside, but inside this place is bright, well kept and friendly. Amenities include kitchen and laundry facilities, TV/VCR and a spacious backyard for hanging out in the sun. Ski packages are available.

Mt Panorama (☎ 250-342-6941, 800-663-2929, W www.panoramaresort.com; full-day adult ticket $49; season Nov-Apr), in the Purcell Mountains 18km southwest of Invermere, has BC's third-highest vertical rise (1220m), after Whistler/Blackcomb and Golden's Kicking Horse. On 1120 hectares of skiable terrain, 10 lifts serve 100-plus runs. You're not going to feel crowded here. The resort also offers Nordic trails and an expansive base village, including slopeside hot pools.

Fairmont Hot Springs is another resort town with the hot springs as its focus. The pool is part of the upscale **Fairmont Hot Springs Resort** (☎ 250-345-6311, 800-663-4979, fax 250-345-6616, W www.fairmont resort.com). A single swim costs $6.50/4.50 adult/child age 4-12. It gets crowded on weekends and public holidays and caters to families.

At Skookumchuk, shortly before Wasa, a gravel road provides access eastward to **Top of the World Provincial Park** (☎ 250-422-4200, open year-round), which has hiking

trails and wilderness camping. Heading south from Skookumchuk, the road forks. If you go left, you'll be heading southeast to Fort Steele. Bearing right will take you to Kimberley.

Kimberley

At 1113m, Kimberley is one of Canada's highest cities. In 1973, the small mountain mining town was revamped to look like a Bavarian alpine village. Most of the downtown section, the Platzl, has been transformed into a small pedestrian mall with lots of oompah music, a pterodactyl-size cuckoo clock, numerous schnitzelhausen and plenty of good German beer. It's hokey, but what the hell. The Visitor Info Centre (☎ 250-427-3666, fax 250-427-5378, 115 Gerry Sorenson Way) is open daily in summer, Monday to Saturday in fall, and weekdays the rest of the year.

The biggest attraction here is **Kimberley Alpine Ski Resort** (☎ 250-427-4881, 800-258-7669, fax 250-427-3927, W www.skikimberley .com; full-day adult ticket $49; season early Dec-mid-Apr). The resort has nine lifts accessing 67 runs on 720 hectares of skiable terrain, plus night skiing, Nordic skiing and summer hiking and mountain biking.

Kimberley SameSun International Hostel (☎ 250-427-7191, 888-562-2783, fax 250-427-7095, W www.samesun.com, 275 Spokane St) Dorm beds $20, private singles/doubles $49/59. SameSun's offering here is much the same as all its other ski-area hostels: the funnest place in town. You may not get a lot of sleep – especially with the rowdy Ozone Pub right downstairs. But you'll meet cool folk and have a blast. The hostel is right on the Platzl and offers a free pancake breakfast.

To the northwest, the provincial **Purcell Wilderness Conservancy** (☎ 250-422-4200) has hiking, fishing and wilderness camping; access is by gravel road off Hwy 95A.

Fort Steele

The heritage park of Fort Steele (☎ 250-426-7352, W www.fortsteele.bc.ca, 9851 Hwy 93/95; adult/youth age 13-18/child age 6-12 $8/4.75/3.25; open daily 9:30am-5:30pm early May-late June & early Sept-early Oct, 9:30am-8pm late June-early Sept), 20km southeast of Wasa on Hwy 93, is a recreation of an East Kootenay town in the late 1800s. Fort Steele was the first Northwest Mounted Police (later to become the RCMP) outpost in western Canada and arose as a commercial, social and administrative center when major silver and lead discoveries were made in 1892. Its fortunes turned when, in 1898, the BC Southern Railway bypassed it in favor of Cranbrook. Fort Steele has more than 60 restored and reconstructed homes and buildings.

Fernie

On its way to Alberta, Hwy 3 goes through Fernie, a ski town sitting between the high peaks of Mt Fernie and Sisters Mountain. Fernie had a devastating fire in 1908, and the town was rebuilt with brick and stone. These fine late 19th- and early 20th-century buildings give the town an appearance unique in the East Kootenays.

At **Fernie Alpine Resort** (☎ 250-423-4655, snow report ☎ 250-423-3555, **w** www.ski fernie.com, 5339 Fernie Ski Hill Rd; adult full-day ticket $56; season early Dec–mid-Apr), 10 lifts access more than 100 trails and more than 1000 hectares of skiable terrain, including five alpine bowls.

HI-Fernie – Raging Elk Hostel (☎ 250-423-6811, fax 250-423-6812, **w** www.raging elk.com, 892 6th Ave) Dorm beds $18/21 members/nonmembers, private rooms available. This HI hostel is central and has ski packages and a free pancake breakfast.

SameSun Hostel (☎ 250-423-4492, 877-562-2783, fax 250-423-6004, **w** www.samesun .com, cnr Hwy 3 & 9th St) Dorm beds $20, private singles/doubles $49/59 & up, larger suites available. This motel-style hostel makes a great base camp for your daytime and nighttime Fernie adventures. Amenities include a pool, hot tub and sauna, Internet access, ski storage, a free pancake breakfast and discount lift tickets.

Cranbrook & Creston

Sitting at the base of the Rocky Mountains, Cranbrook is about 30km southeast of Kimberley on the Crowsnest Hwy. The Visitor Info Centre (☎ 250-426-5914, 800-222-6174, fax 250-426-3873, **w** www.cranbrookchamber .com, 2279 Cranbrook St N) is open year-round. The town is a depressingly workaday place consisting of a main drag that's essentially one huge strip mall, plus an old downtown area with little charm (and some even

less charming lowlifes). Skip it and head on to either Kimberly or Creston.

Near the US border, Creston is the center of a green, fruit-growing district. Just off Canyon, the main street, at 11th Ave, take a look at the murals depicting the region's character. West of town along the highway, the wetlands of the Creston Valley Wildlife Centre are excellent for birding. Farther out is the Kootenay Pass Summit with a provincial park and campground. Grizzlies and caribou frequent the area.

NELSON & AROUND
pop 9600

Nelson, at the junction of Hwy 6 and Hwy 3A, is beautifully situated on the shore of Kootenay Lake surrounded by the Selkirk Mountains. The picturesque town nestled in the hillside has over 350 carefully preserved and restored late 19th- and early 20th-century buildings. Its friendly, laid-back character and location make it the perfect base for exploring the region. The large, active artists' colony adds a cultural and alternative flavor.

Baker and Vernon Sts are the two main downtown thoroughfares. Baker St has many shops and restaurants, while Vernon St has government buildings, including city hall, the courthouse and the post office. The Visitor Info Centre (☎ 250-352-3433, 877-663-5706, fax 250-352-6355, **w** www.discover nelson.com, 225 Hall St) is open daily May to October, weekdays only the rest of the year. The post office (☎ 250-352-3538) is at 514 Vernon St. The municipal library (☎ 250-352-6333, 602 Stanley St) has Internet access for a token fee. The Greyhound bus depot (☎ 250-352-3939, 1112 Lakeside Dr) is in the Chacko Mika Mall.

In town there's a walking trail through **Lakeside Park**, or, using the *Heritage Walking Tour* leaflet from the Visitor Info Centre, you can take a look around the town's historical buildings. From the top of **Gyro Park** there are good views. **Streetcar No 23**, one of the town's originals, has been restored and now follows a track beside the lake from the bridge near Lakeside Park to the wharf at the bottom of Hall St.

Excellent outdoor possibilities abound. Practically in town is the climb to **Pulpit Rock**, affording fine views. **Whitewater Ski & Winter Resort** (☎ 250-354-4944, 800-666-

9420, snow report ☎ 250-352-7669, **W** www
.skiwhitewater.com, Hwy 6; full-day adult
ticket $37; season Dec-Apr), 12km south off
Hwy 6, offers both downhill and cross-
country skiing.

Places to Stay

For B&Bs ask at the Visitor Info Centre.

City Tourist Park (☎/fax 250-352-6075,
High St) Sites $15-20. In Nelson, convenient
camping is available at this basic but well
located park with a great view. Take Vernon
St east from downtown and follow it around
the hill. The park has showers and hookups.

HI-Dancing Bear Inn (☎ 250-352-7573,
888-352-7573, fax 250-352-9818, **W** www
.dancingbearinn.com, 171 Baker St) Dorm
beds $17/20 members/nonmembers; private
rooms start at $34/40. This thoughtfully reno-
vated hostel is central, comfortable and immaculate. It has kitchen and laundry facilities.

Flying Squirrel International Hostel
(☎ 250-352-7285, 866-755-7433, **W** www
.flyingsquirrelhostel.com, 198 Baker St)
Dorm beds $17, semiprivate room $20,
private double $39. Right by the HI-hostel,
this competitor offers decent digs with
similar services.

Heritage Inn (☎ 250-352-5331, 877-568-
0888, fax 250-352-5214, **W** www.heritage
inn.org, 422 Vernon St) Singles/doubles
$65/75 & up. A creaky grande dame built in
1898, this old hotel has unique touches like
squeaky floors that aren't always level,
quirky quotes framed in the hallways and
wonderful historical photos throughout.
Some rooms are right above a noisy pub, and
a bit of smoke seems to waft into the nonsmoking rooms. But all things considered,
this is a classic place to stay. Rates include a
full breakfast in the on-site restaurant.

Best Western Baker St Inn (☎ 250-352-
3525, 888-255-3525, fax 250-352-2995, 153
Baker St) Rooms $119 & up. Down by the
hostels, this modern inn doesn't have the
charm of the Heritage Inn but has all the
contemporary comforts. For best views, get
a room upstairs in back.

Places to Eat

Oso Negro (☎ 250-352-7661, 522 Victoria St)
This classic coffeehouse hides out up the
hill from the tourist heart of town. It's got
the best organic, shade-grown, fair-trade
coffees available and a hip clientele.

The Outer Clove (☎ 250-354-1667, 536
Stanley St) Dinner entrées $13-22. Garlic
lovers will be in heaven at this bistro that
features lots of garlic in everything, from
steak to seafood to international recipes.

All Seasons Cafe (☎ 250-352-0101,
W www.allseasonscafe.com, 620 Herridge
Lane) Dinner entrées $12-27. Ensconced in
the alley between Baker and Victoria Sts,
the All Seasons Cafe offers a superb fine-
dining experience. Food is art here, in both
preparation and presentation. The place
calls itself a 'food and wine shrine,' and
that's pretty accurate. The atmosphere is
comfortably casual, though, with art-filled
ambience.

NORTHEAST OF NELSON

Swimming, hiking, fishing and **camping**
($18.50) are all possible at **Kokanee Creek
Provincial Park** (☎ 250-422-4200 for all parks
in the region), north of town.

A free ferry runs between Balfour and
Kootenay Bay across scenic Kootenay Lake
and the road then travels south along the
lake toward Creston; check out the artisans'
community at **Crawford Bay**.

Ainsworth Hot Springs, on Hwy 31, not
only has the usual pool to soak in but also
hot-water-filled caves. Good exploratory
tours are offered at **Cody Caves** 4km farther
north. Hiking and backcountry camping is
superb in lake-filled **Kokanee Glacier Provincial Park**, where you could also enjoy
backcountry skiing in winter. The two-hour
hike to Kokanee Lake is wonderful and can
be extended to the glacier.

Quiet and attractive **Kaslo** holds many
Victorian-style buildings. Visit the 1898
sternwheeler SS Moyie on Kootenay Lake
and ask the locals how to find nearby
Fletcher's Falls. These secluded, impressive
falls are just a short drive or walk off the
main road.

WEST OF NELSON
Slocan Valley

Heading north from just west of Nelson,
scenic Hwy 6 traverses the Slocan Valley,
the main valley south of Revelstoke, east of
the Okanagan Valley. The dry, picturesque
valley holds a chain of lakes between the
Monashee and Selkirk mountain ranges.
This is an attractive portion of the province
that benefits from not having the high

profile and hence major attention of some of the better-known districts.

The drive up Hwy 6 is beautiful. At one point the road clings precariously to a high cliffside overlooking Slocan Lake. Across the lake is rugged **Valhalla Provincial Park**, which offers hiking trails and wilderness camping mainly accessed by boat; canoes can be rented. **Slocan Lake** provides excellent canoeing. And the **Slocan River**, from the town of Slocan south to the Kootenay River, has Class III rapids in its upper sections and less-demanding water farther down.

Continuing north toward Nakusp, several gorgeous hamlets dot the route, among them **Silverton**, which holds more than its share of artists and galleries.

Nakusp & Around

Quiet Nakusp, sitting on Upper Arrow Lake, is the Slocan Valley's main town, with several modest motels and restaurants. The Nakusp Visitor Info Centre (☎ 250-265-4234, 800-909-8819, fax 250-265-3808, W www.nakusphotsprings.com, 92 W 6th Ave) is open daily in summer, weekdays only the rest of the year. Ask at the Info Centre about trails to undeveloped hot springs in the woods.

McDonald Creek Provincial Park (☎ 250-422-4200, fax 250-422-3326, open Apr-Sept) Sites $12. This park is 10km south of town on Hwy 6. It's a great spot for fishing or just lying around on several kilometers of sandy beach.

About 13km northeast of Nakusp, off Hwy 23, are the tranquil **Nakusp Hot Springs** *(☎ 250-265-4528,* W *www.nakusphotsprings .com, Hot Springs Rd; adult/child age 6-18 $5.75/4.75; open daily year-round except one maintenance week late Apr-early May).* In addition to its two hot pools, the site has *chalets* ($57 & up) and a cramped *campground* with hookups and hot showers ($15-18).

Farther up Hwy 23, 32km north of Nakusp, is **Halcyon Hot Springs** *(☎ 250-265-3554, 888-689-4699,* W *www.halcyon-hot springs.com; adult/senior & student/child $6/5/4; open year-round).* Another developed hot-springs resort, this one has three pools of different temperatures, along with *cabins* ($70), *chalets* ($145 & up) and *camping* ($15-23.50).

Southwest of Nakusp, Hwy 6 heads to Vernon in the Okanagan Valley, going over the 1189m Monashee Pass. Near Vernon, the road goes through beautiful country scenery of small farms and wooded hills. Campgrounds and a few small provincial parks are along this route. North of town, Hwy 23 runs along pretty Upper Arrow Lake to the free ferry at Galena Bay, which connects with the road to Revelstoke.

Castlegar
pop 7500
A sprawling town, Castlegar sits at the confluence of the Columbia and Kootenay Rivers, at the junction of Hwys 3 and 3A. The Visitor Info Centre (☎ 250-365-6313, fax 250-365-5778, W www.castlegar.com, 1995 6th Ave) is open year-round.

Many members of the Russian Christian pacifist sect, the Doukhobors, settled around here at the beginning of the 1900s. Borscht is available at several restaurants.

On Lower Arrow Lake, 2.25-sq-km **Syringa Provincial Park** (☎ 250-422-4200), 19km northwest of Castlegar (Robson exit off Hwy 3A), open from May to September, has hiking, fishing, swimming, sailing, beaches and *camping* ($15).

Trail
An industrial town 27km southwest of Castlegar, Trail is home to Cominco, the world's largest smelter of silver, zinc and lead, whose enormous mishmash of buildings dominates the skyline. Those, together with the houses squeezed along the cliffs by the Columbia River, give the town a strikingly different character – one you might likely wish to avoid.

The Visitor Info Centre (☎ 250-368-3144, fax 250-368-6427, W www.trailchamber.bc.ca, 1199 Bay Ave) is open 9am to 5pm daily in summer, and weekdays only the rest of the year. The Greyhound bus depot (☎ 250-368-8400, 1355 Bay Ave) is right downtown.

Rossland
If you flee Trail upcanyon on Hwy 3B/22, you'll eventually ascend to the beautiful former mining town of Rossland, now a young, hip ski town perched at an elevation of 1038m in the Monashee Range. The Info Centre (☎ 250-362-7722, 888-448-7444; open mid-May–mid-Sept) is on the town's west side where the highways split; also here are a small mining museum and gold-mine tours.

The local ski area is **Red Mountain** (☎ *250-362-5666, 877-969-7669,* W *www .skired.com, Hwy 3B; adult full-day ticket $43; season Dec-Apr),* 5km up Hwy 3B from town. Known for, among other things, its great tree skiing, the area has 480 hectares of skiable terrain. Its five lifts serve 83 runs, with a maximum vertical drop of 870m.

HI-Rossland – Mountain Shadow Hostel (☎ *250-362-7160, 888-393-7160, fax 250-362-7150,* W *www.hihostels.bc.ca, 2125 Columbia Ave)* Dorm beds $17/21 for members/nonmembers, private rooms available. Right downtown, this hostel occupies a mining-era building with laundry and kitchen facilities, and ski and bike lockers. Reservations are essential in winter, when the place fills up with powderhounds.

Mountain Gypsy Cafe (☎ *250-362-3342, 2167 Washington)* Dinner entrées $12-16. Up the hill from downtown, this bright bistro offers great Asian- and Mediterranean-inspired food and great atmosphere. Open daily for lunch and dinner.

Northeastern British Columbia

Northeastern BC is a largely undeveloped, sparsely populated region dominated by the Rocky Mountains to the west and south, and by the Interior Plains to the north and east.

Two major highways connect this region with other parts of the country: the Yellowhead Hwy (Hwy 16) runs east-west between the Alberta border and Prince Rupert in the Pacific Northwest; Hwy 97 connects the south of the province with Dawson Creek where it becomes part of the Alaska Hwy and heads northwest toward the Yukon. The two highways meet at Prince George, the region's largest town. The VIA Rail line follows the Yellowhead Hwy.

Like the province's southeast corner, the area around Dawson Creek is on Mountain Standard Time.

PRINCE GEORGE
pop 72,000
In 1807, Simon Fraser's men cut the first spruce trees down to build Fort George for the North West Company. Since then, vast cutting and milling of the tree earned Prince

George the title 'spruce capital of the world,' though most of the town's spruces sit in piles instead of forests. Prince George, dominated by pulp mills (and the associated stench), is a sprawling and not very interesting or attractive town, but it serves as a useful crossroads and gateway to other northern towns.

Orientation & Information
Hwy 97 from Cache Creek cuts through the center of town on its way north to Dawson Creek (406km) and the Alaska Hwy. The Yellowhead Hwy (Hwy 16) runs through town on its way west to Prince Rupert (724km) and east through Jasper (377km) to Edmonton.

The downtown area is small, with little character. The main roads running east-west are 2nd, 3rd and 4th Aves, parallel to the train tracks. The main north-south thoroughfare is Victoria St, which also forms part of the Yellowhead Hwy; Patricia Blvd, which becomes 15th Ave, is also a major street.

The Visitor Info Centre (☎ 250-562-3700, 800-668-7646, fax 250-563-3584, W www .tourismpg.bc.ca, 1198 Victoria St), on the corner of Patricia Blvd, is open Monday to Saturday in summer, Monday to Friday the rest of the year. A second Info Centre (☎ 250-563-5493) sits 4km southwest of downtown at the junction of Hwy 97 and the Yellowhead Hwy (Hwy 16) and operates daily during summer.

Things to See & Do
Fraser-Fort George Regional Museum (☎ *250-562-1612,* W *www.museum.prince george.com, 970 20th Ave; adult/senior & student/child age 2-12/family $10/9/8/28 with SimEX, $8/6/5/20 without; open 10am-5pm daily in summer, 10am-5pm Wed-Sun in winter)* in Fort George Park, southeast of downtown (follow 20th Ave east of Gorse St), has various large kid-friendly galleries devoted to science, natural history and cultural history. Other highlights include an Internet café and a SimEX full-motion ride simulator.

Prince George is full of parks. Right downtown, **Connaught Hill Park** sits atop the city and provides a good vantage point. The 33-hectare **Cottonwood Island Nature Park**, north of downtown between the

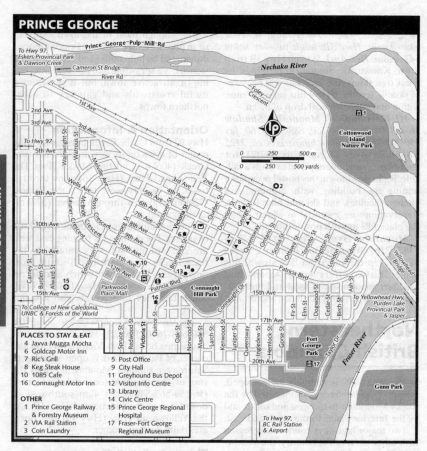

PRINCE GEORGE

PLACES TO STAY & EAT
4 Javva Mugga Mocha
6 Goldcap Motor Inn
7 Ric's Grill
8 Keg Steak House
10 1085 Cafe
16 Connaught Motor Inn

5 Post Office
9 City Hall
11 Greyhound Bus Depot
12 Visitor Info Centre
13 Library
14 Civic Centre
15 Prince George Regional Hospital
17 Fraser-Fort George Regional Museum

OTHER
1 Prince George Railway & Forestry Museum
2 VIA Rail Station
3 Coin Laundry

railway tracks and the river, is a protected riparian forest with a good network of trails; bring bug spray.

Prince George Railway and Forestry Museum (☎ 250-563-7351, 🌐 www.pgrfm .bc.ca, 850 River Rd; adult/senior & student age 13-17/child age 6-12 $6/5/3; open 10am-6pm daily May-Oct), beside Cottonwood Island Nature Park, features a large collection of train memorabilia, including many old cars and cabooses, as well as an antique chainsaw display and a logging arch truck, used to push around logs.

Six companies operate pulp mills in Prince George, and some of them offer **forestry tours** so you can find out – literally – what all the stink is about. These free two-hour tours are organized through the summer-only Visitor Info Centre south of town (☎ 250-563-5493).

Lots of good hiking trails are in the area. The Visitor Info Centre has a few different trail guides; some are free and others are more extensive and for sale. Popular local fishing spots include **Purden Lake Provincial Park**, 16km east on the Yellowhead Hwy (Hwy 16), and **Eskers Provincial Park**, 40km northwest of town (you'll have to hike in here).

Places to Stay

Camping Most campgrounds around Prince George cater to RVs – the tenting sites are generally not great.

Blue Spruce RV Park & Campground (☎ 250-964-7272, fax 250-964-7274, 4433

Kimball Rd) Sites $15.50-21. About 5km southwest of town off the Yellowhead Hwy, Blue Spruce offers full facilities, a store, pool and tenting sites.

Bee Lazee RV Park & Campground *(☎/fax 250-963-7263,* e *drone@pgonline.com, 15910 Hwy 97 S)* Sites $14-18. This place, 15km south on Hwy 97, has free hot showers, a pool, laundry machines and a honey farm.

University Residences From May to mid-August, budget, shared-bath accommodations are available in student residences at ***College of New Caledonia*** *(☎ 250-561-5849, fax 250-561-5832, 3330 22nd Ave)* and ***University of Northern British Columbia*** *(UNBC; ☎ 250-960-6430, University Way).* Expect to pay about $20/30 singles/doubles.

Motels *Grama's Inn (☎ 250-563-7174, 877-563-7174, fax 250-563-7147,* w *www.esthers inn.bc.ca/gramas, 901 Central St)* Singles/doubles $49/56 & up. Out on the Hwy 97 strip, Grama's is a friendly spot (although there's no sign of Grama) with a coffee shop. You can use the pool at nearby Esther's Inn.

Esther's Inn *(☎ 250-562-4131, 800-663-6844, fax 250-562-4145,* w *www.esthersinn.bc .ca, 1151 Commercial Dr)* Singles/doubles $58/66 & up. Behind Grama's, Esther's contains a restaurant and lounge with a Polynesian theme, plus a pool and gym.

Connaught Motor Inn *(☎ 250-562-4441, 800-663-6620, fax 250-562-4441, 1550 Victoria St)* Singles/doubles start at $65/70. The Connaught is across from the Visitor Info Centre. Amenities include an indoor pool, hot tub, sauna and restaurant.

Goldcap Motor Inn *(☎ 250-563-0666, 800-663-8239 in BC, fax 250-563-5775,* w *www.goldcapinn.com, 1458 7th Ave)* Rooms start at $77. The Goldcap is popular with business travelers and has a dining room, lounge and sauna.

Places to Eat
Javva Mugga Mocha (☎ 250-562-3338, 304 George St) Soups $4. At George St and 3rd Ave, this place serves fruit juices, coffees, soups and pies. In nice weather, eat at the outside tables.

1085 Cafe (☎ 250-960-2272, 1085 Vancouver St) Breakfast $3-8, lunch $5-10. This heritage-home-turned-restaurant features reasonable prices and a healthy menu at breakfast and lunch. It has an outdoor patio and local art.

Keg Steak House (☎ 250-563-1768, 582 George St) Dinner entrées $12-24. For dinner, try this popular chain place, which has some pasta and chicken dishes, as well as its signature steaks.

Ric's Grill (☎ 250-614-9096, 547 George St) Dinner entrées $15-30. Right across the street from the Keg, Ric's is big competition with great steaks, ribs, chicken and pastas at reasonable prices. It's a local favorite; reservations are recommended.

Getting There & Away
Prince George Regional Airport (YXS; ☎ 250-963-2400, w www.pgairport.ca) is on Airport Rd off Hwy 97, 14km southeast of downtown. It's served by Air Canada Regional (☎ 888-247-2262), WestJet (☎ 888-937-8538), Central Mountain Air (☎ 888-247-2262), Peace Air (☎ 800-563-3060) and NT Air (☎ 250-963-9611). Flights connect to most anywhere in the province.

The Greyhound bus depot (☎ 250-564-5454, 1566 12th Ave) is near the junction of Victoria St and Patricia Blvd.

The VIA Rail station (☎ 888-842-7245, 1300 1st Ave) is near the top of Queensway. VIA's *Skeena* travels west three times a week to Prince Rupert ($97 one-way, 12 hours) and east three times a week to Jasper ($76 one-way, six hours).

The BC Rail station (☎ 250-561-4033, 800-663-8238), at Terminal Blvd off Hwy 97, is southeast of town, over the Fraser River. The *Cariboo Prospector* runs south three times a week to North Vancouver ($212 one-way, 14 hours). The fare includes three meals.

Getting Around
The Airporter bus (☎ 250-563-2220) will shuttle you to downtown hotels and motels for $8/2.50 adult/child.

Prince George Transit (☎ 250-563-0011) operates local buses. The one-way fare in the central zone is $1.50.

PRINCE GEORGE TO SMITHERS
From Prince George the Yellowhead Hwy (Hwy 16) heads west to Smithers, Terrace and Prince Rupert, from where most people pick up ferries either south to Vancouver Island and Washington State or north to Alaska. The

road travels through a corridor of forest interspersed with lakes, rivers and farmland. (See also the Prince Rupert to New Hazelton section later in this chapter for details.)

The first settlement of any real size is **Vanderhoof**, mainly a service center for the area. East of here, Hwy 27 heads 66km north to **Fort St James National Historic Site** (☎ 250-996-7191), a former Hudson's Bay Company trading post on the southeastern shore of Stuart Lake. The nearby provincial parks at Paarens Beach and Sowchea Bay have *camping* ($9; no showers).

The other towns along the highway have the usual run of campgrounds and motels. Burns Lake is the center of the lakes district, a canoeing and recreation area. You can get a taste of the wilderness by heading north to **Babine Lake**. There are hiking trails in **Red Bluff Provincial Park**.

Smithers, in the pretty Bulkley Valley, is another center for outdoor activity. There's hiking, climbing and skiing on Hudson Bay Mt, 24km south of the junction with the Yellowhead Hwy, and whitewater rafting and canoeing on the Bulkley River. The Visitor Info Centre (☎ 250-847-5072, 800-542-6673, fax 250-847-3337, **W** www.town.smithers.bc.ca, 1411 Court St) is open daily late June to August, weekdays only the rest of the year. Motels line the highway. If the weather is good the road toward Terrace provides spectacular scenery.

PRINCE GEORGE TO DAWSON CREEK

As you travel north from Prince George the mountains and forests give way to gentle rolling hills and farmland, until near Dawson Creek the landscape resembles the prairies of Alberta. In the first 150km the road passes **Summit, Bear and MacLeod Lakes**, with provincial parks and camping along the way. North of MacLeod Lake, Hwy 39 heads north to Mackenzie, which sits on the southern shores of immense **Williston Lake**.

From **Chetwynd** you can take Hwy 29 north past Hudson's Hope (a 20-minute drive from the eastern arm of Williston Lake) to join the Alaska Hwy north of Fort St John.

DAWSON CREEK
pop 11,000
Dawson Creek, 412km north of Prince George on Hwy 97, is notable as the starting point – 'Mile 0' – for the Alaska or Alcan (short for Alaska-Canada) Hwy. The Alaska Hwy from Dawson Creek goes via Watson Lake and Whitehorse in the Yukon all the way to Fairbanks in Alaska.

The Dawson Creek Visitor Info Centre (☎ 250-782-9595, fax 250-782-9538, **e** dctourin@pris.bc.ca, 900 Alaska Ave) can give you the details. It's open daily in summer and weekdays only the rest of the year.

Mile 0 RV Park & Campground (☎ 250-782-2590, fax 250-782-1479, Km 2.5 Alaska Hwy) Sites $10-15. This campground has full facilities, including hot showers and a coin laundry.

Alaska Hotel (☎ 250-782-2625, 10209 10th St) Singles/doubles $35/40. This historic place is Dawson Creek's oldest hotel, once called the Dew Drop Inn. The rooms have been renovated since 1928, but the boardinghouse style remains. The small rooms come with a bed, desk and dresser; the shared bathroom is down the hall. Register for rooms downstairs in the lively pub, where there's live music every night.

George Dawson Inn (☎ 250-782-9151, 800-663-2745, fax 250-782-1617, 11705 8th St) Singles/doubles $68/76 & up. This inn has the nicest rooms in town, plus a restaurant and pub.

DAWSON CREEK TO THE YUKON
Heading northwest from Dawson Creek, the landscape again changes as the prairies are left behind and the Alaska Hwy crosses the Peace River on its way into the foothills of the Rocky Mountains. Except for Fort St John and Fort Nelson, most of the towns on the highway usually have little more than one or two service stations, campgrounds or lodgings.

Fort St John's main function is as a service center for the oil and gas industries and the surrounding farms. The Visitor Info Centre (☎ 250-785-3033, 250-785-6037 in winter, fax 250-785-7181, **W** www.fortstjohnchamber .com, 9923 96th Ave) is open daily in summer and weekdays the rest of the year.

For a look at the area's early days, stop at the worthwhile **Fort St John-North Peace Museum** (☎ 250-787-0430, 9323 100th St; adult/senior/student $3/2.50/2; open 9am-5pm daily in summer (closed on Sunday in winter), which occupies an old schoolhouse. Check out the giant stuffed polar bear and the 1932–48 dentist's office (and you thought going to the dentist now was bad!).

Fort Nelson is home to Canada's largest gas processing plant and BC's largest wood products plant (which is bigger than 13 football fields).

At **Mile 244** (393km from Dawson Creek), past Fort Nelson, the Liard Hwy (Hwy 77) heads north to the Northwest Territories, Fort Simpson and Nahanni National Park.

Continuing up the Alaska Hwy, you'll pass two provincial parks (☎ 250-787-3407). **Stone Mountain Provincial Park** has hiking trails with wilderness camping and a campground ($12). The moose in the park can often be seen eating nonchalantly by the side of the road. The 'stone mountain' in question is Mt St Paul (2127m). **Muncho Lake Provincial Park** has a lot of wildlife (most visibly goats) and several lodging and camping areas ($12). You can go swimming in the emerald-green lake or go hiking. 'Muncho' means 'big lake' in the Tagish language and at 12km long it's one of the largest natural lakes in the Rockies. This 88,420-hectare park is part of the northernmost section of the Rockies which, ending at Liard River 60km northwest, do not continue northward into the Yukon and Alaska. The mountains that do extend northward, the Mackenzies, are geologically different.

SOUTH OF PRINCE GEORGE

South of Prince George, Hwy 97 follows the Goldrush Trail through the northern reaches of the gold rush district known as Cariboo Country.

Quesnel

Quesnel's setting, at the confluence of the Fraser and Quesnel Rivers, and the carefully cultivated flowers along the riverfront trails can't overcome the fact that this is first and foremost a logging town. Pulp mills dominate the townscape and the smells coming from them permeate the air. The observation tower at the town's north end looks over the most concentrated industrial area for wood products in North America. However, it's worth stopping at the Visitor Info Centre (☎ 250-992-8716, 800-992-4922, fax 250-992-2181, 705 Carson Ave), which is open 8am to 8pm daily in summer and 9am to 4pm weekdays other times.

Barkerville Historic Park

This restored gold rush town (☎ 250-994-3332, adult/youth age 13-17/child age 6-12 $8/4.75/2.25; open 8am-8pm daily year-round; full visitor services mid-June–early Sept) is 89km east of Quesnel at the end of Hwy 26.

Today, you can see Barkerville as it was, albeit with a whole lot more fudge for sale than when the miners were here. A hotel, stores and a saloon are among over 100 buildings here. In the Theatre Royal, dancing shows (extra charge) are staged in a family-friendly manner the miners would have jeered. Outside the summer season the park is open and free, but most of the attractions are closed (which may actually make for a more atmospheric visit).

Nearby are three BC Parks *campgrounds* (*Williams Lake* ☎ 250-398-4414) with sites for $12-15; two of the three have showers.

St George Hotel (☎ 250-994-0008, 888-246-7690, fax 250-994-0008, **w** www.stgeorge .travel.bc.ca) Rooms $160 shared bath, $180 private bath, breakfast included. This restored hotel is inside the park and dates from 1898. Three of the seven rooms have private bath, and all are filled with antiques.

You can also stay at Wells, 8km west of Barkerville, which has a commercial *campground* and several *motels*. There's no bus to Barkerville.

Bowron Lake Provincial Park

Surrounded by snowy peaks, this 149,200-hectare park boasts one of the world's best canoe trips. The 116km circular canoe route

---

Barking up the Right Tree

Between 1858 and 1861 the Cariboo Trail, now Hwy 97, was pushed north from Kamloops to Quesnel. It was lined with ramshackle towns that were hastily built by gold prospectors from around the world. In 1862 a Cornishman, Billy Barker, hit the jackpot, making $1000 in the first two days of his claim. Soon Barkerville sprang up to become the largest city west of Chicago and north of San Francisco. The big boom was instrumental in British Columbia becoming a crown colony in 1858.

---

passes through 10 lakes, over sections of three rivers and across several portages. The trip takes seven to 10 days. Backcountry campgrounds are available along the way, and the park service only allows 27 canoes to start the circuit each day. You must bring your own food (or catch your own fish).

Wildlife abounds. You might see moose, black and grizzly bears, caribou and mountain goats. In late summer, you stand a good chance of spotting bears on the upper Bowron River, where they feed on spawning sockeye salmon.

You can paddle the circuit any time from mid-May to October. Most people do it in July and August, but September is also an excellent choice, since that's when the tree leaves change color. Mosquitoes are at their worst in spring.

Before planning your trip, contact Tourism BC (☎ 800-435-5622) to request an information package and to make reservations to do the circuit; you can reserve a spot beginning in January. Once you get to the park, you must go to the Registration Centre and pay a fee of $50 per person. For more information on the park, contact the BC Parks office (☎ 250-398-4414) in Williams Lake.

Access to the park is on a gravel road that leaves Hwy 26 just before you get to Barkerville.

Bowron Lake Provincial Park Campground *(Williams Lake ☎ 250-398-4414, fax 250-398-4686)* Sites $12. Near the Registration Centre is this 25-site vehicle campground with pit toilets and a boat launch.

Bowron Lake Lodge *(☎ 250-992-2733, fax 250-992-1511,* W *www.bowronlakelodge.com, Bowron Lake Rd)* Campsites $20, rooms $60 & up. Open from May to October, this friendly lodge on the lake rents canoes and has a restaurant and lounge.

Becker's Lodge *(☎ 250-992-8864, 800-808-4761, fax 250-992-8893,* W *www.beckers.bc.ca, Bowron Lake Rd)* Camping $15-20, cabins $69 & up. Just up the road, attractive Becker's features a cozy restaurant, nice log chalets and cabins, and canoe rentals. Becker's also leads an eight-day guided canoe tour.

Pacific Northwest

Northwest BC is a huge, little-developed, scarcely populated region whose remote-

ness is one of its main attractions. This largely inaccessible area is one of North America's last true wilderness regions. Various Native Indian peoples have long inhabited the area and to this day they make up a considerable percentage of the permanent residents. The land is dominated by forest, several mountain ranges, and scores of lakes and swift rivers. The Yellowhead Hwy (Hwy 16) connects Prince George and Prince Rupert; the mostly gravel Cassiar Hwy (Hwy 37) heads north to the Yukon.

PRINCE RUPERT
pop 26,000
After Vancouver, Rupert, as it's called, is the largest city on the mainland BC coast. The town is a fishing center for the Pacific Northwest, and its port handles timber, minerals and grain shipments to Asia.

The area has one of the highest precipitation rates in all of Canada. But when it's not raining, misty, foggy or under heavy cloud, the town's setting – surrounded by mountains, sitting at the mouth of the Skeena River, looking out at the fjordlike coastline – is magnificent.

Orientation & Information
Prince Rupert is on Kaien Island and is connected to the mainland by a bridge. The Yellowhead Hwy passes right through downtown, becoming McBride St then 2nd Ave W, which, along with 3rd Ave W, forms the downtown core. McBride St divides the city between east and west. Cow Bay is a historic waterfront area of shops and restaurants just north of downtown. The ferry terminal is in Fairview Bay, 3km southwest of town center.

The Visitor Info Centre (☎ 250-624-5637, 800-667-1994, fax 250-627-0992, 215 Cow Bay Rd, Ste 100) is open daily year-round, 9am to 9pm in summer, variable hours the rest of the year.

The post office (☎ 250-624-2353) is at 365-500 2nd Ave W. Java Dot Cup (☎ 250-622-2822, 516 3rd Ave W) has Internet access ($3.75 an hour). Prince Rupert Regional Hospital (☎ 250-624-2171, 1305 Summit Ave) is southwest of downtown in Roosevelt Park.

Things to See & Do
The **Museum of Northern BC** *(☎ 250-624-3207,* W *www.museumofnorthernbc.com, 100*

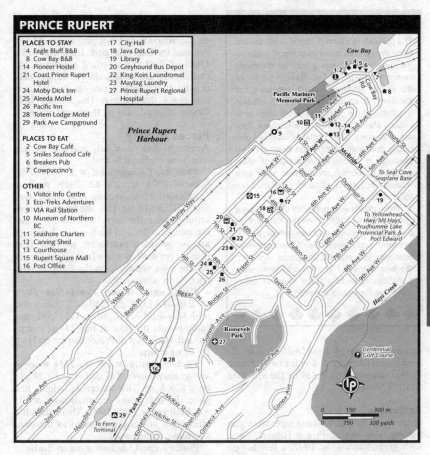

PRINCE RUPER

PLACES TO STAY
4 Eagle Bluff B&B
8 Cow Bay B&B
14 Pioneer Hostel
21 Coast Prince Rupert Hotel
24 Moby Dick Inn
25 Aleeda Motel
26 Pacific Inn
28 Totem Lodge Motel
29 Park Ave Campground

PLACES TO EAT
2 Cow Bay Café
5 Smiles Seafood Café
6 Breakers Pub
7 Cowpuccino's

OTHER
1 Visitor Info Centre
3 Eco-Treks Adventures
9 VIA Rail Station
10 Museum of Northern BC
11 Seashore Charters
12 Carving Shed
13 Courthouse
15 Rupert Square Mall
16 Post Office

17 City Hall
18 Java Dot Cup
19 Library
20 Greyhound Bus Depot
22 King Koin Laundromat
23 Maytag Laundry
27 Prince Rupert Regional Hospital

Prince Rupert Harbour

Cow Bay

Pacific Mariners Memorial Park

To Seal Cove Seaplane Base

To Yellowhead Hwy, Mt Hays, Prudhomme Lake Provincial Park & Port Edward

Roosevelt Park

Centennial Golf Course

To Ferry Terminal

0   150   300 m
0   150   300 yards

BRITISH COLUMBIA

1st Ave W; adult/child $5/1; open 9am-8pm Mon-Sat, 9am-5pm Sun June-Aug, 9am-5pm Mon-Sat Sept-May) occupies a gorgeous post-and-beam building styled after a First Nations longhouse. The incredible massive cedar beams exude a wonderful aroma that will chase away any moths you've picked up on your travels. The area's 10,000 years of human habitation are documented in excellent exhibits, which include a wealth of Haida, Gitksan and Tsimshian art.

You'll see **totems** all around town; two beside City Hall on 3rd Ave flanking the statue of Charlie Hays. (He brought the railroad to town and dreamed of making Prince Rupert a world-class port city. Alas, he perished on the Titanic before his dream could come true.) In summer, the museum offers

guided heritage and totem walking tours around town. To witness totem-building in action, stop by the **Carving Shed**, next door to the courthouse.

Heading out of town, look for the **shoe tree** on the north side of Hwy 16. Weary travelers have nailed more than a hundred shoes to the tree, making it the 'tree for lost soles.'

About 20km south of Prince Rupert, **North Pacific Cannery Village Museum** (☎ 250-628-3538, ⓦ www.district.port edward.bc.ca/northpacific, 1889 Skeena Dr; adult/youth $7.50/5; open 9am-6pm daily May-Sept, as well as many additional weekends through the year), in the town of Port Edward, explores the history of fishing and canning along the Skeena River. The fascinating complex includes a café and B&B

Forbidden Feast

The potlatch (a Chinook jargon word derived from the Nootka word *patschmatl* meaning 'to give' or 'gift') was a feast or ceremony common among the First Nations people of the Pacific Northwest coast, especially the Kwakiutl. Its main purpose was to validate the status of the chief or clan, although individuals also used it to try to enhance their social ranking. The potlatch involved the public exchange of gifts and destruction of property in a competitive display of affluence. A significant social event such as a wedding or funeral was used as an occasion for a potlatch.

The potlatch was prohibited by the federal government in 1884, when the Kwakiutl, at the cost of their own impoverishment, used it to shame and humble their former enemies. However, the practice continued in secret; the ban was lifted in 1951 and small-scale potlatches again take place. They are especially popular among the Haida.

accommodations (☎ 250-628-3538) in an old bunkhouse (starting at $65 for two). Prince Rupert Transit runs buses to the site (see Getting Around).

Activities

More than 70 charter-boat operators run **fishing** trips out of Prince Rupert, some with great success; in 1997, a few happy tourists landed a 106kg (234 lb) halibut. Many charter companies also offer **whale-watching** trips and various harbor tours; try **Seashore Charters** (☎ 250-624-5645, *1st Ave & McBride St*) or ask the Visitor Info Centre for a complete list of operators.

Eco-Treks Adventures (☎ 250-624-8311), on the Cow Bay Pier, offers a variety of guided **kayaking** classes and trips (from $50). It also rents kayaks. Prince Rupert has a huge tide range, with tides rising or falling up to 4 feet an hour. Be sure to get the low-down on the tides before venturing out on the water.

Of the many **hiking** trails in and around town, one path goes up Mt Hays (732m) from the Butze Rapids parking lot, east of town on Hwy 16. On a clear day, you can see local islands, the Queen Charlotte Islands and even Alaska. Beginning at a parking lot on the Yellowhead Hwy, 3km south of town just past the industrial park, trails lead to Mt Oldfield, Tall Trees (you'll see some old cedars) and Butze Rapids. The rapids walk is a flat 4km loop to Grassy Bay; the others are more demanding. The Visitor Info Centre offers details on these and others.

Places to Stay

Accommodations in July and August are sometimes difficult to find.

Park Ave Campground (☎ 250-624-5861, 800-667-1994, fax 250-622-2619, **W** www.tourismprincerupert.com, 1750 Park Ave) Sites $10.50-18.50. This municipal campground, near the ferry terminal, has hot showers, laundry and flush toilets. Tent sites are on wooden platforms so your tent doesn't get soaked when (not *if*) it rains. In summer, on nights when the ferry arrives, it's best to book ahead.

Prudhomme Lake Provincial Park (☎ 250-847-7320, fax 250-847-7659; open mid-May–mid-Sept) Sites $12. You can camp beside the lake at this 24-site campground, 16km east of Prince Rupert on Hwy 16. Bring a tarp.

Pioneer Hostel (☎ 250-624-2334, **W** www.citytel.net/pioneer, 167 3rd Ave E) Dorm beds $20 & up. This venerable lodging has gone through many incarnations since it was built in the early 1900s. These days it's officially a hostel (as opposed to the dive flophouse it once was).

Prince Rupert has over a dozen B&Bs.

Eagle Bluff B&B (☎ 250-627-4955, 201 Cow Bay Rd) Singles/doubles start at $40/50. Eagle Bluff offers five rooms with shared or private bath in a heritage building, right by the marina in Cow Bay.

Cow Bay Bed & Breakfast (☎ 250-627-1804, fax 250-627-1919, **W** www.cowbay.bc.ca, 20 Cow Bay Rd) Singles/doubles start at $75/90. Shared or private bath. Cozy duvets cover every bed in the Northwest Coast-theme rooms here.

Aleeda Motel (☎ 250-627-1367, 888-460-2023, fax 250-624-3132, **W** www.aleedamotel.bc.ca, 900 3rd Ave W) Singles/doubles $58/70 & up. The rooms here are simple but clean and nice.

Pacific Inn (☎ 250-627-1711, 888-663-1999, fax 250-627-4212, **W** www.pacificinn.bc.ca, 909

3rd Ave W) Singles/doubles $69/85 & up. The recently renovated Pacific Inn has a restaurant and large rooms.

Totem Lodge Motel (☎ *250-624-6761, 800-550-0178, fax 250-624-3831,* W *www .tkp-biz.com/totemlodgemotel, 1335 Park Ave)* Singles/doubles start at $79/89. The Totem Lodge is a good choice, but because it's close to the ferry terminal it fills up fast; book early.

Moby Dick Inn (☎ *250-624-6961, 800-663-0822 in Canada and Alaska, fax 250-624-3760,* W *www.mobydickinn.com, 935 2nd Ave W)* Singles/doubles start at $69/79. This large, friendly place has a restaurant and lounge, guest laundry facilities, a hot tub and sauna. Rooms have TVs, fridges and coffeemakers.

Coast Prince Rupert Hotel (☎ *250-624-6711, 800-663-1144, fax 250-624-3288,* W *www.coasthotels.com, 118 6th St)* Singles/doubles start at $98/110. The Coast has good harbor views, a restaurant, lounge and comfortable rooms.

Places to Eat

With fishing a major local industry, it's not surprising to find seafood on just about every menu. Salmon and halibut are headliners.

Smiles Seafood Café (☎ *250-624-3072, 113 Cow Bay Rd)* Most entrées $10-15. Top billing for seafood goes to the storied Smiles, on the waterfront at Cow Bay. It serves a variety of fresh ocean fare, as well as steaks and sandwiches.

Cow Bay Café (☎ *250-627-1212, 205 Cow Bay Rd)* Dinner entrées $12-17. Near Smiles, overlooking the marina, the Cow Bay Café serves up fresh fish every night. The creative menu changes daily, so it's popular with locals as well as tourists. It's closed Sunday.

Breakers Pub (☎ *250-624-5990, 117 George Hills Way)* Meals $8-20. Also in Cow Bay, Breakers makes a worthwhile stop for a meal and a beer. This busy place features an outdoor patio and a huge menu with tasty fresh fish specials. Try the halibut burger ($11).

Cowpuccino's (☎ *250-627-1395, 25 Cow Bay Rd)* This mellow coffeehouse and travelers' hangout maintains the neighborhood's shtick in its name – and with its cow-spotted dumpsters.

Getting There & Away

Air Prince Rupert Airport (YPR; ☎ 250-624-6274) is on Digby Island, across the harbor from town. You must check in for your flight at your airline's downtown terminal two hours before flight time so that you can catch a shuttle bus and ferry (combined ticket $11) to the airport – no last minute showing-up here. Flights are available from Air Canada (☎ 888-247-2262; $28 departure surcharge), Harbour Air (☎ 250-627-1341, 800-689-4234, W www.harbour-air .com), which offers floatplane service from Prince Rupert's Seal Cove Seaplane Base to the Queen Charlotte Islands and small coastal ports, and Hawkair (☎ 866-429-5247, W www.hawkair.net), which flies to Vancouver.

Bus The Greyhound bus depot (☎ 250-624-5090, 112 6th St) has luggage lockers. Buses depart twice daily to Prince George (10½ hours, $96).

Train The VIA Rail station (☎ 250-627-7589, 888-842-7245, 1033 Waterfront St) is near the harbor. This is the western terminus of the *Skeena,* the two-day daylight-only train coming from Jasper, with an overnight stop in Prince George. The three weekly trains arrive in Rupert at 8pm on Monday, Thursday and Saturday; trains depart at 8am on Sunday, Wednesday and Friday.

Ferry From Prince Rupert, Alaska State Ferries runs boats north through the Alaskan Panhandle. The first stop is Ketchikan, but you can go north past Wrangell, Petersburg and Juneau to Skagway.

Alaska State Ferries (☎ 250-627-1744, 800-642-0066, W www.alaska.gov/ferry), also called the Alaska Marine Hwy, maintains an office at the ferry terminal in Fairview Bay, 3km southwest of the center of town via Park Ave. The one-way fare to Skagway (34 hours) is US$143/72/185 adult/child age 2-11/small car; a two-person cabin starts at US$115. Meals are extra. If you're traveling by car or RV, you should book well ahead. You can try going standby, but you may not get on the boat.

BC Ferries (☎ 250-386-3431, 888-223-3779 in BC) sails the *Queen of the North* down the Inside Passage to Port Hardy on Vancouver Island on daytime schedules (15

BRITISH COLUMBIA

hours), departing every other day from mid-May to mid-October. The spectacular cruise along the narrow Inside Passage passes small native villages, islands and inlets. Keep your eyes peeled for the wealth of wildlife, which can include seals and killer, humpback and gray whales. The fare is $106/53/218 adult/child/car.

If you're coming from Port Hardy and you intend to continue north to Alaska by ferry, then you should note that the schedules of BC Ferries and Alaska State Ferries do not coincide; you may get the chance to spend at least one night in Prince Rupert.

BC Ferries also sails across Hecate Strait between Prince Rupert and Skidegate in the Queen Charlotte Islands (from six hours). In summer, boats sail almost daily; in winter, they leave three times a week. The one-way fare is $25/12.50/93 adult/child/car.

Getting Around

City Transit (☎ 250-624-3343) operates buses to all ferry and seaplane terminals. For times, pick up a copy of the *Rider's Guide* from the Visitor Info Centre. The one-way fare on buses is $1; a day pass costs $2.50. The main downtown bus stop is at Rupert Square Mall on 2nd Ave W. Take No 51 east to the seaplane base, or catch the Fairview Bay bus (no number) west to the ferry terminal.

In summer, buses run to the fishing village at Port Edward; the one-way fare to the Cannery Village Museum is $2.50.

PRINCE RUPERT TO NEW HAZELTON

Prince Rupert sits near the mouth of the **Skeena River**, and heading east out of town the Yellowhead Hwy (Hwy 16) follows the river, with some magnificent scenery of lakes, forests and mountains. Camping is possible in provincial parks along the way, and you'll also pass rest areas where you can stop for a while and take it all in.

Terrace, 147km east of Prince Rupert, sitting in a valley surrounded by mountains, is a logging, service and transport center. Hwy 16 becomes Keith Ave through town. The Visitor Info Centre (☎ 250-635-2063, 800-499-1637, **w** www.terracetourism.bc.ca, 4511 Keith Ave), just south and east of downtown, is open 8:30am to 6pm daily July

to September, 8:30am to 4:30pm Monday to Friday the rest of the year. The Greyhound bus depot (☎ 250-635-3680) is nearby at 4620 Keith Ave.

Nisga'a Memorial Lava Bed Provincial Park (☎ 250-847-7320, fax 250-847-7659, *Kalum Lake Rd; open mid-May–Oct*), 80km north of Terrace, preserves a huge, over 250-year-old lava flow. You can go fishing, hiking (guided hikes available by reservation) or *camping* ($12).

The Hazelton area (comprising the distinct towns of New Hazelton, Hazelton and South Hazelton)is the center of some interesting **First Nations sites**. Some totems are west of town at Kitwanga and also farther north at **Kitwanga Fort National Historic Site** (☎ 250-559-8818, Hwy 16; admission free; open year-round), which marks the location of a fort built by the Tsimshian people in the late 18th century. A self-guided trail offers interpretive information. Near the restored pioneer-era Hazelton is **'Ksan Historical Village & Museum** (☎ 250-842-5544, 877-842-5518, *Highlevel Rd; admission $2, admission plus guided tour $8; open daily mid-Apr–mid-Oct & open Mon-Fri with reduced services rest of year*), one of the province's most significant First Nations attractions. The recreated village of the Gitksan people features longhouses, a museum, various outbuildings and totem poles.

CASSIAR HWY

Between Terrace and New Hazelton, Hwy 37 splits off to head for Meziadin Junction and Stewart (221km). The portion of Hwy 37 extending north from Meziadin Junction is known as the Cassiar Hwy and meets the Alaska Hwy in the Yukon 569km north.

The Cassiar is a mostly gravel road and passes through some beautiful countryside. There aren't many service stations along the way, so if you're driving, make sure the vehicle is in good working condition and take spare parts and extra gasoline. Flying gravel can crack the windshield or headlights and dust can severely restrict your vision so treat approaching vehicles with caution, especially logging trucks.

Stewart & Hyder

From Meziadin Junction it's 67km west to Stewart on the Alaskan border. On the way you pass **Bear Glacier**, 49km from Stewart; a rest area provides views of the glacier.

If you're looking for Bumphuque, BC, Stewart is a good bet. It cozies right up with its sister city, Hyder, Alaska, and border formalities are negligible. In fact, 'formalities' of any kind don't exist out here. Life is isolated, independent, surreal. Grizzly bears occasionally roam the streets, but they're not half as formidable as the grizzly locals you'll find in the many local saloons.

This is the gateway to the **Misty Fiords National Monument** in Alaska. At **Fish Creek**, about 3km past Hyder, between late July and September you can see salmon swimming upstream to spawn and bears coming to feed on them.

In Stewart, the Visitor Info Centre (☎ 250-636-9224, 888-366-5999, fax 250-636-2199, **w** www.stewartbc.com, 222 5th Ave) is open mid-May to mid-September.

Rainey Creek Campground (☎ 250-636-2537, fax 250-636-2668, 8th Ave; open mid-May–mid-Sept) Sites $11-18. This municipal campground has hookups, coin-op showers and nature trails.

King Edward Hotel (☎ 250-636-2244, 800-663-3126 in BC, fax 250-636-9160, 5th Ave). Singles/doubles $60/70. The King Edward is part of a small group of affiliated lodgings in Stewart, so if it's full, ask about other options. This one has a restaurant.

Spatsizi Plateau Provincial Wilderness Park

This vast wilderness of more than 675,000 hectares includes the Spatsizi Uplands, the Stikine Plateau and the headwaters of the Stikine River. The park is undeveloped and isolated. From Tatogga Lake Resort at Kilometer 390.2 on the Cassiar Hwy (Hwy 37), drive east 28km on Ealue Lake Rd. It ends at a T intersection with a rough road that parallels the park's western boundary. Turn right here and you'll pass two trailheads (at McEwan Creek and Eaglenest Creek) within the first 30km. From here, access to the park is only on foot, by horse or canoe. You can also arrive via floatplane.

In the park, Gladys Lake Ecological Reserve is home to Stone's sheep, mountain goats, moose, grizzly and black bears, caribou and wolves. The trails are often little more than vague notions across the untouched landscape. There are no campgrounds, although there are some primitive cabins ($10) on Cold Fish Lake for the use of people arriving by floatplane. For more information, contact the BC Parks Skeena District in Smithers (☎ 250-847-7320, fax 250-847-7659).

Iskut, 290km north of Stewart on Hwy 37, has the closest services to the park.

Red Goat Lodge (☎ 250-234-3261, 888-733-4628, fax 250-234-3261, Hwy 37, Km 402.4) Campsites $20-25, singles/doubles $65/85, including full breakfast. This lodge on the shores of Eddontenajon Lake is a haven for travelers, with a campground, B&B rooms, modern cabins and a coin laundry.

Mt Edziza Provincial Park

This park has a volcanic landscape featuring lava flows, cinder cones and fields and an extinct shield volcano. It's accessed by gravel road from Dease Lake to Telegraph Creek and has hiking trails and wilderness camping. The park is mostly west of Hwy 37 and is linked to Spatsizi Plateau Provincial Wilderness Park. The park is undeveloped and the contact information is the same as Spatsizi (above).

Stikine River

The Stikine River, which cuts through the glacier-capped Coast Mountains to Alaska and the Pacific Ocean, is one of the best rivers for wilderness whitewater canoeing. In the upper reaches some rapids are deadly Class V. The section west of the Cassiar Hwy as far as Telegraph Creek is considered unnavigable and you must pre-arrange to be picked up when you reach the Pacific Ocean.

Atlin

This small, remote town in the northwestern corner of the province is reached by road from Whitehorse in the Yukon. See that chapter for details.

QUEEN CHARLOTTE ISLANDS
pop 6000

The Queen Charlotte Islands, sometimes known as the Canadian Galapagos, are a dagger-shaped archipelago of some 154 islands lying 80km off the BC coast and about 50km from Alaska's southern tip. As the only part of Canada that escaped the last Ice Age, the islands are rich in plants and animals markedly different from those of the mainland. Essentially still a wilderness area, the Queen Charlottes are warmed by an ocean current from Japan and hit with 127cm of rain annually. All these factors combine to create a landscape of 1000-year-old spruce and cedar rain forests, abundant animal life and waters teeming with marine life.

The islands have been inhabited continuously for 10,000 years and are the traditional homeland – Haida Gwaii – of the Haida nation, generally acknowledged as the country's prime culture at the time of the arrival of Europeans. The arts of the Haida people – notably their totem poles and carvings in argillate (a black, glasslike stone) – are world renowned. They were also fearsome warriors who dominated the west coast.

Today the Haida are still proud, defiant people. In the 1980s they led an internationally publicized fight to preserve the islands from further logging. A bitter debate raged, but finally the federal government decided to save South Moresby and create Gwaii Haanas National Park Reserve and Haida Heritage Site. Logging still goes on in other parts of the Queen Charlottes.

The three main towns are all on Graham Island. Queen Charlotte City (QCC) is the main commercial and tourism center and is near the ferry dock. Skidegate is a waterfront Haida community and Masset, on the north coast, is a Haida community, commercial center and home to a closed army base. From the Skidegate ferry dock to QCC is 3km, to Masset 135km.

The islands' relative remoteness coupled with the lure of the land and First Nations culture has put the Charlottes on the travelers' map. In conjunction, a number of hostels and services have sprung up to meet the needs of the intrepid. Despite this, it's still all but mandatory to sort out your accommodations in advance and book ahead. It's also important to remember that the Queen Charlottes are a rural and remote place. If you plan to visit the Gwaii Haanas National Park Reserve and Haida Heritage Site – and that's the number one reason for coming to the islands – then understand that a visit takes several days as there are no roads and access is entirely by boat or floatplane. Don't be one of the dullards who hop off the ferry expecting to see everything in a few hours and then depart. You won't.

Information

The main Visitor Info Centre (☎ 250-559-8316, fax 250-559-8952, w www.qcinfo.com, 3220 Wharf St) is in a lovely building on the water in Queen Charlotte City. It is open from 10am to 7pm daily mid-May to early September and 10am to 2pm for about three weeks on either side of that period. Other summer-season-only Info Centres are in Sandspit at the airport (☎ 250-637-5362) and in Masset (☎ 250-626-3982, 1455 Old Beach Rd). These centers have a wealth of knowledge about the islands, and the main office has some good natural history displays. They also have lists of places to rent kayaks, canoes and other gear, including diving equipment.

The *Guide to the Queen Charlotte Islands* is encyclopedic and updated annually. It is widely available for $3.95.

The island has few ATMs. In QCC, you'll find one in the City Centre Store, another in Howler's Pub. The Northern Savings Credit Union operates ATMs in two locations: 106 Causeway in QCC (☎ 250-559-4407) and 1633 Main St in Masset (☎ 250-626-5231). Because the electronic links to the mainland often break down, though, don't count on using ATMs; instead, bring lots of cash.

The post office (☎ 250-559-8349, 117 3rd Ave) is in the same shopping complex in QCC as the City Centre Store.

There's a coin laundry in the City Centre Store complex in QCC. It also has showers, the only public ones at this end of Graham Island.

Queen Charlotte Islands General Hospital (emergency ☎ 250-559-4506, general information ☎ 250-559-4300, 3209 Third Ave) is in QCC. For major emergencies, patients are generally sent to Prince Rupert by air ambulance.

Graham Island

About 80% of the population lives on Graham Island, the only island with any real road system.

Near the ferry terminal in Skidegate is the **Haida Gwaii Museum** (*☎ 250-559-4643, 2nd Beach Rd; adult/child $4/3; open 10am-5pm Mon-Fri, 1pm-5pm Sat & Sun May-Sept & Mon, Wed-Fri 10am-noon & 1pm-5pm, Sat 1pm-5pm rest of year*), with good displays on the area's history, including an excellent collection of Haida works and totem poles.

The Yellowhead Hwy (Hwy 16) heads 110km north from Queen Charlotte past Tlell and Port Clements (the famous golden spruce tree on the banks of the Yakoun River was cut down by a deranged forester in 1997) to Masset. There's good birdwatching at the **Delkatla Wildlife Sanctuary**, off Tow Rd, north of town. Farther along the road are several miles of rugged beaches where bongo-drum-toting backpackers try to set up house in little driftwood shacks. The cold and lack of services soon take their toll. If you try this, make certain your credit card has enough room left to escape.

Much of the island's northeast side between Port Clements and Masset is devoted to **Naikoon Provincial Park** (*☎ 250-557-4390; Hwy 16; open year-round*). The park combines bogland, dunes and beaches. A trail (5km one-way) from the Tlell River bridge at the park's south end (near park headquarters) leads to the wreck of the barge *Pesuta*. North, a 21km loop traverses a good bit of the park to and from Fife Beach from the end of Tow Hill Rd. The beaches in this area feature strong winds, pounding surf and driftwood from across the Pacific. *Camping* is possible ($12).

Gwaii Haanas National Park Reserve & Haida Heritage Site

This huge, remote and wild park (*☎ 250-559-8818,* **W** *www.parkscan.harbour.com/gwaii*) encompasses Moresby Island and scores of smaller islands at the south end of the Queen Charlottes. Ancient Haida villages can be found throughout the park. The most famous – and photographed – is **Ninstints/SGaang Gwaii** (Anthony Island), where rows of totem poles stare eerily out to sea. It was declared a Unesco world heritage site in 1981. Other major sights include **Skedans** on Louise Island and **Hotspring Island**, where you can soak away the bonechilling cold in natural springs.

Access to the park and sights is only by boat or plane. A visit requires a fair amount of advance planning and requires several days. The easiest way to get into the park is with a tour company. The Visitor Info Centre has lists of operators, many of whom are located in Vancouver and Victoria. On the islands, **Queen Charlotte Adventures** (*☎ 250-559-8990, 800-668-4288,* **W** *www.qcislands.net/qciadven, PO Box 196, Queen*

Charlotte, BC V0T 1S0) leads kayak tours of the park. The company has an office on Wharf St in QCC and is active in protecting the preserve's ecology.

Independent travel within the park is not easy and you must come well prepared. Visitation is limited. You should obtain a reservation for park access; call **BC Tourism** (*☎ 250-387-1642, 800-435-5622; reservation fee $15/person, maximum $60/group*). Six standby spaces are available each day, first-come, first-served from the Visitor Info Centre in QCC, beginning at 8am. User fees are $10 per night up to five nights, a flat $60 for six to 14 nights or $80 for over 14 nights. People 17 and under are free. Finally, before entering the park all park visitors must attend a 90-minute orientation session covering ecological, safety and cultural issues.

Places to Stay

Wilderness camping is possible in the forests and on the beaches throughout the islands.

Naikoon Provincial Park (*☎ 250-557-4390*) Sites $12. Naikoon has two excellent campgrounds: Misty Meadows is just off Hwy 16 at the park's south end; Agate Beach is on the north coast off Tow Hill Rd. Both have toilets, firewood and water.

Hayden Turner Campground Sites $5-10. West of QCC (follow Hwy 33 to the end) you'll find this community-run campground with pit toilets, vehicle sites and three walk-in beach sites.

Village of Masset Campground (*☎ 250-626-3995, 888-352-9292, fax 250-626-3968, Tow Hill Rd*) Sites $10-20. Masset has a municipal campground 2km from town. It has full facilities including flush toilets and coin showers.

Sea Raven Motel (*☎ 250-559-4423, 800-665-9606 in BC and AB, fax 250-559-8617,* **W** *www.searaven.com, 3301 3rd Ave*) Singles/doubles start at $45/75. QCC's modern Sea Raven has 29 rooms overlooking the bay.

Copper Beech House B&B (*☎ 250-626-5441, fax 250-626-3706,* **W** *www.copperbeechhouse.com, 1590 Delkatla Rd*) Singles $50-75, doubles $75-100. In Masset, local celebrity and chef extraordinaire David Phillips runs this rambling old house whose backside faces the harbor. Those who stay here, be forewarned: Get

Totem Poles

Totem poles are found along the North Pacific coast, roughly between southern British Columbia and Alaska. Carved on logs of western red cedar by the Haida, Tlingit, Tsimshian and Kwakiutl tribes, totem poles show various animal and human forms stacked on each other, depicting different animal spirits as well as revered and respected supernatural beings.

Although Captain Cook noted totem poles as early as 1778, they didn't become abundant until the native peoples decided to display the wealth they acquired from involvement in the fur trade, around the mid-19th century. Traditional totem poles varied greatly in height, though rarely exceeded 18m. Modern poles can be much taller – the tallest totem pole in the world, at Alert Bay, BC, is 52m.

Totem poles identify a household's lineage in the same way as a family crest might identify an Englishman with a particular lineage, although the totem pole is more of a historical pictograph depicting the entire ancestral history. Like a family crest, totem poles also carry a sense of prestige and prosperity.

If it were possible to 'read' a totem pole, it would be from top to bottom – from present to past. Despite its position, the top figure, which represents the pole's owner, is actually the least important figure on the pole. The largest figure, usually the one at the bottom, is the most important. Loosely associated with individuals and events, the figures have no fixed meanings. A figure might be used to represent a particular person, or it may mark a memorable or adventurous event attributed to a particular creature or spirit. It could also represent a legend.

Because birds, fish and mammals figure so prominently on totem poles, it's possible to identify them without really knowing what they mean. A beak is a dead giveaway for a bird – **raven** has a straight, mid-sized beak and **hawk** has a short down-turned beak that also curves inward. **Eagle** also has a short down-turned beak and looks a lot like the mythical thunderbird, which has curled horns on its head. **Hokw-hokw** is a mythical beast with a very long, slender beak used to burst skulls. **Beaver** looks a lot like **bear**, except for a pair of large incisors and a crosshatched tail.

FRANK CARTER

A few animals appear as if viewed from overhead. **Killer whale** is a good example of this – its fin protrudes from the pole as its head faces downwards. Long-snouted **wolf** also faces downwards, as does **frog**. Pointy-headed **shark** (or dogfish), with a grimacing mouth full of sharp teeth, and the **humpback whale** both face upwards.

The culture of totem poles was largely squashed after the Canadian government outlawed the potlatch ceremony in 1884. Few totem poles remain today because most cedar logs begin to decay within 60 to 80 years, though totem poles in the Queen Charlotte Islands are over 100 years old.

New totem poles are rarely constructed for tribal purposes, and instead are more frequently carved for nontraditional use as public art. Modern totem poles commissioned for college campuses, museums and public buildings no longer recount the lineage of any one household, but instead stand to honor the First Nations peoples and their outstanding artistry.

Phillips talking at night and you might never get to bed. Get him to cook for you and you might never leave. Ask about hostel accommodations in return for chores (like gardening or washing dishes).

Places to Eat

The islands' few restaurants are centered in QCC. Many close from October to April.

Hanging By a Fibre (☎ 250-559-4463, *3207 Wharf St)* Get your coffee and check out the artwork at this café on Wharf St, right in the heart of QCC.

Lam's Cafe (☎ 250-559-4204, 3223 Wharf St) Breakfast $5-10. The place for breakfast is Lam's, just across from the Visitor Info Centre. Formerly Margaret's Cafe, most locals still call it that despite the new owners. You can get bacon, eggs, hash browns and toast for $6.25.

Howler's Bistro (☎ 250-559-8602, 2600 3rd Ave) Dinner entrées $8-19. Howler's features an excellent atmosphere and huge menu, including burgers, pasta dishes and wraps. Downstairs, join others for beer and a game of pool at *Howler's Pub* (☎ 250-559-8600), the only place in town that stays open late.

Hummingbird Café (☎ 250-557-8583, 9 Cedar E) Dinner entrées $14-30. The best place for fresh local seafood is this café, north of QCC in Port Clements. The smoked salmon Caesar salad is a delight.

Getting There & Around

BC Ferries sails between Prince Rupert and Skidegate (from six hours) almost daily in summer and three times a week the rest of the year. The one-way fare is $25/12.50/93 adult/child age 5-11/car. Arriving in Skidegate, as you sail between two islands, you have a vista of rows of mountains receding into the mists; it's wild and verdant.

Ferries make the 20-minute crossing between Graham Island (Skidegate Landing), where most people live, and Moresby Island (Alliford Bay), where the airport is, six times daily year-round. The roundtrip fare is $4.75/2.50/12 adult/child/car.

From Sandspit airport (☎ 250-637-5313), Air Canada Regional (☎ 888-247-2262) offers scheduled flights to the mainland year-round and Harbour Air (☎ 250-559-0052, 800-689-4234) offers flights primarily in summer.

There is no public transportation, although hitchhiking is common, and the paved roads on Graham Island are good for cycling. You'll have to weigh the high cost of local car rental against the cost of bringing a vehicle on the ferry. Budget (☎ 250-637-5688) and Thrifty (☎ 250-637-2299) have offices at the airport. Note that the many gravel roads can take a toll on windshields, so if you're renting sort out breakage coverage in advance. For a taxi at the airport and QCC, try Eagle Cab (☎ 250-559-4461).

Yukon Territory

The Yukon offers an abundance of outdoor opportunities – world-class hiking and mountaineering, cycling, canoeing, rafting, kayaking, camping and fishing – amid a scenic splendor of mountains, forests, fast-flowing rivers and tundra. There are large populations of moose, caribou, bears, sheep, beavers, porcupines, coyotes and wolves, which far outnumber the humans.

The Yukon is between the Northwest Territories and Alaska with British Columbia to the south and the Beaufort Sea to the north. It's a sub-Arctic region about one-third the size of Alaska. Mountain ranges, including some that stretch from the Rockies, almost entirely cover the territory, which is 80% wilderness.

The Alaska Hwy is the main route through the Yukon, and there are a number of other scenic and demanding drives, including the Dempster Hwy, the only north-south road to cross the Arctic Circle. With good road access, transportation and services, costs in the Yukon are reasonable compared to other remote areas of Canada. It's also a great place for kids.

Every year more and more visitors discover the Yukon's rugged charm and beauty during the short summer season or arrive later to strap on skis or snowshoes and experience the extreme winter landscape.

History

When most of North America was encased in ice, the first people to arrive in the region crossed a huge ice-free land bridge linking Asia and the Americas. They followed the woolly mammoths, mastodons and steppe bison. Archeologists date their arrival to the Porcupine River area near Old Crow from between 15,000 and 20,000 years ago. They are considered to be the ancestors of today's Déné (also called Athabaskan) people.

In the 1840s Robert Campbell, a Hudson's Bay Company explorer, was the first European to travel the district. Fur traders, prospectors, whalers and missionaries followed him. Until that point there had been only limited contact between Native Indians and Europeans and many First

Highlights

Granted Territorial Status: 1898
Area: 483,450 sq km
Population: 31,070
Territorial Capital: Whitehorse

- Drive or cycle the Haines Hwy for splendid mountain scenery and wildlife.

- Hike the greenbelt of Kluane National Park or fly over its icy heart.

- Paddle the fast-flowing Yukon River or its tributaries.

- Raft the world-class Alsek and Tatshenshini wilderness rivers.

- Amble down the gold-rush–era streets of Dawson City.

- Experience the Dempster Hwy, a great adventure road, for wide-open tundra and a chance to cross the Arctic Circle.

Nation populations were hit with measles, small pox and influenza.

In 1870 the region became part of the Northwest Territories. But it was in 1896 that the biggest changes began, when gold was found in a tributary of the Klondike River near what became Dawson City. The ensuing gold rush attracted hopefuls from around the world. The population boomed to around 38,000 and transport routes opened up. Towns grew overnight to support the wealth-seekers, who were not prepared for the harsh conditions. First Nation men worked as guides, hunters and freight packers. The women made and sold weather-appropriate clothing. Their traditional patterns of moving with the seasons changed dramatically.

In 1898 the Yukon became a separate territory, with Dawson City the capital, but the city declined as the gold ran out. The construction of the Alaska Hwy in 1942 opened up the territory to development. In 1953 Whitehorse became the capital, for it had the railway and the Alaska Hwy. Mining is still the main industry, followed by tourism.

There are 14 First Nation groups in the Yukon, speaking eight languages. Due to the relative isolation of the territory until WWII, First Nation groups have maintained their relationship to the land and their traditional culture, compared to other groups forced to assimilate in Canada.

Climate

Summers, spanning June, July and August, are short but warm, even hot, with occasional thunderstorms. Many places are only open from May to September because, outside of these months, visitors are few, winters are long, dark and cold and many of the summer residents head south.

On average there are 19 daylight hours in Whitehorse during July; six in January.

Information

Tourist Offices The Yukon has six Visitor Reception Centres (VRCs) in Beaver Creek, Carcross, Dawson City, Haines Junction, Watson Lake and Whitehorse; all are open 8am to 8pm daily mid-May to mid-September. Tourism Yukon (☎ 867-667-5340, fax 867-667-3546, w www.touryukon.com, PO Box 2703, Whitehorse, YT Y1A 2C6). will send free information, including

the annual *Yukon* magazine with specifics on regional activities, events and accommodations. It also distributes an excellent highway map.

Books Poet Robert Service and the writer Jack London both lived and worked in the Yukon during the gold rush, mining raw material for *The Cremation of Sam McGee* and *Call of the Wild.* Perhaps the first guidebook for the region, *The Gold Fields of the Klondike* by John W Leonard, was published in 1897 just months after the discovery was reported. The author provided first-hand accounts and practical tips, shrewdly anticipating the demand for information. The reissued version with original drawings and photographs is interesting.

The Yukon Hiking Guide by Curtis Vos is good for regional trail information. *Yukon's Tombstone Range & Blackstone Uplands* from the Canadian Parks and Wilderness Society covers that area.

Dangers & Annoyances If you're drinking water from lakes or rivers, boil it for at least 10 minutes. The water may contain the intestinal parasite *Giardia lamblia,* which causes giardiasis (see the Health section of the Facts for the Visitor chapter for more). If you're going to be outdoors take plenty of insect repellent. There are 25 varieties of mosquitoes in the Yukon and you will meet many of them. For advice on bear encounters, pick up the *You are in Bear Country* brochure from a VRC.

Although most communities have local emergency numbers, there are two that work anywhere in the territory. For the police dial ☎ 867-667-5555; for medical emergencies dial ☎ 867-667-3333. Hospitals open 24 hours are found in Whitehorse and Watson Lake. In smaller communities there is usually a doctor or nurse on call after hours.

Activities

The Yukon VRCs can supply you with information and answer questions on hiking, canoeing, rafting, cycling, gold prospecting, skiing, fishing and various adventure trips. There are outfitters and tour companies to handle arrangements, but you really don't need an organized trip and you don't need to be wealthy to fully enjoy the Yukon.

YUKON TERRITORY

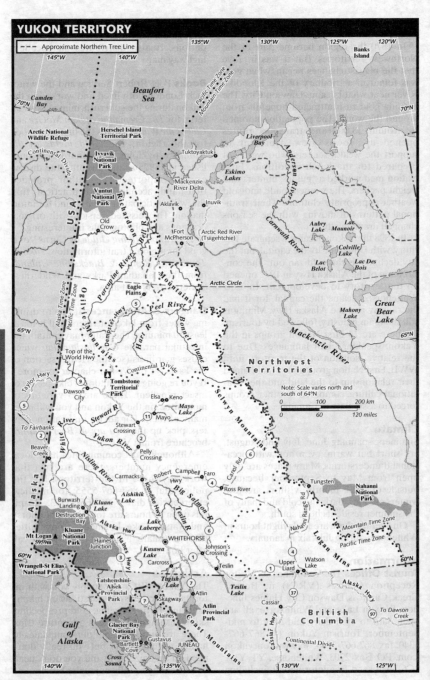

YUKON TERRITORY

- - - Approximate Northern Tree Line

145°W   140°W   135°W   130°W   125°W   120°W

Banks
Island

Beaufort
Sea

Camden
Bay

70°N

Arctic National
Wildlife Refuge

Herschel Island
Territorial Park

Ivvavik
National
Park

Vuntut
National
Park

Old
Crow

Continental Divide

Pacific Time Zone
Mountain Time Zone

Liverpool
Bay

Eskimo
Lakes

Tuktoyaktuk

Mackenzie
River Delta

Aklavik   Inuvik

Fort
McPherson

Arctic Red River
(Tsiigehtchic)

Aubry
Lake

Lac
Maunoir

Colville
Lake

Lac
Belot

Lac Des
Bois

Anderson River

Carnwath River

Richardson Mountains

Porcupine River

Bell R.

USA

Arctic Time Zone
Pacific Time Zone

Arctic Circle

Eagle
Plains

Peel River

Hart R.

Bonnet Plume R.

Mahony
Lake

Great
Bear
Lake

65°N

Ogilvie Mountains

Dempster Hwy

Northwest
Territories

Mackenzie River

Top of the
World Hwy

Continental Divide

Tombstone
Territorial
Park

Note: Scale varies north and
south of 64°N

0   100   200 km

0   60   120 miles

Taylor Hwy

5

Dawson
City

Stewart R.

Elsa   Keno

Mayo
Lake

Selwyn Mountains

11   Mayo

To Fairbanks

2

Beaver
Creek

White River

Nisling River

Yukon River

Stewart
Crossing

2

Pelly
Crossing

Carmacks

Robert Campbell Hwy

Faro

Carol Rd.

6

Ross River

Tungsten

Nahanni
National
Park

Burwash
Landing

Kluane
Lake

Aishihik
Lake

Klondike Hwy

Big Salmon R.

Teslin R.

4

Nahanni Range Rd.

Destruction
Bay

Alaska Hwy

Lake
Laberge

6

Mountain Time Zone
Pacific Time Zone

Mt Logan
5959m

Kluane
National
Park

WHITEHORSE

Logan Mtns

Wrangell-St Elias
National Park

Haines
Junction

3

Kusawa
Lake

Carcross

Johnson's
Crossing

1

Teslin

Upper
Liard

4

Watson
Lake

60°N

Haines Hwy

Tagish
Lake

7

Teslin
Lake

1

Alaska Hwy

Tatshenshini-
Alsek
Provincial Park

7

Skagway

Atlin

Atlin
Provincial
Park

Cassiar

37

To Dawson
Creek

97

Glacier Bay
National
Park

Haines

Bartlett
Cove

Gustavus

JUNEAU

Coast Mountains

Cassiar Hwy

British
Columbia

Continental Divide

Gulf
of
Alaska

Cross
Sound

140°W   135°W   130°W   125°W

Hiking The best known route is the Chilkoot Trail, which begins in Alaska, but Kluane National Park in the territory's southwest corner also has excellent hikes, from short and easy to long and demanding. The Tombstone Mountain area north of Dawson is also good with the North Fork Pass considered the classic hike of the region. N alpine terrain is the MacMillan Pass at the Northwest Territories border, accessible by Canol Rd north from Ross River.

Canoeing Canoeists have many choices, from easy float trips down the waters of the Yukon River and its tributaries to challenging whitewater rivers.

Gentle canoe trips down the Yukon from Whitehorse for a few hours, or 16-day trips all the way to Dawson, are popular. Many people start or end at Carmacks, which is the halfway point, making a shorter eight-day trip. Boat rental and return charges for such an eight-day, one-way trip are about $200 and transportation can be arranged.

Kayaking & Whitewater Rafting The Alsek and Tatshenshini rivers are ranked among the best and wildest in North America. They're found in British Columbia, south of Kluane, and accessible from Haines Junction. Other major areas are the Lapie (near Ross River) and Takhini (north of Whitehorse) rivers.

Fishing For anglers, w www.yukonfishing .com provides regulations and a list of what's where as well as the best time and means to catch your prize salmon, trout or grayling.

Wildlife-Watching Yukon Tourism publishes an excellent *Wildlife Viewing Guide* that details the critters you can expect to see in the territory, many right along the highways.

For an unforgettable introduction into the world of Yukon hunting, pick up the government publication *Hunting Regulations Summary*. Besides telling you how to bag a moose it has a section on determining the sex of caribou that will stay with you long after other memories of your trip fade.

Public Holidays & Special Events

The Yukon Quest In February this 1600km dog sled race goes from Whitehorse to Fairbanks, Alaska.

Kluane Chilkat International Bike Relay Bikers ride 237.8km from Haines Junction to Haines, Alaska, every June.

International Storytelling Festival This June festival in Whitehorse features First Nation participants.

Discovery Day On the third Monday of August, most of the territory shuts down.

Klondike Trail '98 Road Relay In September some 100 running teams of ten each complete the overnight course from Skagway to Whitehorse.

Accommodations

The Yukon government's series of campgrounds along the highways are good; most have drinking water, free firewood and a cooking shelter. Permits are sold at VRCs and stores. There are also private campgrounds, geared toward the recreational vehicle (RV) market, offering hookups, showers and laundry facilities, but some have tent sites. Accommodations prices rise during the short tourist season, so expect to pay more then than you would for comparable accommodations in the south.

Getting Around

The major towns in the Yukon are connected by air and bus (see the Getting There & Away sections for Whitehorse and Dawson City for details).

Driving your own vehicle is the best way to get around, and there are car and RV rental outlets in Whitehorse and car rental in Dawson City.

The road system in the Yukon is fairly extensive, if rough. Remember that many roads are gravel. Most of the Alaska and Klondike Hwys are paved but not necessarily smooth and some parts may be gravel or muck, especially where the never-ending maintenance is taking place. Make certain you are able to change a tire and that you have at least one full-size spare in good condition. Headlights are required to be on at all times on all roads.

Gasoline prices along the highways can be high, so plan your budget accordingly. Generally, along the main routes, there's a service station every 100km, but in some areas there may be nothing for 200km or more. Three places where gasoline is not so expensive are Dawson Creek in British Columbia, Whitehorse and Dawson City.

A good circular trip is to travel the Klondike Hwy (Hwy 2) from Whitehorse to Dawson City, then take the Top of the World Hwy (Hwy 9) to the Alaska border. From the border, take the Taylor Hwy (Hwy 5) south to Tetlin Junction in Alaska where you can follow Hwy 2 to Fairbanks. On the way back take the Alaska Hwy (Hwy 1) southeast past Beaver Creek to Kluane National Park and Haines Junction, then to Whitehorse. This trip, not including a side jaunt to Fairbanks, is 1465km and takes seven to eight days with stops. For a shorter trip, try the Golden Circle loop from Whitehorse to Haines Junction on the Alaska Hwy, then Haines Hwy (Hwy 3) to Haines, Alaska. From here take the car ferry to Skagway and return on the Klondike Hwy to Whitehorse for a total of 579km and four to five days with stops.

For information about road closures due to calamities like floods or major construction, call ☎ 867-456-7623. For Dempster Hwy information call ☎ 800-661-0752.

WHITEHORSE
pop 22,000
Spread along the banks of the Yukon River, Whitehorse is the largest town in the territory. The official city limits cover some 421 sq km, making it one of the largest urban-designated areas in Canada. Despite this, the central core is quite small and it's easy to walk around. Downtown is designed on a grid system and the main traffic routes are 2nd and 4th Aves.

The town sits just off the Alaska Hwy between Dawson Creek in British Columbia (1430km to the east), where the highway starts, and Fairbanks in Alaska (970km west). Despite its growth, Whitehorse still has something of a frontier feel. There's a good local music scene and escaping artists and writers mix with government workers and grizzled old timers. The cafés and restaurants are a welcome sight if you've been out in the backcountry. It's also a good place to repair your windshield.

Information
The VRC (☎ 867-667-3084, 100 Hanson St), open 8am to 8pm daily from mid-May to mid-September with limited winter hours,

provides information on Whitehorse and the Yukon.

Contact the Gay & Lesbian Alliance (☎ 867-667-7857, PO Box 5604, Whitehorse, YT Y1A 5H4) for social activities and information.

The post office (211 Main St) is in the basement of Shoppers Drug Mart and is open 9am to 6pm Monday to Friday and 11am to 4pm Saturday. The public library (☎ 867-667-5239, 2071 2nd Ave) is open 10am to 9pm Monday to Friday, 10am to 6pm Saturday and 1pm to 6pm Sunday; it has free Internet access and provides an updated list of other locations with Internet access in town.

Mac's Fireweed Books (☎ 867-668-2434, fax 867-668-5548, w www.yukonbooks.com, 203 Main St) has a good selection of history, geography and wildlife titles plus a section on First Nation culture. Some German and French books are available. Guidebooks and topographical maps are found downstairs. It's open 8am to midnight daily.

There's a public laundromat (☎ 867-668-5558, 314 Ray St) in the Stop-In Family Hotel that's open 7am to 9pm daily.

Whitehorse General Hospital (☎ 867-393-8700, 5 Hospital Rd) is on the eastern side of the river. To get there, take 2nd Ave east over the Yukon River, then turn north on Hospital Rd.

For police, medical and fire emergencies in Whitehorse, dial ☎ 911.

Things to See & Do
In the town itself there isn't much to see, and what there is can be accomplished in a day.

The dry-docked SS *Klondike* was one of the last and largest sternwheelers used on the Yukon. Built in 1937, it made its final run upriver in 1955 and is now a museum and national historic site (☎ 867-667-4511, *South Access Rd & 2nd Ave; adult/child $4/2.25, includes a guided tour; open 9am-6:30pm daily mid-May–mid-Sept)*.

The log cabin MacBride Museum (☎ 867-667-2709, *1st Ave & Wood St; adult/child $5/3.50; open 10am-6pm daily mid-May–Sept)* with a turf roof has a collection from First Nation cultures, the fur trade, gold-rush days and the construction of the Alaska Hwy. There are also displays of Yukon wildlife and a big canoe.

WHITEHORSE

PLACES TO STAY
3 Stop-In Family Hotel
14 Stratford Motel
19 Westmark Whitehorse Hotel
28 Town & Mountain Hotel
38 Hawkins House B&B
38 High Country Inn
40 Beez Neez Bakpakers
41 Hide on Jeckell Guesthouse
45 Robert Service Campground

PLACES TO EAT
9 Alpine Bakery
10 The Chocolate Claim
15 Tung Lock
16 3 Beans Natural Foods
18 No Pop Sandwich Shop
22 Sam 'n' Andy's
24 Talisman Café

OTHER
1 Whitehorse Subaru
2 Raven's Tale (Westmark Klondike Inn)
4 Whitehorse Transit Bus Stop
5 Qwanlin Mall
6 Greyhound Bus Depot
7 Budget Rent a Car
8 All-West Glass
11 FolkKnits
12 Up North Wilderness Specialists
13 Kanoe People
17 Yukon Historical & Museums Association
20 MacBride Museum
21 Gold Rush Float Tours
23 Royal Bank (ATM)
25 Coast Mountain Sports
26 CIBC Bank (ATM)
27 Alaska Direct Busline
29 Post Office
30 Mac's Fireweed Books
31 Capital Hotel
32 The Old Log Church
33 Visitor Reception Centre
34 Public Library
35 Whitehorse General Hospital
36 Yukon Conservation Society
39 Lions Swimming Pool
42 SS Klondike National Historic Site
43 Yukon Transportation Museum
44 Yukon Beringia Interpretive Centre

To Alaska Hwy North, McIntyre Recreation Center, Yukon Game Farm, Takhini Hot Springs & Klondike Hwy

Kishwoot Island

Two Mile Hill Rd

Quartz Rd

Baxter St

Ray St

Ogilvie St

Cook St

Wheeler St

Black St

Alexander St

Strickland St

Jarvis St

Wood St

Steele St

Main St

Elliott St

Lambert St

Hanson St

Hawkins St

Rogers St

Lowe St

Hoge St

Jeckell St

Taylor St

Drury St

8th Ave

7th Ave

6th Ave

5th Ave

4th Ave

3rd Ave

2nd Ave

1st Ave

Yukon River

Wickstrom Rd

Hospital Rd

Whitehorse Airport

Alaska Hwy

South Access Rd

Waterfront Footpath

Yukon River Trail

To MV Schwatka, Ibex River Valley, Hi Country RV Park & Alaska Hwy South

0   250   500 m
0   250   500 yards

YUKON TERRITORY

Built by the town's first priest in 1900, the **old log church** (☎ 867-668-2555, 303 Elliott St; adult/child $2.50/1; open 10am-6pm daily mid-May–Aug) is the only wooden cathedral in the world and the oldest building in town.

The **Yukon Beringia Interpretive Centre** (☎ 867-667-8855, W www.beringia.com, Kilometer 1473 Alaska Hwy; adult/child $6/4; open 8:30am-7pm daily mid-May–mid-Sept) focuses on Beringia, an area that, during the last Ice Age, encompassed the Yukon, Alaska and eastern Siberia yet was untouched by glaciers. Interactive displays re-create the time. This museum is the most interesting local sight, and it's just south of the airport. From downtown, take the airport bus from Ogilvie St and then walk south for five minutes.

Located close to the Yukon Beringia Interpretive Center, the **Yukon Transportation Museum** (☎ 867-668-4792, 30 Electra Circle; adult/child $4.25/2 or adult $7 with Beringia Centre; open 10am-6pm daily May-Aug) covers the perils and adventures of getting around the Yukon by plane, train, truck and dog sled.

The **Yukon Game Farm** (☎ 867-633-2922, Kilometer 8 Takhini Hot Springs Rd) is 25km northwest of town off the Klondike Hwy. There is a fine selection of northern animals on the rolling 280-hectare spread, which must be visited as part of a Gray Line bus tour (☎ 867-668-3225, Westmark Whitehorse Hotel), which runs at 10:45am and 6pm daily from May to September and costs $21/10.50 adult/child. You may also arrange for pick-up at Takhini Hot Springs; prices are the same.

About 10km off the Klondike Hwy (Hwy 2) north of town in a quiet wooded area are the **Takhini Hot Springs** (☎ 867-633-2706, Kilometer 10 Takhini Hot Springs Rd; adult/child $5.50/4; open 8am-10pm daily). There is also camping at the site (see Places to Stay).

Activities

Around Whitehorse you can go hiking and biking, particularly at **Mt McIntyre Recreation Center**, up Two Mile Hill Rd, **Grey Mountain**, east of town, and along the **Yukon River Trail**, south of town to Fish Ladder and the dam. All along the **Ibex River Valley** west of Whitehorse is good for biking. The hiking trails there become cross-country ski trails in winter. There's a great

swimming pool (☎ 867-668-7665, 4049 4th Ave); call for daily lap and children's swim times year-round.

Whitehorse is the starting place for popular canoe and kayak trips to Carmacks or on to Dawson City. It's an average of eight days to the former and 16 days to the latter. **Kanoe People** (☎ 867-668-4899, fax 867-668-4891, W www.kanoepeople.com, 1st Ave & Strickland St), at the river's edge, can arrange any type of trip (to Carmacks $195/255 in canoe/kayak; to Dawson City $325/450). These prices for unguided trips include an orientation session and drop-off. Bicycle rentals are also available.

Up North Wilderness Specialists (☎ 867-667-7035, fax 867-667-6334, W www.upnorth.yk.ca, 103 Strickland St) offers similar services and competitive prices, with snowmobile trips offered in the winter. Its staff speak German.

Organized Tours

The **Yukon Historical & Museums Association** (☎ 867-667-4704, 3126 3rd Ave) offers downtown walking tours ($2) led by costumed guides four times daily from Monday to Saturday during the summer.

The **Yukon Conservation Society** (☎ 867-668-5678, 302 Hawkins St; open 10am-2pm Mon-Fri July & Aug) arranges free nature hikes in the area, including children's programs.

Gray Line Yukon (☎ 867-668-3225, 201 Wood St in the Westmark Whitehorse Hotel) runs several tours, including the 4½ hour city tour (adult/child $35/17.50) that takes you around town and out to the Yukon Game Farm.

The **MV Schwatka** (☎ 867-668-4716, Schwatka dockside) motors along Schwatka Lake and the Yukon River through Miles Canyon on a pleasant boat ride (adult/child $21/10.50); tours depart 2pm and 7pm daily June to September. Once the most hazardous part of the river journey, this stretch has now been tamed (or ruined) by a dam. This trip can also be combined with the Gray Line Yukon city tour (adult/child $54/27).

Gold Rush Float Tours (☎ 867-633-4836, 1st Ave & Wood St) offers something more adventurous – 2½-hour trips (adult/child $52/29) on re-created gold-rush rafts down the Yukon River. Tours depart daily in summer.

Places to Stay

Camping *Robert Service Campground* (☎ 867-668-3721, e *sercamp@hotmail.com, Robert Service Way*) Tent sites $12. This popular campground along the river is just 1km south of town along the South Access Rd, with showers, firepits and a small store.

Hi Country RV Park (☎ 867-667-7445, fax 867-668-6342, e *hicountryrv@polar com.com, 91374 Alaska Hwy*) RV/tent sites $20/12. At the top of Robert Service Way, this campground in a wooded setting offers hookups, showers, laundry and modem access.

Takhini Hot Springs (☎ 867-633-2706, fax 867-668-2689, w *www.takhinihotsprings .yk.ca, Kilometer 10 Takhini Hot Springs Rd*) RV/tent sites $17.50/12.50. You may camp at these hot springs about 30km northwest of town off the Klondike Hwy.

Yukon Government Campgrounds (☎ 867-667-5648) Sites $8 with firewood. South of Whitehorse on the Alaska Hwy are two campgrounds: Wolf Creek (16km from town), set in a wooded area, and Marsh Lake (50km) with nearby beach access.

Hostels There are two good budget options in Whitehorse.

The Beez Kneez Bakpakers (☎ 867-456-2333, e *hostel@klondiker.com, 408 Hoge St*) Bunks/private room $20/50. This hostel offers a kitchen and Internet access.

Hide on Jeckell Guesthouse (☎ 867-633-4933, w *www.hide-on-jeckell.com, 410 Jeckell*) $20/person. Rates include kitchen facilities, Internet access and strong morning coffee. There's a 10% discount for those arriving by bicycle.

An International Whitehorse Hostel is expected to open across from the VRC in 2002; contact the VRC for updates, as the hostel still hadn't opened at press time.

B&Bs *Hawkins House B&B* (☎ 867-668-7638, fax 867-668-7632, w *www.hawkins house.yk.ca, 303 Hawkins St*) Singles/doubles $129/149, breakfast $7. This lovely Victorian-style establishment has four distinct rooms, each with private bath and balcony.

Motels & Hotels *Stop-In Family Hotel* (☎ 867-668-5558, fax 867-668-5568, e *famhotel@polar.com, 314 Ray St*) Singles/ doubles $75/85 with bath. This well-kept hotel has an elevator, laundry and 24-hour restaurant.

Town & Mountain Hotel (☎ 867-668-7644, 800-661-0522, fax 867-668-5822, w *www.townmountain.com, 401 Main St*) Singles/doubles $69/79 with bath, new rooms with kitchenette $99. The Town & Mountain is a good midrange choice and the new rooms are very comfortable.

Stratford Motel (☎ 867-667-4243, fax 867-668-7432, 401 Jarvis St*) Singles/doubles $69/79. The central Stratford is good; some rooms have kitchenettes.

High Country Inn (☎ 867-667-4471, 800-554-4471, fax 867-668-6457, w *www.high countryinn.yk.ca, 4051 4th Ave*) Rooms $119. The High Country Inn is modern and friendly. Its lively pub has a huge outdoor deck and good barbecue.

Westmark Whitehorse Hotel (☎ 867-668-9700, 800-544-0970, fax 867-668-2789, e *reservations@westmarkwhitehorse.com, 201 Wood St*) Rooms $159. The high-end hotel in town is the Westmark, with nice but unexceptional rooms and good service. Ask about the $129 summer explorer rate.

Places to Eat

Talisman Café (☎ 867-667-2736, 2112 2nd Ave*) Breakfast $6, lunch $6-8, dinner $12. Open 9am-8pm Mon-Fri, 9am-5pm Sat, 9am-3pm Sun. The popular Talisman is tasty for any meal, with good salads and Middle Eastern, Mexican and vegetarian dishes.

No Pop Sandwich Shop (☎ 867-668-3227, 312 Steele St*) Sandwiches $5-7. Open 9am-8:30pm Mon-Thur, 9am-9pm Fri, 10am-7pm Sat, 10am-7pm Sun. This longtime favorite with residents has a patio out back and free Internet access.

The Chocolate Claim (☎ 867-667-2202, 305 Strickland St*) Breakfast & lunch $4-8. Open 7am-7pm Mon-Fri, 7am-6pm Sat. This inviting place has its own bakery with pastries and sandwiches and, as the name implies, fine chocolates.

Sam 'n' Andy's (☎ 867-668-6994, 506 Main St*) Lunch $10, dinner $12-15. Open 11am-11pm daily. Busy Sam 'n' Andy's specializes in Mexican food and big portions. You can have a beer or margarita with your meal in the garden out front.

Tung Lock (☎ 867-668-3298, 404 Wood St*) Lunch $10, dinner $10-20. Open 11am-11pm daily. Of several Chinese restaurants, this one is recommended. Seafood is emphasized, but there is a wide selection of Chinese standards and a few Western dishes.

Alpine Bakery (☎ *867-668-6871, 411 Alexander St*) Prices $2-10. Open 8am-6pm Mon-Sat. This bakery has great bread, rolls and pizza from organic ingredients. The preserves made with Yukon berries are a treat.

Extra Food (☎ *867-667-6251, 303 Ogilvie St*) Open 8:30am-7pm Mon-Sat, until 9pm Thur & Fri, 10am-6pm Sun. For backcountry and paddling provisions, Extra Food in the Qwanlin Mall is the largest supermarket and has a huge bulk-foods section.

3 Beans Natural Foods (☎ *867-668-4908, 308 Wood St*) Open 10am-6pm Mon-Fri, 10am-5:30pm Sat. For good organic, bulk and ethnic food, vitamins and juice, try 3 Beans.

Entertainment

The Raven's Tale (☎ *867-668-6899, 2288 2nd Ave*) Adult/child $19/9.50. Performances 7pm Thur-Sat. This First Nation cultural showcase is staged during the summer at the Westmark Klondike Inn and includes drumming, comedy, storytelling and dance.

Capital Hotel (☎ *867-667-2565, 103 Main St*) This place has a rowdy bar scene and live music almost every night until 2am.

Shopping

Folknits (☎ *867-668-7771, 2151 2nd Ave*) Open 10am-6pm Mon-Sat. Try Folknits for original knitwear and natural fiber yarns, including muskox qiviut.

Coast Mountain Sports (☎ *867-667-4074, 208 Main St*) Open 9:30am-6pm Mon-Sat, until 9pm Thur & Fri, noon-4pm Sunday. Coast Mountain Sports has a large selection of outdoor clothing and equipment, including stove fuel.

Getting There & Away

Air Whitehorse Airport is five minutes west of downtown off the Alaska Hwy. Air Canada (☎ 888-247-2262, w www.air canada.com) has services to/from Vancouver with connections to Edmonton.

Air North (☎ 867-668-2228, 800-661-0407, in the US ☎ 800-764-0407, w www .airnorth.yk.net) connects Whitehorse with Dawson City, Old Crow and Inuvik in the Yukon and Juneau and Fairbanks in Alaska.

First Air (☎ 800-267-1247, w www.firstair .com) flies to Fort Simpson and on to Yellowknife.

You can charter planes with Alkan Air (☎ 867-668-2107, fax 867-667-6117, w www.alkanair.yk.net). In the summer there's a charter service from Frankfurt, Germany, on Condor Air (☎ 800-524-6975, in Frankfurt ☎ 07-939-8800, w www .condoramericas.com).

Bus Whitehorse is the northern end of the road for Greyhound (☎ 867-667-2223, 800-661-8747, w www.greyhound.ca, 2191 2nd Ave), which has services south to Dawson Creek (20 hours, $181), Prince George (28 hours, $232), Vancouver (41 hours, $332) and Edmonton (29 hours, $254). It also provides shipping services.

Dawson City Courier (☎ 867-393-3334) runs daily at 3pm, except Saturday, to Dawson City from the Greyhound Bus Depot (6 hours, $83).

Gray Line of Alaska (☎ 867-668-3225, 800-544-2206, w www.graylineofalaska.com, 201 Wood) operates Alaskon Express buses to Skagway, Haines Junction, Tok, Anchorage and Fairbanks. Trips to Alaska involve an overnight stop so you'll need to add the cost of accommodations. The Anchorage route includes a stop in Beaver Creek, takes two days and costs US$246. Gray Line buses depart from the Westmark Whitehorse Hotel parking lot.

Alaska Direct Busline (☎ 867-668-4833, 800-770-6652, 509 Main St) has buses to Anchorage (18 hours, US$165) and Fairbanks (14 hours, US$140) and points en route such as Haines Junction (two hours, US$40) and Beaver Creek (six hours, $70). This route runs at least once a week in summer and no overnight stop is required. The bus to Skagway is Monday, Tuesday, Thursday & Saturday (three hours, US$50).

For complete details of services to Skagway, including train connections with the White Pass & Yukon, see the Skagway section later in this chapter.

Getting Around

Bus Whitehorse Transit System (☎ 867-668-7433) operates buses Monday to Saturday (no buses on Sunday or public holidays). The one-way fare is $1.50 (exact change) but a day pass for $4 allows unlimited travel. If you're going to the airport take the Hillcrest bus from Qwanlin Mall on Ogilvie St. A bus to Takhini Hot Springs leaves from the same spot.

Car & RV Cars can be rented from the following rental companies; be sure to confirm mileage charges and damage insurance in advance: Budget (☎ 867-667-6200, 800-268-8900, fax 867-667-2732, **w** www.budget.com, 4178 4th Ave); Norcan (☎ 867-668-2137, 800-661-0445, fax 867-633-3110 **w** www.norcan .yk.ca, 213 Range Rd) and Whitehorse Subaru (☎ 867-393-6550, fax 867-393-6551, **e** raman@klondike.com, 2289 2nd Ave). Budget and Norcan have airport service desks and Whitehorse Subaru has the best rates

Klondike Recreational Vehicles (☎ 867-668-2200, fax 867-668-6567, **w** www .klondike-rv.com, 107 Copper Rd) rents all shapes and sizes of RVs from $165-217/day, and you can get them equipped with canoes. They offer one-way rentals to/from Kamloops, British Columbia.

For windshield repair and replacement, try All-West Glass (☎ 867-667-7766, fax 867-667-2513, 4160 4th Ave).

Taxi Try Yellow Cab (☎ 867-668-4811). A trip from the airport into town is about $12.

ALASKA HWY

The Alaska Hwy, the main road in the Yukon, is 2451km long and starts in Dawson Creek, British Columbia. It enters the Yukon in the southeast and passes through Watson Lake, Whitehorse, Haines Junction and Beaver Creek en route to Fairbanks, Alaska. The road is Hwy 97 in British Columbia, Hwy 1 in the Yukon and Hwy 2 in Alaska.

A joint project between the USA and Canada, the highway was built in 1942 as part of the war effort and originally called the Alaska-Canada Military Hwy. The highway is now paved and much tamer than the original, except for a few stretches where road construction is taking place. Here the biggest problems are dust and flying stones from other vehicles, so slow down and keep well to the right. Potholes too can be a problem. A spare tire, fan belt and hose are recommended. Many people attach a bug-and-gravel screen or headlight cover.

Each summer the Alaska Hwy is busy with visitors driving RVs. At times there are 10 of these homes-on-wheels for every car or truck. Services for gasoline, food and lodging occur at regular intervals. Hitchhiking along the highway is good, but be prepared for the occasional long wait and definitely carry a tent, food, water and warm clothing. Don't consider hitchhiking outside of the short summer season.

Watson Lake
pop 1662

Originally named after Frank Watson, a British trapper, Watson Lake is the first town in the Yukon as you head northwest on the Alaska Hwy from British Columbia. The VRC (☎ 867-536-7469, Kilometer 1021 Alaska Hwy) at the junction of the Alaska and Robert Campbell Hwys has a video show on the history of the territory and the Alaska Hwy. It's open 8am to 8pm daily mid-May to mid-September. The town offers campgrounds, motels, gas, ATMs and a Greyhound station. The Watson Lake Library (☎ 867-536-7517) has free Internet access and is open 10am to 8pm Tuesday to Friday, noon to 6pm Saturday.

The town is famous for its **Signpost Forest** just outside the VRC. The first signpost was 'Danville, Illinois' nailed up in 1942 by Carl Lindlay, a homesick US soldier working on the Alaska Hwy. Others added their own signs and now there are over 22,000. You can have your own sign made on the spot.

Twenty-six kilometers west of Watson Lake is the junction with the Cassiar Hwy, which heads south into British Columbia.

Teslin
pop 454

Teslin, on the Nisutlin River 272km west of Watson Lake, began as a trading post in 1903 to serve the Tlingits (lin-**kits**). The Alaska Hwy brought both prosperity and rapid change for this First Nation population. **George Johnston Museum** (☎ 867-390-2550, Kilometer 1294 Alaska Hwy; adult/child $5/3; open 9am-7pm daily mid-May–early Sept) has photographs, displays and artifacts on the Tlingits and the gold-rush days. There's canoeing and camping at nearby Teslin Lake.

Johnson's Crossing & Canol Rd

About 53km north of Teslin is Johnson's Crossing at the junction of the Alaska Hwy and Canol Rd. During World War II, the US army built the Canol pipeline at tremendous human and financial expense to pump oil from Norman Wells in the Northwest Territories to Whitehorse. The only services on Canol Rd (Hwy 6) are in Ross River at the Robert Campbell Hwy (Hwy 4) junction. Canol Rd ends near the Northwest Territories' border. If you want to go any farther you have to hike the demanding **Canol Heritage Trail** (see the Norman Wells section in the Northwest Territories chapter).

Atlin (British Columbia)
pop 400

The small, sleepy town of Atlin, 182km southeast of Whitehorse in British Columbia, is reached by road via the Yukon; take Hwy 7 south from the Alaska Hwy. With forests and glaciers in Atlin Provincial Park and snowcapped mountains rimming the lake, Yukoners head here to **fish**. Atlin is also a pleasant detour for non-anglers with few people and decent **hiking**, lake

canoeing, and **mountain biking** along Warm Springs Rd.

In town, there's gas, groceries, ATMs, a laundromat and the small **Atlin Museum** (☎ 250-651-7552, 3rd St), housed in a 1902 schoolhouse. The museum offers local information and is open from 10am to 6pm Monday to Friday, 11am to 5pm Saturday and Sunday mid-May to mid-September. For more information on the community, visit the website ⓦ www.atlin.net.

There are a number of accommodations options. Try **Brewery Bay Chalet** (☎ 867-651-0040, fax 867-651-0041, ⓔ brewery-bay@atlin.net, McBride Blvd), where rooms with kitchens are $99. **Pine Creek Campground** is 4km from town on Warm Springs Rd; sites cost $5.

Haines Junction
pop 800

Small on the map but large in appeal, Haines Junction makes an excellent base for exploring Kluane National Park or to

---

The Alaska Highway

The construction in 1942 of the Alaska Hwy is considered one of the major engineering feats of the 20th century. Canada and the USA had originally agreed to build an all-weather highway to Fairbanks from the south as early as 1930, but nothing serious was done until WWII. Japan's attack on Pearl Harbor, then its bombing of Dutch Harbor in the Aleutians and occupation of the Aleutian islands of Attu and Kiska, increased Alaska's strategic importance. The US army was told to prepare for the highway's construction a month before Canada's prime minister, WL Mackenzie King, signed the agreement granting the USA permission to do so.

The route chosen for the highway followed a series of existing airfields – Fort St John, Fort Nelson, Watson Lake and Whitehorse – known as the Northwest Staging Route.

Thousands of US soldiers and Canadian civilians, including First Nations, built the 2450km gravel highway between Dawson Creek in British Columbia and Fairbanks in Alaska. They began work on March 9, 1942, and completed it before falling temperatures (in what was to be one of the worst winters in recorded history) could halt the work. Conditions were harsh: sheets of ice rammed the timber pilings; floods during the spring thaw tore down bridges; and bogs swallowed trucks, tractors and other heavy machinery. In the cold months the road crews suffered frostbite, while in the summer they were preyed on by mosquitoes, blackflies and other biting insects.

Despite these hardships, the single-lane pioneer road was completed at the remarkable average rate of 12km a day. The road crews met a little over eight months after construction began at Contact Creek, close to the British Columbia and Yukon border. The highway cost US$135 million, an incredible sum then even as it is now. It was officially opened on November 20 at Soldiers' Summit (Mile 1061) overlooking Kluane Lake in the southwest corner of the Yukon.

The original road had many curves and slopes because, with the bulldozers right behind them, the surveyors didn't have time to pick the best route. In April 1946 the Canadian part of the road (1965km) was officially handed over to Canada. In the meantime private contractors were busy

launch a serious mountaineering, back-country or river trip. Edged by the Kluane Range and surrounding greenbelt, the views are dramatic and access is easy via the Alaska Hwy from Whitehorse (158km) or Tok, Alaska (498km); also by the Haines Hwy (Hwy 3) from Haines, Alaska (237.8km).

The VRC, in the Kluane National Park headquarters building (☎ 867-634-2345, Logan St), is open from 8am to 8pm daily mid-May to mid-September. The VRC has modem hookup and the public library (☎ 867-634-2215) has Internet access 1pm to 5pm Tuesday to Friday and 2pm to 5pm Saturday. The post office, bank, and ATM are inside Madley's Store (☎ 867-634-2200). Madley's, open 8am to 9pm daily, carries everything from fresh berries and smoked salmon to spark plugs and fishing tackle. All shops, lodging and services, including a Shell station (☎ 867-634-2246), are clustered around the Alaska Hwy bend at Haines Hwy.

Alaska Direct Busline (☎ 867-668-4833, 800-770-6652) and Gray Line (☎ 867-668-3225, 800-544-2206, ⓦ www.graylineof alaska.com) operate buses to and from Whitehorse that stop in Haines Junction at least once a week. There is no longer bus service to Haines, Alaska. Note that hitch-hiking can be very slow on Haines Hwy as there are no residents and fewer visitors than on the Alaska Hwy. To reach Haines, Alaska, on public transport go through Whitehorse to Skagway.

Activities Besides the trails in Kluane National Park for **mountain biking**, you can also ride an old stretch of the Alaska Hwy along the Dezadeash River. Take Hume St past the Gateway Hotel and follow the straight ribbon of dirt through the trees. Marshall Creek may stop you from riding to the present Alaska Hwy for a rolling 20km one-way trip. Haines Hwy is popular for **cycling** with a good surface/shoulder and two campgrounds en route to Haines,

The Alaska Highway

widening, graveling and straightening the highway; leveling its steep grades; and replacing temporary bridges with permanent steel ones. In 1949 the Alaska Hwy was opened to full-time civilian travel and for the first time year-round overland travel to Alaska from the south was possible.

The completion of the highway opened the northwest to exploitation of its natural resources, changed settlement patterns and altered the First Nations' way of life forever.

The name of the highway has gone through several incarnations. It has been called the Alaskan International Hwy, the Alaska Military Hwy and the Alcan (short for Alaska-Canada) Hwy. More irreverently, in the early days it was also known as the Oil Can Hwy and the Road to Tokyo. Officially, it is now called the Alaska Hwy but many people still affectionately refer to it simply as the Alcan.

The Alaska Hwy begins at 'Mile 0' in Dawson Creek in northeastern British Columbia and goes to Fairbanks, Alaska, although the official end is at Delta Junction (Mile 1422), about 155km southeast of Fairbanks (Mile 1523).

Milepost signs were set up in the 1940s to help drivers calculate how far they had traveled along the road. Since then improvements, including the straightening of the road, mean that its length has been shortened and the mileposts can't be used literally. On the Canadian side the distance markers are in kilometers. Mileposts are still much in evidence in Alaska, and communities on both sides of the border still use the original mileposts for postal addresses and as reference points.

Until the mid-1970s conditions along the highway were extremely difficult. The highway is now almost completely paved except for stretches where road crews are doing maintenance work on potholes and frost heaves (raised sections of pavement caused by water freezing below). Millions of dollars are spent annually on maintaining and upgrading the road.

Although it's possible to travel the highway year-round, most visitors go between May and September when the weather is warmer and road conditions less hazardous. In winter the road is left mostly to trucks.

Alaska. This scenic 237.8km ride has a gradual 457m elevation gain and is also the course for the Kluane Chilkat International Bike Relay. At Pine Lake campground, 6km east of town on the Alaska Hwy there's good **swimming**, picnic tables and a sandy beach with firepits. **Rock climbing** is possible at nearby Paint Mountain.

Paddlewheel Adventures (☎ 867-634-2683, W www.paddlewheeladventures.com, Logan St), opposite the VRC, arranges Tatshenshini rafting trips ($100/person, includes lunch), Kluane helicopter hikes and other tours and fishing trips at reasonable prices. It rents mountain bikes or canoes ($25/day) and provides local transportation (see the Tatshenshini-Alsek Park section later).

On a sunny day, show up early at the airport for an inspiring 40- to 120-minute flight over the icy heart of Kluane National Park with **Kluane Glacier Tours** (☎ 867-634-2916, fax 867-634-2034, Kilometer 1632 Alaska Hwy), which charges $115 to $325 per person with three passengers; tour leave daily year-round.

You can also land, camp and ski on the glacier below Mt Logan with **Icefield Discovery** (☎ 841-4561, in winter ☎ 867-668-6744, fax 867-633-2018, W www.icefields.ca, Kilometer 1693 Alaska Hwy). Flights leave from the Silver City airstrip from April to September. With four passengers, trips cost $580 per person per night, including food, lodging and some clothing.

Places to Stay & Eat

Pine Lake Campground Sites $8. On the Alaska Hwy 6km from town, this government campground is a good choice, with wooded sites and a day-use area. In town there's *Kluane RV Campground* (☎ 867-634-2709, fax 867-634-2735, Kilometer 1635 Alaska Hwy) Without/with hookups $13/20. The grounds have public showers and a laundromat.

Paddlewheel Cabins (☎ 867-634-2683, Auriol St) Cabin $50. Opposite the Village Bakery, Paddlewheel Adventures has two great, well-equipped cabins with wood stoves, small kitchens and a shared bath.

The Cozy Corner Motel (☎ 867-634-2511, fax 867-634-2119, Alaska Hwy) Singles/doubles $59/69. Open year-around, this motel has standard, clean rooms with baths and good views.

The Raven Motel (☎ 867-634-2500, fax 867-634-2517, e kluaneraven@yknet.yk.ca, 181 Alaska Hwy) Singles/doubles $110/125, including breakfast picnic box. The Raven has deluxe motel rooms with baths, one with disabled access, and a well-known restaurant.

Village Bakery & Deli/Fish Hook Smokehouse (☎ 867-634-2867, Logan St) Prices $4-10. Open 7:30am-9pm daily. Opposite the VRC, this laid-back place with an outdoor deck has delicious pizza, soup and sandwiches. Don't miss the salmon barbecue ($14.95) with live music at 7pm on Monday from June to August.

The Raven (☎ 867-634-2500, 181 Alaska Hwy) Dinner mains $27-35. Open 5:30pm-9pm daily, reservations recommended. For fine French/Italian inspired cuisine and Canadian wines, try the Raven.

Kluane National Park & Reserve

This rugged and magnificent wilderness covers 22,015 sq km in the southwest corner of the Yukon. With British Columbia's Tatshenshini-Alsek Provincial Park to the south and Alaska's Wrangell-St Elias National Park to the west, this is one of the largest protected wilderness areas in the world. Kluane (**kloo-wah-neee**), which is a Unesco world heritage site, gets its name from the Southern Tutchone word for 'lake with many fish.'

There are two information centers operated by Parks Canada. In Haines Junction (☎ 867-634-7250, fax 867-634-7208, W www.parkscanada.gc.ca, PO Box 5495, Haines Junction, YT Y0B 1L0), the facility on Logan St is shared with the Yukon VRC. It's open 9am to 7pm daily from May to September, with limited hours Monday to Friday in winter. There are nature displays, a good introductory video and schedules for free interpretative programs and guided hikes ($10). A second center at Sheep Mountain (Kilometer 1706.8 Alaska Hwy) is open 9am to 5pm daily from mid-May to mid-September and is the starting point for hikes at the north end.

The park consists primarily of the still growing **St Elias Mountains** and the world's largest nonpolar **icefields**. Two-thirds of the park is glacier and interspersed are valleys, glacial lakes, alpine forest, meadows and tundra. The Kluane Ranges (averaging 2500m) are seen along the western edge of the Alaska Hwy. A green belt wraps around the base where most of the animals and vegetation live. Turquoise **Kluane Lake** is the Yukon's largest. Hidden are the immense icefields and the towering peaks with **Mt Logan** (5959m), Canada's highest mountain, and **Mt St Elias** (5488m), the second highest. Partial glimpses of the interior peaks can be found at the Kilometer 1622 viewpoint on the Alaska Hwy from Whitehorse and around the Donjek River Bridge, but the best views are definitely from the air.

The greenbelt area of the park is a great place for **hiking**, either along marked trails or less defined routes. There are about a dozen in each category, some following old mining roads, others traditional First Nation paths. The Parks Canada hiking leaflet has a map and lists the trails with distances and starting points, including possibilities for **mountain biking**. Detailed trail guides and topographical maps are available at the information centers. Talk to the rangers before setting out. They will help select a hike and provide updates on areas that may be closed due to bear activity. **Overnight hikes** require backcountry permits ($5/person/night) and you must have a bear-proof food canister. Parks Canada has 50 canisters provided along with permits on a first-come, first-served basis. The canisters help to gauge the number of people in the park and rangers say they rarely run out. There is also a mandatory orientation talk.

The Sheep Mountain information center is the starting point for **Slims West**, a popular 60km roundtrip trek to **Kaskawulsh Glacier** – one of the few that can be reached on foot. This is a difficult and world-class route that takes from three to five days to complete. An easy overnight trip is the 5.8km (each way) **Bullion Creek** trail. **Sheep Creek** is a moderate 10km day hike. The **Auriol** trail starts 7km south of the town and is a 15km loop above the tree line for some good views. From Kathleen Lake, **King's Throne** is a 5km one-way route with a steep 1220m elevation gain. Great views of the Alsek Valley are waiting at the top.

Fishing is good and wildlife abounds. Most noteworthy are the thousands of Dall sheep that can be seen on Sheep Mountain in April, May and September. There's a large and diverse population of grizzly bears, as well as black bears, moose,

The fishing is good in Kluane.

caribou, goats and 150 varieties of birds, among them eagles and the rare peregrine falcon.

Famous among mountaineers, the internationally renowned **Icefield Ranges** provide excellent climbing on Mt Logan, Mt Kennedy and Mt Hubbard. April, May and June are considered the best months and climbers should contact the park warden well in advance for information and permits (☎ 867-634-7279, fax 867-634-7277).

The only *campground* technically within the park is at Kathleen Lake, 24km south of Haines Junction off the Haines Hwy. Open from mid-June through September, sites are $10 and reservations are not accepted.

Winters are long and can be harsh, though some venture out on skis or snowshoes starting in February. Summers are short and generally temperatures are comfortable from mid-June to mid-September, which is the best time to visit. Note that freezing temperatures can occur at any time, especially in the high country, so bring appropriate clothing and rain gear.

Destruction Bay
pop 50

This small village on the shore of Kluane Lake is 107km north of Haines Junction. Like Haines Junction and Beaver Creek, it started off as a camp and supply depot during the construction of the Alaska Hwy. It was given its present name after a storm tore through the area. There's boating and fishing on Kluane Lake and the village has a gas station and government campground at *Congdon Creek* (Kilometer 1723 Alaska Hwy). Tent camping is not recommended here from mid-July to September because of the area's abundant ripe berries, a principal food source for bears.

Burwash Landing
pop 65

Nineteen kilometers north of Destruction Bay, Burwash Landing predates the Alaska Hwy with a brief gold strike on nearby 4th of July Creek. It's also home of the Kluane First Nation and noted for the **Kluane Museum** (☎ 867-841-5561, *Kilometer 1759 Alaska Hwy; adult/child $3.75/2; open 9am-9pm daily mid-May–early Sept*). The museum features animal exhibits and displays on natural and First Nation history. Burwash Landing has a gas station and there's free camping on the lawn at **Burwash Landing Resort** (☎ 867-841-4441, fax 867-841-4040) just off the highway.

Beaver Creek
pop 112

Beaver Creek, Canada's westernmost town, is on the Alaska Hwy 457km northwest of Whitehorse and close to the Alaska border. The VRC (☎ 867-862-7321, Kilometer 1202 Alaska Hwy) has a wildflower exhibit and information on the Yukon and Alaska from 8am to 8pm daily mid-May to mid-September. The Canadian customs checkpoint is just north of town; the US customs checkpoint is 27km farther west. The border is open 24 hours and is a low-key affair (see the Facts for the Visitor chapter for US border crossing information).

Westmark Inn Beaver Creek (☎ 867-862-7501, 800-544-0920, fax 867-862-7902, 1202 Alaska Hwy) Hostel $20/person with shared bath, single/double rooms with bath $79/99. The nice hostel rooms are a good deal, especially for single travelers. The dining room serves breakfast and dinner.

Snag Lake Campground Sites $8. At Kilometer 1913, this okay government campground has only lake water, which must be treated before using.

Tatshenshini-Alsek Provincial Park (British Columbia)

Tucked along the southern Yukon border west of Hwy 3, this remote and rugged 2.4 million-acre park (☎ 250-847-7320, 867-634-7043, **w** wlapwww.gov.bc.ca/bcparks) is also part of the regional Unesco world heritage site designation. It's home to thousands of bald eagles, rare glacier bears and numerous other species. The park can be viewed and some trails accessed from

abandoned roads along the Haines Hwy (Hwy 3) south of Haines Junction to Klukwan, Alaska. The few trailheads are not marked and there are no facilities of any kind in the park at the present time. Only hunting is regulated.

The best way to visit this area and hike is on a whitewater rafting trip down the Grade III and IV rapids of the 'Tat' run by companies from Haines Junction in the Yukon and Haines, Alaska (see those sections for details). These trips should be booked well in advance. Note that for independent rafters, most of the permits (only one boat in every other day) are issued to commercial companies and there is a long waiting list for the rest. Contact the Kluane National Park office for details. The standard float trip down the Tat is about ten days.

Shorter mountain bike trips in the park can also be arranged (see the Haines (Alaska) section, below).

HAINES (ALASKA)
pop 2400

This pretty harbor town sits on the Lynn Canal at the end of Hwy 3 from Haines Junction in the Yukon. Surrounded by mountains with the salty smell of the sea, Haines is wonderfully quiet compared to other southeastern Alaska towns, as few cruise ships dock here in the summer. There are three state parks and good hiking. Haines is also the departure point for longer raft trips on the Tatshenshini or Alsek in British Columbia, flights to Alaska's Glacier Bay National Park and the Inland Passage on the Alaska Marine Hwy.

The Haines Visitor Bureau (☎ 907-766-2234, fax 907-766-3155, **e** hcvb@haines .ak.us, 122 2nd Ave) has area trail maps available 8am to 6pm Monday to Friday and 10am to 4pm Saturday and Sunday May to September. The US Post Office (☎ 907-766-2930, Mile 0 Haines Hwy), open 9am to 5:30pm Monday to Friday, 10am to 4pm Saturday, is next to Quick Stop Laundry (☎ 907-766-2330). The laundry is open 7am to midnight daily and has coin showers.

The public library (☎ 907-766-2545, 103 Third Ave) is open daily and provides free Internet access. First National Bank of Anchorage (☎ 907-766-2321, 123 Main St) has an ATM and is open 10am to 5pm Monday to Friday.

For police, medical and fire emergencies dial ☎ 911. Haines is on Alaska time, which is one hour earlier than the Yukon. For more coverage of Haines and Skagway, see Lonely Planet's *Alaska*.

Things to See & Do
American Bald Eagle Foundation (☎ *907-766-3094, Haines Hwy & 2nd Ave; adult/child US$3/1, open 9am-5pm daily*) The center features an impressive display of more than 100 species of eagles and a video of the massive annual gathering of bald eagles at Chilkat River.

Fort Seward, the first and for a time the only army post in Alaska, was established in the early 1900s and designated a national historical site in 1972. The **Alaska Indian Arts Center** (☎ 907-766-2160, W www .alaskaindianarts.com, 13 Ft Seward Dr; open 9am-5pm Mon-Fri) in the former post hospital, features five resident artists working in the Tlingit manner. A small gallery sells their work. Commissioned totem poles are usually in progress.

At the **Alaska Chilkat Bald Eagle Preserve**, from Mile 9 to Mile 32 along the Haines Hwy, there is a local population of eagles that congregate by the thousands in November for the late salmon run. There are no facilities; park your vehicle only in turnouts.

South of town on the **Chilkat Peninsula** is the lovely 11.3km **Seduction Point** coastal trail and the steep 4.5km climb to **Mt Riley**; north of Haines is the demanding all-day route to **Mt Ripinsky** summit (1095m). Stop at the visitor bureau for the detailed *Haines is for Hikers* pamphlet before setting out.

Sockeye Cycle Company (☎ *907-766-2869, W www.cyclealaska.com, 24 Portage St*), with locations here and in Skagway, offers mountain bike rentals (US$30/day), advice on routes and guided tours, including the popular Chilkat Pass in Tatshenshini-Alsek Park (US$120/320 day/overnight).

Chilkat Guides (☎ *907-766-2491, fax 907-766-2409, W www.raftalaska.com, Saw Mill Rd*) offers unforgettable wilderness raft trips down the Tatshenshini and Alsek Rivers to the coast of Glacier Bay from July to September. The 10-day Tat trip costs US$1975 per person; the 13-day Alsek is

US$2400/person. In Haines, there's a four-hour daily raft trip (adult/child US$82/41) through the Bald Eagle Preserve that's appropriate for children, though they must be at least seven years old.

Places to Stay & Eat
Portage Cove Sites US$5 with water, privies and firepits. This small waterfront campground for cyclists and walk-ins is 3.2km from the center of town; follow Front St south, which becomes Beach Rd, and around the cove past Fort Seward.

Chilkat State Park Sites US$5 with water, privies and firepits. On the scenic Chilkat Peninsula 11.2km southeast of Haines on Mud Bay Rd, this park has good views of Lynn Canal and of the Davidson and Rainbow Glaciers.

Summer Inn B&B (☎/*fax 907-766-2970, W www.summerinn.wytbear.com, 247 2nd Ave*) Singles/doubles US$70/80 with full breakfast. This B&B is right in town.

Fireweed (☎ *907-766-3838, 37 Blacksmith Rd*) Prices US$4-16. Open 11am-10pm daily. For salads, pasta and pizza on a sunny deck try Fireweed in Ft Seward.

Mountain Market (☎ *907-766-3340, 312 3rd Ave*) Prices US$4-10. Open 7am-7pm Mon-Fri, 7am-5pm Sat & Sun. This busy market has a café with bagels, big sandwiches and Sunday brunch.

Getting There & Away
The best way to reach Haines from the Yukon is by driving the scenic Haines Hwy. Ferries link Haines with Skagway. There is no bus service to Haines Junction from Haines and hitchhiking can be very slow. Instead, take a ferry to Skagway for bus connections to Whitehorse and the Yukon.

Haines-Skagway Water Taxi (☎ 907-766-3395, 888-766-3395, e watertaxi@lynn canal.com, Front & Main Sts) charges US$24/12 adult/child, US$5 for a bike. Boats go daily from the small harbor, mid-May to mid-September.

The Alaska Marine Highway (☎ 907-465-3941, 800-642-0066, fax 907-465-2476, W www.alaska.gov/ferry, Lutak Rd) ferry costs US$19/10 adult/child, plus US$28 for a car. The car and passenger ferry, 7.2km from downtown, goes at least once a day between the two towns in the summer and heads south through the Inland Passage.

GLACIER BAY NATIONAL PARK (ALASKA)

Sixteen tidewater glaciers spill out from the mountains to the sea, making this unusual icy preserve one of the most renowned in the world. The glaciers here are in retreat, revealing plants and animals that fascinate naturalists. The humpback whales are by far the most impressive, but there are also harbor seals, porpoises, orcas and sea otters. Above the waterline are brown and black bears, wolves, moose and 200 species of birds. Most people prefer to kayak the small inlets and bays, particularly Muir, where cruise ships are not allowed. There are few trails except around the park headquarters (☎ 907-697-2627, W www.nps.gov/glba) in Bartlett Cove.

There are a number of expensive inns and cabins in Gustavus, the small village adjacent to the park, but the best place to stay is the free *campground* near park headquarters.

Glacier Bay Lodge (☎ 907-697-2225, 800-622-2042, fax 907-697-2408, W *www.glacierbaylodge.com*) Dorm bunk/double room US$28/165. This lodge at Bartlett Cove has van service to/from Gustavus (US$10) and catamaran service up the bay to park campsites for backpackers and kayakers (US$167.50/person).

The only boat connections to Glacier Bay are from Juneau, Alaska, but it's a quick flight to Gustavus. Skagway Air (☎ 907-766-3233, 907-983-2218, W www.skagwayair.com) has daily service from Haines airport (US$80/150 one-way/roundtrip) and Skagway (US$90/170). Reservations are recommended.

ROBERT CAMPBELL HWY

From Watson Lake, this 588km gravel road (Hwy 4) is an alternative route north to Dawson City; it meets the Klondike Hwy near Carmacks. Named after Robert Campbell, a 19th century explorer and trader with the Hudson's Bay Company, it's a scenic and less traveled route that parallels several major rivers and has few services.

Ross River, 373km from Watson Lake at the junction with the Canol Rd (Hwy 6), is home to the Kaska First Nation and a supply center for the local mining industry. There's a campground and motels in town and a government campground at Lapie Canyon. Little-used Canol Rd goes northeast to the Northwest Territories border and the **Canol Heritage Trail** (see Norman Wells in the Northwest Territories chapter).

Faro, 10km off the Robert Campbell Hwy on the Pelly River, was created in 1968 to support the huge copper, lead and zinc mine in the Anvil Mountains. The mine is currently shut, but has opened and closed several times depending on world markets. There are motels, a campground nearby and some trails around town. Sheep Trail is an 8km roundtrip, others lead to a waterfall or Mount Mye. Wildlife are abundant, particularly Fannin (Dall) sheep.

KLONDIKE HWY

The 716km Klondike Hwy, from Skagway in Alaska, through the northwestern corner of British Columbia and on to Whitehorse and Dawson City, more or less follows the trail some 40,000 gold seekers took in 1898. The highway, open year-round, is paved most of the way but there are some long stretches of gravel where construction is taking place. Smoke and forest fires (or their scorched remains) may be found through the summer but the road is rarely closed. The stretch from Skagway to Carcross is a scenic marvel of lakes and mountains.

Skagway (Alaska)
pop 800

Skagway is a little town that most travelers either love or hate. Although it's in the USA, it can only be reached by car using the Klondike Hwy from the Yukon through British Columbia. It's the starting point for the famed Chilkoot Trail and the White Pass & Yukon Route narrow gauge railroad. Alaska Marine Highway ferries link the town with Haines, Alaska, and points south as far as Prince Rupert, British Columbia, and Bellingham, Washington. It's also the most popular stop for Alaska cruise lines. John Muir described Skagway during the gold-rush era as 'an anthill stirred with a stick.' You'll recall this quote on summer afternoons when cruise ships dump as many as 7500 day-tripping passengers on the narrow streets. To avoid the swarm, plan to visit between Friday and Monday when fewer vessels dock.

From the ferry terminal, the foot and vehicle traffic spills onto Broadway and the center of town. There's a post office, bank with ATM, campgrounds, hotels, restaurants and shops, some selling furs and diamonds. Most of the buildings have been restored and for about eight blocks it's a shoppers delight (or nightmare depending on your perspective). The Klondike Hwy runs into the center from the opposite end.

For police, fire and medical emergencies dial ☎ 911. Skagway is on Alaska time, which is one hour earlier than the Yukon.

Information The Skagway Visitor Bureau (☎ 907-983-2854, fax 907-983-3854, e info skag@aptalaska.net, 245 Broadway) has complete area details and is open 8am to 5pm daily year-round. The US National Park Service (☎ 907-983-2921, Broadway & 2nd St) offers free daily walking tours and the *Skagway Trail Map* for area hikes; visit them 8am to 8pm daily June to August, 8am to 6pm daily May and September. Across the street is the Trail Center (☎ 907-983-3655, 800-661-0486, w www.nps.gov/klgo, Broadway & 2nd). Run by Parks Canada and the US National Park Service, the center provides advice, permits, maps and a list of transportation options to/from the Chilkoot Trail (see Chilkoot Trail, below). It's open 8am to 4:15pm daily from the end May to early September.

Skaguay News Depot & Books (☎ 907-983-3354, 264 Broadway) has a good selection of regional titles and topographical maps available for purchase 8:30am to 8:30pm Monday to Friday and 8:30am to 7:30pm Saturday and Sunday.

Places to Stay & Eat There is free camping, but no water at ***Dyea Campground*** 14km from town on Dyea Rd at the start of the Chilkoot Trail. Near the ferry, try ***Pullen Creek RV Park*** *(☎ 907-983-2768, 800-936-3731, 501 Congress St),* where sites with/without hookups are US$24/18.

Reservations are strongly recommended in Skagway. Two options in town follow.

Skagway Inn B&B *(☎ 907-983-2289, 888-752-4929, fax 907-983-2713, e info@skagway inn.com, Broadway & 7th St)* Rooms $99. Rates include a large breakfast and transportation to the Chilkoot Trail.

Golden North Hotel *(☎ 907-983-2451, fax 907-983-2755, e corrington@msn.com, Broadway & 3rd St)* Singles/doubles US$65/75 with shared bath, US$95/105 with private bath. This place is over 100 years old and was renovated in 1998. There's a brewery on site.

Northern Lights Pizza *(☎ 907-983-3463, Broadway & 4th St)* Prices US$6-16. Open 11am-11pm daily. For strange decor and big portions of Mexican, Greek and Italian food, try this pizzeria.

Stowaway Cafe *(☎ 907-983-3463, 205 Congress St)* Prices US$12-22. Open 11am-10pm Mon-Fri, 4pm-10pm Sat & Sun. Near the harbormaster's office, this cozy cafe with harbor views features fresh seafood and Cajun-style dishes; beware of the lunch stampede from nearby cruise ships during the week.

Getting There & Away From Skagway to Whitehorse on the Klondike Hwy (Hwy 2) is 177km. The road is modern and paved and customs at the border is a no-hassle affair.

The White Pass & Yukon Route (☎ 907-983-2217, 800-343-7373, fax 907-983-2734, w www.whitepassrailroad.com, 2nd Ave & Spring St) costs adult/child US$82/41 one-way, US$95/47.50 with connecting bus to/from Whitehorse. Primarily a tourist train, the White Pass & Yukon offers roundtrip daily sightseeing tours of this truly gorgeous route into Canada that parallels the original White Pass trail. The trains were once the only link to Whitehorse, but now they terminate in Fraser, British Columbia, just over the Canadian border. Trains run mid-may to mid-September.

From Friday to Monday, one train daily goes 32km beyond Fraser to Lake Bennett (adult/child US$128/64, including lunch), which also provides a wonderful return to Skagway for hikers at the end of the Chilkoot Trail (US$65/32.50). Restoration of the tracks from Lake Bennett to Carcross is underway and service is planned along this very scenic stretch.

Several bus companies offer services between Skagway and Whitehorse: Alaska Direct (☎ 907-668-4833, 800-770-6652, US$50, four weekly); Alaska Overland (☎ 907-983-3711, US$30, daily) and Gray Line's Alaskon Express (☎ 907-983-2241, 800-544-2206, US$46, daily).

Skagway is the northern terminus of the Alaska Marine Highway's (☎ 907-465-3941, 800-642-0066, fax 907-465-2476,

W www.alaska.gov/ferry) Inside Passage route through Southeast Alaska and on to Prince Rupert, British Columbia, and Bellingham, Washington. This spectacular voyage can be the highlight of any trip and should be reserved months in advance. (You can try standby but you may not get on.) The schedules vary widely from day to day. The trip from Prince Rupert takes 34 hours. One-way fare is adult/child US$143/72; with a car add US$314; with a berth or cabin add US$51-134, and meals are extra. Most prefer to camp on the deck. (See Haines earlier in this chapter for details on passenger ferries to/from that town.)

Chilkoot Trail

Skagway was the landing point for many in the gold-rush days of the late 1890s. From there began the long, slow, arduous and often deadly haul inland to the Klondike goldfields near Dawson City. One of the main routes from Skagway, the Chilkoot Trail over the Chilkoot Pass, is now extremely popular with hikers.

The well'-marked 53km trail begins near Dyea, 14km northwest of Skagway, then heads northeast following the Taiya River to Lake Bennett in British Columbia, and takes three to five days to hike. It's considered a difficult route with good weather and can be treacherous in bad. You must be in good physical condition and come fully equipped. Layers of warm clothes and rain gear are essential. Single hikers will not have a problem finding company.

Along the trail you'll see hardware, tools and supplies dumped by the gold seekers. At several places there are wooden shacks where you can put up for the night, but these are usually full so a tent and sleeping bag are required. There are 10 designated campgrounds along the route, each with bear caches. The most strenuous part of the trail is over the Chilkoot Pass. The elevation gain on the trail is 1110m.

At the Canadian end you can either take the train from Lake Bennett back to Skagway or you can catch a bus on the Klondike Hwy to Whitehorse or Skagway. Chilkoot Water Charters (☎ 867-821-3209) has a water shuttle ($55, reservations required) on the lake to Carcross, where you can also connect with buses.

The Chilkoot Trail is a primary feature of the **Klondike Gold Rush International Historic Park**, a series of sites managed by both Parks Canada and the US National Park Service that stretches from Seattle, Washington to Dawson City. See the Skagway section above for details on contacting both services, which issue a preparation guide for the trail and an all-but-mandatory trail map (US$2).

Each hiker must obtain one of the 50 permits available each day. Parks Canada/US National Park Service (☎ 867-667-3910, ☎/fax 907-983-3655, W www.nps.gov/klgo) charges $35 for a permit plus $10 for a reservation. The permits must be picked up from the Trail Office in Skagway (see that section). Each day seven permits are issued on a first-come, first-served basis, but it's best to have a reservation to guarantee your camping sites and day over the summit as this is a very popular hiking route.

Carcross
pop 427

Carcross, 74km southeast of Whitehorse, is the first settlement you reach in the Yukon from Skagway on the Klondike Hwy. The site was once a major seasonal hunting camp of the Tagish people, who called the area *'Todezzane,'* or 'blowing all the time.' The present town name is an abbreviation of Caribou Crossing and refers to the local woodland caribou herds. The VRC (☎ 867-821-4431) is in the old train station and provides a walking tour pamphlet of the area buildings, many removed from Bennett by boat when the White Pass & Yukon railway extended north and that town was abandoned in 1900. It's open 8am to 8pm daily mid-May to mid-September.

Two kilometers north of town, **Carcross Desert**, the world's smallest, is the exposed sandy bed of a glacial lake that retreated after the last Ice Age. Strong winds allow little vegetation to grow.

Whitehorse to Carmacks

North of Whitehorse between the Takhini Hot Springs Rd and Carmacks the land is dry and scrubby, although there are some farms with cattle and horses. The Klondike Hwy skirts several lakes where you can go swimming, boating and fishing. The largest is lovely **Lake Laberge** with a beach, 40km north of Whitehorse, followed by **Fox Lake**, 24km farther north, and **Twin Lakes**, 23km south of Carmacks. Each has a government *campground* with shelters and pump water. Near Carmacks the mountains become lower, more rounded hills and the land more forested. On the way to Dawson City, gas stations have taken to selling cinnamon buns the size of bear cubs.

Carmacks
pop 400
Perched on the banks of the Yukon River, Carmacks was once a fueling station for riverboats and a stopover on the overland trail from Whitehorse to Dawson City. Originally known as Tantalus, the town name was changed to Carmacks to honor George Washington Carmack who, along with Skookum Jim and Tagish Charley, discovered gold at Bonanza Creek in 1896 and sparked the Klondike gold rush. There are gas stations, a campground and motels here, as well as a junction for the Campbell Hwy (see the Robert Campbell Hwy section earlier).

North of town about 25km, the **Five Finger Recreation Site** has stairs that lead to a path overlooking rocky outcrops in the Yukon River which caused no end of trouble for riverboats.

Stewart Crossing
pop 50
Once a supply center between Dawson City and Whitehorse, Stewart Crossing sits at the junction of the Klondike Hwy (Hwy 2) and the Silver Trail (Hwy 11), another route taken by prospectors in search of silver. Canoeists can put in here for the

very good, five-day **float trip** down the Stewart River to the Yukon River and on to Dawson City. Though you travel through wilderness, and wildlife is commonly seen, it is a trip suitable for the inexperienced. Canoeists should organize and outfit in Whitehorse or Dawson City (see Activities in those sections).

Silver Trail
The Silver Trail heads northeast to three old mining and fur-trading towns: Mayo, Elsa and Keno. The road is paved as far as Mayo. There are some outdoor possibilities in the area as well as campgrounds and other lodgings, although there are no services in Elsa. **Mt Haldane** is 26km beyond Mayo with a 6km trail to the top and good views. **Keno Hill** in Keno City, with its signposts and distances to cities all over the world, offers more views of the mountains and valleys. There are hiking trails in the vicinity, ranging from 2km to 20km long, providing access to old mining areas and alpine meadows.

Tintina Trench
The Tintina Trench can be seen from a lookout 60km south of Dawson City. The trench, which holds much of the Yukon's mineral wealth, is also its most important geological feature, with sides of the valley revealing evidence of plate tectonics.

DAWSON CITY
pop 2000
Dawson City, a compact town at the confluence of the Yukon and Klondike rivers just 240km south of the Arctic Circle, became

YUKON TERRITORY

The Yukon Cracks Up

The river that gives the Yukon Territory its name begins in a web of tributaries near the Llewellyn Glacier in northwest British Columbia. Although the majority of its 3200km length and its delta are in Alaska, the stretch of the Yukon in the Yukon itself is fabled for its historic and natural wonder.

From the 1890s until after WWII, the river was both a vital and dangerous link from Whitehorse to Dawson City. Its turbulent waters are opaque with glacial silt and mud, which hide submerged hazards. Each April or May the break-up of the frozen waters produces earth-shaking floes that see truck-sized chunks of ice tossed about like toys. Dawson City celebrates this impossible-to-schedule event each year and there is a contest to guess when the first cracks will appear. The break-up is not all fun and games, however. In 1979 an ice jam at Dawson City backed up water and flooded the town.

DAWSON CITY

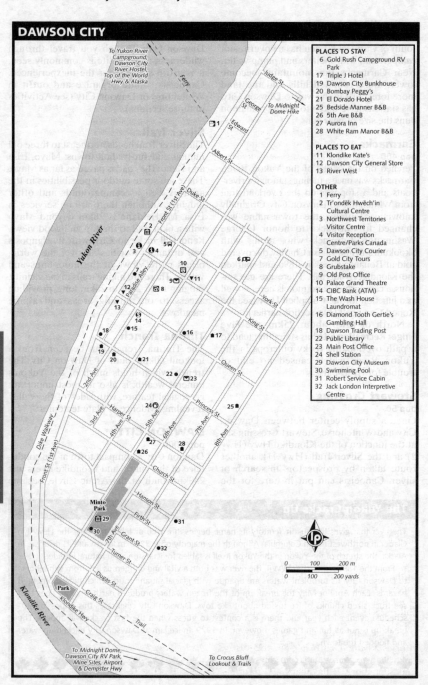

To Yukon River
Campground;
Dawson City
River Hostel
Top of the World
Hwy & Alaska

To Midnight
Dome Hike

To Midnight Dome,
Dawson City RV Park,
Mine Sites, Airport
& Dempster Hwy

To Crocus Bluff
Lookout & Trails

PLACES TO STAY
6 Gold Rush Campground RV Park
17 Triple J Hotel
19 Dawson City Bunkhouse
20 Bombay Peggy's
21 El Dorado Hotel
25 Bedside Manner B&B
26 5th Ave B&B
27 Aurora Inn
28 White Ram Manor B&B

PLACES TO EAT
11 Klondike Kate's
12 Dawson City General Store
13 River West

OTHER
1 Ferry
2 Tr'ondëk Hwëch'in Cultural Centre
3 Northwest Territories Visitor Centre
4 Visitor Reception Centre/Parks Canada
5 Dawson City Courier
7 Gold City Tours
8 Grubstake
9 Old Post Office
10 Palace Grand Theatre
14 CIBC Bank (ATM)
15 The Wash House Laundromat
16 Diamond Tooth Gertie's Gambling Hall
18 Dawson Trading Post
22 Public Library
23 Main Post Office
24 Shell Station
29 Dawson City Museum
30 Swimming Pool
31 Robert Service Cabin
32 Jack London Interpretive Centre

0   100   200 m
0   100   200 yards

the heart of the Klondike gold rush. Once known as 'the Paris of the North' with a population in the west second only to San Francisco, it had deluxe hotels and restaurants, plush river steamers and stores with luxury goods. Many attractions remain from its fleeting but vibrant fling with world fame and some of the original buildings are still standing. Parks Canada is involved in restoring or preserving those considered historically significant and regulations ensure that new buildings are built in sympathy with the old. With unpaved streets and board sidewalks, the town still has a gritty edge-of-the-world feel.

The town is built on permafrost, which begins just a few centimeters down. Buildings have foundations of planks resting on gravel and many show the seasonal effects of heaving. Outside of town are the eerie piles of tailings, which look like the work of mammoth gophers. These huge mounds are actually from gold dredges that sucked up the swampy earth at one end and left it behind sans gold at the other. Some 100 years after the original gold rush, as many as 100 enterprises are still mining for gold in the region around Dawson City.

Summer sees a large influx of tourists and seasonal workers. RVs roam the streets like caribou. Aside from Dawson being a unique and fun place there's a lot to see; a two or three-day visit is not a bad idea.

Orientation & Information

The town is small enough to walk around in a few hours. The Klondike Hwy leads into Front St (also called 1st Ave) along the Yukon River. Just north of town, a free ferry crosses the Yukon River to the Top of the World Hwy and onward to Alaska.

On the corner of Front and King Sts, the VRC (☎ 867-993-5566) is open 8am to 8pm daily from May to September. There's also a Parks Canada counter (☎ 867-993-7200) in the same building open 9am to 8pm. Most of the attractions are national historic sites for which there is a fee, but park passes cover them and are a good value at adult/child $25/12.50, or choose a four-site pack for $15/7.50.

Opposite the VRC is the Northwest Territories Visitor Centre (☎ 867-993-6167), open 9am to 8pm daily from mid-May to mid-September. It has maps and informa-

tion on the Northwest Territories and Dempster Hwy, including road updates.

The main post office (☎ 867-993-5342, 5th Ave & Princess St) is where you pick-up general delivery mail (address it to: General Delivery, Dawson City, YT Y0B 1G0) from 8:30am to 5:30pm Monday to Friday, 9am to noon Saturday. At the beautiful Old Post Office (King St & 3rd Ave) there's a mail drop and stamps for sale noon to 6pm daily mid-May to mid-September.

Grubstake (☎ 867-993-6706, 2nd Ave & King St) has Internet access. At the CIBC Bank (☎ 867-993-5447, 2nd Ave & Queen St) there's an ATM.

The Wash House Laundromat (☎ 867-993-6555, 2nd Ave & Queen St) has laundry (self-service and drop-off) and showers. Stop in 9am to 8pm daily.

For medical emergencies, dial ☎ 867-993-4444; for police, dial ☎ 867-993-5555.

Things to See & Do
Unless otherwise noted, the hours listed below are for the tourist season of May to September. At other times, Dawson City is cold and quiet and most attractions are closed.

Diamond Tooth Gertie's Gambling Hall This hall (☎ 867-993-5575, Queen St & 4th Ave; admission $6; open 7pm-2am daily) is a re-creation of an 1898 saloon, complete with small-time gambling, honky-tonk piano and dancing girls. The casino's winnings go toward town restoration, so go ahead, lose a bundle.

Palace Grand Theatre This large, flamboyant opera house/dance hall, on the corner of 3rd Ave and King St, was built in 1899 by 'Arizona Charlie' Meadows. There are daily guided tours at 2pm (adult/child $5/2.50).

At night, the *Gaslight Follies* presents remarkably corny stage shows vaguely based on the gold-rush era. The box office is across the street from the theater (☎ 867-993-6217; adult/child $15/7.50, shows 8:30pm Mon-Thur, 7pm & 9pm Fri-Sun).

Dawson City Museum This museum (☎ 867-993-5291, 5th Ave; admission $5/4; open 10am-8pm daily) houses a collection of 25,000 gold-rush artifacts. Next door is the old locomotive barn.

Tr'ondëk Hwëch'in Cultural Centre
Inside this beautiful wood building on the riverfront (☎ 867-993-6564, W www.trondek .com, 1st Ave; admission $5; open 10:30am-6pm daily) there's a slide show and interpretative talks on the *Hän Hwëch'in*, or river people, who were the first to inhabit the area. The collection includes traditional artifacts and First Nation regalia. Locally made crafts are for sale.

Robert Service Cabin Called the 'Bard of the Yukon,' Robert W Service lived in this typical gold-rush cabin (8th Ave & Hanson St; admission free; open 10am-4pm daily) from 1909 to 1912. Don't miss the readings of Service's poems at 10am and 1:30pm (adult/child $5/2.50) – cheapskates listen for free from the street.

Jack London Interpretive Centre In 1898 Jack London lived in the Yukon, the setting for his most popular animal stories, including *Call of the Wild* and *White Fang*. At the writer's cabin (8th Ave at Grant St; $2; open 10am-1pm & 2pm-6pm daily), there are talks at 11:15am and 2:30pm daily.

Midnight Dome The quarried face of this hill overlooks the town to the north, but to reach the top you must travel south of town about 1km and turn left off the Klondike Hwy onto New Dome Rd. Continue for about 7km. The Midnight Dome, at 880m above sea level, offers great views of the Ogilvie Mountains, Klondike Valley, Yukon River and Dawson City. From here during the summer solstice, the midnight sun barely sinks below the Ogilvie Mountains to the north before rising again. There's also a steep **trail** from Judge St in town; maps available at the VRC.

Mine Sites There are two national historic sites outside of town that relate to the early gold-mining days. **Dredge No 4** *(Bonanza Creek Rd; adult/child $5/2.50; open 10am-4pm Fri-Wed, 10am-2pm Thur)*, off the Klondike Hwy 13km south of town, is a massive dredging machine that tore up the Klondike Valley and left the tailings, which remain as landscape blight. One kilometer farther south on the highway is **Bear Creek Mining Camp** *(adult/child $5/2.50; open for tours at 1:30pm & 2:30pm*

daily), site of the large community and shop complex which sprang up around the Klondike gold dredges in 1905 and lasted for 60 years.

Ship Graveyard When the Klondike Hwy was completed, the paddlewheel ferries were abandoned. Several were sailed just downstream from town and left to rot on the bank. Now overgrown, they're a fascinating destination for a short hike. Take the ferry across the river, then walk north though the Yukon River Campground for 10 minutes and then another 10 minutes north along the beach.

Activities
Dawson Trading Post *(☎/fax 867-993-5316, e ronryant@yknet.yk.ca, Front St)* sells interesting old mining gadgets, modern camping gear and rents out canoes ($30/day), with longer trips and transportation arranged. One of the main do-it-yourself canoe float trips goes from Dawson three days downstream to Eagle City, Alaska. This trip is good for inexperienced canoeists.

There are numerous trails of all lengths and difficulties, including the 32km **Ridge**

Dawson City's annual gold-panning championship

Road Recreational Trail; the VRC has details. The **swimming pool** (☎ 867-993-7412, 5th Ave) is next to the city museum; call for hours.

Organized Tours

Parks Canada runs excellent walking tours (adult/child $5/2.50) of the town at 9:30am and 1pm daily. Among the highlights are tours of some of the restored buildings as well as details of the now nondescript Paradise Alley, between Front St and 2nd Ave, which was home to 900 prostitutes. You can rent an audiotape tour for the same price as the walking tour.

Gold City Tours (☎ 867-993-5175, fax 867-993-5261, W www.yukonfun.com/e_goldcity .html, Front St), opposite the SS Keno, has a daily city tour and trip to the Bonanza Creek gold mine where you can do some panning (adult/child $37/19). Vans go to Midnight Dome ($11/person) at 11pm daily. The office also books airline tickets and car rentals.

Special Events

Dawson City Music Festival On the third weekend of July, this event features some well-known Canadian musicians. It's very popular – tickets sell out and the city fills up – so reservations are a good idea.

Discovery Day The premier annual event in Dawson City celebrates you-know-what of 1896. On the third Monday in August there are parades, picnics, a demonstration of gold smelting and a demolition derby.

Places to Stay

Most places are open from May to September and fill up in July and August. The VRC will tirelessly search for vacant rooms on busy weekends if you arrive without a reservation.

Camping *Yukon River Campground* Sites $8. This campground is on the western side of the river about 250m up the road to the right after you get off the ferry.

Gold Rush Campground RV Park (☎ 867-993-5247, e goldrush@yukon.net, 5th Ave & York St) RV sites $15. This is one big parking lot downtown for RVs with full facilities.

Dawson City RV Park (☎ 867-993-5142, e dcrvpark@dawsoncity.net, Klondike Hwy)

Klondike Winter

'One December, the mercury dropped below -50[°F] the entire month. There was a flu epidemic that year and there were many deaths...but there would be no burials until the weather moderated. The frozen bodies were stacked in the undertaker's parlor. Indeed, the winter graves had been prepared in the fall, as more people died during the winter than during the summer. There were always a good many standing open for the season. It was a grisly sight to pass the rows of yawning holes waiting for occupants, and to wonder which one of us would rest in them before the long winter was over.'

–Laura Beatrice Berton
I Married the Klondike

Sites $15. This RV park, 1km south of town, has sites with full facilities.

Hostels *Dawson City River Hostel* (☎ 867-993-6823, W www.yukonhostels.com) Tent site $9/person, $7/person for two or more; dorm beds $14/16.50 members/nonmembers, cabins $35/person; cash only. Open mid-May–Sept. This good HI-affiliated hostel is across the river from town and five minutes up the hill from the ferry landing. This is a rustic and funky spot with good views, cabins, a wooded area for tents, cooking shelter and communal bathhouse. There's no electricity and lockers are recommended for your gear.

B&Bs *White Ram Manor B&B* (☎ 867-993-5772, fax 867-993-6509, e pbarthol@ yknet.yk.ca, 7th Ave & Harper St) Singles/doubles $79/89 with breakfast. This roomy pink house has a laundry, Internet access, BBQ and hot tub.

Bedside Manner B&B (☎ 867-993-6948, fax 867-993-5270, 8th Ave & Princess St) Singles/doubles $79/89 with breakfast. This small place offers the same services as the White Ram and airport pick-up.

5th Ave B&B (☎/fax 867-993-5941, W www.5thavebandb.com, 702 5th Ave) Singles/doubles $85/95 with breakfast. Open year-round. This is another homey B&B worth trying near the museum.

Motels, Hotels & Inns Dawson City
Bunkhouse (☎ 867-993-6164, fax 867-993-6051, **W** www.bunkhouse.ca) Singles/doubles without bath $49/59, with bath $79/89. This is a good frontier-style place with clean, basic rooms, but the solid wood construction means it can get noisy.

Triple J Hotel (☎ 867-993-5323, 800-764-3555, fax 867-993-5030, **e** jjj@dawson.net, *Queen St & 5th Ave*) Single/double motel rooms $99/109, hotel or cabin rooms $109/119. Triple J occupies the whole block with dated but clean rooms and cabins with kitchenettes.

El Dorado Hotel (☎ 867-993-5451, 800-661-0518, fax 867-993-5256, **e** eldo@dawson.net, *3rd Ave & Princess St*) Singles/doubles $119/129 & up. Open year-round. The El Dorado has good rooms.

Aurora Inn (☎ 867-993-6860, fax 867-993-5689, **W** www.wildandwooly.yk.net, *5th Ave*) Singles/doubles $109/119, breakfast $9. Open year-round. The Aurora has bright, large rooms and friendly service.

Bombay Peggy's (☎ 867-993-6969, fax 867-993-6199, **W** www.bombaypeggys.com, *2nd Ave & Princess St*) Single/double snugs with shared bath $79/89, rooms with private bath $149/159, suites $169/179. Open year-round. This charming place to stay is a former brothel bearing the name of its madam.

The building was stylishly renovated, including the 'snugs,' which are smaller rooms in the attic, and there's a great pub downstairs.

Places to Eat
Klondike Kate's (☎ 867-993-6527, *King St & 3rd Ave*) Breakfast $5, lunch & dinner $8-15. This busy place has a popular breakfast special, sandwiches, salads, fish and pasta served inside or on the patio.

River West (☎ 867-993-6339, *Front & Queen Sts*) Prices $2-5. The best of several places along Front St, this café has excellent coffee, bagels, soup and sandwiches on delicious bread.

Dawson City General Store (☎ 867-993-5475, *Front & Queen Sts; 8am-8pm Mon-Sat, 9am-8pm Sun*) This is one of the largest supermarkets north of Whitehorse with fresh produce and baked goods.

Many of the hotels have their own dining rooms for steak, seafood or pasta.

Getting There & Away
The airport is 19km east of town off the Klondike Hwy. Air North (☎ 867-668-2228, 800-661-0407, **W** www.airnorth.yk.net) flies to Whitehorse, Old Crow and Inuvik. Fares and schedules vary widely by season. For tickets and transport to the airport contact Gold City Tours (☎ 867-993-6424). They meet most flights ($10/person).

The bus company Dawson City Courier (☎ 867-993-6688, fax 867-993-6010) runs daily, except Saturday, to Whitehorse from 2nd Ave & York St (six hours, $83). Service to Inuvik ($238/person) leaves Tuesday and then returns Thursday, with a minimum of five passengers.

The Parks Highway Express bus (☎ 907-479-3065, 888-600-6001, **e** info@alaskashuttle.com, **W** www.alaskashuttle.com) departs from the VRC to Tok (US$75, five hours) and Fairbanks (US$125, 10 hours) on Wednesday, Friday and Sunday via the Top of the World Hwy. From Fairbanks, there are daily connections to Denali National Park (US$34, 3½ hours), or Wrangell-St. Elias National Park (US$64, six hours). Bike transportation is US$10.

The ferry (☎ 867-993-5441) runs 24 hours a day when the Yukon River is not frozen. It's free and the short trip is worthwhile even if you just go for a ride.

TOP OF THE WORLD HWY
At the northern end of Dawson City's Front St the ferry crosses the Yukon River to the scenic Top of the World Hwy (Hwy 9). Open only in summer, the gravel road can be rough in spots and extends 108km to the Alaska border following the ridge tops. The small customs and immigration checkpoint is open 9am to 9pm daily (Canada time) from June through mid-September. Watch the time and the gas gauge, as you can't cross outside these hours and there are no services at the border.

In Alaska, you'll pass through tiny **Boundary** with a café and gas, then Chicken with services, and along the Taylor Hwy (Hwy 5), which runs south 108km to meet the Alaska Hwy at Tetlin Junction. From here, turn right for Tok, which has motels, camping, road food and a visitor bureau (☎ 907-883-4121, *Alaska Hwy*) that's open 8am to 8pm daily May to September. From Tok, there's a worthwhile detour down the **Richardson**

Hwy as far as Paxson, considered one of the most scenic roads in Alaska, or all the way to **Fairbanks** along the Alaska Hwy.

With less time, turn left at Tetlin Junction and back to Canada through Beaver Creek. The **Tetlin National Wildlife Center** (☎ 907-883-5321) on the Alaska Hwy is an interesting stop before you reach the border and it's open daily 8am to 4:30pm.

DEMPSTER HWY

The Dempster Hwy (Hwy 5 in the Yukon, Hwy 8 in the Northwest Territories) starts 40km southeast of Dawson City off the Klondike Hwy. It heads north over the Ogilvie and Richardson Mountains beyond the Arctic Circle and on to Inuvik in the Northwest Territories near the shores of the Beaufort Sea.

The highway, which opened in 1979, makes road travel along the full length of North America possible. Inuvik is a long way from Dawson City – 747km of gravel road – but the scenery is remarkable: mountains, valleys, rivers and vast open tundra. The highway is open most of the year but the best time to travel is between June and early September when the ferries over the Peel and Mackenzie rivers operate. In winter ice forms a natural bridge over the rivers, which become ice roads. The Dempster is closed during the spring thaw and the winter freeze-up; these vary by the year and can occur from mid-April to June and mid-October to December respectively.

Accommodations and vehicle services along the route are scarce. There is a gas station at the southern start of the highway at **Klondike River Lodge** (☎ 867-993-6892). The lodge will rent jerry cans of gas you can take north and return on the way back. Then it's 370km to Eagle Plains and the next services. The *Eagle Plains Hotel* (☎/fax 867-993-2453) is open year-round and you can get singles/doubles/triples for $112/124/140. The next service station is 180km farther at Fort McPherson in the Northwest Territories. From there it's 216km to Inuvik.

The Yukon government has three *campgrounds* – at Tombstone Mountain (73km from the start of the highway), Engineer Creek (194km) and Rock River (447km) – and there's a Northwest Territories government campground at Nitainlaii Territorial

Park 9km south of Fort McPherson. For maps and information on the road ask at the NWT Visitor Centre (☎ 867-993-6167) in Dawson City.

The road is a test for drivers and cars. Travel with extra gas and tires and expect to use them. For road and ferry reports call ☎ 867-979-2678 or 800-661-0752. Hitchhiking from the start of the highway can be slow though there are many trucks and RVs in the summer. We don't recommend hitchhiking but if you go, definitely carry a tent, warm clothing, rain gear, and enough food and water for the entire trip. Don't hitchhike outside of the short summer season.

TOMBSTONE TERRITORIAL PARK

The Yukon's newest territorial park, Tombstone is 73km up the Dempster Hwy, with a good interpretative center and campground with expansive views. The pointed shape of the prominent peak was a distinctive landmark on First Nation routes and is now an aerial guide for pilots. There are several good **day hikes** leading from the center, as well as longer, more rigorous backcountry trips for experienced wilderness hikers, requiring skilled map reading without established trails. Note that weather can change quickly, so bring appropriate gear even for day hikes. In mid-June there's hiking with some snow pack; July is best for wildflowers, balancing the annoyance of bug season.

It's possible to visit Tombstone as a day trip from Dawson City or to spend the night at the campground (sites $8) to experience a bit of the Dempster and see the headwaters of the Klondike River. All hikers should check in at the center for updates. Currently, permits are not required for the backcountry. There is no telephone at the center; for information ⓔ tombstone@yknet.yk.ca or check out ⓦ www.klondikeweb.com/tombstone. Don't miss the **viewpoint** 1km north up the hill.

VUNTUT NATIONAL PARK

Vuntut, a Gwich'in word meaning 'among the lakes,' was declared a national park in 1993. It's north of the village of Old Crow, the most northerly settlement in the Yukon. Each spring a porcupine caribou herd of 160,000 follows a migration route north across the plain to calving grounds near the Beaufort Sea. In Canada these calving grounds are protected within Ivvavik National Park and extend into Alaska where they are part of the Arctic National Wildlife Refuge.

With its many lakes and ponds, Vuntut National Park is visited by around 500,000 waterbirds each autumn. Archaeological sites contain fossils of ancient animals such as the mammoth, plus evidence of early humans. The only access to the 4345 sq km park is by chartered plane from Old Crow, which itself is reachable only by air. The park has no services or facilities. For more information, contact Parks Canada (☎ 867-777-3248, fax 867-777-4491, ⓦ www.parks canada.gc.ca, Box 1840, Inuvik NT, X0E 0T0).

IVVAVIK NATIONAL PARK

Ivvavik, meaning 'a place for giving birth to and raising the young,' is situated along the Beaufort Sea and adjoining Alaska and covers 10,170 sq km. The park is dominated by the British Mountains and its vegetation is mainly tundra. It's on the migration route of the porcupine caribou and is also a major waterfowl habitat. There are no facilities or services.

Access is by charter plane from either Old Crow or Inuvik. For information contact Parks Canada (see the Vuntut National Park section, above).

HERSCHEL ISLAND TERRITORIAL PARK

Off the coast of Ivvavik is Herschel Island in the Beaufort Sea, below the Arctic Ocean and about 90km south of the packed ice. Rich in plant, bird and marine life, particularly ringed seals and bowhead whales, it was an important area for the Thule. They called it *'Qikiqtaruk,'* or 'it is an island.'

There have been several waves of people through the area, but the Thule, expert whale hunters, were thought to be the first to make a permanent settlement here about 1,000 years ago.

Pauline Cove is deep enough for ocean vessels and protected from the northerly winds and drifting pack ice. As a haven for ships, it became a key port during the last days of the whaling industry when the whales were hunted first for lamp oil and then for baleen. Bowhead whales had the longest bones and were the most desirable for women's corsets. Fashion nearly drove them to extinction. Following the whalers and their families, who numbered about 1500, was an Anglican missionary in 1897, who tried to win converts among the Thule. The whaling station was abandoned around 1907, though the Canadian police continued to use the island as a post until 1964.

The flight across the MacKenzie Delta to reach the island is spectacular. At Pauline Cove, park rangers provide a tour of the historical buildings and lead a hike above the harbor to a hill carpeted with tiny wildflowers in July. The rangers are wonderful hosts and some have family connections to the island. Primitive camping during the short summer season (from late June to August) is possible. There are fire rings, wind shelters, privies and limited water. Access is by chartered plane, usually from Inuvik, 250km southeast. Most visitors spend half a day. For more information contact the Yukon Department of Renewable Resources (☎ 867-667-5648, Box 2703, Whitehorse, YT Y1A 2C6) or the tour companies in Inuvik (see the Northwest Territories chapter).

Northwest Territories

Canada's northern territories stretch from the northern boundaries of the lower provinces to within 800km of the North Pole and from the Atlantic Ocean to the Pacific Ocean. A third ocean, the Arctic, links Alaska and Greenland across the many islands of the far north.

For the most part, this land of the midnight sun is as reputation has it – a barren, treeless tundra that's nearly always frozen. But there are also mountains and forests, abundant wildlife and, even if the season is short, warm summer days with 20 hours of light.

In 1999, this vast region underwent a major political change with the creation of Nunavut (see the following chapter) in the east, which comprises 2.2 million sq km, leaving what is still known as the Northwest Territories (NT) with 1.17 million sq km in the west.

The designation of the Northwest Territories, Nunavut and the Yukon as territories rather than provinces is political. With relatively small populations, they have not been given full status in Parliament.

Along the Mackenzie River and around Great Slave Lake, the people call themselves the Dene, a political entity consisting of several Native Indian groups with different languages. Together with the Inuit, who live mainly in Nunavut, they are the original northern peoples. The term Eskimo is not appreciated by the Inuit and has fallen out of use. The terms Inuit and Dene simply mean 'people.'

Much of the Northwest Territories lies below the tree line. It is a land of thousands of lakes surrounded by forests and tundra. A mere 42,000 people populate this area.

The mighty Mackenzie River, 'Deh Cho,' runs 1800km northwest from Great Slave Lake to the Beaufort Sea and Arctic Ocean. Near its end, it fans out into one of the world's largest deltas, with hundreds of channels and islands over an area of 16,000 sq km. In the rolling hills left by retreating glaciers are rich supplies of oil, gas, diamonds and gold, which fuel the economy. Other sources of income include fish, fur and handicrafts.

Yellowknife is the capital and the main city. Inuvik is the center for First Nations

Highlights

Granted Territorial Status: 1870
Area: 1.17 million sq km
Population: 42,000
Provincial Capital: Yellowknife

- Run the rapids of the Nahanni River.
- Fly over the Mackenzie River Delta.
- Wander the streets of Yellowknife's Old Town, then settle back on the patio at Bullock's Bistro.
- Catch a glimpse of one of the world's largest bison herds at Wood Buffalo National Park.
- Gaze at the wonder of the aurora borealis.

people above the Arctic Circle. Both can be reached by car.

Tourism in the NT (as in Nunavut) is not for the fainthearted. Except for the few parts of the NT that are accessible by car, travelers need plenty of planning, money and time for a trip to this remote area.

For a lot of visitors, a trip to the Northwest Territories means canoeing, fishing, hiking and camping in the national and territorial parks during the short summer season. For others, it means observing the wildlife or even trekking across the tundra in the far north. These activities permit the visitor to see the area's uniqueness and rugged beauty. The NT has every manner of package tour and all-inclusive guided trips (see the *Explorers' Guide,* mentioned in Information, later), but many things can also be done independently, which is much cheaper.

Increasing numbers of travelers are visiting without a prebooked excursion. Facilities and small, modest tour or outfitting businesses are slowly increasing with them.

There are four main areas that can be explored independently. With a car, the Ingraham Trail (Hwy 4) can be explored in any length from a day to several weeks. Many people use the established canoe routes, which vary in difficulty. Although the lakes and waters are calm, be prepared for portages.

The second area to investigate is the Mackenzie River for canoe and boat trips. These can be done from several places, but the primary one is Fort Simpson. Some people spend weeks going all the way to the Beaufort Sea. This area is not for the inexperienced. The waters are swift, and there are no designated campgrounds.

The third area is Nahanni National Park Reserve. Although most of the trips here are prearranged and expensive, you can hire an airplane to reach the park, where there is canoeing, camping and hiking. The headquarters for excursions is Fort Simpson.

Finally, Wood Buffalo National Park has novice and advanced hiking trails, plus a range of canoe routes. Outfitters in Fort Smith rent equipment or organize camping adventures into the park. See Activities, later, for information on outdoor options in the province.

History

The earliest known inhabitants of the Northwest Territories – ancestors of the modern Dene – came to the region from Asia about 14,000 years ago. The Inuit are thought to have arrived about 4000 years ago. The Vikings were the first Europeans here, arriving about AD 1000.

From 1524, British, French and Dutch adventurers began searching for the legendary Northwest Passage – a sea passage from the Atlantic Ocean to the Pacific Ocean and the shortest route from Europe to China and its riches. Many died trying, but the North was mapped out in the process.

The first successful navigation across the North was made in 1906 by Roald Amundsen. Today the route is little used except as a supply line during the very short summer thaw.

With the prospect of wealth from whaling and the fur trade, Europeans began to explore northern Canada in earnest during the 18th and 19th centuries. In their wake came missionaries who built churches, schools and hospitals. Until 1870, when the Canadian government took over, administration of the territories was shared between the Hudson's Bay Company and the British government.

Following the discovery of oil in the 1920s near Fort Norman (now Tulita), a territorial government was set up. In the 1930s, a gold rush and the discovery of radium around Great Bear Lake brought rapid change; WWII brought airfields and weather stations. In the 1950s, the national government began health, welfare and education programs. The 1960s saw accessibility to the territories increase with more roads and airplanes, and Yellowknife became the provincial capital in 1967. The search for oil, gas and minerals changed some areas rapidly. The modernization and development of the region has meant the near-total disappearance of traditional Native Indian lifestyle.

Unlike Nunavut, which is largely populated by the Inuit, the NT's population is split almost equally between Native Indian and non-Native people. There are nine official languages: English, French and seven Native Indian tongues. This heterogeneous mix makes for fractious politics.

Climate

Summers in the southern part of the NT are surprisingly warm, with high temperatures around Yellowknife averaging almost 20°C. Coupled with the long daylight hours, this

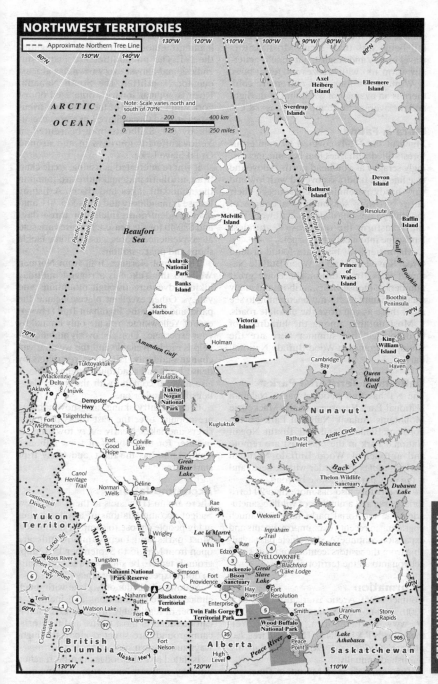

NORTHWEST TERRITORIES

- - - Approximate Northern Tree Line

ARCTIC OCEAN

Note: Scale varies north and south of 70°N

| 0 | 200 | 400 km |
| 0 | 125 | 250 miles |

Axel Heiberg Island

Ellesmere Island

Sverdrup Islands

Devon Island

Bathurst Island

Resolute

Baffin Island

Melville Island

Beaufort Sea

Prince of Wales Island

Gulf of Boothia

Aulavik National Park

Banks Island

Sachs Harbour

Boothia Peninsula

King William Island

Victoria Island

Holman

Cambridge Bay

Gjoa Haven

Queen Maud Gulf

Amundsen Gulf

Tuktoyaktuk

Mackenzie Delta

Aklavik

Inuvik

Paulatuk

Tuktut Nogait National Park

Kugluktuk

Nunavut

Dempster Hwy

Tsiigehtchic

Fort McPherson

Colville Lake

Fort Good Hope

Bathurst Inlet

Arcitc Circle

Back River

Great Bear Lake

Canol Heritage Trail

Norman Wells

Déline

Tulita

Thelon Wildlife Sanctuary

Dubawnt Lake

Continental Divide

Yukon Territory

Rae Lakes

Wekweti

Mackenzie Mtns

Mackenzie River

Wrigley

Lac la Martre

Ingraham Trail

Reliance

Carol Rd

Ross River

Wha Ti

Rae

Edzo

YELLOWKNIFE

Blachford Lake Lodge

Robert Campbell Hwy

Tungsten

Nahanni National Park Reserve

Fort Simpson

Fort Providence

Mackenzie Bison Sanctuary

Great Slave Lake

Teslin

Nahanni Butte

Blackstone Territorial Park

Hay River

Fort Resolution

Watson Lake

Fort Liard

Twin Falls Gorge Territorial Park

Enterprise

Fort Smith

Uranium City

Stony Rapids

Continental Divide

British Columbia

Fort Nelson

Alaska Hwy

Wood Buffalo National Park

Alberta

High Level

Peace River

Peace Point

Lake Athabasca

Saskatchewan

Pacific Time Zone / Mountain Time Zone

Central Time Zone / Mountain Time Zone

weather makes traveling very pleasant. The climate is dry, the average annual rain/snowfall being less than 30cm. Most visitors travel in July and August, but June is generally warm, too, with breezes and fewer bugs.

Winters are long and extremely cold; there is an average of 6½ hours of daylight and the average low temperature is -28°C.

Flora & Fauna

Much of the NT is covered by coniferous forests filled with trees that become increasingly scraggy as you head north. Above the tree line, the tundra is covered with low and very hardy perennials that squeeze their entire growing season into a couple of months. Many boast delicate flowers that can transform the otherwise featureless landscape into a colorful carpet.

Major herds of bison are found around Great Slave Lake and in Wood Buffalo National Park. In addition, there are great numbers of moose, bears, caribou, and many smaller mammals. It's not uncommon to see all of these as you drive the desolate roads.

Most notable among the hundreds of bird species that summer here are the whooping cranes in Wood Buffalo National Park.

National & Territorial Parks

The NT has four national parks. Nahanni National Park Reserve is in the Mackenzie Mountains. Aulavik National Park on the north of Banks Island and Tuktut Nogait National Park in the northeast are remote and untouched. Wood Buffalo National Park straddles the border with Alberta and is the only park accessible by road.

The territory also has more than 20 territorial parks and a number of wildlife sanctuaries. The territorial parks have had much upgrading in recent years; improvements and expansion continue. A $10 vehicle pass, available from the visitors' centers and parks, will get you into all the territorial parks.

Information

Contact NWT Arctic Tourism (☎ 867-873-7200, 800-661-0788, fax 867-873- 4059, ⓦ www.nwttravel.nt.ca, Box 610, Yellowknife, NT X1A 2N5). The good, free *Explorers' Guide* and *Explorers' Map* are published annually.

The entire NT is on Mountain Time.

Activities

Canoeing, kayaking and boating are the leading methods of traveling throughout the NT. The possibilities are just about endless, and almost every town has at least one local outfitter. The South Nahanni River is popular for trips organized out of Fort Simpson. Many of the lakes and tributaries around Great Slave Lake are accessible by car. Sailboats may be rented in Yellowknife for journeys in and around Great Slave Lake.

If you're interested in fishing, arctic char, trout, northern pike and more are found in the abundant lakes and rivers. A fishing license is mandatory and costs $15/30 Canadian resident/nonresident for three days and $20/40 for the season. Licenses are sold at convenience stores, gas stations, tackle shops and police stations.

The Canol Heritage Trail from Norman Wells to the Yukon is a rugged multiday hiking adventure through mountains and valleys. Other excellent places include the parks and along the Ingraham Trail (Hwy 4) east of Yellowknife. You are only limited by your experience. Don't be overly ambitious – help is rarely available and the weather can change suddenly. Hiking is restricted by dense bush and inadequate signage. You'll also have to contend with the three 'Bs' – bugs, bears and bison.

Cross-country skiing and snowmobiling are popular over the vast tracts of frozen rivers and lakes. Nearly every town has an outfitter for these types of trips, although Yellowknife has the most, and many trips start there.

Accommodations

There are no HI hostels in the NT and few budget accommodations of any kind; thus many people choose to camp or use an RV. Most parks and their campgrounds are open from May 15 to September 15. Campgrounds tend to be small, simple and cheap, so don't expect anything fancy.

Yellowknife is the only place with much choice of accommodations and includes a number of reasonably priced B&Bs. Hotels can be found in most towns, and territorial campgrounds are situated along the highways and at town sites.

Isolated seasonal lodges can be reached only by a floatplane from Yellowknife.

Meals can be included and a range of activities is offered, including fishing, canoeing, hiking and hunting.

Getting There & Around

Well-organized package tours have long been the principal means of seeing some aspects of the NT. The *Explorers' Guide* (see Information, earlier) has comprehensive lists of companies and the types of tours they offer.

Air Yellowknife is the transportation hub of the NT and has access to the rest of Canada through Edmonton. Owing to the paucity of roads, most communities have some form of scheduled air service that usually goes through Yellowknife. Air fares are high, and a lack of competition and traffic keeps them that way.

Bus The sole bus link from the rest of the world is provided by Greyhound (☎ 800-661-8747) from Edmonton to Hay River. From here, there is service by Frontier Coachlines (☎ 867-874-2566) to Yellowknife and other places served by road, such as Fort Smith, Fort Providence and Fort Simpson.

Car The Mackenzie Hwy (Hwy 1) north from Edmonton is paved as far as the junction with Hwy 3 just south of the Mackenzie River. From here, Hwy 3 is paved as far as Rae, after which the remaining 98km to Yellowknife is unpaved and frequently under construction. Hwy 2 is paved from Enterprise to Hay River and a stretch of Hwy 5 is paved east to Fort Smith. The rest of the roads are unpaved and are a varying combination of gravel, dirt and mud. Generally all the numbered highways are passable for cars, but it's a good idea to check on local conditions as even the paved roads have washouts. For road conditions, call ☎ 867-874-2208 or ☎ 800-661-0750.

Free ferries link several roads, with the most important one being the Mackenzie River crossing for Hwy 3 near Fort Providence. Travel is interrupted for several weeks during the spring thaw (April or May) and winter freeze (December) when neither the ferries nor ice bridges are usable. For ferry information, call ☎ 867-873-7799 or ☎ 800-661-0750.

Driving in the NT is not especially easy. Distances are long and the drives can be monotonous – there is almost no radio reception and the scenery can be repetitive. Many cars in the NT have damaged windshields from stray rocks; slow down and pull to the right when meeting oncoming traffic. Bring at least one full-service spare tire (not one of those miniature jobs) and know how to change it. Note the distance between services and monitor your gas.

The speed limit on the highways is typically 80 to 100 km/h. The ferries go a lot slower.

You should carry a first-aid kit, flare, water and food. In winter, add a bag of sand, shovel, blankets or sleeping bags, matches and more food. You might want to fit some form of protector over your lights.

YELLOWKNIFE
pop 18,000

Rising out of the wilderness, Yellowknife gets its name from a band of Native Indian peoples who used copper-bladed knives. Although gold was first found here in 1898 by Klondike-bound prospectors, it was not until the discovery of richer veins, first in 1934 and again in 1945, that non-Natives were attracted to the area in large numbers.

Yellowknife is the capital and by far the largest town in the NT. A modern, fast-growing settlement 1508km from Edmonton by road, Yellowknife is essentially a government town. It also acts as the commercial and service center for the region, and people from all over Canada now live and work here. Visitors use Yellowknife as a base for camping and fishing trips, as well as for exploring the rocky landscape and nearby lakes.

Orientation

Yellowknife sits on the northern shores of Great Slave Lake and is connected with the south by Hwy 3, which runs 343km to the junction with the Mackenzie Hwy (Hwy 1). The city is divided into the new (south) and old (north) parts of town, which are connected by Franklin Ave (50th Ave), the main thoroughfare. The new part of town has the shops, businesses, services and hotels, but its utilitarian corrugated-metal architecture won't win any awards. Hilly, residential Old Town, wedged between Back Bay and Yellowknife Bay, is far more interesting, with its history, variety of housing, B&Bs, floatplane bases and views.

YELLOWKNIFE

PLACES TO STAY
1 Blue Raven B&B
2 Island B&B
5 Bayside B&B;
Mary & Friends
Tea Room
6 Prospector B&B
9 Back Bay Boat B&B
13 Explorer Hotel;
Raven Tours
15 Igloo Motor Inn
16 Chateau Nova

PLACES TO EAT
7 Wildcat Café
10 Bullock's Bistro
28 New Country Corner Restaurant
29 Longhini's

OTHER
3 Air Tindi
4 Arctic Excursions
8 Bush Pilot's Monument
12 Gallery of the
Midnight Sun

14 The Arctic Laundromat
17 Legislative Assembly
18 Prince of Wales
Northern Heritage
Centre
19 Northern Frontier
Regional Visitors
Centre
20 Yellowknife Motors
21 RCMP
22 Panda II Mall; Yellowknife
Book Cellar

23 YK Centre; Extra Foods
24 Main Post Office
25 American Express
26 The Map Place
27 The Cave Club
30 Centre Square Mall
(Library; Yellowknife Book
Cellar; Raven Tours)
31 Overlander Sports
32 Frontier Coachlines Stop

Frame Lake lies along downtown's western edge. The 5.2km walking trail around it is a popular jogging spot and a pleasant evening stroll.

Streets run roughly east to west, and avenues run roughly north to south; unfortunately, city planners used the same range of numbers for their street and avenue names.

Information

The Northern Frontier Regional Visitors Centre (☎ 867-873-4262, 877-881-4262, fax 867-873-3654, ⓦ www.northernfrontier.com, 4807 49th St), at 49th Ave, offers a wealth of maps and regional information; the staff is knowledgeable and there are good historical displays. The center is open 8:30am to 6:30pm Monday to Friday and 9am to 5pm Saturday and Sunday from May 1 to September 1; 8:30am to 5:30pm Monday to Friday and noon to 4pm Saturday and Sunday the rest of the year. Ask about the free metered-parking pass for tourists.

There are several banks with ATMs downtown. American Express (☎ 867-873-2121, 5014 Franklin Ave) is in Key West Travel and has member services.

The post office (☎ 867-873-2500, 4902 Franklin Ave), at 49th St, will hold general delivery mail for 15 days. The Yellowknife Public Library (☎ 867-669-3403), in the Centre Square Mall, has free Internet access.

The Yellowknife Book Cellar, in Panda II Mall (☎ 867-920-2220) and Centre Square Mall (☎ 867-920-2005), has a good selection of books on Native Indian culture, the Arctic and the Northwest Territories. Topographical, aeronautical and nautical maps are available from The Map Place (☎ 867-873-8448, 5016 Franklin Ave) on the 2nd floor

To wash your clothes, try Arctic Laundromat (☎ 867-920-2354, 4310 Franklin Ave). The Washtub Ltd (☎ 867-669-0323, 318 Woolgar Ave), west of Frame Lake, has drop-off service for a $15 minimum charge.

Stanton Regional Hospital (☎ 867-669-4111) is a large, full-service facility off Old Airport Rd on Byrne Rd, west of Frame Lake.

For police emergencies dial ☎ 669-1111; for fire and medical emergencies dial ☎ 873-2222.

At night, 50th St between Franklin and 52nd Aves can be an unsavory place as alcohol abuse is rife.

Old Town

Arm yourself with a copy of *Four Historical Walking Tours of Yellowknife* (available at the visitors' center), a superlative illustrated booklet showing the town's many interesting old buildings, and head down Franklin Ave to Old Town. After a recent construction boom, the sights on **Ragged Ass Rd** no longer live up to the promise of the name; still, many small wooden houses remain from the days of the 1934 gold rush.

The Rock is the large nub of land right before the tiny bridge to Latham Island. Walk up the steps to the **Bush Pilot's Monument**. From here you can compare the old and new towns, watch the floatplanes buzzing in and out of the bay, and see the polychromatic houseboats on the lake. Summer sunsets – if you can stay up that late – are often stunning.

At the northern end of Latham Island, **N'Dilo** (pronounced **di**-lo and meaning 'end of the road') is the Dogrib Dene aboriginal community of Yellowknife.

Prince of Wales Northern Heritage Centre

A fine introduction to the Northwest Territories can be found at this museum (☎ 867-873-7551, fax 867-873-0205, ⓦ www.pwnhc.learnnet.nt.ca; admission free; open 10:30am-5:30pm daily June-Aug, 10:30am-5pm Tues-Fri & noon-6pm Sat & Sun Sept-May). Displays focus on the lifestyles of the Dene and Inuit and on European development. The Heritage Centre also has galleries on aviation and the natural sciences, a kid's play area and a cafeteria. The museum is off 48th St near Frame Lake.

Legislative Assembly

In 1993, the NT government coughed up $25 million to build this impressive, igloo-shaped building (☎ 867-669-2230, 800-661-0784, ⓦ www.assembly.gov.nt.ca; admission free; open 8:30am-5pm Mon-Fri). You can wander around or learn about the territories' consensus-style government by joining a free, one-hour tour, given at 10:30am, 1:30pm and 3:30pm Monday to Friday, 1:30pm Sunday June through August and 10:30am Monday to Friday the rest of the year. Excellent collections of Native Indian art can be found throughout the building.

Fred Henne Territorial Park

In this popular local park (☎ 867-873-7184; *open May 15-Sept 15)* off the Mackenzie Hwy opposite the airport, there is sandy **Long Lake Beach** and the 4km **Prospector's Trail**. This excellent walk leads over the Precambrian Shield, through some muskeg and a few swarms of tenacious mosquitoes, to a lake – a microcosm of the far north topography. Get the map from the park office, because it's easy to lose the path.

Activities

The Northern Frontier Regional Visitors Centre (see Information, earlier) maintains a lengthy list of guides and outfitters.

Overlander Sports (☎ 867-873-2474, 5103 51st Ave; *basic canoe day/weekend/week $30/50/150)* has a complete line of outdoor and winter sports gear; in addition, it rents canoes and kayaks. **Narwal Adventure Training & Tours** (☎ 867-873-6443, e *narwal@ssimicro.com),* located right on Back Bay, has canoes and kayaks for the same prices. It also offers lessons. You need to call before you drop by.

There's no shortage of fishing guides; one of the better-known ones is **Bluefish Services** (☎ 867-873-4818, e *greg.tricia@ nt.sympatico.ca).* Four hours of battling northern pike or watching birds on Great Slave Lake costs $75.

Smelly backpackers can opt for a shower ($2.50) at the **Ruth Inch Memorial Pool** (☎ 867-920-5683, 6001 Franklin Ave; *adult/ child $4.25/2.50).* The 25m pool has a wave machine and there are whirlpools and a steam room.

Organized Tours

There is a vast selection of short and long tours offered in and around Yellowknife: walking tours, boat trips, kayak adventures, photography safaris, fishing expeditions and more. See the *Explorers' Guide* for the complete range of options.

Raven Tours (☎ 867-873-4776, w *www .raventours.yk.com),* with offices in the Explorer Hotel and Centre Square Mall, offers a variety of options. It has good daily two-hour boat tours on Great Slave Lake ($30), a basic 2½-hour bus tour of the city ($25), a weekly trip down the Ingraham Trail to Cameron Falls ($40) and aurora viewing tours ($90, four hours).

Ecologist Jamie Bastedo of **Cygnus Eco-tours** (☎/fax 867-873-4782, e *cygnus@inter north.com)* leads recommended nature walks near Yellowknife. A four-hour tour costs about $50 to $60 per person, with a minimum of four people. Jamie sometimes gives free walks that are sponsored by the park department; contact him to find out the schedule.

K&D Kennels (☎ 867-873-2023, fax 867-873-6919, 1519 Curry Dr) is a small family operation that has winter dog-team excursions around Kam Lake. A 30-minute ride costs $45 per person.

Arctic Excursions (☎ 867-669-7216, 3503 McDonald Dr, w *www.arcticx.yk.com)* in Old Town offers charter flights and 30-minute floatplane tours ($275 total for up to five people, or $210 for up to three people). If you're lucky, you'll get the old DeHavilland Beaver, a plane that's been a workhorse of the North for 50 years.

Special Events

Caribou Carnival In March, the locals shake off winter with fireworks, games and contests during three days of festivities. A highlight is the 240km dogsled race on Great Slave Lake.

Festival of the Midnight Sun Held in July, this is a seven-day celebration of northern art and culture.

Folk on the Rocks Held a few days after the Festival of the Midnight Sun, this popular event on the shores of Long Lake draws musicians from all over Canada, as well as Dene drummers and dancers and Inuit throat singers. The cost is $30/50 for one/two days.

Places to Stay

The *Explorers' Guide* contains a complete list of places to stay in Yellowknife and throughout the NT.

Camping *Fred Henne Territorial Park (no direct phone, information* ☎ 867-873-7184) Sites $12. Open May 15-Sept 15. The closest campground to town, off the Mackenzie Hwy opposite the airport, this pleasant park has full facilities, including showers and toilets. If you arrive by bus, ask the driver to drop you off at the entrance. Downtown is easily walkable in under 40 minutes using the trail around Jackfish and Frame lakes.

Those with transportation can also camp along the Ingraham Trail; see Around Yellowknife, later.

The Northern Lights of Yellowknife

A hot show when the weather is cold, the aurora borealis, the famed Northern Lights, can be seen from the Northwest Territories, Nunavut and the Yukon. The best time to see it is during the autumn and winter. It appears in many forms – pillars, streaks, wisps and haloes of vibrating light and sometimes looks like the rippling folds of a curtain. Most often, the aurora borealis glows faintly green or pale rose, but during periods of extreme activity it can flare into bright yellows and crimsons.

The visible aurora is created by solar winds (streams of charged particles from the sun) flowing through the earth's magnetic field in the polar regions. These winds are drawn earthward, where the particles collide with electrons and ions in the ionosphere and create the visible aurora.

The Inuit and other groups attach a spiritual significance to the lights. Some consider it to be a gift from the dead to light the long polar nights, while others believe it to be a storehouse of events past and future.

More than 10,000 Japanese tourists a year visit Yellowknife during the otherwise slow winter season to see the show from a special viewing platform 30km east of town. The lights are thought to bring good luck. **Canadian Ex Aurora Tours** (☎ 867-669-9200, W *www.aurora tour.com*), **Aurora Village** (☎ 867-669-0006, e *morin@arcticdata.nt.ca*) and **Raven Tours** (☎ 867-873-4776, W *www.raventours.yk.com*) have numerous tour packages ($90/night) during the peak viewing season.

B&Bs These are by far the best value accommodations in Yellowknife. The following homes are in the delightful Old Town area. All have shared bathrooms.

Island B&B (☎/fax 867-873-4803, e *island@TheEdge.ca, 34 Morrison Dr*) Singles/doubles from $65/75. This B&B features homemade bread for breakfast, and you can borrow the owner's canoe for a spin around Back Bay.

Blue Raven B&B (☎ 867-873-6328, fax 867-766-3214, e *tmacfoto@internorth.com, 37 Otto Dr*) Singles/doubles $65/80. On Latham Island, Blue Raven has a great sundeck overlooking Yellowknife Bay – a terrific place for watching auroras.

Bayside B&B (☎ 867-920-4686, fax 867-699-8844, e *bryant@ssimicro.com, 3505 McDonald Dr*) Singles/doubles from $65/75. On The Rock by the floatplane terminal, Bayside B&B has terrific views of Yellowknife Bay and features one of the best breakfasts.

Back Bay Boat B&B (☎ 867-873-4080, W *www3.nt.sympatico.ca/backbay, 3530 Ingraham Dr*) Singles/doubles $65/80. This B&B overlooks the boat docks on Back Bay and serves a continental breakfast of bread, cheese and meats.

Prospector B&B (☎ 867-920-7620, fax 867-669-7581, e *info@theprospector.net,*

3506 Wiley Rd) Singles/doubles from $90/125. The Prospector B&B is almost a hotel, with well-equipped rooms and a noted restaurant for fresh fish dinners.

Motels & Hotels Rates at the following places decrease outside the high season.

Igloo Motor Inn (☎ 867-873-8511, fax 867-873-5547, e *iglooinn@internorth.com, 4109 Franklin Ave*) Singles/doubles $85/99. This basic, unexciting motel is halfway between downtown and Old Town. Most of its 34 rooms have kitchenettes.

Chateau Nova (☎ 867-873-9700, 877-839-1236, fax 867-873-9702, W *www.chateaunova .com, 4401 Franklin Ave*) Singles/doubles from $146/161. If you can make it past the ugly exterior, Chateau Nova's common areas and comfortable, new rooms are pleasantly decorated with fascinating historical pictures.

Explorer Hotel (☎ 867-873-3531, 800-661-0892, fax 867-873-2789, W *www.explorer hotel.nt.ca, 4825 49th Ave*) Singles/doubles from $169/184. Looming over downtown is the high-rise Explorer, with comfortable modern rooms and a sushi restaurant.

Places to Eat & Drink

Yellowknife has many places to eat, from fast-food joints and greasy spoons to fine dining on Northern specialties.

Mary & Friends Tea Room (☎ 867-920-4686, 3505 McDonald Dr) Lunch items $5. On the ground floor of the Bayside B&B, you can chow down on whitefish chowder, curried carrot soup and sockeye salmon salad. This cozy tearoom overlooks floatplanes taking off from Yellowknife Bay.

New Country Corner Restaurant (☎ 867-873-3399, 4609 Franklin Ave) Dishes $7-9. Not big on decor, this modest Vietnamese noodle house serves very good meals at reasonable prices.

Longhini's (☎ 867-669-2023, 5022 47th St) Lunch dishes $10-12, dinner $14-26. The best local Italian cooking is at this bustling, cheerful restaurant. Its lunchtime buffet ($11) is deservedly popular.

Wildcat Café (☎ 867-873-8850, Wiley Rd at Doombos Lane) Open June-Sept. This famous café in Old Town is set in an atmospheric 1937 log cabin. Food quality here is inconsistent, because the city licenses the restaurant to a different vendor each summer. Prices and opening hours also change from year to year.

Bullock's Bistro (☎ 867-873-3474, Ingraham Dr at Wiley Rd) Fish $13-24. Often closed Oct. Only the freshest arctic char, whitefish and Great Slave Lake cod make the day's changing menu. There is a good range of beers and they taste even better if you get a table outside. Often crowded, dinner reservations are recommended; expect to wait a while for your food.

Extra Foods is a large supermarket in the YK Centre on 48th St near Franklin Ave.

The Cave Club (☎ 867-920-7011, 5108 Franklin Ave) This subterranean bar is the best place to hear live entertainment, from country to blues to rock.

Shopping

Yellowknife is the distribution center and major retailer of craft items from around the territories. ***Gallery of the Midnight Sun*** (☎ 867-873-8064, 5005 Bryson Dr), just off Franklin Ave, is one of the best places to see a range of crafts. Many more outlets for Native Indian works can be found in the various malls downtown.

Getting There & Away

Air Yellowknife is the hub of air service for much of the NT and western Nunavut. Air fares can be breathtakingly high. Flights to Edmonton provide the major link to the rest of Canada. First Air (☎ 800-267-1247, fax 867-669-6603, ☒ www.firstair.ca) has services to/from Edmonton, Hay River, Fort Simpson, Whitehorse, Inuvik and various Nunavut destinations such as Cambridge Bay, Resolute, Rankin Inlet and Iqaluit.

Canadian North (☎ 867-873-4484, 800-661-1505, ☒ www.canadiannorth.com) flies to/from Edmonton, Norman Wells, Inuvik and various Nunavut destinations such as Cambridge Bay, Rankin Inlet and Iqaluit.

Smaller airlines serve towns in the NT, and they sometimes offer good special fares. Services can be sporadic. Northwestern Air Lease (☎ 867-872-2216, 877-872-2216, ☒ www.nwal.net) serves Fort Smith, Buffalo Airways (☎ 867-873-6112, ☒ www.buffalo airways.com) flies to Hay River, Air Tindi (☎ 867-669-8260, ☒ www.airtindi.com) serves Fort Simpson and North-Wright Airways (☎ 867-587-2288, ☒ north-wright@ nt.sympatico.ca) will deliver you to Norman Wells.

Bus Frontier Coachlines (☎ 867-873-4892) has services to/from Enterprise ($65 one way, seven hours, five weekly) and Hay River ($70 one way, eight hours, five weekly) that connect with Greyhound buses (☎ 800-661-8747) to/from Edmonton. The bus stop in Yellowknife is on the corner of 53rd St and 52nd Ave in front of Bruno's, a scruffy café. However, this location seems to move around a lot, so check with Frontier.

Getting Around

Much of Yellowknife is easily walked. From downtown to Old Town is about 2km, or 25 minutes. The walk to the airport can take about an hour.

Bus The Yellowknife City Transit system is operated by Cardinal Coach Lines (☎ 867-873-4693). Fares are $2/1.50 adults/children. Route No 1 serves the airport, Old Airport Rd and downtown. Route No 2 connects downtown and Old Town. The buses run every half hour, roughly 7am to 7pm Monday to Friday and for just a few hours Saturday.

Car Renting a car in Yellowknife is not cheap. Mileage charges rapidly wipe out the seemingly reasonable daily rates, especially given that many places worth driving to are fairly far away. A small car typically costs about $60/340 per day/week, *plus* 25¢ per kilometer, with 250 free kilometers thrown in with weekly rentals only. If a company tries to talk you up to a four wheel drive, call around – a standard car should be sufficient. Take care to determine your liability, given the high likelihood of windshield and other flying rock damage.

Budget and National have offices at the airport. Yellowknife Motors is most often recommended by locals.

Budget
☎ 867-920-9209, at the airport

National
☎ 867-920-2970, 5118 50th St and at the airport

Yellowknife Motors
☎ 867-873-4414, 49th Ave at 48th St

Taxi Taxis are plentiful in town. Try City Cab (☎ 867-873-4444). A cab from the airport to Old Town costs about $13, and downtown to Old Town costs about $6.

AROUND YELLOWKNIFE
Ingraham Trail
The 70km Ingraham Trail (Hwy 4) extends east of Yellowknife. The first 25km is very rough pavement that is in worse condition than the gravel road that follows. The route reveals superb, hilly, rocky Canadian Shield topography dotted with lakes. There are great views and good fishing, hiking, canoeing, camping and picnicking. *Blue Lake and Rocky Shore,* by Yellowknife naturalist Jamie Bastedo, is an excellent nature guide to the Ingraham Trail and the Yellowknife area.

About 15 minutes from Yellowknife, **Aurora Village** (☎ 867-669-0006, **e** *operations @auroravillage.com*) conveniently rents canoes, powerboats and fishing gear at a put-in point on the Ingraham Trail at Yellowknife River. Canoe rental rates are $15/45/70/190 per hour/day/weekend/week.

Prelude Lake, 30km east of Yellowknife, has *camping (no ☎)*. Tent/RV sites cost $10/15. It's open May 15 to September 15. There is also a beach and a 2.4km nature trail at this busy weekend, family-oriented spot.

At **Hidden Lake Territorial Park**, 47km east of Yellowknife, a popular 1.2km trail leads to Cameron Falls. You can walk over the bridge to the right and crawl to the

brink of this marvelous cascade. Farther down the Ingraham Trail, just before the bridge, a 0.4km trail leads to the Cameron River Ramparts, a smaller but still pretty cousin of Cameron Falls.

At **Reid Lake**, 61km from Yellowknife, you can camp, swim, canoe or fish for pike, whitefish and trout. The *Reid Lake Territorial Park Campground (no ☎)* has spaces for tents/RVs for $10/15. It is busy on weekends; otherwise it's very quiet. There's a good beach and walking trail and some fine campsites on the ridge with views of Pickerel Lake. The campground has pit toilets but no showers, and it's open May 15 to September 15.

The road ends at **Tibbitt Lake**, where, fittingly, there's a stop sign at the end of the road. The lake is good for fishing and is also the start of some fine canoe routes, including a wilderness route to Pensive Lake.

Wilderness Lodges
Numerous remote lodges dot the NT, and several are a short floatplane ride from Yellowknife.

Blachford Lake Lodge (☎ *867-873-3303, fax 867-920-4013,* **w** *www.internorth.com/ blachford, 5009 Bryson Dr)* This is one of the few open year-round. Depending on the season, there's plenty of fishing, canoeing, cross-country skiing, dog mushing and aurora watching. Accommodations range from small rustic cabins to a new, rather plush log-cabin lodge, complete with outside hot tub. Options include the 'economy' service ($649 per person for two days), full meal service ($850, two days) and full meal service with guiding ($1099, two days). The rates include transportation over the 95km to/from Yellowknife by floatplane.

MACKENZIE HWY
TO FORT PROVIDENCE
The first stretch of the Mackenzie Hwy (Hwy 1) follows the Hay River, which flows north into Great Slave Lake. At the border with Alberta, the 60th Parallel Visitors Centre (☎ 867-984-3811) is open 8:30am to 8:30pm daily May 15 to September 15. In addition to road and travel information, it has a small display of arts and crafts. The pleasant, shaded *campground* has showers and sites for $15.

The area between the border and Fort Providence provides the visitor with a good introduction to the uncluttered wildness of the territories. There are some good stops along the way with campgrounds, waterfalls and walking trails.

About 72km north of the border is **Twin Falls Gorge Territorial Park** (☎ *800-661-0788; open May 15-Sept 15)*. The 33m Alexandra Falls is not to be missed. A short trail leads to a platform overlooking the high and wide falls. Stairs nearby lead down to the water and rocky ledges by the lip of the falls. Two kilometers north is the parking lot for the smaller, but still impressive, 15m Louise Falls, where there is overnight *camping* with showers for $15/20 tents/RVs. A 3km walking trail along the Hay River gorge links the two falls and is a very pleasant hike.

Enterprise, with a population of about 90, is the first settlement in the Northwest Territories that you come to. There's a service station, grocery store and a restaurant. *Nature's Rest B&B* (☎ *867-984-3900, 800-279-6171, fax 867-984-3800)*, 1.4km northwest of the Hwys 1 & 2 intersection, has clean, simple rooms from $40/45 singles/doubles. Nonguests can stop here for showers ($6), laundry ($8) or coffee.

From Enterprise, the Mackenzie Hwy is paved to the junction with Hwy 3, which leads to the Mackenzie River ferry at Fort Providence. This portion of the road is also called the Waterfall Route. (Northeast out of Enterprise, Hwy 2 takes you to Hay River.)

About 37km north of Enterprise is the **McNallie Creek Picnic Area**, with a waterfall tumbling into a water-worn bowl of rock. Another 3km north, a parking area offers good views over the plains as far as Great Slave Lake.

Lady Evelyn Falls Territorial Park, 7km off Hwy 1 on the road to Kakisa, is open May 15 to Sept 15. It has a short walking path to the impressive falls, which flow over the edge of an ancient coral reef. Another trail leads to the river beneath the falls, where there's good fishing for whitefish. There's a very fine *campground* ($12) with showers and tall trees presided over by the roar of the falls. It's usually full on weekends with fisherfolk.

The village of **Kakisa**, 13km off Hwy 1, is a small community with nice views of Kakisa Lake, a gas station, convenience store and motel.

Some 105km after Enterprise, Hwy 3 branches north for 31km to the free ferry (☎ 800-661-0750) over the Mackenzie River. It operates 6am to midnight from roughly mid-May to mid-December. There is an ice bridge in the winter and no crossing at all for two to three weeks during the freeze-up and spring thaw.

FORT PROVIDENCE
pop 800

A Slavey community, Fort Providence lies on the banks of the Mackenzie River. The site was settled in 1861 when a Roman Catholic mission was established, followed soon after by a Hudson's Bay Company trading post. The access road is 6km from the ferry and 312km south of Yellowknife; it's another 5km to the village proper. The Fort Providence Visitor Information Centre (☎ 867-699-3410) is on Hwy 3 next to the service station. In town there are benches atop the 10m cliffs overlooking the river. Past the beautiful wooden church, the road leads to the dock. The fishing is very good and pike, walleye and maybe grayling can be caught from shore.

Two kilometers off Hwy 3 on the access road to town is the good *Fort Providence Campground (no ☎)* by the river. It has showers and unpleasant pit toilets. Camping costs $12.

Big River Motel (☎ *867-699-4301, fax 867-699-4327)* Rooms $75. On Hwy 3 near the access road into town, the basic, charmless Big River Motel has a service station and café.

Snowshoe Inn (☎ *867-699-3511, fax 867-699-4300)* Singles/doubles $95/115. In town, the larger Snowshoe Inn has decent modern rooms. The Frontier Coachlines bus stops in front.

NORTH OF FORT PROVIDENCE

Hwy 3 follows the western boundary of the **Mackenzie Bison Sanctuary** for nearly 100km. The sanctuary holds the largest herd of free-ranging, pure wood bison in the world, some of which can occasionally be seen by the side of the road. Hiking is not recommended as there are no trails, it's easy to get lost and the bison can be ill-tempered (possibly due to the enormous swarms of bugs).

The paved and straight road passes through scraggly forests and hilly terrain into the twin Dogrib communities of **Edzo** (214km from Fort Providence) and **Rae**, combined population 1900. In Rae, there is a motel, restaurant, service station and basic convenience store. From here to Yellowknife (98km) you see the rounded and pinkish rock outcrops that form part of the Canadian Shield. This portion of Hwy 3 is unpaved, slow, winding and pretty rough (but manageable in an ordinary car).

HAY RIVER
pop 3800

The town of Hay River sits on the southern shore of Great Slave Lake, 38km north of Enterprise on Hwy 2. This is the heart of Big River Country, which encompasses the area and communities near the Mackenzie, Hay and Slave Rivers and Great Slave Lake. Although it is a bit of a detour from the Mackenzie Hwy, it is a good place to stop.

Hay River has two distinct areas. The old part of town is at the north end on Vale Island; the newer section of town is to the south and will be seen first on arrival by Hwy 2 (called the Mackenzie Hwy in town). This is the commercial center with all the restaurants and stores. The Visitor Information Centre (☎ 867-874-3180) is at Mackenzie Hwy and McBryan Dr. It is open 9am to 9pm daily from mid-May to mid-September. The rest of the year, stop by the town hall for information. The library has free Internet access.

There are a few things to see around this small but busy town. It's a major distribution center where barges load up for trips to settlements along the Mackenzie River and up to the Arctic coast. There is a significant commercial fishery here, including packing and shipping operations. The town operates a vendor's and fish market every Saturday during the summer. The broad sandy **beach** on Vale Island is attractive, and you can fish in the surf. Several kilometers of **trails** wind along the Hay River and across Vale Island.

Across the Hay River, the Dene Reserve operates the **Dene Cultural Institute** (☎ 867-874-8480, W *www.deneculture.org; admission free; open 1pm-5pm Mon-Fri May-Sept)*, 9km from Hwy 5 down Dene Village Rd. This small center offers tours of the Dene village (by appointment only) and has some displays on Dene culture.

Places to Stay & Eat

Hay River Territorial Park Campground (☎ 867-874-3772, *off 104 St on Vale Island)* Tents/RVs $15/20. Open May 15-Sept 15. Near the public beach on Vale Island, this densely wooded campground has hot showers, a barbecue area and flush toilets. It fills up on weekends, but staff will always find an empty spot for you.

Paradise Garden Camp Ground (☎ 867-874-6414, fax 867-874-4422) Tents/RVs $12/20. Some 24km south of Hay River just off Hwy 2, this is a delightful place on a sweeping bend of the Hay River. The sunny campground is in an open field. In summer it sells beautiful organic produce. There's also a kitchen.

Harbour House B&B (☎ 867-874-2233, fax 867-874-2249, 2 Lakeshore Dr) Singles/doubles $50/70. Overlooking the public beach, Harbour House B&B has wonderful views of Great Slave Lake. The best value in town, the rates at this clean beach house include a self-serve continental breakfast and use of the kitchen.

Several motels line the Mackenzie Hwy leading into town.

Caribou Motor Inn (☎ 867-874-6706, fax 867-874-6704, 912 Mackenzie Hwy) Singles/doubles $85/90. The rooms here have garish carpets but firm beds.

Ptarmigan Inn (☎ 867-874-6781, 800-661-0842, fax 867-874-3392, W *www.ptarmigan inn.com, 10J Gagnier St)* Singles/doubles $105/118. Ptarmigan Inn has standard rooms that are a bit worn; its main advantages are its downtown location and its restaurant.

There is a surprising amount of choice here for places to eat, with several situated around the commercial center.

Boardroom Restaurant (☎ 867-874-2111, 891 Mackenzie Hwy) Main dishes $8-13. This is a local favorite, with a large and multicultural choice of Chinese, Northern, Italian and Mexican specialties.

Getting There & Away

Buffalo Airways (☎ 867-874-3333) and First Air (☎ 867-874-2847, 800-267-1247) fly to Yellowknife from the airport on Vale Island. Canadian North (☎ 867-874-2435, 800-661-1505) serves Edmonton.

Greyhound (☎ 867-874-6966, 800-661-8747) has daily bus service to Edmonton ($190, 16 hours). Frontier Coachlines

(☎ 867-874-2566) serves Yellowknife and other places connected by road, such as Fort Smith, Hay River, Fort Providence and Fort Simpson. The bus station is at 39-141 Mackenzie Hwy, just south of the bridge to Vale Island.

FORT SMITH
pop 2600

This sleepy town sits on Hwy 5 on Hwy 5 along the Alberta border, 333km east of Hay River. Stop by the **Northern Life Museum/Fort Smith Visitors Centre** (☎ 867-872-2014, 110 King St; free admission; open 8:30am-6pm Mon-Fri & 1pm-5pm Sat & Sun June-Aug). It has information and exhibits on local history. **Fort Smith Mission Historic Park**, behind St Joseph's Cathedral, is the site of a 1912 Catholic mission.

The nearby Slave River affords several relaxing walking opportunities. From viewpoints at the Rapids of the Drowned and Mountain Rapids, you can watch **white pelicans** serenely surfing in the waves; they nest on seven islands in the middle of the river. *Thebacha Trails*, by Libby Gunn, is a good guide to natural areas near Fort Smith, including Wood Buffalo National Park.

The town acts as a supply center for Wood Buffalo National Park; the entrance to the park is nearby. Get your food in town, as there is nowhere to buy it in the park.

If you want to stay overnight, there are several choices in Fort Smith.

Queen Elizabeth Territorial Park Campground (☎ 867-872-6400) Sites $12. Open May 15-Sept 15. At the end of Teepee Trail 4km west of the town center, this campground lies on the banks of the Slave River. Showers and firewood are available.

Portage Inn (☎ 867-872-2276, 72 Portage Rd) Singles/doubles $115/130. This hotel has large, comfortable rooms with microwaves and stoves.

Pelican Rapids Inn (☎ 867-872-2789, fax 867-872-4727, 152 McDougal Rd) Singles/doubles $120/130. Across from the park visitors center, this inn has standard, overpriced hotel rooms and a serviceable restaurant (most items $7-13).

WOOD BUFFALO NATIONAL PARK
Established in 1922 and nearly 45,000 sq km in size, Wood Buffalo is Canada's largest na-

tional park. Bigger than Switzerland, this wilderness world heritage site lies two-thirds in Alberta and one-third in the Northwest Territories. It is a land of endless boreal forest dappled with bogs and crisscrossed with the shallow delta channels of the Peace and Athabasca rivers. Much of the vast park is inaccessible.

The park is home to one of the world's largest free-roaming bison herds – about 2600 animals – and is the nesting habitat for the only remaining wild migratory flock of whooping cranes. Though rare and endangered, the whooping crane population has

Whooping crane

increased – thanks to international conservation efforts – and attempts are being made to establish a new migratory flock. Moose, caribou, bears, lynx, wolves and many smaller animals abound; more than one million ducks, geese and swans pass by in autumn and spring on their migratory routes. Major features include the Peace-Athabasca Delta, the Salt Plains and karst topography, with underground rivers and sinkholes. Many scenic areas lie a short hike from the road, although some, such as the Peace-Athabasca Delta, are accessible only by boat. Mosquitoes and horseflies can be a serious problem in late June and July – come prepared for battle.

The only year-round road access is from Fort Smith, where there is a Visitors Reception Centre (☎ 867-872-7960, fax 867-872-3910, ⓦ www.parkscanada.gc.ca, Box 750, Fort Smith, NT X0E 0P0) at McDougal Rd and Portage Ave. This center includes a slide show, exhibits and hiking maps (but no topographical maps). It's open daily mid-June to Labour Day and Monday to Friday the rest of the year.

Within the park in Northern Alberta, on the shores of Lake Athabasca, **Fort Chipewyan** is the oldest continuing European settlement in Alberta. There's a Visitors Reception Centre (☎ 780-697-3662) here. The road from Peace Point to Fort Chipewyan is only passable in winter.

Currently, there's no admission fee for the park, but one may be instituted in the near future, very possibly on the day before your arrival.

Activities

Several day-use areas are suitable for **hiking**. The Salt Plains, off Parson's Lake Road, is a 1km walk to a vast plain of salt formed by the evaporation of mineral-laden water seeping out of the earth. Near the Salt River, a short trail leads past a red-sided garter snake pit. The northernmost reptiles in North America, these harmless serpents can be seen entwined in mating balls during the April/May mating season. Nearby, a 16km loop trail leads through boreal forest, salt meadows and along salt flats. The 30-minute walk to Grosbeak Lake – a salt flat strewn with weirdly shaped glacial erratics – is especially worthwhile.

Backcountry hiking, with yet more opportunities to gaze upon bison, is available around Sweetgrass Station. Anyone wishing to visit this area must contact the park well in advance for safety information and backcountry permits (currently free); this area is sometimes closed due to outbreaks of anthrax disease among the animal population. It occurs naturally and periodically and requires some culling of the herd. In winter it is possible to go **skiing** or **showshoeing** on the hiking trails.

Canoeing on the historical fur trade routes along the Athabasca, Peace and Slave Rivers is possible on several backcountry day trips. Contact the park well ahead of time for details and permits. Three outfitters for canoeing and backcountry hiking operate out of Fort Smith (see the park Web site for a list).

You can go **swimming** at Pine Lake.

Places to Stay

There are few comforts in Wood Buffalo National Park, although nearby Fort Smith offers modern accommodations.

Pine Lake Campground (☎ 867-872-7960) Tent sites $10. This small, unstaffed campground, 60km south of Fort Smith, has 24 sites, pump water and a beach. Be prepared to treat the drinking water.

The more adventurous may set off on their own and camp at a beautiful backcountry spot at Rainbow Lakes, if they first obtain a permit from the visitors' center in Fort Smith.

WEST OF GREAT SLAVE LAKE

From the junction with Hwy 3, the Mackenzie Hwy (Hwy 1) continues along a gravel road 300km west to Fort Simpson and beyond. At about two-thirds of the way to Fort Simpson, stop at **Sambaa Deh Falls Territorial Park** (*no* ☎; *open May 15-Sept 15*). This park includes a marvelous waterfall that can be viewed from the road, a fishing spot 10 minutes' walk downstream through multi-hued muskeg (look for the hidden waterfall), and the smaller Coral Falls. The nice, clean *campground* has sites for $12 and showers.

At the junction of the Mackenzie Hwy and Hwy 7, **Checkpoint** has a gas station, a restaurant and a *motel* (☎ 867-695-2953) with simple rooms ($85) in a mobile home.

There is a free ferry (☎ 800-661-0750) across the Liard River just south of Fort Simpson. It runs 8am to 11:45pm from mid-May to late October, replaced by an ice bridge in winter. There's no road connection during the freeze-up and thaw.

Fort Simpson

pop 1300

Established in 1804 as a fur-trading post, Fort Simpson was once district headquarters for the Hudson's Bay Company. Today, most of the people in Fort Smith are Slavey. This is the major town of the Deh Cho region, as the region around the Mackenzie River is known. With its tour operators and charter airlines, it is also the main access point for Nahanni National Park Reserve, 145km west of Fort Simpson. There are ATMs and a bank in town.

Arriving from the south, the Visitors Information Centre (☎ 867-695-3182, [e] vofsvic@shehtah.ca) is at the entrance to town. It's open 9am to 7pm daily May to September. There's a short walk with views along the Mackenzie River on the northern side of town.

The ***Fort Simpson Territorial Campground*** (no ☎), near the Visitors Information Centre, has showers, pit toilets and pleasant campsites for $15/20 tents/RVs.

Bannockland Inn (☎ 867-695-3337, fax 867-695-2555, e *bannockl@cancom.net*) Singles/doubles from $130/140. This spacious B&B, 4.6km east of town, overlooks the intersection of the Mackenzie and Liard Rivers. It's a great place to stay if you have a car or another way into town.

Nahanni Inn (☎ 867-695-2201, fax 867-695-3000, e *nahanmar@cancom.net*) Singles/doubles $125/152. This basic, worn hotel is on the main street (100 St) past the Catholic church. It is one of only two in town and is often full. It has a lounge and restaurant.

First Air (☎ 867-695-2020, 800-267-1247) and Air Tindi (☎ 867-669-8260) serve Yellowknife. Frontier Coachlines (☎ 867-874-2566) serves Hay River.

From Fort Simpson, the Mackenzie Hwy continues 222km north along the Mackenzie River to the small Dene community of Wrigley. Hunting, trapping and fishing remain the basis of this mainly log-cabin village. A winter ice road connects Norman Wells.

Liard Hwy

From a point 63km south of Fort Simpson, the Liard Hwy (Hwy 7) branches west off the Mackenzie Hwy along the Liard River valley toward Nahanni Butte and Fort Liard. The Mackenzie Mountains can be seen to the west. The road then travels south into British Columbia to Fort Nelson, making a circle through British Columbia, the NT and Alberta possible. From Fort Simpson to Fort Nelson the distance is 487km.

Nahanni Butte is a small community (population 80) accessible only by air charter or boat, or by ice road in the winter. There's a café, general store, motel and river taxi services. Most visitors are near the tail end of their trips down the South Nahanni River.

Across from Nahanni Butte and 110km south from the Liard Trail starting point is **Blackstone Territorial Park** (no ☎), with information, short hiking trails and a terrific view of the Mackenzie Mountains and the Liard River. There's also a ***campground***

($15) with showers and flush toilets. The park is open May 15 to September 15. Most trips down the South Nahanni River in the national park end here.

Fort Liard
pop 500

This largely traditional town is well-known for the birch bark baskets, adorned with porcupine quills, made by Dene women. These can be purchased at the Acho Dene Native Crafts shop (☎ 403-770-4161) in the middle of town, which also doubles as the visitors' center.

The town has undergone a boomlet since the opening of the Liard Trail in 1983 and nearby exploration for oil. Before you reach the village, the unstaffed, free ***Hay River Community Campground*** has drinking water, an outhouse and a pretty view of Hay River. The ***Liard Valley General Store & Motel*** (☎ 867-770-4441, fax 867-770-4442) is on the far side of town and charges $95/115 singles/doubles. This place and the only other motel in town are often full, so you'll need to make a reservation.

There are also a café and a service station. The British Columbia border is 38km to the south.

NAHANNI NATIONAL PARK RESERVE

This magnificent wilderness park in the southwestern corner of the territory, close to the Yukon border, is one of the major draws of the NT and attracts visitors from around the world. The 4766-sq-km Nahanni National Park Reserve protects a superb portion of the Mackenzie Mountains and the turbulent South Nahanni River and its spectacular canyons. It is visited mainly by canoeists challenging the whitewaters (considered among the best on the continent) of this renowned 322km Canadian Heritage River. The park has been designated as a Unesco world heritage site because of its dramatic, pristine nature. Only about a thousand visitors come here each year, ensuring that the area remains peaceful and unspoiled. A proposal supported by the Deh Cho First Nations would extend protection to the entire South Nahanni watershed, a sevenfold increase over current park boundaries.

Aside from the mountains, river and canyons, highlights include the waterfalls, particularly **Virginia Falls**, which at 96m is about twice the height of Niagara Falls, and also the hot springs near Rabbitkettle Lake.

Dene stories of giant people and animals associated with this area go back thousands of years. Outsiders have added their own stories since the early 1900s, when the discovery of the decapitated corpses of two brothers looking for gold led to tales of enormous mountain men, wild native tribes, Amazon women and other fanciful horrors. Numerous other miners who died of possible unnatural causes or just disappeared only added to the area's wild reputation. Various place names in the park such as Headless Range, Funeral Range and Deadmen Valley recall this colorful legacy.

Nowadays the wildlife includes large populations of bears, mountain goats, moose, Dall sheep and wolves.

Park information and permits are available in Fort Simpson from the main park office (☎ 867-695-3151, fax 867-695-2446, W www.parkscanada.gc.ca). It is open 8:30am to noon and 1pm to 5pm daily June 15 to Sept 15, and Monday to Friday only the rest of the year. There is a smaller seasonal information office at Blackstone Territorial Park.

The day-use fee for the park is $10, and the overnight park fee is $100 total per trip. There's a very strict quota system for visitors (24 people maximum at the Virginia Falls campground), so contacting the park in advance is essential.

Getting There & Around

With no road access, getting into the park is not cheap. Your choices are a long and difficult overland hike from the Yukon, or by charter airplane. Plane rides are usually part of a guided tour, although you can charter a plane for a self-guided trip.

Air Companies in Fort Simpson provide 'flightseeing' trips into the park via floatplane. A typical six-hour trip will take you over the flat boreal forest dotted with lakes and through steep-walled canyons before landing in the river just above Virginia Falls. You'll then have time to reconnoiter the falls before heading back over the Ram Plateau. This trip costs about $950 for up to three people. If you're alone or traveling as a couple, you *might* be able to find other

travelers to split the costs by phoning the air companies in advance or by asking around at the campground, visitors' center, hotels and restaurants in Fort Simpson.

A cheaper three-hour flight without landing near the falls is available for $750 for up to five people.

The three companies that have floatplanes for landing at the falls are:

Wolverine Air ☎ 867-695-2263, fax 867-695-3400, W www.wolverineair.com

Simpson Air ☎ 867-695-2505, fax 867-695-2925, W www.cancom.net/~simpair

South Nahanni Airways ☎ 867-695-2007, fax 867-695-2943, e snasimp@cancom.net

Float Trips Even a river float trip starts out in a small airplane since there's no other way into the park. Raft, canoe or kayak trips can be arranged with a licensed outfitter or done independently. For independent travel, you need good paddling skills (for Class IV rapids), river rescue abilities, good survival gear and skills relevant to a remote mountain environment. Don't count on help out there. If you lose a canoe through the rapids, you could be in real trouble. Outfitters can take folks with a wider variety of skills.

All trips down the South Nahanni River within the park start at Rabbitkettle Lake or Virginia Falls, because these are the only two places where a plane can land. The 118km from Rabbitkettle Lake to Virginia Falls are through a broad valley with a meandering river and no rapids and take three to four days to complete. Once past the portage around Virginia Falls, it's another 252km to Blackstone Territorial Park, first through steep canyons with rapids and then along the Liard River. This part of the trip requires an average of seven to ten days. The 'classic' trip from Rabbitkettle Lake to Blackstone Territorial Park is 14 days, with nine days paddling and five days for hiking and delays.

The guided canoe and raft trips are excellent but expensive. The prices and nature of the excursions are similar, ranging from $2600 to $3900 and beyond, depending on distance. Different times of the season offer different advantages, so ask for details to best match your interests. Because access to the park is limited, trips should be prebooked, preferably months in advance. The canoe trips are best for people with some basic experience, although you needn't be an advanced whitewater paddler. Raft trips are more relaxing, provide more time to enjoy the scenery and are suitable for all ages. The three licensed companies are:

Black Feather ☎/fax 705-746-4625, ☎ 888-849-7668, **W** www.blackfeather.com

Nahanni River Adventures ☎ 867-668-3180, 800-297-6927, fax 867-668-3056, **W** www.nahanni.com

Nahanni Wilderness Adventures ☎/fax 403-637-3843, ☎ 888-897-5223, **W** www.nahanniwild.com

Independent travelers can contact the guiding companies for assistance with renting canoes or rafts. You'll need to charter an airplane into the park by contacting the companies listed under Air, earlier.

Camping is along the river banks. There are only four designated campgrounds. The campground at Virginia Falls is staffed and has a dock for canoes and floatplanes, as well as composting toilets exposed to the grandeur of nature. The campground at Rabbitkettle Lake is also staffed.

MACKENZIE RIVER VALLEY

The northwestern region of the NT is wide and flat. The Mackenzie River, swollen by water draining from one-fifth of Canada, wends its way across the countryside; in places it is over 3km wide. This is popular canoe and kayak country, with some hearty souls taking advantage of the long summer days to paddle from Fort Providence to Tuktoyaktuk on the Arctic Ocean, a distance of 1800km.

Norman Wells
pop 900

This historic oil town lies on the northern shore of the Mackenzie River halfway between Fort Simpson and Inuvik. You can get more information from the town of Norman Wells (☎ 867-587-2238, **W** www.normanwells.com) or the Norman Wells Historical Centre (☎ 867-587-2415) on Mackenzie Dr that's open noon-6pm in the summer only, which has free displays and videos on the regional geology, arts and crafts, rivers and the Canol Heritage Trail.

The **Great Norman Wells Fossil Hunt** is a week-long series of events each August that focuses on searching for fossils along the river and canyons of the region. Hikers can also explore fossil-laden areas such as **Fossil Canyon** by themselves. Picnicking and canoeing are possible at **Jackfish Lake**. If that doesn't keep you busy, you can always make a trip to the town dump at dusk to watch the black bears.

The town is also used as a jumping-off point for several canoeable rivers, including the Mountain, Keele and Natla. Some of the guide companies listed under Nahanni National Park Reserve, earlier, lead trips here. The friendly folks at **Mountain River Outfitters** (☎/fax 867-587-2698, **W** www.mountainriver.nt.ca) rent canoes, provide transportation back from the rivers and carry Canol Heritage Trail hikers across the Mackenzie River to the start of the trail.

The town's main attraction is the **Canol Heritage Trail**, designated a national historic site, which leads 372km southwest to the Yukon border. From there, a road leads to Ross River and the Yukon highway system. The trail was built at enormous monetary and human cost during WWII to supply oil to Whitehorse; Canol is shorthand for 'Canadian Oil'. The huge project was abandoned, however, in 1947 because the war was over and there were cheaper ways to transport oil. Today the trail is lined with derelict army camps and equipment and should really be designated as a monument to American taxpayers, who forked out over $300 million (in 1945 dollars) for its construction.

The route traverses peaks, canyons and barrens. Wildlife is abundant, and there are numerous deep river crossings along the trail. There are no facilities, although you can sleep in some of the old Quonset huts. Canol Rd (Hwy 6) from Whitehorse meets the trail on the Yukon border. Hiking the whole length takes three to four weeks and most people need to arrange food drops along the way. The beginning of the trail is flat and swampy, so day hikes from Norman Wells are not recommended. Some visitors use helicopters (available in Norman Wells) to reach the most interesting parts of the trail. A couple of dozen stout souls hike the entire trail each year.

Places to Stay & Eat The free *campground* is inconveniently located a few kilometers west of town. Campers often just pitch their tents on the river banks in front of the town proper. No one seems to mind. Of the three hotels, **Rayuka Inn** (☎ 867-587-2354, fax 867-587-2861), in the center of town, is reasonable, centrally located and costs $130 per room.

Both the **Yamouri Inn** and **Mackenzie Valley Hotel** have decent restaurants.

Getting There & Away Canadian North (☎ 867-587-2361, 800-661-1505) stops on its flights between Yellowknife and Inuvik. North-Wright Airways (☎ 867-587-2333) also serves Yellowknife and Inuvik (indirectly), as well as the even more isolated communities along the river. The only road access to Norman Wells is by ice road in the winter.

Inuvik
pop 3500
Inuvik lies on the East Channel of the Mackenzie River 97km south of the Arctic coast. It's the NT's second largest town and the tourism and supply center for the Western Arctic. Founded in 1955 as a government administrative post, Inuvik is a feat of engineering considering the distance that construction materials were brought and the permanently frozen subsoil on which it was built. The population is equally divided between Inuit, Dene and non–First Nations people.

For nearly two months each year from late June, Inuvik has 24 hours of daylight. This is a situation that people soon adapt to, and locals say that the way to tell a new arrival is the aluminum foil in their windows. The first snow falls at the end of August. In early December the sun sets and does not rise until January.

Inuvik has the worn appearance typical of northern towns, but it's a fascinating place and worth the effort and expense to visit.

The Western Arctic Visitors Centre (☎ 867-777-4727, in winter ☎ 867-777-7237, **w** www .town.inuvik.nt.ca, 284 Mackenzie Rd) is open 9am to 8pm daily from mid-May to the end of August. The CIBC Bank (☎ 867-777-2848, 134 Mackenzie Rd) has an ATM. The post office (☎ 867-777-2252, 187 Mackenzie Rd), open 9am to 5:30pm Monday to Friday, also has an ATM (24 hours).

Boreal Books (☎ 867-777-3748, **e** boreal@ permafrost.com, 181 Mackenzie Rd) is a little shop with a big selection of northern books and topographical and river maps. It

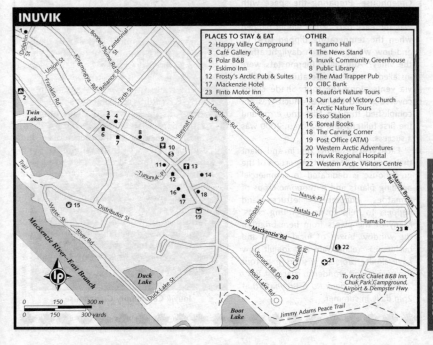

INUVIK

PLACES TO STAY & EAT	OTHER
2 Happy Valley Campground	1 Ingamo Hall
3 Café Gallery	4 The News Stand
6 Polar B&B	5 Inuvik Community Greenhouse
7 Eskimo Inn	8 Public Library
12 Frosty's Arctic Pub & Suites	9 The Mad Trapper Pub
17 Mackenzie Hotel	10 CIBC Bank
23 Finto Motor Inn	11 Beaufort Nature Tours
	13 Our Lady of Victory Church
	14 Arctic Nature Tours
	15 Esso Station
	16 Boreal Books
	18 The Carving Corner
	19 Post Office (ATM)
	20 Western Arctic Adventures
	21 Inuvik Regional Hospital
	22 Western Arctic Visitors Centre

To Arctic Chalet B&B Inn, Chuk Park Campground, Airport & Dempster Hwy is open 9am to 6pm daily. The public library (☎ 867-777-2749, 100 Mackenzie Rd) offers free Internet access and a book exchange. It is open 10am to 6pm and 7pm to 9pm Monday to Thursday, 10am to 6pm Friday and 2pm to 5pm Saturday and Sunday. Inuvik Regional Hospital (☎ 867-777-8000, 285 Mackenzie Rd) is across from the visitors' center.

In town, an Esso station (☎ 867-777-3974, 17 Distributor St) is open 8am to 9pm daily.

Things to See & Do The town landmark is **Our Lady of Victory Church**, or Igloo Church, with a lovely interior created by local artists. Nearby, **The Carving Corner** is

an amiable place where artists create sculptures from ivory and rock. **Chuk Park**, 6km south of town, has a good lookout tower for viewing the sub-Arctic terrain.

But the best reason to come to Inuvik is to get out of town on an Arctic tour. Most involve flights over the **Mackenzie Delta**, a spectacular place of water, squalls (sudden, violent winds often with rain or snow), pingos (huge earth-covered mounds caused by abundant water and frost heaves), wildlife and abandoned trapper's huts on emerald-green banks. Tours start at $159 for three hours and are worth it for the aerial views alone. Photographers should try for a seat at the rear of the plane.

Light, Water & Tomatoes

Satellite television and the Internet connect Inuvik with the world, but try finding a ripe tomato or a fresh cucumber. For Inuvik gardeners, conditions are impossibly harsh, with a short growing season, 24 hours of sunlight and frozen soil to contend with. Canned and frozen food arrive by truck via the rough 747km Dempster Hwy.

So in 1998, a group of enthusiastic gardeners convinced Aurora College to donate the old hockey rink and started the first effort to take local control of the food supply in the northern

communities – the Inuvik Community Greenhouse. Preparing the space with raised planting beds and drip irrigation was the easy part. What would happen when the temperature dipped to 0°C, and how would so much daylight affect the vines? Automatic thermostats were installed and the temperature controlled via vents along the roof. Shade cloths covered sensitive plants. Much was accomplished through trial and error and the first full growing season in 2000 was a success.

Each year residents dig in and plant their own 16 x 16ft plot. A portion of the greenhouse is dedicated to commercial bedding plants and hydroponic crops of tomatoes, cucumbers, lettuces and peppers to help cover operating costs. Many of the plants from here brighten the window boxes of local hotels and businesses. Yellowknife and Iqaluit now have similar projects. Visitors may tour the unique and wonderful space (☎ 867-777-3267, Loucheux Rd & Breynat St) at 2pm daily in summer.

Inuvik Community Greenhouse

SUSAN RIMERMAN

Arctic Nature Tours (☎ 867-777-3300, fax 867-777-3400, e arcticnt@permafrost.com, w www.arcticnaturetours.com, 180 Mackenzie Rd) is next to the Igloo Church. It has the best range of tours to untouched places like Herschel Island ($285 per person), where primitive camping trips at Pauline Cove (see the Yukon chapter) can be arranged ($580 per person, one to three days). Another popular day or overnight trip is to the small village of Tuktoyaktuk ($159/399 one day/ overnight). **Beaufort Nature Tours** (☎/fax 867-777-3067, e tours@permafrost.com, 169 Mackenzie Rd) has similar air tours as well as longer river trips ($65 to $249).

Western Arctic Adventures (☎ 867-777-2594, fax 867-777-4542, e canoe@perma frost.com, 38 Spruce Hill Dr) rents canoes and kayaks for about $200 per week, depending on the destination, and makes logistical arrangements for independent travelers.

Special Events

Sunrise Festival This event (☎ 867-777-2607) brings the locals together in early January for fireworks on the ice to greet the first sunrise after 30 days of darkness.

Great Northern Arts Festival This major show of First Nations art (☎ 867-777-3536, fax 867-777-4445, w www.greatart.nt.ca) happens during the third week of July. Most of the artists travel from remote villages to display and sell their high-quality work. There are evening dance and drumming performances, as well as workshops and demonstrations during the day, some especially for children.

Places to Stay

Chuk Park Campground (☎ 867-777-3613) Tent/RV hookup $10/20. Open Jun-early Sept. This campground, about 6km south of town on the Dempster Hwy, provides hot showers and firewood. There's a good view of the delta and the breeze keeps the mosquitoes down a bit. In town, **Happy Valley Campground** (☎ 867-777-3652, Franklin Road) has the same rates and services, with RV sites and tent platforms, nice views and a coin laundry.

Polar B&B (☎ 867-777-2554, fax 867-777-3668, e islc@permafrost.com, 75 Mackenzie Rd) Singles/doubles $75/85. Polar B&B has four large rooms with shared bath, common area and kitchen, and includes free laundry.

Frosty's Arctic Pub & Suites (☎ 867-777-4839, fax 867-777-7777, 80 Tununuk Place) Rooms $135. Another good choice, Frosty's rooms have kitchenette, private bath and air conditioning. It runs an airport shuttle.

Arctic Chalet B&B Inn (☎ 867-777-3535, fax 867-777-4443, w www.arcticchalet.com, 25 Carn St) Economy cabins $45-85 per person without breakfast, rooms & cabins $98-130 with breakfast. The Arctic Chalet is the best place to stay in Inuvik, with bright cabin-style rooms in a pretty setting. It offers airport pick-up, shared courtesy cars for the 1km trip to town, canoes and fishing gear, and if you're visiting in the winter, you can learn dogsledding.

There are three equally uninspiring hotels in town: **Mackenzie Hotel** (☎ 867-777-2861, fax 867-777-3317, e mack@permafrost.com, 185 Mackenzie Rd) and **Eskimo Inn** (☎ 867-777-2801, fax 867-777-2671, e eskimo@permafrost.com, 133 Mackenzie Rd) have singles/doubles for $149/164. The Eskimo has some rooms with air conditioning. At the east entrance of town, **Finto Motor Inn** (☎ 867-777-2647, fax 867-777-3442, e finto@permafrost.com, 288 Mackenzie Rd) has singles/doubles for $159/174. There are also some renovated rooms, but the price is steep ($189/204).

Places to Eat & Drink For groceries and supplies, visit **The News Stand** (☎ 867-777-4822, 90 Mackenzie Rd), open 8:30am to midnight daily.

Musk ox and caribou burgers are on just about every menu in town. For less meaty fare, try **Café Gallery** (☎ 867-777-2888, 90 Mackenzie Rd) Breakfast & Lunch $3.50-10. Open 8am-6pm Mon-Fri, 12pm-6pm Sat & Sun. This pleasant café has espresso, fresh sandwiches and muffins.

Green Briar Restaurant (☎ 867-777-4671, 185 Mackenzie Rd) Lunch $10-15, dinner $12-20. Open 6pm-9pm Mon-Sat. In the Mackenzie Hotel, Green Briar has fresh Arctic foods and a very popular prime-rib special on Thursday nights for $13.95. There's also a pub, **The Brass Rail** (open 11am-2am Mon-Sat), and **The Zoo** (open 9pm-2am Fri & Sat), a dance club, in the hotel.

Ingamo Hall (☎ 867-777-2166, 20 Mackenzie Rd) Ingamo Hall serves lunch every other Thursday at 1:30pm for village elders. Visitors are welcome, there is no charge and you can hear wonderful stories.

The Mad Trapper Pub (☎ 867-777-3825, 124 Mackenzie Rd) Open 11am-2am Mon-Sat. This raucous pub snares locals and visitors alike.

Getting There & Around Mike Zubko Airport is 14km south of town. Canadian North (☎ 867-777-2951, 800-661-1505, W www.canadiannorth.com) flies to Norman Wells and Yellowknife. First Air (☎ 867-777-2341, 800-267-1247, W www.firstair.com) flies to Yellowknife and Winnipeg. Air North (☎ 867-668-2228, 800-661-0407, W www.airnorth.yk.net) flies to Dawson City, Old Crow and Whitehorse. Aklak Air (☎ 867-777-3777, fax 867-777-3388) has scheduled and charter service to the small Arctic communities.

A taxi for one person to/from the airport costs $25; call United Taxi (☎ 867-777-5050) for pick-up.

There are several car rental outlets available at the airport, including Norcan (☎ 867-777-2346, 800-227-7368, e norcan@permafrost.com). For full details on the 747km Dempster Hwy, see the Yukon chapter.

Aklavik
pop 750
Aklavik, 113km north of the Arctic Circle and about 50km west of Inuvik, is home to the Inuvialuit and the Gwich'in, who have traded and sometimes fought each other in this region over the centuries. Aklavik was for a time the administrative center of the area, but serious flooding and erosion from the Mackenzie Delta prompted the Canadian government to select a new site at Inuvik in the 1950s. Many residents have remained in town, refusing to move to drier land. For local information call the hamlet office (☎ 867-978-2351, fax 867-978-2434, PO Box 88, Aklavik, NT X0E 0A0). The Inuvik tour companies (see earlier) visit Aklavik.

ARCTIC REGION
Inuvik is the base for exploring the tiny villages and remote and wild expanses of the Western Arctic. In comparison with these sparsely settled areas, Inuvik seems like a metropolis.

Tuktoyaktuk
pop 1000
About 137km northeast of Inuvik in Kugmallit Bay on the Arctic coast is Tuktoyaktuk, commonly known as Tuk. Originally the home of the whale-hunting Inuit, it's a land base for some of the Beaufort Sea oil and gas explorations. Pods of beluga whales can be seen in July and early August. The Tuk peninsula has the world's highest concentration of pingos. The hamlet office (☎ 867-977-2286, fax 867-977-2110, W www.tuktoyaktuk.com) can provide more information on the area and services.

There is an old military base here dating from the Cold War, as well as old whaling buildings and two charming little churches dating from the time when the Catholic and Anglican churches battled to proselytize the First Nations people. Land access is limited to winter ice roads, and most tourists arrive by air in the summer as part of half-day trips from Inuvik.

Paulatuk
pop 300
This small Karngmalit community is on the Arctic coast at the southern end of Darnley Bay near the mouth of the Hornaday River, about 400km east of Inuvik. The town's name means 'soot of coal' – one of the main attractions is the **Smoking Hills**, which contain smoldering sulfide-rich slate and seams of coal. For more information, contact the hamlet office (☎ 867-580-3531, fax 867-580-3703).

Paulatuk is the closest settlement to **Tuktut Nogait National Park**, a wild and untouched place about 45km east that is a major calving ground for Bluenose caribou. There are no services or facilities here. For information, contact Parks Canada (☎ 867-580-3233, fax 867-580-3234, W www.parkscanada.gc.ca).

Banks Island
Lying in the Arctic Ocean to the north of Paulatuk, Banks Island may have been first inhabited 3500 years ago. Wildlife is abundant, and this is one of the best places to see musk ox. The island has two bird sanctuaries where you can see flocks of snowgeese and seabirds in the summer. **Sachs Harbour**, also known as Kiaahuk, an

Inuvialuit community of about 150, is the only settlement on the island.

Arctic Nature Tours *(☎ 867-777-3300, fax 867-777-3400,* **w** *www.arcticnature tours.com)* runs a week-long tour to the island from Inuvik that costs about $2800.

Aulavik National Park, on the north of the island, covers 12,300 sq km. It has the world's largest concentration of musk ox as well as badlands, tundra and archaeological sites. For more information, contact Parks Canada.

Nunavut

On April 1, 1999, the territory of Nunavut was created out of what had been the eastern Arctic region of the Northwest Territories (NT), fulfilling a dream of the Native Inuit people to have their own self-governing territory.

Nunavut means 'Our Land' in Inuktitut, the language of the Inuit. They make up 85% of the population and are scattered over the vast stretches of tundra and polar islands. The Inuit are in an uneasy transition between their traditional lives of subsistence hunting of whales and seals and modern lives in towns with schools and jobs. Even when living in towns, Inuit look for time to go out 'on the land' to fish, hunt and live in temporary camps. More than 80% live in government housing; unemployment and other social problems are abundant. Alcohol is severely restricted everywhere and banned entirely in many communities. But after years of existing under the rule from Ottawa and Yellowknife, there is a palpable excitement as the citizens prepare to determine their own destinies.

Nunavut is a wild and isolated place. You can journey from the waters of Hudson Bay all the way to the North Pole, and experience extraordinary places such as Ellesmere and Baffin Islands. Your only real limitations are stamina, time and money, especially money.

History

Nunavut has been inhabited for over 4000 years. The first recorded arrival of Europeans was an expedition led by Martin Frobisher, which landed at Baffin Island in 1576 while looking for the Northwest Passage. Other explorers followed, including John Franklin, who disappeared with 128 crewmen in 1845.

For the next 150 years, the Canadian government was primarily interested in the eastern Arctic for its mineral wealth and strategic position. Large-scale government programs in the 1960s forcibly resettled most of the Inuit in villages away from their nomadic lives.

In 1982, 56% of the voters in the NT approved splitting the territory and creat-

Highlights

Granted Territorial Status: 1999
Area: 2.2 million sq km
Population: 25,000
Provincial Capital: Iqaluit

- Hike the pristine Auyuittuq National Park.
- Explore the magnificent desolation of the lands around Resolute.
- Stay up all night during endless summer days above the Arctic Circle.

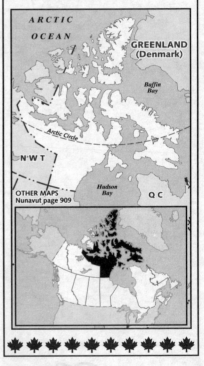

ing Nunavut. There were then several years of wrangling over where to draw the territorial division and how to split up the bureaucracy and infrastructure spoils. In 1993, the Canadian Parliament approved the Nunavut Land Claims Agreement Act, which returned land ownership to Inuit and paved the way for the official creation

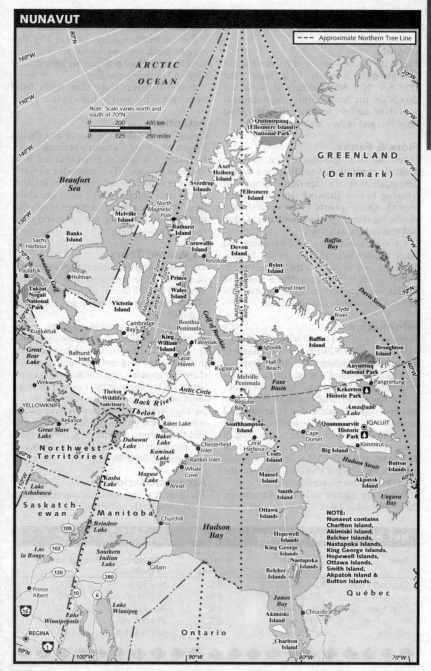

NUNAVUT

--- Approximate Northern Tree Line

ARCTIC OCEAN

Note: Scale varies north and south of 70°N

0   200   400 km
0   125   250 miles

GREENLAND
(Denmark)

Quttinirpaaq
(Ellesmere Island)
National Park

Axel
Heiberg
Island

Sverdrup
Islands

Ellesmere
Island

Beaufort
Sea

Baffin
Bay

Melville
Island

North
Magnetic
Pole

Bathurst
Island

Banks
Island

Sachs
Harbour

Cornwallis
Island

Devon
Island

Bylot
Island

Resolute

Paulatuk

Holman

Prince
of
Wales
Island

Pond Inlet

Greenland Time Zone
Eastern Time Zone

Davis Strait

Tuktut
Nogait
National
Park

Clyde
River

Kugluktuk

Victoria
Island

Cambridge
Bay

Boothia
Peninsula

Gulf of Boothia

Broughton
Island

Baffin
Island

Auyuittuq
National Park

Pangnirtung

Great
Bear
Lake

Bathurst
Inlet

King
William
Island

Taloyoak

Igloolik

Gjoa
Haven

Kugaaruk

Hall
Beach

Kekerten
Historic Park

Amadjuak
Lake

Wekweti

Melville
Peninsula

Foxe
Basin

Qaummaarviit
Historic Park

IQALUIT

YELLOWKNIFE

Thelon
Wildlife
Sanctuary

Back River

Thelon R.

Arctic Circle

Repulse
Bay

Cape
Dorset

Kimmirut

Reliance

Baker Lake

Big Island

Great
Slave
Lake

Dubawnt
Lake

Baker
Lake

Southampton
Island

Hudson Strait

Button
Islands

Northwest
Territories

Kaminak
Lake

Chesterfield
Inlet

Coral
Harbour

Coats
Island

Akpatok
Island

Lake
Athabasca

Kasba
Lake

Maguse
Lake

Rankin Inlet

Whale
Cove

Mansel
Island

Ungava
Bay

Saskatch-
ewan

Manitoba

Arviat

Smith
Island

105

Reindeer
Lake

Churchill

Hudson
Bay

Ottawa
Islands

NOTE:
Nunavut contains
Charlton Island,
Akimiski Island,
Belcher Islands,
Nastapoka Islands,
King George Islands,
Hopewell Islands,
Ottawa Islands,
Smith Island,
Akpatok Island &
Button Islands.

102

Lac
la Ronge

Southern
Indian Lake

Gillam

Hopewell
Islands

King George
Islands

120

280

Nastapoka
Islands

Prince
Albert

10

6

Belcher
Islands

Québec

16

Lake
Winnipegosis

Lake
Winnipeg

James
Bay

REGINA

1

Ontario

Akimiski
Island

Chisasibi

Charlton
Island

of Nunavut. Many towns have reverted to their original Inuit names.

Climate

This is the Arctic – much of Nunavut north of Hudson Bay is covered by ice most of the year. See 'Not All Darkness at Noon' for details on the temperatures and seasonal periods of daylight for five key towns. Most visitors travel in July and early August.

Flora & Fauna

Given the short growing season, only the toughest of plants survive. These are mainly perennials that can experience months of freezing before thawing for some quick growth. Other plants grow very slowly; shrubs the diameter of a thumb might have 400 years of growth rings.

Caribou, musk oxen, wolves, hares and other smaller animals live on the tundra. The seas and islands of the far north are home to seals, walruses, three kinds of whales – beluga, bowhead and narwhal – and the Arctic icon, the polar bear.

Information

Nunavut Tourism (☎ 867-979-6551, ☎ 800-491-7910, fax 867-979-1261, w www.nunavut tourism.com) publishes *The Arctic Traveller*, an excellent annual resource with comprehensive listings of tour and charter operators.

The Nunavut Handbook is an impressive and encyclopedic guide that is written and produced by longtime residents. It is sold throughout Nunavut or can be ordered in advance from Nortext Multimedia (☎ 613-727-5466, 800-263-1452) or from major online bookstores; it's also available on the Web (w www.arctic-travel.com).

Banks are limited to Iqaluit, Cambridge Bay and Rankin Inlet; ATMs are a bit more common. Credit cards may find limited acceptance outside of these three towns.

Expect weather delays even in July. You may be stuck somewhere for several more days than you had planned, so budget your time and money accordingly.

Nunavut covers three time zones, from Mountain in the west to Eastern in the east.

Activities

Canoeing is good on the Kazan and Thelon Rivers, which are Canadian heritage rivers. Kayaking is a natural, given that the Inuit invented the *qajaq*. The season for all water activities is quite short. Fishing is excellent; Arctic char and huge lake trout are abundant. There are myriad hiking and exploring possibilities, but none are easy and most require a guide.

Organized Tours

The vast majority of visitors to Nunavut will be part of some organized tour. *The Arctic Traveller* has full details of the various types of tour operators. Expect to pay thousands of dollars.

Only the most experienced Arctic travelers should consider completely independent travel. The logistics and conditions are just too hard and unforgiving. However, there are growing opportunities for people who wish to organize their own trips using local guides, as opposed to joining a package trip. Many towns now have associations of local guides. Single travelers may find that getting a group together to meet the minimum tour number (typically two to four) can be difficult.

Accommodations

There are few organized campgrounds; plan to be completely self-sufficient. Outside of

Not All Darkness at Noon

Town	24 Hours of Sunshine	Average July Temp	24 Hours of Darkness	Average January Temp
Cambridge Bay	May 20–July 23	8°C	Nov 30–Jan 11	-30°C
Iqaluit	20 hours max	8°C	19½ hours max	-25°C
Pond Inlet	May 5–Aug 7	8°C	Nov 12–Jan 29	-30°C
Rankin Inlet	18 hours max	8°C	21 hours max	-30°C
Resolute	April 29–Aug 13	5°C	Nov 6–Feb 5	-33°C

Iqaluit, choice of lodging is very limited as well. Expect to pay $125 to $310 a night in some very rough-edged hostelries (some lacking windows, others requiring you to share your room); food is also very expensive. The meals at these commercial establishments and on tours tend to be very meaty and fishy. If you have special needs, make arrangements long before you leave home. Once you're out on the ice is not the time to announce 'I'm vegan.'

Getting There & Around

Planes are the only way to get to Nunavut and around once you are there. Iqaluit is linked to Montréal and Ottawa, and Rankin Inlet to Winnipeg. Yellowknife in the NT and Iqaluit are hubs for services to the High Arctic. First Air (☎ 800-267-1247, fax 613-688-2637, **w** www.firstair.ca) and Canadian North (☎ 867-669-4000, 800-661-1505, **w** www.canadiannorth.com) provide flights to the larger towns; otherwise you will have to charter a plane for trips. Airfares are very expensive – a 'cheap' roundtrip fare from Yellowknife to Iqaluit costs $900.

There are no roads of any kind to any place in Nunavut from any other part of Canada. Each town has a few kilometers of roads around it; if necessary, you can usually rent a truck from somebody, hitchhike, or take the town taxi.

In summer, boats are the method of choice to explore bays and islands. In winter, snowmobiles are the quickest – if noisiest – way between two points.

BAFFIN REGION

This region, centered on Baffin Island, stretches north as far as Ellesmere Island at the peak of the Canadian Arctic, not far from Greenland. Not one tree grows here, but many flowers bloom during the short summer. The northern areas are almost completely uninhabited.

Iqaluit

pop 4000

Iqaluit, the capital of Nunavut, is on the east coast of Baffin Island. The name Iqaluit (ee-**kal**-oo-it) means 'the place of fish.' Whatever you do, avoid the English-language habit of inserting a 'u' after the 'q' because that name means something ruder than 'big butt.'

There is not much to see or do here, but a variety of side trips are possible. Most people coming here stop off as part of a package tour en route to somewhere else. Toonik Tyme is a week-long festival in late April that celebrates Inuit culture. Games and contests include igloo-building.

The Unikkaarvik Visitor's Centre (☎ 867-979-4636, fax 867-979-3754) has information on the entire territory and several displays on local life, art and culture there.

There are two banks and numerous stores here. Many of the stores sell local crafts, or bargain hunters can look for the artisans at local restaurants and bars. Arctic Ventures has probably the best selection of Arctic books in the north.

Baffin Regional Hospital (☎ 867-979-7300) is the only full-service health facility in Nunavut.

Things to See & Do You can also see displays on Inuit art and culture at the **Nunatta Sunakkutaangit Museum** (☎ 867-979-5537) adjacent to the visitors' center.

At **Sylvia Grinnell Territorial Park**, a couple of kilometers from town, *inuksuit* (human-like figures made of rocks) mark a number of hiking trails that take you past archaeological sites and out onto the tundra. **Qaummaarviit Historic Park** is 12km by boat or winter dog-sled from Iqaluit. It preserves a settlement of the early Thule Inuit, who used the area as a winter camp intermittently over 750 years. Many of their sod houses and other artifacts are still there. The visitors' center in Iqaluit can put you in touch with someone for transport and a tour ($100 and up/person, four-person minimum; four to five hours).

Eetuk Outfitting and Equipment Rental (☎ 867-979-1984, fax 867-979-1994, **e** eetuk@nunanet.com), in the Arctic Survival Store, can custom design any kind of Arctic journey (all-day boat tour $225/person, four-person minimum).

Inuit Sea Kayaking Adventures (☎ 867-979-0333, fax 867-979-2414, **e** info@qajaq.ca) arranges a peaceful all-day trip around Frobisher Bay, or across it to Qaummaarviit Historic Park, for $250. It is imperative that you rent a survival suit or dry suit at the Arctic Survival Store ($25); the water in the bay is near freezing.

Places to Stay & Eat *Crazy Caribou Bed and Breakfast* (☎/fax 867-979-2449, House No 490, Happy Valley, **w** www.crazy caribouedandbreakfast.com) Singles/doubles $120/135. This is a cozy place, with comfortable rooms and huge breakfasts.

Accommodations By-The-Sea (☎ 867-979-6074, fax 867-979-1830) Singles/doubles $120/140. About 2km from town, you'll be left to yourself in this spacious house in a new suburb with views of the bay.

Discovery Lodge Hotel (☎ 867-979-4433, fax 867-979-6591, **e** disclodg@nunanet .com) Singles/doubles $140/156 and up. This downtown area hotel has some so-so rooms, a few better remodeled rooms and suites, and a good but expensive restaurant.

The Frobisher Inn (☎ 867-979-2222, 877-422-9422, fax 867-979-0427, **e** frobinn@ nunanet.com) Rooms from $195. Up on the hill, the Frobisher is the best hotel in town, with nice, modern rooms and marvelous views of the bay; ask for a bayside room. The hotel has a café, good restaurant and a movie theater.

Getting There & Away Iqaluit's airport (☎ 867-979-5224) is close to town. Canadian North (☎ 867-979-5331, 800-661-1505) flies to Ottawa, Rankin Inlet and Yellowknife. First Air (☎ 867-979-8308, 800-267-1247) services numerous towns in Nunavut as well as Yellowknife, Ottawa and Montréal.

Pangnirtung
pop 1100
Pang, as it's often called, is beautifully set alongside a fjord amid mountains near the entrance to Auyuittuq National Park. It lies at the southern end of Pangnirtung Pass, 40km south of the Arctic Circle, and acts as the jumping-off point for park visitors.

The Angmarlik Interpretive Centre (☎ 867-473-8737, fax 473-8685; open 9am to 9pm daily mid-June to mid-September, 9am to 5 pm Monday to Friday mid-September to mid-June) has displays on Thule and Inuit life, and information on local guides and outfitters. The town has a reputation for its woven tapestries, which can be seen and purchased at the Uqqurmiut Centre for Arts and Crafts.

Two walking trails begin in town. The 6km **Ukama Trail** follows the Duval River and takes about three hours. The highly rec-

ommended 13km **Ikuvik Trail** leads to the top of 671m Mount Duval, and takes about six hours roundtrip. The trail is not always well marked, but it offers superb views of the town and Pangnirtung Fjord. Ask at the interpretive center for a map.

About 50km south of town lies **Kekerten Historic Park**, an old whaling station with an interpretive center. A trail leads around the island past the remains of 19th-century houses, tools and graves. A roundtrip by boat takes 12 hours ($150/person, minimum four people).

The most recommended outfitter is **Ali-vaktuk Outfitting** (☎/fax 867-473-8721). Excursions available include a cruise to Cumberland Sound to see icebergs and seals ($150/person, four minimum) and a day-long fishing trip ($140/person, two minimum).

There's camping at the *Pisuktinu-Tungavik campground ($5)*. The only hotel in town is the *Auyuittuq Lodge* (☎ 867-473-8955, fax 867-473-8611), which has simple rooms with shared baths for $135 per person. In the busy season, you might have to share. A meal plan is an extra $65 per day.

Contact the interpretive center for *home stay* options, where you can bunk with a local Inuit family. This costs about $80/120 singles/doubles without meals, and $125/175 with meals. *Pangnirtung Home Stay* (☎/fax 867-473-8021), run by a gregarious Irish expat, is also a pleasant option for $100/person, including breakfast and use of the kitchen.

From Iqaluit, First Air (☎ 867-979-8308, ☎ 800-267-1247) and Kenn Borek Air (☎ 867-979-0040, fax 867-979-0132, **e** borekyfb@ nunanet.com) fly to Pang ($240 and up).

Auyuittuq National Park
Covering an area of 19,500 sq km, this is one of the world's few national parks north of the Arctic Circle. 'Auyuittuq' (ah-you-**ee**-tuk) means 'the land that never melts.' The park is a beautiful, pristine wilderness of mountains with amazing cliffs, deep valleys, glaciers, fjords and meadows. Most visitors hike along 97km **Akshayuk Pass** between late June and early September, when it's free of snow. You can make day hikes into the park from Pang. You will be crossing many shallow streams of glacial meltwater; an extra pair of shoes will keep your toes from freezing.

Climbers flock to Mount Thor (1500m), which has the tallest uninterrupted cliff face on earth.

Parks Canada (☎ 867-473-8828, fax 867-473-8612, W www.parkscanada.gc.ca) has an office in Pangnirtung next to the Angmarlik Interpretive Centre. The fee for entering the park is $15 for a day trip and $40 for up to three nights. You must check in here before going to the park.

Camping is available wherever you can find a safe and ecologically suitable spot. There are nine emergency shelters along Akshayuk Pass.

You can reach Overlord, an emergency shelter and camping spot at the south end of the park, from Pangnirtung, 30km away. For most of the year, that means a $90 snowmobile ride, plus a $90 ride back if you stay for a while. After the thaw in mid-July, outfitters in Pang will take you by boat ($180 per person roundtrip), or you can hike in for two days. The Angmarlik Interpretive Centre will supply names of outfitters.

Pond Inlet
pop 1200

With scenery that includes mountains, glaciers and icebergs, this town at the northern tip of Baffin Island is also the access point for **Bylot Island**, an island bird sanctuary that is a summer nesting ground for snow geese and home to murres and kittiwakes. The waters around the island are rich in marine life.

Nattinnak Centre (☎ 867-899-8225, fax 867-899-8246) in Pond Inlet has information on the area and outfitters.

Camping is available at *Qilalukat Park*. The *Sauniq Hotel* (☎ 867-899-8928, fax 867-899-8364) charges $155/230 without/with meals per person.

Resolute
pop 200

The logistical center for the far north, Resolute was founded after WWII, when the Canadian government established an air base and moved several Inuit families here to protect territorial claims. The land is like a moonscape, with endless vistas of gray-brown rocks. The remains of several crashed airplanes are near the airport and the remains of centuries-old Thule villages are near the beach. The main reason for visiting Resolute is as part of a trip to natural destinations such

as Bathurst and Ellesmere Islands or to the magnetic and geographic North Poles.

Resolute is not blessed with many activities. If you have a few days here, try local hiking or take a trip to **Beechey Island**, about 100km southwest of Resolute (air charter $3500 for up to 10 people). This desolate place was where the ill-fated Franklin expedition wintered in 1845-46 before vanishing forever. Many traces of these men and their unsuccessful rescuers remain.

Jessco Logistics (☎ 403-282-2268, fax 403-282-2195) handles logistics and support for Arctic travel from its summer base in Resolute. Terry Jesudason organizes all forms of travel from Resolute, and she also manages the *Qausuittuq Inns North* (☎ 867-252-3900, fax 867-252-3766), a delightful family-style lodge with good home-cooked meals for $95/135 per person with shared/private bath.

Because of its important status as a logistical center, Resolute is accessible by air. First Air (☎ 867-979-8308, 800-267-1247) flies to Yellowknife and Iqaluit. Kenn Borek Air (☎ 867-252-3845) serves small High Arctic towns and does charters.

Quttinirpaaq (Ellesmere Island) National Park

This national park, way up at the northern tip of Ellesmere Island 720km from the North Pole, is for wealthy wilderness seekers only. It features **Cape Columbia**, the northernmost point of the North American continent, **Mt Barbeau**, one of the highest peaks on the eastern side of the continent, **Lake Hazen** and numerous glaciers. Around the park are thermal oases where plants and animals survive despite the harsh climate. Adventure tour companies stage through Resolute on the way to the park. The chartered plane from Resolute costs about $15,000 for 10 people. For park information, contact Parks Canada (☎ 867-473-8828, fax 867-473-8612, W www .parcscanada.gc.ca) in Pangnirtung.

KITIKMEOT REGION

This seemingly limitless area of tundra encompasses the Arctic coast of the mainland as well as nearby islands.

Cambridge Bay
pop 1400

In the southeast of Victoria Island, this town is the region's administrative center

NUNAVUT

Two North Poles

The North Pole, the imaginary point at the northern tip of the Earth's axis and about 800km north of Ellesmere Island, lies in an area of permanently frozen water without national jurisdiction. However, the Magnetic North Pole, the direction to which a compass needle points at an angle to true north, is in Canada. Its exact location varies daily. Generally just north of Bathurst Island at about 100 degrees longitude, the pole moves in elliptical circles that can extend over 100km in a 24-hour period. On a yearly basis, the pole has been moving northwest.

You can visit both poles from Resolute. The magnetic pole is about 500km away by air, and flights there are common in spring and summer. The scenery is quite similar to Resolute – lots of rocks and ice. Given that there is no way to see the exact location of the pole, this is just an excuse to go on a jaunt over the High Arctic.

In contrast, the geographic North Pole stays put. Reaching the pole for most people involves a series of charter plane flights to pre-position fuel and supplies for the 1700km journey from Resolute. Because of the instability of the weather, a one-hour visit to the endless expanse of ice at the pole can involve seven to 10 days of travel and delays. The cost ranges from $10,000 to $15,000 per person.

and home to a large military early-warning radar station. Explorers in search of the Northwest Passage often took shelter here; you can see the remains of Roald Amundsen's schooner *Maud* in the harbor. **Mt Pelly** is a 15km walk from town and has good views from its 220m peak. This is a good place to see musk oxen. South across Queen Maud Gulf is the **Queen Maud Bird Sanctuary**, the world's largest migratory bird sanctuary.

The Arctic Coast Visitors Centre (☎ 867-983-2842, fax 867-983-2302) has displays about exploration of the Northwest Passage and organizes tours.

Arctic Islands Lodge (☎ 867-983-2345, fax 867-983-2480, e *ailodge@polarnet.ca*) Singles/doubles $185/260. This lodge has rooms that are swanky by Nunavut standards.

KIVALLIQ REGION

In the south, the Kivalliq Region consists of a vast, rocky, barren plateau laced by streams, rivers and lakes. Its official boundaries incorporate much of Hudson Bay and James Bay. Most of the population lives in Inuit settlements along the western shores of Hudson Bay. The region is good for fishing and canoeing.

Rankin Inlet

pop 2000

Founded in 1955 as a mining center, Rankin Inlet is Kivalliq's largest community and the

government and transport center for the district. From here you can go fishing in the bay or in the many rivers and lakes. **Ijiraliq (Meliadine) River Territorial Historic Park**, 5km from town, is popular for hiking and berry-picking.

In Hudson Bay, about 50km east of Rankin Inlet, is **Marble Island**, a graveyard for James Knight and his crew who sought the Northwest Passage in the 18th century. Some 19th-century whaling ships are there too. You can also hike to the **Ijiraliq Archaeological Site**, at the mouth of the Meliadine River, and explore the 15th-century underground houses of the Thule people.

The Kivalliq Regional Visitors Centre (☎ 867-645-3838, fax 867-645-3904) has area information and historical displays. There are stores and services.

Tara's Bed & Breakfast (☎ 867-645-3478, fax 867-645-3538, e *tarasbb@arctic.ca*) has three rooms with queen-size beds and shared baths for $125/250 singles/doubles. Dinner costs an extra $25.

First Air (☎ 867-979-8308, 800-267-1247) flies to Yellowknife, Winnipeg and Iqaluit from Rankin Inlet. Canadian North (☎ 867-645-3720, 800-661-1505) flies to Yellowknife and Iqaluit. Its commuter affiliate Calm Air flies to numerous small communities in the Kivalliq Region, including Arviat, Baker Lake and Repulse Bay.

Arviat
pop 1100

Arviat, formerly called Eskimo Point, is Nunavut's most southerly settlement. People here still make a living from fishing, hunting and trapping. The Margaret Aniksak Visitors Centre (☎ 867-857-2841) has local information and displays of art from the vibrant community.

From Arviat you can arrange a trip south to **McConnell River Bird Sanctuary**, where from June onwards, about 400,000 snow geese nest, together with snowy owls, Arctic terns, falcons and others.

Baker Lake

Geographically, Baker Lake lies at the center of Canada. It's good for fishing and

is the departure point for canoe or raft trips on the Kazan and Thelon Rivers.

From Baker Lake you can arrange a visit west to the **Thelon Game Sanctuary**, founded in 1927 by the federal government to save the then-endangered musk ox.

The Akumalik Visitors Centre (☎ 867-793-2456) is open in summer only.

Repulse Bay

Sitting on the Arctic Circle at the southern end of Melville Peninsula, Repulse Bay is a natural harbor. For centuries whalers set off from here. You can see beluga or narwhal whales (August is the best time) or take a fishing trip. The **Arviq Hunters and Trappers Association** (*☎ 867-462-4334, fax 867-462-4335*) arranges whale-watching trips.

Language

English and French are the two official languages of Canada. You'll notice both on highway signs, maps, tourist brochures and all types of packaging. In the west of Canada, French isn't as prevalent. Conversely, English can be hard to find in Québec. Indeed, road signs and visitor information there will often be in French only. Outside Montréal and Québec City, the use of some French, or your own version of sign language, will be necessary at least some of the time.

Many immigrants use their mother tongues, as do some groups of Native Indians and Inuit. In some Native Indian communities though, it's now only older members who retain their original indigenous language. Few non–Native Indian Canadians speak any Native Indian or Inuit language, but some words such as igloo, parka, muskeg and kayak are commonly used.

The Inuit languages are interesting for their specialization and use of many words for what appears to be the same thing; for example, the word for 'seal' depends on whether it's old or young, in or out of the water. Famously, there are 20 or so words for 'snow,' describing different consistencies and textures.

CANADIAN ENGLISH

Canada inherited English primarily from the British settlers of the early and mid-1800s. This form of British English remains the basis of Canadian English. There are some pronunciation differences; Britons say 'clark' for clerk, Canadians say 'clurk.' Grammatical differences are few. The Canadian vocabulary has been augmented considerably by the need for new words in a new land, the influence of the Native Indian languages and the heritage of the pioneering French.

Canada has never developed a series of easily detectable dialects such as those of England, Germany or even the USA. There are, though, some regional variations in idiom and pronunciation. In Newfoundland, for example, some people speak with an accent reminiscent of the west country of England (Devon and Cornwall) or Ireland, and some use words such as 'screech' (rum) and 'shooneen' (coward).

The spoken English of the Atlantic Provinces, too, has inflections not heard in the west, and in the Ottawa Valley you'll hear a slightly different sound again, due mainly to the large numbers of Irish who settled there in the mid-1800s. In British Columbia some expressions reflect that province's history; a word like 'leaverite' (a worthless mineral) is a prospecting word derived from the phrase 'Leave 'er right there.'

Canadian English has been strongly influenced by the USA, particularly via the mass media and the historic use of US textbooks and dictionaries in schools. Most spellings follow British English, such as centre, harbour and cheque, but there are some exceptions like tire (rather than tyre) and aluminum (rather than aluminium). US spelling is becoming more common, to the consternation of some. Perhaps the best known difference between US and Canadian English is in the pronunciation of the last letter of the alphabet. In the USA it's pronounced 'zee,' while in Canada it's pronounced 'zed.'

Canadian English as a whole has also developed a few of its own distinctive idioms and expressions. The most recognizable is the interrogative 'eh?,' which sometimes seems to appear at the end of almost every spoken sentence. Although to many non–North Americans, Canadians and Americans may sound the same, there are real differences. Canadian pronunciation of 'ou' is the most notable of these; words like 'out' and 'about' sound more like 'oat' and 'aboat' when spoken by Canadians.

Canadian English has also added to the richness of the global English language, with words like kerosene (paraffin), puck (from ice hockey) and bushed (exhausted), and with moose and muskeg from anglicized Native Indian words.

For those wishing to delve deeper into the topic, there is the excellent *Oxford Dictionary of Canadian English*.

CANADIAN FRENCH

The French spoken in Canada is not, for the most part, the language of France. At times it can be nearly unintelligible to a French person. Although many English (and most French) students in Québec are still taught the French of France, the local tongue is what is known as Québécois or *joual*. For example, while many around the world schooled in Parisian French would say *Quelle heure est-il?* for 'What time is it?,' on the streets of Québec you're likely to hear *Y'est quelle heure?* Most Québécois people will understand a more formal French – it will just strike them as a little peculiar. Remember, too, that broken French can sound as charming as the French speaker's broken English if said with a friendly attitude. Other differences between European French and the Québec version worth remembering (because you don't want to go hungry!) are the terms for breakfast, lunch and dinner. Rather than *petit déjeuner*, *déjeuner* and *diner* you're likely to see and hear *déjeuner*, *diner* and *souper*.

If you have any car trouble, you'll be happy to know that English terms are generally used for parts. Indeed, the word *char* (pronounced 'shar') for car may be heard. Hitchhiking is known not as *auto stop* but as *le pousse* (the thumb).

Announcers and broadcasters on Québec TV and radio tend to speak a more refined, European style of French, as does the upper class. Visitors to the country without much everyday French-speaking experience will have the most luck understanding them. Despite all this, the preservation of French in Québec is a primary concern and fuels the separatist movement.

New Brunswick is, perhaps surprisingly, the only officially bilingual province. French is widely spoken, particularly in the north and east. Again, it is somewhat different from the French of Québec. Nova Scotia and Manitoba also have significant French-speaking populations, and there are pockets in most other provinces.

The following is a short guide to some French words and phrases that may be useful for the traveler. The combinations 'ohn/ehn/ahn' in the phonetic transcriptions are nasal sounds – the 'n' is not pronounced; 'zh' is pronounced as the 's' in 'measure.' Québec French employs a lot of

English words; this may make understanding and speaking the language a little easier.

For a far more comprehensive guide to the language get a copy of Lonely Planet's *French phrasebook* – it's a handy pocket-size book for travelers.

Greetings & Civilities

Hello. (day)	*Bonjour*
	bohn-joor
Hello. (evening)	*Bonsoir.*
	bohn-swar
Hello. (informal)	*Salut.*
	sa-lew
How are you?	*Comment ça va?*
	(often just *Ça va?*)
	commohn sa vah?
I'm fine.	*Ça va bien.*
	sa vah bee-ahn

Basics

Yes.	*Oui.*
	wee
No.	*Non.*
	nohn
Please.	*S'il vous plaît.*
	seel voo pleh
Thank you.	*Merci.*
	mehr-see
Welcome.	*Bienvenu.*
	bee-ahn ven-oo
Excuse me.	*Pardon.*
	par-dohn
Pardon/What?	*Comment?*
	commohn?
	Quoi? (slang)
	kwah?
You're welcome.	*Je vous en prie.*
	zhe voo-zohn pree
How much?	*Combien?*
	kom-bee-ahn?

Language Difficulties

I understand.   *Je comprends.*
                zhe com-prohn
I don't understand.
                Je ne comprends pas.
                zhe neh com-prohn pah
Do you speak English?
                Parlez-vous anglais?
                parlay vooz anglay?
I don't speak French.
                Je ne parle pas francais
                zhe neh parl pah frohn-say

LANGUAGE

Getting Around

bus	*autobus*
	oh-toh-booss
train	*train*
	trahn
plane	*avion*
	a-vee-ohn
train station	*gare*
	gar
platform	*quai*
	kay
bus station	*station d'autobus*
	sta-seeyon d'ohtoh-booss
one-way ticket	*billet simple*
	beeyay sam-pluh
roundtrip ticket	*billet aller et retour*
	beeyay alay eh reh-tour
bicycle	*vélo*
	veh-loh
gasoline (petrol)	*gaz/essence*
	gaz/eh-sohns
lead-free (gas)	*sans plomb*
	sohn plom
self-serve	*service libre*
	sairvees lee-br
Where is ...?	*Où est ...?*
	oo eh ...?

What time does the ... leave/arrive?
A quelle heure part/arrive le ...?
a kel ur pahr/ahreev le ...

Directions

I want to go to ...	*Je veux aller à ...*
	zhe vur ahlay a
left	*à gauche*
	a go-sh
right	*à droit*
	a drwat
straight ahead	*tout droit*
	too drwat
near	*proche*
	prosh
far	*loin*
	lwahn

Signs

Billeterie	Ticket Office
Complet	No Vacancy
Entrée	Entrance
Halte Routière	Rest Stop
Sortie	Exit
Stationnment	Parking

here	*ici*
	ee-see
there	*là*
	lah

Accommodations

hotel	*hôtel*
	o-tell
youth hostel	*auberge de jeunesse*
	o-bairzh de zheuness
bed & breakfast	*un gîte, gîte du passant*
	oon zheet, zheet doo pass-ahn
a room	*une chambre*
	oon shombr
a double room	*une chambre double*
	oon shombr doobl
with a bathroom	*avec salle de bain*
	ahvek sahl de bahn
with a kitchenette	*avec cuisinette*
	ahvek kwee-zee-net
no vacancy, full	*complet*
	cohme-plett

Do you have any rooms available?
Est-ce que vous avez des chambres libres?
ehs-ker voo zah-vay day shombr leebr?

Around Town

bank	*banque*
	bohnk
beach	*plage*
	plazh
the bill	*l'addition/le reçu*
	la-dis-yohn/le reh soo
bridge	*pont*
	pohn
convenience store	*dépanneur*
	day-pahn-nur
grocery store	*épicerie*
	ay-pee-seh-ree
museum	*musée*
	mew-zay
opening hours	*horaires*
	oh-rair
post office	*bureau de poste*
	bew-roh de post
the police	*la police*
	la polees
show/concert	*spectacle*
	spek-tahk'l
toilet	*toilet*
	twah-leh
tourist office	*bureau du tourisme*
	bew-ro doo too-rism
traveler's check	*cheque voyage*
	shek vwoy-yazh

Where is the bathroom?
Où est le toilet?
 oo eh twah-leh?

Food

bakery	*boulangerie*	boo-lohn-zheree
bread	*pain*	pahn
cheese	*fromage*	fro-mahj
fresh fish store	*poissonnerie*	pwa-sohn-eree
fruit	*fruit*	frwee
full, set meal (soup through dessert)	*table d'hôte*	tab'l-doht
restaurant	*restaurant*	rest-a-rohn
snack bar	*casse croûte*	kass krewt
vegetables	*légumes*	lay-gyoom

I'm a vegetarian.
Je suis végétarien/végétarienne (m/f)
 zhe swee vayzhayteh-ryahn/vayzhayteh-ryen

Drinks

water	*eau*	oh
beer	*bière*	bee-yair
milk	*lait*	leh
wine	*vin*	vahn
red wine	*vin rouge*	vahn roozh
white wine	*vin blanc*	vahn blohn

Useful Words

big	*grand*	grond
small	*petit*	peh-tee
much/many	*beaucoup*	boh-coo
expensive	*cher*	share
cheap	*bon marché*	bohn mar-shay
	pas chèr	pa sher

	c'est cheap	seh cheep
before	*avant*	ah-vohn
after	*après*	ah-preh
tomorrow	*demain*	de-mahn
yesterday	*hier*	yeah

Numbers

1	*un*	uhn
2	*deux*	der
3	*trois*	wah
4	*quatre*	cat
5	*cinq*	sank
6	*six*	sease
7	*sept*	set
8	*huit*	weet
9	*neuf*	neuf
10	*dix*	dees
20	*vingt*	vahn
21	*vingt et un*	vahn-teh-un
25	*vingt-cinq*	vahn sank
30	*trente*	tronht
40	*quarante*	car-ohnt
50	*cinquante*	sank-ohnt
60	*soixante*	swa-sohnt
70	*soixante-dix*	wa-sohnt dees
80	*quatre-vingt*	cat-tr' vahn
90	*quatre-vingt-dix*	cat-tr'vahn dees
100	*cent*	sohn
500	*cinq cents*	sank sohn
1000	*mille*	meel

Emergencies

Help!	*Au secours!*	oh say-coor
Call a doctor!	*Appelez un médecin!*	a-pay-lay uhn med-sahn
Call the police!	*Appelez la police!*	a-pay-lay la poh-lees
Leave me alone!	*Laissez-moi tranquille!*	leh-say-mwa tron-kill
I'm lost.	*Je me suis égaré/égarée. (m/f)*	zhe muh swee ay-ga-ray

Glossary

ABM – automated bank machine; same as ATM in the US

Atlantic Provinces – a region that includes Newfoundland, Nova Scotia, Prince Edward Island and New Brunswick

aurora borealis – (also called the northern lights) charged particles from the sun that are trapped in the earth's magnetic field; they appear as colored, waving beams

badlands – a barren, arid region of southern Alberta with unusual features caused by erosion; the rocks in such areas often contain prehistoric fossils

beaver tail – a delicious, large, flat, sugary doughnut sort of thing

boîtes à chanson – generally cheap, casual and relaxed folk clubs, popular in Québec

boreal – an adjective that refers to the Canadian north, as in the boreal forest, the boreal wind, etc

calèche – horse-drawn carriages that can be taken around parts of Montréal and Québec City

ceilidh – (pronounced **kay**-lee) a Gaelic word meaning an informal gathering for song, dance and story; it's sometimes known as a house party and is especially popular in Prince Edward Island

chamber of commerce – an association of businesses and government agencies that represents the interests of a town and often supplies tourist information

dome car – the two-leveled, glass-topped observation car of a train

Doukhobours – a Russian Christian pacifist sect, some of whom settled in Canada during the 19th century

First Nations – a term that denotes Canada's aboriginal peoples; it can be used instead of Native Indians or Native people

fruit leather – a blend of fruit purees dried into thin sheets and pressed together; it's great for backpacking and hiking

hoodoos – fantastically shaped pillars of sandstone rock formed by erosion and found in badland regions, mainly in southern Alberta

ice wine – a fruity, sweet, dessert wine made with grapes that have frozen on the vine; it's a Canadian specialty

impaired – term used to describe someone too drunk to legally drive; the percentage of blood alcohol that qualifies a person for this designation varies by province

interior camping – refers to usually lone, individual campsites accessible only by foot or canoe, generally found in provincial or national parks

Left Coast – a name sometimes applied to coastal British Columbia for the perceived (imagined) left-wing, flaky nature of its residents

loonie – a widely used slang term for the one-dollar coin

Lotto 649 – the country's most popular, highest-paying lottery

Maritime Provinces – also known as the Maritimes, this group includes three provinces: New Brunswick, Nova Scotia and Prince Edward Island

Métis – Canadians of French and Native Indian stock

Mounties – Royal Canadian Mounted Police (RCMP)

muskeg – undrained boggy land most often found in northern Canada

no-see-um – any of various tiny biting insects that are difficult to see and that can annoy travelers when out in the woods or along some beaches; no-see-um netting, a very fine mesh screen on a tent, is designed to keep the insects out

outfitter – a business supplying outdoor/adventure equipment, usually for rent

outports – small, isolated coastal villages of Newfoundland, connected with the rest of the province by boat

permafrost – permanently frozen subsoil that covers the far north of Canada

portage – the process of transporting boats (canoes) and supplies overland between navigable waterways; it can also refer to the overland route used for such a purpose

pingo – in the far north, a huge earth-covered ice hill formed by the upward expansion of underground ice

pop – a popular generic term for a soft drink

Québecois – (also known as *joual*) the local tongue of Québec, where the vast majority of the population is French; the term also refers to the residents of Québec, although it is only applied to the French-speaking locals

RV – recreational vehicle or motor home

screech – a particularly strong rum once available only in Newfoundland, now widely available across Canada, but in diluted form

serviced/unserviced – a serviced campsite includes water and/or electricity and sewage; a plain, unserviced site is geared to tenters

subcompact cars – the smallest cars available either for purchase or rent; they're smaller than compacts, which are one size down from standard cars

taiga – coniferous forests extending across much of subarctic North America and Eurasia

trailer – in Canada, as well as in the USA, this refers to a caravan or a mobile home (house trailer) but can also refer to the type of truck/rig used for transporting goods

tundra – vast, treeless Arctic plains north of the tree line and with a perpetually frozen subsoil

two-four – a case of beer containing 24 bottles

twonie (toonie) – a widely-used slang term for the two-dollar coin

Wet Coast – the name humorously used instead of the West Coast (often by Easterners referring to Vancouver) due to the area's heavy rainfall

Thanks

Many thanks to the travelers who used the last edition and wrote to us with helpful hints, useful advice and anecdotes. Your names follow:

Z Abdullah, Nerea Achutegui, Andrea Adams, Julie Adamson, Amy Agorastos, Sheetal Aiyer, Claire Albrecht, Richard Alderton, Glenn Alger, Helen & Dave Allan, Janet & Dave Allan, Pierre Allard, Nicole Allen, Richard Allen, Myles Anderson, Nils F Anderson, Luc Andre, Nicole Andrews, Eduardo Angel, Wolfgang Angerer, Thierry Antoine, Vanesa Aparicio, Stephanie Appert, Eileen Arandiga, Rosalind Archer, Jarkko Arjatsalo, Sue Asquith, BH Atkins, Brian Back, Hans Bahlmann, Ace Bailey, Steve Bailey, Grace Ann Baker, Jason Baker, Georgia Banks, Michele Barber, Nina Barnaby, Craig Barrack, Greg Barry, Anke Bartels, Cathy Bartlett, Maria Basaraba, Janet Beale, Shayne Beard, Michel Belec, Piet Bels, Verena Berger, Brian & Caryl Bergeron, Shirley Bergert, David Berridge, WJ Best, Luke Biggs, Nancy Evelyn Bikaunieks, Jude A Billard, PR Birch, Jim Bird, Frida Caroline Bjerkan, Julia Black, Sarah Blackwell, Rachel Blair, Bob & Joan Blanchard, Heather Blois, Barbie Bojcun, Phil Munter Bond, David Bonham, Christopher Booth, Michael Borger, Mike Borger, Jack Bornstein, Chris Borthwick, Sarah P Bourque, Simon Bower, Kevin Boyle, Bas & Bertrand Braam, Amy Brandon, Dan Brennan, Michael Briggs, Ashley Bristowe, Joan Brittain, Jack Brondum, Sean Brooks, Michael Brothers, Eliza C Brown, B Gavin Brown, Maxine Brown, Anton Brugman, Claire Brutails, Annette Buckley, Sandra Buhlmann, Larry Buickel, MD Bullen, Dwight Burditt, Ron Burdo, Eugenia Bursey, Marianne Busch, Jonathan Butchard, Claire Butler, Jean Butler, Nicole Caissey, Noel & Rosemary Callow, Cory Camilleri, Blaine Campbell, Kate Campbell, Jonathan Campton, Mark A Canning, Tony & Lena Cansdale, Sharyn Carey, Chris Carlisle, Zahavit Carmel, Ernest Carwithen, Edson Castilho, Vagner Castilho, Robert Catto, Jacky Chalk, Madeline & John Chambers, Sally Chambers, RK Chaplin, Lisa Chapman, Julian Chen, DeWayne Chiasson, Ian Chiclo, Natalie Chow, Ton Christiaanse, Niall GF Christie, Steven Christie, Isabel Chudleigh, Pierre Chum, Wendy & Steve Churchill, Marlene Cirillo, Charles Citroen, Antoni Cladera, Guido Claessen, Dean Clark, Peter Clough, Mike Coburn, Celine Cogneau, M Cohen, David Colburn, Elizabeth Cole, Don Coleman, Paul Collins, Rachel Collis, Maurice Conklin, Conrad, Philip Coo, Katherine Cook, Nathan Cook, Jeremy Copeland, Max Corbeil, Tosja Coronell, Sonja Corradini, Agustin Cot, Elsa Coudon, Peter Court-Hampton, Catrin Cousins, Catherine Cowan, Sara & Brian Cox, Simon Cox, Cilla Craig, Steve Craig, Brian Crawford, Yvette Creighton, Phil Crew, William & Norma Cross, Ken Crossman, Dany Cuello, Valentina Cusnir, Cathy Ann Cwycyshyn, Rod Daldry, Edward Dale, Mary-Camillus Dale, Leonne & Alan Damson, Margaret Darby, Martina D'Ascola, Huw Davies, Louise Davies, Leanne & Alan Dawson, Nicky & Murray Sayers Dawson, M De Souza, Bjorn Debaillie, Leroy W Demery, Petra Dengl, Pierre Devinat, Adri Di Nobile, Julia Dickinson, Martin Dinn, Kerry T Diotte, Tilman Dnrbeck, Alexandra Dodd, Monique Dodinet, Sarah Dodson, Allan Doig, Sandra Dollar, Robert Dorin, Matt Doughty, Allan Douglas, Guy Douglas, Tilman Duerbeck, P Duffy, Judy & Roger Dumm, Jayleen Duncan, Traci Dunlop, Jackie Early, Phillip East, Nadja Eberhardt, Donna Ebert, Hermann Ebsen, Peter Eden, Martin Edwards, Henning Eifler, Frank Eisenhuth, Krispen Elder, Laura Ell, Adriana Ellis-Fragoso, Ben Elliston, Nicholas A Enright, Tore Fagervold, Keith Fairbairn, Paul Falvo, Alan Farleigh, Sandra Farley, Nicole Faubert, Peter Fennick, Joseph Ferigno, Gina Field, Nadine Fillipoff, Raymond Finan, Shaun Finch, Alaric Fish, Sarah Fisher, Mandy Fletcher, Michael Fletcher, Selena Sung Li Foong, Andrew Forbes, Graham Ford, Doreen Forney, Justin Fraser, Suzan Fraser, Magnus Fredrikson, Ben Freeman, Constance Frey, Ingo Friese, Donna Fruin, Derek Galon, Christina Gamouras, Juan Garbajosa, Abraham Garcia, Jennifer Gardner, William Gardner, Alex Garic, Pam Gaskin, Costanza Gechter, Verstrepen Geert, Mathieu Georges, Marg Gibson, Jemma Gilbert, Philip Gilbert, Sandra Gilis, James Gill, James Gilmour, Michele Glover, Javeen Godbeer, Barbara Goldflam, Lisa Goldsworthy, Claudia Gomes, Nigel Goodall, Kristy Goodchild, Hilary Gooding, Katherine Gordon, Ivan Gorman, Paul Goudreau, Peter Gourley, CBT Grace, Kim Graham, Eileen Grant, Anthea Grasty, Andrew Graybill, Ray Greenwood, Ian A Griffin, Wellum & Nonna Gross, Bob Grubb, Judy Grubb, Gilbert

Guinard, Maria Gulliern, Rob & Annemieke Gulmans, Joseph Gumino, Lise Guyot, Alison Hahn, Natalie Haines, Daryl Hal, Nancy Hall, David & Hannah Halliday, Ruth Halsall, Jean-Lou Hamelin, Andrew & Kirsty Hamilton-Wright, Lutz Hankewitz, Ralf Hansen, Mabel Haourt, Janelle Hardy, Kate Hare, Brian Harland, Tony Harminc, John Harper, Roger Harris, Barbara Harrison, Alan Hart, Lorraine Hart, Christopher Harte, Bernice Hartley, Catherine Hartung, John Harvie, Jeff Haslam, Rob Haub, Lilly Haupt, Andy Hay, M Hayden, Nick Hayward, Roland Heere, Sally Heel, Reuben Helms, Laura Henderson, Robert Herritt, Moritz Herrmann, Roger B Hicks, Amy Higginbotham, Dave Higgs, Tim Hildebrandt, TE Hillman, Chris & Sheila Hills, Derrick & Ann Hilton, Abigail Hine, Joan Hirons, Kelley Hishon, Chris Hocking, Pettina Hodgson, Axel Hofer, Fabienne Hoffmann, Kristi Hofman, Clare Holder, Martin Holder, Greg Holland, Samantha Hollier, Sarah Hollingham, John Holman, Henry Hon, Muei Hoon Tan, JP Hope, Rebecca Hope, Margaret Hothi, Janet & Casey Howell, Simon Huang, Paul Hubbard, Keith Hughes, Jane Hunt, Martin Hunt, Paul Hutt, Heidi Ilhren, Cristina Infante, Brent Irvine, Carolyn Irvine, Louis Jacobs, Ed Jager, Marian Jago, Dafydd James, Darlene James, John Jansen, Elfneede Jauelter, Rommary Jenkins, Esther M Jensen, Henrik C Jessen, Geoffrey Joachim, Diana Johns, Bob Johnson, Buffy Johnson, Carolyn Johnson, Margaret Johnson, Pam Johnson, Paul Johnson, Alan Jones, Anita Jones, Lloyd Jones, Margaret Jorstead, Junko Kajino, Jill Kasner, David Kaye, Grant Keddie, Innes Keighren, Steve Kelleher, Pat Kelly, Kieran Kelmar, Madeline Kemna, John Kemp, Dwight Kenney, Don Kerr, Judy Kerr, Steven Kerr, Roger Kershaw, Tarik Khelifi, Barbara Kiepenheuer, Concetta Kincaid, Brian King, Simone Kingston, Mike & Gill Kirkbride, Tyler Kirsh, Hanne Kjeldehl, Wim Klasen, Frank Klimt, Jennifer Klinec, Dayalh Kmeta, Christopher M Knapp, Carla Knoll, Janet Komars, Tim Kong, Airi & George Krause, David Kreindler, Vikram Krishnan, Daniel Kruse, Dave Kruse, Pierre Kruse, Marion Kuehl, M Kulowski Sr, Shiv Kumar, Michelle Labelle, Johannes & Tobias Laengle, Marie-Helene Lagace, Bart Lam, Emmanuel Lambert, Micky Lampe, Denise Lamy, Katrina Lange, Guenter Langergraber, Dany LaRochelle, Hans Latour, Lee Lau, Ron Laufer, Etienne Laverdiere, Al Lawrence, David Lawrence, Denise Le Gal, Pierre L'Ecuyer, Angela Lee, Jessica Lee, Derek Leebosh, Belinda Lees, Peter Lehrke, Caroilne Lemieux, Deborah Leo, Sarah Leonard, Stacie Leptick, Stephen Leslie, Mike B Leussink, James LeVesconte, Lise Levesque, Fabienne Lévy, Bill & Daphne Lewis, Adam Liard, Mark Lightbody, DM Lightfoot, Tan Shuh Lin, Morten Lindow, Kim Linekin, Wai-Ping Lo, Andreas Lober, Edgar H Locke, Raffaella Loi, Clive Long, Robin Longley, Helen Lorimer, Helen Lowe, James Lowenthal, Kris Ludwig, Mark Lunn, Peter Lunt, Derek Lutz, Fiona Lyle, Nick Lynch, Kim Lyons, Carol MacDonald, Peta & Stirling MacDonald, Laurie MacDougall, Eddie Magnusson, Jens Mahlow, Andrew Mair, Maya Malik, John Marett, Edward Marriott, Anne Marsh, Vickie Marsh, Clive & Jean Marshall, James Martin, Alexander Matskevich, Brent Matsuda, Nancy Matthews, Carolyn & WindRider Retreat May, Duncan May, Susan McCain, JR McDermott, Emma McDonald, Pat McDonald, Irma M McDougall, Laura McEachern, Jeremy McElrea, Megan McGlynn, Sue McKinley, Craig McKinnie, Tom McKown, Margaret McLean, Wallace McLean, Fran McQuail, Neil McRae, Judith McRostie, Ryan Medd, Sheila Meehan, Inaki Mendieta, N Merrin, Michael Mersereau, Neal Michael, Nicole Middleton, David Mifsud, Alain Miguelez, Andy Miller, Betty Jean Miller, Ian Mitchinson, Peter W Monteath, Tanya Montebello, Heather Montgomery, Keith Montgomery, Gordon A Moodie, Marcel Moonen, Philip Mooney, Kevin Morai, Stuart Morris, Tom Morrow, Ian Mortimer, Ian Moseley, Dorothy Moszynski, Dominique Mouttet, Mary Movic, Johan Muit, James Mules, Mary Mullane, Andrea Mullin, Liane Munro, Gary Murphy, Anne Murray, Shioko Nagaoka, B Nanser, Jessica Nash, Liz Nash, Daniel Neale, Steve Newcomer, Darlene Newman, Tom Newman, Andrew Newman-Martin, Brian P Nicholas, Brian P Nichols, Alex & Diane Nikolic, Andrew Noblet, Michael Nold, John O'Brien, Etain O'Carroll, Fidelma O'Connor, Keith Odlin, Geni Ogihara, Melinda O'Gorman, Kate O'Hara, Janke Olsson, Jean Yves Paille, Bruce & Ann Palmer, Christine Paquette, Dennis Paradine, Craig Park, Ed Parker, Laura Parker, Dick Parson, Tony Pastachak, Jo Patterson, Graeme Paul Hamilton, Andree Peacock, Jonathon Pease, Richard Pedder, Daiana Pellizzon, Chris Penny, Sophie Percival, Chritopher Perraton, Patrick Perrault, Laure Perrier, Marc Peverini, Uli Pfeiffer, Chris Phillips, Jackey Phillips, Jean-Frantois Pin, Gabriel Pinkstone, Lucy Platt, Helen Pleasance, Vanessa Pocock, Jackie Poole, Paul Poole, Tony & Jill Porco, Erhard Poser, Nina Power, Nina & Tyrone Power, Marcelo

Horacio Pozzo, Antonella Precoma, Simon Preece, Annette Prelle, Nichola & Kevin Prested, Howard Prior, Nancy Prober, Greg Proctor, Marc Prokosch, Martine Proulx, Aljaz & Urska Prusnik, Cindy Puijk, Merissa Quek, Sylrre Quellet, David Quinn, Michel Quintas, Bjorn Anders Radstrom, Linda Rammage, Roger Randall, Shirley Randall, Thomas Rau, Jenny Raven, Reinhard Reading, Margaret Reed, Michael Reine, Pierre Renault, Jane Rennie, Janice G Richards, Judy Roberts, Karen Roberts, Jane Robinson, Yetta Robinson, Bernhard Rock, Scott Rogers, Andrea Rogge, Candace Ross, Derek Ross, Joanne Ross, Susan Ross, T Carter Ross, Louison Rousseau, Duncan Routledge, Gladys Rubatto, Con Ruddock, Carol Rudram, David Rusk, Oxy Rynchus, Ayaka Sakata, Dieter & Sheila Salden, Karlie Salmon, Arnaud Samson, Richard Samuelson, Paul Sands, Andrew Sansbury, Carol & Rick Sarchet, André J Sauvé, Colin Savage, Penny Scheenhouwer, Neil Schlipalius, Simon Schlosser, Erich Schmitt, Sebastian Schmitz, Bruce Schultz, Ruth Schulze, Oliver Schusser, Florian Schweiger, James Scott, Martin Scott, Anthony Sell, Andy Serra, Anne Sevriuk, Anna Shah, Ruth Shannon, Sarah Shaughnessy, SW Shekvadod, Ed Shepard, Edmund Shepard, Ed Shephard, Kerren Sherry, SW Sherwood, Denis Shor, Peggy Shyns, Shreen Sidhu, Constanze Siefarth, Michel Simard, Melissa Simmons, Chris Simon, Andrew Sinclair, Norm Singer, Bronwyn Sivour, Valerie Slade, Jeroen Smeets, Alan Smith, Heather Smith, Heidi Smith, Inga Smith, Jonathan Smith, Rachel & Trevor Smith, Rob Smith, Stephen Smith, Mary Smyth, Kathleen Solose, Ann Soper, David & Jill Spear, Kent Spencer, Patrick Spink, Mike St John, Jane Stalker, Sheila Stam, Jenn Stanley, Gavin Staton, Bryun Stedman, Andrew Steele, Mary Steer, John Steinbachs, Rebecca Stevens, N Stevenson, Mrs JMW & Professor Stewart, John Stigant, Stephy Stoker, Jason Strauss, Stephen Streich, Aruna Subramamian, Arden Sutherland, Anders Svensson, Fabio Sverzut, Eric Swan, O'Rourk Swinney, Sharona Eliahou Taieb, Dorinda Talbot, Calvin

Tam, Kat Tancock, Roy Tanner, Christine Tarrach, Bobby Tehranian, Mike Telford, Rachael Templeton, Reinier ten Veen, Ulrik Terreni, Rowena Thakore, Frank Theissen, Pia Thiemann, Alan & Jo Thomas, Peter Thomas, Carolyn Thompson, Judy & Gary Thompson, Donna Tidey, Glen Timpson, Kerry Tobin, Larissa Tomlinson, Véronique Torche, Travel Girl, Pierre Tremblay, Rhiannon Elizabeth Trevethan, Cathy Tuck, Richard Twigg, F Ubliani, Rosemary & Philip Ulyett, Sam Unruth, Sarah Valair, Joe Valcourt, Maurice Valentine, Jos van den Akker, Marian & Rob van den Heuvel, Sendy & Jeroen Van Heel, Lies Van Nieuwenhove, Hulya van Tangeren, Vanessa Vanclief, Nicole Vandenberg, Sabrina Vandierendonck, Stewart Vanns, Elizabeth E Vans, Oliver Vanzon, S & J Veringer, R Vermaire, Rene Vermaire, Herma & Otto Vermeulan, John Verri, James Vieland, Theo Vlachos, Nichy Vyce, Sally Wade, Aron Wahl, Lary Waldman, Cheryl Walk, Alan Walker, Neil Walker, Naomi Wall, Ron Wallace, Ron W Wallace, Chan Wan Soi, Helen & John Wardle, Julia Warner, Sylvia Warner, Klaus Wartenberg, VA Waters, Lorna Watkins, Linda M Watsham, Tara Watt, Jayne Weber, Bert Weissbach, Claudia Werger, Sarah Rose Werner, Sandra West, Susan Westwood, Michael & Sarah Weyburne, Heather Wharton, Christopher Wheeler, Jennifer Whitman, Mattias Wick, Roma Wiemer, Roy Wiesner, Leonore Wigger, Diederik JD Wijnmalen, Andrew Willers, Edith & Bernard William, Katheen Williams, Olugbala Williams, Pauline Williams, Scott Williams, Paul Williamson, Kim Willoughby, Jeremy Wills, Mary Wills, Alex Wilson, Chris Wilson, Peter Winter, Katherine Wisborg, Andrew Witham, Rhonda Witt, Katrin Wohlleben, Sandra Wolf, Nora & Rick Wolff, Clinton Wong, Jenn Wood, Andrew Wright, Colin & Robyn Wright, Mark Wright, Chandi Wyant, Ingrid Wyles, Scott Wylie, Yildiz Yanmaz, Mary Yearsley, GK Yeoh, Y Yerbury-Nodgron, AL Young, Paul Young, Victoria Young, Wanieta Young, Natacha Zana, Mijke Zengerink, Arlene Zimmerman, Harold & Joyce Zuberman, Wanda Zyla

Index

Abbreviations

AB — Alberta
BC — British Columbia
MB — Manitoba
NB — New Brunswick
NF — Newfoundland & Labrador
NS — Nova Scotia
NT — Northwest Territories
NU — Nunavut
ON — Ontario
PE — Prince Edward Island
QC — Québec
SK — Saskatchewan
YT — Yukon

Text

A

Abénaki 304
Abitibi-Témiscamingue (QC)
  357–9
ABMs 49
Acadian Historic Village (NB)
  581
Acadians
  arts & crafts 469, 488
  festivals 461, 470
  history 350, 430, 432,
    466, 470, 471, 472,
    488, 504, 527, 531,
    569, 580
  museums 350, 528, 570,
    574, 581
  population 461
accommodations 66–9
  B&Bs 68
  camping 66
  efficiencies 68
  farm vacations 69
  guesthouses 68
  hostels 66–7
  hotels 69
  motels 68–9
  tourist homes 68
  university residences 68
  YMCA/YWCA 67–8
activities 62–5. See also
  individual activities
Acute Mountain Sickness
  (AMS) 57
African Lion Safari (ON) 168
Agawa Canyon (ON) 237–8

Ahousat (BC) 797
AIDS. See HIV/AIDS
Air Canada Centre (ON) 126
air travel
  airlines 74, 79
  airports 74
  domestic 79–80
  international 75–6
  tickets 74–5
Aklavik (NT) 906
Alaska 853, 872–6
Alaska Hwy 858, 859,
  867–72
Alberta 647–717, **648, 710**
  accommodations 650–1
  activities 650
  climate 649
  history 647, 649
  parks 650
  tourist office 44
Alberta Legislature (AB) 654
Alberta Railway Museum
  (AB) 664–5
Alcan. See Alaska Hwy
alcoholic beverages 70–1
Alert Bay (BC) 806
Algoma Central Railway
  (ON) 237–8
Algonquin Provincial Park
  (ON) 150, 218–20
Allan Gardens (ON) 111
Alma (NB) 567–8
Alsek River 872
altitude sickness 57
Altona (MB) 602
Ambleside (BC) 740
amethyst 249
Amherst (NS) 477–9, **478**
Amherstburg (ON) 206

Amos (QC) 358–9
amusement parks 104–5,
  274, 674
Anderson, Pamela 29
Anglican Cathedral of St John
  the Baptist (NF) 372
Annapolis Royal (NS) 466–7
Annapolis Valley (NS) 466–8
Anne of Green Gables 503,
  523–4
The Annex (ON) 108, 121–2
Antigonish (NS) 482–3
antiques 101, 126, 164, 313,
  625–6, 657
Apex Mountain Ski Resort
  (BC) 823
aquariums 179–80, 355, 373,
  548, 735–6, 772
Arctic Circle 883, 912, 915
Argentia (NF) 385
art 28–30, 131. See also
  galleries
Art Gallery of Ontario (ON)
  102–3
Arviat (NU) 915
Assiniboine 585, 587, 621,
  649
Assiniboine Park (MB) 594
Athabasca Falls (AB) 700
Athabasca Glacier (AB) 700
Athabaskans. See Dene
Atikaki Provincial Wilderness
  Park (MB) 603
Atikokan (ON) 254–5
Atlin (BC) 853, 868
ATMs. See ABMs
Auclair (QC) 338
aurora borealis 234, 361,
  427–8, 609, 893

Bold indicates maps.

Auyuittuq National Park (NU) 912–3
Avalon Peninsula (NF) 382–5
Avalon Wilderness Reserve (NF) 383
Awenda Provincial Park (ON) 216–7

B

B&Bs. See accommodations
Babine Lake (BC) 846
Backpackers Hostels Canada 67
backpacking. See hiking & backpacking
Baddeck (NS) 499–501
Baffin Region (NU) 911–3
bagels 282
Baie Comeau (QC) 334
Baie St Paul (QC) 324–5
Baie Ste Catherine (QC) 326–7
Baie Verte (NF) 401
Baie Verte Peninsula (NF) 401
Baker Lake (NU) 915
Bancroft (ON) 152
Banff Gondola (AB) 689–90
Banff National Park (AB) 684, 686–701, **685**
Banff Park Museum (AB) 689
Banff Springs Hotel (AB) 689
Banff townsite (AB) 686–96, **687**
  accommodations 692–3
  activities 690–2
  entertainment 695
  history 686, 688
  restaurants 694–5
  transportation 695–6
banks 49, 61
Banks Island 906–7
Barachois Pond Provincial Park (NF) 414
Barkerville Historic Park (BC) 847
Barrie (ON) 207
Barrington (NS) 458
Barry's Bay (ON) 150
Bartlett, Robert 383–4
baseball 71, 73, 100, 126, 288, 600, 663, 757
Basilica Notre Dame de Québec (QC) 311

Basilica of St John the Baptist (NF) 372
Basilique Notre Dame (QC) 269–70
Basin Head (PE) 516
basketball 73, 126
Batchawana Bay (ON) 242–3
bathrooms 56
Bathurst (NB) 581–2
Batoche National Historic Site (SK) 645
The Battlefords (SK) 646
Bay Bulls (NF) 381–2
Bay de Verde (NF) 383, 384
Bay d'Espoir (NF) 400
Bay of Fundy 430, 467, 473, 544, 560, 570–1
Bay St Lawrence (NS) 492
BC Place Stadium (BC) 734
beaches
  BC 737, 738, 776, 795, 800, 811, 812, 822
  MB 603, 612
  NF 415–6
  NS 483
  ON 111, 112, 206, 207, 254
  PE 519
  QC 148–9, 275, 293, 298, 300, 335, 343, 356
bears 34–5, 60, 243, 253–4, 609, 610, 612–3
Beaubears Island (NB) 579
Beaver Creek (YT) 872
Beaverbrook, Lord 579
beavers 34
Bedford Institute of Oceanography (NS) 447
Beechey Island (NU) 913
beer 70. See also brewery tours
Bell, Alexander Graham 186, 500
Bell Island (NF) 381
Belle Côte (NS) 488
Belleville (ON) 163
Belliveau Cove (NS) 461
Beothuk 365, 389, 396, 400
berry-picking 33–4, 162, 228, 622, 638
Berthier sur Mer (QC) 322–3
Berthierville (QC) 301–2
bicycling. See cycling; mountain biking
Big Bras d'Or (NS) 494

Big Muddy Badlands (SK) 634
Big White Ski Resort (BC) 826–7
biosphere reserves 41. See also individual reserves
Bird Islands (NS) 494
Birds Hill Provincial Park (MB) 601
bird-watching 36–7
  AB 667, 674
  BC 801, 855
  MB 601, 609–10, 612
  NB 532, 553, 568
  NF 381, 385
  NS 456, 461, 463, 469, 477, 494
  NT 898, 906
  NU 913, 914, 915
  ON 153, 188, 199, 215–6
  QC 301, 322, 323, 338, 348, 350
  SK 621
bison 36, 40, 616, 644, 665, 666, 712, 888, 896, 898
Black Creek Pioneer Village (ON) 105–6
black settlement 205, 206
Blackfoot 15, 40, 647, 651, 668, 712
Blacks Harbour (NB) 556
Blackstone Territorial Park (NT) 900
Blanc Sablon (QC) 338, 422
Blind River (ON) 235
Blomidon (NS) 469
Blomidon Mountains (NF) 413
Blyth (ON) 207
boats. See cruises; ferries; freighters; sailing
Bobcaygeon (ON) 164
Bon Echo Provincial Park (ON) 161–2
Bonaventure (QC) 350
Bonavista (NF) 386–7
Bonavista Peninsula (NF) 386–90
Bondar, Roberta 239
books 52–3. See also literature
Borden-Carleton (PE) 517–8
border crossings 46, 77, 179, 185, 236, 255
Bouchard, Lucien 18, 259

Bouctouche (NB) 576–7
Boundary (Alaska) 882
Bowron Lake Provincial Park (BC) 847–8
Boyd's Cove (NF) 396
Bracebridge (ON) 218
Brackley Beach (PE) 520
Brandon (MB) 615–6
Brantford (ON) 185–6
brewery tours 181, 374, 436, 560
Bridgetown (NS) 467–8
Bridgewater (NS) 454
Brier Island (NS) 464–5
Brigus (NF) 383–4
British Columbia 718–857, **720–1, 814, 832**
  accommodations 724
  activities 722–4
  climate 719
  history 718–9
  parks 720
  tourist office 44
British North America Act (BNA Act) 17
Brockville (ON) 153
Broken Group Islands (BC) 795
Bromont (QC) 296–7
The Bruce Peninsula (ON) 211–4
Bruce Peninsula National Park (ON) 212
Bruce Trail (ON) 213
buffalo. *See* bison
Bullock's Bistro (NT) 894
bungee jumping 150, 790
Burin (NF) 390–1
Burin Peninsula (NF) 390–2
Burnt Church First Nation (NB) 579–80
Burwash Landing (YT) 872
buses
  alternative 89–90
  within Canada 80–1
  USA-Canada 77
business hours 61–2
Butchart Gardens (BC) 775–6
Bylot Island (NU) 913
Byng Inlet (ON) 221
Bytown Museum (ON) 137

C

CA Pippy Park (NF) 373
CAA 87
Cabano (QC) 338
Cabbagetown (ON) 109
Cabot, John 364, 368, 370, 386, 391, 492
Cabot Trail (NS) 489–90, 492
Cache Creek (BC) 819
Calaway Park (AB) 674
calèches 279, 314
Caledon (ON) 126
Calgary (AB) 668–84, **669, 671**
  accommodations 676–8
  activities 675
  climate 20
  entertainment 680–2
  history 668
  restaurants 678–80
  shopping 682
  special events 675–6
  sports 682
  tours 675
  transportation 682–4
Calgary Science Centre (AB) 672–3
Calgary Stampede 675–6
Calgary Tower (AB) 670, 672
Calgary Zoo (AB) 673–4
Cambridge (ON) 192
Cambridge Bay (NU) 910, 913–4
Campbell, Maria 26
Campbell, Robert 858, 874
Campbell River (BC) 802–3
Campbellton (NB) 582–3
camping. *See* accommodations
Campobello Island (NB) 551–3
Canada Aviation Museum (ON) 138
Canada Olympic Park (AB) 674–5
Canada Science & Technology Museum (ON) 138
Canadian Automobile Association (CAA) 87
Canadian Broadcasting Corporation (CBC) 53
Canadian Craft Museum (BC) 733–4

Canadian Museum of Civilization (QC) 147–8
Canadian Museum of Contemporary Photography (ON) 137
Canadian Museum of Nature (ON) 138
Canadian National Railway (CNR) 81
Canadian Pacific Railway (CPR) 17, 81, 246, 311, 631, 668, 686, 712, 724–5, 734, 833
Canadian Shield 19, 606
Canadian Universities Travel Service 82, 89
Canadian War Museum (ON) 137
Canadian Warplane Heritage Museum (ON) 167
Canal de Lachine (QC) 277
Canal National Historic Site (ON) 238
Canmore (AB) 685–6
canoeing 64
  AB 650, 691
  BC 722, 765, 790, 847–8, 853, 868
  MB 587, 617
  NB 532, 537, 584
  NF 388–9
  NS 432, 465
  NT 888, 892, 895, 899, 901–2, 902
  NU 910
  ON 93, 112, 140, 161, 164–5, 193, 211, 219, 225, 249, 255
  QC 261, 278, 301, 303, 304, 350, 351
  SK 621–2, 638
  YT 861, 864, 877
Canol Heritage Trail (NT) 902
Canol Rd 867–8
Canso (NS) 485–6
Canyon Ste Anne (QC) 322
Cap aux Meules (QC) 354
Cap Chat (QC) 344
Cap des Rosiers (QC) 346
Cap Tourmente National Wildlife Area (QC) 322
Cape Anguille (NF) 415
Cape Breton Highlands National Park (NS) 489–91

Bold indicates maps.

Cape Breton Island (NS) 486–501
Cape Chignecto Provincial Park (NS) 476–7
Cape Columbia (NU) 913
Cape Jourimain (NB) 575–6
Cape Mabou Highlands (NS) 486–7
Cape Merry (MB) 611
Cape North (NS) 492
Cape Onion (NF) 408
Cape Ray (NF) 417–8
Cape Sable Island (NS) 458
Cape St George (NF) 414
Cape St Mary (NS) 461
Cape St Mary's (NF) 385
Cape Scott Provincial Park (BC) 807
Cape Spear (NF) 374
Capilano Suspension Bridge (BC) 739
Caraquet (NB) 580–1
Carbonear Island (NF) 384
Carcross (YT) 876
Cardston (AB) 715
caribou 35, 383, 883–4
Caribou (NS) 480
Carleton (QC) 350
Carleton Martello Tower (NB) 560
Carmacks (YT) 877
Carmanah Walbran Provincial Park (BC) 787
Carr, Emily 774
cars
    border crossings 77
    buying 85–6
    CAA 87
    drive-aways 86
    gasoline 87
    highways & roads 77, 83–4
    insurance 45, 86
    renting 84–5
    road rules 84
    sharing 86–7
Cartier, Jacques 16, 257, 262, 305, 314, 347, 504
carvings 29–30, 323, 401
Casa Loma (ON) 106
casinos 148, 179, 204, 217, 240, 275, 326
Cassiar Hwy 852–3
Castlegar (BC) 842
Cates Park (BC) 740

Cathedral of the Transfiguration (ON) 132
Cathedral Provincial Park (BC) 821
Cathédrale Marie Reine du Monde (QC) 272
Causapscal (QC) 351–2
Cave & Basin National Historic Site (AB) 690
Cavendish (PE) 523–4
caves 150, 164, 350, 801, 804, 841
CBC. See Canadian Broadcasting Corporation
ceilidhs 512
Central Fundy Shore (NB) 564–8
Centre Canadien d'Architecture (QC) 271
Centre Island (ON) 101
Champlain, Samuel de 16, 95, 305, 311–2, 455–6, 466, 467, 475, 548, 557
Change Islands (NF) 396
Chapleau (ON) 243–4
Chaplin Lake (SK) 632
Charlevoix (QC) 323, 324–7, 324
Charlottetown (PE) 507–14, 509
Château de Ramezay (QC) 269
Château Frontenac (QC) 311
Checkpoint (NT) 899
Chemainus (BC) 787–8
Chester (NS) 449–50
Chéticamp (NS) 488–9
Chetwynd (BC) 846
Chibougamau (QC) 361
Chicoutimi (QC) 328–9
Chignecto (NS) 474–7
children, traveling with 45–6, 60
Chilkoot Trail 876
Chinatown
    Montréal 265, 283–4
    Ottawa 144
    Toronto 108, 120–1
    Vancouver 727, 734–5, 751–2
Chinese Cultural Centre (AB) 673
chinook 649
Chisasibi (QC) 360–1
chocolate 152, 545

Chrétien, Jean 18, 22
Christ Church Cathedral (NB) 536–7
Church Point (NS) 461
Churchill (MB) 607–14, **608, 611**
Churchill Falls (NF) 428–9
Citadel National Historic Site (NS) 438
Citadelle (QC) 307
Clarenville (NF) 386
climate 19–21
climbing 64
    AB 650, 691, 698–9, 705
    BC 762, 823
    NF 425
    NS 439
    NU 913
    ON 209
    QC 292–3
    YT 870, 871
clothing
    Native Indian 30
    packing 42
    washing 55–6
CN Tower (ON) 99–100
Coaticook (QC) 301
Cochrane (ON) 232–3
Codroy Valley (NF) 415
Coleman frog 536
Collingwood (ON) 208–9
Columbia Icefield (AB) 700
Comox (BC) 801–2
Conception Bay (NF) 383–4
Confederation Bridge (NB, PE) 504, 506, 575
Confederation Trail (PE) 504, 517, 529
Conne River (NF) 400
consulates 46–7
Cook, Captain James 411, 719, 856
Corner Brook (NF) 411–3, **412**
Cornwall (ON) 152
Corso Italia (ON) 109
Cortes Island (BC) 803–4
Cosmodrôme (QC) 277
costs 49
    accommodations 66
    food 70
cougars 35
Country Harbour (NS) 485
Country Heritage Park (ON) 186

courses 65
Courtenay (BC) 801–2
Cowichan 786
Cowichan Valley (BC) 786–7
coyotes 35, 167
Cranbrook (BC) 840
craters 361–2
Crawford Bay (BC) 841
credit cards 49
Credit River 127
Cree 15, 233–4, 257, 260,
    359, 360, 585, 587, 605,
    619, 621, 622, 634, 642,
    649, 651, 667
Creston (BC) 840
crime 60
Crofton (BC) 787
Crooked Lake Provincial Park
    (SK) 630
Cross, James 258
crown land 38
Crowsnest Pass (AB) 717
cruises 78
Cullen Gardens & Miniature
    Village (ON) 132
curling 628
currency 48
customs 47–8
Cut Knife (SK) 646
cycling 63, 87–8. See also
    mountain biking
    AB 650, 657–8, 675, 691,
        704–5, 716
    BC 722, 741, 743, 777,
        827
    MB 617
    NB 532, 578
    NS 432, 439, 490
    ON 93, 111–2, 140, 160,
        162, 164, 168, 174,
        209
    PE 504
    QC 261, 278, 290, 296,
        298, 314, 320, 329,
        337
    YT 864, 869
Cypress Hills Interprovincial
    Park (AB, SK) 633

D

Dalhousie (NB) 582
The Danforth (ON) 109, 122

Dartmouth (NS) 447–8
Dauphin (MB) 617–8
Davis Inlet (NF) 425
Dawson City (YT) 877–82,
    878
Dawson Creek (BC) 846
Daylight Saving Time 54
debit cards 49
Deep Cove (BC) 740
deer 34
Deer Island (NB) 548–51
Deer Lake (NF) 401–2
Deer Trail (ON) 234–5
Delhi (ON) 198
Dempster Hwy 883
Dene 585, 621, 667, 719,
    858, 886, 897, 900, 903,
    910
Denman Island (BC) 801
Destruction Bay (YT) 871
Detroit (Michigan) 203–4
Devonian Gardens (AB) 672
Diefenbunker (ON) 146
Digby (NS) 461–3
Digby Neck (NS) 463–5
Dildo (NF) 385
Diligent River (NS) 476
Dinosaur Provincial Park (AB)
    40, 711–2
Dinosaur Trail (AB) 709
dinosaurs 475, 633, 666,
    674, 709, 711–2
Dionne quintuplets 222, 224
disabled travelers 59
diving
    BC 722–3, 740, 742,
        776–7, 790, 802, 806,
        812
    NS 439, 452
    ON 213
    QC 348
documents 44–6
dog-sledding 234, 613, 892
Dorcas Bay 212
Doukhobours 629, 630
Drapeau, Jean 263
drinks 70–1
driving. See cars
drugs
    illegal 47–8, 61, 606
    prescription 56
Drumheller (AB) 709, 711
Drummondville (QC) 304–5
Dry Island Buffalo Jump (AB)
    666

Dryden (ON) 254
Duck Lake (SK) 646
ducks 36
Dugald (MB) 601
Duncan (BC) 786–7
Dundarave (BC) 740
Dundurn Castle (ON) 167
Dunlap Observatory (ON)
    132
Durrell (NF) 398
Dyer's Bay (ON) 212

E

eagles, bald 36, 873
East Coast Trail 382
East Point (PE) 516–7
Eastend (SK) 633
Eastern Shore (NS) 483–6
Eastern Townships (QC)
    296–301
economy 22–3
Economy (NS) 475
ecotourism 63
Edmonton (AB) 651–64, **653,
    656**
    accommodations 659–61
    activities 657–8
    day trips 664–6
    entertainment 662–3
    history 651
    restaurants 661–2
    special events 658–9
    sports 663
    transportation 663–4
Edmonton Art Gallery (AB)
    656–7
Edmundston (NB) 542–3
education 25
Edzo (NT) 897
Eel River First Nation (NB)
    582
efficiencies. See accommoda-
    tions
Eganville (ON) 150
eKno communication service
    51
electricity 54, 360, 361
elk 36, 665, 701
Elk Island National Park (AB)
    665
Ellesmere Island (NU) 913
Elliot Lake (ON) 235
Elmira (ON) 191–2
Elmira (PE) 517
Elora (ON) 192–3

Bold indicates maps.

email 51
embassies 46–7
emergencies 61, 919
employment 65
Empress Hotel (BC) 780–1
Enterprise (NT) 896
environmental issues 110,
    198, 225, 391, 496, 541,
    560, 723
Eskimos. *See* Inuit
Espanola (ON) 234
Estevan (SK) 630–1
exchange rates 48
explorers 16, 383–4, 666

F

Fairmont Hot Springs (BC)
    839
farm vacations 69
Faro (YT) 874
Fathom Five National Marine
    Park (ON) 212–3
fauna. *See* wildlife
faxes 51
Fenelon Falls (ON) 164
Fergus (ON) 193–4
Fernie (BC) 840
ferries 77–8, 88–9, 807
Ferryland (NF) 378, 382
Field (BC) 836–7
films 28
fire safety 60
First Nations. *See* Inuit;
    Native Indians
fish 37. *See also* fishing,
    recreational; fishing indus-
    try; salmon
Fish Creek Provincial Park
    (AB) 674
Fisher River (MB) 605
fishing, recreational 64
    AB 675
    BC 722, 723, 777, 802,
        806, 827, 868
    MB 587
    NB 532, 580
    NF 366
    NT 888, 892, 895, 896
    NU 910
    ON 140, 162, 214, 250,
        254, 255
    PE 522
    QC 303, 304, 344, 345,
        350, 352
    SK 622

YT 861, 871
fishing industry 363, 364,
    391, 404, 419
Five Islands Provincial Park
    (NS) 475
flag 21
Fleur de Lys (NF) 401
Flin Flon (MB) 606–7
flora. *See* plants
Fogo Island (NF) 396–7
food 69–70
    costs 70
    French 70
    in Montréal 282
    Native Indian 70
    in Newfoundland 368
football 71, 126, 145, 166,
    167, 287, 599, 628, 663,
    682, 757
forestry 234, 235, 359, 532,
    765, 786, 844
Forillon National Park (QC)
    346–7
Fort Amherst (NF) 370–1
Fort Anne National Historic
    Site (NS) 466
Fort Beauséjour National
    Historic Site (NB) 575
Fort Calgary Historic Park
    (AB) 673
Fort Carlton Historic Park
    (SK) 646
Fort Chipewyan (AB) 899
Fort Edmonton Park (AB)
    654–5
Fort Erie (ON) 185
Fort Frances (ON) 255
Fort Garry (MB) 601
Fort Henry National Historic
    Site (ON) 154
Fort Liard (NT) 900
Fort McMurray (AB) 668
Fort Nelson (BC) 847
Fort Prince of Wales (MB)
    611
Fort Providence (NT) 896
Fort Qu'Appelle (SK) 629
Fort Rodd Hill National
    Historic Park (BC) 775
Fort St John (BC) 846
Fort Simpson (NT) 899–900
Fort Smith (NT) 898
Fort Steele (BC) 839–40
Fort William (ON) 245, 252,
    247

Fort York (ON) 106
Forteau (NF) 423
Fortune (NF) 392
fossils 234, 235, 351, 383,
    475, 666, 674, 709,
    711–2, 837, 902
Fox, Terry 248
Fraser, Simon 17, 719, 843
Fraser River Canyon (BC) 814
Fred Henne Territorial Park
    (NT) 892
Fredericton (NB) 534–40,
    535
freighters 78
French and Indian War 16
French language 916–20
French Shore (NS) 461
Freshwater Resource Centre
    (NF) 373
Frontenac Provincial Park
    (ON) 161
frostbite 56–7
Fundy Isles (NB) 548–56,
    550
Fundy National Park (NB)
    565–7
Fundy Trail Parkway (NB)
    565
fur trade 244, 262, 335, 585,
    601, 649, 651, 666, 719,
    886

G

Gabriola Island (BC) 790
Galiano Island (BC) 811–2
galleries 73
    AB 656–7
    BC 733, 757, 775, 815,
        826, 842
    MB 592, 600
    NB 536
    NF 373, 411–2
    NS 437, 438, 448, 469,
        482
    ON 102–4, 131–2, 136–7,
        167, 175, 187, 196,
        204, 210, 228, 239,
        248
    SK 637–8, 646
Galloping Goose Trail (BC)
    777
gambling. *See* casinos
Gampo Abbey (NS) 491–2
Gander (NF) 394–6
Ganges (BC) 808

Garibaldi Provincial Park (BC)
762
gasoline 87
Gaspé (QC) 347–8
Gaspé Peninsula (QC)
342–52, **343**
Gastown (BC) 727, 734,
751–2
Gatineau (Hull) (QC) 147–8
Gatineau Park (QC) 148–9
gays & lesbians
travelers 59
venues 125–6, 277, 681,
755–6, 783
geese, Canada 36, 243
geography 18–9
Georgian Bay 207–22, **208**
Georgian Bay Islands
National Park (ON) 220
giardiasis 57
Gillam (MB) 607
Gimli (MB) 604
Glace Bay (NS) 498
Glacier Bay National Park
(Alaska) 874
Glacier National Park (BC)
835
Glacier National Park
(Montana). See Waterton-
Glacier International Peace
Park
glaciers 700, 835, 853, 870,
871, 874
Glenbow Museum (AB) 672
GM Place (BC) 734
goats, mountain 36
Godbout (QC) 334
Goderich (ON) 206
Gogama (ON) 231
gold 331, 357–8, 651, 719,
847, 859, 864, 876, 879,
886, 889
Gold River (BC) 804–5
Golden (BC) 835–6
gondolas 689–90, 698, 703,
739
Goods & Services Tax (GST)
49–50
Goose Bay (NF) 426–7
Goulds (NF) 381
government 21–2
Graham Island (BC) 854–5

grain elevators 645
Granby (QC) 296
Grand Bank (NF) 391–2
Grand Banks 391
Grand Beach (MB) 603
Grand Bend (ON) 206
Grand Falls (NB) 542
Grand Falls (NF) 399–400
Grand Manan Island (NB)
553–6
Grand Mère (QC) 303
Grand Métis (QC) 343–4
Grand Pré (NS) 470–1
Grand Pré National Historic
Site (NS) 470
Grand River 193
Grande Anse (NB) 581
Grande Prairie (AB) 667
Grande Vallée (QC) 346
Grandes Bergeronnes (QC)
333
Granville Island (BC) 736,
752
Grasslands National Park (SK)
633–4
Gravenhurst (ON) 217–8
Great Explosion 433, 437
Great Sand Hills (SK) 632
Greektown (ON) 109, 122
Green Park Shipbuilding
Museum (PE) 528
greenhouses 904
Greenwich (PE) 517
Grenfell, Wilfred 409
Gretzky, Wayne 72
Grey Owl 643, 644
Gros Morne National Park
(NF) 39, 402–6
Grosse Île (QC) 322–3, 355
Group of Seven 28–9, 127,
221, 242
Grouse Mountain (BC) 739,
741
Guelph (ON) 186–8
guesthouses. See accommo-
dations
Gulf Islands (BC) 807–13, **809**
Gulf Museum (NF) 415
Guysborough (NS) 486
Gwaii Haanas National Park
Reserve (BC) 855, 857

H

Haida 15, 41, 718, 850, 854,
855, 856

Haines (Alaska) 872–3
Haines Hwy 873
Haines Junction (YT) 868–70
Haliburton Highlands (ON)
150, 165
Halifax (NS) 433–47, **434**
accommodations 440–2
activities 439
climate 20
day trips 447–8
entertainment 443–4
history 433
restaurants 442–3
tours 439–40
transportation 444–7
Hamilton (ON) 165–9
hang-gliding 345
Hanlan's Point (ON) 101
Happy Valley–Goose Bay
(NF) 426–7
Harbour Breton (NF) 401
Harbour Grace (NF) 384
Harbourfront (ON) 100–1,
107–8
Harrington Harbour (QC)
338
Hartland (NB) 541–2
Havre Aubert (QC) 354–5
Havre aux Maisons (QC) 355
Havre St Pierre (QC) 336
Hawke's Bay (NF) 406–7
Hay River (NT) 897–8
Head-Smashed-In Buffalo
Jump (AB) 40, 712
health 56–8
diseases 57–8
environmental hazards
56–7
immunizations 56
insurance 46
water purification 56
Hearst (ON) 231, 237
Heart's Content (NF) 384–5
Hecla Provincial Park (MB)
604
helicopter flights 181, 686
Heritage Park Historical
Village (AB) 673
herons, great blue 36
Herschel Island Territorial
Park (YT) 884
Hewitt, Foster 72
Hidden Lake Territorial Park
(NT) 895
high commissions 46–7

Bold indicates maps.

High Level (AB) 667
hiking & backpacking 63–4, 347
    AB 650, 675, 690–1, 698, 704, 716
    BC 722, 739, 741, 777, 786, 790, 795–6, 802, 804, 827, 836, 850, 868
    MB 587, 602
    NB 532, 554, 557, 566, 584
    NF 366, 375, 382, 388–9, 391, 404, 413–4, 418, 424, 427
    NS 433, 465, 475, 476–7, 484, 485, 486–7, 490, 492
    NT 888, 895, 899, 902
    NU 910, 912
    ON 93, 162, 209, 213, 218, 240, 244
    QC 295, 304, 325, 328, 331, 337, 345, 348
    YT 861, 864, 871, 876, 880–1, 883
Hillsborough (NB) 568
Hinton (AB) 666
Historic Properties (NS) 436
history 14–8, 53. See also individual locations
hitchhiking 88
HIV/AIDS 58
hockey 71, 72, 103, 126, 145, 156, 221, 288, 444, 472, 599, 638, 663, 682, 757
Hockey Hall of Fame (ON) 103
Hockley Valley (ON) 127
holidays 62
homeless people 60
hoodoos 690, 709
Hope (BC) 814
Hopedale (NF) 425
Hopewell Rocks (NB) 568
Hornby Island (BC) 801
Horne Lake Caves Provincial Park (BC) 801
horse racing 126, 185, 513
horseback riding 299, 587, 617, 691, 705, 716
Horseshoe Bay (BC) 740
Horseshoe Canyon (AB) 709
Horseshoe Falls (ON) 176, 178–9

hostels. See accommodations
hot springs
    AB 690, 704
    BC 833–4, 838–9, 841, 842
    SK 641–2
    YT 864
Hot Springs Cove (BC) 796
Hôtel de Ville
    Montréal 269
    Québec City 312
hotels. See accommodations
House of Green Gables (PE) 523–4
houseboats 161, 162, 163–4
Hudson's Bay Company 16, 53, 73, 233, 587, 588, 590, 600, 601, 607–8, 649, 651, 673, 768, 790, 846, 858, 886, 896, 899
Hull (Gatineau) (QC) 147–8
hunting 304, 345, 622
Huntsman Aquarium Museum (NB) 548
Huntsville (ON) 218
Huronia (ON) 207, 215–7
Hurons 215, 262
Hyder (Alaska) 852–3
hydroelectric stations 360, 361
hypothermia 56–7

I

ice hockey. See hockey
Ice Hotel (QC) 316
ice skating. See skating
icebergs 366, 374, 381, 398, 422
Icefields Parkway (AB) 699–701
Ignace (ON) 253–4
Île aux Coudres (QC) 325–6
Île aux Grues (QC) 323
Île d'Anticosti (QC) 336–7
Île de la Grande Entrée (QC) 356
Île d'Entrée (QC) 356
Île d'Orleans (QC) 321
Île du Cap aux Meules (QC) 354
Île du Havre Aubert (QC) 354–5
Île du Havre aux Maisons (QC) 355
Île Notre Dame (QC) 275

Île Ste Hélène (QC) 274–5
Îles de la Madeleine (QC) 352–7, **353**
immigration 24, 322–3, 436
immunizations 56
Indian Arm (BC) 740
Inglewood Bird Sanctuary (AB) 674
Ingonish (NS) 493–4
Ingraham Trail (NT) 895
Innu 257, 259, 333, 335, 336
insects 60–1, 274, 402, 773
insurance
    car 45, 86
    travel 46
International Appalachian Trail 345, 347
International Falls (Minnesota) 255
International Fox Museum & Hall of Fame (PE) 526
Internet
    access 51
    resources 51–2
Inuit
    art 29–30, 104, 147, 292, 310
    history 15, 257, 260, 364, 401, 425
    language 916
    museum 610
    population 15, 24, 259, 260, 361, 365, 903, 908
Inuvik (NT) 903–6, **903**
inventions 23
Invermere (BC) 839
Inverness (NS) 487–8
Iqaluit (NU) 910, 911
Iroquois 15, 92, 257, 262
Irving Eco Center (NB) 576
Irving Nature Park (NB) 560–1
Iskut (BC) 853
Isle aux Morts (NF) 418
itineraries, suggested 43
Ivvavik National Park (YT) 884

J

James Bay (QC) 359–61
Jardin Botanique (QC) 273–4
Jasper National Park (AB) 684, 701–9, **685**
Jasper townsite (AB) 701–9, **702**

Jasper Tramway (AB) 703
Jedore Oyster Pond (NS) 484
Jews 263, 282
Johnson's Crossing (YT) 867–8
Jonquière (QC) 329
Joseph, Chief 185

K

Kakabeka Falls (ON) 253
Kakisa (NT) 896
Kamloops (BC) 815–8, **816**
Kananaskis Country (AB) 684–5
Kapuskasing (ON) 231
Kaslo (BC) 841
Kawartha Lakes (ON) 163, 164–5
kayaking 64
    AB 650
    BC 722, 742, 743, 776, 790, 795, 797, 800, 812, 850
    NB 537, 550, 552, 554, 576, 577, 584
    NF 375, 381
    NS 432–3, 439, 449, 450, 454, 457, 484, 493, 494
    NT 888, 892, 901–2
    NU 910, 911
    ON 112
    PE 504, 506, 520, 522, 528–9
    QC 261, 278, 326–7, 335, 339, 350, 351
    YT 861, 864
Kegasta (QC) 338
Kejimkujik National Park (NS) 465–6
Kelowna (BC) 825–9, **825**
Kenora (ON) 254
Kensington Market (ON) 119
Kentville (NS) 468
Keremeos (BC) 821
Kettle Point (ON) 206
Khyber Centre for the Arts (NS) 438
Killaloe (ON) 150
Killarney Provincial Park (ON) 221–2

Killbear Provincial Park (ON) 221
Kimberley (BC) 839
Kimiwan Birdwalk & Interpretive Centre (AB) 667
King, William Lyon Mackenzie 149, 311
King's Landing Historical Settlement (NB) 540–1
Kingston (ON) 153–9, **155**
Kitchener-Waterloo (ON) 188–91
Kitikmeot Region (NU) 913–4
Kitsilano (BC) 730, 737, 753
Kitwanga Fort National Historic Site (BC) 852
Kivalliq Region (NU) 914–5
Klondike Hwy 874–7
Kluane National Park (YT) 41, 870–1
Knowlton (QC) 297
Komarno (MB) 605
Kootenay National Park (BC) 838
Kortright Waterfowl Park (ON) 188
Kouchibouguac National Park (NB) 577–8
'Ksan Historical Village & Museum (BC) 852
Kwakiutl 850, 856

L

La Broquerie (MB) 602
La Malbaie–Pointe au Pic (QC) 326
La Manche Provincial Park (NF) 382
La Mauricie National Park (QC) 303
La Ronge (SK) 644
La Scie (NF) 401
Labrador 363–7, 420–9, **421**
    accommodations 366
    activities 366
    climate 364
    economy 364
    history 364
    population 364–5
    tourist office 44
    transportation 366–7
Labrador City (NF) 427–8
Labrador Straits 422–5
Lac Brome (QC) 297

Lac la Ronge Provincial Park (SK) 644–5
Lac Memphrémagog (QC) 298–9
Lac St Jean (QC) 329–30
Lachine (QC) 277
lacrosse 71, 126, 169
Lady Evelyn Falls Territorial Park (NT) 896
Ladysmith (BC) 788
LaHave (NS) 454–5
LaHave Islands (NS) 455
Lake District (AB) 667–8
Lake Erie 198–9
Lake Huron 206–7
Lake Louise (AB) 696–9, **697**
Lake Manitoba (MB) 605
Lake Minnewanka (AB) 690
Lake O'Hara (BC) 837
Lake Ontario Waterfront Trail (ON) 164, 168
Lake Superior 242–5
Lake Superior Provincial Park (ON) 243
Lake Winnipeg (MB) 603–5
Lakefield (ON) 165
Lakelands (ON) 207–22, **208**
Landry, Bernard 18, 259
language 52, 395, 916–20
L'Anse Amour (NF) 423
L'Anse au Claire (NF) 422
L'Anse au Loup (NF) 423
L'Anse aux Meadows National Historic Park (NF) 39, 408–9
L'Anse aux Meadows village (NF) 409
L'Anse St Jean (QC) 327
Laporte, Pierre 258
Larch Valley (AB) 698
laundry 55–6
The Laurentians (QC) 290–6
Lawrencetown Beach (NS) 483
Le Pays de la Sagouine (NB) 576
Le Témis (QC) 338
Leamington (ON) 199
legal matters 61
Lennox Island (PE) 528–9
Les Éboulements (QC) 325
lesbians. See gays & lesbians
Lethbridge (AB) 713–5
Lévesque, René 258
Lévis (QC) 322

Bold indicates maps.

Lewisporte (NF) 398–9
Liard Hwy (NT) 900
lighthouses
    BC 740, 775, 793, 800
    NB 583
    NF 370–1, 382, 383, 386,
        397, 404, 407, 417–8,
        423
    NS 448, 456, 459
    ON 199, 212
    PE 516, 529, 530
    QC 350
Liscomb Mills (NS) 485
literature 25–7. See also
    books
Little Current (ON) 214
Little India (ON) 109, 122–3
Little Italy
    Montréal 276
    Ottawa 144
    Toronto 109, 122
Little Manitou Lake (SK) 641
Liverpool (NS) 455–6
lobster 480, 521
London (ON) 199–203, **200**
Long Beach (BC) 794–5
Long Island (NS) 463–4
loons 36
Louisbourg (NS) 498–9
Louiseville (QC) 302
Lower St Lawrence (QC)
    338–42
Loyalists 17, 92, 160, 161,
    257, 349, 350, 457, 531,
    540, 557, 560, 561
Lumsden (SK) 629
Lunenburg (NS) 39–40,
    451–4, **451**
Lyme disease 58
Lynn Canyon Park (BC)
    739–40
lynx 35

M

Mabou (NS) 486–7
Macdonald, John Alexander
    17, 157, 592
Mackenzie, Alexander 17,
    719
Mackenzie, William Lyon 95,
    106, 175
MacKenzie Art Gallery (SK)
    625
Mackenzie Hwy (AB, NT)
    667, 895–6

Mackenzie River 886, 902–6,
    910
Mactaquac (NB) 540–1
Mactaquac Provincial Park
    (NB) 540
magazines 53
Magnetic Hill (NB) 571
Magog (QC) 298
Mahone Bay (NS) 450–1
mail 50
Makkovik (NF) 425
Maligne Canyon (AB) 703–4
Maligne Lake (AB) 704
Maliseet 532, 534, 557
Manitoba 585–618, **586**
    activities 587
    history 585, 587
    parks 587
    tourist office 44
Manitou Beach (SK) 641–2
Manitoulin Island (ON)
    214–5
Manning Provincial Park (BC)
    814–5
Maple Creek (SK) 633
maple syrup 293
maps 42
Mara Lake (BC) 831
Marble Island (NU) 914
Marble Mountain (NF) 413–4
Marconi, Guglielmo 370,
    498
Maritime Museum of the
    Atlantic (NS) 436
Marlbank (ON) 160
Marystown (NF) 390
Mashteuiatsh (QC) 329
Matagami (QC) 359
Matane (QC) 344
Matapédia (QC) 351
Matapédia Valley (QC)
    351–2
Maxville (ON) 152
Mayne Island (BC) 812–3
Maynooth (ON) 152
McGill University (QC) 272
McMichael Collection (ON)
    131–2
McNabs Island (NS) 439
Meadow Lake Provincial Park
    (SK) 646
Meares Island (BC) 796–7
measurements 54–5
Meat Cove (NS) 492–3
Medicine Hat (AB) 712

Meech Lake Accord 18,
    258–9
Meewasin Valley (SK) 637
Mennonite Heritage Village
    (MB) 602
Mennonite Heritage Village
    (SK) 632
Mennonites 187, 188, 191,
    192, 602, 632
Merrickville (ON) 152
Métis 24, 587, 593, 628, 645
metric system 54–5
Micmac. See Mi'kmaq
Midland (ON) 215–6
Miette Hot Springs (AB) 704
Mi'kmaq (Micmac) 257, 347,
    400, 430, 432, 433, 473,
    486, 501, 504, 528–9,
    531, 532, 534, 579–80
Mile End (QC) 265, 275, 277
Miminegash (PE) 529–30
Mingan (QC) 336
Mingan Archipelago National
    Park (QC) 336
mining 225, 227, 231–2,
    235, 249, 357–8, 359,
    381, 391, 401, 426, 427,
    432, 479, 487–8, 498,
    532, 582, 606, 607, 717,
    762, 880
Minister's Island Historic Site
    (NB) 548
Miquelon 392–4
Miramichi (NB) 578–9
Miscouche (PE) 528
Mistaken Point Ecological
    Reserve (NF) 383
Mohawks 162–3, 257, 260,
    290
monasteries 290, 299, 311
Monastery (NS) 483
Moncton (NB) 569–74, **569**
money 48–50
Mont Blanc 433, 437
Mont Jacques Cartier (QC)
    345
Mont Louis (QC) 346
Mont Orford (QC) 299
Mont St Pierre (QC) 345–6
Mont Ste Anne (QC) 322
Mont Tremblant Village (QC)
    294
Montague (PE) 515
Montgomery, Lucy Maud
    503, 523–4, 525

Montmagny (QC) 323
Montréal (QC) 262–90, **263, 266–7, 276**
    accommodations 279–81
    activities 278
    climate 20
    day trips 290–305, **291**
    entertainment 285–7
    history 262–4
    neighborhoods 275, 277
    restaurants 281–5
    shopping 288
    special events 279
    sports 287–8
    suburbs 277–8
    tours 278–9
    transportation 288–90
moose 35, 389
Moose Factory Island (ON) 233–4
Moose Jaw (SK) 631–2
Moose Mountain Provincial Park (SK) 630
Moose Travel 89–90, 113–4
Moosehead Brewery (NB) 560
Moosonee (ON) 233–4
Moraine Lake (AB) 698
Moravians 425
Mormons 715
Morris (MB) 602
Morrisburg (ON) 153
Morrisville (NF) 400
mosquitoes 60–1
motels. See accommodations
mountain biking 63
    BC 722, 802, 823, 868
    NB 566
    ON 209
    QC 261
    YT 869, 871
mountaineering. See climbing
Mounties. See Royal Canadian Mounted Police
Mt Assiniboine Provincial Park (BC) 838
Mt Barbeau (NU) 913
Mt Carleton Provincial Park (NB) 583–4
Mt Edziza Provincial Park (BC) 853
Mt Logan (YT) 19, 41, 871

Mt Mackay (ON) 248–9
Mt Panorama (BC) 839
Mt Pelly (NU) 914
Mt Revelstoke National Park (BC) 832–3
Mt Robson Provincial Park (BC) 818–9
Mt St Elias (YT) 871
Mt Seymour Provincial Park (BC) 740
Mt Washington (BC) 802
Mulroney, Brian 18
Muncho Lake Provincial Park (BC) 847
Murdochville (QC) 346
Musée d'Art Contemporain (QC) 271
Musée de la Civilisation (QC) 312–3
Musée de l'Amérique Française (QC) 311
Musée des Beaux Arts (QC) 271
Musée du Québec (QC) 310
Musée McCord 271–2
Museum of Anthropology (BC) 737
Museum of Man & Nature (MB) 590, 592
music 27–8
Muskoka (ON) 207, 217–8
Musquodoboit Harbour (NS) 483–4
Muttart Conservatory (AB) 656

N

NAFTA 18
Nahanni Butte (NT) 900
Nahanni National Park Reserve (NT) 41, 900–2
Nahanni River 900, 901–2
Naikoon Provincial Park (BC) 855
Nain (NF) 425–6
Nakusp (BC) 842
Nanaimo (BC) 788–92, **789**
Narcisse Wildlife Management Area (MB) 604
Natashquan (QC) 337
national anthem 21
National Gallery (ON) 136–7
national parks 37–8. See also individual parks

Native Indians. See also individual cultures
    archeological sites 636
    art 29–30, 147, 163, 757
    books about 53
    cultural centers & museums 139, 165, 185, 215, 234, 329, 396, 400, 636–7, 638, 689, 771, 786, 806, 815, 817, 852, 854
    cultural rebirth 24–5, 30
    food 70
    history 14–6, 92, 400, 718–9, 854, 858–9
    languages 15, 916
    literature 26
    politics 24, 30
    population 24
    potlatches 850
    religion 30, 31
    reserves 24
    totem poles 771, 786, 849, 852, 856
Neepawa (MB) 617
Neils Harbour (NS) 493
Nelson (BC) 840–1
Netley Marsh (MB) 603
neutrinos 228
New Brunswick 531–84, **533**
    accommodations 532
    activities 532
    climate 531
    history 531
    tourist office 44
    transportation 532–4
New Brunswick Museum (NB) 559
New Carlisle (QC) 349
New Glasgow (NS) 482
New Glasgow (PE) 521–2
New London (PE) 524
New Richmond (QC) 350
New River Provincial Park (NB) 556–7
New World Island (NF) 397
Newcastle (NB) 579
Newcastle Island Provincial Marine Park (BC) 790
Newfoundland 363–420, **365**
    accommodations 366
    activities 366
    climate 364
    economy 364
    history 364

population 364–5
tourist office 44
transportation 366–7
newspapers 53
Newville (NF) 397
Niagara Escarpment (ON) 170
Niagara Falls (ON) 176–84, **177**
Niagara Glen Nature Preserve (ON) 180–1
Niagara Parkway & Recreational Trail (ON) 174–6
Niagara-on-the-Lake (ON) 170–4, **171**
Nicolet (QC) 304
Nipigon (ON) 244
Nisga'a Memorial Lava Bed Provincial Park (BC) 852
Nopoming Provincial Park (MB) 603
Norman Wells (NT) 902–3
Norris Point (NF) 402–3
North Battleford (SK) 646
North Bay (ON) 222, 224
North Cape (PE) 529
North Hatley (QC) 299–300
North Pole 914
North Rustico (PE) 522–3
North Shore (BC) 730, 749
North Shore (QC) 320–2, 330–8
North Sydney (NS) 494–5
North Vancouver (BC) 739–40
northern lights. See aurora borealis
Northern Peninsula (NF) 402–11
Northern Woods & Water Route (NWWR) 605
Northumberland Shore (NB) 575–8
Northwest Territories 885–907, **887**
accommodations 888–9
activities 888
climate 886, 888
flora & fauna 888
history 886
parks 888
tourist office 44
transportation 889
Notre Dame Bay (NF) 396–8
Nova Scotia 430–501, **431**

accommodations 433
activities 432–3
climate 432
history 430, 432
tourist office 44
transportation 433
Nova Scotia Museum of Natural History (NS) 438
nuclear plant 132
Nunavik (QC) 361
Nunavut 908–15, **909**
accommodations 910–1
activities 910
climate 910
flora & fauna 910
history 908, 910
tourist office 44
tours 910
transportation 911

O

Oak Hammock Marsh (MB) 601
observatories 132, 736
Ocean Sciences Centre (NF) 373
Odanak (QC) 304
Odyssium (AB) 657
Officers' Square (NB) 534, 536
oil and gas industries 206, 364, 426, 432, 647, 649, 668, 712, 886
Ojibway 92, 212, 234, 244, 245, 246, 248, 253, 255, 585
Oka (QC) 290
Okanagan Valley (BC) 819–31, **820**
Old Fort William Historical Park (ON) 246, 248
Old Strathcona (AB) 652, 657, **658**
Olympic Village (QC) 273–4
Olympics 263–4, 273–4, 674–5
Onhoúa Chetek8e (QC) 320
Ontario 91–255, **92, 151, 166, 223**
activities 93
conservation areas 133
history 91–2
tourist office 44
Ontario Place (ON) 101–2

Ontario Science Centre (ON) 103
Oratoire St Joseph (QC) 273
orchards 819, 821, 826
Orillia (ON) 217
Orwell (PE) 514
Osoyoos (BC) 821–2
ospreys 36
Ottawa (ON) 133–46, **135**
accommodations 141–3
activities 140
climate 20
day trips 146–50
entertainment 145
history 134
museums & galleries 136–9
restaurants 143–5
sports 145
tours 140
transportation 145–6
Ottawa Locks (ON) 137
Ottawa River 93, 133, 149
Ouimet Canyon Provincial Park (ON) 244–5
outports 419–20
Owen Sound (ON) 209–11

P

Pacific Rim National Park Reserve (BC) 794–6
Pacific Spirit Regional Park (BC) 737–8
packing 42–3
Pangnirtung (NU) 912
Paramount Canada's Wonderland (ON) 104–5
parasailing 822, 827
Parc d'Aiguebelle (QC) 358
Parc de Frontenac (QC) 301
Parc de la Chute Montmorency (QC) 321
Parc de la Gaspésie (QC) 345
Parc de la Gorge (QC) 301
Parc de la Jacques Cartier (QC) 320
Parc de Miguasha (QC) 351
Parc des Champs de Bataille (QC) 307, 310
Parc des Grands Jardins (QC) 325
Parc des Hautes Gorges de la Rivière Malbaie (QC) 326
Parc des Îles de Boucherville (QC) 277–8

Parc du Bic (QC) 339
Parc du Mont Mégantic (QC) 301
Parc du Mont Orford (QC) 299
Parc du Mont Royal (QC) 272–3
Parc du Mont Tremblant (QC) 295
Parc du Saguenay (QC) 327–8
Parc Jean Drapeau (QC) 274–5
Parizeau, Jacques 259
Park Corner (PE) 525
Parksville (BC) 801
Parliament Buildings (BC) 771–2
Parliament Hill (ON) 136
Parrsboro (NS) 475–6
Parry Sound (ON) 221
Partridge Island (NS) 475–6
The Pas (MB) 605–6
passports 44, 61
Paulatuk (NT) 906
Peace River (AB) 667
Peggy's Cove (NS) 448–9
Peguis (MB) 605
Pelee Island (ON) 199
pelicans 898
Pembina Valley (MB) 601
Pembroke (ON) 150
Pender Islands (BC) 810–1
Penetanguishene (ON) 216
Penticton (BC) 822–5
Percé (QC) 348–9
Peterborough (ON) 164
Petit Rocher (NB) 582
Petite Vallée (QC) 346
Petites (NF) 419
Petroglyphs Provincial Park (ON) 164
pets 48
Petty Harbour (NF) 381
Peyto, Bill 688
Peyto Lake (AB) 700
phones 50–1
photography 54, 137
Picton (ON) 163
Pictou (NS) 480–2
Piedmont (QC) 292
Pier 21 Centre (NS) 436–7

Pingualuit (QC) 361
Pisew Falls Provincial Park (MB) 607
Pistolet Bay Provincial Park (NF) 408
Place d'Armes (QC) 269
Place Jacques Cartier (QC) 269
Placentia (NF) 385
planning 42
plants 33–4
The Plateau (QC) 265, 275, 284–5, **276**
Pleasant Bay (NS) 491
Point Pelee National Park (ON) 199
Point Pleasant Park (NS) 438
Point Riche Lighthouse (NF) 407
Pointe à la Croix (QC) 351
Pointe à la Garde (QC) 351
Pointe au Pic (QC) 326
Pointe aux Anglais (QC) 335
Pointe de l'Est (QC) 356
Pointe des Monts (QC) 334
Polar Bear Express 232–3
polar bears 35, 609, 610, 612–3
police 61
politics 21–2
Pond Inlet (NU) 910, 913
population 23–5
porcupines 34
Port Alberni (BC) 792–4
Port Arthur (ON) 245, 251–2, **247**
Port au Choix (NF) 407
Port au Port Peninsula (NF) 414
Port au Port West (NF) 414
Port aux Basques (NF) 415–7, **416**
Port Colborne (ON) 169–70
Port de Grave (NF) 384
Port Dover (ON) 198
Port Dufferin (NS) 484–5
Port Elgin (ON) 211
Port Hardy (BC) 806–7
Port Hastings (NS) 486
Port McNeill (BC) 805
Port Royal National Historic Site (NS) 467
Port Stanley (ON) 198–9
Port Union (NF) 387
Portage la Prairie (MB) 615

Porters Lake Provincial Park (NS) 483
postal services 50
potlatches 850
powwows 114, 186, 214, 250, 473, 626, 629
Prelude Lake (NT) 895
Prescott (ON) 153
Prince Albert (SK) 642–3
Prince Albert National Park (SK) 644
Prince Edward Island 503–30, **505**
 accommodations 506
 activities 504, 506
 climate 504
 history 503–4
 tourist office 44, 504
 transportation 506–7
Prince Edward Island National Park (PE) 518–20, **518–9**
Prince George (BC) 843–5, **844**
Prince of Wales Northern Heritage Centre (NT) 891
Prince Rupert (BC) 807, 848–9, **849**
Prince's Island Park (AB) 673
printmaking 30
Providence Bay (ON) 214
Province House (PE) 508
Provincial Museum of Alberta (AB) 654
provincial parks 38. *See also individual parks*
P'Tit Train du Nord (QC) 290
Pubnico (NS) 458
puffins 37, 494
Pugwash (NS) 479
Pukaskwa National Park (ON) 244

Q

Quadra Island (BC) 803–4
Qualicum Beach (BC) 801
Qu'Appelle Valley (SK) 629
Quartier Latin (QC) 265, 275, 284, **276**
Québec 256–362, **258**
 activities 261–2
 First Nations 259–60
 history 256–9
 parks 260
 separatist movement 17, 18, 22, 258–9

Bold indicates maps.

tourist office 44
Québec City (QC) 39,
    305–20, **306, 308–9**
    accommodations 315–7
    day trips 320–3
    entertainment 318
    history 305–6
    restaurants 317–8
    tours 314–5
    transportation 318–20
Queen Charlotte Islands (BC)
    853–5, 857
Queen Elizabeth Park (BC)
    738
Queenston (ON) 175
Quesnel (BC) 847
Quetico Provincial Park (ON)
    255
Quidi Vidi (NF) 374
Quinte's Isle (ON) 162–3
Quttinirpaaq National Park
    (NU) 913

R

rabies 57–8
radio 53
Radisson (QC) 360
Radium Hot Springs (BC)
    838–9
Rae (NT) 897
rafting
    AB 650, 686, 705
    BC 724, 814, 835, 872
    NT 901–2
    ON 93, 140, 149–50
    QC 149, 262, 279, 290,
        292
    YT 861
Raleigh (NF) 408
Rankin Inlet (NU) 910, 914
rattlesnakes 61
Rawdon (QC) 295–6
razorbills 37
recreational vehicles (RVs) 85
Red Bay (NF) 423–4
Redberry Lake (SK) 645
Reed Deer (AB) 665
Regina (SK) 622–9, **623**
Région Évangéline (PE)
    527–8
Reid Lake (NT) 895
religion 30–1
Repulse Bay (NU) 915
Réserve Faunique des Lau-
    rentides (QC) 320–1

Réserve Faunique du St
    Maurice (QC) 304
Réserve Faunique la
    Vérendrye (QC) 357
reserves. See also individual
    reserves
    biosphere 41
    Native Indian 24
    nature 38
Resolute (NU) 910, 913
restaurants 69–70. See also
    individual cities
Revelstoke (BC) 831–5
Reversing Falls (NB) 560, 561
Reynolds-Alberta Museum
    (AB) 665
rice 644
Richmond (BC) 730, 738–9,
    749
Rideau Canal (ON) 162
Rideau Hall (ON) 139
Rideau Trail (ON) 162
Riding Mountain National
    Park (MB) 617
Riel, Louis 587, 588, 593,
    628, 638, 645
Rimouski (QC) 341–2
Rivière du Loup (QC)
    338–40, **339**
Rivière Éternité (QC) 327
Rivière Rouge (QC) 290
Robert Campbell Hwy 874
Rocher Percé (QC) 348
rock climbing. See climbing
rockhounding 152, 475–6
Rockwood Conservation Area
    (ON) 188
Rocky Harbour (NF) 402–3
Rocky Mountain House
    National Historic Site (AB)
    666
Rocky Mountain Parks (AB,
    BC) 41
Rocky Mountains 19
Roddickton (NF) 408
rodeos 659, 676
Rogers Pass (BC) 835
Roosevelt, Franklin D 551,
    552
Roosevelt Campobello Inter-
    national Park (NB) 552
Rose Blanche (NF) 418
Rosedale (ON) 109
Ross River (YT) 874
Rossland (BC) 842–3

Round-the-World (RTW)
    tickets 75
Route de la Baie James (QC)
    360
Rouyn-Noranda (QC) 358
Royal Botanical Gardens
    (ON) 166–7
Royal British Columbia
    Museum (BC) 771
Royal Canadian Mint (MB,
    ON) 139, 593
Royal Canadian Mounted
    Police 133, 146, 625, 649
Royal Ontario Museum (ON)
    102
Royal Saskatchewan Museum
    (SK) 625
Royal Tyrrell Museum of
    Palaeontology (AB) 709,
    711
rugby 73
rugs 488
RVs 85

S

Sackville (NB) 574–5
safety 60–1
Saguenay (QC) 323, 327–30,
    324
Saguenay–St Lawrence
    Marine Park (QC) 327–8
sailing 162, 254, 439–40,
    452, 500, 722, 742, 822,
    888
St Adèle (QC) 292
St Alban's (NF) 400
St Andrews (NB) 547–9
St Ann (PE) 521–2
St Ann's (NS) 494
St Anthony (NF) 409–11
St Antoine de Padoue (QC)
    302
St Barbe (NF) 408
St Boniface (MB) 590
St Catharines (ON) 169
St Croix Island (NB) 548
St Donat (QC) 295
St Gabriel de Valcartier (QC)
    320
St Jacobs (ON) 191
St Jacques (NB) 543–4
St Jean Port Joli (QC) 323
Saint John (NB) 557–64, **558**
Saint John River Valley (NB)
    540–4

St John's (NF) 367–80, **369, 371**
　accommodations 376–7
　activities 374–5
　day trips 380–5
　entertainment 378–9
　history 368
　restaurants 377–8
　shopping 379
　tours 375
　transportation 379–80
St Joseph (NB) 574
St Joseph Island (ON) 235
St Lawrence (NF) 391
St Lawrence Islands National Park (ON) 161
St Lawrence Market (ON) 108, 120
St Lawrence River 338–42
St Louis de Kent (NB) 577
St Louis du Ha! Ha! (QC) 338
St Lunaire (NF) 408
St Martins (NB) 565
St Marys (ON) 197–8
St Peter's (NS) 501
St Peters (PE) 517
St Pierre 392–4
St Raphaels (ON) 152
St Sauveur des Monts (QC) 292
St Siméon (QC) 326
St Stephen (NB) 544–7, **546**
St Thomas (ON) 203
Ste Agathe des Monts (QC) 293–4
Ste Anne de Beaupré (QC) 321–2
Ste Anne de Portneuf (QC) 334
Ste Anne des Monts (QC) 344–5
Ste Anne du Bocage (NB) 581
Ste Flavie (QC) 343
Ste Rose du Nord (QC) 328
Salish 719, 724, 768
salmon 37, 545, 723, 792, 802, 831
Salmon Arm (BC) 831
Salt Spring Island (BC) 808, 810
Sambaa Deh Falls Territorial Park (NT) 899

Sarnia (ON) 206
Saskatchewan 619–46, **620**
　activities 621–2
　history 621
　parks 621
　tourist office 44
Saskatchewan Landing Provincial Park (SK) 632
Saskatchewan Science Centre (SK) 624–5
Saskatoon (SK) 634–41, **635**
Saturna Island (BC) 813
Sauble Beach (ON) 211
Sault Ste Marie (ON) 235–42, **236**
Sceptre (SK) 632
Science North (ON) 225
Scots Bay (NS) 469
scuba diving. See diving
Sea to Sky Hwy (BC) 762
Searston (NF) 415
Seaside Adjunct Kejimkujik National Park (NS) 456
Secord, Laura 175
Selkirk, Lord 17, 587, 588
Selkirk (MB) 601
senior travelers 59–60
Sept Îles (QC) 335
sexually transmitted diseases (STDs) 58
SGaang Gwaii 41, 855
Shakespeare (ON) 194
Shakespearean Festival 194–5
Shaw, George Bernard 170, 173
Shawinigan (QC) 303
Shelburne (NS) 457–8
Shelburne (ON) 209
Shepody Bay Shorebird Reserve (NB) 568
Sherbrooke (NS) 485
Sherbrooke (QC) 300–1
Sherbrooke Village (NS) 485
ships. See cruises; ferries; freighters
shopping 73
Shubenacadie (NS) 473
Shuswap Lake (BC) 831
Sicamous (BC) 831
Signal Hill National Historic Park (NF) 370
Silver Star Mountain Resort (BC) 830
Silver Trail 877

Silverton (BC) 842
Sioux 245, 253, 649
Sioux Narrows (ON) 255
Six Nations 185, 186
Skagway (Alaska) 874–6
skating
　ice 65, 112, 140, 278
　inline 111–2, 164, 168, 174, 278, 310
skiing & snowboarding 64
　AB 650, 685, 691, 698, 705, 716
　BC 723, 739, 741, 763, 802, 817, 821, 823, 826–7, 830, 834, 835–6, 839, 840, 842–3
　NF 404, 413–4
　NT 888, 899
　ON 93, 138–9, 140, 210
　QC 261–2, 292, 294, 296–8, 299, 303, 310, 322
skunks 34
Skydome (ON) 100, 126
Slate Islands Provincial Park (ON) 244
Slavey 667
Sleeping Giant Provincial Park (ON) 245
Slocan Valley (BC) 841–2
Sloop's Cove (MB) 611
Smithers (BC) 846
Smiths Falls (ON) 152
smoked meat 282
snakes 61, 604–5
snow blindness 56
snowboarding. See skiing & snowboarding
snowmobiling 888
soccer 73
The Soo. See Sault Ste Marie
Sorel-Tracy (QC) 304
Souris (PE) 515–6
South Algonquin area (ON) 150, 152
South Coast (NF) 418–20
South Rustico (PE) 520–1
South Shore (NS) 448–58
South Shore (QC) 322
Southern Bay (NF) 386
souvenirs 73
Spatsizi Plateau Wilderness Park (BC) 853
special events 62

Bold indicates maps.

spelunking. *See* caves
spirits 71
sports 71–3. *See also individ-
    ual sports*
Springdale (NF) 401
Spruce Woods Provincial Park
    (MB) 615
Squamish (BC) 762
Stade Olympique (QC) 273
Stanley Park (BC) 735–6,
    750–1
Station Tremblant (QC) 294
STDs 58
Stephenville (NF) 414
Steveston (BC) 738–9
Stewart (BC) 852–3
Stewart Crossing (YT) 877
Stikine River 853
Stock Market Place (ON) 105
Stone Mountain Provincial
    Park (BC) 847
Stoneham (QC) 320
Strait of Belle Isle 420
Straitsview (NF) 408
Stratford (ON) 194–7, **195**
Strathcona Provincial Park
    (BC) 804
students
    discounts 82
    employment 65
Sudbury (ON) 225–31, **226**
sugar shacks 293
Sugarloaf Provincial Park
    (NB) 583
Summerside (PE) 525–7, **526**
Sun Peaks Resort (BC) 817
sunburn 56
Sunbury Shores Arts &
    Nature Centre (NB) 547–8
Sunrise Trail (NS) 479–83
Sunshine Coast (BC) 764–5
Sunwapta Falls (AB) 700
Supreme Court of Canada
    (ON) 136
surfing 456, 483, 723, 797
Sutton (QC) 297–8
SWAP 65
Swift Current (SK) 632
swimming
    AB 657
    BC 741–2
    MB 595
    NB 577
    NF 403, 412
    NT 892, 899

ON 112, 214, 235
QC 278, 297, 334
YT 864, 870, 881
Sydney (NS) 495–8
Sydney Tar Ponds (NS) 496

T

Tadoussac (QC) 330–3, **331**
Tall Grass Prairie Preserve
    (MB) 602
Tamsworth (ON) 160
Tangier (NS) 484
Tatshenshini River 872
Tatshenshini-Alsek Provincial
    Park (BC) 872
taxes 22–3, 49–50
Taylor Head Provincial Park
    (NS) 484
telegrams 51
Telegraph Cove (BC) 805
telephones 50–1
television 53
Temagami (ON) 224–5
Terra Cotta (ON) 126–7
Terra Nova National Park
    (NF) 388–90
Terrace (BC) 852
Terrace Bay (ON) 244
Terrasse Dufferin (QC) 311–2
territorial parks 38
Teslin (YT) 867
Textile Museum of Canada
    (ON) 103
Thompson, David 17, 666,
    719
Thompson, Tom 131
Thompson (MB) 607
Thousand Islands (ON)
    160–1
Thousand Islands Parkway
    (ON) 160–1
Thule 884
Thunder Bay (ON) 245–53,
    247
Thunderbird Park (BC) 771
Tibbitt Lake (NT) 895
ticks 58
tidal bore 473–4, 570–1
tides 466–7, 544, 560, 568
Tidnish Bridge (NS) 479
Tignish (PE) 529
Tillsonburg (ON) 198
Tilt Cove (NF) 401
time zones 54, **55**
Timmins (ON) 231–2

Tintina Trench (YT) 877
tipping 49
tobacco 198
Tobermory (ON) 212–4
Tofino (BC) 796–9
toilets 56, 378
toll-free numbers 51
Tombstone Territorial Park
    (YT) 883
Tommy Thompson Park (ON)
    110–1
Top of the World Hwy 882–3
Top of the World Provincial
    Park (BC) 839
Torbay (NF) 380
Toronto (ON) 93–130, **94, 96**
    accommodations 115–8
    activities 111–2
    climate 20
    day trips 130–3
    entertainment 123–6
    history 95, 98
    museums & galleries
        102–4
    neighborhoods 107–9
    parks 109–11
    restaurants 118–23
    shopping 126–7
    special events 114–5
    sports 126
    tours 112–4
    transportation 127–30
Toronto Dominion Gallery of
    Inuit Art (ON) 104
Toronto Islands (ON) 101
Toronto Zoo (ON) 104
totem poles 771, 786, 849,
    852, 856
tourist homes. *See* accommo-
    dations
tourist offices 43–4
tours, organized 89–90
Trail (BC) 842
trains
    historic 17, 149, 232–3,
        237–8, 411, 498, 568,
        664–5, 736, 743, 762,
        793, 832, 844
    as transportation 77, 81–3
Trans Canada Trail 63
transportation
    air travel 74–6, 79–80
    bicycles 87–8
    buses 77, 80–1, 89–90
    cars 77, 83–7

cruises 78
ferries 77–8, 88–9
freighters 78
hitchhiking 88
RVs 85
trains 77, 81–3
walking 88
Travel Cuts 82, 89
travel insurance 46
traveler's checks 48–9, 61
trekking. See hiking & back-packing
Trenton (ON) 163–4
Trent-Severn Waterway 163–4
Trepassey (NF) 383
Trinity (NF) 387–8
Trinity Bay (NF) 384–5
Trois Pistoles (QC) 339
Trois Rivières (QC) 302
Tr'ondëk Hwëch'in Cultural Centre (YT) 872
Trout River (NF) 403
Trudeau, Pierre 18, 258
Truro (NS) 473–4
Tuktoyaktuk (NT) 906
Tuktut Nogait National Park (NT) 906
Tunnels of Moose Jaws (SK) 631–2
TV 53
Tweedsmuir Provincial Park (BC) 819
Twillingate Island (NF) 397–8
Twin Falls Gorge Territorial Park (NT) 896
Tyne Valley (PE) 528

U

Ucluelet (BC) 799–801
UFOs 298, 667
Ukrainians 617–8, 637, 651, 657, 665
Ungava Bay 425
University of British Columbia 737–8
University of Toronto (ON) 107, 112–3
Upper Canada Village (ON) 153

USA
border crossings to/from 46, 77, 179, 185, 236, 255
relationship with 18, 22, 916
side trips to 45–6

V

vaccinations 56
Val David (QC) 292–3
Val d'Or (QC) 357–8
Val Morin (QC) 292
Valcourt (QC) 298
Valley Zoo (AB) 655–6
Vancouver, George 719
Vancouver (BC) 724–62, **726, 728–9**
accommodations 745–9
activities 741–2
climate 20, 725
day trips 762–5
entertainment 754–7
history 724–5
restaurants 749–54
shopping 757–8
special events 743–4
sports 757
tours 742–3
transportation 758–62
Vancouver Aquarium Marine Science Centre (BC) 735–6
Vancouver Art Gallery (BC) 733
Vancouver Island (BC) 765–807, **766–7**
Vanderhoof (BC) 846
Vanier Park (BC) 736–7
Veregin (SK) 629, 630
Vernon (BC) 829–30
VIA Rail 81–3
Victoria (BC) 768–86, **769, 772**
accommodations 778–81
activities 776–7
entertainment 783
history 768
restaurants 781–3
shopping 783–4
tours 777–8
transportation 784–6
Victoria (PE) 518
video 54
Vieux Port Montreal 270

Québec City 312–3
Vikings 16, 39, 364, 402, 409, 886
The Village (QC) 265, 277, 284, **276**
Village Historique Val Jalbert (QC) 329
Ville de Mont Tremblant (QC) 294–5
Villeneuve, Gilles 301
Virginia Falls (NT) 901
visas 44–5
Vuntut National Park (YT) 883–4

W

Wabush (NF) 427–8
Wakefield (QC) 149
walking 88
Wanuskewin Heritage Park (SK) 636–7
Wapusk National Park (MB) 612
War of 1812 17, 95, 153, 171, 575
Ward Island (ON) 101
Wasa (BC) 839
Wasaga Beach (ON) 207–8
Wasagaming (MB) 617
Wascana Centre (SK) 624
Waskesiu (SK) 644
water purification 56
Waterfront Park (NS) 469
Waterton-Glacier International Peace Park (AB, Montana) 40–1, 715–7
Watson Lake (YT) 867
Wawa (ON) 243
websites 51–2
Welland (ON) 169
Welland Canal (ON) 169–70
Wells Gray Provincial Park (BC) 818
Wendake (QC) 320
Wentworth (NS) 480
West Coast Trail (BC) 795–6
West Edmonton Mall (AB) 655
West Vancouver (BC) 740, 754
Western Brook Pond (NF) 403–4
Western Development Museum (SK) 637
Westmount (QC) 265

Bold indicates maps.

Wetaskwin (AB) 665
Weyburn (SK) 631
whale-watching 36, 332
    BC 723–4, 776, 797, 805,
        806, 850
    MB 609
    NB 532, 548, 550–1, 552,
        553, 555, 580
    NF 366, 375, 381, 387–8
    NS 433, 452, 463, 488–9,
        491, 492, 493, 553
    NU 915
    QC 262, 326–7, 331–2,
        333, 334
wheat 619, 621, 626, 645
Wheatley (ON) 199
whiskey jacks 36
Whistler (BC) 762–4
White River (ON) 244
Whitehorse (YT) 20, 862–7,
    863
Whiteshell Provincial Park
    (MB) 602–3
whitewater rafting. See
    rafting
whooping cranes 898
Whycocomagh (NS) 501
Whyte Museum of the
    Canadian Rockies (AB)
    689
wildflowers 33
wildlife. See also individual
    species
    photographing 54
    species of 35–7
    in urban environments 110

Wilton (ON) 160
windburn 56
windmills 344
Windsor (NF) 399–400
Windsor (NS) 471–3
Windsor (ON) 203–6
windsurfing 112, 352, 353,
    742, 822, 827
wine 70–1, 169, 172, 174,
    199, 813, 821, 823, 826,
    827
Winnie the Pooh 244
Winnipeg (MB) 587–601,
    588, 591
    accommodations 595–7
    activities 594–5
    climate 20
    day trips 601–2
    entertainment 598–9
    history 587–8
    restaurants 597–8
    shopping 600
    sports 599–600
    transportation 600–1
Winnipeg Beach (MB) 603–4
Witless Bay (NF) 381–2
Wolfe Island (ON) 157
Wolfville (NS) 469–70
wolves 35, 612
women travelers 58–9
Wonderland (ON) 104–5
Wood Buffalo National Park
    (AB, NT) 40, 668, 898–9
Wood Islands (PE) 514–5
Woodstock (NB) 541
Woody Point (NF) 402–3

work 65
world heritage sites 38–41.
    See also individual sites
Writing-on-Stone Provincial
    Park (AB) 715

Y

Yaletown (BC) 727, 751
Yarker (ON) 160
Yarmouth (NS) 458–61, 459
Yellowknife (NT) 889–95,
    890
YMCAs. See accommoda-
    tions
Yoho National Park (BC)
    836–8
York Factory (MB) 611–2
York Redoubt (NS) 438–9
York-Sunbury Historical
    Museum (NB) 536
Yorkton (SK) 629–30
Yorkville (ON) 108
Yukon River 877
Yukon Territory 858–84, 860
    accommodations 861
    activities 859, 861
    climate 859
    history 858–9
    tourist office 44
    transportation 861–2
YWCAs. See accommoda-
    tions

Z

zoos 104, 296, 571, 594,
    638, 655–6, 673–4

Boxed Text

The Acadians 471
The Alaska Highway 868–9
And You Thought He Wasn't Real 244
Barking up the Right Tree 847
Beothuk Indians 400
The Best-Known Canadian of Them All 29
Black Settlement in Ontario 205
Bondar's Not Lost in Space 239
Boundless Riches — Maybe 426
Bridge over Troubled Waters 506
Canada's Coolest Hotel 316
Canadian Means Quality 626
Canadian Universities Travel Service 82
A Christmas Tree for Boston 437
Did You Say What I Thought You Did? 234
Emergencies 919
The Endangered BC Salmon 723
Essential Montréal Experiences 282
Extremely Boring 571
Fluffy White Killers 610
Forbidden Feast 850
Fredericton's Famous Frog 536
The Galloping Goose 777
Glaciers Are Cool, But Icefields Are
    Awesome 700
Going Green 63
The Grand Banks 391
Grey Owl at Home in the Wilderness 643
Having a Whale of a Time 805
High Tea at the Empress 781
Hockey Night in Canada 72
Hotel Hijinks 100
The Inside Passage to Prince Rupert 807
The International Appalachian Trail 347
The Iron Link: An Engineering Marvel 833
Klondike Winter 881
The Legend of the Sleepy Giant 245
The Life & Work of Emily Carr 774
Light, Water & Tomatoes 904
Louis Riel, Hero of the Métis 593
The Magnificent Seven 131
The Mall That Ate... 655
Map Maker, Bible Reader &
    Tireless Trekker 666
Maple Syrup & the Sugar Shack 293

The Mennonites 187
The Mighty Canadian Shield 606
Moose on the Loose 389
The Moravian Church 425
The Naming of Alberta 649
Native Indian Literature 26
Naughtier than the Image? 56
The Niagara Escarpment 170
The Northern Lights of Yellowknife 893
Not a Swiss Watch 367
Not All Darkness at Noon 910
Nothing New about Refugees 161
Not-So-Wild Animals 110
One Park, Two Nations 716
The Pub Crawl 192
A River under Siege 541
St John's on Ice 374
A Shaw Thing 173
Signs 918
Skiing & Snowboarding 210
The Sudbury Basin 225
Sure I'll Try It. What Is It? 368
Symbols & Cymbals 21
That Crazy Mixed-Up Lobster 521
They Call the Wind Chinook 649
Three Little Words 259
The Tides of Funnel-Shaped Fundy 544
Totem Poles 856
Two North Poles 914
The Ultimate Mountain Man 688
The Underground City 264
Up with the Push-Up Bra, Down with the
    Zipper 23
Veregin & the Doukhobours 630
Warning 74
Whale-Watching Galore 553
What Are You Talking About? 395
What I Did on My Holidays 237
What Is It, Where Is It? 228
Wheat Castles of the New World 645
When the Bison Reigned Supreme 616
Who Swims There? 332
The World's First Flush Toilet 378
The Yukon Cracks Up 877

MAP LEGEND

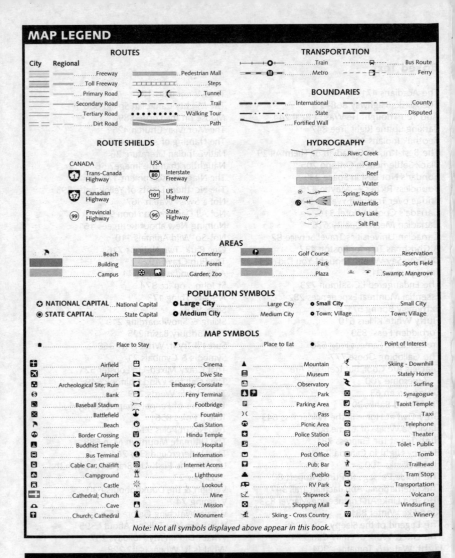

ROUTES

City **Regional**

.... Freeway
.... Toll Freeway
.... Primary Road
.... Secondary Road
.... Tertiary Road
.... Dirt Road
.... Pedestrian Mall
.... Steps
.... Tunnel
.... Trail
.... Walking Tour
.... Path

TRANSPORTATION

.... Train
.... Metro
.... Bus Route
.... Ferry

ROUTE SHIELDS

CANADA

1 Trans-Canada Highway
17 Canadian Highway
99 Provincial Highway

USA

80 Interstate Freeway
101 US Highway
95 State Highway

BOUNDARIES

.... International
.... State
.... Fortified Wall
.... County
.... Disputed

HYDROGRAPHY

.... River; Creek
.... Canal
.... Reef
.... Water
.... Spring; Rapids
.... Waterfalls
.... Dry Lake
.... Salt Flat

AREAS

.... Beach
.... Building
.... Campus
.... Cemetery
.... Forest
.... Garden; Zoo
.... Golf Course
.... Park
.... Plaza
.... Reservation
.... Sports Field
.... Swamp; Mangrove

POPULATION SYMBOLS

○ NATIONAL CAPITAL ... National Capital
◉ STATE CAPITAL ... State Capital
● **Large City** ... Large City
● **Medium City** ... Medium City
● Small City ... Small City
● Town; Village ... Town; Village

MAP SYMBOLS

■ .... Place to Stay
▼ .... Place to Eat
● .... Point of Interest

.... Airfield
.... Airport
.... Archeological Site; Ruin
.... Bank
.... Baseball Stadium
.... Battlefield
.... Beach
.... Border Crossing
.... Buddhist Temple
.... Bus Terminal
.... Cable Car; Chairlift
.... Campground
.... Castle
.... Cathedral; Church
.... Cave
.... Church; Cathedral
.... Cinema
.... Dive Site
.... Embassy; Consulate
.... Ferry Terminal
.... Footbridge
.... Fountain
.... Gas Station
.... Hindu Temple
.... Hospital
.... Information
.... Internet Access
.... Lighthouse
.... Lookout
.... Mine
.... Mission
.... Monument
.... Mountain
.... Museum
.... Observatory
.... Park
.... Parking Area
.... Pass
.... Picnic Area
.... Police Station
.... Pool
.... Post Office
.... Pub; Bar
.... Pueblo
.... RV Park
.... Shipwreck
.... Shopping Mall
.... Skiing - Cross Country
.... Skiing - Downhill
.... Stately Home
.... Surfing
.... Synagogue
.... Taoist Temple
.... Taxi
.... Telephone
.... Theater
.... Toilet - Public
.... Tomb
.... Trailhead
.... Tram Stop
.... Transportation
.... Volcano
.... Windsurfing
.... Winery

Note: Not all symbols displayed above appear in this book.

LONELY PLANET OFFICES

Australia
Locked Bag 1, Footscray, Victoria 3011
☎ 03 8379 8000 fax 03 8379 8111
email talk2us@lonelyplanet.com.au

USA
150 Linden Street, Oakland, California 94607
☎ 510 893 8555, TOLL FREE 800 275 8555
fax 510 893 8572
email info@lonelyplanet.com

UK
10a Spring Place, London NW5 3BH
☎ 020 7428 4800 fax 020 7428 4828
email go@lonelyplanet.co.uk

France
1 rue du Dahomey, 75011 Paris
☎ 01 55 25 33 00 fax 01 55 25 33 01
email bip@lonelyplanet.fr
www.lonelyplanet.fr

World Wide Web: www.lonelyplanet.com *or* AOL keyword: lp
Lonely Planet Images: lpi@lonelyplanet.com.au